PREFACE

This year starts a second century for Black's Law Dictionary—the standard authority for legal definitions since 1891.

Nearly every area of the law has undergone change and development since publication of the Abridged Fifth Edition in 1983. This period has seen particular change and expansion in such areas as tax, finance, commercial transactions, debtor-creditor relations, tort liability, employment, health care, environment, and criminal law. Congress and the states continue to legislate new rights and remedies; the courts continue to define and redefine legal terms; the states are increasingly adopting uniform or model laws and rules; and new causes of action and legal concepts continue unabated.

The vocabulary of the law has likewise continued to change and expand to keep pace. This has necessitated not only a significant expansion of new words and terms for inclusion in this Abridged Sixth Edition, but also a reexamination of all existing entries for currentness of legal usage. Indicative of this growth is that this new edition required the addition or revision of over 4,000 legal words and terms.

Considerable effort has again been made in this new Sixth Edition to provide more than basic definitions of legal words and terms. In those instances where traditional legal concepts and doctrines have over the years been either superseded, modified or supplemented by court decisions or legislation, such developments and changes are fully reflected. Additionally, because so many areas of law and practice are now governed by uniform or model acts and rules, such major sources of law as the Uniform Commercial Code, Restatements of the Law, Model Penal Code, and Federal Rules are fully reflected. Similarly, the growth and importance of federal laws, with their impact on matters that were traditionally state or local in nature, is evidenced with a considerable number of new entries and citations covering federal acts, agencies, departments and courts.

The ever expanding importance of financial terminology to law students, lawyers, and accountants, as well as to college and graduate students, has necessitated the inclusion of numerous new tax, finance, and accounting terms.

Examples of word usages have been added throughout to illustrate how specific terms are used or applied in various legal and business contexts.

Because of the inter-relationship of so many legal words and terms, the number of internal cross-references has been greatly increased throughout the Dictionary.

A number of changes have been made to the pronunciation guides to make this feature even more helpful. A comprehensive explanation of these guides is set forth on pages vii–xiv with a shorter pronunciation Key appearing on the inside front cover.

iii

PREFACE

New and revised words and terms for this Abridged Sixth Edition were prepared by Joseph R. Nolan, Associate Justice, Massachusetts Supreme Judicial Court, and Jacqueline M. Nolan–Haley of Fordham University School of Law. The pronunciation transcription system and guides were prepared by M.J. Connolly, Associate Professor of Linguistics, Boston College. Words and terms of the United Kingdom were revised and updated by Professor Stephen C. Hicks, Suffolk University Law School. Tax and accounting terms were updated and expanded by Martina N. Alibrandi, Certified Public Accountant, Bolton, Massachusetts.

A Final Word of Caution

The language of the law is ever-changing as the courts, Congress, state legislatures, and administrative agencies continue to define, redefine and expand legal words and terms. Furthermore, many legal terms are subject to variations from state to state and again can differ under federal laws. Also, the type of legal issue, dispute, or transaction involved can affect a given definition usage. Accordingly, a legal dictionary should only be used as a "starting point" for definitions. Additional research should follow for state or federal variations, for further or later court interpretations, and for specific applications. Helpful sources for supplemental research are the Unabridged Sixth Edition of Black's Law Dictionary, the multi-volume "Words and Phrases" publication, and WESTLAW.

THE PUBLISHER

St. Paul, Minn.
July, 1991

BLACK'S
LAW DICTIONARY®

Definitions of the Terms and Phrases of
American and English Jurisprudence,
Ancient and Modern

By

HENRY CAMPBELL BLACK, M. A.

ABRIDGED SIXTH EDITION
BY
THE PUBLISHER'S EDITORIAL STAFF

Coauthors

JOSEPH R. NOLAN

Associate Justice, Massachusetts Supreme Judicial Court

and

JACQUELINE M. NOLAN–HALEY

Associate Clinical Professor,
Fordham University School of Law

Contributing Authors

M. J. CONNOLLY
Associate Professor (Linguistics),
College of Arts & Sciences, Boston College

STEPHEN C. HICKS
Professor of Law, Suffolk University
Law School, Boston, MA

MARTINA N. ALIBRANDI
Certified Public Accountant, Bolton, MA

ST. PAUL, MINN.
WEST PUBLISHING CO.
1991

COPYRIGHT © 1983 WEST PUBLISHING CO.
COPYRIGHT © 1991 By WEST PUBLISHING CO.
                 50 West Kellogg Boulevard
                 P.O. Box 64526
                 St. Paul, Mn 55164–0526

Library of Congress Cataloging-in-Publication Data

Black, Henry Campbell, 1850–1927.
   [Law dictionary]
   Black's law dictionary with pronunciations : definitions of the
terms and phrases of American and English jurisprudence, ancient and
modern / by Henry Campbell Black. — Abridged 6th ed. / by the
publisher's editorial staff ; coauthors, Joseph R. Nolan and
Jacqueline M. Nolan-Haley ; contributing authors, M.J. Connolly,
Stephen C. Hicks, Martina N. Alibrandi.
     p.   cm.
  ISBN 0–314–88536–6
   1. Law—United States—Dictionaries. 2. Law—Dictionaries.
I. Nolan, Joseph R. II. Nolan-Haley, Jacqueline M. III. West
Publishing Company. IV. Title. V. Title: Law dictionary.
KF156.B532 1991
340'.03—dc20   91–18715
                                       CIP

ISBN 0–314–88536–6

CONTENTS

*

THE PRONUNCIATION OF LATIN

A majority of the Latin terms in this revised edition of *Black's Law Dictionary*, and also occasional English and foreign terms, have been provided with pronunciation entries. The pronunciations follow a *descriptive* scheme and are based on actual usage rather than on any attempt to *prescribe* a uniform pronunciation. Where alternate pronunciations exist, the philologically more 'appropriate' pronunciation generally receives first listing however. The entries provide an acceptable pronunciation in a transcription system compatible with the major varieties of North American English and extendable to other pronunciations.

Despite its continuing decline as a working language of scholarship and jurisprudence, Latin still supplies a formidable stock of legal terms and phrases. The ability to use a Latin phrase correctly and pronounce it with authority and consistency belongs to the equipment of a well-rounded jurist. Those who actually study Latin today, however, will in all probability learn a pronunciation (either the reformed philological or the Italianate) at variance with the Anglo-Latin system which prevails in legal and medical spheres. Injection of the 'newer' school pronunciations actually serves to increase confusion and uncertainty: Where masculine plural *alumni* and feminine plural *alumnae* were once differentiated in speech as /ələ́mnay/ and /ələ́mniy/ respectively, one widespread variant of the philological pronunciation actually *reverses* the opposition with masculine /ələ́mniy/ and feminine /ələ́mnay/. The status of *amicus curiae*, traditionally pronounced /əmáykəs kyúriyiy/, now has variants /əmíykəs kúriyày/ (adapted philological), /amíykus kúriyèy/ (Italianate), and numerous hybrids. A parliamentarian of the old school, perhaps even well versed in Latin, adjourns a meeting *sine die* /sáyniy dáyiy/ only to have a junior colleague suggest that the 'correct' pronunciation is /síyney díyey/.

Strictly speaking, of course, any attempt at 'correct' pronunciations of foreign terms can at best be only weak approximations. The linguistic contortions of a purist attempting to weave foreign sounds and intonations into the texture of an English sentence usually strike us as pedantic or affected. Although Julius Caesar may have pronounced his name something like /yúwliyus káysar/ and later Romans may have called him /chéyzar/, few speakers of English have place for anything other than the Anglo-Latin /júwl(i)yəs síyzər/.

Three major systems of Latin pronunciation, outlined below, coexist in the English-speaking world. Each has its proper cultural and scholarly context. The *reformed* (or *new*, or *philological*, or *Roman*) pronunciation represents a modification to English speech habits of the reconstructed sounds of Latin as it must have been in the classical period. Philologists, classical historians, and most teachers of Latin employ this pronunciation in their professional activity. *Anglo-Latin* (or English) pronunciation, the form most commonly encountered in law, medicine, the natural sciences, and in general usage, reflects the centuries of sound change that English has undergone. Although it may not possess the authenticity of linguistic reconstruction, the Anglo-Latin system enjoys the authority of a persevering and distinct cultural tradition. The *Italianate* pronunciation derives from the pronunciation of Later Latin and is viewed as the standard in Roman Catholicism (including canon law), in music, in art history, and in medieval studies. There exist, in addition, various *secondary* pronunciations, such as the *Continental* one often used by scholars of Middle English literature and history. Thus, a school master may leave the classroom, where he has just taught his pupils Latin imperatives, including *venite* 'come' /weníyte/ (reformed philological), go to chapel to rehearse with the choir Psalm 95 in Anglican morning prayer, the *Venite* /vənáytiy/ (Anglo-Latin), and then actually sing the text in a Latin setting as /veyníytey èksultéymus.../ (Italianate). Each pronunciation is correct in its own context.

OUTLINE OF LATIN PRONUNCIATIONS

Letter	Reformed Philological	Italianate	Anglo-Latin
a	/a/		/a, æ, ey, ə, o/
b	/b/		
c	/k/	/ch/ before /i, e/ /k/ elsewhere	/s, sh, z, k/
d	/d/		
e	/ey, e/		/e, ey, ə, i, iy/
f	/f/		
g	/ŋ/ before n /g/ elsewhere	/j/ before /i, e/ /g/ elsewhere *gn* pronounced /ny/	/j, g/
h	/h/	/h/ or silent /k/ in *nihil, mihi*	/h/ or silent
i	/i, iy/		/i, iy, ay, ə/
j	/y/		/j/
k	/k/		
l	/l/		
m	/m/		
n	/n, ŋ/		
o	/o, ow/		/o, a, ə, ow/
p	/p/		
qu	/kw/		
r	/r/		
s	/s/	/z/ between vowels /s/ elsewhere	/s, z, sh, zh/
t(h)	/t/	/ts/ before *i* plus vowels except after *s, t, x* /t/ elsewhere	/t, d, sh, ch/ *th* as /Θ/
u	/u, uw, w/	/w/ after *q* or *ng* /uw/ elsewhere	/yuw, uw, u, yə, ə, i, w/

Letter	Reformed Philological	Italianate	Anglo-Latin
v	/w/	/v/	
x	/ks/ x + /ch/ = /ksh/		/ks, gz, z, s/
y	/i, iy/	/iy/ or Gmn ü	/ay, iy, i, y/
z	/z/	/z, dz/	/z/

Attested forms in Anglo-Latin pronunciation sometimes fail to correspond in qualitative or accentual details with the forms we might expect on an etymological or systematic basis. Thus,

bona fide appears as /bównə fáydiy/ instead of */bónə fídiy/

industry appears as /índəstriy/ instead of */ində́striy/

minor appears as /máynər/ instead of */mínər/, etc.

Numerous developments in the sound system of English have tended to override the expected forms. Analogies with sibling or quasi-sibling forms often keep doublets flourishing side by side:

licet 'it is permitted' as /láysət/ (cf. license) or /lísət/ (cf. *licit*)

debet 'one must' as /díybət/ or /débət/ (cf. debit and credit)

capias 'thou shouldst seize' as /kéypiyəs/ (cf. *cape*) or /kǽpiyəs/ (cf. *capture*)

Language traditions usually resolve such conflicts in good time, favoring 'usage' over 'correctness', and then promptly create new conflicts.

TRANSCRIPTION SYSTEM

The transcription system employed for these listings is derived from one of the traditional phonemic analyses of American English (Trager-Smith). The values of the symbols vary with context, i.e., their specific pronunciations depend on the nature of the surrounding sounds. The pronunciation habits of a normal speaker of English will, however, in practically all cases supply the accustomed variants for that speaker's usage if the elements presented in the key are substituted in accordance with the sample indications. This system enables the speakers of a range of dialects to use one and the same transcription and yet produce a pronunciation natural to their speech. For this reason, in addition to the considerations given above concerning the treatment of foreign terms in English, sounds foreign to English have been represented by the customary English substitutes. Thus, for example, the voiceless velar fricative of German *Bach* would be rendered with a simple stop /k/ and French front rounded *eu* with /yuw/. Readers who wish to affect the foreign sounds will find guidance in their own linguistic experience or in the appropriate grammars and dictionaries. Similarly, readers who prefer pronunciations closer to the spelling than those presented here should feel free to substitute their preferences, e.g., restoration of 'full' vowels for unaccented /ə/ or even to pronouncing the *t* in *often*. Finally, readers who already feel secure (or even superior) in their own renderings of words and phrases should retain these. The editors will always appreciate information on local variants and will welcome suggestions for improving the transcriptions.

The rubrics (sets of examples) under any given major symbol should always be applied *in order*. The earlier, more specific contexts take preference over the later, 'elsewhere' variant.

The special symbols

/æ/ (ash)   /ð/ (edh)   /ə/ (schwa)   /ŋ/ (angma)   (Θ/ (theta)

appear respectively after

/a/   /d/   /e/   /n/   /t/

The reader will, of course, be aware that the transcription symbols do not necessarily have the same alphabetic values as in English. Rather, the symbols must be viewed as arbitrary signs, although in many cases their forms will aid the user in remembering and associating the key sounds and symbols.

GUIDE TO PRONUNCIATION SYMBOLS

a

/ay/   as in the bold portions of **aye**, **eye**, **I** /áy/   **lie** /láy/
buy, by, bye /báy/   **high** /háy/   **aisle, isle, I'll** /áyl/
idea /aydíyə/

/aw/   as in **out** /áwt/   **how** /háw/

/ar/   as in **bark** /bárk/   **car** /kár/

/a/   elsewhere as in **father** /fáðər/. In many dialects identical with /o/.

æ

/æ/   as in **cat** /kǽt/

b

/b/   as in **bill** /bíl/

ch

/ch/   as in **ch**ill /chíl/   **ch**ur**ch** /chə́rch/   na**t**ure /néychər/
question /kwés(h)chən/

d

/d/   as in **d**ill /díl/   o**d**or /ówdər/.
In many dialects *better*, *bedder* may both appear as /bédər/.

ð

/ð/   as in **th**is /ðís/   smoo**th** /smúwð/   **th**ou /ðáw/
not to be confused with /Θ/

e

/ey/   as in **th**ey /ðéy/   make /méyk/   sail, sale /séyl/
neigh, nay /néy/

/ehr/   as in **error** /éhrər/   **merry** /méhriy/.
In dialects where /ehr/ is not distinct from /er/ the diacritic /h/
may be ignored.

/er/   as in **th**ere, th**eir** /ðer/   **air, e'er** /ér/

/e/   elsewhere as in **d**ell /dél/   bet /bét/

ə

/əhr/   as in **cur**rent /kə́hrənt/.
In dialects where /əhr/ is not distinct from /ər/ the diacritic /h/
may be ignored.

/ər/   as in **mur**der /mə́rdər/   **were** /wə́r/   mother /máðər/
world /wə́rld/   whirr /(h)wə́r/

/ə́/   /ə́/ (with either primary or secondary stress) as in
but, butt /bə́t/   **blood** /blə́d/   above /əbə́v/

/ə/   elsewhere (unstressed) as in **sofa** /sówfə/   **another** /ənə́ðər/

f

/f/   as in **f**ill, **Ph**il /fíl/   rou**gh** /rə́f/

GUIDE TO PRONUNCIATION SYMBOLS

g

/g/   always 'hard' as in gall /gól/   Gaul /gól/   lag /lǽg/

h

/h/   as silent diacritic in combinations /ehr, əhr, ihr, ohr/
and /ch, sh, zh/
otherwise as in hill /híl/   mousehole /máws-hòwl/

i

/iy/   as in machine /məshíyn/   be, bee, Bea /bíy/   each /íych/
/ihr/ as in irrigate /íhrəgeyt/   spirit /spíhrət.
In dialects where /ihr/ is not distinct from /ir/ the diacritic /h/
may be ignored.
/ir/   as in pier, peer /pír/   hear, here /hír/
/i/   elsewhere as in sit /sít/   pretty /prítiy/

j

/j/   as in Jill /jíl/   general /jén(ə)rəl/   edge /éj/
soldier /sówljər/   carriage /kǽrəj/

k

/k/   as in kill /kíl/   cool /kúwl/

l

/l/   as in Lill /líl/

m

/m/   as in mill /míl/

n

/n/   as in nil /níl/
/ŋ/   as in thing /Ɵíŋ/   singer /síŋər/   finger /fíŋgər/

o

/oy/   as in boy /bóy/   noise /nóyz/
/ow/   as in know /nów/   sew, so, sow (seed) /sów/
/ohr/ as in foreign /fóhrən/   borrow /bóhrow/.
In dialects where /ohr/ is not distinct from /or/ the diacritic /h/
may be ignored.
/or/   as in bore, boar /bór/   course, coarse /kórs/
/o/   elsewhere as in rot, wrought /rót/   wall /wól/
ought, aught /ót/   law /ló/.
Some dialects merge /o/ and /a/ while others treat diphthongal
spellings as /o/ but others as /a/.

p

/p/   as in pill /píl/   lip /líp/

r

/r/   as in rill /ríl/.
See also the coloring function or /r/ in diphthongs /ar, e(h)r,
ə(h)r, i(h)r, o(h)r, ur/.

GUIDE TO PRONUNCIATION SYMBOLS

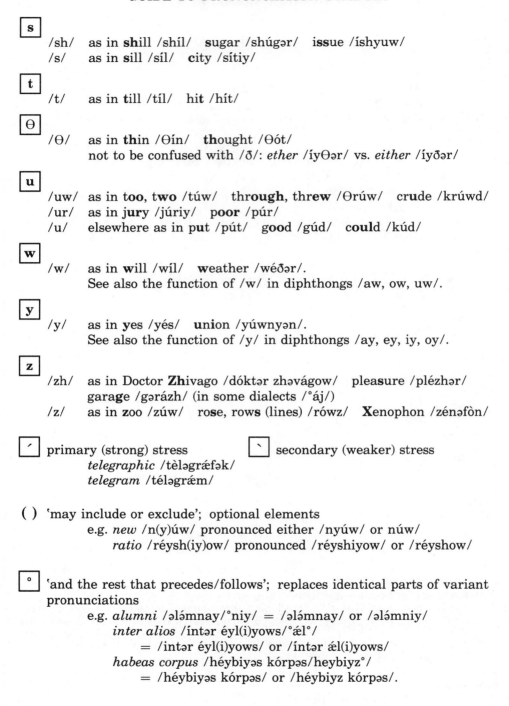

s

/sh/   as in **sh**ill /shíl/   su**g**ar /shúgər/   i**ss**ue /íshyuw/
/s/   as in **s**ill /síl/   **c**ity /sítiy/

t

/t/   as in **t**ill /tíl/   hi**t** /hít/

Θ

/Θ/   as in **th**in /Θín/   **th**ought /Θót/
       not to be confused with /ð/: *ether* /íyΘər/ vs. *either* /íyðər/

u

/uw/   as in **too**, t**wo** /túw/   th**rough**, th**rew** /Θrúw/   cr**u**de /krúwd/
/ur/   as in j**u**ry /júriy/   p**oor** /púr/
/u/   elsewhere as in p**u**t /pút/   g**oo**d /gúd/   c**oul**d /kúd/

w

/w/   as in **w**ill /wíl/   **w**eather /wéðər/.
       See also the function of /w/ in diphthongs /aw, ow, uw/.

y

/y/   as in **y**es /yés/   **u**nion /yúwnyən/.
       See also the function of /y/ in diphthongs /ay, ey, iy, oy/.

z

/zh/   as in Doctor **Zh**ivago /dóktər zhəvágow/   plea**s**ure /plézhər/
       ga**r**a**g**e /gərázh/ (in some dialects /°áj/)
/z/   as in **z**oo /zúw/   ro**s**e, row**s** (lines) /rówz/   **X**enophon /zénəfòn/

´ primary (strong) stress   **`** secondary (weaker) stress
       telegraphic /tèləgrǽfək/
       telegram /téləgræm/

( ) 'may include or exclude'; optional elements
       e.g. *new* /n(y)úw/ pronounced either /nyúw/ or núw/
       ratio /réysh(iy)ow/ pronounced /réyshiyow/ or /réyshow/

° 'and the rest that precedes/follows'; replaces identical parts of variant
pronunciations
       e.g. *alumni* /ələ́mnay/°niy/ = /ələ́mnay/ or /ələ́mniy/
       inter alios /íntər éyl(i)yows/°ǽl°/
              = /íntər éyl(i)yows/ or /íntər ǽl(i)yows/
       habeas corpus /héybiyəs kórpəs/heybiyz°/
              = /héybiyəs kórpəs/ or /héybiyz kórpəs/.

BLACK'S
LAW DICTIONARY®

ABRIDGED SIXTH EDITION

*

A

AAA. Agricultural Adjustment Act; American Accounting Association; American Arbitration Association.

AALS. Association of American Law Schools.

A.B. Able-bodied seaman. For the requirements of able seaman, see 46 U.S.C.A. § 7306 *et seq.* *See* Able-bodied.

Also *artium baccalaureus*, bachelor of arts. In England and U.S., generally written B. A.

A.B.A. American Bar Association.

Ab; Abr. Abridgment.

A.B.A.J. American Bar Association Journal.

Abandon. *See* Abandonment.

Abandoned property. Property intentionally left. Property over which the owner has given up dominion and control with no intention of recovering it. *See also* Abandonment.

Abandonee. A party to whom a right or property is abandoned or relinquished by another. Term is applied to the insurers of vessels and cargoes.

Abandonment. The surrender, relinquishment, disclaimer, or cession of property or of rights. Voluntary relinquishment of all right, title, claim and possession, with the intention of not reclaiming it. The giving up of a thing absolutely, without reference to any particular person or purpose, as vacating property with the intention of not returning, so that it may be appropriated by the next comer or finder. The voluntary relinquishment of possession of thing by owner with intention of terminating his ownership, but without vesting it in any other person. The relinquishing of all title, possession, or claim, or a virtual, intentional throwing away of property.

Term includes both the intention to abandon and the external act by which the intention is carried into effect. In determining whether one has abandoned his property or rights, the intention is the first and paramount object of inquiry, for there can be no abandonment without the intention to abandon.

Time is not an essential element of act, although the lapse of time may be evidence of an intention to abandon, and where it is accompanied by acts manifesting such an intention, it may be considered in determining whether there has been an abandonment.

See also Desertion; Discharge; Release; Waiver.

Actions, in general. Failure to prosecute or bring action within statutorily prescribed period (*see* Limitations *(Statute of limitations))*; failure to object to or submit jury instructions (Fed.R. Civil P. 51); failure to demand jury trial (Fed.R. Civil P. 38).

Adverse possession. To destroy continuity of adverse claimant's possession, there must be an intent to relinquish claim of ownership as well as an act of relinquishment of possession and mere temporary absence is not sufficient.

Assignment of error. Failure to object at trial. Error not presented in brief. Error not supported by point, argument or authority. See Fed.R.Civil Proc. 46 (Exceptions unnecessary).

Children. Desertion or willful forsaking. Foregoing parental duties. *See also* Desertion.

Contracts. To constitute "abandonment" by conduct, action relied on must be positive, decisive, unequivocal, and inconsistent with the existence of the contract. Abandonment is a matter of intent, and implies not only nonperformance, but an intent not to perform which may be inferred from acts which necessarily point to actual abandonment.

Copyright. "Abandonment" of a copyright turns on state of mind of copyright proprietor and occurs whenever he engages in some overt action which manifests his purpose to surrender his rights in the work and to allow the public to enjoy it.

Criminal acts. "Abandonment" can relieve one of criminal responsibility where criminal enterprise is cut short by change of heart, desertion of criminal purpose, change of behavior, and rising revulsion for harm intended, and must occur before criminal act charged is in the process of consummation or has become so inevitable that it cannot reasonably be delayed. See Model Penal Code § 5.01(4) (renunciation of criminal purpose).

Easements. To establish "abandonment" of an easement created by deed, there must be some conduct on part of owner of servient estate adverse to and inconsistent with existence of easement and continuing for statutory period, or nonuser must be accompanied by unequivocal and decisive acts clearly indicating an intent on part of owner of easement to abandon use of it. Permanent cessation of use or enjoyment with no intention to resume or reclaim. Intention and

1

completed act are both essential. A mere temporary or occasional obstruction or use of an easement by the servient owner is not an "abandonment".

Ground for divorce. "Abandonment" as cause for divorce must be willful and intentional without intention of returning, and without consent of spouse abandoned. This ground is commonly termed "desertion" in state divorce statutes. *See also* Desertion.

Inventions. The giving up of rights by inventor, as where he surrenders his idea or discovery or relinquishes the intention of perfecting his invention, and so throws it open to the public, or where he negligently postpones the assertion of his claims or fails to apply for a patent, and allows the public to use his invention.

Leases in general. To constitute an "abandonment" of leased premises, there must be an absolute relinquishment of premises by tenant consisting of act and intention.

Patents. There may be an abandonment of a patent, where the inventor dedicates it to the public use; and this may be shown by his failure to sue infringers, sell licenses, or otherwise make efforts to realize a personal advantage from his patent. A person may not be deprived of a patent as a result of the earlier work of another if that work has been abandoned, supplemented, or concealed. 35 U.S.C.A. § 102(g).

Property. "Abandoned property" in a legal sense is that to which owner has relinquished all right, title, claim, and possession, but without vesting it in any other person, and with no intention of not reclaiming it or resuming its ownership, possession or enjoyment in the future.

Rights in general. The relinquishment of a right. It implies some act of relinquishment done by the owner without regard to any future possession by himself, or by any other person, but with an intention to abandon. *See* Waiver.

Abatable nuisance. A nuisance which is practically susceptible of being suppressed, or extinguished, or rendered harmless, and whose continued existence is not authorized under the law.

Abatare /æbətériy/. To abate.

Abate. To throw down, to beat down, destroy, quash. To do away with or nullify or lessen or diminish. *See also* Abatement; Abatement of action.

Abatement. A reduction, a decrease, or a diminution. The suspension or cessation, in whole or in part, of a continuing charge, such as rent.

Legacies. A proportional diminution or reduction of the pecuniary legacies, when the funds or assets out of which such legacies are payable are not sufficient to pay them in full. Uniform Probate Code, § 3–902. *See* Ademption, *infra,* as to specific legacies and devises.

Nuisance. *See* Nuisance.

Plea in abatement. *See* Plea.

Taxes. Diminution or decrease in the amount of tax imposed. Abatement of taxes relieves property of its share of the burdens of taxation after the assessment has been made and the tax levied.

Abatement of action. An entire overthrow or destruction of the suit so that it is quashed and ended. *See* Dismissal; Vacate.

Pleas in abatement have been abolished by Fed.R. Civil P. 7(c); such being replaced by a motion to dismiss under Rule 41. In certain states however this plea still exists to attack jurisdiction, or service of process, or to allege that a prior action between the same parties concerning the same subject matter is pending.

Abator /əbéytər/. In real property law, a stranger who, having no right of entry, contrives to get possession of an estate of freehold, to the prejudice of the heir or devisee, before the latter can enter, after the ancestor's death. In the law of torts, one who abates, prostrates, or destroys a nuisance.

Abbrochment, *or* **abbroachment** /əbrówchmənt/. The act of forestalling a market, by buying up at wholesale the merchandise intended to be sold there, for the purpose of selling it at retail. *See* Forestalling the market.

Abbuttals. *See* Abuttals.

ABC test. Unemployment compensation law exclusion tests providing that employer is not covered if individuals he employs are free from his control, the services are performed outside employer's places of business, and employees are customarily engaged in independently established trades or professions are known as the "ABC tests". *See* Independent contractor.

ABC transaction. In mining and oil drilling operations, a transfer by which A, the owner, conveys the working interest to B, the operator and developer for cash consideration, reserving a production payment usually larger than the cash consideration paid by B. Later, A sells the reserved production payment to C for cash. The tax advantages of this type of transaction were eliminated by the Tax Reform Act of 1969.

Abdication /æbdəkéyshən/. Renunciation of the privileges and prerogatives of an office. The act of a sovereign in renouncing and relinquishing his government or throne, so that either the throne is left entirely vacant, or is filled by a successor appointed or elected beforehand.

Abduction. The offense of taking away a wife, child, or ward, by fraud and persuasion, or open violence. Model Penal Code, § 212.4. To take away surreptitiously by force in kidnapping. The unlawful taking or detention of any female for purposes of marriage, concubinage, or prostitution. In many states this offense is created by statute and in most cases applies to females under a given age. By statute in some states, abduction includes the withdrawal of a husband from his wife, as where another woman alienates his affection and entices him away and causes him to abandon his wife. *See also* Alienation of affections; Kidnapping.

Abet. To encourage, incite, or set another on to commit a crime. This word is usually applied to aiding in the commission of a crime. To abet another to commit a murder is to command, procure, counsel, encourage, induce, or assist. To facilitate the commission of a crime, promote its accomplishment, or help in advancing or bringing it about. In relation to charge of aiding and abetting, term includes knowledge of the perpetrator's wrongful purpose, and encouragement, promotion or counsel of another in the commission of the criminal offense.

A French word combined of two words "a" and "beter"—to bait or excite an animal.

See also Abettor; Accomplice; Aid and abet.

Abetment. Act of encouraging, inciting or aiding another.

Abettor /əbétər/. An instigator, or setter on; one who promotes or procures a crime to be committed. One who commands, advises, instigates, or encourages another to commit a crime. A person who, being present, incites another to commit a crime, and thus becomes a principal. To be an "abettor" accused must have instigated or advised commission of crime or been present for purpose of assisting in its commission; he must share criminal intent with which crime was committed. *See also* Accessory; Accomplice; Aider and abettor.

Abeyance /əbéyəns/. Lapse in succession during which there is no person in whom title is vested. In the law of estates, the condition of a freehold when there is no person in being in whom it is vested. A condition of being undetermined or in state of suspension or inactivity.

Abide or abide by. To accept the consequences of; to rest satisfied with; to wait for. With reference to an order, judgment, or decree of a court, to perform, to execute.

Abiding conviction. A definite conviction of guilt derived from a thorough examination of the whole case. Used commonly to instruct juries on the frame of mind required for guilt proved beyond a reasonable doubt.

Ability. Capacity to perform an act or service; e. g. to support spouse and family. Financial ability is usually construed as referring to pecuniary

ability. *See also* Able to earn; Capacity; Incapacity.

Ab initio /æb inísh(iy)ow/. Lat. From the beginning; from the first act; from the inception. An agreement is said to be "void ab initio" if it has at no time had any legal validity. A party may be said to be a trespasser, an estate said to be good, an agreement or deed said to be void, or a marriage or act said to be unlawful, *ab initio*. Contrasted in this sense with *ex post facto*, or with *postea*.

Abjuration /æbjəréyshən/. A renunciation or abandonment by or upon oath. The renunciation under oath of one's citizenship or some other right or privilege. *See also* Abjure.

Abjure. To renounce, or abandon, by or upon oath. *See* Abjuration.

Able. *See* Ability.

Able-bodied. As used in a statute relating to service in the militia, this term does not imply an absolute freedom from all physical ailment. It imports an absence of those palpable and visible defects which evidently incapacitate the person from performing the ordinary duties of a soldier. *See also* Able seaman.

Able seaman. A grade of merchant seamen. See 46 U.S.C.A. § 7306 et seq.

Able to earn. Ability to obtain and hold employment means that the person referred to is either able or unable to perform the usual duties of whatever employment may be under consideration, in the manner that such duties are customarily performed by the average person engaged in such employment. *See also* Disability; Gainful employment *or* occupation.

Abnormal loss. In accounting, a decline in units during a production process that is in excess of normal expectations.

Abode. One's home; habitation; place of dwelling; or residence. Ordinarily means "domicile." Living place impermanent in character. The place where a person dwells. Fixed place of residence for the time being. For service of process, one's fixed place of residence for the time being; his "usual place of abode." Fed.R. Civil P. 4. *See* Domicile; Residence.

General abode. See Residence.

Abolish. To do away with wholly; to annul; to repeal; to rescind; to abrogate; to dispense with. Applies particularly to things of a permanent nature, such as institutions, usages, customs, as the abolition of slavery.

Abolishment. *See* Abolish.

Abolition. The destruction, annihilation, abrogation, or extinguishment of anything. *See* Abolish.

Aboriginal title /æbəríjənəl táytəl/. Such title provides original natives of United States exclusive right to occupy lands and waters used by them and their ancestors before United States asserted sovereignty over such areas.

Abortion. The spontaneous or artificially induced expulsion of an embryo or fetus. As used in legal context, usually refers to induced abortion. For the law relating to abortion see Roe v. Wade, 410 U.S. 113, 93 S.Ct. 705, 35 L.Ed.2d 147; Webster v. Reproductive Health Services, 109 S.Ct. 3040, 106 L.Ed.2d 410. *See also* Viability; Viable child.

Abortionist. One who performs abortions.

About. Near in time, quantity, number, quality, or degree. Substantially, approximately, almost, or nearly. When used with reference to time, the term is of flexible significance, varying with the circumstances and the connection in which it is employed. But its use does not necessarily render time immaterial, nor make a contract one terminable at will.

Above. Higher; superior. As, court above; plaintiff or defendant above. *Above all incumbrances* means in excess thereof. Principal, as distinguished from what is auxiliary or instrumental.

Abridge. To reduce or contract; to diminish or curtail. Usually spoken of written language. *See* Abridgment.

Copyright law. To epitomize; to reduce; to contract. It implies preserving the substance, the essence, of a work, in language suited to such a purpose. In making extracts there is no condensation of the author's language, and hence no abridgment. To abridge requires the exercise of the mind; it is not copying. Between a compilation and an abridgment there is a clear distinction. A compilation consists of selected extracts from different authors; an abridgment is a condensation of the views of one author.

Abridgment. Condensation; contraction. An epitome or compendium of another and larger work, wherein the principal ideas of the larger work are summarily contained. Abridgments of the law are brief digests of the law, arranged alphabetically. In this context, the term "digest" *(q.v.)* has generally supplanted that of "abridgment." *See also* Abstract; Headnote; Syllabus.

Abridgment of damages. The right of the court to reduce the damages in certain cases. *See* Remittitur.

Abrogate /æbrəgeyt/. To annul, cancel, revoke, repeal, or destroy. To annul or repeal an order or rule issued by a subordinate authority; to repeal a former law by legislative act, or by usage.

Abrogation /æbrəgéyshən/. The destruction or annulling of a former law, by an act of the legislative power, by constitutional authority, or by us-

age. It stands opposed to *rogation*; and is distinguished from *derogation*, which implies the taking away only some part of a law; from *subrogation*, which denotes the substitution of a clause; from *dispensation*, which only sets it aside in a particular instance; and from *antiquation*, which is the refusing to pass a law. Implied abrogation takes place when the new law contains provisions which are positively contrary to former laws, without expressly abrogating such laws; and also when the order of things for which the law has been made no longer exists.

For "Express abrogation," see that title. *See also* Annul; Repeal.

Abscond /əbskónd/. To go in a clandestine manner out of the jurisdiction of the courts, or to lie concealed, in order to avoid their process. Fleeing from arresting or prosecuting officers of the state. *See* Fugitive.

Absconding debtor. One who absconds from his creditors to avoid payment of debts. A debtor who has intentionally concealed himself from his creditors, or withdrawn himself from the reach of their suits, with intent to frustrate their just demands. Such act was formerly an "Act of bankruptcy" *(q.v.)*.

Absence. The state of being absent, removed, or away from one's domicile, or usual place of residence. Not present at particular time; opposite of appearance at a specified time. *See also* Seven years' absence.

Absent. Being away from; at a distance from; not in company with.

Absentee. One who is absent from his usual place of residence or domicile.

Absentee landlord. Lessor of real property (normally the owner) who does not live on the premises.

Absentee voting. Participation (usually by mail) in elections by qualified voters who, because of serious illness, military service, or absence because of travel or other reasons, are unable to appear at the polls in person on election day. *See also* Proxy with respect to absent voting by stockholder.

Absolute. Complete; perfect; final; without any condition or incumbrance; as an absolute bond *(simplex obligatio)* in distinction from a conditional bond. Unconditional; complete and perfect in itself; without relation to or dependence on other things or persons.

As to *absolute* Conveyance; Covenant; Delivery; Divorce; Estate; Gift; Guaranty; Interest; Legacy; Nuisance; Nullity; Obligation; Property; Right; Rule; Sale; Title, see those titles.

Absolute deed. A document of conveyance without restriction or defeasance; generally used in contradistinction to mortgage deed. *See* Deed.

Absolute law. The true and proper law of nature, immutable in the abstract or in principle, in theory, but not in application; for very often the object, the reason, situation, and other circumstances, may vary its exercise and obligation. *See also* Natural law.

Absolute liability. Responsibility without fault or negligence. Rylands v. Fletcher, 3 H.L. 330. *See* Strict liability.

Absolutely. Completely; wholly; without qualification; without reference or relation to, or dependence upon, any other person, thing, or event. Thus, *absolutely void* means utterly void; that which the law or nature of things forbids to be enforced at all. *Absolutely necessary* may be used to make the idea of necessity more emphatic. Independently or unconditionally, wholly or positively.

Absolutism /ǽbsəl(y)uwtìzəm/. In politics, a system of government in which public power is vested in some person or persons, unchecked and uncontrolled by any law, institution, constitutional device, or coordinate body. A government which is run by a dictator whose power is without restriction and without any checks or balances.

Absolve. To set free, or release, as from obligation, debt, or responsibility. *See also* Amnesty; Pardon; Release.

Absorption /əbzórpshən/. Act or process of absorbing. Term used in collective bargaining agreements to provide seniority for union members if employer's business is merged with another. Partial or complete payment of freight charges by seller or freight carrier. Costs not passed on to customer.

Absorption costing. In accounting, a cost accumulation and reporting method that treats the costs of all manufacturing components (direct materials, direct labor, variable overhead, and fixed overhead) as inventoriable or product cost. The traditional approach to product costing that must be used for external financial statements and tax returns.

Abstention doctrine. Doctrine of "abstention" permits a federal court, in the exercise of its discretion, to relinquish jurisdiction where necessary to avoid needless conflict with the administration by a state of its own affairs. *See also* Certification to state court; Equitable abstention doctrine; Pullman abstention.

Abstract /ǽbstrækt/, *n.* A lesser quantity containing the virtue and force of a greater quantity; an abridgment. A transcript is generally defined as a copy, and is more comprehensive than an abstract. Summary or epitome, or that which comprises or concentrates in itself the essential qualities of a larger thing or of several things. *See* Abridge; Abridgment; Digest; Headnote; Syllabus.

Abstract /əbstrǽkt/, *v.* To take or withdraw from; as, to abstract the funds of a bank. To remove or separate. To summarize or abridge.

Abstraction. Taking from with intent to injure or defraud. "Wrongful abstraction" is unauthorized and illegal taking or withdrawing of funds, etc., and appropriation thereof to taker's benefit.

Abstract of record. A complete history in short, abbreviated form of the case as found in the record, complete enough to show the appellate court that the questions presented for review have been properly reserved. Synopsis or summary of facts, rather than table of contents of transcript. Abbreviated accurate and authentic history of (*e.g.* trial court) proceedings.

Abstract of title. A condensed history of the title to land, consisting of a synopsis or summary of the material or operative portion of all the conveyances, of whatever kind or nature, which in any manner affect said land, or any estate or interest therein, together with a statement of all liens, charges, or liabilities to which the same may be subject, and of which it is in any way material for purchasers to be apprised. An epitome of the record evidence of title, including maps, plats, and other aids. *See also* Torrens title system.

Abstract question. One which does not rest upon existing facts or rights. Hypothetical question. *See also* Hypothetical question; Moot.

Absurdity. Anything which is so irrational, unnatural, or inconvenient that it cannot be supposed to have been within the intention of men of ordinary intelligence and discretion. Obviously and flatly opposed to the manifest truth; inconsistent with the plain dictates of common sense; logically contradictory; nonsensical; ridiculous.

Abuse /əbyúws/, *n.* Everything which is contrary to good order established by usage. Departure from reasonable use; immoderate or improper use. Physical or mental maltreatment. Misuse. Deception. To wrong in speech, reproach coarsely, disparage, revile, and malign. *See* Defamation.

Child abuse. *See* Battered child; Battered Child Syndrome; Child abuse.

Discretion. "Abuse of discretion" is synonymous with a failure to exercise a sound, reasonable, and legal discretion. It is a strict legal term indicating that appellate court is of opinion that there was commission of an error of law by the trial court. It does not imply intentional wrong or bad faith, or misconduct, nor any reflection on the judge but means the clearly erroneous conclusion and judgment—one is that clearly against logic and effect of such facts as are presented in support of the application or against the reasonable and probable deductions to be drawn from the facts disclosed upon the hearing; an improvident exercise of discretion; an error of law. Unreasonable departure from considered precedents and settled judicial custom, constituting error of law. A judgment or decision by an administrative agency or judge which has no foundation in fact or in law. "Abuse of discretion" by trial court is any unreasonable, unconscionable and arbitrary action taken without proper consideration of facts and law pertaining to matter submitted.

Drug abuse. See that title.

Female child. *See* Carnal abuse; Child abuse.

Power. Use of one who possesses it in a manner contrary to law. Improper use of power, distinguished from usurpation of power which presupposes exercise of power not vested in the offender.

Process. Misuse of criminal or civil proceedings against another. The gist of an action for "abuse of process" is improper use or perversion of process after it has been issued. A malicious abuse of legal process occurs where the party employs it for some unlawful object, not the purpose which it is intended by the law to effect. Fundamental elements of this tort are an ulterior purpose, and a willful act in the use of process not proper in the regular conduct of the proceeding. *See also* Malicious abuse of legal process; Malicious use of process.

Spousal abuse. *See* Battered Woman Syndrome.

Abuse /əbyúwz/, *v.* To make excessive or improper use of a thing, or to employ it in a manner contrary to the natural or legal rules for its use. To make an extravagant or excessive use, as to abuse one's authority.

Abusive. Tending to deceive; practicing abuse; prone to ill-treat by coarse, insulting words or harmful acts. Using ill treatment; injurious, improper, hurtful, offensive, reproachful.

Abut. To reach; to touch. To touch at the end; be contiguous; join at a border or boundary; terminate on; end at; border on; reach or touch with an end. The term "abutting" implies a closer proximity than the term "adjacent." No intervening land.

Abuttals /əbə́təlz/. The buttings or boundings of lands, showing to what other lands, highways, or places they belong or are abutting. It has been used to express the end boundary lines as distinguished from those on the sides, as "buttals and sidings".

Abutter. One whose property abuts, is contiguous, or joins at a border or boundary, as where no other land, road, or street intervenes.

Abutting owner. An owner of land which abuts or adjoins. The term usually implies that the relative parts actually adjoin, but is sometimes loosely used without implying more than close proximity. *See* Abut; Adjoining owners.

A.C. *Anno Christi*, the year of Christ.

A/C. Abbreviation used by accountants and bookkeepers meaning "account." As used in a check, it has been held not a direction to the bank to credit the amount of the check to the person named, but rather a memorandum to identify the transaction in which the check was issued.

Academic. Pertaining to college, university, or preparatory school. A question or issue which is not relevant to case or is premature or hypothetical. *See* Academic question; Moot case.

Academic freedom. Right to teach as one sees fit, but not necessarily the right to teach evil. The term encompasses much more than teaching-related speech rights of teachers.

Academic question. An issue which does not require answer or adjudication by court because it is not necessary to case. A hypothetical or moot question. *See* Hypothetical question; Moot case.

Academy. An institution of higher learning. An association of experts in some particular branch of art, literature, law, or science (*e.g.* American Academy of Matrimonial Lawyers). In its original meaning, an association formed for mutual improvement, or for the advancement of science or art; in later use, a species of educational institution, of a level between the elementary school and the college. In current usage, term commonly refers to private high school or one of the service academies (e. g. Air Force Academy).

Accede. To consent; agree.

Accelerated Cost Recovery System. (ACRS). An accounting method whereby the cost of a fixed asset is written off for tax purposes over a prescribed period of time. Instituted by the Economic Recovery Tax Act of 1981, and modified by Tax Reform Act of 1986, the system places assets into one of various recovery periods and prescribes the applicable percentage of cost that can be deducted each year. I.R.C. § 168. *See also* Asset Depreciation Range.

Accelerated depreciation. Various methods of depreciation that yield larger deductions in the earlier years of the life of an asset than the straight-line method. Examples include the double declining-balance and the sum of the years' digits methods of depreciation. *See* Accelerated Cost Recovery System; Depreciation.

Acceleration. The shortening of the time for the vesting in possession of an expectant interest. Hastening of the enjoyment of an estate which was otherwise postponed to a later period. If the life estate fails for any reason the remainder is "accelerated".

Doctrine of "acceleration", as applied to law of property, refers to hastening of owner of future interests toward status of present possession or enjoyment by reason of failure of preceding estate. A remedy used where there has been an anticipatory repudiation or a possibility of a future breach.

Acceleration clause. A provision or clause in a mortgage, note, bond, deed of trust, or other credit agreement, that requires the maker, drawer or other obligor to pay part or all of the balance sooner than the date or dates specified for payment upon the occurrence of some event or circumstance described in the contract. Such clause operates when there has been a default such as nonpayment of principal, interest, failure to pay insurance premiums, or unauthorized transfer. U.C.C. § 1–208 provides that if the provision for acceleration is "at will" such demand must be made only under a "good faith" belief that the prospect of payment is impaired.

Acceleration premium. Increased rate of pay for increased production.

Accept. To receive with approval or satisfaction; to receive with intent to retain. Admit and agree to; accede to or consent to; receive with approval; adopt; agree to. Means something more than to receive, meaning to adopt, to agree to carry out provisions, to keep and retain.

In the capacity of drawee of a bill, means to recognize the draft, and engage to pay it when due. *See* Acceptance.

Acceptance. The taking and receiving of anything in good part, and as it were a tacit agreement to a preceding act, which might have been defeated or avoided if such acceptance had not been made. The act of a person to whom a thing is offered or tendered by another, whereby he receives the thing with the intention of retaining it, such intention being evidenced by a sufficient act. The exercise of power conferred by an offer by performance of some act.

Commercial paper. Acceptance is the drawee's signed engagement to honor the draft as presented. It must be written on the draft, and may consist of his signature alone. It becomes operative when completed by delivery or notification. U.C.C. § 3–410. Certification of a check is acceptance. U.C.C. § 3–411. A draft may be accepted although it has not been signed by the drawer or is otherwise incomplete or is overdue or has been dishonored. U.C.C. § 3–410(2). *See also* Acceptor; Banker's acceptance; Honor.

Contracts. Compliance by offeree with terms and conditions of offer constitute an "acceptance". A

manifestation of assent to terms thereof made by offeree in a manner-invited or required by offer. The offeree's notification or expression to the offeror that he or she agrees to be bound by the terms of the offeror's proposal. A contract is thereby created. The trend is to allow acceptance by any means that will reasonably notify the offeror of the acceptance. *See also* Confirmation; Offer and acceptance.

Insurance. In a contract of insurance, the "acceptance" occurs when insurer agrees to accept application and to issue policy. Delay or inaction on the part of an insurer cannot constitute an "acceptance". More than mere mental resolution or determination on part of insurer to accept application is required; such must be communicated to applicant. Term as applied to policy means assent, acquiescence or agreement to terms and conditions of policy.

Sale of goods. U.C.C. § 2–606 provides three ways a buyer can accept goods: (1) by signifying to the seller that the goods are conforming or that he will accept them in spite of their nonconformity, (2) by failing to make an effective rejection, and (3) by doing an act inconsistent with the seller's ownership. Acceptance of a part of any commercial unit is acceptance of that entire unit.

Types of acceptance.

Conditional. An engagement to pay the draft or accept the offer on the happening of a condition. A "conditional acceptance" is in effect a statement that the offeree is willing to enter into a bargain differing in some respects from that proposed in the original offer. The conditional acceptance is, therefore, itself a counter offer.

Express. An undertaking in direct and express terms to perform the terms of the contract, pay the bill, draft, etc.; an absolute acceptance.

Implied. An undertaking to pay the draft inferred from acts of the drawee of a character which fairly warrant such an inference. In case of a bilateral contract, "acceptance" of an offer need not be expressed, but may be shown by any words or acts indicating the offeree's assent to the proposed bargain.

Qualified. One either conditional or partial, and which introduces a variation in the sum, mode, or place of payment. In contract law, an acceptance based on a variation of the terms of the offer and hence a counteroffer. In negotiable instruments, a variation in the terms of the instrument by the acceptor.

Acceptor. The person (the drawee) who accepts a draft and who engages to be primarily responsible for its payment. One who engages that he will pay the draft according to its tenor at the time of his engagement or as completed pursuant to authority on incomplete instruments. U.C.C. § 3–413.

Acceptor supra protest /əksépter s(y)úwprə prówtèst/. One who accepts a bill which has been protested, for the honor of the drawer or any one of the indorsers.

Access. Freedom of approach or communication; or the means, power, or opportunity of approaching, communicating, or passing to and from. Sometimes importing the occurrence of sexual intercourse; otherwise as importing opportunity of communication for that purpose as between husband and wife.

In real property law, the term denotes the right vested in the owner of land which adjoins a road or other highway to go and return from his own land to the highway without obstruction. "Access" to property does not necessarily carry with it possession. *See* Access, easement of.

For purposes of establishing element of access by defendant in copyright infringement action, "access" is ordinarily defined as opportunity to copy.

Multiple access. The defense of several lovers in paternity actions.

Public records. The right of access to public records includes not only a legal right of access but a reasonable opportunity to avail oneself of the same. *See* Freedom of Information Act.

Accessary. *See* Accessory.

Access, easement of /íyzmənt əv ǽkses/. An easement of access is the right which an abutting owner has of ingress to and egress from his premises, in addition to the public easement in the street.

Accession. Coming into possession of a right or office; increase; augmentation; addition.

The right to all which one's own property produces, whether that property be movable or immovable; and the right to that which is united to it by accession, either naturally or artificially. The right to own things that become a part of something already owned; *e.g.* riparian owners' right to abandoned river beds and rights of alluvion by accretion and reliction. *See* Accretion.

Acquisition of title to personal property by bestowing labor on it which converts it into an entirely different thing or by incorporation of property into a union with other property.

The commencement or inauguration of a sovereign's reign.

International law. The absolute or conditional acceptance by one or several nations of a treaty already concluded between other sovereignties. *See* Adhesion.

Accessions. Goods which are installed in or affixed to other goods. U.C.C. § 9–314(1). *See also* Fixture.

Accessory. Anything which is joined to another thing as an ornament, or to render it more perfect, or which accompanies it, or is connected with it as an incident, or as subordinate to it, or which belongs to or with it. Adjunct or accompaniment. A thing of subordinate importance. Aiding or contributing in secondary way or assisting in or contributing to as a subordinate.

Criminal law. Contributing to or aiding in the commission of a crime. One who, without being present at the commission of a felonious offense, becomes guilty of such offense, not as a chief actor, but as a participator, as by command, advice, instigation, or concealment; either before or after the fact or commission; a *particeps criminis.* Model Penal Code, § 2.06.

One who is not the chief actor in the offense, nor present at its performance, but in some way concerned therein, either *before or after* the act committed. One who aids, abets, commands, or counsels another in the commission of a crime. *See also* Abettor; Aid and abet; Accomplice.

Accessory after the fact. A person who, knowing a felony to have been committed by another, receives, relieves, comforts or assists the felon, in order to enable him to escape from punishment, or the like. 18 U.S.C.A. § 3. *See also* Harbor; Obstructing justice.

Accessory before the fact. One who orders, counsels, encourages, or otherwise aids and abets another to commit a felony and who is not present at the commission of the offense. The primary distinction between the accessory before the fact and the principal in the second degree is presence. Virtually all states have now expressly abrogated the distinction between principals and accessories before the fact; the latter now being classified as principals.

Accessory during the fact. One who stands by without interfering or giving such help as may be in his power to prevent the commission of a criminal offense.

Accessory building. Structures used for benefit of main building; *e.g.* tool shed. Out-buildings.

Accessory contract. An accessory contract is made for assuring the performance of a prior contract, either by the same parties or by others; such as suretyship, mortgage, and pledge.

Accessory obligation. An obligation which is incidental to another or principal obligation; *e.g.* the obligation of a surety.

Accessory use. With reference to zoning law, a use which is dependent on or pertains to principal or main use. A use which is subordinate to, clearly incidental to, customary in connection with, and ordinarily located on same lot with, principal use.

Access to counsel. Right of one to consult with his attorney as guaranteed by the 6th Amendment, U.S.Const. Geders v. U. S., 425 U.S. 80, 96 S.Ct. 1330, 47 L.Ed.2d 592. *See also* Assistance of counsel; Counsel, right to.

Access to courts. Right of person to require fair hearing from judiciary. *See* Fair and impartial trial.

Accident. The word "accident" is derived from the Latin verb "accidere" signifying "fall upon, befall, happen, chance." In an etymological sense anything that happens may be said to be an accident and in this sense, the word has been defined as befalling a change; a happening; an incident; an occurrence or event. In its most commonly accepted meaning, or in its ordinary or popular sense, the word may be defined as meaning: a fortuitous circumstance, event, or happening; an event happening without any human agency, or if happening wholly or partly through human agency, an event which under the circumstances is unusual and unexpected by the person to whom it happens; an unusual, fortuitous, unexpected, unforeseen or unlooked for event, happening or occurrence; an unusual or unexpected result attending the operation or performance of a usual or necessary act or event; chance or contingency; fortune; mishap; some sudden and unexpected event taking place without expectation, upon the instant, rather than something which continues, progresses or develops; something happening by chance; something unforeseen, unexpected, unusual, extraordinary or phenomenal, taking place not according to the usual course of things or events, out of the range of ordinary calculations; that which exists or occurs abnormally, or an uncommon occurrence. The word may be employed as denoting a calamity, casualty, catastrophe, disaster, an undesirable or unfortunate happening; any unexpected personal injury resulting from any unlooked for mishap or occurrence; any unpleasant or unfortunate occurrence, that causes injury, loss, suffering or death; some untoward occurrence aside from the usual course of events. An event that takes place without one's foresight or expectation; an undesigned, sudden, and unexpected event. *See also* Act of God; Casualty; Inevitable accident; Unavoidable accident.

Its synonyms are chance, contingency, mishap, mischance, misfortune, disaster, calamity, catastrophe.

Insurance contract. An accident within accident insurance policies is an event happening without any human agency, or, if happening through such agency, an event which, under circumstances, is unusual and not expected by the person to whom it happens. A more comprehensive term than "negligence," and in its common signification the word means an unexpected happening without intention or design.

Maritime law. "Accidents of navigation" or "accidents of the sea" are such as are peculiar to the sea or to usual navigation or the action of the elements, which do not happen by the intervention of man, and are not to be avoided by the exercise of proper prudence, foresight, and skill. *See also* Perils of the sea.

Unavoidable accident. One which is not occasioned in any degree, either directly or remotely, by the want of such care and prudence as the law holds every man bound to exercise. One which could not have been prevented by exercise of due care by both parties under circumstances prevailing. One which occurs while all persons concerned are exercising ordinary care, which is not caused by fault of any of persons and which could not have been prevented by any means suggested by common prudence. See Restatement, Second, Torts § 8. *See also* Unavoidable accident.

Workers' compensation acts. Within meaning of Worker's Compensation Act is any unforeseen, untoward happening which was not to be reasonably anticipated.

Accident policy. Type of business and personal insurance coverage that insures against loss resulting directly from bodily injuries effected during the term of the policy solely through accidental means.

Accidental cause. That which produces result which is not foreseen; producing an unexpected effect.

Accidental death. One caused by unexpected or unintended means.

Accidental death benefit. Provision in insurance policy encompassing death caused by sudden, unexpected, external force.

Accidental killing. One resulting from an act which is lawful and lawfully done under a reasonable belief that no harm is possible; distinguished from "involuntary manslaughter," which is the result of an unlawful act, or of a lawful act done in an unlawful way.

Accidental means. Injury resulting from unintended, unforseeable, and unexpected cause.

Accident proneness. Tendency towards being involved in or contributing to accidents.

Accommodated party. One to whom the credit of the accommodation party is loaned, and is not necessarily the payee, since the inquiry always is as to whom did the maker of the paper loan his credit as a matter of fact; not third person who may receive advantage. *See also* Accommodation party.

Accommodation /əkòmədéyshən/. An arrangement or engagement made as a favor to another, not upon a consideration received. Something done to oblige, usually spoken of a loan of money or commercial paper; also a friendly agreement or composition of differences. The word implies no consideration. While a party's intent may be to aid a maker of note by lending his credit, if he seeks to accomplish thereby legitimate objects of his own, and not simply to aid maker, the act is not for accommodation. *See* Accommodation maker.

Accommodation bill *or* **note.** *See* Accommodation note or paper.

Accommodation indorsement. *See* Indorsement.

Accommodation indorser. A party who places his name to a note without consideration for purpose of benefiting or accommodating some other party. U.C.C. § 3–415. *See also* Indorsement.

Accommodation lands. Land bought by a builder or speculator, who erects houses thereon, and then leases portions thereof upon an improved ground-rent.

Accommodation line. Insurance policies accepted by insurer because agent or brokers account in general is satisfactory, even though specific policy would otherwise likely not be acceptable.

Accommodation loan. Loan furnished as an act of friendship or assistance without tangible or full consideration; money or credit extended for such reasons.

Accommodation maker. One who puts his name to a note without any consideration with the intention of lending his credit to the accommodated party. U.C.C. § 3–415. *See also* Accommodation party.

Accommodation note or paper. One to which accommodating party has put his name, without consideration, to accommodate some other party, who is to issue it and is expected to pay it. U.C.C. § 3–415.

An accommodation bill or note is one to which the accommodating party, be he acceptor, drawer, or indorser, has put his name, without consideration, for the purpose of benefiting or accommodating some other party who desires to raise money on it, and is to provide for the bill when due.

Accommodation party. One who signs commercial paper in any capacity for purpose of lending his name (*i.e.* credit) to another party to instrument. U.C.C. § 3–415. Such party is a surety.

Accommodation road. A road opened for benefit of certain individuals to go from and to their homes, for service of their lands, and for use of some estates exclusively. *See also* Easement.

Accompany. To go along with. To go with or attend as a companion or associate. To occur in association with.

Accomplice /əkómpləs/. One who knowingly, voluntarily and with common intent unites with the principal offender in the commission of a crime. One who is in some way concerned or associated in commission of crime; partaker of guilt; one who aids or assists, or is an accessory. Model Penal Code, § 2.06(3). Person is liable as an accomplice to the crime of another if he gave assistance or encouragement or failed to perform a legal duty to prevent it with the intent thereby to promote or facilitate commission of the crime. *See also* Abet; Aid and abet; Accessory.

Accomplice liability. Criminal responsibility of one who acts with another before, during or after the perpetration of a crime. Model Penal Code, § 2.06.

Accomplice witness. A person who either as principal, accomplice, or accessory, was connected with crime by unlawful act or omission on his part, transpiring either before, at time of, or after commission of offense, and whether or not he was present and participated in crime.

Accord, *n.* An agreement between two persons, one of whom has a right of action against the other, to settle the dispute. In a debtor/creditor relationship, an agreement between the parties to settle a dispute for some partial payment. It is called an accord because the creditor has a right of action against the debtor. A satisfaction agreed upon between the party injuring and the party injured which, when performed, is a bar to all actions upon this account. *See* Accord and satisfaction; Compromise and settlement; Executory accord; Satisfaction; Settlement.

Accord, *v.* In practice, to agree or concur, as one judge with another. In agreement with. *See* Concur; Concurring opinion.

Accordance. Agreement; harmony; concord; conformity.

Accord and satisfaction. A method of discharging a claim whereby the parties agree to give and accept something in settlement of the claim and perform the agreement, the "accord" being the agreement and the "satisfaction" its execution or performance, and it is a new contract substituted for an old contract which is thereby discharged, or for an obligation or cause of action which is settled, and must have all of the elements of a valid contract.

Accord and satisfaction may also arise in a criminal case. In some jurisdictions, novation is a species of accord and satisfaction.

See Compromise and settlement; Novation; Satisfaction; Settlement.

Affirmative defense. A defense which must be pleaded affirmatively in the defendant's answer. Fed.R.Civ.P. 8(c).

Accord executory. A bilateral agreement of settlement which has not yet been performed (satisfied). Restatement, Second, Contracts, § 281.

Account. A detailed statement of the mutual demands in the nature of debit and credit between parties, arising out of contracts or some fiduciary relation. A statement in writing, of debits and credits, or of receipts and payments; a list of items of debits and credits, with their respective dates. A statement of pecuniary transactions; a record or course of business dealings between parties; a list or statement of monetary transactions, such as payments, losses, sales, debits, credits, accounts payable, accounts receivable, etc., in most cases showing a balance or result of comparison between items of an opposite nature.

See also Accumulated adjustments account; Aging of accounts; Blocked account; Charge account; Community account; Custody account; Contra account; Escrow account; Impound account; Intermediate account; Ledger; Liquidated account; Long account; Margin account; Nominal account; Stated account; Statement of account. For Open account, *see* Open.

Account annexed. Form of simplified statement used in pleading a common count (*e.g.* money had and received) impliedly authorized for use under Fed.R.Civil P. 8(a)(2).

Account balance. Difference between debit and credit sides of an account.

Account debtor. Person who is obligated on an account, chattel paper or general intangible. U.C.C. § 9–105(1)(a).

Account payable. A debt, owed by an enterprise, that arises in the normal course of business dealings and has not been replaced by a note payable of a debtor. For example, bills for materials received but not yet paid. A liability representing an amount owed to a creditor, usually arising from purchase of merchandise or materials and supplies; not necessarily due or past due.

Account receivable. A debt, owed to an enterprise, that arises in the normal course of business dealings and is not supported by negotiable paper. For example, the charge accounts of a department store. But income due from investments (unless investments are the business itself) is not usually shown in accounts receivable. A claim against a debtor usually arising from sales or services rendered; not necessarily due or past due. For accounts receivable insurance, *see* Insurance.

Account rendered. An account made out by the creditor, and presented to the debtor for his examination and acceptance. When accepted, it becomes an account stated.

Account settled. One in which the balance has been in fact paid, thereby differing from an account stated.

Account stated. An agreed balance between parties to a settlement.

Adjunct account. An account that accumulates additions to another account.

Bank account. See Bank.

Book account. See Book.

Closed account. An account to which no further additions can be made on either side, but which remains still open for adjustment and set-off, which distinguishes it from an account stated.

Commercial transactions. In the check collection process, "any account with a bank and includes a checking, time, interest or savings account." U.C.C. § 4–104(1)(a). In secured transactions law, "any right to payment for goods sold or leased or for services rendered which is not evidenced by an instrument or chattel paper, whether or not it has been earned by performance," including ordinary accounts receivable and rights under a ship charter, U.C.C. § 9–106, and also the right to proceeds of a letter of credit. U.C.C. § 5–116(2).

Contra account. An account which serves to reduce the gross valuation of an asset, also known as a valuation allowance. For example, accumulated depreciation serves as a valuation allowance for machinery and equipment. Contrast with *adjunct account, above.*

Control account. A general ledger account that is composed of various subsidiary ledger accounts.

Current account. An open or running or unsettled account between two parties; the antithesis of an account stated.

Mutual accounts. Accounts comprising mutual credits between the parties; or an existing credit on one side which constitutes a ground for credit on the other, or where there is an understanding that mutual debts shall be a satisfaction or set-off *pro tanto* between the parties. A "mutual account" arises when there are items debited and credited on both sides of the account which indicate mutual transactions between the parties.

Open account. An account which has not been finally settled or closed, but is still running or open to future adjustment or liquidation. Open account, in legal as well as in ordinary language, means an indebtedness subject to future adjustment, and which may be reduced or modified by proof.

Real accounts. Accounts whose balances are carried forward from period to period.

Account, *or* **account render.** "Account," sometimes called "account render," was a form of action at common law against a person who by reason of some fiduciary relation (as guardian, bailiff, receiver, etc.) was bound to render an account to another, but refused to do so.

Accountability. State of being responsible or answerable. *See also* Liability.

Accountable. Subject to pay; responsible; liable.

Accountable receipt. An instrument acknowledging the receipt of money or personal property, coupled with an obligation.

Accountant. Person who works in field of accounting and is skilled in keeping books or accounts; in designing and controlling systems of account; in giving tax advice and preparing tax returns.

An accountant authorized under applicable law to practice public accounting, and includes professional accounting association, corporation, or partnership, if so authorized. Bankruptcy Code, § 101.

Certified Public Accountant (CPA). An accountant who has satisfied the statutory and administrative requirements of his or her jurisdiction to be registered or licensed as a public accountant. In addition to passing the Uniform CPA Examination administered by the AICPA, the CPA must meet certain business experience, educational and moral requirements that differ from jurisdiction to jurisdiction. *See also* Auditor.

Cost accountant. See Cost.

Accountant-client privilege. Protection afforded to client from unauthorized disclosure by accountant of materials submitted to or prepared by accountant. *See also* Privileged communications.

Accountant's lien. Possessory right of accountant to papers prepared by him and held until payment is made for his services.

Account book. A book kept by a merchant, trader, professional, or other person, in which are entered from time to time the transactions of his trade, business, or profession. Entries made therein are admissible in evidence as exception to hearsay rule under certain conditions. Fed. Evid.R. 803.

Account for. To pay over to the person entitled thereto. To furnish substantial reasons or convincing explanation, make clear or reveal basic causes.

Accounting. An act or a system of making up or settling accounts, consisting of a statement of account with debits and credits arising from relationship of parties. Rendition of an account, either voluntarily or by order of a court. In the latter case, it imports a rendition of a judgment for the balance ascertained to be due. The term may include payment of the amount due.

In partnership law, is equitable proceeding for a complete settlement of all partnership affairs.

Accounting methods. The methods under which income and expenses are determined for tax purposes. Major accounting methods are the cash basis and the accrual basis. Special methods are available for the reporting of gain on installment sales, recognition of income on construction projects (*i.e.*, the completed-contract and percentage-of-completion methods), and the valuation of inventories (*i.e.* last-in first-out and first-in first-out). The various types of accounting methods appear below:

Accrual method. A method of keeping accounts which shows expenses incurred and income earned for a given period, although such expenses and income may not have been actually paid or received. Right to receive and not the actual receipt determines inclusion of amount in gross income. When right to receive an amount becomes fixed, right accrues. Obligations payable to or by taxpayer are treated as if discharged when incurred. Entries are made of credits and debits when liability arises, whether received or disbursed. *See also* Accrual basis; Accrue *(Taxation)*.

Cash method. The practice of recording income and expense only when cash is received or paid out; used in contradistinction to accrual method. *See* Cash basis accounting.

Completed contract method. A method of reporting profit or loss on certain long-term contracts. Under this method of accounting, gross income and expenses are recognized in the tax year in which the contract is completed. This method should be used only when the conditions or terms of the contract do not permit use of the percent of completion method.

Cost method. The practice of recording the value of assets in terms of their cost. *See also* Cost *(Cost accounting)*.

Fair value method. Valuation of assets at present value, meaning same as actual value or market value.

Flow through method. Type of calculation of depreciation used by regulated utilities for income tax purposes.

Historical-cost method. A method of accounting for short-term debt investments by which securities are initially recorded and subsequently maintained at cost.

Installment method. Procedure applied in reflecting collection of sales price in installments.

Price level accounting. Modern method of valuing assets in a financial statement which requires use of gross national product to reflect current values. *See also* Change in accounting method.

Realized value approach. A method of accounting for by-products or scrap that does not recognize any value for these products until they are sold.

The value recognized upon sale can be treated as other revenue or other income.

See also Absorption costing; Capitalization accounting method; Cash basis accounting; Change in accounting method; Direct costing; Financial accounting; Generally Accepted Accounting Principles; Generally Accepted Auditing Standards; Installment method; Interim statements; Percentage of completion method; Public accounting; Purchase method of accounting; Retail method; T–account; Transactions approach; Trial *(Trial balance)*.

Accounting for profits. Action for equitable relief against one in a fiduciary relation to recover profits taken in breach of relation.

Accounting period. The period of time, usually a year, used by a taxpayer in the determination of income and related tax liability. Unless a fiscal year is chosen, taxpayers must determine and pay their income tax liability by using the calendar year (*i.e.,* January 1 through December 31) as the period of measurement. An example of a fiscal year is July 1 through June 30. A change in accounting periods (*e.g.,* from a calendar year to a fiscal year) generally requires the consent of the Internal Revenue Service. Some new taxpayers, such as a newly formed corporation, are free to select either an initial calendar or a fiscal year without the consent of the Internal Revenue Service. *See* Annual accounting period concept; Fiscal year.

Accounting Research Bulletin (ARB). Statement on recommended accounting procedures issued by the American Institute of Certified Public Accountants' Committee on Accounting Procedure.

Accounting Series Release (ASR). The official pronouncements issued by the Securities and Exchange Commission to clarify accounting and auditing procedures to be followed in reports filed with the SEC.

Account in trust. Account established by an individual to be held in trust for the benefit of another.

Account party. The customer in a letter of credit transaction. Synonymous also with "applicant."

Account payable. *See* Account.

Account receivable. *See* Account.

Accounts receivable insurance. Insurance against loss due to inability to collect outstanding accounts receivable because of damage to or destruction of records.

Accounts receivable turnover. In accounting, an activity ratio that shows the number of times each year a company's receivables turn into cash; computed by dividing net credit sales by average accounts receivable.

Account stated. An agreed balance between parties to a settlement. *See also* Account.

Accredit /əkrédət/. To give official authorization or status. To recognize as having sufficient academic standards to qualify graduates for higher education or for professional practice. In international law: (1) To acknowledge; to receive as an envoy in his public character, and give him credit and rank accordingly. (2) To send with credentials as an envoy. This latter use is now the accepted one.

Accredited law school. Law school which has been approved by the state and the Association of American Law Schools and/or the American Bar Association. In certain states (*e.g.* Calif.) a law school might be accredited by the state, but not by either the AALS or ABA. In most states only graduates of AALS or ABA accredited law schools are permitted to take the state bar exam.

Accredited representative. As respects service of process, representative having general authority to act.

Accretion /əkríyshən/. The act of growing to a thing; usually applied to the gradual and imperceptible accumulation of land by natural causes, as out of the sea or a river.

Civil law. The right of heirs or legatees to unite or aggregate with their shares or portions of the estate the portion of any co-heir or legatee who refuses to accept it, fails to comply with a condition, becomes incapacitated to inherit, or dies before, the testator.

Land. Addition of portions of soil, by gradual deposition through the operation of natural causes, to that already in possession of owner. Accretion of land is of two kinds: By *alluvion, i.e.,* by the washing up of sand or soil, so as to form firm ground; or by *dereliction,* as when the sea shrinks below the usual water-mark. The term "alluvion" is applied to deposit itself, while "accretion" denotes the act. However, the terms are frequently used synonymously. Land uncovered by gradual subsidence of water is not an "accretion" but a "reliction".

Trust property. Receipts other than those ordinarily considered as income.

See Accrue; Alluvion; Avulsion; Reliction.

Accroach. To encroach; to exercise power without authority.

Accrocher /ækrowshéy/. Fr. To delay; retard; put off. *Accrocher un proces,* to stay the proceedings in a suit.

Accrual accounting. *See* Accounting methods.

Accrual basis. A method of accounting that reflects expenses incurred and income earned for any one tax year. In contrast to the cash basis of accounting, expenses do not have to be paid to be deductible nor does income have to be received to be taxable. Unearned income (e. g., prepaid interest and rent) generally is taxed in the year of receipt regardless of the method of accounting used by the taxpayer. *See* Accounting methods.

Accrual, clause of. *See* Accruer, clause of.

Accrual method of accounting. *See* Accounting methods.

Accrue /əkrúw/. Derived from the Latin, "ad" and "creso," to grow to. In past tense, in sense of due and payable; vested. It means to increase; to augment; to come to by way of increase; to be added as an increase, profit, or damage. Acquired; falling due; made or executed; matured; occurred; received; vested; was created; was incurred. To attach itself to, as a subordinate or accessory claim or demand arises out of, and is joined to, its principal.

The term is also used of independent or original demands, meaning to arise, to happen, to come into force or existence; to vest, as in the phrase, "The right of action did not *accrue* within six years." Amy v. Dubuque, 98 U.S. 470, 476, 25 L.Ed. 228. To become a present right or demand; to come to pass. *See also* Vested.

Cause of action. A cause of action "accrues" when a suit may be maintained thereon, and the law in this regard differs from state-to-state and by nature of action (*e.g.* type of breach of contract, tort, etc.). The point in time at which a cause of action "accrues" is important for purposes of running of statute of limitations.

Taxation. Income "accrues" to taxpayer when there arises to him a fixed or unconditional right to receive it. Where taxpayer makes returns on accrual basis, item "accrues" when all events occur which fix amount payable and determine liability of taxpayer.

Accrued alimony. Alimony which is due but not yet paid.

Accrued compensation. Compensation earned but not yet paid.

Accrued depreciation. Formerly called accumulated depreciation. An accumulation of charges made over a period of time for the replacement of a fixed asset. The portion of the useful service life which for tax and financial statement purposes has expired. A loss which is not restored by current maintenance, and which is due to all factors involved causing ultimate retirement of the property, including wear, tear, decay, and inadequacy. *See also* Depreciation *(Accumulated depreciation).*

Accrued dividend. A share of net earnings declared but not yet paid as a dividend.

Accrued expense. Expense incurred but not yet billed for nor paid.

Accrued income. Income which is earned but not yet billed and receivable.

Accrued interest. Interest that has been earned but is not yet received nor receivable.

Accrued liability. An obligation or debt which is properly chargeable in a given accounting period but which is not yet paid or payable.

Accrued right. A matured cause of action, as legal authority to demand redress. *See* Accrue *(Cause of action).*

Accrued salary. Compensation to employee which is incurred by an employer but not yet payable.

Accrued taxes. Taxes which are properly incurred in a given accounting period but not yet paid or payable.

Accruer (*or* **accrual**), **clause of.** An express clause, frequently occurring in the case of gifts by deed or will to persons as tenants in common, providing that upon the death of one or more of the beneficiaries his or their shares shall go to the survivor or survivors. The share of the decedent is then said to *accrue* to the others.

Accruing /əkrúwiŋ/. Inchoate; in process of maturing. That which will or may, at a future time, ripen into a vested right, an available demand, or an existing cause of action. Arising by way of increase or augmentation.

Accounting. Allocation of income and expense, which has been earned or incurred but not yet collected or paid out, to the accounting period in which the income is earned or expense incurred. *See* Accounting methods.

Accruing costs. Costs and expenses incurred after judgment.

Accruing interest. Running or accumulating interest, as distinguished from accrued or matured interest. Interest accumulating daily on the principal debt but not yet paid and payable.

Accruing right. One that is increasing, enlarging, or augmenting.

Acct. Abbreviation for "account", of such universal and immemorial use that the courts will take judicial notice of its meaning.

Accumulated adjustments account. An account that comprises an S corporation's post–1982 income, loss, and deductions for the tax year (including nontaxable income and nondeductible losses and expenses). After the year-end income and expense adjustments are made, the account is reduced by distributions made during the tax year.

Accumulated depreciation. *See* Accrued depreciation.

Accumulated dividend. Dividend due shareholder which has not been paid. *See* Accumulative dividends; Dividend *(Cumulative)*.

Accumulated earnings credit. A deduction allowed in arriving at accumulated taxable income for purposes of determining the accumulated earnings tax. *See* Accumulated earnings tax; Accumulated taxable income.

Accumulated earnings tax. A special tax imposed on corporations that accumulate (rather than distribute via dividends) their earnings beyond the reasonable needs of the business. The accumulated earnings tax is imposed on accumulated taxable income in addition to the corporate income tax. I.R.C. § 531 et seq. *See also* Accumulated taxable income; Excess profits tax.

Accumulated legacy. Portion of distributable estate not yet paid to legatees or donees.

Accumulated profits. Earned surplus or undivided profits. Such include profits earned and invested.

Accumulated surplus. In statutes relative to the taxation of corporations, this term refers to the fund which the company has in excess of its capital and liabilities. *See* Retained earnings.

Accumulated taxable income. The base upon which the accumulated earnings tax is imposed. Basically, it is the taxable income of the corporation as adjusted for certain items (*e.g.*, the Federal income tax, excess charitable contributions, the dividends received deduction) less the dividends paid deduction and the accumulated earnings credit. I.R.C. § 535. *See* Accumulated earnings tax.

Accumulations /əkyùmyəléyshənz/. Increase by continuous or repeated additions, or, if taken literally, means either profit accruing on sale of principal assets, or increase derived from their investment, or both. Adding of interest or income of a fund to principal pursuant to provisions of a will or deed, preventing its being expended.

Accumulations, rule against. A rule rendering an accumulation of income beyond the period of perpetuities void.

Accumulation trust. A trust in which the trustee is directed to accumulate income for a period of time before distribution. *See also* Trust *(Discretionary trust)*.

Accumulative. That which accumulates, or is heaped up; additional. Said of several things joined together, or of one thing added to another.

Accumulative dividends. Same as cumulative dividends; characteristic of preferred stockholders' agreement by which they receive their agreed dividends before common stockholders. Dividends which accumulate from year to year when not paid. *See* Dividend *(Cumulative)*.

Accumulative judgment. Where a person has already been convicted and sentenced, and a second or additional judgment is passed against him, the execution of which is postponed until the completion of the first sentence, such second judgment is said to be *accumulative*. *See also* Accumulative sentence.

Accumulative legacy. A second, double or additional legacy; a legacy given in addition to another given by the same instrument, or by another instrument. *See also* Legacy.

Accumulative sentence. A sentence, additional to others, imposed on a defendant who has been convicted upon an indictment containing several counts, each of such counts charging a distinct offense, or who is under conviction at the same time for several distinct offenses; one of such sentences to begin at the expiration of another. Consecutive sentences. *See* Sentence.

Accusation /æ̀kyəzéyshən/. A formal charge against a person, to the effect that he is guilty of a punishable offense, laid before a court or magistrate having jurisdiction to inquire into the alleged crime. *See* Accuse; Indictment; Information.

Accusatory body. Body such as grand jury whose duty is to hear evidence to determine whether a person should be accused (charged) of a crime; to be distinguished from a traverse or petit jury which is charged with duty of determining guilt or innocence.

Accusatory instrument. A document in which an accusation of crime is set forth like an indictment, information or complaint.

Accusatory part. The "accusatory part" of an indictment is that part where the offense is named.

Accusatory pleading. An indictment or complaint in which a person is accused of crime and on which the government tries such person. Fed. R.Crim.P. 3.

Accusatory procedure. System of American jurisprudence in which the government accuses and bears the burden of proving the guilt of a person for a crime; to be distinguished from inquisitorial system.

Accusatory stage. That stage of criminal proceedings at which right to counsel accrues to accused; such matures when officers have arrested accused, and officers have undertaken process of interrogations that lends itself to eliciting incriminating statements.

Accuse. To bring a formal charge against a person, to the effect that he is guilty of a crime or punishable offense, before a court or magistrate having jurisdiction to inquire into the alleged crime. *See also* Indictment; Information.

Accused. The generic name for the defendant in a criminal case. Person becomes "accused" within meaning of guarantee of speedy trial only at point at which either formal indictment or information has been returned against him, or when he becomes subject to actual restraints on his liberty imposed by arrest, whichever first occurs.

Accuser. The person by whom an accusation is made (*e.g.* State or United States in criminal proceedings). A person who signs and swears to charges, directs charges be brought, or has interest other than official in prosecution of accused.

Accustomed. Habitual; often used; synonymous with usual or customary.

Acid ratio test. Method of financial analysis involving ratio of cash and receivables to current liabilities. Sum of cash, marketable securities, and receivables divided by current liabilities. Also called the "quick ratio."

Acknowledgment. To admit, affirm, declare, testify, avow, confess, or own as genuine. Admission or affirmation of obligation or responsibility. Most states have adopted the Uniform Acknowledgment Act. *See also* Receipt.

Debt. The debtor's acknowledgment of the creditor's demand or right of action that will revive the enforceability of a debt barred by the statute of limitations. Part payment of obligation which tolls statute of limitations is a form of "acknowledgment of debt".

Instruments. Formal declaration before authorized official, by person who executed instrument, that it is his free act and deed. The certificate of the officer on such instrument that it has been so acknowledged. *See also* Attestation clause; Certificate of acknowledgment; Jurat; Notary public; Verification.

Paternity. An avowal or admission that the child is one's own. Recognition of a parental relation, either by a written agreement, verbal declarations or statements, by the life, acts, and conduct of the parties, or any other satisfactory evidence that the relation was recognized and admitted.

A.C.L.U. American Civil Liberties Union.

Acquainted. Having personal, familiar, knowledge of a person, event, or thing. To be "personally acquainted with," and to "know personally," are equivalent terms. When used with reference to a paper to which a certificate or affidavit is attached, it indicates a substantial knowledge of the subject-matter thereof.

Acquest /əkwést/. An estate acquired newly, or by purchase.

Acquêts /àkéy/. In the civil law, property which has been acquired by purchase, gift, or otherwise than by succession. Immovable property which has been acquired otherwise than by succession. Profits or gains of property, as between husband and wife. Civil Code La. art. 2338. The profits of all the effects of which the husband has the administration and enjoyment, either of right or in fact, of the produce of the joint industry of both husband and wife, and of the estates which they may acquire during the marriage, either by donations made jointly to them both, or by purchase, or in any other similar way, even though the purchase be only in the name of one of the two, and not of both. *See* Community property.

Acquiesce /æ̀kwiyés/. To give an implied consent to a transaction, to the accrual of a right, or to any act, by one's mere silence, or without express assent or acknowledgment.

Acquiescence /æ̀kwiyésəns/. Conduct recognizing the existence of a transaction, and intended, in some extent at least, to carry the transaction, or permit it to be carried, into effect. Passive compliance or satisfaction; distinguished from avowed consent on the one hand, and, on the other, from opposition or open discontent. Conduct from which assent may be reasonably inferred. Equivalent to assent inferred from silence with knowledge or from encouragement and presupposes knowledge and assent. Imports tacit consent, concurrence, acceptance or assent.

Acquiescence and *laches* are cognate but not equivalent terms. The former is a submission to, or resting satisfied with, an existing state of things, while laches implies a neglect to do that which the party ought to do for his own benefit or protection. Hence laches may be evidence of acquiescence. Laches imports a merely passive assent, while acquiescence implies active assent. "Acquiescence" relates to inaction during performance of an act while "laches" relates to delay after act is done.

See also Admission; Confession; Estoppel; Nonacquiescence; Ratification.

Administrative agencies. An administrative agency's policy of agreeing to be bound by judicial precedent which is contrary to the agency's interpretation of its organic statute. *Compare* Nonacquiescence.

Agreement by the IRS on the results reached in most of the regular decisions of the U.S. Tax Court; sometimes abbreviated *acq.* or *A.*

Acquiescence, estoppel by. Acquiescence is a species of estoppel. An estoppel arises where party aware of his rights sees other party acting upon mistaken notion of his rights. Injury accruing from one's acquiescence in another's action to his prejudice creates "estoppel". *See also* Estoppel.

Acquire. To gain by any means, usually by one's own exertions; to get as one's own; to obtain by search, endeavor, investment, practice, or purchase; receive or gain in whatever manner; come to have. In law of contracts and of descents, to become owner of property; to make property one's own; to gain ownership of. Sometimes used in the sense of "procure." It does not necessarily mean that title has passed. Includes taking by devise. *See also* Accession; Acquisition; Purchase.

Acquired rights. Those which one does not naturally enjoy, but which are owing to his or her own procurement, as sovereignty, or the right of commanding, or the right of property.

Acquired surplus. Surplus arising from changes of the capital structure of one or more businesses; *e.g.* from the purchase of one business by another business.

Acquisition /ǽkwəzíshən/. The act of becoming the owner of certain property; the act by which one acquires or procures the property in anything. Used also of the thing acquired. *See* Accession; Acquire; Corporate acquisition; Purchase; Tender offer.

Derivative acquisitions are those which are procured from others. Goods and chattels may change owners by act of law in the cases of forfeiture, succession, marriage, judgment, insolvency, and intestacy; or by act of the parties, as by gift or sale.

Original acquisition is that by which a man secures a property in a thing which is not at the time he acquires it, and in its then existing condition, the property of any other individual. It may result from occupancy; accession; intellectual labor—namely, for inventions, which are secured by patent rights; and for the authorship of books, maps, and charts, which is protected by copyrights.

Acquisitive offenses. A generic term to describe all forms of larceny and offenses against the title or possession of property.

Acquit /əkwít/. To set free, release or discharge as from an obligation, burden or accusation. To absolve one from an obligation or a liability; or to legally certify the innocence of one charged with crime. *See also* Acquittal.

Acquittal /əkwítəl/. *Contracts.* A release, absolution, or discharge from an obligation, liability, or engagement.

Criminal law. The legal and formal certification of the innocence of a person who has been charged with crime; a deliverance or setting free a person from a charge of guilt; finding of not guilty. Also, one legally acquitted by a judgment rendered otherwise than in pursuance of a verdict, as where he is discharged by a magistrate because of the insufficiency of the evidence, or the indictment is dismissed by the court or a *nol. pros.* entered. Or, it may occur even though the question of guilt or innocence has never been submitted to a jury, as where a defendant, having been held under an indictment or information, is discharged because not brought to trial within the time provided by statute.

Acquittals in fact are those which take place when the jury, upon trial, finds a verdict of not guilty.

Acquittals in law are those which take place by mere operation of law; as where a man has been charged merely as an accessory, and the principal has been acquitted.

See Autrefois acquit; Jeopardy; Nolle prosequi; Verdict.

Acquittance /əkwítəns/. A written discharge, whereby one is freed from an obligation to pay money or perform a duty. This word, though perhaps not strictly speaking synonymous with "receipt," includes it. A receipt is one form of an acquittance; a discharge is another. A receipt in full is an acquittance, and a receipt for a part of a demand or obligation is an acquittance *pro tanto.*

Acquitted /əkwítəd/. Released; absolved; purged of an accusation. Judicially discharged from accusation; released from debt, etc. Includes both civil and criminal prosecutions. *See* Acquittal.

Acre. A quantity of land containing 160 square rods, 4,840 square yards, or 43,560 square feet of land, in whatever shape. *See* Land measure.

Net acre. The amount of actual acreage that may be used for building lots after installation of streets, sidewalks, etc.

Acre foot. 325,850 gallons, or the amount of water which will cover one acre one foot in depth.

ACRS. *See* Accelerated Cost Recovery System.

Act, *n.* Denotes external manifestation of actor's will. Restatement, Second, Torts § 2. Expression of will or purpose, carrying idea of performance; primarily that which is done or doing; exercise of power, or effect of which power exerted is cause; a performance; a deed. In its most general sense, this noun signifies something done voluntarily by a person; the exercise of an individual's power; an effect produced in the external world by an exercise of the power of a person objectively, prompted by intention, and proximately caused by a motion of the will. In a more technical sense, it means something done voluntarily by a person, and of such a nature that certain legal consequences attach to it. Thus a grantor acknowledges the conveyance to be his "act and deed," the terms being synonymous. It may denote something done by an individual, as a private citizen, or as an officer; or by a body of men, as a legislature, a council, or a court of justice; including not merely physical acts, but also decrees, edicts, laws, judgments, resolves, awards, and determinations. Some general laws made by the Congress of the United States are styled joint resolutions, and these have the same force and effect as those styled acts.

Acts under private signature are those which have been made by private individuals under their hands.

Criminal act. External manifestation of one's will which is prerequisite to criminal responsibility. There can be no crime without some act, affirmative or negative. An omission or failure to act may constitute an act for purpose of criminal law.

Legislative act. An alternative name for statutory law. A bill which has been enacted by legislature into law. When introduced into the first house of the legislature, a piece of proposed legislation is known as a bill. When passed to the next house, it may then be referred to as an act. After enactment the terms "law" and "act" may be used interchangeably. An act has the same legislative force as a joint resolution but is technically distinguishable, being of a different form and introduced with the words "Be it enacted" instead of "Be it resolved."

Acts are either public or private. Public acts (also called general acts, or general statutes, or statutes at large) are those which relate to the community generally, or establish a universal rule for the governance of the whole body politic. Private acts (formerly called special), are those which relate either to particular persons (personal acts) or to particular places (local acts), or which operate only upon specified individuals or their private concerns. Public acts are those which concern the whole community and of which courts of law are bound to take judicial notice.

A "special" or "private" act is one operating only on particular persons and private concerns. A "local act" is one applicable only to a particular part of the legislative jurisdiction.

See also Governmental act; Legislation; Legislative act; Statute.

Private acts are those made by private persons as registers in relation to their receipts and expenditures, schedules, acquittances, and the like.

Public acts are those which have a public authority, and which have been made before public officers, are authorized by a public seal, have been made public by the authority of a magistrate, or which have been extracted and been properly authenticated from public records.

Acting. Doing duty for another. Officiating or holding a temporary rank or position or performing services temporarily; as, an acting captain, manager, president. Performing; operating.

Acting executor. One who assumes to act as executor for a decedent, not being the executor legally appointed or the executor in fact.

Acting officer. Term is used to designate, not an appointed incumbent, but merely a *locum tenens*, who is performing the duties of an office to which he himself does not claim title.

Acting within scope of employment. *See* Scope of employment.

Actio /ǽkshiyow/. Lat. In the civil law, an action or suit; a right or cause of action. Term means both the proceeding to enforce a right in a court and the right itself which is sought to be enforced.

Action. Conduct; behavior; something done; the condition of acting; an act or series of acts.

Term in its usual legal sense means a lawsuit brought in a court; a formal complaint within the jurisdiction of a court of law. The legal and formal demand of one's right from another person or party made and insisted on in a court of justice. An ordinary proceeding in a court of justice by which one party prosecutes another for the enforcement or protection of a right, the redress or prevention of a wrong, or the punishment of a public offense. It includes all the formal proceedings in a court of justice attendant upon the demand of a right made by one person of another in such court, including an adjudication upon the right and its enforcement or denial by the court.

See also Case (*Cases and controversies*); Cause of action; Civil action; Collusive action; Controversy; Counterclaim; Cross-claim; Direct action; Forms of action; Penal action; Petitory action; Plenary action; Proceeding; Suit; Transitory action.

Merger of law and equity. In the federal courts, and most state courts, there is only one form of action—civil action—which embraces all actions formerly denominated suits in equity and actions at law. While there has been a merger of law and equity for procedural purposes, substantive principles of equity still govern. Fed.R.Civ.P. 2.

Types of action. Such term was formerly used to describe action for damages as distinguished from suit in equity for equitable relief. This distinction however has been abolished under Fed. Rules of Civil Procedure and in those states which adopted court rules tracking the Federal Rules. Fed.R.Civ.P. 2.

Action for death. *See* Wrongful death action.

Action in equity. Action in which person seeks equitable relief as distinguished from damages; *e.g.* injunction or specific performance of real estate agreement. Term has been abolished by

Fed. Rules of Civil Procedure (Rule 2) in favor of single form of action—civil action—which embraces both law and equity actions.

Action in personam. *See* In personam.

Action in rem. *See* In rem.

Action on account. An action of assumpsit or debt for recovery of money only for services performed, property sold and delivered, money loaned, or damages for the non-performance of simple contracts, express or implied, when the rights of the parties will be adequately conserved by the payment and receipt of money.

Action quasi in rem. *See* In rem.

Civil actions are such as lie in behalf of persons to enforce their rights or obtain redress of wrongs in their relation to individuals. Fed.R. Civ.P. 2.

Class actions. *See* Class *or* representative action; Derivative action.

Common law actions are such as will lie, on the particular facts, at common law, without the aid of a statute. Actions are called, in common-law practice, *ex contractu* when they arise out of a contract, and *ex delicto* when they arise out of a tort. If a cause of action arises from a breach of promise, the action is "ex contractu", and, if it arises from breach of duty growing out of contract, it is "ex delicto".

Criminal actions are such as are instituted by the sovereign power (*i.e.* government), for the purpose of punishing or preventing offenses against the public.

Local action. *See* Local actions.

Mixed actions partake of twofold nature of real and personal actions, having for their object the demand and restitution of real property and also personal damages for a wrong sustained. In the civil law, an action in which some specific thing was demanded, and also some personal obligation claimed to be performed; or, in other words, an action which proceeded both *in rem* and *in personam.*

Penal actions are such as are brought, either by federal, state, or local authorities or by an individual under permission of a statute, to enforce a penalty imposed by law for the commission of a prohibited act. *See* Criminal.

Personal action. In civil law, an action *in personam* seeks to enforce an obligation imposed on the defendant by his contract or delict; that is, it is the contention that he is bound to transfer some dominion or to perform some service or to repair some loss. In common law, an action brought for the recovery of some debt or for damages for some personal injury, in contradistinction to the old real actions, which related to real property only. An action which can be brought only by the person himself who is in-

jured, and not by his representatives. *See* In personam.

Real actions. At common law, one brought for the specific recovery of lands, tenements, or hereditaments. They are *droitural* when they are based upon the right of property, and *possessory* when based upon the right of possession. They are either writs of right; writs of entry upon disseisin (which lie in the per, the per et cui, or the post), intrusion, or alienation; writs ancestral possessory, as mort d'ancestor, aiel, besaiel, cossinage, or nuper obiit. The former class was divided into *droitural*, founded upon demandant's own seisin, and *ancestral droitural* upon the demandant's claim in respect of a mere right descended to him from an ancestor. Possessory actions were divided in the same way—as to the demandant's own seisin and as to that of his ancestor. Among the civilians, real actions, otherwise called "vindications," were those in which a man demanded something that was his own. They were founded on dominion, or *jus in re.* The real actions of the Roman law were not, like the real actions of the common law, confined to real estate, but they included personal, as well as real, property. *See* In rem.

Statutory actions are such as can only be based upon the particular statutes creating them. Contrast *Common law* actions, *above.*

Transitory actions are those founded upon a cause of action not necessarily referring to or arising in any particular locality. Their characteristic feature is that the right of action follows the person of the defendant. Actions are "transitory" when the transactions relied on might have taken place anywhere, and are "local" when they could not occur except in some particular place; the distinction being in the nature of the subject of the injury, and not in the means used or the place at which the cause of action arises. The test of whether an action is local or transitory is whether the injury is done to a subject-matter which, in its nature, could not arise beyond the locality of its situation, in contradistinction to the subject causing the injury. Actions triable where defendant resides are termed "transitory" and those triable where the subject-matter is situated are termed "local."

Actionable. That for which an action will lie, furnishing legal ground for an action. *See* Cause of action; Justiciable controversy.

Actionable fraud. Deception practiced in order to induce another to part with property or surrender some legal right. A false representation made with an intention to deceive; such may be committed by stating what is known to be false or by professing knowledge of the truth of a statement which is false, but in either case, the essential ingredient is a falsehood uttered with intent to deceive. To constitute "actionable fraud," it must appear that defendant made a material representation; that it was false; that when he made it he knew it was false, or made it recklessly without any knowledge of its truth and as a positive assertion; that he made it with intention that it should be acted on by plaintiff; that plaintiff acted in reliance on it; and that plaintiff thereby suffered injury. Essential elements are representation, falsity, scienter, deception, reliance and injury. *See* Fraud.

Actionable misrepresentation. A false statement respecting a fact material to the contract and which is influential in procuring it. *See* Fraud; Misrepresentation.

Actionable negligence. The breach or nonperformance of a legal duty, through neglect or carelessness, resulting in damage or injury to another. It is failure of duty, omission of something which ought to have been done, or doing of something which ought not to have been done, or which reasonable man, guided by considerations which ordinarily regulate conduct of human affairs, would or would not do. Essential elements are failure to exercise due care, injury, or damage, and proximate cause. *See* Negligence.

Actionable nuisance. Anything wrongfully done or permitted which injures or annoys another in the enjoyment of his legal rights. Anything injurious to health, or indecent, or offensive to the senses, or an obstruction to the free use of property so as to interfere with the comfortable enjoyment of life or property. *See* Nuisance.

Actionable per quod /ǽkshənəbəl pər kwód/. Words actionable only on allegation and proof of special damage. Words not actionable *per se* upon their face, but only in consequence of extrinsic facts showing circumstances under which they were said or the damages resulting to slandered party therefrom. *See* Libelous per quod.

Actionable per se /ǽkshənəbəl pər síy/. Words in themselves libelous or slanderous. Words which law presumes must actually, proximately and necessarily damage defendant for which general damages are recoverable and whose injurious character is a fact of common notoriety, established by the general consent of men, necessarily importing damage. Actions based on such words require no proof of damages. Words actionable per se include imputation of crime, a loathsome disease, unchastity, or words affecting plaintiff's business, trade, profession, office or calling. *See* Libelous per se.

Actionable tort. A tort for which a cause of action exists. To constitute an "actionable tort," there must be a legal duty, imposed by statute or otherwise, owing by defendant to the one injured, and in the absence of such duty damage caused is "injury without wrong" or "damnum absque injuria." *See* Tort.

Actionable words. In law of libel and slander, such words as naturally imply damage. *See* Libel; Slander.

Actionable wrong. A tort committed when a responsible person has neglected to use a reasonable degree of care for protection of another person from such injury as under existing circumstances should reasonably have been foreseen as a proximate consequence of that negligence.

Action ex contractu /ǽkshən èks kəntrǽktyuw/. An action for breach of promise set forth in a contract, express or implied.

Action ex delicto /ǽkshən èks dəlíktow/. An action arising from a breach of duty growing out of contract.

Action for accounting. Action in equity based on inadequacy of legal remedy and particularly applicable to mutual and complicated accounts and where confidential or fiduciary relationship exists. Action to adjust mutual accounts and to strike a balance.

Action for money had and received. Action in assumpsit based upon promise to repay implied by law, and in respect of limitation is a stated or liquidated account. Action brought where one person has received money or its equivalent under such circumstances that in equity and good conscience he ought not to retain it and in justice it belongs to another.

Action for poinding /ǽkshən for píndiŋ/. An action by a creditor to obtain a sequestration of the rents of land and the goods of his debtor for the satisfaction of his debt, or to enforce a distress.

Action in personam /ǽkshən in pərsównəm/. *See* In personam.

Action in rem /ǽkshən in rém/. *See* In rem.

Action of assize /ǽkshən əv əsáyz/. A real action at common law which proved the title of the demandant, merely by showing his ancestor's possession.

Action of assumpsit /ǽkshən əv əsə́mpsət/. *See* Assumpsit.

Action of book debt. A form of common law action for the recovery of claims, such as are usually evidenced by a book-account.

Action of contract. An action brought to enforce rights whereof the contract is the evidence, and usually the sufficient evidence.

Action on the case. A common law species of personal action of formerly extensive application, otherwise called "trespass on the case," or simply "case," from the circumstance of the plaintiff's whole *case or cause of complaint* being set forth at length in the original writ by which formerly it was always commenced. In its most comprehensive signification it includes *assumpsit* as well as an action in form *ex delicto*; though when it is mentioned it is usually understood to mean an action in form *ex delicto*. It is founded on the common law or upon acts of Parliament, and lies generally to recover damages for torts not committed with force, actual or implied; or having been occasioned by force where the matter affected was not tangible, or the injury was not immediate but consequential; or where the interest in the property was only in reversion, in all of which cases trespass is not sustainable. Such form of action no longer exists under Code and Rule pleading. *See* Assumpsit.

Action to quiet title. One in which plaintiff asserts his own estate and declares generally that defendant claims some estate in the land, without defining it, and avers that the claim is without foundation, and calls on defendant to set forth the nature of his claim, so that it may be determined by decree. It differs from a "suit to remove a cloud," in that plaintiff therein declares on his own title, and also avers the source and nature of defendant's claim, points out its defect, and prays that it may be declared void as a cloud on plaintiff's estate. *See* Cloud on title.

Active. That is in action; that demands action; actually subsisting; the opposite of passive. An active debt is one which draws interest. An active trust is a confidence connected with a duty. An active use is a present legal estate.

Active concealment. Term implies a purpose or design to conceal accomplished by words or acts, while passive concealment consists in mere silence where there is a duty to speak. Concealment becomes a fraud where it is effected by misleading and deceptive talk, acts, or conduct, where it is accompanied by misrepresentations, or where, in addition to a party's silence, there is any statement, word, or act on his part which tends affirmatively to a suppression of the truth. Such conduct is designated active concealment.

Active negligence. A term of extensive meaning embracing many occurrences that would fall short of willful wrongdoing, or of crass negligence, for example, all inadvertent acts causing injury to others, resulting from failure to exercise ordinary care; likewise, all acts the effects of which are misjudged or unforeseen, through want of proper attention, or reflection, and hence the term covers the acts of willful wrongdoing and also those which are not of that character.

Active negligence denotes some positive act or some failure in duty of operation which is equivalent of a positive act and is omission of due care and affirmative action by person in control, or negligence occurring in connection with activities conducted on the premises. Difference between "active" and "passive" negligence is that one is only passively negligent if he merely fails to act in fulfillment of duty of care which law imposes upon him, while one is actively negligent if he participates in some manner in conduct or omission which caused injury.

See also Negligence.

Active participant. In criminal law, any person who engages in conduct, either by act or omission, which is an essential element of the crime. *See also* Accessory.

Active trust. *See* Trust.

Activity. An occupation or pursuit in which person is active.

Act malum in se /ǽkt mǽləm in síy/. *See* Malum in se.

Act malum prohibitum /ǽkt mǽləm prəhíbətəm/. *See* Malum prohibitum.

Act of attainder. A legislative act, attainting a person. *See* Attainder.

Act of bankruptcy. Term used under former federal Bankruptcy Act (§ 3), to refer to any act which rendered a person liable to be proceeded against involuntarily as a bankrupt, or for which he could be adjudged bankrupt. The new Bankruptcy Code (1979) no longer provides for specific acts of bankruptcy, but rather provides for involuntary bankruptcy when the debtor, in general, is not paying his debts as they become due. Bankruptcy Code, § 303. *See* Bankruptcy Code; Bankruptcy proceedings.

Act of God. An act occasioned exclusively by forces of nature without the interference of any human agency. A misadventure or casualty is said to be caused by the "act of God," when it happens by the direct, immediate, and exclusive operation of the forces of nature, uncontrolled and uninfluenced by the power of man, and without human intervention, and is of such a character that it could not have been prevented or escaped from by any amount of foresight or prudence, or by any reasonable degree of care or diligence, or by the aid of any appliances which the situation of the party might reasonably require him to use. Any accident produced by any physical cause which is irresistible, such as lightning, tempests, perils of the seas, tornados, earthquakes. *See* Inevitable accident; Perils of the sea; Vis major.

Act of grace. The term is often used to designate a general act of parliament, originating with the crown, such as has often been passed at the commencement of a new reign, or the coming of age or marriage of a sovereign, or at the close of a period of civil troubles, declaring pardon or amnesty to numerous offenders. *See also* Days of grace; Grace period.

Act of insolvency. *See* Act of bankruptcy.

Act of law. The operation of fixed legal rules upon given facts or occurrences, producing consequences independent of the design or will of the parties concerned; as distinguished from "act of parties." Also an act performed by judicial authority which prevents or precludes a party from fulfilling a contract or other engagement.

Act of nature. *See* Act of God.

Act of providence. An accident against which ordinary skill and foresight could not guard. Equivalent to "act of God" (*q.v.*).

Act of sale. An official record of a sale of property, made by a notary who writes down the agreement of the parties as stated by them, and which is then signed by the parties and attested by witnesses.

Act of state. An act done by the sovereign power of a country, or by its delegate, within the limits of the power vested in him. An act of state cannot be questioned or made the subject of legal proceedings in a court of law. *See* Act of state doctrine.

Act of state doctrine. The judicially created act of state doctrine precludes the courts of this country from inquiring into the validity of governmental acts of a recognized foreign sovereign committed within its own territory.

Actor. One who acts. The term is used in the Restatement of Torts, Second, to designate either the person whose conduct is in question as subjecting him to liability toward another, or as precluding him from recovering against another whose tortious conduct is a legal cause of the actor's injury. Sec. 2.

Acts of possession. To constitute adverse possession, acts of possession must be: (1) hostile or adverse, (2) actual, (3) visible, notorious, and exclusive, (4) continuous, and (5) under claim of ownership. *See* Adverse possession.

Actual. Real; substantial; existing presently in fact; having a valid objective existence as opposed to that which is merely theoretical or possible. Opposed to potential, possible, virtual, theoretical, hypothetical, or nominal. Something real, in opposition to constructive or speculative; something existing in act. It is used as a legal term in contradistinction to virtual or constructive as of possession or occupation. *Actually* is opposed to seemingly, pretendedly, or feignedly, as *actually engaged in farming* means really, truly in fact. As to *actual* Bias; Damages; Delivery; Fraud; Malice; Notice; Occupation; Ouster; Possession; Residence; Seisin; Total loss, see those titles.

Actual authority. The power of an agent to bind its principal where such power derives either from express or implied agreement between the principal and the agent. In the law of agency, such authority as a principal intentionally confers on the agent, or intentionally or by want of ordinary care allows the agent to believe himself to possess. Includes both express and implied authority.

Actual bias. *See* Bias.

Actual cash value. The fair or reasonable cash price for which the property could be sold in the market in the ordinary course of business, and not at forced sale. The price it will bring in a fair market after reasonable efforts to find a purchaser who will give the highest price. What property is worth in money, allowing for depreciation. Ordinarily, "actual cash value", "fair market value", and "market value" are synonymous terms. *See* Actual value; Cash value; Fair market value; Fair value.

Actual change of possession. In statutes of frauds, an open, visible and unequivocal change of possession, manifested by the usual outward signs, as distinguished from a merely formal or constructive change.

Actual controversy. Declaratory judgment may be rendered only in cases of "actual controversy" defined as concrete cases touching legal relations of parties having adverse legal interests and susceptible of an immediate and definitive determination of the legal rights of the parties in an adversary proceeding upon the alleged facts. *See also* Case (*Cases and controversies*); Declaratory Judgment Act.

Actual cost. The actual price paid for goods by a party, in the case of a real *bona fide* purchase, which may not necessarily be the market value of the goods. It is a general or descriptive term which may have varying meanings according to the circumstances in which it is used. It imports the exact sum expended or loss sustained rather than the average or proportional part of the cost. Its meaning may be restricted to materials, labor, and overhead or extended to other items.

Actual damages. Compensation for actual injuries or loss. Term used to denote the type of damage award as well as the nature of injury for which recovery is allowed; thus, actual damages flowing from injury in fact are to be distinguished from damages which are nominal, exemplary or punitive. Actual damages are synonymous with compensatory damages. *See also* Damages.

Actual delivery. *See* Delivery.

Actual eviction. An actual expulsion of the tenant out of all or some part of the demised premises. A physical ouster or dispossession from the very thing granted or some substantial part thereof. *See* Constructive eviction; Eviction; Forcible entry and detainer; Summary (*Summary process*).

Actual fraud. *See* Fraud.

Actual loss. One resulting from the real and substantial destruction of the property insured.

Actual malice. *See* Malice.

Actual market value. In custom laws, the price at which merchandise is freely offered for sale to all purchasers; the price which the manufacturer or owner would have received for merchandise, sold in the ordinary course of trade in the usual wholesale quantities. *See also* Market value.

Actual notice. *See* Notice.

Actual possession. *See* Possession.

Actual practice. Active, open and notorious engagement in business, vocation or profession as opposed to casual or clandestine practice.

Actual residence. The abode, where one actually lives, not mere naked legal residence. *See* Domicile; Residence.

Actual trust. *See* Trust.

Actual value. Actual value to be awarded in condemnation proceeding is price that would probably result from negotiations between willing seller and willing buyer. "Actual value," "market value," "fair market value," "just compensation" and the like may be used as convertible terms. "Saleable value," "actual value," "cash value," and other like terms used in directions to tax assessing officers, all mean generally the same thing. *See also* Market value.

Actuarial table /æ̀ktyuwériyəl téybəl/. A form of organized statistical data which indicates the life expectancy of a person and which is admissible in evidence through an expert witness. Such tables are used by insurance companies in determining premiums. *See also* American experience table of mortality; Life tables; Mortality tables.

Actuary /ǽktyuweriy/. A statistician who computes insurance and pension rates and premiums on the basis of experience tables (*e.g.* life expectancy and mortality tables).

Actum /ǽktəm/. Lat. A deed; something done.

Actus /ǽktəs/. In the civil law, an act or action.

Actus reus /ǽktəs ríyəs/. The "guilty act." A wrongful deed which renders the actor criminally liable if combined with mens rea. The *actus reus* is the physical aspect of a crime, whereas the *mens rea* (guilty mind) involves the intent factor.

A.D. An abbreviation of Anno Domini meaning in the year of our Lord.

Adamson Act. Act of Congress (1916) establishing the 8 hour workday. 45 U.S.C.A. § 45.

Adapted. Capable of use. Indicates that the object referred to has been made suitable; has been made to conform to; has been made fit by alteration.

Adaptation right. In copyright law, the exclusive right of the holder of a copyright to prepare "derivative works" based on the copyrighted item.

Add. To unite; attach; annex; join. *See also* Addition; Additional.

Ad damnum /æ̀(d) dǽmnəm/. In pleading, "To the damage." The technical name of that clause of the writ, declaration, or, more commonly, the complaint, which contains a statement of the plaintiff's money loss, or the damages which he claims. Fed.R.Civil P. 8(a).

Such clause informs an adversary of the maximum amount of the claim asserted without being proof of actual injury or of liability.

Added substance. Test for determining whether substance is an "added substance" within meaning of Federal Food, Drug, and Cosmetic Act is whether it occurs naturally in the food. *See also* Foreign substance.

Addendum /ædéndəm/. A thing that is added or to be added; a list or section consisting of added material.

Addict. Any individual who habitually uses any narcotic drug so as to endanger the public morals, health, safety, or welfare, or who is or has been so far addicted to the use of such narcotic drugs as to have lost the power of self-control with reference to his addiction. 21 U.S.C.A. § 802.

Addictive drugs. Any drug, natural or synthetic, which causes periodic or chronic intoxication by its repeated consumption.

Ad diem /æ̀(d) dáyəm/. At a day; at the day. *Ad alium diem,* at another day. *Ad certum diem,* at a certain day. *Solvit ad diem,* he paid at or on the day.

Addition. Implies physical contact, something added to another. Structure physically attached to or connected with building itself. Extension; increase; augmentation. That which has become united with or a part of. *See* Appurtenance; Fixture.

In insurance law, the word "addition", as applied to buildings usually means a part added or joined to a main building; though the term has also been held to apply to buildings appurtenant to some other building though not actually in physical contact therewith.

Additional. This term embraces the idea of joining or uniting one thing to another, so as thereby to form one aggregate.

Additional burden. *See* Eminent domain.

Additional extended coverage. Insurance policy indorsement covering dwellings; covering water damage from plumbing and heating systems, vandalism and malicious mischief, glass breakage, falling trees, ice, snow, etc.

Additional instructions. Charge by judge to jury beyond the original instructions. Frequently required when the jury returns from deliberations with a question concerning the evidence, point of law, or some portion of the original charge.

Additional insurance. Insurance which is added to an existing policy.

Additional insured. Person(s) covered by policy in addition to the named insured; *e.g.* in an automobile liability policy, the "named insured" is usually the purchaser or the owner of the insurance policy, while an "additional insured" or an "insured" is one who is not specifically identified by name in the policy, but enjoys status of an insured under the named insured's policy, for example, as result of being the operator of the named insured's automobile.

Additional legacy. *See* Legacy.

Additional servitude. The imposition of a new and additional easement or servitude on land originally taken by eminent domain proceedings. A use of a different character, for which owner of property is entitled to compensation.

Additional work. Of nature involved in modifications and changes, not independent project. Work which results from a change or alteration in plans concerning work which has to be done under a contract, while "extra work" relates to work which is not included within the contract itself.

Additur /ǽdətər/. The power of trial court to assess damages or increase amount of an inadequate award made by jury verdict, as condition of denial of motion for new trial, with consent of defendant whether or not plaintiff consents to such action. This is not allowed in the Federal system. *Compare* Remittitur.

Add on clause. A clause in an installment sales contract that makes earlier purchases with that firm security for new purchases.

Add on interest. Method of charging interest usually in the financing of certain major types of consumer goods and generally not in real estate financing. Interest is computed on the total amount borrowed and added to the principal. Each payment is then deducted from this total amount.

Addone, addonne /ædówniy/. L. Fr. Given to.

Address. Place where mail or other communications will reach person. Generally a place of business or residence; though it need not be.

Bill of address. Provision in Massachusetts Constitution which provides that judges are subject to removal upon the *address* of a majority of both houses of the legislature with approval of the Governor and the Executive Council.

Equity pleading. Part of a bill wherein is given the appropriate and technical description of the court in which the bill is filed. *See* Caption.

Adduce. To present, bring forward, offer, introduce. Used particularly with reference to evidence.

Adeem /ədíym/. To take away, recall, or revoke. To satisfy a legacy by some gift or substituted disposition, made by the testator, in advance. *See* Ademption.

Ademption /ədém(p)shən/. Extinction or withdrawal of legacy by testator's act equivalent to revocation or indicating intention to revoke. Testator's giving to a legatee that which he has provided in his will, or his disposing of that part of his estate so bequeathed in such manner as to make it impossible to carry out the will. Revocation, recalling, or cancellation of a legacy, according to the apparent intention of the testator, implied by the law from acts done by him in his life, though such acts do not amount to an express revocation of it. *See* Advancement.

Adequate care. Such care as a man of ordinary prudence would himself take under similar circumstances to avoid accident; care proportionate to the risk to be incurred. *See also* Care.

Adequate cause. Sufficient cause for a particular purpose. In criminal law, adequate cause for the passion which reduces a homicide committed under its influence from the grade of murder to manslaughter, means such cause as would commonly produce a degree of anger, rage, resentment, or terror, in a person of ordinary temper, sufficient to render the mind incapable of cool reflection. Insulting words or gestures, or an assault and battery so slight as to show no intention to inflict pain or injury, or an injury to property unaccompanied by violence are not adequate causes. *See* Adequate provocation; Cause; Probable cause; Self-defense.

Adequate compensation. Just value of property taken under power of eminent domain, payable in money, as guaranteed by 5th Amendment. Market value of property when taken. It may include interest and may include the cost or value of the property to the owner for the purposes for which he designed it. Such only as puts injured party in as good a condition as he would have been in if injury had not been inflicted. *See also* Fair market value; Just compensation.

Adequate consideration. Such as is equal, or reasonably proportioned, to the value of that for which it is given. That which is not so disproportionate as to shock our sense of that morality and fair dealing which should always characterize transactions between man and man. Fair and reasonable under circumstances. Reasonably just and equitable. *See* Consideration; Fair consideration; Fair market value; Fair value; Just compensation.

Adequate notice. Notice reasonably calculated to apprise a person of an action, proceeding, or motion. Notice sufficient to permit an objection or defense. Notice reasonably calculated, in all circumstances of given proceeding, to apprise all interested parties of action and opportunity to present their objections. *See* Notice.

Adequate preparation. As used in reference to adequate representation by counsel, embraces full consultation with accused, interviews with witnesses, study of facts and law, and determination of character of defense to be made and policy to be followed during trial.

Adequate protection. Phrase used in several sections of the Bankruptcy Code to describe protection afforded to holders of secured claims. It is meant to preserve secured creditor's position at the time of bankruptcy. More specifically, the lack of adequate protection of the creditor's interest in its collateral is a basis for relief from stay under Code § 362(d)(1); adequate protection is also the standard for creditor protection from sale or use or encumbrance of the collateral under Code sections 363 and 364. While adequate protection is not statutorily defined, section 361 sets out examples of adequate protection.

Adequate provocation. An adequate provocation to cause a sudden transport of passion that may suspend the exercise of judgment and exclude premeditation and a previously formed design is one that is calculated to excite such anger as might obscure the reason or dominate the volition of an ordinary reasonable man. *See* Adequate cause.

Adequate remedy at law. For purposes of rule that a litigant who fails to avail himself of a remedy provided by law and who is subsequently barred from pursuing that remedy because of his own lack of diligence cannot rely on the absence of a remedy at law as a basis for equitable jurisdiction, is one which is as complete, practical and as efficient to the ends of justice and its prompt administration as a remedy in equity, and which is obtainable as of right. A remedy that affords complete relief with reference to the particular matter in controversy, and is appropriate to the circumstances of the case. Such must reach end intended, and actually compel performance of duty in question.

Adhering. Joining, leagued with, cleaving to; as, "adhering to the enemies of the United States." "Adhering" consists in giving to the United States the loyalty due from a citizen. Any intentional act furthering hostile designs of enemies of the United States, or an act which intentionally strengthens or tends to strengthen enemies of the United States, or which weakens or tends to weaken power of the United States to resist and attack such enemies, constitutes "adhering" to such enemies.

Adhesion. Agreement to join; adherence. The entrance of another nation into an existing treaty with respect only to a part of the principles laid down or the stipulations agreed to. Properly speaking, by adhesion the third nation becomes a party only to such parts as are specifically agreed to, and by accession it accepts and is bound by the whole treaty. *See* Accession.

Adhesion contract. Standardized contract form offered to consumers of goods and services on essentially "take it or leave it" basis without affording consumer realistic opportunity to bargain and under such conditions that consumer cannot obtain desired product or services except by acquiescing in form contract. Distinctive feature of adhesion contract is that weaker party has no realistic choice as to its terms. Recognizing that these contracts are not the result of traditionally "bargained" contracts, the trend is to relieve parties from onerous conditions imposed by such contracts. However, not every such contract is unconscionable.

Ad hoc /ǽd hó(w)k/. For this; for this special purpose. An attorney ad hoc, or a guardian or curator ad hoc, is one appointed for a special purpose, generally to represent the client or infant in the particular action in which the appointment is made.

Ad hoc arbitration. Submission of a particular issue to arbitration.

Ad hominem /ǽd hómənəm/. To the person. A term used in logic with reference to a personal argument.

ADI. That amount of a particular chemical which Environmental Protection Agency considers safe for human ingestion every day for seventy years with no ill effects.

Ad idem /ǽd áydəm/. To the same point, or effect. *Ad idem facit*, it makes to or goes to establish the same point.

Ad infinitum /ǽd ìnfináytəm/. Without limit; to an infinite extent; indefinitely.

Adjacent. Lying near or close to; sometimes, contiguous; neighboring. *Adjacent* implies that the two objects are not widely separated, though they may not actually touch, while *adjoining* imports that they are so joined or united to each other that no third object intervenes. *See* Adjoining.

Adjective law. The aggregate of rules of procedure or practice. Also called adjectival law, as opposed to that body of law which the courts are established to administer (called "substantive law"), it means the rules according to which the substantive law is administered; *e.g.* Rules of Civil Procedure. That part of the law which provides a method for enforcing or maintaining rights, or obtaining redress for their invasion. Pertains to and prescribes practice, method, procedure or legal machinery by which substantive law is enforced or made effective. *See also* Procedural law. *Compare* Substantive law.

Adjoining. The word in its etymological sense means touching or contiguous, as distinguished from lying near to or adjacent. To be in contact with; to abut upon. And the same meaning has been given to it when used in statutes. *See* Adjacent.

Adjoining owners. Those persons who own land touching the subject land and who, as a result, have right to notice of proceedings concerning the subject real estate as, for example, in zoning and licensing matters. *See* Abutting owner.

Adjourn /əjə́rn/. To put off; defer; recess; postpone. To postpone action of a convened court or legislative body until another time specified, or indefinitely; the latter being usually called to adjourn *sine die*. To suspend or recess during a meeting, legislature or assembly, which continues in session. Suspending business for a time, delaying. *See* Adjournment.

Adjourned summons. A summons taken out in the chambers of a judge, and afterwards taken into court to be argued by counsel.

Adjourned term. In practice, a continuance, by adjournment, of a regular term. Distinguished from an "additional term," which is a distinct term. A continuation of a previous or regular term. The same term prolonged, wherein power of court over business which has been done, and the entries made at the regular term, continues.

Adjournment. A putting off or postponing of business or of a session until another time or place. The act of a court, legislative body, public meeting, or officer, by which the session or assembly is dissolved, either temporarily or finally, and the business in hand dismissed from consideration, either definitely or for an interval. If the adjournment is final, it is said to be *sine die*. *See also* Recess.

Adjournment day. A further day appointed by the judges at the regular sittings at *nisi prius* to try issue of fact not then ready for trial.

Adjudge /əjə́j/. To pass on judicially, to decide, settle, or decree, or to sentence or condemn. Judgment of a court of competent jurisdiction; equivalent of convicted and sentenced. Implies a judicial determination of a fact, and the entry of a judgment. *See also* Adjudication; Judgment.

Adjudicate /əjúwdəkèyt/. To settle in the exercise of judicial authority. To determine finally. Synonymous with *adjudge* in its strictest sense.

Adjudicated rights. Rights which have been recognized in a judicial or administrative proceeding.

Adjudication /əjùwdəkéyshən/. The legal process of resolving a dispute. The formal giving or pronouncing a judgment or decree in a court proceeding; also the judgment or decision given. The entry of a decree by a court in respect to the parties in a case. It implies a hearing by a court, after notice, of legal evidence on the factual issue(s) involved. The equivalent of a "determination." It contemplates that the claims of all the parties thereto have been considered and set at rest. *See* Administrative adjudication; Judgment.

Adjudicative claims arbitration. This form of dispute resolution is concerned primarily with tort and other claims involving small amounts as distinguished from the traditional categories of arbitration in the fields of labor, commerce and international trade. Designed to relieve courts of burden of handling such cases. *See also* Arbitration.

Adjudicative facts. Factual matters concerning the parties to an administrative proceeding as contrasted with legislative facts which are general and usually do not touch individual questions of particular parties to a proceeding. Facts which concern a person's motives and intent, as contrasted with general policy issues. Those facts that must be found beyond a reasonable doubt by trier of fact before there can be a conviction.

Adjudicatory action. Administrative actions are "adjudicatory" in character when they culminate in final determination affecting personal or property rights. *See also* Adjudicatory hearing; Adjudicatory process.

Adjudicatory hearing. A proceeding before an administrative agency in which the rights and duties of particular persons are adjudicated after notice and opportunity to be heard.

Adjudicatory proceeding. *See* Adjudicatory action; Adjudicatory hearing; Adjudicatory process.

Adjudicatory process. Method of adjudicating factual disputes; used generally in reference to administrative proceedings in contrast to judicial proceedings.

Adjunct /ǽjəŋkt/. Something added to another, but in a subordinate, auxiliary, or dependent position. *See also* Appurtenance.

One associated with another in a subordinate or an auxiliary manner; an associate.

Adjunction /əjə́ŋ(k)shən/. Adding, affixing or attaching to another. Act of adjoining. In civil law, the attachment or union permanently of a thing belonging to one person to that belonging to another. The common law implicitly adopts the civil law doctrines. *See* Accession.

Adjuration /æ̀jəréyshən/. A swearing or binding upon oath.

Adjust. To settle or arrange; to free from differences or discrepancies. To bring to satisfactory state so that parties are agreed, as to adjust amount of loss by fire or controversy regarding property or estate. To bring to proper relations; to settle. To determine and apportion an amount due. Accounts are adjusted when they are settled and a balance is struck. Term is sometimes used in the sense of pay, when used in reference to a liquidated claim. Determination of amount to be paid to insured by insurer to cover loss or damage sustained. *See* Adjuster; Adjustment; Settlement.

Adjustable-rate mortgage (ARM). *See* Mortgage.

Adjusted basis. The cost or other basis of property reduced by depreciation allowed or allowable and increased by capital improvements. *See* Basis.

Adjusted cost basis. For income tax purposes, original cost plus additions to capital less depreciation results in the "adjusted cost basis."

Adjusted current earnings (ACE). An adjustment in computing corporate alternative minimum taxable income. *See also* Alternative minimum tax.

Adjusted gross estate. The gross estate less I.R.C. §§ 2053 and 2054 expenses equals the adjusted gross estate. Generally, I.R.C. §§ 2053 and 2054 expenses include administration expenses, debts of the decedent, and losses incurred during the settlement of the estate. Fifty percent of the adjusted gross estate measures the maximum amount of the marital deduction allowed for death tax purposes. *See* Administration expense; Gross estate; Marital deduction.

Adjusted gross income. A tax determination peculiar to individual taxpayers. Generally, it represents gross income less business expenses, expenses attributable to the production of rent or royalty income, the allowed capital loss deduction, and certain personal expenses. *See also* Gross income.

Adjusted ordinary gross income. A determination peculiar to the personal holding company tax imposed by I.R.C. § 541. Adjusted ordinary gross income is the corporation's gross income less capital gains, § 1231 gains, and certain expenses. I.R.C. § 543(b)(2). *See also* Personal holding company income.

Adjusted present value (APV). A computational method of accounting whereby the value of an asset is determined in two parts by adding the present value without regard to capital structure effects plus the value added by capital structure effects.

Adjuster. One appointed to adjust a matter; to ascertain or arrange or settle. One who makes any adjustment or settlement, or who determines the amount of a claim, as a claim against an insurance company. A representative of the insurer who seeks to determine the extent of the firm's liability for loss when a claim is submitted. A person who acts for the insurance company or the insured in the determination and settlement of claims. "Public" adjusters represent claimants only in presenting their claims to insurer. "Average" adjusters specialize in adjusting marine losses. *See* Claim adjuster; Claimant adjuster; Independent adjuster.

Adjusting entry. An accounting entry made at the end of an accounting period to record previously unrecognized revenue and expenses and changes in assets and liabilities. An adjusting entry can also occur as a result of an error made in a prior period, requiring an adjusting or correcting entry in the current period.

Adjustment. An arrangement; a settlement. In the law of insurance, the adjustment of a loss is the ascertainment of its amount and the ratable distribution of it among those liable to pay it. The settling and ascertaining the amount of the indemnity which the assured, after all allowances and deductions made, is entitled to receive under the policy, and fixing the proportion which each underwriter is liable to pay.

In tax practice, the correction of erroneous determination of deficiency.

Adjustment board. *See* Board of adjustment.

Adjustment bond. *See* Bond.

Adjustment securities. Stocks and bonds which are issued during a corporate reorganization.

Adjutant general /æ̀jədən(t) jén(ə)rəl/. An officer in charge of the National Guard of one of the States. The administrative head of a military unit having a general staff.

Ad litem /æd láytəm/. For the suit; for the purposes of the suit; pending the suit. A guardian *ad litem* is a guardian appointed to prosecute or defend a suit on behalf of a party incapacitated by infancy or otherwise.

Admeasurement /æ̀dmézhərmənt/. Ascertainment by measure; measuring out; assignment or apportionment by measure, that is, by fixed quantity or value, by certain limits, or in definite and fixed proportions.

Admeasurement of dower. A common law remedy which lay for the heir on reaching his majority to rectify an assignment of dower made during his minority, by which the doweress had received more than she was legally entitled to.

Admeasurement, writ of. A common law remedy which lay against persons who usurped more than their share, in the two following cases: Admeasurement of dower, and admeasurement of pasture.

Administer. To manage or conduct. To discharge the duties of an office; to take charge of business; to manage affairs; to serve in the conduct of affairs, in the application of things to their uses; to settle and distribute the estate of a decedent. Also, to give, as an oath; to direct or cause to be taken.

To "administer" a decree is to execute it, to enforce its provisions, to resolve conflicts as to its meaning, to construe and to interpret its language. To "administer" trusts is to manage, direct or superintend affairs of such trusts.

Administration. Management or conduct of an office or employment; the performance of the executive duties of an institution, business, or the like. In public law, the administration of government means the practical management and direction of the executive department, or of the public machinery or functions, or of the operations of the various organs or agencies. Direction or oversight of any office, service, or employment. The term "administration" is also conventionally applied to the whole class of public functionaries, or those in charge of the management of the executive department.

Administration expense. Administrative expenses imply disbursements incidental to the management of the estate which are deductible in computing estate taxes. Deductions are allowed for such expenses or claims only to the extent that they "are allowable by the laws of the jurisdiction" under which the estate is being administered. I.R.C. § 2053.

Administration letters. The instrument by which an administrator or administratrix is authorized by the probate court, surrogate, or other proper officer, to have the charge and administration of the goods and property of an intestate. *See* Administrator.

Administration of estates. The management and settlement of the estate of an intestate decedent, or of a testator who has no executor, performed under the supervision of a court, by a person duly qualified and legally appointed, and usually involving: (1) the collection of the decedent's assets; (2) payment of debts and claims against the estate; (3) payment of estate taxes; (4) distribution of the remainder of the estate among those entitled thereto. The administration of an estate runs from the date of an individual's death until all assets have been distributed and liabilities paid. Such administration is conducted by an administrator or an executor. *See* Administrator; Letters of administration.

Administration of estates is principally of the following kinds:

Ad colligendum bona defuncti. To collect the goods of the deceased. Special letters of administration granted to one or more persons, authorizing them to collect and preserve the goods of the deceased.

Ad prosequendum. An administrator appointed to prosecute or defend a certain action (*e.g.* wrongful death) or actions in which the estate is concerned.

Ancillary administration is auxiliary and subordinate to the administration at the place of the decedent's domicile; it may be taken out in any foreign state or country where assets are locally situated, and is merely for the purpose of collecting such assets and paying debts there.

Cum testamento annexo (CTA). Administration with the will annexed. Administration granted in cases where a testator makes a will without naming any executors; or where the executors who are named in the will are incompetent to act, are deceased, or refuse to act.

De bonis non (DBN). Administration granted for the purpose of administering such of the goods of a deceased person as were not administered by the former executor or administrator.

De bonis non cum testamento annexo (DBNCTA). That which is granted when an executor dies leaving a part of the estate unadministered.

Durante absentia. That which is granted during the absence of the executor and until he has proved the will.

Durante minori ætate. Exists where an infant is made executor, in which case administration with will annexed is granted to another during the minority of such executor, and until he shall attain his lawful age to act.

Foreign administration. That which is exercised by virtue of authority properly conferred by a foreign power.

General administration. The grant of authority to administer upon the entire estate of a decedent, without restriction or limitation, whether under the intestate laws or with the will annexed.

Pendente lite. Administration granted during the pendency of a suit touching the validity of a will.

Public administration is such as is conducted (in some jurisdictions) by an officer called the public administrator, who is appointed to administer in cases where the intestate has left no person entitled to apply for letters.

Special administration. Authority to administer upon some few particular effects of a decedent, as opposed to authority to administer his whole estate.

Administrative. Connotes of or pertains to administration, especially management, as by managing or conducting, directing, or superintending, the execution, application or conduct of persons or things. Particularly, having the character of executive or ministerial action. In this sense, administrative functions or acts are distinguished from such as are judicial.

Administrative acts. Those acts which are necessary to be done to carry out legislative policies and purposes already declared by the legislative body or such as are devolved upon it by the organic law of its existence.

Administrative adjudication. The process by which an administrative agency issues an order, such order being affirmative, negative, injunctive or declaratory in form. Adm. Procedure Act, 5 U.S.C.A. § 551.

Administrative agency. A governmental body charged with administering and implementing particular legislation. Examples are worker's compensation commissions, tax commissioner, public service commissions, Federal Trade Commission, tax commissions, public service commissions, and the like. In addition to "agency", such governmental bodies may be called commissions, corporations (e.g. F.D.I.C.), boards, departments, or divisions.

The term "agency" includes any department, independent establishment, commission, administration, authority, board or bureau of the United States or any corporation in which the United States has a proprietary interest, unless the context shows that such term was intended to be used in a more limited sense. 18 U.S.C.A. § 1.

Administrative authority. The power of an agency or its head to carry out the terms of the law creating the agency as well as to make regulations for the conduct of business before the agency; distinguishable from legislative authority to make laws.

Administrative board. This term is very broad and includes bodies exercising varied functions, some of which involve orders made or other acts done ex parte or without full hearing as to the operative facts, while others are done only after such a notice and hearing, and the functions of the former kind are plainly "administrative" and those of the latter are "quasi judicial." Administrative boards differ from "courts" in that boards frequently represent public interests entrusted to boards, whereas courts are concerned with litigating rights of parties with adverse interests.

Administrative collateral estoppel. Principles of this estoppel doctrine apply when agency is acting in a judicial capacity and resolves disputed issues of fact properly before it which parties have had adequate opportunity to litigate; threshold inquiry is whether earlier proceeding is essential equivalent of judicial proceeding.

Administrative crime. An offense consisting of a violation of an administrative rule or regulation and carrying with it a criminal sanction.

Administrative determination. See Administrative adjudication.

Administrative deviation. Departure from the administrative provisions of a trust by the trustee acting alone or with prior approval of the court.

Administrative discretion. Term means that the doing of acts or things required to be done may rest, in part at least, upon considerations not entirely susceptible of proof or disproof and at times which considering the circumstances and subject-matter cannot be supplied by the Legislature, and a statute confers such discretion when it refers a commission or office to beliefs, expectations, or tendencies instead of facts for the exercise of the powers conferred.

Administrative exhaustion. See Exhaustion of administrative remedies.

Administrative hearing. An oral proceeding before an administrative agency consisting of argument or trial or both. Procedural rules are more relaxed at such hearings as contrasted with civil or criminal trials; e.g. rules governing admissibility of evidence are usually quite liberal. See also Hearing.

Administrative interpretation. Meaning given to a law or regulation by an administrative agency.

Administrative law. Body of law created by administrative agencies in the form of rules, regulations, orders, and decisions to carry out regulatory powers and duties of such agencies.

Administrative law judge. One who presides at an administrative hearing, with power to administer oaths, take testimony, rule on questions of evidence, regulate course of proceedings, and make agency determinations of fact. Formerly called "hearing officer" or "hearing examiner". Adm. Procedure Act, 5 U.S.C.A. § 556.

Administrative Office of United States Courts. Created by the Administrative Office Act of 1939, it is responsible for administration of the Federal court system, as a whole, including the collection of statistics on court business, supervision of administrative personnel in the courts and conducting of financial and management audits of courts.

Administrative officer. Politically, and as used in constitutional law, an officer of the executive department of government, and generally one of inferior rank; legally, a ministerial or executive officer, as distinguished from a judicial officer.

Administrative order. The final disposition of a matter before an administrative agency; product of an administrative adjudication. Such order may be declaratory or it may contain an affirmative or negative command. Adm. Procedure Act, 5 U.S.C.A. § 554.

A regulation issued by an administrative agency interpreting or applying the provisions of a statute. Administrative acts having force of law, designed to clarify or implement a law or policy.

Administrative procedure. Methods and processes before administrative agencies as distinguished from judicial procedure which applies to courts. Procedural rules and regulations of most federal agencies are set forth in the Code of Federal Regulations. *See also* Administrative Procedure Act.

Administrative Procedure Act. *Federal.* Law enacted in 1946 (60 Stat. 237, 5 U.S.C.A.) governing practice and proceedings before federal administrative agencies.

State. Individual states have enacted variations of the federal Act, *e.g.* M.G.L.A. (Mass.) c. 30A. Such acts govern proceedings before state administrative agencies.

Administrative process. In general, the procedure used before administrative agencies; in particular, the means of summoning witnesses before such agencies, *e.g.* subpoena.

Administrative remedy. Procedure for allowing person to assert a right to some kind of relief before an administrative agency. Non-judicial remedy provided by agency, board, commission, or the like. In most instances, all administrative remedies must have been exhausted before a court will take jurisdiction of a case; *e.g.* U.S. District Courts will not consider a social security case unless all hearing, appeal, etc. remedies before the Social Security Administration have been exhausted.

Administrative review. Generally refers to judicial review of administrative proceedings; may also embrace appellate review within the administrative agency itself. Adm. Procedure Act, 5 U.S.C.A. § 557.

Administrative rule. Agency statement of general applicability and continuing effect that interprets law or policy or describes agency's requirements.

Administrative rule-making. Power of an administrative agency to make rules and regulations for proceedings before it. Adm. Procedure Act, 5 U.S.C.A. § 553. *See also* Regulatory Flexibility Act.

Administrative search. Search by regulatory agency to determine if laws have been violated; *e.g.* inspection search of business by Occupational Safety and Health Administration for OSHA violations.

Administrative tribunal. A particular administrative agency before which a matter may be heard or tried as distinguished from a judicial forum.

Administrator(-trix). A person appointed by the court to administer (*i.e.*, manage or take charge of) the assets and liabilities of a decedent (*i.e.*, the deceased). Such person may be a male (*i.e.*, administrator) or a female (*i.e.*, administratrix). If the person performing these probate services is named by the decedent's will, he is designated as the executor, or she the executrix, of the estate. *See also* Executor.

An instrumentality established by law for performing the acts necessary for transfer of effects left by deceased to those who succeed to their ownership.

Domestic. One appointed at the place of the domicile of the decedent; distinguished from a foreign or an ancillary administrator.

Foreign. One appointed or qualified under the laws of a foreign state or country, where the decedent was domiciled.

Public. An official provided for by statute in some states to administer upon the property of intestates in certain cases.

Administrator ad litem /ædmìnəstréytər æd láytəm/. A special administrator appointed by court to supply a necessary party to an action in which deceased or his estate is interested.

Administrator cum testamento annexo (C.T.A.) /ædmìnəstréytər kəm testəméntow ənéksow/. *See* Cum testamento annexo.

Administrator de bonis non (D.B.N.) /ædmìnəstréytər dìy bównəs nòn/. "Administrators de bonis non administratis" are, as the term signifies, persons appointed by the court of probate to administer on the effects of a decedent which have not been included in a former administration.

Administrator pendente lite /ædmìnəstréytər pèndéntey láytiy/. A temporary administrator appointed before an adjudication of intestacy has been made for purpose of preserving assets of the estate.

Administrator with will annexed. One appointed administrator of deceased's estate after executors named in will have refused or are unable to act.

Administratrix /ədmìnəstréytrəks/. A female who administers, or to whom letters of administration have been granted.

Admiralty. *See* Maritime.

Admiralty court. A court exercising jurisdiction over all maritime contracts, torts, injuries, or offenses. Federal district courts have jurisdiction over admiralty and maritime actions. 28 U.S.C.A. § 1333. Procedure in such actions is governed by the Fed.R. Civil P. and Supp. Admiralty Rules. *See also* Saving to suitors clause with respect to admiralty actions in state courts.

Admiralty law. The terms "admiralty" and "maritime" law are virtually synonymous. *See* Maritime law.

Admissible. Pertinent and proper to be considered in reaching a decision. Used with reference to the issues to be decided in any judicial proceeding.

Admissible evidence. As applied to evidence, the term means that the evidence introduced is of such a character that the court or judge is bound to receive it; that is, allow it to be introduced at trial. To be "admissible" evidence must be relevant, and, inter alia, to be "relevant" it must tend to establish material proposition. Admissibility of evidence in federal courts is governed by Federal Rules of Evidence. Many states have similar evidence rules for their trial counts. *See* Evidence; Limited admissibility; Relevant evidence.

Admission. *Admission temporaire.* Admission of goods into country duty-free for processing and eventual export.

Bail. The order of a competent court or magistrate that a person accused of crime be discharged from actual custody upon the taking of bail.

Evidence. Ruling by trial judge that trier of fact, judge or jury, may consider testimony or document or other thing (real evidence) in determining ultimate question. *See* Admissible *(Admissible evidence);* Evidence.

Admissions. Confessions, concessions or voluntary acknowledgments made by a party of the existence of certain facts. More accurately regarded, they are statements by a party, or some one identified with him in legal interest, of the existence of a fact which is relevant to the cause of his adversary.

A voluntary acknowledgement made by a party of the existence of the truth of certain facts which are inconsistent with his claims in an action. An admission is not limited to words, but may also include the demeanor, conduct and acts of the person charged with a crime.

Admissions against interest. A statement made by one of the parties to an action which amounts to a prior acknowledgment by him that one of the material facts relevant to the issues is not as he now claims. Any statements made by or attributable to a party to an action, which constitute admissions against his interest and tend to establish or disprove any material fact in the case.

Admissions by party-opponent. A statement is not hearsay if the statement is offered against a party and is (A) his own statement, in either his individual or a representative capacity, or (B) a statement of which he has manifested his adoption or belief in its truth, or (C) a statement by a person authorized by him to make a statement concerning the subject, or (D) a statement by his agent or servant concerning a matter within the scope of his agency or employment, made during the existence of the relationship, or (E) a statement by a coconspirator of a party during the course and in furtherance of the conspiracy. Fed.Evid.R. 801(d)(2).

Admissions by silence. If a statement is made by another person in the presence of a party to the action, containing assertions of facts which, if untrue, the party would under all the circumstances naturally be expected to deny, his failure to speak has traditionally been receivable against him as an admission. Failure of one not under arrest to respond by denial to accusation of crime, or element of crime, may be construed as admission of guilt if such person understood accusation and could have responded. *See also* Estoppel; Silence.

Adoptive admission. Action by a party in which he approves statement of one for whom he is responsible thereby accepting truth of statement. Silence, actions, or statements which manifest assent to the statements of another person. Such may be received into evidence as admissions of the defendant if it can be shown that the defendant adopted the statements as his own. See Fed.Evid.R. 801(d)(2)(B).

Criminal admissions. A statement by accused, direct or implied, of facts pertinent to issue, and tending, in connection with proof of other facts, to prove his guilt. The avowal of a fact or of circumstances from which guilt may be inferred, but only tending to prove the offense charged, and not amounting to a confession of guilt. A statement by defendant of fact or facts pertinent to issues tending, in connection with proof of other facts or circumstances, to prove guilt, but which is, of itself, insufficient to authorize conviction. Does not include statements which are part of the res gestae.

Discovery practice. Requests for admissions in civil actions are governed by Fed.R. Civil P. 36. Any matter admitted under Rule 36 is conclusively established unless the court on motion permits withdrawal or amendment of the admission. *See* Request *(Request for admission);* Stipulation.

Distinguished from confession. A confession is a statement admitting or acknowledging all facts necessary for conviction of the crime. An admission, on the other hand, is an acknowledgment of a fact or facts tending to prove guilt which falls short of an acknowledgment of all essential elements of the crime. The term "admission" is usually applied to civil transactions and to those matters of fact in criminal cases which do not involve criminal intent, while the term "confession" is generally restricted to acknowledgments of guilt.

Extrajudicial admissions. Those made outside of court.

Implied admissions are those which result from some act or failure to act of the party; *e.g.* part payment of a debt is an admission of liability to pay debt.

Incidental admissions are those made in some other connection, or involved in the admission of some other fact.

Judicial admissions are those made in court by a person's attorney for the purpose of being used as a substitute for the regular legal evidence of the facts at the trial. A formal waiver of proof that relieves opposing party from making proof of admitted fact and bars party who made admission from disputing it. Such as are made voluntarily by a party, which appear of record in the proceedings of the court. Formal acts done by a party or his attorney in court on the trial of a cause for the purpose of dispensing with proof by the opposing party of some fact claimed by the latter to be true.

Pleading. The acknowledgment or recognition by one party of the truth of some matter alleged by the opposite party, made in a pleading, the effect of which is to narrow the area of facts or allegations required to be proved by evidence. Averments in a pleading to which a responsive pleading is required are admitted when not denied in the responsive pleading. Fed.R. Civil P. 8(d).

Quasi admission. See that title.

Request for admission. *See* Request.

Tacit admissions. *See* Tacit admissions.

Admissions tax. Form of tax imposed as part of price of being admitted to a particular function or event.

Admission to sufficient facts. Also called "submission to a finding", means an admission to facts sufficient to warrant a finding of guilty.

Admit. *See* Admission; Admissions.

Admonish /ædmónəsh/. To caution or advise. To counsel against wrong practices, or to warn against danger of an offense. *See* Admonition.

Admonition /ædməníshən/. Any authoritative oral communication or statement by way of advice or caution by the court to the jury respecting their duty or conduct as jurors, the admissibility or nonadmissibility of evidence, or the purpose for which any evidence admitted may be considered by them. Reprimand or cautionary statement addressed to counsel by judge.

Adolescence. That age which follows puberty and precedes the age of majority.

Adopt. To accept, appropriate, choose, or select. To make that one's own (property or act) which was not so originally. To accept, consent to, and put into effective operation; as in the case of a constitution, constitutional amendment, ordinance, court rule, or by-law.

Adoption. Legal process pursuant to state statute in which a child's legal rights and duties toward his natural parents are terminated and similar rights and duties toward his adoptive parents are substituted. To take into one's family the child of another and give him or her the rights, privileges, and duties of a child and heir. The procedure is entirely statutory and has no historical basis in common law. Most adoptions are through agency placements. *See* Adoption by estoppel; De facto adoption; Equitable adoption; Placement; Private placement (*Adoption*).

A contract principle by which a person agrees to assume a contract previously made for his or her benefit. An adoption speaks only from the time such person agrees, in contrast to a "ratification" which relates back to the time the original contract was made. In corporation law, the concept is applied when a newly formed corporation accepts a preincorporation contract made for its benefit by a promoter.

Adoption by estoppel. Equitable adoption of a child by promises and acts which preclude such person and his estate from denying adopted status to child. *See also* Equitable adoption.

Adoption by reference. Statement in writing by which another statement in a separate writing is incorporated by reference. Statement in pleading may be adopted by reference in a different part of same pleading or in another pleading or motion. Fed.R. Civil P. 10(c).

Adoptive act. An act of legislation which comes into operation within a limited area upon being adopted, in manner prescribed therein, by the inhabitants of that area.

A.D.R. *See* Alternative dispute resolution; Asset Depreciation Range.

Ad respondendum /æd rəspondéndəm/. For answering; to make answer. Words used in certain writs employed for bringing a person before the court to make answer in defense in a proceeding, as in *habeas corpus ad respondendum* and *capias ad respondendum, q.v.*

Ad satisfaciendum /æd sætəsfèyshiyéndəm/. To satisfy. The emphatic words of the writ of *capias ad satisfaciendum*, which requires the sheriff to *take* the person of the defendant *to satisfy* the plaintiff's claim.

Ad testificandum /æd tèstəfəkǽndəm/. To testify. Type of writ of habeas corpus used to bring prisoner to court to testify. *See* Habeas corpus.

Adult. One who has attained the legal age of majority; generally 18 years. At civil law, a male who had attained the age of 14; a female who had attained the age of 12. *See* Legal age; Majority.

Adulter /ədə́ltər/. One who corrupts; one who seduces another man's wife. *Adulter solidorum*. A corruptor of metals; a counterfeiter.

Adulteration. The act of corrupting or debasing. The act of mixing something impure or spurious with something pure or genuine, or an inferior article with a superior one of the same kind. The term is generally applied to the act of mixing up with food or drink intended to be sold other matters of an inferior quality, and usually of a more or less deleterious quality. The act, process or omission to act by which food becomes impure and unfit for consumption. Such is prohibited and regulated by federal and state statutes and agencies. *See* Food and Drug Administration; Food, Drug and Cosmetic Act; Foreign substance.

Adulterator /ədə́ltəreydər/. A corrupter. In the civil law, a forger; a counterfeiter.

Adultery /ədə́ltəriy/. Voluntary sexual intercourse of a married person with a person other than the offender's husband or wife, or by a person with a person who is married to another. See *e.g.* Wisc.St. 944.16. This crime, which is variously defined and punished by state statutes, is seldom prosecuted. *See also* Illicit cohabitation.

Open and notorious adultery. To constitute living in open and notorious adultery, the parties must reside together publicly in the face of society, as if conjugal relations existed between them, and their so living and the fact that they are not husband and wife must be known in the community.

Ad valorem tax /ǽd vəlórəm/. According to value. A tax imposed on the value of property. The more common ad valorem tax is that imposed by states, counties, and cities on real estate. Ad valorem taxes, can, however, be imposed upon personal property; *e.g.*, a motor vehicle tax may be imposed upon the value of an automobile and is therefore deductible as a tax. A tax levied on property or an article of commerce in proportion to its value, as determined by assessment or appraisal.

Duties are either *ad valorem* or *specific;* the former when the duty is laid in the form of a percentage on the value of the property; the latter where it is imposed as a fixed sum on each article of a class without regard to its value.

Advance. To move something forward in position, time or place. To pay money or render other value before it is due; to furnish something before an equivalent is received; to loan; to furnish capital in aid of a projected enterprise, in expectation of return from it. To supply beforehand; to

furnish on credit or before goods are delivered or work done; to furnish as a part of a stock or fund; to pay money before it is due; to furnish money for a specific purpose understood between the parties, the money or sum equivalent to be returned; to furnish money or goods for others in expectation of reimbursement.

Money or commodities furnished on credit. A loan, or gift or money advanced to be repaid conditionally; may be equivalent to "pay." *See also* Advances.

Advance bill. Bill of exchange drawn before shipment of goods.

Advancement. Money or property given by a parent to his child or, sometimes, presumptive heir, or expended by the former for the latter's benefit, by way of anticipation of the share which the child will inherit in the parent's estate and intended to be deducted therefrom. It is the latter circumstance which differentiates an advancement from a gift or a loan.

Advance payment. Payments made in anticipation of a contingent or fixed future liability or obligation.

Advances. Moneys paid before or in advance of the proper time of payment; money or commodities furnished on credit; a loan or gift, or money advanced to be repaid conditionally. Payments advanced to the owner of property by a factor or broker on the price of goods which the latter has in his hands, or is to receive, for sale. *See also* Advance.

Advance sheets. Pamphlets (published weekly for National Reporter System) containing the most recently reported opinions of specific courts (*e.g.* Federal Reporter) or the courts of several jurisdictions (*e.g.* Pacific Reporter). The volume and page numbers usually are the same as in the subsequently bound volumes of the respective reporter series, which cover several numbered issues of the advance sheets.

Adventure. A hazardous and striking enterprise. A bold undertaking accompanied by possible hazards, risks and unforeseen events.

A common word in marine insurance policies, used as synonymous, or nearly so, with "perils." A shipment of goods in charge of an agent to be disposed of for the best price obtainable.

Adventure, bill of. In commercial law, a writing signed by a merchant, stating that the property in goods shipped in his name belongs to another, to the adventure or chance of which the person so named is to stand, with a covenant from the merchant to account to him for the produce.

Gross adventure. In maritime law, a loan on bottomry. So named because the lender, in case of a loss, or expense incurred for the common safety, must contribute to the *gross* or general average.

Joint adventure. A commercial or maritime enterprise undertaken by several persons jointly; a limited partnership,—not limited in the statutory sense as to the liability of the partners, but as to its scope and duration. An association of two or more persons to carry out a single business enterprise for profit, for which purpose they combine their property, money, effects, skill, and knowledge. A special combination of two or more persons, where, in some specific adventure, a profit is jointly sought, without any actual partnership or corporate designation. *See also* Joint venture.

Adventurer. One who undertakes uncertain or hazardous actions or enterprises. It is also used to denote one who seeks to advance his own interests by unscrupulous designs on the credulity of others.

Adversary counsel. Such counsel, as required to be appointed in commitment proceedings has the same functions, duties and responsibilities as one would have if one retained by the person involved as his or her own attorney, and such duties include preserving the confidences and secrets of the client, exercising independent professional judgment on behalf of the client, representing the client competently, and representing client zealously within the bounds of the law.

Adversary proceeding. One having opposing parties; contested, as distinguished from an ex parte hearing or proceeding. One of which the party seeking relief has given legal notice to the other party, and afforded the latter an opportunity to contest it. *See also* Case. *Compare* Ex parte.

Adversary system. The jurisprudential network of laws, rules and procedures characterized by opposing parties who contend against each other for a result favorable to themselves. In such system, the judge acts as an independent magistrate rather than prosecutor; distinguished from inquisitorial system.

Adverse. Opposed; contrary; in resistance or opposition to a claim, application, or proceeding. Having opposing interests; having interests for the preservation of which opposition is essential.

Use of land is "adverse", as against owner, if it is not made in subordination to him, is open and notorious and is not wrongful as to him; "adverse" means that one making use shall not recognize in those as against whom it is claimed to be adverse an authority either to prevent or to permit its continuance, and refers to nonrecognition of such authority at time use is made.

As to *adverse* Enjoyment; User; Verdict; Witness, see those titles.

Adverse claim. An alleged right of one person asserted against the interest of another person.

Adverse enjoyment. *See* Adverse possession.

Adverse interest. The "adverse interest" of a witness, so as to permit cross-examination by the party calling him, must be so involved in the event of the suit that a legal right or liability will be acquired, lost, or materially affected by the judgment, and must be such as would be promoted by the success of the adversary of the party calling him. *See also* Adverse witness.

Adverse interest rule. Failure of a party to produce a witness who is within his power to produce and who would naturally have been produced by him, which failure permits inference that evidence of witness would be unfavorable to party's cause.

Adverse opinion. An accounting term used in connection with the issuance of audited financial statements. An adverse opinion states that the entity's financial statements do not present fairly the financial position, results of operations, and changes in financial position in conformity with generally accepted accounting principles (GAAP).

An explanation of the departure from GAAP must be included in the opinion. *See* Opinion (*Accounting*) for "qualified," "unqualified," and "disclaimer" opinions.

Adverse party. A party to an action whose interests are opposed to or opposite the interests of another party to the action.

Appeal. An "adverse party" entitled to notice of appeal is every party whose interest in relation to the judgment or decree appealed from is in conflict with the modification or reversal sought by the appeal. Such term includes the following: Every party interested in sustaining the judgment or decree. All parties appearing against losing party unless reversal of case will not be to party's detriment. Any party who would be prejudicially affected by a modification or reversal of the judgment appealed from. One who has interest in opposing object sought to be accomplished by appeal. Party to record, whose interest in subject-matter of appeal is adverse to reversal or modification of judgment or order appealed from.

Discovery. When the parties exchange pleadings, one asserting a claim for relief against the other, the parties are "adverse," within rule allowing written interrogatories to be served upon any adverse party.

Adverse possession. A method of acquisition of title to real property by possession for a statutory period under certain conditions. It has been described as the statutory method of acquiring title to land by limitation.

Because of the statute of limitations on the bringing of actions for the recovery of land, title can be acquired to real property by adverse possession. In order to establish title in this manner, there must be proof of nonpermissive use which is actual, open, notorious, exclusive and adverse for the statutorily prescribed period. State statutes differ with respect to the required length of possession from an upper limit of 20 years to a lower one of 5 years, with even more extreme time periods covering certain special cases. There may be different periods of time even within a single state, depending on whether or not the adverse possessor has color of title and/or whether or not taxes have been paid. In some cases a longer possession is required against public entities than against individuals.

See also Constructive adverse possession; Hostile; Notorious possession; Possession (*Hostile possession; Open possession*); Prescription; Tacking.

Adverse use. Use without license or permission; an element necessary to acquire title or easement by prescription.

Adverse witness. A witness who gives evidence on a material matter prejudicial to the party then examining him. Commonly used to describe a witness whose testimony is prejudicial or unfavorable to the party who called him and as a result, such witness may be impeached. *See also* Adverse interest; Hostile *or* adverse witness.

Advertise. To advise, announce, apprise, command, give notice of, inform, make known, publish. To call a matter to the public attention by any means whatsoever. Any oral, written, or graphic statement made by the seller in any manner in connection with the solicitation of business and includes, without limitation because of enumeration, statements and representations made in a newspaper or other publication or on radio or television or contained in any notice, handbill, sign, catalog, or letter, or printed on or contained in any tag or label attached to or accompanying any merchandise. As distinguished from other forms of communication means to call a matter to the public attention. False and deceptive advertising is regulated by the Federal Trade Commission and similar state agencies. *See also* Printers Ink Statute.

Comparative advertising. Advertising that specifically compares the advertised brand with other brands of the same product.

Competitive advertising. Advertising that contains basically little information and is used only to allow a producer to maintain a share of the market for that product.

Informative advertising. Advertising that gives information about the suitability and quality of products. To be contrasted with competitive advertising.

Advertisement. Notice given in a manner designed to attract public attention. Information communicated to the public, or to an individual concerned, as by handbills, newspaper, television, billboards, radio.

Advice. View; opinion; information; the counsel given by lawyers to their clients; an opinion expressed as to wisdom of future conduct. *See also* Advise.

The instruction usually given by one merchant or banker to another by letter, informing him of shipments made to him, or of bills or drafts drawn on him, with particulars of date, or sight, the sum, and the payee. Bills presented for acceptance or payment are frequently dishonored for *want of advice.*

Advice of counsel. A defense used in actions for malicious prosecution which requires a finding that defendant presented all facts to his counsel and that he honestly followed counsel's advice.

Advice of credit. Notice by an advising bank of the issuance of a letter of credit.

Advise. To give an opinion or counsel, or recommend a plan or course of action; also to give notice. To encourage, inform, or acquaint. It is different in meaning from "instruct" or "persuade." Where a statute authorizes the trial court to *advise* the jury to acquit, the court has no power to *instruct* the jury to acquit. The court can only counsel, and the jury are not bound by the advice. "Advise" imports that it is discretionary or optional with the person addressed whether he will act on such advice or not.

Advised. Prepared to give judgment, after examination and deliberation. *E.g.* "The court took time to be advised."

Advisedly. With deliberation; intentionally.

Advisement. Consideration; deliberation; consultation. The consultation of a court, after the argument of a cause by counsel, and before delivering their opinion.

Advising bank. A bank which gives notification of the issuance of a [letter of] credit by another bank. U.C.C. § 5–103(1)(e).

Advisory. Counselling, suggesting, or advising, but not imperative or conclusive. A verdict on an issue out of chancery is advisory.

Advisory counsel. Attorney retained to give advice as contrasted with trial counsel.

Advisory jury. In actions in Federal court in which there is no jury trial as of right, court may try case with an advisory jury and its verdict is not binding on court. Fed.R.Civ.P. 39(c). *See also* Jury.

Advisory opinion. Such may be rendered by a court at the request of the government or an interested party indicating how the court would rule on a matter should adversary litigation develop. An advisory opinion is thus an interpretation of the law without binding effect. While the International Court of Justice and some state courts will render advisory opinions the federal courts will not; their jurisdiction being restricted to cases or controversies. *Compare* Declaratory judgment. *See also* Case.

Advisory opinions are also issued by the FTC when there is a question on the legality of proposed business activities.

Advisory trial. *See* Advisory jury.

Advisory verdict. *See* Advisory jury.

Advocacy /ǽdvəkəsiy/. The act of pleading for, supporting, or recommending active espousal.

Advocare /ædvəkériy/. Lat. To defend; to call to one's aid; to vouch; to warrant.

Advocate /ǽdvəkèyt/, *v.* To speak in favor of or defend by argument. To support, vindicate, or recommend publicly.

Advocate /ǽdvəkət/, *n.* One who assists, defends, or pleads for another. One who renders legal advice and aid and pleads the cause of another before a court or a tribunal, a counselor. A person learned in the law, and duly admitted to practice, who assists his client with advice, and pleads for him in open court. An assistant; adviser; a pleader of causes.

Advocating overthrow of government. Such conduct is a federal crime. 18 U.S.C.A. §§ 2384, 2385. *See also* Treason.

Aesthetic value. The artistic worth of something as contrasted with its practical value. Value of property attributable to beauty or improvements or surroundings. *See* Amenity.

A.F.D.C. Aid to Families with Dependent Children.

Affair. (Fr.). A law suit.

Affairs. An inclusive term, bringing within its scope and meaning anything that a person may do. A person's concerns in trade or property; business. That which is done or to be done. General operations carried on by an employer. *See also* Statement of affairs.

Affect. To act upon; influence; change; enlarge or abridge; often used in the sense of acting injuriously upon persons and things. To lay hold of or attack (as a disease does); to act, or produce an effect or result upon; to impress or influence (the mind or feelings); to touch.

Affecting commerce. Any activity which touches or concerns business or industry, favorably or burdensomely; commonly used within context of Labor Management Relations Act regarding a labor dispute which burdens commerce.

The term "affecting commerce" means in commerce, or burdening or obstructing commerce or the free flow of commerce, or having led or tend-

ing to lead to a labor dispute burdening or obstructing commerce or the free flow of commerce. National Labor Relations Act, § 2(7); 29 U.S.C.A. § 152.

The term "industry affecting commerce" means any industry or activity in commerce or in which a labor dispute would burden or obstruct commerce or tend to burden or obstruct commerce or the free flow of commerce. Labor Management Relations Act, § 501(1); 29 U.S.C.A. § 142.

Affection. The making over, pawning, or mortgaging of a thing to assure the payment of a sum of money, or the discharge of some other duty or service. In a medical sense, an abnormal bodily condition.

Affiance. To assure by pledge. An agreement by which a man and woman promise that they will marry each other.

Affiant /əfáyənt/. The person who makes and subscribes an affidavit. The word is used, in this sense, interchangeably with "deponent." But the latter term should be reserved as the designation of one who makes a deposition.

Affidavit /æfədéyvət/. A written or printed declaration or statement of facts, made voluntarily, and confirmed by the oath or affirmation of the party making it, taken before a person having authority to administer such oath or affirmation. *See also* Certification; Jurat; Verification.

Affidavit of defense. An affidavit stating that the defendant has a good defense to the plaintiff's action on the merits; *e.g.* affidavit filed with motion for summary judgment. Fed.R. Civil P. 56(e).

Affidavit of inquiry. By court rule in certain states, substituted service of process may be had on absent defendants if it appears by affidavit of plaintiff's attorney, or other person having knowledge of the facts, that defendant cannot, after diligent inquiry, be served within the state.

Affidavit of merits. One setting forth that the defendant has a meritorious defense (substantial and not technical) and stating the facts constituting the same. *See* Affidavit of defense.

Affidavit of notice. A sworn statement that affiant has given proper notice of hearing to other parties to action.

Affidavit of service. An affidavit intended to certify the service of a writ, notice, summons, or other document or process. In federal courts, if service is made by a person other than a United States Marshall or his deputy, he shall make affidavit thereof. Fed.R. Civil P. 4(g).

Affidavit to hold to bail. An affidavit required in many cases before the defendant in a civil action may be arrested. Such an affidavit must contain a statement, clearly and certainly expressed, by someone acquainted with the fact, of an indebtedness from the defendant to the plaintiff, and must show a distinct cause of action.

Affiliate /əfíliyeyt/. Signifies a condition of being united; being in close connection, allied, associated, or attached as a member or branch.

Affiliate company. Company effectively controlled by another company. A branch, division, or subsidiary. Under Investment Company Act (15 U.S.C.A. § 80a–2), company in which there is ownership (direct or indirect) of 5 percent or more of the voting stock. *See* Controlled company.

Corporations which are related as parent and subsidiary, characterized by identity of ownership of capital stock. *See also* Holding company.

Affiliation. Act or condition of being affiliated, allied, or associated with another person, body, or organization. Imports less than membership in an organization, but more than sympathy, and a working alliance to bring to fruition the proscribed program of a proscribed organization, as distinguished from mere co-operation with a proscribed organization in lawful activities, is essential. It includes an element of dependability upon which the organization can rely which, though not equivalent to membership duty, rests upon course of conduct that could not be abruptly ended without giving at least reasonable cause for charge of breach of good faith. *See also* Association.

The act of imputing or determining the paternity of a child born out of wedlock, and the obligation to maintain it. *See* Paternity suit *or* action.

Affinity /əfínətiy/. A close agreement; relation; spiritual relation or attraction held to exist between certain persons. Relation which one spouse because of marriage has to blood relatives of the other. The connection existing, in consequence of marriage, between each of the married persons and the kindred of the other.

Degrees of relationship by affinity are computed as are degrees of relationship by consanguinity. The doctrine of affinity grew out of the canonical maxim that marriage makes husband and wife one. The husband has the same relation, by affinity, to his wife's blood relatives as she has to them by consanguinity and vice versa.

Affinity is distinguished into three kinds: (1) *Direct*, or that subsisting between the husband and his wife's relations by blood, or between the wife and the husband's relations by blood; (2) *secondary*, or that which subsists between the husband and his wife's relations by marriage; (3) *collateral*, or that which subsists between the husband and the relations of his wife's relations.

In a larger sense, consanguinity or kindred.

Quasi affinity. In the civil law, the affinity which exists between two persons, one of whom has been betrothed to a kinsman of the other, but who have never been married.

Affirm. To ratify, uphold, approve, make firm, confirm, establish, reassert. To make affirmation; to make a solemn and formal declaration or asseveration that an affidavit is true, that the witness will tell the truth, etc., this being substituted for an oath in certain cases. Also, to give testimony on affirmation. *See* Affidavit; Jurat; Verification.

Judgment. In the practice of appellate courts, to *affirm* a judgment, decree, or order, is to declare that it is valid and right and must stand as rendered below; to ratify and reassert it; to concur in its correctness and confirm its efficacy. If the appellate court *remanded* the case, it would be sending it back to the lower court with instructions to correct the irregularities specified in the appellate opinion. If the appellate court *reversed* the court below, it would have changed the result reached below.

Pleading. To allege or aver a matter of fact; to state it affirmatively. The opposite of deny or traverse.

Affirmance. The confirming, or ratifying of a former law, or judgment. The confirmation and ratification by an appellate court of a judgment, order, or decree of a lower court brought before it for review. *See* Affirm.

The ratification or confirmation of a voidable contract or act by the party who is to be bound thereby. The term is in accuracy to be distinguished from *ratification*, which is a recognition of the validity or binding force as against the party ratifying, of some act performed by another person; and from *confirmation*, which would seem to apply more properly to cases where a doubtful authority has been exercised by another in behalf of the person ratifying; but these distinctions are not generally observed.

Affirmant /əfə́rmənt/. A person who testifies on affirmation, or who affirms instead of taking an oath. Used in affidavits and depositions which are *affirmed*, instead of sworn to in place of the word "deponent." *See also* Affirmation; Jurat; Verification.

Affirmation. A solemn and formal declaration or asseveration that an affidavit is true, that the witness will tell the truth, etc.; this being substituted for an oath in certain cases. A solemn religious asseveration in the nature of an oath. *See also* Confirmation; Jurat; Oath; Verification.

Affirmation of fact. A statement concerning a subject-matter of a transaction which might otherwise be only an expression of opinion but which is affirmed as an existing fact material to the transaction, and reasonably induces the other party to consider and rely upon it, as a fact.

Affirmative. That which declares positively; that which avers a fact to be true; that which establishes; the opposite of negative.

As to *affirmative* Plea; Proof; Warranty, see those titles.

Affirmative action programs. Employment programs required by federal statutes and regulations designed to remedy discriminatory practices in hiring minority group members; *i.e.* positive steps designed to eliminate existing and continuing discrimination, to remedy lingering effects of past discrimination, and to create systems and procedures to prevent future discrimination; commonly based on population percentages of minority groups in a particular area. Factors considered are race, color, sex, creed and age.

Affirmative charge. The general "affirmative charge" is an instruction to the jury that, whatever the evidence may be, defendant cannot be convicted under the count in the indictment to which the charge is directed.

Affirmative defense. In pleading, matter asserted by defendant which, assuming the complaint to be true, constitutes a defense to it. A response to a plaintiff's claim which attacks the plaintiff's *legal* right to bring an action, as opposed to attacking the truth of claim. Under the Fed. Rules of Civil Procedure, and also under most state Rules, all affirmative defenses must be raised in the responsive pleading (answer); such defenses include accord and satisfaction, assumption of risk, contributory negligence, duress, statute of limitations, estoppel, etc. See Fed.R. Civil P. 8(c).

Affirmative defenses in criminal cases include insanity, intoxication, self-defense, automatism, coercion, alibi, and duress. See *e.g.* Model Penal Code § 3.01 (justification as affirmative defense).

Affirmative easement. An easement which gives the right to enter or pass over the property of another. *See* Right of way.

Affirmative pregnant. In common law pleading, an affirmative allegation implying some negative in favor of the adverse party.

Affirmative proof. Such evidence of the truth of matters asserted as tends to establish them, regardless of character of evidence offered.

Affirmative relief. Relief, benefit, or compensation which may be due and granted to defendant. Relief for which defendant might maintain an action independently of plaintiff's claim and on which he might proceed to recovery, although plaintiff abandoned his cause of action or failed to establish it. Specific performance *(q.v.)* is a type of affirmative relief that may be granted to plaintiff.

Affirmative statute. A statute couched in affirmative or mandatory terms. One which directs the doing of an act, or declares what shall be done; as

a *negative* statute is one which prohibits a thing from being done, or declares what shall not be done.

Affirmative warranty. *See* Warranty.

Affix. Fix or fasten in any way; to attach physically. To attach to, inscribe, or impress upon, as a signature, a seal, a trade-mark. To attach, add to, or fasten upon, permanently, as in the case of fixtures annexed to real estate. A thing is deemed to be affixed to land when it is attached to it by the roots, as in the case of trees, vines, or shrubs; or imbedded in it, as in the case of walls; or permanently resting upon it, as in the case of buildings; or permanently attached to what is thus permanent, as by means of cement, plaster, nails, bolts, or screws. *See* Fixture.

Affixing. Securely attached.

Affliction. A distress of mind or body; that which causes continuing anguish or suffering.

Affray. A public offense at common law, it is the mutual combat of two or more persons in a public place to the terror of the people. It differs from a riot or duel in not being premeditated. *See also* Disorderly conduct; Dueling; Fight; Riot.

Affreightment /əfreytmənt/. A contract of affreightment is a contract with a ship-owner to hire his ship, or part of it, for the carriage of goods. Such a contract generally takes the form either of a charter-party or of a bill of lading.

Affront /əfrónt/. An insult or indignity; assault, insolence.

A.F.L. American Federation of Labor. Merged with CIO (Congress of Industrial Organizations) in 1955.

Aforementioned. *See* Aforesaid.

Aforesaid. Before, or already said, mentioned, or recited; premised. Preceding; opposite of following.

Aforethought. In criminal law, deliberate; planned; premeditated; prepense. As used in the definition of murder in the first degree, means thought of beforehand and for any length of time, however short, before the doing of the act, and is synonymous with premeditation. *See* Malice aforethought; Premeditation.

A fortiori /èy forshiyóray/. With stronger reason; much more. A term used in logic to denote an argument to the effect that because one ascertained fact exists, therefore another, which is included in it, or analogous to it, and which is less improbable, unusual, or surprising, must also exist.

After. Later, succeeding, subsequent to, inferior in point of time or of priority or preference. Subsequent in time to. On and after.

After-acquired. Acquired after a particular date or event. Thus, a judgment is a lien on after-acquired realty, *i.e.*, land acquired by the debtor after entry of the judgment.

After acquired property. Property of debtor which is acquired after security transaction covering property already owned is perfected. Property acquired after the date of the agreement usually becomes additional security for payment of the indebtedness if an after-acquired property provision is included in the agreement. See UCC § 9–204, and After acquired property clause, *infra*. May also refer to property acquired by testator after execution of will.

In bankruptcy law, with certain exceptions, the bankruptcy estate includes any interest in property that the estate acquires after commencement of the case. Bankruptcy Code § 541(a).

After acquired property clause. A clause in a mortgage or security agreement providing that any property acquired by the borrower after the date of the loan will automatically become additional security for the loan.

After acquired title. Doctrine under which title acquired by grantor who previously attempted to convey title to land which he did not in fact own, inures automatically to benefit of prior grantees. The doctrine provides that, although the sale of another's property is null, the purchaser is entitled to the benefit of any title subsequently acquired by the seller. *See* Estoppel *(Estoppel by deed).*

After born child. Refers to child born after execution of will or to child born after time in which class gift closes. Generally, birth of child after father has executed his will does not revoke will. *See* En ventre sa mere; Heirs; Posthumous child.

After born heirs. A person entitled to property born after the death of the ancestor intestate. *See* Descent; Heirs.

After-discovered. Discovered or made known after a particular date or event.

After-discovered evidence. *See* Evidence.

After-market. Term describing the market for a security after it has been initially sold by the issuer through underwriters.

Afternoon. May mean the whole time from noon to midnight (*e.g.* U.C.C. § 4–104(1)(b)), or it may mean the earlier part of that time as distinguished from evening, or may mean that part of day between noon and evening.

After sight. This term as used in a bill payable so many days after sight, means after legal sight; that is, after legal presentment for acceptance. The mere fact of having seen the bill or known of its existence does not constitute legal "sight."

After the fact. Subsequent to an event from which time is reckoned, *e.g.* accessory after fact is one who harbors, conceals or aids in concealment of the principal felon after the felony has been committed.

Afterthought. A thought composed after the event and with deliberation.

Afterward, afterwards. Subsequent in point of time; synonymous with "thereafter."

Against. Adverse to; contrary. Signifies discord or conflict; opposed to; without the consent of; in conflict with. Sometimes meaning "upon," which is almost, if not altogether, synonymous with word "on."

Against interest. Commonly used to describe a declaration or admission by one, the content of which is adverse to his position, interest or title; *e.g.*, an exception to hearsay rule is a declaration by one against his pecuniary or proprietary interest at the time when it was made. Fed.Evid.Rule 804. *See also* Admission; Declaration *(Declarations against interest).*

Against public interest. An agreement or act which is or has been declared to be adverse to the general good or public welfare; such that a judge may on his own declare void. *See* Public interest.

Against the evidence. *See* Against the weight of the evidence.

Against the form of the statute. Technical words which must be used in framing an indictment for a breach of the statute prohibiting the act complained of. The Latin phrase is *contra forman statuti, q.v.*

Against the law. A decision is "against the law" for purposes of a motion for new trial where the evidence is insufficient in law and without conflict on any material point. Such exists when there is a failure to find on material issue, or when findings are irreconcilable or where evidence is insufficient in law and without conflict on any material point.

Against the peace. A technical phrase used in alleging a breach of the peace.

Against the weight of the evidence. Contrary to the evidence. A finding is "against the manifest weight of the evidence" if an opposite conclusion is clearly evident. For judgement to be considered such, it must appear that conclusions opposite to those reached by the trier of fact are clearly evident. If a verdict is against the weight of the evidence, a new trial may be granted under Fed.R.Civ.P. 59(a). *See also* Directed verdict; Non obstante verdicto; Weight of evidence.

Against the will. Technical words used in framing an indictment for robbery from the person, rape and some other offenses. *See also* Coercion; Duress; Force.

Age. The length of time during which a person has lived. The time at which one attains full personal rights and capacities. In law the term signifies those periods in the lives of persons of both sexes which enable them to do certain acts which, before they had arrived at those periods, they were prohibited from doing. *See e.g.* Age of consent; Age of majority; Legal age; Majority.

Age discrimination act. Federal legislation prohibiting unfair and discriminatory treatment in employment on the basis of age. The Act generally covers individuals at least 40 years of age. Age Discrimination in Employment Act of 1967, as amended. 29 U.S.C.A. § 621 et seq. *See also* Older Workers Benefits Protection Act.

Aged person. One advanced in years; refers to his or her chronological, not mental age.

Agency. A relationship between two persons, by agreement or otherwise, where one (the agent) may act on behalf of the other (the principal) and bind the principal by words and actions. Relation in which one person acts for or represents another by latter's authority, either in the relationship of principal and agent, master and servant, or employer or proprietor and independent contractor. It also designates a place at which business of company or individual is transacted by an agent. The relation created by express or implied contract or by law, whereby one party delegates the transaction of some lawful business with more or less discretionary power to another, who undertakes to manage the affair and render to him an account thereof. Or relationship where one person confides the management of some affair, to be transacted on his account, to other party. Or where one party is authorized to do certain acts for, or in relation to the rights or property of the other. But means more than tacit permission, and involves request, instruction, or command. The consensual relation existing between two persons, by virtue of which one is subject to other's control.

Agency is the fiduciary relation which results from the manifestation of consent by one person to another that the other shall act on his behalf and subject to his control, and consent by the other so to act. Restatement, Second, Agency § 1.

See also Agent; Authority.

Actual agency. Exists where the agent is really employed by the principal.

Administrative agency. *See* Administrative agency.

Agency by estoppel. One created by operation of law and established by proof of such acts of the principal as reasonably lead third person to the conclusion of its existence. Arises where principal, by negligence in failing to supervise agent's affairs, allows agent to exercise powers not grant-

ed to him, thus justifying others in believing agent possesses requisite authority.

Deed of agency. A revocable and voluntary trust for payment of debts.

Del credere. Type of agency in which agent is entrusted with goods, documents or securities and in which he is given broad authority to collect from the buyer and in some cases has been held responsible for the buyer's solvency.

Exclusive agency. An agreement by owner that during life of contract he will not sell property to a purchaser procured by another agent, which agreement does not preclude owner himself from selling to a purchaser of his own procuring, while a contract giving a broker "exclusive sale" is more than such exclusive agency, and is an agreement by the owner that he will not sell the property during the life of the contract to any purchaser not procured by the broker in question. *See also* Exclusive agency.

Executive agency. See that title.

General agency. That which exists when there is a delegation to do all acts connected with a particular trade, business or employment. It implies authority on the part of the agent to act without restriction or qualification in all matters relating to the business of his principal.

Implied agency. One created by act of parties and deduced from proof of other facts. It is an actual agency, proved by deductions or inferences from other facts, and third party need have no knowledge of the principal's acts, nor have relied on them.

One which occurs when agent and principal have no express understanding as to agent's appointment but their conduct suggests agency arrangement, and finding of implied agency depends on facts and circumstances for which principal is responsible which imply that principal intended to create agency.

Intervening agency. See that title.

Mutual agency. A feature of partnerships whereby each partner acts as an agent of the partnership in business transactions.

Ostensible agency. See that title. *See also* Agency by estoppel, above.

Special agency. One in which the agent is authorized to conduct a single transaction or a series of transactions not involving a continuity of service.

Universal agency. One in which agent is empowered to conduct every transaction lawfully delegable by principal to agent.

Agency by operation of law. *See Agency by estoppel* under Agency, *supra.*

Agency coupled with an interest. A relationship known to the law of agency wherein the agent has an interest in the property or subject matter in which he is dealing. This special type of agency relationship will not terminate automatically upon the death of the principal.

Interest in continued existence of power or authority to act with reference to business, where secured by contract and based on consideration moving from agent to principal looking to exercise of power as means of reimbursement, creates agency coupled with an interest. Agent must have an interest or estate in the thing to be disposed of or managed under the power.

Agency in fact. An agency relationship established by agreement of principal and agent as distinguished from one imposed by law; *e.g.* agency by estoppel.

Agency of the United States. A department, division, or administration within the federal government.

Agency relationship. An employment for purpose of representation in establishing legal relations between principal and third persons. *See* Agency; Agent.

Agency shop. A union-security device whereby, in order to continue employment, any nonunion member employee is required to pay to the Union sums equivalent to those paid by union members, either in an amount equal to both union dues and initiation fees, or in an amount equal to dues alone. *See also* Open shop.

Agenda. Memoranda of things to be done, as items of business or discussion to be brought up at a meeting; a program consisting of such items.

Agent. A person authorized by another (principal) to act for or in place of him; one intrusted with another's business. One who represents and acts for another under the contract or relation of agency *(q.v.)*. A business representative, whose function is to bring about, modify, affect, accept performance of, or terminate contractual obligations between principal and third persons. One who undertakes to transact some business, or to manage some affair, for another, by the authority and on account of the latter, and to render an account of it. One who acts for or in place of another by authority from him; a substitute, a deputy, appointed by principal with power to do the things which principal may do. One who deals not only with things, as does a servant, but with persons, using his own discretion as to means, and frequently establishing contractual relations between his principal and third persons.

One authorized to transact all business of principal, or all of principal's business of some particular kind, or all business at some particular place.

See also Agency; Bargaining agent; Corporate agent; Foreign agent; Forwarding agent; Innocent agent; Servant; Soliciting agent; Statutory agent; Subagent; Transfer agent.

Apparent agent or ostensible agent. One whom the principal, either intentionally or by want of ordinary care, induces third persons to believe to be his agent, though he has not, either expressly or by implication, conferred authority on him. A person who, whether or not authorized, reasonably appears to third person, because of manifestations of another, to be authorized to act as agent for such other. Restatement, Second, Agency § 8.

Bargaining agent. See Bargaining agent.

Co-agent. One who shares authority to act for the principal with another agent and who is so authorized by the principal.

Diplomatic agent. One representing government in dealings with foreign government.

Dual agent. See Co-agent, above.

Exclusive agent. The only agent permitted to act for principal in a particular territory or matter, though the principal may act for himself; *i.e.* exclusive sales territory given to agent does not bar principal from selling in this territory.

Foreign agent. See Foreign agent.

General agency business. One not engaged as agent for single firm or person, but holding himself out to public as being engaged in business of being agent.

General agent. One who is authorized to act for his principal in all matters concerning particular business or employment of particular nature. *Compare Special agent, below.*

High managerial agent. An officer of a corporation or any other agent in a position of comparable authority with respect to formulation of corporate policy or the supervision in a managerial capacity of subordinate employees.

Independent agent. One who is an independent contractor exercising his own judgment and subject to the one who hired him only for the result of the work performed.

Insurance agent. See Insurance.

Local agent. One appointed to act as the representative of a corporation and transact its business generally (or business of a particular character) at a given place or within a defined district.

Managing agent. A person who is invested with general power, involving the exercise of judgment and discretion, as distinguished from an ordinary agent or employee, who acts in an inferior capacity, and under the direction and control of superior authority, both in regard to the extent of the work and the manner of executing the same. One who has exclusive supervision and control of some department of a corporation's business, the management of which requires of such person the exercise of independent judgment and discretion, and the exercise of such authority that it may be fairly said that service of summons upon him will result in notice to the corporation.

Mercantile agents. Agents employed for the sale of goods or merchandise are called "mercantile agents," and are of two principal classes,—brokers and factors *(q. v.)*; a factor is sometimes called a "commission agent," or "commission merchant."

Private agent. An agent acting for an individual in his private affairs; as distinguished from a *public* agent, who represents the government in some administrative capacity.

Public agent. An agent of the public, the state, or the government; a person appointed to act for the public in some matter pertaining to the administration of government or the public business.

Real-estate agent. Person whose business it is to sell, or offer for sale, real estate for others, or to rent houses, stores, or other buildings, or real estate, or to collect rent for others.

Special agent. One employed to conduct a particular transaction or piece of business for his principal or authorized to perform a specified act. An agent authorized to conduct a single transaction or a series of transactions not involving continuity of service. *Compare General agent, above.*

Subagent. One authorized by agent to help perform functions for principal. Generally, absent express or implied authority, an agent has no authority to appoint a subagent. The subagent is subject to control by both agent and principal. Restatement, Second, Agency § 5.

Superior agent. See High managerial agent, above.

Transfer agent. Any person who engages on behalf of an issuer of securities or on behalf of itself as an issuer of securities in (A) countersigning such securities upon issuance; (B) monitoring the issuance of such securities with a view to preventing unauthorized issuance, a function commonly performed by a person called a registrar; (C) registering the transfer of such securities; (D) exchanging or converting such securities; or (E) transferring record ownership of securities by bookkeeping entry without physical issuance of securities certificates. Securities Exchange Act of 1934, § 3, 15 U.S.C.A. § 78c.

Undercover agent. See that title.

Universal agent. See Universal agency under topic Agency.

Agent provocateur /éyjənt prəvòkət(y)úr/. A spy; a secret agent hired to penetrate an organization to gather evidence against its members or to incite trouble.

Agent's lien. The legal right agreed in advance to payment from a principal for services rendered by an agent.

Age of consent. Age at which persons may marry without parental approval. Age at which a female is legally capable of agreeing to sexual intercourse and below which age the male commits statutory rape if he has sexual intercourse with her. *See also* Legal age; Majority; Statutory rape.

Age of majority. Age at which a person may contract *sui juris*; now 18 in most jurisdictions. Sometimes referred to as full age; legal age; majority; adulthood. Age at which one may execute a valid will or vote; age at which payments for support by parents may generally be terminated. *See also* Legal age; Majority.

Age of reason. Age at which a child is deemed to be capable of acting responsibly; commonly the age of 7. In general, one between the ages of 7 and 14 is rebuttably presumed to be incapable of committing a crime. Below the age of 7 a child is conclusively presumed to be incapable of committing crime. *See* Infancy.

Aggravate. *See* Aggravation.

Aggravated arson. *See* Arson.

Aggravated assault. A person is guilty of aggravated assault if he: attempts to cause serious bodily injury to another, or causes such injury purposely, knowingly or recklessly under circumstances manifesting extreme indifference to the value of human life; or, attempts to cause or purposely or knowingly causes bodily injury to another with a deadly weapon. Model Penal Code, § 211.1(2). In all jurisdictions statutes punish such aggravated assaults as assault with intent to murder (or rob or kill or rape) and assault with a dangerous (or deadly) weapon more severely than "simple" assaults. *See also* Assault.

Aggravated battery. Unlawful application of force to another characterized by unusual or serious consequences or attending circumstances such as a dangerous weapon. This offense was unknown at common law. *See* Aggravated assault.

Aggravated robbery. *See* Robbery.

Aggravating circumstances. *See* Aggravation.

Aggravation. Any circumstance attending the commission of a crime or tort which increases its guilt or enormity or adds to its injurious consequences, but which is above and beyond the essential constituents of the crime or tort itself. *See* e.g. Aggravated assault.

Aggregate. Entire number, sum, mass, or quantity of something; total amount; complete whole. One provision under will may be the aggregate if there are no more units to fall into that class. Composed of several; consisting of many persons united together; a combined whole. *See also* Joinder.

Aggregate corporation. *See* Corporation.

Aggregate income. Total income of husband and wife who file a joint tax return.

Aggregate theory of partnership. A partnership is the totality of persons engaged in a business and not an entity in itself as in the case of a corporation.

Aggregation /ǽgrəgéyshən/. The combination of two or more elements in patent claims, each of which is unrelated, and each of which performs separately and without cooperation, where combination does not define a composite integrated mechanism. Term means that the elements of a claimed combination are incapable of co-operation to produce a unitary result, and in its true sense does not need prior art patents to support it.

Aggregation doctrine. Rule which precludes totalling of claims for Federal jurisdictional amount purposes.

Aggressor. One who first employs hostile force. The party who first offers violence or offense. He who begins a quarrel or dispute, either by threatening or striking another, that justifies like response.

Aggressor corporation. A corporation that attempts to obtain control of a publicly held corporation, often by a direct cash tender or public exchange offer to shareholders, but also possibly by way of merger, which requires agreement or assent of the target's management. *See* Leveraged buyout; Tender offer.

Aggrieved. Having suffered loss or injury; damnified; injured.

Aggrieved party. One whose legal right is invaded by an act complained of, or whose pecuniary interest is directly and adversely affected by a decree or judgment. One whose right of property may be established or divested. The word "aggrieved" refers to a substantial grievance, a denial of some personal, pecuniary or property right, or the imposition upon a party of a burden or obligation. *See* Party; Standing.

Bankruptcy. A party is "aggrieved," within meaning of Bankruptcy Code, if his property may be diminished, his burden increased, or his rights detrimentally affected by order sought to be reviewed.

Aggrieved person. *See* Aggrieved party.

Aging of accounts. Arranging the accounts (such as receivables or payables) in chronological order and grouping the accounts by intervals, such as accounts outstanding less than 30 days, 30 to 60 days, and so on. The process of classifying accounts receivable by the time elapsed since the claim came into existence for the purpose of estimating the balance of uncollectible accounts as of a given date.

Agist /əjíst/. An ancient law term meant to take in and give feed to the cattle of strangers in the king's forest, and to collect the money due for the same to the king's use.

Agister /əjístər/. A person engaged in the business of pasturing of livestock as a bailee in consideration of an agreed price to be paid by owner of cattle.

Agistment /əjístmənt/. A particular kind of bailment under which a person, for consideration, takes animals for care and pasturing on his land, and the person who cares for the animals has an "agister's lien" on the animals for that care. A contract whereby a person, called an agister, has control of animals and retains possession of land.

Agistor /əjístər/. *See* Agister; Agistment.

Agitator /ǽjəteytər/. One who stirs up; excites; ruffles; perturbs. One who incessantly advocates a social change.

Agony. Extreme physical pain or mental distress.

Agrarian /əgrériyən/. Relating to land, or to a division or distribution of land; as an agrarian law.

Agrarian laws. In Roman law, laws for the distribution among the people, by public authority, of the lands constituting the public domain, usually territory conquered from an enemy. In common parlance the term is frequently applied to laws which have for their object the more equal division or distribution of landed property; laws for subdividing large properties and increasing the number of landholders.

Agree. To concur; come into harmony; give mutual assent; unite in mental action; exchange promises; make an agreement; arrange; to settle. Concur or acquiesce in; approve or adopt. *Agreed or agreed to,* are frequently used (like *accord*), to show the concurrence or harmony of cases; *e.g. Agreed per curiam.* Usually implies some contractual undertaking. To grant or covenant, as when a grantor agrees that no building shall be erected on an adjoining lot; or a mortgagor agrees to cause all taxes to be paid. *See* Agreement; Contract.

Agreed. Settled or established by agreement. Commonly synonymous with "contracted."

Agreed amount clause. Provision in insurance policy that the insured will carry a stated amount of insurance coverage.

Agreed case. *See Case agreed on* under Case.

Agreed judgment. *See* Judgment.

Agreed price. The consideration for sale of goods arrived at by mutual agreement as contrasted with "open price". U.C.C. § 2–305.

Agreed statement of facts. A statement of facts, agreed on by the parties as true and correct, to be submitted to a court for a ruling on the law of the case. *See Case agreed on* under Case. *See also* Declaratory judgment; Stipulation.

Agreed statement on appeal. Narrative statement of facts in case which may be filed on appeal in lieu of report of proceedings below. It is required that all parties agree to content of narrative.

Agreed value. The worth or value of property upon which persons agree beforehand as in a partnership contract in which the parties agree on the value of a partner's interest in a specified amount.

Agreement. A meeting of two or more minds; a coming together in opinion or determination; the coming together in accord of two minds on a given proposition. In law, a concord of understanding and intention between two or more parties with respect to the effect upon their relative rights and duties, of certain past or future facts or performances. The consent of two or more persons concurring respecting the transmission of some property, right, or benefits, with the view of contracting an obligation, a mutual obligation.

A manifestation of mutual assent on the part of two or more persons as to the substance of a contract. Restatement, Second, Contracts, § 3.

The act of two or more persons, who unite in expressing a mutual and common purpose, with the view of altering their rights and obligations. The union of two or more minds in a thing done or to be done; a mutual assent to do a thing. A compact between parties who are thereby subjected to the obligation or to whom the contemplated right is thereby secured.

Although often used as synonymous with "contract", agreement is a broader term; *e.g.* an agreement might lack an essential element of a contract. The bargain of the parties in fact as found in their language or by implication from other circumstances including course of dealing or usage of trade or course of performance. U.C.C. § 1–201(c); Uniform Consumer Credit Code, § 1.301(3).

The writing or instrument which is evidence of an agreement.

See also Binding agreement; Compact; Consent; Contract; Covenant; International agreements; Meeting of minds.

Classification

Conditional agreements. The operation and effect of such depend upon the existence of a supposed state of facts, or the performance of a condition, or the happening of a contingency.

Executed agreements. Such have reference to past events, or which are at once closed and where nothing further remains to be done by the parties.

Executory agreements. Such agreements as are to be performed in the future. They are commonly preliminary to other more formal or important contracts or deeds, and are usually evidenced by memoranda, parol promises, etc.

Express agreements. Those in which the terms and stipulations are specifically declared and avowed by the parties at the time of making the agreement.

Implied agreement. (1) Implied in fact. One inferred from the acts or conduct of the parties, instead of being expressed by them in written or spoken words. (2) Implied in law; more aptly termed a constructive or quasi contract. One where, by fiction of law, a promise is imputed to perform a legal duty, as to repay money obtained by fraud or duress. One inferred by the law where the conduct of the parties with reference to the subject-matter is such as to induce the belief that they intended to do that which their acts indicate they have done.

Parol agreements. At common law, such as are either by word of mouth or are committed to writing, but are not under seal. The common law draws only one great line, between things under seal and not under seal.

Agreement for insurance. An agreement often made in short terms preliminary to the filling out and delivery of a policy with specific stipulations. *See also* Binder.

Agreement not to be performed within a year. An agreement that necessarily must require more than year for performance. Incapable of performance within one year.

Agreement of sale; agreement to sell. An agreement of sale may imply not merely an obligation to sell, but an obligation on the part of the other party to purchase, while an agreement to sell is simply an obligation on the part of the vendor or promisor to complete his promise of sale. It is a contract to be performed in future, and, if fulfilled, results in a sale; it is preliminary to sale and is not the actual sale.

Agricultural lien. A statutory lien to secure money or supplies advanced to an agriculturist to be expended or employed in the making of a crop and attaching to that crop only.

Agricultural Marketing Agreement Act. Federal law passed in 1937 to establish and maintain orderly marketing conditions for farm commodities; enacted to protect purchasing power of farmers. 7 U.S.C.A. § 601 et seq. *See* Parity.

Aguilar-Spinelli test /àgiylár spənéliy/. The "*Aguilar–Spinelli*" test requires that search warrant affidavits disclose both the underlying circumstances necessary to enable the magistrate independently to judge the validity of the informant's conclusion and make some showing of reliability of the informant. Aguilar v. Texas, 378 U.S. 108, 84 S.Ct. 1509, 12 L.Ed.2d 723; Spinelli v. U.S., 393 U.S. 410, 89 S.Ct. 584, 21 L.Ed.2d 637.

AICPA. American Institute of Certified Public Accountants.

Aid. To support, help, assist or strengthen. Act in cooperation with; supplement the efforts of others.

Distinguished from abet. "Aid" within aider and abettor statute means to help, to assist, or to strengthen while "abet" means to counsel, to encourage, to incite or to assist in commission of criminal act.

Aid and abet. Help, assist, or facilitate the commission of a crime, promote the accomplishment thereof, help in advancing or bringing it about, or encourage, counsel, or incite as to its commission. It comprehends all assistance rendered by words, acts, encouragement, support, or presence, actual or constructive, to render assistance if necessary. *See* Abet; Abettor; Accessory; Accomplice; Aider and abettor; Harbor.

Aid and comfort. Help; support; assistance; counsel; encouragement. As an element in the crime of treason (Constitution of the United States, Art. III, § 3), the giving of "aid and comfort" to the enemy may consist in a mere attempt. It is not essential to constitute the giving of aid and comfort that the enterprise commenced should be successful and actually render assistance. An act which intentionally strengthens or tends to strengthen enemies of the United States, or which weakens or tends to weaken power of the United States to resist and attack such enemies. Any intentional act furthering hostile designs of enemies of the United States.

Aid bond. *See* Bond.

Aider and abettor. One who assists another in the accomplishment of a common design or purpose; he must be aware of, and consent to, such design or purpose. One who advises, counsels, procures, or encourages another to commit a crime, himself being guilty of some overt act or advocacy or encouragement of his principal, actually or constructively present when crime is committed, and participating in commission thereof by some act, deed, word, or gesture, and sharing the criminal intent of the principal. One who assists another to commit a crime; may be a

principal, if present, or an accessory before or after fact of crime. The crime must usually be a felony because all parties to misdemeanor are generally principals. *See also* Abettor.

Aider by verdict. The healing or remission, by a verdict rendered, of a defect or error in pleading which might have been objected to before verdict. The presumption of the proof of all facts necessary to the verdict as it stands, coming to the aid of a record in which such facts are not distinctly alleged. Amendment of pleadings to conform to the evidence is provided for by Fed.R.Civil P. 15.

Aiding and abetting. *See* Aid and abet.

Aiding and abetting. Assisting in or otherwise facilitating the commission of a crime. *See* Aider and abettor.

Aiding an escape. Any overt act, intended and useful to assist attempted or completed departure of prisoner from lawful custody before his discharge by due process of law. See *e.g.* Model Pen.Code § 242.6. *See* Accessory (*Accessory after the fact*); Obstructing justice.

Aim a weapon. To point it intentionally. "Aim" denotes direction toward some minute point in an object, while "point" implies direction toward the whole object.

Airbill. A document serving for air transportation as a bill of lading does for marine or rail transportation, and includes an air consignment note or air waybill. U.C.C. § 1–201(6).

Air piracy. Any seizure or exercise of control, by force or violence or threat of force or violence and with wrongful intent, of any aircraft in flight in air commerce. 49 U.S.C.A. § 1472(i).

Air rights. The right to use all or a portion of the air space above real estate. Such right is vested by grant; *e.g.* fee simple, lease, or other conveyance. While commercial airlines have a right to fly over one's land, if such "flight paths" interfere with the owners use of such land, the owner is entitled to recover the extent of actual damage suffered by him. On the other hand, the owner of the land is precluded by state and federal laws from polluting the air.

A.k.a. Also known as. *See* Alias.

Alderman. Municipal officer; member of the legislative body of a municipality. Often called a councilman.

Aleatory contract /éyliyətòriy kóntrækt/. A mutual agreement, of which the effects, with respect both to the advantages and losses, whether to all the parties or to some of them, depend on an uncertain event. Restatement of Contracts, § 291.

Contracts in which promise by one party is conditioned on fortuitous event. A contract, the obligation and performance of which depend upon an uncertain event, such as insurance, engagements to pay annuities, and the like. A contract is aleatory or hazardous when the performance of that which is one of its objects depends on an uncertain event. It is certain when the thing to be done is supposed to depend on the will of the party, or when in the usual course of events it must happen in the manner stipulated.

Aleatory promise. A promise, the performance of which is by its own terms subject to happening of uncertain and fortuitous event or upon some fact existence or past occurrence of which is also uncertain and undetermined.

Aleatory transaction. An event dependent on a fortuitous or uncertain happening. *See* Aleatory contract.

Alford plea. Name derived from North Carolina v. Alford, 400 U.S. 25, 91 S.Ct. 160, 27 L.Ed.2d 162 (1970), in which Supreme Court held that a guilty plea which represented a voluntary and intelligent choice among alternatives available to defendant, especially where he was represented by competent counsel, was not compelled within the meaning of the Fifth Amendment merely because the plea was entered to avoid the possibility of the death penalty. The Supreme Court also held that where strong evidence of actual guilt substantially negated defendant's claim of innocence and provided strong factual basis for the guilty plea, and the state had a strong case of first-degree murder, so that defendant, advised by competent counsel, intelligently concluded that he should plead guilty to second-degree murder rather than be tried for first-degree murder, the court committed no constitutional error in accepting guilty plea despite defendant's claim of innocence.

A.L.I. American Law Institute.

Alias /éyliyəs/. Term used to indicate another name by which a person is known. Short for "alias dictus"; otherwise known as (a. k. a.). When used in connection with a description of a person, it indicates that he has used or been known by another name. *See also* Fictitious name; Name.

Alias dictus /éyliyəs díktəs/. "Otherwise called." (Shorter and more usual form, *alias*). Known by both those names, and is called one or the other. A fictitious name assumed by a person is colloquially termed an "alias". *See also* Alias.

Alias execution. One issued after first has been returned without having accomplished its purpose. A second writ of execution issued to enforce a judgment that was not fully satisfied by the sheriff acting under the first or original writ. *See also* Alias process.

Alias process. A second or further writ, summons, execution or subpoena, used when the first

or earlier process has for any reason failed to accomplish its purpose.

Alias subpoena /éyliyəs səpíynə/. One issued after the first has been returned without having accomplished its purpose.

Alias summons. A summons issued when original has not produced its effect because defective in form or manner of service, and when issued, supersedes the first writ.

Alias tax warrant. One issued after the first has been returned without having accomplished its purpose.

Alias writ. A second or further writ. One issued in a case after another of the same substance has previously been issued; *see e.g.* Alias summons.

Alias writ of execution. *See* Alias execution.

Alibi /ǽləbày/. A defense that places the defendant at the relevant time of crime in a different place than the scene involved and so removed therefrom as to render it impossible for him to be the guilty party. Notice of intention to offer a defense of alibi is governed in federal courts by Fed.R.Crim.P. 12.1.

Alien, *n.* /éyl(i)yən/. A foreign born person who has not qualified as a citizen of the country; but an alien is a person within the meaning of the Fourteenth Amendment due process clause of the U.S. Constitution to same extent as a citizen. Any person not a citizen or national of the United States. 8 U.S.C.A. § 1101. *See also* Resident alien.

Alien *or* **aliene,** *v.* To transfer or make over to another; to convey or transfer the property of a thing from one person to another; to alienate. Usually applied to the transfer of lands and tenements. *See* Alienation.

Alienability. The quality or attribute of being transferrable; *e.g.*, interest in property.

Alienability of future interests. The right of an owner of an interest which vests in possession or enjoyment in the future to transfer such interest beforehand.

Alienable /éyl(i)yənəbəl/. Proper to be the subject of alienation or transfer.

Alienable constitutional rights. Right to a trial by jury, to counsel, and not to incriminate one's self, and related matters are "alienable constitutional rights" which may be waived whenever assertable. *See also* Inalienable rights.

Alienage /éyl(i)yənəj/. The condition or state of an alien.

Alien amy /éyl(i)yən əmíy/. In international law, alien friend. An alien who is the subject or citizen of a foreign government at peace with our own.

Alien and sedition laws. Acts of Congress of July 6 and July 14, 1798, which made it a criminal offense to utter or publish any false, scandalous and malicious writings against the federal government with intent to defame it, or bring it into contempt or disrepute or to excite hatred of people or stir up sedition against it. These short-lived acts tightened residency requirements for citizenships, granted presidential powers to deport and jail aliens, and provided penalties for seditious writings or speech critical of the government. *See also* Sedition.

Alienate /éyl(i)yənèyt/. To convey; to transfer the title to property. *Alien* is very commonly used in the same sense. *See* Alienation.

Alienation /èyl(i)yənéyshən/. In real property law, the transfer of the property and possession of lands, tenements, or other things, from one person to another. The term is particularly applied to absolute conveyances of real property. The voluntary and complete transfer from one person to another. Disposition by will. Every mode of passing realty by the act of the party, as distinguished from passing it by the operation of law. *See also* Restraint on alienation.

Alienation clause. A provision in a document giving a person the right to transfer or forbidding him from transferring the property which is the subject of the document. Provision in fire insurance policy voiding such policy upon transfer of ownership by insured.

Alienation in mortmain. *See* Amortization; Mortmain.

Alienation of affections. Action of "alienation of affections" is a tort based upon willful and malicious interference with marriage relation by third party, without justification or excuse. The elements constituting the cause of action are wrongful conduct of defendant, plaintiff's loss of affection or consortium of spouse and causal connection between such conduct and such loss. Certain states have abolished the right to bring an alienation of affections action. *See* Consortium; Heartbalm statutes.

Alien corporation. A corporation organized under the laws of a foreign country irrespective of where it operates.

Alienee /èyl(i)yəníy/. One to whom an alienation, conveyance, or transfer of property is made. *See* Alienor.

Alien enemy. In international law, an alien who is the subject or citizen of some hostile nation or power. A person who, by reason of owing a permanent or temporary allegiance to a hostile power, becomes, in time of war, impressed with the character of an enemy. Subjects of a foreign nation at war with United States.

Alien immigrant. One who has come into the country from a foreign country and has not yet been naturalized. *See* Alien.

Alienor /éyl(i)yənər/. He who makes a grant, transfer of title, conveyance, or alienation. Correlative of *alienee*.

Alien Registration Act. Act of Congress (1940) which requires annual registration of all aliens over the age of 13. 8 U.S.C.A. §§ 1201(b), 1301, 1302.

Alimony /ǽləməniy/. Derived from Latin "alimonia" meaning sustenance, and means, therefore, the sustenance or support of the wife by her divorced husband and stems from the common-law right of the wife to support by her husband. Allowances which husband or wife by court order pays other spouse for maintenance while they are separated, or after they are divorced (permanent alimony), or temporarily, pending a suit for divorce (pendente lite). Generally, it is restricted to money unless otherwise authorized by statute. But it may be an allowance out of the spouse's estate. Generally, alimony is separable from a binding property settlement agreement. State statutes which provide for payment of alimony only to the wife have been held to be unconstitutional. *See also* Gross alimony; Lump-sum alimony; Palimony; Periodic alimony; Permanent alimony; Rehabilitation *(Alimony)*; Separate maintenance; Trust *(Alimony trust)*.

Alimony in gross, or in a lump sum, is in the nature of a final property settlement, and hence in some jurisdictions is not included in the term "alimony," which in its strict or technical sense contemplates money payments at regular intervals. Refers to those alimony arrangements where entire award is a vested and determined amount and not subject to change.

Alimony pendente lite (temporary alimony). An allowance made pending a suit for divorce or separate maintenance including a reasonable allowance for preparation of the suit as well as for support. *See also* Allowance pendente lite.

Permanent alimony. A provision for the support and maintenance of a wife during her lifetime.

Tax treatment. Alimony and separate maintenance payments are includible in the gross income of the recipient and are deductible by the payor. The payments must be periodic and made in discharge of a legal obligation arising from a marital or family relationship. Child support and voluntary payments are not treated as alimony. I.R.C. §§ 62(10), 71, 215.

Alimony trust. *See* Trust.

Aliquot /ǽləkwòt/. Strictly speaking, means contained in something else an exact number of times. But as applied to resulting trusts, "aliquot" is treated as meaning fractional, and means any definite interest.

Aliquot part rule. A rule which requires that a person intend to acquire a fractional part of the ownership of property before the court can declare a resulting trust in his favor.

Aliter /ǽlətər/. Otherwise; as otherwise held or decided.

Aliunde /èyliyə́ndiy/. Lat. From another source; from elsewhere; from outside.

Evidence aliunde. Evidence from outside, from another source. In certain cases a written instrument may be explained by evidence *aliunde*, that is, by evidence drawn from sources exterior to the instrument itself, *e.g.*, the testimony of a witness to conversations, admissions, or preliminary negotiations. Evidence aliunde (*i.e.*, from outside the will) may be received to explain an ambiguity in a will. *See* Parol evidence.

Aliunde rule /èyliyə́ndiy rúwl/. A verdict may not be impeached by evidence of juror unless foundation for introduction thereof is first made by competent evidence aliunde, or from some other source.

Alius /ǽliyəs/. Lat. Other. The neuter form is *aliud*, something else; another thing.

Alive. As respects birth, it means that child has an independent life of its own for some period, even momentarily, after birth; evidenced by respiration or other indications of life, such as beating of heart and pulsation of arteries (Hydrostatic test); or heart tones in response to artificial respiration, or pulsation of umbilical cord after being severed. *See also* Born alive; Child; Life; Live; Viable child.

In respect of estate matters, a child *en ventre sa mere* is "born" and "alive" for all purposes for his benefit.

ALJ. *See* Administrative law judge.

All. Means the whole of—used with a singular noun or pronoun, and referring to amount, quantity, extent, duration, quality, or degree. The whole number or sum of—used collectively, with a plural noun or pronoun expressing an aggregate. Every member of individual component of; each one of—used with a plural noun. In this sense, all is used generically and distributively. "All" refers rather to the aggregate under which the individuals are subsumed than to the individuals themselves. *See* Both; Entire.

All and singular. All without exception. A comprehensive term often employed in conveyances, wills, and the like, which includes the aggregate or whole and also each of the separate items or components.

Allegation. The assertion, claim, declaration, or statement of a party to an action, made in a

pleading, setting out what he expects to prove. See *e.g.* Fed.R. Civil P. 8. *See also* Charge; Claim; Complaint.

A material allegation in a pleading is one essential to the claim or defense.

Allegation of fact. Generally, narration of transaction by stating details according to their legal effect, and statement of right or liability flowing from certain facts is conclusion of law.

Allegation of faculties. A statement made by the wife of the property of her husband, in order to obtain alimony. *See* Faculties.

Allege /əléj/. To state, recite, claim, assert, or charge; to make an allegation. *See* Allegation.

Alleged. Stated; recited; claimed; asserted; charged.

Allegiance /əlíyjəns/. Obligation of fidelity and obedience to government in consideration for protection that government gives. *See also* Oath of allegiance *or* loyalty.

Allen charge. An instruction advising deadlocked jurors to have deference for each other's views, that they should listen, with a disposition to be convinced, to each other's argument; deriving its name from the case of Allen v. United States, 164 U.S. 492, 17 S.Ct. 154, 41 L.Ed. 528, wherein the instruction was approved. Variously called dynamite charge, shotgun instruction, third degree instruction. The Allen charge is prohibited in certain states; *e.g.* California; and while permissible in others, its use must be carefully examined by trial judge to determine its total effect on jury reaching verdict.

All events test. For accrual method taxpayers, income is earned when: (1) all the events have occurred which fix the right to receive the income and (2) the amount can be determined with reasonable accuracy. Accrual of income cannot be postponed simply because a portion of the income may have to be returned in a subsequent period.

Under this test an accrual basis taxpayer may deduct taxes or any other expense items if all the events fixing the fact of, and amount of, taxpayer's liability have transpired though not paid, and this requires that each taxable year must be treated as a separate unit, and all items of gross income and deductions must be reflected in terms of their posture at close of such year.

All faults. A sale of goods with "all faults" covers, in the absence of fraud on the part of the vendor, all such faults and defects as are not inconsistent with the identity of the goods as the goods described. U.C.C. § 2–316. *See* As is.

All fours. Two cases or decisions which are alike in all material respects, and precisely similar in all the circumstances affecting their determination, are said to be or to run on "all fours."

Alliance. The relation or union between persons or families contracted by intermarriage; affinity. State of being allied.

In international law, a union, association or confederation of two or more states or nations, formed by league or treaty, for the joint prosecution of a war (offensive alliance), or for their mutual assistance and protection in repelling hostile attacks (defensive alliance). The league or treaty by which the association is formed. The act of confederating, by league or treaty, for the purposes mentioned.

The term is also used in a wider sense, embracing unions for objects of common interest to the contracting parties, as the "Holy Alliance" entered into in 1815 by Prussia, Austria and Russia for the purpose of counteracting the revolutionary movement in the interest of political liberalism.

Allision. The running of one vessel into or against another, as distinguished from a collision, *i.e.,* the running of two vessels against each other. But this distinction is not very carefully observed.

Allocable /ǽləkəbəl/. Synonymous with "distributable". In analyzing accounts, the breaking down of a lump sum charged or credited to one account into several parts to be charged or credited to other accounts.

Allocable share of income. Certain entities receive conduit treatment under the Federal income tax law. This means the earned income or loss is not taxed to the entity, but such amounts are allocated to the owners or beneficiaries thereof, regardless of the magnitude or timing of corresponding distributions. The portion of the entity's income that is taxed to the owner or beneficiary is the allocable share of the entity's income or loss for the period. Such allocations are determined by (1) the partnership agreement relative to the partners, (2) a weighted-average stock ownership computation relative to shareholders of an S corporation, and (3) the controlling will or trust instrument relative to the beneficiaries of an estate or trust.

Allocate. In accounting, to assign cost, expense, etc. based on some planned method.

Allocation. Assignment or allotment. In taxation, the assignment of income for various tax purposes. A multistate corporation's nonbusiness income usually is allocated to the state where the nonbusiness assets are located; it is not apportioned with the rest of the entity's income. The income and expense items of an estate or trust are allocated between income and corpus components. Specific items of income, expense, gain, loss, and credit can be allocated to specific partners or shareholders in an S corporation, if a substantial economic nontax purpose for the allocation is established.

Allocation of dividends. In trust accounting, cash dividends are credited or allocated to income; whereas, generally, stock dividends are credited to principal and the basis of the stock on which the dividend has been paid is changed in the portfolio. If the cash dividend is a liquidating dividend, it is commonly allocated to principal.

Allocation of income. When two or more businesses are controlled by the same interests, the Commissioner of Internal Revenue may allocate or distribute income to prevent tax evasion. I.R.C. § 482. In trust accounting, the process by which income is distributed as between principal and income.

Allocation of principal and income. *See* Allocation of dividends; Allocation of income.

Allocatur /ǽləkéytər/. Lat. It is allowed. A word formerly used to denote that a writ or order was allowed. A word denoting the allowance by a master or prothonotary of a bill referred for his consideration, whether touching costs, damages, or matter of account. *A special allocatur* is the special allowance of a writ (particularly a writ of error) which is required in some particular cases.

Allocution /ǽləkyúwshən/. Formality of court's inquiry of defendant as to whether he has any legal cause to show why judgment should not be pronounced against him on verdict of conviction; or, whether he would like to make statement on his behalf and present any information in mitigation of sentence (see e.g. Fed.R.Crim.P. 32(a)).

Allodial /əlówdiyəl/. Free; not holden of any lord or superior; owned without obligation of vassalage or fealty; the opposite of feudal. *See also* Ownership.

Allodium /əlówdiyəm/. Land held absolutely in one's own right, and not of any lord or superior; land not subject to feudal duties or burdens. An estate held by absolute ownership, without recognizing any superior to whom any duty is due on account thereof.

Allograph /ǽləgrǽf/. A writing or signature made for a person by another; opposed to autograph.

Allonge /əlónj/. A piece of paper annexed to a negotiable instrument or promissory note, on which to write endorsements for which there is no room on the instrument itself. Such must be so firmly affixed thereto as to become a part thereof. U.C.C. § 3–202(2).

Allot /əlót/. To apportion, distribute; to divide property previously held in common among those entitled, assigning to each his ratable portion, to be held in severalty. To set apart specific property, a share of a fund, etc., to a distinct party. In the law of corporations, to allot shares, debentures, etc., is to appropriate them to the applicants or persons who have applied for them.

Allotted land. *See* Allotment.

Allotment. A share or portion; that which is allotted; apportionment; division; the distribution of shares in a public undertaking or corporation. Partition; the distribution of land under an inclosure act.

The term ordinarily and commonly used to describe land held by Indians after allotment, and before the issuance of the patent in fee that deprives the land of its character as Indian country. A term of art in Indian law, describing either a parcel of land owned by the United States in trust for an Indian, i.e., a "trust allotment," or owned by an Indian subject to a restriction on alienation in favor of the United States or its officials, i.e., a "restricted fee allotment." In Indian law, means a selection of specific land awarded to an individual allottee from a common holding. *See* Allottee.

Allotment certificate. A document issued to an applicant for shares in a company or public loan announcing the number of shares allotted or assigned and the amounts and due dates of the calls or different payments to be made on the same.

Allottee. One to whom an allotment is made; who receives a ratable share under an allotment. A person to whom land under an inclosure act or shares in a corporation or public undertaking are allotted.

Allow. The word has no rigid or precise meaning, its import varying according to circumstances or context in connection with which it is used. It may mean to bestow or assign to any one as his right or due. To approve of, accept as true, admit, concede, adopt, or fix. To grant something as a deduction or an addition; to abate or deduct; as, to allow a sum for leakage. To sanction, either directly or indirectly, as opposed to merely suffering a thing to be done; to acquiesce in; to suffer; to tolerate. *See also* Acquiescence; Consent.

Allowance. A deduction, an average payment, a portion assigned or allowed; the act of allowing. For Family, see that title.

Allowance pendente lite /əláwəns pendéntiy láytiy/. The court ordered provision for a spouse and children during the pendency of a divorce or separate support proceeding. *See also* Alimony.

Alluvion /əl(y)úwviyən/. That increase of the earth on a shore or bank of a stream or the sea, by the force of the water washing up sand or soil so as to form firm ground, as by a current or by waves, which is so gradual that no one can judge how much is added at each moment of time. "Accretion" denotes the act. However, the terms are frequently used synonymously. Avulsion is sudden and perceptible. *See* Accretion; Avulsion. *Compare* Reliction.

All Writs Act. *See* Writ.

Ally. A nation which has entered into an alliance with another nation. A citizen or subject of one of two or more allied nations.

Alms. Charitable donations. Any species of relief bestowed upon the poor. That which is given by public authority for the relief of the poor.

Almshouse. A house for the publicly or privately supported paupers of a city or county; may also be termed a "mission". In England an almshouse is not synonymous with a workhouse or poorhouse, being supported by private endowment.

Alod, alode, alodes, alodis /ǽləd/. L. Lat. In feudal law, old forms of *alodium* or *allodium* *(q.v.)*. A term used in opposition to *feodum* or *fief*, which means property, the use of which was bestowed upon another by the proprietor, on condition that the grantee should perform certain services for the grantor, and upon the failure of which the property should revert to the original possessor.

Alone. Apart from others; singly; sole.

Along. Lengthwise of, implying motion or at or near, distinguished from across. By, on, up to, or over, according to the subject-matter and context. The term does not necessarily mean touching at all points; nor does it necessarily imply contact.

Also. Besides; as well; in addition; likewise; in like manner; similarly; too; withal. Some other thing; including; further; furthermore; in the same manner; moreover; nearly the same as the word "and" or "likewise."

A.L.T.A. American Land Title Association.

Alter. To make a change in; to modify; to vary in some degree; to change some of the elements or ingredients or details without substituting an entirely new thing or destroying the identity of the thing affected. To change partially. To change in one or more respects, but without destruction of existence or identity of the thing changed; to increase or diminish. *See* Alteration; Amend; Change.

Alteration. Variation; changing; making different. A change of a thing from one form or state to another; making a thing different from what it was without destroying its identity. *See* Alter.

An act done upon an instrument by which its meaning or language is changed. Language different in legal effect, or change in rights, interests, or obligations of parties. It introduces some change into instrument's terms, meaning, language, or details. The term is not properly applied to any change which involves the substitution of a practically new document. An alteration is said to be *material* when it affects, or may possibly affect, the rights of the persons interested in the document. U.C.C. § 3–407. *See also* Fraudulent alteration; Material alteration; Mutilation; Spoliation.

Alteration of contract. A change in the provisions of a contract. If alteration is material, it extinguishes the right of the party who alters it and discharges the other party. The test of whether it is material is whether the rights of the obligee would be varied as to the party making the alteration or to a third party. Restatement of Contracts, § 434.

Alteration of trust. An act by settlor of trust changing the terms of the trust, generally pursuant to a power to alter and amend within the original trust instrument.

Altercation. Warm contentions in words. Dispute or controversy carried on with heat or anger.

Alter ego /óltər íygow/. Second self. Under doctrine of "alter ego", court merely disregards corporate entity and holds individual responsible for acts knowingly and intentionally done in the name of corporation. To establish the "alter ego" doctrine, it must be shown that the stockholders disregarded the entity of the corporation, made corporation a mere conduit for the transaction of their own private business, and that the separate individualities of the corporation and its stockholders in fact ceased to exist. *See also* Instrumentality rule; Piercing the corporate veil.

Alternate legacy. *See* Legacy.

Alternate valuation date. Property passing from a person by death may be valued for estate tax purposes as of the date of death or the alternate valuation date. The alternate valuation date is six months from the date of death or the date the property is disposed of by the estate, whichever comes first. The use of the alternate valuation date requires an affirmative election on the part of the executor or administrator of the estate. I.R.C. §§ 1014(a), 2032.

Alternative. One or the other of two things; giving an option or choice; allowing a choice between two or more things or acts to be done.

Alternative contract. A contract whose terms allow of performance by the doing of either one of several acts at the election of the party from whom performance is due.

Alternative dispute resolution. Term refers to procedures for settling disputes by means other than litigation; e.g., by arbitration, mediation, mini-trials. Such procedures, which are usually less costly and more expeditious, are increasingly being used in commercial and labor disputes, divorce actions, in resolving motor vehicle and medical malpractice tort claims, and in other disputes that would likely otherwise involve court litigation. *See also* Arbitration; Mediation; Mini-trial; Trial *(Summary jury trial)*.

Alternative judgment. *See* Judgment.

Alternative minimum tax (AMT). The tax imposed on individuals, estates, trusts, and, for tax years beginning after 1986, corporations. The tax is designed to ensure that all taxpayers pay at least a minimum amount of taxes. The AMT rate is a fixed percentage of alternative minimum taxable income. I.R.C. §§ 55–59.

Alternative obligation. An obligation allowing the obligor to choose which of two things he will do, the performance of either of which will satisfy the instrument. A promise to deliver a certain thing or to pay a specified sum of money is an example of this kind of obligation.

Alternative pleading. A form of pleading which was formerly prohibited but now recognized under Federal and state Rules of Civ.Proc. by which the pleader sets forth two or more statements by way of claim or defense which are not necessarily consistent with each other. When two or more statements are made in the alternative and one of them if made independently would be sufficient, the pleading is not made insufficient by the insufficiency of one or more of the alternative statements. See Fed.R.Civil P. 8(e)(2).

Alternative relief. Under Fed.Rules Civ.Proc. 8(a) the party seeking a judgment may demand it in the alternative, or in various forms, *e.g.* demand for a money judgment and for equitable relief.

Alternative remainders. Remainders in which disposition of property is made in alternative, one to take effect only in case the other does not, and in substitution of it.

Alternative remedies. *See* Alternative relief.

Alternative writ. A common law writ commanding the person against whom it is issued to do a specified thing, or show cause to the court why he should not be compelled to do it. Under the common-law practice, the first *mandamus* is an alternative writ; but in modern practice this writ is often dispensed with and its place is taken by an order to show cause. *See* Mandamus.

A.M.A. American Medical Association.

Amalgamation /əmǽlgəméyshən/. Union of different races, or diverse elements, societies, unions, associations, or corporations, so as to form a homogeneous whole or new body; interfusion; intermarriage; consolidation; merger; coalescence; as, the amalgamation of stock.

Ambassador. A public officer clothed with high diplomatic powers, commissioned by a government to transact the international business of his government with a foreign government. An Ambassador of the United States is the personal representative of the President and reports to the President through the Secretary of State. Ambassadors have full responsibility for implementing the U.S. foreign policy by any and all U.S. Government personnel within their country of assignment, except those under military commands. Their responsibilities include negotiating agreements between the United States and the host country, explaining and disseminating official U.S. policy, and maintaining cordial relations with that country's government and people. 22 U.S.C.A. § 3942. *See also* Diplomatic agent.

Ambiguity /æmbəgyúwətiy/. Doubtfulness; doubleness of meaning. Duplicity, indistinctness, or uncertainty of meaning of an expression used in a written instrument. Want of clearness or definiteness; difficult to comprehend or distinguish; of doubtful import. For Extrinsic ambiguity, see that title.

Ambiguity exists if reasonable persons can find different meanings in a statute, document, etc.; when good arguments can be made for either of two contrary positions as to a meaning of a term in a document; when application of pertinent rules of interpretation to an instrument as a whole fails to make certain which one of two or more meanings is conveyed by the words employed by the parties.

Ambiguity of language is to be distinguished from unintelligibility and inaccuracy, for words cannot be said to be ambiguous unless their signification seems doubtful and uncertain to persons of competent skill and knowledge to understand them. It does not include uncertainty arising from the use of peculiar words, or of common words in a peculiar sense. It is *latent* where the language employed is clear and intelligible and suggests but a single meaning, but some extrinsic fact or extraneous evidence creates a necessity for interpretation or a choice among two or more possible meanings, as where a description apparently plain and unambiguous is shown to fit different pieces of property. A *patent* ambiguity is that which appears on the face of the instrument, and arises from the defective, obscure, or insensible language used.

Ambiguity upon the factum. An ambiguity in relation to the very foundation of the instrument itself, as distinguished from an ambiguity in regard to the construction of its terms. The term is applied, for instance, to a doubt as to whether a testator meant a particular clause to be a part of the will, or whether it was introduced with his knowledge, or whether a codicil was meant to republish a former will, or whether the residuary clause was accidentally omitted.

Ambiguous. *See* Ambiguity.

Ambulance chaser. A popular name for one who solicits negligence cases for an attorney for a fee or in consideration of a percentage of the recovery. Also, a term descriptive of the practice of some attorneys, on hearing of a personal injury which may have been caused by the negligence or wrongful act of another, of at once seeking out the injured person with a view to securing authority to bring action on account of the injury. *See also* Runner.

Ambulatory. Lat. *ambulare*, to walk about. Movable; revocable; subject to change; capable of alteration.

Ambulatoria voluntas (a changeable will) denotes the power which a testator possesses of altering his will during his life-time.

Ambulatory disposition. A judgment, decree, or sentence which is subject to change, amendment or revocation.

Ambush. To lie in wait, to surprise, to place in ambush.

Ameliorating waste /əmíyl(i)yəreytiŋ wéyst/. An act of lessee, though technically constituting waste, yet in fact resulting in improving instead of doing injury to land. Generally, equity will not enjoin such waste.

Ameliorations /əmìyl(i)yəréyshənz/. Betterments; improvements.

Amenable /əmíynəbəl/°mén°/. Subject to answer to the law; accountable; responsible; liable to punishment. Also means tractable, that may be easily led or governed; formerly applied to a wife who was governable by her husband.

Amend. To improve. To change for the better by removing defects or faults. To change, correct, revise. *See* Amendment.

Amendment. To change or modify for the better. To alter by modification, deletion, or addition.

Practice and pleading. The correction of an error committed in any process, pleading, or proceeding at law, or in equity, and which is done either as of course, or by the consent of parties, or upon motion to the court in which the proceeding is pending. Under Fed.R.Civil P., any change in pleadings, though not necessarily a correction, which a party may accomplish once as a matter of course at any time before a responsive pleading has been served. Such amendment may be necessary to cause pleadings to conform to evidence. Rule 15(a), (b). The amendment relates back to the original pleading if the subject of it arose out of the transaction set forth or attempted to be set forth in the original pleading. Fed.R.Civil P. 15(c). *Compare* Supplemental pleading.

Amendment of judgment. A judgment may be altered or amended for appropriate reasons on motion if served within ten days after entry of judgment. Fed.R.Civ.P. 59(e). See also Rule 60 (Relief from judgment or order).

Amendment of trust. An addition which alters the original terms of a trust, the power to accomplish which may be reserved by the settlor in the original trust instrument.

Amendment on court's own motion. A change or addition to a pleading or other document accomplished by the judge without a prior motion of a party.

Amends. A satisfaction given by a wrongdoer to the party injured, for a wrong committed.

Amenity /əménitiy/. In real property law, such circumstances, in regard to situation, view, location, access to a water course, or the like, as enhance the pleasantness or desirability of the property for purposes of residence, or contribute to the pleasure and enjoyment of the occupants, rather than to their indispensable needs. Extras or intangible items often associated with property. They may be tangible. Often amenities in a condominium include swimming pools, landscaping, and tennis courts.

In the law of *easements*, an "amenity" consists in restraining the owner from doing that on his property which, but for the grant or covenant, he might otherwise lawfully have done. Sometimes called a "negative easement" as distinguished from that class of easements which compel the owner to suffer something to be done on his property by another. A restrictive covenant.

A mensa et thoro /èy ménsə et θórow/. Lat. From table and bed, but more commonly translated, from bed and board. A kind of divorce, which is rather a separation of the parties by law, than a dissolution of the marriage. *See* Separation.

Amerce /əmɔ́rs/. To impose an amercement or fine; to publish by a fine or penalty.

Amercement /əmɔ́rsmənt/. A money penalty in the nature of a fine imposed upon an officer for some misconduct or neglect of duty. At common law, it was assessed by the peers of the delinquent, or the affeerors, or imposed arbitrarily at the discretion of the court or the lord.

American. Of or pertaining to the United States.

American Arbitration Association. National organization of arbitrators from whose panel arbitrators are selected for labor and commercial disputes. The Association has produced a Code of Ethics and Procedural Standards for use and guidance of arbitrators. *See* Arbitration.

American Bar Association. A National association of lawyers, a primary purpose of which is the improvement of lawyers' services and the administration of justice. Membership in the ABA is open to any lawyer who is in good standing in his or her state.

American Bar Foundation. An outgrowth of the American Bar Association involved with sponsoring and funding projects in legal research, education and social studies.

American clause. In marine insurance, a proviso in a policy to the effect that, in case of any subsequent insurance, the insurer shall nevertheless be answerable for the full extent of the sum subscribed by him, without right to claim contribution from subsequent underwriters.

American digest system. *See* Digest.

American experience table of mortality. A series of tables dealing with life insurance, costs and values, varying according to the age of the insured, the period during which the policy has been in force, and the term of the particular policy.

American Federation of Labor. An affiliation of labor unions.

American Institute of Certified Public Accountants (AICPA). A national organization of licensed CPAs.

American Law Institute. Group of American legal scholars who are responsible for the Restatements in the various disciplines of the law and who, jointly with the National Conference of Commissioners on Uniform State Laws, prepare some of the Uniform State Laws, *e.g.* Uniform Commercial Code. *See* Restatement of Law.

American rule. The traditional "American Rule" is that attorney fees are not awardable to the winning party (*i.e.* each litigant must pay his own attorney fees) unless statutorily or contractually authorized; however exceptions exist in that an award may be made to successful party if the opponent has acted in bad faith, vexatiously, wantonly or for oppressive reasons or if the litigation confers a substantial benefit on the members of an ascertainable class and the court's subject matter jurisdiction makes possible an award that will operate to spread the costs proportionately among them. In addition a court may in its discretion award attorney fees in civil rights actions to the prevailing defendant if the action was frivolous, unreasonable or without foundation. Also, a number of federal statutes make provision for awards of attorney fees to prevailing plaintiffs in actions involving violations of various federal laws (e.g., Fair Labor Standards Act, § 16, 29 U.S.C.A. § 216(b)). *See also* Equal Access to Justice Act; Fee.

Americans With Disabilities Act. A federal statute prohibiting discrimination against the disabled in employment, public transportation, telecommunications services, and public accommodations and services operated by private entities. 42 U.S.C.A. §§ 12101–12213.

AMEX. The American Stock Exchange.

Amicable. Friendly; mutually forbearing. Agreed or assented to by parties having conflicting interests or a dispute; as opposed to hostile or adversary.

Amicable action. An action brought and carried on by the mutual consent and arrangement of the parties, to obtain judgment of court on a doubtful question of law, the facts being usually settled by agreement. *See* Case *(Case agreed on)*; Declaratory judgment.

Amicus curiæ /əmáykəs kyúriyiy/əmíykəs kyúriyay/. Means, literally, friend of the court. A person with strong interest in or views on the subject matter of an action, but not a party to the action, may petition the court for permission to file a brief, ostensibly on behalf of a party but actually to suggest a rationale consistent with its own views. Such amicus curiae briefs are commonly filed in appeals concerning matters of a broad public interest; *e.g.* civil rights cases. Such may be filed by private persons or the government. In appeals to the U.S. courts of appeals, such brief may be filed only if accompanied by written consent of all parties, or by leave of court granted on motion or at the request of the court, except that consent or leave shall not be required when the brief is presented by the United States or an officer or agency thereof. Fed.R.App.P. 29. See also Sup.Ct.Rule 37.

Amnesty /ǽmnəstiy/. A sovereign act of forgiveness for past acts, granted by a government to all persons (or to certain classes of persons) who have been guilty of crime or delict, generally political offenses,—treason, sedition, rebellion, draft evasion,—and often conditioned upon their return to obedience and duty within a prescribed time. The 1986 Immigration Reform and Control Act provided amnesty for many undocumented aliens already present in the country.

Included in the concept of pardon is "amnesty," which is similar in all respects to a full pardon, insofar as when it is granted both the crime and punishment are abrogated; however, unlike pardons, an amnesty usually refers to a class of individuals irrespective of individual situations.

A declaration of the person or persons who have newly acquired or recovered the sovereign power in a nation, by which they pardon all persons who composed, supported, or obeyed the government which has been overthrown.

Compare Pardon; Parole.

Express amnesty is one granted in direct terms.

Implied amnesty is one which results when a treaty of peace is made between contending parties.

Among. Mingled with or in the same group or class. Intermingled with. In company or association with. In shares to each of, *e.g.* divided "among" the heirs. In or through the midst of.

Amortization /əmòrtəzéyshən/. In accounting, the allocation (and charge to expense) of the cost or other basis of an intangible asset over its estimated useful life. Intangible assets which have an indefinite life (*e.g.,* goodwill) are not amortizable. Examples of amortizable intangibles include organization costs, patents, copyrights and leasehold interests. A reduction in a debt or fund by periodic payments covering interest and part of principal, distinguished from: (1) depreciation, which is an allocation of the original cost of an asset computed from physical wear and tear as well as the passage of time, and (2) depletion, which is a reduction in the book value of a resource (such as minerals) resulting from conversion into a salable product. The operation of paying off bonds, stock, a mortgage, or other indebtedness, commonly of a state or corporation, by installments, or by a sinking fund. An "amortization plan" for the payment of an indebtedness is one where there are partial payments of the principal, and accrued interest, at stated periods for a definite time, at the expiration of which the entire indebtedness will be extinguished. *Compare* Depreciation. *See also* Discount amortization; Loan amortization schedule.

Amortization reserve. An account created for bookkeeping purposes to extinguish an obligation gradually over a period of time.

Amortized mortgage. Repayment of a mortgage over regular specified time intervals, with equal payments. This would reduce the principal, after any monies owing for interest are applied.

Effective-interest amortization. A method of bond discount and premium amortization by which interest expense (or revenue in the case of investments) is calculated as a constant percentage of bond carrying value.

Negative amortization. This occurs when monthly payments are not large enough to cover all of the interest cost of an adjustable rate mortgage. The interest rate that isn't covered is added to the loan's principal, which then could increase to more than the amount borrowed.

Amortization schedule. A schedule of periodic payments of interest and principal owed on a debt obligation.

Amortize. In accounting, to spread out over a future time period, such as repayment of a loan by installment payments or tax-deductions for depreciation expense. *See also* Amortization.

Amotion /əmówshən/. A putting or turning out, as the eviction of a tenant or a removal from office. Dispossession of lands. Ouster is an *amotion* of possession. A moving or carrying away; the wrongful taking of personal chattels.

In corporation law, the common law procedure by which a director may be removed for cause by the shareholders.

Amount. The whole effect, substance, quantity, import, result, or significance. The sum of principal and interest. *See also* Sum certain.

Amount covered. In insurance, the amount that is insured, and for which underwriters are liable for loss under a policy of insurance.

Amount in controversy. The damages claimed or relief demanded by injured party in dispute; the amount claimed or sued for in litigation. Amount of alleged damages required for diversity jurisdiction in Federal courts. 28 U.S.C.A. § 1332. *See* Jurisdictional amount.

Amount of loss. In insurance, the diminution, destruction, or defeat of the value of, or of the charge upon, the insured subject to the assured, by the direct consequence of the operation of the risk insured against, according to its value in the policy, or in contribution for loss, so far as its value is covered by the insurance. *See* Damages.

Amount realized. The amount received by a taxpayer upon the sale or exchange of property less the cost incurred to transfer the property. The measure of the amount received is the sum of the cash and the fair market value of any property or services received, plus any related debt assumed by the buyer. Determining the amount realized is the starting point for arriving at realized gain or loss. The amount realized is defined in I.R.C. § 1001(b) and accompanying Regulations. *See* Realized gain *or* loss; Recognized gain *or* loss.

Amount to. To reach in the aggregate; to rise to or reach by accumulation of particular sums or quantities.

AMT. *See* Alternative minimum tax.

Amtrak. National Railroad Passenger Corporation.

Amusement tax. A government levy imposed on tickets sold to places of amusement, sporting events, etc.; expressed as a percentage of the price of the ticket. *See also* Luxury tax.

Analogous /ənǽləgəs/. Derived from the Greek ana, up, and logos, ratio. Means bearing some resemblance or likeness that permits one to draw an analogy.

Analogy. Identity or similarity of proportion, where there is no precedent in point. In cases on the same subject, lawyers have recourse to cases on a different subject-matter, but governed by the same general principle. This is reasoning by analogy. The similitude of relations which exist between things compared.

Anarchist. One who professes and advocates the doctrines of anarchy, *q.v.* In the immigration statutes, it includes, not only persons who advocate the overthrow of organized government by force, but also those who believe in the absence of government as a political ideal, and seek the same end through propaganda. *See* 18 U.S.C.A. § 2384.

Anarchy. Absence of government; state of society where there is no law or supreme power; lawlessness or political disorder; destructive of and confusion in government. At its best it pertains to a society made orderly by good manners rather than law, in which each person produces according to his powers and receives according to his needs, and at its worst, the word pertains to a terroristic resistance of all present government and social order. For "criminal anarchy," *see* Criminal.

Anatomical gift. Testamentary donation of a vital organ, or organs, generally for purpose of medical research or transplant. Most states have adopted the Uniform Anatomical Gift Act which authorizes the gift of all or part of a human body after death for specified purposes.

Ancestor. One from whom a person lineally descended or may be descended; a progenitor. A former possessor; the person last seised. A deceased person from whom another has inherited land. Embraces both collaterals and lineals. Correlative of "heir."

Ancestral /ænséstrəl/. Relating to ancestors, or to what has been done by them; as *homage ancestral (q.v.)*. Derived from ancestors.

Ancestral estates are such as are transmitted by descent, and not by purchase; or such as are acquired either by descent or by operation of law. Realty which came to the intestate by descent or devise from a dead ancestor or by deed of actual gift from a living one, there being no other consideration than that of blood. Real estate coming to distributee by descent, gift, or devise from any kinsman. Allotments to members of Indian tribes or their heirs have been treated as an ancestral estate.

Ancestry. Line of descent; persons comprising such. Term which embraces the study of the antecedents of humans and animals; pedigree. May be proved by general reputation.

Ancient. Old; that which has existed from an indefinitely early period, or which by age alone has acquired certain rights or privileges accorded in view of long continuance.

Ancient deed. A deed 30 [or 20] years old and shown to come from a proper custody and having nothing suspicious about it. *See* Ancient writings.

Ancient documents. *See* Ancient writings.

Ancient lights. *See* Lights, ancient.

Ancient records. *See* Ancient writings.

Ancient rent. The rent reserved at the time the lease was made, if the building was not then under lease.

Ancient street. The doctrine is not based upon fact that streets have existed for a long time, but is invoked when it appears that common grantor owning land comprising street in question as well as property in question and other lots has given deeds to lots bounding them by street, thereby not only dedicating the street to public use but at same time creating private easements in the street, which cannot be taken without compensation.

Ancient wall. A wall built to be used, and in fact used, as a party-wall, for more than twenty years, by the express permission and continuous acquiescence of the owners of the land on which it stands.

Ancient water course. A water course is "ancient" if the channel through which it naturally runs has existed from time immemorial independent of the quantity of water which it discharges.

Ancient writings. Documents bearing on their face every evidence of age and authenticity, of age of 30 [or 20] years, and coming from a natural and reasonable official custody. These are presumed to be genuine without express proof, when coming from the proper custody.

Under Federal Rules of Evidence, a document is admissible if it is in such condition as to create no suspicion as to its authenticity, was in a place where it, if authentic, would likely be, and has been in existence 20 years or more at the time it is offered. Fed.Evid.R. 901(b)(8).

Ancillary /ǽnsəlèriy/. Aiding; attendant upon; describing a proceeding attendant upon or which aids another proceeding considered as principal. Auxiliary or subordinate.

Ancillary administration. Administration of estate in state where decedent has property and which is other than where decedent was domiciled. Administration or probate taken out in a second or subsequent jurisdiction to collect assets or to commence litigation on behalf of the estate in that jurisdiction. Ancillary administration of estates is usually governed by state statutes. See e.g., Uniform Probate Code, § 4–101 et seq.

Ancillary attachment. One sued out in aid of an action already brought; its only office being to hold the property attached under it for the satisfaction of the plaintiff's demand.

Ancillary bill *or* **suit.** One growing out of and auxiliary to another action or suit, either at law or in equity, such as a bill for discovery, or a proceeding for the enforcement of a judgment, or to set aside fraudulent transfers of property. One growing out of a prior suit in the same court, dependent upon and instituted for the purpose either of impeaching or enforcing the judgment or decree in a prior suit.

Ancillary claim. Term "ancillary" denotes any claim that reasonably may be said to be collateral to, dependent upon, or otherwise auxiliary to a claim asserted within federal jurisdiction in action. Claim is "ancillary" when it bears a logical relationship to the aggregate core of operative facts which constitutes main claim over which court had independent basis of federal jurisdiction. *See also* Counterclaim *(Compulsory counterclaim).*

Ancillary jurisdiction. Power of court to adjudicate and determine matters incidental to the exercise of its primary jurisdiction of an action.

Under "ancillary jurisdiction doctrine" federal district court acquires jurisdiction of case or controversy as an entirety and may, as incident to disposition of matter properly before it, possess jurisdiction to decide other matters raised by case, though district court could not have taken cognizance of them if they had been independently presented. This doctrine has been codified, as "supplemental jurisdiction", at 28 U.S.C.A. § 1367. *See* Supplemental jurisdiction.

Ancillary legislation. Legislative enactment which is auxiliary to or in aid of other and principal legislation.

Ancillary proceeding. One growing out of or auxiliary to another action or suit, or which is subordinate to or in aid of a primary action, either at law or in equity. In state courts, a procedural undertaking in aid of the principal action; for example, a bill for discovery in aid of a lawsuit or a garnishment proceeding.

Ancillary process. Any process which is in aid of or incidental to the principal suit or action; *e.g.* attachment. *See* Ancillary proceeding.

Ancillary receiver. One appointed in aid of, and in subordination to, a foreign receiver for purpose of collecting and taking charge of assets, as of insolvent corporation, in the jurisdiction where he is appointed.

And. A conjunction connecting words or phrases expressing the idea that the latter is to be added to or taken along with the first. Added to; together with; joined with; as well as; including. Sometimes construed as "or."

"And/or" means either or both of. When expression "and/or" is used, that word may be taken as will best effect the purpose of the parties as gathered from the contract taken as a whole, or, in other words, as will best accord with the equity of the situation.

Anew. To try a case or issue "anew" or "de novo" implies that the case or issue has been heard before. *See* De novo.

Anglo-Saxon law. English law derived from those people who conquered Britain in the 5th and 6th centuries and who dominated England until the Norman Conquest.

Animo /ǽnəmow/. Lat. With intention, disposition, design, will. *Quo animo*, with what intention.

Animus /ǽnəməs/. Lat. Mind; soul; intention; disposition; design; will; that which informs the body. *Animo (q.v.)*, with the intention or design. These terms are derived from the civil law.

Animus donandi /ǽnəməs downǽnday/. The intention of giving. Expressive of the intent to give which is necessary to constitute a gift.

Annex /ənéks/. Derived from the Latin "annectere," meaning to tie or bind to. To attach, and often, specifically, to subjoin. To add to; to unite. The word expresses the idea of joining a smaller or subordinate thing with another, larger, or of higher importance. To consolidate, as school districts. To make an integral part of something larger.

It implies physical connection or physically joined to, yet physical connection may be dispensed with, and things may be annexed without being in actual contact, when reasonably practicable. Something appended to, as a supplementary structure or wing. *See also* Appendant.

Annexation. The act of attaching, adding, joining, or uniting one thing to another; generally spoken of the connection of a smaller or subordinate thing with a larger or principal thing. Term is usually applied with respect to land or fixtures, as: the acquisition of territory or land by a nation, state or municipality; the legal incorporation of a town or city into another town or city.

The attaching an illustrative or auxiliary document to a deposition, pleading, deed, etc., may be called "annexing" it. *See* Exhibit.

In the law relating to fixtures, *actual annexation* includes every movement by which a chattel is joined or united to the property; *constructive annexation* is the union of such things as have been holden parcel of the realty, but which are not actually annexed, fixed, or fastened to the property. *See also* Fixture.

Anniversary. An annual day, recurring each year on the same date; commonly to commemorate an important event. In old-ecclesiastical law, a day set apart in memory of a deceased person. Also called "year day" or "mind day."

Anniversary date. As applied to insurance policy, means yearly recurring date of the initial issuance date.

Anno domini /ǽnow dómənay/. In the year of the Lord. Commonly abbreviated A.D. The computation of time, according to the Christian era, dates from the birth of Christ.

Annotate; Annotated. *See* Annotation.

Annotation /ǽnətéyshən/. A remark, note, case summary, or commentary on some passage of a book, statutory provision, court decision, or the like, intended to illustrate or explain its meaning. *See also* Digest; Headnote.

Civil law. An imperial rescript (*see* Rescript) signed by the emperor. The answers of the prince to questions put to him by private persons respecting some doubtful point of law. Also summoning an absentee, and, as well the designation of a place of deportation.

Statutory. Brief summaries of the law and facts of cases interpreting or applying statutes passed by Congress or state legislatures which are included (normally following text of statute) in annotated statutes or codes.

Announced. A decision is "announced," preventing nonsuit, when court's conclusion on issue tried is made known from bench or by any publication, oral or written, even if judgment has not been rendered.

Annoy. To disturb or irritate, especially by continued or repeated acts; to weary or trouble; to irk; to offend. *See also* Annoyance.

Annoyance. Discomfort; vexation. Not generally synonymous with anguish, inconvenience, or harassment. Such may result from either physical or mental conditions. It includes feeling of imposition and oppression. *See also* Harassment; Nuisance.

Annual /ǽnyuwəl/. Of or pertaining to year; returning every year; coming or happening yearly. Occurring or recurring once in each year; continuing for the period of a year; accruing within the space of a year; relating to or covering the events or affairs of a year. Once a year, without signifying what time in year. *See* Annually.

Annual accounting period concept. In determining a taxpayer's income tax liability, only those transactions taking place during a particular tax year are taken into consideration. For reporting and payment purposes, therefore, the tax life of taxpayers is divided into equal annual accounting periods. *See* Accounting period.

Annual assay. An annual trial of the gold and silver coins of the United States, to ascertain whether the standard fineness and weight of the coinage is maintained. 31 U.S.C.A. § 363.

Annual average earnings. Term used in worker's compensation law to describe a claimant's income both from seasonal and nonseasonal employment, but for inclusion the nonseasonal income is limited to employment of the same class as the seasonal.

Annual depreciation. The annual loss, not restored by current maintenance, which is due to all the factors causing the ultimate retirement of the property. These factors embrace wear and tear, decay, inadequacy, and obsolescence. The annual loss in service value not restored by current maintenance and incurred in connection with the consumption or prospective retirement of property in the course of service from causes known to be in current operation, and whose effect can be forecast with a reasonable approach to accuracy. *See* Depreciation.

Annual exclusion. The amount each year which can be excluded in computing the gift tax on the donor without using the lifetime exemption.

Annually. In annual order or succession; yearly, every year, year by year. At end of each and every year during a period of time. Imposed once a year, computed by the year. Yearly or once a year, but does not in itself signify what time in year.

Annual meeting. The meeting of stockholders each year called to elect officers and directors, to ratify actions of officers and directors and to vote on corporate matters which come before it. Generally, articles of organization or by-laws fix a date for such meeting each year. Annual meetings are required of publicly held corporations.

Annual percentage rate. The actual cost of borrowing money, expressed in form of annual interest rate to make it easy for one to compare cost of borrowing money among several lenders or sellers on credit. Full disclosure of interest rate and other charges is required by the Truth-in-Lending Act *(q.v.)*. Commonly abbreviated APR.

Annual permit. Yearly requirement in certain states for domestic corporations to do business in state. The fee is set according to the capitalization of the corporation.

Annual report. A report for stockholders and other interested parties prepared by corporation once a year; includes a balance sheet, an income statement, a statement of changes in financial position, a reconciliation of changes in owners' equity accounts, a summary of significant accounting principles, other explanatory notes, the auditor's report, and often comments from management about the year's business and prospects for the next year. By law, any public corporation that holds an annual stockholders meeting is required to issue an annual report. *See also* 10–K.

Annual statement. *See* Annual report.

Annual value. The net yearly income derivable from a given piece of property. Its fair rental value for one year, deducting costs and expenses; the value of its use for a year.

Annuitant. The party entitled to receive payments from an annuity contract. *See also* Annuity.

Annuity /ən(y)úwətiy/. A right to receive fixed, periodic payments, either for life or for a term of years. A fixed sum payable to a person at specified intervals for a specific period of time or for life. Payments represent a partial return of capital and a return (interest) on the capital investment. Therefore, an exclusion ratio must generally be used to compute the amount of nontaxable income. Special rules apply to employee retirement plan annuities.

The payment or receipt of a series of equal amounts of money per period for a specified amount of time. In an *ordinary annuity,* payments are made at the end of each period; in an *annuity due,* payments are made at the beginning.

Annuity bond. A bond without a maturity date, that is, perpetually paying interest.

Annuity certain. Payable for specified period; no matter the time of death of the annuitant.

Annuity trust. See that title.

Cash refund annuity. Policy which provides for the lump sum payment at the death of the annuitant of the difference between the total received and the price paid.

Contingent annuity. Funded annuity with payments to commence on the happening of an uncertain event; *e.g.* death of named person other than annuitant. An annuity whose number of payments depends upon the outcome of an event whose timing is uncertain at the time the annuity is set up.

Deferred annuity. Payments begin at some specified future date provided the beneficiary is alive at such date. *See also* Deferred annuity contract.

Equivalent annual annuity. The annual annuity whose present value is equal (equivalent) to a present value of some combination of costs and/or revenues.

Fixed annuity. Annuity that guarantees fixed payments, either for life or for a specified period, to annuitant.

Group annuity contract. A contract to make periodic payments to a member of a group covered by such contract. The usual type is a pension plan providing annuities upon retirement for individual employees under a master contract.

Joint and survivorship annuity. An annuity which is payable to the named annuitants during the period of their joint lives, with the annuity to continue to the survivor when the first annuitant dies.

Joint annuity. An annuity which is paid to the two named persons until the first one dies, at which time the annuity ceases.

Life annuity. Provides for payment of income to annuitant only during his lifetime; even though death is premature.

Private annuity. A contract for periodic payments to the annuitant from private as distinguished from public or life insurance company.

Refund annuity. Annuitant is assured a specified annual sum during his life, with the further assurance that in the event of his premature death there will be paid to his estate an additional amount which represents the difference between the purchase price and the amount paid out during annuitant's life.

Retirement annuity. Policy in which payments to annuitant commence at some future date; *e.g.* after retirement. If annuitant dies in interval or surrender is desired, an agreed upon amount is refunded to annuitant's estate.

Straight annuity. A contract usually by an insurance company to make periodic payments at monthly or yearly intervals; distinguishable from life insurance contract which looks to longevity, while annuity looks to transiency. Straight annuity contract calls for a fixed amount of payment as distinguished from the variable annuity.

Straight life annuity. See *Life annuity; Straight annuity, above.*

Survivorship annuity. See *Joint and survivorship annuity, above.*

Variable annuity. A contract calling for payments to the annuitant in varying amounts depending on the success of the investment policy of the insurance company; unlike a straight annuity which requires the payment of a fixed amount. Purpose of this type of annuity is to offset deflated value of dollar caused by inflation.

Annuity policy. An insurance policy providing for monthly or periodic payments to insured to begin at fixed date and continue through insured's life.

Annuity trust. A form of trust calling for payment of a fixed amount of income regardless of the amount of principal. *See also* Trust *(Annuity trust).*

Annul /ənəl/. To reduce to nothing; annihilate; obliterate; to make void or of no effect; to nullify; to abolish; to do away with. To cancel; destroy; abrogate. To annul a judgment or judicial proceeding is to deprive it of all force and operation, either *ab initio* or prospectively as to future transactions.

Annulment. To nullify, to abolish, to make void by competent authority. An "annulment" differs from a divorce in that a divorce terminates a legal status, whereas an annulment establishes that a marital status never existed. Grounds and procedures for annulment of marriage are governed by state statutes.

Annum /ǽnəm/. Year.

Annus /ǽnəs/. Lat. In civil and old English law, a year; the period of three hundred and sixty-five days. *See* Annual.

Anomalous /ənómələs/. Deviating from common rule, method, or type. Irregular; exceptional; abnormal; unusual.

Anomalous indorser /ənómələs əndórsər/. A stranger to a note, who indorses it after its execution and delivery but before maturity, and before it has been indorsed by the payee.

Anomalous plea /ənómələs plíy/. One which is partly affirmative and partly negative.

Anonymous. Nameless; lacking a name or names; *e.g.* a publication, article, or the like, without any designation of authorship; an unsigned letter; a tip from an unknown service.

Another. Additional. Distinct or different.

Anoysance /ənóyzəns/. Annoyance; nuisance.

Answer. As a verb, the word denotes an assumption of liability, as to "answer" for the debt or default of another.

Discovery. A person who fails to answer, or answers evasively or incompletely, deposition or interrogatory questions, may be compelled to do so under Fed.R. Civil P. 37.

Frivolous answer. See Sham answer, below.

Irrelevant answer. One that has no substantial relation to the controversy; distinguishable from a sham answer. Such may be ordered stricken under Fed.R. Civil P. 12(f).

Pleading. The response of a defendant to the plaintiff's complaint, denying in part or in whole the allegations made by the plaintiff. A pleading by which defendant endeavors to resist the plaintiff's demand by an allegation of facts, either denying allegations of plaintiff's complaint or confessing them and alleging new matter in avoidance, which defendant alleges should prevent recovery on facts alleged by plaintiff. In pleading, under the Codes and Rules of Civil Procedure, the answer is the formal written statement made by a defendant setting forth the grounds of his defense; corresponding to what in actions under the common-law practice is called the "plea." See Fed.R. Civil P. 8 and 12.

Under Fed.R.Civil P. 12, a person may use an answer to set up all defenses, but he also has the option to use a motion to assert certain defenses.

See also Affirmative defense; Defense; Denial; Supplemental answer.

In chancery pleading, the term denotes a defense in writing, made by a defendant to the allegations contained in a bill or information filed by the plaintiff against him.

Sham answer. One sufficient on its face but so clearly false that it presents no real issue to be tried. One good in form, but false in fact and not pleaded in good faith. A frivolous answer, on the other hand, is one which on its face sets up no defense, although it may be true in fact. On motion of a party, the court may order stricken from the pleading any insufficient defense. Fed. R.Civil P. 12(f).

Answerable. *See* Liability.

Ante /æntiy/. Lat. Before. Usually employed in old pleadings as expressive of time, as *præ* (before) was of place, and *coram* (before) of person.

Occurring in a report or a text-book, it is used to refer the reader to a previous part of the book. Synonymous to *"supra"*; opposite of *"post"* or *"infra."*

Antecedent /æntəsíydənt/. Prior in point of time.

Antecedent claim. A preexisting claim. In law of negotiable instruments, a holder takes for value if he takes the instrument for an antecedent claim against any person whether or not the claim is due. U.C.C. § 3–303(b).

Antecedent creditors. Those whose debts are created before the debtor makes a transfer not lodged for record.

Antecedent debt. In contract law, that which may or may not furnish consideration for a new contract to pay. A negotiable instrument given for an antecedent debt is supported by adequate consideration. U.C.C. § 3–408.

In former bankruptcy law, a debt which was incurred before four months prior to filing of bankruptcy petition and hence not a preference. Bankruptcy Act (1898), § 60a.

Antecessor /æntəsésər/. An ancestor *(q.v.)*.

Antedate. To affix an earlier date; to date an instrument as of a time before the time it was written. Such does not affect the negotiability of the instrument. U.C.C. § 3–114.

Antenuptial /æntiynápshəl/. Made or done before a marriage.

Antenuptial agreement. An agreement between prospective spouses made in contemplation of marriage and to be effective upon marriage. Uniform Premarital Agreement Act, § 1. Antenuptial agreements are generally entered into by people about to enter marriage in an attempt to resolve issues of support, distribution of wealth and division of property in the event of the death of either or the failure of the proposed marriage resulting in either separation or divorce. The Uniform Act, which has been adopted by a number of states, sets forth the formalities of execution, amendment or revocation (any of which do not require consideration for enforcement), the matters that can be contracted for, enforcement, etc.

Antenuptial gift. A transfer of property from one party to the marriage to the other before the marriage without consideration.

Antenuptial settlements. *See* Antenuptial agreement; Palimony.

Antenuptial will. A will executed by a person prior to his marriage. Such will is generally deemed revoked unless it appears on the face of the will that it is in contemplation of marriage.

Antichresis /æntəkríyzəs/. In the civil law, a species of mortgage, or pledge of immovables. An agreement by which the debtor gives to the creditor the income from the property which he has pledged, in lieu of the interest on his debt. In the French law, if the income was more than the interest, the debtor was entitled to demand an account of the income, and might claim any excess.

By the law of Louisiana, there are two kinds of pledges,—the pawn and the antichresis. A pawn relates to movables, and the antichresis to immovables. The antichresis must be reduced to writing; and the creditor thereby acquires the right to the fruits, etc., of the immovables, deducting yearly their proceeds from the interest, in the first place, and afterwards from the principal of his debt. He is bound to pay taxes on the property, and keep it in repair, unless the contrary is agreed. The creditor does not become the proprietor of the property by failure to pay at the agreed time, and any clause to that effect is void. He can only sue the debtor, and obtain sentence for sale of the property. The possession of the property is, however, by the contract, transferred to the creditor. La.Civil Code Arts. 3176–3181. The "antichresis" is an antiquated contract, and has been resorted to in Louisiana in but a few instances.

Anticipation. Act of doing or taking a thing before its proper time. To do, take up, or deal with, before another; to preclude or prevent by prior action; to be before in doing.

In conveyancing, the act of assigning, charging, or otherwise dealing with income before it becomes due.

In patent law, an invention is anticipated by prior art when the invention is not new or lacks novelty over that art. Defense of "anticipation" in suit for patent infringement is made out when, except for insubstantial differences, the prior patent contains all of the same elements operating in the same fashion to perform an identical function. Unless all of same elements are found in exactly same situation and are united in same way to perform identical function in a single prior art reference, there is no "anticipation" which will invalidate that patent.

In law of negligence, "anticipation" is not confined to expectation. It means probability, not possibility, as applied to duty to anticipate consequences of conduct attacked as negligent.

Anticipation note. Discount or rebate for prepayment.

Anticipatory assignment of income. See Assignment *(Assignment of income).*

Anticipatory breach of contract. The assertion by a party to a contract that he or she will not perform a future obligation as required by the contract. Such occurs when a party to an executory contract manifests a definite and unequivocal intent prior to time fixed in contract that it will not render its performance under the contract when that time arrives, and in such a case the other party may treat the contract as ended.

The right of one party to a contract to sue for breach before the date set for performance when the other party conveys his intention not to perform (U.C.C. § 2–610), though the repudiating party may retract his repudiation prior to date for performance if the other party has not acted on the repudiation (U.C.C. § 2–611). Some jurisdictions require the aggrieved party to wait for the date for performance before commencing suit.

Anticipatory nuisance. The right in equity to prevent a condition from becoming a nuisance by injunction or other order of the court.

Anticipatory offense. A crime which has as its object a further crime, such as an attempt, a conspiracy, a solicitation, all of which are crimes in themselves.

Anticipatory repudiation. See Anticipatory breach of contract.

Anticipatory search warrant. A warrant based upon an affidavit showing probable cause that at some future time, but not presently, certain evidence of crime will be located at specified place; such warrant is to be distinguished from a premature search.

Anti-deficiency legislation. Statutes which are enacted to provide revenue when a budget deficiency is created.

Antidilutive effect. Result of a transaction that increases earnings per common share (e.g., by decreasing the number of common shares outstanding).

Anti-dilution provision. A provision appearing in convertible securities to guarantee that the conversion privilege is not affected by share reclassifications, share splits, share dividends, or similar transactions that may increase the number of outstanding shares without increasing the corporate capital.

Anti-Dumping Act. *See* Dumping Act.

Anti-dumping duty. Tariff, purpose of which is to prevent imports of goods for sale at a lower price than that charged in the country of origin. *See* Dumping Act.

Antigraphy. A copy or counterpart of a deed.

Anti-lapse statute. Legislation enacted in most jurisdictions to provide for the testamentary passing of property to heirs and next of kin of the designated legatee or devisee if he dies before the testator, thus preventing a lapse of the legacy and the passing of such property through intestacy to the heirs and next of kin of the testator.

Anti manifesto. A term used in international law to denote a proclamation or manifesto published by one of two belligerent powers, alleging reasons why the war is defensive on its part.

Anti-Racketeering Act. Federal act prohibiting robbery, extortion, or other unlawful interference with interstate commerce. *See* Hobbs Act; RICO laws.

Antitrust acts. Federal and state statutes to protect trade and commerce from unlawful restraints, price discriminations, price fixing, and monopolies. Most states have mini-antitrust acts patterned on the federal acts. The principal federal antitrust acts are: Sherman Act (1890); Clayton Act (1914); Federal Trade Commission Act (1914); Robinson-Patman Act (1936). *See* Boycott; Combination in restraint of trade; Hart-Scott-Rodino Antitrust Improvement Act; Per se violations; Price-fixing; Restraint of trade; Rule *(Rule of reason).*

Antitrust Civil Process Act. Federal statute permitting antitrust action by way of a petition in U.S. District Court for an order for enforcement of law. 15 U.S.C.A. § 1314.

Antitrust injury. Such injury, which must be established in order to have standing to bring antitrust claim under Clayton Act, is injury the antitrust laws were designed to prevent and that flows from that which makes a defendant's acts unlawful. The injury should reflect the anticompetitive effect either of the violation or of anticompetitive acts made possible by the violation.

Any. Some; one out of many; an indefinite number. One indiscriminately of whatever kind or quantity. "Any" does not necessarily mean only one person, but may have reference to more than one or to many.

A.O.C. *Anno orbis conditi*, the year of the creation of the world.

A.P.A. Administrative Procedure Act.

Apartment house. A building arranged in several suites of connecting rooms, each suite designed for independent housekeeping, but with certain mechanical conveniences, such as heat, light, or elevator services, in common to all persons occupying the building. A building containing multiple residential rental units. Sometimes called a flat or flat house.

APB. Accounting Principles Board.

A.P.C. Alien Property Custodian.

Apex. The summit or highest point of anything; the top; *e.g.*, in mining law, "apex of a vein." An "apex" is all that portion of a terminal edge of a mineral vein from which the vein has extension downward in the direction of the dip. Or it is the juncture of two dipping limbs of a fissure vein. *See* Apex rule.

Apex juris /éypèks júrəs/. The summit of the law; a legal subtlety; a nice or cunning point of law; close technicality; a rule of law carried to an extreme point, either of severity or refinement. A term used to denote a stricter application of the rules of law than is indicated by the phrase *summum jus (q.v.)*.

Apex rule. In mining law, the mineral laws of the United States give to the locator of a mining claim on the public domain the whole of every vein the apex of which lies within his surface exterior boundaries, or within perpendicular planes drawn downward indefinitely on the planes of those boundaries; and he may follow a vein which thus apexes within his boundaries, on its dip, although it may so far depart from the perpendicular in its course downward as to extend outside the vertical side-lines of his location; but he may not go beyond his end-lines or vertical planes drawn downward therefrom. This is called the apex rule. 30 U.S.C.A. § 26.

A posteriori /èy postìriyóray/. Lat. From the effect to the cause; from what comes after. A term used in logic to denote an argument founded on experiment or observation, or one which, taking ascertained facts as an effect, proceeds by synthesis and induction to demonstrate their cause.

Apparent. That which is obvious, evident, or manifest; what appears, or has been made manifest. That which appears to the eye or mind; open to view; plain; patent. In respect to facts involved in an appeal or writ of error, that which is stated in the record. *See also* Appear on face; Patent.

Apparent agency. *See* Agency.

Apparent authority. In the law of agency, such authority as the principal knowingly or negligently permits the agent to assume, or which he holds the agent out as possessing. Such authority as he appears to have by reason of the actual authority which he has. Such authority as a reasonably prudent man, using diligence and discretion, in view of the principal's conduct, would naturally suppose the agent to possess. Such authority as a principal intentionally or by want of ordinary care causes or allows third person to believe that agent possesses. It includes the power to do whatever is usually done and necessary to be done in order to carry into effect the principal power conferred.

The power to affect the legal relations of another person by transactions with third persons, professedly as agent for the other, arising from and in accordance with the other's manifestations to such third persons. Restatement, Second, Agency § 8.

Apparent danger. As used with reference to the doctrine of self-defense in homicide, means such overt actual demonstration, by conduct and acts, of a design to take life or do some great personal injury, as would make the killing apparently necessary to self-preservation. *See* Self defense.

Apparent defects. Those defects in goods which can be discovered by simple inspection; see U.C.C. § 2–605. Also, may refer to title defects which appear on the record. *See* Patent; Patent defect.

Apparent easement. *See* Easement.

Apparent heir. One whose right of inheritance is indefeasible, provided he outlives the ancestor. To be contrasted with presumptive heir whose claim to inheritance is defeated on the birth of an heir closer in relationship to the ancestor, though at a given point in time the heir presumptive is entitled to the inheritance.

Apparent necessity. *See* Apparent danger.

App. Ct. Appellate Court.

Appeal. Resort to a superior (*i.e.* appellate) court to review the decision of an inferior (*i.e.* trial) court or administrative agency. A complaint to a higher tribunal of an error or injustice committed by a lower tribunal, in which the error or injustice is sought to be corrected or reversed. There are two stages of appeal in the federal and many state court systems; to wit, appeal from trial court to intermediate appellate court and then to Supreme Court. There may also be several levels of appeal within an administrative agency; *e.g.* appeal from decision of Administrative Law Judge to Appeals Council in social security case. In addition, an appeal may be taken from an administrative agency to a trial court (*e.g.* from Appeals Council in social security case to U.S. district court). Also, an appeal may be as of right (*e.g.*

from trial court to intermediate appellate court) or only at the discretion of the appellate court (*e.g.* by writ of certiorari to U.S. Supreme Court). Provision may also exist for joint or consolidated appeals (*e.g.* Fed.R.App.P. 3) and for cross appeals (where both parties to a judgment appeal therefrom).

Appeal was also the name formerly given to the proceeding in English law where a person, indicted of treason or felony, and arraigned for the same, confessed the fact before plea pleaded, and *appealed*, or accused others, his accomplices in the same crime, in order to obtain his pardon. In this case he was called an "approver" or "prover," and the party appealed or accused, the "appellee."

See also Consolidated appeal; Court of Appeals; Courts of Appeals, U.S.; Cross appeal; Interlocutory appeal; Interlocutory Appeals Act; Limited appeal.

Appealable order. A decree or order which is sufficiently final to be entitled to appellate review, as contrasted with an interlocutory order which generally is not appealable until the case has been tried and judgment entered, *e.g.* a denial of motion for summary judgment is not appealable but the allowance of such motion is a final judgment and hence appealable. Fed.R. Civil P. 56.

Appeal bond. The court in its discretion may require the appellant to file a bond or provide other security to ensure payment of costs on appeal. See *e.g.*, Fed.R.App.P. 7.

Appeal in forma pauperis /əpíyl in fórmə pópərəs/. A privilege given indigent person to prosecute an appeal, otherwise and independently allowable, without payment of fees and costs incident to such prosecution. See *e.g.* Fed.R.App.P. 24.

Appeal record. *See* Record (*Record on appeal*).

Appeals council. Body to which appeal is taken from finding and ruling of administrative law judge in social security matters. 42 U.S.C.A. § 405(b).

Appeals courts. *See* Appellate court; Court of Appeals; Court of Customs and Patent Appeals; Court of Military Appeals; Supreme court.

Appear. To be properly before a court; as a fact or matter of which it can take notice. To be in evidence; to be proved. Coming into court by a party to a suit, whether plaintiff or defendant. *See* Appearance.

Appear on face. That which is clear and apparent from a reading of the document. A defect in process or venue which can be gleaned from examining the pleadings and which does not require going outside the record. *See also* Apparent.

Appearance. A coming into court as party to a suit, either in person or by attorney, whether as plaintiff or defendant. The formal proceeding by which a defendant submits himself to the jurisdiction of the court. The voluntary submission to a court's jurisdiction.

In civil actions the parties do not normally actually appear in person, but rather through their attorneys (who enter their appearance by filing written pleadings, or a formal written entry of appearance). Also, at many stages of criminal proceedings, particularly involving minor offenses, the defendant's attorney appears on his behalf. See *e.g.*, Fed.R.Crim.P. 43.

An appearance may be either *general* or *special*; the former is a simple and unqualified or unrestricted submission to the jurisdiction of the court, the latter a submission to the jurisdiction for some specific purpose only, not for all the purposes of the suit. A special appearance is for the purpose of testing or objecting to the sufficiency of service or the jurisdiction of the court over defendant without submitting to such jurisdiction; a general appearance is made where the defendant waives defects of service and submits to the jurisdiction of court.

See also General appearance; Notice to appear.

Appearance by attorney. An act of an attorney in prosecuting an action on behalf of his client. Document filed in court in which attorney sets forth fact that he is representing a party to the action.

Appearance docket. A docket kept by the clerk of the court in which appearances are entered, containing also a brief abstract of all the proceedings in the cause.

Common law classifications. At common law an appearance could be either *compulsory* or *voluntary*, the former where it was compelled by process served on the party, the latter where it was entered by his own will or consent, without the service of process, though process may be outstanding. Also, *optional* when entered by a person who intervened in the action to protect his own interests, though not joined as a party; *conditional*, when coupled with conditions as to its becoming or being taken as a general appearance; *gratis*, when made by a party to the action, but before the service of any process or legal notice to appear; *de bene esse*, when made provisionally or to remain good only upon a future contingency; or when designed to permit a party to a proceeding to refuse to submit his person to the jurisdiction of the court unless it was finally determined that he had forever waived that right; *subsequent*, when made by a defendant after an appearance had already been entered for him by the plaintiff; *corporal*, when the person was physically present in court.

Initial appearance. A court proceeding for a defendant charged with a felony, during which the judge advises the defendant of the charges against him and of his rights, decides upon bail and/or other conditions of release, and sets the date for a preliminary hearing. See *e.g.* Fed.R.Crim.P. 5.

Notice of appearance. A notice given by defendant to a plaintiff that he appears in the action in person or by attorney.

Appearance doctrine. This doctrine is a special rule designed to afford a right of self-defense to defendant based upon which "appears" to the defendant to be a situation which justifies use of force in self-defense. See Self-defense.

Appellant. The party who takes an appeal from one court or jurisdiction to another. Used broadly or nontechnically, the term includes one who sues out a writ of error.

Appellate. Pertaining to or having cognizance of appeals and other proceedings for the judicial review of adjudications. The term has a general meaning, and it has a specific meaning indicating the distinction between original jurisdiction and appellate jurisdiction.

Appellate court. A court having jurisdiction of appeal and review of decisions of lower courts; a court to which causes are removable by appeal, certiorari, error or report. A reviewing court, and, except in special cases where original jurisdiction is conferred, not a "trial court" or court of first instance. See *e.g.* Court of Appeals; Court of Customs and Patent Appeals; Court of Military Appeals; Supreme court.

Appellate division. An intermediate appellate court for hearing civil appeals. See *e.g.,* Mass. G.L. c. 231, § 108. Also, in Mass., a three judge panel to consider appeals of sentences for felonies. Mass.G.L. c. 278, §§ 28A, 28B. In New York, an intermediate appellate court which also has the power to make rules and regulations governing the administration of the courts. See N.Y.Judiciary Law, Article 4, § 70–109. In New Jersey, most civil appeals are to the Appellate Division of the Superior Court.

Appellate jurisdiction. The power vested in an appellate court to review and revise the judicial action of an inferior court, evidenced by an appealable order or an appealable judgment rendered by such court. The power and authority to take cognizance of a cause and proceed to its determination, not in its initial stages (*i.e.* original jurisdiction) but only after it has been finally decided by an inferior court, *i.e.*, the power of review and determination on appeal, writ of error, certiorari, or other similar process. Jurisdiction on appeal; jurisdiction to revise or correct the proceedings in a cause already instituted and acted upon by an inferior court, or by a tribunal having the attributes of a court. Limits of appellate jurisdiction are governed by statutes (*e.g.* 28 U.S.C.A. § 1291 et seq.) or constitutions.

Appellate review. Examination of lower court proceeding by an appellate court brought about by appeal, bill of exceptions, report or certiorari. Such may also embrace review of administrative board's decision by an inferior court; *e.g.* review by federal district court of social security administration decision.

Appellate rules. Rules governing procedure in taking appeals and in practicing before appellate courts; *e.g.* Federal Rules of Appellate Procedure; Massachusetts Rules of Appellate Procedure. See Federal Rules of Appellate Procedure.

Appellee. The party in a cause against whom an appeal is taken; that is, the party who has an interest adverse to setting aside or reversing the judgment. Sometimes also called the "respondent." It should be noted that a party's status as appellant or appellee does not necessarily bear any relation to his status as plaintiff or defendant in the lower court.

Append. To add or attach. See Appendix.

Appendage. Something added as an accessory to or the subordinate part of another thing. See Appendant; Appendix.

Appendant. A thing annexed to or belonging to another thing and passing with it. Something added or attached.

At common law, a thing of inheritance belonging to another inheritance which is more worthy; as an advowson, common, etc., which may be appendant to a manor, common of fishing to a freehold, a seat in a church to a house, etc. It differs from appurtenance, in that appendant must ever be by prescription, *i.e.*, a personal usage for a considerable time, while an appurtenance may be created at this day; for if a grant be made to a man and his heirs, of common in such a moor for his beasts levant or couchant upon his manor, the commons are appurtenant to the manor, and the grant will pass them.

See also Appendix; Appurtenance; Appurtenant.

Appendix. Supplementary materials added to appellate brief; *e.g.* record on appeal. In federal appellate procedure, the appellant is required to file an appendix to the briefs which shall contain the following: (1) the relevant portions of the pleadings, charge, findings or opinion; (2) the judgment, order or decision in question; and (3) any other parts of the record to which the parties wish to direct the particular attention of the court. Fed.R.App.P. 30.

Appertain. To belong to; to have relation to; to be appurtenant to. See Appurtenance; Appurtenant.

Appertaining. Connected with in use or occupancy.

Applicable. Fit, suitable, pertinent, related to, or appropriate; capable of being applied.

Applicable local law. Term used to determine the persons who come within the term heirs and is the law which would be used to ascertain the heirs of the designated ancestor if he had owned the property and had died intestate. Restatement of Law of Property, § 305, Comment e.

Applicant. An applicant, as for letters of administration, is one who is entitled thereto, and who files a petition asking that letters be granted. For purposes of letters of credit, the customer in the credit transaction. Synonymous also with "account party."

Application. A putting to, placing before, preferring a request or petition to or before a person. The act of making a request for something. A petition. The use or disposition made of a thing. A bringing together, in order to ascertain some relation or establish some connection; as the *application* of a rule or principle to a case or fact. An appeal or petition, especially as written or presented; a putting to, placing before; preferring a request or petition to or before a person; the act of making a request for something. *See also,* Apply; Motion; Petition.

Insurance. The preliminary request, declaration, or statement made by a party applying for an insurance policy, such as one on his life, or against fire.

Payments. Appropriation of a payment to some particular debt; or the determination to which of several demands a general payment made by a debtor to his creditor shall be applied.

Purchase money. The disposition made of the funds received by a trustee on a sale of real estate held under the trust.

Application of rules. Refers to area of practice governed by rules of procedure and not left to common law or statutory law.

Apply. To make a formal request or petition, usually in writing, to a court, officer, board, or company, for the granting of some favor, or of some rule or order, which is within his or their power or discretion. For example, to apply for an injunction, for a pardon, for a policy of insurance, or for a receiver. *See* Application; Petition.

To use or employ for a particular purpose; to appropriate and devote to a particular use, object, demand, or subject-matter. Thus, to apply payments to the reduction of interest. *See* Appropriate.

To put, use, or refer, as suitable or relative; to co-ordinate language with a particular subject-matter; as to apply the words of a statute to a particular state of facts.

The word "apply" is used in connection with statutes in two senses. When construing a statute, in describing the class of persons, things, or functions which are within its scope; as that the statute does not "apply" to transactions in interstate commerce. When discussing the use made of a statute, in referring to the process by which the statute is made operative; as where the jury is told to "apply" the statute of limitation if they find that the cause of action arose before a given date.

Appoint. To designate, choose, select, assign, ordain, prescribe, constitute, or nominate. To allot or set apart. To assign authority to a particular use, task, position, or office.

Term is used where exclusive power and authority is given to one person, officer, or body to name persons to hold certain offices. It is usually distinguished from "elect," meaning to choose by a vote of the qualified voters of the city; though this distinction is not invariably observed.

See also Appointment.

Appointee. A person who is appointed or selected for a particular purpose; as the appointee under a power of appointment is the person who is to receive the benefit of the power.

Appointment. The designation of a person, by the person or persons having authority therefor, to discharge the duties of some office or trust. *See* Illusory appointment; Power of appointment.

The exercise of a right to designate the person or persons who are to take the use of real estate. The act of a person in directing the disposition of property, by limiting a use, or by substituting a new use for a former one, in pursuance of a power granted to him for that purpose by a preceding deed, called a "power of appointment"; also the deed or other instrument by which he so conveys. Where the power embraces several permitted objects, and the appointment is made to one or more of them, excluding others, it is called "exclusive."

Appointment may signify an appropriation of money to a specific purpose. It may also mean the arranging of a meeting.

Office or public function. The selection or designation of a person, by the person or persons having authority therefor, to fill an office or public function and discharge the duties of the same. The term "appointment" is to be distinguished from "election." "Election" to office usually refers to vote of people, whereas "appointment" relates to designation by some individual or group.

Appointment, power of. *See* Power of appointment.

Appointor. The person who appoints, or executes a power of appointment; as *appointee* is the person to whom or in whose favor an appointment is made. One authorized by the donor, under the statute of uses, to execute a power.

Apport. L. Fr. In old English law, tax; tallage; tribute; imposition; payment; charge; expenses.

Apportion. To divide and distribute proportionally.

Apportionment /əpórshənmənt/. The process by which legislative seats are distributed among units entitled to representation. Determination of the number of representatives which a State, county, or other subdivision may send to a legislative body. The U.S. Constitution provides for a census every ten years, on the basis of which Congress apportions representatives according to population; but each State must have at least one representative. "Districting" is the establishment of the precise geographical boundaries of each such unit or constituency. Apportionment by state statute which denies the rule of one-man, one-vote is violative of equal protection of laws. Baker v. Carr, 369 U.S. 186, 82 S.Ct. 691, 7 L.Ed.2d 663. *See also* Legislative apportionment; Reapportionment.

The allocation of a charge or cost such as real estate taxes between two parties, often in the same ratio as the respective times that the parties are in possession or ownership of property during the fiscal period for which the charge is made or assessed.

Contracts. The allowance, in case of a severable contract, partially performed, of a part of the entire consideration proportioned to the degree in which the contract was carried out.

Corporate shares. The *pro tanto* division among the subscribers of the shares allowed to be issued by the charter, where more than the limited number have been subscribed for.

Estate taxes. Unless the will otherwise provides, taxes shall be apportioned among all persons interested in the estate. The apportionment is to be made in the proportion that the value of the interest of each person interested in the estate bears to the total value of the interests of all persons interested in the estate. The values used in determining the tax are to be used for that purpose. If the decedent's will directs a method of apportionment of tax different from the method described in the Probate Code, the method described in the will controls. Uniform Probate Code, § 3–916(b).

Incumbrances. Where several persons are interested in an estate, apportionment, as between them, is the determination of the respective amounts which they shall contribute towards the removal of the incumbrance.

Liability. Legal responsibility of parties to a transaction or tort may be distributed or apportioned among them by statute or by agreement. *See* Comparative negligence; Contribution.

Rent. The allotment of shares in a rent to each of several parties owning it. The determination of the amount of rent to be paid when the tenancy is terminated at some period other than one of the regular intervals for the payment of rent.

Representatives. The determination upon each decennial census of the number of representatives in congress which each state shall elect, the calculation being based upon the population. See U.S. Const., Art. 1, § 2; Amend. 14, § 2.

Taxes. The apportionment of a tax consists in a selection of the subjects to be taxed, and in laying down the rule by which to measure the contribution which each of these subjects shall make to the tax. *See also Estate taxes above.*

The assignment of the business income of a multistate corporation to specific states for income taxation. Usually, the apportionment procedure accounts for the property, payroll, and sales activity levels of the various states, and a proportionate assignment of the entity's total income is made thereby, using a three-factor apportionment formula. These activities indicate the commercial domicile of the corporation, relative to that income. Some states exclude nonbusiness income from the apportionment procedure; they *allocate* nonbusiness income to the states where the nonbusiness assets are located.

Apportionment clause. Insurance policy clause which distributes insurance in proportion to the total coverage.

Appraisal. A valuation or an estimation of value of property by disinterested persons of suitable qualifications. The process of ascertaining a value of an asset or liability that involves expert opinion rather than explicit market transactions. *See also* Appraise.

In corporate law, a limited statutory right granted to minority shareholders who object to certain fundamental transactions such as mergers. In an appraisal proceeding a court determines the appraised value of their shares and the corporation pays such appraised value to the shareholder in cash. The Revised Model Business Corporation Act uses the term "dissenters' rights to obtain payment for their shares" to describe this right. An appraisal right exists only to the extent specifically provided by statute. *See* Appraisal remedy.

Appraisal clause. Clause in insurance policy providing that the insurer has the right to demand an appraisal of the loss or damage.

Appraisal remedy. The dissenting shareholder's appraisal remedy is essentially a statutory creation to enable shareholders who object to certain extraordinary matters to dissent and to require the corporation to buy their shares at the value immediately prior to the approval of such matter and thus to withdraw from the corporation. In different jurisdictions, the appraisal remedy often applies to sales of substantially all corporate assets other than in the regular course of business, mergers, and consolidations, more rarely to certain amendments of the articles of incorporation or miscellaneous matters, but usually not to dissolution. The appraisal remedy is often limited to shareholders of record entitled to vote on the matter.

Appraisal rights. *See* Appraisal remedy.

Appraise. To fix or set a price or value upon; to fix and state the true value of a thing, and, usually, in writing. To value property at what it is worth. To "appraise" money means to count. *See also* Appraisal.

Appraisement. A just and true valuation of property. A valuation set upon property under judicial or legislative authority. A valuation or estimation of the value of property. *See also* Appraisal.

Appraiser. A person selected or appointed by competent authority or interested party to make an appraisement; to ascertain and state the true value of goods or real estate. Frequently appointed in probate and condemnation proceedings; also used by condemnation authorities, banks and real estate companies to ascertain market value of real property.

Appreciable. Capable of being estimated, weighed, judged of, or recognized by the mind. Capable of being perceived or recognized by the senses. Perceptible but not a synonym of substantial.

Appreciate. To estimate justly; to set a price or value on. When used with reference to the nature and effect of an act, "appreciate" may be synonymous with "know" or "understand" or "realize."

Appreciation in value. Increase in the market value of an asset (*e.g.*, real estate) over its value at some earlier time. May be due from inflation and/or increased market demand for asset.

Apprehend. To take hold of, whether with the mind (as to conceive, believe, fear, dread, understand, be conscious or sensible of), or actually and bodily (as to seize or arrest a person). *See* Arrest.

Apprehension. The seizure, taking, or arrest of a person on a criminal charge. *See* Arrest.

Civil law. A physical or corporal act (*corpus*), on the part of one who intends to acquire possession of a thing, by which he brings himself into such a relation to the thing that he may subject it to his exclusive control; or by which he obtains the physical ability to exercise his power over the thing whenever he pleases. One of the requisites to the acquisition of judicial possession, and by which, when accompanied by intention, (*animus*) possession is acquired.

Apprendre. A fee or profit taken or received.

Apprenticeship. An apprentice is a person who agrees to work for an employer for a specified time for the purpose of learning the craft, trade or profession in which the employer agrees to instruct him. In a more popular sense the term is used to convey the idea of a learner in any field of employment or business. The requirements of an apprenticeship contract both as to contents and manner of execution are prescribed by statute in a number of states. *See also* Articles of apprenticeship.

The term during which an apprentice is to serve; the *status* of an apprentice; the relation subsisting between an apprentice and his master.

Approach. To come nearer in place or time. An access or a way, passage, or avenue by which a place may be approached.

Approach, right of. In international maritime law, the right of a ship of war, upon the high sea, to draw near to another vessel for the purpose of ascertaining the nationality of the latter. At present the right of approach has no existence apart from the right of visit.

Approbation /ǽprǝbéyshǝn/. Denotes approval and generally includes commendation.

Appropriate. To make a thing one's own; to make a thing the subject of property; to exercise dominion over an object to the extent, and for the purpose, of making it subserve one's own proper use or pleasure. To prescribe a particular use for particular moneys; to designate or destine a fund or property for a distinct use, or for the payment of a particular demand. Also used in the sense of distribute. In this sense it may denote the act of an executor or administrator who distributes the estate of his decedent among the legatees, heirs, or others entitled, in pursuance of his duties and according to their respective rights. *See* Appropriation; Expropriation.

Appropriated surplus. In accounting, portion of surplus set aside for specific purpose other than for existing liability.

Appropriation. The act of appropriating or setting apart; prescribing the destination of a thing; designating the use or application of a fund. In tort law, the act of making a thing one's own or exercising or making use of an object to subserve one's own interest. When the act is wrongful, a tort is committed.

In governmental accounting, an expenditure authorized for a specified amount, purpose, and time. *See Public law (below)* and Appropriation bill.

See also Appropriate; Misappropriation.

Appropriation of land. The act of selecting, devoting, or setting apart land for a particular use or purpose, as where land is appropriated for public buildings, military reservations, or other public uses. Taking of private property for public use in the exercise of the power of eminent domain. In this sense it may refer merely to physical occupation and contemplate payment prior thereto, in contra-distinction to "taking," referring to a legal taking and presupposing payment after damages are due. *See* Condemnation; Eminent domain; Expropriation.

Appropriation of payments. The application of a payment to the discharge of a particular debt. Thus, if a creditor has two distinct debts due to him from his debtor, and the latter makes a general payment on account, without specifying at the time to which debt he intends the payment to apply, it is optional for the creditor to *appropriate* (apply) the payment to either of the two debts he pleases.

Appropriation of water. An appropriation of water flowing on the public domain consists in the capture, impounding, or diversion of it from its natural course or channel and its actual application to some beneficial use private or personal to the appropriator, to the entire exclusion (or exclusion to the extent of the water appropriated) of all other persons. To constitute a valid appropriation, there must be an intent to apply the water to some beneficial use existing at the time or contemplated in the future, a diversion from the natural channel by means of a ditch or canal, or some other open physical act of taking possession of the water, and an actual application of it within a reasonable time to some useful or beneficial purpose.

Public law. The act by which the legislative department of government designates a particular fund, or sets apart a specified portion of the public revenue or of the money in the public treasury, to be applied to some general object of governmental expenditure, or to some individual purchase or expense. Authority given by legislature to proper officers to apply distinctly specified sum from designated fund out of treasury in given year for specified object or demand against state.

Purpose of a *general* appropriation bill is to fund programs that have been separately authorized by other legislation. A *specific* appropriation is an act of the legislature by which a named sum of money has been set apart in the treasury, and devoted to the payment of a particular demand.

Appropriation bill. A measure before a legislative body authorizing the expenditure of public moneys and stipulating the amount, manner, and purpose of the various items of expenditure. Appropriation bills in Congress must originate in the House. U.S.Const. Art. I, Sec. 7. *See also* Appropriation *(Public law).*

Appropriator. One who makes an appropriation; as, an appropriator of water.

Approval. The act of confirming, ratifying, assenting, sanctioning, or consenting to some act or thing done by another. Approval implies knowledge and exercise of discretion after knowledge. *See* Affirm; Approve; Assent; Condonation; Confirmation; Connivance; Consent; Ratification. For *sale on approval, see* Sale.

Approval sales. A buyer may, by agreement, accept goods on approval, and title does not pass until he has indicated his approval. Approval is a condition precedent to passing of title and risk. U.C.C. § 2–326.

Approve. To be satisfied with; to confirm, ratify, sanction, or consent to some act or thing done by another. To sanction officially; to ratify; to confirm; to pronounce good; think or judge well of; admit the propriety or excellence of; be pleased with. Distinguishable from "authorize," meaning to permit a thing to be done in future. To take to one's proper and separate use. To improve; to enhance the value or profits of anything. To inclose and cultivate common or waste land. *See also* Approval; Confirmation; Ratification.

Approved indorsed notes. Notes indorsed by another person than the maker, for additional security, the indorser being satisfactory to the payee. *See* Accommodation paper; Accommodation party.

Approved list. *See,* Legal list.

Approximate. Used in the sense of an estimate merely, meaning more or less, but about and near the amount, quantity, or distance specified. Near to; about; a little more or less; close. "Approximately" is very nearly synonymous with "proximately", meaning very nearly, but not absolutely.

Approximation. Equitable doctrine by which precise terms of charitable trust can be varied under certain circumstances. Applicable to charitable trusts and employed only where on failure of trust the court finds a general charitable intent. Under this doctrine, the general intent of the donor is carried out as nearly as may be even if the particular method pointed out by him cannot be followed. *See* Cy-pres; Equitable doctrine of approximation.

Appurtenance /əpə́rtənəns/. That which belongs to something else; an adjunct; an appendage. Something annexed to another thing more worthy as principal, and which passes as incident to it, as a right of way or other easement to land; an outhouse, barn, garden, or orchard, to a house or messuage. An article adapted to the use of the property to which it is connected, and which was intended to be a permanent accession to the freehold. A thing is deemed to be incidental or appurtenant to land when it is by right used with the land for its benefit, as in the case of a way, or watercourse, or of a passage for light, air, or heat from or across the land of another. *See also* Appendant.

Appurtenant. Belonging to; accessory or incident to; adjunct, appended, or annexed to; answering to *accessorium* in the civil law. Employed in leases for the purpose of including any easements or servitudes used or enjoyed with the demised premises. A thing is "appurtenant" to something else when it stands in relation of an incident to a principal and is necessarily connected with the use and enjoyment of the latter. A thing is deemed to be incidental or *appurtenant* to land when it is by right used with the land for its benefit, as in the case of a way, or water-course, or of a passage for light, air, or heat from or across the land of another. *See also* Easement.

APR. *See* Annual percentage rate.

A prendre /à próndər/. L. Fr. To take; to seize. *Bref à prendre la terre*, a writ to take the land. A right to take something out of the soil of another is a profit *à prendre,* or a right coupled with a profit. Distinguished from an easement. Sometimes written as one word, *apprendre, apprender. See* Profit *(Profit à prendre).*

A priori /èy prayóray/. Lat. From the cause to the effect; from what goes before. A term used in logic to denote an argument founded on analogy, or abstract considerations, or one which, positing a general principle or admitted truth as a cause, proceeds to deduce from it the effects which must necessarily follow.

Aquatic rights. Rights which individuals have to the use of the sea and rivers, for the purpose of fishing and navigation, and also to the soil in the sea and rivers. *See* Riparian rights; Water *(Water rights).*

A quo /èy kwów/. Lat. From which. A court *a quo* (also written "a qua") is a court from which a cause has been removed. The judge *a quo* is the judge in such court. A term used, with the correlative *ad quem* (to which), in expressing the computation of time, and also of distance in space. Thus, *dies a quo,* the day from which and *dies ad quem,* the day to which, a period of time is computed. So, *terminus a quo,* the point or limit from which, and *terminus ad quem,* the point or limit to which, a distance or passage in space is reckoned.

Arable land /ǽrəbəl lǽnd/. That which is fit for plowing or tillage, and thus is distinguishable from swamp land, which is land that is too wet for cultivation.

ARB. *See* Accounting Research Bulletin.

Arbiter /árbətər/. A person chosen to decide a controversy; an arbitrator, referee. A person bound to decide according to the rules of law and equity, as distinguished from an arbitrator, who may proceed wholly at his own discretion, so that it be according to the judgment of a sound man. *See* Arbitrator.

Arbitrage /árbətrəj/. The simultaneous purchase in one market and sale in another of a security or commodity in hope of making a profit on price differences in the different markets. *See* Arbitration of exchange; Arbitragers. For *Arbitrage bond, see* Bond.

Arbitragers /árbətrèyjərz/°zhərz/. Market investors who take off-setting positions in the same or similar securities in order to profit from small price variations. An arbitrager, for example, may buy shares on the Pacific Coast Exchange and simultaneously sell the same shares on the New York Stock Exchange if any price discrepancy occurs between the quotations in the two markets. By taking advantage of momentary disparities in prices between markets, arbitragers perform the economic function of making those markets more efficient.

Arbitrament and award /àrbítrəmənt ǽnd əwórd/. A plea to an action brought for the same cause which had been submitted to arbitration and on which an award had been made.

Arbitrariness. Conduct or acts based alone upon one's will, and not upon any course of reasoning and exercise of judgment.

Arbitrary. In an unreasonable manner, as fixed or done capriciously or at pleasure. Without adequate determining principle; not founded in the nature of things; nonrational; not done or acting according to reason or judgment; depending on the will alone; absolutely in power; capriciously; tyrannical; despotic. Without fair, solid, and substantial cause; that is, without cause based upon the law. Willful and unreasoning action, without consideration and regard for facts and circumstances presented.

Arbitrary and capricious. Characterization of a decision or action taken by an administrative agency or inferior court meaning willful and unreasonable action without consideration or in disregard of facts or law or without determining principle. *See also* Rational basis test.

Arbitrary power. Power to act according to one's own will; especially applicable to power conferred on an administrative officer, who is not furnished any adequate determining principle.

Arbitrary punishment. That punishment which is left to the decision of the judge, in distinction from those defined by statute. *See* Sentence.

Arbitration /àrbətréyshən/. A process of dispute resolution in which a neutral third party (arbitrator) renders a decision after a hearing at which both parties have an opportunity to be heard. Where arbitration is voluntary, the disputing parties select the arbitrator who has the power to render a binding decision.

An arrangement for taking and abiding by the judgment of selected persons in some disputed matter, instead of carrying it to established tribunals of justice, and is intended to avoid the formalities, the delay, the expense and vexation of ordinary litigation. Such arbitration provisions are common in union collective bargaining agreements.

The majority of the states have adopted the Uniform Arbitration Act.

Agreements to arbitrate have been declared to be valid and fully enforceable by statute. 9 U.S. C.A. § 2.

An organization that provides arbitration services is the American Arbitration Association *(q.v.)*.

See also Adjudicative claims arbitration; Alternative dispute resolution; Conciliation; Mediation; Mediation and Conciliation Service; Reference.

Compulsory arbitration is that which occurs when the consent of one of the parties is enforced by statutory provisions. Examples of such are state statutes requiring compulsory arbitration of labor disputes involving public employees. *See* Arbitration clause.

Final offer arbitration. In this type of arbitration, the arbitrator must choose the final offer of either one party or the other and is, therefore, not permitted to compromise.

Voluntary arbitration is by mutual and free consent of the parties.

Arbitration Acts. Federal and state laws which provide for submission of disputes to process of arbitration, including labor grievances and disputes of public employees. An example of a federal Act is Title 9, U.S.C.A. § 1 *et seq.* which governs settlement of disputes involved in maritime transactions and commerce under federal statutes. Most states have arbitration acts, many of which are patterned on the Uniform Arbitration Act. The purpose of such acts, in general, is to validate arbitration agreements, make the arbitration process effective, provide necessary safeguards, and provide an efficient procedure when judicial assistance is necessary.

Arbitration and award. An affirmative defense to the effect that the subject matter of the action has been settled by a prior arbitration. Fed.R. Civil P. 8(c).

Arbitration board. A panel of arbitrators appointed to hear and decide a dispute according to rules of arbitration. *See e.g.* American Arbitration Association.

Arbitration clause. A clause inserted in a contract providing for compulsory arbitration in case of dispute as to rights or liabilities under such contract; *e.g.* disputes arising under union collective bargaining agreement, or disputes between consumer and retailer or manufacturer. The purpose of such clause is to avoid having to litigate disputes that might arise.

Arbitration of exchange. This takes place where a merchant pays his debts in one country by a bill of exchange upon another. The business of buying and selling exchange (bills of exchange) between two or more countries or markets, and particularly where the profits of such business are to be derived from a calculation of the relative value of exchange in the two countries or markets, and by taking advantage of the fact that the rate of exchange may be higher in the one place than in the other at the same time. *See* Arbitrage.

Arbitrator. A neutral person either chosen by the parties to a dispute or appointed by a court, to hear the parties claims and render a decision. Many arbitrators are members of the American Arbitration Association. *See also* Referee; Umpire.

Arbitrium /arbítriyəm/. The decision of an arbiter, or arbitrator; an award; a judgment.

Architect's lien. A lien on real estate created by statute in favor of the architect who drew the plans and supervised the construction of the real estate for purpose of insuring payment of his fee.

Archives. Place where old books, manuscripts, records, etc. are kept.

Archivist /árkəvist/. Custodian of archives.

Area. A surface, a territory, a region. Any plane surface, also the inclosed space on which a building stands. A particular extent of space or surface or one serving a special purpose. In the civil law, a vacant space in a city; a place not built upon. For "common area", *see* Common.

Area bargaining. Negotiation of collective bargaining agreement between a union and more than one employer within a given geographical area.

Area variance. In zoning law, a variance which authorizes deviations from restrictions upon construction and placement of buildings and structures which are employed to serve permitted statutory use. *See also* Variance *(Zoning)*.

Area wide bargaining. *See* Area bargaining.

A rendre /à róndər/. Fr. To render, to yield. That which is to be rendered, yielded, or paid. *Profits à rendre* comprehend rents and services.

Arguendo /àrgyuwéndow/. In arguing; in the course of the argument. A statement or observation made by a judge or attorney as a matter of argument or hypothetical illustration, is said to be made *arguendo*, or in the abbreviated form, *arg.*

Argument. An effort to establish belief by a course of reasoning. In rhetoric and logic, an inference drawn from premises, the truth of which is indisputable, or at least highly probable. *See also* Oral argument.

Argument by counsel. Remarks addressed by attorney to judge or jury on the merits of case or on points of law. Oral presentation to appellate court in which attorney's brief is argued; generally limited in time, order, and content by court rule (see *e.g.* Fed.R.App.P. 34). *See* Opening statement of counsel.

Argument to jury. Closing remarks of attorney to jury in which he strives to persuade jury of merits of case; generally limited in time by rules of court. The argument is not evidence. *See also* Closing argument.

Argumentative. Characterized by argument; controversial; given to debate or dispute. A pleading is so called in which the statement on which the pleader relies is implied instead of being expressed, or where it contains, in addition to proper statements of facts, reasoning or arguments upon those facts and their relation to the matter in dispute, such as should be reserved for presentation at the trial.

Argumentative instruction. A jury instruction which singles out or unduly emphasizes a particular issue, theory, or defense, or one which tends to invade the province of the jury with regard to the weight, probative effect, or sufficiency of the evidence or the inferences to be drawn therefrom.

Argumentative question. A faulty form of examination of witness by propounding a question which suggests answer in a manner favorable to party who advances the question or which contains a statement in place of a question. *See* Leading question.

Arise. To spring up, originate, to come into being or notice; to become operative, sensible, visible, or audible; to present itself. A cause of action or suit "arises", so as to start running of limitation, when party has a right to apply to proper tribunal for relief. *See* Cause of action; Limitation *(Statute of limitations)*.

Arise under. An action "arises under" the laws of the United States, for purposes of federal question jurisdiction, if, and only if, the complaint seeks a remedy expressly granted by a federal statute or if resolution of the issue requires construction of the statute or if the statute embodies a distinct policy which requires that federal legal principles control its disposition. A case "arises" under the Constitution or a law of the United States, so as to be within the jurisdiction of a federal court, whenever its correct decision depends on the construction of either.

Arising out of and in the course of own employment. Workers' compensation acts provide for compensating an employee whose injury is one "arising out of and in the course of the employment." These words describe an injury directly and naturally resulting in a risk reasonably incident to the employment. They mean that there must be some causal connection between the conditions under which the employee worked and the injury which he received.

The words "arising out of employment" refer to the origin of the cause of the injury, while "course of employment" refers to the time, place, and circumstances under which the injury occurred. An injury arises "out of" employment if it arises out of nature, conditions, obligations and incidents of the employment.

See also Course of employment; In the course of employment.

ARM. Adjustable Rate Mortgage. *See* Mortgage.

Armed. Furnished or equipped with weapons of offense or defense.

Armed robbery. An aggravated form of robbery in which the defendant is armed with a dangerous weapon, though it is not necessary to prove that he used the weapon to effectuate the robbery. The taking of property from person or presence of another by use of force or by threatening use of force while armed with a dangerous weapon.

Armistice. A suspending or cessation of hostilities between belligerent nations or forces for a considerable time.

Arm of the sea. A portion of the sea projecting inland, in which the tide ebbs and flows. It is considered as extending as far into the interior of a country as the water of fresh rivers is propelled backwards by the ingress of the tide.

Arms. Anything that a man wears for his defense, or takes in his hands as a weapon. *See also* Bear arms.

Arm's length transaction. Said of a transaction negotiated by unrelated parties, each acting in his or her own self interest; the basis for a fair market value determination. A transaction in good faith in the ordinary course of business by parties with independent interests. Commonly applied in areas of taxation when there are dealings between related corporations, *e.g.* parent and subsidiary. The standard under which unrelated parties, each acting in his or her own best interest, would carry out a particular transaction. For example, if a corporation sells property to its sole shareholder for $10,000, in testing whether $10,000 is an "arm's length" price it must be ascertained for how much the corporation could have sold the property to a disinterested third party in a bargained transaction.

Arms, right to. Right guaranteed by Second Amendment, U.S. Constitution, to keep and bear arms. This right does not, however, permit a person to carry gun in violation of state or federal gun laws.

Army. Armed forces of a nation intended for military service on land.

Regular army. The permanent military establishment, which is maintained both in peace and war according to law. *Compare* Militia.

Around. In the vicinity of; near or close-by.

Arraignment /əhréynmənt/. Procedure whereby the accused is brought before the court to plead to the criminal charge against him in the indictment or information. The charge is read to him and he is asked to plead "guilty" or "not guilty" or, where permitted, "nolo contendere."

Arraignment shall be conducted in open court and shall consist of reading the indictment or information to the defendant or stating to him the substance of the charge and calling on him to plead thereto. He shall be given a copy of the indictment or information before he is called upon to plead. Fed.R.Crim.P. 10.

See also Information; Preliminary hearing; Plea.

Arrangement with creditors. A plan of a debtor for the settlement, satisfaction, or extension of the time of payment of his debts. Chapter 11 of the federal Bankruptcy Code provides for a device whereby, under the protection and supervision of the court, a financially troubled business may work out an agreement with its creditors under a reorganization plan permitting it to stay in business, rather than going bankrupt. Arrangements of individual debtors with their creditors are provided for under Chapter 12 (farmers) and 13 of the Code. *See also* Bankruptcy proceedings *(Business reorganizations; Wage earner's plan)*; Composition with creditors.

Array /əhréy/. The whole body of persons summoned to serve as jurors, from which the final trial jury is selected. Also, the list of jurors impaneled. *See* Jury panel.

Arrears, arrearages. Money which is overdue and unpaid; e.g. overdue mortgage or rent payments.

Term used to describe cumulative preferred stock dividends that have not been declared on time.

Arrest. To deprive a person of his liberty by legal authority. Taking, under real or assumed authority, custody of another for the purpose of holding or detaining him to answer a criminal charge or civil demand.

Arrest involves the authority to arrest, the assertion of that authority with the intent to effect an arrest, and the restraint of the person to be arrested. All that is required for an "arrest" is some act by officer indicating his intention to detain or take person into custody and therby subject that person to the actual control and will of the officer; no formal declaration of arrest is required.

See also Booking; Citizen's arrest; Custodial arrest; False arrest; Lawful arrest; Probable cause; Reasonable grounds; Warrantless arrest.

Citizen's arrest. *See* Citizen's arrest.

Civil arrest. The apprehension of a person by virtue of a lawful authority to answer the demand against him in a civil action. Also includes arrest of a ship or cargo in maritime in rem actions. Fed.R. Civil P., Supp.Admir.R. C(3), D.

Parol arrest. One ordered by a judge or magistrate from the bench, without written complaint or other proceedings, of a person who is present before him, and which is executed on the spot; as in case of breach of the peace in open court.

Privilege from arrest. *See* Privilege.

Rearrest. Right of officer to take without warrant one who has escaped after arrest, or violated parole, or failed to respond to bond for appearance.

Warrantless arrest. Seizure of a person without warrant but based on probable cause that he has committed felony. May also be made for commission of misdemeanor amounting to breach of peace in presence of officer. Wong Sun v. U. S., 371 U.S. 471, 83 S.Ct. 407, 9 L.Ed.2d 441.

Warrant of arrest. *See* Warrant.

Arrest of judgment. The act of staying a judgment, or refusing to render judgment in an action at law and in criminal cases, after verdict, for some matter intrinsic appearing on the face of the record, which would render the judgment, if given, erroneous or reversible. The court on motion of a defendant shall arrest judgment if the indictment or information does not charge an offense or if the court was without jurisdiction of the offense charged. Fed.R.Crim.P. 34.

Arrest record. Official form completed by police department when a person is arrested. Also, cumulative record of instances in which a person has been arrested, commonly maintained by probation office and useful to judge in setting sentences for second, third, etc. offenders.

Arrest warrant. *See* Warrant.

Arret /arét/aréy/. Fr. A judgment, sentence, or decree of a court of competent jurisdiction. The term is derived from the French law, and is used in Canada and Louisiana.

Saisie arrêt is an attachment of property in the hands of a third person.

Arretted /əhrétəd/. Convened before a judge and charged with a crime.

Arrival. To come to, or reach, a particular place. The attainment of an end or state. The act of arriving.

In marine insurance, arrival of a vessel means an arrival for purposes of business, requiring an entry and clearance and stay at the port so long as to require some of the acts connected with business, and not merely touching at a port for advices, or to ascertain the state of the market, or being driven in by an adverse wind and sailing again as soon as it changes.

Arrogation. In the civil law, the adoption of a person who was of full age or *sui juris*.

Arson. At common law, the malicious burning of the house of another. This definition, however, has been broadened by state statutes and criminal codes. For example, the Model Penal Code, § 220.1(1), provides that a person is guilty of arson, a felony of the second degree, if he starts a fire or causes an explosion with the purpose of: (a) destroying a building or occupied structure of another; or (b) destroying or damaging any property, whether his own or another's, to collect insurance for such loss. Other statutes include the destruction of property by other means; *e.g.*, explosion.

In several states, this crime is divided into arson in the first, second, and third degrees, the first degree including the burning of an inhabited dwelling-house in the nighttime; the second degree, the burning (at night) of a building other than a dwelling-house, but so situated with reference to a dwelling-house as to endanger it; the third degree, the burning of any building or structure not the subject of arson in the first or second degree, or the burning of property, his own or another's with intent to defraud or prejudice an insurer thereof. *See Aggravated arson, below.*

Aggravated arson. The burning or blowing up of property when the actor foresees or anticipates the presence of persons at site, or in such close proximity thereto, so that their lives might be endangered by the act.

Arson clause. Clause in insurance policy voiding coverage if fire is set under direction or by insured.

Art. Systematic application of knowledge or skill in effecting a desired result; also an employment, occupation or business requiring such knowledge or skill; a craft, as industrial arts.

In the law of patents, this term means a useful art or manufacture which is beneficial and which is described with exactness in its mode of operation. Such an art can be protected only in the mode and to the extent thus described. It is synonymous with process or method when used to produce a useful result, and may be either a force applied, a mode of application, or the specific treatment of a specific object, and must produce physical effects.

In seduction cases, "art" means the skillful and systematic arrangement of means for the attainment of a desired end.

Artesian basin. A body of water more or less compact, moving through soils with more or less resistance.

Article. A separate and distinct part of an instrument or writing; one of several things presented as connected or forming a whole. A particular object or substance, a material thing or a class of things. Material or tangible object. *See* Articles.

In English ecclesiastical law, a complaint exhibited in the ecclesiastical court by way of libel. The different parts of a libel, responsive allegation, or counter allegation in the ecclesiastical courts.

Articles. A connected series of propositions; a system of rules. The subdivisions of a document, code, book, etc. A specification of distinct matters agreed upon or established by authority or requiring judicial action.

A statute; as having its provisions articulately expressed under distinct heads.

A system of rules established by legal authority; as *articles* of war, *articles* of the navy, *articles* of faith. (*See infra.*)

A contractual document executed between parties, containing stipulations or terms of agreement; as *articles* of agreement, *articles* of partnership.

A naval term meaning employment contract.

In chancery practice, a formal written statement of objections filed by a party, after depositions have been taken, showing ground for discrediting the witnesses.

In ecclesiastical law, a complaint in the form of a libel exhibited to an ecclesiastical court. *See* Article.

Articles of agreement. A written memorandum of the terms of an agreement. *See* Memorandum.

Articles of amendment. Terms and conditions of corporate management enacted subsequent to articles of incorporation. *See* Articles of incorporation.

Articles of apprenticeship. Written agreement between master and minor under which minor agrees to work for master for stated period of time in return for instruction in a trade by the master.

Articles of association. Basic instrument filed with the appropriate governmental agency (*e.g.* Sec. of State) on the incorporation of a business. It sets forth the purposes of the corporation, its duration, the rights and liabilities of shareholders and directors, classes of stock, etc. Such document is referred to as "articles of incorporation" in many states. Certificate (similar to one of incorporation) used by non-stock companies such as charitable and mutual corporations. Articles of association are to be distinguished from a charter, in that the latter is a grant of power from the sovereign or the legislature. *See* Articles of incorporation; Articles of partnership; Certificate of incorporation.

Articles of Confederation. The name of the instrument embodying the compact made between the thirteen original states of the Union, operative from March 1, 1781 to March 4, 1789, before the adoption of the present Constitution.

Articles of dissolution. Document required to be filed with secretary of state (or other designated official) after corporation has settled all its debts and distributed all of its net assets prior to dissolution. See, *e.g.*, Rev.Model Bus.Corp.Act § 14.03.

Articles of impeachment. A formal written allegation of the causes for impeachment; answering the same office as an indictment in an ordinary criminal proceeding. *See* Impeachment.

Articles of incorporation. The basic instrument filed with the appropriate governmental agency (*e.g.*, Sec. of State) on the incorporation of a business; sometimes also called "certificate of incorporation," "articles of organization," "articles of association," or other similar name. The contents thereof are prescribed in the general incorporation statutes (but commonly include the corporation's name, period of existence, purpose and power, authorized number of shares, classes of stock, and other conditions of operation). See *e.g.*, Rev. Model Bus. Corp. Act § 2.02. In many jurisdictions official forms are prescribed. In most jurisdictions, corporate existence begins with the filing, usually with the secretary of state, of the articles or certificate of incorporation. In some jurisdictions, duplicate articles of incorporation are filed, and corporate existence beings with the issue of a formal certificate appended thereto called a "certificate of incorporation." Various conditions precedent to doing business might also be imposed. *See* Articles of association; Certificate of incorporation.

Articles of merger, consolidation, or share exchange. Document filed with Secretary of State setting forth terms and conditions of merger consolidation, or share exchange. See *e.g.*, Rev.Model.Bus.Corp.Act § 11.05.

Articles of partnership. A written agreement by which the parties enter into a partnership upon the terms and conditions therein stipulated.

Articles of war. Codes framed for the government of a nation's army or navy; *e.g.* Code of Military Justice.

Articulated pleading. The stating in separate paragraphs, separately numbered, of each material fact of the petition, complaint, answer, etc. See *e.g.* Fed.R. Civil P. 10(b).

Artifice /ártəfəs/. An ingenius contrivance or device of some kind, and, when used in a bad sense, it corresponds with trick or fraud. It implies craftiness and deceit, and imports some element of moral obliquity. *See also* Scheme *or* artifice to defraud.

Artificer /artífəsər/. One who buys goods in order to reduce them, by his own art or industry, into other forms, and then to sell them.

One who is actually and personally engaged or employed to do work of a mechanical or physical character, not including one who takes contracts for labor to be performed by others, *i.e.* a mechanic or workman as contrasted from the employer of such. One who is master of his art, and whose employment consists chiefly in manual labor. A craftsman; an artisan.

Artificial force. In patent law, a natural force so transformed in character or energies by human power as to possess new capabilities of action; this transformation of a natural force into a force practically new involves a true inventive act.

Artificial persons. Persons created and devised by human laws for the purposes of society and government, as distinguished from natural persons. Corporations are examples of artificial persons.

Artificial presumptions. Also called "legal presumptions;" those which derive their force and effect from the law, rather than their natural tendency to produce belief. *See* Presumption.

Artificial succession. The succession between predecessors and successors in a corporation aggregate or sole.

Artificial water course. *See* Water course.

Artisan. One skilled in some kind of trade, craft, or art requiring manual dexterity; *e.g.* a carpenter, plumber, tailor, mechanic.

Artisan's lien. A possessory lien given to a person who has made improvements and added value to another person's personal property as security for payment for services performed. The statutory right of an artisan to keep possession of the object that he has worked on until he has been paid for such labor.

Art, words of. Words used in a technical sense; words scientifically fit to carry the sense assigned them.

AS or **A/S** or **A/s.** Account sales; also after sight, at sight.

As. Used as an adverb, etc., means like, similar to, of the same kind, in the same manner, in the manner in which. It may also have the meaning of because, since, or it being the case that; in the character or under the name of with significance of in degree; to that extent; so far.

As against; as between. These words contrast the relative position of two persons, with a tacit reference to a different relationship between one of them and a third person. For instance, the temporary bailee of a chattel is entitled to it *as between* himself and a stranger, or *as against* a stranger; reference being made by this form of words to the rights of the bailor.

Ascend. To go up; to pass up or upwards; to go or pass in the ascending line.

Ascendants. Persons with whom one is related in the ascending line; one's parents, grandparents, great-grandparents, etc.

Ascent. Passage upward; the transmission of an estate from the ancestor to the heir in the ascending line.

Aside. On one side; apart. *To set aside*; to annul; to make void.

As is. A sale of goods by sample "as is" requires that the goods be of the kind and quality represented, even though they be in a damaged condition. U.C.C. § 2–313. Use of expression in sales agreement that goods are sold "as is" implies that buyer takes the entire risk as to the quality of the goods involved and he must trust to his own inspection. Implied and express warranties are excluded in sales of goods "as is". U.C.C. § 2–316.

Ask. Demand, request, solicit, petition, appeal, apply for, move for, pray for.

Asking price. The price at which a seller lists his property for sale. Generally connotes a willingness to sell for less than the listed or asking price. May be applied to both real and personal property for sale though more commonly used in sales of real estate.

As per. A term which is not susceptible of literal translation, but which is commonly understood to mean, "in accordance with", or "in accordance with the terms of", or "as by the contract authorized".

Asportation /æspərtéyshən/. The removal of things from one place to another. The carrying away of something; in kidnapping, the carrying away of the victim; in larceny, the carrying away of the victim's property. The carrying away of goods; one of the circumstances requisite to constitute the offense of larceny. The distance away which the property must be moved to constitute the crime need not be substantial; a slight distance will do. But the entire property must be moved.

Asportation was an essential element of common-law kidnapping.

ASPR. Armed Services Procurement Regulations. *See also* Federal Acquisition Regulations.

ASR. Accounting Series Release.

Assassination /əsæsənéyshən/. Murder committed, usually, though not necessarily, for hire, without direct provocation or cause of resentment given to the murderer by the person upon whom the crime is committed; though an assassination of a public figure might be done by one acting alone for personal, social or political reasons. It is a federal crime, punishable as a homicide, to assassinate the President, President-elect, Vice President, or if there is no Vice President, the officer next in order of succession to the office of President, the Vice-President-elect, or any individual who is acting as President under the Constitution. 18 U.S.C.A. § 1751. In addition, advocating the overthrow of the government by assassination of any officer of such government is a crime under 18 U.S.C.A. § 2385.

Assault. Any willful attempt or threat to inflict injury upon the person of another, when coupled with an apparent present ability so to do, and any intentional display of force such as would give the victim reason to fear or expect immediate bodily harm, constitutes an assault. An assault may be committed without actually touching, or striking, or doing bodily harm, to the person of another.

Frequently used to describe illegal force which is technically a battery. For crime of assault victim need not be apprehensive of fear if the outward gesture is menacing and defendant intends to harm, though for tort of assault, element of victim's apprehension is required. It is an unlawful attempt to commit a battery.

In some jurisdictions degrees of the offense are established as first, second and even third degree assault.

See also Aggravated assault; Aggravated battery; Battery; Conditional assault; Felonious assault; Fresh complaint rule; Malicious assault with deadly weapon.

Aggravated assault. One committed with the intention of committing some additional crime; or one attended with circumstances of peculiar outrage or atrocity. This class includes assault with a dangerous or deadly weapon *(q.v.)*.

A person is guilty of aggravated assault if he: (a) attempts to cause serious bodily injury to another, or causes such injury purposely, knowingly or recklessly under circumstances manifesting extreme indifference to the value of human life; or (b) attempts to cause or purposely or knowingly causes bodily injury to another with a deadly weapon. Model Penal Code, § 211.1.

Simple assault. An assault unaccompanied by any circumstances of aggravation. A person is guilty of simple assault if he (a) attempts to cause or purposely, knowingly or recklessly causes bodily injury to another; or (b) negligently causes bodily injury to another with a deadly weapon; or (c) attempts by physical menace to put another in fear of imminent serious bodily injury. Model Penal Code, § 211.1. An unlawful attempt coupled with present ability to commit violent injury on person of another. *See also* Menace.

Assault and battery. Any unlawful touching of another which is without justification or excuse. It is both a tort, as well as a crime. The two crimes differ from each other in that battery requires physical contact of some sort (bodily injury or offensive touching), whereas assault is committed without physical contact. In most jurisdictions, statutes have created aggravated assaults and batteries, punishable as felonies, and worded in various ways. *See* Battery.

Assault with dangerous or deadly weapon. An unlawful attempt or offer to do bodily harm without justification or excuse by use of any instrument calculated to do harm or cause death. An aggravated form of assault as distinguished from a simple assault; *e.g.* pointing loaded gun at one is an assault with dangerous weapon.

Assault with intent to commit manslaughter. An unlawful assault committed in such manner and with such means as would have resulted in commission of crime of manslaughter if person assaulted had died from effects of assault.

Assault with intent to commit murder. To constitute this assault, specific intent to kill, actuated by malice aforethought, must concur.

Assault with intent to commit rape. Crime is constituted by the existence of the facts which bring the offense within the definition of an assault, coupled with an intention to commit the crime of rape.

Assay /əséy/ǽsey/. The proof or trial, by chemical experiments, of the purity or fineness of metals; particularly of the precious metals, gold and silver. Examination and determination as to characteristics (as weight, measure, or quality).

Assayer. One whose business it is to make assays of the precious metals.

Assay office. The U.S. Assay Office, under the Bureau of the Mint, is responsible for the process of assaying gold and silver, required by government, incidental to maintaining the coinage.

Assemblage. A collection of persons. Also the act of coming together. Public address upon public grounds. Combining of adjoining lots into single large lot.

Assembly. The concourse or meeting together of a considerable number of persons at the same place. Also the persons so gathered.

Political assemblies are those required by the constitution and laws: for example, the general assembly.

The lower or more numerous branch of the legislature in many of the states (*e.g.* N.Y.) is also called the "Assembly" or "House of Assembly." *See also* House of Representatives.

Popular assemblies are those where the people meet to deliberate upon their rights; these are guaranteed by the Constitution. *See* Assembly, right of.

Assemblyman. Member of state Assembly *(q.v.)*.

Assembly, right of. Right guaranteed by First Amendment, U.S. Constitution, allowing people to meet for any purpose connected with government; it encompasses meeting to protest governmental policies and actions and the promotion of ideas. *See* Unlawful assembly.

Assembly, unlawful. The congregating of people which results in antisocial behavior of the group, *e.g.* blocking a sidewalk, obstructing traffic, littering streets; but, a law which makes such congregating a crime because people may be annoyed is violative of the right of free assembly. *See* Unlawful assembly.

Assent. Compliance; approval of something done; a declaration of willingness to do something in compliance with a request; acquiescence; agreement. To approve, ratify and confirm. It implies a conscious approval of facts actually known, as distinguished from mere neglect to ascertain facts. Sometimes it is equivalent to "authorize". *See* Approval; Approve; Consent.

Express assent. That which is openly declared.

Implied assent. That which is presumed by law, and proved by conduct of the parties. *See* Consent (*Implied consent*).

Mutual assent. The meeting of the minds of both or all the parties to a contract; the fact that each agrees to all the terms and conditions, in the same sense and with the same meaning as the others.

Assert. To state as true; declare; maintain.

Assertory oath /əsə́rtəriy ówθ/. *See* Oath.

Assess /əsés/. To ascertain; fix the value of. To fix the amount of the damages or the value of the thing to be ascertained. To impose a pecuniary payment upon persons or property. To ascertain, adjust, and settle the respective shares to be contributed by several persons toward an object beneficial to them all, in proportion to the benefit received. To tax.

In connection with taxation of property, means to make a valuation and appraisal of property, usually in connection with listing of property liable to taxation, and implies the exercise of discretion on the part of officials charged with duty of assessing, including the listing or inventory of property involved, determination of extent of physical property, and placing of a value thereon. To adjust or fix the proportion of a tax which each person, of several liable to it, has to pay; to apportion a tax among several; to distribute taxation in a proportion founded on the proportion of burden and benefit. To calculate the rate and amount of taxes. To levy a charge on the owner of property for improvements thereto, such as for sewers or sidewalks.

"Access" is sometimes used as synonymous with "levy".

See also Assessment.

Assessable insurance. Insurance policy under which insured is liable for additional premium if losses are unusually large.

Assessable stock. Stock where the stockholder may have to pay more than his original investment if corporate affairs so require.

Assessed. Term is equivalent to "imposed." To value or appraise.

Assessed valuation. Value on each unit of which a prescribed amount must be paid as property taxes. The worth or value of property established by taxing authorities on the basis of which the tax rate is applied. Commonly, however, it does not represent the true or market value of the property.

Assessment. In a general sense, the process of ascertaining and adjusting the shares respectively to be contributed by several persons towards a common beneficial object according to the benefit received. A valuation or a determination as to value of property. It is often used in connection with assessing property taxes or levying of property taxes. Also the amount assessed. *See also* Assess; Equalization.

Corporations. Installments of the money subscribed for shares of stock, called for from the subscribers by the directors, from time to time as the company requires money, are called "assessments," or, in England, "calls." While the terms "call" and "assessment" are generally used synonymously, the latter term applies with peculiar aptness to contributions above the par value of stock or the subscription liability of the stockholders; whereas "call" or "installments" means action of the board of directors demanding payment of all or portion of unpaid subscriptions.

Damages. Fixing the amount of damages to which the successful party in a suit is entitled after judgment has been taken; also the name given to the determination of the sum which a corporation proposing to take lands for a public use must pay in satisfaction of the demand proved or the value taken.

Insurance. An apportionment made in general average upon the various articles and interests at risk, according to their value at the time and place of being in safety, for contribution for damage and sacrifices purposely made, and expenses incurred for escape from impending common peril.

Special assessment. An assessment in the nature of a tax levied upon property according to benefits conferred on the property. A levy upon the owners of property adjacent to a public improvement (*e.g.*, sidewalks) to defray the capital cost thereof. A tax, intended to offset cost of local improvements such as sewer, water and streets, which is selectively imposed upon beneficiaries. It differs from a general tax in that it is levied for a specific purpose and in an amount proportioned to the direct benefit of the property assessed.

Persons convicted of federal crimes are required to pay special assessments under 18 U.S.C.A. § 3013.

Taxation. The listing and valuation of property for the purpose of apportioning a tax upon it, either according to value alone or in proportion to benefit received. Also determining the share of a tax to be paid by each of many persons; or apportioning the entire tax to be levied among the different taxable persons, establishing the proportion due from each. It fixes the liability of the taxpayer and ascertains the facts and furnishes the data for the proper preparation of the tax rolls.

The process whereby the Internal Revenue Service imposes an additional tax liability. If, for example, the IRS audits a taxpayer's income tax return and finds gross income understated or deductions overstated, it will assess a deficiency in the amount of the tax that should have been paid in light of the adjustments made. *See also,* Deficiency; Deficiency assessment; Jeopardy assessment.

Assessment base. Total assessed value of all property in an assessment district.

Assessment contract. One wherein the payment of the benefit is in any manner or degree dependent on the collection of an assessment levied on persons holding similar contracts. *See also* Assessment insurance.

Assessment district. In taxation, any subdivision of territory, whether the whole or part of any municipality, in which by law a separate assessment of taxable property is made by the officers elected or appointed therefor.

Assessment insurance. Exists when benefit to be paid is dependent upon collection of such assessments as may be necessary for paying the amounts to insured. Type of mutual insurance where the policyholders are assessed whenever there is a loss.

Assessment list. The list of taxable persons and property furnished by the assessor to the board of equalization, board of assessment, or similar body. *See* Assessment roll.

Assessment ratio. For purposes of taxation of property is the ratio of assessed value to fair market value.

Assessment roll. In taxation, the list or roll of taxable persons and property, completed, verified, and deposited by the assessors.

Assessment work. Under the mining laws of the United States, the holder of an unpatented mining claim on the public domain is required, in order to hold his claim, to do labor or make improvements upon it to the extent of at least one hundred dollars in each year. 30 U.S.C.A. § 28. This is commonly called by miners "doing assessment work."

Assessor. An officer chosen or appointed to appraise, value, or assess property. A person learned in some particular science or industry, who sits with the judge on the trial of a cause requiring such special knowledge and gives his advice.

Asset Depreciation Range (ADR). The range of depreciable lives allowed by the Internal Revenue Service for a specified depreciable asset. The ADR system applies to assets placed in service after 1970 and before 1980, at which time the ADR system was replaced by the Accelerated Cost Recovery System (ACRS). However, the ADR system has been revived under The Tax Reform Act of 1986 and is now used to assign class lives to assets depreciated under Modified Accelerated Cost Recovery System (MACRS). *See* Accelerated Cost Recovery System.

Asset dividend. *See* Dividend.

Asset-based financing. Methods of financing in which lenders and equity investors look principally to the cash flow from a particular asset or set of assets for a return on, and the return of, their investment.

Asset–coverage test. In accounting, a bond indenture restriction that permits additional borrowing only if the ratio of assets (typically net tangible assets) to debt (typically long-term debt) does not fall below a specified minimum.

Assets /ǽsets/. Property of all kinds, real and personal, tangible and intangible, including, *inter*

alia, for certain purposes, patents and causes of action which belong to any person including a corporation and the estate of a decedent. The entire property of a person, association, corporation, or estate that is applicable or subject to the payment of his or her or its debts. *See also* Contra asset; Dead asset; Marshalling assets.

Accrued assets. Assets arising from revenues earned but not yet due.

Assets entre mains. L. Fr. Assets in hand; assets in the hands of executors or administrators, applicable for the payment of debts.

Assets per descent. That portion of the ancestor's estate which descends to the heir, and which is sufficient to charge him, as far as it goes, with the specialty debts of his ancestors.

Bankruptcy. The property or effects of debtor in bankruptcy proceedings available for payment of his debts.

Capital assets. For income tax purposes, a capital asset is defined as all property held by a taxpayer (*e.g.* house, car, stocks, bonds), except for certain assets listed in I.R.C. § 1221. Under the tax laws however, a given asset may be treated as a capital asset for one purpose, and as an ordinary asset for another.

Broadly speaking, all assets are capital except those specifically excluded by Internal Revenue Code. Major categories of non-capital assets include: property held for resale in the normal course of business (*i.e.* inventory), trade accounts and notes receivable, depreciable property and real estate used in a trade or business (*i.e.* I.R.C. "§ 1231 assets"). I.R.C. § 1221.

Commercial assets. The aggregate of available property, stock in trade, cash, etc., belonging to a merchant or business.

Current assets. Assets readily convertible into cash, *e.g.* marketable securities, notes, inventories, accounts receivable. *See also Quick assets, below.*

Equitable assets. All assets which are chargeable with the payment of debts or legacies in equity, and which do not fall under the description of legal assets. Those portions of the property which by the ordinary rules of law are exempt from debts, but which the testator has voluntarily charged as assets, or which, being non-existent at law, have been created in equity. They are so called because they can be reached only by the aid and instrumentality of a court of equity, and because their distribution is governed by a different rule from that which governs the distribution of legal assets.

Fixed assets. Assets of a permanent or long-term nature used in operation of business and not intended for sale; *e.g.* property, plant, equipment.

Frozen assets. Assets which are difficult to convert into cash (*e.g.* real estate for which there is no market); also, assets which cannot be used because of legal restriction.

Intangible assets. Assets lacking physical existence; *e.g.* patents, trademarks, organization costs, goodwill.

Legal assets. See Legal assets.

Liquid assets. See Current assets, above.

Monetary assets. Contractual claims to receive a fixed amount of cash in the future; includes cash, accounts receivable, and notes receivable.

Net assets. Excess of assets over liabilities.

Net operating assets. The excess of cash and other assets which will be converted into cash in near future through normal operation over current liabilities.

Nominal assets. Assets whose value is difficult to determine, *e.g.* a judgment or claim; also, book value of asset in contrast to actual value.

Personal assets. Chattels, money, and other personal property belonging to a bankrupt, insolvent, or decedent estate, which go to the assignee or executor. *See also* Personal effects.

Probate assets. Property of a decedent available for the payment of debts and legacies. The estate coming to the heir or personal representative which is chargeable, in law or equity, with the obligations which such heir or representative is required, in his representative capacity, to discharge.

Quick assets. Accounting term used to describe cash and receivables, including notes and sometimes marketable securities, which will be converted into cash as part of normal operations. *See also Current assets, above.*

Real assets. Land and real estate; tangible assets.

Residual assets. Assets that remain after dedicating sufficient assets to meet all senior security-holders' claims in full.

Underlying asset. The asset on which an option contract is based; that is, the asset on which the optionwriter is obligated to transact if the optionholder chooses. The value of an option is contingent upon the value of the underlying asset.

Wasting assets. Assets exhausted through use or loss of value; *e.g.* patents, oil wells, coal deposits.

Assign. To transfer, make over, or set over to another. To appoint, allot, select, or designate for a particular purpose, or duty. To point at, or point out; to set forth, or specify; to mark out or designate; to particularize, as to *assign errors* on a writ of error; to *assign breaches* of a covenant. *See also* Assignment.

Assignability. Quality or legal attribute which permits a thing to be transferred or negotiated.

Assignable. *See* Assignability.

Assignable lease. A lease which contains a provision permitting its transfer by lessee or one which is silent as to lessee's right to transfer his interest and hence a lease which may be transferred. Assignment of lease is distinguishable from sublease to extent, inter alia, that in assigning, lessee transfers his entire estate in the demised premises, whereas in sublease the sublessee acquires something less than the lessee's entire interest. *See also* Assignment *(Assignment of lease).*

Assigned account. Pledge of account receivable to bank or factor as security for loan.

Assigned counsel. An attorney appointed by court to represent an indigent person; most commonly in criminal cases. See U.S. Constitution, Sixth Amendment (right to counsel); Fed.R. Crim.P. 44; 18 U.S.C.A. § 3006A. *See also* Assistance of counsel; Counsel, right to.

Assigned risk. As relating to motor vehicles nuisance, a risk which is not ordinarily acceptable to insurers but for which coverage is required by state statute and which is, therefore, assigned to insurers participating in an assigned risk pool.

Assigned risk plan. In those states having compulsory motor vehicle insurance laws (*i.e.* financial responsibility laws), such statutes provide that persons who are otherwise unable to buy coverage (because of, *e.g.*, poor driving records) may secure insurance through a statutory plan under which insurers are compelled to write coverage for such persons. The insurance is handled through a pool of insurers.

See Financial responsibility acts.

Assignee /æsəgníy/asáyniy/. A person to whom an assignment is made; grantee.

Under U.C.C., assignee is subject to all defenses which may be asserted against assignor by account debtor. U.C.C. § 9–318.

Assignee in fact is one to whom an assignment has been made in fact by the party having the right.

Assignee in law is one in whom the law vests the right; as an executor or administrator.

Assignee clause. A provision in Judiciary Act of 1789 preventing one who could not show diversity of citizenship to bring suit in Federal Court from assigning his claim to one who had the required diversity; modified in 28 U.S.C.A. § 1359 to prevent only assignment made collusively to invoke diversity jurisdiction.

Assignment. The act of transferring to another all or part of one's property, interest, or rights. A transfer or making over to another of the whole of any property, real or personal, in possession or in action, or of any estate or right therein. It includes transfers of all kinds of property including negotiable instruments. The transfer by a party of all of its rights to some kind of property, usually intangible property such as rights in a lease, mortgage, agreement of sale or a partnership. Tangible property is more often transferred by possession and by instruments conveying title such as a deed or a bill of sale. *See also* Collateral assignment.

Assignment for benefit of creditors. A general assignment for benefit of creditors is transfer of all or substantially all of debtor's property to another person in trust to collect any money owing to debtor, to sell property, to distribute the proceeds to his creditors and to return the surplus, if any, to debtor. Under Bankruptcy Act of 1898, such assignment was an "act of bankruptcy" if made within 4 months of bankruptcy. Bankruptcy Act (1898) § 3a(4). *See also* Preferential assignment.

Assignment of account. Transfer to assignee giving him a right to have moneys when collected applied to payment of his debt.

Assignment of counsel. *See* Assigned counsel; Assistance of counsel; Counsel, right to.

Assignment of dower. The act by which the share of a widow in her deceased husband's real estate is ascertained and set apart to her.

Assignment of error. *See* Error.

Assignment of income. A procedure whereby a taxpayer attempts to avoid the recognition of income by assigning the property that generates the income to another. Such a procedure will not avoid the recognition of income by the taxpayer making the assignment if it can be said that the income was earned at the point of the transfer. In this case, usually referred to as an anticipatory assignment of income, the income will be taxed to the person who earns it.

Assignment of lease. Such occurs where lessee transfers entire unexpired remainder of term created by lease as distinguished from sublease which transfers only part of remainder. *See also* Assignable lease.

Assignment of wages. Transfer of right to collect wages from wage earner to creditor; generally, statutes govern the extent to which such assignment may be made.

Assignment with preferences. An assignment for the benefit of creditors, with directions to the assignee to prefer a specified creditor or class of creditors, by paying their claims in full before the others receive any dividend, or in some other manner. More usually termed a "preferential assignment." Such assignments formerly consti-

tuted an "act of bankruptcy" *(q.v.).* *See Assignment for benefit of creditors, above.*

Foreign assignment. An assignment made in a foreign country, or in another state.

General assignment. An assignment made for the benefit of *all* the assignor's creditors, instead of a few only; or one which transfers the *whole* of his estate to the assignee, instead of a part only.

Voluntary assignment. An assignment for the benefit of his creditors made by a debtor voluntarily, as distinguished from a compulsory assignment which takes place by operation of law in proceedings in bankruptcy. Such constitutes an assignment of a debtor's property in trust to pay his debts generally, in distinction from a transfer of property to a particular creditor in payment of his demand, or to a conveyance by way of collateral security or mortgage.

Assignor /əsáynər/. A person who assigns or transfers property to another. *See* Grantor.

Assigns. Assignees; those to whom property is, will, or may be assigned. Used *e.g.* in the phrase, in deeds, "heirs, administrators, and assigns to denote the assignable nature of the interest or right created." It generally comprehends all those who take either immediately or remotely from or under the assignor, whether by conveyance, devise, descent, or act of law.

Assise. *See* Assize.

Assist. To help; aid; succor; lend countenance or encouragement to; participate in as an auxiliary. To contribute effort in the complete accomplishment of an ultimate purpose intended to be effected by those engaged.

Assistance of counsel. Sixth Amendment to Federal Constitution, guaranteeing accused in criminal prosecution "assistance of counsel" for his defense, means effective assistance, as distinguished from bad faith, sham, mere pretense or want of opportunity for conferences and preparation. Fed.R.Crim.P. 44; 18 U.S.C.A. § 3006A; Gideon v. Wainwright, 372 U.S. 335, 83 S.Ct. 792, 9 L.Ed.2d 799; Geders v. U. S., 425 U.S. 80, 96 S.Ct. 1330, 47 L.Ed.2d 592. *See* Access to counsel; Assigned counsel; Counsel, right to; Effective assistance of counsel; Miranda Rule.

Assistance, writ of. *See* Writ of assistance.

Assistant. A deputy, aide, or subordinate; as an assistant assessor. One who stands by and aids or helps another. Ordinarily refers to employee whose duties are to help his superior, to whom he must look for authority to act.

Assize, *or* **assise** (obsolete) /əsáyz/. An ancient species of court, consisting of a certain number of men, usually twelve, who were summoned together to try a disputed cause, performing the functions of a jury, except that they gave a verdict from their own investigation and knowledge and not upon evidence adduced. From the fact that they sat together (*assideo*), they were called the "assize." A court composed of an assembly of knights and other substantial men, with the baron or justice, in a certain place, at an appointed time. The verdict or judgment of the jurors or recognitors of assize.

Associate. Signifies confederacy or union for a particular purpose, good or ill. To join together, as *e.g.* partners. Partner or colleague. *See* Association.

Having subordinate status; *e.g.* associate professor.

Associate justices. Judges of courts, other than the presiding or chief justice.

Association. The act of a number of persons in uniting together for some special purpose or business. It is a term of vague meaning used to indicate a collection or organization of persons who have joined together for a certain or common object. Also, the persons so joining; the state of being associated.

An unincorporated society; a body of persons united and acting together without a charter, but upon the methods and forms used by incorporated bodies for the prosecution of some common enterprise. It is not a legal entity separate from the persons who compose it. *See also* Affiliation.

An organization treated as a corporation for Federal tax purposes even though it may not qualify as such under applicable state law. What is designated as a trust or a partnership, for example, may be classified as an association if it clearly possesses corporate attributes. Corporate attributes include: centralized management, continuity of existence, free transferability of interests, and limited liability. I.R.C. § 7701(a)(3).

To prove "association" with a criminal venture, for purpose of convicting upon evidence that defendant aided and abetted illegal enterprise, there must be evidence to establish defendant shared in principal's criminal intent.

See also Articles of association; Confederacy; Cooperative; Joint stock association *or* company; Non-profit association; Professional association; Unincorporated association.

Partnership association. See Partnership.

Professional association. See Corporation (*Professional corporation*).

Unincorporated association. A confederation of individuals organized for a specific purpose which may or may not be profit making but which is not chartered as a corporation.

Association, freedom of. *See* Assembly, right of.

Association of American Law Schools, The. AALS is literally an association of law schools. After a school has graduated at least three annual classes it is eligible to apply for membership. Compliance with the rules of membership are determined through a three or four person inspection team. Recommendations for admission to membership are made by the Executive Committee, upon advice of the Accreditation Committee. Membership is attained by action of the House of Representatives.

As soon as. This term has a relative meaning according to the thing which is to be done. It may denote merely a reasonable time; or may be equivalent to "whenever", or may mean "immediately".

As soon as may be. Promptly and with due diligence; as soon as was reasonably possible; within a reasonable time; as soon as possible; forthwith; as soon as they conveniently can.

As soon as practicable. Means reasonable time. These words are not synonymous with "as soon as possible"; they mean ordinarily as soon as reasonably can be expected in the particular circumstances; or "in due time". But the words have also been construed as practically synonymous with speedily.

Assume. To pretend. To undertake; engage; promise. To take to or upon one's self. Also taking up, receiving, adopting, taking to oneself, or to put on deceitfully, take appearance of, affect, or outwardly seem. To take on, become bound as another is bound, or put oneself in place of another as to an obligation or liability. *See also* Assumption.

Assumed facts. Facts concerning which no evidence has been introduced at trial and hence no rulings of law or jury instructions are required. In argument, a hypothetical set of facts used to illustrate a point of law. *See* Stipulation.

Assumed name. *See* Alias.

Assumed risk. *See* Assumption of risk.

Assumpsit /əsə́m(p)sət/. Lat. He undertook; he promised.

A promise or engagement by which one person assumes or undertakes to do some act or pay something to another. It may be either oral or in writing, but is not under seal. It is *express* if the promisor puts his engagement in distinct and definite language; it is *implied* where the law infers a promise (though no formal one has passed) from the conduct of the party or the circumstances of the case.

A common law form of action which lies for the recovery of damages for the non-performance of a parol or simple contract; or a contract that is neither of record nor under seal. *See also* Express assumpsit; Non-assumpsit.

Assumpsit for money had and received. Is of equitable character and lies, in general, whenever defendant has received money which in equity and good conscience he ought to pay to plaintiff.

Assumpsit on quantum meruit /əsóm(p)sət òn kwóntəm méruwət/. When a person employs another to do work for him, without any agreement as to his compensation, the law implies a promise from the employer to the workman that he will pay him for his services as much as he may deserve or merit. In such case, the plaintiff may suggest in his declaration that the defendant promised to pay him as much as he reasonably deserved, and then aver that his trouble was worth such a sum of money, which the defendant has omitted to pay. This is called an "assumpsit on quantum meruit". *See also* Quantum meruit.

Assumption. The act of conceding or taking for granted. Laying claim to or taking possession of.

The act or agreement of assuming or taking upon one's self. The undertaking or adoption of a debt or obligation primarily resting upon another, as where the purchaser of real estate "assumes" a mortgage resting upon it, in which case he adopts the mortgage debt as his own and becomes personally liable for its payment. The difference between the purchaser of land assuming a mortgage on it and simply buying subject to the mortgage, is that in the former case he makes himself personally liable for the payment of the mortgage debt, while in the latter case he does not. When he takes the conveyance subject to the mortgage, he is bound only to the extent of the property. Where one "assumes" a lease, he takes to himself the obligations, contracts, agreements, and benefits to which the other contracting party was entitled under the terms of the lease. *See* Assumption of mortgage.

Assumption clause. In mortgages, a provision that the mortgage may not be assumed without written consent of mortgagee. *See* Assumption of mortgage. Also a provision in an instrument of transfer in which the transferee agrees to assume an obligation of the transferor.

Assumption fee. Lender's charge for processing records for new buyer assuming an existing loan (mortgage).

Assumption of care. *See* Good Samaritan doctrine.

Assumption of indebtedness. Exists when person binds himself to pay debt incurred by another. *See also* Subrogation.

Assumption of mortgage. To take or acquire a mortgage or deed of trust from some prior holder. Thus, a purchaser may assume or take over the mortgage of the seller. Often this requires permission of the mortgagee. This is distinguishable from taking equity of redemption subject to mort-

gage because in latter case grantee is not contractually bound to pay mortgage, whereas if he assumes the mortgage, he binds himself to mortgagor to pay the mortgage and to fulfill all other terms and conditions of mortgage. *See also* Assumption.

Assumption of risk. The doctrine of assumption of risk, also known as volenti non fit injuria, means legally that a plaintiff may not recover for an injury to which he assents, *i.e.*, that a person may not recover for an injury received when he voluntarily exposes himself to a known and appreciated danger. The requirements for the defense of volenti non fit injuria are that: (1) the plaintiff has knowledge of facts constituting a dangerous condition, (2) he knows the condition is dangerous, (3) he appreciates the nature or extent of the danger, and (4) he voluntarily exposes himself to the danger. An exception may be applicable even though the above factors have entered into a plaintiff's conduct if his actions come within the rescue or humanitarian doctrine.

A defense to action of negligence which consists of showing that the plaintiff, knowing the dangers and risk involved, chose to act as he did. An affirmative defense which the defendant in a negligence action must plead and prove. Fed.R.Civil P. 8(c). It is not a defense under state workers' compensation laws or in FELA actions. Many states have abolished the defense of assumption of risk in automobile cases with the enactment of no-fault insurance acts or comparative negligence acts.

See also Volenti non fit injuria.

Assurance. The act or action of assuring; *e.g.* a pledge, guaranty, or surety. A declaration tending to inspire full confidence.

The deed or instrument by which real property is conveyed; also, the act of conveying such.

Same as "Insurance"; term used in Canada and England.

Assurance, further, covenant for. *See* Covenant (*Covenant for further assurance*).

Assure. To make certain and put beyond doubt. To declare, aver, avouch, assert, or ensure positively. To declare solemnly; to assure to any one with design of inspiring belief or confidence. Used interchangeably with "insure" in insurance law. In real property documents it means a warranty; and in business documents, generally, it means a pledge or security.

Assured. A person who has been insured by some insurance company, or underwriter, against losses or perils mentioned in the policy of insurance. Ordinarily synonymous with "insured".

Assurer. An insurer against certain perils and dangers; an underwriter; an indemnifier.

Asylum /əsáyləm/. A sanctuary, or place of refuge and protection, where criminals and debtors found shelter, and from which they could not be taken without sacrilege. Shelter; refuge; protection from the hand of justice. The word includes not only place, but also shelter, security, protection. While a foreign country has the right to offer an asylum to fugitives from other countries, there is no corresponding right on the part of the alien to claim asylum. This right of asylum has been voluntarily limited by most countries by treaties providing for the extradition *(q.v.)* of fugitive criminals (international extradition).

In time of war, a place of refuge in neutral territory for belligerent warships.

An institution for the protection and relief of unfortunates, as asylums for the poor, or for the insane; though this term is no longer generally used for such institutions.

Aliens. An alien may be considered for asylum or refugee status in the United States if the alien has a well-founded fear of persecution in his or her home country. To be eligible for either asylum or refugee status, the applicant must qualify as a refugee, as defined by 8 U.S.C.A. § 1101(a)(42). Also, under the Refugee Act of 1980, "an alien physically present in the United States or at a land border or port of entry . . . may be granted asylum in the discretion of the Attorney General if the Attorney General determines that such alien is a refugee . . . ." 8 U.S.C.A. § 1158(a).

At. A term of considerable elasticity of meaning, and somewhat indefinite. A function word to describe or indicate presence or occurrence in, on, or near; or to indicate the means, cause, or manner; or to indicate that with which one is occupied or employed. As used to fix a time, it does not necessarily mean *eo instante* or the identical time named, or even a fixed definite moment. Often expresses simply nearness and proximity, and consequently may denote a reasonable time.

At arm's length. Beyond the reach of personal influence or control. Parties are said to deal "at arm's length" when each stands upon the strict letter of his rights, and conducts the business in a formal manner, without trusting to the other's fairness or integrity, and without being subject to the other's control or overmastering influence. *See* Arm's length transaction.

At bar. Before the court. "The case at bar," etc.

At issue. Whenever the parties come to a point in the pleadings which is affirmed on one side and denied on the other, they are said to be at an issue. Criminal case is "at issue" when defendant enters a plea.

ATLA. American Trial Lawyers Association.

At large. Not limited to any particular place, district, person, matter, or question; open to discussion or controversy; not precluded. Free; unrestrained; not under corporal control, as a ferocious animal so free from restraint as to be liable to do mischief. Fully; in detail; in an extended form.

Elected officials chosen by the voters of the State as a whole rather than from separate congressional or legislative districts.

At law. According to law; by, for, or in law. Particularly in distinction from that which is done in or according to equity; or in titles such as sergeant at law, barrister at law, attorney or counsellor at law.

At least. In deed of trust covenant specifying amount of fire insurance, means at lowest estimate, at smallest concession or claim, in smallest or lowest degree, at smallest number.

At once. In contracts of various kinds the phrase is construed as synonymous with "immediately" and "forthwith," where the subject-matter is the giving of notice. The use of such term does not ordinarily call for instantaneous action, but rather that notice shall be given within such time as is reasonable in view of the circumstances. Likewise, contracts or statutes requiring the performance of a particular act "at once" are usually held to mean simply within a reasonable time. An order to "ship at once" is synonymous with "as soon as possible".

A tort. Without reason; unjustly; wrongfully. *See* Tort.

At par. Said of a bond or preferred stock issued or selling at its face value.

At-risk amount. The taxpayer has an amount at risk in a business or investment venture to the extent that it has subjected personal assets to the risks of the business. Typically, the taxpayer's at-risk amount includes (1) the amount of money or other property that the investor contributed to the venture for the investment, (2) the amount of any of the entity's liabilities for which the taxpayer personally is liable and that relate to the investment, and (3) an allocable share of nonrecourse debts incurred by the venture from third parties in arm's length transactions, with respect to real estate investments. *See* At-risk rules.

At-risk limitation. Generally, a taxpayer can deduct losses relative to a trade or business, S corporation, partnership, or investment asset only to the extent of the at-risk amount.

At-risk rules. The at-risk rules limit a taxpayer's deductible losses to the amount the taxpayer has at risk. Amounts at risk include the cash investment, and the debt for which the taxpayer is personally liable. The objective of the at-risk rules is to prevent investors from sheltering income through losses incurred in activities financed substantially through non-recourse debt. *See also* At-risk amount.

Atrocity. A word implying conduct that is outrageously or wantonly wicked, criminal, vile, cruel; extremely horrible and shocking.

ATS. At suit of.

At sea. Out of the limits of any port or harbor on the sea-coast.

Attach. Seizure of property under a writ of attachment. *See* Attachment.

To bind, fasten, tie, or connect, to make fast or join; its antonyms are separate, detach, remove.

Attaché /ӕtəshéy/ətӕshèy/. A person attached to an embassy, to the office of an ambassador, or to a foreign legation. One connected with an office, *e.g.*, a public office.

Attached. A term describing the physical union of two otherwise independent structures or objects, or the relation between two parts of a single structure, each having its own function. As applied to buildings, the term is often synonymous with "annexed." *See also* Fixture.

Attached account. Account against which court order has been issued; payments can only be made with consent of court.

Attaching creditor. *See* Creditor.

Attachment. The legal process of seizing another's property in accordance with a writ or judicial order for the purpose of securing satisfaction of a judgment yet to be rendered. The act or process of taking, apprehending, or seizing persons or property, by virtue of a writ, summons, or other judicial order, and bringing the same into the custody of the court for the purpose of securing satisfaction of the judgment ultimately to be entered in the action. While formerly the main objective of attachment was to coerce the defendant debtor to appear in court by seizer of his property, today the writ of attachment is used primarily to seize the debtor's property in order to secure the debt or claim of the creditor in the event that a judgment is rendered. The remedy of attachment is governed strictly by state statutes, with such differing considerably as to when attachment is available (the majority of states providing that such is available at or after the commencement of the main action until entry of judgment). Federal courts follow the local rules or statutes relating to attachment. Fed.R.Civil P. 64.

A remedy ancillary to an action by which plaintiff is enabled to acquire a lien upon property or effects of defendant for satisfaction of judgment which plaintiff may obtain.

See also Execution; Garnishment; Levy; Lien of attachment.

Commercial law. When the three basic prerequisites of a security interest exist (agreement, value, and collateral), the security agreement becomes enforceable between the parties and is said to "attach." U.C.C. § 9–203.

Distinguished from execution. See Execution.

Domestic and foreign. In some jurisdictions it is common to give the name "domestic attachment" to one issuing against a resident debtor (upon the special ground of fraud, intention to abscond, etc.), and to designate an attachment against a non-resident, or his property, as "foreign."

Where the defendant is a non-resident, or beyond the territorial jurisdiction of the court, his goods or land within the territory may be seized upon process of attachment; whereby he will be compelled to enter an appearance, or the court acquires jurisdiction so far as to dispose of the property attached. This is sometimes called "foreign attachment." In such a case, the proceeding becomes in substance one in rem against the attached property.

Persons. A writ issued by a court of record, commanding the sheriff to bring before it a person who has been guilty of contempt of court, either in neglect or abuse of its process or of subordinate powers. A capias *(q.v.)*.

Property. A species of mesne process, by which a writ is issued at the institution or during the progress of an action, commanding the sheriff to seize the property, rights, credits, or effects of the defendant to be held as security for the satisfaction of such judgment as the plaintiff may recover. It is principally used against absconding, concealed, or fraudulent debtors. *See e.g.* Mass.R. Civil P. 4.1.

Attachment bond. A bond used to dissolve an attachment so as to free the property subject to the attachment for sale or other disposition; may be surety company bond or personal bond with sureties. Plaintiff then looks to bond for satisfaction of his judgment.

Attachment execution. A name given in some states to a process of garnishment for the satisfaction of a judgment. As to the judgment debtor it is an execution; but as to the garnishee it is an original process—a summons commanding him to appear and show cause, if any he has, why the judgment should not be levied on the goods and effects of the defendant in his hands.

Attachment of risk. Used to describe point in time, generally when title passes, when risk of loss for destruction of property which is subject of sale passes to buyer from seller. U.C.C. § 2–509.

Attain. To reach or come to by progression or motion; to arrive at; as, to attain a ripe old age.

Attainder /ətéyndər/. At common law, that extinction of civil rights and capacities which took place whenever a person who had committed treason or felony received sentence of death for his crime. The effect of "attainder" upon such felon was, in general terms, that all his estate, real and personal, was forfeited.

Bills of attainder. Such special acts of the legislature as inflict capital punishments upon persons supposed to be guilty of high offenses, such as treason and felony, without any conviction in the ordinary course of judicial proceedings. If an act inflicts a milder degree of punishment than death, it is called a "bill of pains and penalties," but both are included in the prohibition in the Constitution (Art. I, Sec. 9). *See also* Bill.

Attempt. In statutes and in cases other than criminal prosecutions an "attempt" ordinarily means an intent combined with an act falling short of the thing intended. It may be described as an endeavor to do an act, carried beyond mere preparation, but short of execution.

Criminal law. An intent to commit a crime coupled with an act taken toward committing the offense. An effort or endeavor to accomplish a crime, amounting to more than mere preparation or planning for it, which, if not prevented, would have resulted in the full consummation of the act attempted, but which, in fact, does not bring to pass the party's ultimate design. The requisite elements of an "attempt" to commit a crime are: (1) an intent to commit it, (2) an overt act toward its commission, (3) failure of consummation, and (4) the apparent possibility of commission.

A person is guilty of an attempt to commit a crime if, acting with the kind of culpability otherwise required for commission of the crime, he: (a) purposely engages in conduct which would constitute the crime if the attendant circumstances were as he believes them to be; or (b) when causing a particular result is an element of the crime, does or omits to do anything with the purpose of causing or with the belief that it will cause such result without further conduct on his part; or (c) purposely does or omits to do anything which, under the circumstances as he believes them to be, is an act or omission constituting a substantial step in a course of conduct planned to culminate in his commission of the crime. Model Penal Code, § 5.01.

Attendant circumstances. Facts surrounding an event; *e.g.* the time, place and declarations of a testator prior to and immediately following execution of his will.

Attest. To bear witness to; to bear witness to a fact; to affirm to be true or genuine; to act as a witness to; to certify; to certify to the verity of a copy of a public document formally by signature; to make solemn declaration in words or writing to support a fact; to signify by subscription of his name that the signer has witnessed the execution of the particular instrument. Also the technical word by which, in the practice in many of the states, a certifying officer gives assurance of the genuineness and correctness of a copy. Thus, an "attested" copy of a document is one which has been examined and compared with the original, with a certificate or memorandum of its correctness, signed by the persons who have examined it. *See* Affirmation; Jurat; Oath; Verification.

Attestation. The act of witnessing an instrument in writing, at the request of the party making the same, and subscribing the name of the witness in testimony of such fact. See Affirmation; Jurat; Oath; Verification.

Attestation clause. That clause (*e.g.* at the end of a will) wherein the witnesses certify that the instrument has been executed before them, and the manner of the execution of the same. A certificate certifying as to facts and circumstances attending execution of will. See Uniform Probate Code, § 2–502.

Attestation of will. Act of witnessing performance of statutory requirements to valid execution. *See* Attestation clause.

Attested copy. *See* Attest.

Attesting witness. One who signs his name to an instrument, at the request of the party or parties, for the purpose of proving and identifying it.

Attestor. One who attests or vouches for. *See also* Witness.

At the market. Order to broker to buy or sell a stock at the current market price, rather than at a specified price. *See* Market order.

Attorn /ətə́rn/. To turn over; to transfer to another money or goods; to assign to some particular use or service. To consent to the transfer of a rent or reversion. To agree to become tenant to one as owner or landlord of an estate previously held of another, or to agree to recognize a new owner of a property or estate and promise payment of rent to him.

Attorney. In the most general sense this term denotes an agent or substitute, or one who is appointed and authorized to act in the place or stead of another. An agent, or one acting on behalf of another. In its most common usage, however, unless a contrary meaning is clearly intended, this term means "attorney at law", "lawyer" or "counselor at law".

"Attorney" means attorney, professional law association, corporation, or partnership, authorized under applicable law to practice law. Bankruptcy Code, § 101.

The word "attorney" includes a party prosecuting or defending an action in person. New York C.P.L.R. § 105.

See also Attorney for government; Attorney General; Barrister; District (*District attorney*); House counsel; Lawyer; Of counsel; Prosecuting attorney; State's attorney; United States Attorney.

Attorney ad hoc. *See* Ad hoc.

Attorney at large. In old practice, an attorney who practiced in all the courts.

Attorney at law. Person admitted to practice law in his respective state and authorized to perform both civil and criminal legal functions for clients, including drafting of legal documents, giving of legal advice, and representing such before courts, administrative agencies, boards, etc.

Attorney ethics. *See* Code of Professional Responsibility; Rules of Professional Conduct.

Attorney fees. *See* American rule; Attorney's lien; Common fund doctrine; Equal Access to Justice Act; Fee; Lodestar Rule; Minimum fee schedules; Retainer.

Attorney in fact. A private attorney authorized by another to act in his place and stead, either for some particular purpose, as to do a particular act, or for the transaction of business in general, not of a legal character. This authority is conferred by an instrument in writing, called a "letter of attorney," or more commonly a "power of attorney." *See* Power of attorney.

Attorney of record. Attorney whose name must appear somewhere in permanent records or files of case, or on the pleadings or some instrument filed in the case, or on appearance docket. Person whom the client has named as his agent upon whom service of papers may be made.

An attorney who has filed a notice of appearance (*e.g.*, through a praecipe) and who hence is formally mentioned in court records as the official attorney of the party. Once an attorney becomes an attorney of record, he often cannot withdraw from the case without court permission.

Every pleading of a party represented by an attorney shall be signed by at least one attorney of record in his individual name, whose address shall be stated. Fed.R. Civil P. 11.

Attorney's license. A formal document issued by a state supreme court, normally after passage of a bar examination, which permits one to practice law in that jurisdiction. Also, a similar document issued by federal courts to attorneys admitted to practice in state courts. Such licenses may be revoked because of disbarment or suspended for attorney misconduct.

Attorney's lien. *See* Attorney's lien.

Letter of attorney. A power of attorney; a written instrument by which one person constitutes an-

other his true and lawful attorney, in order that the latter may do for the former, and in his place and stead, some lawful act. An instrument of writing, appointing an attorney in fact for an avowed purpose and setting forth his powers and duties. It is, in effect, a mere contract of agency. A *general* power authorizes the agent to act generally in behalf of the principal. A *special* power is one limited to particular acts. *See also* Power of attorney.

Power of attorney. The instrument by which authority of one person to act in place and stead of another as attorney in fact is set forth. *See also* Power of attorney.

Practice of law. *See* Practice.

Public attorney. A name sometimes given to an attorney at law, as distinguished from a *private* attorney, or attorney in fact.

Right to attorney. *See* Counsel, right to.

Attorney-client privilege. In law of evidence, client's privilege to refuse to disclose and to prevent any other person from disclosing confidential communications between he and his attorney. Such privilege protects communications between attorney and client made for purpose of furnishing or obtaining professional legal advice or assistance. That privilege which permits an attorney to refuse to testify as to communications from client to him though it belongs to client, not to attorney, and hence client may waive it. In federal courts, state law is applied with respect to such privilege. Fed.Evid. Rule 501. *See also* Client's privilege; Joint defense doctrine.

Attorney for government. Includes the Attorney General, an authorized assistant of the Attorney General, a United States Attorney, an authorized assistant of a United States Attorney and when applicable to cases arising under the laws of Guam means the Attorney General of Guam or such other person or persons as may be authorized by the laws of Guam to act therein. Fed.R. Crim.P. 54(c).

Attorney General. The Attorney General, as head of the Department of Justice and chief law officer of the Federal Government, represents the United States in legal matters generally and gives advice and opinions to the President and to the heads of the executive departments of the Government when so requested. The Attorney General appears in person to represent the Government in the U.S. Supreme Court in cases of exceptional gravity or importance. *See also* Solicitor General.

In each state there is also an attorney general, who is the chief law officer of the state. He gives advice and opinions to the governor and to executive and administrative departments or agencies.

Private Attorney General. The "private attorney general" concept holds that a successful private party plaintiff is entitled to recovery of his legal expenses, including attorney fees, if he has advanced the policy inherent in public interest legislation on behalf of a significant class of persons. *See also* Equal Access to Justice Act.

Attorney general's bill. An indictment presented to grand jury by leave of court without prior complaint before magistrate and holding for court.

Attorney general's opinion. An opinion furnished by U.S. Attorney General to President, members of executive department or governmental agencies on request concerning question of law. Also, opinion rendered by state attorney general to Governor or state agencies on request concerning an interpretation of law.

Attorney, right to. *See* Counsel, right to.

Attorneyship. The office of an agent or attorney.

Attorney's lien. The right of an attorney at law to hold or retain in his possession the money or property of a client until his proper charges have been adjusted and paid. It requires no equitable proceeding for its establishment. Also a lien on funds in court payable to the client, or on a judgment or decree or award in his favor, recovered through the exertions of the attorney, and for the enforcement of which he must invoke the equitable aid of the court.

Charging lien. An attorney's lien, for his proper compensation, on the fund or judgment which his client has recovered by means of his professional aid and services. It is a specific lien covering only the services rendered by an attorney in the action in which the judgment was obtained, whereas a retaining lien is a general lien for the balance of the account between the attorney and his client, and applies to the property of the client which may come into the attorney's possession in the course of his employment.

Retaining lien. The lien which an attorney has upon all his client's papers, deeds, vouchers, etc., which remain in his possession, entitling him to retain them until satisfaction of his claims for professional services. It is a general lien.

Attorney's work product. *See* Work product rule.

Attractive agencies doctrine. *See* Attractive nuisance doctrine.

Attractive instrumentalities doctrine. *See* Attractive nuisance doctrine.

Attractive nuisance doctrine. The doctrine is that person who has an instrumentality, agency, or condition upon his own premises, or who creates such condition on the premises of another, or in a public place, which may reasonably be apprehended to be a source of danger to children, is under a duty to take such precautions as a reasonably prudent man would take to prevent injury to children of tender years whom he knows to be accustomed to resort there, or who may, by reason of something there which may be expected to attract them, come there to play. See Restatement, Second, Torts § 339.

Attribution. Under certain circumstances, the tax law applies attribution rules to assign to one taxpayer the ownership interest of another taxpayer. If, for example, the stock of X Corporation is held 60% by M and 40% by S, M may be deemed to own 100% of X Corporation if M and S are mother and son. In such a case, the stock owned by S is attributed to M. Stated differently, M has a 60% "direct" and a 40% "indirect" interest in X Corporation. It can also be said that M is the "constructive" owner of S's interest.

Att'y. Attorney.

Auction /ókshən/. An auction is a public sale of property to the highest bidder by one licensed and authorized for that purpose. The auctioneer is employed by the seller and is primarily his agent. However, when the property is struck off he is also the agent of the buyer to the extent of binding the parties by his memorandum of sale, thus satisfying the statute of frauds.

A sale by auction is complete when the auctioneer so announces by the fall of the hammer or in other customary manner. Such a sale is with reserve unless the goods are in explicit terms put up without reserve. U.C.C. § 2–328.

Dutch auction. A method of sale by auction which consists in the public offer of the property at a price beyond its value, and then gradually lowering the price until some one becomes the purchaser.

Auctioneer. A person authorized or licensed by law to sell lands or goods of other persons at public auction. One who sells goods at public auction for another on commission, or for a recompense.

Auctioneers differ from *brokers*, in that the latter may both buy and sell, whereas auctioneers can only sell; also brokers may sell by private contract only, and auctioneers by public auction only.

Audit. Systematic inspection of accounting records involving analyses, tests, and confirmations. The investigation and examination of transactions that underlie an organization's financial statements.

The hearing and investigation had before an auditor. An audience; a hearing; an examination in general. A formal or official examination and authentication of accounts, with witnesses, vouchers, etc.

See also Auditor; Generally Accepted Auditing Standards (GAAS).

Audit opinion. Report of certified public accountant after an examination of financial statements, expressing opinion on the fairness of presentation of such statements. The opinion may take one of the following forms: unqualified opinion; qualified opinion; adverse opinion; disclaimer of opinion.

Audit report. A report that presents the auditor's opinion regarding the fairness of the financial statements. *See Audit opinion, above.*

Audit trail. Chain of evidence connecting account balances or other summary results to original transactions and calculations. The flow of events between the original transaction and the account balances in the financial statements.

Correspondence audit. See Correspondence audit.

Desk audit. Review of civil service positions to determine if duties and responsibilities of position fit job classification and pay grade.

Field audit. An audit by the Internal Revenue Service conducted on the business premises of the taxpayer or in the office of the tax practitioner representing the taxpayer. To be distinguished from a correspondence audit or an office audit *(q.v.)*.

Independent audit. One conducted by an outside person or firm not connected in any way with the company being audited. *See also* Audit committee.

Internal audit. Audit performed by personnel of company to assure that internal procedures, operations, and accounting practices are in proper order—in contrast to an audit by outside, independent auditors.

Office audit. See Office (*Office audit*).

Post audits. Audit of the funds spent on a capital project after the project has been completed to assess the efficiency with which the funds were spent; evaluation of the expected future cash flow estimates; and evaluation of abandonment versus continuing the project. The process of gathering information on the actual results of a capital project and comparing them to the expected results.

Tax audit. An examination of books, vouchers and records, or other transactions possessing tax consequences, of a taxpayer conducted by agents of the I.R.S. *See* Correspondence audit; Office (*Office audit*); RAR.

Auditing. *See* Audit.

Audita querela /òdáytə kwəríylə/. The name of a common law writ constituting the initial process in an action brought by a judgment defendant to obtain relief against the consequences of the judgment on account of some matter of defense or discharge arising since its rendition and which could not be taken advantage of otherwise. May also lie for matters arising before judgment where defendant had no opportunity to raise such matters in defense.

This writ has been abolished in most states that have adopted Rules of Civil Procedure, being supplanted by motion for relief from judgment. Rule of Civil Procedure 60(b).

Audit committee. A committee of the board of directors of a corporation usually consisting of outside directors who nominate the independent auditors and discuss their work with them. If the auditors believe certain matters should be brought to the attention of stockholders, the auditors first bring these matters to the attention of the audit committee.

Auditor. One who checks the accuracy, fairness, and general acceptability of accounting records and statements and then attests to them; *e.g.* a Certified Public Accountant.

A State official whose duty is to examine the accounts of state agencies to determine if expenditures were made in accordance with authorizations by the legislature. *See also* General Accounting Office.

An officer of a business who examines and verifies accounts for accuracy.

An officer (or officers) of the court, assigned to state the items of debit and credit between the parties in a suit where accounts are in question, and exhibit the balance. Under the Rules of Civil Procedure in many states, the term "master" is used to describe those persons formerly known as auditors; *e.g.* Mass.R. Civil P. 53. *See* Master; Reference.

Internal auditors. Individuals in large organizations who review and monitor the organization's accounting procedures and controls.

Public auditor. Examines account records of private businesses for a fee.

State auditor. See first general definition above.

Augmented estate. Estate reduced by funeral and administration expenses, homestead allowance, family allowances, exemptions, and enforceable claims to which is added value of property transferred to anyone other than bona fide purchaser and value of property owned by surviving spouse at decedent's death. Uniform Probate Code, § 2–202.

Australian ballot. An official ballot on which the names of all the candidates are printed. Its use is accompanied by safeguards designed to maintain secrecy in voting. The so-called Australian ballot laws, widely adopted in various forms in the United States, have generally been sustained by the courts.

Authentic /oθéntik/. Genuine; true; real; pure; reliable; trustworthy; having the character and authority of an original; duly vested with all necessary formalities and legally attested. Competent, credible, and reliable as evidence.

Authentic act. In the civil law, an act which has been executed before a notary or public officer authorized to execute such functions, or which is testified by a public seal, or has been rendered public by the authority of a competent magistrate, or which is certified as being a copy of a public register.

Authentic copy. A copy which is of such authority as to prove the form and contents of the original from which it is taken. *See also* Authentication.

Authentication /əθèntəkéyshən/. In the law of evidence, the act or mode of giving authority or legal authenticity to a statute, record, or other written instrument, or a certified copy thereof, so as to render it legally admissible in evidence. Verifications of judgments. An attestation made by a proper officer by which he certifies that a record is in due form of law, and that the person who certifies it is the officer appointed so to do. Acts done with a view of causing an instrument to be known and identified. *See also* Verification.

Authentication of a writing means (a) the introduction of evidence sufficient to sustain a finding that it is the writing that the proponent of the evidence claims it is or (b) the establishment of such facts by any other means provided by law. Calif.Evid.Code, § 1400.

The requirement of authentication as a condition precedent to admissibility of evidence is satisfied by evidence sufficient to support a finding that the matter in question is what its proponent claims. Fed.Evid.Rule 901.

Self authentication. Statutes frequently provide that certain classes of writings shall be received in evidence "without further proof." The following fall into this category: (1) deeds, conveyances or other instruments, which have been acknowledged by the signers before a notary public, (2) certified copies of public records, and (3) books of statutes which purport to be printed by public authority. See Fed.Evid.Rule 902.

Author. One who produces, by his own intellectual labor applied to the materials of his composition, an arrangement or compilation new in itself. A beginner or mover of anything; hence efficient cause of a thing; creator; originator; a composer, as distinguished from an editor, translator or compiler.

Authorities. Citations to constitutions, statutes, precedents, judicial decisions, rules, regulations, textbooks, articles, and the like made on the argument of questions of law (*e.g.*, in briefs, motions, etc.) on the trial of causes before a court, in support of the legal positions contended for, or adduced to fortify the opinion of a court or of a text writer upon any question. Authorities may be either primary (*e.g.*, statutes, court decisions, regulations), or secondary (*e.g.*, Restatements, treatises).

Authority. Permission. Right to exercise powers; to implement and enforce laws; to exact obedience; to command; to judge. Control over; jurisdiction. Often synonymous with power. The power delegated by a principal to his agent. The lawful delegation of power by one person to another. Power of agent to affect legal relations of principal by acts done in accordance with principal's manifestations of consent to agent. See Restatement, Second, Agency § 7.

Refers to the precedential value to be accorded an opinion of a judicial or administrative body. A court's opinion is binding authority on other courts directly below it in the judicial hierarchy. Opinions of lower courts or of courts outside the hierarchy are governed by the degree to which it adheres to the doctrine of stare decisis. *See* Stare decisis.

Legal power; a right to command or to act; the right and power of public officers to require obedience to their orders lawfully issued in the scope of their public duties.

See also Actual authority; Apparent authority; Binding authority; Commission; Competent authority; Constructive authority; Control; Credentials; Implied authority; Power; Precedent; Real authority; Scope of authority.

Actual express authority. Actual authority derived from written or spoken words of principal. *See also* Actual authority.

Actual implied authority. Actual authority inferred from words or conducted manifested to agent by principal. *See also* Implied authority.

Apparent authority. That which, though not actually granted, the principal knowingly permits the agent to exercise, or which he holds him out as possessing. The power to affect the legal relations of another person by transactions with third persons, professedly as agent for the other, arising from and in accordance with the other's manifestations to such third persons. Restatement, Second, Agency, § 8. *See Authority by estoppel, below.*

Authority by estoppel. Not actual, but apparent only, being imposed on the principal because his conduct has been such as to mislead, so that it would be unjust to let him deny it. *See Apparent authority, above.*

Authority coupled with an interest. Authority given to an agent for a valuable consideration, or which forms part of a security.

Express authority. That given explicitly, either in writing or orally. *See* Express authority.

General authority. That which authorizes the agent to do everything connected with a particular business. It empowers him to bind his principal by all acts within the scope of his employment; and it cannot be limited by any private direction not known to the party dealing with him.

Implied authority. Actual authority circumstantially proved. That which the principal intends his agent to possess, and which is implied from the principal's conduct. It includes only such acts as are incident and necessary to the exercise of the authority expressly granted.

Incidental authority. Such authority as is necessary to carry out authority which is actually or apparently given, *e.g.* authority to borrow money carries with it as an incidental authority the power to sign commercial paper to effectuate the borrowing.

Inferred authority. *See Incidental authority,* above.

Inherent authority. Such power as reposes in an agent by virtue of the agency itself.

Limited authority. Such authority as the agent has when he is bound by precise instructions.

Naked authority. That arising where the principal delegates the power to the agent wholly for the benefit of the former.

Ostensible authority. *See Apparent authority,* above.

Presumptive authority. *See Implied authority,* above.

Special authority. That which is confined to an individual transaction. Such an authority does not bind the principal, unless it is strictly pursued.

Unlimited authority. That possessed by an agent when he is left to pursue his own discretion.

Authorize. To empower; to give a right or authority to act. To endow with authority or effective legal power, warrant, or right. To permit a thing to be done in the future. It has a mandatory effect or meaning, implying a direction to act.

"Authorized" is sometimes construed as equivalent to "permitted"; or "directed", or to similar mandatory language. Possessed of authority; that is, possessed of legal or rightful power, the synonym of which is "competency."

Authorized capital. *See* Authorized stock issue.

Authorized stock issue. Total number of shares of capital stock which charter or articles of incorporation permits corporation to sell. The shares of all classes a domestic or foreign corporation is authorized to issue. Rev. Model Bus. Corp. Act, § 1.40.

Autocracy /òtókrəsiy/. The name of an unlimited monarchical government. A government at the will of one man (called an "autocrat"), unchecked by constitutional restrictions or limitations.

Autograph. One's handwriting; written with one's own hand.

Automated clearing house (ACH). A collection of regional electronic interbank networks used to process transactions electronically with a guaranteed one-day bank collection float.

Automatic stay. Immediately upon the filing of a voluntary petition under the Bankruptcy Code a stay arises which generally bars all debt collection efforts against the debtor or property of his bankruptcy estate although the collection of postpetition debts against the debtor is not stayed. Code § 362(a). The court need not sign any order to give rise to the stay; the mere filing of the petition, with supporting documentation, with the clerk is sufficient.

Automatism /ətómətìzəm/. Behavior performed in a state of mental unconsciousness or dissociation without full awareness, *i.e.,* somnambulism, fugues. Term is applied to actions or conduct of an individual apparently occurring without will, purpose, or reasoned intention on his part; a condition sometimes observed in persons who, without being actually insane, suffer from an obscuration of the mental faculties, loss of volition or of memory, or kindred affections. "Ambulatory automatism" describes the pathological impulse to purposeless and irresponsible wanderings from place to place often characteristic of patients suffering from loss of memory with dissociation of personality. Automatism may be asserted as a criminal defense to negate the requisite mental state of voluntariness for commission of a crime. See *e.g.* Model Penal Code, § 2.01.

Automobile guest. *See* Family automobile doctrine; Family purpose doctrine; Guest; Guest statute.

Automobile insurance. A comprehensive term which embraces insurance coverage for all risks involved in owning and operating an automobile, such as personal injury protection, property damage to another and to the insured, fire, theft and vandalism. *See* Insurance.

Autonomy. The political independence of a nation; the right (and condition) of power of self-government. The negation of a state of political influence from without or from foreign powers.

Autopsy /ótopsiy/. The dissection of a dead body for the purpose of inquiring into the cause of death. A post mortem examination to determine the cause, seat, or nature of a disease. Such is normally required by statute for deaths by violent, unexplained, or unnatural means. *See also* Inquest.

Autoptic evidence. An exhibit of a thing offered before jury as evidence to be seen through jury's own eyes. *See* Autoptic proference; Demonstrative evidence.

Autoptic proference. Proffering or presenting in open court of articles for observation or inspection of the tribunal. *See* Autoptic evidence; Demonstrative evidence.

Auto theft. A form of larceny, the subject matter of which is a motor vehicle. The taking and carrying away of a motor vehicle from the owner or possessor with intent to deprive him permanently of it. The intent distinguishes larceny from a lesser offense of use without authority. *See also* Joyriding.

Autre /ówtrə/. (Fr.) Another.

Autrefois /òwtrəfwó/. L. Fr. At another time; formerly; before; heretofore.

Autrefois acquit /òwtrəfwó əkíy/°əkwít/. Fr. Formerly acquitted. The name of a plea in bar to a criminal action, stating that the defendant has been once already indicted and tried for the same alleged offense and has been acquitted. *See* Double jeopardy.

Autrefois convict /òwtrəfwó kənvíkt/. Fr. Formerly convicted. A plea by a criminal in bar to an indictment that he has been formerly convicted of the same crime.

Autre vie /ówtrə viy/. Another's life. A person holding an estate for or during the life of another is called a tenant *"pur autre vie,"* or *"pur terme d'autre vie."* *See* Estate pur autre vie.

Auxiliary /ogzíl(iy)əriy/. Aiding; attendant on; ancillary *(q.v.);* as, an auxiliary bill in equity, an auxiliary receiver. Synonymous with "subsidiary."

Available. Suitable; useable; accessible; obtainable; present or ready for immediate use. Having sufficient force or efficacy; effectual; valid.

Aver /əvə́r/, *v.* In pleading, to declare or assert; to set out distinctly and formally; to allege. *See also* Averment.

In old pleading, to avouch or verify; to make or prove true; to make good or justify a plea.

Average. A mean proportion, medial sum or quantity, made out of unequal sums or quantities. In ordinary usage the term signifies the mean between two or more quantities, measures, or numbers. If applied to something which is incapable of expression in terms of measure or amount, it signifies that the thing or person referred to is of the ordinary or usual type.

In maritime law, loss or damage accidentally happening to a vessel or to its cargo during a voyage. Also a small duty paid to masters of ships, when goods are sent in another man's ship, for their care of the goods, over and above the freight. See subdefinitions below.

General average. A contribution by the several interests engaged in a maritime venture to make good the loss of one of them for the voluntary sacrifice of a part of the ship or cargo to save the residue of the property and the lives of those on board, or for extraordinary expenses necessarily incurred for the common benefit and safety of all. The law of general average is part of the maritime law, and not of the municipal law, and applies to maritime adventures only.

Gross average. More commonly called "general average" *(q.v.).* Where loss or damage occurs to a vessel or its cargo at sea, *average* is the adjustment and apportionment of such loss between the owner, the freight, and the cargo, in proportion to their respective interests and losses, in order that one may not suffer the whole loss, but each contribute ratably.

Particular average is a loss happening to the ship, freight, or cargo which is not to be shared by contribution among all those interested, but must be borne by the owner of the subject to which it occurs. It is thus called in contradistinction to *general* average.

Petty average denotes such charges and disbursements as, according to occurrences and the custom of every place, the master necessarily furnishes for the benefit of the ship and cargo, either at the place of loading or unloading, or on the voyage; such as the hire of a pilot for conducting a vessel from one place to another, towage, light money, beaconage, anchorage, bridge toll, quarantine and such like.

Simple average is the same as "particular average" *(q.v.).*

Average clause. A clause providing that similar items in one location or at several locations which are covered by one insurance policy shall each be covered in the proportion that the value in each bears to the value in all.

Average daily balance. Average amount of money that a depositor keeps on deposit in a bank, or average balance on which finance charge is computed on consumer credit account, on any given day.

Average life. The effective maturity of a debt issue, taking into account the effect of sinking fund payments.

Average man test. Used to determine bias of prospective juror who asserts that he is without prejudice but who is so connected with case that ordinary man under circumstances would be biased without recognition of his prejudice.

Average rate of tax. A taxpayer's gross tax liability divided by total taxable income.

Averaging up or down. Practice of purchasing the same security at different price levels, thus realizing a higher or lower average cost than the first purchase. *See* Dollar averaging.

Averment /əvǝrmənt/. In pleading, to allege or assert positively. All averments in pleadings are required to be simple, concise, and direct. Fed.R. Civil P. 8(e).

In old pleading, an offer to prove a plea, or pleading. The concluding part of a plea, replication, or other pleading, containing new affirmative matter, by which the party offers or declares himself "ready to *verify.*"

Aviation Act. Federal law that created Federal Aviation Agency (FAA) which is responsible for regulation of aviation including aircraft safety, aircraft marking, etc. *See* Federal Aviation Administration.

A vinculo matrimonii /ey víŋkyǝlow mæ̀trǝmówniyay/. Lat. From the bond of matrimony. A term descriptive of a kind of divorce, which effects a complete dissolution of the marriage contract. *See* Divorce.

Avoid. To annul; cancel; make void; to destroy the efficacy of anything. To evade; escape.

Avoidable consequences doctrine. Doctrine imposes duty on person injured to minimize damages. The general rule relating to duty of party who has been wronged by breach of contract to mitigate damages; *i.e.* to not sit idly by and allow damages to accumulate. Restatement, Second, Contracts, § 350. This doctrine provides that one injured by tort of another is not entitled to recover damages for any harm that he could have avoided by use of reasonable effort. *See also* Mitigation of damages.

Avoidance. A making void, useless, empty, or of no effect; annulling, cancelling; escaping or evading. *See also* Evasion.

In pleading, the allegation or statement of new matter, in opposition to a former pleading, which, admitting the facts alleged in such former pleading, shows cause why they should not have their ordinary legal effect. Fed.R. Civil P. 8(c). *See also* Affirmative defense; Confession and avoidance.

Avoidance of tax. *See* Tax avoidance.

Avoucher /əváwchǝr/. The calling upon a warrantor of lands to fulfill his undertaking. *See* Voucher.

Avow /əváw/. In pleading, to acknowledge and justify an act done. To make an avowry. *See* Avowal; Avowry; Justification.

Avowal /əváwǝl/. An open declaration. Purpose is to enable the court to know what the witness would have stated in answer to the question propounded, and to inform the court what the interrogator would prove contrary to the testimony given at the trial. *See* Offer of proof.

Avowant. One who makes an avowry.

Avowry /əváwry/. A common law pleading in the action of replevin, by which the defendant *avows*, that is, acknowledges and justifies the taking of the distress or property complained of, where he took it in his own right, and sets forth the reason of it; as for rent in arrear, damage done, etc.

Avulsion /əvǝlshǝn/. A sudden and perceptible loss or addition to land by the action of water, or a sudden change in the bed or course of a stream. The removal of a considerable quantity of soil from the land of one man, and its deposit upon or annexation to the land of another, suddenly and by the perceptible action of water.

Where running streams are the boundaries between states, the same rule applies as between private proprietors, and, if the stream from any cause, natural or artificial, suddenly leaves its old bed and forms a new one by the process known as "avulsion," the resulting change of channel works no change of boundary, which remains in the middle of the old channel though no water may be flowing in it and irrespective of subsequent changes in the new channel.

To constitute "avulsion," rather than "accretion," so as to preclude change in boundary between riparian owners, it is not necessary that soil washed away be identifiable; it being sufficient that change is so sudden that owner of land washed away is able to point out approximately as much land added to opposite bank as he had washed away.

See Accretion; Alluvion; Dereliction; Erosion; Reliction.

Await. Used in old statutes to signify a lying in wait, or waylaying.

Award, v. To grant, concede, or adjudge to. To give or assign by sentence or judicial determination or after careful weighing of evidence. Thus, a jury *awards* damages; the court *awards* an injunction; one *awards* a contract to a bidder. To confer as being deserved or merited.

Award, n. The decision or determination rendered by arbitrators or commissioners, or other private or extrajudicial deciders, upon a controversy submitted to them; also the writing or document embodying such decision. *See also* Final award; Prize.

Away-going crop. A crop sown before the expiration of a tenancy, which cannot ripen until after its expiration to which, however, the tenant is entitled.

A.W.W. Abbreviation for "average weekly wage". Term used in worker's compensation computations.

B

Baby Act. A plea of infancy, interposed for the purpose of defeating an action upon a contract made while the person was a minor, is vulgarly called "pleading the baby act". By extension, the term is applied to a plea of the statute of limitations.

Back, *v.* To indorse; to sign on the back; to sign generally by way of acceptance or approval; to substantiate; to countersign; to assume financial responsibility for.

Back, *adv.* To the rear; backward; in a reverse direction. Also, in arrear.

Backadation. *See* Backwardation.

Backdating. Predating a document or instrument prior to the date it was actually drawn. The negotiability of an instrument is not affected by the fact that it is backdated. U.C.C. § 3–114.

Backhaul. In freight transportation, to carry a shipment back over a segment of a route already covered.

Backing. Indorsement.

Back lands. A term of no very definite import, but generally signifying lands lying back from (not contiguous to) a highway or a water course.

Backlog. Accumulation of unfilled orders.

Back order. An unfilled customer order or commitment, normally occurring because inventory is not sufficient to fill the order upon receipt from the customer.

Back pay award. Difference between wages already paid an employee and higher wages granted retroactively. A determination by a judicial or quasi judicial body that an employee is entitled to accrued but uncollected salary, wages or fringe benefits. Such may be awarded in employment discrimination cases.

Backspread. Less than normal price difference in arbitrage.

Back taxes. Those assessed for a previous year or years and remaining due and unpaid from the original tax debtor.

Back title letter. Letter given by title insurance company to an attorney advising of condition of title as of a certain date. Attorney then starts examination of title as of that date.

Back-to-back loan. A form of loan barter arrangement whereby two firms lend each other funds denominated in different currencies for an agreed period.

Back to work agreement. Agreement between union and employer covering terms and conditions upon which employees will return to work following settlement of strike.

Backwardation (also called Backadation) /bæk-wərdéyshən/. In the language of the stock exchange, this term signifies a consideration paid for delay in the delivery of stock contracted for, when the price is lower for time than for cash.

Backwards. In a policy of marine insurance, the phrase "forwards and backwards at sea" means from port to port in the course of the voyage, and not merely from one terminus to the other and back.

Backwater. Water in a stream which, in consequence of some dam or obstruction below, is detained or checked in its course, or flows back.

Bacon-Davis Act. Federal law (1931) granting Secretary of Labor power to set wage rates on public construction work to meet wages in private sector. 40 U.S.C.A. § 276a.

Bad. Vicious, evil, wanting in good qualities; the opposite of good. Defective, faulty, inferior, or imperfect.

Bad character. Absence of moral virtue; the predominance of evil habits in a person. In law of evidence, such character may be shown to affect credibility of witness by introduction of record of convictions for crimes or by reputation. Fed.Evid.R. 608, 609.

Bad check. A check which is dishonored on presentation for payment because of no, or insufficient, funds or closed bank account. Writing or passing of bad checks is a misdemeanor in most states. Model Penal Code § 224.5. *See also* Check kiting; Worthless (*Worthless check*).

Bad debt. A debt which is uncollectible; a permissible deduction for tax purposes in arriving at taxable income. I.R.C. § 166. Different tax treatment is afforded business and non-business bad debts. A business debt is defined by the Internal Revenue Code as a debt created or acquired in connection with a trade or business of the taxpayer, or a debt which becomes worthless in the taxpayer's trade or business. Loans between related parties (family members) generally are classified as nonbusiness. *See also* Nonbusiness bad debts.

A deduction is permitted if a business account receivable subsequently becomes worthless providing the income arising from the debt was previously included in income. The deduction is allowed only in the year of worthlessness.

Bad-debt loss ratio. The proportion of the total receivables volume that is never collected by a business.

Bad debt reserve. An account used in bookkeeping to reflect the true worth of receivables in the balance sheet by estimating those debts which may not be collected and which ultimately will be written off as bad debts and claimed as a deduction for tax purposes. *See also* Reserve.

Bad faith. The opposite of "good faith," generally implying or involving actual or constructive fraud, or a design to mislead or deceive another, or a neglect or refusal to fulfill some duty or some contractual obligation, not prompted by an honest mistake as to one's rights or duties, but by some interested or sinister motive. Term "bad faith" is not simply bad judgment or negligence, but rather it implies the conscious doing of a wrong because of dishonest purpose or moral obliquity; it is different from the negative idea of negligence in that it contemplates a state of mind affirmatively operating with furtive design or ill will. An intentional tort which results from breach of duty imposed as consequence of relationship established by contract.

Insurance. "Bad faith" on part of insurer is any frivolous or unfounded refusal to pay proceeds of policy; it is not necessary that such refusal be fraudulent. For purposes of an action against an insurer for failure to pay a claim, such conduct imports a dishonest purpose and means a breach of a known duty (*i.e.*, good faith and fair dealing), through some motive of self-interest or ill will; mere negligence or bad judgment is not bad faith.

Badger. To harass, pester, or bedevil persistently especially in a manner likely or designed to confuse, annoy or wear down. *See also* Harassment.

Badges of fraud. A circumstance or other fact accompanying a transfer of property that the courts recognize as an especially reliable indicator of the transferor's actual intention to hinder, delay, or defraud creditors in making the transfer. It is defined as a fact tending to throw suspicion upon a transaction, and calling for an explanation. It is a suspicious circumstance that overhangs a transaction, or appears on the face of the papers. A circumstance which does not alone prove fraud, but which warrants inference of fraud, especially where there is a concurrence of many such badges. Recognized "badges of fraud" include fictitious consideration, false statements as to consideration, transactions different from

usual course of doing business, transfer of all of a debtor's property, insolvency, confidential relationship of parties, and transfers in anticipation of suit or execution.

Bad motive. Intentionally doing a wrongful act knowing at the time that it is wrongful. *See* Bad faith.

Bad title. One which conveys no property to the purchaser of the estate. One which is so radically defective that it is not marketable, and hence such that a purchaser cannot be legally compelled to accept it. *Compare* Marketable title.

Bail, *v.* To procure release of one charged with an offense by insuring his future attendance in court and compelling him to remain within jurisdiction of court. To deliver the defendant to persons who, in the manner prescribed by law, become security for his appearance in court. To set at liberty a person arrested or imprisoned, on security being taken for his appearance on a day and a place certain, which security is called "bail," because the party arrested or imprisoned is delivered into the hands of those who bind themselves for his forthcoming. *See also* Civil bail; Excessive bail; Jump bail; Release on own recognizance.

Bail, *n.* Monetary amount for or condition of pretrial release from custody, normally set by a judge at the initial appearance. The purpose of bail is to ensure the return of the accused at subsequent proceedings. If the accused is unable to make bail, or otherwise unable to be released on his or her own recognizance, he or she is detained in custody. The Eighth Amendment (U.S. Const.) provides that excessive bail shall not be required.

The surety or sureties who procure the release of a person under arrest, by becoming responsible for his appearance at the time and place designated. Those persons who become sureties for the appearance of the defendant in court.

Bail absolute. Sureties whose liability is conditioned upon the failure of the principal to duly account for money coming to his hands as administrator, guardian, etc.

Bail bond. A three-party contract which involves the state, accused and surety and under which surety guarantees the state that accused will appear at subsequent court proceedings.

A written undertaking, executed by the defendant or one or more sureties, that the defendant designated in such instrument will, while at liberty as a result of an order fixing bail and of the execution of a bail bond in satisfaction thereof, appear in a designated criminal action or proceeding when his attendance is required and otherwise render himself amenable to the orders and processes of the court, and that in the event he fails to do so, the signers of the bond will pay to the court (*i.e.* forfeit) the amount of money specified in the order fixing bail. Fed.R.Crim.P. 46; 18 U.S.C.A. § 3141 et seq. *See also* Release on own recognizance.

Cash bail bond. A sum of money, in the amount designated in an order fixing bail, posted by a defendant or by another person on his behalf (surety) with a court or other authorized public officer upon condition that such money will be forfeited if the defendant does not comply with the directions of a court requiring his attendance at the criminal action or proceeding involved and does not otherwise render himself amenable to the orders and processes of the court.

Unsecured bail bond. A bail bond for which the defendant is fully liable upon failure to appear in court when ordered to do so or upon breach of a material condition of release, but which is not secured by any deposit of or lien upon property. *See* Release on own recognizance.

Bail in error. That given by a defendant who intends to bring a writ of error on the judgment and desires a stay of execution in the meantime.

Bail point scale. System whereby a predetermined number of points are given for all positive aspects of the defendant's background. The total number of points determine whether the defendant will be released on his own recognizance or the amount of bail to be set for his release.

Civil bail. See that title.

Bailable. Capable of being bailed; admitting of bail; authorizing or requiring bail.

Bailable action. One in which the defendant is entitled to be discharged from arrest only upon giving bond to answer.

Bailable offense. One for which the prisoner may be admitted to bail.

Bailable process. Such as requires the officer to take bail, after arresting the defendant. That under which the sheriff is directed to arrest the defendant and is required by law to discharge him upon his tendering suitable bail as security for his appearance.

Bail bond. *See* Bail.

Bailee. In the law of contracts, one to whom goods are bailed; one to whom goods are entrusted by a bailor; the party to whom personal property is delivered under a contract of bailment. A species of agent to whom something movable is committed in trust for another. Under U.C.C., a person who by warehouse receipt, bill of lading or other document of title acknowledges possession of goods and contracts to deliver them. The transferee of goods under a bailment, including a warehouseperson or a carrier. U.C.C. § 7–102. *See* Gratuitous bailee.

Bailee for hire. A person to whom possession of personal property is transferred and who is compensated for caring for such property; *e.g.* a mechanic to whom an automobile is entrusted for repairs is a bailee for hire. *See also* Bailment (*Bailment for mutual benefit*).

Bailee policies. Floating insurance policies which cover goods while in possession of bailee without particular description in the policy.

Bailee's lien. Bailee's right (usually statutory) to retain bailed goods for payment of services.

Bailiff. A court officer or attendant who has charge of a court session in the matter of keeping order, custody of the jury, and custody of prisoners while in the court. One to whom some authority, care, guardianship, or jurisdiction is delivered, committed, or intrusted. One who is deputed or appointed to take charge of another's affairs; an overseer or superintendent; a keeper, protector, or guardian; a steward.

A person acting in a ministerial capacity who has by delivery the custody and administration of lands or goods for the benefit of the owner or bailor, and is liable to render an account thereof.

Special bailiff. A deputy sheriff, appointed at the request of a party to a suit, for the special purpose of serving or executing some writ or process in such suit.

Bailiwick /béyləwìk/. A territorial segment over which a bailiff or sheriff has jurisdiction; not unlike a county in today's governmental divisions.

Bailment. A delivery of goods or personal property, by one person (bailor) to another (bailee), in trust for the execution of a special object upon or in relation to such goods, beneficial either to the bailor or bailee or both, and upon a contract, express or implied, to perform the trust and carry out such object, and thereupon either to redeliver the goods to the bailor or otherwise dispose of the same in conformity with the purpose of the trust. The bailee is responsible for exercising due care toward the goods.

Delivery of personalty for some particular use, or on mere deposit, upon a contract, express or implied, that after purpose has been fulfilled it shall be redelivered to the person who delivered it, or otherwise dealt with according to his directions, or kept until he reclaims it, as the case may be.

Generally, no fiduciary relationship is created by a bailment and hence it is not accurate to refer to the transfer as "in trust", because no trustee-beneficiary relationship is created. *See also* Pawn; Pledge.

Actual bailment. One which exists where there is either: (a) an "actual delivery," consisting in giving to the bailee or his agent the real possession of the chattel, or (b) a "constructive delivery," consisting of any of those acts which, although not truly comprising real possession of the goods transferred, have been held by legal construction equivalent to acts of real delivery.

Bailment for hire. A contract in which the bailor agrees to compensate the bailee. *See also* Bailee for hire, *supra;* and *Bailment for mutual benefit, below.*

Bailment for mutual benefit. One in which the parties contemplate some price or compensation in return for benefits flowing from the bailment, necessarily involving an express or implied agreement or undertaking to that effect. For example, delivery of automobile to one who, for a consideration, undertakes to repair it.

Bailment lease. A legal method by which one desiring to purchase an article but unable to pay therefor at the time, may secure possession thereof with the right to use and enjoy it as long as he pays stipulated rentals and becomes absolute owner after completing such installment payments, on payment of an additional sum which may be nominal. This right or option is common in auto lease agreements.

Constructive bailment. One arising where the person having possession of a chattel holds it under such circumstances that the law imposes upon him the obligation to deliver it to another. *See also Involuntary bailment, below.*

Gratuitous bailment. Another name for a depositum or naked bailment, which is made only for the benefit of the bailor and is not a source of profit to the bailee.

Involuntary bailment. One arising by the accidental leaving of personal property in the possession of any person without negligence on the part of its owner. *See Constructive bailment, above.*

Lucrative bailment. One which is undertaken upon a consideration and for which a payment or recompense is to be made to the bailee, or from which he is to derive some advantage. *See Bailment for hire, above.*

Special bailment. In general, a bailment in which by law a bailee is given greater duties and liabilities than those imposed on an ordinary bailee. Innkeepers and common carrier bailees are examples.

Bailor. The party who *bails* or delivers goods to another (bailee) in the contract of bailment. The transferor of goods under a bailment.

Bailout. Various procedures whereby the owners of an entity can obtain its profits with favorable tax consequences. With corporations, for example, the bail-out of corporate profits without dividend consequences might be the desired objective. The alternative of distributing the profits to the shareholders as dividends generally is less attractive, since dividend income is taxed as ordinary income. *See* Preferred stock (*Preferred stock bailout*).

Acquisition of a corporation for the principal purpose of favorable tax consequences by securing benefits of deduction, credit or other allowance which the acquiring corporation would not otherwise enjoy. I.R.C. § 269.

Bailout stock. When preferred stock is issued as a stock dividend and is non-taxable, it is called bailout stock. I.R.C. § 305.

Bait and switch. A deceptive sales practice. Such tactic usually involves advertising a low-priced product to lure customers to a store, then inducing them to buy higher-priced models by failing to stock sufficient quantities of the lower-priced item to satisfy demand, or by disparaging the less-expensive product. Such practices are prohibited by statute in most states. See Model Penal Code § 224.7(5).

Balance. The difference between the sum of debit entries minus the sum of credit entries in an account. If positive, the difference is called a debit balance; if negative, a credit balance.

Often used in the sense of residue or remainder, and, in a general sense, may be defined as what remains or is left over.

See also Average daily balance; Normal balance.

Balance of payments. The difference between all payments made by one nation to all other nations in the world and the payments made to that nation by all other nations. An official accounting record that follows double-entry bookkeeping practices and records all of a country's foreign transactions. The country's exports are recorded as credits and imports as debits.

Balance of power. In international law, a distribution and an opposition of forces, forming one system, so that no nation or country shall be in a position, either alone or united with others, to impose its will on any other nation or country or interfere with its independence. *See also* Separation of powers.

Balance of trade. Part of the balance of payments. It shows the net figure for the value of all the goods imported and exported by one nation. An excess of imports over exports constitutes a trade deficit.

Balance sheet. A statement of financial position of any economic unit, disclosing as at a given moment in time, the value of its assets, liabilities, and equity of the owners in conformity with generally accepted accounting principles. *See also* Profit and loss statement.

Consolidated balance sheet. A statement of financial position which combines the assets, liabilities, and stockholders equity of a parent corporation and its subsidiary.

Net balance. In commercial usage, the balance of the proceeds, as from a sale of stock, after deducting the expenses incident to the sale.

Balancing of interests. Constitutional doctrine invoked when court is examining interplay between state action involving intrastate commerce and federal laws regarding interstate commerce. If there is legitimate state interest and if there is no clear congressional intent to preempt the field, state action will be upheld.

Balancing test. A constitutional doctrine in which the court weighs the right of an individual to certain rights guaranteed by the Constitution with the rights of a state to protect its citizens from the invasion of their rights; used in cases involving freedom of speech and equal protection.

Balancing the equities. Doctrine commonly invoked in cases involving, for example, encroachment of building on another's land in which court will deny equitable relief to offended party in favor of money damages if the encroachment was made innocently and by mistake (not intentionally) and if encroachment is slight as compared with injury to offending party if he is required to remove.

Ballistics /bəlístəks/. The science of gun examination frequently used in criminal cases, especially cases of homicide, to determine the firing capacity of a weapon, its fireability, and whether a given bullet was fired from a particular gun.

Balloon mortgage. A mortgage providing for specific payments at stated regular intervals, with the final payment considerably more than any of the periodic payments.

Balloon note. A form of promissory note which commonly calls for minimum payments of principal, if any, and the payment of interest at regular intervals, but which requires a substantial payment of principal at the end of the term; the final payment frequently representing essentially all the principal.

Balloon payment. The final payment of principal under a balloon note; commonly representing essentially the entire principal. *See* Balloon mortgage; Balloon note.

Ballot. Derived from ballotta, a round bullet, used for casting a vote. Process or means of voting, usually in secret, by written or printed tickets or slips of paper, or voting machine. Piece of paper or levers on voting machine on which the voter gives expression to his choice. A means, or instrumentality, by which a voter secretly indicates his will or choice so that it may be recorded as being in favor of a certain candidate or for or against a certain proposition or measure.

The whole amount of votes cast. Also, list of candidates running for office.

Australian ballot. See Australian ballot.

Joint ballot. In parliamentary practice, an election or vote by ballot participated in by the members of both houses of a legislative assembly sitting together as one body, the result being determined by a majority of the votes cast by the joint assembly thus constituted, instead of by concurrent majorities of the two houses.

Massachusetts ballot. See that title.

Mutilated ballot. One from which the name of the candidate is excised or cut out. One which is without or deprived of some essential or valuable part; greatly shortened ballot.

Office block ballot. A ballot form on which the names of all candidates for a particular office are listed under the office title. Listings are made under various titles regardless of the various party affiliations of the candidates.

Official ballot. Depending on its use in local statutes, this term has a varied meaning. It may refer to a ballot which has been furnished by the clerk; or it may contemplate that a ballot must have been printed under the supervision of a designated member of the electoral board, sealed by the board, and by resolution declared to be one of the official ballots for the election to be held.

Party column ballot. Ballot form on which the names of all candidates of each political party are placed in separate columns under party names and symbols, regardless of the offices sought by the candidates.

Secret ballot. The expression by ballot, voting machine, or otherwise, but in no event by proxy, of a choice with respect to any election or vote taken upon any matter, which is cast in such a manner that the person expressing such choice cannot be identified with the choice expressed.

Ballot-box. A locked box wherein ballots are deposited.

Banc /bǽŋk/báŋk/. Bench; the place where a court permanently or regularly sits; the seat of judgment; as, *banc le roy,* the king's bench; *banc le common pleas,* the bench of common pleas.

The full bench, full court. A "sitting *en banc*" is a meeting of all the judges of a court as distinguished from the sitting of a single judge or panel of judges.

Banishment. A punishment inflicted upon criminals, by compelling them to leave a country for a specified period of time, or for life. Synonymous with exilement or deportation, importing a compulsory loss of one's country. *See also* Deportation.

Bank. A bank is an institution, usually incorporated, whose business it is to receive money on deposit, cash checks or drafts, discount commercial paper, make loans, and issue promissory notes payable to bearer, known as bank notes. U.C.C. § 1–201(4). American commercial banks fall into two main categories: state chartered banks and federally chartered national banks. *See also* Banking.

A bench or seat; the bench of justice; the bench or tribunal occupied by the judges; the seat of judgment; a court. The full bench, or full court; the assembly of all the judges of a court. *See* Banc.

An acclivity; an elevation or mound of earth, especially that which borders the sides of a water course. The land adjacent to a river. That part of a stream which retains the water. The elevation of land which confines the waters of a stream in their natural channel when they rise the highest and do not overflow the banks. A water-washed and relatively permanent elevation or acclivity at the outer line of a river bed which separates the bed from the adjacent upland, and serves to confine the waters within the bed and to preserve the course of the river. The land lying between the edge of the water of a stream at its ordinary low stage and the line which the edge of the water reaches in its ordinary high stage. An elevation of land which confines the waters of a stream when they rise out of the bed. Neither the line of ordinary high-water mark, nor of ordinary low-water mark, nor of a middle stage of water can be assumed as the line dividing the bed from the banks. Banks are fast land, on which vegetation appropriate to such land in the particular locality grows wherever the bank is not too steep to permit such growth, and bed is soil of a different character, and having no vegetation, or only such as exists, when commonly submerged in water. On the borders of navigable streams, where there are levees established according to law, the levees form the "banks of the river."

Advising bank. A bank which gives notification of the issuance of a credit by another bank. U.C.C. § 5–103(e).

Bank acceptance. Draft drawn on and accepted by bank.

Bank-account. A sum of money placed with a bank or banker, on deposit, by a customer, and subject to be drawn out on the latter's check. The statement or computation of the several sums deposited and those drawn out by the customer on checks, entered on the books of the bank and the depositor's passbook. Any account with a bank, including a checking, time, interest or savings account. U.C.C. § 4–104(a). *See also* Joint bank account; Zero balance bank account.

Bank bill. See Bank note, below.

Bank book. A book kept by a customer of a bank, showing the state of his account with it. *See* Passbook.

Bank call. Demand made on bank by state or federal supervisory personnel for examination of balance sheets.

Bank charter. Document issued by appropriate federal or state authority which permits corporation to commence business as a bank.

Bank credit. A credit with a bank by which, on proper credit rating or proper security given to the bank, a person receives liberty to draw to a certain extent agreed upon.

Bank debit. Total of checks and other commercial paper charged to deposit accounts.

Bank deposit. Cash, checks, or drafts placed with bank for credit to depositor's account. Placement of money in bank thereby creating contract between bank and depositor. U.C.C. § 4–103.

Demand deposit. Right to withdraw deposit at any time.

Time deposit. Deposit which is subject to notice (*e.g.* thirty days) before withdrawal.

Bank depositor. One who delivers to or leaves with a bank a sum of money subject to his order.

Bank draft. A check, draft, or other order for payment of money, drawn by an authorized officer of a bank upon either his own bank or some other bank in which funds of his bank are deposited. An order to pay that is similar to a check, except that it is not payable on demand. Instead, a bank draft is payable when the issuing firm accepts it.

Bank note. A promissory note issued by a bank or banker authorized to do so, payable to bearer on demand, and intended to circulate as money. *See* Federal reserve notes.

Bank of circulation. One which issues bank notes payable to bearer. *See Bank of issue, below.*

Bank of deposit. A savings bank or any other bank which receives money on deposit.

Bank of discount. One which lends money on collateral or by means of discounts of commercial paper.

Bank of issue. Bank with authority to issue notes intended to circulate as currency.

Bank rate. Interest rate charged customers on loans. *See* Interest; Legal interest.

Bank statement. Financial statement showing financial condition of bank at a given time. Federal (national banks) and state laws require that such statements be published several times a year.

Also, a document that summarizes the activity in a checking account.

Bank stock. Shares in the capital of a bank; shares in the property of a bank.

Branch banking. *See* Branch bank.

Central banks. Federal Reserve banks.

Collecting bank. Any bank handling the item for collection except the payor bank. U.C.C. § 4–105(d). *See also* Collecting bank.

Commercial bank. *See* Commercial bank.

Confirming bank. A bank which engages either that it will itself honor a credit already issued by another bank or that such a credit will be honored by the issuer or a third bank. U.C.C. § 5–103(f). *See also* Confirming bank.

Correspondent bank. Bank which acts as agent for another bank, or engages in an exchange of services with that bank, in a geographical area to which the other does not have direct access.

Custodian bank. Any bank or trust company which is supervised and examined by state or federal authority having supervision over banks and which is acting as custodian for a clearing corporation. U.C.C. § 8–102(4).

Depository bank. The first bank to which an item is transferred for collection even though it is also the payor bank. U.C.C. § 4–105(a).

Export-import bank. *See* Export-Import Bank.

Federal land bank. *See* Federal Land Banks.

Federal reserve bank. *See* Federal Reserve System.

Intermediary bank. Any bank to which an item is transferred in course of collection except the depositary or payor bank. U.C.C. § 4–105(c). *See also* Intermediary bank.

Land bank. *See* Land bank.

Member bank. *See* Member bank.

Mutual savings bank. *See* Mutual savings bank.

National bank. *See* National bank.

Non-member bank. Bank that is not a member of the Federal Reserve Board and, as such, is only governed by laws of state where chartered.

Payor bank. A bank by which an item is payable as drawn or accepted. U.C.C. § 4–105(b).

Presenting bank. Any bank presenting an item except a payor bank. U.C.C. § 4–105(e).

Remitting bank. Any payor or intermediary bank remitting for an item. U.C.C. § 4–105(f).

Savings and loan bank. *See* Mutual savings bank; Savings and loan association.

Savings bank. Type of bank that receives deposits, and pays interest thereon, and makes certain types of loans (*e.g.* home financing loans), but does not provide checking services. *See* Mutual savings bank; Savings and loan association. *Compare* Commercial bank.

World bank. See that title.

Bankable paper. Notes, checks, bank bills, drafts and other securities for money, received as cash by banks.

Bank bill. *See* Bank *(Bank note).*

Bank clearings. *See* Clearinghouse.

Bank collection float. The time that elapses between when a check is deposited into a bank account and when the funds are available to the depositor (during which period the bank is collecting payment from the payer's bank). *See also* Float.

Banker. In general sense, person that engages in business of banking. In narrower meaning, a private person who keeps a bank; one who is engaged in the business of banking without being incorporated. One who carries on the business of banking by receiving money on deposit with or without interest, by buying and selling bills of exchange, promissory notes, bonds or stock, or other securities, and by loaning money without being incorporated. *See also* Investment banker.

Person who holds stake in gambling game or wager.

Banker's acceptance. A draft accepted by a bank usually for the purpose of financing a sale of goods to or by the bank's customer. A bill of exchange draft payable at maturity that is drawn by a creditor against his or her debtor. Banker's acceptances are short-term credit instruments most commonly used by persons or firms engaged in international trade. They are comparable to short-term government securities (for example, Treasury Bills) and may be sold on the open market at a discount.

Banker's lien. A lien which a banker has by virtue of which he can appropriate any money or property in his possession belonging to a customer to the extinguishment of any matured debt of such customer to the bank, provided such property or money has not been charged, with the knowledge of the bank, with the subservience of a special burden or purpose, or does not constitute a trust fund of which the banker has notice.

Banker's note. A commercial instrument resembling a bank note in every particular except that it is given by a private banker or unincorporated banking institution.

Bank holding company. Any company which has control over any bank or over any company that is or becomes a bank holding company. A company is considered to have control if it directly or indirectly or acting through one or more other persons owns, controls, or has power to vote

25% or more of any class of voting securities of the bank or company; the company controls in any manner the election of a majority of the directors or trustees of the bank or company; or, it is determined that the company directly or indirectly exercises a controlling influence over the management or policies of the bank or company. 12 U.S.C.A. §§ 1841–1850.

Bank Holding Company Act. Federal law which governs any company which directly or indirectly owns or controls, with power to vote, more than 25% of voting shares of each of two or more banks. See 12 U.S.C.A. § 184 et seq.

Banking. The business of banking, as defined by law and custom, consists in the issue of notes payable on demand intended to circulate as money when the banks are banks of issue; in receiving deposits payable on demand; in discounting commercial paper; making loans of money on collateral security; buying and selling bills of exchange; negotiating loans, and dealing in negotiable securities issued by the government, state and national, and municipal and other corporations.

Investment banking. Business of underwriting or distributing bond, stock or other securities issues.

Banking Act of 1933. *See* Glass–Steagall Act.

Banking commission. State regulatory body charged with supervision of banking institutions. *See also* Federal Reserve Board of Governors with respect to regulation of national banks.

Banking day. That part of any day on which a bank is open to the public for carrying on substantially all of its banking functions. U.C.C. § 4–104(c).

Bank reconciliation. A process for determining the amount of cash that a company has control over and reports on its balance sheet.

Bankrupt. The state or condition of a person (individual, partnership, corporation, municipality) who is unable to pay its debts as they are, or become, due. The condition of one whose circumstances are such that he is entitled to take the benefit of the federal bankruptcy laws. The term includes a person against whom an involuntary petition has been filed, or who has filed a voluntary petition, or who has been adjudged a bankrupt. The word "bankrupt" is not used in the federal Bankruptcy Code. "Debtor" is now the term used. See Code § 101.

See Arrangement with creditors; Bankruptcy Code; Bankruptcy proceedings; Composition with creditors; Contemplation of bankruptcy; Insolvency.

Bankruptcy Code. A federal law (11 U.S.C.A.) for the benefit and relief of creditors and their debtors in cases in which the latter are unable or unwilling to pay their debts. The Bankruptcy Code of 1978 substantially revised and replaced the Bankruptcy Act of 1898. Straight bankruptcy is in the nature of a liquidation proceeding and involves the collection and distribution to creditors of all the bankrupt's non-exempt property by the trustee in the manner provided by the Code (Chapter 7). The debtor rehabilitation provisions of the Code (Chapters 11, 12 and 13) differ, however, from the straight bankruptcy in that the debtor looks to rehabilitation and reorganization, rather than liquidation, and the creditor looks to future earnings of the bankrupt, rather than property held by the bankrupt to satisfy their claims; *see, e.g.,* Bankruptcy proceedings (*Business reorganizations, Wage earner's plan*).

Bankruptcy proceedings. General term for the various types of proceedings under the Bankruptcy Code (11 U.S.C.A.) that are initiated either by an insolvent individual or business (termed a voluntary bankruptcy) or by creditors (termed an involuntary bankruptcy) seeking to either have the debtor's remaining assets distributed among the creditors and to thereby discharge the debtor from any further obligation or to restructure and reorganize the insolvent's debt structure. *See* Bankruptcy Code, *supra,* and various types of bankruptcy *below.* *See also* Adequate protection; Automatic stay; Composition with creditors; Core proceeding; Cramdown; Debtor in possession; Workout.

Adjudication of bankruptcy. The judgment or decree of the bankruptcy court that a person against whom a petition in bankruptcy has been filed, or who has filed his voluntary petition, be ordered and adjudged to be a bankrupt. *See Bankruptcy discharge, below.*

Bankruptcy courts. Federal courts which are concerned exclusively with the administration of bankruptcy proceedings and presided over by a bankruptcy judge. Legal bankruptcy is declared by such courts. 28 U.S.C.A. § 151. Bankruptcy courts exercise jurisdiction as generally provided in 28 U.S.C.A. § 1334. See also 11 U.S.C.A. § 105.

Bankruptcy discharge. Order of Bankruptcy Court which discharges debtor from all dischargeable obligations and debts. For effect of, and exceptions to, discharge, see Bankruptcy Code §§ 523, 524, 727.

Bankruptcy distribution. After payment of administration, priority and other debts and expenses of bankrupt estate, trustee in bankruptcy makes pro rata distribution to creditors. See Bankruptcy Code § 726.

Bankruptcy estate. The "bankruptcy estate" is comprised of all legal and equitable interests in property of debtors as of filing of bankruptcy petition. 11 U.S.C.A. § 541 et seq.

Bankruptcy forms. Official forms used in Bankruptcy Court for most matters (*e.g.* petitions, schedules).

Bankruptcy rules. Rules (*i.e.* Federal Rules of Bankruptcy Procedure) governing proceedings in bankruptcy courts; many of which make the Federal Rules of Civil Procedure and Evidence applicable in adversary proceedings.

Bankruptcy schedules. Official forms for listing of debtor's assets, liabilities, and all unsecured creditors.

Bankruptcy trustee. Person appointed by Bankruptcy Court to take charge of debtor estate, to collect assets, to bring suit on debtor's claims, to defend actions against it, and otherwise administer debtor's estate; he has power to examine debtor, to initiate actions to set aside preferences, etc. 11 U.S.C.A. § 321 et seq., 704; 28 U.S.C.A. § 581 et seq.

Business reorganizations (Chapter 11). When a debtor business entity realizes that it will become insolvent or will be unable to pay its debts as they mature, it can petition for reorganization under Chapter 11 of the Bankruptcy Code. The debtor business normally is permitted to continue its operations under court supervision until some plan of reorganization is approved by two-thirds of the creditors. If the business is insolvent at the time a petition for reorganization is filed, a majority of the shareholders must also approve the plan. If agreement cannot be reached, then the court will supervise liquidation proceedings for the business as in any other situation of bankruptcy. *See also Family Farmer Bankruptcy, below.*

Family farmer bankruptcy (Chapter 12). Chapter 12 of the Bankruptcy Code provides special debt repayment relief for a "family farmer with regular income" whose annual income is sufficiently stable and regular to enable such farmer to make payments under a plan as provided under this Chapter.

Involuntary proceedings. Creditors of an insolvent debtor may initiate proceedings under the Bankruptcy Code, thereby in effect forcing the debtor into bankruptcy. *See Straight bankruptcy, below.*

Straight bankruptcy (Chapter 7). A proceeding designed to liquidate the debtor's property, pay off his or her creditors, and discharge the debtor from his or her other debts. It can be either voluntary (started by the debtor himself or herself) or involuntary (started by the debtor's creditors). *Compare Business reorganizations (Chapter 11); Wage earner's plan (Chapter 13),* this topic, which are rehabilitative proceedings.

Voluntary proceedings. A proceeding under the Bankruptcy Code by which a debtor initiates action either to rehabilitate his business (*e.g.,* Chapter 11 reorganization) or to liquidate (*e.g.,* Chapter 7 liquidation).

Wage earner's plan (Chapter 13). Under Chapter 13 of the Bankruptcy Code, any insolvent debtor who is a wage earner (earns wages, salary, or commissions) can formulate and file a plan with the court that provides the debtor with additional time to pay-off unsecured creditors. The debtor's plan must provide that future earnings will be subject to the supervision and control of the trustee until these debts are satisfied. A plan made in good faith and acceptable to the unsecured creditors will be confirmed by the court. Should the wage earner ultimately be unable to pay the debts, Chapter 7 liquidation is still an available alternative.

Bank Secrecy Act. Enacted in 1970, this statute authorizes the Secretary of the Treasury to prescribe by regulation certain recordkeeping and reporting requirements for banks and other financial institutions in the United States. The purpose of the Act is to require the maintenance of records, and the making of certain reports which are highly useful in criminal, tax, or regulatory investigations or proceedings.

Title I of the Act, and the implementing regulations, require financial institutions to maintain records of the identities of their customers, to make microfilm copies of certain checks drawn on them, and to keep records of certain other items. Title II of the Act and its implementing regulations require reports of certain domestic and foreign currency transactions. 12 U.S.C.A. §§ 1730d, 1829b, 1951–1959, and 31 U.S.C.A. §§ 1051–1062, 1081–1083, 1101–1105, 1121–1122.

Banns of matrimony. Public notice or proclamation of a matrimonial contract, and the intended celebration of the marriage of the parties in pursuance of such contract. Such announcement is required by certain religions to be made in a church or chapel, during service, on three consecutive Sundays before the marriage is celebrated. The object is to afford an opportunity for any person to interpose an objection if he knows of any impediment or other just cause why the marriage should not take place.

Bar. The court, in its strictest sense, sitting in full term. The presence, actual or constructive, of the court. Thus a trial *at bar* is one had before the full court, distinguished from a trial had before a single judge at *nisi prius.* So the "case at bar" is the case now before the court and under its consideration; the case being tried or argued.

In another sense, the whole body of attorneys and counsellors, or the members of the legal profession, collectively, who are figuratively called the "bar". They are thus distinguished from the "bench," which term denotes the whole body of judges. Bar associations of attorneys may be either national, state, or local. *See* Bar association. *Compare* Bench.

In the practice of legislative bodies, the outer boundary of the house; therefore, all persons, not being members, who wish to address the house, or are summoned to it, appear *at the bar* for that purpose.

In the law of contracts, an impediment, obstacle, or preventive barrier. Thus, relationship within the prohibited degrees is a *bar* to marriage. In this sense also we speak of the "bar of the statute of limitations."

That which defeats, annuls, cuts off, or puts an end to. Thus, a provision "in bar of dower" is one which has the effect of defeating or cutting off the dower-rights which the wife would otherwise become entitled to in the particular land.

In pleading, a special plea, constituting a sufficient answer to an action at law; so called because it *barred, i.e.,* prevented, the plaintiff from further prosecuting it with effect, and, if established by proof, defeated and destroyed the action altogether. Called a special "plea in bar." It may be further described as a plea or peremptory exception of a defendant to destroy the plaintiff's action. Under Fed.Rules Civ.Proc., pleas in bar are abolished in favor of affirmative pleading of defenses in answer. Rule 8(c). *See* Plea (*Plea in bar*).

With respect to claim preclusion, a valid and final personal judgment on the merits against a claimant precludes (bars) a later suit on the same claim or cause of action. It is the principle that a party may not relitigate a cause of action which has been determined previously.

A judgment rendered in a case is a "bar" to further action in the state in which it was rendered and in all other jurisdictions if the court which rendered it has required jurisdiction and if the subsequent action is brought by a party to first action or his privy. *See* Collateral estoppel doctrine; Double jeopardy; Issue preclusion; Res (*Res judicata*).

A particular part of the court-room; for example, the place where prisoners stand at their trial, hence the expression "prisoner at the bar."

In England, a partition or railing running across a court-room, intended to separate the general public from the space occupied by the judges, counsel, jury, and others concerned in the trial of a cause. In the English courts it is the partition behind which all outer-barristers and every member of the public must stand. Solicitors being officers of the court, are admitted within it; as are also queen's counsel, barristers with patents of precedence, and serjeants, in virtue of their ranks. Parties who appear in person also are placed within the bar on the floor of the court.

Bar admission. Act by which one is licensed to practice before courts of a particular state or jurisdiction after satisfying requirements such as bar examination, period of residency or admission on grounds of reciprocity after period of years as member of bar of another jurisdiction.

Bar association. An association of members of the legal profession. Such associations have been organized on the national (American Bar Association; Federal Bar Association), state, county, and even on city levels (*e.g.,* New York City Bar Ass'n). The first was established in Mississippi in 1825, but it is not known to have had a continued existence. An association of Grafton and Coos counties in New Hampshire had an existence before 1800, and probably a more or less continuous life since then, having finally merged into a state association. Membership may be either compulsory (integrated bar) or voluntary.

Bar integration. *See* Integrated bar.

Bareboat charter. A document under which one who charters or leases a boat becomes for the period of the charter the owner for all practical purposes. Lease of vessel without a crew. One whereby charterer assumes full possession and control of the vessel and constitutes the only form of charter that purports to invest temporary powers of ownership in the charterer.

Bare *or* mere licensee. One whose presence on premises is merely tolerated; while a "licensee" or "invitee" is one who is on the premises by invitation, express or implied.

Bare patent license. A grant of authority to make, use or vend patented product throughout the United States or in a given part thereof, with no right of exclusion.

Bare trustee. One whose trust is to convey, and the time has arrived for a conveyance by him. Trustee of a dry trust; or a trustee to whose office no duties were originally attached, or who, although such duties were originally attached to his office, would, on the requisition of his *cestuis que trust*, be compellable in equity to convey the estate to them or by their direction.

Bargain. A mutual undertaking, contract, or agreement. A contract or agreement between two parties, the one to sell or exchange goods or lands, and the other to buy or exchange them. To negotiate over the terms of a purchase or contract. To come to terms. A bargain is an agreement to exchange promises or to exchange a promise for a performance or to exchange performances. Restatement, Second, Contracts, § 3.

Bargain money. These words in a contract for the sale of land have much the same significance as earnest money.

Catching bargain. A bargain by which money is loaned, at an extortionate or extravagant rate, to an heir or any one who has an estate in reversion or expectancy, to be repaid on the vesting of his interest; or a similar unconscionable bargain with such person for the purchase outright of his expectancy. That kind of fraud often perpetrated upon young, inexperienced, or ignorant people. *See* Unconscionable bargain.

Bargain and sale. In conveyancing, the transferring of the property of a thing from one to another, upon valuable consideration, by way of sale. A contract or bargain by the owner of land, in consideration of money or its equivalent paid, to sell land to another person, called the "bargainee," whereupon a use arises in favor of the latter, to whom the seisin is transferred by force of the statute of uses. The expression "bargain and sale" is also applied to transfers of personalty, in cases where there is first an executory agreement for the sale (the bargain), and then an actual and completed sale.

Bargain and sale deed. A deed that has a recitation of consideration coupled with words of conveyance of real property. It is a form of deed of conveyance without any covenants; a bare conveyance to grantee of whatever interest grantor has at time of the conveyance. *See also* Deed.

Bargainee. The grantee of an estate in a deed of a bargain and sale. The party to a bargain to whom the subject-matter of the bargain or thing bargained for is to go.

Bargaining agent. Union recognized and certified as such by NLRB as the exclusive representative of employees in a bargaining unit.

Bargaining for plea. Commonly referred to as plea bargaining in which defendant seeks a lesser sentence in return for plea of guilty; or an attempt to plead guilty to lesser included offense which carries a less severe penalty. *See* Plea bargaining.

Bargaining unit. Labor union or group of jobs authorized to carry on collective bargaining in behalf of employees. A particular group of employees with a similar community of interest appropriate for bargaining with management on labor relations issues. *See* Collective bargaining unit.

Bargain money. *See* Earnest money.

Bargainor. The person who makes a bargain. The party to a bargain who is to receive the consideration and perform the contract by delivery of the subject matter.

Bargain *or* contract in restraint of trade. Any bargain or contract which purports to limit in any way right of either party to work or to do business. *See also* Restraint of trade.

Bargain sale *or* purchase. A sale of property for less than the fair market value of such property. The difference between the sale or purchase price

and the fair market value of the property is required to be accounted for in terms of its tax consequences. Bargain sales and purchases among members of the same family may lead to gift tax consequences. *See* Dividend *(Constructive dividend).*

Barrator /bǽrətər/. One who commits barratry. *See* Barretor.

Barratry /bǽrətriy/. Also spelled "Barretry." The offense of frequently exciting and stirring up quarrels and suits, either at law or otherwise. *See also* Barretor; Champerty.

In maritime law, an act committed by master or mariners of a vessel for some fraudulent or unlawful purpose contrary to their duty to owner and resulting in injury to owner.

Barred. Obstructed by a bar. Subject to hindrance or obstruction by a bar or barrier which, if interposed, will prevent legal redress or recovery; as, when it is said that a claim or cause of action is "barred by the statute of limitations."

Barrel. A measure of capacity, equal (in England) to 36 imperial gallons. The standard United States measure, except as to barrels of petroleum, equals 31½ gallons.

In agricultural and mercantile parlance, as also in the inspection laws, the term means, *prima facie*, not merely a certain quantity, but, further, a certain state of the article; namely, that it is in a cask.

Barretor /bǽrətər/. A common mover, exciter, or maintainer of suits and quarrels either in courts or elsewhere in the country; a disturber of the peace who spreads false rumors and calumnies, whereby discord and disquiet may grow among neighbors. One who frequently excites and stirs up groundless suits and quarrels, either at law or otherwise. *See also* Champerty.

Barrister. In England, an advocate; a counsellor learned in the law who has been admitted to plead at the bar, and who is engaged in conducting the trial or argument of causes. A person called to the bar by the benchers of Inns of Court, giving exclusive right of audience in the Supreme Court.

Barter. The exchange of goods and productive services for other goods and productive services, without the use of money. *See also* Exchange.

Base, *adj.* Low in place or position; inferior; servile; of subordinate degree; impure, adulterated, or alloyed.

Base, *n.* Bottom, foundation, groundwork, that on which a thing rests. The locality on which a military or naval force relies for supplies or from which it initiates operations; *e.g.* air base; military base; marine base; naval base; submarine base.

Base line. Survey line used in the government survey to establish township lines. Horizontal elevation line used as centerline in a highway survey.

Base pay. Wages, exclusive of overtime, bonuses, etc.

Basic crops. Crops usually subject to government price supports, such as wheat, corn, oats, rice, and similar crops.

Basic or **pioneer patent.** One discovered in new field and recognized by scientific world or industry as startling, unexpected, and unprophesied.

Basis. Fundamental principle; groundwork; support; the foundation or groundwork of anything; that upon which anything may rest or the principal component parts of a thing.

Accounting. Term used in accounting, especially in tax accounting, to describe the value assigned to an asset for the purpose of determining gain (or loss) on the sale or transfer or in determining value in the hands of a donee.

Acquisition cost, or some substitute therefor, of an asset used in computing gain or loss on disposition or retirement. The amount assigned to an asset for income tax purposes. For assets acquired by purchase, the basis would be cost (I.R.C. § 1012). Special rules govern the basis of property received by virtue of another's death (I.R.C. § 1014) or by gift (§ 1015), the basis of stock received on a transfer of property to a controlled corporation (§ 358), the basis of the property transferred to the corporation (§ 362), and the basis of property received upon the liquidation of a corporation (§§ 334 and 338).

Adjusted basis. The cost of property acquired, increased for any capital improvements and decreased by the amount of depreciation allowed or allowable. I.R.C. § 1011.

Carryover basis. The basis of property acquired from a decedent dying after December 1979 is the basis of the property in the hands of the decedent immediately preceding death. The basis is further adjusted for transfers of appreciated property, personal items, and exceptions for small estates. I.R.C. § 1023.

Stepped-up basis. In tax accounting, value placed on property which is acquired in a taxable transaction or purchase. I.R.C. § 1012. The basis of property acquired through inheritance, bequest, or devise from a decedent, is the fair market value of the property on the date of death or the fair market value on the alternate valuation date—six months from the date of death. The value is often higher than in the hands of the decedent, resulting in a stepped-up basis. I.R.C. § 1014.

The basis of assets acquired by gift is the donors basis increased either by the amount of the gift

tax paid (for gifts received before 1977) or the portion of the gift tax paid which is due to the increase in the value of the gift (for gifts received after 1976). I.R.C. § 1015.

Substituted basis. In tax accounting, the basis of property acquired in an exchange in which a gain or loss is not recognized, is the basis of the property transferred, except where the property acquired is subject to a lien. I.R.C. § 1031. *See also* Substituted basis.

See also Accrual basis.

Basis of bargain. That on which any affirmation of fact or promise relating to goods sold is predicated, creating an express warranty. U.C.C. § 2–313(1)(a). *See* Essence of the contract.

Bastard. An illegitimate child; a child born before the lawful marriage of its parents; *i.e.* born out of lawful wedlock. *See also* Illegitimate child.

Bastardy (paternity) proceedings. Court proceeding in which the paternity of a child is determined. The method provided by statute of proceeding against the putative father to secure a proper maintenance of his child born out of wedlock. *See* Paternity suit.

Battered child. A child who is suffering serious physical or emotional injury resulting from abuse inflicted upon him including sexual abuse, or from neglect, including malnutrition, or who is determined to be physically dependent upon an addictive drug at birth. *See also* Child abuse.

Battered Child Syndrome. A medicolegal term which describes diagnosis of medical expert based on scientific studies that when child suffers certain types of continuing injuries that injuries were not caused by accidental means. Upon such finding, it is logical to presume that someone "caring" for the child was responsible for injuries.

Battered Woman Syndrome. A term used to categorize the consequences of physical, sexual, or psychological abuse suffered by a woman at the hands of a spouse or lover, and describe how these factors contribute to her psychological entrapment in the relationship.

Battery. Intentional and wrongful physical contact with a person without his or her consent that entails some injury or offensive touching. Criminal battery, defined as the unlawful application of force to the person of another, may be divided into its three basic elements: (1) the defendant's conduct (act or omission); (2) his "mental state," which may be an intent to kill or injure, or criminal negligence, or perhaps the doing of an unlawful act; and (3) the harmful result to the victim, which may be either a bodily injury or an offensive touching. What might otherwise be a battery may be justified; and the consent of the victim may under some circumstances constitute a defense. The consummation of an unlawful assault.

The actual offer to use force to the injury of another person is *assault;* the use of it is *battery,* which always includes an assault; hence the two terms are commonly combined in the term "assault and battery."

An actor is subject to liability to another for battery if: (a) he acts intending to cause a harmful or offensive contact with the person of the other or a third person, or an imminent apprehension of such a contact, and (b) an offensive contact with the person of the other directly or indirectly results. Restatement, Second, Torts § 18.

See also Assault and battery.

Aggravated battery. An unlawful act of violent injury to the person of another, accompanied by circumstances of aggravation, such as the use of deadly weapon, great disparity between the ages and physical conditions of the parties, or the purposeful infliction of shame and disgrace.

Simple battery. One not accompanied by circumstances of aggravation, or not resulting in grievous bodily injury.

Technical battery. A technical battery occurs when a physician or dentist, in the course of treatment, exceeds the consent given by a patient. Although no wrongful intent is present, and in fact there may be a sincere purpose to aid the patient, recovery is permitted unless there is an emergency. However, if the patient benefits from the battery only nominal damages may be recovered.

Battle of the forms. In commercial law, term used to describe effect of multitude of forms used by buyers and sellers to accept and to confirm terms expressed in other forms. U.C.C. § 2–207.

Bawd /bód/. One who procures opportunities for persons of opposite sexes to cohabit in an illicit manner; who may be, while exercising the trade of a bawd, perfectly innocent of committing in his or her own proper person the crime either of adultery or of fornication. A madam.

Bawdy-house. A house of ill fame; a house of prostitution; a brothel. A house or dwelling maintained for the convenience and resort of persons desiring unlawful sexual connection. A place many may frequent for immoral purposes or a house where one may go for immoral purposes without invitation.

Bay. A bending or curving of the shore of the sea or of a lake, so as to form a more or less inclosed body of water. An opening into the land, or an arm of the sea, where the water is shut in on all sides except at the entrance.

Bayou /báyuw/báyow/. A species of creek or stream common in Louisiana and Texas. An outlet from a swamp, pond, or lagoon, to a river, or the sea.

B.C. An abbreviation for "before Christ," "Bankruptcy Court," "bankruptcy cases," and "British Columbia."

Beach. This term, in its ordinary signification, when applied to a place on tide waters means the space between ordinary high and low water mark; or the space over which the tide usually ebbs and flows. It is a term not more significant of a sea margin than "shore." In common parlance designates that portion of shore consisting generally of sand and pebbles, resulting usually from the action of water, as distinct from the upland, to which it often extends above normal high-water mark. Beach is synonymous with "shore," "strand," or "flats." The term may also include the sandy shore above mean high water which is washed by storms and exceptionally high tides.

To "beach" a ship is to run it upon the beach or shore; this is frequently found necessary in case of a fire, leak, etc.

See Foreshore; Seashore.

Public beach. Beach dedicated by governmental body to the common use of the public, which the unorganized public and each of its members have a right to use while it remains such.

Beams and balance. Instruments for weighing goods and merchandise.

Bear. To support, sustain, or carry. To give rise to, or to produce, something else as an incident or auxiliary. To render, to manage, or direct, or to conduct; to carry on, or maintain. To produce as yield; *e.g.* "bear" interest. One who believes stock prices will decline; opposite of a "bull."

Bear arms. The Second Amendment, U.S. Constitution, provides that the "right of the people to bear arms, shall not be infringed." This right has been restricted however by state and federal laws regulating the transportation, sale, use, and possession of weapons.

Bearer. The person in possession of an instrument, document of title, or security payable to bearer or indorsed in blank. U.C.C. § 1–201(5). When a check, note, draft, etc., is payable to "bearer," it imports that such shall be payable to any person who may present the instrument for payment. *See also* Payable to bearer.

Bearer bond. Bonds payable to the person having possession of them. Such bonds do not require endorsement to transfer ownership but only the transfer of possession.

Bearer document. A document that runs to bearer upon issuance or after a blank indorsement, and that is negotiated by delivery alone. U.C.C. §§ 7–501(1) & (2)(a). Anyone in possession of a bearer document is a holder of it. U.C.C. § 1–201(20).

Bearer instrument. An instrument is payable to bearer when by its terms it is payable to (a) bearer or the order of bearer; or (b) a specified person or bearer; or (c) "cash" or the order of "cash", or any other indication which does not purport to designate a specific payee. U.C.C. §§ 3–111, 3–204(2).

Bearer paper. Commercial paper payable to bearer; *i.e.* to the person having possession of such. *See* Bearer document; Bearer instrument.

Bearer security. A security whose owner is not registered on the books of the issuer. Such security is payable to the holder. *See e.g.,* Bearer bond.

Bearing date. Disclosing a date on its face; having a certain date. Words frequently used in pleading and conveyancing to introduce the date which has been put upon an instrument.

Bear interest. To yield, generate, or produce interest on the principal.

Bear market. A market in which prices are falling or are expected to fall.

Beat, *v.* To strike or hit repeatedly, as with blows. In the criminal law and the law of torts, with reference to assault and battery, the term includes any unlawful physical violence offered to another. *See* Battery.

Beat, *n.* In some of the southern states (as Alabama, Mississippi, South Carolina) the principal legal subdivision of a county, corresponding to towns or townships in other states; or a voting precinct.

Beating. The infliction of extreme force to another. *See* Battery; Corporal punishment.

Bed. The hollow or channel of a water course; the depression between the banks worn by the regular and usual flow of the water. The land that is covered by the water in its ordinary low stage. Area extending between the opposing banks measured from the foot of the banks from the top of the water at its ordinary stage, including sand bars which may exist between the foot of said banks as thus defined. It includes the lands below ordinary high water mark.

Also, the right of cohabitation or marital intercourse; as in the phrase "divorce from bed and board," or *a mensa et thoro.*

Bed and board. Divorce a mensa et thoro. *See* Divorce.

Before. Prior to; preceding; in front of; at the disposal of; in a higher position. In the presence of; under the official purview of; as in a magistrate's jurat, "*before* me personally appeared," etc.

When used as a preposition, does not indicate a period of time as do the prepositions "for," "during," and "throughout," but merely an event or act preceding in time, or earlier than, or previously to, the time mentioned.

Beget. To procreate as the father.

Beggar. One who lives by begging charity, or who has no other means of support than solicited alms.

Begin. To originate; to come into existence; to start; to institute; to initiate; to commence.

Behalf. Benefit, support, defence, or advantage.

Behavior. Manner of having, holding, or keeping one's self; manner of behaving, whether good or bad; conduct; manners; carriage of one's self, with respect to propriety and morals; deportment. *See also* Character; Reputation.

Being struck. Collision, or striking together of two objects, one of which may be stationary. Condition of a person who has been traumatized. Business closed or affected by labor strike. *See also* Strike.

Belief. A conviction of the truth of a proposition, existing subjectively in the mind, and induced by argument, persuasion, or proof addressed to the judgment. A conclusion arrived at from external sources after weighing probability. Conviction of the mind, arising not from actual perception or knowledge, but by way of inference, or from evidence received or information derived from others.

Knowledge is an assurance of a fact or proposition founded on perception by the senses, or intuition; while "belief" is an assurance gained by evidence, and from other persons. "Suspicion" is weaker than "belief," since suspicion requires no real foundation for its existence, while "belief" is necessarily based on at least assumed facts.

Belief-action distinction. The distinction noted in analysis of cases under First Amendment, U.S. Constitution—freedom of speech and religion—to the effect that one is guaranteed the right to any belief he chooses, but when that belief is translated into action, the state also has rights under its police power to protect others from such actions.

Belligerency /bəlíjərənsiy/. In international law, the status of *de facto* statehood attributed to a body of insurgents, by which their hostilities are legalized. The international status assumed by a state (*i.e.* nation) which wages war against another state. Quality of being belligerent; status of a belligerent; act or state of waging war; warfare.

Belligerent /bəlíjərənt/. In international law, as an adjective, it means engaged in lawful war. As a noun, it designates either of two nations which are actually in a state of war with each other, as well as their allies actively co-operating, as distinguished from a nation which takes no part in the war and maintains a strict indifference as between the contending parties, called a "neutral."

As a personality trait, refers to one who is overly assertive, hostile or combative.

Belligerents. A body of insurgents who by reason of their temporary organized government are regarded as conducting lawful hostilities. Also, militia, corps of volunteers, and others, who although not part of the regular army of the state, are regarded as lawful combatants provided they observe the laws of war. *See also* Belligerency; Belligerent.

Bellum /béləm/. Lat. In public law, war. An armed contest between nations; the state of those who forcibly contend with each other. *Jus belli*, the law of war.

Belong. To appertain to; to be the property of; to be a member of; to be appropriate; to own.

Belonging. That which is connected with a principal or greater thing; an appendage, an appurtenance; also, ownership.

Belongings. That which belongs to one; property; possessions; a term properly used to express ownership. *See* Personal effects.

Below. Inferior; of inferior jurisdiction, or jurisdiction in the first instance. The court from which a cause is removed for review is called the "court *below.*" Preliminary; auxiliary or instrumental.

Bail to the sheriff has been called "bail *below,*" as being preliminary to and intended to secure the putting in of bail above, or special bail. *See* Bail.

Below par. *See* Par value.

Ben Avon doctrine. Due process requires opportunity for judicial determination of reasonableness of rates for public utilities set by a Public Service Commission.

Bench. A seat of judgment or tribunal for the administration of justice. The seat occupied by judges in courts. Also, the court itself, or the aggregate of the judges composing a court, as in the phrase "before the full bench." *Compare* Bar.

The judges taken collectively, as distinguished from counsellors and advocates, who are called the bar.

The term, indicating originally the seat of the judges, came to denote the body of judges taken collectively, and also the tribunal itself, as the King's Bench.

Bench and bar. Term refers to judges collectively and attorneys as a whole.

Bench blotter. Record of arrests and other happenings kept by police. *See also* Arrest record; Booking.

Bench conference. A meeting at the judge's bench prior to, during or after a trial or hearing between counsel and the judge to discuss a matter pertaining to such proceeding. Commonly called to discuss questions of evidence out of hearing of jury; it may or may not be made part of the written record of the proceeding.

Bench legislation. *See* Judge-made law.

Bench mark. A mark on a fixed and enduring object, indicating a particular elevation and used as a reference in topographical surveys and tidal observations. Standard unit for basis of comparison.

Bench trial. Trial held before judge sitting without a jury; jury waived trial.

Bench warrant. Process issued by the court itself, or "from the bench," for the attachment or arrest of a person; either in case of contempt, or where an indictment has been found, or to bring in a witness who fails to obey a subpoena.

Bene /bíyniy/. Lat. Well; in proper form; legally; sufficiently.

Beneficial. Tending to the benefit of a person; yielding a profit, advantage, or benefit; enjoying or entitled to a benefit or profit. This term is applied both to estates (as a "beneficial interest") and to persons (as "the beneficial owner").

Beneficial enjoyment. The enjoyment which a man has of an estate in his own right and for his own benefit, and not as trustee for another.

Beneficial estate. An estate in expectancy is one where the right to the possession is postponed to a future period, and is "beneficial" where the devisee takes solely for his own use or benefit, and not as the mere holder of the title for the use of another.

Beneficial holders of securities. In securities law, persons who have the equitable or legal title to shares but who have not registered the shares in their names on the records of the corporation.

Beneficial interest. Profit, benefit, or advantage resulting from a contract, or the ownership of an estate as distinct from the legal ownership or control. When considered as designation of character of an estate, is such an interest as a devisee, legatee, or donee takes solely for his own use or benefit, and not as holder of title for use and benefit of another.

In trust law, refers to interest of the beneficiary in right to income or principal of trust funds, in contrast to trustee who holds legal title.

Beneficial owner. Term applied most commonly to cestui que trust who enjoys ownership of the trust or estate in equity, but not legal title which remains in trustee or personal representative. Equitable as contrasted with legal owner.

One who does not have title to property but has rights in the property which are the normal incident of owning the property. The persons for whom a trustee holds title to property are the beneficial owners of the property, and the trustee has a fiduciary responsibility to them.

Beneficial power. A power which has for its object the donee of the power, and which is to be executed solely for his benefit; as distinguished from a trust power, which has for its object a person other than the donee, and is to be executed solely for the benefit of such person.

Beneficial use. The right to use and enjoy property according to one's own liking or so as to derive a profit or benefit from it, including all that makes it desirable or habitable, as light, air, and access; as distinguished from a mere right of occupancy or possession. Such right to enjoyment of property where legal title is in one person while right to such use or interest is in another.

Beneficiary /bènəfísh(iy)əry/. One who benefits from act of another. A party who will benefit from a transfer of property or other arrangement. Examples include the beneficiary of a trust, the beneficiary of a life insurance policy, and the beneficiary of an estate. *See also* Creditor beneficiary; Primary beneficiary; Third party beneficiary.

Credit. A "beneficiary" of a credit is a person who is entitled under its terms to draw or demand payment. U.C.C. § 5–103(d). *See also* Creditor beneficiary.

Incidental. A person who may derive benefit from performance on contract, though he is neither the promisee nor the one to whom performance is to be rendered. *See also* Incidental beneficiary.

Insurance. The person entitled to take proceeds on death of insured.

Letter of credit. In a letter of credit transaction, the "person who is entitled under its terms [i.e., the terms of the credit] to draw or demand payment." U.C.C. § 5–103(1)(d).

Taxation. One who is assessed as the real owner. *See also* Income beneficiary.

Trust. As it relates to trust beneficiaries, includes a person who has any present or future interest, vested or contingent, and also includes the owner of an interest by assignment or other transfer and as it relates to a charitable trust, includes any person entitled to enforce the trust. Uniform Probate Code, § 1–201. A person named in a trust account as one for whom a party to the account is named as trustee. Uniform Probate Code, § 6–101. Person for whose benefit property is held in trust. Restatement, Second, Trusts § 3.

Will. Person named in will to receive specified property, funds, etc.

Beneficiary association. *See* Benevolent associations.

Beneficiary heir. In the law of Louisiana, one who has accepted the succession under the benefit of an inventory regularly made. Civ.Code La. art. 883. Also, one who may accept the succession with benefit of inventory.

Benefit. Advantage; profit; fruit; privilege; gain; interest. The receiving as the exchange for promise some performance or forbearance which promisor was not previously entitled to receive. Benefits are something to advantage of, or profit to, recipient.

Financial assistance received in time of sickness, disability, unemployment, etc. either from insurance or public programs such as social security.

Contracts. When it is said that a valuable consideration for a promise may consist of a benefit to the promisor, "benefit" means that the promisor has, in return for his promise, acquired some legal right to which he would not otherwise have been entitled. "Benefits" of contract are advantages which result to either party from performance by other.

Eminent domain. It is a rule that, in assessing damages for private property taken or injured for public use, "special benefits" may be set off against the amount of damage found, but not "general benefits." Within the meaning of this rule, general benefits are such as accrue to the community at large, to the vicinage, or to all property similarly situated with reference to the work or improvement in question; while special benefits are such as accrue directly and solely to the owner of the land in question and not to others.

As respects eminent domain law, "general benefits" are those which arise from the fulfillment of the public object which justified taking, while "special benefits" are those which arise from the particular relation of the land in question to the public improvement.

Benefit association. *See* Benefit societies.

Benefit building society. The original name for what is now more commonly called a "building society" *(q.v.).*

Benefit-cost ratio. Such ratio is basically a comparison of anticipated benefits derived from particular public works project with anticipated costs over estimated life span of the project.

Benefit of bargain rule. Under such rule a defrauded purchaser may recover the difference between the real and the represented value of the property purchased. This rule of damages gives damaged party equivalent of what the party would have received if the representations relied upon had been true.

In an action for fraud, plaintiff's recovery is limited to that measured by "out-of-pocket" rule, by which damages are measured by difference between purchase price of property and fair market value of same property on date of sale, unless actionable misrepresentation was warranty of value, in which case plaintiff may recover under "benefit-of-the-bargain" rule by which damages are determined by difference between actual value of property received and its value had representations as made been true.

Benefit of clergy. In its original sense, the phrase denoted the exemption which was accorded to clergymen from the jurisdiction of the secular courts, or from arrest or attachment on criminal process issuing from those courts in certain particular cases. Afterwards, it meant a privilege of exemption from the punishment of death accorded to such persons as were *clerks*, or who could read. This privilege operated greatly to mitigate the extreme rigor of the criminal laws, but was found to involve such gross abuses that parliament began to enact that certain crimes should be felonies "without benefit of clergy," and finally, by the Criminal Law Act of 1827, it was altogether abolished. The act of congress of April 30, 1790, c. 9, § 31, 1 Stat. 119, provided that there should be no benefit of clergy for any capital crime against the United States, and, if this privilege formed a part of the common law of the several states before the Revolution, it no longer exists.

Sometimes used in negative sense, "without benefit of clergy", to describe status of man and woman who live together though not married to each other.

Benefit of counsel. *See* Assistance of counsel; Counsel, right to.

Benefit of discussion. In the civil law, the right which a surety has to cause the property of the principal debtor to be applied in satisfaction of the obligation in the first instance. Civ.Code La. arts. 3045–3051.

Benefit of inventory. In the civil law, the privilege which the heir obtains of being liable for the charges and debts of the succession, only to the value of the effects of the succession, by causing an inventory of these effects within the time and manner prescribed by law. Civil Code La. art. 1032.

Benefit societies. Under this and several similar names, in various states, are corporations which exist to receive periodical payments from members, and hold them as a fund to be loaned or given to members needing pecuniary relief. *See also* Benevolent associations.

Benefits rule. This rule provides that where a benefit, as well as a harm, is conferred by a tort-feasor, the benefits must be weighed against the elements of claimed damage.

Benevolence. The doing of a kind or helpful action towards another, under no obligation except an ethical one. *See also* Benevolent; Charitable; Charity.

Benevolent /bənévələnt/. Philanthropic; humane; having a desire or purpose to do good to men; intended for the conferring of benefits, rather than for gain or profit; loving others and actively desirous of their well being.

This word, as applied to objects or purposes, may refer to those which are in their nature charitable, and may also have a broader meaning and include objects and purposes not charitable in the legal sense of that word. Acts of kindness, friendship, forethought, or good-will might properly be described as benevolent. It has therefore been held that gifts to trustees to be applied for "benevolent purposes" at their discretion, or to such benevolent purposes as they could agree upon, do not create a public charity. But where the word is used in connection with other words explanatory of its meaning, and indicating the intent of the donor to limit it to purposes strictly charitable, it has been held to be synonymous with, or equivalent to, "charitable."

See also Charitable; Charity.

Benevolent associations. Those having a philanthropic or charitable purpose, as distinguished from such as are conducted for profit; specifically, "benefit associations" or "beneficial associations." Another name for a "benefit society," "benevolent society," and "fraternal" or "friendly society." *See also* Benevolent corporation; Charitable corporation.

Benevolent corporation. A nonprofit corporation; created for charitable rather than for business purposes. One that ministers to all; the purpose may be anything that promotes the mental, physical, or spiritual welfare of man. The term may include a corporation to which a bequest is made to be used in the improvement of the social, physical, and economic condition of the employees of a business corporation. *See also* Charitable corporation.

Benevolent society. *See* Benevolent associations; Benevolent corporation.

Bequeath /bəkwíyð/. To give personal property by will to another. It therefore is distinguishable from "devise," which is properly used of realty. But if the context clearly shows the intention of the testator to use the word "bequeath" as synonymous with "devise," it may be held to pass real property. *See* Bequest.

Bequest /bəkwést/. A gift (transfer) by will of personal property; a legacy. Disposition of realty in will is termed "devise." *See also* Charitable bequest; Demonstrative bequest; Devise; General bequest; Legacy.

Conditional bequest. One the taking effect or continuing of which depends upon the happening or non-occurrence of a particular event.

Executory bequest. The bequest of a future, deferred, or contingent interest in personalty.

Residuary bequest. A gift of all the remainder of the testator's personal estate, after payment of debts and legacies, etc.

Specific bequest. One whereby the testator gives to the legatee all his property of a certain class or kind; as all his pure personalty.

Besides. In addition to; moreover; also; likewise.

Best. Of the highest quality; of the greatest usefulness for the purpose intended. Most desirable, suitable, useful, or satisfactory. For example: the "best bid" of interest by a prospective depositary of school funds would not necessarily be the highest bid, but, looking to the solvency of the bidder, the bond tendered, and all the circumstances surrounding the transaction, the safety and preservation of the school fund, the "best bid" might be the lowest bid.

Best-effort basis. With respect to a new securities issue, a commitment by the investment banker or group handling the new issue to sell the securities as an agent of the issuing party, rather than as an underwriting of the entire issue.

Best evidence. Primary evidence, as distinguished from secondary; original, as distinguished from substitutionary; the best and highest evidence of which the nature of the case is susceptible, not the highest or strongest evidence which the nature of the thing to be proved admits of. The original of a written instrument is itself always regarded as the primary or best possible evidence of its existence and contents; a copy, or the recollection of a witness, would be secondary evidence. "Best evidence" or "primary evidence" includes the best evidence which is available to a party and procurable under the existing situation, and all evidence falling short of such standard, and which in its nature suggests there is better evidence of the same fact, is "secondary evidence." *See* Best evidence rule; Original document rule; Primary evidence.

Best evidence rule. Rule which requires that best evidence available be presented in lieu of less satisfactory evidence. This rule prohibits the introduction into evidence of secondary evidence unless it is shown that original document has been lost or destroyed or is beyond jurisdiction of court without fault of the offering party; if original document is lost, then secondary evidence is properly admissible. Fed.R.Evid. 1002 states the basic rule as follows: "To prove the content of a writing, recording, or photograph, the original writing, recording, or photograph is required, except as otherwise provided in these rules or by Act of Congress." As to what constitutes an "original writing", *see* Original.

Bestiality. A sexual connection between a human being and an animal. At common law the term "crime against nature" embraced both "sodomy" and "bestiality". *See* Sodomy.

Bestow. To give, grant, confer, or impart; not necessarily limited in meaning to "devise."

Best use. In eminent domain, the value of property considering its optimum use at a given time and hence the money which should be awarded for such governmental taking; used commonly as "highest and best use". (*q.v.*).

Bet. An agreement between two or more persons that a sum of money or other valuable thing, to which all jointly contribute, shall become the sole property of one or some of them on the happening in the future of an event at present uncertain, or according as a question disputed between them is settled in one way or the other. A contract by which two or more parties agree that a sum of money, or other thing, shall be paid or delivered to one of them on the happening or not happening of an uncertain event. *See* Wager; a term generally synonymous with bet. *See also* Betting book; Betting slips.

Betrothed /bətrowðd/. One who has exchanged promises to marry. The term may be synonymous with "intended wife." *See also* Engagement.

Betrothment, betrothal. Mutual promise of marriage; the plighting of troth; a mutual promise or contract between a man and woman competent to make it, to marry at a future time.

Better Business Bureau. Local, business-supported organizations that promote good business practices, receive complaints about specific businesses, and provide consumers with information about specific firms. The local bureaus are loosely affiliated with a national bureau.

Better equity. *See* Equity.

Betterment. An improvement put upon a property which enhances its value more than mere replacement, maintenance, or repairs. The improvement may be either temporary or permanent. Also applied to denote the additional value which a property acquires in consequence of some public improvement, as laying out or widening a street, etc. *See also* Improvement.

Betterment acts. Statutes which provide that a bona fide occupant of real estate making lasting improvements in good faith shall have a lien upon the estate recovered by the real owner to the extent that his improvements have increased the value of the land. Also called "occupying claimant acts."

Betting. Act of placing a bet or wager. *See* Bet; Gambling; Pari-mutuel betting; Wager.

Betting book. A book kept for registering bets on the result of a race as operated on race track. In a broader sense, the "betting book" is that book which enables the professional bettor to carry on his business, and to promote a race, sporting event, or the like, and it includes the book, the making book and the bookmaker.

Betting slips. Part of gambling paraphernalia consisting of papers on which numbers or names of dogs, horses, teams, etc. to be bet are written and which constitutes evidence for prosecution of illegal gaming.

Between. A space which separates. Strictly applicable only with reference to two things, but this may be understood as including cases in which a number of things are discriminated collectively as two wholes, or as taken in pairs, or where one thing is set off against a number of others. Sometimes used synonymously with "among". As a measure or indication of distance, this word has the effect of excluding the two termini. If an act is to be done "between" two certain days, it must be performed before the commencement of the latter day. In computing the time in such a case, both the days named are to be excluded.

Beyond a reasonable doubt. In evidence means fully satisfied, entirely convinced, satisfied to a moral certainty; and phrase is the equivalent of the words clear, precise and indubitable. In criminal case, the accused's guilt must be established "beyond a reasonable doubt," which means that facts proven must, by virtue of their probative force, establish guilt. *See also* Reasonable doubt.

Beyond control. Anything or any person who, in relationship to another person is out of reach of the latter, either physically, legally or morally; for example, a child who has reached his majority is beyond the legal control of his parents. *See also* Act of God.

Beyond the seas. Beyond the limits of the United States. In England, an expression to indicate that a person was outside the United Kingdom. The Limitation Act of 1939 abolished the old procedure whereby a defendant's absence beyond the seas suspended the operation of the Statutes of Limitations.

B.F. An abbreviation for *bonum factum*, a good or proper act, deed, or decree; signifies "approved."

BFOQ. Bona Fide Occupational Qualification. *See* Bona fide.

BI. Bodily injury.

BIA. Bureau of Indian Affairs.

Biannually. Twice a year; semi-annually.

Bias /báyəs/. Inclination; bent; prepossession; a preconceived opinion; a predisposition to decide a cause or an issue in a certain way, which does not leave the mind perfectly open to conviction. To incline to one side. Condition of mind, which sways judgment and renders judge unable to exercise his functions impartially in particular case. As used in law regarding disqualification of judge, refers to mental attitude or disposition of the judge toward a party to the litigation, and not to any views that he may entertain regarding the subject matter involved.

Actual bias consists in the existence of a state of mind on the part of the juror which satisfies the court, in the exercise of a sound discretion, that the juror cannot try the issues impartially and without prejudice to the substantial rights of the party challenging.

See also Average man test; Discrimination; Prejudice.

Bible. *See* Family Bible.

Bicameral system /bàykǽmərəl sístəm/. A term applied by Jeremy Bentham to the division of a legislative body into two chambers, as in the United States government (Senate and House).

Bid. An offer by an intending purchaser to pay a designated price for property which is about to be sold at auction. An offer to perform a contract for work and labor or supplying materials or goods at a specified price. Public contracts are frequently awarded on basis of submitted, competitive bids. *See also* Firm bid; Invitation to bid; Let; Lowest responsible bidder; Open bid; Sealed bid.

Term may also refer to application for another job by an employee.

Best bid. One that is not necessarily the lowest, but rather fits the best interests of the issuer of the bid; taken into consideration is the solvency of the bidder, quality of his work, reputation, etc.

Bidder. One who makes a bid. One who offers to pay a specified price for an article offered for sale at a public auction or to perform a certain contract for a specified price. As to Responsible bidder see that title.

Biddings. Offers of a designated price for goods or other property put up for sale at auction.

Bidding up. Raising the price for an item being sold at an auction by a series of bids, each higher than the other. If such successive bids are made collusively by persons with an interest in raising the final bid, such practice is unlawful.

Bid in. Property sold at auction is said to be "bid in" by the owner or an incumbrancer or some one else who is interested in it, when he attends the sale and makes the successful bid. This is done so that property is not sold below actual value.

Bid off. One is said to "bid off" a thing when he bids for it at an auction sale, and it is knocked down to him in immediate succession to the bid and as a consequence of it.

By-bidding. In the law relating to sales by auction, this term is equivalent to "puffing." The practice consists in making fictitious bids for the property, under a secret arrangement with the owner or auctioneer, for the purpose of misleading and stimulating other persons who are bidding in good faith.

Competitive bidding. Bids which are submitted as the result of public notice and advertising of an intended sale or purchase.

Letting or awarding of bids. See Let.

Open bid. Offer to perform a contract together with the price, but with right to reduce the price to meet price quoted by others for same job.

Sealed bid. One submitted under seal, and which is not to be opened until a specified time at which all bids are to be opened and compared. Commonly required on construction contracts, to assure independence of bidding.

Upset bid. A bid made after a judicial sale, but before the successful bid at the sale has been confirmed, larger or better than such successful bid, and made for the purpose of upsetting the sale and securing to the "upset bidder" the privilege of taking the property at his bid or competing at a new sale.

Bid and asked. Price quotation for securities that are not frequently traded or are traded on the over-the-counter market. The bid quotation is the highest price a prospective buyer is willing to pay at a particular time; the asked quotation is the lowest price the seller is willing to sell for. Together, the two prices constitute a quotation; the difference between the two prices is the "spread."

Bid bond. Type of bond required in public construction projects which must be filed at the time of the bid and which protects the public agency in the event that the bidder refuses to enter into a contract after the award to him or withdraws his bid before the award. A type of indemnity bond.

Bidder. *See* Bid.

Bid price. In market exchanges, the price a buyer is willing to pay, as contrasted with the price at which a seller is willing to sell; called the "ask price". Also, the amount specified in a bid as the amount for which the bidder will perform the work or buy the property.

Bid quote. Price at which one (usually a broker or dealer) is willing to purchase a security (or commodity).

Bid shopping. The use of the low bid already received by general contractor to pressure other subcontractors into submitting even lower bids.

Biennial /bàyén(i)yəl/. Occurring every two years.

Biennial session. The regular session of most State legislatures, usually held in odd-numbered years; gradually being supplanted by annual sessions.

Biennium /bàyéniyəm/. A two-year period; the period for which appropriations are made in many State legislatures.

Bifurcated trial /báyfərkèytəd tráy(ə)l/. Trial of issues separately, *e.g.* guilt and punishment, or guilt and sanity, in criminal trial.

The trial of the liability issue in a personal injury or wrongful death case separate from and prior to trial of the damages question. The advantage of so doing is that if the liability issue is determined in defendant's favor there is no need to try the damages question, which can be an involved one entailing expensive expert witnesses and other proof.

Compare Severance of actions.

Bigamy /bígəmiy/. The criminal offense of willfully and knowingly contracting a second marriage (or going through the form of a second marriage) while the first marriage, to the knowledge of the offender, is still subsisting and undissolved. The state of a man who has two wives, or of a woman who has two husbands, living at the same time.

A married person is guilty of bigamy, a misdemeanor, if he contracts or purports to contract another marriage, unless at the time of the subsequent marriage: (a) the actor believes that the prior spouse is dead; or (b) the actor and the prior spouse have been living apart for five consecutive years throughout which the prior spouse was not known by the actor to be alive; or (c) a Court has entered a judgment purporting to terminate or annul any prior disqualifying marriage, and the actor does not know that judgment to be invalid; or (d) the actor reasonably believes that he is legally eligible to remarry. Model Penal Code, § 230.1.

In the canon law, the term denoted the offense committed by an ecclesiastic who married two wives successively. It might be committed either by marrying a second wife after the death of a first or by marrying a widow.

See also Polygamy.

Big board. A popular term referring to the board showing the current prices of securities listed on the New York Stock Exchange.

Big eight. A term which refers to the eight largest certified public accounting (CPA) firms in the United States. The ranking of the firms consider such factors as gross receipts, number of staff, etc.

Bilateral contract /bàylǽtərəl kóntrækt/. A term, used originally in the civil law, but now generally adopted, denoting a contract in which both the contracting parties are bound to fulfill obligations reciprocally towards each other; as a contract of sale, where one becomes bound to deliver the thing sold, and the other to pay the price of it. A contract executory on both sides, and one which includes both rights and duties on each side. Contract formed by the exchange of promises in which the promise of one party is consideration supporting the promise of the other as contrasted with a unilateral contract which is formed by the exchange of a promise for an act. *See* Contract. *Compare* Unilateral contract.

Bill. As a legal term, this word has many meanings and applications, the most important of which are set forth below:

Bill of rights. A formal and emphatic legislative assertion and declaration of popular rights and liberties usually promulgated upon a change of government; *e.g.* the famous Bill of Rights of 1688 in English history. Also the summary of the rights and liberties of the people, or of the principles of constitutional law deemed essential and fundamental, contained in many of the American state constitutions. That portion of Constitution guaranteeing rights and privileges to the individual; *i.e.* first ten Amendments of U.S. Constitution.

Commercial transactions. A written statement of the terms of a contract, or specification of the items of a transaction or of a demand. Also, a general name for any item of indebtedness, whether receivable or payable; an account for goods sold, services rendered, or work done. As a verb, as generally and customarily used in commercial transactions, "bill" is synonymous with "charge" or "invoice." *See also Commercial paper; Maritime law, below.*

Bill-book. A book in which an account of bills of exchange and promissory notes, whether payable or receivable, is stated.

Bill-head. A printed form on which merchants and traders make out their bills and render accounts to their customers. *See also* Invoice.

Bill of lading. See Bill of lading, *infra.*

Bill of parcels. A statement sent to the buyer of goods, along with the goods, exhibiting in detail the items composing the parcel and their several prices, to enable him to detect any mistake or omission; an invoice *(q.v.).*

Bill of sale. In contracts, a written agreement, formerly limited to one under seal, by which one person assigns or transfers his right to or interest in goods and personal chattels to another. Legal document which conveys title from seller to buyer.

Bill payable. In a merchant's accounts, all bills which he has accepted, and promissory notes which he has made, are called "bills payable," and are entered in a ledger account under that name, and recorded in a book bearing the same title. *See* Account *(Account payable).*

Bill receivable. In a merchant's accounts, all notes, drafts, checks, etc., payable to him, or of which he is to receive the proceeds at a future date, are called "bills receivable," and are entered in a ledger-account under that name, and also noted in a book bearing the same title. *See* Account *(Account receivable).*

Bill rendered. A bill of items rendered by a creditor to his debtor; an "account rendered," as distinguished from "an account stated."

Commercial paper. A promissory obligation for the payment of money.

Bill broker. Middleman who negotiates purchase or sale of commercial paper.

Bill of credit. A bill or promissory note issued by the government, upon its faith and credit, designed to circulate in the community as money. *See* Federal reserve notes; Treasury bill.

In commercial law, a license or authority given in writing from one person to another, very common among merchants, bankers, and those who travel, empowering a person to receive or take up money of their correspondents abroad. *See also* Letter of credit.

Bill of exchange. An unconditional order in writing addressed by one person to another, signed by the person giving it, requiring the person to whom it is addressed to pay on demand or at a fixed or determinable future time a sum certain in money. A three party instrument in which first party draws an order for the payment of a sum certain on a second party for payment to a third party at a definite future time. Same as "draft" under U.C.C. A check is a demand bill of exchange. *See also* Advance bill; Banker's acceptance; Blank bill; Clean bill; Draft; Time *(Time bill).*

Foreign bill of exchange. A bill of exchange drawn in one country upon another country not governed by the same homogeneous laws, or not governed throughout by the same municipal laws. A bill of exchange drawn in one of the United States upon a person residing in another state is a foreign bill.

Common law pleading and practice.

Bill in equity. The first written pleading in a proceeding in equity. The complaint in a suit in equity.

Bill of costs. A certified, itemized statement of the amount of costs in an action or suit.

Bill of evidence. Stenographer's transcript of testimony heard at trial which may be considered on appeal as bill of exceptions.

Bill of exceptions. A formal statement in writing of the objections or exceptions taken by a party during the trial of a cause to the decisions, rulings, or instructions of the trial judge, stating the objection, with the facts and circumstances on which it is founded, and, in order to attest its accuracy, signed by the judge; the object being to put the controverted rulings or decisions upon the record for the information of the appellate court. Bills of exceptions have been eliminated in civil appeals in jurisdictions which have adopted Rules of Civil Procedure tracking Fed. Rules of Civil Proc. in favor of a straight appeal with no need to claim exception after making objection at trial; *e.g.* Mass.R.Civ.Proc. 46.

Bill of particulars. A written statement or specification of the particulars of the demand for which an action at law is brought, or of a defendant's set-off against such demand (including dates, sums, and items in detail), furnished by one of the parties to the other, either voluntarily or in compliance with a judge's order for that purpose. It is designed to aid the defendant in interposing the proper answer and in preparing for trial, by giving him detailed information regarding the cause of action stated in the complaint. See *e.g.* New York CPLR § 3041 et seq. In jurisdictions which have adopted Rules of Civil Procedure, the bill of particulars has been replaced by various discovery devices (Fed.R. Civil P. 26 et seq.) and by motion for more definite statement (Fed.R. Civil P. 12(e)). See however *Criminal law, below,* with respect to bill of particulars in criminal cases.

Contracts. An obligation; a deed, whereby the obligor acknowledges himself to owe to the obligee a certain sum of money or some other thing.

Criminal law.

Bill of attainder. Legislative acts, no matter what their form, that apply either to named individuals or to easily ascertainable members of a group in such a way as to inflict punishment on them without a judicial trial. An act is a "bill of attainder" when the punishment is death and a "bill of pains and penalties" when the punishment is less severe; both kinds of punishment fall within the scope of the constitutional prohibition. U.S.Const. Art. I, Sec. 9, Cl. 3 (as to Congress); Art. I, Sec. 10 (as to state legislatures).

Bill of indemnity. See Bill of indemnity, *infra.*

Bill of indictment. A formal written document accusing a person or persons named of having committed a felony or misdemeanor, lawfully laid before a grand jury (usually by prosecutor) for their action upon it. *See* Indictment; Presentment.

Bill of pains and penalties. See Bill of attainder, above.

Bill of particulars. Form or means of discovery in which the prosecution sets forth the time, place, manner and means of the commission of the crime as alleged in complaint or indictment. It is one method available to defendant to secure default of charge against him. Fed.R.Crim.P. 7. The purpose of a "bill of particulars" is to give notice to the accused of the offenses charged in the bill of indictment so that he may prepare a defense, avoid surprise, or intelligently raise pleas of double jeopardy and the bar of the statute of limitations.

Equity pleading and practice. The initial pleading of plaintiff or petitioner in equity action in contrast to declaration (complaint) in law actions. Under Rules of Civil Procedure, however, bill has been replaced by complaint for both equitable and legal actions because of merger of law and equity. Fed.R. Civil P. 2.

Legislation. The draft of a proposed law from the time of its introduction in a legislative body through all the various stages in both houses. Once introduced, a federal bill may be considered in any session of a Congress, but it dies at the end of a session, and it must be reintroduced as a new bill if a succeeding Congress is to consider it. The form of a proposed law before it is enacted into law by vote of the legislative body. An "Act" is the appropriate term for it after it has been acted on by, and passed by, the legislature. *See also* Marking up; Omnibus bill.

Appropriations bill. Bill covering raising and expenditure of public funds. Federal appropriations bills must originate in the House of Representatives. Art. I, Sec. 7, U.S. Const. *See also* Appropriation bill.

Authorization bill. Bill authorizing expenditure of public funds.

Clean bill. Bill coming out of legislative committee in amended or redrafted form, making it essentially a new bill.

Engrossed bill. Bill in final form, ready to be voted on by legislature.

Enrolled bill. Bill that has been passed and forwarded to President or Governor for signature or veto.

Private bill. One dealing only with a matter of private personal or local interest. All legislative bills which have for their object some particular or private interest are so termed, as distinguished from such as are for the benefit of the whole community, which are termed "public bills."

Revenue bill. See Appropriations bill, above.

Maritime law.

Bill of adventure. A written certificate by a merchant or the master or owner of a ship, to the effect that the property and risk in goods shipped on the vessel in his own name belong to another person, to whom he is accountable for the proceeds alone.

Bill of entry. Detailed statement by the importer of the nature and value of goods entered at the customhouse. Form filled out by importer for use of customs officer; describes goods, their value, etc. Permits goods to be unloaded from ship.

Bill of health. An official certificate, given by the authorities of a port from which a vessel clears, to the master of the ship, showing the state of the port, as respects the public health, at the time of sailing, and exhibited to the authorities of the port which the vessel next makes, in token that she does not bring disease. If the bill alleges that no contagious or infectious disease existed, it is called a "clean" bill; if it admits that one was suspected or anticipated, or that one actually prevailed, it is called a "touched" or a "foul" bill.

Bill of sight. Customhouse document, allowing a cosignee to see the goods before paying duties.

Negotiable instruments. See Commercial paper, above.

Billing cycle. Period of time in which creditors regularly submit bills to customers or debtors; *e.g.* 30 days.

Bill of address. *See* Address.

Bill of attainder. *See* Attainder; Bill *(Criminal law)*.

Bill of indemnity. A law under which a public official is protected from liability in performance of his official acts including his failure to take his official oath. An initial pleading by which the plaintiff seeks to require another (*e.g.*, insurance company) to discharge his liability to a third person.

Bill of lading. Document evidencing receipt of goods for shipment issued by person engaged in business of transporting or forwarding goods and it includes airbill. U.C.C. § 1–201(6). An instrument in writing, signed by a carrier or his agent, describing the freight so as to identify it, stating the name of the consignor, the terms of the contract for carriage, and agreeing or directing that the freight be delivered to the order or assigns of a specified person at a specified place. It is receipt for goods, contract for their carriage, and is documentary evidence of title to goods.

Bills in a set. A series of bills of lading each bearing a number and providing that a certain bill is valid only if goods have not been delivered against another bill. U.C.C. § 7–304.

Clean bill. One which contains nothing in the margin qualifying the words of the bill of lading itself.

Common law. In common law, the written evidence of a contract for the carriage and delivery of goods sent by sea for a certain freight. A written memorandum, given by the person in command of a merchant vessel, acknowledging the receipt on board the ship of certain specified goods, in good order or "apparent good order," which he undertakes, in consideration of the payment of freight, to deliver in like good order (dangers of the sea excepted) at a designated place to the consignee therein named or to his assigns.

Foul bill. Bill of lading containing notation that goods received by carrier were defective.

Negotiable bill. One which by its terms calls for goods to be delivered to bearer or to order of named persons, or where recognized in overseas trade, if it runs to named persons or assigns. U.C.C. § 7–104(1)(a)(b).

Non-negotiable bill. Document of title in which goods are consigned to named persons. U.C.C. § 7–104(2).

Ocean bill. A negotiable bill of lading used in shipment by water.

On board bill. Bill of lading which shows that loading has been completed.

Order bill. One in which it is stated that goods are consigned to order of any person named therein. *See Negotiable bill, above;* also, Order bill of lading.

Overseas bill. Where the contract contemplates overseas shipment and contains a term C.I.F. or C. & F. or F.O.B. vessel, the seller unless otherwise agreed must obtain a negotiable bill of lading stating that the goods have been loaded on board or, in the case of a term C.I.F. or C. & F., received for shipment. U.C.C. § 2–323(1).

Straight bill. A nonnegotiable bill of lading that specifies a consignee to whom the goods are to be delivered—the carrier is contractually obligated to deliver the goods to that person only.

Through bill. One by which a railroad contracts to transport over its own line for a certain distance carloads of merchandise or stock, there to deliver the same to its connecting lines to be transported to the place of destination at a fixed rate per carload for the whole distance. Embodies undertaking to be performed in part by persons acting as agents for issuer. U.C.C. § 7–302.

Bill of lading acts. The principal acts governing bills of lading are Article 7 of the Uniform Commercial Code, the Federal Bills of Lading Act (49 U.S.C.A. §§ 81–124), and the Carmack Amendment to the Interstate Commerce Act (49 U.S.C.A. § 20(11)). *See also* Harter Act.

Bill of materials. A document that contains information about the product materials components and their specifications (including quality and quantities needed).

Bill of pains and penalties. Statutory provision for punishment without judicial determination of guilt similar to bill of attainder except that punishment is less severe. Prohibited by U.S.Const., Art. I, § 9, cl. 3 (Congress), § 10 (States).

Bill of rights. First ten Amendments to U.S. Constitution providing for individual rights, freedoms, and protections (see Appendix, *infra*). *See also* Bill; Patient's Bill of Rights.

Bill quia timet /bíl kwáyə tímət/. *See* Quia timet.

Bind. To obligate; to bring or place under definite duties or legal obligations, particularly by a bond or covenant. To affect one in a constraining or compulsory manner with a contract or a judgment. So long as a contract, an adjudication, or a legal relation remains in force and virtue, and continues to impose duties or obligations, it is said to be *"binding."* A man is *bound* by his contract or promise, by a judgment or decree against him, by his bond or covenant, by an estoppel, etc.

Binder. A written memorandum of the important terms of contract of insurance which gives temporary protection to insured pending investigation of risk by insurance company or until a formal policy is issued. A receipt for earnest money or a deposit paid to secure the right to purchase real estate at terms that have been agreed upon by both buyer and seller. *See also* Binding receipt; Cover note.

Binding agreement. A contract which is enforceable such as an offer to buy or sell when person to whom it is made accepts it and communicates his acceptance. *See* Contract.

Binding authority. Sources of law that must be taken into account by a judge in deciding a case; for example, statutes or decisions by a higher court of the same state on point. *See* Precedent.

Binding jury instruction. One in which jury is told that if they find certain conditions to be true, they should find for plaintiff or defendant, as case might be. *See* Jury instructions (*Mandatory instruction*).

Binding over. The act by which a court or magistrate requires a person to enter into a recognizance or furnish bail to appear for trial, to keep the peace, to attend as a witness, etc. Also describes act of lower court in transferring case to higher court or to grand jury after a finding of probable cause to believe that defendant committed crime.

Binding receipt *or* **slip.** Term refers to a limited acceptance of an application for insurance given by an authorized agent pending the ascertainment of the company's willingness to assume the burden of the proposed risk, the effect of which is to protect the applicant until the company acts upon the application, and, if it declines to accept the burden, the binding effect of the slip ceases eo instante. *See* Binder.

Bind out. To place one under a legal obligation to serve another; as to *bind out* an apprentice.

Bind over. *See* Binding over.

Birth certificate. A formal document which certifies as to the date and place of one's birth and a recitation of his or her parentage, as issued by an official in charge of such records. Furnishing of such is often required to prove one's age. *See* Birth record.

Birth record. Official statistical data concerning dates and places of persons' birth, as well as parentage, kept by local government officials. *See* Birth certificate.

Biting rule. When first taker of conveyed property under writing submitted for construction is initially conveyed a fee title, it is then incompetent and invalid to modify, qualify, or reduce thereafter the apparent fee title of the first taker so as to reduce it to a life estate, and any gift over after death of first taker is void.

Black acre and white acre. Fictitious names used by the old writers to distinguish one parcel of land from another, to avoid ambiguity, as well as the inconvenience of a fuller description.

Black letter law. An informal term indicating the basic principles of law generally accepted by the courts and/or embodied in the statutes of a particular jurisdiction.

Blacklist. A list of persons marked out for special avoidance, antagonism, or enmity on the part of those who prepare the list or those among whom it is intended to circulate; as where a trades-union "blacklists" workmen who refuse to conform to its rules, or where a list of insolvent or untrustworthy persons is published by a commercial agency or mercantile association. Such practices are prohibited by statute in most states.

Black Lung Benefits Act. Federal statute benefitting coal miners who are stricken with pneumoconiosis, a chronic dust disease of the lung. 30 U.S.C.A. § 902. Benefits under the Act are administered by the Department of Labor.

Blackmail. Unlawful demand of money or property under threat to do bodily harm, to injure property, to accuse of crime, or to expose disgraceful defects. This crime is commonly included under extortion or criminal coercion statutes. See Model Penal Code § 212.5. *See also* Extortion; Shakedown.

Black market. Illegal trading; buying and selling goods which are subject to government rationing or control, including goods which are contraband. *See also* Gray market goods.

Blank. A space left unfilled in a written document, in which one or more words or marks are to be inserted to complete the sense. Also a skeleton or printed form for any legal document, in which the necessary and invariable words are printed in their proper order, with blank spaces left for the insertion of such names, dates, figures, additional clauses, etc., as may be necessary to adapt the instrument to the particular case and to the design of the party using it.

Blank acceptance. An acceptance of a bill of exchange written on the paper before the bill is made, and delivered by the acceptor.

Blank bill. Bill of exchange with payee's name left blank.

Blanket bond. Generic term which may describe a bond covering a number of projects on which performance bonds are required or a bond to dissolve more than one attachment. Any bond used for multiple purposes.

Blanket insurance. *See* Insurance.

Blanket mortgage. Covers two or more assets or properties which are pledged to support the given debt.

A bond issue that is backed by all of the firm's real property.

Blanket policy. *See* Insurance.

Blanket rate. Insurance rate applied when there is more than one property or subject of insurance.

Blanket search warrant. A single warrant authorizing the search of more than one area or the seizure of everything found at a given location without specific authorization in the warrant, the latter being in violation of the requirements of the Fourth Amendment to U.S. Const.

Blank indorsement. The indorsement of a bill of exchange or promissory note, by merely writing the name of the indorser, without mentioning any person to whom the bill or note is to be paid; called "blank," because a blank or space is left *over* it for the insertion of the name of the indorsee, or of any subsequent holder. Otherwise called an indorsement "in blank." Such indorsement causes an instrument, otherwise payable to order, to become payable to bearer and negotiable by delivery alone. U.C.C. § 3–204(2). With respect to a document of title, the signature of a person to whom the document runs in which the

signer specifies no particular person to whom the goods should be delivered. See U.C.C. § 7–501(1).

Blank shares. "Series shares" which may vary in the relative rights and preferences as between different series but which may be fixed in articles of incorporation.

Blasphemy /blǽsfəmiy/. Any oral or written reproach maliciously cast upon God, His name, attributes, or religion.

Blindness. Condition of one who is without sight either wholly or partially. Degrees are recognized for purpose of workers' compensation and social security benefits.

Blind selling. Selling goods without giving buyer opportunity to examine such.

Blind trust. *See* Trust.

Block. A square or portion of a city or town inclosed by streets, whether partially or wholly occupied by buildings or containing only vacant lots. Also used synonymously with "square." The platted portion of a city surrounded by streets. The term need not, however, be limited to blocks platted as such, but may mean an area bounded on all sides by streets or avenues. It must be surrounded on at least three sides by streets, which must be marked on the ground, and not simply indicated as such on a plat. *See also* Lot.

Large amount of stock or bonds sold as a unit in a single trade.

Blockade. Action taken against enemy nation so as to isolate, obstruct and prevent communications, commerce, supplies, and persons from entering into or leaving such nation. Such blockades may be by sea, or land, or both.

Blockage. Recognition in the field of taxation of fact that in some instances a large block of stock cannot be marketed and turned into cash as readily as a few shares. The discount at which a large block of stock sells below the price of a smaller block is blockage. It is generally a phenomenon of shares which do not represent the controlling interest in a corporation. *See* Blockage rule.

Blockage rule. Process of determining value of large blocks of corporate stock for gift and estate tax purposes, based on the postulate that a large block of stock cannot be marketed as readily and as advantageously in price as can a few shares. Application of this rule generally justifies a discount in the fair market value since the disposition of a large amount of stock at any one time may well depress the value of such shares in the market place.

Block book system. An abstract of property assessed for taxes and also of property unrendered and of which owners were unknown, together with maps and plats.

Blocked account. Governmental restrictions on a bank account; usually with reference to transfers to foreign countries.

The President, in times of war or other emergencies, may issue directives to banks to suspend payment of the accounts of enemy nationals.

Blocked currency. Restrictions on use of currency and bank deposits (normally with respect to transfer to other countries) by the government where the currency or deposits are located.

Blocked income. Income earned by foreign taxpayer which is not subject to tax in U.S. because taxpayer is precluded in foreign country from making conversion of foreign earned income to dollars.

Block policy. Insurance policy covering all the property of the insured against most perils.

Block trade. Commonly, a trade involving a large amount of stock.

Block-voting. Exists when a group of shareholders agree to vote their shares in a single block. *See also* Voting trust.

Blood alcohol count. Refers to the standard measure for legal intoxication under state DWI laws. In most states, a person can be charged with "driving while intoxicated" with a blood alcohol level of .10 percent or higher. *See* Breathalyzer test; Driving while intoxicated (DWI).

Blood grouping test. Test used in paternity and illegitimacy cases to determine whether one *could be* father of child. The test does not affirmatively establish paternity but it eliminates one who cannot be adjudicated father. *See also* Blood test evidence; DNA identification.

Blood relations. Kindred; consanguinity; family relationship; relation by descent from a common blood ancestor. A person may be said to be "of the blood" of another who has any, however small a portion, of the blood derived from a common ancestor, thus including half blood as well as whole blood. All persons are of the blood of an ancestor who may, in the absence of other and nearer heirs, take by descent from that ancestor. *See also* Relation.

Half-blood. A term denoting the degree of relationship which exists between those who have the same father or the same mother, but not both parents in common.

Whole blood. Kinship by descent from the same father and mother; as distinguished from *half* blood, which is the relationship of those who have one parent in common, but not both.

Blood test evidence. *See* Blood alcohol count; Blood grouping test; Breathalyzer test; Consent (*Implied consent*); DNA identification; Sobriety check point.

Blotter. *See* Bench blotter.

BLS. Bachelor of Library Science; Bureau of Labor Statistics.

Blue chip investment. Highest quality stock or bond of company with long record of profit growth, minimum risk and satisfactory income or yield; commonly required by trust managers.

Blue laws. Statutes regulating entertainment activities, work, and commerce on Sundays. Such laws have their origin in colonial New England.

Blue list. Daily listing (on blue paper) of municipal bond offerings.

Blue notes. Notes accepted by a life insurance company for the amount of premiums on the policy, which provide for the continuance of the policy in force until the due date of the notes.

Blue ribbon jury. Jury consisting of highly qualified persons.

Blue sky laws. A popular name for state statutes providing for the regulation and supervision of securities offerings and sales, for the protection of citizen-investors from investing in fraudulent companies. Most blue sky laws require the registration of new issues of securities with a state agency that reviews selling documents for accuracy and completeness. Blue sky laws also often regulate securities brokers and salesmen.

A statute called a "Blue Sky Law" because it pertains to speculative schemes which have no more basis than so many feet of blue sky.

Bluff. A high, steep bank, as by a river, the sea, a ravine, or a plain, or a bank or headland with a broad, steep face. To deceive by pretense or appearance of strength.

Board. An official or representative body organized to perform a trust or to execute official or representative functions or having the management of a public office or department exercising administrative or governmental functions.

A committee of persons organized under authority of law in order to exercise certain authorities, have oversight or control of certain matters, or discharge certain functions of a magisterial, representative, or fiduciary character. Thus, "board of aldermen," "board of health," "board of directors," "board of works."

Group of persons with managerial, supervisory, or investigatory functions and power. See types of such boards, *infra*.

Lodging, food, and entertainment, furnished to a guest at an inn or boarding house. As a verb, means to receive food for a reasonable compensation, either with or without lodging.

When used with reference to prisoners, as a basis for the sheriff's fee, board may be equivalent to "necessary food."

Boarder. One that is provided with regular meals, with or without lodging, usually under an express contract.

Board lot. Unit of trade on a stock exchange.

Board of adjustment. Public and quasi judicial agency charged with duty to hear and determine zoning appeals. Also called "Board of Zoning Appeals" in certain cities.

Board of aldermen. The governing body of a municipal corporation. *See* Aldermen.

Board of appeals. A non-judicial, administrative tribunal which reviews decisions made by the hearing officer or by the head of the agency. *See also* Board of review.

Board of audit. A tribunal provided by statute in some states, to adjust and settle the accounts of municipal corporations.

Board of bar overseers. State board which governs licensing and discipline of attorneys.

Board of directors. The governing body of a corporation elected by the stockholders; usually made-up of officers of the corporation and outside (non-company) directors. The board is empowered to elect and appoint officers and agents to act on behalf of the corporation, declare dividends, and act on other major matters affecting the corporation. See *e.g.* Rev.Model Bus.Corp.Act, § 8.01 et seq. *See also* Directors; Outside director.

Staggered board. A corporation's board of directors in which a fraction of the board is elected each year. In staggered boards, members serve two or three years, depending on whether the board is classified into two or three groups.

Board of education. A state or local agency or board organized for government and management of schools in state or municipality. The agency to which state delegates power and duty of controlling schools in school district.

Board of equalization. *See* Equalization.

Board of examiners. A state agency or board appointed to examine the qualifications of applicants for license to practice a trade or profession.

Board of fire underwriters. Unincorporated voluntary associations composed exclusively of persons engaged in business of fire insurance, for consolidation and co-operation in matters affecting the business.

Board of Governors of Federal Reserve System. Seven member board, with fourteen year terms, which governs the twelve Federal Reserve Banks and branches. The Board of Governors determines general monetary, credit, and operating policies for the System as a whole and formulates the rules and regulations necessary to carry out the purposes of the Federal Reserve Act. The Board's principal duties consist of exerting an influence over credit conditions and supervising the Federal Reserve Banks and member banks.

Board of health. A municipal or state board or commission with certain powers and duties relative to preservation and improvement of the public health.

Board of Immigration Appeals. Quasi-judicial agency within the Department of Justice (accountable to Attorney General) which hears appeals from certain decisions of the Immigration and Naturalization Service and reviews actions of the Commissioner of Immigration and Naturalization in deporting and excluding aliens. Most appeals to the Board are from immigration judges' decisions on deportation and exclusion.

Board of pardons. State board, of which the governor is usually a member, authorized to review and grant pardons and clemency to convicted prisoners.

Board of Parole. *See* Parole board.

Board of Patent Appeals and Interferences. Formerly known as the Board of Patent Appeals; consists of Commissioner of Patents, the Deputy Commissioner, the Assistant Commissioners, and the examiners-in-chief whose responsibility is to review adverse decisions of examiners upon applications for patents and to determine priority and patentability of invention in interferences. 35 U.S.C.A. § 7.

Board of regents. A body of officials appointed to direct and supervise an educational institution or, in some states, the educational system of a State.

Board of registration. State boards governing licensing and discipline of professions and quasi-professions in state.

Board of review. Board authorized to review administrative agency decisions and rulings. Body authorized to review alleged improper valuation and assessment of property. In some cities, a board charged with responsibility to review alleged police brutality or excessive force. *See also* Board of appeals.

Board of supervisors. An organized committee, or body of officials, constituting part of the county government, with special charge of the county revenues.

Board of Tax Appeals. The Board of Tax Appeals was a trial court that considered Federal tax matters. This Court is now designated as the U.S. Tax Court.

Board of trade. An organization of merchants, manufacturers, etc., for furthering its commercial interests, advancing its prosperity, etc. Also an organization for the advancement and protection of a particular trade or line of commerce.

An exchange or association engaged in the business of buying or selling commodities; *e.g.* Chicago Board of Trade.

Bodily. Pertaining to or concerning the body; of or belonging to the body or the physical constitution; not mental but corporeal.

Bodily condition. Status of human body at a given point in time as contrasted with state of mind.

Bodily exhibition. Public or semi public showing of private parts of body's anatomy; used in statutes covering obscenity and crimes against public decency; *e.g.* indecent exposure.

Bodily harm. See Bodily injury, below.

Bodily heirs. Heirs begotten or borne by the person referred to; lineal descendants. Progeny or issue, including children, grandchildren, and other lineal descendants. *See* Heir of the body.

Bodily infirmity. A settled disease or ailment that would probably result to some degree in general impairment of physical health and vigor. An ailment or disorder of an established and settled character. Something that amounts to inroad on physical health or impairment of bodily or mental powers. *See also* Disability.

Bodily injury. Generally refers only to injury to the body, or to sickness or disease contracted by the injured as a result of injury; including illness caused by nervous shock or injury resulting from rape or attempted rape. *See also* Disability; Injury.

Body. A person. Used of a natural body, or of an artificial one created by law, as a corporation. Body in the broad sense is the main central or principal part of anything as distinguished from subordinate parts.

The main part of the human body; the trunk. The term however has also been held to embrace all members of the person, including the head and limbs.

Also the main part of an instrument. In deeds it is spoken of as distinguished from the recitals and other introductory parts and signatures; in affidavits, from the title and jurat.

A collection of laws; that is, the embodiment of the laws in one connected statement or collection, called a "body of laws" *(q.v.).*

See also Corpus.

Body corporate. A public or private corporation.

Body execution. Seizure of person by order of court to *e.g.* enforce judgment for payment of money. *See* Capias *(Copias ad satisfaciendum).*

Body heirs. *See* Bodily *(Bodily heirs)*; Heir of the body.

Body of an instrument. The main and operative part of a legal document; the substantive provi-

sions, as distinguished from the recitals, title, jurat, etc.

Body of laws. An organized and systematic collection or codification of laws; *e.g.* United States Code; California Code.

Body of the offense (*or* **crime**). When applied to any particular offense, means that the particular crime charged has actually been committed by some one. The corpus delicti *(q.v.).*

Body politic or **corporate.** A social compact by which the whole people covenants with each citizen, and each citizen with the whole people, that all shall be governed by certain laws for the common good. Also a term applied to a municipal corporation, school district, county or city. State or nation or public associations.

Bogus /bówgəs/. Counterfeit; sham; imitation; as *e.g.* bogus money.

Bogus check. A check given by person upon bank in which he has no funds and which he has no reason to suppose will be honored. Such act is a misdemeanor in most states. *See also* Bad check; Check kiting.

Boilerplate. Language which is used commonly in documents having a definite meaning in the same context without variation; used to describe standard language in a legal document that is identical in instruments of a like nature. *See also* Adhesion contract.

Boiler-room transaction. High-pressure selling of stocks, precious metals, commodities, and other investments of doubtful or risky value, usually over the telephone. Sometimes associated with sales of "hot-issue" securities.

Bolstering. In evidence law, occurs when one item of evidence is improperly used by a party to add credence or weight to some earlier unimpeached piece of evidence offered by the same party.

Bona, *n.* /bównə/. Lat. Goods; property; possessions. In the Roman law, this term was used to designate all species of property, real, personal, and mixed, but was more strictly applied to real estate. In civil law, it includes both personal property (technically so called) and chattels real, thus corresponding to the French *biens (q.v.).* In the common law, its use was confined to the description of movable goods.

Bona, *adj.* /bównə/. Lat. Good. Used in numerous legal phrases of which the following are examples:

Bona fides /bównə fáydiyz/. Good faith; integrity of dealing; honesty; sincerity; the opposite of *mala fides* and of *dolus malus.* See Bona fide.

Bona fide /bównə fáydiy/bównə fayd/. In or with good faith; honestly, openly, and sincerely; without deceit or fraud. Truly; actually; without simulation or pretense. Innocently; in the attitude of trust and confidence; without notice of fraud, etc. Real, actual, genuine, and not feigned. *See also* Good faith.

Bona fide business purpose. In tax law, this term is often used in determining whether a real business purpose in fact existed for carrying out a particular transaction. *See also* Business *(Business purpose).*

Bona fide error. Mistake made unintentionally; inadvertently; in good faith. Within meaning of Truth in Lending Act's exemption from liability for bona fide errors, "bona fide error" is error made in course of good-faith attempt at compliance with Act's requirements.

Bona fide holder for value. An innocent or "bona fide holder for value" of negotiable paper is one who has taken it in good faith for a valuable consideration in the ordinary course of business and when it was not overdue. One who receives negotiable paper in payment of antecedent obligations without notice of prior equities. Under U.C.C. § 3–302, the requirements for a holder in due course are different from a mere bona fide holder for value. *See* Holder in due course.

Bona fide judgment creditor. One who in good faith, without fraud or collusion, recovers a judgment for money honestly due him.

Bona fide occupational qualification (BFOQ). Employment in particular jobs may not be limited to persons of a particular sex, religion, or national origin unless the employer can show that sex, religion, or national origin is an actual qualification for performing the job. The qualification is called a bona fide occupational qualification.

Bona fide possessor. One who not only supposes himself to be the true proprietor of the land, but who is ignorant that his title is contested by some other person claiming a better right to it.

Bona fide purchaser. One who has purchased property for value without any notice of any defects in the title of the seller. One who pays valuable consideration, has no notice of outstanding rights of others, and acts in good faith.

Bona fide purchaser for value is one who, without notice of another's claim of right to, or equity in, property prior to his acquisition of title, has paid vendor a valuable consideration.

One who buys property or to whom a negotiable document of title is transferred in good faith and without notice of any defense or claim to the property or document. U.C.C. § 7–501. One who takes trust property for value and without notice of breach of trust and who is not knowingly part of an illegal transaction. Restatement, Second, Trusts § 284; Uniform Probate Code § 2–202(3).

Bulk transfer. Purchaser from transferee of bulk transfer who takes for value in good faith and without notice of any defect of non-compliance with law. U.C.C. § 6–110.

Investment securities. A purchaser for value in good faith and without notice of any adverse claim who takes delivery of a security in bearer form or of one in registered form issued to him or indorsed to him or in blank. U.C.C. § 8–302.

Bona fide residence. Residence with domiciliary intent, *i.e.*, a home in which the party actually lives.

Bona fide sale. A completed transaction in which seller makes sale in good faith, for a valuable consideration without notice of any reason against the sale.

Bond. A certificate or evidence of a debt on which the issuing company or governmental body promises to pay the bondholders a specified amount of interest for a specified length of time, and to repay the loan on the expiration date. A long-term debt instrument that promises to pay the lender a series of periodic interest payments in addition to returning the principal at maturity. In every case a bond represents debt—its holder is a creditor of the corporation and not a part owner as is the shareholder. Commonly, bonds are secured by a mortgage.

The word "bond" is sometimes used more broadly to refer also to unsecured debt instruments, *i.e.*, debentures. Income bonds are hybrid instruments that take the form of a bond, but the interest obligation is limited or tied to the corporate earnings for the year. Participating bonds are another type of hybrid instruments that take the form of a typical debt instrument but the interest obligation is not fixed so that holders are entitled to receive additional amounts from excess earnings or from excess distributions, depending on the terms of the participating bond.

A written obligation, made by owner of real property, to repay a loan under specific terms, usually accompanied by a mortgage placed on land as security.

See also Debenture.

Specific types of bonds as relating to finance, surety, guaranty, appeals, performance, etc. are set forth below:

Adjustment bond. Bonds issued upon reorganization of corporation.

Annuity bond. See Annuity *(Annuity bond).*

Appeal bond. Bond required to cover costs of appeal in civil cases. See *e.g.* Fed.R.App.P. 7.

Appearance bond. Type of bail bond required to insure presence of defendant in criminal case. *See* Bail *(Bail bond).*

Arbitrage bond. Bond posted to secure performance of arbitrage agreement; a bond which is the subject of arbitrage. *See* Arbitrage.

Attachment bond. See that title.

Bail bond. *See* Bail *(Bail bond).*

Bearer bond. See that title.

Bid bond. See that title.

Blanket bond. See that title.

Bond and mortgage. A species of security, consisting of a bond conditioned for the repayment of a loan of money, and a mortgage of realty to secure the performance of the stipulations of the bond.

Bond coupon. Part of bond which is cut and surrendered for payment of one of successive payments of interest. *See Coupon bond, below.*

Bond creditor. A creditor whose debt is secured by a bond.

Bond discount. The difference between the face amount or obligation of the bond and the current market price of such bond, if selling price is lower than market price.

Bond dividend. See Dividend.

Bond for deed. See Bond for title, below.

Bond for title. An agreement to make title in the future on an executory or incomplete sale. It is not a conveyance of legal title but only a contract to convey and may ripen into an equitable title upon payment of the consideration.

Bond issue. The totality of bonds issued at a given time (for sale to investors). Delivery of instruments as covered by term.

Bond of state or local government. See Municipal bond, below.

Bond premium. The difference between the face amount or obligation of the bond and the selling price of such bond if the selling price is greater than the face amount.

Bottomry bond. Bond secured by mortgage of ships.

Callable bond. *See* Callable bonds.

Carrying value of bond. The face value of a bond minus the unamortized bond discount (or plus the unamortized bond premium).

Chattel mortgage bond. Bonds secured by mortgage on chattels of business.

Closed-end mortgage bond. Debt security with provisions which prohibit the firm from issuing additional bonds with the priority of claim against assets.

Collateral trust bond. A bond secured by collateral deposited with a trustee. The collateral is often the stocks or bonds of companies controlled by the issuing company but may be other securities.

Type of chattel mortgages that are normally secured by common stock and/or bonds issued by subsidiaries of the issuing firm.

Common defeasance bond. One in which the obligor agrees to pay a stipulated amount called a penalty, subject to a condition of defeasance that voids the covenant to pay the specified amount if the condition occurs, and the only covenant or promise to pay by the obligor in such bond is to pay the penalty if the condition is not fulfilled; also known as penalty bond.

Common law bond. That which provides coverage in excess of the minimum statutory requirements with respect to a public works project. *See Performance bond, below.*

Completion bond. A form of surety or guaranty agreement which contains the promise of a third party, usually a bonding company, to complete or pay for the cost of completion of a construction contract if the construction contractor defaults. Bond given to insure public authority that contract once awarded will be completed as awarded within fixed period of time. *See Common law bond; Contract bond; Performance bond; also,* Miller Act.

Consolidated bond. Bond which is sufficiently large in face amount to retire two or more outstanding issues of bonds or securities.

Contract bond. A guarantee of the faithful performance of a construction contract and the payment of all material and labor costs incident thereto. A contract bond covering faithful performance is known as a "performance bond," and one covering payment of labor and materials, a "payment bond." *See also Completion bond above; Performance bond, below.*

Convertible bond. Bond that can, at the option of the holder, be converted into (*i.e.* exchanged for) stock.

Corporate bonds. See that title.

Cost bond. *See Appeal bond, above.*

County bonds. See that title.

Coupon bond. Bond with interest coupons attached. The coupons are clipped as they come due and are presented by the holder for payment of interest.

Debenture bond. Bonds secured by general credit of government or corporation rather than by any specific property; *i.e.* bond which is not secured with collateral. *See also* Debenture.

Deep-discount bond. A bond that is issued at a price significantly below its par value.

Deferred bonds. See that title.

Discharging bond. Same as a delivery bond except that not only does it permit defendant to regain possession of attached property, it also effects a release of the property from the lien of attachment. Another name for this bond is "dissolution bond."

Discount bond. *See* Bond discount.

Executor's bond. A bond that an executor of an estate must furnish in order to serve as the administrator of an estate.

Fidelity bond. Bond covering employer-business for loss due to embezzlement, larceny, or gross negligence by employees.

Fiduciary bond. *See* Fiduciary.

First mortgage bond. Long-term security that has first claim on specified assets.

Foreign bond. An international bond which is denominated in the currency of the country in which it is issued.

General average bond. See that title.

General mortgage bond. A bond which is secured by a blanket mortgage on the company's property, but which may be subordinate to one or more other mortgages.

General obligation bond. A bond secured by the "full faith and credit" of the issuing government and backed by revenues from its taxing power.

Global bonds. Bonds that are designed so as to qualify for immediate trading in any domestic capital market and in the Euromarket.

Gold bond. Formerly, bond containing a clause which required payment of the bonded indebtedness in gold; such clause has since been prohibited. Now bonds are dischargeable by payment in legal tender or money.

Government bond. Evidence of indebtedness issued by the government to finance its operations. Such bonds are backed solely by the credit of the government.

Guaranteed bond. A bond which has interest or principal, or both, guaranteed by a company other than the issuer.

Guaranty bond. Type of bond which combines the features of both the fidelity and surety bond and which is given to secure payment and performance.

Improvement bond. Type of bonds issued by a city, town or special authority to finance improvements within the district, with payment to be made only from the improvement fund.

Income bond. Bonds on which interest is payable only when earned and after payment of interest upon prior mortgages. In some cases unpaid interest on an income bond may accumulate as a claim against the corporation when the bond becomes due. An income bond may also be issued in lieu of preferred stock.

Indemnity bond. See that title.

Indeterminate bond. Callable bond with no set maturity date.

Industrial development bonds. Such bonds are issued by a municipality as a means of attracting private businesses. The bonds are marketed by the municipality and the proceeds used to build the private business facility. Commonly, the business leases the facility from the municipality for a total rent equal to the amount necessary to pay the interest and amortize the principal on the bonds.

Industrial revenue bonds. A specific type of revenue bond whose proceeds are used to finance the purchase or construction of facilities or equipment to be leased to a private corporation. The bonds are backed by the credit of the corporation.

Interest bond. Bond paid in lieu of interest due on other bonds.

Investment grade bonds. Any bond with a rating of BBB or better by the leading bond rating services.

Joint and several bond. A bond the principal and interest of which is guaranteed by two or more persons.

Joint bond. Bond executed by two or more obligors who must be joined in any action on such, as opposed to joint and several bond, on which any or all of obligors may be sued at the option of the obligee.

Judicial bonds. See that title.

Junior bond. Bonds which are subordinate in priority, in principal or interest to another issue.

Junk bond. High yield, high risk bonds of two types: those which were investment-grade when originally issued, but which have subsequently been downgraded and those originally issued as low-grade bonds. The latter group includes bonds issued by low-rated companies to finance operations as well as those issued in connection with corporate takeovers.

Leasehold mortgage bond. A bond secured by a building constructed on leased real estate. This bond is subject to the compliance by the lessee (who issues the bond) with the terms of the lease; upon default in the terms of the lease the lessor of the leased real estate has priority over the holders of the leasehold bonds.

Liability bond. One which is intended to protect the assured from liability for damages or to protect the persons damaged by injuries occasioned by the assured as specified, when such liability should accrue, and be imposed by law, as by a court, as distinguished from an indemnity bond, whose purpose is only to indemnify the assured against actual loss by way of reimbursement for moneys paid or which must be paid.

License bond. The term "License Bond" is used interchangeably with "Permit Bond" to describe bonds required by state law, municipal ordinance, or by regulation as a condition precedent to the granting of a license to engage in a specified business or the grant of a permit to exercise a certain privilege.

Such bonds provide payment to the obligee for the loss or damage resulting from the operations permitted by law, ordinance or regulation, under which the bond is required and for violations by the licensee of the duties and obligations imposed upon him.

Maintenance bond. Bond guaranteeing against defects in workmanship or materials for period of time following completion of work contracted for.

Mortgage bond. A bond secured by a mortgage on a property. The value of the property may or may not equal the value of the so-called mortgage bonds issued against it. *See also Leasehold mortgage bond, above.*

Municipal bond. A bond issued by a state or a political subdivision, such as county, city, town or village. The term also designates bonds issued by state agencies and authorities. In general, interest paid on municipal bonds is exempt from federal income taxes and state and local income taxes within the state of issue. *See also Industrial development bonds; Industrial revenue bonds, above.*

Noncallable bond. Bonds which are neither refundable nor redeemable. Bonds that cannot be redeemed at the option of the issuer.

Obligation bond. Device used by states and municipalities to obtain funds to support projects. The sale of general obligation bonds is the commitment of the state to a debtor relationship with those who purchase the bonds. *See General obligation bond, above.*

Official bond. A bond given by a public officer, conditioned that he shall well and faithfully perform all the duties of the office. The term is sometimes made to include the bonds of executors, guardians, trustees, etc.

Passive bond. Bond which bears no interest.

Payment bond. See Miller Act.

Peace bond. See that title.

Penal bond. See that title.

Performance bond. Type of contract bond which protects against loss due to the inability or refusal of a contractor to perform his contract. Such are normally required on public construction projects.

See Common law bond; Completion bond; Contract bond, above; also, Miller Act.

Perpetual bond. A bond that has no maturity date.

Personal bond. A written document in which the obligor formally recognizes an obligation to pay money or to do a specific act; *e.g.* surrender a lost bank book when it is found.

Premium bond. Bond with selling price above face or redemption value. *See, also, Bond premium, above.*

Pure-discount bond. A bond that will make only one payment of principal and interest. Also called a zero-coupon bond or a single-payment bond.

Put bond. Bond that gives holder right to redeem at specified times before maturity for full face value.

Redeemable bond. See that title.

Redelivery bond. A statutory bond given by a person in whose possession attached property is found in order to regain possession of the property.

Refunding bond. See that title.

Registered bond. A bond which is registered on the books of the issuing company in the name of the owner. It can be transferred only when endorsed by the registered owner.

Removal bond. See that title.

Reorganization bond. See *Adjustment bond, above.*

Replevin bond. Replevin (Replevin bond).

Revenue bond. Bonds issued by a public agency, municipal corporation, or state for purpose of raising revenue. Debt securities issued by municipalities in which the payments must be generated by the project supported by the proceeds from the bonds issued. (*e.g.* earnings of municipal sports complex.)

School bonds. Bonds issued by a city, town or school district for purpose of school construction.

Serial bond. Bond issue consisting of a number of bonds with different maturity dates. Bonds are issued at the same time as distinguished from series bonds which are issued at different times.

Series bonds. Groups of bonds normally issued at different times but under same indenture.

Simple bond. At common law, a bond without penalty; a bond for the payment of a definite sum of money to a named obligee on demand or on a day certain.

Single bond. A deed whereby the obligor obliges himself, his heirs, executors, and administrators, to pay a certain sum of money to the obligee at a day named, without terms of defeasance.

Single-payment bond. A bond that will make only one payment of principal and interest. Also called a pure-discount bond or a zero-coupon bond.

Special tax or assessment bonds. Bonds secured by special levies on taxpayers, usually those in the area immediately benefiting from the project or improvement.

State bond. Bond issued by state, obligating state to make payment.

Straw bond. A bond upon which is used either the names of fictitious persons or those unable to pay the sum guaranteed; generally applied to insufficient bail bonds, improperly taken.

Submission bond. See that title.

Subordinated bonds or debentures. See that title.

Supersedeas bond. See that title.

Suretyship bond. A contractual arrangement between the surety, the principal and the obligee whereby the surety agrees to protect the obligee if the principal defaults in performing the principal's contractual obligations. The bond is the instrument which binds the surety. *See e.g.,* Bail *(Bail bond).*

Tax exempt bond. A bond, the receipt of income from which is not taxable, *e.g.* municipal bond *(q.v.).*

Treasury bonds. Bonds reacquired or unsold by corporation. Bonds issued by U.S. Treasury (*e.g.* U.S. Savings bonds). *See also* Treasury bond.

U.S. Savings bonds. An obligation of the United States designed to afford persons the opportunity to create savings by purchasing the bond at a reduced sum and requiring the purchaser to wait a period of time to redeem at face value.

Zero coupon bond. Treasury bond that has had the interest coupon clipped by the purchaser of the bond. This purchaser sells the remaining bond at a discount from its face value. The deep discount reflects the many years, usually fifteen to thirty, that remain until the bond may be redeemed at face value. The advantage of these long-term investments is the security afforded by United States Government backing.

Bondage. Slavery; involuntary personal servitude; captivity. In old English law, villenage, villein tenure. Such is prohibited by 13th Amendment to U.S. Constitution.

Bond conversion. The act of exchanging convertible bonds for preferred or common stock.

Bond covenant. A contractual provision specified in a bond indenture. *See e.g.* Negative covenant; Negative pledge clause.

Bond discount. Sale of bonds on the market at a price less than the face amount of such.

From the standpoint of the issuer of a bond at the issue date, is the excess of the par value of a bond over its initial sales price; at later dates the excess of par over the sum of (initial) issue price plus the portion of discount already amortized. From the standpoint of a bondholder, is the difference between par value and selling price when the bond sells below par.

Bonded debt. The indebtedness of a business or government which is represented by bonds payable. Indebtedness lawfully contracted for governmental purposes, payable from taxes on all property within municipality.

Bonded warehouse. *See* Warehouse system.

Bond equivalent yield. True interest cost expressed on the basis of a 360–day year.

Bondholders. Creditors of a business, whose evidence of debt is a bond issued by the business.

Bond indenture. The contract between an issuer of bonds and the bondholders. An instrument of secured indebtedness issued by a corporation. *See* Indenture.

Bond premium. The excess of the price of bonds over their face value, and generally reflects the difference between the nominal interest rate borne by such bonds and the actual or effective rate of return determined by the current market.

Bond rating. System of evaluating, appraising and rating the investment value of individual bond issues (*i.e.* a bond's probability of default). Triple A (AAA) bonds have the highest rating. There are several major bond rating companies or services that make such evaluations.

Bond redemption. Retirement of bonds upon payment. *See* Redemption.

Bond refunding. A situation that occurs when a firm redeems a callable bond issue and sells a generally lower interest cost issue to take its place. A bond is refunded when a municipality or state calls in an existing bond, usually when interest rates have dropped, to replace it with lower-cost financing.

Bond retirement. The cancellation of bonds that have been called.

Bondsman. A surety; one who has entered into a bond to give surety for another; *e.g.,* bail bondsman. *See* Bail *(Bail bond).*

Bond value. With respect to a convertible bond, the value the security would have if it were not convertible; the value of the security apart from the value of the conversion option.

Bond yield. *See* Yield.

Bonification. The remission of a tax, particularly on goods intended for export, having the same effect as a bonus or drawback. A device enabling a commodity to be exported and sold in the foreign market as if it had not been taxed.

Bonus. A consideration or premium paid in addition to what is strictly due. A gratuity to which the recipient has no right to make a demand. A premium or extra or irregular remuneration in consideration of offices performed or to encourage their performance. A premium paid to a grantor or vendor. An advance royalty. An extra consideration given for what is received, or something given in addition to what is ordinarily received by, or strictly due, the recipient. Compensation paid to professional athlete in addition to salary for signing with particular team or for specific performance levels. *See also* Bonus stock; Premium.

Bonus share. *See* Bonus stock, *infra.*

Bonus stock. Stock given as premium in connection with (to encourage) the sale of another class of securities; *e.g.* stock issued to the purchasers of bonds as an inducement to them to purchase bonds or loan money.

Par value shares issued without consideration, usually in connection with the issuance of preferred or senior securities, or debt instruments. Bonus shares are considered a species of watered shares and may impose a liability on the recipient equal to the amount of par value.

Booby trap. A concealed or camouflaged device designed to be triggered by an unsuspecting victim; loosely, any device which catches a person off-guard.

Boodle. Term used to designate the money held to be paid or paid as a bribe for corrupt official action.

Book. An assembly or concourse of ideas expressed in words. A literary composition which is printed; a printed composition bound in a volume. The largest subdivisions of a treatise or other literary composition.

A bound volume consisting of sheets of paper, not normally printed, containing manuscript entries; such as a merchant's account-books, dockets of courts, etc. See various types below.

To register or make reservation for transportation, lodging, etc. To set date and time for engagement or appointment.

Book account. A detailed statement, in the nature of debits and credits between entities; an account or record of debits and credits kept in a book. A book in which a detailed history of business transactions is entered; a record of goods sold or services rendered; a statement in detail of the transactions between parties.

Book entry. A notation, generally of figures or numbers, made in an accounting journal, consisting, in double entry bookkeeping, of debits and credits.

Book of original entry. A book maintained to record the day to day transactions of an entity, including the sale and delivery of goods. A book in which a detailed history of business transactions are entered.

Books of account. Books in which merchants, traders, and businessmen generally keep their accounts; including journals, ledgers, and other accounting records. Entries made in the regular course of business. Serial, continuous, and permanent memorials of business affairs.

Book value. The value at which an asset is carried on the balance sheet. Book value is the cost less accumulated depreciation or the valuation allowance. Book value is based on the historical cost of an asset and may vary significantly from the fair market value. The net amount of an asset after reduction by a related reserve. The book value of accounts receivable, for example, would be the amount of the receivables less the reserve for bad debts. *See also* Net book value.

Corporate books. Whatever is kept as written evidence of official doings and business transactions of corporation.

Criminal proceedings. See Booking.

Office book. See Office.

Booked. Engaged, destined, bound to promise or pledge oneself to make an engagement. To have travel, lodging, etc. reservations. To enter charges against accused in police register or blotter. *See* Booking.

Booking. Administrative step taken after an arrested person is brought to the police station, which involves entry of the person's name, the crime for which the arrest was made, and other relevant facts on the police "blotter," and which may also include photographing, fingerprinting, and the like.

A form of gambling commonly associated with number pools horse and dog racing when engaged in away from the track. *See* Bookmaker; Bookmaking.

Booking contract. A contract made by agents who procure contracts for appearance of acts and actors.

Bookkeeping. The art or science of recording business accounts and transactions. *See also* Accounting; Book.

Double entry bookkeeping. Accounting system which requires that in every entry there be a debit and a credit; *e.g.* on cash sale of merchandise, a debit to cash and a credit to sales.

Bookmaker. A gambler who makes book (*i.e.*, partakes in bookmaking) on uncertain future events. One who collects and records bets of others. One who establishes odds on events which are the subject of gambling. In slang, such person is known as "bookie."

Bookmaking. Formerly the collection of sheets of paper or other substances on which entries could be made, either written or printed. The term now commonly denotes the taking and recording or registering of bets or wagers on any trial or contest of speed, skill or power of endurance or selling pools. An operation which involves both the placing of bets and the paying off or collection of debts.

Books and papers. Generic term used to describe all forms of records which are sought in a summons duces tecum, or subject to discovery under Fed.R.Civil P. 26(b)(1), 34, 45, or Fed.R.Crim.P. 16. *See also* Business records exception; Record; Shop-book rule; Subpoena duces tecum.

Book value. *See* Book.

Boot. Term used in tax accounting to describe cash or property other than property qualifying as such for nonrecognition in an exchange of like kind of property under I.R.C. § 1031. As used in connection with reorganization, includes anything received other than stock or securities of a controlled corporation. I.R.C. §§ 355, 356(b).

Cash or property of a type not included in the definition of a nontaxable exchange. The receipt of boot will cause an otherwise taxfree transfer to become taxable to the extent of the lesser of the fair market value of such boot or the realized gain on the transfer.

Cash or other consideration used to balance an otherwise unequal exchange of two properties; *e.g.* machine worth $500 plus $500 for machine worth $1000.

An old Saxon word, equivalent to "estovers".

Bootlegger. One who sells, or keeps for sale, alcoholic beverages in violation of law.

Bootlegging. Illegal manufacture or sale of liquor, cigarettes, records, and the like to evade taxing, licensing, copyright, etc. laws. *See also* Contraband; Gray market goods.

Bootstrap doctrine. The decision of a court on a special as well as a general appearance that it has jurisdiction is not subject of collateral attack but is res judicata.

Bootstrap sale. A means by which the cash or other assets of a business are utilized by the purchaser in acquiring ownership of such business.

An arrangement resulting in tax savings by which a seller converts ordinary income from a business into capital gain from sale of corporate stock.

Booty. Property captured from the enemy in war, on land.

Border. Within rules applicable to border searches includes not only actual border crossing points but also reasonable extended geographic area in immediate vicinity of crossing point. *See also* Border search.

Bordereau /bòrd(ə)rów/. In insurance, summary of transactions between agent and company.

Border search. Search conducted by immigration or customs officials at borders of the country to prevent and to detect illegal entry. Immigration and Nationality Act, 8 U.S.C.A. § 1357. Any person or thing coming into the United States is subject to search by that fact alone, whether or not there be any suspicion of illegality directed to the particular person or thing to be searched. To qualify as a "border search," a search must occur at the border or at the functional equivalent of the border. *See also* Border; Border warrant.

Border warrant. Process issued for search at borders of the country for search and for arrest of illegal immigrants; no warrant necessary for preliminary stop for questioning. *See also* Border search.

Born. Act of being delivered or expelled from mother's body, whether or not placenta has been separated or cord cut.

Born alive. Refers to product of conception after complete expulsion or extraction from mother, irrespective of the duration of the pregnancy, which breathes or shows any other evidence of life such as beating of the heart, pulsation of the umbilical cord or definite movement of voluntary muscles, whether or not the umbilical cord has been cut or the placenta is attached. Each product of such birth is considered live born and fully recognized as a human person. Maine Rev.Stat. Ann., Tit. 22, § 1595. *See also* Viable child.

Born out of wedlock. Children whose parents are not, and have not been, married to each other regardless of marital status of either parent with respect to another. *See* Illegitimate.

Borough /bə́hrə/bə́hrow/. A town or township with a municipal charter. *E.g.* one of the five political divisions of New York City.

Borrow. To solicit and receive from another any article of property, money or thing of value with the intention and promise to repay or return it or its equivalent. If the item borrowed is money, there normally exists an agreement to pay interest for its use. In a broad sense the term means a contract for the use of money. The term may be used to express the idea of receiving something from another for one's own use. The word "loan" is the correlative of "borrow."

Borrowed capital. Term denoting various transactions between corporation and stockholders, but commonly referring to cash dividends declared by corporation and retained by it pursuant to agreement with stockholders for operating business successfully. Moneys due by corporation to another corporation used as its capital.

Borrowed employee. Before person may be considered "borrowed servant," his services must be loaned with his acquiescence or consent and he must become wholly subject to control and direction of second employer, and free during the temporary period from the control of the original employer. Under the "borrowed employee" doctrine, if one to whom an employee is lent is master of servant at very time negligent act occurs, it is upon him, as a special employer, that liability rests, but if one lending employee is his master at very time of injury, then he, as general employer incurs liability.

Borrowed servant. *See* Borrowed employee.

Borrowed statutes. Laws of one state or jurisdiction used by another state in deciding conflicts question involved in choice of law; *e.g.* statute of limitation of state where claim accrued as contrasted with statute of limitation of forum state.

Borrower. He to whom a thing or money is lent at his request. Someone who has, with permission of owner, temporary possession and use of property of another for his own purposes. The person, sometimes referred to as the mortgagor, who obtains a mortgage loan.

Borrowings. Generic term to describe all manners of loans from standpoint of debtor.

Boston interest. Interest computed by using a 30 day month rather than the exact number of days in the month.

Both. The one and the other; the two without the exception of either. The term likewise has a meaning which excludes more than two mentioned subject matters. "Either," may mean "both."

Bottom hole contract. A form of agreement used in drilling for oil or gas and which requires a payment by owners of well to lessee of well upon the drilling to a specified depth.

Bottom land. As used in a contract to convey, means low land formed by alluvial deposits along the river, low-lying ground, a dale, valley, or intervale.

Bottom line. A term used in accounting to describe the net income or loss after income taxes.

Bottomry /bótəmriy/. In maritime law, a contract by which the owner of a ship borrows for the use, equipment, or repair of the vessel, and for a definite term, and pledges the ship (or the keel or *bottom* of the ship, *pars pro toto*) as security; it being stipulated that if the ship be lost in the specified voyage, or during the limited time, by any of the perils enumerated, the lender shall lose his money.

A contract by which a ship or its freightage is hypothecated as security for a loan, which is to be repaid only in case the ship survives a particular risk, voyage, or period. The contract usually in form a bond. When the loan is not made on the ship, but on the goods on board, and which are to be sold or exchanged in the course of the voyage, the borrower's personal *responsibility* is deemed the principal security for the performance of the contract, which is therefore called *"respondentia."*

Bottomry bond. The instrument embodying the contract or agreement of bottomry. Bond with mortgage of ship as security.

Bought. Implies a completed transaction, a vesting of the right of title to and possession of the property sold, and also imports a valuable consideration. *See also* Purchase.

Boulvareism. A bargaining tactic in labor negotiations by which employer chooses a middle ground that both employer and union know will be the probable outcome before the beginning of the bargaining.

Bound. As an *adjective*, denotes the condition of being constrained by the obligations of a bond, contract, covenant, or other moral or legal obligation. *See* Duty; Obligation.

In the law of shipping, "bound to" or "bound for" denotes that the vessel spoken of is intended or designed to make a voyage to the place named.

As a *noun*, denotes a limit or boundary, or a line inclosing or marking off a tract of land. In the phrase "metes and bounds," denotes the natural or artificial marks which indicate their beginning and ending. "Bound" may signify the limit itself, and "boundary" designate a visible mark which indicates the limit. *See* Boundary.

Boundary. Every separation, natural or artificial, which marks the confines or line of division of two contiguous properties. Limits or marks of enclosures if possession be without title, or the boundaries or limits stated in title deed if possession be under a title. *See also* Land boundaries; Metes and bounds; Plat map.

Natural boundary. Any formation or product of nature which may serve to define and fix one or more of the lines inclosing an estate or piece of property.

Private boundary. An artificial boundary set up to mark the beginning or direction of a boundary line.

Public boundary. A natural boundary; a natural object or landmark used as a boundary or as a beginning point for a boundary line.

Bounders. Visible marks or objects at the ends of the lines drawn in surveys of land, showing the courses and distances. *See* Landmark.

Bound over. *See* Binding over.

Bounds. The external or limiting lines, either real or imaginary, of any object or space; that which limits or circumscribes.

Bounty. A gratuity, or an unusual or additional benefit conferred upon, or compensation paid to, a class of persons. A premium given or offered to enlisted men to induce enlistment into public service. Bounty is the appropriate term where services or action of many persons are desired, and each who acts upon the offer may entitle himself to the promised gratuity (*e.g.* killing of dangerous animals). Reward is more proper in the case of a single service, which can be only once performed, and therefore will be earned only by the person or co-operative persons who succeed while others fail (*e.g.* capture of fugitive). *See also* Reward.

Boycott /bóykot/. Concerted refusal to do business with particular person or business in order to obtain concessions or to express displeasure with certain acts or practices of person or business.

A conspiracy or confederation to prevent the carrying on of business, or to injure the business of any one by preventing potential customers from doing business with him or employing the representatives of said business, by threats, intimidation, coercion, etc. Such acts are prohibited by the Sherman Antitrust Act.

Consumer boycott. Practice whereby consumers (*i.e.* customers) refrain from purchasing a particular product in protest of excessive price, offensive actions of manufacturer or producer, etc., or refrain from trading with particular business for similar reasons.

Group boycott. Concerted refusal to deal among traders with the intent or foreseeable effect of exclusion from the market of direct competitors of some of the conspirators; or, concerted refusal to deal with the intent or foreseeable effect of coercion of the trade practices of third parties. Such group boycotts are per se illegal under the Sherman Antitrust Act.

Primary boycott. See that title.

Secondary boycott. A combination to exercise coercive pressure on customers, actual or prospective, to cause them to withhold or withdraw their patronage of a certain business or product. *See also* Secondary boycott.

Bracket creep. The process by which inflation pushes individuals into higher tax brackets.

Black's Law Dictionary Abridged 6th Ed.—4

Brady material. "*Brady* material" is exculpatory information, material to a defendant's guilt or punishment, which government knew about but failed to disclose to defendant in time for trial. Defendant is denied due process if Government suppresses such material. Name is derived from Brady v. U.S., 373 U.S. 83, 83 S.Ct. 1194, 10 L.Ed.2d 215. See Fed.R.Crim.P. 16, 26.2.

Brain death. Numerous states have enacted statutory definitions of death which include brain-related criteria. For example, many states have adopted the Uniform Determination of Death Act. *See* Death.

Characteristics of brain death consist of: (1) unreceptivity and unresponsiveness to externally applied stimuli and internal needs; (2) no spontaneous movements or breathing; (3) no reflex activity; and (4) a flat electroencephalograph reading after 24 hour period of observation. A number of states have adopted this so-called "Harvard" definition of brain death, either by statute or court decision.

See also Death *(Natural Death Acts).*

Branch. An offshoot, lateral extension, or subdivision. Any member or part of a body (*e.g.* executive branch of government), or system; a department. Division, office, or other unit of business located at a different location from main office or headquarters.

A branch of a family stock is a group of persons related by descent from a common ancestor, and related to the main stock by the fact that that common ancestor descends from the original founder or progenitor.

Branch bank. An office of a bank physically separated from its main office, with common services and functions, and corporately part of the bank. Under the National Bank Act, term at very least includes any place for receiving deposits or paying checks or lending money apart from chartered premises.

"Branch banking" is the operation of one banking institution as the instrumentality of another, in which the relationship between them is such that they operate as a single unit. Branch banking is not permitted in certain states.

"Branch office" of a bank or savings bank includes an office, unit, station, facility, terminal, space or receptacle at a fixed location other than a principal office, however designated, at which any business that may be conducted in a principal office of a bank or savings bank may be transacted. Included in this definition are off-premises electronic bank facilities.

Under Uniform Commercial Code, branch bank includes a separately incorporated foreign branch of bank. § 1–201.

Branch of the sea. This term, as used at common law, included rivers in which the tide ebbed and flowed.

Brand. A word, mark, symbol, design, term, or a combination of these, both visual and oral, used for the purpose of identification of some product or service. *See also* Trade name.

Brandeis brief. Form of appellate brief in which economic and social surveys and studies are included along with legal principles and citations and which takes its name from Louis D. Brandeis, former Associate Justice of Supreme Court, who used such brief while practicing law.

Branding. An ancient mode of punishment by inflicting a mark on an offender with a hot iron. A recognized punishment for some military offenses. Marking of cattle for the purpose of identification.

Brassage. Government charge for coining metals; covering only the actual cost. Any profit is termed "Seignorage."

Breach. The breaking or violating of a law, right, obligation, engagement, or duty, either by commission or omission. Exists where one party to contract fails to carry out term, promise, or condition of the contract.

Breach of close. The unlawful or unwarrantable entry on another person's soil, land, or close.

Breach of contract. Failure, without legal excuse, to perform any promise which forms the whole or part of a contract. Prevention or hindrance by party to contract of any occurrence or performance requisite under the contract for the creation or continuance of a right in favor of the other party or the discharge of a duty by him. Unequivocal, distinct and absolute refusal to perform agreement.

Anticipatory breach. See Anticipatory breach of contract.

Breach of warranty. See Breach of warranty.

Constructive breach. Such breach takes place when the party bound to perform disables himself from performance by some act, or declares, before the time comes, that he will not perform. *See also* Anticipatory breach of contract.

Continuing breach. Such breach occurs where the state of affairs, or the specific act, constituting the breach, endures for a considerable period of time, or is repeated at short intervals.

Efficient breach. Modern contract theory which holds that it may be economically efficient to breach a contract and pay damages. Occurs when the breaching party will still profit after compensating the other party for its "expectation interest." This theory is not well accepted.

Material breach. Violation of contract which is substantial and significant and which usually excuses the aggrieved party from further performance under the contract and affords a right to sue for damages.

Partial breach. A violation of a contract as to one part only or to a less significant degree than a material breach and which gives the aggrieved party a right to damages but generally does not excuse his performance.

Rights and remedies. Parts 6 and 7 of U.C.C. Article 2 cover rights and remedies of both buyer and seller on breach of contract by either. *See also* Damages; Performance *(Specific performance).*

Tort action. A tort action may exist for bad faith breach of contract as based on breach of the implied covenant of good faith and fair dealing. Such actions commonly involve insurance contracts.

Breach of covenant. The nonperformance of any covenant agreed to be performed, or the doing of any act covenanted not to be done.

Breach of duty. In a general sense, any violation or omission of a legal or moral duty. More particularly, the neglect or failure to fulfill in a just and proper manner the duties of an office or fiduciary employment. Every violation by a trustee of a duty which equity lays upon him, whether willful and fraudulent, or done through negligence or arising through mere oversight or forgetfulness, is a breach of duty. *See* Non-support.

Breach of privilege. An act or default in violation of the privilege of either house of parliament, of congress, or of a state legislature.

Breach of promise. Violation of a promise; used *e.g.* as an elliptical expression for "breach of promise of marriage."

Breach of the peace. A violation or disturbance of the public tranquillity and order. The offense of breaking or disturbing the public peace by any riotous, forcible, or unlawful proceeding. Breach of the peace is a generic term, and includes all violations of public peace or order and acts tending to a disturbance thereof.

See also Peace; Peace bond.

Breach of trust. Any act done by a trustee contrary to the terms of his trust, or in excess of his authority and to the detriment of the trust; or the wrongful omission by a trustee of any act required of him by the terms of the trust. Also the wrongful misappropriation by a trustee of any fund or property which had been lawfully committed to him in a fiduciary character. Every violation by a trustee of a duty which equity lays upon him, whether willful and fraudulent, or done through negligence, or arising through mere oversight and forgetfulness, is a "breach of trust." The term, therefore, includes every omission and commission in carrying out the trust according to its terms, of care and diligence in protecting and investing the trust property, and of using perfect good faith. A violation by the trustee of any duty which he owes to the beneficiary.

Breach of warranty. In real property law and the law of insurance, the failure or falsehood of an affirmative promise or statement, or the non-performance of an executory stipulation. As used in the law of sales, breach of warranty, unlike fraud, does not involve guilty knowledge, and rests on contract. Under Uniform Commercial Code consists of a violation of either an express or implied warranty relating to title, quality, content or condition of goods sold for which an action in contract will lie. U.C.C. § 2–312 et seq. *See* Warranty.

Breakage. Allowance given by manufacturer to buyer for breakage damage caused while in transit or storage. Also, fractional amounts (*e.g.* pennies) due either party as for example in computing interest on loan or deposits.

Break-even lease rate. The lease rate at which a party to a prospective lease is indifferent between entering and not entering into the lease arrangement.

Breakeven point. In accounting, that level of activity (in units or dollars) at which total revenues equal total costs. That point at which no profit and no loss is experienced on operating activities.

Break-even tax rate. The tax rate at which a party to a prospective transaction is indifferent between entering and not entering into the transaction.

Breaking. Forcibly separating, parting, disintegrating, or piercing any solid substance. In the criminal law as to housebreaking and burglary, it means the tearing away or removal of any part of the premises or of the locks, latches, or other fastenings intended to secure it, or otherwise exerting force to gain an entrance, with criminal intent; or violently or forcibly breaking out of a dwelling, after having unlawfully entered it, in the attempt to escape. Actual "breaking" involves application of some force, though the slightest force is sufficient; *e.g.* an actual "breaking" may be made by unloosening, removing or displacing any covering or fastening of the premises, such as lifting a latch, drawing a bolt, raising an unfastened window, or pushing open a door kept closed by its own weight. Even the opening of a closed and unlocked door or window is sufficient to constitute a "breaking" within terms of statute, so long as it is done with a burglarious intent. *See* Burglary.

Breaking a case. The expression by the judges of a court, to one another, of their views of a case, in order to ascertain how far they are agreed, and as preliminary to the formal delivery of their opinions. Sometimes used by crime investigators to announce the solution of a crime with the apprehension of the principal suspect.

Breaking a close. Unlawful entry upon land of another (common law trespass).

Breaking and entry. Term used to describe the necessary elements of common law burglary which consisted of breaking and entering dwelling of another in nighttime with intent to commit a felony therein. Statutory forms of burglary consist in variations of the common law crime, *e.g.* entering without breaking with intent to commit misdemeanor. *See* Breaking; Burglary.

Breaking bail. Historically, crime committed by bailee who broke open a package (bale) though no crime was committed if he converted the whole package without breaking the bulk. *See* Breaking bulk.

Breaking bulk. The offense committed by a bailee (particularly a carrier) in opening or unpacking the chest, parcel, or case containing goods intrusted to his care, and removing the goods and converting them to his own use. *See also* Breaking bail.

Breathalyzer test. Test to determine content of alcohol in one arrested for operating motor vehicle under influence of liquor. The results of such test, if properly administered, are admissible evidence. *See* Consent (*Implied consent*). *See also* Blood test evidence; Field sobriety tests; Intoxilyzer; Intoximeter.

Breath specimen. Sample of one's breath used in testing for alcoholic content. *See* Breathalyzer test.

Brethren. Plural of brother; though this word, in a will, may include sisters, as well as brothers, of the person indicated; it is not necessarily limited to the masculine gender.

Breve /bríyv(iy)/. L. Lat. A writ. An original writ. A writ or precept of the king issuing out of his courts. A writ by which a person was summoned or attached to answer an action, complaint, etc., or whereby anything was commanded to be done in the courts, in order to justice, etc.

Bribe. Any money, goods, right in action, property, thing of value, or any preferment, advantage, privilege or emolument, or any promise or undertaking to give any, asked, given, or accepted, with a corrupt intent to induce or influence action, vote, or opinion of person in any public or official capacity. See *e.g.* Calif.Penal Code § 7. A gift, not necessarily of pecuniary value, bestowed to influence the conduct of the receiver. *See also* Bribery; Kickback; Solicitation of bribe.

Bribery. The offering, giving, receiving, or soliciting of something of value for the purpose of influencing the action of an official in the discharge of his or her public or legal duties. The corrupt tendering or receiving of a price for official action. The receiving or offering any undue reward by or to any person concerned in the administration of public justice or a public officer to influence his behavior in office. Any gift, advantage, or emolument offered, given, or promised to, or asked or accepted by, any public officer to influence his behavior in office. Model Penal Code § 240.1. The federal statute includes any "officer or employee or person acting for or on behalf of the United States, or any department or agency or branch of government thereof, ... in any official function". 18 U.S.C.A. § 201.

Any direct or indirect action to give, promise or offer anything of value to a public official or witness, or an official's or witness' solicitation of something of value is prohibited as a bribe or illegal gratuity. 18 U.S.C. § 201.

I.R.C. § 162 denies a deduction for bribes or kickbacks.

Commercial bribery. Commercial bribery, as related to unfair trade practices, is the advantage which one competitor secures over his fellow competitors by his secret and corrupt dealing with employees or agents of prospective purchasers.

Bribery at elections. The offense committed by one who gives or promises or offers money or any valuable inducement to an elector, in order to corruptly induce the latter to vote in a particular way or to abstain from voting, or as a reward to the voter for having voted in a particular way or abstained from voting. See 18 U.S.C.A. § 597.

Bridge loan. A loan which is for short duration until more permanent financing is arranged; *e.g.,* person might obtain a bridge loan to purchase real estate and build house before final mortgage financing or the sale of presently held assets can be accomplished; or, firm might utilize bridge loans to finance merger or leveraged buyout until bonds can be issued or other long-term financing secured.

Bridge securities. Type of security issued to finance bridges; usually secured by a lien thereon.

Brief. A written document; a letter; a writing in the form of a letter. A summary, abstract, or epitome. A condensed statement or epitome of some larger document, or of a series of papers, facts and circumstances, or propositions.

A written statement prepared by the counsel arguing a case in court. It contains a summary of the facts of the case, the pertinent laws, and an argument of how the law applies to the facts supporting counsel's position. A summary of a published opinion of a case prepared by law student. *See also* Legal brief.

Appellate brief. Written arguments by counsel required to be filed with appellate court on why the trial court acted correctly (appellee's brief) or incorrectly (appellant's brief). While the contents and form of such briefs are normally prescribed by rule of court, commonly such contain: statement of issues presented for review, statement of the case, an argument (with authorities), a conclusion stating the precise relief sought. See *e.g.* Fed.Rule App.Proc. 28.

Trial brief. Document prepared for and used by attorney at trial which contains, among other things, issues to be tried, synopsis of evidence and witnesses to be presented, and case and statutory authority for the position of counsel at trial. Frequently, copies of the trial briefs are required to be furnished to the trial judge.

Bring. To convey to the place where the speaker is or is to be; to bear from a more distant to a nearer place; to make to come, procure, produce, draw to; to convey, carry or conduct, move. To cause to be, act, or move in a special way. The doing of something effectual. The bringing of someone to account, or the accomplishment of some definite purpose.

Bringing money into court. The act of depositing money in the custody of a court or of its clerk or marshal, for the purpose of satisfying a debt or duty, or to await the result of an interpleader. See *e.g.* Fed.R. Civil P. 67.

Bring into. To import; to introduce.

Bring suit. To "bring" an action or suit has a settled customary meaning at law, and refers to the initiation of legal proceedings in a suit. A suit is "brought" at the time it is commenced. "Brought" and "commenced" in statutes of limitations are commonly deemed to be synonymous. Under the Federal Rules of Civil Procedure, and also most state courts, a civil action is commenced by filing a complaint with the court. Rule 3. *See also* Commence.

Under Fed. Rules of Civil Proc., term "suit" has been replaced by "action". See Rule 2.

Broad interpretation. That interpretation of Constitution or statute which, brushing aside minor objections and trivial technicalities, effectuates intent of act. A meaning given to a constitutional provision or statute which is designed to effectuate the intent of the law as contrasted with a "narrow" interpretation which may fail to do so. Giving to a law a meaning which is not necessarily included in a literal application of the words of the law.

Broadside objection. A general objection interposed without specifying grounds thereof.

Broken lot. Odd lot; less than the usual unit of measurement or unit of sale; *e.g.* less than 100 shares of stock.

Broker. An agent employed to make bargains and contracts for a compensation. A dealer in securities issued by others. A middleman or negotiator between parties. A person dealing with another for sale of property. A person whose business it is to bring buyer and seller together. One who is engaged for others, on a commission, to negotiate contracts relative to property. An agent of a buyer or a seller who buys or sells stocks, bonds, commodities, or services, usually on a commission basis. The term extends to almost every branch of business, to realty as well as personalty.

Ordinarily, the term is applied to one acting for others but is also applicable to one in business of negotiating purchases or sales for himself.

For distinction between "commission merchant" and "broker," *see* Commission merchant. For "Factor" and "broker" as synonymous or distinguishable, *see* Factor. *See also* Commercial broker; Commission broker; Customs broker; Exchange broker; Pawnbroker.

Broker-agent. One licensed to act both as broker and agent.

Broker-dealer. A securities brokerage firm, usually registered with the S.E.C. and with the state in which it does business, engaging in the business of buying and selling securities to or for customers.

Institutional broker. Brokers who trade (buy and sell) securities for institutional clients—mutual funds, banks, pension funds, insurance companies.

Insurance broker. Person who obtains insurance for individuals or companies from insurance companies or their agents. Differs from an insurance agent in that he does not represent any particular company.

Merchandise brokers. Buyers and sellers of goods and negotiators between buyer and seller, but without having the custody of the property.

Money broker. A money-changer; a scrivener or jobber; one who lends or raises money to or for others.

Note broker. Negotiators of the discount or sale of commercial paper.

Real estate broker. Persons who procure the purchase or sale of land, acting as intermediary between vendor and purchaser, and who negotiate loans on real-estate security, manage and lease estates, etc. A broker employed in negotiating the sale, purchase, lease, or exchange of lands on a commission contingent on success. A person engaged in business to such an extent that it is his vocation or partial vocation. *See* Listing.

Securities broker. Brokers employed to buy and sell for their principals stocks, bonds, government securities, etc. Any person engaged in the business of effecting transactions in securities for the account of others, but does not include a bank. Securities Exchange Act of 1934, § 3. A person engaged for all or part of his time in the business of buying and selling securities, who in the transaction concerned, acts for, or buys a security from or sells a security to a customer. U.C.C. § 8–303.

A person who acts as an agent for a buyer or seller, or an intermediary between a buyer and seller, usually charging a commission. A broker who specializes in shares, bonds, commodities or options must be registered with the exchange where the specific securities are traded. A broker should be distinguished from a securities dealer who, unlike the broker, is in the business of buying or selling for his own account. *See also* Broker-dealer, *above*.

Brokerage. The wages or commissions of a broker; also, his business or occupation.

Brokerage contract. A contract of agency, whereby broker is employed to make contracts of kind agreed upon in name and on behalf of his principal, and for which he is paid an agreed commission. A unilateral contract wherein the principal makes an offer which is interpreted as promise to pay broker a commission in consideration of his producing a buyer ready, able, and willing to buy the property on the principal's terms. *See also* Brokerage listing, *infra*.

Brokerage listing. An offer of a unilateral contract, the act requested being the procuring by the broker of a purchaser ready, able and willing to buy upon the terms stated in the offer. *See also* Brokerage contract; Listing.

Brothel /bróθəl/. A bawdy-house; a house of ill fame; a common habitation of prostitutes.

Brother. One person is a brother "of the whole blood" to another, the former being a male, when both are born from the same father and mother. He is a brother "of the half blood" to that other (or half-brother) when the two are born to the same father by different mothers or by the same mother to different fathers.

In the civil law, the following distinctions are observed: Two brothers who descend from the same father, but by different mothers, are called "consanguine" brothers. If they have the same mother, but are begotten by different fathers, they are called "uterine" brothers. If they have both the same father and mother, they are denominated brothers "germane."

Brother-in-law. The brother of one's spouse; the husband of one's sister; the husband of one's spouse's sister.

Brother-sister corporation. More than one corporation owned by the same shareholders. If, for example, C and D each owned one-half of the stock in X Corporation and Y Corporation, X and Y are brother-sister corporations.

Two or more corporations owned and effectively controlled by one or more individuals, and where these corporations are involved, earnings can be transferred between them only through common shareholder or shareholders, who will be subject to progressive individual income tax.

Brown decision. Supreme Court decision which declared racial segregation in public schools to be in violation of equal protection clause of Fourteenth Amendment. Brown v. Board of Education of Topeka, 347 U.S. 483, 74 S.Ct. 686, 98 L.Ed. 873. *See also* Separate but equal doctrine.

Bruton error. Type of error that arises in joint trial by admission of confession of codefendant implicating defendant, where codefendant did not testify and defendant maintained his innocence. Name is derived from Bruton v. U.S., 391 U.S. 123, 88 S.Ct. 1620, 20 L.Ed.2d 476.

B.T.A. *See* Board of Tax Appeals.

Bucketing. Receipt of orders to purchase and sell stock without intention of actually executing such orders.

Bucket shop. An office or place (other than a regularly incorporated or licensed exchange) where persons engage in pretended buying and selling of securities or commodities; *e.g.* broker accepts orders to buy or sell but never actually executes such.

Budget. A statement of estimated revenues and expenses for a specified period of time, generally a year. A balanced budget is one in which revenues equals or exceeds expenditures. Also, sum of money allocated to a particular purpose or project, or for a specified period of time. *See also* Capital *(Capital budget);* Cash budget; Continuous budgeting; Financial budget; Flexible budget; Operating budget; Program budgeting.

Budgeted cost. An expenditure that is planned to occur in the future.

Budgeting. Formalizing of expenditure plans and committing them to written, financial terms. *See also* Budget.

Zero-base budgeting. A comprehensive budgeting process that systematically considers the priorities and alternatives for current and proposed activities in relation to organizational objectives; requires the rejustification of ongoing activities.

Budget slack. Intentional underestimation of revenues and/or overestimation of expenses in a budgeting process for the purpose of including deviations that are likely to occur so that results are still within budget limits.

Budget system. A system by which income and expenditures are balanced for a definite period of time. *See also* Continuous budgeting.

Budget variance. The difference between total actual overhead and budgeted overhead based on standard hours allowed for the production achieved; computed as part of two-variance analysis.

Buffer-zone. Term used in zoning and land use law to describe area separating two different types of zones or classes of areas to make each blend more easily with each other; *e.g.* strip of land between industrial and residential areas.

Buggery. A carnal copulation against nature; a man or a woman with a brute beast, a man with a man, or man unnaturally with a woman. This term is often used interchangeably with "sodomy."

Bugging. Form of electronic surveillance by which conversations may be overheard and recorded; regulated strictly by federal and state statute for use by law enforcement officers. *See also* Eavesdropping; Wiretapping.

Building and loan association. An organization for the purpose of accumulating a fund by subscriptions and savings of its members to assist them in building or purchasing for themselves dwellings or real estate by the loan to them of the requisite money. Quasi public corporations chartered to encourage thrift and promote ownership of homes. Such associations are not commercial banks, nor, in most states, are such classified as savings banks or savings institutions; though in many states such is a special type or variety of savings and loan association. *See also* Savings and loan association.

Building code. Laws, ordinances, or government regulations concerning fitness for habitation setting forth standards and requirements for the construction, maintenance, operation, occupancy, use or appearance of buildings, premises, and dwelling units. While many codes are local in nature and scope, many states have uniform codes which all local municipalities must adhere to. In addition, FHA financed real estate must meet certain building code requirements.

Building lien. The statutory lien of a materialman or contractor for the erection of a building. *See* Mechanic's lien.

Building line. A line established by municipal authority, to secure uniformity of appearance in the streets of the city, drawn at a certain uniform distance from the curb or from the edge of the sidewalk, and parallel thereto, upon which the fronts of all buildings on that street must be placed, or beyond which they are not allowed to project. Often referred to as the "set-back" requirement.

Building loan agreement. An agreement by which one undertakes to advance to another money to be used primarily in erection of buildings.

Such funds are normally used by the borrower to pay the contractor, sub-contractors and materialmen; and such funds are commonly advanced in installments as the structure is completed. The lender's security is normally the structure being erected. Also called interim or construction financing. *See* Bridge loan.

Building permit. Authorization required by local governmental bodies for new building, or major alteration or expansion of existing structures. Building plans, estimated costs, etc., and a fee, are usually required before such is issued. Such permit is normally required to be displayed on the construction site.

Building restrictions. Regulations or restrictions (commonly in zoning ordinances) upon the type of structure that can be constructed on one's property. Such restrictions may also be created in the form of restrictive covenants in deeds. *See* Building code.

Building society. An association in which the subscriptions of the members form a capital stock or fund out of which advances may be made to members desiring them, on mortgage security. *See* Building and loan association.

Bulk. Unbroken packages. Merchandise which is neither counted, weighed, nor measured. The aggregate that forms a body or unit. When used in relation to sale of goods by sample, "bulk" means the whole quantity of goods sold, which is supposed to be fairly represented by the sample.

Bulk mortgage. A mortgage on property in bulk. May describe creation of security interest in several items as a whole or in bulk, or a mortgage of more than one parcel of real estate, though a bulk transfer is not a security interest subject to Art. 9 of U.C.C., § 9–111.

Bulk sale. Any transfer in bulk, and not in the ordinary course of the transferor's business, of a major part of the materials, supplies, merchandise or other inventory of an enterprise. U.C.C. § 6–102(1). Such transfers are regulated by U.C.C. Article 6 to protect creditors of the transferor. *See* Bulk Sales Acts, *infra.*

A sale of substantially all the inventory of a trade or business to one person in one transaction. Under certain conditions, corporations making a bulk sale pursuant to a complete liquidation will recognize neither gain nor loss on such sale. I.R.C. § 337(b)(2).

Bulk Sales Acts. A class of statutes designed to prevent the defrauding of creditors by secret sale in bulk of all or substantially all of a merchant's stock of goods. Individual state bulk sales acts have been superseded by Art. 6 of U.C.C., "Bulk Transfers".

Bulk transfers. *See* Bulk sale; Bulk Sales Acts, *supra.*

Bulletin. An officially published notice or announcement concerning the progress of matters of public importance and interest. A brief news item of immediate publication. The publication (organ) of an institution or association.

Bullion. Gold and silver intended to be coined.

Bullion fund. A fund of public money maintained in connection with the mints, for the purpose of purchasing precious metals for coinage, and also of enabling the mint to make returns of coins to private depositors of bullion without waiting until such bullion is actually coined.

Bull market. Securities term for a market in which prices are rising or are expected to rise.

Bumping. Displacement of a junior employee's position by a senior employee; commonly occurring during periods of layoff. The practice of failing to board ticketed passengers due to oversale of the scheduled flight.

Bunco game /bónkow géym/. Any trick, artifice, or cunning calculated to win confidence and to deceive, whether by conversation, conduct, or suggestion. A swindling game or scheme.

Burden. Capacity for carrying cargo. Something that is carried. Something oppressive or worrisome. A burden, as on interstate commerce, means anything that imposes either a restrictive or onerous load upon such commerce.

Burden of going forward. The onus on a party to a case to refute or to explain as in the case of one who is charged with possession of stolen goods after the government has introduced evidence of the defendant's recent possession of such goods, the inference being that the defendant knew the goods to have been stolen.

Burden of persuasion. The onus on the party with the burden of proof to convince the trier of fact of all elements of his case. In criminal case the burden of the government to produce evidence of all the necessary elements of the crime beyond a reasonable doubt. *See also* Burden of proof.

Burden of producing evidence. The obligation of a party to introduce evidence sufficient to avoid a ruling against him on the issue. Calif.Evid. Code. Such burden is met when one with the burden of proof has introduced sufficient evidence to make out a prima facie case, though the cogency of the evidence may fall short of convincing the trier of fact to find for him. The burden of introducing some evidence on all the required elements of the crime or tort or contract to avoid the direction of a verdict against the party with the burden of proof.

Burden of proof. (Lat. *onus probandi.*) In the law of evidence, the necessity or duty of affirmatively proving a fact or facts in dispute on an issue raised between the parties in a cause. The obligation of a party to establish by evidence a requisite degree of belief concerning a fact in the mind of the trier of fact or the court.

Burden of proof is a term which describes two different concepts; first, the "burden of persuasion", which under traditional view never shifts from one party to the other at any stage of the proceeding, and second, the "burden of going forward with the evidence", which may shift back and forth between the parties as the trial progresses.

The burden of proof may require a party to raise a reasonable doubt concerning the existence or nonexistence of a fact or that he establish the existence or nonexistence of a fact by a preponderance of the evidence, by clear and convincing proof, or by proof beyond a reasonable doubt. Except as otherwise provided by law, the burden of proof requires proof by a preponderance of the evidence. Calif.Evid.Code, § 115.

In a criminal case, all the elements of the crime must be proved by the government beyond a reasonable doubt.

"Burden of establishing" a fact means the burden of persuading the triers of fact that the existence of the fact is more probable than its non-existence. U.C.C. § 1–201(8).

Except in cases of tax fraud, the burden of proof in a tax case generally is on the taxpayer.

See also Beyond a reasonable doubt; Clear and convincing proof; Preponderance of evidence; Reasonable doubt; Shifting the burden of proof.

Bureau /byúrow/. An office for the transaction of business. A name given to the several departments of the executive or administrative branch of government, or their divisions. A specialized administrative unit. Business establishment for exchanging information, making contacts, coordinating activities, etc.

Bureaucracy /byurókrǝsiy/. An organization, such as an administrative agency or the army, with the following general traits: a chain of command with fewer people at the top than at the bottom; well defined positions and responsibilities; fairly inflexible rules and procedures; "red tape"; many forms to be filled out; and delegation of authority downward from level to level.

Bureau of Customs. Federal agency charged with responsibility of collecting importing duties for the Government. It was redesignated as the United States Customs Service in 1973. *See* Customs Service.

Bureau of Land Management. The Bureau of Land Management was established July 16, 1946, by the consolidation of the General Land Office (created in 1812) and the Grazing Service (formed in 1934). The Bureau manages the national resource lands (some 450 million acres) and their resources. It also administers the mineral resources connected with acquired lands and the submerged lands of the Outer Continental Shelf (OCS). It is within the U.S. Dept. of Interior. See 35 U.S.C.A. § 1731 et seq.

Burglar. One who commits burglary.

Burglarious. Of, involving, or related to burglary. The adverb "burglariously" was formerly a pleading requirement in common law burglary indictments.

Burglariously /bǝrglériyǝsliy/. *See* Burglarious.

Burglary. At common law, the crime of burglary consisted of a breaking and entering of a dwelling house of another in the nighttime with the intent to commit a felony therein. The modern statutory definitions of the crime are much less restrictive. For example, they commonly require no breaking and encompass entry at all times of all kinds of structures. In addition, certain state statutes classify the crime into first, second, and even third, degree burglary.

A person is guilty of burglary if he enters a building or occupied structure, or separately secured or occupied portion thereof, with purpose to commit a crime therein, unless the premises are at the time, open to the public or the actor is licensed or privileged to enter. It is an affirmative defense to prosecution for burglary that the building or structure was abandoned. Model Penal Code, § 221.1.

See also Breaking.

Burglary tools. Any implement which may be used to commit burglary though, of itself, it is designed for legitimate use, and possession of which is a crime if accompanied by the intent to use for such illegal purpose and the knowledge of its illegal use.

Burial insurance. A contract based on legal consideration whereby obligor undertakes to furnish obligee or one of latter's relatives at death burial reasonably worth fixed sum.

Bushel. A dry measure, containing four pecks, eight gallons, or thirty-two quarts. But the dimensions of a bushel, and the weight of a bushel of grain, etc., vary in the different states in consequence of statutory enactments.

Business. Employment, occupation, profession, or commercial activity engaged in for gain or livelihood. Activity or enterprise for gain, benefit, advantage or livelihood. Enterprise in which person engaged shows willingness to invest time and capital on future outcome. That which habitually busies or occupies or engages the time, attention, labor, and effort of persons as a principal serious concern or interest or for livelihood or profit.

See also Association; Company; Corporation; Doing business; Joint enterprise; Limited liability company; Partnership; Place of business; Trade.

Business agent. Agent having some general supervision over general affairs. Person employed by union members to represent them in relations with business-employer.

Business bad debt. See Business bad debts.

Business corporation. A corporation organized for the purpose of carrying on a business for profit. *See* Corporation.

Business done in state. Business begun and completed or ended in state.

Business enterprise. Investment of capital, labor and management in an undertaking for profit; one of the recognized attributes is centralized management and control.

Business expense. An expense incurred in connection with carrying on a trade or business, the purpose of which is the production of income. Such expenses are deductible in arriving at taxable income. I.R.C. § 162.

Business gains. Gains from the sale, exchange, or other disposition of property used in a trade or business.

Business guest. One invited to business establishment as a guest and to whom a duty of care is owed generally greater than to a social guest, though such distinctions are becoming less acceptable in the area of torts. *See* Guest.

Business invitee. One who is impliedly invited to premises for transacting business and to whom a duty of due care is owed. One who goes on another's premises at express or implied invitation of owner or occupant for benefit of invitor or for mutual benefit and advantage of both invitor and invitee. *See* Invitee, and *Business visitor, below.*

Business losses. Losses from sale, exchange, or other disposition of property used in trade or business. *See also* Business bad debts.

Business of public character. Business wherein person engaged expressly or impliedly holds himself out as engaged in business of supplying his product or service to public as a class or to limited portion of public.

Business purpose. Term used on occasion to describe the use to which property may be put or not, as in a deed's restrictive covenant. A justifiable business reason for carrying out a transaction. It has long been established that mere tax avoidance is not a business purpose. The presence of a business purpose is of crucial importance in the area of corporate readjustments and certain liquidations.

Business records. Journals, books of account and other records which may be ordered produced as part of discovery in trial or preparation of case and generally given broad interpretation for such purposes; see *e.g.* Fed.R.Civ.Proc. Rules 26(b)(1), 45(b). *See also* Business entry rule; Business records exception.

Business risk. In finance, the risk of default or variability of return arising from the type of business conducted.

Business situs. A situs acquired for tax purposes by one who has carried on a business in the state more or less permanent in its nature. A situs arising when notes, mortgages, tax sale certificates and the like are brought into the state for something more than a temporary purpose, and are devoted to some business use there and thus become incorporated with the property of the state for revenue purposes. A situs arising where possession and control of property right has been localized in some independent business or investment away from owner's domicile so that its substantial use and value primarily attach to and become an asset of the outside business.

Business trust. As distinguished from a joint-stock company, a pure "business trust" is one in which the managers are principals, and the shareholders are cestuis que trust. The essential attribute is that property is placed in the hands of trustees who manage and deal with it for use and benefit of beneficiaries. A "Massachusetts trust" or "common law trust." *See* Massachusetts trust; Real estate investment trust (REIT).

Business usage. See *Business purpose, above.*

Business use of home. Expenses incurred in connection with the use of a taxpayers residence for the purpose of carrying on a trade or business are deductible if the residence is used exclusively and regularly as the taxpayers principal place of business and the place where the taxpayers meet with customers. I.R.C. § 280A.

Business visitor. One who is invited or permitted to enter or remain upon the premises of another for a purpose directly or indirectly connected with the business dealings between them. One who comes on premises at occupant's instance for purposes connected with purpose, business, or otherwise, for which occupant uses premises. *See also* Guest; Invitee, and *Business guest; Business invitee, above.*

Course of business. See Course of dealing; Doing business.

Farming business. See Farming purposes.

Private business. One in which capital, time, attention, labor, and intelligence have been invested for gain and profit for private benefit, purposes and use.

Public business. An element is that the business by its nature must be such that the public must use the same, or the commodities bought and sold in such manner as to affect the community at large as to supply, price, etc. *See* Corporation.

Business bad debts. An obligation obtained in connection with a trade or business which becomes partially or totally worthless. Business bad debts are fully deductible in arriving at taxable income, in contrast with non-business bad debts which are considered casualty losses and limitations apply. *See also* Bad debt.

Business entry. A writing or memorandum of a fact or event made in the regular course of business whose regular course is to make the writing or memorandum at the time of the fact or event or within a reasonable time thereafter.

Business entry rule. Exception to hearsay rule which allows introduction of entries made in usual course of business into evidence though person who made such entry is not in court. Fed.Rules Evid., Rule 803(6); 28 U.S.C.A. § 1732. *See also* Business records exception.

Business judgment rule. This rule immunizes management from liability in corporate transaction undertaken within both power of corporation and authority of management where there is reasonable basis to indicate that transaction was made with due care and in good faith.

Business records exception. An exception to the hearsay exclusion rule that allows original, routine records (whether or not part of a "business") to be used as evidence in a trial even though they are hearsay. Under this exception to hearsay rule, documentary evidence is admissible if identified by its entrant, or one under whose supervision it is kept and shown to be original or first permanent entry, made in routine course of business, at or near time of recorded transaction, by one having both duty to so record and personal knowledge of transaction represented by entry. *See also* Business entry rule.

Business tort. A noncontractual breach of a legal duty by a business directly resulting in damages or injury to another.

"But for" test. Test used in determining tort liability by applying the causative criterion as to whether the plaintiff would not have suffered the wrong "but for" the action of the defendant. Today, largely discredited as a test because of the many modifications necessary in applying it.

Buttals /bátəlz/. The bounding lines of land at the end; abuttals, which see.

Butted and bounded. A phrase sometimes used in conveyancing, to introduce the boundaries of lands. *See* Butts and bounds.

Butts and bounds. A phrase used in conveyancing, to describe the end lines or circumscribing lines of a certain piece of land. The phrase "metes and bounds" has the same meaning.

The angles or points where these lines change their direction. *See* Abuttals; Metes and bounds.

Buy. To acquire the ownership of property by giving an accepted price or consideration therefor; or by agreeing to do so; to acquire by the payment of a price or value; to purchase. To obtain something for a price, usually money. *See also* Purchase.

Buy American acts. Federal and state statutes which require a preference for American made goods over foreign made goods in government contracts. The purpose of such acts is to protect domestic industry, goods and labor. See 41 U.S. C.A. § 10.

Buy and sell agreement. An arrangement, particularly appropriate in the case of a closely-held corporation or a partnership, whereby the surviving owners (*i.e.* shareholders or partners) or the entity (*i.e.*, corporation or partnership) agree to purchase the interest of a withdrawing or deceased owner (*i.e.*, shareholder or partner). The buy and sell agreement provides for an orderly disposition of an interest in a business and is beneficial in setting the value of such interest for death tax purposes.

An agreement between or among part-owners of a business that under stated conditions (usually severance of employment, disability, or death), the person withdrawing or his heirs are legally obligated to sell their interest to the remaining part-owners, and the remaining part-owners are legally obligated to sell at a price fixed in the agreement either on a dollar basis or on a formula for computing the dollar value to be paid.

Entity buy and sell agreement. A buy and sell agreement whereby the entity is to purchase the withdrawing or deceased owner's interest. When the entity is a corporation, the agreement generally involves a stock redemption on the part of the withdrawing shareholder.

See also Cross-purchase buy and sell agreement.

Buy-down. Money that is paid by or on behalf of a homeowner at the time of purchase to reduce the mortgage interest rate and thereby lower monthly payments. Home builders frequently offer buy-downs.

Buyer. One who buys; a purchaser, particularly of chattels. A person who buys or contracts to buy goods. U.C.C. § 2–103(1)(a). *See also* Purchaser.

Buyer in ordinary course of business. A person who in good faith and without knowledge that the sale to him is in violation of the ownership rights or security interest of a third party in the goods buys in ordinary course from a person in the business of selling goods of that kind but does not include a pawnbroker. "Buying" may be for cash or by exchange of other property or on secured or unsecured credit and includes receiving goods or documents of title under a pre-existing contract for sale but does not include a transfer in bulk or as security for or in total or partial satisfaction of a money debt. U.C.C. § 1–201(9).

Buyer's market. Situation where supply is greater than demand.

Buy in. *See* Buying in.

Buying in. Buying of property at auction or tax or mortgage foreclosure sale by original owner or by one with interest in property.

Buying long. Purchase of stocks now with the expectation of selling them for a profit in the future.

Buying on margin. Purchase of security with payment part in cash and part by a loan. Normally, the loan is made by the broker. *See also* Margin account.

Buyout. The purchase of a controlling percentage of a company's shares. A buyout can be accomplished through negotiation, through a tender offer, or through a merger. *See also* Leveraged buyout.

Buyout provision. Provision in partnership agreement permitting partners to purchase departing partner's interest.

By. Before a certain time; beside; close to; in close proximity; in consequence of; not later than a certain time; on or before a certain time; in conformity with; with the witness or sanction of; into the vicinity of and beyond. Through the means, act, agency or instrumentality of.

By-bidder. One employed by the seller or his agent to bid on property with no purpose to become a purchaser, so that bidding thereon may be stimulated in others who are bidding in good faith.

By-bidding. *See* Bid.

By color of office. Acts done "by color of office" are where they are of such a nature that office gives no authority to do them. *See* Color of law; Color of office.

By estimation. In conveyancing, a term used to indicate that the quantity of land as stated is estimated only, not exactly measured; it has the same meaning and effect as the phrase "more or less."

Bylaws. Regulations, ordinances, rules or laws adopted by an association or corporation or the like for its internal governance. Bylaws define the rights and obligations of various officers, persons or groups within the corporate structure and provide rules for routine matters such as calling meetings and the like. Most state corporation statutes contemplate that every corporation will adopt bylaws.

The word is also sometimes used to designate the local laws or municipal statutes of a city or town, though, more commonly the tendency is to employ the word "ordinance" exclusively for this class of enactments, reserving "by-law" for the rules adopted by corporations.

By operation of law. Effected by some positive legal rule or amendment.

By reason of. Because of. By means, acts, or instrumentality of.

Byrnes Act. Federal law prohibiting interstate transportation of strike breakers. 18 U.S.C.A. § 1231.

Bystander. One who stands near; a chance looker-on; hence one who has no concern with the business being transacted. One present but not taking part, looker-on, spectator, beholder, observer.

By virtue of. By force of, by authority of, by reason of. Because of, through, or in pursuance of. For example, money received by an officer by virtue of his office is money which that officer received under the law of his office, and not in violation thereof.

C

CAA. *See* Clean Air Acts.

C.A.B. *See* Civil Aeronautics Board.

Cabinet. The advisory board or counsel of a king or other chief executive; *e.g.* President's Cabinet. The select or secret council of a prince or executive government; so called from the apartment in which it was originally held.

The President's Cabinet is a creation of custom and tradition, going back to the First President, and functions at the pleasure of the President. Its purpose is to advise the President on any matter concerning which he wishes such advice (pursuant to Article II, section 2, of the Constitution). The Cabinet is composed of the heads of the fourteen executive departments—the Secretary of State, the Secretary of the Treasury, the Secretary of Defense, the Attorney General, the Secretary of the Interior, the Secretary of Agriculture, the Secretary of Commerce, the Secretary of Labor, the Secretary of Health and Human Services, the Secretary of Education, the Secretary of Energy, the Secretary of Housing and Urban Development, the Secretary of Veterans Affairs, and the Secretary of Transportation. Certain other officials of the executive branch have been accorded Cabinet rank. The Vice President participates in all Cabinet meetings. Others are invited from time to time for discussion of particular subjects. The Secretary to the Cabinet is designated to provide for orderly handling and followup of matters brought before the Cabinet.

Kitchen cabinet. Informal body of non-cabinet advisors which President turns to for advice.

Cadere /kǽdəriy/. Lat. To end; cease; fail.

C.A.F. Cost and Freight.

Cafeteria plan. Type of fringe benefit plan whereby employee, in addition to receiving certain basic fringe benefits, is permitted to also select and structure certain other types of benefits up to a specified dollar amount.

Cajolery. A deliberate attempt at persuading or deceiving an accused with false promises, inducements or information, into relinquishing his rights and responding to questions posed by law enforcement officers.

Calamity. A state of extreme distress or misfortune, produced by some adverse circumstance or event. Any great misfortune or cause of loss or misery, often caused by natural forces (*e.g.* hurricane, flood, or the like). *See* Act of God; Disaster.

Calculated. Adapted by calculation, forethought or contrivance to accomplish a purpose; likely to produce a certain effect. Thought-out, premeditated. *See* Premeditation.

Calendar. The established order of the division of time into years, months, weeks, and days; or a systematized enumeration of such arrangement; an almanac.

Calendar call. A court session given to calling the cases awaiting trial to determine the present status of each case and commonly to assign a date for trial. *See also* Trial calendar.

Calendar days. A calendar day contains 24 hours; but "calendar days" may be synonymous with "working days." The time from midnight to midnight. So many days reckoned according to the course of the calendar.

Calendar month. Period terminating with day succeeding month, numerically corresponding to day of its beginning, less one.

Calendar week. A block of seven days registered on calendar beginning with Sunday and ending with Saturday. Term may consist of any seven days of given month.

Calendar year. The period from January 1 to December 31 inclusive. Ordinarily calendar year means 365 days except leap year, and is composed of 12 months varying in length. *See also* Accounting period.

Court calendar. A list of cases awaiting trial or other disposition; sometimes called "trial list" or "docket."

Special calendar. A calendar or list of causes, containing those set down specially for hearing, trial, or argument.

Call, *n.* A request or command to come or assemble; a demand for payment of money.

Banking. Demand for repayment of loan.

Contract. As used in contract, means demand for payment of, especially by formal notice.

Conveyance. A visible natural object or landmark designated in a patent, entry, grant, or other conveyance of lands, as a limit or boundary to the land described, with which the points of surveying must correspond. Also the courses and distances designated. *See also* Metes and bounds.

Corporation law. A demand by directors upon subscribers for shares for payment of a portion or installment; in this sense, it is capable of three meanings: (1) The resolution of the directors to levy the assessment; (2) its notification to the persons liable to pay; (3) the time when it becomes payable.

Securities. An option or contract giving the holder the right to purchase a stated number of shares of stock at a specified price on or before a certain fixed date. *See also* Call option; Put.

Call, *v.* To make a request or demand; to summon or demand by name; to demand payment of debt or loan immediately or at a specified time, to demand shareholders to pay additional capital; to redeem bonds before scheduled maturity; to demand the presence and participation of a number of persons by calling aloud their names, either in a pre-arranged and systematic order or in a succession determined by chance.

Callable. Option to pay before maturity on call. A security (*e.g.* bond) issue, all or part of which may be redeemed by the issuing corporation under definite conditions before maturity. The term also applies to preferred shares which may be redeemed by the issuing corporation. *See* Redemption.

Callable bonds. Bonds which may be called for payment before their maturity. A bond for which the issuer reserves the right to pay a specific amount, the call price, to retire the obligation before maturity date. If the issuer agrees to pay more than the face amount of the bond when called, the excess of the payment over the face amount is the call premium. *See also* Redemption.

Call feature. A provision in a bond that allows it to be redeemed by the issuer before maturity. *See* Callable bonds; Redemption.

Call loan. Loan which is callable by lender at any time; usually on 24 hours notice.

Call option. A negotiable instrument whereby writer of option, for a certain sum of money (the "premium"), grants to the buyer of option the irrevocable right to demand, within a specified time, the delivery by the writer of a specified number of shares of a stock at a fixed price (the "exercise" or "striking" price). An option permitting its holder (who has paid a fee for the option) to call for a certain commodity or security at a fixed price in a stated quantity within a stated period. *See* Option.

Call patent. One whose corners are all stakes, or all but one, or whose lines were not run out and marked at time.

Call premium. The difference between a bond's call price and its par value. Amount paid by issuer over par or face value upon calling a security in for payment or redemption.

Call price. The price at which a bond may be retired, or called, prior to its maturity. *See also* Redemption.

Call provision. *See* Call feature.

Calumny /kǽləmniy/. Defamation; slander; false accusation of a crime or offense.

Camera. *See* In camera.

Campaign /kæmpéyn/. All the things and necessary legal and factual acts done by a candidate and his adherents to obtain a majority or plurality of the votes to be cast. Running for office, or candidacy for office. Any organized effort to promote a cause or or to secure some definite result with any group of persons.

Can. As a verb, to be enabled by law, agreement, or custom; to have a right to; to have permission to. Often used interchangeably with "may."

Canal. Artificial waterway used for navigation, drainage or irrigation of land.

Cancel /kǽnsəl/. To obliterate; to strike or cross out. To destroy the effect of an instrument by defacing, obliterating, expunging, or erasing it. To revoke or recall; to annul or destroy, make void or invalid, or set aside. To rescind; abandon; repeal; surrender; waive; terminate. The term is sometimes equivalent to "discharge" or "pay." *See also* Abrogation; Cancellation; Redemption; Rescind; Rescission of contract; Revocation; Termination.

Cancellation. To destroy the force, effectiveness, or validity of. To annul, abrogate, or terminate. Defacement or mutilation of instrument. Words of revocation written across instrument.

A means whereby a holder discharges a party's liability on an instrument by physically demonstrating on the face of the instrument the intention to discharge, as by writing "CANCELLED" across the instrument's face, striking out the party's signature, or destroying or mutilating the signature or the instrument. As applied to documents of title, the term refers to the act of the bailee voiding a negotiable document upon its surrender by the holder in taking possession of the goods.

Occurs when either party puts an end to the contract for breach by the other and its effect is the same as that of "termination" except that the cancelling party also retains any remedy for breach of the whole contract or any unperformed balance. U.C.C. § 2–106(4).

As used in insurance law, term refers to the termination of an insurance policy by an act of either or both of the parties to it, prior to the ending of the policy period.

See also Abrogation; Cancel; Revocation; Termination.

Cancellation clause. A provision in a contract or lease which permits the parties to cancel or discharge their obligations thereunder.

Cancelled check. A check which bears the notation of cancellation of the drawee bank as having been paid and charged to the drawer. Used as evidence of payment of an obligation to the payee.

Cancelli /kænsélay/. The lines drawn on the face of a will or other writing, with the intention of revoking or annulling it.

Candidate. One who seeks or offers himself, or is put forward by others, for an office, privilege, or honor. A nominee.

Cannabis /kǽnəbəs/. Commonly called marihuana; cannabis sativa L embraces all marihuana-producing cannabis. All parts of the plant Cannabis sativa L., whether growing or not; the seeds thereof; the resin extracted from any part of such plant; and every compound, manufacture, salt, derivative, mixture, or preparation of such plant, its seeds or resin, are included in the term "marihuana." 21 U.S.C.A. § 802(16). *See also* Controlled substance; Marihuana.

Canon /kǽnən/. A law, rule, or ordinance in general, and of the church in particular. An ecclesiastical law or statute. A rule of doctrine or discipline. A criterion or standard of judgment. A body of principles, standards, rules, or norms.

In England, a cathedral dignitary, appointed sometimes by the Crown and sometimes by the bishop.

Canon law. A body of Roman ecclesiastical jurisprudence compiled in the twelfth, thirteenth and fourteenth centuries from the opinions of the ancient Latin fathers, the decrees of General Councils, and the decretal epistles and bulls of the Holy See. The canon law is contained in two principal parts,—the decrees or ecclesiastical constitutions made by the popes and cardinals; and the decretals or canonical epistles written by the pope, or by the pope and cardinals, at the suit of one or more persons. As the decrees set out the origin of the canon law, and the rights, dignities, and decrees of ecclesiastical persons, with their manner of election, ordination, etc., so the decretals contain the law to be used in the ecclesiastical courts. The canon law forms no part of the law of England, unless it has been brought into use and acted on there.

Canons of construction. The system of fundamental rules and maxims which are recognized as governing the construction or interpretation of written instruments.

Canons of descent. The legal rules by which inheritances are regulated, and according to which estates are transmitted by descent from the ancestor to the heir.

Canons of ethics. See Code of Professional Responsibility, below.

Canons of judicial ethics. Standards of ethical conduct for members of the judiciary. Such were initially adopted by the American Bar Association and later by most states.

Code of professional responsibility. "Canons" of the Code of Professional Responsibility are statements of axiomatic norms expressing in general terms the standards of professional conduct expected of lawyers in their relationship with the public, the legal system and with the legal profession. Such were initially adopted by the American Bar Association and later by most states. *See* now Model Rules of Professional Conduct, *infra.*

Canvass. The act of examining and counting the returns of votes cast at a public election to determine authenticity. Personal solicitation of votes or survey to determine probable vote outcome.

Canvasser. Any of certain persons, as officers of a state, county, or district, intrusted with the duty of examining the returns of votes cast at an election. *See* Canvass.

One who, in a given town, city, or county, goes from house to house in an effort to take orders for goods; in this sense, to be distinguished from traveling salesmen.

Cap. Term variously applied to statutorily imposed limits on recovery of noneconomic damages in tort actions; to limits on amount interest rates can increase annually on adjustable rate mortgages. *See also* Rate *(Rate cap).*

Capable. Susceptible; competent; qualified; fitting; possessing legal power or capacity. Able, fit or adapted for. *See* Capacity.

Capacity. Legal qualification (*i.e.* legal age), competency, power or fitness. Mental ability to understand the nature and effects of one's acts.

In accounting, a measure of production volume or some other activity base.

Capacity to contract. Legal age and mental ability to enter into contract.

Capacity to sue. The legal ability of a particular individual or entity to sue in, or to be brought into, the courts of a forum.

Criminal capacity. Accountability for committing crime; *e.g.,* child under 7 years of age lacks criminal capacity.

See also Competency; Disability; Earning capacity; Fiduciary capacity; Incapacity; Legal age; Legal capacity to sue; Mental capacity *or* competence; Representative capacity; Standing to sue doctrine; Substantial capacity test; Testamentary (*Testamentary capacity*).

Capacity defense. Generic term to describe lack of fundamental ability to be accountable for actions, as one under duress lacks the capacity to contract and hence when sued on such contract he interposes defense of lack of capacity. Similarly, a child accused of crime committed when he was under age of 7, his defense being lack of criminal capacity. As a defense, it tends to negate some essential element of the action required for responsibility. *See also* Competency proceedings; Competency to stand trial; Defense; Insanity; Intoxication.

Capias /kéypiyəs/kǽpiyəs/. Lat. "That you take." The general name for several species of writs, the common characteristic of which is that they require the officer to take a named defendant into custody.

Capias ad audiendum judicium /kéypiyəs ǽd odiyéndəm juwdísh(iy)əm/. A writ issued, in a case of misdemeanor, after the defendant has appeared and is found guilty, to bring him to hear judgment if he is not present when called.

Capias ad respondendum /kéypiyəs ǽd rèspondéndəm/. A judicial writ (usually simply termed a "capias," and commonly abbreviated to *ca. resp.*) by which actions at law were frequently commenced; and which commands the sheriff to *take* the defendant, and him safely keep, so that he may have his body before the court on a certain day, to *answer* the plaintiff in the action. It notifies defendant to defend suit and procures his arrest until security for plaintiff's claim is furnished.

Capias ad satisfaciendum /kéypiyəs ǽd sætəsféyshiyéndəm/. A writ of execution (usually termed, for brevity, a "ca. sa."), which commands the sheriff to *take* the party named, and keep him safely, so that he may have his body before the court on a certain day, to *satisfy* the damages or debt and damages in certain actions. It deprives the party taken of his liberty until he makes the satisfaction awarded. A body execution enabling judgment creditor in specified types of actions to cause arrest of judgment debtor and his retention in custody until he either pays judgment or secures his discharge as insolvent debtor.

Capita /kǽpətə/. Heads, and, figuratively, entire bodies, whether of persons or animals.

Persons individually considered, without relation to others (polls); as distinguished from *stirpes* or stocks of descent. The term in this sense, making part of the common phrases, *in capita, per capita,* is derived from the civil law.

Capital. Accumulated goods, possessions, and assets, used for the production of profits and wealth. Owners' equity in a business. Often used equally correctly to mean the total assets of a business. Sometimes used to mean capital assets.

In accounting, the amount invested in a business. In economic theory there are several mean-

ings. "Capital" may be used to mean: capital goods, that is, the tools of production; the money available for investment, or invested; the discounted value of the future income to be received from an investment; the real or money value of total assets; money or property used for the production of wealth; sum total of corporate stock.

See also Fixed capital; Floating *or* circulating capital; Impaired capital; Legal capital; Stated capital.

Authorized capital. See Stock *(Authorized stock).*

Capital account. A term used in accounting to describe the equity of a business. In a partnership, each partner has a capital account which represents his contribution or investment in the partnership. In a corporation, the capital account represents the amount invested by shareholders, both as stock and as additional paid-in capital. In a sole proprietorship, the amount contributed by the owner to start the business represents the owner's capital account.

Capital assets. See Assets.

Capital budget. A plan for the acquisition of long-term assets (such as plant and equipment), showing planned expenditures by object and date.

Capital case or crime. One in or for which death penalty may, but need not necessarily, be imposed.

Capital contribution. Cash, property, or services contributed by partners to partnership.

Various means by which a shareholder makes additional funds available to the corporation (*i.e.,* placed at the risk of the business) without the receipt of additional stock. Such contributions are added to the basis of the shareholder's existing stock investment and do not generate income to the corporation. I.R.C. § 118.

Capital costs. Costs for improvements to property; such are depreciable over the useful life of the improvements.

Capital deficiency. A debit balance in a partner's capital account.

Capital expenditure. An outlay of funds for the acquisition or improvement of a fixed asset which extends the life or increases the productivity of the asset. The expenditure for the acquisition of an asset should be capitalized and depreciated over the estimated useful life of the asset. I.R.C. § 263.

Capital gain. The profit realized on the sale or exchange of a capital asset. I.R.C. § 1201. The gain is the difference between the cost or the adjusted basis of an asset and the net proceeds from the sale or exchange of such asset.

Capital gains tax. A provision in the income tax laws that taxes profits from the sale of capital assets at different (lower) rates than the rate applicable to ordinary income.

Capital goods. Durable goods used by business to produce other goods and services; examples of capital goods are machines and equipment.

Capital impairment. Reduction of assets of corporation below aggregate of outstanding shares of capital stock.

Capital improvement. See Capital expenditure, above.

Capital increase. An increase not attributable to earnings.

Capital investment. Acquisition price of a "capital asset"; capital stock, surplus and undivided profits; money spent to increase an asset. *See also Capital expenditure, above.*

Capital lease. A contract that transfers ownership of property to the lessee at the end of the lease term. A contract for the lease of property which possesses the characteristics of a purchase.

Capital leverage. A company's ability to generate an additional return for stockholders by borrowing, then using the borrowed funds to obtain a return greater than the interest rate.

Capital loss. A tax term used in reference to a loss incurred in the sale or exchange of a capital asset. Beginning in 1988, the classification as to short or long term capital losses is no longer relevant.

Capital markets. Financial markets in which long term securities are bought and sold.

Capital offense. See Capital case or crime, above.

Capital outlay. Money expended in acquiring, equipping, and promoting an enterprise. *See also Capital expenditure, above.*

Capital punishment. Punishment by death for capital crimes.

Capital ratio. Ratio of capital to assets.

Capital recovery. Collection of charged-off bad debt previously written off against the allowance for doubtful accounts.

Capital return. In tax accounting, payments received by taxpayer which represent the individual's cost or capital and hence not taxable as income.

Capital stock. The shares of stock representing ownership of a business. The types of stock include preferred stock and common stock. Amount of stock that a corporation may issue; amount subscribed, contributed or secured to be paid in. Corporate assets or property contributed by shareholders. Liability of the corporation to its shareholders, after creditors' claims have been liquidated. Valuation of the corporation as a business enterprise.

Capital stock tax. A state-level tax, usually imposed on out-of-state corporations for the privilege of doing business in the state. The tax may be based on the entity's apportionable income or payroll, or on its apportioned net worth as of a specified date. Such tax was repealed at the federal level by the Revenue Act of 1945, §§ 201, 202.

Capital structure. The composition of a corporation's equities; the relative proportions of short-term debt, long-term debt, and owners' equity. In finance the total of bonds (or long-term money) and ownership interests in a corporation; that is, the stock accounts and surplus. *See also Capitalization.*

Capital surplus. Amounts paid to a corporation in excess of the par value of stock, generally referred to as additional paid-in capital.

An equity or capital account which reflects the capital contributed for shares not allocated to stated capital. The excess of issuance price over the par value of issued shares or the consideration paid for no par shares allocated specifically to capital surplus.

Capital transactions. Purchases, sales and exchanges of capital assets.

Paid-in-capital. Amount paid for stock of corporation that has been sold.

Real capital. Wealth that can be represented in financial terms such as savings account balances, financial securities, and real estate.

Stated capital. The sum of (a) the par value of all shares with par value that have been issued, (b) the amount of the consideration received for all shares without par value that have been issued, except such part of the consideration therefor as may have been allocated to surplus in a manner permitted by law, and (c) such other amounts as have been transferred to stated capital, whether upon the distribution of shares or otherwise, minus all reductions from such sums as have been effected in a manner permitted by law and surplus.

Capitalization /kæpətələzéyshən/. Capitalization represents the total amount of the various securities issued by a corporation. Capitalization may include bonds, debentures, preferred and common stock and surplus. Bonds and debentures are usually carried on the books of the issuing company in terms of their par or face value. Preferred and common shares may be carried in terms of par or stated value. Stated value may be an arbitrary figure decided upon by the directors or it may represent the amount received by the company from the sale of the securities at the time of issuance.

In accounting, to record an expenditure that may benefit a future period as an asset rather than to treat the expenditure as an expense of the period of its occurrence.

See Capitalize; Thin capitalization.

Capitalization accounting method. A method of determining the present value of an asset that is expected to produce a stream of future benefits. This involves *discounting* the stream of expected future benefits at an appropriate rate.

A method of measuring values of realty for purpose of determining values of mortgages by expertly estimating the gross income which property should realize, and separately the expenses reasonably required to carry it, and thus arriving at a fair estimate of net income and using a capitalization figure or factor, expertly chosen. Depreciation must be taken into consideration in use of such method.

Capitalization rate. The rate of interest used in calculating the present value of future periodic payments.

Capitalization ratio. The ratio of the amount of capital raised from a particular source, for example, long-term debt, to the total capitalization of the firm.

Capitalize. To convert periodic payments into an equivalent sum or sum in hand. To compute the present value of income extended over a period of time. To record an expenditure as an asset when the expenditure benefits a period in excess of one year. An example includes improvements to a commercial building. The cost of the improvements is recorded as an asset on the balance sheet and written off over the estimated useful life of the improvement. *See also* Capitalization.

Capita, per /pǝr kǽpǝtǝ/. By heads; by the poll; as individuals. In the distribution of an intestate's personalty, the persons legally entitled to take are said to take *per capita*, that is, equal shares, when they claim, each in his own right, as in equal degree of kindred; in contradistinction to claiming by right of representation, or *per stirpes*. *See* Per capita.

Capitation tax. A poll tax *(q.v.)*. A tax or imposition upon the person. It is a very ancient kind of tribute, and answers to what the Latins called *"tributum,"* by which taxes on persons are distinguished from taxes on merchandise, called *"vectigalia."*

Capitulation /kǝpityǝléyshǝn/. The act or agreement of surrendering upon negotiated or stipulated terms.

Caprice /kǝpríys/. Whim, arbitrary, seemingly unfounded motivation. Disposition to change one's mind impulsively.

Captain of the ship doctrine. This doctrine imposes liability on surgeon in charge of operation for negligence of his assistants during period when those assistants are under surgeon's control, even though assistants are also employees of hospital. This concept is an adaptation of the "borrowed servant" principle in law of agency to operating room of hospital.

Caption /kǽpshǝn/. The heading or introductory part of a pleading, motion, deposition, or other legal instrument which indicates the names of the parties, name of the court, docket or file number, title of the action, etc. Fed.R. Civil P. 10(a).

Captive audience. Any group subject to a speaker or to a performance and which is not free to depart without adverse consequences.

Captor. In international law, one who takes or seizes property in time of war; one who takes the property of an enemy. In a stricter sense, one who takes a prize at sea. The term also designates a belligerent who has captured the person of an enemy.

Capture. Act of catching or controlling by force, threats or strategy. In international law, the taking or wresting of property from one of two belligerents by the other. Also a taking of property by a belligerent from an offending neutral. Capture, in technical language, is a taking by military power; a *seizure* is a taking by civil authority.

Caput /kǽpǝt/. A head; the head of a person; the whole person; the life of a person; one's personality; status; civil condition.

Cardholder. A member of a group such as a union wherein the card is the symbol and identification of membership.

Care. Watchful attention; concern; custody; diligence; discretion; caution; opposite of negligence or carelessness; prudence; regard; preservation; security; support; vigilance. To be concerned with, and to attend to, the needs of oneself or another.

In the law of negligence, the amount of care demanded by the standard of reasonable conduct must be in proportion to the apparent risk. As the danger becomes greater, the actor is required to exercise caution commensurate with it.

There are three degrees of care which are frequently recognized, corresponding (inversely) to the three degrees of negligence, viz.: slight care, ordinary care, and great care. This division into three degrees of care, however, does not command universal assent.

Slight care is such as persons of ordinary prudence usually exercise about their own affairs of slight importance. Or it is that degree of care which a person exercises about his own concerns, though he may be a person of less than common prudence or of careless and inattentive disposition.

Ordinary care is that degree of care which persons of ordinary care and prudence are accustomed to use and employ, under the same or similar circumstances. Or it is that degree of care which may reasonably be expected from a person in the party's situation, that is, reasonable care. *See also* Ordinary.

Reasonable care is such a degree of care, precaution, or diligence as may fairly and properly be expected or required, having regard to the nature of the action, or of the subject-matter, and the circumstances surrounding the transaction. It is such care as an ordinarily prudent person would exercise under the conditions existing at the time he is called upon to act. Substantially synonymous with ordinary or due care.

Great care is such as persons of ordinary prudence usually exercise about affairs of their own which are of great importance; or it is that degree of care usually bestowed upon the matter in hand by the most competent, prudent, and careful persons having to do with the particular subject.

A high degree of care is not the legal equivalent of reasonable care. It is that degree of care which a very cautious, careful, and prudent person would exercise under the same or similar circumstances; a degree of care commensurate with the risk of danger.

Highest degree of care and utmost degree of care have substantially the same meaning. "Highest degree of care" only requires the care and skill exacted of persons engaged in the same or similar business. It means the highest degree required by law where human safety is at stake, and the highest degree known to the usage and practice of very careful, skillful, and diligent persons engaged in the same business by similar means or agencies.

See also Diligence; Due care; Reasonable care; Support.

Careless. Absence of care; negligent; reckless.

Cargare /kargériy/. In old English law, to charge.

Cargo. The load (*i.e.* freight) of a vessel, train, truck, airplane or other carrier. *See* Freight.

Carload. The quantity usually contained in an ordinary freight car used for transporting the particular commodity involved. A commercial unit which by commercial usage is a single whole for purposes of sale and division. U.C.C. § 2–105(6).

Carmack Act. Amendment to Interstate Commerce Act prescribing liability of carrier for loss, damage, or injury to property carried in interstate commerce. 49 U.S.C.A. §§ 10103, 10730, 11707.

Car mile. Movement of loaded freight car one mile.

Carnal /kárnəl/. Pertaining to the body, its passions and its appetites; animal; fleshly; sensual; impure; sexual.

Carnal abuse. An act of debauchery of the female sexual organs by those of the male which does not amount to penetration; the offense commonly called statutory rape consists of carnal abuse. An injury to the genital organs in an attempt at carnal knowledge, falling short of actual penetration. Carnal knowledge of a female child of tender age includes abuse. Carnal abuse and "carnal knowledge" are synonymous in many statutes. *See also* Carnal knowledge.

Carnal knowledge. Coitus; copulation; the act of a man having sexual bodily connections with a woman; sexual intercourse. Carnal knowledge of a child is unlawful sexual intercourse with a female child under the age of consent. It is a statutory crime, usually a felony. Such offense is popularly known as "statutory rape". *See* Rape.

While penetration is an essential element, there is "carnal knowledge" if there is the slightest penetration of the sexual organ of the female by the sexual organ of the male. It is not necessary that the vagina be entered or that the hymen be ruptured; the entering of the vulva or labia is sufficient.

Carnet. An international customs document allowing duty-free temporary exportation of merchandise from one participating country into another participating country, return to the country of origin being contemplated.

Carriage. Transportation of goods, freight or passengers.

Carriage of Goods by Sea Act. Federal act governing the most important of the rights, responsibilities, liabilities and immunities arising out of the relation of issuer to holder of the ocean bill of lading, with respect to loss or damage of goods. 46 U.S.C.A. § 1300 et seq.

Carrier. Individual or organization engaged in transporting passengers or goods for hire.

"Carrier" means any person engaged in the transportation of passengers or property by land, as a common, contract, or private carrier, or freight forwarder as those terms are used in the Interstate Commerce Act, as amended, and officers, agents and employees of such carriers. 18 U.S.C.A. § 831.

See also Certified carriers; Connecting carrier; Contract carrier.

Common carrier. Common carriers are those that hold themselves out or undertake to carry persons or goods of all persons indifferently, or of all who choose to employ it. Those whose occupation or business is transportation of persons or things for hire or reward. Common carriers of passengers are those that undertake to carry all persons indifferently who may apply for passage, so long as there is room, and there is no legal excuse for refusal.

Private carrier. Private carriers are those who transport only in particular instances and only for those they choose to contract with.

Carrier's lien. The right to hold the consignee's cargo until payment is made for the work of transporting it.

Carry. To bear, bear about, sustain, transport, remove, or convey. To have or bear upon or about one's person, as a watch or weapon; locomotion not being essential. As applied to insurance, means "possess" or "hold."

Carry arms or weapons. To wear, bear, or carry them upon the person or in the clothing or in a pocket, for the purpose of use, or for the purpose of being armed and ready for offensive or defensive action in case of a conflict with another person. *See* Bear arms; Carrying concealed weapon.

Carry-back. A provision in the tax law which allows a taxpayer to apply a net operating loss in one year to the three immediately preceding tax years, beginning with the earliest year. A net operating loss must be carried back unless the taxpayer elects to forego the carry-back and carry the loss forward. I.R.C. § 172(b). *Compare* to Carry-over.

Carry costs. A verdict is said to carry costs when the party for whom the verdict is given becomes entitled to the payment of his costs as incident to such verdict. *See also* Costs.

Carrying away. The act of removal or asportation, by which the crime of larceny is completed, and which is essential to constitute it. *See also* Larceny.

Carrying charge. Charge made by creditor, in addition to interest, for carrying installment credit. Under consumer credit protection statutes, full disclosure of all such service charges is required. *See* Truth-in-Lending Act. *See also* Carrying costs.

Carrying concealed weapon. Such act is a criminal offense in most all jurisdictions; though concealment is not universally an element of the crime. See *e.g.* Model Penal Code § 5.06.

Carrying costs. All costs associated with holding items in inventory for a period of time. *See also* Carrying charge; Cost of carrying.

Carry on trade or business. To conduct, prosecute or continue a particular avocation or business as a continuous operation or permanent occupation. The repetition of acts may be sufficient. To hold one's self out to others as engaged in the selling of goods or services.

Term which has multiple meanings depending on the context, but it is commonly used in connection with the degree of activity of a foreign corporation in a given state and the consequent right of that state to regulate such enterprise and the exposure of such foreign corporation to suit within that state. In this connection, so called "long arm" statutes define what constitutes carrying on business.

Carry-over. A provision in the tax law which allows a taxpayer to apply a net operating loss in one year to the years following the loss. Net operating losses incurred after 1975 are carried forward 15 years; and losses incurred prior to 1976 are carried forward five years. I.R.C. § 172(b). *Compare* to Carry-back.

Carry stock. To provide funds or credit for its payment for the period agreed upon from the date of purchase.

Carte blanche /kàrt blónsh/. A white sheet of paper; an instrument signed, but otherwise left blank. A sheet given to an agent, with the principal's signature appended, to be filled up with any contract or engagement as the agent may see fit. Term is commonly used to mean unlimited authority; full discretionary power.

Cartel /kartél/. A combination of producers of any product joined together to control its production, sale, and price, so as to obtain a monopoly and restrict competition in any particular industry or commodity. Such exist primarily in Europe, being restricted in United States by antitrust laws. Also, an association by agreement of companies or sections of companies having common interests, designed to prevent extreme or unfair competition and allocate markets, and to promote the interchange of knowledge resulting from scientific and technical research, exchange of patent rights, and standardization of products.

An agreement between two hostile powers for the delivery of prisoners or deserters, or authorizing certain non-hostile intercourse between each other which would otherwise be prevented by the state of war; for example, agreements for intercommunication by post, telegraph, telephone, railway.

CASB. *See* Cost Accounting Standard Board.

Case. A general term for an action, cause, suit, or controversy, at law or in equity; a question contested before a court of justice; an aggregate of facts which furnishes occasion for the exercise of the jurisdiction of a court of justice. A judicial proceeding for the determination of a controversy between parties wherein rights are enforced or protected, or wrongs are prevented or redressed; any proceeding judicial in its nature.

Criminal act requiring investigation by police. Disease or injury requiring treatment by physician.

Surveillance or inspection of residence, business, etc. by potential burglar or robber.

The word "case" may include applications for divorce, applications for the establishment of highways, applications for orders of support of relatives, and other special proceedings unknown to the common law.

In ordinary usage, the word "case" means "event", "happening", "situation", "circumstances".

A statement of facts involved in a transaction or series of transactions, or occurrence, or other matter in dispute, drawn up in writing in a technical form, for submission to a court or judge for decision or opinion. *See below Case agreed on; Case on appeal; Case reserved; Case stated.*

See also Cause of action.

Case agreed on. A formal written enumeration of the facts in a case, assented to by both parties as correct and complete, and submitted to the court by their agreement, in order that decision may be rendered without a trial, upon the court's conclusions of law upon the facts as stated. For agreed case, or case stated, parties must agree on all material ultimate facts on which their rights are to be determined by law. *See also* Stipulation.

Case made. See Case reserved, below.

Case of actual controversy. The phrase in Federal Declaratory Judgment Act connotes controversy of justiciable nature, excluding advisory decree on hypothetical facts. *See Cases and controversies, below.*

Case of first impression. See First impression case.

Case on appeal. Status of case after it leaves trial court for appellate review and is on appellate docket.

Case reserved. A statement in writing of the facts proved on the trial of a cause, drawn up and settled by the attorneys and counsel for the respective parties under the supervision of the judge, for the purpose of having certain points of law, which arose at the trial and could not then be satisfactorily decided, determined upon full argument before the court *in banc.* This is otherwise called a "special case"; and it is usual for the parties, where the law of the case is doubtful, to agree that the jury shall find a general verdict for the plaintiff, subject to the opinion of the court upon such a case to be made, instead of obtaining from the jury a special verdict.

Cases and controversies. This term, as used in the Constitution of the United States, embraces claims or contentions of litigants brought before the court for adjudication by regular proceedings established for the protection or enforcement of rights, or the prevention, redress, or punishment of wrongs; and whenever the claim or contention of a party takes such a form that the judicial power is capable of acting upon it, it has become a case or controversy. The federal courts will only consider questions which arise in a "case or controversy"; *i.e.*, only justiciable cases. Art. III, Sec. 2, U.S.Const. The case or controversy must be definite and concrete, touching the legal relations of parties having adverse interests. The questions involved must not be moot or academic, nor will the courts consider collusive actions. The facts in controversy, under all the circumstances, must show a substantial issue between the parties having adverse legal interests of sufficient immediacy and reality to warrant issuance of a judgment. *See also* Controversy; Justiciable controversy; Ripeness doctrine; Standing to sue doctrine.

Case stated. See Case agreed on, above.

Case sufficient to go to a jury. A case that has proceeded upon sufficient proof to that stage where it must be submitted to jury and not decided against the state as a matter of law.

Form of action. That category into which a case falls such as contract or tort, though under Rules of Civil Procedure, all actions are "civil" actions. Fed.R. Civil P. 2.

Casebook. Type of book used in law school containing text of leading court decisions in particular field of law (e.g., contracts, torts), together with commentary and other features useful for class discussion and further understanding of subject as prepared by author. *Compare* Hornbook.

Case in chief. That part of a trial in which the party with the initial burden of proof presents his evidence after which he rests.

Case law. The aggregate of reported cases as forming a body of jurisprudence, or the law of a particular subject as evidenced or formed by the adjudged cases, in distinction to statutes and other sources of law. It includes the aggregate of reported cases that interpret statutes, regulations, and constitutional provisions. *See* Common law.

Case or controversy. *See* Case; Standing to sue doctrine.

Case system. A method of teaching or studying the science of the law by a study of the cases historically, or by the inductive method. It was introduced in the Law School of Harvard University in 1869–70 by Christopher C. Langdell, Dane Professor of Law. *See* Casebook.

Caseworker. Generally, a social worker whose clients are called cases and whose work is mainly in the field.

Cash. Money or the equivalent; usually ready money. Currency and coins, negotiable checks, and balances in bank accounts. That which circulates as money. *See* Legal tender; Petty cash.

Cash account. A record, in bookkeeping, of all cash transactions; a summary of moneys received and expended.

Cash bail. Sum of money posted by a criminal defendant to insure his presence in court; used in place of surety bond and real estate. *See* Bail.

Cash basis accounting. A method of accounting that reflects deductions as paid and income as received in any one tax year. That system of accounting which treats as income only cash which is actually received and as expense only cash which is actually paid out, in contrast to accrual basis which records income when due though not received and expense when incurred though not yet paid.

Modified cash basis. A method that utilizes features from both the cash and accrual bases of accounting.

Cash book. In bookkeeping, an account book in which is kept a record of all cash transactions, or all cash received and expended.

Cash breakeven point. In accounting, breakeven point that indicates a sales volume necessary to cover all cash expenses for a period.

Cash budget. A period-by-period statement of opening cash on hand, estimated cash receipts, estimated cash disbursements, and estimated cash balance at the end of each period. A projection of the company's cash receipts and disbursements over some future period of time.

Cash cycle. The time lapse between purchase of materials and collection of accounts receivable for finished product sold.

Cash deficiency agreement. An agreement to invest cash in a project to the extent required to cover any cash deficiency the project may experience.

Cash discount. A deduction from billed price which seller allows for payment within a certain time; *e.g.* 10% discount for payment within 10 days. A discount offered as an incentive for early payment of an invoice.

Cash dividend. That portion of profits and surplus paid to stockholders by a corporation in form of cash. To be contrasted with "stock" dividend.

Cash equivalent. A short-term security that is sufficiently liquid that it may be considered the financial equivalent of cash.

Cash equivalent doctrine. Generally, a cash basis taxpayer does not report income until cash is constructively or actually received. Under the cash equivalent doctrine, cash basis taxpayers are required to report income even though no cash is actually received in a transaction if the equivalent of cash is received *e.g.*, property is received instead of cash in a taxable transaction.

Cash flow. The cash generated from property, business, etc. It is different from net income; cash flow looks to the amount of cash left after all payments are made, whether they are tax deductible or not. Cash receipts minus disbursements from a given asset, or group of assets, for a given period. An analysis of the movement of cash through a venture as contrasted with the earnings of the venture. *See* Incremental cash flow.

Cash flow break-even. The point below which a firm will have insufficient net cash inflow to meet its fixed cost obligations (including such items as fixed salaries and administrative costs, interest and principal payments, and planned cash dividends).

Cash flow from operations. A firm's net cash inflow resulting directly from its regular operations (disregarding extraordinary items such as the sale of fixed assets or transaction costs associated with issuing securities), calculated as the sum of net income plus noncash expenses that were deducted in calculating net income.

Cash flow per common share. The difference between cash flow from operations and preferred stock dividends divided by the number of outstanding common shares.

Free cash flow. Cash flow from operations contributed by a particular capital investment project (*i.e.*, net of salvage value and release of working capital).

Negative cash flow. Refers to a situation where the cash needs of a business exceed its cash intake.

Statement of cash flows. A statement required under generally accepted accounting principles that indicates a firm's cash inflows and cash outflows during the accounting period.

Cashier, *v.* To dismiss dishonorably from service.

Cashier, *n.* Executive officer of bank or trust company responsible for banking transactions. One who collects and records payments at store, restaurant, business, or the like.

Cashiered. Dismissal with ignominy or dishonor, or in disgrace.

Cashier's check. A check drawn by the bank upon itself and issued by an authorized officer of a bank, directed to another person evidencing fact that payee is authorized to demand and receive from the bank, upon presentation, the amount of money represented by the check. *See also* Check.

Cashlite. An amercement or fine; a mulct.

Cash market value. Price which property would bring if offered for sale by one who desired to sell but was under no obligation to sell, and was bought by one who desired to buy but was under no necessity to buy. "Fair market value," "reasonable market value" or "fair cash market value" are synonymous. For Fair market value, and Fair cash market value, see those titles.

Cash out. Exists when seller of property takes the entire amount of equity in cash rather than retaining some interest in property.

Cash position. Degree of liquidity; amount of quick or liquid assets.

Cash price. A price payable in cash at the time of sale of property, in opposition to a barter or a sale on credit.

Cash receipts journal. A special journal used to record all cash received by a business.

Cash sale. A sale for money in hand. A sale conditioned on payment concurrent with delivery. *See* Sale; Time-price differential.

Cash surrender value. The amount of money that an insurance policy would yield if cashed in with the insurance company that issued the policy. The cash surrender value of a life insurance policy is the reserve less a surrender charge. Amount which the insurer will pay upon cancellation of the policy before death. *See* Cash value option.

Cash value. The cash value of an article or piece of property is the price which it would bring at private sale (as distinguished from a forced or auction sale); the terms of sale requiring the payment of the whole price in ready money, with no deferred payments.

Actual value or market value. Clear market value or fair market value. Price property will bring on sale by one desiring, but not compelled, to sell to one desiring but not compelled, to purchase. Saleable value. Value at which property would be taken in payment of just debt from solvent debtor.

See also Actual cash value; Cash surrender value; Fair cash value; Fair market value; Market value.

Cash value option. The right of an owner of life insurance policy to take the cash value of a policy which is a predetermined amount at a given point in time; generally limited to a specified period after default in premium payments.

Cassare. To quash; to render void; to break.

Cast. To deposit formerly or officially, as to cast a ballot. The form in which a thing is constructed. To get rid of; to discard.

Cast away. Rejected; thrown away. Cast ashore or adrift, as a shipwrecked person.

Castle doctrine. A man's home is his castle and, hence, he may use all manner of force including deadly force to protect it and its inhabitants from attack. Doctrine is usually attributed to Coke, Third Institute, 1644, but similar phrases are found in Roman law. *See* Self-defense.

Casual /kǽz(h)yuwəl/. Occurring without regularity, occasional; impermanent, as employment for irregular periods. Happening or coming to pass without design and without being foreseen or expected; unforeseen; uncertain; unpremeditated.

Casual deficiency of revenue. An unforeseen or unexpected deficiency, or an insufficiency of funds to meet some unforeseen and necessary expense.

Casual deficit. A deficit happening by chance or accident and without design.

Casual ejector. The nominal defendant in an action of ejectment.

Casual employment. Employment at uncertain or irregular times. Employment for short time and limited and temporary purpose. Occasional, irregular or incidental employment. Such employee does not normally receive seniority rights nor, if hours worked are below a certain number each week, fringe benefits. By statute in many states, such employment may or may not be subject to workers' compensation at the election of the employer. The test is the nature of the work or the scope of the contract of employment or the continuity of employment.

Casual sale. A sale which is not made customarily or in the regular course of business; an occasional sale.

Casualty /kǽz(h)yuwəltiy/. A serious or fatal accident. A person or thing injured, lost or destroyed. A disastrous occurrence due to sudden, unexpected or unusual cause. Accident; misfortune or mishap; that which comes by chance or without design. A loss from such an event or cause; as by fire, shipwreck, lightning, etc. *See also* Accident; Loss; Unavoidable casualty.

Casualty insurance. *See* Insurance.

Casualty loss. A casualty loss is defined for tax purposes as "the complete or partial destruction of property resulting from an identifiable event of a sudden, unexpected or unusual nature"; *e.g.*, floods, storms, fires, auto accidents. Individuals may deduct business casualty losses in full. Losses include those in a trade or business or incurred in a transaction entered into for a profit. Personal or nonbusiness casualty losses are deductible by individuals as itemized deductions. Such loss deductions are reduced by $100 and 10% of the taxpayer's adjusted gross income.

Casus /kéysəs/. Lat. Chance; accident; an event; a case; a case contemplated.

Casus fortuitus /kéysəs fortyúwətəs/. An inevitable accident, a chance occurrence, or fortuitous event. A loss happening in spite of all human effort and sagacity.

Casus major /kéysəs méyjər/. In the civil law, a casualty; an extraordinary casualty, as fire, shipwreck, etc.

Catals /kǽtəlz/. Goods and chattels.

Catastrophe /kətǽstrəfiy/. A notable disaster; a more serious calamity than might ordinarily be understood from the term "casualty." Utter or complete failure or destruction.

Catching bargain. *See* Bargain.

Catch time charter. One under which compensation is paid for the time the boat is actually used. *See also* Bareboat charter.

Cats and dogs. Colloquial expression for highly speculative securities.

Cattle rustling. Stealing of cattle.

CATV. Community Antenna Television Systems.

Caucasian /kokéyzhən/. Of or pertaining to the white race.

Caucus /kókəs/. A meeting of the legal voters of any political party assembled for the purpose of choosing delegates or for the nomination of candidates for office.

Causa /kózə/kówzə/. Lat. A cause, reason, occasion, motive, or inducement. As used with the force of a preposition, it means by virtue of, on account of, in contemplation of; *e.g. causa mortis*, in anticipation of death. A condition; a consideration; motive for performing a juristic act.

In the Civil and old English law the word signified a source, ground, or mode of acquiring property; hence a title; one's title to property. Thus, *"titulus est justa causa possidendi id quod nostrum est;"* title is the lawful ground of possessing that which is ours. Also a cause; a suit or action pending; *e.g. Causa testamentaria*, a testamentary cause. *Causa matrimonialis*, a matrimonial cause.

See also Cause; Cause of action.

Causal relation. *See* Proximate cause.

Causa mortis /kózə mórtəs/. In contemplation of approaching death.

Causa mortis donatio /kózə mórtəs dənéysh(iy)ow/. *See* Causa mortis gift; Donatio mortis causa.

Causa mortis gift. A gift made by a donor in contemplation of his or her imminent death. If the donor does not die of that ailment, the gift is revoked.

Causa proxima /kózə próksəmə/. The immediate, nearest, or latest cause. The efficient cause; the

one that necessarily sets the other causes in operation. *See* Proximate cause.

Causa proxima non remota spectatur /kózə próksəmə non rəmówtə spektéytər/. An efficient adequate cause being found, it must be considered the true cause unless some other independent cause is shown to have intervened between it and the result. The immediate (or direct), not the remote, cause, is looked at, or considered. For a distinction, however, between immediate and proximate cause, *see* Cause; Proximate cause.

Causa remota /kózə rəmówtə/. A remote or mediate cause; a cause operating indirectly by the intervention of other causes.

Causa sine qua non /kózə sáyniy kwèy nón/. A necessary or inevitable cause; a cause without which the effect in question could not have happened. A cause without which the thing cannot be. With reference to negligence, it is the cause without which the injury would not have occurred. *See* Proximate cause.

Causation. The fact of being the cause of something produced or of happening. The act by which an effect is produced. An important doctrine in fields of negligence and criminal law.

Cause, *v.* To be the cause or occasion of; to effect as an agent; to bring about; to bring into existence; to make to induce; to compel.

Cause, *n.* (Lat. *causa.*) Each separate antecedent of an event. Something that precedes and brings about an effect or a result. A reason for an action or condition. A ground of a legal action. An agent that brings something about. That which in some manner is accountable for condition that brings about an effect or that produces a cause for the resultant action or state.

A suit, litigation, or action. Any question, civil or criminal, litigated or contested before a court of justice. *See* Cause of action.

See also Causa; Causation; Concurrent causes; Contributing cause; Dependent intervening cause; Efficient cause; Efficient intervening cause; Good cause; Immediate cause; Independent intervening cause; Intervening act; Intervening agency; Intervening cause; Legal cause; Natural and probable consequences; Negligence (*Contributory negligence*); Probable cause; Procuring cause; Producing cause; Proximate cause; Remote cause; Sole cause; Sufficient cause.

Direct or immediate cause. See Proximate cause.

Dismissal for cause. See For cause.

Intervening cause. That occurrence which comes between the initial force or occurrence and the ultimate effect. *See also* Intervening act.

Superseding cause. That occurrence or force which not only intervenes, but which also breaks the chain of causation between the initial occurrence and the ultimate effect so as to render the initial force or occurrence causatively harmless.

Cause in fact. That particular cause which produces an event and without which the event would not have occurred. Courts express this in the form of a rule commonly referred to as the "but for" rule: the injury to an individual would not have happened but for the conduct of the wrongdoer. *See* Proximate cause; Res (*Res ipsa loquitur*).

Cause of action. The fact or facts which give a person a right to judicial redress or relief against another. The legal effect of an occurrence in terms of redress to a party to the occurrence. A situation or state of facts which would entitle party to sustain action and give him right to seek a judicial remedy in his behalf. Fact, or a state of facts, to which law sought to be enforced against a person or thing applies. Facts which give rise to one or more relations of right-duty between two or more persons. Failure to perform legal obligation to do, or refrain from performance of, some act. Matter for which action may be maintained. Unlawful violation or invasion of right. The right which a party has to institute a judicial proceeding. *See also* Case; Claim; Failure to state cause of action; Justiciable controversy; New cause of action; Right of action; Severance of actions; Splitting cause of action; Suit.

Cause of injury. That which actually produces it.

Causes célèbres /kówz səléb(rə)/. Celebrated cases. A work containing reports of the decisions of interest and importance in French courts in the seventeenth and eighteenth centuries. Secondarily, a single trial or decision is sometimes called a *"cause célèbre,"* when it is remarkable on account of the parties involved or the unusual, interesting, or sensational character of the facts.

Causeway. A raised roadbed through low lands or across wet ground or water.

Caution. To warn, exhort, to take heed, or give notice of danger.

Cautionary instruction. That part of a judge's charge to a jury in which he instructs them to consider certain evidence only for a specific purpose, *e.g.* evidence that a criminal defendant committed crimes other than the crime for which he is on trial may be admitted to prove a scheme or to show intent as to this crime but not to prove that he committed this particular crime and such evidence requires cautionary instructions. Also, instruction by judge to jury not to be influenced by extraneous matters from outside forces, or to talk about case to anyone outside of trial. Other examples of cautionary instructions are: an instruction to the jurors at the outset of a case against talking with any witness; an instruction on the inherent weakness of eyewitness identifica-

tion; an instruction for the jury not to consider a witness's actions as bearing on the guilt or innocence of any of the defendants.

Cautious. Careful; prudent; circumspect; discreet in face of danger or risk.

C.A.V. An abbreviation for *curia advisari vult*, the court will be advised, will consider, will deliberate.

Caveat /kǽviyət/kéyviyət/. Lat. Let him beware. Warning to one to be careful. A formal notice or warning given by a party interested to a court, judge, or ministerial officer against the performance of certain acts within his power and jurisdiction. This process may be used in the proper courts to prevent (temporarily or provisionally) the proving of a will or the grant of administration, or to arrest the enrollment of a decree in chancery when the party intends to take an appeal, to prevent the grant of letters patent, etc.

Used in writing to warn the reader of an interpretation different from the one proposed or advanced.

See also Warning.

Caveat actor /kǽviyət ǽktər/. Let the doer, or actor, beware.

Caveat emptor /kǽviyət ém(p)tər/kéyviyət°/. Let the buyer beware. This maxim summarizes the rule that a purchaser must examine, judge, and test for himself. This maxim is more applicable to judicial sales, auctions, and the like, than to sales of consumer goods where strict liability, warranty, and other consumer protection laws protect the consumer-buyer. *See also* Warning.

Caveat venditor /kǽviyət véndətər/. Let the seller beware.

C.B.O.E. Chicago Board of Options Exchange. A securities exchange for the public trading of standardized option contracts.

C.C. Various terms or phrases may be denoted by this abbreviation; such as circuit court (or city or county court); criminal cases (or crown or civil or chancery cases); civil code; chief commissioner; and *cepi corpus*, I have taken his body.

C.C.; B.B. I have taken his body; bail bond entered. *See* Capias (*Capias ad respondendum*).

C.C.C. Commodity Credit Corporation.

C.C. & C. I have taken his body and he is held.

C Corporation. A regular corporation governed by Subchapter C of the Internal Revenue Code. Distinguished from S corporations, which fall under Subchapter S of the Code. *See* Corporation.

C.D. Certificate of deposit.

Cease. To stop; to become extinct; to pass away; to suspend or forfeit. To leave off; bring to an end; to come to an end; break off or taper off to a stop; to give over or bring to an end an activity or action.

Cease and desist order. An order of an administrative agency or court prohibiting a person or business firm from continuing a particular course of conduct, *e.g.* Fed. Trade Commission order to business to cease and desist from misbranding or misadvertising its products; or, N.L.R.B. ruling issued in an unfair labor practice case requiring the charged party (respondent) to stop the conduct found illegal and take specified affirmative action designed to remedy the unfair labor practice. *See* Injunction; Restraining order.

Cede. To yield up; to assign; to grant; to surrender; to withdraw. Generally used to designate the transfer of territory from one government to another.

Celebration of marriage /sèləbréyshən əv mǽrəj/. The formal act by which a man and woman take each other for husband and wife, according to law; the solemnization of a marriage. The term is usually applied to a marriage ceremony attended with ecclesiastical functions; *i.e.* a church wedding.

Celler-Kefauver Act. A federal law enacted in 1950 dealing with restrictions on mergers and expanding the Clayton Act of 1914 in this regard.

Censor /sénsər/. One who examines publications, films and the like for objectionable content. Roman officers who acted as census takers, assessors and reviewers of public morals and conduct. Officer of armed forces who reads letters and other communications of servicemen and deletes material considered to be harmful or of a danger to security. *See also* Censorship; Prior restraint.

Censorship. Review of publications, movies, plays, and the like for the purpose of prohibiting the publication, distribution, or production of material deemed objectionable as obscene, indecent, or immoral. Such actions are frequently challenged as constituting a denial of freedom of press and speech. *See also* Obscenity; Prior restraint.

Censure /sénshər/. The formal resolution of a legislative, administrative, or other body reprimanding a person, normally one of its own members, for specified conduct. An official reprimand or condemnation. *See also* Censor; Reprimand.

Census /sénsəs/. The official counting or enumeration of people of a state, nation, district, or other political subdivision. Such contains classified information relating to sex, age, family, social and economic conditions, and public record thereof. The national census has been compiled decennially since 1790, and has increasingly listed a great variety of social and economic data. A primary use of such data is to apportion or reapportion legislative districts. *See also* Census bureau; Federal census.

Census bureau. The Bureau of the Census was established as a permanent office by act of Congress on March 6, 1902 (32 Stat. 51). The major functions of the Bureau are authorized by the Constitution (Art. I, Sec. 2, Cl. 3), which provides that a census of population shall be taken every 10 years, and by laws codified as title 13, U.S. Code. The law also provides that the information collected by the Bureau from individual persons, households, or establishments be kept strictly confidential and be used only for statistical purposes.

Center. This term is often used, not in its strict sense of a geographical or mathematical center, but as meaning the middle or central point or portion of anything. The center of a section of land is the intersection of a straight line from the north quarter corner to the south quarter corner with a straight line from the east quarter corner to the west quarter corner. Similarly, the center of a street intersection refers to the point where the center lines of the two streets cross. The center of the main channel of a river, is the middle of broad and distinctly defined bed of main river.

Center of gravity doctrine. Choice of law questions in conflicts of law are resolved by application of the law of the jurisdiction which has the most significant relationship to or contact with event and parties to the litigation and the issues therein. Term is used synonymously with most significant relationship or grouping of contacts theory.

Central Intelligence Agency. An agency of the Federal government charged with responsibility of coordinating all information relating to security of the country. All such intelligence information, recommendations, etc. are reported to the National Security Council, to whom the CIA is responsible to and under the direction of.

Centralization. Concentration of power and authority in a central organization or government. For example, power and authority over national and international matters is centralized in the federal government.

Centralized management. A concentration of authority among certain persons who may make independent business decisions on behalf of the entity without the need for continuing approval by the owners of the entity. It is a characteristic of a corporation since day-to-day business operations are handled by appointed officers and not by the shareholders.

CEO. Abbreviation for "chief executive officer" of a corporation.

CERCLA. Comprehensive Environmental Response, Compensation, and Liability Act of 1980. *See* Superfund.

Certain. Ascertained; precise; identified; settled; exact; definitive; clearly known; unambiguous; or, in law, capable of being identified or made known, without liability to mistake or ambiguity, from data already given. Free from doubt.

Certainty. Absence of doubt; accuracy; precision; definite. The quality of being specific, accurate, and distinct. *See* Certain.

Cert. den. Certiorari denied. *See* Certiorari.

Certificate /sərtífəkət/. A written assurance, or official representation, that some act has or has not been done, or some event occurred, or some legal formality has been complied with. A written assurance made or issuing from some court, and designed as a notice of things done therein, or as a warrant or authority, to some other court, judge, or officer. A statement of some fact in a writing signed by the party certifying. A declaration in writing. A "certificate" by a public officer is a statement written and signed, but not necessarily sworn to, which is by law made evidence of the truth of the facts stated for all or for certain purposes. A document certifying that one has fulfilled the requirements of and may practice in a field. *See also* Affidavit; Birth certificate; License; Permit.

Certificate in Management Accounting. A professional designation in the area of management accounting that recognizes the successful completion of an examination, acceptable work experience, and continuing education requirements.

Certificate of acknowledgment. The certificate of a notary public, justice of the peace, or other authorized officer, attached to a deed, mortgage, or other instrument, setting forth that the parties thereto personally appeared before him on such a date and acknowledged the instrument to be their free and voluntary act and deed. A verification of the act of the maker of an instrument.

Certificate of amendment. Document filed with state corporation authority (*e.g.* Secretary of State) disclosing amendment to articles of corporate organization or charter or agreement of association.

Certificate of authority. Document issued by state corporation authority (*e.g.* Secretary of State) on application of foreign corporation granting such corporation right to do business in state.

Certificate of competency. Required of business by Small Business Administration to perform a specific government procurement contract.

Certificate of convenience and necessity. Certificate of administrative agency (*e.g.* Public Service Commission; I.C.C.) granting operating authority for utilities and transportation companies.

Certificate of deposit. A written acknowledgment by a bank or banker of a deposit with promise to pay to depositor, to his order, or to some other person or to his order. U.C.C. § 3–104(2)(c). Bank document evidencing existence of a time deposit, normally paying interest.

Certificate of discharge. *See* Satisfaction piece.

Certificate of election. Issued by governor, board of elections, or other competent authority that the person or persons named have been duly elected.

Certificate of good conduct. An official written document which determines that a person is a law-abiding citizen of good repute and character to operate licensed premises, *e.g.* retail liquor store.

Certificate of incorporation. In most states is the document prepared by the Secretary of State that evidences the acceptance of articles of incorporation and the commencement of the corporate existence. In some states the certificate of incorporation is the name given to the document filed with the Secretary of State, i.e., the articles of incorporation. The Revised Model Business Corporation Act has eliminated certificates of incorporation, requiring only a fee receipt. *See also* Articles of incorporation.

Certificate of indebtedness. An obligation sometimes issued by corporations having practically the same force and effect as a bond, though not usually secured on any specific property. It may, however, create a lien on all the property of the corporation issuing it, superior to the rights of general creditors. *Compare* Debenture. In banking, same as a certificate of deposit; as a government security, same as a treasury certificate.

Certificate of insurance. Document evidencing fact that an insurance policy has been written and includes a statement of the coverage of the policy in general terms.

Certificate of interest. An instrument evidencing a fractional or percentage interest in oil and gas production.

Certificate of need. Many states have enacted certificate-of-need laws designed to combat spiraling health care costs and the unnecessary duplication and maldistribution of health care facilities and services. Under these laws, a health care provider seeking to establish or modify a health care facility or to provide new or different institutional health care services must normally apply to the appropriate state agency for a certificate of need.

Certificate of occupancy. Document certifying that premises comply with provisions of zoning and/or building ordinances. Such document, as issued by local government agency, is commonly required before premises can be occupied and title transferred. Document that certifies that what has been done actually conforms substantially to approved plans and specifications.

A number of cities require a "certificate of occupancy" for apartments, which aims at preventing their deterioration in the first place. After each vacancy, the apartment must be newly inspected to make sure it's up to standard.

Certificate of participation. A certificate issued instead of shares of stock to show a proportionate interest in an unincorporated business or in the ownership of debt of a corporation.

Certificate of public convenience and necessity. *See* Certificate of convenience and necessity, *supra.*

Certificate of purchase. A certificate issued by public officer to successful bidder at a judicial sale (such as a tax sale), which will entitle him to a deed upon confirmation of sale by the court, or (as the case may be) if the land is not redeemed within the time limited.

Certificate of redemption. Evidence of redeeming a property by the owner after losing it through a judicial sale.

Certificate of registry. In maritime law, a certificate of the registration of a vessel according to the registry acts, for the purpose of giving her a national character.

Certificate of sale. The same as Certificate of purchase, *supra.*

Certificate of stock. A certificate of a corporation or joint-stock company that named person is owner of designated number of shares of stock. It is merely written evidence of ownership of stock, and of the rights and liabilities resulting from such ownership. It is a document representation of an incorporeal right, and stands on the footing similar to that of other muniments of title.

Certificate of title. Document evidencing ownership; commonly associated with sale of motor vehicles. *See also* Insurance *(Title insurance).*

Certification /sòrtəfəkéyshən/. The formal assertion in writing of some fact. The act of certifying or state of being certified. Formal designation by NLRB that a labor organization represents a majority of employees in a particular bargaining unit. *See* Attestation; Certificate.

Certification mark. The term "certification mark" means any word, name, symbol, or device, or any combination thereof—(1) used by a person other than its owner, or (2) which its owner has a bona fide intention to permit a person other than the owner to use in commerce and files an application to register on the principal register established by the Trademark Act, to certify regional

or other origin, material, mode of manufacture, quality, accuracy, or other characteristics of such person's goods or services was performed by members of a union or other organization. 15 U.S.C.A. § 1127.

Certification of check. *See* Certified check.

Certification of labor union. Declaration by labor board (*e.g.* N.L.R.B.) that a union is bargaining agent for group of employees.

Certification of questions of law. *See* Certification to federal court; Certification to state court.

Certification of record on appeal. Formal acknowledgment of questions for appellate review commonly signed by trial justice.

Certification to federal court. Method of taking case from U.S. Court of Appeals to Supreme Court in which former court may certify any question of law in any civil or criminal case as to which instructions are requested. 28 U.S.C.A. § 1254(2).

Certification to state court. Procedure by which a Federal Court abstains from deciding a state law question until the highest court of the state has had an opportunity to rule on the question so certified by the Federal Court. State statutes and court rules providing for such certification are generally patterned on the "Uniform Certification of Questions of Law Act."

Certified carriers. Carriers using highways of state to whom certificates of public convenience and necessity have been issued.

Certified check. The check of a depositor drawn on a bank on the face of which the bank has written or stamped the words "accepted" or "certified" with the date and signature of a bank official. The check then becomes an obligation of the bank. The certification of a check is a statement of fact, amounting to an estoppel of the bank to deny liability; a warranty that sufficient funds are on deposit and have been set aside. It means that bank holds money to pay check and is liable to pay it to proper party.

Certification of a check is acceptance of check by drawee-bank. Where a holder procures certification the drawer and all prior indorsers are discharged. Unless otherwise agreed a bank has no obligation to certify a check. A bank may certify a check before returning it for lack of proper indorsement. If it does so the drawer is discharged. U.C.C. § 3–411. *Compare* Cashier's check.

Certified copy. A copy of a document or record, signed and certified as a true copy by the officer to whose custody the original is intrusted.

Certified mail. Form of mail similar to registered mail by which sender may require return receipt from addressee.

Certified Management Accounting. A person holding a Certificate in Management Accounting.

Certified public accountant (CPA). *See* Accountant.

Certified question. *See* Certification to federal court; Certification to state court.

Certify. To authenticate or vouch for a thing in writing. To attest as being true or as represented. *See* Certificate; Certification.

Certiorari /sèrsh(iy)ərérạy/sèrshərériy/. Lat. To be informed of. A writ of common law origin issued by a superior to an inferior court requiring the latter to produce a certified record of a particular case tried therein. The writ is issued in order that the court issuing the writ may inspect the proceedings and determine whether there have been any irregularities. It is most commonly used to refer to the Supreme Court of the United States, which uses the writ of certiorari as a discretionary device to choose the cases it wishes to hear. See 28 U.S.C.A. § 1254. The Supreme Court denies most writs of certiorari (i.e. "cert. den."). The trend in state practice has been to abolish such writ. *See also* Writ of certiorari.

Cession /séshən/. The act of ceding; a yielding or giving up; surrender; relinquishment of property or rights. The assignment, transfer, or yielding up of territory by one state or government to another.

In the civil law, an assignment. The act by which a party transfers property to another. The surrender or assignment of property for the benefit of one's creditors.

Cession of goods /séshən əv gúdz/. The surrender of property; the relinquishment that a debtor makes of all his property to his creditors, when he finds himself unable to pay his debts. *See* Bankruptcy proceedings.

Cessment. An assessment, or tax.

Cestui que trust /sétiy kə trə́st/. He who has a right to a beneficial interest in and out of an estate the legal title to which is vested in another. The person who possesses the equitable right to property and receives the rents, issues, and profits thereof; the legal estate of which is vested in a trustee. The beneficiary of a trust.

Cestui que use /sétiy kə yúwz/. He for whose use and benefit lands or tenements are held by another. The *cestui que use* has the right to receive the profits and benefits of the estate, but the legal title and possession (as well as the duty of defending the same) reside in the other.

Cestui que vie /sétiy kə víy/. The person whose life measures the duration of a trust, gift, estate, or insurance contract. Person on whose life insurance is written. The person for whose life any lands, tenements, or hereditaments are held.

Cf. An abbreviated form of the Latin word *confer,* meaning "compare." Directs the reader's attention to another part of the work, to another volume, case, etc., where contrasted, analogous, or explanatory views or statements may be found.

C. & F. *or* **C.F.** Term in sales contract means that the price so includes cost and freight to the named destination. U.C.C. § 2–320(1).

C.F. & I. *or* **C.F.I.** *See* C.I.F.

CFR. Code of Federal Regulations.

C.F.T.C. Commodity Futures Trading Commission.

Ch. This abbreviation most commonly stands for "chapter," or "chancellor," but it may also mean "chancery," or "chief."

Chain. As regards land measure, such equals 66 feet, 100 links, or 4 rods. *See also* Chains and links; Land measure.

Chain-certificate method. Method of authenticating of foreign official record. *See* Fed.R.Civil P. 44(a)(2).

Chain conspiracy. Exists where different activities are carried on with the same subject of the conspiracy in chain-like manner such that each conspirator performs a separate function which serves in the accomplishment of the overall conspiracy.

Chain of custody. In evidence, the one who offers real evidence, such as the narcotics in a trial of drug case, must account for the custody of the evidence from the moment in which it reaches his custody until the moment in which it is offered in evidence, and such evidence goes to weight not to admissibility of evidence. For example, "chain of custody" is proven if an officer is able to testify that he or she took control of the item of physical evidence, identified it, placed it in a locked or protected area, and retrieved the item being offered on the day of trial.

Chain of possession. *See* Chain of custody.

Chain of title. Record of successive conveyances, or other forms of alienation, affecting a particular parcel of land, arranged consecutively, from the government or original source of title down to the present holder. *See* Abstract of title.

Chains and links. Used in real estate measurement; chain is 66′ long or 100 links. *See also* Chain; Land measure.

Chain stores. Number of stores under common name, ownership and management; normally selling same general line of merchandise or products.

Chairman. A name given to the presiding officer of an assembly, public meeting, convention, deliberative or legislative body, board of directors, committee, etc.

Challenge. To object or except to; to prefer objections to a person, right, or instrument; to question formerly the legality or legal qualifications of; to invite into competition; to formally call into question the capability of a person for a particular function, or the existence of a right claimed, or the sufficiency or validity of an instrument; to call or put in question; to put into dispute; to render doubtful. For example, to challenge the personal qualification of a judge or magistrate about to preside at the trial of a cause, as on account of personal interest, his having been of counsel, bias, etc.; or to challenge a juror for cause. *See* Jury challenge; Objection.

Challenge for cause. A request from a party to a judge that a certain prospective juror not be allowed to be a member of the jury because of specified causes or reasons. See *e.g.* 28 U.S.C.A. § 1870.

Challenge to jury array. An exception to the whole panel in which the jury are arrayed, upon account of partiality, or some default in the sheriff or other officer who arrayed the panel or made the return. A challenge to the form and manner of making up the panel. A challenge that goes to illegality of drawing, selecting, or impaneling array. See *e.g.* Fed.R.Crim.P. 6(b) (grand jury).

General challenge. A species of challenge for cause, being an objection to a particular juror, to the effect that the juror is disqualified from serving in any case.

Peremptory challenge. A request from a party that a judge not allow a certain prospective juror to be a member of the jury. No reason or "cause" need be stated for this type of challenge. The number of peremptory challenges afforded each party is normally set by statute or court rule; *e.g.* Fed.R.Crim.P. 24; Fed.R.Civ.P. 47; 28 U.S.C.A. § 1870.

Chamber. A room or apartment in a house. A private repository of money; a treasury. A compartment; a hollow or cavity.

Judges chambers. The private room or office of a judge; any place in which a judge hears motions, signs papers, or does other business pertaining to his office, when he is not holding a session of court. Business so transacted is said to be done "in chambers."

Legislative body. The lower chamber of a bicameral legislature is normally the larger of the two (*e.g.* House of Representatives). The upper chamber is generally the smaller (*e.g.* Senate).

Chamber business. A term applied to all such judicial business as may properly be transacted by a judge at his chambers or elsewhere, as distinguished from such as must be done by the court in session.

Chamber of commerce. A board or association of businessmen and merchants organized to promote the commercial interests of a locality, county, or the like, or a society of a city who meet to promote the general trade and commerce of the locality. Chambers of commerce exist in most cities, and are loosely affiliated with the national organization of the same name. Particular trades may also have their own organizations or boards to promote the interests of their own trade. Organizations with functions similar to that of chambers of commerce may be known under various other names; *e.g.* Board of Trade.

Champertor /chǽmpərtər/. In criminal law, one who makes or brings suits, or causes them to be moved or brought, either directly or indirectly, and maintains them at his own cost, upon condition of having a part of the gains or of the land in dispute. One guilty of champerty *(q.v.)*.

Champertous /chǽmpərtəs/. Of the nature of champerty; affected with champerty.

Champerty /chǽmpərtiy/. A bargain between a stranger and a party to a lawsuit by which the stranger pursues the party's claim in consideration of receiving part of any judgment proceeds; it is one type of "maintenance," the more general term which refers to maintaining, supporting, or promoting another person's litigation. "Maintenance" consists of maintaining, supporting, or promoting the litigation of another. *See also* Maintenance.

Chance. Absence of explainable or controllable causation; accident; fortuity; hazard; result or issue of uncertain and unknown conditions or forces; risk; unexpected, unforeseen, or unintended consequence of an act. The opposite of intention, design, or contrivance. *See* Act of God.

Chancellor. The name given in some states to the judge (or the presiding judge) of a court of chancery. A university president, or chief executive officer of higher education system in certain states.

Chancery. Equity; equitable jurisdiction; a court of equity; the system of jurisprudence administered in courts of equity. *See* Court of Chancery; Equity.

Chance verdict. *See* Verdict.

Chandler Act. Federal act of 1938 making major amendments to Bankruptcy Act (11 U.S.C.A.). Included in amendments was provision for a debtor to arrange payments with creditors without total liquidation of debtor's assets. *See* Bankruptcy Code.

Change, *n.* An alteration; a modification or addition; substitution of one thing for another. Exchange of money against money of a different denomination.

Change, *v.* Alter; cause to pass from one place to another; exchange; make different in some particular; put one thing in place of another; vacate.

Change in accounting method. A change in the taxpayers method of accounting is an overall change in the plan of accounting, *e.g.* a change from the cash to the accrual method, or a change in the method of valuing inventories. Such change normally requires prior approval from the Internal Revenue Service. Generally, a request to the Internal Revenue Service must be filed within 180 days after the beginning of the taxable year of the desired change. In some instances, the permission for change will not be granted unless the taxpayer agrees to certain terms or adjustments which are prescribed by the Internal Revenue Service.

Change in accounting period. *See* Accounting period.

Change in accounting principle. A change from one generally accepted accounting principle to another. *See also* Change in accounting method.

Change of beneficiary. A divesting of beneficial interest held by one person and a vesting of that interest in another.

Change of circumstances. In domestic relations law, condition used to show need for modification of custody or support orders. With reference to custody issues, this term refers to a change relevant to the capacity of the moving party or custodial parent to properly take care of the child. It must be a change which was not contemplated at the time of the original decree and which has occurred since the last custody order and would enhance or have an adverse impact on the welfare of the child. This term is also used interchangeable with "changed circumstances."

Change of domicile. Change of abode or residence and intention to remain.

Change of venue. The removal of a suit begun in one county or district to another county or district for trial, though the term is also sometimes applied to the removal of a suit from one court to another court of the same county or district. In criminal cases a change of venue will be permitted if for example the court feels that the defendant cannot receive a fair trial in a given venue because of prejudice. Fed.R.Crim.P. 21. In civil cases a change *may* be permitted in the interests of justice or for the convenience of the parties. 28 U.S.C.A. §§ 1404(a), 1406(a), 1631. *See also* Forum non conveniens; Venue.

Channel. The bed in which the main stream of a river flows, rather than the deep water of the stream as followed in navigation. The deeper part of a river, harbor or strait. It may also be used as a generic term applicable to any water course, whether a river, creek, slough, or canal.

The "channel" of a river is to be distinguished from a "branch".

A means of expression or communication.

Main channel. That bed of the river over which the principal volume of water flows. The main channel of a navigable stream, called for as a boundary between states, means the "thalweg", or deepest and most navigable channel as it then existed.

Natural channel. The channel of a stream as determined by the natural conformation of the country through which it flows. The floor or bed on which the water flows, and the banks on each side thereof as carved out by natural causes.

Chapter 7 (liquidation) bankruptcy. *See* Bankruptcy proceedings (*Straight bankruptcy*).

Chapter 11 (reorganization) bankruptcy. *See* Bankruptcy proceedings (*Business reorganizations*).

Chapter 12 (farmer) bankruptcy. *See* Bankruptcy proceedings (*Family farmer bankruptcy*).

Chapter 13 (wage earner's) bankruptcy. *See* Bankruptcy proceedings (*Wage earner's plan*).

Character. The aggregate of the moral qualities which belong to and distinguish an individual person; the general result of the one's distinguishing attributes. That moral predisposition or habit, or aggregate of ethical qualities, which is believed to attach to a person, on the strength of the common opinion and report concerning him. A person's fixed disposition or tendency, as evidenced to others by his habits of life, through the manifestation of which his general reputation for the possession of a character, good or otherwise, is obtained. The estimate attached to an individual or thing in the community. The opinion generally entertained of a person derived from the common report of the people who are acquainted with him. Although "character" and "reputation" are often used synonymously, the terms are distinguishable. "Character" is what a man is, and "reputation" is what he is supposed to be in what people say he is. "Character" depends on attributes possessed, and "reputation" on attributes which others believe one to possess. The former signifies reality and the latter merely what is accepted to be reality at present. *See* Bad character; Good character; Reputation.

Class or division to which claim belongs.

Character and habit. The moral traits of a person gleaned from his habitual conduct. *See* Character.

Character evidence. Evidence of person's moral standing in community based on reputation.

Admissibility of character evidence in federal trials is governed by Fed.Evid. Rules 404 and 405, and with respect to witnesses by Rules 607–609.

Characterization. In conflicts, the classification, qualification, and interpretation of laws applicable to a case. Restatement, Second, Conflicts, § 7.

Character witness. *See* Witness.

Charge, *v.* To impose a burden, duty, obligation, or lien; to create a claim against property; to assess; to demand; to accuse; to instruct a jury on matters of law. To impose a tax, duty, or trust. To entrust with responsibilities and duties (*e.g.* care of another). In commercial transactions, to bill or invoice; to purchase on credit. In criminal law, to indict or formally accuse.

Charge, *n.* An incumbrance, lien, or claim; a burden or load; an obligation or duty; a liability; an accusation. A person or thing committed to the care of another. The price of, or rate for, something. *See also* Charged; Charges; Floating charge; Rate; Surcharge.

Charge to jury. The final address by judge to jury before verdict, in which he sums up the case, and instructs jury as to the rules of law which apply to its various issues, and which they must observe. The term also applies to the address of court to grand jury, in which the latter are instructed as to their duties. *See also* Jury instructions.

   General charge. The charge or instruction of the court to the jury upon the case, as a whole, or upon its general features and characteristics.

   Special charge. A charge or instruction given by the court to the jury, upon some particular point or question involved in the case, and usually in response to counsel's request for such instruction.

Criminal law. In a criminal case, the specific crime the defendant is accused of committing. Accusation of a crime by a formal complaint, information or indictment.

Public charge. An indigent. A person whom it is necessary to support at public expense by reason of poverty alone or illness and poverty.

Chargeable. This word, in its ordinary acceptation, as applicable to the imposition of a duty or burden, signifies capable of being charged, subject to be charged, liable to be charged, or proper to be charged.

Charge account. System of purchasing goods and services on credit, under which customer agrees to settle or make payments on his balance within a specified time or periodically. *See* Consumer Credit Protection Act.

Revolving charge account. An arrangement between a seller and a buyer pursuant to which: (1) the seller may permit the buyer to purchase goods or services on credit either from the seller or pursuant to a seller credit card, (2) the unpaid balances of amounts financed arising from purchases and the credit service and other appropri-

ate charges are debited to an account, (3) a credit service charge if made is not precomputed but is computed on the outstanding unpaid balances of the buyer's account from time to time, and (4) the buyer has the privilege of paying the balances in installments. Uniform Consumer Credit Code, § 2.108.

Charge back. The action of a bank in deducting or otherwise revoking a credit given to a customer's account, which credit usually has been given for a check deposited in the account. See U.C.C. §§ 4–212(1) (collecting bank's right of charge back) & 4–212(3) (payor bank's right of charge back).

Charge-back system. In accounting, a transfer pricing system.

Charged. Accusation of crime by complaint, indictment, or information. With respect to "notice", a person is charged with such if he has information sufficient to apprise him of the subject, *e.g.* under land recording acts, a person is charged with notice of a lien or attachment if it is on record.

Charge des affaires, or **charge d'affaires** /shàrzhéy deyz afér(z)/°dàfér(z)/. The title of a diplomatic representative of inferior rank.

Charge-off. Anything manifesting intent to eliminate an item from assets. Write-off of asset or other item, *e.g.* uncollectible account receivable or debt. To treat as a loss or expense an amount originally recorded as an asset; usually the term is used when the charge is not in accord with original expectations. *See* Bad debt.

Charges. The expenses which have been incurred, or disbursements made, in connection with a contract, suit, or business transaction. *See also* Charge; Costs; Fee; Fixed charges.

Charge-sheet. A record kept at a police station to receive the names of the persons brought and given custody, the nature of the accusation, and the name of the accuser in each case.

Charging lien. A lien is a charging lien where the debt is a charge upon the specific property although it remains in the debtor's possession. *See* Floor plan financing.

   The right of an attorney to have expenses and compensation due for services in a suit secured to the attorney in a judgment, decree or award for a client. The lien attaches to judgment but relates back and takes effect from the time of the commencement of services rendered in the action.

Charging order. A statutorily created means for a creditor of a judgment debtor who is a partner of others to reach the debtor's beneficial interest in the partnership, without risking dissolution of the partnership. Uniform Partnership Act, § 28.

Charitable. Having the character or purpose of a charity. The word "charitable", in a legal sense includes every gift for a general public use, to be applied consistent with existing laws, for benefit of an indefinite number of persons, and designed to benefit them from an educational, religious, moral, physical or social standpoint. This term is synonymous with "beneficent", "benevolent", and "eleemosynary". See also Charity; Eleemosynary.

Charitable bequest. A bequest is charitable if its aims and accomplishments are of religious, educational, political, or general social interest to mankind and if the ultimate recipients constitute either the community as a whole or an unascertainable and indefinite portion thereof.

Charitable contributions. Contributions of money, securities, etc. to organizations engaged in charitable purposes. Such contributions are deductible for tax purposes (subject to various restrictions and ceiling limitations) if made to qualified nonprofit charitable organizations. A cash basis taxpayer is entitled to a deduction solely in the year of payment. Accrual basis corporations may accrue contributions at year-end if payment is authorized by the Board of Directors prior to the end of the year and payment is made within time specified by I.R.C. before the end of the year. See also Charitable deduction; Charitable organizations.

Charitable corporation. Non-profit corporation organized for charitable purposes; i.e. for purpose, among other things, of promoting welfare of mankind at large, or of a community, or of some class forming part of it indefinite as to numbers and individuals and is one created for or devoted to charitable purposes. Such corporations must meet certain criteria to receive tax "exempt" status. I.R.C. § 501(c)(3). See Charitable organizations, infra.

Charitable deduction. In taxes, a contribution to a qualified charity or other tax exempt institution for which taxpayer may claim a deduction on his tax return. I.R.C. § 170(c). Also applicable to trusts. I.R.C. § 512(b)(11). As regards tax exempt status of recipient organization, see Charitable organizations. See also Charitable contributions.

Charitable foundation. An organization dedicated to education, health, relief of the poor, etc.; organized for such purposes and not for profit and recognized as such for tax purposes under I.R.C. § 509(a). See also Charitable organizations, infra.

Charitable gift. See Charitable deduction, supra.

Charitable immunity. A doctrine which relieves a charity of liability in tort; long recognized, but currently most states have abrogated or restricted such immunity.

Charitable institution. One which dispenses charity to all who need and apply for it, does not provide gain or profit in private sense to any person connected with it, and does not appear to place obstacles of any character in way of those who need and would avail themselves of charitable benefits it dispenses. Distinctive features are that it has no capital stock or shareholders and earns no profits or dividends; but rather derives its funds mainly from public and private charity and holds them in trust for objects and purposes expressed in its charter.

Charitable organizations. As regards "exempt" tax status, such includes: "Corporations, and any community chest, fund, or foundation, organized and operated exclusively for religious, charitable, scientific, testing for public safety, literary, or educational purposes, or to foster national or international amateur sports competition (but only if no part of its activities involve the provision of athletic facilities or equipment), or for the prevention of cruelty to children or animals, no part of the net earnings of which inures to the benefit of any private shareholder or individual, no substantial part of the activities of which is carrying on propaganda, or otherwise attempting, to influence legislation (except as otherwise provided in subsection (h)), and which does not participate in, or intervene in (including the publishing or distributing of statements), any political campaign on behalf of (or in opposition to) any candidate for public office." I.R.C. § 501(c)(3). See also Benevolent associations; Benevolent corporation; Charitable corporation; Charitable foundation; Charitable institution.

Charitable purpose. Term as used for purpose of tax exemption has as its common element the accomplishment of objectives which are beneficial to community or area, and usually recognized charitable purposes, not otherwise limited by statute, are generally classified as: relief of poverty; advancement of education; advancement of religion; protection of health; governmental or municipal purposes; and other varied purposes the accomplishment of which is beneficial to community.

A gift is for charitable purposes if it is for religious, scientific, charitable, literary, or educational purposes under tax law. I.R.C. § 170(c)(4). These purposes are also required for a trust to qualify as a charitable trust.

See also Charitable deduction; Charitable use.

Charitable remainder. A gift over after an intervening estate to a qualified charity; qualifies as a tax deduction under certain conditions.

Charitable remainder annuity trust. A trust which must pay the noncharitable income beneficiary or beneficiaries a sum certain annually, or more frequently, if desired, which is not less than 5% of the initial net fair market value of all property placed in the trust as finally determined for federal tax purposes. I.R.C. § 664(d)(1).

Charitable trust. One in which property held by a trustee must be used for charitable purposes (advancement of health, religion, etc.). Fiduciary relationship with respect to property arising as a result of a manifestation of an intention to create it, and subjecting the person by whom the property is held to equitable duties to deal with the property for a charitable purpose. Restatement, Second, Trusts, § 348. See Charitable purpose.

Charitable use. Charitable uses are defined as those of religious, educational, political or general social interest to mankind, or as those for the relief of poverty, advancement of education or religion, or beneficial to the community generally. See also Charitable purpose.

Charity. A gift for, or institution engaged in, public benevolent purposes. A gift for benefit of indefinite number of persons under influence of religion or education, relief from disease, assisting people to establish themselves in life, or erecting or maintaining public works. A "charity", in absence of legislative definition, is attempt in good faith, spiritually, physically, intellectually, socially and economically to advance and benefit mankind in general, or those in need of advancement and benefit in particular, without regard to their ability to supply that need from other sources and without hope or expectation, if not with positive abnegation, of gain or profit by donor or by instrumentality of charity. See also Benevolence; Benevolent; Charitable; Charitable organizations.

Public charity. A charity wherein the benefit is conferred on indefinite persons composing the public or some part of the public.

Charlatan /shárlətən/. One who pretends to have more knowledge or skill than he possesses; a quack; a faker.

Chart. A map used by navigators.

Charta /kártə/. In old English law, a charter or deed; an instrument written and sealed; the formal evidence of conveyances and contracts. Also any signal or token by which an estate was held.

The term came to be applied, by way of eminence, to such documents as proceeded from the sovereign, granting liberties or privileges, and either where the recipient of the grant was the whole nation, as in the case of *Magna Charta (q.v.)*, or a public body, or private individual, in which case it corresponded to the modern word "charter."

In the civil law, a paper suitable for inscription of documents or books; hence, any instrument or writing.

See also Charter.

Chartel /kartél/. A variant of "cartel" *(q.v.)*.

Charter, *v.* To hire, rent or lease for a temporary use; *e.g.* to hire or lease a vessel for a voyage.

Charter, *n.* An instrument emanating from the sovereign power, in the nature of a grant, either to the whole nation, or to a class or portion of the people, to a corporation, or to a colony or dependency, assuring to them certain rights, liberties, or powers. Such was the "Great Charter" or *"Magna Charta,"* and such also were the charters granted to certain of the English colonies in America.

A charter differs from a constitution, in that the former is granted by the sovereign, while the latter is established by the people themselves.

A city's organic law. Charter of municipal corporation consists of the creative act of incorporation, together with all those laws in force which relate to the incorporation, whether defining the powers of the corporation or regulating the mode of exercise thereof, and statute does not fail to become part of charter simply because it is not labeled as such.

An act of a legislature creating a business corporation, or creating and defining the franchise of a corporation. Under modern statutes, a charter is usually granted by the state secretary of state, who acts under general statutory authority conferred by the state legislature. Also a corporation's constitution or organic law; that is to say, the articles of incorporation taken in connection with the law under which the corporation was organized. The authority by virtue of which an organized body acts. A contract between the state and the corporation, between the corporation and the stockholders, and between the stockholders and the state. See Corporate charter.

Leasing or hiring of airplane, vessel, or the like. See Charter-party.

Bank charter. Document issued by governmental authority permitting a bank to operate and transact business.

Bareboat charter. Charter where ship owner only provides ship, with charterer providing personnel, insurance and other necessary materials and expenses. See also Bareboat charter.

Charter agreement. See Charter-party.

Charter of affreightment. See Affreightment.

Gross charter. Charter where ship owner provides all personnel and equipment and incurs other expenses such as port costs.

Time charter. Charter wherein vessel is leased for specified time rather than for specified trip or voyage. See also Time (Time charter).

Chartered Life Underwriter (C.L.U.). A designation conferred by the American College of Life Underwriters in recognition of the attainment of certain standards of education and proficiency in the art and science of life underwriting.

Chartered ship. A ship hired or freighted; a ship which is the subject-matter of a charter-party.

Charterer. One who charters (*i.e.*, hires, leases or engages) a vessel, airplane, etc. for transportation or voyage.

Charter-party. A contract by which a ship, or some principal part thereof, is let to a merchant for the conveyance of goods on a determined voyage to one or more places.

The term "charter party" or "charter agreement", often shortened to "charter," designates the document in which are set forth the arrangements and contractual engagements entered into when one person (the "charterer") takes over the use of the whole, or a substantial portion, of a ship belonging to another (the "owner").

Chart of accounts. A detailed listing of a company's accounts and associated account numbers.

Chase. To pursue or follow rapidly with the intention of catching or driving away. *See* Fresh pursuit.

Chattel /chǽtǝl/. An article of personal property, as distinguished from real property. A thing personal and movable. It may refer to animate as well as inanimate property. *See also* Goods; Property (*Personal property*).

Personal chattel. Movable things. Personal property which has no connection with real estate. *See* Goods; Property (*Personal Property*).

Real chattels. Such as concern real property, such as leasehold estates; interests issuing out of, or annexed to, real estate; such chattel interests as devolve after the manner of realty. An interest in real estate less than freehold or fee. *See also* Fixture.

Chattel lien. Chattel liens exist in favor of persons expending labor, skill or materials on any chattel or furnishing storage thereof at request of owner, his agent, reputed owner, or lawful possessor. *See e.g.* Artisan's lien.

Chattel mortgage. A pre-Uniform Commercial Code security device whereby a security interest was taken by the mortgagee in personal property of the mortgagor. A transfer of some legal or equitable right in personal property or creation of a lien thereon as security for payment of money or performance of some other act, subject to defeasance on performance of the conditions. Such security device has generally been superseded by other types of security agreements under U.C.C. Article 9 (Secured Transactions). *See* Secured transaction; Security agreement.

Chattel paper. A writing or writings which evidence both a monetary obligation and a security interest in or a lease of specific goods. In many instances chattel paper will consist of a negotiable instrument coupled with a security agreement. When a transaction is evidenced both by such a security agreement or a lease and by an instrument or a series of instruments, the group of writings taken together constitutes chattel paper. U.C.C. § 9–105(1)(b). *See* Secured transaction; Security agreement.

Chaud-medley /shòwdmédliy/. A homicide committed in the heat of an affray and while under the influence of passion; it is thus distinguished from *chance-medley*, which is the killing of a man in a casual affray in self-defense. It has been said, however, that the distinction is of no great importance. *See* Heat of passion; Homicide.

Cheat, *v.* To deceive and defraud. It necessarily implies a fraudulent intent. The words "cheat and defraud" usually mean to induce a person to part with the possession of property by reason of intentionally false representations relied and acted upon by such person to his harm. They include not only the crime of false pretenses, but also all civil frauds, and include all tricks, devices, artifices, or deceptions used to deprive another of property or other right. *See* Fraud.

Cheat, *n.* Swindling; defrauding. The act of fraudulently deceiving. *See* Fraud.

Check, *v.* To control or restrain; to hold within bounds. To verify or audit, as to examine the books and records of another or a business for accuracy and proper accounting practices. Particularly used with reference to the control or supervision of one department, bureau, office, or person over another.

Check, *n.* A draft drawn upon a bank and payable on demand, signed by the maker or drawer, containing an unconditional promise to pay a sum certain in money to the order of the payee. U.C.C. § 3–104(2)(b).

The Federal Reserve Board defines a check as "a draft or order upon a bank or banking house purporting to be drawn upon a deposit of funds for the payment at all events of a certain sum of money to a certain person therein named or to him or his order or to bearer and payable instantly on demand." It must contain the phrase "pay to the order of."

See also Bad check; Bogus check; Cancelled check; Cashier's check; Depository transfer check (DTC); Draft; Raised check; Registered check; Stale check; Travelers check.

Blank check. Check which is signed by drawer but left blank as to payee and/or amount.

Cashier's check. A bank's own check drawn on itself and signed by the cashier or other authorized official. It is a direct obligation of the bank. One issued by an authorized officer of a bank directed to another person, evidencing that the payee is authorized to demand and receive upon presentation from the bank the amount of money represented by the check. A form of a check by which the bank lends its credit to the purchaser of the check, the purpose being to make it available for immediate use in banking circles. A bill of exchange drawn by a bank upon itself, and accepted by the act of issuance. In its legal effect, it is the same as a certificate of deposit, certified check or draft. An acknowledgment of a debt drawn by bank upon itself. *See also* Certified check.

Memorandum check. A check given by a borrower to a lender, for the amount of a short loan, with the understanding that it is not to be presented at the bank, but will be redeemed by the maker himself when the loan falls due. This understanding is evidenced by writing the word *"Mem."* on the check.

Personal check. An individual's own check drawn on his own account.

Post-dated check. A check which bears a date after the date of its issue. Its negotiability is not affected by being postdated and it is payable on its stated date. U.C.C. § 3–114.

Traveler's check. See Traveler's check.

Checkerboard system. This term, with reference to entries on lands, means one entry built on another, and a third on the second.

Check kiting. Practice of writing a check against a bank account where funds are insufficient to cover it and hoping that before it is deposited the necessary funds will have been deposited. Transfer of funds between two or more banks to obtain unauthorized credit from a bank during the time it takes the checks to clear. In effect, a kite is a bad check used temporarily to obtain credit. *See* Bad check.

Check-off system. Procedure whereby employer deducts union dues directly from pay of employees and remits such sums to union.

Check register. Journal used to record checks issued.

Checks and balances. Arrangement of governmental powers whereby powers of one governmental branch check or balance those of other branches. *See also* Separation of powers.

Chemical analysis. Any form of examination through use of chemicals as in blood tests to determine a person's sobriety, the presence of drugs, etc. *See, e.g.,* Blood test evidence; Breathalyzer test; DNA identification; Intoxilyzer; Intoximeter.

Cheque /chék/. A variant of check *(q.v.)*.

Cherokee Nation. One of the civilized Indian tribes. *See* Indian tribe.

Chicago Board of Trade. Commodities exchange where futures contracts in a large number of agricultural products are transacted.

Chicane /shəkéyn/. Swindling; shrewd cunning. The use of tricks and artifice.

Chickasaw Nation. One of the civilized Indian tribes. *See* Indian tribe.

Chief. One who is put above the rest. Principal; leading; head; eminent in power or importance; the best or most important or valuable of several; paramount; of leading importance.

Declaration in chief is a declaration for the principal cause of action.

Examination in chief is the first examination of a witness by the party who produces him.

Chief clerk. The principal clerical officer of a court, bureau or department, who is generally charged, subject to the direction of his superior officer, with the superintendence of the administration of the business of the office.

Chief executive. *See* Chief magistrate; President.

Chief Judge. *See* Chief Justice.

Chief Justice. The presiding, most senior, or principal judge of a court. *Compare* Associate justices.

Chief magistrate. The head of the executive department of government of a nation, state, or municipal corporation. The President is the chief executive of the United States.

Chief office. Office of paramount importance or the leading office.

Chief use. In customs law, for purposes of determining the proper tariff classification, this refers to the use by users, as a whole, of the type of commodity involved, and not merely individual use.

Child; Children. Progeny; offspring of parentage. Unborn or recently born human being. At common law one who had not attained the age of fourteen years, though the meaning now varies in different statutes; *e.g.* child labor, support, criminal, etc. statutes. The term "child" or "children" may include or apply to: adopted, after-born, or illegitimate child; step-child; child by second or former marriage; issue.

See also Delinquent child; Disobedient child; Foster child; Illegitimate child; Infancy; Juvenile; Minor; Neglected child; Person; Posthumous child; Pretermitted heir; Viable child. For negligence of child, *see* Parental liability.

Childs part. A "child's part," which a widow, by statute in some states, is entitled to take in lieu of dower or the provision made for her by will, is a full share to which a child of the decedent would be entitled, subject to the debts of the estate and the cost of administration up to and including distribution.

Illegitimate child. Child born out of lawful wedlock.

Legitimate child. Child born in lawful wedlock.

Natural child. Child by natural relation or procreation. Child by birth, as distinguished from a child by adoption. Illegitimate children who have been acknowledged by the father.

Posthumous child. One born after the father's death.

Quasi-posthumous child. In the civil law, one who, born during the life of his grandfather, or other male ascendant, was not his heir at the time he made his testament, but who by the death of his father became his heir in his life-time.

Rights of unborn child. The rights of an unborn child are recognized in various different legal contexts; *e.g.* in criminal law, murder includes the unlawful killing of a fetus (Cal.Penal Code § 187), and the law of property considers the unborn child in being for all purposes which are to its benefit, such as taking by will or descent. After its birth, it has been held that it may maintain a statutory action for the wrongful death of the parent. In addition, the child, if born alive, is permitted to maintain an action for the consequences of prenatal injuries, and if he dies of such injuries after birth an action will lie for his wrongful death. While certain states have allowed recovery even though the injury occurred during the early weeks of pregnancy, when the child was neither viable nor quick; other states require that the fetus be viable before a civil damage action can be brought on behalf of the unborn child. *See,* Viable child; Wrongful birth; Wrongful conception; Wrongful life.

Child abuse. Any form of cruelty to a child's physical, moral or mental well-being. Also used to describe form of sexual attack which may or may not amount to rape. Such acts are criminal offenses in most states. *See also* Abuse (*Female child*); Abused and neglected children; Battered child syndrome; Protective order.

Child and dependent care credit. This tax credit is available to individuals who are employed on a full-time basis and maintain a household for a dependent child or disabled spouse or dependent. The amount of the credit is equal to a percentage of the cost of employment-related child and dependent care expenses, up to a stated maximum amount.

Child labor laws. Network of laws on both federal and state levels prescribing working conditions for children in terms of hours and nature of work which may be performed, all designed to protect the child. Included are restrictions on number of hours that teen-agers can work during school year

on school days and weekends; also specific hours during day that they can work. *See also* Fair Labor Standards Act; Working papers.

Children's court. *See* Juvenile courts.

Child support. The legal obligation of parents to contribute to the economic maintenance, including education, of their children; enforceable in both civil and criminal contexts. In a dissolution or custody action, money paid by one parent to another toward the expenses of children of the marriage. *See also* Nonsupport.

Child's income tax. *See* Clifford trust; Kiddie tax.

Child welfare. A generic term which embraces the totality of measures necessary for a child's well being; physical, moral and mental.

Chilling a sale. The act of bidders or others who combine or conspire to suppress fair competition at a sale, for the purpose of acquiring the property at less than its fair value.

Chilling effect doctrine. In constitutional law, any law or practice which has the effect of seriously discouraging the exercise of a constitutional right, *e.g.* the right of appeal. The deterrent effect of governmental action that falls short of a direct prohibition against the exercise of First Amendment rights. To constitute an impermissible chilling effect the constrictive impact must arise from the present or future exercise or threatened exercise of coercive power.

Choate /kówət/. That which has become perfected or ripened as *e.g.* a choate lien *(q.v.).*

Choate lien /kówət líyn/. Lien which is perfected so that nothing more need be done to make it enforcible. Identity of lienor, property subject to lien and amount of lien are all established. The lien must be definite and not merely ascertainable in the future by taking further steps.

Choice of law. In conflicts of law, the question presented in determining what law should govern. There are a number of different choice of law principles used by courts in determining the applicable law to apply; *e.g.* substantive vs. procedure distinction, center of gravity, renvoi, lex fori, grouping-of-contacts, place of most significant relationship. *See also* Conflict of laws.

Choice of law clause. A contractual provision wherein the parties designate the state whose law will govern disputes arising out of their agreement.

Chose /shówz/. Fr. A thing; an article of personal property. A chose is a chattel personal, and is either in action or in possession. *See* Chose in action; Chose in possession, *infra.*

Chose in action. A thing in action; a right of bringing an action or right to recover a debt or money. Right of proceeding in a court of law to procure payment of sum of money, or right to recover a personal chattel or a sum of money by action. A personal right not reduced into possession, but recoverable by a suit at law. A right to personal things of which the owner has not the possession, but merely a right of action for their possession. The phrase includes all personal chattels which are not in possession; and all property in action which depends entirely on contracts express or implied. A right to receive or recover a debt, demand, or damages on a cause of action *ex contractu* or for a tort or omission of a duty. A right to recover by suit a personal chattel. Assignable rights of action ex contractu and perhaps ex delicto. Personalty to which the owner has a right of possession in future, or a right of immediate possession, wrongfully withheld. *See* Cause of action.

Chose in possession. A personal thing of which one has possession. A thing in possession, as distinguished from a thing in action. Taxes and customs, if paid, are a chose in possession; if unpaid, a chose in action. *See also* Chose in action, *supra*.

Chosen freeholders. Name for county or township boards in certain eastern states.

Christian name. The baptismal name as distinct from the surname. The name which is given one after his birth or at baptism, or is afterward assumed by him in addition to his family name. Such name may consist of a single letter.

Chronic /krónək/. With reference to diseases, of long duration, or characterized by slowly progressive symptoms; deepseated and obstinate, or threatening a long continuance;—distinguished from acute.

Churning. Churning occurs when a broker, exercising control over the volume and frequency of trades, abuses his customer's confidence for personal gain by initiating transactions that are excessive in view of the character of account and the customer's objectives as expressed to the broker. As a scheme, the essence of which is deception of a relying customer, churning, as a matter of law, is considered a violation of federal securities law proscribing fraud in connection with the purchase and sale of securities. Securities Exchange Act of 1934, § 10(b), 15 U.S.C.A. § 78j(b).

C.I.A. Central Intelligence Agency.

C.I.F. This term in a sales contract means that the price includes in a lump sum the cost of the goods and the insurance and freight to the named destination.

Cigarette tax. An excise tax imposed on sale of cigarettes by both federal and state governments.

C.I.O. Congress of Industrial Organizations. Merged with AFL (American Federation of Labor) in 1955.

Circa /sárkə/. Lat. About; around; also, concerning; with relation to. Commonly used before a given date when the exact time is not known; as, *circa* 1800. Abbreviated *circ.* or *c.*

Circuit /sárkət/. Judicial divisions of the United States (*e.g.* thirteen judicial circuits wherein U.S. Courts of Appeal sit) or a state, originally so called because the judges traveled from place to place within the circuit, holding court in various locations.

Circuit courts of appeals. Former name for federal intermediate appellate courts, changed in 1948 to present designation of United States Courts of Appeals. See 28 U.S.C.A. §§ 41–48. *See* Courts of Appeals, U.S.

Circuit courts. Courts whose jurisdiction extends over several counties or districts, and of which terms are held in the various counties or districts to which their jurisdiction extends.

In several of the states, the name given to a tribunal, the territorial jurisdiction of which may comprise several counties or districts, and whose sessions are held in such counties or districts alternately. These courts usually have general original jurisdiction.

See also Courts of Appeals, U.S.

Circuity of action. A complex, indirect, or roundabout course of legal proceeding, making two or more actions necessary in order to effect that adjustment of rights between all the parties concerned in the transaction which, by a more direct course, might have been accomplished in a single suit. Former problems of circuity of action have been remedied by Rules of Civil Procedure.

Circular letter of credit. A letter authorizing one person to pay money or extend credit to another on the credit of the writer. *See also* Letter of credit.

Circular notes. Instruments, similar to "letters of credit," drawn by resident bankers upon their foreign correspondents, in favor of persons traveling abroad.

Circulated. A thing is "circulated" when it passes, as from one person or place to another, or spreads, as a report or tale.

Circulation. Transmission from person to person or place to place; *e.g.* interchange of money. Extent or degree of dissemination; *e.g.* total readers or issues sold of given publication.

Circumstances. Attendant or accompanying facts, events or conditions. Subordinate or accessory facts; *e.g.* evidence that indicates the probability or improbability of an event.

As used in a statute for an allowance for the wife in a divorce action, having regard to the "circumstances" of the parties, it includes practically everything which has a legitimate bearing on present and prospective matters relating to the lives of both parties. *See also* Change of circumstances.

See also Extenuating circumstances; Extraordinary circumstances.

Circumstantial evidence. Testimony not based on actual personal knowledge or observation of the facts in controversy, but of other facts from which deductions are drawn, showing indirectly the facts sought to be proved. The proof of certain facts and circumstances in a given case, from which jury may infer other connected facts which usually and reasonably follow according to the common experience of mankind. Evidence of facts or circumstances from which the existence or nonexistence of fact in issue may be inferred. Inferences drawn from facts proved. Process of decision by which court or jury may reason from circumstances known or proved, to establish by inference the principal fact. It means that existence of principal facts is only inferred from circumstances.

The proof of various facts or circumstances which usually attend the main fact in dispute, and therefore tend to prove its existence, or to sustain, by their consistency, the hypothesis claimed. Or as otherwise defined, it consists in reasoning from facts which are known or proved to establish such as are conjectured to exist.

Citation /saytéyshən/. A writ issued out of a court of competent jurisdiction, commanding a person therein named to appear on a day named and do something therein mentioned, or show cause why he should not. An order, issued by the police, to appear before a magistrate or judge at a later date. A citation is commonly used for minor violations (*e.g.* traffic violations); thus avoiding having to take the suspect into immediate physical custody. *See also* Citation of authorities; Cite.

Citation of authorities. The reading, or production of, or reference to, legal authorities and precedents (such as constitutions, statutes, reported cases, and treatises), in arguments to courts, in legal textbooks, law review articles, briefs, motions, and the like to substantiate or fortify the propositions advanced. *See also* Cite.

Citators. A set of books which provide, through letter-form abbreviations or words, the subsequent judicial history and interpretation of reported decisions. The citators also denote the legislative and amendment history, and cases that have cited or construed, constitutions, statutes, rules, regulations, etc. The most widely used set of citators is *Shepard's Citations.*

Cite. To summon; to command the presence of a person; to notify a person of legal proceedings against him and require his appearance thereto. To read or refer to legal authorities, in an argument to a court or elsewhere, in support of propositions of law sought to be established. To name in citation. To mention in support, illustration, or proof of. *See* Citation; Citation of authorities.

Citizen. One who, under the Constitution and laws of the United States, or of a particular state, is a member of the political community, owing allegiance and being entitled to the enjoyment of full civil rights. All persons born or naturalized in the United States, and subject to the jurisdiction thereof, are citizens of the United States and of the state wherein they reside. U.S.Const., 14th Amend. *See* Citizenship.

"Citizens" are members of a political community who, in their associated capacity, have established or submitted themselves to the dominion of a government for the promotion of their general welfare and the protection of their individual as well as collective rights.

Under the diversity statute, which mirrors U.S. Const. Article III's diversity clause, a person is a "citizen of a state" if he or she is a citizen of the United States and a domiciliary of a state of the United States.

Citizen-informant. An eye witness who, with no motive but public service, and without expectation of payment, identifies himself or herself and volunteers information to the police.

Citizen's arrest. A private citizen as contrasted with a police officer may, under certain circumstances, make an arrest, generally for a felony or misdemeanor amounting to a breach of the peace. A private person may arrest another: 1. For a public offense committed or attempted in his presence. 2. When the person arrested has committed a felony, although not in his presence. 3. When a felony has been in fact committed, and he has reasonable cause for believing the person arrested to have committed it. Calif.Penal Code, § 837.

Citizenship. The status of being a citizen. There are four ways to acquire citizenship: by birth in the United States, by birth in U.S. territories, by birth outside the U.S. to U.S. parents, and by naturalization. *See* Corporate citizenship; Diversity of citizenship; Dual citizenship; Federal citizenship; Naturalization.

City. A municipal corporation; in most states, of the largest and highest class. Also, the territory within the corporate limits. A political entity or subdivision for local governmental purposes; commonly headed by a mayor, and governed by a city council.

City council. The principal governmental body of a municipal corporation with power to pass ordinances, levy taxes, appropriate funds, and generally administer city government. The name of a group of municipal officers constituting primarily a legislative and administrative body, but which is often charged with judicial or quasi judicial functions, as when sitting on charges involving the removal of an officer for cause.

City courts. Court which tries persons accused of violating municipal ordinances and has jurisdiction over minor civil or criminal cases, or both.

Civic. Pertaining to a city or citizen, or to citizenship.

Civic enterprise. A project or undertaking in which citizens of a city co-operate to promote the common good and general welfare of the people of the city.

Civil. Of or relating to the state or its citizenry. Relating to private rights and remedies sought by civil actions as contrasted with criminal proceedings.

The word is derived from the Latin civilis, a citizen. Originally, pertaining or appropriate to a member of a *civitas* or free political community; natural or proper to a *citizen*. Also, relating to the community, or to the policy and government of the citizens and subjects of a state.

As to *civil* Bail; Commitment; Commotion; Conspiracy; Contempt; Corporation; Death; Injury; Liberty; Obligation; Officer; Possession; Remedy; Right; and War, see those titles. *See, also,* the titles which follow.

Civil action. Action brought to enforce, redress, or protect private rights. In general, all types of actions other than criminal proceedings.

The term includes all actions, both those formerly known as equitable actions and those known as legal actions, or, in other phraseology, both suits in equity and actions at law.

In the great majority of states which have adopted rules or codes of civil procedure as patterned on the Federal Rules of Civil Procedure, there is only one form of action known as a "civil action." The former distinctions between actions at law and suits in equity, and the separate forms of those actions and suits, have been abolished. Rule of Civil Proc. 2; New York CPLR § 103(a). *Compare* Penal action.

Civil Aeronautics Board. The Civil Aeronautics Board, an independent regulatory commission, was originally established under the Civil Aeronautics Act of 1938. Its functions were terminated or transferred to other agencies beginning in 1966, with remaining functions transferred to Transportation Secretary in 1985. *See* Federal Aviation Administration.

Civil authority clause. Provision in fire insurance policy protecting insured from damages caused by firemen, police, and other civil authorities.

Civil bail. A bond, deposit of money or of property, to secure the release of a person who is under civil arrest for failing to pay a debt which has

been reduced to court order and its effect is to insure payment of such order. *See also* Bail.

Civil Code. *See* Code Civil.

Civil commitment. A form of confinement order used in the civil context for those who are mentally ill, incompetent, alcoholic, drug addicted, etc. as contrasted with the criminal commitment of a sentence. Also applicable to confinement for failing to pay a debt which has been converted to a court order for payment; the failure to pay being contempt of court. *See also* Commitment.

Civil conspiracy. A combination of two or more persons who, by concerted action, seek to accomplish an unlawful purpose or to accomplish some purpose, not in itself unlawful, by unlawful means. *See* Conspiracy.

Civil contempt. A species of contempt of court which generally arises from a wilful failure to comply with an order of court such as an injunction as contrasted with criminal contempt which consists generally of contumelious conduct in the presence of the court. Punishment for civil contempt may be a fine or imprisonment, the object of such punishment being compliance with the order of the court. Such contempt is committed when a person violates an order of court which requires that person in specific and definite language to do or refrain from doing an act or series of acts. It commonly consists of failing to do something ordered by the court in a civil action for the benefit of the opposing litigant, and the proceedings are instituted to compel or coerce obedience to the order or decree. *See also* Contempt.

Civil Damage Acts. *See* Dram Shop Acts.

Civil death. The state of a person who, though possessing natural life, has lost all civil rights and as to them is considered civilly dead. In some states, persons convicted of serious crimes are declared to be civilly dead which means that certain civil rights and privileges of the convicted offender including the right to vote and contract and to sue and be sued are forfeited. *See also* Civil disabilities, *infra.*

A corporation which has formally dissolved or become bankrupt leaving an estate to be administered for the benefit of its shareholders and creditors becomes civilly "dead."

Civil disabilities. Apart from the sentence which is imposed upon a convicted offender, numerous civil disabilities are also often imposed. These disabilities, which adversely affect an offender both during his incarceration and after his release, include denial of such privileges as voting, holding public office, obtaining many jobs and occupational licenses, entering judicially-enforceable agreements, maintaining family relationships, and obtaining insurance and pension benefits. A form of civil disability resulting from a DWI conviction is the revocation or suspension of driver's license. *See also* Civil death.

Civil disobedience. A form of lawbreaking employed to demonstrate the injustice or unfairness of a particular law and indulged in deliberately to focus attention on the allegedly undesirable law. *See* Civil disorder.

Civil disorder. Any public disturbance involving acts of violence by assemblages of three or more persons, which causes an immediate danger of or results in damage or injury to the property or person of any other individual. 18 U.S.C.A. § 232. *See also* Riot.

Civil fraud. In taxation, the specific intent to evade a tax which taxpayer believes to be owing is an essential element of civil fraud. May also be applied to the tort of deceit or fraud in contrast to criminal fraud. *See also* Fraud.

Civilian. Private citizen, as distinguished from such as belong to the armed services, or (in England) the church. One who is skilled or versed in the civil law.

Civilis /sívələs/. Lat. Civil, as distinguished from criminal. *Civilis actio*, a civil action.

Civiliter mortuus /səvílətər mórtyuwəs/. Civilly dead; dead in the view of the law. The condition of one who has lost his civil rights and capacities, and is considered civilly dead in law. *See* Civil death.

Civilization. A law, an act of justice, or judgment which renders a criminal process civil.

A term which covers several states of society; it is relative, and has no fixed sense, but implies an improved and progressive condition of the people, living under an organized government. It consists not merely in material achievements, in accomplishment and accumulation of wealth, or in advancement in culture, science, and knowledge, but also in doing of equal and exact justice.

Civil jury trial. Trial of civil action before a jury rather than before a judge. In suits at common law in Federal court where value in controversy exceeds $20.00, there is constitutional right to jury trial. U.S.Const., 7th Amend.; Fed.R.Civil P. 38. *See also* Jury trial.

Civil law. That body of law which every particular nation, commonwealth, or city has established peculiarly for itself; more properly called "municipal" law, to distinguish it from the "law of nature," and from international law. Laws concerned with civil or private rights and remedies, as contrasted with criminal laws.

The system of jurisprudence held and administered in the Roman empire, particularly as set forth in the compilation of Justinian and his successors,—comprising the Institutes, Code, Digest, and Novels, and collectively denominated the *"Corpus Juris Civilis,"*—as distinguished from the common law of England and the canon law. The civil law (Civil Code) is followed in Louisiana. *See* Code Civil.

Civil liability. The amenability to civil action as distinguished from amenability to criminal prosecution. A sum of money assessed either as general, special or liquidated damages; may be either single, double or treble for violations such as overcharges.

Civil liability acts. *See* Dram Shop Acts.

Civil liberties. Personal, natural rights guaranteed and protected by Constitution; *e.g.* freedom of speech, press, freedom from discrimination, etc. Body of law dealing with natural liberties, shorn of excesses which invade equal rights of others. Constitutionally, they are restraints on government. State law may recognize liberty interests more extensive than those independently protected by the Federal Constitution. *See also* Bill of Rights; Civil Rights Acts; Fundamental rights.

Civil nuisance. At common law, anything done to hurt or annoyance of lands, tenements, or hereditaments of another. *See* Nuisance.

Civil obligation. One which binds in law, and may be enforced in a court of justice.

Civil offense. Term used to describe violations of statutes making the act a public nuisance. Also describes an offense which is malum prohibitum and not considered reprehensible.

Civil office. A non-military public office; one which pertains to the exercise of the powers or authority of government.

Civil officer. *See* Officer.

Civil penalties. Punishment for specific prohibited activities, as usually provided for by statute; *e.g.* violation of antitrust, pollution, or securities laws; usually in the form of fines or money damages. *See* Damages (*exemplary or punitive damages*); Penal action; Statutory penalty; Superfund; Treble damages.

Civil possession. *See* Possession.

Civil procedure. Body of law concerned with methods, procedures and practices used in civil litigation, *e.g.* Federal Rules of Civil Procedure; Title 28 of United States Code.

Civil process. *See* Process.

Civil responsibility. The liability to be called upon to respond to an action at law for an injury caused by a delict or crime, as opposed to criminal responsibility, or liability to be proceeded against in a criminal tribunal.

Civil rights. *See* Civil liberties.

Civil Rights Acts. Federal statutes enacted after Civil War, and more recently in 1957 and 1964, intended to implement and give further force to basic personal rights guaranteed by Constitution. Such Acts prohibit discrimination in employment, education, public accomodations, etc. based on race, color, age, or religion.

Civil rules. *See* Federal Rules of Civil Procedure.

Civil servant. *See* Civil service.

Civil service. Term generally means employment in federal, state, city and town government with such positions filled on merit as a result of competitive examinations. Such employment carries with it certain statutory rights to job security, advancement, benefits, etc. *See* Civil Service Commission; Competitive civil service examination; Merit Systems Protection Board; Office of Personnel Management.

Civil Service Commission. The United States Civil Service Commission (CSC) was created by act of Congress on January 16, 1883. Authority is codified under 5 U.S.C.A. § 1101.

The Civil Service Act was designed to establish a merit system under which appointments to Federal jobs are made on the basis of fitness—as determined by open and competitive examination—rather than personal preference or political considerations. Over the years, additional legislation and Executive orders have broadened the Commission's role to include such Federal personnel management activities as job classification, status and tenure, pay comparability, awards, training, labor-management relations, equal employment opportunity, health and life insurance programs, and retirement. The Commission was reorganized and restructured under the Civil Service Reform Act of 1978. Among the features of the Reform Act were the establishment of an independent and equitable appeals process, protections against abuses of the merit system, and incentives for good work and skilled management. Additionally, the functions of the former Commission were divided between two new agencies—Office of Personnel Management and an independent Merit Systems Protection Board (*q.v.*).

Similar commissions exist in most states covering state and local public employment.

Civil side. When the same court has jurisdiction of both civil and criminal matters, proceedings of the first class are often said to be on the civil side; those of the second, on the criminal side.

Civil suits. *See* Civil action.

Civil trials. Trials of civil as distinguished from criminal cases.

Civil war. In general, any internal armed conflict between persons of same country. War Between the States in which Federal government contended against seceding Confederate states from 1861 to 1865. Also, in England, war between Parliamentarians and Royalists from 1642 to 1652.

Civil year. *See* Year.

C.J. An abbreviation for chief justice; also for circuit judge; Corpus Juris.

C.J.S. Corpus Juris Secundum.

C.L. An abbreviation for civil law.

Claflin trust. A type of trust in which donor or settlor makes specific provisions for termination and the courts respect such provisions by denying the beneficiary the right to terminate. Called an indestructible trust, deriving its name from the case. Claflin v. Claflin, 149 Mass. 19, 20 N.E. 454.

Claim. To demand as one's own or as one's right; to assert; to urge; to insist. A cause of action. Means by or through which claimant obtains possession or enjoyment of privilege or thing. Demand for money or property as of right, *e.g.* insurance claim.

With respect to claims to a negotiable instrument of which a holder in due course takes free, the term "claim" means any interest or remedy recognized in law or equity that creates in the claimant a right to the interest or its proceeds.

Right to payment, whether or not such right is reduced to judgment, liquidated, unliquidated, fixed, contingent, matured, unmatured, disputed, undisputed, legal, equitable, secured, or unsecured; or right to an equitable remedy for breach of performance if such breach gives rise to a right to payment, whether or not such right to an equitable remedy is reduced to judgment, fixed, contingent, matured, unmatured, disputed, undisputed, secured, or unsecured. Bankruptcy Code, § 101.

In conflicts of law, a receiver may be appointed in any state which has jurisdiction over the defendant who owes a claim. Restatement, Second, Conflicts, § 369.

In patent law, a claim is an assertion of what the invention purports to accomplish, and claims of a patent define the invention and the extent of the grant; any feature of an invention not stated in the claim is beyond the scope of patent protection.

See also Antecedent claim; Cause of action; Community debt; Complaint; Counterclaim; Crossclaim; False claim; Joinder; Liability; Liquidated claim; Third party complaint. For proof of claim, *see* Proof; for joinder of claims, *see* Joinder.

Claim adjuster. Independent agent or employee of insurance company who negotiates and settles claims against the insurer. *See* Adjuster; Claimant adjuster.

Claim and delivery. Action at law for recovery of specific personal property wrongfully taken and detained, with damages which the taking or detention has caused. A modification of common-law action of replevin. *See also* Replevin.

Claimant. One who claims or asserts a right, demand or claim. *See* Claim; Plaintiff.

Claimant adjuster. One who will obtain, secure, enforce, or establish a right, claim, or demand for an individual against an insurance company.

Claim check. Form of receipt for bailed or checked property, which normally must be surrendered when such property is recovered.

Claim dilution. A reduction in the likelihood that one or more of the firm's claimants will be fully repaid, including time-value-of-money considerations.

Claim in equity. *See* Equity jurisdiction.

Claim jumping. The location on ground, knowing it to be excess ground, within the staked boundaries of another mining claim initiated prior thereto, because law governing manner of making location had not been complied with, so that location covers the workings of the prior locators. Filing of duplicate mining claims hoping that prior claim will be invalid.

Claim of ownership, right and title. As regards adverse possession, claim of land as one's own to hold it for oneself. Claim of right, claim of title and claim of ownership are synonymous. Claimant's intention to claim in hostility to real owner. Color of title and claim of title are synonymous. Intention of disseisor to appropriate and use land as his own, irrespective of any semblance of color, or right, or title. *See* Adverse possession.

Claim of right doctrine. As contemplated under doctrine of adverse possession is simply that claimant is in possession as owner, with intent to claim the land as his or her own, and not in recognition of or subordination to record title owner. In taxation, a judicially imposed doctrine applicable to both cash and accrual basis taxpayers which holds that an amount is includible in income upon actual or constructive receipt if the taxpayer has an unrestricted claim to such amounts. A payment received under a claim of right is includible in income even though there is a possibility that all or part of it may have to be returned.

Claim preclusion. *See* Res (*Res judicata*).

Claim property bond. A bond filed by a defendant in cases of replevin and of execution to procure return of goods.

Claims Collection Act. Federal Act which requires that each agency of the federal government attempt to collect claims of the government (*e.g.* overpayments) arising out of the activities of the agency.

Claims court. *See* Claims Court, U.S.; Court of Claims; Small Claims Court.

Claims Court, U.S. This federal court was established in 1982 and succeeds to all the original jurisdiction formerly exercised by the Court of Claims, as now provided for in 28 U.S.C.A. 1491 et seq. The court has jurisdiction to render money judgments upon any claim against the United States founded either upon the Constitution, or any act of Congress or any regulation of an executive department, or upon any express or implied in fact contract with the United States or for liquidated or unliquidated damages in cases not sounding in tort. Judgments of the Court are final and conclusive on both the claimant and the United States subject to an appeal as of right to the U.S. Court of Appeals for the Federal Circuit. Authority also rests with the court to furnish reports on any bill that may be referred by either House of Congress. Jurisdiction of the Court is nationwide, and jurisdiction over the parties is obtained when suit is filed and process is served on the United States through the Attorney General. *See also* Court of Claims; Tucker Act.

Clam /klǽm/. Lat. In the civil law, covertly; secretly.

Clandestine. Secret, hidden, concealed; usually for some illegal or illicit purpose. For example, a clandestine marriage is one contracted without observing the conditions precedent prescribed by law, such as publication of banns, procuring a license, or the like.

Class. A group of persons, things, qualities, or activities, having common characteristics or attributes. The order or rank according to which persons or things are arranged or assorted. Securities having similar features. Also, a body of persons uncertain in number.

A "class" within rule relating to class action must be taken in broad colloquial sense of group of people ranked together as having common characteristics, and the function of the enumerated requirements of rule is to assure that from those characteristics there arises a common legal position vis-à-vis the opposing party, the legal right or obligations of which the court can efficiently and fairly adjudicate in a single proceeding.

Class action. *See* Class *or* representative action.

Class directors. System whereby terms of corporate board of directors are staggered, thus making takeover attempt difficult.

Classes of stock. Issuance of common stock in two or more general classes; *e.g.*, Class A and Class B. Normally, only one class has voting rights. *See* Stock.

Class gift. A gift of an aggregate sum to a body of persons uncertain in number at time of gift, to be ascertained at a future time, who are all to take in equal, or other definite proportions, the share of each being dependent for its amount upon the ultimate number.

Classification. Arrangement into groups or categories on the basis of established criteria. The word may have two meanings, one primarily signifying a division required by statutes, fundamental and substantial, and the other secondary, signifying an arrangement or enumeration adopted for convenience only.

Classification of crimes. A grouping of crimes. Taxonomy which may be based on the seriousness of the crime, *e.g.* felony or misdemeanor, or on the nature of the crime, *e.g.* malum prohibitum or malum in se, or on the objects of the crime, *e.g.* crimes against property or crimes against the person. Felonies and misdemeanors are also classified under federal statutes and sometimes in state statutes as Class A, B, etc., with punishments set for each class. 18 U.S.C.A. § 3559. Crimes are also commonly classified into degrees; *e.g.*, first and second degree murder; and also as voluntary or involuntary (*e.g.* manslaughter). *See also* Degrees of crime; Index offenses; Offense.

Classification of risks. Term used in fire insurance to designate the nature and situation of the articles insured, and in accident insurance to the occupation of the applicant.

Classified. Grouped into classes. *See* Classification.

Classified tax. Tax system where different rates are assessed to each group of property.

Class legislation. Legislation limited in operation to certain persons or classes of persons, natural or artificial, or to certain districts of territory or state. Legislation operating upon portion of particular class of persons or things.

The term is applied to enactments which divide the people or subjects of legislation into classes, with reference either to the grant of privileges or the imposition of burdens, upon an arbitrary, unjust, or invidious principle, or which make arbitrary discriminations between those persons or things coming within the same class. Such laws commonly violate equal protection guarantees of Fourteenth Amendment.

Class *or* **representative action.** A class action provides a means by which, where a large group of persons are interested in a matter, one or more may sue or be sued as representatives of the class without needing to join every member of the class. This procedure is available in federal court and in most state courts under Rule of Civil Procedure 23. See also New York C.P.L.R. § 901.

There are general requirements for the maintenance of any class suit. These are that the persons constituting the class must be so numerous that it is impracticable to bring them all before the court, and the named representatives must be such as will fairly insure the adequate representation of them all. In addition, there must be an ascertainable class and there must be a well defined common interest in the questions of law and fact involved affecting the parties to be represented. The trial court must also certify the lawsuit as a class action.

Prior to the revision of Federal Civil Procedure Rule 23 in 1966, there were three categories of class actions, popularly known as "true", "hybrid", and "spurious." These categories no longer exist under present Rule 23.

See Hybrid class action; Spurious class action. *Compare* Multidistrict litigation.

Class voting. *See* Voting group.

Clause /klóz/. A single paragraph or subdivision of a pleading or legal document, such as a contract, deed, will, constitution, or statute. Sometimes a sentence or part of a sentence. *See* Paragraph.

Clausum fregit /klózəm fríyjət/. L. Lat. (He broke the close.) In pleading and practice, technical words formerly used in certain actions of trespass, and still retained in the phrase *quare clausum fregit (q.v.).*

Clayton Act. A Federal law enacted in 1914 as amendment to the Sherman Antitrust Act dealing with antitrust regulations and unfair trade practices. 15 U.S.C.A. §§ 12–27. The Act prohibits price discrimination, tying and exclusive dealing contracts, mergers, and interlocking directorates, where the effect may be substantially to lessen competition or tend to create a monopoly in any line of commerce.

Clean. Irreproachable; innocent of fraud or wrongdoing; free from defect in form or substance; free from exceptions or reservations. It is a very elastic adjective, however, and is particularly dependent upon context.

Clean Air Acts. Federal and state environmental statutes enacted to regulate and control air pollution. See *e.g.* 42 U.S.C.A. § 7401 et seq. *See* Standard of performance.

Clean bill. Bill of exchange without documents attached.

Clean bill of health. One certifying that no contagious or infectious disease exists, or certifying as to healthy conditions generally without exception or reservation. *See* Bill (*Maritime law*).

Clean bill of lading. One without exception or reservation as to the place or manner of stowage of the goods, and importing that the goods are to be (or have been) safely and properly stowed under deck. One which contains nothing in the margin qualifying the words in the bill of lading itself.

Clean hands doctrine. Under this doctrine, equity will not grant relief to a party, who, as actor, seeks to set judicial machinery in motion and obtain some remedy, if such party in prior conduct has violated conscience or good faith or other equitable principle. One seeking equitable relief cannot take advantage of one's own wrong.

Clean Water Acts. Federal and state environmental statutes enacted to regulate and control water pollution. See *e.g.* 33 U.S.C.A. § 1251 et seq.

Clear. Obvious; beyond reasonable doubt; perspicuous; plain. Free from all limitation, qualification, question or shortcoming. Free from incumbrance, obstruction, burden, limitation, etc. Plain, evident, free from doubt or conjecture, unequivocal, also unincumbered. Free from deductions or drawbacks.

In banking, collection of funds on which check is drawn and payment of such funds to holder of check.

Clearance. In maritime law, the right of a ship to leave port. The act of clearing or leaving port. The certificate issued by the collector of a port evidencing the power of the ship to leave port. In contract for exhibition of motion pictures, the interval of time between conclusion of exhibition in one theater and commencement of exhibition at another theater.

Clearance card. A letter given to an employee by his employer, at the time of his discharge or end of service, showing the cause of such discharge or voluntary quittance, the length of time of service, his capacity, and such other facts as would give to those concerned information of his former employment.

Clearance certificate. Issued to ship's captain showing that customs requirements have been made.

Clear and convincing proof. That proof which results in reasonable certainty of the truth of the ultimate fact in controversy. Proof which requires more than a preponderance of the evidence but less than proof beyond a reasonable doubt. Clear and convincing proof will be shown where the truth of the facts asserted is highly probable. *See also* Beyond a reasonable doubt; Burden of proof; Clear evidence or proof.

Clear and present danger doctrine. Doctrine in constitutional law, first formulated in Schenck v. U. S., 249 U.S. 47, 39 S.Ct. 247, 63 L.Ed. 470, providing that governmental restrictions on First Amendment freedoms of speech and press will be upheld if necessary to prevent grave and immediate danger to interests which government may lawfully protect. Speech which incites to unlaw-

ful action falls outside the protection of the First Amendment where there is a direct connection between the speech and violation of the law; this is the "clear and present danger test".

Clear annuity. The devise of an annuity "clear" means an annuity free from taxes or free or clear of legacy or inheritance taxes.

Clear chance. A "clear chance" to avoid accident within meaning of last clear chance doctrine involves the element of sufficient time to appreciate peril of the party unable to extricate himself therefrom, and to take necessary steps to avoid injuring him. *See also* Last clear chance doctrine.

Clear days. If a certain number of clear days be given for the doing of any act, the time is to be reckoned exclusively, as well of the first day as the last.

Clear evidence or proof. Evidence which is positive, precise and explicit, which tends directly to establish the point to which it is adduced and is sufficient to make out a prima facie case. It necessarily means a clear preponderance. It may mean no more than a fair preponderance of proof but may also be construed as requiring a higher degree of proof. It may convey the idea, under emphasis, of certainty, or understood as meaning beyond doubt. *See also* Beyond a reasonable doubt; Clear and convincing proof.

Clearing. The departure of a vessel from port, after complying with the customs and health laws and like local regulations. *See also* Clearance; Clearance certificate.

In banking, a method of making exchanges and settling balances, adopted among banks and bankers. *See* Clearinghouse.

Clearing account. An account containing amounts to be transferred to another account(s) before the end of the accounting period.

Clearing a position. In securities dealing, eliminating a long or short position, leaving no ownership or obligation.

Clearing corporation. A corporation, all of the capital stock of which is held by or for a national securities exchange or association registered under a statute of the U.S., such as the Securities Exchange Act of 1934. U.C.C. § 8–102(3).

Clearinghouse. An association or place where banks exchange checks and drafts drawn on each other, and settle their daily balances. See U.C.C. § 4–104(d).

With respect to a stock or commodities exchange, a facility which provides for the daily clearance of all transactions. With regard to futures transactions, a clearinghouse performs the following functions: confirms that trades made each day are acknowledged by both parties; settles amounts owed daily on futures contracts due to changes in contract prices during the trading session; insures the financial worth of all futures contracts that it has accepted.

Clearing loan. One made to a bond dealer while an issue of bonds is being sold.

Clearings. Method of making exchanges and settling balances among banks and bankers.

Clearing title. Acts or proceedings necessary to render title marketable.

Clear legal right. A right inferable as a matter of law from uncontroverted facts.

Clearly. Visible, unmistakable, in words of no uncertain meaning. Beyond a question or beyond a reasonable doubt; honestly, straightforwardly, and frankly; plainly. Without obscurity, obstruction, entanglement, confusion, or uncertainty. Unequivocal.

Clearly erroneous. For purposes of rule providing that findings of trial court shall not be set aside unless "clearly erroneous," refers to findings when based upon substantial error in proceedings or misapplication of law; or when unsupported by substantial evidence, or contrary to clear weight of evidence or induced by erroneous view of the law. As a basis for appellate review, a finding is "clearly erroneous" when, although there is evidence to support it, the reviewing court on entire evidence is left with definite and firm conviction that a mistake has been committed.

Clearly proved. Proof by preponderance of the evidence. Proof sufficient to satisfy mind of finder of facts that its weight is such as to cause a reasonable person to accept the fact as established. *See* Beyond a reasonable doubt; Clear and convincing proof.

Clear market price. Fair market price. *See* Fair market value.

Clear market value. Sum which property would bring on a fair sale by a willing seller not obliged to sell to a willing buyer not obliged to buy, or fair market value, or cash value. With regard to inheritance tax, highest price obtainable. *See* Fair market value.

Clear reflection of income. The Internal Revenue Service has the authority to redetermine a taxpayer's income using a method which clearly reflects income if the taxpayer's method does not do so. I.R.C. § 446(b). In addition, the I.R.S. may apportion or allocate income among various related business if income is not "clearly reflected". I.R.C. § 482.

Clear residue. Addition of income from funds, used to pay decedent's debts, administration expenses, and general legacies, to residue of estate.

Clear title. Good title; marketable title; one free from incumbrance, obstruction, burden, or limitation. *See* Marketable title.

Clear title of record. Freedom from apparent defects, grave doubts, and litigious uncertainties. Such title as a reasonably prudent person, with full knowledge, would accept. *See* Marketable title; Quiet title action.

Clear view doctrine. *See* Plain view doctrine.

Clemency /klémənsiy/. Kindness, mercy, forgiveness, leniency; usually relating to criminal acts. Used *e.g.* to describe act of governor of state when he commutes death sentence to life imprisonment, or grants pardon. *See also* Amnesty; Executive clemency; Pardon; Reprimand.

Clergy. The whole of clergymen or ministers of religion. Also an abbreviation for "benefit of clergy". *See* Benefit of clergy.

Clergy privilege. Formerly, exemption given to clergy from being tried in civil courts because of availability of trial in canonical court. *See* Benefit of clergy.

Clerical. Pertaining to clergymen; or pertaining to the office or labor of a clerk. *See also* Clerk; Ministerial act.

Clerical error. Generally, a mistake in writing or copying. It may include error apparent on face of instrument, record, indictment or information.

As applied to judgments and decrees is a mistake or omission by a clerk, counsel, judge or printer which is not the result of exercise of judicial function.

Clerical errors may be corrected by the court at any time of its own initiative or on the motion of any party and after such notice, if any, as the court orders. Fed.R. Civil P. 60(a).

Clerk. Officer of court who files pleadings, motions, judgments, etc., issues process, and keeps records of court proceedings. Functions and duties of clerks of court are usually specified by statute or court rules; *e.g.* Fed.R. Civil P. 77, 79.

Person employed in public office whose duties include keeping records or accounts.

One who sells goods, waits on customers, or engages in clerical work such as bookkeeping, copying, transcribing, letter writing, tabulating, stenography, etc.

A *law clerk* assists an attorney or judge with legal research, brief writing, and other legal tasks. Is commonly a recent law school graduate or law student.

Clerkship. The period which formerly must have been spent by a law-student in the office of a practicing attorney before admission to the bar. Term now generally refers to law student who clerks for an attorney, law firm, or judge, or recent law school graduate who clerks for a judge.

Client. An individual, corporation, trust, or estate that employs a professional to advise or assist it in the professional's line of work. Professionals include but are not limited to: attorneys, accountants, architects, etc. A person who employs or retains an attorney, or counsellor, to appear for him in courts, advise, assist, and defend him in legal proceedings, and to act for him in any legal business.

Client security fund. A fund set up by many state bar associations to cover losses incurred by persons as a result of dishonest conduct of member-attorneys.

Client's privilege. Right of client to require attorney to not disclose confidential communications made to him in the attorney-client relationship, including disclosure on the witness stand. *See* Attorney-client privilege; Communication *(Confidential communications).*

Clifford Trust. A trust established for a period of at least 10 years and one day whereby title to income producing assets is transferred and then reclaimed when the trust expires. The objective of a Clifford trust was to shift income from parents in a high income tax bracket to children in a lower bracket. The Tax Reform Act of 1986 repealed the Clifford trust rules for transfers made after March 1, 1986 and the income of the trust is taxed at the grantor's rate. For Clifford trusts established prior to March 2, 1986, income is taxed at the grantor's rate only if the child is under the age of 14. *See also* Kiddie tax.

Clinical tests. Tests involving direct observation of the patient, including laboratory and diagnostic examinations.

Close, *v.* To finish, bring to an end, conclude, terminate, complete, wind up; as, to "close" an account, a bargain, a trial, an estate, or public books, such as tax books.

In accounting, to transfer the balance of a temporary or contra or adjunct account to the main account to which it relates.

To shut up, so as to prevent entrance or access by any person; as in statutes requiring liquor establishments to be "closed" at certain times, which further implies an entire suspension of business. To go out of business. To bar access to. To suspend or stop operations of.

To finalize a real estate transaction. *see* Closing.

Close, *n.* A portion of land, as a field, inclosed as by a hedge, fence, or other visible inclosure, or by an invisible ideal boundary founded on limit of title. The interest of a person in any particular piece of land, whether actually inclosed or not. Final price of stock at end of trading day on securities exchange.

Close, *adj.* Closed or sealed up. Restricted to a particular class. Decided by a narrow margin.

Close copies. Copies of legal documents which might be written closely or loosely at pleasure; as distinguished from *office* copies.

Close *or* closely held corporation. *See* Corporation.

Closed-end investment trust. Trust wherein only original prescribed shares can be distributed.

Closed-end mortgage. A mortgage that does not permit additional borrowing pledging the same collateral nor prepayment. In contrast to open-end mortgage, which allows for the amortization of the mortgage and can be increased to its original mortgage amount.

Closed-end transactions. Credit transaction with a fixed repayment amount and time.

Closed insurance policy. Insurance contract, the terms and rates of which cannot be changed.

Closed primary. Exists where members of each political party participate in nominating candidates of that party, and the voters of one party are not allowed to nominate candidates for another party.

Closed season. The same as "close season" *(q.v.).*

Closed shop. Exists where workers must be members of union as condition of their employment. This practice was made unlawful by the Taft–Hartley Act. *Contrast* Open shop. *See also* Right to work laws.

Closed shop contract. A contract requiring employer to hire only union members and to discharge non-union members and requiring that employees, as a condition of employment, remain union members. "Closed shop" provision in collective bargaining agreement requires membership in the contracting union before a job applicant can be employed and for the duration of his employment.

Closed transaction. Term used in tax law to describe a taxable event which has been consummated. For example, diminution in value of goodwill of business is not a closed transaction so as to permit deduction of the diminution of value as ordinary loss.

Closed union. A labor union whose membership rolls have closed. *See also* Closed shop.

Close-hauled. In admiralty law, this nautical term means the arrangement or trim of a vessel's sails when she endeavors to make progress in the nearest direction possible towards that point of the compass from which the wind blows. But a vessel may be considered as close-hauled, although she is not quite so near to the wind as she could possibly lie.

Close jail execution. A body execution which has indorsed in or upon it the statement that the defendant ought to be confined in close jail.

Closely held corporation. A corporation, the stock ownership of which is not widely dispersed. Rather, a few shareholders are in control of corporate policy and are in a position to benefit personally from such policy. *See also* Corporation *(Close corporation)*.

Close relatives. Kinfolk who bear a close relationship to another such as mother, father, brother, sister, husband, wife and children. *See also* Kin *or* kindred.

Close season. The season of the year or period of time in which the taking of particular game or fish is prohibited, or in which all hunting or fishing is forbidden by law.

Close to. Near; very near; immediately adjoining.

Close writ. *See* Writ.

Closing. As regards sale of real estate, refers to the final steps of the transaction whereat the consideration is paid, mortgage is secured, title is transferred, deed is delivered or placed in escrow, etc. Such closings, which normally take place at a bank or savings and loan institution, are regulated by the federal Real Estate Settlement Procedures Act (RESPA). *See* Closing costs; Closing statement.

Closing argument. The final statements by the attorneys to jury or court summarizing the evidence that they think they have established and the evidence that they think the other side has failed to establish. Such is made before judge's charge to jury. Such does not constitute evidence and may be limited in time by rule of court.

In federal criminal cases, after the closing of evidence the prosecution opens the closing argument; the defense then replies. The prosecution is then permitted to reply in rebuttal. Fed.R. Crim.P. 29.1.

Closing costs. Expenses which must be paid in addition to the purchase price on the sale of real estate. Closing costs with respect to a debt secured by an interest in land include: (a) fees or premiums for title examination, title insurance, or similar purposes including surveys, (b) fees for preparation of a deed, settlement statement, or other documents, (c) escrows for future payments of taxes and insurance, (d) fees for notarizing deeds and other documents, (e) appraisal fees, and (f) credit reports. Uniform Consumer Credit Code, Section 1.301(5). The full disclosure of such costs is regulated by the federal Real Estate Settlement Procedures Act (RESPA). *See also* Closing statement.

Closing entries. In accounting, the entries that accomplish the transfer of balances in temporary accounts to the related balance sheet accounts.

Closing estates. Winding up of estates by paying legacies and inheritances, taxes, and filing necessary probate accounts.

Closing price. The price at which the last transaction before closing (of, for example, stock exchange) took place.

Closing statement. Written analysis of closing (*i.e.* final steps) of real estate transaction setting forth purchase price less deductions for such items as mortgage payoff, tax adjustments, etc. and adding credits to arrive at net amount due seller. Detailed statement is required under federal Real Estate Settlement Procedures Act (RESPA). *See also* Closing; Closing costs; RESPA; Settlement statement.

See Closing argument, *supra*, regarding closing statement at trial.

Cloture. Legislative rule or procedure whereby unreasonable debate (*i.e.* filibuster) is ended to permit vote to be taken.

Cloud on title. An outstanding claim or encumbrance which, if valid, would affect or impair the title of the owner of a particular estate, and on its face has that effect, but can be shown by extrinsic proof to be invalid or inapplicable to the estate in question. A conveyance, mortgage, judgment, tax-levy, etc., may all, in proper cases, constitute a cloud on title. The remedy for removing a cloud on title is usually the means of an action to quiet title. *See* Quiet title action.

C.L.U. Chartered Life Underwriter.

Club. A voluntary, incorporated or unincorporated association of persons for common purposes of a social, literary, investment, political nature, or the like. Association of persons for promotion of some common object, such as literature, science, politics, good fellowship, etc., especially one jointly supported and meeting periodically, and membership is usually conferred by ballot and carries privilege of exclusive use of club quarters, and word also applies to a building, apartment or room occupied by a club.

Clue. Suggestion or piece of evidence which may or may not lead to solution of crime or puzzle.

Cluster housing. Exists where houses are built close together with little individual yard space, but large common area.

Cluster zoning. Such zoning modifies lot size and frontage requirements on certain conditions involving setting aside of land by the developer for parks, schools, or other public needs. *See* Planned unit development (PUD); Zoning.

C/o. Symbol meaning "care of".

Co. A prefix meaning with, in conjunction, joint, jointly, unitedly, and not separately, e.g., cotrustees, co-executors, co-brokers. Also, an abbreviation for "county" and "company."

Co-adjutor /kòwəjúwtər/. An assistant, helper, or ally; particularly a person appointed to assist a bishop who from age or infirmity is unable to perform his duty. Also an overseer (co-adjutor of an executor), and one who disseises a person of land not to his own use, but to that of another.

Co-administrator. One who is a joint administrator (*e.g.* of an estate) with one or more others.

Co-adventurer. One who takes part with others in an adventure or in a venture or business undertaking attended with risk. *See also* Adventure; Joint venture.

Co-agent. *See* Agent.

Co-assignee. One of two or more assignees of the same subject-matter.

Coast. The edge or margin of a country bounding on the sea. The term includes small islands and reefs naturally connected with the adjacent land, and rising above the surface of the water, but not shoals perpetually covered by water. This word is particularly appropriate to the edge of the sea, while "shore" may be used of the margins of inland waters. In precise modern usage, the term "shore" denotes line of low-water mark along mainland, while term "coast" denotes line of shore plus line where inland waters meet open sea.

Coast Guard. The Coast Guard is responsible for enforcing Federal laws on the high seas and navigable waters of the United States and its possessions. Navigation and vessel inspection laws are specific responsibilities. Under provisions of the Federal Boating Act of 1958, Coast Guard boarding teams inspect small boats to insure compliance with required safety measures. The Coast Guard cooperates with other agencies in their law enforcement responsibilities, including enforcement of drug, conservation and marine environmental laws.

Coasting trade. In maritime law, commerce and navigation between different places along the coast of the United States. Commercial intercourse between different districts in different states, different districts in same state, or different places in same district, on sea-coast or on navigable river.

Coast waters. Tide waters navigable from the ocean by sea-going craft, the term embracing all waters opening directly or indirectly into the ocean and navigable by ships coming in from the ocean of draft as great as that of the larger ships which traverse the open seas.

Co-conspirator. One who engages in an illegal confederacy with others. *See* Conspiracy.

Co-conspirator's rule. Under the "co-conspirator exception" to the hearsay rule, acts and declarations of a co-conspirator made in furtherance of the conspiracy are admissible against a defendant even when they are made out of the defendant's presence. *See also* Wharton Rule.

C. O. D. "Collect on delivery." These letters import the carrier's liability to the consignor to collect the cost of the goods from the consignee, and, if not collected, to return the goods to the consignor.

Code. A systematic collection, compendium or revision of laws, rules, or regulations (*e.g.*, Uniform Commercial Code). A private or official compilation of all permanent laws in force consolidated and classified according to subject matter (*e.g.* United States Code). Many states have published official codes of all laws in force, including the common law and statutes as judicially interpreted, which have been compiled by code commissions and enacted by the legislatures (*e.g.* California Code). *See also* Codification.

Code Civil. The code which embodies the civil law of France. It was promulgated in 1804. When Napoleon became emperor, the name was changed to "Code Napoleon," by which it is still often designated though it is now officially styled by its original name of "Code Civil." A great part of the Louisiana Civil Code is derived from the Code Napoleon.

Co-defendant. More than one defendant being sued in the same litigation; or, more than one person charged in same complaint or indictment with same crime.

Code Napoleon. *See* Code Civil.

Code of criminal procedure. Body of federal or state law dealing with procedural aspects of trial of criminal cases; *e.g.* 18 U.S.C.A. § 3001 et seq. Such procedural laws are supplemented by Rules of Criminal Procedure and Rules of Evidence.

Code of ethics. *See* Code of Professional Responsibility.

Code of Federal Regulations. The Code of Federal Regulations (CFR) is the annual cumulation of executive agency regulations published in the daily Federal Register, combined with regulations issued previously that are still in effect. Divided into 50 titles, each representing a broad subject area, individual volumes of the Code of Federal Regulations are revised at least once each calendar year and issued on a staggered quarterly basis. The CFR contains the general body of regulatory laws governing practice and procedure before federal administrative agencies.

Code of Military Justice. This Code, which is uniformly applicable in all its parts to the Army, the Navy, the Air Force, and the Coast Guard, covers both the substantive and the procedural law governing military justice and its administration in all of the armed forces of the United States. The Code established a system of military courts, defines offenses, authorizes punishment, provides broad procedural guidance, and statutory safeguards which conform to the due process safeguards preserved and established by the constitution. As an additional safeguard for an accused person, the Code also provides for a system of automatic appellate review. A Court of Military Review is established within each service to review all court-martial cases where the sentence includes death, a punitive discharge, or confinement for one year or more. Appellate review in this court is automatic. No approved sentence of a courts-martial may be executed unless such findings and sentence are affirmed by a Court of Military Review. In addition, the Court of Military Appeals was established to review certain cases from all the Armed Forces. The latter Court consists of three civilian judges. Automatic review before the Court is provided for all cases in which the sentence, as affirmed by a Court of Military Review, affects a general or flag officer or extends to death. In addition, the Judge Advocate General of each service may direct that a case be reviewed by the Court. An accused may petition the Court for review. 10 U.S.C.A. § 801 et seq.

Uniform Code. Many states have adopted the Uniform Code of Military Justice, and others have adopted acts substantially following the Uniform Code.

Code of Professional Responsibility. The Model Code of Professional Responsibility of the American Bar Association consisted of basic Canons of professional conduct for attorneys together with Ethical Considerations and Disciplinary Rules for each Canon covering specific attorney conduct. Most states adopted similar professional responsibility codes as based on the ABA model. In 1983 the ABA replaced the Code of Professional Responsibility with the Model Rules of Professional Conduct. *See also* Canon; Disciplinary rules; Model Rules of Professional Conduct.

Code pleading. *See* Pleadings.

Codex. Lat. A code or collection of laws; particularly the Code of Justinian. Also a roll of volume, and a book written on paper or parchment.

Codicil. A supplement or an addition to a will; it may explain, modify, add to, subtract from, qualify, alter, restrain or revoke provisions in existing will. Such does not purport to dispose of entire estate or to contain the entire will of testator, nor does it ordinarily expressly or by necessary implication revoke in toto a prior will.

Codification /kòdəfəkéyshən/. The process of collecting and arranging systematically, usually by subject, the laws of a state or country, or the rules and regulations covering a particular area or subject of law or practice; *e.g.* United States Code; Code of Military Justice; Code of Federal Regula-

tions; California Evidence Code. The end product may be called a code, revised code or revised statutes. *See also* Code; Compilation; Compiled statutes.

Co-emption. The act of purchasing the whole quantity of any commodity.

Co-equal. To be or become equal to. To have the same quantity, the same value, the same degree or rank, or the like, with. To be commensurate with.

Coerce /kowárs/. Compelled to compliance; constrained to obedience, or submission in a vigorous or forcible manner. *See* Coercion.

Coercion /kowárshən/. Compulsion; constraint; compelling by force or arms or threat. It may be actual, direct, or positive, as where physical force is used to compel act against one's will, or implied, legal or constructive, as where one party is constrained by subjugation to other to do what his free will would refuse. As used in testamentary law, any pressure by which testator's action is restrained against his free will in the execution of his testament. "Coercion" that vitiates confession can be mental as well as physical, and question is whether accused was deprived of his free choice to admit, deny, or refuse to answer.

A person is guilty of criminal coercion if, with purpose to unlawfully restrict another's freedom of action to his detriment, he threatens to: (a) commit any criminal offense; or (b) accuse anyone of a criminal offense; or (c) expose any secret tending to subject any person to hatred, contempt or ridicule, or to impair his credit or business repute; or (d) take or withhold action as an official, or cause an official to take or withhold action. Model Penal Code, § 212.5.

See also Duress; Extortion; Threat.

Co-executor. One who is a joint executor of an estate with one or more others. *See also* Joint executors.

Cognate offense. An offense which contains some elements not contained in the greater offense but which is related to the greater offense by fact that it is shares several of the elements of the greater offense and is of the same class or category.

Cognizable /kó(g)nəzəbəl/. Capable of being tried or examined before a designated tribunal; within jurisdiction of court or power given to court to adjudicate controversy.

In criminal law, for a group to be "cognizable" so as to render jury selection process which excludes such group unconstitutional, the group must have a definite composition. The defendant must show that the group is defined and limited by some factor, that a common thread or basic similarity in attitude or ideas or experience runs through the group, and that there is a community of interest among members of the group such that the group's interests cannot be adequately represented if the group is excluded from the jury selection process.

Cognizance /kó(g)nəzəns/. Jurisdiction, or the exercise of jurisdiction, or power to try and determine causes; judicial examination of a matter, or power and authority to make it. Judicial notice or knowledge; the judicial hearing of a cause; acknowledgment; confession; recognition.

Cognovit judgment /kògnóvvət/. Confession of judgment by debtor. Written authority of debtor and his direction for entry of judgment against him in the event he shall default in payment. Such provision in a debt instrument or agreement permits the creditor or his attorney on default to appear in court and confers judgment against the debtor. Such agreements are prohibited, or greatly restricted, in many states; though, where permitted, the constitutionality of such has been upheld. *See* Cognovit note; Judgment *(Confession of judgment)*.

Cognovit note. An extraordinary note which authorizes an attorney to confess judgment against person or persons signing it. It is written authority of a debtor and a direction by him for entry of a judgment against him if obligation set forth in note is not paid when due. Such judgment may be taken by any person holding the note, which cuts off every defense which maker of note may otherwise have and it likewise cuts off all rights of appeal from any judgment taken on it. *See* Cognovit judgment; Judgment *(Confession of judgment)*.

C.O.G.S.A. *See* Carriage of Goods by Sea Act.

Cohabitation. To live together as husband and wife. The mutual assumption of those marital rights, duties and obligations which are usually manifested by married people, including but not necessarily dependent on sexual relations. *See also* Notorious cohabitation; Palimony.

Cohabitation agreement. Contract between a man and a woman who are living together in contemplation of sexual relations and out of wedlock, relating to the property and financial relations of the parties. MN.ST. §§ 513.075, 513.076.

Co-heir. One of several to whom an inheritance descends.

Co-heiress. A joint heiress. A woman who has an equal share of an inheritance with another woman.

Cohort analysis. A method used in employment discrimination suits to test for race discrimination whereby all employees who start together at the same level are surveyed over the course of an observation period and their comparative progress in salary and promotion is evaluated.

Coinage clause. Provision in U.S. Constitution granting to Congress the power to coin money, Art. I, § 8, par. 5.

Coinsurance. A relative division of risk between the insurer and the insured, dependent upon the relative amount of the policy and the actual value of the property insured, and taking effect only when the actual loss is partial and less than the amount of the policy; the insurer being liable to the extent of the policy for a loss equal to or in excess of that amount. Insurance policies that protect against hazards such as fire or water damage often specify that the owner of the property may not collect the full amount of insurance for a loss unless the insurance policy covers at least some specified percentage, usually about 80 percent, of the replacement cost of the property.

Coinsurance clause. Provision in insurance policy requiring property owner to carry insurance up to an amount determined in accordance with the provisions of the policy.

Coinsurer. Insurer who shares losses sustained under policy.

COLA. Cost of Living Adjustment. *See* Cost of living clause.

Cold blood. Used in common parlance to designate a willful, deliberate, and premeditated homicide. *See also* Cool state of blood.

Collaboration. The act of working together in a joint project; commonly used in connection with treasonably cooperative efforts with the enemy. *See also* Conspiracy.

Collapsible corporation. A corporation formed or availed of principally for the manufacture, construction, or production of property, for the purchase of property, or for the holding of stock in a corporation so formed or availed of, with a view to the sale or exchange of stock by its shareholders (whether in liquidation or otherwise), or a distribution to its shareholders, before the realization by the corporation of a substantial part of the taxable income to be derived from such property, and the realization by such shareholders of gain attributable to such property. I.R.C. §§ 337(c), 341(b)(1). These I.R.C. provisions prevent the prearranged use of a corporation to convert ordinary income into capital gain.

Collapsible partnership. A partnership formed with the intention to dissolve before any income is realized; however, the amount of money or the fair market value of any property received by a transferror partner in exchange for all or a part of his interest in the partnership attributable to unrealized receivables of the partnership, or inventory items of the partnership which have appreciated substantially in value shall be considered as an amount realized from the sale or exchange of property other than a capital asset. I.R.C. § 751(a).

Collateral, *n.* /kəlǽtərəl/. Property which is pledged as security for the satisfaction of a debt. Collateral is additional security for performance of principal obligation, or that which is by the side, and not in direct line. Property subject to a security interest; includes accounts, contract rights, and chattel paper which have been sold. U.C.C. § 9–105(c). *See also* Collateral security.

Collateral, *adj.* By the side; at the side; attached upon the side. Not lineal, but upon a parallel or diverging line. Additional or auxiliary; supplementary; co-operating; accompanying as a secondary fact, or acting as a secondary agent. Related to, complementary; accompanying as a co-ordinate. As to *collateral* Consanguinity; Descent; Estoppel; Guaranty; Issue; Limitation; Negligence; Power; Proceeding; and Warranty, see those titles. *See also* Pledge; Security.

Collateral act. Formerly, name given to any act (except the payment of money) for the performance of which a bond, recognizance, etc., was given as security.

Collateral actions. Any action which is subsidiary to another action. *See* Collateral attack.

Collateral ancestors. A phrase sometimes used to designate uncles and aunts, and other collateral ancestors, who are not strictly ancestors.

Collateral assignment. Assignment of property as collateral security for loans.

Collateral assurance. That which is made over and above the principal assurance or deed itself.

Collateral attack. With respect to a judicial proceeding, an attempt to avoid, defeat, or evade it, or deny its force and effect, in some incidental proceeding not provided by law for the express purpose of attacking it. An attack on a judgment in any manner other than by action or proceeding, whose very purpose is to impeach or overturn the judgment; or, stated affirmatively, a collateral attack on a judgment is an attack made by or in an action or proceeding that has an independent purpose other than impeaching or overturning the judgment. *Compare* Direct attack.

Collateral consanguinity. Persons are related collaterally when they have a common ancestor. *See also* Collateral heir.

Collateral contract. A contract made prior to or contemporaneous with another contract and if oral and not inconsistent with written contract is admissible within exception to parol evidence rule.

Collateral covenant. A covenant in a deed or other sealed instrument which does not pertain to the granted premises.

Collateral estoppel doctrine. Prior judgment between same parties on different cause of action is an estoppel as to those matters in issue or points controverted, on determination of which finding or verdict was rendered. When an issue of ultimate fact has been determined by a valid judgment, that issue cannot be again litigated between the same parties in future litigation.

As a bar to relitigating an issue which has already been tried between the same parties or their privies, it must be pleaded affirmatively. Fed.R. Civil P. 8(c). It is applicable to criminal cases.

Offensive and defensive collateral estoppel. "Offensive collateral estoppel" is used by plaintiff to prevent relitigation of issues previously lost against another plaintiff by a defendant, in contrast to "defensive collateral estoppel" which prevents relitigation by plaintiff of issues previously lost against another defendant.

See also Administrative estoppel; Defensive collateral estoppel; Direct estoppel; Issue preclusion; Judicial estoppel; Res *(Res judicata)*; Verdict, estoppel by.

Collateral facts. Such as are outside the controversy, or are not directly connected with the principal matter or issue in dispute.

Collateral fraud. *See* Fraud.

Collateral heir. One who is not of the direct line of deceased, but comes from a collateral line, as a brother, sister, an uncle, an aunt, a nephew, a niece, or a cousin of deceased.

Collateral impeachment. *See* Collateral attack.

Collateral inheritance tax. A tax levied upon the collateral devolution of property by will or under the intestate law.

Collateral issues. Question or issues which are not directly involved in the matter.

Collateral kinsmen. Those who descend from one and the same common ancestor, but not from one another.

Collateral line. *See* Descent.

Collateral loan. Loan secured by pledge of specific property.

Collateral matter. A "matter" is "collateral" to the principal issues being tried and therefore unavailable to purposes of impeachment if the matter, as to which error is predicated, could not have been shown in evidence for any purpose independently of the contradiction.

Collateral mortgage. A mortgage designed, not directly to secure an existing debt, but to secure a mortgage note pledged as collateral security for debt or succession of debts.

Collateral negligence. *See* Negligence.

Collateral note. Loan secured by pledge of specific property.

Collateral order doctrine. Doctrine which allows appeal from an interlocutory order which conclusively determines issue completely separate from merits of action, and which cannot be given effective review on appeal from subsequent final judgment; such order is, for purposes of appellate jurisdiction, a "final order."

Collateral promise. A promise ancillary or superadded to the primary (principal) promise of another; the other remaining primarily liable. One in which the promisor is merely acting as surety; the promisor receives no benefit by way of promise and the original debtor remains liable on the debt. A collateral promise is within the statute of frauds and must be in writing.

Collateral relatives. Next of kin who are not in the direct line of inheritance, such as a cousin. *See also* Collateral heir.

Collateral security. A security given in addition to the direct security, and subordinate to it, intended to guaranty its validity or convertibility or insure its performance; so that, if the direct security fails, the creditor may fall back upon the collateral security. Concurrent security for another debt, whether antecedent or newly created and is subsidiary to the principal debt running parallel with and collateral to the debt.

Collateral source rule. Under this rule, if an injured person receives compensation for his injuries from a source wholly independent of the tort-feasor, the payment should not be deducted from the damages which he would otherwise collect from the tort-feasor. In other words, a defendant tortfeasor may not benefit from the fact that the plaintiff has received money from other sources as a result of the defendant's tort, *e.g.* sickness and health insurance.

Collateral trust bonds. Bonds of one corporation secured by its holdings of stocks, bonds, and/or notes of another corporation.

Collateral warranty. Generally applicable to real estate transactions in which a stranger warrants title and hence his warranty runs only to the covenantee, and not with the land.

Collation /kəléyshən/. The comparison of a copy with its original to ascertain its correctness; or the report of the officer who made the comparison. The bringing into the estate of an intestate an estimate of the value of advancements made by the intestate to his or her children in order that the whole may be divided in accordance with the statute of descents. It is synonymous with "hotchpot."

Collect. To gather together; to bring scattered things (assets, accounts, articles of property) into one mass or fund; to assemble. To receive payment.

To collect a debt or claim is to obtain payment or liquidation of it, either by personal solicitation or legal proceedings.

Collectible. Debts, obligations, demands, liabilities that one may be made to pay by means of legal process.

Rare or antique objects, commonly collected for investment.

Collecting bank. In the check collection process, any bank handling the item for collection except the payor bank. U.C.C. § 4–105(d).

Collection. Process through which an item passes in a payor bank. Uniform Commercial Code, Article 4. *See also* Collection indorsement.

Collection float. The time between when a customer mails a check and the firm has use of the funds. *See also* Float.

Collection indorsement. An indorsement on an item that is restrictive because it signifies a purpose of deposit or collection by including words such as "for collection", "for deposit", "pay any bank", or like terms. U.C.C. § 3–205(c). *See also* For collection.

Collection item. An item that a bank takes for its customer's account for which credit is not given until payment for the item is actually received. A documentary draft is ordinarily treated as a collection item.

Collection of illegal fees. Collection by public official of fees in excess of those fixed by law for certain services. *See* Extortion.

Collective bargaining. As contemplated by National Labor Relations Act, is a procedure looking toward making of collective agreements between employer and accredited representative of union employees concerning wages, hours, and other conditions of employment, and requires that parties deal with each other with open and fair minds and sincerely endeavor to overcome obstacles existing between them to the end that employment relations may be stabilized and obstruction to free flow of commerce prevented. National Labor Relations Act § 8(5), 29 U.S.C.A. § 158(5). Negotiation between an employer and organized employees as distinguished from individuals, for the purpose of determining by joint agreement the conditions of employment. *See also* Area bargaining; Labor dispute; Sixty-day notice.

Collective bargaining agreement. Agreement between an employer and a labor union which regulates terms and conditions of employment. The joint and several contract of members of union made by officers of union as their agents establishing, in a general way, the reciprocal rights and responsibilities of employer, employees collectively, and union. Such is enforceable by and against union in matters which affect all members alike or large classes of members, particularly those who are employees of other party to contract. *See also* Collective labor agreement; Trade agreement.

Collective bargaining unit. All of the employees of a single employer unless the employees of a particular department or division have voted otherwise.

Collective labor agreement. *See* Collective bargaining agreement.

Collective mark. The term "collective mark" means a trademark or service mark—(1) used by the members of a cooperative, an association, or other collective group or organization, or (2) which such cooperative, association, or other collective group or organization has a bona fide intention to use in commerce and applies to register on the principal register established by the Trademark Act, and includes marks indicating membership in a union, an association, or other organization. 15 U.S.C.A. § 1127.

Collective work. In copyright law, "collective work" is a work, such as a periodical issue, anthology, or encyclopedia, in which a number of contributions, constituting separate and independent works in themselves, are assembled into a collective whole. Copyright Act, 17 U.S.C.A. § 101. *See also* Compilation.

Collect on delivery. *See* C. O. D.

Collector. One appointed or authorized to receive taxes or other impositions, as: collector of taxes, collector of customs, etc. A person appointed by a private person to collect the debts due him.

Collision. Striking together of two objects, one of which may be stationary. Act or instance of colliding; state of having collided. The term implies an impact or sudden contact of a moving body with an obstruction in its line of motion, whether both bodies are in motion or one stationary and the other, no matter which, in motion.

Colloquium /kəlówkwiyəm/. One of the usual parts of the declaration in an action for slander. It is a general averment that the words complained of were spoken "of and concerning the plaintiff", or concerning the extrinsic matters alleged in the inducement, and its office is to connect the whole publication with the previous statement. An averment in the complaint that the words in question are spoken of or concerning some usage, report, or fact which gives to words otherwise indifferent the peculiar defamatory meaning assigned to them.

Collusion /kəl(y)úwzhən/. An agreement between two or more persons to defraud a person of his rights by the forms of law, or to obtain an object forbidden by law. It implies the existence of fraud of some kind, the employment of fraudulent means, or of lawful means for the accomplishment of an unlawful purpose. A secret combination, conspiracy, or concert of action between two or more persons for fraudulent or deceitful purpose. *See* Conspiracy.

In divorce proceedings, collusion is an agreement between husband and wife that one of them shall commit, or appear to have committed, or be represented in court as having committed, acts constituting a cause of divorce, for the purpose of enabling the other to obtain a divorce. But it also means connivance or conspiracy in initiating or prosecuting the suit, as where there is a compact for mutual aid in carrying it through to a decree. With the enactment of "no-fault" divorce statutes by most states, agreements or acts of collusion are no longer necessary.

Collusive action. An action not founded upon an actual controversy between the parties to it, but brought for purpose of securing a determination of a point of law for the gratification of curiosity or to settle rights of third persons not parties. Such actions will not be entertained for the courts will only decide "cases or controversies". *See also* Collusion.

Collusive joinder. *See* Joinder.

Colony. A dependent political community, consisting of a number of citizens of the same country who have emigrated therefrom to people another, and remain subject to the mother country. Territory attached to another nation, known as the mother country, with political and economic ties; *e.g.* possessions or dependencies of the British Crown (*e.g.* thirteen original colonies of United States).

Colonial charter. A document issued by a colonial government which permits operation of a business or school or college, *e.g.* charters granted by England to institutions or business in this country before War of Independence.

Colonial laws. The body of law in force in the thirteen original colonies before the Declaration of Independence.

Color. An appearance, semblance, or *simulacrum*, as distinguished from that which is real. A *prima facie* or apparent right. Hence, a deceptive appearance; a plausible, assumed exterior, concealing a lack of reality; a disguise or pretext. *See also* Colorable.

Colorable. That which is in appearance only, and not in reality, what it purports to be, hence counterfeit, feigned, having the appearance of truth.

Colorable alteration. One which makes no real or substantial change, but is introduced only as a subterfuge or means of evading the patent or copyright law.

Colorable cause or invocation of jurisdiction. With reference to actions for malicious prosecution, a "colorable cause or invocation of jurisdiction" means that a person, apparently qualified, has appeared before a justice and made a complaint under oath and in writing, stating some facts which in connection with other facts constitute a criminal offense or bear a similitude thereto.

Colorable claim. In bankruptcy law, a claim made by one holding the property as an agent or bailee of the bankrupt; a claim in which as a matter of law, there is no adverseness. *See also* Color.

Colorable imitation. In the law of trademarks, this phrase denotes such a close or ingenious limitation as to be calculated to deceive ordinary persons.

Colorable transaction. One presenting an appearance which does not correspond with the reality, and, ordinarily, an appearance intended to conceal or to deceive.

Color of authority. That semblance or presumption of authority sustaining the acts of a public officer which is derived from his apparent title to the office or from a writ or other process in his hands apparently valid and regular. *See* Color of law; Color of office.

Color of law. The appearance or semblance, without the substance, of legal right. Misuse of power, possessed by virtue of state law and made possible only because wrongdoer is clothed with authority of state, is action taken under "color of state law."

Acts "under color of any law" of a State include not only acts done by State officials within the bounds or limits of their lawful authority, but also acts done without and beyond the bounds of their lawful authority; provided that, in order for unlawful acts of an official to be done "under color of any law", the unlawful acts must be done while such official is purporting or pretending to act in the performance of his official duties; that is to say, the unlawful acts must consist in an abuse or misuse of power which is possessed by the official only because he is an official; and the unlawful acts must be of such a nature or character, and be committed under such circumstances, that they would not have occurred but for the fact that the person committing them was an official then and there exercising his official powers outside the bounds of lawful authority. 42 U.S.C.A. § 1983.

See also Tort *(Constitutional tort).*

Color of office. Pretense of official right to do act made by one who has no such right. An act under color of office is an act of an officer who claims authority to do the act by reason of his office when the office does not confer on him any such authority. *See also* Color of law.

Color of state law. *See* Color of law.

Color of title. The appearance, semblance, or *simulacrum* of title. Also termed "apparent title." Any fact, extraneous to the act or mere will of the claimant, which has the appearance, on its face, of supporting his claim of a present title to land, but which, for some defect, in reality falls short of establishing it. That which is a semblance or appearance of title, but is not title in fact or in law. Any instrument having a grantor and grantee, and containing a description of the lands intended to be conveyed, and apt words for their conveyance, gives color of title to the lands described. Such an instrument purports to be a conveyance of the title, and because it does not, for some reason, have that effect, it passes only color or the semblance of a title.

Color of Title Act. Federal law which gives Secretary of Interior the right to issue a patent for land, exclusive of minerals, to one who has occupied it adversely and under color of right for period of time for a nominal amount of money. 43 U.S.C.A. §§ 1068–1068B.

Com. Abbreviation for "company" or "Commonwealth."

Co-maker. Surety under a loan.

Combination. The union or association of two or more persons for the attainment of some common end. *See* Joint venture. As used in criminal context, means a conspiracy or confederation for unlawful or violent acts. *See* Conspiracy.

Combination in restraint of trade. An agreement or understanding between two or more persons, in the form of a contract, trust, pool, holding company, or other form of association, for the purpose of unduly restricting competition, monopolizing trade and commerce in a certain commodity, controlling its production, distribution, and price, or otherwise interfering with freedom of trade without statutory authority. Such combinations are prohibited by the Sherman Antitrust Act. *See also* Clayton Act; Sherman Antitrust Act.

Combination patent. Patents in which the claimed invention resides in a specific combination or arrangement of elements, rather than in the elements themselves. One in which none of parts or components are new, and none are claimed as new, nor is any portion of combination less than whole claimed as new or stated to produce any given result.

Comfort letter. A letter generally requested by securities underwriters to give "comfort" on the financial information included in an SEC registration statement.

Coming and going rule. *See* Going and coming rule.

Coming to rest doctrine. Under this doctrine with respect to loading and unloading clauses used in automobile liability policies, coverage afforded by loading-unloading clause ceases when goods have actually come to rest and every connection of motor vehicle with process of unloading has ceased.

Comity /kómətiy/. Courtesy; complaisance; respect; a willingness to grant a privilege, not as a matter of right, but out of deference and good will. Recognition that one sovereignty allows within its territory to the legislative, executive, or judicial act of another sovereignty, having due regard to rights of its own citizens. In general, principle of "comity" is that courts of one state or jurisdiction will give effect to laws and judicial decisions of another state or jurisdiction, not as a matter of obligation but out of deference and mutual respect. *See also* Full faith and credit clause.

Comity of nations. The recognition which one nation allows within its territory to the legislative, executive, or judicial acts of another nation, having due regard both to international duty and convenience and to the rights of its own citizens or of other persons who are under the protection of its laws.

Judicial comity. The principle in accordance with which the courts of one state or jurisdiction will give effect to the laws and judicial decisions of another, not as a matter of obligation, but out of deference and respect.

Command. An order, imperative direction, or behest. To direct, with authority. Power to dominate and control.

Commander in Chief. One who holds supreme or highest command of armed forces. By Article II, § 2, of the Constitution it is declared that the President shall be commander in chief of the army and navy of the United States. The term implies supreme control of military operations not only with respect to strategy and tactics, but also in reference to the political and international aspects of the war.

Commence. To initiate by performing the first act or step. To begin, institute or start.

Civil action in most jurisdictions is commenced by filing a complaint with the court. Fed.R. Civil P. 3.

Commencement of building or improvement, within the meaning of mechanic's lien statute, is the visible commencement of actual operations on the ground for the erection of the building, which every one can readily recognize as commencement of a building, and which is done with intention to continue the work until building is completed.

Criminal action is commenced within statute of limitations at time preliminary complaint or information is filed with magistrate in good faith and a warrant issued thereon. A criminal prosecution is "commenced" (1) when information is laid before magistrate charging commission of crime, and a warrant of arrest is issued, or (2) when grand jury has returned an indictment.

Commencement of action. *See* Commence.

Commencement of prosecution. *See* Commence.

Comment. The expression of the judgment passed upon certain alleged facts by a person who has applied his mind to them, and who while so commenting assumes that such allegations of fact are true. The assertion of a fact is not a "comment."

Comment on the evidence. An instruction by judge to jury on the probative value of the evidence. A statement by a trial judge will constitute such a comment only if the trial court's attitude towards the merits of the cause is reasonably inferable from the nature or manner of the judge's statement.

Commerce. The exchange of goods, productions, or property of any kind; the buying, selling, and exchanging of articles. The transportation of persons and property by land, water and air.

Intercourse by way of trade and traffic between different peoples or states and the citizens or inhabitants thereof, including not only the purchase, sale, and exchange of commodities, but also the instrumentalities and agencies by which it is promoted and the means and appliances by which it is carried on, and transportation of persons as well as of goods, both by land and sea. Also interchange of ideas, sentiments, etc., as between man and man.

The term "commerce" means trade, traffic, commerce, transportation, or communication among the several States, or between the District of Columbia or any Territory of the United States and any State or other Territory, or between any foreign country and any State, Territory, or the District of Columbia, or within the District of Columbia or any Territory, or between points in the same State but through any other State or any Territory or the District of Columbia or any foreign country. National Labor Relations Act, § 2.

For purposes of Fair Labor Standards Act, "commerce" means trade, commerce, transportation, transmission, or communication among several states or between any state and any place outside thereof.

See also Affecting commerce; Chamber of commerce; Interstate and foreign commerce; Interstate commerce; Interstate Commerce Act; Interstate Commerce Commission; Intrastate commerce.

Commerce among the states. Transportation and transacting business from one state to another, and also all component parts of such intercourse. *See* Interstate commerce.

Commerce with foreign nations. Commerce between citizens of the United States and citizens or subject governments; commerce which, either immediately or at some stage of its progress, is extraterritorial. The same as *foreign commerce,* which see *below.* Power of Congress to regulate "commerce with foreign nations" comprehends every species of commercial intercourse. U.S.C.A. Const. Art. I, § 8, cl. 3.

Commerce with Indian tribes. Commerce with individuals belonging to such tribes, in the nature of buying, selling, and exchanging commodities, without reference to the locality where carried on, though it be within the limits of a state.

Domestic commerce. Commerce carried on wholly within the limits of the United States, as distinguished from foreign commerce. Also, commerce carried on within the limits of a single state, as distinguished from interstate commerce.

Foreign commerce. Commerce or trade between the United States and foreign countries. The term is sometimes applied to commerce between ports of two sister states not lying on the same coast, *e.g.,* New York and San Francisco.

Internal commerce. Such as is carried on between individuals within the same state, or between different parts of the same state. Now more commonly called "intrastate" commerce.

International commerce. Commerce between states or nations entirely foreign to each other.

Interstate commerce. Such as is carried on between different states of the Union or between points lying in different states. *See* Interstate commerce.

Intrastate commerce. Such as is begun, carried on, and completed wholly within the limits of a single state. Contrasted with "interstate commerce" *(q.v.).*

Commerce clause. The provision of U.S.Const. (Art. I, § 8, cl. 3) which gives Congress exclusive powers over interstate commerce. This power is the basis for a considerable amount of federal legislation and regulation. *See* Commerce; Cooley doctrine; Interstate commerce.

Commerce court. A federal court in existence from 1910 to 1913 which had power to review and enforce determinations of the Interstate Commerce Commission.

Commerce Department. Part of executive branch of federal government headed by cabinet member (Secretary of Commerce) which is concerned with promoting domestic and international business and commerce; may also be a department of state government with similar functions.

Commerce power. *See* Commerce clause.

Commercia belli /kəmǽrs(h)(i)yə bélay/. War contracts. Contracts between nations at war, or their subjects. Agreements entered into by belligerents, either in time of peace to take effect in the event of war, or during the war itself, by which arrangement is made for non-hostile intercourse. They may take the form of armistices, truces, capitulations, cartels, passports, safe-conducts, safeguards.

Commercial /kəmǽrshəl/. Relates to or is connected with trade and traffic or commerce in general; is occupied with business and commerce. Generic term for most all aspects of buying and selling.

Commercial activity. Term includes any type of business or activity which is carried on for a profit. Activity relating to or connected with trade and traffic or commerce in general.

Commercial agency. An office for the collection of debts for clients; also an agency for gathering credit information.

Commercial agent. An officer in the consular service of the United States, of rank inferior to a consul. Also used as equivalent to commercial broker, *see infra.*

Commercial bank. An institution authorized to receive both demand and time deposits, to make loans of various types, to engage in trust services and other fiduciary funds, to issue letters of credit, to accept and pay drafts, to rent safety deposit boxes, and to engage in many similar activities. Formerly, such banks were the only institutions authorized to receive demand deposits, though today many other types of financial institutions are legally permitted to offer checking accounts and other similar services.

Commercial bribery. Illegal payment in exchange for award of a contract or business. A form of corrupt and unfair trade practice in which an employee accepts a gratuity to act against the best interests of his employer. May assume any form of corruption in which an employee is induced to betray his employer or to compete unfairly with a competitor. *See also* Bribery.

Commercial broker. One who negotiates the sale of merchandise without having the possession or control of it, being distinguished in the latter particular from a commission merchant *(q.v.).*

Commercial code. *See* Uniform Commercial Code.

Commercial corporation. One engaged in commerce in the broadest sense of that term.

Commercial credit. A letter of credit used to facilitate sales of goods (especially in international transactions) by insuring payment of the price to the seller-beneficiary upon her compliance with the terms of the credit procured by the buyer-customer.

Commercial credit company. Company which extends credit and finances dealers and manufacturers.

Commercial domicile. *See* Domicile.

Commercial establishment. A place where commodities and goods are exchanged, bought or sold. The term contemplates a profit-making establishment.

Commercial frustration. Excuse of party from performance if contract depends on existence of given person or thing and such person or thing perishes, and if contract is rendered impossible by act of God, the law, or other party. In theory it amounts to no more than a condition or term of a contract which the law implies to take the place of a covenant that it is assumed would have been inserted by the parties had the contingency which arose occurred to them at the time they made the contract. And doctrine is predicated upon premise of giving relief in a situation where parties could not reasonably protect themselves by terms of a contract against happening of subsequent events. Hence doctrine has no application where events were reasonably foreseeable and controllable by the parties. U.C.C. § 2–613. *See* Commercial impracticability; Impossibility *(Impossibility of performance of contract)*.

Commercial impracticability. U.C.C. § 2–615 excuses either party from performing a contract where three conditions exist: (1) a contingency must occur, (2) performance must thereby be made "impracticable," and (3) the nonoccurrence of the contingency must have been a basic assumption on which the contract was made. *See also* Commercial frustration.

Commercial insolvency. Inability of a business to pay its debts as they become due in the regular and ordinary course of business. *See also* Bankrupt; Insolvency.

Commercial instrument. *See* Commercial paper.

Commercial insurance. *See* Insurance.

Commercial law. A phrase used to designate the whole body of substantive jurisprudence (*e.g.* Uniform Commercial Code; Truth in Lending Act) applicable to the rights, intercourse, and relations of persons engaged in commerce, trade, or mercantile pursuits. *See* Uniform Commercial Code.

Commercial letter of credit. *See* Letter of credit.

Commercial loan. Loans made to businesses, as distinguished from personal-consumer credit loans. The direct loan from a bank to a business customer for the purpose of providing funds needed by the customer in its business. *See also* Loan.

Commercial name. *See* Trade name.

Commercial paper. Bills of exchange (*i.e.*, drafts), promissory notes, bank-checks, and other negotiable instruments for the payment of money, which, by their form and on their face, purport to be such instruments. Short-term, unsecured promissory notes, generally issued by large, well-known corporations and finance companies. U.C.C. Article 3 is the general law governing commercial paper. *See also* Bearer instrument; Instrument; Negotiable instruments; Note; Trade acceptance.

Securities law. Commercial paper is a "security" under the Glass–Steagall Act and therefore is subject to its proscriptions on commercial banks marketing "stocks, bonds, debentures, notes, or other securities."

Commercial property. Income producing property (*e.g.* office buildings, apartments, etc.) as opposed to residential property.

Commercial reasonableness. May refer to goods which meet the warranty of merchantability. U.C.C. § 2–314.

In the context of UCC provisions relating to disposition of collateral upon lawful repossession, means that the qualifying disposition of the chattel must be made in a good faith attempt to dispose of the collateral to the parties' mutual best advantage.

Commercial set. Primary documents covering shipment of goods: invoice, bill of lading, bill of exchange, certificate of insurance.

Commercial speech doctrine. Speech that was categorized as "commercial" in nature (*i.e.* speech that advertised a product or service for profit or for business purpose) was formerly not afforded First Amendment freedom of speech protection, and as such could be freely regulated by statutes and ordinances. This doctrine, however, has been essentially abrogated.

Commercial traveler. A drummer; a traveling salesman who simply exhibits samples of goods kept for sale by his principal, and takes orders from purchasers for such goods, which goods are afterwards to be delivered by the principal to the purchasers, and payment for the goods is to be made by the purchasers to the principal on such delivery.

Commercial unit. Means such a unit of goods as by commercial usage is a single whole for purposes of sale and division of which materially impairs its character or value on the market or in use. A commercial unit may be a single article (as a machine) or a set of articles (as a suite of furniture, or an assortment of sizes) or a quantity (as a bale, gross, or carload) or any other unit treated in use or in the relevant market as a single whole. U.C.C. § 2–105(6).

Commercial use. Term implies use in connection with or for furtherance of a profit-making enterprise.

Commingle /kəmíŋgəl/. To put together in one mass; *e.g.* to combine funds or properties into common fund or stock.

Commingling of funds. Act of fiduciary in mingling funds of his beneficiary, client, employer, or ward with his own funds. Such act is generally considered to be a breach of his fiduciary relationship. May be applied to lawyer who mixes client's funds with his own and as a result is subject to disciplinary action under Model Rules of Professional Conduct.

Commissary. One who is sent or delegated to execute some office or duty as the representative of his superior; an officer of the bishop, who exercises spiritual jurisdiction in distant parts of the diocese. A general store, especially on a military base; a lunchroom, especially at a movie or T.V. studio.

Commission. A warrant or authority or letters patent, issuing from the government, or one of its departments, or a court, empowering a person or persons named to do certain acts, or to exercise the authority of an office (as in the case of an officer in the army or navy).

The authority or instructions under which one person transacts business or negotiates for another. In a derivative sense, a body of persons to whom a commission is directed. A body composed of several persons acting under lawful authority to perform some public service. A board or committee officially appointed and empowered to perform certain acts or exercise certain jurisdiction of a public nature or relation; as a "Public Service Commission".

An authority or writ issuing from a court, in relation to a cause before it, directing and authorizing a person or persons named to do some act or exercise some special function; usually to take the depositions of witnesses.

Compensation. The recompense, compensation or reward of an agent, salesman, executor, trustee, receiver, factor, broker, or bailee, when the same is calculated as a percentage on the amount of his transactions or on the profit to the principal. A fee paid to an agent or employee for transacting a piece of business or performing a service. Compensation to an administrator or other fiduciary for the faithful discharge of his duties.

Criminal law. Doing or perpetration of a criminal act.

Commission agent. *See* Commission merchant; Factor.

Commission broker. Member of stock or commodity exchange who executes buy and sell orders.

Commission del credere. In commercial law, exists where an agent of a seller undertakes to guaranty to his principal the payment of the debt due by the buyer. The phrase *"del credere"* is borrowed from the Italian language, in which its signification is equivalent to our word "guaranty" or "warranty."

Commissioned office. Officers in the armed forces who hold their rank by virtue of a commission from the President.

Commissioner. A person to whom a commission is directed by the government or a court. A person with a commission. An officer who is charged with the administration of the laws relating to some particular subject-matter, or the management of some bureau or agency of the government. Member of a commission or board. Specially appointed officer of court.

The administrative head of an organized professional sport.

In the commission form of municipal government, the term is applied to any of the several officers constituting the commission.

Commissioners of bail. Officers appointed to take recognizances of bail in civil cases.

Commissioners of deeds. Officers empowered by the government of one state to reside in another state, and there take acknowledgments of deeds and other papers which are to be used as evidence or put on record in the former state.

County commissioners. See County.

Court Commissioners. Term used variously to designate a lawyer appointed to hear facts and report to court. Specially appointed officer of court. A person appointed to conduct judicial sales. In admiralty, an officer appointed to hear and determine certain issues. *See also* Magistrate *(U.S. (Federal) Magistrates).*

United States Commissioners. The functions of U.S. Commissioners have been taken over by U.S. Magistrates. *See* Magistrate *(U.S. (Federal) Magistrates).*

Commissioner's court. In certain states, such court has jurisdiction over county affairs.

Commission government. A method of municipal government in which the legislative power is in the hands of a few persons.

Commission merchant. A term which is synonymous with "factor." It means one who receives goods, chattels, or merchandise for sale, exchange, or other disposition, and who is to receive a compensation for his services, to be paid by the owner, or derived from the sale, etc., of the goods. One whose business is to receive and sell goods for a commission, being intrusted with the possession of the goods to be sold, and usually selling in his own name. *See also* Factor.

Broker distinguished. A "factor" or "commission merchant" is one who has the actual or technical possession of goods or wares of another for sale, while a "merchandise broker" is one who negotiates the sale of merchandise without having it in his possession or control, being simply an agent with very limited powers.

Commission to examine witnesses. A commission issued out of the court in which an action is pending, to direct the taking of the depositions of witnesses who are beyond the territorial jurisdiction of the court. Fed.R. Civil P. 28.

Commit. To perpetrate, as a crime; to perform as an act; to entrust; to pledge.

To send a person to prison by virtue of a lawful authority, for any crime or contempt, or to a mental health facility, workhouse, reformatory, or the like, by authority of a court or magistrate.

To refer to a committee for action; *e.g.* a legislative bill.

Commitment. A warrant, order, or process by which court or magistrate directs ministerial officer to take person to penal institution or mental health facility. Also, the act of taking or sending to the prison, mental health facility, or the like. A person is committed when he is actually sentenced to confinement by a court as contrasted with a suspended sentence or probation. *See also* Mittimus.

The proceedings directing confinement of a mentally ill or incompetent person for treatment. Commitment proceedings may be either civil or criminal; and voluntary or involuntary. Due process protections are afforded to persons involuntarily committed; *e.g.* periodic judicial review of continued confinement. *See* Civil commitment.

Agreement or pledge to do something; *e.g.* a statement by a lender that a loan will be made under certain terms. Commitments may be of various types, that is, a conditional commitment, subject to certain items being met, or a firm commitment, which is binding on the lender without conditions.

Commitment fee. Amount paid to lender by borrower for loan commitment in addition to interest. Such are common in real estate transactions.

Commitment letter. A lender's written offer to grant a mortgage loan outlining the terms, the amount of the loan, the interest rate and any other conditions. It can also serve as a communication of the lender's decision on the borrower's application.

Committee. A person, or an assembly or board of persons, to whom the consideration, determination, or management of any matter is committed or referred, as by a court or legislature. An individual or body to whom others have delegated or committed a particular duty, or who have

taken on themselves to perform it in the expectation of their act being confirmed by the body they profess to represent or act for.

In legislatures a standing committee considers all bills, resolutions, and other items of legislative business falling within the category of matters over which it has been given jurisdiction. Membership and rank on standing committees are largely determined by the seniority rule. A special (or select) committee investigates and reports on specific matters and terminates when that function has been rendered. A joint committee of a legislative body comprising two chambers is a committee consisting of representatives of each of the two houses, meeting and acting together as one committee.

Committing magistrate. An inferior judicial officer who is invested with authority to conduct the preliminary hearing of persons charged with crime, and either to discharge them for lack of sufficient prima facie evidence or to commit them to jail to await trial or (in some jurisdictions) to accept bail and release them thereon. The term is said to be synonymous with "examining court."

Committitur /kəmítətər/. An order or minute, setting forth that the person named in it *is committed* to the custody of the sheriff.

Commodate. Exists where property is loaned gratuitously by owner for sole benefit, accommodation, and use of borrower, and specific thing loaned is to be returned.

Commodities /kəmódətiyz/. Those things which are useful or serviceable, particularly articles of merchandise movable in trade. Goods, wares, and merchandise of any kind; articles of trade or commerce. Movable articles of value; things that are bought and sold. This word is a broader term than merchandise, and, in referring to commerce may include almost any article of movable or personal property.

Staples such as wool, cotton, etc. which are traded on a commodity exchange and on which there is trading in futures.

Commodity. *See* Commodities.

Commodity Credit Corporation. The Commodity Credit Corporation (CCC) was organized October 17, 1933, pursuant to Executive Order 6340 of October 16, 1933, under the laws of the State of Delaware, as an agency of the United States. From October 17, 1933, to July 1, 1939, the CCC was managed and operated in close affiliation with the Reconstruction Finance Corporation. On July 1, 1939, the CCC was transferred to the Department of Agriculture by the President's Reorganization Plan 1 of 1939. Approval of the Commodity Credit Corporation Charter Act on June 29, 1948 (62 Stat. 1070; 15 U.S.C.A. § 714), subsequently amended, established the CCC, effective July 1, 1948, as an agency and instrumentality of the United States under a permanent Federal charter. The purpose of CCC is to stabilize and protect farm income and prices, to assist in maintaining balanced and adequate supplies of agricultural commodities and their products, and to facilitate the orderly distribution of commodities.

Commodity future. A speculative transaction involving the sale for future delivery of a staple such as wool or cotton at a predetermined price. *See* Futures contract.

Commodity futures contract. *See* Futures contract.

Commodity Futures Trading Commission. An independent agency of the U.S. Government established to administer the Commodity Exchange Act; an Act designed to insure fair practices and honest dealing on the commodity futures exchanges and to provide a measure of control over speculative activity.

Commodity option. *See* Option.

Commodity paper. Commercial documents representing loans secured by bills of lading or warehouse receipts covering commodities.

Commodity rate. With reference to railroads, a rate which applies to a specific commodity alone; —distinguished from a "class rate", meaning a single rate which applies to a number of articles of the same general character.

Common, *n.* Belonging or shared equally by more than one. Of frequent occurrence. Without special or distinguishing characteristics.

An incorporeal hereditament which consists in a profit which one man has in connection with one or more others in the land of another. *See* Profit (*Profit á prendre*).

Tract of land set apart by city or town for use by general public. Formerly, such land was to be used for common pasturage. Now usually called "parks."

Common, *adj.* Usual, ordinary, accustomed; shared among several; owned by several jointly. Belonging or pertaining to many or to the majority. Generally or prevalent, of frequent or ordinary occurrence or appearance; familiar by reason of frequency. Also, usual, customary, and habitual, professed, or confessed, and used indefinitely in various terms implying illegal or criminal conduct, such as common scold, common thief, etc.

As to *common* Bail; Barretor; Carrier; Chase; Council; Debtor; Diligence; Drunkard; Error; Highway; Informer; Intendment of law; Intent; Jury; Labor; Nuisance; Occupant; Property; Seal; Stock; Traverse; see those titles.

Common ancestor. A person through whom two or more persons claim lineage.

Common appearance. The manner in which something generally appears; *e.g.* by common appearance blood is red.

Common area. In law of landlord-tenant, the portion of demised premises used in common by tenants over which landlord retains control (*e.g.* hallways, stairs) and hence for whose condition he is liable, as contrasted with areas of which tenant has exclusive possession. Term also refers to areas in common ownership and use by residents of condominium, subdivision, or planned unit development.

Common carrier. Any carrier required by law to convey passengers or freight without refusal if the approved fare or charge is paid in contrast to private or contract carrier. One who holds himself out to the public as engaged in business of transportation of persons or property from place to place for compensation, and who offers services to the public generally. Such is to be distinguished from a *contract* or *private* carrier. *See* Carrier.

Common counts. Old forms of pleading by which pleader sets forth in account form the basis of his claim such as money had and received, goods sold and delivered, etc. Traditionally, the various forms of action of assumpsit.

Common defense. In joint trial of two or more defendants, a defense asserted by all defendants.

Common design. Community of intention between two or more persons to do an unlawful act. Generally used in criminal context to describe an action taken by two or more persons after joint planning. Actions and declarations of one participant during existence of common design are chargeable to all participants. *See* Combination in restraint of trade; Conspiracy.

Common disaster. Situation in which the insured and beneficiary appear to die simultaneously with no clear indication or evidence of which died first. *See* Simultaneous Death Act.

Common disaster clause. In insurance or will, a clause that provides for an alternative beneficiary in event both the insured (testator) and beneficiary (legatee) die in a common disaster. *See* Simultaneous death clause.

Common enterprise. *See* Joint enterprise.

Common good. Generic term to describe the betterment of the general public.

Common knowledge. Information widely shared by substantial number of people. *See* Judicial notice.

Common repute. The prevailing belief in a given community as to the existence of a certain fact or aggregation of facts.

Common right. A term applied to rights, privileges, and immunities appertaining to and enjoyed by all citizens equally and in common, and which have their foundation in the common law.

Common seller. A common seller of any commodity is one who sells it frequently, usually, customarily, or habitually.

Common sense. Sound practical judgment; that degree of intelligence and reason, as exercised upon the relations of persons and things and the ordinary affairs of life, which is possessed by the generality of mankind, and which would suffice to direct the conduct and actions of the individual in a manner to agree with the behavior of ordinary persons.

Common descriptive name. Generic trademark; as used in the Lanham Act, this refers to a particular genus or class of which an individual article or service is but a member, and suggests the basic nature of the article or services.

Common elements. In condominium law, all portions of a condominium other than the units, *i.e.* physical portion of the condominium designated for separate ownership or occupancy. Uniform Condominium Act, § 1–103(4), (25).

Common enemy doctrine. Under "common enemy doctrine" each landowner has an unqualified right, by operations on his own land, to fend off surface waters as he sees fit without being required to take into account the consequences to other landowners who also have the duty and right to protect themselves as best they can.

Common enterprise. Under securities law, a venture in which the fortunes of an investor are interwoven with and dependent upon the efforts and success of those seeking the investment or of third parties.

Common fund doctrine. This doctrine provides that a private plaintiff, or plaintiff's attorney, whose efforts create, discover, increase, or preserve a fund to which others also have a claim is entitled to recover from the fund the costs of his litigation, including attorneys' fees.

Common humanity doctrine. Where a passenger becomes sick or is injured while en route, carrier owes duty under "common humanity doctrine" to render to passenger such reasonable care and attention as common humanity would dictate.

Common knowledge. Refers to what court may declare applicable to action without necessity of proof. It is knowledge that every intelligent person has, and includes matters of learning, experience, history, and facts of which judicial notice may be taken. *See also* Judicial notice.

Common law. As distinguished from statutory law created by the enactment of legislatures, the common law comprises the body of those principles and rules of action, relating to the government and security of persons and property, which derive their authority solely from usages and customs of immemorial antiquity, or from the judgments and decrees of the courts recognizing, affirming, and enforcing such usages and customs; and, in this sense, particularly the ancient unwritten law of England. In general, it is a body of law that develops and derives through judicial decisions, as distinguished from legislative enactments. The "common law" is all the statutory and case law background of England and the American colonies before the American revolution. It consists of those principles, usage and rules of action applicable to government and security of persons and property which do not rest for their authority upon any express and positive declaration of the will of the legislature.

As distinguished from ecclesiastical law, it is the system of jurisprudence administered by the purely secular tribunals.

Calif. Civil Code, Section 22.2, provides that the "common law of England, so far as it is not repugnant to or inconsistent with the Constitution of the United States, or the Constitution or laws of this State, is the rule of decision in all the courts of this State."

In a broad sense, "common law" may designate all that part of the positive law, juristic theory, and ancient custom of any state or nation which is of general and universal application, thus marking off special or local rules or customs.

For Federal common law, see that title.

As a compound adjective "common-law" is understood as contrasted with or opposed to "statutory," and sometimes also to "equitable" or to "criminal." *See* examples below.

Common-law action. Action governed by common law, rather than statutory, equitable, or civil law.

Common-law assignments. Such forms of assignments for the benefit of creditors as were known to the common law, as distinguished from such as are of modern invention or authorized by statute.

Common-law contempt. A name sometimes applied to proceedings for contempt which are criminal in their nature, as distinguished from those which are intended as purely civil remedies ordinarily arising out of the alleged violation of some order entered in the course of a chancery proceeding.

Common-law copyright. Authors' proprietary interest in his creation before it has been published. An intangible, incorporeal right in an author of literary or artistic productions to reproduce and sell them exclusively and arises at the moment of their creation as distinguished from federal or statutory copyrights which exist for the most part only in published works. Common law copyright is perpetual while statutory copyright is for term of years. Equitable relief is available for violation of common law copyright. The distinction which formerly existed between common law copyrights and statutory copyrights was abolished by the 1976 Copyright Act revision; though § 301 of the new Act specifically preserves common law copyrights accruing prior to January 1, 1978. *See also* Copyright.

Common-law crime. One punishable by the force of the common law, as distinguished from crimes created by statute.

Common-law dedication. *See* Dedication.

Common-law extortion. Corrupt collection of unlawful fee by an office under color of office.

Common-law jurisdiction. Jurisdiction of a court to try and decide such cases as were cognizable by the courts of law under the English common law. The jurisdiction of those courts which exercise their judicial powers according to the course of the common law.

Common-law larceny. *See* Larceny.

Common-law lien. One known to or granted by the common law, as distinguished from statutory, equitable, and maritime liens; also one arising by implication of law, as distinguished from one created by the agreement of the parties. It is a right extended to a person to retain that which is in his possession belonging to another, until the demand or charge of the person in possession is paid or satisfied.

Common-law marriage. One not solemnized in the ordinary way (*i.e.* non-ceremonial) but created by an agreement to marry, followed by cohabitation. A consummated agreement to marry, between persons legally capable of making marriage contract, per verba de præsenti, followed by cohabitation. Such marriage requires a positive mutual agreement, permanent and exclusive of all others, to enter into a marriage relationship, cohabitation sufficient to warrant a fulfillment of necessary relationship of man and wife, and an assumption of marital duties and obligations. Such marriages are invalid in many states; *e.g.* Missouri (after 1921), Indiana (after 1958), Maryland, Massachusetts, Nebraska (after 1939), Nevada, New Hampshire, New Jersey, New Mexico, New York (after 1933), North Dakota, Oregon, South Dakota (after 1959), Virginia, Washington, W. Virginia, Wisconsin, Wyoming.

Common-law state. *See* Community property.

Common-law trademark. One appropriated under common-law rules, regardless of statutes.

Common-law trust. A business trust which has certain characteristics in common with corporations and in which trustees hold the property and manage the business and the shareholders are the trust beneficiaries or cestui que trust; sometimes known as a Massachusetts trust. *See* Massachusetts trust.

Common-law wife. A woman who was party to a common-law marriage; or one who, having lived with a man in a relation of concubinage during his life, asserts a claim, after his death, to have been his wife according to the requirements of the common law.

Common market. An economic union established by the Treaty of Rome, 1957, which originally included Belgium, France, Italy, Luxembourg, the Netherlands and West Germany. Its official title is European Economic Community.

Common nuisance. A nuisance is a "common nuisance" or a "public nuisance", the terms being synonymous, where it affects the rights enjoyed by citizens as part of the public, that is, the rights to which every citizen is entitled. *See also* Nuisance.

Common property. Property held by two or more persons in common with each other; *e.g.* as tenants in common. Portion of rented premises over which landlord retains control but which may be used by tenants such as hallways, stairways, etc. *See also* Community property.

Common right. Right derivative from common law. Right peculiar to certain people is not a common right.

Commons. The class of subjects in Great Britain exclusive of the royal family and the nobility. They are represented in parliament by the House of Commons.

At common law, part of the demesne land of a manor (or land the property of which was in the lord), which, being uncultivated, was termed the "lord's waste," and served for public roads and for common of pasture to the lord and his tenants.

Squares; pleasure grounds and spaces or open places for public use or public recreation owned by towns or cities—in modern usage usually called "parks."

Commons, House of. *See* House (*House of Commons*).

Common stock. Class of corporate stock which represents the residual ownership of the corporation. Holders of common stock have voting powers (to, for example, select directors of corporation) and to participate in the profits of the corporation by way of dividends (but only after preferred stockholders have been paid their dividends). Such stock is last to share in property of corporation on dissolution (after demands of creditors and senior security holders are satisfied).

Common stock equivalents. Securities, including certain types of convertible securities, stock options, and warrants, that are considered to be the substantial equivalent of common stock.

Common stock ratios. Ratios that are designed to measure the relative claims of stockholders to earnings (earnings per share and payout ratio), cash flow (cash flow per share), and equity (book value per share) of a firm.

Common tenancy. Type of tenancy in which tenants hold property in common without right of survivorship. May be holding of unequal shares among tenants. Such tenancy is subject to partition. *See also* Tenancy.

Common thief. One who by practice and habit is a thief. An adjudication of a person which may be made after a person has been convicted more than once of larceny. It generally carries an additional sentence beyond that for larceny. Sometimes known as common and notorious thief.

Common trust fund. One composed of funds contributed by estates, trusts and guardianships, maintained and operated by a bank or trust company for exclusive use of its own estates, trusts and guardianships, under permission of law of state in which it is located and according to rules and regulations promulgated by Federal Reserve System. Type of trust fund in which funds of many persons are commingled for purposes of economy of administration and counselling and in which a bank or other financial institution is trustee; regulated almost entirely by statute. Several states have adopted the Uniform Common Trust Fund Act.

Common wall. *See* Party wall.

Commonwealth. The public or common weal or welfare. This cannot be regarded as a technical term of public law, though often used in political science. It generally designates, when so employed, a republican frame of government,—one in which the welfare and rights of the entire mass of people are the main consideration, rather than the privileges of a class or the will of a monarch; or it may designate the body of citizens living under such a government.

Sometimes it may denote the corporate entity, or the government, of a jural society (or state) possessing powers of self-government in respect of its immediate concerns, but forming an integral part of a larger government (or nation). In this latter sense, it is the official title of several of the United States (as Pennsylvania, Massachusetts, Virginia, and Kentucky), and would be appropriate to them all. In the former sense, the word was used to designate the English government during the protectorate of Cromwell.

Any of the individual States of the United States and the body of people constituting a state or politically organized community, a body politic, hence, a state, especially one constituted by a number of persons united by compact or tacit agreement under one form of government and system of laws.

See Government; Nation; State.

Commotion /kəmówshən/. A condition of turmoil, civil unrest or insurrection. A civil commotion is an uprising among a mass of people which occasions a serious and prolonged disturbance and infraction of civil order not attaining the status of war or an armed insurrection; it is a wild and irregular action of many persons assembled together.

Commune /kómyuwn/, *n.* Small community of people, usually with common interests, who own and share property in common.

Communicate. To bestow, convey, make known, recount, impart; to give by way of information; to talk over; to transmit information. *See also* Utter.

Communication. Information given; the sharing of knowledge by one with another; conference; consultation or bargaining preparatory to making a contract. Intercourse; connection. Act of or system of transmitting information. A "communication" is ordinarily considered to be a deliberate interchange of thoughts or opinions between two or more persons, as distinguished from "res gestae" expressions which are spontaneously or instinctively provoked, or made while under such shock or excitement as to preclude the possibility of design.

Confidential communications. These are certain classes of communications, passing between persons who stand in a confidential or fiduciary relation to each other (or who, on account of their relative situation, are under a special duty of secrecy and fidelity), which the law will not permit to be divulged, or allow them to be inquired into in a court of justice, for the sake of public policy and the good order of society. Examples of such privileged relations are those of husband and wife, doctor and patient, and attorney and client. Such are privileged at the option of the spouse-witness, patient-witness, client-witness. For purpose of rule that the attorney-client privilege is limited to "communication" between the attorney and the client, "communication" is not restricted to oral or written matters but extends to information communicated by the client to the attorney by other means. Fed.Evid.R. 501. *See* Privileged communications.

Libel or slander. As an essential element of tort liability for libel or slander, such communication (*i.e.* publication) may be either printed, written, oral, or conveyed by means of gestures, or exhibition of a picture or statue. *See* Libel; Publication; Slander.

Community. Neighborhood; vicinity; synonymous with locality. People who reside in a locality in more or less proximity. A society or body of people living in the same place, under the same laws and regulations, who have common rights, privileges, or interests. It connotes a congeries of common interests arising from associations—social, business, religious, governmental, scholastic, recreational.

Community account. A bank account consisting of separate and community funds commingled in such manner that neither can be distinguished from the other.

Community antenna television (CATV). System of television reception in which signals from distant stations are picked up by large antenna and transmitted by cable to individual paying customers.

Community debt. One chargeable to the community (of husband and wife) rather than to either of the parties individually.

Community house. A house occupied by two or more persons or families. A tenement.

Community lease. Exists where a number of lessors owning interests in separate tracts execute a lease in favor of a single lessee.

Community of interest. Term as applied to *relation of joint adventure* means interest common to both or all parties, that is, mixture or identity of interest in venture wherein each and all are reciprocally concerned and from which each and all derive material benefit and sustain a mutual responsibility. *See* Joint venture.

In *class actions,* this refers to whatever grievance unites members of the class against the defendant but it must predominate.

In *labor law,* to determine the appropriate bargaining unit, this term includes such factors as bargaining history, operational integration, geographic proximity, common supervision, similarity in job function and degree of employee interchange.

Community of profits. This term, as used in the definition of a partnership (to which a community of profits is essential), means a proprietorship in them as distinguished from a personal claim upon the other associate as much as in the other.

Community property. Property owned in common by husband and wife each having an undivided one-half interest by reason of their marital status. The nine states with community property

systems are Louisiana, Texas, New Mexico, Arizona, California, Washington, Idaho, Nevada, and Wisconsin (with adoption of Uniform Marital Property Act). The rest of the states are classified as common law jurisdictions. The difference between common law and community property systems centers around the property rights possessed by married persons. In a common law system, each spouse owns whatever he or she earns. Under a community property system, one-half of the earnings of each spouse is considered owned by the other spouse.

Community service. A criminal sentence requiring that the offender perform some specific service to the community for some specified period of time.

Commutation /kòmyətéyshən/. Alteration; change; substitution; the act of substituting one thing for another.

In criminal law, the change of a punishment to one which is less severe; as from execution to life imprisonment. The President of the United States has the power to grant reprieves and pardons for offenses against the United States, except in cases of impeachment. U.S. Constitution, Art. 2, Sec. 2, cl. 1. With respect to state offenses, the governor of a state has the power to grant commutations. Compare Amnesty; Pardon.

In commercial law, substituting one form of payment for another.

In civil law, the conversion of the right to receive a variable or periodical payment into the right to receive a fixed or gross payment; a substitution of one sort of payment for another, or of money payment in lieu of a performance of a compulsory duty or labor. Commutation may be effected by private agreement, but it is usually done under a statute.

Commutation of taxes. Payment of a designated lump sum (permanent or annual) for the privilege of exemption from taxes, or the settlement in advance of a specific sum in lieu of an ad valorem tax.

Commutative contract. In civil law, one in which each of the contracting parties gives and receives an equivalent; *e.g.,* the contract of sale. *See* Contract.

Commutative justice. *See* Justice.

Commuted value. The present value of a future interest in property used in taxation and in evaluating damages. Present value of future payments when discounted.

Compact, *n.* An agreement or contract between persons, nations or states. Commonly applied to working agreements between and among states concerning matters of mutual concern. A contract between parties, which creates obligations and rights capable of being enforced, and contemplated as such between the parties, in their distinct and independent characters. A mutual consent of parties concerned respecting some property or right that is the object of the stipulation, or something that is to be done or forborne. *See also* Compact clause; Confederacy; Interstate compact; Treaty.

Compact, *adj.* Closely or firmly united or packed, as the particles of solid bodies; firm; solid; dense, as a compact texture in rocks; also, lying in a narrow compass or arranged so as to economize space; having a small surface or border in proportion to contents or bulk; close, as a compact estate, or a compact order or formation of troops.

Compact clause. Art. I, Section 10, Cl. 3, of U.S. Constitution provides: "No State shall, without the consent of Congress, . . . enter into any Agreement or *Compact* with another State . . . ."

Company. Union or association of persons for carrying on a commercial or industrial enterprise; a partnership, corporation, association, joint stock company.

Company town. A residential and commercial community opened by a company for public use and operated under color of state law. Community exists primarily because of company; with major part of housing and stores owned by company.

Company union. Union whose membership is limited to the employees of a single company. Union under company domination.

Joint stock company. An association of individuals for purposes of profit, possessing a common capital contributed by the members composing it, such capital being commonly divided into shares which each member possesses one or more, and which are transferable by the owner. One having a joint stock or capital, which is divided into numerous transferable shares, or consists of transferable stock. A partnership whereof the capital is divided, or agreed to be divided, into shares so as to be transferable without the express consent of the co-partners.

Limited company. A company in which the liability of each shareholder is limited by the number of shares he has taken, so that he cannot be called on to contribute beyond the amount of his shares. In England, the memorandum of association of such company may provide that the liability of the directors, manager, or managing director thereof shall be unlimited.

Comparables. Properties used as comparisons to determine value of a specific property.

Comparable sales. As evidence of market value of condemned property, sales from a willing seller to a willing buyer of similar property in the vicinity or at about the same time as the taking.

Comparable worth. Term used to describe a class of wage discrimination claims based on the employer's use of different criteria in establishing the wage rates for male- and female-dominated jobs. Several states have enacted laws establishing comparable worth policies and processes for implementing pay adjustments for state employees.

Comparative interpretation. That method of interpretation which seeks to arrive at the meaning of a statute or other writing by comparing its several parts and also by comparing it as a whole with other like documents proceeding from the same source and referring to the same general subject.

Comparative jurisprudence. The study of the principles of legal science by the comparison of various systems of law.

Comparative negligence. Under comparative negligence statutes or doctrines, negligence is measured in terms of percentage, and any damages allowed shall be diminished in proportion to amount of negligence attributable to the person for whose injury, damage or death recovery is sought. Many states have replaced contributory negligence acts or doctrines with comparative negligence. Where negligence by both parties is concurrent and contributes to injury, recovery is not barred under such doctrine, but plaintiff's damages are diminished proportionately, provided his fault is less than defendant's, and that, by exercise of ordinary care, he could not have avoided consequences of defendant's negligence after it was or should have been apparent.

Comparative rectitude. Doctrine wherein relief by divorce is granted to the party least in fault when both have shown grounds for divorce.

Comparative stylistics. An evidential technique focusing on nonidentity of typist of questioned writings. Matter-of-fact solutions are premised on comparisons of the numerous stylistic alternatives in grammar and format, and the individualized habits and routine practices inherent in the repetitive reduction of like writings to paper, with emphasis on typewritings. *See* Fed. and Uniform Rules of Evid. 406 and 901. *See also* Comparative interpretation; Comparison of handwriting; Forensic linguistics.

Comparison of handwriting. A comparison by the juxtaposition of two writings, in order, by such comparison, to ascertain whether both were written by the same person.

A method of proof resorted to where the genuineness of a written document is disputed; it consists in comparing the handwriting of the disputed paper with that of another instrument which is proved or admitted to be in the writing of the party sought to be charged, in order to infer, from their identity or similarity in this respect, that they are the work of the same hand. Expert testimony with respect to such proof is permitted by Fed.Evid. Rule 702, and non-expert testimony is governed by Rule 901.

See also Comparative stylistics.

Compel. To urge forcefully; under extreme pressure. Word "compel" as used in constitutional right to be free from being compelled in a criminal case to be a witness against one's self means to be subjected to some coercion, fear, terror, inducement, trickery or threat—either physically or psychologically, blatantly or subtly; the hallmark of compulsion is the presence of some operative force producing an involuntary response.

Compelling state interest. One which the state is forced or obliged to protect. Term used to uphold state action in the face of attack grounded on Equal Protection or First Amendment rights because of serious need for such state action. Also employed to justify state action under police power of state.

Compensable. Entitled to compensation. *See, e.g.,* Compensable injury.

Compensable death. Within worker's compensation acts is one which results to employee from injury by accident arising out of and in course of employment.

Compensable injury. Such injury within workers' compensation act is one caused by an accident arising out of and in the course of the employment and for which the injured employee is entitled to receive compensation under such law. *See* Workers' Compensation Acts.

Compensate. To make equivalent return to, to recompense, or to pay. *See* Compensation.

Compensating balance. The balance a borrower from a bank is required to keep on deposit as a condition of the loan or for continuing line of credit.

Compensating tax. *See* Use tax.

Compensatio /kòmpənséysh(iy)ow/. Lat. In the civil law, compensation, or set-off. A proceeding resembling a set-off in the common law, being a claim on the part of the defendant to have an amount due to him from the plaintiff deducted from his demand.

Compensatio criminis /kòmpənséysh(iy)ow krímənəs/. (Set-off of crime or guilt). The compensation or set-off of one crime against another; the plea or defense of recrimination in a suit for a divorce; that is, that the complainant is guilty of the same kind of offense with which the respondent is charged.

Compensation. Indemnification; payment of damages; making amends; making whole; giving an equivalent or substitute of equal value. That which is necessary to restore an injured party to his former position. Remuneration for services rendered, whether in salary, fees, or commissions. Consideration or price of a privilege purchased.

Equivalent in money for a loss sustained; equivalent given for property taken or for an injury done to another; giving back an equivalent in either money which is but the measure of value, or in actual value otherwise conferred; recompense in value; recompense or reward for some loss, injury, or service, especially when it is given by statute; remuneration for the injury directly and proximately caused by a breach of contract or duty; remuneration or satisfaction for injury or damage of every description (including medical expenses). An act which a court orders to be done, or money which a court or other tribunal orders to be paid, by a person whose acts or omissions have caused loss or injury to another, in order that thereby the person damnified may receive equal value for his loss, or be made whole in respect of his injury. *See also* Damages.

See also Accrued compensation; Commission; Deferred compensation; Fee; Golden parachute; Incentive pay plans; Profit-sharing plan; Salary; Unreasonable compensation; Wages.

Eminent domain. Payment to owners of lands taken or injured by the exercise of the power of eminent domain. *See* Just compensation.

Unemployment and workers' compensation. Payments to an unemployed or injured worker or his dependents. *See* Workers' Compensation Acts.

Compensation period. Period fixed by unemployment or worker's compensation statutes during which unemployed or injured worker is to receive compensation.

Compensatory damages. *See* Damages.

Compete. To contend emulously; to strive for the position, reward, profit, goal, etc., for which another is striving. To contend in rivalry. *See* Competition.

Competency. In the law of evidence, the presence of those characteristics, or the absence of those disabilities, which render a witness legally fit and qualified to give testimony in a court of justice; applied, in the same sense, to documents or other written evidence. Evidence which is admissible as being able to assist the trier of fact (*i.e.* jury) in determining questions of fact, though it may not be believed. Competency differs from credibility. The former is a question which arises before considering the evidence given by the witness; the latter concerns the degree of credit to be given to his testimony. The former denotes the personal qualification of the witness; the latter his veracity. A witness may be competent, and yet give incredible testimony; he may be incompetent, and yet his evidence, if received, be perfectly credible.

Competency is for the court; credibility for the jury. Yet in some cases the term "credible" is used as an equivalent for "competent". In law of contracts, of legal age without mental disability or incapacity. *See also* Ability; Authority; Capacity; Competent; Competent evidence; Competent witness; Duly qualified; Incompetency; Power; Qualified.

Competency proceedings. Hearings conducted to determine a person's mental capacity. Such may be held within criminal context to determine competency to stand trial, or to be sentenced, or to determine whether at time of offense the accused was legally sane. See *e.g.* 18 U.S.C.A. §§ 4241 et seq. Such may also be held in civil context to determine whether person should be committed for treatment.

Competency to stand trial. A person lacks competency to stand trial if he or she lacks capacity to understand the nature and object of the proceedings, to consult with counsel, and to assist in preparing his or her defense. To be "competent to stand trial" a defendant must have, at time of trial, sufficient present ability to consult with his or her lawyer with a reasonable degree of understanding and a rational as well as factual understanding of the proceedings against him or her. Due process prohibits the government from prosecuting a defendant who is legally incompetent to stand trial. The issue of competency is collateral to the issue of guilt. *See* Insanity.

Competent. Duly qualified; answering all requirements; having sufficient capacity, ability or authority; possessing the requisite physical, mental, natural or legal qualifications; able; adequate; suitable; sufficient; capable; legally fit. A testator may be said to be "competent" if he or she understands (1) the general nature and extent of his property; (2) his relationship to the people named in the will and to any people he disinherits; (3) what a will is; and (4) the transaction of simple business affairs. *See also* Capacity; Competency; Incompetency.

Competent authority. As applied to courts and public officers, this term imports jurisdiction and due legal authority to deal with the particular matter in question.

Competent court. A court, either civil or criminal, having lawful jurisdiction.

Competent evidence. That which the very nature of the thing to be proven requires, as, the production of a writing where its contents are the subject of inquiry. Also, generally, admissible (*i.e.* relevant and material) as opposed to "incompetent" or "inadmissible" evidence. *See also* Competency; Evidence; Relevant evidence.

Competent witness. One who is legally qualified to be heard to testify in a cause. A witness may not testify to a matter unless evidence is introduced sufficient to support a finding that the witness has personal knowledge of the matter. Fed.Evid.R. 602.

As used in statutes relating to the execution of wills, the term means a person who, at the time of making the attestation, could legally testify in court to the facts which he attests by subscribing his name to the will. *See also* Competency.

Competition. Contest between two rivals. The effort of two or more parties, acting independently, to secure the business of a third party by the offer of the most favorable terms; also the relations between different buyers or different sellers which result from this effort. It is the struggle between rivals for the same trade at the same time; the act of seeking or endeavoring to gain what another is endeavoring to gain at the same time. The term implies the idea of endeavoring by two or more to obtain the same object or result. *See also* Compete.

Unfair competition in trade. *See* Combination in restraint of trade; Price-fixing; Sherman Antitrust Act; Unfair competition.

Competitive bidding. Such bidding generally encompasses the submission of bids to complete a project and an award of the contract to the responsible bidder best able to complete the project in a manner which is financially most advantageous to community.

Competitive civil service examination. Examination which conforms to measures or standards which are sufficiently objective to be capable of being challenged and reviewed by other examiners of equal ability and experience. Such exam may be open in which case all may take it or may be promotional in which case only those in service may compete against others in service.

Competitors. Persons endeavoring to do the same thing and each offering to perform the act, furnish the merchandise, or render the service better or cheaper than his rival.

Compilation /kòmpəléyshən/. A bringing together of preexisting statutes in the form in which they were enacted, with the removal of sections which have been repealed and the substitution of amendments in an arrangement designed to facilitate their use. A literary production composed of the works or selected extracts of others and arranged in methodical manner. *Compare* Code; Codification. *See also* Compiled statutes; Revised statutes.

In accounting, a term used in connection with the presentation of financial statements when the accountant has accumulated or compiled the financial information of an entity and does not give assurance that the financial statements are presented in conformity with generally accepted accounting principles. The accountant's responsibility in a compiled set of financial statements is limited to reviewing the statements for obvious errors.

In copyright law, a "compilation" is a work formed by the collection and assembling of preexisting materials or of data that are selected, coordinated, or arranged in such a way that the resulting work as a whole constitutes an original work of authorship. The term "compilation" includes collective works. Copyright Act, 17 U.S. C.A. § 101. *See also* Collective work.

Compile. *See* Compilation.

Compiled statutes. A collection of the statutes existing and in force in a given state, with all laws and parts of laws relating to each subject-matter being brought together under one head and the whole arranged systematically, either under an alphabetical arrangement or some other plan of classification. *Compare* Code; Codification. *See also* Compilation; Revised statutes.

Complainant. One who applies to the courts for legal redress by filing complaint (*i.e.* plaintiff). Also, one who instigates prosecution or who prefers accusation against suspected person.

Complaint. The original or initial pleading by which an action is commenced under codes or Rules of Civil Procedure. *E.g.* Fed.R. Civil P. 3. The pleading which sets forth a claim for relief. Such complaint (whether it be the original claim, counterclaim, cross-claim, or third-party claim) shall contain: (1) a short and plain statement of the grounds upon which the court's jurisdiction depends, unless the court already has jurisdiction and the claim needs no new grounds of jurisdiction to support it, (2) a short and plain statement of the claim showing that the pleader is entitled to relief, and (3) a demand for judgment for the relief to which he deems himself entitled. Relief in the alternative or of several different types may be demanded. Fed.R. Civil P. 8(a). The complaint, together with the summons, is required to be served on the defendant. Rule 4. *See also* Counterclaim; Cross-claim; Supplemental complaint; Third party complaint.

In criminal law, a charge, preferred before a magistrate having jurisdiction, that a person named (or an unknown person) has committed a specified offense, with an offer to prove the fact, to the end that a prosecution may be instituted. The complaint can be "taken out" by the victim, the police officer, the district attorney, or other interested party. Although the complaint charges an offense, an indictment or information may be the formal charging document. The complaint is a written statement of the essential facts constituting the offense charged. In the federal courts, it is to be made upon oath before a magistrate. Fed.R.Crim.P. 3. If it appears from the complaint that probable cause exists that the person named in the complaint committed the alleged crime, a warrant *(q.v.)* for his arrest will be issued. Fed.R.Crim.P. 4.

Complete, *v.* To finish; accomplish that which one starts out to do.

Complete, *adj.* Full; entire; including every item or element of the thing spoken of, without omissions or deficiencies; as, a "complete" copy, record, schedule, or transcript.

Perfect; consummate; not lacking in any element or particular; as in the case of a "complete legal title" to land, which includes the possession, the right of possession, and the right of property (*i.e.* fee simple title).

Completed. Finished; nothing substantial remaining to be done; state of a thing that has been created, erected, constructed or done substantially according to contract.

Completed contract method. A method used in accounting to report profit or loss on long term contracts in the year the contract is complete, except that losses must be recognized in the year incurred. This method differs from the percent of completion method where revenues and expenses are recorded over the life of the contract in accordance with the level of progress. The completed contract method is not allowed for tax purposes for long term contracts entered into after February 28, 1986. The acceptable methods for contracts entered into after February 28, 1986 include; percent of completion and percent of completion—capitalized cost method which combines the elements of the completed contract and percent of completion methods. *See also* Percentage of completion method.

Complete determination of cause. Determination of every issue so as to render decree or judgment res judicata.

Complete in itself. In reference to a legislative act, means covering entire subject; not amendatory.

Completeness rule. Rule of evidence which permits further use of a document to explain portion of document already in evidence. *See also* Open *(Open the door)*.

Complete operation rule. This doctrine holds that an unloading clause in insurance policy covers the entire process involved in the moving of goods from the moment the goods are in the insured's possession and until they are given, at the place of destination, to the party to whom delivery is to be made.

Complete payment. On a contract, the final payment.

Completion. The finishing or accomplishing in full of something theretofore begun. *See also* Substantial performance doctrine.

Completion bond. *See* Bond; Performance bond.

Complex trust. A trust with elaborate provisions as distinguished from a simple trust. May refer to trust in which trustees have complete discretion as to accumulating or distributing trust income, *i.e.* trustee need not distribute income annually, or make distributions other than from income. *See also* Trust.

Compliance. Submission; obedience; conformance.

Complicated. Consisting of many parts or particulars not easily severable in thought; hard to understand or explain; involved, intricate, confused.

Complice. One who is united with others in an ill design; an associate, confederate, accomplice, or accessory *(q.v.)*. *See also* Conspiracy.

Complicity /kəmplísətiy/. A state of being an accomplice; participation in guilt. Involvement in crime as principal or as accessory before fact. May also refer to activities of conspirators. *See* Accomplice; Conspiracy.

Comply. To yield; to accommodate, or to adapt oneself to; to act in accordance with; to accept.

Composed of. Formed of; consisting of.

Composite work. Within Copyright Act means work to which a number of authors have contributed distinguishable parts. Works containing distinguishable parts which are separately copyrightable. *See* Copyright Act §§ 101, 103 (17 U.S.C.A.). *See also* Collective work; Compilation.

Composition deed. An agreement embodying the terms of a composition between a debtor and his creditors.

Composition of matter. In patent law, a substance composed of two or more different substances, without regard to form. A mixture or chemical combination of materials.

Composition with creditors. An agreement, made upon a sufficient consideration, between an insolvent or embarrassed debtor and his creditors, whereby the latter, for the sake of immediate or sooner payment, agree to accept a payment less than the whole amount of their claims, to be distributed *pro rata*, in discharge and satisfaction of the whole. It constitutes an agreement not only between the debtor and his creditors but also one between the creditors themselves that each shall accept the lesser sums from the assets of the embarrassed debtor. Under the former Bankruptcy Act, if such a composition agreement expressly or secretly favored certain creditors, it was considered a preferential transfer and, as

such, treated as an "act of bankruptcy." *See* Act of bankruptcy. Such arrangements are generally provided for under the federal Bankruptcy Code. *See* Bankruptcy proceedings *(Business reorganizations; Wage earner's plan)*.

"Composition" should be distinguished from "accord." The latter properly denotes an arrangement between a debtor and a single creditor for a discharge of the obligation by a part payment or on different terms. The former designates an arrangement between a debtor and the whole body of his creditors (or at least a considerable proportion of them) for the liquidation of their claims by the dividend offered.

See also Arrangement with creditors; Assignment *(Assignment for benefit of creditors)*.

Compos mentis /kómpəs méntəs/. Sound of mind. Having use and control of one's mental faculties.

Compound, *v.* To compromise; to effect a composition with a creditor; to obtain discharge from a debt by the payment of a smaller sum. To put together as elements, ingredients, or parts, to form a whole; to combine, to unite. To form or make up as a composite product by combining different elements, ingredients, or parts, as to combine a medicine. *See* Compounding crime.

Compound, *n.* A combination of two or more elements or things by means of human agency; an artificial or synthetic product.

Compounding a felony. *See* Compounding crime.

Compounding crime. Compounding crime consists of the receipt of some property or other consideration in return for an agreement not to prosecute or inform on one who has committed a crime. There are three elements to this offense at common law, and under the typical compounding statute: (1) the agreement not to prosecute; (2) knowledge of the actual commission of a crime; and (3) the receipt of some consideration.

The offense committed by a person who, having been directly injured by a felony, agrees with the criminal that he will not prosecute him, on condition of the latter's making reparation, or on receipt of a reward or bribe not to prosecute.

The offense of taking a reward for forbearing to prosecute a felony; as where a party robbed takes his goods again, or other amends, upon an agreement not to prosecute.

See Conceal; Misprision of felony; Receiving stolen goods or property; Withholding of evidence.

Compounding period. The time between each interest computation.

Compound interest. Interest that is paid not only on the principal, but also on any interest earned but not withdrawn during earlier periods. Interest upon interest; *i.e.*, when the interest of a sum of money is added to the principal, and then bears interest, which thus becomes a sort of secondary principal.

Compound larceny. *See* Compounding crime; Larceny.

Comprehensive due diligence investigation. The investigation of a firm's business in conjunction with a securities offering to determine the adequacy of disclosure of the firm's business and financial situation and its prospects in the prospectus for the offering. *See also* Offering.

Comprehensive zoning plan. A general plan to control and direct the use and development of property in a municipality or in a large part thereof by dividing it into districts according to the present and potential use of the properties. *See also* Planned unit development (PUD).

Comprint. A surreptitious printing of another book-seller's copy of a work, to make gain thereby, which was contrary to common law, and is illegal. *See* Infringement.

Comprise. To comprehend; include; contain; embrace; cover.

Compromise and settlement. Settlement of a disputed claim by mutual concession to avoid a lawsuit. An arrangement arrived at, either in court or out of court, for settling a dispute upon what appears to the parties to be equitable terms, having regard to the uncertainty they are in regarding the facts or the law and the facts together. An agreement or arrangement by which, in consideration of mutual concessions, a controversy is terminated. *See* Alternative dispute resolution; Arbitration; Mediation; Settlement.

Offer of compromise. See Offer, *n.*

Compromise verdict. One which is reached only by the surrender of conscientious convictions on one material issue by some jurors in return for a relinquishment of matters in their like settled opinion on another issue, and the result is one which does not hold the approval of the entire panel. *See also* Allen charge; Verdict.

Comptroller /kóm(p)trowlǝr/kǝntrówlǝr/kóntr°/. A public officer of a state or municipal corporation, or an officer of a business, charged with certain duties in relation to the fiscal affairs of the same, principally to examine and audit the accounts, to keep records, and report the financial situation from time to time. There are also officers bearing this name in the Treasury Department of the United States.

Comptroller General. Government official (head of G. A. O.) whose main function is to audit governmental agencies.

Comptroller of Currency. The Office of the Comptroller of the Currency was created by act of Congress approved February 25, 1863 (12 Stat. 665), as an integral part of the national banking system. The Comptroller, as the administrator of national banks, is responsible for the execution of laws relating to national banks and promulgates rules and regulations governing the operations of national and District of Columbia banks. Approval of the Comptroller is required for the organization of new national banks, conversion of State-chartered banks into national banks, consolidations or mergers of banks where the surviving institution is a national bank, and the establishment of branches by national banks.

Compulsion. Constraint; objective necessity; duress. Forcible inducement to the commission of an act. The act of compelling or the state of being compelled; the act of driving or urging by force or by physical or moral constraint; subjection to force. The compulsion which will excuse a criminal act must be present, imminent and impending and of such a nature as to induce a well-grounded apprehension of death or serious bodily harm. To constitute "compulsion" or "coercion" rendering payment involuntary, there must be some actual or threatened exercise of power possessed, or supposedly possessed, by payee over payer's person or property, from which payer has no means of immediate relief except by advancing money. *See* Coercion; Duress.

Compulsory, *adj.* Involuntary; forced; coerced by legal process or by force of statute.

Compulsory arbitration. *See* Arbitration.

Compulsory attendance. Refers to legal obligation to attend; *e.g.* school attendance is compulsory up to certain age.

Compulsory counterclaim. *See* Counterclaim.

Compulsory disclosure. Term with variety of meanings; may refer to court order compelling disclosure of matters within scope of discovery rules (see Fed.R. Civil P. 26, 37, 45; Fed.R.Crim.P. 16, 17). May also refer to obligation of public officers or candidates for public office to reveal assets and income from private sources. *See also* Subpoena.

Compulsory insurance. Motor vehicle liability coverage which is required in most states as a condition to registration of such vehicle.

Compulsory license. Licenses created under the Copyright Act to allow certain parties to make certain uses of copyrighted material without the explicit permission of the copyright owner, on payment of a specified royalty. See *e.g.* 17 U.S. C.A. § 115.

Compulsory nonsuit. An involuntary nonsuit. *See* Nonsuit.

Compulsory payment. One not made voluntarily, but exacted by duress, threats, the enforcement of legal process, or unconscionably taking advantage of another. May also refer to legal obligations, such as payment of taxes or support; or to creditor remedies such as garnishment or attachment.

Compulsory process. Process to compel the attendance in court of a person wanted there as a witness or otherwise; including not only the ordinary subpoena, but also a warrant of arrest or attachment if needed. A defendant's right, guaranteed by the federal Constitution, to compel the attendance of witnesses at trial and elicit testimony on behalf of the defense. *See e.g.* Fed.R. Civil P. 45.

The 6th Amend., U.S.Const., provides that the accused shall have the right to "have compulsory process for obtaining witnesses in his favor".

See Bench warrant; Subpoena.

Compulsory removal. A term of art in admiralty law referring to a situation in which a hull has been abandoned by the owner and the hull underwriter, pursuant to government order, must be removed from navigable waters; under those circumstances the protection and indemnity underwriter, absorbing costs which no one else remains liable to pay, must remove the wreck or reimburse the government for removal.

Compulsory sale *or* **purchase.** Term used to characterize the transfer of title to property under the exercise of the power of eminent domain, or by reason of judicial sale for nonpayment of taxes, or the like.

Compulsory self-incrimination. Any form of coercion, physical or psychological, which renders a confession of crime or an admission involuntary, is in violation of the 5th Amend., U.S.Const. and due process clause of 14th Amend. Such practices contravene the very basis of our criminal jurisprudence which is accusatorial not inquisitorial. *See* Confession; Interrogation.

Computation of time. For the purpose of calculating time under the Rules of Civil Procedure, the day of the act or event from which the designated period of time begins to run shall not be included. The last day of the period so computed shall be included, unless it is a Saturday, a Sunday, or a legal holiday, or, when the act to be done is the filing of some paper in court, a day on which weather or other conditions have made the office of the clerk of the district court inaccessible, in which event the period runs until the end of the next day which is not one of the aforementioned days. Fed.R.Civ.P. 6(a); Fed.R.Crim.P. 45.

Computo /kəmpyúwtow/. Lat. To compute, reckon, or account.

Computer fraud. *See* Fraud.

Con. *Adj.* A slang or cant abbreviation for confidence, as a *con* man or a *con* game.

Con. *Prep.* With.

Con-. A prefix meaning with, together.

Conceal. To hide, secrete, or withhold from the knowledge of others. To withhold from utterance or declaration. To cover or keep from sight. To hide or withdraw from observation, or prevent discovery of. *See* Concealment.

See Compounding crime; Harbor; Misprision of felony; Withholding of evidence.

Accessory after the fact. A person who conceals the principal felon or the accessory before the fact is an accessory after the fact if he knows of the felony and of the identity of the felon. See 18 U.S.C.A. § 3. *See also* Accessory.

Concealment. To conceal. A withholding of something which one knows and which one, in duty, is bound to reveal (*e.g.* assets in bankruptcy or divorce proceeding; health condition in insurance application). A "concealment" in law of insurance implies an intention to withhold or secrete information so that the one entitled to be informed will remain in ignorance. *See also* Active concealment; Conceal; Fraudulent concealment.

Concealment may be basis of estoppel. Elements of such estoppel are concealment of material facts with knowledge thereof, ignorance thereof on part of person to whom representations are made, or from whom facts are concealed, intention that such person shall act thereon, and action induced thereby on his part. The doctrine of "estoppel by concealment and suppression" applies only where there has been reduction to practice of invention.

Concentration account. A single centralized account into which funds collected at regional locations (i.e., lock-boxes) are transferred.

Concentration services. Movement of cash from different lock-box locations into a single concentration account from which disbursements and investments are made.

Conception. The beginning of pregnancy. As to human beings, the fecundation of the female ovum by the male spermatozoon resulting in human life capable of survival and maturation under normal conditions. Also, a plan, idea, thought or design.

Conception of invention is formation in mind of inventor of definite and permanent idea of complete and operative invention as it is thereafter to be applied in practice.

Concern. To pertain, relate, or belong to; be of interest or importance to; have connection with; to have reference to; to involve; to affect the interest of.

Concerning, concerned. Relating to; pertaining to; affecting; involving; being substantially engaged in or taking part in.

Concert. A person is deemed to act in concert when he acts with another to bring about some preconceived result. *See* Accomplice; Conspiracy.

Concerted action (*or* **plan**). Action that has been planned, arranged, adjusted, agreed on and settled between parties acting together pursuant to some design or scheme. Mutually contrived or planned activity, as, for example, a joint action by employees, such as a strike or picketing, with the intended purpose of furthering their bargaining demands or other mutual interests. *See* Accomplice; Combination in restraint of trade; Conspiracy; Joint tort-feasors.

Concert of action rule. A rule providing that an agreement by two persons to commit a particular crime cannot be prosecuted as a conspiracy when the crime is of such a nature as to necessarily require participation of two persons for its commission. *See* Wharton Rule.

Concession. A grant, ordinarily applied to the grant of specific privileges by a government; *e.g.*, French and Spanish grants in Louisiana. A voluntary grant, or a yielding to a claim or demand (*e.g.*, when each side in a labor dispute reduces its demands to effect a settlement). A rebate or abatement (*e.g.*, reduced rent for first year as inducement to lease property).

Concessum /kənsésəm/. Accorded; conceded. This term, frequently used in the old reports, signifies that the court admitted or assented to a point or proposition made on the argument.

Conciliation. The adjustment and settlement of a dispute in a friendly, unantagonistic manner. Used in courts before trial with a view towards avoiding trial and in labor disputes before arbitration. *See* Arbitration; Court of Conciliation; Mediation; Pre-trial conference; Settlement.

Concluded. Ended; determined; estopped; prevented from.

Conclusion. The end; the termination; the act of finishing or bringing to a close. The conclusion of a declaration or complaint is all that part which follows the statement of the plaintiff's cause of action. In trial practice, it signifies making the final or concluding address to the jury or the court; *i.e.* the summation; closing argument.

Conclusion against the form of the statute. In common law pleading, the proper form for the conclusion of an indictment for an offense created by statute was the technical phrase "against the form of the statute in such case made and provided"; or, in Latin, *contra formam statuti.*

Conclusion of fact. An inference drawn from the subordinate or evidentiary facts. *See also* Interference.

Conclusion of law. Statement of court as to law applicable on basis of facts found by jury. Finding by court as determined through application of rules of law. The final judgment or decree required on basis of facts found or verdict. Propositions of law which judge arrives at after, and as a result of, finding certain facts in case tried without jury or an advisory jury and as to these he must state them separately in writing. Fed.R. Civil P. 52(a). *See also* Judgment.

Conclusive. Shutting up a matter; shutting out all further evidence; not admitting of explanation or contradiction; putting an end to inquiry; final; irrefutable; decisive. Beyond question or beyond dispute; manifest; plain; clear; obvious; visible; apparent; indubitable; palpable.

As to conclusive proof, *see* Proof.

Conclusive evidence. That which is incontrovertible, either because the law does not permit it to be contradicted, or because it is so strong and convincing as to overbear all proof to the contrary and establish the proposition in question beyond any reasonable doubt. *See* Conclusive presumption; Judicial notice; Presumption; Proof.

Conclusive presumption. Exists when an ultimate fact is presumed to be true upon proof of another fact, and no evidence, no matter how persuasive, can rebut it; an example is the presumption that a child less than a specified age is unable to consent to sexual intercourse. Sometimes referred to as irrebuttable presumption. *See* Presumption.

Concomitant actions. Civil actions which are brought together generally for some type of relief. *See* Joinder.

Concord. An agreement between two persons, one of whom has a right of action against the other, settling what amends shall be made for the breach or wrong. A compromise or an accord.

Concordat. A compact, covenant or convention between two or more independent governments.

An agreement made by a temporal sovereign with the pope, relative to ecclesiastical matters.

Concur. To agree; accord; act together; consent. To agree with the result reached by another, but not necessarily with the reasoning or the logic used in reaching such a result. In the practice of appellate courts, a "concurring opinion" is one filed by one of the judges or justices, in which he agrees with the conclusions or the result of another opinion filed in the case (which may be either the opinion of the court or a dissenting opinion) though he states separately his views of the case or his reasons for so concurring.

In Louisiana law, to join with other claimants in presenting a demand against an insolvent estate.

Concurator /kòŋkyúrətər/. In the civil law, a joint or co-curator, or guardian.

Concurrence. A meeting or coming together; agreement or union in action; meeting of minds; union in design; consent.

Concurrent. Running together; having the same authority; acting in conjunction; agreeing in the same act or opinion; pursuit of same course; contributing to the same event; contemporaneous. Co-operating, accompanying, conjoined, associated, concomitant, joint and equal, existing together, and operating on the same subject. United in agreement.

As to *concurrent* Covenant; Insurance; Lease; Resolution; and Writ, see those titles.

Concurrent causes. Causes acting contemporaneously and together causing injury, which would not have resulted in absence of either. Two distinct causes operating at the same time to produce a given result, which might be produced by either, are "concurrent causes"; but two distinct causes, successive and unrelated in an operation, cannot be concurring, and one will be regarded as the proximate and efficient and responsible cause, and the other will be regarded as the remote cause. *See also* Cause.

Concurrent conditions. Conditions which must occur or be performed at the same time; they are mutually dependent. No obligations arise until these conditions are simultaneously performed. When each party to a transaction is subject to mutual conditions precedent, these are concurrent conditions. *See also* Conditions concurrent.

Concurrent estates. Ownership or possession of property by two or more persons at the same time; *e.g.* joint tenancy, tenancy in common.

Concurrent interests. *See* Concurrent estates.

Concurrent jurisdiction. The jurisdiction of several different tribunals, each authorized to deal with the same subject-matter at the choice of the suitor. Authority shared by two or more legislative, judicial, or administrative officers or bodies to deal with the same subject matter. Jurisdiction exercised by different courts, at same time, over same subject matter, and within same territory, and wherein litigants may, in first instance, resort to either court indifferently. For example, some cases can be heard in a federal or state court. When a case can only be tried in federal court, or only in state court, jurisdiction is "exclusive."

Concurrent liens. Two or more liens or possessory rights in the nature of liens on the same property and possessing the same priority.

Concurrent negligence. Consists of the negligence of two or more persons concurring, not necessarily in point of time, but in point of consequence, in producing a single indivisible injury. *See also* Comparative negligence; Concurrent tortfeasors; Contributory negligence.

Concurrent power. The power of either Congress or the State legislatures, each acting independently of the other, to make laws on the same subject matter.

Concurrent sentences. Two or more terms of imprisonment, all or part of each term of which is served simultaneously and the prisoner is entitled to discharge at the expiration of the longest term specified. The existence of one valid conviction may make unnecessary review of other convictions when concurrent sentences have been given.

Concurrent tortfeasors. Those whose independent, negligent acts combined or concurred at one point in time to injure a third party. *See also* Comparative negligence; Concurrent negligence.

Concurring opinion. A separate opinion delivered by one or more judges which agrees with the decision of the majority of the court but offering own reasons for reaching that decision. *See also* Concur.

Concussion. In the civil law, the unlawful forcing of another by threats of violence to give something of value. It differs from robbery, in this: That in robbery the thing is taken by force, while in concussion it is obtained by threatened violence.

Loss or alteration of consciousness from a direct, closed head injury.

Condemn. To adjudge or sentence. To find or adjudge guilty; especially with reference to pronouncement of sentence of death for capital offense. To declare a building, ship, or the like, unfit for habitation, use or occupation. To adjudge (as an admiralty court) that a vessel is a prize, or that she is unfit for service. To set apart or expropriate property for public use, in the exercise of the power of eminent domain. *See also* Condemnation.

Condemnation /kòndəmnéyshən/. Process of taking private property for public use through the power of eminent domain. "Just compensation" must be paid to owner for taking of such (5th Amend., U.S. Constitution). *See also* Constructive taking; Damages; Eminent domain; Expropriation; Just compensation; Public use; Similar sales; Taking.

Admiralty law. The judgment or sentence of a court having jurisdiction and acting *in rem,* by which: (1) it is declared that a vessel which has been captured at sea as a prize was lawfully so seized and is liable to be treated as prize; or (2) that property which has been seized for an alleged violation of the revenue laws, neutrality laws, navigation laws, etc., was lawfully so seized, and is, for such cause, forfeited to the government; or (3) that the vessel which is the subject of inquiry is unfit and unsafe for navigation.

Civil law. A sentence or judgment which condemns some one to do, to give, or to pay something, or which declares that his claim or pretensions are unfounded.

Excess condemnation. Taking of property not strictly needed for a public use, or taking of more property than is needed for a public use.

Inverse condemnation. Condemnation of property near a parcel so as to cause the parcel to lose much of its value. In such a case the parcel is, in effect, constructively condemned, and just compensation must be paid to the owner, even though formal eminent domain proceedings were not actually taken against that particular parcel.

Quick condemnation. Under this procedure the municipality takes immediate possession of owner's property with estimated just compensation placed in escrow until actual compensation has been ascertained.

Condemnation money. Former term for damages which the party failing in an action was adjudged or *condemned* to pay; sometimes simply called the "condemnation."

Condemnee. Owner of property taken by condemnation.

Condemner. Party taking property by condemnation.

Condition. A future and uncertain event upon the happening of which is made to depend the existence of an obligation, or that which subordinates the existence of liability under a contract to a certain future event. Provision making effect of legal instrument contingent upon an uncertain event. *See also* Constructive condition; Contingency; Contingent; Proviso.

A clause in a contract or agreement which has for its object to suspend, rescind, or modify the principal obligation, or, in case of a will, to suspend, revoke, or modify the devise or bequest. A qualification, restriction, or limitation modifying or destroying the original act with which it is connected; an event, fact, or the like that is necessary to the occurrence of some other, though not its cause; a prerequisite; a stipulation.

A qualification or restriction annexed to a conveyance of lands, whereby it is provided that in case a particular event does or does not happen, or in case the grantor or grantee does or omits to do a particular act, an estate shall commence, be enlarged, or be defeated.

An "estate on condition" arises where an estate is granted, either in fee simple or otherwise, with an express qualification annexed, whereby the estate granted shall either commence, be enlarged, or be defeated, upon performance or breach of such qualification or condition.

In insurance parlance, the printed conditions on the inside of the policy which serve generally as a limitation of risk or of liability or impose various conditions requiring compliance by the insured.

Mode or state of being; state or situation; essential quality; property; attribute; status or rank.

Classification. Conditions are either *express* or *implied,* the former when incorporated in express terms in the deed, contract, lease, or grant; the latter, when inferred or presumed by law, from the nature of the transaction or the conduct of the parties, to have been tacitly understood between them as a part of the agreement, though not expressly mentioned.

They are *possible* or *impossible*: the former when they admit of performance in the ordinary course of events; the latter when it is contrary to the course of nature or human limitations that they should ever be performed.

They are *lawful* or *unlawful*: the former when their character is not in violation of any rule, principle, or policy of law; the latter when they are such as the law will not allow to be made.

They are *consistent* or *repugnant*: the former when they are in harmony and concord with the other parts of the transaction; the latter when they contradict, annul, or neutralize the main purpose of the "contract". Repugnant conditions are also called "insensible".

They are *affirmative* or *negative*: the former being a condition which consists in doing a thing, as provided that the lessee shall pay rent, etc.; the latter being a condition that consists in not doing a thing, as provided that the lessee shall not alien, etc.

They are *precedent* or *subsequent.* A condition *precedent* is one which must happen or be performed before the estate to which it is annexed can vest or be enlarged; or it is one which is to be performed before some right dependent thereon accrues, or some act dependent thereon is performed. A fact other than mere lapse of time which must exist or occur before a duty of immediate performance of a promise arises. A condition *subsequent* is one annexed to an estate already vested, by the performance of which such estate is kept and continued, and by the failure or non-performance of which it is defeated; or it is a condition referring to a future event, upon the happening of which the obligation becomes no longer binding upon the other party, if he chooses to avail himself of the condition. A condition *subsequent* is any condition which divests liability which has already attached on the failure to fulfill the condition as applied in contracts, a provision giving one party the right to divest himself of liability and obligation to perform further if the other party fails to meet condition, *e.g.*, submit dispute to arbitration. In property law, a condition which causes defeasance of estate on failure to perform, *e.g.* fee simple on condition. In lease, a provision giving lessor right to terminate for tenant's failure to perform condition.

Conditions may also be *positive* (requiring that a specified event shall happen or an act be done) and *restrictive* or *negative*, the latter being such as impose an obligation not to do a particular thing, as, that a lessee shall not alien or sub-let or commit waste, or the like.

They may be *single, copulative,* or *disjunctive.* Those of the first kind require the performance of one specified thing only; those of the second kind require the performance of divers acts or things; those of the third kind require the performance of one of several things.

Conditions may also be *independent, dependent,* or *mutual.* They belong to the first class when each of the two conditions must be performed without any reference to the other; to the second class when the performance of one condition is not obligatory until the actual performance of the other; and to the third class when neither party need perform his condition unless the other is ready and willing to perform his, or, in other words, when the mutual covenants go to the whole consideration on both sides and each is precedent to the other.

Conditions may as well be *implied-in-law* or *implied-in-fact.* The former is a condition for performance that exists because of a law or laws; the latter exists because of the contract's nature.

The following varieties may also be noted: A condition *collateral* is one requiring the performance of a collateral act having no necessary relation to the main subject of the agreement. A *compulsory* condition is one which expressly requires a thing to be done, as, that a lessee shall pay a specified sum of money on a certain day or his lease shall be void. *Concurrent* conditions are those which are mutually dependent and are to be performed at the same time or simultaneously. A condition *inherent* is one annexed to the rent reserved out of the land whereof the estate is made, or rather, to the estate in the land, in respect of rent.

Synonymous distinguished. A "condition" is to be distinguished from a *limitation,* in that the latter may be to or for the benefit of a stranger, who may then take advantage of its determination, while only the grantor, or those who stand in his place, can take advantage of a condition. Also, a limitation ends the estate without entry or claim, which is not true of a condition. It also differs from a *conditional limitation.* In determining

whether, in the case of estates greater than estates for years, the language constitutes a "condition" or a "conditional limitation," the rule applied is that, where an estate is so expressly limited by the words of its creation that it cannot endure for any longer time than until the condition happens on which the estate is to fail, this is limitation, but when the estate is expressly granted on condition in deed, the law permits it to endure beyond the time of the contingency happening, unless the grantor takes advantage of the breach of condition, by making entry. It differs also from a *covenant,* which can be made by either grantor or grantee, while only the grantor can make a condition. The chief distinction between a condition subsequent in a deed and a covenant pertains to the remedy in event of breach, which, in the former case, subjects the estate to a forfeiture, and in the latter is merely a ground for recovery of damages. A *charge* is a devise of land with a bequest out of the subject-matter, and a charge upon the devisee personally, in respect of the estate devised, gives him an estate on condition. A condition also differs from a *remainder;* for, while the former may operate to defeat the estate before its natural termination, the latter cannot take effect until the completion of the preceding estate.

Conditional. That which is dependent upon or granted subject to a condition.

As to *conditional* Acceptance; Appearance; Bequest; Contract; Delivery; Devise; Fee; Guaranty; Indorsement; Judgment; Legacy; Limitation; Obligation; Pardon; Privilege; Use; and Zoning, see those titles.

Conditional assault. A threatening gesture with words accompanying it expressing a threat on condition, *e.g.* "your money or your life".

Conditional creditor. In the civil law, a creditor having a future right of action, or having a right of action in expectancy.

Conditional guarantor. Party who guarantees a debtor's payment of debt but only after creditor has exhausted all opportunities for collection.

Conditional indorsement. *See* Indorsement.

Conditional intent. Intent to do or not to do something if some condition exists.

Conditionally privileged communication. One made in good faith on any subject matter in which the person publishing has an interest, or in reference to which he has a duty, if made to a person having a corresponding interest or duty, even though it contains matter which otherwise would be actionable. The essential elements of a conditionally privileged communication are good faith, an interest to be upheld, a statement limited in its scope to such purpose, a proper occasion, and publication in a proper manner to proper persons.

Conditional payment. Payment of an obligation only on condition that something be done. Generally, right is reserved to demand back payment if condition fails.

Conditional promise. In law of contracts, a promise to perform based on condition; held to be valid consideration even if condition fails.

Conditional release. A discharge of obligation based on some condition, the failure of which defeats the release. Term may also be applied to a substituted form of release from custody subject to applicable statutes and rules and regulations of board of parole.

Conditional right. Right to something subject to a condition, *e.g.* parent has right to chastise child on condition that the punishment is reasonable.

Conditional sale contract. Form of sales contract in which seller reserves title until buyer pays for goods or land, at which time, the condition having been fulfilled, title passes to buyer. Such contract under Uniform Commercial Code is a purchase money security agreement. § 9–105(h). *See also* Sale.

Conditional sentence. A sentence to confinement if defendant fails to fulfill conditions of probation.

Conditional will. A will so drawn that it takes effect only on happening of specified contingency which becomes a condition precedent to operation of will.

Condition of employment. Qualification required for a particular job; circumstances under which employment may be secured and maintained. *See also* Probation.

Conditions concurrent. In contract law, conditions which must be performed by each party simultaneously; *e.g.* in a cash sale, payment for the goods and delivery are conditions concurrent. *See also* Concurrent conditions.

Conditions subsequent. Conditions that discharge the duty to perform once they arise; *e.g.* statutes of limitations in contracts.

Conditions of sale. The terms upon which sales are made at auction; usually written or printed and exposed in the auction room at the time of sale.

Condominium /kòndəmíniyəm/. System of separate ownership of individual units in multiple-unit building. A single real property parcel with all the unit owners having a right in common to use the common elements with separate ownership confined to the individual units which are serially designated. An estate in real property consisting of an undivided interest in a portion of a parcel of real property together with a separate fee simple interest in another portion of the same parcel, in essence, condominium ownership is a merger of two estates in land into one: the fee simple ownership of apartment or unit in a condominium project and tenancy in common with other co-owners in the common elements.

The condominium concept was not rooted in English common law and most condominiums in the United States are formed in accordance with specific state enabling statutes. As defined by Uniform Condominium Act (§ 1–103(7)), is: "Real estate, portions of which are designated for separate ownership and the remainder of which is designated for common ownership solely by the owners of those portions. Real estate is not a condominium unless the undivided interests in the common element are vested in the unit owners."

See also Common elements.

Compare Cooperative.

Condonation /kòndənéyshən/. The conditional remission or forgiveness, by means of continuance or resumption of marital cohabitation, by one of the married parties, of a known matrimonial offense committed by the other, that would constitute a cause of divorce; the condition being that the offense shall not be repeated. Condonation to constitute valid defense in divorce action, must be free, voluntary, and not induced by duress or fraud. Condonation means pardon of offense, voluntary overlooking implied forgiveness by treating offender as if offense had not been committed. This defense has been abolished in those jurisdictions which recognize "no fault" divorce.

Condone /kəndówn/. To make condonation of.

Conduce. To contribute to as a result.

Conduct, *v.* To manage; direct; lead; have direction; carry on; regulate; do business.

Conduct, *n.* Personal behavior; deportment; mode of action; any positive or negative act.

An action or omission and its accompanying state of mind, or, where relevant, a series of acts and omissions. Model Penal Code, § 1.13.

See also Disorderly conduct; Tortious.

Conduct, estoppel by. *See* Equitable estoppel.

Conduit concept. An approach the tax law assumes in the tax treatment of certain entities and their owners. The approach permits specified tax characteristics to pass through the entity without losing their identity. Under the conduit concept, for example, long-term capital losses realized by a partnership are passed through as such to the individual partners. The same result does not materialize if the entity is a corporation. Varying forms of the conduit concept are applicable in the case of partnerships, trusts, estates, and Subchapter S corporations.

Confederacy. The association or banding together of two or more persons for the purpose of committing an act or furthering an enterprise which is forbidden by law, or which, though lawful in itself, becomes unlawful when made the object of the confederacy. More commonly called a "conspiracy."

A league or agreement between two or more independent states whereby they unite for their mutual welfare and the furtherance of their common aims. The term may apply to a union so formed for a temporary or limited purpose, as in the case of an offensive and defensive alliance; but it is more commonly used to denote that species of political connection between two or more independent states by which a central government is created, invested with certain powers of sovereignty (mostly external), and acting upon the several component states as its units, which, however, retain their sovereign powers for domestic purposes and some others. See Compact; Federal government.

Confederation. A league or compact for mutual support, particularly of nations, or states. Such was the colonial government during the Revolution. See Confederacy.

Confederation articles. See Articles of Confederation.

Conference. A meeting of several persons for deliberation, for the interchange of opinion, or for the removal of differences or disputes.

In the practice of legislative bodies, when the two houses cannot agree upon a pending measure, each appoints a committee of "conference," and the committees meet and consult together for the purpose of removing differences, harmonizing conflicting views, and arranging a compromise which will be accepted by both houses.

Representative assembly of a denomination; association of athletic teams.

A personal meeting between the diplomatic agents of two or more nations for the purpose of making statements and explanations that will obviate the delay and difficulty attending the more formal conduct of negotiations.

Confess. To admit as true; to assent to; to concede. To admit the truth of a charge or accusation. Usually spoken of charges of tortious or criminal conduct. See Confession.

Confessing error. A plea to an assignment of error, admitting the same.

Confession. A voluntary statement made by a person charged with the commission of a crime or misdemeanor, communicated to another person, wherein he acknowledges himself to be guilty of the offense charged, and discloses the circumstances of the act or the share and participation which he had in it. See 18 U.S.C.A. § 3501.

A statement made by a defendant disclosing his guilt of crime with which he is charged and ex-

cluding possibility of a reasonable inference to the contrary. Voluntary statement made by one who is defendant in criminal trial at time when he is not testifying in trial and by which he acknowledges certain conduct of his own constituting crime for which he is on trial; a statement which, if true, discloses his guilt of that crime.

Confessions are admissible in evidence if given voluntarily. 18 U.S.C.A. § 3501.

See also Interlocking confession; Interrogation; Involuntary confession; Oral confession.

Constitutional protections. See Escobedo Rule; Mallory Rule; Miranda Rule.

Classification of confessions. Confessions are divided into judicial and extrajudicial. The former are such as are made before a magistrate or court in the due course of legal proceedings; they include confessions made in preliminary examinations before magistrates. The latter is one made by the party out of court, or to any person, official or otherwise, when made not in the course of a judicial examination or investigation. See also Extrajudicial.

An *implied* confession is where the defendant does not plead guilty but indirectly admits his guilt by placing himself at the mercy of the court and asking for a light sentence. An *indirect* confession is one inferred from the conduct of the defendant. An *involuntary* confession is one induced by hope, promise, fear, violence, torture, or threat. A *naked* confession is an admission of the guilt of the party, but which is not supported by any evidence of the commission of the crime. A *voluntary* confession is one made spontaneously by a person accused of crime, free from the influence of any extraneous disturbing cause, and in particular, not influenced, or extorted by violence, threats, or promises. It is the product of an essentially free and unconstrained choice by its maker; and, is made with full knowledge of nature and consequences of the confession. For criteria used in determining voluntariness, see 18 U.S.C.A. § 3501(b).

A *judicial confession* is a plea of guilty or some similar action or conduct in court or in a judicial proceeding.

Distinguished from admission. A confession is a statement admitting or acknowledging all facts necessary for conviction of the crime. An admission, on the other hand, is an acknowledgment of a fact or facts tending to prove guilt which falls short of an acknowledgment of all essential elements of the crime.

Confession and avoidance. A plea in confession and avoidance is one which avows and confesses the truth of the averments of fact in the complaint or declaration, either expressly or by implication, but then proceeds to allege new matter which tends to deprive the facts admitted of their ordinary legal effect, or to obviate, neutralize, or *avoid* them.

Confession of judgment. *See* Cognovit judgment; Judgment.

Confessor. A priest who receives auricular confessions of sins from persons under his spiritual charge, and pronounces absolution upon them. The secrets of the confessional were not privileged communications at common law, but are so classified by statute, court decision or court rule in most states. *See* Confidential communication.

Confide. A synonym of the word "trust"; meaning to put into one's trust, keeping, or confidence.

Confidence. Trust; reliance; relation of trust. Reliance on discretion of another. In the construction of wills, this word is considered peculiarly appropriate to create a trust.

Confidence game. Obtaining of money or property by means of some trick, device, or swindling operation in which advantage is taken of the confidence which the victim reposes in the swindler. The elements of the crime of "confidence game" are: (1) an intentional false representation to the victim as to some present fact, (2) knowing it to be false, (3) with intent that the victim rely on the representation, (4) the representation being made to obtain the victim's confidence and thereafter his money and property, (5) which confidence is then abused by defendant.

For distinction between false pretenses and confidence game, *see* False pretenses. *See also* Flimflam.

Confidential. Intrusted with the confidence of another or with his secret affairs or purposes; intended to be held in confidence or kept secret; done in confidence.

Confidential communication. Privileged communications such as those between spouses, physician-patient, attorney-client, confessor-penitent, etc. Such are privileged at the option of the spouse-witness, client-witness and penitent-witness. Confidential communication is statement made under circumstances showing that speaker intended statement only for ears of person addressed; thus if communication is made in presence of third party whose presence is not reasonably necessary for the communication, it is not privileged. State law is applied to such privileged communications in federal court proceedings. Fed.Evid.Rule 501. *See also* Communication; Privileged communications.

Confidentiality. State or quality of being confidential; treated as private and not for publication.

Confidential relation. A fiduciary relation. It is a peculiar relation which exists between client and attorney, principal and agent, principal and surety, landlord and tenant, parent and child, guardian and ward, ancestor and heir, husband and wife, trustee and *cestui que trust,* executors or administrators and creditors, legatees, or distributees, appointor and appointee under powers, and partners and part owners. In these and like cases, the law, in order to prevent undue advantage from the unlimited confidence or sense of duty which the relation naturally creates, requires the utmost degree of good faith in all transactions between the parties. It is not confined to any specific association of parties. It appears when the circumstances make it certain that the parties do not deal on equal terms, but on the one side there is an overmastering influence, or, on the other, weakness, dependence, or trust, justifiably reposed. The mere existence of kinship does not, of itself, give rise to such relation. It covers every form of relation between parties wherein confidence is reposed by one in another, and former relies and acts upon representations of the other and is guilty of no derelictions on his own part. *See also* Fiduciary or confidential relation.

Confinement. State of being confined; shut in; imprisoned; detention in penal institution. Confinement may be by either a moral or a physical restraint, by threats of violence with a present force, or by physical restraint of the person. *See also* Commitment; Solitary confinement.

Confirm. To complete or establish that which was imperfect or uncertain; to ratify what has been done without authority or insufficiently. To make firm or certain; to give new assurance of truth or certainty; to put aside past doubt; to give approval to. *See also* Confirmation.

Confirmation. A contract, or written memorandum thereof, by which that which was infirm, difficult of proof, void, imperfect, or subject to be avoided is ratified, rendered valid and binding, made firm and unavoidable. To give formal approval. Act or process of confirming. *See also* Approval; Ratification; Verification.

A conveyance of an estate or right *in esse,* whereby a voidable estate is made sure and unavoidable, or whereby a particular estate is increased.

The ratification or approval of executive acts by a legislature or one house. In order to be valid, Presidential appointments of important officers of the United States require approval by a majority of the Senate, and treatises must be approved by two-thirds of the Senate. Art. II, § 2, U.S.Const.

A formal memorandum delivered by the customers or suppliers of a company to its independent auditor verifying the amounts shown as receivable or payable. The confirmation document is originally sent by the auditor to the customer.

In bankruptcy, refers to a judicial approval of a Bankruptcy Code Chapter 11, 12, or 13 plan.

Confirmation of sale. The confirmation of a judicial sale by the court which ordered it is a signification in some way (usually by the entry of an order) or the court's approval of the terms, price, and conditions of the sale.

Confirmed credit. In commercial law, means that the credit must carry the direct obligation of an agency which does business in the seller's financial market. U.C.C. § 2–325.

Confirmee /kònfərmíy/. The grantee in a deed of confirmation.

Confirming bank. A bank which engages either that it will itself honor a credit already issued by another bank or that such a credit will be honored by the issuer or a third bank. U.C.C. § 5–103.

Confirmor /kənfírmər/. The grantor in a deed of confirmation.

Confiscate /kónfəskeyt/. To appropriate property to the use of the government. To adjudge property to be forfeited to the public; to seize and condemn private forfeited property to public use. To take property from enemy in time of war. *See also* Confiscation; Forfeiture.

Confiscation /kònfəskéyshən/. Act of confiscating. The seizure of private property by the government without· compensation to the owner, often as a consequence of conviction for crime, or because possession or use of the property was contrary to law. The provisions of due process prohibit the confiscation of property without compensation except where the property is taken in the valid execution of the police power. *See also* Condemnation; Confiscate; Eminent domain; Expropriation; Forfeiture; Seizure.

Confiscatory rates. With respect to utilities, are rates which do not afford a reasonable return on value of property at time it is used in public service; rates which do not afford net return sufficient to preserve utility's property and to attract capital necessary to enable utility to discharge its public duties.

Conflicting evidence. Evidence offered by plaintiff and defendant, or prosecutor and defendant which is inconsistent and cannot be reconciled.

Conflict of authority. A division between two or more courts (generally courts of last resort) on some legal principal or application of law. May also refer to disparity between authorities on a subject. *See also* Choice of law; Conflict of laws.

Conflict of interest. Term used in connection with public officials and fiduciaries and their relationship to matters of private interest or gain to them. Ethical problems connected therewith are covered by statutes in most jurisdictions and by federal statutes on the federal level. The Code of Professional Responsibility and Model Rules of Professional Conduct set forth standards for actual or potential conflicts of interest between attorney and client. Generally, when used to suggest disqualification of a public official from performing his sworn duty, term "conflict of interest" refers to a clash between public interest and the private pecuniary interest of the individual concerned. A situation in which regard for one duty tends to lead to disregard of another.

A conflict of interest arises when a government employee's personal or financial interest conflicts or appears to conflict with his official responsibility. 18 U.S.C.A. § 203 et seq.

Conflict of laws. Inconsistency or difference between the laws of different states or countries, arising in the case of persons who have acquired rights, incurred obligations, injuries or damages, or made contracts, within the territory of two or more jurisdictions. Hence, that branch of jurisprudence, arising from the diversity of the laws of different nations, states or jurisdictions, in their application to rights and remedies, which reconciles the inconsistency, or decides which law or system is to govern in the particular case, or settles the degree of force to be accorded to the law of another jurisdiction, (the acts or rights in question having arisen under it) either where it varies from the domestic law, or where the domestic law is silent or not exclusively applicable to the case in point. Restatement, Second, Conflicts of Law, § 2. *See also* Center of gravity doctrine; Choice of law; Grouping of contacts; Kilberg doctrine; Lex contractus; Lex fori; Lex loci; Lex loci contractus; Renvoi doctrine.

Conformed copy. An exact copy of a document on which has been written explanations of things that could not or were not copied; *e.g.* written signature might be replaced on conformed copy with notation that it was signed by the person whose signature appears on the original.

Conforming. In law of sales, goods or conduct including any part of a performance are conforming or conform to the contract when they are in accordance with the obligations under the contract. U.C.C. § 2–106(2).

Conforming use. In zoning and land use planning, a use of a structure which is in conformity with those uses permitted by the particular zoning classification of the area. *Compare* Nonconforming use.

Conformity. Correspondence in form, manner, or use; agreement; harmony; congruity.

Conformity, Bill of. *See* Bill *(Equity pleading and practice).*

Conformity hearing. Hearing ordered by court to determine whether judgment or decree directed to be prepared by the prevailing party conforms with decision of court. Commonly after court makes its findings it directs prevailing party to draw judgment or decree in conformity with such findings and decision.

Confrontation. In criminal proceedings, the accused has a right to be "confronted with the witnesses against him." This Sixth Amendment right consists of the act of setting a witness face to face with the accused, in order that the latter may make any objection he has to the witness, or that the witness may identify the accused; and, does not mean merely that witnesses are to be made visible to the accused, but imports the constitutional privilege to cross-examine them. In fact, the essence of the right of confrontation is the right to cross-examination. A disruptive defendant may, however, lose his right to be present in the courtroom, and, as a result, lose his right to confront witnesses.

Confrontation clause. *See* Confrontation.

Confusion. This term, as used in the civil law and in compound terms derived from that source, means a blending or intermingling, and is equivalent to the term "merger" as used at common law. To mix or blend so that things cannot be distinguished. The mixing together of fungible goods of two or more owners so that the independent goods cannot be identified. *See also* Commingle.

Confusion of boundaries. The title of that branch of equity jurisdiction which relates to the discovery and settlement of conflicting, disputed, or uncertain boundaries.

Confusion of debts. An obsolete term which refers to a mode of extinguishing a debt, by the concurrence in the same person of two qualities or adverse rights to the same thing which mutually destroy each other. This may occur in several ways, as where the creditor becomes the heir of the debtor, or the debtor the heir of the creditor, or either accedes to the title of the other by any other mode of transfer.

Confusion of goods. Results when goods belonging to two or more owners become intermixed to the point where the property of any of them no longer can be identified except as part of a mass of like goods. *See also* Commingle.

Confusion of rights. A union of the qualities of debtor and creditor in the same person. The effect of such a union is, generally, to extinguish the debt.

Confusion of titles. A civil-law expression, synonymous with "merger," as used in the common law, applying where two titles to the same property unite in the same person.

Con game. A swindle or any arrangement in which a person is deliberately defrauded because of his trust in the one who is swindling. *See also* Confidence game; Flim-flam.

Conglomerate /kənglómərət/. A corporation that has diversified its operations usually by acquiring unrelated enterprises in widely varied industries. Such individual businesses are normally controlled by a single corporate entity.

Conglomerate merger. Merger among firms which operate in separate and distinct markets; *e.g.* merger of companies with different product lines. A merger in which there are no economic relationships between the acquiring and the acquired firm. A combination of two or more companies in which neither competes directly with the other and no buyer-seller relationship exists. A merger other than a horizontal or vertical merger. *See also* Conglomerate; Merger.

Congregate. To come together; to assemble; to meet.

Congregation. An assembly or gathering; specifically, an assembly or society of persons who together constitute the principal supporters of a particular parish, or habitually meet at the same church for religious exercises.

Congress /kóngrəs/. Formal meeting of delegates or representatives. The Congress of the United States was created by Article I, Section 1, of the Constitution, adopted by the Constitutional Convention on September 17, 1787, providing that "All legislative Powers herein granted shall be vested in a Congress of the United States, which shall consist of a Senate and House of Representatives." The first Congress under the Constitution met on March 4, 1789, in the Federal Hall in New York City. The membership then consisted of 20 Senators and 59 Representatives. *See* House of Representatives; Senate.

Congressional apportionment. *See* Apportionment *(Representatives)*.

Congressional committee. A committee of the House of Representatives or of the Senate or a joint committee formed for some particular public purpose.

Congressional district. A geographical unit of a State from which one member of the House of Representatives is elected.

Congressional immunity. *See* Legislative immunity.

Congressional powers. The authority vested in the Senate and House of Representatives to enact laws, etc. as provided in U.S.Const., Art. I.

Congressional Record. Proceedings of Congress are published in the *Congressional Record*, which is issued daily when Congress is in session. Publication of the *Record* began March 4, 1873; it was the first series officially reported, printed, and published directly by the Federal Government. The Daily Digest of the *Congressional Record*, printed in the back of each issue of the *Record*, summarizes the proceedings of that day in each House, and before each of their committees and subcommittees, respectively. The Digest also presents the legislative program for each day, and at the end of the week, gives the program for the following week. Its publication was begun March 17, 1947. Members of Congress are allowed to edit their speeches before printing and may insert material never actually spoken by securing from their respective houses leave to print or to extend their remarks.

Congressman. Strictly, a member of the Congress of the United States. But the common tendency is to apply this term only to a member of the House of Representatives, as distinguished from a senator.

Conjecture. A slight degree of credence, arising from evidence too weak or too remote to cause belief. Supposition or surmise. The idea of a fact, suggested by another fact; as a possible cause, concomitant, or result. An idea or notion founded on a probability without any demonstration of its truth; an idea or surmise inducing a slight degree of belief founded upon some possible, or perhaps probable fact of which there is no positive evidence. An explanation consistent with but not deducible as a reasonable inference from known facts or conditions. In popular use, synonymous with "guess." Also, the bringing together of the circumstances, as well as the result obtained.

Conjugal /kónjəgəl/. Of or belonging to marriage or the married state; suitable or appropriate to the married state or to married persons; matrimonial; connubial.

Conjugal rights. Matrimonial rights; the right which husband and wife have to each other's society, comfort, and affection. *See* Consortium.

Conjunctive denial. Where several material facts are stated conjunctively in the complaint, an answer which undertakes to deny their averments as a whole, conjunctively stated, is called a "conjunctive denial."

Connecting factors. In conflict of laws, legal categories such as the place of making a contract which serve to determine the choice of law in a particular case.

Connecting up doctrine. A thing may be put into evidence (including testimony) subject to its being connected up with later evidence that will show its relevance.

Connivance /kənáyvəns/. The secret or indirect consent or permission of one person to the commission of an unlawful or criminal act by another.

A winking at; voluntary blindness; an intentional failure to discover or prevent the wrong; forbearance or passive consent.

As constituting defense in divorce action, is plaintiff's corrupt consent, express or implied, to offense charged against defendant. This defense has been abolished by many states with the enactment of no-fault divorce laws.

Connive /kənáyv/. To co-operate secretly with, or to have a secret or clandestine understanding with. To take part or co-operate privily with another, to aid or abet. To look upon with secret favor; it implies both knowledge and assent, either active or passive. *See* Connivance.

Consanguineus /kònsəŋgwíniyəs/. Lat. A person related by blood; a person descended from the same common stock.

Consanguinity /kònsæŋgwínətiy/. Kinship; blood relationship; the connection or relation of persons descended from the same stock or common ancestor. Consanguinity is distinguished from "affinity," which is the connection existing in consequence of a marriage, between each of the married persons and the kindred of the other.

Lineal and collateral consanguinity. Lineal consanguinity is that which subsists between persons of whom one is descended in a direct line from the other, as between son, father, grandfather, great-grandfather, and so upwards in the direct ascending line; or between son, grandson, great-grandson, and so downwards in the direct descending line. Collateral consanguinity is that which subsists between persons who have the same ancestors, but who do not descend (or ascend) one from the other. Thus, father and son are related by lineal consanguinity, uncle and nephew by collateral sanguinity.

Conscience. The moral sense; the faculty of judging the moral qualities of actions, or of discriminating between right and wrong; particularly applied to one's perception and judgment of the moral qualities of his own conduct, but in a wider sense, denoting a similar application of the standards of morality to the acts of others. The sense of right and wrong inherent in every person by virtue of his existence as a social entity; good conscience being a synonym of equity. In law, especially the moral rule which requires probity, justice, and honest dealing between man and man, as when we say that a bargain is "against conscience" or "unconscionable," or that the price paid for property at a forced sale was so inadequate as to "shock the conscience." This is also the meaning of the term as applied to the jurisdiction and principles of decision of courts of chancery, as in saying that such a court is a "court of conscience," that it proceeds "according to conscience," or that it has cognizance of "matters of conscience."

Conscience, right of. As used in some constitutional provisions, this phrase is equivalent to religious liberty or freedom of conscience.

Conscientious objector. One who, by reason of religious training and belief, is conscientiously opposed to participation in war. Such person need not be a member of a religious sect whose creed forbids participation in war to be entitled to classification as a conscientious objector. It is sufficient if such person has a conscientious scruple against war in any form. Such objection must however be shown to be sincere. In lieu of active military service, such person is subject to civilian work contributing to the national health, safety or interest. 50 U.S.C.A. App. § 456(J).

Conscription. Compulsory enrollment and induction into military service; drafted.

Consecutive sentences. When one sentence of confinement is to follow another in point of time, the second sentence is deemed to be consecutive. May also be applied to suspended sentences. *Also* called "from and after" sentences. *See also* Sentence.

Consensual contract /kənsénshuwəl kóntrækt/. A term derived from the civil law, denoting a contract founded upon and completed by the mere consent of the contracting parties, without any external formality or symbolic act to fix the obligation. *See also* Contract.

Consensual marriage /kənsénshuwəl mǽrəj/. Marriage resting simply on consent per verba de præsenti, between competent parties. *See also* Common-law marriage.

Consent. A concurrence of wills. Voluntarily yielding the will to the proposition of another; acquiescence or compliance therewith. Agreement; approval; permission; the act or result of coming into harmony or accord. Consent is an act of reason, accompanied with deliberation, the mind weighing as in a balance the good or evil on each side. It means voluntary agreement by a person in the possession and exercise of sufficient mental capacity to make an intelligent choice to do something proposed by another. It supposes a physical power to act, a moral power of acting, and a serious, determined, and free use of these powers. Consent is implied in every agreement. It is an act unclouded by fraud, duress, or sometimes even mistake.

Willingness in fact that an act or an invasion of an interest shall take place. Restatement, Second, Torts, § 10A.

As used in the law of rape "consent" means consent of the will, and submission under the influence of fear or terror cannot amount to real consent. There must be an exercise of intelligence based on knowledge of its significance and moral quality and there must be a choice between resistance and assent. And if woman resists to the point where further resistance would be useless or until her resistance is overcome by force or violence, submission thereafter is not "consent".

See also Acquiescence; Age of consent; Assent; Connivance; Informed consent.

Consent decree. See Decree.

Consent dividends. See Dividend.

Consent judgment. See Judgment.

Express consent. That directly given, either *viva voce* or in writing. It is positive, direct, unequivocal consent, requiring no inference or implication to supply its meaning.

Express or implied consent. Under motor vehicle liability insurance law providing that policy should cover any person responsible for operation of insured vehicle with insured's express or implied consent, words "express or implied consent" primarily modify not the word "operation", but the word "responsible", and imply possession of vehicle with consent of owner and responsibility to him.

Implied consent. That manifested by signs, actions, or facts, or by inaction or silence, which raise a presumption or inference that the consent has been given. An inference arising from a course of conduct or relationship between the parties, in which there is mutual acquiescence or a lack of objection under circumstances signifying assent. For example, when a corporation does business in a state it impliedly consents to be subject to the jurisdiction of that state's courts in the event of tortious conduct, even though it is not incorporated in that state.

Most every state has a statute implying the consent of one who drives upon its highways to submit to some type of scientific test or tests measuring the alcoholic content of the driver's blood. In addition to implying consent, these statutes usually provide that if the result of the test shows that the alcohol content exceeds a specified percentage, then a rebuttable presumption of intoxication arises.

Consent judgment. *See* Judgment.

Consent jurisdiction. Parties may agree in advance to submit their controversy to a given forum, in which case the forum is the consent jurisdiction.

Consent of victim. The submission of a victim is generally no defense to a crime unless, as in the case of rape, the victim's consent negatives an element of the crime itself.

Consent rule. An entry of record by the defendant, confessing the lease, entry, and ouster by the plaintiff in an action of ejectment. A superseded instrument, in which a defendant in an action of ejectment specified for what purpose he intended to defend, and undertook to confess not only the fictitious lease, entry, and ouster, but that he was in possession.

Consent search. A search made by police after the subject of the search has consented; such consent, if freely and intelligently given, will validate a warrantless search. Consent is not freely and voluntarily given in the face of colorably lawful coercion; and questions regarding duress or coercion in a consent search are determined by the totality of the circumstances. See 18 U.S.C.A. § 2236.

Consent to be sued. Agreement in advance to be sued in a particular form. See Cognovit judgment; Judgment *(Confession of judgment).*

Consent to notice. In documents which treat of the requirement of notice, *(e.g.* lease) a party may consent to notice beforehand or agree that notice to some other person will satisfy the requirement of notice to him.

Consequence. The result following in natural sequence from an event which is adapted to produce, or to aid in producing, such result; the correlative of "cause". See also Natural and probable consequences.

Consequential damages. See Damages.

Consequential loss. Losses not directly caused by damage, but rather arising from results of such damage.

Conservator. A guardian; protector; preserver. Appointed by court to manage affairs of incompetent or to liquidate business. Person appointed by a court to manage the estate of one who is unable to manage property and business affairs effectively. Uniform Probate Code §§ 1–201(6), 5–401(2). See also Guardian.

Conserve. To save and protect from loss or damage.

Consider. To fix the mind on, with a view to careful examination; to examine; to inspect. To deliberate about and ponder over. To entertain or give heed to. See also Considered.

Considerable. Worthy of consideration; required to be observed. A "considerable" number, as of persons, does not necessarily mean a very great or any particular number of persons; the term "considerable" being merely relative.

Consideration. The inducement to a contract. The cause, motive, price, or impelling influence which induces a contracting party to enter into a contract. The reason or material cause of a contract. Some right, interest, profit or benefit accruing to one party, or some forbearance, detriment, loss, or responsibility, given, suffered, or undertaken by the other. Restatement, Second, Contracts, §§ 17(1), 71. It is a basic, necessary

element for the existence of a valid contract that is legally binding on the parties.

See also Adequate consideration; Failure of consideration; Fair and valuable consideration; Fair consideration; Good consideration; Inadequate consideration; Love and affection; Past consideration; Valuable consideration; Want of consideration.

Considerations are either *executed* or *executory; express* or *implied; good* or *valuable.* See definitions *below.*

Concurrent consideration. One which arises at the same time or where the promises are simultaneous.

Continuing consideration. One consisting in acts or performances which must necessarily extend over a considerable period of time.

Equitable or moral considerations. Considerations which are devoid of efficacy in point of strict law, but are founded upon a moral duty, and may be made the basis of an express promise.

Executed or executory considerations. The former are acts done or values given before or at the time of making the contract; the latter are promises to give or do something in future.

Express or implied considerations. The former are those which are specifically stated in a deed, contract, or other instrument; the latter are those inferred or supposed by the law from the acts or situation of the parties. Express consideration is a consideration which is distinctly and specifically named in the written contract or in the oral agreement of the parties.

Good consideration. Such as is founded on natural duty and affection, or on a strong moral obligation. A consideration for love and affection entertained by and for one within degree recognized by law. Motives of natural duty, generosity, and prudence come under this class. The term is sometimes used in the sense of a consideration valid in point of law, and it then includes a valuable or sufficient as well as a meritorious consideration. Generally, however, *good* is used in antithesis to *valuable consideration (q.v.).*

Gratuitous consideration. One which is not founded upon any such loss, injury, or inconvenience to the party to whom it moves as to make it valid in law.

Illegal consideration. An act which if done, or a promise which if enforced, would be prejudicial to the public interest or contrary to law.

Implied considerations. See *Express or implied considerations, above.*

Impossible consideration. One which cannot be performed.

Legal consideration. One recognized or permitted by the law as valid and lawful; as distinguished from such as are illegal or immoral. The term is also sometimes used as equivalent to "good" or "sufficient" consideration.

Meritorious consideration. *See Good consideration, above.*

Moral considerations. *See Equitable or moral considerations, above.*

Nominal consideration. One bearing no relation to the real value of the contract or article, as where a parcel of land is described in a deed as being sold for "one dollar," no actual consideration passing, or the real consideration being concealed. This term is also sometimes used as descriptive of an inflated or exaggerated value placed upon property for the purpose of an exchange.

Past consideration. An act done before the contract is made, which is ordinarily by itself no consideration for a promise. As to time, considerations may be of the past, present, or future. Those which are present or future will support a contract not void for other reasons.

Pecuniary consideration. A consideration for an act of forbearance which consists either in money presently passing or in money to be paid in the future, including a promise to pay a debt in full which otherwise would be released or diminished by bankruptcy or insolvency proceedings.

Sufficient consideration. One deemed by the law of sufficient value to support an ordinary contract between parties, or one sufficient to support the particular transaction.

Considered. Deemed; determined; adjudged; reasonably regarded. For example, evidence may be said to have been "considered" when it has been reviewed by a court to determine whether any probative force should be given it.

Consign /kənsáyn/. To deliver goods to a carrier to be transmitted to a designated factor or agent. To deliver or transfer as a charge or trust. To commit, intrust, give in trust. To transfer from oneself to the care of another. To send or transmit goods to a merchant, factor, or agent for sale. To deposit with another to be sold, disposed of, or called for, whereby title does not pass until there is action of consignee indicating sale. *See also* Consignment.

Consignee /kənsàyníy/. One to whom a consignment is made. Person named in bill of lading to whom or to whose order the bill promises delivery. U.C.C. § 7–102(b).

In a commercial use, "consignee" means one to whom a consignment may be made, a person to whom goods are shipped for sale, or one to whom a carrier may lawfully make delivery in accordance with his contract of carriage, or one to whom

goods are consigned, shipped, or otherwise transmitted.

Consignment. The act or process of consigning goods; the transportation of goods consigned; an article or collection of goods sent to a factor; goods or property sent, by the aid of a common carrier, from one person in one place to another person in another place; something consigned and shipped. Entrusting of goods to another to sell for the consignor. A bailment for sale.

The term "consignment", used in a commercial sense, ordinarily implies an agency and denotes that property is committed to the consignee for care or sale.

See also Reconsignment.

Consignment contract. Consignment of goods to another (consignee) for sale under agreement that consignee will pay consignor for any sold goods and will return any unsold goods. A bailment for sale.

Consignment sale. *See* Consignment.

Consignor /kənsáynər/. One who sends or makes a consignment; a shipper of goods. The person named in a bill of lading as the person from whom the goods have been received for shipment. U.C.C. § 7–102(c).

Consolidate. In a general sense, to unite or unify into one mass or body, as to consolidate several small school districts into a large district, or to consolidate various funds. In legislative usage, to consolidate two bills is to unite them into one. The term means something more than to rearrange or redivide.

To make solid or firm; to unite, compress, or pack together and form into a more compact mass, body, or system. To cause to become united and extinguished in a superior right or estate by both becoming vested in the same person.

See also Commingle; Consolidation; Joinder; Merger.

Consolidated appeal. If two or more persons are entitled to appeal from a judgment or order of a district court and their interests are such as to make joinder practicable, they may file a joint notice of appeal, or may join in appeal after filing separate timely notices of appeal, and they may thereafter proceed on appeal as a single appellant. Appeals may be consolidated by order of the court of appeals upon its own motion or upon motion of a party, or by stipulation of the parties to the several appeals. Fed.R.App.P. 3(b).

Consolidated balance sheets. *See* Consolidated financial statements.

Consolidated bonds. Bonds issued to replace two or more existing issues; thus, consolidating debt into single issue.

Consolidated corporations. *See* Consolidation of corporations.

Consolidated financial statements. The financial report of a parent corporation and it's subsidiaries or affiliates which combines the assets, liabilities, revenues, and expenses of all of the entities. In preparing consolidated financial statements, all intercompany transactions are eliminated. *See also* Consolidated tax returns.

Consolidated laws. A compilation of all the laws of a State in force arranged according to subject matter. *See* Code; Codification; Compilation.

Consolidated mortgage. Unification of several outstanding mortgages.

Consolidated securities. An issue of securities sufficiently large to provide the funds to retire two or more outstanding issues of debt securities.

Consolidated tax returns. A procedure whereby certain affiliated corporations may file a single return, combine the tax transactions of each corporation, and arrive at a single income tax liability for the group. The election to file a consolidated return is usually binding on future years. I.R.C. §§ 1501–1505. *See also* Consolidated financial statements.

Consolidation. Act of consolidating, or the status of being consolidated. Unification of two or more actions. *See* Consolidation of actions.

In *corporate law,* the combination of two or more corporations into a newly created corporation. Thus, A Corporation and B Corporation combine to form C Corporation. The Revised Model Business Corporation Act eliminates the consolidation as a distinct type of corporate amalgamation. A consolidation may qualify as a nontaxable reorganization if certain conditions are satisfied. *See also* Consolidation of corporations; Merger.

Consolidation loan. *See* Loan.

Consolidation of actions. The act or process of uniting several actions into one trial and judgment, by order of a court, where all the actions are between the same parties, pending in the same court, and involving substantially the same subject-matter, issues and defenses; or the court may order that one of the actions be tried, and the others decided without trial according to the judgment in the one selected.

When actions involving a common question of law or fact are pending before the court, it may order a joint hearing or trial of any or all the matters in issue in the actions; it may order all the actions consolidated; and it may make such orders concerning proceedings therein as may tend to avoid unnecessary costs or delay. Fed.R. Civil P. 42(a); New York C.P.L.R. § 602.

See also Joinder *(Joinder of claims).*

Consolidation of cases. *See* Consolidation of actions.

Consolidation of corporations. Occurs when two or more corporations are extinguished, and by the same process a new one is created, taking over the assets and assuming the liabilities of those passing out of existence. A unifying of two or more corporations into a single new corporation having the combined capital, franchises, and powers of all its constituents. *See also* Consolidation.

Merger distinguished. In a "merger", one corporation absorbs the other and remains in existence while the other is dissolved, and in a "consolidation" a new corporation is created and the consolidating corporations are extinguished. *See also* Merger.

Consonant statement. A prior declaration of a witness whose testimony has been attacked and whose credibility stands impeached, which the court will allow to be proved by the person to whom the declaration was made in order to support the credibility of the witness and which but for the existence of such impeachment would ordinarily be excluded as hearsay.

Consortium /kənsórsh(iy)əm/. Conjugal fellowship of husband and wife, and the right of each to the company, society, co-operation, affection, and aid of the other in every conjugal relation. Loss of "consortium" consists of several elements, encompassing not only material services but such intangibles as society, guidance, companionship, and sexual relations. Damages for loss of consortium are commonly sought in wrongful death actions, or when spouse has been seriously injured through negligence of another, or by spouse against third person alleging that he or she has caused breaking-up of marriage. It is a separate cause of action belonging to the spouse of the injured married partner and though derivative in the sense of being occasioned by injury to spouse, is a direct injury to the spouse who has lost the consortium. Several states have extended this right of recovery to children of the injured parent. *See also* Alienation of affections.

Consortship. In maritime law, an agreement or stipulation between the owners of different vessels that they shall keep in company, mutually aid, instead of interfering with each other, in wrecking and salvage, whether earned by one vessel or both.

Conspicuous place. Within the meaning of a statute relating to the posting of notices, a "conspicuous place" means one which is reasonably calculated to impart the information in question.

Conspicuous term *or* clause. A term or clause is conspicuous when it is so written that a reasonable person against whom it is to operate ought to have noticed it. For example, printing in italics or boldface or contrasting color, or typing in capitals or underlined, is conspicuous. Rev. Model Bus.Corp. Act, § 1.40. A printed heading in capitals (as: NON–NEGOTIABLE BILL OF LADING) is conspicuous. Language in the body of a form is "conspicuous" if it is in larger or other contrasting type or color. But in a telegram any stated term is "conspicuous."

Whether a term or clause is "conspicuous" or not is for decision by the court. Uniform Consumer Credit Code, § 1.301(6); U.C.C. § 1–201(10). Size of type face alone does not determine whether required disclosure is "conspicuous" for purpose of Truth in Lending Act; rather, location of disclosure, and manner in which it is set off from other information, are also determinative.

Conspiracy /kənspírəsiy/. A combination or confederacy between two or more persons formed for the purpose of committing, by their joint efforts, some unlawful or criminal act, or some act which is lawful in itself, but becomes unlawful when done by the concerted action of the conspirators, or for the purpose of using criminal or unlawful means to the commission of an act not in itself unlawful.

A person is guilty of conspiracy with another person or persons to commit a crime if with the purpose of promoting or facilitating its commission he: (a) agrees with such other person or persons that they or one or more of them will engage in conduct which constitutes such crime or an attempt or solicitation to commit such crime; or (b) agrees to aid such other person or persons in the planning or commission of such crime or of an attempt or solicitation to commit such crime. Model Penal Code, § 5.03.

A conspiracy may be a continuing one; actors may drop out, and others drop in; the details of operation may change from time to time; the members need not know each other or the part played by others; a member need not know all the details of the plan or the operations; he must, however, know the purpose of the conspiracy and agree to become a party to a plan to effectuate that purpose.

There are a number of federal statutes prohibiting specific types of conspiracy. See, *e.g.*, 18 U.S. C.A. § 371.

See also Chain conspiracy; Co-conspirator's rule; Combination in restraint of trade; Confederacy; Seditious conspiracy; Wharton Rule.

Chain conspiracy. Such conspiracy is characterized by different activities carried on with same subject of conspiracy in chain-like manner that each conspirator in chain-like manner performs a separate function which serves in the accomplishment of the overall conspiracy.

Civil conspiracy. The essence of a "civil conspiracy" is a concert or combination to defraud or cause other injury to person or property, which results in damage to the person or property of plaintiff. *See also* Civil conspiracy.

Overthrow of government. See Sedition.

Seditions conspiracy. See Sedition.

Conspiracy in restraint of trade. Term which describes all forms of illegal agreements such as boycotts, price fixing, etc., which have as their object interference with free flow of commerce and trade. *See* Antitrust acts; Clayton Act; Sherman Antitrust Act.

Conspirators. Persons partaking in conspiracy. *See* Conspiracy.

Conspire. To engage in conspiracy. Term carries with it the idea of agreement, concurrence and combination, and hence is inapplicable to a single person or thing, and one cannot agree or conspire with another who does not agree or conspire with him. *See* Conspiracy.

Constable. An officer of a municipal corporation (usually elected) whose duties are similar to those of the sheriff, though his powers are less and his jurisdiction smaller. He is to preserve the public peace, execute the process of magistrates' courts, and of some other tribunals, serve writs, attend the sessions of the criminal courts, have the custody of juries, and discharge other functions sometimes assigned to him by the local law or by statute. Powers and duties of constables have generally been replaced by sheriffs.

Constant purchasing power accounting. An accounting approach used to account for inflation in which historical-cost data are adjusted for changes in the purchasing power of the dollar by using a general price level index.

Constituency. The inhabitants of an electoral district.

Constituent. He who gives authority to another to act for him. The term is used as a correlative to "attorney," to denote one who constitutes another his agent or invests the other with authority to act for him.

It is also used in the language of politics as a correlative to "representative," the constituents of a legislator being those whom he represents and whose interests he is to care for in public affairs; usually the electors of his district.

Constituent elements. The elements of a crime, tort or other type of action. Those matters which must be proved to sustain a cause of action because they constitute the action or crime.

Constituted authorities. Officers properly appointed under a constitution for the government of the people.

Constitution. The organic and fundamental law of a nation or state, which may be written or unwritten, establishing the character and conception of its government, laying the basic principles to which its internal life is to be conformed, organizing the government, and regulating, distributing, and limiting the functions of its different departments, and prescribing the extent and manner of the exercise of sovereign powers. A charter of government deriving its whole authority from the governed. The written instrument agreed upon by the people of the Union (*e.g.* United States Constitution) or of a particular state, as the absolute rule of action and decision for all departments (*i.e.* branches) and officers of the government in respect to all the points covered by it, which must control until it shall be changed by the authority which established it (*i.e.* by amendment), and in opposition to which any act or ordinance of any such department or officer is null and void. The full text of the U.S. Constitution appears at the end of this dictionary.

In a more general sense, any fundamental or important law or edict; as the Novel Constitutions of Justinian; the Constitutions of Clarendon.

Constitutional. Consistent with the constitution; authorized by the constitution; not conflicting with any provision of the constitution or fundamental law of the state. Dependent upon a constitution, or secured or regulated by a constitution; as "constitutional monarchy," "constitutional rights." *Compare* Unconstitutional.

Constitutional convention. A duly constituted assembly of delegates or representatives of the people of a state or nation for the purpose of framing, revising, or amending its constitution. Art. V of U.S. Const. provides that a Constitutional Convention may be called on application of the Legislatures of two-thirds of the states.

Constitutional court. A court named or described and expressly protected by Constitution, or recognized by name or definite description in Constitution (*e.g.* Supreme Court, as provided for in Art. III, Sec. 1 of U.S.Const.) in contrast to legislatively created courts (see *e.g.* Art. I, Sec. 8, cl. 9 of U.S. Const.). Commonly referred to as "Article III" courts in reference to U.S. Constitution. *See also* Legislative courts.

Constitutional freedom. Generic term to describe the basic freedoms guaranteed by the Constitution such as the First Amendment freedoms of religion, speech, press and assembly together with protection under due process clause of the 14th Amendment. *See also* Bill of rights; Constitutional liberty or freedom.

Constitutional law. (1) That branch of the public law of a nation or state which treats of the organization, powers and frame of government, the distribution of political and governmental authorities and functions, the fundamental principles which are to regulate the relations of government and citizen, and which prescribes generally the plan and method according to which the public affairs of the nation or state are to be administered. (2) That department of the science of law which treats of constitutions, their establishment, construction, and interpretation, and of the validity of legal enactments as tested by the criterion of conformity to the fundamental law. (3) A constitutional law is one which is consonant to, and agrees with, the constitution; one which is not in violation of any provision of the constitution of the particular state.

Constitutional liberty or freedom. Such freedom as is enjoyed by the citizens of a country or state under the protection of its constitution. The aggregate of those personal, civil, and political rights of the individual which are guaranteed by the constitution and secured against invasion by the government or any of its agencies. *See also* Bill of rights; Constitutional freedom.

Constitutional limitations. Those provisions of a constitution which restrict the legislature in the types of laws which it may enact. See *e.g.* Art. I, Sec. 9, U.S. Constitution.

Constitutional office. A public position or office which is created by a constitution as distinguished from a statutory office which is created by an enactment of the legislature.

Constitutional officer. A governmental official whose office was created by a constitution; as contrasted with an officer whose position has been created by the legislature. One whose tenure and term of office are fixed and defined by the constitution, as distinguished from the incumbents of offices created by the legislature.

Constitutional powers. *See* Power.

Constitutional protections. Those basic protections guaranteed by the Constitution such as due process, equal protection and the fundamental protections of the First Amendment, such as those touching speech, press and religion. *See* Bill of rights; Constitutional freedom.

Constitutional questions. Those legal issues which require an interpretation of the Constitution for their resolution as distinguished from those of a statutory nature (*e.g.* Fourth Amend. search and seizure issues).

Constitutional right. A right guaranteed to the citizens by the United States Constitution and state constitutions and so guaranteed as to prevent legislative interference therewith. *See also* Constitutional freedom; Constitutional liberty or freedom; Constitutional protections.

Constitutional tort. *See* Tort.

Constraint. Act of constraining; state of being restrained or restricted. A restriction that inhibits the achievement of an objective, the free movement of a person, and the like.

Construction. Interpretation of statute, regulation, court decision or other legal authority. The process, or the art, of determining the sense, real meaning, or proper explanation of obscure, complex or ambiguous terms or provisions in a statute, written instrument, or oral agreement, or the application of such subject to the case in question, by reasoning in the light derived from extraneous connected circumstances or laws or writings bearing upon the same or a connected matter, or by seeking and applying the probable aim and purpose of the provision. Drawing conclusions respecting subjects that lie beyond the direct expression of the term.

The process of bringing together and correlating a number of independent entities, so as to form a definite entity.

The creation of something new, as distinguished from the repair or improvement of something already existing. The act of fitting an object for use or occupation in the usual way, and for some distinct purpose. *See* Construct.

See also Broad interpretation; Comparative interpretation; Contemporaneous construction; Construe; Four corners rule; Interpretation; Last antecedent rule; Literal construction; Statutory construction; Strict construction.

Equitable construction. A construction of a law, rule, or remedy which has regard more to the equities of the particular transaction or state of affairs involved than to the strict application of the rule or remedy; that is, a liberal and extensive construction, as opposed to a literal and restrictive. *See also Strict and liberal construction, below.*

Strict and liberal construction. Strict (or literal) construction is construction of a statute or other instrument according to its letter, which recognizes nothing that is not expressed, takes the language used in its exact and technical meaning, and admits no equitable considerations or implications.

Liberal (or equitable) construction, on the other hand, expands the meaning of the statute to meet cases which are clearly within the spirit or reason of the law, or within the evil which it was designed to remedy, provided such an interpretation is not inconsistent with the language used. It resolves all reasonable doubts in favor of the applicability of the statute to the particular case. It means, not that the words should be forced out of their natural meaning, but simply that they should receive a fair and reasonable interpretation with respect to the objects and purposes of the instrument. *See also Equitable construction, above.*

Construction contract. Type of contract in which plans and specifications for construction are made a part of the contract itself and commonly it is secured by performance and payment bonds to protect both subcontractors and party for whom building is being constructed.

Construction lien. A lien that arises by law and attaches to real estate to secure payment of a person who improved the property through the rendering of labor or other services or the furnishing of materials or other supplies. Another name for this lien is mechanics' lien (*q.v.*).

Construction loan. *See* Loan.

Construction of will. Interpretation which is given to provisions of will and the law to be applied therein when there is conflict as to the meaning intended by the deceased. Such function is commonly performed by Probate Court.

Constructive. That which is established by the mind of the law in its act of *construing* facts, conduct, circumstances, or instruments. That which has not the character assigned to it in its own essential nature, but acquires such character in consequence of the way in which it is regarded by a rule or policy of law; hence, inferred, implied, or made out by legal interpretation; the word "legal" being sometimes used here in lieu of "constructive."

As to *constructive* Bailment; Breaking; Contempt; Conversion; Delivery; Escape; Fraud; Larceny; Seisin; and Treason, see those titles.

Constructive adverse possession. Type of adverse possession which, under certain statutes, is characterized by payment of taxes under color of right, as distinguished from actual adverse possession in which the adverse claimant is in actual possession.

Constructive assent. An assent or consent imputed to a party from a construction or interpretation of his conduct; as distinguished from one which he actually expresses.

Constructive authority. Authority inferred or assumed to have been given because of the grant of some other antecedent authority. *See also* Authority.

Constructive breaking into a house. A breaking made out by construction of law. As where a burglar gains an entry into a house by threats, fraud, or conspiracy.

Constructive condition. Conditions in contracts which are neither expressed nor implied by the words of the contract but are imposed by law to meet the ends of justice. Restatement, Second, Contracts, § 226. The cooperation of the parties to a contract is a constructive condition. In negotiable instruments, a promise or order otherwise unconditional is not made conditional by the fact that the instrument is subject to a constructive condition.   U.C.C. § 3–105(1).

Constructive contract. A species of contracts which arise, not from the intent of the parties, but from the operation of law to avoid an injustice. These are sometimes referred to as quasi contracts or contracts implied in law as contrasted with contracts implied in fact which are real contracts expressing the intent of the parties by conduct rather than by words. An obligation created by law for reasons of justice without regard to expressions of assent by either words or acts. *See also* Contract *(Quasi contract).*

Constructive delivery. The recognition of the act of intending that title to property be transferred to someone, even though the actual, physical delivery of the property is not made (because of difficulty, impossibility) (*e.g.*, the transfer of a key to a safe constructively delivers the contents of the safe). *See also* Delivery.

Constructive desertion. Occurs when one spouse, through misconduct, forces the other to abandon the marital abode. If a spouse is forced to leave the home because of the other's conduct, the former has been constructively deserted.

Constructive dividend. *See* Dividend.

Constructive eviction. Such arises when landlord, while not actually depriving tenant of possession, has done or suffered some act by which premises are rendered untenantable. Any disturbance of the tenant's possession by the landlord whereby the premises are rendered unfit or unsuitable for occupancy in whole or in substantial part for the purposes for which they were leased amounts to a constructive eviction, if the tenant so elects and surrenders his possession. For example, if a tenant vacates the rental property because of the absence of heat or water, he has been constructively evicted.

As the term is used with reference to breach of the covenants of warranty and of quiet enjoyment, it means the inability of the purchaser to obtain possession by reason of a paramount outstanding title.

Constructive filing. The filing of a document with a person who is the only one available to receive it, though he is not the designated person to receive it, is a constructive filing.

Constructive force. As regards robbery, a taking by force is the gist of the crime, but the force may be either actual or constructive. Constructive force is anything which produces fear sufficient to suspend the power of resistance and prevent the free exercise of the will. Actual force is applied to the body; constructive is by threatening words or gestures and operates on the mind.

Constructive fraud. Exists where conduct, though not actually fraudulent, has all actual consequences and all legal effects of actual fraud. Breach of legal or equitable duty which, irrespective of moral guilt, is declared by law to be fraudulent because of its tendency to deceive others or violate confidence. *See also* Fraud.

Constructive intent. Exists where one should have reasonably expected or anticipated a particular result; *e.g.* when one does an act which is wilful and wanton resulting in injury to another, it can be said that he constructively intended the harm.

Constructive knowledge. If one by exercise of reasonable care would have known a fact, he is deemed to have had constructive knowledge of such fact; *e.g.* matters of public record. *See also* Constructive notice.

Constructive loss. One resulting from such injuries to the property, without its destruction, as render it valueless to the assured or prevent its restoration to the original condition except at a cost exceeding its value. *See also* Constructive total loss.

Constructive malice. That type of malice which the law infers from the doing of an evil act; sometimes known as implied malice.

Constructive notice. Such notice as is implied or imputed by law, usually on the basis that the information is a part of a public record or file, as in the case of notice of documents which have been recorded in the appropriate registry of deeds or probate. Notice with which a person is charged by reason of the notorious nature of the thing to be noticed, as contrasted with actual notice of such thing. That which the law regards as sufficient to give notice and is regarded as a substitute for actual notice.

Constructive ownership. *See* Attribution.

Constructive payment. If one charges himself with a payment and the payee has a right to demand it, it can be considered a constructive as contrasted with an actual payment; *e.g.* a check which is mailed in payment though not yet cashed is a constructive payment.

Constructive possession. A person has constructive possession of property if he has power to control and intent to control such item. Exists where one does not have physical custody or possession, but is in a position to exercise dominion or control over a thing.

Constructive receipt of income. As applied to tax laws, is taxable income which is unqualifiedly subject to the demand of taxpayer on cash receipts and disbursements method of accounting, whether or not such income has actually been received in cash. Under this doctrine, income which is subject to unfettered command of taxpayer and which the taxpayer is free to enjoy at his option is taxed to him, despite the fact that the taxpayer has exercised his own choice to turn his back on that income and the doctrine is one by which form of transaction is ignored in order to get to its substance. An example would be accrued interest on a savings account. Under the constructive receipt of income concept, such interest will be taxed to a depositor in the year it is available rather than the year actually withdrawn. The fact that the depositor uses the cash basis of accounting for tax purposes makes no difference.

Constructive service of process. Form of service of process other than actual service; *e.g.* publication in newspaper is constructive service.

Constructive taking. A phrase used in the law to characterize an act not amounting to an actual appropriation of chattels, but which shows an intention to convert them to his use; as if a person intrusted with the possession of goods deals with them contrary to the orders of the owner. With respect to constructive condemnation, *see* Condemnation *(Inverse condemnation).*

Constructive total loss. In insurance, exists whenever insured item of property has lost its total usefulness and insured is deprived of its benefit totally. *See also* Constructive loss.

Constructive transfer. A transfer of an item (*e.g.* a controlled substance), either belonging to an individual or under the individual's control, by some other person or agency at the instance or direction of the individual accused of such constructive transfer.

Constructive trust. Trust created by operation of law against one who by actual or constructive fraud, by duress or by abuse of confidence, or by commission of wrong, or by any form of unconscionable conduct, or other questionable means, has obtained or holds legal right to property which he should not, in equity and good conscience, hold and enjoy.

A constructive trust is a relationship with respect to property subjecting the person by whom the title to the property is held to an equitable duty to convey it to another on the ground that his acquisition or retention of the property is wrongful and that he would be unjustly enriched if he were permitted to retain the property. Restatement, Second, Trusts § 1(e).

Constructive trust ex delicto. A constructive trust which is imposed on property which a fiduciary has claimed or received in violation of his duties.

Constructive willfulness. Intentional disregard of a known duty necessary to the safety of a person, and an entire absence of care for the life, the person, or the property of others, such as exhibits a conscious indifference to consequences.

Construe. To put together; to arrange or interpret the words of an instrument, statute, regulation, court decision or other legal authority. To ascertain the meaning of language by a process of arrangement, interpretation and inference. *See* Construction.

Consuetudo /kònswətyúwdow/. Lat. A custom; an established usage or practice; duties; taxes.

Consul /kónsəl/. An officer of a commercial character, appointed by the different nations to watch over the mercantile and tourist interests of the appointing nation and of its subjects in foreign countries. There are usually a number of consuls in every maritime country, and they are usually subject to a chief consul, who is called a "consul general." A public official residing in a foreign country responsible for developing and protecting the economic interests of his government and looking after the welfare of his government's citizens who may be traveling or residing within his jurisdiction. United States consuls form a part of the Foreign Service and are of various grades: consul general, consul, vice consul, and consular agent.

Consular courts /kóns(y)ələr kórts/. Courts held by the consuls of one country, within the territory of another, under authority given by treaty, for the settlement of civil cases. In some instances they had also a criminal jurisdiction, but in this respect were subject to review by the courts of the home government. The last of the United States consular courts (Morocco) was abolished in 1956.

Consular invoice. Invoice used in foreign trade signed by consul of the country for which the shipment is destined. Such facilitates entry through destination country in that quantity, value, etc. of shipment has been pre-verified.

Consular marriage. A marriage solemnized in a foreign country by a consul or diplomatic agent of the U.S. and held to be valid in some jurisdictions.

Consulate. The residence or headquarters of a foreign consul.

Consul general. Consular officer of highest grade.

Consultation. Act of consulting or conferring; *e.g.* patient with doctor; client with lawyer. Deliberation of persons on some subject. A conference between the counsel engaged in a case, to discuss its questions or arrange the method of conducting it.

An old writ whereby a cause which had been wrongfully removed by prohibition out of an ecclesiastical court to a temporal court was returned to the ecclesiastical court.

Consulto /kənsóltow/. Lat. In the civil law, designedly; intentionally.

Consumer /kəns(y)úwmər/. One who consumes. Individuals who purchase, use, maintain, and dispose of products and services. Users of the final product. A member of that broad class of people who are affected by pricing policies, financing practices, quality of goods and services, credit reporting, debt collection, and other trade practices for which state and federal consumer protection laws are enacted. Consumers are to be distinguished from manufacturers (who produce goods), and wholesalers or retailers (who sell goods). *See also* Purchaser.

A buyer (other than for purposes of resale) of any consumer product, any person to whom such product is transferred during the duration of an implied or written warranty (or service contract) applicable to the product, and any other person who is entitled by the terms of such warranty (or service contract) or under applicable State law to enforce against the warrantor (or service contractor) the obligations of the warranty (or service contract). 15 U.S.C.A. § 2301.

Consumer advocate. One who is given to presenting the position of the consumer or to representing him in judicial, administrative, or legislative proceedings. *See also* Ombudsman.

Consumer credit. Short term loans to individuals for purchase of consumer goods and services.

Consumer Credit Code. A uniform law, adopted by several states, with intent and purpose similar to that of the federal Consumer Credit Protection Act *(q.v.)*.

Consumer Credit Protection Act. Federal and state acts (commonly referred to as Truth-in-Lending Acts) enacted to safeguard the consumer in connection with the utilization of credit by requiring full disclosure of the terms and conditions of finance charges in credit transactions or in offers to extend credit, by restricting the garnishment of wages, and by regulating the use of credit cards. 15 U.S.C.A. § 1601 et seq. In addition to federal and state Truth-in-Lending Acts, several states also require by statute that consumer-loan agreements be written in plain, simplified language. *See also* Annual percentage rate; Equal Credit Opportunity Act; Fair Credit Billing Act; Fair Credit Reporting Acts; Fair Debt Collection Practices Act; Truth-in-Lending Act; Uniform Consumer Credit Code.

Consumer credit sale. Any sale with respect to which consumer credit is extended or arranged by the seller. The term includes any contract in the form of a bailment or lease if the bailee or lessee contracts to pay as compensation for use a sum substantially equivalent to or in excess of the aggregate value of the property and services involved and it is agreed that the bailee or lessee will become, or for no other or for a nominal consideration has the option to become, the owner of the property upon full compliance with his obligations under the contract.

Consumer credit transaction. Credit offered or extended to a natural person, in which the money, property or service which is the subject of the transaction is primarily for personal, family, household or agricultural purposes and for which either a finance charge is or may be imposed or which, pursuant to an agreement, is or may be payable in more than four installments. "Consumer loan" is one type of "consumer credit".

Consumer debt. Debt incurred by an individual primarily for a personal, family, or household purpose. Bankruptcy Code § 101.

Consumer goods. Goods which are used or bought for use primarily for personal, family or household purposes. U.C.C. § 9–109(1). Such goods are not intended for resale or further use in the production of other products. Contrasted with capital goods. *See also* Consumer product.

Consumer lease. Lease of consumer goods; also may be applied to lease of dwelling as contrasted with commercial lease. Article 2A of the U.C.C. is concerned with the formation, construction, effect, and enforcement of the consumer lease contracts, as well as the rights and remedies of both lessor and lessee on default. As defined by U.C.C. § 2A–103 is "a lease that a lessor regularly engaged in the business of leasing or selling makes to a lessee, except an organization, who takes under the lease primarily for a personal, family, or household purpose."

Disclosure of terms in certain types of consumer leases is governed by Federal Consumer Leasing Act (which is fully integrated into the Federal Truth in Lending Act). 15 U.S.C.A. § 1667 et seq.

Consumer Price Index. A price index computed and issued monthly by the Bureau of Labor Statistics of the U.S. Department of Labor. The index attempts to track the price level of a group of goods and services purchased by the average consumer. Widely used to measure changes in cost of maintaining given standard of living. *See* Cost of living clause. *Compare* Producer Price Index.

Consumer product. Any tangible personal property which is distributed in commerce and which is normally used for personal, family, or household purposes (including any such property intended to be attached to or installed in any real property without regard to whether it is so attached or installed). 15 U.S.C.A. § 2301. *See also* Consumer goods.

Consumer Product Safety Commission. An independent federal regulatory agency established by act of October 27, 1972 (86 Stat. 1207) to administer and implement the Consumer Product Safety Act. The Commission has primary responsibility for establishing mandatory product safety standards, where appropriate, to reduce the unreasonable risk of injury to consumers from consumer products. In addition it has authority to ban hazardous consumer products. The Consumer Product Safety Act also authorizes the Commission to conduct extensive research on consumer product standards, engage in broad consumer and industry information and education programs, and establish a comprehensive Injury Information Clearinghouse.

Consumer protection laws. Federal and state statutes governing sales and credit practices involving consumer goods. Such statutes prohibit and regulate deceptive or unconscionable advertising and sales practices, product quality, credit financing and reporting, debt collection, leases, and other aspects of consumer transactions. For examples of such statutes, see Consumer Credit Protection Act; Consumer Product Safety Commission; Deceptive sales practices; Equal Credit Opportunity Act; Fair Credit Billing Act; Fair Credit Reporting Acts; Fair Debt Collection Practices Act; Magnuson–Moss Warranty Act; Truth-in-Lending Act; Uniform Commercial Code; Uniform Consumer Credit Code.

At the federal level, the major regulatory law is the Federal Trade Commission Act. More than half the states have in turn enacted "mini-FTC" laws which, like the federal, prohibit "unfair or deceptive acts or practices."

Consumer report. Document issued by private or governmental body relative to quality of certain products, their dangers and their attributes. Document issued as to certain companies and their practices. See Fair Credit Reporting Acts.

Consumer reporting agency. An agency which acts for monetary fees, dues or on a cooperative nonprofit basis, which regularly engages in whole or in part in gathering or evaluating information on consumers in order to distribute such information to third parties engaged in commerce and which uses a facility of interstate commerce to prepare or distribute the reports. The activities of such agencies are regulated by federal and state laws. See Fair Credit Reporting Acts.

Consumer's cooperative. Group which purchases consumer goods for resale to its members, thus reducing costs by eliminating the middleman's profit.

Consummate /kónsəmèyt/, v. To finish by completing what was intended; bring or carry to utmost point or degree; carry or bring to completion; finish; perfect; fulfill; achieve. See also Consummation.

Consummate lien. A term which may be used to describe the lien of a judgment when a motion for a new trial has been denied (the lien having theretofore been merely inchoate).

Consummation /kònsəméyshən/. The completion of a thing; the completion of a marriage by cohabitation (i.e. sexual intercourse) between spouses.

Consumption. Act or process of consuming; waste; decay; destruction. Using up of anything, as food, natural resources, heat, or time.

Contamination. Condition of impurity resulting from mixture or contact with foreign substance. See also Adulteration; Foreign substance.

Contango /kòntǽŋgow/. A double bargain, consisting of a sale for cash of stock previously bought which the broker does not wish to carry, and a repurchase for the re-settlement several weeks ahead of the same stock at the same price as at the sale plus interest accrued up to the date of that settlement. The rate of interest is called a "contango" and contango days are the days during the settlement when these arrangements are in effect.

Charge by broker for carrying customer's account to next settlement day.

Contemnor /kəntémnər/. One who has committed contempt of court.

Contemplate. To view or consider with continued attention; to regard thoughtfully; to have in view as contingent or probable as an end or intention. To ponder, to study, to plan, to meditate, to reflect. See Consider; Premeditation.

Contemplation. The act of the mind in considering with attention. Continued attention of the mind to a particular subject. Consideration of an act or series of acts with the intention of doing or adopting them. The consideration of an event or state of facts with the expectation that it will transpire. See Consideration; Premeditation.

Contemplation of bankruptcy. Contemplation of the termination of one's business because of the financial inability to continue it. Knowledge of, and action with reference to, a condition of bankruptcy or ascertained insolvency, coupled with an intention to commit what the law formerly declared to be an "act of bankruptcy," or to make provision against the consequences of insolvency, or to defeat the general distribution of assets which would take place under a proceeding in bankruptcy. See Act of bankruptcy; Bankruptcy proceedings.

Contemplation of death. The apprehension or expectation of approaching dissolution; not that general expectation which every mortal entertains, but the apprehension which arises from some presently existing sickness or physical condition or from some impending danger. As applied to transfers of property, the phrase "in contemplation of death" means that thought of death is the impelling cause of transfer and that motive which induces transfer is of sort which leads to testamentary disposition and is practically equivalent to "causa mortis." It has been further held however, that in determining whether transfer by decedent within three years prior to date of death was made in contemplation of death, phrase "contemplation of death" is not restricted in meaning to apprehension that death is imminent; inquiry is whether the "life" as opposed to "death" motives were the dominant controlling or impelling reasons for the transfer. *See also* In contemplation of death.

Contemplation of insolvency. Knowledge of, and action with reference to, an existing or contemplated state of insolvency, with a design to make provision against its results or to defeat the operation of the insolvency laws. *See* Act of bankruptcy; Contemplation of bankruptcy.

Contemporaneous construction. A doctrine which holds that when an administrative body over a long period of time has placed an interpretation upon an ambiguous law, the interpretation of such body is entitled to great weight in the determination of the meaning of the law.

Contemporaneous objection rule. Rule which requires that a specific and timely objection be made to the admission of evidence for the question of its admissibility to be considered on appeal.

Contemporary community standards. In deciding whether allegedly obscene material has any literary, political or scientific value, the proper inquiry is not whether an ordinary member of any given community would find serious literary, artistic, political or scientific value in the material, but whether a reasonable person would find such value in the material taken as a whole.

Contempt. A willful disregard or disobedience of a public authority. *See also* Civil contempt; Common-law contempt; Contempt of Congress; Contempt of court; Direct contempt.

Contempt of Congress. Deliberate interference with duties and powers of Congress. Both houses of Congress may cite an individual for such contempt.

Contempt of court. Any act which is calculated to embarrass, hinder, or obstruct court in administration of justice, or which is calculated to lessen its authority or its dignity. Committed by a person who does any act in willful contravention of its authority or dignity, or tending to impede or frustrate the administration of justice, or by one who, being under the court's authority as a party to a proceeding therein, willfully disobeys its lawful orders or fails to comply with an undertaking which he has given.

Classification

Contempts are, generally, of two kinds, direct and constructive.

Direct contempts are those committed in the immediate view and presence of the court (such as insulting language or acts of violence) or so near the presence of the court as to obstruct or interrupt the due and orderly course of proceedings. These are punishable summarily. They are also called "criminal" contempts, but that term is better used in contrast with "civil" contempts (*see below*).

Constructive (or indirect) contempts are those which arise from matters not occurring in or near the presence of the court, but which tend to obstruct or defeat the administration of justice, and the term is chiefly used with reference to the failure or refusal of a party to obey a lawful order, injunction, or decree of the court laying upon him a duty of action or forbearance. Constructive contempts were formerly called "consequential," and this term is still in occasional use.

Contempts are also classed as civil or criminal. The former are those quasi contempts which consist in the failure to do something which the party is ordered by the court to do for the benefit or advantage of another party to the proceeding before the court, while criminal contempts are acts done in disrespect of the court or its process or which obstruct the administration of justice or tend to bring the court into disrespect. A civil contempt is not an offense against the dignity of the court, but against the party in whose behalf the mandate of the court was issued, and a fine is imposed for his indemnity. But criminal contempts are offenses upon the court such as wilful disobedience of a lawful writ, process, order, rule, or command of court, and a fine or imprisonment is imposed upon the contemnor for the purpose of punishment. Fed.R.Crim.Proc. 42; 18 U.S.C.A. § 402.

A court of the United States has power to punish by fine or imprisonment, at its discretion, such contempt of its authority, and none other, as: (1) misbehavior of any person in its presence or so near thereto as to obstruct the administration of justice; (2) misbehavior of any of its officers in their official transactions; (3) disobedience or resistance to its lawful writ, process, order, rule, decree, or command. 18 U.S.C.A. § 401. *See also* Presence of the court.

Contempt for failure to make discovery is governed by Fed.R. Civil P. 37(b), which provides for imposition of sanctions. *See also* Sanction.

Contempt power. Every court has inherent power to punish one for contempt of its judgments or decrees and for conduct within or proximate to the court which is contemptuous. *See also* Contempt of Congress; Contempt of court; Sanction.

Contempt proceeding. The judicial hearing or trial conducted to determine whether one has been in contempt of court and to make an appropriate disposition. Such proceedings are sui generis and not necessarily connected to or identified with the proceeding out of which the contempt arose.

Contents unknown. Words sometimes annexed to a bill of lading of goods in cases or other packaging. Their meaning is that the carrier only means to acknowledge that the shipment, as evidenced from the external condition of such, is in good order.

Content validation. Content validation of an employment test requires that an analysis of a job involved be undertaken to determine what characteristics are essential for adequate performance of that job and the job analysis is then followed by formulation of a test which accurately reflects presence or absence of these necessary qualities.

Conterminous /kòntárm nəs/. Adjacent; adjoining; having a common boundary; coterminous.

Contest, v. To assert a defense to an adverse claim in a court proceeding. To oppose, resist, or dispute the case made by a plaintiff or prosecutor. To strive to win or hold. To controvert, litigate, call in question, challenge. To defend, as a suit or other proceeding. As used in a no-contest clause in a will, means any legal proceedings designed to thwart testator's wishes. *See* Answer; Defense.

Contestable clause. Provision in an insurance policy setting forth the conditions under which, or the period of time during which, the insurer may contest or void the policy. *See also* Uncontestable clause.

Contested case. A court or administrative proceeding that is opposed by another party or interested person. Within the meaning of the Administrative Procedure Act this means a proceeding including but not restricted to rate making, price fixing, and licensing in which the legal rights, duties or privileges of a party are required by constitution or statute to be determined by an agency after an opportunity for an evidentiary hearing.

Contested election. An election is contested whenever an objection is formally urged against it which, if found to be true in fact, would invalidate it. This is true both as to objections founded upon some constitutional provision and to such as are based on statutes.

Contest of will. *See* Will contest.

Context. The context of a particular sentence or clause in a statute, contract, will, etc., comprises those parts of the text which immediately precede and follow it. The context may sometimes be scrutinized, to aid in the interpretation of an obscure passage. *See* Construction.

Contiguity. Exists where tracts of land touch or adjoin in a reasonably substantial physical sense, but line of demarcation between reasonableness or unreasonableness of a "contiguity" must be determined on the facts of each case.

Contiguous /kəntígyuwəs/. In close proximity; neighboring; adjoining; near in succession; in actual close contact; touching at a point or along a boundary; bounded or traversed by. The term is not synonymous with "vicinal."

Continental. Pertaining or relating to a continent; characteristic of a continent; as broad in scope or purpose as a continent.

Continental Congress. The first national legislative assembly in the United States, which met in 1774, in pursuance of a recommendation made by Massachusetts and adopted by the other colonies. In this Congress all the colonies were represented except Georgia. The delegates were in some cases chosen by the legislative assemblies in the states; in others by the people directly. The powers of the Congress were undefined, but it proceeded to take measures and pass resolutions which concerned the general welfare and had regard to the inauguration and prosecution of the war for independence.

Continental currency. Paper money issued under the authority of the continental congress.

Contingency /kəntínjənsiy/. Something that may or may not happen. Quality of being contingent or casual; the possibility of coming to pass; an event which may occur; a possibility; a casualty. A fortuitous event, which comes without design, foresight, or expectation. *See also* Contingent.

Contingency contract. A contract, part of performance of which at least is dependent on the happening of a contingency. Sometimes used to refer to fee arrangement with attorney who agrees to accept his fee on the contingency of a successful outcome. *See* Fee.

Contingency reserve (*or* **fund**). In accounting, a reserve set up to cover possible or potential losses; *e.g.* possible judgment against company.

A fund created in anticipation of incidental or unforeseen expenditures.

Contingent /kəntínjənt/. Possible, but not assured; doubtful or uncertain; conditioned upon the occurrence of some future event which is itself uncertain, or questionable. Synonymous with provisional. This term, when applied to a use, remainder, devise, bequest, or other legal right or interest, implies that no present interest exists, and that whether such interest or right ever will exist depends upon a future uncertain event.

As to *contingent* Damages; Fee; Legacy; Limitation; Remainder; Trust; Use, and Will, see those titles.

Contingent beneficiary. Person who may or will benefit if primary beneficiary dies or otherwise loses rights as beneficiary; *e.g.* person who will receive life insurance if primary beneficiary dies before insured.

Contingent claim. One which has not accrued and which is dependent on some future event that may never happen.

Contingent debt. One which is not presently fixed, but may become so in the future with the occurrence of some uncertain event. A debt in bankruptcy which may be proved and allowed and which arises out of contract. It does not encompass a tort claim on which no action or suit has been brought prior to adjudication. Term may refer to debt incurred by state to which state pledges its credit and guarantees payment if revenues from funded project prove inadequate. *See also* Contingent claim; Contingent liability.

Contingent estate, interest or right. An estate, interest or right which depends for its effect upon an event which may or may not happen. A contingent estate is one which is conditioned upon the existence of persons who answer the description of takers but who cannot be ascertained until the termination of a precedent or particular estate because the right to take is contingent upon the fact of their being alive or having survived until that time or upon the happening of some other uncertain event.

Contingent fee. *See* Fee.

Contingent fund. One set up by a municipality to pay expense items which will necessarily arise during the year but cannot appropriately be classified under any of the specific purposes for which other taxes are levied. *See also* Contingency reserve.

Contingent interest in personal property. A future interest not transmissible to the representatives of the party entitled thereto, in case he dies before it vests in possession. Thus, if a testator leaves the income of a fund to his wife for life, and the capital of the fund to be distributed among such of his children as shall be living at her death, the interest of each child during the widow's life-time is *contingent*, and in case of his death is not transmissible to his representatives.

Contingent liability. One which is not now fixed and absolute, but which will become so in case of the occurrence of some future and uncertain event. A potential liability; *e.g.* pending lawsuit, disputed claim, judgment being appealed, possible tax deficiency. *See also* Contingent claim; Contingent debt.

Contingent remainder. *See* Remainder.

Continuance. The adjournment or postponement of a session, hearing, trial, or other proceeding to a subsequent day or time; usually on the request or motion of one of the parties. Also the entry of a continuance made upon the record of the court, for the purpose of formally evidencing the postponement, or of connecting the parts of the record so as to make one continuous whole. *Compare* Recess.

Continuing. Enduring; not terminated by a single act or fact; subsisting for a definite period or intended to cover or apply to successive similar obligations or occurrences.

As to *continuing* Breach; Consideration; Conspiracy; Covenant; Damages; Guaranty; and Nuisance, see those titles. *See also* Perpetuity.

Continuing contract. A contract calling for periodic performances over a space of time.

Continuing jurisdiction. A doctrine invoked commonly in child custody or support cases by which a court which has once acquired jurisdiction continues to possess it for purposes of amending and modifying its orders therein.

Continuing offense. Type of crime which is committed over a span of time as, for example, a conspiracy. As to period of statute of limitation, the last act of the offense controls for commencement of the period. A "continuing offense," such that only the last act thereof within the period of the statute of limitations need be alleged in the indictment or information, is one which may consist of separate acts or a course of conduct but which arises from that singleness of thought, purpose or action which may be deemed a single impulse. *See also* Crime; Offense.

Continuity of life or existence. The death or other withdrawal of an owner of an entity does not terminate the existence of such entity. This is a characteristic of a corporation, since the death or withdrawal of a shareholder does not affect the corporation's existence.

Continuous. Uninterrupted; unbroken; not intermittent or occasional; so persistently repeated at short intervals as to constitute virtually an unbroken series. Connected, extended, or prolonged without cessation or interruption of sequence. As to *continuous* Crime and Easement, see those titles.

Continuous budgeting. A process in which there is an ongoing twelve-month budget at all points in time during a budget period; a new budget month (twelve months into the future) is added as each current month expires.

Continuous adverse use. Term is interchangeable with the term "uninterrupted adverse use".

Continuous injury. One recurring at repeated intervals, so as to be of repeated occurrence; not necessarily an injury that never ceases.

Continuous treatment doctrine. Under this doctrine, the time in which to bring a medical malpractice action is stayed when the course of treatment which includes wrongful acts or omissions has run continuously and is related to the same original condition or complaint.

Continuously. Uninterruptedly; in unbroken sequence; without intermission or cessation; without intervening time; with continuity or continuation.

Contour map. Map which shows the configuration and elevation of surface areas with curved lines.

Contra. Against, confronting, opposite to; on the other hand; on the contrary; the reverse of.

Contra account. See Account (Contra).

Contraband. In general, any property which is unlawful to produce or possess. Things and objects outlawed and subject to forfeiture and destruction upon seizure. Goods exported from or imported into a country against its laws. Smuggled goods. Articles, the importation or exportation of which, is prohibited by law. See e.g. 49 U.S.C.A. § 781.

Trafficking in contraband cigarettes is a federal crime. 18 U.S.C.A. § 2341 et seq.

"Contraband per se" is property the mere possession of which is unlawful, while "derivative contraband" is property innocent by itself but used in perpetration of unlawful act.

See also Bootlegging; Counterfeit; Derivative contraband; Gray market goods; Smuggling.

Contraband of war. Certain classes of merchandise, such as arms and ammunition, which, by the rules of international law, cannot lawfully be furnished or carried by a neutral nation to either of two belligerents. If found in transit in neutral vessels, such goods may be seized and condemned for violation of neutrality.

Contra asset. An account used to reduce asset balances in the financial statements.

Contract. An agreement between two or more persons which creates an obligation to do or not to do a particular thing. As defined in Restatement, Second, Contracts § 3: "A contract is a promise or a set of promises for the breach of which the law gives a remedy, or the performance of which the law in some way recognizes as a duty." A legal relationship consisting of the rights and duties of the contracting parties; a promise or set of promises constituting an agreement between the parties that gives each a legal duty to the other and also the right to seek a remedy for the breach of those duties. Its essentials are competent parties, subject matter, a legal consideration, mutuality of agreement, and mutuality of obligation.

Under U.C.C., term refers to total legal obligation which results from parties' agreement as

affected by the Code. Section 1–201(11). As to sales, "contract" and "agreement" are limited to those relating to present or future sales of goods, and "contract for sale" includes both a present sale of goods and a contract to sell goods at a future time. U.C.C. § 2–106(1).

The writing which contains the agreement of parties, with the terms and conditions, and which serves as a proof of the obligation.

Contracts may be classified on several different methods, according to the element in them which is brought into prominence. The usual classifications are as follows:

Blanket contract. Contract covering a number or group of products, goods, or services for fixed period of time.

Certain and hazardous. Certain contracts are those in which the thing to be done is supposed to depend on the will of the party, or when, in the usual course of events, it must happen in the manner stipulated. Hazardous contracts are those in which the performance of that which is one of its objects depends on an uncertain event.

Commutative and independent. Commutative contracts are those in which what is done, given, or promised by one party is considered as an equivalent to or in consideration of what is done, given, or promised by the other. Independent contracts are those in which the mutual acts or promises have no relation to each other, either as equivalents or as considerations.

Conditional contract. A contract whose very existence and performance depends upon the happening of some contingency or condition expressly stated therein. It is not simply an executory contract, since the latter may be an absolute agreement to do or not to do something, but it is a contract whose very existence and performance depend upon a contingency.

Consensual and real. Consensual contracts are such as are founded upon and completed by the mere agreement of the contracting parties, without any external formality or symbolic act to fix the obligation. Real contracts are those in which it is necessary that there should be something more than mere consent, such as a loan of money, deposit or pledge, which, from their nature, require a delivery of the thing (res). In the common law a contract respecting real property (such as a lease of land for years) is called a "real" contract.

Constructive contract. See Constructive contract; also Express and implied; Quasi contract, below.

Cost-plus contract. See Costs.

Divisible and indivisible. The effect of the breach of a contract depends in a large degree upon whether it is to be regarded as indivisible or divisible; i.e. whether it forms a whole, the performance of every part of which is a condition precedent to bind the other party, or is composed of several independent parts, the performance of any one of which will bind the other party *pro tanto*. The only test is whether the whole quantity of the things concerned, or the sum of the acts to be done, is of the essence of the contract. It depends, therefore, in the last resort, simply upon the intention of the parties.

When a consideration is entire and indivisible, and it is against law, the contract is void *in toto*. When the consideration is divisible, and part of it is illegal, the contract is void only *pro tanto*.

Entire and severable. An *entire* contract is one the consideration of which is entire on both sides. The entire fulfillment of the promise by either is a condition precedent to the fulfillment of any part of the promise by the other. Whenever, therefore, there is a contract to pay the gross sum for a certain and definite consideration, the contract is entire. A *severable* contract is one the consideration of which is, by its terms, susceptible of apportionment on either side, so as to correspond to the unascertained consideration on the other side, as a contract to pay a person the worth of his services so long as he will do certain work; or to give a certain price for every bushel of so much corn as corresponds to a sample.

Where a contract consists of many parts, which may be considered as parts of one whole, the contract is entire. When the parts may be considered as so many distinct contracts, entered into at one time, and expressed in the same instrument, but not thereby made one contract, the contract is a separable contract. But, if the consideration of the contract is single and entire, the contract must be held to be entire, although the subject of the contract may consist of several distinct and wholly independent items.

Entire contract clause. A provision in the insurance contract stating that the entire agreement between the insured and insurer is contained in the contract, including the application (if attached), declarations, insuring agreement, exclusions, conditions, and endorsements.

Exclusive contract. See *Requirements contract; Tying contract, below.*

Executed and executory. Contracts are also divided into executed and executory; *executed,* where nothing remains to be done by either party, and where the transaction is completed at the moment that the arrangement is made, as where an article is sold and delivered, and payment therefor is made on the spot; *executory,* where some future act is to be done, as where an agreement is made to build a house in six months, or to do an act on or before some future day, or to lend money upon a certain interest, payable at a future time.

Express and implied. An express contract is an actual agreement of the parties, the terms of

which are openly uttered or declared at the time of making it, being stated in distinct and explicit language, either orally or in writing.

An implied contract is one not created or evidenced by the explicit agreement of the parties, but inferred by the law, as a matter of reason and justice from their acts or conduct, the circumstances surrounding the transaction making it a reasonable, or even a necessary, assumption that a contract existed between them by tacit understanding.

An implied contract is one inferred from conduct of parties and arises where plaintiff, without being requested to do so, renders services under circumstances indicating that he expects to be paid therefor, and defendant, knowing such circumstances, avails himself of benefit of those services. It is an agreement which legitimately can be inferred from intention of parties as evidenced by circumstances and ordinary course of dealing and common understanding of men.

See also Constructive contract; and *Quasi contract, below.*

Gratuitous and onerous. Gratuitous contracts are those of which the object is the benefit of the person with whom it is made, without any profit or advantage received or promised as a consideration for it. It is not, however, the less gratuitous if it proceeds either from gratitude for a benefit before received or from the hope of receiving one thereafter, although such benefit be of a pecuniary nature. Onerous contracts are those in which something is given or promised as a consideration for the engagement or gift, or some service, interest, or condition is imposed on what is given or promised, although unequal to it in value. A gratuitous contract is sometimes called a contract of beneficence.

Investment contract. A contract in which one party invests money or property expecting a return on his investment. See also Investment contract; Security.

Joint and several. A joint contract is one made by two or more promisors, who are jointly bound to fulfill its obligations, or made to two or more promisees, who are jointly entitled to require performance of the same. A contract may be "several" as to any one of several promisors or promisees, if person has a legal right (either from the terms of the agreement or the nature of the undertaking) to enforce his individual interest separately from the other parties. Generally all contracts are joint where the interest of the parties for whose benefit they are created is joint, and separate where that interest is separate.

Mutual interest, mixed, etc. Contracts of "mutual interest" are such as are entered into for the reciprocal interest and utility of each of the parties; as sales, exchange, partnership, and the like.

"Mixed" contracts are those by which one of the parties confers a benefit on the other, receiving something of inferior value in return, such as a donation subject to a charge. Contracts "of beneficence" are those by which only one of the contracting parties is benefited; as loans, deposit and mandate.

Open end contract. Contract (normally sales contract) in which certain terms (*e.g.* order amount) are deliberately left open.

Output contract. A contract in which one party agrees to sell his entire output and the other agrees to buy it; it is not illusory, though it may be indefinite. Such agreements are governed by U.C.C. § 2–306. *See also Requirements contract, below.*

Parol contract. A contract not in writing, or partially in writing. At common law, a contract, though it may be in writing, not under seal. *See* Parol evidence rule.

Personal contract. A contract relating to personal property, or one which so far involves the element of personal knowledge or skill or personal confidence that it can be performed only by the person with whom made, and therefore is not binding on his executor.

Pre-contract. An obligation growing out of a contract or contractual relation, of such a nature that it debars the party from legally entering into a similar contract at a later time with any other person.

Principal and accessory contract. A contract is accessory when it is made to provide security for the performance of an obligation. Suretyship, mortgage, and pledge are examples of such a contract. When the secured obligation arises from a contract, either between the same or other parties, that contract is the principal contract. Civ.Code La. art. 1913.

Quasi contract. Legal fiction invented by common law courts to permit recovery by contractual remedy in cases where, in fact, there is no contract, but where circumstances are such that justice warrants a recovery as though there had been a promise. It is not based on intention or consent of the parties, but is founded on considerations of justice and equity, and on doctrine of unjust enrichment. It is not in fact a contract, but an obligation which the law creates in absence of any agreement, when and because the acts of the parties or others have placed in the possession of one person money, or its equivalent, under such circumstances that in equity and good conscience he ought not to retain it. It is what was formerly known as the contract implied in law; it has no reference to the intentions or expressions of the parties. The obligation is imposed despite, and

frequently in frustration of their intention. *See also* Constructive contract.

In the civil law, a contractual relation arising out of transactions between the parties which give them mutual rights and obligations, but do not involve a specific and express convention or agreement between them. The lawful and purely voluntary acts of a man, from which there results any obligation whatever to a third person, and sometimes a reciprocal obligation between the parties. Civ.Code La. art. 2293.

Record, specialty, simple. Contracts of record are such as are declared and adjudicated by courts of competent jurisdiction, or entered on their records, including judgments, recognizances, and statutes staple. These are not properly speaking contracts at all, though they may be enforced by action like contracts. Specialties, or special contracts, are contracts under seal, such as deeds and bonds. All others are included in the description "simple" contracts; that is, a simple contract is one that is not a contract of record and not under seal; it may be either written or oral, in either case, it is called a "parol" contract, the distinguishing feature being the lack of a seal.

Requirements contract. A contract in which one party agrees to purchase his total requirements from the other party and hence it is binding and not illusory. *See also Output contract, above.*

Shipment contract. See that title.

Special contract. A contract under seal; a specialty; as distinguished from one merely oral or in writing not sealed. But in common usage this term is often used to denote an express or explicit contract, one which clearly defines and settles the reciprocal rights and obligations of the parties, as distinguished from one which must be made out, and its terms ascertained, by the inference of the law from the nature and circumstances of the transaction. A special contract may rest in parol, and does not mean a contract by specialty; it is defined as one with peculiar provisions not found in the ordinary contracts relating to the same subject-matter.

Subcontract. A contract subordinate to another contract, made or intended to be made between the contracting parties, on one part, or some of them, and a third party (*i.e.* subcontractor). One made under a prior contract.

Where a person has contracted for the performance of certain work (*e.g.*, to build a house), and he in turn engages a third party to perform the whole or a part of that which is included in the original contract (*e.g.*, to do the carpenter work), his agreement with such third person is called a "subcontract," and such person is called a "subcontractor." The term "subcontractor" means one who has contracted with the original contractor for the performance of all or a part of the work or services which such contractor has himself contracted to perform.

Tying contract. See Tying arrangement.

Unconscionable contract. One which no sensible man not under delusion, duress, or in distress would make, and such as no honest and fair man would accept. A contract the terms of which are excessively unreasonable, overreaching and one-sided. *See* Adhesion contract; Unconscionability.

Unenforceable contract. An unenforceable contract is one for the breach of which neither the remedy of damages nor the remedy of specific performance is available, but which is recognized in some other way as creating a duty of performance, though there has been no ratification. Restatement, Second, Contracts § 8. When a contract has some legal consequences but may not be enforced in an action for damages or specific performance in the face of certain defenses, such as the Statute of Frauds or a statute of limitations, the contract is said to be "unenforceable."

Unilateral and bilateral. A unilateral contract is one in which one party makes an express engagement or undertakes a performance, without receiving in return any express engagement or promise of performance from the other. Bilateral (or reciprocal) contracts are those by which the parties expressly enter into mutual engagements, such as sale or hire. When the party to whom an engagement is made makes no express agreement on his part, the contract is called unilateral, even in cases where the law attaches certain obligations to his acceptance. Essence of a "unilateral contract" is that neither party is bound until the promisee accepts the offer by performing the proposed act. It consists of a promise for an act, the acceptance consisting of the performance of the act requested, rather than the promise to perform it. *Compare* Bilateral contract.

Usurious contract. See Usurious contract.

Voidable contract. See Voidable contract.

Void contract. See Void contract.

Written contract. A "written contract" is one which in all its terms is in writing. Commonly referred to as a formal contract.

See also Adhesion contract; Agreement; Aleatory contract; Alteration of contract; Bilateral contract; Bottom hole contract; Breach of contract; Collateral contract; Compact; Constructive contract; Contingency contract; Entire output contract; Executory contract; Formal contract; Futures contract; Impairing the obligation of contracts; Indemnity; Installment contract; Integrated contract; Investment contract; Letter contract; Letter of intent; Novation; Oral contract; Parol evidence rule; Privity (*Privity of contract*); Procurement contract; Quasi contract; Requirement contract; Severable contract; Simulated contract; Specialty. For "liberty of contract", *see* Liberty.

Contract carrier. A carrier which furnishes transportation service to meet the special needs of shippers who cannot be adequately served by common carriers. A transportation company that carries, for pay, the goods of certain customers only as contrasted to a common carrier that carries the goods of the public in general.

Contract clause. Provision in U.S.Const., Art. I, Sec. 10, to the effect that no state shall pass a law impairing obligation of contract. Trustees of Dartmouth College v. Woodward, 17 U.S. (4 Wheat.) 518, 4 L.Ed. 629.

Contract, estoppel by. "Estoppel by contract" is intended to embrace all cases in which there is an actual or virtual undertaking to treat a fact as settled. It means party is bound by terms of own contract until set aside or annulled for fraud, accident, or mistake. There are two sorts of "estoppel by contract," estoppel to deny truth of facts agreed on and settled by force of entering into contract, and estoppel arising from acts done under or in performance of contract.

Contract for deed. An agreement by a seller to deliver the deed to the property when certain conditions have been met, such as completion of payments by purchaser. Often such contracts for deed are in turn resold.

Contract for sale of goods. Includes both a contract for present sale of goods and a contract to sell goods at a future time. U.C.C. § 2–106(1).

Contract for sale of land. A contract which calls for conveyance of interest in real estate and requires a writing signed by party sought to be charged as being within Statute of Frauds. *See also* Contract for deed; Contract of sale.

Contract implied in fact. *See* Contract.

Contract implied in law. *See* Contract.

Contract not to compete. An agreement by an employee that he will not for a stated period and within a specific geographical area compete with his employer after termination of his employment. These contracts are enforceable if the time span and area are reasonable.

Contract of affreightment. A contract for hiring a vessel. *See also* Affreightment.

Contract of benevolence. A contract made for the benefit of one of the contracting parties only, as a mandate or deposit.

Contract of guaranty. A promise to pay or an assumption of performance of some duty upon the failure of another who is primarily obligated in the first instance. *See also* Guaranty.

Contract of insurance. Any contract by which one of the parties for a valuable consideration, known as a premium, assumes a risk of loss or liability that rests upon the other, pursuant to a plan for the distribution of such risk, is a contract of insurance, whatever the form it takes or the name it bears. *See* Insurance; Policy of insurance.

Contract of record. A contract which has been declared and adjudicated by a court having jurisdiction, or which is entered of record in obedience to, or in carrying out, the judgments of a court.

Contract of sale. A contract by which one of the contracting parties, called the "seller," enters into an obligation to the other to cause him to have freely, by a title of proprietor, a thing, for the price of a certain sum of money, which the other contracting party, called the "buyer," on his part obliges himself to pay. Agreement under which seller agrees to convey title to property upon payment by buyer under terms of contract. *See also* Contract for deed; Contract for sale of land.

Contractor. One who contracts to do work for another. This term is strictly applicable to any person who enters into a contract, but is commonly reserved to designate one who, for a fixed price, undertakes to procure the performance of works or services on a large scale, or the furnishing of goods in large quantities, whether for the public or a company or individual. Such are generally classified as general contractors (responsible for entire job) and sub-contractors (responsible for only portion of job; *e.g.* plumber, carpenter).

A contractor is a person who, in the pursuit of any independent business, undertakes to do a specific piece of work for another or other persons, using his own means and methods without submitting himself to their control in respect to all its details, and who renders service in the course of an independent occupation representing the will of his employer only as to the result of his work and not as to the means by which it is accomplished.

One who in pursuit of independent business undertakes to perform a job or piece of work, retaining in himself control of means, method and manner of accomplishing the desired result.

See also General contractor; Independent contractor; Prime contractor; Subcontractor.

Contractual obligation. The obligation which arises from a contract or agreement.

Contract under seal. For centuries before the doctrine of consideration was developed, and long before informal contracts were enforced, contracts under seal were enforced. The sealed instrument required no consideration. The required formalities are: a sufficient writing, a seal, and delivery. The seal may be actual, or impressed on the paper, or merely recited by the word "seal" or "L.S."

Contractus. Lat. Contract; a contract; contracts.

Contradiction in terms. A phrase of which the parts are expressly inconsistent, as *e.g.,* "an innocent murder"; "a fee-simple for life."

Contra liability. An account used to reduce liability balances in the financial statements.

Contra revenue. An account that is deducted from revenues and used in the computation of net revenues on the income statement.

Contrary. Against; opposed or in opposition to; in conflict with.

Contrary to law. Illegal; in violation of statute or legal regulations at a given time. In respect of verdict, in conflict with the law contained in court's instructions.

Contrary to the evidence. Against the evidence; against the weight of the evidence. *See also* Against the weight of the evidence.

Contravening equity. A right or equity, in another person, which is inconsistent with and opposed to the equity sought to be enforced or recognized.

Contribute. To lend assistance or aid, or give something, to a common purpose; to have a share in any act or effect; to discharge a joint obligation. As applied to negligence signifies causal connection between injury and negligence, which transcends and is distinguished from negligent acts or omissions which play so minor a part in producing injuries that law does not recognize them as legal causes. *See* Negligence *(Contributory negligence).*

Contributing cause. Generic term used to describe any factor which contributes to a result, though its causal nexus may not be immediate. *See* Cause; Negligence *(Contributory negligence).*

Contributing to delinquency. A criminal offense consisting of an act or omission which tends to make a child delinquent.

Contribution. Right of one who has discharged a common liability to recover of another also liable, the aliquot portion which he ought to pay or bear. Under principle of "contribution," a tort-feasor against whom a judgment is rendered is entitled to recover proportional shares of judgment from other joint tort-feasors whose negligence contributed to the injury and who were also liable to the plaintiff. The share of a loss payable by an insurer when contracts with two or more insurers cover the same loss. The insurer's share of a loss under a coinsurance or similar provision. The sharing of a loss or payment among several. The act of any one or several of a number of co-debtors, co-sureties, etc., in reimbursing one of their number who has paid the whole debt or suffered the whole liability, each to the extent of his proportionate share. A number of states have adopted the Uniform Contribution Among Tortfeasors Act.

In the civil law, a partition by which the creditors of an insolvent debtor divide among themselves the proceeds of his property proportionably to the amount of their respective credits. Division which is made among the heirs of the succession of the debts with which the succession is charged, according to the proportion which each is bound to bear.

In maritime law, where the property of one of several parties interested in a vessel and cargo has been voluntarily sacrificed for the common safety (as by throwing goods overboard to lighten the vessel), such loss must be made good by the contribution of the others, which is termed "general average".

See also General average contribution; Indemnity.

Contribution clause. Insurance clause providing that where more than one policy covers loss, insurers shall share such loss proportionally in accordance with their policy limits.

Contribution margin. In accounting, the difference between selling price and variable cost per unit or in total for level of activity. It indicates the amount of each revenue dollar that remains after variable costs have been covered and that goes toward the coverage of fixed costs and the generation of profits.

Contribution to capital. Funds or property contributed by shareholders as the financial basis for operation of the corporation's business, and signifies resources whose dedication to users of the corporation is made the foundation for issuance of capital stock and which became irrevocably devoted to satisfaction of all obligations of corporation. *See also* Capital.

Contributory, *n.* One who contributes or is required to contribute. A person liable to contribute to the assets of a company which is being wound up, as being a member or (in some cases) a past member thereof.

Contributory, *adj.* Joining in the promotion of a given purpose; lending assistance to the production of a given result. Said of a pension plan where employees, as well as employers, make payments to a pension fund. *See* Pension plan.

As to *contributory* Infringement and Negligence, see those titles.

Contributory cause. *See* Cause; Contributing cause; Negligence *(Contributory negligence).*

Contributory infringement. In patent law, the intentional aiding of one person by another in the unlawful making, selling or using of a patented invention.

Contributory negligence. *See* Negligence.

Contrivance. Any device which has been arranged generally to deceive. An instrument or article designed to accomplish a specific objective and made by use of measure of ingenuity.

Contrive. To devise; to plan; to plot; to scheme.

Control, *v.* To exercise restraining or directing influence over. To regulate; restrain; dominate; curb; to hold from action; overpower; counteract; govern.

Control, *n.* Power or authority to manage, direct, superintend, restrict, regulate, govern, administer, or oversee. The ability to exercise a restraining or directing influence over something. The "control" involved in determining whether principal and agent relationship or master and servant relationship is involved must be accompanied by power or right to order or direct.

As used in statute making it unlawful for any person to possess or "control" any narcotic drug, is given its ordinary meaning, namely, to exercise restraining or directing influence over, and also has been defined to relate to authority over what is not in one's physical possession.

Rule that driver must at all times have automobile under control, means having it under such control that it can be stopped before doing injury to any person in any situation that is reasonably likely to arise under the circumstances.

See also Exclusive control; Immediate control.

Control group. With reference to those whose communications with an attorney on behalf of a corporation are within the attorney-client privilege, this group consists of those persons who have authority to control, or substantially participate in, decisions regarding action to be taken on the advice of a lawyer, or who are authorized members of a group that has such power.

Controlled company. A company, the majority of whose voting stock is held by an individual or corporation. For example, a subsidiary of a parent company. The level of control depends on the amount of stock owned. *See* Controlling interest; Control person.

Controlled foreign corporation. Any foreign corporation in which more than 50 percent of the total combined voting power of all classes of stock entitled to vote or the total value of the stock of the corporation is owned by "U.S. shareholders" on any day during the taxable year of the foreign corporation. For purposes of this definition, a U.S. shareholder is any U.S. person who owns, or is considered as owning, 10 percent or more of the total combined voting power of all classes of voting stock of the foreign corporation. Stock owned directly, indirectly, and constructively is used in this measure.

Controlled group. A controlled group of corporations is required to share the lower-level corporate tax rates and various other tax benefits among the members of the group. A controlled group may be either a brother-sister or a parent-subsidiary group.

Controlled substance. Any drug so designated by law whose availability is restricted; *i.e.*, so designated by federal or state Controlled Substances Acts *(q.v.)*. Included in such classification are narcotics, stimulants, depressants, hallucinogens, and marijuana.

Controlled Substance Acts. Federal and state acts (the latter modeled on the Uniform Controlled Substances Act) the purpose of which is to control the distribution, classification, sale, and use of drugs. The majority of states have such acts. 21 U.S.C.A. § 801 et seq.

Controller. *See* Comptroller.

Controlling interest. A greater-than-50% ownership interest in a subsidiary company. *See* Controlled company.

Control person. In securities law, a person who has actual power or influence over an issuer. One who formulates and directs corporate policy or who is deeply involved in the important business affairs of a corporation. Sales of securities by control persons are subject to many of the requirements applicable to the sale of securities directly by the issuer.

Control premium. Refers to the pricing phenomenon by which shares that carry the power to control a corporation are more valuable per share than the shares that do not carry a power of control. The control premium is often computed not on a per share basis but on the aggregate increase in value of the "control block" over the going market or other price of shares which are not part of the "control block".

Controversy. A litigated question; adversary proceeding in a court of law; a civil action or suit, either at law or in equity; a justiciable dispute. To be a "controversy" under federal constitutional provision limiting exercise of judicial power of United States to cases and controversies there must be a concrete case admitting of an immediate and definitive determination of legal rights of parties in an adversary proceeding upon facts alleged, and claims based merely upon assumed potential invasions of rights are not enough to warrant judicial intervention. In the constitutional sense, it means more than disagreement and conflict; rather it means kind of controversy courts traditionally resolve. This term is important in that judicial power of the courts extends *only* to cases and "controversies." *See* Actual controversy; Case; Cause of action; Justiciable controversy.

Controvert. To dispute; to deny; to oppose or contest; to take issue on.

Contumacious conduct. Wilfully stubborn and disobedient conduct, commonly punishable as contempt of court. *See* Contempt.

Contumacy /kónt(y)əməsiy/. The refusal or intentional omission of a person who has been duly cited before a court to appear and defend the charge laid against him, or, if he is duly before the court, to obey some lawful order or direction made in the cause. In the former case it is called "presumed" contumacy; in the latter, "actual."

Contumely /kóntyəməliy/. Rudeness compounded of haughtiness and contempt; scornful insolence; despiteful treatment; disdain, contemptuousness in act or speech; disgrace.

Convene. To call together; to cause to assemble; to convoke. In the civil law, to bring an action.

Convenience and necessity. *See* Public convenience and necessity.

Convenient. Proper; just; suitable; fit; adapted; proper; becoming appropriate.

Convention. An agreement or compact; *esp.* international agreement, *e.g.* Geneva Convention. An assembly or meeting of members or representatives of political, legislative, fraternal, etc. organizations.

Constitutional convention. *See* Constitution.

Judicial convention. *See* Judicial.

Legislative and political. An assembly of delegates or representatives chosen by the people for special and extraordinary legislative purposes, such as the framing or revision of a state constitution (*i.e.* constitutional convention). Also an assembly of delegates chosen by a political party, or by the party organization in a larger or smaller territory, to nominate candidates for an approaching election.

Public and international law. A pact or agreement between states or nations in the nature of a treaty; usually applied (a) to agreements or arrangements preliminary to a formal treaty or to serve as its basis, or (b) international agreements for the regulation of matters of common interest but not coming within the sphere of politics or commercial intercourse, such as international postage or the protection of submarine cables. An agreement between states relating to trade, finance, or other matters considered less important than those usually regulated by a treaty. *See* Compact; Treaty.

Conventional. Depending on, or arising from, the mutual agreement of parties; as distinguished from *legal*, which means created by, or arising from, the act of the law.

As to *conventional* Estate; Interest; Mortgage; Subrogation; and Trustee, see those titles.

Conventional lien. A lien is conventional where the lien, general or particular, is raised by the express agreement and stipulation of the parties, in circumstances where the law alone would not create a lien from the mere relation of the parties or the details of their transaction.

Conventional loan. Real estate loan (usually from bank or savings and loan association) not involving government participation by way of insurance (FHA) or guarantee (VA). *See* Mortgage (*Conventional mortgage*).

Conventions. This name is sometimes given to compacts or treaties with foreign countries as to the apprehension and extradition of fugitive offenders. *See* Extradition.

Conversation. Manner of living; behavior habits of life; conduct; as in the phrase "chaste life and conversation." Criminal conversation means seduction of another man's wife, considered as an actionable injury to the husband. *See* Criminal (*Criminal conversation*).

Conversion. An unauthorized assumption and exercise of the right of ownership over goods or personal chattels belonging to another, to the alteration of their condition or the exclusion of the owner's rights. Any unauthorized act which deprives an owner of his property permanently or for an indefinite time. Unauthorized and wrongful exercise of dominion and control over another's personal property, to exclusion of or inconsistent with rights of owner. *See also* Embezzlement; Equitable conversion; Fraudulent conversion; Involuntary conversion.

Act of exchanging a convertible security for another security. *See* Convertible securities.

Commercial instruments. An instrument is converted when: a drawee to whom it is delivered for acceptance refuses to return it on demand; or any person to whom it is delivered for payment refuses on demand either to pay or to return it; or it is paid on a forged indorsement. U.C.C. § 3–419(1).

Constructive conversion. An implied or virtual conversion, which takes place where a person does such acts in reference to the goods of another as amount in law to the appropriation of the property to himself.

Direct conversion. The act of actually appropriating the property of another to his own beneficial use and enjoyment, or to that of a third person, or destroying it, or altering its nature, or wrongfully assuming title in himself.

Equitable conversion. The exchange of property from real to personal or from personal to real, which takes place under some circumstances in the consideration of the law, such as, to give effect to directions in a will or settlement, or to stipulations in a contract, although no such change has actually taken place, and by which exchange the

property so dealt with becomes invested with the properties and attributes of that into which it is supposed to have been converted. It is sometimes necessary however for certain purposes of devolution and transfer to regard the property in its changed condition as though the change has not absolutely taken place.

Conversion *or* **convertibility clause.** A provision in an adjustable-rate mortgage that allows the borrower to change from an ARM to a fixed-rate loan at some point during the term. A provision in convertible securities specifying conversion rights. *See* Convertible securities.

Conversion, custodia legis. Converting property in the custody of the court. One who has a lien against property and replevins the same to obtain possession and then sells the property to satisfy the lien before a judgment has entered in the replevin matter, commits conversion by this sale.

Conversion premium. The percentage by which the conversion price in a convertible security exceeds the prevailing common stock price at the time the convertible security is issued.

Conversion price. The contractually specified price per share at which a convertible security can be converted into (exchanged for) shares of common stock.

Conversion ratio. The number of common shares into which a convertible security may be converted. The ratio of the face amount of the convertible security to the conversion price.

Conversion securities. The securities into which convertible securities may be converted. *See* Convertible securities.

Conversion value. The market value of the number of shares into which a convertible security can be converted; i.e., the value of the security as common stock.

Convert. *See* Conversion.

Convertible bond. *See* Bond.

Convertible debt. A bond or debenture or note which under certain conditions and at certain times may be converted into stock by the holder. *See* Convertible securities.

Convertible securities. A bond, debenture or preferred share which may be exchanged by the owner for common stock or another security, usually of the same company, in accordance with the terms of the issue. The ratio between the convertible and conversion securities is fixed at the time the convertible securities are issued, and is usually protected against dilution. *See also* Conversion premium; Conversion price; Conversion ratio.

Forced conversion. Refers to a conversion of a convertible security that follows a call for redemption at a time when the value of the conversion security into which it may be converted is greater than the amount that will be received if the holder permits the security to be redeemed. Normally, a holder of a convertible redeemable security has a period of time after the call for redemption to determine whether or not to exercise the conversion privilege.

Convertible term insurance. Type of term insurance which may be changed to permanent (whole life) insurance carrying loan values, built in values, etc.

Convey. To transfer or deliver to another. To pass or transmit the title to property from one to another. To transfer property or the title to property by deed, bill of sale, or instrument under seal. Used popularly in sense of "assign", "sale", or "transfer". *See* Conveyance.

Conveyance /kɘnvéyɘns/. In its most common usage, transfer of title to land from one person, or class of persons, to another by deed. Term may also include assignment, lease, mortgage or encumbrance of land. Generally, every instrument in writing by which an estate or interest in the realty is created. *See also* Alienation; Demise; Fraudulent conveyance; Involuntary conveyance.

Absolute or conditional conveyance. An absolute conveyance is one by which the right or property in a thing is transferred, free of any condition or qualification, by which it might be defeated or changed, as an ordinary deed of lands, in contradistinction to a mortgage, which is a conditional conveyance.

Fraudulent conveyance. See Fraudulent.

Voluntary conveyance. A conveyance without valuable consideration; such as a deed or settlement in favor of a wife or children.

Conveyancer. One whose business it is to prepare deeds, mortgages, examine titles to real estate, and perform other functions relating to the transfer of real property.

Conveyancing. Act of performing the various functions relating to the transfer of real property such as examination of land titles, preparation of deeds, mortgages, closing agreements, etc.

Convict, *v.* To find a person guilty of a criminal charge, either upon a criminal trial, a plea of guilty, or a plea of nolo contendere. The word was formerly used also in the sense of finding against the defendant in a civil case.

Convict, *n.* One who has been adjudged guilty of a crime and is serving a sentence as a result of such conviction. A prisoner.

Convicted. *See* Conviction.

Conviction. In a general sense, the result of a criminal trial which ends in a judgment or sentence that the accused is guilty as charged. The

final judgment on a verdict or finding of guilty, a plea of guilty, or a plea of nolo contendere, but does not include a final judgment which has been expunged by pardon, reversed, set aside, or otherwise rendered nugatory.

The final consummation of the prosecution including the judgment or sentence, or as is frequently the case, the judgment or sentence itself. The stage of a criminal proceeding where the issue of guilt is determined.

A record of the summary proceedings upon any penal statute before one or more justices of the peace or other persons duly authorized, in a case where the offender has been *convicted* and sentenced.

Summary conviction. The conviction of a person (usually for a minor misdemeanor), as the result of his trial before a magistrate or court, without a jury.

Convincing proof. Such as is sufficient to establish the proposition in question, beyond hesitation, ambiguity, or reasonable doubt, in an unprejudiced mind. *See* Beyond a reasonable doubt; Clear and convincing proof; Proof.

Convoy. An escort for protection, either by land or sea. A naval force for the protection of merchant-ships and others, during the whole voyage, or such part of it as is known to require such protection. An association for a hostile object. In undertaking it, a nation spreads over the merchant vessel an immunity from search which belongs only to a national ship. By joining a convoy every individual ship puts off her pacific character, and undertakes for the discharge of duties which belong only to the military marine, and adds to the numerical, if not to the real strength of the convoy.

Co-obligor. A joint obligor; one bound jointly with another or others in a bond or obligation.

Cool state of blood. In the law of homicide, this term does not mean that the defendant must be calm or tranquil or display the absence of emotion, but rather that the defendant's anger or emotion must not have been such as to disturb defendant's faculties and reason. *See also* Cold blood; Cooling time; Premeditation.

Cooley doctrine. Doctrine which holds that state is deprived of all regulatory power as to subjects which "are in their nature national, or admit only of one uniform system or plan of regulation." Cooley v. Board of Wardens of Port of Philadelphia, 53 U.S. (12 How.) 299, 13 L.Ed. 996. *See also* Preemption.

Cooling off period. A period of time in which no action of a particular sort may be taken by either side in a dispute. For example, a period of a month after a union or a company files a grievance against the other. During this period, the union may not strike and the company may not lock-out the employees. A period of time in which a buyer may cancel a purchase; *e.g.* many states by statute require a three-day cancellation period for door-to-door sales or home improvement contracts. An automatic delay in some states, in addition to ordinary court delays, between the filing of divorce papers and the divorce hearing.

Cooling time. Time to recover "cool blood" after severe excitement or provocation. Time for the mind to become so calm and sedate as that it is supposed to contemplate, comprehend, and coolly act with reference to the consequences likely to ensue.

Cooperate. To act jointly or concurrently toward a common end.

Cooperation. Action of co-operating or acting jointly with another or other. Association of persons for common benefit. In patent law, unity of action to a common end or a common result, not merely joint or simultaneous action.

Cooperation clause. That provision in insurance policies which requires the insured to cooperate with the insurer in defense of a claim. "Co-operation" by insured within a co-operation clause means that there shall be fair and frank disclosure of information reasonably demanded by insurer to enable it to determine whether there is genuine defense.

Cooperative /kowóp(ə)rətəv/. A corporation or association organized for purpose of rendering economic services, without gain to itself, to shareholders or members who own and control it. Type of business that is owned by its member-customers.

Cooperatives vary widely in character and in the manner in which they function. They have been classified along functional lines as follows: (a) consumer cooperatives (including consumer stores, housing cooperatives, utility cooperatives, and health cooperatives); (b) marketing cooperatives; (c) business purchasing cooperatives; (d) workers' productive cooperatives (such as the credit union, mutual savings bank, savings and loan association, and production credit association); (f) insurance cooperatives; (g) labor unions; (h) trade associations; and (i) self-help cooperatives.

The required form for a cooperative may differ in different states; *e.g.* unincorporated association, cooperative association, nonprofit corporation.

See also Consumer's cooperative; Cooperative corporation.

Cooperative apartment. See that title.

Farmer's cooperative. Major function of such cooperative is to market the combined crops, produce or livestock of its farmer-owners. The cooperative attempts to sell crops and livestock at the optimum price. For example, it might store grain until the price of such rises.

Cooperative apartment. Dwelling units in a multi-dwelling complex in which each owner has an interest in the entire complex and a lease of his own apartment, though he does not own his apartment as in the case of a condominium. This is organized in corporate form and is generally treated as a corporation. However, it is somewhat of a legal hybrid in that the stockholder possesses both stock and a lease and the relationship between the tenant shareholder and the owner-cooperative is largely determined by reading together the certificate of incorporation, stock offering prospectus, stock subscription agreement, and proprietary lease.

Cooperative association. *See* Cooperative.

Cooperative corporation. A "cooperative corporation", while having a corporate existence, is primarily an organization for purpose of providing services and profits to its members and not for corporate profit. *See* Cooperative.

Cooperative housing. *See* Cooperative apartment.

Cooperative negligence. *See* Negligence *(Contributory negligence)*.

Coordinate. Equal, of the same order, rank, degree or importance; not subordinate. Adjusted to, in harmony with. As to courts of "coordinate jurisdiction," *see* this term, *infra,* and *also* Jurisdiction.

Coordinate jurisdiction. That which is possessed by courts of equal rank, degree, or authority, equally competent to deal with the matter in question, whether belonging to the same or different systems; concurrent jurisdiction. *See* Jurisdiction.

Coordinate system. A method of land description. It uses a measurement based on an intersection of a defined north-south axis and a defined east-west axis.

Co-owner. Two or more persons who own property, real or personal. Tenants in common of property. Broad term which may describe joint tenants as well.

Coparcenary /kòwparsíynəriy/. Such estate arises where several take by descent from same ancestor as one heir, all coparceners constituting but one heir and having but one estate and being connected by unity of interest and of title. A species of estate, or tenancy, which exists where lands of inheritance descend from the ancestor to two or more persons. It arose in England either by common law or particular custom. By common law, as where a person, seised in fee-simple or fee-tail, dies, and his next heirs are two or more females, his daughters, sisters, aunts, cousins, or their representatives; in this case they all inherit, and these coheirs, are then called "coparceners," or, for brevity, "parceners" only. By particular custom, as where lands descend, as in gavelkind, to all the males in equal degree, as sons, brothers, uncles, etc. An estate which several persons hold as one heir, whether male or female. This estate has the three unities of time, title, and possession; but the interests of the coparceners may be unequal. Today, this type of tenancy is obsolete.

Coparceners /kòwparsíynərz/. Persons to whom an estate of inheritance descends jointly, and by whom it is held as an entire estate.

Coparties. Parties having like status, such as, co-defendants.

"Co-party," within rule (F.R.C.P. 13) providing that a pleading may state as a cross-claim any claim by one party against a co-party arising out of the transaction or occurrence that is the subject matter of the original action, does not mean merely equal party, such as one of several original defendants, but applies to a third-party defendant brought into the case by an original defendant on a theory of liability over.

Copartner. One who is a partner with one or more other persons; a member of a partnership.

Copartnership. A partnership.

Copeland Act. Federal act prohibiting wage kickbacks or rebates being imposed on employees engaged in construction or repair of public buildings or works. See 18 U.S.C.A. § 74.

Coprincipal. One of two or more participants in crime who actually perpetrate crime or are present aiding and abetting person who commits crime. One of two or more persons who has appointed agents whom they have right to control.

Copy; Copying. A transcript, double, imitation, or reproduction of an original writing, painting, instrument, or the like.

Under best evidence rule, a copy may not be introduced until original is accounted for. Certified copies are admissible under statutes in most jurisdictions. Similarly, photographic copies and prints from photographic films are admissible by statute.

Copies of all pleadings, motions and other papers must be served on all parties to action under Fed.R. Civil P. 5(b). Admissions concerning the genuineness of copies of documents are governed by Fed.R. Civil P. 36(a).

A duplicate is admissible in evidence to the same extent as an original unless (1) a genuine question is raised as to the authenticity of the original or (2) in the circumstances it would be unfair to admit the duplicate in lieu of the original. Fed.Evid.R. 1003.

In copyright law, "copying" of a literary work consists in exact or substantial reproduction of the original, using original as a model as distinguished from an independent production of same thing, and a "copy" is that which comes so near to original as to give every person seeing it the idea created by original and must be such that ordinary observation would cause it to be recognized as having been taken from the work of another.

See also Authentication; Authentic copy; Conformed copy; Duplicate.

Examined copies are those which have been compared with the original or with an official record thereof.

Copyhold. In England a species of estate at will, or customary estate, the only visible title to which consisted of the copies of the court rolls, which were made out by the steward of the manor, on a tenant's being admitted to any parcel of land, or tenement belonging to the manor. It was an estate at the will of the lord, yet such a will as was agreeable to the custom of the manor, which customs were preserved and evidenced by the rolls of the several courts baron, in which they were entered. In a larger sense, copyhold was said to import every customary tenure (that is, every tenure pending on the particular custom of a manor), as opposed to free socage, or freehold, which later (since the abolition of knight-service) was considered as the general or common-law tenure of the country. Under the English Law of Property Act of 1922 copyholds were enfranchised and became freehold (or in certain cases leasehold).

Copyright. The right of literary property as recognized and sanctioned by positive law. An intangible, incorporeal right granted by statute to the author or originator of certain literary or artistic productions, whereby he is invested, for a specified period, with the sole and exclusive privilege of multiplying copies of the same and publishing and selling them.

Copyright protection subsists in original works of authorship fixed in any tangible medium of expression, now known or later developed, from which they can be perceived, reproduced, or otherwise communicated, either directly or with the aid of a machine or device. Works of authorship include the following categories: (1) literary works; (2) musical works, including any accompanying words; (3) dramatic works, including any accompanying music; (4) pantomimes and choreographic works; (5) pictorial, graphic, and sculptural works; (6) motion pictures and other audiovisual works; and (7) sound recordings. In no case does copyright protection for an original work of authorship extend to any idea, procedure, process, system, method of operation, concept, principle, or discovery, regardless of the form in which it is described, explained, illustrated, or embodied in such work. Copyright Act, 17 U.S. C.A. § 102.

Prior to the 1976 Copyright Act there was a distinction between common law and statutory protection whereby, generally, common law copyright protected works prior to publication and the federal copyright laws protected works following publication. The 1976 Act attempted to abolish all significant aspects of common law copyright and create a unified protection system by beginning statutory protection as soon as the work was reduced to a concrete form. 17 U.S.C.A. § 102(a). Under the 1976 Act an author is protected as soon as a work is recorded in some concrete way, since the Act protects all expressions upon fixation in a tangible medium. 17 U.S.C.A. § 102(a). Protection under the 1976 Act is secure until fifty years after the death of the author. 17 U.S.C.A. § 302(a).

In addition to injunctive, impoundment, and civil damages relief, criminal penalties are also provided for copyright infringement. 17 U.S.C.A. § 502 et seq.; 18 U.S.C.A. § 2319.

See also Adaptation right; Collective work; Common-law copyright; Compilation; Compulsory license; Created; Derivative work; Descriptive mark; Display; Fair use doctrine; First sale rule; Infringement; Limited publication; Literary property; Literary work; Work made for hire.

Copyright notice. A necessary notice in the form required by law which is placed in each published copy of the work copyrighted. Copyright Act, 17 U.S.C.A. § 401.

Copyright owner. As term is used with respect to any one of the exclusive rights comprised in a copyright, refers to the owner of that particular right. Copyright Act, 17 U.S.C.A. § 101.

Coram /kórəm/. Lat. Before; in presence of. Applied to persons only.

Coram nobis /kórəm nówbəs/. In our presence; before us. "Writ of error coram nobis" is procedural tool whose purpose is to correct errors of fact only, and its function is to bring before the court rendering the judgment matters of fact which, if known at time judgment was rendered, would have prevented its rendition. Its function is to bring attention of court to, and obtain relief from, errors of fact, such as a valid defense existing in facts of case, but which, without negligence on defendant's part, was not made, either through duress or fraud or excusable mistake, where facts did not appear on face of record, and were such as, if known in season, would have prevented rendition of the judgment questioned. The essence of the common law remedy of coram nobis is that it is addressed to the very court which

renders the judgment in which injustice is alleged to have been done, in contrast to appeals or review directed to another court; the words "coram nobis," meaning "our court," as compared to the common-law writ of "coram vobis," meaning "your court," clearly point this up. The writs of coram nobis and coram vobis have been abolished by Fed.R.Civil P. 60(b) and superseded by relief as provided by that rule. *See also* Coram vobis; Error coram nobis; Error coram vobis; Writ of error.

Coram vobis /kórəm vówbəs/. Before you. A writ of error directed by a court of review to the court which tried the cause, to correct an error in fact. *See* Coram nobis; Writ of error.

Core proceeding. For purposes of bankruptcy court jurisdiction, the term "core proceedings" encompasses those proceedings that arise under the Bankruptcy Code (11 U.S.C.A.), including, but not limited to, those proceedings which are specifically defined in 28 U.S.C.A. § 157(b)(2). Determining whether a proceeding is a core or non-core matter requires that a court analyze various causes of action raised by the parties and make findings that they sufficiently affect the debtor-creditor relationship so as to justify the issuance of final judgment.

Co-respondent. A co-defendant. A person summoned to answer a bill, petition, or libel, together with another respondent. Used for example to designate the person charged with adultery with the respondent in a suit for divorce for that cause, and joined as a defendant with such party.

Ordinarily term "co-respondent" denotes one joined as party defendant in equity suit.

Corner. A combination among the dealers in a specific commodity, or outside investors, for the purpose of buying up the greater portion of that commodity which is upon the market or may be brought to market, and holding the same back from sale, until the demand shall so far outrun the limited supply as to advance the price abnormally.

Cornering the market. *See* Corner.

Coroner /kórənər/. Public official, of English origin, charged with duty to make inquiry into the causes and circumstances of any death which occurs through violence or suddenly and with marks of suspicion; *i.e.* unnatural death. The functions and duties of coroners have been diminished having been replaced by medical examiners. *See* Coroner's inquest; Medical examiner.

Coroner's inquest. An inquisition or examination into the causes and circumstances of any death happening by violence or under suspicious conditions, held by the coroner with the assistance of a jury. *See also* Inquest.

Corporal punishment. Physical punishment as distinguished from pecuniary punishment or a fine; any kind of punishment of or inflicted on the body. The term may or may not include imprisonment, according to the context. The Supreme Court has upheld the use of reasonable corporal punishment in schools; though, a number of states, by statute, prohibit paddling of students. Whipping of prisoners has been found to be a form of "cruel and unusual punishment" as prohibited by the 8th Amendment. *See also* Punishment (*Cruel and unusual punishment*).

Corporate. Belonging to a corporation; as a corporate name. Incorporated; as a corporate body.

Corporate acquisition. The takeover of one corporation by another if both parties retain their legal existence after the transaction. An acquisition can be effected via a stock purchase or through a tax-free exchange of stock. *See also* Leveraged buyout; Merger; Reorganization; Takeover bid.

Corporate agent. A natural person or a corporation who is authorized to act for a corporation as for example in the function of accepting service of process. Broadly, term includes all employees and officers of corporation who have power to bind the corporation.

Corporate alter ego, doctrine of. Means that courts, in ignoring form and looking to substance, will regard stockholders as owners of corporation's property, or as the real parties in interest whenever it is necessary to do so to prevent fraud which might otherwise be perpetrated, to redress a wrong which might otherwise go without redress, or to do justice which might otherwise fail. *See* Piercing the corporate veil.

Corporate authorities. The title given in statutes of several states to the aggregate body of officers of a municipal corporation, or to certain of those officers (excluding the others) who are vested with authority in regard to the particular matter spoken of in the statute, as, taxation, bonded debt, regulation of the sale of liquors, etc.

Corporate body. Term is equivalent to "body corporate"; *i.e.* a corporation.

Corporate bonds. Debt securities issued by corporations, typically having a maturity of ten years or longer. A written promise by a corporation to pay a fixed sum of money at some future time named, with stated interest payable at some fixed time or intervals, given in return for money or its equivalent received by the corporation, sometimes secured, and sometimes not.

Corporate charter. Document issued by state agency or authority (commonly Secretary of State) granting corporation legal existence and right to function (*i.e.*, conduct business) as a corporation; or, may mean document filed with Secretary of State on incorporation of a business; *e.g.*, articles

of incorporation. *See also* Charter; Corporate franchise.

Corporate citizenship. Corporate status in the state of incorporation, though a foreign corporation is not a citizen for purposes of the Privileges and Immunities Clause (U.S.Const., Art. IV, § 2).

Corporate crime. Any criminal offense committed by and hence chargeable to a corporation because of activities of its officers or employees (*e.g.*, price fixing, toxic waste dumping). Often referred to as "white-collar" crime.

Corporate domicile. The domicile of a corporation is the state of its incorporation.

Corporate entity. The distinct status of a corporation which sets its existence apart from the status of its shareholders; its capacity to have a name of its own, to sue and be sued in its own name as well as the right to buy, sell, lease and mortgage its property in its own name.

Corporate finance. One of the three areas of the discipline of finance. It deals with the operation of the firm (both the investment decision and the financing decision) from that firm's point of view.

Corporate financial planning. Financial planning conducted by a firm that encompasses preparation of both the long-term financial plan and the short-term financial plan.

Corporate franchise. The right to exist and do business as a corporation. The right or privilege granted by the state or government to the persons forming an aggregate corporation, and their successors, to exist and do business as a corporation and to exercise the rights and powers incidental to that form of organization or necessarily implied in the grant. *See also* Corporate charter.

Corporate liability. *See* Piercing the corporate veil.

Corporate liquidation. *See* Liquidation.

Corporate name. When a corporation is formed, state statutes require that such be given a name and such name is kept on record with the proper state authority (*e.g.* Secretary of State's office). Only by and under such name may the corporation sue or be sued and do all legal acts.

Corporate officers. Those persons who fill the offices which are provided for in the corporate charter such as president, treasurer, etc., though in a broader sense the term includes vice presidents, general manager and other officials of the corporation.

Corporate opportunity doctrine. This doctrine precludes corporate fiduciaries from diverting to themselves business opportunities in which the corporation has an expectancy, property interest or right, or which in fairness should otherwise belong to corporation.

Corporate processing float. The time that elapses between receipt of payment from a customer and the depositing of the customer's check in the firm's bank account; the time required to process customer payments.

Corporate purpose. In reference to municipal corporations, and especially to their powers of taxation, a "corporate purpose" is one which shall promote the general prosperity and the welfare of the municipality; or a purpose necessary or proper to carry into effect the object of the creation of the corporate body or one which is germane to the general scope of the objects for which the corporation was created or has a legitimate connection with those objects and a manifest relation thereto. State statutes commonly require that the articles of incorporation of business corporations state the purpose of the corporation.

Corporate raider. *See* Raider.

Corporate reorganization. *See* Reorganization.

Corporate stock. Term embraces all equity securities issued by a corporation, but not bonds and debentures because these represent debt rather than stock (equity). *See* Stock.

Corporate trustees. Those corporations which are empowered by their charter to act as trustee, such as banks and trust companies.

Corporation. An artificial person or legal entity created by or under the authority of the laws of a state. An association of persons created by statute as a legal entity. The law treats the corporation itself as a person which can sue and be sued. The corporation is distinct from the individuals who comprise it (shareholders). The corporation survives the death of its investors, as the shares can usually be transferred. Such entity subsists as a body politic under a special denomination, which is regarded in law as having a personality and existence distinct from that of its several members, and which is, by the same authority, vested with the capacity of continuous succession, irrespective of changes in its membership, either in perpetuity or for a limited term of years, and of acting as a unit or single individual in matters relating to the common purpose of the association, within the scope of the powers and authorities conferred upon such bodies by law. Dartmouth College v. Woodward, 17 U.S. (4 Wheat.) 518, 636, 657, 4 L.Ed. 629.

See also Brother-sister corporation; Charitable corporation; Charitable organizations; Clearing corporation; Collapsible corporation; Cooperative corporation; Corporation *(S Corporation);* Domestic corporation; Dormant corporation; Foreign corporation; Municipal corporation; Non-profit corporation; Non-stock corporation; Parent company *or* corporation; Person; Public corporations; Registered corporation; Thin corporation.

Classification

According to the accepted definitions and rules, corporations are classified as follows:

Public and private. A public corporation is one created by the state for political purposes and to act as an agency in the administration of civil government, generally within a particular territory or subdivision of the state, and usually invested, for that purpose, with subordinate and local powers of legislation; such as a county, city, town, or school district. These are also sometimes called "political corporations." *See* Municipal corporation.

Private corporations are those founded by and composed of private individuals, for private (usually business) purposes, as distinguished from governmental purposes, and having no political or governmental franchises or duties.

The term "public" corporation is also frequently used to distinquish a business corporation whose shares are traded to and among the general public as opposed to a "private" (or "close" corporation) whose shares are not so traded.

Domestic and foreign. With reference to the laws and the courts of any given state, a "domestic" corporation is one created by, or organized under, the laws of that state; a "foreign" corporation is one created by or under the laws of another state, government, or country. *See also* Domestic corporation.

Subsidiary and parent. Subsidiary corporation is one in which another corporation (called parent corporation) owns at least a majority of the shares, and thus has control.

Other Compound and Descriptive Terms

Acquired corporation. The corporation which disappears as a result of a merger or acquisition.

Acquiring corporation. The offeror in a merger or acquisition.

Aggressor corporation. A corporation that attempts to obtain control of a publicly held corporation, either by a direct cash tender or public exchange offer to shareholders, or by way of merger, which requires the agreement or assent of the target's management. *See* Takeover bid.

Business corporation. One formed for the purpose of transacting business in the widest sense of that term, including not only trade and commerce, but manufacturing, mining, banking, insurance, transportation, and practically every form of commercial or industrial activity where the purpose of the organization is pecuniary profit; contrasted with religious, charitable, educational, and other like organizations, which are sometimes grouped in the statutory law of a state under the general designation of "corporations not for profit."

Brother-sister corporation. See that title.

Close (or closely held) corporation. A corporation whose shares, or at least voting shares, are held by a single shareholder or closely-knit group of shareholders. Generally, there are no public investors and its shareholders are active in the conduct of the business. A close corporation is one which fills its own vacancies or in which power of voting is held through manipulation under fixed and virtually perpetual proxies. A corporation, the stock ownership of which is not widely dispersed. Instead, a few shareholders are in control of corporate policy and are in a position to benefit personally from such policy.

Closely held corporation. See Close corporation, above.

Collapsible corporation. A corporation formed for one specific venture such as a motion picture, or construction of a building, and then collapsed, allowing tax advantages to the shareholders. I.R.C. § 341.

C corporation. A regular corporation governed by Subchapter C of the Internal Revenue Code. Distinguished from S corporations, which fall under Subchapter S of the Code. *See also S corporation below.*

Controlled corporation. A corporation where the majority of stock outstanding is held by one individual or one firm. Where there is complete domination and control of a corporation so that it has no independent identity, a court may disregard the corporate form and extend liability for corporate obligations beyond the confines of a corporation's separate entity whenever it is necessary to prevent fraud or achieve equity.

Corporation de facto. One existing under color of law and in pursuance of an effort made in good faith to organize a corporation under the statute; an association of men claiming to be a legally incorporated company, and exercising the powers and functions of a corporation, but without actual lawful authority to do so. Its elements are a law or charter authorizing such a corporation, an attempt in good faith to comply with law authorizing its incorporation, and unintentional omission of essential requirements of the law or charter, and exercise in good faith of corporate functions under the law or charter. A corporation which has been defectively formed but which is not subject to collateral attack.

Corporation de jure. That which exists by reason of full compliance by incorporators with requirements of an existing law permitting organization of such corporation.

Eleemosynary corporation. Corporation with charitable functions and purposes. *See also* Charitable corporation.

Joint venture corporation. A corporation which has joined with other individuals or corporations within the corporate framework in some specific undertaking commonly found in oil, chemical, electronic and atomic fields.

Municipal corporation. See that title.

Non-stock corporation. Type of corporation where ownership is not recognized by stock; *e.g.* municipal corporation.

Not-for-profit corporation. A corporation formed for some charitable or benevolent purpose and not for profit making and generally organized under special statutes for this purpose. Such corporations are afforded special tax treatment. *See also* Non-profit corporation.

Professional corporation. In most states such may be organized by those rendering personal services to public of a type which requires a license or other legal authorization and which prior to such statutory authorization could not be performed by a corporation. Includes, but is not limited to, public accountants, certified public accountants, chiropractors, osteopaths, physicians, surgeons, dentists, podiatrists, chiropodists, architects, veterinarians, optometrists, and attorneys at law. Tax benefits are one of several reasons for professional incorporation. Incorporation does not alter professional responsibility or privilege nor does it insulate principal from malpractice liability.

Public-service corporations. Those whose operations serve the needs of the general public or conduce to the comfort and convenience of an entire community, such as public transportation, gas, water, and electric light companies. The business of such companies is said to be "affected with a public interest," and for that reason they are subject to legislative regulation and control to a greater extent than corporations not of this character.

S corporation. A small business corporation with a statutorily limited number of shareholders, which, under certain conditions, has elected to have its taxable income taxed to its shareholders at regular income tax rates. I.R.C. § 1361 et seq. Its major significance is the fact that S corporation status usually avoids the corporate income tax, and corporate losses can be claimed by the shareholders. This election is for federal tax purposes only; in terms of legal characteristics under state law, the "S" status corporation is no different than any other regular corporation.

Shell corporation. A corporate frame, containing few, if any, assets, kept alive by required filings, generally for future use.

Subchapter C corporation. A regular corporation subject to the provisions of Subchapter C (§§ 301–386) of the Internal Revenue Code. Distinguished from an S corporation, which is governed by Subchapter S of the Code.

Target corporation. Corporation attempted to be taken over in a tender offer or other type of takeover bid. A corporation viewed as having a good potential for takeover by another corporation or individual.

Corporeal /kərpóriyəl/. A term descriptive of such things as have an objective, material existence; perceptible by the senses of sight and touch; possessing a real body. Opposed to incorporeal and spiritual. There is a distinction between "corporeal" and "corporal." The former term means "possessing a body," that is, tangible, physical, material; the latter means "relating to or affecting a body," that is, bodily, external. Corporeal denotes the nature or physical existence of a body; corporal denotes its exterior or the co-ordination of it with some other body. Hence we speak of "corporeal hereditaments," but of "corporal punishment," "corporal touch," "corporal oath," etc.

Corporeal hereditaments /kərpóriyəl hərédətəmənts/. *See* Hereditaments.

Corporeal property. Such as affects the senses, and may be seen and handled, as opposed to incorporeal property, which cannot be seen or handled, and exists only in contemplation. Thus a house is corporeal, but the annual rent payable for its occupation is incorporeal. Corporeal property is, if movable, capable of manual transfer: if immovable, possession of it may be delivered up. But incorporeal property cannot be so transferred, but some other means must be adopted for its transfer, of which the most usual is an instrument in writing.

Corpse /kórps/. The dead body of a human being.

Corpus /kórpəs/. Lat. Body; an aggregate or mass (of men, laws, or articles); physical substance, as distinguished from intellectual conception; the principal sum or capital, as distinguished from interest or income. The main body or principal of a trust.

A substantial or positive fact, as distinguished from what is equivocal and ambiguous. The *corpus delicti* (body of an offense) is the fact of its having been actually committed.

A corporeal act of any kind (as distinguished from *animus* or mere intention), on the part of him who wishes to acquire a thing, whereby he obtains the physical ability to exercise his power over it whenever he pleases. The word occurs frequently in this sense in the civil law.

As proof, it consists of showing that there exists the object of the crime (dead body in homicide case), and that such resulted from criminal act of some person. In some jurisdictions, it cannot be proved by confession of defendant in the first

instance but only after extrinsic evidence (of the elements) has been offered. In other states, confessional evidence is admissible in the first instance. *See Corpus delicti, below.*

Corpus delicti /kórpəs dəlíktay/. The body of a crime. The body (material substance) upon which a crime has been committed, *e.g.*, the corpse of a murdered man, the charred remains of a house burned down. In a derivative sense, the objective proof or substantial fact that a crime has been committed. The "corpus delicti" of a crime is the body, foundation or substance of the crime, which ordinarily includes two elements: the act and the criminal agency of the act.

Corpus juris /kórpəs júrəs/. A body of law. A term used to signify a book comprehending several collections of law. There are two principal collections to which this name is given; the *Corpus Juris Civilis,* and the *Corpus Juris Canonici.* Also name of an encyclopædic statement of the principles of American law; *e.g. Corpus Juris Secundum.*

Correctional institutions. A generic term describing prisons, jails, reformatories and other places of correction and detention.

Correctional system. Network of governmental agencies concerned with prisons, jails, houses of correction and reformatories; may also refer to pardon and parole systems.

Correction, house of. A prison for the reformation of petty or juvenile offenders.

Correspondence. Interchange of written communications. The letters written by a person and the answers written by the one to whom they are addressed. The agreement of things with one another.

Correspondence audit. An audit conducted by the Internal Revenue Service through the use of the mail. Typically, the I.R.S. writes to the taxpayer requesting the verification of a particular deduction or exemption. The completion of a special form or the remittance of copies of records or other support is all that is requested of the taxpayer. *See also* Audit.

Correspondent. A securities firm, bank or other financial organization which regularly performs services for another in a place or market to which the other does not have direct access. Securities firms may have correspondents in foreign countries or on exchanges of which they are not members. Bank which serves as agent for another bank in performing services; *e.g.* carrying deposit balance or issuing letters of credit for bank in another city.

Correspondent bank. *See* Correspondent.

Corroborate /kəróbəreyt/. To strengthen; to add weight or credibility to a thing by additional and confirming facts or evidence. The testimony of a witness is said to be corroborated when it is shown to correspond with the representation of some other witnesses, or to comport with some facts otherwise known or established. *See* Corroborating evidence.

Corroborating evidence /kəróbəreytiŋ évədəns/. Evidence supplementary to that already given and tending to strengthen or confirm it. Additional evidence of a different character to the same point. In some jurisdictions, corroborating evidence of an accomplice to the crime is given much weight.

Corrupt. Spoiled; tainted; vitiated; depraved; debased; morally degenerate. As used as a verb, to change ones morals and principles from good to bad.

Corruption. An act done with an intent to give some advantage inconsistent with official duty and the rights of others. The act of an official or fiduciary person who unlawfully and wrongfully uses his station or character to procure some benefit for himself or for another person, contrary to duty and the rights of others. *See* Bribe; Extortion.

Corruptly. When used in a statute, this term, generally imports a wrongful design to acquire some pecuniary or other advantage.

Corrupt motive doctrine. Doctrine invoked in assessing crimes like bribery to determine motive of gift or payment.

Corrupt practices acts. Federal and state statutes regulating campaign contributions and expenditures, including disclosure requirements. 2 U.S.C.A. § 231 et seq.

Cosigner. Person who signs a document or instrument along with another, often assuming obligations and providing credit support to be shared with other obligor(s).

Cost. Expense; price. The sum or equivalent expended, paid or charged for something. *See also* Actual cost; Budgeted cost; Current cost; Life-cycle costing; Net cost; Noncash charge; Rate.

Activity-based costing. An accounting system that collects financial and operational data on the basis of the underlying nature and extent of business activities.

Agency cost. In accounting, the incremental cost (to the principal), above what would be incurred in perfect capital and labor markets, of using an agent.

Committed cost. A cost related to the possession of basic plant assets or organizational personnel that an organization must have to operate.

Committed fixed cost. A cost that is related either to the long-term investment in plant and equipment of a business or to the organizational personnel who top management deem permanent; a cost that cannot be changed without long-run detriment to the organization.

Common cost. See Indirect costs, *below.*

Controllable cost. A cost which management has the ability to authorize incurrence or directly influence magnitude.

Conversion cost. The total of direct labor and overhead cost. The cost necessary to transform direct materials into a finished good or service.

Court costs. See Costs (litigation).

Cost accounting. The area of accounting which focuses on the method and system used to compile and analyze the costs of selling and manufacturing products. It includes the method for classifying, summarizing, recording, reporting, and allocating the actual costs incurred and comparing them with the standard costs established. Areas of cost accounting include: job order, process, direct, and standard costing. *See e.g.* Absorption costing; Current cost accounting; Process costing system.

Cost basis. In accounting, the cost basis of an asset is the amount paid for the asset in cash or property. The value placed on an asset in a financial statement in terms of its cost; used in determining capital gains or losses.

Cost bond. See Costs, *infra.*

Cost contract. See Cost-plus contract, *infra.*

Cost depletion. In accounting and taxation, depletion computed in oil production without reference to discovery or percentage depletion.

Current cost. The present cost of replacing an asset with a similar asset in similar condition.

Differential cost. A cost that differs in amount among the alternatives being considered.

Distribution cost. Any cost incurred to market a product or service; all amounts spent on advertising, warehousing, and shipping products to customers

Cost of completion. Measure of damages in breach of contract claim or action.

Engineered cost. Any cost that has been found to bear an observable and known relationship to a quantifiable activity base.

Expired costs. Expenses and losses.

Imputed cost. A value expressing cost which is derived from or based on factors other than actual cost records; estimated costs.

Indirect costs. Costs not readily identifiable with production of specific goods or services, but rather applicable to production activity in general; *e.g.,* overhead allocations for general and administrative activities.

Joint cost. All costs (direct materials, direct labor, and overhead) incurred in a joint process up to the split-off point.

Litigation costs. See Costs (litigation).

Marginal cost. The increase or decrease in total cost that materializes as a result of a variation in output.

Mixed cost. A cost that has both a variable and a fixed element. A cost that neither fluctuates in direct proportion nor remains constant with changes in activity.

Opportunity cost. A potential benefit that is foregone because one course of action is chosen over another.

Opportunity cost of capital. The highest rate of return that could be earned by using capital for the most attractive alternative project available.

Period cost. A cost unrelated to the acquisition or manufacture of inventory; it is expensed when incurred.

Product cost. Any cost associated with making or acquiring inventory; the total of direct materials, direct labor, overhead, and any outside processing costs.

Relevant cost. A cost that is logically associated with a specific problem or decision.

Replacement cost. An appraisal method for determining value by substituting a like property. *See also* Replacement cost.

Relevant costing. A process that compares, to the extent possible and practical, the incremental revenues and incremental costs of alternative decisions.

Setup costs. The direct or indirect labor costs of getting equipment ready for each new production run.

Standard cost. A budgeted or estimated cost to manufacture a single unit of product or perform a single service.

Standard costing system. A product costing system that determines product cost by using standards or benchmarks for quantities and prices of component elements. It allows actual costs to be compared against norms for purposes of cost control.

Sunk cost. A cost that has already been incurred and will not be altered by subsequent decisions.

Target costing. A method of determining what the cost of a product should be based on the estimated selling price of the product less the desired profit.

Transaction cost. Any explicit or implicit cost connected with making a transaction; for example, a commission (explicit) or the time and effort to read and interpret information (implicit).

Transferred-in cost. The cost of transferred-in units that is incurred in a previous manufacturing process.

Unit cost. Cost of a single unit of product or service. Total cost divided by number of units.

Variable costs. Those costs which in the short run vary in close relationship with changes in output, including items such as raw materials, labor directly used in production, and per unit royalties.

Weighted-average process costing. A process costing method under which all goods manufactured during a period are carried at the same unit cost.

Cost Accounting Standard Board (CASB). A body established by Congress in 1970 to promulgate uniform cost accounting standards for defense contractors and federal agencies; disbanded in 1980 and recreated in 1988. Pronouncements still carry weight of law for those organizations that are within its jurisdiction.

Cost allocation. In accounting, the assignment of any indirect cost to one or more cost objects using some reasonable basis.

Cost and freight (C.A.F.). Quoted sales price includes cost of goods and freight but not insurance or other special charges.

Cost avoidance. Finding acceptable alternatives to high-cost items and not spending money for unnecessary goods or services.

Cost center. In business, a responsibility center in which the manager has the authority to incur costs and is evaluated on the basis of how well costs are controlled.

Cost consciousness. A companywide attitude about the topics of cost understanding, cost containment, cost avoidance, and cost reduction.

Cost containment. Minimizing, to the extent possible, period-by-period increases in per-unit variable and total fixed costs.

Cost control system. A logical structure of formal and/or informal activities designed to analyze and evaluate how well expenditures were managed during a period.

Cost flow assumption. In accounting, an assumption regarding the flow of inventory costs through a firm's accounting system.

Co-stipulator. A joint promisor.

Cost object. In accounting, anything to which costs attach or are related; can be a product, department, division, or territory; specified to clarify a point of reference with regard to decision making.

Cost of capital. The annual percent that a utility must receive to maintain its credit, to pay a return to the owners of the enterprise and to insure the attraction of capital in amounts adequate to meet future needs. It involves a calculation of the interest a utility must pay on its borrowed capital (debt) and the cost of attracting and paying investors for its common or preferred stock (equity).

Cost of carrying. In accounting, the variable cost of carrying one unit of inventory in stock for one year; includes the opportunity cost of the capital invested in inventory.

Cost of goods manufactured. The total cost of the goods completed and transferred to finished goods during the period.

Cost of goods sold. The total cost of inventory that a company has sold during an accounting period.

Cost of living clause. A provision, commonly in labor agreements, and also in certain pension, retirement, and disability benefit programs, giving an automatic wage or benefit increase tied in some way to cost-of-living rises in the economy. Cost of living is usually measured by the Consumer Price Index (CPI) *(q.v.)*.

May also exist in certain long term leases where, for example, rent increases are tied to Consumer Price Index.

Cost of ordering. The variable costs associated with preparing, receiving, and paying for an order.

Cost of purchasing. The quoted purchase price of inventory, minus any discounts allowed, plus shipping charges.

Cost pool. A collection of monetary amounts incurred either for the same purpose or at the same organizational level.

Cost-plus contract. One which fixes the amount to be paid the contractor on a basis, generally, of the cost of the material and labor, plus an agreed percentage thereof as profits. Such contracts are used when costs of production or construction are unknown or difficult to ascertain in advance.

Cost reduction. Lowering current costs, especially those that may be in excess of that which is necessary.

Costs (litigation). A pecuniary allowance, made to the successful party (and recoverable from the losing party), for his expenses in prosecuting or defending an action or a distinct proceeding within an action. In federal courts, costs are allowed as a matter of course to the prevailing party unless the court otherwise directs; also, specified fees and certain court expenses may be taxed as

costs. Fed.R.Civil P. 54(d); Fed.R.App.P. 39; 28 U.S.C.A. § 1920. Generally, "costs" do not include attorney fees unless such fees are by a statute denominated costs or are by statute allowed to be recovered as costs in the case.

Fees and charges required by law to be paid to the courts or some of their officers, the amount of which is fixed by statute or court rule; *e.g.* filing and service fees.

See also Closing costs; Fee; Security for costs; Service charge.

Bill of costs. A certified, itemized statement of the amount of costs in an action or suit.

Cost bond, or bond for costs. A bond given by a party to an action to secure the eventual payment of such costs as may be awarded against him. A bond which may be required of an appealing party in a civil case; *e.g.* Fed.R.App.P. 7. Purpose of bond is to cover appellee's costs in event of affirmance of judgment.

Final costs. Such costs as are to be paid at the end of the suit. Costs, the liability for which depends upon the final result of the litigation.

Interlocutory costs. Costs accruing upon proceedings in the intermediate stages of a cause, as distinguished from final costs; such as the costs of motions.

Security for costs. A security which a defendant in an action may require of a plaintiff who does not reside within the jurisdiction of the court, for the payment of such costs as may be awarded to the defendant. *See also Cost bond, above.*

Statutory costs. Amounts awarded for various phases of litigation that are fixed by statute. Word "costs" generally refers to statutory fees to which officers, witnesses, jurors and others are entitled for their services in an action and which statutes authorize to be taxed and included in the judgment. See *e.g.* 28 U.S.C.A. § 1920.

Taxation of litigation costs. See Taxation.

Costs, insurance and freight (C.I.F.). Quoted sales price which includes cost of goods, freight and insurance.

Cost-volume-profit analysis. In accounting, a procedure that examines changes in costs and volume levels and the resulting effects on net income (profit).

Co-sureties /kòwshúrətiyz/. Joint sureties; two or more sureties to the same obligation.

Cotenancy. A tenancy by several distinct titles but by unity of possession, or any joint ownership or common interest with its grantor. The term is broad enough to comprise both tenancy in common and joint tenancy.

Council. An assembly of persons for the purpose of concerting measures of state or municipal policy. The legislative body in the government of cities or boroughs. An advisory body selected to aid the executive; *i.e.* a body appointed to advise and assist the governor in his executive or judicial capacities or both. *See also* City council; Legislative council; Metropolitan council.

Counsel /káwnsəl/. Attorney or counsellor *(q.v.)*.

Advice and assistance given by one person to another in regard to a legal matter, proposed line of conduct, claim, or contention. *See also* Counsel, right to.

The words "counsel" and "advise" may be, and frequently are, used in criminal law to describe the offense of a person who, not actually doing the felonious act, by his will contributed to it or procured it to be done. *See* Accomplice; Aid and abet.

See also Legislative counsel; Of counsel.

Junior counsel. The younger of the counsel employed on the same side of a case, or the one lower in standing or rank, or who is intrusted with the less important parts of the preparation or trial of the cause.

Counsellor. An attorney; lawyer. Member of the legal profession who gives legal advice and handles the legal affairs of client, including, if necessary, appearing on his or her behalf in civil, criminal, or administrative actions and proceedings.

Counsel of record. Attorney whose appearance has been filed with court papers.

Counsel, right to. Constitutional right of criminal defendant to court appointed attorney if he is financially unable to retain private counsel; guaranteed by Sixth and Fourteenth Amendments to U.S. Constitution, and as well by court rule (Fed. R.Crim.P. 44), and statute (18 U.S.C.A. § 3006A). Such right to counsel exists with respect to felonies (Gideon v. Wainright, 372 U.S. 335, 83 S.Ct. 792); misdemeanors when the sentence is to a jail term (Argersinger v. Hemlin, 407 U.S. 25, 92 S.Ct. 2006), and to juvenile delinquency proceedings (In re Gault, 387 U.S. 1, 87 S.Ct. 1428). The extent of this right extends from the time that judicial proceedings have been initiated against the accused, whether by way of formal charge, preliminary hearing, indictment, information, or arraignment through to sentencing and appeal. There is no absolute right to appointed counsel in postconviction proceedings. "Counsel" however within Sixth Amendment does not include a lay person but refers only to person authorized to practice law. *See also* Assistance of counsel; Critical stage; Effective assistance of counsel; Escobedo Rule; Miranda Rule; Public defender.

Count, *v.* In pleading, to declare; to recite; to state a case; to narrate the facts constituting a plaintiff's cause of action. To plead orally; to plead or argue a case in court; to recite or read in court; to recite a count in court.

Count, *n.* In pleading, the plaintiff's statement of a cause of action; a separate and independent claim. Used also to signify the several parts of an indictment, each charging a distinct offense. Fed. R. Crim. P. 7(c)(1), 8. The usual organizational subunit of an indictment.

"Count" and "charge" when used relative to allegations in an indictment or information are synonymous.

An earl.

Common counts. Certain general counts or forms inserted in a declaration in an action to recover a money debt, not founded on the circumstances of the individual case, but intended to guard against a possible variance, and to enable the plaintiff to take advantage of any ground of liability which the proof may disclose, within the general scope of the action.

The various forms of an action of assumpsit. In the action of *assumpsit*, these counts are as follows: For goods sold and delivered, or bargained and sold; for work done; for money lent; for money paid; for money received to the use of the plaintiff; for interest; or for money due on an account stated.

General count. One stating in a general way the plaintiff's claim.

Several counts. Where a plaintiff has several distinct causes of action, he is allowed to pursue them cumulatively in the same action, subject to certain rules which the law prescribes. See *e.g.* Fed.R. Civil P. 8(e).

Special count. As opposed to the common counts, in pleading, a special count is a statement of the actual facts of the particular case, or a count in which the plaintiff's claim is set forth with all needed particularity.

Counter, *adj.* Adverse; antagonistic; opposing or contradicting; contrary.

Counter-affidavit. An affidavit made and presented in contradiction or opposition to an affidavit which is made the basis or support of a motion or application.

Counter-bond. Bond which indemnifies a surety. *See Counter-security below.*

Counterclaim. See that title.

Counter-security. A security given to one who has entered into a bond or become surety for another; a countervailing bond of indemnity.

Counterclaim. A claim presented by a defendant in opposition to or deduction from the claim of the plaintiff. Fed.R. Civil P. 13. If established, such will defeat or diminish the plaintiff's claim. Under federal rule practice, and also in most states, counterclaims are either compulsory (required to be made) or permissive (made at option of defendant).

A counterclaim may be any cause of action in favor of one or more defendants or a person whom a defendant represents against one or more plaintiffs, a person whom a plaintiff represents or a plaintiff and other persons alleged to be liable. New York C.P.L.R. § 3019(a).

For requisite content of counterclaim under Federal Rules of Civil Procedure, *see* Complaint. *Compare* Cross-claim. *See also* Offset; Recoupment; Set-off; Transaction or occurrence test.

Compulsory counterclaim. A pleading shall state as a counterclaim any claim which at the time of serving the pleading the pleader has against any opposing party, if it arises out of the transaction or occurrence that is the subject matter of the opposing party's claim and does not require for its adjudication the presence of third parties of whom the court cannot acquire jurisdiction. But the pleader need not state the claim if (1) at the time the action was commenced the claim was the subject of another pending action, or (2) the opposing party brought suit upon his claim by attachment or other process by which the court did not acquire jurisdiction to render a personal judgment on that claim. Fed.R. Civil P. 13(a).

For claim to constitute a compulsory counterclaim, it must be logically related to original claim and arise out of same subject matter on which original claim is based; many of same factual legal issues, or offshoots of same basic controversy between parties must be involved in a compulsory counterclaim. Tasner v. Billera, D.C. Ill., 379 F.Supp. 809, 813. *See also* Transaction or occurrence test.

Permissive Counterclaim. A pleading may state as a counterclaim any claim against an opposing party not arising out of the transaction or occurrence that is the subject matter of the opposing party's claim. Fed.R. Civil P. 13(b).

Counterfeit /káwntərfit/. To forge; to copy or imitate, without authority or right, and with a view to deceive or defraud, by passing the copy or thing forged for that which is original or genuine. Most commonly applied to the fraudulent and criminal imitation of money or securities. 18 U.S.C.A. § 471 et seq. Counterfeit in common parlance signifies fabrication of false image or representation; counterfeiting an instrument means falsely making it; and in its broadest sense means making of copy without authority or right and with view to deceive or defraud by passing copy as original or genuine. *See also* Bootlegging;

False making; Falsify; Forgery; Gray market goods; Imitation.

Counterfeit coin. Coin not genuine, but resembling or apparently intended to resemble or pass for genuine coin, including genuine coin prepared or altered so as to resemble or pass for coin of a higher denomination.

Counterfeiter. One who unlawfully makes base coin in imitation of the true metal, or forges false currency, or any instrument of writing, bearing a likeness and similitude to that which is lawful and genuine, with an intention of deceiving and imposing upon another.

Counter-feisance. The act of forging.

Countermand. A change or revocation of orders, authority, or instructions previously issued. It may be either express or implied; the former where the order or instruction already given is explicitly annulled or recalled; the latter where the party's conduct is incompatible with the further continuance of the order or instruction, as where a new order is given inconsistent with the former order.

Counteroffer. Statement made by the offeree to the offeror relating to the same matter as the original offer and proposing a substituted bargain differing from that proposed by the original offer. A statement by the offeree which has the legal effect of rejecting the offer and of proposing a new offer to the offeror. Restatement, Second, Contracts, § 59. However, the provisions of U.C.C. § 2–207(1)(2) modifies this principle of contract law as regards sales of goods by providing that the "additional terms are to be construed as proposals for addition to the contract."

Counterpart. In conveyancing, the corresponding part of an instrument; a duplicate or copy. Where an instrument of conveyance, as a lease, is executed in parts, that is, by having several copies or duplicates made and interchangeably executed, that which is executed by the grantor is usually called the "original," and the rest are "counterparts"; although, where all the parties execute every part, this renders them all originals. *See* Duplicate.

Countersign. As a noun, the signature of a secretary or other subordinate officer to any writing signed by the principal or superior to vouch for the authenticity of it. *See also* Attestation.

As a verb, to sign in addition to the signature of another in order to attest the authenticity.

Counter-signature. *See* Countersign.

Counter trade. The exchange of goods for other goods rather than cash. *See also* Barter.

Countervail. To counterbalance; to avail against with equal force or virtue; to compensate for, or serve as an equivalent of or substitute for.

Countervailing equity. *See* Equity.

Country. The territory occupied by an independent nation or people, or the inhabitants of such territory. In the primary meaning "country" denotes the population, the nation, the state, or the government, having possession and dominion over a territory.

Rural, as distinguished from urban areas.

County. The largest territorial division for local government in state. Its powers and importance vary from state to state, and as well within the given state. In certain New England states, it exists mainly for judicial administration. In Louisiana, the equivalent unit is called a parish. Counties are held in some jurisdictions to be municipal corporations, and are sometimes said to be involuntary municipal corporations. Other cases, seeking to distinguish between the two, hold that counties are agencies or political subdivisions of the state for governmental purposes, and not, like municipal corporations, incorporations of the inhabitants of specified regions for purposes of local government. Counties are also said to be merely quasi corporations.

County affairs. Those relating to the county in its organic and corporate capacity and included within its governmental or corporate powers.

County attorney. Attorney employed by county to represent it in civil matters; also, the prosecuting attorney in many counties.

County auditor. County official whose responsibility is examination of accounts and financial records of the county.

County board. The administrative body which governs a county.

County board of equalization. A body created for the purpose of equalizing values of property subject to taxation.

County board of supervisors. A body of town and city officers acting for and on behalf of county in such matters as have been turned over to them by law.

County bonds. Broadly, any bonds issued by county officials to be paid for by a levy on a special taxing district, whether or not coextensive with the county.

County business. All business pertaining to the county as a corporate entity. All business of the county, and any other business of such county connected with or interrelated with the business of any other county properly within the jurisdiction of the county commissioners' court.

County commissioners. Officers of a county, charged with a variety of administrative and executive duties, but principally with the management of the financial affairs of the county, its police regulations, and its corporate business.

Sometimes the local laws give them limited judicial powers. In some states they are called "supervisors".

County courts. The powers and jurisdiction of such courts are governed by state constitutions or statutes; some with strictly administrative, or strictly judicial functions, or a combination of both; some with only criminal jurisdiction, or only civil, or both; some have exclusive jurisdictions, others concurrent jurisdiction; such jurisdictional powers may, in addition, be either general or specific.

County officers. Those whose general authority and jurisdiction are confined within the limits of the county in which they are appointed, who are appointed in and for a particular county, and whose duties apply only to that county, and through whom the county performs its usual political functions. Public officers who fill a position usually provided for in the organization of counties and county governments, and are selected by the county to represent it continuously and as part of the regular and permanent administration of public power in carrying out certain acts with the performance of which it is charged in behalf of the public.

County powers. Such only as are expressly provided by law or which are necessarily implied from those expressed.

County property. That which a county is authorized to acquire, hold, and sell.

County purposes. Those exercised by the county acting as a municipal corporation. As regards the rate of taxation, all purposes for which county taxation may be levied. Test whether a tax is levied for county purposes is whether it is for strictly county uses, for which county or its inhabitants alone would benefit, or is it for a purpose in which entire state is concerned and will profit.

County road. One which lies wholly within one county, and which is thereby distinguished from a state road, which is a road lying in two or more counties.

County-seat. A county-seat or county-town is the chief town of a county, where the county buildings and courts are located and the county business transacted.

County supervisors. *See County commissioners, above.*

County tax. Tax exclusively for county purposes, in which state has no sovereign interest or responsibility, and which has no connection with duties of county in its relation to state.

County-town. The county-seat; the town in which the seat of government of the county is located.

County warrant. An order or warrant drawn by some duly authorized officer of the county, directed to the county treasurer and directing him to pay out of the funds of the county a designated sum of money to a named individual, or to his order or to bearer.

Foreign county. Any county having a judicial and municipal organization separate from that of the county where matters arising in the former county are called in question, though both may lie within the same state or country.

Coupled with an interest. This phrase, in the law of agency, has reference to a writing creating, conveying to, or vesting in the agent an interest in the estate or property which is the subject of the agency, as distinguished from the proceeds or profits resulting from the exercise of the agency.

Coupon equivalent yield. True interest cost expressed on the basis of a 365–day year.

Coupons. Interest and dividend certificates; also those parts of a commercial instrument which are to be cut, and which are evidence of something connected with the contract mentioned in the instrument. They are generally attached to certificates of loan, where the interest is payable at particular periods, and, when the interest is paid, they are cut off and delivered to the payor. That portion of a bond redeemable at a specified date for interest payment.

Coupons are written contracts for the payment of a definite sum of money on a given day, and being drawn and executed in a form and mode for the purpose, that they may be separated from the bonds and other instruments to which they are usually attached, it is held that they are negotiable and that a suit may be maintained on them without the necessity of producing the bonds. Each matured coupon upon a negotiable bond is a separable promise, distinct from the promises to pay the bonds or the other coupons, and gives rise to a separate cause of action.

Coupon bonds. Bonds to which are attached coupons for the several successive installments of interest to maturity.

Coupon notes. Promissory notes with coupons attached, the coupons being notes for interest written at the bottom of the principal note, and designed to be cut off severally and presented for payment as they mature.

Coupon payments. The contractually agreed upon interest payments made by a firm to the bond's owner.

Coupon rate of interest. The interest rate stated on a bond. The coupon rate of interest times the *par*, or principal, value of a bond determines the periodic dollar interest payments received by the bondholder.

The sum of interest payments to be made within one year divided by the par value of the bond. Often called simply coupon or coupon rate.

Coupon securities. Such securities usually provide for the payment of principal to the bearer thereof, and for payment of an installment of interest to the bearer of the respective interest coupons upon presentation thereof upon their respective due dates. Coupon securities are usually in the denomination of $1,000. Ownership of the security and/or coupons is transferred by delivery thereof. Such a security is negotiable under the Uniform Commercial Code. U.C.C. §§ 8–105, 8–302.

Course. In surveying, the direction of a line with reference to a meridian.

Course of business. What is usually and normally done in the management of trade or business. *See also* Course of dealing; Regular course of business.

In worker's compensation acts, the usual course of business of the employer covers the normal operations which form part of the ordinary business carried on, and not including incidental and occasional operations having for their purpose the preservation of the premises or the appliances used in the business.

Commercial paper is said to be transferred, or sales alleged to have been fraudulent may be shown to have been made, "in the course of business," or "in the usual and ordinary course of business," when the circumstances of the transaction are such as usually and ordinarily attend dealings of the same kind and do not exhibit any signs of haste, secrecy, or fraudulent intention.

Course of dealing. A sequence of previous acts and conduct between the parties to a particular transaction which is fairly to be regarded as establishing a common basis of understanding for interpreting their expressions and other conduct. U.C.C. § 1–205(1). *See also* Trade usage; Usage (Usage of trade).

Course of employment. These words as applied to compensation for injuries within the purview of worker's compensation acts, refer to the time, place, and circumstances under which the accident takes place. A worker is in course of employment when, within time covered by employment, he is doing something which he might reasonably do while so employed at proper place. Generally, in order that an injury may arise out of and in the course of employment, it must be received while the worker is doing the duty he is employed to perform and also as a natural incident of the work flowing therefrom as a natural consequence and directly connected therewith.

The expression "in the course of his employment," in the rule that an employer is liable for the torts of an employee done in the course of employment, means while engaged in the service of the employer while engaged generally in the employer's work, as distinguished from acts done when the employee steps outside of employment to do an act for himself or herself not connected with the employer's business. The test as to whether an injury has arisen out of the "course of employment" is whether there is a causal connection between the duties of employment and the injury suffered.

State statutes and decisions differ as to the types and scope of activities which fall within "course of employment".

See also Arising out of and in the course of own employment; Deviation; Scope of employment.

Course of performance. The understandings of performance which develop by conduct without objection between two parties during the performance of an executory contract.

Course of river. The course of a river is a line parallel with its banks. The term is not synonymous with the "current" of the river.

Course of trade. What is customarily or ordinarily done in the management of trade or business. *See also* Course of business.

Course of vessel. In navigation, the "course" of a vessel is her apparent course, and not her heading at any given moment. It is her actual course.

Courses and distances. A method or form for describing real estate in deeds and mortgages by setting forth the distances in one direction as a boundary, followed by other distances and the direction thereof until the entire parcel has been described. *See also* Metes and bounds.

Court. A space which is uncovered, but which may be partly or wholly inclosed by buildings or walls. When used in connection with a street, indicates a short street, blind alley, or open space like a short street inclosed by dwellings or other buildings facing thereon.

A legislative assembly. Parliament is called in the old books a court of the king, nobility, and commons assembled. This meaning of the word has also been retained in the titles of some deliberative bodies, such as the "General Court" of Massachusetts, *i.e.,* the legislature.

The person and suit of the sovereign; the place where the sovereign sojourns with his regal retinue, wherever that may be. The English government is spoken of in diplomacy as the court of St. James, because the palace of St. James is the official palace.

An organ of the government, belonging to the judicial department, whose function is the application of the laws to controversies brought before it and the public administration of justice. The presence of a sufficient number of the members of such a body regularly convened in an authorized place at an appointed time, engaged in the full and regular performance of its functions. A body in the government to which the administration of justice is delegated. A body organized to administer justice, and including both judge and jury. An incorporeal, political being, composed of one or more judges, who sit at fixed times and places, attended by proper officers, pursuant to lawful authority, for the administration of justice. An organized body with defined powers, meeting at certain times and places for the hearing and decision of causes and other matters brought before it, and aided in this, its proper business, by its proper officers, viz., attorneys and counsel to present and manage the business, clerks to record and attest its acts and decisions, and ministerial officers to execute its commands, and secure due order in its proceedings.

The words "court" and "judge," or "judges," are frequently used in statutes as synonymous. When used with reference to orders made by the court or judges, they are to be so understood.

General Classification

Courts may be classified and divided according to several methods, the following being the more usual:

Appellate courts. Such courts review decisions of inferior courts, and may be either intermediate appellate courts (court of appeals) or supreme courts. *See* Court of Appeals; Supreme court.

Article I courts. *See* Legislative courts.

Article III courts. *See* Constitutional court.

Civil and criminal courts. The former being such as are established for the adjudication of controversies between individual parties, or the ascertainment, enforcement, and redress of private rights; the latter, such as are charged with the administration of the criminal laws, and the punishment of wrongs to the public. While in some states there are both civil and criminal courts, in most states the trial court is a *court of general jurisdiction (q.v.)*.

Court above, court below. In appellate practice, the "court above" is the one to which a cause is removed for review, whether by appeal, writ of error, or certiorari; while the "court below" is the one from which the case is removed (normally the trial court).

Court in bank (en banc). A meeting of all the judges of a court, usually for the purposes of hearing arguments on demurrers, motions for new trial, etc., as distinguished from sessions of the same court presided over by a single judge or panel of judges. *See Full court, below.*

Court of competent jurisdiction. One having power and authority of law at the time of acting to do the particular act. One recognized by law as possessing the right to adjudicate a controversy. One having jurisdiction under the Constitution and/or laws to determine the question in controversy.

Court of general jurisdiction. A court having unlimited trial jurisdiction, both civil and criminal, though its judgments and decrees are subject to appellate review. A superior court; a court having full jurisdiction within its own jurisdictional area.

Court of limited jurisdiction. Court with jurisdiction over only certain types of matters; *e.g.* probate or juvenile court. When a court of general jurisdiction proceeds under a special statute, it is a "court of limited jurisdiction" for the purpose of that proceeding, and its jurisdiction must affirmatively appear.

Court of original jurisdiction. Courts where actions are initiated and heard in first instance.

Court of record. A court that is required to keep a record of its proceedings, and that may fine or imprison. Such record imports verity and cannot be collaterally impeached.

De facto court. One established, organized, and exercising its judicial functions under authority of a statute apparently valid, though such statute may be in fact unconstitutional and may be afterwards so adjudged; or a court established and acting under the authority of a *de facto* government.

Equity courts and law courts. The former being such as possess the jurisdiction of a chancellor, apply the rules and principles of chancery (*i.e.* equity) law, and follow the procedure in equity; the latter, such as have no equitable powers, but administer justice according to the rules and practice of the common law. Under Rules of Civil Procedure, however, equity and law have been merged at the procedural level, and as such this distinction no longer exists in the federal courts nor in most state courts, though equity substantive jurisprudence remains viable. Fed.R.Civil P. 2. *See* Court of Chancery; Court of Equity.

Full court. A session of a court, which is attended by all the judges or justices composing it. *See* Court in bank, above.

Spiritual courts. In English law, the ecclesiastical courts, or courts Christian. 3 Bl.Comm. 61. *See* Ecclesiastical courts.

Superior and inferior courts. The former being courts of general original jurisdiction in the first instance, and which exercise a control or supervision over a system of lower courts, either by appeal, error, or *certiorari;* the latter being courts of small or restricted jurisdiction, and subject to the review or correction of higher courts. Sometimes the former term is used to denote a particular group or system of courts of high powers, and all others are called "inferior courts".

Trial courts. Generic term for courts where civil actions or criminal proceedings are first commenced at the state level such are variously called municipal, circuit, superior, district, or county courts. At the federal level, the U.S. district courts are the trial courts.

As to the division of courts according to their *jurisdiction, see* Jurisdiction.

As to several names or kinds of courts not specifically described in the titles immediately following, *see* Admiralty court; Appellate court; Bankruptcy proceedings (*Bankruptcy courts*); Circuit courts; City courts; Claims court; Commonwealth court; Constitutional court; Consular courts; County (*County courts*); Customs court; District (*District courts*); Ecclesiastical courts; Family court; Federal courts; Insular courts; International Court of Justice; Kangaroo court; Legislative courts; Maritime court; Mayor's court; Military courts; Moot court; Municipal courts; Orphan's courts; Police court; Prize courts; Probate court; Superior (*Superior courts*); Supreme court; Surrogate court; Tax court; United States courts.

Court administrator. Generally, a non-judicial officer whose responsibility is the administration of the courts as to budgets, juries, judicial assignments, calendars and non-judicial personnel.

Court calendar. A list of cases for trial or appellate argument prepared for a given period of time as a week, month or even a term of the sitting of the court. Such may include scheduling of motions and other pretrial matters. *See also* Docket.

Court commissioner. A person appointed by a judge to take testimony and find facts or to carry out some specific function connected with a case, such as selling property which is the subject of a petition to partition. *See also* Commissioner; Court administrator; Magistrate; Master; Referee.

Court en banc /kùrt om bóŋk/. *See* Court (*Court in bank*).

Courtesy. *See* Curtesy.

Courthouse. The building occupied for the public sessions of a court, with its various offices. The building occupied and appropriated according to law for the holding of courts.

Court-Martial. An ad hoc military court, convened under authority of government and the Uniform Code of Military Justice, 10 U.S.C.A. § 801 et seq., for trying and punishing offenses in violation of the Uniform Code of Military Justice committed by persons subject to the Code, particularly members of the armed forces. Courts-martial are courts of law and courts of justice although they are not part of the federal judiciary established under Article III of the Constitution.

They are legislative criminal courts established in the armed forces under the constitutional power of congress to regulate the armed forces. Their jurisdiction is entirely penal and disciplinary. They may be convened by the president, secretaries of military departments and by senior commanders specifically empowered by law. The type (*e.g.* summary, special, or general) and composition of courts-martial varies according to the gravity of offenses. Generally they are designed to deal with the internal affairs of the military when summary command discipline is inadequate to achieve corrective results, but they have concurrent jurisdiction with civil courts over a wide range of civil offenses. *See* Courts of Military Review; Court of Military Appeals. *See also* Code of Military Justice.

Court of Admiralty. A court having jurisdiction of admiralty and maritime matters; such jurisdiction being possessed by federal district courts. *See* Admiralty Court.

Court of Appeals. In those states with courts of appeals, such courts are usually intermediate appellate courts (with the highest appellate court being the state Supreme Court). In New York, Maryland, and the District of Columbia, however, such are the highest appellate courts. In West Virginia the Supreme Court of Appeals is the court of last resort. Alabama, Oklahoma, Tennessee, and Texas have Courts of Criminal Appeals, with those in Oklahoma and Texas being the highest appellate courts for criminal matters. Alabama, Oklahoma, and Texas have Courts of Civil Appeals, which are intermediate appellate courts. *See also* Supreme court.

The United States is divided into thirteen federal judicial circuits in each of which there is established a court of appeals known as the United States Court of Appeals for the circuit. Included in these thirteen judicial circuits is the Court of Appeals for the District of Columbia and the Court of Appeals for the Federal Circuit. 28 U.S.C.A. §§ 41, 43. *See* Courts of Appeals, U.S.

Court of Appeals for the Federal Circuit. *See* Courts of Appeals, U.S.

Court of Bankruptcy. Federal court established in each judicial district, as an adjunct to the U.S. district court for such district, with general jurisdiction over bankruptcy matters. 28 U.S.C.A. §§ 151, 1334. *See also* Bankruptcy proceedings.

Court of Chancery. A court administering equity and proceeding according to the forms and principles of equity.

In some of the United States, the title "court of chancery" is applied to a court possessing general equity powers, distinct from the courts of law. Courts of chancery (equity courts) have been abolished by all states that have adopted Rules of Civil Procedure. *See also* Court of Equity.

Court of Civil Appeals. Such exist as intermediate appellate courts in Alabama, Oklahoma, and Texas. The Texas Court of Civil Appeals has appellate jurisdiction of cases decided in district and county courts.

Court of Claims. The federal Court of Claims was established in 1855. The Federal Courts Improvement Act of 1982 abolished this Court and created a new United States Claims Court. Combined with the also abolished United States Court of Customs and Patent Appeals, the former Court of Claims became the new United States Court of Appeals for the Federal Circuit (C.A.F.C.). The "Trial Division" of the former Court of Claims became the newly created U.S. Claims Court. *See* Claims Court, U.S.; Tucker Act.

A number of states also have courts of claims (*e.g.*, Illinois, Michigan, New York, Ohio).

Court of Conciliation. A court which proposes terms of adjustment, so as to avoid litigation; *e.g.* conciliation between debtor and creditor over disputed debt. May also function to aid in resolving marital disputes. *See also* Small claims court.

Court of County Commissioners. In some states, a court of record in each county.

Court of Criminal Appeals. *See* Court of Appeals.

Court of Customs and Patent Appeals. *See* Customs and Patent Appeals Court.

Court of Equity. A court which has jurisdiction in equity, which administers justice and decides controversies in accordance with the rules, principles, and precedents of equity, and which follows the forms and procedure of chancery; as distinguished from a court having the jurisdiction, rules, principles, and practice of the common law. Equity courts have been abolished in all states that have adopted Rules of Civil Procedure; law and equity actions having been merged procedurally into a single form of "civil action". Fed.R. Civil P. 2. *See also* Court of Chancery.

Court of Errors and Appeals. Formerly, the court of last resort in the states of New Jersey and New York.

Court of International Trade. This federal court was originally established as the Board of United States General Appraisers in 1890, and in turn was superseded by the United States Customs Court in 1926. In 1956 the Customs Court was established as an Article III court. The Customs Court Act of 1980 constituted the court as the United States Court of International Trade and revised its jurisdiction. As so reconstituted, the court has jurisdiction over any civil action against the United States arising from federal laws governing import transactions and also jurisdiction to review determinations as to the eligibility of workers, firms, and communities for adjustment assistance under the Trade Act of 1974. Civil actions commenced by the United States to recover customs duties, to recover on a customs bond, or for certain civil penalties alleging fraud or negligence are also within its exclusive jurisdiction. The court is composed of a chief judge and eight judges, not more than five of whom may belong to any one political party.

Court of last resort. Court which handles the final appeal on a matter; *e.g.,* the U.S. Supreme Court for federal cases.

Court of law. In a wide sense, any duly constituted tribunal administering the laws of the state or nation; in a narrower sense, a court proceeding according to the course of the common law and governed by its rules and principles, as contrasted with a "court of equity *(q.v.).*"

Court of Military Appeals. This court was established by Congress in 1950 (10 U.S.C.A. § 867). It is the primary civilian appellate tribunal responsible for reviewing court-martial convictions of all the services. It is exclusively an appellate criminal court. The court, consisting of three civilian judges appointed by the president, is called upon to exercise jurisdiction as to questions of law in all cases extending to death; questions certified to the court by the Judge Advocates General of the armed services, and by the general counsel of the Department of Transportation, acting for the Coast Guard; petitions by accused who have received a sentence of a year or more confinement, and/or a punitive discharge. Decisions of this court are subject to review by the Supreme Court by a writ of certiorari. The Supreme Court may not review by a writ of certiorari, however, any action of this court in refusing to grant a petition for review. 10 U.S.C.A. § 867(3)(h)(i). *See also* Courts of Military Review.

Court of Probate. A court existing in many states having jurisdiction over the probate of wills, the grant of administration, and the supervision of the management and settlement of the estates of decedents, including the collection of assets, the allowance of claims, and the distribution of the estate. In some states the probate courts also have jurisdiction over divorce, custody, adoption and change of name matters and of the estates of minors, including the appointment of guardians and the settlement of their accounts, and of the estates of lunatics, habitual drunkards, and spendthrifts. And in some states these courts possess a limited jurisdiction in civil and criminal cases. They are also called in some jurisdictions "Orphans' courts" (*e.g.* Maryland, Pennsylvania) and "Surrogate's courts" (*e.g.* N.Y.).

Court of Record. *See* Court, *supra.*

Court of Veterans Appeals. The U.S. Court of Veterans Appeals is an Article I court created in 1988 to review decisions of the Board of Veterans' Appeals. Appeals from this Court are to the U.S. Court of Appeals for the Federal Circuit. 38 U.S.C.A. § 4051 et seq.

Court record. *See* Record.

Court reporter. A person who transcribes by shorthand, stenographically takes down, or electronically records testimony during court proceedings, or at trial related proceedings such as depositions. If an appeal is to be taken wherein an official record is required, the reporter prepares an official transcript from his or her record. A reporter may also constitute the person responsible for publication of the opinions of the court; sometimes called "Reporter of Decisions".

Court room. That portion of a courthouse in which the actual proceedings (*i.e.* trial, motions, etc.) take place. *Compare* Chamber.

Court rule. Regulations with the force of law governing practice and procedure in the various courts. They may cover all procedures in a trial court system (*e.g.* Federal Rules of Civil and Criminal Procedure), or govern only procedures before a specific court (*e.g.* U.S. Supreme Court Rules), or only certain aspects of procedure (*e.g.* Federal Rules of Evidence), or they may be so called housekeeping rules which govern internal court practices and procedures. Most states have adopted in whole, or substantially, rules patterned on the Federal Rules of Civil Procedure to govern civil cases. Also, a growing number of states have adopted Rules of Criminal Procedure and Rules of Appellate Procedure modeled after the Federal Rules of Criminal and Appellate Procedure. In addition, a number of states have adopted Rules of Evidence patterned on the Federal Rules of Evidence.

Courts martial. *See* Court-Martial.

Courts of Appeals, U. S. Intermediate appellate courts created by Congress in 1891 and known until 1948 as United States Circuit Courts of Appeals, sitting in eleven numbered circuits, the District of Columbia, and the Court of Appeals for the Federal Circuit. Normally cases are heard by divisions of three judges sitting together, but on certain matters all the judges of a circuit may hear a case. Courts of Appeals have appellate jurisdiction over most cases decided by United States District Courts and review and enforce orders of many federal administrative bodies. The decisions of the courts of appeals are final except as they are subject to discretionary review on appeal by the Supreme Court. 28 U.S.C.A. §§ 41, 43, 1291. *See also* Temporary Emergency Court of Appeals.

Court of Appeals for the Federal Circuit. Federal court, established in 1982, with appellate jurisdiction over actions arising under the laws relating to patents, plant variety protection, copyrights, trademarks, contract and property claims against the United States, appeals from the United States Claims Court, Patent and Trademark Office, the United States Court of International Trade, the Merit Systems Protection Board, the Court of Veterans Appeals, as well as appeals under the Plant Variety Protection Act, the Contract Disputes Act, decisions by the United States International Trade Commission relating to unfair import practices, and decisions by the Secretary of Commerce relating to import tariffs. 28 U.S.C.A. § 1295.

Courts of Military Review. These intermediate appellate criminal courts, formerly constituted as Boards of Review, were established by the Military Justice Act of 1968 (10 U.S.C.A. § 866) to review court-martial convictions of their respective services. These courts are operated by the Army, Air Force, Navy/Marine Corps and the Coast Guard. Each court has one or more panels and each panel is composed of at least three appellate military judges. The court may sit in panels or en banc. The courts possess independent fact-finding powers and may weigh evidence, judge witness credibility, and determine controverted questions of fact, giving due deference to the findings of the trial court. The court reviews cases in which the punishment imposed extends to death, dismissal or punitive discharge, or confinement for one year or more, except when the service member voluntarily waives the right to appeal. The court also possesses extraordinary writs power. Its opinions are subject to review by the United States Court of Military Appeals. *See* Court of Military Appeals.

Courts of record. Those courts whose proceedings are permanently recorded, and which have the power to fine or imprison for contempt.

Courts of the United States. "Court of the United States" includes the Supreme Court of the United States, courts of appeals, district courts, Court of International Trade, and any court created by Act of Congress the judges of which are entitled to hold office during good behavior. 28 U.S.C.A. § 451. Also, the senate sitting as a court of impeachment.

Court system. The network of courts in a particular jurisdiction; *e.g.* trial, appellate, juvenile, land, etc., courts.

Courtyard. A corrupted form of "curtilage", signifying a space of land about a dwelling house, which not only might be inclosed, but within which appurtenant buildings and structures might be erected.

Cousin /kɘ́zɘn/. Kindred in the fourth degree, being the issue (male or female) of the brother or sister of one's father or mother.

Those who descend from the brother or sister of the father of the person spoken of are called "paternal cousins", "maternal cousins" are those who are descended from the brothers or sisters of the mother. Cousins-german are first cousins.

First cousins. Cousins-german; the children of one's uncle or aunt.

Quarter cousin. Properly, a cousin in the fourth degree; but the term has come to express any remote degree of relationship, and even to bear an ironical signification in which it denotes a very trifling degree of intimacy and regard. Often corrupted into "cater" cousin.

Second cousins. Persons who are related to each other by descending from the same great-grandfather or great-grandmother. The children of one's first cousins are his second cousins. These are sometimes called "first cousins once removed."

Coustom. (Fr. Coutum.) Custom; duty; toll; tribute. *See* Custom and usage.

Covenant /kɘ́vɘnɘnt/. An agreement, convention, or promise of two or more parties, by deed in writing, signed, and delivered, by which either of the parties pledges himself to the other that something is either done, or shall be done, or shall not be done, or stipulates for the truth of certain facts. At common law, such agreements were required to be under seal. The term is currently used primarily with respect to promises in conveyances or other instruments relating to real estate.

In its broadest usage, means any agreement or contract.

The name of a common-law form of action *ex contractu,* which lies for the recovery of damages for breach of a covenant, or contract under seal.

General Classification

Covenants may be classified according to several distinct principles of division:

Absolute or conditional. An absolute covenant is one which is not qualified or limited by any condition.

Affirmative or negative. The former are those in which the party binds himself to the existence of a present state of facts as represented or to the future performance of some act; while the latter are those in which the covenantor obliges himself *not* to do or perform some act.

An "affirmative covenant" is an agreement whereby the covenantor undertakes that something shall be done.

Declaratory or obligatory. The former are those which serve to limit or direct uses; while the latter are those which are binding on the party himself.

Dependent, concurrent, and independent. Covenants are either dependent, concurrent, or mutual and independent. The first depends on the prior performance of some act or condition, and, until the condition is performed, the other party is not liable to an action on his covenant. In the second, mutual acts are to be performed at the same time; and if one party is ready, and offers to perform his part, and the other neglects or refuses to perform his, he who is ready and offers has fulfilled his engagement, and may maintain an action for the default of the other, though it is not certain that either is obliged to do the first act. The third sort is where either party may recover damages from the other for the injuries he may have received by a breach of the covenants in his favor; and it is no excuse for the defendant to allege a breach of the covenants on the part of the plaintiff. Mutual and independent covenants are such as do not go to the whole consideration on both sides, but only to a part, and where separate actions lie for breaches on either side to recover damages for the injury sustained by breach.

Covenants are dependent where performance by one party is conditioned on and subject to performance by the other, and in such case the party who seeks performance must show performance or a tender or readiness to perform on his part; but covenants are independent when actual performance of one is not dependent on another, and where, in consequence, the remedy of both sides is by action.

Disjunctive covenants. Those which are for the performance of one or more of several things at the election of the covenantor or covenantee, as the case may be.

Executed or executory. The former being such as relate to an act already performed; while the latter are those whose performance is to be future.

Express or implied. The former being those which are created by the express words of the parties to the deed declaratory of their intention, while implied covenants are those which are inferred by the law from certain words in a deed which imply (though they do not express) them. An implied covenant is one which may reasonably be inferred from whole agreement and circumstances attending its execution. Express covenants are also called covenants "in deed," as distinguished from covenants "in law."

General or specific. The former relate to land generally and place the covenantee in the position of a specialty creditor only; the latter relate to particular lands and give the covenantee a lien thereon.

Inherent and collateral. The former being such as immediately affect the particular property, while the latter affect some property collateral thereto or some matter collateral to the grant or lease. A covenant inherent is one which is conversant about the land, and knit to the estate in the land; as, that the thing demised shall be

quietly enjoyed, shall be kept in repair, or shall not be aliened. A covenant collateral is one which is conversant about some collateral thing that doth nothing at all, or not so immediately, concern the thing granted; as to pay a sum of money in gross, etc.

Joint or several. The former bind both or all the covenantors together; the latter bind each of them separately. A covenant may be both joint and several at the same time, as regards the covenantors; but, as regards the covenantees, they cannot be joint and several for one and the same cause, but must be either joint or several only. Covenants are usually joint or several according as the interests of the covenantees are such; but the words of the covenant, where they are unambiguous, will decide, although, where they are ambiguous the nature of the interests as being joint or several is left to decide.

Principal and auxiliary. The former being those which relate directly to the principal matter of the contract entered into between the parties; while auxiliary covenants are those which do not relate directly to the principal matter of contract between the parties, but to something connected with it.

Real. A real covenant is one which binds the heirs of the covenantor and passes to assignees or purchasers; a covenant the obligation of which is so connected with the realty that he who has the latter is either entitled to the benefit of it or is liable to perform it; a covenant which has for its object something annexed to, or inherent in, or connected with, land or other real property, and runs with the land, so that the grantee of the land is invested with it and may sue upon it for a breach happening in his time.

Transitive or intransitive. The former being those personal covenants the duty of performing which passes over to the representatives of the covenantor; while the latter are those the duty of performing which is limited to the covenantor himself, and does not pass over to his representative.

Other Compound and Descriptive Terms

Continuing covenant. One which indicates or necessarily implies the doing of stipulated acts successively or as often as the occasion may require; as, a covenant to pay rent by installments, to keep the premises in repair or insured, to cultivate land, etc.

Full covenants. As this term is commonly used, it includes: covenants for seisin, for right to convey, against incumbrances, for quiet enjoyment, sometimes for further assurance, and almost always of warranty, this last often taking the place of the covenant for quiet enjoyment, and indeed in many states being the only covenant in practical use.

Restrictive covenant. See that title.

Separate covenant. A several covenant; one which binds the several covenantors each for himself, but not jointly.

Usual covenants. An agreement on the part of a seller of real property to give the usual covenants binds him to insert in the grant covenants of "seisin," "quiet enjoyment," "further assurance," "general warranty," "right to convey," and "against incumbrances." Collectively they are called covenants for title to distinguish them from restrictive covenants. *See Covenants for title, below.*

Specific Covenants

Covenants against incumbrances. A covenant that there are no incumbrances on the land conveyed. A stipulation against all rights to or interests in the land which may subsist in third persons to the diminution of the value of the estate granted.

Covenant appurtenant. A covenant which is connected with land of the grantor, and not in gross. A covenant running with the land and binding heirs, executors and assigns of the immediate parties.

Covenant for further assurance. An undertaking, in the form of a covenant, on the part of the vendor of real estate to do such further acts for the purpose of perfecting the purchaser's title as the latter may reasonably require. This covenant is deemed of great importance, since it relates both to the vendor's title of and to the instrument of conveyance to the vendee, and operates as well to secure the performance of all acts necessary for supplying any defect in the former as to remove all objections to the sufficiency and security of the latter.

Covenant for possession. A covenant by which the grantee or lessee is granted possession.

Covenant for quiet enjoyment. An assurance against the consequences of a defective title, and of any disturbances thereupon. A promise by the landlord or grantor that the tenant or grantee will not be evicted or disturbed by the grantor or a person having a lien or superior title.

Covenants for title. Covenants usually inserted in a conveyance of land, on the part of the grantor, and binding him for the completeness, security, and continuance of the title transferred to the grantee. They comprise covenants for seisin, for right to convey, against incumbrances, or quiet enjoyment, sometimes for further assurance, and almost always of warranty.

Covenant in gross. Such as do not run with the land.

Covenant not to compete. An agreement, generally part of a contract of employment or a contract to sell a business, in which the covenantor agrees for a specific period of time and within a particular area to refrain from competition with the covenantee. Such covenant restrictions must be reasonable in scope and duration or backed by adequate consideration.

Covenant not to sue. A covenant by one who has a right of action at the time of making it against another person, by which he agrees not to sue to enforce such right of action. Such covenant does not extinguish a cause of action and does not release other joint tort-feasors even if it does not specifically reserve rights against them.

Covenant of non-claim. A covenant formerly sometimes employed, particularly in the New England states, and in deeds of extinguishment of ground rents in Pennsylvania, that neither the vendor, nor his heirs, nor any other person, etc., shall claim any title in the premises conveyed.

Covenant of right to convey. An assurance by the covenantor that the grantor has sufficient capacity and title to convey the *estate* which he by his deed undertakes to convey.

Covenant of seisin. An assurance to the purchaser that the grantor has the very estate in quantity and quality which he purports to convey.

Covenant of warranty. An assurance by the grantor of an estate that the grantee shall enjoy the same without interruption by virtue of paramount title.

Covenant running with land. A covenant which goes with the land, as being annexed to the estate, and which cannot be separated from the land, and transferred without it. A covenant is said to run with the land, when not only the original parties or their representatives, but each successive owner of the land, will be entitled to its benefit, or be liable (as the case may be) to its obligation. Or, in other words, it is so called when either the liability to perform it or the right to take advantage of it passes to the assignee of the land. One which touches and concerns the land itself, so that its benefit or obligation passes with the ownership. Essentials of such a covenant are that the grantor and grantee must have intended that the covenant run with the land, the covenant must affect or concern the land with which it runs, and there must be privity of estate between party claiming the benefit and the party who rests under the burden.

Covenant running with title. A covenant which goes with the title. Stipulation in a lease granting to lessee the option of renewing it for another specified period is such a covenant. *See also Covenants for title, above.*

Covenant to convey. A covenant by which the covenantor agrees to convey to the covenantee a certain estate, under certain circumstances.

Covenant to renew. An executory contract, giving lessee the right to renew on compliance with the terms specified in the renewal clause, if any, or, if none, on giving notice, prior to termination of the lease, of his desire to renew, whereupon the contract becomes executed as to him.

Covenant to stand seised. A conveyance adapted to the case where a person seised of land in possession, reversion, or vested remainder, proposes to convey it to his wife, child, or kinsman. In its terms it consists of a covenant by him, in consideration of his natural love and affection, to stand seised of the land to the use of the intended transferee. Before the statute of uses this would merely have raised a use in favor of the covenantee; but by that act this use is converted into the legal estate, and the covenant therefore operates as a conveyance of the land to the covenantee. It is now almost obsolete.

Covenantee /kəvənəntíy/. The party to whom a covenant is made.

Covenantor /kəvənəntər/. The party who makes a covenant.

Cover. To protect by means of insurance; sometimes orally pending issuance of policy. *See also* Binder; Cover note.

The right of a buyer, after breach by a seller, to purchase goods in open market in substitution for those due from the seller if such purchase is made in good faith and without unreasonable delay. The buyer may then recover as damages the difference between the cost of cover and the contract price plus any incidental and consequential damages but less expenses saved in consequence of the seller's breach. U.C.C. § 2–712(1), (2).

Coverage. In insurance, amount and extent of risk contractually covered by insurer. The assumption of risk of occurrence of the event insured against before its occurrence.

Automatic coverage. In insurance, coverage of additional property or for other perils by an existing contract without specific request by the insured.

Coverage ratios. Ratios that are designed to measure a firm's ability to cover its financing charges.

Coverage test. A debt limitation that prohibits the issuance of additional long-term debt if the issuer's interest coverage would, as a result of the issue, fall below some specified minimum.

Cover-all clause. A provision in a document which purportedly embraces all eventualities of which the parties are aware as possibilities.

Cover note. Written statement by insurance agent that coverage is in effect. Distinguished from binder which is prepared by company. *See* Binder.

Covert /kɔ́vərt/kowvɔ́rt/. Covered, protected, sheltered. A covert act is a concealed, not apparent act.

Coverture /kɔ́vərtyər/. The condition or state of a married woman. Sometimes used elliptically to describe the legal disability which formerly existed at common law from a state of coverture whereby the wife could not own property free from the husband's claim or control. Such restrictions were removed by state Married Woman's Property Acts.

Cover-up. To conceal. As a crime, the act of concealing or hiding something wrong or criminal. *See also* Harbor; Misprision of felony.

C.P. An abbreviation for common pleas.

C.P.A. Certified Public Accountant.

C.R. An abbreviation for *curia regis; also* for chancery reports.

Craft. Generally, any boat, ship or vessel.

A trade or occupation of the sort requiring skill and training, particularly manual skill combined with a knowledge of the principles of the art. *Also* the body of persons pursuing such a calling; a guild.

Guile, artful cunning, trickiness. Not a legal term in this sense, though often used in connection with such terms as "fraud" and "artifice."

Craft union. A labor union all of whose members do the same kind of work (*i.e.* trade) such as plumbing or carpentry for different employers and industries.

Cramdown. In bankruptcy, colloquial expression that describes court confirmation of a Bankruptcy Code Chapter 11, 12 or 13 plan, notwithstanding creditor opposition.

Crashworthiness. Doctrine which imposes liability upon a manufacturer in a vehicular collision case for design defects which do not cause the initial accident but which cause additional or more severe injuries when the driver or passenger subsequently impacts with the defective interior or exterior of the vehicle.

Created. In copyright law, a work is "created" when it is fixed in a copy or phonorecord, for the first time; where a work is prepared over a period of time, the portion of it that has been fixed at any particular time constitutes the work as of that time, and where the work has been prepared in different versions, each version constitutes a separate work. Copyright Act, 17 U.S.C.A. § 101.

Credentials /krədénshəlz/. Documentary evidence of a person's authority; commonly in the form of letters, licenses or certificates which on their face indicate the authority and capacity of the bearer.

Credibility. Worthiness of belief; that quality in a witness which renders his evidence worthy of belief. After the competence of a witness is allowed, the consideration of his *credibility* arises, and not before. As to the distinction between *competency* and *credibility, see* Competency. *See also* Character; Reputation.

Credible. Worthy of belief; entitled to credit. *See* Competency; Character; Reputation.

Credible evidence. Evidence to be worthy of credit must not only proceed from a credible source but must, in addition, be "credible" in itself, by which is meant that it shall be so natural, reasonable and probable in view of the transaction which it describes or to which it relates as to make it easy to believe it, and credible testimony is that which meets the test of plausibility.

Credible person. One who is trustworthy and entitled to be believed. In law and legal proceedings, one who is entitled to have his oath or affidavit accepted as reliable, not only on account of his good reputation for veracity, but also on account of his intelligence, knowledge of the circumstances, and disinterested relation to the matter in question. Also one who is competent to testify.

Credible witness. One who is competent to give testimony in court; also one who is worthy of belief. *See* Credibility.

Credibly informed. The statement in a pleading or affidavit, that one is "credibly informed and verily believes" such and such facts, means that, having no direct personal knowledge of the matter in question, he has derived his information in regard to it from authentic sources or from the statements of persons who are not only "credible," in the sense of being trustworthy, but also informed as to the particular matter or conversant with it.

Credit. The ability of a business or person to borrow money, or obtain goods on time, in consequence of the favorable opinion held by the particular lender as to solvency and past history of reliability. Confidence in buyer's ability to meet financial obligations at some future time. Time allowed to the buyer of goods by the seller, in which to make payment for them. The correlative of a *debt;* that is, a debt considered from the creditor's standpoint, or that which is incoming or due *to* one. That which is due to a person, as distinguished from debit, that which is due by him. Claim or cause of action for specific sum of money.

Availability of funds from financial institution or from letter of credit.

"Credit" means the right granted by a creditor to a debtor to defer payment of debt or to incur debt and defer its payment. Uniform Consumer Credit Code, Section 1.301(7).

In accounting, a credit is a component of a journal entry which increases revenues, liabilities, and equity; and decreases assets and expenses.

In taxation, credits reduce the tax liability as computed, as opposed to deductions which reduce the taxable income. Examples of tax credits include; credit for child and dependent care expenses, credit for the elderly or permanently disabled, etc.

See also Confirmed credit; Credit line; Fair Credit Reporting Acts; Installment credit; Investment tax credit; Letter of credit; Notation credit; Open credit; Open-end credit plan; Revocable credit; Revolving credit; Tax credit. *Compare* Debit.

Bank credit. Money that bank owes or will lend individual or person.

Bill of credit. See Bill.

Consumer credit. See Consumer credit; Consumer Credit Code; Consumer Credit Protection Act; Consumer credit sale; Consumer credit transaction; Credit card; Equal Credit Opportunity Act; Fair Credit Billing Act; Fair Credit Reporting Acts; Truth-in-lending Act.

Credit insurance. See Credit insurance.

Extortionate credit. See Extortion; Loansharking.

Line of credit. See Credit line; Line.

Open credit. See Open credit; Open-end credit plan.

Secured credit. See Secured transaction.

Credit advertising. An advertisement which aids, promotes or assists directly or indirectly the extension of credit. Federal and state statutes regulate such advertising.

Credit balance. In accounting, the status of an account when the sum of the credit entries exceeds the sum of the debit entries.

Credit bureau. Establishments which make a business of collecting information relating to the credit, character, responsibility and reputation of individuals and businesses, for the purpose of furnishing the information (*i.e.* credit reports) to subscribers (*i.e.* merchants, banks, suppliers, etc.). Practices of credit bureaus are regulated by federal (*e.g.* Fair Credit Reporting Act) and often state statutes. *See also* Credit rating; Credit report.

Credit card. Any card, plate, or other like credit device existing for the purpose of obtaining money, property, labor or services on credit. The term does not include a note, check, draft, money order or other like negotiable instrument. Federal (*e.g.* Consumer Credit Protection Act) and often state statutes regulate the issuance and use of credit cards.

Credit card crime. A person commits an offense if he uses a credit card for the purpose of obtaining property or services with knowledge that: (1) the card is stolen or forged; or (2) the card has been revoked or cancelled; or (3) for any other reason his use of the card is unauthorized. Model Penal Code, § 224.6.

Credit disclosure. *See* Annual percentage rate; Consumer Credit Protection Act; Truth-in-Lending Act.

Credit insurance. A contract whereby the insurer promises, in consideration of a premium paid, and subject to specified conditions as to the persons to whom credit is to be extended, to indemnify the insured, wholly or in part, against loss that may result from the death, disability, or insolvency of persons to whom he may extend credit within the term of the insurance. The requirement of such, as well as the full disclosure of the terms and cost, is regulated by federal and state consumer protection statutes.

Credit life, accident, and health insurance. Term insurance on lives of debtors, with the creditors of the insured debtor as beneficiary. The amount payable on death of insured debtor is an amount at least sufficient to discharge debtor's indebtedness; and in event of total permanent disability an amount is payable which is at least sufficient to meet installment payments on debtor's indebtedness as they mature during the period of disability.

See also Insurance *(Credit insurance).*

Credit line. In banking and commerce, that amount of money or merchandise which a banker, merchant, or supplier agrees to supply to a person on credit and generally agreed to in advance. *See also* Line *(Line of credit).*

In motion pictures, the preliminary statement which gives the names of the players, producer, director, etc. May also refer to similar acknowledgments of contributors or assistants in authorship of books, production of plays, or the like.

Credit memorandum. A document used by a seller to inform a buyer that the buyer's account receivable is being credited (reduced) because of errors, returns, or allowances.

Creditor. A person to whom a debt is owing by another person who is the "debtor." One who has a right to require the fulfillment of an obligation or contract. One to whom money is due, and, in ordinary acceptation, has reference to financial or business transactions. The antonym of "debtor."

The word is susceptible of latitudinous construction. In its broad sense the word means one who has any legal liability upon a contract, express or implied, or in tort; in its narrow sense, the term is limited to one who holds a demand which is certain and liquidated. In statutes the term has various special meanings, dependent upon context, purpose of statute, etc.

The term "creditor," within the common-law and statutes that conveyances with intent to defraud creditors shall be void, includes every one having right to require the performance of any legal obligation, contract, or guaranty, or a legal right to damages growing out of contract or tort, and includes not merely the holder of a fixed and certain present debt, but every one having a right to require the performance of any legal obligation, contract, or guaranty, or a legal right to damages growing out of contract or tort, and includes one entitled to damages for breach of contract to convey real estate, notwithstanding the abandonment of his action for specific performance.

Under U.C.C., term includes a general creditor, a secured creditor, a lien creditor and any representative of creditors, including an assignee for the benefit of creditors, a trustee in bankruptcy, a receiver in equity and an executor or administrator of an insolvent debtor's or assignor's estate. U.C.C. § 1–201(12).

Under Bankruptcy Code, term includes entity that has a claim against the debtor that arose at the time of or before the order for relief concerning the debtor. Bankruptcy Code, § 101.

"Creditors" subject to Federal Truth in Lending Act are those who regularly extend or arrange for extension to consumers of credit for which a finance charge is required.

Classification

A creditor may be called a "simple contract creditor," a "specialty creditor," a "bond creditor," or otherwise, according to the nature of the obligation giving rise to the debt.

Attaching creditor. One who has caused an attachment to be issued and levied on property of his debtor. *See* Attachment.

Creditor at large. One who has not established his debt by the recovery of a judgment or has not otherwise secured a lien on any of the debtor's property.

Execution creditor. One who, having recovered a judgment against the debtor for his debt or claim, has also caused an execution to be issued thereon. *See* Execution.

Foreign creditor. One who resides in a state or country foreign to that where the debtor has his domicile or his property.

General creditor. A creditor at large *(supra),* or one who has no lien or security for the payment of his debt or claim.

Joint creditors. Persons jointly entitled to require satisfaction of the same debt or demand.

Judgment creditor. See that title.

Junior creditor. One whose claim or demand accrued at a date later than that of a claim or demand held by another creditor, who is called correlatively the "senior" creditor. Creditor whose claim ranks below other creditors in rights to the debtor's property. For example, a creditor with an unperfected security interest in a property is a junior creditor to one holding a perfected security interest.

Lien creditor. A creditor who has acquired a lien on the property involved by attachment, levy or the like and includes an assignee for benefit of creditors from the time of assignment, and a trustee in bankruptcy from the date of the filing of the petition or a receiver in equity from the time of appointment. U.C.C. § 9–301. *See also* Lien creditor.

Preferred creditor. See that title.

Principal creditor. One whose claim or demand exceeds the claims of all other creditors in amount. *See also* Preferred creditor.

Secondary creditors. One whose claim is secondary to preferred creditor(s). *See also Junior creditor, above.*

Secured creditor. See Secured creditor; *also, Lien creditor, above.*

Single creditor. See that title.

Creditor beneficiary. A third person to whom performance of promise comes in satisfaction of legal duty. A creditor who has rights in a contract made by the debtor and a third person, where the terms of the contract obligate the third person to pay the debt owed to the creditor. The creditor beneficiary can enforce the debt against either party.

Where performance of a promise in a contract will benefit a person other than the promisee, that person is a creditor beneficiary if no purpose to make a gift appears from the terms of the promise in view of the accompanying circumstances and performance of the promise will satisfy an actual or supposed or asserted duty of the promisee to the beneficiary, or a right of the beneficiary against the promisee which has been barred by the Statute of Limitations or a discharge in bankruptcy, or which is unenforceable because of the Statute of Frauds. Restatement, Second, Contracts.

Creditor's bill *or* **suit.** Equitable proceeding brought to enforce payment of debt out of property or other interest of debtor which cannot be reached by ordinary legal process. By use of the creditor's bill, a judgment creditor can reach any nonexempt property interest of the debtor that is alienable or assignable under state law. A suit by judgment creditor in equity for purpose of reach-

ing property which cannot be reached by execution at law. A proceeding to enforce the security of a judgment creditor against the property or interests of his debtor. This action proceeds upon the theory that the judgment is in the nature of a lien, such as may be enforced in equity. Under rules of civil procedure, such action is simply a civil action in which demand is made for this type of equitable relief because of the merger of law and equity. Fed.R. Civil P. 2.

Creditor's claim. Generic term to describe any right which a creditor has against his debtor. For recovery in bankruptcy, such must be provable. *See also* Claim.

Creditors' committee. In bankruptcy, a committee of representative creditors elected (in Chapter 7) or appointed (in Chapter 11) to consult with the bankruptcy trustee or United States Trustee, and to perform other services in the interest of the represented creditors. Bankruptcy Code, §§ 705, 1102, 1103.

Creditors' meeting. In bankruptcy, first meeting of creditors and equity security holders, at which time a trustee may be elected and the debtor examined under oath. Bankruptcy Code, § 341. *See also* Meeting of creditors.

Creditors' suit. *See* Creditor's bill *or* suit.

Credit rating. The evaluation of a person's or business' ability and past performance in paying debts. Generally established by a credit bureau and used by merchants, suppliers and bankers to determine whether a loan should be granted or a line of credit given. Credit reporting practices are regulated by the federal Fair Credit Reporting Act.

Credit report. A document from a credit bureau setting forth a credit rating and pertinent financial data concerning a person or a company and used by banks, merchants, suppliers and the like in evaluating a credit risk. Credit reporting practices are regulated by the federal Fair Credit Reporting Act.

Credits. A term of universal application to obligations due and to become due. *See also* Credit; Tax credit.

Credit sale. A sale in which the buyer is permitted to pay for the goods at a later time, as contrasted with a cash sale. Any sale with respect to which consumer credit is extended or arranged by the seller. The term includes any contract in the form of a bailment or lease if the bailee or lessee contracts to pay as compensation for use a sum substantially equivalent to or in excess of the aggregate value of the property and services involved and it is agreed that the bailee or lessee will become, or for no other or for a nominal consideration has the option to become, the owner of the property upon full compliance with his obligations under the contract. *See also* Installment sale.

Credit slip. A document generally given by stores and suppliers when a person returns merchandise and which permits the customer to purchase another item, or receive the equivalent in cash or open credit for future purchases, in return for the credit extended by the slip.

Credit union. Cooperative association that uses money deposited by a closed group of persons (*e.g.* fellow employees) and lends it out again to persons in the same group at favorable interest notes. Credit unions are commonly regulated by state banking boards or commissions.

Crew list. A list of the crew of a vessel or aircraft; one of a ship's or aircraft's papers. This instrument is required by statute and sometimes by treaties. 46 U.S.C.A. §§ 322, 323.

Crier /krǻyər/. An officer of a court, who makes proclamations. His principal duties are to announce the opening of the court and its adjournment and the fact that certain special matters are about to be transacted, to announce the admission of persons to the bar, to call the names of jurors, witnesses, and parties, to announce that a witness has been sworn, to proclaim silence when so directed, and generally to make such proclamations of a public nature as the judges order. An auctioneer (cryer). *See also* Bailiff.

Crim. Con. An abbreviation for "criminal conversation," denoting adultery.

Crime. A positive or negative act in violation of penal law; an offense against the State or United States.

"Crime" and "misdemeanor", properly speaking, are synonymous terms; though in common usage "crime" is made to denote such offenses as are of a more serious nature. In general, violation of an ordinance is not a crime.

A crime may be defined to be any act done in violation of those duties which an individual owes to the community, and for the breach of which the law has provided that the offender shall make satisfaction to the public. A crime or public offense is an act committed or omitted in violation of a law forbidding or commanding it, and to which is annexed, upon conviction, either, or a combination, of the following punishments: (1) death; (2) imprisonment; (3) fine; (4) removal from office; or (5) disqualification to hold and enjoy any office of honor, trust, or profit. While many crimes have their origin at common law, most have been created by statute; and, in many states, such have been codified. In addition, there are both state and federal crimes (as to the latter, see Title 18, U.S.C.A.).

See also Classification of crimes; Compounding crime; Continuing offense; Criminal; Degrees of crime; Elements of crime; Federal crimes; Felony; Inchoate crimes; Instantaneous crime; Lesser included offense; Misdemeanor; Offense; Petty offense; Political crime; Vehicular crimes.

General Classification

Crimes are classified for various purposes, the principal classification being that which divides crimes into felonies and misdemeanors. Other classifications are: (a) crimes which are *mala in se* versus crimes *mala prohibita;* (b) infamous crimes versus crimes which are not infamous; (c) crimes involving moral turpitude versus those which do not involve moral turpitude; (d) major crimes versus petty crimes; and (e) common law crimes versus statutory crimes.

Capital crime. Crime punishable by death.

Common law crimes. Such crimes as are punishable by the force of the common law, as distinguished from crimes created by statute.

Continuous crime. One consisting of a continuous series of acts, which endures after the period of consummation, as, the offense of carrying concealed weapons. In the case of instantaneous crimes, the statute of limitations begins to run with the consummation, while in the case of continuous crimes it only begins with the cessation of the criminal conduct or act.

Crime against law of nations. Term which is understood to include crimes which all nations agree to punish such as murder and rape.

Crime against nature. Deviate sexual intercourse per os or per anum between human beings who are not husband and wife and any form of sexual intercourse with an animal. Model Penal Code, § 213.0. Crime of buggery or sodomy.

Crime against property. Term used to describe a crime, the object of which is property as contrasted with person; *e.g.* larceny.

Crime insurance. See Insurance.

Crime of omission. Any offense, the gravamen of which is the failure to act when there is an obligation to act. May amount to manslaughter if the failure is wilful, wanton and reckless.

Crime of passion. A crime committed in the heat of passion. *See* Heat of passion.

Crime of violence. An offense that has as an element the use, attempted use, or threatened use of physical force against the person or property of another, or any other offense that is a felony and that, by its nature, involves a substantial risk that physical force against the person or property of another may be used in the course of committing the offense. 18 U.S.C.A. § 16. Crimes of violence include voluntary manslaughter, murder, rape, mayhem, kidnaping, robbery, burglary or housebreaking in the nighttime, extortion accompanied by threats of violence, assault with a dangerous weapon or assault with intent to commit any offense punishable by imprisonment for more than one year, arson punishable as a felony, or an attempt or conspiracy to commit any of the foregoing offenses.

Crimes mala in se. Crimes mala in se embrace acts immoral or wrong in themselves, such as burglary, larceny, arson, rape, murder, and breaches of peace.

Crimes mala prohibita. Crimes mala prohibita embrace things prohibited by statute as infringing on others' rights, though no moral turpitude may attach, and constituting crimes only because they are so prohibited.

Felony. See Felony.

Infamous crime. A crime which entails infamy upon one who has committed it. The term "infamous"—*i.e.*, without fame or good report—was applied at common law to certain crimes, upon the conviction of which a person became incompetent to testify as a witness, upon the theory that a person would not commit so heinous a crime unless he was so depraved as to be unworthy of credit. These crimes are treason, felony, and the *crimen falsi.* A crime punishable by imprisonment in the state prison or penitentiary, with or without hard labor, is an infamous crime, within the provision of the fifth amendment of the constitution that "no person shall be held to answer for a capital or otherwise infamous crime unless on a presentment or indictment of a grand jury." It is not the character of the crime but the nature of the punishment which renders the crime "infamous." Whether an offense is infamous depends on the punishment which may be imposed therefor, not on the punishment which was imposed.

Misdemeanor. See Misdemeanor.

Organized crime. Term used to describe that form of crime which is the product of groups and organizations as contrasted with the crime planned and committed by individuals without organizational backing; gambling and narcotics are common subjects of organized crime.

Quasi crimes. This term embraces all offenses not crimes or misdemeanors, but that are in the nature of crimes. A class of offenses against the public which have not been declared crimes, but wrongs against the general or local public which it is proper should be repressed or punished by forfeitures and penalties. This would embrace all *qui tam* actions and forfeitures imposed for the neglect or violation of a public duty. A *quasi* crime would not embrace an indictable offense, whatever might be its grade, but simply forfeitures for a wrong done to the public, whether voluntary or involuntary, where a penalty is given, whether recoverable by criminal or civil process. Also, offenses for which some person other than the actual perpetrator is responsible, the perpetrator being presumed to act by command of the responsible party. Sometimes, injuries which have been unintentionally caused. D.W.I. (driving while intoxicated) offenses are sometimes classified as *quasi* crimes.

Statutory crimes. Those created by statutes, as distinguished from such as are known to, or cognizable by, the common law. See *e.g.* U.S.Code, Title 18.

White-collar crime. Generally included under this classification of crimes are antitrust violations, bribery, computer crime, criminal copyright infringement, environmental crimes, extortion, food and drug violations, government contract fraud, mail and wire fraud, RICO offenses, securities and tax fraud, theft of trade secrets.

Crime Control Acts. Multifaceted legislation designed to curb crime by *e.g.*, legislating new types of crimes, redefining existing crimes, increasing sentences, adding new prosecutors, judges, and prisons, etc. Examples are federal Comprehensive Crime Control Act of 1984; Drug Abuse Act of 1988 (as incorporated in U.S.Code Titles 18 and 21).

Crimen /kráymən/. Lat. Crime. Also an accusation or charge of crime.

Crimen falsi /kráymən fólsay/. Term generally refers to crimes in the nature of perjury or subornation of perjury, false statement, criminal fraud, embezzlement, false pretense, or any other offense which involves some element of deceitfulness, untruthfulness, or falsification bearing on witness' propensity to testify truthfully.

Criminal, *n.* One who has committed a criminal offense; one who has been legally convicted of a crime; one adjudged guilty of crime. *See also* Dangerous criminal; Habitual criminal.

Criminal, *adj.* That which pertains to or is connected with the law of crimes, or the administration of penal justice, or which relates to or has the character of crime. Of the nature of or involving a crime.

Criminal act. Commission of a crime.

Criminal action. Proceeding by which person charged with a crime is brought to trial and either found not guilty or guilty and sentenced. An action, suit, or cause instituted to punish an infraction of the criminal laws. *See also* Indictment; Penal action; Prosecution.

Criminal anarchy. The doctrine that organized government should be overthrown by force and violence or other unlawful means. The advocacy of such doctrine has been made a felony. 18 U.S.C.A. § 2384.

Criminal Appeals Act. Federal Act which allows the United States to appeal to a court of appeals from certain judgments, orders, or rulings of district courts. 18 U.S.C.A. § 3731.

Criminal attempt. Crime of a criminal attempt consists of an attempt to commit the crime and some step or overt act towards commission of the crime. A substantial step towards a criminal offense with specific intent to commit that particular crime. A criminal attempt is defined as an overt act done in pursuance of intent to do a specific thing, tending to the end but falling short of complete accomplishment of it; such overt act must be sufficiently proximate to intended crime to form one of natural series of acts which intent requires for its full execution. *See also* Attempt.

Criminal behavior. Conduct which causes any social harm which is defined and made punishable by law.

Criminal capacity. Legal qualifications necessary to commit a crime such as voluntariness of the act, age and mental condition. *See also* Capacity; Insanity.

Criminal charge. An accusation of crime, formulated in a written complaint, information, or indictment, and taking shape in a prosecution.

Criminal coercion. *See* Coercion.

Criminal conspiracy. An agreement or confederacy of two or more persons to do a criminal or unlawful act or to do a lawful act in an unlawful or criminal manner. In many jurisdictions, an overt act in furtherance of the confederacy is required. *See also* Conspiracy.

Criminal contempt. A crime which consists in the obstruction of judicial duty generally resulting in an act done in the presence of the court; *e.g.* contumelious conduct directed to the judge or a refusal to answer questions after immunity has been granted. Conduct directed against the majesty of the law or the dignity and authority of the court or judge acting judiciously, whereas a "civil contempt" ordinarily consists in failing to do something ordered to be done by a court in a civil action for the benefit of an opposing party therein. *See also* Contempt.

Criminal conversation. Sexual intercourse of an outsider with husband or wife, or a breaking down of the covenant of fidelity. Tort action based on adultery, considered in its aspect of a civil injury to the husband or wife entitling him or her to damages; the tort of debauching or seducing of a wife or husband. Often abbreviated to *crim. con.* Statutes in several states prohibit actions for criminal conversation. *See* Adultery; Alienation of affections; Heart balm statutes.

Criminal forfeiture. The taking by the government of property because of its involvement in a crime; *e.g.* an automobile used to smuggle narcotics; gun used in hunting without license or out of season. *See e.g.* 18 U.S.C.A. § 982; 21 U.S.C.A. § 853. *See also* Confiscate; Forfeiture; Seizure.

Criminal fraud. In taxation, the attempt to evade the payment of lawfully due taxes by willfully filing a false or fraudulent tax return. I.R.C. §§ 7201, 7207. In other contexts, the crime of larceny by false pretenses or larceny by trick. *See also* Fraud.

Criminal gross negligence. Gross negligence is culpable or criminal when accompanied by acts of commission or omission of a wanton or willful nature, showing a reckless or indifferent disregard of the rights of others, under circumstances reasonably calculated to produce injury, or which make it not improbable that injury will be occasioned, and the offender knows or is charged with knowledge of the probable result of his acts; "culpable" meaning deserving of blame or censure. *See also Criminal negligence, below.*

Criminal insanity. *See* Insanity.

Criminal instrumentality rule. Where the wrong is accomplished by a crime, the crime and not the negligent act of the party which made it possible is the "proximate cause".

Criminal intent. The intent to commit a crime; malice, as evidenced by a criminal act; an intent to deprive or defraud the true owner of his property. Includes those consequences which represent the very purpose for which an act is done, regardless of the likelihood of occurrence, or are known to be substantially certain to result, regardless of desire. May be general or specific intent; mens rea. *See also* Knowingly; Mens rea; Premeditation; Specific intent.

Criminal jurisdiction. Power of tribunal to hear and dispose of criminal cases.

Criminal laws. *See* Penal code; Penal laws.

Criminal libel. Criminal libel is the malicious publication of durable defamation. The malicious defamation of a person made public by any printing or writing tending to provoke him to wrath and to deprive him of the benefits of public confidence and social intercourse. It is a misdemeanor at common law and also under modern statutes unless it has been made a felony which is not common. Four elements are included: (1) defamation, (2) durable, (3) publication and (4) malice. It should be noted however that criminal sanctions for defamation of public officials is subject to same constitutional limitations as for civil actions. *See also* Libel.

Criminal mischief. A species of wilful and malicious injury to property made punishable by statutes in most jurisdictions.

Criminal motive. Something in the mind or that condition of the mind which incites to action or induces action, or gives birth to a purpose. Distinguishable from intent which represents the immediate object in view while motive is the ulterior intent.

Criminal negligence. *See Criminal gross negligence, above; also,* Negligence.

Criminal non-support. The wilful and unreasonable failure to support one whom the law requires a person to support (*i.e.* spouse and children). *See* Non-support; Support.

Criminal proceeding. One instituted and conducted for the purpose either of preventing the commission of crime, or for fixing the guilt of a crime already committed and punishing the offender; as distinguished from a "civil" proceeding, which is for the redress of a private injury. Strictly, a "criminal proceeding" means some step taken before a court against some person or persons charged with some violation of the criminal law. *See also* Criminal procedure.

Criminal process. Process which issues to compel a person to answer for a crime or misdemeanor; *e.g.* arrest warrant. *See also* Indictment; Information; Process; Warrant.

Criminal prosecution. An action or proceeding instituted in a proper court on behalf of the public, for the purpose of securing the conviction and punishment of one accused of crime. A proceeding instituted by the state to obtain punishment against the person charged with and found guilty of a public offense; it embraces not only the accusation, whether by indictment or information, and the determination of guilt or innocence, but also, in case of a conviction, the imposition of sentence.

Criminal syndicalism. Any doctrine or precept advocating, teaching or aiding and abetting the commission of crime of sabotage or unlawful acts of force and violence or unlawful methods of terrorism as a means of accomplishing a change in industrial ownership or control or affecting any political change. The advocacy of sabotage, violence, terrorism, or other unlawful methods for revolutionary purposes. *See also* Syndicalism.

Criminal trespass. The offense committed by one who, without license or privilege to do so, enters or surreptitiously remains in any building or occupied structure. Model Penal Code, § 221.2. Offense is committed when a person without effective consent enters or remains on property or in building of another knowingly or intentionally or recklessly when he had notice that entry was forbidden or received notice to depart but failed to do so.

Criminalist. One versed in criminal law, one addicted to criminality, and, also, a psychiatrist dealing with criminality. *See* Recidivist.

Criminalistics. The science of crime detection, based upon the application of chemistry, physics, physiology, psychology, and other sciences. *See also* Criminology.

Criminalization. The rendering of an act criminal (*e.g.* by statutory enactment) and hence punishable by the government in a proceeding in its name.

Criminal justice system. The network of courts and tribunals which deal with criminal law and its enforcement.

Criminal law. The substantive criminal law is that law which for the purpose of preventing harm to society, (a) declares what conduct is criminal, and (b) prescribes the punishment to be imposed for such conduct. It includes the definition of specific offenses and general principles of liability. Substantative criminal laws are commonly codified into criminal or penal codes; *e.g.* U.S.C.A. Title 18, California Penal Code, Model Penal Code. *Compare* Criminal procedure.

Criminal procedure. The rules of law governing the procedures by which crimes are investigated, prosecuted, adjudicated, and punished. Generic term to describe the network of laws and rules which govern the procedural administration of criminal justice; *e.g.* laws and court rules (*e.g.* Rules of Criminal Procedure) governing arrest, search and seizure, bail, etc. *Compare* Criminal law. *See also* Code of criminal procedure.

Criminal protector. An accessory after the fact to a felony. One who aids or harbors a felon after the commission of a crime.

Criminal registration. Statutes in certain jurisdictions require that persons who are convicted felons register with the police so that their presence in the community will be known at all times. Subversive organizations are required to register under 18 U.S.C.A. § 2386.

Criminal sanctions. Punishments attached to conviction of crimes such as fines, restitution, probation and sentences. *See also* Civil death.

Criminal statutes *or* **codes.** Federal and state laws enacted by legislative bodies which define, classify, and set forth punishments for specific crimes; *e.g.* Title 18 of United States Code; Model Penal Code.

Criminate. To charge one with crime; to furnish ground for a criminal prosecution; to implicate, accuse, or expose a person to a criminal charge. A witness cannot be compelled to answer any question which has a tendency to *criminate* him. *See* Incriminate; Self-incrimination.

Criminology. The study of the nature of, causes of, and means of dealing with crime.

Critical evidence. Material evidence of substantial probative force that could induce a reasonable doubt in the minds of enough jurors to avoid a conviction.

Critical stage. Critical stage in a criminal proceeding at which accused is entitled to counsel is one in which a defendant's rights may be lost, defenses waived, privileges claimed or waived, or in which the outcome of the case is otherwise substantially affected. Test of "critical stage" of criminal proceeding as it relates to right to counsel is whether proceeding either requires or offers opportunity to take procedural step which will have prejudicial effects in later proceedings, or whether events transpire that are likely to prejudice ensuing trial. *See also* Counsel, right to; Custodial interrogation.

Crook. A person given to crooked or fraudulent practices; a swindler, sharper, thief, forger, or the like. Term has been defined as a professional rogue; a criminal; or one consorting with criminals; a person recognized by the authorities as belonging to the criminal class.

Crop. Products of the soil, as are annually grown, raised, and harvested. Growing crops are considered "goods" under U.C.C. § 2–105(1). Term includes fruit grown on trees, and grass used for pasturage. *See also* Away going crop; Basic crops; Growing crop.

Crop insurance. *See* Insurance.

Cropper. *See* Sharecropper.

Cross. A mark made by persons who are unable to write, to stand instead of a signature. A mark usually in the form of an **X**, by which voters are commonly required to express their selection. There are four principal forms of the cross: The St. Andrew's cross, which is made in the form of an **X**; the Latin cross, †, as used in the crucifixion; St. Anthony's cross, which is made in the form of a T; and the Greek cross, +, which is made by the intersection at right angles of lines at their center point.

As an adjective, the word is applied to various demands and proceedings which are connected in subject-matter, but opposite or contradictory in purpose or object. *See e.g.* Cross-claim.

Cross-action. An action brought by one who is defendant in a suit against the party who is plaintiff in such suit, or against a co-defendant, upon a cause of action growing out of the same transaction which is there in controversy, whether it be a contract or tort. An independent suit brought by defendant against plaintiff or co-defendant. *See also* Counterclaim; Cross-claim; Cross-complaint.

Cross appeal. An appeal by the appellee. In the federal courts a cross appeal is argued with the initial appeal of the appellant. Fed.R.App.P. 34(d). *See also* Appeal.

Cross-claim. Cross-claims against co-parties are governed in the federal district courts and in most state trial courts by Rule of Civil Procedure 13(g): "A pleading may state as a cross-claim any claim by one party against a co-party arising out of the transaction or occurrence that is the subject matter either of the original action or of a counterclaim therein or relating to any property that is the subject matter of the original action. Such cross-claim may include a claim that the party against whom it is asserted is or may be liable to the cross-claimant for all or part of a claim asserted in the action against the cross-claimant." See also New York C.P.L.R. § 3019(b).

For requisite content of cross-claim under Rules of Civil Procedure, *see* Complaint. *See also* Cross-complaint; Transaction or occurrence test.

Counterclaim distinguished. "Cross-claims" are litigated by parties on the same side of the main litigation, while "counterclaims" are litigated between opposing parties to the principal action.

Cross collateral. Security given by both parties to a contract or undertaking for performance or payment.

Cross-complaint. A defendant or cross-defendant may file a cross-complaint setting forth either or both of the following: (a) Any cause of action he has against any of the parties who filed the complaint against him. (b) Any cause of action he has against a person alleged to be liable thereon, whether or not such person is already a party to the action, if the cause of action asserted in his cross-complaint, (1) arises out of the same transaction, occurrence, or series of transactions or occurrences as the cause brought against him or (2) asserts a claim, right, or interest in the property or controversy which is the subject of the cause brought against him. Calif. Code of Civil Proc. § 428.10. *See also* Cross-claim.

Cross-default. A provision under which default on one debt obligation triggers default on another debt obligation.

Cross-demand. Where a person against whom a demand is made by another, in his turn makes a demand against that other, these mutual demands are called "cross-demands." A *set-off* is a familiar example. *See also* Counterclaim; Cross-claim; Cross-complaint.

Crossed check. *See* Check.

Cross-errors. Errors being assigned by the respondent in a writ of error; the errors assigned on both sides are called "cross-errors."

Cross-examination. The examination of a witness upon a trial or hearing, or upon taking a deposition, by the party opposed to the one who produced him, upon his evidence given in chief, to test its truth, to further develop it, or for other purposes. The examination of a witness by a party other than the direct examiner upon a matter that is within the scope of the direct examination of the witness. Generally the scope of examination is limited to matters covered on direct examination and matters affecting the credibility of the witness; though the court may in its discretion permit inquiry into additional matters as if on direct examination. Fed.R.Civil P. 43(b); Fed.Evid.Rule 611. *Compare* Direct examination; Redirect examination.

Cross interrogatory. A party to an action who has been interrogated may serve cross questions on all other parties. Fed.R. Civil P. 31(a).

Cross-licensing. Permission or right to use a thing or property given in exchange between two or more parties. Exchange of licenses by two or more patent holders in order that each may use or benefit from the patents of the other.

Cross-purchase buy and sell agreement. Under this type of arrangement, the surviving owners of a business agree to buy out the withdrawing owner. Assume, for example, R and S are equal shareholders in T Corporation. Under a cross-purchase buy and sell agreement, R and S would contract to purchase the other's interest should that person decide to withdraw from the business.

Partnership insurance plan wherein each partner individually purchases and maintains enough insurance on the life or lives of other partners to fund the purchase of the others' equity. *See also* Buy and sell agreement.

Cross rates. The exchange rate between two currencies expressed as the ratio of two foreign exchange rates that are both expressed in terms of a common third currency. *See* Foreign exchange rate.

Cross remainder. Cross remainders are remainders which are so limited after particular estates to two or more persons in several parcels of land, or in several undivided shares in the same parcel of land, that, on the determination of the particular estates in any of the several parcels of undivided shares, they remain over to the other grantees, and the reversioner or ulterior remainderman is not let in until the determination of all of the particular estates.

Crown jewel. A particularly profitable or otherwise particularly valuable business unit (or asset) of a firm.

Crown loan. Name for an interest free demand loan, usually from a parent to a child. The borrowed funds are invested and the income from the investment is taxed at the child's rate. This type of loan got its name from Harry Crown of Chicago, who was the first to use it. In 1984, the Supreme Court ruled that the market rate of interest must be imputed on each loan, and treated as a gift subject to gift taxes. *See* Kiddie tax.

Cruel and inhuman treatment. As ground for divorce, consists of unwarranted and unjustifiable conduct on part of defendant causing other spouse to endure suffering and distress, thereby destroying peace of mind and making living with such spouse unbearable, completely destroying real purpose and object of matrimony.

Cruel and unusual punishment. *See* Corporal punishment; Punishment.

Cruelty. The intentional and malicious infliction of physical or mental suffering upon living creatures, particularly human beings; or, as applied to the latter, the wanton, malicious, and unnecessary infliction of pain upon the body, or the feelings and emotions; abusive treatment; inhumanity; outrage.

Chiefly used in the law of divorce, in such phrases as "cruel and abusive treatment," "cruel and barbarous treatment," or "cruel and inhuman treatment" *(q.v.).* In domestic relations, term includes mental injury as well as physical; though, this ground for divorce is of limited importance with the enactment by most states of no-fault divorce laws.

See also Legal cruelty; Mental anguish; Mental cruelty.

Cruelty to animals. The infliction of physical pain, suffering, or death upon an animal, when not necessary for purposes of training or discipline or (in the case of death) to procure food or to release the animal from incurable suffering, but done wantonly, for mere sport, for the indulgence of a cruel and vindictive temper, or with reckless indifference to its pain.

A person commits a misdemeanor if he purposely or recklessly: (1) subjects any animal to cruel mistreatment; or (2) subjects any animal in his custody to cruel neglect; or (3) kills or injures any animal belonging to another without legal privilege or consent of the owner. Model Penal Code, § 250.11.

Cruelty to children. Most jurisdictions have "battered child" statutes in which both emotional and physical injuries are embraced in the term "cruelty." *See also* Child abuse.

Legal cruelty. See Legal cruelty.

C.S.C. Civil Service Commission.

C.T.A. An abbreviation for *cum testamento annexo,* in describing a species of administration.

Culpa /kálpə/. Lat. A term of the civil law, meaning fault, neglect, or negligence. There are three degrees of *culpa, lata culpa,* gross fault or neglect; *levis culpa,* ordinary fault or neglect; *levissima culpa,* slight fault or neglect, and the definitions of these degrees are precisely the same as those in our law. This term is to be distinguished from *dolus,* which means fraud, guile, or deceit.

Culpability /kəlpəbílətiy/. Blameworthiness. Except in cases of absolute liability, a person's criminal culpability requires a showing that he acted purposely, knowingly, recklessly or negligently, as the law may require, with respect to each material element of the offense. Model Penal Code, § 2.02(1).

Culpable conduct /kə́lpəbəl/. Blamable; censurable; criminal; at fault; involving the breach of a legal duty or the commission of a fault. That which is deserving of moral blame. As to *culpable* Homicide; Ignorance; Neglect; Negligence; and Wantonness, see those titles.

Culprit. One accused or charged with commission of crime. Also, commonly used to mean one guilty of a crime or fault.

Cum dividend /kə́m dívədènd/. Means that when a share of stock is sold after a dividend is declared, the buyer has the right to the dividend; *lit.,* with dividend. *See also* Dividend (*Cumulative dividend*).

Cum rights. *Lit.* with rights; a share of stock sold under conditions which permit the buyer to buy new stock of the issuer in a stated amount.

Cum testamento annexo /kə́m testəméntow ənéksow/. L. Lat. With the will annexed. A term applied to administration granted where a testator makes an incomplete will, without naming any executors, or where he names incapable persons, or where the executors so named refuse to act. If the executor has died, an administrator *de bonis non cum testamento annexo* (of the goods not [already] administered upon with the will annexed) is appointed. Often abbreviated d. b. n. c. t. a.

Cumulative /kyúmyələtəv/. Additional; heaping up; increasing; forming an aggregate. The word signifies that two things are to be added together, instead of one being a repetition or in substitution of the other.

As to *cumulative* Dividend, Punishment, and Stock, see those titles.

Cumulative dividend feature. A requirement that any missed preferred or preference stock dividends be paid in full prior to any common dividend payment being made.

Cumulative evidence. Additional or corroborative evidence to the same point. That which goes to prove what has already been established by other evidence. *See also* Corroborating evidence.

Cumulative legacies. Legacies given in addition to a prior legacy, as when one legacy is given in a will and another legacy is given to the same person in a codicil. *See also* Legacy.

Cumulative offense. One which can be committed only by a repetition of acts of the same kind but committed on different days or times.

Cumulative preferred dividend. Dividend on preferred stock which, if declared at the end of a particular year, must be paid before any common stock dividend is paid. *See also* Dividend.

Cumulative preferred stock. *See* Stock.

Cumulative remedy. A remedy created by statute in addition to one which still remains in force.

Cumulative sentence. Any sentence which is to take effect after the expiration of a prior sentence; also known as "from and after" sentence. *See also* Sentence.

Cumulative voting. Type of voting in which a stockholder may cast as many votes for directors as he has shares of stock multiplied by the number of directors to be elected. The stockholder may cast all his votes for one or more but fewer than all the directors on the slate, and hence, minority representation is promoted. It is a method of voting that allows substantial minority shareholders to obtain representation on the board of directors. Cumulative voting is *required* under the corporate laws of some states, while in most states such voting can be included or expressly excluded at the option of the corporation in its articles of incorporation. See, *e.g.,* Rev.Model Bus.Corp. Act § 7.28. *Compare* Noncumulative voting.

A system of minority representation which is used for the election of members of the lower house of the Illinois legislature. Each voter has three votes which he may lump together on one candidate or distribute among two or three candidates as he chooses.

Cura /kyúrə/. Lat. Care; charge; oversight; guardianship. In the civil law a species of guardianship which commenced at the age of puberty (when the guardianship called "tutela" expired), and continued to the completion of the twenty-fifth year.

Curative /kyúrətəv/. Intended to cure (that is, to obviate the ordinary legal effects or consequences of) defects, errors, omissions or irregularities. The word is defined as relating to, or employed in, the cure of diseases; tending to cure; a remedy.

Curative admissibility of evidence. The doctrine of "curative admissibility" allows evidence which is otherwise inadmissible to be presented because similar evidence has been introduced by the adverse party. In some jurisdictions, an opponent may counter or answer evidence which has been admitted without objection though otherwise inadmissible to cure the effect of such evidence. This rule is not of universal application or acceptance.

Curative statute. A law, retrospective in effect, which is designed to remedy some legal defect in previous transactions. A form of retrospective legislation which reaches back into the past to operate upon past events, acts or transactions in order to correct errors and irregularities and to render valid and effective many attempted acts which would otherwise be ineffective for the purpose intended. As applied to conveyances they supply one or more ingredients of a legal act which the parties intended to perform but which they failed to accomplish completely or which they executed only imperfectly.

Curator /kyə́rətər/kyəréytər/. A temporary guardian or conservator appointed by the court to care for the property or person or both of an incompetent, spendthrift, or a minor. One in charge of museum, art gallery, or the like.

In Louisiana, a person appointed to take care of the estate of an absentee.

Curatorship. The office of a curator or guardian. *Compare* Tutorship.

Cure. The act of healing; restoration to health from disease, or to soundness after injury.

Under rule that a vessel and her owner must provide maintenance and "cure" for seaman injured or falling ill while in service, "cure" is care, including nursing and medical attention during such period as the duty continues. *See also* Maintenance and cure.

The right of a seller under U.C.C. to correct a non-conforming delivery of goods to buyer within the contract period. § 2–508.

Term as used in Chapter 13 bankruptcy proceedings (adjustment of debts of an individual) refers to provision in repayment plan for "curing" defaults in debt obligations. Bankruptcy Code § 1322(b)(3).

Cure by verdict. In common law pleading, the rectification or rendering nugatory of a defect in the pleadings by the rendition of a verdict; the court presuming after a verdict, that the particular thing omitted or defectively stated in the pleadings was duly proved at the trial. This function is served by Rule of Civil Procedure 15 which permits amendment of pleadings to conform to the evidence.

Curfew. A law (commonly an ordinance) which imposes on people (particularly children) the obligation to remove themselves from the streets on or before a certain time of night.

Curing title. Removal of defects from land title which render such unmarketable. "Clearing", "curing", "straightening out", or "removing cloud from" title denotes acts or proceedings necessary to render title marketable. *See* Action to quiet title.

Currency. Coined money and such banknotes or other paper money as are authorized by law and do in fact circulate from hand to hand as the medium of exchange. *See also* Blocked currency; Comptroller of Currency; Current money; Legal tender; United States currency.

Currency future. A financial future contract for the delivery of a specified foreign currency.

Currency swap. An agreement to swap a series of specified payment obligations denominated in one currency for a series of specified payment obligations denominated in a different currency.

Current. Running; now in transit; present existence; now in progress; whatever is at present in course of passage, as "the current month." Most recent; up-to-date. A continuous movement in the same direction, as a fluid stream.

The word "current", when used as an adjective, has many meanings, and definition depends largely on word which it modifies, or subject-matter with which it is associated. See *e.g.* usages that follow below.

Current account. An open, running, or unsettled account between two parties.

Current assets. Any property that will be or could be converted into cash in the normal operation of a business or at an earlier date, usually within one year. Short-term assets; *e.g.* cash, accounts receivable, inventory.

Current cost accounting. An approach to accounting for inflation that recognizes price changes in the individual assets owned by an enterprise and restates the assets in terms of their current cost.

Current earnings and profits. A corporate distribution is deemed to be first from the entity's current earnings and profits and then from accumulated earnings and profits. Shareholders recognize dividend income to the extent of the earnings and profits of the corporation. A dividend results to the extent of current earnings and profits even if there is a larger negative balance in accumulated earnings and profits. *See also* Earnings and profits.

Current expenses. Ordinary, regular, recurring, and continuing expenditures for the maintenance of property, the carrying on of a business, an office, municipal government, etc.

Current funds. Cash and other assets readily convertible into cash. Money which circulates as legal tender. Formerly, this phrase meant gold or silver, or something equivalent thereto, and convertible at pleasure into coin money. *See* Current money.

Current income. Income which is due within the present accounting period.

Current liabilities. An obligation that will be paid in the ordinary course of a business or within one year. A current liability is paid by expending a current asset. The phrase "current liability" carries with it the idea of a liability that is presently enforceable.

Current maintenance. The expense occasioned in keeping the physical property in the condition required for continued use during its service life.

Current market value. The value of an asset which may be realized by liquidation within the present accounting period. Present value which may be realized in an arms length transaction between a willing buyer and a willing seller. *See also* Fair market value.

Current money. The currency of the country; whatever is intended to and does actually circulate as currency; every species of coin or currency. In this phrase the adjective "current" is not synonymous with "convertible". It is employed to describe money which passes from hand to hand, from person to person, and circulates through the community, and is generally received. Money is current which is received as money in the common business transactions, and is the common medium in barter and trade. *See also* Currency; Legal tender.

Current obligations. Such as are presently enforceable and not past due. *See also* Current liabilities.

Current price. This term means the same as "market value", "market price", "going price", the price that runs or flows with the market. *See also* Current market value; Fair market value.

Current ratio. In accounting, a measure of liquidity that relates total current assets to total current liabilities.

Current revenues. *See* Current income.

Current use valuation. *See* Special use valuation.

Current value. *See* Current market value; Fair market value.

Current wages. Such as are paid periodically, or from time to time as the services are rendered or the work is performed; more particularly, wages for the current period, hence not including such as are past-due or deferred. *See also* Minimum wage.

Current year. The year now running. Ordinarily, a calendar year in which the event under discussion took place; though the current fiscal year of a business may run from July 1st to June 30th, or some other twelve month period.

Current yield. A bond's annual coupon payment divided by its current market price.

Cursory examination /kɔ́rs(ə)riy əgzæ̀mənéyshən/. An inspection for defects visible or ascertainable by ordinary examination; contrasted from a thorough examination.

Curtesy /kɔ́rtəsiy/. The estate to which by common law a man is entitled, on the death of his wife, in the lands or tenements of which she was seised in possession in fee-simple or in tail during her coverture, provided they have had lawful issue born alive which might have been capable of inheriting the estate. It is a freehold estate for the term of his natural life.

In some jurisdictions, there is no requirement that issue be born of the union. This estate has gradually lost much of its former value and now in some jurisdictions it attaches only to the real estate which the wife owns at death, rather than to the real estate owned by the wife during the marriage, while in most states it has been abolished or otherwise materially altered.

See also Dower.

Initiate and consummate. Curtesy initiate is the interest which a husband has in his wife's estate after the birth of issue capable of inheriting, and before the death of the wife; after her death, it becomes an estate "by the curtesy consummate."

Curtilage /kɔ́rtələj/. A word derived from the Latin cohors (a place enclosed around a yard) and the old French cortilliage or courtillage which today has been corrupted into court-yard. Originally, it referred to the land and outbuildings immediately adjacent to a castle that were in turn surrounded by a high stone wall; today, its meaning has been extended to include any land or building immediately adjacent to a dwelling, and usually it is enclosed some way by a fence or shrubs.

For search and seizure purposes, includes those outbuildings which are directly and intimately connected with the habitation and in proximity thereto and the land or grounds surrounding the dwelling which are necessary and convenient and habitually used for family purposes and carrying on domestic employment.

Custodial account. An account established on behalf of someone else. For example, when a parent opens an account for a minor child, or when a son or daughter opens and controls a bank account of an infirm parent.

Custodial arrest. Confinement or detention by police or government authorities during which a person is entitled to certain warnings as to his rights when questioned. Miranda v. Arizona, 384 U.S. 436, 86 S.Ct. 1602, 16 L.Ed.2d 694. *See* Custodial interrogation.

Custodia legis /kəstówdiyə líyjəs/. In the custody of the law. Doctrine of "custodia legis" provides that when personal property is repossessed under writ of replevin, property is considered to be in custody of the court, though actual possession may be in either of the parties to the replevin action, and that property remains in custody of court until judgment in replevin action finally determines whether replevining party or prior holder is entitled to possession. This doctrine is nothing more than a practical "first come, first serve" method of resolving jurisdictional disputes between two courts with concurrent jurisdiction, and, under such doctrine, court that first secures custody of property administers it.

Custodial interference. A tort recognized in some states for damages resulting from intentional interference with a custodial parent's rights. Though usually arising in the context of parental abduction, the tort has been recognized in cases of unjustified interference by third parties, such as state welfare agencies.

Custodial interrogation. Custodial interrogation, within *Miranda* rule requiring that defendant be advised of his constitutional rights, means questioning initiated by law enforcement officers after person has been taken into custody or otherwise deprived of his freedom in any significant way; custody can occur without formality of arrest and in areas other than in police station. Miranda v. Arizona, 384 U.S. 436, 86 S.Ct. 1602, 16 L.Ed.2d 694. *See* Interrogation; Miranda Rule.

Custodian. General term to describe person or financial institution that has charge or custody of property, securities, papers, assets, etc.

In bankruptcy proceedings, refers to a third party (*e.g.* receiver or trustee) acting under mandatory authority who takes charge of debtor's assets for the benefit of debtor's creditors as a whole. See Bankruptcy Code § 101 (11 U.S.C.A.).

Custody. The care and control of a thing or person. The keeping, guarding, care, watch, inspection, preservation or security of a thing, carrying with it the idea of the thing being within the immediate personal care and control of the person to whose custody it is subjected. Immediate charge and control, and not the final, absolute control of ownership, implying responsibility for the protection and preservation of the thing in custody. Also the detainer of a man's person by virtue of lawful process or authority.

The term is very elastic and may mean actual imprisonment or physical detention or mere power, legal or physical, of imprisoning or of taking manual possession. Within statute requiring that petitioner be "in custody" to be entitled to federal habeas corpus relief does not necessarily mean actual physical detention in jail or prison but rather is synonymous with restraint of liberty. Accordingly, persons on probation or parole or released on bail or on own recognizance have been held to be "in custody" for purposes of habeas corpus proceedings.

See Chain of custody; Custodial interrogation; Custody of children; In custody; Parental Kidnapping Prevention Act; Protective custody.

Custody account. A type of agency account in which the custodian has the obligation to preserve and safekeep the property entrusted to him for his principal.

Custody of children. The care, control and maintenance of a child which may be awarded by a court to one of the parents as in a divorce or separation proceeding. *See also* Guardianship; Parental Kidnapping Prevention Act.

Divided custody. Divided custody is where child lives with each parent part of the year with reciprocal visitation privileges; in divided custody, parent with whom child is living has complete control over child during that period.

Joint custody. Joint custody involves both parents sharing responsibility and authority with respect to the children; it may involve joint "legal" custody and joint "physical" custody. Such includes physical sharing of child in addition to both parents participating in decisions affecting child's life, *e.g.*, education, medical problems, recreation, etc.; "joint custody" does not mean fifty-fifty sharing of time, since each case depends on child's age, parent's availability and desires, and other factors.

Temporary custody. Awarding of custody of a child to a parent temporarily, pending the outcome of a separation or divorce action.

The care, control and maintenance of a child which may be awarded by a court to one of the parents as in a divorce or separation proceeding.

Uniform Child Custody Jurisdiction Act. A uniform law adopted in all states, cf. N.Y. McKinney's Domestic Relations Law, §§ 75–a to 75–z, to deal with multi-state child custody and visitation disputes. Enacted in part to deter parental kidnapping, it generally recognizes jurisdiction in a child's "home state."

Custody of the law. Property is in the custody of the law when it has been lawfully taken by authority of legal process, and remains in the possession of a public officer (as a sheriff) or an officer of a court (as a receiver) empowered by law to hold it. *See* Forfeiture; Seizure.

Custom. Term generally implies habitual practice or course of action that characteristically is repeated in like circumstances. *See also* Custom and usage.

Custom and usage. A usage or practice of the people, which, by common adoption and acquiescence, and by long and unvarying habit, has become compulsory, and has acquired the force of a law with respect to the place or subject-matter to which it relates. It results from a long series of actions, constantly repeated, which have, by such repetition and by uninterrupted acquiescence, acquired the force of a tacit and common consent. An habitual or customary practice, more or less widespread, which prevails within a geographical or sociological area; usage is a course of conduct based on a series of actual occurrences.

Parol evidence rule does not bar evidence of custom or usage to explain or supplement a contract or memorandum of the parties. U.C.C. § 2–203.

Classification. Customs are general, local or particular. *General* customs are such as prevail throughout a country and become the law of that country, and their existence is to be determined by the court. Or as applied to usages of trade and business, a general custom is one that is followed in all cases by all persons in the same business in the same territory, and which has been so long established that persons sought to be charged thereby, and all others living in the vicinity, may be presumed to have known of it and to have acted upon it as they had occasion. *Local* customs are such as prevail only in some particular district or locality, or in some city, county, or town. *Particular* customs are nearly the same, being such as affect only the inhabitants of some particular district.

Usage distinguished. "Usage" is a repetition of acts, and differs from "custom" in that the latter is the law or general rule which arises from such repetition; while there may be usage without custom, there cannot be a custom without a usage accompanying or preceding it. *See also* Usage.

Customarily. Means usually, habitually, according to the customs; general practice or usual order of things; regularly.

Customary. According to custom or usage; founded on, or growing out of, or dependent on, a custom *(q.v.)*; ordinary; usual; common.

Customary interpretation. *See* Interpretation.

Custom duties. *See* Customs duties.

Customer. One who regularly or repeatedly makes purchases of, or has business dealings with, a tradesman or business. Ordinarily, one who has had repeated business dealings with another. A buyer, purchaser, consumer or patron.

In banking, any person having an account with a bank or for whom a bank has agreed to collect items and includes a bank carrying an account with another bank. U.C.C. § 4–104(e). As to letters of credit, a buyer or other person who causes an issuer to issue credit or a bank which procures issuance or confirmation on behalf of that bank's customer. U.C.C. § 5–103(g).

Custom-house. The house or office where commodities are entered for importation or exporta-

tion; where the duties, bounties, or drawbacks payable or receivable upon such importation or exportation are paid or received; and where ships are cleared out, etc. A public establishment for the inspection and assessment of duties on imported goods. *See also* Bureau of Customs; Customs broker; Customs Service.

Custom-house broker. One whose occupation it is, as an agent, to arrange entries and other custom-house papers, or transact business, at any port of entry, relating to the importation or exportation of goods, wares, or merchandise. A person authorized by the commissioners of customs to act for parties, at their option, in the entry or clearance of ships and the transaction of general business.

Customs. This term is usually applied to those taxes which are payable upon goods and merchandise imported or exported. The duties, toll, tribute, or tariff payable upon merchandise exported or imported. Federal agency responsible for assessing imported goods collecting duties. See 19 U.S.C.A. *See also* Customs duties; Custom-house; Customs Service; Tariff.

Customs and Patent Appeals Court. This court was established in 1929 under Article III of the Constitution of the United States as successor to the United States Court of Customs Appeals. The Court was abolished by the Federal Courts Improvement Act of 1982. Matters formerly handled by this Court are now under the jurisdiction of the United States Court of Appeals for the Federal Circuit. *See* Courts of Appeals, U.S. *See also* Court of International Trade.

Customs broker. Licensed agent or broker whose function is to handle the process of clearing goods through customs.

Customs Court. A court created in 1890 as the Board of United States General Appraisers and given this name in 1926. The name of the Court was changed in 1980 to the Court of International Trade. See that Court.

Customs duties. Taxes on the importation and exportation of commodities, merchandise and other goods. The tariff or tax assessed upon merchandise, imported from, or exported to a foreign country. *See* 19 U.S.C.A.

Tax levied by federal government on goods shipped into U.S., though in other countries it may include export taxes as well. *See also* Customs; Tariff.

Customs House. *See* Custom-house; Customs Service.

Customs Service. The United States Customs Service collects the revenue from imports and enforces customs and related laws and also administers the Tariff Act of 1930, as amended, and other customs laws. Some of the responsibilities which the Customs Service is specifically charged with are as follows: properly assessing and collecting customs duties, excise taxes, fees, and penalties due on imported merchandise; interdicting and seizing contraband, including narcotics and illegal drugs; processing persons, carriers, cargo, and mail into and out of the United States; administering certain navigation laws; detecting and apprehending persons engaged in fraudulent practices designed to circumvent customs and related laws; protecting American business and labor by enforcing statutes and regulations such as the Anti-dumping Act; countervailing duty; copyright, patent, and trademark provisions; quotas; and marking requirements for imported merchandise. *See also* Bureau of Customs; Custom-house.

CWA. *See* Clean Water Acts.

CWAS. Contractor Weighted Average Share In Cost Risk.

Cwt. A hundred-weight.

Cy-pres /sìypréy/. As near as (possible). The rule of *cy-pres* is a rule for the construction of instruments in equity, by which the intention of the party is carried out *as near as may be,* when it would be impossible or illegal to give it literal effect. Thus, where a testator attempts to create a perpetuity, the court will endeavor, instead of making the devise entirely void, to explain the will in such a way as to carry out the testator's general intention as far as the rule against perpetuities will allow. So in the case of bequests to charitable uses; and particularly where the language used is so vague or uncertain that the testator's design must be sought by construction.

Equitable power which makes it possible for court to carry out testamentary trust established for particular charitable purpose if testator has expressed general charitable intent, and for some reason his purpose cannot be accomplished in manner specified in the will.

D

Daily balances; average daily balance. The various balances for the different days in the period for which interest is to be paid, and the "average daily balance" for the interest period means the sum of these daily balances divided by the number of days in the interest period.

Damage. Loss, injury, or deterioration, caused by the negligence, design, or accident of one person to another, in respect of the latter's person or property. The word is to be distinguished from its plural, "damages", which means a compensation in money for a loss or damage. An injury produces a right in them who have suffered any damage by it to demand reparation of such damage from the authors of the injury. By damage we understand every loss or diminution of what is a man's own, occasioned by the fault of another. The harm, detriment, or loss sustained by reason of an injury. *See also* Damages; Damage to person; Injury; Loss.

Damages. A pecuniary compensation or indemnity, which may be recovered in the courts by any person who has suffered loss, detriment, or injury, whether to his person, property, or rights, through the unlawful act or omission or negligence of another. A sum of money awarded to a person injured by the tort of another. Restatement, Second, Torts, § 12A. Money compensation sought or awarded as a remedy for a breach of contract or for tortious acts.

Damages may be compensatory or punitive according to whether they are awarded as the measure of actual loss suffered or as punishment for outrageous conduct and to deter future transgressions. Nominal damages are awarded for the vindication of a right where no real loss or injury can be proved. Generally, punitive or exemplary damages are awarded only if compensatory or actual damages have been sustained.

See also Economic loss; Injury; Just compensation; Loss; Pain and suffering.

Actual damages. Real, substantial and just damages, or the amount awarded to a complainant in compensation for his actual and real loss or injury, as opposed on the one hand to "nominal" damages, and on the other to "exemplary" or "punitive" damages. Synonymous with "compensatory damages" and with "general damages."

Benefit-of-the-bargain damages. Difference between the value received and the value of the fraudulent party's performance as represented.

Civil Damage Acts. See Dram Shop Acts.

Compensatory damages. Compensatory damages are such as will compensate the injured party for the injury sustained, and nothing more; such as will simply make good or replace the loss caused by the wrong or injury. Damages awarded to a person as compensation, indemnity, or restitution for harm sustained by him. The rationale behind compensatory damages is to restore the injured party to the position he or she was in prior to the injury. Equivalent of *Actual damages, above.*

Compensatory or actual damages consist of both general and special damages. General damages are the natural, necessary, and usual result of the wrongful act or occurrence in question. Special damages are those "which are the natural, but not the necessary and inevitable result of the wrongful act."

Consequential damages. Such damage, loss or injury as does not flow directly and immediately from the act of the party, but only from some of the consequences or results of such act. Damages which arise from intervention of special circumstances not ordinarily predictable. Those losses or injuries which are a result of an act but are not direct and immediate. Consequential damages resulting from a seller's breach of contract include any loss resulting from general or particular requirements and needs of which the seller at the time of contracting had reason to know and which could not reasonably be prevented by cover or otherwise, and injury to person or property proximately resulting from any breach of warranty. U.C.C. § 2–715(2). *See also* Hadley v. Baxendale, rule of; and *Incidental damages, below.*

Continuing damages. Such as accrue from the same injury, or from the repetition of similar acts, between two specified periods of time.

Criminal damage. Criminal damage to property is by means other than by fire or explosive: (a) Willfully injuring, damaging, mutilating, defacing, destroying, or substantially impairing the use of any property in which another has an interest without the consent of such other person; or (b) Injuring, damaging, mutilating, defacing, destroying, or substantially impairing the use of any property with intent to injure or defraud an insurer or lienholder. *See* Arson.

Direct damages. Direct damages are such as follow immediately upon the act done. Damages which arise naturally or ordinarily from breach of contract; they are damages which, in ordinary course of human experience, can be expected to result from breach.

Excessive damages. Damages awarded by a jury which are grossly in excess of the amount warranted by law on the facts and circumstances of the case; unreasonable or outrageous damages. *See* Remittitur.

Excess liability damages. A cause of action in tort by an insured against his liability carrier for the negligent handling of settlement negotiations which result in a judgment against the insured in excess of his policy limits.

Exemplary or punitive damages. Exemplary damages are damages on an increased scale, awarded to the plaintiff over and above what will barely compensate him for his property loss, where the wrong done to him was aggravated by circumstances of violence, oppression, malice, fraud, or wanton and wicked conduct on the part of the defendant, and are intended to solace the plaintiff for mental anguish, laceration of his feelings, shame, degradation, or other aggravations of the original wrong, or else to punish the defendant for his evil behavior or to make an example of him, for which reason they are also called "punitive" or "punitory" damages or "vindictive" damages. Unlike compensatory or actual damages, punitive or exemplary damages are based upon an entirely different public policy consideration—that of punishing the defendant or of setting an example for similar wrongdoers, as above noted. In cases in which it is proved that a defendant has acted willfully, maliciously, or fraudulently, a plaintiff may be awarded exemplary damages in addition to compensatory or actual damages. Damages other than compensatory damages which may be awarded against person to punish him for outrageous conduct. Such are given as an enhancement of compensatory damages because of wanton, reckless, malicious or oppressive character of acts complained of.

Expectancy damages. As awarded in actions for nonperformance of contract, such damages are calculable by subtracting the injured party's actual dollar position as a result of the breach from that party's projected dollar position had performance occurred. The goal is to ascertain the dollar amount necessary to ensure that the aggrieved party's position after the award will be the same—to the extent money can achieve the identity—as if the other party had performed.

Fee damages. Damages sustained by and awarded to an abutting owner of real property occasioned by the construction and operation of an elevated railroad in a city street, are so called, because compensation is made to the owner for the injury to, or deprivation of, his easements of light, air, and access, and these are parts of the fee.

Foreseeable damages. Loss that the party in breach had reason to know of when the contract was made.

Future damages. Those sums awarded to an injured party for, among other things, residuals or future effects of an injury which have reduced the capability of an individual to function as a whole man, future pain and suffering, loss or impairment of earning capacity, and future medical expenses.

Those damages that flow as a natural and necessary result of the act claimed of, while "special damages" are damages which actually result from the act by reason of the special circumstances of the case and not as a necessary result of the act. *Compare Special damages, below.*

General damages. Such as the law itself implies or presumes to have accrued from the wrong complained of, for the reason that they are its immediate, direct, and proximate result, or such as necessarily result from the injury, or such as did in fact result from the wrong, directly and proximately, and without reference to the special character, condition, or circumstances of the plaintiff.

Hedonic damages. Damages awarded in some jurisdictions for the loss of enjoyment of life, or for the value of life itself, as measured separately from the economic productive value that an injured or deceased person would have had. Compensation to a personal injury victim "for the limitations on the person's life created by the injury." Many courts hold that such loss is included in damages for disability and pain and suffering.

Inadequate damages. Damages are called "inadequate," within the rule that an injunction will not be granted where adequate damages at law could be recovered for the injury sought to be prevented, when such a recovery at law would not compensate the parties and place them in the position in which they formerly stood.

Incidental damages. Under U.C.C. § 2–710, such damages include any commercially reasonable charges, expenses or commissions incurred in stopping delivery, in the transportation, care and custody of goods after the buyer's breach, in connection with the return or resale of the goods or otherwise resulting from the breach. Also, such damages, resulting from a seller's breach of contract, include expenses reasonably incurred in inspection, receipt, transportation and care and custody of goods rightfully rejected, any commercially reasonable charges, expenses or commissions in connection with effecting cover and any other reasonable expense incident to the delay or other breach. U.C.C. § 2–715(1). *See also Consequential damages, above.*

Irreparable damages. In the law pertaining to injunctions, damages for which no certain pecuniary standard exists for measurement. Damages not easily ascertainable at law. With reference to public nuisances which a private party may enjoin, the term includes wrongs of a repeated and continuing character, or which occasion damages estimable only by conjecture, and not by any accurate standard.

Land damages. A term sometimes applied to the amount of compensation to be paid for land taken under the power of eminent domain or for injury to, or depreciation of, land adjoining that taken. *See* Just compensation; *also, Severance damages, below,* this topic.

Limitation of damages. Provision in contract or agreement by which parties agree in advance as to the amount or limit of damages for breach. U.C.C. § 2–718. *See also Liquidated damages and penalties, below.*

Liquidated damages and penalties. The term is applicable when the amount of the damages has been ascertained by the judgment in the action, or when a specific sum of money has been expressly stipulated by the parties to a bond or other contract as the amount of damages to be recovered by either party for a breach of the agreement by the other. The purpose of a penalty is to secure performance, while the purpose of stipulating damages is to fix the amount to be paid in lieu of performance. The essence of a penalty is a stipulation as in terrorem while the essence of liquidated damages is a genuine covenanted preestimate of such damages.

Liquidated damages is the sum which party to contract agrees to pay if he breaks some promise and, which having been arrived at by good faith effort to estimate actual damage that will probably ensue from breach, is recoverable as agreed damages if breach occurs. Such are those damages which are reasonably ascertainable at time of breach, measurable by fixed or established external standard, or by standard apparent from documents upon which plaintiffs based their claim.

Damages for breach by either party may be liquidated in the agreement but only at an amount which is reasonable in the light of the anticipated or actual harm caused by the breach, the difficulties of proof of loss, and the inconvenience or nonfeasibility of otherwise obtaining an adequate remedy. A term fixing unreasonably large liquidated damages is void as a penalty. U.C.C. § 2–718(1).

Compare Unliquidated damages, below.

Mitigation of damages. Although the law of damages contemplates full and just compensation for negligently inflicted injuries, the law likewise prescribes, as a reciprocal principle, that a tortfeasor should not sustain liability for those damages not attributable to the injury producing event. Consequently, a plaintiff may not recover damages for the effects of an injury which reasonably could have been avoided or substantially ameliorated. This limitation on recovery is generally denominated as "mitigation of damages" or "avoidance of consequences." Mitigation of damages or avoidance of consequences arises only after the injury producing event has occurred.

Necessary damages. A term said to be of much wider scope in the law of damages than "pecuniary." It embraces all those consequences of an injury usually denominated "general" damages, as distinguished from special damages; whereas the phrase "pecuniary damages" covers a smaller class of damages within the larger class of "general" damages.

Nominal damages. Nominal damages are a trifling sum awarded to a plaintiff in an action, where there is no substantial loss or injury to be compensated, but still the law recognizes a technical invasion of his rights or a breach of the defendant's duty, or in cases where, although there has been a real injury, the plaintiff's evidence entirely fails to show its amount.

Pecuniary damages. Such as can be estimated in and compensated by money; not merely the loss of money or salable property or rights, but all such loss, deprivation, or injury as can be made the subject of calculation and of recompense in money. Those damages (either general or special) which can be accurately calculated in monetary terms. *See also* Pecuniary loss.

Presumptive damages. A term occasionally used as the equivalent of "exemplary" or "punitive" damages.

Prospective damages. Damages which are expected to follow from the act or state of facts made the basis of a plaintiff's suit; damages which have not yet accrued, at the time of the trial, but which, in the nature of things, must necessarily, or most probably, result from the acts or facts complained of.

Proximate damages. Proximate damages are the immediate and direct damages and natural results of the act complained of, and such as are usual and might have been expected. Remote damages are those attributable immediately to an intervening cause, though it forms a link in an unbroken chain of causation, so that the remote damage would not have occurred if its elements had not been set in motion by the original act or event.

Punitive damages. See *Exemplary or punitive damages, above.*

Remote damages. The unusual and unexpected result, not reasonably to be anticipated from an accidental or unusual combination of circumstances—a result beyond which the negligent party has no control.

Rescissory damages. Such damages contemplate a return of the injured party to the position he occupied before he was induced by wrongful conduct to enter into the transaction. When return of the specific property, right, etc. is not possible (*e.g.* in a stock fraud transaction, the stock is no longer available), the rescissory damages would be the monetary equivalent (*e.g.* value of stock).

Severance damages. In condemnation, where the property condemned constitutes only a part of an owner's interest, the owner is entitled to just compensation, not only for the fair market value of the interest actually taken, but also such additional amount as will be equivalent to the diminution or lowering, if any, of the fair market value of the owner's interest in the land which was not taken, due to the severance therefrom of the interest which was taken.

Special damages. Those which are the actual, but not the necessary, result of the injury complained of, and which in fact follow it as a natural and proximate consequence in the particular case, that is, by reason of special circumstances or conditions. Such are damages which do not arise from wrongful act itself, but depend on circumstances peculiar to the infliction of each respective injury. In contract law, damages not contemplated by the parties at the time of the making of the contract. To be recoverable, they must flow directly and immediately from the breach of contract, and must be reasonably foreseeable. Special damages must be specially pleaded and proved. Fed.R. Civil P. 9(g). *Compare General damages, above.*

Speculative damages. Prospective or anticipated damages from the same acts or facts constituting the present cause of action, but which depend upon future developments which are contingent, conjectural, or improbable.

Statutory damages. Damages resulting from statutorily created causes of actions, as opposed to actions at common law; *e.g.* wrongful death and survival actions; actions under tort claims acts. Under § 504 of the federal Copyright Act, a copyright owner has the right to collect statutory damages in lieu of actual damages for copyright infringement.

Substantial damages. A sum, assessed by way of damages, which is worth having; opposed to nominal damages, which are assessed to satisfy a bare legal right. Considerable in amount and intended as a real compensation for a real injury.

Black's Law Dictionary Abridged 6th Ed.—7

Temporary damages. Damages allowed for intermittent and occasional wrongs, such as injuries to real estate, where cause thereof is removable or abatable.

Treble damages. Damages given by statute in certain types of cases, consisting of the single damages found by the jury, actually tripled in amount. *See e.g.* Section 4 of Clayton Act which provides for treble damages for antitrust violations. 15 U.S.C.A. § 15.

Unliquidated damages. Such as are not yet reduced to a certainty in respect of amount, nothing more being established than the plaintiff's right to recover; or such as cannot be fixed by a mere mathematical calculation from ascertained data in the case. *Compare Liquidated damages and penalties, above.*

Vindictive damages. *See Exemplary or punitive damages, above.*

Damage to person. The measure of injury, physical, mental and emotional, as a result of another's action or omission, whether such action or omission be intentional or negligent. "Damage" and "injury" are commonly used interchangeably, but they are different to extent that injury is what is actually suffered while damage is the measure of compensation for such suffering. *See* Damage; Damages; Injury; Loss.

Damage to property. Injury to property and generally does not include conversion of such property or taking of such property by public authority (*i.e.* eminent domain). *See also* Damage; Damages.

Damnify /dǽmnəfay/. To cause damage or injurious loss to a person or put him in a position where he must sustain it. A surety is "damnified" when a judgment has been obtained against him.

Damnum /dǽmnəm/. Lat. Damage; the loss or diminution of what is a man's own, either by fraud, carelessness, or accident.

Damnum absque injuria /dǽmnəm ǽbskwiy injúriyə/. Loss, hurt, or harm without injury in the legal sense; that is, without such breach of duty as is redressible by a legal action. A loss or injury which does not give rise to an action for damages against the person causing it.

Damnum fatale /dǽmnəm fətéyliy/. Fatal damage; damage from fate; loss happening from a cause beyond human control (*quod ex fato contingit*), or an act of God, for which bailees are not liable; such as shipwreck, lightning, and the like. The civilians included in the phrase "*damnum fatale*" all those accidents which are summed up in the common-law expression, "Act of God or public enemies;" though, perhaps, it embraced some which would not now be admitted as occurring from an irresistible force. *See* Act of God.

Danger. Jeopardy; exposure to loss or injury; peril. *See also* Apparent danger; Dangerous; Hazard; Imminent danger; Peril; Risk.

Danger invites rescue. Term used in law of torts and, in limited manner, in law of crimes to describe where liability is borne by one who creates dangerous condition for one person when another person comes to his rescue and is injured. The liability to the second person is founded on this maxim.

Dangerous. Attended with risk; perilous; hazardous; unsafe. *See also* Danger; Inherently dangerous.

Dangerous condition. Such condition of property for which a public entity may be liable is a condition of property which creates a substantial risk of injury when the property is used with due care in a manner in which it is reasonably foreseeable that it will be used. *See* Attractive nuisance doctrine.

Dangerous criminal. One convicted of a particularly heinous crime or one who has escaped or tried to escape from penal confinement by use of force of an aggravated character. An armed criminal. Such criminals may be segregated within prison.

Dangerous instrumentality. Anything which has the inherent capacity to place people in peril, either in itself (*e.g.* dynamite), or by a careless use of it (*e.g.* boat). Due care must be exercised in using to avoid injury to those reasonably expected to be in proximity. In certain cases, absolute liability may be imposed. *See also* Dangerous weapon; Deadly weapon; Inherently dangerous; Strict liability.

Dangerous machine. A machine is "dangerous" in such sense that the employer is required to guard it, if, in the ordinary course of human affairs, danger may be reasonably anticipated from the use of it without protection.

Dangerous occupation. Term used to describe hazardous work for purposes of worker's compensation laws, and in wage and hour and child labor laws.

Dangerous per se. A thing that may inflict injury without the immediate application of human aid or instrumentality. *See* Inherently dangerous; Strict liability.

Dangerous place. One where there is considerable risk, or danger, or peril; one where accidents or injuries are very apt to occur. *See* Attractive nuisance doctrine.

Dangerous product. *See* Inherently dangerous; Strict liability.

Dangerous-tendency test. Propensity of person or animal to inflict injury; used in dog bite cases to describe viscious habits of dog.

Dangerous weapon. One dangerous to life; one by the use of which a serious or fatal wound or injury may probably or possibly be inflicted. In context of criminal possession of a weapon can be any article which, in circumstances in which it is used, attempted to be used, or threatened to be used, is readily capable of causing death or other serious physical injury. What constitutes a "dangerous weapon" depends not on nature of the object itself but on its capacity, given manner of its use, to endanger life or inflict great bodily harm. As the manner of use enters into the consideration as well as other circumstances, the question is often one of fact for the jury, but not infrequently one of law for the court. *See also* Assault with dangerous or deadly weapon; Dangerous instrumentality; Deadly weapon; Firearm.

Dangers of navigation. *See* Dangers of the river; Dangers of the sea, *infra.*

Dangers of the river. This phrase, as used in bills of lading, means only the natural accidents incident to river navigation, and does not embrace such as may be avoided by the exercise of that skill, judgment, or foresight which are demanded from persons in a particular occupation. It includes dangers arising from unknown reefs which have suddenly formed in the channel, and are not discoverable by care and skill.

Dangers of the sea. The expression "dangers of the sea" means those accidents peculiar to navigation that are of an extraordinary nature, or arise from irresistible force or overwhelming power, which cannot be guarded against by the ordinary exertions of human skill and prudence.

D & O Insurance. Directors and Officers liability insurance. *See* Insurance.

Dartmouth College Case. Dartmouth College v. Woodward, 17 U.S. 518, 4 Wheat. 518, 4 L.Ed. 629, held that a college charter was a contract within the constitutional provision against state legislatures' prohibiting impairment of the obligation of contract. Art. I, Sec. 10, U.S.Const. Although *Dartmouth College* involved a charitable and educational institution, the Supreme Court readily expanded the principles announced in the opinion to corporate charters issued for business purposes. Consequently, the decision protected industrial and financial corporations from much government regulation.

Data. Organized information generally used as the basis for an adjudication or decision. Commonly, organized information, collected for specific purpose.

Date. The specification or mention, in a written instrument, of the time (day, month and year) when it was made (executed). Also the time so specified. In its common and accepted statutory meaning refers simply to day, month and year.

The word is derived from the Latin word "datum" meaning given and is defined as the time given or specified—in some way ascertained and fixed. The time when an instrument was made, acknowledged, delivered or recorded; the clause or memorandum which specifies that fact; and the time from which its operation is to be reckoned.

That part of a deed or writing which expresses the day of the month and year in which it was made or given.

The primary signification of *date* is not time in the abstract, nor time taken absolutely, but time given or specified; time in some way ascertained and fixed. When we speak of the date of a deed, date of issue of a bond or date of a policy, we do not mean the time when it was actually executed, but the time of its execution as given or stated in the deed itself. The date of an item, or of a charge in a book-account, is not necessarily the time when the article charged was, in fact, furnished, but rather the time given or set down in the account, in connection with such charge. And so the expression "the date of the last work done, or materials furnished," in a mechanic's lien law, may be taken, in the absence of anything in the act indicating a different intention, to mean the time when such work was done or materials furnished, as specified in the plaintiff's written claim.

The precise meaning of date, however, depends upon context, since there are numerous instances when it means actual as distinguished from conventional time.

See also Antedate; Backdating; Post-date.

Date of bankruptcy. Under Bankruptcy law, time at which court declares a person a bankrupt. Usually coincides with date of filing in case of voluntary petition. See Bankruptcy Code § 301. *See also* Date of cleavage.

Date of cleavage. The date of filing voluntary petition of bankruptcy and hence the cut-off date as to dischargeability of debts in bankruptcy. Only those debts, with some exceptions, which exist at this time are dischargeable in bankruptcy.

Date of declaration. The date when a dividend is formally declared (approved) by the board of directors.

Date of issue. When applied to notes, bonds, etc., of series, usually means an arbitrary date fixed as beginning of term for which they run, without reference to precise time when convenience or state of market may permit their sale or delivery; date which bonds and stocks bear, and not date

when they were actually issued in sense of being signed and delivered and put into circulation.

The words in life insurance policy have been held not to mean the date of actual execution or the delivery date, but the date set forth in the policy itself.

Date of maturity. Day on which a debt falls due as in the case of a promissory note, bond or other evidence of indebtedness.

Date of payment. The date when a dividend will be distributed to stockholders.

Date of record. Date on which stockholder must have owned shares of stock to be entitled to dividend. *See also* Ex dividend.

Datum /déytəm/. A first principle; a thing given; a date.

Davis-Bacon Act. Federal law which deals with rate of pay for laborers and mechanics on public buildings and public works. 40 U.S.C.A. § 276a.

Day-book. A tradesman's or merchant's account book; a book in which all the occurrences of the day are set down. It is usually a book of original entries.

Day certain. A fixed or appointed day; a specified particular day; a day in term.

Day in court. The right and opportunity afforded a person to litigate his claims, seek relief, or defend his rights in a competent judicial tribunal.

The time appointed for one whose rights are called judicially in question, or liable to be affected by judicial action, to appear in court and be heard in his own behalf. This phrase, as generally used, means not so much the time appointed for a hearing as the opportunity to present one's claims or rights in a proper forensic hearing before a competent tribunal.

A litigant has his "day in court" when he has been duly cited to appear and has been afforded an opportunity to appear and to be heard.

Daylight. *See* Daytime.

Day loan. *See* Loan.

Day order. An order to buy or sell a security or commodity on a particular day and if such sale does not take place, the order expires.

Days of grace. A number of days allowed, as a matter of favor or grace, to a person who has to perform some act, or make some payment (*e.g.*, payment of insurance premium), after the time originally limited for the purpose has elapsed. In life insurance policies most states permit one month or thirty-one days.

In commercial law, a certain number of days (generally three) allowed to the maker or acceptor of a bill, draft, or note, in which to make payment, after the expiration of the time expressed in the paper itself. Originally these days were granted only as a matter of *grace* or favor, but the allowance of them became an established custom of merchants, and was sanctioned by the courts (and in some cases prescribed by statute), so that they are now demandable as of right.

See also Grace period.

Daytime. The time during which there is the light of day, as distinguished from night or night-time. That portion of the full twenty-four hour day in which a man's countenance is visible by natural light and, hence, that portion of the day which is distinguished from nighttime in crime of burglary; nighttime being the period between one hour after sunset and one hour before sunrise. Model Penal Code, § 221.0(2). Word "daytime" as used in statutory crime of breaking and entering a dwelling in the daytime means that time of day when there is sufficient daylight so as to be able to discern the features of another by natural sunlight.

The period between sunrise and sunset. Calif. Penal Code § 7.

Under Fed.R.Crim.Proc. 41(h), relating to search and seizure, "daytime" means the hours from 6:00 a. m. to 10:00 p. m.

See also Nighttime.

D.B.A. Abbreviation for "doing business as."

D.B.E. An abbreviation for *de bene esse (q.v.).*

D.B.N. An abbreviation for *de bonis non*; descriptive of a species of estate administration.

D.C. An abbreviation for "District Court," or "District of Columbia."

DDB. Double-declining-balance depreciation. *See* Depreciation.

Dead. *See* Death.

Dead asset. Worthless asset which has no realizable value; *e.g.* uncollectable account receivable.

Deadbeat. Slang term for one who fails to pay his debts.

Dead freight. The amount paid by a charterer for that part of the vessel's capacity which he does not occupy although he has contracted for it.

Deadlocked. Unable to agree.

Corporation. Deadlock in a closely held corporation arises when a control structure permits one or more factions of shareholders to block corporate action if they disagree with some aspect of corporate policy. A deadlock often arises with respect to the election of directors, *e.g.*, by an equal division of shares between two factions, but may also arise at the level of the board of directors itself. Term as used in statute empowering court to dissolve corporation when directors are deadlocked, means corporation which, because of decision or indecision of stockholders, cannot perform its corporate powers. See Rev.Model

Bus.Corp. Act § 14.30(2) (involuntary dissolution at request of shareholder).

Jury. Jury which cannot agree on verdict; sometimes called "hung jury". Trial court should not repeatedly give an "anti-deadlock" instruction to "deadlocked jury," which is one which trial judge has concluded is genuinely deadlocked, giving due consideration to such things as nature and complexity of trial issues, duration of trial, length of jury deliberations, and representations of jury to court about state of deliberations. *See also* Dynamite instruction.

Deadly force. The degree of force that may result in the death of the person against whom the force is applied. Force likely or intended to cause death or great bodily harm; may be reasonable or unreasonable, depending on the circumstances.

Deadly weapon. Any firearm, or other weapon, device, instrument, material or substance, whether animate or inanimate, which in the manner it is used or is intended to be used is known to be capable of producing death or serious bodily injury. Model Penal Code, § 210.0. See also 18 U.S.C.A. § 921.

Such weapons or instruments as are made and designed for offensive or defensive purposes, or for the destruction of life or the infliction of injury. One which, from the manner used, is calculated or likely to produce death or serious bodily injury.

See also Dangerous weapon; Malicious assault with deadly weapon.

Deadly weapon per se. A weapon which of itself is deadly or one which would ordinarily result in death by its use; *e.g.* gun.

Dead man's statute. An evidential disqualification which renders inadmissible oral promises or declarations of a dead person when offered in support of their claims by those who bring claims against the estate of the dead person. The last vestige of the disqualification of witnesses by reason of interest as this existed at common law, though many states admit such testimony under certain statutory conditions. The standard type of state dead man statute would be applicable under Fed.R.Evid. 601 only if testimony of the witness concerned claims or defenses, or elements thereof, which were governed by state law.

Dead stock. Goods in inventory for which there is no market.

Dead time. Time which does not count for any purpose, *e.g.* time for which a person is not paid wages, or time when employee is not working due to no fault of his own (*e.g.* because of machinery breakdown), or time for which a prisoner does not get credit in serving his sentence.

Dead use. A future use.

Deal, *n.* An arrangement to attain a desired result by a combination of interested parties; the prime object being usually the purchase, sale, or exchange of property for a profit. Also, an act of buying and selling; a bargain to purchase at a favorable price. *See* Bargain.

Deal, *v.* To traffic; to transact business; to bargain or trade. Also, to act between two persons, to intervene, or to have to do with.

As to dealing in futures, *see* Futures contract.

Dealer. In the popular sense, one who buys to sell; not one who buys to keep, or makes to sell. One who purchases goods or property for resale to final customers; a retailer. *See also* Retailer.

The term "dealer" means any person engaged in the business of buying and selling securities for his own account, through a broker or otherwise, but does not include a bank, or any person insofar as he buys or sells securities for his own account, either individually or in some fiduciary capacity, but not as a part of a regular business. Securities Exchange Act of 1934, § 3.

Dealer's talk. The puffing of goods to induce the sale thereof; not regarded in law as fraudulent unless accompanied by some artifice to deceive the purchaser and throw him off his guard or some concealment of intrinsic defects not easily discoverable. *See* Puffing.

Dealings. Transactions in the course of trade or business.

Death. The cessation of life; permanent cessations of all vital functions and signs. Numerous states have enacted statutory definitions of death which include brain-related criteria. For example, many states have adopted, sometimes with variations, the Uniform Determination of Death Act definition: "An individual who has sustained either (1) irreversible cessation of circulatory and respiratory function, or (2) irreversible cessation of all functions of the entire brain, including the brain stem, is dead. A determination of death must be made in accordance with accepted medical standards." See, *e.g.*, Calif.Health & Safety Code, § 7180.

See also Contemplation of death; Presumption of death; Simultaneous Death Act; Wrongful death action.

Brain death. See Brain death; and *Natural Death Acts, below.*

Civil death. See Civil death.

Death benefits. Amount paid under insurance policy on death of insured. A payment made by an employer to the beneficiary or beneficiaries of a deceased employee on account of the death of the employee. A death benefit is also provided for under the Social Security Act.

Death by wrongful act. Statutory action arising from act to which law attaches liability as in the case of serving unwholesome food that results in death, the action for which may be brought by personal representative of deceased. *See also* Wrongful death statutes.

Death certificate. Official document issued by Register of Deaths or some other public official which certifies that a person has died. Generally such certificate specifies the cause of death, and is commonly required to be signed by the attending or an examining physician. Fed.Evid.R. 803(9) provides a hearsay exception for admissibility of death certificates.

Death duty. See Death taxes, below.

Death penalty. Supreme penalty exacted as punishment for murder and other capital crimes. The death penalty has been held to not be, under all circumstances, cruel and unusual punishment within prohibitions of 8th and 14th Amends.; nor does the 6th Amendment require a jury trial on the sentencing issue of life or death.

Death records. Official records of deaths kept by town or city Register of Deaths or by some other public official with like functions. *See Death certificate, above.*

Death sentence. See Death penalty, above.

Death taxes. Generic term to describe all taxes imposed on property or on transfer of property at death of owner. Includes estate and inheritance taxes. *See* Estate tax; Inheritance tax.

Death warrant. A warrant from the proper executive authority appointing the time and place for the execution of the sentence of death upon a convict judicially condemned to suffer that penalty.

Fetal death. See Fetal death.

Instantaneous death. Term to describe death following accident within a very short time such as 15–20 minutes; such concept is important in death actions in which a claim is made for pain and suffering.

Natural death. A death which occurs by the unassisted operation of natural causes, as distinguished not only from "civil death", but also from "unnatural" (*e.g.* violent) death.

Natural Death Acts. Such statutes (*e.g.* Cal. Health & Safety Code § 7185 *et seq.*) authorize an adult to make a written directive instructing his physician to withhold life-sustaining procedures in the event of a terminal condition. In the directive, which is to be executed in a prescribed manner and made a part of the patient's medical records, the declarant directs that if he has been certified by two physicians as being afflicted with a terminal condition, he is to be permitted to die naturally. The Act removes all civil or criminal liability from physicians who act in accordance with its provisions. It has been held that unwritten right of privacy is broad enough to include patient's decision to decline medical treatment in certain circumstances. *See also* Brain death; Health care proxy; Medical directives; Patients Self Determination Act; Power of attorney (*Durable power of attorney*); Will (*Living will*).

Presumptive death. That which is presumed from proof of a long continued absence unheard from and unexplained. The general rule, as provided by state statutes, is that the presumption of the duration of life ceases at the expiration of seven years from the time when the person was last known to be living; and after the lapse of that period there is a presumption of death.

Violent death. One caused or accelerated by the interference of human agency; distinguished from "natural death."

Death action. *See* Wrongful death action.

Death Knell Doctrine. Doctrine which allows immediate appeal from interlocutory order where delay of review until final judgment will cause irreparable loss of substantial rights and where order has practical effect of permanently foreclosing relief on claim.

Death on High Seas Act. Federal Act which provides for a pecuniary recovery for death "caused by wrongful act, neglect or default occurring on the high seas beyond a marine league from the shore of any state [territory or dependency]." 41 U.S.C.A. § 761 *et seq.*

Debarment. To bar, exclude or preclude from having or doing something. Exclusion from government contracting and subcontracting. *See also* Disbarment.

Debasement. Reducing the weight of gold and silver in coins of standard value or of increasing the amount of alloy in such coins. Such has the effect of reducing the intrinsic value.

Debauch /dəbóch/. To corrupt one's manners; to make lewd; to mar or spoil; to entice; and, when used of a woman, to seduce, or corrupt with lewdness. Originally, the term had a limited signification, meaning to entice or draw one away from his work, employment, or duty; and from this sense its application has enlarged to include the corruption of manners and violation of the person. In its modern legal sense, the word carries with it the idea of "carnal knowledge," aggravated by assault, violent seduction, ravishment. *See also* Debauchery.

Debauchery /dəbóchəriy/. In general, excessive indulgence in sensual pleasures; in a narrower sense, sexual immorality or excesses, or the unlawful indulgence of lust.

De bene esse /diy bíyniy ésiy/də bíyniy°/. Conditionally; provisionally; in anticipation of future need. A phrase applied to proceedings which are taken *ex parte* or provisionally, and are allowed to stand as *well done* for the present, but which may be subject to future exception or challenge, and must then stand or fall according to their intrinsic merit and regularity.

Examination de bene esse. A provisional examination of a witness. An examination of a witness whose testimony is important and might otherwise be lost, held out of court and before the trial, with the proviso that the deposition so taken may be used on the trial in case the witness is unable to attend in person at that time or cannot be produced. See *e.g.* Fed.R.Civil P. 26, 27.

Debenture /dəbéntyər/. Long term unsecured debt instrument, issued pursuant to an indenture. A promissory note or bond backed by the general credit and earning history of a corporation and usually not secured by a mortgage or lien on any specific property; *e.g.*, an unsecured bond. Holders of corporate debentures are creditors of the corporation and entitled to payment before shareholders upon dissolution. *See also* Bond; Indenture. *Compare* Secured bond.

Certificate issued by customs to an importer for the deduction or refund of duties on merchandise imported and then exported by such importer.

Convertible debenture. Debenture which may be changed or converted into some other security (*e.g.* stock) usually at the option of the holder.

Convertible subordinated debenture. Debenture which is subject or subordinate to prior payment of other indebtedness but which may be converted into another form of security. *See* False claim.

Sinking fund debenture. Debenture which is secured by periodic payments into sinking fund, commonly managed by trustee for purpose of retiring such debt.

Subordinate debenture. Debenture which is subject to or subordinate to prior payment of other indebtedness.

Debenture bond. Bonds not secured by any specific property but issued against the general credit of a corporation or government.

Debenture indenture. An indenture containing obligations not secured by a mortgage or other collateral; a key instrument in the process of long term debt financing for general business corporations. Its effect is to put the debenture-holder in substantially the same practical position as a bondholder secured by a first mortgage. *See also* Indenture.

Debit /débət/. A sum charged as due or owing. An entry made on the asset or expense side of a ledger or account. The term is used in book-keeping to denote the left side of the ledger, or the charging of a person or an account with all that is supplied to or paid out for him or for the subject of the account. Also, the balance of an account where it is shown that something remains due to the party keeping the account.

As a noun, an entry on the left-hand side of an account. As a verb, to make an entry on the left-hand side of an account. A term used in accounting or book-keeping which results in an increase to an asset and an expense account and a decrease to a liability, revenue, or owner's equity account.

Compare Credit.

Debit balance. Account balance showing money owed to lender or seller. Accounting condition where there is an excess of debit over credit entries.

Debit memorandum. A document prepared by the purchaser for either an allowance or an authorized return of merchandise.

De bonis non /diy bównəs nón/. An abbreviation of *De bonis non administratis (q.v.).*

De bonis non administratis /diy bównəs nòn ədmìnəstréytəs/. Of the goods not administered. When an administrator is appointed to succeed another, who has left the estate partially unsettled, he is said to be granted "administration *de bonis non;*" that is, of the goods not already administered.

Debt. A sum of money due by certain and express agreement. A specified sum of money owing to one person from another, including not only obligation of debtor to pay but right of creditor to receive and enforce payment. Liability on a claim. Bankruptcy Code § 101.

A fixed and certain obligation to pay money or some other valuable thing or things, either in the present or in the future. In a still more general sense, that which is due from one person to another, whether money, goods, or services. In a broad sense, any duty to respond to another in money, labor, or service; it may even mean a moral or honorary obligation, unenforceable by legal action. Also, sometimes an aggregate of separate debts, or the total sum of the existing claims against a person or company. Thus we speak of the "national debt", the "bonded debt" of a corporation, etc.

Active debt. One due to a person. Used in the civil law.

Antecedent debt. See that title.

Bad debt. Uncollectible account receivable. Under National Bank Act, an unsecured debt on which interest or payment is past due for at least six months. *See also* Bad debt; Bad debt reserve.

Bonded debt. Debt represented by bonds. *See* Bonded debt.

Common-law action. The name of a common-law action which lies to recover a certain specific sum of money, or a sum that can readily be reduced to a certainty. It is thus distinguished from *assumpsit,* which lies as well where the sum due is uncertain as where it is certain, and from *covenant,* which lies only upon contracts evidenced in a certain manner.

It is said to lie in the *debet* and *detinet* (when it is stated that the defendant owes and detains), or in the *detinet* (when it is stated merely that he detains). Debt in the *detinet* for goods differs from detinue, because it is not essential in this action, as in detinue, that the specific property in the goods should have been vested in the plaintiff at the time the action is brought.

Consumer debt. See Consumer debt.

Contingent debt. See Contingent debt.

Convertible debt. Debt which may be changed or converted by creditor into another form of security, *e.g.* shares of stock. *See* Debenture *(Convertible debenture).*

Debt by simple contract. A debt or demand founded upon a verbal or implied contract, or upon any written agreement that is not under seal.

Debt of record. A debt which appears to be due by the evidence of a court of record, as by a judgment or recognizance.

Existing debt. See Existing debt.

Floating debt. Short-term or current debt, not represented by securities.

Fraudulent debt. A debt created by fraud. Such a debt implies confidence and deception. It implies that it arose out of a contract, express or implied, and that fraudulent practices were employed by the debtor, by which the creditor was defrauded. *See* False claim.

Funded debt. Debt represented by bonds or other securities.

General debt. See that title.

Hypothecary debt. One which is a lien upon an estate.

Installment debt. Debt which is to be repaid in installments; *e.g.* retail installment contract.

Judgment debt. See Judgment debt.

Legal debts. Those that are recoverable in a court of law, as debt on a bill of exchange, a bond, or a simple contract.

Liquid debt. One which is immediately and unconditionally due. *See also* Liquidated debt.

Mutual debts. Money due on both sides between two persons. Such debts must be due to and from same persons in same capacity. Cross debts in the same capacity and right, and of the same kind and quality.

Passive debt. A debt upon which, by agreement between the debtor and creditor, no interest is payable, as distinguished from *active* debt; *i.e.,* a debt upon which interest is payable. As used in another sense, a debt is "active" or "passive" as regards the person of the creditor or debtor; a passive debt being that which a man owes; an active debt that which is owing to him. In this meaning every debt is both active and passive; active as regards the creditor, passive as regards the debtor.

Preferential debts. See that title.

Privileged debt. One which is to be paid before others in case a debtor is insolvent; *e.g.* secured debt.

Proof of debt. See Proof.

Public debt. That which is due or owing by the government of a municipality, state or nation (*e.g.* government bonds).

Secured debt. Debt secured by collateral; *e.g.* by mortgage, securities, deed, etc. *See* Secured transaction.

Unliquidated debt. See Unliquidated debt.

Debt adjusting. Engagement in the business of making contracts, express or implied, with a debtor whereby the debtor agrees to pay a certain amount of money periodically to the person engaging in the debt adjusting business who shall for a consideration distribute the same among certain specified creditors. *See also* Debt adjustment; Debt pooling; Wage earner's plan.

Debt adjustment. Settlement of dispute regarding debt obligation by compromise and adjustment. Term also refers to adjustment of debts of an individual with regular income as provided for under Chapter 13 of the Bankruptcy Code. *See also* Bankruptcy proceedings; Compromise and settlement; Debt pooling; Wage earner's plan.

Debt cancellation. Under federal tax law, discharge or cancellation of indebtedness ordinarily results in income to debtor when he settles debt for less than amount which he owes. I.R.C. § 61(a)(12). *See* Bankruptcy proceedings.

Debt capacity. Optimal amount of debt in the firm's capital structure.

Debt consolidation. *See* Debt pooling.

Debtee. A person to whom a debt is due; a creditor.

Debt-equity ratio. An amount arrived at by dividing total liabilities by total equity of an entity

(*e.g.,* total liabilities of corporation divided by total shareholders' equity). A high debt ratio is an indication that the entity may have difficulty meeting obligations which come due. A bank may be reluctant to provide financing to an entity with a high debt ratio due to the risks associated with repayment. *See also* Debt ratio; Debt to total assets ratio.

Debt financing. Raising funds by issuing bonds or notes or borrowing from a financial institution. Contrasted with equity financing which is raising funds by issuing and selling stocks. Corporate borrowing of money, generally on a long term basis for acquiring working capital or for retiring current indebtedness.

Debt instrument. Written promise to repay debt; *e.g.,* promissory note, bill, bond, commercial paper.

Debt limitations. Ceiling placed on amount of borrowings by individuals, corporations or governments. Certain state constitutions prohibit deficit spending by government.

Debtor. One who owes a debt to another who is called the creditor; one who may be compelled to pay a claim or demand; anyone liable on a claim, whether due or to become due.

"Debtor" means "the person who owes payment or other performance of the obligation secured, whether or not he owns or has rights in the collateral, and includes the seller of accounts or chattel paper. Where the debtor and the owner of the collateral are not the same person, the term 'debtor' means the owner of the collateral in any provision of the Article dealing with the collateral, the obligor in any provision dealing with the obligation, and may include both where the context so requires." U.C.C. § 9–105(1)(d).

In bankruptcy law, person who files a voluntary petition or person against whom an involuntary petition is filed. Person or municipality concerning which a bankruptcy case has been commenced. Bankruptcy Code, § 101. *See* Bankrupt.

See also Absconding debtor; Joint debtors.

Judgment debtor. One who owes money as a result of a judgment in favor of a creditor.

Debtor in possession. In bankruptcy, refers to a Chapter 11 or 12 debtor who, during the pendency of the case prior to confirmation of the reorganization plan, retains the bankruptcy estate's property in the fiduciary capacity of a trustee. *See also* Bankruptcy proceedings.

Debtor in possession financing. The extension of loans or other financial services to companies that are operating under bankruptcy reorganization. *See also* Debtor in possession.

Debt pooling. Arrangement by which debtor adjusts many debts by distributing his assets among several creditors, who may or may not agree to take less than is owed; or, an arrangement by which debtor agrees to pay in regular installments a sum of money to one creditor who agrees to discharge all his debts. Such activities may constitute unauthorized practice of law (as in *e.g.* Mass.), and formerly could be an act of bankruptcy. *See* Act of bankruptcy; Arrangement with creditors; Assignment (*Assignment for benefit of creditors*); Bankruptcy proceedings; Wage earner's plan.

Debt ratio. Amount of long-term debt divided by total of company's capital. *See also* Debt-equity ratio.

Debt retirement. Repayment of debt.

Debt security. Any form of corporate security reflected as debt on the books of the corporation in contrast to equity securities such as stock; *e.g.* bonds, notes and debentures are debt securities.

Debt service. The interest and charges currently payable on a debt, including principal payments.

Debt to total assets ratio. A coverage ratio that shows the percentage of total capital provided by the creditors of a business; computed as total debt divided by total assets. *See also* Debt-equity ratio.

Decease, *n.* Death; not including civil death. *See* Death.

Decease, *v.* To die; to depart life, or from life.

Deceased. A dead person. *See* Decedent.

Decedent. A deceased person, especially one who has lately died. Etymologically the word denotes a person who is *dying,* but it has come to be used in law as signifying any deceased person, testate or intestate.

Decedent's estate. Property, both real and personal, which person possesses at the time of his death, and title to it descends immediately to his heirs upon his death subject to the control of the probate court for the purposes of paying debts and claims and after distribution the estate ceases to exist.

Deceit. A fraudulent and deceptive misrepresentation, artifice, or device, used by one or more persons to deceive and trick another, who is ignorant of the true facts, to the prejudice and damage of the party imposed upon. To constitute "deceit," the statement must be untrue, made with knowledge of its falsity or with reckless and conscious ignorance thereof, especially if parties are not on equal terms, made with intent that plaintiff act thereon or in a manner apparently fitted to induce him to act thereon, and plaintiff must act in reliance on the statement in the manner contemplated, or manifestly probable, to his injury. *See also* Deception; Fraud; Misrepresentation; Reliance. For larceny by deceit, *see* Larceny.

In old English law, the name of an original writ, and the action founded on it, which lay to recover damages for any injury committed *deceitfully,* either in the name of another (as by bringing an action in another's name, and then suffering a nonsuit, whereby the plaintiff became liable to costs), or by a fraudulent warranty of goods, or other personal injury committed contrary to good faith and honesty. Also the name of a judicial writ which formerly lay to recover lands which had been lost by default by the tenant in a real action, in consequence of his not having been summoned by the sheriff, or by the collusion of his attorney.

Decentralization. Refers to an organizational strategy in which top management grants subordinate managers a significant degree of autonomy and independence in operating and making decisions for their organizational units. *Compare* Centralized management.

Deception. The act of deceiving; intentional misleading by falsehood spoken or acted. Knowingly and willfully making a false statement or representation, express or implied, pertaining to a present or past existing fact. *See also* Bait and switch; Deceit; Fraud; Misrepresentation; Theft (*Theft by deception*).

Deceptive advertising. False and misleading advertising. Advertisement which contains any assertion, representation or statement of fact which is untrue or misleading.

Where the public are not cautious or watchful in their buying habits and are likely to be misled, the legislature may require not only the absence of active deception in advertising, but also affirmative measures to prevent misunderstanding. *See, e.g.,* Mass.G.L. c. 266, § 91; 15 U.S.C.A. § 52 et seq.

See also Deceptive sales practices.

Deceptive sales practices. The Federal Trade Commission and statutes in most states make deceptive sales practices unlawful. Historically, an act was deceptive if it had any tendency to deceive a nontrivial number of customers. A more recent reformulation of the test defines a deceptive act as one which is likely to deceive a consumer acting reasonably in the circumstances. *See, e.g.,* Mass.G.L. c. 93A, § 21(*l*); 15 U.S.C.A. § 45(a)(1).

As term is used in consumer protection statutes, may import less than common law fraud in sale of goods or services though there must be some measure of deceit. A sales practice may be deceptive if it could reasonably be found to have caused person to act differently from way he otherwise would have acted.

Such practices may encompass any type of business practice or action which deceives consumers, but acts or practices which are not among those listed by statute present jury question of whether action was deceptive. *See, e.g.,* Bait and switch.

See also Consumer protection laws; Deceptive advertising.

Decide. To arrive at a determination. To "decide" includes the power and right to deliberate, to weigh the reasons for and against, to see which preponderate, and to be governed by that preponderance. *See* Decision.

Decision. A determination arrived at after consideration of facts, and, in legal context, law. A popular rather than technical or legal word; a comprehensive term having no fixed, legal meaning. It may be employed as referring to ministerial acts as well as to those that are judicial or of a judicial character.

A determination of a judicial or quasi judicial nature. A judgment, decree, or order pronounced by a court in settlement of a controversy submitted to it and by way of authoritative answer to the questions raised before it. The term is broad enough to cover both final judgments and interlocutory orders. And though sometimes limited to the sense of judgment, the term is at other times understood as meaning simply the first step leading to a judgment; or as an order for judgment. The word may also include various rulings, as well as orders, including agency and commission orders.

The findings of fact and conclusions of law which must be in writing and filed with the clerk. "Decision" is not necessarily synonymous with "opinion." A decision of the court is its judgment; the opinion is the reasons given for that judgment, or the expression of the views of the judge. But the two words are sometimes used interchangeably.

See also Decree; Final decision or judgment; Finding; Judgment; Opinion; Order; Unreasonable decision; Verdict.

Decision on merits. A judicial decision determining the validity of a written instrument or passing on a controversy with respect to the interpretation thereof which bars subsequent suit on same cause of action.

Decisive, *or* **decisory, oath.** *See* Oath.

Declarant. A person who makes a declaration.

Declaration. In common-law pleading, the first of the pleadings on the part of the plaintiff in an action at law, being a formal and methodical specification of the facts and circumstances constituting his cause or action. It commonly comprises several sections or divisions, called "counts", and its formal parts follow each other in this general order: Title, venue, commencement, cause of action, counts, conclusion. The declaration, at common law, answers to the "libel" in ecclesiastical and admiralty law, the "bill" in

equity, the "petition" in civil law, the "complaint" in code and rule pleading, and the "count" in real actions. The term "complaint" is used in the federal courts and in all states that have adopted Rules of Civil Procedure.

In law of evidence, an unsworn statement or narration of facts made by party to the transaction, or by one who has an interest in the existence of the facts recounted. Also, similar statements made by a person since deceased, which are admissible in evidence in some cases, contrary to the general rule, *e.g.,* "dying declarations" *(q.v.)*. *See also Declarations against interest, below.*

Listing by person entering United States of merchandise or other goods brought into country by him.

The basic governing document or "constitution" for a condominium.

A document by the owner of property which is recorded in order to establish a legal order upon the property, such as a condominium (by a declaration of condominium or master deed), a system of cross-easements (by a declaration of easements) or a homeowners association (by declaration of covenants, restrictions and easements).

Declarations against interest. An out of court statement by a declarant who is unavailable as a witness is admissible as an exception to the rule against hearsay if the statement was against his interest at the time it was made. Under the common law the statement must have been against the pecuniary or proprietary interest of the declarant. Under Federal Rule of Evidence 804(b)(3) and the law of some states, the statement may also be admitted if it was against the penal interest of the declarant. However, the Federal Rule provides that a statement which tends to expose the declarant to criminal liability and which is "offered to exculpate the accused" is not admissible "unless corroborating circumstances clearly indicate the trustworthiness of the statement."

Such declarations are evidence of the fact declared, and are therefore distinct from admissions, which amount to a waiver of proof. They are statements which, when made, conflict with the pecuniary or proprietary interest of the person making them, or so far tend to subject him to civil or criminal liability, or to render invalid a claim by him against another, that a reasonable man in his position would not have made the statement unless he believed it to be true.

Declaration in chief. A declaration for the principal cause of action. *See* Ad damnum.

Declaration of dividend. The act of a corporation in setting aside a portion of its net or surplus income for distribution among the stockholders according to their respective stock ownership. *See also* Dividend.

Declaration of homestead. Statement required to be filed with proper state or local official or agency showing property ownership for purposes of securing homestead exemption rights. It is merely an act of the owner whereby he avails himself of, and secures, a right or privilege given him by statute; it is neither a conveyance nor a contract, and there is no transfer of, or change in, title, nor any agreement of transfer or change. *See also* Homestead.

Declaration of Independence. A formal declaration or announcement, promulgated July 4, 1776, by the Congress of the United States of America, in the name and behalf of the people of the colonies, asserting and proclaiming their independence of the British crown, vindicating their pretensions to political autonomy, and announcing themselves to the world as a free and independent nation.

Declaration of intention. A declaration made by an alien, as a preliminary to naturalization, before a court of record, to the effect that it is his intention in good faith to become a citizen of the United States, and to renounce forever all allegiance and fidelity to any foreign prince, potentate, state, or sovereignty whereof at the time he may be a citizen or subject. 8 U.S.C.A. § 1445.

Declaration of legitimacy. Formal pronouncement that a person is a legitimate child.

Declaration of pain. Exception to hearsay rule which permits testimony of out of court statement consisting of declarant's exclamation of present pain. Fed.Evid.R. 803(3).

Declaration of right. See Bill of Rights.

Declaration of state of mind. Exception to hearsay rule which permits testimony of out of court statement concerning person's state of mind, *e.g.* "I am sad". Fed.Evid.R. 803(3).

Declaration of trust. The act by which the person who holds the legal title to property or an estate acknowledges and declares that he holds the same in trust to the use of another person or for certain specified purposes. The name is also used to designate the deed or other writing embodying such a declaration.

Declaration of war. A public and formal proclamation by a nation, through its executive or legislative department, that a state of war exists between itself and another nation, and forbidding all persons to aid or assist the enemy.

An act of Congress is necessary to the commencement of a foreign war and is in itself a "declaration" and fixes the date of the war. See Art. I, Sec. 8, cl. 11, U.S. Const. *See also* War clauses.

Dying declarations. Statements made by a person who believes he is about to die in reference to the manner in which he received the injuries of which he is dying, or other immediate cause of his death, and in reference to the person who inflicted such injuries or the connection with such injuries of a person who is charged or suspected of having committed them. Such statements are admissible in evidence as an exception to the hearsay rule in a trial for homicide (and occasionally, at least in some jurisdictions, in other cases) where the killing of the declarant is the crime charged to the defendant.

Generally, the admissibility of such declarations is limited to use in prosecutions for homicide; but is admissible on behalf of accused as well as for prosecution.

In a prosecution for homicide or in a civil action or proceeding, a statement made by a declarant while believing that his death was imminent, concerning the cause or circumstances of what he believed to be his impending death is not excluded by the hearsay rule. Fed.Evid.R. 804(b)(2).

Self-serving declaration. One made by a party in his own interest at some time and place out of court; not including testimony which he gives as witness at the trial.

Declaration date. The day on which directors of a corporation declare a dividend as contrasted with date on which the dividend is actually paid. *See* Ex dividend.

Declaration of estimated tax. A tax payment procedure whereby non-wage earner individuals, and wage earners with other income not subject to withholding, as well as corporations are required to file declarations of estimated tax and make periodic payments of such. This requirement assures current collection of taxes from taxpayers whose incomes are not taxed, or fully taxed, by means of payroll withholdings. I.R.C. §§ 6015, 6154. *See* Estimated tax.

Declaration of Taking Act. Federal law governing taking of private property for public use under eminent domain. 40 U.S.C.A. §§ 58a–258e. *See* Eminent domain.

Declarator of trust. A common law action resorted to against a trustee who holds property upon titles *ex facie* for his own benefit.

Declaratory. Explanatory; designed to fix or elucidate what before was uncertain or doubtful.

Declaratory action. *See* Declaratory judgment.

Declaratory judgment. Statutory (*see* Declaratory Judgment Act) remedy for the determination of a justiciable controversy where the plaintiff is in doubt as to his legal rights. A binding adjudication of the rights and status of litigants even though no consequential relief is awarded. Such judgment is conclusive in a subsequent action between the parties as to the matters declared and, in accordance with the usual rules of issue preclusion, as to any issues actually litigated and determined.

Declaratory Judgment Act. Federal statute enacted in 1934, 28 U.S.C.A. § 2201, which permits bringing of complaint for a declaration of rights if there is an actual controversy between the parties. The judgment is binding as to present and future rights of the parties to the action. See Fed.R.Civil P. 57. Most states have statutes of a like or similar nature; many of which are patterned on The Uniform Declaratory Judgments Act. *See also* Declaratory judgment.

Declaratory part of a law. That which clearly defines rights to be observed and wrongs to be eschewed.

Declaratory relief. *See* Declaratory judgment.

Declaratory statute. One enacted for the purpose of removing doubts or putting an end to conflicting decisions in regard to what the law is in relation to a particular matter. It may either be expressive of the common law, or may declare what shall be taken to be the true meaning and intention of a previous statute, though in the latter case such enactments are more commonly called "expository statutes." A statute enacted to put an end to a doubt as to what is the common law, or the meaning of another statute, and which declares what it is and ever has been.

Declare. To make known, manifest, or clear. To signify, to show in any manner either by words or acts. To publish; to utter; to announce clearly some opinion or resolution. To solemnly assert a fact before witnesses, *e.g.*, where a testator *declares* a paper signed by him to be his last will and testament. *See* Declaration.

De computo /díy kómpyətow/. Writ of account. A writ commanding a defendant to render a reasonable account to the plaintiff, or show cause to the contrary. The foundation of the modern action of account.

Decoy. To inveigle, entice, tempt, or lure; as, to decoy a person within the jurisdiction of a court so that he may be served with process, or to decoy a fugitive criminal to a place where he may be arrested without extradition papers, or to decoy one away from his place of residence for the purpose of kidnapping him and as a part of that act. In all these uses the word implies enticement or luring by means of some fraud, trick, or temptation, but excludes the idea of force. *Compare* Entrapment.

Decoy letter. A letter prepared and mailed for the purpose of detecting a criminal, particularly one who is perpetrating frauds upon the postal or revenue laws.

Decree. The judgment of a court of equity or chancery, answering for most purposes to the judgment of a court of law. A decree in equity is a sentence or order of the court, pronounced on hearing and understanding all the points in issue, and determining the rights of all the parties to the suit, according to equity and good conscience. It is a declaration of the court announcing the legal consequences of the facts found. With the procedural merger of law and equity in the federal and most state courts under the Rules of Civil Procedure, the term "judgment" has generally replaced "decree". See Fed.R. Civil P. 54(a). *See also* Decision; Judgment; Order.

General Classification

Decrees in equity are either *final* or *interlocutory*. A final decree is one which fully and finally disposes of the whole litigation, determining all questions raised by the case, and leaving nothing that requires further judicial action. An interlocutory decree is a provisional or preliminary decree, which is not final and does not determine the suit, but directs some further proceedings preparatory to the final decree. It is a decree pronounced for the purpose of ascertaining matter of law or fact preparatory to a final decree. Where something more than the ministerial execution of the decree as rendered is left to be done, the decree is interlocutory, and not final, even though it settles the equities of the bill.

Consent decree. A judgment entered by consent of the parties whereby the defendant agrees to stop alleged illegal activity without admitting guilt or wrongdoing. Agreement by defendant to cease activities asserted as illegal by government (*e.g.* deceptive advertising practices as alleged by F.T. C.). Upon approval of such agreement by the court the government's action against the defendant is dropped. Also, a decree entered in an equity suit on consent of both parties; it is not properly a judicial sentence, but is in the nature of a solemn contract or agreement of the parties, made under the sanction of the court, and in effect an admission by them that the decree is a just determination of their rights upon the real facts of the case, if such facts had been proved. It binds only the consenting parties; and is not binding upon the court.

Decree nisi /dəkríy náysay/. A provisional decree, which is to be made absolute on motion unless cause be shown against it. Interlocutory judgment or decree in divorce action. In English practice, it is the order made by the court for divorce, on satisfactory proof being given in support of a petition for dissolution of marriage; it remains imperfect for a certain period (which period may be shortened by the court), and then, unless sufficient cause be shown, it is made absolute on motion, and the dissolution takes effect, subject to appeal. It effects a conditional divorce, becoming absolute only upon the happening of a prescribed contingency.

Decree of distribution. An instrument by which heirs receive property of a deceased; it is a final determination of the parties to a proceeding.

Decree of insolvency. One entered in a probate court, declaring the estate in question to be insolvent, that is, that the assets are not sufficient to pay the debts in full. See Bankruptcy proceedings.

Decree of nullity. One entered in a suit for the annulment of a marriage, and adjudging the marriage to have been null and void *ab initio.* See Nullity.

Decree pro confesso. One entered in a court of equity in favor of the complainant where the defendant has made no answer to the bill and its allegations are consequently taken "as confessed." It is merely an admission of the allegations of the bill well pleaded.

Deficiency decree. In a mortgage foreclosure suit, a decree for the balance of the indebtedness after applying the proceeds of a sale of the mortgaged property to such indebtedness.

For *Execution of decree, see* Execution.

Decretal /dəkríytəl/. The granting or denying of remedy sought.

Decretal order /dəkríytəl órdər/. A preliminary order that determines no question upon the merits and establishes no right.

Decriminalization. An official act generally accomplished by legislation, in which an act or omission, formerly criminal, is made non-criminal and without punitive sanctions.

Dedicate. To appropriate and set apart one's private property to some public use; as to make a private way public by acts evincing an intention to do so.

Dedication. The appropriation of land, or an easement therein, by the owner, for the use of the public, and accepted for such use by or on behalf of the public. Such dedication may be express where the appropriation is formally declared, or by implication arising by operation of law from the owner's conduct and the facts and circumstances of the case. A deliberate appropriation of land by its owner for any general and public uses, reserving to himself no other rights than such as are compatible with the full exercise and enjoyment of the public uses to which the property has been devoted. See also Dedication and reservation.

By adverse user. A dedication may arise from an adverse exclusive use by the public under a claim of right with the knowledge, actual or imputed, and acquiescence of the owner.

Common-law or statutory. A common-law dedication is one made as above described, and may be either express or implied. A statutory dedication is one made under and in conformity with the provisions of a statute regulating the subject, and is of course necessarily express. An "express common-law dedication" is one where the intent is expressly manifested, such as by ordinary deeds, recorded plats not executed pursuant to statute or defectively certified so as not to constitute a statutory dedication.

Copyright law. At common law, the creator of a work has the right to copy and profit from it and distribute it or show it to a limited class of persons for a limited purpose without losing such right, and the right continues until the creator allows general publication of the work to occur. A general publication of work occurs when the work is made available to members of the public at large without regard to whom they are or what they propose to do with it, and common law copyright may be lost by general publication or by an unrestricted sale of a single copy. Dedication of work to the public domain is a question of law, not intent of proprietor.

Express or implied. A dedication may be express, as where the intention to dedicate is expressly manifested by a deed or an explicit oral or written declaration of the owner, or some other explicit manifestation of his purpose to devote the land to the public use. An implied dedication may be shown by some act or course of conduct on the part of the owner from which a reasonable inference of intent may be drawn, or which is inconsistent with any other theory than that he intended a dedication.

Statutory dedication. Such occurs when owner of property files or records a plat which marks or notes on plat portions of premises as donated or granted to public; it results in conveyance of dedicated portions in fee simple to public.

Dedication and reservation. The dedicator may impose reasonable conditions, restrictions and limitations, and compliance therewith is essential unless waived. Dedicator may reserve a new right in himself by way of implied grant and may include rights personal or rights appurtenant to the land. At common law, a reservation in a dedication is not perpetual.

Deductible. That which may be taken away or subtracted. In taxation, an item which may be subtracted from gross income or adjusted gross income in determining taxable income (*e.g.*, interest expenses, charitable contributions, certain taxes, etc.). See also Deduction.

The portion of an insured loss to be borne by the insured before he is entitled to recovery from the insurer. See Deductible clause.

Deductible clause. Clause in insurance policy providing that insured will absorb first part of loss (*e.g.* first $100) with insurer paying the excess.

Deduction. That which is deducted; the part taken away; abatement; as deductions from gross income in arriving at net income for tax purposes.

In the civil law, a portion or thing which an heir has a right to take from the mass of the succession before any partition takes place. Civil Code La. art. 1358.

See also Charitable deduction; Deductible; Marital deduction; Orphan's deduction.

Itemized deductions. Those expenses which are allowed as deductions from adjusted gross income, itemized in detail under their appropriate captions, and subtracted to arrive at income subject to tax (*e.g.* taxes, charitable contributions, etc.). I.R.C. §§ 161–188. *See also* Deductible.

Standard deduction. An option available to all individual taxpayers whereby they can deduct a specified amount from adjusted gross income instead of itemizing their deductions. This option is generally used by taxpayers who do not have deductions which exceed the standard deduction assigned to them. The Tax Reform Act of 1986 changed the standard deduction amounts. The standard deduction amounts for 1989 and subsequent years are indexed for inflation.

Deductions in respect of a decedent. Deductions accrued to the point of death but not recognizable on the final income tax return of a decedent because of the method of accounting used. Such items are allowed as deductions on the estate tax return and on the income tax return of the estate or the heir. An example of a deduction in respect of a decedent would be interest expense accrued up to the date of death by a cash basis debtor.

Deed. A conveyance of realty; a writing signed by grantor, whereby title to realty is transferred from one to another. A written instrument, signed, and delivered, by which one person conveys land, tenements, or hereditaments to another.

See also Ancient deed; Bargain and sale deed; Contract for deed; Quitclaim deed; Sheriff's deed; Special warranty deed; Tax deed; Trust (*Trust deed*); Warranty deed.

Deed absolute. Deed which conveys absolute title as contrasted with mortgage deed which is defeasible on fulfillment of mortgage conditions.

Deed indented, or indenture. In common-law conveyancing, a deed executed or purporting to be executed in parts, between two or more parties, and distinguished by having the edge of the paper or parchment on which it is written indented or cut at the top in a particular manner. This was formerly done at the top or side, in a line resembling the teeth of a saw; a formality derived from the ancient practice of dividing chirographs; but the cutting is now made either in a waving line,

or more commonly by notching or nicking the paper at the edge.

Deed in fee. A deed conveying the title to land in fee simple with the usual covenants.

Deed of covenant. Covenants are sometimes entered into by a separate deed, for title, or for the indemnity of a purchaser or mortgagee, or for the production of title-deeds. A covenant with a penalty is sometimes taken for the payment of a debt, instead of a bond with a condition, but the legal remedy is the same in either case.

Deed of distribution. Deed of fiduciary by which real estate of decedent is conveyed.

Deed of gift. A deed executed and delivered without consideration.

Deed of release. One releasing property from the incumbrance of a mortgage or similar pledge upon payment or performance of the conditions. More specifically, where a deed of trust to one or more trustees has been executed, pledging real property for the payment of a debt or the performance of other conditions, substantially as in the case of a mortgage, a deed of release is the conveyance executed by the trustees, after payment or performance, for the purpose of divesting themselves of the legal title and revesting it in the original owner.

Deed of separation. An instrument by which, through the medium of some third person acting as trustee, provision is made by a husband for separation from his wife and for her separate maintenance.

Deed of settlement. A deed formerly used in England for the formation of joint stock companies constituting certain persons trustees of the partnership property and containing regulations for the management of its private affairs. They are now regulated by articles of association.

Deed of trust. An instrument in use in some states, taking the place and serving the uses of a mortgage, by which the legal title to real property is placed in one or more trustees, to secure the repayment of a sum of money or the performance of other conditions. Though differing in form from mortgage, it is essentially a security. *See also* Mortgage; Trust (*Trust deed*).

Deed poll. A deed which is made by one party only. A deed in which only the party making it executes it or binds himself by it as a deed. It was originally so called because the edge of the paper or parchment was *polled* or cut in a straight line, wherein it was distinguished from a deed indented or indenture.

Defeasible deed. A deed containing a condition subsequent the happening of which will cause title to the property to revert to the grantor or to go to some third party.

Gratuitous deed. One made without consideration. *See Deed of gift above.*

Statutory deed. A warranty deed form prescribed by state statute. By statute in such states there are certain warranties and covenants that are legally regarded as being a part of all statutory deeds, although such are not included in the printed form.

Wild deed. A deed not in the chain of title. An instrument which is recorded but, because some previous instrument connecting it to the chain of title has not been recorded, will never be discovered in the indexes.

Deed, estoppel by. "Estoppel by deed" is a bar which precludes one party to a deed and his privies from asserting as against the other party and his privies any right or title in derogation of the deed or from denying the truth of any material facts asserted in it. Such estoppel precludes a party from denying a certain fact recited in deed executed or accepted by him in an action brought on the deed by party who would be detrimentally affected by such denial.

Deem. To hold; consider; adjudge; believe; condemn; determine; treat as if; construe.

Deemed transferor. The person holding an interest in a trust the expiration of which will lead to the imposition of a generation-skipping tax. Assume, for example, GF creates a trust, income payable to S (GF's son) for life and, upon S's death, remainder to GS (GF's grandson). Upon S's death, he will be the "deemed transferor" and the trust will be included in his gross estate for purposes of determining the generation-skipping transfer tax. I.R.S. § 2612. *See* Generation-skipping trust.

Deep pocket. A person or corporation of substantial wealth and resources from which a claim or judgment may be made.

Under the "deep pocket" theory in antitrust law, parent corporation's substantial assets will have an impact on competition in which subsidiary is engaged.

Deep Rock doctrine. A principle in bankruptcy law by which unfair or inequitable claims presented by controlling shareholders of bankrupt corporations may be subordinated to claims of general or trade creditors. The doctrine received its name from the corporate name of the subsidiary involved in the leading case articulating the doctrine.

Deface. To mar or destroy the face (that is, the physical appearance of written or inscribed characters as expressive of a definite meaning) of a written instrument, signature, inscription, etc., by obliteration, erasure, cancellation, or superinscription, so as to render it illegible or unrecognizable. Also used in respect of injury to monument, buildings and other structures. *See* Cancel; Defile; Desecrate; Mutilation; Obliteration.

De facto /díy fǽktow/. In fact, in deed, actually. This phrase is used to characterize an officer, a government, a past action, or a state of affairs which must be accepted for all practical purposes, but is illegal or illegitimate. Thus, an office, position or status existing under a claim or color of right such as a de facto corporation. In this sense it is the contrary of *de jure,* which means rightful, legitimate, just, or constitutional. Thus, an officer, king, or government *de facto* is one who is in actual possession of the office or supreme power, but by usurpation, or without lawful title; while an officer, king, or governor *de jure* is one who has just claim and rightful title to the office or power, but has never had plenary possession of it, or is not in actual possession. A wife *de facto* is one whose marriage is voidable by decree, as distinguished from a wife *de jure,* or lawful wife. But the term is also frequently used independently of any distinction from *de jure;* thus a blockade *de facto* is a blockade which is actually maintained, as distinguished from a mere paper blockade. *Compare* De jure.

As to *de facto* Corporation; Court; Domicile; Government; Merger; and Officer, see those titles.

De facto adoption. An agreement to adopt according to statutory procedures in a given state which will ripen into de jure adoption when the petition is properly presented. An equitable adoption *(q.v.).*

De facto contract /díy fǽktow kóntrækt/. One which has purported to pass the property from the owner to another but is defective in some element.

De facto court. *See* Court.

De facto government. One that maintains itself by a display of force against the will of the rightful legal government and is successful, at least temporarily, in overturning the institutions of the rightful legal government by setting up its own in lieu thereof.

De facto judge. A judge who functions under color of authority but whose authority is defective in some procedural form.

De facto marriage. A marriage in which the parties live together as husband and wife under color of validity but which is defective for reasons of form, etc.

De facto officer. One who, while in actual possession of the office, is not holding such in a manner prescribed by law.

De facto segregation. Segregation which is inadvertent and without assistance of school authorities and not caused by any state action, but rather by social, economic and other determinates. *Compare* De jure segregation.

De facto taking. This type of taking occurs when an entity clothed with power of eminent domain substantially deprives an owner of the use and enjoyment of his property. Such occurs in extraordinary circumstances when entity having power of eminent domain substantially deprives property owner of right to beneficial use and enjoyment of property as consequence of nonappropriative rather than appropriative act.

Defalcation /dìyfolkéyshən/. The act of a defaulter; act of embezzling; failure to meet an obligation; misappropriation of trust funds or money held in any fiduciary capacity; failure to properly account for such funds. Commonly spoken of officers of corporations or public officials.

For purposes of Bankruptcy Code section making nondischargeable a debt resulting from fraud or defalcation by debtor while acting in fiduciary capacity, is failure to meet an obligation, misappropriation of trust funds or money held in any fiduciary capacity, and failure to properly account for such funds.

Also set-off, recoupment or counterclaim. The diminution of a debt or claim by deducting from it a smaller claim held by the debtor or payor. *See* Defalk.

Defalk. To set off one claim against another; to deduct a debt due to one from a debt which one owes. This verb corresponds only to the second meaning of "defalcation" as given above; *i.e.* a public officer or trustee who misappropriates or embezzles funds in his hands is *not* said to "defalk."

Defamation. An intentional false communication, either published or publicly spoken, that injures another's reputation or good name. Holding up of a person to ridicule, scorn or contempt in a respectable and considerable part of the community; may be criminal as well as civil. Includes both libel and slander.

Defamation is that which tends to injure reputation; to diminish the esteem, respect, goodwill or confidence in which the plaintiff is held, or to excite adverse, derogatory or unpleasant feelings or opinions against him. Statement which exposes person to contempt, hatred, ridicule or obloquy. The unprivileged publication of false statements which naturally and proximately result in injury to another.

To recover against a public official or public figure, plaintiff must prove that the defamatory statement was published with malice. Malice as used in this context means that it was published either knowing that it was false or with a reckless disregard as to whether it was true or false. New York Times Co. v. Sullivan, 376 U.S. 254, 84 S.Ct. 710, 11 L.Ed.2d 686.

A communication is defamatory if it tends so to harm the reputation of another as to lower him in the estimation of the community or to deter third persons from associating or dealing with him. The meaning of a communication is that which the recipient correctly, or mistakenly but reasonably, understands that it was intended to express. Restatement, Second, Torts §§ 559, 563.

See also Actionable per quod; Actionable per se; Journalist's privilege; Libel; Slander.

Defamatory. Calumnious; containing defamation; injurious to reputation; libelous; slanderous. *See* Defamation.

Defamatory libel. Written, permanent form of defamation as contrasted with slander which is oral defamation. *See* Libel.

Defamatory per quod /dəfǽmətòriy pər kwód/. In respect of words, those which require an allegation of facts, aside from the words contained in the publication, by way of innuendo, to show wherein the words used libel the plaintiff. *See* Actionable per quod.

Defamatory per se /dəfǽmətòriy pər síy/. In respect of words, those which by themselves, and as such, without reference to extrinsic proof, injure the reputation of the person to whom they are applied. *See* Actionable per se.

Defames /dəféymiyz/. L. Fr. Infamous.

Default. By its derivation, a failure. An omission of that which ought to be done. Specifically, the omission or failure to perform a legal or contractual duty; to observe a promise or discharge an obligation (*e.g.* to pay interest or principal on a debt when due); or to perform an agreement.

Default-judgment. Judgment entered against a party who has failed to defend against a claim that has been brought by another party. Under Rules of Civil Procedure, when a party against whom a judgment for affirmative relief is sought has failed to plead (*i.e.* answer) or otherwise defend, he is in default and a judgment by default may be entered either by the clerk or the court. Fed.R.Civil P. 55. *See also* Judgment.

Defaulter. One who is in default. One who misappropriates money held by him in an official or fiduciary character, or fails to account for such money.

Defeasance /dəfíyzəns/. An instrument which defeats the force or operation of some other deed, estate, or will. A collateral deed made at the same time with a feoffment or other conveyance, containing certain conditions, upon the performance of which the estate then created may be *defeated* or totally undone.

An instrument accompanying a bond, recognizance, or judgment, containing a condition which, when performed, defeats it. *See also* Defeasance clause; Defeasible.

Defeasance clause. That provision in a mortgage which assures the revesting of title in the mortgagor when all the terms and conditions of the mortgage have been met. A clause which permits the mortgagor-borrower to defeat the temporary and conditional conveyance by discharging the debt and thus causing a release of any interests in the real estate.

Defeasible. Subject to be defeated, annulled, revoked, or undone upon the happening of a future event or the performance of a condition subsequent, or by a conditional limitation. An estate which is not absolute, *i.e.*, one which is determinable or subject to an executory limitation or condition subsequent. Usually spoken of estates and interests in land. For instance, a mortgagee's estate is defeasible (liable to be defeated) by the mortgagor's equity of redemption.

Defeasible fee. An estate in fee that is liable to be defeated by some future contingency; *e.g.*, a vested remainder which might be defeated by the death of the remainderman before the time fixed for the taking effect of the devise.

Defeasible title. One that is liable to be annulled or made void, but not one that is already void or an absolute nullity.

Defeasibly vested remainder. Gift over to remainderman which, though not subject to condition precedent as in the case of a contingent remainder, is subject to divestment on the happening of a condition subsequent.

Defeasive. Describes counterclaim which, if it prevails, will defeat right of plaintiffs to recover.

Defeat. To prevent, frustrate, or circumvent; as in the phrase "hinder, delay, or defeat creditors." To overcome or prevail against in any contest; as in speaking of the "defeated party" in an action at law, or "defeated candidate" in an election. To annul, undo, or terminate; as, a title or estate. *See* Defeasible.

Defect. The want or absence of some legal requisite; deficiency; imperfection; insufficiency. The absence of something necessary for completeness or perfection; a deficiency in something essential to the proper use for the purpose for which a thing is to be used. Some structural weakness in part or component which is responsible for damage. In a strict liability action, may consist of a manufacturing flaw, a design defect, or an inadequate warning. *See also* Apparent defects; Defective; Hidden defect; Latent defect.

Design defect. A "design defect" occurs when product is manufactured in conformity with intended design but design itself poses unreasonable dangers to consumers.

Fatal defect. Of such serious nature as to nullify contract.

Latent defect. One which is not apparent to buyer by reasonable observation.

Patent defect. One which is apparent to buyer on normal observation.

Defective. Lacking in some particular which is essential to the completeness, legal sufficiency, or security of the object spoken of; as a "defective" service of process or return of service. A product is "defective" if it is not fit for the ordinary purposes for which such articles are sold and used; or if it is dangerous because it fails to perform in manner to be expected in light of its nature and intended function. *See also* Defect; Defective condition; Warranty.

Defective condition. A product is in a defective condition unreasonably dangerous to the user when it has a propensity for causing physical harm beyond that which would be contemplated by the ordinary user or consumer who purchases it, with the ordinary knowledge common to the foreseeable class of users as to its characteristics. A product is not defective or unreasonably dangerous merely because it is possible to be injured while using it. *See* Defective; Strict liability.

Defective execution. Failure to comply with requirements in executing document with the result that document is legally inadequate or defective.

Defective pleadings. Complaint, answer, cross-claim, counterclaim, etc. which fail to meet minimum standards of sufficiency or accuracy in form or substance. Such defects may usually be cured by amendment. Fed.R.Civil P. 15.

Defective product. *See* Defect; Defective.

Defective record. May refer to record on appeal which does not conform to requisites of appellate rules. May also refer to state of title to real estate based on defects on the record in registry of deeds.

Defective title. With respect to negotiable paper within U.C.C. Article 3 (§ 3–201) the title of a person who obtains instrument or any signature thereto by fraud, duress, or force and fear, or other unlawful means, or for an illegal consideration, or when he negotiates it in breach of faith or under such circumstances as amount to fraud. *See also* Title (*Defective title*); Unmarketable title.

Defective verdict. Verdict lacking legitimacy because of some irregularity or inadequacy and hence one on which a judgment may not be based.

Defect of form. An imperfection in the style, manner, arrangement, or non-essential parts of a legal instrument, plea, indictment, etc., as distinguished from a "defect of substance" *(q.v.)*.

Defect of parties. Insufficiency of the parties before a court in any given proceeding to give it jurisdiction and authority to decide the controversy, arising from the omission or failure to join plaintiffs or defendants who should have been brought in. Rules of Civil Procedure have relaxed some of the former rigidity in requirements of joinder, but not all. Fed.R.Civ.P., Rules 19, 20. *See* Joinder.

Defect of substance. An imperfection in the body or substantive part of a legal instrument, plea, indictment, etc., consisting in the omission of something which is essential to be set forth.

Defend. To prohibit or forbid. To deny. To contest and endeavor to defeat a claim or demand made against one in a court of justice. To oppose, repel, or resist. To protect, to shield, to make a stand for, or uphold by force or argument. To vindicate, to maintain or keep secure, to guaranty, to agree to indemnify. To represent defendant in administrative, civil or criminal proceeding. *See also* Defense.

Defendant. The person defending or denying; the party against whom relief or recovery is sought in an action or suit or the accused in a criminal case. *See also* Joint defendants; Nominal defendant.

Defense. That which is offered and alleged by the party proceeded against in an action or suit, as a reason in law or fact why the plaintiff should not recover or establish what he seeks. That which is put forward to diminish plaintiff's cause of action or defeat recovery. Evidence offered by accused to defeat criminal charge.

With respect to defenses to a commercial instrument of which a holder in due course takes free, the term "defense" means a legally recognized basis for avoiding liability either on the instrument itself or on the obligation underlying the instrument.

A response to the claims of the other party, setting forth reasons why the claims should not be granted. The defense may be as simple as a flat denial of the other party's factual allegations or may involve entirely new factual allegations. In the latter situation, the defense is an affirmative defense. Under Rules of Civil Procedure, many defenses may be raised by motion as well as by answer (Rule 12(b)), while others must be pleaded affirmatively (Rules 8(c), 9). *See* Affirmative defense; Answer; Equitable defense; Justification.

As regards defense to criminal charge, such defenses include alibi, consent, "corporate" liability defenses, de minimis infraction, duress, entrapment, ignorance or mistake, infancy, insanity, intoxication, law enforcement authority, necessity, protection of property, public duty, legal impossibility, self defense and protection of others.

Defense also means the forcible repelling of an attack made unlawfully with force and violence, such as the defense of one's person or property or nation in time of war. *See* Self-defense.

Affidavit of defense. *See* Affidavit.

Frivolous defense. One which at first glance can be seen to be merely pretensive, setting up some ground which cannot be sustained by argument. On motion, such defense may be ordered stricken from the pleadings. Fed.R.Civil P. 12(f).

Legal defense. A defense which is complete and adequate in point of law. A defense which may be set up in court of law, as distinguished from an "equitable defense", which is cognizable only in a court of equity or court possessing equitable powers. This later distinction is no longer applicable with the procedural merger of law and equity under Rules of Civil Procedure.

Meritorious defense. One going to the merits, substance, or essentials of the case, as distinguished from dilatory or technical objections. For purposes of vacating default judgment is defense presumptively established when allegations of defendant's answer, if established on trial, would constitute a complete defense to the action, and defendant need not establish its defense beyond doubt in its pleading.

Partial defense. One which goes only to a part of the cause of action, or which only tends to mitigate the damages to be awarded.

Peremptory defense. A defense which insists that the plaintiff never had the right to institute the suit, or that, if he had, the original right is extinguished or determined.

Personal defense. In negotiable instruments law, a defense which, though not good as against a holder in due course, is good against certain parties, because of their participation in or knowledge of certain transactions or facts from which such defense arises. Such defenses include all defenses that are not real or absolute defenses. U.C.C. § 3–305.

Pretermitted defense. One which was available to a party and of which he might have had the benefit if he had pleaded it in due season, but which cannot afterwards be heard as a basis for affirmative relief.

Real defense. In negotiable instruments law, a defense inherent in the res and therefore good against anyone seeking to enforce the instrument, even a holder in due course. Real defenses include infancy, and such other incapacity, or duress, or illegality of the transaction, as renders the obligation of the party a nullity, and fraud in the factum. These defenses are good even against a holder in due course because, where they exist, no contract was formed. U.C.C. § 3–305(2). *See also* Real defenses.

Self defense.   *See* Self-defense.

Sham defense.   A false or fictitious defense, interposed in bad faith, and manifestly untrue, insufficient, or irrelevant on its face.

Defense attorney.   Lawyer who files appearance in behalf of defendant and represents such in civil or criminal case. *See* Public defender.

Défense bonds.   United States Savings Bonds.

Défense of habitation.   In criminal law, right to use force to defend one's home; interposed in criminal case in defense of crime. *See* Defense of property.

Defense of insanity.   In criminal cases, an affirmative defense interposed to prove that defendant lacked essential mental capacity which is required for criminal responsibility. Model Penal Code, § 4.01. Fed.R.Crim.P. 12.2 requires the defendant to notify the prosecutor prior to trial of intention to assert such defense. *See* Insanity.

Defense of others.   A justification defense available when one harms or threatens another in defense of a person other than oneself. See *e.g.,* Model Penal Code § 3.05. *See also* Self-defense.

Defense of property.   Affirmative defense in criminal case consisting of justified force in protecting one's property though such force must be reasonable under all circumstances.

Defense of self.   *See* Self-defense.

Defensive collateral estoppel.   Doctrine precluding plaintiff from relitigating identical issues by merely switching adversary; thus, defensive collateral estoppel gives plaintiff strong incentive to join all possible defendants in first action if possible. *See also* Collateral estoppel.

Defer.   Delay; put off; remand; postpone to a future time.

Deferment.   A postponement or extension to a later time as in the case of one called to serve in the Armed Forces. See 50 U.S.C.A. § 456.

Deferral.   Act of delaying, postponing or putting off.

Deferral of taxes.   Postponement of taxes from one year to a later year. For example, individuals can defer taxes by contributing money to an individual retirement account (where contributions, as well as any earnings on the contributions, are taxed only when actually withdrawn from the IRA).

Deferral period.   Time span within which payment of expense, premium, interest, or the like, is delayed or in which income is postponed. *See also* Grace period.

Deferred annuity contract.   An agreement in which the terms require payment to begin after a certain period of time has elapsed; e.g., payment will begin when the annuitant reaches the age of 60. *See* Annuity.

Deferred charge.   Expense not recognized currently on the income statement and which is carried on the balance sheet; *e.g.* discount on bonds. Expenditure not recognized as an expense of the period when made but carried forward as an asset to be written off in future periods, such as for advance rent payments or insurance premiums.

Deferred claims.   Claims which are postponed to a future date or to a subsequent accounting period.

Deferred compensation.   Compensation that will be taxed when received and not when earned. An example is contributions by an employer to a qualified pension or profit-sharing plan on behalf of an employee. Such contributions will not be taxed to the employee until the funds are made available or distributed to the employee (*e.g.,* upon retirement). *See* Pension plan.

Nonqualified deferred compensation plans.   Compensation arrangements which are frequently offered to executives. Such plans may include stock options, restricted stock, etc. Generally, an executive may defer the recognition of taxable income to future periods and the employer does not receive a tax deduction until the employee is required to include the compensation in income.

Deferred credits.   In accounting, credits which are required to be spread over subsequent accounting periods such as the premium on bonds issued.

Deferred equity.   A common term for convertible bonds because of their equity component and the expectation that the bond will ultimately be converted into shares of common stock.

Deferred income.   Income received but not yet earned, *i.e.,* prepaid rent or insurance. Deferred income is recorded as a liability on the balance sheet until such time as the income is earned and recorded as revenue.

Deferred interest bonds.   Bonds which carry a provision that interest payments are postponed for a certain period of time.

Deferred lien.   Lien postponed or delayed in its effect until a future time as contrasted with a present lien; usually possessory in nature.

Deferred payments.   Payments of principal or interest postponed to a future time; installment payments. *See also* Deferred income.

Deferred sentence.   A sentence, the pronouncement of which has been postponed. It does not operate as a suspension of sentence. *See* Probation.

Deferred stock.   *See* Stock.

Deferred taxes. A postponement of income taxes that arises from temporary differences.

Deficiency. A lack, shortage, or insufficiency. The amount by which the tax properly due exceeds the sum of the amount of tax shown on a taxpayer's return plus amounts previously assessed or collected as a deficiency, less any credits, refunds or other payments due the taxpayer; *i.e.,* the amount a taxpayer is deficient in his tax payments. *See* Deficiency assessment; Deficiency notice.

That part of a debt secured by mortgage not realized from sale of mortgaged property. A judgment or decree for the amount of such deficiency is called a "deficiency judgment" or "decree." *See* Deficiency judgment.

Deficiency action. *See* Deficiency; Deficiency judgment.

Deficiency assessment. In taxation, the excess of the amount of tax computed by the Internal Revenue Service over the amount computed by the taxpayer. I.R.C. § 6211 et seq. *See also* Deficiency; Deficiency notice; Jeopardy assessment.

Deficiency dividends. *See* Dividend.

Deficiency judgment. In mortgage law, imposition of personal liability on mortgagor for unpaid balance of mortgage debt after foreclosure has failed to yield full amount of due debt. If a foreclosure sale yields less than the mortgage debt, most states permit the mortgagee to obtain a judgment for the difference. Such deficiency judgments are subject, however, to a substantial amount of statutory regulation. May also apply to debt due after repossession of personal property subject to security interest. *See also* Judgment.

Deficiency notice. Notice of tax deficiency (90 day letter) which is mailed to taxpayer by I.R.S. and which is prerequisite to jurisdiction of Tax Court. I.R.C. § 6212. *See also* Ninety day letter.

Deficiency suits. In mortgage law, action to recover difference between debt and amount realized on foreclosure. *See also* Deficiency judgment.

Deficit. An excess of expenditures over revenues. Excess of liabilities and debts over income and assets. A negative balance in the earnings and profits account. Financial loss in operation of business. Something wanting, generally in the accounts of one intrusted with money, or in the money received by him. The term is broad enough to cover defalcation, misappropriation, shrinkage, or costs, and, in its popular meaning, signifies deficiency from any cause.

In accounting, opposite of surplus on the balance sheet. May represent accumulated losses. A negative balance in the earnings and profits account.

Deficit spending. Expenditures in excess of income; usually from borrowed funds rather than from actual revenues or surplus.

Defile. To corrupt purity or perfection of; to debase; to make ceremonially unclean; to pollute; to sully; to dishonor. To debauch, deflower, or corrupt the chastity of a woman. The term does not necessarily imply force or ravishment, nor does it connote previous immaculateness. *See also* Desecrate.

Defilement /dəfáylmənt/. Uncleanness; impurity; corruption of morals or conduct.

Define. To explain or state the exact meaning of words and phrases; to state explicitly; to limit; to determine essential qualities of; to determine the precise signification of; to settle; to establish or prescribe authoritatively; to make clear. To declare that a certain act shall constitute an offense is defining that offense. *See also* Definition.

Definite. Fixed, determined, defined, bounded.

Definite sentence. Sentence calling for imprisonment for specified number of years as contrasted with indeterminate sentence which leaves duration to prison authorities (*e.g.* parole boards) and good behavior of prisoner. Also called "determinate sentence".

Definition. A description of a thing by its properties; an explanation of the meaning of a word or term. The process of stating the exact meaning of a word by means of other words. Such a description of the thing defined, including all essential elements and excluding all nonessential, as to distinguish it from all other things and classes. *See also* Define.

Definitive. That which finally and completely ends and settles a controversy. For example, a definitive sentence or judgment as opposed to an interlocutory judgment. *See* Definite sentence.

Definitive sentence. *See* Definite sentence.

Deflation. Decline in price of goods and services.

Defraud. To make a misrepresentation of an existing material fact, knowing it to be false or making it recklessly without regard to whether it is true or false, intending one to rely and under circumstances in which such person does rely to his damage. To practice fraud; to cheat or trick. To deprive a person of property or any interest, estate, or right by fraud, deceit, or artifice. *See also* Collusion; Deceit; Fraud; Material fact; Misrepresentation.

Intent to defraud means an intention to deceive another person, and to induce such other person, in reliance upon such deception, to assume, create, transfer, alter or terminate a right, obligation or power with reference to property.

Defunct. Having ceased to exist; no longer operative. Deceased; a deceased person. A business which has ceased to function.

Degree. Extent, measure or scope of an action, condition or relation. Legal extent of guilt or negligence. Title conferred on graduates of school, college, or university. The state or civil condition of a person.

The grade or distance one thing may be removed from another; *i.e.,* the distance, or number of removes, which separates two persons who are related by consanguinity. Thus we speak of a brother as being in the second degree of kindred.

Degree of proof. That measure of cogency required to prove a case depending upon the nature of the case. In a criminal case such proof must be beyond a reasonable doubt, whereas in most civil cases such proof is by a fair preponderance of the evidence. *See also* Burden of proof; Proof (*Proof beyond a reasonable doubt*); Preponderance of evidence; Reasonable doubt.

Degrees of crime. A term used to refer to similar conduct that is punished to a greater or a lesser extent depending on the existence of one or more factors. A division or classification of one specific crime into several grades or *stadia* of guilt, according to the circumstances attending its commission. For example, in most states there are degrees of murder as "first" and "second" degree murder. Also, a division of crimes generally. Thus, a *felony* is punishable by imprisonment in state prison whereas a *misdemeanor* carries a maximum punishment of a short term sentence to a jail or house of correction and/or a fine. In some jurisdictions there are also petty misdemeanors. In addition, criminal codes in certain states classify felonies and misdemeanors into classes (*e.g.* class A, B, etc.) with corresponding punishment or sentencing categories. *See also* Classification of crimes; Crime.

Degrees of kin. The relationship between a deceased and the survivors which govern descent and distribution. *See also* Descent.

Degrees of negligence. The different grades of negligence which govern the liability of persons; *e.g.* ordinary negligence as contrasted with gross negligence. *See* Negligence.

De injuria /diy injúriyə/. Of [his own] wrong. In the technical language of common law pleading, a replication *de injuria* is one that may be made in an action of tort where the defendant has admitted the acts complained of, but alleges, in his plea, certain new matter by way of justification or excuse. By this replication the plaintiff avers that the defendant committed the grievances in question "of his own wrong, and without any such cause," or motive or excuse, as that alleged in the plea (*de injuria sua propria absque tali causa);* or, admitting part of the matter pleaded, "without

the rest of the cause" alleged *(absque residuo causœ).* In form it is a species of traverse, and it is frequently used when the pleading of the defendant, in answer to which it is directed, consists merely of matter of excuse of the alleged trespass, grievance, breach of contract, or other cause of action. Its comprehensive character in putting in issue all the material facts of the defendant's plea has also obtained for it the title of the general replication. Such technical pleading no longer exists under current rules practice.

De jure /diy júriy/. Descriptive of a condition in which there has been total compliance with all requirements of law. Of right; legitimate; lawful; by right and just title. In this sense it is the contrary of *de facto (q.v.).* It may also be contrasted with *de gratia*, in which case it means "as a matter of right," as *de gratia* means "by grace or favor." Again it may be contrasted with *de æquitate;* here meaning "by law," as the latter means "by equity."

De jure corporation. Corporation which has been created as result of compliance with all of the constitutional or statutory requirements of state of incorporation.

De jure segregation. Generally refers to segregation directly intended or mandated by law or otherwise issuing from an official racial classification or in other words to segregation which has or had the sanction of law. Term comprehends any situation in which the activities of school authorities have had a racially discriminatory impact contributing to the establishment or continuation of a dual system of schools, while "de facto segregation" is limited to that which is inadvertent and without the assistance or collusion of school authorities. *Compare* De facto segregation.

Delay. To retard; obstruct; put off; postpone; defer; procrastinate; prolong the time of or before; hinder; interpose obstacles; as, when it is said that a conveyance was made to "hinder and delay creditors." The term does not necessarily, though it may, imply dishonesty or involve moral wrong.

Delay rental. Rent, usually on oil and gas leases, paid for additional time in which to utilize land. Periodic payments, usually annual, by oil and gas lessee for privilege of deferring exploration during primary term of lease. It does not depend on oil or gas produced, does not exhaust substance of land, and resembles a bonus payment, which is an advance royalty.

Del credere /dèl kréydərey/. An agreement by which a factor, when he sells goods on credit, for an additional commission (called a *"del credere* commission"), guaranties the solvency of the purchaser and his performance of the contract. Such a factor is called a *"del credere* agent." He is a mere surety, liable to his principal only in case the purchaser makes default. Agent who is obligated to indemnify his principal in event of loss to principal as result of credit extended by agent to third party.

Delectus personæ /dəléktəs pərsówniy/. Lat. Choice of the person. By this term is understood the right of a partner to exercise his choice and preference as to the admission of any new members to the firm, and as to the persons to be so admitted, if any. The doctrine is equally applicable to close and family corporations and is exemplified in the use of restrictions for the transfer of shares of stock.

Delegable duty. An obligation which may be performed by another. Some duties are not delegable such as those which are highly personal, *e.g.*, contract to sing for another. Contract rights are delegable in most instances. See U.C.C. § 2–210(1).

Delegate. A person who is appointed, authorized, delegated or commissioned to act in the stead of another. Transfer of authority from one to another. A person to whom affairs are committed by another.

A person elected or appointed to be a member of a representative assembly. Usually spoken of one sent to a special or occasional assembly or convention. Person selected by a constituency and authorized to act for it at a party or State political convention.

As a verb, it means to transfer authority from one person to another; to empower one to perform a task in behalf of another, *e.g.*, a landlord may delegate his agent to collect rents.

See also Delegable duty; Delegation.

Delegation. A sending away; a putting into commission; the assignment of a debt to another; the intrusting another with a general power to act for the good of those who depute him; a body of delegates. The transfer of authority by one person to another. The act of making or commissioning a delegate.

The body of delegates from a State to a national nominating convention or from a county to a State or other party convention. The whole body of delegates or representatives sent to a convention or assembly from one district, place, or political unit are collectively spoken of as a "delegation."

In civil law, a species of novation which consists in the change of one debtor for another, when he who is indebted substitutes a third person who obligates himself in his stead to the creditor, or to the person appointed by him so that the first debtor is acquitted and his obligation extinguished, and the creditor contents himself with the obligation of the second debtor. Delegation is essentially distinguished from any other species of novation, in this: that the former demands the consent of all three parties, but the latter that only of the two parties to the new debt. Delegation is novation effected by the intervention of another person whom the debtor, in order to be liberated from his creditor, gives to such creditor, or to him whom the creditor appoints; and such person so given becomes obliged to the creditor in the place of the original debtor. *Perfect delegation* exists when the debtor who makes the obligation is discharged by the creditor. *Imperfect delegation* exists when the creditor retains his rights against the original debtor.

Delegation of powers. Transfer of authority by one branch of government in which such authority is vested to some other branch or administrative agency.

U.S. Constitution delegates different powers to the executive, legislative and judicial branches of government. Exercise by the executive branch of the powers delegated to the legislative branch offends this separation and delegation of powers and hence is unconstitutional. Certain powers may not be delegated from one branch of government to another such as the judicial powers or such congressional powers as power to declare war, impeach, or admit new states.

For distinction between delegated powers and various other types of constitutional powers, *see* Power *(Constitutional powers).*

Deliberate, *v.* To weigh, ponder, discuss, regard upon, consider. To examine and consult in order to form an opinion. To weigh in the mind; to consider the reasons for and against; to consider maturely; reflect upon, as to deliberate a question; to weigh the arguments for and against a proposed course of action. *See also* Deliberation.

Deliberate, *adj.* Well advised; carefully considered; not sudden or rash; circumspect; slow in determining. Willful rather than merely intentional. Formed, arrived at, or determined upon as a result of careful thought and weighing of considerations, as a deliberate judgment or plan. Carried on coolly and steadily, especially according to a preconceived design; given to weighing facts and arguments with a view to a choice or decision; careful in considering the consequences of a step; slow in action; unhurried; characterized by reflection; dispassionate; not rash.

By the use of this word, in describing a crime, the idea is conveyed that the perpetrator weighs the motives for the act and its consequences, the nature of the crime, or other things connected with his intentions, with a view to a decision thereon; that he carefully considers all these, and that the act is not suddenly committed. It implies that the perpetrator must be capable of the exercise of such mental powers as are called into use by deliberation and the consideration and weighing of motives and consequences. *See also* Deliberation; Premeditation.

Deliberately. Willfully; with premeditation; intentionally; purposely; in cold blood.

Deliberate speed. Phrase used in mandate to desegregate public schools and means such speed as is consistent with the welfare of all people of the state, with the maintenance of law and order and with the preservation, if possible, of the common school system.

Deliberation. The act or process of deliberating. The act of weighing and examining the reasons for and against a contemplated act or course of conduct or a choice of acts or means.

In the context of jury function means that a properly formed jury, comprised of the number of qualified persons required by law, are within the secrecy of jury room analyzing, discussing and weighing evidence which they have heard with a view to reaching a verdict based upon law applicable to facts of case as they find them to be; such deliberation can only be carried on by a lawful number of jurors in the presence of all.

As used in context of an essential element of first-degree murder, is a weighing in the mind of consequences of course of conduct, as distinguished from acting upon a sudden impulse without exercise of reasoning powers.

For purposes of first-degree murder statute, "deliberation" means intent to kill carried out by defendant in cool state of blood, in furtherance of fixed design for revenge or to accomplish unlawful purpose and not under influence of violent passion, suddenly aroused by lawful or just cause or legal provocation.

See also Deliberate; Premeditation.

Delict. Criminal offense; tort; a wrong.

Delictual fault /dəlíktyuwəl fólt/. An act, productive of obligations, which takes place between persons juridically strangers to each other; it supposes the absence of obligation and its result is the creation of one.

Delictum /dəlíktəm/. Lat. A delict, tort, wrong, injury, or offense. Actions *ex delicto* are such as are founded on a tort, as distinguished from actions on contract.

Delimitation. The act of fixing, marking off, or describing the limits or boundary line of a territory, country, authority, right, statutory exception or the like.

Delinquency. Failure, omission, violation of law or duty. Failure to make payment on debts when due. State or condition of one who has failed to perform his duty or obligation.

Delinquency charges. As used in the commercial credit field, generally refer to specific pecuniary sums that are assessed against the borrower

solely because of his failure to make his payment in timely manner.

Delinquent, *n.* Person who has been guilty of some crime, offense, or failure of duty or obligation.

Delinquent, *adj.* As applied to a debt or claim, it means simply due and unpaid at the time appointed by law or fixed by contract; as due and unpaid taxes or mortgage payments.

Delinquent child. An infant of not more than specified age who has violated criminal laws or engages in disobedient, indecent or immoral conduct, and is in need of treatment, rehabilitation, or supervision. Defined by a state statute as: A child who (A) violates any federal or state law, or municipal or local ordinance; or (B) without just cause runs away from his parental home or other properly authorized and lawful place of abode; or (C) is beyond the control of his parents, parent, guardian or other custodian; or (D) has engaged in indecent or immoral conduct; or (E) has been habitually truant or, while in school, has been continuously and overtly defiant of school rules and regulations; or (F) has violated any lawful order of court. See 18 U.S.C.A. § 5001 et seq. *See also* Disobedient child.

With respect to parental liability for acts of delinquent child, *see* Parental liability.

Delinquent taxes. Past due and unpaid taxes.

Delisting. The process by which the privileges of a security listed on an exchange are suspended for failure to meet the requirements of listing. Such delisting may be permanent or temporary. *See also* Deregistration.

Deliverance. The verdict rendered by a jury.

Delivery. The act by which the res or substance thereof is placed within the actual or constructive possession or control of another. What constitutes delivery depends largely on the intent of the parties. It is not necessary that delivery should be by manual transfer; *e.g.* "deliver" includes mail. Rev. Model Bus. Corp. Act, § 1.40. *See also* Drop shipment delivery; Misdelivery.

Absolute and conditional. An absolute delivery, as distinguished from conditional delivery or delivery in escrow, is one which is complete upon the actual transfer of the instrument from the possession of the grantor. A conditional delivery is one which passes the thing subject to delivery from the possession of the grantor, but is not to be completed by possession of the grantee, or a third person as his agent, until the happening of a specified event. One of the exceptions to parol evidence rule which permits introduction of evidence to the effect that document was delivered on condition that something be done and it is understood that document does not become operative until such action be taken.

Actual and constructive. Actual delivery consists in the giving real possession to the vendee or his servants or special agents who are identified with him in law and represent him. It is a formal immediate transfer of the property to the vendee.

Constructive delivery is a general term, comprehending all those acts which, although not truly conferring a real possession of the thing sold on the vendee, have been held, by construction of law, equivalent to acts of real delivery. A constructive delivery of personalty takes place when the goods are set apart and notice given to the person to whom they are to be delivered, or when, without actual transfer of the goods or their symbol, the conduct of the parties is such as to be inconsistent with any other supposition than that there has been a change in the nature of the holding. "Constructive delivery" is a term comprehending all those acts which, although not truly conferring a real possession of the vendee, have been held by construction of law equivalent to acts of real delivery. *See also Symbolical delivery, below.*

Commercial law. Delivery with respect to instruments, documents of title, chattel paper or securities means voluntary transfer of possession. U.C.C. § 1–201(14).

The act by which seller parts with possession and buyer acquires possession. Delivery occurs whenever seller does everything necessary to put goods completely and unconditionally at buyer's disposal.

Conditional delivery. Issuance of an instrument with the understanding that the instrument is ineffective, that is, the maker or drawer is not liable thereon, unless and until a specified event, *i.e.,* a condition precedent, occurs.

Deed. The final and absolute transfer of a deed, properly executed, to the grantee, or to some person for his use, in such manner that it cannot be recalled by the grantor. Controlling factor in determining if there has been delivery of a deed is the intention of the grantor; to constitute "delivery" the deed must be placed in the hands of the grantee or within his control, with the intention that it is to become presently operative as a conveyance.

Delivery bond. A bond given upon the seizure of goods (as under the revenue laws) conditioned for their restoration to the defendant, or the payment of their value, if so adjudged.

A guaranteed undertaking by a defendant whose property has been seized through attachment promising that, in exchange for return of the property to him pending resolution of the main action, he will surrender the property or its value in satisfaction of judgment against her. Another name for this bond is "forthcoming bond."

Delivery in escrow. Transfer physically of something such as a deed to escrow agent to be held on some condition which is not inconsistent with the primary transaction and which is to be released on the occurrence of some specific event or happening. *See* Escrow.

Delivery order. A written order to deliver goods directed to a warehouseman, carrier or other person who in the ordinary course of business issues warehouse receipts or bills of lading. U.C.C. § 7–102(1)(d). The primary function of the delivery order is to aid in the breaking down into smaller lots of one large lot of goods (whether fungible or otherwise) which is represented by one bill of lading.

Drugs. In the context of illegal transfer of drugs, "deliver" means the actual, constructive, or attempted transfer from one person to another of a controlled substance.

Gift. "Delivery" for purposes of creating a gift consists of irrevocable surrender of dominion and control over the subject matter of the gift.

Second delivery. The legal delivery by the depositary of a deed placed in escrow.

Symbolical delivery. The constructive delivery of the subject-matter of a sale, where it is cumbersome or inaccessible, by the actual delivery of some article which is conventionally accepted as the symbol or representative of it, or which renders access to it possible, or which is the evidence of the purchaser's title to it; as the key of a warehouse, or a bill of lading of goods on shipboard.

Delusion. False, unshakeable belief which is (a) contrary to fact, (b) inappropriate to the person's education, intelligence or culture, and (c) adhered to in spite of tangible evidence that it is false. A reality judgment which cannot be accepted by people of the same class, education, race and period of life as the person who expresses it and which cannot be changed by logical argument or evidence against it. Three common delusions are: (1) delusions of persecution; (2) delusions of grandeur; and (3) delusions of personal unworthiness. The first two are common to schizophrenia. Delusion appears to spring from a distorted world view created by the subject in order to satisfy his inner needs or to reconcile conflicting elements of his personality. *See* Insane delusion.

Demain. *See* Demesne.

Demand, *v.* To claim as one's due; to require; to ask relief. To summon; to call in court.

Demand, *n.* The assertion of a legal right; a legal obligation asserted in the courts. An imperative request preferred by one person to another, under a claim of right, requiring the latter to do or yield something or to abstain from some act. Request for payment of debt or amount due. An asking with authority, claiming or challenging as due.

The seeking after a commodity or service. It is not something static, but necessarily contains the idea of "competition" and a realization that markets are as much limited by sales efforts as by capacity to produce.

See also Call; Liquidated demand; On demand; Payable on demand.

Cross-demand. A demand that is preferred by one party to an action in opposition to a demand already preferred against him by his adversary. *See* Counterclaim; Cross-claim.

Demand clause. Provision in note which allows holder to compel full payment if maker fails to meet any installment. *See Demand note, below.*

Demand deposits. Any bank deposit which the depositor may demand (withdraw) at any time in contrast to time deposit which requires depositor to wait the specified time before withdrawing or pay a penalty for early withdrawal. Funds accepted by bank subject to immediate withdrawal; such represent largest element in money supply of the United States.

Demand draft. Sight draft; draft payable on demand.

Demand instrument. An instrument that is payable on demand, at sight or on presentation. See U.C.C. § 3–108 (when an instrument is payable on demand). *See also Demand note, below.*

Demand loan. Loan which may be called by lender at any time because there is no fixed maturity date. A loan payable upon request by the creditor rather than on a specific date. *See Demand note, below.*

Demand note. A note with no set maturity date which expressly states that it is payable on demand, on presentation, or at sight. A note in which no time for payment is expressed. A note issued, accepted or indorsed when overdue, as regards person so issuing, accepting or indorsing it. *See also Demand instrument, above*; *and* Sight draft.

Legal demand. A demand properly made, as to form, time, and place, by a person lawfully authorized.

Personal demand. A demand for payment of a bill or note, made upon the drawer, acceptor or maker, in person.

Demandant /dəmǽndənt/. The plaintiff or party suing in a real action.

Demarcation. The marking of a boundary line on the ground by physical means or a cartographic representation.

Demeanor /dəmíynər/. As respects a witness or other person, relates to physical appearance; outward bearing or behavior. It embraces such facts as the tone of voice in which a witness' statement is made, the hesitation or readiness with which his answers are given, the look of the witness, his carriage, his evidences of surprise, his gestures, his zeal, his bearing, his expression, his yawns, the use of his eyes, his furtive or meaning glances, or his shrugs, the pitch of his voice, his self-possession or embarrassment, his air of candor or seeming levity.

Demeanor evidence. Species of real evidence consisting of behavior of witness on the witness stand and which may be considered by trier of fact on issue of credibility.

Demesne /dəmíyn/dəméyn/. Domain; dominical; held in one's own right, and not of a superior; not allotted to tenants.

In the language of pleading, own; proper; original. Thus, *son assault demesne,* his own assault, his assault originally or in the first place.

De minimis doctrine. *See* De minimis non curat lex.

De minimis non curat lex /díy mínəməs nòn kyúrət léks/. The law does not care for, or take notice of, very small or trifling matters. The law does not concern itself about trifles. Provision is made under certain criminal statutes for dismissing offenses which are "de minimis." See, *e.g.,* Model Penal Code § 2.12.

De minis /díy mínəs/. Writ of threats. A writ which lay where a person was threatened with personal violence, or the destruction of his property, to compel the offender to keep the peace.

Demise, *v.* To convey or create an estate for years or life. To lease; to bequeath or transmit by succession or inheritance.

Demise, *n.* A conveyance of an estate to another for life, for years, or at will (most commonly for years); a lease. Originally a posthumous grant. Commonly a lease or conveyance for a term of years; sometimes applied to any conveyance in fee, for life, or for years. "Demise" is synonymous with "lease" or "let". The use of the term in a lease imports a covenant for quiet enjoyment; and implies a covenant by lessor of good right and title to make the lease.

Demise charter. Under a demise (or "bareboat") charter, there is but a hiring of the vessel, under which no title passes to the charterer but merely the right to possess and control it for a limited period. One under which control of vessel is taken from owner and vested in the charterer who mans and navigates vessel during rental period. There must be relinquishment of all control over ship, barge or scow.

Demised premises. That property, or portion of a property which is leased to a tenant.

Democracy. That form of government in which the sovereign power resides in and is exercised by the whole body of free citizens directly or indirectly through a system of representation, as distinguished from a monarchy, aristocracy, or oligarchy.

Demolish. To throw or pull down; to raze; to destroy the fabrication of; to pull to pieces; hence to ruin or destroy. To destroy totally or to commence the work of total destruction with the purpose of completing the same.

Demonetization /diymonətəzéyshən/. The disuse of a particular metal for purposes of coinage. The withdrawal of the value of a metal as money. For example, in the United States gold has been demonetized.

Demonstrate. To teach by exhibition of samples; to derive from admitted premises by steps of reasoning which admit of no doubt; to prove indubitably. To show or prove value or merits by operation, reasoning, or evidence.

Demonstration. Description; pointing out. That which is said or written to designate a thing or person. Show or display of attitudes toward a person, cause, or issue.

Demonstrative bequest. A testamentary gift which, by its terms, must be paid from a specific fund; e.g. bequest of one thousand dollars to be paid from testator's shares of stock in X Corporation. Hence, it is partly a general bequest and partly a specific bequest. See also Legacy.

Demonstrative evidence. That evidence addressed directly to the senses without intervention of testimony. Such evidence is concerned with real objects which illustrate some verbal testimony and has no probative value in itself. Real ("thing") evidence such as the gun in a trial of homicide or the contract itself in the trial of a contract case. Evidence apart from the testimony of witnesses concerning the thing. Such evidence may include maps, diagrams, photographs, models, charts, medical illustrations, X-rays.

Demonstrative legacy. See Legacy.

Demonstrator. One who stands, walks or parades in public in support of a cause to inform the public of the legitimacy of the cause and to enlist support for such cause.

Demotion. A reduction to lower rank or grade, or to lower type of position, or to lower pay scale.

Demur /dəmɔ́r/. To present a demurrer; to take an exception to the sufficiency in point of law of a pleading or state of facts alleged. See Demurrer.

Demurrable /dəmɔ́rəbəl/. Subject to a demurrer. A pleading, petition, or the like, is said to be demurrable when it does not state such facts as support the claim, prayer, or defense put forward.

Demurrage /dəmɔ́rəj/. In maritime law, the sum which is fixed by the contract of carriage, or which is allowed, as remuneration to the owner of a ship for the detention of his vessel beyond the number of days allowed by the charter-party for loading and unloading or for sailing. Also the detention of the vessel by the freighter beyond such time. With respect to railroads a charge exacted by a carrier from a shipper or consignee on account of a failure on the latter's part to load or unload cars within the specified time prescribed by the applicable tariffs; the purpose of the charge is to expedite the loading and unloading of cars, thus facilitating the flow of commerce, which is in the public interest. Demurrage is extended freight and is the amount payable for delays by receiver in loading or unloading cargo; it is stipulated damages for detention.

Demurrage lien. Carrier's right to possession of goods for unpaid demurrage charges.

Demurrant /dəmɔ́rənt/. One who demurs; the party who, in pleading, interposes a demurrer.

Demurrer. An allegation of a defendant, which, admitting the matters of fact alleged by complaint or bill (equity action) to be true, shows that as they are therein set forth they are insufficient for the plaintiff to proceed upon or to oblige the defendant to answer; or that, for some reason apparent on the face of the complaint or bill, or on account of the omission of some matter which ought to be contained therein, or for want of some circumstances which ought to be attendant thereon, the defendant ought not to be compelled to answer. The formal mode of disputing the sufficiency in law of the pleading of the other side. In effect it is an allegation that, even if the facts as stated in the pleading to which objection is taken be true, yet their legal consequences are not such as to put the demurring party to the necessity of answering them or proceeding further with the cause. An assertion that complaint does not set forth a cause of action upon which relief can be granted, and it admits, for purpose of testing sufficiency of complaint, all properly pleaded facts, but not conclusions of law. A legal objection to the sufficiency of a pleading, attacking what appears on the face of the document. See Calif. Code of Civil Proc. § 430.10. See also Demurrer to evidence.

By Federal Rules of Civil Procedure (adopted in whole or part in most states) demurrers, pleas and exceptions for insufficiency of a pleading are abolished. Rule 7(c). Every defense in law shall be made by motion or by answer; motions going to jurisdiction, venue, process, or failure to state a claim are to be disposed of before trial, unless the court orders otherwise. While the Federal Rules do not provide for the use of a demurrer, an equivalent to a general demurrer is provided in the motion to dismiss for failure to state a claim on which relief may be granted. Fed.R. Civil P. 12(b). Objections to the pleadings by means of demurrer still exists however in certain states; see *e.g.* Calif. Code of Civil Proc. § 430.10 et seq.

Classification of Demurrers

General demurrer. A *general* demurrer is a demurrer framed in general terms, without showing specifically the nature of the objection, and which is usually resorted to where the objection is to matter of substance. Thus, a demurrer on the ground that the complaint sets forth no cause of action is a general demurrer (see *e.g.* Calif. Code of Civil Proc. § 430.10(e)), and a motion to dismiss a bill on ground that there is no equity apparent on the face thereof or that court has no jurisdiction is treated as a general demurrer.

A general demurrer to an indictment challenges only matters of form and substance appearing on its face. It is one which raises an objection that averments are insufficient in law to support the action or defense without specifying any particular cause or defect, and is sufficient only to reach matters of substance.

The Federal Rules equivalent to a general demurrer is a motion to dismiss for failure to state a claim on which relief may be granted. Fed.R. Civil P. 12(b).

Special demurrer. A *special* demurrer goes merely to structure or form of pleading which it attacks, and usually only to some portion thereof, and must distinctly specify wherein defect lies. It is one which excepts to the sufficiency of the pleadings on the opposite side, and shows specifically the nature of the objection, and the particular ground of the exception. See *e.g.* Calif. Code of Civil Proc. §§ 430.50, 430.60. The Federal Rules analogue of the special demurrer is the motion to make more definite and certain. Fed.R. Civil P. 12(e).

Speaking demurrer. A *speaking* demurrer is one which, in order to sustain itself, requires the aid of a fact not appearing on the face of the pleading objected to, or, in other words, which alleges or assumes the existence of a fact not already pleaded, and which constitutes the ground of objection and is condemned both by the common law and the code system of pleading. A speaking demurrer is one which alleges some new matter, not disclosed by the pleading against which the demurrer is aimed and not judicially known or legally presumed to be true.

Demurrer to evidence. This proceeding is analogous to a demurrer to a pleading. It is an objection or exception by one of the parties in an action at law, to the effect that the evidence which his adversary produced is insufficient in point of law (whether true or not) to make out his case or sustain the issue. The practice has been largely superseded by motions for nonsuit and directed verdict. Thus, a motion to nonsuit, a motion to dismiss at close of plaintiff's evidence for failure to prove essential facts, and a defendant's motion for a directed verdict, made at close of the evidence, have been held to be equivalent to a "demurrer to the evidence" for insufficiency to sustain a verdict for plaintiff. A motion to exclude evidence has the effect of a demurrer to the evidence, the chief points of difference being the stage of the proceeding at which each is available and the consequences resulting from deferring the motion to exclude.

Denationalization. As applied to a person, the act of depriving him of national rights or status. *See* Deportation. As applied to an industry or function, the act of returning it to private ownership and control after a period of national or sovereign ownership and control.

Denial. A traverse in the pleading of one party of an allegation of fact asserted by the other; a defense. A response by the defendant to matter(s) alleged by the plaintiff in the complaint. Under Rules of Civil Procedure, denials must be specific and directed at the particular allegations controverted. Denials may be made in part (*i.e.*, specific denial) or in whole (*i.e.*, general denial), but in the main should be specific and "fairly meet the substance of the averments denied." Fed.R. Civil P. 8(b). Averments in pleadings to which a responsive pleading is required are admitted unless denied. Rule 8(d).

General and specific. In code pleading, a general denial is one which puts in issue all the material averments of the complaint or petition, and permits the defendant to prove any and all facts tending to negative those averments or any of them. A specific denial is a separate denial applicable to one particular allegation of the complaint. An answer by way of a general denial is the equivalent of, and substitute for, the general issue under the common-law system of pleading. It gives to the defendant the same right to require the plaintiff to establish by proof all the material facts necessary to show his right to a recovery as was given by that plea.

Denounce. To declare (an act or thing) to be a crime and prescribe a punishment for it. To pronounce or condemn something as being evil or morally wrong. The word is also used (not technically but popularly) as the equivalent of "accuse" or "inform against."

The term is frequently used in regard to treaties, indicating the act of one nation in giving notice to another nation of its intention to terminate an existing treaty between the two nations.

The French *dénoncer* means to declare, to lodge an information against.

Denouncement. An application to the authorities for a grant of the right to work a mine, either on the ground of new discovery, or on the ground of forfeiture of the rights of a former owner, through abandonment or contravention of the mining law. An application for the acquisition of land for mining purposes, under certain rules prescribed by Mexican laws. The application is called the "denouncement," and, when approved by the Mexican government, is called "concession" or "title," sometimes "patent." It is then a grant given by the government to use the land applied for, for the purpose of mining, and is called the "title."

In Spanish and Mexican law, a judicial proceeding for the forfeiture of land held by an alien.

De novo /diy nówvow/. Anew; afresh; a second time. A *venire de novo* is a writ for summoning a jury for the second trial of a case which has been sent back from above for a new trial.

De novo hearing. *See* Hearing de novo.

De novo trial. Trying a matter anew; the same as if it had not been heard before and as if no decision had been previously rendered.

Density zoning. *See* Zoning.

Deny. To traverse. To give negative answer or reply to. To refuse to grant or accept. To refuse to grant a petition or protest. *See* Denial.

Depart. To go away from; leave; die.

Department. One of the territorial divisions of a country. The term is chiefly used in this sense in France, where the division of the country into departments is somewhat analogous, both territorially and for governmental purposes, to the division of an American state into counties.

One of the major administrative divisions of the executive branch of the government usually headed by an officer of cabinet rank; *e.g.* Department of State. Generally, a branch or division of governmental administration. Also, a division of a business, or of something comparable thereto.

Department of State. *See* State Department.

Departure. A deviation or divergence, from a standard rule, measurement or course of conduct.

A variance between pleading and proof. In common law pleading, the statement of matter in a replication, rejoinder, or subsequent pleading, as a cause of action or defense, which is not pursuant to the previous pleading of the same party, and which does not support and fortify it. Under Rules of Civil Procedure, no provision is made for "departure" but there are liberal amendment provisions. Fed.R. Civil P. 15.

See also Variance.

Depecage. The process whereby different issues in a single case arising out of a single set of facts are decided according to the laws of different states. Under "depecage" choice of law theory, court considers issues on which there is disagreement among the contact states over which rule of law is applicable to each issue.

Dependable, *adj.* Trustworthy or reliable; evidence.

Dependence. A state of looking to another for support, maintenance, food, clothing, comfort and protection of a home and care. *See* Dependent.

Dependency. A territory distinct from the country in which the supreme sovereign power resides, but belonging rightfully to it, and subject to the laws and regulations which the sovereign may think proper to prescribe. It differs from a *colony,* because it is not settled by the citizens of the sovereign or mother state; and from *possession,* because it is held by other title than that of mere conquest. Dependencies of the United States include Puerto Rico, Virgin Islands, Guam and other Pacific islands. See 48 U.S.C.A. § 731 et seq.

A relation between two persons, where one is sustained by another or looks to or relies on aid of another for support or for reasonable necessaries consistent with dependent's position in life. *See* Dependent.

Dependency exemption. An amount which may be subtracted in computing taxable income for each person who qualifies as a dependent of the taxpayer and whose gross income is less than the exemption amount or who is a child of the taxpayer and who has either not attained the age of 19 or who is a full time student. I.R.C. § 151(e).

Dependent, *n.* One who derives his or her main support from another. Means relying on, or subject to, someone else for support; not able to exist or sustain oneself, or to perform anything without the will, power, or aid of someone else. Generally, for workers' compensation purposes, "dependent" is one who relies on another for support or favor and one who is sustained by another. One who has relied upon decedent for support and who has reasonable expectation that such support will continue. *See also* Lawful dependents.

In taxation, a person who receives more than half of his or her support from the taxpayer during the calendar year; is a relative of the taxpayer, *i.e.,* brother, child, parent, aunt, etc.; and is a citizen or resident of the U.S. *See* Dependency exemption.

Dependent, *adj.* Deriving existence, support, or direction from another; conditioned, in respect to force or obligation, upon an extraneous act or fact.

Dependent conditions. Mutual covenants which go to the whole consideration on both sides.

Dependent contract. One which depends or is conditional upon another. One which it is not the duty of the contractor to perform until some obligation contained in the same agreement has been performed by the other party.

Dependent covenant. See Covenant.

Dependent coverage. Provision in life and health insurance for protection of dependents of named insured.

Dependent promise. One which it is not the duty of the promisor to perform until some obligation contained in the same agreement has been performed by the other party.

Dependent intervening cause. A conclusory label used by the common law to refer to a cause that intervenes between the defendant's behavior and a given result such that it is still fair to hold the defendant responsible for the result. *See also* Cause.

Dependent relative revocation. The doctrine which regards as mutually dependent the acts of one destroying a will and thereupon substituting another instrument for distribution of estate, when both acts are result of one plan, so that, if second act, through incompleteness or other defect, fails to accomplish its intended purpose, and it thereby becomes evident that testator was misled when he destroyed his will, act of destruction is regarded as bereft of intent of revocation and way for probate of destroyed will is opened.

Depending. Pending or undetermined; in progress.

In patent law, a convenient means of saying that the parts of a device were so attached as to have a right-angle relationship to each other, not a gravitational hanging of one part upon another.

Deplete. To reduce or lessen, as by use, exhaustion, or waste.

Depletion. An emptying, exhausting or wasting of assets. A reduction during taxable year of oil, gas or other mineral deposits or reserves (*i.e.*, wasting assets) as a result of production. The process by which the cost or other basis of a natural resource (*e.g.*, an oil and gas interest) is recovered upon extraction and sale of the resource.

Depletion allowance. The tax laws allow a depletion allowance (deduction) to owners of oil, gas, mineral, and timber resources as such are exhausted. The two ways to determine the depletion allowance are the *cost* and *percentage* (or statutory) methods. Under the *cost* method, each unit of production sold is assigned a portion of the cost or other basis of the interest. This is determined by dividing the cost or other basis by the total units expected to be recovered. I.R.C. § 611. Under the *percentage* (or statutory) method the

tax law provides a special percentage factor for different types of minerals and other natural resources. Such depletion is based on a percentage of the estimated gross income to be earned during the period from a natural resource, without reference to the cost of the resource. This percentage is multiplied by the gross income from the interest to arrive at the depletion allowance. I.R.C. §§ 613 and 613A. *See also* Amortization.

Depletion allowance. *See* Depletion.

Depletion deduction. *See* Depletion.

Depletion reserve. In accounting, a charge to income to reflect the decrease in value of a wasting asset such as an oil well.

Deponent /dəpównənt/. One who *deposes* (that is, testifies) to the truth of certain facts; one who gives under oath testimony which is reduced to writing; one who makes oath to a written statement. One whose deposition is given. A witness; an affiant. *See* Depose; Deposition.

Deportation. Banishment to a foreign country, attended with confiscation of property and deprivation of civil rights. A punishment derived from the *deportatio (q.v.)* of the Roman law.

The transfer of an alien, excluded or expelled, from the United States to a foreign country. The removal or sending back of an alien to the country from which he came because his presence is deemed inconsistent with the public welfare, and without any punishment being imposed or contemplated. The list of grounds for deportation are set forth at 8 U.S.C.A. § 1251, and the procedures are provided for in §§ 1252–1254. *See also* Banishment. *Compare* Extradition.

Depose. To make a deposition; to give evidence in the shape of a deposition; to make statements which are written down and sworn to; to give testimony which is reduced to writing by a duly-qualified officer and sworn to by the deponent. *See* Deponent; Deposition.

To deprive an individual of a public employment or office against his will. The term is usually applied to the deprivation of all authority of a sovereign.

In ancient usage, to testify as a witness; to give evidence under oath.

Deposit, *v.* To commit to custody, or to lay down; to place; to put; to let fall (as sediment). To lodge for safe-keeping or as a pledge to intrust to the care of another.

Deposit, *n.* A bailment of goods to be kept by the bailee without reward, and delivered according to the object or purpose of the original trust. In general, an act by which a person receives the property of another, binding himself to preserve it and return it in kind. The delivery of chattels by one person to another to keep for the use of the bailor. The giving of the possession of personal property by one person to another, with his consent, to keep for the use, benefit, and safekeeping of the first or of a third person. Something intrusted to the care of another, either for a permanent or a temporary disposition.

Money placed with a person as an earnest or security for the performance of some contract, to be forfeited if the depositor fails in his undertaking. It may be deemed to be part payment, and to that extent may constitute the purchaser the actual owner of the estate.

The act of placing money in the custody of a bank or banker, for safety or convenience, to be withdrawn at the will of the depositor or under rules and regulations agreed on. Also, the money so deposited, or the credit which the depositor receives for it. Deposit, according to its commonly accepted and generally understood meaning among bankers and by the public, includes not only deposits payable on demand and subject to check, but deposits not subject to check, for which certificates, whether interest-bearing or not, may be issued, payable on demand, or on certain notice, or at a fixed future time.

A quantity of ore or other mineral substances occurring naturally in the earth; as, a deposit of gold, oil, etc.

See also Bailment; Certificate of deposit; Earnest money; Escrow; Involuntary deposit; Security deposit. For bank deposit, *see* Bank.

Demand deposit. Bank deposit which may be withdrawn at any time by the depositor, without prior notice to bank. *Compare Time deposit, below.*

Deposit box. Commonly referred to as safe deposit box in which a person may keep valuables. *See* Safe deposit box.

Deposit company. A company whose business is the safe-keeping of securities or other valuables deposited in boxes or safes in its building which are leased to the depositors. *See* Depositary; Depository.

Deposit contract. Agreement between a payor bank and a customer that governs the rights and duties of the parties with respect to funds deposited by the customer in a demand or other account maintained at the bank, and that specifies, among other things, the circumstances under which items drawn against the account are properly payable and properly charged against the account.

Deposit in court. Person who acknowledges liability but is in doubt as to whom the liability runs may pay into court the sum of money representing his liability and be bound by the court's determination of who is entitled to it. See *e.g.* Fed.R. Civil P. 67. May also embrace payment into

court pursuant to court order as in the case of rent pending outcome of eviction case.

Deposit insurance. Insurance coverage (*e.g.* Federal Deposit Insurance Corporation) for bank depositors protecting them from loss resulting from bank failure. *See* Deposit Insurance Corporation.

Deposit of title-deeds. A method of pledging real property as security for a loan, by placing the title-deeds of the land in the keeping of the lender as pledgee. *See* Escrow.

Deposit premium. The initial premium paid by the insured on a provisional basis pending a premium adjustment in the case of policies subject to adjustment.

Deposit ratio. Ratio of total deposits to total capital.

Deposit slip. An acknowledgment that the amount named therein has been received by the bank. It is a receipt intended to furnish evidence as between the depositor and depositary that on a given date there was deposited the sum named therein, the time of deposit, and amount deposited, being also shown.

Time deposit. Bank deposit which is to remain for specified period of time, or on which notice must be given to bank before withdrawal.

Depositary. The party or institution (*e.g.* bank or trust company) receiving a deposit. One with whom anything is lodged in trust, as "depository" is the place where it is put. A trustee; fiduciary; one to whom goods are bailed to be held without recompense. The obligation on the part of the depositary is that he keep the thing with reasonable care, and, upon request, restore it to the depositor, or otherwise deliver it, according to the original trust. This term should not be confused with "depository" which is the physical place of deposit.

Deposit Insurance Act. Federal act creating Federal Deposit Insurance Corporation (F.D.I.C.) to insure deposits of qualifying banks. 12 U.S. C.A. § 1811 et seq. *See* Deposit Insurance Corporation.

Deposit Insurance Corporation. Independent federal agency (Federal Deposit Insurance Corporation) created to insure bank deposits up to a specified amount in national and most state banks, including commercial and savings and loan banks, and to protect depositors from hazards of bank closings. *See* Federal Deposit Insurance Corporation.

Deposit in transit. Receipts entered on company records but not yet processed by the bank.

Deposition. The testimony of a witness taken upon oral question or written interrogatories, not in open court, but in pursuance of a commission to take testimony issued by a court, or under a general law or court rule on the subject, and reduced to writing and duly authenticated, and intended to be used in preparation and upon the trial of a civil action or criminal prosecution. A pretrial discovery device by which one party (through his or her attorney) asks oral questions of the other party or of a witness for the other party. The person who is deposed is called the deponent. The deposition is conducted under oath outside of the courtroom, usually in one of the lawyer's offices. A transcript—word for word account—is made of the deposition. Testimony of witness, taken in writing, under oath or affirmation, before some judicial officer in answer to questions or interrogatories. Fed.R. Civil P. 26 et seq.; Fed.R.Crim.P. 15. *See also* Discovery; Interrogatories.

Oral deposition. Form of discovery by addressing questions orally to person interrogated. Fed.R. Civil Proc. 30.

Written questions. Form of discovery in which written questions are addressed to person interrogated. Fed.R. Civil Proc. 31.

Deposition de bene esse /dèpəzíshən diy bíyniy ésiy/. Testimony to be read at the trial, so far as relevant and competent, as though the witness were present in court.

Depositor. One who makes a deposit. One who delivers and leaves money with a bank on his order or subject to check.

Depository. The place where a deposit *(q.v.)* is placed and kept; *e.g.* bank, savings and loan institutions, credit union, trust company. Place where something is deposited or stored as for safekeeping or convenience; *e.g.* safety deposit box.

This term should not be confused with "depositary" which is the person or institution taking responsibility for the deposit, rather than the place itself.

United States depositories are banks selected and designated to receive deposits of the public funds (*e.g.* taxes) of the United States.

Depository bank. The first bank to which an item is transferred for collection even though it may also be the payor bank. U.C.C. § 4–105(a).

Depository transfer check (DTC). An unsigned, non-negotiable check used to transfer funds from a local collection bank to a concentration bank.

Deprave. To defame; to corrupt morally; vilify; exhibit contempt for. Corrupt, perverted or immoral state of mind.

Depraved. As an adjective means marked by debasement, corruption, perversion or deterioration.

Depraved mind. An inherent deficiency of moral sense and rectitude, equivalent to statutory phrase "depravity of heart" defined as highest grade of malice. A corrupt, perverted, or immoral state of mind. As required for conviction of second-degree murder, is one which is indifferent to the life of others. Such state of mind is equatable with malice in commonly understood sense of ill will, hatred, spite or evil intent.

Depreciable. Assets subject to depreciation; assets that decline in value or usefulness over a period of time through use or obsolescence. An example of depreciable assets includes machinery and equipment; land is a non-depreciable asset. *See* Depreciation.

Depreciable base. The cost of an item of plant and equipment minus any residual value.

Depreciable life. For an asset, the time period over which depreciable cost is to be allocated. For tax returns, depreciable life may be shorter than estimated service life.

Depreciable real property. For tax purposes, defined as tangible property (such as a building) that is attached to land.

Depreciate. To allocate the cost of an asset over its life. *See* Depreciation.

Depreciation /dəpriyshiyéyshən/. In accounting, spreading out the cost of a capital asset over its estimated useful life. Depreciation expense reduces the taxable income of an entity but does not reduce the cash. A decline in value of property caused by wear or obsolescence and is usually measured by a set formula which reflects these elements over a given period of useful life of property. Consistent, gradual process of estimating and allocating cost of capital investments over estimated useful life of asset in order to match cost against earnings. The depreciation expense recorded on the entity's tax return may differ from that recorded on the entity's financial statements. As to *intangible assets, see* Amortization. As to *natural resources, see* Depletion. *See also* Accelerated Cost Recovery System; Accrued depreciation; Annual depreciation; Asset Depreciation Range; Functional depreciation; Recapture of depreciation; Useful life.

Depreciation Methods

Accelerated depreciation. Various methods of depreciation that yield larger deductions in the earlier years of the life of an asset than the straight-line method. Examples include the double declining-balance and the sum of the years' digits methods of depreciation.

Accrued depreciation. See Accrued depreciation, and *Accumulated depreciation, below.*

Accumulated depreciation. Total depreciation recorded on an asset to date. On the balance sheet, the total cost of the asset, less the accumulated depreciation reflects the book value of the asset.

Declining balance method. Under the declining balance method, the annual depreciation allowance is computed by multiplying the undepreciated cost of the asset each year by a uniform rate up to double the straight-line rate or 150 percent, as the case may be.

Double declining method. Spreading the initial cost of a capital asset over time by deducting in each period double the percentage recognized by the straight-line method and applying that double percentage to the undepreciated balance existing at the start of each period. No salvage value is used in the calculation.

Replacement cost method. The amortization or depreciation of an asset in which the value is fixed in terms of replacement cost.

Sinking fund method. A process of recovering the value of an asset by setting up a sinking fund.

Straight-line method. Under the straight-line method of depreciation, the cost or other basis (*e.g.,* fair market value in the case of donated assets) of the asset, less its estimated salvage value, if any, is determined first; then this amount is written off in equal amounts over the period of the estimated useful life of the asset. Taking the initial cost of a capital asset, deducting the expected salvage value at the time it is expected to be discarded, and spreading the difference in equal installments per unit of time over an estimated life of the asset.

Sum-of-the-year's digits method. Under this method, the annual depreciation allowance is computed by multiplying the depreciable cost basis (cost less salvage value) by a constantly decreasing fraction. The numerator of the fraction is represented by the remaining years of useful life of the asset at the beginning of each year, and the denominator is always represented by the sum of the years' digits of useful life at the time of acquisition.

Unit method. A depreciation or amortization method used in which an asset is written off in direct relation to the productivity of the asset. The cost of the asset is divided by the estimated total number of units to be produced. This unit cost is then multiplied by the number of units sold during the year resulting in the depreciation or amortization expense for the year.

Units-of-output depreciation. A depreciation method by which the cost of a depreciable asset, minus residual value, is allocated to the accounting periods benefited based on output (miles, hours, numbers of times used, and so forth).

Depreciation reserve. An account kept on the books, as of a public utility, to offset the depreciation of the property due to time and use. It does not represent the actual depreciation of its properties which is to be deducted from the reproduc-

tion cost new to ascertain the present value for rate purposes; but only what observation and experience suggest as likely to happen, with a margin over. In taxation, when gain is realized on disposition of depreciable property the gain must be reported as ordinary income, not capital gain, to the extent of depreciation previously taken as a deduction. I.R.C. §§ 1245, 1250.

Depredation /dèprədéyshən/. The act of plundering, robbing, or pillaging.

Depression. A period of economic stress; usually accompanied by poor business conditions and high unemployment. A sharp decline in aggregate business activity that persists over an extended period of time. In economic parlance, a "depression" is more severe than a "recession *(q.v.)*."

Deprivation /dèprəvéyshən/. A taking away or confiscation; as the deprivation of a constitutional right or the taking of property under eminent domain without due process of law (*i.e.* without just compensation). See also Deprivation of property.

Deprivation of property. Due process guaranty which is abridged when government takes private property without just compensation except under extraordinary circumstances of the police power, though for deprivation of property there is not required an actual, physical taking for private or public use. Even a temporary deprivation of property constitutes a "deprivation" within meaning of Fourteenth Amendment. See Condemnation; Eminent domain; Expropriation; Just compensation; Taking.

Deprive. As used in the statute proscribing the offense of receiving stolen property means to withhold property from the owner permanently or to use or dispose of the property in a manner that makes recovery of the property by the owner unlikely. See Deprive permanently.

Deprive permanently. To "deprive permanently" means to: (a) Take from the owner the possession, use or benefit of his property, without an intent to restore the same; or (b) Retain property without intent to restore the same or with intent to restore it to the owner only if the owner purchases or leases it back, or pays a reward or other compensation for its return; or (c) Sell, give, pledge or otherwise dispose of any interest in property or subject it to the claim of a person other than the owner.

Deprogramming. As the term has become known, is the process whereby individuals who are members of certain religious groups are subjected to a scheme of brain-washing or mind control in an attempt to dissuade them of their religious beliefs.

Deputize. To appoint a deputy; to appoint or commission one to act as deputy to an officer. In a general sense, the term is descriptive of empowering one person to act for another in any capacity or relation, but in law it is almost always restricted to the substitution of a person appointed to act for an officer of the law.

Deputy. A substitute; a person duly authorized by an officer to exercise some or all of the functions pertaining to the office, in the place and stead of the latter. One appointed to substitute for another with power to act for him in his name or behalf. A substitute for another with power to act for him in his name and behalf in all matters in which principal may act. *Compare* Agent; Guardian.

Deputy consul. See Consul.

Deputy sheriff. One appointed to act in the place and stead of the sheriff in the official business of the latter's office. A *general* deputy (sometimes called "undersheriff") is one who, by virtue of his appointment, has authority to execute all the ordinary duties of the office of sheriff, and who executes process without any special authority from his principal. A *special* deputy, who is an officer *pro hac vice,* is one appointed for a special occasion or a special service, as, to serve a particular writ or to assist in keeping the peace when a riot or tumult is expected or in progress. He acts under a specific and not a general appointment and authority.

Special deputy. One appointed to exercise some special function or power of the official or person for whom he is appointed. *See also Deputy sheriff, above.*

Deregistration. Deregistration of an issuer of securities occurs when the number of securities holders of an issuer registered under section 12 of the Securities Exchange Act of 1934 has declined to the point where registration is no longer required. *See also* Delisting; Registered corporation.

Deregulation. Reduction of government regulation of business to permit freer markets and competition.

Derelict /dérəlikt/. Forsaken; abandoned; deserted; cast away. Personal property abandoned or thrown away by the owner in such manner as to indicate that he intends to make no further claim thereto.

Land left uncovered by the receding of water from its former bed. *See* Dereliction.

A boat or vessel found entirely deserted or abandoned on the sea without hope or intention of recovery or return by the master or crew, whether resulting from wreck, accident, necessity, or voluntary abandonment. When a vessel, without being abandoned, is no longer under the control or direction of those on board (as where part of the crew are dead, and the remainder are physically and mentally incapable of providing for

their own safety), she is said to be *quasi derelict.* When the crew have left their vessel temporarily, with the intention of returning to resume possession, she is not technically a derelict, but is what may be termed a "quasi derelict."

Dereliction /dèrəlíkshən/. The gaining of land from the water, in consequence of the sea, river, or stream shrinking back below the usual water mark; the opposite of *alluvion (q.v.).* Also, land left dry by running water retiring imperceptibly from one of its shores and encroaching on the other. "Dereliction" or "renunciation" of property at sea as well as on land requires both the intention to abandon and external action. *See also* Accretion; Avulsion; Reliction.

Derivative. Coming from another; taken from something preceding; secondary. That which has not its origin in itself, but owes its existence to something foregoing. Anything obtained or deduced from another.

Derivative action. A suit by a shareholder to enforce a corporate cause of action. The corporation is a necessary party, and the relief which is granted is a judgment against a third person in favor of the corporation. An action is a derivative action when the action is based upon a primary right of the corporation, but is asserted on its behalf by the stockholder because of the corporation's failure, deliberate or otherwise, to act upon the primary right. Procedure in such actions in federal courts is governed by Fed.R. Civil P. 23.1. Most states also have similar procedural rules or statutes for such actions.

Term is also used in reference to actions based on injury to another; *e.g.,* action for loss of consortium by husband against third person for injuries to wife. *See* Consortium; *also,* Derivative liability.

Derivative contraband. Items of property not otherwise illegal but subject to forfeiture according to use to which they are put.

Derivative evidence. Evidence which is derived or spawned from other illegally obtained evidence is inadmissible because of the primary taint. *See* Fruit of poisonous tree doctrine.

Derivative jurisdiction doctrine. Under this doctrine, a case is not properly removable unless it is within the subject matter jurisdiction of the state court from which it is removed.

Derivative liability. There are two distinct categories of "derivative liability": in the first category is the action which a plaintiff may institute to redress a wrong done to another; in the second category is the action which a plaintiff may institute to redress a wrong done to himself which is proximately caused by a wrong done to another. *See also* Derivative action; Vicarious liability.

Derivative suit. *See* Derivative action.

Derivative title. The common-law principle, codified repeatedly in the U.C.C., that a transferee of property acquires only the transferor's rights therein.

Derivative tort. Tort liability may be imposed on a principal for wrong committed by agent and to this extent the principal's liability is derivative. *See also* Derivative liability; Vicarious liability.

Derivative work. Under the copyright law, a work based on a pre-existing work, such as a translation, musical arrangement, fictionalization, motion picture version, abridgment or any other form in which a work may be recast, transformed or adapted, is a derivative work. Only the holder of copyright in the underlying work (or one acting with his permission) may prepare a derivative work. The preparation of such a work by any other party constitutes infringement. See Copyright Act, 17 U.S.C.A. § 101.

Derive. To receive from a specified source or origin. To proceed from property, sever from capital, however invested or employed, and to come in, receive or draw by taxpayer for his separate use, benefit, and disposal.

Derived. Received from specified source.

Derogation /dèrəgéyshən/. The partial repeal or abolishing of a law, as by a subsequent act which limits its scope or impairs its utility and force. Distinguished from *abrogation,* which means the entire repeal and annulment of a law.

Derogatory clause. In a will, this is a sentence or secret character, inserted by the testator, of which he reserves the knowledge to himself, with a condition that no will he may make thereafter should be valid, unless this clause be inserted word for word. This is done as a precaution to guard against later wills being extorted by violence, or otherwise improperly obtained. Such a provision is anomalous.

Descend. To pass by succession; as when the estate vests by operation of law in the heirs immediately upon the death of the ancestor. The term, as used in some statutes, includes an acquisition by devise. To pass down from generation to generation. To go or pass to; often used as a word of transfer. As used in wills, the word is often regarded as a general expression equivalent to the words "go to" or "belong to," and as indicating a passing of title by the force of the will rather than of the statute. *See* Descent.

Descendant *or* **descendent.** Those persons who are in the blood stream of the ancestor. Term means those descended from another, persons who proceed from a body of another such as a child or grandchild, to the remotest degree; it is the opposite of "ascendants". In the plural, the term means issue, offspring or posterity in general. Also, all those to whom an estate descends, wheth-

er it be in a direct or collateral line from the intestate. *See* Descent.

Lineal descendant. One who is in the line of descent from the ancestor. The term may include an adopted child.

Descendible. Capable of passing by descent, or of being inherited or transmitted by devise (spoken of estates, titles, offices, and other property).

Descent. Hereditary succession. Succession to the ownership of an estate by inheritance, or by any act of law, as distinguished from "purchase." Title by descent is the title by which one person, upon the death of another, acquires the real estate of the latter as his heir at law. The title by inheritance is in all cases called descent, although by statute law the title is sometimes made to ascend.

The division among those legally entitled thereto of the real property of intestates.

See also Per capita; Per stirpes.

Classification

Descents are of two sorts, *lineal* and *collateral.* Lineal descent is descent in a direct or right line, as from father or grandfather to son or grandson. Collateral descent is descent in a collateral or oblique line, that is, up to the common ancestor and then down from him, as from brother to brother, or between cousins. They are also distinguished into *mediate* and *immediate* descents. But these terms are used in different senses. A descent may be said to be a mediate or immediate descent of the estate or right; or it may be said to be mediate or immediate, in regard to the mediateness or immediateness of the pedigree or consanguinity. Thus, a descent from the grandfather, who dies in possession, to the grandchild, the father being then dead, or from the uncle to the nephew, the brother being dead, is, in the former sense, in law, immediate descent, although the one is collateral and the other lineal; for the heir is in the *per,* and not in the *per* and *cui.* On the other hand, with reference to the line of pedigree or consanguinity, a descent is often said to be immediate, when the ancestor from whom the party derives his blood is immediate, and without any intervening link or degrees; and mediate, when the kindred is derived from him *mediante altero,* another ancestor intervening between them. Thus a descent in lineals from father to son is in this sense immediate; but a descent from grandfather to grandson, the father being dead, or from uncle to nephew, the brother being dead, is deemed mediate; the father and the brother being, in these latter cases, the *medium deferens,* as it is called, of the descent or consanguinity.

Descent was denoted, in the Roman law, by the term *"successio,"* which is also used by Bracton, from which has been derived the *succession* of the Scotch and French jurisprudence.

Line of Descent

The order or series of persons who have descended one from the other or all from a common ancestor, considered as placed in a line of succession in the order of their birth, the line showing the connection of all the blood-relatives.

Collateral line. A line of descent connecting persons who are not directly related to each other as ascendants or descendants, but whose relationship consists in common descent from the same ancestor.

Direct line. A line of descent traced through those persons only who are related to each other directly as ascendants or descendants.

Maternal line. A line of descent or relationship between two persons which is traced through the mother of the younger.

Paternal line. A similar line of descent traced through the father.

Describe. To narrate, express, explain, set forth, relate, recount, narrate, depict, delineate, portray; sketch. Of land, to give the metes and bounds.

Description. A delineation or account of a particular subject by the recital of its characteristic accidents and qualities.

A written enumeration of items composing an estate, or of its condition, or of titles or documents; like an inventory, but with more particularity, and without involving the idea of an appraisement.

An exact written account of an article, mechanical device, or process which is the subject of an application for a patent.

A method of pointing out a particular person by referring to his relationship to some other person or his character as an officer, trustee, executor, etc.

That part of a conveyance, advertisement of sale, etc., which identifies the land or premises intended to be affected.

A fair portrayal of the chief features of the proposed law in words of plain meaning, so that it can be understood by the persons entitled to vote.

That part of affidavit for search warrant describing the place to be searched.

For description of criminal suspect, *see* Lineup.

See also Identification.

Descriptio personæ /dəskrípsh(iy)ow pərsówniy/. Lat. Description of the person. By this is meant a word or phrase used merely for the purpose of identifying or pointing out the person intended, and not as an intimation that the language in connection with which it occurs is to apply to him only in the official or technical character which might appear to be indicated by the word.

In wills, it sometimes happens that the word heir is used as a *descriptio personæ*. A legacy "to the eldest son" of A would be a designation of the person.

Descriptive. Containing a description; serving or aiming to describe; having the quality of representing. *See also* Identification.

Descriptive mark. A trademark which merely describes the goods to which it is affixed. A descriptive mark will only be protected or registrable if the user can demonstrate secondary meaning. *See also* Secondary meaning.

If trademark imparts information directly, it is "descriptive"; if it stands for an idea which requires some operation of the imagination connected with the goods, it is "suggestive"; the information imparted may concern a characteristic, quality or ingredient of the product.

Descriptive term. *See* Descriptive mark.

Desecrate. To violate sanctity of, to profane, or to put to unworthy use. Offense consists of defacing, damaging, polluting or otherwise physically mistreating in a way that the actor knows will outrage the sensibilities of persons likely to observe or discover his action. Model Penal Code, § 250.9. *See also* Deface; Defile; Flag desecration.

Desegregation. The judicial mandate eliminating color of a person as a basis for disqualification to attend the school of his or her choice or to work at place of employment of his or her choice. *See* Brown decision; Discrimination.

Desert. To leave or quit with an intention to cause a permanent separation; to forsake utterly; to abandon. It is essentially willful in nature.

Desertion. The act by which a person abandons and forsakes, without justification, or unauthorized, a station or condition of public, social, or family life, renouncing its responsibilities and evading its duties. A willful abandonment of an employment or duty in violation of a legal or moral obligation.

Criminal desertion is a husband's or wife's abandonment or willful failure without just cause to provide for the care, protection or support of a spouse who is in ill health or necessitous circumstances.

See also Abandonment; Desertion and non-support; Non-support.

Adoption. As used in statute providing that parental consent to adoption is not required when parent has wilfully deserted child evinces settled purpose to forego, abandon, or desert all parental duties and parental rights in child.

Constructive desertion. That arising where an existing cohabitation is put an end to by misconduct of one of the parties, provided such misconduct is itself a ground for divorce. For example, where one spouse, by his or her words, conduct, demeanor, and attitude produces an intolerable condition which forces the other spouse to withdraw from the joint habitation to a more peaceful one.

Divorce law. As a ground for divorce, an actual abandonment or breaking off of matrimonial cohabitation, by either of the parties, and a renouncing or refusal of the duties and obligations of the relation, with an intent to abandon or forsake entirely and not to return to or resume marital relations, occurring without legal justification either in the consent or the wrongful conduct of the other party. The elements of offense of "desertion" as ground for divorce are a voluntary intentional abandonment of one party by the other, without cause or justification and without consent of party abandoned. *See also Constructive desertion, above;* and Desertion and non-support.

Maritime law. The act by which a seaman deserts and abandons a ship or vessel, in which he had engaged to perform a voyage, before the expiration of his time, and without leave. By desertion, in the maritime law, is meant, not a mere unauthorized absence from the ship without leave, but an unauthorized absence from the ship, with an intention not to return to her service, or, as it is often expressed, *animo non revertendi;* that is, with an intention to desert. Desertion, within statute providing for forfeiture of wages of deserting seaman, consists of seaman's unconsented abandonment of duty by quitting ship before termination of engagement specified in articles he signed, without justification and with intention of not returning.

Military law. Any member of the armed forces who—(1) without authority goes or remains absent from his unit, organization, or place of duty with intent to remain away therefrom permanently; (2) quits his unit, organization, or place of duty with intent to avoid hazardous duty or to shirk important service; or (3) without being regularly separated from one of the armed forces enlists or accepts an appointment in the same or another one of the armed forces without fully disclosing the fact that he has not been regularly separated, or enters any foreign armed service except when authorized by the United States; is guilty of desertion. Code of Military Justice, 10 U.S.C.A. § 885.

Non-support. Desertion is frequently accompanied by non-support, which may be a crime. *See also* Desertion and non-support; Non-support.

Obstinate desertion. See Obstinate desertion.

Desertion and non-support. While both desertion and non-support go hand in hand in many cases, they are distinguishable because a man may be guilty of desertion and not guilty of non-support. The converse is also true because a man may be guilty of wilfully failing to support though he remains in the marital home. *See also* Desertion; Non-support.

Deserving. Worthy or meritorious, without regard to condition or circumstances. In no sense of the word is it limited to persons in need of assistance, or objects which come within the class of charitable uses.

Design. To form plan or scheme of, conceive and arrange in mind, originate mentally, plan out, contrive. Also, the plan or scheme conceived in mind and intended for subsequent execution; preliminary conception of idea to be carried into effect by action; contrivance in accordance with preconceived plan. A project, an idea. As a term of art, the giving of a visible form to the conceptions of the mind, or invention.

In evidence, purpose or intention, combined with plan, or implying a plan in the mind.

In patent law, the drawing or depiction of an original plan or conception for a novel pattern, model, shape, or configuration, to be used in the manufacturing or textile arts or the fine arts, and chiefly of a decorative or ornamental character. "Design patents" are contrasted with "utility patents," but equally involve the exercise of the inventive or originative faculty. Design, in the view of the patent law, is that characteristic of a physical substance which, by means of lines, images, configuration, and the like, taken as a whole, makes an impression, through the eye, upon the mind of the observer. The essence of a design resides not in the elements individually, nor in their method of arrangement, but in the total ensemble—in that indefinable whole that awakens some sensation in the observer's mind. Impressions thus imparted may be complex or simple. But whatever the impression, there is attached in the mind of the observer, to the object observed, a sense of uniqueness and character.

Designate. To indicate, select, appoint, nominate, or set apart for a purpose or duty, as to designate an officer for a command. To mark out and make known; to point out; to name; indicate. *See also* Identification.

Designating petition. Means used to designate a candidate for a party nomination at a primary election or for election to party position.

Designation. An addition to a name, as of title, profession, trade, or occupation, to distinguish the person from others. A description or descriptive expression by which a person or thing is denoted in a will without using the name. Also, an appointment or assignment, as to a particular office. The act of pointing out, distinguishing by marks of description, or calling by a distinctive title. *See also* Identification.

Designed. Contrived or taken to be employed for a particular purpose. Fit, adapted, prepared, suitable, appropriate. Intended, adapted, or designated. The term may be employed as indicating a bad purpose with evil intent.

Designedly. Sometimes equivalent to the words "wilfully," "knowingly," "unlawfully," and "feloniously."

Desire. To ask, to request. Sometimes, to empower or authorize. According to context or circumstances, the word may import a request or even a demand, but ordinarily means to wish for more or less earnestly.

This term, used in a will in relation to the management and distribution of property, has been interpreted by the courts with different shades of meaning, varying from the mere expression of a preference to a positive command. The word "desire" may be as effective as if the word "devise" or "bequeath" had been used.

See also Intent.

De son tort /də sówn tór(t)/. L. Fr. Of his own wrong. An *executor de son tort* is an executor of his own wrong. A person who assumes to act as executor of an estate without any lawful warrant or authority, but who, by his intermeddling, makes himself liable as an executor to a certain extent. If a stranger takes upon him to act as executor without any just authority, he is called in law an "executor of his own wrong," *de son tort.*

Despot. This word, in its original and most simple acceptation, signifies *master and supreme lord;* it is synonymous with monarch. A ruler with absolute power and authority, but taken in bad sense, as it is usually employed, it signifies a tyrant. In some nations, despot is the title given to the sovereign, as king is given in others.

Despotism /déspətizəm/. That abuse of government where the sovereign power is not divided, but united and unlimited in the hands of a single man, whatever may be his official title. It is not, properly, a form of government.

"Despotism" is not exactly synonymous with "autocracy," for the former involves the idea of tyranny or abuse of power, which is not necessarily implied by the latter. Every despotism is autocratic; but an autocracy is not necessarily despotic.

Destination. The purpose to which it is intended an article or a fund shall be applied. Act of appointing or setting aside for a purpose. A testator gives a destination to a legacy when he prescribes the specific use to which it shall be put. Place to which something is sent; place set for

end of journey; terminal point to which one directs his course.

Destination bill. Instead of issuing a bill of lading to the consignor at the place of shipment a carrier may at the request of the consignor procure the bill to be issued at destination or at any other place designated in the request. Upon request of anyone entitled as against the carrier to control the goods while in transit and on surrender of any outstanding bill of lading or other receipt covering such goods, the issuer may procure a substitute bill to be issued at any place designated in the request. U.C.C. § 7–305.

Destination contract. Contract between seller and buyer by which risk of loss passes to buyer upon seller's tender of goods at destination. U.C.C. § 2–509(1)(b).

Destitute. Not possessing necessaries of life; in condition of extreme want; bereft; lacking possessions and resources. *See also* Indigent.

Destitute or **necessitous circumstances.** Circumstances in which one needs the necessaries of life, which cover not only primitive physical needs, things absolutely indispensable to human existence and decency, but those things, also, which are in fact necessary to the particular person left without support.

Destroy. Term is susceptible of applications in a variety of contexts, but in general, it means to ruin completely and may include a taking. To ruin the structure, organic existence or condition of a thing; to demolish; to injure or mutilate beyond possibility of use; to nullify.

As used in policies of insurance, leases, and in maritime law, and under various statutes, this term is often applied to an act which renders the subject useless for its intended purpose, though it does not literally demolish or annihilate it.

In relation to wills, contracts, and other documents, the term "destroy" does not import the annihilation of the instrument or its resolution into other forms of matter, but a destruction of its legal efficacy, which may be by cancellation, obliterating, tearing into fragments, etc.

Destructibility. Capability of being destroyed by some action or turn of events or by operation of law. In estates, a characteristic of contingent remainders which requires them to have become vested remainders on or before the time they are to become possessory or else suffer total destruction. *See term below.*

Destructibility of contingent remainders. Doctrine dealing with future interest which may be destroyed by failure of condition. Such destructible future interest as a contingent remainder is subject to Rule Against Perpetuities unlike future interest which is destructible by act of the grantor or owner of present estate.

Destructible trust. Trust susceptible of being terminated or destroyed by happening of certain events or by operation of law.

Detachable warrant. A warrant that can be sold separately from the bond with which it was issued.

Detail, *v.* To enumerate minutely, specify, particularize.

Detail, *n.* An individual part, an item, a particular.

One who belongs to the army, but is only detached, or set apart, for the time to some particular duty or service, and who is liable at any time to be recalled to his place in the ranks.

Detain. To retain as the possession of personalty. To arrest, to check, to delay, to hinder, to hold, or keep in custody, to retard, to restrain from proceeding, to stay, to stop, to withhold. *See* Confinement; Custody.

Detainer. The act (or the juridical fact) of withholding from a person lawfully entitled the possession of land or goods, or the restraint of a man's personal liberty against his will; detention. The wrongful keeping of a person's goods is called an "unlawful detainer" although the original taking may have been lawful. *See also* Forcible detainer; Unlawful detainer.

Request filed by criminal justice agency with institution in which prisoner is incarcerated, asking institution either to hold prisoner for agency or to notify agency when release of prisoner is imminent. Under Interstate Agreement on Detainers, a "detainer" is a notification filed with institution in which prisoner is serving a sentence, advising that he is wanted to face pending criminal charges in another jurisdiction. It must be a formal notice initiated by a prosecuting or law enforcement agency within member state where criminal charges are pending that prisoner is wanted to face criminal charges and notice must be filed with institution in which prisoner is serving a sentence.

Detainment. Act of detaining. This term is used in policies of marine insurance, in the clause relating to "arrests, restraints, and detainments." The last two words are construed as equivalents, each meaning the effect of superior force operating directly on the vessel.

Detection. A discovery or laying open of that which was hidden; investigation.

Detective. One whose business it is to detect criminals or discover matters of secret and pernicious import for the protection of the public. Such may be either a private detective engaged by an individual, or a member of a police force.

Detector. Device which reveals the presence of electric waves or radioactivity or the presence of metal or indicates the presence of eavesdropping equipment ("bug"). *See also* Polygraph; Wiretapping.

Detention. The act of keeping back, restraining or withholding, either accidentally or by design, a person or thing. Detention occurs whenever police officer accosts individual and restrains his freedom to walk away, or approaches and questions individual or stops individual suspected of being personally involved in criminal activity. *See* Confinement; Detain; Detainer; Imprisonment; Preventive detention.

Detention hearing. Judicial or quasi judicial proceeding used to determine the propriety of detaining a person on bail or a juvenile in a shelter facility. *See* Preliminary hearing.

Deter. To discourage or stop by fear. To stop or prevent from acting or proceeding by danger, difficulty, or other consideration which disheartens or countervails the motive for the act.

Deterioration. With respect to a commodity, consists of a constitutional hurt or impairment, involving some degeneration in the substance of the thing, such as that arising from decay, corrosion, or disintegration. With respect to values or prices, a decline. *See also* Depreciation.

Determinable. Liable to come to an end upon the happening of a certain contingency. Susceptible of being determined, found out, definitely decided upon, or settled.

As to determinable Fee and Freehold, see those titles.

Determinate. That which is ascertained; what is particularly designated.

Determinate hospitalization. Fixed period of hospitalization pursuant to civil commitment.

Determinate obligation. *See* Obligation.

Determinate sentence. Sentence to confinement for a fixed period as specified by statute as contrasted with an indeterminate sentence, the duration of which is only partly governed by statute; the duration of the latter, in the main, being governed by behavior of prisoner. *See also* Sentence.

Determination. The decision of a court or administrative agency. It implies an ending or finality of a controversy or suit. To settle or decide by choice of alternatives or possibilities. The ending or expiration of an estate or interest in property, or of a right, power, or authority. The coming to an end in any way whatever.

A "determination" is a "final judgment" for purposes of appeal when the trial court has completed its adjudication of the rights of the parties in the action.

Also, an estimate. As respects an assessment, the term implies judgment and decision after weighing the facts.

See also Determination; Decision; Decree; Finding; Judgment; Opinion.

Determination letter. Document issued by a District Director of Internal Revenue Service, upon request of a taxpayer, giving an opinion as to the tax significance of a past or prospective transaction. Determination letters are most frequently used to clarify employee status, to determine whether a retirement or profit-sharing plan "qualifies" under the Internal Revenue Code, and to determine the tax exempt status of certain non-profit organizations.

Deterrent. Anything which impedes or has a tendency to prevent; *e.g.* punishment is a "deterrent" to crime.

Detinue /détən(y)uw/. A form of action which lies for the recovery, *in specie,* of personal chattels from one who acquired possession of them lawfully, but retains it without right, together with damages for the detention. Possessory action for recovery of personal chattels unjustly detained. *See also* Replevin.

Detour. A temporary turning aside from usual or regular route, course or procedure or from a task or employment. *See also* Deviation.

A temporary road or a longer road in temporary use because of an obstruction or state of disrepair on regularly used road.

Detriment. Any loss or harm suffered in person or property; *e.g.,* the consideration for a contract may consist not only in a payment or other thing of value given, but also in loss or "detriment" suffered by the promisee. In that connection, "detriment" means that the promisee has, in return for the promise, forborne some legal right which he otherwise would have been entitled to exercise, or that he has given up something which he had a right to keep, or done something which he had a right not to do. *See* Consideration; Legal detriment.

Detrimental reliance. Response by promisee by way of act to offer of promisor in a unilateral contract. *See also* Promissory estoppel.

Detriment to promisee. In contracts, consideration offered by promisee to promisor, especially in a unilateral contract which calls for an act from the promisee though the promisor may revoke his offer before the completion of the act. *See also* Consideration.

Devaluation. Reduction in value of a currency or of a standard monetary unit. *See also* Revaluation.

Devest. To deprive or dispossess of a title or right (*e.g.* of an estate).

Deviation. Departure from established or usual conduct or ideology. A change made in the progress of a work from the original terms or design or method agreed upon. A voluntary departure by railroad carrier, without necessity or reasonable cause, from the regular or usual route or from a stipulated or customary mode of carriage. A wandering from the way, variation from the common way, from an established rule, standard, or position.

In employment, departure of employee from his course of employment and duties to employer for purposes entirely personal. Such term comes into use and is applied in workers' compensation cases and in actions against employer by third persons for injuries caused by employee. *See also* Scope of employment.

In insurance, term refers to variance from the risks insured against, as described in the policy, without necessity or just cause, after the risk has begun. Such deviation may void the liability or responsibility of the insurer.

In shipping, a voluntary, unnecessary or unexcused departure without reasonable cause from the course of the voyage insured, or an unreasonable delay in pursuing the voyage, or the commencement of an entirely different voyage.

Deviation doctrine. In wills and trusts, principle which permits variation from terms of trust where circumstances are such that purposes of trust would otherwise be defeated. In agency, principle which permits agent to vary activity slightly from scope of master's permission.

Device. An invention or contrivance; any result of design, as in the phrase "gambling device," which means a machine or contrivance of any kind for the playing of an unlawful game of chance or hazard. A plan or project; a scheme to trick or deceive; a stratagem or artifice, as in the laws relating to fraud and cheating. Also, an emblem, pictorial representation, or distinguishing mark or sign of any kind; as in the laws prohibiting the marking of ballots used in public elections with "any device."

In patent law, a plan or contrivance, or an application, adjustment, shaping, or combination of materials or members, for the purpose of accomplishing a particular result or serving a particular use, chiefly by mechanical means and usually simple in character or not highly complex, but involving the exercise of the inventive faculty. That which is devised, or formed by design; a contrivance; an invention.

Devisable. Capable of being devised.

Devise /dəváyz/. A testamentary disposition of land or realty; a gift of real property by the last will and testament of the donor. When used as a noun, means a testamentary disposition of real or personal property and when used as a verb, means to dispose of real or personal property by will. Uniform Probate Code, § 1–201(7). *See also* Bequest; Executory devise; Legacy.

To contrive; plan; scheme; invent; prepare.

Classification

Devises are *contingent* or *vested;* that is, after the death of the testator. Contingent, when the vesting of any estate in the devisee is made to depend upon some future event, in which case, if the event never occur, or until it does occur, no estate vests under the devise. But, when the future event is referred to merely to determine the time at which the devisee shall come into the use of the estate, this does not hinder the vesting of the estate at the death of the testator. Devises are also classed as *general* or *specific*. A general devise is one which passes lands of the testator without a particular enumeration or description of them; as, a devise of "all my lands" or "all my other lands." In a more restricted sense, a general devise is one which grants a parcel of land without the addition of any words to show how great an estate is meant to be given, or without words indicating either a grant in perpetuity or a grant for a limited term; in this case it is construed as granting a life estate. Specific devises are devises of lands particularly specified in the terms of the devise, as opposed to general and residuary devises of land, in which the local or other particular descriptions are not expressed. For example, "I devise my Hendon Hall estate" is a specific devise; but "I devise all my lands," or, "all my other lands," is a *general* devise or a *residuary* devise. But all devises are (in effect) specific, even residuary devises being so. At common law, all devises of land were deemed to be "specific" whether the land was identified in the devise or passed under the residuary clause. A *conditional* devise is one which depends upon the occurrence of some uncertain event, by which it is either to take effect or be defeated. An *executory* devise of lands is such a disposition of them by will that thereby no estate vests at the death of the devisor, but only on some future contingency. It differs from a remainder in three very material points: (1) That it needs not any particular estate to support it; (2) that by it a fee-simple or other less estate may be limited after a fee-simple; (3) that by this means a remainder may be limited of a chattel interest, after a particular estate for life created in the same. In a stricter sense, a limitation by will of a future contingent interest in lands, contrary to the rules of the common law. A limitation by will of a future estate or interest in land, which cannot, consistently with the rules of law, take effect as a remainder. A future interest taking effect as a fee in derogation of a defeasible fee devised or conveyed to the first taker, when created by will, is an "executory devise," and, when created by deed, is a "condi-tional limitation," and in either event is given effect as a shifting or springing use.

The estates known as a contingent remainder and an "executory devise" are both interests or estates in land to take effect in the future and depend upon a future contingency; an "executory devise" being an interest which the rules of law do not permit to be created in conveyances, but allow in case of wills. It follows a fee estate created by a will. A contingent remainder may be created by will or other conveyance and must follow a particular or temporary estate created by the same instrument of conveyance.

Lapsed devise. A devise which fails, or takes no effect, in consequence of the death of the devisee before the testator; the subject-matter of it being considered as not disposed of by the will.

Residuary devise. A devise of all the residue of the testator's real property, that is, all that remains over and above the other devises. *See also* general definition above.

Devisee /dəvàyzíy/. The person to whom lands or other real property are devised or given by will. In the case of a devise to an existing trust or trustee, or to a trustee on trust described by will, the trust or trustee is the devisee and the beneficiaries are not devisees. Uniform Probate Code, § 1–201(8).

Residuary devisee. The person named in a will, who is to take all the real property remaining over and above the other devises.

Devisor /dəváyzər/. A giver of lands or real estate by will; the maker of a will of lands; a testator.

Devolution. The transfer or transition from one person to another of a right, liability, title, estate, or office. Transference of property from one person to another. *See also* Descent.

In ecclesiastical law, the forfeiture of a right or power (as the right of presentation to a living) in consequence of its non-user by the person holding it, or of some other act or omission on his part, and its resulting transfer to the person next entitled.

Devolve /dəvólv/. To pass or be transferred from one person to another; to fall on, or accrue to, one person as the successor of another; as a title, right, office, liability. The term is said to be peculiarly appropriate to the passing of an estate from a person dying to a person living. *See* Descent; Devolution.

Diagnosis /dàyəgnówsəs/. A medical term, meaning the discovery of the source of a patient's illness or the determination of the nature of his disease from a study of its symptoms. The art or act of recognizing the presence of disease from its symptoms, and deciding as to its character, also the decision reached, for determination of type or condition through case or specimen study or conclusion arrived at through critical perception or scrutiny. A "clinical diagnosis" is one made from a study of the symptoms only, and a "physical diagnosis" is one made by means of physical measure, such as palpation and inspection.

Diagnostic tests. Tests to determine and identify the nature of a disease; including laboratory and exploratory tests.

Dicta /díktə/. Opinions of a judge which do not embody the resolution or determination of the specific case before the court. Expressions in court's opinion which go beyond the facts before court and therefore are individual views of author of opinion and not binding in subsequent cases as legal precedent. *See also* Dictum.

Dictate. To order or instruct what is to be said or written. To pronounce, word by word, what is meant to be written by another. *See* Dictation.

Dictation. In Louisiana, this term is used in a technical sense, and means to pronounce orally what is destined to be written at the same time by another. It is used in reference to nuncupative wills. The dictation of a will refers to the substance, and not the style, and it is sufficient if the will, as written, conveys the identity of thought expressed by the testator, though not the identity of words used by him.

Dictator. One in whom supreme authority in any line is invested, one who rules autocratically, and one who prescribes for others authoritatively, and offer oppressively.

Dictum /díktəm/. A statement, remark, or observation. *Gratis dictum;* a gratuitous or voluntary representation; one which a party is not bound to make. *Simplex dictum*; a mere assertion; an assertion without proof.

The word is generally used as an abbreviated form of *obiter dictum*, "a remark by the way;" that is, an observation or remark made by a judge in pronouncing an opinion upon a cause, concerning some rule, principle, or application of law, or the solution of a question suggested by the case at bar, but not necessarily involved in the case or essential to its determination; any statement of the law enunciated by the court merely by way of illustration, argument, analogy, or suggestion. Statements and comments in an opinion concerning some rule of law or legal proposition not necessarily involved nor essential to determination of the case in hand are obiter dicta, and lack the force of an adjudication. *Dicta* are opinions of a judge which do not embody the resolution or determination of the court, and made without argument, or full consideration of the point, are not the professed deliberate determinations of the judge himself.

Dies /dáyiyz/. Lat. A day; days. Days for appearance in court. Provisions or maintenance for a day. The king's rents were anciently reserved by so many days' provisions.

Die without issue. *See* Dying without issue.

Difference. In an agreement for submission to arbitration, a disagreement or dispute. As respects contract specifications or material described therein, a state of being unlike. Disagreement in opinion, interpretation or conclusion. Instance or cause of disagreement. *See also* Disagreement.

Digest. A collection or compilation, embodying the chief matter of numerous books, articles, court decisions, etc. in one, disposed under proper heads or titles, and usually by an alphabetical arrangement, for facility in reference.

An index to reported cases, providing brief statements of court holdings or facts of cases, which is arranged by subject and subdivided by jurisdiction and courts. *See American Digest System; Special digests, below.*

As a legal term, "digest" is to be distinguished from "abridgment." The latter is a summary or epitome of the contents of a single work, in which, as a rule, the original order or sequence of parts is preserved, and in which the principal labor of the compiler is in the matter of consolidation. A digest is wider in its scope; is made up of quotations or paraphrased passages, and has its own system of classification and arrangement. An "index" merely points out the places where particular matters may be found, without purporting to give such matters *in extenso*. A "treatise" or "commentary" is not a compilation, but an original composition, though it may include quotations and excerpts.

A reference to the "Digest," or "Dig.," is often understood to designate the Digest (or Pandects) of the Justinian collection; that being the digest *par eminence*, and the authoritative compilation of the Roman law.

American Digest System. The American Digest System is a subject classification scheme whereby digests of decisions that were reported chronologically in the various units of the National Reporter System are rearranged by subject, bringing together all cases on a similar point of law. The system divides the subject of law into seven main classes. Each class is then divided into subclasses and then each sub-class into topics. There are over 400 digest topics, each of which corresponds to a legal concept. The system consists of a Century Digest (1658–1896), eight Decennial Digests (1897–1905, 1906–1915, 1916–1925, 1926–1935, 1936–1945, 1946–1955, 1956–1966, and 1966–1976), (the Ninth Decennial Digest, Part 1 (1976–1981), the Ninth Decennial Digest, Part 2 (1981–1986), and the General Digest, 7th Series

(1986 to date). The American Digest System is the master index to all reported case law. *See also* Key number system; *and* Special digests, below.

Special digests. Decisions included in the American Digest System are as well included in special digests covering the federal courts and also in regional, state, and topical digests. The "U.S. Supreme Court Digest" covers decisions of the U.S. Supreme Court. The Federal Digest (cases decided prior to 1939), Modern Federal Practice Digest (1939–1961), West's Federal Practice Digest 2d (1961–1975) and West's Federal Practice Digest 3rd and 4th (1975 to date) cover Federal court cases. Specialty federal digests include the Bankruptcy Digest, the Claims Court Digest, and West's Military Justice Digest. State court decisions from geographical areas are also published in "Regional Digests" (Atlantic, Northwestern, Pacific, Southeastern, Southern Digests; several of these are in 1st and 2d series). *Also,* individual "State Digests" are published for most states. Other specialty digests include West's Education Law Digest and Bankruptcy Digest.

Dilatory /dílət(ò)riy/. Tending or intended to cause delay or to gain time or to put off a decision.

Dilatory defense. In chancery practice, one the object of which is to dismiss, suspend, or obstruct the suit, without touching the merits, until the impediment or obstacle insisted on shall be removed. *See also* Dilatory pleas.

Dilatory exceptions. Such as do not tend to defeat the action, but only to retard its progress.

Dilatory pleas. A class of defenses at common law, founded on some matter of fact not connected with the merits of the case, but such as might exist without impeaching the right of action itself. They were either pleas to the *jurisdiction,* showing that, by reason of some matter therein stated, the case was not within the jurisdiction of the court; or pleas in *suspension,* showing some matter of temporary incapacity to proceed with the suit; or pleas in *abatement,* showing some matter for abatement or quashing the declaration. Under modern civil procedure such defenses are raised by motion or answer. *See* Plea *(plea in abatement).*

Diligence. Vigilant activity; attentiveness; or care, of which there are infinite shades, from the slightest momentary thought to the most vigilant anxiety. Attentive and persistent in doing a thing; steadily applied; active; sedulous; laborious; unremitting; untiring. The attention and care required of a person in a given situation and is the opposite of negligence.

The civil law is in perfect conformity with the common law. It lays down three degrees of diligence,—ordinary *(diligentia);* extraordinary *(exactissima diligentia);* slight *(levissima diligentia).*

There may be a high degree of diligence, a common degree of diligence, and a slight degree of diligence, with their corresponding degrees of negligence. Common or ordinary diligence is that degree of diligence which men in general exercise in respect to their own concerns; high or great diligence is of course extraordinary diligence, or that which very prudent persons take of their own concerns; and low or slight diligence is that which persons of less than common prudence, or indeed of any prudence at all, take of their own concerns.

See also Care.

Diligent. Attentive and persistent in doing a thing; steadily applied; active; sedulous; laborious; unremitting; untiring.

Diligent inquiry. Such inquiry as a diligent man, intent upon ascertaining a fact, would ordinarily make, and it is inquiry made with diligence and good faith to ascertain the truth, and must be an inquiry as full as the circumstances of the situation will permit.

Dillon's Rule. Rule used in construction of statutes delegating authority to local government: " . . . . [A] municipal corporation possesses and can exercise the following powers and no others: First, those granted in express words; second, those necessarily implied or necessarily incident to the powers expressly granted; third, those absolutely essential to the declared objects and purposes of the corporation—not simply convenient, but indispensable . . . ." Merriam v. Moody's Executors, 25 Iowa 163, 170 (1868).

Dilution. In corporate law, refers to the reduction in value of outstanding shares resulting from the issuance of additional shares. The dilution may be of voting power if shares are not issued proportionately to the holdings of existing shareholders, or it may be financial, if shares are issued disproportionately and the price at which the new shares are issued is less than the market or book value of the outstanding shares prior to the issuance of the new shares.

Dilution doctrine. A trademark doctrine protecting strong marks against use by other parties even where there is no competition or likelihood of confusion. Concept is most applicable where subsequent user used the trademark of prior user for a product so dissimilar from the product of the prior user and there is no likelihood of confusion of the products or sources, but where the use of the trademark by the subsequent user will lessen uniqueness of the prior user's mark with the possible future result that a strong mark may become a weak mark.

Diminished capacity doctrine. This doctrine recognizes that although an accused was not suffering from a mental disease or defect when the offense was committed sufficient to exonerate him from all criminal responsibility, his mental capacity may have been diminished by intoxication, trauma, or mental disease so that he did not possess the specific mental state or intent essential to the particular offense charged. *See also* Diminished responsibility doctrine.

Diminished responsibility doctrine /dəmínəsht rəspònsəbílətiy dóktrən/. Term used to refer to lack of capacity to achieve state of mind requisite for commission of crime. The concept of diminished responsibility, also known as partial insanity, permits the trier of fact to regard the impaired mental state of the defendant in mitigation of the punishment or degree of the offense even though the impairment does not qualify as insanity under the prevailing test. A number of courts have adopted the concept. In some jurisdictions, mental retardation and extremely low intelligence will, if proved, serve to reduce first degree murder to manslaughter. *See also* Insanity.

Diminution /dìmən(y)úwshən/. Incompleteness. Act or process of diminishing, taking away, or lessening. A word signifying that the record sent up from an inferior to a superior court for review is incomplete, or not fully certified.

Diminution in value. Rule of damages which provides for difference between "before" and "after" value of property which has been damaged or taken. If breach of contract results in defective or unfinished construction, and loss in value to injured party is not proved with sufficient certainty, the affected party may recover damages based on diminution in market price of property caused by breach. Restatement, Second, Contracts, § 348(2)(a). *See also* Damages (*Expectancy damages*).

Diminution of damages. *See* Mitigation of damages.

Diplomacy. The art and practice of conducting negotiations between foreign governments for the attainment of mutually satisfactory political relations. Negotiation or intercourse between nations through their representatives. The rules, customs, and privileges of representatives at foreign courts.

Diplomatic agent. In international law, a general name for all classes of persons charged with the negotiation, transaction, or superintendence of the diplomatic business of one nation with that of another. *See also* Ambassador.

Diplomatic relations. Established and formal communications and acknowledgment between one country and another in which diplomatic agents are exchanged.

Direct, *v.* To point to; guide; order; command; instruct. To advise; suggest; request.

Direct, *adj.* Immediate; proximate; by the shortest course; without circuity; operating by an immediate connection or relation, instead of operating through a medium; the opposite of *indirect.*

In the usual or natural course or line; immediately upwards or downwards; as distinguished from that which is out of the line, or on the side of it. In the usual or regular course or order, as distinguished from that which diverts, interrupts, or opposes. The opposite of cross, contrary, collateral or remote.

Without any intervening medium, agency or influence; unconditional.

Direct action. An action by insured directly against insurer rather than against tortfeasor's indemnity policy. Action by a stockholder to enforce right of action existing in him as contrasted with a derivative suit in behalf of corporation.

Direct and proximate cause. *See* Direct cause.

Direct attack. A direct attack on a judgment or decree is an attempt, for sufficient cause, to have it annulled, reversed, vacated, corrected, declared void, or enjoined, in a proceeding instituted for that specific purpose, such as an appeal, writ of error, bill of review, or injunction to restrain its execution; distinguished from a collateral attack, which is an attempt to impeach the validity or binding force of the judgment or decree as a side issue or in a proceeding instituted for some other purpose. A direct attack on a judicial proceeding is an attempt to void or correct it in some manner provided by law. *Compare* Collateral attack.

Direct cause. That which sets in motion train of events which brings about result without intervention of any force operating or working actively from new and independent source; or, as one without which the injury would not have happened. *See* Cause; Proximate cause.

Direct charge-off method. A method of accounting for bad debts whereby a deduction is permitted only when an account becomes partially or completely worthless.

Direct contempt. Such contempt consists of contumacious words or acts expressed in presence of court, while "indirect contempt" consists of similar misconduct or other disobedient acts performed outside court's presence. *See also* Contempt.

Direct costs. Costs of direct material and labor, and variable overhead incurred in producing a product.

Direct costing. An accounting method that assigns only variable manufacturing costs (direct materials, direct labor, and variable manufacturing overhead) to products; more appropriately termed variable costing. *See also* Cost.

Direct damages. *See* Damages.

Directed verdict. In a case in which the party with the burden of proof has failed to present a prima facie case for jury consideration, the trial judge may order the entry of a verdict without allowing the jury to consider it, because, as a matter of law, there can be only one such verdict. Fed.R.Civil P. 50(a). In a criminal case, in federal court, the judge may render a judgment of acquittal in favor of defendant (in place of a motion for directed verdict, which has been abolished). Fed. R.Crim.P. 29. A directed verdict may be granted either on the court's own initiative or on the motion of a party. *See also* Verdict.

Direct estoppel. Form of estoppel by judgment where issue has been actually litigated and determined in action between same parties based upon same cause of action. *See also* Collateral estoppel doctrine.

Direct evidence. Evidence in form of testimony from a witness who actually saw, heard or touched the subject of questioning. Evidence, which if believed, proves existence of fact in issue without inference or presumption. That means of proof which tends to show the existence of a fact in question, without the intervention of the proof of any other fact, and is distinguished from circumstantial evidence, which is often called "indirect." Direct evidence means evidence which in the first instance applies directly to the factum probandum, or which immediately points to a question at issue, or is evidence of the precise fact in issue and on trial by witnesses who can testify that they saw the acts done or heard the words spoken which constituted the precise fact to be proved.

Evidence that directly proves a fact, without an inference or presumption, and which in itself, if true, conclusively establishes that fact.

Compare Circumstantial evidence.

Direct examination. The first interrogation or examination of a witness, on the merits, by the party on whose behalf he is called. The first examination of a witness upon a matter that is not within the scope of a previous examination of the witness.

This is to be distinguished from an examination *in pais,* or on the *voir dire,* which is merely preliminary, and is had when the competency of the witness is challenged; from the cross-examination, which is conducted by the adverse party; and from the redirect examination which follows the cross-examination, and is had by the party who first examined the witness.

Compare Cross examination. *See also* Leading question; Redirect examination.

Direct financing. A means whereby a person obtains credit for the purchase or lease of property or services by getting a loan from a bank or other third person who is not the supplier of the property or services.

Direct injury. A wrong which directly results in the violation of a legal right and which must exist to permit a court to determine the constitutionality of an act of Congress.

Direct interest. A direct interest, such as would render the interested party incompetent to testify in regard to the matter, is an interest which is certain, and not contingent or doubtful. A matter which is dependent alone on the successful prosecution of an execution cannot be considered as uncertain, or otherwise than direct, in this sense.

Direction. The act of governing; management; superintendence.

The charge or instruction given by the court to a jury upon a point of law arising or involved in the case, to be by them applied to the facts in evidence. *See* Jury instructions.

The clause of a bill in equity containing the address of the bill to the court.

That which is imposed by directing; a guiding or authoritative instruction; order; command.

The line or course upon which anything is moving or aimed to move.

Direct labor. The gross wages of personnel who work directly on the goods being produced.

Direct line. *See* Descent.

Direct loss. One resulting immediately and proximately from the occurrence and not remotely from some of the consequences or effects thereof. *See* Loss.

Directly. In a direct way without anything intervening; not by secondary, but by direct, means.

Director. One who, or that which directs; as one who directs or regulates, guides or orders; a manager or superintendent, or a chief administrative official. *See* Directors.

Directors. Persons appointed or elected according to law, authorized to manage and direct the affairs of a corporation or company. The whole of the directors collectively form the board of directors.

Board of directors. *See* Board of directors.

Directors liability insurance. *See* Insurance.

Inside director. Director who is an employee, officer or major stockholder of corporation.

Interlocking director. Person who is a director of more than one corporation having allied interests. *See* Interlocking directors.

Outside director. Non-employee director with no, or only minimal, direct interest in corporation.

Directory, *adj.* A provision in a statute, rule of procedure, or the like, which is a mere direction or instruction of no obligatory force, and involving no invalidating consequence for its disregard, as opposed to an imperative or mandatory provision, which must be followed. The general rule is that the prescriptions of a statute relating to the performance of a public duty are so far directory that, though neglect of them may be punishable, yet it does not affect the validity of the acts done under them, as in the case of a statute requiring an officer to prepare and deliver a document to another officer on or before a certain day.

A "directory" provision in a statute is one, the observance of which is not necessary to the validity of the proceeding to which it relates; one which leaves it optional with the department or officer to which it is addressed to obey or not as he may see fit. Generally, statutory provisions which do not relate to essence of thing to be done, and as to which compliance is matter of convenience rather than substance are "directory," while provisions which relate to essence of thing to be done, that is, matters of substance, are "mandatory."

Under a general classification, statutes are either "mandatory" or "directory," and, if mandatory, they prescribe, in addition to requiring the doing of the things specified, the result that will follow if they are not done, whereas, if directory, their terms are limited to what is required to be done. A statute is mandatory when the provision of the statute is the essence of the thing required to be done; otherwise, when it relates to form and manner, and where an act is incident, or after jurisdiction acquired, it is directory merely.

Directory trust. Where, by the terms of a trust, the fund is directed to be vested in a particular manner till the period arrives at which it is to be appropriated, this is called a "directory trust." It is distinguished from a discretionary trust, in which the trustee has a discretion as to the management of the fund.

Directory, *n.* Book containing names, addresses, and occupations of inhabitants of city. Also any list or compilation, usually in book or pamphlet form, of persons, professional organizations, firms or corporations forming some class separate and distinct from others, *e.g.* telephone directory, lawyer's directory, hotel directory, etc.

Direct payment. One which is absolute and unconditional as to the time, amount, and the persons by whom and to whom it is to be made.

Direct placement. With respect to securities offerings, the negotiation by a borrower, such as an industrial or utility company, directly with the lender, such as a life insurance company or group of investors, for sale of an entire issue of securities. No underwriter is involved and the transaction is exempt from SEC filing. This is also called a *private placement* (*q.v.*)

Direct selling. Selling directly to customer rather than to distributor or dealer; or to retailer rather than to wholesaler.

Direct tax. One that is imposed directly upon property, according to its value. It is generally spoken of as a property tax or an ad valorem tax. Distinguishable from an indirect tax which is levied upon some right or privilege.

Disability. The want of legal capability to perform an act. Term is generally used to indicate an incapacity for the full enjoyment of ordinary legal rights; thus, persons under age, insane persons, and convicts are said to be under legal disability. Sometimes the term is used in a more limited sense, as when it signifies an impediment to marriage, or the restraints placed upon clergymen by reason of their spiritual avocations, or lack of legal qualifications to hold office.

As used in connection with workers' compensation acts, disability is a composite of (1) actual incapacity to perform the tasks usually encountered in one's employment and the wage loss resulting therefrom (*i.e.* impairment of earning capacity), and (2) physical impairment of the body that may or may not be incapacitating.

Statutory definition of a "disability," for social security benefits purposes, imposes three requirements: (1) that there be a medically determinable physical or mental impairment which can be expected to result in death or to be of long-continued and indefinite duration; (2) that there be an inability to engage in any substantial gainful employment; and (3) that the inability be by reason of the impairment. 42 U.S.C.A. §§ 416(i)(1), 423(d). Inability to work without some pain or discomfort does not necessarily satisfy test of disability. However, pain by itself or pain in conjunction with other injuries may be the basis for "disability" within meaning of the Social Security Act.

Absence of competent physical, intellectual, or moral powers; impairment of earning capacity; loss of physical function that reduces efficiency; inability to work.

Under Uniform Probate Code, an incapacitated person is one who is impaired by reason of physical disability.

See also Americans with Disabilities Act; Capacity; Civil disabilities; Incapacity; Incompetency; Loss of earning capacity; Permanent injury; Temporary disability; Total disability.

General Classification

Disability may be either *general* or *special;* the former when it incapacitates the person for the performance of all legal acts of a general class, or giving to them their ordinary legal effect; the latter when it debars him from one specific act.

Disability may also be either *personal* or *absolute;* the former where it attaches to the particular person, and arises out of his *status,* his previous act, or his natural or juridical incapacity; the latter where it originates with a particular person, but extends also to his descendants or successors. The term *civil* disability is used as equivalent to *legal* disability, both these expressions meaning disabilities or disqualifications created by positive law, as distinguished from *physical* disabilities. A *physical* disability is a disability or incapacity caused by physical defect or infirmity, or bodily imperfection, or mental weakness or alienation; as distinguished from *civil* disability, which relates to the civil *status* or condition of the person, and is imposed by the law.

Partial disability. Under workers' compensation law, incapacity in part from returning to work performed before accident. Such exists if employee is unable to perform duties in which he was customarily engaged when injured or duties of same or similar character, nature, or description, but is able to engage in gainful activity at some job for which he is fitted by education, training or experience.

Permanent disability. Incapacity forever from returning to work formerly performed before accident, though this incapacity may be either total or partial. *See also* Permanent disability.

Temporary disability. Temporary, as distinguished from permanent, disability is a condition that exists until the injured employee is as far restored as the permanent character of the injuries will permit.

Total disability. Total disability to follow insured's usual occupation arises where person is incapacitated from performing any substantial part of his ordinary duties, though still able to perform a few minor duties and be present at his place of business. "Total disability" within an accident policy does not mean absolute physical disability to transact any business pertaining to insured's occupation, but disability from performing substantial and material duties connected with it. The term may also apply to any impairment of mind or body rendering it impossible for insured to follow continuously a substantially gainful occupation without seriously impairing his health, the disability being permanent when of such nature as to render it reasonably certain to continue throughout the lifetime of insured. *See also* Permanent disability; Wholly disabled.

Disability clause. Provision in insurance policy calling for waiver of premiums during period of disability.

Disability compensation. Payments from public or private funds to one during period of disability and incapacity from work; *e.g.* social security or workers' compensation disability benefits.

Disability insurance. Insurance coverage purchased to protect insured financially during periods of incapacity from working. Often purchased by professionals.

Disability retirement. Plan of retirement which is invoked when person covered is disabled from working to normal retirement age or increased benefits when person retires because of disability.

Disable. Ordinarily, to take away the ability of, to render incapable of proper and effective action. *See* Civil death; Disability.

Disabled person. Person who lacks legal capacity to act *sui juris* or one who is physically or mentally disabled from acting in his own behalf or from pursuing occupation. *See* Civil death; Disability.

Disabling restraints. Restraints on alienation of property which are normally void as against public policy.

Disaffirm. To repudiate; to revoke a consent once given; to recall an affirmance. To refuse one's subsequent sanction to a former act; to disclaim the intention of being bound by an antecedent transaction.

Disaffirmance. The repudiation of a former transaction. The refusal by one who has the legal power to refuse (as in the case of a voidable contract), to abide by his former acts, or accept the legal consequences of them. It may either be "express" (in words) or "implied" from acts inconsistent with a recognition of validity of former transaction.

Disagreement. Difference of opinion or want of uniformity or concurrence of views; as, a disagreement among the members of a jury, among the judges of a court, or between arbitrators.

The refusal by a grantee, lessee, etc., to accept an estate, lease, etc., made to him. The annulling of a thing that had essence before. No estate can be vested in a person against his will. Consequently, no one can become a grantee, etc., without his *agreement.* The law implies such an agreement until the contrary is shown, but his disagreement renders the grant, etc., inoperative.

Disallow. To refuse to allow, to deny the need or validity of, to disown or reject.

Disaster. For common disaster, *see* Common.

Disaster loss. If a casualty is sustained in an area designated as a disaster area by the President of the U.S., the casualty is designated a disaster loss. In such an event, the disaster loss may be treated as having occurred in the taxable year immediately preceding the taxable year in which the disaster actually occurred. Thus, immediate tax benefits are provided to victims of a disaster. *See* Casualty loss.

Disavow /dìsəváw/. To repudiate the unauthorized acts of an agent; to deny the authority by which he assumed to act.

Disbarment. Act of court in suspending attorney's license to practice law. A disbarment proceeding is neither civil nor criminal action; it is special proceeding peculiar to itself, disciplinary in nature, and of summary character resulting from inherent power of courts over their officers. *See also* Debarment.

Disbursement /disbə́rsmənt/. To pay out, commonly from a fund. To make payment in settlement of a debt or account payable.

D.I.S.C. Domestic International Sales Corporation (*q.v.*).

Discharge. To release; liberate; annul; unburden; disincumber; dismiss. To extinguish an obligation (*e.g.* a person's liability on an instrument); terminate employment of person; release, as from prison, confinement or military service.

Discharge is a generic term; its principal species are rescission, release, accord and satisfaction, performance, judgment, composition, bankruptcy, merger.

In contract law, discharge occurs either when the parties have performed their obligations in the contract, or when events, the conduct of the parties, or the operation of law releases the parties from performing.

As applied to demands, claims, rights of action, incumbrances, etc., to discharge the debt or claim is to extinguish it, to annul its obligatory force, to satisfy it. And here also the term is generic; thus a debt, a mortgage, a legacy, may be discharged by payment or performance, or by any act short of that, lawful in itself, which the creditor accepts as sufficient. U.C.C. § 3–601 et seq. governs discharge of commercial instruments. To discharge a person is to liberate him from the binding force of an obligation, debt, or claim.

See also Performance; Release.

Bankruptcy. The release of a debtor from all of his debts which are provable in bankruptcy, except such as are excepted by the Bankruptcy Code. The discharge of the debtor is the step which regularly follows the filing of a petition in bankruptcy and the administration of his estate. By it the debtor is released from the obligation of all his debts which were or might be proved in the proceedings, so that they are no longer a charge upon him, and so that he may thereafter engage in business and acquire property without its being liable for the satisfaction of such former debts. Bankruptcy Code §§ 523, 524. *See also* Bankruptcy proceedings.

Constructive discharge. That which occurs when an employer deliberately makes an employee's working conditions so intolerable that the employee is forced into involuntary resignation.

Contract. To cancel the obligation of a contract; to make an agreement or contract null and inoperative. As a noun, the word means the act or instrument by which the binding force of a contract is terminated, irrespective of whether the contract is carried out to the full extent contemplated (in which case the discharge is the result of *performance*) or is broken off before complete execution.

Criminal law. The act by which a person in confinement, held on an accusation of some crime or misdemeanor, is set at liberty.

Employment. To dismiss from employment; to terminate the employment of a person.

Equity practice. In the process of accounting before a master in chancery, the *discharge* is a statement of expenses and counter-claims brought in and filed, by way of set-off, by the accounting defendant; which follows the *charge* in order.

Jury. To discharge a jury is to relieve them from any further consideration of a cause. This is done when the continuance of the trial is, by any cause, rendered impossible; also when the jury, after deliberation, has rendered a verdict or cannot agree on a verdict.

Military discharge. The release or dismissal of a soldier, sailor, or marine, from further military service, either at the expiration of his term of enlistment, or previous thereto on special application therefor, or as a punishment. An "honorable" discharge is one granted at the end of an enlistment and accompanied by an official certificate of good conduct during the service. A "dishonorable" discharge is a dismissal from the service for bad conduct or as a punishment imposed by sentence of a court-martial for offenses against the military law. There is also in occasional use a form of "discharge without honor," which implies censure, but is not in itself a punishment.

Mortgage. Formal document which recites that a mortgage debt has been satisfied and which is generally recorded in Registry of Deeds (or comparable recording body) or in other appropriate place for recording deeds to real estate.

Dischargeable claim. In bankruptcy, a claim which is barred by bankrupt's discharge if properly scheduled. See Bankruptcy Code § 727.

Disciplinary proceedings. Proceedings which are brought against attorney to secure his or her censure, suspension or disbarment for various acts of unprofessional conduct. Most states have procedural rules governing such proceedings including Disciplinary Rules for attorneys. *See* Code of Professional Responsibility; Disbarment; Disciplinary rules.

Disciplinary rules. Name of the Disciplinary Rules of the ABA Model Code of Professional Responsibility. They stated "the minimum level of conduct below which no lawyer can fall without being subject to disciplinary action." These rules have been superseded by the ABA. Model Rules of Professional Conduct.

Discipline. Instruction, comprehending the communication of knowledge and training to observe and act in accordance with rules and orders.

Correction, chastisement, punishment, penalty. To bring order upon or bring under control.

Disclaimer. The repudiation or renunciation of a claim or power vested in a person or which he had formerly alleged to be his. The refusal, or rejection of an estate or right offered to a person. The disavowal, denial, or renunciation of an interest, right, or property imputed to a person or alleged to be his. Also the declaration, or the instrument, by which such disclaimer is published.

The rejection, refusal, or renunciation of a claim, power, or property. I.R.C. § 2518 sets forth the conditions required to avoid gift tax consequences as the result of a disclaimer.

See also Refusal; Renunciation; Repudiation.

Estates. The act by which a party refuses to accept an estate which has been conveyed to him.

Patents. When the title and specifications of a patent do not agree, or when part of that which it covers is not strictly patentable, because neither new nor useful, the patentee is empowered, with leave of the court, to enter a disclaimer of any part of either the title or the specification, and the disclaimer is then deemed to be part of the letters patent or specification, so as to render them valid for the future.

Pleading. In common law pleading, a renunciation by the defendant of all claim to the subject of the demand made by the plaintiff's bill. *See also* Denial.

Qualified disclaimer. A refusal by a person to accept an interest in property. A qualified disclaimer must be in writing and must be received by the transferor not later than 9 months from the time the interest is created. Once the property is accepted and enjoyed by the individual, the property can not be disclaimed.

Warranty. Words or conduct which tend to negate or limit warranty in sale of goods and which in certain instances must be conspicuous and refer to specific warranty to be excluded. U.C.C. § 2–316.

"Disclaimer of warranties" is means of controlling liability of seller by reducing number of situations in which seller can be in breach of contract terms. *See also* Warranty.

Disclaimer clause. Device used to control seller's liability by reducing number of situations in which seller can be in breach of warranty. *See e.g.* Warranty (*Limited warranty*).

Disclose. To bring into view by uncovering; to expose; to make known; to lay bare; to reveal to knowledge; to free from secrecy or ignorance, or make known. *See* Discovery.

Disclosure. Act of disclosing. Revelation; the impartation of that which is secret or not fully understood.

In patent law, the specification; the statement of the subject-matter of the invention, or the manner in which it operates.

In securities law, the revealing of certain financial and other information believed relevant to investors considering buying securities in some venture; the requirement that sufficient information be provided prospective investors so that they can make an intelligent evaluation of a security. *See* Disclosure principle; Prospectus.

Under Truth in Lending Act "disclosure" is a term of art which refers to the manner in which certain information (*e.g., total* cost of loan), deemed basic to an intelligent assessment of a credit transaction, shall be conveyed to the consumer. 15 U.S.C.A. § 1601 et seq. *See* Disclosure statement.

See Compulsory disclosure; Discovery; Freedom of Information Act; Full disclosure; Subpoena.

Disclosure by parties. Term sometimes used in law of deceit or fraud as to the obligation of parties to reveal fact which is material if its revelation is necessary because of the position of the parties to each other. *See also* Material fact.

Disclosure principle. A principle holding that an entity must provide a complete reporting of all facts important enough to influence the judgment of an informed user of financial information. *See also* Prospectus.

Disclosure statement. The Federal Truth in Lending Act requires that the finance charge, annual percentage rate, number and amount of periodic payments, and other credit terms, be fully disclosed in consumer loan agreements. This is commonly done by means of a disclosure statement which accompanies or is made a part of the agreement. *See also* Truth-in-Lending Act.

Discontinuance /diskəntínyuwəns/. Ending, causing to cease, ceasing to use, giving up, leaving off. Refers to the termination or abandonment of a project, structure, highway, or the like.

The cessation of the proceedings in an action where the plaintiff voluntarily puts an end to it, either by giving notice in writing to the defendant before any step has been taken in the action subsequent to the answer, or at any other time by order of the court of a judge. A non-suit; dismissal. Under Rules practice, "dismissal" is appropriate term for discontinuance; may be voluntary or involuntary and may effect counterclaim, cross claim or third party claim. Costs may be assessed. Fed.R. Civil P. 41. *See* Dismissal.

In common law pleading, that technical interruption of the proceedings in an action which follows where a defendant does not answer the whole of the plaintiff's declaration, and the plaintiff omits to take judgment for the part unanswered.

Discontinuance of an estate. The termination or suspension of an estate-tail, in consequence of the act of the tenant in tail, in conveying a larger estate in the land than he was by law entitled to do.

Discontinued operations. A segment of a business that is sold, abandoned, or otherwise disposed of. *See also* Liquidation.

Discount. In a general sense, an allowance or deduction made from a gross sum on any account whatever. In a more limited and technical sense, the taking of interest in advance.

A deduction from an original price or debt, allowed for paying promptly or in cash. Method of selling securities (*e.g.*, treasury bills) which are issued below face value and redeemed at face value. Difference between a bond's current market price and its face value. Reduction in normal selling price of goods.

The low initial interest rate lenders offer on adjustable-rate mortgages. It usually applies for one or two years. After the discount period ends, the rate usually increases, depending on the index used to determine the interest rate.

To purchase an instrument or other right to the payment of money, usually for an amount less than the face amount or value of the right.

A discount by a bank means a drawback or deduction made upon its advances or loans of money, upon negotiable paper or other evidences of debt payable at a future day, which are transferred to the bank. Although the discounting of notes or bills, in its most comprehensive sense, may mean lending money and taking notes in payment, yet, in its more ordinary sense, the discounting of such means advancing a consideration for a bill or note, deducting or discounting the interest which will accrue for the time the note has to run. Discounting by a bank means lending money upon a note, and deducting the interest or premium in advance. That step in lending transaction where interest on loan is taken in advance by deducting amount therefor for term of loan, giving borrower face value of obligation less interest.

See also Rebate; Rediscount; Rediscount rate.

Black's Law Dictionary Abridged 6th Ed.—8

Quantity discount. Allowed manufacturers or wholesalers for purchases in large amounts. Robinson Patman Act requires that such be justified by savings of seller.

Trade discount. Price reduction to different classes of customers; *e.g.* discount given by lumber dealers to builders and contractors.

Discount amortization. The process of reducing a discount on notes payable (or bonds payable) by recognizing interest expense. Also refers to the process of reducing a discount on bond investments by recognizing interest revenue.

Discount bond. A bond sold for less than face or maturity value. No interest is paid annually, but all interest accrues to the maturity date when it is paid.

Discount broker. A bill broker; one who discounts bills of exchange and promissory notes, and advances money on securities. A securities broker that executes buy and sell orders at rates lower than full service brokers.

Discounting. The process of taking a future amount and bringing it back to its value today. *See also* Discount.

Discount loan. A loan in which the bank deducts the interest in advance at the time the loan is made.

Discounting notes receivable. A means of generating cash by presenting notes receivable to a bank before the maturity date and receiving the maturity value minus a discount (interest) assessed by the bank.

Discount on capital stock. The difference between the par (or stated) value of stock and the issue price, when issuance occurs below par or stated value.

Discount market. Segment of the money market in which banks and other financial institutions trade commercial paper.

Discount period. The period during which the discount stated in an invoice can be claimed.

Discount rate. Percentage of the face amount of commercial paper which a holder pays when he transfers such paper to a financial institution for cash or credit. Rate charged for discounting loan. *See* Discount; Rediscount rate.

The rate of interest used in the process of finding present values (discounting).

The discount rate is the rate charged Federal Reserve System member banks for borrowing from the country's district Federal Reserve banks. The rate, which is set by the Federal Reserve Board, controls the supply of money available to banks for lending and provides a floor for interest rates.

Discount shares. Shares of stock issued as fully paid and nonassessable for less than the full lawful consideration. Par value shares issued for cash less than par value. Discount shares are considered a species of watered shares and may impose a liability on the recipient equal to the difference between the par value and the cash for which such shares were issued.

Discount stock. *See* Discount shares.

Discount yield. Yield on a security sold at a discount.

Discover. To uncover that which was hidden, concealed, or unknown from every one. To get first sight or knowledge of; to get knowledge of what has existed but has not theretofore been known to the discoverer. Under U.C.C., refers to knowledge rather than reason to know. U.C.C. § 1–201(25). *See also* Discovery; Notice.

Discovered peril doctrine. The doctrine of discovered peril (or "last clear chance") is regarded as a limitation of, or an exception to, the general rule of contributory negligence precluding a plaintiff's recovery. It is founded on considerations of public policy, deduced from humanitarian principles, which impose a moral duty upon everyone to avoid injuring another unnecessarily. The three essential elements which comprise the doctrine of discovered peril are: (1) the exposed condition brought about by the negligence of the plaintiff, (2) the actual discovery by defendant or his agents of plaintiff's perilous situation in time to have averted the injury by use of all means at their command commensurate with their own safety, and (3) failure thereafter to use such means. The party raising the issue of discovered peril must also prove that the opposing party's negligent conduct was a proximate cause of the injuries he sustained. *See also* Last clear chance doctrine.

Discovery. In a general sense, the ascertainment of that which was previously unknown; the disclosure or coming to light of what was previously hidden; the acquisition of notice or knowledge of given acts or facts; as, in regard to the "discovery" of fraud affecting the running of the statute of limitations, or the granting of a new trial for newly "discovered" evidence.

International law. As the foundation for a claim of national ownership or sovereignty, discovery is the finding of a country, continent, or island previously unknown, or previously known only to its uncivilized inhabitants.

Mining claim. See Mining location.

Patent law. The finding out some substance, mechanical device, improvement, or application, not previously known. It is something less than invention, and may be the result of industry, application, or be perhaps merely fortuitous.

Trial practice. The pre-trial devices that can be used by one party to obtain facts and information about the case from the other party in order to assist the party's preparation for trial. Under Federal Rules of Civil Procedure (and in states which have adopted rules patterned on such), tools of discovery include: depositions upon oral and written questions, written interrogatories, production of documents or things, permission to enter upon land or other property, physical and mental examinations and requests for admission. Rules 26–37. Term generally refers to disclosure by defendant of facts, deeds, documents or other things which are in his exclusive knowledge or possession and which are necessary to party seeking discovery as a part of a cause of action pending, or to be brought in another court, or as evidence of his rights or title in such proceeding.

In *criminal* proceedings, "discovery" emphasizes right of defense to obtain access to evidence necessary to prepare its own case. Discovery and inspection in federal criminal cases is governed by Fed.R.Crim.P. 16 and 26.2; most states having similar court rule or statutory discovery provisions.

See also Deposition; Fishing trip or expedition; Good cause; Inspection; Interrogatories; Jencks Act or Rule; Perpetuating testimony; Work product rule.

Discovery, bill of. In equity pleading, a bill for the discovery of facts resting in the knowledge of the defendant, or of deeds or writings, or other things in his custody or power; but seeking no relief in consequence of the discovery, though it may pray for a stay of proceedings at law until the discovery is made.

Discovery rule. Under the "discovery rule," limitation statute in malpractice cases does not start to run, *i.e.*, the cause of action does not accrue, until the date of discovery of the malpractice, or the date when, by the exercise of reasonable care and diligence, the patient should have discovered the wrongful act.

Discredit. To destroy or impair the credibility of a person; to impeach; to lessen the degree of credit to be accorded to a witness or document, as by impugning the veracity of the one or the genuineness of the other; to disparage or weaken the reliance upon the testimony of a witness, or upon documentary evidence, by any means whatever. *See* Impeachment.

Discreetly. Prudently; judiciously; with discernment.

Discrepancy. A difference between two things which ought to be identical, as between one writing and another; a variance *(q.v.)*. Also discord, discordance, dissonance, dissidence, unconformity, disagreement, difference.

Discretely. Separately; disjunctively.

Discretion. When applied to public functionaries, discretion means a power or right conferred upon them by law of acting officially in certain circumstances, according to the dictates of their own judgment and conscience, uncontrolled by the judgment or conscience of others. As applied to public officers connotes action taken in light of reason as applied to all facts and with view to rights of all parties to action while having regard for what is right and equitable under all circumstances and law.

In criminal law and the law of torts, it means the capacity to distinguish between what is right and wrong, lawful or unlawful, wise or foolish, sufficiently to render one amenable and responsible for his acts.

Wise conduct and management; cautious discernment, especially as to matters of propriety and self-control; prudence; circumspection; wariness.

See Discretionary acts.

Abuse of discretion. See Abuse (Discretion).

Judicial and legal discretion. These terms are applied to the discretionary action of a judge or court, and mean discretion bounded by the rules and principles of law, and not arbitrary, capricious, or unrestrained. It is not the indulgence of a judicial whim, but the exercise of judicial judgment, based on facts and guided by law, or the equitable decision of what is just and proper under the circumstances. It is a legal discretion to be exercised in discerning the course prescribed by law and is not to give effect to the will of the judge, but to that of the law. The exercise of discretion where there are two alternative provisions of law applicable, under either of which court could proceed. A liberty or privilege to decide and act in accordance with what is fair and equitable under the peculiar circumstances of the particular case, guided by the spirit and principles of the law, and exercise of such discretion is reviewable only for an abuse thereof. For "abuse of discretion", *see* Abuse.

Discretionary account. An account in which customer gives broker discretion, as to purchase and sales of securities or commodities, including selection, timing, and price to be paid or received.

Discretionary acts. Those acts wherein there is no hard and fast rule as to course of conduct that one must or must not take and, if there is clearly defined rule, such would eliminate discretion. Option open to judges and administrators to act or not as they deem proper or necessary and such acts or refusal to act may not be overturned without a showing of abuse of discretion, which

means an act or failure to act that no conscientious person acting reasonably could perform or refuse to perform. One which requires exercise in judgment and choice and involves what is just and proper under the circumstances. *Compare* Ministerial act. *See also* Discretion.

Discretionary fixed cost. A fixed cost that originates from top management's yearly appropriation decisions—for example, advertising expense and research and development expense. *See also* Fixed charges.

Discretionary function. *See* Discretionary acts.

Discretionary power. One which is not imperative or, if imperative, the time, manner, or extent of execution of which is left to donee's discretion. The power to do or to refrain from doing a certain thing.

Discretionary review. Form of appellate review which is not a matter of right but rather occurs only at the discretion of the appellate court; *e.g.* appeal to U.S. Supreme Court. *See* Certiorari.

Discretionary trusts. Such as are not marked out on fixed lines, but allow a certain amount of discretion in their exercise. Those which cannot be duly administered without the application of a certain degree of prudence and judgment. Trusts where the trustee or another party has the right to accumulate (rather than pay out) the income for each year. Depending on the terms of the trust instrument, such income may be accumulated for future distributions to the income beneficiaries or added to corpus for the benefit of the remainderman. *See also* Trust.

Discrimination. In constitutional law, the effect of a statute or established practice which confers particular privileges on a class arbitrarily selected from a large number of persons, all of whom stand in the same relation to the privileges granted and between whom and those not favored no reasonable distinction can be found. Unfair treatment or denial of normal privileges to persons because of their race, age, sex, nationality or religion. A failure to treat all persons equally where no reasonable distinction can be found between those favored and those not favored.

Federal statutes prohibit discrimination in employment on basis of sex, age, race, nationality, religion, or being handicapped; *e.g.* Title VII of 1964 Civil Rights Act, Age Discrimination in Employment Act, Equal Pay Act, Sex Discrimination in Employment Based on Pregnancy Act. Other federal acts, as supplemented by court decisions, prohibit discrimination in voting rights, housing, extension of credit, public education, and access to public facilities.

With reference to common carriers, a breach of the carrier's duty to treat all shippers alike, and afford them equal opportunities to market their product. A carrier's failure to treat all alike under substantially similar conditions.

See also Age Discrimination Act; Bias; Disparate treatment; Equal protection clause; Equal protection of the law; Invidious discrimination; Price discrimination; Protected class; Redlining; Reverse discrimination.

Disentailment. Act of barring the entail created by fee tail conveyance and consisting of a deed absolute in fee simple by the tenant in tail. In this case the grantee took the fee simple and the entail or right of the first born of the tenant in tail took nothing on the death of the tenant in tail.

Disfranchise. To deprive of the rights and privileges of a free citizen; to deprive of chartered rights and immunities; to deprive of any franchise, as of the right of voting in elections, etc. In any election where the party system furnishes the means by which the citizen's right of suffrage is made effective, denial of his party's right to participate in the election accomplishes the "disfranchisement of voters" or compels them, if they vote, to vote for representatives of political parties other than that to which they belong, and the deprivation of the right of selection is a deprivation of the right of franchise.

Disfranchisement. The act of disfranchising. The act of depriving a member of a corporation of his right as such, by expulsion. It differs from amotion *(q.v.)* which is applicable to the removal of an officer from office, leaving him his rights as a member.

In a more popular sense, the taking away of the elective franchise (that is, the right of voting in public elections) from any citizen or class of citizens.

Dishonesty. Disposition to lie, cheat, deceive, or defraud; untrustworthiness; lack of integrity. Lack of honesty, probity or integrity in principle; lack of fairness and straightforwardness; disposition to defraud, deceive or betray.

Dishonor. To refuse to accept or pay a draft or to pay a promissory note when duly presented. An instrument is dishonored when a necessary or optional presentment is duly made and due acceptance or payment is refused, or cannot be obtained within the prescribed time, or in case of bank collections, the instrument is seasonably returned by the midnight deadline; or presentment is excused and the instrument is not duly accepted or paid. U.C.C. § 3–507(1); § 4–210. Includes the insurer of a letter of credit refusing to pay or accept a draft or demand for payment. For bank's liability for wrongful dishonor, see U.C.C. § 4–402. *See also* Notice of dishonor; Protest.

As respects the flag, to deface or defile, imputing a lively sense of shaming or an equivalent acquiescent callousness. *See* Flag desecration.

Disinheritance /disinhéhrətəns/. The act by which the owner of an estate deprives a person, who would otherwise be his heir, of the right to inherit it.

Disinterested witness. One who has no interest in the cause or matter in issue, and who is lawfully competent to testify. An impartial witness.

Disintermediation. When free market interest rates exceed the regulated interest ceiling for time deposits, some depositors withdraw their funds and invest them elsewhere at a higher interest rate (*e.g.* in U.S. Treasury bills). This process is known as "disintermediation."

Disjunctive allegation. A statement in a pleading or indictment which expresses or charges a thing alternatively, with the conjunction "or"; for instance, an averment that defendant "murdered or caused to be murdered", etc., would be of this character.

Disjunctive allegations of indictment are those which charge that defendant did one thing or another, and whenever the word "or" would leave averment uncertain as to which of two or more things is meant, it is inadmissible.

In civil actions, relief in the alternative or of several different types may be demanded. Fed.R. Civ.P. 8(a). *See* Alternative pleading.

Dismiss. To send away; to discharge; to discontinue; to dispose of; to cause to be removed temporarily or permanently; to relieve from duty. To dismiss an action or suit without any further consideration or hearing. *See also* Discharge.

Dismissal. An order or judgment finally disposing of an action, suit, motion, etc., without trial of the issues involved. Such may be either voluntary or involuntary. Fed.R. Civil P. 41.

A release or discharge from employment.

Involuntary dismissal. Under rules practice, may be accomplished on court's own motion for lack of prosecution or on motion of defendant for lack of prosecution or failure to introduce evidence of facts on which relief may be granted. Fed.R. Civil P. 41(b).

Voluntary dismissal. Under rules practice, may be accomplished by plaintiff without leave of court if filed before answer or by stipulation signed by all parties after answer is filed. Fed.R. Civil P. 41(a).

Dismissal and nonsuit. Termination of case because of plaintiff's failure to prosecute or plaintiff's desire to discontinue.

Dismissal compensation. The payment of a specific sum, made by employer to employee for permanently terminating employment. Also called severance or separation pay.

Dismissal for cause. *See* For cause.

Dismissal without prejudice. Term meaning dismissal of action without prejudice to the right of the complainant to sue again on the same cause of action. The effect of the words "without prejudice" is to prevent the decree of dismissal from operating as a bar to a subsequent suit.

Dismissal with prejudice. Term meaning an adjudication on the merits, and final disposition, barring the right to bring or maintain an action on the same claim or cause. It is res judicata as to every matter litigated.

Dismissed for want of equity. A phrase used to indicate a decision on the merits, as distinguished from one based upon some formal defect. The dismissal may be because the averments of complainant's bill have been found untrue in fact, or because they are insufficient to entitle complainant to the relief sought.

Dismortgage /dìsmórgəj/. To redeem from mortgage. *See* Redemption.

Disobedience. *See* Civil disobedience; Civil disorder.

Disobedient child. Child who may be adjudicated delinquent in some jurisdictions under law governing stubborn children. May be subject of petition as child in need of social services. Child who wilfully refuses to honor requests of parents or legal guardian or other person in whose custody he is. *See also* Delinquent child.

Disorder. Turbulent or riotous behavior; immoral or indecent conduct. The breach of the public decorum and morality. *See also* Breach of the peace; Civil disobedience; Civil disorder; Riot; Unlawful assembly.

A slight, partial, and temporary physical ailment. *See* Disability.

Disorderly. Contrary to the rules of good order and behavior; violative of the public peace or good order; turbulent, riotous, or indecent.

Disorderly conduct. A term of loose and indefinite meaning (except when defined by statutes), but signifying generally any behavior that is contrary to law, and more particularly such as tends to disturb the public peace or decorum, scandalize the community, or shock the public sense of morality. An offense against public morals, peace or safety. Disorderly conduct statutes must sufficiently specify the prohibited conduct or they may be held to be unconstitutional.

A person is guilty of disorderly conduct if, with purpose to cause public inconvenience, annoyance or alarm, or recklessly creating a risk thereof, he: (a) engages in fighting or threatening, or in violent or tumultuous behavior; or (b) makes unreasonable noise or offensively coarse utterance, gesture or display, or addresses abusive language to any person present; or (c) creates a hazardous or physically offensive condition by any act which serves no legitimate purpose of the actor. Model Penal Code, § 250.2.

See also Breach of the peace.

Disorderly house. House or place where residents or inhabitants behave in such a manner as to become a nuisance to the neighborhood. One where acts are performed which tend to corrupt morals of community or promote breaches of peace. It has a wide meaning, and includes bawdy houses, gambling houses, houses of prostitution and places of a like character. At common law, it was misdemeanor to keep such house. Under current laws, such activity, generally, would constitute a breach of the peace or disorderly conduct. The *specific* acts (*e.g.* prostitution) might also be crimes.

Disorderly persons. Such as are dangerous or hurtful to the public peace and welfare by reason of their misconduct or vicious habits, and are therefore amenable to police regulation. The phrase is chiefly used in statutes, and the scope of the term depends on local regulations. One who violates peace and good order of society.

Disorderly picketing. *See* Unlawful picketing.

Disparage /dəspǽrəj/. To connect unequally; to match unsuitably. To discredit one's person or property.

Disparagement /dəspǽrəjmənt/. Matter which is intended by its publisher to be understood or which is reasonably understood to cast doubt upon the existence or extent of another's property in land, chattels or intangible things, or upon their quality.

A falsehood that tends to denigrate the goods or services of another party is actionable in a common law suit for disparagement. The same conduct is also actionable under certain state statutes and can form the basis for an F.T.C. complaint. There is no private federal cause of action for disparagement under the Lanham Act.

Disparagement of goods. A statement about a competitor's goods which is untrue or misleading and is made to influence or tends to influence the public not to buy. *See* Disparagement.

Disparagement of title. Actionably tortious detraction from title for which person may be required to respond in damages. Injurious falsehood in which aspersion is cast on person's title to property. Publication made without privilege or justification of matter that is untrue and disparaging to another's property in land, chattels or intangible things under such circumstances as would lead reasonable man to foresee that conduct of third person as purchaser or lessee thereof might be determined thereby and results in pecuniary loss from impairment of vendability thus caused.

Disparaging instructions. Jury charge which tends to detract or defame person or party to litigation.

Disparate treatment. Differential treatment of employees or applicants on the basis of their race, color, religion, sex, national origin, handicap, or veteran's status.

Disparity. Marked difference in quantity or quality between two things or among many things.

Dispatch. A sending off, completion or settlement with speed.

In maritime law, diligence, due activity, or proper speed in the discharge of a cargo; the opposite of delay. *Customary dispatch* is such as accords with the rules, customs, and usages of the port where the discharge is made. *Dispatch money* is in the nature of a reward to charterer of ship for loading or unloading in shorter time than provided for or than stipulated as "lay days". *Quick dispatch* is speedy discharge of cargo without allowance for the customs or rules of the port or for delay from the crowded state of the harbor or wharf.

Dispauper /dispópər/. When a person, by reason of his poverty, is admitted to sue *in formâ pauperis,* and afterwards, before the suit be ended, acquires any lands, or personal estate, or is guilty of anything whereby he is liable to have this privilege taken from him, then he loses the right to sue *in formâ pauperis,* and is said to be dispaupered.

Dispensation. An exemption from some laws; a permission to do something forbidden; an allowance to omit something commanded; the canonistic name for a license. A relaxation of law for the benefit or advantage of an individual. In the United States, no power exists, except in the legislature, to dispense with law; and then it is not so much a dispensation as a change of the law. *See also* Exemption.

Display. An opening or unfolding, exhibition, manifestation, ostentatious show, exhibition for effect, parade.

In copyright law, to "display" a work means to show a copy of it, either directly or by means of a film, slide, television image, or any other device or process or, in the case of a motion picture or other audiovisual work, to show individual images non-sequentially. Copyright Act, 17 U.S.C.A. § 101.

Disportionate. Not pro rata or ratable.

Disposable earnings. That portion of person's income which he is free to spend or invest as he sees fit after payment of taxes and other obligations.

Disposal. Sale, pledge, giving away, use, consumption or any other disposition of a thing. To exercise control over; to direct or assign for a use; to pass over into the control of someone else; to alienate, bestow, or part with.

Dispose of. To alienate or direct the ownership of property, as disposition by will. Used also of the determination of suits. To exercise finally, in any manner, one's power of control over; to pass into the control of someone else; to alienate, relinquish, part with, or get rid of; to put out of the way; to finish with; to bargain away. Often used in restricted sense of "sale" only, or so restricted by context.

Disposing capacity or **mind.** These are alternative or synonymous phrases in the law of wills for "sound mind," and "testamentary capacity" *(q.v.).*

Disposition. Act of disposing; transferring to the care or possession of another. The parting with, alienation of, or giving up property. *See* Bequeath; Testamentary *(Testamentary disposition).*

The final settlement of a matter, and with reference to decisions announced by court, judge's ruling is commonly referred to as disposition, regardless of level of resolution.

In criminal procedure, the sentencing or other final settlement of a criminal case.

With respect to a mental state, means an attitude, prevailing tendency, or inclination.

Disposition hearing. Judicial proceeding in which a criminal defendant is sentenced or otherwise disposed of. *See* Sentencing.

Disposition without trial. The sentencing or other treatment of a criminal defendant who has pleaded guilty or admitted to sufficient facts for finding of guilty without a trial on the merits.

Dispositive facts. Jural facts, or those acts or events that create, modify or extinguish jural relations.

Dispossess. To oust a person from land by legal process (*e.g.,* eviction by landlord). To eject, to exclude from possession of realty. *See* Eviction; Forcible entry and detainer; Process *(Summary process).*

Dispossession. Ouster; a wrong that carries with it the amotion of possession. An act whereby the wrongdoer gets the actual occupation of the land or hereditament. It includes abatement, intrusion, disseisin, discontinuance, deforcement.

Dispossess proceedings. Summary process by a landlord to oust the tenant and regain possession of the premises for nonpayment of rent or other breach of the conditions of the lease. *See also* Ejectment; Eviction; Forcible entry and detainer; Process *(Summary process).*

Disproportionate. Not pro rata or ratable.

Disprove. To refute; to prove to be false or erroneous; not necessarily by mere denial, but by affirmative evidence to the contrary.

Disputable presumption. A species of evidence that may be accepted and acted upon when there is no other evidence to uphold contention for which it stands; and when evidence is introduced supporting such contention, evidence takes place of presumption, and there is no necessity for indulging in any presumption. A rule of law to be laid down by the court, which shifts to the party against whom it operates the burden of evidence merely. *See* Presumption.

Dispute. A conflict or controversy; a conflict of claims or rights; an assertion of a right, claim, or demand on one side, met by contrary claims or allegations on the other. The subject of litigation; the matter for which a suit is brought and upon which issue is joined, and in relation to which jurors are called and witnesses examined. *See* Cause of action; Claim; Controversy; Justiciable controversy; Labor dispute.

Disqualify. To divest or deprive of qualifications; to incapacitate; to render ineligible or unfit, as, in speaking of the "disqualification" of a judge by reason of his interest in the case, of a juror by reason of his holding a fixed preconceived opinion, or of a candidate for public office by reason of non-residence, lack of statutory age, previous commission of crime, etc.

Disregard. To treat as unworthy of regard or notice; to take no notice of; to leave out of consideration; to ignore; to overlook; to fail to observe.

Disregard of corporate entity. To treat a corporation as if it did not exist for tax or certain other liability purposes. In such event, each shareholder would account for an allocable share of all corporate transactions possessing tax or other liability consequences. *See also* Piercing the corporate veil.

Disrepute. Loss or want of reputation; ill character; disesteem; discredit.

Disruptive conduct. Disorderly or contemptuous conduct generally within the framework of a judicial or quasi judicial proceeding. *See* Contempt.

Disseisin /dəsíyzən/. Dispossession; a deprivation of possession; a privation of seisin; a usurpation of the right of seisin and possession, and an exercise of such powers and privileges of ownership as to keep out or displace him to whom these rightfully belong. It is a wrongful putting out of him that is seised of the freehold, not, as in *abatement* or *intrusion,* a wrongful entry, where the possession was vacant, but an attack upon him who is in actual possession, and turning him out. It is an ouster from a freehold in deed, as abatement and intrusion are ousters in law.

When one man invades the possession of another, and by force or surprise turns him out of the occupation of his lands, this is termed a "disseis-

in," being a deprivation of that actual seisin or corporal possession of the freehold which the tenant before enjoyed. In other words, a disseisin is said to be when one enters intending to usurp the possession, and to oust another from the freehold. To constitute an entry a disseisin, there must be an ouster of the freehold, either by taking the profits or by claiming the inheritance.

Equitable disseisin is where a person is wrongfully deprived of the equitable seisin of land, *e.g.,* of the rents and profits.

Disseisin by election is where a person alleges or admits himself to be disseised when he has not really been so.

Dissent /dəsént/. Contrariety of opinion; disagreement with the majority; refusal to agree with something already stated or adjudged or to an act previously performed.

The term is most commonly used to denote the explicit disagreement of one or more judges of a court with the decision passed by the majority upon a case before them. In such event, the non-concurring judge is reported as "dissenting." A dissent may or may not be accompanied by a dissenting opinion.

Dissenter. One who dissents. For shareholder dissenter rights, *see* Appraisal remedy.

Dissipate. To destroy or waste, as to expend funds foolishly. Also, to break up a crowd. *See also* Drain; Spendthrift.

Dissolute. Loosed from restraint, unashamed, lawless, loose in morals and conduct, recklessly abandoned to sensual pleasures, profligate, wanton, lewd, debauched.

Dissolution. Act or process of dissolving; termination; winding up. In this sense it is frequently used in the phrase "dissolution of a partnership." *See Partnership, below,* this topic.

Contracts. The dissolution of a contract is the cancellation or abrogation of it by the parties themselves, with the effect of annulling the binding force of the agreement, and restoring each party to his original rights.

Corporation. The dissolution of a corporation is the termination of its legal existence. This may take place in several ways; as by act of the legislature, by surrender or forfeiture of its charter; by expiration of its charter by lapse of time; by proceedings for winding it up under the law; by loss of all its members or the reduction below the statutory limit; by bankruptcy.

Dissolution of a corporation can be either *voluntary* (initiated and approved by board of directors and shareholders) or *involuntary.* Involuntary dissolutions may be "administrative" (*e.g.,* by state for failure of corporation to file reports or pay certain taxes) or "judicial" (*e.g.,* by attorney general for abuse of corporate authority; by shareholders because of deadlock in managements; by unpaid creditors) or can result from bankruptcy of corporation. Procedures for corporate dissolution are usually provided for in state statutes. See *e.g.* Rev. Model Bus. Corp. Act § 14.01 et seq.

See also Articles of dissolution; Liquidation.

Marriage. The act of terminating a marriage; divorce; but the term does not include annulment. See Divorce.

Partnership. The dissolution of a partnership is the change in the relation of the partners caused by any partner ceasing to be associated in the carrying on as distinguished from the winding up of the business. Uniform Partnership Act, § 29.

Dissolve. To terminate; abrogate; cancel; annul; disintegrate. To release or unloose the binding force of anything. As to "dissolve a corporation," see Dissolution.

Dissolving bond. A bond given to obtain the dissolution of a legal writ or process, particularly an attachment or an injunction, and conditioned to indemnify the opposite party or to abide the judgment to be given.

Dissuade. In criminal law, to advise and procure a person not to do an act.

To dissuade a witness from giving evidence against a person indicted is an indictable offense at common law.

Distinct. Clear to the senses or mind; easily perceived or understood; plain; unmistakable. Evidently not identical; observably or decidedly different.

Distinguished by nature or station; not the same; different in the place or the like; separate; individual; that which is capable of being distinguished; actually divided or apart from other things.

Distinctiveness. An essential element of a device claimed to be a trademark is that it identify the goods of a particular merchant and distinguish them from the goods of others. A word, symbol, shape, or color serving this purpose is said to be distinctive. Certain marks are inherently distinctive while others only acquire distinctiveness over time (*see* Secondary meaning). A distinctive mark may lose its distinctiveness over time and become generic.

Distinguish. To point out an essential difference; to prove a case cited as applicable, inapplicable.

Distinguishing mark. A birth mark, scar, or other like feature which distinguishes a person. A mark on a ballot which takes away its secrecy. Any deliberate marking of ballot by voter that is not made in attempt to indicate his choice of candidates and which is also effective as mark by which his ballot may be distinguished.

In reference to trademark law, *see* Distinctiveness.

Distrain. To take as a pledge property of another, and keep it until he performs his obligation or until the property is replevied by the sheriff. Remedy used to secure an appearance in court, payment of rent, performance of services, etc. Also, any detention of personal property, whether lawful or unlawful, for any purpose. *See* Distraint; Distress.

Distrainer or **distrainor.** He who seizes property under a distress.

Distraint. Seizure; the act of distraining or making a distress. The inchoate right and interest which a landlord has in the property of a tenant located on the demised premises. Upon a tenant's default, a landlord may in some jurisdictions distrain upon the tenant's property, generally by changing the locks and giving notice, and the landlord will then have a lien upon the goods. The priority of the lien will depend on local law. *See* Distress.

Distress. A common-law right of landlord, now regulated by statute, to seize a tenant's goods and chattels in a nonjudicial proceeding to satisfy an arrears of rent.

The taking of goods and chattels out of the possession of a wrong-doer into the custody of the party injured to procure a satisfaction for a wrong committed; as for non-payment of rent. The taking of personal property by way of pledge, to enforce the performance of something due from the party distrained upon. The taking of a defendant's goods, in order to compel an appearance in court.

Certain state statutes, insofar as they authorize distress for rents by landlords, have been held to be unconstitutional.

The seizure of personal property to enforce payment of taxes, to be followed by its public sale if the taxes are not voluntarily paid; also the thing taken by distraining, *i.e.* that which is seized to procure satisfaction.

See Distraint; Landlord's warrant.

Distress warrant. A writ authorizing an officer to make a distraint; particularly, a writ authorizing the levy of a distress on the chattels of a tenant for non-payment of rent. A power of attorney by which landlord delegates exercise of his right to his duly authorized agent.

Distress and danger. The "distress" and "danger" to which a ship needs to be exposed to entitle its rescuer to salvage need not be actual or immediate, or the danger imminent and absolute. It is sufficient if at the time the assistance is rendered, the ship has encountered any damage or misfortune which might possibly expose her to destruction if the services were not rendered, or if a vessel is in a situation of actual apprehension though not of actual danger.

Distressed goods. Goods sold at a distressed sale.

Distressed property. Property that must be sold because of mortgage foreclosure or on probate of insolvent estate.

Distressed sale. Form of liquidation sale (*e.g.* "going out of business" sale) in which the seller receives less for his goods than he would under normal selling conditions.

Distributable net income (DNI). The measure that limits the amount of the distributions from estates and trusts that the beneficiaries thereof will have to include in income. Also, DNI limits the amount that estates and trusts can claim as a deduction for such distributions. I.R.C. § 643(a).

Distribute. To deal or divide out in proportion or in shares. *See* Distribution.

In criminal law, a person "distributes" a dangerous drug when he sells, transfers, gives or delivers to another, or leaves, barters or exchanges with another, or offers or agrees to do the same.

Distributee /dəstríbyuwtíy/. An heir; a person entitled to share in the distribution of an estate. This term is used to denote one of the persons who is entitled, under the statute of distributions, to the personal estate of one who is dead intestate. *See also* Beneficiary.

Distribution. The giving out or division among a number, sharing or parceling out, allotting, dispensing, apportioning.

Corporate. A direct or indirect transfer of money or other property (except its own shares) or incurrence of indebtedness by a corporation to or for the benefit of its shareholders in respect of any of its shares. A distribution may be in the form of a declaration or payment of a dividend; a purchase, redemption, or other acquisition of shares; a distribution of indebtedness; or otherwise. Rev. Model Bus.Corp. Act, § 1.40.

Partnership. A payment by a partnership to a partner. The payment may be in the form of cash or property. A payment to a partner may be out of current earnings or it may be an advance against future earnings to provide cash flow to the partner. A distribution may also consist of the partners' capital in the event of the partners' liquidation. I.R.C. § 731.

Probate. The apportionment and division, under authority of a court, of the remainder of the estate of an intestate, after payment of the debts and charges, among those who are legally entitled to share in the same. *See* Distributive share.

Securities offering. A public offering of securities of an issuer, whether by an underwriter, statutory underwriter or by the issuer itself. Such offering may be *controlled, i.e.* an offering to the public of securities by selling stockholders or an issuer through a broker-dealer acting as an underwriter for such persons pursuant to a formal underwriting arrangement; or *uncontrolled, i.e.* an offering to the public of securities by selling stockholders on a random basis through any number of brokers who are willing to assist such persons; or an offering to the public by such persons without the use of a broker.

Statutes of distribution. State laws prescribing the manner of the distribution of the estate of an intestate among his heirs or relatives.

Trust. The amount paid or credited to the beneficiaries of a trust. The payment may be in the form of cash or property and is generally income to the beneficiary. I.R.C. § 643(a).

Distribution in kind. A transfer of property "as is." If, for example, a corporation distributes land to its shareholders, a distribution in kind has taken place. A sale of land followed by a distribution of the cash proceeds would not be a distribution in kind of the land. *See also* Like-kind exchange.

Distribution in liquidation. Distribution of assets upon dissolution of corporation. Liquidating dividend is amount distributed in complete or partial liquidation of corporation and such amount is treated as in full payment for the stock of the corporation. I.R.C. § 331(a). *Compare* Nonliquidating distribution.

Distributive. That which exercises or accomplishes distribution; that which apportions, divides, and assigns in separate items or shares.

Distributive clause. That provision in trust which governs distribution of income and ultimate distributions or gifts over.

Distributive deviation. Distribution of principal to income beneficiaries for whom income is inadequate, without the consent of the remaindermen who are entitled to receive the entire principal at a later time under the terms of the trust.

Distributive finding of the issue. The jury are bound to give their verdict for that party who, upon the evidence, appears to them to have succeeded in establishing his side of the issue. But there are cases in which an issue may be found distributively, *i.e.,* in part for plaintiff, and in part for defendant. Thus, in an action for goods sold and work done, if the defendant pleaded that he never was indebted, on which issue was joined, a verdict might be found for the plaintiff as to the goods, and for the defendant as to the work. *See also* Comparative negligence.

Distributive justice. *See* Justice.

Distributive share. The share or portion which a given heir receives on the legal distribution of an intestate estate; or from a dissolved partnership. Sometimes, by an extension of meaning, the share or portion assigned to a given person on the distribution of any estate or fund, as, under an assignment for creditors or under insolvency proceedings.

Distributor. Any individual, partnership, corporation, association, or other legal relationship which stands between the manufacturer and the retail seller in purchases, consignments, or contracts for sale of consumer goods. A wholesaler, jobber or other merchant middleman authorized by a manufacturer or supplier to sell chiefly to retailers and commercial users. *See also* Dual distributor.

District. One of the territorial areas into which an entire state or country, county, municipality or other political subdivision is divided, for judicial, political, electoral, or administrative purposes.

The circuit or territory within which a person may be compelled to appear. Circuit of authority; province.

As to Fire; Judicial; Land; Levee; Metropolitan; Mineral; Mining; Road; School; and Tax *(districts)* see those titles.

Congressional district. Geographical district of state which may send (vote) a representative to U.S. Congress.

District attorney. Under the state governments, the prosecuting officer who represents the state in each of its judicial districts. Also, the prosecuting officer of the United States government in each of the federal judicial districts. In some states, where the territory is divided, for judicial purposes, into sections called by some other name than "districts," the same officer is denominated "prosecuting attorney", "county attorney" or "state's attorney." *See also* United States Attorney; Prosecutor.

District clerk. The clerk of a district court of either a state or the United States.

District courts. Each state is comprised of one or more federal judicial districts, and in each district there is a district court. 28 U.S.C.A. § 81 *et seq.* The United States district courts are the trial courts with general Federal jurisdiction over cases involving federal laws or offenses and actions between citizens of different states. Each State has at least one district court, though many have several judicial districts (*e.g.* northern, southern, middle districts) or divisions. There is also a United States district court in the District of Columbia. In addition, the Commonwealth of Puerto Rico has a United States district court with jurisdiction corresponding to that of district courts in the various States. Only one judge is usually required to hear and decide a case in a district court, but in some kinds of cases it is

required that three judges be called together to comprise the court (28 U.S.C.A. § 2284). In districts with more than one judge, the judge senior in commission who has not reached his seventieth birthday acts as the chief judge. *See* Diversity of citizenship; Federal question jurisdiction.

Also, name for inferior state courts of record having general jurisdiction.

District judge. The judge of a United States district court; also, in some states, the judge of a district court of the state.

Legislative district. Geographical district which may send (vote) a representative to the state legislature.

Districting. Term refers to defining lines of electoral districts. The establishment of the precise geographical boundaries of each such unit or constituency. *See* Apportionment; Reapportionment.

District of Columbia. A territory situated on the Potomac river, and being the seat of government of the United States. It was originally ten miles square, and was composed of portions of Maryland and Virginia ceded by those states to the United States; but in 1846 the tract coming from Virginia was retroceded. Legally it is neither a state nor a territory, but is made subject, by the Constitution, to the exclusive jurisdiction of Congress.

Disturb. To throw into disorder; to move from a state of rest or regular order; to interrupt a settled state of; to throw out of course or order.

Disturbance. Any act causing annoyance, disquiet, agitation, or derangement to another, or interrupting his peace, or interfering with him in the pursuit of a lawful and appropriate occupation or contrary to the usages of a sort of meeting and class of persons assembled that interferes with its due progress or irritates the assembly in whole or in part. *See* Disturbance of peace; Riot.

At common law, a wrong done to an incorporeal hereditament by hindering or disquieting the owner in the enjoyment of it. Blackstone enumerated five types of such disturbances: Disturbances of franchises, common, tenure, ways, and patronage.

Disturbance of peace. Interruption of the peace, quiet, and good order of a neighborhood or community, particularly by unnecessary and distracting noises. Conduct which tends to annoy all good citizens and which does in fact annoy anyone present not favoring it. In some jurisdictions (*e.g.* Calif.) term includes an affray. "Breach of the peace" and "disturbing the peace" are synonymous terms. *See also* Breach of the peace; Disorderly conduct; Riot.

Disturbance of public meetings. It was a misdemeanor at common law to be guilty of conduct which tended to disturb a public assembly, though the prosecution, in most instances, was required to prove that the disturbance was caused wantonly or wilfully. In most jurisdictions there is statutory crime for such conduct and the disturbance need not be so turbulent as to constitute a riot.

Disturbance of public or religious worship. Any acts or conduct which interfere with the peace and good order of an assembly of persons lawfully met together for religious exercises.

Diversion. A turning aside or altering the natural course or route of a thing. The term is chiefly applied to the unauthorized change or alteration of a water course to the prejudice of a lower riparian, or to the unauthorized use of funds.

Diversion program. A disposition of a criminal defendant either before or after adjudication of guilt in which the court directs the defendant to participate in a work or educational program as part of a probation.

Diversity /dəvə́rsətiy/. In criminal pleading at common law, a plea by the prisoner in bar of execution, alleging that he was not the same who was attainted, upon which a jury was immediately impaneled to try the collateral issue thus raised, viz., the identity of the person, and not whether he was guilty or innocent, for that had been already decided.

Diversity jurisdiction. See Diversity of citizenship.

Diversity of citizenship. A phrase used with reference to the jurisdiction of the federal courts, which, under U.S.Const. Art. III, § 2, extends to cases between citizens of different states, designating the condition existing when the party on one side of a lawsuit is a citizen of one state, and the party on the other side is a citizen of another state, or between a citizen of a state and an alien. The requisite jurisdictional amount must, in addition, be met. 28 U.S.C.A. § 1332. See Outcome test.

Manufactured diversity. The improper or collusive creation of diversity of citizenship for the sole or primary purpose of obtaining federal court jurisdiction. Such a practice is prohibited by 28 U.S.C.A. § 1359.

Divert /dəvə́rt/. To turn aside; to turn out of the way; to alter the course of things. Usually applied to water-courses or to the unauthorized use of funds. See Diversion.

Divest. Equivalent to devest (q.v.).

Divestiture /dəvéstətyər/. In anti-trust law, the order of court to a defendant (e.g. corporation) to divest itself of property, securities or other assets. A firm's act of selling off one or more of its parts, such as a subsidiary, a plant, or certain assets that create productive capacity. Divestiture is sometimes mandated by the courts in merger and monopolization cases.

Divestment. In property law, the cutting short of an interest prior to its normal termination. Restatement, Second, Property, § 16. The complete loss of an interest in land (total divestment) or the partial loss of it by virtue of others sharing it (partial divestment).

Divide. To cut into parts, disunite, separate, keep apart. The term is synonymous with distribute.

Divided court. Appellate court whose opinion or decision is not unanimous in a particular case. See also Division of opinion.

Divided custody. See Custody.

Dividend. The distribution of current or accumulated earnings to the shareholders of a corporation pro rata based on the number of shares owned. Dividends are usually issued in cash. However, they may be issued in the form of stock or property. The dividend on preferred shares is generally a fixed amount; however, on common shares the dividend varies depending on such things as the earnings and available cash of the corporation, as well as future plans for the acquisition of property and equipment by the corporation. See also Allocation of dividends; Date of declaration; Date of payment.

Accumulated dividend. A cumulative dividend which has not been paid when due.

Asset dividend. Dividend paid in the form of an asset of the company; normally a product. See Property dividend, below.

Bond dividend. Type of dividend distribution which is rare but one in which the shareholder receives bonds instead of scrip, property or money.

Cash dividend. See that title.

Consent dividend. For purposes of avoiding or reducing the penalty tax on the unreasonable accumulation of earnings or the personal holding company tax, a corporation may declare a consent dividend. In a consent dividend no cash or property is distributed to the shareholders although the corporation obtains a dividends paid deduction. The consent dividend is taxed to the shareholders and increases the basis in their stock investment. I.R.C. § 565.

Constructive dividend. A taxable benefit derived by a shareholder from his or her corporation although such benefit was not designated as a dividend. Examples include unreasonable compensation, excessive rent payments, bargain purchases of corporate property, and shareholder use of corporate property. The pass-through of undistributed taxable income (i.e., UTI) to the shareholders of a Subchapter S corporation sometimes is referred to as a constructive dividend. Constructive dividends generally are a problem limited to closely-held corporations.

If a stockholder has an unqualified right to a dividend, such a dividend is called constructive for tax purposes though he does not actually receive it because it is subject to his demand and the corporation has set it aside for this purpose.

Cumulative dividend. A typical feature of preferred stock that requires any past-due preferred stock dividends to be paid before any common stock dividends can be paid. A dividend that if not paid annually (or periodically as provided in the stock certificate) will ultimately have to be paid before any common stock dividend can be paid. The arrearage is said to accumulate. *See also* Cumulative dividend feature.

Deferred dividend. One declared, but due to be paid at some future date.

Deficiency dividend. Once the IRS has established a corporation's liability for the personal holding company tax in a prior year, the tax may be reduced or avoided by the issuance of a deficiency dividend under I.R.C. § 547. The deficiency dividend procedure is not available in cases where the deficiency was due to fraud with intent to evade tax or to a willful failure to file the appropriate tax return (§ 547(g)). Nor does the deficiency dividend procedure avoid the usual penalties and interest applicable for failure to file a return or pay a tax.

Dividend addition. Something added to the policy in the form of paid-up insurance, and does not mean unapportioned assets or surplus. The term does not refer to dividends added directly to the loan value.

Ex-dividend. Term used by stock brokers, meaning that a sale of corporate stock does not carry with it the seller's right to receive his proportionate share of a dividend already declared and shortly payable. *See* Ex dividend.

Extra dividend. One paid in addition to regular dividends; normally because of exceptional profits of corporation during dividend period.

Extraordinary dividend. See that title.

Liquidation dividend. See that title.

Nimble dividends. Dividends paid out of current earnings at a time when there is a deficit in earned surplus (or other financial account from which dividends may be paid). Some state statutes do not permit nimble dividends. These statutes require current earnings to be applied against prior deficits rather than being used to pay a current dividend.

Noncumulative dividends. See that title.

Passed dividend. Dividend not paid when due by company which has history of paying regular dividends.

Preferred dividend. One paid on the preferred stock of a corporation. A dividend paid to one class of shareholders in priority to that paid to another.

Property dividend. Consists of a portion of corporate property paid to shareholders instead of cash or corporate stock. *See Asset dividend, above.*

Scrip dividend. One paid in scrip, or in certificates of the ownership of a corresponding amount of capital stock of the company thereafter to be issued. Dividend paid in a short term promissory note which, in effect, divides profits but enables the corporation to postpone actual distribution of cash.

Stock dividend. A dividend paid in the form of stock rather than cash. A stock dividend is usually expressed as a percentage of the number of shares already held by the shareholder. A corporation normally elects to issue a stock dividend in order to conserve cash. The tax advantage of a stock dividend to a shareholder is that a stock dividend is taxable at the time of sale, while a cash dividend is taxable when received.

Tax treatment. A nondeductible distribution to the shareholders of a corporation. A dividend constitutes gross income to the recipient if it is from the current or accumulated earnings and profits of the corporation. *See* Current earnings and profits. *See also* Dividend received deduction, *infra.*

Unpaid dividend. Dividends declared by a corporation, but not yet paid. Unpaid dividends are a liability on the balance sheet of a corporation.

Year-end dividend. Type of extra dividend paid at end of fiscal year with amount dependent on profits. *See also Extra dividend, above.*

Dividend growth method. A method of computing the cost of common stock equity that indicates the rate of return that common shareholders expect to earn in the form of dividends on a company's common stock.

Dividend limitation. A bond covenant that restricts in some way the firm's ability to pay cash dividends.

Dividend payout ratio. A profitability ratio; annual dividends per share divided by earnings per share.

Dividend policy. A firm's policy that governs that portion of the firm's earnings and cash flow that should be paid out to the firm's common stockholders in the form of cash dividends.

Dividend income. Species of gross income derived from dividend distribution and subject to tax. I.R.C. §§ 61(a)(7), 301(c).

Dividend rate. Dividends paid per common share per annum.

Dividend reinvestment plan. A company-sponsored program that enables common stockholders to pool their dividends (plus, in many cases, supplementary cash) for reinvestment in shares of the firm's common stock.

Dividend rights. A shareholder's right to receive per share dividends identical to other shareholders. *See also* Dividend.

Dividends in arrears. Dividends that have been omitted on cumulative preferred stock. *See also* Dividend.

Dividend payout ratio. A profitability ratio; annual dividend per share divided by earnings per share. *See also* Dividend yield.

Dividend received deduction. A deduction allowed a corporate shareholder for dividends received from a domestic corporation. As a result of the Tax Reform Act of 1986, corporations are allowed an 80% deduction for dividends received in 1987, and a deduction of 70% for dividends received after 1987. However, if the corporation owns more than 80% of the stock of the distributing corporation, the deduction allowed is 80%. I.R.C. §§ 243–246.

Dividend yield. The current annual dividend divided by the market price per share.

Divine laws. Those ascribed to God. *See* Natural law.

Divine right of kings. The right of a king to rule as posited by the patriarchal theory of government, especially under the doctrine that no misconduct and no dispossession can forfeit the right of a monarch or his heirs to the throne, and to the obedience of the people. This theory was in its origin directed, not against popular liberty, but against papal and ecclesiastical claims to supremacy in temporal as well as spiritual affairs.

Divisible. That which is susceptible of being divided.

Divisible contract. One which is in its nature and purposes susceptible of division and apportionment, having two or more parts in respect to matters and things contemplated and embraced by it, not necessarily dependent on each other nor intended by the parties so to be.

Divisible divorce. Decree of divorce may be divided as between provisions for support and alimony and provisions dissolving the marriage. Doctrine applied in cases under full faith and credit clause in connection with effect of foreign divorce on support provisions.

Divisible obligation. *See* Obligation.

Divisible offense. One that includes one or more offenses of lower grade, *e.g.*, murder includes assault, battery, assault with intent to kill, and other offenses. *See* Lesser included offense.

Division. Act of distributing among a number. Portion of territorial area marked off for a particular purpose. Operating or administrative unit of government, court, business, or school system. Condition of being divided in opinion. Major military unit. Separation of members of a legislative body to take a vote. *See also* Range.

Divisional securities. Special type of securities issued to finance particular projects.

Division of opinion. In the practice of appellate courts, this term denotes such a disagreement among the judges that there is not a majority in favor of any one view, and hence no decision can be rendered on the case. But it also commonly denotes a division into two classes, one of which may comprise a majority of the judges; as when we speak of a decision having proceeded from a "divided court." *See also* Divided court.

Division of powers. *See* Separation of powers.

Division order. A direction and authorization to purchaser of oil to distribute purchase price in specified manner; its purpose is to assure that purchaser pays only those parties who are entitled to payment.

Divorce. The legal separation of man and wife, effected by the judgment or decree of a court, and either totally dissolving the marriage relation, or suspending its effects so far as concerns the cohabitation of the parties.

   See also Alimony; Equitable distribution; Ex parte divorce; Legislative divorce; Living separate and apart; Mail order divorce; Mexican divorce; Migratory divorce; Rabbinical divorce.

Divisible divorce. Decree of divorce may be divided as between provisions for support and alimony and provisions dissolving the marriage. Doctrine applied in cases under Full Faith and Credit Clause in connection with effect of foreign divorce on support provisions.

Divorce a mensa et thoro /dəvórs èy ménsə èt θórow/. A divorce from table and bed, or from bed and board. A partial or qualified divorce, by which the parties are separated and forbidden to live or cohabit together, without affecting the marriage itself.

Divorce a vinculo matrimonii /dəvórs èy víŋkyəlow mætrəmówniyay/. A divorce from the bond of marriage. A total, absolute divorce of husband and wife, dissolving the marriage tie, and releasing the parties wholly from their matrimonial obligations.

Divorce by consent (no-fault). Type of no-fault divorce in which parties are not required to prove fault or grounds for divorce beyond a showing of irretrievable breakdown of marriage or irreconcilable differences. The majority of states have no-fault divorce statutes in one form or another.

See, *e.g.,* Uniform Marriage and Divorce Act, §§ 302, 305.

Divorce from bed and board. *See Divorce a mensa et thoro, above.*

Foreign divorce. A divorce obtained out of the state or country where the marriage was solemnized.

Limited divorce. A divorce from bed and board; or a judicial separation of husband and wife not dissolving the marriage tie. *See also* Separation of spouses.

Migratory divorce. Term used to describe a divorce secured by a spouse or spouses who leave(s) his/their domicile and move(s) to, or reside(s) temporarily in, another state or country for purpose of securing the divorce. *See also* Ex parte divorce.

No-fault divorce. *See Divorce by consent, above.*

Divorce proctors. Person, generally an attorney, appointed to protect children or the interests of the state in a divorce action. Uniform Marriage and Divorce Act, § 310.

Divulge /dəvə́lj/. To disclose or make known, as to divulge secret or classified information.

D. J. An abbreviation for "District Judge."

DNA identification. DNA profiling or fingerprinting is an analysis of Deoxyribonucleic Acid (DNA) resulting in the identification of an individual's patterned chemical structure of genetic information. A method of determining distinctive patterns in genetic material in order to identify the source of a biological specimen, such as blood, tissue or hair. A forensic technique used in criminal cases to identify, or rule out, crime suspect and in paternity cases to identify, or rule out, father of child. See *e.g.* Ann. Code of Md., Cts. & Jud. Proc. § 10–915.

Dock, *v.* To curtail or diminish, as to dock a person's wages for, *e.g.* lateness or poor work.

Dock, *n.* The cage or inclosed space in a criminal court where prisoners stand when brought in for trial.

Dockage. A charge against vessels for the privilege of mooring to the wharves or in the slips. A pecuniary compensation for the use of a dock while a vessel is undergoing repairs. *See also* Demurrage; Moorage.

Docket, *v.* To abstract and enter in a book. To make a brief entry of any proceeding in a court of justice in the docket.

Docket, *n.* A minute, abstract, or brief entry; or the book containing such entries. A formal record, entered in brief, of the proceedings in a court of justice. A book containing an entry in brief of all the important acts done in court in the conduct of each case, from its inception to its conclusion. The name of "docket" or "trial dock-

et" is sometimes given to the list or calendar of causes set to be tried at a specified term, prepared by the clerks for the use of the court and bar.

General Classification

An *appearance* docket is one in which the appearances in actions are entered, containing also a brief abstract of the successive steps in each action. A *bar* docket is an unofficial paper consisting of a transcript of the docket for a term of court, printed for distribution to members of the bar. An *execution* docket is a list of the executions sued out or pending in the sheriff's office. A *judgment* docket is a list or docket of the judgments entered in a given court, methodically kept by the clerk or other proper officer, open to public inspection, and intended to afford official notice to interested parties of the existence or lien of judgments. *See also* Judgment docket; Preferred dockets.

Civil docket. Fed.R. Civil P. 79(a), and analogous state rules, requires that the clerk keep a "civil docket" of all actions pending before the court. Actions shall be assigned consecutive file numbers. The file number of each action shall be noted on the folio of the docket whereon the first entry of the actions is made. All papers filed with the clerk, all process issued and returns made thereon, all appearances, orders, verdicts, and judgments shall be entered chronologically in the civil docket on the folio assigned to the action and shall be marked with its file number. The entry of an order or judgment shall show the date the entry is made. When in an action trial by jury has been properly demanded or ordered the clerk shall enter the word "jury" on the folio assigned to that action.

Docket fee. An attorney's fee, of a fixed sum, chargeable with or as a part of the costs of the action, for the attorney of the successful party; so called because chargeable on the docket, not as a fee for making docket entries.

Dock receipt. Also known as dock warrant. A type of interim certificate issued by maritime shipping company upon delivery of goods at the dock, often entitling the designated person to have a bill of lading issued to him. Trade usage may in some cases entitle such paper to be treated as a document of title. If the receipt actually represents a storage obligation undertaken by the shipping company, then it is a warehouse receipt. *See also* Document *(Document of title)*; Warehouse receipt.

Dock sale. Exists where a purchaser uses its owned or rented vehicles to take possession of the product at the seller's shipping dock. In most states, the sale is apportioned to the operating state of the purchaser, rather than the seller.

Dock warrant. *See* Dock receipt.

Doctor-patient privilege. In law of evidence, right of patient to exclude from evidence communications made by him to his physician; recognized in most jurisdictions but sometimes limited; *e.g.* to communications to psychotherapist.

Doctrinal interpretation. *See* Interpretation.

Doctrine. A rule, principle, theory, or tenet of the law; as, *e.g.* Abstention doctrine; Clean hands doctrine, etc.

Document. An instrument on which is recorded, by means of letters, figures, or marks, the original, official, or legal form of something, which may be evidentially used. In this sense the term "document" applies to writings; to words printed, lithographed, or photographed; to maps or plans; to seals, plates, or even stones on which inscriptions are cut or engraved. In the plural, the deeds, agreements, title-papers, letters, receipts, and other written instruments used to prove a fact. As used as a verb, to support with documentary evidence or authorities.

Within meaning of the best evidence rule, document is any physical embodiment of information or ideas; *e.g.* a letter, a contract, a receipt, a book of account, a blueprint, or an X-ray plate. *See also* Documentary evidence.

See also Instrument.

Ancient documents. Deeds, wills, and other writings more than thirty years (twenty years under Fed.Evid.R. 803(16)) old are so called; they are presumed to be genuine without express proof, when coming from the proper custody.

Commercial law. Under U.C.C., any paper including document of title, security, invoice, certificate, notice of default and the like. U.C.C. § 5–103. *See also* Documentary draft.

Conflicts of law. (1) Whether a right is embodied in a document is determined by the law which governs the right. (2) As between persons who are not both parties to the conveyance, (a) the effect of a conveyance of a right embodied in a document depends upon the effect of the conveyance of the document; and (b) the effect of a conveyance of an interest in a document in which a right is embodied is determined by the law that would be applied by the courts of the state where the document was at the time of the conveyance. These courts would usually apply their own local law in determining such questions. Restatement, Second, Conflicts, § 249.

Document of title. A written description, identification or declaration of goods "which in the regular course of business or financing is treated as adequately evidencing that the person in possession of it is entitled to receive, hold and dispose of the document and the goods it covers. To be a document of title a document must purport to be issued by or addressed to a bailee and purport to cover goods in the bailee's possession which are either identified or are fungible portions of an identified mass." U.C.C. § 1–201(15). Examples are: bill of lading, dock warrant, dock receipt, warehouse receipt or order for the delivery of goods. Id. *See also* Order document; Order instrument.

Foreign document. One which was prepared or executed in, or which comes from, a foreign state or country.

Judicial documents. Proceedings relating to litigation. They are divided into (1) judgments, decrees, and verdicts; (2) depositions, examinations, and inquisitions taken in the course of a legal process; (3) writs, warrants, pleadings, etc., which are incident to any judicial proceedings.

Public document. A state paper, or other instrument of public importance or interest, issued or published by authority of congress or a state legislature. Also any document or record, evidencing or connected with the public business or the administration of public affairs, preserved in or issued by any department of the government. One of the publications printed by order of congress or either house thereof. Broadly any document open to public inspection.

Documentary credit. Credit which is extended on documents of title or other legal documents.

Documentary draft. A "documentary draft" or a "documentary demand for payment" is one the honor of which is conditioned upon the presentation of a document or documents. "Document" means any paper including document of title, security, invoice, certificate, notice of default and the like. U.C.C. § 5–103(b).

Any negotiable or non-negotiable draft with accompanying documents, securities or other papers to be delivered against honor of the draft. U.C.C. § 4–104(f).

Check with accompanying documents which are to be delivered when payment is made is "documentary draft."

Documentary evidence. Evidence derived from conventional symbols (such as letters) by which ideas are represented on material substances. Such evidence as is furnished by written instruments, inscriptions, documents of all kinds, and also any inanimate objects admissible for the purpose, as distinguished from "oral" evidence, or that delivered by human beings viva voce. *See also* Authentication; Document.

Documentary instructions. Term for written agreement between importer and exporter covering disposition of the various documents relating to the shipment, and disposition of the goods.

Documentary originals rule. *See* Best evidence.

Documentary stamp. Stamp required by federal (prior to 1968) and state law to be affixed to deeds and other documents of transfer before they may be recorded, the cost of which is generally governed by the consideration recited in the document. Federal Revenue Stamps were abolished in 1968.

Documentation. *See* Authorities.

DOD. Department of Defense.

DOE. Department of Energy.

Doe, John. The name of the fictitious plaintiff in certain types of actions; *e.g.* ejectment action. *See also* John Doe.

Dogma. Definite authoritative opinions or tenets. Formally stated and proclaimed doctrines on faith or morals. In the civil law, a word occasionally used as descriptive of an ordinance of the senate.

DOHSA. Death on High Seas Act.

Doing business. Within statutes on service of process on foreign corporations, means equivalent to carrying on, conducting or managing business. A foreign corporation is "doing business", making it amenable to process within state, if it does business therein in such a manner as to warrant the inference that it is present there. Or that it has subjected itself to the jurisdiction and laws in which the service is made. The doing of business is the exercise in the state of some of the ordinary functions for which the corporation was organized. What constitutes "doing business" depends on the facts in each particular case. The general rule is that the business need only have certain "minimum contacts" with the state to make it amenable to process in that state. International Shoe Co. v. State of Washington, 326 U.S. 310, 66 S.Ct. 154, 90 L.Ed. 95. And, such contacts may be as minimal as selling a single insurance contract. McGee v. International Life Insurance Co., 355 U.S. 220, 78 S.Ct. 199, 2 L.Ed.2d 223; Hanson v. Denckla, 357 U.S. 235, 78 S.Ct. 1228, 2 L.Ed.2d 1283. *See also* Long arm statutes; Minimal contacts; Transacting business.

The determination as to what constitutes "doing business" may differ as to whether the term is being used with reference to amenability to service of process or to taxation, and also may vary in definition from state to state.

Dollar averaging. Investment term for practice of purchasing a fixed dollar amount of a given security at regular intervals. *See also* Averaging up or down.

Dolus /dówləs/. In the civil law, guile; deceitfulness; malicious fraud. A fraudulent address or trick used to deceive some one; a fraud. Any subtle contrivance by words or acts with a design to circumvent.

Such acts or omissions as operate as a deception upon the other party, or violate the just confidence reposed by him, whether there be a deceitful intent *(malus animus)* or not.

Domain. The complete and absolute ownership of land; a paramount and individual right of property in land. Also the real estate so owned. The inherent sovereign power claimed by the legislature of a state, of controlling private property for public uses, is termed the "right of eminent domain." *See* Condemnation; Eminent domain.

National domain is sometimes applied to the aggregate of the property owned directly by a nation. Public domain embraces all lands, the title to which is in the United States, including as well land occupied for the purposes of federal buildings, arsenals, dock-yards, etc., as land of an agricultural or mineral character not yet granted to private owners.

Sphere of influence. Range of control or rule; realm.

Dombrowski doctrine. Rule enunciated in Dombrowski v. Pfister, 380 U.S. 479, 85 S.Ct. 1116, 14 L.Ed.2d 22, to the effect that a person is entitled to an injunction in a federal court to prevent state officers from prosecuting or threatening to prosecute him under a state statute which is so broad and vague that it interferes with rights guaranteed by the First Amendment, U.S. Constitution.

Domesday, domesday-book /dówmzdey búk/dúwmzdey°/. (Sax.) An ancient record made in the time of William the Conqueror, and later remaining in the English exchequer, consisting of two volumes of unequal size, containing minute and accurate surveys of the lands in England. The work was begun by five justices in each county in 1081, and finished in 1086.

Domestic, *n.* A household servant.

Domestic, *adj.* Pertaining, belonging, or relating to a home, a domicile, or to the place of birth, origin, creation, or transaction.

As to *domestic* Administrators; Attachment; Commerce; Corporation; Creditor; Factor; Fixture; Judgment; and Manufacture, see those titles.

Domestic animals. Such as are habituated to live in or about the habitations of men, or such as contribute to the support of a family. Tamed animals; *e.g.* horses, sheep, dogs.

Domestic authority. The right of parents and, by extension, the right of teachers, to discipline and compel obedience to their lawful commands from their children. *See* Corporeal punishment.

Domestic bill. Draft which is payable in the state in which it is drawn, as contrasted with a foreign bill which is payable in another state.

Domestic corporation. When a corporation is organized and chartered in a particular state, it is considered a domestic corporation of that state. Term is used in contrast to foreign corporation which has been incorporated in another state, territory or country. For tax purposes, a corporation created or organized in the U.S. or under the law of the U.S. or any state or territory. I.R.C. § 7701(a)(4). *Compare* Foreign corporation.

Domestic courts. Those existing and having jurisdiction at the place of the party's residence or domicile.

Domestic exports. Goods originally grown, produced, or manufactured in the United States, in contrast to goods originally imported and then re-exported.

Domestic International Sales Corporation (DISC). A U.S. corporation, usually a subsidiary, whose income is primarily attributable to exports. Income tax on a certain percentage of a DISC's income is usually deferred resulting, generally, in a lower overall corporate tax for the parent than would otherwise be incurred. I.R.C. § 991 et seq.

Domestic jurisdiction. Power of court over a person or action within its district or state.

Domestic relations. That branch or discipline of the law which deals with matters of the household or family, including divorce, separation, custody, support and adoption.

Domicile. A person's legal home. That place where a man has his true, fixed, and permanent home and principal establishment, and to which whenever he is absent he has the intention of returning. Generally, physical presence within a state and the intention to make it one's home are the requisites of establishing a "domicile" therein. The permanent residence of a person or the place to which he intends to return even though he may actually reside elsewhere. A person may have more than one residence but only one domicile. The legal domicile of a person is important since it, rather than the actual residence, often controls the jurisdiction of the taxing authorities and determines where a person may exercise the privilege of voting and other legal rights and privileges. The established, fixed, permanent, or ordinary dwellingplace or place of residence of a person, as distinguished from his temporary and transient, though actual, place of residence. It is his legal residence, as distinguished from his temporary place of abode; or his home, as distinguished from a place to which business or pleasure may temporarily call him. *See also* Abode; Residence.

"Citizenship," "habitancy," and "residence" are severally words which in particular cases may mean precisely the same as "domicile," while in other uses may have different meanings.

"Residence" signifies living in particular locality while "domicile" means living in that locality with intent to make it a fixed and permanent home.

For purpose of federal diversity jurisdiction, "citizenship" and "domicile" are synonymous.

Commercial domicile. A domicile acquired by the maintenance of a commercial establishment. A concept employed to permit taxation of property or activity of nonresident corporation by state in which managerial activities occurred in quantity and character sufficient to avoid contention of nonresident corporation that taxation of its activities and property located outside bounds of taxing state amounted to deprivation of property without due process.

Corporate domicile. Place considered by law as center of corporate affairs and place where its functions are discharged. *See also Commercial domicile, above.*

Domicile of choice. The essentials of "domicile" of choice are the fact of physical presence at a dwelling place and the intention to make that place home.

Domicile of origin. The home of the parents. That which arises from a man's birth and connections. The domicile of the parents at the time of birth, or what is termed the "domicile of origin," constitutes the domicile of an infant, and continues until abandoned, or until the acquisition of a new domicile in a different place.

Domicile of succession. As distinguished from a commercial, political, or forensic domicile, the actual residence of a person within some jurisdiction, of such a character as shall, according to the well-established principles of public law, give direction to the succession of his personal estate.

Domicile of trustee. Jurisdiction which appoints trustee is domicile of trustee.

Elected domicile. The domicile of parties fixed in a contract between them for the purposes of such contract.

Foreign domicile. A domicile established by a citizen or subject of one sovereignty within the territory of another.

Matrimonial domicile. The place where a husband and wife have established a home, in which they reside in the relation of husband and wife, and where the matrimonial contract is being performed.

Municipal domicile. One which as distinguished from "national domicile" and "quasi national domicile" (see those titles, *infra*), has reference to residence in a county, township, or municipality.

National domicile. The domicile of a person, considered as being within the territory of a particular nation, and not with reference to a particular locality or subdivision of a nation.

Natural domicile. The same as domicile of origin or domicile by birth.

Necessary domicile. That kind of domicile which exists by operation of law, as distinguished from voluntary domicile or domicile of choice.

Quasi national domicile. One involving residence in a state. *See also National domicile, above.*

Domiciled /dómǝsǝld/dómǝsàyld/. Established in a given domicile; belonging to a given state or jurisdiction by right of domicile.

Domiciliary /dòmǝsíl(i)yǝriy/. Pertaining to domicile; relating to one's domicile. Existing or created at, or connected with, the domicile of a suitor or of a decedent.

Domiciliary administration. Administration of estate in state where person was domiciled at time of death is deemed principal or primary administration and is ordinarily termed "domiciliary administration."

Domiciliate /dòmǝsíliyeyt/. To establish one's domicile; to take up one's fixed residence in a given place. To establish the domicile of another person whose legal residence follows one's own.

Dominant estate *or* **tenement** /dómǝnǝnt ǝstéyt/. Land that benefits from easement on another (usually adjacent) property. That to which a servitude or easement is due, or for the benefit of which it exists. A term used in the civil and Scotch law, and later in ours, relating to servitudes, meaning the tenement or subject in favor of which the service is constituted; as the tenement over which the servitude extends is called the "servient tenement." That particular parcel of land that is benefited as a result of an easement on a servient estate.

Possessor of dominant estate is entitled to benefit of uses authorized by easement. In such case, easement is said to be appurtenant to dominant estate. *See also Servient tenement.*

Dominant tenant. The person who holds the benefit of an easement.

Dominant theme. Within meaning of requirement that before any material can be found to be obscene the dominant theme of material taken as a whole must appeal to prurient interest in sex means prevailing, governing, influencing or controlling idea. *See also Obscene; Obscenity.*

Dominion. Perfect control in right of ownership. The word implies both title and possession and appears to require a complete retention of control over disposition. Title to an article of property which arises from the power of disposition and the right of claiming it.

Sovereignty; as the dominion of the seas or over a territory.

In the civil law, with reference to the title to property which is transferred by a sale of it,

dominion is said to be either "proximate" or "remote," the former being the kind of title vesting in the purchaser when he has acquired both the ownership and the possession of the article, the latter describing the nature of his title when he has legitimately acquired the ownership of the property but there has been no delivery.

See also Ownership; Title.

Donated stock. Securities given to a corporation by its own stockholders commonly for resale.

Donated surplus. Contribution of assets to a corporation generally in the form of stock from its stockholders.

Donatio /dòwnéysh(iy)ow/. Lat. A gift. A transfer of the title to property to one who receives it without paying for it. The act by which the owner of a thing voluntarily transfers the title and possession of the same from himself to another person, without any consideration.

By the civil law (adopted into the English and American law) donations are either *inter vivos* (between living persons) or *mortis causa* (in anticipation of death). As to these forms, see *infra.* A *donatio* or gift as between living persons is called *donatio mera* or *pura* when it is a simple gift without compulsion or consideration, that is, resting solely on the generosity of the donor, as in the case of most charitable gifts. It is called *donatio remuneratoria* when given as a reward for past services, but still not under any legal compulsion, as in the case of pensions and land-grants. It is called *donatio sub modo* (or *modalis*) when given for the attainment of some special object or on condition that the donee shall do something not specially for the benefit of the donor, as in the case of the endowment of hospitals, colleges, etc., coupled with the condition that they shall be established and maintained. The following terms are also used: *Donatio conditionalis,* a conditional gift; *donatio relata,* a gift made with reference to some service already done, *donatio stricta et coarctura,* a restricted gift, as an estate tail.

Donatio causa mortis. A gift of personal property made by a party in expectation of death, then imminent, subject to condition that donor die as anticipated; establishment of gift calls for proof of delivery. *See* Donatio mortis causa.

Donatio inter vivos /dòwnéysh(iy)ow íntǝr váyvows/. A gift between the living. The ordinary kind of gift by one person to another. A term derived from the civil law. A donation *inter vivos* (between living persons) is an act by which the donor divests himself at present and irrevocably of the thing given in favor of the donee who accepts it.

There are three kinds of "donations inter vivos", namely, "gratuitous donations", "onerous donations", and "remunerative donations", the first being based on mere liberality, the second being burdened with charges imposed by the donee, and the third being recompense for services rendered.

Donatio mortis causa /dòwnéysh(iy)ow mórtəs kózə/. A gift made by a person in sickness, who, apprehending his death, delivers, or causes to be delivered, to another the possession of any personal goods, to keep as his own in case of the donor's decease. The civil law defines it to be a gift under apprehension of death; as when anything is given upon condition that, if the donor dies, the donee shall possess it absolutely, or return it if the donor should survive or should repent of having made the gift, or if the donee should die before the donor. A gift in view of death is one which is made in contemplation, fear, or peril of death, and with intent that it shall take effect only in case of the death of the giver. A donation *mortis causa* (in prospect of death) is an act to take effect when the donor shall no longer exist, by which he disposes of the whole or a part of his property, and which is revocable. *See* Contemplation of death.

Donation. A gift *(q.v.)*. *See* Donatio.

Donative trust. Type of trust created by transfer of property in trust as gift for benefit of another person or by proper declaration of legal owner of property that he will hold it in trust for another's benefit and does not require payment of any consideration by the beneficiary.

Donee. The recipient of a gift. One to whom a gift is made or a bequest given. One who is invested with a power of appointment; the party executing a power, otherwise called the "appointer." He to whom lands or tenements are given in tail. In old English law, he to whom lands were given; the party to whom a *donatio* was made.

Donee beneficiary. A person not a party to a contract but to whom the benefits of a contract flow as a direct result of an intention to make a gift to that person. In a third party contract, the person who takes the benefit of the contract though there is no privity between him and the contracting parties.

Where performance of a promise in a contract will benefit a person other than the promisee, that person is a "donee beneficiary" if it appears from the terms of the promise in view of the accompanying circumstances that the purpose of the promisee in obtaining the promise is to make a gift to the beneficiary or to confer upon him a right against the promissor to some performance not due from the promisee to the beneficiary.

Donee of power. The person to whom the settlor or donor of a power of appointment gives such power to be exercised. In the case of a special power, in favor of a limited class such as members

of a family, or, in the case of a general power, in favor of any one including the donee himself.

Donor. The party conferring a power. One who makes a gift. One who creates a trust. He who gives lands or tenements to another in tail. In old English law, he by whom lands were given to another; the party making a *donatio*.

Doomsday-book. *See* Domesday-book.

Door closing doctrine. The principle invoked when a loop-hole in a law is closed by a statute or decision.

Dormancy. Lapse in the executability of a judgment, and also in the effectiveness of the judgment lien, which is cured through revival of the judgment.

Dormant claim. One which is in abeyance.

Dormant corporation. An inactive but legal corporation which is capable of being activated, but is presently not operating.

Dormant execution. One which a creditor delivers to the sheriff with directions to levy only, and not to sell, until further orders, or until a junior execution is received.

Dormant judgment. One which has not been satisfied, nor extinguished by lapse of time, but which has remained so long unexecuted that execution cannot now be issued upon it without first reviving the judgment, or one which has lost its lien on land from the failure to issue execution on it or take other steps to enforce it within the time limited by statute. *See* Judgment; Revival.

Dormant partner. *See* Partner.

Dot. (A French word, adopted in Louisiana.) The fortune, portion, or dowry which a woman brings to her husband by the marriage.

DOT. Department of Transportation.

Dotal property /dówtəl própərtiy/. In the civil law, in Louisiana, property which the wife brings to the husband to assist him in bearing the expenses of the marriage establishment. Extradotal property, otherwise called "paraphernal property," is that which forms no part of the dowry. *See also* Community.

Dotation /dòwtéyshən/. The act of giving a dowry or portion; endowment in general, including the endowment of a hospital or other charitable institution.

Double assessment. The imposition of same tax, by same taxing power, upon same subject matter.

Double commissions. Commissions or fees paid by both seller and buyer or paid to the same person in different capacities, such as executor and trustee.

Double costs. *See* Costs.

Double creditor. One who has a lien on two funds.

Double damages. *See* Damages.

Double entry. A system of bookkeeping, in which the entries are posted twice into the ledger, once as a credit and once as a debit.

Double (or multiple) hearsay. Hearsay statements which contain further hearsay statements within them. A statement made outside of court is hearsay when introduced in court to prove the truth of the statement. However, certain exceptions permit the introduction of hearsay if the out-of-court statement was made on the personal knowledge of the declarant as in the case of a declaration of a deceased person. If such statement of the deceased person was not made on his personal knowledge, the hearsay would be double or totem pole hearsay.

An out-of-court admission of a defendant repeated by a non-testifying co-conspirator.

Double indemnity. Payment of twice the basic benefit in event of loss resulting from specified causes or under specified circumstances. Provision in life insurance contract requiring payment of twice the face amount of the policy by the insurer in the event of death by accidental means.

Double insurance. Exists where the same person is insured by several insurers separately in respect to the same subject and interest.

Double jeopardy. Fifth Amendment guarantee, enforceable against states through Fourteenth Amendment, protects against second prosecution for same offense after acquittal or conviction, and against multiple punishments for same offense. The evil sought to be avoided is double trial and double conviction, not necessarily double punishment. *See also* Former jeopardy; Jeopardy; Same evidence test.

Double patenting. A doctrine of patent law which prevents single patentee from obtaining two patents on same invention. The test respecting "double patenting" is whether the claims of both patents, when properly construed in the light of the descriptions given, define essentially the same things. Occurs only when claims of two patents issued to one applicant are the same.

Double plea, double pleading. *See* Duplicity; Plea; Pleadings.

Double proof. Species of evidence required for conviction of certain crimes in which the government must offer corroboration.

Double recovery. Recovery which represents more than the total maximum loss which all parties have sustained.

Double standard. Set of principles which permit greater opportunity for one class of people than another and commonly based on differences such as sex, race or color and hence invidious standards which may offend equal protection of law to the discriminated minority. *See* Discrimination.

Double taxation. The taxing of the same item or piece of property twice to the same person, or taxing it as the property of one person and again as the property of another, but this does not include the imposition of different taxes concurrently on the same property or income (*e.g.* federal and state income taxes), nor the taxation of the same piece of property to different persons when they hold different interests in it or when it represents different values in their hands, as when both the mortgagor and mortgagee of property are taxed in respect to their interests in it, or when a tax is laid upon the profits of a corporation and also upon the dividends paid to its shareholders. "Double taxation" means taxing twice for the same purpose in the same year some of the property in the territory in which the tax is laid without taxing all of it. To constitute "double taxation," two taxes must be imposed on same property by same governing body during same taxing period and for same taxing purpose.

Term also refers to the structure of taxation under the Internal Revenue Code which subjects income earned by a corporation to an income tax at the corporate level and a second tax at the shareholder level if the same income is distributed to shareholders in the form of dividends.

Double use. In patent law, an application of a principle or process, previously known and applied, to some new use, but which does not lead to a new result or the production of a new article.

Double will. A will in which two persons join, each leaving his property and estate to the other, so that the survivor takes the whole. *See* Reciprocal wills.

Doubt, *v.* To question or hold questionable.

Doubt, *n.* Uncertainty of mind; the absence of a settled opinion or conviction; the attitude of mind towards the acceptance of or belief in a proposition, theory, or statement, in which the judgment is not at rest but inclines alternately to either side.

Reasonable doubt. This is a term often used, probably quite well understood, but not easily defined. It does not mean a mere possible doubt, because everything relating to human affairs, and depending on moral evidence, is open to some possible or imaginary doubt. It is that state of the case which, after the entire comparison and consideration of all the evidence, leaves the minds of jurors in that condition that they cannot say they feel an abiding conviction to a moral certainty of the truth of the charge. If upon proof there is reasonable doubt remaining, the accused is entitled to the benefit of it by an acquittal; for it is not sufficient to establish a probability, though a strong one, arising from the doctrine of chances, that the fact charged is more likely to be true than the contrary, but the evidence must establish the truth of the fact to a reasonable and moral certainty, *i.e.* a certainty that convinces and directs the understanding and satisfies the reason and judgment of those who are bound to act conscientiously upon it. This is proof beyond reasonable doubt; because if the law, which mostly depends upon considerations of a moral nature, should go further than this, and require absolute certainty, it would exclude circumstantial evidence altogether.

Proof "beyond a reasonable doubt" is not beyond all possible or imaginary doubt, but such proof as precludes every reasonable hypothesis except that which it tends to support. It is proof "to a moral certainty"; such proof as satisfies the judgment and consciences of the jury, as reasonable men, and applying their reason to the evidence before them, that the crime charged has been committed by the defendant, and so satisfies them as to leave no other reasonable conclusion possible.

A "reasonable doubt" is such a doubt as would cause a reasonable and prudent man in the graver and more important affairs of life to pause and hesitate to act upon the truth of the matter charged. But a reasonable doubt is not a mere possibility of innocence, nor a caprice, shadow, or speculation as to innocence not arising out of the evidence or the want of it.

See also Reasonable doubt.

Doubtful title. One as to the validity of which there exists some doubt, either as to matter of fact or of law; one which invites or exposes the party holding it to litigation. Distinguished from a "marketable" title, which is of such a character that the courts will compel its acceptance by a purchaser who has agreed to buy the property or has bid it in at public sale. *See* Marketable title.

Dovetail seniority. Combining two or more seniority lists (usually of different companies being merged) into a master seniority list, with each employee keeping the seniority he had previously acquired even though he may thereafter be employed by a new employer.

Dowable /dáwəbəl/. Subject to be charged with dower; as dowable lands. Entitled or entitling to dower. Thus, a dowable interest in lands is such as entitles the owner to have such lands charged with dower.

Dowager /dáwəjər/. A widow who is endowed, or who has a jointure in lieu of dower. Widow holding property or a title received from her deceased husband. In England, this is a title or addition given to the widows of princes, dukes, earls, and other noblemen, to distinguish them

from the wives of the heirs, who have right to bear the title.

Dower. The provision which the law makes for a widow out of the lands or tenements of her husband, for her support and the nurture of her children. A species of life-estate which a woman is, by law, entitled to claim on the death of her husband, in the lands and tenements of which he was seised in fee during the marriage, and which her issue, if any, might by possibility have inherited. The life estate to which every married woman is entitled on death of her husband, intestate, or, in case she dissents from his will, one-third in value of all lands of which husband was beneficially seized in law or in fact, at any time during coverture.

Dower has been abolished in the majority of the states and materially altered in most of the others.

See also Curtesy; Election (*Law of wills*); Election by spouse; Inchoate dower.

Dow Jones Average. A stock market performance indicator that consists of the price movements in the top 30 industrial companies in the United States.

Down payment. The portion of purchase price which is generally required to be paid at time purchase and sale agreement is signed and is generally paid in cash or its equivalent. An amount of money paid to the seller at the time of sale, which represents only a part of the total cost. *See also* Earnest money.

Dowry. The property which a woman brings to her husband in marriage; also sometimes called a "portion."

Dr. An abbreviation for "doctor". Also, in commercial usage, for "debtor," indicating the items or particulars in a bill or in an account-book chargeable against the person to whom the bill is rendered or in whose name the account stands, as opposed to "Cr." ("Credit" or "creditor"), which indicates the items for which he is given credit.

Draft. A written order by the first party, called the drawer, instructing a second party, called the drawee (such as a bank), to pay money to a third party, called the payee. An order to pay a sum certain in money, signed by a drawer, payable on demand or at a definite time, and to order or bearer. An unconditional order to pay money drawn by drawer on drawee to the order of the payee; same as a bill of exchange. U.C.C. § 3–104. *See also* Check; Documentary draft; Redraft; Sight draft; Trade acceptance.

A tentative, provisional, or preparatory writing out of any document (as a will, contract, lease, etc.) for purposes of discussion and correction, which is afterwards to be prepared in its final form.

Compulsory conscription of persons into military service.

Also, a small arbitrary deduction or allowance made to a merchant or importer, in the case of goods sold by wright or taxable by weight, to cover possible loss of weight in handling or from differences in scales.

Bank draft. One drawn by one bank on another.

Clean draft. One which has no shipping documents attached.

Documentary draft. One to which various shipping documents are attached.

Overdraft. Writing a check for more money than is in account.

Sight draft. One which is payable on presentation or demand. UCC § 3–108.

Time draft. One payable a certain number of days after sight or after presentation for acceptance. The number of days must be specified. UCC § 3–109.

Draft board. Federal agency that registers, classifies and selects men for compulsory military service. *See also* Selective Service System.

Draftsman. Any one who draws or frames a legal document, *e.g.,* a will, conveyance, pleading, etc. One who draws plans and specifications for machinery, structures, etc.

Dragnet clause. Provision in a mortgage in which mortgagor gives security for past and future advances as well as present indebtedness. A type of mortgage provision that attempts to make the mortgaged real estate security for other, usually unspecified, debts that the mortgagor may already or in the future owe to the mortgagee. While it is a species of future advances mortgage, the mortgagor and mortgagee rarely have in mind any specific future advances.

Drago doctrine. The principle asserted by Luis Drago, Minister of Foreign Affairs of the Argentine Republic, in a letter to the Argentine Minister at Washington, December 29, 1902, that the forcible intervention of states to secure the payment of public debts due to their citizens from foreign states is unjustifiable and dangerous to the security and peace of the nations of South America. The subject was brought before the Conference by the United States and a Convention was adopted in which the contracting powers agreed, with some restrictive conditions, not to have recourse to armed force for the recovery of contract debts claimed by their nationals against a foreign state. *See* Calvo doctrine.

Drain, *v.* To conduct water from one place to another, for the purpose of drying the former. To make dry; to draw off water; to rid land of its superfluous moisture by adapting or improving natural water courses and supplementing them,

when necessary, by artificial ditches. To "drain," in its larger sense, includes not only the supplying of outlets and channels to relieve the land from water, but also the provision of ditches, drains, and embankments to prevent water from accumulating.

To totally consume or exhaust.

Drain, *n.* A trench or ditch to convey water from wet land; a channel through which water may flow off. The word has no technical legal meaning. Any hollow space in the ground, natural or artificial, where water is collected and passes off, is a ditch or drain.

Also, sometimes, the easement or servitude (acquired by grant or prescription) which consists in the right to drain water through another's land. *See* Drainage rights.

Public drainage way. The land reserved or dedicated for the installation of storm water sewers or drainage ditches, or required along a natural stream or watercourse for preserving the channel and providing for the flow of water to safeguard the public against flood damage, sedimentation, and erosion.

Drainage district. A political subdivision of the state, created for the purpose of draining and reclaiming wet and overflowed land, as well as to preserve the public health and convenience.

Drainage rights. A landowner may not obstruct or divert the natural flow of a watercourse or natural drainage course to the injury of another. In urban areas, "natural drainage course" is narrowly interpreted to include only streams with well-defined channels and banks. In rural areas, the term is more broadly construed, apparently including the flow and direction of diffused surface waters.

Dramatic composition. In copyright law, a literary work setting forth a story, incident, or scene from life, in which, however, the narrative is not related, but is represented by a dialogue and action; may include a descriptive poem set to music, or a pantomime.

Dram-shop. A drinking establishment where liquors are sold to be drunk on the premises; a bar or saloon.

Dram Shop Acts. Many states have Dram Shop or Civil Liability Acts which impose liability on the seller of intoxicating liquors (which may or may not include beer), when a third party is injured as a result of the intoxication of the buyer where the sale has caused or contributed to such intoxication. Some acts apply to gifts as well as sales. Such acts protect the third party not only against personal injuries and property damages resulting directly from affirmative acts of the intoxicated man, such as resulting from negligent operation of vehicle or assault and battery, but also against the loss of family support due to such injuries.

Draw, *v.* To draw a firearm or deadly weapon is to point it intentionally. To draw a bead on; to bring into line with the bead or fore sight of a rifle and the hind sight; to aim at.

The act of a drawer in creating a draft. To draw a bill of exchange, check, or draft, is to write (or cause it to be written) and sign it; to make, as a note.

To compose and write out in due form, as, a deed, complaint, petition, memorial, etc.

To draw a jury is to select the persons who are to compose it, either by taking their names successively, but at hazard, from the jury box, or by summoning them individually to attend the court. *See* Impanel.

In old criminal practice, to drag (on a hurdle) to the place of execution. Anciently no hurdle was allowed, but the criminal was actually dragged along the road to the place of execution. A part of the ancient punishment of traitors was to be thus drawn.

To withdraw money; *i.e.,* to take out money from a bank, treasury, or other depository in the exercise of a lawful right and in a lawful manner. To periodically advance money on a construction loan agreement or against future sales commissions. *See also* Drawing account.

Drawback. In the customs laws, an allowance made by the government upon the duties due on imported merchandise when the importer, instead of selling it here, re-exports it; or the refunding of such duties if already paid. This allowance amounts, in some cases, to the whole of the original duties; in others, to a part only. See 19 U.S.C.A. § 1313.

Drawee. The person on whom a bill or draft is drawn. A person to whom a bill of exchange or draft is directed, and who is requested to pay the amount of money therein mentioned. The drawee of a check is the bank on which it is drawn.

When drawee accepts, he engages that he will pay the instrument according to its tenor at the time of his engagement or as completed. U.C.C. § 3–413(1).

Drawer. The person who draws a bill or draft. The drawer of a check is the person who signs it. The person who creates or executes a draft, that is, issues it, and in signing the instrument gives the order to pay contained therein.

The drawer engages that upon dishonor of the draft and any necessary notice of dishonor or protest, he will pay the amount of the draft to the holder or to any indorser who takes it up. The drawer may disclaim this liability by drawing without recourse. U.C.C. § 3–413(2).

Drawing account. Fund of money from which salesperson or other employees may draw in anticipation of future earnings or commissions; may be used to pay current expenses.

Drawing lots. An act in which selection is based on pure chance and in which the result depends upon the particular lot which is drawn. *See also* Lottery.

Drawlatches /drólæchəz/. Thieves; robbers.

Drayage. A charge for the local transportation of property. Similar to cartage.

Dred Scott Case. The case in which the United States Supreme Court held that descendants of Africans who were imported into this country, and sold as slaves, were not included nor intended to be included under the word "Citizens" in the Constitution, whether emancipated or not, and remained without rights or privileges except such as those which the government might grant them. Dred Scott v. Sandford, 60 U.S. (19 How.) 393, 15 L.Ed. 691.

Driving while intoxicated (DWI). An offense committed by one who operates a motor vehicle while under the influence of intoxicating liquor or drugs. A showing of complete intoxication is not required. State statutes specify levels of blood alcohol content at which a person is presumed to be under the influence of intoxicating liquor. *See also* Blood alcohol count; Blood test evidence; Breathalyzer test; Consent (*Implied consent*); Drunk-o-meter; Field sobriety tests; Intoxilyzer; Intoximeter; Sobriety checkpoint.

Droit Fr. /dr(w)ó, Engl. /dróyt/. In French law, right, justice, equity, law, the whole body of law; also a right.

This term exhibits the same ambiguity which is discoverable in the German equivalent, *"recht"* and the English word *"right."* On the one hand, these terms answer to the Roman *"jus,"* and thus indicate law in the abstract, considered as the foundation of all rights, or the complex of underlying moral principles which impart the character of justice to all positive law, or give it an ethical content. Taken in this abstract sense, the terms may be adjectives, in which case they are equivalent to "just," or nouns, in which case they may be paraphrased by the expressions "justice," "morality," or "equity." On the other hand, they serve to point out *a* right; that is, a power, privilege, faculty, or demand, inherent in one person, and incident upon another. In the latter signification, *droit* (or *recht* or *right*) is the correlative of "duty" or "obligation." In the former sense, it may be considered as opposed to wrong, injustice, or the absence of law. *Droit* has the further ambiguity that it is sometimes used to denote the existing body of law considered as one whole, or the sum total of a number of individual laws taken together. *See* Jus; Right.

A person was said to have *droit droit, plurimum juris,* and *plurimum possessionis,* when he had the freehold, the fee, and the property in him.

In old English law, law; right; a writ of right.

Autre droit. The right of another.

Droit de détraction /drwó də dèytraksyówn/. A tax upon the removal from one state or country to another of property acquired by succession or testamentary disposition; it does not cover a tax upon the succession to or transfer of property. *Cf.* Duties of detraction.

Droit moral. A European doctrine of "artistic integrity" that gives artists the right to prevent others from altering their work without permission. Non-pecuniary right based upon the dual relationship between society and its artists, and the artist and his work. The basic rights sought to be protected under this concept comprise: the right to create; the right to disclose or publish; the right to withdraw from publication; the right to be identified with the work; and, the right to integrity with respect to the work, including the right to object to the mutilation or distortion of the work.

Drop-letter. A letter addressed for delivery in the same city or district in which it is posted.

Drop shipment delivery. Shipment of goods directly from manufacturer to dealer or consumer rather than first to wholesaler, though wholesaler still earns profit because he took order for such.

Drop shipper. Type of wholesaler described above.

Drug. An article intended for use in the diagnosis, cure, mitigation, treatment, or prevention of disease in man or other animals and any article other than food intended to affect the structure or any function of the body of man or other animals. 21 U.S.C.A. § 321(g)(1). The general name of substances used in medicine; any substance, vegetable, animal, or mineral, used in the composition or preparation of medicines; any substance used as a medicine. *See* Controlled Substance Acts.

Drug abuse. State of chronic or periodic intoxication detrimental to the individual and to society, produced by the repeated consumption of a drug, natural or synthetic. *See also* Addict; Drug dependence.

The voluntary, habitual, and excessive use of drugs is a ground for divorce in many states.

Drug addict. A person subject to drug abuse. *See* Addict; Drug abuse; Drug dependence.

Drug dependence. Habituation to, abuse of, and/or addiction to a chemical substance. *See* Addict.

Drummer. A term applied to commercial agents who travel for wholesale merchants and supply the retail trade with goods or take orders for goods to be shipped to the retail dealer. Term most commonly refers to traveling salesmen. *See also* Commercial traveler.

Drunkenness. State of intoxication. The condition of a person whose mind is affected by the consumption of intoxicating drinks; the state of one who is "drunk." The effect produced upon the mind or body by drinking intoxicating liquors to such an extent that the normal condition of the subject is changed and his capacity for rational action and conduct is substantially lessened. *See also* Driving while intoxicated; Intoxication.

While some states have decriminalized public drunkenness (*e.g.* Mass.), there is no constitutional infirmity in a criminal statute which penalizes being drunk in public.

Drunk-o-meter. Device used for measuring blood alcohol content by chemical analysis of the breath. The results of such tests are generally used in prosecutions for drunk driving or operating a vehicle under the influence of liquor. *See also* Blood alcohol count; Breathalyzer test; Consent (*Implied consent*); Driving while intoxicated; Field sobriety tests; Intoxilyzer; Intoximeter.

Dry hole agreement. In oil and gas law, a support agreement in which the contributing party agrees to make a cash contribution in exchange for geological or drilling information, if a dry hole is drilled.

Dry hole clause. A provision in an oil and gas lease specifying what a lessee must do to maintain the lease for the remainder of the primary term after drilling an unproductive well. A dry hole clause is intended to make clear that the lease may be maintained by payment of delay rentals for the remainder of the primary term.

Dry mortgage. One which creates a lien on land for the payment of money, but does not impose any personal liability upon the mortgagor, collateral to or over and above the value of the premises.

Dry receivership. Receivership wherein there is no equity to be administered for general creditors, even if action is in statutory form.

Dry rent. Rent seck; a rent reserved without a clause of distress.

Dry state. State wherein sale of intoxicating liquors is prohibited.

Dry trust. A passive trust; one which requires no action on the part of the trustee beyond turning over money or property to the *cestui que trust.*

DSAT. Debt Service After Tax.

DSP. Debt Service Parity.

Dual capacity doctrine. Under this doctrine employer normally shielded from tort liability by exclusive remedy of workers' compensation law may become liable in tort to his employee if he occupies, in addition to his capacity as employer, a second capacity that confers on him obligations independent of those imposed on him as employer.

Dual citizenship. Citizenship in two different countries. Status of citizens of United States who reside within a state; *i.e.,* persons who are born or naturalized in the U.S. are citizens of the U.S. and the state wherein they reside.

Dual court system. Term descriptive of Federal and State court systems of United States.

Dual distributor. A firm that sells goods simultaneously to buyers on two different levels of the distribution chain—such as a manufacturer who sells directly to both wholesalers and retailers—is called a dual distributor.

Dual listing. *See* Listed security.

Dual pricing arrangement. In accounting, allows a selling division to record the transfer of goods or services at one price (e.g., a market or negotiated market price) and a buying division to record the transfer at another price (e.g., a cost-based amount).

Dual purpose doctrine. The dual purpose doctrine is that if the work of an employee creates a necessity for travel, he is in the course of his employment while doing that work even though at the same time he is serving some purpose of his own. Doctrine is that injury during trip which serves both business and personal purpose is within course of employment if trip involves performance of service for employer which would have caused trip to be taken by someone even if it had not coincided with personal journey.

Duces tecum /d(y)úwsiyz tíykəm/. (Lat. Bring with you.) The name of certain species of writs, of which the *subpoena duces tecum* is the most usual, requiring a party who is summoned to appear in court to bring with him some document, piece of evidence, or other thing to be used or inspected by the court. *See* Subpoena duces tecum.

Due. Just; proper; regular; lawful; sufficient; reasonable, as in the phrases "due care," "due process of law," "due notice."

Owing; payable; justly owed. That which one contracts to pay or perform to another; that which law or justice requires to be paid or done.

Owed, or owing, as distinguished from payable. A debt is often said to be *due* from a person where he is the party owing it, or primarily bound to pay, whether the time for payment has or has not arrived. The same thing is true of the phrase "due and owing."

Payable. A bill or note is commonly said to be *due* when the time for payment of it has arrived.

The word "due" always imports a fixed and settled obligation or liability, but with reference to the time for its payment there is considerable ambiguity in the use of the term, the precise signification being determined in each case from the context. It may mean that the debt or claim in question is now (presently or immediately) matured and enforceable, or that it matured at some time in the past and yet remains unsatisfied, or that it is fixed and certain but the day appointed for its payment has not yet arrived. But commonly, and in the absence of any qualifying expressions, the word "due" is restricted to the first of these meanings, the second being expressed by the term "overdue," and the third by the word "payable."

Due and proper care. That degree of care which is required of one for prevention of the accident. *See* Due care.

Due and reasonable care. Care which reasonably prudent man would exercise under same or similar circumstances. *See* Due care.

Due bill. Written acknowledgment of a debt, or promise to pay. *See* IOU.

Due care. Just, proper, and sufficient care, so far as the circumstances demand; the absence of negligence. That degree of care that a reasonable person can be expected to exercise to avoid harm reasonably foreseeable if such care is not taken. That care which an ordinarily prudent person would have exercised under the same or similar circumstances. "Due care" is care proportioned to any given situation, its surroundings, peculiarities, and hazards. It may and often does require extraordinary care. "Due care," "reasonable care," and "ordinary care" are often used as convertible terms.

This term, as usually understood in cases where the gist of the action is the defendant's negligence, implies not only that a party has not been negligent or careless, but that he has been guilty of no violation of law in relation to the subject-matter or transaction which constitutes the cause of action.

Due compensation. Term as used in eminent domain is the value of land taken and the damages, if any, which result to owner as a consequence of the taking without considering either general benefits or injuries. *See* Just compensation.

Due consideration. To give such weight or significance to a particular factor as under the circumstances it seems to merit, and this involves discretion. As regards sufficient consideration in contract law, *see* Consideration.

Due course holder. *See* Holder in due course.

Due course of law. This phrase is synonymous with "due process of law," or "the law of the land," and the general definition thereof is "law in its regular course of administration through courts of justice". *See* Due process of law.

Due date. In general, the particular day on or before which something must be done to comply with law or contractual obligation.

Due diligence. *See* Diligence.

Due influence. Influence obtained by persuasion and argument or by appeals to the affections. *See also* Coercion; Duress.

Dueling. The fighting of two persons, one against the other, at an appointed time and place, upon a precedent quarrel. If death results, the crime is murder. It differs from an affray in this, that the latter occurs on a sudden quarrel, while the former is always the result of design.

Due negotiation. Transferring a negotiable document of title under such conditions that the transferee takes the document and the goods free of certain claims enforceable against the transferor. See U.C.C. §§ 7–501(4) & 7–502(1). Due negotiation is the good faith purchase exception to the doctrine of derivative title as applied to documents.

Due notice. Sufficient, legally prescribed notice. Notice reasonably intended, and with the likelihood of, reaching the particular person or public. No fixed rule can be established as to what shall constitute "due notice." "Due" is a relative term, and must be applied to each case in the exercise of the discretion of the court in view of the particular circumstances. *See* Notice.

Due-on-encumbrance clause. Mortgage language that gives the mortgagee the option to accelerate the mortgage debt in the event the mortgagor further encumbers or mortgages the real estate without mortgagee's consent.

Due-on-sale clause. A provision usually found in a note or mortgage whereby the entire debt becomes immediately due and payable at mortgagee's option upon sale of mortgaged property. Such clauses are generally used to prevent subsequent purchasers from assuming existing loans at lower than current market rates. The validity of such provisions has been upheld by the Supreme Court.

Due posting. Stamping and placing letter in United States mail.

Due process clause. Two such clauses are found in the U.S. Constitution, one in the 5th Amendment pertaining to the federal government, the other in the 14th Amendment which protects persons from state actions. There are two aspects: procedural, in which a person is guaranteed fair procedures and substantive which protects a person's property from unfair governmental interference or taking. Similar clauses are in most state constitutions. *See* Due process of law.

Due process of law. Law in its regular course of administration through courts of justice. Due process of law in each particular case means such an exercise of the powers of the government as the settled maxims of law permit and sanction, and under such safeguards for the protection of individual rights as those maxims prescribe for the class of cases to which the one in question belongs. A course of legal proceedings according to those rules and principles which have been established in our systems of jurisprudence for the enforcement and protection of private rights. To give such proceedings any validity, there must be a tribunal competent by its constitution—that is, by the law of its creation—to pass upon the subject-matter of the suit; and, if that involves merely a determination of the personal liability of the defendant, he must be brought within its jurisdiction by service of process within the state, or his voluntary appearance. Pennoyer v. Neff, 95 U.S. 733, 24 L.Ed. 565. Due process of law implies the right of the person affected thereby to be present before the tribunal which pronounces judgment upon the question of life, liberty, or property, in its most comprehensive sense; to be heard, by testimony or otherwise, and to have the right of controverting, by proof, every material fact which bears on the question of right in the matter involved. If any question of fact or liability be conclusively presumed against him, this is not due process of law.

An orderly proceeding wherein a person is served with notice, actual or constructive, and has an opportunity to be heard and to enforce and protect his rights before a court having power to hear and determine the case. Phrase means that no person shall be deprived of life, liberty, property or of any right granted him by statute, unless matter involved first shall have been adjudicated against him upon trial conducted according to established rules regulating judicial proceedings, and it forbids condemnation without a hearing. The concept of "due process of law" as it is embodied in Fifth Amendment demands that a law shall not be unreasonable, arbitrary, or capricious and that the means selected shall have a reasonable and substantial relation to the object being sought. Fundamental requisite of "due process" is the opportunity to be heard, to be aware that a matter is pending, to make an informed choice whether to acquiesce or contest, and to assert before the appropriate decision-making body the reasons for such choice. Aside from all else, "due process" means fundamental fairness and substantial justice.

Embodied in the due process concept are the basic rights of a defendant in criminal proceedings and the requisites for a fair trial. These rights and requirements have been expanded by Supreme Court decisions and include, timely notice of a hearing or trial which informs the accused of the charges against him or her; the opportunity to confront accusers and to present evidence on one's own behalf before an impartial jury or judge; the presumption of innocence under which guilt must be proven by legally obtained evidence and the verdict must be supported by the evidence presented; the right of an accused to be warned of constitutional rights at the earliest stage of the criminal process; protection against self-incrimination; assistance of counsel at every critical stage of the criminal process; and the guarantee that an individual will not be tried more than once for the same offense (double jeopardy).

See also Procedural due process; Substantive due process.

Due process rights. All rights which are of such fundamental importance as to require compliance with due process standards of fairness and justice. Procedural and substantive rights of citizens against government actions that threaten the denial of life, liberty, or property. *See* Due process of law.

Due proof. Within insurance policy requirements, term means such a statement of facts, reasonably verified, as, if established in court, would prima facie require payment of the claim, and does not mean some particular form of proof which the insurer arbitrarily demands. Sufficient evidence to support or produce a conclusion; adequate evidence. *See* Burden of proof; Proof.

Due regard. Consideration in a degree appropriate to demands of the particular case.

Dues. Certain payments, rates or taxes. As applied to clubs and other membership organizations, refers to sums paid toward support and maintenance of same and as a requisite to retain membership.

Due to. Expressions "sustained by," "caused by," "due to," "resulting from," "sustained by means of," "sustained in consequence of," and "sustained through" have been held to be synonymous.

D.U.I. The crime of driving under the influence of alcohol or drugs. *See* Driving while intoxicated.

Duly. In due or proper form or manner; according to legal requirements. Regularly; properly; suitable; upon a proper foundation, as distinguished from mere form; according to law in both form and substance. *See* Due process of law.

Duly qualified. Being "duly qualified" to fill an office, in the constitutional sense and in the ordinary acceptation of the words, means that the officer shall possess every qualification; that he shall in all respects comply with every requisite before entering on duties of the office; and that

he shall be bound by oath or affirmation to support the Constitution, and to perform the duties of the office with fidelity.

Dumb-bidding. In sales at auction, when the minimum amount which the owner will take for the article is written on a piece of paper, and placed by the owner under an object, and it is agreed that no bidding shall avail unless equal to that, this is called "dumb-bidding."

Dummy, *n.* One who purchases property and holds legal title for another, usually to conceal the identity of the true owner; a straw man (*q.v.*).

Dummy, *adj.* Sham; make-believe; pretended; imitation. Person who serves in place of another, or who serves until the proper person is named or available to take his place (*e.g.* dummy corporate directors; dummy owners of real estate).

Dummy corporation. Corporation formed for sham purposes and not for conduct of legitimate business; *e.g.* formed for sole reason of avoiding personal liability.

Dummy director. One to whom (usually) a single share of stock in a corporation is transferred for the purpose of qualifying him as a director of the corporation, in which he has no real or active interest. One who is a mere figurehead and in effect discharges no duties.

Dummy stockholder. One who holds shares of stock in his name for the benefit of the true owner whose name is generally concealed. *See also* Street name.

Dump. To put or throw down with more or less of violence; to unload. To drop down; to deposit something in a heap or unshaped mass. To sell abroad at less than price sold at home. *See* Dumping Act.

Dumping. The act of selling in quantity at a very low price or practically regardless of the price; also, selling goods abroad at less than the market price at home. *See* Dumping Act.

The act of forcing a product such as cotton on the market during the short gathering season.

Dumping Act. Federal antidumping law which provides that the Secretary of Treasury is required to notify U.S. International Trade Commission (USITC) whenever he determines that foreign merchandise is being or is likely to be sold in U.S. or elsewhere at less than its fair value and the USITC shall determine the injury to U.S. industry. If such imports are determined to be injurious to domestic sales of like products, such imports may be ordered stopped. 19 U.S.C.A. § 1673.

Dun. A demand for payment (*e.g.* dun letter) to a delinquent debtor.

Duopoly /d(y)uwópəliy/. A condition in the market in which there are only two producers or sellers of a given product.

Duosony /d(y)uwósəniy/. A condition of the market in which there are only two buyers of a given product.

Duplicate, *v.* To douple, repeat, copy, make, or add a thing exactly like a preceding one; reproduce exactly.

Duplicate, *n.* A "duplicate" is a counterpart produced by the same impression as the original, or from the same matrix, or by means of photography, including enlargements and miniatures, or by mechanical or electronic re-recording, or by chemical reproduction, or by other equivalent techniques which accurately reproduces the original. Fed.R.Evid. 1001.

That which exactly resembles or corresponds to something else; another, correspondent to the first; hence, a copy; transcript; counterpart; an original instrument repeated; a document the same as another in essential particulars. The term is also frequently used to signify a new original, made to take the place of an instrument that has been lost or destroyed, and to have the same force and effect. *See also* Copy.

Duplicate taxation. *See* Double taxation.

Duplicate will. A term used where a testator executes two copies of his will, one to keep himself, and the other to be deposited with another person. Upon application for probate of a duplicate will, both copies must be deposited in the registry of the court of probate. The execution of duplicate wills is undesirable because if the testator desires to revoke his will, he must be careful to comply with the laws of revocation as to both wills. *See also* Reciprocal wills.

Duplicitous /d(y)ùwplísətəs/. A pleading which joins in one and the same count different grounds of action of different nature, or of the same nature, to enforce a single right to recovery, or which is based on different theories of the defendant's liability. Such duplicity was not permitted in common law pleading, but is allowed under Rule of Civil Procedure 8(e). In an information, the joinder of separate and distinct offenses in one and the same count. *See e.g.* Fed.R.Crim.P. 8(a). *See also* Duplicity.

Duplicitous appeal. Appeal from two separate judgments or from judgment and order or from two independent orders, both of which are appealable.

Duplicity. The technical fault in common law pleading of uniting two or more causes of action in one count in a writ, or two or more grounds of defense in one plea, or two or more breaches in a replication, or two or more offenses in the same count of an indictment, or two or more incongruous subjects in one legislative act, or two or more controverted ultimate issues submitted in a single special issue. Such duplicity of pleading in civil actions is permitted under Rule of Civil Procedure 8(e).

Rule of "duplicity" prohibits the simultaneous charging of several distinct, unrelated crimes in one indictment. The joining in a single count of two or more distinct and separate offenses. *See e.g.* Fed.R.Crim.P. 8(a). *See also* Multiplicity of actions or suits.

Deliberate deception or double dealing.

Durable goods. *See* Goods.

Durable leases. Leases reserving a rent payable annually, with right of re-entry for nonpayment of the same, and for the term "as long as grass grows or water runs," or equivalent terms.

Durable power of attorney. *See* Power of attorney.

Duration. Extent, limit or time. The portion of time during which anything exists.

Interest. The period of time during which an interest in property lasts.

Trust. The period of time during which a trust exists before its termination.

Duress. Any unlawful threat or coercion used by a person to induce another to act (or to refrain from acting) in a manner he or she otherwise would not (or would). Subjecting person to improper pressure which overcomes his will and coerces him to comply with demand to which he would not yield if acting as free agent. Application of such pressure or constraint as compels man to go against his will, and takes away his free agency, destroying power of refusing to comply with unjust demands of another.

A condition where one is induced by wrongful act or threat of another to make a contract or perform a tortious act under circumstances which deprive him of exercise of his free will. Includes any conduct which overpowers will and coerces or constrains performance of an act which otherwise would not have been performed.

Duress may be a defense to a criminal act, breach of contract, or tort because an act to be criminal or one which constitutes a breach of contract or a tort must be voluntary to create liability or responsibility.

A contract entered into under duress by physical compulsion is void. Also, if a party's manifestation of assent to a contract is induced by an improper threat by the other party that leaves the victim no reasonable alternative, the contract is voidable by the victim. Restatement, Second, Contracts §§ 174, 175.

As a defense to a civil action, it must be pleaded affirmatively. Fed.R.Civil P. 8(c).

As an affirmative defense in criminal law, one who, under the pressure of an unlawful threat from another human being to harm him (or to harm a third person), commits what would otherwise be a crime may, under some circumstances, be justified in doing what he did and thus not be guilty of the crime in question. See Model Penal Code § 2.09.

See also Coercion; Economic duress; Extortion; Undue influence.

Duress of goods. Exists where the act consists of a tortious seizure or detention of property from the person entitled to it, and requires some act as a condition for its surrender.

Durham rule. The irresistible impulse test of criminal responsibility. The rule states that when there is some evidence that the accused suffered from a diseased or defective mental condition at the time the unlawful act was committed the accused is not criminally responsible if it is found beyond a reasonable doubt that the act was the product of such mental abnormality. Durham v. United States, C.A.D.C., 214 F.2d 862, 875. This test of criminal responsibility (as first adopted in 1954 by the Court of Appeals of the District of Columbia in the cited case) was rejected by the same Court in 1972 when it adopted the ALI criterion of insanity of Model Penal Code § 4.01(1). This same Model Penal Code test has also been adopted by a number of other courts. *See* Insanity.

During. Throughout the course of; throughout the continuance of; in the time of; after the commencement and before the expiration of.

During the hours of service. Within workers' compensation law, means working-hours plus reasonable periods for ingress and egress. *See also* Course of employment.

During the trial. Period beginning with swearing of jury and ending with rendition of verdict. Period commencing with presentation of indictment by grand jury to court and terminating with final judgment.

Dutch auction. *See* Auction.

Dutch lottery. Also known as the "class lottery." As distinguished from the "Genoese lottery" *(q.v.)*, it is a scheme in which the number and value of the prizes are regularly estimated, all the ticket holders are interested at once in the play, and chance determines whether a prize or a blank falls to a given number.

Duties. In its most usual signification this word is the synonym of imposts or customs; *i.e.* tax on imports; but it is sometimes used in a broader sense, as including all manner of taxes, charges, or governmental impositions. *See also* Customs; Most favored nation clause; Tariff; Toll; Tonnage-duty.

Duties of detraction. Taxes levied upon the removal from one state to another of property acquired by succession or testamentary disposition. *Cf.* Droit de détraction.

Duties on imports /d(y)úwtiyz òn impòrts/. This term signifies not merely a duty on the act of importation, but a duty on the thing imported. It is not confined to a duty levied while the article is entering the country, but extends to a duty levied after it has entered the country. *See* Customs duties.

Duty. A human action which is exactly conformable to the laws which require us to obey them. Legal or moral obligation. An obligation that one has by law or contract. Obligation to conform to legal standard of reasonable conduct in light of apparent risk. Obligatory conduct or service. Mandatory obligation to perform. An obligation, recognized by the law, requiring actor to conform to certain standard of conduct for protection of others against unreasonable risks. *See also* Legal duty; Obligation.

A thing due; that which is due from a person; that which a person owes to another. An obligation to do a thing. A word of more extensive signification than "debt," although both are expressed by the same Latin word *"debitum."* Sometimes, however, the term is used synonymously with debt.

Those obligations of performance, care, or observance which rest upon a person in an official or fiduciary capacity; as the *duty* of an executor, trustee, manager, etc.

In negligence cases term may be defined as an obligation, to which law will give recognition and effect, to comport to a particular standard of conduct toward another, and the duty is invariably the same, one must conform to legal standard of reasonable conduct in light of apparent risk. The word "duty" is used throughout the Restatement of Torts to denote the fact that the actor is required to conduct himself in a particular manner at the risk that if he does not do so he becomes subject to liability to another to whom the duty is owed for any injury sustained by such other, of which that actor's conduct is a legal cause. Restatement, Second, Torts § 4. *See* Care; Due care.

In its use in jurisprudence, this word is the correlative of *right*. Thus, wherever there exists a right in any person, there also rests a corresponding duty upon some other person or upon all persons generally.

It also denotes a tax or impost due to the government upon the importation or exportation of goods. See 19 U.S.C.A. *See also* Customs; Customs duties; Tariff; Toll; Tonnage-duty.

Judicial duty. *See* Judicial.

Duty free. Products or merchandise of foreign origin that are not subject to import or export taxes. *See* Customs duties.

Duty of tonnage. A charge upon a vessel as an instrument of commerce for entering, lying in or leaving a port, and includes all taxes and duties, regardless of name or form.

Duty of water. Such a quantity of water necessary when economically conducted and applied to land without unnecessary loss as will result in the successful growing of crops.

Duty to act. Obligation to take some action to prevent harm to another and for failure of which there may or may not be liability in tort depending upon the circumstances and the relationship of the parties to each other. *See* Emergency doctrine; Humanitarian doctrine.

Duty to mitigate. Obligation of non-breaching party in contract to minimize damages. *See* Mitigation of damages.

Dwell. To have an abode; to reside; to inhabit; to live in a place. More than mere physical presence is sometimes required. It must be in conformity with law. To abide as a permanent residence or for a time. Term is synonymous with inhabit, live, sojourn, reside, stay, rest. *See also* Domicile; Residence.

Dwelling. The house or other structure in which a person or persons live; a residence; abode; habitation; the apartment or building, or group of buildings, occupied by a family as a place of residence. Structure used as place of habitation.

In conveyancing, includes all buildings attached to or connected with the house. In criminal law (*e.g.* burglary), means a building or portion thereof, a tent, a mobile home, a vehicle or other enclosed space which is used or intended for use as a human habitation, home or residence.

Under statute prohibiting breaking and entering a "dwelling house" the test for determining if a building is such a house is whether it is used regularly as a place to sleep.

Dwelling defense. In most jurisdictions, a person in his dwelling is permitted to use even deadly force to protect himself, his household and the house itself from attack on the principle that a person's house is his castle. Model Penal Code §§ 3.11, 3.06(3)(d).

D.W.I. In genealogical tables, a common abbreviation for "died without issue." Also, abbreviation for offense of "driving while intoxicated" *(q.v.)*.

Dyer Act. National Motor Vehicle Theft Act (1919) which makes it a criminal offense to transport a stolen motor vehicle in interstate or foreign commerce knowing it to be stolen or to receive or conceal such a motor vehicle in interstate or foreign commerce knowing it to be stolen, though knowledge of its interstate transportation is not essential to guilt. 18 U.S.C.A. §§ 2311–2313.

Dying declaration. *See* Declaration.

Dying without issue. Dying without a child either before or after the decedent's death. At common law this phrase imports an indefinite failure of issue, and not a dying without issue surviving at the time of the death of the first taker. But this rule has been changed in many decisions, with many states having held that the expression "dying without issue," and like expressions, have reference to the time of the death of the party, and not to an indefinite failure of issue. *See also* Failure of issue.

Dying without children imports not a failure of issue at any indefinite future period, but a leaving no children at the death of the legatee. The law favors vesting of estates, and limitation such as "dying without issue," refers to a definite period, fixed in will, rather than to an indefinite failure of issue. Where context is such as to show clearly that testator intended the phrase "die without issue" to mean that, if first taker die without issue during life of testator, the second taker shall stand in his place and prevent a lapse, the words "die without issue" are taken to mean death during life of testator.

Dynamite instruction. Further instruction given by the trial judge to jury when the jury have reported an inability to agree on a verdict in a criminal case. In the further instructions, the judge advises them of their obligation to consider the opinions of their fellow jurors and to yield their own views where possible. Allen v. United States, 164 U.S. 492, 17 S.Ct. 154, 41 L.Ed. 528. This type of jury instruction (also called "Allen charge") is prohibited in certain states; *e.g.* California. *See also* Allen charge.

E

Each. A distributive adjective pronoun, which denotes or refers to every one of the persons or things mentioned; every one of two or more persons or things, composing the whole, separately considered. "Each" is synonymous with "all" and agrees in inclusiveness but differs in stress; "all" collects and "each" distributes.

Earlier maturity rule. The rule under which bonds first maturing are entitled to priority when sale of security is not sufficient to satisfy all obligations.

Ear-mark. A mark put upon a thing to distinguish it from another. Originally and literally, a mark upon the ear; a mode of marking sheep and other animals.

Property is said to be *ear-marked* when it can be identified or distinguished from other property of the same nature.

To set apart from others.

Ear-mark rule. Rule that through the process of commingling money or deposit with the funds of a bank it loses its identity, with the resultant effect of defeating the right of preference over general creditors.

Earn. To acquire by labor, service or performance. Earned means to merit or deserve, as for labor or service. To do that which entitles one to a reward, whether the reward is received or not; to acquire by labor, service or performance.

Earned income. Income from services (*e.g.*, salaries, wages, or fees); distinguished from passive, portfolio, and other unearned income. See I.R.C. § 911. In taxation, term generally is meant to include all income not representing return on capital. *See also* Earnings; Income.

Earned income credit. A refundable tax credit on earned income up to a certain amount for low income workers who maintain a household for dependent children. The amount of the credit is reduced dollar for dollar if earned income (or adjusted gross income) is greater than a specified amount.

Earned premium. In insurance, that portion of the premium properly allocable to policy period which has expired. An "earned premium" is difference between premium paid by insured and portion returnable to him by insurance company on cancellation of policy during its term.

Earned surplus. Retained earnings. That species of surplus which has been generated from profits as contrasted with paid-in surplus. Term relates to net accumulation of profits; it is a part of surplus that represents net earnings, gains or profits, after deduction of all losses, but has not been distributed as dividends, or transferred to stated capital or capital surplus, or applied to other purposes permitted by law.

Earner. One whose personal efforts produce income (*e.g.* wage earner) or who owns property which produces it, or combination of both.

Earnest. The payment of a part of the price of goods sold, or the delivery of part of such goods, for the purpose of binding the contract. A token or pledge passing between the parties, by way of evidence, or ratification of the sale. *See* Earnest money.

Earnest money. A sum of money paid by a buyer at the time of entering a contract to indicate the intention and ability of the buyer to carry out the contract. Normally such earnest money is applied against the purchase price. Often the contract provides for forfeiture of this sum if the buyer defaults. A deposit of part payment of purchase price on sale to be consummated in future. Import of term in real estate contract is that when comparatively small sum is paid down, it is an assurance that party is in earnest and good faith and that if his being in earnest and good faith fails, it will be forfeited. *See also* Binder; Down payment.

Earning capacity. Term refers to capability of worker to sell his labor or services in any market reasonably accessible to him, taking into consideration his general physical functional impairment resulting from his accident, any previous disability, his occupation, age at time of injury, nature of injury and his wages prior to and after the injury. Term does not necessarily mean the actual earnings that one who suffers an injury was making at the time the injuries were sustained, but refers to that which, by virtue of the training, the experience, and the business acumen possessed, an individual is capable of earning.

"Earning capacity" of husband or wife for purpose of determining amount of support which he or she may be required to pay spouse is not that amount which an individual could theoretically earn but is amount which individual could realistically earn under circumstances, including health, age, mental and physical condition and training.

Fitness, readiness and willingness to work, considered in connection with opportunity to work.

Earning power. *See* Earning capacity.

Earnings. Income. That which is earned; *i.e.*, money earned from performance of labor, services, sale of goods, etc. Revenue earned by an individual or business. Earnings generally include but are not limited to: salaries and wages, interest and dividends, and income from self-employment. Term is broader in meaning than "wages." *See also* Commissions; Compensation; Dividend; Gross earnings; Income; Premium; Real earnings; Retained earnings; Salary; Wages.

Gross earnings. Total income from all sources without considering deductions, personal exemptions, or other reductions of income in order to arrive at taxable income. *See also* Gross income.

Net earnings. Net earnings (income) is the excess of gross income over expenses incurred in connection with the production of such income. For tax purposes, net earnings is the number used to determine taxable income. For accounting purposes, net earnings is generally determined after deduction of income taxes. *See also* Net income.

Surplus earnings. *See* Surplus.

Earnings and profits. A tax concept peculiar to corporate taxpayers which measures economic capacity to make a distribution to shareholders that is not a return of capital. Such a distribution will result in dividend income to the shareholders to the extent of the corporation's current and accumulated earnings and profits. *See also* Accumulated earnings tax; Accumulated taxable income.

Earnings deficiency. The condition that exists when a partnership incurs a net loss or has insufficient earnings to cover salary and interest allowances.

Earnings per share. One common measure of the value of common stock. The figure is computed by dividing the net earnings for the year (after interest and prior dividends) by the number of shares of common stock outstanding.

Fully diluted earnings per share. Earnings per share calculated under the assumption that all convertible securities have been converted into common equity and all stock options have been exercised.

Earnings report. Businesses' statement of profit and loss; commonly issued quarterly by publically-held companies.

Earnout agreement. An agreement whereby a business seller accepts a lump sum up front, with the ultimate purchase price being determined by the company's future profits. Typically, the sell-er stays on for a period to help manage the company.

Ear-witness. In the law of evidence, one who attests or can attest anything as heard by himself. *See also* Voiceprint.

Easement. A right of use over the property of another. Traditionally the permitted kinds of uses were limited, the most important being rights of way and rights concerning flowing waters. The easement was normally for the benefit of adjoining lands, no matter who the owner was (an easement appurtenant), rather than for the benefit of a specific individual (easement in gross). The land having the right of use as an appurtenance is known as the dominant tenement and the land which is subject to the easement is known as the servient tenement.

A right in the owner of one parcel of land, by reason of such ownership, to use the land of another for a special purpose not inconsistent with a general property in the owner.

An interest which one person has in the land of another. A primary characteristic of an easement is that its burden falls upon the possessor of the land from which it issued and that characteristic is expressed in the statement that the land constitutes a servient tenement and the easement a dominant tenement. An interest in land in and over which it is to be enjoyed, and is distinguishable from a "license" which merely confers personal privilege to do some act on the land.

See also Affirmative easement; Non-continuous easement; Prescriptive easement.

Access easement. *See* Access.

Affirmative easement. One where the servient estate must permit something to be done thereon, as to pass over it, or to discharge water on it.

Apparent easement. One the existence of which appears from the construction or condition of one of the tenements, so as to be capable of being seen or known on inspection.

Appendent easement. *See* Appurtenant easement, below.

Appurtenant easement. An easement that benefits a particular tract of land. An incorporeal right which is attached to a superior right and inheres in land to which it is attached and is in the nature of a covenant running with the land. There must be a dominant estate and servient estate. An easement interest which attaches to the land and passes with it. An "incorporeal right" which is attached to and belongs with some greater and superior right or something annexed to another thing more worthy and which passes as incident to it and is incapable of existence separate and apart from the particular land to which it is annexed.

Discontinuing easement. Discontinuous, non-continuous, or non-apparent easements are those the enjoyment of which can be had only by the interference of man, as, a right of way or a right to draw water.

Easement by estoppel. Easement which is created when landlord voluntarily imposes apparent servitude on his property and another person, acting reasonably, believes that servitude is permanent and in reliance upon that belief does something that he would not have done otherwise or refrains from doing something that he would have done otherwise.

Easement by implication. Easement created by law and grounded in court's decision in reference to particular transaction in land where owner of two parcels had so used one parcel to the benefit of other parcel that on selling the benefited parcel purchaser could reasonably have expected, without further inquiries, that these benefits were included in sale.

Easement by prescription. A mode of acquiring an easement in property by immemorial or long-continued enjoyment, and refers to personal usage restricted to claimant and his ancestors or grantors. The uninterrupted use of the land must generally be for the same statutory period of time as for adverse possession.

Easement in gross. An easement in gross is not appurtenant to any estate in land or does not belong to any person by virtue of ownership of estate in other land but is mere personal interest in or right to use land of another; it is purely personal and usually ends with death of grantee. Easements that do not benefit a particular tract of land (*e.g.* utility easements).

Easement of access. Right of ingress and egress to and from the premises of a lot owner to a street appurtenant to the land of the lot owner.

Easement of convenience. One which increases the facility, comfort, or convenience of the enjoyment of the dominant estate, or of some right connected with it.

Easement of natural support. Easement which creates right of lateral support to land in its natural condition entitling the holder thereof to have his land held in place from the sides by neighboring land. *See also* Support (*n*).

Easement of necessity. One in which the easement is indispensable to the enjoyment of the dominant estate. Such arises by operation of law when land conveyed is completely shut off from access to any road by land retained by grantor or by land of grantor and that of a stranger.

Equitable easements. The special easements created by derivation of ownership of adjacent proprietors from a common source, with specific intentions as to buildings for certain purposes, or

with implied privileges in regard to certain uses, are sometimes so called. A name frequently applied to building restrictions in a deed.

Exclusive easement. Grant of "exclusive easement" conveys unfettered rights to owner of easement to use that easement for purposes specified in grant to exclusion of all others.

Flowage easement. Common law right of lower land to allow water from higher land to flow across it.

Implied easement. One which the law imposes by inferring the parties to a transaction intended that result, although they did not express it. An easement resting upon the principle that, where the owner of two or more adjacent lots sells a part thereof, he grants by implication to the grantee all those apparent and visible easements which are necessary for the reasonable use of the property granted, which at the time of the grant are used by the owner of the entirety for the benefit of the part granted. One not expressed by parties in writing but arises out of existence of certain facts implied from the transaction.

Intermittent easement. One which is usable or used only at times, and not continuously.

Light and air easement. An easement obtained from an adjoining land owner to protect against the obstruction of light and air which would result if a building or structure was constructed on the grantor's property.

Negative easement. Those where the owner of the servient estate is prohibited from doing something otherwise lawful upon his estate, because it will affect the dominant estate (as interrupting the light and air from the latter by building on the former). As to *Reciprocal negative easement,* see that title *below.*

Private or public easements. A private easement is one in which the enjoyment is restricted to one or a few individuals, while a public easement is one the right to the enjoyment of which is vested in the public generally or in an entire community; such as an easement of passage on the public streets and highways or of navigation on a stream.

Quasi easement. An "easement," in the proper sense of the word, can only exist in respect of two adjoining pieces of land occupied by different persons, and can only impose a negative duty on the owner of the servient tenement. Hence an obligation on the owner of land to repair the fence between his and his neighbor's land is not a true easement, but is sometimes called a "*quasi* easement."

Reciprocal negative easement. If the owner of two or more lots, so situated as to bear the relation, sells one with restrictions of benefit to the land retained, the servitude becomes mutual, and, during the period of restraint, the owner of the lot or lots retained can do nothing forbidden to the owner of the lot sold; this being known as the doctrine of "reciprocal negative easement."

Reserved easement. An easement created by the grantor of property, benefitting the retained property and burdening the granted property.

Secondary easement. One which is appurtenant to the primary or actual easement. Every easement includes such "secondary easements," that is, the right to do such things as are necessary for the full enjoyment of the easement itself.

EAT. Abbreviation for *earnings after taxes.*

Eaves-drip. The drip or dropping of water from the eaves of a house on the land of an adjacent owner; the easement of having the water so drip, or the servitude of submitting to such drip; the same as the *stillicidium* of the Roman law.

Eavesdropping. Eavesdropping is knowingly and without lawful authority: (a) Entering into a private place with intent to listen surreptitiously to private conversations or to observe the personal conduct of any other person or persons therein; or (b) Installing or using outside a private place any device for hearing, recording, amplifying, or broadcasting sounds originating in such place, which sounds would not ordinarily be audible or comprehensible outside, without the consent of the person or persons entitled to privacy therein; or (c) Installing or using any device or equipment for the interception of any telephone, telegraph or other wire communication without the consent of the person in possession or control of the facilities for such wire communication. Such activities are regulated by state and federal statutes, and commonly require a court order.

At common law, the offense of listening under walls or windows, or the *eaves* of a house, and thereupon to frame slanderous and mischievous tales. It was a misdemeanor at common law.

See also Pen register; Wiretapping.

Ebb and flow. The coming in and going out of tide. An expression used formerly to denote the limits of admiralty jurisdiction.

EBIT. Abbreviation for *earnings before interest and taxes* (also called *operating earnings*).

Ecclesiastical /əkliyziyǽstəkəl/. Pertaining to anything belonging to or set apart for the church, as distinguished from "civil" or "secular," with regard to the world.

Ecclesiastical courts (called, also, "Courts Christian"). A generic name for certain courts having cognizance mainly of spiritual matters. A system of courts in England, held by authority of the sovereign, and having jurisdiction over matters pertaining to the religion and ritual of the established church, and the rights, duties, and discipline of ecclesiastical persons as such. They are as follows: The Archdeacon's Court (now practically obsolete), Consistory Court, Provincial Courts (*i.e.* Court of Arches of Canterbury and Chancery Court of York), Court of Faculties, and Court of Final Appeal (Judicial Committee of the Privy Council). Modern jurisdiction is limited to matters of ecclesiastical discipline and church property.

Ecclesiastical jurisdiction. Jurisdiction over ecclesiastical cases and controversies; such as appertains to the ecclesiastical courts.

Ecclesiastical law. The body of jurisprudence administered by the ecclesiastical courts of England; derived, in large measure, from the canon and civil law. As now restricted, it applies mainly to the affairs, and the doctrine, discipline, and worship, of the established church.

Ecology. In general, the study or science of the relationships between organisms and their environments; study of the environment. *See* Ecosystems.

Economic discrimination. Any form of discrimination within the field of commerce such as a boycott of a particular product or price fixing. *See* Boycott; Price discrimination; Price-fixing.

Economic duress. Defense of "economic duress," or business compulsion, arises where one individual, acting upon another's fear of impending financial injury, unlawfully coerces the latter to perform an act in circumstances which prevent his exercise of free will. For example, threatening not to complete a contract for a particular essential part unless the buyer agrees to another production contract.

Economic entity. A group of companies that function as a single entity to pursue the objectives of operational efficiency and profit.

Economic life. Useful or profitable life of property, which may be shorter than the physical life. *See also* Economic obsolescence.

Economic loss. In a products' liability action, recovery of damages for "economic loss" includes recovery for costs of repair and replacement of defective property which is the subject of the transaction, as well as commercial loss for inadequate value and consequent loss of profits or use.

Economic obsolescence. Loss of desirability and useful life of property due to economic developments (*e.g.* deterioration of neighborhood or zoning change) rather than deterioration (functional obsolescence). Term as used with respect to valuation of property for taxation is a loss of value brought about by conditions that environ a structure such as a declining location or down-grading of a neighborhood resulting in reduced business volume. *See also* Obsolescence.

Economic production run. An estimate of the number of units to produce at one time that minimizes the total costs of setting up a production run and carrying a unit in stock for one year.

Economics of scale. The marginal cost of production decreases as a plant's scale of operations increases.

Economic strike. Refusal to work because of dispute over wages, hours or working conditions or other conditions of employment. An economic strike is one neither prohibited by law nor by collective bargaining agreement nor caused by employer unfair labor practices, but is typically for purpose of enforcing employer compliance with union collective bargaining demands, and economic strikers possess more limited reinstatement rights than unfair labor practice strikers. *See also* Strike.

Economy. Frugality; prudent expenditure of money or use of resources. Not synonymous with "parsimony." Includes that which pertains to the satisfaction of man's needs. Economic structure of country.

Ecosystems. The totality of cycles and processes which constitute the ecology system.

Edict. A formal decree, command, or proclamation. A positive law promulgated by the sovereign of a country, and having reference either to the whole land or some of its divisions, but usually relating to affairs of state. It differs from a "public proclamation," in that it enacts a new statute, and carries with it the authority of law, whereas the latter is, at most, a declaration of a law before enacted. In Roman law, sometimes, a citation to appear before a judge. A "special edict" was a judgment in a case; a "general edict" was in effect a statute. *See* Decree; Mandate.

Edition. The total number of copies of a publication printed from a single typesetting or at one specified time. May also refer to the form which a publication takes such as a hardbound or paperback edition. Also, the means of identifying the various versions of a given publication; *e.g.* first, second, etc. edition. One of the several issues of a newspaper for a single day.

Editor. One who directs or supervises the policies, content and contributions of a newspaper, magazine, book, work of reference, or the like. The term is held to include not only the person who writes, edits or determines the content for publication, but he who publishes a paper, book, etc. and puts it in circulation.

Edmunds Act. An act of Congress of March 22, 1882, punishing polygamy.

Educational expenses. Employees may deduct education expenses as ordinary and necessary business expenses provided such items were incurred for either of two reasons: (1) to maintain or improve existing skills required in present job or (2) to meet the express requirements of the employer or the requirements imposed by law to retain employment status. Such expenses are not deductible if the education is (1) required to meet the minimum educational requirements for the taxpayer's existing job or (2) the education qualifies the individual for a new trade or business.

Educational institution. A school, seminary, college, university, or other educational establishment, not necessarily a chartered institution. As used in a zoning ordinance, the term may include not only buildings, but also all grounds necessary for the accomplishment of the full scope of educational instruction, including those things essential to mental, moral, and physical development.

Educational purposes. Term as used in constitutional and statutory provisions exempting property so used from taxation, includes systematic instruction in any and all branches of learning from which a substantial public benefit is derived, and is not limited to such school properties as would relieve some substantial educational burden from the state.

E.E.O.C. Equal Employment Opportunity Commission.

Effect, *v.* To do; to produce; to make; to bring to pass; to execute; enforce; accomplish.

Effect, *n.* That which is produced by an agent or cause; result; outcome; consequence. The result which an instrument between parties will produce in their relative rights, or which a statute will produce upon the existing law, as discovered from the language used, the forms employed, or other materials for construing it. The operation of a law, of an agreement, or an act. The phrases "take effect," "be in force," "go into operation," etc., are used interchangeably.

With effect. With success; as, to prosecute an action with effect.

Effecting loan. To bring about a loan. To accomplish, fulfill, produce or make a loan. It means the result or consequence of bringing into operation a loan; while "renewal" is not a loan, but an extension of the time of payment.

Effective annual rate. An annual measure of the time value of money that fully reflects the effects of compounding.

Effective assistance of counsel. Conscientious, meaningful representation wherein accused is advised of his rights and honest, learned and able counsel is given a reasonable opportunity to perform task assigned to him. Benchmark for judging any claim of ineffectiveness of counsel must be whether counsel's conduct so undermined proper functioning of adversarial process that trial cannot be relied on as having produced a just result. As required by 6th Amendment for criminal defendant, does not mean errorless counsel, and not counsel judged ineffective by hindsight, but counsel reasonably likely to render and rendering reasonably effective assistance; this necessarily involves inquiry into actual performance of counsel in conducting defense, based on totality of circumstances of entire record. 18 U.S.C.A. § 3006A. *See* Assistance of counsel; Counsel, right to.

Effective call price. The strike price in an optional redemption provision plus the accrued interest to the redemption date.

Effective date. Date on which contract, law, insurance policy, or the like, takes effect.

Effective possession. *See* Constructive possession.

Effective procuring cause. The "effective procuring cause" of sale of realty is ordinarily the broker who first secures the serious attention of the customer and is instrumental in bringing the parties together. *See* Cause; Efficient cause; Proximate cause.

Effective rate. A measure of the time value of money that fully reflects the effects of compounding.

Effective rate of return. The real or actual yield on investments as distinguished from the quoted yield. *See also* Rate (*Rate of return*).

Effects. Personal estate or property; though the term may include both real and personal property. *See* Personal effects.

Efficiency. Performing tasks to produce the best yield at the lowest cost from the resources available. The degree to which a satisfactory relationship occurs when comparing outputs to inputs.

Efficiency variance. The difference between total budgeted overhead at actual hours and total budgeted overhead at standard hours allowed for the production achieved; computed as part of three-variance analysis; same as variable overhead efficiency variance.

Efficient. Causing an effect; particularly the result or results contemplated. Adequate in performance or producing properly a desired effect.

Efficient capital market. A market in which new information is very quickly (within at most a few hours) accurately reflected in share prices.

Efficient cause. The working cause; that cause which produces effects or results. An intervening cause, which produces results which would not have come to pass except for its interposition, and for which, therefore, the person who set in motion the original chain of causes is not responsible.

The cause which originates and sets in motion the dominating agency that necessarily proceeds through other causes as mere instruments or vehicles in a natural line of causation to the result. That cause of an injury to which legal liability attaches. The "proximate cause." The phrase is practically synonymous with "procuring cause." The immediate agent in the production of an effect.

The proximate cause of an injury is the efficient cause, the one that necessarily sets the other causes in operation, and, where a wrongful act puts other forces in operation which are natural and which the act would reasonably and probably put in action, the party who puts in force the first efficient cause will be responsible in damages for the injury proved, although immediately resulting from the other force so put in motion.

See also Proximate cause.

Efficient intervening cause. An intervening efficient cause is a new and independent force, which breaks the causal connection between the original wrong and the injury, and is the proximate and immediate cause of the injury. Thus, the original negligent actor is not liable for an injury that could not have been foreseen or reasonably anticipated as the probable consequence of his negligent act, and would not have resulted from it had not the intervening efficient cause interrupted the natural sequence of events, turned aside their course, and produced the injury. *See also* Intervening cause; Proximate cause.

Effluent. Liquid waste which is discharged into a lake, river, etc.

Efflux /éfləks/. The running, as of a prescribed period of time to its end; expiration by lapse of time. Particularly applied to the termination of a lease by the expiration of the term for which it was made.

Effluxion of time /əfləkshən əv táym/. When this phrase is used in leases, conveyances, and other like deeds, or in agreements expressed in simple writing, it indicates the conclusion or expiration of an agreed term of years specified in the deed or writing, such conclusion or expiration arising in the natural course of events, in contradistinction to the determination of the term by the acts of the parties or by some unexpected or unusual incident or other sudden event.

Effort. An attempt; an endeavor; a struggle directed to the accomplishment of an object. To try.

Effraction /əfrǽkshən/. A breach made by the use of force.

Effractor /əfrǽktər/. One who breaks through; one who commits a burglary.

E.g. An abbreviation of *exempli gratia*. For the sake of an example.

Ego /íygow/. I; myself. This term is used in forming genealogical tables, to represent the person who is the object of inquiry. *See also* Alter ego.

Egress /íygrès/. The path or opening by which a person goes out; exit. The means or act of going out.

Eighteenth Amendment. The amendment to the U.S. Constitution added in 1919 which prohibited the manufacture, sale, transportation and exportation of intoxicating liquors in all the States and Territories of the United States and which was repealed in 1933 by the Twenty-first Amendment.

Eighth Amendment. The amendment to the U.S. Constitution added in 1791 which prohibits excessive bail, excessive fines and cruel and unusual punishment.

Eight hour laws. Statutes (*e.g.* Adamson Act; Fair Labor Standards Act) which established eight hours as the length of a day's work, prohibited work beyond this period, and required payment of overtime for work in excess of this period. *See* Wage and hour laws.

Either. Each of two; the one and the other; one or the other of two alternatives; one of two. Often used, however, with reference to more than two, in which case it may mean "each" or "any"; but does not mean "all".

Eject. To cast, or throw out; to oust, or dispossess; to put or turn out of possession. To expel or thrust forcibly, as disorderly patrons.

Ejection. A turning out of possession.

Ejectment. At common law, this was the name of a mixed action (springing from the earlier personal action of *ejectione firmœ*) which lay for the recovery of the possession of land, and for damages for the unlawful detention of its possession. The action was highly fictitious, being in theory only for the recovery of a term for years, and brought by a purely fictitious person, as lessee in a supposed lease from the real party in interest. The latter's title, however, had to be established in order to warrant a recovery, and the establishment of such title, though nominally a mere incident, was in reality the object of the action. Hence this convenient form of suit came to be adopted as the usual method of trying titles to land.

The common law action for ejectment has been materially modified by statute in most states and may come under the title of action to recover possession of land, action for summary process, action for eviction, or forcible entry and detainer action.

Ejectment is an action to restore possession of property to the person entitled to it. Not only must the plaintiff establish a right to possession in himself, but he must also show that the defendant is in wrongful possession. If the defendant has only trespassed on the land, the action is for trespass (*i.e.* damages).

See also Eviction; Forcible entry and detainer; Process (*Summary process*).

Ejector. One who ejects, puts out, or dispossesses another.

Ejectum /əjéktəm/. That which is thrown up by the sea. Also jetsam, wreck, etc.

Ejusdem generis /iyjə́sdəm jénərəs/. Of the same kind, class, or nature. In the construction of laws, wills, and other instruments, the "ejusdem generis rule" is, that where general words follow an enumeration of persons or things, by words of a particular and specific meaning, such general words are not to be construed in their widest extent, but are to be held as applying only to persons or things of the same general kind or class as those specifically mentioned. The rule, however, does not necessarily require that the general provision be limited in its scope to the identical things specifically named. Nor does it apply when the context manifests a contrary intention.

Under "ejusdem generis" canon of statutory construction, where general words follow the enumeration of particular classes of things, the general words will be construed as applying only to things of the same general class as those enumerated.

Elder title. A title of earlier date, but coming simultaneously into operation with a title of younger origin, is called the "elder title," and prevails.

Eldest. Oldest; first born; one with greatest seniority.

Elected. The word "elected," in its ordinary signification, carries with it the idea of a vote, generally popular, sometimes more restricted, and cannot be held the synonym of any other mode of filling a position.

Election. The act of choosing or selecting one or more from a greater number of persons, things, courses, or rights. The choice of an alternative. The internal, free, and spontaneous separation of one thing from another, without compulsion, consisting in intention and will. The selection of one person from a specified class to discharge certain duties in a state, corporation, or society. An expression of choice by the voters of a public body politic, or as a means by which a choice is made by the electors. With respect to the choice of persons to fill public office or the decision of a particular public question or public policy the term means in ordinary usage the expression by vote of the will of the people or of a somewhat numerous body of electors. "Election" ordinarily has reference to a choice or selection by electors, while "appointment" refers to a choice or selection by an individual.

The choice which is open to a debtor who is bound in an alternative obligation to select either one of the alternatives.

The choice, by the prosecution, upon which of several counts in an indictment (charging distinct offenses of the same degree, but not parts of a continuous series of acts) it will proceed.

Obligation imposed upon party to choose between two inconsistent or alternative rights or claims in cases where there is clear intention of the person from whom he derives one that he should not enjoy both.

See also Certificate of election; Equitable election; Free and clear.

Election at large. Election in which a public official is selected from a major election district rather than a minor subdivision within the larger unit.

Election of defenses. The selection of a particular defense on which to rest in contesting a claim or in defending a criminal charge.

Election of remedies. The liberty of choosing (or the act of choosing) one out of several means afforded by law for the redress of an injury, or one out of several available forms of action. An "election of remedies" arises when one having two coexistent but inconsistent remedies chooses to exercise one, in which event he loses the right to thereafter exercise the other. Doctrine provides that if two or more remedies exist which are repugnant and inconsistent with one another, a party will be bound if he has chosen one of them. Under Rule of Civil Procedure 8(a): "Relief in the alternative or of several different types may be demanded." *See also* Alternative pleading; Alternative relief; Choice of law; Equitable election.

General election. One for a definite purpose, regularly reoccurring at fixed intervals without any requirements other than the lapse of time. One at which the officers to be elected are such as belong to the general government; that is, the general and central political organization of the whole state, as distinguished from an election of officers for a particular locality only. Also, one held for the selection of an officer after the expiration of the full term of the former officer; thus distinguished from a *special* election, which is one held to supply a vacancy in office occurring before the expiration of the full term for which the incumbent was elected.

One that regularly recurs in each election precinct of the state on a day designated by law for the selection of officers, or is held in such entire territory pursuant to an enactment specifying a single day for the ratification or rejection of one or more measures submitted to the people by the Legislature, and not for the election of any officer.

One that is held throughout the entire state or territory. An election for the choice of a national, state, judicial, district, municipal, county or township official, required by law to be held regularly at a designated time, to fill a new office or a vacancy in an office at the expiration of the full term thereof.

In statutes, the term may include a primary election.

See also Popular election and *Regular election, below.*

Law of wills. A widow's election is her choice of whether she will take what is provided for her in her husband's will or rather her statutorily prescribed share; that is, whether she will accept the provision made for her in the will, and acquiesce in her husband's disposition of his property, or disregard it and claim what the law allows her. An "election under the will" means that a legatee or devisee under a will is put to the choice of accepting the beneficial interest offered by the donor in lieu of some estate which he is entitled to, but which is taken from him by the terms of the will. *See also* Election by spouse; Equitable election.

Off-year election. Election conducted at a time other than the presidential election year.

Popular election. Election by people as a whole, rather than by a select group.

Presidential election. See U.S.Const. Amends. XII, XX, XXII–XXVI.

Primary election. An election by the voters of a ward, precinct, or other small district, belonging to a particular party, of representatives or delegates to a convention which is to meet and nominate the candidates of their party to stand at an approaching municipal or general election. Also, an election to select candidates for office by a political organization, the voters being restricted to the members or supporters of such organization. An election, preliminary in nature, the purpose being to narrow in number the candidates that will appear on the final, official ballot.

Recall election. Election where voters have opportunity to remove public official from elected office.

Regular election. One recurring at stated times fixed by law. A general, usual, or stated election. When applied to elections, the terms "regular" and "general" are used interchangeably and synonymously. The word "regular" is used in reference to a general election occurring throughout the state. *See also General election, above.*

Special election. An election for a particular emergency or need, conducted in the interval between regularly scheduled elections in order to fill a vacancy arising by death of the incumbent of the office, decide a question submitted on an initiative referendum, or recall petition, etc. In determining whether an election is special or general, regard must be had to the subject-matter as well as date of the election, and, if an election occurs throughout state uniformly by direct operation of law, it is a "general election," but, if it depends on employment of special preliminary proceeding peculiar to process which may or may not occur, and the election is applicable only to a restricted area less than whole state, it is a "special election."

Election board. A board of inspectors or commissioners appointed in each election precinct by government (*e.g.* county or city) authorities responsible for determining whether individual voters are qualified, supervising the polling, and often ascertaining and reporting the results. Local, city or town agency which is charged with the conduct of elections.

Election by spouse. Statutory provision that a surviving spouse may choose as between taking that which is provided for her in her husband's will, claiming dower or taking her statutorily prescribed share. Such election may be presented if the will leaves the spouse less than she would otherwise receive by statute. This election may also be taken if the spouse seeks to set aside a will which contains a provision to the effect that an attempt to contest the will defeats the rights of one to take under the will. *See also* Election *(Law of wills)*; Equitable election.

Election contest. A contest in behalf of one who has failed of success in election against right of one who has been declared or determined by proper authority to have been successful. Election contest involves matter of going behind election returns and inquiring into qualifications of electors, counting of ballots, and other matters affecting validity of ballots.

Election district. A subdivision of territory, whether of state, county, or city, the boundaries of which are fixed by law, for convenience in local or general elections.

Election, doctrine of. When a third person has contracted with an agent without knowing of the agency, and thereafter the third person discovers the agency and the identity of the principal, the third person may enforce the contract against the agent or against the principal at his election, but not against both. This is known as the doctrine of election. *See* Election.

Election dower. A name sometimes given to the provision which a law or statute makes for a widow in case she "elects" to reject the provision made for her in the will and take what the statute accords. *See* Election *(Law of wills)*; Election by spouse.

Election, estoppel by. An estoppel which arises by a choice between inconsistent remedies. *See* Election *(Election of remedies)*.

An estoppel predicated on a voluntary and intelligent action or choice of one of several things which is inconsistent with another, the effect of the estoppel being to prevent the party so choosing from afterwards reversing his election or disputing the state of affairs or rights of others resulting from his original choice.

The doctrine of "estoppel by election" against beneficiary who has elected to take favorable provisions of will from objecting to other provisions of will applies only where will undertakes to bestow a gift and also deprive donee of a prior existing right, thus confronting devisee with alternative of accepting devise and renouncing prior right or of retaining latter and renouncing devise.

Election of remedies. *See* Election.

Election returns. The report made to the board of canvassers or election board of the number of votes cast for each candidate or proposition voted upon by those charged by law with the duty of counting or tallying the votes for or against the respective candidates or propositions.

Elective. Dependent upon choice; bestowed or passing by election. Also pertaining or relating to elections; conferring the right or power to vote at elections.

Elective franchise. The right of voting at public elections. The privilege of qualified voters to cast their ballots for the candidates they favor at elections authorized by law as guaranteed by Fifteenth and Nineteenth Amendments to Constitution, and by federal voting rights acts. *See* Voting Rights Act.

Elective office. One which is to be filled by popular election. One filled by the direct exercise of the voters' franchise in contrast to an appointive office.

Elective share. *See* Election *(Law of wills)*; Election by spouse.

Elector. A duly qualified voter; one who has a vote in the choice of any officer; a constituent. One who elects or has the right of choice, or who has the right to vote for any functionary, or for the adoption of any measure. In a narrower sense, one who has the general right to vote, and the right to vote for public officers. One authorized to exercise the elective franchise. *See* Voting Rights Act.

One of the persons chosen to comprise the "electoral college" *(q.v.)*.

Also, the title of certain German princes who had a voice in the election of the Holy Roman Emperors. The office of elector in some instances became hereditary and was connected with territorial possessions.

Sometimes, one who exercises the right of election in equity.

Registered qualified elector. One possessing the constitutional qualifications, and registered under the registration statute.

Electoral. Pertaining to electors or elections; composed or consisting of electors. *See* Electoral college.

Electoral college. The college or body of electors of a state chosen to elect the president and vice-president; also, the whole body of such electors, composed of the electoral colleges of the several states. See U.S.Const. Amend. XII.

Electoral process. Generic term for methods by which persons are elected to public office; voting.

Electronic funds transfers. A transaction with a financial institution by means of a computer, telephone or electronic instrument (*e.g.* automatic tellers or cash machines). An electronic funds transfer is typically initiated by a bank customer (the originator) who requests the bank to transfer credit to the account, usually in another bank, of another person (the beneficiary). Such transactions are governed by federal and state laws. See 15 U.S.C.A. § 1693 et seq.; U.C.C. Art. 4A.

Electronic surveillance. *See* Eavesdropping; Wiretapping.

Eleemosynary /èləmósənè(h)riy/èliyəmózənè(h)riy/. Relating or devoted to charity; given in charity; having the nature of alms. *See* Charity; Charitable.

Eleemosynary corporation. A private corporation created for charitable and benevolent purposes. Charitable corporation. *See also* Charitable organizations.

Eleemosynary defense. Term used to describe defense available in some jurisdictions for charitable corporations and institutions when they are sued in tort; though such tort immunity has been abrogated or greatly restricted in many states.

Element. Material; substance; ingredient; factor. *See* Elements of crime.

Also, one of the simple substances or principles of which, according to early natural philosophers, the physical universe is composed, the four elements pointed out by Empedocles being fire, air, water, earth. *See* Elements.

Elements. The forces of nature. Violent or severe weather. The ultimate undecomposable parts which unite to form anything. Popularly, fire, air, earth, and water, anciently supposed to be the four simple bodies of which the world was composed. Often applied in a particular sense to wind and water, as "the fury of the elements." Fire and water as elements included in the expression "damages by the elements" means the same thing as "damages by the act of God."

Elements of crime. Those constituent parts of a crime which must be proved by the prosecution to sustain a conviction. A term used by the common law to refer to each component of the actus reus, causation, and the mens rea that must be proved in order to establish that a given offense has occurred. The term is more broadly defined by the Model Penal Code in § 1.13(9) to refer to each component of the actus reus, causation, the mens rea, any grading factors, and the negative of any defense.

Eleventh Amendment. The Amendment to the U.S. Constitution, added in 1798, which provides that the judicial power of the U.S. shall not extend to any suit in law or equity, commenced or prosecuted against one of the United States by citizens of another state, or by citizens or subjects of any foreign state.

Eligible. Fit and proper to be chosen; qualified to be elected. Capable of serving, legally qualified to serve. Capable of being chosen, as a candidate for office. Also, qualified and capable of holding office. *See also* Capacity; Competency; Duly qualified; Qualified.

Eligibility. Qualification for an office, e position, or specific status. Commonly refers to "legal" qualification. *See also* Eligible.

Elimination entry. In accounting, an entry made on the consolidated work sheet to eliminate intercompany transactions from consolidated financial statements.

Elkins Act. Federal Act (1903) which strengthened the Interstate Commerce Act by prohibiting rebates and other forms of preferential treatment to large shippers.

Elopement. The act of running away, leaving without permission, or escaping from custody. An unmarried couple's act of secretly leaving home for the purpose of getting married.

At common law, the act of a wife who voluntarily deserts her husband to go away with and cohabit with another man.

Elsewhere. In another place; in any other place. The term does not always mean literally any other place whatever, but may be more or less limited by the context.

In shipping articles, this term, following the designation of the port of destination, must be construed either as void for uncertainty or as subordinate to the principal voyage stated in the preceding words.

Eluviation /əl(y)ùwviyéyshən/. Movement of soil caused by excessive water in soil.

Emancipated minor. A person under 18 years of age who is totally self-supporting.

Emancipation. A surrender and renunciation of the correlative rights and duties touching the care, custody and earnings of a child. The term is principally used with reference to the emancipation of a minor child by its parents, which involves an entire surrender of the right to the care, custody, and earnings of such child as well as a renunciation of parental duties. The emancipation may be express, as by voluntary agreement of parent and child, or implied from such acts and conduct as import consent, and it may be conditional or absolute, complete or partial. Complete emancipation is entire surrender of care, custody, and earnings of child, as well as renunciation of parental duties. And a "partial emancipation" frees a child for only a part of the period of minority, or from only a part of the parent's rights, or for some purposes, and not for others.

There is no fixed age when a child becomes emancipated (though it is usually upon reaching majority); it does not automatically occur on reaching majority.

Emancipation proclamation. An executive proclamation, issued January 1, 1863, by Abraham Lincoln, declaring that all persons held in slavery in certain designated states and districts were and should remain free.

Embargo /əmbárgow/. A proclamation or order of government, usually issued in time of war or threatened hostilities, prohibiting the departure of ships or goods from some or all ports until further order. Government order prohibiting commercial trade with individuals or businesses of other specified nations. Legal prohibition on commerce.

The temporary or permanent sequestration of the property of individuals for the purposes of a government, *e.g.,* to obtain vessels for the transport of troops, the owners being reimbursed for this forced service.

Embassador. *See* Ambassador.

Embassy /émbəsiy/ or **Embassage** /émbəsəj/. Mission, function, business, or official residence of an ambassador. Body of diplomatic representatives headed by ambassador. *See* Ambassador.

Embezzlement. The fraudulent appropriation of property by one lawfully entrusted with its possession. To "embezzle" means willfully to take, or convert to one's own use, another's money or property, of which the wrongdoer acquired possession lawfully, by reason of some office or employment or position of trust. The elements of "offense" are that there must be relationship such as that of employment or agency between the owner of the money and the defendant, the money alleged to have been embezzled must have come into the possession of defendant by virtue of that relationship and there must be an intentional and fraudulent appropriation or conversion of the money. The fraudulent conversion of the property of another by one who has lawful possession of

the property and whose fraudulent conversion has been made punishable by statute. For federal crimes involving embezzlement, see 18 U.S.C.A. § 641 et seq. *See also* Conversion. *Compare* Theft.

Emblements /émbləmənts/. Crops annually produced by labor of tenant. Corn, wheat, rye, potatoes, garden vegetables, and other crops which are produced annually, not spontaneously, but by labor and industry. The doctrine of emblements denotes the right of a tenant to take and carry away, after his tenancy has ended, such annual products of the land as have resulted from his own care and labor. *See* Fructus industriales.

Embraceor /əmbréysər/. A person guilty of the offense of embracery *(q.v.).*

Embracery /əmbréysəriy/. The crime of attempting to influence a jury corruptly to one side or the other, by promises, persuasions, entreaties, entertainments, *douceurs,* and the like. The person guilty of it is called an "embraceor." This is both a state and federal (18 U.S.C.A. §§ 1503, 1504) crime, and is commonly included under the offense of "obstructing justice". *See* Obstructing justice.

Emergency. A sudden unexpected happening; an unforeseen occurrence or condition; perplexing contingency or complication of circumstances; a sudden or unexpected occasion for action; exigency; pressing necessity. Emergency is an unforeseen combination of circumstances that calls for immediate action without time for full deliberation. *See also* Emergency doctrine; Sudden emergency doctrine.

Emergency Court of Appeals. Court created during World War II to review orders of the Price Control Administrator. It was abolished in 1953. This court was established again in 1970 under Section 211 of the Economic Stabilization Act to handle primarily wage and price control matters.

Emergency doctrine. Under the doctrine variously referred to as the "emergency," "imminent peril," or "sudden peril" doctrine, when one is confronted with a sudden peril requiring instinctive action, he is not, in determining his course of action, held to the exercise of the same degree of care as when he has time for reflection, and in the event that a driver of a motor vehicle suddenly meets with an emergency which naturally would overpower the judgment of a reasonably prudent and careful driver, so that momentarily he is thereby rendered incapable of deliberate and intelligent action, and as a result injures a third person, he is not negligent, provided he has used due care to avoid meeting such an emergency and, after it arises, he exercises such care as a reasonably prudent and capable driver would use under the unusual circumstances.

In an emergency situation when medical service is required for an adult who by virtue of his physical condition is incapable of giving consent, or with respect to a child, whose parent or other guardian is absent, and thus incapable of giving consent, the law implies the consent required to administer emergency medical services. This is a good defense to an action of tort for an alleged battery.

Emigrant /émagrant/. One who leaves his country for any reason, with intention to not return, with design to reside elsewhere. *Compare* Immigrant.

Emigration. The act of removing from one country to another, with intention to not return. It is to be distinguished from "expatriation" which means the abandonment of one's country and renunciation of one's citizenship in it, while emigration denotes merely the removal of person and property to another country. The former is usually the consequence of the latter. Emigration is also sometimes used in reference to the removal from one section to another of the same country. *See also* Deportation; Immigration.

Emigré. Person forced to emigrate for political reasons. *See also* Deportation.

Eminent domain /émanant daméyn/. The power to take private property for public use by the state, municipalities, and private persons or corporations authorized to exercise functions of public character. Fifth Amendment, U.S. Constitution.

In the United States, the power of eminent domain is founded in both the federal (Fifth Amend.) and state constitutions. The Constitution limits the power to taking for a public purpose and prohibits the exercise of the power of eminent domain without just compensation to the owners of the property which is taken. The process of exercising the power of eminent domain is commonly referred to as "condemnation", or, "expropriation".

The right of eminent domain is the right of the state, through its regular organization, to reassert, either temporarily or permanently, its dominion over any portion of the soil of the state on account of public exigency and for the public good. Thus, in time of war or insurrection, the proper authorities may possess and hold any part of the territory of the state for the common safety; and in time of peace the legislature may authorize the appropriation of the same to public purposes, such as the opening of roads, construction of defenses, or providing channels for trade or travel. Eminent domain is the highest and most exact idea of property remaining in the government, or in the aggregate body of the people in their sovereign capacity. It gives a right to resume the possession of the property in the manner directed

by the constitution and the laws of the state, whenever the public interest requires it.

See also Adequate compensation; Condemnation; Constructive taking; Damages; Expropriation; Fair market value; Just compensation; Larger parcel; Public use; Taking.

Expropriation. The term "expropriation" (used *e.g.* in Louisiana) is practically synonymous with the term "eminent domain".

Partial taking. The taking of part of an owner's property under the laws of eminent domain. Compensation must be based on damages or benefits to the remaining property, as well as the part taken. *See* Condemnation.

Emissary /émaseriy/. A person sent upon a mission as the agent of another; also a secret agent sent to ascertain the sentiments and designs of others, and to propagate opinions favorable to his employer. *See* Ambassador; Diplomatic agent.

Emission. The discharge, ejection or throwing out of; *e.g.* a pollutant from a factory or any secretion or other matter from the body.

Emission standards. Limits on discharges of impurities into the air.

Emit. To put forth or send out; to issue. "No state shall *emit* bills of credit." Art. 1, § 10, U.S. Const.

To give forth with authority; to give out or discharge; to put into circulation. *See* Bill (*Bill of credit*).

Emolument /amólyamant/. The profit arising from office, employment, or labor; that which is received as a compensation for services, or which is annexed to the possession of office as salary, fees, and perquisites. Any perquisite, advantage, profit, or gain arising from the possession of an office.

Empanel. *See* Impanel.

Empirical. That which is based on experience, experiment, or observation.

Emplead. To indict; to prefer a charge against; to accuse.

Employ. To engage in one's service; to hire; to use as an agent or substitute in transacting business; to commission and intrust with the performance of certain acts or functions or with the management of one's affairs; and, when used in respect to a servant or hired laborer, the term is equivalent to hiring, which implies a request and a contract for a compensation. To make use of, to keep at work, to entrust with some duty. *See also* Employment.

Employed. Performing work under an employer-employee relationship. Term signifies both the act of doing a thing and the being under contract or orders to do it. To give employment to; to have employment.

Employee. A person in the service of another under any contract of hire, express or implied, oral or written, where the employer has the power or right to control and direct the employee in the material details of how the work is to be performed. One who works for an employer; a person working for salary or wages.

Generally, when person for whom services are performed has right to control and direct individual who performs services not only as to result to be accomplished by work but also as to details and means by which result is accomplished, individual subject to direction is an "employee".

"Servant" is synonymous with "employee". However, "employee" must be distinguished from "independent contractor," "officer," "vice-principal," "agent," etc.

The term is often specially defined by statutes (*e.g.* workers' compensation acts; Fair Labor Standards Act), and whether one is an employee or not within a particular statute will depend upon facts and circumstances.

In corporation law, "employee" includes an officer but not a director. A director may accept duties that make him also an employee. Rev. Model Bus.Corp. Act, § 1.40.

For Executive employees, see that title. *See also* Borrowed employee; Fellow servant; Independent contractor; Line employee; Servant.

Staff employee. An employee responsible for providing advice, guidance, and service to line personnel.

Employee pro hac vice. *See* Borrowed employee.

Employee Retirement Income Security Act. *See* E.R.I.S.A.

Employee Stock Ownership Plan (ESOP). A type of qualified profit sharing plan that invests in securities of the employer. Such plans acquire shares of the employer-corporation for the benefit of employees usually through contributions of the employer to the plan. In a noncontributory ESOP, the employer usually contributes its shares to a trust and receives a deduction for the fair market value of such stock. Generally, the employee recognizes no income until the stock is sold after its distribution to him or her upon retirement or other separation from service. Special tax benefits are provided to companies with such benefits. *See also* Profit-sharing plan.

Employer. One who employs the services of others; one for whom employees work and who pays their wages or salaries. The correlative of "employee." *See also* Master. *Compare* Independent contractor.

Employer's liability acts. Statutes (*e.g.*, Federal Employer's Liability Act; Workers' Compensation Acts) defining or limiting the occasions and the extent to which public and private employers shall be liable in damages (compensation) for injuries to their employees occurring in the course of their employment, and particularly abolishing the common-law rule that the employer is not liable if the injury is caused by the fault or negligence of a fellow servant and also the defenses of contributory negligence and assumption of risk. *See also* Federal Employer's Liability Act; Insurance; Workers' Compensation Acts.

Employment. Act of employing or state of being employed; that which engages or occupies; that which consumes time or attention; also an occupation, profession, trade, post or business. Includes the doing of the work and a reasonable margin of time and space required in passing to and from the place where the work is to be done. Activity in which person engages or is employed; normally, on a day-to-day basis. *See also* Casual employment; Course of employment; Seasonal employment.

Discrimination. *See* Discrimination; Disparate treatment.

Employment agency. Business operated by a person, firm or corporation engaged in procuring, for a fee, employment for others and employees for employers. The fee may be paid by either the employer or the employee, depending upon the terms of the agreement. *See also* Finder.

Employment at will. This doctrine provides that, absent express agreement to contrary, either employer or employee may terminate their relationship at any time, for any reason. Such employment relationship is one which has no specific duration, and such a relationship may be terminated at will by either the employer or the employee, for or without cause. *See also* Whistle blower acts; Wrongful discharge.

Employment contract. An agreement or contract between employer and employee in which the terms and conditions of one's employment are provided.

Emporium /əmpóriyəm/. A place for wholesale trade in commodities carried by sea. The name is sometimes applied to a seaport town, but it properly signifies only a particular place in such a town.

Empower. A grant of authority rather than a command of its exercise. *See* Power.

Emptor /ém(p)tər/. Lat. A buyer or purchaser. Used in the maxim *"caveat emptor,"* let the buyer beware; *i.e.,* the buyer of an article must be on his guard and take the risks of his purchase. *See* Caveat emptor.

Empty chair doctrine. Under this doctrine, a trial justice may charge a jury that it may infer from litigant's unexplained failure to produce an available witness who would be expected to give material testimony in litigant's behalf that witness, had he occupied empty chair, would have testified adversely to litigant.

Enable. To give power to do something; to make able. In the case of a person under disability as to dealing with another, "enable" has the primary meaning of removing that disability; not of conferring a compulsory power as against that other.

Enabling Act. *See* Enabling statute.

Enabling clause. That portion of a statute or constitution which gives to governmental officials the power and authority to put it into effect and to enforce such. *See* Enacting clause; Enforcement powers.

Enabling power. When the donor of a power, who is the owner of the estate, confers upon persons not seised of the fee the right of creating interests to take effect out of it, which could not be done by the donee of the power unless by such authority, this is called an "enabling power." *See also* Power of appointment.

Enabling statute. Term applied to any statute enabling persons or corporations, or administrative agencies to do what before they could not. It is applied to statutes which confer new powers. *See also* Enabling clause.

Enact. To establish by law; to perform or effect; to decree. The common introductory formula in making statutory laws is, *"Be it enacted."* *See* Enacting clause.

Enacting clause. A clause at the beginning of a statute which states the authority by which it is made. That part of a statute which declares its enactment and serves to identify it as an act of legislation proceeding from the proper legislative authority. Various formulas are used for this clause, such as "Be it enacted by the people of the state of Illinois represented in general assembly," "Be it enacted by the Senate and House of Representatives of the United States of America in Congress assembled," "The general assembly do enact," etc. *See also* Enabling clause; Preamble.

Enactment. The method or process by which a bill in the Legislature becomes a law.

En autre droit /ən ówtrə dróyt/òn ówtrə dr(w)ó/. In the right of another.

En banc /ən bǽŋk/òn bóŋk/. L. Fr. In the bench. Full bench. Refers to a session where the entire membership of the court will participate in the decision rather than the regular quorum. In other countries, it is common for a court to have more members than are usually necessary to hear an appeal. In the United States, the Circuit Courts of Appeal usually sit in panels of judges but for important cases may expand the bench to a larger number, when they are said to be sitting *en banc*. See Fed.R.App.P. 35. Similarly, only one of the judges of the U.S. Tax Court will typically hear and decide on a tax controversy. However, when the issues involved are unusually novel or of wide impact, the case will be heard and decided by the full court sitting *en banc*. An appellate court in which all the judges who are necessary for a quorum are sitting as contrasted with a session of such court presided over by a single justice or panel of justices.

En bloc /òn blók/. As a unit; as a whole.

Enclose. *See* Inclose.

Enclosure /ənklówzhər/. *See* Inclosure.

Encourage. In criminal law, to instigate; to incite to action; to give courage to; to inspirit; to embolden; to raise confidence; to make confident; to help; to forward; to advise. *See* Aid and abet.

Encroach. To enter by gradual steps or stealth into the possessions or rights of another; to trespass or intrude. To gain or intrude unlawfully upon the lands, property, or authority of another.

Encroachment. An illegal intrusion in a highway or navigable river, with or without obstruction. An encroachment upon a street or highway is a fixture, such as a wall or fence, which illegally intrudes into or invades the highway or incloses a portion of it, diminishing its width or area, but without closing it to public travel.

In the law of easements, where the owner of an easement alters the dominant tenement, so as to impose an additional restriction or burden on the servient tenement, he is said to commit an encroachment.

Encumbrance. Any right to, or interest in, land which may subsist in another to diminution of its value, but consistent with the passing of the fee by conveyance. A claim, lien, charge, or liability attached to and binding real property; *e.g.* a mortgage; judgment lien; mechanics' lien; lease; security interest; easement or right of way; accrued and unpaid taxes. If the liability relates to a particular asset, the asset is encumbered.

While encumbrances usually relate to real property, a purchaser of personal property is provided with a warranty of title against unknown encumbrances. U.C.C. § 2–312.

Encumbrancer. A lien or mortgage holder; one who has a legal claim against an estate.

Endeavor. To exert physical and intellectual strength toward the attainment of an object. A systematic or continuous effort. As used in statute relating to corruptly endeavoring to influence, obstruct, or impede due administration of justice, describes any effort or assay to accomplish evil purpose the statute was enacted to prevent.

End lines. In mining law, the end lines of a claim, as platted or laid down on the ground, are those which mark its boundaries on the shorter dimension, where it crosses the vein, while the "side lines" are those which mark its longer dimension, where it follows the course of the vein. But with reference to extra-lateral rights, if the claim as a whole crosses the vein, instead of following its course, the end lines will become side lines and vice versa.

End of will. Point in will at which dispositive provisions terminate. Such is normally followed by attestation clauses.

Endorsement. *See* Indorsement.

Endorsee. *See* Indorsee.

Endorser. *See* Indorser.

Endow. To give a dower; to bestow upon; to make pecuniary provision for.

Endowment. Transfer, generally as a gift, of money or property to an institution for a particular purpose such as a gift to a hospital for medical research. The act of establishing a fund, or permanent pecuniary provision, for the maintenance of a public institution, charity, college, etc. The bestowment of money as a permanent fund, the income of which is to be used in the administration of a proposed work.

Endowment insurance. *See* Insurance.

Endowment policy. *See* Policy of insurance *(Endowment policy).*

Enelow–Ettelson Rule. This Rule provides that an order staying federal court proceedings pending the determination of an equitable defense is an injunction appealable under 28 U.S.C.A. § 1292(a)(1) if the proceeding stayed was an action that could have been maintained as an action at law before the merger of law and equity.

Enemy. Adversary; *e.g.* military adversary.

Enemy alien. An alien residing or traveling in a country which is at war with the country of which he is a national. Enemy aliens may be interned or restricted.

Enemy belligerent. Citizens who associate themselves with the military arm of an enemy government and enter the United States bent on hostile acts.

Enemy's property. In international law, and particularly in the usage of prize courts, this term designates any property which is engaged or used in illegal intercourse with the public enemy, whether belonging to an ally or a citizen, as the illegal traffic stamps it with the hostile character and attaches to it all the penal consequences.

Public enemy. A nation at war with the United States; also every citizen or subject of such nation. Term however does not generally include robbers, thieves, private depredators, or riotous mobs. The term has acquired, in the vocabulary of journalism and civic indignation, a more extended meaning, denoting a particularly notorious offender against the criminal laws, especially one who seems more or less immune from successful prosecution, or a social, health or economic condition or problem affecting the public at large, which is difficult to abate or control.

Energy, Department of. The Department of Energy (DOE) provides the framework for a comprehensive and balanced national energy plan through the coordination and administration of the energy functions of the Federal Government. The Department is responsible for the research, development, and demonstration of energy technology; the marketing of Federal power; energy conservation; the nuclear weapons program; regulation of energy production and use; pricing and allocation; and a central energy data collection and analysis program.

Enfeoff /ènfǐyf/ənféf/. To invest with an estate by feoffment. To make a gift of any corporeal hereditaments to another. *See* Feoffment.

Enfeoffment /ənfíyfmənt/. The act of investing with any dignity or possession; also the instrument or deed by which a person is invested with possessions.

Enforce. To put into execution; to cause to take effect; to make effective; as, to enforce a particular law, a writ, a judgment, or the collection of a debt or fine; to compel obedience to. *See e.g.* Attachment; Execution; Garnishment.

Enforcement. The act of putting something such as a law into effect; the execution of a law; the carrying out of a mandate or command. *See also* Enforcement powers.

Enforcement of Foreign Judgments Act. One of the uniform laws adopted by several states which gives the holder of a foreign judgment essentially the same rights to levy and execution on his judgment as the holder of a domestic judgment. The Act defines a "foreign judgment" as any judgment, decree, or order of a court of the United States or of any other court which is entitled to full faith and credit in the state. *See also* Full faith and credit clause.

Enforcement powers. The 13th, 14th, 15th, 19th, 23rd, 24th, and 26th Amendments to U.S.Const. each contain clauses granting to Congress the power to enforce by appropriate legislation the provisions of such Amendments.

Enfranchisement. The act of making free (as from slavery); giving a franchise or freedom to; investiture with privileges or capacities of freedom, or municipal or political liberty. Conferring the privilege of voting upon classes of persons who have not previously possessed such. *See also* Franchise.

Engage. To employ or involve one's self; to take part in; to embark on.

Engaged in commerce. To be "engaged in commerce" for purposes of Fair Labor Standards Act and Federal Employers' Liability Act, an employee must be actually engaged in the movement of commerce or the services he performs must be so closely related thereto as to be for all practical purposes an essential part thereof, rather than an isolated local activity. *See also* Commerce.

Engagement. A contract or agreement characterized by exchange of mutual promises; *e.g.* engagement to marry.

Engagement to marry. A promise or undertaking by a man to marry a woman, for breach of which, formerly, there was a cause of action in many jurisdictions. These actions today have lost favor and are not available in most states. Such actions were called heart balm suits. *See* Heart balm statutes.

Engrossment. To copy in final draft. Drafting of resolution or bill just prior to final vote upon same in legislature. Buying up or securing enough of a commodity to obtain a monopoly, so as to resell at higher price; *i.e.* to corner market in such commodity. Preparing deed for execution.

Enhanced. Made greater; *e.g.* in value or attractiveness. This word, taken in an unqualified sense, is synonymous with "increased," and comprehends any increase of value, however caused or arising.

Enjoin. To require; command; positively direct. To require a person, by writ of injunction, to perform, or to abstain or desist from, some act. *See* Injunction; Restraining order.

Enjoy. To have, possess, and use with satisfaction; to occupy or have benefit of.

Enjoyment. The exercise of a right; the possession and fruition of a right, privilege or incorporeal hereditament. Comfort, consolation, contentment, ease, happiness, pleasure and satisfaction. Such includes the beneficial use, interest and purpose to which property may be put, and implies right to profits and income therefrom.

Adverse enjoyment. The possession or exercise of an easement under a claim of right against the owner of the land out of which such easement is derived.

Quiet enjoyment. Covenant for. *See* Covenant.

Enlarge. To make larger; to increase; to extend a time limit; to grant further time. Also to set at

liberty one who has been imprisoned or in custody.

Enlargement of time. Extension of time allowed for performing an act that is otherwise to be done within time specified by court rule or order. See, *e.g.*, Fed.R.Civil P. 6(b).

Enlistment. Voluntary entry into one of the armed services other than as a commissioned officer. "Enlistee" voluntarily submits himself to military authority by virtue of his enlistment while "inductee" does not.

En masse /òn mǽs/°más/. Fr. In a mass; in a lump; in bulk; at wholesale.

Enoc Arden doctrine. The legal principles involved when a person leaves his spouse under such circumstances and for such a period of time as to make the other spouse believe that he is dead with the result that the remaining spouse marries another only to discover later the return of her first husband. Generally, in most states, it is safer for the remaining spouse to secure a divorce before marrying again.

Enroll. To register; to record; to enter on the rolls of a court; to transcribe.

Enrolled. Registered; recorded. Generally speaking, terms "registered" and "enrolled" are used to distinguish certificates granted to two classes of vessels; registry is for purpose of declaring nationality of vessel engaged in foreign trade, and enrollment evidences national character of a vessel engaged in coasting trade or home traffic.

Enrolled bill. The final copy of a bill or joint resolution which has passed both houses of a legislature and is ready for signature. In legislative practice, a bill which has been duly introduced, finally passed by both houses, signed by the proper officers of each, approved by the governor (or President) and filed by the secretary of state.

Enrolled bill rule. Under "enrolled bill rule" it is conclusively presumed that statute, as authenticated and deposited in Secretary of State's office, is precisely same as enacted by Legislature and courts will not go behind enrolled bill. Under this rule, once an election which is had on question of adoption of statute is sanctioned by law and is held, it is then too late to question the steps or legal procedure by which the measure got on the ballot.

Enrollment. Act of recording, enrolling, or registering.

Enrollment of vessels. The recording and certification of vessels employed in coastwise or inland navigation; as distinguished from the "registration" of vessels employed in foreign commerce.

En route /òn rúwt/. Fr. On the way; in the course of a voyage or journey; in course of transportation.

Entail, *v.* To settle or limit the succession to real property; to create an estate tail.

Entail, *n.* A fee abridged or limited to the issue, or certain classes of issue, instead of descending to all the heirs.

Entailed. Settled or limited to specified heirs, or in tail.

Entailed money. Money directed to be invested in realty to be entailed.

Entailment. An interference with and curtailment of the ordinary rules pertaining to devolution by inheritance; a limitation and direction by which property is to descend different from the course which it would take if the creator of the entailment, grantor or testator, had been content that the estate should devolve in regular and general succession to heirs at law in the statutory order of precedence and sequence.

Enter. To form a constituent part; to become a part or partaker; to impenetrate; share or mix with, as, tin "enters" into the composition of pewter. To go or come into a place or condition; to make or effect an entrance; to cause to go into or be received into.

In the law of real property, to go upon land for the purpose of taking possession of it. In strict usage, the entering is preliminary to the taking possession but in common parlance the entry is now merged in the taking possession. *See* Entry.

To place anything before a court, or upon or among the records, in a formal and regular manner, and usually in writing; as to "enter an appearance," to "enter a judgment." In this sense the word is nearly equivalent to setting down formally in writing, in either a full or abridged form. *See* Appearance; Docket; Entering judgments; Entry.

Entering. Generally synonymous with "recording".

Entering judgments. The formal entry of the judgment on the rolls or records (*e.g.* civil docket) of the court, which is necessary before bringing an appeal or an action on the judgment. The entering of judgment is a ministerial act performed by the clerk of court by means of which permanent evidence of judicial act in rendering judgment is made a record of the court. Under some statutes or court rules, the entering consists merely in the filing of a judgment with the clerk, while under others the entry of a judgment consists in the recording of it in the judgment book or civil docket. Fed.R.Civil P. 55, 58, 79.

Entry of judgment differs from rendition of judgment. "Rendition" of a judgment is the judicial act of the court in pronouncing the sentence of the law upon the facts in controversy. The "entry" is a ministerial act, which consists in entering upon the record a statement of the final conclusion reached by the court in the matter, thus furnishing external and incontestable evidence of the sentence given, and designed to stand as a perpetual memorial of its action.

Enterprise. A business venture or undertaking.

As used in the anti-racketeering statute (RICO), it includes any individual, partnership, corporation, association, or other legal entity, and any union or group of individuals associated in fact although not a legal entity. 18 U.S.C.A. § 1961(4). Additionally, it must be an ongoing organization, and an entity separate from the pattern of activity in which it engages. *See also* RICO laws.

To find an "enterprise" under the Fair Labor Standards Act, there must be related activities, unified operation or common control, and common business purpose. See 29 U.S.C.A. § 203(r).

See also Common enterprise; Joint enterprise.

Enterprise liability. Imposition of liability upon each member in industry who manufactures or produces product which causes injury or harm to a consumer and apportionment of liability of each member of industry by reference to that member's share of market for product. Such theory (also known as "industry wide liability"), shifts responsibility to industry for causing injury, because of concert of action by manufacturers through their trade association or their collective action, where specific injury-causing product cannot be identified. A defendant may exculpate itself by proving it did not manufacture the particular product at issue.

Term also refers to criminal liability imposed on a corporation, partnership, unincorporated association, or other artificial "person." See *e.g.,* Model Penal Code § 2.07.

Entertainment expenses. Such expenses are deductible only if they are directly related or associated with business. Various restrictions and documentation requirements have been imposed by the Internal Revenue Code and Regulations upon the deductibility of entertainment expenses to prevent abuses.

Entice. To wrongfully solicit, persuade, procure, allure, attract, draw by blandishment, coax or seduce. To lure, induce, tempt, incite, or persuade a person to do a thing. Enticement of a child is inviting, persuading or attempting to persuade a child to enter any vehicle, building, room or secluded place with intent to commit an unlawful sexual act upon or with the person of said child.

Entire. Whole; without division, separation, or diminution; unmingled; complete in all its parts; not participated in by others.

Entire balance of my estate. The residue.

Entire blood. Relations of the "entire blood" are those derived not only from the same ancestor, but from the same couple of ancestors. *See* Blood relations.

Entire contract. *See* Contract.

Entire controversy doctrine. Doctrine requires that a party who has elected to hold back from first proceeding on a related component of the controversy among the parties be barred from thereafter raising it in a subsequent proceeding. Under this doctrine, "entire controversy," rather than its constituent causes of action, is the unit of litigation and joinder of all such causes of action, is compulsory under penalty of forfeiture.

Entire day. This phrase signifies an undivided day, not parts of two days. An entire day must have a legal, fixed, precise time to begin, and a fixed, precise time to end. A day, in contemplation of law, comprises all the twenty-four hours, beginning and ending at twelve o'clock at night; *e.g.,* in a statute requiring the closing of all liquor establishments during "the entire day of any election," etc., this phrase means the natural day of twenty-four hours, commencing and terminating at midnight. *See also* Day.

Entire interest. The whole interest or right, without diminution. *See* Fee simple.

Entire loss of sight. In respect of one eye, or both, means substantial blindness, not necessarily absolute. *See* Blindness.

Entire output contract. Promise to deliver one's entire output (*i.e.* production) to the other. If no other detriment can be located, it will be found in the promisor's having surrendered his privilege of selling elsewhere. Such agreements are governed by U.C.C. § 2–306.

Entire tenancy. A sole possession by one person, called "severalty," which is contrary to several tenancy, where a joint or common possession is in one or more.

Entirety. The whole, in contradistinction to a moiety or part only. When land is conveyed to husband and wife, they do not take by moieties, but both are seised of the *entirety*. Parceners, on the other hand, have not an *entirety* of interest, but each is properly entitled to the whole of a distinct moiety. *See* Estate by the entirety.

The word is also used to designate that which the law considers as one whole, and not capable of being divided into parts. Thus, a judgment, it is held, is an *entirety*, and, if void as to one of the two defendants, cannot be valid as to the other. Also, if a contract is an *entirety*, no part of the

consideration is due until the whole has been performed.

Entire use, benefit, etc. These words in the *habendum* of a trust-deed for the benefit of a married woman are equivalent to the words "sole use," or "sole and separate use," and consequently her husband takes nothing under such deed.

Entitle. In its usual sense, to entitle is to give a right or legal title to. To qualify for; to furnish with proper grounds for seeking or claiming. In ecclesiastical law, to entitle is to give a title or ordination as a minister.

Entitlement. Right to benefits, income or property which may not be abridged without due process; *e.g.* social security benefits.

Entity. A real being; existence. An organization or being that possesses separate existence for tax purposes. Examples would be corporations, partnerships, estates and trusts. The accounting entity for which accounting statements are prepared may not be the same as the entity defined by law.

"Entity" includes corporation and foreign corporation; not-for-profit corporation; profit and not-for-profit unincorporated association; business trust, estate, partnership, trust, and two or more persons having a joint or common economic interest; and state, United States, and foreign government. Rev. Model Bus.Corp. Act, § 1.40.

An existence apart, such as a corporation in relation to its stockholders.

Entity includes person, estate, trust, governmental unit. Bankruptcy Code, § 101.

See also Legal entity.

Entity assumption. An assumption that a business is viewed as a unit that is separate and apart from its owners and from other firms.

Entrap. To catch, to entrap, to ensnare; hence, to catch by artifice. To involve in difficulties or distresses; to catch or involve in contradictions.

Entrapment. The act of officers or agents of the government in inducing a person to commit a crime not contemplated by him, for the purpose of instituting a criminal prosecution against him. According to the generally accepted view, a law enforcement official, or an undercover agent acting in cooperation with such an official, perpetrates an entrapment when, for the purpose of obtaining evidence of a crime, he originates the idea of the crime and then induces another person to engage in conduct constituting such a crime when the other person is not otherwise disposed to do so.

A public law enforcement official or a person acting in cooperation with such an official perpetrates an entrapment if for the purpose of obtaining evidence of the commission of an offense, he induces or encourages another person to engage in conduct constituting such offense by either: (a) making knowingly false representations designed to induce the belief that such conduct is not prohibited; or (b) employing methods of persuasion or inducement which create a substantial risk that such an offense will be committed by persons other than those who are ready to commit it. Model Penal Code, § 2.13.

See also Predisposition.

Entrepreneur /òntrəprənə́r/°n(y)u(wə)r/. One who, on his own, initiates and assumes the financial risks of a new enterprise and who undertakes its management.

Entrust. To give over to another something after a relation of confidence has been established. To deliver to another something in trust or to commit something to another with a certain confidence regarding his care, use or disposal of it.

Entrusting. The transfer of possession of goods to a merchant who deals in goods of that type and who may in turn transfer such goods and all rights therein to a purchaser in the ordinary course of business. U.C.C. § 2–403(2)(3).

Entry. The act of making or entering a record; a setting down in writing of particulars; or that which is entered; an item. Generally synonymous with "recording." *See also* Enroll.

Enter, in practice, means to place anything before court, or upon or among records, and is nearly equivalent to setting down formally in writing, either in full or abridged form but it may be used as meaning simply to file or duly deposit. *See also* Docket.

Passage leading into a house or other building or to a room; a vestibule.

The act of a merchant, trader, or other businessman in recording in his account-books the facts and circumstances of a sale, loan, or other transaction. The books in which such memoranda are first (or originally) inscribed are called "books of original entry," and are *prima facie* evidence for certain purposes.

In copyright law, depositing with the register of copyrights the printed title of a book, pamphlet, etc., for the purpose of securing copyright on the same. Copyright Act, § 408 (17 U.S.C.A.).

In immigration law, any coming of an alien into the U.S., from a foreign part or place or from an outlying possession, whether voluntary or otherwise. 8 U.S.C.A. § 1101.

In criminal law, entry is the unlawful making one's way into a dwelling or other house, for the purpose of committing a crime therein. In cases of burglary, the least entry with the whole or any part of the body, hand, or foot, or with any instrument or weapon, introduced for the purpose of committing a felony, is sufficient to complete the offense. *See also* Breaking.

In customs law, the entry of imported goods at the custom house consists in submitting them to the inspection of the revenue officers, together with a statement or description of such goods, and the original invoices of the same, for the purpose of estimating the duties to be paid thereon.

See also False entry; Forcible entry; Illegal entry; Journal entry.

Entry of judgment. See Entering judgments.

Open entry. An entry upon real estate, for the purpose of taking possession, which is not clandestine nor effected by secret artifice or stratagem, and (in some states by statute) one which is accomplished in the presence of two witnesses.

Re-entry. The resumption of the possession of leased premises by the landlord on the tenant's failure to pay the stipulated rent or otherwise to keep the conditions of the lease. *See* Ejectment.

Right of entry. See Right of entry.

Entry in regular course of business. A record setting forth a fact or transaction made by one in the ordinary and usual course of one's business, employment, office or profession, which it was the duty of the enterer in such manner to make, or which was commonly and regularly made, or which it was convenient to make, in the conduct of the business to which such entry pertains.

Entry of judgment. *See* Entering judgments.

Entry, right of. *See* Right of entry.

Enumerated. This term is often used in law as equivalent to "mentioned specifically," "designated," or "expressly named or granted"; as in speaking of "enumerated" governmental powers, items of property, or articles in a tariff schedule.

Enumerated powers. The powers specifically delegated by the Constitution to some branch or authority of the national government, and which are not denied to that government or reserved to the States or to the people. The powers specifically given to Congress are enumerated in Article I of U.S. Constitution. *See also* Power *(Constitutional powers)*.

Enure. To operate or take effect. To serve to the use, benefit, or advantage of a person. A release to the tenant for life *enures* to him in reversion; that is, it has the same effect for him as for the tenant for life. Often written "inure."

En ventre sa mere /òn vóntrə sà mér/. L. Fr. In its mother's womb. A term descriptive of an unborn child. For some purposes the law regards an infant *en ventre* as in being. It may take a legacy; have a guardian; an estate may be limited to its use, etc.

En vie /òn víy/. L. Fr. In life; alive.

Environment. The totality of physical, economic, cultural, aesthetic, and social circumstances and factors which surround and affect the desirability and value of property and which also affect the quality of peoples' lives. The surrounding conditions, influences or forces which influence or modify.

Environmental impact statements. Documents which are required by federal and state laws to accompany proposals for major projects and programs that will likely have an impact on the surrounding environment. See 42 U.S.C.A. § 4332. Statement required by the National Environmental Policy Act to be developed by federal agencies for every recommendation or report on proposals for legislation and other major federal actions significantly affecting the quality of the human environment. *See also* National Environmental Policy Act.

Environmental Protection Agency. The federal Environmental Protection Agency was created in 1970 to permit coordinated and effective governmental action on behalf of the environment. EPA endeavors to abate and control pollution systematically, by proper integration of a variety of research, monitoring, standard setting, and enforcement activities. As a complement to its other activities, EPA coordinates and supports research and antipollution activities by State and local governments, private and public groups, individuals, and educational institutions. EPA also reinforces efforts among other Federal agencies with respect to the impact of their operations on the environment, and it is specifically charged with making public its written comments on environmental impact statements and with publishing its determinations when those hold that a proposal is unsatisfactory from the standpoint of public health or welfare or environmental quality. *See also* National Environmental Policy Act.

Envoy. A diplomat of the rank of minister or ambassador sent by a country to the government of a foreign country to execute a special mission or to serve as a permanent diplomatic representative.

E.O.E. Abbreviation for "errors and omissions excepted"; a term commonly included in accounts and financial statements.

E.O.M. End of month. Payment terms in sale contract.

Eo nomine /íyow nómaniy/. Lat. Under or by that name; by that appellation. An "eo nomine" designation is one which describes commodity by a specific name, usually one well known to commerce. Ordinarily, use is not a criteria in determining whether merchandise is embraced within eo nomine provision, but use may be considered in determining identity of eo nomine designation.

EPA. Environmental Protection Agency.

E pluribus unum /iy pl(y)úrabas yúwnam/. One out of many. The motto of the United States of America.

E.P.S. Earnings per share.

Equal. Alike; uniform; on the same plane or level with respect to efficiency, worth, value, amount, or rights. Word "equal" as used in law implies not identity but duality and the use of one thing as the measure of another.

Equal Access to Justice Act. This 1980 Act entitles certain prevailing parties to recover attorney and expert witness fees, and other expenses, in actions involving the United States, unless the Government action was substantially justified. 5 U.S.C.A. § 504; 28 U.S.C.A. § 2412. *See also* American rule; Prevailing party; Substantially justified.

Equal and uniform taxation. Taxes are said to be "equal and uniform" when no person or class of persons in the taxing district, whether it be a state, county, or city, is taxed at a different rate than are other persons in the same district upon the same value or the same thing, and where the objects of taxation are the same, by whomsoever owned or whatsoever they may be.

Equal Credit Opportunity Act. Federal Act prohibiting a creditor from discriminating against any applicant on the basis of race, color, religion, national origin, age, sex or marital status with respect to any aspect of a credit transaction. 15 U.S.C.A. § 1691 et seq.

Equal degree. Persons are said to be related to a decedent "in equal degree" when they are all removed by an equal number of steps or degrees from the common ancestor.

Equal Employment Opportunity Commission. The Equal Employment Opportunity Commission (EEOC) was created by Title VII of the Civil Rights Act of 1964 (78 Stat. 241; 42 U.S.C.A. § 2000a), and became operational July 2, 1965. The purposes of the Commission are to end discrimination based on race, color, religion, age, sex, or national origin in hiring, promotion, firing, wages, testing, training, apprenticeship, and all other conditions of employment; and to promote voluntary action programs by employers, unions, and community organizations to put equal employment opportunity into actual operation.

Equality. The condition of possessing substantially the same rights, privileges, and immunities, and being liable to substantially the same duties. "Equality" guaranteed under equal protection clause is equality under the same conditions and among persons similarly situated; classifications must not be arbitrary and must be based upon some difference in classes having substantial relation to legitimate objects to be accomplished. *See*

Equal protection clause; Equal protection of the law.

Equalization. The act or process of making equal or bringing about conformity to a common standard. The process of equalizing assessments or taxes, as performed by "boards of equalization" in various states, consists in comparing the assessments made by the local officers of the various counties or other taxing districts within the jurisdiction of the board and reducing them to a common and uniform basis, increasing or diminishing by such percentage as may be necessary, so as to bring about, within the entire territory affected, a uniform and equal ratio between the assessed value and the actual cash value of property. The term is also applied to a similar process of leveling or adjusting the assessments of individual taxpayers, so that the property of one shall not be assessed at a higher (or lower) percentage of its market value than the property of another. The process of determining that property of a certain nature is generally placed on the assessment rolls at a certain percentage of its true and full value. *See also* Equal protection of the law.

Equalization board. Local governmental agency whose function is to supervise the equalization of taxes as among various properties and as among various districts to bring about an equitable distribution of tax burdens.

Equalization of taxes. *See* Equalization.

Equalize. To make equal, to cause to correspond, or be like in amount or degree, as compared with something.

Equally divided. Provision in will that property shall be "equally divided," or divided "share and share alike" means that the property shall be divided per capita and not per stirpes. However, these phrases may be so modified by other parts of the will as to require distribution per stirpes.

Equal Pay Act. Federal law which mandates same pay for all persons who do same work without regard to sex, age, etc. For work to be "equal" within meaning of Act, it is not necessary that jobs be identical but only that they be substantially equal. 29 U.S.C.A. § 206.

Equal protection clause. That provision in 14th Amendment to U.S. Constitution which prohibits a State from denying to any person within its jurisdiction the equal protection of the laws. This clause requires that persons under like circumstances be given equal protection in the enjoyment of personal rights and the prevention and redress of wrongs. *See also* Equal protection of the law.

Equal protection of the law. The constitutional guarantee of "equal protection of the laws" means that no person or class of persons shall be denied the same protection of the laws which is enjoyed by other persons or other classes in like circumstances in their lives, liberty, property, and in their pursuit of happiness. 14th Amend., U.S. Const. Doctrine simply means that similarly situated persons must receive similar treatment under the law.

The equal protection of the laws of a state is extended to persons within its jurisdiction, within the meaning of the constitutional requirement, when its courts are open to them on the same conditions as to others, with like rules of evidence and modes of procedure, for the security of their persons and property, the prevention and redress of wrongs, and the enforcement of contracts; when they are subjected to no restrictions in the acquisition of property, the enjoyment of personal liberty, and the pursuit of happiness, which do not generally affect others; when they are liable to no other or greater burdens and charges than such as are laid upon others; and when no different or greater punishment is enforced against them for a violation of the laws.

"Equal protection," with respect to classification for taxation purposes, does not require identity of treatment, but only (1) that classification rests on real and not feigned differences, (2) that the distinction have some relevance to purpose for which classification is made, and (3) that the different treatments be not so disparate, relative to difference in classification, as to be wholly arbitrary.

Equal Rights Amendment. Proposed amendment to U.S. Constitution which provided that: "Equality of rights under the law shall not be denied or abridged by the United States or by any State on account of sex." Such amendment failed to receive ratification by the required number of states.

Equal Time Act. This Act requires that if licensee of broadcasting facility permits a legally qualified candidate for public office to use facility for broadcasting, he shall afford equal opportunities to all other such candidates for that office. 47 U.S.C.A. § 315.

Equip. To furnish for service or against a need or exigency; to fit out; to supply with whatever is necessary to efficient action in any way. Synonymous with furnish.

Equipment. Furnishings, or outfit for the required purposes. Whatever is needed in equipping; the articles comprised in an outfit; equippage.

Under U.C.C., goods include "equipment" if they are used or bought for use primarily in business (including farming or a profession) or by a debtor who is a non-profit organization or a governmental subdivision or agency or if the goods are not included in the definitions of inventory, farm products or consumer goods. U.C.C. § 9–109(2).

Equipment trust. Financing device commonly used by railroads by which equipment is purchased from the manufacturer by a trustee who provides a substantial portion of the purchase price, the railroad providing the balance. The trustee then leases the equipment to the railroad which pays a rental fee consisting of interest, amortization for serial retirement and trustee's fee.

Equipment trust certificate. A type of security, generally issued by a railroad, to pay for new equipment. Title to the equipment, such as a locomotive, is held by a trustee until the notes are paid off. An equipment trust certificate is usually secured by a first claim on the equipment.

Equitable. Just; conformable to the principles of justice and right. Existing in equity; available or sustainable by action in equity, or upon the rules and principles of equity. *See* Equitable action.

As to *equitable* Assets; Construction; Conversion; Easement; Ejectment; Estate; Fraud; Garnishment; Levy; Mortgage; Title, and Waste, see those titles.

Equitable abstention doctrine. A court may refrain from exercising jurisdiction which it possesses in the interest of comity between courts and between states as in the case of actions involving the affairs of a foreign corporation or foreign land. Doctrine also applies to case of Federal court's refraining from interfering with decision of state administrative agency's decision on a local matter.

Equitable action. One seeking an equitable remedy or relief; though in the federal and most state courts, with the procedural merger of law and equity, there is now *procedurally* only one type of action—a "civil action." Fed.R. Civil P. 2.

Equitable adjustment theory. In settlement of federal contract disputes, contracting officer should make fair adjustment within a reasonable time before contractor is required to settle with his subcontractors, suppliers and other creditors.

Equitable adoption. Refers to situation involving oral contract to adopt child, fully performed except that there was no statutory adoption, and in which rule is applied for benefit of child in determination of heirship upon death of person contracting to adopt. In certain jurisdictions, a child has rights of inheritance from person who has contracted to adopt him but has not done so.

Equitable assignment. An assignment which, though invalid at law, will be recognized and enforced in equity; *e.g.*, an assignment of a chose in action, or of future acquisitions of the assignor. In order to work an "equitable assignment", there

must be an absolute appropriation by the assignor of the debt or fund sought to be assigned.

Equitable benefit doctrine. This doctrine allows bankruptcy court to grant preferred status to claims for service rendered by persons other than bankruptcy officers, to extent that services benefited estate, where person is acting primarily for benefit of estate as a whole.

Equitable conversion. The doctrine that, since equity regards as done what out to be done, once parties have executed a binding contract for the sale of land, equitable title vests in the purchaser and the vendor holds legal title only as security for payment of the balance of the purchase price. A doctrine commonly applied when death intervenes between the signing of an agreement to sell real estate and the date of transfer of title resulting in treating land as personalty and personalty as land under certain circumstances. It takes place when a contract for sale of realty becomes binding on parties. *See also* Conversion.

Equitable defense. Formerly, a defense which was only available in a court of equity. With the procedural merger of law and equity however, equitable defenses can be raised along with legal defenses in same action. Fed.R. Civil P. 8.

Equitable distribution. No-fault divorce statutes in certain states (*e.g.* New Jersey) grant courts the power to distribute equitably upon divorce all property legally and beneficially acquired during marriage by husband and wife, or either of them, whether legal title lies in their joint or individual names.

Equitable doctrine of approximation. This doctrine differs from "Cy pres doctrine" in purpose and application. The last mentioned doctrine applies where an apparent charitable intention has failed, whether by an incomplete disposition at the outset or by subsequent inadequacy of the original object, and its purpose is to give a cy pres or proximate application to testator's intention, whereas the "equitable doctrine of approximation" merely authorizes a court to vary the details of administration, in order to preserve the trust, and carry out the general purpose of the donor. *See also* Approximation.

Equitable election. Under this doctrine, a person cannot accept benefits accruing to him by a will and at the same time refuse to recognize validity of will in other respects, but doctrine may not be applied to prejudice of third parties. The choice to be made by a person who may, under a will or other instrument, have either one of two alternative rights or benefits, but not both. The obligation imposed upon a party to choose between two inconsistent or alternative rights or claims, in cases where there is clear intention of the person from whom he derives one that he should not enjoy both. A choice shown by an overt act between two inconsistent rights, either of which may be asserted at the will of the chooser alone. *See also* Election *(Law of wills)*.

Equitable estoppel. The doctrine by which a person may be precluded by his act or conduct, or silence when it is his duty to speak, from asserting a right which he otherwise would have had. The effect of voluntary conduct of a party whereby he is precluded from asserting rights against another who has justifiably relied upon such conduct and changed his position so that he will suffer injury if the former is allowed to repudiate the conduct.

Elements or essentials of such estoppel include change of position for the worse by party asserting estoppel; conduct by party estopped such that it would be contrary to equity and good conscience for him to allege and prove the truth; false representation or concealment of facts; ignorance of party asserting estoppel of facts and absence of opportunity to ascertain them; injury from declarations, acts, or omissions of party were he permitted to gainsay their truth; intention that representation should be acted on; knowledge, actual or constructive, of facts by party estopped; misleading person to his prejudice; omission, misconduct or misrepresentation misleading another. It is based on some affirmative action, by word or conduct, of the person against whom it is invoked, and some action of the other party, relying on the representations made.

Estoppel in pais and equitable estoppel are convertible terms.

Equitable interest. The interest of a beneficiary under a trust is considered equitable as contrasted with the interest of the trustee which is a legal interest because the trustee has legal as contrasted with equitable title. Restatement, Second, Trusts, § 2f. *See also* Equitable ownership.

Equitable lien. A right, not existing at law, to have specific property applied in whole or in part to payment of a particular debt or class of debts. Such type lien arises either from a written contract which shows an intention to charge some particular property with a debt or obligation or is implied and declared by a court of equity out of general considerations of right and justice as applied to relations of the parties and circumstances of their dealings.

Equitable life estate. An interest in real or personal property which lasts for the life of the holder of the estate and which is equitable as contrasted with legal in its creation as in the case of a beneficiary of a trust who has a life estate under the trust.

Equitable mortgage. An agreement to post certain property as security before the security agreement is formalized. A catchall term to connote all of the transactions which, despite peculiarities of form or appearance of nonsecured transaction, are given effect of mortgage when examined by court with equitable powers. For example, if a person transfers property by deed absolute to his creditor as security for a debt with the mutual understanding that such property will be reconveyed by the creditor on the repayment of the debt, a court will consider such a deed a mortgage, though an innocent purchaser for value from the creditor can cut off the equitable rights of the debtor. *See also* Mortgage.

Equitable owner. One who is recognized in equity as owner of the property, because real and beneficial use and title belong to him, even though bare legal title is invested in another.

Equitable ownership. The ownership interest of one who has equitable as contrasted with legal ownership of property as in the case of a trust beneficiary. Ownership rights which are protected in equity. *See also* Equitable interest.

Equitable recoupment. Rule of the law which diminishes the right of a party invoking legal process to recover a debt, to the extent that he holds money or property of his debtor, to which he has no moral right, and it is ordinarily a defensive remedy going only to mitigation of damages. This doctrine provides that, at least in some cases, a claim for a refund of taxes barred by a statute of limitations may nevertheless be recouped against a tax claim of the government.

Equitable redemption. The act or process by which a mortgagor redeems his property after payment of the mortgage debt. The purchase of the equity of redemption after foreclosure has commenced. *See* Equity of redemption.

Equitable relief. That species of relief sought in a court with equity powers as, for example, in the case of one seeking an injunction or specific performance instead of money damages.

Equitable rescission. Rescission decreed by court of equity, as distinguished from "legal rescission" which is effected by restoration or offer to restore.

Equitable restraint doctrine. Under this doctrine, federal courts will not intervene to enjoin a pending state criminal prosecution absent a strong showing of bad faith and irreparable injury.

Equitable right. Right cognizable within court of equity as contrasted with legal right enforced in court of law; though under rules practice in most states and in the federal courts there has been a merger procedurally between actions at law and equity. Fed.R. Civil P. 2.

Equitable servitudes. Building restrictions and restrictions on the use of land which may be enforced in equity. If there is a scheme in their creation, a subsequent owner may enforce them by injunctive relief against another subsequent owner. Such are broader than covenants running with the land because they are interests in land.

Equitable subrogation. Legal fiction through which person who pays debt for which another is primarily responsible is substituted, or subrogated, to all rights and remedies of other.

Equitable title. *See* Equitable ownership.

Equitable waste. Injury to the corpus of property inconsistent with good management or husbandry and recognized by a court of equity but not by a court of law.

Equitas sequitur legem /íykwətǽs sékwətər líyjəm/. Equity follows the law.

Equity. Justice administered according to fairness as contrasted with the strictly formulated rules of common law. It is based on a system of rules and principles which originated in England as an alternative to the harsh rules of common law and which were based on what was fair in a particular situation. One sought relief under this system in courts of equity rather than in courts of law. The term "equity" denotes the spirit and habit of fairness, justness, and right dealing which would regulate the intercourse of men with men. Equity is a body of jurisprudence, or field of jurisdiction, differing in its origin, theory, and methods from the common law; though procedurally, in the federal courts and most state courts, equitable and legal rights and remedies are administered in the same court. *See* Equity, courts of.

A system of jurisprudence collateral to, and in some respects independent of, "law"; the object of which is to render the administration of justice more complete, by affording relief where the courts of law are incompetent to give it, or to give it with effect, or by exercising certain branches of jurisdiction independently of them.

A stockholders' proportionate share (ownership interest) in the corporation's capital stock and surplus. The extent of an ownership interest in a venture. In this context, equity refers not to a legal concept but to the financial definition that an owner's equity in a business is equal to the business's assets minus its liabilities.

Value of property or an enterprise over and above the indebtedness against it (*e.g.*, market value of house minus mortgage). *See Real estate, below.*

Accounting. Paid-in capital plus retained earnings.

Countervailing equity. A contrary and balancing equity; an equity or right opposed to that which is sought to be enforced or recognized, and which ought not to be sacrificed or subordinated to the latter, because it is of equal strength and justice, and equally deserving of consideration.

Investment. Ownership interest of shareholders in corporation (as opposed to bond or other debt interests). *See* Stock.

Latent or secret equity. An equitable claim or right, the knowledge of which has been confined to the parties for and against whom it exists, or which has been concealed from one or several persons interested in the subject-matter.

Natural equity. A term sometimes employed in works on jurisprudence, possessing no very precise meaning, but used as equivalent to justice, honesty, or morality in business relations, or man's innate sense of right dealing and fair play. Inasmuch as equity, as now administered, is a complex system of rules, doctrines, and precedents, and possesses, within the range of its own fixed principles, but little more elasticity than the law, the term "natural equity" may be understood to denote, in a general way, that which strikes the ordinary conscience and sense of justice as being fair, right, and equitable, in advance of the question whether the technical jurisprudence of the chancery courts would so regard it.

Perfect equity. An equitable title or right which lacks nothing to its completeness as a legal title or right except the formal conveyance or other investiture which would make it cognizable at law; particularly, the equity or interest of a purchaser of real estate who has paid the purchase price in full and fulfilled all conditions resting on him, but has not yet received a deed or patent.

Real estate. The remaining interest belonging to one who has pledged or mortgaged his property, or the surplus of value which may remain after the property has been disposed of for the satisfaction of liens. The amount or value of a property above the total liens or charges. The difference between the fair market value and debt in property; thus, an equity of $5,000 may come about by having fair market value property of $20,000 with debt of $15,000. The term came from the development in English courts of equity of the right of an owner of property to redeem his property even after a foreclosure, which right came to be known as the equity of redemption. The existence of the right was predicated on the property being of far greater value than the debt owed to the party that foreclosed.

Statement of owner's equity. A financial statement that discloses the changes in owner's equity during an accounting period.

Statement of stockholders' equity. A financial statement that discloses the changes in all stockholders' equity accounts maintained by a business.

Equity acts in personam. A basic principle of law of equity to the effect that equity grants relief in the form of personal decrees as contrasted with law which awards money damages. A necessary corollary of this principle is that equity requires personal jurisdiction to grant its relief.

Equity, bill in. The name given to the original pleading in an equity case. However, under current rules practice in most states, the "bill" has been replaced by a complaint with the procedural merger of law and equity. Fed.R. Civil P. 2.

Equity capital. Funds furnished by owners of company in return for stock or other evidence of ownership. *See* Equity.

Equity contribution agreement. An agreement to contribute equity to a project under certain specified conditions.

Equity, courts of. Courts which administer justice according to the system of equity, and according to a peculiar course of procedure or practice. Frequently termed "courts of chancery." With the procedural merger of law and equity in the federal and most state courts, equity courts have been abolished.

Equity financing. Raising of capital by corporation by issuing (selling) stock. This is contrasted with "debt financing" which is the raising of capital by issuing bonds or borrowing money.

Equity follows the law. Equity adopts and follows the rules of law in all cases to which those rules may, in terms, be applicable. Equity, in dealing with cases of an equitable nature, adopts and follows the analogies furnished by the rules of law. A leading maxim of equity jurisprudence, which, however, is not of universal application, but liable to many exceptions.

Equity jurisdiction. In a general sense, the jurisdiction belonging to a court of equity, but more particularly the aggregate of those cases, controversies, and occasions which form proper subjects for the exercise of the powers of a chancery court.

In the federal and most state courts there has been a merger procedurally between law and equity actions (*i.e.*, the same court has jurisdiction over *both* legal and equitable matters) and, hence, a person seeking equitable relief brings the same complaint as in a law action and simply demands equitable relief instead of (or in addition to) money damages. Fed.R. Civil P. 2.

"Equity jurisdiction," in its ordinary acceptation, as distinguished on the one side from the general power to decide matters at all, and on the other from the jurisdiction "at law" or "common-law jurisdiction," is the power to hear certain kinds and classes of civil causes according to the principles of the method and procedure adopted by the court of chancery, and to decide them in accordance with the doctrines and rules of equity jurisprudence, which decision may involve either the determination of the equitable rights, estates, and interests of the parties to such causes, or the granting of equitable remedies. In order that a cause may come within the scope of the equity jurisdiction, one of two alternatives is essential; either the primary right, estate, or interest to be maintained, or the violation of which furnishes the cause of action, must be equitable rather than legal; or the remedy granted must be in its nature purely equitable, or if it be a remedy which may also be given by a court of law, it must be one which, under the facts and circumstances of the case, can only be made complete and adequate through the equitable modes of procedure.

Equity jurisprudence. That portion of remedial justice which is exclusively administered by courts of equity as distinguished from courts of common law. More generally speaking, the science which treats of the rules, principles, and maxims which govern the decisions of a court of equity, the cases and controversies which are considered proper subjects for its cognizance, and the nature and form of the remedies which it grants.

Equity loan. Line of credit made available by banks to homeowners with the extent of such credit based on, and secured with, built-up equity in borrower's home. *See* Equity (*Real estate*).

Equity looks upon that as done which ought to have been done. Equity will treat the subject-matter, as to collateral consequences and incidents, in the same manner as if the final acts contemplated by the parties had been executed exactly as they ought to have been; not as the parties might have executed them.

Equity method. A method of accounting for long-term investments in common stock, where the investment account includes the acquisition cost and a share of the investee's net income, net losses, and dividends.

Equity of a statute. By this phrase is intended the rule of statutory construction which admits within the operation of a statute a class of cases which are neither expressly named nor excluded, but which, from their analogy to the cases that are named, are clearly and justly within the spirit and general meaning of the law; such cases are said to be "within the equity of the statute."

Equity of partners. A term used to designate the right of each partner to have the firm's property applied to the payment of the firm's debts.

Equity of redemption. The right of the mortgagor of property to redeem the same (*i.e.*, save from foreclosure) after it has been forfeited, at law, by a breach of the condition of the mortgage (*i.e.*, default in mortgage payments), upon paying the amount of debt, interest and costs. *See* Foreclosure; Redemption.

Equity ratio. Stockholders' equity divided by total assets.

Equity security. A security that represents an equity ownership interest in a corporation, rather than debt. Equity securities are usually considered to be common and preferred shares. *See* Stock. *Compare* Bond.

As defined in Bankruptcy Code § 101, term includes: (A) share in a corporation, whether or not transferable or denominated "stock", or similar security; (B) interest of a limited partner in a limited partnership; or (C) warrant or right, other than a right to convert, to purchase, sell, or subscribe to a share, security, or interest of a kind specified in subparagraph (A) or (B).

Equity shares. Shares of any class of stock, whether or not preferred as to dividends or assets, having unlimited dividend rights. *See* Stock.

Equity term. An equity term of court is one devoted exclusively to equity business, that is, in which no criminal cases are tried nor any cases requiring the impaneling of a jury. *See* Equity, courts of.

Equity to a settlement. The equitable right of a wife, when her husband sues in equity for the reduction of her equitable estate to his own possession, to have the whole or a portion of such estate settled upon herself and her children. Also a similar right recognized by the equity courts as directly to be asserted against the husband. Also sometimes called the "wife's equity."

Equivalent, *adj.* Equal in value, force, measure, volume, power, and effect or having equal or corresponding import, meaning or significance; alike, identical.

Equivalents doctrine. In patent infringement law, doctrine of "equivalents" means that if two devices do the same work in substantially the same way and accomplish substantially the same result, they are the same, even though they differ in name, form or shape. A doctrine which declares that a device infringes a patented invention if it does the same work as the invention in substantially the same way, even if it is outside the literal terms of the claims of the patent. The doctrine prevents parties from infringing patents with impunity by making merely trivial changes in an invention. The more significant the patented invention the greater the scope of this doctrine.

Equivocal. Having a double or several meanings or senses. Synonymous with "ambiguous". *See* Ambiguity.

ERA. *See* Equal Rights Amendment.

Erasure. The obliteration of words or marks from a written instrument by rubbing, scraping, or scratching them out. Also the place in a document where a word or words have been so removed. The term is sometimes used for the removal of parts of a writing by any means whatever, as by cancellation; but this is not an accurate use.

Erasure of record. Procedure by which a person's criminal record may be sealed or destroyed if certain conditions are met. This is commonly provided for by statute for juvenile records. Within statute providing that all police and court records shall be erased upon acquittal of the accused, word "erased" means at the very least nondisclosure. *See also* Expungement of record.

Erie v. Tompkins. The landmark case holding that in an action in the Federal court, except as to matters governed by the U.S. Constitution and Acts of Congress, the law to be applied in any case is the law of the State in which the Federal Court is situated. 304 U.S. 64, 58 S.Ct. 817, 82 L.Ed. 1188. This case overruled Swift v. Tyson, 41 U.S. 1, 16 Pet. 1, 10 L.Ed. 865, which held that there was a body of federal general common law to be applied in such cases.

E.R.I.S.A. Employee Retirement Income Security Act. Federal Act governing the funding, vesting, administration, and termination of private pension plans. This Act also established the Pension Benefit Guaranty Corporation. 29 U.S.C.A. § 1001 et seq.

Erosion. To wear away by the action of water, wind, or other elements. The gradual eating away of the soil by the operation of currents or tides. Distinguished from *submergence,* which is the disappearance of the soil under the water and the formation of a navigable body over it. *See* Avulsion. *Compare* Accretion.

Errant. Wandering; itinerant; applied to justices on circuit, and bailiffs at large, etc.

Erratum /ərǽtəm/əréytəm/. Lat. Error. Used in the Latin formula for assigning errors, and in the reply thereto, "in nullo est erratum," *i.e.,* there was no error, no error was committed.

Erroneous. Involving error; deviating from the law. This term is not generally used as designating a corrupt or evil act. *See* Error.

Erroneous assessment. Refers to an assessment that deviates from the law and is therefore invalid, and is a defect that is jurisdictional in its nature, and does not refer to the judgment of the assessing officer in fixing the amount of valuation of the property.

Erroneous judgment. One rendered according to course and practice of court, but contrary to law, upon mistaken view of law, or upon erroneous application of legal principles.

Erroneous *or* **illegal tax.** One levied without statutory authority, or upon property not subject to taxation, or by some officer having no authority to levy the tax, or one which in some other similar respect is illegal.

Error. A mistaken judgment or incorrect belief as to the existence or effect of matters of fact, or a false or mistaken conception or application of the law. Such a mistaken or false conception or application of the law to the facts of a cause as will furnish ground for a review of the proceedings upon a writ of error. A mistake of law, or false or irregular application of it, such as vitiates the proceedings and warrants the reversal of the judgment. An act involving a departure from truth or accuracy; a mistake; an inaccuracy; as, an error in calculation.

Error is also used as an elliptical expression for "writ of error"; as in saying that *error* lies; that a judgment may be reversed *on error*. *See* Writ of error.

See also Ignorance; Mistake; Plain error rule.

Assignment of errors. A specification of the errors upon which the appellant will rely in seeking to have the judgment of the lower court reversed, vacated, modified, or a new trial ordered. See *e.g.* Fed.R.App. P. 28.

Clerical error. See Clerical error.

Error apparent of record. Plain, fundamental error that goes to the foundation of the action irrespective of the evidence; an obvious misapprehension of the applicable law.

Fundamental error. In appellate practice, error which goes to the merits of the plaintiff's cause of action, and which will be considered on review, whether assigned as error or not, where the justice of the case seems to require it. Error of such character as to render judgment void. Error so grave that, if not rectified, would result in denial of fundamental due process. Error in law apparent on the face of the record; *e.g.* court lacked jurisdiction. Such error is presented, for example, where error in court's instruction to jury goes to very basis of case so that charge fails to state and apply law under which accused is prosecuted. *See Reversible error, below. See also* Plain error rule.

Harmful error. Error which more probably than improbably affected the verdict or judgment prejudicially to the party complaining. *See Fundamental error; Reversible error, this topic. See also* Plain error rule.

Harmless error. In appellate practice, an error committed in the progress of the trial below, but which was not prejudicial to the rights of the party assigning it, and for which, therefore, the court will not reverse the judgment, as, where the error was neutralized or corrected by subsequent proceedings in the case, or where, notwithstanding the error, the particular issue was found in that party's favor, or where, even if the error had not been committed, he could not have been legally entitled to prevail. Error which is not suffi-

cient in nature or effect to warrant reversal, modification, or retrial. Fed.R.Crim.P. 52 provides: "Any error, defect, irregularity or variance which does not affect substantial rights shall be disregarded." *See also* Harmless error doctrine.

Invited error. In appellate practice, the principle of "invited error" is that if, during the progress of a cause, a party requests or moves the court to make a ruling which is actually erroneous, and the court does so, that party cannot take advantage of the error on appeal or review.

Reversible error. In appellate practice, such an error as warrants the appellate court in reversing the judgment before it; substantial error, that which reasonably might have prejudiced the party complaining. *See Fundamental error, above. See also* Plain error rule.

Error coram nobis /éhrər kórəm nówbəs/. Error committed in the proceedings "before us"; *i.e.,* error assigned as a ground for reviewing, modifying, or vacating a judgment in the same court in which it was rendered. A writ to bring before the court that pronounced judgment errors in matters of fact which had not been put in issue or passed on and were material to validity and regularity of legal proceeding itself. *See* Coram nobis.

Error coram vobis /éhrər kórəm vówbəs/. Error in the proceedings "before you"; words used in a writ of error directed by an appellate court to the court which tried the cause. *See* Coram vobis.

Error in fact. Error in fact occurs when, by reason of some fact which is unknown to the court and not apparent on the record (*e.g.,* infancy, or death of one of the parties), it renders a judgment void or voidable. Such occurs when some fact which really exists is unknown, or some fact is supposed to exist which really does not.

Error in law. An error of the court in applying the law to the case on trial, *e.g.,* in ruling on the admission of evidence, or in charging the jury. *See also* Error.

Error of fact. *See* Error in fact.

Error of law. *See* Error in law.

Errors and omissions insurance. *See* Insurance.

Errors excepted /éhrərz əkséptəd/. A phrase appended to an account stated, in order to excuse slight mistakes or oversights.

Error, writ of. *See* Writ of error.

Escalation clause. *See* Escalator clause.

Escalator clause. In union contract, a provision that wages will rise or fall depending on some standard like the cost of living index. In lease, provision that rent may be increased to reflect increase in real estate taxes, operating costs, and even increases in Consumer Price Index. In construction contract, clause authorizing contractor to increase contract price should costs of labor or materials increase.

Clause in leases or contracts executed subject to price control regulations. Under this clause, in the case of a lease, the landlord is authorized to collect the maximum rent permissible under rent regulations in force at time of execution of the lease. The escalator part of the clause of the lease consists in the provision that in the event that the rent regulations are modified during the term of the lease, the tenant will pay the increased rental following the allowance thereof. *See also* Cost of living clause.

Escape. Leaving physical confinement without permission. The departure or deliverance out of custody of a person who was lawfully imprisoned before he is entitled to his liberty by the process of law. The voluntarily or negligently allowing any person lawfully in confinement to leave. To flee from; to avoid; to get away, as to flee to avoid arrest. The voluntary departure from lawful custody by a prisoner with the intent to evade the due course of justice. See 18 U.S.C.A. § 751 et seq.

Escape clause. Provision in a contract, insurance policy, or other legal document permitting party or parties to avoid liability or performance under certain conditions. For example, international tariff containing clause that tariff will be changed if imports covered by such cause harm to domestic industries producing like goods; clause in insurance policy that provides for avoidance of liability when there is other valid insurance; clause in door-to-door sale contract giving purchaser three day period to cancel.

Escape period. Term generally applied to provision in union contracts in connection with maintenance of membership clauses permitting workers to withdraw from the union during a certain period near the end of the contract period and before the start of the next contract period.

Escheat /əs(h)chíyt/. A reversion of property to the state in consequence of a want of any individual competent to inherit.

Escobedo Rule /èskəbíydow ruwl/. Under this rule, where police investigation begins to focus on a particular suspect, the suspect is in custody, the suspect requests and is denied counsel, and the police have not warned him of his right to remain silent, the accused will be considered to have been denied assistance of counsel and no statement elicited during such interrogation may be used in a criminal trial. Escobedo v. State of Illinois, 378 U.S. 478, 490, 491, 84 S.Ct. 1758, 12 L.Ed.2d 977. *See also* Effective assistance of counsel; Miranda Rule.

Escrow. A legal document (such as a deed), money, stock, or other property delivered by the grantor, promisor or obligor into the hands of a third person, to be held by the latter until the happening of a contingency or performance of a condition, and then by him delivered to the grantee, promisee or obligee. A system of document transfer in which a deed, bond, stock, funds, or other property is delivered to a third person to hold until all conditions in a contract are fulfilled; *e.g.* delivery of deed to escrow agent under installment land sale contract until full payment for land is made.

Escrow account. A bank account generally held in the name of the depositor and an escrow agent which is returnable to depositor or paid to third person on the fulfillment of escrow condition; *e.g.* funds for payment of real estate taxes are commonly paid into escrow account of bank-mortgagor by mortgagee.

Escrow contract. Agreement between buyer, seller, and escrow holder setting forth rights and responsibilities of each.

Escrow deposit. *See* Escrow account.

ESOP. *See* Employee Stock Ownership Plan.

Espera /éspərə/. A period of time fixed by law or by a court within which certain acts are to be performed, *e.g.,* the production of papers, payment of debts, etc.

Espionage. Espionage, or spying, has reference to the crime of "gathering, transmitting or losing" information respecting the national defense with intent or reason to believe that the information is to be used to the injury of the United States, or to the advantage of any foreign nation. 18 U.S.C.A. § 793. *See* Internal security acts.

Espionage Act. Federal law which punishes espionage, spying, and related crimes. 18 U.S.C.A. § 793 *et seq.*

Esq. Abbreviation for Esquire.

Esquire /éskway(ə)r/əskwáy(ə)r/. In English law, a title of dignity next above gentleman, and below knight. Also a title of office given to sheriffs, serjeants, and barristers at law, justices of the peace, and others.

In United States, title commonly appended after name of attorney; *e.g.* John J. Jones, Esquire.

Essence. That which is indispensable. The gist or substance of any act; the vital constituent of a thing; that without which a thing cannot be itself.

Essence of the contract. Any condition or stipulation in a contract which is mutually understood and agreed by the parties to be of such vital importance that a sufficient performance of the contract cannot be had without exact compliance with it is said to be "of the essence of the contract." *See also* Basis of bargain.

Essential. Indispensably necessary; important in the highest degree; requisite. That which is required for the continued existence of a thing.

Essential governmental duties. Those duties which framers of Constitution intended each member of union would assume in functioning under form of government guaranteed by Constitution.

Establish. This word occurs frequently in the Constitution of the United States, and it is there used in different meanings: (1) To settle firmly, to fix unalterably; as to establish justice, which is the avowed object of the Constitution. (2) To make or form; as to establish uniform laws governing naturalization or bankruptcy. (3) To found, to create, to regulate; as: "Congress shall have power to establish post-offices." (4) To found, recognize, confirm, or admit; as: "Congress shall make no law respecting an establishment of religion." (5) To create, to ratify, or confirm, as: "We, the people . . . do ordain and establish this Constitution." *See also* Establishment clause.

To settle, make or fix firmly; place on a permanent footing; found; create; put beyond doubt or dispute; prove; convince. To enact permanently. To bring about or into existence.

Establishment. An institution or place of business, with its fixtures and organized staff. State of being established.

Establishment clause. That provision of the First Amendment to U.S. Constitution which provides that "Congress shall make no law respecting an establishment of religion, or prohibiting the free exercise thereof . . . ". Such language prohibits a state or the federal government from setting up a church, or passing laws which aid one, or all, religions, or giving preference to one religion, or forcing belief or disbelief in any religion. Everson v. Board of Education, 330 U.S. 1, 67 S.Ct. 504, 91 L.Ed. 711; McCollum v. Brd. of Education, 333 U.S. 203, 68 S.Ct. 461, 92 L.Ed. 649. *See also* Freedom of religion.

Estate. The degree, quantity, nature, and extent of interest which a person has in real and personal property. An estate in lands, tenements, and hereditaments signifies such interest as the tenant has therein. The condition or circumstance in which the owner *stands* with regard to his property. In this sense, "estate" is commonly used in conveyances in connection with the words "right," "title," and "interest," and is, in a great degree, synonymous with all of them.

When used in connection with probate proceedings, term encompasses totality of assets and liabilities of decedent, including all manner of property, real and personal, choate or inchoate, corporeal or incorporeal.

The total property of whatever kind that is owned by a decedent prior to the distribution of that property in accordance with the terms of a will, or, when there is no will, by the laws of inheritance in the state of domicile of the decedent. It means, ordinarily, the whole of the property owned by anyone, the realty as well as the personalty. As used in connection with the administration of decedents' estates, term includes property of a decedent, trust or other person as such property exists from time to time during the administration, and hence may include probate assets as well as property passing by intestacy. Uniform Probate Code, § 1–201(11).

In its broadest sense, the social, civic, or political condition or standing of a person; or a class of persons considered as grouped for social, civic, or political purposes.

Common Law Classifications

Estates may be either *absolute* or *conditional*. An absolute estate is a full and complete estate, or an estate in lands not subject to be defeated upon any condition. In this phrase the word "absolute" is not used legally to distinguish a fee from a life-estate, but a qualified or conditional fee from a fee simple. A conditional estate is one, the existence of which depends upon the happening or not happening of some uncertain event, whereby the estate may be either originally created, or enlarged, or finally defeated. Estates are also classed as *executed* or *executory*. The former is an estate whereby a present interest passes to and resides in the tenant, not dependent upon any subsequent circumstance or contingency. They are more commonly called "estates in possession." An estate where there is vested in the grantee a present and immediate right of present or future enjoyment. An executory estate is an estate or interest in lands, the vesting or enjoyment of which depends upon some future contingency. Such estate may be an *executory devise,* or an *executory remainder,* which is the same as a contingent remainder, because no present interest passes. A *contingent* estate is one which depends for its effect upon an event which may or may not happen, as, where an estate is limited to a person not yet born. *Conventional* estates are those freeholds not of inheritance or estates for life, which are created by the express acts of the parties, in contradistinction to those which are legal and arise from the operation of law. A *dominant* estate, in the law of easements, is the estate for the benefit of which the easement exists, or the tenement whose owner, as such, enjoys an easement over an adjoining estate. An *expectant* estate is one which is not yet in possession, but the enjoyment of which is to begin at a future time; a present or vested contingent right of future enjoyment. Examples are remainders and reversions. A *future* estate is an estate which is not now vested in the grantee, but is to commence in possession at some future time. It includes remainders, reversions, and estates limited to commence *in futuro* without a particular estate to support them, which last are not good at common law, except in the case of chattel interests. An estate limited to commence in possession at a future day, either without the intervention of a precedent estate, or on the determination by lapse of time, or otherwise, of a precedent estate created at the same time. A *particular* estate is a limited estate which is taken out of the fee, and which precedes a remainder; as an estate for years to A., remainder to B. for life; or an estate for life to A., remainder to B. in tail. This precedent estate is called the "particular estate," and the tenant of such estate is called the "particular tenant." A *servient* estate, in the law of easements, is the estate upon which the easement is imposed or against which it is enjoyed; an estate subjected to a burden or servitude for the benefit of another estate. A *settled* estate, in English law, is one created or limited under a settlement; that is, one in which the powers of alienation, devising, and transmission according to the ordinary rules of descent are restrained by the limitations of the settlement. A *vested* estate is one in which there is an immediate right of present enjoyment or a present fixed right of future enjoyment; an estate as to which there is a person in being who would have an immediate right to the possession upon the ceasing of some intermediate or precedent estate. An *original* estate is the first of several estates, bearing to each other the relation of a particular estate and a reversion. An original estate is contrasted with a *derivative* estate; and a derivative estate is a particular interest carved out of another estate of larger extent.

As to Homestead; Movable; Real; Residuary; Separate, and Trust (*estate*), see those titles. *See also* Augmented estate; Beneficial estate; Gross estate; Joint estate; Landed estate *or* property; Life estate; Net estate; Residuary estate; Vested estate.

For the names and definitions of the various kinds of estates in land, see the different titles below.

Bankruptcy estate. *See* Bankruptcy proceedings.

Equitable estate. An interest recognized only in equity such as the beneficial interest of a beneficiary of a trust.

Future estate. An estate or interest in which title or possession or both is deferred to a future time. *See* Future interests.

Legal estate. An estate or interest in property which is recognized and enforced in law, not merely in equity.

Qualified estate. Interests in real property which are not absolute and unconditional including fee

tail, estates on condition, estates on limitation, and estates on conditional limitation.

Small estate. In some jurisdictions, there is an informal procedure for administration of small estates of decedents less structured than ordinary probate and administration. Normally, the services of an attorney are not required. Uniform Probate Code, § 3–1201 *et seq.*

Estate at sufferance. The interest of a tenant who has come rightfully into possession of lands by permission of the owner, and continues to occupy the same after the period for which he is entitled to hold by such permission. The estate arises where one comes into possession of land by lawful title, but keeps it afterwards without any title at all, and the original entry need not have been under lease or as a tenant of the dispossessing landlord.

Estate at will. A species of estate less than freehold, where lands and tenements are let by one man to another, to have and to hold at the will of the lessor; and the tenant by force of this lease obtains possession. Or it is where lands are let without limiting any certain and determinate estate. The estate arises where lands or tenements are expressly demised by one person to another to be held during the joint wills of both parties, or it may arise by implication of law wherever one person is put in possession of another's land with the owner's consent, but under an agreement which does not suffice to create in the tenant an estate of freehold or for years.

Estate by entirety. *See* Estate by the entirety.

Estate by purchase. One acquired in any other method than descent. *See also* Purchase.

Estate by the curtesy. *See* Curtesy.

Estate by the entirety. Called also estate in entirety, or estate by the entireties. An estate in joint tenancy, plus the unity of the marital relation. A form of co-ownership of realty or personalty held by husband and wife in which there is unity of estate, unity of possession and unity of control of entire property, and on death of one, survivor takes estate under original conveyance. A common-law estate, based on the doctrine that husband and wife are one, and that a conveyance of real property to husband and wife creates but one estate. An estate held by husband and wife together so long as both live, and, after the death of either, by the survivor. It is an estate held by husband and wife by virtue of a title acquired by them jointly after marriage. A creature of the common law created by legal fiction based wholly on the common-law doctrine that husband and wife are one, and hence a conveyance to husband and wife created only one estate, and each was owner of the whole estate, and neither could dispose of it without the consent of the other, and on the death of one survivor was the owner in fee simple.

Type of joint estate which may be held only by two persons who are married to each other at the time that the estate is created and which does not admit of partition, though, on divorce, it automatically becomes an estate in common unless the parties provide otherwise.

An "estate by entireties" resembles a "joint tenancy" in that there is a right of survivorship in both, but such an estate is distinguishable from a joint tenancy in that the latter may be invested in any number of natural persons each of whom is seized of an undivided moiety of the whole, whereas a "tenancy by entirety" is vested in two persons only, who in law are regarded as only one, and each of whom becomes seized of the estate as a whole.

See also Community property; Entirety; Tenancy *(Joint tenancy)*.

Estate for life. *See* Life estate.

Estate for years. A species of estate less than freehold, where a man has an interest in lands and tenements, and a possession thereof, by virtue of such interest, for some fixed and determinate period of time; as in the case where lands are leased for the term of a certain number of years, agreed upon between the lessor and the lessee. Blackstone calls this estate a "contract" for the possession of lands or tenements for some determinate period. Estates for years embrace all terms limited to endure for a definite and ascertained period, however short or long the period may be; they embrace terms for a fixed number of weeks or months or for a single year, as well as for any definite number of years, however great. Also called "tenancy for a term".

Estate freeze. An estate planning tool for owners of closely-held businesses in which the owner exchanges his common stock for preferred stock paying a fixed cash dividend and having a fixed cash value, with the common stock then given to the owner's children. The owner gets a fixed pension for life (the dividend), while any future increases in the company's value accrue to the children, thus escaping estate tax. I.R.C. §§ 2701–2704.

Estate from period to period. An estate continuing for successive periods of a year, or successive periods of a fraction of a year, unless it is terminated. Also called "tenancy from period to period"; or "periodic estate".

Estate from year to year. An example of an "estate for years" *(q.v.)*. It exists in cases where the parties stipulate for it, and also where the parties by their conduct have placed themselves in the relation of landlord and tenant without adopting any other term. If a tenant has been allowed to hold over after the expiration of his term in such a way as to preclude the possibility of his becoming a tenant on sufferance, it is a tenancy from year to year. It was originally a development of a tenancy at will, by which the tenancy was terminable only at the time of the year at which it began, and on notice.

Estate in common. An estate in lands held by two or more persons, with interests accruing under different titles; or accruing under the same title, but at different periods; or conferred by words of limitation importing that the grantees are to take in distinct shares. *See also* Tenancy *(Tenancy in common)*.

Estate in coparcenary /əstéyt ən kowpárs(ə)nəriy/. *See* Coparcenary.

Estate in dower. *See* Dower.

Estate in expectancy. One which is not yet in possession, but the enjoyment of which is to begin at a future time. An estate giving a present or vested contingent right of future enjoyment. One in which the right to pernancy of the profits is postponed to some future period. Such are estates in remainder and reversion.

Estate in fee simple. *See* Fee simple.

Estate in fee-tail. *See* Tail, estate in.

Estate in joint tenancy. *See* Tenancy.

Estate in lands. Property one has in lands, tenements or hereditaments, or conditions or circumstances in which tenant stands as to his property. *See* Estate.

Estate in remainder. *See* Remainder.

Estate in reversion. *See* Reversion *or* estate in reversion.

Estate in severalty /əstéyt ən sévrəltiy/. An estate held by a person in his own right only, without any other person being joined or connected with him in point of interest, during his estate. This is the most common and usual way of holding an estate.

Estate less than freehold. An estate for years, estate at will, or estate at sufferance.

Estate of freehold. *See* Freehold.

Estate of inheritance. An estate which may descend to heirs. A species of freehold estate in lands, otherwise called a "fee," where the tenant is not only entitled to enjoy the land for his own life, but where, after his death, it is passed by the law upon the persons who successively represent him *in perpetuum*, according to a certain established order of descent. *See* Estate.

Estate on condition. *See* Estate upon condition.

Estate on conditional limitation. An estate conveyed to one person so that, upon occurrence or failure of occurrence of some contingent event, whether conditional or limitative, the estate shall depart from original grantee and pass to another.

Estate on limitation /əstéyt òn lìmətéyshən/. An estate originated by the use of words denoting duration of time, such as while, during, so long as, and the like and when designated limitative event happens, such estate ends naturally without any re-entry and property reverts to grantor. Sometimes referred to as "base fee", "qualified fee", "determinable fee", or "fee simple defeasible".

Estate planning. That branch of the law which, in arranging a person's property and estate, takes into account the laws of wills, taxes, insurance, property, and trusts so as to gain maximum benefit of all laws while carrying out the person's own wishes for the disposition of his property upon his death.

Estate pur autre vie /əstéyt pər ówtrə váy/. See Pur autre vie.

Estate subject to a conditional limitation. The distinction between an estate upon condition subsequent and an "estate subject to a conditional limitation" is that in former words creating condition do not originally limit term, but merely permit its termination upon happening of contingency, while in latter words creating it limit continuation of estate to time preceding happening of contingency.

Estate tail. See Tail, estate in.

Estate tail, quasi. When a tenant for life grants his estate to a man and his heirs, as these words, though apt and proper to create an estate tail, cannot do so, because the grantor, being only tenant for life, cannot grant *in perpetuum*, therefore they are said to create an estate tail *quasi,* or improper.

Estate tax. A tax imposed on the right to transfer property by death. Thus, an estate tax is levied on the decedent's estate and not on the heir receiving the property. A tax levied on right to transmit property, while "inheritance tax" is levied on right to receive property. The tax is based on value of the whole estate less certain deductions. I.R.C. § 2001 *et seq. See also* Alternate valuation date; Inheritance tax; Unified transfer tax.

Many states have adopted the "Uniform Interstate Compromise of Death Taxes Act" or the "Uniform Interstate Arbitration of Death Taxes Act."

Estate upon condition. An estate in lands, the existence of which depends upon the happening or not happening of some uncertain event, whereby the estate may be either originally created, or enlarged, or finally defeated. An estate having a qualification annexed to it, by which it may, upon the happening of a particular event, be created, or enlarged, or destroyed.

Estate upon condition expressed. An estate granted, either in fee-simple or otherwise, with an express qualification annexed, whereby the estate granted shall either commence, be enlarged, or be defeated upon performance or breach of such qualification or condition. An estate which is so expressly defined and limited by the words of its creation that it cannot endure for any longer time than till the contingency happens upon which the estate is to fail.

Estate upon condition implied. An estate having a condition annexed to it inseparably from its essence and constitution, although no condition be expressed in words.

Estimate. A valuing or rating by the mind, without actually measuring, weighing, or the like. A rough or approximate calculation only. Act of appraising or valuing. Determination of approximate cost or return.

This word is used to express the mind or judgment of the speaker or writer on the particular subject under consideration. It implies a calculation or computation, as to *estimate* the gain or loss of an enterprise.

Estimated tax. Federal and state tax laws require a quarterly payment of estimated taxes due from corporations, trusts, estates, non-wage employees, and wage employees with income not subject to withholding. Individuals must remit at least 100% of their prior year tax liability or 90% of their current year tax liability in order to avoid an underpayment penalty. Corporations must pay at least 90% of their current year tax liability in order to avoid an underpayment penalty. Additional taxes due, if any, are paid on taxpayer's annual tax return. I.R.C. § 6015. *See also* Declaration of estimated tax.

Estimated useful life. The period over which an asset will be used by a particular taxpayer. Although such period cannot be longer than the estimated physical life of an asset, it could be shorter if the taxpayer does not intend to keep the asset until it wears out. Assets such as goodwill do not have an estimated useful life. The estimated useful life of an asset is essential in calculating depreciation and amortization as well as any allowable investment tax credit.

Estin doctrine. The principle of law enunciated in Estin v. Estin, 334 U.S. 541, 68 S.Ct. 1213, 92 L.Ed. 1561 to the effect that a divorce decree is divisible and, while full faith and credit must be given to a decree as to the termination of the marriage, no full faith and credit is required as to that portion of the decree ordering support for the wife unless the court entering the order had personal jurisdiction of the husband.

Estop. To stop, bar, or impede; to prevent; to preclude. *See* Embargo; Estoppel; Injunction.

Estoppel /əstópəl/. Term means that party is prevented by his own acts from claiming a right to detriment of other party who was entitled to rely on such conduct and has acted accordingly. A principle that provides that an individual is barred from denying or alleging a certain fact or state facts because of that individual's previous conduct, allegation, or denial. A doctrine which holds that an inconsistent position, attitude or course of conduct may not be adopted to loss or injury of another. See Restatement, Agency, Second, § 8B.

Estoppel is a bar or impediment which precludes allegation or denial of a certain fact or state of facts, in consequence of previous allegation or denial or conduct or admission, or in consequence of a final adjudication of the matter in a court of law. It operates to put party entitled to its benefits in same position as if thing represented were true. Under law of "estoppel" where one of two innocent persons must suffer, he whose act occasioned loss must bear it. Elements or essentials of estoppel include change of position of parties so that party against whom estoppel is invoked has received a profit or benefit or party invoking estoppel has changed his position to his detriment.

Estoppel is or may be based on acceptance of benefits; actual or constructive fraudulent conduct; admissions or denials by which another is induced to act to his injury; agreement on and settlement of facts by force of entering into contract; assertion of facts on which another relies; assumption of position which, if not maintained, would result in injustice to another; concealment of facts; conduct or acts amounting to a representation or a concealment; consent to copyright infringement, whether express or implied from long acquiescence with knowledge of the infringement; election between rights or remedies; inaction; laches; language or conduct which has induced another to act.

Estoppels at common law are sometimes said to be of three kinds: (1) by deed; (2) by matter of record; (3) by matter in pais. The first two are also called legal estoppels, as distinguished from the last kind, known as equitable estoppels.

For Acquiescence, estoppel by; Collateral attack; Collateral estoppel doctrine; Contract, estoppel by; Deed, estoppel by; Direct estoppel; Election, estoppel by; Equitable estoppel; In pais, estoppel by; Judgment, estoppel by; Judicial estoppel; Laches, estoppel by; Legal estoppel; Negligence, estoppel by; Promissory estoppel; Quasi estoppel; Record, estoppel by; Representation, estoppel by; Silence, estoppel by; and Verdict, estoppel by, see those titles. See also Authority (*Authority by estoppel*).

Acts and declarations. An "estoppel by acts and declarations" is such as arises from the acts and declarations of a person by which he designedly induces another to alter his position injuriously to himself.

Equitable estoppel. (*See Estoppel in pais, below*).

Estoppel by deed. A grantor in a warranty deed who does not have title at the time of the conveyance but who subsequently acquires title is estopped from denying that he had title at the time of the transfer and such after-acquired title inures to the benefit of the grantee or his successors. *See also* Deed, estoppel by.

Estoppel by judgment. Term means that when a fact has been agreed on, or decided in a court of record, neither of the parties shall be allowed to call it in question, and have it tried over again at any time thereafter, so long as judgment or decree stands unreversed. Final adjudication of material issue by a court of competent jurisdiction binds parties in any subsequent proceeding between or among them, irrespective of difference in forms or causes of action. Sometimes referred to as issue preclusion. *See also* Collateral estoppel doctrine; Judgment, estoppel by. *Compare* Res (*Res judicata*).

Estoppel certificate. A signed statement by a party, such as a tenant or a mortgagee, certifying for the benefit of another party that a certain statement of facts is correct as of the date of the statement, such as that a lease exists, that there are no defaults and that rent is paid to a certain date. Delivery of the statement by the tenant prevents (estops) the tenant from later claiming a different state of facts.

Estoppel in pais. The doctrine by which a person may be precluded by his act or conduct, or silence when it is his duty to speak, from asserting a right which he otherwise would have had. *See also* Equitable estoppel; In pais, estoppel.

Misrepresentation. See Representation, estoppel by.

Pleading. Pleader must allege and prove not only that person sought to be estopped made misleading statements and representations but that pleader actually believed and relied on them and was misled to his injury thereby.

Under rules practice in most states, and in the federal courts, estoppel is an affirmative defense which must be pleaded. Fed.R. Civil P. 8(c).

Ratification distinguished. The substance of "estoppel" is the inducement of another to act to his prejudice. The substance of "ratification" is confirmation after conduct. By ratification party is bound because he intended to be, while under "estoppel" he is bound because other party will be prejudiced unless the law treats him as legally bound. *See* Ratification.

Res judicata distinguished. A prior judgment between same parties, which is not strictly res judicata because based upon different cause of action, operates as an "estoppel" only as to matters actually in issue or points controverted. In a later action upon a different cause of action a judgment operates as an "estoppel" only as to such issues in second action as were actually determined in the first action. The doctrine of "res judicata" is a branch of law of "estoppel". The plea of "res judicata" is in its nature an "estoppel" against the losing party from again litigating matters involved in previous action, but the plea does not have that effect as to matters transpiring subsequently. *See* Res *(Res judicata)*.

Waiver distinguished. Waiver is voluntary surrender or relinquishment of some known right, benefit or advantage; estoppel is the inhibition to assert it. In insurance law, however, the two terms are commonly used interchangeably. *See* Waiver.

Estover /əstówvər/. The right or privilege which a tenant has to furnish himself with so much wood from the demised premises as may be sufficient or necessary for his fuel, fences, and other agricultural operations.

An allowance made to a person out of an estate or other thing for his or her support, as for food and raiment.

An allowance (more commonly called "alimony") granted to a woman divorced *a mensa et thoro,* for her support out of her husband's estate.

Estray /əstréy/. An estray is an animal that has escaped from its owner, and wanders or strays about; usually defined, at common law, as a wandering animal whose owner is unknown. An animal cannot be an estray when on the range where it was raised, and permitted by its owner to run, and especially when the owner is known to the party who takes it up.

The term is also used of flotsam at sea.

Estuary /és(h)chəwèhriy/. That part of the mouth or lower course of a river flowing into the sea which is subject to tide; especially, an enlargement of a river channel toward its mouth in which the movement of the tide is very prominent.

Et. And. The introductory word of several Latin and law French phrases formerly in common use.

Et al. /èt ǽl/. An abbreviation for *et alii,* "and others." The singular is "et alius" *(q.v.).* It may also mean "and another" in the singular.

The abbreviation et al. (sometimes in the plural written *et als.*) is often affixed to the name of the person first mentioned, where there are several plaintiffs, grantors, persons addressed, etc.

Et cetera (or **etc.**) /et sétərə/. And others; and other things; and others of like character; and others of the like kind; and the rest; and so on; and so forth. In its abbreviated form *(etc.)* this

phrase is frequently affixed to one of a series of articles or names to show that others are intended to follow or understood to be included. So, after reciting the initiatory words of a set formula, or a clause already given in full, *etc.* is added, as an abbreviation, for the sake of convenience. And other things of like kind or purpose as compared with those immediately theretofore mentioned.

Ethics. Of or relating to moral action, conduct, motive or character; as, ethical emotion; also, treating of moral feelings, duties or conduct; containing precepts of morality; moral. Professionally right or befitting; conforming to professional standards of conduct.

Legal ethics. See Canon *(Canons of judicial ethics)*; Code of Professional Responsibility; Legal ethics.

Et non /èt nón/. Lat. And not. A technical phrase in pleading, which introduces the negative averments of a special traverse. It has the same force and effect as the words *absque hoc,* "without this," and is occasionally used instead of the latter.

Et seq. /èt səkwéntiyz/et səkwénsh(iy)ə/. An abbreviation for *et sequentes* (masculine and feminine plural) or *et sequentia* (neuter), "and the following." Thus a reference to "p. 1, *et seq.*" means "page first and the following pages." Also abbreviated "et sqq.," which is preferred by some authorities for a reference to more than one following page.

Et ux /èd ə́ks(ər)/. An abbreviation for *et uxor,—* "and wife." Where a grantor's wife joins him in the conveyance, it is sometimes expressed (in abstracts, etc.) to be by "A. B. *et ux.*"

Euclidian zoning. *See* Zoning.

Eurobanks. Banks that participate in the European currency markets by accepting deposits and providing loans in foreign currencies.

Eurobond. An international bond which is issued outside the country in whose currency the bonds are denominated.

Eurodollar /yúrowdòlər/. U.S. dollars that have been deposited in European banks or European branches of U.S. banks.

Euthanasia /yùwθənéyzhə/. The act or practice of painlessly putting to death persons suffering from incurable and distressing disease as an act of mercy. *See also* Brain death; Death *(Natural Death Acts)*; Will *(Living will)*.

Evarts Act. *See* Judiciary Acts.

Evasion. An act of eluding, dodging, or avoiding, or avoidance by artifice. A subtle endeavoring to set aside truth or to escape the punishment of the law.

Tax "evasion" is to be distinguished from tax "avoidance," the former meaning the illegal nonpayment of taxes due, the latter referring to the legal reduction or nonpayment of taxes through allowable deductions, exemptions, etc.

Evasive. Tending or seeking to evade; elusive; shifting; as an *evasive* argument or plea. If a pleading to which a responsive pleading is required is evasive, a party may make motion for a more definite statement. Fed.R.Civil P. 12(e).

Evasive answer. One which consists in refusing either to admit or to deny a matter in a direct, straight-forward manner as to which the person is necessarily presumed to have knowledge. Under Fed.R.Civil P. 37, an evasive answer is considered and treated as a failure to answer, for which a party may on motion seek a court order compelling answers to discovery questions.

Evening. The closing part of the day and beginning of the night; in a strict sense, from sunset till dark. In common speech, the latter part of the day and the earlier part of the night, until bedtime. The period between sunset or the evening meal and ordinary bedtime. *See also* Nighttime.

Event. The consequence of anything; the issue or outcome of an action as finally determined; that in which an action, operation, or series of operations, terminates. Noteworthy happening or occurrence. Something that happens.

Distinguished from an act in that an act is the product of the will whereas an event is an occurrence which takes place independent of the will such as an earthquake or flood.

See also Fortuitous event.

Evergreen contract. A contract which renews itself from year to year in lieu of notice by one of the parties to the contrary.

Every. Each one of all; all the separate individuals who constitute the whole, regarded one by one. The term is sometimes equivalent to "all"; and sometimes to "each".

Evict. In civil law, to recover anything from a person by virtue of the judgment of a court or judicial sentence. *See* Eviction.

Eviction. Dispossession by process of law; the act of depriving a person of the possession of land or rental property which he has held or leased. Act of turning a tenant out of possession, either by re-entry or legal proceedings, such as an action of ejectment. Deprivation of lessee of possession of premises or disturbance of lessee in beneficial enjoyment so as to cause tenant to abandon the premises (the latter being constructive conviction).

See also Actual eviction; Constructive eviction; Ejectment; Forcible entry and detainer; Notice to quit; Partial eviction; Process (*Summary process*); Retaliatory eviction.

Evidence. Any species of proof, or probative matter, legally presented at the trial of an issue, by the act of the parties and through the medium of witnesses, records, documents, exhibits, concrete objects, etc., for the purpose of inducing belief in the minds of the court or jury as to their contention. Testimony, writings, or material objects offered in proof of an alleged fact or proposition. That probative material, legally received, by which the tribunal may be lawfully persuaded of the truth or falsity of a fact in issue.

Testimony, writings, material objects, or other things presented to the senses that are offered to prove the existence or nonexistence of a fact. Calif.Evid.Code.

All the means by which any alleged matter of fact, the truth of which is submitted to investigation, is established or disproved. Any matter of fact, the effect, tendency, or design of which is to produce in the mind a persuasion of the existence or nonexistence of some matter of fact. That which demonstrates, makes clear, or ascertains the truth of the very fact or point in issue, either on the one side or on the other. That which tends to produce conviction in the mind as to existence of a fact. The means sanctioned by law of ascertaining in a judicial proceeding the truth respecting a question of fact.

As a part of procedure "evidence" signifies those rules of law whereby it is determined what testimony should be admitted and what should be rejected in each case, and what is the weight to be given to the testimony admitted. *See* Evidence rules.

For Presumption as evidence, *see* Presumption; Proof; Testimony; View.

See also Aliunde; Autoptic evidence; Best evidence; Beyond a reasonable doubt; Circumstantial evidence; Competent evidence; Conclusive evidence; Conflicting evidence; Corroborating evidence; Critical evidence; Cumulative evidence; Demeanor (*Demeanor evidence*); Demonstrative evidence; Derivative evidence; Direct evidence; Documentary evidence; Exemplars; Extrajudicial evidence; Extraneous evidence; Extrinsic evidence; Fabricated evidence; Fact; Fair preponderance of evidence; Hearsay; Illegally obtained evidence; Immaterial evidence; Incompetent evidence; Incriminating evidence; Inculpatory; Independent source rule; Indirect evidence; Indispensable evidence; Inference; Laying foundation; Legal evidence; Legally sufficient evidence; Limited admissibility; Material evidence; Mathematical evidence; Moral evidence; Narrative evidence; Newly discovered evidence; Offer of proof; Opinion evidence *or* testimony; Oral evidence; Original document rule; Parol evidence rule; Partial evidence; Past recollection recorded; Perpetuating testimony; Physical fact rule; Positive evidence; Preliminary evidence; Preponderance of evidence; Presumption; Presumptive evidence; Prima facie evidence; Primary evidence; Prior inconsistent statements; Privileged evidence; Probable evidence; Probative evidence; Probative facts; Proof; Proper evidence; Real evidence; Reasonable inference rule; Rebuttal evidence; Relevant evidence; Satisfactory evidence; Scintilla of evidence rule; Secondary evidence; Second-hand evidence; State's evidence; Substantive evidence; Sufficiency of evidence; View; Weight of evidence; Withholding of evidence.

There are, generally speaking, two types of evidence from which a jury may properly find the truth as to the facts of a case. One is direct evidence—such as the testimony of an eyewitness. The other is indirect or circumstantial evidence—the proof of a chain of circumstances pointing to the existence or non-existence of certain facts. As a general rule, the law makes no distinction between direct and circumstantial evidence, but simply requires that the jury find the facts in accordance with the preponderance of all the evidence in the case, both direct and circumstantial.

Autoptic evidence. Type of evidence presented in court which consists of the thing itself and not the testimony accompanying its presentation. Articles offered in evidence which the judge or jury can see and inspect. Real evidence as contrasted with testimonial evidence; *e.g.* in contract action, the document purporting to be the contract itself, or the gun in a murder trial. *See* Demonstrative evidence.

Character evidence. Evidence of a person's character or traits is admissible under certain conditions in a trial, though, as a general rule, evidence of character traits are not competent to prove that a person acted in conformity therewith on a particular occasion. Fed.Evid.R. 404.

Curative admissibility. See Curative.

Exculpatory evidence. A defendant in a criminal case is entitled to evidence in possession or control of the government if such evidence tends to indicate his innocence or tends to mitigate his criminality if he demands it and if the failure to disclose it results in a denial of a fair trial. Disclosure of evidence by the government is governed by Fed.R.Crim.P. 16.

Expert evidence. Testimony given in relation to some scientific, technical, or professional matter by experts, *i.e.,* persons qualified to speak authoritatively by reason of their special training, skill, or familiarity with the subject. *See also* Expert witness.

Identification evidence. See Exemplars.

Illegally obtained evidence. See Exclusionary Rule; Fruit of poisonous tree doctrine; Mapp v. Ohio; Miranda Rule; McNabb-Mallory Rule; Motion to suppress.

Inculpatory evidence. Evidence tending to show a person's involvement in a crime; incriminating evidence. *See* Incriminating evidence.

Irrelevant evidence. Evidence is irrelevant if it is not so related to the issues to be tried and if it has no logical tendency to prove the issues. *See* Irrelevancy. *Compare Relevant evidence, below.*

Material evidence. See Relevant evidence, below.

Original evidence. See Original; Original document rule.

Preponderance of the evidence. A standard of proof (used in many civil suits) which is met when a party's evidence on a fact indicates that it is "more likely than not" that the fact is as the party alleges it to be. *See* Fair preponderance of evidence.

Proffered evidence. Evidence, the admissibility or inadmissibility of which is dependent upon the existence or nonexistence of a preliminary fact. Calif.Evid.Code.

Relevant evidence. Evidence having any tendency to make the existence of any fact that is of consequence to the determination of the action more probable or less probable than it would be without the evidence. Fed.Evid.R. 401. Evidence, including evidence relevant to the credibility of a witness or hearsay declarant, having any tendency in reason to prove or disprove any disputed fact that is of consequence to the determination of the action. Calif.Evid.Code. Evidence which bears a logical relationship to the issues in a trial or case. *See* Material evidence.

Tangible evidence. Physical evidence; evidence that can be seen or touched, *e.g.,* documents, weapons. Testimonial evidence is evidence which can be heard, *e.g.,* the statements made by anyone sitting in the witness box. *See* Demonstrative evidence.

Testimonial evidence. Communicative evidence as distinguished from demonstrative or physical evidence.

Evidence by inspection. Such evidence as is addressed directly to the senses without intervention of testimony. Tangible, physical evidence. *See* Demonstrative evidence.

Evidence codes. Statutory provisions governing admissibility of evidence and burden of proof at hearings and trials (*e.g.* California Evidence Code). *See also* Evidence rules, *infra.*

Evidence completed. Exists where both sides have offered testimony and rested, or where plaintiff has rested and defendant has made motion for finding on plaintiff's case and stands on motion and declines to offer evidence.

Evidence, law of. The aggregate of rules and principles regulating the burden of proof, admissibility, relevancy, and weight and sufficiency of evidence in legal proceedings. *See* Evidence codes; Evidence rules.

Evidence of debt. A term applied to written instruments or securities for the payment of money, importing on their face the existence of a debt. *See* Bond; Debenture; Mortgage.

Evidence of insurability. Medical examination, records, and the like, required by insurer to establish a potential insurers qualification, or lack thereof, for particular insurance.

Evidence of title. A deed or other document establishing the title to property, especially real estate. *See* Deed.

Evidence reasonably tending to support verdict. Means evidence that is competent, relevant, and material, and which to rational and impartial mind naturally leads, or involuntarily tends to lead, to conclusion for which there is valid, just, and substantial reason. *See also* Evidence to support findings.

Evidence rules. Rules which govern the admissibility of evidence at hearings and trials, *e.g.*, Federal Rules of Evidence; Uniform Rules of Evidence. A number of states have adopted evidence rules as patterned on the Federal Rules of Evidence. In certain states evidence rules are codified (*e.g.*, California Evidence Code) or otherwise set forth in statutes (*e.g.*, state statutes commonly govern admissibility of privileged communications).

Evidence to support findings. Substantial evidence or such relevant evidence as a reasonable mind might accept as adequate to support a conclusion and enough to justify, if the trial were to a jury, a refusal to direct a verdict when the conclusion sought to be drawn from it is one of fact for jury. *See also* Ultimate facts.

Evident. Clear to the understanding and satisfactory to the judgment; manifest; plain; obvious; conclusive. Noticeable; apparent to observation.

Proof evident. See Proof.

Evidentiary / èvədénsh(ə)riy / °chəriy / °iyèriy /. Having the quality of evidence; constituting evidence; evidencing. Pertaining to the rules of evidence or the evidence in a particular case.

Evidentiary facts. Those facts which are necessary for determination of the ultimate facts; they are the premises upon which conclusions of ultimate facts are based. Facts which furnish evidence of existence of some other fact.

Evidently. Means in an evident manner; perceptibly, clearly, obviously, plainly. It is employed to express the idea of full-proof conviction.

Evolution statute. Legislative enactment which forbids teaching of evolution in schools and which has been held unconstitutional as violative of the Establishment Clause of First Amend., U.S.Const. Epperson v. Arkansas, 393 U.S. 97, 89 S.Ct. 266, 21 L.Ed.2d 228.

Ex /éks/. A latin preposition meaning from, out of, by, on, on account of, or according to.

A prefix, denoting removal, cessation or former. Prefixed to the name of an office, relation, *status,* etc., it denotes that the person spoken of once occupied that office or relation, but does so no longer, or that he is now *out* of it. Thus, *ex*-mayor, *ex*-partner, *ex*-judge.

A prefix which is equivalent to "without," "reserving," or "excepting." In this use, probably an abbreviation of "except." Thus, *ex*-interest, *ex*-coupons, *ex*-dividend.

Also used as an abbreviation for "exhibit."

Exaction. The wrongful act of an officer or other person in compelling payment of a fee or reward for his services, under color of his official authority, where no payment is due. *See also* Extortion.

Examination. An investigation; search; inspection; interrogation.

Abstract of title. An investigation of the abstract of title made by or for a person who intends to purchase real estate, to ascertain the history and present condition of the title to such land, and its status with reference to liens, incumbrances, clouds, etc. to determine if marketable title exists.

Bankruptcy. Questioning of bankrupt during course of bankruptcy proceedings (first meeting of creditors) concerning extent of his debts and assets, conduct of his business, the cause of his bankruptcy, his dealings with his creditors and other persons, the amount, kind, and whereabouts of his property, and all matters which may affect the administration and settlement of his estate. Bankruptcy Code, § 343.

Criminal procedure. An investigation by a magistrate of a person who has been charged with crime and arrested, or of the facts and circumstances which are alleged to have attended the crime, in order to ascertain whether there is sufficient ground to hold him to bail for his trial by the proper court. The preliminary hearing to determine whether person charged with having committed a crime should be held for trial. *See* Court of Inquiry; Examining court; Examining trial; Interrogation; Preliminary hearing.

Discovery. See Deposition; Discovery; Interrogatories.

Invention. An inquiry made at the patent-office, upon application for a patent, into the novelty and utility of the alleged invention, and as to its interfering with any other patented invention. 35 U.S.C.A. § 131 et seq.

Witnesses. The examination of a witness consists of the series of questions put to him by a party to the action, or his counsel, or opposing counsel, for the purpose of bringing before the court and jury in legal form the knowledge which the witness has of the facts and matters in dispute, or of probing and sifting his evidence previously given.

See also Cross-examination; Direct examination; Leading question; Preliminary hearing; Recross examination; Redirect examination; Re-examination; Separate examination. As regards examination of witnesses prior to trial, *see* Deposition; Interrogatories. As regards compulsory examination, *see* Subpoena.

Examined copy. A copy of a record, public book, or register, and which has been compared with the original.

Examiner. Officer or other person authorized to conduct an examination (*e.g.* bank examiner) or appointed by court to take testimony of witnesses.

An officer appointed by the court to take testimony in causes pending in that court; *e.g.* a master, auditor, referee.

An officer in the patent-office charged with the duty of examining the patentability of inventions for which patents are asked.

See also Auditor; Inspector; Master; Referee.

Examiners, bar. Persons appointed in states to test law graduates to ascertain their qualifications to practice law. Such test is called "bar examination." *See* Bar admission.

Examining board. Generally, a board composed of public or quasi public officials who are responsible for conducting tests and examinations for those applying for occupational, professional, etc. licenses.

Examining court. A lower court which conducts preliminary examinations to determine probable cause and set bail before a criminal defendant is bound over to the grand jury. *See* Court of inquiry; Exclusionary hearing; Grand jury; Preliminary hearing.

Examining trial. A preliminary hearing to determine whether there exists probable cause for binding one over to the grand jury. See also Preliminary hearing.

Ex bonis /èks bównəs/. Of the goods or property. A term of the civil law, distinguished from *in bonis,* as being descriptive of or applicable to property not in actual possession.

Ex cathedra /èks kǽθədrə/°kəθíydrə/. From the chair. Originally applied to the decisions of the popes from their *cathedra,* or chair. Hence, authoritative; having the weight of authority.

Except. But for; only for; not including; other than; otherwise than; to leave out of account or consideration. *See* Exception.

Excepting. As used in a deed, the terms "reserving" and "excepting" are used interchangeably, and their technical meaning will give way to the manifest intent. The words "reserving" and "excepting," although strictly distinguishable, may be used interchangeably or indiscriminately.

Exceptio /əksépsh(iy)ow/. An exception, plea, or objection. In civil law, a plea by which the defendant admits the cause of action, but alleges new facts which, provided they be true, totally or partially answer the allegations put forward on the other side; thus distinguished from a mere traverse of the plaintiff's averments. In this use, the term corresponds to the common-law plea in confession and avoidance. A species of defense allowed in cases where, though the action as brought by the plaintiff was in itself just, yet it was unjust as against the particular party sued.

Exception. Act of excepting or excluding from a number designated or from a description; that which is excepted or separated from others in a general rule or description; a person, thing, or case specified as distinct or not included; an act of excepting, omitting from mention or leaving out of consideration. Express exclusion of something from operation of contract or deed. An "exception" operates to take something out of thing granted which would otherwise pass or be included. Such excludes from the operation of conveyance the interest specified and it remains in grantor unaffected by conveyance.

Objection to order or ruling of trial court. A formal objection to the action of the court, during the trial of a cause, in refusing a request or overruling an objection; implying that the party excepting does not acquiesce in the decision of the court, but will seek to procure its reversal, and that he means to save the benefit of his request or objection in some future proceeding. Under rules practice in the federal and most state courts, the need for claiming an exception to evidence or to a ruling to preserve appellate rights has been eliminated in favor of an objection. Fed.R. Civil P. 46.

See also Challenge; Dilatory exceptions; General exception; Objection; Peremptory exceptions; Reservation; Special exception.

Bill of exceptions. See Bill.

Deed. An exception withdraws from operation of deed part of thing granted which would otherwise pass to grantee.

Insurance policy. An exclusion of one or more risks. The object of an exception is to exclude that which otherwise would be included, to take special cases out of a general class, or to guard against misinterpretation.

"Reservation" and "proviso" compared. A "reservation" creates some new right in grantor while an "exception" withholds from grant title to some part of property which would otherwise pass. A reservation does not affect the description of the property conveyed, but retains to the grantor some right upon the property, as an easement, whereas an exception operates upon the description and withdraws from the description the excepted property. *Compare also* Variance.

Statutory laws. An exception in a statute is a clause designed to reserve or exempt some individuals from the general class of persons or things to which the language of the act in general attaches. The office of an "exception" in a statute is to except something from the operative effect of a statute or to qualify or restrain the generality of the substantive enactment to which it is attached, and it is not necessarily limited to the section of the statute immediately following or preceding. Two statutes relating to same subject must be read together, and provisions of one having special application to particular subject will be deemed an "exception" to other statute general in its terms. *See* Grandfather clause.

Exceptional circumstances. Conditions which are out of the ordinary course of events; unusual or extraordinary circumstances. For example, lack of original jurisdiction to hear and determine a case constitutes "exceptional circumstance" as basis for raising question for the first time on habeas corpus.

Excess. Act or amount which goes beyond that which is usual, proper, or necessary. Degree or amount by which one thing or number exceeds another. *See also* Excessive.

Excess clause. An "excess clause" in insurance policy limits liability to the amount of loss in excess of the coverage provided by other insurance. In insurance policy, such clause provides for insurer's liability up to limits of policy covering excess loss only after exhaustion of other valid insurance. *See also* Excess insurance; Excess policy.

Excess condemnation. Taking more property under condemnation than is actually needed. *See* Condemnation.

Excess insurance. That amount of insurance coverage which is beyond the dollar amount of coverage of one carrier but which is required to pay a particular loss as distinguished from "other insurance" which may be used to pay or contribute to the loss. *See also* Excess clause; Excess policy.

Excess jurisdiction. Such exists where a court, having jurisdiction of persons and subject matter of the case before it, exceeds its power in trial of such case by dealing with matters about which it is without power or authority to act; and error in court's ruling is not synonymous with ruling in excess of jurisdiction. *See* Excess of jurisdiction.

Excessive. Greater than what is usual or proper. A general term for what goes beyond just measure or amount. Tending to or marked by excess, which is the quality or state of exceeding the proper or reasonable limit or measure.

Excessive assessment. A tax assessment grossly disproportionate as compared with other assessments.

Excessive bail. The 8th Amendment to the U.S. Constitution, as well as the constitutions of the various states, prohibits excessive bail. Refers to bail in a sum more than will be reasonably sufficient to prevent evasion of the law by flight or concealment; bail which is per se unreasonably great and clearly disproportionate to the offense involved, or shown to be so by the special circumstances of the particular case. Bail set at higher figure than amount reasonably calculated to fulfill purpose of assuring that accused will stand trial and submit to sentence if found guilty is "excessive" under 8th Amendment.

Excessive damages. *See* Damages.

Excessive fine *or* **penalty.** The 8th Amendment to the U.S. Constitution, as well as the constitutions of the various states, prohibits excessive fines. A state may not constitutionally imprison a person for inability to pay a fine if he would not have been imprisoned on a showing of ability to pay the fine and on payment of the fine. Any fine or penalty which seriously impairs the capacity of gaining a business livelihood. *See* Corporal punishment; Excessive punishment; Punishment.

Excessive force. That amount of force which is beyond the need and circumstances of the particular event or which is not justified in the light of all the circumstances as in the case of deadly force to protect property as contrasted with protecting life. *See* Self defense.

Excessively. To excess.

Excessive punishment. Any sentence or fine which is not commensurate with the gravity of the offense or the criminal record of the defendant. Excessive punishments under 8th Amendment are those which by their length or severity are greatly disproportionate to offenses charged. Excessive length of a sentence may be cruel and unusual punishment within the meaning of the prohibition in the 8th Amendment, U.S. Constitution. *See* Corporal punishment; Excessive fine *or* penalty; Punishment.

Excessive verdict. A verdict which is result of passion or prejudice. The test of whether a verdict is "excessive" is whether the amount thereof is such as to shock the conscience of the court. *See* Remittitur.

Excess limits. Insurance coverage against losses in excess of specified limit. *See* Excess insurance; Excess policy.

Excess of jurisdiction. A case in which court has initially proceeded properly within its jurisdiction but steps out of jurisdiction in making of some order or in the doing of some judicial act. Acts which exceed defined power of court in any instance. A departure by a court from those recognized and established requirements of law, however close apparent adherence to mere form in method of procedure, which has the effect of depriving one of a constitutional right. *See also* Excess jurisdiction; Lack of jurisdiction.

Excess policy. One that provides that the insurer is liable only for the excess above and beyond that which may be collected on other insurance. *See also* Excess clause; Excess insurance.

Excess profits tax. Tax levied on profits which are beyond the normal profits of a business and generally imposed in times of national emergency such as war to discourage profiteering. The Internal Revenue Code also imposes a tax on corporations who accumulate an unreasonable surplus of profits rather than paying such out as dividends. I.R.C. § 531 et seq. *See* Accumulated earnings tax.

Exchange. To barter; to swap. To part with, give or transfer for an equivalent. To transfer goods or services for something of equal value. Act of giving or taking one thing for another. Contract by terms of which specific property is given in consideration of the receipt of property other than money. Mutual grant of equal interests, the one in consideration of the other. Transaction in which one piece of property, usually something other than money or its equivalent, is given in return for another piece of property. The criterion in determining whether a transaction is a sale or an exchange is whether there is a determination of value of things exchanged, and if no price is set for either property it is an "exchange".

Commerce or trade in goods, currency, or commercial paper.

Any organization, association, or group of persons, incorporated or not, which constitutes, maintains, or provides a market place or facilities for bringing together purchasers and sellers of securities, and includes the market place and facilities maintained by such an exchange. A major stock and bond exchange is the New York Stock Exchange. Similar exchanges exist for the trading of commodities; *e.g.* New York Commodities Exchange; Minneapolis Grain Exchange; Chicago Board of Trade. Trading in securities is controlled by the Securities and Exchange Commis-

sion; trading in commodities by the Commodity Futures Trading Commission.

For Arbitration of exchange; First of exchange, and Owelty *(Owelty of exchange)*, see *those titles.* For Bill of exchange, see Bill. See also Barter; Sale or exchange.

Commercial law. A negotiation by which one person transfers to another funds which he has in a certain place, either at a price agreed upon or which is fixed by commercial usage. The process of settling accounts or debts between parties residing at a distance from each other, without the intervention of money, by exchanging orders or drafts, called bills of exchange. The payment of debts in different places by an exchange or transfer of credits. The profit which arises from a maritime loan, when such profit is a percentage on the money lent, considering it in the light of money lent in one place to be returned in another, with a difference in amount in the sum borrowed and that paid, arising from the difference of time and place.

Conveyancing. A mutual grant of equal interests (in lands or tenements), the one in consideration of the other.

Like kind exchange. See Like-kind exchange.

Exchange broker. One who negotiates bills of exchange drawn on foreign countries or on other places in the same country. One who makes and concludes bargains for others in matters of money or merchandise.

Exchange offer. In a bilateral contract, such constitutes part of the consideration for the ultimate contract when such offer is accepted.

Exchange rate. The value of one country's money in terms of the value of another country's currency (*e.g.*, dollar vs. pound). Price at which the currency of one country can be converted into that of another country. *See also* Foreign exchange rate; Rate *(Rate of exchange)*.

Exchange ratio. The number of shares an acquiring company must give, or *exchange*, for each share of an acquired company in a merger.

Exchequer /ĕkschékər/. That department of the English government which has charge of the collection of the national revenue; the treasury department.

Excise tax. A tax imposed on the performance of an act, the engaging in an occupation, or the enjoyment of a privilege. A tax on the manufacture, sale, or use of goods or on the carrying on of an occupation or activity, or a tax on the transfer of property. In current usage the term has been extended to include various license fees and practically every internal revenue tax except the income tax (*e.g.*, federal alcohol and tobacco excise taxes, I.R.C. § 5001 et seq.)

Excited utterance. In evidence, a statement relating to a startling event or condition made while the declarant was under the stress of excitement caused by the event or condition. It is an exception to the hearsay rule. Fed.Evid. Rule 803(2). *See also* Fresh complaint rule; Res gestæ; Spontaneous declarations.

Exclusion. Denial of entry or admittance.

In taxation, item of income that is excluded from gross income (*i.e.*, not taxed) because of particular I.R.C. provision; *e.g.*, gifts and inheritance (I.R.C. § 102); qualified scholarships (I.R.C. § 117). *Compare* Deduction.

Evidence. The action by the trial judge in which he excludes from consideration by the trier of fact whatever he rules is not admissible as evidence. *See also* Exclusionary Rule.

Gift tax. The amount which a donor may transfer by gift each year without tax consequences. I.R.C. § 2503(b).

Insurance. In insurance policy, "exclusion" is provision which eliminates coverage where were it not for exclusion, coverage would have existed. Provision in policy specifying the situations, occurrences or persons not covered by the policy.

Witness. A trial judge may, under certain circumstances, sequester witnesses and require that they be kept apart from other witnesses until they are called to testify.

Exclusionary hearing. Pre-trial hearing at which alleged illegally obtained evidence is reviewed by trial judge to determine whether such is admissable at trial. *See* Fed.R.Crim.P. 12(b)(3). *See also* Exclusionary Rule.

Exclusionary Rule. This rule commands that where evidence has been obtained in violation of the search and seizure protections guaranteed by the U.S. Constitution, the illegally obtained evidence cannot be used at the trial of the defendant. Under this rule evidence which is obtained by an unreasonable search and seizure is excluded from admissibility under the Fourth Amendment, and this rule has been held to be applicable to the States. Mapp v. Ohio, 367 U.S. 643, 81 S.Ct. 1684, 6 L.Ed.2d 1081.

"Good faith exception" to exclusionary rule provides that evidence is not to be suppressed under such rule where that evidence was discovered by officers acting in good faith and in reasonable, though mistaken, belief that they were authorized to take those actions. United States v. Leon, 468 U.S. 897, 104 S.Ct. 3405, 82 L.Ed.2d 677. This exception recognizes that officers who have acted with objective good faith have right to rely upon issuing magistrate's determination that substantial basis existed for finding probable cause.

See also Counsel, right to; Escobedo Rule; Exclusionary hearing; Fruit of poisonous tree doctrine;

Good faith exception to exclusionary rule; Illegally obtained evidence; Independent source rule; Inevitable discovery rule; Miranda Rule; Motion to suppress; Suppression hearing; Suppression of evidence.

Exclusionary zoning. Any form of zoning ordinance which tends to exclude specific classes of persons or businesses from a particular district or area. *See also* Zoning.

Exclusive. Appertaining to the subject alone, not including, admitting, or pertaining to any others. Sole. Shutting out; debarring from interference or participation; vested in one person alone. Apart from all others, without the admission of others to participation.

Exclusive agency. Grant to agent of exclusive right to sell within a particular market or area. A contract to give an "exclusive agency" to deal with property is ordinarily interpreted as not precluding competition by the principal generally, but only as precluding him from appointing another agent to accomplish the result. The grant of an "exclusive agency to sell," that is, the exclusive right to sell the products of a wholesaler in a specified territory, ordinarily is interpreted as precluding competition in any form within designated area. *See also* Agency; Exclusive agency listing.

Exclusive agency listing. Agreement between a property owner and a real estate broker whereby the owner promises to pay a fee or commission to broker if his real property is sold during the listing period, regardless of whether the broker is responsible for the sale. *See also* Agency; Exclusive right (*Exclusive right to sell*); Listing.

Exclusive agent. An agent who has exclusive right to sell within a particular market or area. *See also* Agent; Exclusive agency.

Exclusive contract. A contract by which one binds himself to sell to or buy from only one person for his total requirements. *See* Entire output contract; Exclusive dealing arrangements; Requirement contract.

Exclusive control. Essential prerequisite to application of doctrine of *res ipsa loquitur* is that person to be charged have "exclusive control," connoting that no other person or entity had any control of instrumentality causing harm. Under this rule, where a thing is shown to be under management of defendant or his servants, and accident is such as in ordinary course does not happen if those having management use proper care, it affords reasonable evidence in absence of explanation that the accident arose from want of care. *See also* Res (*Res ipsa loquitur*).

Exclusive dealing arrangements. A form of vertical integration by contract under which a buyer agrees to purchase all its needs of a particular product from the seller—*i.e.*, the buyer agrees not to deal in the same product with a different supplier. At common law, generally agreements to deal exclusively with one seller or buyer were upheld, but under the Sherman Act as well as the Clayton and Federal Trade Commission Acts, such agreements are usually illegal. *See also* Exclusive contract; Requirement contract.

Exclusive franchise. *See* Exclusive agency.

Exclusive jurisdiction. That power which a court or other tribunal exercises over an action or over a person to the exclusion of all other courts. That forum in which an action must be commenced because no other forum has the jurisdiction to hear and determine the action. For example, by statute, actions brought under the Securities Exchange Act *must* be brought in federal district court.

Exclusive and concurrent jurisdiction. The federal courts have original and exclusive jurisdiction over certain actions (*e.g.* controversies between two or more states) and concurrent jurisdiction with that of state courts in others (*e.g.* actions between citizens of different states).

Exclusive license. Exclusive right granted by patent holder to licensee to use, manufacture, and sell patented article. Permission to do thing and contract not to give leave to any one else to do same thing. A license which binds licensor not to enlarge thereafter the scope of other licenses already granted, or increase the number of licenses. *See also* Exclusive agency; License.

Exclusive licensee. One granted exclusive right and license to use, manufacture, and sell patented article. One having exclusive right to use patented method and apparatus in designated territory.

Exclusive listing. *See* Exclusive agency listing.

Exclusively. Apart from all others; only; solely; substantially all or for the greater part. To the exclusion of all others; without admission of others to participation; in a manner to exclude.

Exclusive ownership. Ownership free from any kind of legal or equitable interest in any one else. *See* Fee simple.

Exclusive possession. With respect to adverse possession, means that adverse possessor must show an exclusive dominion over the land and an appropriation of it to his own use and benefit, and not for another. Possession may be "exclusive" so as to entitle possessor to title by adverse possession, notwithstanding that the land is subject to exercise of easement by private party. *See also,* Adverse possession.

Exclusive right. One which only the grantee thereof can exercise, and from which all others are prohibited or shut out.

Exclusive right to sell. An "exclusive right to sell" agreement listing real property for sale prohibits the owner from selling his property either by himself or through another broker without liability while the property is listed with the original broker. *See* Exclusive agency listing.

Exclusive use. As used in law authorizing registration of trademarks, means exclusive use not only of specific mark but also any other confusingly similar mark or term.

As essential element of acquisition of easement by prescription, means that exercise of right shall not be dependent upon similar right in others, but use may be shared with owner of servient estate. Exclusive use, for purpose of establishing a right in easement by adverse user, does not mean use to exclusion of use by all others, but exclusive use under claim of right requires only that right claimed by adverse user be not dependent on right of any one else to use way and may be established by common user thereof with owner of servient land and without any subjective claim of right.

Ex contractu /éks kəntrǽkt(y)uw/. From or out of a contract. In both the civil and the common law, rights and causes of action are divided into two classes,—those arising *ex contractu* (from a contract), and those arising *ex delicto* (from a delict or tort). Where cause of action arises from breech of a promise set forth in contract, the action is *"ex contractu"*, but where it arises from a breech of duty growing out of contract, it is *"ex delicto"*. *See also* Ex delicto.

Exculpate /ékskəlpeyt/əkskǽlpeyt/. Term is employed in sense of excuse or justification.

Exculpatory /ekskǽlpət(ò)riy/. Clearing or tending to clear from alleged fault or guilt; excusing. *See* Exculpatory statement or evidence. *Compare* Incriminate.

Exculpatory clause. A contract clause which releases one of the parties from liability for his or her wrongful acts. A provision in a document which protects a party from liability arising, in the main, from negligence; such clause is common in leases, contracts and trusts. Such clause in favor of a trustee in will implies that trustee has power which he purports to execute, and it exculpates him where this power is exercised in good faith. *See also* Hold harmless agreement.

Exculpatory statement or evidence. A statement or other evidence which tends to justify, excuse or clear the defendant from alleged fault or guilt. Declarations against declarant's interest which indicate that defendant is not responsible for crimes charged. Evidence which extrinsically tends to establish defendant's innocence of crimes charged as differentiated from that which although favorable, is merely collateral or impeaching. For purposes of rule constraining State from disposing of potentially exculpatory evidence, is evidence which clears or tends to clear accused person from alleged guilt. *Compare* Incriminating evidence.

Ex curia /èks kyúriyə/. Out of court; away from the court.

Excusable. Admitting of excuse or palliation. Justifiable, pardonable, allowable, defensible. As used in the law, this word implies that the act or omission spoken of is on its face unlawful, wrong, or liable to entail loss or disadvantage on the person chargeable, but that the circumstances attending it were such as to constitute a legal "excuse" for it, that is, a legal reason for withholding or foregoing the punishment, liability, or disadvantage which otherwise would follow. *See* Justification; Legal excuse.

Excusable assault. One committed by accident or misfortune in doing any lawful act by lawful means, with ordinary caution and without any unlawful intent. *See e.g.* Self-defense.

Excusable homicide. *See* Homicide.

Excusable neglect. In practice, and particularly with reference to the setting aside of a judgment taken against a party through his "excusable neglect," this means a failure to take the proper steps at the proper time, not in consequence of the party's own carelessness, inattention, or willful disregard of the process of the court, but in consequence of some unexpected or unavoidable hindrance or accident, or reliance on the care and vigilance of his counsel or on promises made by the adverse party. As used in rule (*e.g.* Fed.R.Civil P. 6(b)) authorizing court to permit an act to be done after expiration of the time within which under the rules such act was required to be done, where failure to act was the result of "excusable neglect", quoted phrase is ordinarily understood to be the act of a reasonably prudent person under the same circumstances. For purposes of motion to vacate judgment, "excusable neglect" is that neglect which might have been the act of a reasonably prudent person under the circumstances.

Excuse. A reason alleged for doing or not doing a thing. A matter alleged as a reason for relief or exemption from some duty or obligation. That which is offered as a reason for being excused, or a plea offered in extenuation of a fault or irregular deportment. It is that plea or statement made by the accused which arises out of the state of facts constituting and relied on as the cause. *See also* Defense.

Ex-date. Ex-dividend date. *See* Ex dividend.

Ex delicto /èks dəliktow/. From a delict, tort, fault, crime, or malfeasance. In both the civil and the common law, obligations and causes of action are divided into two classes—those arising *ex contractu* (out of a contract), and those *ex*

delicto. The latter are such as grow out of or are founded upon a wrong or tort, e.g., trespass, trover, replevin. *See also* Ex contractu.

Where cause of action arises from breach of a promise set forth in contract, the action is "ex contractu", but where it arises from a breach of duty growing out of contract, it is "ex delicto".

Ex delicto trusts. Trusts which are created for illegal purposes, the most common of which are trusts created to prevent creditors of the settlor from collecting their claims out of the property.

Ex dividend. A synonym for "without dividend." The buyer of a stock selling ex-dividend does not receive the recently declared dividend. Said of a stock at the time when the declared dividend becomes the property of the person who owned the stock on the record date. The payment date follows the ex-dividend date. When stock is sold ex dividend, the seller, not the buyer, has the right to the next dividend which has been declared but not paid. The ex dividend date is a matter of agreement or of convention to be established by the securities exchange. On the first day shares are traded without the right to receive a dividend, the price will normally decline by approximately the amount of the dividend. Such shares are often referred to as "trading ex dividend."

Ex-dividend date. The date on which the right to the most recently declared dividend no longer goes along with the sale of the stock.

Ex dolo malo /èks dówlo mǽlow/. Out of fraud; out of deceitful or tortious conduct. A phrase applied to obligations and causes of action vitiated by fraud or deceit.

Execute. To complete; to make; to sign; to perform; to do; to follow out; to carry out according to its terms; to fulfill the command or purpose of. To perform all necessary formalities, as to make and sign a contract, or sign and deliver a note. *See also* Execution.

Executed. Completed; carried into full effect; already done or performed; signed; taking effect immediately; now in existence or in possession; conveying an immediate right or possession. Act or course of conduct carried to completion. Term imports idea that nothing remains to be done. The opposite of *executory*. *See also* Execution.

Executed consideration. A consideration which is wholly performed. An act done or value given before the making of the agreement.

Executed contract. Contract which has been fully performed by the parties. If performed in part, it is partially executed (executory); if entirely performed, it is fully or wholly executed. *See also* Contract; Executory contract.

Executed estate. Estate in property which is vested. *See* Estate.

Executed gift. *See* Gift.

Executed note. Promissory note which has been signed and delivered.

Executed remainder. *See* Remainder.

Executed sale. *See* Sale.

Executed trust. *See* Trust.

Executed use. *See* Use.

Execution. Carrying out some act or course of conduct to its completion. Completion of an act. Putting into force. The completion, fulfillment, or perfecting of anything, or carrying it into operation and effect.

Execution of contract includes performance of all acts necessary to render it complete as an instrument and imports idea that nothing remains to be done to make complete and effective contract. *See* Execution of instrument.

Execution upon a money judgment is the legal process of enforcing the judgment, usually by seizing and selling property of the debtor. Form of process whereby an official (usually a sheriff) is directed by way of an appropriate judicial writ to seize and sell so much of the debtor's nonexempt property as is necessary to satisfy a judgment. Process of carrying into effect the directions in a decree or judgment. *See* Writ of execution, below.

In criminal law, refers to carrying out of death sentence (capital punishment).

Body execution. An order of court which commands the officer to take the body of the defendant or debtor; generally to bring him before court to pay debt. A capias.

Writ of execution. Formal process issued by court generally evidencing the debt of the defendant to the plaintiff and commanding the officer to take the property of the defendant in satisfaction of the debt. Unless the court directs otherwise, the process to enforce a money judgment shall be a writ of execution. Fed.R. Civil P. 69. A writ of execution is a written demand to bailiff, directing him to execute the judgment of the court. Process issuing from a court in a civil action authorizing the sheriff or other competent officer to carry out the court's decision in favor of the prevailing party.

For "Testatum execution", *see* Testatum. *See also* Alias execution; Attachment execution; Dormant execution; General execution; Judgment execution; Junior execution; Lien of execution; Special execution.

Execution creditor. *See* Creditor.

Executioner. Person who executes (*i.e.* carries out) capital punishment.

Execution lien. An execution lien may be created by service of execution, levy upon real estate, and filing of a certificate of levy in the proper office of county in which real estate is located. *See* Execution.

Execution of instrument. Completion of instrument, including signing and delivery. Execution includes performance of all acts necessary to render instrument complete and of every act required to give instrument validity or to carry it into effect. Execution of written contract includes signing, unconditional delivery by promisor, and acceptance by promisee.

Execution of judgment *or* **decree.** *See* Execution; Judgment execution.

Execution sale. A sale by a sheriff or other ministerial officer under the authority of a writ of execution which he has levied on property of the debtor. *See also* Execution; Judicial sale.

Executive. As distinguished from the legislative and judicial departments (*i.e.* branches) of government, the executive department is that which is charged with the detail of carrying the laws into effect and securing their due observance. *See also* Executive department; Executive powers.

The word "executive" is also used as an impersonal designation of the chief executive officer of a state or nation. Term also refers to upper level management of business. *See also* Executive employees.

Executive agency. A department of the executive branch of government such as the Army and Air Force Exchange Service whose activities are subject to statutes and whose contracts are subject to judicial review.

Executive agreement. A treaty-like agreement with another country in which the President may bind the country without submission to the Senate (as in the case of a treaty). Executive Agreements prevail over contrary state law. Even though there is no express constitutional authority for such agreements, their constitutional validity has been long established.

Executive clemency. The power of the chief executive (*i.e.* President or a governor) to pardon or commute a criminal sentence as, for example, the power to reduce the death penalty to life imprisonment. Art. II, § 2, U.S.Const. *See also* Clemency.

Executive committee. In business, the body which directly manages the operations between meetings of the board of directors; commonly consisting of the principal officers and directors.

Executive department. That branch of government charged with carrying out the laws enacted by the legislature. The President is the chief executive officer of the country and the governor is chief executive officer of a state. Used to describe that branch of the government in contrast to the other two branches; *i.e.* legislative and judicial. See Art. II, U.S.Const.

Executive employees. Persons whose duties include some form of managerial authority, actually directing the work of other persons. Persons whose duties relate to active participation in control, supervision and management of business, or who administer affairs, or who direct, manage, execute or dispense. The term carries the idea of supervision of or control over ordinary employees.

Executive officer. An officer of the executive department of government; one in whom resides the power to execute the laws; one whose duties are to cause the laws to be executed and obeyed. Officers who are neither judicial nor legislative are executive officers. One who assumes command or control and directs course of business, or some part thereof, and who outlines duties and directs work of subordinate employees. President and vice president of corporation are executive officers.

Executive order. An order or regulation issued by the President or some administrative authority under his direction for the purpose of interpreting, implementing, or giving administrative effect to a provision of the Constitution or of some law or treaty. To have the effect of law, such orders must be published in the Federal Register.

Executive pardon. An executive act of grace exempting an individual from punishment for a crime he has committed. Such presidential power is authorized by Art. II, § 2, U.S.Const. Similar powers are afforded to governors by state constitutions. *See also* Executive clemency; Pardon.

Executive powers. Authority vested in executive department of federal or state government to execute laws. The enumerated powers of the President are provided for in Article II of the U.S. Const. Executive powers of governors are provided for in state constitutions. The executive powers vested in governors by state constitutions include the power to execute the laws, that is, to carry them into effect, as distinguished from the power to make the laws and the power to judge them. *See also* Executive order.

Executive privilege. This privilege, based on constitutional doctrine of separation of powers, exempts the executive from disclosure requirements applicable to the ordinary citizen or organization where such exemption is necessary in the discharge of highly important executive responsibilities involved in maintaining governmental operations, and extends not only to military and diplomatic secrets but also to documents integral to an appropriate exercise of the executive's domestic decisional and policy making functions, that is, those documents reflecting the frank expression necessary in intra-governmental advisory and deliberative communications. 5 U.S.C.A. § 552(b)(1). However, need for confidentiality of high level communications cannot, without more, sustain an absolute unqualified presidential privilege of immunity from judicial process under all circumstances. U. S. v. Nixon, 418 U.S. 683, 94 S.Ct. 3090, 3106, 3107, 41 L.Ed.2d 1039. As term is generally employed, relates to matters of national security and foreign policy. *See also* Privilege.

Executive session. Executive session of a board or governmental body is a session closed to the public, and at which only such selected persons as the board or other body may invite are permitted to be present.

Executor(-trix) /əgzékətər/. A person appointed by a testator to carry out the directions and requests in his will, and to dispose of the property according to his testamentary provisions after his decease.

"Personal representative" includes "executor." Uniform Probate Code, § 1–201. *Compare* Administrator(-trix).

For Co-executor; General executor; Instituted executor; Joint executors; Limited executor; Special executor and Substituted executor, see those titles.

Executor creditor. *See* Creditor.

Executor de son tort. *See* De son tort.

Executorship. Office held by an executor.

Executory /əgzékyətòriy/. That which is yet to be fully executed or performed; that which remains to be carried into operation or effect; incomplete; depending upon a future performance or event. The opposite of *executed*.

As to *executory* Bequest; Contracts; Devise; Estates; Remainder; Trust, and Use, see those titles.

Executory accord. An agreement embodying a promise, express or implied, to accept at some future time a stipulated performance in satisfaction or discharge, in whole or in part, of any present claim, cause of action or obligation, and a promise, express or implied, to render such performance. Two principal categories of compromise agreements are "executory accord", providing for acceptance in future of stated performance in satisfaction of claim, and "substituted contract" which itself is accepted as substitution for and extinguishment of existing claim.

Executory consideration. A consideration which is to be performed after the contract for which it is a consideration is made.

Executory contract. A contract that has not as yet been fully completed or performed. A contract the obligation (performance) of which relates to the future. In context of Bankruptcy Code, is contract under which obligation of both bankrupt and other party to contract are so far unperformed that failure of either to complete performance would constitute material breach excusing performance of either. *Compare* Executed contract.

Executory devise. Devise of a future estate, and, if the executory devisee dies before the event happens, the estate goes to the heir at the time of the event, and not to the heir at the time of the death of the devisee. The happening of the contingency determines who is to take the estate, and until that time no one has an interest to transmit. By the earlier common law it was an established rule that a devise of lands, without words of limitation, conferred upon the devisee an estate for life only. An exception was soon recognized in the case of a will, so that an estate in fee could be given without the use of the technical words required in a conveyance or deed. The gift in such case was known as an "executory devise."

Executory interests. A general term, comprising all future estates and interests in land or personalty, other than reversions and remainders. A future interest held by a third person (not the grantor) which either cuts short (shifting) or begins some time after (springing) the natural termination of the preceding estate.

A contingent future interest which: (a) cannot qualify as a remainder; (b) is always in favor of a conveyee, and; (c) takes effect when the contingency happens as a springing use or shifting use under the Statute of Uses (1535), or Statute of Wills (1540).

Executory judgment. Court decision that has not yet been carried out; *e.g.,* order to defendant to pay plaintiff which has not as yet been fulfilled.

Executory limitation. A limitation of a future interest by deed or will; if by will, it is also called an "executory devise."

Executory process. A civil law process which can be resorted to in the following cases, namely: (1) When the right of the creditor arises from an act importing confession of judgment, and which contains a privilege or mortgage in his favor; (2) when the creditor demands the execution of a judgment which has been rendered by a tribunal different from that within whose jurisdiction the execution is sought. An accelerated procedure, summary in nature, by which holder of a mortgage or privilege evidenced by an authentic act importing a confession of judgment seeks to effect an ex parte seizure and sale of the subject property, without previous citation, contradictory hearing or judgment.

Executory promise. A promise that has not yet been performed by the promisor doing whatever act was promised.

Executory sale. *See* Sale.

Executory trust. Under this type of trust a further conveyance or settlement is to be made by the trustee. The test as to whether a trust is an "executory trust" is to determine whether settlor has acted as his own conveyancer and defines precisely the settlement to be made, and, if he has, the word "heirs" is one of limitation, and if he has not, the trust is executory, and the word "heirs" is a word of purchase, and the persons coming within such definition have an interest in the property.

Executory unilateral accord. An offer to enter a contract.

Executory warranties. Such arise where insured undertakes to perform some executory stipulation, as that certain acts will be done, or that certain facts will continue to exist.

Executress /əgzékyətrəs/. A female executor.

Executrix /əgzékyətriks/. Female executor. A woman who has been appointed by will to execute such will or testament. *See* Executor(-trix).

Exemplars /əgzémplərz/. Nontestimonial identification evidence taken from defendant; *e.g.* fingerprints, blood samples, voiceprints, lineup identification, handwriting samples.

Exemplary damages /əgzémpləriy dǽmǝjəz/. Damages on an increased scale, awarded to plaintiff over and above actual or ordinary damages, where wrong done to plaintiff was aggravated by circumstances of violence, oppression, malice, fraud, or wanton and wicked conduct on part of defendant. *See also* Damages *(Exemplary or punitive damages).*

Exemplification. An official transcript of a document from public records, made in form to be used as evidence, and authenticated or certified as a true copy. *See* Certified copy.

Exemplified copy. Copy of document which has been authenticated. *See* Certified copy.

Exempt. To release, discharge, waive, relieve from liability. To relieve, excuse, or set free from a duty or service imposed upon the general class to which the individual exempted belongs; as to exempt from military service.

To relieve certain classes of property from liability to sale on execution, or from taxation, or from bankruptcy or attachment.

See also Exemption; Exemption laws.

Exempt income. Income that is not subject to state and/or federal taxation. Certain income may be exempt from federal but not from state taxation, and vice versa (*e.g.,* tax exempt bond interest). *See also* Exemption.

Exemption. Freedom from a general duty or service; immunity from a general burden, tax, or charge. Immunity from service of process or from certain legal obligations, as jury duty, military service, or the payment of taxes. *See also* Immunity.

A privilege allowed by law to a judgment debtor, by which he may retain property to a certain amount or certain classes of property, free from all liability to levy and sale on execution, attachment, or bankruptcy. *See* Exemption laws; Non-leviable.

Property exempt in bankruptcy proceedings is provided for under Bankruptcy Code § 522. *See* Exemption laws.

In taxation, an exemption is an amount allowed as a deduction from adjusted gross income in arriving at taxable income. There are two types of exemptions allowed; personal and dependency exemptions. Exemptions are allowed as follows; the taxpayer, the taxpayer's spouse, the taxpayer who is 65 or older or who is blind, the taxpayer's dependent children for whom the taxpayer provides more that one half of the dependent's support. I.R.C. § 151. *See also* Dependency exemption.

Exemption equivalent. The maximum value of assets that can be transferred to another party without incurring any Federal gift or estate tax because of the application of the unified tax credit.

Exemption laws. A privilege allowed by law to a judgment debtor, by which he may hold property to a certain amount, or certain classes of property, free from all liability to levy and sale on execution or attachment. Laws enacted by individual states describing the property of the debtor that cannot be attached by a judgment creditor or trustee in bankruptcy to satisfy a debt. See Bankruptcy Code § 522.

Exempt organization. An organization that is either partially or completely exempt from Federal income taxation. I.R.C. § 501. *See* Charitable organizations.

Exempt property. Real estate of religious, educational, and charitable organizations, as well as of federal, state and local government which is not subject to real estate taxes. With respect to property that is exempt in bankruptcy, attachment, etc., proceedings, *see* Exemption; Exemption laws.

Exempt securities. Securities exempt from registration requirements of federal and state securities laws. *See also* Registration of securities.

Exempt transactions. Those dealings in securities which fall outside the scope of Securities Act of 1933 and Securities Exchange Act.

Exercise. To make use of. Thus, to exercise a right or power is to do something which it enables

the holder to do; *e.g.* exercising option to purchase stock.

When an optionholder enforces the sale on the terms specified in an option contract. Also called *put* (to exercise a put option) or *call* (to exercise a call option).

To put in action or practice, to carry on something, to transact or execute. *See* Performance.

Exercise clause. *See* Free exercise clause.

Exercise price. The price for which the asset will be exchanged in an option contract if the option is exercised. Also called strike price.

Exercise value. The value to an optionholder of exercising the option. Sometimes called intrinsic value.

Exercised dominion. Open acts and conduct relative to land as evidence claim of the right of absolute possession, use, and ownership. *See* Dominion.

Ex facie /èks féys(h)iyiy/. From the face; apparently; evidently. A term applied to what appears on the face of a writing.

Ex facto /èks fǽktow/. From or in consequence of a fact or action; actually. Usually applied to an unlawful or tortious act as the foundation of a title, etc. Sometimes used as equivalent to *"de facto."*

Ex gratia /èks gréysh(iy)ə/. Out of grace; as a matter of grace, favor, or indulgence; gratuitous. A term applied to anything accorded as a favor; as distinguished from that which may be demanded *ex debito*, as a matter of right.

Exhaustion of administrative remedies /əgzóstyən əv ədmínəstrətəv rémədiyz/. This doctrine requires that where an administrative remedy is provided by statute, relief must first be sought by exhausting such remedies before the courts will act. The doctrine requires the party to use all available agency administrative procedures before resorting to courts for relief and requires that a party not only initially raise the issue in the administrative forum, but requires party to proceed through the entire proceeding to a final decision on the merits of the entire controversy. *See also* Primary jurisdiction.

Exhaustion of state remedies. Federal courts require that state remedies be exhausted in certain classes of cases in order to give state courts as a matter of comity the opportunity to make the initial determination as to all claims, federal or state, raised in those cases. Under this doctrine, a petition for habeas corpus by a state prisoner will be entertained by a federal court only after all state remedies have been exhausted. 28 U.S. C.A. § 2254. However, exhaustion of state remedies is not required in Civil Rights § 1983 (42

U.S.C.A.) actions. *See also* Abstention doctrine; Comity.

Exhibit, *v.* To show or display; to offer or present for inspection. To produce anything in public, so that it may be taken into possession. To present; to offer publicly or officially; to file of record. To administer; to cause to be taken, as medicines. To submit to a court or officer in course of proceedings.

Exhibit, *n.* A paper or document produced and exhibited to a court during a trial or hearing, or to a person taking depositions, or to auditors, arbitrators, etc., as a voucher, or in proof of facts, or as otherwise connected with the subject-matter, and which, on being accepted, is marked for identification and annexed to the deposition, report, or other principal document, or filed of record, or otherwise made a part of the case.

Paper, document, chart, map, or the like, referred to and made a part of an affidavit, pleading or brief.

An item of physical/tangible evidence which is to be or has been offered to the court for inspection.

Exhibits may be included as a part of the appendix to appellate briefs. See Fed.R.App.P. 30(e).

Exhibition. *See* Exhibit.

Exhibitionism. Indecent exposure of sexual organs. *See* Indecent.

Exhumation /èks(h)yuwméyshən/ègz(y)uw°/. Disinterment; the removal from the earth of anything previously buried therein, particularly a human corpse.

Ex hypothesi /èks hàypóθəsay/. By the hypothesis; upon the supposition; upon the theory or facts assumed.

Exigence /égzəjəns/ *or* **exigency** /égzəjənsiy/əgzí-°/. Demand, want, need, imperativeness. Something arising suddenly out of the current state of events; any event or occasional combination of circumstances, calling for immediate action or remedy; a pressing necessity; a sudden and unexpected happening or an unforeseen occurrence or condition. State of being urgent or exigent; pressing need or demand; also, case requiring immediate attention, assistance, or remedy; critical period or condition, pressing necessity. *See* Exigent circumstances, *infra.*

Exigency of a bond. That which the bond demands or exacts, *i.e.,* the act, performance, or event upon which it is conditioned.

Exigency of a writ. The command or imperativeness of a writ; the directing part of a writ; the act or performance which it commands.

Exigent circumstances. Situations that demand unusual or immediate action. "Exigent circum-

stances" in relation to justification for warrantless arrest or search refers generally to those situations in which law enforcement agents will be unable or unlikely to effectuate an arrest, search or seizure for which probable cause exists unless they act swiftly and without seeking prior judicial authorization. Exception to rule requiring search warrant is presence of exigent or emergency-like circumstances as for example presence of weapons in a motor vehicle stopped on highway and such exigent circumstances permit warrantless search and seizure. Where there are exigent circumstances in which police action literally must be "now or never" to preserve the evidence of the crime, it is reasonable to permit action without prior evaluation. *See also* Probable cause.

Exigent search. *See* Exigent circumstances.

Exile /égzayl/éksayl/. Banishment; the person banished. As noun, expulsion from country; expatriation. As verb, to expel from country; to banish. *See also* Deportation.

Exist. To live; to have life or animation; to be in present force, activity, or effect at a given time, as in speaking of "existing" contracts, creditors, debts, laws, rights, or liens. To be or continue to be.

Existing claim. Claim which has arisen and is pending.

Existing debt. To have an "existing debt" it is sufficient if there is an absolute debt owing though the period for its payment may not yet have arrived. A tax may be a "debt" within meaning of agreement to assume "existing debts". Within provision of Uniform Fraudulent Conveyance Act which defines "insolvency", an "existing debt" is an existing legal liability, whether matured or unmatured, liquidated or unliquidated, absolute, fixed or contingent.

Exit /égzət/. Lat. It goes forth. This word is used in docket entries as a brief mention of the issue of process. Thus, *"exit fi. fa."* denotes that a writ of *fieri facias* has been issued in the particular case. The *"exit* of a writ" is the fact of its issuance.

Way out; opposite of entrance. *See* Egress.

Ex lege /èks líyjiy/. By the law; by force of law; as a matter of law.

Ex maleficio /èks mæləfish(i)yow/. Defined variously as from or growing out of wrongdoing; tortious; tortiously; growing out of, or founded on, misdoing or tort; on account of misconduct; by virtue of or out of an illegal act. Synonymous with "malfeasance". This term is frequently used in the civil law as the synonym of *"ex delicto" (q.v.),* and is thus contrasted with *"ex contractu".* In this sense it is of more rare occurrence in the common law.

Ex mero motu /èks mírow mówtuw/. Of his own mere motion; of his own accord; voluntarily and without prompting or request.

Ex officio /èks əfísh(iy)ow/. From office; by virtue of the office; without any other warrant or appointment than that resulting from the holding of a particular office. Powers may be exercised by an officer which are not specifically conferred upon him, but are necessarily implied in his office; these are *ex officio*. Thus, a judge has *ex officio* the powers of a conservator of the peace.

Ex officio justices. Judges who serve in a particular capacity by reason of their office as a judge who serves on a commission or board because the law requires a particular judge to serve thereon and not because he is selected for such post. May also refer to one who exercises judicial functions by reason of his office.

Ex officio services /èks əfísh(iy)ow sə́rvəsəs/. Services which the law annexes to a particular office and requires the incumbent to perform.

Exonerate /əgzónəreyt/. To exculpate.

Exoneration /əgzònəréyshən/. The removal of a burden, charge, responsibility, or duty. Right to be reimbursed by reason of having paid that which another should be compelled to pay while "indemnity" generally is based upon contract, express or implied, and means compensation for loss already sustained.

Equitable right of a surety, confirmed by statute in many states, to proceed by action in court to compel the principal debtor, against whom the surety will have a right of reimbursement, to satisfy the obligation where it would be inequitable for the surety to be compelled to perform, and thereby suffer the inconvenience and temporary loss which a payment by her will entail, if the principal debtor can satisfy the obligation. See Restatement of Security § 112 (1941).

Ex parte /èks pártiy/. On one side only; by or for one party; done for, in behalf of, or on the application of, one party only.

A judicial proceeding, order, injunction, etc., is said to be *ex parte* when it is taken or granted at the instance and for the benefit of one party only, and without notice to, or contestation by, any person adversely interested.

"Ex parte," in the heading of a reported case, signifies that the name following is that of the party upon whose application the case is heard.

Ex parte divorce. Divorce proceeding in which only one spouse participates or one in which the other spouse does not appear. The validity of such divorce depends upon the nature of the notice given to the absent spouse.

Ex parte hearing. Hearings in which the court or tribunal hears only one side of the controversy.

Ex parte injunction. An injunction which issues from a court which has heard only one side, the moving side, of the controversy. *See* Injunction; Temporary restraining order.

Ex parte investigation. An investigation conducted about a person who is not personally contacted or questioned.

Ex parte materna /èks pártiy mətə́rnə/. On the mother's side; of the maternal line.

Ex parte paterna /èks pártiy pətə́rnə/. On the father's side; of the paternal line.

Ex parte proceeding. Any judicial or quasi judicial hearing in which only one party is heard as in the case of a temporary restraining order.

Ex parte revocation. The withdrawal or revocation of a license or other authority from a person without that person's participation or without notice and opportunity to be heard and defend.

Expatriation /ekspèytriyéyshən/. The voluntary act of abandoning or renouncing one's country, and becoming the citizen or subject of another.

Expect. To await; to look forward to something intended, promised, or likely to happen.

Expectancy. That which is expected or hoped for. The condition of being deferred to a future time, or of dependence upon an expected event. Contingency as to possession or enjoyment. With respect to the time of their enjoyment, estates may either be in possession or in expectancy; and of expectancies there are two sorts,—one created by the act of the parties, called a "remainder;" the other by act of law, called a "reversion." Expectancy as applied to property, is contingency as to possession, that which is expected or hoped for. At most it is a mere hope or expectation, contingent upon the will and pleasure of the landowner, and hardly reaches the height of a property right, much less a vested right, because where there is no obligation, there is no right. It is a possibility for which a party may under certain circumstances properly hope for or expect.

Expectancy of life. With respect to life annuities, the share or number of years of life which a person of a given age may, upon an equality of chance, expect to enjoy. *See* Actuarial table; Mortality tables.

Expectancy tables. *See* Actuarial table; Mortality tables.

Expectant. Contingent as to enjoyment. Having relation to, or dependent upon, a contingency. *See* Contingent.

Expectant estates. *See* Estate in expectancy.

Expectant heir /əkspéktənt ér/. A person who has the expectation of inheriting property or an estate, but small present means.

Expectant right. A contingent right, not vested; one which depends on the continued existence of the present condition of things until the happening of some future event. A right is contingent, not vested, when it comes into existence only on an event or condition which may not happen.

Expectation of life. *See* Actuarial table; Expectancy of life; Mortality tables.

Expected future cash flows. Projected future cash flows associated with an asset or decision.

Expected future rate of return. The rate of return that is expected to be earned on an asset in the future. Also called simply the expected or internal rate of return. *See* Rate (*Rate of return*).

Expedient. Apt and suitable to end in view. Whatever is suitable and appropriate in reason for the accomplishment of a specified object.

Expedited Funds Availability Act. Federal law that requires banks to make check deposits available more quickly than the longer holding period that banks formerly required. 12 U.S.C.A. § 4002.

Expedition. A sending forth or setting forth for the execution of some object of consequence. Speed or promptness in performance. An important journey or excursion for a specific purpose; as, a military or exploring expedition; also, the body of persons making such an excursion. A journey, march, or voyage generally of several or many persons for definite purpose, such as a military or exploring expedition or a trading expedition to the African coast. The word carries an implication of a military exploit or of an exploration into remote regions or over new routes.

Expeditious /èkspədíshəs/. Possessed of, or characterized by, expedition or efficiency and rapidity in action; performed with, or acting with, expedition; quick; speedy.

Expel. In regard to trespass and other torts, this term means to eject, to put out, to drive out, and generally with an implication of the use of force. *See also* Ejectment; Eviction.

Expend. To pay out, lay out, consume, use up; normally implying receiving something in return.

Expendable. That which is consumed in its use over a short period of time such as expenses for day to day operations which are charged as expenses to current income as contrasted with payments for long term or capital improvements. Not essential or critical to preserve.

Expenditure. Spending or payment of money; the act of expending, disbursing, or laying out of money; payment. *Compare* Appropriation. *See also* Expense. As regards *Capital expenditure, see* Capital.

Expense. That which is expended, laid out or consumed. An outlay; charge; cost; price. The expenditure of money, time, labor, resources, and thought. That which is expended in order to secure benefit or bring about a result. *See also* Costs; Fee.

Accrued expense. One which has been incurred in a given period but not yet paid.

Business expense. One which is directly related to one's business as contrasted with expenses incurred for personal and family reasons. *See Tax deduction, below.*

Current expense. Normal expense incurred, for example, in daily operations of a business. *See Operating expenses, below.*

Operating expenses. The cost of operating a business, such as rent, wages, utilities, and similar day to day expenses, as well as taxes, insurance, and a reserve for depreciation.

Ordinary expense. *See* Ordinary.

Out of pocket expenses. A direct expense which requires the immediate outlay of cash in contrast to an accrued expense.

Prepaid expense. Payment of rent, interest, insurance, or similar expenses, prior to actual due date for payment. I.R.C. §§ 162, 213. Costs that are deductible from current income as opposed to capital expenditures. Cash basis as well as accrual basis taxpayers are generally required to capitalize prepayments for rent, insurance, etc. that cover more than one year. Deductions are taken during the period the benefits are received.

Tax deduction. Certain expenses such as those directly related to production of income are deductions from gross income for tax purposes.

Expense in carrying on business. In tax law, refers to usual or customary expenditure in course of conducting business during the year. *See* Ordinary (*Ordinary expenses*).

Expense ratio. Proportion or ratio of expenses to income.

Expenses of administration. As used in Internal Revenue Code, means obligations incurred after decedent's death by his representatives in administering his estate. *See* Administration expense.

Expenses of receivership. Includes allowances to receivers' counsel, master's fees, appraisers' fees, auditors' fees, and rent and other expenses incurred by receivers in conducting business.

Experience. A state, extent, or duration of being engaged in a particular study or work; the real life as contrasted with the ideal or imaginary. A word implying skill, facility, or practical wisdom gained by personal knowledge, feeling, and action, and also the course or process by which one attains knowledge or wisdom.

Experience rating. In insurance, a method of determining rates by using the loss experience of the insured over a period of time.

Expert. One who is knowledgeable in specialized field, that knowledge being obtained from either education or personal experience. One who by reason of education or special experience has knowledge respecting a subject matter about which persons having no particular training are incapable of forming an accurate opinion or making a correct deduction. One who by habits of life and business has peculiar skill in forming opinion on subject in dispute. *See* Expert testimony; Expert witness.

Expert testimony. Opinion evidence of some person who possesses special skill or knowledge in some science, profession or business which is not common to the average man and which is possessed by the expert by reason of his special study or experience. Testimony given in relation to some scientific, technical, or professional matter by experts, *i.e.*, persons qualified to speak authoritatively by reason of their special training, skill, or familiarity with the subject. Evidence of persons who are skilled in some art, science, profession, or business, which skill or knowledge is not common to their fellow men, and which has come to such experts by reason of special study and experience in such art, science, profession, or business.

If scientific, technology, or other specialized knowledge will assist the trier of fact to understand the evidence or to determine a fact in issue, a witness qualified as an expert by knowledge, skill, experience, training, or education, may testify thereto in the form of an opinion or otherwise. Fed.Evid.R. 702, 703. *See also* Expert witness; Opinion evidence or testimony.

Expert witness. One who by reason of education or specialized experience possesses superior knowledge respecting a subject about which persons having no particular training are incapable of forming an accurate opinion or deducing correct conclusions. A witness who has been qualified as an expert and who thereby will be allowed (through his/her answers to questions posted) to assist the jury in understanding complicated and technical subjects not within the understanding of the average lay person. One possessing, with reference to particular subject, knowledge not acquired by ordinary persons. One skilled in any particular art, trade, or profession, being possessed of peculiar knowledge concerning the same, and one who has given subject in question particular study, practice, or observation. One who by habits of life and business has peculiar skill in forming opinion on subject in dispute. For admissibility of testimony and court appointment of expert witnesses, see Fed.Evid.Rules 702–706. *See also* Expert testimony; Hypothetical question.

Expiration. Cessation; termination from mere lapse of time, as the expiration date of a lease, insurance policy, statute, and the like. Coming to close; termination or end.

Term as used in insurance policy, refers to termination of the policy by lapse of time covering the policy period, while "cancellation" refers to termination of the policy by act of either or both parties prior to ending of the policy period.

Expiration date. The date on which a financial security will cease to exist. Also called maturity date.

Expire. *See* Expiration.

Explicit. Not obscure or ambiguous, having no disguised meaning or reservation. Clear in understanding.

Exploitation /èksploytéyshən/. Act or process of exploiting, making use of, or working up. Utilization by application of industry, argument, or other means of turning to account, as the exploitation of a mine or a forest. Taking unjust advantage of another for one's own advantage or benefit (*e.g.* paying low wages to illegal aliens).

Exploration. The examination and investigation of land supposed to contain valuable minerals, by drilling, boring, sinking shafts, driving tunnels, and other means, for the purpose of discovering the presence of ore and its extent.

Export, *v.* To carry or to send abroad. To send, take, or carry an article of trade or commerce out of the country. To transport merchandise or goods from one country to another in the course of trade. To carry out or convey goods by sea. Transportation of goods from United States to foreign country. The Constitution gives Congress the power to regulate exports through its grant of power to regulate trade with foreign nations. Art. I, Sec. 8, Cl. 3. *See also* Re-export.

Export, *n.* Products manufactured in one country, and then shipped and sold in another. A thing or commodity exported. More commonly used in the plural.

Exportation. The act of sending or carrying goods and merchandise from one country to another.

Export declaration. Document which contains details of export shipment and required by federal law.

Export drafts. When a domestic seller and foreign buyer complete a trade transaction, the actual exchange of documents for payment is usually handled by banks. To carry out the financial end of the transaction, the parties often use an "export draft" or "bill of exchange." An export draft is an unconditional order, drawn by the seller upon the buyer, directing the buyer to pay the face amount of the draft, either when it is presented (a sight draft) or at a specified future date (a time draft or usance). The draft is usually made payable to the order of the seller—or to the order of the seller's bank.

Export-Import Bank. Independent agency of federal government whose function is to aid in financing exports and imports.

Export quotas. Amounts of specific goods which may be exported. Such quotas are set by the federal government for purposes of national defense, economic stability, price support, etc.

Exports clause. Provision in U.S.Const., Art. I, Sec. 10, Cl. 2, limiting power of states to impose duties or imposts on imports or exports.

Export tax. Tax levied upon merchandise and goods shipped out of a country. Tax levied upon right to export or upon goods because of fact that they are being exported or intended to be exported. *See also* Customs duties; Domestic International Sales Corporation (DISC).

Expose, *v.* To show publicly; to display; to offer to the public view, as, to "expose" goods to sale, to "expose" a tariff or schedule of rates, to "expose" misconduct of public or quasi-public figures.

To place in a position where the object spoken of is open to danger, or where it is near or accessible to anything which may affect it detrimentally; as, to "expose" a child, or to expose oneself or another to a contagious disease or to danger or hazard of any kind.

For *indecent exposure, see* Indecent.

Exposé /əkspówz/èkspowzéy/. Fr. A statement; account; recital; explanation. The term is used in diplomatic language as descriptive of a written explanation of the reasons for a certain act or course of conduct. Exposure of discreditable matter concerning a person, government, etc.

Expository statute. A law that is enacted to explain the meaning of a previously enacted law. Such statutes are often expressed thus: "The true intent and meaning of an act passed * * * be and is hereby declared to be"; "the provisions of the act shall not hereafter extend"; or "are hereby declared and enacted not to apply", and the like. This is a common mode of legislation.

Ex post facto /éks pòwst fǽktow/. After the fact; by an act or fact occurring after some previous act or fact, and relating thereto; by subsequent matter; the opposite of *ab initio.* Thus, a deed may be good *ab initio,* or, if invalid at its inception, may be confirmed by matter *ex post facto.*

Ex post facto law /éks pòwst fǽktow ló/. A law passed after the occurrence of a fact or commission of an act, which retrospectively changes the legal consequences or relations of such fact or deed. A law is unconstitutionally "ex post facto" if it deprives the defendant of a defense to crimi-

nal liability that he had prior to enactment of the law. Art. I, § 9 (Cl.3) and § 10 of U.S.Const. prohibit both Congress and the states from passing any *ex post facto* law. Most state constitutions contain similar prohibitions against *ex post facto* laws.

A law which provides for the infliction of punishment upon a person for an act done which, when it was committed, was innocent; a law which aggravates a crime or makes it greater than when it was committed; a law that changes the punishment or inflicts a greater punishment than the law annexed to the crime when it was committed; a law that changes the rules of evidence and receives less or different testimony than was required at the time of the commission of the offense in order to convict the offender; a law which, assuming to regulate civil rights and remedies only, in effect imposes a penalty or the deprivation of a right which, when done, was lawful; a law which deprives persons accused of crime of some lawful protection to which they have become entitled, such as the protection of a former conviction or acquittal, or of the proclamation of amnesty; every law which, in relation to the offense or its consequences, alters the situation of a person to his disadvantage.

Exposure. The act or state of exposing or being exposed. *See* Exposé.

For *Indecent exposure, see* Indecent.

Exposure of child. Placing child in such a place or position as to leave it unprotected against danger to its health or life or subject it to the peril of severe suffering or serious bodily harm.

Exposure of person. In criminal law, such an intentional exposure, in a public place, of the naked body or the private parts as is calculated to shock the feelings of chastity or to corrupt the morals of the community. *See also* Indecent (*Indecent exposure*).

Express. Clear; definite; explicit; plain; direct; unmistakable; not dubious or ambiguous. Declared in terms; set forth in words. Directly and distinctly stated. Made known distinctly and explicitly, and not left to inference. Manifested by direct and appropriate language, as distinguished from that which is inferred from conduct. The word is usually contrasted with "implied."

As to *express* Condition; Consent; Consideration; Contract; Covenant; Dedication; Emancipation; Invitation; Malice; Notice; Obligation; Trust; Waiver; and Warranty, see those titles.

Express abrogation. Abrogation by express provision or enactment; the repeal of a law or provision by a subsequent one, referring directly to it. Abrogation that is literally pronounced by the law either in general terms, as when a final clause abrogates or repeals all laws contrary to the provisions of the new one, or in particular terms, as when it abrogates certain preceding laws which are named.

Express active trust. *See* Trust.

Express assumpsit /əksprés əsə́m(p)sət/. An undertaking to do some act, or to pay a sum of money to another, manifested by express terms. An undertaking made orally, by writing not under seal, or by matter of record, to perform act or to pay sum of money to another. *See also* Assumpsit.

Express authority. Authority delegated to agent by words which expressly authorize him to do a delegable act. Authority which is directly granted to or conferred upon agent in express terms. That authority which principal intentionally confers upon his agent by manifestations to him.

Express common-law dedication. *See* Dedication.

Express conditions. *See* Condition.

Express contract. *See* Contract.

Expressed. Means stated or declared in direct terms; set forth in words; not left to inference or implication. *See* Express.

Expression, freedom of. One of the basic freedoms guaranteed by the First Amendment of U.S. Const. and by most state constitutions. Such is equivalent to freedom of speech, press, or assembly.

Expressio unius est exclusio alterius /əksprésh(iy)ow yənáyəs èst əksklúwz(h)(i)yow òltəráyəs/. A maxim of statutory interpretation meaning that the expression of one thing is the exclusion of another.

Expressio unius personæ est exclusio alterius /əksprésh(iy)ow yənáyəs pərsówniy èst əksklúwz(h)(i)yow òltəráyəs/. The mention of one person is the exclusion of another.

Expressly. In an express manner; in direct or unmistakable terms; explicitly; definitely; directly. The opposite of impliedly.

Express malice. Express malice for purposes of first degree murder includes malice, formed design or intention to kill or to do great bodily harm, and sedate and deliberate mind of which that intention is the product. As used with respect to libel, means publication of defamatory material in bad faith, without belief in the truth of the matter published, or with reckless disregard of the truth or falsity of the matter. *See also* Malice.

Express permission. Within statute respecting automobile owner's liability, includes prior knowledge of intended use and affirmative and active consent thereto.

Express private trust. *See* Trust.

Express repeal. Abrogation or annulment of previously existing law by enactment of subsequent statute declaring that former law shall be revoked or abrogated.

Express republication. Occurs with respect to will when testator repeats ceremonies essential to valid execution, with avowed intention of republishing will.

Express request. That which occurs when one person commands or asks another to do or give something, or answers affirmatively when asked whether another shall do a certain thing.

Express terms. Within provision that qualified acceptance, in "express terms," varies effect of draft, "express terms" means clear, unambiguous, definite, certain, and unequivocal terms.

Express trust. *See* Trust.

Express warranty. *See* Warranty.

Expropriation. A taking, as of privately owned property, by government under eminent domain. This term is also used in the context of a foreign government taking an American industry located in the foreign country. In Louisiana, the word has the same general meaning as eminent domain.

A voluntary surrender of rights or claims; the act of divesting oneself of that which was previously claimed as one's own, or renouncing it. In this sense it is the opposite of "appropriation."

See also Condemnation; Eminent domain.

Expulsion. A putting or driving out. Ejectment; banishment; a cutting off from the privileges of an institution or society permanently. The act of depriving a member of a corporation, legislative body, assembly, society, commercial organization, etc., of his membership in the same, by a legal vote of the body itself, for breach of duty, improper conduct, or other sufficient cause. Also, in the law of torts and of landlord and tenant, an eviction or forcible putting out. *See* Deportation; Ejectment; Eviction; Expel; Forcible entry and detainer; Process (*Summary process*).

Expunge /əkspə́nj/. To destroy; blot out; obliterate; erase; efface designedly; strike out wholly. The act of physically destroying information—including criminal records—in files, computers, or other depositories.

Expungement of record. Process by which record of criminal conviction is destroyed or sealed after expiration of time. Some states also provide for expungement of criminal records if arrested person is not convicted (*e.g.* N.J.S.A. 2C:52–6) or in the event of unlawful arrest. *See also* Erasure (*Erasure of record*).

Expurgation /èkspərgéyshən/. The act of purging or cleansing, as where a book is published without its obscene passages.

Expurgator /ékspərgèytər/. One who corrects by expurging.

Ex quasi contractu /èks kwéysày kəntrǽktyuw/. From *quasi* contract.

Ex rel. *See* Ex relatione.

Ex relatione /èks rəlèyshiyówniy/. Upon relation or information.

Legal proceedings which are instituted by the attorney general (or other proper person) in the name and behalf of the state, but on the information and at the instigation of an individual who has a private interest in the matter, are said to be taken "on the relation" *(ex relatione)* of such person, who is called the "relator." Such a cause is usually entitled thus: "State *ex rel.* Doe *v.* Roe."

In the books of reports, when a case is said to be reported *ex relatione,* it is meant that the reporter derives his account of it, not from personal knowledge, but from the relation or narrative of some person who was present at the argument.

Ex rights. Literally, without rights. A stock sells *ex rights* when stock purchasers no longer receive the rights along with the shares purchased. Such stock is sold without privileged subscription rights to a current new issue by a corporation. Refers to the date on which a purchaser of publicly traded shares is not entitled to receive rights that have been declared on the shares.

Ex-rights date. The date on which a share of common stock begins trading ex-rights.

Ex ship. Words in a contract for the sale of goods denoting that risk of loss shall pass to the buyer upon the goods leaving the ship. Buyer is responsible for any subsequent landing charges. UCC § 2–322. *See also* Ship.

Ex tempore /èks témpəriy/. From or in consequence of time; by lapse of time. *Ex diuturno tempore,* from length of time. Without preparation or premeditation.

Extend. Term lends itself to great variety of meanings, which must in each case be gathered from context. It may mean to expand, enlarge, prolong, lengthen, widen, carry or draw out further than the original limit; *e.g.,* to extend the time for filing an answer, to extend a lease, term of office, charter, railroad track, etc. To stretch out or to draw out. *See also* Extension; Renewal.

Extended. A lengthening out of time previously fixed and not the arbitrary setting of a new date. Stretched, spread, or drawn out.

Extended coverage clause. Provision in insurance policy which carries protection for hazards beyond those covered (or excluded) in the basic policy. *See also* Omnibus clause.

Extended warranty. *See* Warranty (*Extended service warranty*).

Extension. An increase in length of time specified in contract (*e.g.* of expiration date of lease, or due date of note). *See also* Grace period.

A part constituting an addition or enlargement, as an annex to a building or an extension to a house. Addition of existing facilities. Enlargement of main body; addition of something smaller than that to which it is attached; to cause to reach or continue as from point to point; to lengthen or prolong. That property of a body by which it occupies a portion of space.

Commercial law. An allowance of additional time for the payment of debts. An agreement between a debtor and his creditors, by which they allow him further time for the payment of his liabilities. A creditor's indulgence by giving a debtor further time to pay an existing debt. *See* Bankruptcy proceedings.

Lease. The word "extension," when used in its proper and usual sense in connection with a lease, means a prolongation of the previous leasehold estate. The distinction between "extension" and "renewal" of lease is chiefly that, in the case of renewal, a new lease is requisite, while, in the case of extension, the same lease continues in force during additional period upon performance of stipulated act. An option for renewal implies giving of new lease on same terms as old lease, while an option for extension contemplates a continuance of old lease for a further period.

Patents. Extension of life of patent for an additional statutorily allowed period.

Taxes. Request for additional time to file income tax return beyond due date.

Time. Extensions of time for performing an act that is otherwise to be done within time specified by court rule or order in civil actions is governed by Fed.R. Civil P. 6, in criminal actions by Fed.R. Crim.P. 45, and in appeals by Fed.R.App.P. 26.

Extension agreements. Those agreements which provide for further time in which performance of the basic agreement may be performed. *See e.g.* Warranty (*Extended service warranty*).

Extension or renewal of note. Takes place when parties agree upon valuable consideration for maturity of debt on day subsequent to that provided in original contract.

Extensive. Widely extended in space, time, or scope; great or wide or capable of being extended.

Extent. Amount; scope; range; magnitude.

Extenuate /əkstényuweyt/. To lessen; to palliate; to mitigate.

Extenuating circumstances. Such as render a delict or crime less aggravated, heinous, or reprehensible than it would otherwise be, or tend to palliate or lessen its guilt. Such circumstances may ordinarily be shown in order to reduce the punishment or damages. In contract law, unusual or extraordinary events that prevent performance within specified time (*e.g.*, strike by workers or suppliers). *See also* Extraordinary circumstances; Mitigating circumstances.

Extenuation. That which renders a crime or tort less heinous than it would be without it. It is opposed to aggravation. *See* Extenuating circumstances.

External. Apparent, outward, visible from the outside, patent, exterior, capable of being perceived. Acting from without, as the external surface of a body; physical or corporeal, as distinguished from mental or moral.

Exterritoriality. The privilege of those persons (such as foreign ministers) who, though temporarily resident within a country, are not subject to the operation of its laws. The exemption from the operation of the ordinary laws of the country accorded to foreign monarchs temporarily within the country and their retinue, to diplomatic agents and the members of their household, and to others of similar position and rank. *See* Capitulation.

Extinct. Extinguished. No longer in existence or use. Lacking a claimant. *See* Extinguishment.

Extinguish. To bring or put an end to. To terminate or cancel. To put out, quench, stifle, as to extinguish a fire or flame. *See also* Cancellation; Termination.

Extinguishment. The destruction or cancellation of a right, power, contract, or estate. The annihilation of a collateral thing or subject in the subject itself out of which it is derived. *See* Cancellation.

Term is sometimes confounded with "merger," though there is a clear distinction between them. "Merger" is only a mode of extinguishment, and applies to estates only under particular circumstances; but "extinguishment" is a term of general application to rights, as well as estates. "Extinguishment" connotes the end of a thing, precluding the existence of future life therein; in "mergers" there is a carrying on of the substance of the thing, except that it is merged into and becomes a part of a separate thing with a new identity.

Extinguishment of debts. This takes place by payment; by accord and satisfaction; by novation, or the substitution of a new debtor; by merger, when the creditor recovers a judgment or accepts a security of a higher nature than the original obligation; by a release; by bankruptcy; and where one of the parties, debtor or creditor,

makes the other his executor. *See also* Bankruptcy proceedings.

Extinguishment of legacy. This occurs in case the identical thing bequeathed is not in existence, or has been disposed of so that it does not form part of the testator's estate, at the time of his death. *See* Ademption.

Extinguishment of lien. Discharge by operation of law.

Extinguishment of rent. If a person has a yearly rent of lands, and afterwards purchases those lands, so that he has as good an estate in the land as in the rent, the rent is extinguished. Rent may also be extinguished by conjunction of estates, by confirmation, by grant, by release, and by surrender.

Extinguishment of ways. This is usually effected by unity of possession, as if a man had a way over the close of another, and he purchased that close, the way is extinguished.

Extort. To compel or coerce, as a confession or information by any means serving to overcome one's power of resistance, thus making the confession or admission involuntary. To gain by wrongful methods; to obtain in an unlawful manner, as to compel payments by means of threats of injury to person, property, or reputation. To exact something wrongfully by threats or putting in fear. The natural meaning of the word "extort" is to obtain money or other valuable thing either by compulsion, by actual force, or by the force of motives applied to the will, and often more overpowering and irresistible than physical force. *See also* Extortion.

Extortion. The obtaining of property from another induced by wrongful use of actual or threatened force, violence, or fear, or under color of official right. 18 U.S.C.A. § 871 et seq.; § 1951.

A person is guilty of theft by extortion if he purposely obtains property of another by threatening to: (1) inflict bodily injury on anyone or commit any other criminal offense; or (2) accuse anyone of a criminal offense; or (3) expose any secret tending to subject any person to hatred, contempt or ridicule, or to impair his credit or business repute; or (4) take or withhold action as an official, or cause an official to take or withhold action; or (5) bring about or continue a strike, boycott or other collective unofficial action, if the property is not demanded or received for the benefit of the group in whose interest the actor purports to act; or (6) testify or provide information or withhold testimony or information with respect to another's legal claim or defense; or (7) inflict any other harm which would not benefit the actor. Model Penal Code, § 223.4.

See also Blackmail; Hobbs Act; Loansharking; Shakedown. With respect to *Larceny by extortion*, *see* Larceny. *Compare* Coercion. For the distinction between *extortion* and *exaction, see* Exaction.

Extortionate credit. *See* Loansharking.

Extra /ékstrə/. A Latin preposition, occurring in many legal phrases, and meaning beyond, except, without, out of, outside. Additional.

Extract, *v.* To draw out or forth; to pull out from a fixed position.

Extract, *n.* A portion or segment of a writing.

Extradition. The surrender by one state or country to another of an individual accused or convicted of an offense outside its own territory and within the territorial jurisdiction of the other, which, being competent to try and punish him, demands the surrender. U.S.Const., Art. IV, § 2; 18 U.S.C.A. § 3181 *et seq.* Most states have adopted the Uniform Criminal Extradition Act. *See also* Fugitive Felon Act; Fugitive from justice; Interstate rendition; Rendition.

Extra dividend. Dividend paid by corporation in cash or stock beyond that which is regularly paid. *See also* Ex dividend; Extraordinary dividend.

Extrajudicial /èkstrəjuwdíshəl/. That which is done, given, or effected outside the course of regular judicial proceedings. Not founded upon, or unconnected with, the action of a court of law, as *e.g.* extrajudicial evidence, or an extrajudicial oath.

That which, though done in the course of regular judicial proceedings, is unnecessary to such proceedings, or interpolated, or beyond their scope; as an extrajudicial opinion *(dictum).*

That which does not belong to the judge or his jurisdiction, notwithstanding fact that he takes cognizance of it.

See also Alternative dispute resolution; Self-help.

Extrajudicial confession /èkstrəjuwdíshəl kənféshən/. *See* Confession.

Extrajudicial evidence. That which is used to satisfy private persons as to facts requiring proof.

Extrajudicial oath. One taken not in the course of judicial proceedings, or taken without any authority of law, though taken formally before a proper person.

Extrajudicial statement. Any utterance, written or oral, made outside of court. It is governed by the hearsay rule and its exceptions when offered in court as evidence.

Extra judicium /ékstrə jədish(iy)əm/. Extrajudicial; out of the proper cause; out of court; beyond the jurisdiction. *See* Extrajudicial.

Extra jus /ékstrə jə́s/. Beyond the law; more than the law requires.

Extralateral right. In mining law, the right of the owner of a mining claim duly located on the

public domain to follow, and mine, any vein or lode the apex of which lies within the boundaries of his location on the surface, notwithstanding the course of the vein on its dip or downward direction may so far depart from the perpendicular as to extend beyond the planes which would be formed by the vertical extension downwards of the side lines of his location.

Extramural /èkstrəmyúrəl/. As applied to the powers of a municipal corporation, its "extramural" powers are those exercised outside the corporate limits, as distinguished from "intramural".

Extranational. Beyond the territorial and governing limits of a country. *See also* Extraterritorial.

Extraneous evidence. With reference to a contract, deed, will, or any writing, extraneous evidence is such as is not furnished by the document itself, but is derived from outside sources; the same as evidence *aliunde. See also* Aliunde; Immaterial evidence; Parol evidence rule.

Extraneous offense. One that is extra, beyond, or foreign to the offense for which the party is on trial.

Extraneous questions. Issues which are beyond or beside the point to be decided. *See* Irrelevancy.

Extraordinary. Out of the ordinary; exceeding the usual, average, or normal measure or degree; beyond or out of the common order, method, or rule; not usual, regular, or of a customary kind; remarkable; uncommon; rare; employed for an exceptional purpose or on a special occasion. Beyond or out of the common order or method; exceeding the ordinary degree; not ordinary; unusual; employed for an exceptional purpose or on a special occasion. The word is both comprehensive and flexible in meaning.

Extraordinary average. In admiralty law, a contribution by all the parties concerned in a commercial voyage, either as to the vessel or cargo, toward a loss sustained by some of the parties in interest for the benefit of all.

Extraordinary care. Synonymous with greatest care, utmost care, highest degree of care. *See* Care; Diligence; Negligence.

Extraordinary circumstances. Factors of time, place, etc., which are not usually associated with a particular thing or event; out of the ordinary factors. *See also* Extenuating circumstances; Mitigating circumstances.

The "extraordinary circumstances" justifying federal equitable intervention in pending state criminal prosecution must be extraordinary in the sense of creating an extraordinary pressing need for immediate federal equitable relief, not merely in the sense of presenting a highly unusual factual situation.

Extraordinary danger. Danger or risk of employment, not ordinarily incident to the service. *See also* Extraordinary hazard; Extraordinary risk.

Extraordinary dividend. Dividend of corporation which is nonrepetitive and generally paid at irregular time because of some unusual corporate event (*e.g.* unusually high profits). An "extraordinary dividend" is distinguished from an "ordinary dividend" or "regular dividend" in that it is not declared from ordinary profits arising out of regular course of business of corporation and is generally declared by reasons of unusually large income or unexpected increment in capital assets due to fortuitous conditions or circumstances occurring outside of activities and control of corporation but advantageous to corporation either in stepping up its product and sales or in giving added value to its property. *See also* Extra dividend.

Cash disbursements by "wasting asset" companies are apportioned as "extraordinary dividends" where they represent, in part at least, distribution of proceeds of capital assets.

Extraordinary expenses. An expense characterized by its unusual nature and infrequency of occurrence; *e.g.* plant abandonment, goodwill write-off, large product liability judgment.

This term in a constitutional provision that the state may incur indebtedness for extraordinary expenses, means other than ordinary expenses and such as are incurred by the state for the promotion of the general welfare, compelled by some unforeseen condition which is not regularly provided for by law, such as flood, famine, fire, earthquake, pestilence, war, or any other condition that will compel the state to put forward its highest endeavors to protect the people, their property, liberty, or lives.

Extraordinary flood. A flood whose unexplained occurrences is not foreshadowed by the usual course of nature, and whose magnitude and destructiveness could not have been anticipated or provided against by the exercise of ordinary foresight. One of such unusual occurrence that it could not have been foreseen by men of ordinary experience and prudence.

Extraordinary gain or loss. A gain or loss that is both unusual and infrequent; *e.g.*, gain from sale of a significant segment of a business, loss resulting from an earthquake.

Extraordinary grand jury. Such jury is limited in scope of its investigation and may not go beyond terms of executive proclamation, and examination of witness must be confined within those terms, and must not be used as a means of disclosing or intermeddling with extraneous matters.

Extraordinary hazard. One not commonly associated with a job or undertaking. If hazards are increased by what other employees do, and injured employee has no part in increasing them, they are "extraordinary". *See also* Extraordinary risk.

Extraordinary remedies. The writs of *mandamus, quo warranto, habeas corpus,* and some others are often classified or termed "extraordinary remedies," in contradistinction to the ordinary remedy by civil action.

Under Rules practice in the federal courts and most states, most extraordinary "writs" have been abolished. In any action seeking relief formerly obtainable under any such writ, the procedure shall follow that of a regular action. See Fed.R. Civ.P. 60(b), 81(b).

Extraordinary repairs. Within the meaning of a lease, such repairs as are made necessary by some unusual or unforeseen occurrence which does not destroy the building but merely renders it less suited to the use for which it was intended. In lease provisions for "extraordinary" repairs, word "extraordinary" means beyond or out of common order of rule, not the usual, customary or regular kind, not ordinary.

Extraordinary risk. A risk lying outside of the sphere of the normal, arising out of conditions not usual in the business. It is one which is not normally and necessarily incident to the employment, and is one which may be obviated by the exercise of reasonable care by the employer. *See also* Extraordinary hazard.

Extraordinary session. A legislative session, called usually by the governor, which meets in the interval between regular sessions to handle specific legislation. In most states such sessions are limited to the consideration of matters specified in the governor's call. *See also* Extra session, *supra.*

Extraordinary writs. *See* Extraordinary remedies.

Extrapolation. The process of estimating an unknown number outside the range of known numbers. Term sometimes used in cases when a court deduces a principle of law from another case.

Extra session. After a Legislature has adjourned or prorogued, it may be recalled for an additional session by the Governor to deal with matters which could not be considered during the regular term. Also, a court may provide additional court sessions to eliminate or reduce a case backlog. *See also* Extraordinary session.

Extraterritorial. Beyond the physical and juridical boundaries of a particular state or country. *See* Extraterritoriality.

Extraterritoriality. The extraterritorial operation of laws; that is, their operation upon persons, rights, or jural relations, existing beyond the limits of the enacting state or nation, but still amenable to its laws. A term used, especially formerly, to express, in lieu of the word exterritoriality the exemption from the obligation of the laws of a state granted to foreign diplomatic agents, warships, etc. The term is used to indicate jurisdiction exercised by a nation in other countries by treaty, or by its own ministers or consuls in foreign lands. Crime is said to be extraterritorial when committed in a state or country other than that of the forum in which the party is tried.

Extraterritorial jurisdiction. Juridical power which extends beyond the physical limits of a particular state or country. *See* Long arm statutes.

Extra vires /ékstrə váyriyz/. Beyond powers.

Extra work. As used in connection with construction contract, means work done not required in performance of the contract, *i.e.* something done or furnished in addition to or in excess of the requirement of the contract. Work entirely outside and independent of contract—something not required or contemplated in its performance.

Extra work, for which a contractor is entitled to charge additional compensation, depends on construction of the original contract, and generally means only labor and materials not contemplated by or embraced in terms of the original contract. Such work is usually defined as being work not foreseen at time of entrance into contract. Materials and labor not contemplated by the contract, but which are required by changes in the plans and specifications made after the contract had been entered into, are "extra work".

Extreme. At the utmost point, edge, or border; most remote. Last; conclusive. Greatest, highest, strongest, or the like. Immoderate; violent.

Extreme case. One in which the facts or the law or both reach the outer limits of probability; desperate.

Extreme cruelty. As grounds for divorce, may consist of personal injury or physical violence or it may be acts or omissions of such character as to destroy peace of mind or impair bodily or mental health of person upon whom inflicted or be such as to destroy the objects of matrimony.

Extremis /(ìn) əkstríyməs/. When a person is sick, beyond the hope of recovery, and near death, he is said to be in *extremis*. *See also* In extremis.

Extremity. The furthest point, section, or part. Limb of the body (hand or foot). Extreme danger or need. Desperate act or measure.

Extrinsic. Foreign; from outside sources; *dehors*. As to *Extrinsic fraud, see* Fraud.

Extrinsic ambiguity. In a written contract, such is an uncertainty which does not arise by the terms of the instrument itself, but is created by some collateral matter not appearing in the instrument.

Extrinsic evidence. External evidence, or that which is not contained in the body of an agreement, contract, and the like. Evidence which does not appear on the face of a document, but which is available from other sources such as statements by the parties and other circumstances surrounding the transaction. Extrinsic evidence is also said to be evidence not legitimately before the tribunal in which the determination is made. *See* Parol evidence rule.

Extrinsic fraud. *See* Fraud.

Ex warrants. A security is traded "ex warrants" when sold without warrants which have been retained by seller.

Eyewitness. A person who can testify as to what he has seen from personal observation. One who saw the act, fact, or transaction to which he testifies. Distinguished from an ear-witness *(auritus)*.

Eyewitness identification. Type of evidence by which one who has seen the event testifies as to the person or persons involved from his own memory of the event. *See also* Lineup.

F

F. Under the old English criminal law, this letter was branded upon felons upon their being admitted to clergy; as also upon those convicted of fights or frays, or falsity.

Federal Reporter, First Series. *See* Federal Reporter.

F.2d. Federal Reporter, Second Series. *See* Federal Reporter.

F.A.A. *See* Federal Aviation Administration. In maritime insurance means: "Free of all average", denoting that the insurance is against total loss only.

Fabricate. To invent; to devise falsely. *See also* Counterfeit; Forgery.

Fabricated evidence. Evidence manufactured or arranged after the fact, and either wholly false or else warped and discolored by artifice and contrivance with a deceitful intent. To fabricate evidence is to arrange or manufacture circumstances or *indicia,* after the fact committed, with the purpose of using them as evidence, and of deceitfully making them appear as if accidental and undesigned. To devise falsely or contrive by artifice with the intention to deceive. Such evidence may be wholly forged and artificial, or it may consist in so warping and distorting real facts as to create an erroneous impression in the minds of those who observe them and then presenting such impression as true and genuine. *See also* Fabricated fact; Perjury.

Fabricated fact. In the law of evidence, a fact existing only in statement, without any foundation in truth. An actual or genuine fact to which a false appearance has been designedly given; a physical object placed in a false connection with another, or with a person on whom it is designed to cast suspicion. *See also* Deceit; False fact; Fraud; Perjury.

Face. The surface of anything, especially the front, upper, or outer part or surface. That which particularly offers itself to the view of a spectator. The words of a written paper in their apparent or obvious meaning, as, the face of a note, bill, bond, check, draft, judgment record, or contract. The face of a judgment for which it was rendered exclusive of interest.

Face amount. The face amount of an instrument is that shown by the mere language employed, and excludes any accrued interest. *See* Face of instrument; Face value.

Face amount insured by the policy. Within statute relating to extended life insurance, means the amount which is, in all events, payable under the policy as straight life insurance without regard to additional features such as accident or disability insurance. *See also* Face value.

Face of instrument. That which is shown by the language employed, without any explanation, modification, or addition from extrinsic facts or evidence. Thus, if the express terms of the paper disclose a fatal legal defect, it is said to be "void on its face." Regarded as an evidence of debt, the face of an instrument is the principal sum which it expresses to be due or payable, without any additions in the way of interest or costs. *See also* Face value.

Face of judgment. The sum for which it was rendered, exclusive of interest.

Face of record. The entire record in a case, not merely what the judgment recites. Every part of trial proceedings reserved in courts of record under direction of court for purpose of its records. In a criminal case, means the indictment and the verdict. *See also* Record.

Face value. The value of an insurance policy, bond, note, mortgage, or other security, as given on the certificate or instrument, payable upon maturity of the instrument. The face value is also the amount on which interest or coupon payments are calculated. Thus, a 10% bond with face value of $1000 pays bondholders $100 per year. Face value is also often referred to as the par value or nominal value of the instrument. The value which can be ascertained from the language of the instrument without aid from extrinsic facts or evidence. *See also* Face amount. *Compare* Market value.

Facias /féys(h)(i)yəs/. That you cause.

Occurring in the phrases *"scire facias"* (that you cause to know), *"fieri facias"* (that you cause to be made), etc. Used also in the phrases *Do ut facias* (I give that you may do), *Facio ut facias* (I do that you may do), two of the four divisions of considerations made by Blackstone.

Facilitate. To free from difficulty or impediment. Within statute prohibiting use of facilities of interstate commerce with intent to promote, manage, facilitate, or carry on unlawful activity

409

means to make easy or less difficult. *See also* Facilitation; Facilities.

Facilitation. In criminal law, the act of making it easier for another to commit crime; *e.g.* changing of cars to evade police officer who has suspect under surveillance and thus to enable a clandestine transfer of contraband to take place would constitute "facilitation" within forfeiture statute. *See also* Accomplice; Aid and abet.

Facilities. That which promotes the ease of any action, operation, transaction, or course of conduct. The term normally denotes inanimate means rather than human agencies, though it may also include animate beings such as persons, people and groups thereof.

The term embraces anything which aids or makes easier the performance of the activities involved in the business of a person or corporation.

Facility. Something that is built or installed to perform some particular function, but it also means something that promotes the ease of any action or course of conduct. *See also* Facilities.

Facility of payment clause. Provision in insurance policy providing for appointment by insured and beneficiary of persons authorized to receive payment. It confers on insurer an option as to whom it will make payment.

Facsimile /fæksíməliy/. An exact copy, preserving all the marks of the original.

Facsimile signature. One which has been prepared and reproduced by some mechanical or photographic process. Many states have adopted the Uniform Facsimile Signatures of Public Officials Act.

Fact. A thing done; an action performed or an incident transpiring; an event or circumstance; an actual occurrence; an actual happening in time or space or an event mental or physical; that which has taken place. A fact is either a state of things, that is, an existence, or a motion, that is, an event. The quality of being actual; actual existence or occurrence.

Evidence. A circumstance, event or occurrence as it actually takes or took place; a physical object or appearance, as it usually exists or existed. An actual and absolute reality, as distinguished from mere supposition or opinion. A truth, as distinguished from fiction or error. "Fact" means reality of events or things the actual occurrence or existence of which is to be determined by evidence. Under Rule of Civil Procedure 41(b), providing for motion for dismissal at close of plaintiff's evidence in nonjury case on ground that upon the facts and the law plaintiff has shown no right to relief, the "facts" referred to are the prima facie facts shown by plaintiff's evidence viewed in light most favorable to him.

Fact and law distinguished. "Fact" is very frequently used in opposition or contrast to "law". Thus, questions of *fact* are for the jury; questions of *law* for the court. *E.g.* fraud *in fact* consists in an actual intention to defraud, carried into effect; while fraud imputed by *law* arises from the person's conduct in its necessary relations and consequences. A "fact", as distinguished from the "law", may be taken as that out of which the point of law arises, that which is asserted to be or not to be, and is to be presumed or proved to be or not to be for the purpose of applying or refusing to apply a rule of law. Law is a principle; fact is an event. Law is conceived; fact is actual. Law is a rule of duty; fact is that which has been according to or in contravention of the rule. *See* E.g. Fact question.

See also Adjudicative facts; Collateral facts; Dispositive facts; Evidentiary facts; Fabricated fact; Fact question; Finding (*Finding of fact*); Material fact; Principal (*Principal fact*); Ultimate facts.

Fact finder. Person or persons appointed by business, government, or by court to investigate, hear testimony from witnesses, or otherwise determine and report facts concerning a particular event, situation, or dispute (*e.g.*, jury; administrative hearing officer). *See also* Trier of fact.

Fact finding board. A group or committee appointed by business, labor organization, government, or similar body to investigate and report facts concerning some event or situation.

The right or capacity of taking by will; called *"factio passiva."*

Fact material to risk. *See* Material fact.

Facto /fǽktow/. In fact; by an act; by the act or fact. *Ipso facto,* by the act itself; by the mere effect of a fact, without anything superadded, or any proceeding upon it to give it effect.

Facto et animo /fǽktow èt ǽnəmow/. In fact and intent.

Factor. At common law, a commercial agent, employed by a principal to sell merchandise consigned to him for that purpose, for and in behalf of the principal, but usually in his own name, being entrusted with the possession and control of the goods, and being remunerated by a commission, commonly called "factorage." A commercial agent to whom the possession of personalty is entrusted by or for the owner, to be sold, for a compensation, in pursuance of the agent's usual trade or business, with title to goods remaining in principal and the "factor" being merely a bailee for the purposes of the agency.

A firm (typically a finance company) that purchases a firm's receivables at a discount and is responsible for processing and collecting the balances of these accounts. Financier who generally lends money and takes in return an assignment of accounts receivable or some other security. *See* Factoring.

See also Commission merchant; Jobber.

Any circumstance or influence which brings about or contributes to a result such as a factor of production.

Broker and factor distinguished. A factor differs from a "broker" in that he is entrusted with the possession, management, and control of the goods (which gives him a special property in them); while a broker acts as a mere intermediary without control or possession of the property. A factor may buy and sell in his own name, as well as in that of the principal, while a broker, as such, cannot ordinarily buy or sell in his own name.

Factorage /fǽkt(ə)rəj/. The wages, allowance, or commission paid to a factor for his services. The business of a factor.

Factor analysis. A statistical procedure that seeks to explain a certain phenomenon (e.g., the actual rate of return on common stock) in terms of the behavior of a specified set of predictive factors.

Factoring. Sale of accounts receivable of a firm to a factor at a discounted price. The purchase of accounts receivable from a business by a factor who thereby assumes the risk of loss in return for some agreed discount. *See* Factor.

Factorizing process. A process by which the effects of a debtor are attached in the hands of a third person. More commonly termed "trustee process", "garnishment", and process by "foreign attachment".

Factor's lien. The right (usually provided by statute) of a factor to keep possession of his principal's merchandise until the latter has settled his account with him.

Factory acts. Laws enacted for the purpose of regulating the hours of work, and the health and safety conditions. *See e.g.* Child labor laws; Fair Labor Standards Act; Occupational Safety and Health Act; Wage and hour laws.

Factory prices. The prices at which goods may be bought at the factories, as distinguished from the prices of goods bought in the market after they have passed into the hands of wholesalers or retailers.

Fact question. Those issues in a trial or hearing which concern facts or events and whether such occurred and how they occurred as contrasted with issues and questions of law. Fact questions are for the jury, unless the issues are presented at a bench trial, while law questions are decided by the judge. Fact questions and their findings are generally not appealable though rulings of law are subject to appeal.

Facts. *See* Fact.

Facts in issue. Those matters of fact on which the plaintiff proceeds by his action, and which the defendant controverts in his defense. Under civil rule practice in the federal courts, and in most state courts, the facts alleged in the initial complaint are usually quite brief, with the development of additional facts being left to discovery and pretrial conference.

Factum /fǽktəm/. A fact, event, deed, act, doing. A statement of facts.

Faculties /fǽkəltiyz/. Abilities; powers; capabilities. In the law of divorce, the capability of the husband to render a support to the wife in the form of alimony, whether temporary or permanent, including not only his tangible property, but also his income and his ability to earn money. *See* Allegation of faculties.

Fail. Fault, negligence, or refusal. Fall short; be unsuccessful or deficient. Fading health. *See* Extremis.

Fail also means: involuntarily to fall short of success or the attainment of one's purpose; to become insolvent and unable to meet one's obligations as they mature; to become or be found deficient or wanting; to keep or cease from an appointed, proper, expected, or required action; to lapse, as a legacy which has never vested or taken effect; to leave unperformed; to omit; to neglect; to be wanting in action. *See also* Failure; Lapse.

Failing circumstances. Insolvency, that is, the lack of sufficient assets to pay one's debts as they become due. A person (or a corporation or institution) is said to be in failing circumstances when he is about to fail, that is, when he is actually insolvent and is acting in contemplation of giving up his business because he is unable to carry it on. *See also* Bankruptcy; Failure to meet obligations.

Failure. Abandonment or defeat. Failure of duty or obligation. Lapse. Deficiency, want, or lack; ineffectualness; inefficiency as measured by some legal standard; an unsuccessful attempt. *See also* Fail; Lapse.

Failure of consideration. As applied to notes, contracts, conveyances, etc., this term does not necessarily mean a want of consideration, but implies that a consideration, originally existing and good, has since become worthless or has ceased to exist or been extinguished, partially or entirely. It means that sufficient consideration was contemplated by the parties at time contract was entered into, but either on account of some innate defect in the thing to be given or nonperformance in whole or in part of that which the promisee agreed to do or forbear nothing of value can be or is received by the promisee. Such consists of neglect, refusal, or failure of one of the parties to perform or furnish agreed-upon consideration.

Failure of evidence. *See* Failure of proof.

Failure of issue. Dying without children. The failure at a fixed time, or the total extinction, of issue to take an estate limited over by an executory devise. A definite failure of issue is when a precise time is fixed by the will for the failure of issue, as in the case where there is a devise to one, but if he dies without issue or lawful issue living at the time of his death, etc. An indefinite failure of issue is the period when the issue or descendants of the first taker shall become extinct, and when there is no longer any issue of the issue of the grantee, without reference to any particular time or any particular event. *See also* Dying without issue.

Failure of justice. The defeat of a particular right, or the failure of reparation for a particular wrong, from the lack or inadequacy of a legal remedy for the enforcement of the one or the redress of the other. The term is also colloquially applied to the miscarriage of justice which occurs when the result of a trial is so palpably wrong as to shock the moral sense. *See also* Miscarriage of justice.

Failure of proof. Inability or failure to prove the cause of action or defense in its entire scope and meaning. Where evidence is such as would support either of two contradictory inferences, or presumptions, respecting the ultimate facts, there is a "failure of proof". *See* Directed verdict; Failure to state cause of action; Non obstante veredicto; Summary judgment.

Failure of record. Failure of the defendant to produce a record which he has alleged and relied on in his plea.

Failure of title. The inability or failure of a vendor to make good title to the whole or a part of the property which he has contracted to sell. *See also* Cloud on title; Curing title; Marketable title.

Failure of trust. The lapsing or nonefficiency of a proposed trust, by reason of the defect or insufficiency of the deed or instrument creating it, or on account of illegality, indefiniteness, or other legal impediment.

Failure otherwise than upon merits. Phrase imports some action by court by which plaintiff is defeated without a trial upon the merits; *e.g.* judgment on pleadings, summary judgment.

Failure to make delivery. Misdelivery or nondelivery. This phrase is fully adequate to cover all cases where delivery has not been made as required.

Failure to meet obligations. Inability or failure to pay debts as due. For example, bank's failure to pay depositors on demand constitutes "failure to meet obligations" in most cases. Where bank closed its doors and ceased to transact business or make transfers of capital stock, and thereafter ordinary deposits could not be drawn out and checks in process of collection were dishonored, returned unpaid, was "failure to meet obligations". *See also* Bankruptcy; Failing circumstances; Insolvency.

Failure to state cause of action. Failure of the plaintiff to allege sufficient facts in the complaint to maintain action. In other words, even if the plaintiff proved all the facts alleged in the complaint, the facts would not establish a cause of action entitling the plaintiff to recover against the defendant. The motion to dismiss for failure to state a cause of action is sometimes referred to as (a) a demurrer (*e.g.* California) or (b) a failure to state a claim upon which relief can be granted. Fed.R.Civ.P. 12(b). *See also* Directed verdict; Summary judgment.

Failure to testify. In a criminal trial, defendant is not required to testify and such failure may not be commented on by judge or prosecution because of protection of Fifth Amendment, U.S.Const. *See also* Self-incrimination.

Fair. Having the qualities of impartiality and honesty; free from prejudice, favoritism, and self-interest. Just; equitable; even-handed; equal, as between conflicting interests. *See also* Equitable; Reasonable.

A gathering of buyers and sellers for purposes of exhibiting and sale of goods; usually accompanied by amusements, contests, entertainment, and the like.

Fair and impartial jury. Jury chosen to hear evidence and render verdict without any fixed opinion concerning the guilt, innocence or liability of defendant. Means that every member of the jury must be a fair and impartial juror. Denotes jurors who are not only fair and impartial, but also qualified. *See* Fair and impartial trial; Impartial jury.

Fair and impartial trial. A hearing by an impartial and disinterested tribunal; a proceeding which hears before it condemns, which proceeds upon inquiry, and renders judgment only after trial consideration of evidence and facts as a whole. A basic constitutional guarantee contained implicitly in the Due Process Clause of Fourteenth Amendment, U.S. Constitution.

One where accused's legal rights are safeguarded and respected. A fair and impartial trial by a jury of one's peers contemplates counsel to look after one's defense, compulsory attendance of witnesses, if need be, and a reasonable time in the light of all prevailing circumstances to investigate, properly prepare, and present the defense. *See also* Impartial jury.

Fair and proper legal assessment. Such as places the value of property on a fair, equal, and uniform basis with other property of like character and value throughout the county and state. *See also* Equalization.

Fair and reasonable value. *See* Fair market value; Fair value; Just compensation.

Fair and valuable consideration. One which is a substantial compensation for the property conveyed, or which is reasonable, in view of the surrounding circumstances and conditions and market value of comparable properties in same vicinity, in contradistinction to an inadequate consideration. *See also* Adequate consideration; Fair consideration; Fair market value; Fair value; Just compensation.

Fair cash market value. Terms "cash market value", "fair market value", "reasonable market value" or "fair cash market value" are substantially synonymous.

Fair cash value. The phrase is practically synonymous with "reasonable value," "fair market value," and "actual cash value," meaning the fair or reasonable cash price for which the property can be sold on the market. Fair cash value for property tax purposes is interpreted as meaning "fair market value" or price that property would bring at a sale where both parties are willing, ready and able to do business and under no duress to do so. The price which someone will pay for it in open market. *See also* Fair market value; Fair value; Just compensation.

Fair comment. A form of qualified privilege applied to news media publications relating to discussion of matters which are of legitimate concern to the community as a whole because they materially affect the interests of all the community. A term used in the defense of libel actions, applying to statements made by a writer (*e.g.*, news media) in an honest belief of their truth, relating to official acts, even though the statements are not true in fact. Fair comment must be based on facts truly stated, must not contain imputations of corrupt or dishonorable motives except as warranted by the facts, and must be honest expression of writer's real opinion. *See also* Fairness *or* equal time doctrine.

Fair competition. Open, equitable, just competition, which is fair as between competitors and as between any of them and his customers. *See* Antitrust acts; Clayton Act; Price-fixing; Sherman Antitrust Act.

Fair consideration. A fair equivalent. One which, under all the circumstances, is honest, reasonable, and free from suspicion. Full and adequate consideration. Good-faith satisfaction of an antecedent debt. One which fairly represents the value of the property transferred. One which is not disproportionate to the value of the property conveyed. A term of fraudulent conveyance law describing whatever is given in exchange for

a conveyance of debtor's property whenever the exchange involves property or other things having substantially equivalent values. *See also* Adequate consideration; Fair cash value; Fair market value; Fair value; Just compensation.

Fair Credit Billing Act. Federal Act designed to facilitate settlement of billing error disputes and to make credit card companies more responsible for the quality of merchandise purchased by cardholders. 15 U.S.C.A. § 1666 et seq.

Fair Credit Reporting Acts. *Federal Act.* This law represents the first Federal regulation of the vast consumer reporting industry, covering all credit bureaus, investigative reporting companies, detective and collection agencies, lenders' exchanges, and computerized information reporting companies. The purpose of this Act is to insure that consumer reporting activities are conducted in a manner that is fair and equitable to the affected consumer, upholding his right to privacy as against the informational demands of others. The consumer is given several important rights, including the right to notice of reporting activities, the right to access to information contained in consumer reports, and the right to correction of erroneous information that may have been the basis for a denial of credit, insurance, or employment. 15 U.S.C.A. § 1681 et seq. *See also* Consumer reporting agency.

State Acts. Typical state acts cover consumer's rights against credit investigatory agencies; prohibit reporting of obsolete information; require that person giving credit disclose to consumer that report is being obtained, and require reporting agency to make copy available to consumer.

Fair Debt Collection Practices Act. Federal act, the purpose of which is to eliminate abusive debt collection practices by debt collectors, to insure that those debt collectors who refrain from using abusive debt collection practices are not competitively disadvantaged, and to promote consistent state action to protect consumers against debt collection abuses. This act also applies to debt collection practices of attorneys. 15 U.S.C.A. § 1692(e). Most states also have statutes regulating debt collection practices.

Fair equivalent. As used in statute providing that fair consideration is given for property exchanged at fair equivalent means value at time of conveyance. "Equivalent" means equal in worth or value; "fair" means equitable as a basis for exchange; reasonable; a fair value.

Fair hearing. One in which authority is fairly exercised; that is, consistently with the fundamental principles of justice embraced within the conception of due process of law. Contemplated in a fair hearing is the right to present evidence, to cross examine, and to have findings supported by evidence. See *e.g.* APA, 5 U.S.C.A. § 556.

Statutes and regulations establish procedures to assure fair hearings for various types of administrative proceedings. For example, fair hearing of an alien's right to enter the United States means a hearing before the immigration officers in accordance with the fundamental principles that inhere in due process of law, and implies that alien shall not only have a fair opportunity to present evidence in his favor, but shall be apprised of the evidence against him, so that at the conclusion of the hearing he may be in a position to know all of the evidence on which the matter is to be decided; it being not enough that the immigration officials meant to be fair.

See also Fair and impartial trial; Full hearing.

Fair knowledge or skill. A reasonable degree of knowledge or measure of skill.

Fair Labor Standards Act. Federal Act (1938) which set a minimum standard wage (periodically increased by later statutes) and a maximum work week of 40 hours in industries engaged in interstate commerce. Such Act also regulates hours of work, and type of work, that can be performed by teen-agers. The Act created the Wage and Hour Division in the Department of Labor. 29 U.S.C.A. § 201 et seq. *See also* Child labor laws; Minimum wage; Wage and hour laws.

Fairly. Equitably, honestly, impartially, reasonably. Justly; rightly. With substantial correctness. "Fairly merchantable" conveys the idea of mediocrity in quality, or something just above it. *See also* Equitable; Fair.

Fair market price. *See* Fair market value.

Fair market value. The amount at which property would change hands between a willing buyer and a willing seller, neither being under any compulsion to buy or sell and both having reasonable knowledge of the relevant facts. By fair market value is meant the price in cash, or its equivalent, that the property would have brought at the time of taking, considering its highest and most profitable use, if then offered for sale in the open market, in competition with other similar properties at or near the location of the property taken, with a reasonable time allowed to find a purchaser. The price that the asset would bring by bona fide bargaining between well-informed buyers and sellers at the date of acquisition. Usually the fair market price will be the price at which bona fide sales have been consummated for assets of like type, quality, and quantity in a particular market at the time of acquisition. *See also* Fair value.

Fairness *or* **equal time doctrine.** This doctrine imposes affirmative responsibilities on the broadcaster to provide coverage of issues of public importance which is adequate and which fairly reflects differing viewpoints. In fulfilling its "Fairness Doctrine" obligations, broadcaster must provide free time for the presentation of opposing views if a paid sponsor is unavailable and must initiate programming on public issues if no one else seeks to do so. Refers to section of Federal Communications Act which provides that major advocates of both sides of political and public issues should be given fair or equal opportunity to broadcast their viewpoints. 47 U.S.C.A. § 315. *See also* Equal Time Act.

Fair on its face. A document "fair on its face" is one which cannot be shown to be illegal without extraneous evidence. A process fair on its face does not mean that it must appear to be perfectly regular or in all respects in accord with proper practice and after the most approved form, but that it shall apparently be process lawfully issued and such as the officer may lawfully serve, and a process is fair on its face which proceeds from a court, magistrate, or body having authority of law to issue process of that nature and which is legal in form and on its face contains nothing to notify or fairly apprise the officer that it is issued without authority.

Fair persuasion. Argument, exhortation, or entreaty addressed to a person without threat of physical harm or economic loss, or persistent molestation or harassment or material and fraudulent misrepresentations. *Compare* Duress; Undue influence.

Fair play. Equity, justice and decency in dealings with another. *See* Arm's length transaction; Equity.

Fair preponderance of evidence. Evidence sufficient to create in the minds of the triers of fact the conviction that the party upon whom is the burden has established its case. The greater and weightier evidence; the more convincing evidence. Such a superiority of evidence on one side that the fact of its outweighing the evidence on the other side can be perceived if the whole evidence is fairly considered. Such evidence as when weighed with that which is offered to oppose it, has more convincing power in the minds of the jury. The term conveys the idea of something more than a preponderance. The term is not a technical term, but simply means that evidence which outweighs that which is offered to oppose it, and does not necessarily mean the greater number of witnesses. *See also* Burden of proof; Preponderance of evidence.

Fair rate of return. Amount of profits that a public utility is permitted to earn as determined by public utility commissions. Such is based on the need of the utility to maintain service to customers, finance expenditures for improvements and expansion, pay dividends to shareholders, etc. *See also* Fair return on investment.

Fair representation. Refers to the duty of a union to represent fairly all its members, both in the conduct of collective bargaining and in the enforcement of the resulting agreement, and to serve the interests of all members without hostility or discrimination toward any and to exercise its discretion with complete good faith and honesty and to avoid arbitrary conduct.

Fair return on investment. A "fair return" is to be largely measured by usual returns in like investments in the same vicinity over the same period of time. Reasonable profit on sale or holding of investment assets. A fair return on value of property used and useful in carrying on the enterprise, performing the service or supplying the thing for which the rates are paid. Term is generally used in reference to setting of rates for public utilities. *See also* Fair rate of return.

Fair sale. In foreclosure and other judicial proceedings, this means a sale conducted with fairness and impartiality as respects the rights and interests of the parties affected. A sale at a price sufficient to warrant confirmation or approval when it is required.

Fair trade laws. State statutes which permit manufacturers or distributors of namebrand goods to fix minimum retail prices. Following a series of court decisions striking down such statutes, Congress in 1976 repealed such statutes.

Fair trial. *See* Fair and impartial trial.

Fair use doctrine. A privilege in others than the owner of a copyright to use the copyrighted material in a reasonable manner without the owner's consent, notwithstanding the monopoly granted to the owner. To determine whether fair use has been made of copyrighted material, the nature and objects of the selections made, the quantity and value of material used and extent to which the use may diminish the value of the original work must be considered.

Fair use involves a balancing process by which a complex of variables determine whether other interests should override the rights of creators. The Copyright Act explicitly identifies four interests: (1) the purpose and character of the use, including its commercial nature; (2) the nature of the copyrighted work; (3) the proportion that was "taken"; and (4) the economic impact of the "taking." 17 U.S.C.A. § 107.

Fair value. Present market value. Price which a seller, willing but not compelled to sell, would take, and a purchaser, willing but not compelled to buy, would pay. Such a price as a capable and diligent business man could presently obtain from the property after conferring with those accustomed to buy such property; the amount the property would bring at a sale on execution shown to have been in all respects fair and reasonable; the fair market value of the property as

between one who wants to purchase and one who wants to sell the property. Where no definite market value can be established and expert testimony must be relied on, fair valuation is the amount which the property ought to give to a going concern as a fair return, if sold to some one who is willing to purchase under ordinary selling conditions. In determining "fair valuation" of property, court should consider all elements entering into the intrinsic value, as well as the selling value, and also the earning power of the property.

Among elements to be considered in arriving at "fair value" or "fair cash value" of stock of a stockholder who dissents from a sale of corporate assets are its market value, net asset value, investment value, and earning capacity.

"Actual value," "market value," "fair value," and the like, are commonly used as convertible terms. *See also* Fair market value.

Fait accompli. Fact or deed accomplished, presumably irreversible.

Faith. Confidence; credit; reliance. Thus, an act may be said to be done "on the faith" of certain representations.

Belief; credence; trust. Thus, the Constitution provides that "full faith and credit" shall be given to the judgments of each state in the courts of the others.

Purpose; intent; sincerity; state of knowledge or design. This is the meaning of the word in the phrases "good faith" and "bad faith." *See* Good faith.

Faithful. Honest; loyal; trustworthy; reliable; allegiant; conscientious. As used in the rule that executors must be "faithful," means that they must act in good faith. *See also* Good faith.

Faithfully. Conscientious diligence or faithfulness in meeting obligations, or just regard of adherence to duty, or due observance of undertaking of contract. Diligently, and without unnecessary delay. Truthfully, sincerely, accurately.

As used in bonds of public and private officers, this term imports not only honesty, but also a punctilious discharge of all the duties of the office, requiring competence, diligence, and attention, without any malfeasance or nonfeasance, aside from mere mistakes.

Fake. To make or construct falsely. A "faked alibi" is a made, manufactured, or false alibi. Something that is not what it purports to be; counterfeit. An imposter. *See* Counterfeit; Forgery.

Faker. A swindler; an imposter.

Fall. To come within limits, scope, or jurisdiction of something. To decrease in value. To recede, as a depression or recession in the economy.

Fallow-land. Land plowed, but not sown, and left uncultivated for a time after successive crops. Land tilled, but left unseeded during the growing season.

False. Not true. Term also means: artificial; counterfeit; assumed or designed to deceive; contrary to fact; deceitful; deliberately and knowingly false; designedly untrue; erroneous; hypocritical; sham; feigned; incorrect; intentionally untrue; not according to truth or reality; not genuine or real; uttering falsehood; unveracious; given to deceit; dishonest; wilfully and intentionally untrue.

The word has two distinct and well-recognized meanings: (1) intentionally or knowingly or negligently untrue; (2) untrue by mistake or accident, or honestly after the exercise of reasonable care. A thing is called "false" when it is done, or made, with knowledge, actual or constructive, that it is untrue or illegal, or is said to be done falsely when the meaning is that the party is in fault for its error. A statement (including a statement in a claim or document), is "false" if it was untrue by the person making it, or causing it to be made.

See also Alteration; Bogus; Counterfeit; Falsely; False representation; Falsify; Forgery; Fraud; Misrepresentation; Perjury.

False action. *See* Feigned action.

False and fraudulent. *See* False representation; Fraud.

False answer. In pleading, a sham answer; one which is false in the sense of being a mere pretense set up in bad faith and without color of fact. Such answer may be ordered stricken on motion. Fed.R. Civil P. 12(f).

False arrest. A species of false imprisonment, consisting of the detention of a person without his or her consent and without lawful authority. Such arrest consists in unlawful restraint of an individual's personal liberty or freedom of locomotion. An arrest without proper legal authority is a false arrest and because an arrest restrains the liberty of a person it is also false imprisonment. The gist of the tort is protection of the personal interest in freedom from restraint of movement. Neither ill will nor malice are elements of the tort, but if these elements are shown, punitive damages may be awarded in addition to compensatory or nominal damages. *See also* Imprisonment *(False imprisonment)*; Malicious prosecution.

False checks. Offense of obtaining money by means and use of a check upon a bank, in which the drawer at the time had no funds or credit with which to meet the same, and which he had no reason to believe would honor such check upon presentation at said bank for payment. *See also* Kiting.

False claim. A statement or a claim which is not true.

False Claims Act. Federal act providing for civil and criminal penalties against individuals who knowingly present or cause to be presented to the government a false claim or bill, or deliver less property to the government than what is billed for, or make or use a false record to decrease an obligation to the government. The statute provides for enforcement of its provisions either by the U.S. Attorney General or in "qui tam" actions by private persons. 18 U.S.C.A. §§ 286, 287; 31 U.S.C.A. §§ 3729–3733. *See also* Qui tam action.

False entry. An untrue statement of items of account by written words, figures, or marks. One making an original false entry makes a false entry in every book which is made up in regular course from the entry or entries from the original book of entry.

An entry in books of a bank or trust company which is intentionally made to represent what is not true or does not exist, with intent either to deceive its officers or a bank examiner or to defraud the bank or trust company.

False fact. In the law of evidence, a feigned, simulated, or fabricated fact; a fact not founded in truth, but existing only in assertion; the deceitful semblance of a fact. *See* Fabricated fact; Perjury.

Falsehood. A statement or assertion known to be untrue, and intended to deceive. A willful act or declaration contrary to the truth. It is committed either by the wilful act of the party, or by dissimulation, or by words. A fabrication. *See* False; False fact; Perjury.

False impersonation. The criminal offense of falsely representing some other person and acting in the character thus unlawfully assumed, in order to deceive others, and thereby gain some profit or advantage, or enjoy some right or privilege belonging to the one so personated, or subject him to some expense, charge, or. liability. To impersonate another falsely, and in such assumed character to do any act whereby any benefit might accrue to the offender or to another person. *See also* Impersonation; Personate.

False implication libel. Type of libel action by public figure against news media alleging that news article created a false impression or implication even though each statement, taken separately, was true.

False imprisonment. Tort of unlawful detainment of another. *See* False arrest; Imprisonment; Probable cause.

False instrument. A counterfeit document; one made in the similitude of a genuine instrument and purporting on its face to be such. *See also* Counterfeit; False making; Forgery.

False light privacy. Where an invasion of privacy tort action is brought against the media because a report has been published that is false (*i.e.* that defendant made plaintiff appear other than plaintiff actually is), the privacy plaintiff will be required to show, if the report was newsworthy, that the publication was made with actual malice.

Falsely. In a false manner, erroneously, not truly, perfidiously or treacherously. Knowingly affirming without probable cause.

The word, particularly in a criminal statute, suggests something more than a mere untruth and includes perfidiously or treacherously or with intent to defraud. Commonly used in the sense of designedly untrue and deceitful, and as implying an intention to perpetrate some treachery or fraud. As applied to making or altering a writing in order to make it forgery, implies that the paper or writing is not genuine; that in itself it is false or counterfeit.

See also Counterfeit; False; Forgery.

False making. An essential element of forgery, where material alteration is not involved. Term has reference to manner in which writing is made or executed rather than to its substance or effect. A falsely made instrument is one that is fictitious, not genuine, or in some material particular something other than it purports to be and without regard to truth or falsity of facts stated therein. See also Counterfeit; False entry; Forgery.

False misrepresentation. See False representation.

False oath. To defeat discharge in bankruptcy "false oath" must contain all the elements involved in "perjury" at common law, namely, an intentional untruth in matter material to a material issue. It must have been knowingly and fraudulently made. See also False swearing; Perjury.

False personation. See False impersonation.

False plea. See Sham pleading.

False pretenses. Illegally obtaining money, goods, or merchandise from another by fraud or misrepresentation. As a statutory crime, although defined in slightly different ways in the various jurisdictions, consists generally of these elements: (1) an intent to defraud; (2) the use of false pretenses or representations regarding any existing facts; and (3) the accomplishment of the intended fraud by means of such false pretenses. Such representation may be implied from conduct or may consist of concealment or non-disclosure where there is duty to speak, and may consist of any acts, work, symbol or token calculated and intended to deceive.

Other definitions include: false representation of existing fact or condition by which a party obtains property of another; false representation

of existing fact, whether by oral or written words or conduct, calculated to deceive, intended to deceive, and does in fact deceive, whereby one person obtains value from another without compensation; false representation of existing or past fact calculated to induce confidence on part of one to whom representation is made, and accompanied by or blended with a promise to do something in future; false representation of existing fact, made with knowledge of falsity, with intent that party to whom it is made should act upon it, and acted upon by such party to his detriment; false representation of past or existing fact, made with knowledge of falsity, with intent to deceive and defraud, and which is adapted to deceive person to whom made.

Under Model Penal Code § 223.3, a person is guilty of "theft by deception" if he purposely obtains property of another by deception.

Larceny distinguished. In crime of larceny owner has no intention to part with his property, although he may intend to part with possession, while in false pretenses the owner does intend to part with the property but it is obtained from him by fraud. The intention of owner of property not to part with title when relinquishing possession of property is vital point to be determined in distinguishing between "larceny by fraud" and obtaining property by "false pretenses".

False representation. For purposes of the common-law tort of fraudulent misrepresentation, such may be either an affirmative misrepresentation or a failure to disclose a material fact when a duty to disclose that fact has arisen. To maintain an action for damages for "false representation," the plaintiff, in substance, must allege and must prove by a preponderance of the evidence the following elements: (1) that representation was made; (2) that it was false; (3) that the defendant knew it was false, or else made it without knowledge as a positive statement of known fact; (4) that the plaintiff believed the representation to be true; (5) that the plaintiff relied on and acted upon the representation; (6) that the plaintiff was thereby injured; and (7) the amount of the damages. See also Deceit; False statement; Fraud; Material fact; Reliance.

False return. See Return.

False statement. Statement knowingly false, or made recklessly without honest belief in its truth, and with purpose to mislead or deceive. An incorrect statement made or acquiesced in with knowledge of incorrectness or with reckless indifference to actual facts and with no reasonable ground to believe it correct. Such are more than erroneous or untrue and import intention to deceive.

Under statutory provision making it unlawful for officer or director of corporation to make any false statement in regard to corporation's financial condition, the phrase means something more than merely untrue or erroneous, but implies that statement is designedly untrue and deceitful, and made with intention to deceive person to whom false statement is made or exhibited.

The federal criminal statute governing false statements applies to three distinct offenses: falsifying, concealing, or covering up a material fact by any trick, scheme or device; making false, fictitious, or fraudulent statements or representations; and making or using any false documents or writing. 18 U.S.C.A. § 1001.

See also Deceit; False representation; Fraud; Material fact; Perjury; Reliance.

False swearing. A person who makes a false statement under oath or equivalent affirmation, or swears or affirms the truth of such a statement previously made, when he does not believe the statement to be true, is guilty of a misdemeanor if: (a) the falsification occurs in an official proceeding; or (b) the falsification is intended to mislead a public servant in performing his official function. Model Penal Code, § 241.2.

The essential elements of crime consist in willfully, knowingly, absolutely and falsely swearing under oath or affirmation on a matter concerning which a party could legally be sworn and on oath administered by one legally authorized to administer it. It must appear that matter sworn to was judicially pending or was being investigated by grand jury, or was a subject on which accused could legally have been sworn, or on which he was required to be sworn. See also False oath; Perjury.

False token. In criminal law, a false document or sign of the existence of a fact, in general, used for the purpose of fraud. Device used to obtain money by false pretenses. See Counterfeit; False weights.

False verdict. See Verdict.

False weights. False weights and measures are such as do not comply with the standard prescribed by the state or government, or with the custom prevailing in the place and business in which they are used.

Falsi crimen /fólsay kráymən/. Fraudulent subornation or concealment, with design to darken or hide the truth, and make things appear otherwise than they are. It is committed (1) by words, as when a witness swears falsely; (2) by writing, as when a person antedates a contract; (3) by deed, as selling by false weights and measures. See Crimen falsi.

Falsification. See Falsify.

Falsify. To counterfeit or forge; to make something false; to give a false appearance to anything. To make false by mutilation, alteration, or addition; to tamper with, as to falsify a record or document. The word "falsify" may be used to convey two distinct meanings—either that of being intentionally or knowingly untrue, made with intent to defraud, or mistakenly and accidentally untrue. See also Alteration; Counterfeit; False; Forgery.

To disprove; to prove to be false or erroneous; to avoid or defeat. Spoken of verdicts, appeals, etc.

Falsifying a record. It is a crime, under state and federal statutes, for a person, knowing that he has no privilege to do so, to falsify or otherwise tamper with public records with purpose to deceive or injure anyone or to conceal any wrongdoing. See, e.g., Model Penal Code, § 224.4; 18 U.S.C.A. §§ 1506, 2071, 2073.

Falsity. Term implies more than erroneous or untrue; it indicates knowledge of untruth.

Falsus /fólsəs/. Lat. False; fraudulent; erroneous; deceitful; mistaken.

Falsus in uno, falsus in omnibus /fólsəs in yúwnow, fólsəs in ómnəbəs/. False in one thing, false in everything. The doctrine means that if testimony of a witness on a material issue is willfully false and given with an intention to deceive, jury may disregard all the witness' testimony. The maxim deals only with weight of evidence. It does not relieve jury from passing on credibility of the whole testimony of a false swearing witness or excuse jury from weighing the whole testimony.

Familiar. Fair or reasonable knowledge of, or acquaintance with. Closeness; intimacy.

Familiarity. Close or reasonable acquaintance with or knowledge of.

Family. The meaning of word necessarily depends on field of law in which word is used, purpose intended to be accomplished by its use, and facts and circumstances of each case. Most commonly refers to group of persons consisting of parents and children; father, mother and their children; immediate kindred, constituting fundamental social unit in civilized society. A collective body of persons who live in one house and under one head or management. A group of blood-relatives; all the relations who descend from a common ancestor, or who spring from a common root. A group of kindred persons. Husband and wife and their children, wherever they may reside, and whether they dwell together or not.

As used in context of uninsured motorist insurance coverage, "family" is not confined to those who stand in a legal or blood relationship, but rather should include those who live within the domestic circle of, and are economically dependent on, the named insured (e.g. foster child or ward).

Descent and descendants. The word may mean all descendants of a common progenitor; or, those who are of the same lineage, or descend from one common progenitor.

Homestead and exemption laws. To constitute family there must be one whom law designates or recognizes as head of family who by natural ties or by legal or moral obligation is under duty to support others of the household. To constitute persons living with another in same house a "family", it must appear that they are being supported by that other in whole or in part, and are dependent on him therefor, and that he is under a natural or moral obligation to render such support. *See also* Dependent.

Household. Those who live in same household subject to general management and control of the head thereof. Family and household are substantially synonymous terms for certain purposes.

Wills. As respects construction of will, the word "family" denotes a group of persons related to each other by marriage or blood living together under a single roof and comprising a household whose head is usually the father or husband, but the word is not one of inflexible meaning and its significance to a large extent depends upon the context and the purpose for which it is employed. For example, the word "family" has been held to include those who have left father's home and have married and established their own homes when context and purpose indicate such significance should be attributed to the word.

When the word "family" is used to designate those entitled to receive a legacy, the intended meaning of the word depends upon the context of the will and upon a showing as to whom were the objects of the testator's bounty by reason of kinship or friendship.

Family allowance. Consists of certain amount of decedent's property allocated for the support of the widow and children during the period of estate administration.

Family arrangement. A term denoting an agreement between a father and his children, or between the heirs of a deceased father, to dispose of property, or to partition it in a different manner than that which would result if the law alone directed it, or to divide up property without administration. In these cases, frequently, the mere relation of the parties will give effect to bargains otherwise without adequate consideration. *See also* Family settlement.

Family automobile doctrine. In a number of jurisdictions, when an automobile is maintained by the owner thereof for the general use and convenience of his or her family, such owner is liable for the negligence of a member of the family, having general authority to drive the car, while it is being used as such family car; that is,

for the pleasure or convenience of the family or a member of it. This doctrine has been rejected, superseded, or limited in its application, in most states.

The doctrine rests upon the basis that the automobile is furnished by the husband in his individual capacity and as common-law head of the family for the use of the family, and not as the agent of the community. Under the doctrine, a father furnishing automobile for pleasure and convenience of family makes the use of automobile by family his business and any member of family driving automobile with father's express or implied consent is the father's agent and the father is liable for the member's negligence.

See also Family group; Family purpose doctrine, which are synonymous terms.

Family Bible. A Bible containing a record of the births, marriages, and deaths of the members of a family.

Family car doctrine. *See* Family automobile doctrine.

Family council. *See* Family arrangement.

Family court. Such courts exist in several states. While the jurisdiction of such courts will differ somewhat from state to state, typically this court will have jurisdiction over: (1) child abuse and neglect proceedings, (2) support proceedings, (3) proceedings to determine paternity and for support of children born out of wedlock, (4) proceedings permanently to terminate custody by reason of permanent neglect, (5) proceedings concerning juvenile delinquency and whether a person is in need of supervision, and (6) family offenses proceedings. The family court may be a division or department of a court of general jurisdiction.

Family disturbance. Generic term used to describe any crime, tort or disorder within or touching the family.

Family division or department. *See* Family court.

Family expense statutes. State statutes which permit charge against property of husband or wife for debts connected with family support and maintenance such as rent, food, clothing, and tuition.

As used in tax law, expenses incurred for personal, living or family purposes for which no deduction may be claimed. I.R.C. § 262.

Family group. Within purview of the family automobile doctrine, is not confined to persons related to the owner, but includes members of the collective body of persons living in his household for whose convenience the car is maintained and who have authority to use it. *See also* Family;

Family automobile doctrine; Family purpose doctrine, which are synonymous terms.

Family law. Branch or specialty of law, also denominated "domestic relations" law, concerned with such subjects as adoption, annulment, divorce, separation, paternity, custody, support and child care. *See also* Family court.

Family partnership. In tax law, partnership consisting of members of family and such members shall include only a spouse, ancestors, lineal descendants, and any trusts for the benefit of such persons. I.R.C. § 704(e).

Family purpose doctrine. Under this doctrine where one purchases and maintains automobile for comfort, convenience, pleasure, entertainment and recreation of one's family, any member thereof operating automobile will be regarded as agent or servant of the owner and owner will be held liable for injuries sustained by third person by reason of negligent operation of vehicle by member of family. This doctrine has been rejected, or limited in its application, in many states. *See also* Family automobile doctrine and Family group, which are synonymous terms.

Family service rule. *See* Family automobile doctrine.

Family settlement. An agreement between members of a family settling the distribution of family property among them. An arrangement or an agreement, between heirs of a deceased person, by which they agree on distribution or management of estate without administration by court having jurisdiction of such administration proceedings. A term of practically the same signification as "family arrangement" *(q.v.)*.

Fanciful terms. In trademark law, those terms that are "coined," having no independent meaning; they may be registered as trademarks even if they have not acquired secondary meaning.

Fannie Mae. *See* Federal National Mortgage Association.

FAR. *See* Federal Acquisition Regulations.

Fare. A voyage, journey, or passage. The transportation charge paid by passenger. A paying passenger.

As used in connection with interstate transportation means a rate of charge for the carriage of passengers, as approved by the proper governmental agency.

Farm, n. A tract of land devoted to agriculture, pasturage, stock raising, or some allied industry. Includes dairy, stock, and poultry farms.

The original meaning of the word was rent; a term; a lease of lands; a leasehold interest, and by a natural transition it came to mean the land out of which the rent or lease issued.

A letting out of the collection of taxes and revenues for a fixed sum.

See also Farmer.

Farm, v. To lease or let; to demise or grant for a limited term and at a stated rental. To carry on business or occupation of farming.

Farm Credit Administration. An independent federal agency, responsible for supervising and coordinating activities of the cooperative Farm Credit System. The System is comprised of Federal land banks and Federal land bank associations, Federal intermediate credit banks and production credit associations, and banks for cooperatives. Initially capitalized by the United States, the entire system is now owned by its users. *See also* Farmers Home Administration; Federal farm credit system.

Farm crossing. A roadway over or under a railroad track for the purpose of reaching land cut off by the track.

Farmer. One engaged in agricultural pursuits as a livelihood or business. *See also* Husbandman.

As defined in Bankruptcy Code, is person who received more than 80 percent of his gross income during the taxable year immediately preceding commencement of bankruptcy proceeding from a farming operation owned or operated by such person. Bankruptcy Code § 101. *See also* Bankruptcy proceedings *(Family farmer bankruptcy)*.

Farmer bankruptcy. *See* Bankruptcy proceedings *(Family farmer bankruptcy)*.

Farmers Home Administration (FmHA). A division of the Department of Agriculture engaged in making direct mortgage loans to farmers and also home mortgage insurance and guarantee programs in rural areas and small towns. *See also* Farm Credit Administration; Federal farm credit system.

Farming operation. As defined in Bankruptcy Code, term includes farming, tillage of the soil, dairy farming, ranching, production or raising of crops, poultry, or livestock, and production of poultry or livestock products in an unmanufactured state. Bankruptcy Code § 101.

Farming products. Agricultural products which have a situs of their production upon the farm and which are brought into condition for uses of society by labor of those engaged in agricultural pursuits as contradistinguished from manufacturing or other industrial pursuits.

Crops or livestock or supplies used or produced in farming operations or products of crops or livestock in their unmanufactured states, if they are in the possession of a debtor engaged in farming operations. U.C.C. § 9–109(3).

Farming purposes. These words are not limited in meaning to mere cultivation of soil and maintenance of improvements thereon for such purposes, but include raising of livestock, as well as production of farm crops directly from soil. *See* Farming operation.

Farm labor *or* **laborer.** *See* Farmer.

Farm let. Technical words in a lease creating a term for years. Operative words in a lease, which strictly mean to let upon payment of a certain rent in farm; *i.e.,* in agricultural produce.

Farm out. To let for a term at a stated rental. To turn over for performance or care. To exhaust farm land by continuous raising of single crop.

Farmout agreement. An agreement by which one who owns an oil and gas lease agrees to assign to another an interest in the lease in return for drilling and testing operations on the lease. Under standard "farmout agreement" farmout operator drills at his own expense and upon completion of commercial well becomes owner of working interest and usually operates well or arranges for its operation, the assignor retaining a royalty.

Farm products. *See* Farming products.

F.A.S. "Free alongside ship." Delivery term under which the seller is obligated to deliver goods to a specified loading dock and bears expense and risk of loss up to that point. Term used in sales price quotations, indicating that the price includes all costs of transportation and delivery of the goods alongside the ship. See U.C.C. § 2–319(2).

FASB. *See* Financial Accounting Standards Board.

Fatal errors. As grounds for new trial, mean harmful errors; reversible errors. Such only as may reasonably be held to have worked substantial injury or prejudice to complaining party. Such errors generally afford party right to new trial, as contrasted with "harmless" errors which do not. *See* Error; Plain error rule.

Fatal injury. A term embracing injuries resulting in death, which, as used in accident and disability insurance policies is distinguished from "disability," which embraces injuries preventing the insured from performing the work in which he is usually employed, but not resulting in death.

Fatal variance. A variance in indictment tending to mislead defendant in making defense or one preventing plea of former jeopardy. A "variance" occurs when facts proved at trial are different from those alleged in the indictment; however, variance constitutes grounds for reversing a conviction only when it affects defendant's "substantial rights," that is, when the variance deprives a defendant of sufficiently specific information to prepare a defense and to be protected against surprise at trial, and prevents him from asserting

his constitutional protection against double jeopardy. It must be misleading or serve so as to substantially and materially mislead the adverse party. *See also* Variance.

Father. A male parent. He by whom a child is begotten. Natural father; procreator of a child. For Putative father, see that title.

As used in law, this term may (according to the context and the nature of the instrument) include a putative as well as a legal father, also a stepfather, an adoptive father, or a grandfather, but is not as wide as the word "parent," and cannot be so construed as to include a female.

Father-in-law. The father of one's wife or husband.

Fatico hearing. An adversarial sentencing hearing at which the court considers allegedly illegal conduct for which a defendant was not convicted and did not plead guilty. United States v. Fatico, 603 F.2d 1053, at 1057, note 9 (2d Cir.1979). If the government proves its allegations by a preponderance of the evidence, the court may consider such conduct in determining an appropriate sentence for the crime for which the defendant was convicted.

Fault. Negligence; an error or defect of judgment or of conduct; any deviation from prudence, duty, or rectitude; any shortcoming, or neglect of care or performance resulting from inattention, incapacity, or perversity; a wrong tendency, course, or act; bad faith or mismanagement; neglect of duty. Under general liability principles, is a breach of a duty imposed by law or contract. The term connotes an act to which blame, censure, impropriety, shortcoming or culpability attaches.

Wrongful act, omission or breach. U.C.C. § 1–201(16).

See also Negligence; No fault; Pari delicto; Tort.

Fauntleroy doctrine. In Fauntleroy v. Lum, 210 U.S. 230, 28 S.Ct. 641, 52 L.Ed. 1039, the U.S. Supreme Court held that a state must give full faith and credit to a judgment of a sister state if such state had jurisdiction to render it even though the judgment is based on an original cause of action which is illegal in the state in which enforcement is sought.

Favored nation. *See* Most favored nation clause.

Favoritism. Invidious preference and selection based on friendship and factors other than merit. *See* Nepotism; Patronage.

F.B.I. *See* Federal Bureau of Investigation.

F.C.A. *See* Farm Credit Administration.

F.C.C. *See* Federal Communications Commission.

F.C.I.C. Federal Crop Insurance Corporation. *See* Insurance.

F.D.A. *See* Food and Drug Administration.

F.D.I.C. *See* Federal Deposit Insurance Corporation.

Fealty /fíy(ə)ltiy/. In feudal law, fidelity; allegiance to the feudal lord of the manor; the feudal obligation resting upon the tenant or vassal by which he was bound to be faithful and true to his lord, and render him obedience and service. This fealty was of two sorts: that which is general, and is due from every subject to his prince; the other special, and required of such only as in respect of their fee are tied by this oath to their landlords.

Fear. Apprehension of harm; dread; consciousness of approaching danger. Mental response to threat. Profound reverence and awe.

Within Hobbs Act extortion definition, includes fear of economic loss as well as of physical harm.

Feasance /fíyzəns/. A doing; the doing of an act; a performing or performance. *See* Malfeasance; Misfeasance; Nonfeasance.

Feasible. Capable of being done, executed, affected or accomplished. Reasonable assurance of success. *See* Possible.

Featherbedding. The name given to employee practices which create or spread employment by unnecessarily maintaining or increasing the number of employees used, or the amount of time consumed, to work on a particular job. Most of these practices stem from a desire on the part of employees for job security in the face of technological improvements.

F.E.C.A. *See* Federal Employees' Compensation Act.

Fed. *See* Federal Reserve System.

Federal. Belonging to the general government or union of the states. Founded on or organized under the Constitution of the United States. Pertaining to the national government of the United States. Of or constituting a government in which power is distributed between a central authority (*i.e.* federal government) and a number of constituent territorial units (*i.e.* states). *See also* Federal government.

A league or compact between two or more states, to become united under one central government. *See* Federation.

Federal Acquisition Regulations. Federal regulations governing government contracting methods, requirements, and procedures. 48 CFR (Ch. 1).

Federal Acts. Statutes enacted by Congress, relating to matters within authority delegated to federal government by U.S. Constitution. *Compare* State law.

Federal agency. Any executive department, military department, government corporation, government-controlled corporation or other establishment in the executive branch of government including the Executive office of the President or any independent regulatory agency. 5 U.S.C.A. § 552(f).

Federal agency securities. Debt securities issued by a federal agency and backed to varying degrees by the federal government.

Federal Aviation Administration. The Federal Aviation Administration (FAA), formerly the Federal Aviation Agency, became a part of the Department of Transportation in 1967 as a result of the Department of Transportation Act (80 Stat. 932). The Federal Aviation Administration is charged with regulating air commerce to foster aviation safety; promoting civil aviation and a national system of airports; achieving efficient use of navigable airspace; developing and operating a common system of air traffic control and air navigation for both civilian and military aircraft; and developing and implementing programs and regulations to control aircraft noise, sonic boom, and other environmental effects of civil aviation.

Federal Bureau of Investigation. The FBI (established in 1908) is charged with investigating all violations of Federal laws with the exception of those which have been assigned by legislative enactment or otherwise to some other Federal agency. The FBI's jurisdiction includes a wide range of responsibilities in the criminal, civil, and security fields. Among these are espionage, sabotage, and other subversive activities; kidnaping; extortion; bank robbery; interstate transportation of stolen property; civil rights matters; interstate gambling violations; fraud against the Government; and assault or killing the President or a Federal officer. Cooperative services of the FBI for other duly authorized law enforcement agencies include fingerprint identification, laboratory services, police training, and the National Crime Information Center.

Federal census. A census of each state or territory or of a certain state or of any subdivision or portion of any state, provided it is taken by and under the direction and supervision of the Census Bureau of the United States, and approved and certified by it as the census of that state or subdivision. *See* Census.

Federal citizenship. Rights and obligations accruing by reason of being a citizen of the United States. State or status of being a citizen of the United States.

A person born or naturalized in the United States and subject to the jurisdiction thereof is a citizen of the United States and of the State wherein he resides. Fourteenth Amend., U.S. Const.

See also Citizenship; Naturalization.

Federal common law. A body of decisional law developed by the federal courts. The application of this body of common law is limited by the *Erie* doctrine and by the Rules of Decision Act, which provides that except for cases governed by the Constitution, the treaties of the United States, or acts of Congress, federal courts are to apply state law. Areas in which federal common law have been developed include federal "proprietary" interests, admiralty and foreign relations. Erie R. Co. v. Tompkins, 304 U.S. 64, 58 S.Ct. 817, 82 L.Ed. 1188. *See also* Erie v. Tompkins; Rules of Decision Act; Swift v. Tyson Case.

Federal Communications Commission. The Federal Communications Commission was created by the Communications Act of 1934 to regulate interstate and foreign communications by wire and radio in the public interest. It was assigned additional regulatory jurisdiction under the provisions of the Communications Satellite Act of 1962. The scope of its regulatory powers includes radio and television broadcasting) telephone, telegraph, and cable television operation; two-way radio and radio operators; and satellite communication.

Federal courts. The courts of the United States (as distinguished from state, county, or city courts) as created either by Art. III of U.S.Const., or by Congress. *See* specific courts; *e.g.,* Courts of Appeals, U.S.; Claims Court, U.S.; District *(District courts)*; Supreme court; Three-judge courts.

Federal crimes. Those acts which have been made criminal by federal law. There are no federal common law crimes though many federal statutes have incorporated the elements of common law crimes. Most federal crimes are codified in Title 18 of the United States Code; though other Code Titles also include specific crimes. Such crimes (*e.g.,* RICO offenses, tax evasion, interstate kidnapping) are prosecuted in federal courts.

Federal Deposit Insurance Corporation. The FDIC is an independent agency within the executive branch of the Government. It insures, up to the statutory limitation, deposits in qualified banks and savings associations. 12 U.S.C.A. § 1811.

Federal Employees' Compensation Act. Type of workers' compensation plan for federal employees by which payments are made for death or disability sustained in performance of duties of employment. 5 U.S.C.A. § 8101 *et seq.*

Federal Employer's Liability Act. Federal workers' compensation law which protects employees of railroads engaged in interstate and foreign commerce. 45 U.S.C.A. § 51 *et seq.* Payments are made for death or disability sustained in performance of duties of employment.

Federal Energy Regulatory Commission. The successor agency to the Federal Power Commission responsible for administering the Natural Gas Act and the Natural Gas Policy Act.

Federal farm credit system. Consists of the Federal land banks, the Federal land bank associations, the Federal intermediate credit banks, the production credit associations, the banks for cooperatives, and such other institutions as may be made part of the system. The farm credit system as a whole is regulated by the Farm Credit Administration, an independent executive agency which sets policy and exercises supervisory authority. 12 U.S.C.A. §§ 2001–2260. *See also* Farm Credit Administration.

Federal funds. Uncommitted reserves that a bank has available to sell to other banks.

Federal government. The system of government administered in a nation formed by the union or confederation of several independent states.

In strict usage, there is a distinction between a *confederation* and a *federal government.* The former term denotes a league or permanent alliance between several states, each of which is fully sovereign and independent, and each of which retains its full dignity, organization, and sovereignty, though yielding to the central authority a controlling power for a few limited purposes, such as external and diplomatic relations. In this case, the component states are the units, with respect to the confederation, and the central government acts upon them, not upon the individual citizens. In a *federal government,* on the other hand, the allied states form a union (*e.g.* United States),— not, indeed, to such an extent as to destroy their separate organization or deprive them of *quasi* sovereignty with respect to the administration of their purely local concerns, but so that the central power is erected into a true national government, possessing sovereignty both external and internal, —while the administration of national affairs is directed, and its effects felt, not by the separate states deliberating as units, but by the people of all, in their collective capacity, as citizens of the nation. The distinction is expressed, by the German writers, by the use of the two words *"Staatenbund"* and *"Bundesstaat;"* the former denoting a league or confederation of states, and the latter a federal government, or state formed by means of a league or confederation.

See also Federal.

Federal grand jury. *See* Jury.

Federal Home Loan Bank Board. The federal agency formerly charged with regulating federal savings and loan associations and the Federal Home Loan Bank system. Abolished in 1989, its functions are now performed by the Office of Thrift Supervision and the Federal Housing Finance Board. *See also* Federal Housing Finance Board; Office of Thrift Supervision.

Federal Home Loan Banks. Banks created under the Federal Home Loan Bank Act of 1932, for the purpose of keeping a permanent supply of money available for home financing. The banks are controlled by the Federal Housing Finance Board. Savings and loans, insurance companies, and other similar companies making long term mortgage loans may become members of the Federal Home Loan Bank System, and thus may borrow from one of twelve regional banks throughout the country.

Federal Home Loan Mortgage Corporation. A federal agency which purchases first mortgages (both conventional and federally insured) from members of the Federal Reserve System, and the Federal Home Loan Bank System. Commonly called "Freddie Mac."

Federal Housing Administration. This federal agency, established by Congress in 1934, insures mortgage loans made by FHA-approved lenders on homes that meet FHA standards in order to make mortgages more desirable investments for lenders.

Federal Housing Finance Board. An independent agency in the executive branch charged with supervising the system of Federal Home Loan Banks. *See also* Federal Home Loan Banks.

Federal instrumentality. A means or agency used by the federal government to implement or carry out a federal law or function. *See* Administrative agency.

Federal Insurance Contributions Act. Federal Act imposing social security tax on employees, self employed, and employers. Under the F.I.C.A. the employer matches the tax paid by the employee. These taxes fund the social security and medicare programs.

Federalism. The federal (national) government and individual state government principle of organization. Term which includes interrelationships among the states and relationship between the states and the federal government. *See also* Federal.

Federalist Papers. A series of 85 essays by Alexander Hamilton, James Madison and John Jay, expounding and advocating the adoption of the Constitution of the United States. All but six of the essays were first published in the "Independent Journal" of New York City from October, 1787, to April, 1788.

Federal Judicial Code. This Code, comprising Title 28 of the United States Code, is concerned with the organization, jurisdiction, venue, and procedures of the federal court system. Also covered by this Code is the Department of Justice as well as court officers and personnel.

Federal jurisdiction. Powers of federal courts founded on U.S. Constitution (Article III) and Acts of Congress (*e.g.* Title 28 of United States Code). *See* Diversity of citizenship; Federal question jurisdiction.

Federal Land Banks. Regional banks established by Congress, and regulated by U.S. Farm Credit Administration, to provide mortgage loans to farmers. *See* Federal farm credit system; Federal Home Loan Banks.

Federal laws. *See* Federal Acts.

Federal Maritime Commission. The Federal Maritime Commission regulates the waterborne foreign and domestic offshore commerce of the United States, assures that United States international trade is open to all nations on fair and equitable terms, and guards against unauthorized monopoly in the waterborne commerce of the United States. This is accomplished through maintaining surveillance over steamship conferences and common carriers by water; assuring that only the rates on file with the Commission are charged; approving agreements between persons subject to the Shipping Act; guaranteeing equal treatment to shippers and carriers by terminal operators, freight forwarders, and other persons subject to the shipping statutes; and ensuring that adequate levels of financial responsibility are maintained for indemnification of passengers or oil spill cleanup.

Federal Mediation and Conciliation Service. The Federal Mediation and Conciliation Service helps prevent disruptions in the flow of interstate commerce caused by labor-management disputes by providing mediators to assist disputing parties in the resolution of their differences. The Service can intervene on its own motion or by invitation of either side in a dispute. Mediators have no law enforcement authority and rely wholly on persuasive techniques. The Service also helps provide qualified third party neutrals as factfinders or arbitrators.

Federal National Mortgage Association. Organized in 1938 to provide a secondary mortgage market for purchase and sale of mortgages guaranteed by Veterans Administration and those insured under Federal Housing Administration. The short name for this association is "Fannie Mae".

Federal Power Commission. The Federal Power Commission was terminated in 1977, with its functions of regulating the interstate energy industry taken over by the Department of Energy, and, within the DOE, by the Federal Energy Regulatory Commission.

Federal pre-emption. The U.S. Constitution and acts of Congress have given to the federal government exclusive power over certain matters such as interstate commerce and sedition to the exclusion of state jurisdiction. Occurs where federal law so occupies the field that state courts are prevented from asserting jurisdiction. *See also* Preemption.

Federal Privacy Act. *See* Privacy laws.

Federal question jurisdiction. Cases arising under Constitution of United States, Acts of Congress, or treaties, and involving their interpretation and application, and of which jurisdiction is given to federal courts, are commonly described as involving a "federal question." See U.S.Const., Art. III, Sec. 2, and 28 U.S.C.A. § 1331 with respect to "federal question" jurisdiction of federal courts.

Federal Register. The Federal Register, published daily, is the medium for making available to the public Federal agency regulations and other legal documents of the executive branch. These documents cover a wide range of Government activities. An important function of the Federal Register is that it includes proposed changes (rules, regulations, standards, etc.) of governmental agencies. Each proposed change published carries an invitation for any citizen or group to participate in the consideration of the proposed regulation through the submission of written data, views, or arguments, and sometimes by oral presentations. Such regulations and rules as finally approved appear thereafter in the Code of Federal Regulations.

Federal regulations. *See* Code of Federal Regulations; Federal Register.

Federal Reporter. The Federal Reporter (consisting of a First and Second series) publishes opinions of the below listed federal courts:

1880–1932

Circuit Court of Appeals

District Courts

U.S. Court of Customs and Patent Appeals

Court of Claims of the U.S.

Court of Appeals of the District of Columbia

1932–present

U.S. Courts of Appeals

1932–1982

U.S. Court of Customs and Patent Appeals

1942–61, 1972–present

U.S. Emergency Court of Appeals

1960–1982

U.S. Court of Claims (Claims Court decisions published in U.S. Claims Court Reporter 1983 to present)

See also Federal Supplement.

Federal Reserve Act. Law which created Federal Reserve banks which act as agents in maintaining money reserves, issuing money in the form of bank notes, lending money to banks, and supervising banks. Administered by Federal Reserve Board *(q.v.)*.

Federal Reserve Banks. *See* Federal Reserve Act; Federal Reserve Board of Governors; Federal Reserve System.

Federal Reserve Board of Governors. The seven-member Board of Governors, appointed by the President and confirmed by the Congress, sets reserve requirements for member banks, reviews and approves the discount-rate actions of regional Federal Reserve Banks, sets ceilings on the rates of interest that banks can pay on time and savings deposits, and issues regulations. Members also sit on the Federal Open Market Committee— the principal instrument for implementing the Board's national monetary policy.

Federal reserve notes. Form of currency issued by Federal Reserve Banks in the likeness of non-interest bearing promissory note payable to bearer on demand. The federal reserve note (*e.g.* one, five, ten, etc. dollar bill) is the most widely used paper currency. Such have replaced silver and gold certificates which were backed by silver and gold. Such reserve notes are direct obligations of the United States.

Federal Reserve System. Network of twelve central banks to which most national banks belong and to which state chartered banks may belong. Membership rules require investment of stock and minimum reserves. The Federal Reserve System was established in 1913 to give the country an elastic currency, provide facilities for discounting commercial paper and to improve the supervision of banking.

The System consists of five parts: the Board of Governors in Washington; the 12 Federal Reserve Banks, their branches and other facilities situated throughout the country; the Federal Open Market Committee; the Federal Advisory Council; and the member commercial banks, which include all national banks and State-chartered banks that have voluntarily joined the System.

Federal Rules Act. Act of 1934 granting U.S. Supreme Court power to adopt Federal Rules of Civil Procedure. See 28 U.S.C.A. §§ 2071, 2072. Additional power to prescribe rules is provided for by 28 U.S.C.A. § 2075 (Bankruptcy Rules), § 2072 (Evidence Rules) and 28 U.S.C.A. §§ 2071–2074 for other procedural rules for cases in U.S. district or courts of appeals.

Federal Rules Decisions. A unit of the National Reporter System which publishes federal court decisions which construe or apply the Federal Rules of Civil, Criminal and Appellate Procedure, as well as Federal Rules of Evidence. Also included are articles relating to federal court practice and procedure.

Federal Rules of Appellate Procedure. These rules govern procedure in appeals to United States courts of appeals from the United States district courts and the Tax Court of the United States; in proceedings in the courts of appeals for review or enforcement of orders of administrative agencies, boards, commissions and officers of the United States; and in applications for writs or other relief which a court of appeals or a judge thereof is competent to give. Certain states have adopted rules patterned on such federal rules to govern practice in their appellate courts.

Federal Rules of Bankruptcy Procedure. *See* Rules of Bankruptcy Procedure.

Federal Rules of Civil Procedure. Body of procedural rules which govern all civil actions in U.S. District Courts and after which most states have modeled their own rules of civil procedure. These rules were promulgated by the U.S. Supreme Court in 1938 under power granted by Congress, and have since been frequently amended. Such rules also govern adversary proceedings in the bankruptcy courts; and, Supplemental Rules, in addition to main body of rules, govern admiralty and maritime actions. See 28 U.S.C.A. §§ 2071-2074.

Federal Rules of Criminal Procedure. Procedural rules which govern all criminal proceedings in the U.S. District Courts, and, where specified, before U.S. Magistrates. Such rules were promulgated by the U.S. Supreme Court in 1945 under power granted by Congress, and have since been frequently amended. Several states have adopted criminal procedural rules patterned on the federal criminal rules. See 28 U.S.C.A. §§ 2071-2074.

Federal Rules of Evidence. Rules which govern the admissibility of evidence at trials in the Federal District Courts, Bankruptcy Courts, and before U.S. Magistrates. Many states have adopted Evidence Rules patterned on these federal rules. See 28 U.S.C.A. §§ 2072-2074.

Federal statutes. *See* Federal Acts.

Federal Supplement. The Federal Supplement publishes opinions of the below listed federal courts:

1932–present

U.S. District Courts

1932–1960

U.S. Court of Claims

1949–present

U.S. Customs Court (vol. 135). (Renamed Court of International Trade in 1980)

See also Federal Reporter.

Federal Tort Claims Act. The government of the United States may not be sued in tort without its consent. That consent was given in the Federal Tort Claims Act (1946), which largely abrogated the federal government's immunity from tort liability and established the conditions for suits and claims against the federal government. The Act (28 U.S.C.A. §§ 1346(b), 2674) preserves governmental immunity with respect to the traditional categories of intentional torts, and with respect to acts or omissions which fall within the "discretionary function or duty" of any federal agency or employee. *See also* Sovereign immunity.

Federal Trade Commission. Agency of the federal government created in 1914. The Commission's principal functions are to promote free and fair competition in interstate commerce through prevention of general trade restraints such as price-fixing agreements, false advertising, boycotts, illegal combinations of competitors and other unfair methods of competition. *See also* Clayton Act; Robinson-Patman Act; Sherman Antitrust Act.

Federal Unemployment Tax Act (FUTA). *See* Tax (*Unemployment tax*).

Federal Warranty Act. *See* Magnuson–Moss Warranty Act.

Federation. A joining together of states or nations in a league or association; the league itself. *See also* Compact; Federal; Federal government; United States.

An unincorporated association of persons for a common purpose.

Fee. A charge fixed by law for services of public officers or for use of a privilege under control of government. A recompense for an official or professional service or a charge or emolument or compensation for a particular act or service. A fixed charge or perquisite charged as recompense for labor; reward, compensation, or wage given to a person for performance of services or something done or to be done.

See also Base; Commitment fee; License fee *or* tax; Poundage fees; Retainer.

Attorney fees. Charge to client for services performed (*e.g.* hourly fee, flat fee, contingency fee). Such fees must be "reasonable" (see *e.g.* Model Rules of Professional Conduct, Rule 1.5(a)). Numerous federal statutes provide for the award of attorney fees to the prevailing party; *e.g.*, 25% of award in social security disability claim actions. *See Contingent fees, below; also,* American rule; Attorney's lien; Equal Access to Justice Act; Fee splitting; Minimum fee schedules; Retainer; Suit (*Suit money*).

Contingent fees. Arrangement between attorney and client whereby attorney agrees to represent client with compensation to be a percentage of the amount recovered; *e.g.*, 25% if the case is settled, 30% if case goes to trial. Frequently used in personal injury actions. Such fee arrangements are often regulated by court rule or statute depending on the type of action and amount of recovery; and are not permitted in criminal cases (see, *e.g.,* ABA, Model Rules of Professional Conduct, Rule 1.5(c), (d)).

Court fees. Those amounts paid to court or one of its officers for particular charges that typically are delineated by statute, such as docket fees, marshal's charges and witness fees. See *e.g.* 28 U.S.C.A. § 1911 et seq. *See also* Cost; Docket *(Docket fee).*

Docket fees. See Court fees above; also Docket.

Estates

An interest in land which (a) is or may become possessory; and (b) is ownership measured in terms of duration. Restatement of Property § 9. *See also* Fee simple.

Ordinarily, word "fee" or "fee simple" is applied to an estate in land, but term is applicable to any kind of hereditament, corporeal or incorporeal, and is all the property in thing referred to or largest estate therein which person may have.

Base fee. A determinable or qualified fee; an estate having the nature of a fee, but not a fee simple absolute. *See Determinable fee, below.*

Conditional fee. An estate restrained to some particular heirs, exclusive of others, as to the heirs of a man's body, by which only his lineal descendants were admitted, in exclusion of collateral; or to the heirs male of his body, in exclusion of heirs female, whether lineal or collateral. It was called a "conditional fee," by reason of the condition expressed or implied in the donation of it that, if the donee died without such particular heirs, the land should revert to the donor. The term includes a fee that is either to commence or determine on some condition; and is sometimes used interchangeably with "base fee," that is, one to determine or be defeated on the happening of some contingent event or act.

Determinable fee. Also called a "base" or "qualified" fee. One which has a qualification subjoined to it, and which must be determined whenever the qualification annexed to it is at an end. An estate in fee which is liable to be determined by some act or event expressed on its limitation to circumscribe its continuance, or inferred by law as bounding its extent. An estate which may last forever is a "fee," but if it may end on the happening of a merely possible event, it is a "determinable," or "qualified fee."

Fee damages. See Damages.

Fee expectant. A name sometimes applied to an estate created where lands are given to a man and his wife and the heirs of their bodies.

Fee simple. See Fee simple.

Fee simple defeasible. Title created in trustees where legal title in fee simple to active trust estate is by will placed in trustees who are required to distribute property in fee simple upon happening of event. Also called a "determinable fee", "base fee", or "qualified fee".

Qualified fee. See Determinable fee, above.

Feed. To lend additional support; to strengthen *ex post facto.* Similarly, a subsequent title acquired by the mortgagor is said "to feed the mortgage."

Feeder organization. An entity that carries on a trade or business for the benefit of an exempt organization. However, such a relationship does not result in the feeder organization itself being tax-exempt. I.R.C. § 502.

Fee interest. *See* Fee; Fee simple; Fee tail.

Fee simple. Typically, words "fee simple" standing alone create an *absolute* estate in devisee and such words followed by a condition or special limitation create a *defeasible* fee. *See also* Fee.

Absolute. A fee simple absolute is an estate limited absolutely to a person and his or her heirs and assigns forever without limitation or condition. An absolute or fee-simple estate is one in which the owner is entitled to the entire property, with unconditional power of disposition during one's life, and descending to one's heirs and legal representatives upon one's death intestate. Such estate is unlimited as to duration, disposition, and descendibility.

Conditional. Type of transfer in which grantor conveys fee simply on condition that something be done or not done. A defeasible fee which leaves grantor with right of entry for condition broken, which right may be exercised by some action on part of grantor when condition is breached.

At common law an estate in fee simple conditional was a fee limited or restrained to some particular heirs, exclusive of others. But the statute "De donis" converted all such estates into estates tail.

Defeasible. Type of fee grant which may be defeated on the happening of an event. An estate which may last forever, but which may end upon the occurrence or nonoccurrence of a specified event, is a "fee simple defeasible".

Determinable. A "fee simple determinable" is created by conveyance which contains words effective to create a fee simple and, in addition, a provision for automatic expiration of estate on occurrence of stated event.

Fee simple title. *See* Fee simple.

Fee splitting. Division of legal fees between attorney who handles matters and attorney who referred such to him or her. Referrals commonly occur when referring attorney lacks expertise, or experience to effectively handle the particular matter.

Fee tail. A freehold estate in which there is a fixed line of inheritable succession limited to the issue of the body of the grantee or devisee, and in which the regular and general succession of heirs at law is cut off.

An estate tail; an estate of inheritance given to a man and the heirs of his body, or limited to certain classes of particular heirs. For the varieties and special characteristics of this kind of estate, see Tail, Estate in.

Feigned /féynd/. Fictitious; pretended; supposititious; simulated.

Feigned accomplice. One who pretends to consult and act with others in the planning or commission of a crime, but only for the purpose of discovering their plans and confederates and securing evidence against them. See Informer.

Feigned action. An action, now obsolete, brought on a pretended right, when the plaintiff has no true cause of action, for some illegal purpose. In a feigned action the words of the writ are true. It differs from *false action*, in which case the words of the writ are false.

FELA. See Federal Employer's Liability Act.

Fellow-heir. A co-heir; partner of the same inheritance.

Fellow servant. One who works for and is controlled by the same employer; a co-worker. Those engaged in the same type of work, under the control of a common employer. Employees who derive authority and compensation from the same common employer, and are engaged in the same general business. When persons are employed and paid by the same employer, and their duties are such as to bring them into such relation that negligence of one in doing his work may injure other in performance of his, then they are engaged in the same common businesses, and are "fellow servants." See also Employee; Fellow servant rule.

Fellow servant rule. A common law doctrine, now generally abrogated by workers' compensation acts and Federal Employers' Liability Act, that in an action for damages brought against an employer by an injured employee the employer may allege that the negligence of another fellow employee was partly or wholly responsible for the accident resulting in the injury and, thus reducing or extinguishing his own liability.

Felon /félən/. Person who commits or has committed a felony *(q.v.)*.

Felonious /fəlówn(i)yəs/. A technical word of law which means done with intent to commit crime,

i.e. criminal intent. Of the grade or quality of a felony, as, for example, a felonious assault *(q.v.)*. Malicious; villainous; traitorous; malignant. Proceeding from an evil heart or purpose. Wickedly and against the admonition of the law; unlawfully. *See also* Felony; Feloniously.

Felonious assault. Such an assault upon the person as, if consummated, would subject the party making it, upon conviction, to the punishment of a felony, that is, to imprisonment. Aggravated assault as contrasted with simple assault. *See also* Assault.

Felonious entry. Type of statutory burglary. *See* Burglary.

Felonious homicide. Killing of human being without justification or excuse. *See* Homicide; Manslaughter; Murder; Premeditation.

Felonious intent. An act of the will in which one forms a desire to commit a felony. As applied to crime of larceny, the intent which exists where a person knowingly takes and carries away the personal property of another without any claim or pretense of right with the intent wholly and permanently to deprive the owner of his property.

Feloniously. *See* Felonious.

Felonious taking. As used in the crimes of larceny and robbery, it is the taking with intent to steal.

Felony. A crime of a graver or more serious nature than those designated as misdemeanors; *e.g.*, aggravated assault (felony) as contrasted with simple assault (misdemeanor). Under many state statutes, any offense punishable by death or imprisonment for a term exceeding one year. See, *e.g.*, Model Penal Code § 1.04(2); 18 U.S.C.A. § 1. The federal and many state criminal codes define felony status crimes, and in turn also have various classes of felonies (*e.g.*, Class A, B, C, etc.) or degrees (*e.g.*, first, second, third) with varying sentences for each class. See, *e.g.*, 18 U.S.C.A. § 3559; Model Penal Code § 6.01.

Felony, compounding of. See Compounding crime.

Forcible felony. Forcible felony includes any treason, murder, voluntary manslaughter, rape, robbery, burglary, arson, kidnapping, aggravated battery, aggravated sodomy and any other felony which involves the use or threat of physical force or violence against any person.

Misprision of felony. See Misprision.

Reducible felony. A felony upon conviction of which the offender may be punished as for a misdemeanor, upon recommendation of the jury.

Felony murder doctrine. At common law, one whose conduct brought about an unintended death in the commission or attempted commission of a felony was guilty of murder (*e.g.* a homicide committed during an armed robbery). While some states still follow the common law rule, today the law of felony murder varies substantially throughout the country, largely as a result of efforts to limit the scope of the rule. Jurisdictions have limited the rule in one or more of the following ways: (1) by permitting its use only as to certain types of felonies; (2) by more strict interpretation of the requirement of proximate or legal cause; (3) by a narrower construction of the time period during which the felony is in the process of commission; (4) by requiring that the underlying felony be independent of the homicide. See e.g. Model Penal Code § 210.2.

Feme covert /fém kɔ́vərt/. A married woman. Generally used in reference to the former legal disabilities of a married woman, as compared with the condition of a *feme sole*.

Feme sole /fém sówl/. A single woman, including those who have been married, but whose marriage has been dissolved by death or divorce, and, for most purposes, those women who are judicially separated from their husbands.

Fence, n. A hedge, structure, or partition, erected for the purpose of inclosing a piece of land, or to divide a piece of land into distinct portions, or to separate two contiguous estates. An enclosure about a field or other space, or about any object; especially an enclosing structure of wood, iron or other materials, intended to prevent intrusion from without or straying from within.

A colloquial characterization of a receiver of stolen property; one who receives and sells stolen goods. *See* Receiving stolen goods or property.

Fencing patents. Patents procured in an effort to broaden the scope of the invention beyond the article or process which is actually intended to be manufactured or licensed.

Feneration /fènəréyshən/. Usury; the gain of interest; the practice of increasing money by lending. Sometimes applied to interest on money lent. *See* Interest.

Feoffment /féfmənt/fíyfˀ/. The gift of any corporeal hereditament to another, operating by transmutation of possession, and requiring, as essential to its completion, that the seisin be passed, which might be accomplished either by investiture or by livery of seisin. A gift of a freehold interest in land accompanied by livery of seisin. The essential part is the livery of seisin. Also the deed or conveyance by which such corporeal hereditament is passed.

Feoffment to uses /féfmənt tə yúwsəz/fíyfˀ/. A feoffment of lands to one person to the use of another. In such case the feoffee was bound in conscience to hold the lands according to the use, and could himself derive no benefit. Sometimes such feoffments were made to the use of the

feoffer. The effect of such conveyance was entirely changed by the statute of uses.

Feoffment with livery of seisin. An early English method of conveyance by which the transferor met the transferee at or near the land to be transferred and handed over a twig or clod while reciting to witnesses that the transfer was being made.

Feoffor /féfər/fíyfər/. The person making a feoffment, or enfeoffing another in fee.

Feræ naturæ /fíriy nətyúriy/. Lat. Of a wild nature or disposition. Animals which are by nature wild are so designated, by way of distinction from such as are naturally tame, the latter being called "*domitæ naturæ.*"

FERC. *See* Federal Energy Regulatory Commission.

Ferry. Commercial transportation of people, vehicles, goods, etc. across body of water. Also, boat or vessel used in such transportation. In law it is treated as a franchise, and defined as the exclusive right to carry passengers and freight across a river, lake or arm of the sea, or to connect a continuous line of road leading from one side of the water to the other.

Ferry franchise. The public grant of a right to maintain a ferry at a particular place; a right conferred to land at a particular point and secure toll for the transportation of persons and property from that point across the stream.

Fetal death. The death of a child not yet born. Death in utero of a fetus weighing 500 grams or more. This weight corresponds roughly to a fetus of twenty weeks or more (gestational age), *i.e.* a viable fetus.

Death is defined in the following context: after expulsion, the fetus does not breathe or show any other evidence of life, such as the beating of the heart, pulsation of the umbilical cord, or definite movement of voluntary muscles.

Feticide /fíytəsàyd/. Destruction of the fetus; the act by which criminal abortion is produced. The killing of an unborn child. *See also* Abortion.

Fetus /fíytəs/. An unborn child. The unborn offspring of any viviparous animal; specifically the unborn offspring in the post embryonic period after major structures have been outlined (in man from seven or eight weeks after fertilization until birth).

Feudal /fyúwdəl/. Pertaining to feuds or fees; relating to or growing out of the feudal system or feudal law; having the quality of a feud, as distinguished from "allodial."

Feudal courts. In the 12th century a lord *qua* lord had the right to hold a court for his tenants. In the 13th century, they became of less importance for three reasons: The feudal principle would have led to a series of courts one above the other, and the dominions of the large landowners were usually scattered, so that great feudal courts became impossible. The growth of the jurisdiction of the king's court removed the necessity for feudal courts. All the incidents of the feudal system came to be regarded in a commercial spirit—as property. Its jurisdiction became merely appendant to landowning.

Feudalism. The feudal system; the aggregate of feudal principles and usages. The social, political, and economic system that dominated the major European nations between the ninth and fifteenth centuries. The system was based upon a servile relationship between a "vassal" and a "lord." The vassal paid homage and service to the lord and the lord provided land and protection to the vassal. *See also* Feudal system.

Feudal law. The body of jurisprudence relating to feuds; the real-property law of the feudal system; the law anciently regulating the property relations of lord and vassal, and the creation, incidents, and transmission of feudal estates.

The body of laws and usages constituting the "feudal law" was originally customary and unwritten, but a compilation was made in the twelfth century, called "Feodarum Consuetudines," which has formed the basis of later digests. The feudal law prevailed over Europe from the twelfth to the fourteenth century, and was introduced into England at the Norman Conquest, where it formed the entire basis of the law of real property until comparatively modern times. Survivals of the feudal law, to the present day, so affect and color that branch of jurisprudence as to require a certain knowledge of the feudal law in order to better comprehend modern tenures and rules of real-property law.

See also Feudal system.

Feudal possession. The equivalent of "seisin" under the feudal system.

Feudal system. The system of feuds. A political and social system which prevailed throughout Europe during the eleventh, twelfth, and thirteenth centuries, and is supposed to have grown out of the peculiar usages and policy of the Teutonic nations who overran the continent after the fall of the Western Roman Empire, as developed by the exigencies of their military domination, and possibly furthered by notions taken from the Roman jurisprudence.

It was introduced into England, in its completeness, by William I, A.D. 1085, though it may have existed in a rudimentary form among the Saxons before the Conquest. It formed the entire basis of the real-property law of England in medieval times; and survivals of the system, in modern days, so modify and color that branch of jurisprudence, both in England and America, that many

of its principles require for their complete understanding a knowledge of the feudal system. The feudal system originated in the relations of a military chieftain and his followers, or king and nobles, or lord and vassals, and especially their relations as determined by the bond established by a grant of *land* from the former to the latter. From this it grew into a complete and intricate complex of rules for the tenure and transmission of real estate, and of correlated duties and services; while, by tying men to the land and to those holding above and below them, it created a close-knit hierarchy of persons, and developed an aggregate of social and political institutions.

Feudal tenures. The tenures of real estate under the feudal system, such as knight-service, socage, villenage, etc.

Feudum /fyúwdəm/. L. Lat. A feud, fief, or fee. A right of using and enjoying forever the lands of another, which the lord grants on condition that the tenant shall render fealty, military duty, and other services. It is not properly the land, but a right in the land.

Few. Not many; of small number. An indefinite expression for a small or limited number. Indicating a small number of units or individuals which constitute a whole. A relative term of great elasticity of meaning.

F.G.A. In marine insurance means: "Free from general average"; also, sometimes, "foreign general average." The precise meaning of this abbreviation must be gathered from the context. *See* Average; General average contribution.

FHA. *See* Federal Housing Administration.

FHLB. *See* Federal Home Loan Banks.

FHLMC. *See* Federal Home Loan Mortgage Corporation.

Fiancer. L. Fr. To pledge one's faith.

Fiat /fáyæt, fáyət/. (Lat. "Let it be done.") A command or order to act. Arbitrary or authoritative order or decision. In old English practice, a short order or warrant of a judge or magistrate directing some act to be done; an authority issuing from some competent source for the doing of some legal act. *See* Order.

FICA. Federal Insurance Contributions Act *(q.v.)*. The law that sets "Social Security" taxes and benefits.

Fiction of law. An assumption or supposition of law that something which is or may be false is true, or that a state of facts exists which has never really taken place. An assumption, for purposes of justice, of a fact that does not or may not exist. A rule of law which assumes as true, and will not allow to be disproved, something which is false, but not impossible. *See also* Legal fiction.

These assumptions are of an innocent or even beneficial character, and are made for the advancement of the ends of justice. They secure this end chiefly by the extension of procedure from cases to which it is applicable to other cases to which it is not strictly applicable, the ground of inapplicability being some difference of an immaterial character.

Fictitious. Founded on a fiction; having the character of a fiction; pretended; counterfeit. Feigned, imaginary, not real, false, not genuine, nonexistent. Arbitrarily invented and set up, to accomplish an ulterior object.

Fictitious action. An action brought for the sole purpose of obtaining the opinion of the court on a point of law, not for the settlement of any actual controversy between the parties. *See* Declaratory judgment; Feigned action.

Fictitious name. A counterfeit, alias, feigned, or pretended name taken by a person, differing in some essential particular from his true name (consisting of Christian name and patronymic), with the implication that it is meant to deceive or mislead. *See also* Alias.

Fictitious payee. Negotiable instrument is drawn to fictitious payee whenever payee named in it has no right to it, and its maker does not intend that such payee shall take anything by it; whether name of payee used by maker is that of person living or dead or one who never existed is immaterial. The test is not whether the named payee is "fictitious" but whether the signer intends that he shall have no interest in the instrument. U.C.C. § 3–405.

Fictitious plaintiff. A person appearing in the writ, complaint, or record as the plaintiff in a suit, but who in reality does not exist, or who is ignorant of the suit and of the use of his name in it. It is a contempt of court to sue in the name of a fictitious party.

Fictitious promise. *See* Promise.

Fidelity and guaranty insurance. A contract of fidelity or guaranty insurance is one whereby the insurer, for a valuable consideration, agrees, subject to certain conditions, to indemnify the insured against loss consequent upon the dishonesty or default of a designated person. Guaranty insurance, used in its broad sense, also includes credit insurance, and title insurance, as well as the numerous forms of surety bonds.

The contract partakes of the nature both of insurance and of suretyship. Hence, even in the absence of terms so providing, the contract is avoided by the failure of the insured to disclose to the insurer, at the time of making the contract, any known previous acts of dishonesty on the part of the employee, or any dishonest practices that may occur during the currency of the policy. But the insured is not required to give notice of mere irregularities not involving moral turpitude; nor, in the absence of agreement to that effect, does the insured owe to the insurer any duty of watching the conduct and accounts of the employee concerned.

Fidelity bond. Contract of fidelity insurance. A guaranty of personal honesty of officer furnishing indemnity against his defalcation or negligence. A contract whereby, for a consideration, one agrees to indemnify another against loss arising from the want of honesty, integrity, or fidelity of an employee or other person holding a position of trust. *See also* Bond; Fidelity and guaranty insurance; Insurance.

Fidelity insurance. *See* Fidelity and guaranty insurance; Insurance.

Fides /fáydiyz/. Lat. Faith; honesty; confidence; trust; veracity; honor. Occurring in the phrases *"bona fides"* (good faith), *"mala fides"* (bad faith), and *"uberrima fides"* (the utmost or most abundant good faith).

Fides est obligatio conscientiæ alicujus ad intentionem alterius /fáydiyz èst òbləgéysh(iy)ow kònshiyénshiyiy æləkyúwjəs æd intènshiyównəm oltəráyəs/. A trust is an obligation of conscience of one to the will of another.

Fiducial. An adjective having the same meaning as "fiduciary;" as, in the phrase "public or fiducial office."

Fiduciary /fəd(y)úwsh(iy)əry/. The term is derived from the Roman law, and means (as a noun) a person holding the character of a trustee, or a character analogous to that of a trustee, in respect to the trust and confidence involved in it and the scrupulous good faith and candor which it requires. A person having duty, created by his undertaking, to act primarily for another's benefit in matters connected with such undertaking. As an adjective it means of the nature of a trust; having the characteristics of a trust; analogous to a trust; relating to or founded upon a trust or confidence.

A term to refer to a person having duties involving good faith, trust, special confidence, and candor towards another. A fiduciary "includes such relationships as executor, administrator, trustee, and guardian." ABA Code of Judicial Conduct, Canon 3C(3)(b). A lawyer is also in a fiduciary relationship with the client.

A person or institution who manages money or property for another and who must exercise a standard of care in such management activity imposed by law or contract; *e.g.* executor of estate; receiver in bankruptcy; trustee. A trustee, for example, possesses a fiduciary responsibility to the beneficiaries of the trust to follow the terms of the trust and the requirements of applicable state law. A breach of fiduciary responsibility would make the trustee liable to the beneficiaries for any damage caused by such breach.

The status of being a fiduciary gives rise to certain legal incidents and obligations, including the prohibition against investing the money or property in investments which are speculative or otherwise imprudent.

Many states have adopted the Uniform Fiduciaries Act, and the Uniform Management of Institutional Funds Act.

See also Fiduciary capacity; Fiduciary or confidential relation.

Foreign fiduciary. A trustee, executor, administrator, guardian or conservator appointed by a jurisdiction other than the one in which he is acting.

Fiduciary bond. Type of surety bond required by court to be filed by trustees, administrators, executors, guardians, and conservators to insure proper performance of their duties.

Fiduciary capacity. One is said to act in a "fiduciary capacity" or to receive money or contract a debt in a "fiduciary capacity," when the business which he transacts, or the money or property which he handles, is not his own or for his own benefit, but for the benefit of another person, as to whom he stands in a relation implying and necessitating great confidence and trust on the one part and a high degree of good faith on the other part. The term is not restricted to technical or express trusts, but includes also such offices or relations as those of an attorney at law, a guardian, executor, or broker, a director of a corporation, and a public officer.

Fiduciary contract. An agreement by which a person delivers a thing to another on the condition that he will restore it to him.

Fiduciary debt. A debt founded on or arising from some confidence or trust as distinguished from a "debt" founded simply on contract.

Fiduciary duty. A duty to act for someone else's benefit, while subordinating one's personal interests to that of the other person. It is the highest standard of duty implied by law (*e.g.,* trustee, guardian).

Fiduciary heir. The Roman laws called a fiduciary heir the person who was instituted heir, and who was charged to deliver the succession to a person designated by the testament.

Fiduciary *or* confidential relation. A very broad term embracing both technical fiduciary relations and those informal relations which exist wherever one person trusts in or relies upon another. One founded on trust or confidence reposed by one person in the integrity and fidelity of another. Such relationship arises whenever

confidence is reposed on one side, and domination and influence result on the other; the relation can be legal, social, domestic, or merely personal. *See also* Confidential communication.

Fiduciary shield doctrine. Equitable doctrine which holds that actions taken by individual defendants solely in their capacity as corporate officers could not provide the basis for the exercise of jurisdiction over their persons, absent circumstances making such exercise appropriate. This doctrine confers jurisdictional immunity upon corporate officials, even though their conduct be tortious as long as the actions taken were in the interests of the corporation and not purely personal and the corporation is not merely a shell for the individual and does not lack sufficient assets to respond.

Field audit. *See* Audit.

Field book. A description of the courses and distances of the lines, and of the corners of the lots of the town as they were surveyed, and as they appear by number and division on the town plan.

Field Code. The original New York Code brought into being by David Dudley Field in 1848 calling for simplification of civil procedure. This Code served as the model for future state civil procedure codes and rules.

Field notes. A description of a survey.

Field sobriety tests. In determining reasonable grounds for DWI arrest, many police departments use field sobriety tests in which a suspect is requested to step from his vehicle and engage in a number of physical acts which are designed to test the person's coordination for the purpose of determining intoxication. The finger-to-nose test, picking up coins, walking a line, reciting the alphabet, and other similar activities have become a fairly common part of DWI arrest procedure. *See* Sobriety checkpoint.

Field warehouse financing agreement. A loan agreement in which the inventory that is being pledged as collateral is segregated from the company's other inventories and stored on its premises under the control of a field warehouse company. *See also* Field warehousing.

Field warehouse receipt. Document issued by warehouseman evidencing receipt of goods which have been stored. Such may be used as collateral for loans. *See also* Field warehousing; Warehouse receipt.

Field warehousing. Arrangement whereby wholesaler, manufacturer, or merchant finances his business through pledge of goods remaining on his premises and it is limited type of warehousing as distinguished from public warehouse. An arrangement whereby a pledgor may have necessary access to the pledged goods, while the goods are actually in the custody and control of a third person, acting as a warehouseman on the pledgor's premises. Field warehousing is often employed as a security device in inventory financing where the financer or secured party desires to maintain close control over the borrower's inventory and have the advantages of being a pledgee of the property. The device is employed in financing manufacturers or wholesalers in seasonal industries and is also useful where the manufactured products must be aged or cured or where they are accumulated over a period of time and then disposed of all at once.

Fieri /fáyəray/. Lat. To be made; to be done. *See* In fieri.

Fieri facias (Fi. Fa.) /fáyəray féys(h)(i)yəs/. Lat. Means that you "cause (it) to be done." Judicial writ directing sheriff to satisfy a judgment from the debtor's property. In its original form, the writ directed the seizure and sale of goods and chattels only, but eventually was enlarged to permit levy on real property, too; largely synonymously with modern writ of execution.

Fieri feci /fáyəray fíysay/. Means I have caused to be made. The return made by a sheriff or other officer to a writ of *fieri facias,* where he has collected the whole, or a part, of the sum directed to be levied. The return, as actually made, is expressed by the word "Satisfied" indorsed on the writ.

Fi. Fa. /fáy féy/. An abbreviation for *fieri facias (q.v.).*

FIFO. First-in, first-out. A method of accounting for inventory which assumes that goods are sold in the order in which they are purchased, *i.e.,* the oldest items sold first. The other common inventory costing methods include LIFO (last-in, first-out), specific identification, and average cost. *Contrast with* Last-in, first-out (LIFO).

Modified FIFO method. A process costing method that uses FIFO to compare a cost per equivalent unit but, in transferring units out of a department, the costs of the beginning inventory units and the units started and completed are combined and averaged.

FIFRA. Federal Insecticide, Fungicide, and Rodenticide Act. 7 U.S.C.A. §§ 136–136y.

Fifteenth Amendment. Amendment to U.S. Constitution, ratified by the States in 1870, guaranteeing all citizens the right to vote regardless of race, color, or previous condition of servitude. Congress was given the power to enforce such rights by appropriate legislation.

Fifth Amendment. Amendment to U.S. Constitution providing that no person shall be required to answer for a capital or otherwise infamous offense unless on indictment or presentment of a grand jury except in military cases; that no person will suffer double jeopardy; that no person will be compelled to be a witness against himself; that no person shall be deprived of life, liberty or property without due process of law and that private property will not be taken for public use without just compensation.

Fifth degree of kinship. The degree of kinship between a deceased intestate and the children of decedent's first cousin, sometimes designated as "first cousins once removed", is in the "fifth degree".

Fight. A hostile encounter, affray, or altercation; a physical or verbal struggle for victory; pugilistic combat. *See also* Affray.

Fighting words doctrine. The First Amendment doctrine that holds that certain utterances are not constitutionally protected as free speech if they are inherently likely to provoke a violent response from the audience. Words which by their very utterance inflict injury or tend to incite an immediate breach of the peace, having direct tendency to cause acts of violence by the persons to whom, individually, remark is addressed. The test is what persons of common intelligence would understand to be words likely to cause an average addressee to fight.

The "freedom of speech" protected by the Constitution is not absolute at all times and under all circumstances and there are well-defined and narrowly limited classes of speech, the prevention and punishment of which does not raise any constitutional problem, including the lewd and obscene, the profane, the libelous, and the insulting or "fighting words" which by their very utterance inflict injury or tend to incite an immediate breach of the peace.

Filching /fílchiŋ/fílshiŋ/. To steal money, commonly of little value, secretly or underhandedly.

File, n. A record of the court. A paper is said to be filed when it is delivered to the proper officer, and by him received to be kept on file as a matter of record and reference. But, in general, "file," or "the files," is used loosely to denote the official custody of the court or the place in the offices of a court where the records and papers are kept. The "file" in a case includes the original complaint and all pleadings and papers belonging thereto. *See also* Docket; Record.

File, v. To lay away and arrange in order, pleadings, motions, instruments, and other papers for preservation and reference. To deposit in the custody or among the records of a court. To deliver an instrument or other paper to the proper officer or official for the purpose of being kept on file as a matter of record and reference in the proper place. It carries the idea of permanent preservation as a public record. *See also* Record.

Constructive filing. See that title.

Filing officer. The person in charge of the office responsible for receiving legal papers and documents that are required to be publicly filed (*e.g.*, office or department of Secretary of State in which a financing statement must be filed to perfect a security interest under the Uniform Commercial Code. U.C.C. § 9–401).

Filing with court. Delivery of legal document to clerk of court or other proper officer with intent that it be filed with court. Fed.R.Civil P. 5 requires that all papers after the complaint required to be served upon a party shall be filed with the court (*i.e.*, clerk or judge) either before service or within a reasonable time thereafter.

Filed. *See* File.

Filed rate doctrine. Doctrine which forbids a regulated entity from charging rates for its services other than those properly filed with the appropriate federal regulatory authority.

File wrapper. The written record of the preliminary negotiations between an applicant and the Patent Office for a patent monopoly contract.

File wrapper estoppel doctrine. Under this doctrine, an applicant who has limited or modified a claim in order to avoid its rejection by the Patent Office may not later expand his claim by including the excluded matter, or its equivalent, or by omitting the limitations period. Doctrine means that the inventor had earlier given up certain claims with respect to his patent that he is now attempting to assert through the doctrine of equivalents in order to establish a basis for his charge that the patent has been infringed. *See also* Prosecution history estoppel.

Filiation /filiyéyshən/. Judicial determination of paternity. The relation of child to father.

In the civil law, the descent of son or daughter, with regard to his or her father, mother, and their ancestors.

Filiation proceeding. A special statutory proceeding in the nature of a civil action to enforce a civil obligation or duty specifically for the purpose of establishing parentage and the putative father's duty to support his illegitimate child. *See also* action.

Filibuster. Tactics designed to obstruct and delay legislative action by prolonged and often irrelevant speeches on the floor of the House or Senate. *See also* Cloture; a means of cutting off filibustering.

Filing. Process of recording document in a public office to provide notice of a legal interest. *See* Constructive filing; File.

Filing status. One of four categories used by an individual in preparing his or her income taxes. The four categories include: (1) single, (2) head of household, (3) married filing a joint return, (4) married filing separate returns. The taxpayer's filing status determines the tax rate schedule to be used in calculating the individual's tax liability. The filing status with the most advantageous rate schedule is "married filing a joint return."

Filiolus (or **filious**) /filiyówləs/. In old records, a godson.

Filius /filiyəs/. Lat. A son; a child. As distinguished from heir, *filius* is a term of nature, *hæres* a term of law. In the civil law the term was used to denote a child generally. A distinction was sometimes made, in the civil law, between *"filii"* and *"liberi";* the latter word including grandchildren *(nepotes),* the former not.

Fill. To make full; to complete; to satisfy or fulfill; to possess and perform the duties of; to occupy the whole capacity or extent of, so as to leave no space vacant. To execute customer's order to buy or sell a security or commodity.

Final. Last; conclusive; decisive; definitive; terminated; completed. As used in reference to legal actions, this word is generally contrasted with "interlocutory." For res judicata purposes, a judgment is "final" if no further judicial action by court rendering judgment is required to determine matter litigated. *See also* Final decision or judgment.

As to *final* Cost; Decree; Injunction; Judgment; Order; Process; Recovery; Sentence, and Settlement, see those titles.

Final appealable order or judgment. One that disposes of all issues and all parties in the case and leaves nothing for further determination. *See also* Final decision or judgment.

Final architect's certificate. One which is issued after a job is done and which finally determines the rights of the parties as to money and disputes.

Final award. One which conclusively determines the matter submitted and leaves nothing to be done except to execute and carry out terms of award. *See* Final decision or judgment.

Final decision or judgment. One which leaves nothing open to further dispute and which sets at rest cause of action between parties. One which settles rights of parties respecting the subject-matter of the suit and which concludes them until it is reversed or set aside. Also, a decision from which no appeal or writ of error can be taken. Judgment is considered "final," and thus appealable only if it determines the rights of the parties and disposes of all of the issues involved so that no future action by the court will be necessary in order to settle and determine the entire controversy.

"Final decision" which may be appealed (to Court of Appeals under 28 U.S.C.A. § 1291) is one that ends litigation on merits and leaves nothing for courts to do but execute judgment. In criminal case, is imposition of sentence. *See also* Final decision rule; Final disposition; Interlocutory Appeals Act; Judgment *(Final judgment)*; Res *(Res judicata)*.

Final decision rule. Appeals to federal courts of appeals from U.S. district courts must be from "final decisions" of district courts. 28 U.S.C.A. § 1291. In other words, the courts of appeals lack jurisdiction over nonfinal judgments. The object of this restriction is to prevent piecemeal litigation which would otherwise result from the use of interlocutory appeals. *See* Interlocutory Appeals Act.

Final decree. *See* Final decision or judgment.

Final determination. *See* Final decision or judgment.

Final disposition. Such a conclusive determination of the subject-matter that after the award, judgment, or decision is made nothing further remains to fix the rights and obligations of the parties, and no further controversy or litigation can arise thereon. It is such an award that the party against whom it is made can perform or pay it without any further ascertainment of rights or duties. *See* Final decision or judgment.

Final hearing. Describes that stage of proceedings relating to the determination of a subject matter upon its merits as distinguished from those of preliminary or interlocutory nature.

Finality rule. *See* Final decision rule.

Final judgment. *See* Final decision or judgment; Judgment.

Final judgment rule. *See* Final decision rule.

Final order. One which terminates the litigation between the parties and the merits of the case and leaves nothing to be done but to enforce by execution what has been determined. *See also* Final decision or judgment.

Final passage. The vote on a passage of a bill or resolution in either house of the legislature after it has received the prescribed number of readings and has been subjected to such action as is required by the fundamental law governing the body or its own rule.

Final payment. The point at which monetary credit given for an item cannot be revoked under U.C.C. Article 4, which describes four means of final payment occurs. See U.C.C. § 4–213(1).

Final settlement. In probate proceeding, a direct adjudication that the estate is fully administered; that the administrator has completely executed his trust and has accounted for all moneys received as the law requires.

With respect to final settlement in a real estate transaction, *see* Closing.

Final submission. Exists when nothing remains to be done in proceedings to render submission of case complete. Where the whole case, both requested instructions and evidence, is submitted to the court for its ruling and the court takes the case under advisement, there is a "final submission" of the entire case.

Finance. As a verb, to supply with funds through the payment of cash or issuance of stocks, bonds, notes, or mortgages; to provide with capital or loan money as needed to carry on business. Finance is concerned with the value of the assets of the business system and the acquisition and allocation of the financial resources of the system. *See also* Asset–based financing; Corporate finance; Off-balance-sheet financing.

Finance charge. The consideration for privilege of deferring payments of purchase price. The amount however denominated or expressed which the retail buyer contracts to pay or pays for the privilege of purchasing goods or services to be paid for by the buyer in installments; it does not include the amounts, if any, charged for insurance premiums, delinquency charges, attorney's fees, court costs, collection expenses or official fees. All charges incident to or condition of credit. Such costs are regulated by state and federal "truth-in-lending" statutes which require full disclosure of finance charges on credit agreements, billing statements, and the like. *See* Truth-in-Lending Act.

Finance committee. A committee of the U.S. Senate with functions and powers similar to that of the Ways and Means Committee of the House. In business, an executive level committee, commonly made up of members of board of directors, responsible for major financial decisions of business.

Finance company. Non-bank company that makes loans to individuals and businesses. Its capital comes from banks and other financial institutions and money markets—rather than from deposits. The primary types of finance companies are: consumer (or small loan) finance companies; sales finance (acceptance) companies, that purchase installment financing paper from *e.g.* automobile dealers; and, commercial finance or credit companies that make loans to manufacturers and wholesalers.

Finance lease. A lease in which the lessor does not select, manufacture or supply the goods, but enters into a contract with a third party supplier to acquire goods specifically for the purpose of leasing them to the lessee. U.C.C. § 2A–103.

Financial. Fiscal. Relating to finances.

Financial accounting. An area of accounting concerned primarily with external reporting; that is, reporting the results of financial activities to parties outside the firm.

Financial Accounting Standards Board. Independent board with responsibility to establish and interpret Generally Accepted Accounting Principles.

Financial budget. A budget that aggregates monetary details from the operating budgets; such includes the cash and capital budgets of a company as well as the pro forma financial statements.

Financial control. The day-to-day management of the firm's costs and expenses in order to control them in relation to the budgeted amounts.

Financial institutions. An insured bank; a commercial bank or trust company; a private banker; an agency or branch of a foreign bank in the United States; an insured institution as defined in the National Housing Act; a thrift institution; a broker or dealer registered with the Securities and Exchange Commission; a broker or dealer in securities or commodities; an investment banker or investment company; a currency exchange; an issuer, redeemer, or cashier of travelers' checks, checks, money orders, or similar instruments; an operator of a credit card system; an insurance company; a dealer in precious metals, stones or jewels; a pawnbroker; a loan or finance company; a travel agency; a licensed sender of money; a telegraph company. 31 U.S.C.A. § 5312. See also Uniform Probate Code, § 6–101(3).

Financial interest. An interest equated with money or its equivalent.

Financial intermediary. An institution (such as a bank) or individual that makes transactions that transform funds from one form (such as a savings deposit) into another form (such as a loan).

Financial leverage. The use of debt financing. *See also* Leverage.

Financially able. Solvent; credit worthy; able to pay debts and expenses as due. Means purchaser must be able to command the necessary funds to close the transaction within the required time. A prospective purchaser is "financially able" if he or she has the capability to make downpayment and all deferred payments required under a proposed contract of sale. *See also* Financial responsibility acts; Solvency.

Financial markets. Markets for the exchange of capital in the economy, including stock, bond, commodity and foreign exchanges.

Financial position. A determination of the resources owned by a company and the claims on those resources at a particular point in time.

Financial ratios. Ratios that can be calculated from a firm's financial statements that enhance the understanding of the firm's financial performance and financial position.

Financial reports. *See* Annual report; Financial statement; Profit and loss statement.

Financial responsibility. Term commonly used in connection with motor vehicle insurance equivalents. *See also* Financial responsibility acts.

Financial responsibility acts. State statutes which require owners of motor vehicles to produce proof of financial accountability as a condition to acquiring a license and registration so that judgments rendered against them arising out of the operation of the vehicles may be satisfied.

Financial responsibility clause. Provision in automobile insurance policy stating that the insured has at least the minimum amount of coverage required by state financial responsibility laws.

Financial security. A standardized financial asset such as common stock, preferred stock, bond, convertible bond, or financial future.

Financial statement. Any report summarizing the financial condition or financial results of a person or organization on any date or for any period. Financial statements include the balance sheet and the income statement and sometimes the statement of changes in financial position. *See also* Annual report; Footnotes.

Consolidated statement. Financial statements that include the accounts of both a parent company and controlled subsidiaries. *See also* Consolidated financial statements.

Financial worth. The value of one's property less what he owes, or the value of his resources less his liabilities.

Financier. A person or financial institution employed in the economical management and application of money. One skilled in matters appertaining to the judicious investment, loaning, and management of money affairs. Person or institution that financially backs business ventures.

Financing agency. A bank, finance company or other person who in the ordinary course of business makes advances against goods or documents of title or who by arrangement with either the seller or the buyer intervenes in ordinary course to make or collect payment due or claimed under the contract for sale, as by purchasing or paying the seller's draft or making advances against it or by merely taking it for collection whether or not documents of title accompany the draft. "Financing agency" includes also a bank or other person who similarly intervenes between persons who are in the position of seller and buyer in respect to the goods. U.C.C. § 2–104.

Financing statement. A document setting out a secured party's security interest in goods. A document designed to notify third parties, generally prospective buyers or lenders, that there may be an enforceable security interest in the property of the debtor. It is merely evidence of the creation of a security interest, and usually is not itself a security agreement.

Under the Uniform Commercial Code, a financing statement is used under Article 9 to reflect a public record that there is a security interest or claim to the goods in question to secure a debt. The financing statement is filed by the security holder with the Secretary of State, or similar public body, and as such becomes public record. When the document is filed with the appropriate government agency, all potential lenders and third parties are put on constructive notice of the security interest. *See also* Secured transaction; Security interest.

Find. To come upon by seeking or by effort. To discover; to determine; to locate; to ascertain and declare. *See also* Found; Locate.

To announce a conclusion upon a disputed fact or state of facts; as a jury is said to "find a will." To determine a controversy in favor of one of the parties; as a jury "finds for the plaintiff." *See also* Finding.

Finder. An intermediary who contracts to find, introduce and bring together parties to a business opportunity, leaving ultimate negotiations and consummation of business transaction to the principals. With respect to a securities issue, refers to one who brings together an issuer and an underwriter; in connection with mergers, refers to one who brings two companies together. May also refer to one who secures mortgage financing for borrower; or one who locates a particular type of executive or professional for a corporation; or one who locates a particular type of business acquisition for a corporation.

Finder's fee. Amount charged for bringing together parties to business opportunity (*e.g.*, lender and borrower) or bringing issuer and underwriter together, or for performing other types of services described under "finder" supra. A finder's fee for a securities issue may be stock or a combination of cash and stock.

Finder's fee contract. An arrangement by which an intermediary finds, introduces, and brings together parties to a business opportunity, leaving the ultimate negotiation and consummation of the business transaction to the principals.

Finding. The result of the deliberations of a jury or a court. A decision upon a question of fact reached as the result of a judicial examination or investigation by a court, jury, referee, coroner, etc. A recital of the facts as found. The word commonly applies to the result reached by a judge or jury. *See also* Decision; Judgment; Verdict.

Finding of fact. Determinations from the evidence of a case, either by court or an administrative agency, concerning facts averred by one party and denied by another. A determination of a fact by the court, averred by one party and denied by the other, and founded on evidence in case. A conclusion by way of reasonable inference from the evidence. Also the answer of the jury to a specific interrogatory propounded to them as to the existence or non-existence of a fact in issue. Conclusion drawn by trial court from facts without exercise of legal judgment. *Compare* Conclusion of law; *and Finding of law, below.*

Findings of fact shall not be set aside unless clearly erroneous. Fed.R. Civil P. 52(a). The court may amend, or make additional findings, on motion of a party. Fed.R. Civil P. 52(b).

A *general* finding by a court is a general statement that the facts are in favor of a party or entitle him to judgment. It is a complete determination of all matters, and is a finding of every special thing necessary to be found to sustain the general finding.

A *special* finding is a specific setting forth of the ultimate facts established by the evidence and which are determinative of the judgment which must be given. It is only a determination of the ultimate facts on which the law must be determined. A special finding may also be said to be one limited to the fact issue submitted.

Finding of law. Term applies to rulings of law made by court in connection with findings of fact; such findings or rulings of law are subject to appellate review. *See also* Conclusion of law. *Compare Finding of fact, above.*

Fine, n. A pecuniary punishment or penalty imposed by lawful tribunal upon person convicted of crime or misdemeanor. See *e.g.* 18 U.S.C.A. § 3571. It may include a forfeiture or penalty recoverable in a civil action, and, in criminal convictions, may be in addition to imprisonment. A fine constitutes a "sentence" as defined in Rules of Criminal Procedure. *See also* Penalty.

Fine, v. To impose a pecuniary punishment or mulct. To sentence a person convicted of an offense to pay a penalty in money.

In imposing fines, modern statutes require the court to consider the ability of the defendant to pay, the burden such will have on dependents of the defendant, and the effect such fine will have on the ability of the defendant to make restitution to the victim. *E.g.*, Model Penal Code § 7.02(3)(b); 18 U.S.C.A. § 3571.

Fine print. Term or expression referring to disclaimer or avoidance type provisions in insurance policies, financing agreements, and the like, that are typeset in small type and so located in the document so as to not be readily noticed by the insured, borrower, etc. State and federal disclosure laws have greatly curtailed this practice. *Compare* Conspicuous term *or* clause.

Fingerprints. The distinctive pattern of lines on human fingertips, often used as a method of identification in criminal cases. For genetic fingerprinting, *see* DNA identification.

FIO. "Free in and out". Term in a bill of lading means that the shipper supervises and pays for both loading and discharge of cargo.

FIOS. "Free in and out stowage". Term indicates that the vessel does not pay for the costs of loading, stowage or discharge.

Fire. To dismiss or discharge from a position or employment.

Firearm. An instrument used in the propulsion of shot, shell, or bullets by the action of gunpowder exploded within it. A weapon which acts by force of gunpowder. This word comprises all sorts of guns, fowling-pieces, blunderbusses, pistols, etc. In addition, grenade shells, fuses, and powder may be considered "firearm" even though disassembled.

The term "firearm" means any weapon which is designed to or may readily be converted to expel any projectile by the action of an explosive; or the frame or receiver of any such weapon. 18 U.S.C.A. §§ 232(4), 921(3).

Firearms Acts. Statutes (federal and state) imposing criminal penalties for illegal possession, sale and use of firearms; *e.g.* possession without license; carrying concealed weapon. See 18 U.S.C.A. § 921 et seq.; Model Penal Code § 5.07.

Firebug. A popular phrase referring to persons guilty of the crime of arson; commonly understood to mean an incendiary, pyromaniac, or arsonist. *See* Arson.

Fire district. One of the districts into which a city may be divided for the purpose of more efficient service by the fire department.

Fire insurance. *See* Insurance.

Fireman's Rule. Doctrine which holds that professionals, whose occupations by nature expose them to particular risks, may not hold another negligent for creating the situation to which they respond in their professional capacity.

Fire marshal *or* **warden.** Official whose duties include supervision of firefighting and fire prevention for a state, county, city or town.

Fire ordeal. *See* Ordeal.

Fire sale. Sale of merchandise at reduced prices because of damage by fire or water; commonly, any sale at reduced prices, especially one brought about by an emergency. Fire sales are often regulated by statute or ordinance to protect the public-buyer from deceptive sales practices.

Firm. Business entity or enterprise. Unincorporated business. Partnership of two or more persons. *See also* Firm name.

Binding; fixed; final; definite. *See* Confirmation; Firm offer.

Firm bid. Offer which contains no conditions which may defeat acceptance and which by its terms remains open and binding until accepted or rejected.

Firmly. A statement that an affiant "firmly believes" the contents of the affidavit imports a strong or high degree of belief, and is equivalent to saying that he "verily" believes it. The operative words in a bond or recognizance, that the obligor is held and "firmly bound," are equivalent to an acknowledgment of indebtedness and promise to pay.

Firm name. The name or title under which company transacts its business.

Firm offer. As defined by U.C.C. is an offer by a merchant to buy or sell goods in a signed writing which by its terms give assurance that it will be held open. Such is not revocable for lack of consideration during the time stated or if no time is stated for a reasonable time, but in no event may such period of irrevocability exceed three months; but any such term of assurance on a form supplied by the offeree must be separately signed by the offeror. U.C.C. § 2–205. A binding, definite offer that is irrevocable for an agreed upon time.

FIRPTA. Under this Act (Foreign Investment in Real Property Tax Act), gains or losses realized by nonresident aliens and non-U.S. corporations on the disposition of U.S. real estate create U.S. source income and are subject to U.S. income tax.

First. Preceding all others; foremost; used as an ordinal of one, as earliest in time or succession or foremost in position; in front of or in advance of all others. Initial; senior; leading; chief; entitled to priority or preference above others.

As to *first* Cousin, and Mortgage, see those titles.

First Amendment. Amendment to U.S. Constitution guaranteeing basic freedoms of speech, religion, press, and assembly and the right to petition the government for redress of grievances. The various freedoms and rights protected by the First Amendment have been held applicable to the states through the due process clause of the Fourteenth Amendment.

First blush rule. This rule, whereby a verdict may be set aside as excessive only if it is so to such an extent as to cause the mind at first blush to conclude that it was returned under influence of passion or prejudice on part of jury, is a mechanism to assist trial court in performing its responsibility when called upon to decide whether award is so excessive as to appear to have been given under influence of passion or prejudice.

First-class. Of the most superior or excellent grade or kind; belonging to the head or chief or numerically precedent of several classes into which the general subject is divided; *e.g.* first class mail, first class airline ticket.

First-class title. A marketable title, shown by a clean record, or at least not depending on presumptions that must be overcome or facts that are uncertain. *See also* Clear title; Marketable title.

First degree murder. Murder committed with deliberately premeditated malice aforethought, or with extreme atrocity or cruelty, or in the commission or attempted commission of a crime punishable with death or imprisonment for life, is murder in the first degree. Distinction between "first degree murder" and "second degree murder" is a presence of a specific intent to kill. *See also* Murder; Premeditation.

Firsthand knowledge. Information or knowledge gleaned directly from its source; *e.g.* eyewitness to a homicide.

A lay witness may not testify to a matter unless evidence is introduced sufficient to support a finding that he has personal knowledge of the matter. Federal Rules Evid. 602. If testimony purports to be based on observed facts but is in fact mere repetition of the statement of another, the proper objection is lack of first-hand knowledge. *Compare* Hearsay.

First heir. The person who will be first entitled to succeed to the title to an estate after the termination of a life estate or estate for years.

First impression case. First examination. First presentation of question of law to a court for examination or decision. A case is said to be "of the first impression" when it presents an entirely novel question of law for the decision of the court, and cannot be governed by any existing precedent.

First in, first out. *See* FIFO.

First lien. One which takes priority or precedence over all other charges or encumbrances upon the same piece of property, and which must be satisfied before such other charges are entitled to participate in the proceeds of its sale. *See also* First mortgage.

First meeting. As used in a statute providing that, for insulting words or conduct to reduce homicide to manslaughter, killing must occur immediately or at "first meeting" after slayer is informed thereof, quoted words mean first time parties are in proximity under such circumstances as would enable slayer to act in the premises.

First meeting of creditors. In bankruptcy, the initial meeting called by the court for the examination of the bankrupt (*i.e.* debtor). Bankruptcy Code, § 341.

First mortgage. The senior mortgage which, by reason of its position, has priority over all junior encumbrances. The holder of the first or senior mortgage has priority right to payment on default. *See also* Mortgage.

First of exchange. Where a set of bills of exchange is drawn in duplicate or triplicate, for greater safety in their transmission, all being of the same tenor, and the intention being that the acceptance and payment of any one of them (the first to arrive safely) shall cancel the others of the set, they are called individually the "first of exchange," "second of exchange," etc.

First offender. One who has never before been convicted of a crime and, hence, one generally given special consideration in the disposition of his case. For example, first offenders of less serious crimes often receive suspended sentences or are placed on probation.

First policy year. In insurance, the year beginning with the first issuance of the insurance policy. This phrase in a statute eliminating suicide of insured after such year as defense, means year for which policy, annually renewed, was first issued.

First purchaser. In the law of descent, this term signifies the ancestor who first acquired (in any other manner than by inheritance) the estate which still remains in his family or descendants.

First refusal. A right to elect to take specified property at the same price and on the same terms and conditions as those contained in a good faith offer by a third person if the owner manifests a willingness to accept the offer. *See also* Right of first refusal.

First sale rule. Under this doctrine, a copyright holder who conveys title to a particular copy of a copyrighted work relinquishes exclusive right to vend that particular copy; although holder's other rights remain intact, vendee holds right to distribute the transferred copy in whatever manner vendee chooses.

First vested estate. Refers to first estate to vest in heirs after death of ancestor.

Fiscal. In general, having to do with financial matters; *i.e.* money, taxes, public or private revenues, etc. Belonging to the fisc, or public treasury. Relating to accounts or the management of revenue. Of or pertaining to the public finances of a government or private finances of business.

Fiscal agent. Generally, a bank which collects and disburses money and serves as a depository of private and public funds in behalf of another.

Fiscal officers. Those charged with the collection and distribution of public money, as, the revenues of a state (State Treasurer), county, or municipal corporation. In private corporation, officers directly charged with duty to oversee financial transactions such as treasurer and comptroller.

Fiscal period. In accounting, a period of time for which financial statements are prepared such as a year, a month or a quarter. *See also* Accounting period; Fiscal year.

Fiscal year. A period of twelve consecutive months chosen by a business as the accounting period for annual reports. A corporation's accounting year. Due to the nature of a particular business, some companies do not use the calendar year for their bookkeeping. A typical example is the department store which finds December 31 too early a date to close its books after Christmas sales. For that reason many stores close their accounting year January 31. Their fiscal year, therefore, runs from February 1 of one year through January 31 of the next. The fiscal year of other companies may run from July 1 through the following June 30. Most companies, though, operate on a calendar year basis. *See also* Accounting period.

Fishing trip *or* **expedition.** Using the courts to find out information beyond the fair scope of the lawsuit. The loose, vague, unfocused questioning of a witness or the overly broad use of the discovery process. Discovery sought on general, loose, and vague allegations, or on suspicion, surmise, or vague guesses. The scope of discovery may be restricted by protective orders as provided for by Fed.Rule Civil P. 26(c).

Fit. Suitable or appropriate. Conformable to a duty. Adapted to, designed, prepared. Words "fit" and "proper" on issue of custody in divorce cases are usually interpreted as meaning moral fitness.

Fitness for particular purpose. Where the seller at the time of contracting has reason to know any particular purpose for which the goods are required and that the buyer is relying on the seller's skill or judgment to select or furnish suitable goods, there is, unless excluded or modified, an implied warranty that the goods shall be fit for such purpose. U.C.C. § 2–315. *See also* Warranty.

Fix. Adjust or regulate; determine; settle; make permanent. Term imports finality; stability; certainty; definiteness. *See also* Firm.

To liquidate or render certain. To fasten a liability upon one. To transform a possible or contingent liability into a present and definite liability.

The illegal injection of a narcotic.

Fixed. Prices are "fixed" when they are mutually agreed upon. *See* Fixed prices; Price-fixing.

In copyright law, a work is "fixed" in a tangible medium of expression when its embodiment in a copy or phonorecord, by or under the authority of the author, is sufficiently permanent or stable to permit it to be perceived, reproduced, or otherwise communicated for a period of more than transitory duration. A work consisting of sounds, images, or both, that are being transmitted, is "fixed" for purposes of this title if a fixation of the work is being made simultaneously with its transmission. Copyright Act, 17 U.S.C.A. § 101.

Fixed assets. Tangible property used in operating a business which will not be consumed or converted into cash or its equivalent during the current accounting period; *e.g.* plant, machinery, land, buildings, fixtures. Contrasted with liquid assets; *e.g.* cash, securities.

Fixed bail. Setting the amount and terms of bail.

Fixed capital. The amount of money which is permanently invested in the business. May also refer to capital invested in fixed assets (land, buildings, machinery, etc.). Cost of total plant and general equipment.

Fixed charges. Costs that do not vary with changes in output and would continue even if firm produced no output at all, such as most management expenses, interests on bonded debt, depreciation, property taxes, and other irreducible overhead.

Fixed costs. *See* Discretionary fixed cost; Fixed charges.

Fixed debt. A more or less permanent form of debt commonly evidenced by bonds or debenture. *See also* Fixed indebtedness; Fixed liabilities.

Fixed expenses. *See* Fixed charges.

Fixed fee. Term commonly used in construction contracts which provide for payment of costs plus a predetermined amount as a fee.

Fixed income. That species of income which does not fluctuate over a period of time such as interest on bonds and debentures or dividends from preferred stock as contrasted with dividend income from common stock. May also refer to income received by retiree from pension, annuity, or other form of fixed retirement benefit or income.

Fixed indebtedness. An established or settled indebtedness; not contingent. *See* Fixed debt; Fixed liabilities.

Fixed liabilities. Those certain and definite as to both obligation and amount; *e.g.* interest on bonds or mortgage. Long term liabilities. *See also* Fixed debt.

Fixed opinion. A conviction, bias, or prejudgment as to guilt or liability disqualifying juror to impartially consider whole evidence and apply free from bias law as given in charge by court.

Fixed price contract. Type of contract in which buyer agrees to pay seller a definite, predetermined price, regardless of costs.

Fixed-price basis. An offering of securities at a fixed price.

Fixed prices. Prices established (*i.e.* mutually agreed upon) between wholesalers or retailers for sale or resale of materials, goods, or products. Agreements to fix prices are generally prohibited by state and federal statutes. *See* Price-fixing.

Fixed rate loan. Loan is which interest rate does not change depending on market conditions.

Fixed salary. One which is definitely ascertained and prescribed as to amount and time of payment, and does not depend upon the receipt of fees or other contingent emoluments; though not necessarily a salary which cannot be changed by competent authority. Established or settled, to remain for a time.

Fixture. An article in the nature of personal property which has been so annexed to the realty that it is regarded as a part of the real property. That which is fixed or attached to something permanently as an appendage, and not removable.

A thing is deemed to be affixed to real property when it is attached to it by roots, imbedded in it, permanently resting upon it, or permanently attached to what is thus permanent, as by means of cement, plaster, nails, bolts, or screws.

Goods are fixtures when they become so related to particular real estate that an interest in them arises under real estate law; *e.g.*, a furnace affixed to a house or other building; counters permanently affixed to the floor of a store; a sprinkler system installed in a building. U.C.C. § 9–313(1)(a).

Agricultural fixtures. Those annexed for the purpose of farming.

Trade fixtures. Articles placed in or attached to leased property by the tenant, to facilitate the trade or business for which he occupies the premises, or to be used in connection with such business, or promote convenience and efficiency in conducting it. Such personal property as merchants usually possess and annex to the premises occupied by them to enable them to store, handle, and display their goods, which are generally removable without material injury to the premises. Unlike regular fixtures, *trade* fixtures are not considered part of the realty.

FKA. Formerly known as.

Flaco. A place covered with standing water.

Flag. A national standard on which are certain emblems; an ensign; a banner. It is carried by soldiers, ships, etc., and commonly displayed at forts, businesses and many other suitable places.

In common parlance, the word "flag," when used as denoting a signal, does not necessarily mean the actual use of a flag, but by figure of speech the word is used in the secondary sense and signifies a signal given as with a flag, that is to say, as by a waving of the hand for the purpose of communicating information.

Flag desecration. Flagrant misuse of flag by such acts as mutilation, defacement, or burning. Statutes making such acts criminal offenses (*e.g.* 18 U.S.C.A. § 700 (1989)) have been held to be unconstitutional as violating the freedom of expression protection of the First Amendment. *See also* Desecrate.

Flag, law of. In maritime law, the law of that nation or country whose flag is flown by a particular vessel. A shipowner who sends his vessel into a foreign port gives notice by his flag to all who enter into contracts with the master that he intends the law of that flag to regulate such contracts, and that they must either submit to its operation or not contract with him.

Flag of convenience. Practice of registering a merchant vessel with a country that has favorable (*i.e.* less restrictive) safety requirements, registration fees, etc.

Flag of the United States. By the act entitled "An act to establish the flag of the United States," (Rev.St. §§ 1791, 1792), it was provided that, "from and after the fourth day of July next, the flag of the United States be thirteen horizontal stripes, alternate red and white; that the union be twenty stars, white in a blue field; that, on the admission of every new state into the Union, one star be added to the union of the flag; and that such addition shall take effect on the fourth day of July then next succeeding such admission." See 4 U.S.C.A. §§ 1, 2.

Flag of truce. A white flag displayed by one of two belligerent parties to notify the other party that communication and a cessation of hostilities are desired.

Flagrant necessity /fléygrənt nəsésətiy/. A case of urgency rendering lawful an otherwise illegal act, as an assault to remove a man from impending danger.

Flash check. A check drawn upon a banker by a person who has no funds at the banker's and knows that such is the case. Such act is a crime. Also called check kiting (*q.v.*).

Flat. A place covered with water too shallow for navigation with vessels ordinarily used for commercial purposes. The space between high and low water mark along the edge of an arm of the sea, bay, tidal river, etc.

A floor or separate division of a floor, fitted for housekeeping and designed to be occupied by a single family. An apartment on one floor. A floor or story in a building. A building, the various floors of which are fitted up as flats, either residential or business.

In insurance, a policy without coinsurance provision; a provision for termination of renewal policy within short period after anniversary date without charge to insured.

In finance, stock is sold flat when no provision is made for adjusting accrued dividends.

Flat bond. Bond which includes accrued interest in the price.

Flat money. Paper money which is not backed by gold or silver but issued by order of the government. Also called "fiat" money. *See* Federal reserve notes.

Flat rate. Fixed amount paid each period without regard to actual amount of electricity, gas, etc. used in that particular period.

Flat tax. In its pure form, a flat tax would eliminate all exclusions, deductions, and credits and impose a one-rate tax on gross income. *See also* Tax.

Flee from justice. Removing one's self from or secreting one's self within jurisdiction wherein offense was committed to avoid arrest; or leaving one's home, residence, or known place of abode, or concealing one's self therein, with intent, in either case, to avoid arrest, detention, or punishment for some criminal offense. *See also* Extradition; Flight from prosecution; Fugitive.

Fleet. A place where the tide flows; a creek, or inlet of water.

Flee to the wall. A metaphorical expression, used in connection with homicide done in self-defense, signifying the exhaustion of every possible means of escape, or of averting the assault, before killing the assailant. *See* Self-defense.

Fleet policy. In insurance, a blanket policy which covers a number of vehicles owned by the same insured.

Flexible budget. A series of individual budgets that present costs according to their behavior at different levels of activity. *See also* Budget.

Flight from prosecution. The evading of the course of justice by voluntarily withdrawing one's self in order to avoid arrest or detention, or the institution or continuance of criminal proceedings, regardless of whether one leaves jurisdiction. Also comprehends continued concealment. Such is considered to exist when an accused departs from the vicinity of the crime under circumstances such as to indicate a sense of fear, or of guilt or to avoid arrest, even before the defendant has been suspected of the crime. See *e.g.* 18

U.S.C.A. §§ 1073, 1074. *See also* Escape; Flee from justice; Fugitive.

Flim-flam. A form of bunco or confidence game. Procedure variously known as "flim-flam", "faith and trust" or "confidence game" essentially is performed by two operators, ostensibly strangers to each other, by persuading victim to turn over to one of operators a sum of money to demonstrate his trustworthiness as prerequisite to obtaining some easy money and, after victim has turned over his money, operators disappear and victim receives nothing.

Flipping. Colloquial term for refinancing of consumer loans.

Float. The delay in processing transactions by banks and others which may permit the interest-free use of funds for brief periods. Checks that have been credited to the depositor's bank account, but not yet debited to the drawer's bank account. The time between when a check is written and when such check is actually deducted from bank account. In banking practice, checks and other items in the process of collection. "Float" in a checking account occurs when someone writes a check without sufficient funds, then covers the check before it returns to the bank for payment. *See also* Bank collection float; Collection float; Corporate processing float; Kiting; Mail float.

In manufacturing, the amount of goods in the process of production, usually measured in terms of the number of units in process divided by the number of finished units produced per average day and expressed as, for example, "six days float." In finance, the unsold part of a security issue or the number of shares actively traded.

To let a given currency "float" is to allow it to freely establish its own value as against other currencies (*i.e.* exchange rate) by the law of supply and demand.

In land law, especially in the western states, a certificate authorizing the entry, by the holder, of a certain quantity of land not yet specifically selected or located.

Floatage. *See* Flotsam.

Floater policy. In insurance, policy which is issued to cover items which have no fixed location such as jewelry or other items of personal property worn or carried about by the insured. *See also* Floating policy.

Floating charge. A continuing charge on the assets of the company creating it, but permitting the company to deal freely with the property in the usual course of business until the security holder shall intervene to enforce his claim. *See also* Floating lien.

Floating debt. Liabilities (exclusive of bonds) payable on demand or at an early date; *e.g.* accounts payable; bank loans.

Floating easement. Easement for right-of-way which, when created, is not limited to any specific area on servient tenement.

Floating interest rate. Rate of interest that is not fixed but which varies depending upon the existing rate in the money market.

Floating lien. A security interest retained in collateral even when the collateral changes in character, classification, or location. An inventory loan in which the lender receives a security interest or general claim on all of a company's inventory. Security interest under which borrower pledges security for present and future advances. Such security is not only in inventory or accounts of the debtor in existence at the time of the original loan, but also in his after-acquired inventory or accounts. U.C.C. § 9–204(4).

Floating *or* **circulating capital**. Capital retained for the purpose of meeting current expenditures. The capital which is consumed at each operation of production and reappears transformed into new products. Capital in the form of current, as opposed to fixed, assets.

Floating policy. Insurance policy intended to supplement specific insurance on property and attaches only when the latter ceases to cover the risk, and the purpose of such policy is to provide indemnity for property which cannot, because of its frequent change in location and quantity, be covered by specific insurance. *See also* Floater policy.

Floating stock. The act or process by which stock is issued and sold. *See also* Issue.

Floating zone. A concept in zoning whereby land use is predetermined by reserving specified portions of an entire area for particular uses while not immediately assigning particular parcels to a certain use. Such a zone has no defined boundaries. It is conceived as floating over the entire area where it may eventually be established. *See also* Zoning.

Flood. An inundation of water over land not usually covered by it. Water which inundates area of surface of earth where it ordinarily would not be expected to be. *See also* Act of God.

Flood insurance. *See* Insurance.

Floodplain. Land adjacent to rivers, which, because of its level topography, floods when river overflows.

Floor. A term used metaphorically, in parliamentary practice, to denote the exclusive right to address the body in session. A member who has been recognized by the chairman, and who is in order, is said to "have the floor", until his remarks are concluded. Similarly, the "floor of the house" means the main part of the hall where the members sit, as distinguished from the galleries, or from the corridors or lobbies.

Trading area where stocks and commodities are bought and sold on exchanges.

The lower limit; *e.g.* minimum wages; lowest price stock will be permitted to fall before selling.

Floor broker. Member of stock or commodity exchange who is employee of member firm and executes trades for clients.

Floor plan financing. Arrangement for the lending of money to an automobile dealer, or other supplier of goods, so that he may purchase cars, or other articles, to include in his inventory; the loan being secured by the automobiles or other goods while in the dealer's possession, and is gradually reduced as the cars or other merchandise are sold. *See* Floor plan rule.

Floor plan rule. Rule by which an owner who has placed an automobile on the floor of a retail dealer's showroom for sale is estopped to deny the title of an innocent purchaser from such dealer in the ordinary retail dealing, without knowledge of any conflicting claim.

Floor trader. Member of stock or commodity exchange who trades on floor for his own account.

Flotation cost. The cost of selling a new issue of securities.

Floterial district /flòwtíriyəl dístrəkt/. Term used to refer to a legislative district which includes within its boundaries several separate districts or political subdivisions which independently would not be entitled to additional representation but whose conglomerate population entitles the entire area to another seat in the particular legislative body being apportioned.

Flotsam, flotsan /flótsəm/. A name for the goods which float upon the sea when cast overboard for the safety of the ship, or when a ship is sunk. Distinguished from "jetsam" (goods deliberately thrown over to lighten ship) and "ligan".

Flowage. The natural flow or movement of water from an upper estate to a lower one is a servitude which the owner of the latter must bear, though the flowage be not in a natural water course with well defined banks.

Flowage easement. *See* Easement.

Flower bond. Type of U.S. Savings Bond which may be cashed in at par to pay Federal estate taxes.

Flowing lands. Term imports raising and setting back water on another's land, by a dam placed across a stream or water course which is the natural drain and outlet for surplus water on such land.

Flow tide. High tide. *See* Tide.

FLSA. *See* Fair Labor Standards Act.

Fluctuating clause. Type of escalator provision which is inserted in some long term contracts to allow for increase in costs during the contract period. *See also* Escalator clause.

Flume. Primarily a stream or river, but usually used to designate an artificial channel applied to some definite use, and may mean either an open or a covered aqueduct.

Fly-power. A written assignment in blank, whereby, on being attached to a stock certificate, the stock may be transferred.

FMC. Federal Maritime Commission.

FMCS. Federal Mediation and Conciliation Service.

FMW. Fair market value.

FNMA. Federal National Mortgage Association.

FOB. Free on board some location (for example, FOB shipping point; FOB destination). A delivery term which requires a seller to ship goods and bear the expense and risk of loss to the F.O.B. point designated. The invoice price includes delivery at seller's expense to that location. Title to goods usually passes from seller to buyer at the FOB location. U.C.C. § 2–319(1).

FOIA. Freedom of Information Act.

Food and Drug Administration. An agency within the Department of Health and Human Services established to set safety and quality standards for foods, drugs, cosmetics, and other household substances sold as consumer products. Among the basic tasks of the FDA are research, inspection and licensing of drugs for manufacturing and distribution. This agency is in charge of administering Food, Drug and Cosmetic Act *(q.v.)*.

Food, Drug and Cosmetic Act. Federal Act of 1938 prohibiting the transportation in interstate commerce of adulterated or misbranded food, drugs and cosmetics. Act is administered by Food and Drug Administration.

Foot-frontage rule. Under rule, assessment is confined to actual frontage on line of improvement, and depth of lot, number or character of improvements, or value thereof, is immaterial.

Footnotes. A supplemental, yet integral, part of financial statements that provides an expansion of the information contained in the body of the statements.

Footprints. In the law of evidence, impressions made upon earth, snow, or other surface by the feet of persons, or by their shoes, boots, or other foot covering.

For. In behalf of, in place of, in lieu of, instead of, representing, as being which, or equivalent to which, and sometimes imports agency. During; throughout; for the period of, as, where a notice is required to be published "for" a certain number of weeks or months. Duration, when put in connection with time.

In consideration for; as an equivalent for; in exchange for; in place of; as where property is agreed to be given "for" other property or "for" services.

Belonging to, exercising authority or functions within, as where one describes himself as "a notary public in and for the said county."

By reason of; with respect to; for benefit of; for use of; in consideration of. The cause, motive or occasion of an act, state or condition. Used in sense of "because of," "on account of," or "in consequence of." By means of, or growing out of.

It connotes the end with reference to which anything is, acts, serves, or is done. In consideration of which, in view of which, or with reference to which, anything is done or takes place. In direction of; with view of reaching; with reference to needs, purposes or uses of; appropriate or adapted to; suitable to purpose, requirement, character or state of.

For account of. Language introducing name of person entitled to receive proceeds of indorsed note or draft.

Forbearance. Refraining from doing something that one has a legal right to do. Giving of further time for repayment of obligation or agreement not to enforce claim at its due date. A delay in enforcing a legal right. Act by which creditor waits for payment of debt due him by debtor after it becomes due.

Refraining from action. The term is used in this sense in general jurisprudence, in contradistinction to "act." As regards forbearance as a form of consideration, *see* Consideration.

For cause. With respect to removal from office "for cause", means for reasons which law and public policy recognize as sufficient warrant for removal and such cause is "legal cause" and not merely a cause which the appointing power in the exercise of discretion may deem sufficient. They do not mean removal by arbitrary or capricious action but there must be some cause affecting and concerning ability and fitness of official to perform duty imposed on him. The cause must be one in which the law and sound public policy will recognize as a cause for official no longer occupying his office.

Force. Power, violence, compulsion, or constraint exerted upon or against a person or thing. Power dynamically considered, that is, in motion or in action; constraining power, compulsion; strength directed to an end. Commonly the word occurs in such connections as to show that unlawful or wrongful action is meant; *e.g.* forcible entry.

Power statically considered; that is at rest, or latent, but capable of being called into activity upon occasion for its exercise. Efficacy; legal validity. This is the meaning when we say that a statute or a contract is "in force."

See also Constructive force; Excessive force; Intervening force; Reasonable force.

Deadly force. Force which the actor uses with the purpose of causing or which he knows to create a substantial risk of causing death or serious bodily harm. Purposely firing a firearm in the direction of another person or at a vehicle in which another person is believed to be constitutes deadly force. A threat to cause death or serious bodily harm, by the production of a weapon or otherwise, so long as the actor's purpose is limited to creating an apprehension that he will use deadly force if necessary, does not constitute deadly force. Model Penal Code, § 3.11.

Unlawful force. Force, including confinement, which is employed without the consent of the person against whom it is directed and the employment of which constitutes an offense or actionable tort or would constitute such offense or tort except for a defense (such as the absence of intent, negligence, or mental capacity; duress; youth; or diplomatic status) not amounting to a privilege to use the force. Assent constitutes consent, within the meaning of this Section, whether or not it otherwise is legally effective, except assent to the infliction of death or serious bodily harm. Model Penal Code, § 3.11(1). *See also* Battery.

Force and arms. A phrase used in common law pleading in declarations of trespass and in indictments, but now unnecessary, to denote that the act complained of was done with violence.

Force and fear. Called also *"vi metuque"* means that any contract or act extorted under the pressure of force *(vis)* or under the influence of fear *(metus)* is voidable on that ground, provided, of course, that the force or the fear was such as influenced the party.

Forced heirs. Those persons whom the testator or donor cannot deprive of the portion of his estate reserved for them by law, except in cases where he has a just cause to disinherit them (*e.g.*, person's spouse). *See* Election by spouse.

Forced sale. A sale made at the time and in the manner prescribed by law, in virtue of execution issued on a judgment already rendered by a court of competent jurisdiction; a sale made under the process of the court, and in the mode prescribed by law. A sale which is not the voluntary act of the owner, such as to satisfy a debt, whether of a mortgage, judgment, tax lien, etc. Sale brought about in shorter time than normally required because of creditor's action. For comparable sale purposes in eminent domain proceedings, "forced sales" are those occurring as result of legal process, such as tax sale. *See also* Fire sale; Fore-

closure; Judicial sale; Sale (*Tax-sale*); Sheriff's sale.

Force majesture /fórs màzhəstyúr/. Includes lightnings, earthquakes, storms, flood, sunstrokes, freezing, etc., wherein latter two can be considered hazards in contemplation of employer within compensation acts. *See also* Act of God; Vis major.

Force majeure /fórs màzhúr/°məzhə́r/. Fr. In the law of insurance, superior or irresistible force. Such clause is common in construction contracts to protect the parties in the event that a part of the contract cannot be performed due to causes which are outside the control of the parties and could not be avoided by exercise of due care. An oil and gas lease clause that provides that the lessee will not be held to have breached the lease terms while the lessee is prevented by *force majeure* (literally, "superior force") from performing. Typically, such clauses specifically indicate problems beyond the reasonable control of the lessee that will excuse performance. *See also* Act of God; Vis major.

Force majeure risk. As used in project financing, the risk that there will be an interruption of operations for a prolonged period after the project has been completed due to fire, flood, storm, or some other factor beyond the control of the project's sponsors.

Forces /fórsəz/. The military and naval power of the country.

Forcible. Effected by force used against opposition or resistance; obtained by compulsion or violence.

Forcible detainer. A summary, speedy and adequate statutory remedy for obtaining possession of premises by one entitled to actual possession. Exists where one originally in rightful possession of realty refuses to surrender it at termination of his possessory right. Forcible detainer may ensue upon a peaceable entry, as well as upon a forcible entry; but it is most commonly spoken of in the phrase "forcible entry and detainer." *See also* Ejectment; Eviction; Forcible entry and detainer; Process (*Summary process*).

Forcible entry. At common law, violently taking possession of lands and tenements with menaces, force, and arms, against the will of those entitled to the possession, and without the authority of law. Entry accompanied with circumstances tending to excite terror in the occupant, and to prevent him from maintaining his rights. Angry words and threats of force may be sufficient.

Every person is guilty of forcible entry who either (1) by breaking open doors, windows, or other parts of a house, or by any kind of violence or circumstance of terror, enters upon or into any real property; or (2) who, after entering peaceably upon real property, turns out by force, threats, or menacing conduct the party in possession. Code Civil Proc.Cal. § 1159.

In many states, an entry effected without consent of rightful owner, or against his remonstrance, or under circumstances which amount to no more than a mere trespass, is now technically considered "forcible," while a detainer of the property consisting merely in the refusal to surrender possession after a lawful demand, is treated as a "forcible" detainer, the "force" required at common law being now supplied by a mere fiction.

See Ejectment; Eviction; Forcible detainer; Forcible entry and detainer; Process (*Summary process*).

Forcible entry and detainer. A summary proceeding for restoring to possession of land by one who is wrongfully kept out or has been wrongfully deprived of the possession. An action to obtain possession or repossession of real property which had been transferred from one to another pursuant to contract; such proceeding is not an action to determine ownership of title to property. *See also* Ejectment; Eviction; Forcible detainer; Process (*Summary process*).

Forcible rape. Aggravated form of statutory rape made punishable by statute. *See also* Rape.

Forcible trespass. An invasion of the rights of another with respect to his personal property, of the same character, or under the same circumstances, which would constitute a "forcible entry and detainer" of real property at common law. It consists in taking or seizing the personal property of another by force, violence, or intimidation or in forcibly injuring it. There must be actual violence used, or such demonstration of force as is calculated to intimidate or tend to a breach of the peace. It is not necessary that the person be actually put in fear.

For collection. A form of indorsement on a note or check where it is not intended to transfer title to it or to give it credit or currency, but merely to authorize the transferee to collect the amount of it. Such an indorsement is restrictive. U.C.C. § 3–205(c).

Fordal /fórdəl/. A butt or headland, jutting out upon other land.

Forebearance. *See* Forbearance.

Foreclose /fòrklówz/. To shut out; to bar; to terminate. Method of terminating mortgagor's right of redemption. *See also* Foreclosure.

Foreclosure /fòrklówzhər/. To shut out, to bar, to destroy an equity of redemption. A termination of all rights of the mortgagor or his grantee in the property covered by the mortgage. The process by which a mortgagor of real or personal property, or other owner of property subject to a lien, is deprived of his interest therein. A pro-

ceeding in equity whereby a mortgagee either takes title to or forces the sale of the mortgagor's property in satisfaction of a debt. Procedure by which mortgaged property is sold on default of mortgagor in satisfaction of mortgage debt. If proceeds from sale fail to pay debt in full, mortgagee creditor may obtain a Deficiency judgment (*q.v.*).

A default under a security interest in personal property can be foreclosed by a judicial sale of collateral. U.C.C. § 9–501.

In common usage, refers to enforcement of lien, trust deed, or mortgage in any method provided by law.

See also Equity of redemption.

Statutory foreclosure. The term is sometimes applied to foreclosure by execution of a power of sale contained in the mortgage, without recourse to the courts, as it must conform to the provisions of the statute regulating such sales.

Strict foreclosure. A decree of strict foreclosure of a mortgage finds the amount due under the mortgage, orders its payment within a certain limited time, and provides that, in default of such payment, the debtor's right and equity of redemption shall be forever barred and foreclosed; its effect is to vest the title of the property absolutely in the mortgagee, on default in payment, without any sale of the property.

Foreclosure decree. Properly speaking, a decree ordering the strict foreclosure of a mortgage; but the term is also loosely and conventionally applied to a decree ordering the sale of the mortgaged premises and the satisfaction of the mortgage out of the proceeds.

Foreclosure sale. A sale of mortgaged property to obtain satisfaction of the mortgage out of the proceeds, whether authorized by a decree of the court or by a power of sale contained in the mortgage. *See also* Deficiency judgment; Forced sale.

Foreign. Belonging to another nation or country; belonging or attached to another jurisdiction; made, done, or rendered in another state or jurisdiction; subject to another jurisdiction; operating or solvable in another territory; extrinsic; outside; extraordinary. Nonresident person, corporation, executor, etc.

As to *foreign* Administrator(-trix); Assignment; Attachment; Bill (*Bill of exchange*); Charity; Commerce; Corporation; County; Creditor; Divorce; Document; Domicile; Factor; Judgment; Jury; Minister; Plea; Port; and State, see those titles.

Foreign agent. Person who registers with the federal government as a lobbyist representing the interests (*e.g.* import quotas, tourism, foreign aid)

of a foreign nation or corporation. See 22 U.S.
C.A. § 611 et seq.

Foreign bill of exchange. Bill of exchange
which is drawn in one state or country and payable in another state or country. *See also* Bill
(*Bill of exchange*).

Foreign coins. Coins issued as money under the
authority of a foreign government.

Foreign commerce. Trade between persons in
the United States and those in a foreign country.
See also Commerce; Foreign trade.

Foreign consulate. The office or headquarters of
a consul who represents a foreign country in the
United States.

Foreign corporation. A corporation doing business in one state though chartered or incorporated in another state is a foreign corporation as to
the first state, and, as such, is required to consent
to certain conditions and restrictions in order to
do business in such first state. Rev. Model Bus.
Corp. Act § 1.40. Under federal tax laws, a foreign corporation is one which is not organized
under the laws of one of the states or territories of
the United States. I.R.C. § 7701(a)(5). Service of
process on foreign corporations is governed by
Fed.R.Civil P. 4. *See also* Corporation; Controlled
foreign corporation.

U.S. owned foreign corporation. A foreign corporation in which 50 percent or more of the total
combined voting power or total value of the stock
of the corporation is held directly or indirectly by
U.S. persons. A U.S. corporation is treated as a
U.S.-owned foreign corporation if dividend or interest income paid by such corporation is classified as foreign source under I.R.C. § 861.

Foreign Corrupt Practices Act (FCPA). Federal
law that prohibits bribes and questionable payments to foreign firms, governments, and political
officials and makes such payments a criminal
offense. 15 U.S.C.A. §§ 78dd–1, 78dd–2.

Foreign courts. The courts of a foreign state or
nation. In the United States, this term is frequently applied to the courts of one of the states
when their judgments or records are introduced
in the courts of another.

Foreign currency risk. The risk that the value
of one currency expressed in terms of another
currency (the foreign exchange rate) may fluctuate over time.

Foreign currency transaction. An exchange
that could generate a foreign currency gain or
loss for a U.S. taxpayer.

Foreign diplomatic *or* consular offices. Officials appointed by a foreign government to protect
the interest of its nationals in the United States.
See also Foreign agent.

Foreign earned income exclusion. The Internal
Revenue Code allows exclusions for earned income generated outside the United States, and for
related housing expenses, to alleviate any tax
base and rate disparities among countries.

Foreigner. Person belonging to or under citizenship of another country.

Foreign exchange. Conversion of the money of
one country into its equal of another country.
Process by which money of one country is used to
pay balances due in another country.

Foreign exchange market. Institution through
which foreign currencies are bought and sold.

Foreign exchange rate. The rate or price for
which the currency of one country may be exchanged for the money of another country. *See
also* Cross rates; Float.

Foreign exchange risk. *See* Foreign currency risk.

Foreign immunity. The immunity of a foreign
sovereign, its agencies or instrumentalities, from
suit in United States courts. Federal court jurisdiction is limited to claims falling within one of
the enumerated exceptions to the Foreign Sovereign Immunities Act of 1976. 28 U.S.C.A.
§§ 1602–1607.

Foreign Investment in Real Property Tax Act.
See FIRPTA.

Foreign judgment. *See* Judgment.

Foreign jurisdiction. Any jurisdiction foreign to
that of the forum; *e.g.* of a sister state or another
country. Also the exercise by a state or nation of
jurisdiction beyond its own territory. Long-arm
service of process is a form of such foreign or
extraterritorial jurisdiction. See 28 U.S.C.A.
§ 1330. *See also* Foreign service of process.

Foreign laws. The laws of a foreign country, or
of a sister state. In conflicts of law, the legal
principles of jurisprudence which are part of the
law of a sister state or nation. Foreign laws are
additions to our own laws, and in that respect are
called *"jus receptum"*.

Foreign money. The currency or medium of exchange of a foreign country. *See also* Foreign
exchange.

Foreign national. A person owing permanent
allegiance to a country other than the United
States. *See also* National.

Foreign personal holding company (FPHC). A
foreign corporation in which (1) 60 percent or
more of the gross income for the taxable year is
FPHC income and (2) more than 50 percent of the
total combined voting power or the total value of
the stock is owned, directly or indirectly, by five
or fewer individuals who are U.S. persons (the
U.S. group) at any time during the taxable year.
The 60 percent of gross income test drops to 50

percent or more after the 60 percent requirement has been met for one tax year, until the foreign corporation does not meet the 50 percent test for three consecutive years or the stock ownership requirement is not met for an entire tax year.

Foreign personal representative. A personal representative of another jurisdiction. Uniform Probate Code, § 1–201(14).

Foreign proceeding. Proceeding, whether judicial or administrative and whether or not under bankruptcy law, in a foreign country in which the debtor's domicile, residence, principal place of business, or principal assets were located at the commencement of such proceeding, for the purpose of liquidating an estate, adjusting debts by composition, extension, or discharge, or effecting a reorganization. Bankruptcy Code § 101. *See also* Foreign jurisdiction; Foreign service of process.

Foreign receiver. An official receiver appointed by a court of another state or nation.

Foreign representative. Duly selected trustee, administrator, or other representative of an estate in a foreign proceeding. Bankruptcy Code § 101.

Foreign sales corporation. An entity qualifying for a partial exemption of its gross export receipts from U.S. tax.

Foreign service. The United States Foreign Service conducts relations with foreign countries through its representatives at embassies, missions, consulates general, consulates, and consular agencies throughout the world. These representatives and agencies report to the State Department.

Foreign service of process. Service of process for the acquisition of jurisdiction by a court in the United States upon a person in a foreign country is prescribed by Fed.R.Civil P. 4(i) and 28 U.S.C.A. § 1608. Service of process on foreign corporations is governed by Fed.R.Civil P. 4(d)(3).

Foreign states. Nations which are outside the United States. Term may also refer to another state; *i.e.* a sister state.

The term "foreign nations," as used in a statement of the rule that the laws of foreign nations should be proved in a certain manner, should be construed to mean all nations and states other than that in which the action is brought; and hence one state of the Union is foreign to another, in the sense of that rule.

Foreign substance. Substance occurring in any part of the body or organism where it is not normally found, usually introduced from without. Within rule that a cause of action against physician who leaves a foreign substance in body does not begin until patient discovers or should have discovered the presence of such substance in-

cludes drugs and medicine which are introduced into the body and which are not organically connected or naturally related.

Foreign tax credit or deduction. A U.S. citizen or resident who incurs or pays income taxes to a foreign country on income subject to U.S. tax may be able to claim some of these taxes as a deduction or a credit against the U.S. income tax. I.R.C. §§ 27 and 901–905.

Foreign trade. Commercial interchange of commodities between different countries; export and import trade. *See also* Foreign commerce.

Foreign trade zone. Areas within the United States, but outside the customs zone, where foreign merchandise may be brought without formal customs entry and payment of duty for virtually any legal purpose including storage, grading, sampling, cleaning, or packaging. Duties are paid when the products enter the U.S. market. *See also* Free port.

Foreign will. Will of person not domiciled within state at time of death.

Foreman *or* **foreperson.** The presiding member of a grand or petit jury, who speaks or answers for the jury.

Person designated by employer-management to direct work of employees; superintendent, overseer.

Forensic. Belonging to courts of justice.

Forensic engineering. The application of the principles and practice of engineering to the elucidation of questions before courts of law. Practice by legally qualified professional engineers who are experts in their field, by both education and experience, and who have experience in the courts and an understanding of jurisprudence. A forensic engineering engagement may require investigations, studies, evaluations, advice to counsels, reports, advisory opinions, depositions and/or testimony to assist in the resolution of disputes relating to life or property in cases before courts, or other lawful tribunals.

Forensic linguistics. A technique concerned with in-depth evaluation of linguistic characteristics of text, including grammar, syntax, spelling, vocabulary and phraseology, which is accomplished through a comparison of textual material of known and unknown authorship, in an attempt to disclose idiosyncracies peculiar to authorship to determine whether the authors could be identical. U.S. v. Clifford, C.A.Pa., 704 F.2d 86. See Fed. Evid.R. 901. *See also* Comparative interpretation; Comparative stylistics; Comparison of handwriting.

Forensic medicine. That science which teaches the application of every branch of medical knowledge to the purposes of the law; hence its limits are, on the one hand, the requirements of the law, and, on the other, the whole range of medicine. Anatomy, physiology, medicine, surgery, chemistry, physics, and botany lend their aid as necessity arises; and in some cases all these branches of science are required to enable a court of law to arrive at a proper conclusion on a contested question affecting life or property.

Forensic pathology. That branch of medicine dealing with diseases and disorders of the body in relation to legal principles and cases.

Forensic psychiatry. That branch of medicine dealing with disorders of the mind in relation to legal principles and cases.

Foreseeability. The ability to see or know in advance; *e.g.* the reasonable anticipation that harm or injury is a likely result from certain acts or omissions. In tort law, the "foreseeability" element of proximate cause is established by proof that actor, as person of ordinary intelligence and prudence, should reasonably have anticipated danger to others created by his negligent act. That which is objectively reasonable to expect, not merely what might conceivably occur. *See also* Assumption of risk.

Foreseeable consequences. *See* Foreseeability.

Foreshore. The strip of land that lies between the high and low water marks and that is alternately wet and dry according to the flow of the tide. According to the medium line between the greatest and least range of tide (spring tides and neap tides). *See also* Shore.

Foresight. Heedful thought for the future; reasonable anticipation of result of certain acts or omissions. *See* Foreseeability.

Forfeit /fórfət/. To lose, or lose the right to, by some error, fault, offense, or crime; or to subject, as property, to forfeiture or confiscation. To lose, in consequence of breach of contract, neglect of duty, or offense, some right, privilege, or property to another or to the State. To incur a penalty; to become liable to the payment of a sum of money, as the consequence of a certain act. It can be a loss of position or personal right, as well as property.

To lose an estate, a franchise, or other property belonging to one, by the act of the law, and as a consequence of some misfeasance, negligence, default, or omission. It is a deprivation (that is, against the will of the losing party), with the property either transferred to another or resumed by the original grantor.

See also Forfeiture; Seizure.

Forfeitable. Liable to be forfeited; subject to forfeiture for non-user, neglect, crime, etc.

Forfeiture /fórfətyər/. A comprehensive term which means a divestiture of specific property without compensation; it imposes a loss by the taking away of some preexisting valid right without compensation. A deprivation or destruction of a right in consequence of the nonperformance of some obligation or condition. Loss of some right or property as a penalty for some illegal act. Loss of property or money because of breach of a legal obligation (*e.g.* default in payment).

Forfeiture of property (including money, securities, and real estate) is one of the penalties provided for under various federal and state criminal statutes (*e.g.*, RICO and Controlled Substances Acts). Such forfeiture provisions apply to property used in the commission of a crime under the particular statutes, as well as property acquired from the proceeds of the crime. See, *e.g.*, 18 U.S.C.A. §§ 981, 982, 28 U.S.C.A. §§ 2461–2465 (criminal and civil forfeiture), 21 U.S.C.A. § 853 (forfeiture in drug cases).

See also Confiscate; Default; Divestiture; Foreclosure; Forfeit; Seizure.

Forfeiture of bond. A failure to perform the condition upon which obligor was to be excused from the penalty in the bond. With respect to a bail bond, occurs when the accused fails to appear for trial.

Forge. To fabricate by false imitation. To fabricate, construct, or prepare one thing in imitation of another thing, with the intention of substituting the false for the genuine, or otherwise deceiving and defrauding by the use of the spurious article. To counterfeit or make falsely. Especially, to make a spurious written instrument with the intention of fraudulently substituting it for another, or of passing it off as genuine; or to fraudulently alter a genuine instrument to another's prejudice; or to sign another person's name to a document, with a deceitful and fraudulent intent. *See* Counterfeiter; Forgery; Fraud.

Forgery. The false making or the material altering of a document with the intent to defraud. A signature of a person that is made without the person's consent and without the person otherwise authorizing it. A person is guilty of forgery if, with purpose to defraud or injure anyone, or with knowledge that he is facilitating a fraud or injury to be perpetrated by anyone, the actor: (a) alters any writing of another without his authority; or (b) makes, completes, executes, authenticates, issues or transfers any writing so that it purports to be the act of another who did not authorize that act, or to have been executed at a time or place or in a numbered sequence other than was in fact the case, or to be a copy of an original when no such original existed; or (c) utters any writing which he knows to be forged in a manner specified in paragraph (a) or (b). Model Penal Code, § 224.1. See also MPC § 241.7, "Tampering with or Fabricating Physical Evidence."

Crime includes both act of forging handwriting of another and act of uttering as true and genuine any forged writing knowing same to be forged with intent to prejudice, damage or defraud any person. Crime is committed when one makes or passes a false instrument with intent to defraud, and the element of loss or detriment is immaterial. The false making of an instrument, which purports on face of it to be good and valid for purposes for which it was created, with a design to defraud any person or persons.

See also Alteration; Counterfeit; False making; Falsify; Fraud; Imitation; Raised check; Utter; Uttering a forged instrument.

Evidence. The fabrication or counterfeiting of evidence. The artful and fraudulent manipulation of physical objects, or the deceitful arrangement of genuine facts or things, in such a manner as to create an erroneous impression or a false inference in the minds of those who may observe them.

For hire *or* **reward.** To transport passengers or property for a fare, charge, or rate to be paid by such passengers, or persons for whom such property is transported, to owner or operator. *See also* Carrier.

Form. A model or skeleton of an instrument to be used in a judicial proceeding or legal transaction, containing the principal necessary matters, the proper technical terms or phrases and whatever else is necessary to make it formally correct, arranged in proper and methodical order, and capable of being adapted to the circumstances of the specific case or transaction.

In contradistinction to "substance," "form" means the legal or technical manner or order to be observed in legal instruments or juridical proceedings, or in the construction of legal documents or processes. Antithesis of "substance."

Form of the statute. This expression means the words, language, or frame of a statute, and hence the inhibition or command which it may contain; used in the phrase (in criminal pleading) "against the form of the statute in that case made and provided."

Forms of action. This term is the general designation of the various species or kinds of personal actions known to the common law, such as trover, trespass, debt, assumpsit, etc., and also to the general classification of actions as those in "equity" or "law". These differ in their pleadings and evidence, as well as in the circumstances to which they are respectively applicable. Under Rules of Civil Procedure (applicable in federal and most state courts) there is now only one form of action known as a "civil action," Fed.R.Civ.Proc., Rule 2. *See also* Forms of action.

Matter of form. In pleadings, indictments, affidavits, conveyances, etc., matter of form (as distinguished from matter of substance) is all that relates to the mode, form, or style of expressing the facts involved, the choice or arrangement of words, and other such particulars, without affecting the substantial validity or sufficiency of the instrument, or without going to the merits.

Form 10–K. Financial reporting form required to be filed annually with SEC by publicly traded corporations.

Form 10–Q. Financial reporting form required to be filed quarterly with SEC by publicly traded corporations. Such is less comprehensive than Form 10–K.

Forma. Lat. Form; the prescribed form of judicial proceedings.

Formal. Relating to matters of form; as, "formal defects"; inserted, added, or joined *pro forma*. *See* Form; Parties.

Formal contract. A *written* contract or agreement as contrasted with an *oral* or informal contract or agreement. Historically, a formal contract was under seal; though this is generally no longer required. *See also* Contract.

Formality. The conditions, in regard to method, order, arrangement, use of technical expressions, performance of specific acts, etc., which are required by the law in the making of contracts or conveyances, or in the taking of legal proceedings, to insure their validity and regularity. Term generally refers to "procedure" in contrast to "substance".

Formal parties. *See* Parties.

Forma pauperis /fórmə pópərəs/. *See* Appeal in forma pauperis; In forma pauperis.

Formed action. An action for which a set form of words is prescribed, which must be strictly adhered to. Such are now generally obsolete. *See* Forms of action.

Formed design. In criminal law, and particularly with reference to homicide, this term means a deliberate and fixed intention to kill, whether directed against a particular person or not. *See also* Premeditation.

Former adjudication. An adjudication in a former action. Either a final determination of the rights of the parties or an adjudication of certain questions of fact. *See* Res (*Res judicata*).

Former jeopardy. Also called "double jeopardy." Plea of "former jeopardy," that a person cannot be tried for an offense more than once, is fundamental common law and constitutional right of defendant, affording protection against the defendant being again tried for the same offense, and not against the peril of second punishment. Fifth

Amendment of U.S.Const. However, prosecution by both the state and federal governments is not barred by the constitutional protection against double jeopardy. *See also* Double jeopardy.

Former proceedings. Term used in reference to action taken earlier and its result in determining whether present proceeding is barred by res judicata.

Former recovery. Recovery in a former action. *See* Res (*Res judicata*).

Former statements. As used in evidence, declarations made by a party or witness at an earlier time. Fed.Evid.R. 613.

Former testimony. In evidence, testimony given by party or witness at an earlier trial or hearing and which, under certain conditions, may be used in present proceeding. Fed.Evid.R. 613.

Forms of action. Forms of action governed common law pleading and were the procedural devices used to give expression to the theories of liability recognized by the common law. Failure to analyze the cause of action properly, to select the proper theory of liability and to choose the appropriate procedural mechanism or forms of action could easily result in being thrown out of court. A plaintiff had to elect his remedy in advance and could not subsequently amend his pleadings to conform to his proof or to the court's choice of another theory of liability. According to the relief sought, actions have been divided into three categories: real actions were brought for the recovery of real property; mixed actions were brought to recover real property and damages for injury to it; personal actions were brought to recover debts or personal property, or for injuries to personal, property, or contractual rights. The common law actions are usually considered to be eleven in number: trespass, trespass on the case, trover, ejectment, detinue, replevin, debt, covenant, account, special assumpsit, and general assumpsit.

Under the Rules of Civil Procedure (applicable in the federal and most state courts) there is now only one form of action known as a "civil action". Fed.R.Civil P., Rule 2.

Formula. In common-law practice, a set form of words used in judicial proceedings. In the civil law, an action.

Formula basis. A method of selling a new issue of common stock in which the Securities and Exchange Commission declares the registration statement effective based on a price formula, rather than a specific price.

Formula instruction. A jury instruction intended to be complete statement of law upon which jury may base verdict. An instruction which advises the jury that under certain facts therein hypothesized their verdict should be for one of the parties. *See* Jury instructions.

Fornication. Sexual intercourse other than between married persons. Further, if one of the persons be married and the other not, it is fornication on the part of the latter, though adultery for the former. In some jurisdictions, however, by statute, it is adultery on the part of both persons if the woman is married, whether the man is married or not. This offense, which is variously defined by state statutes, is very seldom enforced. *See also* Adultery; Illicit cohabitation.

Forswear /fòrswér/. In criminal law, to make oath to that which the deponent knows to be untrue. This term is wider in its scope than "perjury," for the latter, as a technical term, includes the idea of the oath being taken before a competent court or officer, and relating to a material issue, which is not implied by the word "forswear." *See* Perjury.

For that. In pleading, words used to introduce the allegations of a declaration. "For that" is a positive allegation; "For that whereas" is a recital. Such words are not required in federal court pleadings nor in the majority of states that have adopted Rules of Civil Procedure.

For that whereas. In pleading, formal words introducing the statement of the plaintiff's case, by way of recital, in his declaration, in all actions except trespass. In trespass, where there was no recital, the expression used was, "For that." Such words are not required in federal court pleadings nor in the majority of states that have adopted Rules of Civil Procedure.

Forthcoming bond. A bond conditioned on the forthcoming of property to answer such judgment as may be entered. If the property be forthcoming, no liability ensues. A bond given to a sheriff who has levied on property, conditioned that the property shall be forthcoming, *i.e.*, produced, when required. On the giving of such bond, the goods are allowed to remain in the possession of the debtor.

Forthwith. Immediately; without delay; directly; within a reasonable time under the circumstances of the case; promptly and with reasonable dispatch. Within such time as to permit that which is to be done, to be done lawfully and according to the practical and ordinary course of things to be performed or accomplished. The first opportunity offered.

Fortior /fórshiyər/. Lat. Stronger. A term applied, in the law of evidence, to that species of presumption, arising from facts shown in evidence, which is strong enough to shift the burden of proof to the opposite party. *See* A fortiori.

Fortiori /fòrshiyóray/. *See* A fortiori.

Fortuitous /fortyúwətəs/. Happening by chance or accident. Occurring unexpectedly, or without known cause. Accidental; undesigned; adventitious. Resulting from unavoidable physical causes.

Fortuitous collision /fortyúwədəs kəlízhən/. In maritime law, the accidental running foul of vessels.

Fortuitous event /fortyúwədəs əvént/. An event happening by chance or accident. That which happens by a cause which cannot be resisted. An unforeseen occurrence, not caused by either of the parties, nor such as they could prevent. For purposes of an all risk insurance policy, an event which occurs accidentally, as a lay-person, and not a technician or scientist, would understand that term. It is an event which happens by chance, unexpectedly, or without known cause; one which is undesigned or unplanned.

Forty. In land laws and conveyancing, in those regions where grants, transfers, and deeds are made with reference to the subdivisions of the government survey, this term means forty acres of land in the form of a square, being the tract obtained by quartering a section of land (640 acres) and again quartering one of the quarters.

Forum /fórəm/. Lat. A court of justice, or judicial tribunal; a place of jurisdiction; a place of litigation; an administrative body. Particular place where judicial or administrative remedy is pursued. *See also* Venue.

Forum actus /fórəm ǽktəs/. The forum of the act. The forum of the place where the act was done which is now called in question.

Forum contractus /fórəm kəntrǽktəs/. The forum of the contract; the court of the place where a contract is made; the place where a contract is made, considered as a place of jurisdiction.

Forum conveniens /fórəm kənvíyn(i)yènz/. The state or judicial district in which an action may be most appropriately brought, considering the best interest of the parties and the public. *Compare* Forum non conveniens.

Forum non conveniens /fórəm nòn kənvíyn(i)yènz/. Term refers to discretionary power of court to decline jurisdiction when convenience of parties and ends of justice would be better served if action were brought and tried in another forum. See 28 U.S.C.A. § 1404.

The rule is an equitable one embracing the discretionary power of a court to decline to exercise jurisdiction which it has over a transitory cause of action when it believes that the action may be more appropriately and justly tried elsewhere. The doctrine presupposes at least two forums in which the defendant is amenable to process and furnishes criteria for choice between such forums. In determining whether doctrine

should be applied, court should consider relative ease of access to sources of proof, availability of compulsory process for attendance of unwilling witnesses, cost of obtaining attendance of willing witnesses, possibility of view of premises, and all other practical problems that make trial easy, expeditious and inexpensive. *See also* Change of venue; Forum conveniens.

Forum selection clause. A clause in a contract preselecting a particular forum, such as a given state, country, court or administrative proceeding, for the resolution of a dispute. Usually upheld unless the clause is designed to discourage litigation.

Forum shopping. Such occurs when a party attempts to have his action tried in a particular court or jurisdiction where he feels he will receive the most favorable judgment or verdict.

For use. For the benefit or advantage of another. Thus, where an assignee is obliged to sue in the name of his assignor, the suit is entitled "A. *for use* of B. v. C." For enjoyment or employment without destruction. A loan "for use" is one in which the bailee has the right to use and enjoy the article, but without consuming or destroying it, in which respect it differs from a loan "for consumption."

For value. *See* Holder.

For value received. *See* Value *(Value received)*.

Forward. To send forward; to send toward the place of destination; to transmit. To ship goods by common carrier. *See* Forwarder.

Forward contract. An agreement to sell a commodity at a fixed future date but at a price set at the time the contract is written.

Forward discount. The difference between the spot foreign exchange rate and the forward exchange rate when the spot rate exceeds the forward rate.

Forwarder. Person or business whose business it is to receive goods for further handling by way of warehousing, packing, carload shipping, delivery, etc. *See* Forwarding agent; Freight forwarder.

Forward exchange rate. Foreign exchange rate for a forward trade.

Forwarding agent. Freight forwarder who assembles less than carload shipments (small shipments) into carload shipments, thus taking advantage of lower freight rates. Company or individual whose business it is to receive and ship merchandise for others. *See* Forwarder.

Forward premium. The difference between the forward exchange rate and the spot foreign exchange rate when the forward rate exceeds the spot rate.

Forward rate. The rate of exchange between two currencies being bought and sold for delivery at a future date.

Forward trade. The purchase or sale of a foreign currency, commodity, or other item for future delivery based on a price that is agreed to today.

For whom it may concern. Salutation used when particular name of addressee or recipient is unknown. Phrase creates presumption of intention on part of named insured to cover any persons who may have an insurable interest in the property.

Foster child. Child whose care, comfort, education and upbringing has been left to persons other than his natural parents. *See* Foster parent.

Foster home. A home for children without parents or who have been taken from their parents.

Foster parent. One who has performed the duties of a parent to the child of another by rearing the child as his or her own child. *See* Foster child.

Foul bill of lading. Type of bill of lading which shows on its face that the goods were damaged or that there was a shortage at the time of shipment.

Found. A person is said to be "found" within a state for purposes of service of process when actually present therein. But only if a person is in a place voluntarily and not by reason of plaintiff's fraud, artifice, or trick for purpose of obtaining service. It does not necessarily mean physical presence; *e.g.* defendant who, after removal of action for breach of contract to federal court, entered general appearance, defended on the merits, and filed counterclaim, was "found" in the district. As applied to a corporation it is necessary that it be doing business in such state through an officer or agent or by statutory authority in such manner as to render it liable then to suit and to constructive or substituted service of process. A corporation is "found" in a district for venue purposes if it is subject to personal jurisdiction in that district. *See also* Locate; Service (*Service of process*).

Foundation. Permanent fund established and maintained by contributions for charitable, educational, religious, research, or other benevolent purpose. An institution or association given to rendering financial aid to colleges, schools, hospitals, and charities and generally supported by gifts for such purposes.

The founding or building of a college or hospital. The incorporation or endowment of a college or hospital is the foundation; and he who endows it with land or other property is the founder.

Preliminary questions to witness to establish admissibility of evidence. "Laying foundation" is a prerequisite to the admission of evidence at trial. It is established by testimony which identifies the evidence sought to be admitted and connects it with the issue in question. See, *e.g.*, Fed.Evid.R. 104. *See* Laying foundation.

See also Charitable foundation; Endowment.

Founded. Based upon; arising from, growing out of, or resting upon; as in the expressions "founded in fraud," "founded on a consideration," "founded on contract," and the like.

Founded on. To serve as a base or basis for.

Founder. The person who endows an eleemosynary corporation or institution, or supplies the funds for its establishment. *See* Foundation.

Four corners. The face of a written instrument.

Four corners rule. Under "four corners rule", intention of parties, especially that of grantor, is to be gathered from instrument as a whole and not from isolated parts thereof.

401(k) plan. A savings plan established by corporations for the benefit of employees. Such a plan allows employees to defer pre-tax income on a certain portion of their gross salary and invest the funds in stocks, bonds, or other investment tools. In addition, many companies match a percentage of the employees' contributions. The contributions and earnings from such are accumulated tax free until such time as the funds are withdrawn. There is a penalty for early withdrawal, with some exceptions such as death or disability of the employee. I.R.C. § 401(k).

Fourteenth Amendment. The Fourteenth Amendment of the Constitution of the United States, ratified in 1868, creates or at least recognizes for the first time a citizenship of the United States, as distinct from that of the states; forbids the making or enforcement by any state of any law abridging the privileges and immunities of citizens of the United States; and secures all "persons" against any state action which results in either deprivation of life, liberty, or property without due process of law, or, in denial of the equal protection of the laws. This Amendment also contains provisions concerning the apportionment of representatives in Congress. *See also* Due process of law; Equal protection clause.

Fourth Amendment. Amendment of the U.S. Constitution guaranteeing people the right to be secure in their homes and property against unreasonable searches and seizures and providing that no warrants shall issue except upon probable cause and then only as to specific places to be searched and persons and things to be seized. *See* Probable cause; Search (and other cross-references thereunder).

Fourth estate. The journalistic profession (*i.e.* the press). Term has its source from a reference to the reporters' gallery of the British Parliament whose influence on public policy was said to equal that of Parliament's three traditional estates, the clergy, nobility, and commons.

Fourth market. Over-the-counter market in which transactions in financial securities are made directly between institutions.

F.P.A. In maritime insurance: "Free from particular average". *See* Average.

F.P.R. Federal Procurement Regulations. *See now* Federal Acquisition Regulations.

Fraction. A breaking, or breaking up; a fragment or broken part; a portion of a thing, less than the whole.

Fractional. As applied to tracts of land, particularly townships, sections, quarter sections, and other divisions according to the government survey, and also mining claims, this term means that the exterior boundary lines are laid down to include the whole of such a division or such a claim, but that the tract in question does not measure up to the full extent or include the whole acreage, because a portion of it is cut off by an overlapping survey, a river or lake, or some other external interference. Any irregular division whether containing more or less than conventional amount of acreage.

Fractional share. Unit of stock less than a full share. This term comes into use with a stock dividend in an instance for example where an owner of 75 shares receives a 10% stock dividend. That part or portion of a share of stock indicated on a right or warrant as subject to purchase by the exercise of such right.

Fractional share formula. *See* Marital deduction.

Framed. Incrimination of person on false or fabricated evidence. *Compare* Entrapment.

Frame-up. Conspiracy or plot, especially for evil purpose, as to incriminate person on false evidence. *See* Entrapment.

Franchise. A special privilege to do certain things conferred by government on individual or corporation, and which does not belong to citizens generally of common right; *e.g.*, right granted to offer cable television service.

A privilege granted or sold, such as to use a name or to sell products or services. The right given by a manufacturer or supplier to a retailer to use his products and name on terms and conditions mutually agreed upon.

In its simplest terms, a franchise is a license from owner of a trademark or trade name permitting another to sell a product or service under that name or mark. More broadly stated, a "franchise" has evolved into an elaborate agreement under which the franchisee undertakes to conduct a business or sell a product or service in accordance with methods and procedures prescribed by the franchisor, and the franchisor un-

dertakes to assist the franchisee through advertising, promotion and other advisory services. Term also refers to such business as owned by franchisee. State and Federal laws regulate business franchising. *See also* Franchised dealer.

Corporate franchise. See that title. *See also* Charter.

Elective franchise. The right of suffrage; the right or privilege of voting in public elections. Such right is guaranteed by Fifteenth, Nineteenth, and Twenty-fourth Amendments to U.S. Constitution.

Exclusive franchise. *See* Exclusive agency.

General and special. The charter of a corporation is its "general" franchise, while a "special" franchise consists in any rights granted by the public to use property for a public use but with private profit.

Sports franchise. As granted by a professional sports association, it is a privilege to field a team in a given geographic area under the auspices of the league that issues it. It is merely an incorporeal right.

Tax treatment. A franchise is an agreement which gives the transferee the right to distribute, sell, or provide goods, services, or facilities, within a specified area. The cost of obtaining a franchise may be amortized over the life of the agreement. In general, a franchise is a capital asset and results in capital gain or loss if all significant powers, rights or continuing interests are transferred pursuant to the sale of a franchise.

Franchise agreement. Generally, an agreement between a supplier of a product or service or an owner of a desired trademark or copyright (franchisor), and a reseller (franchisee) under which the franchisee agrees to sell the franchisor's product or service or to do business under the franchisor's name. State and federal laws regulate the content of franchise agreements.

Franchise appurtenant to land. Usually a franchise is not regarded as real property or land and is not included in the term "tenement;" but it is sometimes characterized or classified as real property or as property of the nature of real property when exercised in connection with real property, and is, in terms, classified as real property, real estate, or land by some statutes.

Franchise clause. Provision in casualty insurance policy to the effect that the insurer will pay those claims only over a stated amount and that the insured is responsible for all damage under the agreed amount. This clause differs from a deductible provision in that the insured bears the loss in every claim up to the deductible amount whereas, under the franchise clause, once the claim exceeds the agreed amount, the insurer pays the entire claim.

Franchised dealer. A retailer who sells the product or service of a manufacturer or supplier under a franchise agreement which generally protects the territory for the retailer and provides advertising and promotion support to him. *See* Franchise.

Franchisee. Person or company that is granted franchise by a franchisor.

Franchise tax. A tax upon the privilege of existing or the privilege of doing certain things. An annual tax on the privilege of doing business in a state; it is not a direct tax on income. A tax on the franchise of a corporation, that is, on the right and privilege of carrying on business in the character of a corporation, for the purposes for which it was created, and in the conditions which surround it.

Though the value of the franchise, for purposes of taxation, may be measured by the amount of business done, or the amount of earnings or dividends, or by the total value of the capital or stock of the corporation in excess of its tangible assets, a franchise tax is not a tax on either property, capital, stock, earnings, or dividends.

Franchisor. Person or company that grants a franchise to a franchisee.

Frank, v. To send matter through the public mails free of postage, by a personal or official privilege. *See* Franking privilege.

Franking privilege. The privilege of sending certain matter through the public mails without payment of postage, in pursuance of a personal or official privilege. The privilege granted to members of Congress to send out a certain amount of mail under signature without charge. See 39 U.S.C.A. § 3210 et seq.

F.R.A.P. *See* Federal Rules of Appellate Procedure.

Fraternal. Brotherly; relating or belonging to a fraternity or an association of persons formed for mutual aid and benefit, but not for profit.

Fraternal benefit association *or* society. One whose members have adopted the same, or a very similar, calling, avocation, or profession, or who are working in unison to accomplish some worthy object, and who for that reason have joined themselves together as an association or society to aid and assist one another, and to promote the common cause. A society or voluntary association organized and carried on for the mutual aid and benefit of its members, not for profit; which ordinarily has a lodge system, a ritualistic form of work, and a representative government, makes provision for the payment of death benefits, and (sometimes) for benefits in case of accident, sickness, or old age, the funds therefor being derived from dues paid or assessments levied on the members.

Fraternal insurance. The form of life (or accident) insurance furnished by a fraternal beneficial association, consisting in the payment to a member, or his heirs in case of death, of a stipulated sum of money, out of funds raised for that purpose by the payment of dues or assessments by all the members of the association.

Fraternal lodge. *See* Fraternal benefit association *or* society.

Fratricide /frǽtrəsáyd/. One who has killed a brother or sister; also the killing of a brother or sister.

Fraud. An intentional perversion of truth for the purpose of inducing another in reliance upon it to part with some valuable thing belonging to him or to surrender a legal right. A false representation of a matter of fact, whether by words or by conduct, by false or misleading allegations, or by concealment of that which should have been disclosed, which deceives and is intended to deceive another so that he shall act upon it to his legal injury. Anything calculated to deceive, whether by a single act or combination, or by suppression of truth, or suggestion of what is false, whether it be by direct falsehood or innuendo, by speech or silence, word of mouth, or look or gesture. A generic term, embracing all multifarious means which human ingenuity can devise, and which are resorted to by one individual to get advantage over another by false suggestions or by suppression of truth, and includes all surprise, trick, cunning, dissembling, and any unfair way by which another is cheated. "Bad faith" and "fraud" are synonymous, and also synonyms of dishonesty, infidelity, faithlessness, perfidy, unfairness, etc.

Elements of a cause of action for "fraud" include false representation of a present or past fact made by defendant, action in reliance thereupon by plaintiff, and damage resulting to plaintiff from such misrepresentation.

As distinguished from negligence, it is always positive, intentional. It comprises all acts, omissions, and concealments involving a breach of a legal or equitable duty and resulting in damage to another. And includes anything calculated to deceive, whether it be a single act or combination of circumstances, whether the suppression of truth or the suggestion of what is false, whether it be by direct falsehood or by innuendo, by speech or by silence, by word of mouth, or by look or gesture. Fraud, as applied to contracts, is the cause of an error bearing on a material part of the contract, created or continued by artifice, with design to obtain some unjust advantage to the one party, or to cause an inconvenience or loss to the other.

See also Actionable fraud; Bad faith; Badges of fraud; Cheat; Civil fraud; Collusion; Constructive fraud; Criminal *(Criminal fraud)*; Deceit; False pretenses; False representation; Intrinsic fraud; Mail fraud; Material fact; Misrepresentation; Promissory fraud; Reliance; Scheme *or* artifice to defraud.

Actionable fraud. See Actionable fraud.

Actual or constructive fraud. Fraud is either *actual* or *constructive*. Actual fraud consists in deceit, artifice, trick, design, some direct and active operation of the mind; it includes cases of the intentional and successful employment of any cunning, deception, or artifice used to circumvent or cheat another. It is something said, done, or omitted by a person with the design of perpetrating what he knows to be a cheat or deception. Constructive fraud consists in any act of commission or omission contrary to legal or equitable duty, trust, or confidence justly reposed, which is contrary to good conscience and operates to the injury of another. Or, as otherwise defined, it is an act, statement or omission which operates as a virtual fraud on an individual, or which, if generally permitted, would be prejudicial to the public welfare, and yet may have been unconnected with any selfish or evil design. Or, constructive frauds are such acts or contracts as, though not originating in any actual evil design or contrivance to perpetrate a positive fraud or injury upon other persons, are yet, by their tendency to deceive or mislead other persons, or to violate private or public confidence, or to impair or injure the public interests, deemed equally reprehensible with actual fraud. Constructive fraud consists in any breach of duty which, without an actually fraudulent intent, gains an advantage to the person in fault, or any one claiming under him, by misleading another to his prejudice, or to the prejudice of any one claiming under him; or, in any such act or omission as the law specially declares to be fraudulent, without respect to actual fraud.

Computer fraud. A scheme that involves a computer to aid and abet in a fraud or embezzlement. *See e.g.* 18 U.S.C.A. § 1030.

Extrinsic fraud. Fraud which is collateral to the issues tried in the case where the judgment is rendered. Type of deceit which may form basis for setting aside a judgment as for example a divorce granted ex parte because the plaintiff-spouse falsely tells the court he or she is ignorant of the whereabouts of the defendant-spouse.

Fraud by concealment. Misrepresentation to induce another to enter into a contract by not telling the other party an important fact which would affect the decision to enter into the contract.

Fraud in fact or in law. Fraud is also classified as *fraud in fact* and *fraud in law*. The former is actual, positive, intentional fraud. Fraud disclosed by matters of fact, as distinguished from

constructive fraud or fraud in law. Fraud in law is fraud in contemplation of law; fraud implied or inferred by law; fraud made out by construction of law, as distinguished from fraud found by a jury from matter of fact; constructive fraud *(q.v.)*. *See also Fraud in the factum; Legal or positive fraud, below.*

Fraud in the execution. Misrepresentation that deceives the other party as to the nature of a document evidencing the contract.

Fraud in the factum. Misrepresentation as to the nature of a writing that a person signs with neither knowledge nor reasonable opportunity to obtain knowledge of its character or essential terms. See U.C.C. § 3–305(2)(c). *See also Fraud in fact or in law, above.*

Fraud in the inducement. Fraud connected with underlying transaction and not with the nature of the contract or document signed. Misrepresentation as to the terms, quality or other aspects of a contractual relation, venture or other transaction that leads a person to agree to enter into the transaction with a false impression or understanding of the risks, duties or obligations she has undertaken.

Intrinsic fraud. That which pertains to issue involved in original action or where acts constituting fraud were, or could have been, litigated therein. Perjury is an example of intrinsic fraud.

Larceny. See Larceny *(Larceny by fraud or deception)*.

Legal or positive fraud. Fraud is also said to be *legal* or *positive*. The former is fraud made out by legal construction or inference, or the same thing as constructive fraud. Positive fraud is the same thing as actual fraud. *See also* Legal fraud.

Mail and wire fraud. Criminal offense of using mails or interstate wires to create or in furtherance of a scheme or artifice to defraud, or for obtaining money or property by means of false or fraudulent pretenses. 18 U.S.C.A. §§ 1341, 1343.

Statute of frauds. See Frauds, Statute of.

Tax fraud. Federal offense of willfully attempting to evade or defeat the payment of taxes due and owing. I.R.C. § 7201. Tax fraud falls into two categories: civil and criminal. Under civil fraud, the IRS may impose as a penalty an amount equal to 75 percent of the underpayment. I.R.C. § 6653(b). Fines and/or imprisonment are prescribed for conviction of various types of criminal tax fraud. I.R.C. §§ 7201–7207. Both civil and criminal fraud require a specific intent on the part of the taxpayer to evade the tax; mere negligence is not enough. Criminal fraud requires the additional element of willfulness (*i.e.,* done deliberately and with evil purpose). In practice, it becomes difficult to distinguish between the degree of intent necessary to support criminal, rather than civil, fraud. In either situation, the IRS has the burden of proving fraud.

Fraud on court. A scheme to interfere with judicial machinery performing task of impartial adjudication, as by preventing opposing party from fairly presenting his case or defense. Finding of fraud on the court is justified only by most egregious misconduct directed to the court itself such as bribery of a judge or jury to fabrication of evidence by counsel and must be supported by clear, unequivocal and convincing evidence. It consists of conduct so egregious that it undermines the integrity of the judicial process.

Frauds, Statute of. This is the common designation of a very celebrated English statute (29 Car. II, c. 3), passed in 1677, which has been adopted, in a more or less modified form, in nearly all of the United States. Its chief characteristic is the provision that no suit or action shall be maintained on certain classes of contracts or engagements unless there shall be a note or memorandum thereof in writing signed by the party to be charged or by his authorized agent (*e.g.*, contracts for the sale of goods priced at $500 or more; contracts for the sale of land; contracts which cannot, by their terms, be performed within a year; and contracts to guaranty the debt of another). Its object was to close the door to the numerous frauds and perjuries. It is more fully named as the "statute of frauds and perjuries."

Uniform Commercial Code. U.C.C. § 2–201 provides that a contract for the sale of goods for the price of $500 or more is not enforceable by way of action or defense unless there is some writing sufficient to indicate that a contract for sale has been made between the parties and signed by the party against whom enforcement is sought or by his authorized agent or broker.

Fraudulent. Based on fraud; proceeding from or characterized by fraud; tainted by fraud; done, made, or effected with a purpose or design to carry out a fraud. *See also* False and fraudulent; Fraud.

A statement, or claim, or document, is "fraudulent" if it was falsely made, or caused to be made, with the intent to deceive.

To act with "intent to defraud" means to act willfully, and with the specific intent to deceive or cheat; ordinarily for the purpose of either causing some financial loss to another, or bringing about some financial gain to oneself.

Fraudulent alienation. In a general sense, the transfer of property with an intent to defraud creditors, lienors, or others. In a particular sense, the act of an administrator who wastes the assets of the estate by giving them away or selling at a gross undervalue. *See* Fraudulent conveyance.

Fraudulent alienee /frɔ́dyələnt èyl(i)yəníy/. One who knowingly receives from an administrator assets of the estate under circumstances which make it a fraudulent alienation on the part of the administrator.

Fraudulent alteration. A change in the terms of an instrument, document or other paper made with a dishonest and deceitful purpose to acquire more than one was entitled to under the original terms of the paper. *See also* Alteration; Forgery; Raised check.

Fraudulent banking. Receipt of deposit by banker who knows that bank is insolvent at the time.

Fraudulent claims. *See* False claim.

Fraudulent concealment. The hiding or suppression of a material fact or circumstance which the party is legally or morally bound to disclose. The employment of artifice planned to prevent inquiry or escape investigation and to mislead or hinder the acquisition of information disclosing a right of action; acts relied on must be of an affirmative character and fraudulent. The test of whether failure to disclose material facts constitutes fraud is the existence of a duty, legal or equitable, arising from the relation of the parties; failure to disclose a material fact with intent to mislead or defraud under such circumstances being equivalent to an actual "fraudulent concealment." Fraudulent concealment justifying a rescission of a contract is the intentional concealment of some fact known to the party charged, which is material for the party injured to know to prevent being defrauded; the concealment of a fact which one is bound to disclose being the equivalent of an indirect representation that such fact does not exist. *See* Material fact.

Fraudulent conversion. Receiving into possession money or property of another and fraudulently withholding, converting, or applying the same to or for one's own use and benefit, or to use and benefit of any person other than the one to whom the money or property belongs. *See* Conversion.

Fraudulent conveyance. A conveyance or transfer of property, the object of which is to defraud a creditor, or hinder or delay him, or to put such property beyond his reach. Conveyance made with intent to avoid some duty or debt due by or incumbent on person making transfer.

In bankruptcy law, refers to a gift or transfer of the bankrupt's property for little or no consideration at a time when the debtor is insolvent, or one which renders debtor's capital unreasonably small, or one made by debtor who believes that he will not be able to meet maturing obligations, or one made with actual intent to hinder, delay or defraud his creditors. Such fraudulent conveyances may be avoided by the trustee. Bankruptcy Code § 548.

For a conveyance to be a "fraudulent conveyance" under Uniform Fraudulent Conveyance Act, there must be actual intent to hinder, delay, or defraud creditors, or grantor must be insolvent or be rendered insolvent by conveyance, and conveyance must be made without fair consideration. Many states have enacted this Uniform Act.

Fraudulent intent. Such intent exists where one, either with a view of benefitting oneself or misleading another into a course of action, makes a representation which one knows to be false or which one does not believe to be true. *See* Fraud; Fraudulent misrepresentation.

Fraudulent misrepresentation. A false statement as to material fact, made with intent that another rely thereon, which is believed by other party and on which he relies and by which he is induced to act and does act to his injury, and statement is fraudulent if speaker knows statement to be false or if it is made with utter disregard of its truth or falsity. As basis for civil action, establishment of representation, falsity, scienter, deception, and injury, are generally required. *See also* Deceit; Fraud; Material fact; Misrepresentation.

Fraudulent preferences. *See* Preference.

Fraudulent pretense. Crime which consists of a false pretense, obtaining property of value thereby, and an intent to cheat and defraud. *E.g.,* credit purchases made without requisite intent or ability to pay.

Fraudulent sale. *See* Sale.

Fraudulent transfers. *See* Fraudulent conveyance.

Fray /fréy/. *See* Affray.

F.R.B. *See* Federal Reserve Board of Governors.

F.R.C.P. *See* Federal Rules of Civil Procedure.

F.R.D. *See* Federal Rules Decisions.

Freddie Mac. *See* Federal Home Loan Mortgage Corporation.

Free. Not subject to legal constraint of another. *See also* Freedom.

Free alongside ship (FAS). In price quotations, means that the price includes all costs of transportation and delivery of the goods alongside of the ship. See U.C.C. § 2–319(2–4).

Free and clear. The title to property is said to be "free and clear" when it is not incumbered by any liens; but it is said that an agreement to convey land "free and clear" is satisfied by a conveyance passing a good (*i.e.* marketable) title.

Free course. In admiralty law, a vessel having the wind from a favorable quarter is said to sail on a "free course," or said to be "going free" when

she has a fair (following) wind and her yards braced in.

Freedom. The state of being free; liberty; self-determination; absence of restraint; the opposite of slavery.

The power of acting, in the character of a moral personality, according to the dictates of the will, without other check, hindrance, or prohibition than such as may be imposed by just and necessary laws and the duties of social life. *See* Liberty.

The prevalence, in the government and constitution of a country, of such a system of laws and institutions as secure civil liberty to the individual citizen.

Freedom of association. Right to peaceably assemble as guaranteed by First Amendment of U.S. Constitution. *See* Association.

Freedom of choice. As used in context of freedom of choice to attend school of choice in unitary, integrated school system, devoid of any de jure segregation, means the maximum amount of freedom and clearly understood choice in bona fide unitary system where schools are not white schools or Negro schools, but just schools. With respect to punishment, loss of freedom of choice is a natural by-product of the detention process and should not be considered "punishment" in the constitutional sense.

Freedom of contract. A basic right reserved to the people by the Constitution (Art. I, § 10) that a state cannot violate even under sanction of direct legislative act. *See also* Impairing the obligation of contracts; Liberty (*Liberty of contract*).

Freedom of expression. Right guaranteed by First Amendment of U.S. Constitution; includes freedom of religion, speech, and press. *See also* Liberty.

Freedom of Information Act. The Freedom of Information Act (5 U.S.C.A. § 552) provides for making information held by Federal agencies available to the public unless it comes within one of the specific categories of matters exempt from public disclosure. Virtually all agencies of the executive branch of the Federal Government have issued regulations to implement the Freedom of Information Act. These regulations inform the public where certain types of information may be readily obtained, how other information may be obtained on request, and what internal agency appeals are available if a member of the public is refused requested information. This Act is designed to prevent abuse of discretionary power of federal agencies by requiring them to make public certain information about their workings and work product.

Freedom of press. Right to publish and distribute one's thoughts and views without governmental restriction as guaranteed by First Amendment of U.S. Constitution. Such right includes freedom from prior restraint of publication. There is little difference between "freedom of speech" and "freedom of press." *See* Censor; Censorship; Gag order; Liberty *(Liberty of the press)*; Prior restraint.

Freedom of religion. Freedom to individually believe and to practice or exercise one's belief. This First Amendment protection embraces the concept of freedom to believe and freedom to act, the first of which is absolute, but the second of which remains subject to regulation for protection of society. Such freedom means not only that civil authorities may not intervene in affairs of church; it also prevents church from exercising its authority through state. *See also* Establishment clause; Free exercise clause; Liberty *(Religious liberty)*.

Freedom of speech. Right guaranteed by First Amendment of U.S. Constitution to express one's thoughts and views without governmental restrictions. *See also* Fighting words doctrine; Liberty *(Liberty of speech)*; Speech or debate clause.

Free election. Exists where each voter is allowed to cast his ballot as his own conscience dictates.

Free enterprise. The right to conduct a legitimate business for profit, under usual laws of supply and demand, without undue government interference.

Free exercise clause. First Amendment to U.S. Constitution provides that "Congress shall make no law respecting an establishment of religion, or prohibiting the free exercise thereof." *See also* Establishment clause; Freedom of religion; Liberty.

Freehold. An estate for life or in fee. A "freehold estate" is a right of title to land. An estate in land or other real property, of uncertain duration; that is, either of inheritance or which may possibly last for the life of the tenant at the least (as distinguished from a leasehold); and held by a free tenure (as distinguished from copyhold or villeinage).

An estate to be a freehold must possess these two qualities: (1) Immobility, that is, the property must be either land or some interest issuing out of or annexed to land; and (2) indeterminate duration, for, if the utmost period of time to which an estate can endure be fixed and determined, it cannot be a freehold.

Freehold *in deed* is the real possession of land or tenements in fee, fee-tail, or for life. Freehold *in law* is the right to such tenements before entry. The term has also been applied to those offices which a man holds in fee or for life.

Determinable freeholds are estates for life, which may determine upon future contingencies before the life for which they are created expires, as if an estate be granted to a woman during her widowhood, or to a man until he be promoted to a benefice.

Freehold in law is a freehold which has descended to a man, upon which he may enter at pleasure, but which he has not entered on.

Freeholder. One having title to realty; either of inheritance or for life; either legal or equitable title. A person who possesses a freeholder estate; *i.e.* the owner of a freehold.

Free on board (FOB). The term "F.O.B." is an abbreviation for "free on board" and means that seller will deliver subject matter contracted for, on certain conveyance, without expense to buyer. In sales price quotation, means generally that the seller assumes all responsibilities and costs up to the point of delivery, including insurance, transportation, etc. See U.C.C. § 2–319.

Free port. An area or section of a port set aside for handling of foreign goods without entering customs. *See also* Foreign trade zone.

Free press. *See* Freedom of press.

Free shareholders. The free shareholders of a building and loan association are subscribers to its capital stock who are not borrowers from the association.

Free ships. In international law, ships of a neutral nation. The phrase "free ships shall make free goods" is often inserted in treaties, meaning that goods, even though belonging to an enemy, shall not be seized or confiscated, if found in neutral ships.

Free tenure. Tenure by free services; freehold tenure.

Free time. Period that railroad car or vessel may remain unloaded before demurrage charges begin.

Free trade. A situation where all commodities can be freely imported and exported without special taxes or restrictions being levied.

Free trade zone. *See* Foreign trade zone.

Freeze-out. Refers to a process, usually in a closely held corporation, by which minority shareholders are prevented from receiving any direct or indirect financial return from the corporation in an effort to persuade them to liquidate their investment in the corporation on terms favorable to the controlling shareholders. The use of corporate control vested in the statutory majority of shareholders or the board of directors to eliminate minority shareholders from the enterprise or to reduce to relevant insignificance their voting power or claims on corporate assets. It implies a purpose to force upon the minority shareholder a change which is not incident to any other business goal of the corporation. *See also* Squeeze-out.

Freight. The price or compensation paid for the transportation of goods by a carrier. Name also applied to goods transported by such carriers. *See also* Freight rate.

Dead freight. Money payable by a person who has chartered a ship and only partly loaded her, in respect of the loss of freight caused to the ship-owner by the deficiency of cargo.

Freight booking. Making of specific arrangements for the transportation of goods in advance. *See* Forwarding agent; Freight forwarder.

Freighter. One who charters a ship to transport cargo; also, the vessel so chartered. The party by whom a vessel is engaged or chartered; otherwise called the "charterer." In French law, the owner of a vessel is called the "freighter" *(fréteur);* the merchant who hires it is called the "affreighter" *(affréteur).*

Freight forwarder. One who in the ordinary course of business assembles and consolidates small shipments into a single lot and assumes responsibility for transportation of such property from point of receipt to point of destination. Freight forwarders collect and consolidate less than carload or less than truckload shipments and secure common carrier transportation for the long haul movement of property owned by individual shippers by carload or truckload.

Freight mile. The equivalent of one ton of goods (*i.e.* freight) carried one mile.

Freight rate. The transportation charge for goods carried based on number of pieces carried, or the weight, or the mileage, or the value of the goods, or a combination thereof.

Frequent /frəkwént/, *v.* To visit often; to resort to often or habitually.

Frequenter /frəkwéntər/. Any person not an employee who may go in or be in place of employment or public building under circumstances which render him other than trespasser. An employee of an independent contractor working upon the premises of an owner is a "frequenter" working in a place of employment.

Fresh. Immediate; recent; following without any material interval.

Fresh complaint rule. The fresh complaint rule provides that in certain sexual assault cases proof that the alleged victim complained of the criminal act within a reasonable time after it occurred to a person she would ordinarily turn to for help or advice is admissible to bolster the credibility of the victim.

Fresh pursuit. Refers to common-law right of police officer to cross jurisdictional lines in order to arrest a felon. Several states have adopted the Uniform Extra-Territorial Arrest on Fresh Pursuit Act. Basically, the law permits a police officer, of a state which has enacted the Act, to enter a state, which has enacted a similar Act, if he is in fresh pursuit and he can continue in fresh pursuit, of a person in order to arrest him on the ground that he had committed a felony in the state of the pursuing officer. The officer has the same powers of arrest and to hold in custody as the law enforcement officials of the state that he has entered.

Also refers to Fourth Amendment doctrine allowing warrantless searches and arrests where police pursue a fleeing suspect into a protected area.

One from whom property has been taken may use reasonable force to retake it if such force is used immediately after the taking. Sometimes referred to as hot pursuit.

Fresh start adjustment. For persons dying after 1976, normally the decedent's income tax basis in property will carry over to the estate of heirs. The "fresh start" adjustment, however, permits an addition to basis for the appreciation attributable to the period from the date the property was acquired by the decedent to December 31, 1976. The "fresh start" adjustment is only allowed for purposes of determining income tax gain on the later disposition of the property by the estate or heirs. I.R.C. § 1023.

Friend. One favorably disposed. Varying in degree from greatest intimacy to acquaintance more or less casual. One that seeks society or welfare of another whom one holds in affection, respect or esteem or whose companionship and personality are pleasurable; acquaintance, intimate, or confidant. *See also* Next friend.

Friendly suit. A suit brought by a creditor against an executor or administrator, being really a suit by the executor or administrator, in the name of a creditor, against himself, in order to compel the creditors to take an equal distribution of the assets. Also any suit instituted by agreement between the parties to obtain the opinion of the court upon some doubtful question in which they are interested. *See also* Amicable action; Declaratory judgment. *Compare* Adversary proceeding.

Friendly takeover. A corporate takeover that is approved or favored by the target company. *See* Takeover bid. *Compare* Hostile takeover.

Friend of the court. *See* Amicus curiæ.

Fringe benefits. Side, non-wage benefits which accompany or are in addition to a person's employment such as paid insurance, recreational facilities, sick leave, profit-sharing plans, paid holidays and vacations, etc. that are not in the form of cash. Such benefits are in addition to regular salary or wages and are a matter of bargaining in union contracts. *See also* Cafeteria plan; Pension plan; Perquisites.

Frisk. Contact of the outer clothing of a person to detect by the sense of touch whether a concealed weapon is being carried. A pat-down search of a suspect by police, designed to discover weapons for purpose of insuring safety of officer and others nearby, and not to recover contraband or other evidence for use at subsequent trial. The scope of a frisk has been limited by the courts to be less than a full-scale search. In determining whether a police officer had a basis for initiating a frisk, there are two matters to be considered. One concerns whether the officer had a sufficient degree of suspicion that the party frisked was armed and dangerous, and the other whether the officer was rightfully in the presence of the party frisked so as to be endangered if that person was armed. Terry v. Ohio, 392 U.S. 1, 88 S.Ct. 1868, 20 L.Ed.2d 889. *See also* Stop and frisk.

Frivolous. Of little weight or importance. A pleading is "frivolous" when it is clearly insufficient on its face, and does not controvert the material points of the opposite pleading, and is presumably interposed for mere purposes of delay or to embarrass the opponent. A claim or defense is frivolous if a proponent can present no rational argument based upon the evidence or law in support of that claim or defense. Frivolous pleadings may be amended to proper form, or ordered stricken, under federal and state Rules of Civil Procedure.

Frivolous action. Groundless lawsuit with little prospect of success; often brought to embarrass or annoy the defendant. *See* Failure to state cause of action.

Frivolous appeal. One in which no justiciable question has been presented and appeal is readily recognizable as devoid of merit in that there is little prospect that it can ever succeed. In federal practice, if a court of appeals determines that an appeal is "frivolous," it may award damages and single or double costs to the appellee. Fed.R. App.P. 38.

From. As used as a function word, implies a starting point, whether it be of time, place, or condition; and meaning having a starting point of motion, noting the point of departure, origin, withdrawal, etc., as he traveled "from" New York to Chicago. One meaning of "from" is "out of". Word "from" or "after" an event or day does not have an absolute and invariable meaning, but each should receive an inclusion or exclusion construction according to intention with which such word is used. Words "from" and "to," used in contract, may be given meaning to which reason

and sense entitles them, under circumstances of case.

From person. Includes taking from presence of person assaulted as well as taking of property in actual contact with person of one robbed.

From, through, *or* **under.** The term refers to origin or devolution of property, and unless some title to or interest therein has been derived by assignment or otherwise from party adverse to decedent's estate, statute barring testimony is inapplicable.

From time to time. Occasionally, at intervals, now and then. *See* From.

Front. Forepart, as opposed to the back or rear. Any side or face of a building is a front, although the word is more commonly used to denote the entrance side. As applied to a bare lot, it is that side of lot towards which, in ordinary circumstances, house, when built, will most likely face, and very general usage of building houses with their main entrance toward shorter street line results in common understanding that this is side intended when front of lot is referred to.

Frontage. Linear distance of property along street, highway, river, or lake. Extent of front along road or street. The line of property on a public street. Space available for erection of buildings, and does not include cross streets or space occupied by sidewalk or any ornamental spaces in plat between sidewalks and curb. The expense of local improvements made by municipal corporations (such as paving, curbing, and sewering) is generally assessed on abutting property owners in proportion to the "frontage" of their lots on the street or highway, and an assessment so levied being called a "frontage assessment."

Front foot. Measurement used in assessing and apportioning cost of public improvements; *e.g.* curbs, sewers, sidewalks, streets. As respects assessment, synonymous with "abutting foot." *See also* Frontage.

Front-foot rule. One by which cost of improvement is to be apportioned among several properties in proportion to their frontage on improvement and without regard to benefits conferred.

Frontier. In international law, that portion of the territory of any country which lies close along the border line of another country, and so "fronts" or faces it. Border between two countries. The term means something more than the boundary line itself, and includes a tract or strip of country, of indefinite extent, contiguous to the line.

Front wages. Type of prospective compensation paid to a victim of job discrimination without harm to incumbent employees until the victim achieves the position that he would have attained but for the illegal and discriminatory act. *See also* Back pay award.

Frozen account. An account in which no activity is permitted until a court order is lifted.

Frozen assets. Those assets of a business which cannot be readily sold without injuring the capital structure of the business in contrast to liquid assets which are readily convertible into cash.

Frozen deposits. Bank deposits that cannot be withdrawn because, for example, the financial institution is bankrupt or insolvent. In general, taxpayers are not required to report interest on frozen deposits.

Fructus /frɔ́ktəs/. Lat. In the civil law, fruit, fruits; produce; profit or increase; the organic productions of a thing. The right to the fruits of a thing belonging to another. The compensation which a man receives from another for the use or enjoyment of a thing, such as interest or rent.

Fructus industriales /frɔ́ktəs əndə̀striyéyliyz/. Industrial fruits, or fruits of industry. Those fruits of a thing, as of land, which are produced by the labor and industry of the occupant, as crops of grain; as distinguished from such as are produced solely by the powers of nature. Emblements are so called in the common law. Annual crops obtained by yearly labor and cultivation. Term includes those plants which are sown annually and grown primarily by manual labor such as wheat, corn and vegetables.

Fructus legis /frɔ́ktəs liyjəs/. The fruit of the law, i.e. execution.

Fructus naturales /frɔ́ktəs næ̀tyəréyliyz/. Those products which are produced by the powers of nature alone; as wool, metals, milk, the young of animals. Term includes any plant which has perennial roots, such as trees, shrubs and grasses.

Fruit and the tree doctrine. The courts have held that an individual who earns income from his property or services cannot assign that income to another to avoid taxation. For example, a father cannot assign his earnings from commissions to his son and escape income tax on such amount. See Kiddie tax.

Fruit of poisonous tree doctrine. Evidence which is spawned by or directly derived from an illegal search or illegal interrogation is generally inadmissible against the defendant because of its original taint, though knowledge of facts gained independently of the original and tainted search is admissible. Wong Sun v. U. S., 371 U.S. 471, 83 S.Ct. 407, 9 L.Ed.2d 441. This doctrine is to the effect that an unlawful search taints not only evidence obtained at the search, but facts discovered by process initiated by the unlawful search. This doctrine is generally applied to cases involving searches in violation of the Fourth Amendment to the Constitution right against unlawful searches and seizures, but it can be applied to searches in violation of a statutory right. See Exclusionary Rule.

Fruits of crime. In the law of evidence, material objects acquired by means and in consequence of the commission of crime, and sometimes constituting the subject-matter of the crime. See also Fruit of poisonous tree doctrine.

Frustration of contract. This doctrine provides, generally, that where existence of a specific thing is, either by terms of contract or in contemplation of parties, necessary for performance of a promise in the contract, duty to perform promise is discharged if thing is no longer in existence at time for performance. See U.C.C. § 2–615. See also Commercial impracticability; Impossibility.

Frustration of purpose doctrine. A court-created doctrine under which a party to a contract will be relieved of his or her duty to perform when the objective purpose for performance no longer exists (due to reasons beyond that party's control). This doctrine excuses a promisor in certain situations when the objectives of contract have been utterly defeated by circumstances arising after formation of agreement, and performance is excused under this rule even though there is no impediment to actual performance. See also Frustration of contract.

F.Supp. Federal Supplement. A unit of the National Reporter System covering cases decided in the U.S. district courts and U.S. Court of International Trade. See Federal Supplement.

F.T.C. See Federal Trade Commission.

Fuero /fwérow/. In Spanish law, a law; a code.

Fugitive. One who flees; used in criminal law with the implication of a flight, evasion, or escape from arrest, prosecution, or imprisonment. See Extradition; Fugitive from justice; Rendition.

Fugitive Felon Act. A federal statute which makes it a felony to flee across the state line for the purpose of avoiding prosecution or confinement for a state felony or attempted felony, or to avoid giving testimony in a state felony case. 18 U.S.C.A. § 1073. See Extradition.

Fugitive from justice. A person who, having committed a crime, flees from jurisdiction of court where crime was committed or departs from his usual place of abode and conceals himself within the district. A person who, having committed or been charged with crime in one state, has left its jurisdiction and is found within territory of another state when it is sought to subject him to criminal process of former state. See 18 U.S.C.A. §§ 1073, 1074. See also Extradition; Harbor; Rendition.

Fugitive slave law. Acts of Congress passed in 1793 and 1850 (prior to abolition of slavery) providing for the surrender and deportation of slaves who escaped from their masters and fled into the territory of another state, generally a "free" state.

Full. Abundantly provided, sufficient in quantity or degree, complete, entire, and detailed. Having no open space. Ample, perfect, mature, not wanting in any essential quality.

Full age. The age of legal majority; legal age.

Full answer. In pleading, a complete and meritorious answer, not wanting in any essential requisite.

Full blood. Relations of the "full blood," "whole blood," or "entire blood" are those derived not only from the same ancestor, but from the same couple of ancestors.

Full cash value. For property tax purposes, that which is synonymous with market value; that estimate of value which is derived annually by the use of standard appraisal methods and techniques. *See* Fair market value.

Full copy. In equity practice, a complete and unabbreviated transcript of a bill or other pleading, with all indorsements, and including a copy of all exhibits.

Full court. In practice, a court *en banc*. A court duly organized with all the judges present. Court containing permissible complement of judges, as distinguished from a lesser quorum or panel. *See* En banc.

Full cousin. Son or daughter of one's uncle or aunt.

Full covenants. *See* Covenant.

Full coverage. Type of insurance protection which covers all losses with no deductible amount and which covers to the full amount.

Full crew laws. Laws which regulate the number of railroad employees who are required to operate trains.

Full defense. In common law pleading, the formula of defense in a plea, stated at length and without abbreviation, thus: "And the said C.D., by E.F., his attorney, comes and defends the force (or wrong) and injury when and where it shall behoove him, and the damages, and whatsoever else he ought to defend, and says," etc. Such technical pleading is no longer required under federal or state Rules of Civil Procedure.

Full disclosure. Term used in variety of legal contexts, *e.g.* a fiduciary who participates in a transaction for his own benefit is required to fully reveal the details of such. In consumer law, the obligation to reveal all details of a transaction to the consumer; *e.g.* federal and state Truth-in-Lending Acts. Also, federal election laws require candidates to make full disclosure of the extent and source of their campaign contributions. *See also* Compulsory disclosure; Disclosure.

Full faith and credit clause. The clause of the U.S. Constitution (Art. IV, Sec. 1) which provides that the various states must recognize legislative acts, public records, and judicial decisions of the other states within the United States. There are exceptions to this, a major one being that a state need not recognize a divorce decree of a state where neither spouse was a legal resident. Doctrine means that a state must accord the judgment of a court of another state the same credit that it is entitled to in the courts of that state. A judgment or record shall have the same faith, credit, conclusive effect, and obligatory force in other states as it has by law or usage in the state from whence taken. *See also* Comity; Fauntleroy doctrine.

Full hearing. Embraces not only the right to present evidence, but also a reasonable opportunity to know the claims of the opposing party, and to meet them. One in which ample opportunity is afforded to all parties to make, by evidence and argument, a showing fairly adequate to establish the propriety or impropriety from the standpoint of justice and law of the step asked to be taken. *See also* Fair hearing.

Full indorsement. *See* Indorsement.

Full jurisdiction. Complete jurisdiction over a given subject-matter or class of actions without any exceptions or reservations. *See* Jurisdiction.

Full life. Life in fact and in law.

Full name. The first, middle and surname of a person, or the first name, middle initial and surname. May also refer to name under which a person is known in the community.

Full-paid stock. Stock on which no further payments can be demanded by the issuing company.

Full powers. A document issued by the government of a nation empowering its diplomatic agent to conduct special business with a foreign government.

Full proof. In the civil law, proof by two witnesses, or a public instrument. Evidence which satisfies the minds of the jury of the truth of the fact in dispute, to the entire exclusion of every reasonable doubt. *See* Prima facie; Proof.

Full right. The union of a good title with actual possession.

Full settlement. Implies an adjustment of all pending matters, the mutual release of all prior obligations existing between the parties.

Full value. *See* Fair market value.

Function. Derived from Latin "functus," the past participle of the verb "fungor" which means to perform, execute, administer. The nature and proper action of anything; activity appropriate to any business or profession. Office; duty; fulfillment of a definite end or set of ends by the correct adjustment of means. The occupation of an office. By the performance of its duties, the officer is said to fill his function. The proper activities or duties of municipality.

Functional depreciation. Such results from necessary replacement of equipment before it is worn out, by reason of invention and improved machinery, equipment, etc. which render more efficient and satisfactory service. *See* Depreciation; Functional obsolescence.

Functional discount. Such as occurs where a supplier charges different prices to purchasers at different functional levels of distribution and where the higher price is charged to the purchaser at the level farther from the supplier in the chain of distribution, *i.e.,* the retailer is charged more than the wholesaler. Such is permissible under the Robinson-Patman Act.

Functionality. Under trademark law, doctrine allowing protection to a shape, configuration or color scheme only if it is non-functional. Functionality exists if the design or color is so superior to available alternatives that competition would be hindered by giving the first user exclusive rights.

Functional obsolescence. The need for replacement because a structure or equipment has become inefficient or out-moded because of improvements developed since its original construction or production. The loss of value due to inherent deficiencies within the property.

With respect to valuation of property for taxation, is loss of value brought about by the failure or inability to deliver full service, and includes any loss of value by reason of shortcomings or undesirable features contained within the property itself and is a loss of utility and failure to function due to inadequacies of design and deficiencies in the property.

See also Economic obsolescence; Obsolescence.

Functionary. A public officer or employee. An officer of a private corporation is also sometimes so called.

Functus officio /fə́ŋktəs əfísh(iy)ow/. Lat. A task performed. Having fulfilled the function, discharged the office, or accomplished the purpose, and therefore of no further force or authority. Applied to an officer whose term has expired and who has consequently no further official authority; and also to an instrument, power, agency, etc., which has fulfilled the purpose of its creation, and is therefore of no further virtue or effect.

Fund *or* **funds.** To capitalize with a view to the production of interest. Also, to put into the form of bonds, stocks, or other securities, bearing regular interest, and to provide or appropriate a fund

or permanent revenue for the payment thereof. An asset or group of assets set aside for a specific purpose. To fund a debt is to pledge a specific fund to keep down the interest and reduce the principal.

A generic term and all-embracing as compared with term "money," etc., which is specific. A sum of money or other liquid assets set apart for a specific purpose, or available for the payment of general debts, claims, or expenses.

In the plural, this word has a variety of slightly different meanings, as follows: moneys and much more, such as notes, bills, checks, drafts, stocks and bonds, and in broader meaning may include property of every kind. Money in hand, assets, cash, money available for the payment of a debt, legacy, etc. Corporate stocks or government securities; in this sense usually spoken of as the "funds." Assets, securities, bonds, or revenue of a state or government appropriated for the discharge of its debts. Generally, working capital; sometimes used to refer to cash or to cash and marketable securities.

See also Contingent fund; Current funds; Funded; Funding; General fund; Mutual fund; Revolving fund.

Funded debt. As applied to states or municipal corporations, a funded debt is one for the payment of which (interest and principal) some fund is appropriated, either specifically, or by provision made for future taxation and the *quasi* pledging in advance of the public revenue. As applied to the financial management of corporations (and sometimes of estates in course of administration or properties under receivership) funding means the borrowing of a sufficient sum of money to discharge a variety of floating or unsecured debts, or debts evidenced by notes or secured by bonds but maturing within a short time, and creating a new debt in lieu thereof, secured by a general mortgage, a series of bonds, or an issue of stock, generally maturing at a more remote period, and often at a lower rate of interest. The new debt thus substituted for the pre-existing debts is called the "funded debt." This term is very seldom applied to the debts of a private individual; but when so used it must be understood as referring to a debt embodied in securities of a permanent character and to the payment of which certain property has been applied or pledged. *See also* Funded.

Fund in court. As used in the rule providing for allowance of costs out of a "fund in court," this is a term of art and is applied where the plaintiffs' actions have created, preserved or increased property to the benefit of a class of which the plaintiff is not a member.

Funding system. The practice of borrowing money to defray the expenses of government, and creating a "sinking fund," designed to keep down interest, and to effect the gradual reduction of the principal debt. *See Sinking fund, below.*

General fund. This phrase, in many states, is a collective designation of all the assets of the state which furnish the means for the support of government and for defraying the discretionary appropriations of the legislature. Such are distinguished from assets of a special character, such as the school fund. *See also* General fund.

General revenue fund. As used in connection with municipal finances, term refers to the fund out of which the usual, ordinary, running, and incidental expenses of a municipality are paid.

No funds. This term denotes a lack of assets or money for a specific use. It is the return made by a bank to a check drawn upon it by a person who has no deposit to his credit there; also by an executor, trustee, etc., who has no assets for the specific purpose.

Public funds. An untechnical name for (1) the revenue or money of a government, state, or municipal corporation; (2) the bonds, stocks, or other securities of a national or state government. Money, warrants, or bonds, or other paper having a money value, and belonging to the state, or to any county, city, incorporated town or school district. The term applies to funds of every political subdivision of state wherein taxes are levied for public purposes.

Revolving fund. Usually, a renewable credit over a defined period. In simple parlance it relates usually to a situation where a banker or merchant extends credit for a certain amount which can be paid off from time to time and then credit is again given not to exceed the same amount. It may also mean a fund, which, when reduced, is replenished by new funds from specified sources. Term may refer to a revolving charge account.

Sinking fund. The aggregate of sums of money (as those arising from particular taxes or sources of revenue) set apart and invested, usually at fixed intervals, for the extinguishment of the debt of a government or corporation, by the accumulation of interest. A fund arising from particular taxes, imposts, or duties, which is appropriated towards the payment of the interest due on a public loan and for the gradual payment of the principal. A fund created for extinguishing or paying a funded debt.

Sinking fund tax. A tax raised to be applied to the payment of interest on, and principal of public loan.

Fundamental error. *See* Error; Plain error rule.

Fundamental fairness doctrine. Due process of law as applied to judicial procedure. *See* Due process of law.

Fundamental law. The law which determines the constitution of government in a nation or state, and prescribes and regulates the manner of its exercise. The organic law of a nation or state; its constitution.

Fundamental rights. Those rights which have their source, and are explicitly or implicitly guaranteed, in the federal Constitution and state constitutions. *See e.g.,* Bill of rights.

Challenged legislation that significantly burdens a "fundamental right" (examples include First Amendment rights, privacy, and the right to travel interstate) will be reviewed under a stricter standard of review. A law will be held violative of the due process clause if it is not closely tailored to promote a compelling or overriding interest of government. A similar principle applies under Equal Protection law.

Funded. Said of a pension plan or other obligation when funds have been set aside for meeting the obligation when it becomes due. *See also* Fund *(Funded debt).*

Funded pension plan. One containing sufficient funds as contributed by a corporation to meet current and future retirement benefit obligations. The Employee Retirement Income Security Act (ERISA) regulates funding of pension plans.

Funding. Process of financing capital expenditures by issuing long term debt obligations or by converting short term obligations into long term obligations to finance current expenses. Allocation of money to investments or other type of reserve fund to meet future expenses for pension, welfare, or other benefits. ERISA specifies the requirements for funding of qualified retirement plans. *See also* Fund; Funded.

Fungibles. Goods which are identical with others of the same nature, such as grain and oil. With respect to goods or securities, those of which any unit is, by nature or usage of trade, the equivalent of any other like unit, U.C.C. § 1–201(17); § 8–107(1); *e.g.,* a bushel of wheat or other grain; common shares of the same company.

A product which has no important characteristics that identify it as coming from a particular supplier.

Movable goods which may be estimated and replaced according to weight, measure, and number. Things belonging to a class, which do not have to be dealt with *in specie.*

Where a thing which is the subject of an obligation (which one man is bound to deliver to another) must be delivered *in specie,* the thing is not fungible; that very individual thing, and not another thing of the same or another class, in lieu of it, must be delivered. Where the subject of the obligation is a thing of a given class, the thing is said to be fungible; *i.e.,* the delivery of any object which answers to the generic description will satisfy the terms of the obligation.

Furlong. A measure of length, being forty poles, or one-eighth of a mile.

Furlough /fə́rlow/. A leave of absence; *e.g.* a temporary leave of absence to one in the armed service of the country; an employee placed in a temporary status without duties and pay because of lack of work or funds or for other non-disciplinary reasons. 5 U.S.C.A. § 7511(a)(5). Also the document granting leave of absence.

Furnish. To supply, provide, or equip, for accomplishment of a particular purpose. As used in the liquor laws, "furnish" means to provide in any way, and includes giving as well as selling. As used in the Controlled Substances Act, means to provide or supply and connotes a transfer of possession.

Further. Not a word of strict legal or technical import, and may be used to introduce negation or qualification of some precedent matter, but generally when used as an adverb it is word of comparison, and means "additional," and is equivalent to "moreover, or furthermore, something beyond what has been said or likewise, or also." Wider, or fuller, or something new. Occasionally it may mean any, future, or other.

Further advance. A second or subsequent loan of money to a mortgagor by a mortgagee, either upon the same security as the original loan was advanced upon, or an additional security. Equity considers the arrears of interest on a mortgage security converted into principal, by agreement between the parties, as a further advance. *See also* Future advance clause; Future advances.

Furtherance. Act of furthering, helping forward, promotion, advancement, or progress.

Further assurance, covenant for. *See* Covenant.

Further hearing, *or* **further proceedings.** Hearing at another time; additional hearing; new trial; or other proceedings directed by appellate court. Not a new proceeding but rather a continuation of an existing proceeding.

Further instructions. Additional instructions given to jury after they have once been instructed and have retired. Such may be requested by jury during course of deliberations when, for example, the jury is uncertain as to the applicable law.

Further maintenance of action, plea to. A plea grounded upon some fact or facts which have arisen since the commencement of the suit, and which the defendant puts forward for the purpose of showing that the plaintiff should not further maintain his action. Such plea is obsolete under federal and state Rules of Civil Procedure.

Future acquired property. *See* After acquired property.

Future advance clause. A clause in an open-end mortgage or deed of trust which allows the borrower to borrow additional sums at a future time, secured under the same instrument and by the same real property security.

Future advances. Money lent after a security interest has attached and secured by the original security agreement. U.C.C. § 9–204(5). *See also* Further advance.

Future damages. *See* Damages.

Future earnings. Earnings which, if it had not been for injury, could have been made in future, but which were lost as result of injury.

Future estate. *See* Estate.

Future goods. Goods which are not both existing and identified. A purported present sale of such goods operates as a contract to sell. U.C.C. § 2–105(2).

Future interests. Interests in real or personal property, a gift or trust, or other things in which the privilege of possession or of enjoyment is in the future and not present. An interest that will come into being at some future point in time. It is distinguished from a present interest which is already in existence. Assume, for example, that D transfers securities to a newly created trust. Under the terms of the trust instrument, income from the securities is to be paid each year to W for her life, with the securities passing to S upon W's death. W has a present interest in the trust since she is currently entitled to receive the income from the securities. S has a future interest since he must wait for W's death to benefit from the trust.

Future performance. In contracts, execution which is due in the future; deferred performance.

Futures contract. A present right to receive at a future date a specific quantity of a given commodity for a fixed price. Commodity futures contracts are commitments to buy or sell commodities at a specified time and place in the future. The price is established when the contract is made in open auction on a futures exchange. Only a small percentage of futures trading actually leads to delivery of a commodity, for a contract may change hands or be liquidated before the delivery date. Participants fall into two categories: commercial hedgers who use futures to minimize price risks inherent in their marketing operations and speculators who, employing venture capital, seek profits through price changes. Both purchase contracts with only a small margin payment. Futures prices are an indication of the direction of prices based on current market conditions. Such exchanges and transactions are regulated by the federal Commodity Futures Trading Commission. *See also* Option.

Currency futures contract. Futures contracts that allow one to purchase or sell a specified currency at a specified price on a specified settlement date. *See also* Currency future.

Futures market. Commodity exchanges where futures contracts are traded (*e.g.*, Chicago Board of Trade).

Futures trading. The buying and selling of futures contracts, usually on commodity exchanges. *See* Futures contract.

Future value (or terminai value). The value at some future point in time of a present amount of money, or a series of payments, evaluated at the appropriate interest (growth) rate.

G

GAAP. *See* Generally Accepted Accounting Principles.

GAAS. *See* Generally Accepted Auditing Standards.

Gag order. An unruly defendant at trial may constitutionally be bound and gagged to prevent further interruptions in the trial. Term may also refer to an order by the court, in a trial with a great deal of notoriety, directed to attorneys and witnesses, to not discuss the case with reporters—such order being felt necessary to assure the defendant of a fair trial. Term also refers to orders of the court directed to reporters to not report court proceedings, or certain aspects thereof. Such latter type orders have been struck down by the Supreme Court as being an unconstitutional obstruction of freedom of the press. *See also* Jury *(Sequestration of jury).*

Gain. Profits; winnings; increment of value. Difference between receipts and expenditures; pecuniary gain. Difference between cost and sale price. Appreciation in value or worth of securities or property.

Excess of revenues over expenses from a specific transaction. Frequently used in the context of describing a transaction not part of a firm's typical, day-to-day operations.

See also Acquire; Acquisition; Capital (*Capital gain*); Includible gain; Income; Profit; Realized gain *or* loss; Return.

Gainful. Profitable, advantageous, or lucrative.

Gainful employment *or* occupation. In general, any calling, occupation, profession or work which one may or is able to profitably pursue. Within disability clause of policy, term means ordinary employment of particular insured, or such other employment, if any, as insured may fairly be expected to follow.

Gallagher agreements. *See* Mary Carter agreement.

Gallon. A liquid measure containing 231 cubic inches, or four quarts; the standard gallon of the United States. The imperial gallon contains about 277, and the ale gallon 282, cubic inches. The metric equivalent is 3.785 liters.

Gallows. A scaffold; a beam laid over either one or two posts, from which persons sentenced to capital punishment are hanged.

Gambler. One who follows or practices games of chance or skill, with the expectation and purpose of thereby winning money or other property. *See* Gambling.

Gambling. Making a bet. Such occurs when there is a chance for profit if a player is skillful and lucky. A play for value against an uncertain event in hope of gaining something of value. It involves, not only chance, but a hope of gaining something beyond the amount played. Gambling consists of a consideration, an element of chance, and a reward. The elements of gambling are payment of a price for a chance to win a prize. Gambling is regulated by state and federal statutes. See *e.g.* 18 U.S.C.A. §§ 1081 et seq. *See also* Bet; Bookmaking; Game of chance; Gaming; Lottery; Wager.

Gambling device. Tangible means, instrument, contrivance, or thing with or by which money may be lost or won, as distinguished from the game itself. A machine, implement, or contrivance of any kind for the playing of an unlawful game of chance or hazard.

Gambling place. Any place, room, building, vehicle, vessel, tent or location which is used for any of the following: Making and settling bets; receiving, holding, recording or forwarding bets or offers to bet; conducting lotteries or policy games; playing games of chance for money or other property; or playing gambling devices. See 18 U.S.C.A. § 1081.

Gambling policy. In life insurance, one issued to a person, as beneficiary, who has no pecuniary interest in the life insured. Otherwise called a "wager policy." Such policies are generally illegal or not otherwise written by insurance companies because of the absence of an insurable interest.

Game. Wild birds and beasts. The word includes all game birds, game fowl, and game animals. A sport, pastime or contest. A contrivance which has for its object to furnish sport, recreation, or amusement. *See* Gaming.

Game laws. Federal and state laws passed for the preservation of wildlife, usually forbidding the killing or capturing of specified game either entirely or during certain seasons, or by certain described means, or by restricting the number and type of game that may be killed or trapped in season. See 16 U.S.C.A. § 661 et seq., 18 U.S.C.A. § 41 et seq. *See also* Lacey Act; Open season.

Game of chance. A game in which chance rather than skill determines the outcome. *See also* Gaming; Lottery.

Gaming. The practice or act of gambling. An agreement between two or more persons to play together at a game of chance for a stake or wager which is to become the property of the winner, and to which all contribute. The elements of gaming are the presence of price or consideration, chance, and prize or reward. *See* Gambling.

Gaming contracts. *See* Wager.

Gaming device. *See* Gambling device.

Gaming house. *See* Gambling place.

Gang. Any company of persons who go about together or act in concert; in modern use, mainly for criminal purposes.

Gangster. A member of a gang of criminals, thieves, or the like.

GAO. General Accounting Office.

Gaol /jéy(ə)l/. A now obsolete term (of English origin) for a prison for temporary confinement; a jail; a place for the confinement of offenders against the law. As distinguished from "prison," it is said to be a place for temporary or provisional confinement, or for the punishment of the lighter offenses and misdemeanors. *See also* Jail.

Garnish, *v.* To warn or summon. To issue process of garnishment against a person.

Garnishee. One garnished; a person against whom process of garnishment is issued; one who has money or property in his possession belonging to a defendant, or who owes the defendant a debt, which money, property, or debt is attached. A person who owes a debt to a judgment debtor, or a person other than the judgment debtor who has property in his possession or custody in which a judgment debtor has an interest.

Garnishment. A proceeding whereby a plaintiff creditor, *i.e.,* garnishor, seeks to subject to his or her claim the property or money of a third party, *i.e.,* garnishee, owed by such party to defendant debtor, *i.e.,* principal defendant. Satisfaction of an indebtedness out of property or credits of debtor in possession of, or owing by, a third person. An ancillary remedy in aid of execution to obtain payment of a judgment. It is an incident to or an auxiliary of judgment rendered in principal action, and is resorted to as a means of obtaining satisfaction of judgment by reaching credits or property of judgment debtor. This proceeding is called "trustee process" in certain states.

Due process requirements of Fourteenth Amendment, U.S.Const., requires notice and an opportunity to be heard before pre-judgment garnishment of wages. Sniadach v. Family Finance Corp. of Bay View et al., 395 U.S. 337, 89 S.Ct. 1820, 23 L.Ed.2d 349. Garnishment is regulated by both state and federal (*e.g.* Consumer Credit Protection Act) statutes.

See also Attachment execution; Lien of garnishment; Trustee *(Trustee process)*.

Garnishor. Creditor who initiates garnishment for the purpose of reaching property or credits of a debtor held or owed by a third person who is the garnishee.

Gasoline tax. Excise imposed on sale of gasoline by both Federal and state governments.

GATT. General Agreement on Tariffs and Trade. A multi-lateral international agreement that requires foreign products to be accorded no less favorable treatment under the laws than that accorded domestic products.

Gault, Application of. Landmark Supreme Court case guaranteeing to a defendant in a juvenile proceeding the right of confrontation, the privilege against self incrimination, prior notice of the complaint, and the right to counsel. Application of Gault, 387 U.S. 1, 87 S.Ct. 1428, 18 L.Ed.2d 527.

Gdn. Equivalent to guardian.

Genealogy /jiyniyólǝjiy/. The summary history or table of a family, showing how the persons there named are connected together.

General. From Latin word genus. It relates to the whole kind, class, or order. Pertaining to or designating the genus or class, as distinguished from that which characterizes the species or individual; universal, not particularized, as opposed to special; principal or central, as opposed to local; open or available to all, as opposed to select; obtaining commonly, or recognized universally, as opposed to particular; universal or unbounded, as opposed to limited; comprehending the whole or directed to the whole, as distinguished from anything applying to or designed for a portion only. Extensive or common to many.

A statute is "general" when it operates uniformly on all persons and things of a class and such classification is natural, reasonable, and appropriate to purpose sought to be accomplished.

As a noun, the word is the title of a principal officer in the army, usually one who commands a whole army, division, corps, or brigade. In the United States army, the rank of "general" is one of the highest, next to the commander in chief (*i.e.* President), and is only occasionally created. The officers next in rank are lieutenant general, major general, and brigadier general.

As to *general* Acceptance; Administration of estates; Agent; Appearance; Assignment; Average; Benefit; Challenge; Character; Charge; Covenant; Creditor; Customs; Damages; Demurrer; Denial; Deposit; Devise; Election; Finding; Franchise; Fund *or* funds; Guaranty; Guardian; Insurance; Intent; Issue; Legacy; Letter of credit; Malice;

Meeting; Monition; Mortgage; Occupant; Orders; Owner; Partnership; Power; Power of appointment; Property; Replication; Restraint of trade; Retainer; Return; Rule; Session; Ship; Statute; Tail; Tenancy; Term; Traverse; Usage; Verdict; Warrant; and Warranty, see those titles.

General Accounting Office. The General Accounting Office of the federal government has the following basic purposes: assist the Congress, its committees, and its members to carry out their legislative and oversight responsibilities, consistent with its role as an independent nonpolitical agency in the legislative branch; carry out legal, accounting, auditing, and claims settlement functions with respect to Federal Government programs and operations as assigned by the Congress; and make recommendations designed to make Government operations more efficient and effective. The GAO is under the control and direction of the Comptroller General of the United States and the Deputy Comptroller General of the United States, appointed by the President with the advice and consent of the Senate for a term of 15 years.

General appearance. Consent to the jurisdiction of the court and a waiver of all jurisdictional defects except the competency of the court. An appearance by defendant in an action that has the effect of waiving any threshold defenses of lack of territorial authority to adjudicate or lack of notice. *See* Appearance.

General assembly. Title of legislative body in many states. *See also* Legislature.

The policy making body of the United Nations. It is composed of from one to five delegates from each member nation, although each member nation has but one vote.

General assignment for benefit of creditors. A transfer of legal and equitable title to all debtor's property to trustee, with authority to liquidate debtor's affairs and distribute proceeds equitably to creditors. *See also* Assignment (*Assignment for benefit of creditors*).

General average. *See* Average; General average contribution.

General average bond. Type of bond required by master of ship as security for general average contribution before master delivers the cargo.

General average contribution. Such arises from an ancient maritime doctrine making all participants in a maritime venture ratably responsible for losses incurred for their common good. Contribution by all parties in sea venture to make good loss sustained by one of their number on account of sacrifices voluntarily made of part of ship or cargo to save residue, or for extraordinary expenses necessarily incurred by one or more of parties for general benefit of all interests embarked in general enterprise. *See also* Average (*General average*).

General average loss. Loss at sea commonly sustained when cargo is thrown overboard to save ship. Such loss is generally shared by shipowner and owners of cargo. *See* General average contribution; Jettison.

General average statement. Statement of account and admission on shipowner's part as to amount due cargo owner.

General bequest. One not segregated or withdrawn from estate under terms of will but to be paid in money or property as latter directs. Gift payable out of general assets of estate, not amounting to a bequest of particular thing or money.

General circulation. That of a general newspaper only, as distinguished from one of a special or limited character. It is not determined by number of subscribers but by the diversity of subscribers and general nature of subject matter.

General contractor. One who contracts for the construction of an entire building or project, rather than for a portion of the work. The general contractor hires subcontractors (*e.g.* plumbing, electrical, etc.), coordinates all work, and is responsible for payment to subcontractors. Also called "prime" contractor.

General Court. The name given to the legislature of Massachusetts and of New Hampshire in colonial times, and subsequently by their constitutions; so called because the colonial legislature of Massachusetts grew out of the general court or meeting of the Massachusetts Company.

General court martial. *See* Court-Martial.

General credit. The character of a witness as one generally worthy of credit. A distinction is sometimes made between this and "particular credit," which may be affected by proof of particular facts relating to the particular action. *See also* General reputation.

General debt. Debt of a governmental unit legally payable from general revenues and backed by the full faith and credit of the governmental unit.

General denial. *See* General plea.

General election. An election held in the state at large. A regularly recurring election to select officers to serve after the expiration of the full terms of their predecessors. *See also* Election.

General estate. Customarily, the entire estate held by a person in his individual capacity.

General exception. General exception is an objection to a pleading, or any part thereof, for want of substance, while a special exception is an objection to the form in which a cause of action is stated. Exception taken at trial of case in which the exceptor does not specify the grounds or limitations of his objection. *See also* Demurrer.

General execution. A writ commanding an officer to satisfy a judgment out of any personal property of the defendant. If authorizing him to levy only on certain specified property, the writ is sometimes called a "special" execution.

General executor. One whose power is not limited either territorially or as to the duration or subject of his trust. One who is to have charge of the whole estate, wherever found, and administer it to a final settlement.

General fund. Assets and liabilities of a nonprofit entity not specifically earmarked for other purposes. The primary operating fund of a governmental unit not designated for any specific purpose. *See also* General revenue; Fund *or* funds.

General improvement. One which exists where primary purpose and effect of improvement is to benefit public generally, though it may incidentally benefit property owners in particular locality.

General indorsement. *See* Indorsement.

General intangibles. Any personal property (including things in action) other than goods, accounts, contract rights, chattel paper, documents, instruments, and money. U.C.C. § 9–106.

General interest. In regard to admissibility of hearsay evidence, a distinction is sometimes made between "public" and "general" interest, the term "public" being strictly applied to that which concerns every member of the state, and the term "general" being confined to a lesser, though still a considerable, portion of the community.

General jurisdiction. Such as extends to all controversies that may be brought before a court within the legal bounds of rights and remedies; as opposed to *special* or *limited* jurisdiction, which covers only a particular class of cases, or cases where the amount in controversy is below a prescribed sum, or which is subject to specific exceptions. The terms "general" and "special," applied to jurisdiction, indicate the difference between a legal authority extending to the whole of a particular subject and one limited to a part; and, when applied to the terms of court, the occasion upon which these powers can be respectively exercised. A court of "general jurisdiction" is one which takes cognizance of all cases, civil or criminal, of a particular nature. *See also* Jurisdiction.

General Land Office. Formerly an office of the United States government, being a division of the Department of the Interior, having charge of all executive action relating to the public lands, including their survey, sale or other disposition, and patenting; originally constituted by Act of Congress in 1812. The General Land Office and the U.S. Grazing Service were consolidated into the Bureau of Land Management under the Department of the Interior by 1946 Reorganization Plan No. 3, § 403. *See* Bureau of Land Management.

General law. A law that affects the community at large. A general law as contradistinguished from one that is special or local, is a law that embraces a class of subjects or places, and does not omit any subject or place naturally belonging to such class. A law, framed in general terms, restricted to no locality, and operating equally upon all of a group of objects, which, having regard to the purposes of the legislation, are distinguished by characteristics sufficiently marked and important to make them a class by themselves, is not a special or local law, but a general law. A law that relates to a subject of a general nature, or that affects all people of state, or all of a particular class (*e.g.* General Laws of Massachusetts). *Compare* Private law; Special law.

General ledger. An accounting term used to describe the book or other instrument which summarizes an entity's financial accounts. The general ledger is the source from which the entity's trial balance and financial statements are prepared. The general ledger contains a separate account for each of the assets, liabilities, revenues and expenses of the entity.

General lien. A general lien is a right to detain a chattel, etc., until payment be made, not only of any debt due in respect of the particular chattel, but of any balance that may be due on general account in the same line of business.

Generally Accepted Accounting Principles (GAAP). The conventions, rules and procedures necessary to define accepted accounting practices at a particular time; includes both broad and specific guidelines. The source of such principles is the Financial Accounting Standards Board.

Generally Accepted Auditing Standards (GAAS). The standards, as opposed to particular procedures, promulgated by the AICPA which concern the auditor's professional qualities and the judgment exercised by him in the performance of his examination and in his report.

General manager. One having general direction and control of corporation's affairs, and who may do everything which corporation could do in transaction of its business. A manager for all general purposes of the corporation.

General partner. One of two or more persons who associate to carry on business as co-owners for profit and who are personally liable for all debts of the partnership. Uniform Partnership Act, § 6(1), (15). To be contrasted with "limited" partner who is liable only to the extent of his or her contributed capital. May also be the managing partner of a limited partnership who is responsible for operations of partnership. *See* Partner.

General plea. Type of pleading such as a general denial which controverts *all* of the averments of the preceding pleading (*e.g.* of the complaint). See Fed.R. Civil P. 8(b).

General power of appointment. One exercisable in favor of any person the donee may select.

General publication. In copyright law, "general publication" is such disclosure, communication, circulation, exhibition or distribution of subject of copyright tendered or given to one or more members of general public as implies abandonment of right of common-law copyright or its dedication to public, whereas "limited publication" is one which communicates knowledge of its contents under conditions expressly or impliedly precluding its dedication to public.

General reputation. In evidence, testimony concerning the repute in which a person is held in the community; *e.g.* peaceable, law abiding citizen.

Criminal defendant may show his good character by proof of his "real character", that is, those peculiar qualities which individual is supposed to possess and which distinguish him from others and denote what a person really is, not what he is reputed to be, or by proof of his "general reputation" which is based on speech of his associates and is sum of opinions generally entertained concerning what is reputed or understood to be the estimate of person's character in community in which he moves or resides.

See Character; Reputation.

General revenue. Fund from which all lawful obligations of a state or municipality are payable in the absence of a provision calling for payment from a special fund (*e.g.*, special fund for the benefit of the courts).

General Services Administration. Federal agency created to manage government property and records. The GSA supervises construction and operation of buildings, procurement and distribution of supplies, disposal of surplus property, traffic and communications facilities, stockpiling of strategic and critical materials, and management of automatic data processing resources program.

General taxes. Those imposed by and paid to government which return taxpayer no special benefit other than the protection afforded him and his property by government, and promotion of programs which have for their benefit the welfare of all. A tax, imposed solely or primarily for purpose of raising revenue and merely granting person taxed right to conduct business or profession.

General welfare. General term used to describe the government's concern for the health, peace, morals, and safety of its citizens.

General welfare clause. The provision of the U.S. Constitution (Art. I, Sec. 8, Cl. 1) which declares that Congress may tax and pay debts in order to provide for the "general welfare of the United States."

General words. Such words of a descriptive character as are used in conveyances in order to convey, not only the specific property described but also all kinds of easements, privileges, and appurtenances which may possibly belong to the property conveyed. Such words are in general unnecessary; but are properly used when there are any easements or privileges reputed to belong to the property not legally appurtenant to it.

Generation. May mean either a degree of removal in computing descents, or a single succession of living beings in natural descent. Average span of time between birth of parents and that of their offspring. Group of people born and living contemporaneously.

Generation-skipping transfer. Transfer of assets more than a single generation removed from the transferor (*e.g.*, from grandfather to grandchild). *See* Generation-skipping transfer tax; Generation-skipping trust.

Generation-skipping transfer tax. The 1986 Tax Reform Act imposes a generation-skipping transfer tax on (1) transfers under trusts (or similar arrangements) having beneficiaries in more than one generation below that of the transferor, and (2) direct transfers to beneficiaries more than one generation below that of the transferor. The tax is imposed (with certain exemptions) on the occurrence of any one of three taxable events: a taxable termination, a taxable distribution (including distributions of income) and a direct skip, that is, an outright transfer to or for the benefit of a person at least two generations below that of the transferor. I.R.C. §§ 2601 et seq. *See* Generation-skipping trust.

Generation-skipping trust. A trust established to transfer assets more than a single generation removed from the transferor. *See* Deemed transferor; Generation-skipping transfer tax.

Generic. Relating to or characteristic of a whole group or class; general, as opposed to specific or special.

Generic mark or term. Within the purview of trademark law, this term means a lack of distinctiveness necessary for name or mark to be given federal trademark law protection. Generic marks are marks which include words which embrace entire class of products or services, not all of which necessarily emanate from same source.

A "generic term" is one which is commonly used as name or description of a kind of goods and it is generally accepted that a generic term is incapable of achieving trade name protection.

Generic name. The "established name" of a drug; its chemical name, a common name, or an official name used in an official compendium. *See also* Name.

Generic drug laws. Laws which permit pharmacists to substitute generic drugs for brand name drugs under specified conditions. Most states have passed such laws. The purpose of these laws ostensibly is to make available to consumers less expensive generic drugs in lieu of more expensive brand-name drugs.

Genetic fingerprinting. *See* DNA identification.

Geneva Convention. An international agreement for the conduct of nations at war drafted in 1864 and ratified by nearly every country. It provides, among other things, that a belligerent shall give proper care to enemy sick or wounded, that the Red Cross shall be the emblem of the sanitary service; and that hospitals and ambulances with their personnel shall be respected and protected. Revisions have brought the convention into accord with newer scientific discoveries and methods of warfare.

Gentlemen's agreement. Generally an unsigned and unenforceable agreement made between parties who expect its performance because of good faith.

Gentrification. A term used in land development to describe a trend whereby previously underdeveloped areas become revitalized as persons of relative affluence invest in homes and begin to upgrade the neighborhood economically.

Genuine. As applied to notes, bonds, and other written instruments, this term means that they are truly what they purport to be, and that they are free of forgery or counterfeiting. U.C.C. § 1–201(18).

Genuine issue. Genuine issues which will preclude entry of summary judgment are issues which can be sustained by substantial evidence. As used in rule that burden of proving absence of material fact so that no "genuine issue" is left for jury determination is on movant for summary judgment, means a real as opposed to a false or colorable issue. A "genuine issue of fact" exists, precluding rendition of summary judgment, where there is the slightest doubt as to the facts, so long as the fact in doubt is a material one which has legal probative force as to a controlling issue. See Fed.R.Civil P. 56(c).

Geodetic survey system. A system of nationwide survey marks (bench) at longitude and latitude points, created by the federal government. A scientific method of integrating all real estate within the continental United States into one unified system.

Geographic market. In antitrust law, that part of a relevant market that identifies the physical area in which a firm might have market power. It is the territorial area in which businessmen effectively compete.

Germane /jərméyn/. In close relationship, appropriate, relative, pertinent. Relevant to or closely allied.

Gerrymander /jéhriymǽndər/géhr°/. A name given to the process of dividing a state or other territory into the authorized civil or political divisions, but with such a geographical arrangement as to accomplish an ulterior or unlawful purpose, as, for instance, to secure a majority for a given political party in districts where the result would be otherwise if they were divided according to obvious natural lines.

Gestation. The time during which a woman carries a fetus in her womb, from conception to birth. But, as used in medical authorities, this phrase does not mean the actual number of days from conception to birth.

Gideon v. Wainwright. Landmark Supreme Court decision which held that provision guaranteeing a criminal defendant the assistance of counsel under the Sixth Amendment, U.S.Const., is binding on the states in state proceedings through the due process provision of the Fourteenth Amendment. 372 U.S. 335, 83 S.Ct. 792, 9 L.Ed.2d 799. *See also* Counsel, right to; Effective assistance of counsel.

Gift. A voluntary transfer of property to another made gratuitously and without consideration. Essential requisites of "gift" are capacity of donor, intention of donor to make gift, completed delivery to or for donee, and acceptance of gift by donee.

In tax law, a payment is a gift if it is made without conditions, from detached and disinterested generosity, out of affection, respect, charity or like impulses, and not from the constraining force of any moral or legal duty or from the incentive of anticipated benefits of an economic nature.

An *absolute gift,* or gift inter vivos, as distinguished from a testamentary gift, or one made in contemplation of death, is one by which the donee becomes in the lifetime of the donor the absolute owner of the thing given, whereas a *donatio mortis causa* leaves the whole title in the donor, unless the event occurs (the death of the donor) which is to divest him.

The only important difference between a "gift" and a "voluntary trust" is that in the case of a gift the thing itself passes to the donee, while in the case of a trust the actual, beneficial, or equitable title passes to the cestui que trust, and the legal title is transferred to a third person, or retained by the person creating it.

See also Anatomical gift; Animus donandi; Annual exclusion; Endowment; Symbolic delivery; Taxable gift; Vested gift.

Antenuptial gift. Voluntary transfer of property before a marriage from one spouse to another, commonly made in exchange for a waiver of rights to property after the marriage.

Class gift. See Class gift.

Gift in contemplation of death. See Gift causa mortis; Gifts within three years of death.

Split gift. See Gift splitting election.

Testamentary gift. Voluntary transfer of property to take effect upon the death of the donor.

Gift causa mortis /gíft kózə mórtəs/. A gift of personal property made in expectation of donor's death and on condition that donor die as anticipated. A gift causa mortis is effected only if the following conditions are met: the donor must be stricken with some disorder which makes death imminent, death of donor must ensue as a result of the disorder existing at time the gift was made without any intervening perfect recovery, gift must have been made to take effect only in event of donor's death by his existing disorder, and there must have been an actual delivery of the subject of the donation to the donee. *See also* Gifts within three years of death.

Gift deed. A deed for a nominal sum or for love and affection.

Gift enterprise. A scheme for the division or distribution of articles to be determined by chance amongst those who have taken shares in the scheme. A sporting artifice by which, for example, a merchant or tradesman sells his wares for their market value, but, by way of inducement, gives to such purchaser a ticket which entitles him to a chance to win certain prizes to be determined after the manner of a lottery.

Gift inter vivos /gíft íntər váyvows/. Gifts between the living, which are perfected and become absolute during lifetime of donor and donee. An immediate, voluntary, and gratuitous transfer of personalty by one to another. The essentials of an inter vivos gift are: (1) donative intention; (2) delivery to donee; in the case of a chose in action not capable of delivery, the donor must during his lifetime strip himself of all dominion over the thing taken; (3) acceptance by donee.

Gift in trust. Gift made in such manner that the donee acquires legal title for the beneficial enjoyment of the cestui que trust.

Gift over. A gift to one for life, and from and after his death to another. Broadly, any transfer of property to take effect after the termination of an intermediate estate or estates such as a life estate, *e.g.* to A for life, remainder to B.

Gift splitting election. A special election for Federal gift tax purposes whereby husband and wife can treat a gift by one of them to a third party as being made one-half by each. The major advantage of the election is that it enables the parties to take advantage of the nonowner spouse's annual exclusion and unified credit. I.R.C. § 2513.

Gifts (or Transfers) to Minors Act. A Uniform Act adopted by most states providing for a means of transferring property (usually stocks and bonds) to a minor. The designated custodian of the property has the legal right to act on behalf of the minor without the necessity of a guardianship. Generally, the custodian possesses the right to change investments (*e.g.*, sell one type of stock and buy another), apply the income from the custodial property to the minor's support, and even terminate the custodianship. In this regard, however, the custodian is acting in a fiduciary capacity on behalf of the minor. The custodian could not, for example, appropriate the property for his or her own use because it belongs to the minor. During the period of the custodianship, the income from the property is taxed to the minor. The custodianship terminates when the minor reaches legal age. One of the primary reasons for making gifts to minors pursuant to the requirements of the Uniform Act had been to receive favorable tax treatment; however, the Tax Reform Act of 1986 reduced the tax benefits of such income shifting.

This uniform act has been replaced by and renamed the Uniform Transfers to Minors Act. *See* Transfers to Minors Act.

Gifts within three years of death. Some taxable gifts automatically are included in the gross estate of the donor if death occurs within three years of the gift. I.R.C. § 2035.

Gift tax. A tax imposed on the transfer of property by gift. Such tax is imposed upon the donor of a gift and is based on the fair market value of the property on the date of the gift. *See also* Gift splitting election; Tax.

Gift to a class. A gift of aggregate sum to body of persons uncertain in number at time of gift, to be ascertained at future time, who are all to take in equal shares, or some other definite proportion; share of each being dependent for its amount upon ultimate number taking. *See also* Class gift.

Gilt edge. As applied to commercial paper, a colloquialism, meaning of the best quality or highest price, first class; but not implying that a note which is not gilt edge is not collectible, or that the maker is irresponsible. Also, a bond or other security issue with the highest rating (*i.e.* highest investment quality).

Ginnie Mae. Government National Mortgage Association; and the securities guaranteed by that agency.

Gist /jist/. In common law pleading, the essential ground or object of the action in point of law, without which there would be no cause of action. The cause for which an action will lie or the ground or foundation of a suit without which it would not be maintainable; the essential ground or object of the suit without which there is no cause of action. This term is no longer used in those states that have adopted Rules of Civil Procedure, nor in the federal courts.

Give. To transfer ownership or possession without compensation. To bestow upon another gratuitously or without consideration. *See also* Gift.

Give and bequeath. These words, in a will, import a benefit in point of right, to take effect upon the decease of the testator and proof of the will, unless it is made in terms to depend upon some contingency or condition precedent.

Give bail. To furnish or post bail or security for one's appearance. *See* Bail.

Give color. To admit an apparent or colorable right in the opposite party. In common law pleading, a plea of confession and avoidance had to give color to the affirmative averments of the complaint, or it would be fatally defective. The "giving color" was simply the absence of any denials, and the express or silent admission that the declaration, as far as it went, told the truth. *See* Color.

Give judgment. To render, pronounce, or declare the judgment of the court in an action at law; not spoken of a judgment obtained by confession. *See* Rendition of judgment.

Give notice. To communicate to another, in any proper or permissible legal manner, information or warning of an existing fact or state of facts or (more usually) of some intended future action; *e.g.* tenant giving landlord thirty day notice of termination of tenancy; employee giving employer two weeks notice of intention to quit; to give notice of appeal to appellee. *See also* Notice.

Giver. A donor; person who makes a gift.

Give time. Extending the period at which, by the contract between them, the principal debtor was originally liable to pay the creditor. *See* Forbearance.

Give way. In the rules of navigation, one vessel is said to "give way" to another when she deviates from her course in such a manner and to such an extent as to allow the other to pass without altering her course.

Glass–Steagall Act. Also known as the Banking Act of 1933, restricts the securities-related business of commercial banks in order to protect depositors. Such Act, which prohibits commercial banks from owning brokerage firms or engaging in certain types of brokerage business, applies both to national banks and to state-chartered banks that are members of the Federal Reserve System. 12 U.S.C.A. § 378.

Gloss. An interpretation, consisting of one or more words, interlinear or marginal; an annotation, explanation, or comment on any passage in the text of a work, for purposes of elucidation or amplification.

G.N.M.A. Government National Mortgage Association (Ginnie Mae).

GNP. Gross National Product.

Go. To be dismissed from a court. To issue from a court. "The court said a *mandamus* must *go.*"

Go bail. To assume the responsibility of a surety on a bail-bond.

Go hence. To depart from the court; with the further implication that a suitor who is directed to "go hence" is dismissed from further attendance upon the court in respect to the suit or proceeding which brought him there, and that he is finally denied the relief which he sought, or, as the case may be, absolved from the liability sought to be imposed upon him.

Going. In various compound phrases (as those which follow) this term implies either motion, progress, active operation, or present and continuous validity and efficacy.

Going and coming rule. Under this rule, employees who suffer injuries while going to and returning from work are generally excluded from the benefits of workers' compensation acts. Such injuries, generally, are not compensable because they do not arise out of or in the course of the employment.

Going before the wind. In the language of mariners and in the rules of navigation, a vessel is said to be going "before the wind" when the wind is free as respects her course, that is, comes from behind the vessel or over the stern, so that her yards may be braced square across. She is said to be "going off large" when she has the wind free on either tack, that is, when it blows from some point abaft the beam or from the quarter.

Going concern. An enterprise which is being carried on as a whole, and with some particular object in view. The term refers to an existing solvent business, which is being conducted in the usual and ordinary way for which it was organized. When applied to a corporation, it means that it continues to transact its ordinary business. A firm or corporation which, though financially embarrassed, continues to transact its ordinary business.

Going concern value. The value of a firm, assuming that the firm's organization and assets remain intact and are used to generate future income and cash flows. The value which inheres in a company where its business is established, as distinguished from one which has yet to establish its business. The value of the assets of a business as an operating, active concern, rather than merely as items of property (book value of assets alone) which would be the case in a liquidation sale. Such value includes goodwill.

Going into effect of act. Becoming operative as a law.

Going off large. *See* Going before the wind.

Going price. The prevalent market price; the current market value of the article in question at the time and place of sale. *See* Fair market value.

Going private. Process by which a publically owned company becomes a privately held company. Causing of a class of equity securities to be delisted from a national securities exchange or the causing of a class of equity securities which is authorized to be quoted in an inter-dealer quotation system of a registered national securities exchange to cease to be so authorized. Nearly all attempts to go private utilize variations of one or more of a limited number of basic techniques. These include (in probable order of frequency): (1) A cash tender offer to purchase all outstanding publically held shares by the issuer, its management or an affiliated entity; (2) a merger or consolidation of the issuer with, or the sale of its assets to, another corporation controlled by management of the issuer; (3) an exchange offer (almost always involving a debt security) by the issuer, its management or an affiliated entity; and (4) a reverse stock split. *See also* Leveraged buyout.

Going public. Term used to describe the process by which a corporation issues its first stock for public purchase. Also, when a private corporation becomes a public corporation. Said of a business when its shares become traded to the general public, rather than being closely held by relatively few stockholders.

Going short. *See* Short sale.

Going value. *See* Going concern value.

Gold bond. One payable in gold coin or its equivalent, which means any money acceptable to United States government in payment of debts due it.

Gold clause. Provision formerly found in contracts, bonds and mortgages calling for payment in gold, though such clause is void today.

Golden parachute. A slang term for a termination agreement which shelters executives from the effects of a corporate change in control. Such an agreement generally provides for substantial bonuses and other benefits for top management and certain directors who may be forced to leave the target company or otherwise voluntarily leave upon a change in control. A special tax is imposed on golden parachute payments. I.R.C. § 4999. *See also* Silver parachute.

Golden Rule argument. This type of argument, by which jurors are urged to place themselves or members of their families or friends in place of person who has been offended and to render verdict as if they or either of them or member of their families or friends was similarly situated, is improper in both civil and criminal cases.

Gold standard. A monetary system in which every form of currency is convertible on demand into its legal equivalent in gold or gold coin. The United States adopted the gold standard in 1900 and terminated it in 1934.

Good. Valid; sufficient in law; effectual; unobjectionable; sound; responsible; solvent; able to pay an amount specified.

Of a value corresponding with its terms; collectible. A note is said to be "good" when the payment of it at maturity may be relied on.

Good and clear record title, free from all incumbrances. A title which on the record itself can be again sold as free from obvious defects and substantial doubts; it differs from a "good, marketable title," which is an actual title, but which may be established by evidence independently of the record. *See* Marketable title.

Good and valid. Reliable, sufficient, and unimpeachable in law; adequate; responsible.

Good and workmanlike manner. In a manner generally considered skillful by those capable of judging such work in the community of the performance.

Good behavior. Orderly and lawful conduct; behavior such as is proper for a peaceable and law-abiding citizen. A term is used in an order suspending sentence upon a defendant during good behavior, means merely conduct conformable to law, or to the particular law theretofore breached.

Under some state penal systems, each day of "good behavior" by a prisoner reduces his or her sentence by one day. *See also* Goodtime allowance.

Good cause. Term generally means a substantial reason amounting in law to a legal excuse for failing to perform an act required by law. Legally sufficient ground or reason. Phrase "good cause" depends upon circumstances of individual case, and finding of its existence lies largely in discretion of officer or court to which decision is committed. It is a relative and highly abstract term, and its meaning must be determined not only by verbal context of statute in which term is employed but also by context of action and procedures involved in type of case presented. *See also* Probable cause.

Alimony modification. "Good cause" for modification or revocation of orders for alimony means material and substantial change in circumstances and depends upon circumstances of individual case.

Discovery. "Good cause" for discovery is present if information sought is material to moving party's trial preparation. Such requirement for discovery and production of documents is ordinarily satisfied by a factual allegation showing that requested documents are necessary to establishment of the movant's claim or that denial of production would cause moving party hardship or injustice. Under a 1970 amendment to Fed.R.Civil P. 34, however, "good cause" is no longer required to be shown for production of documents and things. Federal Rule 35(a) does, however, require that "good cause" be shown for order requiring physical or mental examination, as does Rule 26(c) for protective orders to restrict scope of discovery.

Unemployment compensation. "Good cause" for leaving employment, so as not to render one ineligible for unemployment compensation benefits, must be objectively. related to the employment and be such cause as would compel a reasonably prudent person to quit under similar circumstances.

Good character. Sum or totality of virtues of a person which generally forms the basis for one's reputation in the community, though his reputation is distinct from his character. *See* Character; Reputation.

Good conduct. *See* Certificate of good conduct.

Good consideration. Any benefit conferred, or agreed to be conferred, upon the promisor, by any other person, to which the promisor is not lawfully entitled, or any prejudice suffered, or agreed to be suffered, by such person, other than such as the person is at the time of consent lawfully bound to suffer, as an inducement to the promisor, is a good consideration for a promise. That consideration or detriment which the law considers valid and to this extent "good" does not refer to moral goodness. *See* Consideration; Valuable consideration.

Good faith. Good faith is an intangible and abstract quality with no technical meaning or statutory definition, and it encompasses, among other things, an honest belief, the absence of malice and the absence of design to defraud or to seek an unconscionable advantage, and an individual's personal good faith is concept of his own mind

and inner spirit and, therefore, may not conclusively be determined by his protestations alone. Honesty of intention, and freedom from knowledge of circumstances which ought to put the holder upon inquiry. An honest intention to abstain from taking any unconscientious advantage of another, even through technicalities of law, together with absence of all information, notice, or benefit or belief of facts which render transaction unconscientious. In common usage this term is ordinarily used to describe that state of mind denoting honesty of purpose, freedom from intention to defraud, and, generally speaking, means being faithful to one's duty or obligation. *See* Bona fide. *Compare* Bad faith.

Bankruptcy law. "Good faith" as used in statute requiring debtor to propose Chapter 13 plan in good faith has a meaning consisting of two elements: honesty of purpose and full and complete disclosure of the financial facts of the debtor.

Commercial law. Honesty in fact in the conduct or transaction concerned. U.C.C. § 1–201(19). In the case of a merchant, honesty in fact and the observance of reasonable commercial standards of fair dealing in the trade. U.C.C. § 2–103(1)(b).

Insurance law. "Good faith" required of a liability insurer in determining whether to accept settlement within policy limits implies honesty, fair dealing and full revelation; while "bad faith" implies dishonesty, fraud and concealment. *Compare* Bad faith.

Good faith bargaining. In labor law, requirement of "good faith bargaining" imposes upon employer and employee organization obligation to come to the bargaining table with an open mind and sincere desire to reach agreement. Such necessarily entails the earnest efforts of both sides to resolve a controversy.

Good faith exception to exclusionary rule. *See* Exclusionary Rule.

Good faith purchaser. A purchaser who buys without notice of circumstance which would put a person of ordinary prudence on inquiry as to the title, or as to an impediment on the title, of a seller. Sometimes used interchangeably with a "buyer in ordinary course of business" when the seller is a merchant. U.C.C. §§ 1–201(9), 2–403.

Good health. A relative term, meaning a condition of body and mind that ordinary affairs of life may be attended to without serious strain upon the vital powers. As employed in insurance contracts, ordinarily means a reasonably good state of health. It means that the applicant has no grave, important, or serious disease, and is free from any ailment that seriously affects the general soundness and healthfulness of the system. A mere temporary indisposition not tending to weaken or undermine constitution does not render a person in "bad health." It does not mean a condition of perfect health.

Good jury. A jury of which the members are selected from the list of special jurors.

Good, merchantable abstract of title. An abstract showing a good title, clear from incumbrances, and not merely an abstract of matters of record affecting the title, made by one engaged in the business of making abstracts in such form as is customary, as passing current among persons buying and selling real estate and examining titles. *See also* Marketable title.

Good moral character. As a prerequisite to the admission to the practice of law, an absence of proven conduct or acts which have been historically considered as manifestation of moral turpitude.

Good order. Goods or property are in "good order" when they are in acceptable condition under all the circumstances. *See* Merchantability.

Good record title. A "good record title," without words of limitation, means that the proper records shall show an unincumbered, fee-simple title, the legal estate in fee, free and clear of all valid claims, liens, and incumbrances. *See also* Marketable title.

Good repute. An expression, synonymous with and meaning only "of good reputation." *See* Reputation.

Goods. A term of variable content and meaning. It may include every species of personal property or it may be given a very restricted meaning. Items of merchandise, supplies, raw materials, or finished goods. Sometimes the meaning of "goods" is extended to include all tangible items, as in the phrase "goods and services."

All things (including specially manufactured goods) which are movable at the time of identification to the contract for sale other than the money in which the price is to be paid, investment securities and things in action. Also includes the unborn of animals and growing crops and other identified things attached to realty as fixtures. U.C.C. § 2–105(1). All things treated as movable for the purposes of a contract of storage or transportation. U.C.C. § 7–102(1)(f). In context of U.C.C., includes used goods.

As used with reference to secured transactions, goods include all things which are movable at the time the security interest attaches or which are fixtures, but does not include money, documents, instruments, accounts, chattel paper, general intangibles, or minerals or the like (including oil and gas) before extraction. "Goods" also includes standing timber which is to be cut and removed under a conveyance or contract for sale, the unborn young of animals, and growing crops. U.C.C. § 9–105(h).

See also Confusion of goods; Future goods; Identification of goods.

Capital goods. The equipment and machinery used in production of other goods or services.

Consumer goods. Goods which are used or bought for use primarily for personal, family or household purposes. U.C.C. § 9–109(1). *See also* Consumer goods.

Durable goods. Goods which have a reasonably long life and which are not generally consumed in use; *e.g.* refrigerator.

Finished goods. The inventory of completed production that is owned by a firm.

Fungible goods. Goods, every unit of which is similar to every other unit in the mass; *e.g.* uniform goods such as coffee, grain, etc. U.C.C. § 1–201(17).

Hard goods. Consumer durable goods. *See Durable goods, above.*

Soft goods. Generally consumer goods such as wearing apparel, curtains, etc., in contrast to hard goods (*e.g.* appliances).

Good Samaritan doctrine. One who sees a person in imminent and serious peril through negligence of another cannot be charged with contributory negligence, as a matter of law, in risking his own life or serious injury in attempting to effect a rescue, provided the attempt is not recklessly or rashly made. Under this doctrine, negligence of a volunteer rescuer must worsen position of person in distress before liability will be imposed. This protection from liability is provided by statute in most states.

Goods and chattels. This phrase is a general denomination of personal property, as distinguished from real property. In the law of wills, the term "goods and chattels" will, unless restrained by the context, pass all the personal estate.

Goods available for sale. In accounting, the beginning balance of inventory plus net purchases.

Goods on consignment. Merchandise in the hands of sales agents. The agents possess the merchandise; ownership, however, remains with the consignor. *See also* Consignment.

Goods sold and delivered. A phrase frequently used in the action of *assumpsit,* when the sale and delivery of goods furnish the cause.

Goods, wares, and merchandise. A general and comprehensive designation of such chattels and goods as are ordinarily the subject of commerce and sales. The phrase is used in the statute of frauds, and is sometimes found in pleadings and other instruments.

Goodtime allowance. "Good time" credit is awarded for good conduct and reduces period of sentence which prisoner must spend in prison although it does not reduce the period of the sentence itself. Credit allowed on the sentence which is given for satisfactory conduct in prison. Introduced as an incentive for inmates, it has become practically automatically awarded. It may reduce the minimum or maximum sentence or both. *See also* Good behavior.

Good title. One free from reasonable doubt, that is, not only a valid title in fact, but one that can again be sold to a reasonable purchaser or mortgaged to a person of reasonable prudence. A title free from litigation, palpable defects and grave doubts. *See also* Marketable title.

Goodwill. The favor which the management of a business wins from the public. The favorable consideration shown by the purchasing public to goods or services known to emanate from a particular source. Property of an intangible nature, commonly defined as the expectation of continued public patronage.

The custom of patronage of any established trade or business; the benefit or advantage of having established a business and secured its patronage by the public. And as property incident to business sold, favor vendor has won from public, and probability that all customers will continue their patronage. It means every positive advantage that has been acquired by a proprietor in carrying on his business, whether connected with the premises in which the business is conducted, or with the name under which it is managed, or with any other matter carrying with it the benefit of the business.

The excess of cost of an acquired firm or operating unit over the current or fair market value of net assets of the acquired unit. Informally used to indicate the value of good customer relations, high employee morale, a well-respected business name, etc. which are expected to result in greater than normal earning power.

The ability of a business to generate income in excess of normal rate on assets, due to superior managerial skills, market position, new product technology, etc. The capacity to earn profits in excess of a normal rate of return due to establishment of favorable community reputation and consumer identification of the business name.

As applied to law firms, term refers to ability to attract clients as result of firm's name, location, or the reputation of lawyers.

For accounting purposes, goodwill has no basis unless it is purchased. In the purchase of a business, goodwill generally is the difference between the purchase price and the value of the assets acquired. Goodwill is an intangible asset and cannot be amortized for tax purposes. *See also* Amortization.

Go to. In a statute, will, or other instrument, a direction that property shall "go to" a designated person means that it shall pass or proceed to such person, vest in and belong to him.

Go to protest. Commercial paper is said to "go to protest" when it is dishonored by non-payment or non-acceptance. *See also* Protest.

Govern. To direct and control the actions or conduct of, either by established laws or by arbitrary will; to direct and control, rule, or regulate, by authority. To be a rule, precedent, law or deciding principle for.

Governing body. Governing body of institution, organization or territory means that body which has ultimate power to determine its policies and control its activities.

Government. From the Latin *gubernaculum*. Signifies the instrument, the helm, whereby the ship to which the state was compared, was guided on its course by the "gubernator" or helmsman, and in that view, the government is but an agency of the state, distinguished as it must be in accurate thought from its scheme and machinery of government.

In the United States, government consists of the executive, legislative, and judicial branches in addition to administrative agencies. In a broader sense, includes the federal government and all its agencies and bureaus, state and county governments, and city and township governments.

The system of polity in a state; that form of fundamental rules and principles by which a nation or state is governed, or by which individual members of a body politic are to regulate their social actions. A constitution, either written or unwritten, by which the rights and duties of citizens and public officers are prescribed and defined, as a monarchical government, a republican government, etc. The sovereign or supreme power in a state or nation. The machinery by which the sovereign power in a state expresses its will and exercises its functions; or the framework of political institutions, departments, and offices, by means of which the executive, judicial, legislative, and administrative business of the state is carried on.

The whole class or body of officeholders or functionaries considered in the aggregate, upon whom devolves the executive, judicial, legislative, and administrative business of the state.

In a colloquial sense, the United States or its representatives, considered as the prosecutor in a criminal action; as in the phrase, "the government objects to the witness."

The regulation, restraint, supervision, or control which is exercised upon the individual members of an organized jural society by those invested with authority; or the *act* of exercising supreme political power or control.

See also De facto government; Federal government; Judiciary; Legislature; Seat of government.

Federal government. The government of the United States of America, as distinguished from the governments of the several states.

Local government. The government or administration of a particular locality; especially, the governmental authority of a municipal corporation, as a city or county, over its local and individual affairs, exercised in virtue of power delegated to it for that purpose by the general government of the state or nation.

Mixed government. A form of government combining some of the features of two or all of the three primary forms, viz., monarchy, aristocracy, and democracy.

Republican government. One in which the powers of sovereignty are vested in the people and are exercised by the people, either directly, or through representatives chosen by the people, to whom those powers are specially delegated.

Governmental. Of, pertaining to, or proceeding from government.

Governmental act. An act in exercise of police power or in exercise of constitutional, legislative, administrative, or judicial powers conferred on federal, state or local government for benefit of public. A step physically taken by persons capable of exercising the sovereign authority of the foreign nation. Any action of the federal government, or of a state, within its constitutional power. *See also* Governmental activity; Governmental functions.

Governmental activity. A function of government in providing for its own support or in providing services to the public; *e.g.* taxation and the collection of taxes. Generally, when a municipality's activity is for advantage of state as a whole, or is in performance of a duty imposed by sovereign power, activity is "public" and "governmental." *See* Governmental act; Governmental functions.

Governmental agency. A subordinate creature of federal, state or local government created to carry out a governmental function or to implement a statute or statutes. For example, the Federal Trade Commission was created and functions to implement and enforce the Federal Trade Commission Act and various other federal antitrust and consumer protection laws. *See also* Administrative agency; Governmental subdivision.

Governmental agents. Those performing services and duties of a public character for benefit of all citizens of community. The term includes public school officials, firemen and policemen.

Governmental body. *See* Administrative agency; Governmental agency; Governmental subdivision.

Governmental corporation. Corporation organized to perform a governmental function. *See e.g.* Federal Deposit Insurance Corporation.

Governmental duties. Those duties of a municipality that have reference to some part or element of the state's sovereignty granted it to be exercised for the benefit of the public, and all other duties are "proprietary". Those duties that the framers of the Constitution intended each member of the union of states would assume in order adequately to function under the form of government guaranteed by the Constitution. *See also* Governmental functions.

Governmental facility. A building or institution provided by the government to care for a specified need, such as a courthouse or county jail.

Governmental functions. The functions of a municipality which are essential to its existence, in sense of serving public at large, and are to be distinguished from those which are private, which are not necessary to its existence, and which enure to advantage of its inhabitants. Activities which are carried on by city, pursuant to state requirement, in discharge of state's obligation for health, safety or general welfare of public generally, or which are voluntarily assumed by city for benefit of public generally rather than for its own citizens, are performed in governmental capacity and as "governmental function". *See* Governmental act; Governmental activity.

Governmental immunity. *See* Federal Tort Claims Act; Sovereign immunity.

Governmental instrumentality. Any agency constitutionally or legislatively created. For purposes of the doctrine that federal agencies or instrumentalities are immune from special assessments by state and local governments, a governmental instrumentality is that which performs an important governmental function. *See* Administrative agency; Governmental agency; Governmental subdivision.

Governmental interests. In conflicts of law, term used to describe the particular governmental policies of a jurisdiction in terms of whether its law or another law should be applied in a choice of law issue.

Governmental powers. The totality of power which reposes in a government enabling it to carry out its proper functions as a sovereign. General powers of federal government are enumerated in U.S. Constitution; powers of state governments in state constitutions; municipal governments in charters.

Governmental privileges. *See* Governmental secrets.

Governmental purpose. One which has for its objective the promotion of the public health, safety, morals, general welfare, security, prosperity and contentment of the inhabitants of a given political division. *See also* Governmental functions.

Governmental secrets. In evidence, a privilege exists which protects the government from revealing military or diplomatic secrets or other information the disclosure of which would be contrary to the public interest. *See also* Executive privilege.

Governmental subdivision. An agency created to carry out a governmental purpose or function. *See* Administrative agency; Governmental agency.

Governmental trusts. Type of charitable trust used for erection and maintenance of public buildings and for the promotion of purposes which are of a character sufficiently beneficial to the community to justify permitting property to be devoted forever to their accomplishment. Restatement, Second, Trusts, §§ 373, 374.

Government bonds. *See* Bond.

Government contract. *See* Procurement contract.

Government de facto. A government of fact. A government actually exercising power and control, as opposed to the true and lawful government; a government not established according to the constitution of the nation, or not lawfully entitled to recognition or supremacy, but which has nevertheless supplanted or displaced the government *de jure*. A government deemed unlawful, or deemed wrongful or unjust, which, nevertheless, receives presently habitual obedience from the bulk of the community.

Government de jure /gávǝrnmǝnt diy júriy/. A government of right; the true and lawful government; a government established according to the constitution of the nation, and lawfully entitled to recognition and supremacy and the administration of the nation, but which is actually cut off from power or control. A government deemed lawful, or deemed rightful or just, which, nevertheless, has been supplanted or displaced; that is to say, which receives not presently (although it received formerly) habitual obedience from the bulk of the community.

Government immunity. *See* Governmental immunity.

Government instrumentality doctrine. The doctrine that government instrumentalities are tax exempt.

Government National Mortgage Association. Agency of Federal government (division of HUD) which is primarily engaged in purchasing on the secondary market federally subsidized residential mortgages originated by local lenders, and also in guaranteeing payment of securities backed by residential mortgages. Referred to as "Ginnie Mae."

Government of laws. Fundamental principle of American jurisprudence which requires decisions of courts to be based on laws, statutory and common law, irrespective of the character of the litigants and the personal predelictions of the judges.

Government securities. Direct debt obligations of U.S. government; *see e.g.,* Treasury bill; Treasury bond; Treasury note.

Government survey. General mapping out by government of towns, sections, quarter sections, etc.; sometimes known as a congressional survey. *See also* Government survey system.

Government survey system. A type of legal description whereby the United States is generally divided into checks or tracts of ground. These are further broken down by smaller descriptions, such as metes and bounds. *See also* Government survey; Metes and bounds.

Government tort. A wrong perpetrated by the government through an employee or agent or instrumentality under its control which may or may not be actionable depending upon whether there is governmental tort immunity. Tort actions against the federal government are governed by the Federal Tort Claims Act; many states also have Tort Claims Acts. *See* Federal Tort Claims Act; Sovereign immunity.

Governor. The chief executive official of a state in the United States, and territories of the United States; and also of the chief magistrate of some colonies, provinces, and dependencies of other nations. Governors serve terms ranging from two to four years; are usually restricted to two terms in office; possess veto powers, powers to call special sessions of legislature, powers to pardon and reprieve, and many other appointive, administrative, and financial powers.

Go without day. Words used to denote that a party is dismissed by the court. Party is said to go without day, because there is no day appointed for the party to appear again.

GPO. Government Printing Office. Such office prints and publishes laws, regulations, forms, etc. of federal government.

Grace. A favor or indulgence as distinguished from a right. *See also* Days of grace; Grace, days of; Grace period; Of grace.

Grace, days of. Time of indulgence granted to an acceptor or maker for the payment of his bill of exchange or note. It was originally a gratuitous favor (hence the name), but custom has rendered it a legal right. *See also* Days of grace; Grace period.

Grace period. In insurance law, a period beyond the due date of premium (usually 30 or 31 days) during which insurance is continued in force and during which payment may be made to keep policy in good standing. The grace period for payment of premium does not contemplate free insurance or operate to continue the policy in force after it expires by agreement of the parties. May also refer to period of time provided for in a loan agreement during which default will not occur even though payment is overdue.

Grade, *v.* To establish a level by mathematical points and lines, and then to bring the surface of the street or highway to the level by the elevation or depression of the natural surface to the line fixed. To bring property to the level of an abutting highway.

Grade, *n.* Used in reference to streets: (1) The line of the street's inclination from the horizontal; (2) a part of a street inclined from the horizontal. The hypothetical line to which the work is to be constructed.

Quality, value, relative position, rank, status, or standing.

"Grades of crime" in legal parlance are understood as higher or lower in grade or degree, according to the measure of punishment attached and meted out on conviction and the consequences resulting to the party convicted; *e.g.* first, second or, third degree murder. *See* Classification of crimes; Graded offense.

Grade crossing. A place where a railroad is crossed at grade by a public or private road, or by another railroad, or where one highway crosses another.

Graded offense. One for which offender is subject to a more severe penalty for a higher grade than for a lower grade of offense according to terms of statute; *e.g.*, first degree murder, as opposed to second or third degree; aggravated as opposed to simple assault. Most state criminal statutes provide for degrees of crimes with corresponding differing punishments or sentences. *See* Classification of crimes.

Graduated lease. A type of lease arrangement which provides that rent will vary depending upon future contingencies, such as the amount of traffic or gross income produced.

Graduated payment mortgages (GPM). *See* Mortgage.

Graduated tax. Tax structured so that the rate increases as the amount of income of taxpayer increases.

Graft. The popular meaning is the fraudulent obtaining of public money unlawfully by the corruption of public officers. Advantage or personal gain received because of peculiar position or superior influence of one holding position of trust and confidence without rendering compensatory services, or dishonest transaction in relation to public or official acts, and sometimes implies theft, corruption, dishonesty, fraud, or swindle, and always want of integrity. See *e.g.* 18 U.S.C.A. § 201 et seq. *See also* Bribery.

A term used in equity to denote the confirmation, by relation back, of the right of a mortgagee in premises to which, at the making of the mortgage, the mortgagor had only an imperfect title, but to which the latter has since acquired a good title.

Grain. In Troy weight, the twenty-fourth part of a pennyweight. Any kind of corn sown in the ground.

Grain rent. A payment for the use of land in grain or other crops; the return to the landlord paid by sharecroppers or persons working the land on shares.

Gramm–Rudman–Hollings amendment. Federal law (1986) setting balanced budget goals and requiring automatic reductions in federal expenditures (with certain programs exempted) if Congress fails to meet such annual goals.

Grand, *n.* Jargon term for one thousand dollars.

As to *grand* Assize, *or* assise; Distress; Jury; Larceny, see those titles.

Grandchild. Generally, child of one's child. Descendant of second degree.

Grandfather. The father of either of one's parents.

Grandfather clause. Provision in a new law or regulation exempting those already in or a part of the existing system which is being regulated. An exception to a restriction that allows all those already doing something to continue doing it even if they would be stopped by the new restriction. A clause introduced into several of the constitutions of the southern states, limiting the right to vote to those who can read and write any article of the constitution of the United States, and have worked or been regularly employed in some lawful employment for the greater part of the year next preceding the time they offer to register unless prevented from labor or ability to read or write by physical disability, or who own property assessed at three hundred dollars upon which the taxes have been paid; but excepting those who have served in the army or navy of the United States or in the Confederate States in time of war, their lawful descendants in every degree, and persons of good character who understand the duties and obligations of citizenship under a republican form of government.

One of the original purposes of the "grandfather" clause of the Motor Carrier Act was to permit the continued operation of carrier businesses already established prior to passage of the Act.

Grand jury. *See* Jury.

Grand jury investigation. Investigations conducted by a grand jury into possible wrongdoing. Generally, such are conducted under the aegis of the prosecuting official and they may or may not result in indictments. *See* Jury *(Grand jury).*

Grand larceny. *See* Larcency.

Grandmother. The mother of either of one's parents.

Granger Cases. A name applied to six cases decided by the supreme court of the United States in 1876, which are reported in Munn v. Illinois, 94 U.S. 113, 24 L.Ed. 77; Chicago, B. & Q. R. Co. v. Iowa, 94 U.S. 155, 24 L.Ed. 94; Peik v. Ry. Co., 94 U.S. 164, 24 L.Ed. 97; Chicago, M. & St. P. R. Co. v. Ackley, 94 U.S. 179, 24 L.Ed. 99; Winona & St. Peter R. Co. v. Blake, 94 U.S. 180, 24 L.Ed. 99; those most frequently cited being Munn v. Illinois, and C., B. & Q. R. Co. v. Iowa. They are so called because they arose out of an agitation commenced by the grangers which resulted in the enactment of statutes for the regulation of the tolls and charges of common carriers, warehousemen, and the proprietors of elevators. The enforcement of these acts was resisted and their constitutionality questioned. The supreme court affirmed the common-law doctrine that private property appropriated by the owner to a public use is thereby subjected to public regulation. They also held that the right of regulation was not restrained by the prohibition of the fourteenth amendment of the federal constitution against the taking by the states of private property without due process of law.

Grangia /gréynj(iy)ə/. A grange.

Grant. To bestow or confer, with or without compensation, a gift or bestowal by one having control or authority over it, as of land or money.

A conveyance; *i.e.* transfer of property real or personal by deed or writing. A generic term applicable to all transfers of real property, including transfers by operation of law as well as voluntary transfers. A technical term made use of in deeds of conveyance of lands to import a transfer. A deed for an incorporeal interest such as a reversion.

As distinguished from a mere license, a grant passes some estate or interest, corporeal or incorporeal, in the lands which it embraces.

To give or permit as a right or privilege; *e.g.* grant of route authority to a public carrier.

By the word "grant," in a treaty, is meant not only a formal grant, but any concession, warrant, order, or permission to survey, possess, or settle, whether written or parol, express, or presumed from possession. Such a grant may be made by law, as well as by a patent pursuant to a law.

Land grant. See Land grant.

Office grant. See Office.

Private land grant. A grant by a public authority vesting title to public land in a private (natural) person.

Public grant. A grant from the public; a grant of a power, license, privilege, or property, from the state or government to one or more individuals, contained in or shown by a record, conveyance, patent, charter, etc.

Grant and to freight let. Operative words in a charter party, implying the placing of the vessel at the disposition of the charterer for the purposes of the intended voyage, and generally, transferring the possession.

Grant, bargain, and sell. Operative words in conveyances of real estate.

Grantee. One to whom a grant is made.

Grant-in-aid. Sum of money given by a governmental agency to a person or institution for a specific purpose such as education or research.

Granting clause. That portion of a deed or instrument of conveyance which contains the words of transfer of a present interest. For example, the clause in an oil and gas lease that spells out what rights are given by the lessor to the lessee. Typically, an oil and gas lease granting clause will specify kinds of uses permitted and substances covered by the lease.

Grant of patent. Written transfer of rights to an invention or of a right to use or sell the thing patented. *See also* License; Patent.

Grant of personal property. A method of transferring personal property, distinguished from a gift by being always founded on some consideration or equivalent. Its proper legal designation is an "assignment," or "bargain and sale."

Grantor. The person by whom a grant is made. A transferor of property. The creator of a trust is usually designated as the grantor of the trust. *See also* Settlor.

Grantor-grantee index. Master index, as kept in county recorder's office, to all recorded instruments. Such index contains the volume and page number where the specific instrument can be located in the record books.

Grantor retained income trust (GRIT). Commonly referred to as a "Grit," it is an estate tax planning tool involving the placement of the settlor's residence in a trust, to be gifted away only if the settlor survives the trust term. Assuming survival, the full value of the residence is removed from the settlor's estate at cost of only the present value of the gift at the time the trust was created. I.R.C. § 2036.

Grantor's lien. Lien which exists for payment of purchase money when title is transferred. Such lien arises when vendor has conveyed title to vendee without receiving full consideration.

Grantor trusts. Trusts whereby the grantor retains control over the income or corpus, or both, to such an extent that such grantor will be treated as the owner of the property and its income for income tax purposes. The result is that the income and deductions attributable to the trust is taxable to the grantor and not to the beneficiary who receives it. I.R.C. §§ 671–677. *See also* Clifford Trust; Reversionary interest.

Gratification. A gratuity; a recompense or reward for services or benefits, given voluntarily, without solicitation or promise. *See* Gift; Gratuity.

Gratis /gréytəs/grǽtəs/. Without reward or consideration. Done or received freely or gratuitously. *See* Gift; Gratuity.

Gratis dictum /gréytəs díktəm/. A voluntary assertion; a statement which a party is not legally bound to make, or in which he is not held to precise accuracy.

Gratuitous. Given or granted without valuable or legal consideration. A term applied to deeds of conveyance and to bailments and other contracts.

As to *gratuitous* Bailment; Contract; Deposit, see those titles. *See also* Gratis.

Gratuitous bailee. Person to whom possession of personal property is transferred and who furnishes no consideration for such transfer and hence is required to use great care to avoid liability for negligence. One responsible for goods entrusted to him or her when goods are damaged or lost through one's gross negligence. *See also* Bailee.

Gratuitous guest. In motor vehicle law, a person riding at invitation of owner or authorized agent without payment of a consideration or fare. *See* Guest; Guest statute.

Gratuitous licensee. Person who has permission though not an invitation to come on to the property of another and who has furnished no consideration for such permission. He is not an invitee, though, because of the permission, he is not a trespasser.

Gratuitous passenger. *See* Gratuitous guest; Guest.

Gratuitous promise. Promise made by one who has not received consideration for it. The absence of consideration makes such unenforceable as legal contracts.

Gratuity. Something acquired or otherwise received without bargain or inducement. Something given freely or without recompense; a gift. Something voluntarily given in return for a favor or especially a service, hence, a bounty; a tip; a bribe. *See also* Gift; Honorarium; Tip.

Gravamen /grəvéymən/. The material part of a grievance, complaint, indictment, charge, cause of action, etc. The burden or gist of a charge; the grievance or injury specially complained of.

Gray market goods. Foreign-manufactured goods, bearing a valid United States trademark, that are imported without the consent of the U.S. trademark holder.

The gray market arises in three general contexts. In the first case, despite a domestic firm's having purchased from an independent foreign firm the rights to register and use the latter's trademark as a U.S. trademark and to sell its foreign manufactured products here, the foreign firm imports the trademarked goods and distributes them here, or sells them abroad to a third party who imports them here.

In the second case, domestic firms register the trademark in the U.S. for goods which are manufactured abroad by an affiliated manufacturer. The foreign affiliate may be a subsidiary of the U.S. firm, the parent company or an unincorporated manufacturing division of the U.S. firm. The gray market arises when the trademark holder or its foreign affiliate sells trademarked articles overseas which are then imported into the U.S. by a third party without authorization of the U.S. trademark holder.

In the third case, the domestic holder of a U.S. trademark authorizes an independent foreign manufacturer to use that trademark in a particular foreign location. The foreign manufacturer or a third party then imports and distributes the foreign made goods.

Gray's inn. An inn of court. *See* Inns of Court.

Great. Considerable in magnitude, power, importance, intensity or degree. As used in various compound legal terms, this word generally means extraordinary, that is, exceeding the common or ordinary measure or standard, in respect to physical size, or importance, dignity, etc.

For *presumption great, see* Proof. As to *great* Care; Pond; Seal; Tithes; see those titles.

Great bodily injury. Bodily injury which involves a substantial risk of death, serious permanent disfigurement, or protracted loss or impairment of function of any part of an organ of the body. Term as used in statute stating when an assault and battery becomes aggravated, is not susceptible of precise definition, but implies an injury of a graver and more serious character than ordinary battery.

Great charter. *Magna Carta (q.v.).*

Great-grandchildren. Children of one's grandchildren.

Great writ of liberty. The writ of "habeas corpus and subjiciendum", issuing at common law out of courts of Chancery, King's Bench, Common Pleas, and Exchequer. *See* Habeas corpus.

Greenback. The popular name applied to United States paper currency.

Green card. Registration card issued to alien as evidence of the alien's status as a permanent resident of the United States.

Greenmail. In corporate takeovers, term that refers to payment by target company to buy back shares owned by potential acquirer at a premium over market. The acquirer in exchange agrees not to pursue its hostile takeover bid. A special tax is imposed on greenmail payments. I.R.C. § 5881.

Green River ordinance. Type of local licensing law which protects persons from unwanted peddlers and salespersons who call on homes and business establishments. Green River v. Bunger, 50 Wyo. 52, 70, 58 P.2d 456, 462.

Grievance. In labor law, a complaint filed by an employee, or by his or her union representative, regarding working conditions and for resolution of which there is procedural machinery provided in the union contract. An injury, injustice or wrong which gives ground for complaint because it is unjust, discriminatory, and oppressive. *See* Complaint.

Grieved. Aggrieved.

GRIT. *See* Grantor retained income trust.

Gross. Great; culpable; general; absolute. A thing *in gross* exists in its own right, and not as an appendage to another thing. Before or without diminution or deduction. Whole; entire; total; as the gross sum, amount, weight—opposed to net. Not adjusted or reduced by deductions or subtractions. *Contrast* with Net.

Out of all measure; beyond allowance; flagrant; shameful; as a gross dereliction of duty, a gross injustice, gross carelessness or negligence. Such conduct as is not to be excused.

As to *gross* Adventure; Average; Fault, see those titles.

Gross alimony. The terms "alimony in gross" and "gross alimony" are applied to an amount agreed upon or determined in full or in lieu of all alimony, and such amount is frequently payable in installments. *See also* Alimony.

Gross earnings. Total income and receipts of a person or business before deductions and expenses. *See* Gross income.

Gross estate. Income subject to federal income tax. The property owned by a decedent that will be subject to the Federal estate tax. It can be distinguished from the probate estate which is property actually subject to administration by the administrator or executor of an estate. I.R.C. §§ 2031–2044. *See also* Adjusted gross estate.

Gross income. Under I.R.C. Section 61(a) gross income means all income from whatever source derived, including (but not limited to) the following items: (1) Compensation for services, including fees, commissions, and similar items; (2) Gross income derived from business; (3) Gains derived from dealings in property; (4) Interest; (5) Rents; (6) Royalties; (7) Dividends; (8) Alimony and separate maintenance payments; (9) Annuities; (10) Income from life insurance and endowment contracts; (11) Pensions; (12) Income from discharge of indebtedness; (13) Distributive share of partnership gross income; (14) Income in respect of a decedent; and (15) Income from an interest in an estate or trust. *See also* Gross profit.

In the case of a manufacturing or merchandising business, gross income means gross profit (*i.e.*, gross sales or gross receipts less cost of goods sold).

Adjusted gross income. A determination peculiar to individual taxpayers. Generally, it represents gross income less business expenses, expenses attributable to the production of rent or royalty income and the long-term capital gain deduction.

Gross income multiplier. Valuation technique used to estimate the valuation of real property. For example, the gross income times a given gross income multiplier to produce the estimated value.

Gross income tax. Levy on total receipts of business without allowance for expenses and deductions. Any tax imposed on gross receipts; may include retail sales tax and general sales tax.

Gross interest. Total interest payment by borrower including administrative, service, and insurance charges.

Gross lease. *See* Lease.

Gross margin. The difference between the amount of sales after returns and allowances and the cost of goods sold.

Gross misdemeanor. Classification of a type of crime which, while not a felony, is ranked as a serious misdemeanor.

Gross National Product (GNP). The market value within a nation for a year of all goods and services produced as measured by final sales of goods and services to individuals, corporations, and governments plus the excess of exports over imports. The total market value of the output of all goods and services of a country without double-counting, divided into four main categories: consumption, gross private domestic investment, government purchases of goods and services, and net exports (exports minus imports).

Gross neglect of duty. Type of serious nonfeasance or failure to attend to one's duties, either public or private. *See* Desertion; Non-support.

Gross negligence. *See* Negligence.

Gross premium. Net (insurance) premium plus loading for expenses and contingencies; *i.e.,* the net premium represents the cost of insurance.

Gross profit. The difference between sales and the cost of goods sold before allowance for operating expenses and income taxes. *See also* Gross income.

Gross profit margin. The ratio of gross profit to net sales.

Gross profit method. In accounting, an inventory estimation method based on a company's gross profit rate; that is, gross profit expressed as a percentage of net sales.

Gross receipts. The total amount of money or the value of other considerations received from selling property or from performing services. *See also* Gross income.

Gross receipts tax. *See* Gross income tax.

Gross revenue. Receipts of a business before deductions for any purpose except those items specifically exempted. *See also* Gross income.

Gross sales. Total of all sales at invoice prices, not reduced by discounts, allowances, returns, commissions, or other adjustments.

Gross spread. In finance, the difference between the price paid by an investment banker for an issue and the price paid by the buying public.

Gross up. To add back to the value of the property or income received the amount of the tax that has been paid. For gifts made within three years of death, any gift tax paid on the transfer is added to the gross estate. I.R.C. § 2035. Process by which U.S. corporations add pre-foreign tax income in federal income tax returns in order to acquire credit against federal taxes for foreign income taxes paid.

Ground. Soil; earth; the earth's surface appropriated to private use and under cultivation or susceptible of cultivation.

A foundation or basis; points relied on; *e.g.* "ground" for bringing civil action, or charging criminal defendant, or foundation for admissibility of evidence. *See also* Ground of action.

Ground lease. A lease of vacant land, or land exclusive of any buildings on it, or unimproved real property. Usually a net lease. *See also* Ground rent; Lease.

Groundless. *See* Frivolous.

Ground of action. The basis of a suit; the foundation or fundamental state of facts on which an action rests (*e.g.* negligence; breach of contract);

the real object of the plaintiff in bringing his suit. *See also* Cause of action.

Ground rent. Rent paid to owner of land for use of property; normally to construct building on such. Generally, rent is paid for a long-term lease (*e.g.* 99 year lease) with lessor retaining title to land. Such long-term lease is commonly renewable. Office buildings, hotels, and similar large structures in cities are commonly built on land under such types of ground leases.

A perpetual rent reserved to himself and his heirs, by the grantor of land in fee-simple, out of the land conveyed. It is in the nature of an emphyteutic rent. Also, in English law, rent paid on a building lease.

Ground water. Water in the subsoil or of a spring or shallow well.

Group annuity. Type of pension plan for employees under a master plan or contract in which employer each year buys a deferred annuity for each qualified employee. The individual members of the group hold certificates as evidence of their coverage.

Group boycott. A concerted refusal by traders to deal with other traders. Occurs when competitors combine to exclude a would-be competitor by threatening to withhold their business from firms that deal with the potential competitor. Such is a per se violation of Sherman Antitrust Act because it restrains freedom of parties to the boycott independently to decide whether to deal with boycotted party. A single trader's refusal to deal with another does not constitute a group boycott.

Grouping of contacts. In conflict of laws, when choice-of-law issue arises, court will apply the law of the jurisdiction most intimately concerned with the outcome of the litigation; also known as "center of gravity" approach or doctrine. *See also* Center of gravity doctrine.

Group life insurance. A contract of group life insurance is one between insurer and employer for benefit of employees. In its nature, group life insurance is similar, if not identical, with that form of insurance known as "term" life insurance. *See* Group policy; Insurance.

Group libel. *See* Libel.

Group policy. A contract of insurance whereby persons, usually employees of a business enterprise, are insured in consideration of a determined payment per period, so long as the person remains in employment and the premiums are paid. The employer holds a master policy from the insurer, and each employee participant holds a certificate as evidence of coverage. *See also* Insurance.

Growing crop. A crop in the process of growth; though decisions differ as to whether such must be above the surface of the soil, and as to whether matured crops are "growing" crops. The cases as well differ as to whether pasturage grass is a growing crop. Growing crops are personal property. *See* U.C.C. §§ 2–105, 2–107.

Growth rate. An estimate of the increase expected in dividends (or in market value) per share of stock.

Growth stock. Type of security characterized by the prospect of increase in market value, but not necessarily with a good dividend return.

Grub stake. In mining law, a contract between two parties by which one undertakes to furnish the necessary provisions, tools, and other supplies, and the other to prospect for and locate mineral lands and stake out mining claims thereon, the interest in the property thus acquired inuring to the benefit of both parties, either equally or in such proportion as their agreement may fix.

G.S.A. General Services Administration.

Guarantee. One to whom a guaranty is made. This word is also used, as a noun, to denote the contract of guaranty or the obligation of a guarantor, and, as a verb, to denote the action of assuming the responsibilities of a guarantor.

Guarantee clause. That provision in a contract, deed, mortgage, etc. by which one person promises to pay the obligation of another. Also, the provision in Art. IV, § 4, U.S.Const., in which the federal government guarantees to every state a republican form of government and the protection of the federal government in the event of domestic violence.

Guaranteed annual wage. Provision in labor agreement in which employer agrees to pay an employee a certain basic sum of money each year, even though the employee has an hourly or weekly salary arrangement.

Guaranteed payment. *See* Payment guaranteed.

Guaranteed sale. A guarantee in a real estate listing agreement which states that after a specified length of time, if the subject property has not been sold, the real estate firm will buy it, under particular terms and conditions, usually at a substantial discount from the listed price.

Guaranteed stock. *See* Stock.

Guarantee stock. Guarantee stock of a building and loan association is a fixed non-withdrawal investment which guarantees to all other investors in the association a fixed rate of dividend or interest.

Guarantor. One who makes a guaranty. Person who becomes secondarily liable for another's debt or performance in contrast to a strict surety who is primarily liable with the principal debtor. One

who promises to answer for a debt, default or miscarriage of another. *See also* Surety.

For purposes of U.C.C. Article 3, a party to an instrument who, by adding words to her signature, makes either a guaranty of collectibility or a guaranty of payment. A guarantor is usually also an accommodation party.

Guaranty, *v.* To undertake collaterally to answer for the payment of another's debt or the performance of another's duty, liability, or obligation; to assume the responsibility of a guarantor; to warrant. *See* Guaranty, *n.*

Guaranty, *n.* A collateral agreement for performance of another's undertaking. An agreement in which the guarantor agrees to satisfy the debt of another (the debtor), only if and when the debtor fails to repay (secondarily liable). An undertaking or promise that is collateral to primary or principal obligation and that binds guarantor to performance in event of nonperformance by the principal obligor.

A promise to answer for payment of debt or performance of obligation if person liable in first instance fails to make payment or perform obligation. An undertaking by one person to be answerable for the payment of some debt, or the due performance of some contract or duty, by another person, who himself remains liable to pay or perform the same. A promise to answer for the debt, default, or miscarriage of another person. *See* Guaranty of payment.

A guaranty is a contract that some particular thing shall be done exactly as it is agreed to be done, whether it is to be done by one person or another, and whether there be a prior or principal contractor or not. A guarantor of a bill or note is said to be one who engages that the note shall be paid, but is not an indorser or surety.

The contract of a guarantor is the guarantor's own separate contract. It is in the nature of a warranty by guarantor that the thing guaranteed to be done by the principal shall be done, not merely an engagement jointly with the principal to do the thing. *See* Suretyship, *contract of.*

Synonyms

The terms *guaranty* and *suretyship* are sometimes used interchangeably; but they should not be confounded. The distinction between contract of suretyship and contract of guaranty is whether or not the undertaking is a joint undertaking with the principal or a separate and distinct contract; if it is the former it is one of "suretyship", and if the latter, it is one of "guaranty".

Guaranty and *warranty* are derived from the same root, and are in fact etymologically the same word, the "g" of the Norman French being interchangeable with the English "w." They are often used colloquially and in commercial transactions as having the same signification, as where a piece of machinery or the produce of an estate is "guarantied" for a term of years, "warranted" being the more appropriate term in such a case. A distinction is also sometimes made in commercial usage, by which the term "guaranty" is understood as a collateral warranty (often a conditional one) against some default or event in the future, while the term "warranty" is taken as meaning an absolute undertaking *in præsenti*, against the defect, or for the quantity or quality contemplated by the parties in the subject-matter of the contract. But in strict legal usage the two terms are widely distinguished in this, that a warranty is an absolute undertaking or liability on the part of the warrantor, and the contract is void unless it is strictly and literally performed, while a guaranty is a promise, entirely collateral to the original contract, and not imposing any primary liability on the guarantor, but binding him to be answerable for the failure or default of another. *See* Warranty.

Absolute guaranty. An unconditional undertaking by a guarantor that debtor will pay debt or perform the obligation. An unconditional promise of payment or performance of principal contract on default of principal debtor or obligor.

Collateral guaranty. A contract by which the guarantor undertakes, in case the principal fails to do what he has promised or undertaken to do, to pay damages for such failure; distinguished from an engagement of suretyship in this respect, that a surety undertakes to do the very thing which the principal has promised to do, in case the latter defaults.

Conditional guaranty. One which depends upon some extraneous event, beyond the mere default of the principal, and generally upon notice of the guaranty, notice of the principal's default, and reasonable diligence in exhausting proper remedies against the principal. One which is not immediately enforceable against the guarantor upon default of the principal but one in which the creditor must take some action in order that liability arise.

Continuing guaranty. A guaranty which is not limited to a particular transaction but which is intended to cover future transactions until revoked. One relating to a future liability of the principal, under successive transactions, which either continue the principal's liability or from time to time renew it after it has been satisfied.

Special guaranty. A guaranty which is available only to the particular person to whom it is offered or addressed; as distinguished from a *general* guaranty, which will operate in favor of any person who may accept it.

Guaranty company. A corporation authorized to transact the business of entering into contracts of guaranty and suretyship; as one which, for fixed premiums, becomes surety on judicial bonds, fidelity bonds, and the like.

Guaranty bond. *See* Bond.

Guaranty clause. *See* Guarantee clause.

Guaranty fund. Statutes have made provision for depositors' guaranty funds to be raised, in whole or in part, by assessments on banks and to be used to pay the depositors of an insolvent bank. Most bank deposits are insured to a specified limit by the Federal Deposit Insurance Corporation (*q.v.*).

Guaranty insurance. *See* Insurance.

Guaranty of payment. A party to an instrument who, by adding "payment guaranteed" or equivalent words to signature, affects contract of liability on the instrument such that, regardless of the capacity in which he signs, he "engages that if the instrument is not paid when due he will pay it according to its tenor without resort by the holder to any other party." U.C.C. § 3–416(1). A person who makes a guaranty of payment is a guarantor, specifically a guarantor of payment.

Guardage. A state of wardship.

Guardian. A person lawfully invested with the power, and charged with the duty, of taking care of the person and managing the property and rights of another person, who, for defect of age, understanding, or self-control, is considered incapable of administering his own affairs. One who legally has responsibility for the care and management of the person, or the estate, or both, of a child during its minority. *See also* Next friend.

Classification

A *testamentary* guardian is one appointed by the deed or last will of the child's father or mother; while a guardian *by election* is one chosen by the infant in a case where he or she would otherwise be without one.

A *general* guardian is one who has the general care and control of the person and estate of a ward; while a *special* guardian is one who has special or limited powers and duties with respect to a ward, *e.g.*, a guardian who has the custody of the estate but not of the person, or vice versa, or a guardian *ad litem*.

A *domestic* guardian is one appointed at the place where the ward is legally domiciled; while a *foreign* guardian derives authority from appointment by the courts of another state, and generally has charge only of such property as may be located within the jurisdiction of the power appointing him.

A *guardian ad litem* is a special guardian appointed by the court in which a particular litigation is pending to represent an infant, ward or unborn person in that particular litigation, and the status of guardian ad litem exists only in that specific litigation in which the appointment occurs.

A *guardian by estoppel* is one who assumes to act as guardian without legal authority; similar to a *guardian de son tort (see below)*.

A *guardian by statute or testamentary guardian* is a guardian appointed for a child by the deed or last will of the father, and who has the custody both of his person and estate until the attainment of full age. This kind of guardianship is founded on the English statute of 12 Car. II, c. 24, and has been extensively adopted in this country.

A *guardian for nurture* is the father, or, at his decease, the mother, of a child. This kind of guardianship at common law extended only to the person, and ended when the infant arrived at the age of fourteen.

With respect to a child born out of wedlock, the child's mother was the guardian by nurture and had the sole right to the custody and control of her child. Today, statutes have superseded the common law in this regard.

A *guardian de son tort*, sometimes described as "quasi guardian" or "guardian by estoppel," is one who assumes to act as guardian without valid authority. Similar to *guardian by estoppel (see above)*.

Natural guardian. At common law, the father of the child, or the mother if the father be dead. In most states, statutes have superseded this rule and mothers and fathers are equal in their rights of guardianship over their children. *E.g.*, N.Y. Dom.Rel.L. § 81.

Guardianship. The office, duty, or authority of a guardian. Also the relation subsisting between guardian and ward. A legal arrangement under which one person (a guardian) has the legal right and duty to care for another (the ward) and his or her property. A guardianship is established because of the ward's inability to legally act on his or her own behalf [e.g., because of minority (he or she is not of age) or mental or physical incapacity]. *See* Guardian; Ward.

Guest. A person receiving lodging for pay at an inn, motel, or hotel on general undertaking of keeper thereof. A traveler who lodges with the consent of the keeper or owner.

A person who is received and entertained at one's home, club, etc., and who is not a regular member. *See also* Social guest.

A "guest" in an automobile is one who takes ride in automobile driven by another person, merely for his own pleasure or on his own business, and without making any return or conferring any benefit on automobile driver. Guest is used to denote one whom owner or possessor of vehicle invites or permits to ride with him as gratuity, without any financial return except such slight benefits as are customarily extended as part of ordinary courtesies of road. *See* Guest statute.

Business guest. See Business.

Guest statute. Many states have statutes referred to as "automobile guest statutes," which provide that operators of automobiles shall only be liable for injuries to guests carried gratuitously for gross or willful negligence, willful or wanton misconduct, or the like, with a further provision in some statutes continuing liability for want of ordinary care in case of hosts operating automobiles while intoxicated. In recent years however there has been a trend towards repealing or delimiting such statutes.

While a typical guest statute excludes all nonpaying guests from suing the host-driver or owner for damages arising out of the host-driver's ordinary negligence, certain statutes are more narrow in their scope; *e.g.* precluding only those guests without payment who are related within the second degree of consanguinity or affinity to the owner or operator from suing.

A "guest," under provisions of guest statute, is a recipient of the voluntary hospitality of the driver or owner, that is, one who is invited or permitted by owner or possessor of automobile to ride with owner-possessor as a gratuity.

Guild. A voluntary association of persons, pursuing the same trade, art, profession or business, such as printers, goldsmiths, artists, wool merchants, etc., united under a distinct organization of their own, analogous to that of a corporation, regulating the affairs of their trade or business by their own laws and rules, and aiming, by cooperation and organization, to protect and promote the interests of their common vocation.

Guilt. In criminal law, that quality which imparts criminality to a motive or act, and renders the person amenable to punishment by the law. Responsibility for offense. That disposition to violate the law which has manifested itself by some act already done. The opposite of innocence.

Guilty. Having committed a crime or other breach of conduct; justly chargeable with a crime; responsible for a crime or tort or other offense or fault. The word used by an accused in pleading or otherwise answering to an indictment when he confesses to the crime of which he is charged, and by the jury in convicting a person on trial for a particular crime. The connotation of such word is "evil," "wrongdoing," or "culpability."

Guilty plea. Formal admission in court as to guilt of having committed criminal act charged which a defendant may make if he or she does so intelligently and voluntarily; *i.e.*, accused can only make such plea after he or she has been fully advised of rights and court has determined that accused understands such rights and is making plea voluntarily. Fed.R.Crim.P. 11. It is equivalent to and is binding as a conviction after trial on the merits, and it has the same effect in law as a verdict of guilt and authorizes imposition of punishment prescribed by law. *See also* Alford plea; Nolo contendere; Plea; Plea bargaining.

Guilty verdict. Formal pronouncement by jury that they adjudge the defendant guilty of the offense charged.

Gun. Portable firearm such as a rifle, pistol, revolver, shotgun, carbine, etc. *See also* Firearm.

Gun control laws. Laws which regulate the sale and use of guns and firearms in a variety of ways such as prohibitions against carrying concealed weapons or requiring a license to buy or possess a handgun or any type of firearm. *e.g.* N.Y. Penal Law §§ 265.11, 265.12; M.G.L.A. (Mass.) Ch. 140; 18 U.S.C.A. §§ 921–928.

H

H. Abbreviation for House, as in House of Representatives, House Report, House Bill.

H.A. An abbreviation for *hoc anno,* this year, in this year.

Habeas corpus /héybiyəs kórpəs/héybiyz°/. Lat. (You have the body.) The name given to a variety of writs (of which these were anciently the emphatic words), having for their object to bring a party before a court or judge. In common usage, and whenever these words are used alone, they are usually understood to mean the *habeas corpus ad subjiciendum* (see *infra*). The primary function of the writ is to release from unlawful imprisonment. The office of the writ is not to determine prisoner's guilt or innocence, and only issue which it presents is whether prisoner is restrained of his liberty by due process.

A form of collateral attack. An independent proceeding instituted to determine whether a defendant is being unlawfully deprived of his or her liberty. It is not an appropriate proceeding for appeal-like review of discretionary decisions of a lower court. For federal habeas corpus procedures, see 28 U.S.C.A. § 2241 et seq.

Initially, the writ only permitted a prisoner to challenge a state conviction on constitutional grounds that related to the jurisdiction of the state court. But the scope of the inquiry was gradually expanded, and the writ now extends to all constitutional challenges.

See also Post-conviction remedies with respect to review of sentence of federal prisoner.

Habeas corpus acts. The English statute of 31 Car. II, c. 2, is the original and prominent *habeas corpus* act. It was amended and supplemented by St. 56 Geo. III, c. 100. Similar statutes have been enacted in all the United States. This act is regarded as the great constitutional guaranty of personal liberty. See Art. I, § 9, U.S.Const.; 28 U.S.C.A. § 2241 et seq.

Habeas corpus ad prosequendum /héybiyəs kórpəs æd pròsəkwéndəm/. A court issues a writ of "habeas corpus ad prosequendum" when it is necessary to bring a person who is confined for some other offense before the issuing court for trial.

Habeas corpus ad respondendum /héybiyəs kórpəs æd rèspondéndəm/. A writ which is usually employed in civil cases to remove a person out of the custody of one court into that of another, in order that he may be sued and answer the action in the latter.

Habeas corpus ad subjiciendum /héybiyəs kórpəs æd səbjìs(h)iyéndəm/. A writ directed to the person detaining another, and commanding him to produce the body of the prisoner, or person detained. This is the most common form of habeas corpus writ, the purpose of which is to test the legality of the detention or imprisonment; not whether he is guilty or innocent. This writ is guaranteed by U.S.Const. Art. I, § 9, and by state constitutions. See 28 U.S.C.A. § 2241 et seq. for federal habeas corpus procedures.

Habeas corpus ad testificandum /héybiyəs kórpəs æd tèstəfəkǽndəm/. The writ, meaning "you have the body to testify", used to bring up a prisoner detained in a jail or prison to give evidence before the court.

Habendum clause /həbéndəm klòz/. Portion of deed beginning with the words "To have and to hold". The clause usually following the granting part of the premises of a deed, which defines the extent of the ownership in the thing granted to be held and enjoyed by the grantee. The office of the "habendum" is properly to determine what estate or interest is granted by the deed, though office may be performed by the premises, in which case the habendum may lessen, enlarge, explain, or qualify, but not totally contradict or be repugnant to, estate granted in the premises.

Habit. A disposition or condition of the body or mind acquired by custom or a usual repetition of the same act or function. The customary conduct, to pursue which one has acquired a tendency, from frequent repetition of the same acts. A regular practice of meeting a particular kind of situation with a certain type of conduct, or a reflex behavior in a specific set of circumstances. Course of behavior of a person regularly repeated in like circumstances. Evidence of a specific habit may be admissible to show specific conduct or acts within the sphere of the developed habit. Fed.Evid. R. 406. *See also* Custom and usage; Habitual.

Habitable. *See* Habitability.

Habitability. Condition of premises which permits inhabitant to live free of serious defects to health and safety.

Warranty of habitability. Under "implied warranty of habitability," applicable to new housing,

491

the builder-vendor warrants that he has complied with the building code of the area in which the structure is located and that the residence was built in a workmanlike manner and is suitable for habitation. In most states, either by statute or case law, every landlord is held to impliedly warrant that the residential premises rented are fit for human habitation (*i.e.* free of violations of building and sanitary codes) at the time of the inception of the tenancy, and will continue as such during the term. See Uniform Residential Landlord and Tenant Law, § 2.104. *See also* Constructive eviction; Home Owners Warranty.

Habitable repair. A covenant by a lessee to "put the premises into habitable repair" binds him to put them into such a state that they may be occupied, not only with safety, but with reasonable comfort, for the purposes for which they are taken. *See* Habitability.

Habitancy. That fixed place of abode to which a person intends to return habitually when absent. Settled dwelling in a given place; fixed and permanent residence there. Place of abode; settled dwelling; residence; house.

It is difficult to give an exact definition of "habitancy." In general terms, one may be designated as an "inhabitant" of that place which constitutes the principal seat of his residence, of his business, pursuits, connections, attachments, and of his political and municipal relations. The term, therefore, embraces the fact of residence at a place, together with the intent to regard it and make it a home. The act and intent must concur.

See also Domicile; Residence.

Habitation. Place of abode; dwelling place; residence.

In the civil law, the right of a person to live in the house of another without prejudice to the property. It differed from a usufruct, in that the usufructuary might apply the house to any purpose, as of a business; whereas the party having the right of habitation could only use it for the residence of himself and family.

See Domicile; Habitancy; Residence.

Habitual. Customary, usual, of the nature of a habit. Synonyms are customary, common, regular; while its antonyms are unusual, unwonted, extraordinary, rare. Formed or acquired by or resulting from habit; frequent use or custom. *See also* Habit.

Habitual criminal. A recidivist *(q.v.).* A legal category created by statute in many states by which more severe penalties can be imposed on offenders who have multiple felony convictions. In general, habitual offender statutes (which differ from state-to-state) impose greater sentences on offender for repeated crimes, with life imprisonment being imposed upon commission of sever-

al felonies. (see *e.g.* 21 U.S.C.A. § 848 re repeated drug offenses). The criminal history of a defendant is an important factor in imposing sentence under federal sentencing guidelines. 18 U.S.C.A. § 3553. See also Model Penal Code § 7.03.

Habitual drunkenness *or* **intoxication.** One who frequently and repeatedly becomes intoxicated by excessive indulgence in intoxicating liquor so as to acquire a fixed habit and an involuntary tendency to become intoxicated as often as the temptation is presented, even though he remains sober for days or even weeks at a time. A person given to inebriety or the excessive use of intoxicating drink, who has lost the power or the will, by frequent indulgence, to control his appetite for it. The custom or habit of getting drunk; the constant indulgence in stimulants, whereby intoxication is produced; not the ordinary use, but the habitual use of them; the habit should be actual and confirmed, but need not be continuous, or even of daily occurrence. That degree of intemperance from the use of intoxicating drinks which disqualifies the person a great portion of the time from properly attending to business, or which would reasonably inflict a course of great mental anguish upon the innocent party.

Habitually. Customarily; by frequent practice or use. It does not mean entirely or exclusively. *See* Habitual.

Hadley v. Baxendale, rule of. Under the rule of *Hadley v. Baxendale,* "special" or "consequential" damages (as opposed to "general" damages which so obviously result from a breach that all contracting parties are deemed to have contemplated them) will only be awarded if they were in the parties' contemplation, at the time of contracting, as a probable consequence of a breach of contract. *See also* Damages *(Consequential damages).*

Hague Tribunal /héyg trəbyúwnəl/. The Court of Arbitration established by the Hague Peace Conference of 1899. The object of the establishment was to facilitate the immediate recourse to arbitration for the settlement of international differences by providing a permanent court, "accessible at all times, and acting, in default of agreement to the contrary between the parties, in accordance with the rules of procedure inserted in the present convention." The court was given jurisdiction over all arbitration cases, provided the parties did not agree to institute a special tribunal. An international Bureau was likewise established to serve as a registry for the court and to be the channel of communications relative to the meetings of the court. The court, although called "permanent," is really so only in the fact that there is a permanent list of members from among whom the arbitrators in a given case are selected. At the Second Hague Conference of 1907, apart from minor changes made in the court, it was provided that, of the two arbitrators appointed by each of the parties, only one should be a national of the appointing state.

Half. One of two equal parts into which anything may be divided. A moiety.

Half blood. *See* Blood relations.

Half brother; half sister. Persons who have the same father, but different mothers; or the same mother, but different fathers.

Halfway house. Loosely structured residential facility designed to rehabilitate persons who have recently left a medical care facility or prison or who, for personal reasons, need help in readjusting. Such houses, for example, assist a recently discharged prisoner in making the often difficult transition from prison to civilian life.

Half year. In legal computation, the period of one hundred and eighty-two days; the odd hours being rejected.

Hallmark. An official stamp affixed by the goldsmiths upon articles made of gold or silver as an evidence of genuineness, and hence used to signify any mark of genuineness.

Hammer. Metaphorically, a forced sale or sale at public auction. "To bring to the hammer", *i.e.* to put up for sale at auction. "Sold under the hammer", *i.e.* sold by an officer of the law or by an auctioneer. *See also* Forced sale.

Hammurabi, Code of. Set of laws once considered the oldest promulgation of laws in human history prepared by Babylonian king, 1792–1750 B.C. (circa).

Hand. A measure of length equal to four inches, used in measuring the height of horses.

A person's signature.

In anatomical usage the hand, or manus, includes the phalanges, or fingers and thumb; the metacarpus, or hand proper; and the carpus, or wrist; but in popular usage the wrist is often excluded.

An instrumental part; *e.g.* "he had a hand in the crime". One who performs some work or labor; *e.g.* a "hired hand". To give assistance; *e.g.* to lend a "hand". To deliver; *e.g.* to "hand over".

In the plural, the term may be synonymous with "possession"; as, the "hands" of an executor, garnishee, etc.

In old English law, an oath.

For the meaning of the term   Clean hands doctrine, see that title.

Handbill. A written or printed notice displayed, handed out, or posted, to inform those concerned of something to be done or some event. Posting and distribution of handbills is regulated by ordinance or statute in most localities.

Hand down. To announce or file an opinion in a cause. Used originally and properly of the opinions of appellate courts transmitted to the court below; but in later usage the term is employed more generally with reference to any decision by a court upon a case or point reserved for consideration.

Handle. To control, direct, to deal with, to act upon, to perform some function with regard to or to have passed through one's hands. To buy and sell, or to deal or trade in. To manage or operate.

Hand money. Money paid in hand to bind a bargain; earnest money, when it is in cash.

Handsel. Handsale, or earnest money.

Handwriting. The chirography of a person. The cast or form of writing peculiar to a person, including the size, shape, and style of letters, tricks of penmanship, and whatever gives individuality to his writing, distinguishing it from that of other persons. Anything written by hand; an instrument written by the hand of a person, or a specimen of his writing.

Handwriting, considered under the law of evidence, includes not only the ordinary writing of one able to write, but also writing done in a disguised hand, or in cipher, and a mark made by one able or unable to write. For nonexpert opinion as to genuineness of handwriting, as based on familiarity not required for purposes of litigation, see Fed.Evid. R. 901(b)(2).

Handwriting exemplars. Samples of one's handwriting required in criminal cases involving forgery, kidnapping, etc., for comparison purposes.

Compelling grand jury witness to produce handwriting and printing exemplars, to be used solely as standard of comparison in order to determine whether witness was author of certain writings, does not violate Fifth Amendment privilege although privilege might be asserted if government should seek more than physical characteristics of handwriting as by seeking to obtain written answers to incriminating questions or a signature on incriminating statement. U.S. Const. Amend. 5.

Hanging. As a form of capital punishment, means suspension by neck until dead. Such means of capital punishment is seldom used in United States.

Hangman. An executioner. One who executes condemned criminals by hanging.

Happiness. Comfort, consolation, contentment, ease, enjoyment, pleasure, satisfaction. The constitutional right of men to pursue their "happiness" means the right to pursue any lawful business or vocation, in any manner not inconsistent with the equal rights of others, which may increase their prosperity, or develop their faculties, so as to give to them their highest enjoyment.

Harassment. As defined in federal statute providing for a civil action to restrain harassment of a victim or witness, is "a course of conduct directed at a specific person that causes substantial emotional distress in such person and serves no legitimate purpose." 18 U.S.C.A. § 1514(c)(1). Term is used in a variety of legal contexts to describe words, gestures and actions which tend to annoy, alarm and abuse (verbally) another person; *e.g.*, the use of "obscene or profane language or language the natural consequence of which is to abuse the hearer or reader" is unlawful harassment under the Federal Fair Debt Collection Practices Act. 15 U.S.C.A. § 1692(d)(2).

Sexual harassment by employers against employees is recognized as a cause of action under Title VII of the Civil Rights Act of 1964, 42 U.S.C.A. § 2000e et seq. *See also* Sexual harassment.

A person commits a petty misdemeanor if, with purpose to harass another, he: (1) makes a telephone call without purpose of legitimate communication; or (2) insults, taunts or challenges another in a manner likely to provoke violent or disorderly response; or (3) makes repeated communications anonymously or at extremely inconvenient hours, or in offensively coarse language; or (4) subjects another to an offensive touching; or (5) engages in any other course of alarming conduct serving no legitimate purpose of the actor. Model Penal Code, § 250.4.

The federal Fair Debt Collection Practices Act prohibits debt collectors from using such harassment tactics as threats, abusive language, or telephone excesses. 15 U.S.C.A. § 1692c et seq.

Harbor, *n.* A haven, or a space of deep water so sheltered by the adjacent land and surroundings as to afford a safe anchorage for ships. A port or haven for ships; a sheltered place, natural or artificial, on the coast of a sea, lake, or other body of water. A place of security and comfort; a refuge.

Harbor, *v.* To afford lodging to, to shelter, or to give a refuge to. To clandestinely shelter, succor, and protect improperly admitted aliens. To receive clandestinely and without lawful authority a person for the purpose of so concealing him that another having a right to the lawful custody of such person shall be deprived of the same. Or, in a less technical sense, it is the reception of persons improperly. It may be aptly used to describe the furnishing of shelter, lodging, or food clandestinely or with concealment, and under certain circumstances, may be equally applicable to those acts divested of any accompanying secrecy. . Harboring a criminal is a crime under both federal and state statutes, and a person who harbors a criminal is an accessory after the fact. See, *e.g.*, 18 U.S.C.A. §§ 2, 1071, 1072; Model Penal Code,

§ 242.3. *See also* Accessory *(Accessory after the fact)*; Aid and abet.

Harboring a criminal. *See* Harbor.

Harbor line. A line marking the boundary of a certain part of a public water which is reserved for a harbor. The line beyond which wharves and other structures cannot be extended.

Hard cases. A phrase used to indicate judicial decisions which, to meet a case of hardship to a party, are not entirely consonant with the true principle of the law. It is said of such: "Hard cases make bad law."

Hard goods. Durable merchandise (*e.g.*, appliances, furniture, hardware).

Hard labor. A punishment, additional to mere imprisonment, sometimes imposed upon convicts sentenced to a penitentiary for serious crimes, or for misconduct while in prison.

Hard money. Lawful coined money (as contrasted with paper currency).

Hardship. In general, privation, suffering, adversity. As used in zoning statutes as grounds for variance, it refers to fact that zoning ordinance or restriction as applied to a particular property is unduly oppressive, arbitrary or confiscatory.

The severity with which a proposed construction of the law would bear upon a particular case, founding, sometimes, an argument against such construction, which is otherwise termed the "argument *ab inconvenienti.*" *See* Hard cases.

Harm. The existence of loss or detriment in fact of any kind to a person resulting from any cause. *See also* Damages; Injury; Physical injury.

Harmful. As used in connection with foods, means noxious, hurtful, pernicious, likely to cause illness or damage. *See also* Adulteration.

As used in connection with errors committed at trial, it means that rights were seriously affected; an appellate court will consider harmful error but not harmless error. *See also* Error; Harmless error doctrine; Plain error rule.

Harmless error doctrine. The doctrine that minor or harmless errors during a trial do not require reversal of the judgment by an appellate court. An error which is trivial or formal or merely academic and was not prejudicial to the substantial rights of the party assigning it, and in no way affected the final outcome of the case. An error is "harmless" if reviewing court, after viewing entire record, determines that no substantial rights of defendant were affected and that error did not influence or had only very slight influence on verdict. Doctrine which permits an appellate court to affirm a conviction in spite of such type error appearing in the record.

Harmless error is not a ground for granting a new trial or for setting aside a verdict or for vacating, modifying or otherwise disturbing a judgment or order, unless such refusal appears to the court inconsistent with substantial justice. Fed.R.Civil P. 61. Any error, defect, irregularity or variance which does not affect substantial rights will be disregarded by court. Fed.R. Crim.P. 7(c), 52.

See also Error.

Harmonic plane. The zero adopted by the United States Coast and Geodetic Survey of the Department of Commerce upon which its tidal tables, charts, and maps are based. It is an arbitrary plane, and, in Puget Sound, is the lowest plane of the tide recognized by that department.

Harmonize. See Harmony.

Harmony. The phrase "in harmony with" is synonymous with "in agreement, conformity, or accordance with."

Harter Act. A name commonly applied to the act of Congress of February 13, 1893, c. 105, providing: (§ 1) that agreements in a bill of lading relieving the owner, etc., of a vessel sailing between the United States and foreign ports, from liability for negligence or fault in proper loading, storage, custody, care, or delivery of merchandise, are void (46 U.S.C.A. § 190); (§ 2) that no bill of lading shall contain any agreement whereby the obligations of the owner to exercise due diligence, properly equip, man, provision and outfit a vessel and make it seaworthy, and whereby the obligations of the master, etc., carefully to handle, store, care for and deliver the cargo, are in any way lessened, weakened or avoided (46 U.S.C.A. § 191); (§ 3) that if the owner shall exercise due diligence to make such vessel in all respects seaworthy and properly manned, equipped and supplied, neither the vessel nor her owners, etc., shall be liable for loss resulting from faults or errors in navigation or management, nor for losses arising from dangers of the sea, acts of God, or public enemies, or the inherent defect of the thing carried, or insufficiency of package, or seizure under legal process, or any act or omission of the shipper of the goods, or from saving or attempting to save life at sea, or deviation in rendering such service (46 U.S.C.A. § 192).

Hart–Scott–Rodino Antitrust Improvement Act. A (1976) procedural statute that gives states attorneys general the right to sue as parens patriae for injuries suffered by consumers in the state, provides for premerger notification, and generally strengthens the antitrust enforcement powers of the Department of Justice.

Hashish. Drug which is formed of resin scraped from the flowering top of the cannabis plant, as distinguished from marijuana which consists of the chopped leaves and stems of the cannabis plant.

Hatch Act. Federal statute which prohibits federal, state, and local employees from partaking in certain types of political activities. 5 U.S.C.A. § 7324.

Hat money. In maritime law, primage; a small duty paid to the captain and mariners of a ship.

Haul. To pull or draw with force; to drag; to transport by hauling.

Have. Imports ownership, and has been defined to mean "to keep," "to hold in possession," "to own." To bear (children).

Have and hold. A common phrase in conveyancing, derived from the habendum et tenendum of the old common law.

Hawker. An itinerant or traveling salesman who carries goods about in order to sell them, and who actually sells them to purchasers, in contradistinction to a trader who has goods for sale and sells them in a fixed place of business. A hawker or peddler usually sells his goods in the public streets, or from door-to-door, and commonly is required to have a license.

Formerly, a peddler who used beast of burden to carry wares and who cried out merits of wares in street. See Hawking; Peddler.

Hawking. The act of offering goods for sale from door-to-door, or on the streets by outcry or by attracting the attention of persons by exposing goods in a public place, or by placards, labels, or signals. The business of peddling or hawking is distinct from that of a manufacturer selling his own products, and those who raise or produce what they sell, such as farmers and butchers, are not peddlers or hawkers.

Hazard. A risk or peril, assumed or involved, whether in connection with contract relation, employment, personal relation, sport or gambling. A danger or risk lurking in a situation which by change or fortuity develops into an active agency of harm. Exposure to the chance of loss or injury. A game of chance or wagering.

In insurance law, the risk, danger, or probability that the event insured against may happen, varying with the circumstances of the particular case.

See also Dangerous; Extraordinary hazard; Risk.

Moral hazard. In fire insurance, the risk or danger of the destruction of the insured property by fire, as measured by the character and interest of the insured owner, his habits as a prudent and careful man or the reverse, his known integrity or his bad reputation, and the amount of loss he would suffer by the destruction of the property or the gain he would make by suffering it to burn and collecting the insurance.

Hazardous. Exposed to or involving danger; perilous; risky; involving risk of loss.

The terms "hazardous", "extra-hazardous", "specially hazardous", and "not hazardous" are well-understood technical terms in the business of insurance, having distinct and separate meanings. *See* Extraordinary hazard.

Hazardous contract. *See* Contract.

Hazardous employment. High risk and extra perilous work. When used in context of workers' compensation, it refers to employment which requires employer to carry workers' compensation coverage or its equivalent regardless of the number of employees.

Hazardous insurance. Insurance effected on property which is in unusual or peculiar danger of destruction by fire, or on the life of a person whose occupation exposes him to special or unusual perils.

Hazardous negligence. *See* Negligence.

Hazardous substance. A solid waste, or combination of solid wastes, which because of its quantity, concentration or physical, chemical, or infectious characteristics may cause, or significantly contribute to an increase in mortality or an increase in serious irreversible, or incapacitating reversible, illness or pose a substantial present or potential hazard to human health or the environment when improperly treated, stored, transported, or disposed of, or otherwise managed. 42 U.S.C.A. § 6903(5).

Includes certain flammable, toxic or radioactive substances. Under the Federal Hazardous Substance Act, a substance may be a "hazardous substance" if it meets the statutory definition or has been so defined by regulation. See 15 U.S. C.A. § 1261(f) et seq.

Hazard pay. Special compensation for work under unpleasant or unsafe conditions.

H.B. House Bill; a bill in the process of going through the House of Representatives on its way to becoming a law.

He. Properly a pronoun of the masculine gender, but usually used and construed in statutes to include both sexes as well as corporations.

Head. Chief; leading; principal; the upper part or principal source of a stream.

The principal person or chief of any agency, bureau, organization, corporation, or firm.

Head money. A sum of money reckoned at a fixed amount for each head (person) in a designated class. Particularly (1) a capitation or poll tax. (2) A bounty offered by the laws of the United States for each person on board an enemy's ship or vessel, at the commencement of a naval engagement, which shall be sunk or destroyed by a ship or vessel of the United States of equal or inferior force, the same to be divided among the officers and crew in the same manner as prize money. A similar reward is offered by the British statutes. (3) The tax or duty imposed by act of congress of Aug. 3, 1882, on owners of steamships and sailing vessels for every immigrant brought into the United States. Head Money Cases, 112 U.S. 580, 5 S.Ct. 247, 28 L.Ed. 798. (4) A bounty or reward formerly paid to one who pursued and killed a bandit or outlaw and produced his head as evidence; the offer of such a reward being popularly called "putting a price on his head". *See* Bounty; Capitation tax; Poll-tax; Reward.

Headnote. A brief summary of a legal rule or significant facts in a case, which, among other headnotes applicable to the case, precedes the printed opinion in reports. A syllabus to a reported case; a summary of the points decided in the case, which is placed at the head or beginning of the opinion. *See also* Digest; Syllabus.

Head of household. An individual who actually supports and maintains in one household one or more individuals who are closely connected with him by blood relationship, relationship by marriage, or by adoption, and whose right to exercise family control and provide for the dependent individuals is based upon some moral or legal obligation.

A taxpayer classification which, generally, describes an unmarried individual (other than a surviving spouse) who provides a home for his or her dependent(s). I.R.C. § 2(b). The Internal Revenue Code provides for preferential treatment for those individuals that qualify as a head of household. The head of household status entitles the taxpayer to use income tax rates which are lower than those applicable to other unmarried individuals, but higher than those applicable to surviving spouses and married persons filing a joint return.

A term used in homestead and exemption laws to designate a person who maintains a family; a householder. Not necessarily a husband or father, but any person who has charge of, supervises, supports, maintains, and manages the affairs of the household or the collective body of persons residing together and constituting the family. The term may thus include an abandoned wife maintaining minor children or a bachelor supporting his parents.

Head of stream. The highest point on the stream which furnishes a continuous stream of water, not necessarily the longest fork or prong. The source of a stream. *See also* Headstream.

Headright. An interest in trust funds arising from mineral income from land held or once held by an Indian tribe as well as the right to any royalties or interest. Under the Allotment Act (Act Cong. June 28, 1906 [34 Stat. 539]), creating a trust fund from all tribal funds which included funds from sale of tribal lands, funds allowed on claims against the United States and received from tribal oil, gas, and mineral rights, each allottee owned his pro rata share of the trust fund, and this pro rata beneficial interest is commonly called a "headright."

Headstream. Stream that is the source of a river. *See also* Head of stream.

Head tax. Tax of flat amount per person. *See* Capitation tax; Poll-tax.

Health. State of being hale, sound, or whole in body, mind or soul, well being. Freedom from pain or sickness. *See* Healthy.

Bill of health. See Bill.

Board of health. See Board.

Health laws. Laws, ordinances, or codes prescribing sanitary, clean air, etc. standards and regulations, designed to promote and preserve the health of the community and working conditions of businesses. *See e.g.* Clean Air Acts; Occupational Safety and Health Act.

Health officer. The officer charged with the execution and enforcement of health laws, *e.g.* Surgeon General. The powers and duties of health officers are regulated by federal, state and local laws.

Public health. As one of the objects of the police power of the state, the "public health" means the prevailingly healthful or sanitary condition of the general body of people or the community in mass, and the absence of any general or widespread disease or cause of mortality. The wholesome sanitary condition of the community at large. Many cities have "Public Health Departments" or agencies of similar function and status. Federal laws dealing with health are administered by the Department of Health and Human Services.

Sound health. See Sound.

Health care proxy. Document in which patients designate a surrogate who has legal authority to make medical decisions if they are too incapacitated to make such. This type proxy is permitted by statute in a number of states. *See also* Medical directives; Patient Self Determination Act; Will (*Living will*).

Health Maintenance Organization (HMO). Groups of participating health care providers (physicians, hospitals, clinics) that provide medical services to enrolled members of group health insurance plan.

Healthy. Free from disease, injury, or bodily ailment, or any state of the system peculiarly susceptible or liable to disease or bodily ailment.

Hearing. A proceeding of relative formality (though generally less formal than a trial), generally public, with definite issues of fact or of law to be tried, in which witnesses are heard and evidence presented. It is a proceeding where evidence is taken to determine issue of fact and to render decision on basis of that evidence. The parties proceeded against or otherwise involved have right to be heard, in much the same manner as a trial and such proceedings may terminate in final order. *See e.g.* 5 U.S.C.A. § 556.

It is frequently used in a broader and more popular significance to describe whatever takes place before magistrates clothed with judicial functions and sitting without jury at any stage of the proceedings subsequent to its inception (*see Preliminary hearing, below*), and to hearings before administrative agencies as conducted by a hearing examiner or Administrative Law Judge. As to the later type, it consists of any confrontation, oral or otherwise, between an affected individual and an agency decision-maker sufficient to allow individual to present his case in a meaningful manner.

The introduction and admissibility of evidence is usually more lax in a hearing than in a civil or criminal trial (*see e.g.,* 42 U.S.C.A. § 405(b) which provides for admissibility of evidence at social security hearings that would otherwise be inadmissible at regular trial).

Hearings are extensively employed by both legislative and administrative agencies and can be adjudicative or merely investigatory. Adjudicative hearings can be appealed in a court of law. Congressional committees often hold hearings prior to enactment of legislation; these hearings are then important sources of legislative history.

See also Administrative hearing; Detention hearing; Fair hearing; Full hearing; Omnibus hearing.

Ex parte hearing. See Ex parte.

Final hearing. See Final.

In criminal law. The examination of a person charged with a crime or misdemeanor, and of the witnesses for or against the accused; *See Preliminary hearing, below.*

Preliminary examination. The examination of a person charged with crime, before a magistrate or judge. *See Preliminary hearing, below.*

Preliminary hearing. In criminal law, is synonymous with "preliminary examination". The hearing given to a person accused of crime, by a magistrate or judge, exercising the functions of a committing magistrate, to ascertain whether there is sufficient evidence to warrant and require the commitment and holding to bail of the persons accused. It is in no sense a trial for the determination of accused's guilt or innocence, but simply a course of procedure whereby a possible abuse of power may be prevented, and accused discharged or held to answer, as the facts warrant. *See* Fed.R.Crim.P. 5(c), 5.1. *See also* Exclusionary hearing; Suppression hearing.

Probable cause hearing. See *preliminary hearing, above.*

Unfair hearing. See that title.

Hearing de novo /híriŋ dìy nówvow/. Generally, a new hearing or a hearing for the second time, contemplating an entire trial in same manner in which matter was originally heard and a review of previous hearing. Trying matter anew the same as if it had not been heard before and as if no decision had been previously rendered. On hearing "de novo" court hears matter as court of original and not appellate jurisdiction.

Hearing examiner. Generally, a civil service employee of an administrative agency whose responsibility is to conduct hearings on matters within the agency's jurisdiction. See *e.g.* 5 U.S.C.A. § 556(b). Now called "Administrative Law Judge" (*q.v.*) in the federal government.

Hearing officer. See Administrative law judge.

Hearsay. A term applied to that species of testimony given by a witness who relates, not what he knows personally, but what others have told him, or what he has heard said by others. A statement, other than one made by the declarant while testifying at the trial or hearing, offered in evidence to prove the truth of the matter asserted. Fed.R.Evid. 801(c). Hearsay includes any statement made outside the present proceeding which is offered as evidence of the truth of matters asserted therein. Also included as hearsay is nonverbal conduct which is intended to be the equivalent of a spoken assertion. Such conduct is called assertive conduct. Under Fed.R.Evid. Rule 801(a) conduct which was not intended as an assertion at the time it was done is not hearsay. Such conduct is called nonassertive conduct. Fed. R.Evid. Rule 801(c) also provides that assertions which are offered to prove something other than the matter asserted are not hearsay.

Hearsay evidence is testimony in court of a statement made out of the court, the statement being offered as an assertion to show the truth of matters asserted therein, and thus resting for its value upon the credibility of the out-of-court asserter. Evidence not proceeding from the personal knowledge of the witness, but from the mere repetition of what he has heard others say. That which does not derive its value solely from the credit of the witness, but rests mainly on the veracity and competency of other persons. The very nature of the evidence shows its weakness, and, as such, hearsay evidence is generally inadmissible unless it falls within one of the many exceptions which provides for admissibility (*see e.g.*, Fed.R.Evid. 803, 804).

See *also* Double (*or* multiple) hearsay.

Heart balm statutes. State statutes abolishing right of action for alienation of affections, breach of promise to marry, criminal conversation, and seduction of person over legal age of consent.

Heat of passion. A term used by the common law to refer to the condition of a defendant who can assert provocation as a basis for mitigating murder to manslaughter. Refers to passion or anger suddenly aroused at the time by some immediate and reasonable provocation, by words or acts of one at the time. As sufficient to reduce killing from murder to voluntary manslaughter means any intense or vehement emotional excitement of the kind prompting violent and aggressive action, which would cause an ordinary person to act on impulse without reflection. The term includes an emotional state of mind characterized by anger, rage, hatred, furious resentment or terror. See *also* Hot blood.

Hedge fund. Mutual funds that utilize various types of hedging techniques for their investments. See Hedging.

Hedger. A commodities trader with an interest in the cash market for the commodity, who deals in futures contracts as a means of transferring risks which he or she faces in the cash market. See Hedging.

Hedging. A means by which traders and exporters of grain or other products, and manufacturers who make contracts in advance for the sale of their goods, secure themselves against the fluctuations of the market by counter-contracts for the purchase or sale of an equal quantity of the product or of the material of manufacture. A means by which a party who deals in the purchase of commodities in large quantities for actual delivery at some future time insures itself against unfavorable changes in the price of such commodities by entering into compensatory arrangements or counterbalancing transactions on the other side. A transaction where an identified forward exchange contract is locked into an identified agreement to purchase or sell goods in the future.

Safeguarding one's self from loss on a bet or speculation by making compensatory arrangements on the other side.

For various types of *hedging* techniques, *see* Arbitrage; Call option; Futures contract; Option; Put option; Short sale.

Cross-hedging. The use of a futures contract on one financial instrument to hedge a position in a different financial instrument.

Hedonic damages. See Damages.

Heedless. Term is almost as strong as word "reckless" and includes the element of disregard of the rights or safety of others. Thoughtless; inconsiderate.

Heir /ér/. See Heirs.

Heir apparent. An heir whose right of inheritance is indefeasible, provided he outlive the ancestor; as in England the eldest son, or his issue, who must, by the course of the common law, be heir to the father whenever he happens to die. One who, before the death of the ancestor, is next in the line of succession, provided he be heir to the ancestor whenever he happens to die. *See also* Apparent heir.

Heir at law. At common law, he who, after his ancestor dies intestate, has a right to all lands, tenements, and hereditaments which belonged to him or of which he was seised. The same as "heir general."

A deceased person's "heirs at law" are those who succeed to his estate of inheritance under statutes of descent and distribution, in absence of testamentary disposition, and not necessarily his heirs at common law, who are persons succeeding to deceased's realty in case of his intestacy.

As the term is used in wrongful death statute, means lineal descendants.

See also Descent; Heir, legal.

Heir beneficiary. In the civil law, one who has accepted the succession under the benefit of an inventory regularly made.

Heirs are divided into two classes, according to the manner in which they accept the successions left to them, to-wit, unconditional and beneficiary heirs. Unconditional heirs are those who inherit without any reservation, or without making an inventory, whether their acceptance be express or tacit. Beneficiary heirs are those who have accepted the succession under the benefit of an inventory regularly made. Civ.Code La. art. 883. If the heir apprehend that the succession will be burdened with debts beyond its value, he accepts with benefit of inventory, and in that case he is responsible only for the value of the succession. *See* Beneficiary.

Heir by adoption. By statute in most all jurisdictions, an adopted child takes all the rights of succession to intestate property as those of a natural born child unless a contrary intention is clearly expressed. Statutes differ however as to whether such adopted child may in addition inherit from its natural parents or family.

Heir collateral. One who is not lineally related to the decedent, but is of collateral kin; *e.g.*, his uncle, cousin, brother, nephew.

Heir conventional. In the civil law, one who takes a succession by virtue of a contract or settlement entitling him thereto.

Heirdom /érdəm/. Succession by inheritance.

Heiress /érəs/. A female heir to a person having an estate of inheritance. When there are more than one, they are called "co-heiresses," or "co-heirs."

Heir expectant. *See* Heir apparent.

Heir, forced. One who cannot be disinherited. *See* Forced heirs.

Heir, legal. The person to whom the law would give the decedent's property, real and personal, if he should die intestate. In legal strictness, the term signifies one who would inherit real estate, but it is also used to indicate one who would take under the statute of distribution. *See also* Descent; Heir at law; Heirs.

Heirless estate. The property of one who dies intestate leaving no heirs in which case there generally is escheat *(q.v.)*.

Heirlooms /érlùwmz/. In general, valued possessions of great sentimental value passed down through generations within a family.

Heir of the blood. An inheritor who succeeds to the estate by virtue of consanguinity with the decedent, either in the ascending or descending line, including illegitimate children, but excluding husbands, wives, and adopted children. *See* Blood relations.

Heir of the body. An heir begotten or borne by the person referred to, or a child of such heir; any lineal descendant of the decedent, excluding a surviving husband or wife, adopted children, and collateral relations; bodily heir. May be used in either of two senses: In their unrestricted sense, as meaning the persons who from generation to generation become entitled by descent under the entail; and in the sense of heirs at law, or those persons who are descendants of him whom the statute of descent appoints to take intestate estate.

Heir presumptive. The person who, if the ancestor should die immediately, would, in the present circumstances of things, be his heir, but whose right of inheritance may be defeated by the contingency of some nearer heir being born; as a brother or nephew, whose presumptive succession may be destroyed by the birth of a child.

Heir, pretermitted. One who, except for an unambiguous act of the ancestor, would take his property on his death. *See also* Pretermitted heir.

Heirs /érz/. At common law, the person appointed by law to succeed to the estate in case of intestacy. One who inherits property, whether real or personal. A person who succeeds, by the rules of law, to an estate in lands, tenements, or hereditaments, upon the death of his ancestor, by descent and right of relationship. One who would receive his estate under statute of descent and distribution. Moreover, the term is frequently used in a popular sense to designate a successor to property either by will or by law. Word "heirs" is no longer limited to designated character of estate as at common law.

See also Descent.

Bodily laws. *See* Heir of the body.

Civil law. A universal successor in the event of death. He who actively or passively succeeds to the entire property or estate, rights and obligations, of a decedent, and occupies his place.

The term is indiscriminately applied to all persons who are called to the succession, whether by the act of the party or by operation of law. The person who is created universal successor by a will is called the "testamentary heir;" and the next of kin by blood is, in cases of intestacy, called the "heir at law," or "heir by intestacy." The executor of the common law in many respects corresponds to the testamentary heir of the civil law. Again, the administrator in many respects corresponds with the heir by intestacy. By the common law, executors and administrators have no right except to the personal estate of the deceased; whereas the heir by the civil law is authorized to administer both the personal and real estate. The term "heir" has several significations. Sometimes it refers to one who has formally accepted a succession and taken possession thereof; sometimes to one who is called to succeed, but still retains the faculty of accepting or renouncing, and it is frequently used as applied to one who has formally renounced.

Collateral heir. See that title.

Joint heirs. Co-heirs. The term is also applied to those who are or will be heirs to both of two designated persons at the death of the survivor of them, the word "joint" being here applied to the ancestors rather than the heirs.

Known heirs. See that title.

Lawful heirs. *See* Descent; Heir at law; Heir, legal.

Legitimate heirs. Children born in lawful wedlock and their descendants, not including collateral heirs or issue in indefinite succession.

Lineal heir. *See* Lineal heir.

Natural heirs. Heirs by consanguinity as distingushed from heirs by adoption, and also as distinguished from collateral heirs.

Right heir. This term was formerly used, in the case of estates tail, to distinguish the preferred heir, to whom the estate was limited, from the heirs in general, to whom, on the failure of the preferred heir and his line, the remainder over was usually finally limited. With the abolition of estates tail, the term has fallen into disuse, but when still used, in modern law, it has no other meaning than "heir at law."

Heirs and assigns. Ordinarily words of limitation and not of purchase. At common law, the words were essential to conveyance granting title in fee simple, and though they are unnecessary

for that or any purpose under statute when used in wills or deeds, words still have that meaning.

Heirship /érshəp/. The quality or condition of being heir, or the relation between the heir and his ancestor. It is a legal right, regulated by law, to be enjoyed subject to the provisions of the statute.

Heirs per stirpes. *See* Per stirpes.

Heir testamentary. In the civil law, one who is named and appointed heir in the testament of the decedent. This name distinguishes him from a *legal* heir (one upon whom the law casts the succession), and from a *conventional* heir (one who takes it by virtue of a previous contract or settlement).

Held. In reference to the decision of a court, means decided. In context of kidnapping offense, connotes a state or degree of physical restraint. *See also* Hold; Judgment.

Henceforth /hénsfòrθ/. A word of futurity, which, as employed in legal documents, statutes, and the like, always imports a continuity of action or condition from the present time forward, but excludes all the past.

Hepburn Act. The name commonly given to an act of Congress (1906), amending §§ 1, 6, 14, 15, 16 and 20 of the Interstate Commerce Act. Such Act increased the jurisdiction of the I.C.C. to include pipelines; prohibited free passes except to employees; prohibited common carriers from transporting any products, except timber, in which they had an interest; required joint tariffs and uniform system of accounts.

Herd, *n.* An indefinite number, more than a few, of cattle, sheep, horses, or other animals of the larger sorts, assembled and kept together as one drove and under one care and management.

Herd, *v.* To tend, take care of, manage, and control a herd of cattle or other animals, implying something more than merely driving them from place to place.

Hereafter. A word of futurity, used in statutes and legal documents as indicative of future time, excluding both the present and the past.

Hereditaments /hərédətəmənts/hèhrədítəmənts/. Things capable of being inherited, be it corporeal or incorporeal, real, personal, or mixed, and including not only lands and everything thereon but also heirlooms, and certain furniture which, by custom, may descend to the heir together with the land. Things which may be directly inherited, as contrasted with things which go to the personal representative of a deceased.

Corporeal hereditaments. Substantial permanent objects which may be inherited. The term "land" will include all such.

Incorporeal hereditaments. Anything, the subject of property, which is inheritable and not tangible or visible. A right issuing out of a thing corporate (whether real or personal) or concerning or annexed to or exercisable within the same. A right growing out of, or concerning, or annexed to, a corporeal thing, but not the substance of the thing itself.

Hereditary /hərédət(èh)riy/. That which is the subject of inheritance. Genetically transmitted or transmittable from parent to offspring.

Hereditary succession. Inheritance by law; title by descent. The title whereby a person, on the death of his ancestor, acquires his estate by right of representation as his heir at law. *See* Descent.

Heredity /hərédətiy/. Inheritance. That biological law by which all living beings tend to repeat themselves in their descendants. The transmission through genes of characteristics from parents to children.

Heretofore. This word simply denotes time past, in distinction from time present or time future, and has no definite and precise signification beyond this.

Hereunder. A word of reference in a document or law, directing attention to matter therein which follows in such document or is contained therein.

Heritable bond /héhrətəbəl bónd/. A bond for a sum of money to which is added, for further security of the creditor, a conveyance of land or heritage to be held by the creditor as pledge.

Heritable security /héhrətəbəl səkyúrədiy/. Security constituted by heritable property.

Heritage /héhrətəj/. In the civil law, every species of immovable which can be the subject of property; such as lands, houses, orchards, woods, marshes, ponds, etc., in whatever mode they may have been acquired, either by descent or purchase.

Hermeneutics /hərmən(y)úwtəks/. The science or art of construction and interpretation. By the phrase "legal hermeneutics" is understood the systematic body of rules which are recognized as applicable to the construction and interpretation of legal writings.

Heroin. Narcotic drug which is a derivative of opium and whose technical name is diacetyl-morphine. It is classified as a Class A substance for criminal purposes and the penalty for its unlawful manufacture, distribution, sale, or possession is severe. 21 U.S.C.A. § 841.

He who comes into a court of equity must come with clean hands. *See* Clean hands doctrine.

He who seeks equity must do equity. This expression means that the party asking the aid of a court for equitable relief must stand in a conscientious relation toward his adversary and the transaction from which his claim arises must be fair and just and the relief must not be harsh and oppressive upon defendant. This maxim provides that court will not confer equitable relief on party seeking its aid, unless he has acknowledged and conceded or will admit and provide for all equitable rights, claims, and demands justly belonging to adverse party and growing out of or necessarily involved in subject matter of controversy. *See also* Clean hands doctrine.

HHS. Federal Department of Health and Human Services.

Hidden asset. Asset carried on books at a substantially reduced or understated value; its market value being greater than its book value.

Hidden defect. Type of deficiency in property which is not discoverable by reasonable inspection and for which a lessor or seller is generally liable if such defect causes harm to a user, and for which a purchaser is provided a right to revoke a prior acceptance. U.C.C. § 2–608(1)(b). *See also* Defect; Latent defect.

Hidden tax. Tax built into ultimate selling price that was incurred at a prior manufacturing or distribution stage.

Hierarchy /háy(ə)ràrkiy/híyər°. Originally, government by a body of priests. Now, the body of officers in any church or ecclesiastical institution, considered as forming an ascending series of ranks or degrees of power and authority, with the correlative subjection, each to the one next above. Derivatively, any body of persons organized or classified according to authority, position, rank, or capacity.

High. This term, as used in various compound legal phrases, is sometimes merely an addition of dignity, not importing a comparison; but more generally it means exalted, either in rank or location, or occupying a position of superiority, and in a few instances it implies superiority in respect to importance, size, or frequency or publicity of use, *e.g.,* "high seas," "highway."

As to *high* Bailiff; Constable; Crime; Justice; License; Prerogative writs; Probability; Sea; Sheriff; Tide; Treason; Water-mark, see those titles.

High degree of negligence. *See* Negligence *(Gross negligence).*

Highest and best use. In real estate valuation (*e.g.* in condemnation proceedings) the use of land or buildings which will bring the greatest economic return over a given time. This method of valuation requires expert to determine what condemned property's fair market value would realistically be if owner were hypothetically allowed to adapt his property to its most advantageous and valuable use.

Highest court. Court of last resort; a court whose decision is final and cannot be appealed because there is no higher court to further consider such matter; *e.g.* U.S. Supreme Court is highest federal court.

Highest degree of care. That degree of care that a very careful and prudent person would use under same or similar circumstances. A standard of care exacted in some jurisdictions of common carriers of passengers. The standard is relative, not absolute, and is sometimes regarded as no more than reasonable care measured by the circumstances.

High seas. That portion of ocean which is beyond the territorial jurisdiction of any country. The "high seas" lie seaward of a nation's territorial sea, which is the bank of water that extends up to three miles out from the coast. See 18 U.S.C.A. § 3241 for jurisdiction of federal courts over crimes committed on high seas. *See also* Sea; Territorial waters.

High water line *or* **mark.** The line on the shore to which high tide rises under normal weather conditions. High-water mark is generally computed as a mean or average high tide and not as extreme height of water. High water mark of navigable river is line to which high water ordinarily reaches and is not line reached by water in unusual floods; it is that line below which soil is unfit for vegetation or agricultural purposes.

Highway. A free and public roadway, or street; one which every person has the right to use. In popular usage, refers to main public road connecting towns or cities. The entire width between boundaries of every publicly maintained way when any part is open to use of the public for purposes of vehicular traffic. In broader sense, refers to any main route on land, water, or in the air.

The term, as generally understood, does not have a restrictive or a static meaning, but it denotes ways laid out or constructed to accommodate modes of travel and other related purposes that change as customs change and as technology develops, and the term "highway," as it is generally understood, includes areas other than and beyond the boundaries of the paved surface of a roadway.

Commissioners of Highways. Public officers appointed in states, counties and municipalities to take charge of constructing, altering, repairing, maintaining, and vacating of highways within their respective jurisdictions.

Common highway. A road to be used by the community at large for any purpose of transit or traffic. *See Public highway, below.*

Highway acts, or laws. The body or system of laws governing the laying out, construction, repair, and use of highways.

Highway crossing. A place where the track of a railroad crosses the line of a highway.

Highway robbery. See Hijacking; Robbery.

Highway tax or toll. A tax or fee for and applicable to the construction and repair of highways. See Toll.

Public highway. One under the control of and maintained by public authorities for use of the general public; including every public street, road or highway. Calif.Code Pub.Utilities, § 3509.

Hijacking. Robbery of goods while in transit, commonly from trucks. May involve robbery of only goods, or of both vehicle and goods. May also refer to commandeering an airplane. See 18 U.S.C.A. §§ 1951, 2117. *See also* Piracy.

Hire, *v.* To purchase the temporary use of a thing, or to arrange for the labor or services of another for a stipulated compensation. *See also* Employ; Rent. *Compare* Lease.

Hire, *n.* Compensation for the use of a thing, or for labor or services. Act of hiring. A bailment in which compensation is to be given for the use of a thing, or for labor and services about it.

Hirer. One who hires a thing, or the labor or services of another person. *See also* Employer.

Hiring. *See* Hire.

Hiring at will. A general or indefinite hiring with right to terminate such at will of employer. *See* Employment at will.

Hiring hall. Agency or office operated by union, by employer and union, or by state or local employment service, to provide and place employees for specific jobs.

His. This pronoun, generically used, may refer to a person of either sex. Its use in a written instrument, in referring to a person whose Christian name is designated therein by a mere initial, is not conclusive that the person referred to is a male; it may be shown by parol that the person intended is a female.

Historical cost. In accounting, acquisition or original cost; *e.g.* original construction cost of building.

Historic bay. Those bays over which a coastal nation has traditionally asserted and maintained dominion with the acquiescence of foreign nations.

Historic preservation. An ordinance which prohibits the demolition or exterior alteration of certain historic buildings or of all buildings in an historic district. *See* Historic site.

Historic site. Any building, structure, area or property that is significant in the history, architecture, archeology or culture of a State, its communities or the Nation and has been so designated pursuant to statute. Such structures are commonly statutorily protected and cannot be altered without permission of the appropriate authorities. See, *e.g.,* 16 U.S.C.A. § 461 et seq.

Hit and run accident. Collision generally between motor vehicle and pedestrian or with another vehicle in which the operator of vehicle leaves scene without identifying himself and without giving certain other information to other motorist and police as usually required by statute. Such an act is a crime.

Most states by statute require that motorists involved in accidents to stop at the scene and provide certain information to police and other drivers and passengers involved.

Hitherto. In legal use, this term always restricts the matter in connection with which it is employed to a period of time already passed.

HLA test. A system of tissue typing for determining the probability of paternity and which involves the drawing of blood. *See also* DNA identification.

HMO. *See* Health Maintenance Organization.

Hoarding. Act of holding and acquiring goods in short supply beyond the reasonable needs of the person so holding. *See also* Profiteering.

Hobbs Act. Federal anti-racketeering act making it a crime to interfere with interstate commerce by extortion, robbery, or physical violence. 18 U.S.C.A. § 1951. Racketeering offenses are defined in 18 U.S.C.A. § 1961. *See* Racketeering; RICO laws.

Hobby. An activity not engaged in for profit. The IRC restricts the amount of losses that an individual can deduct with respect to hobby activities so that such transactions cannot be used to offset income from other sources. I.R.C. § 183. *See* Hobby loss.

Hobby loss. A nondeductible loss arising from a personal hobby as contrasted with an activity engaged in for profit. Generally, the law provides a presumption that an activity is engaged in for profit if gross profits are earned during any 2 or more years during a 5 year period. I.R.C. § 183.

Hold, *v.* 1. To possess in virtue of a lawful title; as in the expression, common in grants, "to have and to hold," or in that applied to notes, "the owner and holder."

2. To be the grantee or tenant of another; to take or have an estate from another. Properly, to have an estate on condition of paying rent, or performing service.

3. To adjudge or decide, spoken of a court, particularly to declare the conclusion of law reached by the court as to the legal effect of the facts disclosed. *See* Holding.

4. To maintain or sustain; to be under the necessity or duty of sustaining or proving; as when it is said that a party "holds the affirmative" or negative of an issue in a cause.

5. To bind or obligate; to restrain or constrain; to keep in custody or under an obligation; as in the phrases "hold to bail," "hold for court," "held and firmly bound," etc.

6. To administer; to conduct or preside at; to convoke, open, and direct the operations of; as to hold a court, hold pleas, etc.

7. To prosecute; to direct and bring about officially; to conduct according to law; as to hold an election.

8. To possess; to occupy; to be in possession and administration of; as to hold office.

9. To keep; to retain; to maintain possession of or authority over.

See also Ownership; Possession.

Hold over. To retain possession as tenant of property leased, after the end of the term. To continue in possession of an office and continue to exercise its functions, after the end of the officer's lawful term.

Hold pleas. To hear or try causes.

Hold, *n.* In old English law, tenure. A word constantly occurring in conjunction with others, as *freehold, leasehold, copyhold,* etc., but rarely met with in the separate form.

Holder. The holder of a bill of exchange, promissory note, check, or other commercial paper, is the person who has legally acquired possession of the same, by indorsement or delivery, and who is entitled to receive payment of the instrument. Person who is in possession of a document of title or an instrument or an investment security drawn, issued or endorsed to him or to his order, or to bearer or in blank. U.C.C. § 1–201(20).

Holder for value. A holder who has given a valuable consideration for the document of title, instrument or investment security which he has in his possession. A holder takes an instrument for value: (a) to the extent that the agreed consideration has been performed or that he acquires a security interest in, or a lien on, the instrument otherwise than by legal process; or (b) when he takes the instrument in payment of, or as security for, an antecedent claim against any person whether or not the claim is due; or (c) when he gives a negotiable instrument for it or makes an irrevocable commitment to a third person. U.C.C. § 3–303.

Holder in due course. In commercial law, a holder of an instrument who took it for value, in good faith and without notice of any claim or defense against it, U.C.C. § 3–302(1), and who can enforce the instrument free from all claims and personal defenses. U.C.C. § 3–305. A payee may be a holder in due course. A holder does not become a holder in due course of an instrument by purchase of it at a judicial sale or by taking it under legal process, or by acquiring it in taking over an estate, or by purchasing it as part of a bulk transaction not in regular course of business of the transferor. A purchaser of a limited interest can be a holder in due course only to the extent of the interest purchased.

A holder in due course of a consumer credit contract (*i.e.* consumer paper) is subject to all claims and defenses which the debtor (buyer) could assert against the seller of the goods or services obtained pursuant to the credit contract or with the proceeds thereof. 16 CFR § 433.1 et seq.

Compare Bona fide *(Bona fide purchaser)*. *See also* Real defenses.

Holder in good faith. One who takes property or an instrument without knowledge of any defect in its title.

Hold harmless agreement. A contractual arrangement whereby one party assumes the liability inherent in a situation, thereby relieving the other party of responsibility. Such agreements are typically found in leases, and easements. Agreement or contract in which one party agrees to hold the other without responsibility for damage or other liability arising out of the transaction involved. *See also* Guaranty; Indemnity; Surety.

Holding. The legal principle to be drawn from the opinion (decision) of the court. Opposite of dictum *(q.v.)*. It may refer to a trial ruling of the court upon evidence or other questions presented during the trial. Also, general term for property, securities, etc. owned by person or corporation. *See also* Decision; Dicta.

Holding company. A company that usually confines its activities to owning stock in, and supervising management of, other companies. A holding company usually owns a controlling interest in the companies whose stock it holds. In order for a corporation to gain the benefits of tax consolidation, including tax free dividends and the ability to share operating losses, the holding company must own 80% or more of the voting stock of the corporation. I.R.C. § 243. *See also* Investment company.

Personal holding company. A closely held corporation which receives personal holding company income. Personal holding income includes but is not limited to: dividends, interest, rents, royalties, etc. If a company comes within the definition of a personal holding company, it may be subject to the regular corporate tax, as well as a personal holding company tax on the undistributed personal holding company income. The tax is imposed to prevent individuals from accumulating income in the corporation and not subjecting the individuals to the personal income tax on the earnings. *See also* Holding company tax; Personal holding company.

Holding company tax. Tax on undistributed personal holding company income after allowable deductions for dividends paid, etc. I.R.C. § 545.

Holding gains and losses. The difference between an asset's acquisition cost and current cost.

Holding period. In taxation, that period of time in which a capital asset must be held to determine whether gain or loss from its sale or exchange is long term or short term. I.R.C. §§ 1222–1223.

Holdings. Extent of ownership of investments (real estate, securities, etc.).

Holdover tenant. A tenant who remains in possession after the expiration of a lease, or after a tenancy at will has been terminated.

Holiday. A religious festival; a day set apart for commemorating some important event in history; a day of exemption from labor. A day upon which the usual operations of business and government are suspended and the courts closed, and, generally, no legal process is permitted to be served. In addition to national holidays (*e.g.* Fourth of July), there are also state holidays (*e.g.* "Bunker Hill" holiday in Massachusetts).

Legal holiday. *See* Legal holiday.

Public holiday. A legal holiday *(q.v.)*.

Statutory holidays. Most states observe the same holidays as those observed by the federal government (*see* 5 U.S.C.A. § 6103). There are variations however, *e.g.*, several states do not celebrate Columbus Day, several states do not observe the National Memorial Day, while many other states have special holidays commemorating historical events, the birthdays of state or regional heros, religious festival days, or other occasions deemed worthy of celebration. *See also* Legal holiday.

Holograph /hó(w)ləgrǽf/. A will or deed written entirely by the testator or grantor with his own hand and not witnessed (attested). State laws vary widely with respect to the status of self-written "holographic" wills. Some states categorically refuse to recognize any will not meeting the formal statutory requirements relating to attestation clause, witnesses, etc. Others will recognize a holographic will if all or certain portions are in the handwriting of the testator. And many states that do not recognize holographic wills executed by their own citizens within their borders will nevertheless recognize such wills if valid under other jurisdictions. Under the Uniform Probate Code (as adopted by several states), such will is valid, whether or not witnessed, if the signature and the material provisions are in the handwriting of the testator. § 2–503.

Holographic will. *See* Holograph.

Homage /(h)ómǝj/. In feudal law, a service (or the ceremony of rendering it) which a tenant was bound to perform to his lord on receiving investiture of a fee, or succeeding to it as heir, in acknowledgment of the tenure. It is described as the most honorable service of reverence that a free tenant might do to his lord.

Home. One's own dwelling place; the house in which one lives, especially the house in which one lives with his family; the habitual abode of one's family; a dwelling house. That place in which one in fact resides with the intention of residence, or in which he has so resided, and with regard to which he retains residence or to which he intends to return. Place where a person dwells and which is the center of his domestic, social and civil life. Restatement of Conflicts, Second, § 12. As relating to deductions of expenses for carrying on a trade or business while living away from home, "home" within I.R.C. § 162(a)(2) is defined as taxpayer's principal place of business. *See also* Domicile; Residence; Tax home.

Home loan bank. *See* Federal Home Loan Banks.

Home office. As applied to a corporation, its principal office or corporate headquarters.

Homeowner's association. An association of people who own homes in a given area, formed for the purpose of improving or maintaining the quality of the area.

An association formed by a land developer or the builder of condominiums or planned unit developments to provide management for and maintenance of property in which they own undivided, common interest. The builder's participation as well as the duties of the association are controlled by statute in certain states. Such non-profit associations are commonly formed pursuant to a restrictive covenant or a declaration of restrictions.

Homeowner's equity loan. *See* Equity loan.

Homeowners policy. In insurance, multi-peril type policy available to homeowners, combining coverage for fire, water, burglary, liability, etc.

Home Owners Warranty (HOW). A warranty and insurance protection program offered by many home builders in the United States. The program was developed by the Home Owners Warranty Corporation, a subsidiary of the National Association of Home Builders. The major provisions of the program are that a new home is protected for ten years against major structural defects. Similar warranty protection is provided by statute in many states.

Home port. In maritime law, the home port of a vessel is either the port where she is registered or enrolled, or the port at or nearest to which her owner usually resides, or, if there be more than one owner, the port at or nearest to which the husband, or acting and managing owner resides. But for some purposes any port where the owner happens at the time to be with his vessel is its home port. Under the shipping laws, every vessel has what is called her "home port," to which she belongs, and which constitutes her legal abiding place or residence, regardless of her actual absence therefrom. *See also* Port.

Home port doctrine. Under this doctrine vessels engaged in interstate and foreign commerce are taxable at their home port only, and no other jurisdiction, including those ports visited by the vessel during its voyages, has power to tax it.

Home rule. State constitutional provision or type of legislative action which results in apportioning power between state and local governments by providing local cities and towns with a measure of self government if such local government accepts terms of the state legislation. *See also* Local option.

Home rule charter. The organizational plan or framework of a municipal corporation, analogous to a constitution of a state or nation, drawn by the municipality itself and adopted by popular vote of its people.

Homestead. The dwelling house and the adjoining land where the head of the family dwells; the home farm. The fixed residence of the family, with the land, usual and customary appurtenances, and buildings surrounding the main house.

Technically, and under the modern homestead laws, an artificial estate in land, devised to protect the possession and enjoyment of the owner against the claims of his creditors, by withdrawing the property from execution and forced sale, so long as the land is occupied as a home. *See* *Homestead exemption laws, below.*

Homestead corporations. Corporations organized for the purpose of acquiring lands in large tracts, paying off incumbrances thereon, improving and subdividing them into homestead lots or parcels, and distributing them among the shareholders, and for the accumulation of a fund for such purposes.

Homestead entry. See Entry.

Homestead exemption laws. Laws passed in most states allowing a householder or head of a family to designate a house and land as his homestead, and exempting the same homestead from execution by creditors for his general debts (in, for example, bankruptcy proceedings). Property tax reductions or exemptions (for all or part of the tax) are also available in some states for homesteaded property. Statutory requirements to establish a homestead may include a formal declaration to be recorded annually.

Homestead right. The personal right to the beneficial, peaceful and uninterrupted use of the home property free from claims of creditors.

Probate homestead. A homestead set apart by the probate court for the use of a surviving husband or wife and the minor children out of the common property, or out of the real estate belonging to the deceased.

Homicidal. Pertaining, relating, or impelling to homicide, as a homicidal mania.

Homicide. The killing of one human being by the act, procurement, or omission of another. A person is guilty of criminal homicide if he purposely, knowingly, recklessly or negligently causes the death of another human being. Criminal homicide is murder, manslaughter or negligent homicide. Model Penal Code, § 210.1; 18 U.S.C.A. § 1111 et seq. *See* Manslaughter; Murder.

Homicide is not necessarily a crime. It is a necessary ingredient of the crimes of murder and manslaughter, but there are other cases in which homicide may be committed without criminal intent and without criminal consequences, as, where it is done in the lawful execution of a judicial sentence, in self-defense, or as the only possible means of arresting an escaping felon. The term "homicide" is neutral; while it describes the act, it pronounces no judgment on its moral or legal quality. *See Excusable homicide; Justifiable homicide, below.*

Classification

Homicide is ordinarily classified as "justifiable," "excusable," and "felonious." For the definitions of these terms, and of some other compound terms, see *below.*

Culpable homicide. Described as a crime varying from the very lowest culpability, up to the very verge of murder.

Excusable homicide. The killing of a human being, either by misadventure or in self-defense. Such homicide consists of a perpetrator's acting in a manner which the law does not prohibit, such as self-defense or accidental homicide. *See* Justification; Self-defense; also *Justifiable homicide, below.*

Felonious homicide. The wrongful killing of a human being, of any age or either sex, without justification or excuse in law; of which offense there are two degrees, manslaughter and murder.

Homicide by misadventure. The accidental killing of another, where the slayer is doing a lawful act, unaccompanied by any criminally careless or reckless conduct. The same as "homicide *per infortunium.*" *See* Manslaughter.

Homicide by necessity. A species of justifiable homicide, because it arises from some unavoidable necessity, without any will, intention, or desire, and without any inadvertence or negligence in the party killing, and therefore without any shadow of blame. *See* Justification; Self-defense.

Homicide per infortunium. Homicide by misfortune, or accidental homicide; as where a man doing a lawful act without any intention of hurt, accidentally kills another; a species of excusable homicide. *See* Negligent homicide.

Homicide se defendendo. Homicide in self-defense; the killing of a person in self-defense upon a sudden affray, where the slayer had no other possible (or, at least, probable) means of escaping from his assailant. A species of excusable homicide. *See* Self defense.

Justifiable homicide. Such as is committed intentionally, but without any evil design, and under such circumstances of necessity or duty as render the act proper, and relieve the party from any shadow of blame; as where a sheriff lawfully executes a sentence of death upon a malefactor, or where the killing takes place in the endeavor to prevent the commission of felony which could not be otherwise avoided, or, as a matter of right, such as self-defense or other causes provided for by statute. *See* Justification; Self-defense; also *Excusable homicide, above.*

Negligent homicide. Criminal homicide constitutes negligent homicide when it is committed negligently. Model Penal Code, § 210.4. *See* Negligent homicide; also *Vehicular homicide, below.*

Reckless homicide. See that title.

Vehicular homicide. The killing of a human being by the operation of an automobile, airplane, motorboat or other motor vehicle in a manner which creates an unreasonable risk of injury to the person or property of another and which constitutes a material deviation from the standard of care which a reasonable person would observe under the same circumstances.

Honor, *v.* To accept a bill of exchange, or to pay a note, check, or accepted bill, at maturity and according to its tenor. To pay or to accept and pay, or where a credit so engages to purchase or discount a draft complying with the terms of the draft. U.C.C. § 1–201(21). *See also* Dishonor.

Honor, *n.* In old English law, a seigniory of several manors held under one baron or lord paramount. Also those dignities or privileges, degrees of nobility, knighthood, and other titles, which flow from the crown as the fountain of honor.

In America, the customary title of courtesy given to judges, and occasionally to some other officers; as, "his honor," "your honor," "honorable".

Act of honor. When a bill has been protested, and a third person wishes to take it up, or accept it, for the "honor" (credit) of one or more of the parties, the notary draws up an instrument, evidencing the transaction, which is called by this name. Such acts of honor have been eliminated by the U.C.C.

Office of honor. As used in constitutional and statutory provisions, this term denotes a public office of considerable dignity and importance, to which important public trusts or interests are confided, but which is not compensated by any salary or fees, being thus contrasted with an "office of profit."

Honorable discharge. A formal final judgment passed by the government upon the entire military record of a soldier, and an authoritative declaration by the government that he has left the service in a status of honor. Full veterans benefits are only given to those with an "honorable discharge" status.

Honorarium /ònərériyəm/. In the civil law, an honorary or free gift; a gratuitous payment, as distinguished from hire or compensation for service.

A voluntary reward for that for which no remuneration could be collected by law. A voluntary donation, in consideration of services which admit of no compensation in money.

A payment of money or anything of value made to a person for services rendered for which fees cannot legally or are not traditionally made. Federal laws place restrictions on the payment of honoraria to members of Congress. 2 U.S.C.A. § 31–1. *See also* Gratuity.

Honorary. As applied to public offices and other positions of responsibility or trust, this term means either that the office or title is bestowed upon the incumbent as a mark of honor or compliment, without intending to charge him with the active discharge of the duties of the place, or else that he is to receive no salary or other compensation in money, the honor conferred by the incumbency of the office being his only reward. In other contents or usages, it means attached to or growing out of some honor or dignity or honorable office, or else it imports an obligation or duty growing out of honor or trust only, as distinguished from legal accountability.

Honorary trust. *See* Trust.

Honorary trustees. Trustees to preserve contingent remainders, so called because they are bound, in honor only, to decide on the most proper and prudential course.

Hope, *v.* A desire or expectation. As used in a will, this term is a precatory word, rather than mandatory or dispositive, but it is sufficient, in proper cases, to create a trust in or in respect to the property spoken of.

Horizontal agreements. Agreements among competitors at same level of distribution. *See* Horizontal restraints of trade.

Horizontal analysis. In accounting, the calculation of dollar and percentage changes for corresponding items in comparative financial statements.

Horizontal merger. A combination of two or more companies that compete directly with each other. Merger of one company with another company producing same product or similar product and selling it in same geographic market. *See* Merger. *Compare* Vertical merger.

Horizontal price-fixing. Agreements between producers, wholesalers, or retailers as to sale or resale prices. Price fixing among businesses on the same level the effect of which is to eliminate competition based on price. Such agreements are prohibited by federal and state antitrust laws. *See also* Price-fixing.

Horizontal property acts. Statutes dealing with cooperatives and condominiums.

Horizontal restraints of trade. A restraint of trade involving businesses at the same level of operation. A "horizontal restraint" is an agreement between competitors to refuse to deal with one or more persons, while a "vertical restraint" involves combinations of parties on different levels of the distribution system. Both types of restraints constitute per se violations of Sherman Anti-trust Act. *See also* Horizontal price-fixing.

Hornbook. A primer; a book explaining the basics, fundamentals or rudiments of any science or branch of knowledge. The phrase "hornbook law" is a colloquial designation of the rudiments or general principles of law.

Popular reference to a series of textbooks which review various fields of law in summary, narrative form, as opposed to casebooks which are designed as primary teaching tools and include many reprints of court opinions.

Hostage. An innocent person held captive by one who threatens to kill or harm him if his demands are not met. A person who is given into the possession of the enemy, in time of war, his freedom (or life) to stand as security for the performance of some contract or promise made by the belligerent power giving the hostage with the other.

Hostage taking is a federal crime. 18 U.S.C.A. § 1203.

Term, when used with reference to person and in context in which it is used in kidnapping statute, implies unlawful taking, restraining or confining of person with intent that person, or victim, be held as security for performance, or forbearance, of some act by third person. *See* Kidnapping.

Hostile. Having the character of an enemy; standing in the relation of an enemy. Feeling or displaying enmity or antagonism such as a hostile witness. *See* Hostile *or* Adverse witness.

Within requirement for adverse possession that possession be asserted in hostile manner, "hostile" means that it is asserted against claim of ownership of all others, including record owner, but does not mean that adverse possessor display a subjective evil intent or emotion against title owner. *See also* Adverse possession; Notorious possession.

Hostile embargo. One laid upon the vessels of an actual or prospective enemy.

Hostile fire. In fire insurance law, a fire which breaks out in place not anticipated; fire which escapes into area not expected. One which becomes uncontrollable or breaks out from where it was intended to be and becomes hostile element.

Hostile *or* adverse witness. A witness who manifests so much hostility or prejudice under examination in chief that the party who has called him, or his representative, is allowed to cross-examine him, *i.e.,* to treat him as though he had been called by the opposite party. When a party calls a hostile witness, an adverse party, or a witness identified with an adverse party, interrogation may be by leading questions. Fed.Evid. R. 611. *See also* Adverse witness.

Hostile possession. *See* Possession.

Hostile takeover. Takeover that is opposed by management of target company. *See* Takeover bid. *Compare* Friendly takeover.

Hot blood. In criminal law, condition of one whose passions have been aroused to an uncontrollable degree and whose homicide may be reduced, therefore, from murder to manslaughter. *See also* Heat of passion; Manslaughter.

Hot cargo. In labor law, goods produced or handled by employer with whom union has dispute.

Hot cargo agreement. Voluntary agreement between union and neutral employer by which latter agrees to exert pressure on another employer with whom union has a dispute; by, for example, ceasing or refraining from handling, using, selling, transporting or otherwise dealing in any of the products of any other employer the union has labeled as unfair or "hot". *See* Landrum-Griffin Act.

Hotchpot. The blending and mixing property belonging to different persons, in order to divide it equally. Anciently applied to the mixing and blending of lands given to one daughter in frank marriage, with those descending to her and her sisters in fee-simple, for the purpose of dividing the whole equally among them; without which the daughter who held in frank marriage could have no share in the lands in fee-simple.

Hotchpot, or the *putting in hotchpot,* is applied in modern law to the throwing the amount of an advancement made to a particular child, in real or personal estate, into the common stock, for the purpose of a more equal division, or of equalizing the shares of all the children. This answers to or resembles the *collatio bonorum,* or *collation* of the civil law.

Hotelkeeper's lien. A possessory or statutory lien allowing the hotelkeeper or innkeeper to take the personal property of a guest, brought into the hotel, as security for nonpayment of the guest's bill.

Hot issue. *See* Issue *(Securities).*

Hot pursuit. *See* Fresh pursuit.

Hour. The twenty-fourth part of a natural day; sixty minutes of time.

Office hours. See Office.

Hours of labor. Time period in which employees work and which is governed in part by state and federal (*e.g.* Adamson Act; Fair Labor Standards Act) laws enacted under police power insofar as such legislation deals with the safety and welfare of laborers and the public. *See* Child labor laws; Fair Labor Standards Act; Wage and hour laws.

House. Structure that serves as living quarters for one or more persons or families. *See also* Curtilage; Domicile; Home; Residence.

A legislative assembly, or (where the bicameral system obtains) one of the two branches of the legislature; as the "house of lords" or "house of representatives". Also a quorum of a legislative body.

The name "house" is also given to some collections of persons other than legislative bodies, to some public institutions, and (colloquially) to commercial firms or joint-stock companies (*e.g.* publishing or securities businesses).

Bawdy house. A brothel; a house maintained for purposes of prostitution.

Disorderly house. See that title.

Duplex house. A double house.

Dwelling house. See Dwelling.

House-burning. See Arson.

House of Commons. One of the constituent houses of the British parliament, composed of representatives of the counties, cities, and boroughs. The lower house, so called because the commons of the realm, that is, the knights, citizens, and burgesses returned to parliament, representing the whole body of the commons, sit there. Its jurisdiction is limited to bills of attainder and pains and penalties, and breach of privileges of the House and its members. *See also House of Lords, below.*

House of correction. A reformatory. A place for the confinement of juvenile offenders, or those who have committed crimes of lesser magnitude.

House of Delegates. The official title of the lower branch of the legislative assembly of several of the states, *e.g.,* Maryland and Virginia.

House of ill fame. A bawdy house; house of prostitution; a brothel; a dwelling allowed by its chief occupant to be used as a resort of persons desiring unlawful sexual intercourse. *See* Bawdy-house.

House of Lords. The upper chamber of the British parliament. It comprises the lords spiritual and the lords temporal, and a certain number of Scottish peers. The House of Lords is also the court of final appeal in most civil cases and has jurisdiction over impeachment. *See House of Commons, above.*

House of Representatives. See House of Representatives.

House of worship. A building or place set apart for and devoted to the holding of religious services or exercises or public worship; a church or chapel or place similarly used.

Housebreaking. Burglary. Breaking and entering a dwelling-house with intent to commit any felony therein. *See* Burglary.

Under some statutes housebreaking may consist in "breaking out" of a house after access had been gained without breaking.

House counsel. Lawyer who acts as attorney for business though carried as an employee of that business and not as an independent lawyer. Generally, such lawyer advises business on day to day matters. Larger businesses have legal departments with attorneys assigned to specialized areas of law affecting their particular business; *e.g.* labor law, taxes, personal injury litigation, corporate law, etc.

Household, *adj.* Belonging to the house and family; domestic.

Household, *n.* A family living together. Those who dwell under the same roof and compose a family. Term is generally synonymous with "family" for insurance purposes, and includes those who dwell together as a family under the same roof. Generally, the term as used in auto-

mobile policies is synonymous with "home" and "family."

For Family, see that title.

Householder. The occupier of a house. More correctly, one who keeps house with his or her family; the head or master of a family. One who has a household; the head of a household. *See also* Head of household.

House of delegates. When used in connection with the American Bar Association, the House of Delegates is the body in which is vested the control and administration of the ABA. See ABA Constitution, Art. VI.

House of prostitution. *See* Bawdy-house.

House of Representatives. The House of Representatives of Congress comprises 435 representatives. The number representing each State is determined by population but every State is entitled to at least one representative. Members are elected by the people by district for 2-year terms, all terms running for the same period. Representatives must be at least 25 years of age, citizens of United States for at least seven years, and live in the state they represent. Art. I, § 2 of U.S.Const.

Housing code. *See* Building code.

Housing courts. Such courts, as existing in a number of cities, deal primarily with landlord and tenant matters, including disputes concerning maintenance of premises, terms of lease, building and fire codes, and the like.

HOW. *See* Home Owners Warranty.

H.R. House of Representatives; House Report.

H.R. 10 Plans. *See* Keogh Plan.

Huckster /hə́kstər/. A petty hawker or peddler.

HUD. Department of Housing and Urban Development.

Humanitarian doctrine. Doctrine evolved from Missouri (Wonnack v. Missouri Pacific R. Co., 337 Mo. 1160, 88 S.W.2d 368) in which a plaintiff is relieved of responsibility for his negligence if he can show that the defendant (generally one operating a train or motor vehicle while plaintiff is pedestrian) had last opportunity to avoid the accident. It is only when plaintiff comes into a position of imminent, impending and immediate danger in which injury to plaintiff is reasonably certain if the existing circumstances remain unchanged that the "humanitarian doctrine" seizes upon the situation and imposes upon defendant a duty to thereafter exercise proper care to avoid the threatened injury. Only a very few states follow this doctrine.

See also Immediate danger; Imminent peril; Last clear chance doctrine.

Hundred. Under the Saxon organization of England, each county or shire comprised of an indefinite number of *hundreds,* each hundred containing ten *tithings,* or groups of ten families of freeholders or frankpledges. The hundred was governed by a high constable, and had its own court; but its most remarkable feature was the corporate responsibility of the whole for the crimes or defaults of the individual members.

Hundred Court. In English law, a larger court-baron, being held for all the inhabitants of a particular *hundred,* instead of a manor. The free suitors were the judges, and the steward the registrar, as in the case of a court-baron. It was not a court of record, and resembled a court-baron in all respects except that in point of territory it was of greater jurisdiction. These courts no longer exist.

Hundredweight. A denomination of weight containing, according to the English system, 112 pounds; but in this country, generally, it consists of 100 pounds avoirdupois.

Hung jury. A jury so irreconcilably divided in opinion that they cannot agree upon any verdict by the required unanimity. *See* Deadlocked (*Jury*); Dynamite instruction.

Hurdle rate. A preestablished rate of return against which other rates of return are measured in evaluating projects using the internal rate of return. *See also* Rate (*Rate of return*).

Hurt. In such phrases as "to the hurt or annoyance of another," or "hurt, molested, or restrained in his person or estate," this word is not restricted to physical injuries, but includes also mental pain, as well as discomfort or annoyance. *See also* Damage; Injury.

Husband. A married man; one who has a lawful wife living. The correlative of "wife."

Husbandman. A farmer, a cultivator or tiller of the ground. The word "farmer" is colloquially used as synonymous with "husbandman", but originally meant a tenant who cultivates *leased* ground.

Husband of a ship. *See* Ship.

Husbandry. Agriculture; farming; cultivation of the soil for food. Farming, in the sense of operating land to raise crops and livestock. Care of household. Careful management of resources.

Husband-wife privilege. Term refers to privilege extended to confidential marital communications. While state statutes vary, in general such provide that a spouse has a privilege to refuse to disclose, and to prevent the other from disclosing, a confidential communication made while spouses were married. There are certain exceptions to this privilege, the major one being where one spouse is the victim of a crime by the other.

Husband-wife tort actions. The common law rule, carried forward by statute in many states, prohibits tort actions between spouses. The current trend however is to abolish this interspousal immunity doctrine, thus permitting such suits between spouses. Some states have abolished the doctrine only insofar as automobile tort actions. *See also* Consortium.

Hush-money. A colloquial expression to designate a bribe to hinder information; pay to secure silence.

Hybrid class action. Term refers to type of actions where the right to be enforced is several but the object of the action is the adjudication of claims which do or may affect specific property in the action. *See* Class *or* Representative action.

Hybrid securities. Securities that have some of the attributes of both debt securities and equity securities. Type of security which, in the form of a debenture, contains elements of indebtedness and elements of equity stock.

Hypnosis. The act of inducing artificially a state of sleep or trance in a subject by means of verbal suggestion by the hypnotist or by the subject's concentration upon some object. It is generally characterized by extreme responsiveness to suggestions from the hypnotist.

A state of heightened concentration with diminished awareness of peripheral events. A majority of states have held that hypnotically induced testimony is admissible in a criminal trial. Some courts hold, however, that hypnotically refreshed testimony must satisfy the standard of acceptability for scientific evidence before it is admissible in a criminal trial.

Hypothecate /həpóθəkèyt/. To pledge property as security or collateral for a debt. Generally, there is no physical transfer of the pledged property to the lender, nor is the lender given title to the property; though he has the right to sell the pledged property upon default. *See also* Pledge; Rehypothecation.

Hypothesis /həpóθəsəs/. A supposition, assumption, or theory; a theory set up by the prosecution, on a criminal trial, or by the defense, as an explanation of the facts in evidence, and a ground for inferring guilt or innocence, as the case may be, or as indicating a probable or possible motive for the crime.

Hypothetical question. A hypothetical question is a form of question framed in such a manner as to call for an opinion from an expert based on a series of assumptions claimed to have been established as fact by the evidence in a case. It is a device which is used at trial to enable an expert witness to express an opinion concerning facts about which he did not have personal knowledge. It should be so framed as to recite all the facts in evidence which are relevant to the formation of an opinion and then, assuming the facts recited to be true, the witness should be asked whether he is able to form an opinion therefrom and if so to state his opinion. Federal Rules of Evidence 705 and 703 eliminate the requirement that a hypothetical question must be used in Federal Court, but either the court or the questioner may decide that one should be used.

I

Ib. *See* Ibidem.

Ibidem /íbədəm/əbáydəm/. Lat. In the same place; in the same book; on the same page, etc. Abbreviated to *"ibid."* or *"ib."*

I.C.C. Interstate Commerce Commission.

Id. *See* Idem.

I.D. Identification.

Idem /áydəm/. Lat. The same; used to indicate a reference previously made. According to Lord Coke, *"idem"* has two significations, *sc., idem syllabis seu verbis* (the same in syllabus or words), and *idem re et sensu* (the same in substance and in sense).

Idem sonans /áydəm sównænz/. Sounding the same or alike; having the same sound. A term applied to names which are substantially the same, though slightly varied in the spelling, as "Lawrence" and "Lawrance," and the like. Under the rule of "idem sonans," variance between allegation and proof of a given name is not material if the names sound the same or the attentive ear finds difficulty in distinguishing them when pronounced.

Identical. Exactly the same for all practical purposes.

Identification. Proof of identity. The proving that a person, subject, or article before the court is the very same that he or it is alleged, charged, or reputed to be; as where a witness recognizes the prisoner as the same person whom he saw committing the crime; or where handwriting, stolen goods, counterfeit coin, etc., are recognized as the same which once passed under the observation of the person identifying them.

The requirement of identification as a condition precedent to admissability is satisfied by evidence sufficient to support a finding that the matter in question is what its proponent claims. Fed. Evid.R. 901.

See also Authentication; Blood test evidence; DNA identification; Eyewitness identification; Lineup; Mug book; Voice identification; Voiceprint.

Identification of goods. Exists when goods are shipped, marked or otherwise designated for the buyer. The buyer obtains a special property and an insurable interest in goods by identification of existing goods as goods to which the contract refers even though the goods so identified are non-conforming and he has an option to return or reject them. Such identification can be made at any time and in any manner explicitly agreed to by the parties. U.C.C. § 2–501.

Identity. *Evidence.* Sameness; the fact that a subject, person, or thing before a court is *the same* as it is represented, claimed, or charged to be. *See* Authentication; Identification.

Patent Law. Such sameness between two designs, inventions, combinations, etc., as will constitute the one an infringement of the patent granted for the other. To constitute "identity of invention," and therefore infringement, not only must the result obtained be the same, but, in case the means used for its attainment is a combination of known elements, the elements combined in both cases must be the same, and combined in the same way, so that each element shall perform the same function; provided that the differences alleged are not merely colorable according to the rule forbidding the use of known equivalents. "Identity of design" means sameness of appearance, or, in other words, sameness of effect upon the eye,—not the eye of an expert, but of an ordinary intelligent observer.

Identity of interests. In civil procedure, an amendment (addition) of a party will be allowed if the party sought to be joined is so closely related in business operations or other activities that the institution of an action against one serves as notice of litigation to the other, and hence the amendment will relate back. Fed.R. Civil P. 15(c). *See also* Identity of parties; Privity.

Identity of parties. Refers to condition of persons in relation to each other so that a former judgment against one bars action against others because of res adjudicata; hence, same parties and those in privity are so barred. *See* Res (*Res judicata*).

Id est /íd èst/. Lat. That is. Commonly abbreviated *"i.e."*

I.e. An abbreviation for *"id est,"* that is; that is to say.

If. In deeds and wills, this word, as a rule, implies a condition precedent, unless it be controlled by other words.

I.F.B. Invitation for Bids.

Ignoramus /ìgnəréyməs/. Lat. "We are ignorant;" "We ignore it." Formerly the grand jury wrote this word on bills of indictment when, after having heard the evidence, they thought the accusation against the prisoner was groundless, intimating that, though the facts might possibly be true, the truth did not appear to them; but now they usually write in English the words "No bill", "Not a true bill," or "Not found," if that is their verdict. But they are still said to *ignore* the bill.

Ignorance. The want or absence of knowledge, unaware or uninformed.

Ignorance *of law* is want of knowledge or acquaintance with the laws of the land in so far as they apply to the act, relation, duty, or matter under consideration. Ignorance *of fact* is want of knowledge of some fact or facts constituting or relating to the subject-matter in hand.

In criminal law, ignorance as to a fact may be a defense, but ignorance as to law generally is no defense. See Model Penal Code, § 2.04.

See also Mistake *(Mistake of fact and law)*.

Ignore. To be ignorant of, or unacquainted with. To disregard willfully; to refuse to recognize; to decline to take notice of.

To reject as groundless, false or unsupported by evidence; as when a grand jury *ignores* a bill of indictment.

Illegal. Against or not authorized by law. Unlawful *(q.v.)*.

Illegal contract. Contract is illegal where its formation or performance is expressly forbidden by a civil or criminal statute or where penalty is imposed for doing act agreed upon. *See* Void contract.

Illegal entry. An alien is guilty of illegal entry if: (1) he enters the country at the wrong time or place, or (2) eludes an examination by immigration officers, or (3) obtains entry by fraud, or (4) knowingly enters into a marriage for the purpose of evading any provision of the immigration laws. 8 U.S.C.A. § 1325. *See* Border search.

Illegal interest. Usury; interest at a higher rate than the law allows.

Illegality /iləgǽlətiy/. That which is contrary to the principles of law, as contradistinguished from mere rules of procedure.

Illegally obtained evidence. Evidence which is obtained in violation of defendant's rights because officers had no warrant and no probable cause to arrest or because the warrant was defective and no valid grounds existed for seizure without a warrant. Evidence secured in violation of statutes or constitutional guarantee against unreasonable searches; U.S. Constitution, 4th Amendment. Such evidence is inadmissible in criminal trial of victim of such search. Mapp v. Ohio, 367 U.S. 643, 81 S.Ct. 1684, 6 L.Ed.2d 1081. *See* Exclusionary Rule; Fruit of poisonous tree doctrine; Suppression hearing; Suppression of evidence.

Illegal per se. Unlawful in and of itself and not because of some extraneous circumstance, *e.g.* a contract to assassinate a public official. *See* Per se violations.

Illegal trade. Such traffic or commerce as carried on itn violation of federal, state, or local laws; *e.g.* trade in violation of antitrust laws; trade in stolen goods.

Illegitimacy /iləjítəməsiy/. The condition before the law, or the social status, of a child born out of wedlock; condition of one whose parents were not intermarried at the time of his or her birth.

Illegitimate /iləjítəmət/. That which is contrary to law; term is usually applied to children born out of lawful wedlock. *See* Illegitimate child.

Illegitimate child. Child who is born at a time when his parents, though alive, are not married to each other. Such child however is legitimate if they were married after his conception and before his birth. An illegitimate child has a constitutionally protected right to inherit from his or her father. *See also* Person.

Ill fame. Evil repute; notorious bad character. Houses of prostitution, gaming houses, and other such disorderly places are called "houses of ill fame," and a person who frequents them is a person of ill fame.

Illicit /əlísət/. Not permitted or allowed; prohibited; unlawful; illegal; as an illicit trade, illicit intercourse.

Illicit cohabitation. The living together as man and wife of two persons who are not lawfully married, with the implication that they habitually practice fornication. At common law and by statutes in many states, living together either in adultery or fornication is a crime, though at common law such cohabitation had to be open and notorious so as to cause a public scandal. Such statutes are seldom enforced. *See* Adultery.

Illicit connection. Unlawful sexual intercourse. *See* Illicit relations.

Illicit distillery. One carried on in violation of the laws of the United States relating to the distribution and taxation of spirituous liquor.

Illicit relations. Any form of unlawful sexual intercourse such as fornication or adultery. *See* Illicit cohabitation.

Illicit trade. Policies of marine insurance usually contain a covenant of warranty against "illicit trade", meaning thereby trade which is forbidden, or declared unlawful, by the laws of the country where the cargo is to be delivered.

Illinois land trust. *See* Land trust.

Illiteracy. The condition of one who cannot read or write and, in general, of one who is unlettered or unlearned.

Illness. Sickness, disease or disorder of body or mind. In insurance law, a disease or ailment of such a character as to affect the general soundness and healthfulness of the system seriously, and not a mere temporary indisposition which does not tend to undermine or weaken the constitution of the insured. For mental illness, *see* Insanity. *See also* Serious illness.

Illusion /əl(y)uwzhən/. Distorted or misinterpreted sensory impression which, in contrast to hallucinations, arises from an actual stimulus, *i.e.,* shadow is taken to be a man, specks on window are seen as a swarm of mosquitos. Prevalent in delirious states. The misinterpretation of a real, external sensory experience.

Illusory /əl(y)úwsəriy/°uwz°/. Deceiving by false appearances; nominal, as distinguished from substantial; fallacious; illusive.

Illusory appointment. Nominal, overly restrictive or conditional transfer of property under power of appointment; lacking in substantial existence.

Illusory contract. An expression cloaked in promissory terms, but which, upon closer examination, reveals that the promisor has not committed himself in any manner. *See also* Illusory promise.

Illusory promise. A purported promise that actually promises nothing because it leaves to speaker the choice of performance or nonperformance. When promise is illusory, there is no actual requirement upon promisor that anything be done because promisor has an alternative which, if taken, will render promisee nothing. When provisions of supposed promise leave promisor's performance optional or entirely within discretion, pleasure and control of promisor, the promise is illusory.

An illusory promise is an expression cloaked in promissory terms, but which, upon closer examination, reveals that the promisor has really not committed himself to anything. If performance of an apparent promise is entirely optional with the provisor, the promise is illusory.

Illusory tenant. A straw man who, as landlord's alter ego, subleases apartment to permit landlord to circumvent or evade obligations under rent laws, or prime tenant who is individual entrepreneur trafficking in stabilized or controlled apartments which he subleases as business.

Illusory trust. Where a settlor *in form* either declares himself trustee of, or transfers to a third party, property in trust, but by the terms of the trust, or by his dealings with the trust property, *in substance* exercises so much control over the trust property that it is clear that he did not intend to relinquish any of his rights in the trust property, the trust is invalid as illusory. A trust

arrangement which takes the form of a trust, but because of powers retained in the settlor has no real substance and in reality is not a completed trust.

Imbargo. An old form of "embargo" *(q.v.).*

Imbezzle. An occasional or obsolete form of "embezzle" *(q.v.).*

Imbracery. *See* Embracery.

Imitation. The making of one thing in the similitude or likeness of another; as, counterfeit coin is said to be made "in imitation" of the genuine. That which is made or produced as a copy; an artificial likeness; a counterfeit; simulating something superior.

An imitation of a trademark is that which so far resembles the genuine trademark as to be likely to induce the belief that it is genuine, whether by the use of words or letters similar in appearance or in sound, or by any sign, device, or other means. The test of "colorable imitation" is, not whether a difference may be recognized between the names of two competing articles when placed side by side, but whether the difference will be recognized by the purchaser with no opportunity for comparison.

See Counterfeit; Forgery.

Immaterial. Not material, essential, or necessary; not important or pertinent; not decisive; of no substantial consequence; without weight; of no material significance. *See also* Impertinence; Irrelevancy: Irrelevant allegation. *Compare* Material; Material fact; Relevant.

Immaterial averment. In pleading, an averment alleging with needless particularity or unnecessary circumstances what is material and necessary, and which might properly have been stated more generally, and without such circumstances and particulars; or, in other words, a statement of unnecessary particulars in connection with and as descriptive of what is material. Such immaterial matter may be ordered stricken from the pleading. Fed.R.Civil P. 12(f). *See also* Irrelevant allegation.

Immaterial evidence. Evidence which lacks probative weight and is unlikely to influence the tribunal in resolving the issue before it. Such evidence is commonly objected to by opposing counsel, and disallowed by the court. *See also* Irrelevancy. *Compare* Relevant evidence.

Immaterial facts. Those which are not essential to the right of action or defense. *See* Immaterial averment. *Compare* Material fact.

Immaterial issue. In pleading, an issue taken on an immaterial point; that is, a point not proper to decide the action.

Immaterial variance. Discrepancy between the pleading and proof of a character so slight that the adverse party cannot say that he was misled thereby. One in which difference between allegations and proof is so slight and unimportant that adverse party is not misled or prejudiced in maintaining his defense. *See also* Variance.

Immediacy. The state or quality of being immediately and directly perceived; urgency; occurring without delay.

Immediate. Present; at once; without delay; not deferred by any interval of time. In this sense, the word, without any very precise signification, denotes that action is or must be taken either instantly or without any considerable loss of time. A reasonable time in view of particular facts and circumstances of case under consideration. Next in line or relation; directly connected; not secondary or remote. Not separated in respect to place; not separated by the intervention of any intermediate object, cause, relation, or right. Thus we speak of an action as prosecuted for the "immediate benefit" of A., of a devise as made to the "immediate issue" of B., etc.

Immediate cause. The last of a series or chain of causes tending to a given result, and which, of itself, and without the intervention of any further cause, directly produces the result or event. A cause may be immediate in this sense, and yet not "proximate;" and conversely, the proximate cause (that which directly and efficiently brings about the result) may not be immediate. The familiar illustration is that of a drunken man falling into the water and drowning. His intoxication is the proximate cause of his death, if it can be said that he would not have fallen into the water when sober; but the immediate cause of death is suffocation by drowning. *See also* Proximate cause.

Immediate control. Such constant control as would enable driver to instantly govern vehicle's movements, including the power to stop within a distance in which such a vehicle, in good mechanical condition, driven by a reasonably skillful driver, and traveling at a lawful rate of speed, could be stopped.

Immediate danger. Definition of "immediate danger" as part of humanitarian doctrine contemplates that there be some inexorable circumstance, situation or agency bearing down on plaintiff with reasonable probability of danger prior to negligent act of defendant. *See also* Imminent danger; Imminent peril.

Immediate descent. *See* Descent.

Immediate family. Term generally referring to one's parents, wife or husband, children, and brothers and sisters.

Immediately. Without interval of time, without delay, straightway, or without any delay or lapse of time. When used in contract is usually construed to mean "within a reasonable time having due regard to the nature of the circumstances of the case", although strictly, it means "not deferred by any period of time". The words "immediately" and "forthwith" have generally the same meaning. They are stronger than the expression "within a reasonable time" and imply prompt, vigorous action without any delay.

Immediate notice. As required by insurance policy as for proof of loss means within a reasonable time.

Immemorial. Beyond human memory; time out of mind.

Immemorial usage. A practice which has existed time out of mind; custom; prescription.

Immigrant. An alien in a country except, in United States, one within a specified class within the Immigration and Nationality Act. 8 U.S.C.A. § 1101(a)(15). One who leaves a country to permanently settle in another.

Immigration. The coming into a country of foreigners for purposes of permanent residence. The correlative term "emigration" denotes the act of such persons in leaving their former country.

Immigration and Nationality Act. A comprehensive federal law which deals with immigration, naturalization and exclusion of aliens. 8 U.S.C.A. § 1101 *et seq.*

Immigration and Naturalization Service. Such Service is responsible for administering the immigration and naturalization laws relating to the admission, exclusion, deportation, and naturalization of aliens. Specifically, the Service inspects aliens to determine their admissibility into the United States; adjudicates requests of aliens for benefits under the law; guards against illegal entry into the United States; investigates, apprehends, and removes aliens in this country in violation of the law; and examines alien applicants wishing to become citizens.

Immigration Appeals Board. The Board of Immigration Appeals, the highest administrative tribunal in the immigration field, is charged with the interpretation and administration of the immigration laws. The Board has jurisdiction, defined by regulation, to hear appeals from certain decisions of the Immigration and Naturalization Service. Most of the cases reaching the Board consist of appeals from formal orders of the Service's Immigration Judges entered in due process deportation hearings against aliens. These usually also involve applications by aliens for discretionary relief from deportation.

Imminent. Near at hand; mediate rather than immediate; close rather than touching; impending; on the point of happening; threatening; menacing; perilous. Something which is threatening to happen at once, something close at hand, something to happen upon the instant, close although not yet touching, and on the point of happening.

Imminent danger. In relation to homicide in self-defense, this term means immediate danger, such as must be instantly met, such as cannot be guarded against by calling for the assistance of others or the protection of the law. Or, as otherwise defined, such an appearance of threatened and impending injury as would put a reasonable and prudent man to his instant defense. *See* Self-defense.

Imminently dangerous article. One that is reasonably certain to place life or limb in peril.

Imminent peril. Such peril under humanitarian doctrine means certain, immediate, and impending, and not remote, uncertain, or contingent; and likelihood or bare possibility of injury is not sufficient to create "imminent peril." That position of danger to the plaintiff in which—if the existing circumstances remain unchanged—injury to him is reasonably certain. Doctrine is properly applied only in cases where an unexpected physical danger is presented so suddenly as to deprive driver of his power of using reasonable judgment, and a party will be denied benefit of the doctrine where that party's negligence causes or contributes to creation of the perilous situation. *See also* Emergency doctrine; Humanitarian doctrine.

Immoderate /imódərət/. Exceeding just, usual, or suitable bounds; not within reasonable limits.

Immoral. Contrary to good morals; inconsistent with the rules and principles of morality; inimical to public welfare according to the standards of a given community, as expressed in law or otherwise. Morally evil; impure; obscene; unprincipled; vicious; or dissolute.

Immoral act *or* **conduct.** Within rules authorizing disbarment of attorney is that conduct which is willful, flagrant, or shameless, and which shows a moral indifference to the opinions of the good and respectable members of the community.

Immoral consideration. One contrary to good morals, and therefore invalid. Contracts based upon an immoral consideration are generally void.

Immoral contracts. Contracts founded upon considerations *contra bonos mores* are void.

Immorality. That which is *contra bonos mores.* *See* Immoral.

Immovables. In the civil law, property which, from its nature, destination, or the object to which it is applied, cannot move itself, or be removed.

In conflicts of law, refers to land and those things so firmly attached thereto that they may be regarded as part of it and the law of the situs

governs in choice of law. Restatement, Second, Conflict of Laws, § 223.

Immunity. Exemption, as from serving in an office, or performing duties which the law generally requires other citizens to perform; *e.g.* exemption from paying taxes. Freedom or exemption from penalty, burden, or duty. Special privilege. *See also* Exemption; Foreign immunity; Judicial immunity; Legislative immunity; Parent-child immunity; Privilege; Sovereign immunity.

Governmental tort immunity. The federal, and derivatively, the state and local governments are free from liability for torts committed except in cases in which they have consented by statute to be sued; *e.g.* Federal Tort Claims Act; state tort claims acts. Most states, either by statute or court decision, have abolished or greatly restricted the doctrine of sovereign immunity at both the state and local levels.

The Supreme Court has held that local governments can be sued directly under 42 U.S.C.A. § 1983 for monetary, declaratory, or injunctive relief where "the action that is alleged to be unconstitutional implements or executes a policy statement, ordinance, regulation, or decision officially adopted and promulgated by that body's officers." Monell v. Department of Social Services of N. Y., 429 U.S. 1071, 97 S.Ct. 807, 50 L.Ed.2d 789. A state law that immunizes government conduct otherwise subject to suit under 42 U.S. C.A. § 1983 is preempted.

See also Color of law; Federal Tort Claims Act; Official immunity doctrine; Sovereign immunity.

Immunity from prosecution. By state and federal statutes, a witness may be granted immunity from prosecution for his or her testimony (*e.g.* before grand jury). States either adopt the "use" or the "transactional" immunity approach. The federal government replaced the later with the former approach in 1970. The distinction between the two is as follows: "Use immunity" prohibits witness' compelled testimony and its fruits from being used in any manner in connection with criminal prosecution of the witness; on the other hand, "transactional immunity" affords immunity to the witness from prosecution for offense to which his compelled testimony relates. See 18 U.S.C.A. §§ 6001–6005.

Protection from prosecution must be commensurate with privilege against self incrimination, but it need not be any greater and hence a person is entitled only to protection from prosecution based on the use and derivative use of his testimony; he is not constitutionally entitled to protection from prosecution for everything arising from the illegal transaction which his testimony concerns (transactional immunity).

Interspousal immunity. See Husband-wife tort actions.

Qualified immunity. Affirmative defense which shields public officials performing discretionary functions from civil damages if their conduct does not violate clearly established statutory or constitutional rights of which reasonable person would have known.

Property law. A freedom on the part of one person against having a given legal relation altered by a given act or omission to act on the part of another person. Restatement of Property, § 4.

Immunization. The condition of being, or the act rendering one, immunized or protected, especially from communicable diseases.

Impacted area. An area whose school population has been burdened because of attendance by a large number of federal employees' children and which may at the same time be losing school tax revenue because of the United States Government's immunity from land taxes.

Impact rule. Rule formerly prevailing in many jurisdictions which required a blow or impact from without as a condition for recovering damages in negligence for emotional distress. Such rule has been abandoned in most jurisdictions today.

Impair. To weaken, to make worse, to lessen in power, diminish, or relax, or otherwise affect in an injurious manner. To diminish in quality, value, excellence or strength, and not every change that affects contract constitutes an impairment.

Impaired capital. Condition of a business when the surplus account shows a negative balance and hence the capital is reduced below its value from when the stock was issued (*i.e.* less than the stated or par value of business' capital stock).

Impairing the obligation of contracts. A law which impairs the obligation of a contract is one which renders the contract in itself less valuable or less enforceable, whether by changing its terms and stipulations, its legal qualities and conditions, or by regulating the remedy for its enforcement.

To "impair the obligation of a contract", within prohibition of Art. I, § 10, U.S.Const., is to weaken it, lessen its value, or make it worse in any respect or in any degree, and any law which changes the intention and legal effect of the parties, giving to one a greater and to the other a less interest or benefit, or which imposes conditions not included in the contract or dispenses with the performance of those included, impairs the obligation of the contract.

A statute "impairs the obligation of a contract" when by its terms it nullifies or materially changes existing contract obligations.

Impanel. The act of the clerk of the court in making up a list of the jurors who have been selected for the trial of a particular cause. All the steps of ascertaining who shall be the proper jurors to sit in the trial of a particular case up to the final formation. *See also* Jury-list; Jury panel.

Impartial. Favoring neither; disinterested; treating all alike; unbiased; equitable, fair, and just.

Impartial expert. Person appointed by tribunal for unbiased opinion on matter addressed to the court (*e.g.,* an appraiser in a condemnation case). Commonly, Worker's Compensation Board will appoint an impartial physician to examine and report his findings to Board. Similar usage of experts is made in social security disability hearings (*e.g.,* vocational expert). Also, a court may appoint an expert witness (see *e.g.,* Fed.R.Evid. 706).

Impartial jury. The provision of the Bill of Rights (Sixth Amendment to Const. of U.S.) requiring that the accused shall have a fair trial by an impartial jury, means that the jury must be not partial, not favoring one party more than another, unprejudiced, disinterested, equitable, and just, and that the merits of the case shall not be prejudged. Term refers to a jury which is of impartial frame of mind at beginning of trial, is influenced only by legal and competent evidence produced during trial, and bases its verdict upon evidence connecting defendant with the commission of the crime charged.

For Fair and impartial jury, and Fair and impartial trial, see those titles.

Impeach. To accuse; to charge a liability upon; to sue. To dispute, disparage, deny, or contradict; as, to impeach a judgment or decree, or impeach a witness; or as used in the rule that a jury cannot "impeach their verdict". To proceed against a public officer for crime or misfeasance, before a proper court, by the presentation of a written accusation called "articles of impeachment". *See* Impeachment.

Impeachment. A criminal proceeding against a public officer, before a *quasi* political court, instituted by a written accusation called "articles of impeachment"; for example, a written accusation by the House of Representatives of the United States to the Senate of the United States against the President, Vice President, or an officer of the United States, including federal judges. Such federal power of impeachment is provided for in Art. II, § 4 of the Constitution. Under Art. I, § 2, cl. 5, the House of Representatives "shall have the sole Power of Impeachment", and under § 3, cl. 6, "The Senate shall have the sole Power to try all Impeachments". A two thirds vote of the Senate is required for impeachment.

Articles of impeachment. The formal written allegation of the causes for an impeachment, answering the same purpose as an indictment in an ordinary criminal proceeding. Under the above cited constitutional provisions, Articles of Impeachment are initiated by the House of Representatives with the trial conducted by the Senate. *See also* Address (*Bill of address*).

Collateral impeachment. *See* Collateral attack.

Impeachment of verdict. Attack on verdict because of alleged improprieties in the jury's deliberations or conduct.

Impeachment of witness. To call in question the veracity of a witness, by means of evidence adduced for such purpose, or the adducing of proof that a witness is unworthy of belief. In general, though there are variations from state to state, a witness may be impeached with respect to prior inconsistent statements, contradiction of facts, bias, or character. A witness, once impeached, may be rehabilitated with evidence supporting credibility.

Fed.R.Civil P. 32(a)(1) permits the use at trial of a witness's prior deposition to discredit or impeach testimony of the deponent as a witness.

Fed.Evid.R. 607 provides that the "credibility of a witness may be attached by any party, including the party calling him." Rule 608 governs impeachment by evidence of character and conduct of witness, and Rule 609 impeachment by evidence of conviction of crime.

See also Address (*Bill of address*); Cross-examination; Jenks Act *or* Rule; Prior inconsistent statements.

Impede. To obstruct; hinder; check; delay.

Impediments /impédəmənts/. Disabilities, or hindrances to the making of contracts, such as infancy, want of reason, etc.

Impediment to marriage. Legal obstacle to contracting a valid marriage such as relationship of blood within prohibited degree of consanguinity between parties. *See also* Impediments.

Imperative. Mandatory. *See* Directory.

Imperfect. As used in various legal compound terms, this word means defective or incomplete; wanting in some legal or formal requisite; wanting in legal sanction or effectiveness; as in speaking of imperfect "obligations," "ownership," "rights," "title," "usufruct," or "war." See those nouns.

Impersonation. False impersonation is representing oneself to be a public officer or employee or a person licensed to practice or engage in any profession or vocation for which a license is required by state law with knowledge that such representation is false. The act of pretending or representing oneself to be another, commonly a crime if the other is a public official or police officer. See 18 U.S.C.A. § 911 et seq. *See also* Personate.

Impertinence. Irrelevancy; the fault of not properly pertaining to the issue or proceeding. The introduction of any matters into a bill, complaint, answer, or other pleading or proceeding in a suit, which are not properly before the court for decision, at any particular stage of the suit. *See* Impertinent; Irrelevancy.

A question propounded to a witness, or evidence offered or sought to be elicited, is called "impertinent" when it has no logical bearing upon the issue, is not necessarily connected with it, or does not belong to the matter in hand. *See also* Immaterial evidence.

Impertinent. That which does not belong to a pleading, interrogatory, or other proceeding; out of place; superfluous; irrelevant. A term applied to matter not necessary to constitute the cause of action or ground of defense. Such matter may be ordered stricken from the pleading. Fed.R.Civil P. 12(f). *See also* Immaterial averment; Irrelevancy; Surplusage.

Implead. To sue; to prosecute. To bring a new party into action on ground that new party is, or may be, liable to party who brings him in, for all or part of the subject matter claim. Fed.R.Civil P. 14. *See* Third-party practice.

Impleader. Procedure by which party is impleaded. *See* Implead; Third-party practice; Vouching-in. *Compare* Interpleader; Joinder.

Implements /impləmənts/. Such things as are used or employed for a trade, or furniture of a house. Particularly applied to tools, utensils, instruments of labor; as the implements of trade or of farming.

Implication. Intendment or inference, as distinguished from the actual expression of a thing in words. In a will, an estate may pass by mere *implication*, without any express words to direct its course.

An inference of something not directly declared, but arising from what is admitted or expressed. Act of implying or condition of being implied.

"Implication" is also used in the sense of "inference"; *i.e.*, where the existence of an intention is inferred from acts not done for the sole purpose of communicating it, but for some other purpose. *See also* Inference.

Implied. This word is used in law in contrast to "express"; *i.e.*, where the intention in regard to the subject-matter is not manifested by explicit and direct words, but is gathered by implication or necessary deduction from the circumstances, the general language, or the conduct of the parties. Term differs from "inferred" to the extent that the hearer or reader "infers" while the writer or speaker "implies".

As to *implied* Abrogation; Agency; Agreement; Assumpsit; Condition; Confession; Consent; Consideration; Contract; Covenant; Dedication; Easement; Invitation; Malice; Notice; Obligation; Power; Trust; Use; Waiver; and Warranty, see those titles.

Implied assertions. Statements which, while not expressed, may be deduced from what is written or spoken.

Implied authority. In law of agency, power given by principal to agent which necessarily follows from the express authority given though such power is not expressly asserted. The power of an agent to act on behalf of his principal which is inferred from the responsibilities imposed on the agent or necessary to carry out an agent's express authority. Actual authority may be either express or implied, "implied authority" being that which is necessary, usual and proper to accomplish or perform the main authority expressly delegated to an agent.

Implied consent. *See* Consent.

Implied intent. Intent which necessarily arises from language used in an instrument or from conduct of parties.

Implied promise. Fiction which the law creates to render one liable on contract theory so as to avoid fraud or unjust enrichment. *See also* Equitable estoppel.

Implied reservation. Type of easement created by grantor for benefit of land retained by him and not included in conveyance.

Implied reservation of water doctrine. When Federal Government withdraws its land from public domain and reserves it for a federal purpose, the government, by implication, reserves appurtenant water then unappropriated to the extent needed to accomplish the purpose of the reservation. However, it reserves only that amount of water necessary to fulfill the purpose of the reservation, and no more.

Implied warranty. *See* Warranty.

Import. A product manufactured in a foreign country, and then shipped to and sold in this country. *See also* Importation.

Importation. The act of bringing goods and merchandise into a country from a foreign country. *See* Customs duties.

Importer. Person who brings (*i.e.*, imports) goods into country from foreign country and pays customs duties. *See* Customs duties.

Import-export clause. Provision in U.S. Constitution, Art. I, § 10, cl. 2, to the effect that no state shall, without the consent of Congress, lay imposts or duties on imports or exports, except what may be absolutely necessary for executing its inspection laws.

Import quota. A quantitative restriction on the importation of an article into the United States. 19 U.S.C.A. § 22.53(a)(3)(C). The establishment of a quota is one of the remedies available to the President upon his determination that an imported article threatens serious injury to a domestic industry. *See also* Dumping; Most favored nation clause.

Imports clause. *See* Import-export clause.

Importunity. Pressing solicitation; urgent request; application for a claim or favor which is urged with troublesome frequency or pertinacity.

Impose. To levy or exact as by authority; to lay as a burden, tax, duty or charge.

Imposition. An impost; tax; contribution. Unreasonable request or burden. Act of imposing.

Impossibility. That which, in the constitution and course of nature or the law, no person can do or perform.

Impossibility is of the following several sorts:

An act is *physically* impossible when it is contrary to the course of nature. Such an impossibility may be either *absolute, i.e.,* impossible in any case, (*e.g.,* to stop earth rotation) or *relative* (sometimes called "impossibility in fact"), *i.e.,* arising from the circumstances of the case (*e.g.,* for A. to make a payment to B., he being a deceased person). To the latter class belongs what is sometimes called "*practical* impossibility," which exists when the act *can* be done, but only at an excessive or unreasonable cost. An act is *legally* or juridically impossible when a rule of law makes it impossible to do it; *e.g.,* for A. to make a valid will before his majority. This class of acts must not be confounded with those which are possible, although forbidden by law, as to commit a theft. An act is *logically* impossible when it is contrary to the nature of the transaction, as where A. gives property to B. expressly for his own benefit, on condition that he transfers it to C. *See also* Legal impossibility.

Impossibility of performance of contract. A doctrine under which a party to a contract is relieved of his or her duty to perform when performance has become impossible or totally impracticable (through no fault of the party). As a defense to nonperformance, such arises when performance is not possible because of, for example, destruction of subject of contract or death of person necessary for performance or where act contracted for has become illegal. The doctrine of "impossibility of performance" is an exception to the general rule that the promisor must either perform, or pay damages for his failure to perform, no matter how burdensome his performance has become because of unforeseen circumstances. While the doctrine has evolved around various specific categories, one basic part of the doctrine is that the impossibility of performance must be objective rather than merely subjective.

It is now recognized that a thing is impossible in legal contemplation when it is not practicable; and a thing is impracticable when it can only be done at an excessive and unreasonable cost. When the issue is raised, the court is asked to construct a condition of performance based on changed circumstances, a process which involves at least three reasonably definable steps. First, a contingency—something unexpected—must have occurred. Second, the risk of the unexpected occurrence must not have been allocated either by agreement or by custom. Finally, occurrence of the contingency must have rendered performance commercially impracticable. Although impossibility or impracticability of performance may arise in many different ways, the tendency has been to classify the cases into several categories. These are: 1) Destruction, deterioration or unavailability of the subject matter or the tangible means of performance; 2) Failure of the contemplated mode of delivery or payment; 3) Supervening prohibition or prevention by law; 4) Failure of the intangible means of performance and 5) Death or illness. The basic U.C.C. sections dealing with impossibility of performance are §§ 2–613, 2–615, 2–616. *See* in this regard, Commercial frustration; Commercial impracticability; Frustration of contract; Impracticability.

Impossible contract. One which the law will not hold binding upon the parties, because of the natural or legal impossibility of the performance by one party of that which is the consideration for the promise of the other.

Imposter. One who pretends to be somebody other than who he is, with intent to deceive; a faker, charlatan; mountebank. One who poses as another to obtain benefits under a negotiable instrument. *See also* Impersonation; Personate.

Impostor rule. Refers to a UCC Article 3 provision, § 3–405(1)(a), that renders effective any person's indorsement of a check drawn payable to an impostor.

Imposts. Taxes, duties, or impositions levied for divers reasons. Generic term for taxes. *See* Customs duties; Duty; Excise tax.

Impotence. The inability to have sexual intercourse; it is not sterility. Properly used of the male. Impotency as a ground for divorce means want of *potentia copulandi* or incapacity to consummate the marriage, and not merely incapacity for procreation.

Impound. To shut up stray animals or distrained goods in a pound. To seize and take into the custody of the law or of a court. Thus, a court will sometimes *impound* a suspicious document produced at a trial or a vehicle, funds, records, or other items used in commission of a crime. The term, in its application to funds, means to take or retain in the custody of the law, and that obli-

gation, as is an escrow, is to hold and deliver property intact. *See also* Confiscate; Forfeiture; Seizure; Sequestered account.

Impound account. Accumulated funds (normally collected monthly from mortgagor or trustor) held by a lender for payment of taxes, insurance, or other periodic debts against real property. The lender pays the tax bill, premium, etc. from the accumulated funds when due. *See also* Escrow.

Impoundment. Action, or inaction, by President or other offices of U.S. Government, that precludes the obligation or expenditure of budget authority by Congress.

Impracticability. The term "impracticability" in federal rule (Fed.R.Civ.P. 23) providing for class action if class is so numerous that joinder of all members is impracticable does not mean "impossibility" but only the difficulty of inconvenience of joining all members of the class.

Commercial impracticability. A broadened interpretation of the doctrine of impossibility which holds that a party to a contract for the sale of goods will be relieved of his or her duty to perform when the premise (*e.g.*, existence of certain goods) on which the contract was based no longer exists due to unforeseeable events. See U.C.C. § 2–615. *See also* Commercial frustration; Commercial impracticability; Impossibility.

Impression, case of first. *See* First impression case.

Imprest fund. Petty cash fund used by business for small, routine expenses.

Imprest money. Money paid on enlisting or impressing soldiers or sailors.

Impretiabilis /əmprèshiyéybələs/. Lat. Beyond price; invaluable.

Imprimatur /ímprəméytər/. Lat. Let it be printed. A license or allowance, granted by the constituted authorities, giving permission to print and publish a book. This allowance was formerly necessary, in England, before any book could lawfully be printed, and in some other countries is still required.

Imprison. To put in a prison; to put in a place of confinement. To confine a person, or restrain his liberty, in any way.

Imprisonment. The detention of a person contrary to his will. The act of putting or confining a person in prison. The restraint of a person's personal liberty; coercion exercised upon a person to prevent the free exercise of his powers of locomotion. It is not a necessary part of the definition that the confinement should be in a place usually appropriated to that purpose; it may be in a locality used only for the specific occasion; or it may take place without the actual application of any physical agencies of restraint (such as locks or bars), as by verbal compulsion and the display of available force. Every confinement of the person is an "imprisonment," whether it be in a prison, or in a private house, or even by forcibly detaining one in the public streets. Any unlawful exercise or show of force by which person is compelled to remain where he does not wish to be. *See also* Solitary confinement.

False imprisonment. The unlawful arrest or detention of a person without warrant, or by an illegal warrant, or a warrant illegally executed, and either in a prison or a place used temporarily for that purpose, or by force and constraint without confinement. False imprisonment consists in the unlawful detention of the person of another, for any length of time, whereby he is deprived of his personal liberty. The unlawful detention of the occupant of an automobile may be accomplished by driving so rapidly that he cannot alight.

A person commits a misdemeanor if he knowingly restrains another unlawfully so as to interfere substantially with his liberty. Model Penal Code, § 212.3.

The tort of "false imprisonment" is the nonconsensual, intentional confinement of a person, without lawful privilege, for an appreciable length of time, however short. Restatement, Second, Torts § 35.

See also False arrest; False imprisonment.

Improbable. Unlikely to be true, or to occur, not to be readily believed.

Improper. Not suitable; unfit; not suited to the character, time, and place. Not in accordance with fact, truth, or right procedure and not in accord with propriety, modesty, good taste, or good manners.

Improve. To meliorate, make better, to increase the value or good qualities of, mend, repair, as to "improve" a street by grading, parking, curbing, paving, etc.

Improved land. Real estate whose value has been increased by landscaping and addition of sewers, roads, utilities, and the like.

Improved value. Appraisal term encompassing the total value of land and improvements rather than the separate values of each.

Improvement. A valuable addition made to property (usually real estate) or an amelioration in its condition, amounting to more than mere repairs or replacement, costing labor or capital, and intended to enhance its value, beauty or utility or to adapt it for new or further purposes. Generally has reference to buildings, but may also include any permanent structure or other development, such as a street, sidewalks, sewers, utilities, etc. An expenditure to extend the useful life of an asset or to improve its performance over that of the original asset. Such expenditures are capitalized as part of the asset's cost. *Contrast* with Maintenance *and* Repair. *See also* Betterment; Internal improvements; Leasehold improvements.

In the law of patents, an addition to, or modification of, a previous invention or discovery, intended or claimed to increase its utility or value. It includes two necessary ideas: the idea of a complete and practical operative art or instrument and the idea of some change in such art or instrument not affecting its essential character but enabling it to produce its appropriate results in a more perfect or economical manner.

Improvement bonds. *See* Bond.

Improvidence. As used in a statute excluding one found incompetent to execute the duties of an administrator by reason of improvidence, means that want of care and foresight in the management of property which would be likely to render the estate and effects of the intestate unsafe, and liable to be lost or diminished in value, in case the administration should be committed to the improvident person.

Improvidently. A judgment, decree, rule, injunction, etc., when given or rendered without adequate consideration by the court, or without proper information as to all the circumstances affecting it, or based upon a mistaken assumption or misleading information or advice, is sometimes said to have been "improvidently" given or issued.

Impulse. Sudden urge or inclination; thrusting or impelling force within a person. *See also* Insanity; Irresistible impulse.

Impunity. Exemption or protection from penalty or punishment. *See also* Immunity.

Imputability. The state or condition rendering one chargeable for an act. Liability or responsibility for conduct or omission. *See* Liability.

Imputed. As used in legal phrases, this word means attributed vicariously; that is, an act, fact, or quality is said to be "imputed" to a person when it is ascribed or charged to him, not because he is personally cognizant of it or responsible for it, but because another person is, over whom he has control or for whose acts or knowledge he is responsible. *See also* Estoppel.

Imputed cost. *See* Cost.

Imputed income. *See* Income.

Imputed interest. *See* Interest.

Imputed knowledge. This phrase is sometimes used as equivalent to "implied notice," *i.e.*, knowledge attributed or charged to a person because the facts in question were open to his discovery and it was his duty to inform himself as to them. In law of agency, notice of facts brought to the attention of an agent within the scope of his authority or employment is chargeable to his principal in most cases. *See* Imputed notice.

Imputed negligence. The negligence of one person may be chargeable to another depending upon the relationship of the parties, as for example, the negligence of an agent acting within the scope of his employment is chargeable to the principal. Negligence which is not directly attributable to the person himself, but which is the negligence of a person who is in privity with him, and with whose fault he is chargeable. *See also* Negligence.

Imputed notice. Information as to a given fact or circumstance charged or attributed to a person, and affecting his rights or conduct on the ground that actual notice was given to some person whose duty was to report it to the person to be affected, as, his agent or his attorney of record. *See also* Notice.

In. In the law of real estate, this preposition is used to denote the fact of seisin, title, or possession, and serves as an elliptical expression for some such phrase as "in possession," or as an abbreviation for "*in*titled" or "*in*vested with title."

An elastic preposition in other cases, expressing relation of presence, existence, situation, inclusion, action, etc.; inclosed or surrounded by limits, as in a room; also meaning for, in and about, on, within etc.; and is synonymous with expressions "in regard to", "respecting", "with respect to", and "as is".

In action. Attainable or recoverable by action; not in possession. A term applied to property of which a party has not the possession, but only a right to recover it by action. Things in action are rights of personal things, which nevertheless are not in possession. *See* Chose in action.

Inadequate. Insufficient; disproportionate; lacking in effectiveness or in conformity to a prescribed standard or measure.

Inadequate consideration. One not adequate or equal in value to the thing conveyed.

Inadequate damages. *See* Damages.

Inadequate price. A term applied to indicate the want of a sufficient consideration for a thing sold, or such a price as would ordinarily be entirely incommensurate with its intrinsic value.

Inadequate remedy at law. Within the meaning of the rule that equity will not entertain a suit if there is an adequate remedy at law, this does not mean that there must be a failure to collect money or damages at law, but the remedy is considered inadequate if it is, in its nature and character, unfitted or not adapted to the end in view, as, for instance, when the relief sought is preventive (*e.g.* injunction) rather than compensatory. *Compare* Adequate remedy at law.

Inadmissible. That which, under the established rules of law, cannot be admitted or received; *e.g.,* parol evidence to contradict a written contract; evidence obtained from illegal search and seizure; certain types of hearsay evidence.

Inadvertence. Heedlessness; lack of attention; want of care; carelessness; failure of a person to pay careful and prudent attention to the progress of a negotiation or a proceeding in court by which his rights may be affected. Used chiefly in statutory and rule enumerations of the grounds on which a judgment or decree may be vacated or set aside; as, "mistake, inadvertence, surprise, or excusable neglect." Fed.R. Civil P. 60(b).

Inalienable /inéyl(i)yənəbəl/. Not subject to alienation; the characteristic of those things which cannot be bought or sold or transferred from one person to another, such as rivers and public highways, and certain personal rights; *e.g.,* liberty.

Inalienable interests. Type of interest in property which cannot be sold or traded.

Inalienable rights. Rights which are not capable of being surrendered or transferred without the consent of the one possessing such rights; *e.g.,* freedom of speech or religion, due process, and equal protection of the laws. *See* Bill of rights.

Inauguration. The act of installing or inducting into office with formal ceremonies, as the coronation of a sovereign, the inauguration of a president or governor, or the consecration of a prelate. A word applied by the Romans to the ceremony of dedicating a temple, or raising a man to the priesthood, after the *augurs* had been consulted.

In banc. *See* En banc.

In being. In existence or life at a given moment of time, as, in the phrase "life or lives in being" in the rule against perpetuities. An unborn child may, in some circumstances be considered as "in being."

In blank. A term applied to the indorsement of a bill or note where it consists merely of the indorser's name, without restriction to any particular indorsee. U.C.C. § 3–204(2).

Inboard. In maritime law, and particularly with reference to the stowage of cargo, this term is contrasted with "outboard." It does not necessarily mean under deck, but is applied to a cargo so piled or stowed that it does not project over the "board" (side or rail) of the vessel.

In bulk. As a whole; as an entirety, without division into items or physical separation in packages or parcels. *See also* Bulk.

Inc. Incorporated.

In cahoots /in kəhúwts/. Jointly interested in property; or, common participants in enterprise or illegal act.

In camera /in kǽm(ə)rə/. In chambers; in private. A judicial proceeding is said to be heard *in camera* either when the hearing is had before the judge in his private chambers or when all spectators are excluded from the courtroom. *See also* In chambers.

In camera inspection. Under certain circumstances, a trial judge may inspect a document which counsel wishes to use at trial in his chambers before ruling on its admissibility or its use; *e.g.* grand jury testimony. See, *e.g.*, Fed.R.Crim. P. 14.

In camera proceedings. Trial or hearing held in a place not open to the public such as the judge's lobby or chambers.

Incapacitated person. Any person who is impaired by reason of mental illness, mental deficiency, physical illness or disability, advanced age, chronic use of drugs, chronic intoxication, or other cause (except minority) to the extent that he lacks sufficient understanding or capacity to make or communicate responsible decisions concerning his person. Uniform Probate Code, § 5–101. *See also* Incapacity.

Incapacity. Want of legal, physical, or intellectual capacity; want of power or ability to take or dispose; want of legal ability to act. Inefficiency; incompetency; lack of adequate power. The quality or state of being incapable, want of capacity, lack of physical or intellectual power, or of natural or legal qualification; inability, incapability, disability, incompetence. *See also* Incompetency; Partial incapacity.

Legal incapacity. This expression implies that the person in view has the right vested in him, but is prevented by some impediment from exercising it; as in the case of minors, committed persons, prisoners, etc. *See* Civil death; Minority.

Total incapacity. In workers' compensation acts, such disqualification from performing the usual tasks of a worker that he or she cannot procure and retain employment. Incapacity for work is total not only so long as the injured employee is unable to do any work of any character, but also while he remains unable, as a result of his injury, either to resume his former occupation or to procure remunerative employment at a different occupation suitable to his impaired capacity. Such period of total incapacity may be followed by a period of partial incapacity, during which the injured employee is able both to procure and to perform work at some occupation suitable to his then-existing capacity, but less remunerative than the work in which he was engaged at the time of his injury. That situation constitutes "partial

incapacity." Synonymous with "total disability." *See* Disability.

In capita /in kǽpətə/. To the heads; by heads or polls. Persons succeed to an inheritance *in capita* when they individually take equal shares. So challenges to individual jurors are challenges *in capita,* as distinguished from challenges to the array. *See also* Challenge; Per capita.

Incarceration /inkàrsəréyshən/. Imprisonment; confinement in a jail or penitentiary. *See* Imprisonment.

In case. If; in the event.

Incendiary /insénd(i)yəriy/. A house-burner; one guilty of arson (an arsonist); one who maliciously and willfully sets another person's building on fire.

Incentive pay plans. Compensation programs whereby wages increase as productivity increases above a set standard or base.

Incentive stock option. An option granted to an employee of a corporation to purchase stock of such corporation at a specified price for a specified period of time. Generally, there are no tax consequences until such time as the stock is sold.

Inception. Commencement; opening; initiation. The beginning of the operation of a contract or will, or of a note, mortgage, lien, etc.; the beginning of a cause or suit in court.

Incest. The crime of sexual intercourse or cohabitation between a man and woman who are related to each other within the degrees wherein marriage is prohibited by law.

A person is guilty of incest, a felony of the third degree, if he knowingly marries or cohabits or has sexual intercourse with an ancestor or descendant, a brother or sister of the whole or half blood [or an uncle, aunt, nephew or niece of the whole blood]. "Cohabit" means to live together under the representation or appearance of being married. The relationships referred to herein includes blood relationships without regard to legitimacy, and relationship of parent and child by adoption. Model Penal Code, § 230.2.

Incestuous adultery. The elements of this offense are that defendant, being married to one person, has had sexual intercourse with another related to the defendant within the prohibited degrees.

In chambers. While a common meaning of word "chambers" is room adjacent to courtroom in which judge performs the duties of his office when court is not in session, it also connotes fact that judicial action was taken when court was not in session. Thus, when judge performs judicial act while court is not in session in the matter acted upon, it is said that he acted "in chambers" whether the act was performed in the judge's chambers, the library, at his home, or elsewhere. *See also* In camera.

In charge of. Means in the care or custody of, under control of, or intrusted to the management or direction of. *See* Guardian; Ward.

In chief. Principal; primary; directly obtained. A term applied to the evidence obtained from a witness upon his examination in court by the party producing him; *i.e.* direct examination of witness. *See* Case in chief.

Tenure in chief, or *in capite,* is a holding directly of the king or chief lord.

Inchmaree clause. In marine insurance, provision in policy protecting one from perils resulting from negligence of master, or from any latent defect in machinery or hull, charterer, mariners, engineers and pilots.

Inchoate /inkówət/. Imperfect; partial; unfinished; begun, but not completed; as a contract not executed by all the parties.

Inchoate crimes. An incipient crime which generally leads to another crime. An assault has been referred to as an inchoate battery, though the assault is a crime in and of itself. The Model Penal Code classifies attempts, solicitation and conspiracy as such. §§ 5.01–5.03.

Inchoate dower. A wife's interest in the lands of her husband during his life, which may become a right of dower upon his death. A contingent claim or possibility of acquiring dower by outliving husband and arises, not out of contract, but as an institution of law constituting a mere chose in action incapable of transfer by separate grant but susceptible of extinguishment, which is effected by wife joining with husband in deed, which operates as release or satisfaction of interest and not as conveyance.

Inchoate instrument. Instruments which the law requires to be registered or recorded are said to be "inchoate" prior to registration, in that they are then good only between the parties and privies and as to persons having notice.

Inchoate interest. An interest in real estate which is not a present interest, but which may ripen into a vested estate, if not barred, extinguished, or divested.

Inchoate lien. The lien of a judgment, from the day of its entry, subject to be defeated by its vacation, becoming a consummate lien if the motion for a new trial is thereafter overruled; such lien then relating back to the original entry of the judgment.

Inchoate right. In patent law, the right of an inventor to his invention while his application is pending which matures as "property" when the patent issues.

Incident. Something dependent upon, appertaining or subordinate to, or accompanying something else of greater or principal importance, something arising or resulting from something else of greater or principal importance. Used both substantively and adjectively of a thing which, either usually or naturally and inseparably, depends upon, appertains to, or follows another that is more worthy. Used as a noun, it denotes anything which inseparably belongs to, or is connected with, or inherent in, another thing, called the "principal". Also, less strictly, it denotes anything which is usually connected with another, or connected for some purposes, though not inseparably. Thus, the right of alienation is incident to an estate in fee-simple, though separable in equity.

Incident of ownership. An element of ownership or degree of control over a life insurance policy. The retention by an insured of an incident of ownership in a life insurance policy will cause the policy proceeds to be included in the insured's gross estate upon death. I.R.C. § 2042(2).

In estate taxation, if decedent retains control or right in property, as for example the right to change beneficiary of insurance policy, the property falls into his gross estate for estate tax purposes.

Incidental. Depending upon or appertaining to something else as primary; something necessary, appertaining to, or depending upon another which is termed the principal; something incidental to the main purpose.

Incidental beneficiary. Person who may derive benefit from performance of contract, though he is neither the promisee nor the one to whom performance is to be rendered. A person who is a donee or creditor (third party) beneficiary of a contract is entitled, in certain circumstances, to enforce such contract. Since there will often be many people indirectly or even directly benefitted by any given contractual performance, the term "incidental beneficiary" is used to describe those persons who would benefit by the performance but who were not intended by the parties to be benefitted and who thus cannot enforce the contract.

A person is not a beneficiary of a trust if the settlor does not manifest an intention to give him a beneficial interest, although he may incidentally benefit from the performance of the trust. Restatement, Second, Trusts, § 126.

Incidental damages. *See* Damages.

Incidental powers. This term, within the rule that a corporation possesses only those powers which its charter confers upon it, either expressly or as incidental to its existence, means such powers as are directly and immediately appropriate to the execution of the powers expressly granted and exist only to enable the corporation to carry out the purpose of its creation. *Compare* Inherent powers.

Incident to arrest. A search can be "incident to arrest" only if it is substantially contemporaneous with the arrest and is confined to the immediate vicinity of the arrest. *See also* Search incident to arrest.

Incidental to employment. *See* Risk incident to employment.

Incidental use. In zoning, use of premises which is dependent on or affiliated with the principal use of such premises.

Incite /insáyt/. To arouse; urge; provoke; encourage; spur on; goad; stir up; instigate; set in motion; as, to "incite" a riot. Also, generally, in criminal law to instigate, persuade, or move another to commit a crime; in this sense nearly synonymous with "abet."

Inciter. In criminal law, an aider or abettor; an accessory.

Inclose. To surround; to encompass; to bound; fence, or hem in, on all sides. To shut up.

Inclosure. In old English law, act of freeing land from rights of common, commonable rights, and generally all rights which obstruct cultivation and the productive employment of labor on the soil.

Land surrounded by some visible obstruction. An artificial fence around one's estate. *See* Close.

Include. (Lat. *Inclaudere,* to shut in, keep within.) To confine within, hold as in an inclosure, take in, attain, shut up, contain, inclose, comprise, comprehend, embrace, involve. Term may, according to context, express an enlargement and have the meaning of *and* or *in addition to,* or merely specify a particular thing already included within general words theretofore used. "Including" within statute is interpreted as a word of enlargement or of illustrative application as well as a word of limitation.

Included offense. In criminal law, a crime which is part of another crime; *e.g.* included in every murder is assault and battery. One which is established by proof of the same or less than all of the facts, or a less culpable mental state, or both, than that which is required to establish commission of offense charged. To be an "included offense", all elements of the lesser offense must be contained in the greater offense, the greater containing certain elements not contained in the lesser. It is impossible to commit a greater offense without necessarily committing included offense. The defendant may be found guilty of an offense necessarily included in the offense charged. Fed.R.Crim. P. 31.

Includible gain. I.R.C. § 644 imposes a built-in gains tax on trusts that sell or exchange property at a gain within two years after the date of its transfer in trust by the transferor.

Inclusionary approach. Under the "inclusionary approach", evidence of prior crimes, wrongs, or acts is admissible for any purpose other than to show defendant's criminal propensity, as long as it is relevant to some disputed issue in trial, and satisfies probative-prejudice balancing test.

Inclusive. Embraced; comprehended; comprehending the stated limits or extremes. Opposed to "exclusive."

Inclusive survey. In land law, one which includes within its boundaries prior claims excepted from the computation of the area within such boundaries and excepted in the grant.

Incognito. Status of person who appears or travels without disclosing his true identity.

Income. The return in money from one's business, labor, or capital invested; gains, profits, salary, wages, etc.

The gain derived from capital, from labor or effort, or both combined, including profit or gain through sale or conversion of capital. Income is not a gain accruing to capital or a growth in the value of the investment, but is a gain, a profit, something of exchangeable value, proceeding from the property, severed from the capital, however invested or employed, and coming in, being derived, that is, received or drawn by the recipient for his separate use, benefit, and disposal. The true increase in amount of wealth which comes to a person during a stated period of time. That which comes in or is received from any business, or investment of capital, without references to outgoing expenditures.

See also Allocation of income; Blocked income; Clear reflection of income; Constructive receipt of income; Deferred income; Earned income; Earnings; Fixed income; Gross income; Income averaging; Income basis; Income in respect of decedent; Income tax; Net income; Net operating income; Personal income; Profit; Real income; Split income; Taxable income and *Unearned income, below.*

Accrued income. Income earned during a certain accounting period but not received.

Adjusted gross income. The difference between the taxpayers' gross income and allowable adjustments. Adjustments include but are not limited to; contributions to an individual retirement account, alimony payments and reimbursed employee business expenses. I.R.C. § 162.

Deferred income. Income received before it is earned, such as rents received in one accounting period for use of the premises in the following period.

Earned income. Income derived from one's own labor or through active participation in a business as distinguished from income from, for example, dividends or investments. *See also* Earnings.

Fixed income. That type of income which is stable over a considerable period of time such as a pension or annuity.

Gross income. The total income of a business or individual before deductions; including salary, commissions, royalties, gains from dealings in property, interest, dividends, etc. I.R.C. § 61.

Imputed income. Value assigned to property or income, sometimes artificially for tax purposes, as in the case of a non-interest bearing or low interest bearing loan between persons or organizations related to each other. I.R.C. § 483. The value of property enjoyed by the taxpayer as part of his salary; *e.g.* use of home provided by employer to employee.

The monetary value of goods and services which someone produces and is consumed within the immediate family unit as well as the monetary value of the use of property which someone within the family unit owns. Imputed income is not included in gross income.

Investment income. See Unearned income, below.

Net (business) income. The profit of a business arrived at by deducting operating expenses and taxes from gross receipts. Income after costs and taxes.

Nonoperating income. Income of a business from investments and not from operations.

Operating income. Income derived from operations of business in contrast to income from investments.

Ordinary income. See Ordinary.

Personal income. In taxation, the total of income received by individuals from all sources.

Unearned income. Income derived from investments, such as dividends and interest, as distinguished from income derived from personal labor.

Income received but not yet earned. Normally, such income is taxed when received, even for accrual basis taxpayers.

Income averaging. Method of computing tax by averaging an individual's current income with that of the three preceding years. Income averaging was common with individuals such as athletes, or actors whose income may be very high in a given year in contrast to prior years. The tax benefits of income averaging were repealed with the Tax Reform Act of 1986.

Income basis. Method of computing the rate of return on a security based on the dividend or interest and on the price paid rather than on its face or par value.

Income beneficiary. The party entitled to income from property. A typical example would be a trust where A is to receive the income for life with corpus or principal passing to B upon A's death. In this case, A would be the income beneficiary of the trust.

Income bond. *See* Bond.

Income exclusions. Items of income which are not subject to federal taxes. An example of such includes interest earned on municipal bonds, as well as money or property received by gift or inheritance.

Income in respect of decedent. Income earned by a decedent at the time of death but not reportable on the final income tax return because of the method of accounting utilized. Typically it includes any accrued income to date of death for cash basis decedent/taxpayer. Such income is included in the gross estate and will be taxed to the eventual recipient (*i.e.*, either the estate or heirs). The recipient will, however, be allowed an income tax deduction for the death tax attributable to the income. I.R.C. § 691.

In estate taxation, term refers to inclusion of certain income in estate as if it had been collected by decedent in his or her lifetime; *e.g.* payments received toward satisfaction of a right or expectancy created almost entirely through the efforts or status of the decedent and which, except for his death and without further action on his part, the decedent would have realized as gross income.

Income property. Property which produces income; *e.g.* rental property. Such property can be either residential, commercial, or industrial.

Income security. Government programs to maintain the income of people, including Social Security, government pensions, unemployment compensation, welfare, food stamps, disability benefits, subsidized housing, and energy assistance. Medicare and Medicaid are categorized as health programs.

Income shifting. An attempt by a taxpayer to transfer income to a taxpayer who is subject to a lower tax rate, such as to one or several family members in an effort to reduce the transferors' tax liability. The Tax Reform Act of 1986 has reduced the benefits of income shifting by such regulations as taxing children under the age of 14 on unearned income (interest and dividends) at the parents' highest rate. *See* Kiddie tax.

Income splitting. *See* Joint tax return.

Income statement. The statement of revenues, expenses, gains, and losses for the period ending with net income (or loss) for the period. A financial statement that indicates how a firm performed during a period of time. *See also* Balance *(Balance sheet);* Earnings report; Profit and loss statement.

Income tax. A tax on the annual profits arising from property, business pursuits, professions, trades, or offices. A tax on a person's income, wages, salary, commissions, emoluments, profits, and the like, or the excess thereof over a certain amount. Tax levied by the U.S. Government, and by some state governments, on an individual, corporation, or other taxable unit's income. *See also* Tax.

Income tax deficiency. Such exists whenever taxpayer has failed to pay sufficient taxes on income, notwithstanding lack of determination by commissioner or his agents. 26 U.S.C.A. § 6211 et seq. *See* Deficiency notice; Ninety (90) day letter.

Income tax return. Forms required by federal and state taxing authority to be completed by taxpayer, disclosing all items necessary for computation of tax and the computation itself. *See also* Return.

Income tax withholdings. The portion of an employee's gross earnings withheld by the employer to satisfy federal (and sometimes state and local) income tax laws.

In commerce. The words "in commerce" normally mean in interstate commerce. *See* In commerce test; Interstate commerce.

In commerce test. Jurisdiction under the Sherman Act is conferred if the acts complained of occur in the flow of commerce or if those acts, though local in nature, substantially affect interstate commerce. With the "in commerce test," the impact on interstate commerce is judged according to a qualitative standard, even insubstantial activity placed directly in the flow of commerce satisfies the jurisdictional requirements.

In common. Shared in respect to title, use, or enjoyment; without apportionment or division into individual parts. Held by several for the equal advantage, use, or enjoyment of all. *See* Condominium.

Incommunicado. A person accused of a crime who does not have the right of communicating with other than the ones in charge of his custody or the one investigating the crime.

Incommutable. Not capable of or entitled to be commuted. *See* Commutation.

Incompatibility. Incapability of existing or being exercised together. As ground for divorce, refers to such deep and irreconcilable conflict in personalities or temperments of parties as makes it impossible for them to continue normal marital relationship. Such conflict of personalities and dispositions must be so deep as to be irreconcilable and irremediable. Such condition is a ground for divorce in states with no-fault divorce statutes. *See* Irretrievable breakdown of marriage.

Incompetency. Lack of ability, knowledge, legal qualification, or fitness to discharge the required duty or professional obligation. A relative term which may be employed as meaning disqualification, inability or incapacity and it can refer to lack of legal qualifications or fitness to discharge the required duty and to show want of physical or intellectual or moral fitness. *See also* Guardian; Incapacity; Insanity; Non compos mentis. *Compare* Competency.

Incompetent evidence. Evidence which is not admissible under the established rules of evidence; *e.g.* Fed.Rules of Evidence. Evidence which the law does not permit to be presented at all, or in relation to the particular matter, on account of lack of originality or of some defect in the witness, the document, or the nature of the evidence itself. *See e.g.* Hearsay. *See also* Inadmissible.

Incomplete transfer. A transfer made by a decedent during lifetime which, because of certain control or enjoyment retained by the transferor, will not be considered complete for Federal death tax purposes. Thus, some or all of the fair market value of the property transferred will be included in the transferor's gross estate. I.R.C. §§ 2036–2038. *See also* Revocable transfer.

Inconclusive. That which may be disproved or rebutted; not shutting out further proof or consideration. Applied to evidence and presumptions. *See* Presumption.

In conjunction with /in kənjə́ŋkshən wíθ/. In association with.

Inconsistent. Mutually repugnant or contradictory. Contrary, the one to the other, so that both cannot stand, but the acceptance or establishment of the one implies the abrogation or abandonment of the other; as, in speaking of "inconsistent defenses," or the repeal by a statute of "all laws inconsistent herewith."

Inconsistent statement. *See* Prior inconsistent statements.

In contemplation of death. In taxation and property law, a transaction, commonly a transfer or gift of property, made by the donor with a view towards his death. For federal estate tax purposes, a transfer made within three years of the decedent's death is deemed to be made in contemplation of death and the value of the property is included in his or her estate for such tax purposes. I.R.C. § 2035(b). *See also* Contemplation of death.

Incontestability clause. A clause in a life or health insurance policy providing that after the policy has been in force for a given length of time (*e.g.* two or three years) the insurer shall not be able to contest it as to statements contained in the application; and, in the case of health insurance, the provision also states that no claim shall be denied or reduced on the grounds that a condition not excluded by name at the time of issue existed prior to the effective date.

Inconvenience. In the rule that statutes should be so construed as to avoid "inconvenience," this means, as applied to the public, the sacrifice or jeopardizing of important public interests or hampering the legitimate activities of government or the transaction of public business, and, as applied to individuals, serious hardship or injustice.

Incorporate. To create a corporation; to confer a corporate franchise upon determinate persons. *See* Incorporation.

To declare that another document shall be taken as part of the document in which the declaration is made as much as if it were set out at length therein. *See* Incorporation by reference.

Incorporation. The act or process of forming or creating a corporation. The formation of a legal or political body, with the quality of perpetual existence and succession, unless limited by the act of incorporation. Incorporation procedure and requisites are governed by state statutes; a number of which are patterned on the Model Business Corporation Act. *See also* Incorporator.

In the civil law, the union of one domain to another.

See also Articles of incorporation; Certificate of incorporation.

Incorporation by reference. The method of making one document of any kind become a part of another separate document by referring to the former in the latter, and declaring that the former shall be taken and considered as a part of the latter the same as if it were fully set out therein. If the one document is copied at length in the other, it is called "actual incorporation."

Incorporator. Person who joins with others to form a corporation and the successors of those who actually sign the papers of incorporation. The person or persons who execute the articles of incorporation. In modern corporation statutes only a single incorporator is required. Under such statutes the role of the incorporator is largely limited to the act of execution of the articles of incorporation, and restrictions on who may serve as incorporators have largely been eliminated. See, *e.g.*, Rev. Model Bus. Corp. Act, § 2.01.

Incorporeal /ìnkərpóriyəl/. Without body; not of material nature; the opposite of "corporeal" *(q.v.)*.

Incorporeal chattels. A class of incorporeal rights growing out of or incident to things *personal;* such as patent-rights and copyrights.

Incorporeal hereditaments. *See* Hereditaments.

Incorporeal property. In the civil law, that which consists in legal right merely. The same as choses in action at common law.

Incorporeal rights. Rights to intangibles, such as legal actions, rather than rights to property (rights to possession or use of land).

Incorporeal things. Things that have no body, but are comprehended by the understanding, such as rights of inheritance, servitudes, obligations, and right of intellectual property.

Incorrigible /inkórəjəbəl/. Incapable of being corrected, reformed, amended, or improved. With respect to juvenile offenders, unmanageable by parents or guardians. *See* Delinquent child; Disobedient child.

Incorruptible /ìnkərə́ptəbəl/. That which cannot be affected by immoral or debasing influences, such as bribery or the hope of gain or advancement.

Increase. Enlargement, growth, development, increment, addition, accession, extension, production, profit, interest, issue. The produce of land; the offspring of animals.

Increment /íŋkrəmənt/. An increasing in quantity, number, value, etc. That which is gained or added; the act or process of increasing, augmenting, or growing; enlargement, that which is added; increase; opposed to decrement.

Incremental cash flow. Net increase in the firm's cash flow attributable to a particular capital investment project after allowing for any negative impact the project may have on existing product sales or corporate expenses. The difference between free cash flow with the project and free cash flow without it.

Incremental cost. Additional or increased costs. The additional cost of producing or selling a contemplated quantity of output. For example, as applied to cost of gas, includes cost of gas to distributors plus transportation costs and taxes.

Incremental revenue. In accounting, the additional revenue resulting from a contemplated sale.

Incriminate /inkrímeneyt/. To charge with crime; to expose to an accusation or charge of crime; to involve oneself or another in a criminal prosecution or the danger thereof; as, in the rule that a witness is not bound to give testimony which would tend to incriminate him. *See* Inculpatory; Self-incrimination.

Incriminating admission. An acknowledgment of facts tending to establish guilt.

Incriminating circumstance. A fact or circumstance, collateral to the fact of the commission of a crime, which tends to show either that such a crime has been committed or that some particular person committed it.

Incriminating evidence. Evidence which tends to establish guilt of the accused or from which, with other evidence, his or her guilt may be inferred. *See also* Inculpatory. *Compare* Exculpatory statement or evidence.

Incrimination. *See* Incriminate; Self-incrimination.

Incriminating statement. A statement which tends to establish guilt of the accused or from which, with other facts, his guilt may be inferred, or which tends to disprove some defense. *See* Self-incrimination.

Incroachment /inkrówchmənt/. An unlawful gaining upon the right or possession of another. *See* Encroachment; Trespass.

Inculpate /inkəlpeyt/inkəlpeyt/. To impute blame or guilt; to accuse; to involve in guilt or crime. *See* Incriminate.

Inculpatory /inkəlpət(ò)riy/. In the law of evidence, going or tending to establish guilt; that which tends to incriminate. While a "confession" admits commission of a crime, an "inculpatory statement" admits a fact, circumstance or involvement which tends to establish guilt or from which guilt may be inferred. *See also* Incriminate; Incriminating evidence. *Compare* Exculpatory statement or evidence.

Incumbent /inkə́mbənt/. A person who is in present possession of an office, and it is not limited, qualified or restricted by the method by which one attained office. One who is legally authorized to discharge the duties of an office.

Incumber. *See* Encumbrance.

Incumbrance. *See* Encumbrance.

Incumbrances, covenant against. *See* Covenant.

Incur. To have liabilities cast upon one by act or operation of law, as distinguished from contract, where the party acts affirmatively. To become liable or subject to, to bring down upon oneself, as to incur debt, danger, displeasure and penalty, and to become through one's own action liable or subject to.

Incurred risk. A defense to a claim of negligence, separate and distinct from defense of contributory negligence. It contemplates acceptance of a specific risk of which the plaintiff has actual knowledge. *See also* Assumption of risk.

In custodia legis /in kəstówd(i)yə líyjəs/. In the custody or keeping of the law, as when a defendant's property is seized through the remedy of attachment and is held by the sheriff pending resolution of the main action between the parties.

In custody. A suspect is "in custody" for purpose of determining necessity of *Miranda* warnings if police, by word or by conduct, have manifested to suspect that he is not free to leave. Such custody exists when the suspect has been deprived of his freedom in a significant way, and the place where the interrogation takes place does not conclusively establish presence or absence of custody. *See also* Miranda Rule.

Indebtedness. The state of being in debt, without regard to the ability or inability of the party to pay the same. The owing of a sum of money upon a certain and express agreement. Obligations yet to become due constitute indebtedness, as well as those already due. And in a broad sense and in common understanding the word may mean anything that is due and owing. *See also* Debt.

Indecent. Offensive to common propriety; offending against modesty or delicacy; grossly vulgar; obscene; lewd; unseemly; unbecoming; indecorous; unfit to be seen or heard. *See* Obscene.

Indecent assault. The act of a male person taking indecent liberties with the person of a female, without her consent and against her will, but with no intent to commit the crime of rape.

Indecent exhibition. Any exhibition *contra bonos mores,* as the taking a dead body for the purpose of dissection or public exhibition.

Indecent exposure. Exposure to sight of the private parts of the body in a lewd or indecent manner in a public place. It is an indictable offense at common law, and by statute in most states. Term refers to exhibition of those private parts which instinctive modesty, human decency or self-respect require shall be kept covered in presence of others. Exposure of person becomes indecent when it occurs at such time and place where reasonable person knows or should know his act will be open to observation of others.

A person commits a misdemeanor if, for the purpose of arousing or gratifying sexual desire of himself or of any person other than his spouse, he exposes his genitals under circumstances in which he knows his conduct is likely to cause affront or alarm. Model Penal Code, § 213.5.

Indecent liberties. In the statutory offense of "taking indecent liberties with the person of a female child," this phrase means such liberties as the common sense of society would regard as indecent and improper. According to some authorities, it involves an assault or attempt at sexual intercourse, but according to others, it is not necessary that the liberties or familiarities should have related to the private parts of the child. *See* Obscene.

Indecent publications. Such as are offensive to modesty and delicacy; obscene; lewd; tending to the corruption of morals. *See* Obscene.

Public indecency. This phrase has no fixed legal meaning, is vague and indefinite, and cannot, in itself, imply a definite offense. The courts, by a kind of judicial legislation, in England and the United States, have usually limited the operation of the term to public displays of the naked person, the publication, sale, or exhibition of obscene books and prints, or the exhibition of a monster,—acts which have a direct bearing on public morals, and affect the body of society. *See* Obscene; also, *Indecent exposure, above.*

Indefeasible /ìndəfíyzəbəl/. That which cannot be defeated, revoked, or made void. This term is usually applied to an estate or right which cannot be defeated.

Indefinite. Without fixed boundaries or distinguishing characteristics; not definite, determinate, or precise. Term is more synonymous with temporary than with permanent; indefinite contemplates that condition will end at unpredictable time, whereas "permanent" does not contemplate that condition will cease to exist.

Indefinite failure of issue. A failure of issue not merely at the death of the party whose issue are referred to, but at any subsequent period, however remote. A failure of issue whenever it shall happen, sooner or later, without any fixed, certain, or definite period within which it must happen.

Indefinite legacy. *See* Legacy.

Indefinite number. A number which may be increased or diminished at pleasure.

In delicto /ìn dəlíktow/. In fault. *See* In pari delicto.

Indemnification. In corporate law, the practice by which corporations pay expenses of officers or directors who are named as defendants in litigation relating to corporate affairs. In some instances corporations may indemnify officers and directors for fines, judgments, or amounts paid in settlement as well as expenses. *See also* Indemnify; Indemnity; Insurance *(Directors' and officers' (D&0) liability insurance).*

Indemnify /indémnəfày/. To restore the victim of a loss, in whole or in part, by payment, repair, or replacement. To save harmless; to secure against loss or damage; to give security for the reimbursement of a person in case of an anticipated loss falling upon him. To make good; to compensate; to make reimbursement to one of a loss already incurred by him. Several states by statute have provided special funds for compensating crime victims. *See also* Contribution; Hold harmless agreement; Indemnity; Reparation; Restitution; Subrogation.

Indemnity /indémnədiy/. Reimbursement. An undertaking whereby one agrees to indemnify another upon the occurrence of an anticipated loss. A contractual or equitable right under which the entire loss is shifted from a tortfeasor who is only technically or passively at fault to another who is primarily or actively responsible. *Compare* Contribution; Subrogation. *See also* Double indemnity; Exoneration; Indemnify.

The benefit payable under an insurance policy.

The term is also used to denote the compensation given to make a person whole from a loss already sustained; as where the government gives indemnity for private property taken by it for public use. *See* Condemnation; Eminent domain; Expropriation; Just compensation.

Indemnity against liability. As contrasted with indemnity against loss, which is an obligee's right to compensation for a loss already sustained, it is an obligee's right to indemnification at the time a liability arises. The claim arises upon the obligor's default, regardless of whether the obligee has suffered loss. *See also* Subrogation.

Indemnity bond. An undertaking given by an obligor to reimburse an obligee for any loss suffered due to the conduct of the obligor or a third person.

Indemnity insurance. *See* Insurance.

Indemnity policy. *See Indemnity insurance* and *Liability insurance* under Insurance.

Indent, n. A certificate or indented certificate issued by the government of the United States at the close of the Revolution for the principal or interest of the public debt.

Indenture /indéntyər/. In business financing, a written agreement under which bonds and debentures are issued, setting forth form of bond, maturity date, amount of issue, description of pledged assets, interest rate, and other terms. Typically, the contract is entered into between the corporation and an indenture trustee whose responsibility is to protect the bondholders. The indenture often constitutes a mortgage on specified corporate property to secure the bonds. *See* Debenture; Trust indenture; Trust Indenture Act.

In real estate conveyancing, a deed to which two or more persons are parties, and in which these enter into reciprocal and corresponding grants or obligations towards each other; whereas a deed-poll is properly one in which only the party making it executes it, or binds himself by it as a deed, though the grantors or grantees therein may be several in number. *See* Indent, *v.*

In bankruptcy law, indenture means mortgage, deed of trust, or indenture, under which there is outstanding a security, other than a voting-trust certificate, constituting a claim against the debtor, a claim secured by a lien on any of the debtor's property, or an equity security of the debtor. Bankruptcy Code, § 101.

Indenture of trust. *See* Trust indenture.

Indenture trustee. Person or institution named in a trust indenture and charged with holding legal title to the trust property and with carrying out the terms of the indenture. Trustee under an indenture. Bankruptcy Code, § 101.

Independence. The state or condition of being free from dependence, subjection, or control. Political independence is the attribute of a nation or state which is entirely autonomous, and not subject to the government, control, or dictation of any exterior power.

Independent. Not dependent; not subject to control, restriction, modification, or limitation from a given outside source.

When the occurrence or nonoccurrence of one event has no effect on the probability of the occurrence or nonoccurrence of the other.

Independent adjuster. A person, firm or corporation who holds himself or itself out for employment as claims adjuster to more than one insurance company, is not a regular employee of the company, does not work exclusively for one company and is paid in each case assigned for time consumed and expenses incurred.

Independent advice. Concerning a trust deed or will which must be shown where a fiduciary relationship exists, means that the donor had the preliminary benefit of conferring fully and privately upon the subject of his intended gift with a person who was not only competent to inform him correctly as to its legal effect, but who was, furthermore, so disassociated from the interests of the donee as to be in a position to advise with the donor impartially and confidentially as to the consequences to himself of his proposed benefaction.

Independent contract. *See* Contract.

Independent contractor. Generally, one who, in exercise of an independent employment, contracts to do a piece of work according to his own methods and is subject to his employer's control only as to end product or final result of his work. One who renders service in course of self employment or occupation, and who follows employer's desires only as to results of work, and not as to means whereby it is to be accomplished.

An independent contractor is a person who contracts with another to do something for him but who is not controlled by the other nor subject to the other's right to control with respect to his physical conduct in the performance of the undertaking. He may or may not be an agent. Restatement, Second, Agency, § 2.

Independent counsel. The Ethics in Government Act, 28 U.S.C.A. § 591 et seq., provides for a Special Division with authority to appoint independent counsel to investigate possible criminal misconduct by high level government officials. The constitutionality of this Act was upheld in

Morrison v. Olson et al., 487 U.S. 654, 108 S.Ct. 2597, 101 L.Ed.2d 569.

Independent covenant. *See* Covenant.

Independent intervening cause. A conclusory label used by the common law to refer to a cause that intervenes between the defendant's behavior and a given result such that it is regarded as unfair to hold the defendant responsible for the result. *See also* Intervening cause.

Independent projects. In accounting, a set of capital investment projects that can be evaluated independently; acceptance or rejection of one does not affect acceptance or rejection of any of the others.

Independent review. An internal control feature that involves the review and evaluation of accounting controls by an independent external auditor.

Independent source rule. In connection with evidence, if the evidence to be introduced can be traced to a source independent of the originally illegally obtained fruits of interrogation or arrest, it is admissible. Wong Sun v. U. S., 371 U.S. 471, 83 S.Ct. 407, 9 L.Ed.2d 441. This exception to exclusionary rule allows admission of evidence which was gained through independent source as well as tainted source.

Independent variable. In accounting, an activity measure that, when changed, will cause consistent, observable changes in a specified cost (the dependent variable); a variable used as the basis of predicting the value of a dependent variable.

Indestructible trust. A trust which, inter alia, does not permit the invasion of principal by the trustees but which provides for income to A for life, with remainder to A's son's issue and for failure to A's daughter or issue.

Indeterminate. That which is uncertain, or not particularly designated.

Indeterminate conditional release. Type of release from penal confinement after fulfillment of conditions but subject to revocation for breach of conditions of release. *See also* Parole.

Indeterminate obligation. *See* Obligation.

Indeterminate sentence. A sentence to imprisonment for the maximum period defined by law, subject to termination by the parole board or other agency at any time after service of the minimum period. Such a sentence is invalid unless specifically authorized by statute.

A sentence of imprisonment the duration of which is not fixed by the court but is left to the determination of penal authorities within minimum and maximum time limits fixed by the court of law. *See also* Sentence; Sentencing guidelines.

Index. A book containing references, alphabetically arranged, to the contents of a series or collection of documents or volumes; or a section (normally at the end) of a single volume or set of volumes containing such references to its contents.

Statistical indexes are also used to track or measure changes in the economy (*see, e.g.,* Consumer Price Index) and movement in stock markets (*e.g.,* Standard & Poor's Index). Such indexes are usually keyed to a base year, month, or other period of comparison.

In mortgage financing, term used to determine adjustable-rate mortgage interest rates after the discount period ends. Common indexes for ARMs are one-year Treasury securities and the national average cost of funds to savings and loan associations.

Index fund. *See* Mutual fund.

Indexing. Adjusting or tying wages, pensions, mortgages, or other debt issues to some measure of inflation (*e.g.,* Consumer Price Index) to preserve the purchasing power of future benefits and investment earnings.

Index offenses. The term designating the eight classes of offenses reported annually by the FBI in its Uniform Crime Reports. They include: murder, forcible rape, robbery, burglary, aggravated assault, larceny over a specified amount, arson, and motor vehicle theft. *See also* Classification of crimes.

Index options. *See* Option.

Indian Claims Commission. The Indian Claims Commission hears and determines claims against the United States on behalf of any Indian tribe, band, or other identifiable group of American Indians residing within the United States.

Indian country. Part of public domain set apart for use, occupancy and protection of Indian peoples. *See* Indian lands; Indian reservation; Indian tribal property.

Indian lands. Real property ceded to the U.S. by Indians, commonly to be held in trust for Indians. *See* Indian country; Indian reservation; Indian tribal property; Indian tribe.

Indian reservation. A part of public domain set aside by proper authority for use and occupation of tribe or tribes of Indians, and under superintendence of the government which retains title to the land.

Indian title. Claim of Indian tribes of right, because of immemorial occupancy, to occupy certain territory to exclusion of any other Indians. Permissive right of occupancy granted by federal government to aboriginal possessors of the land; it is mere possession not specifically recognized as ownership and may be extinguished by federal government at any time.

Indian tribal property. Property in which an Indian tribe has a legally enforceable interest. Such term refers to real property, the title to which is vested in United States but held in trust for the Indian tribe. Such property, depending on context in which the term is used, may or may not be "public property" of the United States. *See* Indian lands; Indian reservation.

Indian tribe. A separate and distinct community or body of the aboriginal Indian race of men found in the United States. Within meaning of Indian Nonintercourse Act is a body of Indians of the same or similar race, united in a community under one leadership or government, and inhabiting a particular, though sometimes ill-defined, territory.

For purpose of statute governing federal court jurisdiction of actions brought by Indian tribe or band, "Indian tribes or bands" are separate communities of citizens of Indian descent, possibly with a common racial origin, possessing the power of a sovereign to regulate their internal and social relations.

Indication. In the law of evidence, a sign or token; a fact pointing to some inference or conclusion. *See* Inference.

Indicative evidence. This is not evidence properly so called, but the mere suggestion of evidence proper, which may possibly be procured if the suggestion is followed up. *See* Inference.

Indicia /indís(h)(i)yə/. Signs; indications. Circumstances which point to the existence of a given fact as probable, but not certain. For example, "*indicia* of partnership" are any circumstances which would induce the belief that a given person was in reality, though not ostensibly, a member of a given firm. *See* Circumstantial evidence.

The term is much used in the civil law in a sense nearly or entirely synonymous with circumstantial evidence. It denotes facts which give rise to inferences, rather than the inferences themselves.

Indicia of title. Generally, a document evidencing title to property, real or personal; *e.g.* carbon copy of bill of sale to automobile.

Indict /indáyt/. *See* Indictment.

Indictable offense /indáytəbəl/. Subject to being indicted. An offense, the nature of which is proper or necessary to be prosecuted by process of indictment. Indictable offenses embrace common-law offenses or statutory offenses the punishments for which are infamous. *See also* Indictment.

Indicted /indáytəd/. Charged in an indictment with a criminal offense. *See* Indictment; Jury.

Indictee /indaytíy/. A person indicted.

Indictment /indáytmənt/. An accusation in writing found and presented by a grand jury, legally convoked and sworn, to the court in which it is impaneled, charging that a person therein named has done some act, or been guilty of some omission, which by law is a public offense, punishable on indictment. A formal written accusation originating with a prosecutor and issued by a grand jury against a party charged with a crime. An indictment is referred to as a "true bill", whereas failure to indict is called a "no bill".

An indictment is merely a charge which must be proved at trial beyond a reasonable doubt before defendant may be convicted. An indictment is only an accusation; it is the physical means by which a defendant is brought to trial. Its sole purpose is to identify defendant's alleged offense, and it is not evidence that offense charged was committed and may not be considered as evidence by jury during its deliberations.

An offense which may be punished by death shall be prosecuted by indictment. An offense which may be punished by imprisonment for a term exceeding one year or at hard labor shall be prosecuted by indictment or, if indictment is waived, it may be prosecuted by information. Any other offense may be prosecuted by indictment or by information. Fed.R.Crim.P. 7.

See also Grand jury; Information; Presentment; True bill.

Joinder of indictments. See Joinder.

Joint indictment. When several offenders are joined in the same indictment, as when principals in the first and second degree, and accessories before and after the fact, are all joined in the same indictment.

In diem /in dáyəm/. For a day; for the space of a day. *See also* Per diem.

Indifferent. Impartial; unbiased; disinterested.

Indigent /índəjənt/. In a general sense, one who is needy and poor, or one who has not sufficient property to furnish him a living nor anyone able to support him to whom he is entitled to look for support. Term commonly used to refer to one's financial ability, and ordinarily indicates one who is destitute of means of comfortable subsistence so as to be in want.

Indigent defendant. A person indicted or complained of who is without funds or ability to hire a lawyer to defend him is, in most instances, entitled to appointed counsel to represent him at every stage of the criminal proceedings, through appeal, consistent with the protection of the Sixth and Fourteenth Amendments to U.S.Const. Gideon v. Wainwright, 372 U.S. 335, 83 S.Ct. 792, 9 L.Ed.2d 799; Fed.R.Crim.P. 44; 18 U.S.C.A. § 3006A. Provision also may be made for waiver of court costs and fees for indigent defendants in appealing a case (*e.g.* Fed.R.App.P. 24); and, the financial condition of the defendant will be considered in imposing fines (see 18 U.S.C.A. § 3572). *See also* Counsel, right to; Effective assistance of counsel; In forma pauperis; Pauper's oath.

Indignity /indígnətiy/. In the law of divorce, a species of cruelty addressed to the mind, sensibilities, self-respect, or personal honor of the subject, rather than to the body. "Indignities" justifying grant of divorce may consist of vulgarity, unmerited reproach, habitual contumely, studied neglect, intentional incivility, manifest disdain, abusive language, or malignant ridicule. *See* Mental cruelty.

Indirect. Not direct in relation or connection; not having an immediate bearing or application; not related in the natural way. Circuitous, not leading to aim or result by plainest course or method or obvious means, roundabout, not resulting directly from an act or cause but more or less remotely connected with or growing out of it. Almost always used in law in opposition to "direct," though not the only antithesis of the latter word, as the terms "collateral" and "cross" are sometimes used in contrast with "direct."

As to *indirect* Confession; Contempt; Cost, and Tax, see those titles.

Indirect attack. *See* Collateral attack.

Indirect evidence. Such evidence which only tends to establish the issue by proof of various facts sustaining by their consistency the hypothesis claimed. It consists of both inferences and presumptions. Proof of collateral circumstances, from which a fact in controversy, not directly attested to by direct evidence (witnesses or documents), may be inferred. Proof of some other fact or facts from which, taken either singly or collectively, existence of particular fact in question may be inferred as necessary or probable consequence. *See also* Circumstantial evidence; Inference; Presumption.

Indirect labor. The wages of factory employees who do not work directly on the product; treated in accounting as part of factory overhead.

Indirect materials. Minor materials (such as glue, varnish, and nails) used in manufacturing a product; treated in accounting as part of factory overhead.

Indirect tax. A tax upon some right or privilege or corporate franchise; *e.g.* privilege tax; franchise tax. A tax laid upon the happening of an event as distinguished from its tangible fruits.

Indispensable. That which cannot be spared, omitted, or dispensed with.

Indispensable evidence. That without which a particular fact cannot be proved.

Indispensable parties. One without whose presence no adequate judgment can be entered determining rights of parties before a court. Those who have such an interest in the controversy that the court cannot render a final decree without affecting their interests. Those who must be joined because nonjoinder prejudices their rights and those of parties already joined such that the action cannot continue without them. Those without whom the action cannot proceed, and must be joined even if by such joinder the court loses jurisdiction over the controversy. Fed.R.Civil P. 19. *See* Joinder *(Joinder of parties)*; Necessary parties; Parties.

Individual. As a noun, this term denotes a single person as distinguished from a group or class, and also, very commonly, a private or natural person as distinguished from a partnership, corporation, or association; but it is said that this restrictive signification is not necessarily inherent in the word, and that it may, in proper cases, include artificial persons. *See also* Person.

As an adjective, "individual" means pertaining or belonging to, or characteristic of, one single person, either in opposition to a firm, association, or corporation, or considered in his relation thereto.

Individual assets. In the law of partnership, property belonging to a member of a partnership as his separate and private property, apart from the assets or property belonging to the firm as such or the partner's interest therein.

Individual debts. Such as are due from a member of a partnership in his private or personal capacity, as distinguished from those due from the firm or partnership.

Individually. Separately and personally, as distinguished from jointly or officially, and as opposed to collective or associate action or common interest.

Individual proprietorship. *See* Sole proprietorship.

Individual retirement account (I.R.A.). Individuals with earned income are permitted, under certain circumstances, to set aside a limited amount of such income per year for a retirement account. The amount so set aside can be deducted by the taxpayer and is subject to income tax only upon withdrawal. The Internal Revenue Code limits the amount of this contribution that can be deducted for adjusted gross income depending upon (1) whether the taxpayer or spouse is an active participant in an employer-provided qualified retirement plan and (2) the magnitude of the taxpayer's adjusted gross income before the IRA contribution is considered. I.R.C. § 219. Specific statutory requirements are established for the establishment of the trust or custodial account, contributions, and withdrawal of such amounts with penalties provided for failure to comply. I.R.C. § 408(a). *See also* Keogh Plan.

Indivisible. Not susceptible of division or apportionment; inseparable; entire. Thus, a contract, covenant, consideration, etc., may be divisible or indivisible; *i.e.,* separable or entire. *See also* Contract.

Indorsee /əndòrsíy/indorsíy/. The person to whom or for whose benefit an instrument, document or other commercial paper is indorsed, usually referring to the indorser's transferee.

Indorsee in due course. An indorsee in due course is one who, in good faith, in the ordinary course of business, and for value, before its apparent maturity or presumptive dishonor, and without knowledge of its actual dishonor, acquires a negotiable instrument duly indorsed to him, or indorsed generally, or payable to the bearer.

Indorsement /əndórsmənt/. The act of a payee, drawee, accommodation indorser, or holder of a bill, note, check, or other negotiable instrument, in writing his name upon the back of the same, with or without further or qualifying words, whereby the property in the same is assigned and transferred to another. U.C.C. § 3–202 *et seq.*

The signature on an instrument of a person who has the liability thereon of an indorser. Any signature in an ambiguous capacity is an indorsement. U.C.C. § 3–402. As applied to documents, the term means the signature thereon of a person to whose order the document runs.

An indorsement must be written by or on behalf of the holder and on the instrument or on a paper so firmly affixed thereto as to become a part thereof. An indorsement is effective for negotiation only when it conveys the entire instrument or any unpaid residue. If it purports to be of less it operates only as a partial assignment. U.C.C. § 3–202.

Accommodation indorsement. In the law of negotiable instruments, one made by a third person without any consideration, but merely for the benefit of the holder of the instrument, or to enable the maker to obtain money or credit on it. Unless otherwise explained, it is understood to be a loan of the indorser's credit without restriction. Accommodation indorser is not liable to party accommodated. U.C.C. § 3–415.

Blank indorsement. One made by the mere writing of the indorser's name on the back of the note or bill, without mention of the name of any person in whose favor the indorsement is made, but with the implied understanding that any lawful holder may fill in his own name above the indorsement if he so chooses. An indorsement in blank specifies no particular indorsee and may consist of a mere signature. An instrument payable to order and indorsed in blank becomes payable to bearer and may be negotiated by delivery alone until specially indorsed. The holder may convert a blank indorsement into a special indorsement by writing over the signature of the indorser in blank any contract consistent with the character of the indorsement. U.C.C. § 3–204(2), (3).

Collection indorsement. See that title.

Conditional indorsement. An indorsement that is restrictive because it purports to limit when the instrument can be paid or further transferred, or to condition payment or further transfer on the occurrence of a specified event. One by which the indorser annexes some condition (other than the failure of prior parties to pay) to his liability. The condition may be either present or subsequent. Special indorsement with additional words of condition. U.C.C. § 3–205(a).

Full indorsement. One by which the indorser orders the money to be paid to some particular person by name; it differs from a blank indorsement, which consists merely in the name of the indorser written on the back of the instrument.

General indorsement. See *Blank indorsement,* above.

Irregular indorsement. An indorsement out of the chain of title which is ordinarily added to an instrument prior to delivery to the payee. Also known as an anomalous indorsement. *E.g.,* M makes a note payable to P; M is the maker and P is the payee. If when the note is executed by M, I also signs in the margin of the instrument, or on the back of it, I's indorsement is irregular. An irregular indorsement is notice of accommodation status. U.C.C. § 3–415(4).

Qualified indorsement. One which restrains or limits, or qualifies or enlarges, the liability of the indorser, in any manner different from what the law generally imports as his true liability, deducible from the nature of the instrument. A transfer of a bill or promissory note to an indorsee, without any liability to the indorser. Such is accomplished by adding after signature words such as "without recourse" or the like. U.C.C. §§ 3–414(1), 3–417(2)(3).

Restrictive indorsement. One which stops the negotiability of the instrument, or which contains such a definite direction as to the payment as to preclude the indorsee from making any further transfer of the instrument. An indorsement is restrictive which either: (a) is conditional; or (b) purports to prohibit further transfer of the instrument; or (c) includes the words "for collection",

"for deposit", "pay any bank", or like terms signifying a purpose of deposit or collection; or (d) otherwise states that it is for the benefit or use of the indorser or of another person. U.C.C. § 3–205.

Special indorsement. An indorsement that specifies a person to whom or to whose order the instrument is thereafter payable, U.C.C. § 3–204(1), or, in the case of a document, as the person to whom or to whose order the goods should be delivered. Any instrument specially indorsed becomes payable to the order of the special indorsee and may be further negotiated only by his indorsement.

Trust indorsement. An indorsement of an instrument that is restrictive because it states that it is for the benefit or use of the indorser or of another person. U.C.C. § 3–205(d).

Unauthorized indorsement. One made without actual, implied or apparent authority and includes a forgery. U.C.C. § 3–404.

Without recourse. See *Qualified indorsement,* above.

Indorser /əndórsər/. Person who indorses; *i.e.,* being the payee or holder, writes his name on the back of a negotiable instrument. One who signs his name as payee on the back of a check to obtain the cash or credit represented on its face.

A signer of an instrument who engages to pay it only upon dishonor and any necessary notice of dishonor and protest. U.C.C. § 3–414(1). As applied to documents, the term means the person who signs a document that runs to her order.

Induce. To bring on or about, to affect, cause, to influence to an act or course of conduct, lead by persuasion or reasoning, incite by motives, prevail on. *See also* Seduce.

Inducement. In contracts, the benefit or advantage which the promisor is to receive from a contract is the inducement for making it. To cause party to choose one course of conduct rather than another.

In criminal law, motive; that which leads or tempts to the commission of crime. For purposes of entrapment defense, may be defined as government conduct which creates substantial risk that undisposed person or otherwise law-abiding citizen would commit the offense. *See* Entrapment.

Induct. To put in enjoyment or possession, especially to introduce into possession of an office or benefice, with customary ceremonies. To bring in, initiate; to put formally in possession; to enter formerly into military service; to inaugurate or install. *See* Induction.

Induction. Act or process of inducting; *e.g.* process of inducting civilian into military service.

Industrial development bonds. *See* Bond.

Industrial disease. In law of workers' compensation, is physical disorder which is caused by or is incident to particular employment or occupation. *See also* Occupational disease.

Industrial goods. Goods which are destined and designed to produce other goods as contrasted with consumer goods.

Industrial relations. Labor relations. Term includes all phases of relations between employer and employee, including collective bargaining, safety, employee benefits, etc.

Industrial revenue bond. *See* Bond.

Industry. Any department or branch of art, occupation, or business conducted as a means of livelihood or for profit; especially, one which employs much labor and capital and is a distinct branch of trade.

Term is susceptible of more than one meaning: it may be defined in terms of end uses for which various products compete; it may also denote an aggregate of enterprises employing similar production and marketing facilities and producing products having markedly similar characteristics.

Industry wide liability. *See* Enterprise liability.

Inebriate /əníybriyət/. A person under the influence of or addicted to the use of intoxicating liquors.

Ineligibility. Disqualification or legal incapacity to be elected to an office or appointed to a particular position. Thus, an alien or naturalized citizen is ineligible to be elected president of the United States. This incapacity arises from various causes, and a person may be incapable of being elected to one office who may be elected to another; the incapacity may also be perpetual or temporary. *See also* Incapacity.

In equity. In a court of equity, as distinguished from a court of law; in the purview, consideration, or contemplation of equity; according to the doctrines of equity. *See* Equitable; Equity.

Inescapable peril. Within last clear chance doctrine, means peril which the plaintiff is helpless to avoid by his own efforts, but which requires action on part of defendant to avert it. *See* Last clear chance doctrine.

In esse /in ésiy/. In being. Actually existing. Distinguished from *in posse*, which means "that which is not, but may be." A child before birth is *in posse;* after birth, *in esse.*

In evidence. Included in the evidence already adduced. The "facts in evidence" are such as have already been proved in the cause.

Inevitable. Incapable of being avoided; fortuitous; transcending the power of human care, foresight, or exertion to avoid or prevent, and therefore suspending legal relations so far as to excuse from the performance of contract obligations, or from liability for consequent loss.

Inevitable accident. An unavoidable accident; one produced by an irresistible physical cause; an accident which cannot be prevented by human skill or foresight, but results from natural causes, such as lightning or storms, perils of the sea, inundations or earthquakes, or sudden death or illness. By irresistible force is meant an interposition of human agency, from its nature and power absolutely uncontrollable.

An accident is "inevitable", so as to preclude recovery on ground of negligence, if person by whom it occurs neither has nor is legally bound to have sufficient power to avoid it or prevent its injuring another.

The highest degree of caution that can be used is not required. It is enough that it is reasonable under the circumstances; such as is usual in similar cases, and has been found by long experience to be sufficient to answer the end in view,—the safety of life and property. Inevitable accident is only when the disaster happens from natural causes, without negligence or fault on either side, and when both parties have endeavored, by every means in their power, with due care and caution, and with a proper display of nautical skill, to prevent the occurrence of the accident.

See also Act of God; Unavoidable accident.

Inevitable discovery rule. An exception to the exclusionary rule which permits evidence to be admitted in a criminal case, even though it was obtained unlawfully, when the government can show that discovery of the evidence by lawful means was inevitable.

Inexcusable neglect. Such neglect which will preclude setting aside of default judgment, implies something more than the unintentional inadvertence or neglect common to all who share the ordinary frailties of mankind.

In execution and pursuance of /in èksəkyúwshən ænd pərs(y)úwəns òv/. Words used to express the fact that the instrument is intended to carry into effect some other instrument, as in case of a deed in execution of a power.

In extremis /in əkstríyməs/. In extremity; in the last extremity; in the last illness. *Agens in extremis,* being in extremity. Declarations *in extremis,* dying declarations. In extremis does not always mean in articulo mortis. *See also* Extremis.

In fact. Actual, real; as distinguished from implied or inferred. Resulting from the acts of parties, instead of from the act or intendment of law.

Infamous /ínfəməs/. Shameful or disgraceful. Possessing notorious reputation. Famous or well known in a derogatory sense.

Infamous crime. *See* Crime.

Infamous punishment. *See* Punishment.

Infamy /ínfəmiy/. Condition of being infamous. A qualification of a man's legal status produced by his conviction of an infamous crime and the consequent loss of honor and credit, which, at common law, rendered him incompetent as a witness, and by statute in some jurisdictions entails other disabilities. *See* Civil death.

Infancy. Minority; the state of a person who is under the age of legal majority,—at common law, twenty-one years; now, generally 18 years. According to the sense in which this term is used, it may denote the condition of the person merely with reference to his years, or the contractual disabilities which non-age entails, or his status with regard to other powers or relations.

At common law, children under the age of seven are conclusively presumed to be without criminal capacity, those who have reached the age of fourteen are treated as fully responsible, while as to those between the ages of seven and fourteen there is a rebuttable presumption of criminal incapacity. Many states have made some change by statute in the age of criminal responsibility for minors. In addition, all jurisdictions have adopted juvenile court legislation providing that some or all criminal conduct by those persons under a certain age (usually eighteen) must or may be adjudicated in the juvenile court rather than in a criminal prosecution.

See also Child; Children; Minor.

Infant. *See* Child; Children; Infancy; Minor.

Infanticide /ínfǽntəsàyd/. The murder or killing of an infant soon after its birth. The fact of the birth distinguishes this act from "feticide" or "procuring abortion," which terms denote the destruction of the *fetus* in the womb.

Infeoffment /infíyfmənt/°féf°/. The act or instrument of feoffment.

Inference. In the law of evidence, a truth or proposition drawn from another which is supposed or admitted to be true. A process of reasoning by which a fact or proposition sought to be established is deduced as a logical consequence from other facts, or a state of facts, already proved or admitted. A logical and reasonable conclusion of a fact not presented by direct evidence but which, by process of logic and reason, a trier of fact may conclude exists from the established facts. Inferences are deductions or conclusions which with reason and common sense lead the jury to draw from facts which have been established by the evidence in the case.

See also Necessary inference; Reasonable inference rule. *Compare* Presumption.

Inference on inference, rule of. Means that one presumption or inference may not be based upon another.

Inferential. In the law of evidence, operating in the way of inference; argumentative. Presumptive evidence is sometimes termed "inferential".

Inferential facts. Such as are established not directly by testimony or other evidence, but by inferences or conclusions drawn from the evidence. *See* Inference.

Inferior. One who, in relation to another, has less power and is below him; one who is bound to obey another. He who makes the law is the superior; he who is bound to obey it, the inferior.

Inferior court. This term may denote any court subordinate to the chief appellate tribunal in the particular judicial system (*e.g.* trial court); but it is also commonly used as the designation of a court of special, limited, or statutory jurisdiction, whose record must show the existence and attaching of jurisdiction in any given case, in order to give presumptive validity to its judgment.

Infidelity. Unfaithfulness in marriage; usually referring to commission of adultery by one spouse.

In fieri /in fáyəray/. In being made; in process of formation or development; hence, incomplete or inchoate. Legal proceedings are described as *in fieri* until judgment is entered.

Infirm. Weak, feeble. Lacking moral character or weak of health. The testimony of an "infirm" witness may be taken *de bene esse* in some circumstances. *See also* Incapacity.

Infirmity. Disability; feebleness. In an application for insurance is an ailment or disease of a substantial character, which apparently in some material degree impairs the physical condition and health of the applicant and increases the chance of his death or sickness and which if known, would have been likely to deter the insurance company from issuing the policy. *See also* Disability; Incapacity.

Inflation. An overall rise in prices which results in a decline in the real value of the dollar.

Inflation rate. Rate of change in prices of goods and services as measured for a particular period. The primary indexes for measuring the rate of change are the Consumer Price Index and Producer Price Index.

Influence. Power exerted over others. To affect, modify or act upon by physical, mental or moral power, especially in some gentle, subtle, and gradual way. *See also* Coercion; Duress; Undue influence.

Informal. Deficient in legal form; inartificially drawn up.

Informal contract. A contract that does not require a specified form or formality for its validity. Generally refers to an oral contract as contrasted with a written contract or specialty instrument. *See* Contract.

Informality. Want of legal form.

Informal proceedings. Proceedings less formal than a normal trial; *e.g.* small claims or conciliation court, administrative hearings, etc. Those conducted without prior notice to interested persons by an officer of the Court acting as registrar for probate of a will or appointment of a personal representative. Uniform Probate Code, § 1–201(19).

Informant. *See* Informer.

In forma pauperis /in fórmə pópərəs/. In the character or manner of a pauper. Describes permission given to a poor person (*i.e.* indigent) to proceed without liability for court fees or costs. An indigent will not be deprived of his rights to litigate and appeal; if the court is satisfied as to his indigence he may proceed without incurring costs or fees of court. Fed.R.App.P. 24. *See also* Counsel, right to; Indigent defendant; Pauper's oath.

Information. An accusation exhibited against a person for some criminal offense, without an indictment. An accusation in the nature of an indictment, from which it differs only in being presented by a competent public officer on his oath of office, instead of a grand jury on their oath. A written accusation made by a public prosecutor, without the intervention of a grand jury. Function of an "information" is to inform defendant of the nature of the charge made against him and the act constituting such charge so that he can prepare for trial and to prevent him from being tried again for the same offense.

While Fifth Amendment of U.S. Constitution requires federal government to prosecute infamous crimes only upon presentment of grand jury indictment, in most states the information may be used in place of grand jury indictment to bring a person to trial. As regards federal crimes, see Fed.R.Crim.P. 7. *See also* Arraignment; Indictment; Preliminary hearing. As to joinder of informations, *see* Joinder.

Information and belief. A standard legal term which is used to indicate that the allegation is not based on the firsthand knowledge of the person making the allegation, but that person nevertheless, in good faith, believes the allegation to be true. A request for a search warrant may be based upon information and belief. *See* Probable cause.

Informed consent. A person's agreement to allow something to happen (such as surgery) that is based on a full disclosure of facts needed to make the decision intelligently; *i.e.,* knowledge of risks involved, alternatives, etc. Informed consent is the name for a general principle of law that a physician has a duty to disclose what a reasonably prudent physician in the medical community in the exercise of reasonable care would disclose to his patient as to whatever grave risks of injury might be incurred from a proposed course of treatment, so that a patient, exercising ordinary care for his own welfare, and faced with a choice of undergoing the proposed treatment, or alternative treatment, or none at all, may intelligently exercise his judgment by reasonably balancing the probable risks against the probable benefits.

Informer. An undisclosed person who confidentially discloses material information of a law violation, thereby supplying a lead to officers for their investigation of a crime. This does not include persons who supply information only after being interviewed by police officers, or who give information as witnesses during course of investigation. Rewards for information obtained from informers is provided for by 18 U.S.C.A. § 3059. *See also* Citizen-informant.

Informer's privilege. The government's privilege to withhold from disclosure the identity of persons who furnish information on violations of law to officers charged with enforcement of that law. In the exercise of its power to formulate evidentiary rules for federal criminal cases, the Supreme Court has consistently declined to hold that an informer's identity need always be disclosed in a federal criminal trial or in a preliminary hearing. A defendant is entitled to a veracity hearing if he makes a substantial preliminary showing that an affiant knowingly and intentionally, or with reckless disregard for the truth, included in a warrant affidavit a false statement necessary to the finding of probable cause. However, the deliberate falsity or reckless disregard whose impeachment is permitted is only that of the affiant, not of any nongovernmental informant.

In foro /in fórow/. In a (or the) forum, court, or tribunal.

Infra /infrə/. (Lat.) Below, under, beneath, underneath. The opposite of *supra*, above. Thus, we say, *primo gradu est*—supra, *pater, mater,* infra, *filius, filia*: in the first degree of kindred in the ascending line, above is the father and the mother, below, in the descending line, son and daughter.

Infraction. A breach, violation, or infringement; as of a law, a contract, a right or duty. A violation of a statute for which the only sentence authorized is a fine and which violation is expressly designated as an infraction.

Infringement /infrínjmənt/. A breaking into; a trespass or encroachment upon; a violation of a law, regulation, contract, or right. Used especially of invasions of the rights secured by patents, copyrights, and trademarks. *See also* Encroachment; Trespass.

Contributory infringement. The intentional aiding of one person by another in the unlawful making or selling of a patented invention; usually done by making or selling one part of the patented invention, or one element of the combination, with the intent and purpose of so aiding.

Criminal infringement. Any person who infringes a copyright willfully and for purposes of commercial advantage or private financial gain is subject to a fine and/or imprisonment. Copyright Act, § 506 (17 U.S.C.A.).

Infringement of copyright. Unauthorized use of copyrighted material; *i.e.* use without permission of copyright holder. In determining whether there is a copyright infringement, and not a "fair use" exemption, the factors to be considered include: (1) the purpose and character of the use, including whether such use is of a commercial nature or is for nonprofit educational purposes; (2) the nature of the copyrighted work; (3) the amount and substantiality of the portion used in relation to the copyrighted work as a whole; and (4) the effect of the use upon the potential market for or value of the copyrighted work. Copyright Act, § 107 (17 U.S.C.A.).

Remedies for copyright infringement include injunctive relief, impounding and disposition of infringing articles, and recovery of actual damages and profits. In lieu of actual damages, the federal Copyright Act provides for statutory damages which will vary as to whether the infringement was willful or unintentional. Copyright Act, § 504 (17 U.S.C.A.).

See also Fair use doctrine.

Infringement of patent. The unauthorized making, using, or selling for practical use, or for profit, of an invention covered by a valid claim of a patent during the life of the patent. It may involve any one or all of the acts of making, using, and selling. To constitute infringement of a patent claim there must be present in the infringing device or combination every element of such claim or its equivalent, so combined as to produce substantially the same result operating in substantially the same way. See 35 U.S.C.A. § 100 et seq. *See also* Contributory infringement.

Infringement of trademark. The unauthorized use, or colorable imitation of the mark already appropriated by another, on goods of a similar class. It exists if words or designs used by defendant are identical with or so similar to plaintiff's that they are likely to cause confusion, or deceive or mislead others. One who affixes the trademark of another to similar articles in such way that his use of it is liable to cause confusion in the

trade, or is calculated to mislead purchasers and induce them to buy infringer's articles as goods of the other thus depriving the latter of the full benefit of his property. See 15 U.S.C.A. § 1051 et seq. *See also* Likelihood of confusion.

Infringer. One who infringes the rights secured by copyright, patent or trademark holders. *See* Infringement.

In futuro /in f(y)ətyúrow/. In future; at a future time; the opposite of *in præsenti.*

In genere /in jénəriy/. In kind; in the same *genus* or class; the same in quantity and quality, but not individually the same. *See* Generic; In pari materia.

Ingress. The act, or right of, entering. Access; entrance.

In gross. In a large quantity or sum; without deduction, division, or particulars; by wholesale. At large, in one sum; not annexed to or dependent upon another thing. Common in gross is such as is neither appendant nor appurtenant to land, but is annexed to a man's person. *See also* In bulk.

For easement in gross, *see* Easement.

Ingrossing. The act of making a fair and perfect copy of any document from a rough draft of it, in order that it may be executed or put to its final purpose. *See* Engrossment.

Inhabit. Synonymous with dwell, live, reside, sojourn, stay, rest. *See also* Domicile; Residence.

Inhabitant. One who resides actually and permanently in a given place, and has his domicile there.

The words "inhabitant," "citizen," and "resident," as employed in different constitutions to define the qualifications of electors, means substantially the same thing; and, in general, one is an inhabitant, resident, or citizen at the place where he has his domicile or home. But the terms "resident" and "inhabitant" have also been held not synonymous, the latter implying a more fixed and permanent abode than the former, and importing privileges and duties to which a mere resident would not be subject. A corporation can be an inhabitant only in the state of its incorporation. *See also* Domicile; Residence.

In hac parte /in hæc pártiy/. In this behalf; on this side.

In hæc verba /in híyk vérbə/. In these words; in the same words.

Inhere /inhír/. To exist in and inseparable from something else; to stick fast. To be inherent.

Inherently dangerous. Danger inhering in instrumentality or condition itself at all times, so as to require special precautions to prevent injury; not danger arising from mere casual or collateral negligence of others with respect thereto under particular circumstances. An object which has in itself the potential for causing harm or destruction, against which precautions must be taken. Dangerous per se, without requiring human intervention to produce harmful effects; *e.g.,* explosives.

Product is "inherently dangerous" where danger of an injury arises from product itself, and not from defect in product. Work is "inherently dangerous" when in ordinary course of events its performance would probably, and not merely possibly, cause injury if proper precautions are not taken.

See also Dangerous instrumentality; Dangerous weapon; Strict liability.

Inherent *or* **latent defect.** Fault or deficiency in a thing, no matter the use made of such, which is not easily discoverable and which is fixed in the object itself and not from without. *See also* Latent defect; Strict liability.

Inherent powers /inhírənt páwərz/. An authority possessed without its being derived from another. A right, ability, or faculty of doing a thing, without receiving that right, ability, or faculty from another. Powers originating from the nature of government or sovereignty, *i.e.,* powers over and beyond those explicitly granted in the Constitution or reasonably to be implied from express grants; *e.g.* in the foreign policy area, the Executive's inherent powers have been held to confer authority upon the President to settle the claims of American nationals against a foreign state as part of a diplomatic agreement. *See also* Power. *Compare* Incidental powers.

Inherent powers of court. The "inherent power" of a court is that which is necessary for the proper and complete administration of justice and such power is resident in all courts of superior jurisdiction and essential to their existence; *e.g.,* sentencing and contempt powers; power to enjoin vexatious litigation.

Inherent right. One which abides in a person and is not given from something or someone outside itself. A right which a person has because he is a person. *See* Inalienable rights.

Inheretrix /inhéhrətriks/. The old term for "heiress".

Inherit /inhéhrət/. To take or receive by inheritance; to take by descent as a matter of law as heir on death of ancestor; though this item has also come to mean to receive by devise (*i.e.,* by will). Acquisition of property by descent and distribution. The word is also used in its popular sense as the equivalent of to take or receive. *See also* Descent; Inheritance.

Inheritance /inhéhrədəns/. That which is inherited or to be inherited. Property which descends to heir on the intestate death of another. An estate or property which a person has by descent, as heir to another, or which he may transmit to another, as his heir. *See* Bequest; Descent; Heirs; Inherit; Legacy.

Inheritance tax. Tax imposed in some states upon the privilege of receiving property from a decedent at death as contrasted with an estate tax which is imposed on the privilege of transmitting property at death. A tax on the transfer or passing of estates or property by legacy, devise, or intestate succession; not a tax on the property itself, but on the right to acquire it by descent or testamentary gift. *Compare* Estate tax.

Inhibition /in(h)əbíshən/. Restraining or holding back.

Inhuman treatment. In the law of divorce, such mental or physical cruelty or severity as endangers the life or health of the party to whom it is addressed, or creates a well-founded apprehension of such danger. The phrase commonly employed in statutes is "cruel and inhuman treatment," from which it may be inferred that "inhumanity" is an extreme or aggravated "cruelty." Such treatment commonly constitutes a ground for divorce. *See also* Cruel and inhuman treatment; Cruelty; Mental cruelty.

In infinitum /ìn infənáytəm/. Infinitely; indefinitely. Imports indefinite succession or continuance.

In initio /ìn ənísh(iy)ow/. In or at the beginning. *In initio litis,* at the beginning, or in the first stage of the suit.

Initial. That which begins or stands at the beginning. The first letter of a person's name.

Initial appearance. After arrest, the first appearance of the accused before a judge or magistrate. *See* Arraignment; Preliminary hearing.

Initial carrier. In the law of bailments, the carrier who first receives the goods and begins the process of their transportation, afterwards delivering them to another carrier for the further prosecution or completion of their journey. But it has also been defined as the one contracting with the shipper, and not necessarily the one whose line constitutes the first link in transportation.

Initial determination. With respect to social security benefit claims, refers to first determination of agency of claimants' application for benefits. Several levels of appeal are provided for from an initial claim denial. 42 U.S.C.A. § 405(b).

Initiate. Commence; start; originate; introduce; inchoate. *Curtesy initiate* is the interest which a husband has in the wife's lands after a child is born who may inherit, but before the wife dies. To propose for approval—as schedule of rates.

Initiative. An electoral process whereby designated percentages of the electorate may initiate legislative or constitutional changes through the filing of formal petitions to be acted on by the legislature or the total electorate. The power of the people to propose bills and laws, and to enact or reject them at the polls, independent of legislative assembly. Not all state constitutions provide for initiative. *See also* Referendum.

Injunction. A court order prohibiting someone from doing some specified act or commanding someone to undo some wrong or injury. A prohibitive, equitable remedy issued or granted by a court at the suit of a party complainant, directed to a party defendant in the action, or to a party made a defendant for that purpose, forbidding the latter from doing some act which he is threatening or attempting to commit, or restraining him in the continuance thereof, such act being unjust and inequitable, injurious to the plaintiff, and not such as can be adequately redressed by an action at law. A judicial process operating in personam, and requiring person to whom it is directed to do or refrain from doing a particular thing. Generally, it is a preventive and protective remedy, aimed at future acts, and is not intended to redress past wrongs. Fed.R.Civil P. 65. *See also* Temporary restraining order.

Interlocutory injunction. Interlocutory injunctions are those issued at any time during the pendency of the litigation for the short-term purpose of preventing irreparable injury to the petitioner prior to the time that the court will be in a position to either grant or deny permanent relief on the merits. In accordance with their purpose, interlocutory injunctions are limited in duration to some specified length of time, or at the very outside, to the time of conclusion of the case on the merits. Within the category of interlocutory injunctions there are two distinct types which must be considered individually. The first is generally referred to as a preliminary injunction, and includes any interlocutory injunction granted after the respondent has been given notice and the opportunity to participate in a hearing on whether or not that injunction should issue. The second is generally referred to as a temporary restraining order, and differs from a preliminary injunction primarily in that it is issued ex parte, with no notice or opportunity to be heard granted to the respondent. Temporary restraining orders supply the need for relief in those situations in which the petitioner will suffer irreparable injury if relief is not granted immediately, and time simply does not permit either the delivery of notice or the holding of a hearing. Fed.R.Civil P. 65. *See also* Injury (*Irreparable injury*); Temporary restraining order.

Mandatory injunction. One which (1) commands the defendant to do some positive act or particu-

lar thing; (2) prohibits him from refusing (or persisting in a refusal) to do or permit some act to which the plaintiff has a legal right; or (3) restrains the defendant from permitting his previous wrongful act to continue operative, thus virtually compelling him to undo it.

Permanent injunction. One intended to remain in force until the final termination of the particular suit.

Perpetual injunction. An injunction which finally disposes of the suit, and is indefinite in point of time.

Preliminary injunction. An injunction granted at the institution of a suit, to restrain the defendant from doing or continuing some act, the right to which is in dispute, and which may either be discharged or made perpetual, according to the result of the controversy, as soon as the rights of the parties are determined. Fed.R.Civil P. 65.

Preventive injunction. One which prohibits the defendant from doing a particular act or commands him to refrain from it.

Prohibitory injunction. An order of a court in the form of a judgment which directs one not to do a certain thing; sometimes called a restraining order. *See* Restraining order.

Provisional injunction. Another name for a preliminary or temporary injunction or an injunction pendente lite.

Restraining order. See Order; Restraining order; Temporary restraining order.

Temporary injunction. A preliminary or provisional injunction, or one granted pendente lite; as opposed to a final or perpetual injunction. A provisional remedy to preserve subject matter of controversy pending trial. It is one which operates until dissolved by interlocutory order or until final hearing on matter. *See also* Temporary restraining order.

In jure /in júriy/. In law; according to law.

Injure. To violate the legal right of another or inflict an actionable wrong. To do harm to, damage, or impair. To hurt or wound, as the person; to impair the soundness of, as health; to damage. As applied to a building, "injure" means to materially impair or destroy any part of the existing structure. *See* Injury; Tort.

Injuria /ənjúr(i)yə/. Lat. Injury; wrong; the privation or violation of right.

Injuria absque damno /ənjúr(i)yə ǽbskwiy dǽmnow/. Injury or wrong without damage. A wrong done, but from which no loss or damage results, and which, therefore, will not sustain an action.

Injurious exposure. Such exposure as will render employer liable for occupational disease of employee, is concentration of toxic material which would be sufficient to cause disease in event of prolonged exposure to such concentration regardless of length of exposure required actually to cause the disease. *See also* Occupational disease.

Injurious falsehood. In law of slander and libel, a defamation which does actual damage. *See* Libel; Slander.

Injurious words /ənjúriyəs wə́rdz/. Slander, or libelous words. *See* Libel; Slander.

Injury. Any wrong or damage done to another, either in his person, rights, reputation, or property. The invasion of any legally protected interest of another. Restatement, Second, Torts, § 7.

Absolute injuries. Injuries to those rights which a person possesses as being a member of society.

Accidental injury. A bodily injury by accident.

Within worker's compensation acts, one which occurs in the course of the employment, unexpectedly, and without the affirmative act or design of the employee; it being something which is unforeseen and not expected by the person to whom it happens. Any injury to an employee in the course of his employment due to any occurrence referable to a definite time, and of the happening of which he can give notice to his employer, regardless of whether the injury is a visible hurt from external force, or disease or infection induced by sudden and castastrophic exposure. The term is to receive a broad and liberal construction with a view to compensating injured employés where injury resulted through some accidental means, was unexpected and undesigned and may be the result of mere mischance or miscalculation as to effect of voluntary action.

See also Accident; Compensable injury; Continuous injury; Damages; Disability; Great bodily injury; Harm; Loss; Malicious injury; Pain and suffering; Pecuniary injury.

Bankruptcy law. Willful and malicious conversion is an "injury" within meaning of Bankruptcy Code section stating that individual is not discharged from debt for willful and malicious "injury" by debtor. Bankruptcy Code § 523.

Bodily injury. Physical pain, illness or any impairment of physical condition. "Serious bodily injury" means bodily injury which creates a substantial risk of death or which causes serious, permanent disfigurement, or protracted loss or impairment of the function of any bodily member or organ. Model Penal Code, § 210.0.

Civil injury. Injuries to person or property, resulting from a breach of contract, delict, or criminal offense, which may be redressed by means of a civil action. An infringement or privation of the civil rights which belong to individuals considered as individuals.

Injury in fact. Such as is required to give a plaintiff standing to sue means concrete and certain harm and, to warrant granting of standing, there must also be reason to think that the harm can be redressed by relief the court can grant.

Irreparable injury. This phrase does not mean such an injury as is beyond the possibility of repair, or beyond possible compensation in damages, or necessarily great damage, but includes an injury, whether great or small, which ought not to be submitted to, on the one hand, or inflicted, on the other; and which, because it is so large or so small, or is of such constant and frequent occurrence, or because no certain pecuniary standard exists for the measurement of damages, cannot receive reasonable redress in a court of law. Wrongs of a repeated and continuing character, or which occasion damages that are estimated only by conjecture, and not by any accurate standard, are included. The remedy for such is commonly in the nature of injunctive relief. "Irreparable injury" justifying an injunction is that which cannot be adequately compensated in damages or for which damages cannot be compensable in money. Contrast *Reparable injury, below. See* Injunction; Temporary restraining order.

Permanent injury. An injury that, according to every reasonable probability, will continue throughout the remainder of one's life.

Personal injury. In a narrow sense, a hurt or damage done to a man's *person,* such as a cut or bruise, a broken limb, or the like, as distinguished from an injury to his property or his reputation. The phrase is chiefly used in this connection with actions of tort for negligence and under worker's compensation statutes. But the term is also used (usually in statutes) in a much wider sense, and as including any injury which is an invasion of personal rights, and in this signification it may include such injuries to the person as libel or slander, criminal conversation, malicious prosecution, false imprisonment, and mental suffering.

In workers' compensation acts, "personal injury" means any harm or damage to the health of an employee, however caused, whether by accident, disease, or otherwise, which arises in the course of and out of his employment, and incapacitates him in whole or in part. The occurrence of disability or impairment. Such includes the aggravation of a preexisting injury.

Private injuries. Infringements of the private or civil rights belonging to individuals considered as individuals.

Public injuries. Breaches and violations of rights and duties which affect the whole community as a community.

Real injury. A *real injury* is inflicted by any act by which a person's honor or dignity is affected.

Relative injuries. Injuries to those rights which a person possesses in relation to the person who is immediately affected by the wrongful act done.

Reparable injury. An injury, the damage from which is merely in the nature of pecuniary loss, and can be exactly and fully repaired by compensation in money. Contrast *Irreparable injury, above.*

Unknown injury rule. Under this rule, release of claims for personal injuries may be avoided on the ground of mutual mistake if parties at the time of signing the agreement were mistaken as to the existence of injury, as opposed to unknown consequences of known injuries.

Verbal injury. See Libel; Slander.

Injustice. The withholding or denial of justice. In law, almost invariably applied to the act, fault, or omission of a court, as distinguished from that of an individual. "Fraud" is deception practiced by the party; "injustice" is the fault or error of the court. They are not equivalent words in substance, or in a statute authorizing a new trial on a showing of fraud or injustice.

In kind. Of the same species or category. In the same kind, class, or genus. A loan is returned "in kind" when not the identical article, but one corresponding and equivalent to it, is given to the lender. *See* Distribution in kind; In genere; Like-kind exchange.

Inland. Within a country, state or territory; within the interior part of a land mass.

Inland bill of exchange. A bill of which both the drawer and drawee reside within the same state or country. Otherwise called a "domestic bill," and distinguished from a "foreign bill." *See* Bill.

Inland marine insurance. *See* Insurance.

Inland navigation. Within the meaning of the legislation of congress upon the subject, this phrase means navigation upon inland waters *(q.v.).*

Inland trade. Trade wholly carried on at home; as distinguished from foreign commerce. *See* Commerce.

Inland waters. Such waters as canals, lakes, rivers, watercourses, inlets and bays, within, or partly within, the United States, exclusive of the open sea, though the water in question may open or empty into the ocean.

Inlaw. To place under the protection of the law.

In law. In the intendment, contemplation, or inference of the law; implied or inferred by law; existing in law or by force of law. *See* In fact.

In laws. Persons related by marriage rather than blood; *e.g.* relationship of parents of wife to husband.

Inlet. A narrow strip of water running into the land or between islands.

In lieu of /in lyúw əv/. Instead of; in place of; in substitution of. It does not mean "in addition to."

In limine /in líməniy/. On or at the threshold; at the very beginning; preliminarily. Any motion, whether used before or during trial, by which exclusion is sought of anticipated prejudicial evidence. *See* Motion in limine.

In litem /in láytəm/. For a suit; to the suit.

In loco /in lówkow/. In place; in lieu; instead; in the place or stead.

In loco parentis /in lówkow pəréntəs/. In the place of a parent; instead of a parent; charged, factitiously, with a parent's rights, duties, and responsibilities.

"Loco parentis" exists when person undertakes care and control of another in absence of such supervision by latter's natural parents and in absence of formal legal approval, and is temporary in character and is not to be likened to an adoption which is permanent.

Inmate. A person confined to a prison, penitentiary, or the like. A person who lodges or dwells in the same house with another, occupying different rooms, but using the same door for passing in and out of the house.

Innavigability. In insurance law, the condition of being *innavigable (q.v.).* The term is also applied to the condition of streams which are not large enough or deep enough, or are otherwise unsuited, for navigation.

Innavigable. As applied to streams, not capable of or suitable for navigation; impassable by ships or vessels. As applied to vessels in the law of marine insurance, it means unfit for navigation; so damaged by misadventures at sea as to be no longer capable of making a voyage. *Compare* Navigable waters.

Innocence. The absence of guilt. *See also* Presumption of innocence.

Innocent. Free from guilt; acting in good faith and without knowledge of incriminatory circumstances, or of defects or objections. *See* Not guilty.

Innocent agent. In criminal law, one who, being ignorant of any unlawful intent on the part of his principal, is merely the instrument of the guilty party in committing an offense; one who does an unlawful act at the solicitation or request of another, but who, from defect of understanding or ignorance of the inculpatory facts, incurs no legal guilt.

Innocent party. Person who did not consciously or intentionally participate in event, transaction, etc.

Innocent purchaser. One who, by an honest contract or agreement, purchases property or acquires an interest therein, without knowledge, or means of knowledge sufficient to charge him in law with knowledge, of any infirmity in the title of the seller. Person is "innocent purchaser" when he purchases without notice, actual or constructive, of any infirmity and pays valuable consideration and acts in good faith. *See also* Good faith purchaser.

Innocent trespass. A trespass to land, committed, not recklessly, but through inadvertence or mistake, or in good faith, under an honest belief that the trespasser was acting within his legal rights.

Innocent trespasser. One who enters another's land unlawfully, but inadvertently or unintentionally, or in the honest, reasonable belief of his own right so to do, and removes sand or other material therefrom, is an "innocent trespasser." Restatement, Second, Torts, § 164.

Inns of Court. These are certain private unincorporated associations, in the nature of collegiate houses, located in London, and invested with the exclusive privilege of calling people to the bar; that is, conferring the rank or degree of a barrister. They were founded probably about the beginning of the fourteenth century. The principal inns of court are the Inner Temple, Middle Temple, Lincoln's Inn, and Gray's Inn. (The two former originally belonged to the Knights Templar; the two latter to the earls of Lincoln and Gray respectively.) These bodies now have a "common council of legal education," for giving lectures and holding examinations. The inns of chancery, distinguishable from the foregoing, but generally classed with them under the general name, are the buildings known as "Clifford's Inn," "Clement's Inn," "New Inn," "Staples' Inn," and "Barnard's Inn." They were formerly a sort of collegiate houses in which law students learned the elements of law before being admitted into the inns of court, but they have long ceased to occupy that position. The Inns of Court (governed by officers called "benchers") hold the exclusive privilege of conferring the degree of barrister-at-law which is required to practice as an advocate or counsel in the superior courts.

Innuendo /ìnyuwéndow/. This Latin word (commonly translated "meaning") was the technical beginning of that clause in a declaration or indictment for slander or libel in which the meaning of the alleged libelous words was explained, or the application of the language charged to the plaintiff was pointed out; hence it gave its name to the whole clause. Indirect or subtle implication in words or expression, usually derogatory.

In pleading a libel action is a statement by plaintiff of construction which he puts upon words which are alleged to be libelous and which meaning he will induce jury to adopt at trial. Its function is to set a meaning upon words or language of doubtful or ambiguous import which alone would not be actionable.

In pais /ìn péy(s)/. This phrase, as applied to a legal transaction, primarily means that it has taken place without legal proceedings. Thus a widow was said to make a request *in pais* for her dower when she simply applied to the heir without issuing a writ. So conveyances are divided into those by matter of record and those by matter *in pais*. In some cases, however, "matters *in pais*" are opposed not only to "matters of record," but also to "matters in writing," *i.e.*, deeds, as where estoppel by deed is distinguished from estoppel by matter *in pais*.

In pais, estoppel /əstópəl in péy(s)/. An estoppel not arising from deed or record or written contract. The doctrine is that a person may be precluded by his act or conduct or silence, when it is his duty to speak, from asserting a right which he otherwise would have had. The effect of a party's voluntary conduct whereby he is precluded from asserting rights as against another person who has in good faith relied upon such conduct and has been led thereby to change his condition for the worse and who acquires some corresponding right of property or contract.

Elements or fundamentals of "estoppel in pais" include admission, statement, or act inconsistent with claim afterwards asserted; change of position to loss or injury of party claiming estoppel; circumstances such that party estopped knew or should have known facts to be otherwise or pretended to know facts which he did not know; false representation or concealment of material facts; inducement to alter position; intention that false representation or concealment be acted on; knowledge of facts, by party to be estopped; lack of knowledge or means of knowledge of party claiming estoppel; misleading of one person by another person to his prejudice or injury; prejudice or loss or injury to party claiming estoppel; reliance by one party on belief induced by other party.

See also Equitable estoppel; Estoppel.

In pari causa /ìn pæray kózə/°péray°/. In equal fault or guilt; equally culpable or criminal. A common law defense that prohibited a plaintiff from suing if it had been a participant in the contract or conspiracy that led to the violation of law at issue. As a general rule, the defense of *in pari delicto* is not recognized in the antitrust laws. *See also* Unclean hands doctrine.

In pari delicto /ìn pæray dəlíktow/°péray°/. In equal fault; equally culpable or criminal; in a case of equal fault or guilt. A person who is *in pari delicto* with another differs from a *particeps* *criminis* in this, that the former term always includes the latter, but the latter does not always include the former.

In pari materia /ìn pǽray mətír(i)yə/. Upon the same matter or subject. Statutes "in pari materia" are those relating to the same person or thing or having a common purpose. This rule of statutory construction, that statutes which relate to the same subject matter should be read, construed and applied together so that the legislature's intention can be gathered from the whole of the enactments, applies only when the particular statute is ambiguous.

In perpetuity /ìn pərpətyúwətiy/. Endless duration; lasting; forever.

In person. A party, plaintiff or defendant, who sues out a complaint, writ or other process, or appears to conduct his case in court himself, instead of through a solicitor or counsel, is said to act and appear *in person*. *See* In personam; Pro se.

In personam /ìn pərsównəm/. Against the person. Action seeking judgment against a person involving his personal rights and based on jurisdiction of his person, as distinguished from a judgment against property (*i.e.* in rem). Type of jurisdiction or power which a court may acquire over the defendant himself in contrast to jurisdiction over his property. *See also* In personam jurisdiction; In rem; Jurisdiction in personam.

In personam jurisdiction. Power which a court has over the defendant himself in contrast to the court's power over the defendant's interest in property (quasi in rem) or power over the property itself (in rem). A court which lacks personal jurisdiction is without power to issue an in personam judgment. Pennoyer v. Neff, 95 U.S. 714, 24 L.Ed. 565. *See also* In rem; Jurisdiction in personam.

In præsenti /ìn prəzéntay/. At the present time. Used in opposition to *in futuro*.

In propria persona /ìn prówpriyə pərsównə/. In one's own proper person. It was formerly a rule in pleading that pleas to the jurisdiction of the court must be plead *in propria persona*, because if pleaded by attorney they admit the jurisdiction, as an attorney is an officer of the court, and he is presumed to plead after having obtained leave, which admits the jurisdiction. *See* Pro se.

Inquest. The inquiry by a coroner or medical examiner, sometimes with the aid of a jury, into the manner of the death of any one who has been killed, or has died suddenly under unusual or suspicious circumstances, or by violence, or while in prison.

A body of men appointed by law to inquire into certain matters. The grand jury is sometimes called the "grand inquest." The judicial inquiry made by a jury summoned for the purpose is called an "inquest." The finding of such men, upon an investigation, is also called an "inquest."

See also Inquisition.

Coroner's inquest. See Coroner.

Inquest, arrest of. See Arrest.

Inquest jury. See Jury.

Inquiry court. *See* Inquest.

Inquiry notice. Information which is charged to a person where a duty is imposed upon him by law to make a reasonable investigation; the information which such investigation would have revealed is imputed to such person.

Inquisition /ìnkwəzíshən/. An inquiry or inquest; particularly, an investigation of certain facts made by a sheriff, together with a jury impaneled by him for the purpose. The instrument of writing on which their decision is made is also called an inquisition. In its broadest sense, "inquisition," includes any judicial inquiry. *See* Inquest.

Inquisition after death. *See* Inquest.

In re /ìn ríy/. In the affair; in the matter of; concerning; regarding. This is the usual method of entitling a judicial proceeding in which there are not adversary parties, but merely some *res* concerning which judicial action is to be taken, such as a bankrupt's estate, an estate in the probate court, a proposed public highway, etc. It is also sometimes used as a designation of a proceeding where one party makes an application on his own behalf, but such proceedings are more usually entitled *"Ex parte _____."*

In rem /ìn rém/. A technical term used to designate proceedings or actions instituted *against the thing*, in contradistinction to personal actions, which are said to be *in personam*.

"In rem" proceedings encompass any action brought against person in which essential purpose of suit is to determine title to or to affect interests in specific property located within territory over which court has jurisdiction. It is true that, in a strict sense, a proceeding *in rem* is one taken directly against property, and has for its object the disposition of property, without reference to the title of individual claimants; but, in a larger and more general sense, the terms are applied to actions between parties, where the direct object is to reach and dispose of property owned by them, or of some interest therein. Such are cases commenced by attachment against the property of debtors, or instituted to partition real estate, foreclose a mortgage, or enforce a lien. Pennoyer v. Neff, 95 U.S. 714, 24 L.Ed. 565. In the strict sense of the term, a proceeding "in rem" is one which is taken directly against property or one which is brought to enforce a right in the thing itself.

See also In personam; In rem jurisdiction; Quasi in rem jurisdiction.

Judgment in rem. See that title.

Quasi in rem. A term applied to proceedings which are not strictly and purely *in rem,* but are brought against the defendant personally, though the real object is to deal with particular property or subject property to the discharge of claims asserted; for example, foreign attachment, or proceedings to foreclose a mortgage, remove a cloud from title, or effect a partition. An action in which the basis of jurisdiction is the defendant's interest in property, real or personal, which is within the court's power, as distinguished from in rem jurisdiction in which the court exercises power over the property itself, not simply the defendant's interest therein.

In rem jurisdiction. Refers to an action that is taken directly against the defendant's property. The term may be contrasted with *in personam* jurisdiction. Power over a thing possessed by a court which allows it to seize and hold the object for some legal purpose; *e.g.* boat on which narcotics are found. *See also* Forfeiture; Jurisdiction in rem; Quasi in rem jurisdiction.

In respect of decedent. *See* Income in respect of decedent.

Inroll. A form of "enroll," used in the old books. *See* Enroll.

Inrollment. *See* Enrollment.

I.N.S. Immigration and Naturalization Service.

Insane delusion. A conception of a disordered mind which imagines facts to exist of which there is no evidence and belief in which is adhered to against all evidence and argument to contrary, and which cannot be accounted for on any reasonable hypothesis.

Insanity. The term is a social and legal term rather than a medical one, and indicates a condition which renders the affected person unfit to enjoy liberty of action because of the unreliability of his behavior with concomitant danger to himself and others. The term is more or less synonymous with mental illness or psychosis. In law, the term is used to denote that degree of mental illness which negates the individual's legal responsibility or capacity.

Insanity as Defense to Crime

There are various tests used by the courts to determine criminal responsibility, or lack thereof, of a defendant who asserts the defense that he or she was insane at the time of the crime. A frequently used test as provided in Section 4.01 of the Model Penal Code is as follows: "A person is not responsible for criminal conduct if at the time of such conduct as a result of mental disease or defect he lacks substantial capacity either to appreciate the criminality (wrongfulness) of his conduct or to conform his conduct to the requirements of law." Under this test there must be a sufficient causal link between the defendant's mental disease or defect and his inability to control his behavior. This test, as defined by the American Law Institute, has been adopted (sometimes with slight modifications) by a number of states and also in most federal courts. See 18 U.S.C.A. § 4241.

If a defendant intends to rely upon the defense of insanity at the time of the alleged crime, he is required to notify the attorney for the government of such intention. Fed.R.Crim.P. 12.2; 18 U.S.C.A. § 4242.

It is an affirmative defense to a prosecution under any Federal statute that, at the time of the commission of the acts constituting the offense, the defendant, as a result of a severe mental disease or defect, was unable to appreciate the nature and quality or the wrongfulness of his acts. Mental disease or defect does not otherwise constitute a defense. 18 U.S.C.A. §§ 17(a), 4241.

In certain states, once the insanity defense is made the burden is on the prosecution to prove that the defendant is mentally competent, while in others the burden is on the defense to prove the defendant is insane. In federal criminal cases, the defendant has the burden of proving the defense of insanity by clear and convincing evidence. 18 U.S.C.A. § 17.

See also Automatism; Diminished responsibility doctrine; Durham rule; Irresistible impulse; M'Naghten Rule and Right and wrong test, for various other tests used by courts to determine criminal responsibility of defendant who asserts insanity defense. *See also* Competency; Incompetency; Insane delusion; Lucid interval; Sanity hearing; Substantial capacity test; Uncontrollable impulse.

Insanity as Affecting Capacity

Capacity to make a will includes an intelligent understanding of the testator's property, its extent and items, and of the nature of the act he is about to perform, together with a clear understanding and purpose as to the manner of its distribution and the persons who are to receive it. Lacking these, the testator is not mentally competent. The presence of insane delusions is not inconsistent with testamentary capacity, if they are of such a nature that they cannot reasonably be supposed to have affected the dispositions made by the will; and the same is true of the various forms of monomania and of all kinds of eccentricity and personal idiosyncrasy. But imbecility, senile dementia, and all forms of systematized mania which affect the understanding and judgment generally disable the person from making a valid will. To constitute "senile dementia," incapacitating one to make a will, there must be such a failure of the mind as to deprive the testator of intelligent action. *See also* Capacity.

As a ground for voiding or annulling a contract or conveyance, insanity does not mean a total deprivation of reason, but an inability, from defect of perception, memory, and judgment, to do the act in question or to understand its nature and consequences. The insanity must have entered into and induced the particular contract or conveyance; it must appear that it was not the act of the free and untrammeled mind, and that on account of the diseased condition of the mind the person entered into a contract or made a conveyance which he would not have made if he had been in the possession of his reason.

Most state statutes provide for annulment of a marriage because of insanity. Insanity sufficient to justify the annulment of a marriage means such a want of understanding at the time of the marriage as to render the party incapable of assenting to the contract of marriage. Also, under most state statutes, insanity, if sufficient in degree and/or duration, constitutes a ground for divorce. In general, the same degree of mental capacity which enables a person to make a valid deed or will is sufficient to enable him to marry.

As a ground for restraining the personal liberty of the person (*i.e.* commitment), it may be said in general that the form of insanity from which he suffers should be such as to make his going at large a source of danger to himself or to others, though this matter is largely regulated by statute, and in many places the law permits the commitment of persons whose insanity does not manifest itself in homicidal or other destructive forms of mania, but who are incapable of caring for themselves and their property or who are simply fit subjects for treatment in hospitals and other institutions specially designed for the care of such patients. *See* Commitment.

To constitute insanity such as will authorize the appointment of a guardian or conservator, there must be such a deprivation of reason and judgment as to render him incapable of understanding and acting with discretion in the ordinary affairs of life; a want of sufficient mental capacity to transact ordinary business and to take care of and manage his property and affairs.

Insanity as a plea or proceeding to avoid the effect of the statute of limitations means practically the same thing as in relation to the appointment of a guardian. On the one hand, it does not require a total deprivation of reason or absence of understanding. On the other hand, it does not include mere weakness of mind short of imbecility. It means such a degree of derangement as renders the subject incapable of understanding the nature of the particular affair and

his rights and remedies in regard to it and incapable of taking discreet and intelligent action. The time of sanity required in order to allow the statute to begin to run is such as will enable the party to examine his affairs and institute an action, and is for the jury.

There are a few other legal rights or relations into which the question of insanity enters, such as the capacity of a witness or of a voter; but they are governed by the same general principles. The test is capacity to understand and appreciate the nature of the particular act and to exercise intelligence in its performance. A witness must understand the nature and purpose of an oath and have enough intelligence and memory to relate correctly the facts within his knowledge. So a voter must understand the nature of the act to be performed and be able to make an intelligent choice of candidates. In either case, eccentricity, feeble-mindedness not amounting to imbecility, or insane delusions which do not affect the matter in hand, do not disqualify.

Inscribed. Entered (*e.g.* a name) on a list or in a register. Type of government bonds, such as Series E, whose records are kept by the Federal Reserve Bank rather than by the Treasury Dept.

Inscription. In evidence, anything written or engraved upon a metallic or other solid substance, intended for great durability; as upon a tombstone, pillar, tablet, medal, ring, etc.

The entry of a mortgage, lien, or other document at large in a book of public records; corresponding to "recording" or "registration."

In civil law, an engagement which a person who makes a solemn accusation of a crime against another enters into that he will suffer the same punishment, if he has accused the other falsely, which would have been inflicted upon him had he been guilty.

Insecure. Unsafe and dangerous. Not secure or safe; not certain. Impairment or loss of security. *See* Acceleration clause; Insecurity clause.

Insecurity clause. Provision in contract that allows a creditor to make an entire debt come due if there is good reason to believe that the debtor cannot or will not pay. *See also* Acceleration clause.

Insider. With respect to federal regulation of purchase and sale of securities, refers to anyone who has knowledge of facts not available to the general public (*e.g.*, officers, directors, key employees, relatives). 15 U.S.C.A. § 78p(a). An insider is liable for insider stock trading under section 10(b) of the Securities Exchange Act of 1934 and SEC Rule 10b–5 only where he or she fails to disclose material non-public information before trading on it and thus makes secret profits. In determining whether a person, not a director or officer, is a corporate "insider" who as a purchaser of stock has a duty to disclose material facts unknown to seller, the test is whether he had such a relationship to corporation that he had access to information which should be used only for corporate purposes and not for personal benefit of anyone. *See also* Insider information; Insider reports; Insider trading; Rule 10b–5; Short swing profits; Tippees.

For purposes of Bankruptcy Code, "insider" is entity or person with sufficiently close relationship with debtor that his conduct is made subject to closer scrutiny than those dealing at arm's length with debtor. Bankruptcy Code § 101.

Insider information. Information about a company's financial situation that is obtained by insiders (officers, directors, employees, etc.), before the public obtains it. True inside information is usually only known by corporate officials or other "insiders." SEC rules and court decisions restrict stock trading by insiders on the basis of such information. *See also* Insider; Insider trading; Tippees.

Insider reports. Monthly reports required by Securities and Exchange Commission from directors, officers and stockholders of their transactions in stock of which they own more than 10% of such shares. 15 U.S.C.A. § 78p(a).

Insider trading. Term refers to transactions in shares of publicly held corporations by persons with inside or advance information on which the trading is based. Usually the trader himself is an insider with an employment or other relation of trust and confidence with the corporation. Such transactions must be reported monthly to Securities and Exchange Commission (*see* Insider reports).

The Supreme Court has established rules governing liability for insider trading under section 10(b) of the Securities Exchange Act of 1934 and SEC Rule 10b–5. Two elements for establishing a violation of section 10(b) and Rule 10b–5 by corporate insiders are the existence of a relationship affording access to inside information intended to be available only for a corporate purpose, and the unfairness of allowing a corporate insider to take advantage of that information by trading without disclosure. *See* Insider.

Insignia /insígn(i)yə/. Ensigns or arms; distinctive marks; badges; *indicia;* characteristics.

Insinuation. To hint or suggest doubt or suspicion.

In solido /in sólədow/. In the civil law, for the whole; as a whole. An obligation *in solido* is one where each of the several obligors is liable for the whole; that is, it is joint and several. Possession *in solidum* is exclusive possession. When several persons obligate themselves to the obligee by the terms *"in solido,"* or use any other expressions

which clearly show that they intend that each one shall be separately bound to perform the whole of the obligation, it is called an "obligation *in solido*" on the part of the obligors.

Insolvency. The condition of a person or business that is insolvent; inability or lack of means to pay debts. Such a relative condition of a person's or entity's assets and liabilities that the former, if all made immediately available, would not be sufficient to discharge the latter. Under bankruptcy law, the condition of a person or firm that is unable to pay debts as they fall due, or in the usual course of trade or business. Financial condition such that businesses' or person's debts are greater than aggregate of such debtor's property at a fair valuation. In general, state insolvency laws have been superseded by the Federal Bankruptcy Code (11 U.S.C.A.). *See* Bankruptcy proceedings.

"Insolvency" under the Bankruptcy Code is defined in § 101.

"Technical" insolvency is a situation in which a firm is unable to meet its current obligations as they come due, even though the value of its assets may exceed its liabilities.

Under U.C.C., a person is insolvent who either has ceased to pay his debts in the ordinary course of business or cannot pay his debts as they fall due or is insolvent within the meaning of the Federal Bankruptcy Law. U.C.C. § 1–201(23).

Insolvency proceeding. Any proceeding intended to liquidate or rehabilitate the estate of the person involved, including any assignment for the benefit of creditors and any chapter proceeding under federal bankruptcy law. U.C.C. § 1–201(22). *See* Bankruptcy proceedings.

Insolvency risk. The risk that a firm will be unable to discharge its debt. Also called bankruptcy risk.

In specie /in spíys(h)iy(iy)/. Specific; specifically. Thus, to decree performance *in specie* is to decree specific performance. In kind; in the same or like form. A thing is said to exist *in specie* when it retains its existence as a distinct individual of a particular class.

Inspectator. A prosecutor or adversary.

Inspection. To examine; scrutinize; investigate; look into; check over; or view for the purpose of ascertaining the quality, authenticity or conditions of an item, product, document, residence, business, etc. Word has broader meaning than just looking, and means to examine carefully or critically, investigate and test officially, especially a critical investigation or scrutiny. *See also* Freedom of Information Act; In camera inspection; Privacy laws.

Discovery practice. Rights of parties in civil actions to inspect papers, documents, land, etc. of opposing party are governed by Fed.R. Civil P. 26 and 34. Similar rights of prosecutor and defendant in criminal cases are governed by Fed.R. Crim.P. 16. Under discovery rules and statutes, "inspection" is sufficiently broad to include testing of evidence, and is not necessarily confined to visual observation but is ordinarily understood to embrace tests and examinations. *See also* Inspection of documents; Jencks Act or Rule; Subpoena duces tecum.

Reasonable inspection. As relates to duty of employer to provide employee with proper instrumentalities with which to work, does not mean such an inspection as would necessarily or infallibly disclose a defect if one existed, but only such inspection as reasonably prudent man, in the exercise of ordinary care, would make.

Inspection laws. Laws authorizing and directing the inspection and examination of various kinds of merchandise intended for sale, especially food, with a view to ascertaining its fitness for use, and excluding unwholesome or unmarketable goods from sale that do not conform to standards prescribed by regulations, and directing the appointment of official inspectors for that purpose; *e.g.* grain or meat inspection laws. State and federal inspection laws may also be concerned with employment safety conditions (*e.g.* Occupational Safety and Health Act (OSHA)); building construction safety (*e.g.* building ordinances); health conditions of restaurants or food processors; and safety conditions of motor vehicles. *See* Food and Drug Administration; Occupational Safety and Health Administration.

If a resident refuses permission to a fire, health, building, etc. inspector to inspect the premises, a search warrant will be required. A warrant is likewise required for inspection of business premises by OSHA inspectors.

See also Freedom of Information Act; Inspection rights; Inspection searches; Privacy laws.

Inspection of documents. This phrase refers to the right of a party, in a civil action, to inspect and make copies of documents which are essential or material to the maintenance of his cause, and which are either in the custody of an officer of the law or in the possession of the adverse party. Fed.R. Civil P. 26, 34 and 37. Such opportunity for inspection in criminal cases is afforded both the prosecutor and defendant under Fed.R. Crim.P. 16. *See also* Subpoena duces tecum.

Inspection rights. Buyer of goods has right to inspect them before payment or acceptance at any reasonable place and time and in any reasonable manner. U.C.C. § 2–513(1). *See also* Inspection.

With respect to discovery in civil actions, Fed.R. Civil P. 26 and 34 affords a party the right to inspect documents, records, land, etc. of the other party. Similar rights are afforded the prosecutor

and defendant under Fed.R.Crim.P. 16. *See also* Inspection of documents; Subpoena duces tecum.

Inspection searches. Administrative searches conducted by local or state authorities for health or building law enforcement must be based on a warrant issued on probable cause. A warrant is likewise required for inspection of business premises by OSHA inspectors. An exception to the warrant requirement is in cases involving closely regulated industries where the commercial operator's privacy interest is adequately protected by detailed regulatory schemes authorizing warrantless inspections. *See also* Inspection laws.

Inspector. The name given to certain officers whose duties are to examine and inspect things over which they have jurisdiction. Officers whose duty it is to examine the quality of certain articles of merchandise, food, weights and measures, working conditions of business, structural soundness of building, etc.; *e.g.* federal grain or meat inspectors; OSHA inspectors; building inspectors; health inspectors. *See also* Inspection laws.

Inspector general. Various agencies of the federal government have an office of Inspector General whose primary function is to conduct and supervise audits and investigations relating to programs and operations of the particular agency. 5 U.S.C.A.App.

Install. To place in a seat, give a place to; to set, place, or instate in an office, rank, or order, etc. To set up or fix in position for use or service.

Installation. The ceremony of inducting or investing with any charge, office, or rank, as the placing a bishop into his see, a dean or prebendary into his stall or seat, or a knight into his order. The act by which an officer is put in public possession of the place he is to fill. The President of the United States, or a governor, is installed into office, by being sworn agreeably to the constitution and laws.

Installment. Partial payment of a debt or collection of a receivable. Different portions of the same debt payable at different successive periods as agreed. Partial payments on account of a debt due. *See* Installment loan.

Installment contract. Type of agreement calling for periodic performances and payments.

An "installment contract" is one which requires or authorizes the delivery of goods in separate lots to be separately accepted, even though the contract contains a clause "each delivery is a separate contract" or its equivalent. U.C.C. § 2–612.

See Installment land contract; Installment sale; Retail installment contract.

Installment credit. Commercial arrangement in which buyer undertakes to pay in more than one payment and seller agrees to sell on such basis and in which a finance charge may be exacted.

Such agreements are commonly subject to statutory disclosure regulation; *e.g.* Truth-in-Lending laws. *See also* Annual percentage rate.

Installment land contract. Type of contract by which buyer is required to make periodic payments towards purchase price of land and only on the last payment is the seller required to deliver a deed. Also called a "contract for deed" or "long-term land contract." *See also* Land contract.

Installment loan. A loan made to be repaid in specified, usually equal, amounts over a certain number of months. The contract specifies the amount and method of payment. Consumer installment loan contracts are subject to disclosure requirements of Truth-in-Lending Act *(q.v.)*. *See also* Annual percentage rate; Balloon payment; Installment credit; Installment sale.

Installment method. A method of accounting enabling a taxpayer to spread the recognition of gain on the sale of property over the payout period. Under this elective procedure, the seller computes the gross profit percentage from the sale (*i.e.,* the gain divided by the selling price) and applies it to each payment received to arrive at the gain to be recognized. Effective for tax years beginning after 1987, a restriction has been placed on the use of the installment method and dealers in real estate or personal property are not permitted to use the installment method to report gains from the sale of property. I.R.C. § 453.

Installment note. *See* Installment loan.

Installment plan. Commercial sales arrangement by which goods are sold and buyer pays for them in periodic payments. *See also* Installment contract; Installment credit; Installment loan; Installment sale.

Installment receivable. Amounts due an entity from sales made on an installment plan. Such plans require specified, uniform payments over a predetermined number of months.

Installment sale. Commercial arrangement by which buyer makes initial down payment and signs a contract for payment of the balance in installments over a period of time. In accounting for such sales, the seller may either account for the profits on basis of each installment payment received or the entire amount in the period of the sale; in latter case, reserves are established for bad debts, collection expenses and costs of reconditioning returned merchandise. *See also* Installment contract; Installment credit; Installment loan; Installment method; Truth-in-Lending Act.

Retail installment sale. The sale of goods or the furnishing of services by a retail seller to a retail buyer for a deferred payment price payable in installments. Retail installment sales contracts are governed with respect to disclosure of terms

and finance charges by Truth-in-Lending Act *(q.v.)*. *See also* Annual percentage rate.

Instant. Present, current, as instant case.

Instantaneous crime. One which is fully consummated or completed in and by a single act (such as arson or murder) as distinguished from one which involves a series or repetition of acts.

Instantaneous death. *See* Death.

Instanter /instǽntər/. Immediately; instantly; forthwith; without delay. Trial *instanter* was had where a prisoner between attainder and execution pleaded that he was not the same who was attainted. When a party was ordered to plead *instanter,* he was required to plead the same day. The term was usually understood to mean within twenty-four hours.

Instantly. Immediately; directly; without delay; at once.

Instigate /ínstəgeyt/. To stimulate or goad to an action, especially a bad action; one of its synonyms is "abet". *See* Aid and abet; Entrapment.

Instigation /ìnstəgéyshən/. Incitation; urging; solicitation. The act by which one incites another to do something, as to commit some crime or to commence a suit. *See* Aid and abet; Entrapment; Incite.

In stirpes /ìn stə́rpiyz/. In the law of intestate succession, according to the roots or stocks; by representation; as distinguished from succession *per capita*. *See* Per capita; Per stirpes.

Institute, *v.* To inaugurate or commence, as to institute an action. To set up; to originate; to initiate; to start; to introduce. To nominate, constitute, or appoint, as to institute an heir by testament. *See* Institution.

Institute, *n.* Act of instituting; something that is instituted. A principle recognized as authoritative; also the organization which drafts and authors such authoritative principles; *e.g.* American Law Institute. *See also* Institution.

Instituted executor. An instituted executor is one who is appointed by the testator without any condition.

Institute of Certified Management Accountants. An affiliate organization of the National Association of Accountants that administers the CMA Examination, monitors the work experience of CMA candidates, and reviews the continuing education requirements of CMAs.

Institutes. A name sometimes given to textbooks containing the elementary principles of jurisprudence, arranged in an orderly and systematic manner. For example, the Institutes of Justinian, of Gaius, of Lord Coke.

Institution. The commencement or inauguration of anything, as the commencement of an action.

The first establishment of a law, rule, rite, etc. Any custom, system, organization, etc., firmly established. An elementary rule or principle. *See also* Institute.

An establishment, especially one of eleemosynary or public character or one affecting a community. An established or organized society or corporation. It may be private in its character, designed for profit to those composing the organization, or public and charitable in its purposes, or educational (*e.g.* college or university). A foundation, as a literary or charitable institution.

Civil law. The appointment of an heir; the act by which a testator nominates one or more persons to succeed him in all his rights active and passive.

Political law. A law, rite, or ceremony enjoined by authority as a permanent rule of conduct or of government. An organized society, established either by law or the authority of individuals, for promoting any object, public or social.

A system or body of usages, laws, or regulations, of extensive and recurring operation, containing within itself an organism by which it effects its own independent action, continuance, and generally its own further development. Its object is to generate, effect, regulate, or sanction a succession of acts, transactions, or productions of a peculiar kind or class. We are likewise in the habit of calling single laws or usages "institutions," if their operation is of vital importance and vast scope, and if their continuance is in a high degree independent of any interfering power.

Practice. Commencement of civil action or criminal prosecution. *See* Commence.

Public institution. One which is created and exists by law or public authority, for benefit of public in general; *e.g.*, a public hospital, charity, college, university, etc.

Institutional investors. Large investors, such as mutual funds, pension funds, insurance companies, and others who largely invest other people's money.

Institutional lender. Banks, savings and loan associations, and other businesses which make loans in the ordinary course of business, rather than individuals, credit unions, or companies which may make loans to employees.

Instruct. To convey information as a client to an attorney, or as an attorney to a counsel, or as a judge to a jury. To authorize one to appear as advocate; to give a case in charge to the jury.

Instructions to jury. *See* Jury instructions.

Instrument. A formal or legal document in writing, such as a contract, deed, will, bond, or lease. A writing that satisfies the requisites of negotiability prescribed by U.C.C. Art. 3. A negotiable instrument (defined in U.C.C. § 3–104), or a security (defined in U.C.C. § 8–102) or any other writing which evidences a right to the payment of money and is not itself a security agreement or lease and is of a type which is in ordinary course of business transferred by delivery with any necessary indorsement or assignment. U.C.C. § 9–105(1).

Anything reduced to writing, a document of a formal or solemn character, a writing given as a means of affording evidence. A document or writing which gives formal expression to a legal act or agreement, for the purpose of creating, securing, modifying, or terminating a right. A writing executed and delivered as the evidence of an act or agreement. Anything which may be presented as evidence to the senses of the adjudicating tribunal.

Incomplete instrument. A paper whose contents show, at the time of signing, that it is intended to become an instrument but that is not an instrument because a necessary element is missing. See U.C.C. § 3–115(1).

See also Bearer instrument; Bill; Commercial paper; Negotiable instruments; Note.

Instrumental. Serviceable, helpful; serving as a means or agent; something by which an end is achieved.

Instrumentality. Something by which an end is achieved; a means, medium, agency.

Instrumentality rule. Under this rule, corporate existence will be disregarded where a corporation (subsidiary) is so organized and controlled and its affairs so conducted as to make it only an adjunct and instrumentality of another corporation (parent corporation), and parent corporation will be responsible for the obligations of its subsidiary.

The so-called "instrumentality" or "alter ego" rule states that when a corporation is so dominated by another corporation that the subservient corporation becomes a mere instrument and is really indistinct from controlling corporation, then the corporate veil of dominated corporation will be disregarded, if to retain it results in injustice.

Instrument of appeal. The document by which an appeal is brought in an English matrimonial cause from the president of the probate, divorce, and admiralty division to the full court. It is analogous to a petition.

Instrument of evidence. Instruments of evidence are the *media* through which the evidence of facts, either disputed or required to be proved, is conveyed to the mind of a judicial tribunal; and they comprise persons and living things as well as writings. Demonstrative evidence.

Insubordination. State of being insubordinate; disobedience to constituted authority. Refusal to obey some order which a superior officer is entitled to give and have obeyed. Term imports a wilful or intentional disregard of the lawful and reasonable instructions of the employer.

Insufficiency of evidence to support verdict. This phrase in a motion for new trial, motion for directed verdict, or for judgment notwithstanding the verdict, means that there is some evidence, but not enough in light of the evidence to the contrary to support a verdict. It does not mean that evidence is factually insufficient to support affirmative finding on an issue, but that there is no evidence to warrant submission of the issue. *See also* Directed verdict; Dismissal; Judgment *(Judgment notwithstanding verdict)*. *Compare* Sufficiency of evidence.

Insufficient. Not sufficient; inadequate to some need, purpose, or use; wanting in needful value, ability, or fitness; incompetent; unfit, as insufficient food; insufficient means. It is the antonym of "sufficient."

Insufficient funds. Bank term meaning that the drawers deposit balance is less than the amount of the check drawn on such account. *See* Bad check.

Insular courts. Federal courts established by Congress with jurisdiction over insular possessions of the United States.

Insular possessions. Island territories of the U.S., *e.g.* Puerto Rico.

Insulation period. The sixty days immediately preceding the expiration of a collective bargaining agreement when no representation petition may be filed. This is to permit the employer and incumbent union the opportunity to negotiate a new contract without rival claims for recognition.

Insurable. Capable of being insured against loss, damage, illness, death, etc.; proper to be insured as based on standards of insurer; affording a sufficient ground for insurance. *Compare* Noninsurable risk.

Insurable interest. Such a real and substantial interest in specific property as will prevent a contract to indemnify the person interested against its loss from being a mere wager policy. Such an interest as will make the loss of the property of pecuniary damage to the insured. A right, benefit, or advantage arising out of the property or dependent thereon, or any liability in respect thereof, or any relation thereto or concern therein, of such a nature that it might be so affected by the contemplated peril as to directly damnify the insured. Generally, an "insurable interest" exists where insured derives pecuniary benefit or advantage by preservation and continued existence of property or would sustain pecuniary loss from its destruction.

In the case of life insurance, a reasonable expectation of pecuniary benefit from the continued life of another; also, a reasonable ground, founded upon the relation of the parties to each other, either pecuniary or of blood or affinity, to expect some benefit or advantage from the continuance of the life of the assured.

Insurable value. Value of property for insurance purposes. Based on the value of the property, less indestructible parts (land) for fire insurance. For title insurance purposes, the sales price (market value) is used.

Insurance. A contract whereby, for a stipulated consideration, one party undertakes to compensate the other for loss on a specified subject by specified perils. The party agreeing to make the compensation is usually called the "insurer" or "underwriter;" the other, the "insured" or "assured;" the agreed consideration, the "premium;" the written contract, a "policy;" the events insured against, "risks" or "perils;" and the subject, right, or interest to be protected, the "insurable interest." A contract whereby one undertakes to indemnify another against loss, damage, or liability arising from an unknown or contingent event and is applicable only to some contingency or act to occur in future. An agreement by which one party for a consideration promises to pay money or its equivalent or to do an act valuable to other party upon destruction, loss, or injury of something in which other party has an interest.

See also Additional insurance; Insurable interest; Liability limits; Lloyd's insurance; Lloyd's of London; Loss; Named insured; Partial limitation; Participation; Policy of insurance; Premium; Pro rata clause; Reinsurance; Replacement insurance; Self-insurance.

Classification

Accident insurance. Form of insurance which undertakes to indemnify the assured against expense, loss of time, and suffering resulting from accidents causing him physical injury, usually by payment at a fixed rate per month while the consequent disability lasts, and sometimes including the payment of a fixed sum to his heirs in case of his death by accident within the term of the policy. *See also, Casualty insurance below.*

Accounts receivable insurance. Insurance coverage designed to protect against inability to collect because of damage to records which support the accounts.

Additional insured. A person other than the named insured, such as the insured's spouse, who is protected under the terms of the contract.

Air travel insurance. Form of life insurance which may be purchased by air travelers according to the terms of which the face value of the policy is paid to the named beneficiary in the event of death resulting from a particular flight.

All-risk insurance. Type of insurance policy which ordinarily covers every loss that may happen, except by fraudulent acts of the insured. Type of policy which protects against all risks and perils except those specifically enumerated.

Annuity insurance. An insurance contract calling for periodic payments to the insured or annuitant for a stated period or for life.

Assessment insurance. A species of mutual insurance in which the policyholders are assessed as losses are incurred. A contract by which payments to insured are not unalterably fixed, but dependent on collection of assessments necessary to pay amounts insured, while an "old-line policy" unalterably fixes premiums and definitely and unchangeably fixes insurer's liability.

Automobile insurance may embrace insurance against loss of or damage to a motor vehicle caused by fire, windstorm, theft, collision, or other insurable hazards, and also against legal liability for personal injuries or damage to property resulting from operation of the vehicle. Policy of indemnity to protect the operator and owner from liability to third persons as a result of the operation of the automobile. *See also Collision insurance;* and *No-fault auto insurance, below,* this topic.

Business insurance. Type of insurance which protects a business on the disability or death of a key employee. *See also Key man life insurance, below.*

Business interruption insurance. Type of insurance which protects a business from losses due to inability to operate because of fire or other hazards.

Cargo insurance. Insures risk that cargo will not be delivered in the same condition in which it was initially shipped.

Casualty insurance. That type of insurance that is primarily concerned with losses caused by injuries to persons and legal liability imposed upon the insured for such injury or for damage to the property of others.

Coinsurance. Provision in a policy that the liability of the insurer is limited to that proportion of the loss which the amount of insurance bears to a particular percentage of the value of property at the time of the loss. *See also Coinsurance.*

Collision insurance. A form of automobile insurance that covers loss to the insured vehicle from its collision with another vehicle or object, but not covering bodily injury or liability also arising out of the collision. Type of coverage which protects insured for damage to his own property in an accident as contrasted with liability insurance which protects him in an action or claim for loss to another's property.

See also Convertible collision insurance, below.

Commercial insurance. Indemnity agreements, in the form of insurance bonds or policies, whereby parties to commercial contracts are to a designated extent guaranteed against loss by reason of a breach of contractual obligations on the part of the other contracting party. To this class belong policies of contract credit and title insurance.

Comprehensive insurance. See *All-risk insurance, above.*

Concurrent insurance. Insurance coverage under two or more similar policies of varying dates and amounts.

Convertible collision insurance. Type of collision coverage generally carrying lower premium but requiring higher premium after first loss or claim; an alternative form of deductible collision coverage.

Convertible insurance. A policy that may be changed to another form by contractual provision and without evidence of insurability. Usually used to refer to term life insurance convertible to permanent insurance.

Convertible life insurance. Generally a form of term life insurance which gives the insured the right to change policy to permanent life insurance without medical examination.

Cooperative insurance. Type of non-stock mutual insurance in which the policyholders are the owners; may be assessable or nonassessable.

Credit insurance. Type of insurance protection against losses due to death, disability, insolvency or bankruptcy of debtor. Policy covers balance of debt due, with proceeds payable to creditor. Commonly offered by banks and other lenders. Terms and conditions of such are regulated by federal and state statutes; *e.g.* Truth-in-Lending laws. *See also* Credit insurance.

Crime insurance. Type of insurance which protects insured from losses due to criminal acts against insured such as burglary, etc. Such insurance is sponsored by federal government for residents of certain high-crime localities.

Crop insurance. Insurance coverage against financial loss due to destruction of agricultural products resulting from rain, hail, and other elements of nature. Such insurance is sponsored by Federal Crop Insurance Corporation.

Decreasing term insurance. A term insurance policy where the premiums are uniform throughout its life, but the face value of the policy declines. Sometimes called a home protection plan because the face value declines much in the same way a mortgage due on a house declines. A form of life insurance that provides a death benefit of amount declining throughout the term of the contract to zero at the end of the term.

Deposit insurance. Federally sponsored (Federal Deposit Insurance Corp.) insurance coverage against loss of deposits due to bank or savings and loan closings.

Directors' and officers' (D & O) liability insurance. Such insures corporate directors and officers against claims based on negligence, failure to disclose, and to a limited extent, other defalcations. Such insurance provides coverage against expenses and to a limited extent fines, judgments and amounts paid in settlement.

Disability insurance. See Disability insurance.

Employer's liability insurance. In this form of insurance the risk insured against is the liability of the assured to make compensation or pay damages for an accident, injury, or death occurring to a servant or other employee in the course of his employment, either at common law or under statutes imposing such liability on employers. Coverage which protects employer as to claims not covered under worker's compensation insurance.

Endowment insurance. Type of protection which combines life insurance and investment so that if the insured outlives the policy the face value is paid to him. If he does not outlive it, the face value is paid to his beneficiary.

Errors and omissions insurance. Insurance that indemnifies the insured for any loss sustained because of an error or oversight on his part.

Excess insurance. Coverage against loss in excess of a stated amount or in excess of coverage provided under another insurance contract.

Extended term insurance. A non-forfeiture provision in most policies which continues the existing amount of life insurance for as long a period of time as the contract's cash value will purchase term coverage.

Family income insurance. Type of term insurance designed to give maximum coverage during the period of maximum family dependency.

Fidelity insurance. Form of insurance in which the insurer undertakes to guaranty the fidelity of an officer, agent, or employee of the assured, or rather to indemnify the latter for losses caused by dishonesty or a want of fidelity on the part of such a person. *See also* Fidelity and guaranty insurance.

Fire insurance. A contract of insurance by which the underwriter, in consideration of the premium, undertakes to indemnify the insured against all losses in his houses, buildings, furniture, ships in port, or merchandise, by means of accidental fire happening within a prescribed period. *See also* Loss payable clause; Pro rata distribution clause.

First party insurance. Insurance which applies to the insured's own property or person.

Fleet policy insurance. Type of blanket policy covering a number of vehicles of the same insured; *e.g.* covers pool or fleet of vehicles owned by business.

Floater insurance. A form of insurance that applies to moveable property whatever its location, if within the territorial limits imposed by the contract.

Flood insurance. Insurance indemnifying against loss by flood damage. Required by lenders in areas designated as potential flood areas. The insurance is privately issued but federally subsidized.

Fraternal insurance. The form of life or accident insurance furnished by a fraternal beneficial association, consisting in the undertaking to pay to a member, or his heirs in case of death, a stipulated sum of money, out of funds raised for that purpose by the payment of dues or assessments by all the members of the association.

Government insurance. Life insurance underwritten and offered by Federal government to war veterans. *See also National service life insurance; War risk insurance, below.*

Group health insurance. Provides protection to employees or other members covered under group policy for hospital, surgical and other medical expenses.

Group insurance. A form of insurance whereby individual lives of a group of persons, usually employees, are in consideration of a flat periodical premium based on average age and paid either by employer in whole or partially by both employer and employee, insured each in a definite sum so long as insured remains in such employment and the premiums are paid. Coverage of number of individuals by means of single or blanket policy. Type of insurance (life, medical, dental, automobile, legal) offered to employees or other homogeneous group under a single master policy. Generally, each employee receives a certificate of participation instead of a policy.

Group term life insurance. Life insurance coverage permitted by an employer for a group of employees. Such insurance is renewable on a year-to-year basis and does not accumulate in value (*i.e.,* no cash surrender value is built up). The premiums paid by the employer on such insurance are not taxed to an employee on coverage of up to a specified amount per year.

Guaranty or fidelity insurance. A contract whereby one, for a consideration, agrees to indemnify another against loss arising from the want of integrity or fidelity of employees and persons holding positions of trust, or embezzlements by them, or against the insolvency of debtors, losses in trade, loss by non-payment of notes, or against breaches of contract.

Hail insurance. Type of insurance which provides protection against loss of crops, grain, etc. because of hail storms. *See also Crop insurance, above.*

Health insurance. A contract or agreement whereby an insurer is obligated to pay or allow a benefit of pecuniary value with respect to the bodily injury, disablement, sickness, death by accident or accidental means of a human being, or because of any expense relating thereto, or because of any expense incurred in prevention of sickness, and includes every risk pertaining to any of the enumerated risks.

Homeowners insurance. Policy insuring individuals against any, some, or all of the risks of loss to personal dwellings or the contents thereof or the personal liability pertaining thereto.

Hull insurance. Marine or aviation insurance covering loss to vessel or plane or its machinery or equipment.

Indemnity insurance. Insurance which provides indemnity against loss, in contrast to contracts which provide for indemnity against liability. The latter are known as liability contracts or policies, and the former as indemnity contracts or policies.

Inland marine insurance. Originally, a form of insurance protection for goods transported other than on the ocean. Now, term applies to a variety of coverages on floating personal property and to general liability as a bailee.

Joint life insurance. Form of life insurance on two or more persons and payable on the death of the first to die.

Key man life insurance. Type of life insurance written on the life of an important or key officer or employee in a business organization. The business is the beneficiary and is entitled to the proceeds on his death. *See also* Key man insurance.

Last survivor insurance. Life insurance on two or more persons, the benefits of which are payable on the death of the last survivor.

Lease insurance. Protects against the loss sustained through the termination of a lease by hazards specifically insured against such as, for example, fire.

Level premium insurance. Type of insurance in which the cost is spread evenly over the premium paying period.

Liability insurance. Insurance that covers suits against the insured for such damages as injury or death to other drivers or passengers, property

damage, and the like. It is insurance for those damages for which the driver can be held liable.

Liability insurance is that form of insurance which indemnifies against liability on account of injuries to the person or property of another. It is distinguished from "indemnity insurance" (see that title, *above*), and may be issued to cover the liability of, for example, carriers, contractors, employers, landlords, manufacturers, drivers. *See also* Liability limits.

Life insurance. A contract between the holder of a policy and an insurance company (*i.e.*, the carrier) whereby the company agrees, in return for premium payments, to pay a specified sum (*i.e.*, the face value or maturity value of the policy) to the designated beneficiary upon the death of the insured.

That kind of insurance in which the risk contemplated is the death of a particular person; upon which event (if it occurs within a prescribed term, or, according to the contract, whenever it occurs) the insurer engages to pay a stipulated sum to the legal representatives of such person, or to a third person having an insurable interest in the life of such person.

See also Life insurance proceeds; Life insurance trust; *Term insurance* (this topic).

Group life insurance. Type of life insurance commonly offered by companies to their employees in which there is a master insurance contract providing life insurance benefits to each covered employee who holds a certificate indicating his participation. *See also Group term life insurance, above.*

Limited payment life insurance. Type of life insurance for which premiums are payable for a definite period after which the policy is fully paid.

Straight life insurance or whole life insurance is insurance for which premiums are collected so long as the insured may live, whereas, term insurance is insurance which promises payment only within a stipulated term covered by the policy; though such term policies are commonly renewed each term. The premium for whole life insurance remains the same whereas the premium for term insurance increases with the age of the insured, *i.e.* as the risk increases. Also, whole life policies build up cash reserves, whereas term policies do not. *See also Term insurance, below.*

Universal life insurance. Insurance over a specified period of time, which builds a cash value for policyholders over time. This coverage emphasizes the separation of the portion of the premium that is used to cover the insurance protection from the portion of the premium allocated to an investment that is used to build the policy's cash value. Investments are usually selected with a view to maximizing the rate of return.

Variable life insurance. A distinct type of whole-life insurance in which some amount of death benefit is guaranteed by the insurer, but the total death benefit and the cash-value of the insurance before death depend on the investment performance of that portion of the premium which is allocated to a separate fund. Some variable-life insurance policies allow the insured to decide how the separate account is to be invested.

Whole life insurance. A life insurance policy in which the insured pays a level premium for his or her entire life and in which there is a constantly accumulating cash value against which the insured can withdraw or borrow. Sometimes referred to as straight life insurance.

Limited policy insurance. Type of coverage which offers protection against specific perils or accidents and against no others.

Major medical insurance. Insurance protection against large medical, surgical and hospital expenses of the insured.

Malpractice insurance. Type of liability insurance which protects professional people (*e.g.* doctors, lawyers, accountants) against claims of negligence brought against them.

Manual rating insurance. Type of insurance in which the premium is set from a manual classifying types of risk on a general basis such as a particular industry without reference to the individual case.

Marine insurance. A contract whereby one party, for a stipulated premium, undertakes to indemnify the other against certain perils or sea-risks to which his ship, freight, and cargo, or some of them, may be exposed during a certain voyage, or a fixed period of time. An insurance against risks connected with navigation, to which a ship, cargo, freightage, profits, or other insurable interest in movable property may be exposed during a certain voyage or a fixed period of time. *See also Inland marine insurance, above.*

Mortgage insurance. Insurance from which the benefits are intended by the policyowner to pay off the balance due on a mortgage upon the death of the insured or to meet the payments on a mortgage as they fall due in case of the death or disability of the insured. Insurance against loss to the mortgagees in the event of default and a failure of the mortgaged property to satisfy the balance owing plus costs of foreclosure.

National service life insurance. Life insurance on servicemen. The contract is between the U.S. Government and private insurers for benefit of servicemen.

No-fault auto insurance. Type of automobile insurance in which claims for personal injury (and sometimes property damage) are made against the claimant's own insurance company (no matter who was at fault) rather than against the insurer of the party at fault. Under such state "no-fault" statutes only in cases of serious personal injuries and high medical costs may the injured bring an action against the other party or his insurer. No-fault statutes vary from state to state in terms of scope of coverage, threshold amounts, threshold types (*e.g.* monetary or verbal), etc.

Nonassessable insurance. Type of insurance in which the rate of premium is guaranteed and no additional assessments may be made against the policyholder.

Old line life insurance. Insurance on a level or flat rate plan where, for a fixed premium payable without condition at stated intervals, a certain sum is to be paid upon death without condition.

Ordinary life insurance. Whole life and permanent insurance as distinguished from term, group and industrial insurance.

Paid-up insurance. Insurance policy on which all premiums have been paid and on which no further premiums are due and for which benefits company is liable.

Participating insurance. Type of insurance issued by a mutual company on which policyholder may participate in dividend distributions.

Partnership insurance. Life insurance on lives of partners designed to enable surviving partners to buy out deceased partner's estate. Life or health insurance sold to a partnership, usually for guaranteeing business continuity in case of disability or death of a partner.

Patent insurance. Insurance against loss due to infringement of the insured's patent, or due to claim of infringement of the other's patent by the insured.

Product liability insurance. Type of liability coverage which protects manufacturers and suppliers from claims for accidents arising out of the use of their products.

Profits insurance. Policy that pays the insured for loss of profits he would have had if the damage or loss had not occurred.

Public liability insurance. Insurance liability protection against claims arising out of the insured's property, conduct or the conduct of his agent.

Reciprocal insurance. Type of insurance plan administered by an exchange rather than an insurance company and in which each insured is the insurer of the other members of the plan.

Renewable term insurance. Type of term insurance in which the premiums are level during each term, but increases at each *new* term with the age of the insured. The insured generally has the right to renew for additional terms without a medical examination.

Retirement income insurance. Type of insurance in which the insurer guarantees payment of the policy if the insured dies before a certain age and an annuity if the insured survives beyond the specified period.

Self insurance. Plan in which the insured (*e.g.* business) places aside in a fund sufficient sums to cover liability losses that may be sustained. Commonly, under such plan the business will self-insure itself up to a certain amount and then carry regular liability insurance to cover any excesses.

Single premium insurance. Type of policy on which the insured makes but one premium payment.

Social insurance. A comprehensive welfare plan established by law, generally compulsory in nature, and based on a program which spreads the cost of benefits among the entire population rather than on individual recipients. The federal government began to use social insurance programs in 1935 with the passage of the Social Security Act. The basic federal and state approaches to social insurance presently in use are: Old Age, Survivors, and Disability Insurance (*i.e.* social security); Medicare and Medicaid; unemployment insurance; and worker's compensation.

Split dollar insurance. Type of insurance in which the insurer divides the premium dollar between life insurance protection and investment for the benefit of the insured.

Step-rate premium insurance. Type of insurance in which the premium may vary from time to time at the option of the insurer.

Surety and fidelity insurance. Form of insurance which more approximates a bond which protects the insured against dishonesty of employees, agents and the public.

Term insurance. Form of pure life insurance having no cash surrender or loan value and generally furnishing insurance protection for only a specified or limited period of time; though such policy is usually renewable from term to term. *See also Convertible life; Decreasing term; Extended term; Family income; Group term; Renewable term insurance, above.*

Title insurance. A policy issued by a title company after searching the title, representing the state of that title and insuring the accuracy of its search against claims of title defects. Insurance against loss or damage resulting from defects or failure of title to a particular parcel of realty, or from the enforcement of liens existing against it

at the time of the insurance. This form of insurance is taken out by a purchaser of the property or one loaning money on mortgage, and is furnished by companies specially organized for the purpose, and which keep complete sets of abstracts or duplicates of the records, employ expert title-examiners, and prepare conveyances and transfers of all sorts. A "certificate of title" furnished by such a company is merely the formally expressed professional opinion of the company's examiner that the title is complete and perfect (or otherwise, as stated), and the company is liable only for a want of care, skill, or diligence on the part of its examiner; whereas an "insurance of title" warrants the validity of the title in any and all events. It is not always easy to distinguish between such insurance and a "guaranty of title" given by such a company, except that in the former case the maximum limit of liability is fixed by the policy, while in the latter case the undertaking is to make good any and all loss resulting from defect or failure of the title. *See also* Back title letter.

Trust insurance. A trust, the res of which consists in whole or in part of insurance policies.

Unemployment insurance. Form of taxation collected from business to fund unemployment payments and benefits.

War risk insurance. Insurance offered by the federal government to protect persons against wartime loss of vessels and property on the high seas, and death or injury while in the armed forces. Insurance covering damage caused by acts of war. War risk insurance refers to those contracts which were brought into being by the United States government during the first World War to replace ordinary life and accident insurance which was no longer available to those in the hazardous occupation of military service. *See also National service life insurance, above.*

Workers' compensation insurance. Type of protection purchased by employers to cover payments to employees who are injured in accidents arising out of and in the course of their employment; governed by statutes in all jurisdictions. *See also Employer's liability insurance, above.*

Other Insurance Terms

Aviation clause. Insurance clause limiting the liability of the insurer in case of death or injury is connected in a specified degree with aviation.

Blanket policy. Policy covering more than one type of property in one location, or one or more types of property at more than one location.

Claims made policy. Under this type policy the insured is indemnified for claims made during the policy period regardless of when the acts giving rise to those claims occur. Also called "discovery" policy. *Compare Occurrence policy, below.*

Comprehensive coverage. A simple and convenient form of indemnity now commonly available in contracts of automobile insurance. It includes not only the conventional coverages against loss caused by fire, theft, wind, water, or malicious mischief, but is generally designed to protect against all damage to the insured vehicle except collision or upset.

Concurrent insurance. That which to any extent insures the same interest against the same casualty, at the same time, as the primary insurance, on such terms that the insurers would bear proportionately the loss happening within the provisions of both policies.

Contract of insurance. See Contract of insurance.

Discovery policy. See *Claims made policy, above.*

Excess insurance. See *Excess insurance, above.*

General and special insurance. In marine insurance, a general insurance is effected when the perils insured against are such as the law would imply from the nature of the contract considered in itself and supposing none to be specified in the policy. In the case of special insurance, further perils (in addition to implied perils) are expressed in the policy.

Insurance adjuster. One undertaking to ascertain and report the actual loss to the subject-matter of insurance due to the peril insured against. The adjuster also settles claims against the insurer. Such adjuster may be employed either by the insurer or the insured. See Adjuster.

Insurance agent. Person authorized to represent insurer in dealing with third parties in matters relating to insurance. An agent employed by an insurance company to solicit insurance business. Agents of insurance companies are called "general agents" when clothed with the general oversight of the companies' business in a state or large section of country, and "local agents" when their functions are limited and confined to some particular locality. *See also Insurance broker, below.*

Insurance binder. A memorandum of the insurance coverage agreement. It extends temporary protection pending issuance of the formal policy, while the insurer is investigating the risks and setting appropriate premium rates.

Insurance broker. One who acts as middleman between insured and company, and who solicits insurance from public under no employment from any special company and places order of insurance with company selected by insurer or, in absence of any selection, with company selected by such broker. Broker is agent for insured though at same time for some purposes he may be

agent for insurer, and his acts and representations within scope of his authority as such agent are binding on insured. An "insurance agent" is tied to his company, whereas an "insurance broker" is an independent middleman not tied to a particular company.

Insurance commissioner. A public officer in most states, whose duty is to supervise the business of insurance as conducted in the state by foreign and domestic companies, for the protection and benefit of policy-holders, and especially to issue licenses, approve rates, make periodical examinations into the condition of such companies, and receive, file, and publish periodical statements of their business as furnished by them.

Insurance company. A corporation or association whose business is to make contracts of insurance. They are generally either mutual companies or stock companies. A "mutual" insurance company is one whose fund for the payment of losses consists not of capital subscribed or furnished by outside parties, but of premiums mutually contributed by the parties insured, or in other words, one in which all persons insured become members of the association and contribute either cash or assessable premium notes, or both, to a common fund, out of which each is entitled to indemnity in case of loss. A "stock" company is one organized according to the usual form of business corporations, having a capital stock divided into shares, which, with current income and accumulated surplus, constitutes the fund for the payment of losses, policy-holders paying fixed premiums and not being members of the association unless they also happen to be stockholders. *See also* Joint-stock insurance company.

Insurance contract. See Policy of insurance.

Insurance policy. See Policy of insurance.

Insurance pool. Combining together of several insurers to share premiums and losses so as to spread risks.

Insurance premium. The consideration paid by insured to insurer for insurance protection. *See* Premium.

Insurance rating. Process by which the premium for a policy is set after considering the risks involved.

Insurance trust. An agreement between insured and trustee, whereby proceeds of policy are paid directly to trustee for investment and distribution to designated beneficiaries in manner and at such time as insured has directed in trust agreement. *See also* Trust.

Insuring clause. Provision in insurance policy or bond which recites the agreement of the insurer to protect the insured against some form of loss or damage.

Interinsurance. Insurance system whereby several individuals, partnerships, or corporations, through common attorney in fact, underwrite one another's risks against loss under agreement that underwriters act separately and severally. It is distinguishable from all other forms of insurance, in that every insured is interinsurer, and every insurer is insured.

Loss. See Loss.

Mutual insurance company. See that term.

Occurrence policy. This type policy provides for indemnity, regardless of when claim is made or reported, if act giving rise to the claim occurred during policy period. *Compare Claims made policy, above.*

Over-insurance. Insurance effected upon property, either in one or several companies, to an amount which, separately or in the aggregate, exceeds the actual value of the property. *See Excess insurance, above.*

Policy of insurance. See that title.

Reinsurance. Insurance of an insurer; a contract by which an insurer procures a third person (usually another insurance company) to insure it against loss or liability, or a portion of such, by reason of the original insurance.

Standard policy. A form of insurance contract which is required, or recommended, to be issued in a particular state. Such is regulated by various state statutes and administrative officials.

Umbrella policy. A form of insurance protection against losses in excess of the amount covered by other liability insurance policies. Type of supplemental or excess liability policy that provides coverage above basic or normal limits of liability.

Under-insurance. Insurance coverage for less than the value of the property. Under such policy, coverage for loss or damage to property will be reduced by percentage of under-insurance.

Underwriter. Party (insurer) who assumes a risk in return for the payment of a premium. *See* Insurer; Underwriter.

Insure. To make sure or secure, to guarantee, as, to insure safety to any one. To engage to indemnify a person against pecuniary loss from specified perils or possible liability. To provide insurance. *See also* Underwrite.

Insured. The person who obtains or is otherwise covered by insurance on his health, life, or property. The "insured" in a policy is not limited to the insured named in the policy, but applies to anyone who is insured under the policy. The owner of a policy of insurance.

Insurer. The underwriter or insurance company with whom a contract of insurance is made. The one who assumes risk or underwrites a policy, or

the underwriter or company with whom contract of insurance is made. *See also* Underwriter.

Insurgent. One who participates in an insurrection; one who opposes the execution of law by force of arms, or who rises in revolt against the constituted authorities. An enemy.

Insurrection. A rebellion, or rising of citizens or subjects in resistance to their government. Insurrection consists in any combined resistance to the lawful authority of the state, with intent to cause the denial thereof, when the same is manifested, or intended to be manifested, by acts of violence. It is a federal crime to incite, assist, or engage in a rebellion or insurrection against the United States. 18 U.S.C.A. § 2383. *See also* Internal security acts.

Intangible asset. Property that is a "right" such as a patent, copyright, trademark, etc., or one which is lacking physical existence, such as goodwill. A nonphysical, noncurrent asset which exists only in connection with something else, such as the goodwill of a business. An intangible asset generally has a life longer than one year, and is amortized over the period benefited, not to exceed forty years. *See* Amortization; Intangible property.

Intangible drilling costs. Costs incurred incident to and necessary for the drilling and preparation of oil or gas wells for production that have no salvage value. Under I.R.C. § 263, such costs may be deducted in the year paid rather than capitalized and depreciated.

Intangible property. As used chiefly in the law of taxation, this term means such property as has no intrinsic and marketable value, but is merely the representative or evidence of value, such as certificates of stock, bonds, promissory notes, copyrights, and franchises. *See* Intangible asset. *Compare* Tangible property.

Intangibles. Property that is a "right" such as a patent, copyright, trademark, etc., or one which is lacking physical existence; such as goodwill. *See* Amortization; General intangibles; Intangible asset.

Intangibles tax. In certain states such tax is imposed on every resident for right to exercise following privileges: (a) Signing, executing and issuing intangibles; (b) selling, assigning, transferring, renewing, removing, consigning, mailing, shipping, trading in and enforcing intangibles; (c) receiving income, increase, issues and profits of intangibles; (d) transmitting intangibles by will or gift or under state laws of descent; (e) having intangibles separately classified for taxes.

Intangible value. Nonphysical value of such assets as patents, copyrights, goodwill.

Integral. Term in ordinary usage means part or constituent component necessary or essential to complete the whole.

Integrated agreement. *See* Integrated contract; Integrated writing.

Integrated bar. The act of organizing the bar of a state into an association, membership in which is a condition precedent to the right to practice law. Integration is generally accomplished by enactment of a statute conferring authority upon the highest court of the state to integrate the bar, or by rule of court in the exercise of its inherent power.

A "unified bar" or an "integrated bar" is qualitatively different from a "voluntary bar"; membership in a unified or integrated bar is compulsory, whereas membership in a voluntary bar is voluntary, and in effect, one is not at liberty to resign from a unified bar, for, by so doing, one loses the privilege to practice law.

Integrated contract. Contract which contains within its four corners the entire agreement of the parties and parol evidence tending to contradict, amend, etc., is inadmissible; the parties having made the contract the final expression of their agreement.

An agreement is integrated where the parties thereto adopt the writing or writings as the final and complete expression of the agreement and an "integration" is the writing or writings so adopted. *See* Integrated writing.

Partial integration. Such exists where only a certain part of transaction is embodied in writing and the remainder is left in parol.

Integrated property settlements. Contract commonly made on separation or divorce of spouses wherein the parties intend that the contract become part of the court order, decree or judgment.

Integrated writing. The writing or writings adopted by the parties to an agreement as the final and complete expression of the agreement. Restatement, Second, Contracts, § 209. *See also* Integrated contract.

Integration. The act or process of making whole or entire. Bringing together different groups (as races) as equals.

Horizontal integration. Combination of two or more businesses of the same type such as manufacturers of the same type of products. Such combinations may violate antitrust laws under certain conditions. *See also* Merger.

Vertical integration. Combination of two or more businesses on different levels of operation such as manufacturing, wholesaling and retailing the same product. *See also* Merger.

Integrity. As used in statutes prescribing the qualifications of public officers, trustees, etc., this term means soundness or moral principle and character, as shown by one person dealing with others in the making and performance of con-

tracts, and fidelity and honesty in the discharge of trusts; it is synonymous with "probity," "honesty," and "uprightness."

Intelligibility. In pleading, the statement of matters of fact directly (excluding the necessity of inference or argument to arrive at the meaning) and in such appropriate terms, so arranged, as to be comprehensible by a person of common or ordinary understanding. "Each averment of a pleading shall be simple, concise, and direct." Fed.R. Civil P. 8(e).

Intemperance. A lack of moderation. Habitual intemperance is that degree of intemperance from the use of intoxicating liquor which disqualifies the person a great portion of the time from properly attending to business, or which would reasonably inflict a course of great mental anguish upon an innocent party. Habitual or excessive use of liquor. *See* Intoxication.

Intend. To design, resolve, propose. To plan for and expect a certain result. To apply a rule of law in the nature of presumption; to discern and follow the probabilities of like cases. *See also* Intent.

Intended use doctrine. In determining "intended use" for which products must be reasonably safe, manufacturer has duty to take into consideration the environment in which product will be used. In product liability cases, two factors are considered: the marketing scheme of the maker, and the foreseeability of the risks which are inherent in the product when used for the purposes intended.

Intendment of law. The true meaning, the correct understanding or intention of the law. A presumption or inference made by the courts.

Common intendment. The natural and usual sense; the common meaning or understanding; the plain meaning of any writing as apparent on its face without straining or distorting the construction.

Intent. Design, resolve, or determination with which person acts. A state of mind in which a person seeks to accomplish a given result through a course of action. As used in intentional torts, "intent" is desire to bring about result that will invade interests of another. A mental attitude which can seldom be proved by direct evidence, but must ordinarily be proved by circumstances from which it may be inferred. A state of mind existing at the time a person commits an offense and may be shown by act, circumstances and inferences deducible therefrom.

The word "intent" is used throughout the Restatement of Torts, 2nd, to denote that the actor desires to cause consequences of his act, or that he believes that the consequences are substantially certain to result from it. Sec. 8A. *See* Intentional tort.

Intent and motive should not be confused. Motive is what prompts a person to act, or fail to act. Intent refers only to the state of mind with which the act is done or omitted.

See also Aforethought; Constructive intent; Intention; Larcenous intent; Legislative intent; Malice aforethought; Manifestation of intention; Mens rea; Predatory intent; Premeditation; Presumed intent; Scienter; Specific intent; Willful.

Common intent. The natural sense given to words.

Criminal intent. See Criminal; Knowingly; Mens rea; Premeditation.

General intent. In criminal law, the intent to do that which the law prohibits. It is not necessary for the prosecution to prove that the defendant intended the precise harm or the precise result which eventuated.

Objective intent. The intent attributed to a person who appears to a reasonable third person to be making an offer to contract.

Specific intent. In criminal law, the intent to accomplish the precise act which the law prohibits; *e.g.* assault with intent to rape.

Transferred intent. In tort law, if A, intending to strike B, misses B and hits C instead, the intent to strike B is transferred and supplies the necessary intent for the tort against C. *See also* Transferred intent doctrine.

Intention. Determination to act in a certain way or to do a certain thing. Meaning; will; purpose; design. "Intention," when used with reference to the construction of wills and other documents, means the sense and meaning of it, as gathered from the words used therein. When used with reference to civil and criminal responsibility, a person who contemplates any result, as not unlikely to follow from a deliberate act of his own, may be said to intend that result, whether he desires it or not. *See also* Four corners rule; Intent; Intentionally.

Intentional. *See* Intent; Intention.

Intentionally. To do something purposely, and not accidentally or involuntarily. Person acts "intentionally" if he desires to cause consequences of his act or he believes consequences are substantially certain to result. *See also* Intent; Intention.

Intentional tort. A tort in which the actor is expressly or impliedly judged to have possessed intent or purpose to injure.

Intent to kill. An element in certain aggravated assaults and batteries which requires the prosecution to prove the intent to kill in addition to the other elements of the assault and battery. *See* Aggravated assault; Malice aforethought; Premeditation.

Inter /íntər/. Lat. Among; between.

Inter alia /íntər éyl(i)yə/°ǽliyə/. Among other things. A term anciently used in pleading, especially in reciting statutes, where the whole statute was not set forth at length. *Inter alia enactatum fuit,* among other things it was enacted.

Intercept. As used in federal wiretapping statute, means the aural acquisition of the contents of any wire or oral communication through the use of any electronic, mechanical, or other device. 18 U.S.C.A. § 2510. *See* Eavesdropping; Interception; Wiretapping.

Interception. Within Federal Communications Act, prohibiting interception of communication by wire or radio, indicates taking or seizure by the way or before arrival at destined place, and does not ordinarily connote obtaining of what is to be sent before, or at the moment, it leaves the possession of the proposed sender, or after, or at the moment, it comes into possession of intended receiver. Communications Act of 1934, § 605, 47 U.S.C.A. § 605. *See* Eavesdropping; Wiretapping.

Interchangeably. By way of exchange or interchange. This term properly denotes the method of signing deeds, leases, contracts, etc., executed in duplicate, where each party signs the copy which he delivers to the other.

Intercompany transaction. A transaction between two affiliated companies such as a parent and a subsidiary.

Intercourse. Communication; literally, a *running* or passing *between* persons or places; commerce; sexual relations.

Interdict /íntərdìkt/. A prohibitory decree.

Interest. The most general term that can be employed to denote a right, claim, title, or legal share in something. In its application to real estate or things real, it is frequently used in connection with the terms "estate," "right," and "title." More particularly it means a right to have the advantage accruing from anything; any right in the nature of property, but less than title.

The word "interest" is used throughout the Restatement of Torts, Second, to denote the object of any human desire. Sec. 1.

The word "interest" is used in the Restatement of Property both generically to include varying aggregates of rights, privileges, powers and immunities and distributively to mean any one of them. Sec. 5.

"Interest" which may disqualify a judge from hearing a suit is a personal proprietary or pecuniary interest or one affecting individual rights of the judge, and liability, gain or relief to judge must turn on outcome of suit.

See also Add on interest; Adverse interest; Against interest; Beneficial interest; Community of interest; Compelling state interest; Compound interest; Conflict of interest; Contingent interest in personal property; Coupons; Equitable interest; Executory interests; Future interests; Identity of interests; Insurable interest; Leasehold interest; Legal interest; Lessee's interest; Lessor's interest; New York interest; Ownership; Pecuniary interest; Possessory interest; Public interest; Security interest; Senior interest; Terminable interest; Usury; Vested interest.

Absolute interest. Person has absolute interest in property when such is so completely vested in individual that no contingency can deprive him of it without his consent. So, too, he is the owner of such absolute interest who must necessarily sustain the loss if the property is destroyed. *See also* Fee simple; Title.

Easement. An easement is an "interest" in land and involves the title. *See* Easement.

For use of money. Interest is the compensation allowed by law or fixed by the parties for the use or forbearance of borrowed money. Basic cost of borrowing money or buying on installment contract. Payments a borrower pays a lender for the use of the money. Cost of using credit or funds of another. A corporation pays interest on its bonds to the bondholders.

Accrued interest. Interest earned but not yet paid. *See also* Accruing interest.

Accumulated interest. Interest on bonds and other debts which is due or overdue but not yet paid.

Boston interest. *See* Boston interest.

Compound interest. Interest upon interest; *i.e.* interest paid on principal plus accrued interest. Exists where accrued interest is added to the principal sum, and the whole treated as a new principal for the calculation of the interest for the next period. Interest added to principal as interest becomes due and thereafter made to bear interest.

Conventional interest. Interest at the rate agreed upon and fixed by the parties themselves, as distinguished from that which the law would prescribe in the absence of an explicit agreement.

Excessive interest. *See* Usury.

Ex-interest. In the language of stock exchanges, a bond or other interest-bearing security is said to be sold "ex-interest" when the seller reserves to himself the interest already accrued and payable (if any) or the interest accruing up to the next interest day.

Gross interest. The total interest paid by the borrower which includes administrative costs and expenses to lender.

Interest rate. *See* Interest rate.

Interest upon interest. *See* Compound interest, above.

Legal interest. *See* Legal interest.

New York interest. Computation of interest on the exact number of days in a month and not on a thirty day month. *See also* Boston interest.

Nominal interest. The interest stated on the security and not the rate based on the price of the security.

Ordinary interest. Interest computed entirely on the principal with no interest computed on the interest past due.

Simple interest. That which is paid for the principal or sum lent, at a certain rate or allowance, made by law or agreement of parties. Interest calculated on principal where interest earned during periods before maturity of the loan is neither added to the principal nor paid to the lender. That paid on the principal lent as distinguished from compound interest which is interest paid on unpaid interest. Difference between "simple interest" and "compound interest" is that "simple interest" does not merge with principal and thus does not become part of base on which future interest is calculated.

Imputed interest. In taxation, taxable income resulting from the purchase at a bargain of assets for less than their fair value; such occurs when one is so placed as to take advantage of an opportunity not available to others. An estimated charge for interest for use of capital though no cash payment is provided. *See also* Cost (*Imputed cost*).

For certain long-term sales of property, the IRS has the authority to convert some of the gain from the sale into interest income if the contract does not provide for a minimum rate of interest to be paid by the purchaser. The application of this procedure has the effect of forcing the seller to recognize less long-term capital gain and more ordinary income (*i.e.*, interest income). I.R.C. § 483. *See also* Cost (*Imputed cost*).

Insurance. *See* Insurable interest.

Intervention. Word "interest" as used in provision of Federal Rule of Civil Procedure that on timely application anyone shall be permitted to intervene in an action when representation of his "interest" by existing parties is or may be inadequate and he is or may be bound by judgment in action means specific legal or equitable interest in case. See Fed.R.Civil P. 24.

Interest sufficient to support intervention as of right must be significant, must be direct rather than contingent, and must be based on a right which belongs to the proposed intervenor rather than to an existing party to the suit. An "interest" in the subject of an action so as to render the holder thereof a necessary party or a proper intervenor does not include a mere, consequential, remote or conjectural possibility of being in some manner affected by the result of the action but must be such a direct claim upon the subject matter of the action that the holder will either gain or lose by direct operation of the judgment to be rendered.

Penalty. Interest as a penalty is exaction for past-due obligations; it is compensation for delay in payment (*e.g.* interest impose by IRS on overdue taxes). *See also* Penalty.

Interest allowances. A consideration used in the division of net income of many partnerships. The allowances recognize differences in capital provided to the firm by the partners.

Interest coverage ratio. The ratio of earnings before interest and income taxes to interest expense.

Interested party. For purposes of administrative hearing, are those who have a legally recognized private interest, and not simply a possible pecuniary benefit.

Interest equalization tax. Tax imposed on each acquisition by a U.S. person of stock of a foreign issuer, or of a debt obligation of a foreign obligor if such obligation has a period remaining to maturity of a year or more. I.R.C. § 4911(a). This tax expired in 1974.

Interest-free loans. Bona fide loans that carry no interest (or a below-market rate). If made in a nonbusiness setting, the imputed interest element is treated as a gift from the lender to the borrower. If made by a corporation to a shareholder, a constructive dividend could result. In either event, the lender may have interest income to recognize. I.R.C. § 7872.

Interest rate. The percentage of an amount of money which is paid for its use for a specified time. Commonly expressed as an annual percentage rate (APR). Federal and state laws regulate interest rate amounts and disclosures on consumer loans. *See* Annual percentage rate; Truth-in-Lending Act; Usury.

Contract interest rate. The interest rate printed on the face of a bond certificate.

Effective interest rate. The actual rate on a bond, which may be different from the contract interest rate.

Lock rate. An interest rate established at the time of the mortgage application and guaranteed for a specified period, usually until closing. A rate can be "locked" for varying periods—30, 60 or 90 days, in most cases.

Nominal interest rate. The periodic rate of interest that is stated in a loan agreement or security. Frequently the *effective interest rate* is greater than the nominal rate because of factors like the frequency of compounding and the deduction of interest in advance.

Prime rate. The most favorable interest rates charged by a commercial bank on short-term loans to its best (*i.e.* most credit worthy) customers.

Real interest rate. The inflation-adjusted rate charged for borrowing funds.

Variable interest rate. A flexible rate of interest which increases or decreases according to current market rates.

Interest rate parity. A theory of relative exchange rates that states that the difference in interest rates in two currencies for a stated period should just offset the difference between the spot foreign exchange rate and the forward exchange rate corresponding to that period.

Interest rate swap. An agreement to swap interest payment obligations.

Interest tax shield. The reduction in income taxes that results from the tax-deductibility of interest.

Interfere. To check; hamper; hinder; infringe; encroach; trespass; disturb; intervene; intermeddle; interpose. To enter into, or to take part in, the concerns of others.

Interference. A Patent and Trademark Office proceeding to determine priority of invention between two or more parties claiming patentably indistinct subject matter. An interference may be between two or more patent applicants or one or more patentees and at least one patent applicant. It may be declared *sua sponte* by the Patent and Trademark Office or requested by a patent applicant. An interference is decided by the Board of Patent Appeals. 35 U.S.C.A. § 135. *See also* Infringement.

Interference with business relationship. The elements of this tort are the existence of a business relationship under which the plaintiff has legal rights, an intentional and unjustified interference with that relationship by defendant, and damage to plaintiff as result of breach of that business relationship.

Interference with contractual relationship. This tort has four elements: existence of valid contract, defendant's knowledge of that contract, defendant's intentional procuring of breach of that contract and damages.

Interim /íntərəm/. Lat. In the meantime; meanwhile; temporary; between. An assignee *ad interim* is one appointed between the time of bankruptcy and appointment of the regular assignee. *See also* Interlocutory.

Interim financing. A short-term loan secured to cover interim costs associated with building construction, corporate takeovers, or the like, until permanent financing (*e.g.,* mortgage, bonds) is obtained. Also called a bridge loan.

Interim officer. One appointed to fill the office during a temporary vacancy, or during an interval caused by the absence or incapacity of the regular incumbent.

Interim order. One made in the meantime, and until something is done.

Interim receipt. A receipt for money paid by way of premium for a contract of insurance for which application is made. If the risk is rejected, the money is refunded, less the *pro rata* premium.

Interim statements. In accounting, statements issued for periods less than the regular, annual accounting period. Most corporations are required to issue interim statements on a quarterly basis.

Interinsurance exchange /intərinshúrəns əkschéynj/. Reciprocal exchange (*q.v.*).

Interior Department. Executive level department of federal government overseeing agencies concerned with Indian affairs, mining, fish and wildlife, geologic research, land management, national parks and monuments, territories, flood control, conservation, public works, and related areas. *See also* Bureau of Land Management.

Interlineation. The act of writing between the lines of an instrument; also what is written between lines. *See also* Interpolate.

Interlocking confession. Confessions which are substantially the same and consistent concerning the major elements of the crime involved. They are admissible in joint trials.

Interlocking directors. Persons who serve simultaneously on the boards of directors of two or more corporations that have dealings with each other. Federal antitrust law prohibits interlocking directors of competing businesses (15 U.S.C.A. § 19); such directors may also create problems involving fiduciary duties.

Interlocutory /intərlók(y)ətəriy/. Provisional; interim; temporary; not final. Something intervening between the commencement and the end of a suit which decides some point or matter, but is not a final decision of the whole controversy. An interlocutory order or decree is one which does not finally determine a cause of action but only decides some intervening matter pertaining to the cause, and which requires further steps to be taken in order to enable the court to adjudicate the cause on the merits.

As to *interlocutory* Costs; Decree; Injunction; Judgment; Order; and Sentence, see those titles. *See also* Intermediate order.

Interlocutory appeal. An appeal of a matter which is not determinable of the controversy, but which is necessary for a suitable adjudication of the merits. *See also* Final decision rule.

Interlocutory Appeals Act. Federal Act which grants discretion to the courts of appeals to review any interlocutory order whatever in a civil case if the trial (*i.e.* federal district court) judge, in making the order, has stated in writing that the order involves a controlling question of law as to which there is substantial ground for difference of opinion and that an immediate appeal from the order may materially advance the ultimate termination of litigation. 28 U.S.C.A. § 1292.

Interlocutory decision. Any decision prior to a final decision. *See* Interlocutory. *Compare* Final decision or judgment.

Interloper. Persons who interfere or intermeddle into business to which they have no right. Persons who enter a country or place to trade without license. One who meddles in affairs which are none of his business and for which he has no responsibility; an intruder; an intermeddler. Encroachment on rights of others.

Intermarriage. *See* Miscegenation.

Intermeddle. To interfere wrongly with property or the conduct of business affairs officiously or without right or title. *See also* Interfere; Interloper.

Not a technical legal term, but sometimes used with reference to the acts of an executor *de son tort* or a *negotiorum gestor* in the civil law.

Intermediary. An arbitrator or mediator. A broker; one who is employed to negotiate a matter between two parties, and who for that purpose may be agent of both; *e.g.* insurance broker. *See also* Finder.

Intermediary bank. Any bank to which an item is transferred in the course of collection except the depositary or payor bank. U.C.C. § 4–105(c).

Intermediate. Intervening; interposed during the progress of a suit, proceeding, business, etc., or between its beginning and end. *See* Interlocutory; Intervention.

Intermediate account. In probate law, an account of an executor, administrator, or guardian filed subsequent to his first or initial account and before his final account. An account filed with the court for the purpose of disclosing the acts of the person accounting and the state or condition of the fund in his hands, and not made the subject of a final judicial settlement.

Intermediate courts. Those courts which have general jurisdiction, either trial or appellate or both, but which are below the court of last resort in the jurisdiction.

Intermediate order. An order made between the commencement of the action and its final determination, incident to and during its progress, which does not determine the cause but only some intervening matter relating thereto; one that is not directly appealable. *See* Interlocutory.

Intermediation. A financial term which refers to the placement of funds with a bank or other financial institution, also known as an intermediary, with the objective of investing such funds in stocks, bonds, etc.

Intermittent easement. *See* Easement.

Intermittent stream. A stream, the flow of which in the state of nature is interrupted either from time to time during the year or at various places along its course, or both.

Intermixture of goods. Confusion of goods; the confusing or commingling together of goods belonging to different owners in such a way that the property of no particular owner can be separately identified or extracted from the mass. *See also* Confusion of goods.

Intern. To restrict or confine a person or group of persons, particularly in time of war (*e.g.* enemy aliens). An advanced student or recent graduate in a professional field; *e.g.* one trained in a profession allied to medicine who undergoes a period of practical clinical experience prior to practicing his profession. *See also* Internment.

Internal. Relating to the interior; comprised within boundary lines; of interior concern or interest; domestic, as opposed to foreign.

Internal act. That which transpires within a person or organization or government as contrasted with a happening outside such.

Internal audit. *See* Audit.

Internal affairs of corporation. In conflicts, the rights and liabilities of a corporation are determined by the local law of the state which has the most significant relationship to the occurrence and the parties. Restatement, Second, Conflicts, § 302(1). Such affairs are generally left to courts of the state of incorporation.

Internal commerce. *See* Commerce.

Internal control. A plan of organization and policies and procedures to: safeguard assets; provide accurate and reliable accounting data; promote operational efficiency, and; encourage adherence to managerial policies.

Internal financing. Financing of business from funds generated from normal operations in contrast to financing from borrowed funds or stock issues.

Internal improvements. With reference to governmental policy and constitutional provisions restricting taxation or the contracting of public debts, this term means works of general public utility or advantage, designed to promote facility of intercommunication, trade, and commerce, the transportation of persons and property, or the development of the natural resources of the state, such as railroads, public highways, turnpikes, and canals, bridges, the improvement of rivers and harbors, systems of artificial irrigation, and the improvement of water powers; but it does not include the building and maintenance of state institutions.

Internal police. A term sometimes applied to the police power, or power to enact laws in the interest of the public safety, health, and morality, which is inherent in the legislative authority of each state, is to be exercised with reference only to its domestic affairs and its own citizens, and is not surrendered to the federal government. *See also* Police power.

Internal rate of return. In accounting, a discounted cash flow method of evaluating long-term projects that derives the actual return on an investment.

Internal revenue. Governmental revenues from internal sources by way of taxes as contrasted with revenues from customs and foreign sources.

Internal Revenue Code (I.R.C.). That body of law which codifies all federal tax laws including income, estate, gift, excise, etc. taxes. Such laws comprise Title 26 of the U.S. Code, and are implemented by the Internal Revenue Service and through it by Treasury Regulations; Revenue Rulings, etc. Because of the extensive revisions to the tax statutes that occurred with the Tax Reform Act of 1986, Title 26 of the U.S. Code is now known as the Internal Revenue Code of 1986.

Internal Revenue Service. The Internal Revenue Service (I.R.S.) is responsible for administering and enforcing the internal revenue laws, except those relating to alcohol, tobacco, firearms, explosives, and wagering. It is a part of the Department of the Treasury. Basic I.R.S. activities include providing taxpayer service and education; determination, assessment, and collection of internal revenue taxes; determination of pension plan qualification and exempt organization status; and preparation and issuance of rulings and regulations to interpret the provisions of the Internal Revenue Code.

Internal security. That branch of law and government (*e.g.* CIA, FBI) dealing with measures to protect the country from subversive activities.

Internal security acts. Federal Acts (Smith Act, 18 U.S.C.A. §§ 2385, 2386; McCarran Act, 50 U.S.C.A. § 781 et seq.) controlling and making illegal subversive activities of communist organizations and other groups whose purpose is to overthrow or disrupt the government.

Internal waters. Such as lie wholly within the body of the particular state or country. *See also* Inland waters.

International agreements. Treaties and other agreements of a contractual character between different countries or organizations of states (foreign) creating legal rights and obligations between the parties. *See e.g.* GATT.

International commerce. *See* Commerce.

International Court of Justice. Judicial arm of the United Nations. It has jurisdiction to give advisory opinions on matters of law and treaty construction when requested by the General Assembly, Security Council or any other international agency authorized by the General Assembly to petition for such opinion. It has jurisdiction, also, to settle legal disputes between nations when voluntarily submitted to it. Its judgments may be enforced by the Security Council. Its jurisdiction and powers are defined by statute, to which all member states of the U.N. are parties. Judges of such court are elected by the General Assembly and Security Council of U.N.

International jurisdiction. Power of a court or other organization to hear and determine matters between different countries or persons of different countries or foreign states. *See* International Court of Justice.

International law. Those laws governing the legal relations between nations. Rules and principles of general application dealing with the conduct of nations and of international organizations and with their relations inter se, as well as with some of their relations with persons, whether natural or juridical. Restatement Foreign Relations (Third) § 101. Body of consensual principles which have evolved from customs and practices civilized nations utilize in regulating their relationships and such customs have great moral force. International customs and treaties are generally considered to be the two most important sources of international law. *See e.g.* GATT.

International Monetary Fund. Agency of United Nations established to stabilize international exchange and promote balanced international trade. *See also* World Bank.

International Shoe Case. Due process requires that a foreign corporation be "present" within a state by a measure of minimal activity within the state for suits to be maintained against it in the state. International Shoe Co. v. State of Washington, etc., 326 U.S. 310, 66 S.Ct. 154, 90 L.Ed. 95. See also McGee v. International Life Ins. Co., 355 U.S. 220, 78 S.Ct. 199, 2 L.Ed.2d 223; Hanson v.

Denckla, 357 U.S. 235, 78 S.Ct. 1228, 2 L.Ed.2d 1283. *See* Minimum contacts.

International Trade Court. *See* Court of International Trade.

Internment. The detainment or confinement of enemy aliens or persons suspected of disloyalty in specially designated areas; *e.g.* Japanese during World War II.

Inter partes /íntər pártiyz/. Between parties. Instruments in which two persons unite, each making conveyance to, or engagement with, the other, are called "papers *inter partes*."

Judgment inter partes. *See* Judgment in personam *or* inter partes.

Interplea /íntərpliy/. A plea by which a person sued in respect to property disclaims any interest in it and demands that rival claimants shall litigate their titles between themselves and relieve him from responsibility. *See* Interpleader.

A statutory proceeding, serving as a substitute for the action of replevin, by which a third person intervenes in an action of attachment, sets up his own title to the specific property attached, and seeks to recover the possession of it.

Interpleader. An equitable proceeding to determine the rights of rival claimants to property held by a third person having no interest therein. When two or more persons claim the same thing (or fund) of a third, and he, laying no claim to it himself, is ignorant which of them has a right to it, and fears he may be prejudiced by their proceeding against him to recover it, he may join such claimants as defendants and require them to interplead their claims so that he may not be exposed to double or multiple liability. A defendant exposed to similar liability may obtain such interpleader by way of cross-claim or counterclaim. Interpleader in federal court is governed by the federal Interpleader Act, 28 U.S.C.A. § 1335, and Fed.R. Civil P. 22. Similar statutes and court rules govern interpleader in state courts.

Statutory interpleader. A federal statutory right (28 U.S.C.A. § 1335) whereby disinterested stakeholder from whom several people claim same proceeds may require claimants to litigate matter among themselves without embroiling stakeholder.

Interpol. International Criminal Police Organization; a coordinating group for international law enforcement.

Interpolate /intэ́rpəleyt/. To insert (additional or false) words in a complete instrument or document, thus altering meaning of such. *See also* Interlineation.

Interpolated terminal reserve. The method used in valuing insurance policies for gift and estate tax purposes when the policies are not paid-up at the time of their transfer.

Interpolation /intɜ̀rpəléyshən/. The act of interpolating; the words interpolated. The process of finding a term between two other terms in a series. *See also* Interlineation; Interpretation.

Interposition /intərpəzíshən/. The doctrine that a state, in the exercise of its sovereignty, may reject a mandate of the federal government deemed to be unconstitutional or to exceed the powers delegated to the federal government. The doctrine denies constitutional obligation of states to respect Supreme Court decisions with which they do not agree. The concept is based on the 10th Amendment of the Constitution of the United States reserving to the states powers not delegated to the United States. Historically, the doctrine emanated from Chisholm v. Georgia, 2 U.S. (Dall.) 419, wherein the state of Georgia, when sued in the Supreme Court by a private citizen of another state, entered a remonstrance and declined to recognize the court's jurisdiction. The U.S. Supreme Court rejected this doctrine of interposition in Cooper v. Aaron, 358 U.S. 1, 78 S.Ct. 1401, 3 L.Ed.2d 5.

Interpret. To construe; to seek out the meaning of language; to translate orally from one tongue to another.

Interpretation. The art or process of discovering and ascertaining the meaning of a statute, will, contract, or other written document. The discovery and representation of the true meaning of any signs used to convey ideas.

It is said to be either "legal," which rests on the same authority as the law itself, or "doctrinal," which rests upon its intrinsic reasonableness. Legal interpretation may be either "authentic," when it is expressly provided by the legislator, or "usual," when it is derived from unwritten practice. Doctrinal interpretation may turn on the meaning of words and sentences, when it is called "grammatical," or on the intention of the legislator, when it is described as "logical." When logical interpretation stretches the words of a statute to cover its obvious meaning, it is called "extensive;" when, on the other hand, it avoids giving full meaning to the words, in order not to go beyond the intention of the legislator, it is called "restrictive."

As to *strict* and *liberal* interpretation, *see* Construction. *See also* Broad interpretation; Last antecedent rule.

Construction distinguished. In the strict usage of this term, "construction" is a term of wider scope than "interpretation;" for, while the latter is concerned only with ascertaining the sense and meaning of the subject-matter, the former may also be directed to explaining the legal effects and consequences of the instrument in question.

Hence interpretation precedes construction, but stops at the written text. Interpretation and construction of written instruments are not the same. A rule of construction is one which either governs the effect of an ascertained intention, or points out what the court should do in the absence of express or implied intention, while a rule of interpretation is one which governs the ascertainment of the meaning of the maker of the instrument.

These two terms are however, commonly used interchangeably.

Interpretation clause. A section of a statute which defines the meaning of certain words occurring frequently in the other sections.

Interpreter. A person sworn at a trial to interpret the evidence of a foreigner or a deaf person to the court.

Interpretative rule. Rule which is promulgated by administrative agency to interpret, clarify or explain statutory regulations under which agency operates.

Interrogation. In criminal law, the process of questions propounded by police to person arrested or suspected to seek solution of crime. Such person is entitled to be informed of his rights, including right to have counsel present, and the consequences of his answers. If the police fail or neglect to give these warnings, the questions and answers are not admissible in evidence at the trial or hearing of the arrested person. Miranda v. State of Arizona, 384 U.S. 436, 86 S.Ct. 1602, 16 L.Ed.2d 694. As conceptualized in the *Miranda* decision of the United States Supreme Court, constitutionally protected interrogation must reflect a measure of compulsion above and beyond that inherent in custody itself. *See also* Confession; Custodial interrogation; Exclusionary Rule; Investigatory interrogation; Miranda Rule.

Custodial interrogation. Questioning initiated by law enforcement officers after a person has been taken into custody or otherwise deprived of his freedom of action in any significant way. *See also* Miranda Rule.

Interrogatories /intərógət(ò)riyz/. A set or series of written questions drawn up for the purpose of being propounded to a party, witness, or other person having information of interest in the case.

A pretrial discovery device consisting of written questions about the case submitted by one party to the other party or witness. The answers to the interrogatories are usually given under oath, *i.e.*, the person answering the questions signs a sworn statement that the answers are true. Fed.R. Civil P. 33.

The court may submit to the jury, together with appropriate forms for a general verdict, written interrogatories upon one or more issues of fact the decision of which is necessary to a verdict. See Fed.R. Civil P. 49.

See also Deposition; Discovery; Special interrogatories.

In terrorem /ìn tèhrórəm/. Lit. In fright or alarm or terror. In terror or warning; by way of threat. Applied to legacies given upon condition that the recipient shall not dispute the validity or the dispositions of the will; such a condition being usually regarded as a mere threat. *See* In terrorem clause.

In terrorem clause. A provision in a document such as a lease or will designed to frighten a beneficiary or lessee into doing or not doing something; *e.g.* clause in a will providing for revocation of a bequest or devise if the legatee or devisee contests the will. A condition "in terrorem" is a provision in a will which threatens beneficiaries with forfeiture of their legacies and bequests should they contest validity or dispositions of will. Such provisions are unenforceable in many states.

Interruption. A break in continuity or uniformity. The occurrence of some act or fact, during the period of prescription, which is sufficient to arrest the running of the statute of limitations. It is said to be either "natural" or "civil," the former being caused by the act of the party; the latter by the legal effect or operation of some fact or circumstance. Interruption of the possession is where the right is not enjoyed or exercised continuously; interruption of the right is where the person having or claiming the right ceases the exercise of it in such a manner as to show that he does not claim to be entitled to exercise it.

Intersection. As applied to a street or highway means the space occupied by two streets at the point where they cross each other. Space common to both streets or highways, formed by continuing the curb lines.

Point of intersection of two roads is the point where their middle lines intersect. But the term may also mean the point which each of two approaching vehicles will reach at the same moment. "Intersection" may also apply where street or highway runs into but without crossing another; *e.g.* a "T" intersection.

Inter se *or* **inter sese** /íntər síy(siy)/. Lat. Among or between themselves; used to distinguish rights or duties between two or more parties from their rights or duties to others.

Interspousal. Between husband and wife.

Interspousal immunity. *See* Husband-wife tort actions.

Interstate. Between two or more states; between places or persons in different states; concerning or affecting two or more states politically or territorially. *Compare* Intrastate commerce.

Interstate agreements. *See* Interstate compact.

Interstate and foreign commerce. Commerce between a point in one State and a point in another State, between points in the same State through another State or through a foreign country, between points in a foreign country or countries through the United States, and commerce between a point in the United States and a point in a foreign country or in a Territory or possession of the United States, but only insofar as such commerce takes place in the United States. The term "United States" means all the States and the District of Columbia. 49 U.S.C.A. § 10102.

Interstate commerce. Traffic, intercourse, commercial trading, or the transportation of persons or property between or among the several states of the Union, or from or between points in one state and points in another state; commerce between two states, or between places lying in different states. It comprehends all the component parts of commercial intercourse between different states. *See* Balancing of interests.

Interstate Commerce Act. The act of congress of February 4, 1887 (49 U.S.C.A. § 10101 *et seq.*), designed to regulate commerce between the states, and particularly the transportation of persons and property, by carriers, between interstate points.

Interstate Commerce Commission. The Interstate Commerce Commission regulates interstate surface transportation, including trains, trucks, buses, water carriers, freight forwarders, transportation brokers, and a coal slurry pipeline. The regulatory laws vary depending on the type of transportation; however, they generally involve certification of carriers seeking to provide transportation for the public, rates, adequacy of service, purchases, and mergers. The Commission assures that the carriers it regulates will provide the public with rates and services that are fair and reasonable. 49 U.S.C.A. § 10301 et seq.

Interstate compact. A voluntary agreement between two or more states which is designed to meet common problems of the parties concerned. Compacts on major matters must receive the consent of the U.S. Congress as specified in Article I, Section 10 of the Constitution. They usually relate to such things as conservation, boundary problems, education, port control, flood control, water rights, and penal matters.

Interstate extradition. The reclamation and surrender, according to due legal proceedings, of a person who, having committed a crime in one of the states of the Union, has fled into another state to evade justice or escape prosecution. Art. IV, § 2, U.S.Const.; 18 U.S.C.A. § 3181 et seq. *See* Extradition; Interstate rendition.

Interstate Land Sales Full Disclosure Act. Federal Act (15 U.S.C.A. § 1701 *et seq.*), the purpose of which is to provide purchasers and lessees of undeveloped land with the information they need in order to make an informed decision with regard to the land being sold or leased. As indicated by its title, this is a "disclosure" act.

Interstate law. That branch of law which affords rules and principles for the determination of controversies between citizens of different states in respect to mutual rights or obligations, in so far as the same are affected by the diversity of their citizenship or by diversity in the laws or institutions of the several states.

Interstate rendition. Right of one state to demand from asylum state surrender of a fugitive from justice from the demanding state when the fugitive is found in the asylum state. Art. IV, § 2, U.S.Const. Nearly all states have adopted the Uniform Criminal Extradition Act. *See* Extradition; Interstate extradition; Rendition.

Interval ownership. Type of ownership of second (*i.e.* vacation) home whereby the property is owned for only an interval (*e.g.* two weeks or a month) of the year. Each owner receives a deed covering his interval period. *See also* Timesharing.

Intervening act. Such act of third person in order to break chain of causation and obviate liability for original breach of duty must be a superseding cause and one which original wrongdoer was not bound to anticipate as the natural or ordinary result of his acts. *See also* Intervening cause; Superseding cause.

Intervening agency. To render an original wrong a remote cause, an "intervening agency" must be independent of such wrong, adequate to produce the injury, so interrupting the natural sequence of events as to produce a result different from what would have been produced, and one that could not have been reasonably expected from the original wrong. An independent "intervening agency" which will protect the original wrongdoer must be the efficient cause of the injury of which complaint is made, and not a negligent act or omission of such agency concurring with or succeeding the original negligence permitted by the original wrongdoer to continue and which in the natural course of events results in such injury. In short, the result prevented by the intervening agency must be the injury complained of, and not the requital for that injury. *See also* Intervening cause.

Intervening cause. In tort law, as will relieve of liability for an injury, is an independent cause which intervenes between the original wrongful act or omission and the injury, turns aside the natural sequence of events, and produces a result which would not otherwise have followed and which could not have been reasonably anticipated. An act of an independent agency which destroys the causal connection between the negligent act of the defendant and the wrongful injury; the independent act being the immediate cause, in which case damages are not recoverable because the original wrongful act is not the proximate cause. An "intervening efficient cause" is a new and independent force which breaks the causal connection between the original wrong and injury, and itself becomes direct and immediate cause of injury.

In criminal law, a cause which comes between an antecedent and a consequence; it may be either independent or dependent, but in either case it is sufficient to negate criminal responsibility.

See also Intervening act; Intervening agency; Superseding cause.

Intervening damages. *See* Damages.

Intervening force. One which actively operates in producing harm to another after defendant's act or omission has been committed. Intervening force will not break a causal connection if that force was itself probable or foreseeable by the original wrongdoer. *See also* Intervening agency; Intervening cause.

Intervenor. An intervenor is a person who voluntarily interposes in an action or other proceeding with the leave of the court. *See* Intervention.

Intervention. The procedure by which a third person, not originally a party to the suit, but claiming an interest in the subject matter, comes into the case, in order to protect his right or interpose his claim. The grounds and procedure are usually defined by various state statutes or Rules of Civil Procedure; *e.g.,* Fed.R. Civil P. 24; 28 U.S.C.A. § 2403. Intervention may exist either as a matter of right (Rule 24(a)) or at the discretion of the court (Rule 24(b)).

Inter vivos /íntər váyvows/. Between the living; from one living person to another. Where property passes by conveyance, the transaction is said to be *inter vivos,* to distinguish it from a case of succession or devise. So an ordinary gift from one person to another is called a "gift *inter vivos,*" to distinguish it from a gift made in contemplation of death *(mortis causa)* or a testamentary gift.

Inter vivos gift. Gift made when donor is living and provides that gift take effect while donor is living as contrasted with testamentary gift which is to take effect on death of donor (testator).

Inter vivos transfer. A transfer of property during the life of the owner. To be distinguished from testamentary transfers where the property passes at death. *See e.g.* Inter vivos gift.

Inter vivos trust. Trust created during lifetime of settlor and to become effective in his lifetime as contrasted with a testamentary trust which takes effect at death of settlor or testator. *See also* Trust.

Intestable. One who has not testamentary capacity; *e.g.*, an infant, lunatic, or person civilly dead.

Intestacy /intéstəsiy/. The state or condition of dying without having made a valid will, or without having disposed by will of a part of his property.

Intestate. To die without a will. A person is said to die intestate when he dies without making a will, or dies without leaving anything to testify what his wishes were with respect to the disposal of his property after his death. Under such circumstances, state law prescribes who will receive the decedent's property. The laws of intestate succession generally favor the surviving spouse, children, and grandchildren and then move to parents and grandparents and to brothers and sisters.

The word is also often used to signify the person himself. Thus, in speaking of the property of a person who died intestate, it is common to say "the intestate's property;" *i.e.*, the property of the person dying in an intestate condition. *Compare* Testate.

Intestate laws. State statutes which provide and prescribe the devolution of estates of persons who die without disposing of their estates by will. *See* Descent.

Intestate succession. A succession is called "intestate" when the deceased has left no will or when his will has been revoked or annulled as irregular. In such case the property of the deceased will be disposed of under the laws of descent and distribution. *See* Intestate.

In testimonium /in tèstəmówn(i)yəm/. Lat. In witness; in evidence whereof.

In the course of employment. The phrase "in the course of" employment, as used in workers' compensation acts, relates to time, place and circumstances under which accident occurred, and means injury happened while worker was at work in his or her employer's service. *See also* Arising out of and in the course of own employment; Course of employment.

In-the-money. An option with a positive exercise value. For a call option, this is when the value of the underlying asset exceeds the strike price. For a put option, this is when the value of the underlying asset is less than the strike price.

Intimacy /íntəməsiy/. As generally applied to persons, it is understood to mean a proper, friendly relation of the parties, but it is frequently used to convey the idea of an improper relation.

Intimate. Close in friendship or acquaintance, familiar, near, confidential. To communicate indirectly; to hint or suggest.

Intimation. In the civil law, a notification to a party that some step in a legal proceeding is asked or will be taken. Particularly, a notice given by the party taking an appeal, to the other party, that the court above will hear the appeal.

Intimidation. Unlawful coercion; extortion; duress; putting in fear.

To take, or attempt to take, "by intimidation" means willfully to take, or attempt to take, by putting in fear of bodily harm. Such fear must arise from the willful conduct of the accused, rather than from some mere temperamental timidity of the victim; however, the fear of the victim need not be so great as to result in terror, panic, or hysteria. *See* Coercion; Extortion; Duress.

Intitle. An old form of *"entitle."*

Into. A preposition signifying to the inside of; within. It expresses entrance, or a passage from the outside of a thing to its interior, and follows verbs expressing motion. It has been held equivalent to, or synonymous with, "at," "inside of," and "to," and has been distinguished from the words "from" and "through."

In toto /in tówtow/. In the whole; wholly; completely; as the award is void *in toto*.

Intoxicated. Affected by an intoxicant, under the influence of an intoxicating liquor. *See* Intoxication.

Intoxicating liquor. Any liquor intended for use as a beverage or capable of being so used, which contains alcohol, either obtained by fermentation or by the additional process of distillation, in such proportion that it will produce intoxication when imbibed in such quantities as may practically be drunk.

Intoxication. Term comprehends situation where, by reason of taking intoxicants, an individual does not have the normal use of his physical or mental faculties, thus rendering him incapable of acting in the manner in which an ordinarily prudent and cautious man, in full possession of his faculties, using reasonable care, would act under like conditions.

A disturbance of mental or physical capacities resulting from the introduction of substances into the body. Model Penal Code, § 2.08.

The fact that a person charged with a crime was in an intoxicated condition at the time the alleged crime was committed is a defense only if such condition was involuntarily produced and rendered such person substantially incapable of knowing or understanding the wrongfulness of his conduct and of conforming his conduct to the requirements of law. An act committed while in a state of voluntary intoxication is not less criminal by reason thereof, but when a particular intent or other state of mind is a necessary element to constitute a particular crime, the fact of intoxication may be taken into consideration in determining such intent or state of mind.

Under most state statutes dealing with driving while intoxicated, "intoxication" includes such by alcohol or by drug or by both. *See* Driving while intoxicated; Sobriety checkpoint.

Confirmed habits of intoxication caused by voluntary and excessive use of liquor is a ground for divorce under many state divorce statutes.

See also Habitual drunkenness *or* intoxication; Intemperance.

Public intoxication. Public intoxication is being on a highway or street or in a public place or public building while under the influence of intoxicating liquor, narcotics or other drug to the degree that one may endanger himself or other persons or property, or annoy persons in his vicinity.

Voluntary intoxication. The voluntary introduction of any substances into the body which the defendant knows or should know are likely to have intoxicating effects. The Model Penal Code (§ 2.08) uses the term "self-induced intoxication" to refer to this idea. Evidence of voluntary or self-induced intoxication can be admitted in some circumstances but not others.

Intoxilyzer. Breath analysis. A device used to measure the concentration of alcohol in the blood of motorists suspected of driving while under the influence of intoxicating liquor. *See* Breathalyzer test; Intoximeter.

Intoximeter. A trade name for scientific breath testing device that operates on assumption that concentration of blood alcohol bears fixed relation to concentration of alcohol in the deep lung, or alveolar air. Also commonly called breathalyzer test. *See* Breathalyzer test.

Intra /íntrə/. Lat. In; near; within. *"Infra"* or *"inter"* has taken the place of *"intra"* in many of the more modern Latin phrases.

Intraliminal /ìntrəlímənəl/. In mining law, the term "intraliminal rights" denotes the right to mine, take, and possess all such bodies or deposits of ore as lie within the four planes formed by the vertical extension downward of the boundary lines of the claim; as distinguished from "extraliminal," or more commonly "extralateral," rights.

Intramural. Within the walls. Existing within. The confines of an institution or governmental body. The powers of a municipal corporation are "intramural" and "extramural"; the one being the powers exercised within the corporate limits, and the other being those exercised without.

In transitu /in trǽnzət(y)uw/. In transit; on the way or passage; while passing from one person or place to another. In the course of transportation.

Intra-period tax allocation. In accounting, the practice of relating income tax expense to the items that give rise to the tax.

Intrastate commerce. Commerce within a state, as opposed to commerce between states (*i.e.* interstate). *See also* Balancing of interests; Commerce. *Compare* Interstate commerce.

Intra vires /íntrə váyriyz/. An act is said to be *intra vires* ("within the power") of a person or corporation when it is within the scope of his or its powers or authority. It is the opposite of *ultra vires (q.v.).*

Intrinsic. Internal; inherent. Pertaining to the essential nature of a thing.

Intrinsic evidence. Evidence brought out by the examination of the very witness testifying. *Compare* Circumstantial evidence; Extrinsic evidence.

Intrinsic fraud. That fraud which occurs within framework of actual conduct of trial and pertains to and affects determination of issues presented therein, and it may be accomplished by perjury, or by use of false or forged instruments, or by concealment or misrepresentation of evidence. Fraud is "intrinsic fraud" where judgment is founded on fraudulent instruments or perjured evidence or the fraudulent actions pertain to an issue involved in original action and litigated therein.

Species of fraud which renders the document void as, for example, an instrument signed by one who had neither knowledge nor reasonable opportunity to obtain knowledge of its character or its essential terms, is not enforceable even by a holder in due course because such fraud is intrinsic. U.C.C. § 3–305(2)(c).

Intrinsic value. The true, inherent and essential value of thing, not depending upon accident, place or person but same everywhere and to everyone. The value of the thing itself, rather than any special features which make its market value different (*e.g.* value of silver in coin).

Introduction. The part of a writing which sets forth preliminary matter, or facts tending to explain the subject.

Intruder. One who enters upon land without either right of possession or color of title. In a more restricted sense, a stranger who, on the death of the ancestor, enters on the land, unlawfully, before the heir can enter. Also one who intrudes on office and assumes to exercise its functions without legal title or color of right thereto. *See* Encroachment; Intrusion; Trespass.

Intrusion. Act of wrongfully entering upon or taking possession of property of another. *See also* Encroachment; Trespass.

Intrust. To confer a trust upon; to deliver to another something in trust or to commit something to another with a certain confidence regarding his care, use or disposal of it. *See also* Bailment; Fiduciary; Trust.

Inundation. To flood or swamp. The overflow of waters by coming out of their natural bed or confines. *See also* Backwater; Flood; Water course.

Inure /inyúr/. To take effect; to result. In property law, to come to the benefit of a person or to fix his interest therein.

Inurement /inyúrmənt/. Useful, beneficial; serving to the use or benefit of a person or thing.

Invalid. Vain; inadequate to its purpose; not of binding force or legal efficacy; lacking in authority or obligation. *See also* Illegal; Void; Voidable.

Invasion. An encroachment upon the rights of another. The incursion of an army for conquest or plunder. Act of invading; intrusion; encroachment.

Invasion of privacy. The unwarranted appropriation or exploitation of one's personality, publicizing one's private affairs with which public has no legitimate concern, or wrongful intrusion into one's private activities, in such a manner as to cause mental suffering, shame or humiliation to person of ordinary sensibilities. Violation of right which one has to be left alone and unnoticed if he so chooses. Such invasion by an individual or the government may constitute an actionable tort; though public figures have less protection than private persons. *See* Eavesdropping; Privacy laws.

Inveigle. To lure or entice or lead astray, by false representations or promises, or other deceitful means.

Invent. To find out something new. To devise, contrive, and produce something not previously known or existing, by the exercise of independent investigation and experiment; particularly applied to machines, mechanical appliances, compositions, and patentable inventions of every sort. To create. *See also* Invention; Patent.

Invention. In patent law, the act or operation of finding out something new; the process of contriving and producing something not previously known or existing, by the exercise of independent investigation and experiment. Also the article or contrivance or composition so invented.

Invention is a concept; a thing involved in the mind; it is not a revelation of something which exists and was unknown, but is creation of something which did not exist before, possessing elements of novelty and utility in kind and measure different from and greater than what the art might expect from skilled workers. The finding out—the contriving, the creating of something which did not exist, and was not known before,

and which can be made useful and advantageous in the pursuits of life, or which can add to the enjoyment of mankind. Not every improvement is invention; but to entitle a thing to protection it must be the product of some exercise of the inventive faculties and it must involve something more than what is obvious to persons skilled in the art to which it relates. Mere adaptation of known process to clearly analogous use is not invention.

For *Examination of invention, see* Examination. *See also* Patent; Reduced to practice.

Inventor. One who invents or has invented. One who finds out or contrives some new thing; one who devises some new art, manufacture, mechanical appliance, or process; one who invents a patentable contrivance. *See* Invention.

Inventory. A detailed list of articles of property; a list or schedule of property and other assets, containing a designation or description of each specific article; quantity of goods or materials on hand or in stock; an itemized list of the various items or articles constituting a collection, estate, stock in trade, etc., with their estimated or actual values. In law, the term is often applied to such a list made by an executor, administrator, or trustee in bankruptcy.

In accounting, refers to segment of financial statement reflecting value of businesses' raw materials, work in process, and finished goods. The two primary types of inventory accounting methods are First-in, first-out, and Last-in, first-out. *See* FIFO and LIFO.

Goods held for sale or lease or furnished under contracts of service; also, raw materials, work in process or materials used or consumed in a business. U.C.C. § 9–109(4). Also, written schedule of such goods.

Merchandise inventory. Goods held by a merchandising business for resale to others.

Physical inventory accounting. The process of counting or measuring the goods in a company's possession upon conclusion of an accounting period.

Weighted-average method of accounting. A method of accounting for inventory under a periodic inventory system that requires the computation of a weighted-average cost for goods purchased or manufactured. The average is used to value the ending inventory and to determine cost of goods sold.

Inventory search. An inventory search is not an independent legal concept but rather an incidental administrative step following arrest and preceding incarceration. To determine whether such search is unreasonable, the court balances its intrusion on the individual's Fourth Amendment interests against its promotion of legitimate governmental interests. See Fed.R.Crim.P. 41.

Inventory turnover ratio. In accounting, an activity ratio that lends insight into a firm's inventory management policies; computed by dividing the cost of goods sold by average inventory.

Inverse condemnation. An action brought by a property owner seeking just compensation for land taken for a public use, against a government or private entity having the power of eminent domain. It is a remedy peculiar to the property owner and is exercisable by him where it appears that the taker of the property does not intend to bring eminent domain proceedings. Such an action might result, for example, where use and value of property adjacent to new airport or freeway is materially diminished.

Inverse order of alienation doctrine. Under this doctrine, mortgage or other lienor, where land subject to lien has been aliened in separate parcels successively, shall satisfy his lien out of land remaining in grantor or original owner if possible, and, if that be insufficient, he shall resort to parcels aliened in inverse order of their alienation.

Invest. *See* Investment.

Investee. A company whose shares have been acquired by an investor.

Investigate. To follow up step by step by patient inquiry or observation. To trace or track; to search into; to examine and inquire into with care and accuracy; to find out by careful inquisition; examination; the taking of evidence; a legal inquiry. *See also* Discovery; Inspection.

Investigation. The process of inquiring into or tracking down through inquiry, inspection, observation, and search.

Investigatory interrogation. An "investigatory interrogation" outside scope of *Miranda* Rule is questioning of persons by law enforcement officers in a routine manner in an investigation which has not reached an accusatory stage and where such persons are not in legal custody or deprived of their freedom of action in any significant way. *See also* Interrogation; Sobriety checkpoint.

Investigatory powers. Authority conferred on governmental agencies to inspect and compel disclosure of facts germane to the investigation. *See also* Inquest; Inspection laws; Search warrant; Subpoena.

Investigatory stop. Such stop, which is limited to brief, nonintrusive detention during a frisk for weapons or preliminary questioning, is considered a "seizure" sufficient to invoke Fourth Amendment safeguards, but because of its less intrusive character requires only that the stopping officer have specific and articulable facts sufficient to give rise to reasonable suspicion that a person has committed or is committing a crime. *See also* Sobriety checkpoint; Stop and frisk.

Investing activities. Those activities that involve investment of an entity's resources.

Investitive fact /invéstətəv fǽkt/. The fact by means of which a right comes into existence; *e.g.*, a grant of a monopoly; the death of one's ancestor.

Investiture /invéstətyər/. A ceremony which accompanied the grant of lands in the feudal ages, and consisted in the open and notorious delivery of possession in the presence of the other vassals, which perpetuated among them the *æra* of their new acquisition at the time when the art of writing was very little known; and thus the evidence of the property was reposed in the memory of the neighborhood, who, in case of disputed title, were afterwards called upon to decide upon it.

Investment. An expenditure to acquire property or other assets in order to produce revenue; the asset so acquired. The placing of capital or laying out of money in a way intended to secure income or profit from its employment. To purchase securities of a more or less permanent nature, or to place money or property in business ventures or real estate, or otherwise lay it out, so that it may produce revenue or gain (or both) in the future. *See also* Investment contract.

To clothe one with the possession of a fief or benefice. *See* Investiture.

For *capital investment*, *see* Capital. *See also* Legal investments; Legal list; Prudent Man Rule.

Investment advisor. Any person who, for compensation, engages in the business of advising others, either directly or through publications or writings, as to the value of securities or as to the advisability of investing in, purchasing, or selling securities, or who, for compensation and as a part of a regular business, issues or promulgates analyses or reports concerning securities. Uniform Securities Act, § 401(f).

Investment Advisors Act. Federal statute which regulates activities of those who furnish investment advice and counselling. 15 U.S.C.A. § 80b. The Act is administered by the Securities and Exchange Commission which, among other things, requires registration of investment advisors.

Investment banker. A financial institution that underwrites and sells new securities. In general, investment bankers assist firms in obtaining new financing. An underwriter, the middleman or broker between the corporation issuing new securities and the public. The usual practice is for one or more investment bankers to buy outright from a corporation a new issue of stocks or bonds. The group forms a syndicate to sell the securities to individuals and institutions. Investment bankers also distribute very large blocks of stocks or bonds—perhaps held by an estate. Thereafter the market in the security may be over-the-counter or on a stock exchange. *See also* Underwriter.

Investment banking. Underwriting and selling primarily new issues of stocks and bonds to investors. *See* Investment banker.

Investment bill. Type of bill of exchange purchased at a discount and intended to be held to maturity in the form of an investment.

Investment company. Any issuer which: (1) is or holds itself out as being engaged primarily, or proposes to engage primarily, in the business of investing, reinvesting, or trading in securities; (2) is engaged or proposes to engage in the business of issuing face-amount certificates of the installment type, or has been engaged in such business and has any such certificates outstanding; or (3) is engaged or proposes to engage in the business of investing, reinvesting, owning, holding, or trading in securities, and owns or proposes to acquire investment securities having a value exceeding 40 percentum of the value of such issuer's total assets (exclusive of Government securities and cash items) on an unconsolidated basis. Investment Company Act, § 3.

A company or trust which uses its capital to invest in other companies. The most common kind of investment company is the mutual fund. An investment company differs from a holding company in that the latter seeks control of the ventures in which it invests while an investment company seeks the investment for its own sake and normally diversifies its investments. There are two principal types: the closed-end and the open-end, or mutual fund. Shares in closed-end investment companies are readily transferable in the open market and are bought and sold like other shares. Capitalization of these companies remains the same unless action is taken to change. Open-end funds sell their own new shares to investors, stand ready to buy back their old shares, and are not listed. Open-end funds are so called because their capitalization is not fixed; they issue more shares as demanded. *See also* Mutual fund.

Investment Company Act. Federal statute passed in 1940 which regulates investment companies. 15 U.S.C.A. § 80a–1 et seq. *See* Investment company.

Investment contract. A contract, transaction or scheme whereby a person invests his money in a common enterprise and is led to expect profits solely from the efforts of the promoter or a third party. The placing of capital or laying out of money in a way intended to secure income or profit from its employment.

To fall within scope of the federal securities acts an "investment contract" must involve three elements: (1) an investment of money, (2) in a common enterprise, and (3) an expectation of profits solely from the efforts of others.

Investment credit. *See* Investment tax credit.

Investment grade rating. A long-term debt rating in one of the four highest rating categories (Aaa, Aa, A, or Baa from Moody's Investors Service and AAA, AA, A, or BBB from Standard & Poor's).

Investment indebtedness. Debt incurred to carry or acquire investments by the taxpayer in assets that will produce portfolio income. Limitations are placed upon interest deductions that are incurred with respect to such debt (*i.e.*, generally to the corresponding amount of investment income).

Investment property. Generally, any property purchased for the primary purpose of profit. The profit may be from income or from resale.

Investment security. Under U.C.C., an instrument issued in bearer or registered form as a type commonly recognized as a medium for investment and evidencing a share or other interest in the property or enterprise of the issuer. § 8–102(1)(a). *See also* Investment contract; Security.

Investment tax credit. Federal legislation designed to stimulate investment by business in capital goods and equipment by allowing a percentage of the purchase price as a credit against individual and corporate taxes due and not merely as a deduction from taxable income. The Tax Reform Act of 1986 generally repealed this credit retroactively for most property placed in service after January 1, 1986. *See also* Recapture of investment tax credit.

Investment trust. A company which sells its own stock and invests the money in stocks, real estate, and other investments. *See also* Investment company; Mutual fund; Real estate investment trust.

Invidious discrimination. Term "invidious" in context of claim that difference in treatment amounts to "invidious" discrimination in violation of the Fourteenth Amendment, means arbitrary, irrational and not reasonably related to a legitimate purpose.

In vinculis /ìn víŋk(y)ələs/. In chains; in actual custody. Applied also, figuratively, to the condition of a person who is compelled to submit to terms which oppression and his necessities impose on him.

Inviolability /invàyələbílədiy/. The attribute of being secured against violation. Safe from trespass or assault.

Inviolate. Intact; not violated; free from substantial impairment.

Invitation. In the law of negligence, and with reference to trespasses on realty, invitation is the act of one who solicits or incites others to enter upon, remain in, or make use of, his property or structures thereon, or who so arranges the property or the means of access to it or of transit over it as to induce the reasonable belief that he expects and intends that others shall come upon it or pass over it. Thus the proprietor of a store, theatre or amusement park "invites" the public to come upon his premises for such purposes as are connected with its intended use.

The differences in duties of care owed as between and among licensees, business guests and social guests have been eliminated in many jurisdictions so that today reasonable care is owed to all lawful visitors and this phrase includes all but trespassers.

An invitation may be *express*, when the owner or occupier of the land by words invites another to come upon it or make use of it or of something thereon; or it may be *implied* when such owner or occupier by acts or conduct leads another to believe that the land or something thereon was intended to be used as he uses them, and that such use is not only acquiesced in by the owner or occupier, but is in accordance with the intention or design for which the way or place or thing was adapted and prepared and allowed to be used. *See also* Attractive nuisance doctrine; Invitee.

Invitation to bid. Type of advertisement used by one who desires bids to be submitted for a particular job; it usually contains sufficient specifications to permit an intelligent bid.

Invited error. Doctrine of "invited error" provides that when the court acquiesces in course of conduct urged by defendant, defendant is estopped on appeal from raising as error that conduct or its result. *See also* Error.

Invitee. A person is an "invitee" on land of another if (1) he enters by invitation, express or implied, (2) his entry is connected with the owner's business or with an activity the owner conducts or permits to be conducted on his land and (3) there is mutuality of benefit or benefit to the owner. Person who is on property of another for economic benefit of owner or for the economic benefit of both parties.

The leading English case of Indermaur v. Dames laid down the rule that as to those who enter premises upon business which concerns the occupier, and upon his invitation express or implied, the latter is under an affirmative duty to protect them, not only against dangers of which he knows, but also against those which with reasonable care he might discover. The case has been accepted in all common law jurisdictions, and the invitee, or as he is sometimes called the business visitor, is placed upon a higher footing than a licensee. The typical example, of course, is the customer in a store. There is however a conflict of decisions as to whether certain visitors are to be included in the definition of invitee. The minority view is that there must be some economic benefit to the occupier before his duty to the visitor attaches. The majority view holds however that the basis of liability is not any economic benefit to the occupier, but a representation to be implied when he encourages others to enter to further a purpose of his own, that reasonable care has been exercised to make the place safe for those who come for that purpose; *e.g.* persons attending free public lectures, persons using municipal parks, playgrounds, libraries and the like. The element of "invitation" however must exist.

See also Guest; Licensee; Public invitee.

Invoice. A written account, or itemized statement of merchandise shipped or sent to a purchaser, consignee, factor, etc., with the quantity, value or prices and charges annexed, and may be as appropriate to a consignment or a memorandum shipment as it is to a sale. Document showing details of a sale or purchase transaction. A list sent to a purchaser, factor, consignee, etc., containing the items, together with the prices and charges of merchandise sent or to be sent to him. A writing made on behalf of an importer, specifying the merchandise imported, and its true cost or value. *See also* Consular invoice.

Invoice book. A book in which invoices are copied.

Invoice price. List price minus applicable trade discounts.

Involuntary. Without will or power of choice; opposed to volition or desire. An involuntary act is that which is performed with constraint *(q.v.)* or with repugnance, or without the will to do it. An action is involuntary, then, which is performed under duress, force, or coercion. *See* Coercion; Duress.

As to *Involuntary* Dismissal; Indebtedness; Nonsuit; and Trust, see those titles. For *Involuntary bankruptcy, see* Bankruptcy proceedings.

Involuntary alienation. A loss of or parting with property by attachment, levy, sale for taxes or other debts. *See also* Involuntary conveyance.

Involuntary confession. Confession is "involuntary" if it is not the product of an essentially free and unrestrained choice of its maker or where maker's will is overborne at the time of the confession. Term refers to confessions that are extracted by any threats of violence, or obtained by direct or implied promises, or by exertion of improper influence.

An involuntarily obtained confession cannot be used in prosecuting a defendant. Such a confession is inadmissible both because it is likely to be unreliable and because of society's aversion to forced confessions, even if true. Coercive activity is a necessary predicate to the finding that a confession is not voluntary within the meaning of the Due Process Clause of the 14th Amendment. See 18 U.S.C.A. § 350. *See also* Confession; Interrogation; Self-incrimination.

Involuntary conversion. The loss or destruction of property through theft, casualty, or condemnation. Any gain realized on an involuntary conversion can, at the taxpayer's election, be considered nonrecognizable for Federal income tax purposes if the owner reinvests the proceeds within a prescribed period of time in property that is similar or related in service or use. I.R.C. § 1033.

Involuntary conversion for federal income tax purposes must result from (1) destruction of property in whole or in part; or (2) theft; or (3) actual seizure; or (4) requisition or condemnation or threat or imminence of requisition or condemnation.

See also Condemnation.

Involuntary conveyance. A transfer of real property without the consent of the owner, such as in a divorce, in condemnation, etc. *See also* Involuntary alienation; Sheriff's sale.

Involuntary deposit. In the law of bailments, one made by the accidental leaving or placing of personal property in the possession of another, without negligence on the part of the owner, or, in cases of fire, shipwreck, inundation, riot, insurrection, or the like extraordinary emergencies, by the owner of personal property committing it out of necessity to the care of any person.

Involuntary discontinuance. A discontinuance is involuntary where, in consequence of technical omission, mispleading, or the like, the suit is regarded as out of court, as where the parties undertake to refer a suit that is not referable, or omit to enter proper continuances.

Involuntary lien. A lien, such as a tax lien, judgment lien, etc., which attaches to property without the consent of the owner, rather than a mortgage lien, to which the owner agrees.

Involuntary liquidation preference. A premium that must be paid to preferred stockholders if the issuer of the stock is forced into involuntary liquidation.

Involuntary manslaughter. The unlawful killing of a human being in the commission of an unlawful act not amounting to felony, or in the commission of a lawful act which might produce death in an unlawful manner, or without due caution and circumspection. An unlawful homicide, unintentionally caused by an act which constitutes such disregard of probable harmful consequences to another as to constitute wanton or reckless conduct. *See also* Manslaughter.

Involuntary payment. One obtained by fraud, oppression, or extortion, or to avoid the use of force to coerce it, or to obtain the release of the person or property from detention.

Involuntary servitude. The condition of one who is compelled by force, coercion, or imprisonment, and against his will, to labor for another, whether he is paid or not. Slavery, peonage, or compulsory labor for debts; all of which are prohibited by the 13th Amendment, U.S.Const.

Involuntary transfer. *See* Involuntary conveyance.

Involuntary trust. An implied trust which arises because the law imposes trust-like consequences on certain transactions where, for example, an agent breaches his fiduciary duty and buys property in his own name which rightfully should have been purchased for the benefit of his principal (constructive trust) or A supplies the funds for purchase of property by B with the understanding that A will own it but title will be taken in the name of B (resulting trust).

In witness whereof /in wítnəs (h)wèróv/. The initial words of the concluding clause in deeds: "In witness whereof the said parties have hereunto set their hands", etc. A translation of the Latin phrase *"in cujus rei testimonium"*.

IOLTA. Interest on Lawyers' Trust Accounts. In some states, lawyers turn over such interest to public service institutions (*e.g.*, Mass.).

Iota. The minutest quantity possible. Iota is the smallest Greek letter. The word "jot" is derived therefrom.

IOU. A memorandum of debt, consisting of these letters ("I owe you"), a sum of money and the debtor's signature, is termed an "IOU".

Ipso facto /ípsow fǽktow/. By the fact itself; by the mere fact. By the mere effect of an act or a fact.

IRA. Individual Retirement Account.

IRAN. Individual Retirement Annuity.

IRB. Individual Retirement Bond.

I.R.C. Internal Revenue Code.

I.R.D. Income in respect of decedent.

Iron-safe clause. A clause in policies of fire insurance, requiring the insured to preserve his books and inventory in an iron or fireproof safe, or in some secure place not exposed to a fire which would destroy the building. This provision casts on the insured the responsibility for the loss of books and records if due to the wrongful act or negligence of himself or his employees in failing to comply with the requirement.

IRR. Internal Rate of Return.

Irrational. Unreasonable, foolish, illogical, absurd; a person may be irrational in such sense, and still not be insane in the legal sense.

Irreconcilable differences. No-fault ground for dissolution of marriage under many state divorce statutes. *See also* Irretrievable breakdown of marriage.

Irrecusable /ìrəkyúwzəbəl/. A term used to indicate a certain class of contractual obligations recognized by the law which are imposed upon a person without his consent and without regard to any act of his own. They are distinguished from recusable obligations which are the result of a voluntary act on the part of a person on whom they are imposed by law. A clear example of an irrecusable obligation is the obligation imposed on every man not to strike another without some lawful excuse. A recusable obligation is based upon some act of a person bound, which is a condition precedent to the genesis of the obligation. These terms were first suggested by Prof. Wigmore in 8 Harv.Law Rev. 200.

Irregular. Not regular; not according to established law, method, or usage; not conformable to nature, to rules of moral rectitude, or to established principles; not normal, disorderly. As to *irregular* Deposit; Indorsement; Process; and Succession, see those titles.

Irregularity. The doing or not doing that, in the conduct of a suit at law, which, conformably with the practice of the court, ought or ought not to be done. Violation or nonobservance of established rules and practices. The want of adherence to some prescribed rule or mode of proceeding; consisting either in omitting to do something that is necessary for the due and orderly conducting of a suit, or doing it in an unseasonable time or improper manner. The technical term for every defect in mechanics of proceedings, or the mode of conducting an action or defense, as distinguishable from defects in pleadings (see *e.g.* Fed.R.Civ. P. 32(d), irregularities in taking of depositions). Term is not synonymous with "illegality."

In Canon law, any impediment which prevents a man from taking holy orders.

Irregular judgment. One rendered contrary to the method of procedure and practice allowed by the law in some material respect.

Irrelevancy. The absence of the quality of relevancy, as in evidence or pleadings. The quality or state of being inapplicable or impertinent to a fact or argument. Irrelevancy, in an answer, consists in statements which are not material to the decision of the case; such as do not form or tender any material issue. Such irrelevancy in pleadings may be stricken on motion of party. Fed.R.Civil P. 12(f). *See also* Immaterial; Irrelevant allegation; Irrelevant evidence.

Irrelevant allegation. One which has no substantial relation to the controversy between the parties to the suit, and which cannot affect the decision of the court. The test of any allegation being whether it tends to constitute a cause of action or a defense.

An allegation is irrelevant, where the issue made by its denial has no effect upon the cause of action or no connection with the allegation. In this connection, "redundant" is almost a synonym for "irrelevant". Irrelevant matters may be stricken from pleadings on motion of party. Fed. R.Civil P. 12(f).

Irrelevant answer. *See* Answer.

Irrelevant evidence. Not relevant; immaterial; not relating or applicable to the matter in issue; not supporting the issue or fact to be proved. Evidence is irrelevant where it has no tendency to prove or disprove any issue of fact involved. Irrelevant evidence is commonly objected to and disallowed at trial. Fed.Evid.R. 402. *See also* Immaterial; Impertinence; Irrelevancy.

Irreparable damages. *See* Damages.

Irreparable harm. *See* Injury (*Irreparable injury*).

Irreparable injury. *See* Damages; Injunction; Injury (*Irreparable injury*).

Irresistible force. A term applied to such an interposition of human agency as is, from its nature and power, absolutely uncontrollable; as the inroads of a hostile army. *See also* Act of God.

Irresistible impulse. As used as insanity defense, an "irresistible impulse" means an impulse to commit an unlawful or criminal act which cannot be resisted or overcome because mental disease has destroyed the freedom of will, the power of self-control, and the choice of actions. The "irresistible impulse" test for insanity is a test which is broader than the M'Naghten test. Under the "irresistible impulse" test a person may avoid criminal responsibility even though he is capable of distinguishing between right and wrong, and is fully aware of the nature and quality of his acts, provided that he establishes that he was unable to refrain from acting. *See also* Insanity; M'Naghten Rule.

Irretrievable breakdown of marriage. As a no-fault ground for divorce means a condition in which either or both spouses are unable or unwilling to cohabit as husband and wife and for which there are no prospects for reconciliation. In some jurisdictions, it is the sole ground for so-called no-fault divorce. *See also* Irreconcilable differences.

Irrevocable. That which cannot be revoked or recalled.

Irrevocable letter of credit. A confirmed irrevocable letter of credit, irrevocable letter, or a confirmed credit is a contract to pay on compliance with its terms, and needs no formal acknowledgment or acceptance other than is therein stated. *See also* Letter of credit.

Irrevocable offer. An offer which cannot be revoked or recalled by the offeror without liability. U.C.C. 2–205. *See* Firm offer.

Irrevocable trust. *See* Trust.

Irrigation district. A public and quasi-municipal corporation authorized by law in several states, comprising a defined region or area of land which is susceptible of one mode of irrigation from a common source and by the same system of works. These districts are created by proceedings in the nature of an election under the supervision of a court, and are authorized to purchase or condemn the lands and waters necessary for the system of irrigation proposed and to construct necessary canals and other works, and the water is apportioned ratably among the landowners of the district.

I.R.S. Internal Revenue Service.

Is. This word, although normally referring to the present, often has a future meaning, but is not synonymous with "shall have been." It may have, however, a past signification, as in the sense of "has been."

Island. A piece of land surrounded by water. Land in a navigable stream which is surrounded by water only in times of high water is not an island within the rule that the state takes title to newly formed islands in navigable streams.

Isolated sale. Isolated sale which does not entail implied warranty of merchantability is one which occurs only once or at least very infrequently within ordinary course of business.

Issuable. Leading or tending to, or producing, an issue; relating to an issue or issues.

Issuable defense. In common law pleading, a technical expression meaning a plea to the merits, properly setting forth a legal defense, as distinguished from a plea in abatement, or any plea going only to delay the case.

Issuable plea. In common law pleading, a plea to the merits; a traversable plea. A plea such that the adverse party can join issue upon it and go to trial. It is true a plea in abatement is a plea, and if it be properly pleaded, issues may be found on it. In the ordinary meaning of the word "plea", and of the word "issuable," such pleas may be called "issuable pleas," but, when these two words are used together, "issuable plea," or "issuable defense," they have a technical meaning, to-wit, pleas to the merits.

Issue, *v.* To send forth; to emit; to promulgate; as, an officer issues orders, process issues from a court. To put into circulation; as, the treasury issues notes. To send out, to send out officially; to deliver, for use, or authoritatively; to go forth as authoritative or binding. When used with reference to writs, process, and the like the term is ordinarily construed as importing delivery to the proper person, or to the proper officer for service, etc. With respect to securities, refers to act or process of offering stocks or bonds for sale to public or institutional investors.

In financial parlance the term "issue" has two phases of meaning. "Date of issue" when applied to notes, bonds, etc., of a series, usually means the arbitrary date fixed as the beginning of the term for which they run, without reference to the precise time when convenience or the state of the market may permit of their sale or delivery. When the securities are delivered to the purchaser, they will be "issued" to him, which is the other meaning of the term. *See also* "Securities", below.

Issue, *n.* The act of issuing, sending forth, emitting or promulgating; the giving a thing its first inception; as the issue of an order or a writ.

See also Date of issue.

Pleading and Practice

A single, certain, and material point, deduced by the allegations and pleadings of the parties, which is affirmed on the one side and denied on the other. A fact put in controversy by the pleadings; such may either be issues of law or fact. An "issue" is a disputed point or question to which parties to action have narrowed their several allegations and upon which they are desirous of obtaining either decision of court on question of law or of court or jury on question of fact.

Real or *feigned.* A real or actual issue is one formed in a regular manner in a regular suit for the purpose of determining an actual controversy. A feigned issue is one made up by direction of the court, upon a supposed case, for the purpose of obtaining the verdict of a jury upon some question of fact collaterally involved in the cause. Such issues are generally ordered by a court of equity, to ascertain the truth of a disputed fact. They are also used in courts of law, by the consent of the parties, to determine some disputed rights without the formality of pleading; and by this practice much time and expense are saved in the decision of a cause. The name is a misnomer, inasmuch as the *issue* itself is upon a real, material point in question between the parties, and the circumstances only are fictitious.

Ultimate issue. Signifies either such an issue as within itself is sufficient and final for the disposition of the entire case or one which in connection with other issues will serve such end.

See also Failure of issue; Genuine issue; Issue of fact; Issue of law; Issue preclusion; Lawful issue; Legal issue; Ultimate issue.

Commercial Transactions

Issue. The first delivery of an instrument to a holder or remitter. U.C.C. § 3–102(1)(a). The term also applies to documents and refers to the first delivery of a document by the person who created it. See U.C.C. § 7–102(1)(g) (definition of "issuer"). Also describes the act of the issuer of a letter of credit in sending the credit for the purpose of establishing it.

Descendant's Estates

All persons who have descended from a common ancestor. Offspring; progeny; descent; lineage; lineal descendants. In this sense, the word includes not only a child or children, but all other descendants in whatever degree, and it is so construed generally in deeds. But, when used in wills, it is, of course, subject to the rule of construction that the intention of the testator, as ascertained from the language used by him; and hence issue may, in such a connection, be restricted to children, or to descendants living at the death of the testator, where such an intention clearly appears.

The term "issue" and "descendants" have been held to be co-extensive and interchangeable.

"Issue" within its normal usage in wills connotes at least all progeny or blood descendants.

The word "issue" in a will is generally a word of limitation, and when so used, is sometimes said to be equivalent to "heirs of the body". But it has been pointed out in other cases that this word is not as strong a word of limitation as the words "heirs of the body", and yields readily to a context indicating its use as a work of purchase.

Formerly, this term included only legitimate issue. This limitation, however, is changing as a result of Supreme Court cases which prohibit unjustified discrimination against children born out of wedlock. In New York, for example, an illegitimate child shares in the intestate estate of the father. N.Y.EPTL 4–1.2(a)(2)(c).

Many state intestacy statutes provide that an adopted child is "issue" of his or her adopted parents.

Securities

Any of a corporation's or government's securities offered for sale at a certain time to the public, or the act or process of distributing (*i.e.* offering) such for sale by a corporation or government entity. A class or series of bonds, debentures, etc., comprising all that are emitted at one and

the same time. *See also* Distribution; Issuer; Offering; Prospectus; Underwriter; When issued.

Hot issue. A public offering where securities, after their initial sale to the public, are resold in the open market at prices substantially higher than the original public offering price.

New issue. A stock or bond sold by a corporation for the first time. Proceeds may be used to retire outstanding securities of the company, for new plant or equipment, or for additional working capital. *See also* New issue.

Issue of fact. An issue of fact arises when a fact is maintained by one party and is controverted by the other in the pleadings. An issue which arises upon a denial in the answer of a material allegation of the complaint or in the reply of a material allegation in the answer.

Issue of law. An issue of law arises where evidence is undisputed and only one conclusion can be drawn therefrom. An issue of law arises upon a demurrer to the complaint, cross-complaint, or answer, or to some part thereof; or, upon a motion to strike. Calif.C.C.P. § 589.

In making motion for summary judgment, party must show that only issues of law exist for court to consider; *i.e.* must show that there is no genuine issue of material facts. Fed.R.Civil P. 56.

In pleading, an issue upon matter of law, or consisting of matter of law, being produced by a demurrer on the one side, and a joinder in demurrer on the other. The term "issue" may be so used as to include one of law raised by demurrer to the complaint, as well as one raised by answer.

Issue preclusion. Term means that when a particular issue has already been litigated, further litigation of same issue is barred. As it relates to civil actions, concept of "issue preclusion" is in substance that any fact, question or matter in issue and directly adjudicated or necessarily involved in determination of action before court of competent jurisdiction in which judgment or decree is rendered on merits, is conclusively settled by judgment therein and cannot be relitigated in any future action between parties or privies, either in same court or court of concurrent jurisdiction, while judgment remains unreversed or unvacated by proper authority, regardless of whether claim or cause of action, purpose or subject matter of two suits is same. *See also* Collateral estoppel doctrine; Res (*Res judicata*).

Issuer. Corporation, governmental bodies, and other entities that issue and distribute securities. With respect to obligations on or defenses to investment securities "issuer" includes a person who: (a) places or authorizes the placing of his name on a security (otherwise than as authenticating trustee, registrar, transfer agent or the like) to evidence that it represents a share, participation or other interest in his property or in an enterprise or to evidence his duty to perform an obligation evidenced by the security; or (b) directly or indirectly creates fractional interests in his rights or property which fractional interests are evidenced by securities; or (c) becomes responsible for or in place of any other person described as an issuer in this section. U.C.C. § 8–201(1). Every person who issues or proposes to issue any securities; generally the legal entity owning the securities and which has the responsibility for causing the same to be offered publicly or privately. *See also* Issue *(Securities).*

As regards letters of credit, means a bank or other person issuing a credit. U.C.C. § 5–103(1)(c).

As regards documents of title, means a bailee who issues a document except that in relation to an unaccepted delivery order it means the person who orders the possessor of goods to deliver. Issuer includes any person for whom an agent or employee purports to act in issuing a document if the agent or employee has real or apparent authority to issue documents, notwithstanding that the issuer received no goods or that the goods were misdescribed or that in any other respect the agent or employee violated his instructions. U.C.C. § 7–102(g).

Item /áytəm/. Also; likewise; in like manner; again; a second time. This word was formerly used to mark the beginning of a new paragraph or division after the first, whence is derived the common application of it to denote a separate or distinct particular of an account or bill. One of the portions, equal or unequal, into which anything is divided, or regarded as divided; something less than a whole; a number, quantity, mass, or the like, regarded as going to make up, with others or another, a larger number, quantity, mass, etc., whether actually separate or not; a piece, fragment, fraction, member or constituent. A separate entry in an account or a schedule, or a separate particular in an enumeration of a total. An "item" in an appropriation is an indivisible sum of money dedicated to a stated purpose.

For commercial paper purposes, a negotiable or non-negotiable writing for the payment of money that is collected through the collection process governed by U.C.C. Article 4. U.C.C. § 4–104(1)(g).

Itemize. To set down by items. To state each item or article separately. Used commonly with reference to tax accounting.

Itemized deductions. Certain personal expenditures allowed by the Internal Revenue Code as deductions from adjusted gross income if an individual taxpayer chooses not to use the standard deduction and total itemized deductions exceed the standard deduction. Examples include certain medical expenses, interest on home mortgages, state income taxes, and charitable contributions.

Itinerant. Wandering or traveling from place to place; formerly applied to justices who made circuits. Also applied in various statutory and municipal laws (in the sense of traveling from place to place) to certain classes of merchants, traders, and salesmen.

Itinerant peddling. The going about of a merchant from place to place, meeting and dealing with his customers where he finds them. *See* Hawker.

Itinerant vendor. This term is variously defined in statutes; *e.g.,* a person engaged in transient business either in one locality or in traveling from place to place selling goods. *See also* Hawker; Peddler.

Ius cogens. A peremptory norm of general international law. For the purposes of the present convention, a peremptory norm of general international law is a norm accepted and recognized by the international community of states as a whole as a norm from which no derogation is permitted and which can be modified only by a subsequent norm of general international law having the same character. (cf. Vienna Convention on the Law of Treaties, 1958, Article 53.)

J

J. The initial letter of the words "judge" and "justice," for which it frequently stands as an abbreviation. Thus, "J.A.," judge advocate; "J.J.," junior judge; "L.J.," law judge; "A.L.J.," administrative law judge; "P.J.," president judge; "F.J.," first judge; "A.J.," associate judge; "C.J.," chief justice or judge; "J.P.," justice of the peace; "JJ.," judges or justices.

J.A.G. Judge Advocate General.

Jail. A gaol; a prison. A building designated by law, or regularly used, for the confinement of persons held in lawful custody. A place of confinement that is more than a police station lockup and less than a prison. It is usually used to hold persons either convicted of misdemeanors (minor crimes) or persons awaiting trial or as a lockup for intoxicated and disorderly persons. *See also* Gaol; Lockup; Prison.

Jail credit. Refers to time spent by criminal defendant in confinement awaiting trial that will be deducted from his or her final sentence. *See also* Goodtime allowance.

Jail delivery. *See* Gaol.

Jailer. A keeper or warden of a prison or jail.

Jailhouse lawyer. Inmate of a penal institution who spends his time reading the law and giving legal assistance and advice to inmates, especially to those who are illiterate.

Jail liberties. *See* Gaol.

Jason clause. Clause in bills of lading which obligates cargo owners to contribute in general average in cases of danger, damage, or disaster resulting from faults or errors in navigation or in management of vessel, her machinery or appurtenances, provided that shipowner shall have exercised due diligence to make vessel in all respects seaworthy, and to have her properly manned, equipped, and supplied.

J.D. Short for "Juris Doctor" or "Doctor of Jurisprudence." This is now the basic law degree, replacing the "LL.B." in the late 1960's.

Jencks Act *or* **Rule.** A criminal defendant in a Federal Court is entitled to access to government documents for assistance in cross-examination of witnesses in order to impeach for prior inconsistent statements. Jencks v. U. S., 353 U.S. 657, 77 S.Ct. 1007, 1 L.Ed.2d 1103. Following this case, a federal statute was enacted to the same effect; 18 U.S.C.A. § 3500. See also Fed.R.Crim.P. 26.2.

Jeopardy. Danger; hazard; peril.

The danger of conviction and punishment which the defendant in a criminal action incurs when a valid indictment has been found, and a petit jury has been impaneled and sworn to try the case and give a verdict in a court of competent jurisdiction. The condition of a person when he is put upon trial, before a court of competent jurisdiction, upon an indictment or information which is sufficient in form and substance to sustain a conviction, and a jury has been charged with his deliverance. For purpose of constitutional prohibition against double jeopardy, a court proceeding which may result in incarceration places a person, adult or juvenile, in "jeopardy."

The terms "jeopardy of life and liberty for the same offense," "jeopardy of life or limb," "jeopardy for the same offense," "in jeopardy of punishment," and other similar provisions used in the various constitutions, are to be construed as meaning substantially the same thing.

See also Double jeopardy; Former jeopardy; Legal jeopardy.

Jeopardy assessment. If the Internal Revenue Service believes that the collection of a tax deficiency is in jeopardy due to delay, the IRS may assess and collect the tax immediately and without the usual formalities. I.R.C. § 6861.

Jetsam /jétsəm/. Goods which, by the act of the owner, have been voluntarily cast overboard from a vessel, in a storm or other emergency, to lighten the ship. *See also* Jettison.

Jettison /jétəsən/. The act of throwing overboard from a vessel part of the cargo, in case of extreme danger, to lighten the ship. The thing or things so cast out; jetsam. A carrier by water may, when in case of extreme peril it is necessary for the safety of the ship or cargo, throw overboard, or otherwise sacrifice, any or all of the cargo or appurtenances of the ship. Throwing property overboard for such purpose is called "jettison," and the loss incurred thereby is called a "general average loss." *See also* Jetsam.

J.N.O.V., *Abr.* Judgment non obstante veredicto; judgment notwithstanding verdict. *See* Non obstante veredicto.

Job. The whole of a thing which is to be done. A specific task or piece of work to be done for a set fee or compensation. Employment position. Criminal act (*e.g.* robbery).

Jobber. One who buys and sells goods for others. One who buys or sells on the stock exchange; a dealer in stocks, shares, or securities. One who buys and sells articles in bulk and resells them to dealers. A merchant buying and selling in job lots. In general, a middleman in the sale of goods; one who buys from a wholesaler and sells to a retailer. Person who does piecework. *See also* Agent; Broker; Factor; Middleman; Wholesaler.

Job cost record. A source document used in job order costing that provides virtually all financial information about a particular job. The set of job cost records for uncompleted jobs makes up the subsidiary ledger for work in process.

Job order costing. A system of product costing used by an entity that provides limited quantities of identifiable, unique products or services; focus of recordkeeping is on individual jobs.

John Doe. A fictitious name frequently used to indicate a person for the purpose of argument or illustration, or in the course of enforcing a fiction in the law. The name which was usually given to the fictitious lessee of the plaintiff in the mixed action of ejectment. He was sometimes called "Goodtitle." So the Romans had their fictitious personages in law proceedings, as *Titius, Seius.*

The name "John Doe" is, and for some centuries has been, used in legal proceedings as a fictitious name to designate a party until his real name can be ascertained. When "John Doe" is used in a search warrant, case report, textbook, or other legal document, it refers to an unknown or nonexistent person.

John Doe summons. A summons used when the defendant's name is unknown and which is therefore made out to John Doe. After the true name of the defendant is known, it is substituted.

Join. To unite; to come together; to combine or unite in time, effort, action; to enter into an alliance.

Joinder. Joining or coupling together; uniting two or more constituents or elements in one; uniting with another person in some legal step or proceeding; union; concurrence.

The consent to an agreement or document by a party who has an interest in the subject matter of the agreement or document, but who is not himself an active party to the agreement or document.

Collusive joinder. The joinder of a defendant, commonly a nonresident, for purpose of removal to or conferring jurisdiction on a Federal Court.

Compulsory joinder. A person must be joined in an action if complete relief cannot be afforded the parties without his joinder or if his interest is such that grave injustice will be done without

him. Fed.R.Civ.P. 19(a). *See Joinder of parties, below.*

Joinder in demurrer. In common law pleading, when a defendant in an action tenders an issue of law (called a "demurrer"), the plaintiff, if he means to maintain his action, must accept it, and this acceptance of the defendant's tender, signified by the plaintiff in a set form of words, is called a "joinder in demurrer."

Joinder in issue. In common law pleading, a formula by which one of the parties to a suit joins in or accepts an issue in fact tendered by the opposite party. Also called *"similiter".*

Joinder in pleading. In common law pleading, accepting the issue, and mode of trial tendered, either by demurrer, error, or issue, in fact, by the opposite party.

Joinder of claims. Under rules practice, a party asserting a claim to relief as an original claim, counterclaim, cross claim or third party claim may join as many claims as he has against an opposing party whether they are legal or equitable. Fed.R.Civ.P. 18(a); New York C.P.L.R. § 601.

Joinder of defendants. Two or more defendants may be charged in the same indictment or information if they are alleged to have participated in the same act or transaction or in the same series of acts or transactions constituting an offense or offenses. Such defendants may be charged in one or more counts together or separately and all of the defendants need not be charged in each count. Fed.R.Crim.Proc. 8(b).

Joinder of error. In proceedings on a writ of error in criminal cases, the joinder of error is a written denial of the errors alleged in the assignment of errors. It answers to a joinder of issue in an action.

Joinder of indictments or informations. The court may order two or more indictments or informations or both to be tried together if the offenses, and the defendants if there is more than one, could have been joined in a single indictment or information. The procedure shall be the same as if the prosecution were such single indictment or information. Fed.R.Crim.P. 13.

Joinder of issue. The act by which the parties to a cause arrive at that stage of it in their pleadings, that one asserts a fact to be so, and the other denies it.

Joinder of offenses. Two or more offenses may be charged in the same indictment or information in a separate count for each offense if the offenses charged, whether felonies or misdemeanors or both, are of the same or similar character or are based on the same act or transaction or on two or more acts or transactions connected together or constituting parts of a common scheme or plan. Fed.R.Crim.Proc. 8(a).

Joinder of parties. The act of uniting as parties to an action all persons who have the same rights or against whom rights are claimed, as either co-plaintiffs or co-defendants. Fed.R.Civil P. 19 and 20.

Necessary and indispensible parties. Prior to 1966 the federal, and most state, courts used classifications to determine if a person should or must be joined in an action. The label "indispensible" was used if the connection to the action of the absentee party was so close that the action should be dismissed unless the party was joined. The label "necessary" was used if the party was one who ought to be joined if this was possible. These classifications proved unsatisfactory and in 1966 Fed.Rule of Civil Proc. 19 was replaced with a new Rule 19, "Joinder of Persons needed for Just Adjudication." Rule 19(a) defines the class of persons who are needed for just adjudication. If an absentee meets this test, and is subject to process, the court must require that he be joined. If the absentee is needed for just adjudication and is not subject to process, Rule 19(b) states the factors to be considered in deciding whether to proceed in his absence or to dismiss the action.

Proper parties. If a party has some relation to the action, but it is not so close as to make him a person needed for just adjudication within Rule of Civil Proc. 19(a), he is a "proper" party, and the plaintiff has an option whether to join him if the tests of Rule 20 are met.

Joinder of remedies. Whenever a claim is one theretofore cognizable only after another claim has been prosecuted to a conclusion, the two claims may be joined in a single action; but the court will grant relief in that action only in accordance with the relative substantive rights of the parties. In particular, a plaintiff may state a claim for money and a claim to have set aside a conveyance fraudulent as to him, without first having obtained a judgment establishing the claim for money. Fed.R.Civ.P. 18(b).

Misjoinder. The improper joining together of parties to a suit, as plaintiffs or defendants, or of different causes of action. Misjoinder, however, is not a ground for dismissal. The improper party is merely dropped on motion of any party or on courts own motion. Fed.R.Civil P. 21. Relief from prejudicial joinder of offenses or defendants in an indictment or information is permitted under Fed.R.Crim.P. 14.

Nonjoinder. The omission to join some person as party to a suit, whether as plaintiff or defendant, who ought to have been so joined. An omitted party may be added on motion of any party or on courts own motion. Fed.R.Civil P. 21.

Permissive joinder. All persons may join in one action as plaintiffs if they assert any right to relief jointly, severally, or in the alternative in respect of or arising out of the same transaction, occurrence, or series of transactions or occurrences and if any question of law or fact common to all these persons will arise in the action. All persons (and any vessel, cargo or other property subject to admiralty process in rem) may be joined in one action as defendants if there is asserted against them jointly, severally, or in the alternative, any right to relief in respect of or arising out of the same transaction, occurrence, or series of transactions or occurrences and if any questions of law or fact common to all defendants will arise in the action. A plaintiff or defendant need not be interested in obtaining or defending against all the relief demanded. Judgment may be given for one or more of the plaintiffs according to their respective rights to relief, and against one or more defendants according to their respective liabilities. Fed.R.Civ.P. 20(a).

Joint. United; combined; undivided; done by or against two or more unitedly; shared by or between two or more; coupled together in interest or liability.

The term is used to express a common property interest enjoyed or a common liability incurred by two or more persons. Thus, it is one in which the obligors (being two or more in number) bind themselves jointly but not severally, and which must therefore be prosecuted in a joint action against them all; distinguished from "joint and several" obligation.

As to *joint* Annuity; Ballot; Committee; Contract; Covenant; Creditor; Custody; Fiat; Fine; Indictment; Obligation; Obligee; Obligor; Owner; Rate; Resolution; Session; Tenancy; Tenant; Trespass; Trespasser; Trustee; Will, see those titles. As to *Joint stock company, see* Company.

Joint account. An account (*e.g.* bank or brokerage account) in two or more names.

Joint action. An action brought by two or more as plaintiffs or against two or more as defendants. *See* Joinder.

Joint adventure. Any association of persons to carry out a single business enterprise for profit, for which purpose they combine their property, money, effects, skill, and knowledge. A "joint adventure" exists where there is a special combination of two or more persons jointly seeking to profit in some specific venture without actual partnership or corporate designation; it is an association of persons to carry out a single business enterprise for profit, for which purpose they combine their property, money, effects, skill, and knowledge. *See also* Community of interest; Joint enterprise; Joint venture.

Joint and several contracts. Contracts in which the parties bind themselves both individually and as a unit (jointly).

Joint and several liability. Describes the liability of copromisors of the same performance when each of them, individually, has the duty of fully performing the obligation, and the obligee can sue all or any of them upon breach of performance. A liability is said to be joint and several when the creditor may demand payment or sue one or more of the parties to such liability separately, or all of them together at his option. A joint and several bond or note is one in which the obligors or makers bind themselves both jointly and individually to the obligee or payee, so that all may be sued together for its enforcement, or the creditor may select one or more as the object of his suit.

Term also refers to the liability of joint tort-feasors (*i.e.*, liability that an individual or business either shares with other tortfeasors or bears individually without the others). *See* Contribution; Indemnity; Joint liability; Joint tort-feasors; Liability.

Such liability permits the Internal Revenue Service to collect a tax from one or all of several taxpayers. A husband and wife that file a joint income tax return usually are collectively or individually liable for the full amount of the tax liability. I.R.C. § 6013.

Joint authorship. As to literary property, such exists where there is a common design to the execution of which several persons contribute. Mere alterations, additions or improvements, whether with or without the sanction of the author, will not entitle the person making them to claim to be a joint author of the work. Joint labor in furtherance of a common design.

Joint bank account. An account in the names of two or more persons who have equal right to it, generally with the right of survivorship.

Joint cause of action. *See* Joinder.

Joint debtors. Persons united in a joint liability or indebtedness. Two or more persons jointly liable for the same debt.

Joint debtors' acts. Statutes enacted in many of the states, which provide that judgment may be given for or against one or more of several defendants, and that, "in an action against several defendants, the court may, in its discretion, render judgment against one or more of them, leaving the action to proceed against the others, whenever a several judgment is proper". The name is also given to statutes providing that where an action is instituted against two or more defendants upon an alleged joint liability, and some of them are served with process, but jurisdiction is not obtained over the others, the plaintiff may still proceed to trial against those who are before the court, and, if he recovers, may have judgment against all of the defendants whom he shows to be jointly liable.

Joint defendants. Persons who are sued and tried together. In criminal law, persons who are indicted for the same crime and tried together. *See* Joinder; Trial.

Joint defense doctrine. This doctrine generally allows defendant to assert attorney-client privilege to protect his statements made in confidence not to his own lawyer, but to attorney for codefendant for common purpose related to defense of both.

Joint enterprise. Also called "common enterprise". The joint prosecution of common purpose under such circumstances that each has authority express or implied to act for all in respect to the control, means or agencies employed to execute such common purpose. The necessary elements are: (1) an agreement among the group's members, either express or implied; (2) a common purpose that the group intends to carry out; (3) community of pecuniary interest among members of the group in that purpose; and (4) an equal right to a voice in control and direction of the enterprise which gives an equal right of control. *See also* Joint adventure; Joint venture.

Joint estate. Joint estate involves unity of interest, unity of title, unity of time, and unity of possession, and joint tenants must have the same interest accruing under the same conveyance, commencing at the same time, and held under the same undivided possession. *See also* Joint tenancy.

Joint executors. Co-executors; two or more who are joined in the execution of a will. *See also* Co-executor.

Joint indictment. *See* Indictment.

Joint inventions. Such as are made when two or more persons jointly work or collaborate in devising and putting into practical form the subject-matter of patent.

Joint liability. Liability that is owed to a third party by two or more other parties together. One wherein joint obligor has right to insist that co-obligor be joined as a codefendant with him, that is, that they be sued jointly. *See* Contribution; Indemnity; Joinder; Joint and several liability; Joint tort-feasors; Liability.

Joint lives. This expression is used to designate the duration of an estate or right which is granted to two or more persons to be enjoyed so long as they both (or all) shall live. As soon as one dies, the interest determines.

Jointly. Unitedly, combined or joined together in unity of interest or liability. In a joint manner;

in concert; not separately; in conjunction. To be or become liable to a joint obligation. Participated in or used by two or more, held or shared in common.

Jointly acquired property. Property accumulated by joint industry of husband and wife during marriage. *See also* Community property; Marital property.

Jointly and severally. *See* Joint and several contracts; Joint and several liability.

Jointly owned property. *See* Community property; Joint bank account; Joint possession; Tenancy.

Joint negligence. In case of "joint negligence" of several people, proximately causing accident, they act together in concert and either do something together which they should not do or fail to do something which they are together obligated to do under circumstances. *See also* Comparative negligence; Contribution; Joint tort-feasors; Negligence *(Contributory negligence)*.

Joint offense. One offense committed by two or more persons jointly. Crime committed by the participation of two or more persons. *See* Accomplice; Aid and abet; Conspiracy.

Joint ownership. *See* Tenancy *(Joint tenancy)*.

Joint policy. Insurance on lives of spouses, for benefit of survivor.

Joint possession. Exists where two or more persons share actual or constructive possession.

Joint rate. *See* Joint through rate; Rate.

Jointress, jointuress. A woman who has an estate settled on her by her husband, to hold during her life, if she survives him.

Joint return. *See* Joint tax return.

Joint-stock association *or* **company.** An unincorporated business enterprise with ownership interests represented by shares of stock. This type enterprise was recognized at common law and by statute is generally treated as a corporate entity for certain purposes. Such entities bear a resemblance to both a corporation and a partnership. They appear to be like corporations to the extent that they have capital stock, but are not treated as corporations in many jurisdictions.

Joint-stock company. *See* Joint-stock association *or* Company.

Joint-stock insurance company. *See* Stock insurance company.

Joint tax return. Tax return filed for federal or state taxes by a husband and wife together and each is individually liable. Such return includes the income of both spouses, though one spouse need not have any income. It is usually more beneficial from a tax standpoint for spouses to file a joint return than as "married filing separately".

Joint tenancy. *See* Tenancy.

Joint through rate. Transportation charge applicable from a point on one transportation line to a point on another transportation line. Occurs when freight is to be shipped to its destination by more than one carrier.

Joint tort. Where two or more persons owe to another the same duty and by their common neglect such other is injured, the tort is "joint." *See* Contribution; Joint negligence; Joint tort-feasors.

Joint tort-feasors. Term refers to two or more persons jointly or severally liable in tort for the same injury to person or property. Those persons who have acted in concert in their tortious conduct and are, accordingly, jointly and severally liable. Those who act together in committing wrong, or whose acts if independent of each other, unite in causing single injury. Several states have adopted the Uniform Contribution Among Tortfeasors Act. *See also* Contribution.

Joint trial. The trial of two or more persons for the same or similar offenses conducted within the framework of one trial. *See also* Joinder; Trial.

Jointure. A freehold estate in lands or tenements secured to the wife, and to take effect on the decease of the husband, and to continue during her life at the least, unless she be herself the cause of its determination. Property provision for wife, made prior to marriage, in lieu of dower.

Joint venture. A legal entity in the nature of a partnership engaged in the joint undertaking of a particular transaction for mutual profit. An association of persons or companies jointly undertaking some commercial enterprise; generally all contribute assets and share risks. It requires a community of interest in the performance of the subject matter, a right to direct and govern the policy in connection therewith, and duty, which may be altered by agreement, to share both in profit and losses.

A one-time grouping of two or more persons in a business undertaking. Unlike a partnership, a joint venture does not entail a continuing relationship among the parties. A joint venture is treated like a partnership for Federal income tax purposes. I.R.C. § 7701(a).

See also Community of interest; Joint adventure; Joint enterprise. *Compare* Corporation; Partnership.

Joint venture corporation. *See* Corporation.

Joint verdict. Jury verdict covering more than one party to the action and combining two or more verdicts in one. *See also* Verdict.

Joint will. *See* Will.

Joint work. In copyright law, a "joint work" is a work prepared by two or more authors with the intention that their contributions be merged into inseparable or interdependent parts of a unitary whole. Copyright Act, 17 U.S.C.A. § 101.

Jones Act. Federal statute passed in 1920 which provides that a seaman injured in the course of his employment by the negligence of the owner, master or fellow crew members can recover damages for his injuries. 46 U.S.C.A. § 688. Similar remedies are available under the Act to the personal representative of a seaman killed in the course of his employment. *See also* Longshore and Harbor Workers' Compensation Act.

Journal. A daily book; a book in which entries are made or events recorded from day to day. The place where transactions are recorded as they occur. The book of original entry.

In maritime law, the journal (otherwise called "log" or "log-book") is a book kept on every vessel, which contains a brief record of the events and occurrences of each day of a voyage, with the nautical observations, course of the ship, account of the weather, etc. In the system of double-entry bookkeeping, the journal is an account-book into which are transcribed, daily or at other intervals, the items entered upon the day-book, for more convenient posting into the ledger. In the usage of legislative bodies, the journal is a daily record of the proceedings of either house. It is kept by the clerk, and in it are entered the appointments and actions of committees, introduction of bills, motions, votes, resolutions, etc., in the order of their occurrence.

Journal entry. A recording in an accounting journal of equal debits and credits, with, when necessary, an explanation of the transaction.

Reversing entry. A journal entry made on the first day of the following period that is the exact opposite of an adjustment.

Journal entry rule. Regularity of enactment of statute may be inquired into by examining legislative journals.

Journalists' privilege. In the law of defamation, a publisher is protected in actions of defamation if the publication constitutes fair comment on the subject of public officers and employees in matters of public concern. Such privilege is qualified and hence is lost on proof of malice which, in this context, consists in publishing material either knowing it to be false or heedless in the reckless disregard of whether it is true or false when, in fact, it is false. New York Times Co. v. Sullivan, 376 U.S. 254, 84 S.Ct. 710, 11 L.Ed.2d 686. *See also* Libel; Shield laws.

Journalizing. The process of recording transactions in a journal in the form of debits and credits.

Journeyman. A craftsman who has progressed through an apprenticeship and is qualified in his trade.

Joyriding. The temporary taking of an automobile without intent to deprive owner permanently of the vehicle. Called in some jurisdictions the crime of use of motor vehicle without authority which is commonly a misdemeanor in contrast to larceny of motor vehicle which is a more serious offense.

J.P. Justice of the Peace.

Judge. An officer so named in his commission, who presides in some court; a public officer, appointed to preside and to administer the law in a court of justice; the chief member of a court, charged with the control of proceedings and the decision of questions of law or discretion. A public officer who, by virtue of his office, is clothed with judicial authority. Presiding officer of court. Any officer authorized to function as or for judge in doing specified acts.

"Judge", "justice", and "court" are often used synonymously or interchangeably.

See also Magistrate.

Judge advocate. An officer of the Judge Advocate General's Corps of the Army or the Navy or an officer of the Air Force or the Marine Corps who is designated as a judge advocate. 10 U.S.C.A. § 801.

In American usage, the term "judge advocate" no longer refers to any of the parties involved in a court-martial. Instead, it refers to the principal legal adviser on the staff of a military commander (usually with a more definitive title, such as Staff Judge Advocate, Post Judge Advocate, or Command Judge Advocate) or, more broadly, to any officer in the Judge Advocate General's Corps or Department (*i.e.,* branch) of one of the U.S. armed forces. British usage is different.

Judge advocate corps. Staff of Judge Advocate General.

Judge Advocate General. Senior legal officer and chief legal advisor of the Army, Navy, and Air Force and, except when the Coast Guard is operating as a service in the Navy, the General Counsel of the Department of Transportation. 10 U.S.C.A. § 801.

Judge de facto. One who holds and exercises the office of a judge under color of lawful authority and by a title valid on its face, though he has not full right to the office, as where he was appointed under an unconstitutional statute, or by an usurper of the appointing power, or has not taken the oath of office.

Judge-made law. A phrase used to indicate judicial decisions which construe away the meaning of statutes, or find meanings in them the legislature never intended. It is perhaps more common-ly used as meaning, simply, the law established by judicial precedent and decisions. Laws having their source in judicial decisions as opposed to laws having their source in statutes or adminis-trative regulations.

Judge pro tempore /jəj pròw témpəriy/. One appointed for the term or some part thereof, dur-ing which time he exercises all the functions of the regular judge. As opposed to a special judge who is appointed to act in a particular case, such judge is appointed to act during the absence of the regular judge and exercises all of the powers of the regular judge during that period.

Judge's minutes, or **notes.** Memoranda usually taken by a judge, while a trial is proceeding, of the testimony of witnesses, or documents offered or admitted in evidence, of offers of evidence, and whether it has been received or rejected, and the like matters.

Judge trial. Trial conducted before a judge with-out a jury. Jury waived trial; bench trial; non-jury trial.

Judgment. A sense of knowledge sufficient to comprehend nature of transaction. An opinion or estimate. The formation of an opinion or notion concerning some thing by exercising the mind upon it.

The official and authentic decision of a court of justice upon the respective rights and claims of the parties to an action or suit therein litigated and submitted to its determination. The final decision of the court resolving the dispute and determining the rights and obligations of the par-ties. The law's last word in a judicial controver-sy, it being the final determination by a court of the rights of the parties upon matters submitted to it in an action or proceeding. Conclusion of law upon facts found or admitted by the parties or upon their default in the course of the suit. Deci-sion or sentence of the law, given by a court of justice or other competent tribunal, as the result of proceedings instituted therein. Decision or sentence of the law pronounced by the court and entered upon its docket, minutes or record. De-termination of a court of competent jurisdiction upon matters submitted to it. Determination or sentence of the law, pronounced by a competent judge or court, as the result of an action or proceeding instituted in such court, affirming that, upon the matters submitted for its decision, a legal duty or liability does or does not exist.

Term "judgment" under rules practice includes "decree". Fed.R.Civ.P. 54(a). Terms "decision" and "judgment" are commonly used interchange-ably. "Sentence" and "judgment" are synon-ymous in criminal action and appeal from sen-tence is same as appeal from judgment.

The term "judgment" is also used to denote the reason which the court gives for its decision; but this is more properly denominated an "opinion."

An award may be in the nature of, or equiva-lent of, a judgment. Also, an order may be a judgment.

See also Amendment of judgment; Decree; En-tering judgments; Judgment in rem; Judgment qua-si in rem; Rendition of judgment; Sentence; Sim-ulated judgment; Vacation of judgment; Void judg-ment.

Specific Types of Judgments

Agreed judgment. A judgment entered on agree-ment of the parties, which receives the sanction of the court, and it constitutes a contract between the parties to the agreement, operates as an adju-dication between them and when court gives the agreement its sanction, becomes a judgment of the court. *See also Consent judgment, below.*

Alternative judgment. One that by its terms might be satisfied by doing either of several acts at the election of the party or parties against whom the judgment is rendered and from whom performance is by the judgment required. A judgment for one thing or another which does not specifically and in a definite manner determine the rights of the parties.

Appealable judgment. One which disposes of all parties and issues in case. *See also Final judg-ment, below.*

Arrest of judgment. See Arrest of judgment.

Cognovit judgment. See Cognovit judgment; *also, Confession of judgment, below.*

Conditional judgment. One whose force depends upon the performance of certain acts to be done in the future by one of the parties; as, one which may become of no effect if the defendant appears and pleads according to its terms, or one which orders the sale of mortgaged property in a fore-closure proceeding unless the mortgagor shall pay the amount decreed within the time limited.

Confession of judgment. At common law, judg-ment entered where defendant, instead of enter-ing plea, confessed action, or withdrew plea and confessed action. Judgment where a defendant gives the plaintiff a cognovit or written confession of the action by virtue of which the plaintiff enters judgment. The act of a debtor in permit-ting judgment to be entered against him by his creditor, for a stipulated sum, by a written state-ment to that effect or by warrant of attorney, without the institution of legal proceedings of any kind; voluntary submission to court's jurisdiction. Such agreements for confession of judgment are void in many states; *e.g.* Mass.G.L. c. 231, § 13A.

The negotiability of an instrument is not affected by a term authorizing a confession of judgment if the instrument is not paid when due. U.C.C. § 3–112.

See also Cognovit judgment.

Consent judgment. A judgment, the provisions and terms of which are settled and agreed to by the parties to the action. *See also* Decree *(Consent decree)*; and *Agreed judgment, above.*

Contradictory judgment. A judgment which has been given after the parties have been heard, either in support of their claims or in defense. Used in Louisiana to distinguish such judgments from those rendered by default.

Declaratory judgment. See Declaratory judgment.

Default and inquiry, judgment by. It establishes right of action of kind properly pleaded in complaint, determines right of plaintiff to recover at least nominal damages and costs, and precludes defendant from offering any evidence on execution of inquiry to show that plaintiff has no right of action. Such type judgment is obsolete.

Default judgment. A judgment rendered in consequence of the non-appearance of the defendant. Fed.R.Civil P. 55(a). One entered upon the failure of a party to appear or plead at the appointed time. The term is also applied to judgments entered under statutes or rules of court, for want of affidavit of defense, plea, answer, and the like, or for failure to take some required step in the cause.

Judgments rendered on defendant's default are: Judgment *by default;* Judgment by *non sum informatus;* judgment *nil dicit.* Judgments rendered on plaintiff's default are: Judgment of *non pros.* (from *non prosequitur)* and judgment of *nonsuit* (from *non sequitur,* or *ne suit pas).*

Deficiency judgment. A judgment in favor of a creditor for the difference between the amount of the indebtedness and the amount derived from the judicial sale held in order to satisfy the indebtedness. *See also* Deficiency judgment.

Demurrer, judgment on. Such concludes party demurring, because by demurring, a party admits the facts alleged in the pleadings of his adversary and relies on their insufficiency in law. *See* Demurrer.

Dismissal, judgment of. See Dismissal.

Domestic judgment. A judgment is *domestic* in the courts of the same state or country where it was originally rendered; in other states or countries it is called *foreign. See Foreign judgment, below.*

Dormant judgment. One which has not been satisfied or extinguished by lapse of time, but which has remained so long unexecuted that execution cannot now be issued upon it without first reviv-

ing the judgment. Or one which has lost its lien on land from the failure to issue execution on it or take other steps to enforce it within the time limited by statute.

Execution of judgment. See Execution of judgment *or* decree.

Face of judgment. See Face of judgment.

Final judgment. One which puts an *end* to an action at law by declaring that the plaintiff either has or has not entitled himself to recover the remedy he sues for. So distinguished from *interlocutory* judgments. A judgment which disposes of the subject-matter of the controversy or determines the litigation as to all parties on its merits. A judgment which terminates all litigation on the same right. Appeals in federal courts will only lie from "final" judgments. 28 U.S.C.A. § 1291. *See* Final decision *or* judgment; Final decision rule.

Foreign judgment. One rendered by the courts of a state or country politically and judicially distinct from that where the judgment or its effect is brought in question. One pronounced by a tribunal of a foreign country, or of a sister state. Several states have adopted the Uniform Foreign Money Judgments Recognition Act, and also the Uniform Enforcement of Foreign Judgments Act.

General verdict subject to a special case, judgment on. Exists where at the trial the parties agree on the facts and the only question is one of law and a verdict pro forma is taken and the jury find for the plaintiff generally but subject to the opinion of the court on a special case.

In personam or inter partes judgment. See Personal judgment below. See also Judgment in personam or inter partes.

In rem judgment. See Judgment in rem.

Interlocutory judgment. One given in the progress of a cause upon some plea, proceeding, or default which is only intermediate and does not finally determine or complete the suit. One which determines some preliminary or subordinate point or plea, or settles some step, question, or default arising in the progress of the cause, but does not adjudicate the ultimate rights of the parties, or finally put the case out of court. Thus, a judgment or order passed upon any provisional or accessory claim or contention is, in general, merely interlocutory, although it may finally dispose of that particular matter. An "interlocutory judgment" is one which reserves or leaves some further question or direction for future determination. *See* Interlocutory appeal.

Judgment notwithstanding verdict. See Non obstante veredicto.

Judgment of conviction. A judgment of conviction shall set forth the plea, the verdict or findings, and the adjudication and sentence. If the defendant is found not guilty or for any other reason is entitled to be discharged, judgment shall be entered accordingly. The judgment shall be signed by the judge and entered by the clerk. Fed.R.Crim.P. 32(b).

Judgment on pleadings. After the pleadings are closed but within such time as not to delay the trial, any party may move for judgment on the pleadings. If, on a motion for judgment on the pleadings, matters outside the pleadings are presented to and not excluded by the court, the motion shall be treated as one for summary judgment and disposed of as provided in Rule 56, and all parties shall be given reasonable opportunity to present all material made pertinent to such a motion by Rule 56. Fed.R.Civ.P. 12(c). This device resembles closely a demurrer to the extent that it attacks the pleadings on the same basis as a demurrer.

Junior judgment. One which was rendered or entered after the rendition or entry of another judgment, on a different claim, against the same defendant.

Merits, judgment on. One rendered after argument and investigation, and when it is determined which party is in the right, as distinguished from a judgment rendered upon some preliminary or formal or merely technical or procedural point, or by default and without trial. A decision that was rendered on the basis of the evidence and facts introduced. Normally, a judgment based solely on some procedural error is not a judgment on the merits. The latter kind of judgment is often referred to as a "dismissal without prejudice." A party who has received a judgment on the merits cannot bring the same suit again. A party whose case has been dismissed without prejudice can bring the same suit again so long as the procedural errors are corrected (*i.e.,* cured) in the later action.

For res judicata purposes is one which determines the rights and liabilities of the parties based on the ultimate fact as disclosed by the pleadings or issues presented for trial.

Money judgment. One which adjudges the payment of a sum of money, as distinguished from one directing an act to be done or property to be restored or transferred. A judgment, or any part thereof, for a sum of money or directing the payment of a sum of money. For enforcement or satisfaction of money judgment, *see* Execution. Several states have adopted the Uniform Foreign Money Judgments Recognition Act.

Nihil dicit judgment. See Nihil dicit.

Nil capiat per breve or per billa (that he take nothing by his writ, or by his bill). A judgment in favor of the defendant upon an issue raised upon a declaration or peremptory plea.

Nil dicit, judgment by. Judgment for plaintiff rendered when defendant has appeared but has failed to answer or when answer has been withdrawn or abandoned and no further defense is made. At common law, it may be taken against defendant who omits to plead or answer whole or any separable substantial portion of declaration. It amounts to judgment by confession with reference to cause of action states. Under current rules practice, such judgment is substantially identical with default judgment. *See also* Nihil dicit.

Nisi. At common law, judgment nisi was a judgment entered on the return of the nisi prius record, which, according to the terms of the postea indorsed thereon was to become absolute unless otherwise ordered by the court within the first four days of the next succeeding term. *See also* Nisi; Show cause order.

Nolle prosequi, judgment of. One entered against plaintiff when, after appearance and before judgment, he declares that he will not further prosecute his suit. *See also* Nolle prosequi.

Non obstante veredicto. See Non obstante veredicto.

Non pros. (Non prosequitur [he does not follow up, or pursue]). *See* Non prosequitur.

Nonsuit. See Nonsuit.

Notwithstanding verdict. See Non obstante verdicto.

Nunc pro tunc. Judgment given effect as of a date in the past. One entered on a day subsequent to the time at which it should have been entered, as of the latter date. *See* Nunc pro tunc.

Offer of judgment. Before trial, a party defending against a claim may serve upon the adverse party an offer to allow judgment to be taken against him for the money or property or to the effect specified in his offer, with costs then accrued. If after service of the offer the adverse party serves written notice that the offer is accepted, either party may then file the offer and notice of acceptance together with proof of service thereof and thereupon the clerk shall enter judgment. Fed.R. Civil P. 68.

Personal judgment. One imposing on the defendant a personal liability to pay it, and which may therefore be satisfied out of any of his property which is within the reach of process, as distinguished from one which may be satisfied only out of a particular fund or the proceeds of particular property. Judgments in which court has personal jurisdiction over parties.

Repleader, judgment of. See Repleader.

Respondeat ouster. When the issue in law arises on a dilatory plea, and is determined for the plaintiff, the judgment is only that the defendant "do answer over," called a judgment of *respondeat ouster;* it is interlocutory only.

Retraxit. See Retraxit.

Revival of judgment. See Revival.

Summary judgment. See Summary judgment.

Verdict, judgment on. The most usual of the judgments upon facts found, and is for the party obtaining the verdict. *See also* Verdict.

Judgment book. A book required to be kept by the clerk, among the records of the court, for the entry of judgments. Such is called a "civil docket" or "criminal docket" in the federal and many state courts. Fed.R.Civil P. 79; Fed.R.Crim.P. 55. *See also* Judgment docket.

Judgment creditor. A person in whose favor a money judgment has been entered by a court of law and who has not yet been paid. One who has obtained a judgment against his debtor, under which he can enforce execution. A person in whose favor a money judgment is entered or a person who becomes entitled to enforce it. Owner of an unsatisfied judgment. For purpose of Internal Revenue Code, term is used in conventional sense of judgment of court of record. *Cf.* U.C.C. 9–301(3) (lien creditor). *Compare* Judgment debtor. *See also* Attachment; Execution *(Writ of execution)*; Judgment lien.

Judgment debt. A monetary obligation which is either evidenced by a written record, or brought about by successful legal action against the debtor. A debt, whether on simple contract or by specialty, for the recovery of which judgment has been entered, either upon a *cognovit* or upon a warrant of attorney or as the result of a successful action. *See also* Judgment debtor.

Judgment debtor. A person against whom judgment has been recovered, and which remains unsatisfied. The term has been construed to include a judgment debtor's successors in interest. *Compare* Judgment creditor. *See also* Attachment; Execution *(Writ of execution)*; Judgment lien.

Judgment docket. A list or docket of the judgments entered in a given court, methodically kept by the clerk or other proper officer, open to public inspection, and intended to afford official notice to interested parties of the existence or lien of judgments. See Fed.R.Civ.P. 79; Fed.R.Crim.P. 55. *See also* Docket; Judgment book.

Judgment, estoppel by. The estoppel raised by the rendition of a valid judgment by a court having jurisdiction. The essence of estoppel by judgment is that there has been a judicial determination of a fact. It rests upon principles forbidding one to relitigate matter in dispute between parties which has been determined by competent court, on ground that record of judgment imports absolute verity. Where subsequent proceeding is on same cause of action between same parties a former adjudication is conclusive. Ordinarily, "estoppel" of judgment does not extend to matters not expressly adjudicated; and, a judgment or decree without prejudice does not work an "estoppel". *See also* Collateral estoppel doctrine; Issue preclusion; Judicial estoppel; Res *(Res judicata)*.

Judgment execution. The formal or written evidence of the judgment which commands the officer to seize the goods and property of the judgment debtor to satisfy the judgment. Procedure on execution is governed by Fed.R.Civil P. 69. *See* Execution.

Judgment file. The docket in which the entry of a judgment is recorded and preserved as a permanent court record. Fed.R.Civ.P. 79; Fed.R. Crim.P. 55. *See also* Docket; Judgment docket.

Judgment in personam or **inter partes** /jójmənt ìn pərsównəm/°íntər pártiyz/. A judgment against a particular person, as distinguished from a judgment against a thing or a right or *status*. *See also* Judgment *(Personal judgment)*.

Judgment in rem. An adjudication pronounced upon the status of some particular thing or subject matter, by a tribunal having competent authority. It is founded on a proceeding instituted against or on some thing or subject matter whose status or condition is to be determined; or, one brought to enforce a right in the thing itself. It operates directly upon the property. It is a solemn declaration of the status of some person or thing. It is binding upon all persons in so far as their interests in the property are concerned. *See also* Judgment quasi in rem.

Judgment in retraxit /jójmənt ìn rətrǽksət/. A judgment which is usually based upon and follows a settlement out of court, and like a judgment on the merits is a bar and estops plaintiff from again proceeding in another suit on same cause of action. *See* Retraxit.

Judgment lien. An encumbrance that arises by law when a judgment for the recovery of money is docketed and that attaches to the debtor's real estate located in the county where the judgment is docketed. A lien binding the real estate of a judgment debtor, in favor of the holder of the judgment, and giving the latter a right to levy on the property for the satisfaction of his judgment to the exclusion of other adverse interests subsequent to the judgment. Right to subject property of judgment debtor to satisfaction of judgment. A charge on or attachment of property of one who owes a debt and is subject to a judgment thereon. *See also* Execution.

Judgment note. A promissory note (also called cognovit note) embodying an authorization to an attorney, or to a designated attorney, or to the holder, or the clerk of the court, to enter an appearance for the maker and confess a judgment against him for a sum therein named, upon default of payment of the note. Such are invalid in many states. *See* Cognovit note; Judgment *(Confession of judgment).*

Judgment of his peers. A term of expression borrowed from Magna Charta meaning trial by jury.

Judgment proof. Descriptive of all persons against whom judgments for money recoveries are of no effect; *e.g.,* persons who are insolvent, who do not have sufficient property within the jurisdiction of the court to satisfy the judgment, or who are protected by statutes which exempt wages and property from execution.

Judgment quasi in rem. A judgment based on the court's jurisdiction over the defendant's interest in property within the jurisdiction of the court and not on the court's jurisdiction over the person of the defendant (in personam) or over the thing itself (in rem).

Judgment record. In English practice, a parchment roll, on which are transcribed the whole proceedings in the cause, deposited and filed of record in the treasury of the court, after signing of judgment. In American practice, the record is signed, filed, and docketed by the clerk. *See* Fed.R.Civil P. 79. *See also* Docket; Judgment docket.

Judgment recovered. A plea by a defendant that the plaintiff has already recovered that which he seeks to obtain by his action. This was formerly a species of sham plea, often put in for the purpose of delaying a plaintiff's action. Under current rules practice, the defense of prior judgment would be raised as an affirmative defense. Fed.R. Civ.P. 8(c).

Judgment roll. *See* Roll.

Judicature. The state or profession of those officers who are employed in administering justice; the judiciary. A judicatory, tribunal, or court of justice. Jurisdiction; the right of judicial action; the scope or extent of jurisdiction.

Judices /júwdəsiyz/. Lat. Judges.

Judicial. Belonging to the office of a judge; as judicial authority. Relating to or connected with the administration of justice; as a judicial officer. Having the character of judgment or formal legal procedure; as a judicial act. Proceeding from a court of justice; as a judicial writ, a judicial determination. Involving the exercise of judgment or discretion; as distinguished from *ministerial.*

Of or pertaining or appropriate to the administration of justice, or courts of justice, or a judge thereof, or the proceedings therein; as, judicial power, judicial proceedings.

As to *judicial* Action; Confession; Discretion; Document; Estoppel; Evidence; Factor; Mortgage; Notice; Process; Record; Sale; Sequestration; Writ, see those titles. As to Quasi judicial, see that title.

Judicial act. An act which involves exercise of discretion or judgment. It is also defined as an act by court or magistrate touching rights of parties or property brought before it or him by voluntary appearance, or by prior action of ministerial officers. An act by member of judicial department in construing law or applying it to a particular state of facts. An act of administrative board if it goes to determination of some right, protection of which is peculiar office of courts. An act which imposes burdens or confers privileges according to finding of some person or body whether a general rule is applicable or according to discretionary judgment as to propriety. An act which undertakes to determine a question of right or obligation or of property as foundation on which it proceeds. The action of judge in trying a cause and rendering a decision.

Rendition or pronouncement of a judgment is a judicial act and entry thereof a ministerial act. But if there are matters requiring exercise of court's discretion, entry of decree is judicial act.

For purposes of judicial immunity, an act is "judicial" if it is a function normally performed by a judge, and parties dealt with judge in his judicial capacity.

See also Decision; Decree; Judgment; Order.

Judicial action. An adjudication upon rights of parties who in general appear or are brought before tribunal by notice or process, and upon whose claims some decision or judgment is rendered. Action of a court upon a cause, by hearing it, and determining what shall be adjudged or decreed between the parties, and with which is the right of the case.

Judicial activism. Judicial philosophy which motivates judges to depart from strict adherence to judicial precedent in favor or progressive and new social policies which are not always consistent with the restraint expected of appellate judges. It is commonly marked by decisions calling for social engineering and occasionally these decisions represent intrusions into legislative and executive matters. *See also* Judicial self-restraint.

Judicial acts. *See* Judiciary Acts.

Judicial admission. *See* Admission.

Judicial Article. Article III of the U.S.Const. which creates the U.S. Supreme Court; vests in Congress the right to create inferior courts; provides for life tenure for Federal Court judges; and specifies the powers and jurisdiction of the Federal Courts. *See* Federal Judicial Code; Judicial branch; Judicial power; Judicial system; Judiciary Acts.

Judicial authority. The power and authority appertaining to the office of a judge. Jurisdiction; the official right to hear and determine questions in controversy.

Judicial bonds. Generic term for bonds required by court for appeals, costs, attachment, injunction, etc.

Judicial branch. Branch of state and federal government whose function it is to interpret, construe, apply, and generally administer and enforce the laws. This branch, together with the executive and legislative branches forms our tripartite form of federal and state government. See U.S. Constitution, Article III. *See* Judicial Article; Judicial power; Judicial system; Judiciary Acts.

Judicial business. Such as involves the exercise of judicial power, or the application of the mind and authority of a court to some contested matter, or the conduct of judicial proceedings, as distinguished from such ministerial and other acts, incident to the progress of a cause, as may be performed by the parties, counsel, or officers of the court without application to the court or judge. *See* Judicial act; Judicial action.

Judicial Code. *See* Federal Judicial Code.

Judicial cognizance. Judicial notice, or knowledge upon which a judge is bound to act without having it proved in evidence. *See* Judicial notice.

Judicial comity. Principle in accordance with which courts of one state or jurisdiction give effect to laws and judicial decisions of another state out of deference and respect, not obligation. *See also* Full faith and credit clause.

Judicial council. Provision is made in 28 U.S. C.A. § 332 for the Chief Judge of each Circuit Court of Appeal to call a council of all the judges of the circuit twice each year. The primary function of the councils is to assure expeditious and effective administration of the business of the courts.

Judicial cy pres /jədíshəl sìy préy/. Doctrine of "judicial cy pres" is a principle of construction based on a judicial finding of donor's intention as applied to new conditions. When only minor features of a trust for charity become impossible or impracticable of performance and it cannot properly be said that general scheme of testator has failed, doctrine of "judicial cy pres" operates to avoid failure of charity. *See also* Cy-pres.

Judicial decision. Application by a court or tribunal exercising judicial authority of competent jurisdiction of the law to a state of facts proved, or admitted to be true, and a declaration of the consequences which follow. *See also* Decision; Decree; Judgment; Opinion; Order.

Judicial department. *See also* Judicial branch.

Judicial dictum /juwdíshəl díktəm/. A dictum made by a court or judge in the course of a judicial decision or opinion. Expression of opinion by court on question directly involved, argued by counsel and deliberately passed on by court, which is not necessary to decision in the case. *See* Dictum.

Judicial discretion. Term is a broad and elastic one which is equated with sound judgment of court to be exercised according to rules of law. The option the trial judge has in doing or not doing a thing that cannot be demanded by a litigant as an absolute right. A sound judgment which is not exercised arbitrarily, but with regard to what is right and equitable in circumstances and law, and which is directed by the reasoning conscience of the trial judge to a just result. *See also* Discretion; Judicial duty.

Judicial district. One of the circuits or precincts into which a state is commonly divided for judicial purposes; a court of general original jurisdiction being usually provided in each of such districts, and the boundaries of the district marking the territorial limits of its authority; or the district may include two or more counties, having separate and independent county courts, but in that case they are presided over by the same judge. Term is also used to describe or refer to federal judicial districts of the various states. See 28 U.S.C.A. § 81 et seq.

Judicial duty. One that requires exercise of judgment or choice of alternatives in its performance. One that requires exercise of judgment or decision of a question of fact. One that requires use of discretion or examination of evidence and decision of questions of law and fact. One that legitimately pertains to an officer in judicial department. *See also* Judicial act; Judicial action; Judicial discretion.

Judicial errors. Errors into which the court itself falls are "judicial errors." An error of this character occurs when the judgment rendered is erroneous in some particular, requiring it to be changed. *See* Error.

Judicial estoppel. Under doctrine of "judicial estoppel," a party is bound by his judicial declarations and may not contradict them in a subsequent proceeding involving same issues and parties. Under this doctrine, a party who by his pleadings, statements or contentions, under oath, has assumed a particular position in a judicial proceeding is estopped to assume an inconsistent position in a subsequent action. It is the doctrine of the conclusiveness of the judgments. *See also* Collateral estoppel doctrine; Issue preclusion; Judgment, estoppel by; Res *(Res judicata)*.

Judicial evidence. The means, sanctioned by law, of ascertaining in a judicial proceeding the truth respecting a question. *See* Evidence.

Judicial foreclosure. *See* Foreclosure sale.

Judicial function. The exercise of the judicial faculty or office. The capacity to act in the specific way which appertains to the judicial power, as one of the powers of government. The term is used to describe generally those modes of action which appertain to the judiciary as a department of organized government, and through and by means of which it accomplishes its purposes and exercises its peculiar powers. *See also* Judicial act; Judicial action; Judicial business.

Judicial immunity. The absolute protection from civil liability arising out of the discharge of judicial functions which every judge enjoys. Under doctrine of "judicial immunity," a judge is not subject to liability for any act committed within the exercise of his judicial function; the immunity is absolute in that it is applicable even if the actions of the judicial official are taken in bad faith. However, a person may be given injunctive relief and an award of attorneys' fees under the Civil Rights Act (42 U.S.C.A. §§ 1983, 1988).

Judicial knowledge. Knowledge of that which is so notorious that everybody, including judges, knows it, and hence need not be proved. *See* Judicial notice.

Judicial legislation. *See* Judge-made law.

Judicial lien. One obtained by judgment, levy, sequestration, or other legal or equitable process or proceeding. Within meaning of Bankruptcy Code lien avoidance section, is charge against or interest in property to secure payment of debt, obtained by judgment or other legal proceedings. Bankruptcy Code § 101. *See also* Lien.

Judicial notice. The act by which a court, in conducting a trial, or framing its decision, will, of its own motion or on request of a party, and without the production of evidence, recognize the existence and truth of certain facts, having a bearing on the controversy at bar, which, from their nature, are not properly the subject of testimony, or which are universally regarded as established by common notoriety, *e.g.,* the laws of the state, international law, historical events, the constitution and course of nature, main geographical features, etc. The cognizance of certain facts which judges and jurors may properly take and act upon without proof, because they already know them. Such notice excuses party having burden of establishing fact from necessity of producing formal proof. Fed.Evid.Rule 201.

Judicial oath. *See* Oath.

Judicial office. Offices which relate to the administration of justice; and which should be exercised by persons of sufficient skill and experience in the duties which appertain to them. A general term including courts of record and courts not of record.

Judicial officer. A judge or magistrate. The term, in the popular sense, applies generally to any officer of a court, but in the strictly legal sense applies only to an officer who determines causes between parties or renders decision in a judicial capacity. One who exercises judicial function. A person in whom is vested authority to decide causes or exercise powers appropriate to a court.

Judicial opinion. A term synonymous with what has been adjudged or decreed and final in its character. *See* Decision; Decree; Judgment; Opinion; Order.

Judicial order. One which involves exercise of judicial discretion and affects final result of litigation. *See also* Decision; Decree; Judgment; Order.

Judicial power. The authority exercised by that department of government which is charged with declaration of what law is and its construction. The authority vested in courts and judges, as distinguished from the executive and legislative power. Courts have general powers to decide and pronounce a judgment and carry it into effect between two persons and parties who bring a case before it for decision; and also such specific powers as contempt powers, power to control admission and disbarment of attorneys, power to adopt rules of court, etc.

A power involving exercise of judgment and discretion in determination of questions of right in specific cases affecting interests of person or property, as distinguished from ministerial power involving no discretion. Inherent authority not only to hear and determine controversies between adverse parties, but to make binding orders or judgments. Power to decide and pronounce a judgment and carry it into effect between persons and parties who bring a case before court for decision. Power that adjudicates upon and protects the rights and interests of persons or property, and to that end declares, construes and applies the law.

The primary source of powers of federal courts is provided in Art. III of U.S.Const., and Judiciary Act of 1789 (Title 28 of U.S.Code). *See* Judiciary Acts.

Judicial proceeding. Any proceeding wherein judicial action is invoked and taken. Any proceeding to obtain such remedy as the law allows. Any step taken in a court of justice in the prosecution or defense of an action. A general term for proceedings relating to, practiced in, or proceeding from, a court of justice; or the course prescribed to be taken in various cases for the determination of a controversy or for legal redress or relief. A proceeding in a legally constituted court. A proceeding wherein there are parties, who have opportunity to be heard, and wherein the tribunal proceeds either to a determination of facts upon evidence or of law upon proved or conceded facts. *See also* Trial.

Judicial question. One proper for the determination of a court of justice, as distinguished from moot questions or from such questions as belong to the decision of the legislative or executive departments of government and with which the courts will not interfere, called "political" or "legislative" questions. *See also* Case *(Cases and controversies).*

Judicial records. Dockets or records of judicial proceedings; *e.g.* a judgment is a judicial record. Fed.R.Civil P. 79. *See* Docket; Judgment docket; Judgment record.

Judicial remedy. Such as is administered by the courts of justice, or by judicial officers empowered for that purpose by the constitution and laws of the state or nation. *See also* Remedy.

Judicial reprieve. *See* Reprieve.

Judicial review. Power of courts to review decisions of another department or level of government. Marbury v. Madison, 5 U.S. (1 Cranch) 137, 177, 2 L.Ed. 60. Form of appeal from an administrative body to the courts for review of either the findings of fact, or of law, or of both. May also refer to appellate court review of decisions of trial court or of an intermediate appellate court. *See also* Appeal.

Judicial Review Act. Federal statute which sets forth scope of review of decisions of federal administrative agencies. 28 U.S.C.A. §§ 2341–2351.

Judicial sale. Sale conducted under a judgment, order, or supervision of a court as in a sale under a petition for partition of real estate or an execution or a foreclosure sale. One which must be based upon an order or a decree of a court directing the sale. A sale in a bankruptcy proceeding is a "judicial sale". *See also* Execution sale; Foreclosure sale; Sale; Sheriff's sale; Tax sale.

Judicial self-restraint. Self-imposed discipline by judges in deciding cases without permitting themselves to indulge their own personal views or ideas which may be inconsistent with existing decisional or statutory law. *See also* Judicial activism.

Judicial separation. A separation of man and wife by decree of court, less complete than an absolute divorce. A "limited divorce" or a "divorce a mensa et thoro." *See* Separation of spouses; Separation order.

Judicial system. Entire network of courts in a particular jurisdiction. The federal judicial system consists of the Supreme Court, Courts of Appeals, District Courts, and specialized courts such as the Claims Court; Bankruptcy Courts, etc. See 28 U.S.C.A. § 1 et seq.; Art. III, U.S. Const. *See also* Judicial Article; Judiciary *(n).*

Judiciary, *adj.* /jədísh(iy)əriy/. Pertaining or relating to the courts of justice, to the judicial department of government, or to the administration of justice.

Judiciary, *n.* That branch of government invested with the judicial power; the system of courts in a country; the body of judges; the bench. That branch of government which is intended to interpret, construe and apply the law. *See also* Judicial system.

Judiciary Acts. The Judiciary Article (Art. III) of the U.S. Constitution created a Supreme Court and "such inferior courts as the Congress may from time to time ordain or establish". The First Congress established such inferior federal courts under the Judiciary Act of 1789. Subsequent major judiciary acts include the following: Act of 1875 granting federal question jurisdiction; Act of 1891 (Evarts Act) establishing circuit courts of appeals and fixing the outline of the contemporary scheme of federal appellate review; Act of 1911 enacting the Federal Judicial Code (which was recodified in 1948 and 1958); Act of 1925 (Judges' Bill), and 1988, further narrowing the scope of discretionary review by certiorari of the Supreme Court. *See also* Federal Judicial Code.

Judiciously. Directed by sound judgment.

Judicium /jədís(h)(i)yəm/. Lat. Judicial authority or jurisdiction; a court or tribunal; a judicial hearing or other proceeding; a verdict or judgment; a proceeding before a judex or judge.

Jump bail. To abscond, withdraw, leave the jurisdiction, or secrete one's self, in violation of the obligation of a bail bond. *See* Forfeiture of bond.

Junior. Younger. Lower in rank, tenure, preference, or position.

This has been held to be no part of a man's name, but an addition by use, and a convenient distinction between a father and son of the same name.

As to *junior* Barrister; Counsel; Creditor; Judgment; Partner; Security; Writ, see those titles.

Junior execution. One which was issued after the issuance of another execution, on a different judgment, against the same defendant.

Junior interest. A legal right which is subordinate to another's right as applied to property; *e.g.* a second mortgage is subordinate to a first mortgage. *See also* Creditor *(Junior creditor).*

Junior lien. Lien which is subordinate to prior lien. *See* Lien.

Junior mortgage. A mortgage which is subordinate to another mortgage, called the priority, prior, or senior mortgage. *See also* Mortgage.

Junior security issue. Debt or equity issue that is subordinate to another security issue in terms of interest, principal, dividends, payment on dissolution, etc. *See also* Security.

Junk bond. *See* Bond.

Junket. An arrangement or arrangements the primary purpose of which is to induce any person to gamble at a licensed casino and pursuant to which, and as consideration for which, a certain portion of the cost of transportation, food, lodging, and entertainment for said person is directly or indirectly paid by a casino licensee or employee or agent thereof.

Jura /júrə/. Lat. Plural of "jus." Rights; laws.

Jural /júrəl/. Pertaining to natural or positive right, or to the doctrines of rights and obligations; as "jural relations." Of or pertaining to jurisprudence; juristic; juridical.

Recognized or sanctioned by positive law; embraced within, or covered by, the rules and enactments of positive law; Founded in law; organized upon the basis of a fundamental law, and existing for the recognition and protection of rights.

The term "jural society" is used as the synonym of "state" or "organized political community."

Jural cause. A matter or item involving law as contrasted with social obligations or ethics. A judicial matter.

Jurat /júrət/. Certificate of officer or person before whom writing was sworn to. In common use term is employed to designate certificate of competent administering officer that writing was sworn to by person who signed it. The clause written at the foot of an affidavit, stating when, where, and before whom such affidavit was sworn. *See also* Affidavit; Verification.

Juration /jəréyshən/. The act of swearing; the administration of an oath.

Juridical /jərídəkəl/. Relating to administration of justice, or office of a judge.

Regular; done in conformity to the laws of the country and the practice which is there observed.

Juridical day. Day on which court is in session.

Juris /júrəs/. Lat. Of right; of law.

Jurisdiction. A term of comprehensive import embracing every kind of judicial action. It is the power of the court to decide a matter in controversy and presupposes the existence of a duly constituted court with control over the subject matter and the parties. Jurisdiction defines the powers of courts to inquire into facts, apply the law, make decisions, and declare judgment. The legal right by which judges exercise their authority. It exists when court has cognizance of class of cases involved, proper parties are present, and point to be decided is within powers of court. Power and authority of a court to hear and determine a judicial proceeding; and power to render particular judgment in question. The right and power of a court to adjudicate concerning the subject matter in a given case. The term may have different meanings in different contexts.

Areas of authority; the geographic area in which a court has power or types of cases it has power to hear.

Scope and extent of jurisdiction of federal courts is governed by 28 U.S.C.A. § 1251 et seq.

For Ancillary; Appellate; Concurrent; Continuing; Coordinate; Criminal; Equity; Exclusive; Foreign; General; Legislative; Limited *or* special jurisdiction; Military; Pendent jurisdiction; Plenary; Primary; Probate; Special; Subject-matter Summary; Supplemental; and Territorial, see those titles. *See also* Excess jurisdiction; Jurisdiction in personam; Jurisdiction in rem; Jurisdiction of the subject matter; Jurisdiction quasi in rem; Lack of jurisdiction. For *original jurisdiction, see* Original. For *diversity jurisdiction, see* Diversity of citizenship. For *federal question jurisdiction, see* Federal question jurisdiction. For *jurisdiction over nonresidents* or *foreign corporations, see* Long arm statutes; Minimum contacts.

Jurisdictional. Pertaining or relating to jurisdiction; conferring jurisdiction; showing or disclosing jurisdiction; defining or limiting jurisdiction; essential to jurisdiction.

Jurisdictional amount. Required amount involved in the particular case to give court jurisdiction; sum of all claims that are properly joined; value of the object sought to be attained in the litigation. The jurisdiction of the trial court is commonly limited by the amount in controversy in the particular action; *e.g.* the requisite jurisdictional amount for diversity of citizenship jurisdiction in the federal district courts is set forth in 28 U.S.C.A. § 1332.

Jurisdictional dispute. The competing claims made to an employer by different unions that each of their members are entitled to perform certain specific work. There must be evidence of a threat of coercive action for the N.L.R.B. to conduct a hearing and make an assignment of the work.

Jurisdictional facts. Those matters of fact which must exist before the court can properly take jurisdiction of the particular case, as, that the defendant has been properly served with process, that the amount in controversy exceeds a certain sum, that the parties are citizens of different states, etc. *See* Jurisdictional statement; Jurisdiction clause.

Jurisdictional limits. The constitutional or statutory parameters within which judicial power may be exercised such as limits based on the monetary value of the action. *See* Jurisdictional amount.

Jurisdictional plea. Form of answer addressed to the issue of whether the court has the power over the defendant or over the subject matter of the litigation; *e.g.* Fed.R.Civ.P. 12(b)(1), (2).

Jurisdictional statement. In some states, a statement required to set forth the amount claimed to be in controversy so as to permit a court of general jurisdiction to hear the case without remanding it to an inferior court. *See also* Jurisdiction clause.

Jurisdiction clause. A pleading which sets forth a claim for relief, whether an original claim, counterclaim, crossclaim, or third party claim, shall contain "a short and plain statement of the grounds upon which the court's jurisdiction depends, unless the court already has jurisdiction and the claim needs no new grounds to support it." Fed.R.Civ.P. 8(a).

In equity practice, that part of a bill which is intended to give jurisdiction of the suit to the court, by a general averment that the acts complained of are contrary to equity, and tend to the injury of the complainant, and that he has no remedy, or not a complete remedy, without the assistance of a court of equity, is called the "jurisdiction clause."

See also Jurisdictional statement.

Jurisdiction in personam. Power which a court has over the defendant's person and which is required before a court can enter a personal or in personam judgment. Pennoyer v. Neff, 95 U.S. 714, 24 L.Ed. 565. It may be acquired by an act of the defendant within a jurisdiction under a law by which the defendant impliedly consents to the personal jurisdiction of the court, *e.g.* operation of a motor vehicle on the highways of state confers jurisdiction of operator and owner on courts of state. A judgment in personam brings about a merger of the original cause of action into the judgment and thereafter the action is upon the judgment and not on the original cause of action. *See also* In personam; Jurisdiction over person.

Jurisdiction in rem. Power of a court over a thing so that its judgment is valid as against the rights of every person in the thing, *e.g.* a judgment or decree of registration of title to land. *See also* In rem; Jurisdiction quasi in rem.

Jurisdiction of the person. *See* Jurisdiction in personam.

Jurisdiction of the subject matter. Power of a particular court to hear the type of case that is then before it. Term refers to jurisdiction of court over class of cases to which particular case belongs; jurisdiction over the nature of the cause of action and relief sought; or the amount for which a court of limited jurisdiction is authorized to enter judgment.

A court is without authority to adjudicate a matter over which it has no jurisdiction even though the court possesses jurisdiction over the parties to the litigation; *e.g.* a court of limited criminal jurisdiction has no power to try a murder indictment and its judgment therein would be void and of no effect because it lacks subject matter jurisdiction.

Jurisdiction over person. The legal power of the court to render a personal judgment against a party to an action or a proceeding. *See* Jurisdiction in personam.

Jurisdiction quasi in rem. *See* Quasi in rem jurisdiction.

Juris doctor. *See* J.D.

Juris et de jure /júrəs èt dìy júriy/. Of law and of right.

Juris privati /júrəs prəvéytay/. Of private right; subjects of private property.

Jurisprudence. The philosophy of law, or the science which treats of the principles of positive law and legal relations.

In the proper sense of the word, "jurisprudence" is the science of law, namely, that science which has for its function to ascertain the principles on which legal rules are based, so as not only to classify those rules in their proper order, and show the relation in which they stand to one another, but also to settle the manner in which new or doubtful cases should be brought under the appropriate rules. Jurisprudence is more a formal than a material science. It has no direct concern with questions of moral or political policy, for they fall under the province of ethics and legislation; but, when a new or doubtful case arises to which two different rules seem, when taken literally, to be equally applicable, it may be, and often is, the function of jurisprudence to consider the ultimate effect which would be produced if each rule were applied to an indefinite number of similar cases, and to choose that rule which, when so applied, will produce the greatest advantage to the community.

For Comparative jurisprudence and Medical jurisprudence, see those titles. For *equity jurisprudence, see* Equity.

Jurist. One who is versed or skilled in law; answering to the Latin *"jurisperitus"* (q.v.). A judge; a legal scholar.

The term is commonly applied to those who have distinguished themselves by their writings on legal subjects or to judges.

Juristic /jərístək/. Pertaining or belonging to, or characteristic of, jurisprudence, or a jurist, or the legal profession.

Juristic act. One designed to have a legal effect, and capable thereof. An act of a private individual directed to the origin, termination, or alteration of a right.

Juror. Member of jury. In addition to regular jurors, term includes special and alternate jurors.

Alternate juror. Additional juror impanelled in case of sickness or disability of another juror; generally in trials of expectedly long duration. Fed.R.Civil P. 47(b).

Juror designate. A juror who has been drawn as a juror.

Juror's book. A list of persons qualified to serve on juries. *See also* Jury-list.

Jury. A certain number of men and women selected according to law, and *sworn (jurati)* to inquire of certain matters of fact, and declare the truth upon evidence to be laid before them. This definition embraces the various subdivisions of juries; as *grand jury, petit jury, common jury, special jury, coroner's jury, sheriff's jury (q.v.).*

A jury is a body of persons temporarily selected from the citizens of a particular district, and invested with power to present or indict a person for a public offense, or to try a question of fact. *See also* Trier of fact.

Advisory jury. A body of jurors impanelled to hear a case in which the parties have no right to a jury trial. The judge remains solely responsible for the findings and he may accept or reject the jury's verdict. Fed.R.Civil P. 39(c). *See also* Advisory jury.

Blue ribbon jury. Jury not drawn from the community at large, but one selected from unusually qualified people; an exceptional jury.

Challenge to jury. *See* Jury challenge.

Common jury. The ordinary kind of jury (*i.e.* petit jury) by which issues of fact are generally tried, as distinguished from a *special jury (q.v.).*

Deadlocked jury. *See* Hung jury, below.

Fair and impartial jury. *See* Fair and impartial jury.

Foreign jury. A jury obtained from a county or jurisdiction other than that in which issue was joined.

Grand jury. A jury of inquiry who are summoned and returned by the sheriff to each session of the criminal courts, and whose duty is to receive complaints and accusations in criminal cases,

hear the evidence adduced on the part of the state, and find bills of indictment in cases where they are satisfied a trial ought to be had. They are first sworn, and instructed by the court. This is called a "grand jury" because it comprises a greater number of jurors than the ordinary trial jury or "petit jury." At common law, a grand jury consisted of not less than twelve nor more than twenty-three men.

Body of citizens, the number of whom varies from state to state, whose duties consist in determining whether probable cause exists that a crime has been committed and whether an indictment (true bill) should be returned against one for such a crime. If the grand jury determines that probable cause does not exist, it returns a "no bill." It is an accusatory body and its function does not include a determination of guilt.

Federal grand jury. Every grand jury impaneled before any federal district court shall consist of not less than sixteen nor more than twenty-three persons. If less than sixteen of the persons summoned attend, they shall be placed on the grand jury, and the court shall order the marshal to summon, either immediately or for a day fixed, from the body of the district, and not from the bystanders, a sufficient number of persons to complete the grand jury. 18 U.S.C.A. § 3321; Fed.R.Crim.P. 6.

See also Extraordinary grand jury; Inquest; Special grand jury.

Hung jury. A jury which is unable to agree on a verdict after a suitable period of deliberation; a deadlocked jury. The result is a mistrial of the case. *See* Dynamite instruction.

Impanelling of jury. *See* Impanel; Jury challenge; Striking a jury.

Impartial jury. *See* Impartial jury.

Inquest jury. A jury of inquest is a body of persons summoned from the citizens of a particular district before the sheriff, coroner, or other ministerial officers, to inquire of particular facts. *See* Inquest.

Jury instructions. *See* Jury instructions.

Jury size. While at common law, and traditionally, a jury consisted of 12 members, there is no constitutional infirmity or deficiency in a jury of less than twelve; and it is common for state and Federal district court juries to consist of six persons for civil cases, instead of twelve (*e.g.* Dist. of Mass.). Also, in federal district courts, and many state courts, the parties may stipulate that the jury shall consist of any number less than twelve. Fed.R.Civil P. 48; Fed.R.Crim.P. 23. For size of federal grand jury, *see Federal grand jury, above.*

Jury tampering. The unauthorized communication with a juror for the purpose of exerting improper influence. It is proscribed by Federal and state statutes. *Cf.* 18 U.S.C.A. §§ 1503, 1504; N.Y. McKinney's Penal Law § 215.25.

Petit jury. The ordinary jury for the trial of a civil or criminal action; so called to distinguish it from the grand jury.

Polling of jury. See Polling the jury.

Sequestration of jury. In some cases of great notoriety, the trial judge will order the jury to be isolated from the public (*e.g.* confined to area of hotel while trial not in session) for the duration of the trial to prevent tampering and exposure to trial publicity. In these cases the jurors are always in the custody of the court.

Special jury. A jury ordered by the court, on the motion of either party, in cases of unusual importance or intricacy. Called, from the manner in which it is constituted, a "struck jury." See Striking a jury.

At common law, a jury composed of persons above the rank of ordinary freeholders; usually summoned to try questions of greater importance than those usually submitted to common juries.

Traverse jury. See Traverse.

Trial jury. The jury participating in the trial of a given case; or a jury summoned and impaneled for the trial of a case, and in this sense a petit jury as distinguished from a grand jury. A body of persons returned from the citizens of a particular district before a court or officer of competent jurisdiction, and sworn to try and determine, by verdict, a question of fact.

Jury-box. The place in court (strictly an inclosed place) where the jury sits during the trial of a cause.

Jury challenge. *Challenge for cause.* In most jurisdictions, each party to the litigation has right to a certain number of peremptory challenges to jurors at the time of impanelling. In addition, a party has the right to challenge a juror by furnishing a satisfactory reason why such juror should not be seated such as bias or knowledge of the case. Unlike the peremptory challenge for which no reason need be given, the party challenging a juror for cause must satisfy the trial judge that his reasons are compelling. See *e.g.* Fed.R.Crim.P. 24. *See also* Challenge.

Challenge to array. A challenge to the entire jury venire based on such grounds as systematic exclusion of women, blacks, young persons, etc. in the selection process.

Peremptory challenge. A challenge to a juror at the time of impanelling for which no reason need be advanced; in most jurisdictions each party is entitled to a certain number of such challenges in addition to challenges for cause. See *e.g.* Fed.R. Crim.P. 24.

Jury commissioner. An officer charged with the duty of selecting the names to be put into the jury wheel, or of drawing the panel of jurors for a particular term of court. Local official responsible for collecting lists of qualified prospective jurors for submission to court.

Jury instructions. A direction given by the judge to the jury concerning the law of the case; a statement made by the judge to the jury informing them of the law applicable to the case in general or some aspect of it; an exposition or the rules or principles of law applicable to the case or some branch or phase of it, which the jury are bound to accept and apply. Attorneys for both sides normally furnish judge with suggested instructions. Fed.R.Civil P. 51; Fed.R.Crim.P. 30. Many states and federal courts have model or pattern jury instructions which are required to be used, or substantially followed, by the trial judge.

See also Allen charge; Argumentative instruction; Cautionary instruction; Charge *(Charge to jury)*; Dynamite instruction; Formula instruction; Golden Rule argument. For *request for instructions, see* Request.

Additional instructions. If during the course of deliberations the jury is unclear about a particular point of law or aspect of the evidence it may request the court for additional or supplementary instructions.

Mandatory instruction. A mandatory instruction unequivocally charges the jury that if jurors find from preponderance of evidence that certain set of facts exists, jurors must find for one party and against the other. Instructions which attempt to set up a factual situation and direct jury to a certain result and they are to be distinguished from instructions which merely state propositions of law without incorporating a factual situation.

Peremptory instruction. An instruction given by a court to a jury which the latter must obey implicitly; as an instruction to return a verdict for the defendant, or for the plaintiff, as the case may be. *See also Mandatory instruction, above.*

Jury-list. A paper containing the names of jurors impaneled to try a cause, or the names of all the jurors summoned to attend court. *See also* Jury panel.

Jury of matrons. *See* Matrons, jury of.

Jury panel. The group of prospective jurors who are summoned to appear on a stated day and from which a grand jury or petit jury is chosen. *See* Impanel, Jury-list.

Jury polling. *See* Polling the jury.

Jury process. The process by which a jury is summoned in a cause, and by which their attendance is enforced. *See also* Impanel.

Jury questions. In general, term refers to questions of fact which are peculiarly within the province of the jury as contrasted with questions of law which must be decided by the judge. Term may also refer to special questions or interrogatories which the court may direct to the jury for a special verdict. Fed.R.Civil P. 49. *See also* Fact question; Special interrogatories; Voir dire.

Jury Selection and Service Act. Federal Act (1968) to insure non-discrimination in federal jury selection and service. 28 U.S.C.A. § 1861.

Jury summation. *See* Closing argument.

Jury trial. Trial of matter or cause before jury as opposed to trial before judge. Such right is guaranteed with respect to criminal cases by Art. III, Sec. 2, cl. 3 of U.S.Const., and with respect to "suits at common law, where the value in controversy shall exceed twenty dollars" by the Seventh Amendment. Such right is also preserved by rule of court (*e.g.* Fed.R.Civil P. 38) and by the Fifth Amendment which provides *inter alia* for indictment by grand jury, and the Sixth Amendment which contains further specifications respecting jury trial in criminal cases. In addition, state constitutions provide for right to jury trial and the Supreme Court has held that the Fourteenth Amendment guarantees a right of jury trial in all state criminal cases which—were they to be tried in federal court—would come within the Sixth Amendment's guarantee.

The right to "jury trial" of controverted issues implies a trial by an impartial and qualified jury. *See* Impartial jury.

See also Trial.

Jury wheel. Physical device or electronic system for the storage and random selection of the names or identifying numbers of prospective jurors. A machine containing the names of persons qualified to serve as grand and petit jurors, from which, in an order determined by the hazard of its revolutions, are drawn a sufficient number of such names to make up the panels for a given term of court.

Jurywoman. Member of a jury of matrons.

Jus /jŭs/. Lat. In Roman law, right; justice; law; the whole body of law; also a right.

Jus civile /jŭs sívəliy/. Civil law. The system of law peculiar to one state or people. Particularly, in Roman law, the civil law of the Roman people, as distinguished from the *jus gentium*. The term is also applied to the body of law called, emphatically, the "civil law." *See also* Civil law.

Jus naturale /jŭs nætyəréyliy/. The natural law, or law of nature; law, or legal principles, supposed to be discoverable by the light of nature or abstract reasoning, or to be taught by nature to all nations and men alike; or law supposed to govern men and peoples in a state of nature, *i.e.,* in advance of organized governments or enacted laws. *See* Natural law.

Just. Conforming to or consonant with what is legal or lawful. Legally right; lawful; equitable; in accordance with law and justice. *See also* Equitable.

Justa causa /jŭstə kózə/. In the civil law, a just cause; a lawful ground; a legal transaction of some kind.

Just cause. Fair, adequate, reasonable cause. Legitimate cause; legal or lawful ground for action; such reasons as will suffice in law to justify the action taken. A cause outside legal cause, which must be based on reasonable grounds, and there must be a fair and honest cause or reason, regulated by good faith. As used in statutory sense is that which to an ordinary intelligent person is justifiable reason for doing or not doing a particular act. *See* Cause of action.

Just compensation. Compensation which is fair to both the owner and the public when property is taken for public use through condemnation (eminent domain). Consideration is taken of such criteria as the cost of reproducing the property, its market value, and the resulting damage to the remaining property of the owner. The Fifth Amendment to the U.S. Constitution provides that no private property shall be taken for public use, without "just compensation." Within Fifth Amendment provision that private property shall not be taken for public use without just compensation, "just compensation" means the full monetary equivalent of the property taken.

As regards property taken for public use, the term is comprehensive and includes all elements. It means a settlement which leaves one no poorer or richer than he was before the property was taken. It requires that the owner be put in as good position pecuniarily as he would otherwise have been if the property had not been taken.

Market value at time of taking; *i.e.* highest price for which property considered at its best and most profitable use can be sold in open market by willing seller to willing buyer, neither acting under compulsion and both exercising reasonable judgment. *See also* Adequate compensation; Similar sales.

Just debts. As used in a will or a statute, this term means legal, valid, and incontestable obligations, not including such as are barred by the statute of limitations or voidable at the election of the party.

Justice, v. To do justice, to see justice done; to summon one to do justice.

Justice, n. Title given to judges, particularly to judges of U.S. and state supreme courts, and as well to judges of appellate courts. The U.S. Supreme Court, and most state supreme courts are composed of a chief justice and several associate justices.

Proper administration of laws. In jurisprudence, the constant and perpetual disposition of legal matters or disputes to render every man his due.

See also Miscarriage of justice; Obstructing justice.

Justice Department. One of the executive departments of the federal government, headed by the Attorney General. The chief purposes of the Department of Justice are to enforce the federal laws, to furnish legal counsel in federal cases, and to construe the laws under which other departments act. It conducts all suits in the Supreme Court in which the United States is concerned, supervises the federal penal institutions, and investigates and detects violations against federal laws. It represents the government in legal matters generally, rendering legal advice and opinions, upon request, to the President and to the heads of the executive departments. The Attorney General supervises and directs the activities of the U.S. attorneys and marshals in the various judicial districts. *See* Attorney General.

Justice of the peace. A judicial magistrate (of English origin) of inferior rank having (usually) jurisdiction limited to that prescribed by statute in civil matters (*e.g.* performance of marriages) and jurisdiction over minor criminal offenses, committing more serious crimes to higher courts. Trend in most states has been to abolish office and courts of justice of the peace, transferring their powers and functions to other courts; *e.g.* municipal or district courts.

Justicer /jə́stəsər/. The old form of *justice*.

Justiciability. *See* Justiciable controversy.

Justiciable /jəstísh(iy)əbəl/. Matter appropriate for court review. *See* Justiciable controversy.

Justiciable controversy. A controversy in which a present and fixed claim of right is asserted against one who has an interest in contesting it; rights must be declared upon existing state of facts and not upon state of facts that may or may not arise in future. A question as may properly come before a tribunal for decision. Courts will only consider a "justiciable" controversy, as distinguished from a hypothetical difference or dispute or one that is academic or moot. Term refers to real and substantial controversy which is appropriate for judicial determination, as distinguished from dispute or difference of contingent, hypothetical or abstract character. *Compare* Political questions. *See* Case; Cause of action; Controversy.

Justifiable. Rightful; defensible; warranted or sanctioned by law; that which can be shown to be sustained by law, as justifiable homicide. *See* Homicide; Justifiable homicide.

Justifiable cause. Justifiable cause for prosecution is well-founded belief of person of ordinary caution, prudence, and judgment in existence of facts essential to prosecution. *See also* Probable cause.

Justifiable homicide. Killing of another in self-defense when danger of death or serious bodily injury exists. Such homicide generally connotes only the use of force which is necessary, or which reasonably appears to be necessary, to resist other party's misconduct; and use of excessive force destroys the justification. An act which the law positively enjoins upon the perpetrator or positively permits him to perform, such as a capital crime execution or the prevention of a crime or escape by a proper officer. *See* Self-defense.

Justification. Just, lawful excuse or reason for act or failing to act. Explanation with supporting data.

As defense in criminal and tort law, term means maintaining or showing a sufficient reason in court why the defendant did what he is called upon to answer or, just cause or lawful excuse for act, reasonable excuse. See Model Penal Code § 3.01 et seq. *See* Self defense.

Term is not widely used in torts where, instead, defenses and privileges are more commonly asserted.

See also Legal excuse; Necessity; Self-defense.

Justness. Conformity to truth, propriety, accuracy, or the like.

Just prior. Immediately preceding; just before; without appreciable lapse of time before. It means before the time and connotes nearness in point of time. Some period of time before.

Just title. By the term "just title," in cases of prescription, is meant a title which the possessor may have received from any person whom he honestly believed to be the real owner, provided the title was such as to transfer the ownership of the property. One good against all the world. *See* Marketable title.

Just value. In taxation, the fair, honest, and reasonable value of property, without exaggeration or depreciation; its actual market value. *See also* Fair market value.

Juvenile. A young person who has not yet attained the age at which he or she should be treated as an adult for purposes of criminal law. In some states, this age is seventeen. Under the federal Juvenile Delinquency Act, a "juvenile" is a person who has not attained his eighteenth birthday. 18 U.S.C.A. § 5031. A term which may be, though not commonly is, applied to a person who has not reached his or her legal majority for purposes of contracting, marrying, etc. In law, the terms "juvenile" and "minor" are usually used in different contexts; the former used when referring to young criminal offenders, the latter to legal capacity or majority. *See also* Minor; Youthful offenders.

Juvenile courts. A court having special jurisdiction, of a paternal nature, over delinquent, dependent, and neglected children. In juvenile court proceedings, due process requires that juveniles have right to notice of charges, to counsel, to confrontation and cross-examination of witnesses, and to privilege against self-incrimination. In re Gault, 387 U.S. 1, 87 S.Ct. 1428, 18 L.Ed.2d 527.

Juvenile delinquency. Participation in illegal behavior by a minor who falls under a statutory age limit. *See also* Delinquent child.

Juvenile delinquent. *See* Delinquent child.

Juvenile offenders. *See* Delinquent child.

K

Kangaroo court. Term descriptive of a sham legal proceeding in which a person's rights are totally disregarded and in which the result is a foregone conclusion because of the bias of the court or other tribunal.

Keep, *v.* To continue. To have or retain in one's power or possession; not to lose or part with; to preserve or retain. To maintain, carry on, conduct, or manage; as, to "keep" a bawdy house, gaming table, nuisance, or the like. To maintain, tend, harbor, feed, and shelter; as, to "keep" a dangerous animal.

To maintain continuously and methodically for the purposes of a record; as, to "keep" books. Thus to "keep" records of court means, not only to preserve the manual possession of the records, books, and papers, but to correctly transcribe therein the proceedings of the court.

To maintain continuously and without stoppage or variation; as, when a vessel is said to "keep her course," that is, continue in motion in the same general direction in which she was previously sailing. To maintain, to cause to continue without essential change of condition. To take care of and to preserve from danger, harm, or loss.

See also Maintain.

Keeper. A custodian, manager, or superintendent; one who has the care, custody, or management of any thing or place; one who has or holds possession of anything. *See* Bailment; Custodian; Depository.

Keeping a lookout. Being watchful of movements of driver's own vehicle, as well as other vehicles and pedestrians. *See* Lookout.

Keeping books. Preserving an intelligent record of a merchant's or tradesman's affairs with such reasonable accuracy and care as may properly be expected from a person in that business. *See* Accounting.

Keeping the peace. Avoiding a breach of the peace; dissuading or preventing others from breaking the peace.

Keep in repair. When a lessee is bound to keep the premises in repair, he must have them in repair at all times during the term; and, if they are at any time out of repair, he is guilty of a breach of the covenant. *See* Habitability.

Kefauver-Cellar Act. Federal anti-merger statute enacted in 1950 prohibiting the acquisition of assets of one company by another (generally in the same line of business) when the effect is to lessen competition. 15 U.S.C.A. §§ 18, 21.

Kentucky Rule. In the allocation of dividends by trustees as between income and principal, all dividends whether paid in cash or stock are regarded as income though in most jurisdictions accepting this rule a dividend paid in the stock of the issuing corporation is considered principal and brings about an adjustment in the basis of such stock in the portfolio.

Keogh Plan. A designation for retirement plans available to self-employed taxpayers (also referred to as H.R.10 plans). Such plans extend to the self-employed tax benefits similar to those available to employees under qualified pension and profit sharing plans. Yearly contributions to the plan (up to a certain amount) are tax deductible. *See also* Individual retirement account.

Ketubah. The Jewish "Ketubah" is a marriage contract or marriage settlement.

Key man insurance. Type of insurance coverage purchased by companies to protect them on the death or disability of a valued employee or by partnership to provide for funds with which to buy out the interest of such partner on his death or disability.

Key number system. A standard legal research tool in which each point of law derived from reported cases is topically arranged in a digest and assigned a "key" number. Once the key number for a relevant point of law is determined, generally through a digest index, a researcher may look under that topic, in either a digest or on WESTLAW, for topically related cases. *See also* Digest *(American Digest System)*.

Kickback. Payment back by seller of a portion of the purchase price to buyer or public official to induce purchase or to improperly influence future purchases or leases. Such payments are not tax deductible as ordinary and necessary expenses. I.R.C. § 162.

Under federal statute kickbacks are a criminal offense in connection with a contract for construction or repair of a public building or a building financed by loans from the government. 18 U.S.C.A. § 874. Such acts are also generally prohibited by state commercial bribery statutes. *See also* Bribery.

Kiddie tax. A tax imposed on unearned income (in excess of a minimal amount) of a child under the age of 14. Such income is taxed at the parents' highest rate. The Tax Reform Act of 1986 instituted the "kiddie tax" in an effort to stop the shifting of income producing assets within families (*i.e.*, from parents to minor children) which, prior to the TRA, resulted in substantial tax savings to upper bracket parents. I.R.C. § 1(i).

Kidnapping. At common law, the forcible abduction or stealing and carrying away of a person from own country to another. The unlawful seizure and removal of a person from own country or state against his will. In American law, the intent to send the victim out of the country does not constitute a necessary part of the offense; the unlawful taking and carrying away of a human being by force or fraud or threats or intimidation and against his will being the essential elements. At common law kidnapping was a misdemeanor, but under modern statutes such crime is a felony. 18 U.S.C.A. § 1201.

A person is guilty of kidnapping if he unlawfully removes another from his place of residence or business, or a substantial distance from the vicinity where he is found, or if he unlawfully confines another for a substantial period in a place of isolation, with any of the following purposes: (a) to hold for ransom or reward, or as a shield or hostage; or (b) to facilitate commission of any felony or flight thereafter; or (c) to inflict bodily injury on or to terrorize the victim or another; or (d) to interfere with the performance of any governmental or political function. Model Penal Code, § 212.1.

With respect to federal kidnapping act, *see* Lindbergh Act. *See also* Abduction; Hostage; Parental Kidnapping Prevention Act; Ransom.

Child-stealing. Child-stealing statutes commonly provide a penalty for any one who shall lead, take, entice or detain a child under a specified age with intent to keep or conceal it from its parent, guardian, or other person having lawful care or control thereof.

Kidnapping for ransom. One who detains another for the purpose of extorting money from him or from another person as the price of his release is guilty of the felony of kidnapping for ransom. 18 U.S.C.A. § 1201.

Simple kidnapping. Kidnapping which is not in some aggravated form, such as holding for ransom, is commonly referred to as "simple kidnapping."

Kilberg doctrine. In conflicts of law, a rule to the effect that the forum is not bound by the law of the place of the death as to the limitations on damages for wrongful death because such law is procedural and hence the law of the forum governs on this issue.

Kill, *v.* To deprive of life; to destroy the life of an animal or person. The word "homicide" expresses the killing of a human being. *See also* Homicide; Manslaughter; Murder.

Killing by misadventure. Accidental killing of a person where the slayer is doing a lawful act, unaccompanied by any criminal carelessness or reckless conduct. Excusable homicide occurring where one engaged in doing lawful act, without intention to do harm and, with proper precaution to avoid danger, unfortunately kills another. *See also* Accidental killing; Manslaughter.

Kind. Class, grade, or sort. Genus; generic class; description. *See* In kind; Like-kind exchange; Sample.

Kindred. *See* Kin or kindred; Next of kin.

King. The sovereign, ruler, or chief executive magistrate of a state or nation whose constitution is of the kind called "monarchical" is thus named if a man; if it be a woman, she is called "queen."

The word expresses the idea of one who rules singly over a whole people or has the highest executive power; but the office may be either hereditary or elective, and the sovereignty of the king may or may not be absolute, according to the constitution of the country.

King's (Queen's) Bench. One of the superior courts of common law in England, being so called because the king (or queen) used formerly to sit there in person, the style of the court being *"coram ipso rege."*

It was called the "queen's bench" in the reign of a queen, and during the protectorate of Cromwell it was styled the "upper bench." It consisted of a chief justice and three puisne justices, who were by their office the sovereign conservators of the peace and supreme coroners of the land. It was a remnant of the *aula regis*, and was not originally fixed to any certain place, but might follow the king's person, though for some centuries past it usually sat at Westminster. It had a very extended jurisdiction both in criminal and civil causes; the former in what was called the "crown side" or "crown office," the latter in the "plea side," of the court. Its civil jurisdiction was gradually enlarged until it embraced all species of personal actions. By the Judicature Act of 1873 the jurisdiction of this court was assigned to the Queens Bench Division of the High Court of Justice.

Kin or kindred. Relation or relationship by blood or consanguinity. Relatives by blood; by birth. May be either lineal (ascending or descending) or collateral. *See also* Blood relations; Heirs; Next of kin.

Kinsfolk. Relations; those who are of the same family.

Kinship. Relationship by blood. *See* Kin *or* Kindred.

Kinsman /kínzmən/. A man of the same race or family.

Kinswoman. A female relation.

Kiting. The wrongful practice of taking advantage of the float, the time that elapses between the deposit of a check in one bank and its collection at another. Method of drawing checks by which the drawer uses funds which are not his by drawing checks against deposits which have not yet cleared through the banks. "Kiting" consists of writing checks against a bank account where funds are insufficient to cover them, hoping that before they are presented the necessary funds will be deposited. *See also* Float.

Knight. In English law, the next personal dignity after the nobility. Of knights there are several orders and degrees. The first in rank are knights of the Garter, instituted by Richard I and improved by Edward III in 1344; next follows a knight banneret; then come knights of the Bath, instituted by Henry IV, and revived by George I; and they were so called from a ceremony of bathing the night before their creation. The last order are knights bachelors, who, though the lowest, are yet the most ancient, order of knighthood; for we find that King Alfred conferred this order upon his son Athelstan. Other degrees of knights include Knight of the Order of St. Michael and St. George (instituted in 1345), Knight of the Thistle (reestablished in 1703), and Knight of the Most Excellent Order of the British Empire (instituted in 1917).

Knock and announce rule. This rule for execution of arrest and search warrants requires that police knock and announce their authority and purpose before entering into home. A peace officer, whether he arrests by virtue of warrant or by virtue of his authority to arrest without warrant on probable cause, can break door of house to effect arrest only after first stating his authority and purpose for demanding admission. The officer may break open any outer or inner door or window of a house, or any part of a house, or anything therein, to execute a search warrant, if, after notice of his authority and purpose, he is refused admittance or when necessary to liberate himself or a person aiding him in the execution of the warrant. 18 U.S.C.A. § 3109.

Knock down. To assign to a bidder at an auction by a knock or blow of the hammer. Property is said to be "knocked down" when the auctioneer, by the fall of his hammer, or by any other audible or visible announcement, signifies to the bidder that he is entitled to the property on paying the amount of his bid, according to the terms of the sale. "Knocked down" and "struck off" are synonymous terms.

Knock-off. Slang name for product that looks like similar popular product, but costing less. *See also* Gray market goods.

Know. To have knowledge; to possess information, instruction, or wisdom. To perceive or apprehend; to understand. The word "familiar" is equivalent. *See* Knowingly; Knowledge; Notice; Scienter.

Know all men. A form of public address, of great antiquity, and with which many written instruments, such as bonds, letters of attorney, etc., still commence.

Knowingly. With knowledge; consciously; intelligently; willfully; intentionally. An individual acts "knowingly" when he acts with awareness of the nature of his conduct. Act is done "knowingly" or "purposely" if it is willed, is product of conscious design, intent or plan that it be done, and is done with awareness of probable consequences.

A person acts knowingly with respect to a material element of an offense when: (i) if the element involves the nature of his conduct or the attendant circumstances, he is aware that his conduct is of that nature or that such circumstances exist; and (ii) if the element involves a result of his conduct, he is aware that it is practically certain that his conduct will cause such a result. Model Penal Code, § 2.202.

The use of the word in an indictment is equivalent to an averment that the defendant knew what he was about to do, and, with such knowledge, proceeded to do the act charged.

See also Intent; Knowledge; Scienter.

Knowingly and willfully. This phrase, in reference to violation of a statute, means consciously and intentionally.

Knowledge. Acquaintance with fact or truth. It has also been defined as act or state of knowing or understanding; actual notice or information; assurance of fact or proposition founded on perception by senses, or intuition; clear perception of that which exists, or of truth, fact or duty; notice or knowledge sufficient to excite attention and put person on guard and call for inquiry; state of being or having become aware of fact or truth.

In commercial law, the level of a person's awareness of information at which the person actually knows the information. See U.C.C. § 1–201(25).

When knowledge of the existence of a particular fact is an element of an offense, such knowledge is established if a person is aware of a high probability of its existence, unless he actually believes that it does not exist. Model Penal Code, § 2.202.

Knowledge consists in the perception of the truth of affirmative or negative propositions, while "belief" admits of all degrees, from the slightest suspicion to the fullest assurance. The difference between them is ordinarily merely in the degree, to be judged of by the court, when addressed to the court; by the jury, when addressed to the jury.

See also Constructive knowledge; Imputed knowledge; Knowingly; Notice; Scienter.

Actual knowledge. Positive, in contrast to imputed or inferred, knowledge of a fact. For notice purposes, "actual knowledge" embraces those things of which the one sought to be charged has express information and those things which a reasonably diligent inquiry and exercise of the means of information at hand would have disclosed.

Agency relationship. Unless the parties have otherwise agreed, a principal or agent, with respect to the other, should know what a person of ordinary experience and intelligence would know, and in addition, what he would know if, having the knowledge and intelligence which he has or which he purports to have, he were to use due care in the performance of his duties to the other. Restatement, Second, Agency, § 10.

Carnal knowledge. See Carnal knowledge.

Knowledge of another's peril. One has "knowledge of peril of another," within doctrine of discovered peril, whenever it reasonably appears from the known facts and circumstances that the latter is pursuing a course which will probably terminate in serious bodily injury to him, and that he probably will pursue it to the end.

Personal knowledge. Knowledge of the truth in regard to a particular fact or allegation, which is original, and does not depend on information or hearsay. Personal knowledge of an allegation in an answer is personal knowledge of its truth or falsity; and if the allegation is a negative one, this necessarily includes a knowledge of the truth or falsity of the allegation denied. In the law of evidence means something which the witness actually saw or heard, as distinguished from something he learned from some other person or sources.

Reason to know. The words "reason to know" are used throughout the Restatement of Torts to denote the fact that the actor has information from which a person of reasonable intelligence or of the superior intelligence of the actor would infer that the fact in question exists, or that such person would govern his conduct upon the assumption that such fact exists. Restatement, Second, Torts, § 12.

Should know. The words "should know" are used throughout the Restatement of Torts to denote the fact that a person of reasonable prudence and intelligence or of the superior intelligence of the actor would ascertain the fact in question in the performance of his duty to another, or would govern his conduct upon the assumption that such fact exists. Restatement, Second, Torts, § 12.

Known. Familiar; perceived; recognized; understood; especially, when used absolutely, familiar to all; generally understood or perceived. Term may, according to context, refer to both actual and constructive knowledge.

Known heirs. In a statute relating to the sale of property of unknown heirs, it has been held to mean those persons who are known, and whose right to inherit, or the extent of whose right, to inherit, is dependent on the non-existence of other persons nearer or as near as the ancestor in the line of descent.

Ku Klux Act. Federal statute which creates civil liability for interfering with a person's civil rights. 42 U.S.C.A. § 1985(3).

L

L. This letter, as a Roman numeral, stands for the number "fifty." It is also used as an abbreviation for "law," "*liber*," (a book) "lord," and some other words of which it is the initial.

Label. Anything appended to a larger writing, as a codicil.

An affixation to or marking on a manufactured product, giving information as to its nature or quality, or the contents of a material, package or container, or the name of the maker, etc. The informational content of such labels is often governed by federal and state laws; *e.g.* Fair Packaging and Labeling Act. 15 U.S.C.A. § 1457.

Labor. Work; toil; service; mental or physical exertion. Term in its ordinary use is synonymous with "employment," "job" or "position." Term normally refers to work for wages as opposed to work for profits; though the word is sometimes construed to mean service rendered or part played in production of wealth, and includes superintendence or supervision of work.

See also Farm labor *or* laborer; Indirect labor; Laborer.

Labor agreement. *See* Labor contract.

Labor a jury. To tamper with a jury; to endeavor to influence them in their verdict, or their verdict generally. Jury tampering is a crime. See *e.g.* 18 U.S.C.A. §§ 1503, 1504.

Labor contract. Contract between employer and employees (*i.e.* union) which governs working conditions, wages, fringe benefits, and grievances. *See* Collective bargaining agreement; Master agreement; More favorable terms clause.

Labor dispute. Term generally includes any controversy between employers and employees concerning terms, tenure, hours, wages, fringe benefits, or conditions of employment, or concerning the association or representation of persons in negotiating, fixing, maintaining, changing, or seeking to arrange terms or conditions or employment. National Labor Relations Act, § 2(9). However, not every activity of labor organization and not even every controversy in which it may become involved is "labor dispute" within National Labor Relations Act.

Laborer. The word ordinarily denotes one who subsists by physical labor. One who, as a means of livelihood, performs work and labor for another. Person who follows any legitimate employ-

ment or discharges the duties of any office. *See* Farm labor *or* laborer; Labor.

Laborers' lien. Species of non-possessory lien which gives preference to laborer who works on job for payment of his wages ahead of general creditors. Such liens are generally governed by state statutes. *See* Mechanic's lien.

Labor-management relations. Term used to describe broad spectrum of activities which concern relationship of employees to employers both union and non-union. *See* Fair Labor Standards Act; Labor-Management Relations Act; National Labor Relations Act; National Labor Relations Board; Wage and hour laws.

Labor-Management Relations Act. Federal statute (Taft-Hartley Act) which regulates certain union activities, permits suits against unions for proscribed acts, prohibits certain strikes and boycotts and provides machinery for settling strikes which involve national emergencies. 29 U.S.C.A. § 141 et seq.

Labor organization. Any organization of any kind, or any agency or employee representation committee, group, association, or plan so engaged in which employees participate and which exists for the purpose, in whole or in part, of dealing with employers concerning grievances, labor disputes, wages, rates of pay, hours, or other terms or conditions of employment, and any conference, general committee, joint or system board, or joint council so engaged which is subordinate to a national or international labor organization, other than a State or local central body. National Labor Relations Act, § 2(5); 29 U.S.C.A. § 152(5).

A combination of workers usually, but not necessarily, of the same trade or of several allied trades, for securing by united action, the most favorable conditions as regards wages, hours of labor, etc., for its members.

See also Closed shop; Labor union; Open shop.

Labor picketing. The act of patrolling in motion at or near employer or customer entrances; usually carrying placards with a terse legend communicating the gist of the union's claims. Certain forms are prohibited. Landrum-Griffin Act, § 8(b)(7). *See also* Picketing.

Labor rate variance. The difference between the actual rate (or actual weighted average rate) paid to labor for the period and the standard rate for all hours actually worked during the period; actual labor cost minus (actual hours times standard rate).

Labor relations acts. State and federal laws that regulate relations between employers and employees; *e.g.* Fair Labor Standards Act; Equal Pay Act. *See* Labor-management relations.

Labor Relations Board. *See* National Labor Relations Board.

Labor standards. *See* Fair Labor Standards Act

Labor union. A combination or association of workers organized for purpose of securing favorable wages, improved labor conditions, better hours of labor, etc., and righting grievances against employers. Such unions normally represent trades, crafts, and other skilled workers (*e.g.* plumbers, truck drivers). *See also* Labor organization; Union.

Lacey Act. An act of Congress, May 25, 1900, under which the states may enforce game laws against animals, birds, etc., imported from other states or countries. See 16 U.S.C.A. § 661 et seq. *See also* Game laws.

Laches /lǽchəz/léychəz/lǽshəz/. "Doctrine of laches," is based upon maxim that equity aids the vigilant and not those who slumber on their rights. It is defined as neglect to assert a right or claim which, taken together with lapse of time and other circumstances causing prejudice to adverse party, operates as bar in court of equity. The neglect for an unreasonable and unexplained length of time under circumstances permitting diligence, to do what in law, should have been done.

Unreasonable or unexplained delay in asserting right which works disadvantage to another. Knowledge, unreasonable delay, and change of position are essential elements. Laches requires an element of estoppel or neglect which has operated to prejudice of defendant. *See also* Equitable estoppel.

Laches, estoppel by /əstópəl bày lǽchəz/. A failure to do something which should be done or to claim or enforce a right at a proper time. A neglect to do something which one should do, or to seek to enforce a right at a proper time. An element of the doctrine is that the defendant's alleged change of position for the worse must have been induced by or resulted from the conduct, misrepresentation, or silence of the plaintiff. A species of "equitable estoppel" or "estoppel by matter in pais." *See* Equitable estoppel; In pais, estoppel; Laches.

Lack of jurisdiction. The phrase may mean lack of power of a court to act in a particular manner or to give certain kinds of relief. It may consist in court's total want of power to act at all, or lack of power to act in particular case because conditions essential to exercise of jurisdiction have not been complied with, or may consist of lack of jurisdiction over subject matter or over person. *See* Jurisdiction.

Lading, bill of. *See* Bill of lading.

Laissez-faire /lésey fér/. Expresses a political-economic philosophy of the government of allowing the marketplace to operate relatively free of restrictions and intervention.

Lake. A considerable body of standing water in a depression of land or expanded part of a river. An inland body of water or naturally enclosed basin serving to drain surrounding country; or a body of water of considerable size surrounded by land; a widened portion of a river or a lagoon.

Lame duck. An elected officeholder who is to be succeeded by another, between the time of the election and the date that his successor is to take office. A speculator in stock who has overbought and cannot meet his commitments.

Lame Duck Amendment. Twentieth Amendment to U. S. Constitution, abolishing the short congressional term.

Lame duck session. Legislative session conducted after election of new members but before they are installed and hence one in which some participants are voting for the last time as elected officials because of failure to become reelected or voluntary retirement.

Land. In the most general sense, comprehends any ground, soil, or earth whatsoever; including fields, meadows, pastures, woods, moors, waters, marshes, and rock. In its more limited sense, "land" denotes the quantity and character of the interest or estate which a person may own in land. It may include any estate or interest in lands, either legal or equitable, as well as easements and incorporeal hereditaments. The land is one thing, and the estate in land is another thing, for an estate in land is a time in land or land for a time.

Land is the material of the earth, whatever may be the ingredients of which it is composed, whether soil, rock, or other substance, and includes free or occupied space for an indefinite distance upwards as well as downwards, subject to limitations upon the use of airspace imposed, and rights in the use of airspace granted, by law. Calif.Civil Code, § 659. *See* Air rights.

The term may be used interchangeably with "property"; it may include anything that may be classed as real estate or real property.

See also Lands; Ownership; Parcel; Partition; Property *(Real property)*; Real estate.

Accommodation lands. *See* Accommodation lands.

Bounty lands. *See* Bounty.

Demesne lands. *See* Demesne.

General land office. *See* General Land Office.

Land patent. *See* Patent.

Mineral lands. *See* Mineral lands.

Public lands. *See* Public lands.

Tide lands. *See* Tide.

Land bank. A federally created bank under the Federal Farm Loan Act and organized to make loans on farm security at low interest rates. May also describe program in which land is retired from agricultural production for use in conservation or in tree cultivation and as such is sometimes called a Soil Bank. *See* Federal Home Loan Banks.

Land boundaries. Limits of land holdings described by linear measurements of the borders, or by points of the compass, or by stationary markers. *See* Landmark; Land measure; Legal description; Lot line; Metes and bounds; Plat map.

Land certificate. An obligation of government entitling owner to secure designated quantity of land by following the requirements of law. It contains a description of the land as it appears on the register and the name and address of the proprietor, and is *prima facie* evidence of the truth of the matters therein set forth. *See also* Land warrant.

Land contract *See* Land sale contract.

Land damages. *See* Damages.

Land department. *See* Bureau of Land Management; Interior Department.

Land descriptions. *See* Land boundaries.

Land district. A division of a state or territory, created by federal authority, in which is located a United States land office, with a "register of the land office" and a "receiver of public money," for the disposition of the public lands within the district.

Landed. Consisting in real estate or land; having an estate in land.

Landed estate *or* **property.** A colloquial or popular phrase to denote real property. Landed estate ordinarily means an interest in and pertaining to lands. Real estate in general, or sometimes, by local usage, suburban or rural land, as distinguished from real estate situated in a city.

Landed securities. Mortgages or other encumbrances affecting land.

Land gabel. A tax or rent issuing out of land.

Land grant. A donation of public lands to a subordinate government, a corporation, or an individual; as, from the United States to a state, or

to a railroad company to aid in the construction of its road. *See also Land patent* under Patent.

Land improvements. *See* Improvement.

Landing. A place on a river or other navigable water for loading and unloading of goods, or for the reception and delivery of passengers or pleasure boats. The terminus of a road on a river or other navigable water for these purposes. Act or process of coming back to land after voyage or flight. *See also* Port.

Land, law of. *See* Law of the land.

Landlocked. An expression applied to a piece of land belonging to one person and surrounded by land belonging to other persons, so that it cannot be approached except over their land. Access to such land will normally be via an easement from surrounding landowner.

Landlord. He of whom lands or tenements are holden. The owner of an estate in land, or a rental property, who has leased it to another person, called the "tenant." Also called "lessor."

Landlord and tenant relationship. A phrase used to denote the familiar legal relation existing between lessor and lessee of real estate. The relation is contractual. A lease (or agreement therefor) of lands for a term of years, from year to year, for life, or at will creates the relation. The relation exists where one person occupies premises of another in subordination to other's title or rights and with his permission or consent. There must be reversion in landlord, an estate in tenant, transfer of possession and control of premises, and, generally, a contract, express or implied. *See also* Lease.

Landlord's warrant. A distress warrant; a warrant from a landlord to levy upon the tenant's goods and chattels, and sell the same at public sale, to compel payment of the rent or the observance of some other stipulation in the lease. *See* Distraut; Distress. *See also* Habitability (*Warranty of habitability*).

Land management. *See* Bureau of Land Management.

Landmark. A feature of the land, monument, marker, or other erection set up on the boundary line of two adjoining estates, to fix such boundary. The removing of a landmark is a wrong for which an action lies. Building or site having historical significance. *See also* Monument.

Landmark decision. A decision of the Supreme Court that significantly changes existing law. *See e.g.,* Brown decision; Miranda Rule.

Land measure.

1 mile—80 chains, 320 rods, 1,760 yards or 5,280 feet.

16½ feet—1 rod, perch or pole.

1 chain—66 feet, 100 links or 4 rods.

1 link—7.92 inches.

25 links—1 rod.

4 rods—1 chain.

144 square inches—1 square foot.

9 square feet—1 square yard.

30¼ square yards—1 square rod.

160 square rods—1 acre.

10,000 square links—1 square chain.

10 square chains—1 acre.

1 acre—208.708 feet by 208.708 feet.

1 acre—43,560 square feet.

1 acre—4,840 square yards.

1 acre—160 square rods.

640 acres—1 square mile or section.

36 square miles or sections—1 township.

See also Land boundaries; Survey.

Land offices. Government offices, administered by Bureau of Land Management, established principally in the Western States, for the transaction of local business relating to the survey, location, settlement, pre-emption, and sale of the public lands. A former primary function of these offices was to administer land grants.

Land patent. An instrument conveying a grant of public land; also, the land so conveyed. See also Patent.

Land-poor. Term used to describe person that owns a substantial amount of land, but is nonetheless short of cash to pay bills because, for example, land is unproductive, market for crops depressed, etc.

Landrum-Griffin Act. Federal statute enacted in 1959, known as the Labor-Management Reporting and Disclosure Act, designed to curb corruption in union leadership and undemocratic conduct of internal union affairs as well as to outlaw certain types of secondary boycotts and "hot cargo" provisions in collective bargaining agreements. 29 U.S.C.A. § 401 et seq.

Lands. This term, the plural of "land," is said, at common law, to be a word of less extensive signification than either "tenements" or "hereditaments." But in some of the states it has been provided by statute that it shall include both those terms. See also Land.

Land sale contract. Contract for the purchase and sale of land upon execution of which title is transferred. Term commonly refers to an installment contract for the sale of land whereby purchaser (vendee) receives the deed from the owner (vendor) upon payment of final installment. The vendor/seller finances the sale for the buyer and retains legal title to the property (deed) as security for payment of contract price. May also be called "contract for deed", or "installment land contract".

Lands, public. See Public lands.

Lands, tenements, and hereditaments. The technical and most comprehensive description of real property, as "goods and chattels" is of personalty. The term refers to property in land. Under ancient law, the words comprehended only freehold estate and did not apply to easements or other incorporeal hereditaments.

Land tax. Property tax. A tax laid upon the legal or beneficial owner of real property, and apportioned upon the assessed value of his land. A tax on land. See Property tax.

Land tenant. The person actually in possession of land. See Tenant.

Land trust. Property ownership arrangement whereby, pursuant to statute, trustee holds legal and equitable title to trust, and beneficiary, who has personal property interest, retains power of direction over trustee and power to manage and receive income from trust property. A land trust (also called Illinois Land Trust) is a trust in which corpus consists of real estate and in which deed to trustee appears to confer upon him full powers to deal with real estate and complete legal and equitable title to trust property. So far as public records are concerned, trustee's powers are complete. Such powers, however, are in fact restricted by a trust agreement mentioned in the deed in trust. Such trust agreements typically vest in beneficiary full powers of management and control. However, beneficiary cannot deal with property as if no trust existed. Such trusts generally continue for a definite term. Unlike trustees under classical testamentary or inter vivos trust, trustees under land trust may be personally liable.

Land trust certificate. Instrument granting participation in benefits of ownership of property, while trustee retains title. See Land Trust.

Land use planning. Generic term used to describe activities such as zoning, control of real estate developments and use, environmental impact studies and the like. Many states have land use planning laws which are implemented by local zoning and land use laws and ordinances. See also Master plan; Planned unit development; Zoning.

Land warrant. A warrant issued at the local land offices of the United States to purchasers of public lands, on the surrender of which at the general land office at Washington, they receive a conveyance from the general government. See Land certificate.

The evidence which the state, on good consideration, gives that the person therein named is entitled to the quantity of land therein specified, the bounds and description of which the owner of the warrant may fix by entry and survey, in the section of country set apart for its location and satisfaction.

Language. Any means of conveying or communicating ideas; specifically, human speech, or the expression of ideas by written characters or by means of sign language. The letter, or grammatical import, of a document or instrument, as distinguished from its spirit; as "the language of the statute." As to *offensive language, see* Offensive language.

Lanham Trademark Act. Federal statute enacted in 1946 which revised federal trademark law and registration process. Purposes of Act (15 U.S.C.A. § 1501 et seq.), are to protect the public so it may buy a product bearing a particular trademark with confidence that it will get the product it wants. It also protects the holder of the mark's investment in time and money from its misappropriation by pirates and others. *See also* Likelihood of confusion.

Lapse, *v.* To glide; to pass slowly, silently, or by degrees. To slip; to deviate from the proper path. To fall or fail. *See also* Expiration; Termination.

Lapse, *n.* The termination or failure of a right or privilege through neglect to exercise it within some limit of time, or through failure of some contingency.

Failure to vest a bequest or devise by reason of death of devisee of legatee prior to death of testator. The death of a legatee before the testator causes the legacy to lapse and to fall into the residue unless there is a statute which provides for its disposition as, for example, if the legatee is a child or relation of the testator, the legacy passes to the issue of the legatee.

The expiration of a right either by the death of the holder or upon the expiration of a period of time. Thus, a power of appointment lapses upon the death of the holder if such holder has not exercised the power during life or at death (*i.e.,* through a will).

Termination of insurance policy because of failure to pay the premium.

In the law of wills, the failure of a testamentary gift.

See also Anti-lapse statute.

Lapsed devise. *See* Devise.

Lapsed legacy. *See* Legacy.

Lapsed policy. Insurance policy on which there has been default in payment of premiums. Policy remaining in force according to statutory provisions after such default (normally a 30 or 31 day grace period on non-payment of premiums is provided).

Lapse patent. A patent for land issued in substitution for an earlier patent to the same land, which was issued to another party, but has lapsed in consequence of his neglect to avail himself of it.

Lapse statutes. Those state statutory enactments which prevent the lapse or passing into the residue or by intestacy of legacies and devises when the legatee or devisee predeceases the testator, and which commonly provide that, if the legatee or devisee is a child or other relation of the testator, the legacy or devise passes to the issue of such legatee or devisee.

Larcenous /lársənəs/. Having the character of larceny; as a "larcenous taking." Contemplating or intending larceny; as a "larcenous purpose."

Larcenous intent. A larcenous intent exists where a man knowingly takes and carries away the goods of another without any claim or pretense of right, with intent wholly to deprive the owner of them or convert them to his own use.

Larceny /lársəniy/. Felonious stealing, taking and carrying, leading, riding, or driving away another's personal property, with intent to convert it or to deprive owner thereof. The unlawful taking and carrying away of property of another with intent to appropriate it to use inconsistent with latter's rights. The essential elements of a "larceny" are an actual or constructive taking away of the goods or property of another without the consent and against the will of the owner or possessor and with a felonious intent to convert the property to the use of someone other than the owner.

Obtaining possession of property by fraud, trick or device with preconceived design or intent to misappropriate, convert or steal.

Common-law distinctions between obtaining money under false pretenses, embezzlement, and larceny no longer exist in many states; all such crimes being embraced within general definition of "larceny." Some states classify larceny as either grand or petit, depending on the property's value.

See also Burglary; Robbery; Shoplifting; Stolen; Theft.

Compound larceny. Larceny or theft accomplished by taking the thing stolen either from one's person or from his house; otherwise called "mixed" larceny, and distinguished from "simple" or "plain" larceny, in which the theft is not aggravated by such an intrusion either upon the person or the dwelling. Sometimes referred to as larceny from the person.

Constructive larceny. One where the felonious intent to appropriate the goods to his own use, at the time of the asportation, is made out by construction from the defendant's conduct, although, originally, the taking was not apparently felonious.

False pretenses and larceny distinguished. See False pretenses.

Grand larceny. Taking and carrying away the personal property of another to a value in excess of $100.00 (or whatever the cut-off amount may be in a given jurisdiction) with the intent to feloniously deprive the owner or possessor of it permanently. Distinguished from *petit larceny (q.v.)* only by the value of the property stolen.

Larceny by bailee. The crime of larceny committed where any person, being a bailee of any property, shall fraudulently take or convert the same to his own use, or to the use of any other person except the owner thereof, although he shall not break bulk or otherwise determine the bailment.

Larceny by extortion. A person is guilty of theft if he purposely obtains property of another by threatening to: (1) inflict bodily injury on anyone or commit any other criminal offense; or (2) accuse anyone of a criminal offense; or (3) expose any secret tending to subject any person to hatred, contempt or ridicule, or to impair his credit or business repute; or (4) take or withhold action as an official, or cause an official to take or withhold action; or (5) bring about or continue a strike, boycott or other collective unofficial action, if the property is not demanded or received for the benefit of the group in whose interest the actor purports to act; or (6) testify or provide information or withhold testimony or information with respect to another's legal claim or defense; or (7) inflict any other harm which would not benefit the actor. Model Penal Code, § 223.4. *See also* Extortion.

Larceny by fraud or deception. A person is guilty of theft if he purposely obtains property of another by deception. A person deceives if he purposely: (1) creates or reinforces a false impression, including false impressions as to law, value, intention or other state of mind; but deception as to a person's intention from the act alone that he did not subsequently perform the promise; or (2) prevents another from acquiring information which would affect his judgment of a transaction; or (3) fails to correct a false impression which the deceiver previously created or reinforced, or which the deceiver knows to be influencing another to whom he stands in a fiduciary or confidential relationship; or (4) fails to disclose a known lien, adverse claim or other legal impediment to the enjoyment of property which he transfers or encumbers in consideration for the property obtained, whether such impediment is or is not valid, or is or is not a matter of official record. Model Penal Code, § 223.3.

Larceny by trick. See *Larceny by fraud or deception, above.*

Larceny from the person. Act of taking property from the person by merely lifting it from the person or pocket. Larceny committed where the property stolen is on the person or in the immediate charge or custody of the person from whom the theft is made, but without such circumstances of force or violence as would constitute robbery, including pocket-picking and such like crimes.

Larceny of auto. See Auto theft.

Larceny of property lost, mislaid, or delivered by mistake. A person who comes into control of property of another that he knows to have been lost, mislaid, or delivered under a mistake as to the nature or amount of the property or the identity of the recipient is guilty of theft if, with purpose to deprive the owner thereof, he fails to take reasonable measures to restore the property to a person entitled to have it. Model Penal Code, § 223.5.

Mixed larceny. Otherwise called "compound" or "complicated larceny;" that which is attended with circumstances of aggravation or violence to the person, or taking from a house.

Petit (Petty) larceny. Larceny of things or goods whose value is below a statutorily set amount (*e.g.* $100). The value at common law was twelve pence. *Compare Grand larceny, above.*

Simple larceny. Felonious or wrongful taking and carrying away of personal goods of another with intent to steal, unattended by acts of violence. Larceny which is not complicated or aggravated with acts of violence. Larceny from the person, or with force and violence, is called "compound" larceny.

Larger parcel. A term used in eminent domain proceedings, signifying that the parcel taken is not a complete parcel but part of a "larger parcel"; the owner, therefore is entitled to damages from the severance as well as the value of the parcel taken. Unity of ownership, use, and contiguity must be present, although federal courts and some states do not require contiguity where there is a strong unity of use.

Larons /lérənz/. In old English law, thieves.

Lascivious /ləsíviyəs/. Tending to excite lust; lewd; indecent; obscene; sexual impurity; tending to deprave the morals in respect to sexual relations; licentious. Conduct which is wanton, lewd, and lustful, and tending to produce voluptuous or lewd emotions. *See* Lewd; Obscene.

Lascivious cohabitation. The offense committed by two persons (not married to each other) who live together in one habitation as man and wife and practice sexual intercourse. Such offense, where it still exists, is seldom enforced.

Last, *adj.* Latest; ultimate; final; most recent.

Last antecedent rule. A canon of statutory construction that relative or qualifying words or phrases are to be applied to the words or phrases immediately preceding, and as not extending to or including other words, phrases, or clauses more remote, unless such extension or inclusion is clearly required by the intent and meaning of the context, or disclosed by an examination of the entire act.

Last clear chance doctrine. This doctrine permits a plaintiff in a negligence action to recover, notwithstanding his own negligence, on a showing that the defendant had the last clear chance to avoid the accident. Under the doctrine of last clear chance (or "discovered peril" doctrine), as applied in automobile law, a plaintiff may recover from a defendant motorist for injuries or damages suffered, notwithstanding his own contributory negligence, where, as stated in terms of the essential elements of the doctrine, plaintiff was in a place of peril of which he was unaware or from which he was unable to extricate himself, the motorist discovered or had the opportunity to discover plaintiff's peril, and the motorist had the opportunity to avoid the accident through the exercise of reasonable care. The last clear chance doctrine is not recognized in every jurisdiction and is subject to limitations in others. There are many variant forms and applications of this doctrine in the jurisdictions which apply it. *See also* Discovered peril doctrine.

Last illness. The illness terminating in person's death.

Last-in, first-out (LIFO). A method of identifying and valuing inventories which assumes that last goods purchased are the first ones sold and therefore the goods left in inventory at the end of the year are assumed to be those first purchased. A method of accounting for inventory which assumes that the most recent purchases are sold first. In times of inflation, the LIFO method results in a lower net income figure and lower inventory valuation than the FIFO method. This is due to the current costs being matched against current revenues and older costs and dollars which remain in inventory. *Compare* FIFO.

Last resort, court of. A court from which there is no further appeal is called the "court of last resort." For example, the United States Supreme Court.

Last sickness. *See* Last illness.

Last will. Term used alone or with "and testament" to designate the instrument which ultimately fixes the disposition of real and personal property at death. Usually used in reference to most recent will of deceased. *See* Will.

Lata culpa /léytə kə́lpə/. Lat. In the law of bailment, gross fault or neglect; extreme negligence or carelessness *(nimia negligentia)*.

Late. Defunct; existing recently, but now dead. Formerly; recently; lately.

Latent. Hidden; concealed; dormant; that which does not appear upon the face of a thing; as, a latent ambiguity or defect.

Latent ambiguity. A defect which does not appear on the face of language used or an instrument being considered. It arises when language is clear and intelligible and suggests but a single meaning, but some extrinsic fact or some extraneous evidence creates a necessity for interpretation or a choice between two or more possible meanings.

That species of uncertainty or ambiguity in an instrument which is not apparent from a reading of it but which is revealed when the terms of the instrument are applied or made operative; *e.g.* in a bill of lading goods are to be delivered at "Essex Railroad Wharf", and there are two such wharfs with the same name. Parol evidence is admissible to prove the intention of the party drawing the instrument.

Parol evidence may be admitted to explain terms of contract, but not to contradict. See U.C.C. § 2–202.

See also Ambiguity. *Compare* Patent ambiguity.

Latent deed. A deed kept for twenty years or more in a strongbox or other secret place.

Latent defect. A hidden or concealed defect. One which could not be discovered by reasonable and customary observation or inspection; one not apparent on face of goods, product, document, etc.

Defect of which owner has no knowledge, or which, in exercise of reasonable care, he should have had no knowledge. One which cannot be discovered by observation or inspection made with ordinary care. A latent defect in the title of a vendor of land is one not discoverable by inspection made with ordinary care, even though a matter of public record.

Latent equity. *See* Equity.

Lateral support. The right of lateral and subjacent support is the right to have land supported by the adjoining land or the soil beneath. The right of a landowner to the natural support of his land by adjoining land. The adjoining owner has the duty not to change his land (such as lowering it) so as to cause this support to be weakened or removed.

Laundering. Term used to describe investment or other transfer of money flowing from racketeering, drug transactions, and other illegal sources into legitimate channels so that its original source cannot be traced. Money laundering is a federal crime. 18 U.S.C.A. § 1956.

Law. That which is laid down, ordained, or established. A rule or method according to which phenomena or actions co-exist or follow each other. Law, in its generic sense, is a body of rules of action or conduct prescribed by controlling authority, and having binding legal force. That which must be obeyed and followed by citizens subject to sanctions or legal consequences is a law. Law is a solemn expression of the will of the supreme power of the State. Calif.Civil Code, § 22.

The "law" of a state is to be found in its statutory and constitutional enactments, as interpreted by its courts, and, in absence of statute law, in rulings of its courts (*i.e.* case law).

The word may mean or embrace: body of principles, standards and rules promulgated by government constitution or constitutional provision; statute or enactment of legislative body; administrative agency rules and regulations; judicial decisions, judgments or decrees; municipal ordinances; or, long established local custom which has the force of law.

With reference to its origin, "law" is derived either from judicial precedents, from legislation, or from custom.

As to the different kinds of law, or law regarded in its different aspects, *see* Absolute law; Adjective law; Administrative law; Bankruptcy Code; Canon (*Canon law*); Case law; Civil law; Commercial law; Common law; Conclusion of law; Conflict of laws; Constitutional law; Criminal law; Custom and usage; Ecclesiastical law; Edict; Enabling statute; Equity; Evidence, law of; Flag, law of; Foreign laws; General law; International law; Local law; Maritime; Maritime law; Marque, law of; Martial law; Mercantile law; Military law; Moral law; Municipal law; Natural law; Ordinance; Organic law; Parliamentary law; Penal laws; Positive law; Private law; Probate; Procedural law; Prospective law; Public law; Remedial laws and statutes; Retrospective law; Revenue law or measure; Road (*Law of the road*); Roman law; Special law; Statute; Substantive law; Unwritten law; War; Written law.

For "facts" and "law" as distinguishable, *see* Fact. For *practice of law*, *see* Practice.

Law department. Department having charge of law business of government. *See* Judicial branch.

Law enforcement officer. Those whose duty it is to preserve the peace. *See also* Police officer; Sheriff.

Lawful. Legal; warranted or authorized by the law; having the qualifications prescribed by law; not contrary to nor forbidden by the law; not illegal.

The principal distinction between the terms "lawful" and "legal" is that the former contemplates the substance of law, the latter the form of law. To say of an act that it is "lawful" implies that it is authorized, sanctioned, or at any rate not forbidden, by law. To say that it is "legal" implies that it is done or performed in accordance with the forms and usages of law, or in a technical manner. In this sense "illegal" approaches the meaning of "invalid." For example, a contract or will, executed without the required formalities, might be said to be invalid or illegal, but could not be described as unlawful. Further, the word "lawful" more clearly implies an ethical content than does "legal." The latter goes no further than to denote compliance, with positive, technical, or formal rules; while the former usually imports a moral substance or ethical permissibility. A further distinction is that the word "legal" is used as the synonym of "constructive," which "lawful" is not. Thus "legal fraud" is fraud implied or inferred by law, or made out by construction. "Lawful fraud" would be a contradiction of terms. Again, "legal" is used as the antithesis of "equitable." Thus, we speak of "legal assets," "legal estate," etc., but not of "lawful assets," or "lawful estate." But there are some connections in which the two words are used as exact equivalents. Thus, a "lawful" writ, warrant, or process is the same as a "legal" writ, warrant, or process.

See also Legal; Legitimate; Valid.

Lawful age. Full age, legal age, majority; generally 18 years of age, though the "lawful age" for certain acts (*e.g.* drinking, driving motor vehicle, etc.) may vary from state to state. *See also* Capacity; Legal age.

Lawful arrest. The taking of a person into legal custody either under a valid warrant or on probable cause for believing that he has committed a crime or under civil process which permits his arrest; *e.g.* capias for arrest of debtor. Term is used in connection with right to search a person and his immediate surroundings without a warrant as an incident of the arrest. Chimel v. California, 395 U.S. 752, 89 S.Ct. 2034, 23 L.Ed.2d 685. *See* Arrest; Probable cause; Search; Search-warrant.

Lawful authorities. Those persons who have right to exercise public power, to require obedience to their lawful commands, to command or act in the public name; *e.g.* police.

Lawful cause. Legitimate reason for acting, based on the law or on the evidence in a particular case as contrasted with acting on a whim or out of prejudice, or for a reason not recognized by the law. *See also* Cause of action.

Lawful damages. Such damages as the law fixes and are ascertainable in a court of law. *See* Damages.

Lawful dependents. Term generally associated with allowances or benefits from public (*e.g.* Social Security benefits) or private funds to those who qualify as dependents and whose dependency is within the terms of the law which govern the distribution. Term is also used with respect to tax exemptions for dependents. *See also* Dependent; Legal dependent.

Lawful discharge. Such a discharge in insolvency as exonerates the debtor from his debts; *e.g.* discharge pursuant to bankruptcy proceeding.

Lawful entry. An entry on real estate, by one out of possession, under claim or color of right and without force or fraud. An entry of premises pursuant to a search warrant. *See* Ejection; Eviction; Process (*Summary process*); Search Warrant.

Lawful goods. Property which may be legally held, sold, or exported; non-contraband property.

Lawful heirs. *See* Heirs.

Lawful issue. As used in will the words primarily and generally mean descendants, including descendants more remote than children. At common law, the term includes only those who were children of legally recognized subsisting marriage. Lawful descendants; lineal descendants by blood; heirs. *See* Descendant; Heirs; Issue.

Lawful man. A freeman, unattainted, and capable of bearing oath; a *legalis homo*.

Lawful money. Money which is a legal tender in payment of debts. *See* Legal tender.

Lawful representatives. Where real property is involved as subject-matter, term includes or means legal heirs. Where personal property is involved the term, when not qualified by context, is limited to executors and administrators.

Law latin. The corrupt form of the Latin language employed in the old English lawbooks and legal proceedings.

Lawless. Not subject to law; not controlled by law; not authorized by law; not observing the rules and forms of law.

Law list or directory. A publication compiling the names and addresses of those engaged in the practice of law and information of interest to the legal profession often including listings of courts, court calendars, lawyers engaged in specialized fields (as admiralty or patent law), public officers, stenographers, handwriting experts, private investigators, and sometimes abstracts of law. National legal directories include the "Law Directory", as published by Martindale–Hubbell and "West's Legal Directory." There are also law listings or directories for most states and for many of the larger cities.

Law merchant. Body of law governing commercial transactions which had its origin in common law of England regulating merchants. See U.C.C. § 1–103. *See also* Commercial law; Mercantile law; Uniform Commercial Code.

Law of a general nature. One which relates to a subject that may exist throughout the state; one whose subject-matter is common to all the people.

Law of capture. Under this doctrine, landowner does not own migratory substances underlying his land, but has exclusive right to drill for, produce, or otherwise gain possession of such substances, subject only to restrictions and regulations pursuant to police power.

Law of evidence. *See* Evidence, law of.

Law of marque. *See* Marque, law of.

Law of nations. *See* International law.

Law of nature. *See* Natural law.

Law of the case. This term, as generally used, designates the principle that if an appellate court has passed on a legal question and remanded the cause to the court below for further proceedings, the legal question thus determined by the appellate court will not be differently determined on a subsequent appeal in the same case where the facts remain the same. Doctrine which provides that an appellate court's determination on a legal issue is binding on both the trial court on remand and an appellate court on a subsequent appeal given the same case and substantially the same facts.

Jury instructions. It has been held that jury instructions are the "law of the case" where appealing defendant accepted instructions as correct; where such were approved on former appeal and given at second trial; where instructions were not challenged in any manner or in any particular.

See also Collateral estoppel; Res judicata.

Law of the flag. *See* Flag, law of.

Law of the land. Due process of law (*q.v.*). Body of law consisting of court decisions, statutes, and treaties. See U.S. Const., Art. VI, § 2. By the law of the land is most clearly intended the general law which hears before it condemns, which proceeds upon inquiry, and renders judgment only after trial. The meaning is that every citizen shall hold his life, liberty, property, and immunities under the protection of general rules which govern society. *See also* Due process of law; Law.

Law of the road. *See* Road (*Law of the road*).

Law questions. Issues or questions in a case which do not require findings of fact but are addressed to the judge for application of the law. In those instances wherein the law depends on the facts, the factual questions are first decided and then the law is applied to the facts as found by the judge or jury. *Compare* Fact question.

Law reporters *or* **reports.** Published volumes containing the decisions and opinions of state and federal courts; *e.g.* National Reporter System. Commonly such decisions are first published in advance sheets and thereafter in bound reports or reporter volumes. Law reports or reporters may be either official (published by the state or federal government) or unofficial (published by private publisher). *See e.g.* Federal Reporter.

Law review. A periodic publication of most law schools containing lead articles on topical subjects by law professors, judges or attorneys, and case summaries by law review member-students. Normally only honor or top law students are members of the law review staff.

Laws. Rules promulgated by government as a means to an ordered society. Strictly speaking, session laws or statutes and not decisions of court; though in common usage refers to both legislative and court made law, as well as to administrative rules, regulations and ordinances. *See also* Law.

Law School Admissions Test. *See* LSAT.

Laws of the several states. As used in statute requiring federal courts to apply laws of the several states, includes not only state statutory law, but also state decisions on questions of general law. Erie R. Co. v. Tompkins, 304 U.S. 64, 58 S.Ct. 817, 822, 82 L.Ed. 1188. See Erie v. Tompkins.

Laws of war. *See* War.

Law spiritual. The ecclesiastical law, or law Christian. *See also* Ecclesiastical law.

Lawsuit. A vernacular term for a suit, action, or cause instituted or depending between two private persons in the courts of law. A suit at law or in equity; an action or proceeding in a civil court; a process in law instituted by one party to compel another to do him justice. *See also* Action; Cause of action.

Lawyer. A person learned in the law; as an attorney, counsel, or solicitor; a person licensed to practice law. Any person who prosecutes or defends causes in courts of record or other judicial tribunals of the United States, or of any of the states, or whose business it is to give legal advice or assistance in relation to any cause or matter whatever. *See also* Attorney; House counsel. For *right to attorney, see* Counsel, right to.

Lay, *n.* A share of the profits of a fishing or whaling voyage, allotted to the officers and seamen, in the nature of wages. *See also* Lay system.

Lay, *adj.* Relating to persons or things not clerical or ecclesiastical; a person not in ecclesiastical orders. Also non-professional. *See also* Layman.

Lay, *v.* To state or allege in pleading.

Layaway. To hold goods for future sale. An agreement by a retail seller with a consumer to retain specified consumer goods for sale to the consumer at a specified price, in earnest of which sale the consumer has deposited with the retail seller an agreed upon sum of money, and any other terms and conditions not contrary to law which are mutually agreed upon.

Lay damages. To state at the conclusion of the complaint declaration the amount of damages which the plaintiff claims. *See* Ad damnum.

Lay days. In the law of shipping, days allowed without penalty to charter-parties for loading and unloading the cargo.

Laying foundation. In law of evidence, the practice or requirement of introducing evidence of things necessary to make further evidence relevant, material or competent; *e.g.* the hypothetical question propounded before an expert is permitted to render his opinion. See Fed. Evid.R. 104. *See also* Foundation.

Laying the venue. Stating in the complaint or declaration the district or county in which the plaintiff proposes that the trial of the action shall take place.

Lay judge. A judge who is not learned in the law, *i.e.,* not a lawyer; employed in some of the states as assessors or assistants to the presiding judges in the *nisi prius* courts or courts of first instance. Many justices of the peace are, or were, not lawyers.

Layman. One of the people, and not one of the clergy; one who is not of a particular profession (*i.e.* non-lawyer).

Layoff. A termination of employment at the will of employer. Such may be temporary (*e.g.* caused by seasonal or adverse economic conditions) or permanent.

Lay system. As applied to fishing vessels, exists where the fish caught are sold at auction and from the proceeds is deducted charges for supplies furnished and balance distributed to the master and the crew.

Lay witness. Person called to give testimony who does not possess any expertise in the matters about which he testifies. Used in contrast to expert witness who may render an opinion based on his expert knowledge if proper foundation is laid. Generally, such non-expert testimony in the form of opinions or inferences is limited to those opinions or inferences which are (a) rationally based on the perception of the witness (*i.e.* first-hand knowledge or observation) and (b) helpful to a clear understanding of his testimony or the determination of a fact at issue. Fed.Evid.R. 701. *See* Opinion evidence *or* testimony. *Compare* Expert witness.

LEAA. Law Enforcement Assistance Act.

Lead counsel. The counsel on either side of a litigated action who is charged with the principal management and direction of the party's case, as distinguished from his juniors or subordinates, is said to "lead in the cause," and is termed the "leading counsel" on that side. May also refer to chief or primary attorney in class action or multidistrict litigation.

Leading case. Among the various cases that are argued and determined in the courts, some, from their important character, have demanded more than usual attention from the judges, and from this circumstance are frequently looked upon as having settled or determined the law upon all points involved in such cases, and as guides for subsequent decisions, and from the importance they thus acquire are familiarly termed "leading cases." *See e.g.* Marbury v. Madison.

Leading object rule. If the leading object or main purpose of a person's promise to answer for the debt of another is the promisor's own benefit, such promise need not be in writing as required by the statute of frauds; sometimes known as the "main purpose" doctrine.

Leading question. One which instructs witness how to answer or puts into his mouth words to be echoed back; one which suggests to witness answer desired, or a question admitting of being answered by a simple "yes" or "no".

Leading questions are usually deemed improper on the direct examination of a witness except as may be necessary to develop the witnesses' testimony. Ordinarily leading questions are permitted on cross-examination. When a party calls a hostile witness, an adverse party, or a witness identified with an adverse party, interrogation may be by leading questions. Fed.Evid.R. 611(c).

Even on direct examination, leading questions may be permitted if the witness is very young, mentally disabled, or unfamiliar with the language spoken. And may, in certain circumstances, also be permitted to facilitate a witness's introduction of subject of inquiry; *e.g.*, police officer may be led as to activities leading up to events in dispute in order to save time.

League. An association or treaty of alliance between different nations, states, organizations, sports teams, or parties. *See also* Compact; Treaty.

A measure of distance, varying in different countries (equal to about three statute miles).

Leakage. The waste or diminution of a liquid caused by its leaking from the cask, barrel, or other vessel in which it was placed. Also an allowance made to an importer of liquids, at the custom-house, in the collection of duties, for his loss sustained by the leaking of the liquid from its cask or vessel.

Lean. To incline in opinion or preference. A court is sometimes said to "lean against" a doctrine, construction, or view contended for, whereby it is meant that the court regards it with disfavor or repugnance, because of its inexpedience, injustice, or inconsistency.

Learn. To gain knowledge or information of; to ascertain by inquiry, study, or investigation.

Learned. Possessing learning; erudite; versed in the law; informed. In statutes prescribing the qualifications of judges, "learned in the law" designates one who has received a regular legal education, the almost invariable evidence of which is the fact of his admission to the bar.

Learning. Legal doctrine.

Learning curve. A model that helps to predict how labor time will decrease as people become more experienced at performing a task and eliminate the inefficiencies associated with unfamiliarity.

Lease. Any agreement which gives rise to relationship of landlord and tenant (real property) or lessor and lessee (real or personal property). A contract for exclusive possession of lands, tenements or hereditaments for life, for term of years, at will, or for any interest less than that of lessor, usually for a specified rent or compensation. Contract wherein one lets to the other a certain space, property or building for specified unit of time, generally a week, month or year. Agreement under which owner gives up possession and use of his property for valuable consideration and for definite term and at end of term owner has absolute right to retake, control and use property.

When used with reference to tangible personal property, word "lease" means a contract by which one owning such property grants to another the right to possess, use and enjoy it for specified period of time in exchange for periodic payment of a stipulated price, referred to as rent.

The Federal Consumer Leasing Act provides for certain disclosure requirements in consumer leases. 15 U.S.C.A. § 1667 et seq. In addition, certain states require that consumer (*e.g.* residential) leases be written in "plain language." See McKinney's (N.Y.) Consol.Laws, Gen.Obl., § 5–702.

See also U.C.C. Article 2A with respect to consumer leases.

The person who conveys is termed the "lessor," and the person to whom conveyed, the "lessee;" and when the lessor conveys lands or tenements to a lessee, he is said to lease, demise, or let them. The word when used as verb, means to transfer for term specified therein from lessor to lessee property therein demised, also to let, to farm out, to rent.

See also Assignable lease; Community lease; Consumer lease; Demise; Finance lease; Graduated lease; Ground lease; Mining lease; Net lease; Operating lease; Percentage lease; Sale and leaseback; Sandwich lease; Under-lease. For *Extension of lease, see* Extension. *Compare* License.

Concurrent lease. One granted for a term which is to commence before the expiration or other determination of a previous lease of the same premises made to another person; or, in other words, an assignment of a part of the reversion, entitling the lessee to all the rents accruing on the previous lease after the date of his lease and to appropriate remedies against the holding tenant.

Direct lease. A lease arrangement under which the manufacturer of an asset leases it (directly) to some entity.

Full-service lease. A lease in which the lessor agrees to pay all costs of maintaining the leased item in good working condition, the cost of insurance, and any property taxes.

Graduated lease. Lease that takes into consideration future increases in operating expenses. In a graduated lease there must be a base year on which an increase is judged. With inflation and continuing increases in taxes, energy costs, and other expenses, this type lease has become more popular than the fixed-straight lease.

Gross lease. Lease in which lessee pays a flat sum for rent out of which the lessor is required to pay all expenses such as taxes, water, utilities, insurance, etc.

Index lease. A lease arrangement that provides for increases in rent according to increases in the consumer price index. *See also* Graduated lease.

Long term lease. See Ground rent.

Master lease. A main lease controlling subsequent leases or subleases.

Mineral lease. Lease in which the lessee acquires the right to work a mine of oil or gas, etc. The rent is commonly based on the amount or value of the mineral withdrawn.

Mining lease. See Mining.

Month to month lease. Tenancy where no lease is involved, rent being paid monthly. Statutes often require one month's notice to landlord of intent to terminate such tenancy.

Net lease. Lease which requires the tenant to pay, in addition to rent, the expenses of the leased property, *e.g.* taxes, insurance, maintenance, etc.

Net-net-net lease. Lease in which the lessee pays all the expenses including mortgage interest and amortization leaving the lessor with an amount free of all claims.

Parol lease. A lease of real estate not evidenced by writing, but resting in an oral agreement.

Percentage lease. A percentage lease is one in which the amount of rent is based upon a percentage of the gross or net profits of the lessee's business, or of his gross sales, with a stipulated minimum rent. Such leases are mainly used where location of the property is an important part of its value (*e.g.* in shopping center).

Perpetual lease. A lease of lands which may last without limitation as to time; a grant of lands in fee with the reservation of a rent in fee; a fee-farm.

Proprietary lease. Lease used in cooperative form of ownership in which lessee acquires right to possession.

Sublease, or underlease. One executed by the lessee to a third person, conveying the same estate for a shorter term than that for which the lessee holds it. *See also* Sublease.

Top lease. A lease granted on property already subject to an oil and gas lease. Generally, a top lease grants rights if and when the existing lease expires.

True lease. A contract that qualifies as a valid lease agreement under the Internal Revenue Code.

Leaseback. Transaction whereby transferor sells property and later leases it back. In a sale-leaseback situation, for example, R would sell property to S and subsequently lease such property from S. Thus, R becomes the lessee and S the lessor.

Leasehold. Historically classified as a chattel real, a species of personalty, it is a tenant/lessee's possessory estate in land, granted by a landlord/lessor who holds an estate of larger duration in the same land. The four principal types of leasehold estates are the estate for years, periodic tenancy, tenancy at will, and tenancy at sufferance. *See also* Chattel.

Leasehold improvements. Improvements made by lessee to leased property such as parking lot or driveway. The term is used in condemnation proceedings to determine the portion of the award to which the lessee is entitled.

Leasehold interest. The interest of the lessor or the lessee under a lease contract. U.C.C.

§ 2A–103. The interest which the lessee has in the value of the lease itself in condemnation award determination. The difference between the total remaining rent under the lease, and the rent lessee would currently pay for similar space for the same time period. *See also* Leasehold value; No bonus clause.

Leasehold mortgage. *See* Mortgage.

Leasehold mortgage bond. *See* Bond.

Leasehold value. The value of a leasehold interest. Usually applies to a long term lease when market rental for similar space is higher than rent paid under the lease. Some states allow the lessee to claim the leasehold value against the landlord in eminent domain proceedings, unless specifically prohibited by the lease itself. Other states, by statute, do not allow for such a claim. *See also* Leasehold interest; No bonus clause.

Lease rate. The payment per period stated in a lease contract.

Lease with option to purchase. A lease under which the lessee has the right to purchase the property. The price and terms of the purchase must be set forth for the option to be valid. The option may run for the length of the lease period.

Leave, *v.* To give. To allow or cause to remain; to let remain, unmoved or undone; to refrain from or neglect taking, doing, or changing; to let stay or continue; to let be without interference; to suffer to remain subject to another's action, control, or the like; to suffer to be undisturbed in action. To give or dispose of by will; to bequeath or devise. To put, place, deposit, deliver, or the like.

Leave, *n.* Permission or authorization to do something.

Willful departure with intent to remain away, and not temporary absence with intention of returning. *See also* Desertion.

Leave and license. A defense to an action in trespass setting up the consent of the plaintiff to the trespass complained of.

Leave no issue. Not survived by a child or children or their descendants.

Leave of absence. Temporary absence from employment or duty with intention to return during which time remuneration and seniority are not normally affected. *See also* Furlough; Sick leave.

Leave of court. Permission obtained from a court to take some action which, without such permission, would not be allowable; as, to receive an extension of time to answer complaint. Fed.R. Civil P. 6.

Ledger /léjər/. A book of accounts, often referred to as a general ledger, in which a business records transactions; there being two parallel columns in each account, one for the debit entries, the other for the credits. Into this book are posted the items from the books of original entry or journals. The principal book of accounts of a business establishment in which all the transactions of each day are entered under appropriate heads so as to show at a glance the debits and credits of each account. *See also* Journal.

Subsidiary ledger. A group of lower-level accounts that compose a general ledger account.

Left. To let remain or have remaining at death; to transmit, bequeath or give by will. *See also* Bequest; Devise; Leave; Legacy.

Legacy. A disposition of personalty by will. A bequest.

In a technical sense and strictly construed, "legacy" is a gift or bequest by will of personal property, whereas a "devise" is a testamentary disposition of real estate, but such distinction will not be permitted to defeat the intent of a testator, and such terms may be construed interchangeably or applied indifferently to either personalty or real estate if the context of the will shows that such was the intention of the testator.

See also Ademption; Bequest; Cumulative legacies; Devise; Legatee; Vested legacy.

Absolute legacy. One given without condition and intended to vest immediately.

Accumulative legacy. A second, double, or additional legacy; a legacy given in addition to another given by the same instrument, or by another instrument.

Additional legacy. One given to the same legatee in addition to (and not in lieu of) another legacy given before by the same will or in a codicil thereto.

Alternate legacy. One by which the testator gives one of two or more things without designating which.

Conditional legacy. One which is liable to take effect or to be defeated according to the occurrence or non-occurrence of some uncertain event.

Contingent legacy. A legacy given to a person at a future uncertain time, that may or may not arrive; as "at his age of twenty-one," or "if" or "when he attains twenty-one." A legacy made dependent upon some uncertain event. A legacy which has not vested.

Cumulative legacies. These are legacies so called to distinguish them from legacies which are merely repeated. In the construction of testamentary instruments, the question often arises whether, where a testator has twice bequeathed a legacy to the same person, the legatee is entitled to both, or only to one of them; in other words, whether the second legacy must be considered as a mere repetition of the first, or as cumulative, *i.e.,* additional.

In determining this question, the intention of the testator, if it appears on the face of the instrument, prevails.

Demonstrative legacy. A bequest of a certain sum of money, with a direction that it shall be paid out of a particular fund. It differs from a specific legacy in this respect: that, if the fund out of which it is payable fails for any cause, it is nevertheless entitled to come on the estate as a general legacy. And it differs from a general legacy in this: that it does not abate in that class, but in the class of specific legacies. A bequest of a certain sum of money, stock, or other property, payable out of a particular fund of property or security, but it can neither amount to a gift of the corpus nor serve the purpose of releasing the estate from liability in event particular fund or property should fail. A legacy of quantity is ordinarily a general legacy; but there are legacies of quantity in the nature of specific legacies, as of so much money, with reference to a particular fund for payment. This kind of legacy is called by the civilians a "demonstrative legacy," and it is so far general and differs so much in effect from one properly specific that, if the fund be called in or fail, the legatee will not be deprived of his legacy, but be permitted to receive it out of the general assets; yet the legacy is so far specific that it will not be liable to abate with general legacies upon a deficiency of assets.

General legacy. A pecuniary legacy which is payable out of general assets of estate of testator, being bequest of money or other thing in quantity and not separated or distinguished from others of the same kind. One so given as not to amount to a bequest of a particular thing or particular money of the testator, distinguished from others of the same kind; one of quantity merely, not specific. *Compare Specific legacy, below.*

Indefinite legacy. One which passes property by a general or collective term, without enumeration of number or quantity; as, a bequest of "all" the testator's "goods," or his "bank stock."

Lapsed legacy. Where the legatee dies before the testator, or before the legacy is payable, the bequest is said to *lapse.* Such legacy then falls into residue unless there is an anti-lapse statute in which case the legacy passes to the issue of the legatee. *See Lapse statutes.*

Modal legacy. A bequest accompanied by directions as to the mode or manner in which it shall be applied for the legatee's benefit, *e.g.,* a legacy to A. to buy him a house.

Pecuniary legacy. A bequest of a sum of money, or of an annuity. It may or may not specify the fund from which it is to be drawn. It is none the less a pecuniary legacy if it comprises the specific pieces of money in a designated receptacle, as a purse or chest.

Residuary legacy. A bequest of all the testator's personal estate not otherwise effectually disposed of by his will. A bequest of "all the rest, residue, and remainder" of the personal property after payment of debts and satisfaction of the particular legacies. Legacy containing assets after other legacies and estate debts and costs of administration have been paid.

Special legacy. A "specific legacy" *(q.v.)* is sometimes so called.

Specific legacy. One which operates on property particularly designated. A legacy or gift by will of a particular specified thing, as of a horse, a piece of furniture, a term of years, and the like. In a strict sense, a legacy of a particular chattel, which is specified and distinguished from all other chattels of the testator of the same kind; as of a horse of a certain color. A legacy of a quantity of chattels described collectively; as a gift of all the testator's pictures. A legacy is specific, when it is limited to a particular thing, subject, or chose in action, so identified as to render the bequest inapplicable to any other; as the bequest of a horse, a picture, or jewel, or a debt due from a person named, and, in special cases, even of a sum of money. *Compare General legacy, above.*

Trust legacy. A bequest of personal property to trustees to be held upon trust; as, to pay the annual income to a beneficiary for life.

Universal legacy. In the civil law, a testamentary disposition by which the testator gives to one or several persons the whole of the property which he leaves at his decease.

Void legacy. Term formerly used to describe legacy given to one who died before execution of will. Now, such legacy is considered a lapsed legacy and is treated as such. *See* Legacy *(Lapsed legacy).*

Legacy *or* **succession tax.** An excise on privilege of taking property by will or inheritance or by succession on death of owner. *See also* Inheritance tax.

Legal. 1. Conforming to the law; according to law; required or permitted by law; not forbidden or discountenanced by law; good and effectual in law; of or pertaining to the law; lawful. *See* Lawful; Valid.

2. Proper or sufficient to be recognized by the law; cognizable in the courts; competent or adequate to fulfill the requirements of the law.

3. Cognizable in courts of law, as distinguished from courts of equity; construed or governed by the rules and principles of law, in contradistinction to rules of equity. With the merger in most states of law and equity courts, this distinction generally no longer exists. Fed.R.Civil Proc. 2.

4. Posited by the courts as the inference or imputation of the law, as a matter of construction,

rather than established by actual proof; *e.g.,* legal malice.

    5. Created by law.

    As to *legal* Consideration; Damages; Debt; Defense; Demand; Disability; Discretion; Estate; Incapacity; Irregularity; Mortgage; Process; Relevancy; Remedy; Reversion, and Tender, see those titles.

Legal acumen /líygəl əkyúwmən/. The doctrine of legal acumen is that if a defect in, or invalidity of, a claim to land is such as to require legal acumen to discover it, whether it appears upon the face of the record or proceedings, or is to be proved aliunde, then the powers or jurisdiction of a court of equity may be invoked to remove the cloud created by such defect or invalidity.

Legal age. The age at which the person acquires full capacity to make his own contracts and deeds and transact business generally (age of majority) or to enter into some particular contract or relation, as the "legal age of consent" to marriage. The age at which a person may enter into binding contracts or commit other legal acts. In most states a minor reaches legal age or majority (*i.e.,* becomes of age) at age 18; though for certain acts (*e.g.* drinking) it may be higher, and for others (*e.g.* driving) it may be lower. *See also* Capacity; Majority.

Legal aid. Country-wide system administered locally by which legal services are rendered to those in financial need and who cannot afford private counsel. *See* Counsel, right to; Indigent; Legal Services Corporation; Public defender.

Legal assets. That portion of the assets of a deceased party which by law is directly liable, in the hands of his executor or administrator, to the payment of debts and legacies. Such assets as can be reached in the hands of an executor or administrator, by a suit at law against him.

Legal brief. Document containing brief statement of facts of case, issues and arguments; used most commonly on appeal, but also used at trial level (trial brief) when requested by trial judge. Content of appellate briefs is usually governed by court rules; *e.g.* Fed.R.App.P. 28–32. *See also* Brief.

Legal capacity to sue. Right to come into court. It is not necessary in pleadings to aver the capacity of a party to sue or be sued, except to the extent required to show the jurisdiction of the court. A party desiring to raise the issue of lack of capacity shall do so by specific negative averment. Fed.R.Civil P. 9(a). *See also* Capacity; Standing to sue doctrine.

Legal capital. Par or stated value of issued capital stock. The amount of contributed capital that, according to state law, must remain permanently in the firm as protection for creditors. Property sufficient to balance capital stock liability.

Legal cause. Proximate cause *(q.v.).* Substantial factor in bringing about harm. In conflicts, denotes fact that the manner in which the actor's tortious conduct has resulted in another's injury is such that the law holds the actor responsible unless there is some defense to liability. Restatement, Second, Conflicts, § 160, Comment a.

    The words "legal cause" are used throughout the Restatement of Torts to denote the fact that the causal sequence by which the actor's tortious conduct has resulted in an invasion of some legally protected interest of another is such that the law holds the actor responsible for such harm unless there is some defense to liability. Restatement, Second, Torts, § 9.

    See also Cause; Cause of action.

Legal conclusion. A statement of legal duty without stating fact from which duty arises. A particular statement which would be considered a statement of fact in everyday conversation might, nevertheless, be considered a "legal conclusion" when used in connection with a legal proceeding if the truth of the fact stated is one of the ultimate issues to be determined in such proceeding. *See also* Decision; Judgment.

Legal cruelty. Such as will warrant the granting of a divorce to the injured party, as distinguished from such kinds or degrees of cruelty as do not. Such conduct on the part of a spouse as will endanger the life, person, or health (bodily or mental) of his or her spouse, or create a reasonable apprehension of bodily or mental hurt; such acts as render cohabitation unsafe, or are likely to be attended with injury to the person or to the health of the spouse. *See also* Cruelty; Mental cruelty.

Legal custody. Restraint of or responsibility for a person according to law, such as a guardian's authority over the person or property, or both, of his ward. *See also* Commitment; Custody; Guardian; Ward.

Legal death. *See* Brain death; Civil death.

Legal defeasance. The deposit of cash and permitted securities, as specified in the bond indenture, into an irrevocable trust sufficient to enable the issuer to discharge fully its obligations under the bond indenture.

Legal dependent. Dependent according to law. The term imports right to invoke aid of law to require support. *See* Dependent; Lawful dependents; Support; Ward.

Legal description. A description of real property by government survey, metes and bounds, or lot numbers of a recorded plat including a description of any portion thereof subject to an easement or reservation, if any. Such must be complete enough that a particular parcel of land can be located and identified. *See* Land boundaries; Metes and bounds.

Legal detriment. Legal detriment to promisee means that promisee changed his legal position, or assumed duties or liabilities not theretofore imposed on him on reliance of actions of promisor. Term refers to giving up something which immediately prior thereto the promisee was privileged to retain, or doing or refraining from doing something which he was then privileged not to do, or not to refrain from doing. *See also* Consideration; Detriment.

Legal discretion. *See* Discretion.

Legal distributees. As used in will, term is construed to mean persons who would be entitled to take under the law.

Legal duty. An obligation arising from contract of the parties or the operation of the law; *e.g.* legal duty of parents to support children. That which the law requires to be done or forborne to a determinate person or the public at large, correlative to a vested and coextensive right in such person or the public, and the breach of which constitutes negligence. An obligation recognized by law which requires an actor to conform to a certain standard of conduct for the protection of others against unreasonable risk. *See also* Legal obligation; Support.

Legal entity. Legal existence. An entity, other than a natural person, who has sufficient existence in legal contemplation that it can function legally, be sued or sue and make decisions through agents as in the case of corporations.

Legal estoppel. Estoppel by deed or record, as distinguished from estoppel by matter in pais. It excludes evidence of the truth and the equity of the particular case to support a strict rule of law on grounds of public policy. *See also* Estoppel.

Legal ethics. Usages and customs among members of the legal profession, involving their moral and professional duties toward one another, toward clients, and toward the courts. That branch of moral science which treats of the duties which a member of the legal profession owes to the public, to the court, to his professional brethren, and to his client. Most states have adopted the Model Rules of Professional Conduct of the American Bar Association. *See also* Canon.

Legal evidence. A broad general term meaning all admissible evidence, including both oral and documentary, but with a further implication that it must be of such a character as tends reasonably and substantially to prove the point, not to raise a mere suspicion or conjecture. *See also* Admissible; Evidence; Relevant evidence.

Legal excuse. Doctrine by which one seeks to avoid the consequences of his own conduct by showing justification for acts which would otherwise be considered negligent or criminal; *e.g.* killing of another in self defense. *See also* Excusable; Justification; Legal impossibility; Self-defense.

Legal fiction. Assumption of fact made by court as basis for deciding a legal question. A situation contrived by the law to permit a court to dispose of a matter, though it need not be created improperly; *e.g.* fiction of lost grant as basis for title by adverse possession.

Legal fraud. Contracts or acts as, though not originating in actual evil design to perpetrate fraud, yet by their tendency to mislead others or to violate confidence, are prohibited by law. Breach of some legal or equitable duty which, irrespective of moral guilt, the law declares fraudulent because of its tendency to deceive others, to violate confidence, or to injure public interests. Misrepresentation of a material fact made wilfully to deceive, or recklessly without knowledge, and acted on by the opposite party to his damages constitutes "legal fraud."

Synonymous with "constructive fraud". For definition of *Constructive fraud, see* Fraud.

Legal heirs. As used in will, term means decedent's next of kin. Persons entitled under laws of descent and distribution. Person to whom law would give decedent's property if decedent died intestate. "Heirs at law," "lawful heirs," "legal heirs," and similar expressions are synonymous. *See also* Heirs; Legal issue.

Legal holiday. A day designated by law as exempt from judicial proceedings, service of process, demand and protest of commercial paper, etc. A day designated by legislative enactment for purpose within meaning of term "holiday." Fed.R. Civil P. 6(a), 77(c).

The legal or practical effect of a day being a "legal holiday" varies from state to state. A "holiday" may in some states be a day on which service of process is invalid, on which all or only some businesses are closed, on which state offices may or may not be closed. The statutes should be consulted in individual cases, as well as local custom, to determine if a "holiday" affects some particular contemplated action. *See also* Holiday.

Legal impossibility. As defense to criminal charge, occurs when the actions which the defendant performs or sets in motion, even if fully carried out as he desires, would not constitute a crime, whereas "factual impossibility" occurs when the objective of the defendant is proscribed by the criminal law but a circumstance unknown to the actor prevents him from bringing about that objective. Defense of "legal impossibility" may be established only where a defendant's actions, if fully performed, would not constitute a crime, while "factual impossibility" can serve as a defense only where circumstances unknown to the actor prevent his commission of an offense. *See also* Impossibility.

Legal injury. Violation or invasion of legal right. *See* Injury; Tort.

Legal insanity. *See* Insanity.

Legal interest. A rate of interest fixed by statute as either the maximum rate of interest permitted to be charged by law, or a rate of interest to be applied when the parties to a contract intend an interest rate to be paid but do not fix the rate in the contract. Even in the latter case, frequently this rate is the same as the statutory maximum rate permitted. Term may also be used to distinguish interest in property or in claim cognizable at law in contrast to equitable interest. *See also* Legal owner; Usury.

Legal investments. Those investments sometimes called "legal lists" in which banks and other financial institutions may invest. State statutes often provide that trust funds be invested only in high grade, "legal list," securities. *See also* Legal list; Prudent Man Rule.

Legal issue. When used in will and unexplained by context, means descendants. In proper context, may refer to legal question which is at the foundation of a case and which requires decision by court. *See* Issue; Legal heirs.

Legality, *or* **legalness.** Lawfulness.

Legalization. The act of legalizing or making legal or lawful. *See* Legalize.

Legalize. To make legal or lawful. To confirm or validate what was before void or unlawful. To add the sanction and authority of law to that which before was without or against law. *See also* Legitimate, *v.*

Legalized nuisance. A structure, erection, or other thing which would constitute a nuisance at common law, but which cannot be objected to by private persons because constructed or maintained under direct and sufficient legislative authority. Such, for example, are hospitals or recreational areas maintained by cities.

Legal jeopardy. A person is in "legal jeopardy" when he is put upon trial before a court of competent jurisdiction upon an indictment or information which is sufficient in form and substance to sustain a conviction, and a jury has been "charged with his deliverance," and a jury is thus charged when they have been impaneled and sworn. *See also* Jeopardy.

Legal liability. A liability which courts recognize and enforce as between parties litigant. *See also* Legally liable; Legal negligence; Liability; Strict liability.

Legal life estate. Interest in real or personal property for the life of the holder and enforceable at law in contrast to equitable life estate.

Legal list. A list of investments selected by various states in which certain institutions and fiduciaries, such as insurance companies and banks, may invest. Legal lists are often restricted to high quality securities meeting certain specifications. *See also* Legal investments; Prudent Man Rule.

Legally. Lawfully; according to law.

Legally adopted. Adopted in accordance with laws of state.

Legally committed. Refers to accused who has been committed by magistrate who has jurisdiction to hold examination and who has actually heard evidence and determined probable cause exists for holding defendant. *See also* Commitment.

Legally competent. Words "legally competent" in statute prescribing qualifications of executor mean fit or qualified to act according to judicial standards essential to proper course of justice. *See also* Capacity.

Legally constituted court. One known to and recognized by law. *See* Constitutional court.

Legally contributing cause of injury. Substantial factor in bringing about injury. *See also* Cause; Contributing cause; Proximate cause.

Legally liable. Liable under law as interpreted by courts. Liability imposed by law or liability which law fixes by contract. *See* Liability; Strict liability.

Legally sufficient consideration. Consideration which the law recognizes as legally adequate to support a valid contract. *See* Consideration.

Legally sufficient evidence. Competent, pertinent evidence coming from a legal source. Evidence is "legally sufficient to sustain finding", if supported by substantial evidence, and record as whole does not clearly, convincingly, or even, possibly, indisputably require contrary conclusion. *See* Evidence; Relevant evidence.

Legally sufficient tender. A tender made under circumstances that fulfill obligations assumed by vendors. *See* Legal tender.

Legal malice. Such consists of either an express intent to kill or inflict great bodily harm, or of a wickedness of disposition, hardness of heart, cruelty, recklessness of consequences and a mind regardless of social duty which indicates an unjustified disregard for the likelihood of death or great bodily harm and an extreme indifference to the value of human life.

An expression used as the equivalent of "constructive malice," or "malice in law." Inference of malice which can be reasonably drawn from wrongful act. Intentional doing of a wrongful act without just cause. For purposes of determining punitive damages, standard for "legal malice" is that there be wrongful act intentionally committed and without just cause or excuse. *See also* Malice.

Legal malpractice. *See* Malpractice.

Legal monopoly. *See* Monopoly.

Legal name. Under common law consists of one Christian name and one surname, and the insertion, omission, or mistake in middle name or initial is immaterial. The "legal name" of an individual consists of a given or baptismal name, usually assumed at birth, and a surname deriving from the common name of the parents.

Legal negligence. Negligence per se; the omission of such care as ordinarily prudent persons exercise and deem adequate to the circumstances of the case. In cases where the common experience of mankind and the common judgment of prudent persons have recognized that to do or omit certain acts is productive of danger, the doing or omission of them is "legal negligence." Failure to perform duty law imposes on one person for benefit of another. *See also* Strict liability.

Legal newspaper. Newspapers published nationally and in major cities containing summaries of important court decisions, recently enacted or pending legislation or regulatory changes, and, locally, notices of bankruptcy, probate, foreclosure, divorce, etc. proceedings, and also news of general interest to the legal profession.

Legal notice. Such notice as is adequate in point of law; notice as the law requires to be given for the specific purpose or in the particular case. Such legal notice is typically required to be published a specified number of times in a legal and/or general circulation newspaper; may also be required to be posted in designated area in court house. *See also* Notice.

Legal obligation. A legal obligation against state is an obligation which would form basis of judgment against state in court of competent jurisdiction should Legislature permit state to be sued. In its broadest sense, any duty imposed by law; *e.g.* duty of parent to support children. *See also* Legal duty; Support.

Legal owner. The term has come to be used in technical contrast to the equitable owner, and not as opposed to an illegal owner. The legal owner has title to the property, although the title may actually carry no rights to the property other than a lien.

Legal opinion. A document in which an official such as a state attorney general, a city solicitor or a private attorney, renders his or her understanding of the law as applied to the assumed facts. It may or may not serve as protection to one acting on it, depending on the nature of it and the law governing such opinions. It may concern the state of a real estate title on which a buyer or lender may act.

Legal personal representative. Generally, when applied by testator to personalty, signifies "executors and administrators" and when applied to realty those upon whom law casts real estate immediately upon death of ancestor. As respects delivery of deposit on behalf of deceased seaman, means the public administrator, or executor or administrator appointed in state where seaman resided. *See* Legal representative.

Legal possessor. One who, but for the reservation of strict legal title in conditional vendor, or the giving of a strict legal title in a conditional vendor, or the giving of a strict legal title to a chattel mortgagee, would have the status of a full and unqualified owner. One who has the legal right to possession of property as contrasted with the owner of such property who has legal title. *See* Legal owner.

Legal prejudice. Legal prejudice which will defeat plaintiff's motion to dismiss is such as deprives defendant of substantive rights of property, or concerns his defense, which will not be available or may be endangered in a second suit.

Legal presumption. For *presumption of law, see* Presumption.

Legal privity. Term, within rule that defense of usury is personal to debtor and those in legal privity with him, means those upon whom title or interest is cast by law. An agent and his principal are in legal privity to each other. *See also* Privity.

Legal proceedings. Term includes all proceedings authorized or sanctioned by law, and brought or instituted in a court or legal tribunal, for the acquiring of a right or the enforcement of a remedy.

Legal rate of interest. *See* Legal interest; Usury.

Legal representative. The term in its broadest sense, means one who stands in place of, and represents the interests of, another. A person who oversees the legal affairs of another. Examples include the executor or administrator of an estate and a court appointed guardian of a minor or incompetent person.

Term, which is almost always held to be synonymous with term "personal representative," means, in accident cases, member of family entitled to benefits under wrongful death statute.

Legal rescission. Rescission by act of parties. *See also* Rescind; Rescission of contract; Void; Voidable.

Legal reserve. Liquid assets which life insurance companies are required by statute to set aside and maintain to assure payment of claims and benefits. In banking, that amount of percentage of bank deposits which must by law be maintained in cash or equally liquid assets to meet the demands of depositors.

Legal residence. The place of domicile or permanent abode, as distinguished from temporary residence. Permanent fixed place of abode which person intends to be his residence and to which he intends to return despite temporary residences elsewhere or despite temporary absences. Place recognized by law as residence of person. *See also* Domicile; Residence.

Legal right. Natural rights, rights existing as result of contract, and rights created or recognized by law.

Legal secretary. An employee of an attorney or law office whose responsibilities include the typing of legal documents, memoranda and correspondence, the keeping of records and files, giving and receiving notices, and such other duties as required by her or his employer in the practice of law.

Legal separation. A court order arranging the terms (custody, support, etc.) under which a married couple will live separately. *See also* Divorce *(divorce a mensa et thoro);* Separate maintenance; Separation of spouses.

Legal Services Corporation. The Legal Services Corporation was established by the Legal Services Corporation Act of 1974 (42 U.S.C.A. § 2996) to provide financial support for legal assistance in noncriminal proceedings to persons financially unable to afford legal services. The Corporation provides financial assistance to qualified programs furnishing legal assistance to eligible clients and makes grants to and contracts with individuals, firms, corporations, organizations, and State and local governments for the purpose of providing legal assistance to these clients.

Legal subdivisions. Divisions of land which result from application of ordinary methods used in making of a government survey.

Legal subrogation. A right arising by operation of law: where one having liability, right, or fiduciary relation pays another's debt under circumstances equitably entitling former to rights, remedies or securities held by creditor; where person pays in performance of legal duty imposed by contract, statute, or rule of law or where payment is favored by public policy; where person secondarily liable pays debt and becomes subrogated to creditor's rights; where person who pays stands

in situation of a surety or is compelled to pay to protect his own right or property. *See* Subrogation.

Legal tender. All coins and currencies of the United States (including Federal Reserve notes and circulating notes of Federal Reserve banks and national banking associations), regardless of when coined or issued, are legal tender for all debts, public and private, public charges, taxes, duties, and dues. 31 U.S.C.A. § 392. *See also* United States currency.

Seller of goods may demand payment by legal tender but he is required to give an extension of time reasonably necessary to procure it. U.C.C. § 2–511(2).

Legal tender cases. Two cases upholding the constitutionality of the Acts of Congress in 1862 and 1863 calling for the issuance of paper money. Knox v. Lee, 79 U.S. (12 Wall.) 457, 20 L.Ed. 287, Juilliard v. Greenman, 110 U.S. 421, 4 S.Ct. 122, 28 L.Ed. 204.

Legal title. One cognizable or enforceable in a court of law, or one which is complete and perfect so far as regards the apparent right of ownership and possession, but which carries no beneficial interest in the property, another person being equitably entitled thereto; in either case, the antithesis of "equitable title." It may also mean appearance of title as distinguished from complete title; or full and absolute title or apparent right of ownership with beneficial or equitable title in another. A tax title, which is prima facie valid, is a "legal title". *See* Title.

Legal usufruct /líygəl yúwzəfrəkt/. Usufructs established by operation of law; *e.g.,* the usufruct collated for surviving spouse in necessitous circumstances. *See also* Usufruct.

Legal voter. A person meeting constitutional requirements and who is registered. A person invested by law with right to vote. A person qualified by U.S. Constitution and laws of state to vote.

Legal willfulness. Intentional disregard of known duty necessary to safety of person or property of another and entire absence of care for life, person or property of others.

Legatee /lègətíy/. The person to whom a legacy in a will is given. The term may be used to denominate those who take under will without any distinction between realty and personalty; though commonly it refers to one who takes *personal* property under a will. *See* Legacy.

Residuary legatee. The person to whom a testator bequeaths the residue of his personal estate, after the payment of such other legacies as are specifically mentioned in the will.

Legation. An embassy; a diplomatic minister and his suite. The persons commissioned by one government to exercise diplomatic functions at the court of another, including the minister, secretaries, attachés, interpreters, etc., are collectively styled the "legation" of their government. The word also denotes the official residence of a foreign minister.

Legator /ləgéytər/. One who makes a will, and leaves legacies.

Legislate. To enact laws or pass resolutions via legislation, in contrast to court-made law.

Legislating. Enactment of laws by Congress or state legislatures.

Legislation. The act of giving or enacting laws; the power to make laws; the act of legislating; preparation and enactment of laws; the making of laws via legislation, in contrast to court-made laws. Formulation of rule for the future. Laws enacted by lawmaking body (e.g. by Congress or state legislature). See also Act (Legislative act); Bill; Class legislation; Statute.

Legislative. Making or giving laws; pertaining to the function of law-making or to the process of enactment of laws. Actions which relate to subjects of permanent or general character are "legislative". Making or having the power to make a law or laws.

Legislative act. Enactment of laws. Law (i.e. statute) passed by legislature in contrast to court-made law. One which prescribes what the law shall be in future cases arising under its provisions. See Statute.

Legislative apportionment. Amend. XIV, § 2, of U.S.Const. provides that representatives to congress "shall be apportioned among the several states according to their respective numbers, counting the whole number of persons in each state." Equal protection under the Fourteenth Amendment of the U.S. Constitution requires the allocation of representatives on a population basis and a justiciable issue is presented when a claim is made that states are denying right of representation to its citizens. Baker v. Carr, 369 U.S. 186, 82 S.Ct. 691, 7 L.Ed.2d 663. See also Apportionment; Reapportionment.

Legislative council. A legislative agency used in some states which is composed of legislators and other selected officials who study legislative problems and plan legislative strategy between regular legislative sessions.

Legislative counsel. A person or agency specially charged with assisting legislators in fulfilling their legislative tasks. Legislative counsel handles problems of research, drafting bills, legislative hearings, and other technical legislative details.

Legislative courts. Courts created by legislature (e.g. Art. I, Sec. 8, Cl. 9 of U.S. Const.) in contrast to those created by constitution (e.g. Art. III of U.S.Const.). In many states almost all courts are created by Legislature, though court of last resort is commonly creature of its constitution. Compare Constitutional court.

Legislative department. That department of government (i.e. Congress, consisting of Senate and House of Representatives; Art. I of U.S. Const.) whose appropriate function is the making or enactment of laws, as distinguished from the judicial department (Article III), which interprets and applies the laws, and the executive department (Article II), which carries them into execution and effect. See also Legislature.

Legislative districting. The apportionment or division of a legislative body into territorial districts. See Apportionment; Legislative apportionment; Reapportionment.

Legislative divorce. A divorce decreed by an act of the legislature as to one particular couple and not by judicial decree. While legislative divorces once existed in New England states, and parliamentary divorces once were granted in England, such have long been superseded by judicial divorces.

Legislative functions. The determination of legislative policy and its formation as rule of conduct. The formation and determination of future rights and duties. See also Legislative power.

Legislative history. The background and events, including committee reports, hearings, and floor debates, leading up to enactment of a law. Such history is important to courts when they are required to determine the legislative intent of a particular statute. Legislative histories of major statutes are published in U.S.Code, Congressional and Administrative News.

Legislative immunity. The Constitution grants two immunities to Congressmen, first, that except for treason, felony, and a breach of the peace, they are "privileged from Arrest during their Attendance" at sessions of their body, and, second, that "for any Speech or Debate in either House, they shall not be questioned in any other Place." (Art. I, § 6, cl. 1). The first immunity is of little practical value, for its exceptions withdraw all criminal offenses and arrests therefor from the privilege, and it does not apply to the service of any process in a civil or criminal matter. The second immunity is liberally construed and includes not only opinion, speeches, debates, or other oral matter, but also voting, making a written report or presenting a resolution, and in general to whatever a congressman feels necessary to transact the legislative functions and business. Even a claim of a bad motive does not destroy the immunity, for it is the public good which is thereby served.

Legislative intent. Such is looked to when court attempts to construe or interpret a statute which is ambiguous or inconsistent. *See also* Legislative history.

Legislative investigations. Legislatures are empowered to make investigations as an incident of their legislative authority; included are powers of subpoena, cross examination, etc.

Legislative jurisdiction. The sphere of authority of a legislative body to enact laws and to conduct all business incidental to its law-making function. Art. I of U.S. Constitution.

Legislative officer. A member of the legislative body or department of a state or municipal corporation. One of those whose duties relate mainly to the enactment of laws, such as members of congress and of the several state legislatures. These officers are confined in their duties by the constitution generally to make laws, though sometimes, in cases of impeachment, one of the houses of the legislature exercises judicial functions somewhat similar to those of a grand jury, by presenting to the other articles of impeachment, and the other house acts as a court in trying such impeachment.

Legislative power. The lawmaking powers of a legislative body, whose functions include the power to make, alter, amend and repeal laws. In essence, the legislature has the power to make laws and such power is reposed exclusively in such body though it may delegate rule making and regulatory powers to departments in the executive branch. It may not, however, delegate its law making powers nor is the judicial branch permitted to obtrude into its legislative powers. The enumerated powers of Congress are provided for in Article I of the U.S. Constitution.

Legislative rule. A rule issued by an administrative agency pursuant to statutory authority implementing statute that has force and effect of law. Those rules that are promulgated pursuant to congressional delegation of power to issue rules and regulations that have force of law and are binding on courts because they are source of law that court and agency must enforce.

Legislator. One who makes laws; a member of a federal, state or municipal lawmaking body; senator, representative, assemblyman.

Legislature. The department, assembly, or body of persons that makes statutory laws for a state or nation. At the federal level, and in most states, the legislature is bicameral in structure, usually consisting of two branches; *i.e.* upper house (Senate) and lower house (House of Representatives or Assembly). Legislative bodies at the local levels are variously called city councils, boards of aldermen, etc. *See* Chamber; Congress; House of Rep-

resentatives; Legislative department; Legislative districting; Senate.

Legitimacy. Lawful birth; the condition of being born in wedlock; the opposite of illegitimacy or bastardy.

Legitimate, *v.* To make lawful; to confer legitimacy; *e.g.*, to place a child born before marriage on the legal footing of those born in lawful wedlock.

Legitimate, *adj.* That which is lawful, legal, recognized by law, or according to law; as, legitimate children, legitimate authority, lawful power, legitimate sport or amusement. Real, valid, or genuine. *See* Presumption of legitimacy.

Legitimation. The making legitimate or lawful that which was not originally so; especially the statutory procedure of legalizing (legitimating) the status of an illegitimate child. Such is usually necessary to assure inheritance rights to child.

Lemon laws. Laws enacted in many states governing rights of purchasers of new and used motor vehicles which do not function properly and which have to repeatedly be returned to the dealer for repairs. Such laws give redress to purchasers and permit refund of purchase price after certain steps are taken and opportunity has been given dealer to correct defects.

Le mort saisit le vif. Doctrine of "le mort saisit le vif" requires that there can be no gap in seisin, and on death of de cujus, legal title immediately vests in heirs of deceased, and that is not to say that doctrine is so narrow as to exclude unknown heirs or absent heirs at date of death.

Lend. To give or put out for hire or compensation. To part with a thing of value to another for a time fixed or indefinite, yet to have some time in ending, to be used or enjoyed by that other; the thing itself or the equivalent of it to be given back at the time fixed, or when lawfully asked for, with or without compensation for the use as may be agreed upon. Term "lend" when used in a will means to "give" or "devise." To provide money to another for a period of time, usually with interest charge to be incurred by borrower. *See also* Loan.

Lender. He from whom a thing or money is borrowed. The bailor of an article loaned. A bank or other lending institution; a mortgagee.

Lenity Rule. This rule provides that where there is ambiguity in the language of a statute concerning multiple punishment, ambiguity should be resolved in favor of lenity in sentencing.

Lesion /líyzhən/. Damage; injury; detriment; sore; wound. Any change in the structure of an organ due to injury or disease, whether apparent or diagnosed as the cause of a functional irregularity or disturbance.

In the civil law, the injury suffered by one who does not receive a full equivalent for what he gives in a commutative contract. Inequality in contracts.

Lessee. One who rents property from another. In the case of real estate, the lessee is also known as the tenant. He to whom a lease is made. He who holds an estate by virtue of a lease. One who has been given possession of land which is exclusive even of the landlord, except as the lease permits his entry, and except right to enter to demand rent or to make repairs. *See also* Tenant.

A person who acquires the right to possession and use of goods under a lease. Unless the context clearly indicates otherwise, the term includes a sublessee. U.C.C. § 2A–103.

Lessee's interest. The appraised value of a lessee's interest in order to determine its worth for assignment or sale. In appraising the value of a potential sublease or assignment (sale) of the lease, the value is the market value of the property, less the interest of the lessor. The lessor's interest would be largely determined by the ratio of the return on the lease to the market value without the lease.

Lesser included offense. One which is composed of some, but not all elements of a greater offense and which does not have any element not included in greater offense so that it is impossible to commit greater offense without necessarily committing the lesser offense. One that does not require proof of any additional element beyond those required by the greater offense. One which must necessarily be included in the greater offense. One which includes some of the elements of the crime charged in the information without the addition of any element irrelevant to the original charge. When it is impossible to commit a particular crime without concomitantly committing, by the same conduct, another offense of lesser grade or degree, the latter is, with respect to the former, a "lesser included offense". In any case in which it is legally possible to attempt to commit a crime, such attempt constitutes a lesser included offense with respect thereto. The defendant may be found guilty of an offense necessarily included in the offense charged. Fed.R.Crim.P. 31. *See also* Necessarily included offense.

Lessor. He who grants a lease. One who rents property to another. In the case of real estate, the lessor is also known as the landlord. One who has leased land for a definite or indefinite period, by a written or parol lease, irrespective of whether a statute of fraud requires the lease to be in writing. *See also* Landlord.

A person who transfers the right to possession and use of goods under a lease. Unless the context clearly indicates otherwise, the term includes a sublessor. U.C.C. § 2A–103.

Lessor's interest. The present value of the future income under the lease, plus the present value of the property after the lease expires (reversion).

Let, *v.* *Contracts.* To award to one of several persons, who have submitted proposals (bids) therefor, the contract for erecting public works or doing some part of the work connected therewith, or rendering some other service to government for a stipulated compensation. Letting the contract is the choosing one from among the number of bidders, and the formal making of the contract with him. The letting, or putting out, is a different thing from the invitation to make proposals; the letting is subsequent to the invitation. It is the act of awarding the contract to the proposer, after the proposals have been received and considered.

Conveyancing. To demise or lease a certain property. *See* Lease.

Let, *n.* In old conveyancing, hindrance; obstruction; interruption.

Lethal. Deadly, mortal, fatal.

Lethal weapon. A deadly weapon *(q.v.)*.

Letter. A communication inclosed, sealed, stamped, carried and delivered by private or U.S. Postal service.

A commission, patent, or written instrument containing or attesting the grant of some power, authority, or right.

The word appears in this generic sense in many compound phrases known to commercial law and jurisprudence; *e.g.,* letter of attorney, letter missive, letter of credit, letters patent. The plural is frequently used.

Metaphorically, the verbal expression; the strict literal meaning. The *letter* of a statute, as distinguished from its *spirit,* means the strict and exact force of the language employed, as distinguished from the general purpose and policy of the law.

As to *letters of* Administration; Advice; Attorney; Credit; Recommendation, see those titles. As to *Letters patent, see* Patent.

Letter contract. In federal contract law, a written contractual instrument with sufficient provisions to permit contractor to begin performance.

Letter of administration. *See* Letters of administration.

Letter of advice. Drawer's communication to the drawee that a described draft has been drawn. U.C.C. § 3–701(1).

Letter of attornment. A letter from a grantor to a tenant, stating that the property has been sold, and directing rent to be paid to the grantee (new owner).

Letter of comment. Letters of comment are sent out by the S.E.C. in most cases as a means of informing registrants of securities offerings of the respects in which a registration statement is deemed not to meet the disclosure and other requirements of the Securities Exchange Act and the forms and regulations thereunder. A letter of comment may not be sent out, however, where the circumstances are such that an investigatory or stop order proceeding is deemed more appropriate.

Letter of credence. In international law, the document which accredits an ambassador, minister, or envoy to the courts or government to which he is sent; *i.e.,* certifies to his appointment and qualification, and bespeaks credit for his official actions and representations.

Letter of credit. An engagement by a bank or other person made at the request of a customer that the issuer will honor drafts or other demands for payment upon compliance with the conditions specified in the credit. A credit may be either revocable or irrevocable. The engagement may be either an agreement to honor or a statement that the bank or other person is authorized to honor. U.C.C. § 5–103. Letters of credit are intended generally to facilitate purchase and sale of goods by providing assurance to the seller of prompt payment upon compliance with specified conditions or presentation of stipulated documents without the sellers having to rely upon the solvency and good faith of the buyer.

See also Advice of credit.

Commercial letter. Type of letter of credit used by buyer of merchandise who sends it to bank in district in which he is to buy and seller then presents his bill of sale, etc. to obtain payment. *See also* Commercial credit.

Confirmed letter. Type of letter of credit in which local bank gives its guarantee that seller's draft will be honored if the bank which issued letter fails to honor it.

Export letter. Type of letter of credit forwarded to seller or exporter advising him that a credit has been established in his favor by a foreign bank and further consenting to honor the seller's or exporter's draft for the goods.

General and special. A general letter of credit is one addressed to any and all persons, without naming any one in particular, while a special letter of credit is addressed to a particular individual, firm, or corporation by name.

Import letter. Type of letter of credit issued by a foreign bank to a local seller permitting him to draw draft on the foreign bank against shipment of the merchandise.

Irrevocable letter. Type of letter of credit in which issuing bank guarantees that it will not withdraw the credit or cancel the letter before the expiration date. A letter of credit which cannot be modified or revoked as regards the customer or the beneficiary without his or her consent.

Open credit. See Open letter of credit.

Revocable letter. Letter of credit in which the issuing bank reserves the right to cancel and withdraw from the transaction upon appropriate notice.

Revolving credit. See Revolving credit.

Standby letter. A letter of credit which commits the issuer to honor the credit not upon evidence of performance by the beneficiary, as by presenting evidence of the shipment of goods to the customer, but upon evidence or a mere declaration of the customer's default in the underlying transaction with the beneficiary.

Straight credit. A letter of credit that does not run in favor of purchasers of drafts drawn thereunder.

Time credit. A letter of credit that is duly honored by the issuer accepting drafts drawn thereunder. Essentially synonymous with "usance credit" and "acceptance credit."

Transferable credit. A letter of credit that authorizes the beneficiary to assign the right to draw thereunder.

Traveler's letter. Type of letter of credit used by one traveling abroad in which the issuing bank authorizes payment of funds to holder in the local currency by a local bank. The holder signs a check on the issuing bank and the local bank forwards it to the issuing bank for its credit.

Letter of exchange. A bill of exchange *(q.v.).*

Letter of intent. A letter of intent is customarily employed to reduce to writing a preliminary understanding of parties who intend to enter into contract or who intend to take some other action such as merger of companies.

Letter of marque and reprisal. An authorization formerly granted in time of war by a government to the owner of a private vessel to capture enemy vessels and goods on the high seas. Art. I, Sec. 8 of U.S.Const. The signatory powers to the Declaration of Paris in 1856 agreed to stop issuing such authorizations.

Letter of recall. A document addressed by the executive of one nation to that of another, informing the latter that a minister sent by the former has been recalled. May also refer to letter sent by manufacturer of product to purchasers requesting that they bring product, automobile, etc. into dealer to repair or replace item.

Letter of the law. Expression used to denote the exact, strict interpretation of a statute, ordinance, regulation, or law.

Letter patent. *See* Letters patent.

Letter ruling. A written statement which is issued to a taxpayer by Office of Assistant Commissioner of I.R.S. in which interpretations of tax laws are made and applied to a specific set of facts. Such is issued in response to request for ruling by a private party of tax implications of a particular transaction.

Letters. In probate practice, includes letters testamentary, letters of guardianship, letters of administration, and letters of conservatorship. Uniform Probate Code, § 1–201(23). *See* Letters of administration.

Letters of administration. Formal document issued by probate court appointing one an administrator of an estate.

Letters of administration C.T.A. Document issued by probate court appointing one administrator cum testamento annexo (with the will annexed) by reason of the failure of the named executor to qualify.

Letters of administration D.B.N. Document issued by probate court appointing one administrator de bonis non (concerning goods—not already administered) because of failure of named executor to complete the probate of the estate.

Letters of administration D.B.N. C.T.A. Document issued by probate court to one who is thereby authorized to administer estate in place of named executor in accordance with will of testator. *See* Letters of Administration C.T.A.; Letters of Administration D.B.N.

Letters of guardianship. A commission placing ward's property in the care of officer of court as custodian.

Letters patent /létərz péytənt/°pǽt°/. An instrument issued by a government to the patentee, granting or confirming a right to the exclusive possession and enjoyment of land, or of a new invention or discovery. *See also* Land patent; Patent.

Letters rogatory /létərz rógət(ə)riy/. A request by one court of another court in an independent jurisdiction, that a witness be examined upon interrogatories sent with the request. The medium whereby one country, speaking through one of its courts, requests another country, acting through its own courts and by methods of court procedure peculiar thereto and entirely within the latter's control, to assist the administration of justice in the former country.

A formal communication in writing, sent by a court in which an action is pending to a court or judge of a foreign country, requesting that the testimony of a witness resident within the jurisdiction of the latter court may be there formally taken under its direction and transmitted to the first court for use in the pending action. Fed.R. Civil P. 28; 28 U.S.C.A. §§ 1781, 1782.

This process was also in use, at an early period, between the several states of the Union. The request rests entirely upon the comity of courts towards each other.

Letters testamentary. The formal instrument of authority and appointment given to an executor by the proper court, empowering him to enter upon the discharge of his office as executor. It corresponds to letters of administration granted to an administrator.

Letter stock. Stock not registered under the Securities Act of 1933, where the buyer gives the seller a letter stating the buyer intends to hold for investment purposes and does not contemplate reoffering the stock to others.

Letting. Leasing or awarding. *See also* Lease; Let.

Letting out. The act of leasing property or awarding a contract. *See* Let.

Levee /léviy/. An embankment or artificial mound of earth constructed along the margin of a river, to confine the stream to its natural channel or prevent inundation or overflow. Also, a landing place on a river or lake; a place on a river or other navigable water for lading and unlading goods and for the reception and discharge of passengers to and from vessels lying in the contiguous waters, which may be either a wharf or pier or the natural bank.

Levee district. A municipal subdivision of a state (which may or may not be a public corporation) organized for the purpose, and charged with the duty, of constructing and maintaining such levees within its territorial limits as are to be built and kept up at public expense and for the general public benefit.

Level rate, legal reserve policy. Insurance which seeks to build up a reserve which will equal face value of policy at the end of insured's life.

Leverage. The ability to finance an investment with a small amount of one's own funds, such as a down payment, with the balance consisting of borrowed funds. The use of a smaller investment to generate a larger rate of return through borrowing.

The amount of money borrowed by party in business in excess of money or assets invested personally in the business. Term refers to the advantages that may accrue to a business through the use of debt obtained from third persons (*e.g.* banks or outside investors) in lieu of contributed capital. Such debt improves the earnings allocable to contributed capital if the business earns more on each dollar invested than the interest cost of borrowing funds.

The effect on common stockholders of the requirements to pay bond interest and preferred stock dividends before payment of common stock dividends.

Leveraged buyout. Method of purchasing outstanding stock of publicly held corporation by management or outside investors, with financing consisting primarily of funds borrowed from investment bankers or brokers. The initial and subsequent long term capital used for the buyout is usually secured by the target company's assets with repayment generated from the company's retained or future earnings, sales of certain of its assets, and the like. For a type of employee buyout method, see Employee Stock Ownership Plan. See also Aggressor corporation; Going private.

Leveraged lease. A type of financial lease in which the lessor borrows a high percentage of the cost of the leased asset on a nonrecourse basis from lenders. This is also sometimes called a third-party equity lease or a tax lease.

Leverage ratio. The ratio of the value of the firm's debt to the total value of the firm.

Leviable /léviyəbəl/. That which may be levied. That which is a proper or permissible subject for a levy; as, a "leviable interest" in land.

Levy, *v.* To assess; raise; execute; exact; tax; collect; gather; take up; seize. Thus, to levy (assess, exact, raise, or collect) a tax; to levy (raise or set up) a nuisance; to levy (acknowledge) a fine; to levy (inaugurate) war; to levy an execution, *i.e.,* to levy or collect a sum of money on an execution.

Levy, *n.* A seizure. The obtaining of money by legal process through seizure and sale of property; the raising of the money for which an execution has been issued.

The process whereby a sheriff or other state official empowered by writ or other judicial directive actually seizes, or otherwise brings within her control, a judgment debtor's property which is taken to secure or satisfy the judgment.

In reference to taxation, the word may mean the legislative function and declaration of the subject and rate or amount of taxation; or the rate of taxation rather than the physical act of applying the rate to the property; or the formal order, by proper authority declaring property subject to taxation at fixed rate at its assessed valuation; or the ministerial function of assessing, listing and extending taxes; or the extension of the tax; or the doing of whatever is necessary in order to authorize the collector to collect the tax. When used in connection with authority to tax, denotes exercise of legislative function, whether state or local, determining that a tax shall be imposed and fixing amount, purpose and subject of the exaction. The qualified electors "levy" a tax when they vote to impose it.

See also Assess; Assessment; Tax.

Equitable levy. The lien in equity created by the filing of a creditor's bill to subject real property of the debtor, and of a lis pendens, is sometimes so called. The right to an equitable lien is sometimes called an "equitable levy."

Levying war. In criminal law, the assembling of a body of men for the purpose of effecting by force a treasonable object; and all who perform any part, however minute, or however remote from the scene of action, and who are leagued in the general conspiracy, are considered as engaged in levying war, within the meaning of the constitution. Art. III, § 3, U.S. Constitution. *See also* Insurrection.

The words include forcible opposition, as the result of a combination of individuals, to the execution of any public law of the United States; and to constitute treason within the Federal Constitution, there must be a combination of individuals united for the common purpose of forcibly preventing the execution of some public law and the actual or threatened use of force by the combination to prevent its execution.

Lewd /l(y)uwd/. Obscene, lustful, indecent, lascivious, lecherous. The term imports a lascivious intent. It signifies that form of immorality which has relation to moral impurity; or that which is carried on in a wanton manner. Given to unlawful indulgence of lust, eager for sexual indulgence. *See also* Indecent *(Indecent exposure)*; Lascivious; Lewdness; Obscene; Obscenity.

Lewd and lascivious cohabitation. Within criminal statutes, the living together of a man and woman not married to each other as husband and wife. Also called "illicit cohabitation". Where existing, such statutes are seldom enforced. *See also* Lewdness.

Lewd house. *See* Bawdy-house

Lewdness. Gross and wanton indecency in sexual relations so notorious as to tend to corrupt community's morals. Licentiousness; that form of immorality which has relation to sexual impurity. Moral turpitude. Open and public indecency. Sensuality; debauchery.

Any act which the actor knows is likely to be observed by others who would be affronted or alarmed and hence it is a criminal offense. Model Penal Code, § 251.1. Lewdness is specifically made an offense under some state statutes, and is included under more general clauses in others.

See also Indecent *(Indecent exposure)*; Lascivious; Obscene; Obscenity.

Lewd person. One who is lawless, bad, vicious, unchaste, indecent, obscene, lascivious.

Lex /léks/. Lat. In medieval jurisprudence, a body or collection of various laws peculiar to a given nation or people; not a code in the modern sense, but an aggregation or collection of laws not codified or systematized. Also, a similar collection of laws relating to a general subject, and not peculiar to any one people.

In modern American and English jurisprudence, a system or body of laws, written or unwritten, or so much thereof as may be applicable to a particular case or question, considered as being local or peculiar to a given state, country, or jurisdiction, or as being different from the laws or rules relating to the same subject-matter which prevail in some other place.

In old English law, a body or collection of laws, and particularly the Roman or civil law. Also a form or mode of trial or process of law, as the ordeal or battel, or the oath of a party with compurgators, as in the phrases *legem facere, legem vadiare*, etc. Also used in the sense of legal rights or civil rights or the protection of the law, as in the phrase *legem amittere*.

In Roman law, a law; the law.

This term was often used as the synonym of *jus*, in the sense of a rule of civil conduct authoritatively prescribed for the government of the actions of the members of an organized jural society.

Lex is used in a purely juridical sense, law, and not also right; while *jus* has an ethical as well as a juridical meaning, not only law, but right. *Lex* is usually concrete, while *jus* is abstract. In English we have no term which combines the legal and ethical meanings, as do *jus* and its French equivalent, *droit*.

In a more limited and particular sense, it was a resolution adopted by the whole Roman *"populus"* (patricians and plebeians) in the *comitia*, on the motion of a magistrate of senatorial rank, as a consul, a prætor, or a dictator. Such a statute frequently took the name of the proposer; as the *lex Falcidia, lex Cornelia*, etc.

A rule of law which magistrates and people had agreed upon by means of a solemn declaration of consensus.

In a somewhat wider and more generic sense, a law (whatever its origin) or the aggregate of laws, relating to a particular subject-matter, thus corresponding to the meaning of the word "law" in some modern phrases, such as the "law of evidence," "law of wills," etc.

Other specific meanings of the word in Roman jurisprudence were as follows: Positive law, as opposed to natural. That system of law which descended from the Twelve Tables, and formed the basis of all the Roman law. The terms of a private covenant; the condition of an obligation.

A form of words prescribed to be used upon particular occasions.

Lex actus /léks ǽktəs/. In conflicts, the law of the transaction; this governs in choice of law situation.

Lex contractus /léks kəntrǽktəs/. In conflicts, the law of the place where the contract was formed, though the term today has undergone changes from the time that substantive questions of law were decided by the law of the place of the making while procedural questions were decided by the law of the forum.

Lex fori /léks fóray/. The law of the forum, or court; that is, the positive law of the state, country, or jurisdiction of whose judicial system the court where the suit is brought or remedy sought is an integral part. Substantive rights are determined by the law of the place where the action arose, "lex loci," while the procedural rights are governed by the law of the place of the form, "lex fori." *See* Lex loci contractus.

LEXIS. A computer-assisted legal research service provided by Mead Data Central. LEXIS provides on-line access to a database of legal information including federal and state caselaw, statutes, and administrative, regulatory, and secondary materials.

Lex loci /léks lówsay/. The law of the place. This may be of several descriptions but, in general, *lex loci* is only used for *lex loci contractus (q.v.).*

The "lex loci" furnishes the standard of conduct; it governs as to all matters going to the basis of the right of action itself. The substantive rights of parties to action are governed by "lex loci" or law of place where rights were acquired or liabilities incurred. *Compare* Lex fori.

Lex loci actus /léks lówsay ǽktəs/. The law of the place where the act was done.

Lex loci contractus /léks lówsay kəntrǽktəs/. Used sometimes to denote the law of the place where the contract was made, and at other times to denote the law by which the contract is to be governed (*i.e.* place of its performance), which may or may not be the same as that of the place where it was made. The earlier cases do not regard this distinction.

Lex loci delictus /léks lówsay dəlíktəs/. The law of the place where the crime or wrong took place. The "lex loci delicti", or "place of the wrong", is the state where the last event necessary to make an actor liable for an alleged tort takes place. More fully expressed by the words *lex loci delicti commissi* (law of the place where a tort is committed), usually written more briefly as *lex loci delicti*, or, sometimes, simply *lex delicti*.

Lex loci domicilii /léks lówsay dòməsíliyay/. The law of the place of domicile.

Lex naturale /léks nÃ¦tyÉ™réyliy/. Natural law. *See* Jus naturale.

Ley /léy/. L. Fr. (A corruption of *loi.*) Law; the law. For example, *Termes de la Ley*, Terms of the Law. In another, and an old technical, sense, ley signifies an oath, or the oath with compurgators; as, il tend sa *ley* aiu pleyntiffe. *See also* Lex.

In Spanish law, a law; the law; law in the abstract.

L.H.W.C.A. Longshore and Harbor Workers' Compensation Act.

Liability. The word is a broad legal term of the most comprehensive significance, including almost every character of hazard or responsibility, absolute, contingent, or likely. It has been defined to mean: all character of debts and obligations; amenability or responsibility; an obligation one is bound in law or justice to perform; an obligation which may or may not ripen into a debt; any kind of debt or liability, either absolute or contingent, express or implied; condition of being actually or potentially subject to an obligation; condition of being responsible for a possible or actual loss, penalty, evil, expense, or burden; condition which creates a duty to perform an act immediately or in the future; duty to pay money or perform some other service; that which one is under obligation to pay, or for which one is liable; the state of being bound or obliged in law or justice to do, pay, or make good something; the state of one who is bound in law and justice to do something which may be enforced by action.

All the claims against a corporation. Liabilities include accounts and wages and salaries payable, dividends declared payable, accrued taxes payable, fixed or long-term liabilities such as mortgage bonds, debentures and bank loans.

See also Current liabilities; Derivative liability; Employer's liability acts; Enterprise liability; Legal liability; Liable; Limitation of liability acts; Malpractice; Monetary liabilities; No fault; Parental liability; Personal liability; Product liability; Several liability; Strict liability; Vicarious liability.

Absolute liability. See Strict liability.

Accrued liability. Obligation which has been incurred but not yet paid; *e.g.* taxes, rent.

Children. See Parental liability.

Contingent liability. A liability not yet fixed but dependent on events to occur in the future (*e.g.* a pending law suit).

Fixed liability. One fixed as to time, amount, etc.; *e.g.* mortgage.

Joint and several liability. Responsible together and individually. The person who has been harmed can sue and recover from both wrongdoers or from either one of the wrongdoers (if he goes after both of them, he does not, however,

receive double compensation). *See also* Joint and several liability; Joint tort-feasors.

Joint liability. Liability for which more than one person is responsible. *See also* Contribution; Joint liability; Joint tort-feasors.

Liability bond. See Bond.

Long term liabilities. Obligations expected to be paid after one year or the operating cycle, whichever is longer.

Primary liability. A liability for which a person is directly responsible as contrasted with one which is contingent or secondary.

Secondary liability. A liability in the nature of a contigent claim such as the liability of a guarantor as contrasted with that of a strict surety or comaker. A guarantor's liability does not arise until the principal debtor has failed to pay the creditor.

Liability created by statute. One depending for its existence on the enactment of a statute, and not on the contract of the parties. One which would not exist but for the statute.

Liability for damages. Liability for an amount to be ascertained by trial of the facts in particular cases.

Liability imposed by law. Liability imposed in a definite sum by a final judgment against assured. Total liability imposed by law upon a person.

Liability insurance. Contract by which one party promises on consideration to compensate or reimburse other if he shall suffer loss from specified cause or to guaranty or indemnify or secure him against loss from that cause. That type of insurance protection which indemnifies one from liability to third persons as contrasted with insurance coverage for losses sustained by the insured. *See also* Insurance.

Liability limits. The sum beyond which a liability insurance company does not protect the insured on a particular policy. Most policies covering liability for bodily injury have two limits, a limit of liability to any one person, and, subject to the personal limit, another and usually higher limit for any single accident, where more than one person is involved.

Liable. Bound or obliged in law or equity; responsible; chargeable; answerable; compellable to make satisfaction, compensation, or restitution. Obligated; accountable for or chargeable with. Condition of being bound to respond because a wrong has occurred. Condition out of which a legal liability might arise. Justly or legally responsible or answerable.

Exposed or subject to a given contingency, risk, or casualty, which is more or less probable. Exposed, as to damage, penalty, expense, burden, or anything unpleasant or dangerous. *See also* Liability.

Future possible or probable happening which may not actually occur, and relates to an occurrence within the range of possibility. In all probability. *See also* Contingency; Contingent.

Libel /láybəl/. A method of defamation expressed by print, writing, pictures, or signs. In its most general sense, any publication that is injurious to the reputation of another. A false and unprivileged publication in writing of defamatory material. A maliciously written or printed publication which tends to blacken a person's reputation or to expose him to public hatred, contempt, or ridicule, or to injure him in his business or profession.

Accusation in writing or printing against the character of a person which affects his reputation, in that it tends to hold him up to ridicule, contempt, shame, disgrace, or obloquy, to degrade him in the estimation of the community, to induce an evil opinion of him in the minds of rightthinking persons, to make him an object of reproach, to diminish his respectability or abridge his comforts, to change his position in society for the worse, to dishonor or discredit him in the estimation of the public, or his friends and acquaintances, or to deprive him of friendly intercourse in society, or cause him to be shunned or avoided, or where it is charged that one has violated his public duty as a public officer. Almost any language which upon its face has a natural tendency to injure a man's reputation, either generally or with respect to his occupation.

States are free to fashion their own law of defamation of a private person so long as they do not impose liability without fault.

There can be no presumption of malice or bad faith consistent with freedom of the press under First Amend., U.S.Const. if plaintiff is a public figure. Malice must be proved on a showing that defendant published material either knowing it to be false or recklessly without regard as to whether it is true or false. N. Y. Times v. Sullivan, 376 U.S. 254, 84 S.Ct. 710, 11 L.Ed.2d 686.

See also Actionable per quod; Actionable per se; Criminal *(Criminal libel)*; Defamation; False implication libel; False light privacy; Innuendo; Libelous per quod; Libelous per se; Malice; Obscene libel; Privilege; Publication; Seditious libel; Single publication rule; Trade libel. *Compare* Slander.

Constitutional privilege. Prior to New York Times v. Sullivan, 376 U.S. 254, 84 S.Ct. 710, 11 L.Ed.2d 686 (1964), media comment on the conduct of public officials or public figures was free from liability for libel only in certain limited circumstances, usually difficult to prove at trial. If a statement of fact was involved, it had to be substantially true; if a comment or opinion was

involved, it had to be based on true facts which fully and fairly justified the comment or opinion. The United States Supreme Court, however, in a series of decisions beginning with New York Times Co. v. Sullivan, imposed constitutional limitations on State libel laws, based upon the First Amendment guarantees of freedom of speech and press. In New York Times, the Supreme Court eroded the prior common law libel standard of strict liability, holding that misstatements of fact or unjustified comments or opinions published by the media about the conduct of public officials were constitutionally privileged, unless the false or unjustified material was published with "actual malice," *i.e.,* with actual knowledge of falsity or with reckless disregard of probable falsity. By requiring a public official plaintiff to prove actual malice on the part of defendant, the burden of proving that the material was false was shifted to plaintiff, contrary to the common law rule which presumed falsity.

Group libel. The holding up of a group to ridicule, scorn or contempt to a respectable and considerable part of the community. The plaintiff must prove that he is a member of the group.

Pleadings. Formerly, the initiatory pleading in an admiralty action, corresponding to the declaration, bill or complaint. Since 1966 the Federal Rules of Civil Procedure and Supp. Admiralty Rules have governed admiralty actions and as such, admiralty actions are now commenced by complaint.

Libelant /láybələnt/. Formerly, the complainant or party who files a libel in an ecclesiastical or admiralty case, corresponding to the plaintiff in actions at law. *See* Libel *(Pleadings).*

Libelee /làybəlíy/. Formerly, a party against whom a libel has been filed in an ecclesiastical court or in admiralty, corresponding to the defendant in actions at law. *See* Libel *(Pleadings).*

Libelous /láybləs/. Defamatory; of the nature of a libel; constituting or involving libel. *See also* Libel.

Libelous per quod /láybləs pər kwód/. Expressions "libelous per quod" are such as require that their injurious character or effect be established by allegation and proof. They are those expressions which are not actionable upon their face, but which become so by reason of the peculiar situation or occasion upon which the words are written. Publications which are susceptible of two reasonable interpretations, one of which is defamatory and the other is not, or publications which are not obviously defamatory, but which become so when considered in connection with innuendo, colloquium, and explanatory circumstances. *Compare* Actionable per quod.

Libelous per se /láyblǝs pǝr síy/. A publication is libelous *per se* when the words are of such a character that an action may be brought upon them without the necessity of showing any special damage, the imputation being such that the law will presume that any one so slandered must have suffered damage. To render words "libelous per se," the words must be of such character that a presumption of law will arise therefrom that the plaintiff has been degraded in the estimation of his friends or of the public or has suffered some other loss either in his property, character, reputation, or business or in his domestic or social relations. When a publication is "libelous per se", that is, defamatory on its face, it is actionable per se; *i.e.* one need not prove that he received any injury as a result of the publication in order to recover damages, and in such a case general damages for loss of personal or business reputation are recoverable and no averments or proof of special damages are necessary. *Compare* Actionable per se.

Liber, *adj.* /láybǝr/. Lat. Free; open and accessible, as applied to courts, places, etc.; of the state or condition of a freeman, as applied to persons. Exempt from the service or jurisdiction of another.

Liberal /líb(ǝ)rǝl/. Free in giving; generous; not restrained or narrow-minded; not literal or strict.

Liberal construction *or* **interpretation** /líb(ǝ)rǝl kǝnstrǝ́kshǝn/°ǝntǝ̀rprǝtéyshǝn/. *See* Construction.

Liberty. Freedom from all restraints except such as are justly imposed by law. Freedom from restraint, under conditions essential to the equal enjoyment of this same right by others; freedom regulated by law. The absence of arbitrary restraint, not immunity from reasonable regulations and prohibitions imposed in the interests of the community.

The "liberty" guaranteed and protected by constitutional provisions denotes not only freedom from unauthorized physical restraint, but embraces also the freedom of an individual to use and enjoy his faculties in all lawful ways, acquire useful knowledge, marry, establish a home, and bring up children, worship God according to the dictates of his own conscience, live and work where he chooses, engage in any of the common and lawful occupations of life, enter into all contracts which may be proper and essential to carrying out successfully the foregoing purposes, and generally to enjoy those privileges long recognized at common law as essential to the orderly pursuit of happiness by free people. *See also* Liberty *interest, below.*

Also, a franchise or personal privilege, being some part of the sovereign power, vested in an individual, either by grant or prescription.

The term is used in the expression, rights, liberties, and franchises, as a word of the same general class and meaning with those words and privileges. This use of the term is said to have been strictly conformable to its sense as used in Magna Charta and in English declarations of rights, statutes, grants, etc.

In a derivative sense, the place, district, or boundaries within which a special franchise is enjoyed, an immunity claimed, or a jurisdiction exercised. In this sense, the term is commonly used in the plural; as the "liberties of the city."

Civil liberty. The liberty of a member of society, being a man's natural liberty, so far restrained by human laws (and no further) as is necessary and expedient for the general advantage of the public. The power of doing whatever the laws permit. The greatest amount of absolute liberty which can, in the nature of things, be equally possessed by every citizen in a state. Guaranteed protection against interference with the interests and rights held dear and important by large classes of civilized men, or by all the members of a state, together with an effectual share in the making and administration of the laws, as the best apparatus to secure that protection. *See* Civil rights.

Liberty interest. An interest recognized as protected by the due process clauses of state and federal constitutions. U.S.C.A. Const.Amend. 5, 14. Generally included are liberties guaranteed by the first eight amendments of the United States Constitution, as well as interests created when states either legislatively or administratively impose limitations on their discretion and require that a specific standard prevail in decision making.

Liberty of a port. In marine insurance, a license or permission incorporated in a marine policy allowing the vessel to touch and trade at a designated port other than the principal port of destination.

Liberty of conscience. Liberty for each individual to decide for himself what is to him religious. *See, also, Religious liberty,* as defined below.

Liberty of contract. The ability at will, to make or abstain from making, a binding obligation enforced by the sanctions at the law. The right to contract about one's affairs, including the right to make contracts of employment, and to obtain the best terms one can as the result of private bargaining. It includes the corresponding right to accept a contract proposed. There is, however, no absolute freedom of contract. The government may regulate or forbid any contract reasonably calculated to affect injuriously public interest. It means freedom from arbitrary or unreasonable restraint, not immunity from reasonable regulation to safeguard public interest; or the right to make contracts with competent persons on a plane of relative parity or freedom of choice and within the limits allowed or not forbidden by law. See Art. I, § 10, U.S. Constitution.

Liberty of speech. Freedom accorded by the Constitution (First Amendment of U.S.Const.) or laws to express opinions and facts by word of mouth, uncontrolled by any censorship or restrictions of government. As used in Constitution, "freedom of speech" means freedom of speech as it was understood by the common law when the Constitution was adopted. *See* however Clear and present danger doctrine. *See also* Symbolic speech.

Liberty of the globe. In marine insurance, a license or permission incorporated in a marine policy authorizing the vessel to go to any part of the world, instead of being confined to a particular port of destination.

Liberty of the press. The right to print and publish the truth, from good motives and for justifiable ends, as guaranteed by First Amendment of U.S. Constitution. The right to print without any previous license, subject to the consequences of the law. The right to publish whatever one may please; and to be protected against any responsibility for so doing except so far as such publications, from their blasphemy, obscenity, or scandalous character, may be a public offense, or as by their falsehood and malice they may injuriously affect the standing, reputation, or pecuniary interests of individuals. Immunity from previous restraints or [from] censorship. *See* Censor; Censorship; Prior restraint.

Personal liberty. The right or power of locomotion; of changing situation, or moving one's person to whatsoever place one's own inclination may direct, without imprisonment or restraint, unless by due course of law.

Political liberty. Liberty of the citizen to participate in the operations of government, and particularly in the making and administration of the laws.

Religious liberty. Freedom, as guaranteed by First Amendment of U.S. Constitution, from constraint, or control in matters affecting the conscience, religious beliefs, and the practice of religion. Freedom to entertain and express any or no system of religious opinions, and to engage in or refrain from any form of religious observance or public or private religious worship, not inconsistent with the peace and good order of society and the general welfare. *See also* Freedom of religion; Religion.

License. A personal privilege to do some particular act or series of acts on land without possessing any estate or interest therein, and is ordinarily revocable at the will of the licensor and is not assignable. The permission by competent author-

ity to do an act which, without such permission, would be illegal, a trespass, a tort, or otherwise not allowable. Certificate or the document itself which gives permission. Leave to do thing which licensor could prevent. Permission to do a particular thing, to exercise a certain privilege or to carry on a particular business or to pursue a certain occupation.

See also Bare *or* mere license; Certificate; Compulsory license; Exclusive license; Franchise; Licensee; Marriage license; Permit.

Executed license. That which exists when the licensed act has been done.

Executory license. That which exists where the licensed act has not been performed.

Express license. One which is granted in direct terms.

Implied license. One which is presumed to have been given from the acts of the party authorized to give it.

License bond. See Bond.

Patents. A written authority granted by the owner of a patent to another person empowering the latter to make or use the patented article for a limited period or in a limited territory. A permission to make, use or sell articles embodying invention. A transfer which does not affect the monopoly, except by estopping licensor from exercising his prohibitory powers in derogation of privileges conferred upon licensee. An assignment by the patentee to another of rights less in degree than the patent itself. Any right to make, use, or sell the patented invention, which is less than an undivided part interest in the patent itself. Any transfer of patent rights short of assignment. Language used by owner of patent, or any conduct on his part exhibited to another, from which that other may properly infer that owner consents to his use of patent, on which the other acts, constitutes a license. Transfer of exclusive right to do merely two of the three rights under patent to make, use, and vend invention. *See also* Patent.

Pleading. The defense of justification to an action of trespass that the defendant was authorized by the owner of the land to commit the trespass complained of. License is an affirmative defense which must be pleaded by defendant. Fed.R.Civil P. 8(c).

Real property. A license is ordinarily considered to be a mere personal or revocable privilege to perform an act or series of acts on the land of another. A privilege to go on premises for a certain purpose, but does not operate to confer on, or vest in, licensee any title, interest, or estate in such property. Such privilege is unassignable.

A license is distinguished from an "easement," which implies an interest in the land, and a "lease," or right to take the profits of land. It may be, however, and often, is, coupled with a grant of some interest in the land itself, or right to take the profits.

Simple license. One revocable at the will of the grantor; *i.e.,* one not coupled with a grant.

Streets and highways. A permit to use street is a mere license revocable at pleasure. The privilege of using the streets and highways by the operation thereon of motor carriers for hire can be acquired only by permission or license from the state or its political subdivisions.

Trade, business or calling. Authority or permission to do or carry on some trade or business which would otherwise be unlawful. Permission conferred by proper authority to pursue certain trade, profession, or calling. A license confers upon licensee neither contractual nor vested rights. *See also* Franchise.

Trademark. Permission to use a trademark in an area where the purported owner's goods have not become known and identified by his use of mark is a naked "license". *See* Trademark.

Licensee. A person who has a privilege to enter upon land arising from the permission or consent, express or implied, of the possessor of land but who goes on the land for his own purpose rather than for any purpose or interest of the possessor. For duty of care purposes, one who is privileged to enter or remain upon land by virtue of possessor's consent, whether given by invitation or permission.

Person to whom a license has been granted.

Formerly, the duty owed to a licensee was that of refraining from wilful, wanton and reckless conduct. This rule has been changed and now, in most jurisdictions, the occupier of land owes the licensee the duty of reasonable or due care.

See also Exclusive licensee; Invitee.

Licensee by invitation. A person who goes upon the lands of another with express or implied invitation to transact business with the owner or occupant or do some act to his advantage or to the mutual advantage of both the licensee and the owner or occupant. An invitee (*q.v.*).

Licensee by permission. One who, for his own convenience, curiosity, or entertainment, goes upon the premises of another by the owner's or occupant's permission or sufferance.

License fee *or* **tax.** Charge imposed by governmental body for the granting of a privilege. Charge or fee imposed primarily for the discouragement of dangerous employments, the protection of the safety of the public, or the regulation of relative rights, privileges, or duties as between individuals. Price paid to governmental or municipal authority for a license to engage in and pursue a particular calling or occupation. Tax on

privilege of exercising corporate franchise. The term "license tax" includes both charge imposed under police power for privilege of obtaining license to conduct particular business, and tax imposed upon business for sole purpose of raising revenue; "license tax" being defined as sum exacted for privilege of carrying on particular occupation. Where a fee is exacted and something is required or permitted in addition to the payment of the sum, either to be done by the licensee, or by some regulation or restriction imposed on him, then the fee is a "license fee". A license fee is charge made primarily for regulation, with the fee to cover cost and expenses of supervision or regulation. *See also* Franchise tax.

License tax. *See* License fee *or* tax.

Licensing. The sale of a license permitting the use of patents, trademarks, or other technology to another firm. *See also* Cross-licensing.

Licensing involves the many procedures administrative agencies perform in conjunction with issuance of various types of licenses.

Licensing power. The authority in a governmental body to grant a license to pursue a particular activity; *e.g.* license to sell liquor.

Licensor /láysənsər/. The person who gives or grants a license.

Lie, *n.* A falsehood uttered for the purpose of deception; an intentional statement of an untruth designed to mislead another; anything which misleads or deceives; it means an untruth deliberately told; the uttering or acting of that which is false for the purpose of deceiving; intentional misstatement. *See* Perjury.

Lie, *v.* To subsist; to exist; to be sustainable; to be proper or available. Thus the phrase "an action will not *lie* " means that an action cannot be sustained, or that there is no ground upon which to found the action.

Lie detector. *See* Polygraph.

Lien /líy(ə)n/. A claim, encumbrance, or charge on property for payment of some debt, obligation or duty. Qualified right of property which a creditor has in or over specific property of his debtor, as security for the debt or charge or for performance of some act. Right or claim against some interest in property created by law as an incident of contract. Right to enforce charge upon property of another for payment or satisfaction of debt or claim. Right to retain property for payment of debt or demand. Security for a debt, duty or other obligation. Tie that binds property to a debt or claim for its satisfaction. The word is a generic term and, standing alone, includes liens acquired by contract or by operation of law.

A change against or interest in property to secure payment of a debt or performance of an obligation. Bankruptcy Code § 101.

Lien *by operation of law.* Exists where the law itself, without the stipulation of the parties, raises a lien, as an implication or legal consequence from the relation of the parties or the circumstances of their dealings. Liens of this species may arise either under the rules of common law or of equity or under a statute. In the first case they are called "common-law liens;" in the second, "equitable liens;" in the third, "statutory liens."

See also Agent's lien; Architect's lien; Artisan's lien; Attorney's lien; Banker's lien; Charging Lien; Chattel lien; Common-law lien; Concurrent liens; Deferred lien; Equitable lien; Execution lien; Factor's lien; First lien; Floating lien; General lien; Inchoate lien; Involuntary lien; Judgment lien; Judicial lien; Laborers' lien; Maritime lien; Materialman's lien; Mechanic's lien; Municipal lien; Retaining lien; Second lien; Secret lien; Special lien; Statutory lien; Tax lien; Vendor's lien; Warehousemen's lien.

Lien account. Such statement of claims as fairly apprises property owner and public of nature and amount of demand asserted as lien.

Lien creditor. One whose debt or claim is secured by a lien on particular property, as distinguished from a "general" creditor, who has no such security. A creditor who has acquired a lien on the property involved, by attachment, levy or the like, and includes an assignee for benefit of creditors from the time of assignment, and a trustee in bankruptcy from the date of the filing of the petition, or a receiver in equity from the time of appointment. U.C.C. § 9–301(3). *See also* Creditor.

Lienee /liyniy/. One whose property is subject to a lien.

Lien of attachment. An encumbrance on property seized through the pre-judgment remedy of attachment that is inchoate when it first arises, usually upon the sheriff's levy of the property, and that becomes final and perfected upon judgment for the attaching creditor in the action who caused attachment to issue. For purposes of priority against third parties' claims to the property, a lien of attachment perfected by judgment dates from the time the lien first arose. *See* Attachment.

Lien of execution. An encumbrance that attaches by operation of law to a judgment debtor's real and personal property when the property is subjected to execution process and that gives the execution creditor a priority over subsequent transferees of the property and also over prior unrecorded conveyances of interests in the property. *See* Attachment; Execution.

Lien of garnishment. Encumbrance on property of a debtor held by a garnishee that attaches in favor of the garnishing creditor when garnishment summons is served upon the garnishee and that also impounds credits owed by the garnishee to the debtor so that they must be paid to the garnishing creditor. *See* Garnishment.

Lienor /liy(ə)nər/. The person having or owning a lien; one who has a right of lien upon property of another.

Lien waiver. A waiver of mechanic's lien rights, signed by subcontractors so that the owner or general contractor can receive a draw on a construction loan.

Lie to. To adjoin.

Life. That state of animals, humans, and plants or of an organized being, in which its natural functions and motions are performed, or in which its organs are capable of performing their functions. The interval between birth and death. The sum of the forces by which death is resisted.

"Life" protected by the Federal Constitution includes all personal rights and their enjoyment of the faculties, acquiring useful knowledge, the right to marry, establish a home, and bring up children, freedom of worship, conscience, contract, occupation, speech, assembly and press.

See also Natural life; Useful life; Viability; Viable child; Wrongful life.

Life annuity. An engagement to pay an income yearly during the life of some person; also the sum thus promised. An annuity, depending on the continuance of an assigned life or lives, is sometimes called a life annuity. *See also* Annuity.

Life beneficiary. One who receives payments or other rights from a trust for his or her lifetime.

Life care contract. An agreement in which one party is assured of care and maintenance for his natural life in consideration of a transfer of property to the other party. Such contracts exist, for example, between elderly persons and nursing homes.

Life-cycle costing. The accumulation of costs for activities that occur over the entire life cycle of a product from inception to abandonment by the manufacturer and consumer.

Life estate. An estate whose duration is limited to the life of the party holding it, or some other person. *See also* Life interest.

A legal arrangement whereby the beneficiary (*i.e.,* the life tenant) is entitled to the income from the property for his or her life. Upon the death of the life tenant, the property will go to the holder of the remainder interest or to the grantor by reversion.

Life expectancy. The period of time in which a person of a given age and sex is expected to live according to statistical (*i.e.* actuarial) tables. *See also* Actuarial table; Life tables.

Life in being. A phrase used in the common-law and statutory rules against perpetuities, meaning the remaining duration of the life of a person who is in existence at the time when the deed or will takes effect.

Life insurance. *See* Insurance.

Life insurance proceeds. Generally, life insurance proceeds paid to a beneficiary upon the death of the insured are exempt from Federal income tax. An exception is provided where a life insurance contract has been transferred for valuable consideration to another individual who assumes ownership rights. In such case the proceeds are income to the assignee to the extent that the proceeds exceed the amount paid for the policy plus any subsequent premiums paid. Insurance proceeds may be subject to the Federal estate tax if the decedent retained any incidents of ownership in the policy prior to death or if the proceeds are payable to his estate. I.R.C. §§ 101 and 2042.

Life insurance reserves. Fund which, together with future premiums and interest, will be sufficient to pay future claims.

Life insurance trust. Type of trust, the res of which consists in whole or in part of life insurance policies owned by the trustees and payable to the trust on the death of the insured. A device commonly used in estate planning.

Life interest. A claim or interest in real or personal property, not amounting to ownership, and limited by a term of life, either that of the person in whom the right is vested or that of another. *See also* Life estate.

Life-land, *or* **life-hold.** Land held on a lease for lives.

Life of a writ. The period during which a writ (execution, etc.) remains effective and can lawfully be served or levied, terminating with the day on which, by law or by its own terms, it is to be returned into court.

Life or limb. The phrase "life or limb" within constitutional provision that no person shall be subject for the same offense to be twice put in jeopardy of life or limb is not construed strictly but applies to any criminal penalty. Fifth Amend., U.S.Const.

Life policy. *See* Insurance *(Life insurance).*

Life sentence. *See* Sentence.

Life sustaining procedures. Such procedures which may be suspended on a court order or pursuant to a living will (or other type of medical care directive) in case of, for example, a comatose and terminally ill individual, are medical procedures which utilize mechanical or other artificial means to sustain, restore, or supplant a vital function, which serve only or primarily to prolong the moment of death, and where, in the judgment of the attending and consulting physicians, as reflected in the patient's medical records, death is imminent if such procedures are not utilized. *See also* Health care proxy; Medical directives; Patient Self Determination Act; Power of Attorney *(Durable power of attorney);* Right to die laws; Will *(Living will).*

Life tables. Statistical *(i.e.* actuarial) tables exhibiting the probable proration of persons who will live to reach different ages. Such tables are used for many purposes, such as the computation of the present value of annuities, dower rights, etc.; and for the computation of damages resulting from injuries which destroy the earning capacity of a person, or those resulting from the death of a person to those who are dependent upon him. *See also* Actuarial tables.

Life tenancy. An estate in real property in which the tenant has a freehold interest for his life or for the life of another *(pur autre vie).*

Life tenant. One who holds an estate in lands for the period of his own life or that of another certain person.

LIFO. *See* Last-in, first-out.

Light, right to. A privilege or easement to have light admitted into one's building by the openings made for that purpose, without obstruction or obscuration by the walls of adjacent or neighboring structures. *See also* Easement *(Light and air easement).*

Lights, ancient. English doctrine under which a landowner acquired, by uninterrupted use for 20 years, an easement or right by prescription over adjoining land for the unobstructed passage of light and air.

Like. Equal in quantity, quality, or degree or exactly corresponding. Also means having the same, or nearly the same, appearance, qualities, or characteristics; resembling another; same manner; similar or substantially similar.

Like-kind exchange. An exchange of property held for productive use in a trade or business or for investment (except inventory and stocks and bonds) for other investment or trade or business property. Unless cash is received, the exchange is nontaxable. I.R.C. § 1031. Test for determining whether exchanged properties are of "like kind," such that gain from the exchange is not recognized for federal income tax purposes, is whether the property is of the same nature or character and a mere difference in grade or quality does not disqualify the exchange. *See also* Boot.

Like-kind property. *See* Like-kind exchange.

Likelihood. Probability. The word imports something less than reasonably certain. *See* Likely.

Likelihood of confusion. Touchstone of trademark infringement under Lanham Trade–Mark Act is "likelihood of confusion," or whether substantial number of ordinarily prudent purchasers are likely to be misled or confused as to source of different product. Factors to be considered in determining "likelihood of confusion" are the degree of resemblance between the marks in appearance, pronunciation, translation and suggestiveness, the intent of the second user in adopting the allegedly infringing mark, similarity of circumstances and conditions surrounding the purchase of the goods involved and the degree of care likely to be exercised by purchasers.

Likely. Probable. In all probability. It is a word of general usage and common understanding, broadly defined as of such nature or so circumstantial as to make something probable and having better chance of existing or occurring than not.

Limine. *See* Motion in limine.

Limit, *v.* To abridge, confine, restrain, and restrict. To mark out; to define; to fix the extent of. Thus, to limit an estate means to mark out or to define the period of its duration, and the words employed in deeds for this purpose are thence termed "words of limitation," and the act itself is termed "limiting the estate."

Limit, *n.* A bound; a restriction; a restraint; a circumscription. Boundary, border, or outer line of thing. Extent of power, right or authority conferred.

Limitation. Restriction or circumspection; settling an estate or property. A certain time allowed by a statute for bringing litigation (*see* Statute of limitations, below). The provisions of state constitution are not a "grant" but a "limitation" of legislative power. *See also* Proviso.

Corporations. Under statute providing that all corporations expiring by their own "limitation" shall for certain purposes be continued as bodies corporate for a term of three years, the word "limitation" is an act of limiting, a restriction of power, a qualification.

Estates. The restriction or circumscription of an estate, in the conveyance by which it is granted, in respect to the interest of the grantee or its duration. The specific curtailment or confinement of an estate, by the terms of the grant, so that it cannot endure beyond a certain period or a designated contingency. A "limitation" on a grant determines an estate upon the happening of the event itself without the necessity of doing any act to regain the estate, such as re-entry. A limitation, whether made by the express words of the party or existing in intendment of law, circumscribes the continuance of time for which the property is to be enjoyed, and by positive and certain terms, or by reference to some event which possibly may happen, marks the period at which the time of enjoyment shall end.

Collateral limitation. One which gives an interest in an estate for a specified period, but makes the right of enjoyment to depend on some collateral event, as an estate to A. till B. shall go to Rome.

Conditional limitation. A condition followed by a limitation over to a third person in case the condition be not fulfilled or there be a breach of it. A conditional limitation is where an estate is so expressly defined and limited by the words of its creation that it cannot endure for any longer time than till the contingency happens upon which the estate is to fail. Between conditional limitations and estates depending on conditions subsequent there is this difference: that in the former the estate determines as soon as the contingency happens; but in the latter it endures until the grantor or his heirs take advantage of the breach.

In landlord and tenant law, a provision in a lease which gives a landlord added protection by enabling the landlord to end the term before its natural expiration date. Such exists, for example, when lease provides that it shall terminate upon the happening of an event without any further election, entry, or re-entry.

Contingent limitation. When a remainder in fee is limited upon any estate which would by the common law be adjudged a fee tail, such a remainder is valid as a contingent limitation upon a fee, and vests in possession on the death of the first taker without issue living at the time of his death.

Limitation in law. A limitation in law, or an estate limited, is an estate to be holden only during the continuance of the condition under which it was granted, upon the determination of which the estate vests immediately in him in expectancy.

Limitation over. This term includes any estate in the same property created or contemplated by the conveyance, to be enjoyed after the first estate granted expires or is exhausted. Thus, in a gift to A. for life, with remainder to the heirs of his body, the remainder is a "limitation over" to such heirs.

Special limitation. A qualification serving to mark out the bounds of an estate, so as to determine it *ipso facto* in a given event, without action, entry, or claim, before it would, or might, otherwise expire by force of, or according to, the general limitation.

Title by limitation. A prescriptive title; one which is indefeasible because of the expiration of the time prescribed by the statute of limitations for the bringing of actions to test or defeat it.

Words of limitation. In a conveyance or will, words which have the effect of marking the duration of an estate are termed "words of limitation." Thus, in a grant to A. and his heirs, the words "and his heirs" are words of limitation, because they show that A. is to take an estate in fee-simple and do not give his heirs anything.

Limitation of actions. *See* Statute of limitations, below.

Statute of limitations. Statutes of the federal government and various states setting maximum time periods during which certain actions can be brought or rights enforced. After the time period set out in the applicable statute of limitations has run, no legal action can be brought regardless of whether any cause of action ever existed.

A statute prescribing limitations to the right of action on certain described causes of action or criminal prosecutions; that is, declaring that no suit shall be maintained on such causes of action, nor any criminal charge be made, unless brought within a specified period of time after the right accrued. See *e.g.* 28 U.S.C.A. §§ 2401, 2501 (statutes of limitation for actions against U.S. government). In criminal cases, however, a statute of limitation is an act of grace, a surrendering by sovereign of its right to prosecute. See *e.g.* 18 U.S.C.A. § 3281 et seq. (statutes of limitations for federal criminal prosecutions). *See also* Laches; Statute *(Statute of repose).*

Statute of repose compared. While statutes of limitation are sometimes called "statutes of repose," the former bars right of action unless it is filed within a specified period of time after injury occurs, while "statute of repose" terminates any right of action after a specific time has elapsed, regardless of whether there has as yet been an injury. *See also* Statute *(Statute of repose).*

Words of limitation. Words that limit or define the interest in land that a grantee receives such as "and his heirs." Language in a deed indicating how long the estate granted is to endure.

Limitation of liability acts. State and federal statutes that limit liability for certain types of damages (*e.g.*, pain and suffering) or limit liability of certain persons or groups (*e.g.*, liability of corporate directors for acts of corporation), or limit time period in which action can be maintained (*see* Limitation *(Statute of limitations))*. *See also* Cap; Federal Tort Claims Act; Sovereign Immunity; No-fault.

Limitation of prosecutions. *See* Limitation *(Statute of limitations).*

Limitations, statute of. *See* Limitation *(Statute of limitations).*

Limited. Restricted; bounded; prescribed. Confined within positive bounds; restricted in duration, extent, or scope.

As to *limited* Company; Divorce; Fee; and Partnership, see those titles.

Ltd. A designation following a corporate business name and indicating its corporate and limited liability status. It is found most commonly after British and Canadian corporate names, though it is sometimes used in the United States.

Limited administration. Administration powers and duties of a temporary character, granted for a particular period, or for a special or particular purpose. *See e.g.* Limited executor.

Limited admissibility. In law of evidence, testimony or things may be admitted into evidence for a restricted purpose, and the trial judge should so instruct the jury at the time of its admission; *e.g.* prior contradictory statements are admissible to impeach but not admissible for the truth of the statements. However, if the evidence has multiple purposes, one being in violation of a constitutional protection for a criminal defendant, such evidence should not be admitted.

Similarly, evidence may frequently be competent as against one party, but not as against another, in which event the practice is to admit the evidence, with an instruction, if requested, that the jury are to consider it only as to the party against whom it is competent. Fed.Evid.R. 105.

Limited appeal. An appeal from only adverse portions of a decree; such is limited to the particular portions of the decree appealed from. *See also* Interlocutory appeal; Interlocutory Appeals Act.

Limited court. Where special authority, in derogation of common law, is conferred by statute on a court of general jurisdiction, it becomes an "inferior or limited court". For example, a probate court is a court of limited jurisdiction. *See* Limited *or* special jurisdiction.

Limited divorce. A divorce decree or judgment may be restricted to a dissolution of the marriage with no provision for support. In another sense, term refers to a divorce a mensa et thoro (from bed and board) with no right to remarry.

Limited executor. An executor whose appointment is qualified by limitations as to the time or place wherein, or the subject-matter whereon, the office is to be exercised; as distinguished from one whose appointment is absolute, *i.e.*, certain and immediate, without any restriction in regard to the testator's effects or limitation in point of time.

Limited guaranty. Such a guaranty as is ordinarily restricted in its application to a single transaction.

Limited liability. *See* Limitation of liability acts.

Limited liability company. A form of business organization, authorized by statute in certain states, characterized by limited liability, management by members or managers, and limitations on the transferability of ownership interests.

Limited *or* **special jurisdiction.** Jurisdiction of court which is confined to particular types of cases or actions, or which can be exercised only under the limitations and circumstances prescribed by the statute. A court's power over an action is governed generally by statute and some courts have limited authority or power and the limitation is in terms of the nature of the case (*e.g.* probate courts), or the amount in controversy (*e.g.* small claims court), or the type of crime with which the defendant is charged or the age of the accused (*e.g.* juvenile courts). *See also* Limited court.

Limited owner. A tenant for life, or by the curtesy, or other person not having absolute ownership.

Limited partner. A person who has been admitted to a limited partnership as a limited partner in accordance with the partnership agreement. Uniform Partnership Act, § 101. A partner whose liability to third party creditors of the partnership is limited to the amount invested by such partner in the partnership. *See* Limited partnership. *Compare* General partner.

Limited partnership. Type of partnership comprised of one or more general partners who manage business and who are personally liable for partnership debts, and one or more limited partners who contribute capital and share in profits but who take no part in running business and incur no liability with respect to partnership obligations beyond contribution.

A partnership formed by two or more persons under the provisions of the Uniform Limited Partnership Act, having as members one or more general partners and one or more limited partners. The limited partners, as such, are not bound by the obligations of the partnership. Uniform Limited Partnership Act § 101(7). Most all states have adopted the Uniform Limited Partnership Act.

See also General partner; Limited partner.

Master limited partnership. A standard limited partnership in which its interests are publicly traded. "Master" merely refers to the two tier form often employed to meet state law requirements as to limited liability.

Limited payment plan. A policy upon a "limited payment plan" is a paid-up policy, and insurance upon which no further premium is to be paid.

Limited policy. Insurance policy specifically excluding certain classes or types of loss.

Limited power of appointment. Power of appointment is limited when it is exercisable only in favor of persons or a class of persons designated in the instrument creating the power. *See also* Power of appointment.

Limited publication. Copyrighted material loses its protected status if it is published without notice of copyright; an exception to such doctrine exists for material whose publication can be characterized as "limited," but to qualify as a "limited publication," the publication must communicate the contents of a manuscript to a definitely selected group and for a limited purpose without the right of diffusion, reproduction, distribution or sale. Circulation must be restricted both as to persons and purpose or it cannot be called a private or limited publication.

Limit order. Requests by customers to purchase or sell securities at the market price existing when the order reaches the exchange floor. A restriction on the sale or purchase of a security placed by a customer with a broker, limiting the price at which the customer is willing to buy or sell.

Lincoln's Inn /línkənz ín/. An inn of court. *See* Inns of Court.

Lindbergh Act. Federal law which punishes kidnapping for ransom or reward when the victim is transported from one state to another or to a foreign country. The failure to release the victim within 24 hours creates a rebuttable presumption that such person has been transported in interstate or foreign commerce. 18 U.S.C.A. § 1201.

Line. A demarcation, border, or limit. The boundary or line of division between two estates. Person's trade, occupation or business. Carrier's route.

Building line. See Building line.

Collateral line. See Descent.

Descent. See Descent.

Direct line. See Descent.

Line by line budget. A detailed itemization of all expenditures by budget line.

Line item veto. See Veto.

Line of credit. A margin or fixed limit of credit granted by one to another, typically from bank, retailer, or credit card issuer to customer, to the full extent of which the latter may avail himself in his dealings with the former, but which he must not exceed; usually intended to cover a series of transactions, in which case, when the customer's line of credit is nearly or quite exhausted, he is expected to reduce his indebtedness by payments before drawing upon it further. The maximum borrowing power (*i.e.* credit limit) of a person from a financial institution, credit card issuer, or the like. Agreement with bank or number of banks for short-term borrowings on demand.

Line of duty. In military law and usage, an act is said to be done, or an injury sustained, "in the line of duty," when done or suffered in the performance or discharge of a duty incumbent upon the individual in his character as a member of the military or naval forces. An injury suffered or disease contracted by a sailor is considered to have been in "line of duty" unless actually caused by something for which sailor is responsible which intervenes between his performance of duty and the injury or disease. Phrase in Federal Tort Claims Act, as applicable to military and naval personnel, has no broader significance than "scope of employment" as used in master and servant cases.

Maternal line. *See* Maternal line.

Paternal line. *See* Paternal line.

Public utilities. *See* Public utility.

Lineage /lín(i)yəj/. Race; progeny; family, ascending or descending. Line of descent from an ancestor, hence, family, race, stock. *See also* Descent.

Lineal /líniyəl/. That which comes in a line; especially a direct line, as from father to son. Collateral relationship is not called "lineal," though the expression "collateral line," is not unusual. Proceeding in direct or unbroken line, hereditary, unbroken in course; distinguished from collateral, as lineal descent, lineal succession, having an ancestral basis or right. *See also* Descent.

Lineal consanguinity /líniyəl kònsæŋgwínətiy/. That kind of consanguinity which subsists between persons of whom one is descended in a *direct line* from the other; as between a particular person and his father, grandfather, great-grandfather, and so upward, in the direct ascending line; or between the same person and his son, grandson, great-grandson, and so downwards in the direct descending line. *See* Descent.

Lineal descendent. A person in the direct line of descent such as a child or grandchild as contrasted with a collateral descendent such as a niece.

Lineal descent. *See* Descent.

Lineal heir /líniyəl é(yə)r/. One who inherits in a line either ascending or descending from a common source as distinguished from a collateral heir. The words "lineal heirs" like "heirs of the body" mean all lineal descendants to the remotest posterity and are words of "inheritance" and not of "purchase", unless the instrument clearly shows that they were used in a restricted sense to denote "children". *See also* Heirs.

Lineals. Blood relatives of decedent.

Lineal warranty. A warranty by an ancestor from whom the title did or might have come to the heir.

Line employee. An employee who is directly responsible for achieving an organization's goals and objectives.

Line of credit. *See* Line (*Line of credit*).

Lines and corners. In deeds and surveys, boundary-lines and their angles with each other.

Lineup. A police identification procedure by which the suspect in a crime is exhibited, along with others with similar physical characteristics, before the victim or witness to determine if he can be identified as having committed the offense. To be accepted as valid, the lineup must meet certain standards and be free of undue suggestiveness. U. S. v. Wade, 388 U.S. 218, 87 S.Ct. 1926, 18 L.Ed.2d 1149. If the standards are met, the person who has identified the defendant may so testify at trial. "Lineup" involves and requires lining up of a number of individuals from which one of those lined up may or may not be identified as committer of a crime and there cannot be a one-man lineup.

Post-indictment lineups are considered to be a "critical stage" of criminal proceedings at which the accused has the constitutional right to be represented by counsel. Gilbert v. California, 388 U.S. 263, 87 S.Ct. 1951, 18 L.Ed. 1178.

Compare Show-up.

Link. A unit in a connected series; anything which serves to connect or bind together the things which precede and follow it. Thus, we speak of a "link in the chain of title." Something which binds together, or connects, separate things; a part of a connected series; a tie, a bond.

As a unit of land measurement, *see* Land measure.

Link-in-chain. The 5th Amendment (U.S.Const.) privilege against self incrimination protects a witness not only from the requirement of answering questions which might call for directly incriminating answers but also from answers which might tie or link the defendant to criminal activity in the chain of evidence. Immunity also protects one from such result.

Liquid. Said of a business with a substantial amount (the amount is unspecified) of working capital, especially quick assets. *See also* Liquidity.

Liquid assets. Cash, or assets readily convertible to cash.

Liquidate. To pay and settle. To convert assets to cash. To ascertain the amount, or the several amounts, of the liabilities of the debtor and apportion the assets toward discharge of the indebtedness. To assemble and mobilize the assets, settle with the creditors and the debtors and apportion the remaining assets, if any, among the stockholders or owners. To gather in the assets, convert them into cash and distribute them according to the legal rights of the parties interested. *See also* Bankruptcy proceedings; Liquidation; Settle; Settlement.

Liquidated. Ascertained; determined; fixed; settled; made clear or manifest. Cleared away; paid; discharged. Adjusted, certain, or settled. Made certain or fixed by agreement of parties or by operation of law. *See also* Liquidate; Liquidated claim; Liquidation; Settle; Settlement.

Liquidated account. An account whereof the amount is certain and fixed, either by the act and agreement of the parties or by operation of law.

Liquidated claim. Claim, amount of which has been agreed on by parties to action or is fixed by operation of law. A claim which can be determined with exactness from parties' agreement or by arithmetical process or application of definite rules of law, without reliance on opinion or discretion.

Liquidated damages. *See* Damages.

Liquidated debt. A debt is liquidated when it is certain what is due and how much is due. That which has been made certain as to amount due by agreement of parties or by operation of law. *Compare* Unliquidated debt.

Liquidated demand. A demand the amount of which has been ascertained or settled by agreement of the parties, or otherwise. Amount claimed is a "liquidated demand" if it is susceptible of being made certain in amount by mathematical calculations from factors which are or ought to be in possession or knowledge of party to be charged.

Liquidating distribution. A distribution by a partnership or corporation that is in complete liquidation of the entity's trade or business activities. Typically, such distributions generate capital gain or loss to the investors without regard, for instance, to the earnings and profits of the corporation or to the partnership's basis in the distributed property. They can, however, lead to recognized gain or loss at the corporate level. *See also* Liquidating dividend; Liquidation.

Liquidating dividend. A distribution of assets in the form of a dividend from a corporation that is reducing capital or going out of business. Such a payment may arise, for example, when management decides to sell off certain company assets and distribute the proceeds to the shareholders. Such a distribution may not be from current or retained earnings. *See also* Liquidating distribution.

Liquidating partner. The partner who upon the dissolution or insolvency of the firm, is appointed to settle its accounts, collect assets, adjust claims, and pay debts.

Liquidating trust. A trust, the object of which is liquidation as soon as possible.

Liquidation. The act or process of settling or making clear, fixed, and determinate that which before was uncertain or unascertained. Payment, satisfaction, or collection; realization on assets and discharge of liabilities. Winding up or settling with creditors and debtors.

With respect to winding up of affairs of corporation, is process of reducing assets to cash, discharging liabilities and dividing surplus or loss. Occurs when a corporation distributes its net assets to its shareholders and ceases its legal existence.

The settling of financial affairs of a business or individual, usually by liquidating (turning to cash) all assets for distribution to creditors, heirs, etc. It is to be distinguished from dissolution which is the end of the legal existence of a corporation. Liquidation may precede or follow dissolution, depending upon statutes.

See also Bankruptcy proceedings; Distressed sale; Distribution in liquidation; Liquidate; Liquidated; Receivership.

One month liquidation. A special election available to certain shareholders of a corporation which determines how the distributions received in liquidation by the electing shareholders will be treated for Federal income tax purposes. In order to qualify for the election, the corporation must be completely liquidated within the time span of any one calendar month. I.R.C. § 333.

Partial liquidation. A partial liquidation occurs when some of the corporation's assets are distributed to its shareholders (usually on a pro rata basis) and the corporation continues doing business in a contracted form. Distributions of cash or property beyond the amount of earned surplus of a corporation is a partial liquidation.

Tax implications. In a complete or partial liquidation of a corporation, amounts received by the shareholders in exchange for their stock are usually treated as a sale or exchange of the stock resulting in capital gain or loss treatment. Special rules apply to one month liquidations, twelve month liquidations, and the liquidation of a subsidiary.

Twelve-month liquidation. A provision of the Internal Revenue Code that requires a corporation selling property within the 12-month period from the adoption of a plan of liquidation to its complete liquidation to recognize no gain or loss on such sales. Generally, inventory is not included within the definition unless a bulk sale occurs. See I.R.C. § 337.

Liquidation dividend. Act or operation in winding up affairs of firm or corporation, a settling with its debtors and creditors, and an appropriation and distribution to its stockholders ratably of the amount of profit and loss. *See also* Liquidating dividend.

Liquidation price. A price paid for property sold to liquidate a debt. Usually less than market value since there is pressure to sell or a forced sale, either of which does not usually bring the highest price. *Compare* Going concern value.

Liquidation rights. The rights of a firm's securityholders in the event the firm liquidates.

Liquidator. A person appointed to carry out the winding up of a company. In England and Canada, a receiver who liquidates a corporation on dissolution.

Liquid debt /líkwəd dét/. A debt immediately and unconditionally due. *See* Liquidated debt.

Liquidity. The status or condition of a person or a business in terms of his or its ability to convert assets into cash. The degree to which an asset can be acquired or disposed of without danger of intervening loss in nominal value. Money is the most liquid asset.

With respect to securities markets, refers to the market characteristic of a security or commodity with enough units outstanding and traded to allow large transactions to occur without a substantial variation in price. Most shares traded at the New York Stock Exchange have liquidity.

Liquidity ratios. Ratios that measure the ability of a business to meet current debts as the obligations come due.

Liquor. Alcoholic beverage made by distillation; to be contrasted with wines which are made by fermentation. *See also* Intoxicating liquor.

Liquor offenses. Generic term describing crimes connected with the use, sale or abuse of intoxicating liquor or the absence of a license to sell liquor (*e.g.* federal liquor traffic offenses, 18 U.S.C.A. § 1261 et seq.). *See* Dram Shop Acts; Driving while intoxicated.

Lis /lís/. Lat. A controversy or dispute; a suit or action at law.

Lis alibi pendens /lís ǽləbay péndènz/. A suit pending elsewhere. The fact that proceedings are pending between a plaintiff and defendant in one court in respect to a given matter is a ground for preventing the plaintiff from taking proceedings in another court against the same defendant for the same object arising out of the same cause of action.

Lis pendens /lís péndènz/. A pending suit. Jurisdiction, power, or control which courts acquire over property in litigation pending action and until final judgment.

A common-law doctrine, now codified in many states so as to condition its effect on the filing of a notice, that binds a purchaser or encumbrancer of property to the results of any pending lawsuit which may affect the title to, any lien on, or possession of the property. Purpose of "lis pendens" is to notify prospective purchasers and encumbrancers that any interest acquired by them in property in litigation is subject to decision of court and while it is simply a notice of pending litigation the effect thereof on the owner of property is constraining.

Notice of lis pendens. A notice filed on public records for the purpose of warning all persons that the title to certain property is in litigation, and that they are in danger of being bound by an adverse judgment. The notice is for the purpose of preserving rights pending litigation. This is termed a "notice of pendency" in New York. CPLR § 6501.

List. A docket or calendar of cases ready for trial or argument, or of motions ready for hearing. Entering in an official list or schedule; as, to list property for taxation, to put into a list or catalogue, to register, to list a property with a real estate broker. Official registry of voters. *See also* Docket; Listing.

Listed. Included in a list; put on a list; *e.g.* on a list of taxable persons or property. *See* Listing.

Listed security. A security of a company that has met the registration requirements of the SEC and has been accepted for trading on a securities exchange, having complied with the rules of the stock exchange on which it is traded. Such requirements include submitting periodic financial reports and consenting to certain supervision. "Unlisted" securities are traded on the over-the-counter markets. *See also* Listing (*Securities*); Offering.

Dual listing. Listing of a security on more than one security exchange.

Listed security exchanges. Organized secondary security markets that operate at designated places of business. The New York Stock Exchange (NYSE) is an example of a listed security exchange.

Listing. *Real estate.* An agreement between an owner of real property and a real estate agent, whereby the agent agrees to attempt to secure a buyer or tenant for specific property at a certain price and terms in return for a fee or commission.

LISTING   644

The various types of real estate listings are as follows:

An *open* or *general listing* is the right to sell that may be given to more than one agent at a time. An *exclusive agency listing* is the right of one agent to be the only one other than the owner who may sell the property during a period of time. An *exclusive authorization to sell listing* is a written contract that gives one agent the sole right to sell the property during a time period. This means that even if the owner finds the buyer, the agent will get a commission. *Multiple listing* occurs when an agent with an exclusive listing shares information about the property sale with many members of a real estate association and shares the sale commission with an agent who finds the buyer. A *net listing* is an arrangement in which the seller sets a minimum price he or she will take for the property and the agent's commission is the amount the property sells for over that minimum selling price. *Nonexclusive listing* exists when the real estate broker has an exclusive listing as opposed to other agents, but the owner may sell the property without using an agent, and not be liable to pay a commission. Also called an agency agreement. An *open listing* obligates a seller to pay a commission when a specified broker makes a sale, but which reserves the right of the seller to sell his own property without paying a commission. Such listings may be given to any number of brokers on the same property.

See also Brokerage listing; Multiple listing; Open listing.

Securities. In securities, the contract between a firm and a stock exchange covering the trading of that firm's securities on the stock exchange. *See also* Listed security; Offering.

Taxation. "Listing property for taxation" is the making of a schedule or inventory of such property, whereby owner makes statement of property in response to assessor's inquiries. The word listing ordinarily implies an official listing of the persons and property to be taxed, and a valuation of the property of each person as a basis of apportionment.

Listing agent. The broker's representative who obtains a listing agreement with the seller, as opposed to the selling agent who may represent another broker.

Listing agreement. *See* Listing.

List of creditors. Documentation in the form of a list with names and addresses and amounts owed to creditors, required as a schedule in bankruptcy proceedings.

List price. The published or advertised price of goods which may change after negotiation and be reduced by a discount or rebate for prompt payment or volume purchase.

Lite pendente /láytiy pəndéntiy/. Lat. Pending the suit. *See also* Lis pendens.

Literacy. Term as generally defined requires both ability to read and ability to write a language.

Literacy test. Test required in certain states as a precondition to right to vote. Such tests are unconstitutional if invidiously discriminatory. The Voting Rights Act of 1965 suspended such tests in states where less than half the adult population were registered or had voted in the previous election.

Literal /lítərəl/. According to language; following expression in words. A literal construction of a document adheres closely to its words, without making differences for extrinsic circumstances; a literal performance of a condition is one which complies exactly with its terms.

Literal construction. The interpretation of a document according to its words alone without any consideration of the intent of the parties who drafted or signed it beyond the fact that they used such language.

Literary /lítərehriy/. Pertaining to literature; connected with authors and the study or use of books and writings.

Literary composition. An original result of mental production, developed in a series of written or printed words, arranged for an intelligent purpose, in an orderly succession of expressive combinations. *See also* Literary work.

Literary property. The right which entitles an author and his assigns to all the use and profit of his composition, to which no independent right is, through any act or omission on his or their part, vested in another person. The exclusive right of owner to possess, use and dispose of intellectual productions. The term denotes the corporal property in which an intellectual production is embodied; and it may consist of letters, lectures, sermons or addresses. *See also* Copyright; Literary work.

Literary work. Under Copyright Act, "literary works" are works, other than audiovisual works, expressed in words, numbers, or other verbal or numerical symbols or indicia, regardless of the nature of the material objects, such as books, periodicals, manuscripts, phonorecords, film, tapes, disks, or cards in which they are embodied. 17 U.S.C.A. § 101.

Literate. A person is literate if he can read and write a language. Knowledgable and educated.

Litigant. A party to a lawsuit (*i.e.* plaintiff or defendant); one engaged in litigation; usually spoken of active parties, not of nominal ones.

Litigate /lítəgeyt/. To dispute or contend in form of law; to settle a dispute or seek relief in a court of law; to carry on a lawsuit. To bring into or engage in litigation; the act of carrying on a suit in a law court; a judicial contest; hence, any controversy that must be decided upon evidence in a court of law. To make the subject of a lawsuit; to contest in law; to prosecute or defend by pleadings, evidence, and debate in a court. *See also* Adjudge; Adjudication.

Litigation /lìtəgéyshən/. A lawsuit. Legal action, including all proceedings therein. Contest in a court of law for the purpose of enforcing a right or seeking a remedy. A judicial contest, a judicial controversy, a suit at law.

Litigious /lətíjəs/. That which is the subject of a law-suit or action; that which is contested in a court of law. In another sense, "litigious" signifies fond of litigation; prone to engage in suits.

Litre /líytər/. Fr. A measure of capacity in the metric system, being a cubic decimetre, equal to 61.022 cubic inches, or 2.113 American pints, or 1.76 English pints.

Littering. Littering is dumping, throwing, placing, depositing or leaving, or causing to be dumped, thrown, deposited or left any refuse of any kind or any object or substance which tends to pollute, mar or deface, into, upon or about: (a) Any public street, highway, alley, road, right-of-way, park or other public place, or any lake, stream, watercourse, or other body of water, except by direction of some public officer or employee authorized by law to direct or permit such acts; or (b) Any private property without the consent of the owner or occupant of such property.

Littoral. Belonging to shore, as of seas, oceans and great lakes.

Littoral land. Land bordering ocean, sea, or lake.

Littoral rights. Rights concerning properties abutting an ocean, sea or lake rather than a river or stream (riparian). Littoral rights are usually concerned with the use and enjoyment of the shore.

Live, *adj.* Having or possessing life. *See also* Alive; Life.

Live, *v.* To live in a place, is to reside there, to abide there, to occupy as one's home. *See also* Domicile; Living; Residence.

Livelihood. Means of support or subsistence.

Livelode. Maintenance; support.

Livery /lív(ə)riy/. In old English law, delivery of possession of their lands to the king's tenants *in capite* or tenants by knight's service. A writ which could be sued out by a ward in chivalry, on reaching his majority, to obtain delivery of the

possession of his lands out of the hands of the guardian.

Act of delivering legal possession of property. *See* Livery of seisin.

A particular dress or garb appropriate or peculiar to certain persons, as the members of a guild, or, more particularly, the servants of a nobleman or gentleman.

The privilege of a particular guild or company of persons, the members thereof being called "livery-men."

A contract of hiring out of work-beasts, particularly horses, to the use of the hirer. It is commonly used in the compound, "livery-stable." Feeding, stabling, and care of horses for pay. Rental of vehicles, boats, etc. Word "livery" as used in automobile policy excluding coverage for automobile while being used as a livery conveyance means the hiring out of horses and carriages or a concern offering vehicles of various kinds for rent.

Livery of seisin /lív(ə)riy əv síyzən/. The appropriate ceremony, at common law, for transferring the corporal possession of lands or tenements by a grantor to his grantee. It was livery *in deed* where the parties went together upon the land, and there a twig, clod, key, or other symbol was delivered in the name of the whole. Livery *in law* was where the same ceremony was performed, not upon the land itself, but in sight of it.

Lives in being. As used in rule against perpetuities, means any lives in being at any time future interest is created, regardless of personal interest therein.

Livestock. Domestic animals used or raised on a farm. The term in its generic sense includes all domestic animals, including fur bearing animals raised in captivity.

Livestock insurance. *See* Insurance.

Living. Existing, surviving, or continuing in operation. Also means to abide, to dwell, to reside and literally signifies the pecuniary resources by means of which one exists. *See also* Alive; Domicile; Life; Residence; Viable.

Living apart. To live in a separate abode. *See also* Living separate and apart.

Living at time of another's death. Remaining in life after such other person's death (*e.g.* surviving spouse). *See* Survivor.

Living in open and notorious adultery. To constitute, parties must dwell together openly and notoriously as if conjugal relation existed between them. The parties must reside together in face of society as if conjugal relations existed between them, and fact of their so living and that they are not husband and wife must be known in community in which they reside.

Living issue. Living children.

Living separate and apart. Exists where the spouses have come to a parting of the ways and have no present intention of resuming marital relations and taking up life together under the same roof, not where they are residing temporarily in different places for economic or social reasons. This is a no-fault ground for divorce in many states when the spouses have lived apart for the statutorily prescribed period.

Living together. As respects court's right to allow suit money to wife in divorce action, means dwelling together in same house, eating at same table, the two parties holding themselves out to world and conducting themselves toward each other as husband and wife.

Living trust. Trust which is operative during life of settlor; an active or inter vivos trust.

Living will. *See* Will.

Living with husband. Means to dwell, to reside, to make one's abiding place or home with him, and may also mean to cohabit. Living together as husband and wife in ordinary acceptation of words in common understanding; maintaining a home and living together in same household or actually cohabiting under conditions which would be regarded as constituting a family relation.

L.J. An abbreviation for "Law Judge;" also for "Law Journal."

LL. The reduplicated form of the abbreviation "L." for "law," used as a plural. It is generally used in citing old collections of statute law; as "LL. Hen. I."

L.L. (Also L.Lat.) and **L.F.** (also L.Fr.) are used as abbreviations of the terms "Law Latin" and "Law French."

LL.B., LL.M., and LL.D. Abbreviations used to denote, respectively, the three academic degrees in law,—bachelor, master, and doctor of laws; the latter commonly being an honorary degree. *See also* J.D.

Lloyd's association. *See* Lloyd's underwriters.

Lloyd's insurance. Under this type of insurance, insurers are such as individuals and not as a corporate insurance company and the liability for loss is several and not joint. The "Lloyds' Plan," contemplates individual liability of the several underwriters. *See also* Lloyd's of London; Lloyd's underwriters; London Lloyds.

Lloyd's of London. An association in the city of London, originally for the transaction of marine insurance, the members of which underwrite one another's policies. An insurance mart in London at which individual underwriters gather to quote rates and write insurance on the widest variety of risks. *See also* London Lloyds.

Lloyd's underwriters. Any aggregation of individuals, who under a common name engage in the business of insurance for profit through an attorney-in-fact having authority to obligate the underwriters severally, within such limits as may be lawfully specified in the power of attorney, on contracts of insurance made or issued by such attorney-in-fact, in the name of such aggregation of individuals, to and with any person or persons insured. N.Y.Consol. Laws, Insurance § 425.

Load. The portion of the offering price of shares of mutual fund open-end investment companies that covers sales commissions and all other costs of distribution.

Load fund. *See* Load; Mutual Fund.

Loading. The act of putting a load on or in; as to load a car or a vessel.

The difference between gross and net premiums on insurance policies. In insurance, that portion of the premium used for meeting selling and administrative expenses beyond that portion required to meet the liability reserve. In an open-end investment company, that portion of the price of the share added to cover selling expenses.

Loaf. To spend time in idleness, to lounge or loiter about or along. *See also* Malinger.

Loan. A lending. Delivery by one party to and receipt by another party of sum of money upon agreement, express or implied, to repay it with or without interest. Anything furnished for temporary use to a person at his request, on condition that it shall be returned, or its equivalent in kind, with or without compensation for its use.

Bailment without reward, consisting of the delivery of an article by the owner to another person, to be used by the latter gratuitously, and returned either *in specie* or in kind. A borrowing of money or other personal property by a person who promises to return it.

"Loan" includes: (1) the creation of debt by the lender's payment of or agreement to pay money to the debtor or to a third party for the account of the debtor; (2) the creation of debt by a credit to an account with the lender upon which the debtor is entitled to draw immediately; (3) the creation of debt pursuant to a lender credit card or similar arrangement; and (4) the forbearance of debt arising from a loan. Uniform Consumer Credit Code, § 3–106.

See also Back-to-back loan; Conventional loan; Equity loan; Fixed rate loan; Morning loan; Participation loan. For *term loan, see* Term.

Amortized loan. One which calls for periodic payments which are applied first to interest and then to principal as provided by the terms of the note.

Bridge loan. Short term loan needed to cover down payment and costs associated with purchase or construction of new home pending sale of existing home. *See* Bridge loan; *also* Construction loan, below.

Call loan. One which is payable on demand or call by the lender.

Collateral loan. One which is secured by property or securities. *See* Secured loan.

Commercial loan. Generally a short term loan for 30 to 90 days given by financial institutions.

Commodity loan. One which is secured by a commodity such as cotton or wool in the form of a warehouse receipt or other negotiable instrument.

Consolidation loan. A borrowing in which the proceeds of the loan are used to pay off other individual loans and create a more manageable debt.

Construction loan. Short-term interim loan for financing cost of building construction. Payments are made periodically as work is completed with repayment usually made from permanent mortgage funds secured by completed structure. Also referred to as *bridge loan, above.*

Consumer loan. One which is made or extended to a natural person for family, household, personal or agricultural purposes and generally governed by truth-in-lending statutes and regulations.

Day loan. One made to a broker on a day to day basis to finance his daily transactions.

Demand loan. One on which the lender may make demand or call at any time for repayment. *See also Call loan, above.*

Equity loan. See that topic.

Installment loan. One which is repaid according to its terms over a period of time in installments.

Non-performing loan. An outstanding loan that is not being repaid, *i.e.* neither payments on interest or principal are being made.

Non-recourse loan. Loans made to farmers by a government organization in exchange for a particular commodity; *e.g.* wheat or corn. They are called nonrecourse because the government can never demand payment for the loan.

Personal loan. One which is generally for a short period of time for personal as contrasted with commercial purposes. It may be secured or unsecured. *See also Consumer loan, above.*

Secured loan. One which is secured by property or securities. *See also Collateral loan, above.*

Short-term loan. One which runs for a period of less than a year and which is commonly evidenced by a note or other negotiable instrument.

Time loan. One which is made for a fixed period of time and which generally may not be repaid before the expiration of such time (without penalty) as distinguished from a call or demand loan.

Transaction loan. A loan extended for the purpose of financing a particular specified transaction. *See also Bridge loan, above.*

Loan amortization schedule. A schedule that breaks down each payment on a loan into an interest component and a principal repayment component.

Loan association. *See* Building and loan association.

Loan certificates. Certificates issued by a clearing-house to the associated banks to a specified per cent. of the value of the collaterals deposited by the borrowing banks with the loan committee of the clearing-house. Documents issued by a borrower to evidence participation in a loan for an extended term; formerly used by municipalities. These have been replaced, in the main, by coupon bonds. *See also* Certificate of indebtedness.

Loan commitment. Commitment to borrower by lending institution that it will loan a specific amount at a certain rate on a particular piece of real estate. Such commitment is usually limited to a specified time period (*e.g.* four months), which is commonly based on the estimated time that it will take the borrower to construct or purchase the home contemplated by the loan. *See also* Mortgage commitment.

Loaned employee *or* **servant.** Loaned servant is an employee who is loaned or hired out to another employer for some specific service or particular transaction and who is under exclusive control of that employer who may then be held vicariously liable for acts of employee under ordinary principles of respondeat superior. Whether an employee should be regarded as a "loaned employee" in the service of a special employer, or whether he should be regarded as remaining in the service of his general employer, depends upon in whose work the employee was engaged at the time of injury.

Loaned servant doctrine. Under the "loaned servant doctrine", when one lends his employee to another for a particular employment, employee, for anything done in that employment, must be dealt with as employee of one to whom he is lent. This doctrine provides that if employer loans employee to another for performance of some special service, then that employee, with respect to that special service, may become employee of party to whom his services have been loaned. In order for employee to be a "loaned servant", it is not essential that general employer relinquish full control over his employee, or that special employee be completely subservient to borrower.

Loan for consumption. An agreement by which one person delivers to another a certain quantity of things which are consumed by the borrower, with the obligation to return as much of the same kind and quality. *See also* Loan for use.

Loan for exchange. A contract by which one delivers personal property to another, and the latter agrees to return to the lender a similar thing at a future time, without reward for its use. Cal.Civil Code § 1902.

Loan for use. An agreement by which a person delivers a thing to another, to use it according to its natural destination, or according to the agreement, under the obligation on the part of the borrower, to return it after he shall be done using it. Civ.Code La. art. 2893. A contract by which one gives to another the temporary possession and use of personal property, and the latter agrees to return the same thing to him at a future time, without reward for its use. Cal.Civil Code, § 1884.

Loan participation. Loan provided by a group of lenders to a single borrower, which spreads the default risk of the loan among all lenders in the group.

Loan ratio. The ratio, expressed as a percentage, of the amount of a loan to the value or selling price of real property. Usually, the higher the percentage, the greater the interest charged. Maximum percentages for banks, savings and loan, or government insured loans, is set by statute. *See also* Loan-to-value ratio.

Loansharking. Practice of lending money at excessive and usurious interest rates, with the threat or employment of extortionate means to enforce repayment of the loan. Such activities are termed "extortionate credit transactions" under Federal Criminal Code. 18 U.S.C.A. § 891 *et seq.*

Loan-to-value ratio. The percentage of purchase price to be financed with a mortgage. Common ratios are 80 and 90 percent. A down payment covers the rest of the purchase price.

Loan value. The maximum amount which can be safely lent on property or life insurance consistent with the lender's rights to protection in the event of the borrower's default.

Lobbying. All attempts including personal solicitation to induce legislators to vote in a certain way or to introduce legislation. It includes scrutiny of all pending bills which affect one's interest or the interests of one's clients, with a view towards influencing the passage or defeat of such legislation. Federal, and most state, statutes require that lobbyists be registered. *See* Lobbying acts.

Lobbying acts. Federal and state statutes governing conduct of lobbyists; *e.g.* Federal Regulation of Lobbying Act requires that lobbyists register with House and Senate and file quarterly reports of amount and source of payments received for lobbying activities. See 12 U.S.C.A. § 261 et seq.

Lobbyist. One who makes it a business to procure the passage or defeat of bills pending before a legislative body. *See also* Lobbying; Lobbying acts.

Local. Relating to place, expressive of place; belonging or confined to a particular place. Distinguished from "general," "personal," "widespread" and "transitory."

As to *local* Allegiance; Customs; Government; Tax and Venue, see those titles.

Local act. *See* Local law.

Local actions. Term embraces all actions in which the subject or thing sought to be recovered is in its nature local. Action which must be brought in jurisdiction of act or subject matter, as opposed to transitory action. Actions are "local" when the transactions on which they are based could not occur except in some particular place. One wherein all principal facts on which it is founded are of a local nature; as where possession of land is to be recovered, or damages for an actual trespass, or for waste affecting land, because in such case the cause of action relates to some particular locality, which usually also constitutes the venue of the action. A "transitory action" may be brought in any court of general jurisdiction in any district wherein defendant can be found and served with process, whereas in a "local action" the plaintiff must bring suit in the court designated, if not statutorily required to do otherwise. *Compare* Transitory action.

Local agent. An agent at a given place or within a definite district. An agent may be a general agent as to his powers, although he represents the company only in a particular locality or within a limited territory, and in the latter aspect is called a "local agent". An agent placed in charge of corporation's local business for purpose of winding it up. One appointed to act as the representative of a corporation and transact its business generally (or business of a particular character) at a given place or within a defined district. One who represents corporation in promotion of business for which it was incorporated, in county in which suit is filed. One who stands in shoes of corporation in relation to particular matters committed to his care and represents corporation in its business in either a general or limited capacity. A "local agent" to receive and collect money means an agent residing either permanently or temporarily within the state for purpose of his agency. By statute or court rule in most states, service of process on a foreign corporation may be made on a local agent of such corporation. See Fed.R.Civil P. 4; New York C.P.L.R. §§ 308, 318.

Local and special legislation. Term applies to special or particular places or special and particular person, and is distinguished from general statute in operation and relation to classes of persons or subjects.

Local assessment. A charge in the nature of tax, levied to pay the whole or part of the cost of local improvements (*e.g.* sewers, sidewalks) and assessed upon the various parcels of property specially benefited thereby. *See also* Local improvement assessment.

Local courts. Courts whose jurisdiction is limited to a particular territory or district. The expression usually signifies the courts of the state, in opposition to the United States courts, or to municipal or county courts in contrast to courts with state-wide jurisdiction.

Local government. City, county, or other governing body at a level smaller than a state. Local government has the greatest control over real property, zoning, and other local matters.

Local improvement. A public improvement made in a particular locality, by which the real property adjoining or near such locality is specially benefited.

Local improvement assessment. A charge placed upon lands within a given district to pay the benefits which the respective parcels of land derive from the improvement. An assessment for construction of improvement; *e.g.* sewers.

Locality. A definite region in any part of space; geographical position. Place; vicinity; neighborhood; community. *See also* Situs.

Locality of a lawsuit. Place where judicial authority may be exercised. *See* Venue.

Local law. A local law is one which relates or operates over a particular locality instead of over the whole territory of the state. One which relates to particular persons or things or to particular persons or things of a class or which operates on or over a portion of a class instead of all of the class.

The law of a particular jurisdiction as contrasted with the law of a foreign state. Term is used in conflicts to describe the power of the forum to determine questions of procedure while acknowledging the law of the situs to govern substantive questions. As used in the Restatement of this subject, the "local law" of a state is the body of standards, principles and rules, exclusive of its rules of conflict of laws, which the courts of that state apply in the decision of controversies brought before them. Restatement, Second, Conflicts, § 4(1).

Local option. An option of self-determination available to a municipality or other governmental unit to determine a particular course of action without specific approval from state officials. Local option is often used in local elections to determine whether the selling and consumption of alcoholic beverages will be permitted in local areas. Such is also used in many states to permit home rule elections for determining the structures of local governmental units. *See also* Home rule.

Local rules. Those promulgated in view of local physical conditions in the state, the character of the people, their peculiar customs, usages, and beliefs. Term may also refer to court rules adopted by individual U.S. district courts which supplement Federal Rules of Civil Procedure. See Fed.R.Civil P. 83.

Local statute. *See* Local law.

Local usage. A practice or method of dealing regularly observed in a particular place and such that it may be considered by the court under certain circumstances in interpreting a document. See U.C.C. § 1–205(2), (3). *See also* Custom and usage.

Locate. To find. To discover by survey. Also means to ascertain place in which something belongs. To ascertain and fix the position of something, the place of which was before uncertain or not manifest, as to locate the calls in a deed. To decide upon the place or direction to be occupied by something not yet in being, as to locate a road. To define location or limits; or designate site or place. To settle or become situated or established.

Located. Having a physical presence or existence in a place.

Location. Site or place where something is or may be located. Act of locating. *See also* Situs.

Mining law. The act of appropriating a mining claim (parcel of land containing precious metal in its soil or rock) according to certain established rules. It usually consists in placing on the ground, in a conspicuous position, a notice setting forth the name of the locator, the fact that it is thus taken or located, with the requisite description of the extent and boundaries of the parcel. In a secondary sense, the mining claim covered by a single act of appropriation or location. The act or series of acts whereby the boundaries of the claim are marked, etc., but it confers no right in the absence of discovery, both being essential to a valid claim. *See also* Mining claim; Mining location.

Real property. The designation of the boundaries of a particular piece of land, either upon record or on the land itself. The finding, surveying and marking out the bounds of a particular tract of land or mining claims. *See* Locative calls.

Locative calls. In a deed, patent, or other instrument containing a description of land, locative calls are specific calls, descriptions, or marks of location, referring to landmarks, physical objects, or other points by which the land can be exactly located and identified.

In harmonizing conflicting calls in a deed or survey of public lands, courts will ascertain which calls are locative and which are merely directory, and conform the lines to the locative calls; "directory calls" being those which merely direct the neighborhood where the different calls may be found, whereas "locative calls" are those which serve to fix boundaries.

Locator /lówkèytər/ləkéytər/. One who locates land, or sets the boundaries of a mining claim, or intends or is entitled to locate. *See* Finder; Location.

Lockbox. A collection and processing service provided to firms by banks, which collect payments from a dedicated postal box that the firm directs its customers to send payment to. The banks make several collections per day, immediately process the payments, and deposit the funds into the firm's bank account.

Lockdown. Temporary confinement of prisoners in their cells as security measure following escape, riot or other emergency. Permissible by compelling necessities of prison administration.

Locked in. A predicament of one who has profits on securities which he owns but which he is unwilling to sell because of the liability for capital gains. A fixed rate of return on an investment or savings instrument, or an interest rate on a loan, rate is assured for a specified period of time.

Lockout. Employer's withholding of work from employees in order to gain concession from them; it is employer's counterpart of employee's strike. Refusal by employer to furnish available work to its regular employees, whether refusal is motivated by employer's desire to protect itself against economic injury, by its desire to protect itself at bargaining table, or by both.

Lockup. A place of detention in a police station, court or other facility used for persons awaiting trial. *See also* Lockdown.

In corporate law, a slang term that refers to the setting aside of securities for purchase by friendly interests in order to defeat or make more difficult a takeover attempt. A lockup option is a takeover defensive measure permitting a friendly suitor to purchase divisions of a corporation for a set price when any person or group acquires a certain percentage of corporation's shares. To be legal, such agreement must advance or stimulate the bidding process, so as to best serve the interests of the shareholders through encouraged competition. *See also* Poison pill; Porcupine provisions; White knight.

Loco parentis /lówkow pəréntəs/. *See* In loco parentis.

Locus /lówkəs/. A place; the place where a thing is done.

Locus contractus /lówkəs kəntrǽktəs/. The place of a contract; the place where a contract is made. The place where the last act is performed which makes an agreement a binding contract.

Locus contractus regit actum /lówkəs kəntrǽktəs ríyjət ǽktəm/. The place of the contract governs the act. *See* Lex loci.

Locus criminis /lówkəs krímənəs/. The locality of a crime; the place where a crime was committed.

Locus delicti /lówkəs dəlíktay/. The place of the offense; the place where an offense was committed. State where last event necessary to make actor liable occurs.

Locus in quo /lówkəs ìn kwów/. The place in which. The place in which the cause of action arose, or where anything is alleged, in pleadings, to have been done. The phrase is most frequently used in actions of trespass *quare clausum fregit.*

Locus standi /lówkəs stǽnday/. A place of standing; standing in court. A right of appearance in a court of justice, or before a legislative body, on a given question.

Lode. Any zone or belt of mineralized rock lying within boundaries clearly separating it from neighboring rock.

Lodestar Rule. In determining amount of statutorily authorized attorneys' fees, "lodestar" is equal to number of hours reasonably expended multiplied by prevailing hourly rate in community for similar work and is then adjusted to reflect other factors such as contingent nature of suit and quality of representation. *See also* Equal Access to Justice Act; Fee.

Lodger. Person who rents a furnished room or rooms.

Lodging house. A house where lodgings are let. Building containing furnished apartments which are let out by the week or by the month, without meals, or with limited meals.

Logbook. A ship's or aircraft's journal containing a detailed account of the ship's course, with a short history of every occurrence during the voyage.

Log rolling. A legislative practice of embracing in one bill several distinct matters, none of which, perhaps, could singly obtain the assent of the legislature, and then procuring its passage by a combination of the minorities in favor of each of the measures into a majority that will adopt them all.

Practice of including in one statute or constitutional amendment more than one proposition, inducing voters to vote for all, notwithstanding they might not have voted for all if amendments or statutes had been submitted separately.

Loiter /lóytər/. To be dilatory; to be slow in movement; to stand around or move slowly about; to stand idly around; to saunter; to lag behind; to linger or spend time idly. Traditionally includes acts constituting vagrancy and as such, many loitering ordinances have been struck as unconstitutionally vague. *See also* Vagrancy.

London Lloyds. Voluntary association of merchants, shipowners, underwriters, and brokers, which writes no policies, but, when broker for one wishing insurance posts particulars of risk, underwriting members wishing to so subscribe name and share of total that each wishes to take, and policy is issued when total is reached containing names of underwriters bound thereby and name of attorney in fact who handles insurance affairs of the group. *See* Lloyd's of London.

Long. In various compound legal terms (see *infra*) this word carries a meaning not essentially different from its signification in the vernacular.

Long account. An account involving numerous separate items or charges, on one side or both, or the statement of various complex transactions, such as a court of equity will refer to a master, referee or commissioner.

Long arm statutes. Various state legislative acts which provide for personal jurisdiction, via substituted service of process, over persons or corporations which are nonresidents of the state and which voluntarily go into the state, directly or by agent, or communicate with persons in the state, for limited purposes, in actions which concern claims relating to the performance or execution of those purposes, *e.g.* transacting business in the state, contracting to supply services or goods in the state, or selling goods outside the state when the seller knows that the goods will be used or consumed in the state. See International Shoe Co. v. State of Washington, 326 U.S. 310, 316, 66 S.Ct. 154, 158, 90 L.Ed. 95. *E.g.* in New York, as to a cause of action arising from any of the following acts, the court may exercise personal jurisdiction over any nondomiciliary, or his executor or administrator, who in person or through agent: (1) Transacts any business within state; (2) commits tortious act other than defamation within state; (3) commits tortious act, other than defamation, outside state causing injury to person or property within state, if such nondomiciliary regularly does or solicits business, or engages in any other persistent course of conduct, or derives substantial revenue from goods used or consumed or services rendered within state; or (4) owns, uses, or possesses real property within state.

N.Y.Consol. Laws, CPLR § 302. See also Mass.G. L.A. c. 223A. *See also* Minimum contacts; Service *(Service of process).*

Longevity pay. Extra compensation for longevity in actual service in the army or navy.

Long position. The status of one who owns securities which he holds in expectation of a rise in the market or for income as contrasted with one who goes in and out of the market on a short point spread.

In the language of the stock exchange, a broker or speculator is said to be "long" on stock, or as to a particular security, when he has in his possession or control an abundant supply of it, or a supply exceeding the amount which he has contracted to deliver, or, more particularly, when he has bought a supply of such stock or other security for future delivery, speculating on a considerable future advance in the market price. A trader is said to be "long" on the market when he takes the full price risk; *i.e.* gains if the market price goes up, and loses if it goes down.

Longshore and Harbor Workers' Compensation Act. Federal Act (33 U.S.C.A. § 901 et seq.) designed to provide workers' compensation benefits to employees, other than seamen, or private employers any of whose employees work in maritime employment upon the navigable waters of the United States (including any adjoining pier, wharf, dry dock, terminal, building way, marine railway, or other adjoining area customarily used by an employer in loading, unloading, repairing, or building a vessel). The principal employments subject to the Act are stevedoring and ship service operations. The Act is administered by the Office of Workers' Compensation Programs.

Longshoreman. A maritime laborer, such as a stevedore or loader, who works about wharves of a port. Person who loads and unloads ships.

For federal compensation act covering seamen, *see* Jones Act.

Long term capital gain. *See* Capital *(Capital gain).*

Long term capital loss. *See* Capital *(Capital loss).*

Long term debt. Term generally refers to debt with a maturity date beyond one year.

Long-term debt ratio. The ratio of long-term debt to total capitalization.

Long-term financial plan. In accounting, financial plan covering two or more years of future operations.

Long term financing. A mortgage or deed of trust for a term of one year or more, as distinguished from construction, interim, or other short term loans.

Long-term securities. With regard to a new securities issue, typically means a security with an initial maturity of 10 years or more. With regard to the balance sheet, long-term indicates a remaining maturity of one year or longer.

Long ton. A measure of weight equivalent to 20 hundred-weight of 112 pounds each, or 2,240 pounds, as distinguished from the "short" ton of 2,000 pounds.

Lookout. The exercise of ordinary diligence requires that the driver of a motor vehicle be on the lookout for other travelers so that he may avoid placing himself or them in peril. As variously expressed, the rule requires that a motorist maintain a reasonable and proper lookout, which implies being watchful of the movements of the driver's own vehicle as well as of the movements of other traffic; a careful lookout; an efficient lookout; a vigilant watch ahead. A lookout must be made from the most effective place reasonably possible. The failure of a motorist to exercise ordinary care with respect to lookout, proximately resulting in injury or damage, may constitute negligence. That watchfulness which prudent and reasonable person must maintain for his own safety and safety of others taking into consideration circumstances with which he is immediately concerned or confronted.

Generally, a "lookout" is a person, other than pilot, who has duty of observing sounds, lights, echoes and obstructions to navigation and he is generally stationed on the bow of the vessel.

See also Proper lookout.

Loophole. In taxation, a provision in the tax code by which a taxpayer may legally avoid or reduce his income taxes. For example, prior to the Tax Reform Act of 1986, a tax shelter was an effective loophole in reducing an individual's taxes; however, with the change in the law, the advantages of such shelters have been substantially reduced.

Lord. A feudal superior or proprietor; one who granted a feudal estate in land to a tenant; one of whom a fee or estate is held.

A title of honor or nobility belonging properly to the degree of baron, but applied also to the whole peerage, as in the expression "the House of Lords." *See* House *(House of Lords).*

A title of office, as lord mayor, lord commissioner, etc.

Lord Campbell Act. An act which fixes the maximum amount recoverable for wrongful death. Most states have such statutes. *See* Wrongful death statutes.

In England, also refers to the Libel Act of 1843 which permits the defendant in a libel action to assert the defense of truth and that the publication was made for the benefit of the public.

Lord Mansfield's Rule. Such rule renders inadmissible testimony by either spouse on the question of whether the husband had access to the wife at time of conception. This Rule has been abandoned by several states as having outlived its original policy foundations.

Lordship. In English law, dominion, manor, seigniory, domain; also a title of honor used to a nobleman not being a duke. It is also the customary titulary appellation of the judges, and some other persons in authority and office.

Lose. To bring to destruction; to ruin; to destroy; to suffer the loss of; to be deprived of; to part with, especially in an accidental or unforeseen manner; as to lose an eye. *See also* Lost; Mislay.

Loss. Loss is a generic and relative term. It signifies the act of losing or the thing lost; it is not a word of limited, hard and fast meaning and has been held synonymous with, or equivalent to, "damage", "damages", "deprivation", "detriment", "injury", and "privation".

It may mean expenses exceeding costs; actual losses; bad and uncollectible accounts; damage; a decrease in value of resources or increase in liabilities; depletion or depreciation or destruction of value; deprivation; destruction; detriment; failure to keep that which one has or thinks he has; injury; ruin; shrinkage in value of estate or property; state or fact of being lost or destroyed; that which is gone and cannot be recovered or that which is withheld or that of which a party is dispossessed; unintentional parting with something of value.

The word in insurance policy in its common usage means a state of fact of being lost or destroyed, ruin or destruction.

See also Abnormal loss; Actual loss; Capital *(Capital loss)*; Casualty loss; Consequential loss; Constructive loss; Constructive total loss; Damages; Direct loss; Disaster loss; General average loss; Hobby loss; Net operating loss; Pain and suffering; Partial loss; Pecuniary injury; Pecuniary loss; Reasonable certainty, rule of; Total loss. As to loss of consortium, *see* Consortium; salvage loss, *see* Salvage; proof of loss, *see* Proof. *Compare* Profit.

Disability benefits. State workers' compensation laws, social security, and disability insurance contracts provide disability benefits for partial or permanent loss of use of limbs, eyes, etc.

Loss carry-back. *See* Carry-back.

Loss carry-over *(or* **Carry forward).** *See* Carry-over.

Loss leader. Item sold by a merchant at very low price and sometimes below cost in order to attract people to store with the hope that they will buy additional items on which a profit will be made. *See also* Bait and switch.

Loss of bargain. Under "loss of bargain" rule, applicable in common-law contract actions brought for misrepresentations in the nature of breaches of warranty, damages are measured by difference between value of goods as warranted and value as received.

Loss of consortium. *See* Consortium.

Loss of earning capacity. Damage to one's ability to earn wages in the future and recoverable as element of damage in tort actions. It is not the same as loss of earnings though loss of actual earnings is competent evidence of loss of earning capacity. A person unemployed at the time of the accident has an earning capacity though he has no earnings.

Loss of profits. Type of UCC damages that allows seller to collect profit that would otherwise have been made on sale if buyer had not breached. *See e.g.,* U.C.C. § 2–708(2).

Loss payable clause. A clause in a fire insurance policy, listing the priority of claims in the event of destruction of the property insured. Generally, a mortgagee, or beneficiary under a deed of trust, is the party appearing in the clause, being paid to the amount owing under the mortgage or deed of trust before the owner is paid. A provision in property insurance contracts that authorizes payments to persons other than the insured to the extent that they have an insurable interest in the property.

Loss payee. Person named in insurance policy to be paid in event of loss or damage to property insured.

Loss ratio. In insurance, the proportion between premiums collected and loss payments made. In finance, loan losses of a bank or the receivable losses of a business compared to the assets of that class.

Loss reserve. That portion of insurance company's assets set aside for payment of losses which will probably arise or which have arisen but have not been paid.

Lost. An article is "lost" when the owner has lost the possession or custody of it, involuntarily and by any means, but more particularly by accident or his own negligence or forgetfulness, and when he is ignorant of its whereabouts or cannot recover it by an ordinarily diligent search. *See also* Lost property.

As applied to ships and vessels, the term means "lost at sea," and a vessel lost is one that has totally gone from the owners against their will, so that they know nothing of it, whether it still exists or not, or one which they know is no longer within their use and control, either in consequence of capture by enemies or pirates, or an unknown foundering, or sinking by a known storm, or collision, or destruction by shipwreck.

Lost corner. A point of survey whose position cannot be determined beyond reasonable doubt either from traces of the original marks or from acceptable evidence, and whose location can be restored only by reference to one or more independent corners. *See* Corner.

Lost papers. Papers or documents which have been so mislaid that they cannot be found after diligent search.

Lost profits. *See* Loss of profits.

Lost property. Property which the owner has involuntarily parted with, through neglect, carelessness or inadvertence, and does not know where to find or recover it, not including property which he has intentionally concealed or deposited in a secret place for safe-keeping. Distinguishable from mislaid property which has been deliberately placed somewhere and forgotten. The majority of the states have adopted the Uniform Disposition of Unclaimed Property Act. *Compare* Property *(Mislaid property)*.

A person who comes into control of property of another that he knows to have been lost, mislaid, or delivered under a mistake as to the nature or amount of the property or the identity of the recipient is guilty of theft if, with purpose to deprive the owner thereof, he fails to take reasonable measures to restore the property to a person entitled to have it. Model Penal Code § 223.5.

Lost will. A will which was once executed but cannot be found at death of testator. The contents can be proved by parol in many jurisdictions, though in some states there is a rebuttable presumption that a will once in existence has been revoked if it cannot be found at testator's death.

Lot. A number of associated persons or things taken collectively.

Real estate. A share; one of several parcels into which property is divided. Any portion, piece, division or parcel of land. Fractional part or subdivision of block, according to plat or survey; portion of platted territory measured and set apart for individual and private use and occupancy.

A lot is commonly one of several other contiguous parcels of land making up a block. Real property is typically described by reference to lot and block numbers on recorded maps and plats.

Local zoning laws commonly require minimum lot sizes for residential and commercial building.

See also Minimum lot; Nonconforming lot; Parcel.

Sales. In sales, a parcel or single article which is the subject matter of a separate sale or delivery whether or not it is sufficient to perform the contract. U.C.C. § 2–105(5).

Securities. In securities and commodities market, a specified number of shares or specific quantity of a commodity designated for trading. *See* Odd lot; Odd lot doctrine.

Lot book. Plat book.

Lot line. A boundary of a tract of land used to describe such land and often used in description of contiguous land.

Lottery /lótəriy/. A chance for a prize for a price. A scheme for the distribution of a prize or prizes by lot or chance, the number and value of which is determined by the operator of lottery. Essential elements of a lottery are consideration, prize and chance and any scheme or device by which a person for a consideration is permitted to receive a prize or nothing as may be determined predominantly by chance.

An unlawful gambling scheme in which (a) the players pay or agree to pay something of value for chances, represented and differentiated by numbers or by combinations of numbers or by some other media, one or more of which chances are to be designated the winning ones; and (b) the winning chances are to be determined by a drawing or by some other method based upon the element of chance; and (c) the holders of the willing chances are to receive something of value. New Jersey Criminal Code, N.J.S. § 2C:37–1.

A number of states, by statute, provide for state-run lotteries (*e.g.* Mass.G.L. Ch. 10, § 22 et seq.).

The advertising and sending of lottery tickets through the mails and by other instrumentalities of interstate commerce is prohibited by federal law. 18 U.S.C.A. § 1301 et seq., 1953. Though most states also have similar laws prohibiting such activities, these federal laws do not apply to state-run lotteries. 18 U.S.C.A. § 1307.

See also Dutch lottery; Gambling; Game of chance; Sweepstakes.

Love and affection. Such is a sufficient consideration when a gift is contemplated, but is not considered "valuable" consideration where such is required. *See* Nudum pactum.

Lower of cost or **market.** A basis for inventory valuation where the inventory value is set at the lower of acquisition cost or current replacement cost (market).

Lowest responsible bidder. Bidder who not only has lowest price which conforms with the specifications, but also is financially able and competent to complete work as evidenced by prior performance.

Low-water mark. Line on the shore marking the lowest ebb of the tide. *See also* Water-mark.

Loyal. Legal; authorized by or conforming to law. Also faithful in one's political relations; giving faithful support and allegiance to one's sovereign or to the existing government. Faithful support to cause, ideal, office, or person.

Loyalty. Adherence to law. Faithfulness to one's office or sovereign or to the existing government.

Loyalty oath. An oath whereby an individual declares his allegiance to his government and its institutions and disclaims any support of foreign ideologies or associations. Such oaths as are required of various classifications of public officials and persons working in "sensitive" government positions. See *e.g.* Art. II, § 1, cl. 7; Art. VI, cl. 3, U.S.Const. However, oaths too vague to specify clearly what constitutes seditious acts and utterances have been declared unconstitutional. *See also* Oath.

L.R. An abbreviation for "Law Reports."

L.S. An abbreviation for *"Locus sigilli,"* the place of the seal; *i.e.,* the place where a seal is to be affixed, or a scroll which stands instead of a seal.

LSAT. Law School Admission Test. This test is given to law school applicants. The LSAT is a half-day multiple choice test designed to measure certain basic reasoning abilities important in the study of law, general academic ability and command of written English. It provides two scores: an LSAT score and a writing ability (WA) score. The LSAT portion measures the ability to understand and reason with a variety of verbal, quantitative, and symbolic materials. The writing ability portion measures the use of standard English to express ideas clearly and precisely. The test is intended to supplement the undergraduate record and other information about the student in the assessment of potential for law school work. It covers a broad range of disciplines, measures skills acquired over a long period of time, and gives no advantage to students with particular specializations.

Ltd. Limited.

Lucid. Easily understood; clear; rational; sane.

Lucid interval. A temporary cure; temporary restoration to sanity. Intervals occurring in the mental life of an insane person during which he is completely restored to the use of his reason, or so far restored that he has sufficient intelligence, judgment, and will to enter into contractual relations, or perform other legal acts, without disqualification by reason of his disease. With respect to marriage, refers to period of time during which person had sufficient mental capacity to know and understand nature and consequence of marriage relation, and the reciprocal and mutual duties and obligations thereof. In connection with wills, a period of time within which an insane person enjoys the restoration of his faculties sufficiently to enable him to judge his act. *See also* Insanity.

Lucrative. Yielding gain or profit; profitable; bearing or yielding a revenue or salary.

Lucrative bailment. *See* Bailment.

Lumping sale. As applied to judicial sales, this term means a sale in mass, as where several distinct parcels of real estate, or several articles of personal property, are sold together for a "lump" or single gross sum. *See* Bulk sale.

Lump-sum alimony. Settlement or payment of money or property in divorce action made in single payment instead of installments. Sometimes called "alimony in gross." *See* Alimony.

Lump-sum distribution. Single payment of the entire amount due at one time rather than in installments. Such distributions often occur from qualified pension or profit-sharing plans upon the retirement or death of a covered employee.

Lump-sum payment. A single payment in contrast to installments; *e.g.* single premium payment for life insurance; a single lump sum divorce settlement; or single worker's compensation payment in lieu of future monthly installment payments. *See also* Alimony.

Lump-sum purchase. The purchase of a number of assets together for a single amount.

Luxury tax. Generic term for excise imposed on purchase of items which are not necessaries; *e.g.* tax on liquor or cigarettes.

Lying by. A person who, by his presence and silence at a transaction which affects his interests, may be fairly supposed to acquiesce in it, if he afterwards propose to disturb the arrangement, is said to be prevented from doing so by reason that he has been lying by. *See also* Acquiescence; Estoppel; Ratification.

Lying in wait. Lying in ambush; lying hidden or concealed for the purpose of making a sudden and unexpected attack upon a person when he shall arrive at the scene. For purposes of aggravating circumstance, elements necessary to constitute "lying in wait" are watching, waiting and concealment from person killed with intent to kill or inflict bodily injury upon that person. In some jurisdictions, where there are several degrees of murder, lying in wait is made evidence of that deliberation and premeditated intent which is necessary to characterize murder in the first degree.

Lynch law. A term descriptive of the action of unofficial persons, organized bands, or mobs, who seize persons charged with or suspected of crimes, or take them out of the custody of the law, and inflict summary punishment upon them, without legal trial, and without the warrant or authority of law.

M

M. This letter, used as a Roman numeral, stands for one thousand.

Machination /mæ̀kənéyshən/mǽsh°/. The act of planning or contriving a scheme for executing some purpose, particularly an evil purpose; an artful design formed with deliberation. *See also* Artifice; Scheme.

Made. Filed; executed. Produced or manufactured artificially.

Made known. Where a process or other legal paper has been actually served upon a defendant, the proper return is that its contents have been "made known" to him. A crime is "made known" to an officer when facts which come to knowledge of the officer are such as to indicate to him that it is his official duty to act or to see that an investigation of the alleged crime is instituted within his jurisdiction. *See also* Notice.

Magisterial /mæ̀jəstíriyəl/. Relating or pertaining to the character, office, powers, or duties of a magistrate or of the magistracy.

Magisterial precinct. In some American states, a local subdivision of a county, defining the territorial jurisdiction of justices of the peace and constables; also called magisterial district.

Magistracy /mǽjəstrəsiy/. This term may have a more or less extensive signification according to the use and connection in which it occurs. In its widest sense it includes the whole body of public functionaries, whether their offices be legislative, judicial, executive, or administrative. In a more restricted (and more usual) meaning, it denotes the class of officers who are charged with the application and execution of the laws. In a still more confined use, it designates the body of judicial officers of the lowest rank, and more especially those who have jurisdiction for the trial and punishment of petty misdemeanors or the preliminary steps of a criminal prosecution, such as police judges and justices of the peace. The term also denotes the office of a magistrate. *See also* Magistrate.

Magistrate. A public civil officer, possessing such power—legislative, executive, or judicial—as the government appointing him may ordain. In a narrower sense, an inferior judicial officer, such as a justice of the peace.

U.S. (Federal) Magistrates. A judicial officer (called U.S. Magistrate Judges since 1991), appointed by judges of federal district courts, having many but not all of the powers of a judge. 28 U.S.C.A. §§ 631–639. Generally exercising duties formerly performed by U.S. Commissioners, magistrates may be designated to hear a wide variety of motions and other pretrial matters in both criminal and civil cases. With the consent of the parties, they may conduct civil or misdemeanor criminal trials. However, magistrates may not preside over felony trials or over jury selection in felony cases.

For Chief magistrate; Committing magistrate; and Police magistrates, see those titles.

Magistrate's courts. The jurisdiction of these courts of limited jurisdiction differs from state to state. Such may be divisions of courts of general jurisdiction, and may have concurrent jurisdiction with other courts. Commonly their jurisdiction is restricted to the handling of minor offenses, small claims or preliminary hearings.

Magna Carta /mǽgnə kártə/. The great charter. The name of a charter (or constitutional enactment) granted by King John of England to the barons, at Runnymede, on June 15, 1215, and afterwards, with some alterations, confirmed in parliament by Henry III and Edward I. This charter is justly regarded as the foundation of English constitutional liberty. Among its thirty-eight chapters are found provisions for regulating the administration of justice, defining the temporal and ecclesiastical jurisdictions, securing the personal liberty of the subject and his rights of property, and the limits of taxation, and for preserving the liberties and privileges of the church. *Magna Carta* is so called, partly to distinguish it from the *Charta de Foresta*, which was granted about the same time, and partly by reason of its own transcendent importance.

Magna culpa /mǽgnə kə́lpə/. Great fault; gross negligence.

Magnuson-Moss Warranty Act. Federal statute (15 U.S.C.A. § 2301 *et seq.*) requiring that written warranties as to consumer products must fully and conspicuously disclose in simple and readily understood language the terms and conditions of such warranty, including whether the warranty is a full or limited warranty according to standards set forth in the Act.

Mail. *See* Mailed; Registered mail.

Mailable. Suitable or admissible for transmission by the mail; belonging to the classes of articles which, by the laws and postal regulations, may be sent by mail. *Compare* Non-mailable.

Mailbox rule. In contract law, unless otherwise agreed or provided by law, acceptance of offer is effective when deposited in mail if properly addressed.

Mailed. A letter, package, or other mailable matter is "mailed" when it is properly addressed, stamped with the proper postage, and deposited in a proper place for receipt of mail.

Under rules practice in some jurisdictions, an action is deemed commenced when the complaint and appropriate entry fee is deposited in the mails under either certified or registered mail procedure; *e.g.* Mass.R.Civ.P. 3.

Mail float. The time elapsed while an invoice or payment of an invoice is in the mail.

Mail fraud. The use of the mails to defraud is a federal offense requiring the government to prove a knowing use of the mails to execute the fraudulent scheme. Elements of "mail fraud" are a scheme to defraud and the mailing of a letter for the purpose of executing the scheme. See 18 U.S.C.A. §§ 1341, 1342. *See* Using mail to defraud.

Mail order divorce. Divorce obtained by parties who are not physically present nor domiciled in the jurisdiction which purports to grant divorce (*e.g.* Mexican divorce). Such divorces are not recognized because of the complete absence of the usual bases for divorce jurisdiction.

Maim. To cripple or mutilate in any way. To inflict upon a person any injury which deprives him of the use of any limb or member of the body, or renders him lame or defective in bodily vigor. To inflict bodily injury; to seriously wound or disfigure; disable. *See also* Mayhem.

At common law, to deprive a person of a member or part of the body, the loss of which renders him less capable of fighting, or of defending himself; to commit mayhem (*q.v.*).

Main. Principal, leading, primary, chief. Most important in size, extent, rank, importance, strength or utility.

Main channel. The main channel of a river is that bed over which the principal volume of water flows. The deeper or more navigable channel of river.

Main purpose doctrine. The Statute of Frauds requires contracts to answer for the debt, default or misdoing of another to be in writing to be enforceable. However, if the main purpose of the promisor's undertaking is his own benefit or protection, such promise need not be in writing. The "main purpose rule" is that whenever the main purpose and object of promisor is not to answer

for another but to subserve some purpose of his own, his promise is not within statute of frauds, although it may be in form a promise to pay debt of another and although performance of promise may incidentally have effect of extinguishing liability of another.

Maintain. The term is variously defined as acts of repairs and other acts to prevent a decline, lapse or cessation from existing state or condition; bear the expense of; carry on; commence; continue; furnish means for subsistence or existence of; hold; hold or keep in an existing state or condition; hold or preserve in any particular state or condition; keep from change; keep from falling, declining, or ceasing; keep in existence or continuance; keep in force; keep in good order; keep in proper condition; keep in repair; keep up; preserve; preserve from lapse, decline, failure, or cessation; provide for; rebuild; repair; replace; supply with means of support; supply with what is needed; support; sustain; uphold. Negatively stated, it is defined as not to lose or surrender; not to suffer or fail or decline.

To "maintain" an action is to uphold, continue on foot, and keep from collapse a suit already begun, or to prosecute a suit with effect. To maintain an action or suit may mean to commence or institute it; the term imports the existence of a cause of action. Maintain, however, is usually applied to actions already brought, but not yet reduced to judgment. In this connection it means to continue or preserve in or with; to carry on.

The words "maintains" and "maintaining" in statutes prohibiting maintenance of a liquor nuisance denote continuous or recurrent acts approaching permanence. The term "maintaining government" means providing money to enable government to perform duties which it is required by law to perform.

See also Maintenance; Repair.

Maintained. Carried on; kept possession and care of; kept effectively; commenced and continued.

Maintainor. In criminal law, one who maintains or seconds a cause pending in litigation between others, either by disbursing money or otherwise giving assistance. One who is guilty of *maintenance (q.v.)*.

Maintenance. The upkeep or preservation of condition of property, including cost of ordinary repairs necessary and proper from time to time for that purpose. *See also* Maintain.

Sustenance; support; assistance; aid. The furnishing by one person to another, for his or her support, of the means of living, or food, clothing, shelter, etc., particularly where the legal relation of the parties is such that one is bound to support the other, as between father and child, or husband and wife. The supplying of the necessaries of life. While term primarily means food, clothing and shelter, it has also been held to include such items as reasonable and necessary transportation or automobile expenses, medical and drug expenses, utilities and household expenses. *See also* Separate maintenance; Support.

Assets. Expenditures undertaken to preserve an asset's service potential for its originally-intended life; these expenditures are treated as periodic expenses or product costs. Contrast with Improvement. *See also* Maintain; Repair.

Lawsuits. An officious intermeddling in a lawsuit by a non-party by maintaining, supporting or assisting either party, with money or otherwise, to prosecute or defend the litigation. The offense committed by a maintainor *(q.v.)*. *See also* Champerty.

Seamen. See Maintenance and cure.

Maintenance and cure. Contractual form of compensation given by general maritime law to seaman who falls ill while in service of his vessel. Seaman is entitled to maintenance and cure if he is injured or becomes ill in service or vessel, without regard to negligence of his employer or to unseaworthiness of ship; and "maintenance" is a per diem living allowance for food and lodging and "cure" is payment for medical, therapeutic and hospital expenses; and employer's duty to pay maintenance and cure continues until seaman has reached "maximum cure." *See also* Cure.

Maintenance assessment *or* **fee.** Charge for purpose of keeping an improvement in working order or a residential property in habitable condition.

A monthly charge for maintaining and repairing the commonly owned areas in a condominium building, subdivision or planned unit development.

Maintenance call. *See* Margin call.

Major. A person of full age; one who is no longer a minor; one who has attained the management of his own concerns and the enjoyment of his civic rights. *See also* Adult; Legal age; Majority.

Major and minor fault rule. Vessel guilty of gross fault has burden of showing that other vessel committed a plain fault. Where fault on part of one vessel is established by uncontradicted testimony and such fault is, of itself, sufficient to account for the disaster, it is not enough for such vessel to raise a doubt with regard to management of other vessel and any reasonable doubt with regard to propriety of conduct of such other vessel should be resolved in its favor.

Major crimes. A loose classification of serious crimes such as murder, rape, armed robbery, etc. *See* Felony.

Major (or minor) dispute. Major disputes within Railway Labor Act are those concerned with formation of collective bargaining agreements or with efforts to secure such agreements and look to acquisition of rights of future rather than to rights which vested in past; and, "minor disputes" are those arising where there is existing agreement and there has been no effort to bring about formal change in terms or to create new agreement but dispute relates to application of particular provision. *Compare* Minor dispute.

Majority. Full age; legal age; age at which a person is no longer a minor. The age at which, by law, a person is capable of being legally responsible for all his or her acts (*e.g.* contractual obligations), and is entitled to the management of his or her own affairs and to the enjoyment of civic rights (*e.g.* right to vote). The opposite of minority. Also the *status* of a person who is a major in age. *See* Adult; Capacity; Legal age.

The greater number. The number greater than half of any total.

Majority opinion. The opinion of an appellate court in which the majority of its members join. May also refer to a view of a legal principle in which most jurisdictions concur. *See also* Opinion.

Majority rule. Rule by the choice of the majority of those who actually vote, irrespective of whether a majority of those entitled participate. *See also* Majority vote.

Majority stockholder. One who owns or controls more than 50 percent of the stock of a corporation, though effective control may be maintained with far less than 50 percent if most of the stock is widely held. In close corporation, majority shareholders may owe fiduciary, partner-like duties to minority shareholders.

Majority vote. Vote by more than half of voters for candidate or other matter on ballot. When there are only two candidates, he who receives the greater number of the votes cast is said to have a majority; when there are more than two competitors for the same office, the person who receives the greatest number of votes has a *plurality,* but he has not a majority unless he receives a greater number of votes than those cast for all his competitors combined.

As regards voting by stockholders, means majority per capita when the right to vote is per capita, and a majority of stock when each share of stock is entitled to a vote, each particular case being determined by provisions of charter regulating voting.

Majority voting. A system of voting for directors of a corporation in which each shareholder has one vote for each director and a simple majority can elect each director. *See also* Voting stock rights.

Make. To cause to exist. To form, fashion, or produce. To do, perform, or execute; as to make an issue, to make oath, to make a presentment. To do in form of law; to perform with due formalities; to execute in legal form; as to make answer, to make a return or report.

To execute as one's act or obligation; to prepare and sign; to issue; to sign, execute, and deliver; as to make a conveyance, to make a note. To conclude, determine upon, agree to, or execute; as to make a contract.

To cause to happen by one's neglect or omission; as to make default. To make acquisition of; to procure; to collect; as to make the money on an execution or to make a loan. To have authority or influence; to support or sustain; as in the phrase, "This precedent makes for the plaintiff."

Make a contract. To agree upon, and conclude or adopt, a contract. In case of a written contract, to reduce it to writing, execute it in due form, and deliver it as binding. *See* Contract.

Make an award. To form and publish a judgment on the facts.

Make default. To fail or be wanting in some legal duty; particularly to omit the entering of an appearance when duly summoned in an action at law or other judicial proceeding. To neglect to obey the command of a subpœna, etc. *See also* Default.

Make *or* **buy decision.** In accounting, comparison of the cost of internally manufacturing a component of a final product (or providing a service function) with the cost of purchasing it from outside suppliers or from another division of the company at a specified transfer price.

Maker. One who makes, frames, executes, or ordains; as a "lawmaker," or the "maker" of a promissory note. One who signs a note to borrow and, as such, assumes obligation to pay note when due. The person who creates or executes a note, that is, issues it, and in signing the instrument makes the promise of payment contained therein. One who signs a check; in this context, synonymous with drawer. U.C.C. § 3–413(1). One who issues a promissory note or certificate of deposit (*i.e.*, one who promises to pay a certain sum to the holder of the note or CD). *See* Draft; Drawer.

Accommodation maker. See Accommodation.

Making law. Court decision that establishes new law on a particular matter or subject. *See also* First impression case.

Making record. The preparation of an appellate record. May also refer to the process of trying a case with a view towards an eventual appeal in which the record of the trial is important. In the later instance care is taken during trial to make all appropriate objections so that such become part of the record on appeal.

Mal. A prefix meaning bad, wrong, fraudulent; as maladministration, malpractice, malversation, etc.

Mala /mǽlə/. Lat. Bad; evil; wrongful.

Maladministration /mæ̀lədmìnəstréyshən/. This term is used interchangeably with *misadministration,* and both words mean "wrong administration."

Mala fides /mǽlə fáydiyz/. Bad faith. The opposite of *bona fides (q.v.). Malâ fide,* in bad faith. *Malæ fidei possessor,* a possessor in bad faith.

Mala in se /mǽlə in síy/. Wrongs in themselves; acts morally wrong; offenses against conscience.

Malapportionment. An improper or unconstitutional apportionment of legislative districts. *See* Gerrymander; Legislative apportionment.

Mala praxis /mǽlə prǽksəs/. Malpractice; unskillful management or treatment. Particularly applied to the neglect or unskillful management of a physician, surgeon, or apothecary. *See* Malpractice.

Mala prohibita /mǽlə prəhíbətə/. Prohibited wrongs or offenses; acts which are made *offenses* by positive laws, and *prohibited* as such. Acts or omissions which are made criminal by statute but which, of themselves, are not criminal. Generally, no criminal intent or mens rea is required and the mere accomplishment of the act or omission is sufficient for criminal liability. Term is used in contrast to *mala in se* which are acts which are wrongs in themselves such as robbery.

Malconduct /mælkóndəkt/. Ill conduct, especially dishonest conduct, maladministration, or, as applied to officers, official misconduct. *See* Malfeasance; Misfeasance.

Malefaction /mæ̀ləfǽkshən/. A crime; an offense.

Malefactor /mǽləfæ̀ktər/. He who is guilty, or has been convicted, of some crime or offense.

Malfeasance /mælfíyzən(t)s/. Evil doing; ill conduct. The commission of some act which is positively unlawful; the doing of an act which is wholly wrongful and unlawful; the doing of an act which person ought not to do at all or the unjust performance of some act which the party had no right or which he had contracted not to do. Comprehensive term including any wrongful conduct that affects, interrupts or interferes with the performance of official duties. Malfeasance is a wrongful act which the actor has no legal right to do, or any wrongful conduct which affects, interrupts, or interferes with performance of official duty, or an act for which there is no authority or warrant of law or which a person ought not to do at all, or the unjust performance of some act, which party performing it has no right, or has contracted not, to do. It differs from "misfeasance" and "nonfeasance" (q.v.).

Malice. The intentional doing of a wrongful act without just cause or excuse, with an intent to inflict an injury or under circumstances that the law will imply an evil intent. A condition of mind which prompts a person to do a wrongful act willfully, that is, on purpose, to the injury of another, or to do intentionally a wrongful act toward another without justification or excuse. A conscious violation of the law (or the prompting of the mind to commit it) which operates to the prejudice of another person. A condition of the mind showing a heart regardless of social duty and fatally bent on mischief. Malice in law is not necessarily personal hate or ill will, but it is that state of mind which is reckless of law and of the legal rights of the citizen.

In murder, that condition of mind which prompts one to take the life of another without just cause, legal justification, or provocation. A willful or corrupt intention of the mind. It includes not only anger, hatred and revenge, but also every other unlawful and unjustifiable motive.

As requirement to sustain award of punitive damages, is wrongful act done intentionally without just cause or excuse.

As used in Bankruptcy Code (§ 523(a)(6)) provision excepting from discharge liabilities for willful and malicious injuries to another entity or property of another entity does not require personal hatred or ill will, but requires that debtor know his act will harm another and proceed in face of such knowledge.

In libel and slander, as to privileged communications, "malice" involves an evil intent or motive arising from spite or ill will; personal hatred or ill will; or culpable recklessness or a willful and wanton disregard of the rights and interests of the person defamed. In a libel case it consists in intentionally publishing, without justifiable cause, any written or printed matter which is injurious to the character of another. Malice may be defined, insofar as defamation is concerned, as acting in bad faith and with knowledge of falsity of statements. In the context of a libel suit brought by a public figure, it consists in publishing the false defamation knowing it to be false or with a reckless disregard of whether it is true or false. New York Times Co. v. Sullivan, 376 U.S. 254, 84 S.Ct. 710, 11 L.Ed.2d 686. See also Libel; Slander.

In the law of malicious prosecution, it means that the prosecution was instituted primarily because of a purpose other than that of bringing an offender to justice. It is the intentional doing of a wrongful act without legal justification, and may be inferred from the absence of probable cause; it does not necessarily involve hatred or ill will. See also Malicious prosecution.

Actual malice. Express malice, or malice in fact. In libel law, "actual malice" can be established either by proving the publication was made with the knowledge of its falsity of its contents or with reckless disregard of whether it was false or not. Such will be found where an intent to inflict harm through falsehood is established. See also Malice in fact.

Constructive malice. Implied malice; malice inferred from acts; malice imputed by law; malice which is not shown by direct proof of an intention to do injury (express malice), but which is inferentially established by the necessarily injurious results of the acts shown to have been committed. See also Implied malice, below.

Express malice. Actual malice; malice in fact; ill will or wrongful motive. A deliberate intention to commit an injury, evidenced by external circumstances. See also Express malice; Malice in fact.

Implied malice. Malice inferred by legal reasoning and necessary deduction from the res gestæ or the conduct of the party. Malice inferred from any deliberate cruel act committed by one person against another, however sudden. What is called "general malice" is often thus inferred. See also Constructive malice, above; and Malice in law.

Legal malice. See Legal malice; Malice in law.

Particular malice. Malice directed against a particular individual. Ill will; a grudge; a desire to be revenged on a particular person. See also Special malice, below.

Preconceived malice. Malice prepense or aforethought. See Malice aforethought; Premeditation.

Premeditated malice. An intention to kill unlawfully, deliberately formed in the mind as the result of a determination meditated upon and fixed before the act. See Malice aforethought; Premeditation.

Special malice. Particular or personal malice; that is, hatred, ill will, or a vindictive disposition against a particular individual.

Universal malice. By this term is not meant a malicious purpose to take the life of all persons, but it is that depravity of the human heart which determines to take life upon slight or insufficient provocation, without knowing or caring who may be the victim.

Malice aforethought. A predetermination to commit an act without legal justification or excuse. A malicious design to injure. The intentional doing of an unlawful act which was determined upon before it was executed. An intent, at the time of a killing, willfully to take the life of a human being, or an intent willfully to act in callous and wanton disregard of the consequences to human life; but "malice aforethought" does not necessarily imply any ill will, spite or hatred towards the individual killed. *See also* Premeditation.

Malice in fact. Express or actual malice. Ill will towards a particular person; an actual intention to injure or defame such person. It implies desire or intent to injure, while "malice in law," or "implied malice," means wrongful act done intentionally, without just cause or excuse, and jury may infer it. *See* Malice *(Actual malice)*. *Compare* Malice in law.

Malice in law. The intentional doing of a wrongful act without just cause or excuse. Implied, inferred, or legal malice. As distinguished from malice in fact, it is presumed from tortious acts, deliberately done without just cause, excuse, or justification, which are reasonably calculated to injure another or others. *See also* Legal malice. *Compare* Malice in fact.

Malicious /məlíshəs/. Characterized by, or involving, malice; having, or done with, wicked, evil or mischievous intentions or motives; wrongful and done intentionally without just cause or excuse or as a result of ill will. *See also* Malice; Willful.

Malicious abandonment. In criminal law, the desertion of a wife or husband without just cause.

Malicious abuse of legal process. Wilfully misapplying court process to obtain object not intended by law. The wilful misuse or misapplication of process to accomplish a purpose not warranted or commanded by the writ. The malicious perversion of a regularly issued process, whereby a result not lawfully or properly obtained on a writ is secured; not including cases where the process was procured maliciously but not abused or misused after its issuance. The employment of process where probable cause exists but where the intent is to secure objects other than those intended by law. The tort requires a perversion of court process to accomplish some end which the process was not designed to accomplish, and does not arise from a regular use of process, even with ulterior motives. *See also* Abuse *(Process)*; Malicious prosecution. *Compare* Malicious use of process.

Malicious accusation. Procuring accusation or prosecution of another from improper motive and without probable cause. *See* Malicious prosecution.

Malicious act. A wrongful act intentionally done without legal justification or excuse; an unlawful act done willfully or purposely to injure another.

Malicious arrest. *See* Malicious prosecution.

Malicious assault with deadly weapon. Form of aggravated assault in which the victim is threatened with death or serious bodily injury from the defendant's use of a deadly weapon.

The element of malice can be inferred from the nature of the assault and the selection of the weapon.

Malicious injury. An injury committed against a person at the prompting of malice or hatred towards him, or done spitefully or wantonly. The willful doing of an act with knowledge it is liable to injure another and regardless of consequences. Injury involving element of fraud, violence, wantonness and willfulness, or criminality. An injury that is intentional, wrongful and without just cause or excuse, even in the absence of hatred, spite or ill will. Punitive damages may be awarded to plaintiff for such injury.

Malicious killing. Any intentional killing without a legal justification or excuse and not within the realm of voluntary manslaughter.

Maliciously. Imports a wish to vex, annoy, or injure another, or an intent to do a wrongful act, and may consist in direct intention to injure, or in reckless disregard of another's rights. *See also* Malice; Malicious.

Malicious mischief. Willful destruction of personal property of another, from actual ill will or resentment towards its owner or possessor. Though only a trespass at the common law, it is now a crime in most states.

Malicious motive. Any motive for instituting a prosecution, other than a desire to bring an offender to justice. *See* Malicious prosecution.

Malicious prosecution. One begun in malice without probable cause to believe the charges can be sustained. An action for damages brought by person, against whom civil suit or criminal prosecution has been instituted maliciously and without probable cause, after termination of prosecution of such suit in favor of person claiming damages.

One who takes an active part in the initiation, continuation or procurement of civil proceedings against another is subject to liability to the other for wrongful civil proceedings if: (a) he acts without probable cause, and primarily for a purpose other than that of securing the proper adjudication of the claim in which the proceedings are based, and (b) except when they are ex parte, the proceedings have terminated in favor of the person against whom they are brought. Restatement, Second, Torts, § 674.

Elements of a cause of action for malicious prosecution are: (1) commencement of prosecution of proceedings against present plaintiff; (2) its legal causation by present defendant; (3) its termination in favor of present plaintiff; (4) absence of probable cause for such proceedings; (5) presence of malice therein; and (6) damage to plaintiff by reason thereof.

In addition to the tort remedy for malicious criminal proceedings, the majority of states also permit tort actions for malicious institution of civil actions.

See also Advice of counsel; False arrest; Malicious abuse of legal process.

Malicious trespass. The act of one who maliciously or mischievously injures or causes to be injured any property of another or any public property.

Malicious use of process. Utilization of process to intimidate, oppress or punish a person against whom it is sued out. Exists where plaintiff proceeds maliciously and without probable cause to execute object which law intends process to subserve. It has to do with the wrongful initiation of such process, while "abuse of civil process" is concerned with perversion of a process after it is issued. See also Abuse (Process). Compare Malicious abuse of legal process.

Malinger /məlíŋgər/. To feign sickness or any physical disablement or mental lapse or derangement, especially for the purpose of escaping the performance of a task, duty, or work, or for purpose of continuing to receive disability payments. Person who consciously feigns or simulates mental or physical illness for gain.

Mallory Rule. Rule derived from case of the same name in which the court held that a confession given by one who had been detained an unreasonable time before being brought before magistrate was inadmissible though it was otherwise voluntary and trustworthy. Mallory v. U. S., 354 U.S. 449, 77 S.Ct. 1356, 1 L.Ed.2d 1479. Also known as McNabb-Mallory Rule (q.v.).

Maloney Act. Amendment passed in 1938 to Securities Exchange Act requiring registration of brokers in over-the-counter securities.

Malpractice. Professional misconduct or unreasonable lack of skill. This term is usually applied to such conduct by doctors, lawyers, and accountants. Failure of one rendering professional services to exercise that degree of skill and learning commonly applied under all the circumstances in the community by the average prudent reputable member of the profession with the result of injury, loss or damage to the recipient of those services or to those entitled to rely upon them. It is any professional misconduct, unreasonable lack of skill or fidelity in professional or fiduciary duties, evil practice, or illegal or immoral conduct. See also Discovery rule; Standard of care.

Legal malpractice. Consists of failure of an attorney to use such skill, prudence, and diligence as lawyers of ordinary skill and capacity commonly possess and exercise in performance of tasks which they undertake, and when such failure proximately causes damage it gives rise to an action in tort.

Medical malpractice. In medical malpractice litigation, negligence is the predominant theory of liability. In order to recover for negligent malpractice, the plaintiff must establish the following elements: (1) the existence of the physician's duty to the plaintiff, usually based upon the existence of the physician-patient relationship; (2) the applicable standard of care and its violation; (3) a compensable injury; and, (4) a causal connection between the violation of the standard of care and the harm complained of. See also Captain of the ship doctrine; Continuous treatment doctrine; Discovery rule; Maltreatment.

Maltreatment. In reference to the treatment of his patient by a surgeon, this term signifies improper or unskillful treatment; it may result either from ignorance, neglect, or willfulness; but the word does not necessarily imply that the conduct of the surgeon, in his treatment of the patient, is either willfully or grossly careless. See also Malpractice (Medical malpractice).

Malum /mǽləm/, adj. Lat. Wrong; evil; wicked; reprehensible.

Malum in se /mǽləm in síy/. A wrong in itself; an act or case involving illegality from the very nature of the transaction, upon principles of natural, moral, and public law. An act is said to be malum in se when it is inherently and essentially evil, that is, immoral in its nature and injurious in its consequences, without any regard to the fact of its being noticed or punished by the law of the state. Such are most or all of the offenses cognizable at common law (without the denouncement of a statute); as murder, larceny, etc. Compare Malum prohibitum.

Malum prohibitum /mǽləm prəhíbətəm/. A wrong prohibited; a thing which is wrong because prohibited; an act which is not inherently immoral, but becomes so because its commission is expressly forbidden by positive law; an act involving an illegality resulting from positive law. Compare Malum in se.

Manage. To control and direct, to administer, to take charge of. To conduct; to carry on the concerns of a business or establishment. Generally applied to affairs that are somewhat complicated and that involve skill and judgment.

Management. Government, control, superintendence, physical or manual handling or guidance; act of managing by direction or regulation, or administration, as management of family, or of household, or of servants, or of great enterprises, or of great affairs. Discretionary power of direction.

Management fee. The portion of the gross underwriting spread that compensates the securities firms who manage a public offering for their management efforts.

Manager. One who has charge of corporation and control of its business, or of its branch establishments, divisions, or departments, and who is vested with a certain amount of discretion and independent judgment. A person chosen or appointed to manage, direct, or administer the affairs of another person or of a business, sports team, or the like. The designation of "manager" implies general power and permits reasonable inferences that the employee so designated is invested with the general conduct and control of his employer's business. *See also* General manager.

Also one of the persons appointed on the part of the House of Representatives to prosecute impeachments before the Senate.

Managing agent. *See* Agent.

Mandamus /mændéyməs/. Lat. We command. This is the name of a writ (formerly a high prerogative writ) which issues from a court of superior jurisdiction, and is directed to a private or municipal corporation, or any of its officers, or to an executive, administrative or judicial officer, or to an inferior court, commanding the performance of a particular act therein specified, and belonging to his or their public, official, or ministerial duty, or directing the restoration of the complainant to rights or privileges of which he has been illegally deprived. A writ issuing from a court of competent jurisdiction, commanding an inferior tribunal, board, corporation, or person to perform a purely ministerial duty imposed by law. Extraordinary writ which lies to compel performance of ministerial act or mandatory duty where there is a clear legal right in plaintiff, a corresponding duty in defendant, and a want of any other appropriate and adequate remedy. *See also* Ministerial act.

The U.S. District Courts have original jurisdiction of any action in the nature of mandamus to compel an officer or employee of the United States or any agency thereof to perform a duty owed to the plaintiff. 28 U.S.C.A. § 1361.

Mandamus has traditionally issued in response to abuses of judicial power. Thus, where a district judge refuses to take some action he is required to take or takes some action he is not empowered to take, mandamus will lie. The Supreme Court may issue a writ of mandamus in aid of the appellate jurisdiction that might otherwise be defeated by the unauthorized action of the court below.

The remedy of mandamus is a drastic one, to be invoked only in extraordinary situations. The writ has traditionally been used in the federal courts only to confine an inferior court to a lawful exercise of its prescribed jurisdiction or to compel it to exercise its authority when it is its duty to do so.

Pleading. Like most of the extraordinary writs, the *writ* of mandamus has been abolished under rules practice in favor of a complaint or motion in the nature of mandamus which accomplishes the same object; *e.g.* Federal or Mass.R.Civ.P. 81(b).

Mandatary /mǽndətèhriy/. He to whom a mandate, charge, or commandment is given; also, he that obtains a benefice by *mandamus*.

Mandate. A command, order, or direction, written or oral, which court is authorized to give and person is bound to obey. A judicial command or precept proceeding from a court or judicial officer, directing the proper officer to enforce a judgment, sentence, or decree. A precept or order issued upon the decision of an appeal or writ of error, directing action to be taken, or disposition to be made of case, by inferior court. Official mode of communicating judgment of appellate court to lower court, directing action to be taken or disposition to be made of cause by trial court. *See also* Decree; Order.

A bailment of property in regard to which the bailee engages to do some act without payment. Agreement to perform services for another without pay.

A contract by which a lawful business is committed to the management of another, and by him undertaken to be performed gratuitously. The mandatary is bound to the exercise of slight diligence, and is responsible for gross neglect.

A mandate, procuration, or letter of attorney is an act by which one person gives power to another to transact for him and in his name one or several affairs. *See also* Power of attorney.

Mandatory /mǽndət(ə)riy/. *adj.* Containing a command; preceptive; imperative; peremptory; obligatory.

Mandatory injunction /mǽndət(ə)riy injə́ŋkshən/. *See* Injunction.

Mandatory instructions. *See* Jury instructions.

Mandatory presumption. *See* Presumption.

Mandatory sentencing. *See* Sentence.

Mandatory statutes. Generic term describing statutes which require and not merely permit a course of action. They are characterized by such directives as "shall" and not "may."

A "mandatory" provision in a statute is one the omission to follow which renders the proceedings to which it relates void, while a "directory" provision is one the observance of which is not necessary to validity of the proceeding. It is also said that when the provision of a statute is the essence of the thing required to be done, it is mandatory; otherwise, when it relates to form and manner, and where an act is incident, or after jurisdiction acquired, it is directory merely.

Manhood. The status of one who has reached his legal majority which in most jurisdictions is 18. Formerly, it was the age of 21. When this status is achieved, a person may act sui juris. *See also* Legal age; Majority.

Mania /méyniyə/. *See* Insanity.

Manifest. Evident to the senses, especially to the sight, obvious to the understanding, evident to the mind, not obscure or hidden, and is synonymous with open, clear, visible, unmistakable, indubitable, indisputable, evident, and self-evident. In evidence, that which is clear and requires no proof; that which is notorious.

Document used in shipping and warehousing containing a list of the contents, value, origin, carrier and destination of the goods to be shipped or warehoused. A written document required to be carried by merchant vessels, containing an account of the cargo, with other particulars, for the facility of the customs officers. See 19 U.S. C.A. § 1431 et seq. List of passengers and cargo kept by vessel and aircraft.

Manifestation of intention. In trusts and wills, the external expression of intention as distinguished from the undisclosed internal intention. Restatement of Trusts, Second, § 2, comment g.

Manifest necessity. Doctrine of "manifest necessity" which will authorize granting of mistrial in criminal case, and preclude defendant from successfully raising plea of former jeopardy, contemplates a sudden and overwhelming emergency beyond control of court and unforeseeable, and it does not mean expediency. Such exists where, due to circumstances beyond control of parties and court, it becomes no longer possible to conduct trial, or to reach a fair result based upon the evidence.

Manifesto /mænəféstow/. A formal written declaration, promulgated by a sovereign, or by the executive authority of a state or nation, proclaiming its reasons and motives for declaring a war, or for any other important international action. Public declaration or proclamation of political or social principals.

Manifest weight of evidence. The word "manifest", in rule that appellate court cannot substitute its opinion for that of trial court as to facts unless trial court's finding is manifestly against the weight of the evidence, means unmistakable, clear, plain, or indisputable, and requires that an opposite conclusion be clearly evident.

Manipulation. Series of transactions involving the buying or selling of a security for the purpose of creating a false or misleading appearance of active trading or to raise or depress the price to induce the purchase or sale by others. Such acts are prohibited by Sec. 10(b) of the Securities Exchange Act of 1934, 15 U.S.C.A. § 78i, j. *See also* Wash sale.

Term as used in provision in Securities Exchange Act of 1934 [15 U.S.C.A. § 78n(e)] prohibiting use of manipulative practices in tender offers connotes conduct designed to deceive or defraud investors by controlling or artificially affecting price of securities.

Mankind. The race or species of human beings. In law, females, as well as males, are included under this term.

Mann Act. Federal statute (White Slave Traffic Act, 18 U.S.C.A. § 2421) making it a crime to transport a woman or girl in interstate or foreign commerce for the purpose of prostitution or debauchery, or for any other immoral purpose.

Manner. A way, mode, method of doing anything, or mode of proceeding in any case or situation. *See also* Custom and usage.

Manor. A house, dwelling, seat, or residence.

Manorial system. A medieval system of land ownership by lords of the manor for whom serfs and some freemen toiled in the soil in return for protection from the lord. *See also* Manor.

Manslaughter. The unjustifiable, inexcusable and intentional killing of a human being without deliberation, premeditation and malice. The unlawful killing of a human without any deliberation, which may be involuntary, in the commission of a lawful act without due caution and circumspection.

Criminal homicide constitutes manslaughter when: (a) it is committed recklessly; or (b) a homicide which would otherwise be murder is committed under the influence of extreme mental or emotional disturbance for which there is reasonable explanation or excuse. The reasonableness of such explanation or excuse shall be determined from the viewpoint of a person in the actor's situation under the circumstances as he believes them to be. Model Penal Code, § 210.3.

The heat of passion, which will reduce a murder to manslaughter, must be such passion as would be aroused naturally in the mind of the ordinary reasonable person under the same or similar circumstances, as shown by the evidence in the case.

See also Adequate cause; Assault with intent to commit manslaughter; Hot blood; Negligent manslaughter; Sudden heat of passion.

There are various types or degrees of manslaughter recognized by federal and state statutes:

Involuntary manslaughter. Such exists where a person in committing an unlawful act not felonious or tending to great bodily harm, or in committing a lawful act without proper caution or requisite skill, unguardedly or undesignedly kills another. Model Penal Code, § 210.3(1)(a); 18 U.S. C.A. § 1112. *Compare* Accidental killing.

Voluntary manslaughter. Manslaughter committed voluntarily upon a sudden heat of the passions; as if, upon a sudden quarrel, two persons fight, and one of them kills the other. Model Penal Code, § 210.3(1)(b); 18 U.S.C.A. § 1112. It is the unlawful taking of human life without malice and under circumstances falling short of willful, premeditated, or deliberate intent to kill and approaching too near thereto to be justifiable homicide.

The absence of intention to kill or to commit any unlawful act which might reasonably produce death or great bodily harm is the distinguishing feature between voluntary and involuntary homicide.

Manual. Of, or pertaining to, the hand or hands; done, made, or operated by or used with the hand or hands; or as manual labor. Performed by the hand; used or employed by the hand; held in the hand. *See also* Manual labor.

Manual delivery. Delivery of personal property sold, donated, mortgaged, etc., by passing it into the "hand" of the purchaser or transferee, that is, by an actual and corporeal change of possession.

Manual labor. Work done with the hand. Labor performed by hand or by the exercise of physical force, with or without the aid of tools, machinery or equipment, but depending for its effectiveness chiefly upon personal muscular exertion rather than upon skill, intelligence or adroitness.

Manufacture. *v.* From Latin words manus and factura, literally, put together by hand. Now it means the process of making products by hand, machinery, or other automated means. Meaning of word "manufacture," which is defined as the making of goods or wares by manual labor or by machinery, especially on a large scale, has expanded as workmanship and art have advanced, so that now nearly all artificial products of human industry, nearly all such materials as have acquired changed conditions or new and specific combinations, whether from the direct action of the human hand, from chemical processes devised and directed by human skill, or by the employment of machinery, are commonly designated as "manufactured."

Manufacture. *n.* The process or operation of making goods or any material produced by hand, by machinery or by other agency; anything made from raw materials by the hand, by machinery, or by art. The production of articles for use from raw or prepared materials by giving such materials new forms, qualities, properties or combinations, whether by hand labor or machine.

In patent law, any useful product made directly by human labor, or by the aid of machinery directed and controlled by human power, and either from raw materials, or from materials worked up into a new form. Also the process by which such products are made or fashioned.

Manufacturer. One who by labor, art, or skill transforms raw material into some kind of a finished product or article of trade. Any individual, partnership, corporation, association, or other legal relationship which manufactures, assembles, or produces goods.

Manufactured diversity. The improper or collusive creation of diversity of citizenship for the sole or primary purpose of obtaining federal court jurisdiction. Such a practice is prohibited by 28 U.S.C.A. § 1359. *See also* Diversity of citizenship.

Manufacturers liability doctrine. The foundation for the liability under this doctrine is knowledge of the danger attending use of manufactured or assembled product and negligence in failing to give appropriate warning, or negligence in failing to discover and appreciate the danger, and the probable consequences that injury will proximately result from the use of such product for the purposes for which it was intended. *See* Product liability; Strict liability.

Manuscript. An author's work product which is submitted to the publisher either in his own hand, typewritten, on word processing disk, or the like. Lit., written by hand. A writing that has not as yet been printed and published.

Many. The word "many" is defined as consisting of a great number, numerous, not few. Many is a word of very indefinite meaning, and, though it is defined to be numerous and multitudinous, it is also recognized as synonymous with "several", "sundry", "various" and "divers".

Map. A representation of the earth's surface, or of some portion of it, showing the relative position of the parts represented, usually on a flat surface. *See also* Plat map.

Mapp v. Ohio. Landmark Supreme Court case decided in 1961 in which it was ruled that evidence illegally obtained by state officers is not admissible in a state trial if appropriate motions are filed to suppress. The rationale for the rule is that the 4th Amendment (U.S.Const.) protection against unreasonable search and seizure is applicable to the states under and through the 14th Amendment. Mapp v. Ohio, 367 U.S. 643, 81 S.Ct. 1684, 6 L.Ed.2d 1081.

Marbury v. Madison. Landmark case decided in 1803 in which the Supreme Court established the right of the judicial branch to pass on the constitutionality of an act of Congress, thereby establishing the functions and prerogatives of the judiciary in its relation to the legislative branch.

Marbury v. Madison, 5 U.S. (1 Cranch) 137, 2 L.Ed. 60.

Margin. The edge or border; the edge of a body of water where it meets the land. As applied to a boundary line of land, the "margin" of a river, creek, or other watercourse means the center of the stream. But in the case of a lake, bay, or natural pond, the "margin" means the line where land and water meet.

In finance, difference between market value of loan collateral and face value of loan.

A sum of money, or its equivalent, placed in the hands of a broker by the principal or person on whose account a purchase or sale of securities is to be made, as a security to the former against losses to which he may be exposed by subsequent fluctuations in the market value of the stock. The amount paid by the customer when he uses his broker's credit to buy a security. *See also* Margin account; Margin transaction.

In commercial transactions the difference between the purchase price paid by a middleman or retailer and his selling price, or difference between price received by manufacturer for its goods and costs to produce. Also called gross profit margin. *See also* Profit; Remargining.

Margin account. Securities industry's method of extending credit to customers. Under such practice customer purchases specified amount of stock from securities firm by advancing only portion of purchase price, with brokerage firm extending credit or making loan for balance due, and firm maintains such stock as collateral for loan and charges interest on balance of purchase price. Margin account requirements are specified by regulations of Federal Reserve Board. See 15 U.S.C.A. § 78g. *See also* Margin transaction.

Margin call. A demand by a broker to put up money or securities upon purchase of a stock, or, if the stock is already owned on margin, to increase the money or securities in the event the price of the stock has or is likely to fall since purchase. The last process (of maintaining the minimum required margin) is remargining. *See* Margin requirement.

Margin list. List of Federal Reserve Board which limits the loan value of a bank's stock to a certain per cent (*e.g.* 50%) of its market value. When a bank is not on the margin list, no limit is placed on the value of its stock for use as collateral.

Margin profit. *See* Margin; Profit.

Margin requirement. The percentage of the purchase price that must be deposited with a broker to purchase a security on margin. The margin requirement is set or adjusted by the Federal Reserve Board.

Margin trading. *See* Margin; Margin account; Margin transaction.

Margin transaction. The purchase of a stock or commodity with payment in part in cash (called the margin) and in part by a loan. Usually the loan is made by the broker effecting the purchase. *See also* Margin account.

Marihuana, mariguana, marijuana /mǽrə(h)wónə/. An annual herb, cannabis sativa, having angular rough stem and deeply lobed leaves. The bast fibres of cannabis are the hemp of commerce. A drug prepared from "cannabis sativa," designated in technical dictionaries as "cannabis" and commonly known as marijuana, marihuana, marajuana, or maraguana.

"Marihuana" means all parts of the plant Cannabis sativa L., whether growing or not; the seeds thereof; the resin extracted from any part of the plant; and every compound, manufacture, salt, derivative, mixture, or preparation of the plant, its seeds or resin. It does not include the mature stalks of the plant, fiber produced from the stalks, oil or cake made from the seeds of the plant, any other compound, manufacture, salt, derivative, mixture, or preparation of the mature stalks (except the resin extracted therefrom), fiber, oil, or cake, or the sterilized seed of the plant which is incapable of germination. Uniform Controlled Substances Act, 21 U.S.C.A. § 802. *See also* Cannabis.

Marihuana is also commonly referred to as "pot", "grass", "tea", "weed" or "Mary-Jane"; and in cigarette form as a "joint" or "reefer".

Marine. Naval; relating or pertaining to the sea; native to or formed by the sea, such as marine life; transacted at sea; doing duty or service on the sea. The mercantile and naval shipping of a country. Concerned with navigation and commerce of the sea; *i.e.* maritime matters. Member of U.S. Marine Corps. *See also* Maritime.

Marine belt. That portion of the main or open sea, adjacent to the shores of a given country, over which the jurisdiction of its municipal laws and local authorities extends. Territorial waters, defined by international law as extending out three miles from the shore. *See also* Territorial waters.

Marine carrier. By statutes of several states this term is applied to carriers plying upon the ocean, arms of the sea, the Great Lakes, and other navigable waters within the jurisdiction of the United States.

Marine contract. One relating to maritime affairs, shipping, navigation, marine insurance, affreightment, maritime loans, or other business to be done upon the sea or in connection with navigation. *See e.g.* Bareboat charter.

Marine insurance. *See* Insurance.

Marine interest. Interest, allowed to be stipulated for at an extraordinary rate, for the use and risk of money loaned on *respondentia* and bottomry bonds.

Marine league /mɔríyn líyg/. A measure of distance commonly employed at sea, being equal to one-twentieth part of a degree of latitude, or three geographical or nautical miles.

Mariner. A seaman or sailor; one engaged in navigating vessels upon the sea; persons employed aboard ships or vessels.

Marine risk. The perils of the sea; the perils necessarily incident to navigation.

Mariner's will. A nuncupative or oral will permitted in some jurisdictions for the sailor who is actually at sea at the time of making the will. Generally, such will affects personal property only.

Marital /mǽrətəl/məráytəl/. Relating to, or connected with, the *status* of marriage; pertaining to a husband; incident to a husband.

Marital agreements. Contracts between parties who are either on the threshold of marriage or on the verge of separation, though, in general, the term refers to all agreements between married people. Such agreements are primarily concerned with the division and ownership of marital property. In some jurisdictions, the contract must be made through a third person if the law does not permit the spouses to contract directly with each other. A number of states have adopted the Uniform Premarital Agreement Act. *See also* Antenuptial agreement; Equitable distribution; Marriage settlement; Post-nuptial agreement.

Marital communications privilege. In most jurisdictions private communications between the spouses during the marriage are privileged at the option of the witness spouse and hence inadmissible in a trial. In some jurisdictions the communications are disqualified, and hence not admissible, even with the consent of the witness spouse. This privilege is subject to certain limitations; *e.g.* prosecutions for crimes committed by one spouse against the other or against the children of either; also, communications made in letter dictated by husband to stenographer to his wife is not within privilege; presence of third party and intent that third party communicate message destroys privilege. *See also* Husband-wife privilege.

Marital deduction. A deduction allowed upon the transfer of property from one spouse to another. The deduction is allowed under the Federal gift tax for lifetime (*i.e.,* inter vivos) transfers and also under the Federal estate tax for testamentary transfers. There is no ceiling on the estate tax marital deduction for decedents dying after 1981. I.R.C. §§ 2056, 2523. *See also* Pecuniary formulas.

Marital deduction trust. In estate planning, a device in the form of a trust utilized to gain the maximum benefit of the marital deduction by dividing the property in half. Commonly, one half of the property is transferred to the marital deduction trust and the other half is disposed of in a trust or like arrangement with a view towards having it escape taxation in the estate of the surviving spouse. As a result of a change in the law with respect to the estate of decedents dying after 1981, the marital deduction trust is generally not used. The law provides that there is no monetary ceiling on the estate tax marital deduction for decedents dying after 1981.

Marital portion. In Louisiana, the name given to that part of a deceased husband's estate to which the widow is entitled.

Marital privileges. Those rights, immunities and advantages which attach to the state of marriage such as the right to connubial relations and the right to hold property as husband and wife. *See also* Marital communications privilege.

Marital property. Term used to describe property of spouses subject to equitable distribution upon termination of marriage. Property purchased or otherwise accumulated by spouses while married to each other and which, in most jurisdictions, on dissolution of the marriage is divided in proportions as the court deems fit. *See* Community property; Equitable distribution; Property; Separate property.

Marital rights and duties. Those arising from marriage contract and constituting its object, and therefore embracing what the parties agree to perform towards each other and to society. Rights of husband and wife to a specified share of other's personal estate upon death of other. *See* Marital agreements.

Maritime. Pertaining to navigable waters, *i.e.* to the sea, ocean, great lakes, navigable rivers, or the navigation or commerce thereof.

All work occurring on navigable waters is "maritime" within meaning of Longshore and Harbor Workers' Compensation Act.

See also Federal Maritime Commission; Marine; Maritime court; Navigable waters.

Maritime Administration. An agency within the Department of Commerce which promotes and regulates the activities of the U.S. merchant marine, directs emergency operations related to merchant marine activities, establishes specifications for shipbuilding and design, determines routes, and manages other areas of merchant operations. The Maritime Act of 1981 transferred the Maritime Administration to the Department of Transportation. *See also* Maritime Commission.

Maritime belt. That part of the sea which, in contradistinction to the open sea, is under the sway of the riparian states. *See also* Marine belt; Territorial waters.

Maritime bills. *See* Bill *(Maritime Law)*.

Maritime cause of action. A case arising on the sea, ocean, great lakes, or navigable rivers, or from some act or contract concerning the commerce and navigation thereof. An action based upon an injury to a passenger of a vessel while on navigable waters and caused by negligence comes within scope of "maritime cause of action" within original jurisdiction of federal District Court. *See also* Maritime jurisdiction; Maritime law; Maritime tort; Navigable waters.

Maritime Commission. The Federal Maritime Commission regulates the waterborne foreign and domestic offshore commerce of the United States, assures that United States international trade is open to all nations on fair and equitable terms, and guards against unauthorized monopoly in the waterborne commerce of the United States. This is accomplished through maintaining surveillance over steamship conferences and common carriers by water; assuring that only the rates on file with the Commission are charged; approving agreements between persons subject to the Shipping Acts of 1916 and 1984; guaranteeing equal treatment to shippers and carriers by terminal operators, freight forwarders, and other persons subject to the shipping statutes; and ensuring that adequate levels of financial responsibility are maintained for indemnification of passengers or oil spill cleanup. *See also* Maritime Administration.

Maritime contract. A contract relating to business of navigation. A contract whose subject-matter has relation to the navigation of the seas or to trade or commerce to be conducted by navigation or to be done upon the sea or in ports. One having reference to maritime services or maritime transactions. As regards right to jury trial in contract disputes, see 28 U.S.C.A. § 1873.

Maritime court. A court exercising jurisdiction in maritime causes; one which possesses the powers and jurisdiction of a court of admiralty. *See* Admiralty court; Maritime jurisdiction.

Maritime interest. An expression equivalent to "marine interest" *(q.v.)*.

Maritime jurisdiction. Jurisdiction over maritime causes is granted to Federal district courts. 28 U.S.C.A. § 1333. Procedure in maritime actions is governed by the Federal Rules of Civil Procedure and Supp. Admiralty Rules. *See* Admiralty court.

Maritime law. That which the Congress has enacted or the Federal courts, sitting in admiralty, or in the exercise of their maritime jurisdiction, have declared and would apply. That system of law which particularly relates to marine commerce and navigation, to business transacted at sea or relating to navigation, to ships and shipping, to seamen, to the transportation of persons and property by sea, and to marine affairs generally. The law relating to harbors, ships, and

seamen, divided into a variety of subject areas, such as those concerning harbors, property of ships, duties and rights of masters and seamen, contracts of affreightment, average, salvage, etc. It extends to civil marine torts and injuries, illegal dispossession or withholding of possession from the owners of ships, municipal seizures of ships, etc.

Substantively, in the United States, it is federal law, and jurisdiction to administer it is vested in the federal courts, though not to the entire exclusion of the courts of the states. *See* Maritime jurisdiction.

Maritime lien. A privileged claim on a vessel for some service rendered to it to facilitate its use in navigation, or an injury caused by it in navigable waters, to be carried into effect by legal process in the admiralty court. A special property right in a ship given to a creditor by law as security for a debt or claim subsisting from the moment the debt arises with right to have the ship sold and debt paid out of proceeds. Such a lien is a proprietary interest or right of property in the vessel itself, and not a cause of action or demand for personal judgment against the owner. The lien is enforced by a direct proceeding against the vessel or other property in which it exists. See Supp. Admiralty Rule C.

Any person furnishing repairs, supplies, towage, use of dry dock or marine railway, or other necessaries, to any vessel, whether foreign or domestic, upon the order of the owner of such vessel, or of a person authorized by the owner, shall have a maritime lien on the vessel, which may be enforced by suit in rem, and it shall not be necessary to allege or prove that credit was given to the vessel. Federal Maritime Lien Act, § 971.

Maritime loan. A contract or agreement by which one, who is the lender, lends to another, who is the borrower, a certain sum of money, upon condition that if the thing upon which the loan has been made should be lost by any peril of the sea, or *vis major*, the lender shall not be repaid unless what remains shall be equal to the sum borrowed; and if the thing arrive in safety, or in case it shall not have been injured but by its own defects or the fault of the master or mariners, the borrower shall be bound to return the sum borrowed, together with a certain sum agreed upon as the price of the hazard incurred.

Maritime prize. *See* Prize.

Maritime service. In admiralty law, a service rendered upon the seas, ocean, great lakes, or a navigable river, and which has some relation to commerce or navigation,—some connection with a vessel employed in trade, with her equipment, her preservation, or the preservation of her cargo or crew.

Maritime tort. Civil wrongs committed on navigable waters. As regards right to jury trial, see 28 U.S.C.A. § 1873. *See* Jones Act; Longshore and Harbor Workers' Compensation Act.

Maritus /məráytəs/mǽrətəs/. Lat. A husband; a married man.

Mark. A character, usually in the form of a cross, made as a substitute for his signature by a person who cannot write, in executing a conveyance, will or other legal document. It is commonly made as follows: A third person writes the name of the marksman, leaving a blank space between the Christian name and surname; in this space the latter traces the mark, or crossed lines, and above the mark is written "his" (or "her"), and below it, "mark." *See* Cross.

The sign, writing, or ticket put upon manufactured goods to distinguish them from others, appearing thus in the compound, "trade-mark."

A token, evidence, or proof; as in the phrase "a mark of fraud."

In trademark law, the term "mark" includes any trademark, service mark, collective mark, or certification mark. 15 U.S.C.A. § 1127. *See also* Trademark.

A weight used in several parts of Europe, and for several commodities, especially gold and silver.

Monetary unit, *e.g.* German Deutsche mark.

The word is sometimes used as another form of *"marque,"* a license of reprisals.

See also Bench mark; Certification mark; Collective mark.

Markdown. Reduction in selling price.

Marked money. Term used to describe money given by undercover agent who buys contraband or gives bribe in money, or ransom money given to kidnapper, or money given to bank robber, which bears a tell-tale mark for use in identifying and connecting the money to the perpetrator of the crime.

Market. Place of commercial activity in which goods, commodities, securities, services, etc., are bought and sold. The region in which any commodity or product can be sold; the geographical or economic extent of commercial demand. A public time and appointed place of buying and selling; also purchase and sale. It differs from the *forum*, or market of antiquity, which was a public marketplace on one side only, or during one part of the day only, the other sides being occupied by temples, theaters, courts of justice, and other public buildings.

In a limited sense, "market" is the range of bid and asked prices reported by brokers making the market in over-the-counter securities.

By the term "market" is also understood the demand there is for any particular article; as, "the cotton market is depressed." Is also an abbreviated term for "stock" or "commodity" markets.

See also Common market; Current market value; Negotiated markets.

Geographic market. In antitrust context, that geographic area in which a product is sold and in which there is or is not competition. It generally implies agreement allocating different areas to each competitor with the understanding that the other competitors will not sell in those areas. A relevant "geographic market" for purposes of assessing monopoly power is the territorial area in which businessmen effectively compete. Within broad geographic market, well-defined submarkets may exist which, in themselves, constitute "geographic markets" for antitrust purposes. *See also Product market; Relevant market, below.*

Listed market securities. The market value of a security as reflected by transactions of that security on the floor of an exchange.

Open market. A market wherein supply and demand are expressed in terms of a price.

Product market. In antitrust context, a market in which competitors agree among themselves to limit the manufacture or sales of products so as to prevent competition among themselves.

Public market. A market which is not only open to the resort of the general public as purchasers, but also available to all who wish to offer their wares for sale, stalls, stands, or places being allotted to those who apply, to the limits of the capacity of the market, on payment of fixed rents or fees.

Relevant market. In antitrust context, it may refer to geographic area in which competitors agree to respect the rights of others to sell a product. It may also refer to product markets in which competitors agree among themselves to limit the manufacture or sales of products so as to prevent or limit competition among themselves. *See also* Relevant market.

Thin market. A market for publicly traded securities in which the number of transactions and/or the number of securities offered for sale or purchase at any one time are relatively few. In a thin market a single substantial purchase or sale order may cause a significant price movement.

Marketability. Salability. The probability of selling property, goods, securities, services, etc., at a specific time, price, and terms.

Marketable. Salable. Such things as may be sold in the market; those for which a buyer may be found; merchantable.

Marketable securities. Stocks and bonds held of other companies that can be readily sold on stock exchanges or over-the-counter markets and that the company plans to sell as cash is needed. Classified as current liquid assets and as part of working capital.

Marketable title. A title which is free from encumbrances and any reasonable doubt as to its validity, and such as a reasonably intelligent person, who is well informed as to facts and their legal bearings, and ready and willing to perform his contract, would be willing to accept in exercise of ordinary business prudence. Such a title as is free from reasonable doubt in law and in fact; not merely a title valid in fact, but one which readily can be sold or mortgaged to a reasonably prudent purchaser or mortgagee; one acceptable to a reasonable purchaser, informed as to the facts and their legal meaning, willing to perform his contract, in the exercise of that prudence which businessmen usually bring to bear on such transactions; one under which a purchaser may have quiet and peaceful enjoyment of the property; one that is free from material defects, or grave doubts, and reasonably free from litigation.

Marketable title is one which is free from reasonable doubt and will not expose party who holds it to hazards of litigation. One that may be freely made the subject of resale.

A marketable title to land is such a title as a court, when asked to decree specific performance of the contract of sale, will compel the vendee to accept as sufficient. It is said to be not merely a defensible title, but a title which is free from plausible or reasonable objections.

See also Merchantable title. *Compare* Unmarketable title.

Marketable Title Acts. Many states have adopted Marketable Title Acts the purpose of which is to simplify land title transactions through making it possible to determine marketability by limited title searches over some reasonable period of the immediate past (*e.g.* 40 yrs.) and thus avoid the necessity of examining the record back into distant time for each new transaction.

Market geld. The toll of a market.

Market making. Regarding securities in over the counter trading, the process consisting of bid and ask quotations which results in the establishment of a market for such securities. *See* Bid and asked.

Market order. An order to buy or sell on a stock or commodity exchange at the current (best) price when the order reaches the floor of the exchange. Requests by customers to purchase or sell securities at the market price existing when the order reaches the exchange floor.

Market portfolio. A value-weighted portfolio of every asset in a market.

Market power. Term for purposes of the Sherman Act, is the ability to raise prices significantly above the competitive level without losing all of one's business; the ability to raise prices above those which would be charged in a competitive market. *See* Market share.

Market price. The price at which a seller is ready and willing to sell and a buyer ready and willing to buy in the ordinary course of trade. The price actually given in current market dealings; price established by public sales or sales in the way of ordinary business. The actual price at which given stock or commodity is currently sold, or has recently been sold in open market, that is, not at forced sale, but in the usual and ordinary course of trade and competition between sellers and buyers equally free to bargain, as established by records of late sales. In the case of a security, market price is usually considered the last reported price at which the stock or bond sold.

Market price is synonymous with market value, and means the price actually given in current market dealings, or the price at which the supply and demand are equal. The point of intersection of supply and demand in the market. *See also* Market value.

Market quotations. The latest (most current) prices at which securities or commodities have been bought and sold on an exchange or other market.

Market share. The percentage of a market that is controlled by a firm. A 20 percent share of market means that the firm has captured 20 percent of the actual sales in the market. *See* Market power.

Market structure. Refers to the broad organizational characteristics of a market. The major characteristics are seller concentration, product differentiation, and barriers to entry.

Market value. The price property would command in the open market. The highest price a willing buyer would pay and a willing seller accept, both being fully informed, and the property being exposed for a reasonable period of time. The market value may be different from the price a property can actually be sold for at a given time (market price). The market value of an article or piece of property is the price which it might be expected to bring if offered for sale in a fair market; not the price which might be obtained on a sale at public auction or a sale forced by the necessities of the owner, but such a price as would be fixed by negotiation and mutual agreement, after ample time to find a purchaser, as between a vendor who is willing (but not compelled) to sell and a purchaser who desires to buy but is not compelled to take the particular article or piece of property. *See also* Actual market value; Cash value; Clear market value; Fair cash market value; Fair market value; Market price.

Marking up. The process wherein a legislative committee goes through a bill section by section, revising its language and amending the bill as desired. Extensive revision may lead to the introduction of a clean bill under a new number. May also refer to procedure by which a case is placed on the trial calendar; *e.g.* "marking up for trial."

Markon. An amount originally added to cost to obtain list price. Usually expressed as a percentage of cost. Further increases in list price are called markups; decreases are called markdowns. *See also* Markup.

Markup. An amount originally added to cost. Usually expressed as a percentage of selling price. Also refers to an increase above an originally-established retail price. *See* Margin; Marking up; Markon.

Marque and reprisal, letters of /létərz əv márk ənd rəpráyzəl/. These words, "marque" and "reprisal," are frequently used as synonymous, but, taken in their strict etymological sense, the latter signifies a "taking in return;" the former, the passing the frontiers *(marches)* in order to such taking. Letters of marque and reprisal are grantable, by the law of nations, whenever the subjects of one state are oppressed and injured by those of another, and justice is denied by that state to which the oppressor belongs; and the party to whom these letters are granted may then seize the bodies or the goods of the subjects of the state to which the offender belongs, until satisfaction be made, wherever they happen to be found. Reprisals are to be granted only in case of a clear and open denial of justice. At the present day, in consequence partly of treaties and partly of the practice of nations, the making of reprisals is confined to the seizure of commercial property on the high seas by public cruisers, or by private cruisers specially authorized thereto. Article I, Sec. 8, of U.S.Const. grants Congress the power to grant Letters of Marque and Reprisal.

Marque, law of /ló əv márk/. A sort of law of reprisal, which entitles him who has received any wrong from another and cannot get ordinary justice to take the shipping or goods of the wrong-doer, where he can find them within his own bounds or precincts, in satisfaction of the wrong.

Marriage. Legal union of one man and one woman as husband and wife. Marriage, as distinguished from the agreement to marry and from the act of becoming married, is the legal status, condition, or relation of one man and one woman united in law for life, or until divorced, for the discharge to each other and the community of the duties legally incumbent on those whose association is founded on the distinction of sex. A con-

tract, according to the form prescribed by law, by which a man and woman capable of entering into such contract, mutually engage with each other to live their whole lives (or until divorced) together in state of union which ought to exist between a husband and wife. The word also signifies the act, ceremony, or formal proceeding by which persons take each other for husband and wife.

See also Banns of matrimony; Common-law marriage; Consensual marriage; Voidable marriage; Void marriage.

Ceremonial marriage. Marriage which follows all the statutory requirements of blood tests, license, waiting period, and which has been solemnized before an official (religious or civil) capable of presiding at the marriage.

Informal marriage. A marriage in which promises are exchanged between the parties without an official ecclesiastical representative present. In most cases, the law requires consummation of the marriage to consider such valid. *See* Consensual marriage.

Marriage in jest. A marriage in jest is subject to annulment for lack of requisite consent and intention to marry.

Mixed marriage. A marriage between persons of different nationalities or religions; or, more particularly, between persons of different racial origin; as between a white person and a negro or an Indian. *See* Miscegenation.

Plural marriage. In general, any bigamous or polygamous union, but particularly, a second or subsequent marriage of a man who already has one wife living under system of polygamy. Such marriages are prohibited.

Proxy marriage. Marriage contracted or celebrated by one or more agents rather than by the parties themselves.

Putative marriage. One contracted in good faith and in ignorance (on one or both sides) of some existing impediment on the part of at least one of the contracting parties. Such marriages are recognized in very few jurisdictions.

Marriage articles. Articles of agreement between parties contemplating marriage, intended as preliminary to a formal marriage settlement, to be drawn after marriage. *See also* Marital agreements; Marriage settlement.

Marriage broker. One who for a consideration brings a woman and man together in marriage.

Such activity is void and illegal as against public policy.

Marriage ceremony. The form, religious or civil, for the solemnization of a marriage.

Marriage certificate. An instrument which certifies a marriage, and is executed by the person officiating at the marriage; it is not intended to be signed by the parties, but is evidence of the marriage.

Marriage license. A license or permission granted by public authority to persons who intend to intermarry, usually addressed to the minister or magistrate who is to perform the ceremony, or, in general terms, to any one authorized to solemnize marriages. By statute in most jurisdictions, it is made an essential prerequisite to the lawful solemnization of the marriage.

Marriage portion. Dowry; a sum of money or other property which is given to or settled on a woman on her marriage.

Marriage promise. Betrothal; engagement to intermarry with another.

Marriage records. Those documents kept by a state, city or town official which are permanent records of marriages and which include the names of the spouses, the maiden name of the wife, their addresses and the date of the marriage. From these documents certificates of marriages are prepared.

Marriage settlement. An agreement in contemplation of marriage in which each party agrees to release or modify property rights which would otherwise arise from the marriage. A written agreement in the nature of a conveyance, called a "settlement," which is made in contemplation of a proposed marriage and in consideration thereof, either by the parties about to marry, or one of them, or by a parent or relation on their behalf, by which the title to certain property is settled, *i.e.,* fixed or limited to a prescribed course of succession; the object being, usually, to provide for the wife and children. Thus, the estate might be limited to the husband and issue, or to the wife and issue, or to husband and wife for their joint lives, remainder to the survivor for life, remainder over to the issue, or otherwise. Such settlements may also be made after marriage, in which case they are called "postnuptial." *See also* Antenuptial agreement; Marital agreements; Palimony; Post-nuptial agreement.

Married woman. A woman who has a husband living and not divorced; a *feme covert*.

Marshal. The President is required to appoint a U.S. Marshal to each judicial district. It is the responsibility of U.S. marshals to execute all lawful writs, process and orders issued under authority of the United States. In executing the laws of the United States within a state, the marshal may exercise the same powers which a sheriff of the State may exercise in executing the laws thereof. 28 U.S.C.A. §§ 561, 569, 570.

Also, in some of the states, this is the name of a law officer in certain cities having powers and duties corresponding generally to those of a constable or sheriff. Administrative head of city police or fire department.

See also Provost-Marshal.

Marshalling assets. Also known as marshalling assets and securities, marshalling of liens or marshalling of remedies, it is an equitable doctrine requiring a senior creditor, having two funds to satisfy his debt, to resort first to the one fund which is not subject to the demand of a junior creditor of the common debtor, to avoid the inequity which would result from an election of the senior creditor to satisfy its demand out of the only fund available to the junior creditor, thereby excluding the junior creditor from any satisfaction.

The arrangement or ranking of assets in a certain order towards the payment of debts.

Under the common law, a doctrine whereby encumbered lands, which are sold to different persons at different times by conveyances the grantees and the person holding the lien, are chargeable in equity with the encumbrance in the inverse order of their alienation.

Martial law /márshəl ló/. Exists when military authorities carry on government or exercise various degrees of control over civilians or civilian authorities in domestic territory. Such may exist either in time of war or when civil authority has ceased to function or has become ineffective. A system of law, obtaining only in time of actual war and growing out of the exigencies thereof, arbitrary in its character, and depending only on the will of the commander of an army, which is established and administered in a place or district of hostile territory held in belligerent possession, or, sometimes, in places occupied or pervaded by insurgents or mobs, and which suspends all existing civil laws, as well as the civil authority and the ordinary administration of justice. *See also* Military government; Military law.

Mary Carter agreement. The term "Mary Carter Agreement" arises from the agreement popularized by the case of Booth v. Mary Carter Paint Co., Fla.App. 1967, 202 So.2d 8, and now is used rather generally to apply to any agreement between the plaintiff and some, but less than all, defendants whereby the parties place limitations on the financial responsibility of the agreeing defendants, the amount of which is variable and usually in some inverse ratio to the amount of recovery which the plaintiff is able to make against the nonagreeing defendant or defendants. Such agreements are held to be void as against public policy in certain states, while in others are permissible if disclosed to the jury.

Mason and Dixon Line. The boundary line between Pennsylvania on the north and Maryland on the south, celebrated before the extinction of slavery as the line of demarcation between the slave and the free states. It was run by Charles Mason and Jeremiah Dixon, commissioners in a dispute between the Penn Proprietors and Lord Baltimore. The line was carried 244 miles from the Delaware river where it was stopped by Indians. A resurvey was made in 1849, and in 1900 a new survey was authorized by the two states.

Massachusetts ballot. The office-block type of Australian ballot in which, under each office, the names of candidates, with party designations, are printed in alphabetical order.

Massachusetts rule. As regards sending out checks through banks for collection, the "Massachusetts rule" is that each bank that receives the item acts as an agent for the depositor; but in some other states, the "New York rule" prevails, under which only the bank first receiving the item is responsible to, or is the agent of, the depositor, the other banks being the agent of the bank, in the process of the collection.

Massachusetts trust. A business organization wherein property is conveyed to trustees and managed for benefit of holders of certificates like corporate stock certificates. A "Massachusetts business trust" is an unincorporated association organized under Massachusetts law for purpose of investing in real estate in much the same manner as a mutual fund invests in corporate securities. *See also* Common-law trust; Real estate investment trust; Trust estates as business companies.

Master. A principal who employs another to perform service in his affairs and who controls or has right to control physical conduct of other in performance of the service. Restatement, Second, Agency, § 2. One who stands to another in such a relation that he not only controls the results of the work of that other but also may direct the manner in which such work shall be done.

One having authority; one who rules, directs, instructs, or superintends; a head or chief; an instructor; an employer. *See* various "Master" titles *below*.

One who has reached the summit of his trade and who has the right to hire apprentices and journeymen.

Fed.R.Civil P. 53, and analogous state rules, provide for the appointment by the court of a master to assist it in specific judicial duties as may arise in a case. The master's powers and duties depend upon the terms of the order of reference and the controlling court rule, and may include taking of testimony, discovery of evidence and other acts or measures necessary for the performance of his duties specified in the order of reference. The master is required to prepare a report of his proceedings for the court. In the federal courts the appointment of a master is the "exception rather than the rule", while under many state rules, the court has more liberal powers to appoint such. *See also* Reference.

Special master. A master appointed to act as the representative of the court in some particular act or transaction, as, to make a sale of property under a decree. A federal judge may appoint a U.S. magistrate to serve as a special master. 28 U.S.C.A. § 636.

Master agreement. The omnibus labor agreement reached between a union and the leaders of the industry or a trade association. It becomes the pattern for labor agreements between the union and individual employers.

Master and servant. The relation of master and servant exists where one person, for pay or other valuable consideration, enters into the service of another and devotes to him his personal labor for an agreed period. The relation exists where the employer has the right to select the employee, the power to remove and discharge him and the right to direct both what work shall be done and the manner in which it shall be done. Restatement, Second, Agency § 2. Such term has generally been replaced by "employer and employee". *Compare* Agency; Independent contractor.

Master budget. In accounting, the comprehensive set of all budgetary schedules and the pro forma financial statements of an organization.

Master deed *or* **lease.** Conveyancing document used by owners or lessees of condominiums.

Master in chancery. An officer of a court of chancery who acts as an assistant to the judge or chancellor. His duties are to inquire into such matters as may be referred to him by the court, examine causes, take testimony, take accounts, compute damages, etc., reporting his findings to the court in such shape that a decree may be made; also to take oaths and affidavits and acknowledgments of deeds. In modern practice, many of the functions of a master are performed by clerks, commissioners, auditors, and referees, and in those states that have merged law and equity courts in adopting Rules of Civil Procedure the office has been superseded. *See* Master.

Master lease. *See* Lease; Sublease.

Master Limited Partnership (MLP). A publicly-traded limited partnership.

Master of a ship. In maritime law, the commander of a merchant vessel, who has the chief charge of her government and navigation and the command of the crew, as well as the general care and control of the vessel and cargo, as the representative and confidential agent of the owner. He is commonly called the "captain."

Master plan. Term used in land use control law, zoning and urban redevelopment to describe the omnibus plan of a city or town for housing, industry and recreational facilities and their impact on environmental factors. *See also* Planned unit development.

Master policy. An insurance policy which covers a group of persons as in health or life insurance written as group insurance. Generally, there is only one master policy and the participants have only certificates evidencing their participation.

Master's report. The formal report or statement made by a master in chancery of his decision on any question referred to him, or of any facts or action he has been directed to ascertain or take.

The document filed with the court after a master has heard the evidence and made his findings. The report should contain his findings and conclusions of law where necessary. Fed.R.Civil P. 53(e).

Master-servant rule. Under this rule, master (employer) is liable for conduct of servant (employee) which occurs while servant is acting within scope of his employment or within scope of his authority. *See also* Fellow servant; Respondeat superior; Servant.

Material. Important; more or less necessary; having influence or effect; going to the merits; having to do with matter, as distinguished from form. Representation relating to matter which is so substantial and important as to influence party to whom made is "material." *See* Material fact; Relevant.

Material allegation. An allegation is said to be material when it forms a substantive part of the case presented by the pleading. A material allegation in a pleading is one essential to the claim or defense, and which could not be stricken from the pleading without leaving it insufficient.

Material alteration. A material alteration in any written instrument is one which changes its tenor, or its legal meaning and effect; one which causes it to speak a language different in effect from that which it originally spoke. A material alteration of a deed is one which effects a change in its legal effect.

Any alteration of an instrument is material which changes the contract of any party thereto in any respect, including any such change in: (a) the number or relations of the parties; or (b) an incomplete instrument, by completing it otherwise than as authorized; or (c) the writing as signed, by adding to it or by removing any part of it. U.C.C. § 3–407(1). The term is defined similarly when applied to other kinds of commercial paper.

Material breach. *See* Breach of contract.

Material evidence. That quality of evidence which tends to influence the trier of fact because of its logical connection with the issue. Evidence which has an effective influence or bearing on question in issue. "Materiality" of evidence refers to pertinency of the offered evidence to the issue in dispute. Evidence which is material to question in controversy, and which must necessarily enter into the consideration of the controversy, and which by itself or in connection with other evidence is determinative of the case.

To establish *Brady* violation requiring reversal of a conviction, defendant must show that prosecution has suppressed evidence, that such evidence was favorable to defendant or was exculpatory, and that evidence was material; evidence is "material" if there is reasonable probability that, but for failure to produce such evidence, outcome of case would have been different. Brady v. Maryland, 373 U.S. 83, 83 S.Ct. 1194, 10 L.Ed.2d 215.

See also Evidence; Relevancy; Relevant evidence.

Material fact. *Contracts.* One which constitutes substantially the consideration of the contract, or without which it would not have been made. *See also* Reliance.

Insurance. A fact which, if communicated to the agent or insurer, would induce him either to decline the insurance altogether, or not accept it unless a higher premium is paid. One which necessarily has some bearing on the subject-matter. A fact which increases the risk, or which, if disclosed, would have been a fair reason for demanding a higher premium. Any fact the knowledge or ignorance of which would naturally influence the insurer in making or refusing the contract, or in estimating the degree and character of the risk, or in fixing the rate.

Pleading and practice. One which is essential to the case, defense, application, etc., and without which it could not be supported. One which tends to establish any of issues raised. The "material facts" of an issue of fact are such as are necessary to determine the issue. Material fact is one upon which outcome of litigation depends. *See also* Material allegation.

Securities. To be a "material" fact within the Securities Act of 1933, it must concern information about which an average prudent investor ought reasonably be informed before purchasing a security. Within purview of Securities Act provision rendering it unlawful for any person in connection with offer, sale or purchase of any security, directly or indirectly, to make any untrue statement of material fact, or fail to disclose a material fact, is one which a reasonable person would attach importance to in determining his or her choice of action in the transaction. Or, stated alternatively, a fact is deemed "material" if its disclosure would have been viewed by a reasonable investor as having significantly altered the "total mix" of information made available. An omitted fact is material if there is a substantial likelihood that a reasonable shareholder would consider it important in deciding how to vote. *See also* Reliance; Rule 10b–5.

Summary judgment. In determining what constitutes a genuine issue as to any material fact for purposes of summary judgment, an issue is "material" if the facts alleged are such as to constitute a legal defense or are of such nature as to affect the result of the action. See Fed.R.Civil P. 56(c).

A fact is "material" and precludes grant of summary judgment if proof of that fact would have effect of establishing or refuting one of essential elements of a cause of action or defense asserted by the parties, and would necessarily affect application of appropriate principle of law to the rights and obligations of the parties.

Materiality. In accounting, a concept dictating that an accountant must judge the impact and importance of each transaction (or event) to determine its proper handling in the accounting records. Minor items are treated in the most expedient manner possible.

Materialman. A person who has furnished materials or supplies used in the construction or repair of a building, structure, etc.

Materialman's lien. By statute in most states, a person who furnishes material for the construction, improvement or alteration of a building or other structure has a priority for payment of his claim based on his lien as a supplier of such materials. *See also* Mechanic's lien.

Material representation *or* **misrepresentation.** A misrepresentation is "material" if it relates to a matter upon which plaintiff could be expected to rely in determining to engage in the conduct in question. In law of deceit, a statement or undertaking of sufficient substance and importance as to be the foundation of an action if such representation is false. *See also* Material fact; Representation.

Material witness. A person who can give testimony relating to a particular matter no one else, or at least very few, can give. In an important criminal case, a material witness may sometimes be held by the government against his or her will. He may be the victim or an eye witness. *See also* Witness.

Maternal. That which belongs to, or comes from, the mother; as maternal authority, maternal relation, maternal estate, maternal line.

Maternal line. A line of descent or relationship between two persons which is traced through the mother of the younger.

Maternal property. That which comes from the mother of the party, and other ascendants of the maternal stock.

Maternity. The character, relation, state, or condition of a mother.

Mathematical evidence. Demonstrative evidence; such as establishes its conclusions with absolute necessity and certainty. It is used in contradistinction to *moral* evidence.

Matricide /mǽtrəsàyd/. The murder of a mother; or one who has slain his mother.

Matriculate /mətríkyəleyt/. To enroll; to enter in a register; specifically, to enter or admit to membership in a body or society, particularly in a college or university, by enrolling the name in a register. To go through the process of admission to membership, as by examination and enrollment, in a society or college.

Matrimonial. Of or pertaining to matrimony or the estate of marriage.

Matrimonial action. Term that includes actions for a separation, for an annulment or dissolution of a marriage, for a divorce, for a declaration of the nullity of a void marriage, for a declaration of the validity or nullity of a foreign judgment of divorce and for a declaration of the validity or nullity of a marriage. See *e.g.* New York C.P.L.R. § 105. *See also* Annulment; Custody; Divorce; Equitable distribution; Separation of spouses.

Matrimonial cohabitation. The living together of a man and woman ostensibly as husband and wife. Also the living together of those who are legally husband and wife, the term carrying with it, in this sense, an implication of mutual rights and duties as to sharing the same habitation. *See* Palimony.

Matrimonial domicile. Place where parties live together as husband and wife either actually or constructively.

Matrimonial res /mǽtrəmówn(i)yəl ríyz/. The marriage state.

Matrimony. Marriage *(q.v.)*, in the sense of the relation or *status,* not of the ceremony.

Matrons, jury of. Jury impaneled to determine if a woman condemned to death is pregnant. In common-law practice, a jury of twelve matrons or discreet women, impaneled upon a writ *de ventre inspiciendo,* or where a female prisoner, being under sentence of death, pleaded her pregnancy as a ground for staying execution. In the latter case, such jury inquired into the truth of the plea.

Matter. Substantial facts forming basis of claim or defense; facts material to issue; substance as distinguished from form; transaction, event, occurrence; subject-matter of controversy. *See* Issue; Material fact; Matter in issue; Subject-matter.

Matter in controversy *or* **in dispute.** Subject of litigation; matter on which action is brought and issue is joined and in relation to which, if issue be one of fact, testimony is taken. Rights which plaintiffs assert and seek to have protected and enforced. *See also* Cause of action; Issue; Matter in issue; Subject-matter.

Matter in issue. That matter on which plaintiff proceeds by his action, and which defendant controverts by his pleadings; not including facts offered in evidence to establish the matters in issue. That ultimate fact or state of facts in dispute upon which the verdict or finding is predicated. *See also* Matter in controversy *or* in dispute.

Matter in pais /mǽtər in péy/. Matter of fact that is not in writing; thus distinguished from matter in deed and matter of record; matter that must be proved by parol evidence.

Matter of fact. That which is to be ascertained by the senses, or by the testimony of witnesses describing what they have perceived. Distinguished from matter of law and matter of opinion. *See also* Demonstrative evidence; Fact.

Matter of form. *See* Form.

Matter of law. Whatever is to be ascertained or decided by the application of statutory rules or the principles and determinations of the law, as distinguished from the investigation of particular facts.

Matter of record. Any judicial matter or proceeding entered on the records of a court, and to be proved by the production of such record. It differs from matter in deed, which consists of facts which may be proved by specialty.

Matter of record, estoppel by. *See* Record, estoppel by.

Matter of substance. That which goes to the merits. The opposite of matter of form.

Matured claim. Claim which is unconditionally due and owing. *See* Liquidated claim; Ripeness doctrine.

Maturity date. The date on which the principal amount of a note, draft, acceptance, bond, or other debt instrument becomes due and payable.

Maturity value. The amount which is due and payable on the maturity date of an obligation.

Maxim /mǽksəm/. Maxims are but attempted general statements of rules of law and are law only to extent of application in adjudicated cases. An established principle or proposition. A principle of law universally admitted as being a correct statement of the law, or as agreeable to reason.

Principles invoked in equity jurisdiction; *e.g.* "equity treats as done what ought to be done."

The various maxims of law appear in alphabetical order throughout this dictionary.

Maximum. The highest or greatest amount, quality, value, or degree.

May. An auxiliary verb qualifying the meaning of another verb by expressing ability, competency, liberty, permission, possibility, probability or contingency. Word "may" usually is employed to imply permissive, optional or discretional, and not mandatory action or conduct. Regardless of the instrument, however, whether constitution, statute, deed, contract or whatever, courts not infrequently construe "may" as "shall" or "must" to the end that justice may not be the slave of grammar. However, as a general rule, the word "may" will not be treated as a word of command unless there is something in context or subject matter of act to indicate that it was used in such sense. In construction of statutes and presumably also in construction of federal rules word "may" as opposed to "shall" is indicative of discretion or choice between two or more alternatives, but context in which word appears must be controlling factor.

Mayhem /méy(h)əm/. Mayhem at common law required a type of injury which permanently rendered the victim less able to fight offensively or defensively; it might be accomplished either by the removal of (dismemberment), or by the disablement of, some bodily member useful in fighting. Today, by statute, permanent disfigurement has been added; and as to dismemberment and disablement, there is no longer a requirement that the member have military significance. In many states the crime of mayhem is treated as aggravated assault. *See also* Maim.

May not. A phrase used to indicate that a person is not permitted to do or to perform some act, *e.g.* a person may not be allowed to sit for the bar examination in certain states without specific academic credits. "May not" speaks to permission, whereas "cannot" generally deals with ability.

Mayor. A governmental figure who is generally the principal administrative officer of a city or other municipal area. The position of mayor varies from city to city. In some cities the mayor is essentially a ceremonial figure, while in others he is a major executive official. In some instances he is popularly elected and in others, such as in the commission plan, he is selected from within the administrative council to serve as a presiding officer and ceremonial figure. Duties of mayor are usually prescribed by statute or municipal charter.

Mayoralty /méy(ə)rəltiy/. The office or dignity of a mayor.

Mayor's court. A court established in some cities, in which the mayor sits with the powers of a police judge or committing magistrate in respect to offenses committed within the city (*e.g.* traffic or ordinance violations) and sometimes with civil jurisdiction in small causes, or other special statutory powers.

McCarran Act. A federal statute which permits a state to regulate and to tax foreign insurance companies which do business within the state. 15 U.S.C.A. § 1011 *et seq. See also* Internal security acts.

McNabb-Mallory Rule. The rule which requires that a suspect be promptly brought before a magistrate or else incriminating statements made by him during the illegal detention will be suppressed. McNabb v. U. S., 318 U.S. 332, 63 S.Ct. 608, 87 L.Ed. 819, and Mallory v. U. S., 354 U.S. 449, 77 S.Ct. 1356, 1 L.Ed.2d 1479. "McNabb Rule" is that there must be reasonable promptness in taking prisoner before committing magistrate, or confession obtained during period between arrest and commitment is inadmissible in prosecution of party arrested, and that rule applies to voluntary as well as involuntary confessions. See also Fed.R.Crim.P. 5(a); 18 U.S.C.A. § 3501. *See also* Confession.

McNaghten Rule. *See* M'Naghten Rule.

M.D. An abbreviation for "Middle District," in reference to the division of the United States into judicial districts; *e.g.* U.S. District Court for middle district of Ohio. Also an abbreviation for "Doctor of Medicine" or "Medical Doctor."

Meadow. A tract of low or level land producing grass which is mown for hay. A tract which lies above the shore, and is overflowed by spring and extraordinary tides only, and yields grasses which are good for hay.

Mean *or* **mesne.** A middle between two extremes, whether applied to persons, things, or time. Average, having an intermediate value between two extremes or between the several successive values of variable quantity during one cycle of variation.

Meander /miyǽndər/. To meander means to follow a winding or flexuous course; and when it it said, in a description of land, "thence with the meander of the river," it must mean a meandered line,—a line which follows the sinuosities of the river,—or, in other words, that the river is the boundary between the points indicated.

This term is used in some jurisdictions with the meaning of surveying and mapping a stream according to its meanderings, or windings and turnings. *See* Meander lines.

Meander lines. Lines run in surveying particular portions of the public lands which border on navigable rivers, not as boundaries of the tract, but for the purpose of defining the sinuosities of the banks of the stream, and as the means of ascertaining the quantity of land in the fraction subject to sale, and which is to be paid for by the purchaser. In preparing the official plat from the field notes, the meander line is represented as the border line of the stream, and shows that the watercourse, and not the meander line as naturally run on the ground, is the boundary.

Mean high tide. The "mean high tide" or "ordinary high tide" is a mean of all the high tides, and the average to be used should be, if possible, the average of all the high tides over a period of 18.6 years.

Mean high water mark. The point on the shore which the average high tide will reach.

Meaning. That which is, or is intended to be, signified or denoted by act or language; signification; sense; import. *See also* Construction.

Mean lower low tide. The average of lower low tides over a fixed period of time.

Mean low tide. The average of all low tides both low and lower low over a fixed period of time.

Mean low water mark. The point on the shore which the average low tide will reach.

Mean reserve. The mean of the reserve at the beginning of the policy year, after the premium for such year is paid, and the terminal reserve at end of such policy year.

Means. That through which, or by the help of which, an end is attained; something tending to an object desired; intermediate agency or measure; necessary condition or co-agent; instrument. Under insurance policy, equivalent to cause.

Enactments and initiative and referendum measures.

Resources; available property; money or property, as an available instrumentality for effecting a purpose, furnishing a livelihood, paying a debt, or the like.

Measure. That by which extent or dimension is ascertained, either length, breadth, thickness, capacity, or amount. The rule by which anything is adjusted or proportioned. *See* Land measure; Metes and bounds; Survey.

Measure of damages. The rule, or rather the system of rules, governing the adjustment or apportionment of damages as a compensation for injuries in actions at law. *See* Damages.

Measure of value. In the ordinary sense of the word, "measure" would mean something by comparison with which we may ascertain what is the value of anything. When we consider, further, that value itself is relative, and that two things are necessary to constitute it, independently of the third thing, which is to measure it, we may define a "measure of value" to be something by comparing with which any two other things we may infer their value in relation to one another. *See* Value.

Mechanical equivalent. If two devices do the same work in substantially the same way, and accomplish substantially the same result, they are "mechanical equivalents." A device which may be substituted or adopted, instead of another, by any person skilled in the particular art from his knowledge of the art, and which is competent to perform the same functions or produce the same result, without introducing an original idea or changing the general idea of means. The test of equivalency is whether the substituted element operates in substantially the same way to produce substantially the same result. *See also* Equivalent.

Mechanical process. *See* Process.

Mechanic's lien. A claim created by state statutes for the purpose of securing priority of payment of the price or value of work performed and materials furnished in erecting, improving, or repairing a building or other structure, and as such attaches to the land as well as buildings and improvements erected thereon. Such lien covers materialmen, tradesmen, suppliers, and the like, who furnish services, labor, or materials on construction or improvement of property. *See also* Commence *(Commencement of building or improvement)*; Lien waiver; Stop notice statute.

Mechanic's lienor. The term "mechanic's lienor" means any person who under local law has a lien on real property (or on the proceeds of a contract relating to real property) for services, labor, or materials furnished in connection with the construction or improvement of such property. I.R.C. § 6323(h).

Mediate descent. *See* Descent.

Mediate powers. Those incident to primary powers given by a principal to his agent. For example, the general authority given to collect, receive, and pay debts by or to the principal is a primary power. In order to accomplish this, it is frequently required to settle accounts, adjust disputed claims, resist those which are unjust, and answer and defend suits. These subordinate powers are sometimes called "mediate powers."

Mediate testimony. Secondary evidence *(q.v.)*.

Mediation. Private, informal dispute resolution process in which a neutral third person, the mediator, helps disputing parties to reach an agreement. The mediator has no power to impose a decision on the parties. *See also* Alternative dispute resolution; Arbitration; Conciliation.

Also, the friendly interference of a neutral nation in the controversies of others, for the purpose, by its influence and by adjusting their difficulties, of keeping the peace in the family of nations.

Mediation and Conciliation Service. An independent department of the federal government charged with trying to settle labor disputes by conciliation and mediation. 29 U.S.C.A. § 172 *et seq.*

The Federal Mediation and Conciliation Service represents the public interest by promoting the development of sound and stable labor-management relationships; preventing or minimizing work stoppages by assisting labor and management to settle their disputes through mediation; advocating collective bargaining, mediation, and voluntary arbitration as the preferred processes for settling issues between employers and representatives of employees; developing the art, science, and practice of dispute resolution; and fostering constructive joint relationships of labor and management leaders to increase their mutual understanding and solution of common problems. *See also* American Arbitration Association; National Mediation Board.

Mediator. Neutral third person who helps disputing parties to reach agreement through the mediation process. *See also* Arbitrator; Referee.

Medicaid. A form of public assistance sponsored jointly by the federal and state governments providing medical aid for people whose income falls below a certain level. *See also* Medicare.

Medical. Pertaining, relating or belonging to the study and practice of medicine, or the science and art of the investigation, prevention, cure, and alleviation of disease.

Medical care. The term "medical care" is defined broadly in the Internal Revenue Code (I.R.C. § 213) and more comprehensively in the regulations. It includes expenses for doctors, nurses and other medical services, as well as payments for operations, hospitals, institutional care and transportation necessary to obtain medical care. The basic test for the allowance of medical deductions is whether the expense was incurred and paid primarily for the prevention or alleviation of a physical or mental defect or illness. *See also* Medical expenses.

Medical deduction. *See* Medical expenses.

Medical directive. Document which expresses a patients wishes regarding various types of medical treatment in several different situations where the patient may become incapacitated and thus unable to make or communicate such decisions on their own. The medical directive also can grant a power to make such medical care decisions to another by means of a durable power of attorney or health care proxy. *See also* Health care proxy; Patient Self Determination Act; Will *(Living will)*.

Medical evidence. Evidence furnished by doctors, nurses, and other medical personnel testifying in their professional capacity as experts, or by standard treatises on medicine or surgery. Fed. Evid.R. 702, 703. *See* Expert witness.

Medical examiner. Public officer charged with responsibility of investigating all sudden, unexplained, unnatural or suspicious deaths reported to him, including the performance of autopsies and assisting the state in criminal homicide cases. Term may also include a physician who conducts examinations for insurance companies and other institutions. The medical examiner has replaced the coroner in many states. *See also* Coroner.

Medical expenses. Medical expenses, including medicines and drugs and health insurance premiums, of an individual and his or her dependents are allowed as an itemized deduction to the extent that such amounts (less insurance reimbursements) exceed a certain percent of adjusted gross income. I.R.C. § 213. *See also* Medical care.

Medical jurisprudence. The science which applies the principles and practice of the different branches of medicine to the elucidation of doubtful questions in a court of law. Otherwise called "forensic medicine" *(q.v.)*. A sort of mixed science, which may be considered as common ground to the practitioners both of law and medicine.

Medical malpractice. *See* Malpractice.

Medicare. Federal Act (Health Insurance for the Aged Act) to provide hospital and medical insurance for aged persons under Social Security Act. 42 U.S.C.A. § 1395 et seq. *See also* Medicaid (state provided medical assistance).

Medico-legal. Relating to the law concerning medical questions. *See* Forensic medicine.

Medium of exchange. Anything which serves to facilitate the exchange of things by providing a common basis of measurement such as money, checks, drafts, etc. *See* Legal tender.

Medium-term notes. Unsecured notes, similar to commercial paper, that are registered with the SEC and whose maturities range from 9 months to 30 years.

Medley /médliy/. An affray; a sudden or casual fighting; a hand to hand battle; a *mêlée*. *See* Chaud-medley.

Meeting. A coming together of persons; an assembly. Particularly, in law, an assembling of a number of persons for the purpose of discussing and acting upon some matter or matters in which they have a common interest; *e.g.* in corporate law, a meeting of the board of directors or of the stockholders.

Annual meeting. See Regular meeting, below.

Called meeting. In the law of corporations, a meeting not held at a time specially appointed for it by the charter or by-laws, but assembled in pursuance of a "call" or summons proceeding from some officer, committee or group of stockholders, or other persons having authority in that behalf.

Family meeting. See Family.

General meeting. A meeting of all the stockholders of a corporation, all the creditors of a bankrupt, etc.

Regular meeting. In the law of public and private corporations, a meeting (of directors, trustees, stockholders, etc.) held at the time and place appointed for it by statute, by-law, charter or other positive direction. This is commonly termed the "annual" meeting of such group.

Special meeting. In the law of corporations, a meeting called for special purposes; one limited to particular business; a meeting for those purposes of which the parties have had special notice.

Stated meeting. A meeting held at a stated or duly appointed time and place; a regular meeting *(q.v.)*.

Town meeting. See Town.

Meeting of creditors. *See* Creditor's meeting.

Meeting of minds. As essential element of contract, is mutual agreement and assent of parties to contract to substance and terms. It is an agreement reached by the parties to a contract and expressed therein, or as the equivalent of mutual assent or mutual obligation. The "meeting of the minds" required to make a contract is not based on secret purpose or intention on the part of one of the parties, stored away in his mind and not brought to the attention of the other party, but must be based on purpose and intention which has been made known or which from all the circumstances should be known. A subjective understanding is not required; it suffices that the conduct of the contracting parties indicates an agreement to the terms of the alleged contract.

Megalopolis. Heavily populated continuous urban area including many cities.

Member. One of the persons constituting a family, partnership, association, corporation, guild, court, legislature, or the like.

A part or organ of the body; especially a limb or other separate part.

Member bank. A bank which has become affiliated with (*i.e.* purchased stock in) one of the Federal Reserve banks. Member of Federal Reserve System (which includes all nationally chartered banks and any state-chartered banks that have been accepted for membership). *See* Federal Reserve System.

Member firm. In securities and commodities trading, a brokerage firm that is a member of a particular exchange (*e.g.* member of New York Stock Exchange).

Member of Congress. A member of the Senate or House of Representatives of the United States. In popular usage, particularly the latter.

Member of crew. To qualify as a "member of the crew" and thus as a "seaman" under the Jones Act, one must be more or less permanently attached to a vessel or fleet, must be one whose duties serve naturally and primarily as an aid to navigation in the broadest sense, and the vessel must be in the navigation.

Memorandum /mèmərǽndəm/. Lat. To be remembered; be it remembered. A formal word with which the body of a record in the Court of King's Bench anciently commenced.

An informal record, note or instrument embodying something that the parties desire to fix in memory by the aid of written evidence, or that is to serve as the basis of a future formal contract or deed. A brief written statement outlining the terms of an agreement or transaction. Informal interoffice communication.

Under portion of statute of frauds providing that a contract not to be performed within a year is invalid unless the contract, or some memorandum of the contract, is in writing and subscribed by the party to be charged or his agent, the word "memorandum" implies something less than a complete contract, and the "memorandum" functions only as evidence of the contract and need not contain every term, so that a letter may be a sufficient "memorandum" to take a case out of the statute of frauds.

This word is used in the statute of frauds as the designation of the written agreement, or note or evidence thereof, which must exist in order to bind the parties in the cases provided. The memorandum must be such as to disclose the parties, the nature and substance of the contract, the consideration and promise, and be signed by the party to be bound or his authorized agent. See U.C.C. § 2–201. *See also* Contract.

Memorandum articles. In the law of marine insurance, this phrase designates the articles of merchandise which are usually mentioned in the memorandum clause *(q.v.),* and for which the underwriter's liability is thereby limited.

Memorandum check. *See* Check.

Memorandum clause. In a policy of marine insurance the memorandum clause is a clause inserted to prevent the underwriters from being liable for injury to goods of a peculiarly perishable nature, and for minor damages. It might begin, for example, as follows: "N. B. Corn, fish, salt, fruit, flour, and seed are warranted free from average, unless general, or the ship be stranded," —meaning that the underwriters are not to be liable for damage to these articles caused by seawater or the like.

Memorandum decision. A court's decision that gives the ruling (what it decides and orders done), but no opinion (reasons for the decision).

Memorandum in error. A document alleging error in fact, accompanied by an affidavit of such matter of fact.

Memorandum sale. *See* Sale.

Memorial. A document presented to a legislative body, or to the executive, by one or more individuals, containing a petition or a representation of facts.

In practice, a short note, abstract, memorandum, or rough draft of the orders of the court, from which the records thereof may at any time be fully made up. *See* Memorandum decision.

Menace. To threaten; make threats. An unlawful threat of duress or injury to the person, property or character of another. Menace may constitute a ground for divorce, or duress such as would vitiate a contract. *See also* Assault.

Mens /ménz/. Lat. Mind; intention; meaning; understanding; will.

Mensa et thoro /ménsə èt θórow/. From bed and board. *See* Divorce.

Mens legis /ménz líyjəs/. The mind of the law; that is, the purpose, spirit, or intention of a law or the law generally.

Mens rea /ménz ríyə/. As an element of criminal responsibility: a guilty mind; a guilty or wrongful purpose; a criminal intent. Guilty knowledge and wilfulness. *See* Model Penal Code § 2.02. *See also* Actus reus, Criminal *(Criminal intent)*; Knowledge; Knowingly; Premeditation; Specific intent.

Mental. Relating to or existing in the mind; intellectual, emotional, or psychic, as distinguished from bodily or physical.

Mental anguish. When connected with a physical injury, this term includes both the resultant mental sensation of pain and also the accompanying feelings of distress, fright, and anxiety. As an element of damages implies a relatively high degree of mental pain and distress; it is more than mere disappointment, anger, worry, resentment, or embarrassment, although it may include all of these, and it includes mental sensation of pain resulting from such painful emotions as grief, severe disappointment, indignation, wounded pride, shame, despair and/or public humiliation. In other connections, and as a ground for divorce or for compensable damages or an element of damages, it includes the mental suffering resulting from the excitation of the more poignant and painful emotions, such as grief, severe disappointment, indignation, wounded pride, shame, public humiliation, despair, etc. *See also* Mental cruelty.

Mental capacity *or* **competence.** Term contemplates the ability to understand the nature and effect of the act in which a person is engaged and the business he or she is transacting. Such a measure of intelligence, understanding, memory, and judgment relative to the particular transaction (*e.g.* making of will or entering into contract) as will enable the person to understand the nature, terms, and effect of his or her act. *See also* Capacity; Insanity.

Mental cruelty. A course of conduct on the part of one spouse toward the other spouse which can endanger the mental and physical health and efficiency of the other spouse to such an extent as to render continuance of the marital relation intolerable. As a ground for divorce, is conduct which causes embarrassment, humiliation and anguish so as to render life miserable and unendurable or to cause a spouse's life, person or health to become endangered. *See also* Indignity; Mental anguish.

Mental disease *or* **defect.** *See* Insanity.

Mental incapacity; mental incompetency. Such is established when there is found to exist an essential privation of reasoning faculties, or when a person is incapable of understanding and acting with discretion in the ordinary affairs of life. *See* Incapacity; Insanity.

Mental reservation. A silent exception to the general words of a promise or agreement not expressed, on account of a general understanding on the subject. But the word has been applied to an exception existing in the mind of the one party only, and has been degraded to signify a dishonest excuse for evading or infringing a promise.

Mental state. Capacity or condition of one's mind in terms of ability to do or not do a certain act. *See* Mental capacity *or* competence.

Mental suffering. *See* Mental anguish; Mental cruelty.

Mercantile /márkəntàyl/°əl/. Of, pertaining to, or characteristic of, merchants, or the business of merchants; having to do with trade or commerce or the business of buying and selling merchandise; trading; commercial; conducted or acting on business principles. *See also* Commercial.

Mercantile agencies. *See* Credit bureau.

Mercantile law. An expression substantially equivalent to commercial law. It designates the system of rules, customs, and usages generally recognized and adopted by merchants and traders, and which, either in its simplicity or as modified by common law or statutes, constitutes the law for the regulation of their transactions and the solu-

tion of their controversies. The Uniform Commercial Code is the general body of law governing commercial or mercantile transactions. *See* Commercial law; Uniform Commercial Code.

Mercantile paper. *See* Commercial paper; Negotiable instruments.

Mercantile specialty. A writing that is not payable to order or to bearer but is otherwise negotiable. See U.C.C. § 3–805 (making Article 3 applicable to instruments lacking words of negotiability).

Merchandise. All goods which merchants usually buy and sell, whether at wholesale or retail; wares and commodities such as are ordinarily the objects of trade and commerce. But the term is generally not understood as including real estate, and is rarely applied to provisions such as are purchased day by day for immediate consumption (*e.g.* food).

Stock of merchandise. *See* Stock.

Merchandise broker. One who negotiates the sale of merchandise without having it in his possession or control, being simply an agent with very limited powers. *See* Broker. *Compare* Factor.

Merchant. One who is engaged in the purchase and sale of goods; a trafficker; a retailer; a trader. Term commonly refers to person who purchases goods at wholesale for resale at retail; *i.e.* person who operates a retail business (retailer).

A person who deals in goods of the kind or otherwise by his occupation holds himself out as having knowledge or skill peculiar to the practices or goods involved in the transaction or to whom such knowledge or skill may be attributed by his employment of an agent or broker or other intermediary who by his occupation holds himself out as having such knowledge or skill. U.C.C. § 2–104(1).

A man who traffics or carries on trade with foreign countries, or who exports and imports goods and sells them by wholesale. Merchants of this description are commonly known by the name of "shipping merchants."

Commission merchant. *See* Commission merchant.

Factor. See that title.

Law merchant. *See* Commercial law; Mercantile law.

Statute merchant. *See* Statute.

Merchantability /mèrchəntəbílətiy/. Means that the article sold shall be of the general kind described and reasonably fit for the general purpose for which it shall have been sold, and where the article sold is ordinarily used in but one way, its fitness for use in that particular way is impliedly warranted unless there is evidence to the contrary. *See also* Fitness for particular purpose; Merchantable; Warranty.

Merchantable /mə́rchəntəbəl/. Goods, to be "merchantable," must be fit for the ordinary purposes for which such goods are to be used, and conform to any promises or affirmations of fact made on the container or label. Within § 2–314 of the U.C.C. creating implied warranty of merchantability, term "merchantable" implies that the goods sold conform to ordinary standards of care and that they are of average grade, quality and value of similar goods sold under similar circumstances.

Goods to be merchantable must be at least such as: pass without objection in the trade under the contract description; and in the case of fungible goods, are of fair average quality within the description; and are fit for the ordinary purposes for which such goods are used; and run, within the variations permitted by the agreement, of even kind, quality and quantity within each unit and among all units involved; and are adequately contained, packaged, and labeled as the agreement may require; and conform to the promises or affirmations of fact made on the container or label if any. U.C.C. § 2–314(2).

See also Fitness for particular purpose; Warranty *(Implied warranty of merchantability or fitness for particular purpose)*.

Merchantable title. A good and marketable title in fee simple, free from litigation, palpable defects, and grave doubts; a title which will enable the owner not only to hold it in peace but to sell it to a person of reasonable prudence. Good record title acceptable to a knowledgeable buyer not being under duress to purchase. One that can be held without reasonable apprehension of being assailed and readily transferable in market. *See also* Marketable title; Warranty *(Warranty of title)*.

Merchant appraiser. *See* Appraiser.

Merchant seaman. A sailor employed in a private vessel, as distinguished from one employed in the navy or public ships.

Mercy. In criminal law, the discretion of a judge, within the limits prescribed by law, to remit altogether the punishment to which a convicted person is liable, or to mitigate the severity of his sentence; as when a jury recommends the prisoner to the *mercy* of the court.

Mercy killing. Euthanasia. The affirmative act of bringing about immediate death allegedly in a painless way and generally administered by one who thinks that the dying person wishes to die because of a terminal or hopeless disease or condition. *See also* Brain death; Death *(Natural Death Acts)*; Medical directive; Right to die laws; Will *(Living will)*.

Mere evidence rule. In search and seizure, it was once the rule that in a lawful search the officer had a right to seize instrumentalities and fruits of the crime but no right to seize other items (*e.g.* clothing of the suspect) which are mere evidence. This rule no longer prevails. *See* Fruit of poisonous tree doctrine.

Merely. Without including anything else; purely; only; solely; absolute; wholly.

Meretricious /mèhrətríshəs/. Of the nature of unlawful sexual connection. The term is descriptive of the relation sustained by persons who contract a marriage that is void by reason of legal incapacity.

Merger. The fusion or absorption of one thing or right into another; generally spoken of a case where one of the subjects is of less dignity or importance than the other. Here the less important ceases to have an independent existence.

Contract law. The extinguishment of one contract by its absorption into another, and is largely a matter of intention of the parties.

Corporations. An amalgamation of two corporations pursuant to statutory provision in which one of the corporations survives and the other disappears. The absorption of one company by another, the former losing its legal identity, and latter retaining its own name and identity and acquiring assets, liabilities, franchises, and powers of former, and absorbed company ceasing to exist as separate business entity. It differs from a consolidation wherein all the corporations terminate their existence and become parties to a new one.

The antitrust laws seek not only to control existing monopolies but also to discourage the acquisition of market power. Historically, mergers have provided an important route to positions of market dominance. Accordingly, Congress has required all mergers, whether vertical, horizontal, or conglomerate, to be scrutinized under the provisions of section 7 of the Clayton Act. 15 U.S. C.A. § 18. *See also* Kefauver-Celler Act; Hart-Scott-Rodino Antitrust Improvement Act.

Accounting methods. See Pooling of interests; Purchase method of accounting.

Cash merger. A merger transaction in which certain shareholders or interests in a corporation are required to accept cash for their shares while other shareholders receive shares in the continuing enterprise. Modern statutes generally authorize cash mergers, though courts test such mergers on the basis of fairness and, in some states, business purpose.

Conglomerate merger. Merger of corporations which are neither competitors nor potential or actual customers or suppliers of each other. One in which there are no economic relationships between the acquiring and the acquired firm. A *conglomerate* merger is one that is neither vertical nor horizontal and can be any of three types. A *geographic extension* merger occurs when the acquiring firm, by merger, extends its dominance to an adjacent geographic market. A *product extension* merger occurs when the merger joins firms in related product markets. A "pure" conglomerate merger occurs when the two merging firms operate in unrelated markets having no functional economic relationship. These categories are not mutually exclusive: for example, a merger may have both horizontal and vertical aspects.

Defacto merger. A transaction that has the economic effect of a statutory merger but is cast in the form of an acquisition of assets or an acquisition of voting stock and is treated by a court as if it were a statutory merger. Occurs where one corporation is absorbed by another, but without compliance with statutory requirements for a merger.

Down stream merger. The merger of a parent corporation into its subsidiary.

Horizontal merger. Merger between business competitors, such as manufacturers of the same type products or distributors selling competing products in the same market area. *See also* Vertical merger.

Short form merger. A number of states provide special rules for the merger of a subsidiary corporation into its parent where the parent owns substantially all of the shares of the subsidiary. This is known as a "short-form" merger. Short-form mergers under such special statutes may generally be effected by: (a) adoption of a resolution of merger by the parent corporation, (b) mailing a copy of the plan of merger to all shareholders of record of the subsidiary, and (c) filing the executed articles of merger with the secretary of state and his issuance of a certificate of merger. This type of merger is less expensive and time consuming than the normal type merger. See *e.g.* Rev. Model Bus. Corp. Act § 11.04.

Reverse subsidiary merger. A merger involving a subsidiary of the acquiror and acquiree in which the acquiree is the surviving entity (and becomes a subsidiary of the acquiror).

Stock merger. Merger involving the purchase by one company of the stock of another company. *See also Short form merger, above.*

Subsidiary merger. A merger involving a subsidiary of the acquiror and an acquiree in which the subsidiary of the acquiror is the surviving entity.

Triangular merger. A method of amalgamation of two corporations by which the disappearing corporation is merged into a subsidiary of the surviving corporation and the shareholders of the disappearing corporation receive shares of the surviving corporation. In a reverse triangular merger the subsidiary is merged into the disappearing corporation so that it becomes a wholly owned subsidiary of the surviving corporation.

Up stream merger. A merger of a subsidiary corporation into its parent. *See Short form merger, above.*

Vertical merger. Union with corporate customer or supplier.

Criminal law. When a man commits a major crime which includes a lesser offense, or commits a felony which includes a tort against a private person, the latter is merged in the former.

Divorce law. Substitution of rights and duties under judgment or decree for those under property settlement agreement.

Judgments. A valid and personal judgment merges the original claim in the judgment and thereafter suit is brought on the judgment and not on the original claim. Restatement of Judgments § 45, comment a.

Law and equity. Under Rules of Civil Procedure, there is now only one form of action, the "civil action," in which the parties may be given both legal and equitable relief. Fed.R.Civil P. 2.

Property interests. It is a general principle of law that where a greater estate and a less coincide and meet in one and the same person, without any intermediate estate, the less is immediately annihilated, or, in the law phrase, is said to be *merged;* that is, sunk or drowned, in the greater. Thus, if there be tenant for years, and the reversion in fee-simple descends to or is purchased by him, the term of years is *merged* in the inheritance, and shall never exist any more. Similarly, a lesser interest in real estate merges into a greater interest when lessee purchases leased property.

Sentences. If a defendant is charged in two duplicitous indictments with commission of two crimes, he may be sentenced on conviction of the more serious crime but not on both indictments, *e.g.* possession of marihuana and possession of the same marihuana at the same time and place with intent to sell.

Title. See Property interests, above.

Merger clause. A provision in a contract to the effect that the written terms may not be varied by prior or oral agreements because all such agreements have been merged into the written document. See U.C.C. § 2–202.

Meridians. These are imaginary north and south lines which are used in the Governmental Survey System. These intersect the base line to form a starting point for the measurement of land under that system.

Meritorious /mèhrətór(i)yəs/. Possessing or characterized by "merit" in the legal sense of the word. *See* Merits.

Meritorious cause of action. This description is sometimes applied to a person with whom the ground of action, or the consideration, originated or from whom it moved. For example, where a cause of action accrues to a woman while single, and is sued for, after her marriage, by her husband and herself jointly, she is called the "meritorious cause of action."

Meritorious consideration. One founded upon some moral obligation; a valuable consideration in the second degree.

Meritorious defense. *See* Defense.

Merits. As a legal term, refers to the strict legal rights of the parties. The substance, elements, or grounds of a cause of action or defense. *See* Ground of action; Judgment *(Merits, judgment on)*.

Merit system. System used by federal and state governments for hiring and promoting governmental employees to civil service positions on basis of competence. *See also* Civil service; Merit Systems Protection Board.

Merit Systems Protection Board. As successor to the U.S. Civil Service Commission, this Board has responsibility for hearing and adjudicating appeals by Federal employees of adverse personnel actions, such as removals, suspensions, and demotions. It also resolves cases involving reemployment rights, the denial of periodic step-increases in pay, actions against administrative law judges, and charges of merit system violations. The Board has the authority to enforce its decisions and to order corrective and disciplinary actions. An employee or applicant for employment involved in an appealable action that also involves an allegation of discrimination may ask the Equal Employment Opportunity Commission to review a Board decision. Final decisions and orders of the Board can be appealed to the U.S. Court of Appeals for the Federal Circuit.

Mesne /míyn/. Intermediate; intervening; the middle between two extremes, especially of rank or time.

As to *mesne* Conveyance and Process, see those titles.

Mesne process. *See* Process.

Mesne profits. Intermediate profits; *i.e.,* profits which have been accruing between two given periods. Value of use or occupation of land during time it was held by one in wrongful possession and is commonly measured in terms of rents and profits. *See also* Profit.

Message. Any notice, word, or communication, no matter the mode and no matter how sent, from one person to another.

President's message. An annual communication from the president of the United States to Congress, made at or near the beginning of each session, embodying his views on the state and exigencies of national affairs, suggestions and recommendations for legislation, and other matters. U.S.Const. art. 2, § 3.

Messenger. One who bears messages or errands; a ministerial officer employed by executive officers, legislative bodies, and courts of justice, whose service consists principally in carrying verbal or written communications or executing other orders.

Meter. An instrument of measurement; as a coal-meter, a gas-meter, a land-meter.

The basic metric unit of length; equivalent to 39.37 inches. *See also* Metric system.

Meter rate. Rate applied to charge for utility services based upon quantity used; *e.g.* kilowatt hours of electricity.

Metes and bounds /míyts ən báwndz/. The boundary lines of land, with their terminal points and angles. A way of describing land by listing the compass directions and distances of the boundaries. It is often used in connection with the Government Survey System. *See also* Land measure.

Method. The mode of operating, or the means of attaining an object. In patent law, "engine" and "method" mean the same thing, and may be the subject of a patent. Method, properly speaking, is only placing several things, or performing several operations, in the most convenient order, but it may signify a contrivance or device.

Metric system. A decimal system of weights and measures based on the meter as a unit length and the kilogram as a unit mass. Derived units include the liter for liquid volume, the stere for solid volume, and the are for area.

Metropolitan /mètrəpólətən/. Of or pertaining to a city or metropolis and the cluster of towns surrounding it. In ecclesiastical matters, the head of a province or an archbishop.

Metropolitan council. Official or quasi-official body appointed or elected by voters in the city and towns which comprise the metropolitan area. The powers and duties of such council are set by statute. Created to provide unified administration of functions and services common to cities and towns within metropolitan area; *e.g.* sewage disposal, public transportation, water supply.

Metropolitan district. A special district embracing parts or the whole of several contiguous cities or other areas, created by a State to provide unified administration of one or more functions; *e.g.,* sewage disposal, water supply, metropolitan transit.

Mexican divorce. Term used to describe divorce decree in Mexico either by mail order or by the appearance of one spouse who never acquires a Mexican domicile. In both cases, the divorce is not entitled to recognition in the United States.

Middle line of main channel. The equidistant point in the main channel of the river between the well-defined banks on either shore.

Middleman. One who merely brings parties together in order to enable them to make their own contracts.

An agent between two parties; an intermediary who performs the office of a broker or factor between seller and buyer, producer and consumer, land-owner and tenant, etc. One who has been employed as an agent by a principal, and who has employed a subagent under him by authority of the principal, either express or implied.

A person who is employed both by the seller and purchaser of goods, or by the purchaser alone, to receive them into his possession, for the purpose of doing something in or about them. One who buys at one price from a manufacturer for resale at a higher price.

See also Broker; Finder; Jobber.

Middle of the river. The phrases "middle of the river" and "middle of the main channel" are equivalent expressions, and both mean the main line of the channel or the middle thread of the current.

Midnight deadline. A term of the check collection process applicable to a bank, meaning "midnight on its next banking day following the banking day on which it receives the relevant item or notice or from which the time for taking action commences to run, whichever is later." U.C.C. § 4–104(1)(h).

Might, *v.* The past tense of the word "may". Equivalent to "had power" or "was possible" or "have the physical or moral opportunity to be contingently possible."

Migration. Movement from one place to another; from one country or region to another country or region.

Migratory divorce. Term used to describe a divorce secured by a spouse who leaves his or her domicile and moves to, or resides temporarily in, another state or country for purpose of securing the divorce. *See also* Mexican divorce.

Migratory game. Generally applied to birds which move from one place to another in season.

Mile. A measure of length or distance, containing 8 furlongs, or 1,760 yards, or 5,280 feet; or 1,609 meters. This is the measure of an ordinary or statute mile; but the nautical or geographical mile contains 6,080 feet. *See* Land measure.

Mileage. Allowance for traveling expenses at certain rate per mile. Especially to members of legislative bodies, witnesses, sheriffs, and bailiffs. *See also* Per diem.

Mileage tax. License tax imposed upon intrastate business of transportation for compensation on public roads of state.

Military. Pertaining to war or to the army; concerned with war. Also the whole of military forces, staff, etc. under the Department of Defense.

Military appeals. *See* Court of Military Appeals.

Military base. *See* Base.

Military boards. A military board is a body of persons appointed to act as a fact finding agency or as an advisory body to the appointing authority. A military board may be appointed to investigate, advise, administer or adjudicate. Military boards may act as investigating committees to determine the cause of property damage, injury, or death, or to inquire into loss or misappropriation of property or funds. Boards may also act as administrative tribunals to examine the applicable facts, hear evidence, and make determination concerning personnel matters such as promotion, separation, and retirement.

Military bounty land. *See* Bounty.

Military commissions. Courts whose procedure and composition are modeled upon courts-martial, being the tribunals by which alleged violations of martial law are tried and determined. The membership of such commissions is commonly made up of civilians and army officers. They are probably not known outside of the United States, and were first used by General Scott during the Mexican war.

Military court of inquiry. A military court of special and limited jurisdiction, convened to investigate specific matters. 10 U.S.C.A. § 935. Proceedings do not include a trial of issues in which anyone is formally a party; its traditional function has been to investigate and advise whether further proceedings shall be had.

Military courts. Courts convened subject to the Code of Military Justice (10 U.S.C.A. § 801 *et seq.*); *e.g.* Courts-martial, Court of Military Review, Military Court of Inquiry; Court of Military Appeals.

Military government. Such as is exercised by military commander under direction of President in time of foreign war without the boundaries of the United States, or in time of rebellion and civil war within states or districts occupied by rebels. Such supersedes local law. *See* Martial law.

Military jurisdiction. There are under the Constitution, three kinds of military jurisdiction: one to be exercised both in peace and war; another to be exercised in time of foreign war without the boundaries of the United States or in time of rebellion and civil war within states or districts occupied by rebels treated as belligerents; and a third to be exercised in time of invasion or insurrection within the limits of the United States or during rebellion within the limits of states maintaining adhesion to the National Government, when the public danger requires its exercise. The first of these may be called jurisdiction under "military law" and is found in acts of Congress prescribing rules and articles of war, or otherwise providing for the government of the national forces; the second may be distinguished as "military government" superseding, as far as may be deemed expedient the local law, and exercised by the military commander under the direction of the President, with the express or implied sanction of Congress; while the third may be denominated "martial law", and is called into action by Congress, or temporarily when the action of Congress cannot be invited, and in the face of justifying or excusing peril, by the President in times of insurrection or invasion, or of civil or foreign war, within districts or localities where ordinary law no longer adequately secures public safety and private rights.

Military justice. *See* Code of Military Justice; Court Martial; Court of Military Appeals.

Military law. A system of regulations for the government of armed forces. That branch of the laws which respects military discipline and the government of persons employed in the military service. Military law is distinct from martial law, in that it applies only to persons in the military or naval service of the government; whereas, martial law, when once established, applies alike to citizens and soldiers and supersedes civil law. *See* Code of Military Justice.

Military offenses. Those offenses which are cognizable by the military courts, as insubordination, sleeping on guard, desertion, etc. *See* Code of Military Justice; Court Martial.

Military office. *See* Office.

Military officer. *See* Officer.

Military Review, Courts of. Each armed service has a Court of Military Review which reviews courts-martial decisions. 10 U.S.C.A. § 866. Further appeal is to the U.S. Court of Military Appeals. *See* Court of Military Appeals.

Militia /məlíshə/. The body of citizens in a state, enrolled for discipline as a military force, but not engaged in actual service except in emergencies, as distinguished from regular troops or a standing army.

Militiamen /məlíshəmən/. Comprehends every temporary citizen-soldier who in time of war or emergency enters active military service of the country.

Mill. One-tenth of one cent. Many states use a mill rate to compute property taxes. *See* Mill rate.

Miller Act. Federal statute which requires the posting of performance and payment bonds before an award may be made for a contract beyond a certain amount for construction, alteration or repair of a public building or public work of the U.S. government. 40 U.S.C.A. §§ 270a–270f.

Miller-Tydings Act. Federal Act (15 U.S.C. § 1) granting anti-trust exemption to State laws which permitted resale price maintenance agreements (fair trade laws). This exemption was repealed in 1975.

Mill power. An expression designating a unit of water power. It is the descriptive term used to rate water power for the purpose of renting it. It indicates the amount of power due to a stated quantity of water used on the particular fall. It is a term of practical convenience in defining the quantity and weight of water available for use by the lessee. The actual amount of horse power developed may vary with the efficiency of the water wheels and other appliances supplied by the lessee.

Mill privilege. The right of a riparian proprietor to erect a mill on his land and to use the power furnished by the stream for the purpose of operating the mill, with due regard to the rights of other owners above and below him on the stream.

Mill rate. Tax applied to real property. Each mill represents $1 of tax assessment per $1000 of property value assessment. *See also* Mill.

Mill site. A parcel of land on or contiguous to a water-course, suitable for the erection and operation of a mill operated by the power furnished by the stream. Specifically, in mining law, a parcel of land constituting a portion of the public domain, located and claimed by the owner of a mining claim under the laws of the United States (or purchased by him from the government and patented), not exceeding five acres in extent, not including any mineral land, not contiguous to the vein or lode, and occupied and used for the purpose of a mill or for other uses directly connected with the operation of the mine; or a similar parcel of land located and actually used for the purpose of a mill or reduction plant, but not by the owner of an existing mine nor in connection with any particular mining claim. See 30 U.S. C.A. § 42.

Mind. In its legal sense, "mind" means only the ability to will, to direct, to permit, or to assent.

Mind and memory. A phrase applied to testators, denoting the possession of mental capacity to make a will. In other words, one ought to be capable of making his will, with an understanding of the nature of the business in which he is engaged, a recollection of the property he means to dispose of, of the persons who are the objects of his bounty, and the manner in which it is to be distributed between them. *See also* Capacity.

Mind, state of. Evidence is admissible to show a person's state of mind when this issue is material and relevant to the case; *e.g.* statements indicating despair may be admissible on issue of suicide. Fed.Evid.R. 803(3). *See also* Mental state.

Mine. An excavation in the earth from which ores, coal, or other mineral substances are removed by digging or other mining methods, and in its broader sense it denotes the vein, lode, or deposit of minerals. It may include open cut, strip, or hydraulic methods of mining.

Mineral, *adj.* Relating to minerals or the process and business of mining; bearing or producing valuable minerals.

Mineral, *n.* Any valuable inert or lifeless substance formed or deposited in its present position through natural agencies alone, and which is found either in or upon the soil of the earth or in the rocks beneath the soil.

Any natural constituent of the crust of the earth, inorganic or fossil, homogeneous in structure, having a definite chemical composition and known crystallization. The term includes all fossil bodies or matters dug out of mines or quarries, whence anything may be dug, such as beds of stone which may be quarried.

The word is not a definite term and is susceptible of limitations or extensions according to intention with which it is used. In its ordinary and common meaning is a comprehensive term including every description of stone and rock deposit whether containing metallic or nonmetallic substances. Standing alone it might by itself embrace the soil, hence include sand and gravel, or, under a strict definition, it might be limited to metallic substances. The term "mineral" as it is used in the public land laws is more restricted than it is when used in some other respects. Its definition has presented many difficulties. It has been held that for purposes of mining laws, a mineral is whatever is recognized as mineral by the standard authorities on the subject.

Mineral deed. A realty conveyance involving a severance from fee of present title to minerals in place, either effecting such severance in first instance or conveying part of such mineral ownership previously severed from the fee.

Mineral district. A term occasionally used in acts of congress, designating in a general way those portions or regions of the country where valuable minerals are mostly found, or where the business of mining is chiefly carried on, but carrying no very precise meaning and not a known term of the law.

Mineral land entry. *See* Entry.

Mineral lands. Lands containing deposits of valuable, useful, or precious minerals in such quantities as to justify expenditures in the effort to extract them, and which are more valuable for the minerals they contain than for agricultural or other uses. Lands on which metals or minerals have been discovered in rock in place. Such lands include not merely metaliferous lands, but all such as are chiefly valuable for their deposits of mineral character, which are useful in arts or valuable for purposes of manufacture; and, embrace not only those which the lexicon defines as "mineral", but, in addition, such as are valuable for deposits of marble, slate, petroleum, asphaltum, and even guano.

Mineral lease. An agreement permitting use of land to explore, and then, if mineral is discovered, giving right to take mineral either for definite term or so long as it can be produced in paying quantities upon reserved royalty. A mineral lease so characterized as a real right, is merely a contract which permits the lessee to explore for minerals on the land of the lessor in consideration of the payment of a rental and/or bonuses. *See also* Mining lease.

Mineral lode. A mineral bed of rock with definite boundaries in a general mass of the mountain and also any zone or belt of mineralized rock lying within boundaries clearly separating it from the neighboring rock.

Mineral right. An interest in minerals in land, with or without ownership of the surface of the land. A right to take minerals or a right to receive a royalty.

Mineral royalty. Income received from lessees of mineral land. The term is distinguished from mineral interest. *See also* Mineral lease; Royalty.

Mineral servitude. The right to exploit or develop minerals.

Minimal contacts. *See* Minimum contacts.

Mini-maxi. An underwriting arrangement with a broker requiring the broker to sell the minimum on an all-or-none basis and the balance on a best-efforts basis.

Minimum charge. The lowest tariff which may be charged to a customer of a public utility or common carrier regardless of the amount of service rendered.

Minimum. The least quantity assignable, admissible or possible in given case and is opposed to maximum.

Minimum contacts. A doctrine referring to the minimum due process requirement for subjecting a non-resident civil defendant to a court's personal jurisdiction. The defendant must have sufficient contacts with the forum state such that maintenance of the suit does not offend traditional notions of fair play and substantial justice. International Shoe Co. v. State of Washington, 326 U.S. 310, 66 S.Ct. 154, 90 L.Ed. 95. It exists when a defendant takes purposeful and affirmative action, the effect of which is to cause business activity, foreseeable by the defendant, in the forum state. *See also* Doing business; Long arm statutes.

Minimum fee schedules. Schedules of fees which may be charged by lawyers and published generally by bar associations for guidance of the members of the local bar. The trend has been to abolish such schedules as being in violation of the anti-trust laws.

Minimum lot. The least amount of square footage required for a lot to be approved under local zoning laws.

Minimum royalty clause. Provision in royalty agreement which prescribes a fixed obligation of the licensee regardless of whether the invention is used or not.

Minimum sentence. The least severe sentence which a judge may impose. *See* Sentence.

Minimum tax. *See* Alternative minimum tax.

Minimum wage. The minimum hourly rate of compensation for labor, as established by federal statute and required of employers engaged in businesses which affect interstate commerce. 29 U.S.C.A. § 206 et seq. Most states also have similar statutes governing minimum wages (*e.g.,* Mass.G.L. ch. 151). The least wage on which an ordinary individual can be self-sustaining and obtain the ordinary requirements of life. *See also* Fair Labor Standards Act.

Mining. The process or business of extracting from the earth the precious or valuable metals, either in their native state or in their ores.

Mining claim. A parcel of land, containing precious metal in its soil or rock, and appropriated by an individual, according to established rules, by the process of "location." 30 U.S.C.A. § 21 *et seq.*

A mining claim on public lands is a possessory interest in land that is mineral in character and as respects which discovery within the limits of the claim has been made.

See also Mining location; Placer claim.

Mining district. A section of country usually designated by name and described or understood as being confined within certain natural boundaries, in which the precious metals (or their ores) are found in paying quantities, and which is

worked therefor, under rules and regulations prescribed or agreed upon by the miners therein. *See also* Mining location.

Mining lease. A lease of a mine or mining claim or a portion thereof, to be worked by the lessee, usually under conditions as to the amount and character of work to be done, and reserving compensation to the lessor either in the form of a fixed rent or a royalty on the tonnage of ore mined, and which (as distinguished from a license) conveys to the lessee an interest or estate in the land, and (as distinguished from an ordinary lease) conveys not merely the temporary use and occupation of the land, but a portion of the land itself, that is, the ore in place and unsevered and to be extracted by the lessee. *See also* Mineral lease.

Mining location. The act of appropriating and claiming, according to certain established rules and local customs, a parcel of land of defined area, upon or in which one or more of the precious metals or their ores have been discovered, and which constitutes a portion of the public domain, with the declared intention to occupy and work it for mining purposes under the implied license of the United States. Also the parcel of land so occupied and appropriated. Essential to any valid location is the discovery of a valuable mineral deposit. Upon making a valid location the locator has vested rights in the land which are property in the true sense of the word. Once the land is patented, the land is private property. *See also* Location (*Mining law*).

Mining partnership. An association of several owners of a mine for co-operation in working the mine. Generally, where the parties co-operate in developing a lease for oil and gas, each agreeing to pay his part of the expenses and to share in the profits or losses, a "mining partnership" exists. A special type of partnership different in many respects from ordinary or trading partnerships.

Mining rent. Consideration given for a mining lease, whether such lease creates a tenancy, conveys a fee, or grants an incorporeal right or a mere license.

Minister. Person acting as agent for another in performance of specified duties or orders. A person ordained according to the usages of some church or associated body of Christians for the preaching of the gospel and filling the pastoral office. In England, holder of government office; *e.g.* Prime Minister.

Foreign minister. An ambassador, minister, or envoy from a foreign government.

International law. An officer appointed by the government of one nation as a mediator or arbitrator between two other nations who are engaged in a controversy, with their consent, with a view to effecting an amicable adjustment of the dispute.

A general name given to the diplomatic representatives sent by one state to another, including ambassadors, envoys, and residents.

Public law. One of the highest functionaries in the organization of civil government, standing next to the sovereign or executive head, acting as his immediate auxiliary, and being generally charged with the administration of one of the great bureaus or departments of the executive branch of government. In England, otherwise called a "cabinet minister," "secretary of state," or "secretary of a department".

Public minister. A general term comprehending all the higher classes of diplomatic representatives,—as ambassadors, envoys, residents,—but not including the commercial representatives, such as consuls.

Ministerial act. /mìnəstír(i)yəl/. That which is done under the authority of a superior; opposed to *judicial.* That which involves obedience to instructions, but demands no special discretion, judgment, or skill. An act is "ministerial" when its performance is positively commanded and so plainly prescribed as to be free from doubt. Official's duty is "ministerial" when it is absolute, certain and imperative, involving merely execution of a specific duty arising from fixed and designated facts.

One which a person or board performs under a given state of facts in a prescribed manner in obedience to the mandate of legal authority without regard to or the exercise of his or their own judgment upon the propriety of the act being done. *Compare* Discretionary acts. *See also* Mandamus.

Ministerial duty. One regarding which nothing is left to discretion—a simple and definite duty, imposed by law, and arising under conditions admitted or proved to exist.

Ministerial function. A function as to which there is no occasion to use judgment or discretion. *See also* Ministerial act.

Ministerial office. *See* Office.

Ministerial officer. One whose duties are purely ministerial, as distinguished from executive, legislative, or judicial functions, requiring obedience to the mandates of superiors and not involving the exercise of judgment or discretion.

Ministerial power. *See* Power.

Ministerial trust. *See* Trust.

Mini-trial. A private, voluntary, informal form of dispute resolution in which attorneys for each disputant make a brief presentation of his or her best case before officials for each side who have authority to settle. Usually, a neutral, third-party advisor is present at the hearing. Following the attorneys' presentations, the principals attempt to settle the dispute. The neutral third-party may be asked to render a non-binding advisory opinion regarding the outcome of the dispute if it were litigated.

Minor. An infant or person who is under the age of legal competence. A term derived from the civil law, which described a person under a certain age as *less than* so many years. In most states, a person is no longer a minor after reaching the age of 18 (though state laws might still prohibit certain acts until reaching a greater age; *e.g.* purchase of liquor). *See also* Delinquent child; Infancy; Juvenile; Legal age; Majority.

Also, less; of less consideration; lower; a person of inferior condition.

Minor deviation rule. Under "minor deviation rule" for determining when the deviation from purpose and use for which permission to drive insured vehicle is granted will preclude coverage under omnibus clause of policy, if bailee's use is not gross, substantial, or major violation, even though it may have amounted to deviation, protection is still afforded to bailee under omnibus clause.

Minor dispute. A "minor dispute" within the meaning of the Railway Labor Act is one which relates to the interpretation of an existing labor management contract and is directed to rights already vested, in contrast to a major dispute, which involves the formation of the collective bargaining agreement or the substantial alteration of an existing agreement and which involves the acquisition of rights. *Compare* Major (or minor) dispute.

Minor fact. In the law of evidence, a relative, collateral, or subordinate fact; a circumstance. *Compare* Material fact.

Minority. The state or condition of a minor; infancy. Opposite of "majority." *See* Minor. *Compare* Legal age; Majority.

The smaller number of votes of a deliberative assembly; opposed to majority *(q.v.).*

In context of Constitution's guarantee of equal protection, "minority" does not have merely numerical denotation but refers to identifiable and specially disadvantaged group.

Minority interest. A stock or investment interest in a company or venture that is less than a controlling or majority interest.

Minority opinion. *See* Opinion.

Minority stockholder. Those stockholders of a corporation who hold so few shares in relation to the total outstanding that they are unable to control the management of the corporation or to elect directors.

Minor offenses. *See* Petty offense.

Minors' estates. Property of those who have not reached their legal majority and which must be administered after their death or during their lives under a court appointed fiduciary.

Mint. The place designated by law where bullion is coined into money under authority of the government.

Mintage /míntəj/. The charge or commission taken by the mint as a consideration for coining into money the bullion which is brought to it for that purpose; the same as "seigniorage."

Also that which is coined or stamped as money; the product of the mint.

Mint-mark. The masters and workers of the English mint, in the indentures made with them, agreed "to make a privy mark in the money they make, of gold and silver, so that they may know which moneys were of their own making." After every trial of the pix, having proved their moneys to be lawful, they were entitled to their *quietus* under the great seal, and to be discharged from all suits or actions.

Mint-master. One who manages the coinage.

Minutes. Memoranda or notes of a transaction or proceeding. Thus, the record of the proceedings at a meeting of directors or shareholders of a company is called the "minutes."

A memorandum of what takes place in court, made by authority of the court. *See also* Record; Transcript.

Minutes book. A book kept by the clerk or prothonotary of a court for entering memoranda of its proceedings. A record of all actions authorized at corporate board of directors' or stockholders' meeting.

Miranda hearing. A pre-trial proceeding to determine whether there has been compliance with the requirements of the Miranda Rule *(q.v.)*. The outcome will decide whether the prosecution will be permitted to introduce into evidence statements of the defendant made during custodial interrogation. *See* Miranda Rule; Suppression hearing.

Miranda Rule /mərǽndə rúwl/. Prior to any custodial interrogation (that is, questioning initiated by law enforcement officers after a person is taken into custody or otherwise deprived of his freedom in any significant way) the person must be warned: 1. That he has a right to remain silent; 2. That any statement he does make may be used as evidence against him; 3. That he has a right to the presence of an attorney; 4. That if he cannot afford an attorney, one will be appointed for him prior to any questioning if he so desires.

Unless and until these warnings or a waiver of these rights are demonstrated at the trial, no evidence obtained in the interrogation may be used against the accused. Miranda v. Arizona, 384 U.S. 436, 444, 478, 479, 86 S.Ct. 1602, 1612, 1630, 16 L.Ed.2d 694.

See also In custody; Interrogation.

Misadventure. A mischance or accident; a casualty caused by the act of one person inflicting injury upon another. Homicide "by misadventure" occurs where a person, doing a lawful act, without any intention of harm, hurt, unfortunately kills another.

Misapplication. Improper, illegal, wrongful, or corrupt use of application of funds, property, etc. *See also* Misappropriation.

Misappropriation. The unauthorized, improper, or unlawful use of funds or other property for purpose other than that for which intended. Misappropriation of a client's funds is any unauthorized use of client's funds entrusted to an attorney, including not only stealing but also unauthorized temporary use for lawyer's own purpose, whether or not he derives any personal gain or benefit therefrom. Term may also embrace the taking and use of another's property for sole purpose of capitalizing unfairly on good will and reputation of property owner. *See* Model Rules of Professional Conduct. *See also* Embezzlement.

Misbehavior. Ill conduct; improper or unlawful behavior. Such as to support contempt conviction is conduct inappropriate to particular role of actor, be he judge, juror, party, witness, counsel or spectator.

Misbranding. False or misleading labeling. Such practices are prohibited by federal and state statutes; *e.g.* Fair Packaging and Labeling Act.

Miscarriage /məskǽrəj/mískǽrəj/. Poor management or administration; mismanagement.

Miscarriage of justice. Decision or outcome of legal proceeding that is prejudicial or inconsistent with substantial rights of party.

As used in constitutional standard of reversible error, "miscarriage of justice" means a reasonable probability of more favorable outcome for the defendant. A miscarriage of justice, warranting reversal, should be declared only when the court, after examination of entire cause, including the evidence, is of the opinion that it is reasonably probable that a result more favorable to appealing party would have been reached in absence of the error.

Miscarriage of justice from erroneous charge to jury, under statute declaring that no judgment shall be set aside or new trial granted on basis of error which does not result in such miscarriage, results only when an erroneous charge is reasonably calculated to confuse or mislead.

Miscegenation /məsèjənéyshən/mísəjə°/. Mixture of races. Term formerly applied to marriage between persons of different races. Statutes prohibiting marriage between persons of different races have been held to be invalid as contrary to equal protection clause of Constitution.

Mischarge. An erroneous charge; a charge, given by a court to a jury, which involves errors for which the judgment may be reversed.

Mischief. In legislative parlance, the word is sometimes used to signify the evil or danger which a statute is intended to cure or avoid.

In the phrase "malicious mischief," *(q.v.)* it imports a wanton or reckless injury to persons or property.

A person is guilty of criminal mischief if he: (a) damages tangible property of another purposely, recklessly, or by negligence in the employment of fire, explosives, or other dangerous means, or (b) purposely or recklessly tampers with tangible property of another so as to endanger person or property; or (c) purposely or recklessly causes another to suffer pecuniary loss by deception or threat. Model Penal Code, § 220.3.

Misconduct. A transgression of some established and definite rule of action, a forbidden act, a dereliction from duty, unlawful behavior, willful in character, improper or wrong behavior; its synonyms are misdemeanor, misdeed, misbehavior, delinquency, impropriety, mismanagement, offense, but not negligence or carelessness. Term "misconduct" when applied to act of attorney, implies dishonest act or attempt to persuade court or jury by use of deceptive or reprehensible methods. Misconduct, which renders discharged employee ineligible for unemployment compensation, occurs when conduct of employee evinces willful or wanton disregard of employer's interest, as in deliberate violations, or disregard of standards of behavior which employer has right to expect of his employees, or in carelessness or negligence of such degree or recurrence as to manifest wrongful intent or evil design. *See also* Wanton misconduct.

Misconduct in office. Any unlawful behavior by a public officer in relation to the duties of his office, willful in character. Term embraces acts which the office holder had no right to perform, acts performed improperly, and failure to act in the face of an affirmative duty to act. *See also* Malfeasance; Misfeasance.

Miscontinuance. In practice, an improper continuance; want of proper form in a continuance; the same with "discontinuance."

Misdate. A false or erroneous date affixed to a paper or document.

Misdelivery. Delivery of mail, freight, goods, or the like, to person other than authorized or specified recipient. The delivery of property by a carrier or warehouseman to a person not authorized by the owner or person to whom the carrier or warehouseman is bound by his contract to deliver it. In commercial law, refers to a bailee surrendering goods to someone other than the person entitled to them under a document covering the goods.

Misdemeanant /misdəmíynənt/. A person guilty of a misdemeanor; one sentenced to punishment upon conviction of a misdemeanor.

Misdemeanor /misdəmíynər/. Offenses lower than felonies and generally those punishable by fine, penalty, forfeiture or imprisonment otherwise than in penitentiary. Under federal law, and most state laws, any offense other than a felony is classified as a misdemeanor. 18 U.S. C.A. §§ 1, 19, 3401. Certain states also have various classes of misdemeanors (*e.g.* Class A, B, etc.). See Fed.R.Crim.P. 58 with respect to "Procedure for Misdemeanors and Other Petty Offenses". *See also* Degrees of crime; Infraction; Petty offense.

Misdescription. An error or falsity in the description of the subject-matter of a contract which deceives one of the parties to his injury, or is misleading in a material or substantial point. In commercial law, refers to a bailee inaccurately identifying, in a document of title, the goods received from the bailor. *See also* Misrepresentation.

Misdirection. An error made by a judge in instructing the jury upon the trial of a cause.

Misfeasance /misfíyzəns/. The improper performance of some act which a person may lawfully do. "Nonfeasance" means the omission of an act which a person ought to do; "misfeasance" is the improper doing of an act which a person might lawfully do; and "malfeasance" is the doing of an act which a person ought not to do at all. *Compare* Malfeasance.

Misfeazance. *See* Misfeasance.

Misfortune. An adverse event, calamity, or evil fortune, arising by accident (or without the will or concurrence of him who suffers from it), and not to be foreseen or guarded against by care or prudence. In its application to the law of homicide, this term always involves the further idea that the person causing the death is not at the time engaged in any unlawful act. *See also* Accident.

Misjoinder. *See* Joinder.

Mislaid property. *See* Property.

Mislay. To deposit in a place not afterwards recollected; to lose anything by forgetfulness of the place where it was laid.

Misleading. Delusive; calculated to lead astray or to lead into error. A Judge's instructions which are of such a nature as to be misunderstood by the jury, or to give them a wrong impression, are said to be "misleading." *See also* Deception; Deceit; Misrepresentation.

Misnomer. Mistake in name; giving incorrect name to person in accusation, indictment, pleading, deed or other instrument. Under rules practice in some states, such is ground for dismissal by motion. In most states, however, as well as in the federal courts, such misnomer can be corrected by amendment of the pleadings.

When a misnomer occurs in a deed, the normal procedure is to prepare and record a correction deed. Commonly, a quit claim deed is used for this purpose.

Mispleading. Pleading incorrectly, or omitting anything in pleading which is essential to the support or defense of an action, is so called; as in the case of a plaintiff not merely stating his title in a defective manner, but setting forth a title which is essentially defective in itself; or if, to an action of debt, the defendant pleads "not guilty" instead of *nil debet*. Rules of Civil Procedure (in effect in the federal and many state courts) permit liberal amendment of incorrect or deficient pleadings. See Fed.R.Civil P. 15.

Misprision. A word used to describe an offense which does not possess a specific name. But more particularly and properly the term denotes either: (1) a contempt against the sovereign, the government, or the courts of justice, including not only contempts of court, properly so called, but also all forms of seditious or disloyal conduct and leze-majesty; (2) maladministration of public office; neglect or improper performance of official duty, including peculation of public funds; (3) neglect of light account made of a crime, that is, failure in the duty of a citizen to endeavor to prevent the commission of a crime, or, having knowledge of its commission, to fail to reveal it to the proper authorities.

Concealment of crime. See Misprision of felony.

Negative misprision. The concealment of something which ought to be revealed; that is, misprision in the third of the specific meanings given above.

Positive misprision. The commission of something which ought not to be done; that is, misprision in the first and second of the specific meanings given above.

Misprision of felony. The offense of concealing a felony committed by another, but without such previous concert with or subsequent assistance to the felon as would make the party concealing an accessory before or after the fact. Elements of the crime are that the principal committed and completed the felony alleged, that the defendant had full knowledge of that fact, that the defen-

dant failed to notify the authorities, and that defendant took an affirmative step to conceal the crime.

Whoever, having knowledge of the actual commission of a felony cognizable by a court of the United States, conceals and does not as soon as possible make known the same to some judge or other person in civil or military authority under the United States, is guilty of the federal crime of misprision of felony. 18 U.S.C.A. § 4.

See also Obstructing justice.

Misprision of treason. The bare knowledge and concealment of an act of treason or treasonable plot by failing to disclose it to the appropriate officials; that is, without any assent or participation therein, for if the latter elements be present the party becomes a principal. 18 U.S.C.A. § 2382.

Misreading. Reading a deed or other instrument to an illiterate or blind man (who is a party to it) in a false or deceitful manner, so that he conceives a wrong idea of its tenor or contents.

Misrepresentation. Any manifestation by words or other conduct by one person to another that, under the circumstances, amounts to an assertion not in accordance with the facts. An untrue statement of fact. An incorrect or false representation. That which, if accepted, leads the mind to an apprehension of a condition other and different from that which exists. Colloquially it is understood to mean a statement made to deceive or mislead.

As amounting to actual legal fraud consists of material representation of presently existing or past fact, made with knowledge of its falsity and with intention that other party rely thereon, resulting in reliance by that party to his detriment.

In a limited sense, an intentional false statement respecting a matter of fact, made by one of the parties to a contract, which is material to the contract and influential in producing it. A "misrepresentation," which justifies the rescission of a contract, is a false statement of a substantive fact, or any conduct which leads to a belief of a substantive fact material to proper understanding of the matter in hand, made with intent to deceive or mislead.

See also Deceit; Deception; False; Fraud; Material fact; Reliance.

Insurance law. A statement of something as a fact which is untrue and material to the risk, and which assured states knowing it to be untrue and with intent to deceive, or which insured states positively as true, not knowing it to be true, and which has a tendency to mislead. One that would influence a prudent insurer in determining whether or not to accept the risk, or in fixing the amount of the premium in the event of such acceptance. *See also* Material fact.

Mistake. Some unintentional act, omission, or error arising from ignorance, surprise, imposition, or misplaced confidence. A state of mind not in accord with reality. A mistake exists when a person, under some erroneous conviction of law or fact, does, or omits to do, some act which, but for the erroneous conviction, he would not have done or omitted. It may arise either from unconsciousness, ignorance, forgetfulness, imposition, or misplaced confidence. *See also* Error; Ignorance.

Mistake of fact is a mistake not caused by the neglect of a legal duty on the part of the person making the mistake, and consisting in (1) an unconscious ignorance or forgetfulness of a fact, past or present, material to the contract; or (2) belief in the present existence of a thing material to the contract which does not exist, or in the past existence of such a thing which has not existed.

A *mistake of law* happens when a party, having full knowledge of the facts, comes to an erroneous conclusion as to their legal effect. It is a mistaken opinion or inference, arising from an imperfect or incorrect exercise of the judgment, upon facts; and necessarily presupposes that the person forming it is in full possession of the facts. The facts precede the law, and the true and false opinion alike imply an acquaintance with them. The one is the result of a correct application of legal principles, which every man is presumed to know, and is called "law;" the other, the result of a faulty application, and is called a "mistake of law."

In criminal law, ignorance or mistake as to a matter of fact or law is a defense if: (a) the ignorance or mistake negatives the purpose, knowledge, belief, recklessness or negligence required to establish a material element of the offense; or (b) the law provides that the state of mind established by such ignorance or mistake constitutes a defense. Model Penal Code, § 2.04(1).

Mutual mistake is where the parties have a common intention, but it is induced by a common or mutual mistake. "Mutual" as used in the expression mutual mistake of fact expresses a thought of reciprocity and distinguishes it from a mistake which is a common mistake of both parties. There is something of the thought of a common mistake because it must affect both parties. Mistake of fact as ground for relief may be neither "mutual" nor common in the strict sense because it may be wholly the mistake of one of the parties, the other being wholly ignorant both of the fact upon the faith of which the other has mistakenly acted and that the other has acted upon such an understanding of the fact situation.

Unilateral mistake. A mistake by only one party to an agreement and generally not a basis for relief by rescission or reformation.

Mistrial. An erroneous, invalid, or nugatory trial. A trial of an action which cannot stand in law because of want of jurisdiction, or a wrong drawing of jurors, or disregard of some other fundamental requisite before or during trial. Trial which has been terminated prior to its normal conclusion. A device used to halt trial proceedings when error is so prejudicial and fundamental that expenditure of further time and expense would be wasteful if not futile. The judge may declare a mistrial because of some extraordinary event (*e.g.* death of juror, or attorney), for prejudicial error that cannot be corrected at trial, or because of a deadlocked jury.

A mistrial is equivalent to no trial and is a nugatory trial while "new trial" recognizes a completed trial which for sufficient reasons has been set aside so that the issues may be tried de novo.

Misuse. As defense in products liability action, requires use of product by injured party in a manner neither intended nor reasonably foreseeable by manufacturer.

Mitigating circumstances. Such as do not constitute a justification or excuse for the offense in question, but which, in fairness and mercy, may be considered as extenuating or reducing the degree of moral culpability. For example, mitigating circumstances which will reduce degree of homicide to manslaughter are the commission of the killing in a sudden heat of passion caused by adequate legal provocation.

Those that affect basis for award of exemplary damages, or reduce actual damages by showing, not that they were never suffered, but that they have been partially extinguished.

In actions for libel and slander, refer to circumstances bearing on defendant's liability for exemplary damages by reducing moral culpability, or on liability for actual damages by showing partial extinguishment thereof. The "mitigating circumstances" which the statute allows defendant in libel action to prove are those which tend to show that defendant in speaking the slanderous words acted in good faith, with honesty of purpose, and not maliciously.

See also Comparative negligence; Extenuating circumstances; Extraordinary circumstances.

Mitigation. To make less severe. Alleviation, reduction, abatement or diminution of a penalty or punishment imposed by law.

Mitigation of damages. Doctrine of "mitigation of damages," sometimes called doctrine of avoidable consequences, imposes on party injured by breach of contract or tort duty to exercise reasonable diligence and ordinary care in attempting to minimize his damages, or avoid aggravating the injury, after breach or injury has been inflicted and care and diligence required of him is the same as that which would be used by man of ordinary prudence under like circumstances. Mitigation of damages is an affirmative defense and applies when plaintiff fails to take reasonable actions that would tend to mitigate his injuries. See Restatement, Contracts § 336(1); U.C.C. § 2–603. *See also* Avoidable consequences doctrine.

Mitigation of punishment. A judge may reduce or order a lesser sentence in consideration of such factors as the defendant's past good behavior, his family situation, his cooperation with the police and kindred factors. *See also* Sentence.

Mittimus /mítəməs/. The name of a precept in writing, issuing from a court or magistrate, directed to the sheriff or other officer, commanding him to convey to the prison the person named therein, and to the jailer, commanding him to receive and safely keep such person until he shall be delivered by due course of law. Transcript of minutes of conviction and sentence duly certified by court clerk.

Mixed. Formed by admixture or commingling; partaking of the nature, character, or legal attributes of two or more distinct kinds or classes.

As to *mixed* Action; Contract; Government; Jury; Larceny; Marriage; Nuisance; Policy; Presumption; Property; Tithes; and War, see those titles.

Mixed laws. A name sometimes given to those which concern both persons and property.

Mixed question of law and fact. A question depending for solution on questions of both law and fact, but is really a question of either law or fact to be decided by either judge or jury. This phrase may mean either those which arise from the conflict of foreign and domestic laws, or questions arising on a trial involving both law and fact.

Mixed subjects of property. Such as fall within the definition of things real, but which are attended, nevertheless, with some of the legal qualities of things personal, as emblements, fixtures, and shares in public undertakings, connected with land. Besides these, there are others which, though things personal in point of definition, are, in respect of some of their legal qualities, of the nature of things real; such are animals *feræ naturæ,* charters and deeds, court rolls, and other evidences of the land, together with the chests in which they are contained, ancient family pictures, ornaments, tombstones, coats of armor, with pennons and other ensigns, and especially heirlooms.

MLP. *See* Master Limited Partnership.

M'Naghten Rule. The test applied in a number of the states for the defense of insanity. This test, as prescribed by statute or case law, has a number of variations in the respective states applying such. Under M'Naghten test or rule, an accused is not criminally responsible if, at the time of committing the act, he was laboring under such a defect of reason from disease of the mind as not to know the nature and quality of the act he was doing, or if he did know it that he did not know he was doing what was wrong. M'Naghten's Case, 8 Eng.Rep. 718 (1843). State v. Johnson, 383 A.2d 1012, 1022.

The standard under the "M'Naghten insanity" test to determine whether a person is sane is did the defendant have sufficient mental capacity to know and understand what he was doing, and did he know and understand that it was wrong and a violation of the rights of another. To be "sane" and thus responsible to the law for the act committed, the defendant must be able to both know and understand the nature and quality of his act and to distinguish between right and wrong at the time of the commission of the offense.

See also Insanity, *supra,* regarding other tests used by courts in determining criminal responsibility.

Mob. An assemblage of many people, acting in a violent and disorderly manner, defying the law, and committing, or threatening to commit, depredations upon property or violence to persons.

The word, in legal use, is practically synonymous with "riot," but the latter is the more correct term.

Mode. The manner in which a thing is done; as the mode of proceeding, the mode of process.

Model. A preliminary pattern or representation of something to be made or something already made. A *facsimile* of something invented, made on a reduced scale, in compliance with the patent laws. A replication of something made to scale. Style or design of product or item. *See also* Sample.

Model act. Statute proposed by the National Conference of Commissioners of Uniform State Laws or other organization for adoption by state legislatures, *e.g.* Uniform Commercial Code; Model Penal Code; Model Probate Code; Model Business Corporation Act. Frequently, the state adopting the model act will modify it to some extent to meet its own needs or may adopt only a portion of such. *See also* Uniform Laws *or* Acts.

Model jury instructions. *See* Jury instructions.

Model Rules of Professional Conduct. Rules adopted by the American Bar Association in 1983, with technical amendments adopted in 1987, which provide comprehensive treatment of professional conduct in the form of rules as to what an attorney may and may not do in dealing with the court, opposing counsel, his/her client and third persons. These Rules, which replace the former ABA Code of Professional Responsibility, have been adopted by many states (usually by the state supreme court) to govern conduct of attorneys admitted to practice in the state.

Moderator. A chairman or president of an assembly. A person appointed to preside at a popular meeting. The presiding officer of town meetings in New England is so called.

Modification. A change; an alteration or amendment which introduces new elements into the details, or cancels some of them, but leaves the general purpose and effect of the subject-matter intact. *See* Amendment.

Modify. To alter; to change in incidental or subordinate features; enlarge, extend; amend; limit, reduce. Such alteration or change may be characterized, in quantitative sense, as either an increase or decrease. *See* Modification.

Modus /mówdəs/. Lat. In Civil law, manner; means; way.

Criminal pleading. The *modus* of an indictment is that part of it which contains the narrative of the commission of the crime; the statement of the mode or manner in which the offense was committed.

Modus operandi /mówdəs òpərǽnday/. Method of operating or doing things (M.O.). Term used by police and criminal investigators to describe the particular method of a criminal's activity. It refers to pattern of criminal behavior so distinct that separate crimes or wrongful conduct are recognized as work of same person.

Moiety /móyədiy/. The half of anything. Joint tenants are said to hold by moieties. *See also* Community property. *Compare* Entirety.

Moiety acts. A name sometimes applied to penal and criminal statutes which provide that half the penalty or fine shall inure to the benefit of the informer.

Monarchy /mónərkiy/. A government in which the supreme power is vested in a single person. Where a monarch is invested with absolute power, the monarchy is termed "despotic;" where the supreme power is virtually in the laws, though the majesty of government and the administration are vested in a single person, it is a "limited" or "constitutional" monarchy. It is hereditary where the regal power descends immediately from the possessor to the next heir by blood, as in England; or elective, as was formerly the case in Poland.

Monetary. The usual meaning is "pertaining to coinage or currency or having to do with money", but it has been held to include personal property.

Monetary bequest. A transfer by will of cash. It is often designated as a pecuniary bequest.

Monetary liabilities. Contractual claims to pay a fixed amount of cash in the future; includes accounts payable, salaries payable, and bonds payable. *See also* Debt.

Money. In usual and ordinary acceptation it means coins and paper currency used as circulating medium of exchange, and does not embrace notes, bonds, evidences of debt, or other personal or real estate.

A medium of exchange authorized or adopted by a domestic or foreign government as a part of its currency. U.C.C. § 1–201(24).

See also Currency; Current money; Flat money; Legal tender; Near money; Scrip.

Public money. Revenue received from federal, state, and local governments from taxes, fees, fines, etc. *See* Revenue.

Money-bill. A legislative act by which revenue is directed to be raised, for any purpose or in any shape whatsoever, either for governmental purposes, and collected from the whole people generally, or for the benefit of a particular district, and collected in that district, or for making appropriations. All federal revenue bills must arise in the House of Representatives, but the Senate may propose or concur with amendments as on other bills. Art. I, Sec. 7, U.S.Const.

Money demand. A claim for a fixed and liquidated amount of money, or for a sum which can be ascertained by mere calculation; in this sense, distinguished from a claim which must be passed upon and liquidated by a jury, called "damages."

Moneyed corporation. *See* Corporation.

Money had and received. In common law pleading, the technical designation of a form of declaration in *assumpsit*, wherein the plaintiff declares that the defendant *had and received* certain money, etc.

Gist of action for "money had and received" is that defendant has received money which, in equity and good conscience, should have been paid to plaintiff and under such circumstances that he ought to pay it over.

Money judgment. A final order, decree or judgment of a court by which a defendant is required to pay a sum of money in contrast to a decree or judgment of equity in which the court orders some other type of relief; *e.g.* injunction or specific performance. *See also* Judgment. For enforcement of money judgments, *see* Execution.

Money laundering. *See* Laundering.

Money lent. In common law pleading, the technical name of a declaration in an action of *assumpsit* for which the defendant promised to pay the plaintiff for money lent.

Money market. The financial market for dealing in short term debt instruments such as U.S. Treasury bills, commercial paper, and bankers' acceptances, in contrast to the capital market which furnishes long term financing.

Money order. A type of negotiable draft issued by banks, post offices, telegraph companies and express companies and used by the purchaser as a substitute for a check. Form of credit instrument calling for payment of money to named payee, and involving three parties: remitter, payee, and drawee. Money order may encompass nonnegotiable as well as negotiable instruments and may be issued by a governmental agency, a bank, or private person or entity authorized to issue it, but essential characteristic is that it is purchased for purpose of paying a debt or to transmit funds upon credit of the issuer of the money order.

Money-order office. One of the post-offices authorized to draw or pay money orders.

Money paid. In common law pleading, the technical name of a declaration in *assumpsit*, in which the plaintiff declares for money paid for the use of the defendant. *See also* Money had and received.

Money-purchase plan. A pension plan where the employer contributes a specified amount of cash each year to each employee's pension fund. Benefits ultimately received by the employee are not specifically defined but depend on the rate of return on the cash invested.

Money supply. The amount of money in the economy at any point in time. Such consists of funds in circulation as well as in checking accounts. Money has been categorized into 4 groups based upon liquidity, as follows:

M–1 is generally funds in circulation, checking accounts, drafts.

M–2 includes M–1 as well as mutual funds, overnight repurchase agreements, and savings accounts.

M–3 includes M–2 as well as longer term repurchase agreements and time deposits in excess of $100,000.

L includes M–3 as well as banker's acceptances, T-bills and similar longer term investments.

Moniment /mónəmənt/. A memorial, superscription, or record.

Monition /məníshən/. In admiralty, formerly the summons to appear and answer, issued on filing the libel; which was either a simple monition *in personam* or an attachment and monition *in rem*. With the unification of the Admiralty Rules and Federal Rules of Civil Procedure in 1966, the monition was abolished.

General monition. In civil law practice, a monition or summons to all parties in interest to appear and show cause against the decree prayed for.

Practice. A monition is a formal order of the court commanding something to be done by the person to whom it is directed, and who is called the "person monished." Thus, when money is decreed to be paid, a monition may be obtained commanding its payment. In ecclesiastical procedure, a monition is an order monishing or warning the party complained against to do or not to do a certain act "under pain of the law and contempt thereof." A monition may also be appended to a sentence inflicting a punishment for a past offense; in that case the monition forbids the repetition of the offense.

Monocracy /mənókrəsiy/. A government by one person.

Monocrat /mónəkræt/. A monarch who governs alone; an absolute governor.

Monogamy /mənógəmiy/. The marriage of one wife only, or the state of such as are restrained to a single wife. The term is used in opposition to "bigamy" and "polygamy."

Monopoly /mənóp(ə)ly/. A privilege or peculiar advantage vested in one or more persons or companies, consisting in the exclusive right (or power) to carry on a particular business or trade, manufacture a particular article, or control the sale of the whole supply of a particular commodity. A form of market structure in which one or only a few firms dominate the total sales of a product or service.

"Monopoly", as prohibited by Section 2 of the Sherman Antitrust Act, has two elements: possession of monopoly power in relevant market and willful acquisition or maintenance of that power, as distinguished from growth or development as a consequence of a superior product, business acumen, or historic accident. A monopoly condemned by the Sherman Act is the power to fix prices or exclude competition, coupled with policies designed to use or preserve that power.

It is "monopolization" in violation of Sherman Antitrust Act for persons to combine or conspire to acquire or maintain power to exclude competitors from any part of trade or commerce, provided they also have such power that they are able, as group, to exclude actual or potential competition and provided that they have intent and purpose to exercise that power.

See also Market; Relevant market.

Legal monopoly. Exclusive right granted by governmental unit to business to provide such services as electric and telephone service. The rates and services of such utilities are in turn regulated by the government.

Natural monopoly. A natural monopoly is one resulting where one firm of efficient size can produce all or more than market can take at remunerative price. One which is created from circumstances over which the monopolist has no power. For example, a market for a particular product may be so limited that it is impossible to profitably produce such except by a single plant large enough to supply the whole demand.

Monopoly power. The "monopoly power" which must exist in order to establish a violation of Sherman Antitrust Act may be defined as the power to fix prices, to exclude competitors, or to control the market in the relevant geographical area in question. *See also* Market; Monopoly; Relevant market.

Monopsony. A condition of the market in which there is but one buyer for a particular commodity.

Month to month tenancy. *See* Tenancy.

Monument. Anything by which the memory of a person, thing, idea, art, science or event is preserved or perpetuated. A tomb where a dead body has been deposited.

In real-property law and surveying, monuments are visible marks or indications left on natural or other objects indicating the lines and boundaries of a survey. Any physical object on ground which helps to establish location of boundary line called for; it may be either natural (*e.g.* trees, rivers, and other land features) or artificial (*e.g.* fences, stones, stakes, or the like placed by human hands). *See also* Natural monument.

Moonlighting. Working at another job after hours of regular job.

Moorage. A sum charged for use of mooring facilities. Act of mooring vessel.

Mooring. Anchoring or making fast to the shore or dock. The securing or confining a vessel in a particular station, as by cables and anchors or by a line or chain run to the wharf.

Moot. A subject for argument; unsettled; undecided. A moot point is one not settled by judicial decisions.

Moot case. A case is "moot" when a determination is sought on a matter which, when rendered, cannot have any practical effect on the existing controversy. Question is "moot" when it presents no actual controversy or where the issues have ceased to exist.

Generally, an action is considered "moot" when it no longer presents a justiciable controversy because issues involved have become academic or dead. Case in which the matter in dispute has already been resolved and hence, one not entitled to judicial intervention unless the issue is a recurring one and likely to be raised again between the parties. A case becomes "moot" when the issues presented are no longer "live" or the parties lack a legally cognizable interest in the outcome. *See* Mootness doctrine.

Moot court. A court held (normally in law schools) for the arguing of moot or hypothetical cases.

Mootness doctrine. The principle that when the matter in dispute has already been resolved, there is no actual controversy that would be affected by a judicial decision, and federal courts will not exercise their jurisdiction over such matters. *See* Moot case.

Moral. Pertains to character, conduct, intention, social relations, etc.

1. Pertaining or relating to the conscience or moral sense or to the general principles of right conduct.

2. Cognizable or enforceable only by the conscience or by the principles of right conduct, as distinguished from positive law.

3. Depending upon or resulting from probability; raising a belief or conviction in the mind independent of strict or logical proof.

4. Involving or affecting the moral sense; as in the phrase "moral insanity."

Moral actions. Those only in which persons have knowledge to guide them, and a will to choose for themselves.

Moral certainty. That degree of assurance which induces a man of sound mind to act, without doubt, upon the conclusions to which it leads. A high degree of impression of the truth of a fact, falling short of absolute certainty, but sufficient to justify a verdict of guilty, even in a capital case. Such signifies a probability sufficiently strong to justify action on it; a very high degree of probability, although not demonstrable, as a certainty. It has also been used as indicating a conclusion of the mind established beyond a reasonable doubt.

Moral consideration. *See* Consideration.

Moral duress. Consists in imposition, oppression, undue influence, or the taking of undue advantage of the business or financial stress or extreme necessity or weakness of another. *See also* Coercion; Duress.

Moral evidence. As opposed to "mathematical" or "demonstrative" evidence, this term denotes that kind of evidence which, without developing an absolute and necessary certainty, generates a high degree of probability or persuasive force. It is founded upon analogy or induction, experience of the ordinary course of nature or the sequence of events, and the testimony of men.

Moral fraud. This phrase is one of the less usual designations of "actual" or "positive" fraud or "fraud in fact," as distinguished from "constructive fraud" or "fraud in law." It means fraud which involves actual guilt, a wrongful purpose, or moral obliquity.

Moral hazard. *See* Hazard.

Moral law. The law of conscience; the aggregate of those rules and principles of ethics which relate to right and wrong conduct and prescribe the standards to which the actions of men should conform in their dealings with each other. *See also* Natural law.

Moral obligation. *See* Obligation.

Moral turpitude. The act of baseness, vileness, or the depravity in private and social duties which man owes to his fellow man, or to society in general, contrary to accepted and customary rule of right and duty between man and man. Act or behavior that gravely violates moral sentiment or accepted moral standards of community and is a morally culpable quality held to be present in some criminal offenses as distinguished from others. The quality of a crime involving grave infringement of the moral sentiment of the community as distinguished from statutory mala prohibita. *See also* Turpitude.

Moratorium /mòhrətór(i)yəm/. A term designating suspension of all or of certain legal remedies against debtors, sometimes authorized by law during financial distress. A period of permissive or obligatory delay; specifically, a period during which an obligor has a legal right to delay meeting an obligation. Delay or postponement of a legal obligation or an action or proceeding. *See* Injunction; Restraining order.

More favorable terms clause. A provision in a labor-management contract by which the union agrees not to make more favorable agreements with other and competing employers.

More or less. About; substantially; or approximately; implying that both parties assume the risk of any ordinary discrepancy. The words are intended to cover slight or unimportant inaccuracies in quantity; and are ordinarily to be interpreted as taking care of unsubstantial differences or differences of small importance compared to the whole number of items transferred.

Moreover. In addition thereto, also, furthermore, likewise, beyond this, besides this.

Morgue /mórg/. A place where the bodies of persons found dead are kept for a limited time and exposed to view, to the end that their relatives or friends may identify them.

Morning loan. An unsecured loan to permit the borrower, generally a stockbroker, to carry on his business for the day.

Mortal. Destructive to life; causing or occasioning death; exposing to or deserving death, especially spiritual death; deadly; fatal, as, a mortal wound, or mortal sin; of or pertaining to time of death.

Mortality. The relative incidence of death.

Mortality tables. A means of ascertaining the probable number of years any man or woman of a given age and of ordinary health will live. A mortality table expresses, on the basis of the group studied, the probability that, of a number of persons of equal expectations of life who are living at the beginning of any year, a certain number of deaths will occur within that year.

Such tables are used by insurance companies to determine the premium to be charged for those in the respective age groups.

Mortgage /mórgəj/. A mortgage is an interest in land or real property created by a written instrument providing security for the performance of a duty or the payment of a debt.

At common law, an estate created by a conveyance absolute in its form, but intended to secure the performance of some act, such as the payment of money, and the like, by the grantor or some other person, and to become void if the act is performed agreeably to the terms prescribed at the time of making such conveyance. Such a mortgage today is called an equitable mortgage. The mortgage operates as a conveyance of the legal title to the mortgagee, but such title is subject to defeasance on payment of the debt or performance of the duty by the mortgagor.

The above definitions are applicable to the common-law (*i.e.* estate or title) conception of a mortgage. Such conception is still applicable in certain states. But in many other states, a mortgage is regarded as a mere lien, and not as creating a title or estate. It is a pledge or security of particular property for the payment of a debt or the performance of some other obligation, whatever form the transaction may take, but is not now regarded as a conveyance in effect, though it may be cast in the form of a conveyance. Still other states have adopted a hybrid or intermediate theory or category of mortgage.

See also Assumption of mortgage; Balloon mortgage; Bulk mortgage; Chattel mortgage; Collateral mortgage; Conversion *or* convertibility clause; Deed (*Deed of trust*); Due-on-sale clause; Release (*Release of mortgage*); Ship Mortgage Act; Submortgage; Title theory; Trust (*Trust deed*); Union mortgage clause. For *Bona fide mortgage,* see Bona fide.

Adjustable rate mortgage (ARM). A mortgage in which the interest rate is not fixed but is tied to an index and is periodically adjusted as the rate index moves up or down. Such ARM mortgages commonly provide for an option to convert to a fixed rate mortgage. *See also* Cap; Conversion *or* convertibility clause.

Amortized mortgage. One in which the mortgagor pays the current interest charge as well as a portion of principal in his periodic payment.

Balloon-payment mortgage. Mortgage requiring interest payments for a specified period and full payment of principal (a balloon payment) at the end of the period.

Blanket mortgage. One which conveys title to or creates a lien on all the borrower's assets or a substantial portion of them rather than on a specific asset.

Chattel mortgage. Mortgage secured by personal property. *See* Chattel mortgage.

Closed-end mortgage. One in which neither the property mortgaged nor the amount borrowed may be altered during the term of the mortgage.

Consolidated mortgage. A single mortgage given to replace or to combine several outstanding mortgages.

Construction draw mortgage. Type of mortgage used to finance building construction.

Conventional mortgage. The conventional mortgage is a contract by which a person binds the whole of his property, or a portion of it only, in favor of another, to secure the execution of some engagement, but without divesting himself of possession. It is distinguished from the "legal" mortgage, which is a privilege which the law alone in certain cases gives to a creditor over the property of his debtor, without stipulation of the parties. This last is very much like a general lien at common law, created by the law rather than by the act of the parties, such as a judgment lien.

Conventional home mortgage. The common security device used by those who wish to purchase a home by transferring to the bank or other financial institution a lien or defeasible legal title in return for the price or part of the price of the home. A non-FHA or VA home loan; *i.e.* not backed by government insurance or security. The mortgage is conventional in that the lender looks only to the credit of the borrower and the security of the property, and not to the additional backing of another such as would be the case with an FHA insured mortgage.

Direct reduction mortgage. An amortized mortgage. One on which principal and interest payments are paid at the same time (usually monthly) with interest being computed on the remaining balance.

Equitable mortgage. A specific lien upon real property to secure the payment of money or the performance of some other obligation, which a court of equity will recognize and enforce, in accordance with the clearly ascertained intent of the parties to that effect, but which lacks the essential features of a legal mortgage, either because it grows out of the transactions of the parties without any deed or express contract to give a lien, or because the instrument used for that purpose is wanting in some of the characteristics of a common-law mortgage, or, being absolute in form, is accompanied by a collateral reservation of a right to redeem, or because an explicit agreement to give a mortgage has not been carried into effect.

FHA mortgage. One in which the loan has been insured in whole or in part by the Federal Housing Administration.

First mortgage. The first (in time or right) of a series of two or more mortgages covering the same property and successively attaching as liens upon it. Also, in a more particular sense, a mortgage which is a first lien on the property, not only as against other mortgages, but as against any other charges or incumbrances. Also called "senior" mortgage.

First mortgage bonds. Bonds the payment of which is secured by a first mortgage on property.

Fixed-rate mortgage. Such mortgage specifies an interest rate that remains fixed for the life of the mortgage regardless of market conditions. *Compare Adjustable rate mortgage, above.*

Future advances mortgage. A term used to describe a present mortgage transaction where part of the loan proceeds will not be paid out until a future date.

General mortgage. Mortgages are sometimes classified as general and special, a mortgage of the former class being one which binds all property, present and future, of the debtor (sometimes called a "blanket" mortgage); while a special mortgage is limited to certain particular and specified property.

Graduated payment adjustable rate mortgage (GPARM). A mortgage format that combines the features of the graduated payment mortgage (GPM) and the adjustable rate mortgage (ARM).

Graduated payment mortgage (GPM). A mortgage loan that carries monthly payments which increase annually by a specified percentage during the early years of the loan and then remain constant thereafter. *See also Adjustable rate mortgage, above.*

Growing equity mortgage (GEM). A mortgage loan that is fully amortized over a significantly shorter term than the traditional 25 or 30 year mortgage, and which may have payments which increase each year.

Joint mortgage. One which is given to or by two or more mortgagees jointly.

Judicial mortgage. In the law of Louisiana, the lien resulting from judgments, whether rendered on contested cases or by default, whether final or provisional, in favor of the person obtaining them. Civ.Code La. art. 3321.

Junior mortgage. One which ranks below another mortgage of the name property in the value of the security, and is subordinate to senior mortgages in its rights.

Leasehold mortgage. Mortgage secured by lessee's interest in leased property.

Legal mortgage. A term used in Louisiana. The law alone in certain cases gives to the creditor a mortgage on the property of his debtor, without it being requisite that the parties should stipulate it. That is called "legal mortgage." It is also called a *tacit* mortgage, because it is established by the law without the aid of any agreement. Civ.Code La. art. 3311.

Mortgage of goods. See Chattel mortgage.

Open-end mortgage. A mortgage permitting the mortgagor to borrow additional money under the same mortgage, with certain conditions, usually as to the assets of the mortgagor.

Package mortgage. A package mortgage is used to include not only the real property but many items of personal property incident to the real property, such as stoves, refrigerators, and the like.

Purchase money mortgage. Generally, any mortgage given to secure a loan made for the purpose of acquiring the land on which the mortgage is given; more particularly, a mortgage given to the seller of land to secure payment of a portion of the purchase price. A mortgage given, concurrently with a conveyance of land, by the vendee to the vendor, on the same land, to secure the unpaid balance of the purchase price.

Reverse annuity mortgage (RAM). A mortgage format under which the mortgage loan proceeds are disbursed periodically over a long time period to provide regular income for the borrower-mortgagor. The loan will usually be repaid in a lump sum when the mortgagor dies or the property is sold.

Second mortgage. One which takes rank immediately after a first mortgage on the same property, without any intervening liens, and is next entitled to satisfaction out of the proceeds of the property. Properly speaking, however, the term designates the second of a series of mortgages, not necessarily the second lien. For instance, the lien of a judgment might intervene between the first and second mortgages; in which case, the second mortgage would be the third lien. Also called "junior" mortgage. *See also* Wraparound mortgage *infra.*

Senior mortgage. One which ranks ahead of another mortgage in terms of rights in the security. *See also First mortgage, above.*

Shared appreciation mortgage (SAM). A mortgage format that gives the lender the right to recover, as "contingent interest", some agreed-upon percentage of the property's appreciation in value measured when it is sold or at some other future fixed date.

Shared-equity mortgage (SEM). A mortgage format under which a purchaser-occupant and another person (often a relative) become co-owners and co-mortgagors of real estate. Usually the non-occupant owner pays all or a substantial part of the monthly payments and is entitled to share in any appreciation when the real estate is sold.

Straight mortgage. One in which the mortgagor is obligated to pay interest during the term of the mortgage and a final payment of principal at the end of the term in contrast to an amortized mortgage.

Tacit mortgage. See Legal mortgage, above.

VA Mortgage. Home mortgage loan provided to veterans and their spouses which is guaranteed by the Veterans Administration.

Variable rate mortgage. A long-term mortgage contract which includes a provision permitting the lending institution to adjust, upward and downward, the contract's interest rate in response to changes in money market rates and the conditions of demand for mortgages.

Wraparound mortgage. See Wraparound mortgage.

Mortgage banker. A person or firm engaged in the business of dealing in mortgages including their original placement, servicing, refinancing, and resale to other investors. Normally such banker uses its own funds as opposed to a commercial or savings and loan bank which uses primarily funds of depositors. While some mortgage bankers do provide long term (permanent) financing, the majority specialize in short term and interim financing.

Mortgage bond. Bonds for which real estate or personal property is pledged as security that the bond will be paid as stated in its terms. May be first, second, refunding, and so on.

Mortgage broker. Person or firm who functions as intermediary between borrower and lender in securing loan, or places loans with investors.

Mortgage certificate. Document evidencing participation in a large mortgage held by the mortgagee for the benefit of the certificate holders.

Mortgage clause. Provision in fire insurance policies protecting the mortgagee as his interest may appear.

Mortgage commitment. A formal written communication by a lender, agreeing to make a mortgage loan on specific property, specifying the loan's amount, length of time, and other conditions. Because of interest rate fluctuations, such commitments normally have time limitations. *See also* Loan commitment.

Mortgage company. A firm engaged in the business of originating and closing mortgages which are then assigned or sold to investors.

Mortgage contingency clause. Clause in an agreement for sale of real estate conditioning the purchaser's performance on his obtaining a mortgage from a third party.

Mortgage discount. The difference between the principal amount of a mortgage and the amount it actually sells for. Sometimes called points, loan brokerage fee, or new loan fee.

Mortgagee /mòrgəjíy/. Person that takes, holds, or receives a mortgage.

Mortgagee in possession. A mortgagee of real property who is in possession of it with the agreement or assent of the mortgagor, express or implied, and in recognition of his mortgage and because of it, and under such circumstances as to make the satisfaction of his lien an equitable prerequisite to his being dispossessed.

Mortgage foreclosure. *See* Foreclosure.

Mortgage guarantee insurance. A type of insurance which guarantees to the mortgagee a given portion of the loss if the mortgagee suffers a loss due to nonpayment on the loan. *See* Federal Housing Administration; Insurance.

Mortgage insurance. *See* Insurance.

Mortgage lien. Encumbrances on property of mortgagor which secures debt obligation. In some states, the mortgagor retains legal title until foreclosure and the mortgagee has a security interest called a lien which is recognized ahead of other claims to the property.

Mortgage loan. A loan secured by a mortgage on real estate in which the borrower is the mortgagor and the lender the mortgagee. *See* Mortgage.

Mortgage market. Conditions which exist as to demand for purchase of mortgages generally by financial institutions which use mortgages as part of their investment portfolio.

Mortgage point. A percentage of the mortgage, generally 1%, charged by the mortgagee up front as a cost of financing.

Mortgage servicing. The responsibilities (which may be undertaken by a service company hired by the original lender) of mortgage lending, such as collecting installment payments, releasing liens, initiating foreclosure upon default, etc.

Mortgage warehousing. System under which mortgage company holds loans which would ordinarily be sold, in order to sell later at a lower discount. These mortgages are used as collateral security with a bank to borrow new money to loan.

Mortgaging out. The process by which a mortgagor secures one hundred percent financing of his purchase. He purchases property with no money of his own but entirely with mortgage money.

Mortgagor /mórgəjər/. One who, having all or some part of title to property, by written instrument pledges that property for some particular purpose such as security for a debt. The party who mortgages the property; the debtor. That party to a mortgage who gives legal title or a lien to the mortgagee to secure the mortgage loan.

Mortis causa /mórtəs kózə/. Lat. By reason of death; in contemplation of death. Thus used in the phrase *"Donatio mortis causa"* (q.v.).

Mortmain /mórtmèyn/. A term applied to denote the alienation of lands or tenements to any corporation, sole or aggregate, ecclesiastical or temporal. These purchases having been chiefly made by religious houses, in consequence of which lands became perpetually inherent in one "dead hand", this occasioned the general appellation of "mortmain" to be applied to such alienations.

Mortmain acts. These acts had for their object to prevent lands getting into the possession or control of religious corporations, or, as the name indicates, *in mortua manu*. After numerous prior acts dating from the reign of Edward I, it was enacted by the statute 9 Geo. II, c. 36 (called the "Mortmain Act" *par excellence*), that no lands should be given to charities unless certain requisites should be observed. Some traces of these laws remained until 1960.

Mortuary tables. *See* Actuarial table; Mortality tables.

Most favored nation clause. A clause found in most treaties providing that the citizens or subjects of the contracting nations may enjoy the privileges accorded by either party to those of the most favored nations. The general design of such clauses is to establish the principle of equality of international treatment. The test of whether this principle is violated by the concession of advantages to a particular nation is not the form in which such concession is made, but the condition on which it is granted; whether it is given for a price, or whether this price is in the nature of a substantial equivalent, and not of a mere evasion. The United States has generally taken the stand that reciprocal commercial concessions are given for a valuable consideration and are not within the scope of this clause. *See also* Reciprocal trade agreements.

A primary effect of "most favored nation" status is lower import tariffs or duties.

Most suitable use valuation. For gift and estate tax purposes, property that is transferred normally is valued in accordance with its most suitable or highest and best use. Thus, if a farm is worth more as a potential shopping center, this value will control even though the transferee (*i.e.*, the donee or heir) continues to use the property as a farm. For an exception to this rule concerning the valuation of certain kinds of real estate transferred by death, *see* Special use valuation.

Mother-in-law. The mother of one's wife or of one's husband.

Motion. In parliamentary law, the formal mode in which a member submits a proposed measure or resolve for the consideration and action of the meeting.

An application made to a court or judge for purpose of obtaining a rule or order directing some act to be done in favor of the applicant. It is usually made within the framework of an existing action or proceeding and is ordinarily made on notice, but some motions may be made without notice. One without notice is called an ex parte motion. Written or oral application to court for ruling or order, made before (*e.g.* motion to dismiss) during (*e.g.* motion for directed verdict), or after (*e.g.* motion for new trial) trial. For requisite form of motions, see Fed.R.Civil P. 7(b).

See also Speaking motion.

Motion for judgment notwithstanding verdict. A motion that judgment be entered in accordance with the movant's earlier motion for a directed verdict and notwithstanding the contrary verdict actually returned by the jury. See Fed.R.Civil P. 50(b).

Motion for judgment on pleadings. Under Fed. R.Civil P. 12(c) any party may move after the pleadings are closed for judgment thereon. It is a device for disposing of cases when the material facts are not in dispute and only questions of law remain. *See also* Summary judgment.

Motion for more definite statement. If a pleading is so vague or ambiguous that a party cannot reasonably be required to frame a responsive pleading, such party may move for a more definite statement. Fed.R.Civil P. 12(e).

Motion for new trial. A request that the judge set aside the judgment or verdict and order a new trial on the basis that the trial was improper or unfair due to specified prejudicial errors that occurred, because of newly discovered evidence, etc. Fed.R.Civil P. 59; Fed.R.Crim.P. 33. *See also* Plain error rule.

Motion in arrest of judgment. *See* Arrest of judgment.

Motion in bar. One which, if allowed, will absolutely bar the action; *e.g.* plea of double jeopardy.

Motion in limine. A pretrial motion requesting court to prohibit opposing counsel from referring to or offering evidence on matters so highly prejudicial to moving party that curative instructions cannot prevent predispositional effect on jury. Purpose of such motion is to avoid injection into

trial of matters which are irrelevant, inadmissible and prejudicial and granting of motion is not a ruling on evidence and, where properly drawn, granting of motion cannot be error. *See also* Motion to suppress; Suppression hearing.

Motion to dismiss. A motion requesting that a complaint be dismissed because it does not state a claim for which the law provides a remedy, or is in some other way legally insufficient. One which is generally interposed before trial to attack the action on the basis of insufficiency of the pleading, of process, venue, joinder, etc. Fed.R. Civil P. 12(b). *See also* Demurrer.

Motion to strike. On motion of either party, the court may order stricken from any pleading any insufficient defense, or any redundant, immaterial, impertinent or scandalous matter. Fed.R.Civil P. 12(f).

Motion to suppress. Device used to eliminate from the trial of a criminal case evidence which has been secured illegally, generally in violation of the Fourth Amendment (search and seizure), the Fifth Amendment (privilege against self incrimination), or the Sixth Amendment (right to assistance of counsel, right of confrontation etc.), of U.S. Constitution. See Fed.R.Crim.P. 12(b) and 41(f); *also* Motion in limine; Suppression hearing.

Motive. Cause or reason that moves the will and induces action. An idea, belief or emotion that impels or incites one to act in accordance with his state of mind or emotion. The circumstance tending to establish the requisite mens rea for a criminal act and is the inducement which impels or leads the mind to indulge in a criminal act.

In common usage intent and "motive" are not infrequently regarded as one and the same thing. In law there is a distinction between them. "Motive" is said to be the moving course, the impulse, the desire that induces criminal action on part of the accused; it is distinguished from "intent" which is the purpose or design with which the act is done, the purpose to make the means adopted effective.

As to *criminal motive, see* Criminal; Mens rea. *See also* Intent.

Motor Carrier Act. Federal statute (administered by ICC) which regulated (routes, rates, etc.) motor carriers of freight and passengers in interstate commerce. 49 U.S.C.A. § 301 *et seq.* This Act was repealed in 1983 when motor carriers became deregulated.

Movable. That which can be changed in place, as movable property; or in time, as movable feasts or terms of court. *Compare* Fixture.

Movable estate. A term equivalent to "personal estate" or "personal property."

Movable freehold. A term applied by Lord Coke to real property which is capable of being increased or diminished by natural causes; as where the owner of seashore acquires or loses land as the waters recede or approach.

Movables. Things movable; movable or personal chattels which may be annexed to or attendant on the person of the owner, and carried about with him from one place to another. Things which may be carried from one place to another whether they move by themselves or whether they are inanimate objects capable of being moved by extraneous power.

Movant. One who moves; one who makes a motion before a court; the applicant for a rule or order.

Move. To make an application to a court for a rule or order, or to take action in any matter. The term comprehends all things necessary to be done by a litigant to obtain an order of the court directing the relief sought. *See* Motion.

To propose a resolution, or recommend action in a deliberate body.

To pass over; to be transferred, as when the consideration of a contract is said to "move" from one party to the other.

To occasion; to contribute to; to tend or lead to.

Movent. An alternative spelling of *movant.*

Move out. To vacate; to yield up possession.

Moving-average method. In accounting, a perpetual inventory costing system under which a new average cost is computed after each purchase.

Moving expenses. A tax deduction is permitted to employees and self-employed persons for expenses incurred in moving to a new job location, provided certain tests are met.

Moving papers. Such papers as are made the basis of some motion in court proceedings, *e.g.* a motion for summary judgment with supporting affidavits.

Mrs. /mísəz/. Title of courtesy prefixed to name of woman to indicate that she is or has been married.

Ms. /miz/. Title prefixed to a woman's name which does not indicate whether she is married or single but simply indicates that she is a woman.

Mug book. Collection of pictures or "mug shots" of suspects in criminal cases kept by police and FBI and displayed to victim or witnesses in order to obtain identification of criminal offender. *See also* Lineup.

Mugshot. Photograph of person's face taken on being booked into custody; usually used as an official photograph by police officers.

Mulct /mə́lkt/. A penalty or punishment imposed on a person guilty of some offense, tort, or misdemeanor, usually a pecuniary fine or condemnation in damages. A forfeit, fine, or penalty. To sentence to a pecuniary penalty or forfeiture as a punishment; fine; hence to fine unjustly; to punish.

Formerly, an imposition laid on ships or goods by a company of trade for the maintenance of consuls and the like.

Multa /mə́ltə/. A fine or final satisfaction, anciently given to the king by the bishops, that they might have power to make their wills, and that they might have the probate of other men's wills, and the granting of administration. Called, also, *multura episcopi.*

A fine imposed *ex arbitrio* by magistrates on the *præsides probinciarum.*

Multicraft union. A labor union which craftsmen in different trades may join.

Multidistrict litigation. When civil actions involving one or more common (and often complex) questions of fact are pending in several different federal district courts, such actions may be transferred to one district for coordinated and consolidated management and trial under a single judge. 28 U.S.C.A. § 1407. The types of cases in which massive filings of multidistrict litigation are reasonably certain to occur include not only civil antitrust actions but also, common disaster (air crash) actions, patent and trademark suits, products liability actions and securities law violation actions, among others. Such cases are assigned and transferred by a Judicial Panel on Multidistrict Litigation, and are governed by the "Manual for Complex Litigation" and "Rules of Procedure of the Judicial Panel on Multidistrict Litigation."

Multifarious issue. A multifarious issue is one that inquires about several different facts when each fact should be inquired about in a separate issue. *See* Multifariousness.

Multifariousness /mə̀ltəfér(i)yəsnəs/. In equity pleading, the misjoinder of causes of action in a bill. The fault of improperly joining in one bill distinct and independent matters, and thereby confounding them; as, for example, the uniting in one bill of several matters perfectly distinct and unconnected against one defendant (more commonly called misjoinder of claims), or the demand of several matters of a distinct and independent nature against several defendants, in the same bill.

This problem does not generally arise in the federal courts or in the majority of state courts, for Rule of Civil Procedure 8(e) permits pleading of inconsistent claims or defenses and Rule 18(a) permits liberal joinder of independent or alternative claims. Civil Rule 18 permits a party to join, either as independent or as alternate claims, as many claims, legal, equitable, or maritime, as he has against an opposing party.

Legislation. The joining, in a single legislative act, of dissimilar and discordant subjects, which, by no fair intendment, can be considered as having a legitimate connection or relation to the subject of the act.

Multilateral agreement. An agreement among more than two persons, firms, or governments.

Multinational corporation. In a strict sense this term is descriptive of a firm which has centers of operation in many countries in contrast to an "international" firm which does business in many countries but is based in only one country, though the terms are often used interchangeably.

Multiple access. The defense of several lovers in paternity actions.

Multiple counts. A civil pleading (*e.g.* complaint) or a criminal indictment which contains several separate causes of action or crimes within the framework of one pleading. Joinder of multiple claims against opposing party is permitted under Fed.R.Civil P. 18. Joinder of offenses is provided for in Fed.R.Crim.P. 8.

Multiple evidence. That which is admissible for a specific purpose to which it must be confined and inadmissible to prove a different fact.

Multiple listing. An agreement between the owner of real estate and a broker in which the broker will permit other brokers to sell property for a percentage of his commission or on some other basis satisfactory to the brokers. Device used by real estate brokers to give wide exposure to properties listed for sale whereby each cooperating broker informs all other participating brokers of properties listed with him. *See also* Listing.

Multiple offenses. A single act may be an offense against two statutes, and if each statute requires proof of an additional fact which the other does not, an acquittal or conviction under either statute does not exempt the defendant from prosecution and punishment under the other. If there is identity between the two charges, the defendant may not be punished for both, though he may be punished for the more serious.

Multiple-party accounts. A multiple-party account is any of the following types of account: (i) a joint account, (ii) a P.O.D. account, or (iii) a trust account. It does not include accounts established for deposit of funds of a partnership, joint venture, or other association for business purposes, or accounts controlled by one or more persons as the duly authorized agent or trustee for a corporation, unincorporated association, charitable or civic organization or a regular fiduciary or trust account where the relationship is established other than by deposit agreement. Uniform Probate Code, § 6–101(5).

Multiple sentences. If a defendant has been found guilty of more than one offense, he may be given consecutive ("on and after") sentences. *See also* Sentence.

Multiplicity /məltəplísətiy/. A state of being many. That quality of a pleading which involves a variety of matters or particulars. A multiplying or increasing.

Multiplicity of actions *or* **suits.** Numerous and unnecessary attempts to litigate the same right. A phrase descriptive of the situation where several different suits or actions are brought upon the same issue. The actions must be against a single defendant. Under Civil Rules practice such claims should properly be joined or maintained as a single class action. Fed.R.Civil P. 23.

Term "multiplicity" refers to the practice of charging the commission of a single offense in several counts. This practice is prohibited because single wrongful act cannot furnish basis for more than one criminal prosecution. Federal Rules of Criminal Procedure have been drafted to discourage this practice.

See Collateral estoppel doctrine; Duplicity; Final decision rule; Multiple counts; Res (*Res judicata*).

Multistate corporation. A corporation that has operations in more than one state; from which issues commonly arise relative to the assignment of appropriate amounts of the entity's taxable income to the states in which it has a presence. *See* UDITPA.

Multitude. An assemblage of many people.

Municipal. In narrower, more common, sense, it means pertaining to a local governmental unit, commonly, a city or town or other governmental unit. In its broader sense, it means pertaining to the public or governmental affairs of a state or nation or of a people. Relating to a state or nation, particularly when considered as an entity independent of other states or nations.

Municipal action. Exercise of governmental power by a municipal board, agency, or other body, or by a municipal officer.

Municipal affairs. A term referring to the internal business affairs of a municipality. The term is frequently used in constitutional and statutory provisions concerning the power to legislate as to the concerns of municipalities. And it has come to include public service activities, such as supplying water to the inhabitants, the construction of a reservoir for their benefit, the sale and distribution of electrical energy, and the establishment and operation of transportation service, which were once regarded as being of a strictly private nature. *See also* Municipal function.

Municipal aid. A contribution or assistance granted by a municipal corporation towards the execution or progress of some enterprise, undertaken by private parties, but likely to be of benefit to the municipality; *e.g.,* urban redevelopment projects.

Municipal authorities. As used in statutes contemplating the consent of such authorities, the term means the consent by the legislative authorities of the city acting by ordinance; for example, in a town, the members of the town board.

Municipal bonds. Evidences of indebtedness (debt obligations) issued by state or local government entities, negotiable in form, payable at designated future time, and intended for sale in market with object of raising money for municipal expense, which is beyond immediate resources of reasonable taxation, as distinguished from temporary evidences of debt, such as vouchers, certificates of indebtedness, orders, or drafts drawn by one officer on another and similar devices for liquidating current obligations in anticipation of collection of taxes. A bond issued by a village, town, city, county, state, or other public body. Interest on such bonds is generally exempt from federal income taxes and from some state income taxes. Sometimes referred to as "tax exempts."

Municipal charter. A legislative enactment conferring governmental powers of the state upon its local agencies.

Municipal corporation. A legal institution formed by charter from sovereign (*i.e.* state) power erecting a populous community of prescribed area into a body politic and corporate with corporate name and continuous succession and for the purpose and with the authority of subordinate self-government and improvement and local administration of affairs of state. A body corporate consisting of the inhabitants of a designated area created by the legislature with or without the consent of such inhabitants for governmental purposes, possessing local legislative and administrative power, also power to exercise within such area so much of the administrative power of the state as may be delegated to it and possessing limited capacity to own and hold property and to act in purveyance of public conveniences.

Municipal corporation is a body politic and corporate, created to administer the internal concerns of the district embraced with its corporate limits, in matters peculiar to such place and not common to the state at large. A municipal corporation has a dual character, the one public and the other private, and exercises correspondingly twofold functions and duties—one class consisting of those acts performed by it in exercise of delegated sovereign powers for benefit of people generally, as arm of state, enforcing general laws made in pursuance of general policy of the state, and the other consisting of acts done in exercise of power of the municipal corporation for its own benefit, or for benefit of its citizens alone, or

citizens of the municipal corporation and its immediate locality.

See also Public corporations.

Quasi municipal corporations. Bodies politic and corporate, created for the sole purpose of performing one or more municipal functions. Public corporations organized for governmental purposes and having for most purposes the status and powers of municipal corporations (such as counties, townships, school districts, drainage districts, irrigation districts, etc.), but not municipal corporations proper, such as cities and incorporated towns.

Municipal corporation de facto. One which exists when there is (1) some law under which a corporation with the powers assumed might lawfully have been created; (2) a colorable and bona fide attempt to perfect an organization under such a law; (3) user of the rights claimed to have been conferred by the law.

Municipal courts. In the judicial organization of several states, courts are established under this name with territorial authority confined to the city or community in which they are established. Such courts usually have a criminal jurisdiction corresponding to that of a police court, and, in some cases, possess civil jurisdiction in small causes. In certain cities, small claims or traffic courts are under the jurisdiction of the municipal court.

Municipal domicile. Sometimes used in contradistinction to "national domicile" and "quasi national domicile" to refer to residence in a county, township, or municipality; called also "domestic domicile."

Municipal election. One at which municipal officers are chosen.

Municipal function. One created or granted for the special benefit and advantage of the urban community embraced within the corporate boundaries.

Municipal functions are those which specially and peculiarly promote the comfort, convenience, safety and happiness of the citizens of the municipality, rather than the welfare of the general public. Under this class of functions are included, in most jurisdictions, the proper care of streets and alleys, parks and other public places, and the erection and maintenance of public utilities and improvements generally.

Municipal government. Instrumentalities of state for purpose of local government. This term, in certain state constitutions, embraces the governmental affairs of counties, and includes all forms of representative municipal government— towns, cities, villages, etc. *See also* Municipality.

Municipality. A legally incorporated or duly authorized association of inhabitants of limited area for local governmental or other public purposes. A body politic created by the incorporation of the people of a prescribed locality invested with subordinate powers of legislation to assist in the civil government of the state and to regulate and administer local and internal affairs of the community. A city, borough, town, township or village. Also, the body of officers taken collectively, belonging to a city, who are appointed to manage its affairs and defend its interests.

Political subdivision or public agency or instrumentality of a State. Bankruptcy Code § 101.

See also Person (*Municipalities*).

Municipal law. That which pertains solely to the citizens and inhabitants of a state, and is thus distinguished from political law, commercial law, and international law. In its more common and narrower connotation however it means those laws which pertain to towns, cities and villages and their local government.

Municipal lien. A lien or claim existing in favor of a municipal corporation against a property owner for his proportionate share of a public improvement, made by the municipality, whereby his property is specially and individually benefited.

Municipal officer. One who holds an office of a municipality; *e.g.* mayor, city manager.

Municipal ordinance. A law, rule, or ordinance enacted or adopted by a municipal corporation for the proper conduct of its affairs or the government of its inhabitants; *e.g.* zoning or traffic ordinances, building codes. Particularly a regulation under a delegation of power from the state.

Municipal purposes. Public or governmental purposes as distinguished from private purposes. It may comprehend all activities essential to the health, morals, protection, and welfare of the municipality.

Municipal securities. The evidences of indebtedness issued by cities, towns, counties, townships, school-districts, and other such territorial divisions of a state. They are of two general classes: (1) Municipal warrants, orders, or certificates; (2) municipal bonds.

The term "municipal securities" means securities which are direct obligations of, or obligations guaranteed as to principal or interest by, a State or any political subdivision thereof, or any agency or instrumentality of a State or any political subdivision thereof, or any municipal corporate instrumentality of one or more States, or any security which is an industrial development bond (as defined in § 103(c)(2) of the Internal Revenue Code) the interest on which is excludable from gross income. Securities Exchange Act of 1934, § 3.

See Municipal bonds; Municipal warrants.

Municipal warrants. A municipal warrant or order is an instrument drawn by an officer of a municipality upon its treasurer, directing him to pay an amount of money specified therein to the person named or his order, or to bearer.

Muniments of title /myúwnəmənts əv táydəl/. Documentary evidence of title. The instruments of writing and written evidences which the owner of lands, possessions, or inheritances has, by which he is enabled to defend the title of his estate. *See* Deed.

The records of title transactions in the chain of title of a person purporting to create the interest in land claimed by such person and upon which he relies as a basis for the marketability of his title, commencing with the root of title and including all subsequent transactions.

Under "muniment of title doctrine" when ownership of property has been litigated between individuals and title has been adjudicated in one of the parties, the losing party cannot relitigate the matter with those who rely upon the title of the winning party.

Murder. The unlawful killing of a human being by another with malice aforethought, either express or implied. The crime is defined by statute in most states (*e.g.* Calif. Penal Code, § 187). The Model Penal Code definition is as follows:

Criminal homicide constitutes murder when: (a) it is committed purposely or knowingly; or (b) it is committed recklessly under circumstances manifesting extreme indifference to the value of human life. Such recklessness and indifference are presumed if the actor is engaged or is an accomplice in the commission of, or an attempt to commit, or flight after committing or attempting to commit robbery, rape or deviate sexual intercourse by force or threat of force, arson, burglary, kidnapping or felonious escape. Model Penal Code, § 210.2.

See also Assassination; Assault with intent to commit murder; Felony murder doctrine; Homicide; Manslaughter.

Degrees of murder. In most states murder is divided into two degrees, for the purpose of imposing a more severe penalty for some murders than for others. All murder which shall be perpetrated by means of poison, or by lying in wait, or by any other kind of wilful, deliberate and premeditated killing, or which shall be committed in the perpetration of, or attempt to perpetrate any arson, rape, robbery or burglary, are commonly deemed *murder of the first degree*; and all other kinds of murder are deemed *murder of the second degree*. This general pattern has been followed in most of the states although slight changes have been made in a few of these. Some, for example, have omitted any reference to "poison", while a few have added "torture" to "poison". To the felony-murder clause of the statute several have added "mayhem" and sometimes the inclusion of some other felony may be found, such as kidnapping, sodomy or larceny. In certain states there is also the crime of murder in the third degree. For the definition of first and second degree murder under the federal criminal code, see 18 U.S.C.A. § 1111.

Depraved heart murder. Killing of a human being accomplished by extreme atrocity; malice is inferred from the act of atrocity. Extremely negligent conduct, which creates what a reasonable man would realize to be not only an unjustifiable but also a very high degree of risk of death or serious bodily injury to another or to others—though unaccompanied by any intent to kill or do serious bodily injury—and which actually causes the death of another, may constitute murder.

Serial murder. A pattern of murder in which a single individual selects victims either at random or because they share some characteristic.

Must. This word, like the word "shall," is primarily of mandatory effect; and in that sense is used in antithesis to "may". But this meaning of the word is not the only one, and it is often used in a merely directory sense, and consequently is a synonym for the word "may" not only in the permissive sense of that word, but also in the mandatory sense which it sometimes has.

Muster. To assemble together troops and their arms, whether for inspection, drill, or service in the field. To take recruits into the service in the army and inscribe their names on the muster-roll or official record. To summon together; to enroll in service. In the latter sense the term implies that the persons mustered are not already in the service.

Muster-roll. In maritime law, a list or account of a ship's company, required to be kept by the master or other person having care of the ship, containing the name, age, national character, and quality of every person employed in the ship. At time of war it is of great use in ascertaining the ship's neutrality.

Mute. Speechless; dumb; that cannot or will not speak.

Mutilation. As applied to written documents, such as wills, court records, and the like, this term means rendering the document imperfect by the subtraction from it of some essential part, as, by cutting, tearing, burning, or erasure, but without totally destroying it. See U.C.C. § 3–407. Also, the alteration in the writing, as in a negotiable instrument, so as to make it another and different instrument and no longer evidence of the contract which the parties made. *See also* Alteration; Deface; Spoliation.

In criminal law, the depriving a man of the use of any of those limbs which may be useful to him in fight, the loss of which amounts to *mayhem.* See Maim; Mayhem.

It is a federal crime to mutilate public records (18 U.S.C.A. § 2071), coins (§ 331), passports (§ 1543).

Mutinous. Insubordinate; disposed to mutiny; tending to incite or encourage mutiny.

Mutiny, v. To rise against lawful or constituted authority, particularly in the naval or military service.

Mutiny, n. In criminal law, an insurrection of soldiers or seamen against the authority of their commanders; a sedition or revolt in the army or navy. One is guilty of mutiny who with intent to usurp or override lawful military authority refuses in concert with any other person or persons to obey orders or otherwise do his duty or creates any violence or disturbance. 10 U.S.C.A. § 894. (Uniform Code of Military Justice, Art. 94.) *See also* Desertion.

Mutual. Common to both parties. Interchangeable; reciprocal; each acting in return or correspondence to the other; given and received;—spoken of an engagement or relation in which like duties and obligations are exchanged; *e.g.,* the marital relation.

As to *mutual* Account; Assent; Condition; Contract; Covenant; Credits; Debt; Insurance; Mistake; Promise; and Testament, see those titles. *See also* Mutuality.

Mutual affray. A fight in which both parties willingly enter and is similar to a duel. *See* Affray.

Mutual agreement. A meeting of the minds on a specific subject, and a manifestation of intent of the parties to do or refrain from doing some specific act or acts. *See* Agreement; Contract; Mutuality; Treaty.

Mutual association. *See* Savings and loan association.

Mutual benefit association. One based on reciprocal contracts and requires that a member receive benefits as a matter of right. Commonly a fraternal or social organization which provides insurance for its members on an assessment basis.

Mutual benefit insurance. Type of insurance offered to members of a mutual benefit association commonly characterized by assessment of members to meet claims. *See* Mutual benefit association.

Mutual company. A corporation in which shares are held exclusively by members to whom profits are distributed as dividends in proportion to the business which the members did with the company (*e.g.* state-chartered mutual savings banks, federal savings and loan associations). One in which the members are both the insurers and the insured (mutual insurance companies).

Mutual demands. Those between the same parties and due in the same capacity or right.

Mutual fund. A fund managed by an investment company in which money is raised through the sale of stock and subsequently invested in publicly traded securities. The investment performance of the mutual fund depends on the performance of the underlying investments. Each mutual fund tends to have an investment objective such as; a growth fund strives for capital appreciation in the portfolio; an income fund looks for a stream of income over the life of the investment.

There are two general types of mutual funds; "open-end" in which capitalization is not fixed and more shares may be sold at any time, and "closed-end" in which capitalization is fixed and only the number of shares originally authorized may be sold.

See also Investment company; Load; Open-end investment company.

Closed-end funds. Mutual funds that do not repurchase their shares from investors; the shares are sold in a secondary market, such as on a stock exchange.

Growth funds. Mutual funds that are composed of stocks of companies that are still experiencing growth; the objective is to generate an increase in investment value, with less concern about the provision of steady income. *Compare* with *Income funds, below.*

Income funds. Mutual fund consisting of securities that provide periodic dividends or coupon payments; they usually consist of coupon bonds; they are designed to provide investors with a stable income. *Compare* with *Growth funds, above.*

Index fund. A mutual fund whose portfolio is designed to match the performance of a broad-based index such as Standard & Poor's Index and whose performance therefore mirrors the market as reflected by the index.

Load fund. Mutual fund in which a charge (load) is made at time of purchase of shares to cover administrative and commission expenses.

Money market funds. Mutual fund that invests in money market securities.

No-load fund. A mutual fund that has no service charge (load) for buying its shares.

Open-end funds. Mutual funds that are willing to repurchase their shares from investors at any time.

Mutual insurance company. Type of insurance company in which there is no capital stock and in which the policy holders are the sole owners. A cooperative enterprise in which members are both insurers and insureds, whose business is conducted for benefit of policy holders. *See also* Stock insurance company.

Mutuality. Reciprocation; interchange. An acting by each of two parties; an acting in return. "Mutuality of contract" means that obligation rests on each party to do or permit doing of something in consideration of other party's act or promise; neither party being bound unless both are bound. Called, also, mutuality of obligation.

As to *mutuality of* Assent, Mistake, etc., see those titles.

Mutuality doctrine. Doctrine in equity to the effect that equitable relief will be denied a party to a contract on a showing that the plaintiff is not bound to the same extent as the defendant in fulfilling the contract. In another context, it refers to the obligation of a meeting of the minds before a contract can be found. *See* Mutuality of obligation.

Mutuality of estoppel. This doctrine dictates that a judgment will not be held conclusive in favor of one person unless it would be conclusive against him had the case been decided the other way.

Mutuality of obligation. Mutuality of obligation requires that unless both parties to a contract are bound, neither is bound. Such obligation as pertaining to executory contract requires that each party to agreement be bound to perform, and if it appears that one party was never bound to do the acts which formed the consideration for promise of the other, there is lack of mutuality of obligation and other party is not bound. *See* Mutuality doctrine.

Mutuality of remedy. In equity, one party to a contract may not have equitable relief if he is not bound by the contract to the same extent as the other party, or if his remedy is not co-extensive. Generally, specific performance will be granted only where there is "mutuality of remedy", which means that right to performance must be mutual.

Mutual mistake. As justifying reformation of an instrument is one common to both or all parties, where each party labors under the same misconception respecting a material fact, the terms of the agreement, or the provision of a written instrument designed to embody such an agreement. Mutual mistake with regard to contract, justifying reformation, exists where there has been a meeting of the minds of the parties and an agreement actually entered into but the agreement in its written form does not express what was really intended by the parties.

Mutual relief association. An insurer, chartered under a designated statute, having no capital stock, having relief funds created and sustained by assessments made upon the members, which files reports with insurance commissioner evidencing that it is not conducted for profit of its officers.

Mutual rescission. An agreement between the parties to cancel their contract, releasing the parties from further obligations under the contract. The object of the agreement is to restore the parties to positions they would have occupied had no contract ever been made. *See also* Rescission of contract.

Mutual savings bank. A bank organized by depositors, whose interest is shown by certificates of deposit, for the purpose of furnishing a safe depositary for money of members. It need not be incorporated or under supervision unless state law so requires. A banking institution in which the depositors are the owners and which has no capital stock. *See also* Savings and Loan Association.

Mutual wills. Those made as the separate wills of two people which are reciprocal in provisions. Or those executed pursuant to agreement or compact between two or more persons to dispose of their property in particular manner, each in consideration of the other's doing so. *See* Reciprocal wills.

Mysterious disappearance. Term refers to theft insurance policy provision covering any disappearance or loss under unknown, puzzling or baffling circumstances which arouse wonder, curiosity or speculation, or circumstances which are difficult to understand or explain.

N

N.A. An abbreviation for *"non allocatur"*; it is not allowed. Also sometimes used as abbreviation for "not available" or "not applicable".

Naked. Bare; wanting in necessary conditions; incomplete, as a naked contract *(nudum pactum)*, *i.e.*, a contract devoid of consideration, and therefore invalid; or, simple, unilateral, comprising but a single element, as a naked authority, *i.e.*, one which is not coupled with any interest in the agent, but subsists for the benefit of the principal alone.

As to *naked* Confession; Deposit; Option; Possession; Possibility; Power; Promise; and Trust, see those titles.

Naked contract. *See* Nudum pactum.

Name. The designation of an individual person, or of a firm or corporation. Word or combination of words used to distinguish person or thing or class from others.

A person's "name" consists of one or more Christian or given names and one surname or family name. It is the distinctive characterization in words by which one is known and distinguished from others, and description, or abbreviation, is not the equivalent of a "name."

See also Alias; Christian name; Corporate name; Fictitious name; Full name; Generic (*Generic name*); Legal name; Nickname; Street name; Tradename.

Corporate name. Most states require corporations doing business under an assumed or fictitious name to register, record, or register and record, the name with state, county, or state and county officials.

Distinctive name. As used in regulation of United States Department of Agriculture, a trade, arbitrary, or fancy name which clearly distinguishes a food product, mixture, or compound from any other. *See also* Tradename.

Generic name. The general or nontrademark name of a product. For example, the trade names of a particular type of fiber may be Antron, Cantrece, Qiana; but the generic name of that fiber is nylon. *See also* Generic.

Named insured. In insurance, the person specifically designated in the policy as the one protected and, commonly, it is the person with whom the contract of insurance has been made.

Namely. A difference, in grammatical sense, in strictness exists between the words namely and including. Namely imports interpretation, *i.e.*, indicates what is included in the previous term; but including imports addition, *i.e.*, indicates something not included.

Narcoanalysis. Process whereby a subject is put to sleep, or into a semi-somnolent state by means of chemical injections and then interrogated while in this dreamlike state.

Narcotic. Generic term for any drug which dulls the senses and commonly becomes addictive after prolonged use. An addictive or otherwise harmful drug, the manufacture, importation, sale, or possession of which is statutorily prohibited. 21 U.S.C.A. § 801 et seq.

NAR. National Association of Realtors.

Narrative evidence. Testimony from a witness which he is permitted to give without the customary questions and answers; *e.g.* when witness explains in detail what happened without interruption.

NASA. National Aeronautics and Space Administration.

NASD. The National Association of Securities Dealers, Inc. An association of brokers and dealers empowered to regulate the over-the-counter securities business. The Association has the power to expel members who have been declared guilty of unethical practices.

NASDAQ. National Association of Securities Dealers Automated Quotations. An information system which gives price quotations on securities traded over-the-counter to brokers and dealers. The system is automated.

Nation. A people, or aggregation of men, existing in the form of an organized jural society, usually inhabiting a distinct portion of the earth, speaking the same language, using the same customs, possessing historic continuity, and distinguished from other like groups by their racial origin and characteristics, and generally, but not necessarily, living under the same government and sovereignty.

In American constitutional law the word "state" is applied to the several members of the American Union, while the word "nation" is applied to the whole body of the people embraced within the jurisdiction of the federal government.

National. Pertaining or relating to a nation as a whole. Commonly applied in American law to institutions, laws, or affairs of the United States or its government, as opposed to those of the several states. "National" contemplates an activity with a nationwide scope. *See also* Federal.

A person owing permanent allegiance to a state. 8 U.S.C.A. § 1101.

The term "national" as used in the phrase "national of the United States" is broader than the term "citizen". *See also* Foreign national.

National Association of Accountants (NAA). An organization composed of accountants working primarily in areas such as industry and government. The NAA's Management Accounting Practices Committee develops Statements on Management Accounting.

National bank. A bank incorporated and doing business under the laws of the United States, whose charter is approved by the Comptroller of the Currency as distinguished from a *state* bank, which derives its powers from the authority of a particular state. Most such banks are members of the Federal Reserve System and the Federal Deposit Insurance Corporation. *See* Member bank.

National currency. Legal tender; that which circulates as money. Notes issued by national banks, and by the United States government. *See* Currency; Federal reserve notes; Legal tender.

National debt. The money owing by government to some of the public or to financial institutions, consisting of such obligations as Treasury bills, notes, and bonds, the interest of which is paid out of the taxes raised by the whole of the public (*i.e.* out of general revenues).

National defense. A generic concept that refers to the military and naval establishments and the related activities of national preparedness and includes all matters directly and reasonably connected with the defense of the nation against its enemies. Implicit in the term is the notion of defending those values and ideals which set this nation apart.

National domain. *See* Domain.

National domicile. *See* Domicile.

National Environmental Policy Act. Federal Act setting forth declaration of national environmental policy and goals. Major provision requires that every federal agency submit an environmental impact statement with every legislative recommendation or program affecting the quality of the environment. 42 U.S.C.A. § 4321 et seq. *See* Environmental impact statements.

National government. The government of a whole nation, as distinguished from that of a state, local or territorial division of the nation, and also as distinguished from that of a league or confederation. Commonly referred to as the "federal government".

National Guard. Organization of men maintained as a reserve for the U.S. Army and Air Force. Members serve on a state-wide basis but are subject to being activated for federal service as well as for state emergencies.

Nationality. That quality or character which arises from the fact of a person's belonging to a nation or state. Nationality determines the political *status* of the individual, especially with reference to allegiance; while domicile determines his civil *status*. Nationality arises either by birth or by naturalization. *See also* Naturalization.

Nationality Act. Shortened name for Immigration and Nationality Act which is a comprehensive federal statute embracing such matters as immigration, naturalization and admission of aliens. 8 U.S.C.A. § 1101 *et seq.*

Nationalization. The acquisition and control of privately owned business by government. *See also* Denationalization.

National Labor Relations Act. A federal statute known as the Wagner Act of 1935 and amended by the Taft-Hartley Act of 1947; it is comprehensive legislation regulating the relations between employers and employees, including supervised elections, and establishing National Labor Relations Board. 29 U.S.C.A. § 151 et seq.

National Labor Relations Board. The National Labor Relations Board is an independent agency created by the National Labor Relations Act of 1935 (Wagner Act), as amended by the acts of 1947 (Taft-Hartley Act) and 1959 (Landrum-Griffin Act). 29 U.S.C.A. § 153.

The Board has two principal functions under the act: preventing and remedying unfair labor practices by employers and labor organizations or their agents, and conducting secret ballot elections among employees in appropriate collective-bargaining units to determine whether or not they desire to be represented by a labor organization. The Board also conducts secret ballot elections among employees who have been covered by a union-shop agreement to determine whether or not they wish to revoke their union's authority to make such agreements; in jurisdictional disputes, decides and determines which competing group of workers is entitled to perform the work involved; and conducts secret ballot elections among employees concerning employers' final settlement offers in national emergency labor disputes.

National Mediation Board. The National Mediation Board was created on June 21, 1934, by an act of Congress amending the Railway Labor Act (48 Stat. 1185, 45 U.S.C.A. § 154).

The Board's major responsibilities are: (1) the mediation of disputes over wages, hours, and working conditions which arise between rail and air carriers and organizations representing their employees, and (2) the investigation of representation disputes and certification of employee organizations as representatives of crafts or classes of carrier employees.

National origin. In equal employment opportunities provisions of Civil Rights Act, term "national origin" on its face refers to country where person was born, or, more broadly, country from which his or her ancestors came, and was not intended to embrace requirement of United States citizenship.

National Service Life Insurance. Special type of life insurance for military and naval personnel during and after their service created by the National Service Life Insurance Act of 1940 and containing highly favorable rates and terms.

Nations, law of. See International law.

Native. A natural-born subject or citizen; a citizen by birth; one who owes his domicile or citizenship to the fact of his birth within the country referred to. The term may also include one born abroad, if his parents were then citizens of the country, and not permanently residing in foreign parts.

Native born. See Native.

Natural. Untouched by man or by influences of civilization; wild; untutored, and is the opposite of the word "artificial". The juristic meaning of this term does not differ from the vernacular, except in the cases where it is used in opposition to the term "legal;" and then it means proceeding from or determined by physical causes or conditions, as distinguished from positive enactments of law, or attributable to the nature of man rather than to the commands of law, or based upon moral rather than legal considerations or sanctions.

As to *natural* Allegiance; Boundary; Channel; Child; Children; Day; Death; Domicile; Equity; Guardian; Heirs; Infancy; Liberty; Obligation; Person; Possession; Presumption; Right; Succession, and Water course, see those titles.

Natural affection. Such as naturally subsists between near relatives, as a father and child, brother and sister, husband and wife. This is regarded in law as a good consideration. See Nudum pactum.

Natural and probable consequences. Those consequences that a person by prudent human foresight can anticipate as likely to result from an act, because they happen so frequently from the commission of such an act that in the field of human experience they may be expected to happen again.

Natural born citizen. Persons who are born within the jurisdiction of a national government, i.e., in its territorial limits, or those born of citizens temporarily residing abroad. See Naturalization clause.

Natural consequences. See Natural and probable consequences.

Natural death. Death from causes other than accident or violence. Also called death from natural causes.

Natural Death Acts. See Right to die laws; Will *(Living will)*.

Natural flood channel. A channel beginning at some point on banks of stream and ending at some other point lower down stream, through which flood waters naturally flow at times of high water.

Naturalization. The process by which a person acquires nationality after birth and becomes entitled to the privileges of U.S. citizenship. 8 U.S. C.A. § 1401 *et seq.*

In the United States collective naturalization occurs when designated groups are made citizens by treaty (as Louisiana Purchase), or by a law of Congress (as in annexation of Texas and Hawaii). Individual naturalization must follow certain steps: (a) petition for naturalization by a person of lawful age who has been a lawful resident of the United States for 5 years; (b) investigation by the Immigration and Naturalization Service to determine whether the applicant can speak and write the English language, has a knowledge of the fundamentals of American government and history, is attached to the principles of the Constitution and is of good moral character; (c) hearing before a U.S. District Court or certain State courts of record; and (d) after a lapse of at least 30 days a second appearance in court when the oath of allegiance is administered.

Naturalization clause. The Fourteenth Amendment to the U.S. Constitution, Section 1, provides that all persons born or naturalized in the United States, and subject to the jurisdiction thereof, are citizens of the United States, and of the State wherein they reside.

Naturalization courts. Both federal and state courts of record have jurisdiction over naturalization matters. 8 U.S.C.A. § 1421.

Naturalized citizen. One who, being an alien by birth, has received U.S. citizenship under naturalization laws. 8 U.S.C.A. § 1421 et seq.

Natural law. This expression, "natural law," or *jus naturale,* was largely used in the philosophical speculations of the Roman jurists of the Antonine age, and was intended to denote a system of rules and principles for the guidance of human conduct which, independently of enacted law or of the systems peculiar to any one people, might be discovered by the rational intelligence of man, and would be found to grow out of and conform to his *nature,* meaning by that word his whole mental, moral, and physical constitution. The point of departure for this conception was the Stoic doctrine of a life ordered "according to nature," which in its turn rested upon the purely supposititious existence, in primitive times, of a "state of nature;" that is, a condition of society in which men universally were governed solely by a rational and consistent obedience to the needs, impulses, and promptings of their true nature, such nature being as yet undefaced by dishonesty, falsehood, or indulgence of the baser passions. In ethics, it consists in practical universal judgments which man himself elicits. These express necessary and obligatory rules of human conduct which have been established by the author of human nature as essential to the divine purposes in the universe and have been promulgated by God solely through human reason.

Natural life. The period of a person's existence considered as continuing until terminated by physical dissolution or death occurring in the course of nature; used in contradistinction to that juristic and artificial conception of life as an aggregate of legal rights or the possession of a legal personality, which could be terminated by "civil death" *(q.v.),* that is, that extinction of personality which resulted from entering a monastery or being attainted of treason or felony.

Natural monument. Objects permanent in character which are found on the land as they were placed by nature, such as streams, lakes, ponds, shores, and beaches; sometimes including highways and streets, walls, fences, trees, hedges, springs, and rocks, and the like.

Natural objects. In interpretation of boundaries term includes mountains, lakes, rivers, etc. *See also* Natural monument.

Natural resources. Any material in its native state which when extracted has economic value. Timberland, oil and gas wells, ore deposits, and other products of nature that have economic value. The cost of natural resources is subject to depletion. Often called "wasting assets."

The term includes not only timber, gas, oil, coal, minerals, lakes, and submerged lands, but also, features which supply a human need and contribute to the health, welfare, and benefit of a community, and are essential to the well-being thereof and proper enjoyment of property devoted to park and recreational purposes.

Natural rights. Those which grow out of nature of man and depend upon his personality and are distinguished from those which are created by positive laws enacted by a duly constituted government to create an orderly civilized society.

Nature. A kind, sort, type, order; general character.

Nautical. Pertaining to ships or to the art of navigation or the business of carriage by sea. *See also* Marine.

Nautical mile. *See* Mile.

Naval. Appertaining to the navy *(q.v.).*

Naval base. *See* Base.

Naval law. The system of regulations and principles for the government of the navy. *See* Code of Military Justice.

Navigable. *See* Navigable waters.

Navigable in fact. Streams or lakes are navigable in fact when they are used or are susceptible of being used in their natural and ordinary condition as highways for commerce over which trade and travel are or may be conducted in the customary modes of trade and travel on water. *See also* Navigable waters.

Navigable river *or* **stream.** At common law, a river or stream in which the tide ebbs and flows, or as far as the tide ebbs and flows. But as to the definition in American law, *see* Navigable waters.

Navigable sea. The "navigable sea" is divided into three zones: (1) nearest to the nation's shores are its internal or "inland waters"; (2) beyond the inland waters, and measured from their seaward edge, is a belt known as the marginal or "territorial sea"; and (3) outside the territorial sea are the "high seas".

Navigable waters. Those waters which afford a channel for useful commerce. Any body of water, navigable in fact, which by itself or by uniting with other waters forms a continuous highway over which commerce may be carried on with other states or countries. In determining whether water is "navigable," the factual inquiry is whether the water has capability of use by the public for the purpose of transportation and commerce.

A water is "navigable," for purposes of admiralty jurisdiction, provided that it is used or susceptible of being used as an artery of commerce. Rivers are "navigable" in fact when they are used, or are susceptible of being used, in their ordinary condition as highways for commerce over which trade and travel are or may be conducted in the customary modes of trade and travel on water.

Navigate. To journey by water; to go in a vessel; to sail or manage a vessel; to use the waters as a highway for commerce or communication; to ply. To direct one's course through any medium; to steer, especially to operate an airplane or airship.

Navigation. The act or the science or the business of traversing the sea or other navigable waters in ships or vessels.

Rules of navigation. Rules and regulations adopted by commercial nations to govern the steering and management of vessels approaching each other at sea so as to avoid the danger of collision or fouling.

N.B. An abbreviation for *"nota bene,"* mark well, observe; also *"nulla bona,"* no goods.

N.D. An abbreviation for "Northern District," *e.g.* U.S. District Court for Northern District of N.Y.

Near. Proximate; close-by; about; adjacent; contiguous; abutting. The word as applied to space is a relative term without positive or precise meaning, depending for its signification on the subject-matter in relation to which it is used and the circumstances under which it becomes necessary to apply it to surrounding objects. Closely akin or related by blood; as, a near relative. Close to one's interests and affections, etc.; touching or affecting intimately, as one's near affairs, friends. Not far distant in time, place or degree; not remote; adjoining.

Near money. Liquid assets which are readily convertible into money.

Neat, net. The clear weight or quantity of an article, without the bag, box, keg, or other thing in which it may be enveloped.

Necessaries. An article which a party actually needs. Things indispensable, or things proper and useful, for the sustenance of human life.

Necessaries include food, drink, clothing, medical attention, and a suitable place of residence, and they are regarded as necessaries in the absolute sense of the word. However, liability for necessaries is not limited to articles required to sustain life; it extends to articles which would ordinarily be necessary and suitable, in view of the rank, position, fortune, earning capacity, and mode of living of the individual involved.

See also Necessary; Necessitous circumstances; Support.

Necessaries, doctrine of. One who sells goods to a wife or child may charge the husband or father if the goods are required for their sustenance or support.

Necessarily included offense. For a lesser offense to be "necessarily included" in offense charged, within lesser included offense rule, it must be such that the greater offense cannot be committed without also committing the lesser. "Lesser offense" is "necessarily included" in a graver offense if the greater of the offenses includes all the legal and factual elements of the lesser. *See* Fed.R.Crim.P. 31(c). *See also* Lesser included offense.

Necessary. This word must be considered in the connection in which it is used, as it is a word susceptible of various meanings. It may import absolute physical necessity or inevitability, or it may import that which is only convenient, useful, appropriate, suitable, proper, or conducive to the end sought. It is an adjective expressing degrees, and may express mere convenience or that which is indispensable or an absolute physical necessity. It may mean something which in the accomplishment of a given object cannot be dispensed with, or it may mean something reasonably useful and proper, and of greater or lesser benefit or convenience, and its force and meaning must be determined with relation to the particular object sought.

In eminent domain proceedings, it means land reasonably requisite and proper for accomplishment of end in view, not absolute necessity of particular location.

With respect to taxation (*i.e.* deduction of necessary expenses is carrying on trade or business), means appropriate and helpful in furthering the taxpayer's business or income producing activity. I.R.C. §§ 162(a) and 212. *See also* Ordinary (*Ordinary expenses*).

As to *necessary* Damages; Deposit; Domicile; Implication; Repair; and Way, see those titles. *See also* Necessaries; Necessity.

Necessary and proper. Term meaning appropriate and adapted to carrying into effect given object.

Necessary and proper clause. Art. I, § 8, par. 18 of U.S. Constitution, which authorizes Congress to make all laws necessary and proper to carry out the enumerated powers of Congress and all other powers vested in the government of the United States or any department or officer thereof. *See* Penumbra doctrine.

These words are not limited to such measures as are absolutely and indispensably necessary, without which the powers granted must fail of execution, but they include all appropriate means which are conducive or adapted to the end to be accomplished, and which, in the judgment of Congress will most advantageously effect it. The "necessary and proper" clause of the federal Constitution is not a grant of power but a declaration that Congress possesses all of the means necessary to carry out its specifically granted powers.

Necessary inference. One which is inescapable or unavoidable from the standpoint of reason. *See also* Inference.

Necessary parties. In pleading and practice, those persons who must be joined in an action because, *inter alia,* complete relief cannot be given to those already parties without their joinder. Fed.R.Civil P. 19(a).

Necessary parties are those who must be included in action either as plaintiffs or defendants, unless there is a valid excuse for their nonjoinder. Those persons who have such an interest in controversy that a final judgment or decree cannot be made without either affecting their interests or leaving the controversy in such a condition that its final adjudication may be wholly inconsistent with equity and good conscience. A "necessary party" is one whose joinder is required in order to afford the plaintiff the complete relief to which he is entitled against the defendant who is properly suable in that county.

See also Indispensable parties; Joinder; Parties.

Necessitas /nəsésətæs/. Lat. Necessity; a force, power, or influence which compels one to act against his will.

Necessitas culpabilis /nəsésətæs kəlpéybələs/. Culpable necessity; unfortunate necessity; necessity which, while it excuses the act done under its compulsion, does not leave the doer entirely free from blame. The necessity which compels a man to kill another in self-defense is thus distinguished from that which requires the killing of a felon. *See also* Justification; Self-defense.

Necessities. *See* Necessaries.

Necessitous /nəsésətəs/. Indigent or pressed by poverty. *See* Indigent.

Necessitous circumstances /nəsésətəs sárkəmstænsəz/. Needing the necessaries of life, which cover not only primitive physical needs, things absolutely indispensable to human existence and decency, but those things, also, which are in fact necessary to the particular person left without support. In the civil code of Louisiana the words are used relative to the fortune of the deceased and to the condition in which the claimant lived during the marriage. *See also* Necessaries; Non-support; Support.

Necessity. Controlling force; irresistible compulsion; a power or impulse so great that it admits no choice of conduct. That which makes the contrary of a thing impossible. The quality or state of being necessary, in its primary sense signifying that which makes an act or event unavoidable. Quality or state of fact of being in difficulties or in need; a condition arising out of circumstances that compels a certain course of action.

A person is excused from criminal liability if he acts under a duress of circumstances to protect life or limb or health in a reasonable manner and with no other acceptable choice. *See* Justification; Self-defense.

See also Irresistible impulse; Necessaries; Necessary.

Need. A relative term, the conception of which must, within reasonable limits, vary with the personal situation of the individual employing it. Term means to have an urgent or essential use for (something lacking); to want, require. *See* Necessaries.

Needful. Necessary, requisite, essential, indispensable. *See* Necessaries.

Needless. In a statute against "needless" killing or mutilation of any animal, this term denotes an act done without any useful motive, in a spirit of wanton cruelty, or for the mere pleasure of destruction.

Needy. Indigent, necessitous, very poor. *See* Indigent.

Ne exeat /níy éksiyət/. A writ which forbids the person to whom it is addressed to leave the country, the state, or the jurisdiction of the court. It is the nature of civil bail, the purpose of which is to prevent the frustration of a plaintiff's equitable claims by insuring the continued physical presence of the defendant within the court's jurisdiction. Sometimes a ne exeat writ is issued only to restrain a person from leaving the jurisdiction, and sometimes it is issued against a person who is removing or attempting to remove property beyond the jurisdiction.

Negative. A denial; a proposition by which something is denied; a statement in the form of denial. Two negatives do not make a good issue.

As to *negative* Covenant; Easement; Servitude; Statute; and Testimony, see those titles.

Negative averment. As opposed to the traverse or simple denial of an affirmative allegation, a negative averment is an allegation of some substantive fact, *e.g.,* that premises are not in repair, which, although negative in form, is really affirmative in substance, and the party alleging the fact of non-repair must prove it. An averment in some of the pleadings in a case in which a negative is asserted.

Negative condition. One by which it is stipulated that a given thing shall not happen.

Negative covenant. A provision in an employment agreement or a contract of sale of a business which prohibits the employee or seller from competing in the same area or market. Such restriction must be reasonable in scope and duration.

In terms of a bond, a covenant that limits or prohibits altogether certain actions unless the bondholders agree.

Negative easement. A right in owner of dominant tenement to restrict owner of servient tenement in exercise of general and natural rights of property. An easement which restrains a landowner from making certain use of his land which he might otherwise have lawfully done but for that restriction and such easements arise principally by express grant or by implication.

Negative evidence. Testimony that an alleged fact did not exist. *See* Rebuttal evidence.

Negative pledge clause. A bond covenant that requires the borrower to grant lenders a lien equivalent to any liens that may be granted in the future to any other currently unsecured lenders.

Negative pregnant. In pleading, a negative implying also an affirmative. Such a form of negative expression as may imply or carry within it an affirmative. A denial in such form as to imply or express an admission of the substantial fact which apparently is controverted; or a denial which, although in the form of a traverse, really admits the important facts contained in the allegations to which it relates. It occurs in responsive pleading where the denial is stated in the very words employed in the complaint and negative pregnant is condemned because it is pregnant with alternative admissions to allegations of the complaint.

Neggildare. To claim kindred.

Neglect. May mean to omit, fail, or forbear to do a thing that can be done, or that is required to be done, but it may also import an absence of care or attention in the doing or omission of a given act. And it may mean a designed refusal, indifference, or unwillingness to perform one's duty.

The term is used in the law of bailment as synonymous with "negligence." But the latter word is the closer translation of the Latin *"negligentia."*

An omission to do or perform some work, duty, or act. Failure to perform or discharge a duty, covering positive official misdoing or official misconduct as well as negligence.

See also Excusable neglect; Negligence.

Culpable neglect. Such neglect which exists where the loss can fairly be ascribed to the party's own carelessness, improvidence, or folly.

Willful neglect. Intentional, purposeful neglect. For example, the neglect of the husband to provide for his family the common necessaries of life, he having the ability to do so; or it is the failure to do so by reason of idleness, profligacy, or dissipation. *See also* Necessaries.

Neglected child. A child is "neglected" when his parent or custodian, by reason of cruelty, mental incapacity, immorality or depravity, is unfit properly to care for him, or neglects or refuses to provide necessary physical, affectional, medical, surgical, or institutional or hospital care for him, or he is in such condition of want or suffering, or is under such improper care or control as to endanger his morals or health. *See* Non-support.

Negligence. The omission to do something which a reasonable man, guided by those ordinary considerations which ordinarily regulate human affairs, would do, or the doing of something which a reasonable and prudent man would not do.

Negligence is the failure to use such care as a reasonably prudent and careful person would use under similar circumstances; it is the doing of some act which a person of ordinary prudence would not have done under similar circumstances or failure to do what a person of ordinary prudence would have done under similar circumstances. Conduct which falls below the standard established by law for the protection of others against unreasonable risk of harm; it is a departure from the conduct expectable of a reasonably prudent person under like circumstances.

The term refers only to that legal delinquency which results whenever a man fails to exhibit the care which he ought to exhibit, whether it be slight, ordinary, or great. It is characterized chiefly by inadvertence, thoughtlessness, inattention, and the like, while "wantonness" or "recklessness" is characterized by willfulness. The law of negligence is founded on reasonable conduct or reasonable care under all circumstances of particular case. Doctrine of negligence rests on duty of every person to exercise due care in his conduct toward others from which injury may result.

See also Actionable negligence; Active negligence; Cause; Comparative negligence; Concurrent negligence; Fault; Imputed negligence; Invitation; Joint negligence; Laches; Legal negligence; Palsgraf Rule; Parental liability; Product liability; Reasonable man doctrine *or* standard; Reckless; Simple negligence; Standard of care; Strict liability; Supervening negligence.

Actionable negligence. See Actionable negligence.

Active negligence. See Active negligence.

Collateral negligence. Doctrine which holds that: An employer of an independent contractor, unless he is himself negligent, is not liable for physical harm caused by any negligence of the contractor if (a) the contractor's negligence consists solely in the improper manner in which he does the work, and (b) it creates a risk of such harm which is not inherent in or normal to the work, and (c) the employer had no reason to contemplate the contractor's negligence when the contract was made. Restatement, Second, Torts § 426.

Comparative negligence. See Comparative negligence.

Concurrent negligence. Arises where the same injury is proximately caused by the concurrent wrongful acts or omissions of two or more persons acting independently. *See also* Concurrent negligence.

Contributory negligence. The act or omission amounting to want of ordinary care on part of complaining party, which, concurring with defendant's negligence, is proximate cause of injury. Conduct by a plaintiff which is below the standard to which he is legally required to conform for his own protection and which is a contributing cause which cooperates with the negligence of the defendant in causing the plaintiff's harm.

Conduct for which plaintiff is responsible amounting to a breach of duty which law imposes on persons to protect themselves from injury, and which, concurring and cooperating with actionable negligence for which defendant is responsible, contributes to injury complained of as a proximate cause.

The defense of contributory negligence has been replaced by the doctrine of comparative negligence *(q.v.)* in many states. *See also Exceptions and limitations, below.*

It is an affirmative defense which must be pleaded and proved by defendant. Fed.R.Civil P., Rule 8(c).

Doctrine is also applicable to one who through his own negligence has contributed to material alteration of a negotiable instrument. U.C.C. § 3–406.

Criminal negligence. Criminal negligence which will render killing a person manslaughter is the omission on the part of the person to do some act which an ordinarily careful and prudent man would do under like circumstances, or the doing of some act which an ordinarily careful, prudent man under like circumstances would not do by reason of which another person is endangered in life or bodily safety; the word "ordinary" being synonymous with "reasonable" in this connection.

Negligence of such a character, or occurring under such circumstances, as to be punishable as a crime by statute; or (at common law) such a flagrant and reckless disregard of the safety of others, or wilful indifference to the injury liable to follow, as to convert an act otherwise lawful into a crime when it results in personal injury or death.

A wanton or reckless disregard for human life; a degree of carelessness amounting to a culpable disregard of rights and safety of others. That species of want of care by which a person may be criminally liable. It varies from jurisdiction to jurisdiction and is called culpable negligence in some. However, it generally refers to conduct which is not intentional and ordinarily not wilful, wanton and reckless.

See Negligent homicide; Negligently; Negligent manslaughter.

Culpable negligence. Failure to exercise that degree of care rendered appropriate by the particular circumstances, and which a man of ordinary prudence in the same situation and with equal experience would not have omitted.

Degrees of negligence. While there are degrees of care, and failure to exercise proper degree of care is "negligence," most courts hold that there are no degrees (*e.g.* slight, ordinary, gross) of negligence, except in bailment cases or under automobile guest statutes. The prevailing view is that there are no "degrees" of care in negligence, as a

matter of law; there are only different amounts of care as a matter of fact. To the extent that the degrees of negligence survive, they are described below.

Exceptions ar   limitations. The general rule in automobile accident cases that contributory negligence bars recovery for the injuries sustained is subject to various exceptions and limitations. Thus the defense of contributory negligence may be inapplicable where defendant's negligence is of a gross or willful character. Moreover, application of the doctrine of contributory negligence is limited by the last clear chance doctrine or similar doctrines, or by comparative negligence statutes.

Gross negligence. The intentional failure to perform a manifest duty in reckless disregard of the consequences as affecting the life or property of another.

It is materially more want of care than constitutes simple inadvertence. It is an act or omission respecting legal duty of an aggravated character as distinguished from a mere failure to exercise ordinary care. It amounts to indifference to present legal duty and to utter forgetfulness of legal obligations so far as other persons may be affected. It is a heedless and palpable violation of legal duty respecting the rights of others. The element of culpability which characterizes all negligence is in gross negligence magnified to a high degree as compared with that present in ordinary negligence. Gross negligence is a manifestly smaller amount of watchfulness and circumspection than the circumstances require of a person of ordinary prudence. It falls short of being such reckless disregard of probable consequences as is equivalent to a wilful and intentional wrong. Ordinary and gross negligence differ in degree of inattention, while both differ in kind from wilful and intentional conduct which is or ought to be known to have a tendency to injure.

Gross negligence consists of conscious and voluntary act or omission which is likely to result in grave injury when in face of clear and present danger of which alleged tortfeasor is aware. That entire want of care which would raise belief that act or omission complained of was result of conscious indifference to rights and welfare of persons affected by it. Indifference to present legal duty and utter forgetfulness of legal obligations, so far as other persons may be affected, and a manifestly smaller amount of watchfulness and circumspection than the circumstances require of a person of ordinary prudence.

Hazardous negligence. Such careless or reckless conduct as exposes one to very great danger of injury or to imminent peril.

Imputed negligence. Refers to doctrine that places upon one person responsibility for the negligence of another; such responsibility or liability is imputed by reason of some special relationship of the parties, such as parent and child, husband and wife, driver and passenger, owner of vehicle and driver, bailor and bailee, master and servant, joint enterprise, and parent and custodian of a child.

Generally the doctrine of imputed negligence, as applied to automobile accidents, visits on one person legal responsibility for the negligent conduct of another. The doctrine applies only in limited classes of cases, as where there is a right to control in the relationship of master and servant, principal and agent, or a joint enterprise. The independent negligence of one person ordinarily is not imputable to another person except where the relation between the persons gives rise to an express or implied agency in the person committing the act of negligence.

See also Respondeat superior; Vicarious liability.

Legal negligence. *See* Legal negligence.

Ordinary negligence. The omission of that care which a person of common prudence usually takes of his own concerns. Failure to exercise care of an ordinarily prudent person in same situation. A want of that care and prudence that the great majority of mankind exercise under the same or similar circumstances. Wherever distinctions between gross, ordinary and slight negligence are observed, "ordinary negligence" is said to be the want of ordinary care.

Ordinary negligence is based on fact that one ought to have known results of his acts, while "gross negligence" rests on assumption that one knew results of his acts, but was recklessly or wantonly indifferent to results. The distinction between "ordinary negligence" and "gross negligence" is that the former lies in the field of inadvertence and the latter in the field of actual or constructive intent to injure.

Passive negligence. Failure to do something that should have been done. It is negligence which permits defects, obstacles, or pitfalls to exist on premises; that is, negligence which causes dangers arising from physical condition of land.

Difference between "active" and "passive" negligence is that one is only passively negligent if he merely fails to act in fulfillment of duty of care which law imposes upon him, while one is actively negligent if he participates in some manner in conduct or omission which caused injury.

Per se negligence. The unexcused violation of a statute which is applicable is per se or automatic negligence in some states. *See also* Negligence per se.

Slight negligence. A failure to exercise great care. Slight negligence is defined to be only an absence of that degree of care and vigilance which persons of extraordinary prudence and foresight are accustomed to use.

Subsequent negligence. Exists where defendant sees plaintiff in a position of danger and fails to exercise due and proper precaution to prevent injury to plaintiff.

Tax negligence. I.R.C. § 6653(a) imposes a penalty on taxpayers who show negligence or intentional disregard of rules and regulations with respect to the underpayment of certain taxes.

Wilful, wanton or reckless negligence. These terms are customarily treated as meaning essentially the same thing. The usual meaning assigned to "wilful," "wanton" or "reckless," according to taste as to the word used, is that the actor has intentionally done an act of an unreasonable character in disregard of a risk known to him or so obvious that he must be taken to have been aware of it, and so great as to make it highly probable that harm would follow. It usually is accompanied by a conscious indifference to the consequences, amounting almost to willingness that they shall follow; and it has been said that this is indispensable. The result is that "wilful," "wanton" or "reckless" conduct tends to take on the aspect of highly unreasonable conduct, or an extreme departure from ordinary care, in a situation where a high degree of danger is apparent. As a result there is often no clear distinction at all between such conduct and "gross" negligence, and the two have tended to merge and take on the same meaning, of an aggravated form of negligence, differing in quality rather than in degree from ordinary lack of care. It is at least clear, however, that such aggravated negligence must be more than any mere mistake resulting from inexperience, excitement, or confusion, and more than mere thoughtlessness or inadvertence, or simple inattention.

"Wantonness" constituting gross and wanton negligence within automobile guest statute indicates a realization of imminence of danger and a reckless disregard, complete indifference, and unconcern of probable consequences of the wrongful act.

Negligence, estoppel by. Equitable estoppel can arise when one through culpable negligence induces another to believe certain facts to exist and the other reasonably relies and acts on such belief. Imposition of an estoppel in such setting is designed to assure that the loss is borne by the party who made the injury possible or who could have prevented it.

Negligence in law. "Actionable negligence" or "negligence in law" grows out of nonobservance of a duty prescribed by law. *See also* Negligence per se; Strict liability.

Negligence per se. A form of ordinary negligence that results from violation of a statute. Conduct, whether of action or omission, which may be declared and treated as negligence without any argument or proof as to the particular surrounding circumstances, either because it is in violation of a specific statute or valid municipal ordinance, or because it is so palpably opposed to the dictates of common prudence that it can be said without hesitation or doubt that no careful person would have been guilty of it. As a general rule, the violation of a public duty, enjoined by law for the protection of person or property, so constitutes. *See also* Strict liability.

Negligent. *See* Negligence.

Negligent entrustment. Negligence consisting of entrusting dangerous article to another whom lender knows, or should know, is likely to use it in a manner involving unreasonable risk of harm to others.

Negligent homicide. The criminal offense committed by one whose negligence is the direct and proximate cause of another's death. Criminal homicide constitutes negligent homicide when it is committed negligently. Model Penal Code § 210.4(1). Killing of a human being by criminal negligence. La.Rev.St. § 14:32. Although an intentional act is required, it is not necessary, unlike the crime of involuntary manslaughter, that a defendant realize the risk of death involved in his conduct. *See also* Homicide *(Vehicular homicide)*; Negligent manslaughter.

Negligently. A person acts negligently with respect to a material element of an offense when he should be aware of a substantial and unjustifiable risk that the material element exists or will result from his conduct. The risk must be of such a nature and degree that the actor's failure to perceive it, considering the nature and purpose of his conduct and the circumstances known to him, involves a gross deviation from the standard of care that a reasonable person would observe in the actor's situation. Model Penal Code, § 2.02. *See also* Negligence.

Negligently done. The doing of an act where ordinary care required that it should not have been done at all, or that it should have been done in some other way, and where the doing of the act was not consistent with the exercise of ordinary care under the circumstances. *See* Negligence.

Negligent manslaughter. A statutory crime in some jurisdictions consisting of an unlawful and unjustified killing of a person by negligence but without malice. *See also* Negligent homicide; Vehicular homicide.

Negligent offense. One which ensues from a defective discharge of a duty, which defect could have been avoided by the exercise of that care which is usual, under similar circumstances, with prudent persons of the same class.

Negligent violation of statute. One occasioned by or accompanied with negligent conduct.

Negotiability /nəgòwsh(iy)əbílətiy/. Legal character of being negotiable *(q.v.)*. A term referring to a set of circumstances, described by law, under which a transferee of property can acquire rights therein that are better or greater than the rights of the transferor. *See also* Words of negotiability.

Negotiable /nəgówsh(iy)əbəl/. Legally capable of being transferred by endorsement or delivery. Usually said of checks and notes and sometimes of stocks and bearer bonds. *See* Commercial paper; Negotiable instruments; Non-negotiable.

Negotiable bond. Type of bond which may be transferred by negotiation from original holder to another.

Negotiable certificate of deposit (CD). Security issued by large commercial banks and other depository institutions as a short-term source of funds; it typically specifies a fixed interest rate and has a maturity of one year or less.

Negotiable document of title. A document of title providing by its terms that the goods are to be delivered to bearer or to the order of a named person or, where recognized in overseas trade, that runs to a named person or assigns. U.C.C. § 7–104(1).

Negotiable instruments. A written and signed unconditional promise or order to pay a specified sum of money on demand or at a definite time payable to order or bearer. U.C.C. 3–104(1). To be negotiable within the meaning of U.C.C. Article 3, an instrument must meet the requirements set out in Section 3–104: (1) it must be a writing signed by the maker or drawer; it must contain an (2) unconditional (3) promise (example: note) or order (example: check) (4) to pay a sum certain in money; (5) it must be payable on demand or at a definite time; (6) it must be payable to the bearer or to order (examples of instruments payable to order are (a) "Pay to the order of Daniel Dealer," and (b) "Pay Daniel Dealer or order"); and (7) it must not contain any other promise, order, obligation, or power given by the maker or drawer except as authorized by Article 3. *See also* Commercial paper; Negotiation.

Negotiable Order of Withdrawal. *See* N.O.W. account.

Negotiable words. Words and phrases which impart the character of negotiability to bills, notes, checks, etc., in which they are inserted; for instance, a direction to pay to A. "or order" or "bearer". *See* Negotiable instruments.

Negotiate /nəgówshiyèyt/. To transact business; to bargain with another respecting a transaction; to conduct communications or conferences with a view to reaching a settlement or agreement. It is that which passes between parties or their agents in the course of or incident to the making of a contract and is also conversation in arranging terms of contract.

To communicate or confer with another so as to arrive at the settlement of some matter. To meet with another so as to arrive through discussion at some kind of agreement or compromise about something. To discuss or arrange a sale of bargain; to arrange the preliminaries of a business transaction. Also to sell or discount negotiable paper, or assign or transfer it by indorsement and delivery. To conclude by bargain, treaty, or agreement.

See also Negotiation.

Negotiated markets. Markets in which each transaction is separately negotiated between buyer and seller (*i.e.*, an investor and a dealer).

Negotiated offering. Offering of securities for which the terms, including underwriters' compensation, have been negotiated between the issuer and the underwriters. *See also* Offering.

Negotiated plea. The effect of plea bargaining in which the criminal defendant agrees to plead guilty to the charge or to a reduced charge in return for a recommendation from the prosecutor of a disposition less severe than possible under the particular statute. *See e.g.* Fed.R.Crim.P. 11(e). *See* Plea bargaining.

Negotiating bank. A bank that purchases drafts drawn by the beneficiary of a negotiation credit.

Negotiation /nəgòws(h)iyéyshən/. The transfer of an instrument in such form that the transferee becomes a holder. If the instrument is payable to order it is negotiated by delivery with any necessary indorsement; if payable to bearer it is negotiated by delivery. U.C.C. § 3–202(1). The act by which a check or promissory note is put into circulation by being passed by one of the original parties to another person. The term also describes the same process with respect to documents of title. See U.C.C. § 7–501.

Negotiation is process of submission and consideration of offers until acceptable offer is made and accepted. The deliberation, discussion, or conference upon the terms of a proposed agreement; the act of settling or arranging the terms and conditions of a bargain, sale, or other business transaction.

See also Due negotiation; Negotiate.

N.E.I. An abbreviation for *"non est inventus,"* he is not found.

Neighbor. One who lives in close proximity to another.

Neighborhood. A place near; an adjoining or surrounding district; a more immediate vicinity; vicinage.

It is not synonymous with territory or district, but is a collective noun, with the suggestion of proximity, and refers to the units which make up its whole, as well as to the region which comprehends those units. A district or locality, especially when considered with relation to its inhabitants or their interests. In ordinary and common usage "locality" is synonymous in meaning with "neighborhood," and neither connote large geographical areas with widely diverse interests.

As used with reference to a person's reputation, "neighborhood" means in general any community or society where person is well known and has established a reputation.

Neither party. An abbreviated form of docket entry, meaning that, by agreement, neither of the parties will further appear in court in that suit. Such is used as a form of judgment in some states where a case has been settled.

Nemo /níymow/. Lat. No one; no man. The initial word of many Latin phrases and maxims, among which are the following:

NEPA. National Environmental Policy Act. 42 U.S.C.A. § 4321 et seq.

Nephew. The son of one's brother or sister, or one's brother-in-law or sister-in-law.

Nepotism /népətizəm/. Bestowal of patronage by public officers in appointing others to positions by reason of blood or marital relationship to appointing authority. Term is also used to refer to preferential hiring or promotion of relative by management of company.

Net. That which remains after all allowable deductions, such as charges, expenses, discounts, commissions, taxes, etc., are made.

Net assets. A term used in accounting which is arrived at by subtracting a company's total liabilities from total assets. *See* Net worth.

Net asset value (N.A.V.). The market value of a share of stock in a mutual fund. The net asset value is arrived at by deducting total liabilities (accounts payable, notes payable, etc.) from total assets (cash, securities, etc.) and dividing such amount by the number of shares outstanding.

The net asset value of a corporation, for stock appraisal purposes, is the share which stock represents in the value of the net assets of the corporation including all property and value, whether realty or personalty, tangible or intangible, goodwill, and the corporation's value as a going concern. *See also* Book (*Book value*); Net worth.

Net balance. In reference to the sale of goods, the proceeds from the sale, after deducting expenses associated with the sale (commissions, etc.)

Net book value. The current book value of an asset or liability; that is, its original book value net of any accounting adjustments such as depreciation.

Net cash flow. Cash inflow minus cash outflow. It is often measured as income after tax plus non-cash expenses associated with a particular investment project (*i.e.*, depreciation, amortization, etc.).

Net cost. The actual cost of an item. Net cost is arrived at by deducting any income or financial gain from the total cost. As used in insurance, it represents the total premiums paid less the dividends received and cash surrender value.

Net earnings. *See* Earnings.

Net estate. Under estate tax statute the term means that which is left of the gross estate after the deduction of proper and lawful items in the course of settlement. In general, the net estate is the gross estate less the following allowable deductions: (a) funeral expenses; (b) claims against the estate; and (c) unpaid mortgages or indebtedness on property which is included in the gross estate.

Net income. Income subject to taxation after allowable deductions and exemptions have been subtracted from gross income. The excess of all revenues and gains for a period over all expenses and losses of the period.

Net income for income tax purposes is what remains out of gross income after subtracting ordinary and necessary expenses incurred in efforts to obtain or to keep it.

See also Distributable net income; Net profits; Taxable income.

Net interest. Pure interest which is theoretical and excludes overhead and risks from cost of capital.

Net investment. The net cash outlay required at the beginning of an investment project.

Net lease. Lease in which provision is made for the lessee to pay, in addition to rent, such additional expenses as the taxes, insurance and maintenance charges. *See also* Escalator clause; Net rent.

Net level annual premium. An amount which, if exacted from a group of insurance policyholders and increased by interest, will yield a sum sufficient to satisfy all death claims. The result is generally referred to as the "net" or "net level premium" of the policy.

Net listing. A type of listing contract whereby the broker is only entitled to a commission to the extent that sales price exceeds the given amount. For example, a net listing of $15,000 where the property sold for $18,000 would result in a $3,000 commission. *See also* Listing; Multiple listing; Net sale contract.

Net loss. Any deficit from operations, plus any shrinkage in value of plant investment. The excess of all expenses and losses for a period over all revenues and gains of the period. Negative net income.

Net national product. In a given period of time, the gross national product less allowance for capital consumption. *See also* Gross National Product.

Net operating assets. The assets, net of depreciation and bad debts, employed in the ordinary course of business. Hence excludes investments in stocks and bonds owned by a manufacturing company, for example.

Net operating income. Income generated from the operations of a business reduced by operating expenses. Expenses not considered operating expenses include: interest, depreciation, and income taxes.

Net operating loss. The excess of operating expenses over revenues. Items such as interest expenses and dividends are not considered ordinary business expenses, and, therefore are excluded in calculating the net operating loss. I.R.C. § 172(c).

Net position. In securities and commodity trading, the difference between contracts long and contracts short held by a trader.

Net premium. In life insurance, this term is used to designate that portion of the premium which is intended to meet the cost of the insurance, both current and future. Its amount is calculated upon the basis of the mortality tables and upon the assumption that the company will receive a certain rate of interest upon all its assets; it does not include the entire premium paid by the assured, but does include a certain sum for expenses.

Net present value (NPV). The present value of the stream of net cash flows resulting from a project, discounted at the firm's cost of capital, minus the project's net investment. It is used to evaluate, rank, and select from among various investment projects.

Net adjusted present value. The adjusted present value minus the initial cost of an investment.

Net present value method. In accounting, a process that uses the discounted cash flows of a project to determine whether the rate of return on that project is equal to, higher than, or lower than the desired rate of return.

Net price. The lowest price, after deducting all deductions, discounts, etc.

Net proceeds. Gross proceeds, less charges which may be rightly deducted.

Net profit margin. A percent arrived at by dividing income after cost of goods sold, operating expenses and taxes by total revenues.

Net profits. Profits after deduction of all expenses; may be classified as net before or after taxes. Deducting the cost of goods sold from sales gives the *gross profit*. Deducting the operating expenses (overhead) from gross profit gives the *operating profit*. Deducting income taxes from operating profits gives the *net profit*. *See also* Net income.

Net realizable value. For receivables, the amount of cash expected from the collection of present customer balances. For inventory, an item's selling price minus completion and disposal costs.

A method of accounting for by-products or scrap which requires that the net realizable value of these products be treated as a reduction in the cost of the primary products.

Net rent. Basic rent charge plus additional monthly charges for taxes, utilities and maintenance. *See also* Net lease.

Net return. *See* Net income; Net profits.

Net revenues. *See* Net income; Net profits.

Net sale contract. One in which the principal agrees to accept a specified net price for property to be sold, and the agent's compensation for negotiating a sale is to be any amount received in excess of the specified figure. *See also* Net listing.

Net sales. Gross sales minus returns, allowances, rebates, and discounts.

Net salvage value. The sum of after-tax cash flows, excluding operating revenues and expenses, connected with the termination of a capital budgeting project.

Net settlement. The accounting or bookkeeping balance that results when banks exchange items drawn on each other.

Net single premium. Aggregate of future yearly costs of insurance, severally discounted to age from which computation is made.

Premium which, if exacted from a group of policyholders and immediately invested at the assumed rate of interest, will yield in the aggregate a sum exactly sufficient to pay all death claims as they mature providing the mortality rate is in accord with the table used.

Net tonnage. The cubic contents of the interior of a vessel, when the spaces occupied by the crew and by propelling machinery are deducted, numbered in tons.

Net value. In insurance, accumulation of balances of past net premiums not absorbed in carrying risk. "Net valuation" portion of life insurance premium is amount of reserve necessary, under proper interest and mortality calculations, to properly fund policy for payment of future claims.

Net weight. The weight of an article or collection of articles, after deducting from the gross weight the weight of the boxes, coverings, casks, etc., containing the same. The weight of an animal dressed for sale, after rejecting hide, offal, etc.

Net worth. The amount by which assets exceed liabilities. Remainder after deduction of liabilities from assets. Difference between total assets and liabilities of individual, corporation, etc.

The total assets of a person or business less the total liabilities (amounts due to creditors). In the case of a corporation net worth includes both capital stock and surplus; in the case of a partnership or single proprietorship it is the original investment plus accumulated and reinvested profits.

Net worth of a corporation may be determined by subtracting liabilities from assets or by adding the capital account and surplus account as reflected in the general ledger of a corporation.

See also Book *(Book value);* Net asset value.

Net worth method. An approach used by the Internal Revenue Service to reconstruct the income of a taxpayer who fails to maintain adequate records. Under this approach, the gross income for the year is the increase in net worth of the taxpayer (*i.e.,* assets in excess of liabilities) with appropriate adjustment for nontaxable receipts and nondeductible expenditures. The net worth method often is used when tax fraud is suspected.

Net yield. The rate of return on an investment after deducting all costs, losses and charges for management.

Neutral. Indifferent; unbiased; impartial; not engaged on either side; not taking an active part with either of the contending sides. In an international war, the principal hostile powers are called "belligerents;" those actively co-operating with and assisting them, their "allies;" and those taking no part whatever, "neutrals."

Neutrality. The state of a nation which takes no part between two or more other nations at war.

Neutrality laws. Acts of Congress which forbid the fitting out and equipping of armed vessels, the enlisting of troops, or the engaging in other specified activities; for the aid of either of two belligerent powers with which the United States is at peace. See 22 U.S.C.A. § 441 et seq.

Neutrality proclamation. A proclamation by the President of the United States, issued on the outbreak of a war between two powers with both of which the United States is at peace, announcing the neutrality of the United States and warning all citizens to refrain from any breach of the neutrality laws.

Neutralization. Erasure or cancellation of unexpected harmful testimony by showing either by cross-examination or other witnesses that the witness has made a statement in conflict with his testimony. *See also* Impeachment.

Neutral principles doctrine. Doctrine applied in the resolution of church property disputes which holds that court must refrain from resolving dispute on basis of religious doctrine and practice and must rely exclusively on objective, well-established concepts of trust and property law familiar to lawyers and judges; documents, including religious documents, pertinent to dispute must be scrutinized in purely secular terms.

Neutral property. Property which belongs to citizens of neutral powers, and is used, treated, and accompanied by proper *insignia* as such.

New. As an element in numerous compound terms and phrases of the law, this word may denote novelty, or the condition of being previously unknown or of recent or fresh origin, but ordinarily it is a purely relative term and is employed in contrasting the date, origin, or character of one thing with the corresponding attributes of another thing of the same kind or class.

In order to be "new", as that word is used in the patent laws, the achievement must be either one that produces an unusual or improved or advanced result, which was unknown to the same prior art at the time of the claimed invention; or the achievement must be one that produces an old result in an unusual and substantially more efficient, or more economical way.

New and useful. The phrase used in the patent laws to describe the two qualities of an invention or discovery which are essential to make it patentable, viz., novelty, or the condition of having been previously unknown, and practical utility. To accomplish a new and useful result it is not necessary that result before unknown should be brought about, but it is sufficient if an old result is accomplished in a new and more effective way. An invention achieves a new result, where a function which had been performed by other means was performed to an efficient degree by an association of means never before combined, though all of them were old, and some of the changes seemed to be only in degree. *See also* Patentable.

New assets. In the law governing the administration of estates, this term denotes assets coming into the hands of an executor or administrator after the expiration of the time when, by statute, claims against the estate are barred so far as regards recourse against the assets with which he was originally charged.

New assignment. Under common law practice, where the declaration in an action is ambiguous, and the defendant pleads facts which are literally an answer to it, but not to the real claim set up by the plaintiff, the plaintiff's course is to reply by way of new assignment; *i.e.,* allege that he brought his action not for the cause supposed by the defendant, but for some other cause to which the plea has no application.

New cause of action. With reference to the amendment of pleadings, this term may refer to a new state of facts out of which liability is claimed to arise, or it may refer to parties who are alleged to be entitled under the same state of facts, or it may embrace both features. Amended and supplemental pleadings are permitted under Fed.R. Civil P. 15.

New for old. In making an adjustment of a partial loss under a policy of marine insurance, the rule is to apply the old materials towards the payment of the new, by deducting the value of them from the gross amount of the expenses for repairs, and to allow the deduction of one-third *new for old* upon the balance. *See also* Partial loss.

New inn. An inn of chancery.

New issue. A security being offered to the public for the first time. The distribution of new issues is usually subject to SEC rules. New issues may be initial public offerings by previously private companies or additional securities offered by public companies.

Newly discovered evidence. Evidence of a new and material fact, or new evidence in relation to a fact in issue, discovered by a party to a cause after the rendition of a verdict or judgment therein. Testimony discovered after trial, not discoverable before trial by exercise of due diligence.

Newly discovered evidence such as will support motion for new trial or to reopen for amended findings refers to evidence of facts existing at the time of trial of which the aggrieved party was excusably ignorant. To constitute newly discovered evidence for which new trial may be granted, evidence must pertain to facts in existence at time of trial, and not to facts that have occurred subsequently.

On motion, the court may relieve a party from a judgment or order because of newly discovered evidence which by due diligence could not have been discovered in time to move for a new trial. Fed.R.Civ.P. 60(b).

Motions for new trial or relief from judgment or order based on newly discovered evidence must generally be made within a specified time period; see *e.g.* Fed.R.Civil P. 59, 60; Fed.R.Crim.P. 33.

New matter. In pleading, matters of fact not previously alleged by either party in the pleadings, involving, generally, new issues with new facts to be proved. Amended and supplemental pleadings are permitted under Fed.R.Civil P. 15 to add new matter. *See also* Newly discovered evidence.

In patent law, "new matter" is matter involving a departure from or in addition to the original disclosure. Such matter may not be introduced into a patent application by way of amendment or continuation application. 35 U.S.C.A. § 132.

New promise. *See* Promise.

Newsman's privilege. The alleged constitutional right (freedom of speech and press) of a newsman to refuse to disclose the sources of his information. *See* Shield laws.

Newspaper. A publication, usually in sheet form, intended for general circulation, and published regularly at short intervals, containing information and editorials on current events and news of general interest.

Official newspaper. One designated by a state or municipal legislative body, or agents empowered by them, in which the public acts, resolves, advertisements, and notices are required to be published. *See also* Legal newspaper.

New trial. *See* Motion for new trial; Plain error rule; Trial; Venire facias.

New York interest. System of computing interest by using the exact number of days in a month and not 30 days uniformly.

New York Stock Exchange. An unincorporated association of member firms which handle the purchase and sale of securities for themselves and customers. It is the oldest and largest stock exchange in the country.

New York Times v. Sullivan. Landmark case in which the U.S. Supreme Court held that the constitutional guarantee of a free press and free speech require a public official who sues for defamation to prove malice on the part of the defendant in the publication of the matter. Malice in this context is the publishing of the material knowing it to be false or with a reckless disregard of its falsity. 376 U.S. 254, 279–280, 84 S.Ct. 710–726, 11 L.Ed.2d 686. *See also* Libel.

Next. Nearest; closest; immediately following.

Next devisee /nékst dəvàyzíy/°dèvəzíy/. Person to whom remainder is given by will.

Next eventual estate. Estate taking effect upon happening of the event terminating accumulation.

Next friend. One acting for benefit of infant, or other person not sui juris (person unable to look after his or her own interests or manage his or her own lawsuit), without being regularly appointed guardian. A "next friend" is not a party to an action, but is an officer of the court, especially appearing to look after the interests of the minor or the disabled person whom he represents. Such person is not substantially different in many jurisdictions from "guardian ad litem"; their functions being generally the same. *See also* Guardian; Parens patriæ.

Next-in, first-out (NIFO). An inventory valuation method whereby the cost of goods sold is based on the replacement cost, rather than the actual cost of the goods. This method is not a generally accepted accounting principle; therefore it is not commonly used. *Compare* Last-in, first-out (LIFO); First-in, first-out (FIFO).

Next of kin. In the law of descent and distribution, this term denotes the persons nearest of kindred to the decedent, that is, those who are most nearly related by blood; but it is sometimes construed to mean only those who are entitled to take under the statute of distributions (*i.e.* statutory distributees). See *e.g.* N.Y. Estates, Powers & Trusts § 2–1.1.

The term "next of kin" is used with two meanings; (1) nearest blood relations according to law of consanguinity and (2) those entitled to take under statutory distribution of intestate's estates, and term is not necessarily confined to relatives by blood, but may include a relationship existing by reason of marriage, and may well embrace persons, who in natural sense of word, and in contemplation of Roman law, bear no relation of kinship at all.

Within wrongful death statutes, means those who inherit from decedent under law of descents and distributions.

Nexus. A multistate corporation's taxable income can be apportioned to a specific state only if the entity has established a sufficient presence, or nexus, with that state. State law, which often follows the Uniform Division of Income for Tax Purposes Act (UDITPA), specifies various activities that lead to such nexus in various states. *See also* UDITPA.

NGRI. Not guilty by reason of insanity. *See* Insanity; M'Naghten Rule.

Nickname. A short name; one *nicked* or cut off for the sake of brevity, without conveying an idea of opprobrium, and frequently evincing the strongest affection or the most perfect familiarity.

Niece. The daughter of one's brother or sister, or of one's brother-in-law or sister-in-law.

NIFO. *See* Next-in, first-out. *Compare* Last-in, first-out (LIFO), and First-in, first-out (FIFO).

Nighttime. Generally, in absence of statutory provision to contrary, "nighttime," within definition of burglary, is, as was held at common law, that period between sunset and sunrise during which there is not enough daylight to discern a man's face. The rule is often followed that "nighttime" begins thirty minutes after sunset and ends thirty minutes before sunrise, Model Penal Code, § 221.0(2); or, that period of time from one hour after sunset to one hour before sunrise.

The common-law definition is still adhered to in some states (*e.g.* Calif. Penal Code § 7: "The period between sunset and sunrise.") but in others "night" has been defined by statute (see *e.g.* Model Penal Code definition above).

Nihil /náy(h)əl/. Lat. Nothing. Often contracted to *"nil."* The word standing alone is the name of an abbreviated form of return to a writ made by a sheriff or constable, the fuller form of which would be *"nihil est"* or *"nihil habet,"* according to circumstances.

Nihil dicit /náy(h)əl dísət/°dáy°/. He says nothing. The name of the judgment which may be taken as of course against a defendant who omits to plead or answer the plaintiff's declaration or complaint within the time limited. In some jurisdictions it is otherwise known as judgment "for want of a plea."

Judgment taken against party who withdraws his answer is *judgment nihil dicit,* which amounts to confession of cause of action stated, and carries with it, more strongly than judgment by default, admission of justice of plaintiff's case. *See also* Nil dicit judgment.

Nihil est /náy(h)əl èst/. There is nothing. A form of return made by a sheriff when he has been unable to serve the writ.

Nihil habet /náy(h)əl héybət/. He has nothing. The name of a return made by a sheriff to a *scire facias* or other writ which he has been unable to serve on the defendant.

Nil /níl/. Lat. Nothing. A contracted form of *"nihil,"* which see.

Nil debet /níl débət/. He owes nothing. The form of the general issue in all actions of debt on simple contract.

Nil dicit judgment. Judgment entered against defendant, in proceeding in which he is in court but has not filed an answer; all error of pleading being waived, court examines petition only to determine if it attempts to state cause of action within court's jurisdiction. *See also* Nihil dicit.

Nil ligatum /níl ləgéytəm/. Nothing bound; that is, no obligation has been incurred.

Nineteenth Amendment. Known as the women's suffrage amendment to the U.S. Const., it provides that the right of citizens of the U.S. to vote shall not be denied or abridged by the U.S. or by any state on account of sex. The 19th Amendment was ratified in 1920. *See also* Twenty-Sixth Amendment.

Ninety (90) day letter. Statutory notice sent by I.R.S. to taxpayer of tax deficiency. During the 90 day period after the mailing of such notice the taxpayer may either pay the tax and seek a refund or not pay the tax and challenge such alleged deficiency on petition to the Tax Court. I.R.C. §§ 6212, 6213. Notice of Commissioner's determination of tax liability must, absent jeopardy, precede assessment. *See also* Thirty-day letter.

Ninth Amendment. This amendment to the U.S. Const. provides that the enumeration in the Constitution of certain rights, shall not be construed to deny or disparage others retained by the people.

Nisi /náysay/. Lat. Unless. The word is often affixed, as a kind of elliptical expression, to the words "rule," "order," "decree," "judgment," or "confirmation," to indicate that the adjudication spoken of is one which is to stand as valid and operative *unless* the party affected by it shall appear and show cause against it, or take some other appropriate step to avoid it or procure its revocation. Thus a "decree *nisi*" is one which will definitely conclude the defendant's rights unless, within the prescribed time, he shows cause to set it aside or successfully appeals. The word, in this sense, is opposed to "absolute." And when a rule *nisi* is finally confirmed, for the defendant's failure to show cause against it, it is said to be "made absolute." *See also* Show cause order.

Nisi decree. An interim decree or order which will ripen into a final decree unless something changes, or some event takes place. Conditional device decree. *See also* Nisi.

Nisi prius /náysay práyəs/. The *nisi prius* courts are such as are held for the trial of issues of fact before a jury and one presiding judge. In America the phrase was formerly used to denote the forum (whatever may be its statutory name) in which the cause was tried to a jury, as distinguished from the appellate court.

Nisi prius clause /nàysay práyəs klóz/. In practice, a clause entered on the record in an action at law, authorizing the trial of the cause at *nisi prius* in the particular county designated. It was first used by way of continuance.

Nisi prius roll /nàysay práyəs rówl/. In practice, the roll or record containing the pleadings, issue, and jury process of an action, made up for use in the *nisi prius* court.

NKA. Now known as.

N.L.R.A. National Labor Relations Act.

N.L.R.B. National Labor Relations Board.

No-action clause. Provision commonly found in liability insurance policies to the effect that the insurer is not liable to the insured and that no action may be brought against the insurer by the insured until an action has been brought and the insured has either paid the amount to the third person or until a judgment has been rendered fixing the amount due or until an agreement has been reached.

No-action letter. Letter written by attorney for governmental agency (*e.g.* S.E.C.) to effect that, if facts are as represented in request for ruling, he will advise agency not to take action because the facts do not warrant prosecution.

No arrival, no sale. Provision in sales contract that if goods do not arrive at destination buyer acquires no property therein and does not become liable for price.

No award. The name of a plea in an action on an award, by which the defendant traverses the allegation that an award was made.

Nobility. In English law, a division of the people, comprehending dukes, marquises, earls, viscounts, and barons. These had anciently duties annexed to their respective honors. They are created either by writ, *i.e.*, by royal summons to attend the house of peers, or by letters patent, *i.e.*, by royal grant of any dignity and degree of peerage; and they enjoy many privileges, exclusive of their senatorial capacity. Since 1963 no new hereditary ennoblements have been created.

No bill. This phrase, endorsed by a grand jury on the indictment, is equivalent to "not found", "no indictment", or "not a true bill". It means that, in the opinion of the jury, evidence was insufficient to warrant the return of a formal charge. *See e.g.* Fed.R.Crim.P. 6(f). *See* Indictment.

No bonus clause. In states where applicable, a clause under the eminent domain section of a lease, giving the lessee the right to recover only the value of his physical improvements in the event of a taking, and not the value of his leasehold interest (the difference between the fixed rent of the lease and current market rental value).

No contest clause. Provision in a will to the effect that the legacy or devise is given on condition that no action is taken to contest the will; and if such action is initiated, the legacy or devise is forfeited. *See also* Non-contestability clause.

No evidence. Under the rule that the court may render judgment non obstante veredicto if directed verdict would have been proper, the term "no evidence" does not mean literally no evidence at all; "no evidence" comprehends those situations wherein by the application of established principles of law the evidence is deemed legally insufficient to establish an asserted proposition of fact. "No evidence" points may be sustained only when (1) evidence of a vital fact is completely absent;

(2) rules of law or evidence bar court from giving weight to only evidence offered to prove a vital fact; (3) no more than a mere scintilla of evidence is offered to prove a vital fact; and (4) the evidence conclusively establishes the opposite of the vital fact. *See* Non obstante veredicto.

No eyewitness rule. The principle by which one who is charged with the burden of showing freedom from contributory negligence is assumed to have acted with due care for his own safety in the absence of eyewitnesses or of any obtainable evidence to the contrary. The "no eyewitness rule" is that where there is no obtainable direct evidence of what decedent did or failed to do immediately before injury, trier of facts may infer that decedent was in exercise of ordinary care for his own safety.

No fault. A type of automobile insurance, in force in many states, in which each person's own insurance company pays for injury or damage up to a certain limit regardless of whether its insured was actually at fault. *See* Insurance.

Also, popular name for a type of divorce in which a marriage can be ended on a mere allegation that it has "irretrievably" broken down or because of "irreconcilable" differences between the spouses. Under such statutory ground for dissolution of marriage, which exists in most all states, fault on the part of either spouse need not be shown or proved. *See* Irretrievable breakdown of marriage.

No fault insurance. *See* Insurance; No fault.

No funds. Endorsement marked on check when a check is drawn on bank in which the drawer has no funds with which to cover check. *See also* Fund *or* funds.

N.O.I.B.N. Abbreviation, used under terms of tariffs, meaning not otherwise indexed by name.

No limit order. An order to buy or sell securities in which there is no stipulation as to price.

Nolle prosequi /nóliy prósəkwày/. Lat. A formal entry upon the record, by the plaintiff in a civil suit, or, more commonly, by the prosecuting attorney in a criminal action, by which he declares that he "will no further prosecute" the case, either as to some of the defendants, or altogether. The voluntary withdrawal by the prosecuting attorney of present proceedings on a criminal charge. Commonly called "nol pros".

No-load fund. A type of mutual fund which charges little or nothing for administrative and selling expenses in the sale of its shares. *See* Mutual fund.

Nolo contendere /nówlow kənténdəriy/. Latin phrase meaning "I will not contest it"; a plea in a criminal case which has a similar legal effect as pleading guilty. Type of plea which may be entered with leave of court to a criminal complaint or indictment by which the defendant does not admit or deny the charges, though a fine or sentence may be imposed pursuant to it. Fed.R. Crim.P. 11(a), 12(a). The principal difference between a plea of guilty and a plea of nolo contendere is that the latter may not be used against the defendant in a civil action based upon the same acts. As such, this plea is particularly popular in antitrust actions (*e.g.* price fixing) where the likelihood of civil actions following in the wake of a successful antitrust prosecution is very great.

A defendant may plead nolo contendere only with the consent of the court. Such a plea shall be accepted by the court only after due consideration of the views of the parties and the interest of the public in the effective administration of justice. Fed.R.Crim.P. 11(b).

Nominal. Titular; existing in name only; not real or substantial; connected with the transaction or proceeding in name only, not in interest. Not real or actual; merely named, stated, or given, without reference to actual conditions; often with the implication that the thing named is so small, slight, or the like, in comparison to what might properly be expected, as scarcely to be entitled to the name; *e.g.*, a nominal price.

Nominal account. In accounting, an income statement account which is closed into surplus at the end of the year when the books are balanced.

Nominal annual rate. An effective rate per period multiplied by the number of periods in a year.

Nominal capital. Very small or negligible capital, whose use in particular business is incidental. Capital in name only and which is not substantial; not real or actual; merely named, stated, or given, without reference to actual conditions.

Nominal consideration. *See* Consideration.

Nominal damages. *See* Damages.

Nominal defendant. A person who is joined as defendant in an action, not because he is immediately liable in damages or because any specific relief is demanded as against him, but because his connection with the subject-matter is such that the plaintiff's action would be defective, under the technical rules of practice, if he were not joined. *See also* Parties.

Nominal interest rate. The rate of interest stated in a security as opposed to the actual interest yield that is based upon the price at which the interest-bearing property is purchased and the length of time to maturity of the obligation.

Nominal partner. A person who appears to be a partner in a firm, or is so represented to persons dealing with the firm, or who allows his name to appear in the style of the firm or to be used in its

business, in the character of a partner, but who has no actual interest in the firm or business.

Nominal party. *See* Nominal defendant; Parties.

Nominal payee rule. Refers to a U.C.C. Article 3 provision, § 3–405(1)(b), which renders effective any person's indorsement of an instrument drawn by a person who intends the payee to have no interest in the instrument.

Nominal trust. A dry or passive trust in which the duties of the trustee are minimal and in which the beneficiary has virtual control.

Nominate. To name, designate by name, appoint, or propose for election or appointment.

Nomination. An appointment or designation of a person to fill an office or discharge a duty. The act of suggesting or proposing a person by name as a candidate for an office.

Nominee /nòmǝníy/. One who has been nominated or proposed for an office. One designated to act for another in his or her place.

A form of securities registration widely used by institutional investors to avoid onerous requirements of establishing the right of registration by a fiduciary.

One designated to act for another as his representative in a rather limited sense; *e.g.* stock held by brokerage firm in street name to facilitate transactions even though customer is actual owner of securities. It is used sometimes to signify an agent or trustee. It has no connotation, however, other than that of acting for another, in representation of another, or as the grantee of another.

Nominee trust. An arrangement for holding title to real property under which one or more persons or corporations, pursuant to a written declaration of trust, declare that they will hold any property that they acquire as trustees for the benefit of one or more undisclosed beneficiaries.

Non. Lat. Not. The common prefix of negation.

Non-ability. Want of ability to do an act in law, as to sue. A plea founded upon such cause.

Non-acceptance. A buyer's right under a contract of sale to reject the goods because of nonconformance with the contract. U.C.C. § 2–601(a). Failure or refusal of a drawee to accept a draft or bill. The refusal to accept anything.

Non-access. Absence of opportunities for sexual intercourse between husband and wife; or the absence of such intercourse. Defense interposed by alleged father in paternity cases.

Nonacquiescence. An administrative agency's policy of declining to be bound by judicial precedent which is contrary to the agency's interpretation of its organic statute, until the Supreme Court has ruled on the issue. At its most extreme, it is the policy of disregarding the decisions of federal courts within the circuit in which they sit when those decisions conflict with the Secretary's own policies. A more limited version is an agency's refusal to give nationwide effect to the holdings of a particular court of appeals. Sometimes abbreviated as non-acqu. or NA. *Compare* Acquiescence.

Non-admission. The refusal of admission.

Non-age. Lack of requisite legal age. A minor. In general, the legal status of a person who is under eighteen years of age. *See* Minor.

Non-ancestral estate. Realty coming to deceased in any way other than by descent or devise from a now dead ancestor, or by deed of actual gift from a living one, there being no other consideration than that of blood. One acquired by purchase or by act or agreement of the parties, as distinguished from one acquired by descent or by operation of law.

Non-apparent easement. A non-continuous or discontinuous easement. *See* Easement.

Non-appearance. A failure of appearance; the omission of the defendant to appear within the time limited. *See* Default.

Non-assessable. This word, placed upon a certificate of stock, does not cancel or impair the obligation to pay the amount due upon the shares created by the acceptance and holding of such certificate. At most its legal effect is a stipulation against liability from further assessment or taxation after the entire subscription of one hundred per cent. shall have been paid.

Non assumpsit /nón əsə́m(p)sət/. The general issue in the action of *assumpsit;* being a plea by which the defendant avers that "he did not undertake" or promise as alleged by the plaintiff. *See* Assumpsit.

Non-bailable. Not admitting of bail; not requiring bail.

Nonbusiness bad debts. A bad debt loss not incurred in connection with a creditor's trade or business (*e.g.,* family loans). *See* Bad debt.

Non-cancellable /nón kǽnsələbəl/. Such provision in insurance policy precludes insurer from cancelling policy after an illness or accident, so long as the premium has been paid.

Noncash charge. A cost, such as depreciation, depletion, and amortization, that does not involve any cash outflow.

Non cepit /nón síypət/. He did not take. The general issue in replevin, where the action is for the wrongful *taking* of the property; putting in issue not only the taking, but the *place* in which the taking is stated to have been made.

Non-commissioned. A non-commissioned officer of the armed services is an officer who holds his

rank, not by commission from the executive authority, but by appointment by a superior officer.

Non compos mentis /nón kómpəs méntəs/. Lat. Not sound of mind; insane. This is a very general term, embracing all varieties of mental infirmity. *See* Incompetency; Insanity.

Nonconforming lot. A lot the area, dimension or location of which was lawful prior to the adoption, revision or amendment of a zoning ordinance, but now fails to conform to the requirements of the zoning district in which it is located by reason of such adoption, revision, or amendment.

Nonconforming use. A structure the size, dimension or location of which was lawful prior to the adoption, revision or amendment of a zoning ordinance, but which fails to conform to the requirements of the zoning district in which it is located by reasons of such adoption, revision or amendment. A use which does not comply with present zoning provisions but which existed lawfully and was created in good faith prior to the enactment of the zoning provision.

Uses permitted by zoning statutes or ordinances to continue notwithstanding that similar uses are no longer permitted in area in which they are located. *See also* Variance.

Non-contestability clause. Clause in insurance policy that precludes insurer from contesting policy on basis of fraud or mistake after a specified period of time (*e.g.,* two years) when insured has acted thereon to his detriment by payments of premiums and foregoing other insurance. *See also* Incontestability clause.

Non-continuous easement. "Continuous easement" is one which may be enjoyed without any act by party claiming it, while "noncontinuous easement," such as right of way, is one to enjoyment of which party's act is essential. A non-apparent or discontinuous easement. *See* Easement.

Noncontribution clause. In fire insurance policies, a provision that only the interests of the owner and first mortgagee are protected under the policy.

Non culpabilis /nón kəlpéybələs/. Lat. In pleading, not guilty. It is usually abbreviated *"non cul."* See Not guilty.

Noncumulative dividends. Commonly incident to preferred stock if a dividend is "passed" (not paid) in a particular year or period; such passed dividends are gone forever and there is no obligation to pay such when the next dividend is paid.

Noncumulative voting. Also called "straight" voting, such voting rights limit a shareholder to voting no more than the number of shares he owns for a single candidate. In noncumulative voting, a majority shareholder will elect the entire board of directors. *Compare* Cumulative voting.

Non-delivery. Neglect, failure, or refusal to deliver goods, on the part of a carrier, vendor, bailee, etc. Refers to a bailee who refuses to, or is unable to, surrender goods to a person entitled under a document of title covering them.

Non detinet /nón détənət/. Lat. He does not detain.

The name of the general issue in the action of detinue. The general issue in the action of replevin, where the action is for the wrongful detention only.

Non-direction. Omission on the part of a judge to properly instruct the jury upon a necessary conclusion of law.

Non-dischargeable debts. Types of debts that are not discharged in bankruptcy proceedings (*e.g.* taxes).

Non-disclosure. A failure to reveal facts, which may exist when there is no "concealment." *See* Fraud; Material fact; Misrepresentation.

Nonfeasance /nónfíyzəns/. Nonperformance of some act which person is obligated or has responsibility to perform; omission to perform a required duty at all; or, total neglect of duty. As respects public officials, "nonfeasance" is substantial failure to perform a required legal duty, while "misfeasance" is the doing in a wrongful manner that which the law authorizes or requires a public officer to do.

There is a distinction between "nonfeasance" and "misfeasance" or "malfeasance"; and this distinction is often of great importance in determining an agent's liability to third persons. "Nonfeasance" means the total omission or failure of an agent to enter upon the performance of some distinct duty or undertaking which he has agreed with his principal to do; "misfeasance" means the improper doing of an act which the agent might lawfully do, or, in other words, it is the performing of his duty to his principal in such a manner as to infringe upon the rights and privileges of third persons; and "malfeasance" is a doing of an act which he ought not to do at all.

Compare Malfeasance; Misfeasance; Non-performance.

Non-forfeitable. Not subject to forfeiture. *See also* Non-leviable.

Non-freehold estates. All estates in real property without seisin; hence, all estates except the fee simple, fee tail and life estates are non-freehold.

Non-functional. A feature of goods is "non-functional" if it does not affect their purpose, action or performance, or the facility or economy of processing, handling or using them. In effect a mere form of merchandising or a business method. A feature if, when omitted, nothing of substantial value in the goods is lost.

Noninsurable risk. A hazard or risk for which insurance will not be written because not subject to evaluation by actuarial computations; such risk being too uncertain. *Compare* Insurable.

Non-intercourse. The refusal of one state or nation to have commercial dealings with another; similar to an embargo *(q.v.)*.

The absence of access, communication, or sexual relations between husband and wife. *See* Non-access.

Non-intervention will. A term sometimes applied to a will which authorizes the executor to settle and distribute the estate without the intervention of the court and without giving bond.

Non-issuable pleas. Those upon which a decision would not determine the action upon the merits, as a plea in abatement.

Non-joinder. *See* Joinder.

Non-judicial day. Day on which process cannot ordinarily issue or be executed or returned, and on which courts do not usually sit. *See e.g.* Fed.R. Civil P. 77(c).

Non-leviable /nón léviyəbəl/. Not subject to be levied upon. Property exempt from seizure, forfeiture or sale in bankruptcy, attachment, garnishment, etc. Non-leviable assets are assets upon which an execution cannot be levied. *See also* Exemption; Homestead.

Nonliquidating distribution. A payment made by a partnership or corporation to the entity's owner when the entity's legal existence does not cease thereafter. *Compare* Distribution in liquidation.

Non-mailable. A term applied to all letters and parcels which are by law excluded from transportation in the United States mails, whether on account of the size of the package, the nature of its contents, its obscene character, or for other reasons. *See e.g.* 18 U.S.C.A. § 1715 et seq.

Non-medical policy. Insurance policy issued without medical examination of an applicant.

Non-merchantable title. The title to realty need not be bad in fact to render it "non-merchantable", but it is sufficient, if an ordinarily prudent man with knowledge of facts and aware of legal questions involved would not accept it in ordinary course of business. *Compare* Merchantable title.

Nonmonetary items. Asset, liability, and owner's equity items whose prices can change over time; for example, land, equipment, inventory, and warranty obligations.

Non-navigable. At common law, streams or bodies of water not affected by tide were "non-navigable". Bodies of water other than navigable waters *(q.v.)*.

Non-negotiable. Not negotiable; not capable of passing title or property by indorsement and delivery. Any document of title that is not a negotiable document. An instrument which may not be transferred by indorsement and delivery or by delivery alone, though it may be assigned. The transferee does not become a holder unless it is negotiated. *Compare* Negotiable.

Non obstante /nón əbstǽntiy/. Lat. Notwithstanding.

Words anciently used in public and private instruments, intended to preclude, in advance, any interpretation contrary to certain declared objects or purposes.

Non obstante veredicto /nón əbstǽntiy vèhrədík-tow/. Notwithstanding the verdict. A judgment entered by order of court for the plaintiff (or defendant) although there has been a verdict for the defendant (or plaintiff). Judgment *non obstante veredicto* in its broadest sense is a judgment rendered in favor of one party notwithstanding the finding of a verdict in favor of the other party. A motion for a directed verdict is a prerequisite to a subsequent grant of judgment notwithstanding the verdict. Fed.R. Civil P. 50. *See also* No evidence.

Judgment *non obstante veredicto* originally, at common law, was a judgment entered for plaintiff "notwithstanding the verdict" for defendant; which could be done only, after verdict and before judgment, where it appeared that defendant's plea confessed the cause of action and set up matters in avoidance which, although verified by the verdict, were insufficient to constitute a defense or bar to the action. But either by statutory enactment or because of relaxation of the early common-law rule, the generally prevailing rule now is that either plaintiff or defendant may have a judgment *non obstante veredicto* in proper cases.

Nonpayment. The neglect, failure, or refusal of payment of a debt or evidence of debt when due.

Non-performance. Neglect, failure, or refusal to do or perform an act stipulated or contracted to be done. Failure to keep the terms of a contract or covenant, in respect to acts or doings agreed upon. The failure or neglect to render performance called for in a contract, rendering the non-performer liable in damages or subject to a decree or judgment of specific performance. *See also* Nonfeasance.

Non-profit association. A group organized for purposes other than generating profit, such as a charitable, scientific, or literary organization. *See also* Non-profit corporation.

Non-profit corporation. A corporation no part of the income of which is distributable to its members, directors or officers. Corporation organized for other than profit-making purposes. Corporations may be organized under the Revised Model Non-Profit Corporation Act (1986) "for any lawful activity unless a more limited purpose is set forth in the articles of incorporation". Id. § 3.01(A).

For purposes of federal income taxation, an organization may be exempt as an "exempt organization" if it is organized and operated exclusively for one or more of the following purposes: (a) religious, (b) charitable, (c) scientific, (d) testing for public safety, (e) literary, (f) educational, (g) prevention of cruelty to children or animals, or (h) to foster national or international sports. See I.R.C. § 501(c) for a list of exempt organizations.

Non pros /nón prós/. Abbreviation of non prosequitur *(q.v.)*.

Non prosequitur /nón prəsékwətər/. Lat. He does not follow up, or pursue. If, in the proceedings in an action at law, the plaintiff neglects to take any of those steps which he ought to take within the time prescribed by the practice of the court for that purpose, the defendant may enter judgment of *non pros.* against him, whereby it is adjudged that the plaintiff does not follow up *(non prosequitur)* his suit as he ought to do, and therefore the defendant ought to have judgment against him. Under current rules practice, such failure would result in a dismissal of the action or in a default judgment for defendant. Fed.R. Civil P. 41, 55.

Nonrecourse. Status of person who holds an instrument which gives him no legal right against prior endorsers or the drawer to compel payment if the instrument is dishonored. *See also* Recourse; Without recourse; With recourse.

Nonrecourse debt. Debt secured by the property that it is used to purchase. The purchaser of the property is not personally liable for the debt upon default. Rather, the creditor's recourse is to repossess the related property. Nonrecourse debt generally does not increase the purchaser's at-risk amount.

Nonrecourse loan. Type of security loan which bars the lender from action against other assets of the borrower if the security value of the specified collateral for the loan falls below the amount required to repay the loan. It is used by the U.S. in loans to farmers on surplus crops.

Non-residence. Residence beyond the limits of the particular jurisdiction.

In ecclesiastical law, the absence of spiritual persons from their benefices.

Non-resident. One who does not reside within jurisdiction in question; not an inhabitant of the state of the forum. Special rules govern service of process on non-residents; *e.g.* Fed.R. Civil P. 4(e). *See* Long arm statutes.

For the distinction between "residence" and "domicile," *see* Domicile.

Non-resident alien. One who is neither a resident nor a citizen of the United States. Citizenship is determined under the federal immigration and naturalization laws (U.S.Code Title 8.)

Non-resident decedent. Decedent domiciled in another jurisdiction at the time of his death. Uniform Probate Code, § 1–201(26).

Non-resident motorist statutes. State laws governing the liability and obligations of non-residents who use the state's highways.

Non-sane. *See* Insanity.

Non sequitur /nón sékwətər/. Lat. It does not follow.

Non-stock corporation. Species of corporation in which the members hold no shares of stock as in the case of mutual companies and religious and charitable corporations. Ownership is through the membership charter or agreement rather than through the usual issuance of stock.

Nonsuit. A term broadly applied to a variety of terminations of an action which do not adjudicate issues on the merits. Name of a judgment given against the plaintiff when he is unable to prove a case, or when he refuses or neglects to proceed to trial and leaves the issue undetermined. Type of judgment rendered against party in legal proceeding on his inability to maintain his cause in court, or when he is in default in prosecuting his suit or in complying with orders of court.

A plaintiff suffers a "non-suit" when a court order finally terminates the cause without prejudice.

Action in form of a judgment taken against a plaintiff who has failed to appear to prosecute his action or failed to prove his case. Under civil rules practice, the applicable term is "dismissal". Fed.R. Civil P. 41.

See also Default-judgment; Directed verdict; Dismissal.

Judgment of nonsuit (*i.e.* "dismissal") is of two kinds,—*voluntary* and *involuntary*. When plaintiff abandons his case, and consents that judgment go against him for costs, it is *voluntary*. Fed.R. Civil P. 41(a). But when he, being called, neglects to appear, or when he has given no evidence on which a jury could find a verdict, or when his case is put out of court by some adverse ruling precluding a recovery, it is *involuntary*. Rule 41(b).

A *peremptory* nonsuit is a compulsory or involuntary nonsuit, ordered by the court upon a total failure of the plaintiff to substantiate his claim by evidence.

Non-support. The failure or neglect unreasonably to support those to whom an obligation of support is due; *e.g.* duty of parents to support children; duty to support spouse. Such failure to support is a criminal offense in most states. See *e.g.* Model Penal Code § 230.5.

Nonsupport of a child is a parent's failure, neglect or refusal without lawful excuse to provide for the support and maintenance of his or her child in necessitous circumstances. Nonsupport of a spouse is an individual's failure without just cause to provide for the support of his or her spouse in necessitous circumstances.

See also Necessitous circumstances; Reciprocal Enforcement of Support Act; Support.

Non-tenure. A common law plea in a real action, by which the defendant asserts, either as to the whole or as to some part of the land mentioned in the plaintiff's declaration, that he does not hold it.

Non-term. The vacation between two terms of a court.

Non-user. Neglect to use. Neglect to use a franchise; neglect to exercise an office. Neglect or omission to use an easement or other right. A right acquired by use may be lost by non-user.

Non vult /nón vólt/. Lit. He does not wish (to contend). A plea similar to nolo contendere *(q.v.)* and carrying the implications of a plea of guilty.

Non vult contendere /nòn vólt kənténdəriy/. Lat. He (the defendant in a criminal case) will not contest it. A plea legally equivalent to that of guilty, being a variation of the form *"nolo contendere" (q.v.),* and sometimes abbreviated *"non vult."*

Non-waiver agreement. Such agreement reserves to insurer every right under policy not previously waived, and to the insured every right which had not been forfeited.

No par. Said of stock without a par value.

No protest. Term used to describe the waiver of any right of protest when an instrument is not paid. Protest of dishonor is necessary, unless excused, to charge a drawer and endorser on any draft payable outside the United States. U.C.C. §§ 3–501(3), 509, 511.

No recourse. No access to; no return; no coming back upon; no assumption of any liability whatsoever; no looking to the party using the term for any reimbursement in case of loss or damage or failure of consideration in that which was the cause, the motive, or the object, of the undertaking or contract.

Normal. According to, constituting, or not deviating from an established norm, rule, or principle; conformed to a type, standard or regular form; performing the proper functions; regular; average; natural.

Normal balance. In accounting, the type of balance (debit or credit) usually found in a ledger account; for example, assets usually have debit balances, liabilities normally have credit balances, and so forth.

Normally. As a rule; regularly; according to rule, general custom, etc.

Norris-La Guardia Act. Federal statute restricting the use of injunctions by federal courts in labor disputes.

Northwest territory. A name formerly applied to the territory northwest of the Ohio river.

No-strike clause. Provision commonly found in public service labor-management agreements to the effect that the employees will not strike for any reason; with labor disputes to be resolved by binding arbitration.

Notarial /nòwtériyəl/. Taken by a notary; performed by a notary in his official capacity; belonging to a notary and evidencing his official character, as, a notarial seal.

Notarial acts. Official acts of notary public *(q.v.)*.

Notarial will. A will executed by the testator in the presence of a Notary Public and two witnesses.

Notary public. A public officer whose function it is to administer oaths; to attest and certify, by his hand and official seal, certain classes of documents, in order to give them credit and authenticity in foreign jurisdictions; to take acknowledgments of deeds and other conveyances, and certify the same; and to perform certain official acts, chiefly in commercial matters, such as the protesting of notes and bills, the noting of foreign drafts, and marine protests in cases of loss or damage. One who is authorized by the state or federal government to administer oaths, and to attest to the authenticity of signatures.

Notation credit. A credit which specifies that any person purchasing or paying drafts drawn or demands for payment made under it must note the amount of the draft or demand on the letter or advise of credit. U.C.C. § 5–108(1).

Note, *v.* To make a brief written statement; to enter a memorandum, as to note an exception.

Note, *n.* An instrument containing an express and absolute promise of signer (*i.e.* maker) to pay to a specified person or order, or bearer, a definite sum of money at a specified time. The borrower's legally binding written promise to repay a debt to a lender on a specified date. An instrument that is a promise to pay other than a certificate of deposit. U.C.C. § 3–104(2)(d). Two party instrument made by the maker and payable to payee which is negotiable if signed by the maker and contains an unconditional promise to pay sum certain in money, on demand or at a definite time,

to order or bearer. U.C.C. § 3–104(1). A note not meeting these requirements may be assignable but not negotiable.

An abstract; a memorandum; an informal statement in writing.

See also Balloon note; Judgment note; Promissory note; Treasury note.

Circular note. See Letter of credit.

Collateral note. Two party instrument containing promise to pay and secured by pledge of property such as securities, real estate, etc.

Demand note. Note payable on demand as contrasted with a time note which is payable at a definite time in the future.

Installment note. One of a series of notes payable at regular intervals or a single note calling for payment in installments at fixed periods of time.

Joint and several note. A note signed by persons as makers who agree to be bound both jointly and severally; *i.e.* they may be joined in a suit or they may be sued separately.

Joint note. Note evidencing an indebtedness in which two or more persons agree to be liable jointly and for payment of which all such persons must be joined in an action to recover.

Mortgage note. A note evidencing a loan for which real estate has been offered as security.

Negotiable note. To qualify as negotiable, the note must be signed by the maker, contain an unconditional promise to pay a sum certain in money and be payable on demand or at a definite time to order or bearer. U.C.C. § 3–104(1).

Secured note. A note for which security in the form of either real or personal property has been pledged or mortgaged. *See also Collateral note, above.*

Time note. Note payable at a definite future time as contrasted with a demand note.

Unsecured note. Note evidencing an indebtedness for which no security has been pledged or mortgaged.

Note of protest. A memorandum of the fact of protest, indorsed by the notary upon the bill, at the time, to be afterwards written out at length. *See* Protest.

Note *or* **memorandum.** Under statute of frauds, an informal minute or memorandum made on the spot. It must contain all the essential elements and substantial parts of the contract.

Notes payable. In bookkeeping, an account reflecting the aggregate indebtedness evidenced by promissory notes; the notes themselves are liabilities.

Notes receivable. In bookkeeping, an account containing evidence of indebtedness for which promissory notes have been given to the account of the party making the entry; the notes themselves are assets. *See also* Discounting notes receivable.

Not found. These words, indorsed on a bill of indictment by a grand jury, have the same effect as the indorsement "Not a true bill", "No bill," or *"Ignoramus."*

Not-for-profit corporation. *See* Non-profit corporation.

Not guilty. Plea entered by the accused to criminal charge. If the defendant refuses to plead, the court will enter a plea of not guilty. *See e.g.* Fed.R.Crim.P. 11. Also, the form of the verdict in criminal cases where the jury acquits the defendant; *i.e.* finds him "not guilty". For defense of not guilty by reason of insanity, *see* Insanity.

In common law pleadings, a plea of the general issue in the actions of trespass and case.

Notice. Information; the result of observation, whether by the senses or the mind; knowledge of the existence of a fact or state of affairs; the means of knowledge. Intelligence by whatever means communicated. Any fact which would put an ordinarily prudent person on inquiry. That which imparts information to one to be notified.

Notice in its legal sense is information concerning a fact, actually communicated to a person by an authorized person, or actually derived by him from a proper source, and is regarded in law as "actual" when the person sought to be affected by it knows thereby of the existence of the particular fact in question. It is knowledge of facts which would naturally lead an honest and prudent person to make inquiry, and does not necessarily mean knowledge of all the facts. In another sense, "notice" means information, an advice, or written warning, in more or less formal shape, intended to apprise a person of some proceeding in which his interests are involved, or informing him of some fact which it is his right to know and the duty of the notifying party to communicate.

Fed.R. Civil P. 5(a) requires that every written notice be served upon each of the parties.

A person has notice of a fact if he knows the fact, has reason to know it, should know it, or has been given notification of it. Restatement, Second, Agency § 9.

Notice may be either (1) statutory, *i.e.*, made so by legislative enactment; (2) actual, which brings the knowledge of a fact directly home to the party; or (3) constructive. Constructive notice may be subdivided into: *(a)* Where there exists actual notice of matter, to which equity has added constructive notice of facts, which an inquiry after such matter would have elicited; and *(b)* where there has been a designed abstinence from inquiry for the very purpose of escaping notice.

See also Adequate notice; Charged; Due notice; Immediate notice; Imputed notice; Judicial notice; Knowledge; Legal notice; Publication; Reasonable notice.

Actual notice. Actual notice has been defined as notice expressly and actually given, and brought home to the party directly. The term "actual notice," however, is generally given a wider meaning as embracing two classes, express and implied; the former includes all knowledge of a degree above that which depends upon collateral inference, or which imposes upon the party the further duty of inquiry; the latter imputes knowledge to the party because he is shown to be conscious of having the means of knowledge. In this sense actual notice is such notice as is positively proved to have been given to a party directly and personally, or such as he is presumed to have received personally because the evidence within his knowledge was sufficient to put him upon inquiry.

Averment of notice. The statement in a pleading that notice has been given.

Commercial law. A person has "notice" of a fact when: (a) he has actual knowledge of it; or (b) he has received a notice or notification of it; or (c) from all the facts and circumstances known to him at the time in question he has reason to know that it exists. A person "knows" or has "knowledge" of a fact when he has actual knowledge of it. "Discover" or "learn" or a word or phrase of similar import refers to knowledge rather than to reason to know. The time and circumstances under which a notice or notification may cease to be effective are not determined by the U.C.C. U.C.C. § 1–201(25).

A person "notifies" or "gives" a notice or notification to another by taking such steps as may be reasonably required to inform the other in ordinary course whether or not such other actually comes to know of it. A person "receives" a notice or notification when: (a) it comes to his attention; or (b) it is duly delivered at the place of business through which the contract was made or at any other place held out by him as the place for receipt of such communications. U.C.C. § 1–201(26).

Under the Uniform Commercial Code, the law on "notice," actual or inferable, is precisely the same whether the instrument is issued to a holder or negotiated to a holder.

Constructive notice. Constructive notice is information or knowledge of a fact imputed by law to a person (although he may not actually have it), because he could have discovered the fact by proper diligence, and his situation was such as to cast upon him the duty of inquiring into it. Every person who has actual notice of circumstances sufficient to put a prudent man upon inquiry as to a particular fact, has constructive notice of the fact itself in all cases in which, by prosecuting such inquiry, he might have learned such fact.

Constructive "notice" includes implied actual notice and inquiry notice.

Express notice. Express notice embraces not only knowledge, but also that which is communicated by direct information, either written or oral, from those who are cognizant of the fact communicated. *See also Actual notice, above.*

Implied notice. Implied notice is one of the varieties of actual notice (not constructive) and is distinguished from "express" actual notice. It is notice inferred or imputed to a party by reason of his knowledge of facts or circumstances collateral to the main fact, of such a character as to put him upon inquiry, and which, if the inquiry were followed up with due diligence, would lead him definitely to the knowledge of the main fact. "Implied notice" is a presumption of fact, relating to what one can learn by reasonable inquiry, and arises from actual notice of circumstances, and not from constructive notice. Or as otherwise defined, implied notice may be said to exist where the fact in question lies open to the knowledge of the party, so that the exercise of reasonable observation and watchfulness would not fall to apprise him of it, although no one has told him of it in so many words.

Personal notice. Communication of notice orally or in writing (according to the circumstances) directly to the person affected or to be charged, as distinguished from constructive or implied notice, and also from notice imputed to him because given to his agent or representative. *See Actual notice; Express notice, above.*

Public notice. Notice given to the public generally, or to the entire community, or to all whom it may concern. Such must commonly be published in a newspaper of general circulation. *See also* Publication.

Reasonable notice. Such notice or information of a fact as may fairly and properly be expected or required in the particular circumstances.

Notice of action. *See* Lis pendens.

Notice of appeal. A document giving notice of an intention to appeal filed with the appellate court and served on the opposing party. *See e.g.* Fed.R. App.P. 3.

Notice of appearance. *See* Appearance.

Notice of deficiency. *See* Ninety (90) day letter.

Notice of dishonor. Notice of dishonor may be given to any person who may be liable on the instrument by or on behalf of the holder or any party who has himself received notice, or any other party who can be compelled to pay the instrument. In addition an agent or bank in whose hands the instrument is dishonored may give notice to his principal or customer or to another agent or bank from which the instrument was received. U.C.C. § 3–508(1). *See also* Dishonor.

Notice of issue. *See* Notice of trial.

Notice of lis pendens /nówtəs əv lís péndənz/. *See* Lis pendens.

Notice of motion. A notice in writing, entitled in a cause, stating that on a certain day designated, a motion will be made to the court for the purpose or object stated. Such notice is required to be served upon all parties. Fed.R. Civil P. 5(a).

Notice of orders *or* **judgments.** Immediately upon the entry of an order or judgment the clerk shall serve notice of the entry by mail upon each party who is not in default for failure to appear, and shall make a note in the docket of the mailing. Fed.R. Civil P. 77(d). *See also* Fed.R.Crim.P. 49(c).

Notice of pendency. *See* Lis pendens.

Notice of protest. *See* Protest.

Notice of tax deficiency. *See* Ninety (90) day letter.

Notice of trial. A notice given by one of the parties in an action to the other, after an issue has been reached, that he intends to bring the cause forward for trial at the next term of the court.

Notice race statutes. In some jurisdictions, in recording of documents of title to real estate, the first grantee or mortgagee to record in the chain of title without actual notice of a prior unrecorded deed or mortgage prevails. Also known as Race-Notice Statute. *See also* Notice recording statutes; Recording acts.

Notice recording statutes. An unrecorded conveyance or other instrument is invalid as against a subsequent bona fide purchaser (creditor or mortgagee if the statute so provides) for value and without notice. Under this type of statute the subsequent bona fide purchaser prevails over the prior interest whether the subsequent purchaser records or not. Insofar as the subsequent purchaser is concerned, there is no premium on his race to the recorder's office. His priority is determined upon his status at the time he acquires his deed or mortgage. *See also* Recording acts.

Notice to appear. Shorthand expression for the form of summons or order of notice in which the defendant is ordered to appear and show cause why judgment should not be entered against him. Fed.R. Civil P. 4(b). *See also* Show cause order; Summons.

Notice to creditors. Formal notification in bankruptcy proceeding to creditors of the bankrupt that a meeting will be held, or that proof of claims must be filed on or before a certain date, or that an order for relief has been granted. See Bankruptcy Code, § 342.

Notice to plead. A notice which, in the practice of the federal courts, and most state courts, is prerequisite to the taking judgment by default. It proceeds from the plaintiff, and warns the defendant that he must plead to the declaration or complaint within a prescribed time. Such notice is required in the summons. Fed.R. Civil P. 4(b).

Notice to produce. Document by which party to civil or criminal action requests opposing party to submit specified papers, evidence, etc. needed for preparation of case and use at trial. See *e.g.* Fed.R.Civil P. 30(b); Fed.R.Crim.P. 15(a), 26.2. 18 U.S.C.A. § 3500. *See* Discovery; Inspection of documents.

Notice to quit. A written notice given by a landlord to his tenant, stating that the former desires to repossess himself of the demised premises, and that the latter is required to quit and remove from the same at a time designated, either at the expiration of the term, if the tenant is in under a lease, or immediately, if the tenancy is at will or by sufferance. The term is also sometimes applied to a written notice given by the tenant to the landlord, to the effect that he intends to quit the demised premises and deliver possession of the same on a day named.

Notification. *See* Notice; Notify.

Notify. To give notice to; to inform by words or writing, in person or by message, or by any signs which are understood; to make known. To "notify" one of a fact is to make it known to him; to inform him by notice. *See* Notice.

Not later than. "Within" or "not beyond" time specified.

Not less than. The smallest or lowest degree, at the lowest estimate; at least.

Notoriety /nòwtəráyədiy/. The state of being notorious or universally well known.

Notorious /nowtóriyəs/. Generally known and talked of; well or widely known; forming a part of common knowledge, or universally recognized. Open; generally or commonly known and spoken of.

Notorious cohabitation. The statutory offense in some jurisdictions committed by two persons who live together openly while not being married to each other. Such laws are seldom enforced.

Notorious insolvency. A condition of insolvency which is generally known throughout the community or known to the general class of persons with whom the insolvent has business relations.

Notorious possession. As a requisite of adverse possession, such possession that is so conspicuous that it is generally known and talked of by the public or the people in the neighborhood. Possession or character of holding in its nature having such elements of notoriety that the owner may be presumed to have notice of it and of its extent. *See also* Adverse possession.

Not satisfied. A return sometimes made by sheriffs or constables to a writ of execution; but it is not a technical formula, and has been criticized by the courts as ambiguous and insufficient. *See* Nulla bona.

Not to be performed within one year. The clause "not to be performed within one year" includes any agreement which by a reasonable interpretation in view of all the circumstances does not admit of its performance, according to its language and intention, within one year from the time of its making.

N.O.V. *See* Non obstante veredicto.

Novation. A type of substituted contract that has the effect of adding a party, either as obligor or obligee, who was not a party to the original duty. Substitution of a new contract, debt, or obligation for an existing one, between the same or different parties. The substitution by mutual agreement of one debtor for another or of one creditor for another, whereby the old debt is extinguished. A novation substitutes a new party and discharges one of the original parties to a contract by agreement of all parties. See Restatement of Contracts, Second, § 280.

The requisites of a novation are a previous valid obligation, an agreement of all the parties to a new contract, the extinguishment of the old obligation, and the validity of the new one.

In the civil law, there are three kinds of novation: where the debtor and creditor remain the same, but a new debt takes the place of the old one; where the debt remains the same, but a new debtor is substituted; where the debt and debtor remain, but a new creditor is substituted.

Novelty. In order that there may be "novelty" so as to sustain a patent, the thing must not have been known to any one before; mere novelty of form being insufficient. An invention or discovery is new or possesses requisite element of "novelty" if it involves the presence of some element, or the new position of an old element in combination, different from anything found in any prior structure. Novelty, in respect to design terminology, is present when the average observer takes the new design for a different and not just a modified already existing design. An objection to a patent or claim for a patent on the ground that the invention is not new or original is called an objection "for want of novelty."

Now. At this time, or at the present moment; or at a time contemporaneous with something done. At the present time.

"Now" as used in a statute ordinarily refers to the date of its taking effect, but the word is sometimes used, not with reference to the moment of speaking but to a time contemporaneous with something done, and may mean at the time spoken of or referred to as well as at the time of speaking.

Word "now" used in will normally refers to time of testator's death; but, in light of context, may apply to date of will.

N.O.W. account. Negotiable Order of Withdrawal account. Form of interest bearing checking account.

N.P. An abbreviation for "notary public."

NPV. *See* Net present value.

N.R. An abbreviation for "New Reports;" also for "not reported," and for "nonresident."

N.S. An abbreviation for "New Series;" also for "New Style."

NSF Check. Banking term meaning that there are "not sufficient funds" to cover check drawn on account. A check that is dishonored on presentment for payment because the drawer does not have sufficient funds in his or her account to cover its payment. *See also* Overdraft.

N.T.S.B. National Transportation Safety Board.

Nude pact. One without consideration; an executory contract without a consideration; a naked promise.

Nudum pactum /n(y)úwdəm pǽktəm/. A voluntary promise, without any other consideration than mere goodwill, or natural affection.

A naked pact; a bare agreement; a promise or undertaking made without any consideration for it.

Nugatory /n(y)úwgətəriy/. Futile; ineffectual; invalid; destitute of constraining force or vitality. A legislative act may be "nugatory" because unconstitutional.

Nuisance. Nuisance is that activity which arises from unreasonable, unwarranted or unlawful use by a person of his own property, working obstruction or injury to right of another, or to the public, and producing such material annoyance, inconvenience and discomfort that law will presume resulting damage. That which annoys and disturbs one in possession of his property, rendering its ordinary use or occupation physically uncomfortable to him; *e.g* smoke, odors, noise, or vibration. The term is incapable of exhaustive definition which will fit all cases, as it is very comprehensive and includes everything that endangers life or health, gives offense to senses, violates laws of decency, or obstructs reasonable and comfortable use of property. An offensive, annoying, unpleasant, or obnoxious thing or practice; a cause or source of annoyance, especially a continuing or repeated invasion or disturbance of another's right, or anything that works a hurt, inconvenience or damage.

Nuisances are commonly classed as *public, private,* and *mixed.* A *public* nuisance is one which affects an indefinite number of persons, or all the residents of a particular locality, or all people coming within the extent of its range or operation, although the extent of the annoyance or damage inflicted upon individuals may be unequal. Maintaining a *public* nuisance is by act, or by failure to perform a legal duty, intentionally causing or permitting a condition to exist which injures or endangers the public health, safety or welfare. An invasion of a person's interest in the private use and enjoyment of land by any type of liability-forming conduct is termed a *private* nuisance. It is a tort against a private person, and actionable by him as such. As distinguished from public nuisance, a *private* nuisance includes any wrongful act which destroys or deteriorates the property of an individual or of a few persons or interferes with their lawful use or enjoyment thereof, or any act which unlawfully hinders them in the enjoyment of a common or public right and causes them a special injury different from that sustained by the general public. Therefore, although the ground of distinction between public and private nuisances is still the injury to the community at large or, on the other hand, to a single individual, it is evident that the same thing or act may constitute a public nuisance and at the same time a private nuisance. A *mixed* nuisance is of the kind last described; that is, it is one which is both public and private in its effects,—public because it injures many persons or all the community, and private in that it also produces special injuries to private rights.

See also Anticipatory nuisance; Attractive nuisance doctrine; Common nuisance; Legalized nuisance; Offensive; Private nuisance; Public nuisance.

Abatement of a nuisance. The removal, stoppage, prostration, or destruction of that which causes a nuisance, whether by breaking or pulling it down, or otherwise removing, destroying, or effacing it. *See also* Abatable nuisance.

Absolute nuisance. Nuisance grounded in conduct which is intentional, rather than negligent. *Compare Qualified nuisance, below.*

Actionable nuisance. *See* Actionable.

Common nuisance. One which affects the public in general, and not merely some particular person; a public nuisance.

Continuing nuisance. An uninterrupted or periodically recurring nuisance; not necessarily a constant or unceasing injury, but a nuisance which occurs so often and is so necessarily an incident of the use of property complained of that it can fairly be said to be continuous.

Maintaining a nuisance. To "maintain" a nuisance means something more than having knowledge of its existence; it means, in addition, preserving and continuing its existence either by some positive act or by acquiescence.

Permanent nuisance. A nuisance of such a character that its continuance is necessarily an injury which will continue without change. One that cannot be readily abated at small expense.

Qualified nuisance. As distinguished from an "absolute nuisance," may consist of anything lawfully done or permitted to be done, so as to create a potential and reasonable risk of damage, which in due course results in injury to another. *Compare, Absolute nuisance, above.*

Temporary nuisance. A nuisance which can be corrected by the expenditure of labor or money.

Nuisance at law. *See* Nuisance per se.

Nuisance in fact. Acts, occupations or structures which are not nuisances per se but may become nuisances by reason of the circumstances of the location and surroundings or manner in which it is performed or operated.

Nuisance per accidens /n(y)úwsəns pər ǽksədènz/. *See* Nuisance in fact.

Nuisance per se /n(y)úwsəns pər síy/. An act, occupation, or structure which is a nuisance at all times and under all circumstances, regardless of location or surroundings; as, things prejudicial to public morals or dangerous to life or injurious to public rights; distinguished from things declared to be nuisances by statute, and also from things which constitute nuisances only when considered with reference to their particular location or other individual circumstances. The difference between a "nuisance per se" and a "nuisance per accidens" is that in the former, injury in some form is certain to be inflicted, while in the latter, the injury is uncertain or contingent until it actually occurs.

Null and void. Naught; of no validity or effect. The words when used in a contract or statute are often construed as meaning "voidable." "Null and void" means that which binds no one or is incapable of giving rise to any rights or obligations under any circumstances, or that which is of no effect. *See also* Void; Voidable.

Nulla bona /nə́lə bównə/. Lat. No goods. The name of the return made by the sheriff to a writ of execution, when he has not found any goods of the defendant within his jurisdiction on which he could levy.

Nullification. The state or condition of being void; without legal effect or status. Also, the act which produces such effect. *See* Void.

Jury in criminal case possesses de facto power of "nullification," to acquit defendant regardless of strength of evidence against him.

Nullity. Nothing; no proceeding; an act or proceeding in a cause which the opposite party may treat as though it had not taken place, or which has absolutely no legal force or effect.

Nullity of marriage. The entire invalidity of a supposed, pretended, or attempted marriage, by reason of relationship or incapacity of the parties or other diriment impediments. An action seeking a decree declaring such an assumed marriage to be null and void is called a suit of "nullity of marriage." It differs from an action for divorce, because the latter supposes the existence of a valid and lawful marriage. *See* Annulment.

Numbers game. "Numbers" or the numbers game is that game wherein the player wagers or plays that on a certain day a certain series of digits will appear or "come out" in a series such as the United States Treasury balance or parimutuel payoff totals of particular races at a certain racetrack for the day used as a reference, and though number of digits is fixed, usually at three, any player is free to select any number or quantity of numbers within the range of those digits, and designate amount of his wager upon each, and in such game neither number of players nor amount of money wagered nor total amount of payoffs can be predicted in any one day. Federal and state laws regulate such activities (see *e.g.* 18 U.S.C.A. § 1953). *See also* Lottery.

Nunc pro tunc /nə́nk pròw tə́nk/. Lat. Now for then. A phrase applied to acts allowed to be done after the time when they should be done, with a retroactive effect, *i.e.,* with the same effect as if regularly done. Nunc pro tunc entry is an entry made now of something actually previously done to have effect of former date; office being not to supply omitted action, but to supply omission in record of action really had but omitted through inadvertence or mistake.

Nunc pro tunc merely describes inherent power of court to make its records speak the truth, *i.e.,* to correct record at later date to reflect what actually occurred at trial. Nunc pro tunc signifies now for then, or, in other words, a thing is done now, which shall have same legal force and effect as if done at time when it ought to have been done.

Fed.R.Civ.P. 15(b) permits amendment of pleadings to conform to evidence. Clerical mistakes in judgments, orders, or other parts of the record can be made by the court under Rule 60(a).

Nuncupate /nə́ŋkyəpèyt/. To declare publicly and solemnly.

Nuncupative will. An oral will declared or dictated by the testator in his last sickness before a sufficient number of witnesses, and afterwards reduced to writing. A will made by the verbal declaration of the testator, and usually dependent merely on oral testimony for proof. Such wills are invalid in certain states, and in others are valid only under certain circumstances.

Nuptial /nə́pshəl/. Pertaining to marriage; constituting marriage; used or done in marriage.

Nurture. To give nourishment to, to feed; to bring up, or train; to educate. The act of taking care of children, bringing them up, and educating them.

N.Y.S.E. New York Stock Exchange.

O

OASDI. Old Age, Survivors' and Disability Insurance. *See* Social Security Administration.

Oath. Any form of attestation by which a person signifies that he is bound in conscience to perform an act faithfully and truthfully, *e.g.* President's oath on entering office, Art. II, Sec. 1, U.S.Const. An affirmation of truth of a statement, which renders one willfully asserting untrue statements punishable for perjury. An outward pledge by the person taking it that his attestation or promise is made under an immediate sense of responsibility to God. A solemn appeal to the Supreme Being in attestation of the truth of some statement. An external pledge or asseveration, made in verification of statements made, or to be made, coupled with an appeal to a sacred or venerated object, in evidence of the serious and reverent state of mind of the party, or with an invocation to a supreme being to witness the words of the party, and to visit him with punishment if they be false. In its broadest sense, the term is used to include all forms of attestation by which a party signifies that he is bound in conscience to perform the act faithfully and truly. In a more restricted sense, it excludes all those forms of attestation or promise which are not accompanied by an imprecation.

See also Affirmation; Attestation; False swearing; Jurat; Loyalty oath; Pauper's oath; Verification.

Affirmation in lieu of oath. Fed.R.Civil P. 43 provides that whenever an oath is required under the rules, a solemn affirmation may be accepted in lieu thereof. See also Art. II, Sec. 1, and Art. VI, U.S.Const.

Assertory oath. One relating to a past or present fact or state of facts, as distinguished from a "promissory" oath (*see infra*) which relates to future conduct; particularly, any oath required by law other than in judicial proceedings and upon induction to office, such, for example, as an oath to be made at the custom-house relative to goods imported.

Extrajudicial oath. One not taken in any judicial proceeding, or without any authority or requirement of law, though taken formally before a proper person.

False oath. See False swearing; Perjury.

Judicial oath. One taken in some judicial proceeding or in relation to some matter connected with judicial proceedings. One taken before an officer in open court, as distinguished from a "non-judicial" oath, which is taken before an officer ex parte or out of court. *See also Witnesses, below.*

Loyalty oath. See Oath of allegiance.

Oath of office. Various declarations of promises, made by persons who are about to enter upon the duties of a public office, concerning their performance of that office. An oath of office is required, by federal and state constitutions, and by various statutes, to be made by major and minor officials. See *e.g.* 28 U.S.C.A. § 544 (U.S. attorneys). *See also* Oath of allegiance; and *Official oath, below.*

Official oath. One taken by an officer when he assumes charge of his office, whereby he declares that he will faithfully discharge the duties of the same, or whatever else may be required by statute in the particular case. See Art. VI, U.S. Const. *See also Oath of office, above.*

Poor debtor's oath. See Pauper's oath.

Promissory oaths. Oaths which bind the party to observe a certain course of conduct, or to fulfill certain duties, in the future, or to demean himself thereafter in a stated manner with reference to specified objects or obligations; such, for example, as the oath taken by a high executive officer, a legislator, a judge, a person seeking naturalization, an attorney at law. A solemn appeal to God, or, in a wider sense, to some superior sanction or a sacred or revered person in witness of the inviolability of a promise or undertaking. *Compare Assertory oath, above.*

Voluntary oath. Such as a person may take in extrajudicial matters, and not regularly in a court of justice, or before an officer invested with authority to administer the same.

Witnesses. Before testifying, every witness shall be required to declare that he will testify, truthfully, by oath or affirmation administered in a form calculated to awaken his conscience and impress his mind with his duty to do so. Fed. Evid.R. 603. *See also Affirmation in lieu of oath, above.*

Oath of allegiance *or* loyalty. An oath by which a person promises and binds himself to bear true allegiance to a particular sovereign or government (*e.g.*, the United States), and to support its

Constitution, administered generally to certain public officers or officials, to members of the armed services, to attorneys on being admitted to the bar, to aliens applying for naturalization (8 U.S. C.A. § 1448), etc. Such oaths which are not overbroad have been upheld. As to oath of allegiance to the Constitution as required of President, members of Congress, and executive and judicial officers, see Art. II, Sec. 1, and Art. VI, U.S. Const. It is commonly provided that an affirmation may be given in lieu of an oath.

Obedience. Compliance with a command, prohibition, or known law and rule of duty prescribed. The performance of what is required or enjoined by authority, or the abstaining from what is prohibited, in compliance with the command or prohibition.

Obiter /ó(w)bətər/. Lat. By the way; in passing; incidentally; collaterally.

Obiter dictum /ó(w)bətər díktəm/. Words of an opinion entirely unnecessary for the decision of the case. A remark made, or opinion expressed, by a judge, in his decision upon a cause, "by the way," that is, incidentally or collaterally, and not directly upon the question before him, or upon a point not necessarily involved in the determination of the cause, or introduced by way of illustration, or analogy or argument. Such are not binding as precedent. *See* Dicta; Dictum.

Obit sine prole /ówbət sáyniy prówliy/. Lat. [He] died without issue.

Object, *v.* In legal proceedings, to object (*e.g.*, to the admission of evidence) is to interpose a declaration to the effect that the particular matter or thing under consideration is not done or admitted with the consent of the party objecting, but is by him considered improper or illegal, and referring the question of its propriety or legality to the court. *See also* Objection.

Object, *n.* End aimed at, the thing sought to be accomplished; the aim or purpose, the thing sought to be attained.

Anything which comes within the cognizance or scrutiny of the senses, especially anything tangible or visible. That which is perceived, known, thought of, or signified; that toward which a cognitive act is directed. The term includes whatever may be presented to the mind as well as to the senses; whatever, also, is acted upon or operated upon affirmatively, or intentionally influenced by anything done, moved, or applied thereto. It may be used as having the sense of effect.

See also Intent; Motive.

Objection. Act of objecting; that which is, or may be, presented in opposition; an adverse reason or argument; a reason for objecting or opposing; a feeling of disapproval.

The act of a party who objects to some matter or proceeding in the course of a trial, or an argument or reason urged by him in support of his contention that the matter or proceeding objected to is improper or illegal. Used to call the court's attention to improper evidence or procedure. Such objections in open court are important so that such will appear on the record for purposes of appeal. See Fed.Evid.R. 103(a)(1), Fed.R.Civil P. 46, and Fed.R.Crim.P. 51. *See also* Contemporaneous objection rule; Object *(v).*

Objection to jury. See Challenge.

Objective. In cost accounting, a desired quantifiable achievement for a period of time.

Objective intent. *See* Intent.

Objective symptom. Those which a surgeon or physician discovers from an examination of his patient; "subjective symptoms" being those which he learns from what his patient tells him.

Objectivity principle. A principle requiring that accounting information be free from bias and verifiable by an independent party, such as an external auditor.

Object of an action. Legal relief to prevent or redress the wrong. The thing sought to be obtained by the action; the remedy demanded or the relief or recovery sought or prayed for; not the same thing as the cause of action or the subject of the action.

Object of a statute. Aim, intent or purpose of its enactment. End or design which it is meant to accomplish, while the "subject" is the matter to which it relates and with which it deals. Matter or thing forming groundwork of statute.

Objects of a power. Those among whom donee is given power to appoint.

Obligate. To bind or constrain; to bind to the observance or performance of a duty; to place under an obligation. To bind one's self by an obligation or promise; to assume a duty; to execute a written promise or covenant; to make a writing obligatory.

Obligatio ex contractu /òbləgéysh(iy)ow èks kəntrǽkt(y)uw/. An obligation arising from contract, or an antecedent *jus in personam.*

Obligatio ex delicto, *or* **obligatio ex maleficio** /òbləgéysh(iy)ow èks dəlíktow/°mǽləfísh(iy)ow/. An obligation founded on wrong or tort, or arising from the invasion of a *jus in rem.*

Obligation. A generic word, derived from the Latin substantive "obligatio," having many, wide, and varied meanings, according to the context in which it is used. That which a person is bound to do or forbear; any duty imposed by law, promise, contract, relations of society, courtesy, kindness, etc. Law or duty binding parties to perform their agreement. An undertaking to perform. That which constitutes a legal or moral duty and which renders a person liable to coercion and punishment for neglecting it; a word of broad meaning, and the particular meaning intended is to be gained by consideration of its context. An obligation or debt may exist by reason of a judgment as well as an express contract, in either case there being a legal duty on the part of the one bound to comply with the promise. Liabilities created by contract or law (*i.e.* judgments). As legal term word originally meant a sealed bond, but it now extends to any certain written promise to pay money or do a specific thing. A formal and binding agreement or acknowledgment of a liability to pay a certain sum or do a certain thing. The binding power of a vow, promise, oath, or contract, or of law, civil, political, or moral, independent of a promise; that which constitutes legal or moral duty.

See also Contract; Duty; Liability.

Absolute obligation. One which gives no alternative to the obligor, but requires fulfillment according to the engagement.

Contractual obligation. One which arises from a contract or agreement. *See* Contract; Impairing the obligation of contracts; Obligation of a contract.

Current obligation. *See* Current obligations.

Divisible or indivisible obligation. A divisible obligation is one which, being a unit, may nevertheless be lawfully divided, with or without the consent of the parties. An indivisible obligation is one which is not susceptible of division.

Express or implied obligation. Express or conventional obligations are those by which the obligor binds himself in express terms to perform his obligation, while implied obligations are such as are raised by the implication or inference of the law from the nature of the transaction.

Failure to meet obligations. *See* Failure to meet obligations.

Joint or several obligation. A joint obligation is one by which two or more obligors bind themselves jointly for the performance of the obligation. A several obligation is one where the obligors promise, each for himself, to fulfill the engagement.

Moral obligation. A duty which is valid and binding in conscience and according to natural justice, but is not recognized by the law as adequate to set in motion the machinery of justice; that is, one which rests upon ethical considerations alone, and is not imposed or enforced by positive law. A duty which would be enforceable by law, were it not for some positive rule, which, with a view to general benefit, exempts the party in that particular instance from legal liability. *See also* Love and affection.

Simple or conditional obligation. Simple obligations are such as are not dependent for their execution on any event provided for by the parties, and which are not agreed to become void on the happening of any such event. Conditional obligations are such as are made to depend on an uncertain event.

Obligation of a contract. That which the law in force when contract is made obliges parties to do or not to do, and the remedy and legal means to carry it into effect. The "obligation of a contract" is the duty of performance. The term includes everything within the obligatory scope of the contract, and it includes the means of enforcement. *See also* Contract; Impairing the obligation of contracts.

Obligatory writing. *See* Writing obligatory.

Obligee /òbləjíy/. A promisee. The person in favor of whom some obligation is contracted, whether such obligation be to pay money or to do or not to do something. The party to whom someone else is obligated under a contract. Thus, if C loans money to D, C is the obligee and D is the obligor under the loan. The party to whom a bond is given.

Obligor /óbləgər/òbləgór/. A promisor. The person who has engaged to perform some obligation. Person obligated under a contract or bond.

Obliteration. To destroy; wipe or rub out; erase. Erasure or blotting out of written words. A method of revoking a will or a clause therein if accompanied by the required intent to revoke. *See also* Alteration; Deface; Spoliation.

Oblivion. Act of forgetting, or fact of having forgotten; forgetfulness. Official ignoring of offenses. Amnesty, or general pardon, as, an act of oblivion. State or fact of being forgotten. *See* Amnesty; Pardon.

Obloquy /óbləkwiy/. Censure and reproach. Blame, reprehension, being under censure, a cause or object of reproach, a disgrace.

Obscene. Objectionable or offensive to accepted standards of decency. Basic guidelines for trier of fact in determining whether a work which depicts or describes sexual conduct is obscene is whether the average person, applying contemporary community standards would find that the work, taken as a whole, appeals to the prurient interest, whether the work depicts or describes, in a patently offensive way, sexual conduct specifically defined by the applicable state law, and whether the work, taken as a whole, lacks serious literary, artistic, political, or scientific value. A state may choose to define obscenity offense in terms of "contemporary community standards" without further specification or may choose to define standards in more precise geographic terms. *See also* Censor; Censorship; Contemporary community standards; Dominant theme; Lewd; Obscenity; Pornographic; Prurient interest.

Obscene libel. That type of defamation which holds up a person to ridicule, scorn or contempt to a considerable and respectable class in the community by printed words or configurations of a lewd and lascivious nature.

Obscenity. The character or quality of being obscene; conduct tending to corrupt the public morals by its indecency or lewdness.

Material is obscene if, considered as a whole, its predominant appeal is to prurient interest, that is, a shameful or morbid interest, in nudity, sex or excretion, and if in addition it goes substantially beyond customary limits of candor in describing or representing such matters. Predominant appeal shall be judged with reference to ordinary adults unless it appears from the character of the material or the circumstances of its dissemination to be designed for children or other specially susceptible audience. Undeveloped photographs, molds, printing plates, and the like, shall be deemed obscene notwithstanding that processing or other acts may be required to make the obscenity patent or to disseminate it. Model Penal Code, § 251.4.

Federal laws prohibit the mailing, transportation for sale or distribution, importation, and broadcasting of obscene matters. 18 U.S.C.A. § 1461 et seq.

See also Censor; Censorship; Lewd; Obscene; Pander (*Pandering of obscenity*); Profanity.

Obscure. When applied to words, statements or meanings, it signifies not perspicuous, not clearly expressed, vague, hard to understand.

Observe. To perform that which has been prescribed by some law or usage. To adhere to or abide by.

Obsolescence. Condition or process of falling into disuse. The diminution in value of property caused by changes in technology, public taste, and new inventions rendering the property less desirable on the market. A decline in market value of an asset caused by improved alternatives becoming available that will be more cost-effective; such decline in market value is unrelated to physical changes in the asset itself. The process whereby property, because of causes other than physical deterioration, loses its economic usefulness to taxpayer. *See also* Economic obsolescence; Functional obsolescence.

Obsolescent. Becoming obsolete; going out of use; not entirely disused, but gradually becoming so. *See* Obsolescence.

Obsolete. That which is no longer used. Disused; neglected; not observed. *See also* Obsolescence.

The term is applied to statutes which have become inoperative by lapse of time, either be-

cause the reason for their enactment has passed away, or their subject-matter no longer exists, or they are not applicable to changed circumstances, or are tacitly disregarded by all men, yet without being expressly abrogated or repealed.

Obstante /əbstǽntiy/. Withstanding; hindering. *See* Non obstante.

Obstinate desertion. "Obstinate" as used of desertion, which is a ground for divorce, means determined, fixed, persistent. Persisted in against the willingness of the injured party to have it concluded.

Obstriction. Obligation; bond.

Obstruct. To hinder or prevent from progress, check, stop, also to retard the progress of, make accomplishment of difficult and slow. To be or come in the way of or to cut off the sight of an object. To block up; to interpose obstacles; to render impassable; to fill with barriers or impediments, as to obstruct a road or way. To impede; to interpose impediments to the hindrance or frustration of some act or service, as to obstruct an officer in the execution of his duty. As applied to navigable waters, to "obstruct" them is to interpose such impediments in the way of free and open navigation that vessels are thereby prevented from going where ordinarily they have a right to go or where they may find it necessary to go in their maneuvers.

Obstructing justice. Impeding or obstructing those who seek justice in a court, or those who have duties or powers of administering justice therein. The act by which one or more persons attempt to prevent, or do prevent, the execution of lawful process. The term applies also to obstructing the administration of justice in any way—as by hindering witnesses from appearing, assaulting process server, influencing jurors, obstructing court orders or criminal investigations. Any act, conduct, or directing agency pertaining to pending proceedings, intended to play on human frailty and to deflect and deter court from performance of its duty and drive it into compromise with its own unfettered judgment by placing it, through medium of knowingly false assertion, in wrong position before public, constitutes an obstruction to administration of justice. See 18 U.S.C.A. § 1501 et seq.; Model Penal Code § 242.1 et seq. *See also* Misprision of felony; Obstructing process; Withholding of evidence.

Obstructing mails. Federal offense consisting of interfering with the mails. 18 U.S.C.A. § 1701.

Obstructing proceedings of legislature. The term embraces not only things done in the presence of the legislature, but those done in disobedience of a committee.

Obstructing process. In criminal law, the act by which one or more persons attempt to prevent or do prevent the execution of lawful process. Obstructing legal process or official duty is knowingly and willfully obstructing, resisting or opposing any person authorized by law to serve process or order of a court, or in the discharge of any official duty. *See e.g.* 18 U.S.C.A. § 1501 et seq. *See also* Obstructing justice.

Obstruction. A hindrance, obstacle, or barrier. Delay, impeding or hindering. *See also* Obstruct.

Obstruction to navigation. Any unnecessary interference with the free movements of vessels.

Obtain. To get hold of by effort; to get possession of; to procure; to acquire, in any way. *See also* False pretenses.

Obtaining money or property by false pretenses. *See* False pretenses.

Obvious. Easily discovered, seen, or understood; readily perceived by the eye or the intellect; plain; patent; apparent; evident; clear; manifest.

Patent. Whether a patent is "obvious" must be determined by considering the scope and content of the prior art, the differences between the prior art and the claims at issue and the level of ordinary skill in the pertinent art.

Obvious danger. Apparent in exercise of ordinary observation and disclosed by use of eyes and other senses. Plain and apparent to a reasonably observant person.

Obvious risk. One so plain that it would be instantly recognized by a person of ordinary intelligence. Within an accident policy, one which would be plain and apparent to a reasonably prudent and cautious person in the use of his faculties. It does not mean an unnecessary risk. *See* Assumption of risk.

Occasion, *n.* That which provides an opportunity for the causal agency to act. Meaning not only particular time but carrying idea of opportunity, necessity, or need, or even cause in a limited sense. Condition of affairs; juncture entailing need; exigency; or juncture affording ground or reason for something.

Occasion, *v.* To cause or bring about by furnishing the condition or opportunity for the action of some other cause. To give occasion to, to produce; to cause incidentally or indirectly; bring about or be the means of bringing about or producing.

Occupancy. Taking possession of property and use of the same; said *e.g.* of a tenant's use of leased premises. Period during which person owns, rents, or otherwise occupies real property or premises. Occupancy is a mode of acquiring property by which a thing which belongs to nobody becomes the property of the person who took possession of it with the intention of acquiring a right of ownership in it. The taking possession of things which before belonged to nobody, with an intention of appropriating them to one's own use. To constitute occupancy, there must be a taking of a thing corporeal, belonging to nobody, with an intention to becoming the owner of it. *See also* Occupant; Occupation; Possession.

Term also refers to the constitutional concept of "occupancy of the field" when the federal government has so claimed for its jurisdiction a particular sphere that state action is no longer allowed; *e.g.* sedition and espionage laws. *See* Preemption.

In international law, the taking possession of a newly discovered or conquered country with the intention of holding and ruling it.

See also Adverse possession; Certificate of occupancy; Occupant; Occupation; Occupy; Possession.

Occupant. Person in possession. Person having possessory rights, who can control what goes on on premises. One who has actual use, possession or control of a thing. One who takes the first possession of a thing of which there is no owner. One who occupies and takes possession. Person who acquires title by occupancy. *See also* Occupancy; Occupation; Possession.

Occupation. Possession; control; tenure; use. The act or process by which real property is possessed and enjoyed. Where a person exercises physical control over land.

That which principally takes up one's time, thought, and energies, especially, one's regular business or employment; also, whatever one follows as the means of making a livelihood. Particular business, profession, trade, or calling which engages individual's time and efforts; employment in which one regularly engages or vocation of his life.

Actual occupation. An open, visible occupancy as distinguished from the constructive one which follows the legal title. *See also* Adverse possession.

Occupational. Of or pertaining to an occupation, trade or work.

Occupational disease. A disease (as black lung disease incurred by miners) resulting from exposure during employment to conditions or substances detrimental to health. Impairment of health not caused by accident but by exposure to conditions incidental to and arising out of or in the course of one's employment. Such disease may be found if there is substantial evidence that either employment conditions specifically affected the employee in a matter resulting in contraction of disease, or employment conditions generally tend, to a reasonable medical probability, to cause a particular disease or condition in a given class of workers.

A disease is compensable under workers' compensation statute as being an "occupational" disease where: (1) the disease is contracted in the course of employment; (2) the disease is peculiar to the claimant's employment by its causes and the characteristics of its manifestation or the conditions of employment result in a hazard which distinguishes the employment in character from employment generally; and (3) the employment creates a risk of contracting the disease in a greater degree and in a different manner than in the public generally.

Compensation for such is provided by state workers' compensation acts and such federal acts as the Black Lung Benefits Act.

Occupational hazard. A risk of accident or disease which is peculiar to a particular calling or occupation. *See also* Injurious exposure.

Occupational Safety and Health Act. Federal law (1970) administered by the Occupational Safety and Health Administration enacted to reduce the incidence of personal injuries, illnesses, and deaths among working men and women in the United States which result from their employment. 29 U.S.C.A. § 651 et seq.

Occupational Safety and Health Administration. Federal agency, established pursuant to the Occupational Safety and Health Act of 1970, to develop and promulgate occupational safety and health standards; develop and issue regulations; conduct investigations and inspections to determine the status of compliance with safety and health standards and regulations; and issue citations and propose penalties for noncompliance with safety and health standards and regulations.

Occupational Safety and Health Review Commission. An independent federal adjudicatory agency established by the Occupational Safety and Health Act to adjudicate enforcement actions initiated under the Act when they are contested by employers, employees, or representatives of employees. 29 U.S.C.A. § 661.

Occupation tax. A tax imposed upon an occupation or the prosecution of a business, trade, or profession; not a tax on property, or even the capital employed in the business, but an excise tax on the business itself; to be distinguished from a "license tax," which is a fee or exaction for the privilege of engaging in the business, not for its prosecution. An occupation tax is form of excise tax imposed upon persons for privilege of carrying on business, trade or occupation.

Occupy. To take or enter upon possession of; to hold possession of; to hold or keep for use; to possess; to tenant; to do business in; to take or hold possession. Actual use, possession, and cultivation. *See* Occupancy; Occupant; Occupation; Possession.

Occupying claimant. An occupant claiming right under statute to recover for improvements he has placed on the land subsequently found not to be his. *See* Occupying Claimant Acts.

Occupying Claimant Acts. Statutes providing for the reimbursement of a *bona fide* occupant and claimant of land, on its recovery by the true owner, to the extent to which lasting improvements made by him have increased the value of the land, and generally giving him a lien therefor.

Occur. To happen; to meet one's eye; to be found or met with; to present itself; to appear; hence, to befall in due course; to take place; to arise.

Occurrence. A coming or happening. Any incident or event, especially one that happens without being designed or expected (from *e.g.* standpoint of insured). Within meaning of insurance provision requiring notice of a reportable occurrence to insurer as soon as practicable, "occurrence" means incident which was sufficiently serious to lead a person of ordinary intelligence and prudence to believe that it might give rise to a claim for damages covered by policy. *See also* Accident; Act of God; Event.

Ocean. The main or open sea; the high sea; that portion of the sea which does not lie within the body of any country and is not subject to the territorial jurisdiction or control of any country, but is open, free, and common to the use of all nations. Body of salt water that covers over 70% of earth's surface.

Odal right /ówdǝl ráyt/. An allodial right.

Odd lot. An amount of stock less than the established 100-share unit or 10-share unit of trading: from 1 to 99 shares for the great majority of issues, 1 to 9 for so-called inactive stocks. *Compare* Round lot.

Odd lot dealer. A broker who combines odd lots of securities from multiple buy orders or sell orders into round lots and executes transactions in those round lots.

Odd lot doctrine. Doctrine which permits finding of total disability where claimant is not altogether incapacitated for any kind of work but is nevertheless so handicapped that he will not be able to obtain regular employment in any well-known branch of the competitive labor market absent superhuman efforts, sympathetic friends or employers, a business boom, or temporary good luck. Under the "odd-lot doctrine", worker's compensation claimant will be considered to be totally disabled if it appears probable that claimant cannot sell his services in a competitive labor market.

Odd lot order. Order for less than 100 shares of stock.

Of. A term denoting that from which anything proceeds; indicating origin, source, descent, and the like; as, he is of noble blood. Associated with or connected with, usually in some causal relation, efficient, material, formal, or final. The word has been held equivalent to after; at, or belonging to; in possession of; manufactured by; residing at; from.

Of age. *See* Legal age; Majority.

Of counsel. A phrase commonly applied in practice to the counsel employed by a party in a cause, and particularly to one employed to assist in the preparation or management of an action, or its presentation on appeal, but who is not the principal attorney of record for the party. United States attorney is "of counsel" to United States in all criminal prosecutions brought within his district, for purposes of mandatory judicial disqualification statute requiring judge to disqualify himself in any case in which he has been of counsel.

Term is also used to refer to retired or semi-retired member of a law firm, or outside attorney that only does occasional or special legal work for the firm.

Of course. As a matter of right. Any action or step taken in the course of judicial proceedings which will be allowed by the court upon mere application, without any request or contest, or which may be effectually taken without having to apply to the court for leave to take such action; e.g. Fed.R. Civil P. 15(a) permits a party to amend his pleadings once as a matter "of course" at any time before a responsive pleading is served.

Off-balance-sheet financing. Financing not required to be reported on the firm's balance sheet.

Off-board. This term may refer to transactions over-the-counter in unlisted securities, or to a transaction involving listed shares which was not executed on a national securities exchange.

Offender. Commonly used in statutes to indicate person implicated in the commission of a crime and includes person guilty of a misdemeanor or traffic offense.

Offense. A felony or misdemeanor; a breach of the criminal laws; violation of law for which penalty is prescribed. The word "offense," while sometimes used in various senses, generally implies a felony or a misdemeanor infringing public as distinguished from mere private rights, and punishable under the criminal laws, though it may also include the violation of a criminal statute for which the remedy is merely a civil suit to recover the penalty. An act clearly prohibited by the lawful authority of the state, providing notice through published laws.

Criminal offenses may be classified into general categories as felonies and misdemeanors and as offenses against the person (*e.g.* murder, manslaughter), against habitation and occupancy (*e.g.* burglary, arson), against property (*e.g.* larceny),

against morality and decency (*e.g.* adultery), against public peace, against government (*e.g.* treason). *See e.g.* 18 U.S.C.A. § 1. Also, for sentencing purposes, offenses may be classified by letter grades, as *e.g.* class A, B, C, etc. felonies or misdemeanors. *See e.g.* 18 U.S.C.A. § 3559.

See also Anticipatory offense; Civil offense; Continuing offense; Crime; Degrees of crime; Delict; Felony; Graded offense; Included offense; Index offenses; Joint offense; Lesser included offense; Misdemeanor; Multiple offenses; Petty offense; Same offense; Tort.

Continuing offense. A transaction or a series of acts set on foot by a single impulse, and operated by an unintermittent force, no matter how long a time it may occupy. Conspiracy is an example of a continuing offense. *See e.g.* 18 U.S.C.A. § 3237; 21 U.S.C.A. § 848.

Criminal offense. Includes misdemeanors as well as felonies. It is an offense which subjects the offender to imprisonment, and/or fine. *See* Crime; Degrees of crime; Felony; Misdemeanor.

Joinder of offenses. *See* Joinder.

Same offense. As used in a provision against double jeopardy, the term means the same crime, not the same transaction, acts, circumstances, or situation.

Second offense. One committed after conviction for a first offense. It is the previous conviction, and not the indictment, which is the basis of the charge of a second offense.

Offensive. In the law relating to nuisances and similar matters, this term means noxious, causing annoyance, discomfort, or painful or disagreeable sensations. In ordinary use, the term is synonymous with "obnoxious" and means objectionable, disagreeable, displeasing and distasteful.

Offensive language. Language adapted to give offense; displeasing or annoying language. *See* Defamation; Libel; Slander.

Offensive weapon. As occasionally used in criminal law and statutes, a weapon primarily meant and adapted for attack and the infliction of injury, but practically the term includes anything that would come within the description of a "deadly" or "dangerous" weapon *(q.v.)*.

Offer, *v.* To bring to or before; to present for acceptance or rejection; to hold out or proffer; to make a proposal to; to exhibit something that may be taken or received or not. To attempt or endeavor; to make an effort to effect some object, as, to offer to bribe; in this sense used principally in criminal law.

In trial practice, to "offer" evidence is to state its nature and purport, or to recite what is expected to be proved by a given witness or document, and demand its admission. *See* Offer of proof.

Offer, *n.* A proposal to do a thing or pay an amount, usually accompanied by an expected acceptance, counter-offer, return promise or act. A manifestation of willingness to enter into a bargain, so made as to justify another person in understanding that his assent to that bargain is invited and will conclude it. Restatement, Second, Contracts, § 24. A promise; a commitment to do or refrain from doing some specified thing in the future. An act on the part of one person whereby that person gives to another the legal power of creating the obligation called contract. The offer creates a power of acceptance permitting the offeree by accepting the offer to transform the offeror's promise into a contractual obligation. *See also* Offer and acceptance.

An attempt; endeavor.

With respect to securities, the price at which a person is ready to sell. Opposed to bid, the price at which one is ready to buy. *See also* Offering.

See also Bid; Counteroffer; Firm offer; Issue; Offer and acceptance; Offer of proof; Promise; Proposal; Tender; Utter.

Irrevocable offer. One which may not be withdrawn after it has been communicated without the consent of the offeree.

Public exchange offer. A technique by which an aggressor corporation seeks to obtain control over a target corporation by offering to exchange a package of its securities for the target corporation's voting shares. Usually, a specified number of target corporation shares must be presented for exchange before the exchange will take place.

Offer and acceptance. In a bilateral contract, the two elements which constitute mutual assent, a requirement of the contract. In a unilateral contract, the acceptance is generally the act or performance of the offeree, though, in most jurisdictions, a promise to perform is inferred if the offeree commences the undertaking and the offeror attempts to revoke before the offeree has had an opportunity to complete the act. *See also* Offer; Parol evidence rule.

Offeree. In contracts, the person to whom an offer is made by the offeror.

Offering. An issue of securities offered for sale to the public or private group. Securities offerings are generally of two types: primary (proceeds going to the company for some lawful purpose) and secondary (where the funds go to a person other than the company; *i.e.,* selling stockholders). Primary offerings are also termed "new issues" as they involve the issuance of securities not previously offered and sold. *See also* Comprehensive due diligence investigation; Issue; Letter of comment; Negotiated offering; Prospectus; Red herring; Registration statement; Secondary distribution; Secondary offering; Tombstone ad; Underwrite.

Interstate offerings. A public securities offering made or which may be made to residents of more than one state. Such offerings are regulated by federal securities laws and regulations.

Intrastate offerings. A restricted public securities offering which is made by an issuer organized under the laws of a state, doing its principal business in such state, and offered solely to bona fide residents of such state with substantially all of the proceeds of the offering remaining in the state.

Private offerings. An offering made to a limited number of persons, who are so well-informed concerning the affairs of a company, through the possession of information which would be found in a registration statement, that they do not require the protection afforded by the disclosure provisions of the Securities Act of 1933. Sale of unregistered stock which is exempt from securities laws. *See also* Private offering.

Public offerings. The offering of securities at random and in general to anyone who will buy, and whether solicited or unsolicited. Sale of stock to the public in contrast to a "private" offering or placement. Public offerings are generally regulated by federal and state laws and regulations. *See also* Underwrite.

Undigested offering. Newly issued shares and bonds that remain undistributed because there is insufficient public demand at the offer price. *See also* Underwrite.

Offering circular. An offering circular is required to be filed with the S.E.C. and distributed with any securities offerings. The content of such is similar to the prospectus *(q.v.)* and is governed by S.E.C. rules and regulations. *See also* Prospectus.

Offering memorandum. A document prepared to outline the terms of securities to be offered in a private placement. *See also* Offering.

Offering price. Per share price at which new or secondary offering of stock is sold.

Offering statement. *See* Offering circular.

Offer of compromise. An offer to settle a dispute or difference amicably for the purpose of avoiding a lawsuit and without admitting liability. A tender or offer to settle or compromise a claim. The fact that such offer has been made is generally not admissible at the trial of the action as an admission of liability. See Fed.Evid. Rule 408.

Offer of judgment. *See* Judgment.

Offer of proof. At a trial or hearing, when an objection to a question has been sustained, the party aggrieved by the ruling may indicate for the record (out of the presence of the jury) the answer which would have been given if the question had not been excluded. The appellate court is then in a position to determine from the record the correctness of the ruling and the prejudice in its exclusion, if any. See Fed.Evid.Rule 103(a)(2).

Offeror. In contracts, the party who makes the offer and looks for acceptance from the offeree.

Office. A right, and correspondent duty, to exercise a public trust. A public charge or employment. An employment on behalf of the government in any station or public trust, not merely transient, occasional, or incidental. The most frequent occasions to use the word arise with reference to a duty and power conferred on an individual by the government; and, when this is the connection, "public office" is a usual and more discriminating expression. But a power and duty may exist without immediate grant from government, and may be properly called an "office;" as the office of executor. Here the individual acts towards legatees in performance of a duty, and in exercise of a power not derived from their consent, but devolved on him by an authority which *quoad hoc* is superior.

An "assigned duty" or "function." Synonyms are "post", "appointment", "situation", "place", "position", and "office" commonly suggests a position of (especially public) trust or authority. Also right to exercise a public function or employment, and to take the fees and emoluments belonging to it. A public charge or employment, and he who performs the duties of the office is an officer. Although an office is an employment, it does not follow that every employment is an office. A man may be employed under a contract, express or implied, to do an act, or to perform a service, without becoming an officer. But, if the duty be a continuing one, which is defined by rule prescribed by the government, which an individual is appointed by the government to perform, who enters upon the duties appertain to his status, without any contract defining them, it seems very difficult to distinguish such a charge or employment from an office, or the person who performs the duty from an officer. In the constitutional sense, the term implies an authority to exercise some portion of the sovereign power, either in making, executing, or administering the laws.

A place for the regular transaction of business or performance of a particular service.

As to various *particular offices, see* Home office; Land offices; Public office, etc.

County office. Public office filled by the electorate of the entire county.

Judicial office. See Judicial.

Lucrative office. See Lucrative.

Ministerial office. One which gives the officer little or no discretion as to the matter to be done, and requires him to obey mandates of a superior. It is a general rule that a judicial office cannot be exercised by a deputy, while a ministerial office may.

Office audit. An audit by the Internal Revenue Service of a taxpayer's return which is conducted in the agent's office. It may be distinguished from a correspondence audit or a field audit. *See also* Audit.

Office copy. A copy or transcript of a deed or record or any filed document, made by the officer having it in custody or under his sanction, and by him sealed or certified.

Office grant. A designation of a conveyance made by some officer of the law to effect certain purposes, where the owner is either unwilling or unable to execute the requisite deeds to pass the title; such, for example, as a tax-deed.

Office hours. That portion of the day during which offices are usually open for the transaction of business.

Office of honor. See Honor.

Principal office. The principal office of a corporation is its headquarters, or the place where the chief or principal affairs and business of the corporation are transacted. Usually it is the office where the company's books are kept, where its meetings of stockholders are held, and where the directors, trustees, or managers assemble to discuss and transact the important general business of the company; but no one of these circumstances is a controlling test. Synonymous with "principal place of business," being the place where the principal affairs of a corporation are transacted.

The office (in or out of the state of incorporation) so designated in the annual report where the principal executive offices of a domestic or foreign corporation are located. Rev.Model Bus. Corp.Act, § 1.40.

Public office. The right, authority, and duty created and conferred by law, by which for a given period, either fixed by law or enduring at the pleasure of the creating power, an individual is invested with some portion of the sovereign functions of government for the benefit of the public. An agency for the state, the duties of which involve in their performance the exercise of some portion of the sovereign power, either great or small.

State office. Public offices to be filled by the electorate of the entire state.

Office-block ballot. A form of ballot in which the names of candidates, with or without party designations, are grouped under the offices for which they are contesting; also called "Massachusetts" ballot.

Office in home expense. In taxation, employment and business-related expenses attributable to use of one's residence for his or her business.

Office of Personnel Management. Created in 1978, the Office of Personnel Management is responsible for the nationwide recruiting and examining of applicants for positions in the Federal civil service. The OPM also administers the Qualifications Review Board examining process for career Senior Executive Service appointments and examines for administrative law judges. Personnel investigations are used in support of the selection and appointment processes.

Office of Thrift Supervision. An office in the Treasury Department charged with providing for the examination, safe and sound operation, and regulation of savings associations.

Officer. Person holding office of trust, command or authority in corporation, government, armed services, or other institution or organization.

In corporations, a person charged with important functions of management such as president, vice president, treasurer, etc.

In determining whether one is an "officer" or "employee," important tests are the tenure by which a position is held, whether its duration is defined by the statute or ordinance creating it, or whether it is temporary or transient or for a time fixed only by agreement; whether it is created by an appointment or election, or merely by a contract of employment by which the rights of the parties are regulated; whether the compensation is by a salary or fees fixed by law, or by a sum agreed upon by the contract of hiring.

For definitions of the various classes and kinds of officers, see the titles Commissioned office; Constitutional; Corporate; Executive; Fiscal; Judicial; Legislative; Municipal; Naval; Non-commissioned; Peace; Public; State; Subordinate.

Civil officer. The word "civil," as regards civil officers, is commonly used to distinguish those officers who are in public service but not of the military. Hence, any officer of the United States who holds his appointment under the national government, whether his duties are executive or judicial, in the highest or the lowest departments of the government, with the exception of officers of the armed services.

Military officer. Commissioned officer in armed services. Officer who has command in armed forces.

Officer de facto. As distinguished from an officer de jure; this is the designation of one who is in the actual possession and administration of the office, under some colorable or apparent authority, although his title to the same, whether by election or appointment, is in reality invalid or at least formally questioned. One who actually assumes and exercises duties of public office under color of known and authorized appointment or election, but who has failed to comply with all requirements of law prescribed as precedent to performance of duties of the office.

Officer de jure. One who is in all respects legally appointed and qualified to exercise the office. One who is clothed with the full legal right and title to the office; he is one who has been legally elected or appointed to an office, and who has qualified himself to exercise the duties thereof according to the mode prescribed by law.

Officer of justice. A general name applicable to all persons connected with the administration of the judicial department of government, but commonly used only of the class of officers whose duty is to serve the process of the courts, such as sheriffs, constables, bailiffs, marshals, sequestrators, etc.

Officer of the United States. An officer nominated by the President and confirmed by the senate or one who is appointed under an act of congress, by the President alone, a court of law, or a head of a department. *See also* United States officer.

Public officer. An officer of a public corporation; that is, one holding office under the government of a municipality, state, or nation. One occupying a public office created by law. One of necessary characteristics of "public officer" is that he performs public function for public benefit and in so doing he be vested with exercise of some sovereign power of state.

Warrant officer. Officer of armed forces, with rank between commissioned and non-commissioned officer, holding rank by virtue of warrant.

Official, *n.* An officer; a person invested with the authority of an office. *See also* Officer.

Official, *adj.* Pertaining to an office; invested with the character of an officer; proceeding from, sanctioned by, or done by, an officer. Authorized act.

As to *official* Bond; Liquidator; Logbook; Newspaper; Oath; Use, see those titles.

Official act. One done by an officer in his official capacity under color and by virtue of his office. Authorized act.

Official misconduct. Any unlawful behavior by a public officer in relation to the duties of his office, willful in its character, including any willful or corrupt failure, refusal, or neglect of an officer to perform any duty enjoined on him by law. *See* Malfeasance; Misfeasance.

Official bond. Type of fidelity bond required to be posted by certain public officials to indemnify the government, municipality or court in the event of defalcation by the officer.

Official Gazette. Weekly publication of U.S. Patent and Trademark Office containing patent and trademark notices and applications, as well as mark registrations.

Official immunity doctrine. Doctrine of "official immunity" provides that government officials enjoy an absolute privilege from civil liability should the activity in question fall within the scope of their authority and if the action undertaken requires the exercise of discretion, and this rule of immunity is not limited to the highest executive officers of the government. *See* Sovereign immunity.

Official map. In zoning and land use, the authorized map for the determination of proper land use in the city or town, showing the zones and areas and their authorized uses.

Official record. Records kept in the performance of official duty by an officer even if not specifically required by statute.

Fed.Evid.R. 803(8) provides, without regard to availability of the declarant, a hearsay exception for: "Records, reports, statements, or data compilations, in any form, of public offices or agencies . . . ." Proof of official records at trial is governed by Fed.R.Civil P. 44 and Fed.Evid.R. 1005. Admissibility of official records at administrative proceedings is governed by the Official Records Act *(q.v.)*.

Official Records Act. Federal statute applicable to cases in which the Federal Rules of Evidence do not apply *(i.e.* administrative proceedings) providing that books and records of account and minutes of any department or agency of the U.S. shall be admissible to prove the act or transaction as a memorandum of which it was made or kept. Properly authenticated copies are equally admissible with the originals. 28 U.S.C.A. § 1733(a).

Official reports *or* **reporters.** Publication of court decisions as directed by statute; *e.g.* United States Supreme Court Reports. 28 U.S.C.A. § 411. *See* Reports *or* reporters.

Officialty. The court or jurisdiction of which an official is head.

Of force. In force; in effect; extant; not obsolete; existing as a binding or obligatory power.

Offset. A deduction; a counterclaim; a contrary claim or demand by which a given claim may be lessened or canceled. A claim that serves to counterbalance or to compensate for another claim. *See also* Counterclaim; Recoupment; Setoff.

Type of entry in bookkeeping which counters the effect of a prior entry. *See* Offset account.

Offset account. In bookkeeping, a ledger account which has a corresponding account to be washed against it when the books are closed.

Offshore transactions. Refers to transactions in locations outside the United States, *e.g.* 31 CFR § 540.401.

Offspring. Children; issue.

Of grace. This phrase had its origin in an age when kings dispensed their royal favors at the hands of chancellors. A term applied to any permission or license granted to a party in the course of a judicial proceeding which is not claimable as a matter of course or of right, but is allowed by the favor or indulgence of the court. *See* Act of grace; Grace period.

Of record. Recorded; entered on the records; existing and remaining in or upon the appropriate records; *e.g.* a mortgage to be "of record" must normally be recorded in the county in which it is properly and legally recordable for purpose of constructive notice. *See also* Attorney *(Attorney of record)*; Court *(Court of record)*; Record.

Of right. As a matter of course. *See* Of course; Right.

Of the blood. A technical legal phrase meaning to be descended from the person referred to or from the same common stock and from a common ancestor. *See* Blood relations; Descent; Next of kin.

Oil and gas lease. Grant of right to extract oil and/or gas from land.

O.K. A conventional symbol often used in commercial practice and occasionally in indorsements on legal documents, signifying "correct," "approved," "accepted," "satisfactory," or "assented to." *See* Okay.

Okay. The colloquial expression means correct, all right, to approve, and is of such common usage that it immediately conveys to the mind of person to whom it is addressed that a proposition submitted is agreed to. *See also* O.K.

Old Age, Survivors' and Disability Insurance. A system established under the Federal Social Security Act providing for retirement, disability, widows', widowers', and dependent benefits. Such program is funded by employer, employee and self-employed contributions. 42 U.S.C.A. § 301 et seq. *See* Social Security Administration.

Older Workers Benefits Protection Act. Enacted as an amendment to the federal Age Discrimination Employment Act, 29 U.S.C.A. §§ 621 et seq., this Act requires a company to give benefits to older workers *(i.e.,* those over 40) that cost at least as much as the benefits given to younger workers. *See also* Age discrimination act.

Oligarchy /ólǝgàrkiy/. A form of government wherein the administration of affairs is lodged in the hands of a few persons.

Oligopoly /òləgópəliy/. Economic condition where only a few companies sell substantially similar or standardized products. Oligopoly markets often exhibit the lack of competition, high prices and low output of monopoly markets. *See also* Conscientious parallelism; Monopoly.

Olograph /óləgræf/. An instrument (*e.g.*, a will) wholly written by the person from whom it emanates. *See* Holograph.

Ombudsman /ómbədzmən/. An official or semi official office or person to which people may come with grievances connected with the government. The ombudsman stands between, and represents, the citizen before the government.

Omission. The neglect to perform what the law requires. The intentional or unintentional failure to act which may or may not impose criminal liability depending upon the existence, vel non, of a duty to act under the circumstances. *See also* Neglect.

Omittance /əmítəns/. Forbearance; omission.

Omnibus bill /ómnəbəs bíl/. A legislative bill including in one act various separate and distinct matters, and frequently one joining a number of different subjects in one measure in such a way as to compel the executive authority to accept provisions which he does not approve or else defeat the whole enactment.

In equity pleading, a bill embracing the whole of a complex subject-matter by uniting all parties in interest having adverse or conflicting claims, thereby avoiding circuity or multiplicity of action.

Omnibus clause. Clause in a will or decree of distribution passing all property not specifically mentioned or known of at the time.

Such a clause in automotive liability policy extends coverage thereunder to person using automobile owned by named insured with express or implied permission of the latter.

Omnibus hearing. Hearing at which there are many unrelated matters on the agenda for discussion and consideration.

On. Upon; as soon as; near to; along; along side of; adjacent to; contiguous to; at the time of; following upon; in; during; at or in contact with upper surface of a thing.

On account. Sale on credit. In part payment; in partial satisfaction of an account. The phrase is usually contrasted with "in full." *See also* Account *(Open account)*.

On account of whom it may concern. When a policy of insurance expresses that the insurance is made "on account of whom it may concern," it will cover all persons having an insurable interest in the subject-matter at the date of the policy and who were then contemplated by the party procuring the insurance.

On all fours. A judicial decision exactly in point with another as to result, facts, or both. A phrase used to express the idea that a particular case in litigation is in all points similar to another. The one is said to be on all fours with the other when the facts are similar and the same questions of law are involved. *See* Stare decisis.

On call. There is no legal difference between an obligation payable "when demanded" or "on demand" and one payable "on call" or "at any time called for." In each case the debt is payable on demand. *See* On demand.

Once in jeopardy. A phrase used to express the condition of a person charged with crime, who has once already, by legal proceedings, been put in danger of conviction and punishment for the same offense. *See also* Jeopardy.

On default. In case of default; upon failure of stipulated action or performance; upon the occurrence of a failure, omission, or neglect of duty. *See* Default.

On demand. Note payable on request. If no due date is stated in note, such is payable on demand. Instruments payable "on demand" include those payable at sight or on presentation and those in which no time for payment is stated. U.C.C. § 3–108. *See also* Demand.

One person, one vote. Expression used to describe state legislative districting which gives equal legislative representation to all citizens of all places. The rule was established in Reynolds v. Sims, 377 U.S. 533, 568, 84 S.Ct. 1362, 1385, 12 L.Ed.2d 506, which required that the seats in both houses of a bicameral state legislature be apportioned on a population basis. *See also* Apportionment; Reapportionment.

Onerous /ównərəs/. A contract, lease, share, or other right is said to be "onerous" when the obligations attaching to it unreasonably counterbalance or exceed the advantage to be derived from it, either absolutely or with reference to the particular possessor. Unreasonably burdensome or one-sided. *See* Unconscionability.

Onerous contract. *See* Adhesion contract; Contract; Unconscionability.

Onerous gift. A gift made subject to certain charges imposed by the donor on the donee.

Onerous title. A title acquired by the giving of a valuable consideration, as the payment of money or rendition of services or the performance of conditions or assumption or discharge of liens or charges.

One sided. *See* Adhesion contract; Unconscionability.

On file. Filed; entered or placed upon the files; existing and remaining upon or among the proper files. *See also* Of record.

Only. Solely; merely; for no other purpose; at no other time; in no otherwise; along; of or by itself; without anything more; exclusive; nothing else or more.

Onomastic /ònəmǽstək/. A term applied to the signature of an instrument, the body of which is in a different handwriting from that of the signature.

On or about. A phrase used in reciting the date of an occurrence or conveyance, or the location of it to escape the necessity of being bound by the statement of an exact date, or place; approximately; about; without substantial variance from; near. For purpose of pleading, term "on or about," with respect to specified date, means generally in time around date specified.

On or about the person. As used in statutes making it an offense to carry a weapon "on or about" the person, it is generally held that the word "on" means connected with or attached to, and that "about" is a comprehensive term having a broader meaning than "on," and conveying the idea of being nearby, in close proximity, within immediate reach, or conveniently accessible. *See also* On the person.

On or before. These words, inserted in a stipulation to do an act or pay money, entitle the party stipulating to perform at any time before the day; and upon performance, or tender and refusal, he is immediately vested with all the rights which would have attached if performance were made on the day.

On sale. In context of patent law, an invention may be placed "on sale" in two ways: first, it may be placed on sale by an actual and completed transaction and, alternatively, an invention is placed "on sale" whenever its inventor or his company engages in any activity to sell the invention, including making an offer for sale; under the first situation, an inventor must construct a physical specimen of his invention and deliver it to a third party who accepts it.

Onset date. A term of art used by the Social Security Administration that marks the commencement of a period of disability for purposes of disability payments.

On the brief. Phrase which refers to the names of all persons who participated in writing the brief, whether or not such persons are attorneys of record.

On the merits. *See* Judgment *(Merits, judgment on)*; Merits.

On the person. In common parlance, when it is said that someone has an article on his person, it means that it is either in contact with his person or is carried in his clothing. *See also* On or about the person.

Onus /ównəs/. Lat. A burden or load; a weight. Burden of responsibility or proof. The lading, burden, or cargo of a vessel. A charge; an incumbrance. *Cum onere (q.v.)*, with the incumbrance.

OPEC. Organization of Petroleum Exporting Countries.

Open, *v.* To render accessible, visible, or available; to submit or subject to examination, inquiry, or review, by the removal of restrictions or impediments.

Open a case. In practice, to open a case is to begin it; to make an initiatory explanation (*i.e.* opening statement) of its features to the court, jury, referee, etc., by outlining the nature of the occurrence or transaction on which it is founded, the questions involved, and the character and general course of the evidence to be adduced. *See also* Opening statement of counsel.

Open a judgment. To lift or relax the bar of finality and conclusiveness which it imposes so as to permit a re-examination of the merits of the action in which it was rendered. This is done at the instance of a party showing good cause why the execution of the judgment would be inequitable. It so far annuls the judgment as to prevent its enforcement until the final determination upon it. Fed.R.Civil P. 60 governs relief from judgment because of mistakes, inadvertence, excusable neglect, newly discovered evidence, fraud, etc.

Open the door. If one party to litigation puts in evidence part of document or correspondence or conversation which is detrimental to the opposing party, the latter may introduce balance of document, correspondence or conversation in order to explain or rebut adverse inferences which might arise from the fragmentary or incomplete character of evidence introduced by his adversary. *See also* Fed.Evid. R. 106.

Open, *adj.* Patent; visible; apparent; notorious; exposed to public view; not clandestine; not closed, settled, fixed, or terminated.

As an element of adverse possession, *see* Open and notorious.

As to *open* Corporation; Entry; Insolvency; Lewdness; Policy; Possession; Verdict, see those titles.

Open account. An unpaid or unsettled account; an account with a balance which has not been ascertained, which is kept open in anticipation of future transactions. Type of credit extended by a seller to buyer which permits buyer to make purchases without a note or security and it is based on an evaluation of the buyer's credit. A contractual obligation which may be modified by subsequent agreement of the parties, either by expressed assent or implied from the conduct of the parties, provided the agreement changing the contractual obligation is based upon independent consideration. *See also* Open credit; Open-end credit plan.

Open and notorious. Acts on the land of another sufficient to alert the owner of a claim to his land which may ripen into title under adverse possession. *See also* Adverse possession; Notorious possession.

Behavior which is "open and notorious" for purposes of statute prohibiting adultery is behavior which is prominent, conspicuous and generally known and recognized by the public. The prohibition of open and notorious adultery is meant to protect the public from conduct which disturbs the peace, tends to promote breaches of the peace, and openly flouts accepted standards of morality in the community.

Open bid. An offer to perform a contract, generally of a construction nature, in which the bidder reserves the right to reduce his bid to compete with a lower bid.

Open bulk. In the mass; exposed to view; not tied or sealed up.

Open court. Common law requires a trial in open court; "open court" means a court to which the public have a right to be admitted. This term may mean either a court which has been formally convened and declared open for the transaction of its proper judicial business, or a court which is freely open to spectators. For accused's right to an open/public trial, *see* Public trial. *See also e.g.* Fed.R.Crim.P. 10 (arraignment), R. 26 (testimony of witnesses).

Open credit. Line of credit extended up to a certain amount by a merchant, bank or supplier so as to permit borrowings or purchases to such amount without posting security or reestablishing credit limit. *See also* Open account; Open-end credit plan.

Open-end contract. Contract which permits buyer to make purchases over a period of time without change in the price or terms by the seller.

Open-end credit plan. Credit extended pursuant to a plan providing for and contemplating continuing or repetitive transactions on credit. For purposes of Truth in Lending Act, "open end credit plan" is one in which credit terms are initially established with the opening of the account, but no fixed amount of debt is incurred at that time with purchases made from time to time instead being added to the outstanding balance in the account; each new purchase represents an additional extension of credit. Examples are credit cards and "revolving charges" where one can pay a part of what he owes each month on several different purchases.

Open-end investment company. A mutual fund which will buy back its shares at net asset value

and which is continuously offering to sell new shares to the public. *See* Mutual fund.

Open-end investment trust. Type of trust in which the trustees are permitted to make on-going investments for its portfolio.

Open-end lease. Lease with no fixed termination date.

Open-end mortgage. A mortgage that allows the borrowing of additional sums, usually providing that at least the stated ratio of assets to the debt must be maintained. A mortgage which provides for future advances on the given mortgage and increases the amount of the existing mortgage.

Open-end transaction. Generic term to describe a loose transaction in which the parties may add to or amend the original bargain or agreement. It may include an open-end mortgage or open-end credit arrangement.

Open fields doctrine. This doctrine permits police officers to enter and search a field without a warrant. The term "open fields" may include any unoccupied or undeveloped area outside of the curtilage.

Opening statement of counsel. Outline or summary of nature of case and of anticipated proof presented by attorney to jury at start of trial, before any evidence is submitted. Its purpose is to advise the jury of facts relied upon and of issues involved, and to give jury a general picture of the facts and the situations so that jury will be able to understand the evidence. Opening statement in criminal case is outline of facts which prosecution in good faith expects to prove.

Open letter of credit. An unrestricted letter of credit which will be paid on a simple draft without the need of documentary title. *See also* Letter of credit.

Open listing. A type of real estate listing contract whereby any agent who has a right to participate in the open listing is entitled to a commission if he produces the sale. *See also* Listing.

Open market purchase. The purchase of securities in one or more transactions arranged in the open market.

Open mortgage clause. *See* Union mortgage clause.

Open order. An order to buy securities or commodities at or below or above a certain price and such order remains viable until canceled by the customer.

Open price term. The parties if they so intend can conclude a contract for sale even though the price is not settled. In such a case the price is a reasonable price at the time for delivery if: (a) nothing is said as to price; or (b) the price is left to be agreed by the parties and they fail to agree;

or (c) the price is to be fixed in terms of some agreed market or other standard as set or recorded by a third person or agency and it is not so set or recorded. U.C.C. § 2–305.

Open sea. The expanse and mass of any great body of water, as distinguished from its margin or coast, its harbors, bays, creeks, inlets.

Open possession. *See* Notorious possession; Open and notorious.

Open season. That portion of the year wherein the laws for the preservation of game and fish permit the killing of a particular species of game or the taking of a particular variety of fish.

Open shop. A business in which union and non-union workers are employed indiscriminately. Business in which union membership is not a condition of securing or maintaining employment. *See* Right to work laws. *Contrast* Closed shop.

Open space. Any parcel or area of land or water essentially unimproved and set aside, dedicated, designated or reserved for public or private use or enjoyment or for the use and enjoyment of owners and occupants of land adjoining or neighboring such open spaces.

Common open space. An open space area within or related to a site designated as a development and designed and intended for the use or enjoyment of residents and owners of the development. Common open space may contain such complementary structures and improvements as are necessary and appropriate for the use or enjoyment of residents and owners of the development.

Open trial. *See* Public trial.

Open union. A labor union without restrictive membership provisions. *See also* Open shop.

Operate. To perform a function, or operation, or produce an effect. *See* Operation.

Operating activities. Company activities primarily related to the production and sale of goods and services, and that enter into the determination of net income.

Operating budget. A collection of individual budgets that combine to form a part of a firm's integrated business plan, usually for the next year. It is normally composed of a *sales budget* and a *production budget.*

Operating cycle. The period of time it takes a firm to buy merchandise inventory, sell the inventory, and collect the related receivables.

Operating expenses. Those expenses required to keep the business running, *e.g.* rent, electricity, heat. Expenses incurred in the course of ordinary activities of an entity.

Operating lease. A lease agreement, usually cancellable, which provides the lessee with the use of an asset for a period of time which is considerably shorter than the useful life of the asset. Unlike a capital lease, the lessee in an operating lease does not assume the economic risks of ownership, and the lessor generally provides all of the maintenance and services on the leased asset.

Operating leverage. The proportionate relationship between a company's variable and fixed costs.

Operating margin. Net operating income divided by sales for the period.

Operating profit. Deducting the cost of goods sold from sales gives gross profit. Deducting the operating expense (overhead) from the gross profit gives the operating profit.

Operating profit margin. The ratio of operating income to net sales. *See also* Profit margin.

Operating risk. Risk that is created by operating leverage. Also called business risk.

Operation. Exertion of power; the process of operating or mode of action; an effect brought about in accordance with a definite plan; action; activity. In surgical practice, the term may be defined as an act or succession of acts performed upon the body of a patient, for his relief or restoration to normal conditions, by the use of surgical instruments as distinguished from therapeutic treatment by the administration of drugs or other remedial agencies.

Operation of law. This term expresses the manner in which rights, and sometimes liabilities, devolve upon a person by the mere application to the particular transaction of the established rules of law, without the act or co-operation of the party himself.

Operative part. That part of a conveyance, or of any instrument intended for the creation or transference of rights, by which the main object of the instrument is carried into effect. It is distinguished from introductory matter, recitals, formal conclusion, etc.

Operative words. In a deed or lease, such are the words which effect the transaction intended to be consummated by the instrument.

Opiate. Any substance having an addiction-forming or addiction-sustaining liability similar to morphine or being capable of conversion into a drug having addiction-forming or addiction-sustaining liability.

OPIC. Overseas Private Investment Corporation.

Opinion. A document prepared by an attorney for his client, embodying his understanding of the law as applicable to a state of facts submitted to him for that purpose; *e.g.* an opinion of an attorney as to the marketability of a land title as determined from a review of the abstract of title and other public records.

The statement by a judge or court of the decision reached in regard to a cause tried or argued before them, expounding the law as applied to the case, and detailing the reasons upon which the judgment is based.

An expression of the reasons why a certain decision (the judgment) was reached in a case. A *majority* opinion is usually written by one judge and represents the principles of law which a majority of his colleagues on the court deem operative in a given decision; it has more precedential value than any of the following. A *separate opinion* may be written by one or more judges in which he or they concur in or dissent from the majority opinion. A *concurring opinion* agrees with the result reached by the majority, but disagrees with the precise reasoning leading to that result. A *dissenting or minority opinion* disagrees with the result reached by the majority and thus disagrees with the reasoning and/or the principles of law used by the majority in deciding the case. A *plurality opinion* is agreed to by less than a majority as to the reasoning of the decision, but is agreed to by a majority as to the result. A *per curiam opinion* is an opinion "by the court" which expresses its decision in the case but whose author is not identified. A *memorandum opinion* is a holding of the whole court in which the opinion is very concise.

In *accounting*, a document prepared by a certified public accountant regarding the audited financial statements of an entity. There are four types of opinions:

Unqualified: The financial statements are presented fairly in accordance with generally accepted accounting principles (GAAP) and are presented in a manner consistent with the prior year. An unqualified opinion is considered a clean opinion.

Qualified: The financial statements are presented fairly in accordance with GAAP applied on a basis consistent with the prior year, "except for" a particular transaction, or "subject to" a certain event.

Disclaimer: The CPA is unable to render an opinion on the financial statements due to insufficient competent evidential matter.

Adverse: The financial statements are not presented fairly in conformity with GAAP, or do not present fairly the financial position, results of operation, and changes in the financial position of the entity. An adverse opinion is uncommon and generally results when the CPA is unable to convince the client to present the financial statements fairly and in conformity with GAAP. *See also* Adverse opinion.

See also Audit *(Audit opinion).*

See also Advisory opinion; Letter ruling; Majority opinion; Opinion evidence *or* testimony; Plurality; Slip opinion; Title opinion; Unqualified opinion.

Opinion evidence *or* testimony. Evidence of what the witness thinks, believes, or infers in regard to facts in dispute, as distinguished from his personal knowledge of the facts themselves. The rules of evidence ordinarily do not permit witnesses to testify as to opinions or conclusions. An exception to this rule exists as to "expert witnesses". Witnesses who, by education and experience, have become expert in some art, science, profession, or calling, may state their opinions as to relevant and material matter, in which they profess to be expert, and may also state their reasons for the opinion.

By expert witness. If scientific, technical, or other specialized knowledge will assist the trier of fact to understand the evidence or to determine a fact in issue, a witness qualified as an expert by knowledge, skill, experience, training, or education, may testify thereto in the form of an opinion or otherwise. Fed.Evid. Rule 702. *See also* Expert testimony; Expert witness.

By lay witness. If the witness is not testifying as an expert, his testimony in the form of opinions or inferences is limited to those opinions or inferences which are (a) rationally based on the perception of the witness and (b) helpful to a clear understanding of his testimony or the determination of a fact in issue. Fed.Evid. Rule 701.

Opposite party. Within statutes providing that opposite party shall be incompetent to testify as to matters equally within knowledge of deceased is one whose personal and financial interests, either immediate or remote, are antagonistic to like interests of protected party. *See* Parties.

Opposition. Act of opposing or resisting; antagonism; state of being opposite or opposed; antithesis. Also, a position confronting another or placing in contrast; that which is or furnishes an obstacle to some result. Political party opposed to ministry or administration; or might be construed to include peaceful and orderly opposition to government.

Oppression. The misdemeanor committed by a public officer, who under color of his office, wrongfully inflicts upon any person any bodily harm, imprisonment, or other injury. An act of cruelty, severity, unlawful exaction, or excessive use of authority. An act of subjecting to cruel and unjust hardship; an act of domination.

Oppression which justifies award of punitive damages means act of cruelty, severity, unlawful exaction, or excessive use of authority and results from acts done in manner which violates right of another person with unnecessary harshness or severity as by misuse or abuse of authority or power.

See Coercion; Cruelty; Threat.

Oppressor. A public officer who unlawfully uses his authority by way of oppression *(q.v.)*.

Option. Right of election to exercise a privilege. Contract made for consideration to keep an offer open for prescribed period. A right, which acts as a continuing offer, given for consideration, to purchase or lease property at an agreed upon price and terms, within a specified time. An option is an agreement which gives the optionee the power to accept an offer for a limited time. An option to purchase or to sell is not a contract to purchase or sell, as optionee has the right to accept or to reject the offer, in accordance with its terms, and is not bound.

An option contract is a promise which meets the requirements for the formation of a contract and limits the promisor's power to revoke an offer. Restatement, Second, Contracts, § 25.

A privilege existing in one person, for which he has paid money, which gives him the right to *buy* certain commodities or certain specified securities from another person, if he chooses, at any time within an agreed period, at a fixed price, or to *sell* such commodities or securities to such other person at an agreed price and time. If the option gives the choice of buying or not buying, it is denominated a "call." If it gives the choice of selling or not, it is called a "put." If it is a combination of both these, and gives the privilege of *either* buying or selling or not, it is called a "straddle" or a "spread eagle."

The sale or exchange of an option to buy or sell property results in capital gain or loss if the property is a capital asset.

See also Call; Cash value option; In-the-money; Local option; Option to purchase; Put; Striking price.

Commodity futures option. The right—but not the obligation—to buy or sell a futures contract at a specified price within a fixed period, say, three, six, nine months or longer. The option buyer pays a premium to the dealer for this right, plus the usual commission and nothing else. The option buyer does not have to be concerned about margin calls. All he can lose is the premium paid and commission.

Commodity option. A right that is purchased by the option holder entitling him either to buy ("call option") from or to sell ("put option") at a stated price and within a stated time an underlying physical commodity (such as a specific quantity of gold, a train carload of coffee, etc.), or a commodity futures contract relating to that commodity. The price paid for the option right is referred to as the "premium," and the price at which the option purchaser is entitled to buy or sell the underlying commodity for futures contract is referred to as the "striking price." "Exercise" is the decision of an option holder to require

performance by the grantor of his obligation with respect to the underlying commodity or futures contract. The period during which an option may be exercised is specified in the contract. The "exercise date" or "expiration date" is the final day on which the option holder may exercise the option.

Foreign currency option. An option that conveys the right to buy (in the case of a call option) or sell (put option) a specified amount of a specified foreign currency at a specified price within a specified time period.

Index option. A type of security in which the holder has the right to buy or sell, for a specified price at a specified future date, a theoretical interest in stocks making up the index. The option is exercised in cash, in an amount equal to the difference between the closing level of the index on the exercise date and the exercise price of the option, multiplied by the index "multiplier."

Naked options. Options sold by investors granting others the right to buy stock from them even though they own no stock to back up those commitments.

Option premium. The consideration paid to keep a contractual offer to buy or sell open for a specified period of time.

Stock option. The right to buy stock in the future at a price fixed in advance. *See also* Stock.

Incentive stock option. See Qualified stock option, below.

Non-qualified stock option. Stock option which does not meet the qualifications of a restricted stock option. *See Restricted stock option, below.*

Qualified stock option. An option to purchase shares provided to an employee of the corporation under terms that qualify the option for special tax treatment under the Internal Revenue Code. I.R.C. § 421 et seq.

Restricted stock option. A right granted to an employee prior to 1964 which allows such an employee to buy stock at a fixed price established in advance. The options are restricted with respect to the option price, time of exercise, amount owned by the optionee, non-transferability, and minimum holding period. Restricted stock options were replaced by Qualified Stock Options in 1964, and Incentive Stock Options in 1981. I.R.C. § 424.

Time value of an option. The difference between the market value of an option and its exercise value.

Optionee. One who receives an option.

Optionholder. The person in the long position side of an option transaction; the owner.

Option spread. In securities trading, the difference between the option price and the fair market value of the stock at the time of exercise of the stock option.

Option to purchase. A bilateral contract in which one party is given the right to buy the property within a period of time for a consideration paid to the seller. A right acquired by contract to accept or reject a present offer within a limited or reasonable time and is simply a contract by which the owner of property agrees with another person that he shall have the right to buy his property at a fixed price within a certain time. *See also* Option.

Optionwriter. The person in the short position side of an option transaction; the person with the obligation; the seller of the option.

Opus /ówpəs/. Lat. Work; labor; the product of work or labor.

Or, *conj.* A disjunctive particle used to express an alternative or to give a choice of one among two or more things. It is also used to clarify what has already been said, and in such cases, means "in other words," "to-wit," or "that is to say." The word "or" is to be used as a function word to indicate an alternative between different or unlike things. In some usages, the word "or" creates a multiple rather than an alternative obligation; where necessary in interpreting an instrument, "or" may be construed to mean "and."

Oral. Uttered by the mouth or in words; spoken, not written.

Oral argument. Presentation of reasons for affirmance, reversal, modification, etc. by appellee and appellant before appellate court; generally limited in time by court rule; *e.g.* Fed.R.App.P. 34.

Statement before court in support of, or in objection to, motion or other legal relief sought.

Oral confession. Statement given orally by defendant in which he admits the commission of the crime. Its admissibility in evidence is dependent upon its voluntariness, the condition of the defendant at the time of the confession, the length of time during which the defendant was held by the police before being brought before a magistrate and other factors. Federal courts generally hold that the burden of establishing the constitutional admissibility of a confession rests upon the prosecution. *See also* Confession; Miranda Rule; Self incrimination.

Oral contract. One which is partly in writing and partly depends on spoken words, or none of which is in writing; one which, so far as it has been reduced to writing, is incomplete or expresses only a part of what is intended, but is completed by spoken words; or one which, originally written, has afterwards been changed orally. *See also* Contract (*Parol contract*).

Oral evidence. Evidence given by word of mouth; the oral testimony of a witness. *See* Parol evidence.

Oral pleading. Pleading by word of mouth, in the actual presence of the court. This was the ancient mode of pleading in England, and continued to the reign of Edward III. *See also* Motion.

Oral trust. The transfer of property in trust informally through an oral declaration in contrast to a formal trust which is in writing. Real estate trusts may not be created orally. *See* Frauds, Statute of.

Oral will. *See* Nuncupative will.

Ordain. To institute or establish; to make an ordinance; to enact a constitution or law. To confer on a person the holy orders of priest or deacon.

Ordeal. The most ancient species of trial, in Saxon and old English law, being peculiarly distinguished by the appellation of *"judicium Dei,"* or "judgment of God," it being supposed that supernatural intervention would rescue an innocent person from the danger of physical harm to which he was exposed in this species of trial. The ordeal was of two sorts,—either fire ordeal or water ordeal; the former being confined to persons of higher rank, the latter to the common people.

Order. A mandate; precept; command or direction authoritatively given; rule or regulation. Direction of a court or judge made or entered in writing, and not included in a judgment, which determines some point or directs some step in the proceedings. An application for an order is a motion.

In commercial law, a designation of the person to whom a bill of exchange or negotiable promissory note is to be paid. An "order" is a direction to pay and must be more than an authorization or request. It must identify the person to pay with reasonable certainty. It may be addressed to one or more such persons jointly or in the alternative but not in succession. U.C.C. § 3–102(1)(b). With respect to documents of title, is a direction to deliver goods to a specified person or to his or her order.

Term is also used to designate a rank, class, or division of men; as the order of nobles, order of knights, order of priests, etc.

See also Appealable order; Back order; Decision; Decree; Executive order; Intermediate order; Judgment; Limit order; Payable to order; Percentage order; Restraining order.

Day order. Order from a customer to a broker to buy or sell a security on the particular day and such order is automatically cancelled at the end of that day.

Discretionary order. An order from a customer to a broker to sell a security at a price deemed acceptable by the broker.

Final order. One which either terminates the action itself, or finally decides some matter litigated by the parties, or operates to divest some right; or one which completely disposes of the subject-matter and the rights of the parties. *See also* Final decision rule.

General orders. Orders or rules of court, promulgated for the guidance of practitioners and the regulation of procedure in general, or in some general branch of its jurisdiction; as opposed to a rule or an order made in an individual case. General orders have generally been replaced by rules of court.

Interlocutory order. An order which decides not the cause, but only settles some intervening matter relating to it or affords some temporary relief (*e.g.* temporary restraining order).

Limit order. An order from a customer to a broker in which the customer places a lower limit on the price at which the security may be sold and a ceiling on the price at which the security may be bought.

Market order. An order from a customer to a broker to buy or to sell a security at the market price then prevailing and hence the order must be executed promptly.

Money order. See Money.

Open order. An order from a customer to a broker to buy or to sell a security and the order remains in force until it is either executed or cancelled by the customer.

Percentage order. See that title.

Restraining order. An order which may issue upon the filing of an application for an injunction forbidding the defendant to do the threatened act until a hearing on the application can be had. Though the term is sometimes used as a synonym of "injunction," a restraining order is properly distinguishable from an injunction, in that the former is intended only as a restraint upon the defendant until the propriety of granting an injunction, temporary or perpetual, can be determined, and it does no more than restrain the proceedings until such determination. Fed.R. Civil P. 65. *See also* Injunction; Restraining order; Temporary restraining order.

Speaking order. An order which contains matter which is explanatory or illustrative of the mere direction which is given by it.

Stop order. Order by customer to stockbroker to wait until the market price of the particular security reaches a specified figure, and then to "stop" the transaction by either selling or buying, as the case may be.

Stop payment order. Order from the drawer of a check to the drawee bank to stop payment on a check which has been drawn and given to the payee or lost.

Order bill of lading. A negotiable bill of lading directing that the goods be delivered to the person named or his order upon indorsement.

Order document. A document of title that runs to a named person, either because the document was so issued or because the document was specially indorsed, which can therefore be negotiated only by the named person indorsing it. See U.C.C. § 7–501(1)–(3).

Order instrument. A negotiable instrument that is payable to order either because the instrument was so issued, or because the instrument was specially indorsed. See U.C.C. §§ 3–110 (when instruments originally payable to order); 3–204(1).

Order nisi. A provisional or conditional order, allowing a certain time within which to do some required act, on failure of which the order will be made absolute.

Order of filiation. An order made by a court or judge having jurisdiction, fixing the paternity of a child born out of wedlock upon a given man, and requiring him to provide for its support.

Order paper. A negotiable instrument which is payable to a specific payee or to any person the payee, by his or her indorsement, designates. See U.C.C. § 3–104(1)(d); § 3–110. *See also* Order document; Order instrument.

Orders. The directions as to the course and purpose of a voyage given by the owner of the vessel to the captain or master. For other meanings, *see* Order.

Orders to pay. Checks and drafts.

Order to show cause. *See* Show cause order.

Ordinance. A rule established by authority; a permanent rule of action; a law or statute. In its most common meaning, the term is used to designate the enactments of the legislative body of a municipal corporation. It designates a local law of a municipal corporation, duly enacted by the proper authorities, prescribing general, uniform, and permanent rules of conduct relating to the corporate affairs of the municipality. An ordinance is the equivalent of a municipal statute, passed by the city council, or equivalent body, and governing matters not already covered by federal or state law. Ordinances commonly govern zoning, building, safety, etc. matters of municipality.

The name has also been given to certain enactments, more general in their character than ordinary statutes, and serving as organic laws, yet not exactly to be called "constitutions." Such was the

"Ordinance for the government of the North-West Territory," enacted by congress in 1787.

See also Municipal ordinance. Compare Resolution.

Ordinary, *n.* At common law, one who had exempt and immediate jurisdiction in causes ecclesiastical. Also a bishop; and an archbishop is the ordinary of the whole province, to visit and receive appeals from inferior jurisdictions. Also a commissary or official of a bishop or other ecclesiastical judge having judicial power; an archdeacon; officer of the royal household.

In American law, a judicial officer, in several of the states, clothed by statute with powers in regard to wills, probate, administration, guardianship, etc.

Former term for a public house where food and lodging were furnished to the traveler and his beast, at fixed rates, open to whoever may apply for accommodation, and where intoxicating liquor was sold at retail.

In the civil law, a judge who has authority to take cognizance of causes in his own right, and not by deputation.

Ordinary, *adj.* Regular; usual; normal; common; often recurring; according to established order; settled; customary; reasonable; not characterized by peculiar or unusual circumstances; belonging to, exercised by, or characteristic of, the normal or average individual.

As to *ordinary* Care; Diligence; Negligence, see those titles. *See also* Extraordinary.

Ordinary and necessary expenses. The phrase "ordinary and necessary expenses", as found in business deduction section of Internal Revenue Code, implies that the expenses are reasonable and bear proximate relation to management of property held for production of income. "Ordinary" means normal and expected and "necessary" means appropriate and helpful. For an item to qualify as an "ordinary and necessary expense" deductible under Internal Revenue Code section, five requirements must be met: item must be paid or incurred during taxable year, must be for carrying on any trade or business, must be an expense, must be necessary, and must be ordinary. *See also* Necessary; and *Ordinary expenses, below.*

Ordinary calling. Those things which are repeated daily or weekly in the course of business.

Ordinary care. That degree of care which ordinarily prudent and competent person engaged in same line of business or endeavor should exercise under similar circumstances, and in law means same as "due care" and "reasonable care." That care which reasonably prudent persons exercise in the management of their own affairs, in order to avoid injury to themselves or their property, or the persons or property of others. Ordinary care

is not an absolute term, but a relative one. Thus, in deciding whether ordinary care was exercised in a given case, the conduct in question must be viewed in the light of all the surrounding circumstances, as shown by the evidence in the case. *See also* Care.

Ordinary course of business. The transaction of business according to the common usages and customs of the commercial world generally or of the particular community or (in some cases) of the particular individual whose acts are under consideration. Term used in connection with sales made by a merchant as part of his regular business and in contrast with a sale in bulk which is regulated by statute, *e.g.* U.C.C. § 6–102(1). In general, any matter which transpires as a matter of normal and incidental daily customs and practices in business.

Ordinary dangers incident to employment. Those commonly and usually pertaining to and incident to it, which a reasonably prudent person might anticipate, and do not include danger by acts of negligence, unless habitual and known to the servant.

Ordinary expenses. Common and accepted in the general business in which the taxpayer is engaged. It comprises one of the tests for the deductibility of normal and expected expenses incurred or paid in connection with a trade or business; for the production or collection of income; for the management, conservation, or maintenance of property held for the production of income; or in connection with the determination, collection, or refund of any tax. I.R.C. § 162(a). *See also* Necessary; and *Ordinary and necessary expenses, above.*

Ordinary income. As tax term used in connection with a business, means earnings from the normal operations or activities of a business. In terms of an individual, ordinary income is income from such sources as wages, commissions, interest, etc.

Ordinary loss. A loss on the sale or exchange of an item used in a trade or business which is not considered a capital asset. In taxation, ordinary losses reduce ordinary income such as; salaries, interest, etc., while capital losses serve to reduce capital gains and those in excess of capital gains may reduce ordinary income up to a certain amount.

Ordinary negligence. The failure to use that degree of care which the ordinary or reasonably prudent person would have used under the circumstances and for which the negligent person is liable. Term is used in contradistinction to gross negligence which is more serious and a more flagrant lack of care. *See also* Negligence, and *Ordinary care, above.*

Ordinary persons. Men of ordinary care and diligence in relation to any particular thing.

Ordinary proceeding. Such a proceeding as was known to the common law and was formerly conducted in accordance with the proceedings of the common-law courts, and as is generally known under the current Rules of Civil Procedure and Codes to be such a proceeding as is started by the issuance of a summons, and results in a judgment enforceable by execution.

Ordinary repairs. Such as are necessary to make good the usual wear and tear or natural and unavoidable decay and keep the property in good condition. *Compare* Improvements.

Ordinary risks. Those incident to the business, and do not imply the result of the employer's negligence. The expression "extraordinary risks" *(q.v.)* is generally used to describe risks arising from the negligence of the employer, and they are generally held not to be assumed unless known or obvious.

Ordinary seaman. A sailor who is capable of performing the ordinary or routine duties of a seaman, but who is not yet so proficient in the knowledge and practice of all the various duties of a sailor at sea as to be rated as an "able" seaman.

Ordinary services of administrators include all the services incident to the closing and distribution of an estate, and not merely the receiving and disbursing of the funds and to justify an allowance of further compensation the administrator must have rendered services of an extraordinary character necessary to the protection of the estate, and, if he employs another to perform services which he is required to perform under the law, he cannot charge such services as an expense of administration.

Ordinary skill in an art. That degree of skill which persons engaged in that particular art usually employ; not that which belongs to a few persons only, of extraordinary endowments and capacities.

Ordinary written law. Law made, within constitutional restrictions, by the Legislature; *i.e.* statutes.

Organic Act. An act of Congress conferring powers of government upon a territory. Statute creating an administrative agency.

A statute by which a municipal corporation is organized and created is its "organic act" and the limit of its power, so that all acts beyond the scope of the powers there granted are void.

Organic law. The fundamental law, or constitution, of a state or nation, written or unwritten. That law or system of laws or principles which defines and establishes the organization of its government. *See also* Organic Act.

Organization. As term is used in commercial law, includes a corporation, government or governmental subdivision or agency, business trust, estate, trust, partnership or association, two or more persons having a joint or common interest, or any other legal or commercial entity. U.C.C. § 1–201(28). *See also* Charitable organizations.

Organization chart. A document that depicts the functions, divisions, and positions of the employee/jobs in a company and how they are related; also indicates the lines of authority and responsibility.

Organizational expenses. In taxation, those expenses associated with the organization of a business prior to the beginning of operations; *e.g.* state incorporation fees and legal costs.

Organize. To establish or furnish with organs; to systematize; to put into working order; to arrange in order for the normal exercise of its appropriate functions.

Organized exchange. A securities marketplace where purchasers and sellers regularly gather to trade securities according to the formal rules adopted by the exchange (*e.g.*, New York Stock Exchange).

Organized labor. Segments of labor force represented by unions; *e.g.* AFL–CIO.

Original. Primitive; first in order; bearing its own authority, and not deriving authority from an outside source; as *original* jurisdiction, *original* writ, etc. As applied to documents, the original is the first copy or archetype; that from which another instrument is transcribed, copied, or imitated. *See also Original evidence, below.*

In copyright law means that the work owes its creation or origin to the author and this in turn means that the work must not consist in actual copying.

Original bill. In equity pleading, a bill which relates to some matter not before litigated in the court by the same persons standing in the same interests. The ancient mode of commencing actions in the English court of King's bench. *See* Bill.

Original contractor. One who for a fixed price agrees with owner to perform certain work or furnish certain material.

Original cost. Total of all costs associated with acquisition of an asset.

Original entry. The first entry of an item of an account made by a merchant or other person in his account-books, as distinguished from entries posted into the ledger or copied from other books.

Original estates. See Estate.

Original evidence. An original document, writing, or other material object introduced in evidence as distinguished from a copy of it or from extraneous evidence of its content or purport.

An "original" of a writing or recording is the writing or recording itself or any counterpart intended to have the same effect by a person executing or issuing it. An "original" or a photograph includes the negative or any print therefrom. If data are stored in a computer or similar device, any printout or other output readable by sight shown to reflect the data accurately, is an "original". Fed.Evid.R. 1001(3). *See also* Copy; Duplicate.

Original inventor. In patent law, a pioneer in the art; one who evolves the original idea and brings it to some successful, useful and tangible result; as distinguished from an improver.

Original jurisdiction. Jurisdiction to consider a case in the first instance. Jurisdiction of court to take cognizance of a cause at its inception, try it, and pass judgment upon the law and facts. Distinguished from *appellate* jurisdiction.

Original package. A package prepared for interstate or foreign transportation, and remaining in the same condition as when it left the shipper, that is, unbroken and undivided. A package of such form and size as is used by producers or shippers for the purpose of securing both convenience in handling and security in transportation of merchandise between dealers in the ordinary course of actual commerce. *See also* Original package doctrine.

Original plat. The first plat of a town from the subsequent additions, and "original town" is employed in the same way.

Original process. See Process.

Original promise. An original promise, without the statute of frauds, is one in which the direct and leading object of the promisor is to further or promote some purpose or interest of his own, although the incidental effect may be the payment of the debt of another.

Original writ. See Writ.

Single original. An original instrument which is executed singly, and not in duplicate.

Original document rule. The best evidence of the contents of a document is the original of that document. The party bearing the burden of proving the contents of a document is required to introduce the original unless he is excused from its production because of its nonavailability and in this instance, secondary evidence is admissible. There are no degrees of secondary evidence. *See also* Best evidence.

Original issue. The first issue of stocks or bonds of a particular kind or series.

Original package doctrine. In Brown v. Maryland, 25 U.S. (12 Wheat.) 419, 6 L.Ed. 678, a

landmark case under the commerce clause of the U.S.Const., the Supreme Court held that a state was free to levy a tax or license fee on imports only after the original package had been broken because at this juncture the goods no longer were in the flow of interstate commerce and therefore no longer subject to federal regulation.

Origination clause. Article I, Section 7 or U.S. Constitution provides that "All Bills for raising Revenue shall originate in the House of Representatives." *See* Revenue bills.

Origination fee. Charge to borrower (of *e.g.,* mortgage loan) to cover costs of issuing loan, including credit and title checks, property appraisals, etc.

ORP. Ordinary, reasonable and prudent (man or woman). *See* Negligence. The standard of care on which negligence cases are based. *See* Reasonable man doctrine *or* standard; Reasonable woman standard.

Orphan /órfən/. Any person (but particularly a minor or infant) who has lost both (or, sometimes, one) of his or her parents.

Orphan's courts. Courts in several New England states with probate jurisdiction.

Orphan's deduction. Deduction from the taxable estate of the decedent permitted if the decedent does not have a surviving spouse, and is survived by a minor child who, immediately after the death of the decedent, has no known parent. The amount of the deduction is governed by I.R.C. § 2057.

O.S. An abbreviation for "Old Style," or "Old Series."

OSHA. Occupational Safety and Health Act.

Ostensible agency. An implied or presumptive agency, which exists where one, either intentionally or from want of ordinary care, induces another to believe that a third person is his agent, though he never in fact employed him. It is, strictly speaking, no agency at all, but is in reality based entirely upon estoppel. *See also* Agency *(Agency by estoppel.)*

Ostensible authority. Such authority as a principal, intentionally or by want of ordinary care, causes or allows a third person to believe that the agent possesses.

Ostensible ownership. Apparent ownership derived from conduct or words. Theory of "ostensible ownership" estops an owner of property who clothes another with apparent title from later asserting his title against an innocent third party who has been induced to deal with apparent owner.

Ostensible partner. *See* Partner.

OTB. Off-track betting.

O.T.C. *See* Over-the-counter market.

Other. Different or distinct from that already mentioned; additional, or further. Following an enumeration of particular classes "other" must be read as "other such like," and includes only others of like kind and character.

Other income. In taxation, income from sources other than in the operation of a business. An example of "other income" of a corporation includes, but is not limited to, interest and dividend income.

Otherwise. In a different manner; in another way, or in other ways.

Ought. This word, though generally directory only, will be taken as mandatory if the context requires it.

OUI. Abbreviation for state statutes involving operation of motor vehicle while under influence of liquor or drugs. See Driving while intoxicated.

Oust. To put out; to eject; to remove or deprive; to deprive of the possession or enjoyment of an estate or franchise.

Ouster. A putting out; dispossession; amotion of possession. A species of injuries to things real, by which the wrong-doer gains actual occupation of the land, and compels the rightful owner to seek his legal remedy in order to gain possession. An "ouster" is a wrongful dispossession or exclusion of a party from real property and involves a question of intent. Notorious and unequivocal act by which one cotenant deprives another of right to common and equal possession and enjoyment of property. See also Ejectment.

Outbuilding. Something used in connection with a main building. A small building appurtenant to a main building, and generally separated from it; e.g. outhouse; storage shed. See also Outhouse.

Outcome test. In a diversity of citizenship action in the federal court, the result should be the same as if the action had been commenced in the state court.

Outer continental shelf. All lands lying submerged seaward and not including lands beneath navigable waters. The subsoil and sea bed of such lands are subject to the jurisdiction and control of the United States. 43 U.S.C.A. § 1331.

Outgo. Expenditures.

Outhouse. A building subservient to, yet distinct from, the principal dwelling, located either within or without the curtilage. A smaller or subordinate building connected with a dwelling, usually detached from it and standing at a little distance from it, not intended for persons to live in, but to serve some purpose of convenience or necessity; as a barn, outside privy, a dairy, a toolhouse, and the like. Under statutes, such a building may be subservient to and adjoin a business building as well as a dwelling house. See also Outbuilding.

Outlaw. In English law, one who is put out of the protection or aid of the law. Popularly, a person violating the law; a fugitive.

Outlot. In early American land law (particularly in Missouri), a lot or parcel of land lying outside the corporate limits of a town or village but subject to its municipal jurisdiction or control. Term now generally refers to an area of land on a plat which is to be used for a purpose other than a building site.

Out-of-court settlement. The phrase is used with reference to agreements and transactions in regard to a pending suit which are arranged or take place between parties or their counsel privately and without being referred to the judge or court for authorization or approval. Thus, a case which is compromised, settled, and withdrawn by private agreement of the parties, after its institution, is said to be settled "out of court." See Settlement (Structured settlement).

Out-of-pocket expenses. Said of an expenditure usually paid for with cash. An incremental cost.

Out-of-pocket loss. As measure of damages, is the difference between the value of what the purchaser parted with (i.e., the purchase price paid by him) and the value of what he has received (i.e., the actual market value of the goods). Also called "out-of-pocket loss rule."

Out of term. At a time when no term of the court is being held; in the vacation or interval which elapses between terms of the court.

Out of the state. In reference to rights, liabilities, or jurisdictions arising out of the common law, this phrase is equivalent to "beyond sea" (q.v.). In other connections, it means physically beyond the territorial limits of the particular state in question, or constructively so, as in the case of a foreign corporation. But a foreign corporation maintaining an agent within the state is not deemed to be "out of the state," within various statutes dealing with jurisdiction over foreign corporations "doing business" within state.

Output contract. See Contract; Entire output contract.

Outrage. A grave injury; injurious violence. The tort of "outrage" (intentional infliction of serious mental distress) requires that defendant engage in outrageous and extreme conduct which results in intentionally or recklessly inflicted severe emotional distress.

Outright. Free from reserve or restraint; direct; positive; down-right; altogether; entirely; openly.

Outside. To the exterior of; without; outward from.

Outside director. A member of a corporate board of directors who is not an employee or company officer and does not participate in the corporation's day-to-day management. Outside directors, however, may include investment bankers, attorneys, or others who provide advice or services to incumbent management and thus have financial ties with management.

Outstanding. Remaining undischarged; unpaid; uncollected; as an outstanding debt. Constituting an effective obligation. When said of stock, the shares issued less treasury stock. When said of checks, it means a check issued but not yet presented for payment; a check that did not clear the drawer's bank prior to the bank statement date.

Existing as an adverse claim or pretension; not united with, or merged in, the title or claim of the party; as an outstanding title.

Outstanding and open account. In legal and commercial transactions it is an unsettled debt arising from items of work and labor, goods sold and delivered, and other open transactions, not reduced to writing, and subject to future settlement and adjustment and usually disclosed by account books of the owner of the demand and does not include express contracts or obligations which have been reduced to writing such as bonds, bills of exchange, or notes.

Outstanding balance. Current amount owed on debt.

Outstanding checks. Checks written but not yet processed by the bank. *See* Float.

Outstanding shares. Stock shares issued by a firm and held by the stockholders.

Ovelty /ów(v)əltiy/. In old English law, equality.

Over. Above; overhead; more than; in excess of.

Continued;—sometimes written on one page or sheet to indicate a continuation of matter on a separate page or sheet.

In conveyancing, the word is used to denote a contingent limitation intended to take effect on the failure of a prior estate. Thus, in what is commonly called the "name and arms clause" in a will or settlement there is generally a proviso that if the devisee fails to comply with the condition the estate is to go to some one else. This is a limitation or gift over.

Overbreadth doctrine. This doctrine, which derives from First Amendment, serves to invalidate legislation so sweeping that, along with its allowable proscriptions, it also restricts constitutionally protected rights of free speech, press or assembly. The doctrine requires that a statute be invalidated if it is fairly capable of being applied to punish people for constitutionally protected speech or conduct. A law is void on its face if it "does not

aim specifically at evils within the allowable area of [government] control, but . . . sweeps within its ambit other activities that constitute an exercise" of protected expressive or associational rights. Thornhill v. Alabama, 310 U.S. 88, 97, 60 S.Ct. 296, 84 L.Ed. 460. A plausible challenge to a law as *void for overbreadth* can be made only when (1) the protected activity is a significant part of the law's target, and (2) there exists no satisfactory way of severing the law's constitutional from its unconstitutional applications so as to excise the latter clearly in a single step from the law's reach.

Overcharge. With respect to public carriers or public utilities, a charge collected above a lawful tariff rate; a charge of more than is permitted by law. As regards interest rates, *see* Usury.

Overdraft. A check written on a checking account containing less funds than the amount of the check. Term may also refer to the condition which exists when vouchers or purchase orders are drawn in amounts in excess of budgeted or appropriated amount. *See also* Kiting; NSF check.

Overdraw. To draw upon a person or a bank in an amount in excess of the funds remaining to the drawer's credit with the drawee, or to an amount greater than what is due. *See also* Overdraft.

Overdue. Due and more than due; delayed or unpaid. The circumstance of an instrument that has not been paid despite arrival of the time for paying it, as by arrival of a date specified for payment or by acceleration or demand. A negotiable instrument or other evidence of debt is overdue when the day of its maturity is past and it remains unpaid.

A vessel is said to be overdue when she has not reached her destination at the time when she might ordinarily have been expected to arrive.

Overflowed lands. Those that are covered by nonnavigable waters (not including lands between high and low water mark of navigable streams or bodies of water, nor lands covered and uncovered by ordinary daily ebb and flow of normal tides of navigable waters).

Overhaul. To inquire into; to review; to disturb. To examine thoroughly, as machinery, with a view to repairs.

Overhead. All administrative or executive costs incident to the management, supervision, or conduct of the capital outlay, or business; distinguished from "operating charges," or those items that are inseparably connected with the productive end and may be seen as the work progresses, and are the subject of knowledge from observation. Continuous expenses of a business; the expenses and obligations incurred in connection with operation; expenses necessarily incurred in organization, office expenses, engineering, inspection, supervision, and management during construction; and general expenditures in financial or industrial enterprise which cannot be attributed to any one department or product, excluding cost of materials, labor, and selling.

Any cost not specifically or directly associated with the production of identifiable goods and services. Sometimes called "burden" or "indirect costs" and, in Britain, "oncosts." Frequently limited to manufacturing overhead.

Applied overhead. In accounting, the amount of overhead that has been assigned to work in process as a result of productive activity; credits for this amount are to a manufacturing overhead account.

Factory overhead. All factory-related costs other than direct materials used and direct labor.

Underapplied overhead. In accounting, the actual overhead of a period in excess of the amount of overhead applied to work in process.

Volume variance. A fixed overhead variance that represents the difference between budgeted fixed overhead and fixed overhead applied to production of the period.

Over-insurance. *See* Double insurance.

Overissue. To issue in excessive quantity; to issue in excess of fixed legal limits. Thus, "overissued stock" of a corporation is capital stock issued in excess of the amount limited and prescribed by the charter or certificate of incorporation. U.C.C. § 8–104(2). *See also* Oversubscription.

Overlying right. Right of owner of land to take water from ground underneath for use on his land within basin or watershed. Right is based on ownership of land and is appurtenant thereto.

Overreaching. In connection with commercial and consumer transactions, is that which results from an inequality of bargaining power or other circumstances in which there is an absence of meaningful choice on the part of one of the parties. *See also* Adhesion contract; Unconscionability.

Overreaching clause. In a resettlement, a clause which saves the powers of sale and leasing annexed to the estate for life created by the original settlement, when it is desired to give the tenant for life the same estate and powers under the resettlement. The clause is so called because it provides that the resettlement shall be overreached by the exercise of the old powers. If the resettlement were executed without a provision to this effect, the estate of the tenant for life and the annexed powers would be subject to any charges for portions, etc., created under the original settlement.

Override. An estate carved out of working interest under an oil or gas lease. Commissions paid to managers on sales made by subordinates. Provision in real estate brokers listing agreement giving him right to certain commission for a reasonable period of time after expiration of listing in event owner sells to purchaser with whom broker negotiated during term of listing.

Overriding royalty. As applied to an existing oil and gas lease is a given percentage of the gross production payable to some person other than the lessor or persons claiming under him. Royalty interest carved out of working interest created by oil and gas lease, and is interest in oil and gas produced at surface free of expense of production and its outstanding characteristic is that its duration is limited by duration of lease under which it is created.

Overrule. To supersede; annul; reverse; make void; reject by subsequent action or decision. A judicial decision is said to be overruled when a later decision, rendered by the same court or by a superior court in the same system, expresses a judgment upon the same question of law directly opposite to that which was before given, thereby depriving the earlier opinion of all authority as a precedent. The term is not properly applied to conflicting decisions on the same point by co-ordinate or independent tribunals. It also signifies that a majority of the judges of a court have decided against the opinion of the minority, in which case the minority judges are said to be overruled. *See* Reverse; Vacate.

To refuse to sustain, or recognize as sufficient, an objection made in the course of a trial, as to the introduction of particular evidence, etc.

Overseer /ówvərsi(yə)r/òwvərsíyər/. A superintendent or supervisor; a public officer whose duties involve general superintendence of routine affairs. Member of a University board.

Oversubscription. Condition which exists when there are more orders or subscriptions for corporate stock offering than can be issued. *See also* Overissue.

Overt. Open; manifest; public; issuing in action, as distinguished from that which rests merely in intention or design.

Market overt. *See* Market.

Overt act. An open, manifest act from which criminality may be implied. An outward act done in pursuance and manifestation of an intent or design. An open act, which must be manifestly proved.

An overt act essential to establish an attempt to commit a crime is an act done to carry out the intention, and it must be such as would naturally effect that result unless prevented by some extraneous cause. It must be something done that directly moves toward the crime, and brings the accused nearer to its commission than mere acts of preparation or of planning, and will apparently result, in the usual and natural course of events, if not hindered by extraneous causes, in the commission of the crime itself.

In reference to the crime of treason, and the provision of the federal Constitution that a person shall not be convicted thereof unless on the testimony of two witnesses to the same "overt act," the term means a step, motion, or action really taken in the execution of a treasonable purpose, as distinguished from mere words, and also from a treasonable sentiment, design, or purpose not issuing in action. It is an act in furtherance of the crime. One which manifests the intention of the traitor to commit treason.

An overt act which will justify the exercise of the right of self-defense is such as would manifest to the mind of a reasonable person a present intention to kill him or do him great bodily harm.

An overt act which completes crime of conspiracy to violate federal law is something apart from conspiracy and is an act to effect the object of the conspiracy, and need be neither a criminal act, nor crime that is object of conspiracy, but must accompany or follow agreement and must be done in furtherance of object of agreement.

Overtake. To come or catch up with in a course of motion. To catch up with and pass.

Over-the-counter market. Refers to the broad securities market consisting of brokers who purchase or sell securities by computer hook-up or telephone rather than through the facilities of a securities exchange. At one time completely unorganized, the over-the-counter market is now relatively organized with computerized quotation and transaction reporting services. *See* NASD; NASDAQ.

Overtime. Work done after regular working hours; beyond the regular fixed hours.

Overtime wage. Portion of wages paid employee for services rendered beyond regularly fixed working hours.

Overture. An opening; a proposal.

Overt word. An open, plain word, not to be misunderstood. *See* Unequivocal.

Owe. To be bound to do or omit something, especially to pay a debt. May also refer to a moral or social obligation.

Owelty /ówəltiy/. Equality; an equalization charge.

Owing. Unpaid. A debt, for example, is owing while it is unpaid, and whether it be due or not.

Own. To have a good legal title; to hold as property; to have a legal or rightful title to; to have; to possess.

Owner. The person in whom is vested the ownership, dominion, or title of property; proprietor. He who has dominion of a thing, real or personal, corporeal or incorporeal, which he has a right to enjoy and do with as he pleases, even to spoil or destroy it, as far as the law permits, unless he be prevented by some agreement or covenant which restrains his right.

The term is, however, a nomen generalissimum, and its meaning is to be gathered from the connection in which it is used, and from the subject-matter to which it is applied. The primary meaning of the word as applied to land is one who owns the fee and who has the right to dispose of the property, but the term also includes one having a possessory right to land or the person occupying or cultivating it.

The term "owner" is used to indicate a person in whom one or more interests are vested for his own benefit. The person in whom the interests are vested has "title" to the interests whether he holds them for his own benefit or for the benefit of another. Thus the term "title," unlike "ownership," is a colorless word; to say without more that a person has title to certain property does not indicate whether he holds such property for his own benefit or as trustee. Restatement, Second, Trusts, § 2, Comment (d); Restatement of Property, § 10.

See also Ownership.

Beneficial owner. See Beneficial owner; *also Equitable owner, below.*

Equitable owner. One who is recognized in equity as the owner of property, because the real and beneficial use and title belong to him, although the bare legal title is vested in another, *e.g.,* a trustee for his benefit. One who has a present title in land which will ripen into legal ownership upon the performance of conditions subsequent. There may therefore be two "owners" in respect of the same property, one the nominal or legal owner, the other the beneficial or equitable owner. *See also* Beneficial owner.

General and beneficial owner. The person whose interest is primarily one of possession and enjoyment in contemplation of an ultimate absolute ownership;—not the person whose interest is primarily in the enforcement of a collateral pecuniary claim, and does not contemplate the use or enjoyment of the property as such. *See also* Beneficial owner.

General owner. He who has the primary or residuary title to it; as distinguished from a *special* owner, who has a special interest in the same thing, amounting to a qualified ownership, such, for example, as a bailee's lien. One who has both the right of property and of possession.

Joint owners. Two or more persons who jointly own and hold title to property, *e.g.,* joint tenants, and also partners and tenants in common. In its most comprehensive sense, the term embraces all cases where the property in question is owned by two or more persons regardless of the special nature of their relationship or how it came into being. An estate by entirety is a "joint ownership" of a husband and wife as at common law notwithstanding legislative enactments touching joint tenancy. *See also* Joint estate; Tenancy.

Legal owner. One who is recognized and held responsible by the law as the owner of property. In a more particular sense, one in whom the legal title to real estate is vested, but who holds it in trust for the benefit of another, the latter being called the "equitable" owner.

Part owners. Joint owners; co-owners; those who have shares of ownership in the same thing. *See Joint owners, above.*

Record owner. This term, particularly used in statutes requiring notice of tax delinquency or sale, means the owner of record, not the owner described in the tax roll; the owner of the title at time of notice.

Reputed owner. One who has to all appearances the title to, and possession of, property; one who, from all appearances, or from supposition, is the owner of a thing. He who has the general credit or reputation of being the owner or proprietor of goods.

Riparian owner. See Riparian.

Sole and unconditional owner. An expression commonly used in fire insurance policies, in which the word "sole" means that no one else has any interest in the property as owner, and "unconditional" means that the quality of the estate is not limited or affected by any condition. To be "unconditional and sole," the interest or ownership of the insured must be completely vested, not contingent or conditional, nor in common or jointly with others, but of such nature that the insured must alone sustain the entire loss if the property is destroyed; and this is so whether the title is legal or equitable. It is sufficient to satisfy the requirements of "sole and unconditional ownership" that the insured is the sole equitable owner and has the full equitable title. It is enough that the insured is equitably entitled to immediate and absolute legal ownership. The term contemplates beneficial and practical proprietorship and not necessarily technical title.

Special owner. One who has a special interest in an article of property, amounting to a qualified ownership of it, such, for example, as a bailee's lien; as distinguished from the *general* owner, who has the primary or residuary title to the same thing. Some person holding property with the consent of, and as representative of, the actual owner.

Owner's equity (capital). The owner's net worth of "interest" in the assets of a business; equal to the company's net assets (assets minus liabilities). *See also* Equity.

Ownership. Collection of rights to use and enjoy property, including right to transmit it to others. The complete dominion, title, or proprietary right in a thing or claim. The entirety of the powers of use and disposal allowed by law.

The right of one or more persons to possess and use a thing to the exclusion of others. The right by which a thing belongs to some one in particular, to the exclusion of all other persons. The exclusive right of possession, enjoyment, and disposal; involving as an essential attribute the right to control, handle, and dispose.

Ownership of property is either absolute or qualified. The ownership of property is absolute when a single person has the absolute dominion over it, and may use it or dispose of it according to his pleasure, subject only to general laws. The ownership is qualified when it is shared with one or more persons, when the time of enjoyment is deferred or limited, or when the use is restricted. Calif.Civil Code, §§ 678–680.

There may be ownership of all inanimate things which are capable of appropriation or of manual delivery; of all domestic animals; of all obligations; of such products of labor or skill as the composition of an author, the goodwill of a business, trademarks and signs, and of rights created or granted by statute. Calif.Civil Code, § 655.

In connection with burglary, "ownership" means any possession which is rightful as against the burglar.

See also Equitable ownership; Exclusive ownership; Hold; Interest; Interval ownership; Ostensible ownership; Owner; Possession; Title.

Oyer /óyər/. In old English practice, hearing; the hearing a deed read, which a party sued on a bond, etc., might pray or demand, and it was then *read* to him by the other party; the entry on the record being, *"et ei legitur in hœc verba"* (and it is read to him in these words).

A *copy* of a bond or specialty sued upon, given to the opposite party, in lieu of the old practice of reading it.

Oyer and terminer /óyər ən tə́rmənər/. A half French phrase applied in England to the assizes, which are so called from the commission of *oyer and terminer* directed to the judges, empowering them to "inquire, *hear, and determine* " all treasons, felonies, and misdemeanors. This commission is now issued regularly, but was formerly used only on particular occasions, as upon sudden outrage or insurrection in any place. In the United States, certain higher criminal courts were called "courts of oyer and terminer."

Oyez /óyeyz/°(t)s/. Hear ye. A word used in courts by the public crier to command attention when a proclamation is about to be made. Usually pronounced "O yes."

P

P.A. Professional Association.

PAC. Political Action Committee. Committees, clubs, associations or other groups of persons formed to receive contributions for use in election campaigns. The organization, registration, reporting, and other activities of such organizations is regulated by federal and state laws. See *e.g.,* 2 U.S.C.A. § 431 et seq.

Pace. A measure of length containing two feet and a half, being the ordinary length of a step. The geometrical pace is five feet long, being the length of two steps, or the whole space passed over by the same foot from one step to another.

Pacifist. One who seeks to maintain peace and to abolish war. One who refuses or is unwilling for any purpose to bear arms because of conscientious considerations, and who is disposed to encourage others in such refusal. A conscientious objector.

Pack. To decide by false appearances; to counterfeit; to delude; to put together in sorts with a fraudulent design. To pack a jury is to use unlawful, improper, or deceitful means to have the jury made up of persons favorably disposed to the party so contriving, or who have been or can be improperly influenced to give the verdict he seeks. The term imports the improper and corrupt selection of a jury sworn and impaneled for the trial of a cause.

Package. *See* Parcel.

Packing list. Document which contains the contents, weight and other information concerning the package to be shipped. It accompanies the package and is available for inspection.

Pact. A bargain; compact; agreement. An agreement between two or more nations or states usually less elaborate than a treaty but nearly equivalent thereto. *See also* Compact; Pactum; Treaty.

Pactum /pǽktəm/. Lat. *Civil law.* A pact. An agreement or convention without specific name, and without consideration, which, however, might, in its nature, produce a civil obligation.

Nudum pactum. A bare or naked pact or agreement; a promise or undertaking made without any consideration for it, and therefore not enforceable.

Paid-in-capital. Money or property given to a corporation in exchange for the corporation's capital stock; as distinguished from capital obtained

from the earnings of or donations to the corporation. *See also* Paid-in surplus.

Paid-in-surplus. The amount paid for the stock of a corporation in excess of its par or stated value. *See* Capital *(Capital surplus)*; Paid-in-capital; Surplus *(Paid-in surplus).*

Paid-up insurance. Insurance coverage for which no additional premiums are due.

Paid-up stock. Shares of stock for which full payment has been received by the corporation.

Pain and suffering. Term used to describe not only physical discomfort and distress but also mental and emotional trauma which are recoverable as elements of damage in torts. Recovery for pain and suffering is restricted by statute in certain states. *See* Cap; Damages.

Pairing-off. In the practice of legislative bodies, a species of negative proxies, by which two members, who belong to opposite parties or are on opposite sides with regard to a given question, mutually agree that they will both be absent from voting, either for a specified period or when a division is had on the particular question. By this mutual agreement a vote is neutralized on each side of the question, and the relative numbers on the division are precisely the same as if both members were present. It is said to have originated in the house of commons in Cromwell's time.

Palimony. Term has meaning similar to "alimony" except that award, settlement or agreement arises out of nonmarital relationship of parties (*i.e.* nonmarital partners). It has been held that courts should enforce express contracts between nonmarital partners except to the extent the contract is explicitly founded on the consideration of meretricious sexual services, despite contention that such contracts violate public policy; that in the absence of express contract, the court should inquire into the conduct of the parties to determine whether that conduct demonstrates implied contract, agreement of partnership or joint venture, or some other tacit understanding between the parties, and may also employ the doctrine of quantum meruit or equitable remedies such as constructive or resulting trust, when warranted by the facts of the case. Marvin v. Marvin, 557 P.2d 106, 18 Cal.3d 660, 134 Cal.Rptr. 815.

Palm off. Refers to the conduct of selling goods as the goods of another or doing business as the business of another such that the public is misled by the conduct and believes it is purchasing the goods of another or doing business with someone other than the actual seller.

Palm prints. The impression made by a person's palm on a smooth surface. They may be used for purpose of identification in criminal cases.

Palpable. Easily perceptible, plain, obvious, readily visible, noticeable, patent, distinct, manifest.

Palsgraf Rule. The rule derived from the case of Palsgraf v. Long Island R. Co., 248 N.Y. 339, 162 N.E. 99, to the effect that one who is negligent is liable only for the harm or injury which is within the orbit of foreseeability and not for every injury which follows from his negligence. *See also* Foreseeability. *Compare* Strict Liability.

Pandects /pǽndekts/. A compilation of Roman law, consisting of selected passages from the writings of the most authoritative of the older jurists, methodically arranged, prepared by Tribonian with the assistance of sixteen associates, under a commission from the emperor Justinian. This work, which is otherwise called the "Digest," because in his compilation the writings of the jurists were reduced to order and condensed *quasi digestiœ*, comprises fifty books, and is one of the four great works composing the *Corpus Juris Civilis*. It was first published in A.D. 533, when Justinian gave to it the force of law.

Pander, *n.* One who caters to the lust of others; a male bawd, a pimp, or procurer.

Pander, *v.* To pimp; to cater to the gratification of the lust of another. To entice or procure a female, by promises, threats, fraud, or artifice, to enter any place in which prostitution is practiced, for the purpose of prostitution. Pandering is established when evidence shows that accused has succeeded in inducing his victim to become engaged in prostitution.

Pandering of obscenity. Business of purveying textual, pictorial or graphic matter openly advertised to appeal to prurient interest of customers, or potential customers, by either blatant and explicit advertising or subtle and sophisticated advertising. Such conduct is not protected by the First Amendment.

Panderer. One who solicits for prostitute. A pimp.

P & L. *See* Profit (*Profit and loss*); Profit and loss statement.

Panel. A list of jurors summoned to serve in a particular court, or for the trial of a particular action. Group of judges (smaller than the entire court) which decides a case; *e.g.* a nine member appellate court might be divided into three, three member panels with each panel hearing and de-

ciding cases. May also refer to members of a commission.

See also Impanel; Jury-list; Jury panel.

Paper. A written or printed document or instrument. A document filed or introduced in evidence in a suit at law, as, in the phrase "papers in the case" and in "papers on appeal." Any writing or printed document, including letters, memoranda, legal or business documents, and books of account, as in the constitutional provision which protects the people from unreasonable searches and seizures in respect to their "papers" as well as their houses and persons. A written or printed evidence of debt, particularly a promissory note or a bill of exchange, as in the phrases "accommodation paper" and "commercial paper" *(q.v.)*. *See also* Bearer paper; Chattel paper; Commercial paper; Document; Instrument.

Paper money. Bills drawn by a government against its own credit, engaging to pay money, but which do not profess to be immediately convertible into specie, and which are put into compulsory circulation as a substitute for coined money. *See* Federal reserve notes; Legal tender.

Paper patent. Term used derisively to refer to a discovery or invention which has never been put to commercial use nor recognized in the trade.

Paper profit (*or loss*). An unrealized profit (or loss) on a security or other investment still held. Paper profits (or losses) become realized profits (or losses) only upon the sale of the security.

Paper standard. A money system based on pure paper which is not convertible into gold or other metal of intrinsic value.

Par. In commercial law, equal; equality. An equality subsisting between the nominal or face value of a bill of exchange, share of stock, etc., and its actual selling value. When the values are thus equal, the instrument or share is said to be "at par;" if it can be sold for more than its nominal worth, it is "above par;" if for less, it is "below par." *See also* Par of exchange; Par value *or* stated value.

Any standard or norm of conduct which is expected of people.

Paragraph. A distinct part of a discourse or writing; any section or subdivision of writing or chapter which relates to particular point, whether consisting of one or many sentences.

A part or section of a statute, pleading, affidavit, will, trust, etc., which contains one article, the sense of which is complete.

Fed.R.Civil P. 10(b) provides that: "All averments of claim or defense shall be made in numbered paragraphs, the contents of each of which shall be limited as far as practicable to a statement or of a single set of circumstances; and a paragraph may be referred to by number in all succeeding pleadings ...."

Paralegal. A person with legal skills, but who is not an attorney, and who works under the supervision of a lawyer in performing various tasks relating to the practice of law or who is otherwise authorized by law to use those legal skills. Paralegal courses leading to degrees in such specialty are now afforded by many schools.

Parallel citation. A citation reference to the same case printed in two or more different reports. See *e.g.* the case citation to U.S. Supreme Court decisions in this Dictionary.

Paramount. Above; upwards. Higher; superior; pre-eminent; of the highest rank or nature.

Paramount equity. An equitable right or claim which is prior, superior, or preferable to that with which it is compared.

Paramount title. In the law of real property, properly one which is superior to the title with which it is compared, in the sense that the former is the source or origin of the latter. It is, however, frequently used to denote a title which is simply better or stronger than another, or will prevail over it. But this use is scarcely correct, unless the superiority consists in the seniority of the title spoken of as "paramount."

Paramour. In general, a lover; but term is used commonly in connection with a person of either sex in an adulterous alliance.

Paraphernalia /pærəfərnéyl(i)yə/. The separate property of a married woman, other than that which is included in her dowry, or dos. Those goods which a woman is allowed to have, after the death of her husband, besides her dower, consisting of her apparel and ornaments, suitable to her rank and degree. Those goods which a wife could bequeath by her testament.

Paraphernal property /pærəfərnəl própərdiy/. See Paraphernalia.

Paraprofessional. One who assists a professional person though not a member of the profession himself; *e.g.* a paralegal *(q.v.)* who assists a lawyer.

Parcel, *v.* To divide an estate.

Parcel, *n.* A small package or bundle.

A part or portion of land. A part of an estate. "Parcel" as used with reference to land generally means a contiguous quantity of land in the possession of an owner. A contiguous quantity of land in possession of, owned by, or recorded as property of the same claimant person or company. Term may be synonymous with "lot." *See also* Tract of land.

Parcels. A description of property, formally set forth in a conveyance, together with the boundaries thereof, in order to provide for easy identification.

Parcenary /pársənèhriy/. The state or condition of holding title to lands jointly by parceners, before the common inheritance has been divided.

Parcener /pársənər/. A joint heir; one who, with others, holds an estate in co-parcenary *(q.v.)*.

Parchment. Sheep-skins dressed for writing, so called from *Pergamus*, Asia Minor, where they were invented. Used for deeds, and used for writs of summons in England previous to the Judicature Act of 1875. The skin of a lamb, sheep, goat, young calf, or other animal, prepared for writing on; also, any of various papers made in imitation thereof.

Par delictum /pár dəlíktəm/. (In pari delicto.) Equal guilt.

Pardon. An executive action that mitigates or sets aside punishment for a crime. An act of grace from governing power which mitigates the punishment the law demands for the offense and restores the rights and privileges forfeited on account of the offense. A pardon releases offender from entire punishment prescribed for offense and from disabilities consequent on his conviction; it reinstates his civil liberties.

The power to pardon for non-federal crimes is generally invested in state governors, while the President has the power to pardon for federal offenses (Art. II, Sec. 2, U.S.Const.).

See also Amnesty; Board of pardons; Clemency; Commutation; Condonation; Parole; Reprieve.

Types of Pardons

Absolute or unconditional pardon. One which frees the criminal without any condition whatever. That which reaches both the punishment prescribed for the offense and the guilt of the offender. It obliterates in legal contemplation the offense itself. It goes no further than to restore the accused to his civil rights and remit the penalty imposed for the particular offense of which he was convicted in so far as it remains unpaid.

Conditional pardon. One to which a condition is annexed, performance of which is necessary to the validity of the pardon. A pardon which does not become operative until the grantee has performed some specific act, or where it becomes void when some specific event transpires. One granted on the condition that it shall only endure until the voluntary doing of some act by the person pardoned, or that it shall be revoked by a subsequent act on his part, as that he shall leave the state and never return.

Executive pardon. See Executive pardon.

Full pardon. One freely and unconditionally absolving party from all legal consequences, direct and collateral, of crime and conviction.

General pardon. One granted to all the persons participating in a given criminal or treasonable offense (generally political), or to all offenders of a given class or against a certain statute or within certain limits of time. But "amnesty" is the more appropriate term for this. It may be express, as when a general declaration is made that all offenders of a certain class shall be pardoned, or implied, as in case of the repeal of a penal statute. *See* Amnesty.

Partial pardon. That which remits only portion of punishment or absolves from only portion of legal consequences of crime.

Unconditional pardon. Pardon that frees a prisoner without any conditions attached. A full pardon.

Pardon attorney. Official of Justice Department who considers applications for federal pardons and makes recommendations for the exercise of Presidential clemency.

Parens /pǽrènz/pér°/. Lat. In Roman law, a parent; originally and properly only the father or mother of the person spoken of; but also, by an extension of its meaning, any relative, male or female, in the line of direct ascent.

Parens patriæ /pǽrènz pǽtriyiy or /pérènz péytriyiy/. "Parens patriae," literally "parent of the country," refers traditionally to role of state as sovereign and guardian of persons under legal disability, such as juveniles or the insane; and, in child custody determinations, when acting on behalf of the state to protect the interests of the child. It is the principle that the state must care for those who cannot take care of themselves, such as minors who lack proper care and custody from their parents. It is a concept of standing utilized to protect those quasi-sovereign interests such as health, comfort and welfare of the people, interstate water rights, general economy of the state, etc.

Parens patriæ originates from the English common law where the King had a royal prerogative to act as guardian to persons with legal disabilities such as infants. In the United States, the *parens patriæ* function belongs with the states.

State attorney generals have *parens patriæ* authority to bring actions on behalf of state residents for anti-trust offenses and to recover on their behalf. 15 U.S.C.A. § 15c. *See also* Hart-Scott-Rodino Antitrust Improvement Act.

The use of this power to deprive a person of freedom has been limited by laws and decisions. *See also* Surrogate parent.

Parent. The lawful father or mother of a person. In common and ordinary usage the word comprehends much more than mere fact of who was responsible for child's conception and birth and is commonly understood to describe and refer to person or persons who share mutual love and affection with a child and who supply child support and maintenance, instruction, discipline and guidance.

By statute, "parent" has been defined to include (1) either the natural father or the natural mother of a child born of their valid marriage to each other, if no subsequent judicial decree has divested one or both of them of their statutory coguardianship as created by their marriage; (2) either the adoptive father or the adoptive mother of a child jointly adopted by them, if no subsequent judicial decree has divested one or both of them of their statutory coguardianship as created by the adoption; (3) the natural mother of an illegitimate child, if her position as sole guardian of such a child has not been divested by a subsequent judicial decree; (4) a child's putative blood parent who has expressly acknowledged paternity and contributed meaningfully to the child's support; (5) any individual or agency whose status as guardian of the person of the child has been established by judicial decree.

Includes any person entitled to take, or who would be entitled to take if the child died without a will, as a parent under the Uniform Probate Code by intestate succession from the child whose relationship is in question and excludes any person who is only a stepparent, foster parent, or grandparent. Uniform Probate Code, § 1–201(28).

See also Adoption; Loco parentis; Parens patriæ; Parent company *or* corporation; Surrogate parent.

Parentage. Kindred in the direct ascending line. The state or condition of being a parent.

Parental consent. Consent required of minor from parent to marry or undertake other legal obligations.

Parental Kidnapping Prevention Act. Federal law which imposes a duty on the states to enforce a child custody determination entered by a court of a sister state if the determination is consistent with provisions of the Act. 28 U.S.C.A. § 1738A.

Parental liability. By statute in certain states, the parents may be held liable up to a specified amount for damages caused to property of others by their children if such damage is found to have resulted from negligent control of parent over acts of child.

Parental rights. The sum total of the rights of the parent or parents in and to the child as well as the rights of the child in and to the parent or parents. The following are "parental rights" protected to varying degrees by constitution: physical possession of child, which, in case of custodial parent, includes day-to-day care and companionship of child; right to discipline child, which includes right to inculcate in child parent's moral and ethical standards; right to control and manage minor child's earnings; right to control and manage minor child's property; right to be supported by adult child; right to have child bear parent's name; and right to prevent adoption of child without parents' consent.

Parent-child immunity. In some jurisdictions a parent is immune from liability for negligence in an action brought by his or her child, though the trend has been to abolish or restrict such immunity.

Parent company *or* **corporation.** Company owning more than 50 percent of the voting shares, or otherwise a controlling interest, of another company, called the subsidiary. *Compare* Holding company.

Parenticide /pəréntəsàyd/. One who murders a parent; also the crime so committed.

Pari delicto /pǽray dəlíktow/. Lat. In equal fault; in a similar offense or crime; equal in guilt or in legal fault. "Pari delicto" doctrine rests on rule that courts will not enforce an invalid contract and that no party can recover in any action where it is necessary for him to prove an illegal contract in order to make out his case. Under this doctrine transgressor will not be allowed to profit from his own wrongdoing and party is barred from recovering damages if his losses are substantially caused by activities which the law forbade him to engage in. *See* In pari delicto.

Pari-mutuel betting /pæriy myúwty(u)wəl bétiŋ/. A form of wagering, generally on the outcome of horse or dog races, whereby all bets made on a particular race are pooled and then paid, less a management fee, to holders of winning tickets. Such betting is allowed in most states, though it is heavily regulated. *Cf.* New York McKinney's Racing, Pari-mutuel Wagering and Breeding Law, § 101 et seq.

Parish. In Louisiana, a territorial governmental division of the state corresponding to what is elsewhere called a "county."

Par items. Items which a drawee bank will remit to another bank without charge.

Parity. Equality in amount or value. Equivalence of prices of farm products in relation to those existing at some former date (base period) or to the general cost of living. Parity prices are important in establishing government price support programs for farmers.

Equivalence of prices of goods or services in two different markets.

The relationship between two currencies such that they are exchangeable for each other at the par or official rate of exchange. *See* Exchange rate.

Parity ratio. A relationship developed between the index of prices received by farmers for their crops and the index of costs of the farmers for the items which they buy.

Parliament. The supreme legislative assembly of Great Britain and Ireland, consisting of the king or queen and the three estates of the realm, viz., the lords spiritual, the lords temporal, and the commons.

High Court of Parliament. In English law, the English parliament, as composed of the house of peers and house of commons; or the house of lords sitting in its judicial capacity.

Parliamentary. Relating or belonging to, connected with, enacted by or proceeding from, or characteristic of, the English parliament in particular, or any legislative body in general.

Parliamentary law. The general body of enacted rules (*e.g.* Roberts Rules of Order) and recognized usages which governs the procedure of legislative assemblies and other deliberative bodies such as meetings of stockholders and directors of corporations, town meetings, boards, clubs, and the like.

Parliamentary taxes. *See* Tax.

Par of exchange. The precise equality or equivalency of any given sum or quantity of money of one country, and the like sum or quantity of money of any other foreign country into which it is to be exchanged. The par of the currencies of any two countries means the equivalence of a certain amount of the currency of the one in the currency of the other. *See* Exchange rate.

Parol. A word; speech; hence, oral or verbal. Expressed or evidenced by speech only; as opposed to by writing or by sealed instrument.

As to *parol* Agreement; Arrest; Demurrer; Lease; and Promise; see those titles.

Parol contract. An oral contract as distinguished from a written or formal contract. *See also* Oral contract.

Parole /pərówl/. Release from jail, prison or other confinement after actually serving part of sentence. Conditional release from imprisonment which entitles parolee to serve remainder of his term outside confines of an institution, if he satisfactorily complies with all terms and conditions provided in parole order.

The granting, denying, revocation, and supervision of parole for federal prisoners rests in the U.S. Parole Commission. Most states have similar boards or commissions. *See* Parole board *or* commission.

In military law, a promise given by a prisoner of war, when he has leave to depart from custody, that he will return at the time appointed, unless discharged. An engagement by a prisoner of war, upon being set at liberty, that he will not again take up arms against the government by whose forces he was captured, either for a limited period or while hostilities continue.

Compare Amnesty; Pardon.

Parole board *or* **commission.** The state and federal administrative bodies empowered to decide whether inmates shall be conditionally released from prison before completion of their sentences. Called "Correctional Boards" in some states.

The U.S. Parole Commission consists of nine members, appointed by the President by and with the advice and consent of the Senate. It has sole authority to grant, modify, or revoke paroles of all U.S. prisoners. It is responsible for the supervision of parolees and prisoners released upon the expiration of their sentences with allowances for statutory good time. U.S. probation officers supervise parolees and mandatory releases.

The former federal Board of Parole was abolished in 1976 with its functions transferred to the U.S. Parole Commission. With implementation of the 1987 federal Sentencing Guidelines, the federal parole system will be phased out and replaced by release under the supervision of the judge who imposed the sentence—rather than by a parole board.

Parolee. Ex-prisoner who has been placed on parole.

Parole officers. Parole system is administered by parole officers whose duties include supervision of parolees. Normally, parolees must periodically report to such officers.

Parol evidence. Oral or verbal evidence; that which is given by word of mouth; the ordinary kind of evidence given by witnesses in court. In a particular sense, and with reference to contracts, deeds, wills, and other writings, parol evidence is the same as extraneous evidence or evidence *aliunde. See also* Aliunde; Extraneous evidence; Oral evidence.

Parol evidence rule. This evidence rule seeks to preserve integrity of written agreements by refusing to permit contracting parties to attempt to alter import of their contract through use of contemporaneous oral declarations. Under this rule when the parties to a contract embody their agreement in writing and intend the writing to be the final expression of their agreement, the terms of the writing may not be varied or contradicted by evidence of any prior written or oral agreement in the absence of fraud, duress, or mutual mistake. But rule does not forbid a resort to parol evidence not inconsistent with the matters stated in the writing. Also, as regards sales of goods, such written agreement may be explained or supplemented by course of dealing or usage of trade or by course of conduct, and by evidence of consistent additional terms unless the court finds the writing to have been intended also as a com-

plete and exclusive statement of the terms of the agreement. U.C.C. § 2–202.

This rule is also applicable to wills and trusts.

Parricide /pǽrəsayd/. The crime of killing one's father; also a person guilty of killing his father.

Part. An integral portion, something essentially belonging to a larger whole; that which together with another or others makes up a whole. A portion, share, or purpart. One of two duplicate originals of a conveyance or covenant, the other being called "counterpart." Also, in composition, partial or incomplete; as part payment, part performance.

Partial. Relating to or constituting a part; not complete; not entire or universal; not general or total.

Partial account. An account of an executor, administrator, guardian, etc., not exhibiting his entire dealings with the estate or fund from his appointment to final settlement, but covering only a portion of the time or of the estate.

Partial average. Another name for particular average. *See* Average.

Partial eviction. That which takes place when the possessor is deprived of only a portion of his rights in the premises. Such may result in constructive eviction.

Partial evidence. That which goes to establish a detached fact, in a series tending to the fact in dispute. It may be received, subject to be rejected as incompetent, unless connected with the fact in dispute by proof of other facts; for example, on an issue of title to real property, evidence of the continued possession of a remote occupant is partial, for it is of a detached fact, which may or may not be afterwards connected with the fact in dispute.

Partial incapacity. Such occurs when injury disables a worker to perform part of the usual tasks of his job, though such disablement does not prevent him from procuring and retaining employment reasonably suitable to his physical condition and ability to work, or when because of his injury he is only able to perform labor of a less remunerative class than he performed before the injury, and as a consequence he suffers a depression or reduction in his earning capacity.

Partial limitation. Provision found in some insurance policies in which the insurer agrees to pay a total loss if the actual loss exceeds a certain amount.

Partial loss. A loss of a part of a thing or of its value, or any damage not amounting (actually or constructively) to its entire destruction; as contrasted with *total* loss. Partial loss is one in which the damage done to the thing insured is not so complete as to amount to a total loss, either actual or constructive. In every such case the underwriter is liable to pay such proportion of the sum which would be payable on total loss as the damage sustained by the subject of insurance bears to the whole value at the time of insurance. Partial loss implies a damage sustained by the ship or cargo, which falls upon the respective owners of the property so damaged; and, when happening from any peril insured against by the policy, the owners are to be indemnified by the underwriters, unless in cases excepted by the express terms of the policy. *See also* New for old.

Partial payment. *See* Payment.

Partial release. Clause in blanket mortgage directing mortgagee to release specified parcels from lien upon payment of certain sum.

Partial taking. *See* Eminent domain.

Partial verdict. *See* Verdict.

Particeps criminis /pártəsèps krímənəs/. A participant in a crime; an accomplice. One who shares or co-operates in a criminal offense, tort or fraud. *See* Accomplice.

Participate /pərtísəpèyt/. To receive or have a part or share of; to partake of; experience in common with others; to have or enjoy a part or share in common with others. To partake, as to "participate" in a discussion, or in a pension or profit sharing plan. To take equal shares and proportions; to share or divide, as to participate in an estate. To take as tenants in common.

Participation. Provision in insurance policies by which the insured shares or participates in each loss incurred and covered by the policy on a specified percentage basis. Sometimes loosely referred to as coinsurance but latter term is not strictly applicable.

To prove "participation" in a criminal enterprise, for purpose of convicting for aiding and abetting, there must be evidence to establish that defendant engaged in some affirmative conduct, that is, that defendant committed an overt act designed to aid in success of the venture; proof of mere negative acquiescence will not suffice.

Participation loan. As a loan risk safeguard, and because of statutory and regulatory limitations on the amount which a single bank may lend to a single borrower, two or more banks will join in larger loans with each bank lending a portion of the amount to the borrower. Such loans are usually arranged for and serviced by a "lead" bank-lender.

Participation mortgage. Type of mortgage where lender participates in profits of venture beyond or in addition to normal interest rate.

Particular. Relating to a part or portion of anything; separate; sole; single; individual; specific; local; comprising a part only; partial in extent;

not universal. Opposed to general. Of, or pertaining to, a single person, class or thing.

As to *particular* Average; Customs; Estate; Malice; and Partnership, see those titles.

Particularity. In a pleading, affidavit, or the like, is the detailed statement of particulars.

Particular lien. A right to retain a thing for some charge or claim growing out of, or connected with, the identical thing. Right to retain property of another on account of labor employed or money expended on that specific property, and such lien may arise by implication of law, usages of a trade, or by express contract. *See e.g.* Artisan's lien.

Particulars. The details of a claim, or the separate items of an account. When these are stated in an orderly form, for the information of a defendant, the statement is called a "bill of particulars". *See* Particulars of criminal charges.

Particulars, bill of. *See* Bill *(Bill of particulars)*; Particulars of criminal charges.

Particulars of criminal charges. A prosecutor, when a charge is general, is frequently ordered to give the defendant a statement of the specific acts charged (bill of particulars). Fed.R.Crim.P. 7. *See* Bill *(Bill of particulars)*.

Particulars of sale. When property such as land, houses, shares, reversions, etc., is to be sold by auction, it is usually described in a document called the "particulars," copies of which are distributed among intending bidders. They should fairly and accurately describe the property.

Particular tenant. The tenant of a particular estate. *See* Estate.

Parties. The persons who take part in the performance of any act, or who are directly interested in any affair, contract, or conveyance, or who are actively concerned in the prosecution and defense of any legal proceeding. *See also* Party.

In the Roman civil law, the parties were designated as *"actor" and "reus".* In civil actions they are called "plaintiff" and "defendant"; in equity, "complainant", or "plaintiff", and "defendant"; in admiralty practice, "libelant" and "respondent" or "libelee"; in appeals, "appellant" and "respondent" or "appellee", or sometimes, "plaintiff in error" and "defendant in error"; in criminal proceedings, "State of ____," or "United States of America", and "defendant".

See also Coparties; Identity of parties; Indispensable parties; Interpleader; Intervention; Joinder; Necessary parties; Party; Proper party; Real party in interest; Substitution of parties; Third-party practice.

Indispensible parties. See Joinder.

Joinder of parties. See Joinder.

Necessary parties. *See* Joinder; Necessary parties.

Parties to crime. *See* Accessory; Accomplice; Principal.

Proper parties. *See* Joinder.

Real party in interest. *See* Party.

Parties and privies. Parties to a deed or contract are those with whom the deed or contract is actually made or entered into. By the term "privies," as applied to contracts, is frequently meant those between whom the contract is mutually binding, although not literally parties to such contract. Thus, in the case of a lease, the lessor and lessee are both parties and privies, the contract being literally made between the two, and also being mutually binding; but, if the lessee assign his interest to a third party, then a privity arises between the assignee and the original lessor, although such assignee is not literally a party to the original lease.

Parties in interest. *See* Party *(Real party in interest).*

Partisan. An adherent to a particular party or cause as opposed to the public interest at large.

Partition. The dividing of lands held by joint tenants, coparceners, or tenants in common. And, in a less technical sense, any division of real or personal property between co-owners, resulting in individual ownership of the interests of each. Division between several persons of property which belongs to them as co-owners; it may be compulsory (judicial) or voluntary. Partition severs unity of possession.

Commonly, the court will order the property sold and the proceeds divided instead of ordering a physical partition of the property.

Partner. A member of partnership or firm; one who has united with others to form a partnership in business. *See also* General partner; Partnership.

Dormant partners. Those whose names are not known or do not appear as partners, but who nevertheless are silent partners, and partake of the profits, and thereby become partners, either absolutely to all intents and purposes, or at all events in respect to third parties. Dormant partners, in strictness of language, mean those who are merely passive in the firm, whether known or unknown, in contradistinction to those who are active and conduct the business of the firm, as principals. *See also* Silent partner.

Full or general partner. A partner who participates fully in the profits, losses and management of the partnership and who is personally liable for its debts.

Junior partner. A partner whose participation in the firm is limited as to both profits and management. *See also* Limited partner, below.

Limited partner. A partner whose participation in the profits is limited by an agreement and who is not liable for the debts of the partnership beyond his capital contribution. *See also* Partnership *(Limited partnership).*

Liquidating partner. The partner who, upon the dissolution or insolvency of the firm, is appointed to settle its accounts, collect assets, adjust claims, and pay debts.

Nominal partner. One whose name appears in connection with the business as a member of the firm, but who has no real interest in it.

Ostensible partner. One whose name appears to the world as such, or who is held out to all persons having dealings with the firm in the character of a partner, whether or not he has any real interest in the firm.

Principal partner. A partner with a 5 percent or greater interest in partnership capital or profits. I.R.C. § 706(b)(3).

Quasi partner. One who has joined with others in a business which appears to be a partnership but who is not actually a partner, *e.g.* joint adventurer.

Secret partner. *See Dormant partners, above.*

Silent partner. *See Dormant partners, above.*

Special partner. A member of a limited partnership, who furnishes certain funds, and whose liability extends no further than the fund furnished. A partner whose responsibility is restricted to the amount of his investment.

Surviving partner. The partner who, on the dissolution of the firm by the death of his copartner, occupies the position of a trustee to settle up its affairs.

Partnership. A business owned by two or more persons that is not organized as a corporation. A voluntary contract between two or more competent persons to place their money, effects, labor, and skill, or some or all of them, in lawful commerce or business, with the understanding that there shall be a proportional sharing of the profits and losses between them. An association of two or more persons to carry on, as co-owners, a business for profit. Uniform Partnership Act, § 6(1). Nearly all states have adopted the Uniform Partnership Act.

For income tax purposes, a partnership includes a syndicate, group, pool, or joint venture, as well as ordinary partnerships. In an ordinary partnership, two or more parties combine capital and/or services to carry on a business for profit as co-owners. I.R.C. § 7701(a)(2). *See also Limited partnership* and *Tiered partnership, below.*

Partnerships are treated as a conduit and are, therefore, not subject to taxation. The various items of partnership income, gains and losses, etc.

flow through to the individual partners and are reported on their personal income tax returns.

Articles of partnership. See that title.

Collapsible partnership. See that title.

Commercial partnership. See Trading partnership.

Family partnership. One which family members control by being partners. Children may be partners but for tax purposes they should be given complete control over their interests; otherwise, the entire profits will be considered income of the active adult partners. *See also* Family partnership.

General partnership. A partnership in which the parties carry on all their trade and business, whatever it may be, for the joint benefit and profit of all the parties concerned, whether the capital stock be limited or not, or the contributions thereto be equal or unequal. One in which all the partners share the profits and losses as well as the management equally, though their capital contributions may vary.

Implied partnership. One which is not a real partnership but which is recognized by the court as such because of the conduct of the parties; in effect, the parties are estopped from denying the existence of a partnership.

Limited partnership. A partnership consisting of one or more general partners, jointly and severally responsible as ordinary partners, and by whom the business is conducted, and one or more special partners, contributing in cash payments a specific sum as capital to the common stock, and who are not liable for the debts of the partnership beyond the fund so contributed. *See also* Limited partnership.

Mining partnership. See that title.

Particular partnership. One existing where the parties have united to share the benefits of a single individual transaction or enterprise.

Partnership assets. Property of any kind belonging to the firm as such (not the separate property of the individual partners) and available to the recourse of the creditors of the firm in the first instance.

Partnership at will. One designed to continue for no fixed period of time, but only during the pleasure of the parties, and which may be dissolved by any partner without previous notice.

Partnership by estoppel. Two or more persons who hold themselves out as partners to a third person, when in fact they are not partners, are barred from claiming they are not partners.

Partnership debt. One due from the partnership or firm as such and not (primarily) from one of the individual partners.

Partnership in commendam. A partnership formed by a contract by which one person or partnership agrees to furnish another person or partnership a certain amount, either in property or money, to be employed by the person or partnership to whom it is furnished, in his or their own name or firm, on condition of receiving a share in the profits, in the proportion determined by the contract, and of being liable to losses and expenses to the amount furnished and no more.

Secret partnership. One where the existence of certain persons as partners is not avowed to the public by any of the partners. *See* Partner *(Dormant partners).*

Special partnership. At common law, one formed for the prosecution of a special branch of business, as distinguished from the general business of the parties, or for one particular venture or subject. A joint adventure under state statutes; such are usually considered "limited partnerships".

Statutory partnership association. A statutory creation in some states (*e.g.* Michigan, New Jersey, Ohio) which resembles a corporation more than a partnership, but which has many attributes of the limited partnership.

Subpartnership. One formed where one partner in a firm makes a stranger a partner with him in his share of the profits of that firm. It is not a partnership but an arrangement in which the subpartner shares in the profits and losses of a partner.

Tiered partnership. An ownership arrangement wherein one partnership (the parent or first tier) is a partner in one or more partnerships (the subsidiary/subsidiaries or second tier). Frequently, the first tier is a holding partnership and the second tier is an operating partnership.

Trading partnership. See that title.

Universal partnership. One in which the partners jointly agree to contribute to the common fund of the partnership the whole of their property, of whatever character, and future, as well as present.

Partnership agreement. The document embodying the terms and conditions of a partnership and sometimes referred to as the articles of partnership.

Partnership articles. *See* Articles of partnership.

Partnership association. Type of business association which resembles in part a partnership and a joint stock company. Its salient feature is the limited liability of the members and is seldom used today.

Partnership certificate. A document evidencing the participation of the partners in a partnership and commonly furnished to financial institutions when the partnership borrows money.

Partnership insurance. *See* Insurance.

Part performance. A plaintiff who renders partial performance of a contract relying on the promised performance of the other party may successfully resist the defense of the statute of frauds under certain conditions. In order to establish part performance taking an oral contract for the sale of realty out of the statute of frauds, the acts relied upon as part performance must be of such a character that they can reasonably be naturally accounted for in no other way than that they were performed in pursuance of the contract, and they must be in conformity with its provisions. See U.C.C. § 2–201(3). *See also* Performance.

Party, *n.* A person concerned or having or taking part in any affair, matter, transaction, or proceeding, considered individually. A "party" to an action is a person whose name is designated on record as plaintiff or defendant. Term, in general, means one having right to control proceedings, to make defense, to adduce and cross-examine witnesses, and to appeal from judgment.

"Party" is a technical word having a precise meaning in legal parlance; it refers to those by or against whom a legal suit is brought, whether in law or in equity, the party plaintiff or defendant, whether composed of one or more individuals, and whether natural or legal persons; all others who may be affected by the suit, indirectly or consequently, are persons interested but not parties. *See also* Nominal defendant; Parties; Prevailing party.

For indispensable parties, joinder of parties, necessary parties, proper parties, *see* Joinder.

Party aggrieved. Under statutes permitting any party aggrieved to appeal, is one whose right has been directly and injuriously affected by action of court. One whose pecuniary interest in subject matter of an action is directly and injuriously affected or whose right of property is either established or divested by complained of decision.

To be "party aggrieved" by judgment, appellant's interest must be immediate, pecuniary and substantial and not nominal or remote consequence of judgment. *See also* Aggrieved party.

Party in interest. Primary meaning ascribed this term in bankruptcy cases is one whose pecuniary interest is directly affected by the bankruptcy proceeding. *See also Real party in interest, below.*

Party to be charged. A phrase used in the statute of frauds, meaning the party against whom the contract is sought to be enforced. The party to be charged in the action—that is, the defendant.

Political party. A body of voters organized for the purpose of influencing or controlling the policies and conduct of government through the nomination and election of its candidates to office. *See also* Political party.

Real party in interest. Fed.R. Civil P. 17(a) provides that every action shall be prosecuted by the "real party in interest." The adoption of this rule was intended to change the common law rule which permitted suit to be brought only in the name of the person having the legal title to the right of action, and thus precluded suit by persons who had only equitable or beneficial interests. Under the rule the "real party in interest" is the party who, by the substantive law, possesses the right sought to be enforced, and not necessarily the person who will ultimately benefit from the recovery. This is illustrated by the further language of the rule stating that executors, administrators, and other named representatives may sue in their own name without joining with them the party for whose benefit the action is brought.

Third parties. A term used to include all persons who are not parties to the contract, agreement, or instrument of writing by which their interest in the thing conveyed is sought to be affected. *See also* Beneficiary.

In civil actions, a defendant, as a third-party plaintiff, may cause a summons and complaint to be served upon a person not a party to the action who is or may be liable to him for all or part of the plaintiffs' claim against him. A similar right is afforded to the plaintiff when a counterclaim is asserted against him. Fed.R. Civil P. 14. *See* Third party complaint; Third-party practice.

Party wall. A wall erected on a property boundary as a common support to structures on both sides, which are under different ownerships. A wall built partly on the land of one owner, and partly on the land of another, for the common benefit of both in supporting the construction of contiguous buildings. A division wall between two adjacent properties belonging to different persons and used for mutual benefit of both parties, but it is not necessary that the wall should stand part upon each of two adjoining lots, and it may stand wholly upon one lot.

In the primary and most ordinary meaning of the term, a party-wall is (1) a wall of which the two adjoining owners are tenants in common. But it may also mean (2) a wall divided longitudinally into two strips, one belonging to each of the neighboring owners; (3) a wall which belongs entirely to one of the adjoining owners, but is subject to an easement or right in the other to have it maintained as a dividing wall between the two tenements (the term is so used in some of the English building acts); or (4) a wall divided longitudinally into two moieties, each moiety being subject to a cross-easement in favor of the owner of the other moiety.

Par value. The face or stated value of a share of stock or bond. With reference to mortgages or trust deeds, the value of the mortgage based on the balance owing, without discount.

In the case of a common share, par means an arbitrary or nominal dollar amount assigned to the share by the issuing company. Par value may also be used to compute the dollar amount of the common shares on the balance sheet. Par value has little significance so far as market value of common stock is concerned. Many companies today issue no-par stock but give a stated per share value on the balance sheet. In the case of preferred shares and bonds, however, par is important. It often signifies the dollar value upon which dividends on preferred stocks, and interest on bonds, are figured. In the case of bonds and stock, the face value appearing on the certificate is the par value. Those stocks not containing such a statement have no par value.

Bonds are issued at or very near par value, and subsequently trade at either a discount or a premium to this figure, based on the direction of interest rates. Bonds mature at par.

Par value *or* **stated value.** The Revised Model Business Corporation Act and the statutes of many states have eliminated the concept of par value.

Pass, *v.* To utter or pronounce, as when the court *passes* sentence upon a prisoner. Also to proceed; to be rendered or given, as when judgment is said to *pass* for the plaintiff in a suit.

In legislative parlance, a bill or resolution is said to *pass* when it is agreed to or enacted by the house, or when the body has sanctioned its adoption by the requisite majority of votes; in the same circumstances, the body is said to *pass* the bill or motion. *See also* Passage.

When an auditor appointed to examine into any accounts certifies to their correctness, he is said to *pass* them; *i.e.,* they pass through the examination without being detained or sent back for inaccuracy or imperfection.

The term also means to examine into anything and then authoritatively determine the disputed questions which it involves. In this sense a jury is said to *pass upon* the rights or issues in litigation before them.

In the language of conveyancing, the term means to move from one person to another; *i.e.* to be transferred or conveyed from one owner to another.

To publish; utter; transfer; circulate; impose fraudulently. This is the meaning of the word when the offense of *passing* counterfeit money or a forged paper is spoken of.

"Pass," "utter," "publish," and "sell" are in some respects convertible terms, and, in a given case, "pass" may include utter, publish, and sell. The words "uttering" and "passing," used of notes, do not necessarily import that they are transferred as genuine. The words include any delivery of a note to another for value, with intent that it shall be put into circulation as money. When used in connection with negotiable instrument means to deliver, to circulate, to hand from one person to another. *See* Delivery; Negotiation; Transfer; Utter.

Pass, *n.* Permission to pass; a license to go or come; a certificate, emanating from authority, wherein it is declared that a designated person is permitted to go beyond certain boundaries which, without such authority, he could not lawfully pass. Also a ticket issued by a railroad or other transportation company, authorizing a designated person to travel free on its lines, between certain points or for a limited time.

Passage. Act of passing; transit; transition. A way over water or land or through the air. An easement giving the right to pass over a piece of private water. Travel by sea; a voyage over water; the carriage of passengers by water; price paid for such carriage.

Enactment; the act of carrying a bill or resolution through a legislative or deliberative body in accordance with the prescribed forms and requisites. The emergence of the bill in the form of a law, or the motion in the form of a resolution. Passage may mean when bill has passed either or both houses of legislature or when it is signed by President or Governor.

Passbook. Document issued by a bank in which the customer's transactions (*i.e.* savings deposits and withdrawals) are recorded.

Passenger. In general, a person who gives compensation to another for transportation. The word passenger has however various meanings, depending upon the circumstances under which and the context in which the word is used; sometimes it is construed in a restricted legal sense as referring to one who is being carried by another for hire; on other occasions, the word is interpreted as meaning any occupant of a vehicle other than the person operating it.

The essential elements of "passenger" as opposed to "guest" under guest statute are that driver must receive some benefit sufficiently real, tangible, and substantial to serve as the inducing cause of the transportation so as to completely overshadow mere hospitality or friendship; it may be easier to find compensation where the trip has commercial or business flavor.

A person whom a common carrier has contracted to carry from one place to another, and has, in the course of the performance of that contract, received under his care either upon the means of conveyance, or at the point of departure of that means of conveyance.

Passenger mile. In statistics of transportation, a unit of measure equal to the transport of one passenger over one mile of route.

Passim /pǽsəm/. Lat. Everywhere. Often used to indicate a very general reference to a book or legal authority.

Passion. In the definition of manslaughter as homicide committed without premeditation but under the influence of sudden "passion" or "heat of passion", this term means any of the emotions of the mind known as rage, anger, hatred, furious resentment, or terror, rendering the mind incapable of cool reflection. *See also* Heat of passion.

Passive. As used in law, this term means inactive; permissive; consisting in endurance or submission, rather than action; and in some connections it carries the implication of being subjected to a burden or charge.

As to *passive* Debt; Negligence; Title; Trust and Use; see those titles.

Passive activity. A term, introduced with the Tax Reform Act of 1986, generally refering to a trade or business activity in which a taxpayer does not materially participate. Such activities are subject to limitations on the deduction of losses and credits. An example is an investment in a limited partnership. *See* Passive income; Passive loss.

Passive income. Income earned in an activity in which an individual does not materially participate. An example is income from an interest in a limited partnership in contrast to "active income" which is salaries and wages, or earnings from a trade or business. *See also* Passive loss.

Passive investment income. As defined in I.R.C. § 1362(d)(3)(D), passive investment income means gross receipts from royalties, certain rents, dividends, interest, annuities, and gains from the sale or exchange of stock and securities.

Passive loss. In tax law, any loss from (1) activities in which the taxpayer does not materially participate, (2) rental activities (with certain exceptions for individuals who actively participate in rental activities), or (3) tax shelter activities. The deductibility of passive losses are limited based upon when the activity was acquired, as well as the type of activity involved. Any passive losses which are limited in the year incurred are fully deductible in the year the investment activity is disposed. Passive loss limitations were phased in beginning in 1987. *See also* Passive activity; Passive income; Portfolio income.

Passport. A document identifying a citizen, in effect requesting foreign powers to allow the bearer to enter and to pass freely and safely, recognizing the right of the bearer to the protection and good offices of American diplomatic and consular offices. A passport is evidence of permission from sovereign to its citizen to travel to foreign countries and to return to land of his allegiance, as well as request to foreign powers that such citizen be allowed to pass freely and safely. *See also* Visa.

Any travel document issued by competent authority showing the bearer's origin, identity, and nationality if any, which is valid for the entry of the bearer into a foreign country. 8 U.S.C.A. § 1101.

In international law. A license or safe-conduct, issued during the progress of a war, authorizing a person to remove himself or his effects from the territory of one of the belligerent nations to another country, or to travel from country to country without arrest or detention on account of the war.

Maritime. A document issued to a neutral merchant vessel, by her own government, during the progress of a war, to be carried on the voyage, to evidence her nationality and protect her against the cruisers of the belligerent powers. This paper is otherwise called a "pass," "sea-pass," "sea-letter," "sea-brief." It usually contains the captain's or master's name and residence, the name, property, description, tonnage, and destination of the ship, the nature and quantity of the cargo, the place from whence it comes, and its destination, with such other matters as the practice of the place requires.

Past consideration. In contracts, a detriment suffered by a contracting party at a time antecedent to the formation of a contract and hence, except in unusual cases, is not legally sufficient consideration to support a contract. In law of negotiable instruments, past consideration is sufficient to support a note or other negotiable instrument.

Past recollection recorded. Under this evidence rule, a memorandum or record concerning a matter about which a witness once had knowledge but now has insufficient recollection to enable him to testify fully and accurately, shown to have been made or adopted by the witness when the matter was fresh in his memory and to reflect that knowledge correctly, is not excluded by the hearsay rule, even though the declarant is available as a witness. If admitted, the memorandum or record may be read into evidence but may not itself be received as an exhibit unless offered by an adverse party. Fed.Evid.R. 803(5).

Under this doctrine, a written report or other document is properly admissible into evidence if witness has testified that on examination of the document he has no independent recollection of the matters contained therein.

Patent, *adj.* /péytənt/. Open; manifest; evident; unsealed. Used in this sense in such phrases as "patent ambiguity," "patent writ," "letters patent."

Letters patent. Open letters, as distinguished from letters close. An instrument proceeding from the government, and conveying a right, authority, or grant to an individual, as a patent for a tract of land, or for the exclusive right to make and sell a new invention. *See* Letters patent; Patent and Trademark Office.

Patent, *n.* /pǽtənt/. A grant of some privilege, property, or authority, made by the government or sovereign of a country to one or more individuals.

The instrument by which a state or government grants public lands to an individual.

A grant of right to exclude others from making, using or selling one's invention and includes right to license others to make, use or sell it. A grant from the government conveying and securing for an inventor the exclusive right to make, use, and sell an invention for seventeen years. 35 U.S.C.A. § 154. *See* Board of Patent Appeals and Inferences; Patent and copyright clause; Patent and Trademark Office.

See also Basic *or* pioneer patent; Combination patent; File wrapper estoppel; Identity; Invent; Invention; Lapse patent; Letters patent; License; New and useful; Novelty; Official Gazette; On sale; Paper patent; Process patent; Prosecution history estoppel; Public use; Scope of a patent; Shop right rule; Useful; Utility.

Design patent. The unique appearance or design of an article of manufacture may be protected against duplication by a design patent if it is original, non-obvious and ornamental. Design patents may be issued for both surface ornamentation or the overall configuration of an object. Such patents last for a term of 14 years. Material that is eligible for design patent protection may also be copyrightable. 35 U.S.C.A. § 171.

Land patent. A muniment of title issued by a government or state for the conveyance of some portion of the public domain.

Mining claims. The instrument by which title to mining claims is conveyed by the federal government subject to any existing liens and any vested and accrued water rights and in conformity with conditions imposed by state statutes.

Patent pending. Designation (often abbreviated "Pat. Pend.") describing the legal status of patent application, after patent application has been filed and while patent examination is being conducted by U.S. Patent and Trademark Office to determine whether the claimed invention is in fact new, useful and non-obvious.

Patent-right. A right secured by patent; usually meaning a right to the exclusive manufacture, use and sale of an invention or patented article.

Patent-right dealer. Any one whose business it is to sell, or offer for sale, patent-rights.

Patent suit. A suit with issues affecting the validity, enforcement or infringement of a patent.

Pioneer patent. A patent for an invention covering a function never before performed, or a wholly novel device, or one of such novelty and importance as to mark a distinct step in the progress of the art, as distinguished from a mere improvement or perfecting of what has gone before. *See* Novelty.

Plant patent. A patent granted to person who invents or discovers and asexually reproduces any distinct and new variety of plant, including cultivated sports, mutants, hybrids, and newly found seedlings, other than a tuber propagated plant or a plant found in an uncultivated state. 35 U.S. C.A. § 161.

Reissued patent. A patent may be reissued whenever it is, through error without any deceptive intention, deemed wholly or partly inoperative or invalid, by reason of a defective specification or drawing, or by reason of the patentee claiming more or less than he had a right to claim in the patent. 35 U.S.C.A. § 251.

Tax treatment. A patent is an identifiable intangible asset which may be amortized over the remaining life of the patent. The sale of a patent usually results in capital gain treatment. I.R.C. § 1235. If developed internally by a company, the development costs are expensed as incurred under generally accepted accounting principles.

Utility patent. The customary type of patent issued to any novel, non-obvious, and useful machine, article of manufacture, composition of matter or process. This is one of three types of patents provided for by the statute, the others being design and plant patents. *See also* Utility.

Patentable. Suitable to be patented; entitled by law to be protected by the issuance of a patent. And to be patentable, a device must embody some new idea or principle not before known, and it must be a discovery as distinguished from mere mechanical skill or knowledge. *See* New and useful; Novelty.

Patent ambiguity. An ambiguity apparent on face of instrument and arising by reason of any inconsistency or inherent uncertainty of language used so that effect is either to convey no definite meaning or confused meaning. *See also* Ambiguity. *Compare* Latent ambiguity.

Patent and copyright clause. Art. I, Sec. 8, cl. 8, U.S. Constitution, which provides for promoting the progress of science and useful arts, by securing for limited times to authors and inventors the exclusive right to their respective writings and discoveries.

Patent and Trademark Office. Federal agency in the Department of Commerce headed by the Commissioner of Patents and Trademarks. In addition to the examination of patent and trademark applications, issuance of patents, and registration of trademarks, the Patent and Trademark Office (PTO) sells printed copies of issued documents; records and indexes documents transferring ownership; maintains a scientific library and search files containing over 20 million documents, including U.S. and foreign patents and U.S. trademarks; provides search rooms for the public to research their applications; hears and decides appeals from prospective inventors and trademark applicants; participates in legal proceedings involving the issue of patents or trademark registrations; helps represent the United States in international efforts to cooperate on patent and trademark policy; compiles the Official Gazettes—a weekly list of all patents and trademarks issued by the PTO; and maintains a roster of agents and attorneys qualified to practice before the PTO.

Patent appeals. *See* Board of Patent Appeals and Interferences.

Patent defect. In sales of personal property, one which is plainly visible or which can be discovered by such an inspection as would be made in the exercise of ordinary care and prudence. U.C.C. § 2–605(1).

A patent defect in a legal description is one which cannot be corrected on its face, and a new description must be used. *Compare* Latent defect.

Patentee. He to whom a patent has been granted. The term is usually applied to one who has obtained letters patent for a new invention.

Patent infringement. The unauthorized making, using or selling of an invention covered by a valid claim of a patent during the term or extended term of the patent. See 35 U.S.C.A. § 271. Liability also exists for actively inducing infringement and for contributory infringement. 35 U.S. C.A. § 271(b), (c). *See also* Infringement.

Patent medicine. A packaged health remedy for public use, protected by letters patent and sold over-the-counter without a physician's prescription.

Patent pooling. An arrangement in which a number of manufacturers agree to an interchange of patent licenses among the members of the pooling group.

Paternal. That which belongs to the father or comes from him.

Paternal line. A line of descent or relationship between two persons which is traced through the father.

Paternal power. The authority lawfully exercised by parents over their children. This phrase is also used to translate the Latin *"patria potestas" (q.v.)*.

Paternal property. That which descends or comes to one from his father, grandfather, or other ascendant or collateral on the paternal side of the house.

Paternity. The state or condition of a father; the relationship of a father.

Paternity suit *or* **action.** A court action to determine whether a person is the father of a child born out of wedlock for the purpose, commonly, of enforcing support obligations. *See also* HLA test; Multiple access.

Pater patriæ /péytər pǽtriyiy/. Father of the country. *See* Parens patriæ.

Pathologist. One trained in the scientific study of disease, its causes, development and consequences.

Pathology. The science or doctrine of diseases. That part of medicine which explains the nature of diseases, their causes, and their symptoms.

Patient. Person under medical or psychiatric treatment and care. Person may be "patient" and physician-patient privilege may apply, where physician attends person for purpose of giving professional aid, even though person attended is unconscious or unaware of physician's presence and does not consent, or actually objects to being treated.

Patient-physician privilege. The right of one who is a patient to refuse to divulge, or have divulged by his physician, the communications made between he and his physician. This privilege is provided for by statute in most states, and, where recognized, it belongs to the patient and not to the physician and hence, it may be waived by the patient.

Patient's bill of rights. A general statement of patient rights voluntarily adopted by most health care providers, covering matters such as access to care, patient dignity and confidentiality, personal safety, consent to treatment and explanation of charges. Similar rights have been statutorily adopted in several states (cf. Minn.Stat. § 144.651) and by the federal government (cf. Developmentally Disabled Assistance and Bill of Rights Act of 1975, 42 U.S.C.A. § 6010). *See also* Patients Self Determination Act.

Patients Self Determination Act. Federal Act which requires hospitals, nursing homes, health maintenance organizations, hospices and home health-care companies to inform patients on admission if their state laws permit them to refuse treatment that would prolong their lives if they become incapacitated. *See also* Health care proxy; Medical directives; Will *(Living will)*.

Pat. Pend. *See* Patent *(Patent pending)*.

Patricide /pǽtrəsàyd/. One who has killed his or her father. The act of killing one's father.

Patrimonial /pæ̀trǝmówn(i)yǝl/. Pertaining to a patrimony; inherited from ancestors, but strictly from the direct male ancestors.

Patrimony /pǽtrǝmǝniy/. Such estate as has descended in the same family. Estates which have descended or been devised in a direct line from the father, and, by extension, from the mother or other ancestor. It has been held that the word is not necessarily restricted to property inherited directly from the father.

Patrimony is the total mass of existing or potential rights and liabilities attached to a person for the satisfaction of his economic needs and it is always attached to a natural or juridical person. Patrimony of a debtor is totality of assets and liabilities susceptible of pecuniary evaluation; as practical matter, debtor's patrimony consists of assets which are subject to execution for benefit of creditor.

Patrolman. A policeman assigned to duty in patrolling a certain beat or district; also the designation of a grade or rank in the organized police force of large cities, a patrolman being generally a private in the ranks, as distinguished from sergeants, lieutenants, etc. *See also* Police officer.

Patron. In ordinary usage one who protects, countenances, or supports some person or thing or business. One who habitually extends material assistance; a regular business customer; a protector or benefactor.

Patronage /pǽtrǝnǝj/péytr°/. Collective term to describe the customers of a business. Also, the practice of a public official in making appointments to public (non-civil service) offices and to confer honors. The right of appointing to office, considered as a perquisite, or personal right; not in the aspect of a public trust.

Patronize /péytrǝnayz/pǽtr°/. To act as a patron, extend patronage, countenance, encourage, favor.

Pattern. A reliable sample of traits, acts or other observable features characterizing an individual.

The words "pattern or practice" within the Civil Rights Act provision which permits the Attorney General to seek relief when there is a pattern or practice of resistance to the Act is more than isolated or accidental instance of conduct in violation of the Act; it means an intentional, regular or repeated violation of the right granted by the Act.

Pattern of racketeering activity. As used in the racketeering statute (RICO), 18 U.S.C.A. § 1962, a "pattern of racketeering activity" includes two or more related criminal acts that amount to, or threaten the likelihood of, continued criminal activity. A single illegal scheme can constitute a "pattern of racketeering activity," so long as the racketeering acts meet the "continuity plus rela-

tionship" requirement. A combination of specific factors, such as the number of unlawful acts, the length of time over which the acts were committed, the similarity of the acts, the number of victims, the number of perpetrators, and the character of the unlawful activity can be considered in determining whether a pattern existed. *See also* RICO laws.

Pauper /pópǝr/. A person so poor that he must be supported at public expense. A suitor who, on account of poverty, is allowed to sue or defend without being chargeable with costs; also, an indigent criminal defendant who has a right to assigned defense counsel. Fed.R.Crim.P. 44; Fed.R. App.P. 24; 18 U.S.C.A. § 3006A; 28 U.S.C.A. § 1915. *See* Counsel, right to; Indigent; In forma pauperis; Pauper's oath.

Dispauper. To deprive one of the status of a pauper and of any benefits incidental thereto: particularly, to take away the right to sue *in forma pauperis* because the person so suing, during the progress of the suit, has acquired money or property which would enable him to sustain the costs of the action.

Pauper's oath. Affidavit, verification, or oath by person seeking public assistance, appointment of counsel, waiver of court fees, or other free services or benefits, that he or she is in fact impoverished and as such unable to pay for such. *See e.g.* 28 U.S.C.A. § 1915. *See also* Poverty affidavit.

Pawn, *v.* To deliver personal property to another in pledge, or as security for a debt or sum borrowed.

Pawn, *n.* A bailment of goods to a creditor, as security for some debt or engagement; a pledge; a deposit of personal property made to a pawnbroker as security for a loan. That sort of bailment when goods or chattels are delivered to another as security to him for money borrowed of him by the bailor.

Also the specific chattel delivered to the creditor as a pledge.

See Bailment; Pledge.

Pawnbroker. A person whose business is to lend money, usually in small sums, on security of personal property deposited with him or left in pawn.

Pawnee. The person receiving a pawn, or to whom a pawn is made; the person to whom goods are delivered by another in pledge.

Pawnor. The person pawning goods or delivering goods to another in pledge.

Pay, *n.* Compensation; wages; salary; commissions; fees. The act or fact of paying or being paid. *See* Discharge; Payment.

Pay, *v.* To discharge a debt by tender of payment due; to deliver to a creditor the value of a debt, either in money or in goods, for his acceptance.

U.C.C. §§ 2–511, 3–604. To compensate for goods, services or labor. *See also* Discharge; Payment.

Payable. Capable of being paid; suitable to be paid; admitting or demanding payment; justly due; legally enforceable. A sum of money is said to be payable when a person is under an obligation to pay it. Payable may therefore signify an obligation to pay at a future time, but, when used without qualification, term normally means that the debt is payable at once, as opposed to "owing."

Payable after sight. Means that instrument is payable after acceptance of bill or protest for nonacceptance.

Payable on demand. Instruments payable on demand include those payable at sight or on presentation and those in which no time for payment is stated. U.C.C. § 3–108.

Payables. *See* Account (*Account payable*).

Payable to bearer. A negotiable instrument is payable to bearer when by its terms it is payable to (a) bearer or the order of bearer; or (b) a specified person or bearer; or (c) "cash" or the order of "cash", or any other indication which does not purport to designate a specific payee. U.C.C. § 3–111. *See also* Negotiation.

Payable to order. A negotiable instrument is payable to order when by its terms it is payable to the order or assigns of any person therein specified with reasonable certainty, or to him or his order, or when it is conspicuously designated on its face as "exchange" or the like and names a payee. U.C.C. § 3–110. *See also* Negotiation.

Pay any bank. After an item has been indorsed with the words "pay any bank" or the like, only a bank may acquire the rights of a holder: (a) until the item has been returned to the customer initiating collection; or (b) until the item has been specially indorsed by a bank to a person who is not a bank. U.C.C. § 4–201(2).

Payback method. An accounting method of analysis that measures the amount of time necessary to recover a project's initial cash investment.

Payback period. The amount of time it takes for the initial investment outlay to be recovered, without consideration for the time value of money.

Paydown. Repayment of loan but in an amount less than entire principal of loan. *See also* Payment, (*Part payment*).

Payee. The person in whose favor a bill of exchange, promissory note, or check is made or drawn; the person to whom or to whose order a bill, note, or check is made payable; the person to whom an instrument is payable upon issuance. The entity to whom a cash payment is made or who will receive the stated amount of money on a check. One to whom money is paid or is to be paid. *See* Draft; Fictitious payee.

Payer, *or* **payor.** One who pays, or who is to make a payment; particularly the person who is to make payment of a check, bill or note. Correlative to "payee."

Payment. The fulfilment of a promise, or the performance of an agreement. A discharge of an obligation or debt, and part payment, if accepted, is a discharge pro tanto.

In a more restricted legal sense payment is the performance of a duty, promise, or obligation, or discharge of a debt or liability, by the delivery of money or other value by a debtor to a creditor, where the money or other valuable thing is tendered and accepted as extinguishing debt or obligation in whole or in part. Also the money or other thing so delivered. U.C.C. §§ 2–511, 3–604.

Payment is a delivery of money or its equivalent in either specific property or services by one person from whom it is due to another person to whom it is due. A discharge in money or its equivalent of an obligation or debt owing by one person to another, and is made by debtor's delivery to creditor of money or some other valuable thing, and creditor's receipt thereof, for purpose of extinguishing debt.

Under Internal Revenue Code provision allowing deduction for charitable contribution of which payment is made within taxable year, "payment" need not be in money, but subject matter must have been placed beyond dominion and control of donor.

The execution and delivery of negotiable papers is not payment unless it is accepted by the parties in that sense. U.C.C. § 3–410.

See also Compulsory payment; Conditional payment; Constructive payment; Down payment; Final payment; Guaranty of payment; Installment credit; Installment loan; Installment sale; Involuntary payment; Liquidation; Lump-sum payment; Pay.

Affirmative defense. Payment is an affirmative defense which must be pleaded under Fed.R. Civil P. 8(c). It is a plea in avoidance.

Balloon payment. *See* Balloon payment.

Part payment. The reduction of any debt or demand by the payment of a sum less than the whole amount originally due.

The rule of partial payments is to apply the payment, in the first place, to the discharge of the interest then due. If the payment exceeds the interest, the surplus goes toward discharging the principal, and the subsequent interest is to be computed on the balance of principal remaining due. If the payment be less than the interest, the surplus of the interest must not be taken to augment the principal; but interest continues on the former principal until the period of time when the payments, taken together, exceed the interest then due, to discharge which they are applied, and the surplus, if any, is to be applied towards the discharge of the principal, and the interest is to be computed on the balance as aforesaid, and this process continues until final settlement.

Payment into court. The act of a defendant in depositing the amount which he admits to be due, with the proper officer of the court, for the benefit of the plaintiff and in answer to his claim. Fed.R. Civil P. 67.

Voluntary payment. A payment made by a debtor of his own will and choice, as distinguished from one exacted from him by process of execution or other compulsion.

Payment bond. *See* Miller Act; Performance bond.

Payment date. Date on which dividends will be paid to shareholders.

Payment guaranteed. "Payment guaranteed" or equivalent words added to a signature mean that the signer engages that if the instrument is not paid when due he will pay it according to its tenor without resort by the holder to any other party. U.C.C. § 4–416.

Payment in due course. With respect to negotiable instruments, means payment at or after the instrument's maturity date to the holder in good faith and without notice that the title is defective. Under the former Negotiable Instruments Law, a negotiable instrument could be discharged by payment in due course by or on behalf of the principle debtor. The Uniform Commercial Code § 3–603 eliminates any reference to payment in due course. It is now covered by § 3–601(3).

Payment into court. The deposit of funds or other things capable of delivery with the court during the pendency of a lawsuit. Fed.R.Civil P. 67.

Payor. The person by whom a bill or note has been or should have been paid.

Payor bank. A bank by which an item is payable as drawn or accepted, U.C.C. § 4–105(b), which includes the drawee of a check. Term includes drawee bank and also bank at which item is payable if item constitutes order on bank to pay.

Payout ratio. A firm's dividends divided by its earnings.

Payroll register. A journal-like record that summarizes a firm's entire payroll.

Payroll tax. A tax on an employees' salary or on the income of a self-employed individual. Federal and state income taxes are paid by the employee or the self-employed individual; social security taxes are paid both by the employer and employee and paid solely by the self-employed individual. Unemployment taxes are paid by the employer.

PBGC. *See* Pension Benefit Guaranty Corporation.

P.C. An abbreviation for "Pleas of the Crown;" sometimes also for "Privy Council," "Parliamentary Cases," "Patent Cases," "Practice Cases," "Penal Code," "Political Code," or "Professional Corporation."

Peace. For purposes of breach of the peace statute, peace is that state and sense of safety which is necessary to the comfort and happiness of every citizen, and which government is instituted to secure. Term, within law of breach of the peace, means tranquility enjoyed by citizens of the municipality or community where good order reigns among its members.

Articles of the peace. *See* Articles.

Bill of peace. *See* Bill.

Breach of peace. *See* Breach.

Conservator of the peace. *See* Conservator.

Justice of the peace. See that title.

Peace officers. This term is variously defined by statute in the different states; but generally it includes sheriffs and their deputies, constables, marshals, members of the police force of cities, and other officers whose duty is to enforce the local government laws and ordinances and preserve the public peace. In general, any person who has been given general authority to make arrests. Generally a "peace officer" is a person designated by public authority to keep the peace and arrest persons guilty or suspected of crime and he is a conservator of the peace, which term is synonymous with the term "peace officer". *See also* Police officer.

Peaceable. Free from the character of force, violence, or trespass; as, a "peaceable entry" on lands. *Peaceable possession* of real estate is such as is acquiesced in by all other persons, including rival claimants, and not disturbed by any forcible attempt at ouster nor by adverse suits to recover the possession or the estate. *Compare* Adverse possession.

Peace bond. Type of surety bond required by a judge or magistrate of one who has threatened to breach the peace or has a history of such misconduct.

Peace officer. *See* Police officer.

Peck. A measure of two gallons; a dry measure.

Peculation. The unlawful appropriation, by a depositary of public funds, of the property of the government intrusted to his care, to his own use, or that of others. The fraudulent misappropriation by one to his own use of money or goods intrusted to his care.

Pecuniary /pəkyúwn(i)yəriy/. Monetary; relating to money; financial; consisting of money or that which can be valued in money.

As to *pecuniary* Consideration; Damages; and Legacy; see those titles.

Pecuniary benefits. Benefits that can be valued in money. Pecuniary benefits available to parents by reason of death of an adult child encompass those benefits, including money, that can be reasonably estimated in money, such as labor, services, kindness and attention of child to parents.

Pecuniary bequest. A bequest of money to an heir by a decedent. A bequest of money to a legatee by a testator. Also known as a monetary bequest. *See* Bequest.

Pecuniary consideration. *See* Consideration.

Pecuniary damages. *See* Damages; Pecuniary loss.

Pecuniary formulas. In federal estate taxation, a gift to a surviving spouse of an amount equal to the maximum marital deduction to which the estate is entitled, less the value of any other interests passing to the surviving spouse that qualify for the marital deduction. *See also* Marital deduction.

Pecuniary injury. Within meaning of wrongful death statute providing that damages may be awarded "taking into consideration the pecuniary injury or injuries resulting from such death to the surviving party or parties entitled to the judgment," term "pecuniary injury" means a reasonable expectation of pecuniary benefits from the continued life of the deceased. Such compensation includes damages for deprivation of support, of companionship, guidance, advice, love and affection of deceased. *See also* Consortium; Damages *(Pecuniary damages);* Loss; Pecuniary loss.

Pecuniary interest. A direct financial interest in an action or other matter as would, for example, require a judge to disqualify himself from sitting on a case if he owned stock in corporate party.

Pecuniary legacy. *See* Legacy.

Pecuniary loss. A loss of money, or of something by which money or something of money value may be acquired. As applied to a dependent's loss from death pecuniary loss means the reasonable expectation of pecuniary benefit from the continued life of the deceased: such includes loss of services, training, nurture, education, guidance, and society.

Pecuniary loss within Wrongful Death Act means what the life of decedent was worth, in a pecuniary sense, to the survivors, including loss of care, love, and affection.

See also Pecuniary injury.

Peddler. An itinerant trader; person who goes about seeking sales and deliveries of articles to possible customers. A person who sells small goods which he carries with him in traveling about from place to place, and whose activities generally require that he be licensed by the city or town within which he peddles. *See also* Hawker.

Pederasty /pédəræstiy/. In criminal law, the unnatural carnal copulation of male with male, particularly of a man with a boy; a form of sodomy *(q.v.).*

Pedestrian. While "pedestrians" are ordinarily understood to be persons traveling on foot, they may be on roller skates, ice skates, stilts or crutches. The statutory definition of "pedestrian" is broad enough to include persons standing upon the highway as well as those traversing it. Person on foot does not cease to be "pedestrian" within policy covering injuries sustained while a pedestrian merely because he is not in motion.

Pedigree /pédəgriy/. Lineage, descent, and succession of families; line of ancestors from which a person descends; genealogy. An account or register of a line of ancestors. Family relationship.

Evidence. The "pedigree exception" to hearsay rule allows consideration of hearsay evidence regarding a person's family relationship as proof of existence of the relationship. Statements of fact concerning genealogy are not excluded by the hearsay rule, even though the declarant is available as a witness. Fed.Evid.R. 803.

Peeping Tom. As used in reference to, *e.g.,* "Peeping Tom" statute, has commonly understood meaning as one who sneaks up to window and peeps in for purpose of spying on and invading privacy of inhabitants.

Peer Review Organizations. A Peer Review Organization in the medicare program is essentially an enforcement agent of the federal government for purposes of Health and Human Services regulations under which the PRO monitors compliance with Health and Human Services' rules affecting private hospitals seeking compensation from the agency.

Peers /pírz/. Equals; those who are a man's equals in rank and station; thus "trial by a jury of his peers" means trial by jury of citizens. For *Judgment of his peers, see* Judgment.

Peg. To fix the price of something, as the government may stabilize the price of gold by offering to buy all the gold offered at a stated price. Speculators in stocks may peg the price of securities by frequent buying and selling at the pegged price, though today such manipulation is illegal.

Penal. Punishable; inflicting a punishment; containing a penalty, or relating to a penalty.

Penal action. In its broadest context, it refers to criminal prosecution. More particularly, it refers to a civil action in which a wrongdoer is subject to a fine or penalty payable to the aggrieved party (*e.g.* punitive damages).

The word "penal" is inherently a much broader term than "criminal" since it pertains to any punishment or penalty and relates to acts which are not necessarily delineated as criminal. Action is essentially "penal" if amount sought to be recovered is arbitrarily exacted for some act or omission of the defendant.

An action upon a penal statute; an action for the recovery of a penalty given by statute. In a broad sense, the term has been made to include all actions in which there may be a recovery of exemplary or vindictive damages, as suits for libel and slander, or in which special, double, or treble damages are given by statute, such as actions to recover money paid as usury or for violation of antitrust laws. But in a more particular sense it means (1) an action on a statute which gives a certain penalty to be recovered by any person who will sue for it, or (2) an action in which the judgment against the defendant is in the nature of a fine or is intended as a punishment, actions in which the recovery is to be compensatory in its purpose and effect not being penal actions but civil suits, though they may carry special damages by statute. *See* Damages (*Exemplary or punitive damages, Treble damages*).

Penal bill. An instrument formerly in use, by which a party bound himself to pay a certain sum or sums of money, or to do certain acts, or, in default thereof, to pay a certain specified sum by way of penalty; thence termed a "penal sum." These instruments have been superseded by the use of a bond in a penal sum, with conditions. *See* Penal bond.

Penal bond. A promise to pay a named sum of money, the penalty, in the event of nonperformance, with a condition underwritten that, if a stipulated collateral thing, other than the payment of money, be done or forborne, the obligation shall be void. Bond conditioned upon forfeiture of penalty for its breach. *See* Penalty.

Penal clause. A secondary obligation entered into for purpose of enforcing performance of a primary obligation, and nature of penalty is by way of compensation for damages and not as punishment for failure to perform obligation. Also a clause in a statute declaring a penalty for a violation of the preceding clauses. *See* Penalty clause.

Penal code. Bringing together and codification of substantive criminal laws of state or federal government; *e.g.* California Penal Code; Title 18 of U.S. Code. Several state Penal or Criminal Codes are patterned on the A.L.I. Model Penal Code. *See also* Penal laws.

Penal institutions. Generic term to describe all places of confinement for those convicted of crime such as jails, prisons, workhouses, houses of correction, and other correctional institutions.

Penal laws. Term, in general, refers to state and federal statutes that define criminal offenses and specify corresponding fines and punishment. Statutes imposing a penalty, fine, or punishment for certain offenses of a public nature or wrongs committed against the state. *See also* Penal code.

Penal statutes. *See* Penal code; Penal laws.

Penal sum. A sum agreed upon in a bond, to be forfeited if the condition of the bond is not fulfilled. *See also* Penal bond; Penalty.

Penalty. An elastic term with many different shades of meaning; it involves idea of punishment, corporeal or pecuniary, or civil or criminal, although its meaning is generally confined to pecuniary punishment.

The sum of money which the obligor of a bond undertakes to pay in the event of his omitting to perform or carry out the terms imposed upon him by the conditions of the bond. A penalty is a sum inserted in a contract, not as a measure of compensation for its breach, but rather as punishment for default, or by way of security for actual damages which might be sustained by reason of nonperformance. The sum a party agrees to pay in the event of a contract breach, but which is fixed, not as a pre-estimate of probable actual damages, but as a punishment, the threat of which is designed to prevent the breach.

A penalty is a sum of money which the law exacts payment of by way of punishment for doing some act which is prohibited or for not doing some act which is required to be done. A statutory liability imposed on wrongdoer in amount which is not limited to damages suffered by party wronged. *See also* Damages (*Exemplary or punitive damages*), (*Treble damages*).

See also Fine; Forfeiture; Penal action; Punishment; Statutory penalty.

Penalty clause. Provision in contract, loan agreement, savings instrument or the like providing penalties for default, late or missed payments, early withdrawals, etc. Such clauses are generally not enforceable by the courts. A provision for liquidated damages, however, will be enforced by the courts but the liquidated damages must be a reasonable estimate at the time of contracting of the likely damages from breach. Whether a provision for damages is a penalty clause or a liquidated damages clause is a question of law.

Pendency. Suspense; the state of being pendent or undecided; the state of an action, etc., after it has been begun, and before the final disposition of it. *See* Pending.

Pendens /péndènz/. Lat. Pending; as *lis pendens,* a pending suit.

Pendente lite /pendéntiy láytiy/. Lat. Pending the lawsuit; during the actual progress of a suit; during litigation. Matters "pendente lite" are contingent on outcome of litigation.

Pendent jurisdiction. A principle applied in federal courts that allows state created causes of action arising out of the same transaction to be joined with a federal cause of action even if diversity of citizenship is not present. Pendent jurisdiction is discretionary matter whereby federal court may allow assertion of nonfederal claim for which no independent jurisdictional ground exists along with recognized federal claim between same parties who are properly before the court, provided relationship between federal claim and state claim permits conclusion that entire action before court comprises but one constitutional case. The doctrine permits federal court under some circumstances to determine state cause of action which otherwise would have to be heard in state court; if state court would be without authority to award damages under state law, the doctrine can give the federal district court no greater power to do so. The doctrine has been codified as "supplemental jurisdiction" at 28 U.S.C.A. § 1367. *See* Supplemental jurisdiction.

Pending. Begun, but not yet completed; during; before the conclusion of; prior to the completion of; unsettled; undetermined; in process of settlement or adjustment. Awaiting an occurrence or conclusion of action, period of continuance or indeterminacy. Thus, an action or suit is "pending" from its inception until the rendition of final judgment.

An action is "pending" after it is commenced by either filing a complaint with the court or by the service of a summons.

See also Pendente lite.

Penetration. A term used in criminal law, and denoting (in cases of alleged rape) the insertion of the male part into the female parts to however slight an extent; and by which insertion the offense is complete without proof of emission.

Penitentiary. A prison, correctional institution, or other place of confinement where convicted felons are sent to serve out the term of their sentence.

Pennoyer Rule. A rule to the effect that a court which has no personal jurisdiction over a defendant may not issue an in personam judgment or decree against him. Pennoyer v. Neff, 95 U.S. 714, 24 L.Ed. 565.

Penny stocks. Low-priced stock issues often highly speculative, selling at less than $1 a share.

Pennyweight. A Troy weight, equal to twenty-four grains, or one-twentieth part of an ounce.

Penology. The science of prison management and rehabilitation of criminals.

Pen register. A mechanical device that records the numbers dialed on a telephone by monitoring the electrical impulses caused when the dial on the telephone is released. It does not overhear oral communications and does not indicate whether calls are actually completed; thus, there is no recording or monitoring of the conversation. For regulation of use of pen registers, see 18 U.S.C.A. § 3121 et seq. *See also* Wiretapping.

Pension. Retirement benefit paid regularly (normally, monthly), with the amount of such based generally on length of employment and amount of wages or salary of pensioner. Deferred compensation for services rendered. *See also* Pension plan; Vested pension.

Pension Benefit Guaranty Corporation. Federal agency established by Employee Retirement Income Security Act of 1974 (ERISA), to guarantee payment of insured benefits if covered employee retirement plans terminate without sufficient assets to pay such benefits. 29 U.S.C.A. § 1302.

Pensioner. Recipient or beneficiary of a pension plan.

Pension fund. Fund established by corporations, unions, governmental bodies, etc. to pay pension benefits to its retired workers. *See* Pension plan.

Pension plan. A plan established and maintained by an employer primarily to provide systematically for the payment of definitely determinable benefits to his employees, or their beneficiaries, over a period of years (usually for life) after retirement. Retirement benefits are measured by, and based on, such factors as years of service and compensation received by the employees. The Employees Retirement Income Security Act (ERISA) governs plan qualification, operation, and administration, and specifically such matters as participation requirements, funding, vesting and filing and reporting with the Internal Revenue Service and Labor Department. Pension benefits under qualified plans are guaranteed by the Pension Benefit Guaranty Corporation.

A stated allowance out of the public treasury granted by government to an individual, or to his representatives, for his valuable services to the country, or in compensation for loss or damage sustained by him in the public service.

See also Individual retirement account; Keogh Plan; Money-purchase plan; Pension trust; Supplementary Employee Retirement Plan (SERP).

Contributory pension plan. A plan funded with both employer and employee contributions.

Defined-contribution plan. Pension plan that provides benefits as determined by the accumulated contributions and the return on the fund's investment performance; the contributions are specified, but the benefits are not.

Defined pension plan. A pension plan where the employer promises specific benefits to each employee. The employer's cash contributions and pension expense are adjusted in relation to investment performance of the pension fund. Sometimes called a "fixed-benefit" pension plan.

Funded pension plan. See Funded.

Noncontributory plan. A pension plan where only the employer makes payments to fund the plan. *Compare Contributory pension plan, above.*

Qualified pension plan. An employer-sponsored plan that meets the requirements of I.R.C. § 401. If these requirements are met, none of the employer's contributions to the plan are taxed to the employee until distributed to him or her (§ 402). The employer will be allowed a deduction in the year the contributions are made (§ 404).

Pension trust. Type of funded pension plan in which the employer transfers to trustees an amount sufficient to cover cost of pensions to employees who are the beneficiaries of the trust.

Penumbra doctrine. The implied powers of the federal government predicated on the Necessary and Proper Clause of the U.S.Const., Art. I, Sec. 8(18), permits one implied power to be engrafted on another implied power.

Peonage /píyənəj/. A condition of servitude (prohibited by 13th Amendment) compelling persons to perform labor in order to pay off a debt.

People. A state; as the people of the state of New York. A nation in its collective and political capacity. The aggregate or mass of the individuals who constitute the state. In a more restricted sense, and as generally used in constitutional law, the entire body of those citizens of a state or nation who are invested with political power for political purposes. *See also* Citizen; Person.

Per /pɔ́r/. Lat. By, through, or by means of.

Per annum /pɔ̀r ǽnəm/. By the year; annually; yearly.

P/E ratio. *See* Price earnings ratio.

Per autre vie /pɔ̀r ówtrə víy/°váy/. L. Fr. For or during another's life; for such period as another person shall live.

Per capita /pɔ̀r kǽpədə/. Lat. By the heads or polls; according to the number of individuals; share and share alike. This term, derived from the civil law, is much used in the law of descent and distribution, and denotes that method of dividing an intestate estate by which an equal share is given to each of a number of persons, all of whom stand in equal degree to the decedent, without reference to their stocks or the right of representation. It is the antithesis of *per stirpes* (q.v.). A division "per capita" means by a number of individuals equally or share and share alike.

Per cent. An abbreviation of the Latin *"per centum,"* meaning by the hundred, or so many parts in the hundred, or so many hundredths.

Percentage depletion. *See* Depletion.

Percentage lease. A lease, usually on a retail business property, using a percentage of the gross or net sales to determine the rent. There is usually a minimum or "base" rental, in the event of poor sales.

Percentage of completion method. A method of reporting income or loss on certain long-term contracts. Under this method of accounting, revenue is recognized gradually throughout the construction period. *See also* Completed contract method.

Percentage order. A market or limited price order to buy (or sell) a stated amount of a certain stock after a fixed number of shares of such stock have traded.

Perception. Taking into possession. Thus, perception of crops or of profits is reducing them to possession. As used with respect to money, it means the counting out and payment of a debt. Seeing, noticing or otherwise comprehending.

Percolate /pɔ́rkəleyt/. As used in the cases relating to the right of land-owners to use water on their premises, designates any flowage of sub-surface water other than that of a running stream, open, visible, clearly to be traced.

Percolation test. The test to determine the capability of the soil to absorb and drain water, both for construction and septic systems.

Per curiam /pɔ̀r kyúriyəm/. Lat. By the court. A phrase used to distinguish an opinion of the whole court from an opinion written by any one judge. Sometimes it denotes an opinion written by the chief justice or presiding judge, or to a brief announcement of the disposition of a case by court not accompanied by a written opinion.

Per diem /pɔ̀r dáyəm/°díyəm/. By the day; an allowance or amount of so much per day. For example, state legislators are often given a per diem allowance to cover expenses while attending legislature sessions. Generally, as used in connection with compensation, wages or salary, means pay for a day's service.

Peremption /pərém(p)shən/. A nonsuit; also a quashing or killing.

Peremptory /pərém(p)təriy/. Imperative; final; decisive; absolute; conclusive; positive; not admitting of question, delay, reconsideration or of any alternative. Self-determined; arbitrary; not requiring any cause to be shown.

As to *peremptory* Defense; Jury instructions; Mandamus; Nonsuit; Plea; and Writ, see those titles.

Peremptory challenge. The right to challenge a juror without assigning, or being required to assign, a reason for the challenge. In most jurisdictions each party to an action, both civil and criminal, has a specified number of such challenges and after using all his peremptory challenges he is required to furnish a reason for subsequent challenges. Fed.R.Crim.P. 24; 28 U.S.C.A. § 1870 (civil cases). *See also* Challenge; Jury challenge.

Peremptory day. A day assigned for trial or hearing in court, absolutely and without further opportunity for postponement.

Peremptory exceptions. In the civil law, any defense which denies entirely the ground of action. Those exceptions which tend to the dismissal of the action.

Peremptory instruction. *See* Jury instruction.

Peremptory rule. In practice, an absolute rule; a rule without any condition or alternative of showing cause. Ruling made by a trial judge or hearing magistrate "on the spot" and without taking the matter under advisement.

Perfect *or* perfected. Complete; finished; executed; enforceable; without defect; merchantable; marketable. Brought to a state of perfection.

As to *perfect* Equity; Obligation; Ownership; Title; and Usufruct, see those titles.

Perfect attestation clause. One that asserts performance of all acts required to be done to make valid testamentary disposition.

Perfected. *See* Perfect *or* perfected; Perfection of security interest.

Perfecting bail. Term describing certain qualifications of a property character being required of persons who tender themselves as bail, when such persons have justified, *i.e.*, established their sufficiency by satisfying the court that they possess the requisite qualifications; a rule or order of court is made for their allowance, and the bail is then said to be perfected, *i.e.*, the process of giving bail is finished or completed.

Perfect instrument. An instrument such as a deed or mortgage is said to become perfect or perfected when recorded (or registered) or filed for record, because it then becomes good as to all the world.

Perfection of security interest. In secured transactions law, the process whereby a security interest is protected, as far as the law permits, against competing claims to the collateral, which usually requires the secured party to give public notice of the interest as by filing in a government office (*e.g.* in office of Secretary of State). Perfection of a security interest deals with those steps legally required to give a secured party a superior interest in subject property against debtor's creditors.

The minimum meaning of this term in connection with a security interest is that the secured party has done whatever is necessary in the way of giving notice to make his security interest effective at least against lien creditors of the debtor. Depending upon the type of collateral and the method of perfection, it may mean more; *e.g.* it may mean that the interest is good even against all purchasers. The methods for attaining perfection are stated in U.C.C. Sections 9–302 through 9–306. In most cases the secured party may obtain perfection either by filing (*i.e.* with Secretary of State) or by taking possession of the collateral. When the collateral is held by a bailee who has not issued a negotiable document of title, perfection by notification is possible; *e.g.* the secured party may obtain perfection by notifying the bailee of the secured party's interest. For a few special situations the Code provides that a security interest is perfected without any of the above actions on the part of the secured party. Such perfection is called automatic perfection, or perfection by attachment.

Perfect trust. An executed trust (*q.v.*).

Perform. To perform an obligation or contract is to execute, fulfill, or accomplish it according to its terms. This may consist either in action on the part of the person bound by the contract or in omission to act, according to the nature of the subject-matter; but the term is usually applied to any action in discharge of a contract other than payment. *See* Performance.

In copyright law, to "perform" a work means to recite, render, play, dance, or act it, either directly or by means of any device or process or, in the case of a motion picture or other audiovisual work, to show its images in any sequence or to make the sounds accompanying it audible. Copyright Act, 17 U.S.C.A. § 101.

Performance. The fulfillment or accomplishment of a promise, contract, or other obligation according to its terms, relieving such person of all further obligation or liability thereunder. *See also* Execute; Execution; Part performance; Payment; Substantial performance doctrine.

Non performance. *See* Commercial frustration; Default; Impossibility.

Part performance. The doing some portion, yet not the whole, of what either party to a contract has agreed to do.

Part performance of an obligation, either before or after a breach thereof, when expressly accepted by the creditor in writing, in satisfaction, or rendered in pursuance of an agreement in writing for that purpose, though without any new consideration, extinguishes the obligation.

As regards the sale of goods, the statute of frauds requirement is dispensed with by partial performance for the goods which have been accepted or for which payment has been made and accepted. U.C.C. § 2–201(3). *See also* Part performance.

Specific performance. The remedy of requiring exact performance of a contract in the specific form in which it was made, or according to the precise terms agreed upon. The actual accomplishment of a contract by a party bound to fulfill it. The doctrine of specific performance is that, where money damages would be an inadequate compensation for the breach of an agreement, the contractor or vendor will be compelled to perform specifically what he has agreed to do; *e.g.* ordered to execute a specific conveyance of land. See Fed.R. Civil P. 70.

With respect to sale of goods, specific performance may be decreed where the goods are unique or in other proper circumstances. The decree for specific performance may include such terms and conditions as to payment of the price, damages, or other relief as the court may deem just. U.C.C. §§ 2–711(2)(b), 2–716.

As the exact fulfillment of an agreement is not always practicable, the phrase may mean, in a given case, not literal, but substantial performance.

Performance bond. Surety bond which guarantees that contractor will fully perform contract and guarantees against breach of contract. Proceeds of bond are used to complete contract or compensate for loss in the event of nonperformance. *See also* Bond; Bid bond; Miller Act.

Peril. The risk, hazard, or contingency insured against by a policy of insurance. In general, the cause of any loss such as may be caused by fire, hail, etc. *See also* Imminent peril.

Perils of the lakes. As applied to navigation of the Great Lakes, this term has the same meaning as "perils of the sea (*q.v.*)."

Perils of the sea. In maritime and insurance law, natural accidents peculiar to the sea, which do not happen by the intervention of man, nor are to be prevented by human prudence. Hence to recover on marine policy insuring against loss by perils of sea, vessel must be seaworthy when it is sent to sea. Perils of the sea are from (1) storms and waves; (2) rocks, shoals, and rapids; (3) other obstacles, though of human origin; (4) changes of climate; (5) the confinement necessary at sea; (6) animals peculiar to the sea; (7) all other dangers peculiar to the sea. All losses caused by the action of wind and water acting on the property insured under extraordinary circumstances, either directly or mediately, without the intervention of other independent active external causes, are losses by "perils of the sea or other perils and

dangers," within the meaning of the usual clause in a policy of marine insurance. In an enlarged sense, all losses which occur from maritime adventure may be said to arise from the perils of the sea; but underwriters are not bound to this extent. They insure against losses from extraordinary occurrences only; such as stress of weather, winds and waves, lightning, tempests, etc. These are understood to be meant by the phrase "the perils of the sea," in a marine policy, and not those ordinary perils which every vessel must encounter.

Peril of the sea within a marine policy envisions extraordinary and unusual perils which vessel may not reasonably expect to encounter; circumstances which are ordinarily encountered such as predictable winds, tides, wave actions and conditions of the water do not fall within such classification. Under Carriage of Goods by Sea Act, "perils of the sea" are understood to mean those perils which are peculiar to sea and which are of extraordinary nature or arise from irresistible force or overwhelming power, and which cannot be guarded against by ordinary exertions of human skill and prudence.

Period. Any point, space, or division of time.

Periodic. Recurring at fixed intervals; to be made or done, or to happen, at successive periods separated by determined intervals of time, as periodic payments of interest on a bond, or periodic alimony payments.

Periodic alimony. A form of support alimony which may be modified for changed circumstances of either party. An allowance payable by one spouse to the other at intermittent times, usually by the week or by the month, in a definite amount over a definite or indefinite period of time. An award of periodic alimony is appropriate according to the needs of the spouse requesting alimony and the corresponding ability of the other spouse to pay. This is also known in some jurisdictions as permanent alimony. State statutes which provide for alimony payments only from husbands, and not wives, have been held unconstitutional. *See also* Alimony; Permanent alimony.

Periodic tenancy. Generic term descriptive of a tenancy from week to week, month to month, or year to year.

Periodic tenancy is one continuing tenancy subject to termination at various rental periods rather than a series of individual and new tenancies. An estate that continues for successive periods unless terminated at end of a period by notice.

Peripheral rights. Those rights which surround or spring from other rights.

Perish. To come to an end; to cease to be; to die.

Perishable. Subject to speedy and natural decay (*e.g.* fruits, vegetables, dairy products, meat). But, where the time contemplated is necessarily long, the term may embrace property liable merely to material depreciation in value from other causes than such decay.

Perishable commodity. A relative term used to describe a product, like fruit or fresh vegetables, which quickly deteriorates in quality and value.

Perishable goods. Goods which quickly decay and lose their value if not put to their intended use within a short period of time.

Perjury. In criminal law, the willful assertion as to a matter of fact, opinion, belief, or knowledge, made by a witness in a judicial proceeding as part of his evidence, either upon oath or in any form allowed by law to be substituted for an oath, whether such evidence is given in open court, or in an affidavit, or otherwise, such assertion being material to the issue or point of inquiry and known to such witness to be false. A false statement knowingly made in a proceeding in a court of competent jurisdiction or concerning a matter wherein an affiant is required by law to be sworn as to some matter material to the issue or point in question.

A person is guilty of perjury if in any official proceeding he makes a false statement under oath or equivalent affirmation, or swears or affirms the truth of a statement previously made, when the statement is material and he does not believe it to be true. Model Penal Code, § 241.1. See also 18 U.S.C.A. §§ 1621, 1623.

Subornation of perjury is procuring another to commit perjury. See 18 U.S.C.A. § 1622.

For unsworn declarations under penalty of perjury, see 28 U.S.C.A. § 1746.

See also False swearing; Two witness rule.

Perks. *See* Perquisites.

Permanent. Continuing or enduring in the same state, status, place, or the like, without fundamental or marked change, not subject to fluctuation, or alteration, fixed or intended to be fixed; lasting; abiding; stable; not temporary or transient. Generally opposed in law to "temporary," but not always meaning "perpetual."

As to *permanent* Injunction; Nuisance; and Trespass; see those titles.

Permanent abode. A domicile or fixed home, which the party may leave as his interest or whim may dictate, but which he has no present intention of abandoning. *See also* Domicile; Residence.

Permanent alimony. An allowance for the support and maintenance of a spouse during his or her lifetime, and its purpose is to provide nourishment, sustenance and the necessities of life to a former spouse who has neither the resources nor ability to be self-sustaining. *See also* Alimony; Periodic alimony.

Permanent disability. Generally, permanent disability is one which will remain substantially the same during remainder of workers' compensation claimant's life. A permanent disability is one which causes impairment of earning capacity, impairment of normal use of member, or competitive handicap in open labor market.

Within insurance policies does not mean that disability must continue throughout life of insured, but it connotes idea that disability must be something more than temporary, and at least presumably permanent.

See also Disability; Permanent injury.

Permanent employment. As provided for by contract, means only that employment is to continue indefinitely and until either party wishes to sever relation for some good reason.

Permanent financing. Long term loan which replaces bridge or interim financing; *e.g.,* mortgage loan used to repay construction loan.

Permanent injury. One where situation has stabilized and permanent damage is reasonably certain. Physical or mental impairment or disability which will last throughout life, or injury reasonably certain to be followed by permanent impairment of earning capacity or one producing permanent irremediable pain. *See also* Permanent disability.

Permanent law. An act which continues in force for an indefinite time.

Permission. A license to do a thing; an authority to do an act which, without such authority, would have been unlawful. An act of permitting, formal consent, authorization, leave, license or liberty granted, and it has a flexible meaning depending upon the sense in which it is used. *See also* Authority; Certificate; License; Permit.

Permissions. Negations of law, arising either from the law's silence or its express declaration.

Permissive. Allowed; allowable; that which may be done. Lenient; tolerant.

Permissive counterclaim. Federal Rule of Civil Procedure 13(b) grants defendant unqualified right to interpose "permissive counterclaim"; one that does not arise out of same transaction or occurrence furnishing subject matter of plaintiff's claim, and court possesses no discretion to reject it. *See also* Counterclaim.

Permissive use. *See* Use.

Permissive waste. *See* Waste.

Permit, *v.* To suffer, allow, consent, let; to give leave or license; to acquiesce, by failure to prevent, or to expressly assent or agree to the doing of an act.

Permit, *n.* In general, any document which grants a person the right to do something. A license or grant of authority to do a thing. A written license or warrant, issued by a person in authority, empowering the grantee to do some act not forbidden by law, but not allowable without such authority.

A license or instrument granted by the officers of excise (or customs), certifying that the duties on certain goods have been paid, or secured, and permitting their removal from some specified place to another.

See also Building permit; Certificate; License; Special use permit.

Permit card. A document given by a union to a non-union member which allows an employer to hire him for a job for which the union is unable to supply sufficient members.

Permutation /pɜ̀rmyətéyshən/. The exchange of one movable subject for another; barter.

Pernancy. Taking; a taking or receiving; as of the profits of an estate. Actual pernancy of the profits of an estate is the taking, perception, or receipt of the rents and other advantages arising therefrom.

Perpetration. The act of one committing a crime either with his own hands, or by some means or instrument or through some innocent agent.

Perpetrator /pɜ́rpətrèytər/. Generally, this term denotes the person who actually commits a crime or delict, or by whose immediate agency it occurs.

Perpetual /pərpétyuwəl/. Never ceasing; continuous; enduring; lasting; unlimited in respect of time; continuing without intermission or interval.

As to *perpetual* Injunction; Lease; and Statute, see those titles.

Perpetual succession. That continuous existence which enables a corporation to manage its affairs, and hold property without the necessity of perpetual conveyances, for the purpose of transmitting it. By reason of this quality, this artificial person remains, in its legal entity and personality, the same, though frequent changes may be made of its members. See Corporation.

Perpetuating testimony. Means or procedure permitted by federal and state discovery rules for preserving for future use the testimony of witness, which might otherwise be lost or unavailable before the trial in which it is intended to be used. Fed.R. Civil P. 27(a) (depositions before trial).

Perpetuities, rule against. See Perpetuity; Rule (Rule against perpetuities).

Perpetuity /pɜ̀rpətyúwədiy/. Continuing forever. Legally, pertaining to real property, any condition extending the inalienability or property beyond the time of a life or lives in being plus twenty one years. A perpetuity is a limitation which takes the subject-matter of the perpetuity out of com-

merce for a period greater than a life or lives in being and 21 years thereafter, plus ordinary period of gestation. See also Rule (Rule against perpetuities).

Perquisites /pɜ́rkwəzəts/. Emoluments, privileges, fringe benefits, or other incidental profits or benefits attaching to an office or employment position in addition to regular salary or wages. Shortened term "Perks" is used with reference to such extraordinary benefits afforded to business executives (e.g. free cars, club memberships, insurance, etc.). See also Fringe benefits.

Per quod /pər kwód/. Lat. Whereby. When the declaration in an action of tort, after stating the acts complained of, goes on to allege the consequences of those acts as a ground of special damage to the plaintiff, the recital of such consequences is prefaced by these words, *"per quod,"* whereby; and sometimes the phrase is used as the name of that clause of the declaration or complaint.

At the common law, "per quod" acquired two meanings in the law of defamation: when used in the frame of reference of slander it meant proof of special damages was required and when used in the frame of reference of libel it meant that proof of extrinsic circumstances was required. See also Libelous per quod.

Words "actionable per quod" are those not actionable per se upon their face, but are only actionable in consequence of extrinsic facts showing circumstances under which they were said or the damages resulting to slandered party therefrom.

See also Actionable per quod.

Per sample /pər sǽmpəl/. By sample. A purchase so made is a collateral engagement that the goods shall be of a particular quality. U.C.C. § 2–313(1)(c).

Per se /pər síy/°séy/. Lat. By itself; in itself; taken alone; by means of itself; through itself; inherently; in isolation; unconnected with other matters; simply as such; in its own nature without reference to its relation.

In law of defamation, certain words and phrases that are actionable as slander or libel in and of themselves without proof of special damages, e.g. accusation of crime. Used in contrast to defamation per quod which requires proof of special damage. See Actionable per se; Libelous per se; Slanderous per se.

See also Negligence per se; Per se doctrine; Per se violations.

Per se doctrine. Under the "per se doctrine," if an activity is blatant in its intent and pernicious in its effect, a court need not inquire into the reasonableness of the same before determining that it is a violation of the antitrust laws. *See* Per se violations.

Per se violations. In anti-trust law, term that implies that certain types of business agreements, such as price-fixing, are considered inherently anti-competitive and injurious to the public without any need to determine if the agreement has actually injured market competition. *See* Per se doctrine; Rule *(Rule of reason).*

Person. In general usage, a human being (*i.e.* natural person), though by statute term may include labor organizations, partnerships, associations, corporations, legal representatives, trustees, trustees in bankruptcy, or receivers. See *e.g.* National Labor Relations Act, § 2(1), 29 U.S.C.A. § 152; Uniform Partnership Act, § 2.

Scope and delineation of term is necessary for determining those to whom Fourteenth Amendment of Constitution affords protection since this Amendment expressly applies to "person."

Aliens. Aliens are "persons" within meaning of Fourteenth Amendment and are thus protected by equal protection clause against discriminatory state action.

Bankruptcy Code. "Person" includes individual, partnership, and corporation, but not governmental unit. 11 U.S.C.A. § 101.

Commercial law. An individual or organization. U.C.C. § 1–201(30).

Corporation. A corporation is a "person" within meaning of Fourteenth Amendment equal protection and due process provisions of United States Constitution. The term "persons" in statute relating to conspiracy to commit offense against United States, or to defraud United States, or any agency, includes corporation.

In corporate law, "person" includes individual and entity. Rev.Model Bus.Corp.Act, § 1.40.

Foreign government. Foreign governments otherwise eligible to sue in U.S. courts are "persons" entitled to bring treble-damage suit for alleged antitrust violations under Clayton Act, Section 4.

Illegitimate child. Illegitimate children are "persons" within meaning of the Equal Protection Clause of the Fourteenth Amendment, and also within scope of wrongful death statute.

Interested person. Includes heirs, devisees, children, spouses, creditors, beneficiaries and any others having a property right in or claim against a trust estate or the estate of a decedent, ward or protected person which may be affected by the proceeding. It also includes persons having priority for appointment as personal representative, and other fiduciaries representing interested persons. The meaning as it relates to particular persons may vary from time to time and must be determined according to the particular purposes

of, and matter involved in, any proceeding. Uniform Probate Code, § 1–201(20).

Labor unions. Labor unions are "persons" under the Sherman Act, the Clayton Act, and also under Bankruptcy Code.

Minors. Minors are "persons" under the United States Constitution, possessed of rights that governments must respect.

Municipalities. Municipalities and other government units are "persons" within meaning of 42 U.S.C.A. § 1983. Local government officials sued in their official capacities are "persons" for purposes of Section 1983 in those cases in which a local government would be suable in its own name. *See* Color of law.

Definition of "person" or "persons" covered by antitrust laws includes cities, whether as municipal utility operators suing as plaintiffs seeking damages for antitrust violations or as operators being sued as defendants.

Protected person. One for whom a conservator has been appointed or other protective order has been made. Uniform Probate Code, § 5–103(18).

Resident alien. A resident alien is a "person" within the meaning of the due process and equal protection clauses of the Fourteenth Amendment.

Unborn child. Word "person" as used in the Fourteenth Amendment does not include the unborn. Roe v. Wade, 410 U.S. 113, 93 S.Ct. 705, 729, 35 L.Ed.2d 147. Unborn child is a "person" for purpose of remedies given for personal injuries, and child may sue after his birth. In some jurisdictions a viable fetus is considered a person within the meaning of the state's wrongful death statute, and within the meaning of the state's vehicular homicide statute. *See also* Child; Children *(Rights of unborn child)*; Unborn child; Viable child.

University. A state university is a "person", within in meaning of 42 U.S.C. § 1983.

Person aggrieved. To have standing as a "person aggrieved" under equal employment opportunities provisions of Civil Rights Act, or to assert rights under any federal regulatory statute, a plaintiff must show (1) that he has actually suffered an injury, and (2) that the interest sought to be protected by the complainant is arguably within the zone of interests to be protected or regulated by the statute in question.

As contemplated by federal rule governing standing to object to alleged illegal search and seizure is one who is the victim of the search and seizure, as distinguished from one who claims prejudice only through the use of evidence gathered in a search directed at someone else.

Test of whether a petitioner is a "person aggrieved" and thereby entitled to seek review of an order of referee in bankruptcy is whether his property may be diminished, his burden increased or his rights detrimentally affected by order sought to be reviewed.

See also Aggrieved party; Standing to sue doctrine.

Personal. Appertaining to the person; belonging to an individual; limited to the person; having the nature or partaking of the qualities of human beings, or of movable property.

As to *personal* Action; Assets; Chattel; Contract; Covenant; Credit; Demand; Disability; Franchise; Injury; Judgment; Knowledge; Liberty; Notice; Obligation; Property; Replevin; Representative; Right; Security; Service; Servitude; Statute; Tax; Tithes; Tort; and Warranty, see those titles.

Personal and dependency exemption. *See* Exemption.

Personal belongings. In probate law, term is a broad classification and in absence of restriction may include most or all of the testator's personal property. *See also* Personal effects.

Personal defenses. In commercial law, term usually refers to defenses that cannot be asserted against a holder in due course in enforcing an instrument. Also refers to defenses of a principal debtor against a creditor that cannot be asserted derivatively by a surety.

Personal effects. Articles associated with person, as property having more or less intimate relation to person of possessor; "effects" meaning movable or chattel property of any kind. Usual reference is to such items as the following owned by a decedent at the time of death: clothing, furniture, jewelry, stamp and coin collections, silverware, china, crystal, cooking utensils, books, cars, televisions, radios, etc.

Term "personal effects" when employed in a will enjoys no settled technical meaning and, when used in its primary sense, without any qualifying words, ordinarily embraces such tangible property as is worn or carried about the person, or tangible property having some intimate relation to the person of the testator or testatrix; where it is required by the context within which the term appears, it may enjoy a broader meaning.

Personal expenses. Expenses of an individual for personal purposes that are not deductible unless specifically provided for under the tax Code. I.R.C. § 262.

Personal holding company. Type of corporation subject to special Personal Holding Company Tax (I.R.C. § 541 et seq.) on undistributed income so as to preclude use of such organization by individuals in high tax brackets to avoid taxes. Typically, such corporations have a limited number of shareholders and the major sources of revenue are from passive income such as dividends, interest, annuities, royalties, rent, and the like.

Personal holding company income. Income as defined by I.R.C. § 543. Such income includes interest, dividends, certain rents and royalties, income from the use of corporate property by certain shareholders, income from certain personal service contracts, and distributions from estates and trusts. Such income is relevant in determining whether a corporation is a personal holding company and is therefore subject to the penalty tax on personal holding companies.

Personal holding company tax. Federal tax imposed on personal holding companies and designed to force the distribution of corporate earnings through the threat of a penalty tax on the corporation. I.R.C. § 541.

Personal injury. *See* Injury.

Personal judgment. *See* Judgment *(Personal judgment).*

Personal income. The income which an individual earns or receives. *See* Income.

Personal jurisdiction. The power of a court over the person of a defendant in contrast to the jurisdiction of a court over a defendant's property or his interest therein; *in personam* as opposed to *in rem* jurisdiction. *See* In personam jurisdiction.

Personal liability. A kind of responsibility for the payment or performance of an obligation which exposes the personal assets of the responsible person to payment of the obligation. *See e.g.* Surety.

The liability of the stockholders in corporations, under certain statutes, by which they may be held individually responsible for the debts of the corporation, either to the extent of the par value of their respective holdings of stock, or to twice that amount, or without limit, or otherwise, as the particular statute directs. This may be required by state statute of stockholders of a new corporation that is undercapitalized.

Personal property. *See* Property.

Personal property tax. Tax on such items of personal property as household furniture, jewelry, etc. levied by local or state governments.

Personal recognizance. *See* Release on own recognizance.

Personalty. Personal property; movable property; chattels; property that is not attached to real estate. *See also* Property *(Personal property).*

Quasi personalty. Things which are movable in point of law, though fixed to things real, either actually, as emblements *(fructus industriales),* fixtures, etc.; or fictitiously, as chattels-real, leases for years, etc.

Persona non grata /pərsównə nòn grǽtə/°gréytə/. Person not wanted; an undesirable person. In international law and diplomatic usage, a person not acceptable (for reasons peculiar to himself) to the court or government to which it is proposed to accredit him in the character of an ambassador or minister.

Personate /pə́rsənèyt/. To assume the person (character) of another, without his consent or knowledge, in order to deceive others, and, in such feigned character, to fraudulently do some act or gain some advantage, to the harm or prejudice of the person counterfeited. To pass one's self off as another having a certain identity. *See also* Impersonation.

Person in loco parentis /pə́rsən in lówkow pəréntəs/. In place of parent. One who has assumed status and obligations of parent without formal adoption. *See* In loco parentis.

Per stirpes /pə̀r stə́rpiyz/. Lat. By roots or stocks; by representation. This term, derived from the civil law, is much used in the law of descents and distribution, and denotes that method of dividing an intestate estate where a class or group of distributees take the share which their deceased would have been entitled to, had he or she lived, taking thus by their right of representing such ancestor, and not as so many individuals. It is the antithesis of *per capita (q.v.)*.

Persuade. To induce one by argument, entreaty, or expostulation into a determination, decision, conclusion, belief, or the like; to win over by an appeal to one's reason and feelings, as into doing or believing something; to bring oneself or another to belief, certainty or conviction; to argue into an opinion or procedure.

Persuasion. The act of persuading; the act of influencing the mind by arguments or reasons offered, or by anything that moves the mind or passions, or inclines the will to a determination. For Fair persuasion, see that title.

Pertain. To belong or relate to, whether by nature, appointment, or custom.

Pertinent /pə́rtənənt/. Applicable; relevant. Evidence is called "pertinent" when it is directed to the issue or matters in dispute, and legitimately tends to prove the allegations of the party offering it; otherwise it is called "impertinent." A pertinent hypothesis is one which, if sustained, would logically influence the issue. *See* Material; Relevant.

Per year. In a contract, is equivalent to the word "annually." *See* Annual.

Petit /pétiy/pətíy(t)/. Fr. Small; minor; inconsiderable. Used in several compounds, and sometimes written "petty." As to *petit* Jury; Larceny; and Treason, see those titles.

Petition. A written address, embodying an application or prayer from the person or persons preferring it, to the power, body, or person to whom it is presented, for the exercise of his or their authority in the redress of some wrong, or the grant of some favor, privilege, or license. A formal written request addressed to some governmental authority. The right of the people to petition for redress of grievances is guaranteed by the First Amendment, U.S. Constitution.

A written request to a board for action on some matter therein laid before it. For example, a formal paper filed with the N.L.R.B. seeking a secret ballot election among a certain group of employees (bargaining unit).

A formal written application to a court requesting judicial action on a certain matter. A recital of facts which give rise to a cause of action. An application made to a court *ex parte*, or where there are no parties in opposition, praying for the exercise of the judicial powers of the court in relation to some matter which is not the subject for a suit or action, or for authority to do some act which requires the sanction of the court; as for the appointment of a guardian, for leave to sell trust property, etc. Formerly, in equity practice the original pleading was denominated a petition or bill. Today, in almost all jurisdictions, whether in law or equity, the initial pleading is a complaint.

Written request to the court for an order after notice. Uniform Probate Code, §§ 1–201(31), 5–103(15).

Petitioner. One who presents a petition to a court, officer, or legislative body. The one who starts an equity proceeding or the one who takes an appeal from a judgment. In legal proceedings commenced by petition, the person against whom action or relief is prayed, or who opposes the prayer of the petition, is called the "respondent." *See also* Plaintiff.

Petition in bankruptcy. A document filed in a court of bankruptcy, or with the clerk, by a debtor seeking the relief provided under the various chapters of the Bankruptcy Code. This is the manner in which a bankruptcy case is commenced. See Bankruptcy Code, § 301 et seq.

Petitioning creditor. The creditor at whose instance an adjudication of bankruptcy is made against a debtor.

Petit jury. *See* Jury.

Petit larceny. *See* Larceny.

Petitory action /pétət(ə)riy ǽkshən/. A droitural action; that is, one in which the plaintiff seeks to establish and enforce, by an appropriate legal proceeding, his right of property, or his title, to the subject-matter in dispute; as distinguished from a *possessory* action, where the right to the possession is the point in litigation, and not the mere right of property. In admiralty, suits to try title to property independent of questions concerning possession are referred to as "petitory suits," which suits must be based on a claim of legal title; the assertion of a mere equitable interest is not sufficient.

In Louisiana, an action brought by an alleged owner out of possession against one having possession to determine ownership, in which plaintiff must recover on strength of his own title, not on weakness of defendant's title.

Petty. Small, minor, of less or inconsiderable importance. The English form of *"petit,"* and sometimes used instead of that word in such compounds as "petty jury," "petty larceny," and "petty treason."

See Misdemeanor; Petit. As to *petty* Average; Constable; Jury; Larceny; and Session, see those titles.

Petty cash. Currency maintained for expenditures that are conveniently made with cash on hand. A fund used by business to pay small expenses for such items as travel, stationery, etc. Sometimes called imprest fund, it is operated by a voucher system in which the person desiring the money submits a voucher properly authorized and receives the cash.

Petty larceny. *See* Larceny.

Petty offense. A minor crime, the maximum punishment for which is generally a fine or short term in jail or house of correction. In some states, it is a classification in addition to misdemeanor and felony. See *e.g.* 18 U.S.C.A. § 19.

A six month sentence is the constitutional dividing line between serious offenses for which a trial by jury must be afforded and petty offenses. In contempt cases, it is the sentence actually imposed, rather than the penalty authorized by law which is determinative.

See also Infraction; Misdemeanor.

Petty officers. Inferior officers in the naval service, of various ranks and kinds, corresponding to the non-commissioned officers in the army.

Peyote. A type of cactus called mescal, found in Mexico and southwestern U.S. It contains button-like tubercles that are dried and chewed as an hallucinatory drug. Mescaline is an alkaloid of it.

Phantom stock plan. An employee benefit plan in which benefits are determined by reference to the performance of the corporation's common shares. A deferred compensation unit plan for corporate executives and employees which credits to the unit account of the employee so-called excess market appreciation measured by the difference between the market value of the corporate stock at the time of termination of employ-

ment and the market value when the employee entered into the plan.

P.H.V. An abbreviation for *"pro hac vice,"* for this turn, for this purpose or occasion.

Phylasist. A jailer.

Physical. Relating or pertaining to the body, as distinguished from the mind or soul or the emotions. Material, substantive, having an objective existence, as distinguished from imaginary or fictitious; real, having relation to facts, as distinguished from moral or constructive.

Physical cruelty. As used in divorce law means actual personal violence, or such a course of physical treatment as endangers life, limb or health, and renders cohabitation unsafe.

Physical depreciation. Reduction in value of structure due to actual wear and tear or physical deterioration. *See* Depreciation.

Physical disability. *See* Disability.

Physical fact. In the law of evidence, a fact having a physical existence, as distinguished from a mere conception of the mind; one which is visible, audible, or palpable, such as the sound of a pistol shot, a man running, impressions of human feet on the ground. *See* Demonstrative evidence.

Physical fact rule. In evidence, a judge is required to take case from jury if plaintiff's evidence as to physical facts leads to an impossibility in the light of undisputed physical laws. An appellate court is not bound by findings which violate physical laws. *See also* Impossibility.

The physical fact rule is that if a driver does not see that which he could or should have seen, he is guilty of negligence as a matter of law.

Physical force. Force applied to the body; actual violence.

Physical harm. These words are used throughout the Restatement of Torts to denote the physical impairment of the human body, or of land or chattels. Restatement, Second, Torts, § 7. *See also* Physical injury.

Physical impossibility. Practical impossibility according to the knowledge of the day. *See* Impossibility; Physical fact rule.

Physical incapacity. In the law of marriage and divorce, impotence, inability to accomplish sexual coition, arising from physical imperfection or malformation.

Physical injury. Bodily harm or hurt, excluding mental distress, fright, or emotional disturbance. *See also* Physical cruelty; Physical harm.

Physical necessity. A condition in which a person is absolutely compelled to act in a particular way by overwhelming superior force; as distinguished from *moral* necessity, which arises where there is a duty incumbent upon a rational being to perform, which he ought at the time to perform. *See* Necessity.

Physician-patient privilege. *See* Patient-physician privilege.

P.I. Physical injury.

Picketing. Term refers to presence at an employer's business by one or more employees and/or other persons to publicize labor dispute, influence employees or customers to withhold their work or business, respectively, or show union's desire to represent employees; picketing is usually accompanied by patrolling with signs. Patrolling the entrance of a business by members of a labor union in order to inform other employees and the public of the existence of a strike and to influence or deter them from entering. *See also* Labor picketing; Secondary picketing; Unlawful picketing. *Compare* Boycott.

Peaceable picketing, in which laboring men and women have right to participate during labor dispute, means tranquil conduct, conduct devoid of noise or tumult, the absence of a quarrelsome demeanor, and a course of conduct that does not violate or disturb the public peace. It connotes peaceable methods of presenting a cause to the public in the vicinity of the employer's premises.

Pickpocket. A thief who secretly steals money or other property from the person of another.

Piercing the corporate veil. Judicial process whereby court will disregard usual immunity of corporate officers or entities from liability for wrongful corporate activities; *e.g.* when incorporation exists for sole purpose of perpetrating fraud. The doctrine which holds that the corporate structure with its attendant limited liability of stockholders may be disregarded and personal liability imposed on stockholders, officers and directors in the case of fraud or other wrongful acts done in name of corporation. The court, however, may look beyond the corporate form only for the defeat of fraud or wrong or the remedying of injustice. *See also* Instrumentality rule.

Pilfer /pílfər/. To pilfer, in the plain and popular sense, means to steal. *See* Larceny; Theft.

Pilferage /pílf(ə)rəj/. Petty larceny; stealing of small items, generally of stored goods.

Pilferer /pílfərər/. One who steals petty things, or a small part of a thing.

Pillage /píləj/. Plunder; the forcible taking of private property by an invading or conquering army from the enemy's subjects.

Pimp. One who obtains customers ("tricks") for a whore or prostitute. *See also* Pander.

Pioneer patent. *See* Patent.

Piracy. Those acts of robbery and depredation upon the high seas which, if committed on land, would have amounted to a felony. Brigandage committed on the sea or from the sea. Whoever, on the high seas, commits the crime of piracy as defined by the law of nations, and is afterwards brought into or found in the United States, shall be imprisoned for life. 18 U.S.C.A. § 1651. *See also* Air piracy.

The term is also applied to the illegal reprinting or reproduction of copyrighted matter or to unlawful plagiarism from it; and, similarly, to the unlawful reproduction or distribution of property protected by patent and trademark laws. *See also* Infringement; Plagiarism.

Pirate. One guilty of the crime of piracy.

PITI. Principal, interest, taxes and insurance; the most common components of monthly mortgage payments.

P.J. An abbreviation for "presiding judge" (or justice).

PKPA. *See* Parental Kidnapping Prevention Act.

P.L. An abbreviation for "Pamphlet Laws" or "Public Laws."

Placard. An edict; a declaration; a manifesto. Also an advertisement or public notification.

Place, n. This word is a very indefinite term. It is applied to any locality, limited by boundaries, however large or however small. It may be used to designate a country, state, county, town, or a very small portion of a town. The extent of the locality designated by it must generally be determined by the connection in which it is used. In its primary and most general sense means locality, situation, or site, and it is also used to designate an occupied situation or building. *See also* Site; Situs.

Place, v. To arrange for something as to place a mortgage or to place an order. *See also* Placement.

Placement. The act of selling a new issue of securities or arranging a loan or mortgage. The act of finding employment for a person as in the case of an employment agency. *See also* Finder; Offering.

Place of abode. One's residence or domicile *(q.v.)*.

Place of business. The location at which one carries on his business or employment. Under many state statutes, service of process may be made at one's place of business and jurisdiction may be acquired by a court whose territorial district includes one's place of business. *See also* Domicile.

Place of contract. The place (country or state) in which a contract is made, and whose law must determine questions affecting the execution, validity, and construction of the contract.

Place of delivery. The place where delivery is to be made of goods sold. If no place is specified in the contract, the articles sold must, in general, be delivered at the place where they are at the time of the sale. See U.C.C. §§ 2–503, 2–504.

Placer /pléysər/. In mining law, a superficial deposit of sand, gravel, or disintegrated rock, carrying one or more of the precious metals, along the course or under the bed of a watercourse, ancient or current, or along the shore of the sea. Under the acts of congress, the term includes all forms of mineral deposits, except veins of quartz or other rock in place. 30 U.S.C.A. § 35.

Placer claim. A mining claim located on the public domain for the purpose of placer mining, that is, ground within the defined boundaries which contains mineral in its earth, sand, or gravel; ground which includes valuable deposits not "in place," that is, not fixed in rock, or which are in a loose state.

Plagiarism /pléyjərizəm/. The act of appropriating the literary composition of another, or parts or passages of his writings, or the ideas or language of the same, and passing them off as the product of one's own mind. If the material is protected by copyright, such act may constitute an offense of copyright infringement.

To be liable for plagiarism it is not necessary to exactly duplicate another's literary work, it being sufficient if unfair use of such work is made by lifting of substantial portion thereof, but even an exact counterpart of another's work does not constitute plagiarism if such counterpart was arrived at independently.

See also Copyright; Fair use doctrine; Infringement.

Plagiarist /pléyjərəst/, *or* **plagiary** /pléyjiyèhriy/. One who publishes the thoughts and writings of another as his own.

Plain error rule. This rule that plain errors affecting substantial rights may be considered on motion for new trial or on appeal though not raised in trial court if manifest injustice or miscarriage of justice has resulted, is invoked on case to case basis, but there must be sound, substantial manifestation, a strong, clear showing, that injustice or miscarriage of justice will result if the rule is not invoked. For there to be "plain error" warranting reversal absent objection, there must be legal impropriety affecting defendant's substantial rights, sufficiently grievous to justify notice by reviewing court and to convince it that, of itself, error possessed clear capacity to bring about unjust result. Doctrine which encompasses those errors which are obvious and highly prejudicial, which affect the substantial rights of the accused, and which, if uncorrected, would be an affront to the integrity and reputation of judicial proceedings.

Plain meaning rule. A rule used to interpret statutes which says that the court will interpret words in the statute according to their usual or "plain" meaning as understood by the general public.

Plain sight rule. *See* Plain view doctrine.

Plaintiff. A person who brings an action; the party who complains or sues in a civil action and is so named on the record. A person who seeks remedial relief for an injury to rights; it designates a complainant. The prosecution (*i. e.* State or United States) in a criminal case.

Plaintiff in error. In current nomenclature, "appellant" is the accepted word to indicate the party who seeks appellate review, and not *plaintiff in error,* as formerly.

Plain view doctrine. In search and seizure context, objects falling in plain view of officer who has the right to be in position to have that view are subject to seizure without a warrant and may be introduced in evidence. Under this doctrine, warrantless seizure of incriminating evidence may be permitted when police are lawfully searching specified area if it can be established that police had prior justification for intrusion into area searched, that police inadvertently came across item seized, and that it was immediately apparent to the police that the item seized was evidence. However, the plain view doctrine may not be used to extend a general exploratory search from one object to another until something incriminating at last emerges.

Plan. A delineation; a design; a draft, form or representation. The representation of anything drawn on a plane, as a map or chart; a scheme; a sketch. Also, a method of design or action, procedure, or arrangement for accomplishment of a particular act or object. Method of putting into effect an intention or proposal. *See also* Planning.

Planned unit development (PUD). An area with a specified minimum contiguous acreage to be developed as a single entity according to a plan, containing one or more residential clusters or planned unit residential developments and one or more public, quasi-public, commercial or industrial areas in such ranges of ratios of nonresidential uses to residential uses as shall be specified in the zoning ordinance.

Area of land controlled by landowner to be developed as a single entity for a number of dwelling units, and commercial and industrial uses, if any, the plan for which does not correspond in lot size, bulk or type of dwelling or commercial or industrial use, density, lot coverage and required open space to the regulations established in any one or more districts, created from time to time, under the provisions of a municipal zoning ordinance enacted pursuant to the conventional zoning enabling act of the state.

Planning. In municipal law, term connotes systematic development of municipality to promote general welfare and prosperity of its people with greatest efficiency and economy, while zoning is concerned primarily with use of property.

Planning board *or* **commission.** The agency of a local government which recommends approval or disapproval of proposed building projects, real estate developments, and the like, in their jurisdiction. A higher authority such as the city council usually makes the final decision based on the recommendation of such board or commission.

Plat *or* **plot.** A map of a specific land area such as a town, section, or subdivision showing the location and boundaries of individual parcels of land subdivided into lots, with streets, alleys, easements, etc., usually drawn to a scale. *See also* Plat map.

Platform. A statement of principles and of policies adopted by a political party convention as a basis for the party's appeal for public support.

Plat map. A plat which gives legal descriptions of pieces of property by lot, street, and block numbers. A plat map is generally drawn after the property has been described by some other means, such as a Government Survey System. Once a plat map is set, legal descriptions are defined by referring to the given map, in a lot and block description.

Play-debt. Debt contracted by gaming.

Plea. In common law pleading (now obsolete with adoption of Rules of Civil Procedure) a pleading; any one in the series of pleadings. More particularly, the first pleading on the part of the defendant. In the strictest sense, the answer which the defendant in an action at law made to the plaintiff's declaration, and in which he set up matter of *fact* as defense, thus distinguished from a demurrer, which interposed objections on grounds of *law.*

In equity pleading (now obsolete with adoption of Rules of Civil Procedure) a special answer showing or relying upon one or more things as a cause why the suit should be either dismissed or delayed or barred. A short statement, in response to a bill in equity, of facts which, if inserted in the bill, would render it demurrable.

Affirmative plea. In equity pleading, one which sets up a single fact, not appearing in the bill, or sets up a number of circumstances all tending to establish a single fact, which fact, if existing, destroys the complainant's case. Such is obsolete under Rules of Civil Procedure. *See* Affirmative defense.

Common pleas. In common law pleading, common causes or suits; civil actions brought and prosecuted between subjects or citizens, as distinguished from criminal cases. Such are obsolete under Rules of Civil Procedure.

Criminal pleas. The defendant's response to a criminal charge (guilty, not guilty, or nolo contendere). If a defendant refuses to plead or if a defendant corporation fails to appear, the court shall enter a plea of not guilty. Fed.R.Crim.P. 11(a). *See also* Alford plea; Arraignment; Guilty plea; Insanity; Nolo contendere; Not guilty; Plea bargaining; Standing mute.

Dilatory pleas. See Dilatory.

Double plea. In common law pleading, one having the technical fault of duplicity; one consisting of several distinct and independent matters alleged to the same point and requiring different answers. This does not present any problem under Rules of Civil Procedure which permits party to plead as many separate claims or defenses, regardless of consistency. Fed.R.Civil P. 8(e)(2).

False plea. A sham plea *(q.v. infra).*

Insanity plea. See Insanity.

Negative plea. In equity pleading, one which does not undertake to answer the various allegations of the bill, but specifically denies some particular fact or matter the existence of which is essential to entitle the complainant to any relief. Abolished under Rules of Civil Procedure. *See* Denial.

Peremptory pleas. In common law pleading, "pleas in bar" are so termed in contradistinction to that class of pleas called "dilatory pleas." The former, viz., peremptory pleas, are usually pleaded to the merits of the action, with the view of raising a material issue between the parties; while the latter class, viz., dilatory pleas, are generally pleaded with a view of retarding the plaintiff's proceedings, and not for the purpose of raising an issue upon which the parties may go to trial and settle the point in dispute. Peremptory pleas are also called "pleas in bar," while dilatory pleas are said to be in abatement only. Abolished under Rules of Civil Procedure.

Plea agreements. See Plea bargaining.

Plea in abatement. In common law pleading, a plea which, without disputing merits of plaintiff's claim, objects to place, mode, or time of asserting it. It allows plaintiff to renew suit in another place or form, or at another time, and does not assume to answer action on its merits, or deny existence of particular cause of action on which plaintiff relies. A plea in abatement sets forth facts extrinsic to merits which affect only manner in which action is framed or circumstances under which it is sought to be prosecuted, and does not destroy the right of action but merely suspends or postpones its prosecution. In states which have adopted rules patterned on the Federal Rules of Civil Procedure, the plea in abatement has been replaced by a motion. *See, e.g.,* Fed.R.Civ.P. 12(b). See Abatement of action.

Plea in bar. A plea which goes to *bar* the plaintiff's action; that is, to defeat it absolutely and entirely. A plea in bar sets forth matters which per se destroy right of action and bar its prosecution absolutely, such as bar of statute of limitations or constitutional guarantee against self-incrimination. A plea in bar is one that denies a plaintiff's right to maintain the action and which, if established, will destroy the action.

Plea of confession and avoidance. In common law pleading, one which admits that plaintiff had a cause of action, but which avers that it has been discharged by some subsequent or collateral matter. Abolished under Rules of Civil Procedure. *See* Affirmative defense.

Plea of guilty. A confession of guilt in open court. *See also Criminal pleas, above,* and Guilty plea.

Plea of nolo contendere /plíy əv nówlow kənténdəriy/. *See* Nolo contendere.

Sham plea. A false plea; a plea of false or fictitious matter, subtly drawn so as to entrap an opponent, or create delay. A vexatious or false defense, resorted to under the old system of pleading for purposes of delay and annoyance. Such a plea may be ordered stricken on motion under Rules of Civil P. 12(f).

Special plea. In common law pleading, a special kind of plea in bar, distinguished by this name from the general issue, and consisting usually of some new affirmative matter, though it may also be in the form of a traverse or denial. Abolished under Rules of Civil Procedure.

Plea agreement. *See* Plea bargaining.

Plea bargaining. The process whereby the accused and the prosecutor in a criminal case work out a mutually satisfactory disposition of the case subject to court approval. It usually involves the defendant's pleading guilty to a lesser offense or to only one or some of the counts of a multi-count indictment in return for a lighter sentence than that possible for the graver charge. Plea bargaining procedures in the federal courts are governed by Fed.R.Crim.P. 11(e).

Plead. To make, deliver, or file any pleading; to conduct the pleadings in a cause. To interpose any pleading in a civil action. More particularly, to deliver in a formal manner the defendant's answer to the plaintiff's declaration, complaint or to the indictment, as the case may be. *See* Pleadings.

Pleader. A person whose business it was to draw pleadings. Formerly, when pleading at common law was a highly technical and difficult art, there was a class of men known as "special pleaders not at the bar," who held a position intermediate between counsel and attorneys. In current usage, the pleader is the party asserting a particular pleading.

Pleadings. The formal allegations by the parties to a lawsuit of their respective claims and defenses, with the intended purpose being to provide notice of what is to be expected at trial.

Rules or Codes of Civil Procedure. Unlike the rigid technical system of common law pleading, pleadings under federal and state rules or codes of civil procedure have a far more limited function, with determination and narrowing of facts and issues being left to discovery devices and pre-trial conferences. In addition, the rules and codes permit liberal amendment and supplementation of pleadings.

The Field Code *(q.v.)* of New York was the first major state effort to simplify pleading requirements. This was followed by similar state civil procedure codes, and by the Federal Rules of Civil Procedure at the federal level.

Under rules of civil procedure the pleadings consist of a complaint, an answer, a reply to a counterclaim, an answer to a cross-claim, a third party complaint, and a third party answer. Fed.R.Civil P. 7(a).

For *amendment of pleadings, see* Amendment. For *judgment on pleadings, see* Judgment. *See also* Affirmative defense; Alternative pleading; Defective pleadings; Responsive pleading; Supplemental pleading; Variance.

Affirmative pleadings. *See* Affirmative defense.

Common law pleading. The system of rules and principles, established in the common law, according to which the pleadings or responsive allegations of litigating parties were framed with a view to preserve technical propriety and to produce a proper issue.

The process performed by the parties to a suit or action, in alternately presenting written statements of their contention, each responsive to that which precedes, and each serving to narrow the field of controversy, until there evolves a single point, affirmed on one side and denied on the other, called the "issue," upon which they then go to trial.

The individual allegations of the respective parties to an action at common law proceeded from them alternately in the order and under the following distinctive names: The plaintiff's *declaration,* the defendant's *plea,* the plaintiff's *replication,* the defendant's *rejoinder,* the plaintiff's *surrejoinder,* the defendant's *rebutter,* the plaintiff's *surrebutter;* after which they have no distinctive names.

Pleading Fifth Amendment. *See* Self-incrimination.

Plead over. To pass over, or omit to notice, a material allegation in the last pleading of the opposite party; to pass by a defect in the pleading of the other party without taking advantage of it. In another sense, to plead the general issue, after one has interposed a demurrer or special plea which has been dismissed by a judgment of *respondeat ouster*. Obsolete under Rules of Civil Procedure.

Plea in abatement. *See* Plea *(Plea in abatement)*.

Plea negotiations. *See* Plea bargaining.

Plebiscite /plébəsàyt/°sət/°sìyt/. A vote of the people expressing their choice for or against a proposed law or enactment, submitted to them, and which, if adopted, will work a change in the constitution, or which is beyond the powers of the regular legislative body. *See also* Referendum.

Pledge. A bailment, pawn, or deposit of personal property to a creditor as security for some debt or engagement. Personal property transferred to pledgee as security for pledgor's payment of debt or other obligation. A pledge, considered as a transaction, is a bailment or delivery of goods or property by way of security for a debt or engagement, or as security for the performance of an act. Another definition is that a pledge is a security interest in a chattel or in an intangible represented by an indispensable instrument (such as formal, written evidence of an interest in an intangible so representing the intangible that the enjoyment, transfer, or enforcement of the intangible depends upon possession of the instrument), the interest being created by a bailment for the purpose of securing the payment of a debt or the performance of some other duty. A pledge is a promise or agreement by which one binds himself to do or forbear something. A lien created by delivery of personal property by owner to another, upon express or implied agreement that it shall be retained as security for existing or future debt.

Much of the law of pledges has been replaced by the provisions for secured transactions in Article 9 of the U.C.C.

See also Bailment; Collateral; Hypothecate; Pawn; Secured transaction; Security. *Compare* Assignment.

Pledgee. The party to whom goods are pledged, or delivered in pledge. A person holding property as collateral security for his own benefit.

Pledgery. Suretyship, or an undertaking or answering for another.

Pledges. In common law pleading, those persons who became sureties for the prosecution of the suit. Their names were anciently appended at the foot of the declaration. In time it became purely a formal matter, because the plaintiff was no longer liable to be amerced for a false claim, and the fictitious persons John Doe and Richard Roe became the universal pledges, or they might be omitted altogether; or inserted at any time before judgment; they are now omitted.

Pledgor /pléjər/. The party delivering goods in pledge; the party pledging.

Plenary. Full, entire, complete, absolute, perfect, unqualified.

Plenary action. A complete and formal hearing or trial on the merits as distinguished from a summary hearing which is commonly less strict and more informal.

Plenary confession. A full and complete confession. An admission or confession, whether in civil or criminal law, is said to be "plenary" when it is, if believed, conclusive against the person making it.

Plenary jurisdiction. Full and complete jurisdiction or power of a court over the subject matter as well as the parties to a controversy. *See also* Jurisdiction.

Plenary powers. Authority and power as broad as is required in a given case.

Plenary proceedings. *See* Plenary action.

Plenary session. A meeting of all members of a deliberative body, as distinguished from a meeting of a committee of the same body.

Plenary suit. One that proceeds on formal pleadings. *See also* Plenary action.

Plot. *See* Plat *or* Plot.

Plottage. A term used in appraising land values and particularly in eminent domain proceedings to designate the additional value given to city lots by the fact that they are contiguous, which enables the owner to utilize them as large blocks of land. Plottage is a recognized concept in the field of eminent domain, referring to an added increment of value which may accrue to two or more vacant and unimproved contiguous parcels of land held in one ownership because of their potentially enhanced marketability by reason of their greater use adaptability as a single unit; simplistically stated, an assemblage of vacant and unimproved contiguous parcels held in one ownership may have a greater value as a whole than the sum of their values as separate constituent parcels and, hence, plottage value may be considered in determining fair market value.

Plow back. To retain earnings for continued investment in the business. To reinvest the earnings and profits into the business instead of paying them out as dividends or withdrawals by partners or proprietor.

Plunder, *v.* To pillage or loot. To take property from persons or places by open force, and this may be in course of a war, or by unlawful hostility, as in the case of pirates or robbers. The term is also used to express the idea of taking property from a person or place, without just right, but not expressing the nature or quality of the wrong done.

Plunder, *n.* Personal property belonging to an enemy, captured and appropriated on land; booty. Also the act of seizing such property. *See* Booty; Prize.

Plunderage. In maritime law, the embezzlement of goods on board of a ship is so called.

Plural. Containing more than one; consisting of or designating two or more.

Plurality /plúrǽlədiy/. The excess of the votes cast for one candidate over those cast for any other. Where there are only two candidates, he who receives the greater number of the votes cast is said to have a *majority;* when there are more than two competitors for the same office, the person who receives the greatest number of votes has a *plurality,* but he has not a majority unless he receives a greater number of votes than those cast for all his competitors combined, or, in other words, more than one-half of the total number of votes cast.

An opinion of an appellate court in which more justices join than in any concurring opinion (though not a majority of the court) is a plurality opinion as distinguished from a majority opinion in which a larger number of the justices on the panel join than not.

Plural marriage. *See* Marriage; Polygamy.

Pluries fi. fa. /pl(y)úriyiyz fáy(əray) féy(shiyəs)/. A writ issued where other commands of the court have proved ineffectual. Process that issues in the third instance, after the first and the alias have been ineffectual.

Pluries writs of execution. Third and subsequent writs of execution issued to enforce a judgment that was not satisfied by the sheriff acting under the original and alias writs of execution.

P.M. An abbreviation for "postmaster;" also for *"post-meridiem,"* afternoon.

P.O. An abbreviation of "public officer;" "police officer;" or "post-office."

Poach. To steal or destroy game on another's land. *See* Poaching.

Poaching. In criminal law, the unlawful entry upon land for the purpose of taking or destroying fish or game. The illegal taking or killing of fish or game.

Pocket veto. The act of the President in retaining a legislative bill without approving or rejecting it at the end of the legislative session and, in effect, vetoing it by such inactivity. See U.S. Constitution, Art. I, Sec. 7, Cl. 2.

P.O.D. account. An account payable on request to one person during lifetime and on his death to one or more P.O.D. payees, or to one or more persons during their lifetimes and on the death of all of them to one or more P.O.D. payees. Uniform Probate Code, § 6–101(11).

Point. A distinct proposition or question of law arising or propounded in a case. *See also* Issue.

In the case of shares of stock, a point means $1. In the case of bonds a point means $10, since a bond is quoted as a percentage of $1,000. In the case of market averages, the word point means merely that and no more. If, for example, the Dow-Jones Industrial Average rises from 870.25 to 871.25, it has risen a point. A point in this average, however, is not equivalent to $1.

Real estate financing. The word "point" as used in home mortgage finance industry denotes a fee or charge equal to one percent of principal amount of loan which is collected by lender at time the loan is made. It is a fee or charge which is collected only once, at inception of loan, and is in addition to constant long-term stated interest rate on face of loan.

Point reserved. When, in the progress of the trial of a cause, an important or difficult point of law is presented to the court, and the court is not certain of the decision that should be given, it may *reserve* the point, that is, decide it provisionally as it is asked by the party, but reserve its more mature consideration for the hearing on a motion for a new trial, when, if it shall appear that the first ruling was wrong, the verdict will be set aside. The point thus treated is technically called a "point reserved."

Points. *See* Point.

Points of law. Those distinct propositions of law on which each side relies in a lawsuit, and on which the court bases its decision (opinion) on.

Point system. The "point system", with respect to suspension of license of operator of a motor vehicle, automatically fixes penalty points following conviction of moving traffic violations and provides for mandatory suspension of the driver's license of a person who has accumulated a statutorily prescribed number of points within a year involved.

Poisonous tree doctrine. Doctrine refers to an illegal arrest or search which leads officers to evidence seized in a proper manner that may be inadmissible because of the taint of the original illegality. Sometimes also referred to as "fruit of poisonous tree" doctrine (*q.v.*).

Poison pill. A defensive tactic used by a company that is a target of an unwanted takeover to make its shares or financial condition less attractive to an acquirer. For instance, a firm may issue a new series of preferred shares that give shareholders the right to compel their redemption at a premium price after a takeover. *See also* Lockup; Porcupine provisions; White knight.

Pole. A measure of length, equal to five yards and a half.

Police. Branch of the government which is charged with the preservation of public order and tranquillity, the promotion of the public health, safety, and morals, and the prevention, detection, and punishment of crimes. *See also* Internal police; Peace *(Peace officers)*; Sheriff.

Police court. The name of an inferior court in several of the states, which has jurisdiction over minor offenses and city ordinances, concurrent jurisdiction in certain matters with justices of the peace, and the powers of a committing magistrate in respect to more serious crimes, and, in some states, a limited jurisdiction for the trial of civil causes.

Police jury. In Louisiana, the governing bodies of the parishes, which are political subdivisions of the state, comparable to counties in other states.

Police justice. A magistrate charged exclusively with the duties incident to the common-law office of a conservator or justice of the peace; the prefix "police" serving merely to distinguish them from justices having also civil jurisdiction.

Police magistrate. An inferior judicial officer having jurisdiction of minor criminal offenses, breaches of police regulations, and the like; so called to distinguish them from magistrates who have jurisdiction in civil cases also, as justices of the peace.

Police officer. One of the staff of persons employed in cities and towns to enforce the municipal laws and ordinances for preserving the peace, safety, and good order of the community. Also called "policeman" or "policewoman"; "patrolman" or "patrolwoman", or "peace officer". *See also* Peace *(Peace officers)*.

Police power. An authority conferred by the American constitutional system in the Tenth Amendment, U.S. Const., upon the individual states, and, in turn, delegated to local governments, through which they are enabled to establish a special department of police; adopt such laws and regulations as tend to prevent the commission of fraud and crime, and secure generally the comfort, safety, morals, health, and prosperity of its citizens by preserving the public order, preventing a conflict of rights in the common intercourse of the citizens, and insuring to each an uninterrupted enjoyment of all the privileges conferred upon him or her by the general laws.

The power of the State to place restraints on the personal freedom and property rights of persons for the protection of the public safety, health, and morals or the promotion of the public convenience and general prosperity. The police power is subject to limitations of the federal and State constitutions, and especially to the requirement of due process. Police power is the exercise of the sovereign right of a government to promote order, safety, security, health, morals and general welfare within constitutional limits and is an essential attribute of government.

Policy. The general principles by which a government is guided in its management of public affairs, or the legislature in its measures.

A general term used to describe all contracts of insurance. *See* Policy of insurance.

This term, as applied to a law, ordinance, or rule of law, denotes its general purpose or tendency considered as directed to the welfare or prosperity of the state or community.

A species of "lottery" whereby the chance is determined by numbers; "numbers game" also being a lottery. Policy is a lottery or game of chance where bettors select numbers to bet on and place the bet with a policy writer. *See* Lottery.

Public policy. That principle of the law which holds that no subject can lawfully do that which has a tendency to be injurious to the public or against the public good. The principles under which the freedom of contract or private dealings is restricted by law for the good of the community. The term "policy," as applied to a statute, regulation, rule of law, course of action, or the like, refers to its probable effect, tendency, or object, considered with reference to the social or political well-being of the state. Thus, certain classes of acts are said to be "against public policy," when the law refuses to enforce or recognize them, on the ground that they have a mischievous tendency, so as to be injurious to the interests of the state, apart from illegality or immorality.

Policyholder. The person who owns the policy of insurance whether he is the insured or not. In most states, any person with an insurable interest may be a policyholder.

Policy of insurance. An instrument in writing, by which one party (insurer), in consideration of a premium, engages to indemnify another (insured) against a contingent loss, by making him a payment in compensation, whenever the event shall happen by which the loss is to accrue. Contract whereby insurer, in return for premiums, engages, on happening of designated event, to pay certain sum as provided. The evidence delivered to the insured of the contract of the insurer, and ordinarily, of itself, constitutes complete evidence of the contract.

The written instrument in which a contract of insurance is set forth.

See also Face of policy; Floater policy; Homeowners policy; Master policy.

Assessable policy. A policy under which a policyholder may be held liable for losses of the insurance company beyond its reserves.

Blanket policy. A policy of fire insurance which contemplates that the risk is shifting, fluctuating, or varying, and is applied to a class of property rather than to any particular article or thing.

The term "specific" as applied in insurance phraseology is frequently used in contrast with "blanket insurance" and denotes coverage of a particular piece of property or property at a specific location, as contrasted with blanket insurance which covers the same and other property in several different locations.

Class of life insurance policies. Those policies issued in the same calendar year, upon the lives of persons of the same age, and on the same plan of insurance.

Endowment policy. A policy which agrees to pay to the insured, if living at the expiration of a certain period, a specified amount of money, and in the event of his death in the interim, agrees to pay the face amount of the policy to his designated beneficiary.

Extended policy. A policy which provides protection beyond the time when premiums are no longer paid.

Floater policy. A policy of fire insurance not applicable to any specific described goods, but to any and all goods which may at the time of the fire be in a certain building.

Incontestable policy. A policy which contains a provision to the effect that the company after the policy has been in force cannot contest, challenge or cancel the policy on the basis of statements made in the application. The period of contestability may be one, two or three years.

Interest policy. One where the assured has a real, substantial, and assignable interest in the thing insured; as opposed to a wager policy.

Master policy. In group life, medical, etc. insurance, the single policy under which the participants are covered. The individuals covered by the master policy receive a certificate indicating their participation.

Mixed policy. A policy of marine insurance in which not only the time is specified for which the risk is limited, but the voyage also is described by its local termini; as opposed to policies of insurance for a particular voyage, without any limits as to time, and also to purely time policies, in which there is no designation of local termini at all.

Open policy. One in which the value of the subject insured is not fixed or agreed upon in the policy as between the assured and the underwriter, but is left to be estimated in case of loss. The term is opposed to "valued policy," in which the value of the subject insured is fixed for the purpose of the insurance, and expressed on the face of the policy. But this term is also sometimes used to describe a policy in which an aggregate amount is expressed in the body of the policy, and the specific amounts and subjects are to be indorsed from time to time.

Paid-up policy. In life insurance, a policy on which no further payments are to be made in the way of annual premiums.

Participating policy. A policy commonly found in mutual insurance companies and in some stock companies in which the insured participates in the profits by receiving dividends or rebates from future premiums.

Policy loan. An advancement on life policy without a personal obligation on the part of the policyholder as to repayment. A loan made by an insurance company which takes the policy's cash reserve as security for the loan.

Policy reserves. Funds held by insurance company specifically to meet its policy obligations.

Term policy. In life insurance, a policy which gives protection for a specified period of time but no cash or reserve value is created in the policy. See Insurance.

Time policy. In fire insurance, one made for a defined and limited time, as, one year. In marine insurance, one made for a particular period of time, irrespective of the voyage or voyages upon which the vessel may be engaged during that period.

Valued policy. See that title.

Voyage policy. A policy of marine insurance effected for a particular voyage or voyages of the vessel, and not otherwise limited as to time.

Wager policy. An insurance upon a subject-matter in which the party assured has no real, valuable, or insurable interest. A mere wager policy is that in which the party assured has no interest in the thing assured, and could sustain no possible loss by the event insured against, if he had not made such wager. Such policies are generally illegal, or not otherwise written, because the insured does not have an insurable interest.

Policy value. The amount of cash available to the policyholder on the surrender or cancellation of the insurance policy.

Policy year. In insurance, the year which commences with the date of the commencement or anniversary of the policy.

Political. Pertaining or relating to the policy or the administration of government, state or national. Pertaining to, or incidental to, the exercise of the functions vested in those charged with the conduct of government; relating to the management of affairs of state, as political theories; of or pertaining to exercise of rights and privileges or the influence by which individuals of a state seek to determine or control its public policy; having to do with organization or action of individuals, parties, or interests that seek to control appointment or action of those who manage affairs of a state.

Political action committees. *See* PAC.

Political corporation. A public or municipal corporation; one created for political purposes, and having for its object the administration of governmental powers of a subordinate or local nature.

Political crime. In general, any crime directly against the government; *e.g.* treason; sedition. It includes any violent political disturbance without reference to a specific crime. *See also* Political offenses.

Political law. That branch of jurisprudence which treats of the science of politics, or the organization and administration of government. More commonly called "Political science."

Political liberty. *See* Liberty.

Political offenses. As a designation of a class of crimes usually excepted from extradition treaties, this term denotes crimes which are incidental to and form a part of political disturbances; but it might also be understood to include offenses consisting in an attack upon the political order of things established in the country where committed, and even to include offenses committed to obtain any political object. Under extradition treaties is an offense committed in the course of and incidental to a violent political disturbance, such as war, revolution and rebellion; an offense is not of a political character simply because it was politically motivated. *See also* Political crime; Terrorism.

Political office. *See* Office.

Political party. An association of individuals whose primary purposes are to promote or accomplish elections or appointments to public offices, positions, or jobs. A committee, association, or organization which accepts contributions or makes expenditures for the purpose of influencing or attempting to influence the election of presidential or vice presidential electors or of any individual whose name is presented for election to any federal, state, or local elective public office, whether or not such individual is elected. Cal. Rev. & Tax Code § 24434(b)(1)(C).

Political questions. Questions of which courts will refuse to take cognizance, or to decide, on account of their purely political character, or because their determination would involve an encroachment upon the executive or legislative powers.

"Political question doctrine" holds that certain issues should not be decided by courts because their resolution is committed to another branch of government and/or because those issues are not capable, for one reason or another, of judicial resolution.

A matter of dispute which can be handled more appropriately by another branch of the government is not a "justiciable" matter for the courts. However, a state apportionment statute is not such a political question as to render it nonjusticiable. Baker v. Carr, 369 U.S. 186, 208–210, 82 S.Ct. 691, 705–706, 7 L.Ed.2d 663.

Compare Justiciable controversey.

Political rights. Those which may be exercised in the formation or administration of the government. Rights of citizens established or recognized by constitutions which give them the power to participate directly or indirectly in the establishment or administration of government.

Political subdivision. A division of the state made by proper authorities thereof, acting within their constitutional powers, for purpose of carrying out a portion of those functions of state which by long usage and inherent necessities of government have always been regarded as public.

Political trial. Term loosely applied to trials in which the parties represent fundamentally different political convictions and in which the parties or one of them attempts to litigate their political beliefs.

Politics. The science of government; the art or practice of administering public affairs.

Polity. The form of government; civil constitution.

Poll, *v.* To single out, one by one, of a number of persons. To examine each juror separately, after a verdict has been given, as to his concurrence in the verdict. *See* Polling the jury.

Poll, *n.* A head; an individual person; a register of persons. In the law of elections, a list or register of heads or individuals who may vote in an election; the aggregate of those who actually cast their votes at the election, excluding those who stay away.

Polling the jury. A practice whereby the jurors are asked individually whether they assented, and still assent, to the verdict. To poll a jury is to call the names of the persons who compose a jury and require each juror to declare what his verdict is before it is recorded. This may be accomplished by questioning them individually or by ascertaining fact of unanimous concurrence by general question, and once concurrence has been determined, the polling is at an end.

If upon the poll there is not unanimous concurrence, the jury may be directed to retire for further deliberations or may be discharged. Fed.R. Crim.P. 31.

Polls. The place where electors cast in their votes.

Poll-tax. A capitation tax; a tax of a specific sum levied upon each person within the jurisdiction of the taxing power and within a certain class (as, all males of a certain age, etc.) without reference to his property or lack of it. A tax upon the privilege of being; it is a sum levied upon persons without regard to property, occupation, income or ability to pay.

Poll taxes as a prerequisite to voting in federal elections are prohibited by the 24th Amendment and as to state elections such were held to be unconstitutional in Harper v. Virginia Bd. of Elections, 383 U.S. 663, 86 S.Ct. 1079, 16 L.Ed.2d 169.

Po. lo. suo. An old abbreviation for the words *"ponit loco suo"* (puts in his place), used in warrants of attorney.

Pollute. To corrupt or defile. The contamination of soil, air and water by noxious substances and noises. *See also* Pollution.

Pollution. Contamination of the environment by a variety of sources including but not limited to hazardous substances, organic wastes and toxic chemicals. Pollution is legally controlled and enforced through various federal and state laws and agencies, including common law nuisance laws. Examples of federal laws are the Clean Water Act, 33 U.S.C.A. § 1251 et seq. and the Clean Air Act, 31 U.S.C.A. § 7401 et seq. *See also* Environmental Protection Agency; Hazardous substance; Superfund; Toxic waste.

Polyandry /póliyǽndriy/. The civil condition of having more husbands than one to the same woman; a social order permitting plurality of husbands.

Polygamy /pəlígəmiy/. The offense of having several wives or husbands at the same time, or more than one wife or husband at the same time. Bigamy literally means a second marriage distinguished from a third or other; while polygamy means many marriages,—implies more than two. Polygamy is a crime in all states.

A person is guilty of polygamy, a felony of the third degree, if he marries or cohabits with more than one spouse at a time in purported exercise of the right of plural marriage. The offense is a continuing one until all cohabitation and claim of marriage with more than one spouse terminates. This section does not apply to parties to a polygamous marriage, lawful in the country of which they are residents or nationals, while they are in transit through or temporarily visiting this State. Model Penal Code, § 230.1.

Polygraph. Also known as a lie detector, it is an electro-mechanical instrument used to determine whether an examinee is truthfully answering questions. It simultaneously measures and records certain physiological changes in the human body which it is believed are involuntarily caused by an examinee's conscious attempt to deceive an interrogator. Though historically inadmissible on grounds of unreliability, polygraph evidence is increasingly being admitted if, for example, the parties stipulate in advance to its admission or it is being offered to impeach or corroborate witness testimony.

With certain exceptions, employers engaged in commerce are statutorily prohibited from requiring employees or prospective employees to submit to a polygraph test. Employee Polygraph Protection Act of 1988, 29 U.S.C.A. § 2001 et seq.

See also Lie detector.

Polyopsony. The condition of a market characterized by the fewness of buyers. The fewness has an effect on the price of the materials or products.

Polypoly. A market condition characterized by the fewness of sellers where this has a direct effect on prices.

Pomerene Bills of Lading Act. Federal Bills of Lading Act, 49 U.S.C.A. §§ 81–124. *See* Bill of lading acts.

Pond. A body of stagnant water without an outlet, larger than a puddle and smaller than a lake; or a like body of water with a small outlet.

Pool. A combination of persons or corporations engaged in the same business, or for the purpose of engaging in a particular business or commercial or speculative venture, where all contribute to a common fund, or place their holdings of a given stock or other security in the hands and control of a managing member or committee, with the object of eliminating competition as between the several members of the pool, or of establishing a monopoly or controlling prices or rates by the weight and power of their combined capital, or of raising or depressing prices on the stock market, or simply with a view to the successful conduct of an enterprise too great for the capital of any member individually, and on an agreement for the division of profits or losses among the members, either equally or pro rata. Also, a similar combination not embracing the idea of a pooled or contributed capital, but simply the elimination of destructive competition between the members by an agreement to share or divide the profits of a given business or venture, as, for example, a contract between two or more competing railroads to abstain from "rate wars" and (usually) to maintain fixed rates, and to divide their earnings from the transportation of freight in fixed proportions. Such type pooling arrangements are illegal under the Sherman Antitrust Act. *See also* Cartel; Trust.

In various methods of gambling, a "pool" is a sum of money made up of the stakes contributed by various persons, the whole of which is then wagered as a stake on the event of a race, game, or other contest, and the winnings (if any) are divided among the contributors to the pool pro rata. Or it is a sum similarly made up by the contributions of several persons, each of whom then makes his guess or prediction as to the event of a future contest or hazard, the successful bettor taking the entire pool. Such pools are distinct from the practice of bookmaking.

A body of standing water, without a current or issue, accumulated in a natural basin or depression in the earth, and not artificially formed. *See* Pond.

Pooling agreement. A contractual arrangement among shareholders relating to the voting of their shares. So long as such agreement is limited to voting as shareholders, it is enforceable.

Pooling of interests. A method of accounting for mergers in which the acquired company's assets are recorded on the acquiring company's books at their cost when originally acquired. No goodwill account is created under the pooling method.

Poor debtors' oath. *See* Pauper's oath; Poverty affidavit.

Popular sense. In reference to the construction of a statute, this term means that sense which people conversant with the subject-matter with which the statute is dealing would attribute to it.

Porcupine provisions. Defensive provisions in articles of incorporation or bylaws designed to make unwanted takeover attempts impossible or impractical without the consent of the target's management. *See also* Lockup; Poison pill; White knight.

Pornographic. That which is of or pertaining to obscene literature; obscene; licentious. Material is pornographic or obscene if the average person, applying contemporary community standards, would find that the work taken as a whole appeals to the prurient interest and if it depicts in a patently offensive way sexual conduct and if the work taken as a whole lacks serious literary, artistic, political or scientific value. Miller v. California, 413 U.S. 15, 24–25, 93 S.Ct. 2607, 2615, 37 L.Ed.2d 419. *See also* Dominant theme; Obscene; Pander *(Pandering of obscenity)*; Prurient interest.

Pornography. *See* Pornographic.

Port. A place for the loading and unloading of the cargoes of vessels, and the collection of duties or customs upon imports and exports. A place, on the seacoast, great lakes, or on a river, where ships stop for the purpose of loading and unloading cargo, or for purpose of taking on or letting off passengers, from whence they depart, and where they finish their voyage. A port is a place intended for loading or unloading goods; hence includes the natural shelter surrounding water, as also sheltered water produced by artificial jetties, etc.

Foreign port. One exclusively within the jurisdiction of a foreign nation, hence one without the United States. But the term is also applied to a port in any state other than the state where the vessel belongs or her owner resides. Port other than home port.

Free port. See that title.

Home port. The port at which a vessel is registered or enrolled or where the owner resides.

Port of call. Port at which ships usually stop on a route or voyage.

Port of delivery. The port which is to be the terminus of any particular voyage, and where the vessel is to unlade or deliver her cargo, as distinguished from any port at which she may touch, during the voyage, for other purposes.

Port of departure. The port from which vessel clears and departs upon start of voyage. As used in the United States statutes requiring a ship to procure a bill of health from the consular officer at the place of departure, is not the last port at which the ship stops while bound for the United States, but the port from which she cleared.

Port of destination. The port at which a voyage is to end. In maritime law and marine insurance, the term includes both ports which constitute the termini of the voyage; the home port and the foreign port to which the vessel is consigned as well as any usual stopping places for the receipt or discharge of cargo.

Port of discharge. In a policy of marine insurance, means the place where the substantial part of the cargo is discharged, although there is an intent to complete the discharge at another basin.

Port of entry. One of the ports designated by law, at which a custom-house or revenue office is established for the execution of the laws imposing duties on vessels and importations of goods. Port where immigrants arrive. 8 U.S.C.A. § 1221.

Port-risk. In marine insurance, a risk upon a vessel while lying in port, and before she has taken her departure upon another voyage. *See also* Port risk insurance.

Port toll. The toll paid for bringing goods into a port.

Portal-to-Portal Act. Federal statute regulating pay for non-productive time required of employee to reach place of employment and to return in some instances. 29 U.S.C.A. §§ 216, 251–262.

Port authority. Governmental agency authorized by a state or the federal government to regulate and plan traffic through a port, and also commonly charged with responsibility of encouraging or securing businesses to locate on land or areas served by port. Sometimes such authorities also have responsibility over establishment and maintenance of airports, bridges, tollways, and surface transportation in metropolitan area of port; *e.g.* New York Port Authority, which is operated jointly by New York and New Jersey under an interstate compact.

Portfolio. In investments, the collective term for all the securities (which may consist of various types) held by one person or institution.

Portfolio income. Income from interest, dividends, rentals, royalties, capital gains, or other investment sources. Portfolio income is not considered passive income, therefore net passive losses cannot be used to offset net portfolio income. *See also* Passive investment income; Passive loss.

Portion. An allotted part; a share, a parcel; a division in a distribution; a share of an estate or the like, received by gift or inheritance. *See* Per capita; Per stirpes.

Port risk insurance. In contradistinction to voyage or time insurance, means insurance upon a vessel while lying in port, and before she has taken her departure on another voyage.

Position. Extent of person's investment in a particular security or market.

Position of United States. Phrase "the position of the United States" within meaning of section of Equal Access to Justice Act (5 U.S.C.A. § 504; 28 U.S.C.A. § 2412) permitting government, when it loses a case, to avoid liability for attorney fees if it can show that its "position" was substantially justified refers to the arguments relied upon by the government in litigation. *See also* Equal Access to Justice Act.

Positive. Laid down, enacted, or prescribed. Express or affirmative. Direct, absolute, explicit. As to *positive* Condition; Fraud; Proof; and Servitude, see those titles.

Positive evidence. Direct evidence. Eye witness testimony. Direct proof of the fact or point in issue; evidence which, if believed, establishes the truth or falsehood of a fact in issue, and does not arise from any presumption. It is distinguished from circumstantial evidence. *See also* Evidence.

Positive law. Law actually and specifically enacted or adopted by proper authority for the government of an organized jural society. *See also* Legislation.

Posse /pósiy/. Lat. A possibility. A thing is said to be *in posse* when it may possibly be; *in esse* when it actually is. Group of people acting under authority of police or sheriff and engaged in searching for a criminal or in making an arrest. Same as Posse comitatus *(q.v.)*.

Posse comitatus /pósiy kòmətéytəs/. Lat. The power or force of the county. The entire population of a county above the age of fifteen, which a sheriff may summon to his assistance in certain cases, as to aid him in keeping the peace, in pursuing and arresting felons, etc.

Possess. To occupy in person; to have in one's actual and physical control; to have the exclusive detention and control of; to have and hold as property; to have a just right to; to be master of; to own or be entitled to.

Term "possess," under narcotic drug laws, means actual control, care and management of the drug. Defendant "possesses" controlled substance when defendant knows of substance's presence, substance is immediately accessible, and defendant exercises "dominion or control" over substance.

See also Hold; Possession.

Possessio /pəzésh(iy)ow/. Lat. *Civil law.* That condition of fact under which one can exercise his power over a corporeal thing at his pleasure, to the exclusion of all others. This condition of fact is called "detention," and it forms the substance of possession in all its varieties.

Possession. Having control over a thing with the intent to have and to exercise such control. The detention and control, or the manual or ideal custody, of anything which may be the subject of property, for one's use and enjoyment, either as owner or as the proprietor of a qualified right in it, and either held personally or by another who exercises it in one's place and name. Act or state of possessing. That condition of facts under which one can exercise his power over a corporeal thing at his pleasure to the exclusion of all other persons.

The law, in general, recognizes two kinds of possession: actual possession and constructive possession. A person who knowingly has direct physical control over a thing, at a given time, is then in actual possession of it. A person who, although not in actual possession, knowingly has both the power and the intention at a given time to exercise dominion or control over a thing, either directly or through another person or persons, is then in constructive possession of it. The law recognizes also that possession may be sole or joint. If one person alone has actual or constructive possession of a thing, possession is sole. If two or more persons share actual or constructive possession of a thing, possession is joint.

Generally, "possession" within context of title insurance policies refers to open, visible and exclusive use.

See also Adverse possession; Constructive possession; Exclusive possession; Hold; Notorious possession; Occupancy; Repossession.

Actual possession. Exists where the thing is in the immediate occupancy and physical control of the party. *See also* general definition above.

Constructive possession. Possession not actual but assumed to exist, where one claims to hold by virtue of some title, without having the actual occupancy, as, where the owner of a tract of land, regularly laid out, is in possession of a part, he is constructively in possession of the whole. *See also* general definition above.

Criminal law. Possession as necessary for conviction of offense of possession of controlled substances with intent to distribute may be constructive as well as actual; as well as joint or exclusive. The defendants must have had dominion and control over the contraband with knowledge of its presence and character. *See also* Possess.

Possession, as an element of offense of stolen goods, is not limited to actual manual control upon or about the person, but extends to things under one's power and dominion.

To constitute "possession" of a concealable weapon under statute proscribing possession of a concealable weapon by a felon, it is sufficient that defendant have constructive possession and immediate access to the weapon.

Dispossession. The act of ousting or removing one from the possession of property previously held by him, which may be tortious and unlawful, as in the case of a forcible amotion, or in pursuance of law, as where a landlord "dispossesses" his tenant at the expiration of the term or for other cause by the aid of judicial process. *See* Dispossess proceedings; Ejectment; Eviction; Process (*Summary process*).

Hostile possession. This term, as applied to an occupant of real estate holding adversely, is not construed as implying actual emnity or ill will, but merely means that he claims to hold the possession in the character of an owner, and therefore denies all validity to claims set up by any and all other persons. *See* Adverse possession.

Open possession. Possession of real property is said to be "open" when held without concealment or attempt at secrecy, or without being covered up in the name of a third person, or otherwise attempted to be withdrawn from sight, but in such a manner that any person interested can ascertain who is actually in possession by proper observation and inquiry. *See* Adverse possession.

Unity of possession. Joint possession of two rights by several titles, as where a lessee of land acquires the title in fee-simple, which extinguishes the lease. The term also describes one of the essential properties of a joint estate, each of the tenants having the entire possession as well of every parcel as of the whole.

Possession is nine-tenths of the law. This adage is not to be taken as true to the full extent, so as to mean that the person in possession can only be ousted by one whose title is nine times better than his, but it places in a strong light the legal truth that every claimant must succeed by the strength of his own title, and not by the weakness of his antagonist's.

Possessor. One who possesses; one who has possession. *See also* Occupant.

Possessory. Relating to possession; founded on possession; contemplating or claiming possession.

Possessory action. See next title.

Possessory action. An action which has for its immediate object to obtain or recover the actual *possession* of the subject-matter; as distinguished from an action which merely seeks to vindicate the plaintiff's *title,* or which involves the bare right only; the latter being called a "petitory" action; *e.g.* summary process action to dispossess tenant for non-payment of rent. A "possessory action" is one brought by a possessor of immovable property to be maintained in his possession when his possession has been disturbed or to be restored to possession from which he has been evicted. *See also* Ejectment; Eviction; Process (*Summary process*).

An action founded on possession. Trespass for injuries to personal property is called a "possessory" action, because it lies only for a plaintiff who, at the moment of the injury complained of, was in actual or constructive, immediate, and exclusive possession.

Admiralty practice. One which is brought to recover the possession of a vessel, had under a claim of title.

Possessory claim. The title of a pre-emptor of public lands who has filed his declaratory statement but has not paid for the land.

Possessory interest. Right to exert control over specific land to exclusion of others. Right to possess property by virtue of an interest created in the property though it need not be accompanied by title; *e.g.* right of a tenant for years.

A possessory interest in land exists in a person who has (a) a physical relation to the land of a kind which gives a certain degree of physical control over the land, and an intent so to exercise such control as to exclude other members of society in general from any present occupation of the land; or (b) interests in the land which are substantially identical with those arising when the elements stated in Clause (a) exist. Restatement, Property, § 7.

Possessory lien. A lien is possessory where the creditor has the right to hold possession of the specific property until satisfaction of the debt or performance of an obligation.

Possessory warrant. The proceeding by possessory warrant is a summary remedy for the recovery of a personal chattel which has been taken by fraud, violence, enticement, or seduction from the possession of the party complaining or which, having been in his recent possession, has disappeared and is believed to be in the possession of the party complained against. The purpose of the proceeding is to protect and quiet the possession of personalty, but only as against acts which are inhibited by statute.

Possibility. An uncertain thing which may happen. A contingent interest in real or personal estate.

It is either *near* (or *ordinary*), as where an estate is limited to one after the death of another, or *remote* (or *extraordinary*), as where it is limited to a man, provided he marries a certain woman, and that she shall die and he shall marry another.

See also Impossibility; Probability.

Possibility coupled with an interest. An expectation recognized in law as an estate or interest, such as occurs in executory devises and shifting or springing uses. Such a possibility may be sold or assigned.

Possibility of reverter. Future estate left in creator or in his successors in interest upon simultaneous creation of estate that will terminate automatically within a period of time defined by occurrence of specified event. The interest which remains in a grantor or testator after the conveyance or devise of a fee simple determinable and which permits the grantor to be revested automatically of his estate on breach of the condition.

Possible. Capable of existing, happening, being, becoming or coming to pass; feasible, not contrary to nature of things; neither necessitated nor precluded; free to happen or not; contrasted with impossible. In another sense, the word denotes improbability, without excluding the idea of feasibility. It is also sometimes equivalent to "practicable" or "reasonable," as in some cases where action is required to be taken "as soon as possible." *See also* Potential.

Post. Lat. After; as occurring in a report or a textbook, term is used to send the reader to a subsequent part of the book. Same as "infra."

Post, *n.* Military establishment where body of troops is stationed; also place where soldier is stationed.

Post, *v.* To bring to the notice or attention of the public by affixing to a post or wall, or putting up in some public place; to display in a conspicuous manner; to announce, publish or advertise by use of placard. To place in mails. In accounting, to transfer an entry from an original record to a ledger. As regards posting of bail, *see* Bail. *See also* Posting.

Post-act. An after-act; an act done afterwards.

Postage. Charges for postal service.

Postal. Relating to the mails; pertaining to the post-office.

Postal order. A money order. A letter of credit furnished by the government, at a small charge, to facilitate the transmission of money.

Post-closing trial balance. An internal report that examines ledger account balances after the closing process has been completed to determine if total debits equal total credits. *See also* Trial (*Trial balance*).

Post-conviction remedies. *Federal.* A federal prisoner, attacking the constitutionality of his sentence, may move the court which imposed the sentence to vacate, set aside or correct the same. This motion, under 28 U.S.C.A. § 2255, must normally be made before the prisoner can seek habeas corpus relief.

State. Almost every state has one or more post-conviction procedures that permit prisoners to challenge at least some constitutional violations. A substantial group of states have adopted special post-conviction statutes or court rules, roughly similar to section 2255 of 28 U.S.C.A., that encompass all constitutional claims. Others, following the federal habeas corpus statute, have held that at least some constitutional violations are jurisdictional defects cognizable under a common law or statutory writ of habeas corpus. The writ of coram nobis is also viewed in several states as an appropriate remedy for presenting certain types of constitutional claims. In addition, several states have adopted the Uniform Post Conviction Procedure Act.

See also Habeas corpus.

Post-date. To date an instrument as of a time later than that at which it is really made. The negotiability of an instrument is not affected by the fact that it is post-dated. U.C.C. § 3–114.

Post-dated check. A check issued before the stated date of the instrument. One delivered prior to its date, generally payable at sight or on presentation on or after day of its date. *See* Post-date.

Post diem /pówst dáyəm/. After the day; as, a plea of payment *post diem,* after the day when the money became due.

Posted waters. Waters flowing through or lying upon inclosed or cultivated lands, which are preserved for the exclusive use of the owner or occupant by his posting notices (according to the statute) prohibiting all persons from shooting, trapping, or fishing thereon, under a prescribed penalty.

Posteriority /pəstèhriyóhrətiy/. This is a word of comparison and relation in tenure, the correlative of which is the word "priority." Thus, a man who held lands or tenements of two lords was said to hold of his more ancient lord by priority, and of his less ancient lord by posteriority. It has also a general application in law consistent with its etymological meaning, and, as so used, it is likewise opposed to priority.

Posterity /postéhrətiy/. All the descendants of a person in a direct line to the remotest generation.

Post facto /pòwst fǽktow/. After the fact. See Ex post facto.

Post-factum, or **postfactum** /pòwstfǽktəm/. An afteract; an act done afterwards; a post-act.

Post hoc /pòwst hǽk/. Lat. After this; after this time; hereafter.

Posthumous. That which is done after the death of a person as the publication of a book after the death of the author, or the birth of a child after the death of its father.

Posthumous child /póstyəməs cháyld/. Child born after the death of his or her father. See Unborn child.

Posthumous work /póstyəməs wɘ́rk/. Work on which original copyright has been taken out by someone to whom literary property passed before publication.

Posting. In accounting, the act of transferring an original entry to a ledger. The act of mailing a document. Form of substituted service of process consisting of displaying the process in a prominent place when other forms of service are unavailing.

The process of posting of a check means the usual procedure followed by a payor bank in determining to pay an item and in recording the payment including one or more of the following or other steps as determined by the bank: verification of any signature; ascertaining that sufficient funds are available; affixing a "paid" or other stamp; entering a charge or entry to a customer's account; correcting or reversing an entry or erroneous action with respect to the item. U.C.C. § 4–109.

In connection with trespass statutes, the act of placing or affixing signs on private property in a manner to give notice of the trespass.

Post-mortem /pòwstmórtəm/. After death; pertaining to matters occurring after death. A term generally applied to an autopsy or examination of a dead body, to ascertain the cause of death, or to the inquisition for that purpose by the coroner.

Post-nuptial /pòwstnə́pshəl/. After marriage.

Post-nuptial agreement. Agreements or settlements made after marriage between spouses still married to determine the rights of each in the others' property in the event of divorce or death. They take the form of separation agreements, property settlements in contemplation of a separation or divorce, or property settlements where there is no intention of the parties to separate. Compare Pre-nuptial agreement; Separation agreement.

Post-nuptial settlement. See Post-nuptial agreement.

Postpone. To put off; defer; delay; continue; adjourn; as when a hearing is postponed. Also to place after; to set below something else; as when an earlier lien for some reason postponed to a later lien. The term carries with it the idea of deferring the doing of something or the taking effect of something until a future or later time.

Post-trial discovery. Under rules procedure, a party may take depositions pending appeal to perpetuate the testimony of witness for use in the event of further proceedings in the trial court. Fed.R.Civil P. 27(b).

Post-trial motions. Generic term to describe those motions which are permitted after trial such as motion for new trial (Fed.R.Civil P. 59), and motion for relief from judgment (Rule 60).

Post-trial remedies. See Post-conviction remedies; Post-trial motions.

Potentia /pəténsh(iy)ə/. Lat. Possibility; power.

Potential. Existing in possibility but not in act. Naturally and probably expected to come into existence at some future time, though not now existing; for example, the future product of grain or trees already planted, or the successive future installments or payments on a contract or engagement already made. Things having a "potential existence" may be the subject of mortgage, assignment, or sale. See Possible.

Pound. A place, inclosed by public authority, for the detention of stray animals; e.g. dog pound. Place where impounded property is held until redeemed.

A pound-overt is said to be one that is open overhead; a pound-covert is one that is closed, or covered over, such as a stable or other building.

A measure of weight, equal to 16 avoirdupois ounces or 7,000 grains; the pound troy 12 ounces or 5,760 grains.

Basic monetary unit of United Kingdom; also called pound sterling.

Poundage fees. A fee awarded to the sheriff in the nature of a percentage commission upon monies recovered pursuant to a levy or execution or attachment. The money which an owner of animals (or other property) impounded must pay to obtain their release.

In old English law, a subsidy to the value of twelve pence in the *pound*, granted to the king, of all manner of merchandise of every merchant, as well denizen as alien, either exported or imported.

Pound breach. The common law offense of breaking a pound, for the purpose of taking out the cattle or goods impounded.

Pour-over. Provision in a will which directs the distribution of property into a trust. Also, a similar provision in a trust which directs property into a will.

Pour-over trust. *See* Pour-over; Trust.

Pour-over will. *See* Pour-over.

Poverty. The state or condition of being poor. *See also* Indigent.

Poverty affidavit. An affidavit, made and filed by person seeking public assistance, appointment of counsel, waiver of court fees, or other free services or benefits, that he or she is in fact, financially unable to pay for such.

Document signed under oath which may be the basis of a court's permitting one to proceed in forma pauperis. See *e.g.* 28 U.S.C.A. § 1915; Fed. R.App.P., Form 4. Leave to proceed on appeal in forma pauperis from district court to court of appeals is governed by Fed.R.App.P. 24.

See also Pauper's oath.

Power. The right, ability, authority, or faculty of doing something. Authority to do any act which the grantor might himself lawfully perform.

A power is an ability on the part of a person to produce a change in a given legal relation by doing or not doing a given act. Restatement, Second, Agency, § 6; Restatement, Property, § 3.

In a restricted sense a "power" is a liberty or authority reserved by, or limited to, a person to dispose of real or personal property, for his own benefit, or benefit of others, or enabling one person to dispose of interest which is vested in another.

See also Authority; Beneficial power; Capacity; Concurrent power; Control; Delegation of powers; Donee of power; Enumerated powers; Executive powers; Governmental powers; Judicial power; Legislative power; Police power; Right.

Appendant or appurtenant powers. Those existing where the donee of the power has an estate in the land and the power is to take effect wholly or in part out of that estate, and the estate created by its exercise affects the estate and interest of the donee of the power.

Collateral powers. Those in which the donee of the power has no interest or estate in the land which is the subject of the power. Also called *naked powers.*

Constitutional powers. The right to take action in respect to a particular subject-matter or class of matters, involving more or less of discretion, granted by the constitution to the several departments or branches of the government, or reserved to the people. Powers in this sense are generally classified as legislative, executive, and judicial *(q.v.);* and further classified as enumerated (or express), implied, inherent, resulting, or sovereign powers.

Commerce powers. Power of Congress to regulate commerce with foreign nations, and among the several states. Art. I, § 8, Cl. 3, U.S.Const.

Enforcement powers. The 13th, 14th, 15th, 19th, 23rd, 24th, and 26th Amendments each contain a section providing, in these or equivalent words, that "Congress shall have the power to enforce by appropriate legislation, the provisions of this article."

Enumerated or express powers. Powers expressly provided for in Constitution; *e.g.,* U.S.Const. Art. I, § 8.

Implied powers. Such as are necessary to make available and carry into effect those powers which are expressly granted or conferred, and which must therefore be presumed to have been within the intention of the constitutional or legislative grant. *See Enforcement powers, above; also Necessary and proper powers, below.* See also Penumbra doctrine.

Inherent powers. Powers which necessarily inhere in the government by reason of its role as a government; *e.g.* conducting of foreign affairs. *See also* Supremacy clause.

Necessary and proper powers. Art. I, § 8, Cl. 18 gives Congress power "To make all laws which shall be necessary and proper for carrying into execution the foregoing powers (*i.e.* those enumerated in clauses 1–17), and all other powers vested by this Constitution in the Government of the United States, or in any Department or Officer thereof." *See also* Penumbra doctrine.

Preemptive powers. See Preemption; Supremacy clause.

Reserved or residual state powers. The powers not delegated to the United States by the Constitution, nor prohibited by it to the States, are reserved to the States respectively, or to the people. 10th Amend., U.S.Const.

Resulting powers. Those powers which "result from the whole mass of the powers of the National Government and from the nature of political society." American Ins. Co. v. Canter, 26 U.S. (1 Pet.) 516, 7 L.Ed. 242.

Spending power. Power of Congress "to pay the debts and provide for the common defense and general welfare of the United States." Art. I, § 8, Cl. 1, U.S.Const.

Taxing power. Power of Congress "to lay and collect taxes, duties, imports and excises." Art. I, § 8, Cl. 1.

Corporate powers. The right or capacity of a corporation to act or be acted upon in a particular manner or in respect to a particular subject; as, the power to have a corporate seal, to sue and be sued, to make by-laws, to carry on a particular business or construct a given work.

General and special powers. A power is general when it authorizes the alienation in fee, by means of a conveyance, will, or charge, of the lands embraced in the power to any alienee whatsoever. It is special (1) when the persons or class of persons to whom the disposition of the lands under the power is to be made are designated, or (2) when the power authorizes the alienation, by means of a conveyance, will, or charge, of a particular estate or interest less than a fee.

General and special powers in trust. A general power is in trust when any person or class of persons other than the grantee of such power is designated as entitled to the proceeds or any portion of the proceeds or other benefits to result from the alienation. A special power is in trust (1) when the disposition or charge which it authorizes is limited to be made to any person or class of persons other than the holder of the power, or (2) when any person or class of persons other than the holder is designated as entitled to any benefit from the disposition or charge authorized by the power.

Implied powers. Powers not granted in express terms but existing because they are necessary and proper to carry into effect some expressly granted power. *See also Constitutional powers, above.*

Inherent powers. Those which are enjoyed by the possessors of natural right, without having been received from another. Such are the powers of a people to establish a form of government, of a father to control his children. Some of these are regulated and restricted in their exercise by law, but are not technically considered in the law as powers.

Inherent agency power is a term used in the Restatement of Agency to indicate the power of an agent which is derived not from authority, apparent authority or estoppel, but solely from the agency relation and exists for the protection of persons harmed by or dealing with a servant or other agent. Restatement, Second, Agency § 8A.

Naked power. One which is simply collateral and without interest in the donee, which arises when, to a mere stranger, authority is given of disposing of an interest, in which he had not before, nor has by the instrument creating the power, any estate whatsoever.

Power of revocation. A power which is to divest or abridge an existing estate.

Powers in gross. Those which give a donee of the power, who has an estate in the land, authority to create such estates only as will not attach on the interest limited to him or take effect out of his interest, but will take effect after donee's estate has terminated.

Real property law. An authority to do some act in relation to real property, or to the creation or revocation of an estate therein, or a charge thereon, which the owner granting or reserving such power might himself perform for any purpose. An authority expressly reserved to a grantor, or expressly given to another, to be exercised over lands, etc., granted or conveyed at the time of the creation of such power. *See* Power of alienation.

For other compound terms, such as Power of appointment; Power of sale; etc., see the following titles.

Power coupled with an interest. A right or power to do some act, together with an interest in the subject-matter on which the power is to be exercised. It is distinguished from a *naked* power, which is a mere authority to act, not accompanied by any interest of the donee in the subject-matter of the power.

Power of acceptance. Capacity of offeree, upon acceptance of terms of offer, to create binding contract.

Power of alienation. The power to sell, transfer, assign or otherwise dispose of property.

Power of appointment. A power or authority conferred by one person by deed or will upon another (called the "donee") to appoint, that is, to select and nominate, the person or persons who are to receive and enjoy an estate or an income therefrom or from a fund, after the testator's death, or the donee's death, or after the termination of an existing right or interest.

A power of appointment may be exercisable by deed or by will depending upon the terms established by the donor of the power, and is defined, generally, as power or authority given to person to dispose of property, or interest therein, which is vested in person other than donee of the power.

Powers are either: *Collateral*, which are given to strangers; *i.e.*, to persons who have neither a present nor future estate or interest in the land. These are also called simply "collateral," or powers not coupled with an interest, or powers not being interests. Or they are powers relating to the land. These are called *"appendant"* or *"appurtenant,"* because they strictly depend upon the estate limited to the person to whom they are given. Thus, where an estate for life is limited to a man, with a power to grant leases in possession, a lease granted under the power may operate wholly out of the life-estate of the party executing it, and must in every case have its operation out of his estate during his life. Such an estate must be created, which will attach on an interest actually vested in himself. Or they are called *"in gross,"* if given to a person who had an interest in the estate at the execution of the deed creating the power, or to whom an estate is given by the deed, but which enabled him to create such estates only as will not attach on the interest limited to him. Of necessity, therefore, where a man seised in fee settles his estate on others, reserving to himself only a particular power, the power is in gross.

An important distinction is established between *general* and *particular* powers. By a general power we understand a right to appoint to whomsoever the donee pleases including himself or his estate. By a particular power it is meant that the donee is restricted to some objects designated in the deed or will creating the power.

A general power is *beneficial* when no person other than the grantee has, by the terms of its creation, any interest in its execution. A general power is *in trust* when any person or class of persons, other than the grantee of such power, is designated as entitled to the proceeds, or any portion of the proceeds, or other benefits to result from the alienation.

When a power of appointment among a class requires that each shall have a share, it is called a "distributive" or "non-exclusive" power; when it authorizes, but does not direct, a selection of one or more to the exclusion of the others, it is called an "exclusive" power, and is also distributive; when it gives the power of appointing to a certain number of the class, but not to all, it is exclusive only, and not distributive. A power authorizing the donee either to give the whole to one of a class or to give it equally among such of them as he may select (but not to give one a larger share than the others) is called a "mixed" power.

For the estate tax and gift tax effects of powers of appointment, see I.R.C. §§ 2041 and 2514.

See also General power of appointment; Illusory appointment; Limited power of appointment.

Special power of appointment. A power of appointment that cannot be exercised in favor of the donee or his or her estate but may be exercised only in favor of identifiable person(s) other than the donee. *See also* Limited power of appointment.

Testamentary power. A power of appointment that can only be exercised through a will (*i.e.,* upon the death of the holder).

Power of attorney. An instrument in writing whereby one person, as principal, appoints another as his agent and confers authority to perform certain specified acts or kinds of acts on behalf of principal. An instrument authorizing another to act as one's agent or attorney. The agent is attorney in fact and his power is revoked on the death of the principal by operation of law. Such power may be either general (full) or special (limited).

Durable power of attorney. Exists when person executes a power of attorney which will become or remain effective in the event he or she should later become disabled. Uniform Probate Code § 5–501. *See also* Health care proxy; Medical directives; Patients Self Determination Act; Will (*Living will*).

Power of disposition. Every power of disposition is deemed absolute, by means of which the donee of such power is enabled in his life-time to dispose of the entire fee for his own benefit; and, where a general and beneficial power to devise the inheritance is given to a tenant for life or years, it is absolute, within the meaning of the statutes of some of the states. *See* Power of appointment.

Power of sale. A clause commonly inserted in mortgages and deeds of trust, giving the mortgagee (or trustee) the right and power, on default in the payment of the debt secured, to advertise and sell the mortgaged property at public auction (but without resorting to a court for authority), satisfy the creditor out of the net proceeds, convey by deed to the purchaser, return the surplus, if any, to the mortgagor, and thereby divest the latter's estate entirely and without any subsequent right of redemption.

Power of termination. The interest left in the grantor or testator after the conveyance or devise of a fee simple on condition subsequent or conditional fee, *e.g.* "to A on condition that the property be used for church purposes." When such property is no longer used for church purposes, the grantor may enter or commence an action for entry based on the breach of the condition. However, he is not automatically revested. He must enter or commence an action.

P.P. An abbreviation for *"propria persona,"* in his proper person, in his own person, and for *per procuration* (*q.v.*).

P.P.I. Policy proof of interest, *i.e.,* in the event of loss, the insurance policy is to be deemed sufficient proof of interest.

Practicable, practicably. Practicable is that which may be done, practiced, or accomplished; that which is performable, feasible, possible; and the adverb practicably means in a practicable manner. Within liability policy providing that when accident occurred, written notice should be given by or on behalf of insured to insurer or any of its authorized agents as soon as practicable, "practicable" was held to mean feasible in the circumstances.

Practice. Repeated or customary action; habitual performance; a succession of acts of similar kind; custom; usage. Application of science to the wants of men. The exercise of any profession.

The form or mode or proceeding in courts of justice for the enforcement of rights or the redress of wrongs, as distinguished from the substantive law which gives the right or denounces the wrong. The form, manner, or order of instituting and conducting an action or other judicial proceeding, through its successive stages to its end, in accordance with the rules and principles laid down by law or by the regulations and precedents of the courts. The term applies as well to the conduct of criminal as to civil actions, to proceedings in equity as well as at law, and to the defense as well as the prosecution of any proceeding.

Practice of law. The rendition of services requiring the knowledge and the application of legal principles and technique to serve the interests of another with his consent. It is not limited to appearing in court, or advising and performing of services in the conduct of the various shapes of litigation, but embraces the preparation of pleadings, and other papers incident to actions and special proceedings, and in larger sense includes legal advice and counsel and preparation of legal instruments by which legal rights and obligations are established. A person engages in the "practice of law" by maintaining an office where he is held out to be an attorney, using a letterhead describing himself as an attorney, counseling clients in legal matters, negotiating with opposing counsel about pending litigation, and fixing and collecting fees for services rendered by his associate.

Practice of medicine. The treatment of injuries as well as the discovery of the cause and nature of disease, and the administration of remedies, or the prescribing of treatment therefor.

Routine practice, evidence. Evidence of the routine practice of an organization is relevant to prove that the conduct of the organization on a particular occasion was in conformity with the routine practice. Fed.Evid.R. 406.

Practice acts. Statutes that govern practice and procedure in courts (*e.g.,* Title 28, United States Code; Georgia Civil Practice Act). Such acts are frequently supplemented with court rules (*e.g.,* Fed.Rules of Civil Procedure).

Practice court. *See* Moot court.

Practices. A succession of acts of a similar kind or in a like employment. For routine practices as constituting relevant evidence, *see* Practice supra.

Practitioner. A person who is engaged in the exercise or employment of any art or profession as contrasted with one who teaches such. *See* Practice.

Præcipe /présəpiy/. Lat. In practice, an original writ drawn up in the alternative, commanding the defendant to do the thing required, or show the reason why he had not done it. It includes an order to the clerk of court to issue an execution on a judgment already rendered.

A paper upon which the particulars of a writ are written. It is filed in the office out of which the required writ is to issue. Also an order, written out and signed, addressed to the clerk of a court, and requesting him to issue a particular writ.

Prædial /príydiyəl/. That which arises immediately from the ground: as, grain of all sorts, hay, wood, fruits, herbs, and the like.

Prayer. The request contained in a bill in equity that the court will grant the process, aid, or relief which the complainant desires. Also, by extension, the term is applied to that part of the bill which contains this request. Under modern rules practice, the pleader does not pray for relief, but, rather, demands it. Fed.R.Civil P. 8(a). *See* Prayer for relief.

Prayer for relief. That portion of a complaint (more properly called "demand for relief") in a civil action which sets forth the requested relief or damages to which the pleader deems himself entitled. This is a requisite element of the complaint. Fed.R.Civil P. 8(a).

Preamble. A clause at the beginning of a constitution or statute explanatory of the reasons for its enactment and the objects sought to be accomplished. Generally, a preamble is a declaration by the legislature of the reasons for the passage of the statute and is helpful in the interpretation of any ambiguities within the statute to which it is prefixed. It has been held however to not be an essential part of act, and neither enlarges nor confers powers.

Preappointed evidence. The kind and degree of evidence prescribed in advance (as, by statute) as requisite for the proof of certain facts or the establishment of certain instruments. It is opposed to *casual* evidence, which is left to grow naturally out of the surrounding circumstances.

Preauthorized checks (PACs). Checks that are authorized by the payer in advance and are written either by the payee or the payee's bank and then deposited in the payee's bank account.

Precarious /prəkériyəs/. Liable to be returned or rendered up at the mere demand or request of another; hence, held or retained only on sufferance or by permission; and, by an extension of meaning, doubtful, uncertain, dangerous, very liable to break, fail, or terminate.

Precarious loan. A bailment by way of loan which is not to continue for any fixed time, but may be recalled at the mere will and pleasure of the lender (*e.g.* a demand loan). A loan, the repayment of which is in doubt or uncertain. A non-performing loan.

Precatory /prékət(ə)riy/. Having the nature of prayer, request, or entreaty; conveying or embodying a recommendation or advice or the expression of a wish, but not a positive command or direction.

Precatory trust. A trust created by certain words, which are more like words of entreaty and permission than of command or certainty. Examples of such words, which the courts have held sufficient to constitute a trust, are "wish and request," "have fullest confidence," "heartily beseech," and the like. *See* Trust.

Precatory words. Words of entreaty, request, desire, wish, or recommendation, employed in wills, as distinguished from direct and imperative terms. Mere precatory words or expressions in a trust or will are ineffective to dispose of property. There must be a command or order as to the disposition of property.

Precaution /prəkóshən/. Previous action; proven foresight; care previously employed to prevent mischief or to secure good result; or a measure taken beforehand; an active foresight designed to ward off possible problems, accidents, liability, or secure good results.

Precedence /présədəns/ *or* **precedency** /présədənsiy/. The act or state of going before; adjustment of place. The right of being first placed in a certain order. *See also* Preference; Precedent; Priority.

Precedent /présədənt/. An adjudged case or decision of a court, considered as furnishing an example or authority for an identical or similar case afterwards arising or a similar question of law. Courts attempt to decide cases on the basis of principles established in prior cases. Prior cases which are close in facts or legal principles to the case under consideration are called precedents. A rule of law established for the first time by a court for a particular type of case and thereafter referred to in deciding similar cases. *See also* Stare decisis.

A course of conduct once followed which may serve as a guide for future conduct. *See* Custom and usage; Habit.

Precedent condition. Such as must happen or be performed before an estate can vest or be enlarged. *See* Condition.

Precept /príysept/. An order, writ, warrant, or process. An order or direction, emanating from authority, to an officer or body of officers, commanding him or them to do some act within the scope of their powers. An order in writing, sent out by a justice of the peace or other like officer, for the bringing of a person or record before him. Precept is not to be confined to civil proceedings, and is not of a more restricted meaning than "process." It includes warrants and processes in criminal as well as civil proceedings.

Rule imposing standard of conduct or action.

Precept of attachment. An order to attach the goods and property of the defendant issued by a court generally after the action has been commenced when a writ of attachment has not been used.

Precinct /príysiŋkt/. A constable's or police district. A small geographical unit of government. An election district created for convenient localization of polling places. A county or municipal subdivision for casting and counting votes in elections.

Precipe /présəpiy/. Another form of the name of the written instructions to the clerk of court; also spelled "præcipe" (*q.v.*).

Precipitation /prəsipətéyshən/. Hastening occurrence of event or causing to happen or come to crisis suddenly, unexpectedly or too soon.

Preclude /prəkl(y)úwd/. Estop. To prohibit or prevent from doing something; *e.g.* injunction.

Preclusion order. Under Fed.R.Civil P. 37(b)(2)(B), a party to an action who fails to comply with an order for discovery may be precluded from supporting or opposing designated claims or defenses.

Precontract. A contract or engagement made by a person, which is of such a nature as to preclude him from lawfully entering into another contract of the same nature.

Predatory intent. In purview of Robinson-Patman Act, means that alleged price discriminator must have at least sacrificed present revenues for purpose of driving competitor out of market with hope of recouping losses through subsequent higher prices. *See also* Predatory pricing.

Predatory pricing. As antitrust violation, consists of pricing below appropriate measure of cost for purpose of eliminating competitors in short run and reducing competition in long run. An inference to be drawn from predatory pricing is that defendant is acting with anticompetitive intent. *See also* Predatory intent.

Predecease. To die before another person.

Predecessor. One who goes or has gone before; the correlative of "successor." One who has filled an office or station before the present incumbent.

Applied to a body politic or corporate, in the same sense as "ancestor" is applied to a natural person.

Predial servitude /príydiyəl sɔ́rvət(y)uwd/. A charge laid on an estate for the use and utility of another estate belonging to another owner. A charge on one estate for the stipulated benefit of another estate; the benefit must be attributable to any person who may own the dominant estate at any time. To exist, there must be two different estates, servient and dominant, belonging to different owners, with benefit to dominant estate.

Predisposition. For purposes of entrapment defense, may be defined as defendant's inclination to engage in illegal activity for which he has been charged, *i.e.,* that he is ready and willing to commit the crime. It focuses on defendant's state of mind before government agents suggest that he commit crime. *See also* Premeditation.

Predominant. Something greater or superior in power and influence to others with which it is connected or compared.

Preemption /priyém(p)shən/. Doctrine adopted by U.S. Supreme Court holding that certain matters are of such a national, as opposed to local, character that federal laws preempt or take precedence over state laws. As such, a state may not pass a law inconsistent with the federal law. Examples are federal laws governing interstate commerce. *See also* Federal pre-emption; Supremacy clause.

As applied to state action versus local action, "preemption" means that where legislature has adopted scheme for regulation of given subject, local legislative control over such phases of subject as are covered by state regulation ceases.

Preemption claimant. One who has settled upon land subject to pre-emption, with the intention to acquire title to it, and has complied, or is proceeding to comply, in good faith, with the requirements of the law to perfect his right to it. *See* Preemption right.

Preemption doctrine. *See* Preemption.

Preemption entry. *See* Entry.

Preemption right. A privilege accorded by the government to the actual settler upon a certain limited portion of the public domain, to purchase such tract at a fixed price to the exclusion of all other applicants. One who, by settlement upon the public land, or by cultivation of a portion of it, has obtained the right to purchase a portion of the land thus settled upon or cultivated, to the exclusion of all other persons.

Preemptive right. The privilege of a stockholder to maintain a proportionate share of ownership by purchasing a proportionate share of any new stock issues. An existing stockholder in most jurisdictions has the right to buy additional shares of a new issue to preserve his equity before others have a right to purchase shares of the new issue. The purpose of such rights is to protect shareholders from dilution of value and control when new shares are issued. In modern corporation statutes, preemptive rights may be limited or denied. *See also* Stock.

Pre-existing duty. A common law rule which holds that where a party does or promises to do what he or she is already legally obligated to do, there exists no sufficient consideration to support this new promise. The Uniform Commercial Code has eliminated the "pre-existing duty" rule in sales contracts. UCC § 209–(1).

Prefer. To bring before; to prosecute; to try; to proceed with. Thus, preferring an indictment signifies prosecuting or trying an indictment.

To give advantage, priority, or privilege; to select for first payment, as to prefer one creditor over others.

Preference. The paying or securing to one or more of his creditors, by an insolvent debtor, the whole or a part of their claim, to the exclusion or detriment of the rest. The act of an insolvent debtor who, in distributing his property or in assigning it for the benefit of his creditors, pays or secures to one or more creditors the full amount of their claims or a larger amount than they would be entitled to receive on a *pro rata* distribution. It imports the relation of existing creditors having equal equities at the time of the transfer whereby the rights of one are advanced over those of another.

In bankruptcy law, a transfer by an insolvent debtor to one or more of his or her creditors whereby the creditor to whom the property was transferred is put in a better position than other creditors with respect to their priority claims to the assets of the insolvent. The bankruptcy trustee may disallow such preferential payments or transfers of property. Bankruptcy Code § 547. *See also* Secured creditor; Voidable preference.

Preference share. Stock giving its holder a preference, either as to receipt of dividends, or as to payment in case of winding up, or both. A security that ranks junior to preferred stock but senior to common stock in the right to receive payments from the firm; essentially junior preferred stock. *See also* Preferred stock.

Preferential assignment. An assignment of property for the benefit of creditors, made by an insolvent debtor, in which it is directed that a preference (right to be paid first in full) shall be given to a creditor or creditors therein named over other creditors. Such assignments are controlled by statute in most states, normally requiring recording, filing of schedules of assets and liabilities, giving notice to creditors, etc. Most all state statutes prohibit preferential assignments as being fraudulent conveyances. *See* Preference.

Preferential claim. *See* Preferential debts.

Preferential debts. In bankruptcy, those debts which are payable in preference to all others; as, wages of employees and administrative costs. Such debts are classified according to priority of claim. See Bankruptcy Code § 507. *See also* Priority; Privileged debts.

Preferential dividend. *See* Preferred stock.

Preferential shop. A place of employment in which union members are given preference over nonunion members in matters of employment by agreement with the employer. A labor situation in a business in which preference is given to union men in hiring and layoff, but nonunion men may be hired when members of the union are not available. *See* Right to work laws.

Preferential tariff. A tariff which imposes lower rates of duty on goods imported from some countries ("preferred countries") than on the same goods imported from other countries. *See also* Most favored nation clause.

Preferential transfer. *See* Preference; Preferential assignment.

Preferred. Possessing or accorded a priority, advantage, or privilege. Generally denoting a prior or superior claim or right of payment as against another thing of the same kind or class; *e.g.* creditor with perfected security interest.

Preferred creditor. Creditor with preferential right to payment over junior creditors; *e.g.* creditor with perfected security interest has priority over unsecured creditor. U.C.C. § 9–301. *See also* Preferential debts.

Preferred dividend. *See* Dividend.

Preferred dockets. Lists of preference cases prepared by the clerks when the cases are set for trial. For example, because of the constitutional right to a speedy trial in criminal cases, criminal dockets are normally given preference over civil dockets.

Preferred stock. Stock shares that have preferential rights to dividends or to amounts distributable on liquidation, or to both, ahead of common shareholders. Preferred shares are usually entitled only to receive specified limited amounts as dividends or on liquidation. If preferred shares are entitled to share in excess distributions with common shareholders on some defined basis, they are participating preferred shares. Participating preferred shares may also be called class A common, or some similar designation to reflect its open-ended rights. *See also* Stock.

Callable. Preferred stock which is subject by its terms to being called in for payment at a predetermined price.

Cumulative dividend. If a dividend is passed, it must be paid to the preferred stockholders before the common stockholders receive their current dividend, and hence, the dividends accumulate in connection with this type of preferred stock.

Non-cumulative dividend. Once a preferred dividend is passed in a particular period, the right to that dividend has passed though the preferred stockholder is entitled to his dividend in the next period before the common stockholders receive their dividend.

Participating. That type of preferred stock which is entitled to additional dividends beyond its stated dividend after the common stock dividend has been paid.

Preferred stock bailout. A procedure whereby the issuance, sale, and later redemption or a preferred stock dividend was used by a shareholder to obtain long-term capital gains without any loss of voting control over the corporation. In effect, therefore, the shareholder was able to bail-out corporate profits without suffering the consequences of dividend income treatment. This procedure led to the enactment by Congress of I.R.C. § 306 which, if applicable, converts the prior long-term capital gain on the sale of the stock to ordinary income. Under these circumstances, the amount of ordinary income is limited to the shareholder's portion of the corporation's earnings and profits existing when the preferred stock was issued as a stock dividend. However, the enactment of the Tax Reform Act of 1986 has changed the impact of I.R.C. § 306 substantially due to the repeal of the favorable tax treatment previously given to long term capital gains.

Prior. Preferred stock which takes precedence over other issues of preferred stock of the same corporation.

Preferred stockholders. Beneficial holders of preferred stock shares.

Preferred stockholders' contract. Term used to describe the provisions of the articles of incorporation, the bylaws, or the resolution of the board of directors, creating and defining the rights of holders of the preferred shares in question. Preferred shareholders have only very limited statutory or common law rights outside of the preferred shareholders' contract.

Pregnant negative. *See* Negative pregnant.

Prejudice. A forejudgment; bias; partiality; preconceived opinion. A leaning towards one side of a cause for some reason other than a conviction of its justice.

See also Average man test; Bias; Discrimination.

Evidence. Within rule allowing exclusion of relevant evidence if probative value is substantially outweighed by danger of unfair prejudice, means undue tendency to move tribunal to decide on improper basis. *See* Fed.Evid.R. 403.

Of judge. That which disqualifies judge is condition of mind, which sways judgment and renders judge unable to exercise his functions impartially in particular case. It refers to mental attitude or disposition of the judge toward a party to the litigation, and not to any views that he may entertain regarding the subject matter involved.

Speedy trial. Prejudice with respect to right to speedy trial means actual prejudice to defendant's ability to present effective defense, and such prejudice is not confined to merely an impairment of the defense but includes any threat to what has been termed an accused's significant stakes, psychological, physical and financial, in the prompt termination of a proceeding which may ultimately deprive him of life, liberty or property.

Without prejudice. Where an offer or admission is made "without prejudice," or a motion is denied or a bill in equity dismissed "without prejudice," it is meant as a declaration that no rights or privileges of the party concerned are to be considered as thereby waived or lost, except in so far as may be expressly conceded or decided. *See also* Dismissal without prejudice; Dismissal with prejudice.

Prejudicial error. Error substantially affecting appellant's legal rights and obligations. One which affects or presumptively affects the final results of the trial. Such may be ground for new trial and reversal of judgment. Fed.R.Civil P. 59. *See also* Error; Plain error rule.

Prejudicial publicity. Due process requires that all parties to an action, civil or criminal, receive a trial by an impartial jury or tribunal free from outside influences. Extensive newspaper, radio and television coverage of a criminal trial may deprive the defendant of a fair trial. *See* Gag order; Trial *(Trial by news media).*

Preliminary. Introductory; initiatory; preceding; temporary and provisional; as preliminary examination, injunction, articles of peace, etc.

Preliminary complaint. In some states, a court without jurisdiction to hear a criminal case on its merits may issue a preliminary complaint or process and conduct a probable cause or bind over hearing on such complaint.

Preliminary evidence. Such evidence as is necessary to commence a hearing or trial and which may be received conditionally in anticipation of other evidence linking it to issues in the case. *See* Foundation.

Preliminary examination. *See* Preliminary hearing.

Preliminary hearing. The hearing by a judge to determine whether a person charged with a crime should be held for trial. A hearing held in felony cases prior to indictment during which the state is required to produce sufficient evidence to establish that there is probable cause to believe (a) that a crime has been committed and (b) that the defendant committed it. *See* Fed.R.Crim.P. 5.1.

Preliminary hearing before magistrate is, basically, a first screening of the charge; its function is not to try the defendant, nor does it require the same degree of proof or quality of evidence as is necessary for an indictment or for conviction at trial. Its function is to determine whether there is sufficient evidence to hold an accused for trial.

Indigent defendants have a right to be represented by counsel at a preliminary examination.

Compare Arraignment. *See also* Information.

Preliminary injunction. A preliminary injunction should be granted only upon a clear showing by party seeking the extraordinary remedy of (1) probable success upon a trial on the merits, and (2) likely irreparable injury to him unless the injunction is granted, or (3) if his showing of probable success is limited but he raised substantial and difficult issues meriting further inquiry, that the harm to him outweighs the injury to others if it is denied. *See* Fed.R.Civil P. 65. *See also* Injunction.

Preliminary prospects. *See* Red herring.

Preliminary warrant. In some jurisdictions, a warrant or order to bring a person to court for a preliminary hearing (*q.v.*) on probable cause.

Premarital agreements. *See* Antenuptial agreements.

Premeditate. To think of an act beforehand; to contrive and design; to plot or lay plans for the execution of a purpose. *See* Deliberate; Premeditation.

Premeditated design. In homicide cases, the mental purpose, the formed intent, to take human life. Premeditated murder is murder in the first degree.

Premeditatedly. Thought of beforehand, for any length of time, however short.

Premeditation. The act of meditating in advance; deliberation upon a contemplated act; plotting or contriving; a design formed to do something before it is done. Decision or plan to commit a crime, such as murder, before committing it. A prior determination to do an act, but such determination need not exist for any particular period before it is carried into effect. Thought of beforehand for any length of time, however short.

Premeditation is one of the elements of first degree murder, and in this context, means that defendant acts with either the intention or the knowledge that he will kill another human being when such intention or knowledge precedes the killing by a length of time to permit reflection. *See also* Deliberate; Deliberation; Malice aforethought; Willful.

Premises. That which is put before; that which precedes; the foregoing statements. Thus, in logic, the two introductory propositions of the syllogism are called the "premises," and from them the conclusion is deduced. So, in pleading, the expression "in consideration of the premises" means in consideration of the matters hereinbefore stated.

In conveyancing. That part of a deed which precedes the *habendum*, in which are set forth the names of the parties with their titles and additions, and in which are recited such deeds, agreements, or matters of fact as are necessary to explain the reasons upon which the present transaction is founded; and it is here, also, the consideration on which it is made is set down and the certainty of the thing granted.

In equity pleading. The stating part of a bill. It contains a narrative of the facts and circumstances of the plaintiff's case, and the wrongs of which he complains, and the names of the persons by whom done and against whom he seeks redress. In most states equity pleading is obsolete, having been replaced by notice pleading under Rules of Civil Procedure. *See* Complaint.

In estates and property. Land with its appurtenances and structures thereon. Premises is an elastic and inclusive term, and it does not have one definite and fixed meaning; its meaning is to be determined by its context and is dependent on circumstances in which used, and may mean a room, shop, building, or any definite area.

A dwelling unit and the structure of which it is a part and faculties and appurtenances therein and grounds, areas, and facilities held out for the use of tenants generally or whose use is promised to the tenant. Uniform Residential Landlord and Tenant Act, 1.301(a).

In criminal law. The term as used in a search warrant includes land, buildings, and appurtenances thereto.

In workers' compensation acts. "Premises" of the employer as used in workers' compensation acts is not restricted to the permanent site of the statutory employer's business nor limited to property owned or leased by him but contemplates any place under the exclusive control of employer where his usual business is being carried on or conducted.

Premium. A reward for an act done. *See also* Bonus.

A bounty or bonus; a consideration given to invite a loan or a bargain, as the consideration

paid to the assignor by the assignee of a lease, or to the transferer by the transferee of shares of stock, etc. So stock is said to be "at a premium" when its market price exceeds its nominal or face value. The excess of issue (or market) price over par value. *See* Par.

In granting a lease, part of the rent is sometimes capitalized and paid in a lump sum at the time the lease is granted. This is called a "premium."

The sum paid or agreed to be paid by an insured to the underwriter (insurer) as the consideration for the insurance. The price for insurance protection for a specified period of exposure.

See also Earned premium; Net premium; Net single premium.

Advance premium. Payment made at the start of the period covered by the insurance policy.

Premium note. A promissory note given by the insured for part or all of the amount of the premium.

Securities. The amount by which a preferred stock or bond may sell above its par (face) value. In the case of a new issue of bonds or stocks, premium is the amount the market price rises over the original selling price. Also refers to a charge sometimes made when a stock is borrowed to make delivery on a short sale. May refer, also, to redemption price of a bond or preferred stock if it is higher than face value.

Unearned premium. Portion of original premium not yet earned by insurance company and therefore due policyholder if the policy should be cancelled. In accounting, the account which reflects that portion of a premium that has been paid for insurance coverage which has not yet been extended. The basic insurance reserve in the casualty insurance business. Since policyholders typically pay the full premium in advance, the premium is wholly "unearned" when the primary insurer receives it. See I.R.C. § 801(c).

Premium bond. *See* Bond.

Premium loan. Loan made for purpose of paying an insurance premium and secured by the policy.

Premium on capital stock. The difference between the par (or stated) value of stock and the issue price, when issuance occurs above par or stated value.

Premium tax. Tax paid by insurer on gross insurance premiums sold in state.

Prenatal injuries. *See* Child; Children.

Prender, prendre /préndər/próndr(ə)/. L. Fr. To take. The power or right of taking a thing without waiting for it to be offered. *See* A prendre.

Pre-nuptial agreement. One entered into by prospective spouses prior to marriage but in contemplation and in consideration thereof; by it, the property or other financial rights of one or both of the prospective spouses are determined or are secured to one or both of them or their children. A number of states have adopted the Uniform Premarital Agreement Act which prescribes the content, execution, amendment, etc. of such agreements. *See also* Antenuptial agreement; Marital agreements; Post-nuptial agreement.

Prepaid expense. An expense paid before it is currently due. In accounting, an expenditure for a benefit not yet enjoyed, *e.g.* pre-paid insurance premiums from the standpoint of the insured. Cash basis as well as accrual basis taxpayers are generally required to capitalize prepayments for rent, insurance, etc. that cover more than one year. Deductions are taken during the period the benefits are received.

Prepaid income. In accounting, income received but not yet earned; also referred to as deferred revenue.

Prepaid interest. Interest paid before the time it is earned.

Prepaid legal services. System, which may be an employee fringe benefit, by which persons may pay premiums to cover future legal services much the same as payments are made for future medical expenses. Such plan may be either open-ended whereby the person can secure legal services from the attorney of his choice, or closed-end whereby he must secure the services of a particular attorney, group of attorneys, or list of attorneys.

"Open panel" legal services is a plan in which legal services are paid for in advance (usually by a type of insurance) and members can choose their own lawyer. Under a "closed panel", however, all legal services are performed by a group of attorneys previously selected by the insurer, union, etc.

Preparation. With respect to criminal offense, consists in devising or arranging means or measures necessary for its commission, while attempt is direct movement toward commission after preparations are made. *See also* Aid and abet.

Prepare. To provide with necessary means; to make ready; to provide with what is appropriate or necessary.

Prepayment. Payment of debt obligation or expense before it is due.

Prepayment clause. Provision in mortgage or note giving borrower right to pay off the indebtedness before it becomes due. *See also* Prepayment penalty.

Prepayment penalty. A penalty under a note, mortgage, or deed of trust, imposed when the loan is paid before its due date. Consideration to terminate loan at borrower's election before maturity. *See also* Penalty clause.

Prepayments. Assets representing expenditures for future benefits. Rent and insurance premiums paid in advance are usually classified as current prepayments.

Prepense. Forethought; preconceived; premeditated.

Preponderance of evidence. As standard of proof in civil cases, is evidence which is of greater weight or more convincing than the evidence which is offered in opposition to it; that is, evidence which as a whole shows that the fact sought to be proved is more probable than not. With respect to burden of proof in civil actions, means greater weight of evidence, or evidence which is more credible and convincing to the mind. That which best accords with reason and probability. The word "preponderance" means something more than "weight"; it denotes a superiority of weight, or outweighing. The words are not synonymous, but substantially different. There is generally a "weight" of evidence on each side in case of contested facts. But juries cannot properly act upon the weight of evidence, in favor of the one having the *onus*, unless it overbear, in some degree, the weight upon the other side.

That amount of evidence necessary for the plaintiff to win in a civil case. It is that degree of proof which is more probable than not.

Preponderance of evidence may not be determined by the number of witnesses, but by the greater weight of all evidence, which does not necessarily mean the greater number of witnesses, but opportunity for knowledge, information possessed, and manner of testifying determines the weight of testimony.

See also Fair preponderance of evidence.

Prerogative /prərógətəv/. An exclusive or peculiar right or privilege. The special power, privilege, immunity, right or advantage vested in an official person, either generally, or in respect to the things of his office, or in an official body, as a court or legislature.

Prerogative writs. In English law, the name was given to certain judicial writs issued by the courts only upon proper cause shown, never as a mere matter of right, the theory being that they involved a direct interference by the government with the liberty and property of the subject, and therefore were justified only as an exercise of the extraordinary power (prerogative) of the crown. In America, issuance is now generally regulated by statute, and such are generally referred to as extraordinary writs or remedies.

Such writs have been abolished in the federal and most state courts with the adoption of Rules of Civil Procedure. The relief formerly available by such writs is now available by appropriate action or motion under the Rules of Civil Procedure. See Rule 81. These writs are the writs of mandamus, procedendo, prohibition, quo warranto, habeas corpus, and certiorari.

Pres /préy/. L. Fr. Near. *Cy pres*, so near; as near. *See* Cy-pres.

Prescribe. To assert a right or title to the enjoyment of a thing, on the ground of having hitherto had the uninterrupted and immemorial enjoyment of it.

To lay down authoritatively as a guide, direction, or rule; to impose as a peremptory order; to dictate; to point, to direct; to give as a guide, direction, or rule of action; to give law. To direct; define; mark out.

In a medical sense "prescribe" means to direct, designate, or order use of a particular remedy, therapy, medicine, or drug.

Prescription. A direction of remedy or remedies for a disease, illness, or injury and the manner of using them. Also, a formula for the preparation of a drug or medicine.

Prescription is a peremptory and perpetual bar to every species of action, real or personal, when creditor has been silent for a certain time without urging his claim.

Acquisition of a personal right to use a way, water, light and air by reason of continuous usage. *See also* Prescriptive easement.

International law. Acquisition of sovereignty over a territory through continuous and undisputed exercise of sovereignty over it during such a period as is necessary to create under the influence of historical development the general conviction that the present condition of things is in conformity with international order.

Real property law. The name given to a mode of acquiring title to incorporeal hereditaments by immemorial or long-continued enjoyment. Prescription is the term usually applied to incorporeal hereditaments, while "adverse possession" is applied to lands. *See* Hereditaments.

See also Adverse possession; Prescriptive easement.

Prescriptive easement. A right to use another's property which is not inconsistent with the owner's rights and which is acquired by a use, open and notorious, adverse and continuous for the statutory period (*e.g.* twenty years). To a certain extent, it resembles title by adverse possession but differs to the extent that the adverse user acquires only an easement and not title. To create an easement by "prescription," the use must have been open, continuous, exclusive, and under claim of right for statutorily prescribed period with

knowledge or imputed knowledge of the owner. *See also* Adverse possession.

Presence. Act, fact, or state of being in a certain place and not elsewhere, or within sight or call, at hand, or in some place that is being thought of. The existence of a person in a particular place at a given time particularly with reference to some act done there and then. Besides actual presence, the law recognizes *constructive* presence, which latter may be predicated of a person who, though not on the very spot, was near enough to be accounted present by the law, or who was actively co-operating with another who was actually present.

Presence of an officer. An offense is committed in "presence" or "view" of officer, within rule authorizing arrest without warrant, when officer sees act constituting it, though at distance, or when circumstances within his observation give probable cause for belief that defendant has committed offense, or when he hears disturbance created by offense and proceeds at once to scene, or if offense is continuing, or has not been fully consummated when arrest is made.

Presence of defendant. In the trial of all felonies, the defendant or accused has the right to be present at every stage of the criminal proceeding unless he wilfully and without justification absents himself or by his conduct renders it impossible to conduct the trial. In many states, this rule does not obtain as to misdemeanors. Fed.R. Crim.P. 43 specifies when the presence of the defendant is required and not required.

Presence of the court. A contempt is in the "presence of the court," if it is committed in the ocular view of the court, or where the court has direct knowledge of the contempt. *See also* Contempt of court.

Presence of the testator. Will is attested in presence of testator if witnesses are within range of any of testator's senses. *See* Attestation.

Present, *n.* A gift; a gratuity; anything presented or given.

Present, *adj.* Now existing; at hand; relating to the present time; considered with reference to the present time. *See also* Presentment.

Pre-sentence hearing. Procedural step prior to sentencing at which a judge may examine the presentence report and all other relevant material before imposing sentence. Sentencing is a "critical stage" of a criminal prosecution requiring assistance of appointed counsel. *See* Pre-sentence investigation; Pre-sentence report.

Pre-sentence investigation. Investigation of the relevant background of a convicted offender, usually conducted by a probation officer attached to a court, designed to act as a sentencing guide for the sentencing judge. See *e.g.* 18 U.S.C.A. § 3552; Fed.R.Crim.P. 32(c). *See also* Pre-sentence report.

Pre-sentence report. The report prepared from the presentence investigation, which is designed to assist the judge in passing sentence on a convicted defendant. Presentence reports vary in scope and focus, but typically contain at least the following items: (1) complete description of the situation surrounding the criminal activity; (2) offender's educational background; (3) offender's employment background; (4) offender's social history; (5) residence history of the offender; (6) offender's medical history; (7) information about environment to which the offender will return; (8) information about any resources available to assist the offender; (9) probation officer's view of the offender's motivations and ambitions; (10) full description of the defendant's criminal record; and, (11) recommendation as to disposition. See *e.g.,* 18 U.S.C.A. § 3552 and Fed.R.Crim.P. 32(c) with regard to presentence reports in federal criminal cases.

Presenter. Any person presenting a draft or demand for payment for honor under a credit even though that person is a confirming bank or other correspondent which is acting under an issuer's authorization. U.C.C. § 5–112(3). *See also* Presentment.

Presenting bank. Any bank presenting an item except a payor bank, U.C.C. § 4–105(e), i.e., a bank that demands of a drawee or other payor that she pay or accept a draft or other instrument.

Presently. Immediately; now; at once. A right which may be exercised "presently" as opposed to one in reversion or remainder.

Presentment. The written notice taken by a grand jury of any offense, from their own knowledge or observation, without any bill of indictment laid before them at the suit of the government. A presentment is an accusation, initiated by the grand jury itself, and in effect an instruction that an indictment be drawn. A written accusation of crime made and returned by the grand jury upon its own initiative in the exercise of its lawful inquisitorial powers, is in the form of a bill of indictment, and in practice is signed individually by all the grand jurors who return it. *See also* Indictment; Information; Presenter.

The production of a negotiable instrument to the drawee for his acceptance, or to the drawer or acceptor for payment; or of a promissory note to the party liable, for payment of the same. Presentment is a demand for acceptance or payment made upon the maker, acceptor, drawee or other payor by or on behalf of the holder. U.C.C. § 3–504(1).

Presentment warranty. *See* Warranty.

Present recollection recorded. A witness may use any document which helps revive or "jog" his memory of a past event and such document does not thereby become evidence. His testimony is the evidence though the opponent is entitled to see and examine the document and to impeach the credibility of the witness with it. Fed.Evid.R. 612. *See also* Past recollection recorded.

Present recollection revived. The use by a witness of some writing or other object to refresh his recollection so that he may testify about past events from present recollection. *See also* Present recollection recorded.

Present value. Time value of money. Current value of a future payment, or series of payments, discounted at some compound or discount rate. The amount as of a date certain of one or more sums payable in the future, discounted to the date certain. See, *e.g.,* U.C.C. § 2A–103.

Present value index. A ratio that compares the present value of net cash inflows to the present value of the net investment.

Preservation. Keeping safe from harm; avoiding injury, destruction, or decay; maintenance. It is not creation, but the saving of that which already exists, and implies the continuance of what previously existed. *See* Maintenance.

Preside. To occupy the place of authority as of president, chairman, moderator, etc. To direct, control or regulate proceedings as chief officer, moderator, etc. To possess or exercise authority. To preside over a court is to "hold" it,—to direct, control, and govern it as the chief officer. A judge may "preside" whether sitting as a sole judge or as one of several judges.

President. One placed in authority over others; a chief officer; a presiding or managing officer; a governor, ruler, or director. The chairman, moderator, or presiding officer of a legislative or deliberative body, appointed to keep order, manage the proceedings, and govern the administrative details of their business.

Presidential electors. A body of electors chosen in the different states, whose sole duty it is to elect a president and vice-president of the United States. Each state appoints, in such manner as the legislature thereof may direct, a number of electors equal to the whole number of senators and representatives to which the state is entitled in congress. Const.U.S. Art. 2, § 1; Amendment XII. The usual method of appointment is by general ballot, so that each voter in a state votes for the whole number of electors to which his state is entitled. *See* Electoral college.

Presidential powers. *See* Executive powers.

President of the United States. The official title of the chief executive officer of the federal government in the United States.

Press. The aggregate of publications issuing from the press, or the giving publicity to one's sentiments and opinions through the medium of printing; as in the phrase "liberty of the press." Freedom of the press is guaranteed by the First Amendment. *See* Liberty.

Presume. To assume beforehand. In a more technical sense, to believe or accept upon probable evidence. *See* Presumption.

Presumed intent. A person is presumed to intend the natural and probable consequences of his voluntary acts. The government is not required in crimes to prove that a defendant intended the precise consequences of his act and his criminal intent can be inferred from his act.

Presumption. An inference in favor of a particular fact. A presumption is a rule of law, statutory or judicial, by which finding of a basic fact gives rise to existence of presumed fact, until presumption is rebutted. A legal device which operates in the absence of other proof to require that certain inferences be drawn from the available evidence.

A presumption is an assumption of fact that the law requires to be made from another fact or group of facts found or otherwise established in the action. A presumption is not evidence. A presumption is either conclusive or rebuttable. Every rebuttable presumption is either (a) a presumption affecting the burden of producing evidence or (b) a presumption affecting the burden of proof. Calif.Evid.Code, § 600.

In all civil actions and proceedings not otherwise provided for by Act of Congress or by the Federal Rules of Evidence, a presumption imposes on the party against whom it is directed the burden of going forward with evidence to rebut or meet the presumption, but does not shift to such party the burden of proof in the sense of the risk of nonpersuasion, which remains throughout the trial upon the party on whom it was originally cast. Federal Evidence Rule 301.

See also Disputable presumption; Inference; Juris et de jure; Presumptive evidence; Prima facie; Raise a presumption.

Commercial law. A presumption means that the trier of fact must find the existence of the fact presumed unless and until evidence is introduced which would support a finding of its non-existence. U.C.C. § 1–201(31).

Conclusive presumptions. A conclusive presumption is one in which proof of basic fact renders the existence of the presumed fact conclusive and

irrebuttable. Such is created when a jury is charged that it must infer the presumed fact if certain predicate facts are established. Few in number and often statutory, the majority view is that a conclusive presumption is in reality a substantive rule of law, not a rule of evidence. An example of this type of presumption is the rule that a child under seven years of age is presumed to be incapable of committing a felony. The Federal Evidence Rules (301, 302) and most state rules of evidence are concerned only with rebuttable presumptions. *Compare Rebuttable presumption, below.*

Conflicting presumptions. See Inconsistent presumptions below.

Inconsistent presumptions. If presumptions are inconsistent, the presumption applies that is founded upon weightier considerations of policy. If considerations of policy are of equal weight neither presumption applies. Uniform Rules of Evidence. Rule 301(b).

Irrebuttable presumption. See Conclusive presumptions, above.

Mandatory presumption. See Conclusive presumptions, above.

Permissive presumption. One which allows, but does not require, trier of fact to infer elemental fact from proof by prosecutor of basic one, and which places no burden of any kind on defendant.

Presumptions of fact. Such are presumptions which do not compel a finding of the presumed fact but which warrant one when the basic fact has been proved. The trend has been to reject the classifications of presumptions of "fact" and presumptions of "law". *See* Inference.

Presumptions of law. A presumption of law is one which, once the basic fact is proved and no evidence to the contrary has been introduced, compels a finding of the existence of the presumed fact. The presumption of law is rebuttable and in most cases the adversary introduces evidence designed to overcome it. The trend has been to reject the classifications of presumptions of "law" and presumptions of "fact."

Procedural presumption. One which is rebuttable, which operates to require production of credible evidence to refute the presumption, after which the presumption disappears.

Rebuttable presumption. A presumption that can be overturned upon the showing of sufficient proof. In general, all presumptions other than conclusive presumptions are rebuttable presumptions. Once evidence tending to rebut the presumption is introduced, the force of the presumption is entirely dissipated and the party with the burden of proof must come forward with evidence to avoid a directed verdict. *Compare Conclusive presumptions, above.*

Statutory presumption. A presumption, either rebuttable or conclusive, which is created by statute in contrast to a common law presumption; *e.g.* I.R.C. § 6062 (individual's name on tax return is prima facie evidence of his authority to sign return).

Presumption of death. A presumption which arises upon the disappearance and continued absence of a person from his customary location or home for an extended period of time, commonly 7 years, without any apparent reason for such absence.

Presumption of innocence. A hallowed principle of criminal law to the effect that the government has the burden of proving every element of a crime beyond a reasonable doubt and that the defendant has no burden to prove his innocence. It arises at the first stage of the criminal process but it is not a true presumption because the defendant is not required to come forward with proof of his innocence once evidence of guilt is introduced to avoid a directed verdict of guilty.

Presumption of innocence succinctly conveys the principle that no person may be convicted of a crime unless the government carries the burden of proving his guilt beyond a reasonable doubt but it does not mean that no significance at all may be attached to the indictment.

Presumption of legitimacy. Whenever it is established in an action that a child was born to a woman while she was the lawful wife of a specified man, the party asserting the illegitimacy of the child has the burden of producing evidence and the burden of persuading the trier of fact beyond reasonable doubt that the man was not the father of the child. Model Code of Evidence, Rule 703.

Presumption of survivorship. A presumption of fact, to the effect that one person survived another, applied for the purpose of determining a question of succession or similar matter, in a case where the two persons perished in the same catastrophe, and there are no circumstances extant to show which of them actually died first, except those on which the presumption is founded, viz., differences of age, sex, strength, or physical condition.

Presumption of validity. In patent law, the holder of a patent is entitled to a statutory presumption of validity. 35 U.S.C.A. § 282.

Presumptive. Resting on presumption; created by or arising out of presumption; inferred; assumed; supposed; as, "presumptive" damages, evidence, heir, notice, or title.

Presumptive evidence. Prima facie evidence or evidence which is not conclusive and admits of explanation or contradiction; evidence which must be received and treated as true and suffi-cient until and unless rebutted by other evidence, *i.e.,* evidence which a statute says shall be presumptive of another fact unless rebutted. *See* Presumption; Prima facie evidence.

Presumptive trust. Trust raised by implication of law and presumed always to have been contemplated by parties; intention as to which is to be found in nature of transaction but not expressed in deed or instrument of conveyance, and is thus distinguished from "constructive trust." Also called "Resulting trust."

Pretax earnings. Net income before income taxes.

Pretend. To feign or simulate; to hold that out as real which is false or baseless.

Pretense. *See* False pretenses.

Pretermission. The state of one who is pretermitted, as an heir or child of the testator. The act of omitting a child or heir from a will.

Pretermission statute. Those laws of the various states which make provision for children and heirs who have been omitted from the will of the father or ancestor. Commonly the child takes the same share of the estate which he would have taken if the testator had died intestate unless the omission was intentional and not occasioned by accident or mistake. *See* Pretermitted heir.

Pretermit /priytərmít/. To pass by, to omit or to disregard, *e.g.,* failure of testator to mention his children in his will.

Pretermitted heir /priytərmítəd ér/. A child or other descendant omitted by a testator. Where a testator unintentionally fails to mention in his will, or make provision for, a child, either living at the date of the execution of the will or born thereafter, a statute may provide that such child, or the issue of a deceased child, shall share in the estate as though the testator had died intestate. *See* Pretermission statute.

Pretext. Ostensible reason or motive assigned or assumed as a color or cover for the real reason or motive; false appearance, pretense. *See* False pretenses.

Pre-trial conference. Procedural device used prior to trial to narrow issues to be tried, to secure stipulations as to matters and evidence to be heard, and to take all other steps necessary to aid in the disposition of the case. Such conferences between opposing attorneys may be called at the discretion of the court. The actions taken at the conference are made the subject of an order which controls the future course of the action. Fed.R. Civil P. 16. *See* Pre-trial order.

Criminal cases. At any time after the filing of the indictment or information the court upon motion of any party or upon its own motion may order one or more conferences to consider such matters as will promote a fair and expeditious trial. At the conclusion of a conference the court shall prepare and file a memorandum of the matters agreed upon. No admissions made by the defendant or his attorney at the conference shall be used against the defendant unless the admissions are reduced to writing and signed by the defendant and his attorney. Fed.R.Crim.P. 17.1.

Pre-trial discovery. Those devices which may be used by the parties to an action prior to trial to discover evidence and otherwise prepare for trial such as interrogatories, depositions, requests for admission of fact, etc. provided for under rules of procedure and statutes; *e.g.* Fed.R.Civil P. 26–37. *See* Discovery.

Pre-trial diversion. A system of recent origin by which certain defendants in criminal cases are referred to community agencies prior to trial while their criminal complaints or indictments are held in abeyance. The defendant may be given job training, counselling, and education. If he responds successfully within a specified period (*e.g.* 90 days, more or less), the charges against him are commonly dismissed.

Pre-trial hearing. *See* Pre-trial conference.

Pre-trial intervention. A program that diverts selected criminal defendants from the normal prosecution process in order that they can be rehabilitated and returned to the community as productive citizens with no criminal record. Upon successfully completing the PTL program the pending criminal charges are dismissed. See *e.g.* N.J.Court Rule 3:28.

Pre-trial order. An order embodying the terms and stipulations agreed upon at the pre-trial conference or hearing. This order governs the conduct of the trial and binds the parties unless, for good cause shown, the trial judge modifies it. Fed.R.Civil P. 16.

Prevail. To be or become effective or effectual, to be in force, to obtain, to be in general use or practice, to be commonly accepted or adopted; to exist. To succeed; to win.

Prevailing party. The party to a suit who successfully prosecutes the action or successfully defends against it, prevailing on the main issue, even though not necessarily to the extent of his original contention. The one in whose favor the decision or verdict is rendered and judgment entered. This may be the party prevailing in interest, and not necessarily the prevailing person. To be such does not depend upon the degree of success at different stages of the suit, but whether, at the end of the suit, or other proceeding, the party who has made a claim against the other, has successfully maintained it.

As used in Federal Civil Procedure Rule 54(d), which provides that costs shall be allowed as of course to prevailing party unless court otherwise directs, "prevailing party" means a party who has obtained some relief in an action, even if that party has not sustained all of his or her claims.

The interpretation of this term is important as regards attorney fees in that by statute in certain cases (*e.g.*, civil rights) attorney fees are awarded to the prevailing party. See *e.g.*, 42 U.S.C.A. § 1988. *See also* Equal Access to Justice Act.

Prevent. To hinder, frustrate, prohibit, impede, or preclude; to obstruct; to intercept. To stop or intercept the approach, access, or performance of a thing. *See* Injunction; Restraining order.

Preventive detention. Confinement imposed generally on a defendant in criminal case who has threatened to escape or otherwise violate the law while awaiting trial or disposition, or of a mentally ill person who may harm himself or others. See *e.g.* 18 U.S.C.A. § 3142. The term is also used to describe the improper use of bail. *See also* Commitment; Preventive justice.

Preventive injunction. *See* Restraining order.

Preventive justice. The system of measures taken by government with reference to the direct prevention of crime. It generally consists in obliging those persons whom there is probable ground to suspect of future misbehavior to give full assurance to the public that such offense as is apprehended shall not happen, by requiring pledges or securities to keep the peace, or for their good behavior (*e.g.* peace bonds).

Preventive remedy. *See* Injunction; Restraining order.

Previous. Antecedent; prior; before. Sometimes limited in meaning to "next prior to" or "next preceding".

Previously taxed income (PTI). Before the Subchapter S Revision Act of 1982, the undistributed taxable income of an S corporation was taxed to the shareholders as of the last day of the corporation's tax year and usually could be withdrawn by the shareholders without tax consequences at some later point in time. The role of PTI has been taken over by the accumulated adjustments account.

Price. The cost at which something is obtained. Something which one ordinarily accepts voluntarily in exchange for something else. The consideration given for the purchase of a thing. Amount which a prospective seller indicates as the sum for which he is willing to sell; market value. The amount of money given or set as the amount to be given as a consideration for the sale of a specified thing. The term may be synonymous with cost, and with value, as well as with consideration, though price is not always identical either with consideration. The consideration given for the purchase of a thing. Amount which a prospective seller indicates as the sum for which he is willing to sell; market value. The term may be synonymous with cost, and with value, as well as with consideration, though price is not always identical either with consideration.

See also Asking price; Fair market value; Going price; Liquidation price; Open price term.

Support price. A minimum price set by the government for a particular agricultural raw commodity. For example, the support price of wheat may be set at, say $2 per bushel. That means that the farmer never has to sell his or her wheat below that support price. *See also* Parity.

Target price. Prices set by the government for particular agricultural commodities such as wheat and corn. If the actual market price falls below the target price, farmers get a subsidy from the government for the difference. *See* Parity.

Unit pricing. Pricing of food products expressed in a well-known unit such as ounces or pounds.

Price discrimination. Exists when a buyer pays a price that is different from the price paid by another buyer for an identical product or service. Price discrimination is prohibited if the effect of this discrimination may be to lessen substantially or injure competition, except where it was implemented to dispose of perishable or obsolete goods, was the result of differences in costs incurred, or was given in good faith to meet an equally low price of a competitor. Clayton Act, § 2. *See also* Predatory intent; Robinson-Patman Act.

Price earnings ratio. The market price per share of a company's common stock divided by the company's annual earnings per share. For example, a stock selling for $50 per share, and earnings of $5 per share, is said to be selling at a price earnings ratio of 10 to 1.

Price-fixing. A combination formed for the purpose of and with the effect of raising, depressing, fixing, pegging, or stabilizing the price of a commodity. The cooperative setting of price levels or range by competing firms, which would otherwise be set by natural market forces. Such agreements are in violation of the Sherman Antitrust Act. Price-fixing within intent of Sherman Act is either horizontal (dealing with arrangements among competitors, as between competing retailers) or vertical (attempting to control resale price, as agreements between manufacturer and retailer).

Minimum fee schedules proposed and enforced by state bar associations are within orbit of prohibited price-fixing under Sherman Act.

See also Horizontal price-fixing; Peg; Per se violations; Predatory intent; Resale price maintenance; Vertical price-fixing contract.

Price index. A number representing average prices as a percent of the average prevailing at some other time (called the base or base year).

Price leadership. A market condition in which a leader in the industry establishes a price and the others in the field follow suit by adopting that price as their own. Price leadership implies a set of industry practices or customs under which list price changes are normally announced by a specific firm accepted as the leader by others, who follow the leader's initiatives. Such practices have been held to not be in violation of the antitrust laws in the absence of a showing of confederated action or an intent to monopolize.

Price supports. A device used generally by the federal government to keep prices (normally commodity prices) from falling below a predesignated level by such means as loans, subsidies, and government purchases. *See also* Parity; Price.

Priest-penitent privilege. In evidence, the recognition of the seal of confession which bars testimony as to the contents of a communication from one to his confessor. Nearly all states provide for this privilege by statute.

Prima facie /práymə féyshiy(iy)/. Lat. At first sight; on the first appearance; on the face of it; so far as can be judged from the first disclosure; presumably; a fact presumed to be true unless disproved by some evidence to the contrary. *See also* Presumption.

Prima facie case. Such as will prevail until contradicted and overcome by other evidence. A case which has proceeded upon sufficient proof to that stage where it will support finding if evidence to contrary is disregarded.

A prima facie case consists of sufficient evidence in the type of case to get plaintiff past a motion for directed verdict in a jury case or motion to dismiss in a nonjury case; it is the evidence necessary to require defendant to proceed with his case. Courts use concept of "prima facie case" in two senses: (1) in sense of plaintiff producing evidence sufficient to render reasonable a conclusion in favor of allegation he asserts; this means plaintiff's evidence is sufficient to allow his case to go to jury, and (2) courts use "prima facie" to mean not only that plaintiff's evidence would reasonably allow conclusion plaintiff seeks, but also that plaintiff's evidence compels such a conclusion if the defendant produces no evidence to rebut it.

Prima facie evidence. Evidence good and sufficient on its face. Such evidence as, in the judgment of the law, is sufficient to establish a given fact, or the group or chain of facts constituting the party's claim or defense, and which if not rebutted or contradicted, will remain sufficient. Evidence which, if unexplained or uncontradicted, is sufficient to sustain a judgment in favor of the issue which it supports, but which may be contradicted by other evidence.

That quantum of evidence that suffices for proof of a particular fact until the fact is contradicted by other evidence; once a trier of fact is faced with conflicting evidence, it must weigh the prima facie evidence with all of the other probative evidence presented. Evidence which, standing alone and unexplained, would maintain the proposition and warrant the conclusion to support which it is introduced. An inference or presumption of law, affirmative or negative of a fact, in the absence of proof, or until proof can be obtained or produced to overcome the inference. *See also* Presumptive evidence.

Prima facie tort. The infliction of intentional harm, resulting in damage, without excuse or justification, by an act or series of acts which would otherwise be lawful. *See also* Strict liability.

Primary. First; principal; chief; leading. First in order of time, or development, or in intention. As to *primary* Conveyance; Election; and Obligation, see those titles.

Primary activity. Concerted action such as a strike or picketing directed against the employer with whom it has a dispute. *Compare* Secondary picketing.

Primary beneficiary. In life insurance, the person named in the policy who is to receive the proceeds on the death of the insured if such person is alive. If deceased, the proceeds are payable to a secondary beneficiary also designated as such in the policy. *Compare* Secondary beneficiary.

Primary boycott. Action by a union by which it tries to induce people not to use, handle, transport or purchase goods of an employer with which the union has a grievance. *Compare* Secondary boycott. *See also* Boycott.

Primary election. A preliminary election for the nomination of candidates for office or of delegates to a party convention, designed as a substitute for party conventions. Such elections are classified as closed or open depending on whether or not tests of party affiliation are required. *See also* Closed primary; Election.

Primary evidence. Primary evidence means original or first-hand evidence; the best evidence that the nature of the case admits of; the evidence which is required in the first instance, and which must fail before secondary evidence can be admitted. That evidence which the nature of the case or question suggests as the proper means of ascertaining the truth. It is the particular means of proof which is the most natural and satisfactory of which the case admits, and includes the best evidence which is available to a party and procurable under the existing situation, and all evidence

falling short of such standard, and which in its nature suggests there is better evidence of the same fact, is "secondary evidence." *Compare* Secondary evidence. *See also* Best evidence.

Primary insurance coverage. Coverage whereby, under terms of policy, liability attaches immediately upon happening of occurrence that gives rise to liability.

Primary jurisdiction. Doctrine of "primary jurisdiction" provides that where the law vests in an administrative agency the power to decide a controversy or treat an issue, the courts will refrain from entertaining the case until the agency has fulfilled its statutory obligation. The doctrine does not involve jurisdiction in the technical sense, but it is a doctrine predicated on an attitude of judicial self-restraint and is applied when the court feels that the dispute should be handled by an administrative agency created by the legislature to deal with such problems. *See also* Exhaustion of administrative remedies.

Primary liability. In commercial law, a description of the nature of a signer's engagement, *i.e.*, his or her contract liability, on an instrument which means that he or she is obligated to pay without someone else refusing to pay. Ordinarily, the liability of a maker or acceptor is primary.

Primary market. In finance, the market where the initial sale by the issuer of new securities occurs; in contrast with secondary market where previously issued securities are traded. *Compare* Secondary market.

Primary obligation. In contract law, the foundational requirement of a contracting party from which other obligations may spring; *e.g.* in a contract of sale, the buyer's primary obligation is to purchase the goods.

Primary powers. The principal authority given by a principal to his agent. It differs from "mediate powers."

Primary purpose. That which is first in intention; which is fundamental. The principal or fixed intention with which an act or course of conduct is undertaken.

Prime. To stand first or paramount; to take precedence or priority of; to outrank.

Prime contractor. The party to a building contract who is charged with the total construction and who enters into sub-contracts for such work as electrical, plumbing and the like. Also called "general contractor."

Prime cost. The true price paid for goods upon a *bona fide* purchase.

Prime interest rate. Usually defined as the lowest rate of interest from time to time charged by a specific lender to its most credit worthy customers for short term unsecured loans. The prime rate is often used as the floor or base rate for setting interest rates on other loans (*e.g.* consumer loans).

Prime maker. The person who signs a negotiable instrument such as a note and becomes primarily liable thereon.

Prime tenant. *See* Tenant.

Primogeniture /pràymǝjénǝtyǝr/. The state of being the first-born among several children of the same parents; seniority by birth in the same family. The superior or exclusive right possessed by the eldest son, and particularly, his right to succeed to the estate of his ancestor, in right of his seniority by birth, to the exclusion of younger sons.

Principal, *adj.* Chief; leading; most important or considerable; primary; original. Highest in rank, authority, character, importance, or degree.

As to *principal* Challenge; Contract; Obligation; and Office, see those titles.

Principal fact. In the law of evidence, a fact sought and proposed to be proved by evidence of other facts (termed "evidentiary facts") from which it is to be deduced by inference. A fact which is the principal and ultimate object of an inquiry, and respecting the existence of which a definite belief is required to be formed.

Principal residence. See that title.

Principal, *n.* The source of authority or right. A superintendent, as of a school.

An amount of money that has been borrowed or invested. The capital sum of a debt or obligation, as distinguished from interest or other additions to it. An amount on which interest is charged or earned. Amount of debt, not including interest. The face value of a note, bond, mortgage, etc. that must be repaid as distinct from the interest that is paid thereon. Capital sum placed at interest, due as a debt, or use as a fund, as distinguished from interest or profit.

See also Coprincipal; Undisclosed principal.

Criminal law. One who is present at and participates in the crime charged or who procures an innocent agent to commit the crime. A chief actor or perpetrator, or an aider and abettor actually or constructively present at the commission of the crime, as distinguished from an "accessory." At common law, a principal in the first degree is he that is the actor or absolute perpetrator of the crime; and, in the second degree, he who is present, aiding and abetting the principal in the first degree. The distinction between principals in the first and second degrees has been abrogated in the Model Penal Code and by many state codes.

A "principal" differs from an "accessory before the fact" only in the requirement of presence during commission of crime.

Whoever commits an offense against the United States or aids, abets, counsels, commands, induces or procures its commission, is punishable as a principal. Also, whoever willfully causes an act to be done which if directly performed by him or another would be an offense against the United States, is punishable as a principal. 18 U.S.C.A. § 2.

Principal in the first degree. A principal in the first degree may simply be defined as the criminal actor; the one who actually commits a crime, either by his own hand, or by an inanimate agency, or by an innocent human agent. He is the one who, with the requisite mental state, engages in the act or omission concurring with the mental state which causes the criminal result.

Principal in the second degree. To be a principal in the second degree, one must be present at the commission of a criminal offense and aid, counsel, command, or encourage the principal in the first degree in the commission of that offense. This requirement of presence may be fulfilled by constructive presence. A person is constructively present when he is physically absent from the situs of the crime but aids and abets the principal in the first degree at the time of the offense from some distance.

Investments. The person for whom a broker executes an order, or a dealer buying or selling for his own account. The term "principal" may also refer to a person's capital or to the face amount of a bond.

Law of agency. The term "principal" describes one who has permitted or directed another (*i.e.* agent or servant) to act for his benefit and subject to his direction and control, such that the acts of the agent become binding on the principal. Principal includes in its meaning the term "master", a species of principal who, in addition to other control, has a right to control the physical conduct of the species of agents known as servants, as to whom special rules are applicable with reference to harm caused by their physical acts.

If, at the time of a transaction conducted by an agent, the other party thereto has notice that the agent is acting for a principal and of the principal's identity, the principal is a *disclosed* principal. If the other party has notice that the agent is or may be acting for a principal but has no notice of the principal's identity, the principal for whom the agent is acting is a *partially disclosed* principal. If the other party has no notice that the agent is acting for a principal, the one for whom he acts is an *undisclosed* principal. Restatement, Second, Agency, § 4.

Law of guaranty and suretyship. The person primarily liable, for whose performance of his obligation the guarantor or surety has become bound.

Principal and surety. Relationship between accommodation maker and party accommodated on promissory note is that of "principal and surety."

Trust law. Property as opposed to income. The term is often used to designate the corpus of a trust. If, for example, G places real estate in trust with income payable to A for life and the remainder to B upon A's death, the real estate is the principal or corpus of the trust. *See also* Kentucky Rule. The majority of states have adopted the Uniform Principal and Income Act.

Vice principal. A vice principal is an employee to whom the master delegates those absolute or nondelegable duties cast upon a master for protection of his employees, and who is in charge of the master's business or any department thereof, and whose duties are exclusively supervision, direction and control of the work of subordinate employees engaged therein, whose duty it is to obey him. Vice principal is servant who, in addition to his authority to direct and supervise work of those under him, has authority to hire and discharge a subordinate servant.

Principal residence. The residence (which may be a single family home, trailer, condominium, or houseboat) where the taxpayer resides most of the time. For tax purposes, capital gains may be deferred on the sale of the taxpayer's principal residence if a new residence is purchased within a certain period of time. *See also* Domicile; Residence.

Principle. A fundamental truth or doctrine, as of law; a comprehensive rule or doctrine which furnishes a basis or origin for others; a settled rule of action, procedure, or legal determination. A truth or proposition so clear that it cannot be proved or contradicted unless by a proposition which is still clearer. That which constitutes the essence of a body or its constituent parts. That which pertains to the theoretical part of a science.

Printers Ink Statute. A model statute drafted in 1911 and adopted with some variations in a number of states making it a misdemeanor to advertise a representation that is untrue, deceptive or misleading.

Prior, *adj.* Earlier; elder; preceding; preferable or preferred; superior in rank, right, or time; as, a prior lien, mortgage, or judgment.

Prior art. In patent law, includes any relevant knowledge, acts, descriptions and patents which pertain to, but predate, invention in question. Anything in tangible form that may properly be relied on by patent office in patent cases in support of rejection on matter of substance, not form, of claim in pending application for patent. Prior art may also be relied on by a court to hold a patent claim invalid, *i.e.*, not novel or not unobvious. 35 U.S.C.A. § 102.

Prior creditor. Generally, the creditor who is accorded priority in payment from the assets of his debtor. *See* Preferential debts; Preferred creditor.

Prior inconsistent statements. In evidence, prior statements made by the witness which contradict statements made on the witness stand may be introduced to impeach the witness after a foundation has been laid and an opportunity given to the witness to affirm or deny whether such prior statements were made. Such impeachment may be made through the witness himself or through another witness who heard the prior statements or by means of inconsistent prior depositions (Fed. R.Civil P. 32(a)). Such prior inconsistent statements are not admissible to prove the truth of the matter asserted but only to impeach the credibility of the witness. See Fed.Evid.R. 613(b). *See also* Declaration *(Declaration against interest)*; Impeachment.

Priority. Precedence, going before. A legal preference or precedence. The relative ranking of competing claims to the same property. When two persons have similar rights in respect of the same subject-matter, but one is entitled to exercise his right to the exclusion of the other, he is said to have priority. The order in which claims may be satisfied out of the sale of real property or other assets (*see e.g.* Mortgage *(First mortgage)*). *See also* Preferential debts.

In bankruptcy, refers to secured claims that by statute receive more favorable treatment than other unsecured claims. In a Bankruptcy Code Chapter 7 distribution, priority claims must be paid first. In a Chapter 11 plan, priority claims must be paid in full.

Priority of liens. Liens are ranked in the order in which they are perfected and those which are perfected first are said to be priority liens. For priority of security interests, see U.C.C. § 9–301 et seq.

Prior jeopardy. *See* Jeopardy.

Prior lien. This term commonly denotes a first or superior lien, and not one necessarily antecedent in time.

Prior restraint. A system of "prior restraint" is any scheme which gives public officials the power to deny use of a forum in advance of its actual expression. In constitutional law, the First Amendment, U.S.Const., prohibits the imposition of a restraint on a publication before it is published. The person defamed is left to his remedy in libel. Near v. Minnesota, 283 U.S. 697, 51 S.Ct. 625, 75 L.Ed. 1357. Any system of prior restraints of expression bears a heavy presumption against its constitutional validity, and the Government carries a heavy burden of showing justification for imposition of such a restraint.

New York Times Co. v. U.S., 403 U.S. 713, 91 S.Ct. 2140, 29 L.Ed.2d 822.

Prior restraints on speech and publication are the most serious and least tolerable infringement on First Amendment Rights. Three exceptions are recognized: a publication creating a "clear and present danger" to the country, Schenck v. U.S., 249 U.S. 47, 52, 39 S.Ct. 247, 249, 63 L.Ed. 470; obscene publications, and publications which invade the zone of personal privacy.

A prohibited prior restraint is not limited to the suppression of a thing before it is released to the public; rather, an invalid prior restraint is an infringement upon constitutional right to disseminate matters that are ordinarily protected by the First Amendment without there first being a judicial determination that the material does not qualify for First Amendment protection.

See also Censor; Censorship.

Prior use doctrine. Between two public bodies, property already devoted to a public use may not be taken for another public use in absence of express legislative authority.

Prison. A public building or other place for the confinement of persons, whether as a punishment imposed by the law or otherwise in the course of the administration of justice. A state or federal correctional institution for incarceration of felony offenders for terms of one year or more. The words "prison" and "penitentiary" are used synonymously to designate institutions for the imprisonment of persons convicted of the more serious crimes, as distinguished from reformatories and county or city jails. See also Jail.

Prison breaking, or breach. The common-law offense of one who, being lawfully in custody, escapes from the place where he is confined, by the employment of force and violence. This offense is to be distinguished from "rescue" (q.v.), which is a deliverance of a prisoner from lawful custody by a third person, and from "escape" which is an unauthorized departure of a prisoner from legal custody without the use of force. The trend however of modern statutes is to abandon these common-law distinctions based upon the presence or absence of force, and substitute other factors to determine the grade of the offense; with "prison breaking" generally referring to escaping from prison or jail by any means. See e.g. 18 U.S.C.A. § 751 et seq.

Prisoner. One who is deprived of his liberty. One who is kept against his will in confinement or custody in a prison, penitentiary, jail, or other correctional institution, as a result of conviction of a crime or awaiting trial.

Prisoner at the bar. An accused person, while on trial before the court, is so called. One accused of crime, who is actually on trial, is in legal effect a "prisoner at the bar," notwithstanding he has given bond for his appearance at the trial. He is a "prisoner" if held in custody either under bond or other process of law, or when physically held under arrest, and when actually on trial he is a "prisoner at the bar."

Privacy laws. Those federal and state statutes which prohibit an invasion of a person's right to be left alone (e.g. to not be photographed in private), and also restrict access to personal information (e.g. income tax returns, credit reports); and overhearing of private communications (e.g. electronic surveillance). Some provide for equitable relief in the form of injunction to prevent the invasion of privacy while others specifically call for money damages and some provide for both legal and equitable protection. See e.g. Fair Credit Reporting Act (15 U.S.C.A. § 1681n–p). See also Privacy, right of.

The federal Privacy Act (5 U.S.C.A. § 552a) provides for making known to the public the existence and characteristics of all personal information systems kept by every Federal agency. The Act permits an individual to have access to records containing personal information on that individual and allows the individual to control the transfer of that information to other Federal agencies for nonroutine uses. The Act also requires all Federal agencies to keep accurate accountings of transfers of personal records to other agencies and outsiders, and to make the accountings available to the individual. The Act further provides for civil remedies for the individual whose records are kept or used in contravention of the requirements of the Act.

Breach of privacy is knowingly and without lawful authority: (a) Intercepting, without the consent of the sender or receiver, a message by telephone, telegraph, letter or other means of private communications; or (b) Divulging, without the consent of the sender or receiver, the existence or contents of such message if such person knows that the message was illegally intercepted, or if he illegally learned of the message in the course of employment with an agency in transmitting it. Kansas Criminal Code 21–4002. See Eavesdropping; Wiretapping.

Privacy, right of. The right to be let alone; the right of a person to be free from unwarranted publicity; and right to live without unwarranted interference by the public in matters with which the public is not necessarily concerned. Term "right of privacy" is generic term encompassing various rights recognized to be inherent in concept of ordered liberty, and such right prevents governmental interference in intimate personal relationships or activities, freedoms of individual to make fundamental choices involving himself, his family, and his relationship with others. The right of an individual (or corporation) to withhold himself and his property from public scrutiny, if he so chooses.

It is said to exist only so far as its assertion is consistent with law or public policy, and in a proper case equity will interfere, if there is no remedy at law, to prevent an injury threatened by the invasion of, or infringement upon, this right from motives of curiosity, gain or malice. While there is no right of privacy found in any specific guarantees of the Constitution, the Supreme Court has recognized that zones of privacy may be created by more specific constitutional guarantees and thereby impose limits upon governmental power. See Warren and Brandeis, The Right to Privacy, 4 Harv.L.Rev. 193.

Tort actions for invasion of privacy fall into four general classes: *Appropriation,* consisting of appropriation, for the defendant's benefit or advantage, of the plaintiff's name or likeness; *Intrusion,* consisting of intrusion upon the plaintiff's solitude or seclusion, as by invading his home, eavesdropping, as well as persistent and unwanted telephone calls; *Public disclosure of private facts,* consisting of a cause of action in publicity, of a highly objectionable kind, given to private information about the plaintiff, even though it is true and no action would lie for defamation; *False light in the public eye,* consisting of publicity which places the plaintiff in a false light in the public eye.

See also False light privacy; Invasion of privacy.

Private. Affecting or belonging to private individuals, as distinct from the public generally. Not official; not clothed with office.

As to *private* Act; Agent; Bill; Boundary; Business; Carrier; Corporation; Detective; Dwelling; Easement; Examination; Ferry; Nuisance; Pond; Property; Prosecutor; Right; Road; Sale; Seal; Statute; Trust; War; Way; and Wrong, see those titles.

Private bank. An unincorporated banking institution owned by an individual or partnership and, depending upon state statutes, subject to or free from state regulation.

Private bill. Legislation for the special benefit of an individual or a locality. Many State constitutions prohibit such legislation except by general law. *See also* Private law.

Privateer /pràyvətír/. A vessel owned, equipped, and armed by one or more private individuals, and duly commissioned by a belligerent power to go on cruises and make war upon the enemy, usually by preying on his commerce. A private vessel commissioned by a nation by the issue of a letter of marque to its owner to carry on all hostilities by sea, presumably according to the laws of war. Formerly a state issued letters of marque to its own subjects, and to those of neutral states as well, but a privateersman who accepted letters of marque from both belligerents was regarded as a pirate. By the Declaration of Paris (April, 1856), privateering was abolished, but the United States, Spain, Mexico, and Venezuela did not accede to this declaration. It has been thought that the constitutional provision empowering Congress to issue letters of marque deprives it of the power to join in a permanent treaty abolishing privateering. *See* Piracy.

Piracy and privateering are federal offenses. 18 U.S.C.A. § 1651 *et seq.*

Private foundations. An organization which is operated privately for the advancement of charitable or education projects. An organization generally exempt from taxation that is subject to additional statutory restrictions on its activities and on contributions thereto. Excise taxes may be levied on certain prohibited transactions, and the Internal Revenue Code places more stringent restrictions on the deductibility of contributions to private foundations. I.R.C. § 509. *See also* Charitable organizations; Foundation.

Private international law. A name used by some writers to indicate that branch of the law which is now more commonly called "Conflict of laws" *(q.v.).*

Private law. That portion of the law which defines, regulates, enforces, and administers relationships among individuals, associations, and corporations. As used in contradistinction to public law, the term means all that part of the law which is administered between citizen and citizen, or which is concerned with the definition, regulation, and enforcement of rights in cases where both the person in whom the right inheres and the person upon whom the obligation is incident are private individuals. *See also* Private bill; Special law. *Compare* Public law.

Private letter ruling. A written statement issued to the taxpayer by the Internal Revenue Service in which interpretations of the tax laws are made and applied to a specific set of facts. Function of the letter ruling, usually sought by the taxpayer in advance of a contemplated transaction, is to advise the taxpayer regarding the tax treatment he can expect from the I.R.S. in the circumstances specified by the ruling. *See also* Letter ruling.

Private nuisance. A private nuisance is generally anything that by its continuous use or existence works annoyance, harm, unreasonable interference, inconvenience or damage to another landowner in the enjoyment of his property. A nuisance affecting a single individual or definite small number of persons in enjoyment of private rights not common to the public. It is only a tort, and the remedy therefor lies exclusively with the individual whose rights have been disturbed. *See also* Nuisance. *Compare* Public nuisance.

Private offering. *See* Offering; Private placement.

Private person. Term sometimes used to refer to persons other than those holding public office or in military services.

Private placement. *Adoption.* In adoption cases, the placement of a child for adoption by the mother or parents themselves or by an intermediary like a lawyer or doctor, rather than by an adoption agency. Also sometimes called a "direct" placement.

Securities. The sale of a stock or bond issued directly to private persons, institutional investors, etc., outside of a public offering. Securities Act (1933), § 4(2). *See also* Direct placement; Offering.

Private ruling. *See* Letter ruling; Private letter ruling.

Privation /prəvéyshən/. A taking away or withdrawing.

Privies /príviyz/. Those who are partakers or have an interest in any action or thing, or any relation to another.

Privilege. A particular and peculiar benefit or advantage enjoyed by a person, company, or class, beyond the common advantages of other citizens. An exceptional or extraordinary power or exemption. A peculiar right, advantage, exemption, power, franchise, or immunity held by a person or class, not generally possessed by others.

In tort law, the ability to act contrary to another individual's legal right without that individual having legal redress for the consequences of that act; usually raised by the actor as a defense.

An exemption from some burden or attendance, with which certain persons are indulged, from a supposition of law that the stations they fill, or the offices they are engaged in, are such as require all their time and care, and that, therefore, without this indulgence, it would be impracticable to execute such offices to that advantage which the public good requires. That which releases one from the performance of a duty or obligation, or exempts one from a liability which he would otherwise be required to perform, or sustain in common with all other persons. *See also* Exemption; Immunity.

See also Doctor-patient privilege; Executive privilege; Husband-wife privilege; Journalist's privilege; Legislative immunity; Marital communications privilege; Newsmen's privilege; Patient-physician privilege; Priest-penitent privilege; Privileged communications; Right; State secrets privilege.

Attorney-client, doctor-patient, etc. privilege. See Privileged communications.

Communications. See Privileged communications.

Deliberative process privilege. This governmental privilege permits government to withhold documents that reflect advisory opinions, recommen- dations and deliberations comprising part of a process by which government decisions and policies are formulated, and was developed to promote frank and independent discussion among those responsible for making governmental decisions and to protect against premature disclosure of proposed agency policies or decisions.

Discovery. When interrogatories, depositions or other forms of discovery seek information which is otherwise privileged, the party from whom it is sought may claim his privilege. Fed.R.Civil P. 26; Fed.R.Crim.P. 16. *See also* Protective order; Work product rule.

Evidence. See Privileged communications; Privileged evidence.

Executive privilege. The protection afforded to confidential presidential communications. However, the generalized need for confidentiality of high level communications cannot sustain an absolute unqualified presidential privilege. U. S. v. Nixon, 418 U.S. 683, 94 S.Ct. 3090, 41 L.Ed.2d 1039. *See also* Executive privilege.

Journalist's privilege. See Journalist's privilege; Newsmen's privilege; Shield laws.

Libel and slander. An exemption from liability for the speaking or publishing of defamatory words concerning another, based on the fact that the statement was made in the performance of a political, judicial, social, or personal duty. The privilege is either *absolute* or *conditional*. The former protects the speaker or publisher without reference to his motives or the truth or falsity of the statement. This may be claimed in respect, for instance, to statements made in legislative debates, in reports of military officers to their superiors in the line of their duty, and statements made by judges, witnesses, and jurors in trials in court. Conditional privilege (called also "qualified privilege") will protect the speaker or publisher unless actual malice and knowledge of the falsity of the statement is shown. This may be claimed where the communication related to a matter of public interest, or where it was necessary to protect one's private interest and was made to a person having an interest in the same matter.

For defense of "constitutional privilege" in libel actions, *see* Libel.

Maritime law. An allowance to the master of a ship of the same general nature with primage, being compensation, or rather a gratuity, customary in certain trades, and which the law assumes to be a fair and equitable allowance, because the contract on both sides is made under the knowledge of such usage by the parties.

Privilege from arrest. A privilege extended to certain classes of persons, either by the rules of international law, the policy of the law, or the necessities of justice or of the administration of government, whereby they are exempted from arrest on civil process, and, in some cases, on criminal charges, either permanently, as in the case of a foreign minister and his suite, or temporarily, as in the case of members of the legislature, parties and witnesses engaged in a particular suit, etc. Art. I, § 6, U.S.Const. *See also* Immunity.

Privilege tax. A tax on the privilege of carrying on a business or occupation for which a license or franchise is required.

Torts. Privilege is the general term applied to certain rules of law by which particular circumstances justify conduct which otherwise would be tortious, and thereby defeat the tort liability (or defense) which, in the absence of such circumstances, ordinarily would follow from that conduct. In other words, even if all of the facts necessary to a prima facie case of tort liability can be proved, there are additional facts present sufficient to establish some privilege, and therefore defendant has committed no tort. Privileges thus differ from other defenses, such as contributory negligence, which operate to bar plaintiff's recovery but do not negate the tortious nature of defendant's conduct. Conversely, plaintiff's privilege may defeat a defense which defendant otherwise might have had. The term and concept of privilege apply primarily to the intentional torts, but also appear in other areas, such as defamation. *See Libel and slander, above.*

A privilege may be based upon: (a) the consent of the other affected by the actor's conduct, or (b) the fact that its exercise is necessary for the protection of some interest of the actor or of the public which is of such importance as to justify the harm caused or threatened by its exercise, or (c) the fact that the actor is performing a function for the proper performance of which freedom of action is essential. Restatement, Second, Torts, § 10.

Privileges may be divided into two general categories: (1) consent, and (2) privileges created by law irrespective of consent. In general, the latter arise where there is some important and overriding social value in sanctioning defendant's conduct, despite the fact that it causes plaintiff harm.

Privilege is an affirmative defense which must be pleaded by defendant. Fed.R.Civil P. 8(c).

Writ of privilege. A common law process to enforce or maintain a privilege; particularly to secure the release of a person arrested in a civil suit contrary to his privilege.

Privilege against self-incrimination. The privilege derived from the Fifth Amendment, U.S. Const., and similar provisions in the constitutions of states. It requires the government to prove a criminal case against the defendant without the aid of the defendant as a witness against himself, though it protects only communications, not physical evidence such as handwriting and fingerprints. It is invocable by any witness who is called to the witness stand against his wishes whether the proceeding be a trial or grand jury hearing or a proceeding before an investigating body, but it is waived when the witness voluntarily takes the witness stand. *See also* Immunity; Link-in-chain.

Privileged. Possessing or enjoying a privilege; exempt from burdens; entitled to priority or precedence.

Privileged communications. Those statements made by certain persons within a protected relationship such as husband-wife, attorney-client, priest-penitent and the like which the law protects from forced disclosure on the witness stand at the option of the witness, client, penitent, spouse. In federal courts, the extent and scope of the specific privilege is to be governed by federal common law or state rules governing evidentiary privileges. Fed.Evid. Rule 501. *See also* Accountant-client privilege; Attorney-client privilege; Communication; Conditionally privileged communication; Journalist's privilege; Privilege.

Privileged debts. Those which an executor or administrator, trustee in bankruptcy, and the like, may pay in preference to others; such as funeral expenses, servants' wages, and doctors' bills during last sickness, etc. *See also* Preferential debts; Priority.

Privileged evidence. In addition to privileged communications *(q.v.)*, privileged evidence may also include governmental secrets or records, identity of informer, grand jury proceedings, certain types of accident reports, and attorney's work product.

Privileges and immunities clause. There are two Privileges and Immunities Clauses in the federal Constitution and Amendments, the first being found in Art. IV, and the second in the 14th Amendment, § 1, second sentence, clause 1. The provision in Art. IV states that "The Citizens of each State shall be entitled to all Privileges and Immunities of Citizens in the several States," while the 14th Amendment provides that "No State shall make or enforce any law which shall abridge the privileges or immunities of citizens of the United States.

The purpose of these Clauses is to place the citizens of each State upon the same footing with citizens of other states, so far as the advantages resulting from citizenship in those states is concerned; to insure that a citizen of State A who ventures into State B be accorded the same privileges that the citizens of State B enjoy. Pursuing a common calling, plying a trade, and doing business in another state are examples of "privileges" protected by the privileges and immunities clause of the Federal Constitution. *See also* Full faith and credit clause.

Privity. In its broadest sense, "privity" is defined as mutual or successive relationships to the same right of property, or such an identification of interest of one person with another as to represent the same legal right. Derivative interest founded on, or growing out of, contract, connection, or bond of union between parties; mutuality of interest. Thus, the executor is in privity with the testator, the heir with the ancestor, the assignee with the assignor, the donee with the donor, and the lessee with the lessor.

Privity signifies that relationship between two or more persons is such that a judgment involving one of them may justly be conclusive upon other, although other was not party to lawsuit.

Private knowledge; joint knowledge with another of a private concern; cognizance implying a consent or concurrence. *See* Insider; Legal privity; Privy.

Horizontal privity. Such privity is not, in reality, a state of privity but rather one of nonprivity. The term refers to those who are not in the distributive chain of a product but who, nonetheless, use the product and retain a relationship with the purchaser, such as a member of the purchaser's family. See also U.C.C. § 2–318.

Privity of contract. That connection or relationship which exists between two or more contracting parties. It was traditionally essential to the maintenance of an action on any contract that there should subsist such privity between the plaintiff and defendant in respect of the matter sued on. However, the absence of privity as a defense in actions for damages in contract and tort actions is generally no longer viable with the enactment of warranty statutes (see *e.g.* U.C.C. § 2–318 below), acceptance by states of doctrine of strict liability *(q.v.)*, and court decisions (*e.g.* MacPherson v. Buick Motor Co., 217 N.Y. 382, 111 N.E. 1050) which have extended the right to sue for injuries or damages to third party beneficiaries, and even innocent bystanders.

U.C.C. § 2–318 provides three Alternative provisions (A–C) covering third party beneficiaries of express or implied warranties. Most states have enacted Alternative A: "A seller's warranty whether express or implied extends to any natural person who is in the family or household of his buyer or who is a guest in his home if it is reasonable to expect that such person may use, consume or be affected by the goods and who is injured in person by breach of the warranty. A seller may not exclude or limit the operation of this section." Other states have further broadened this model provision. For example Massachusetts U.C.C. § 2–318 provides: "Lack of privity between plaintiff and defendant shall be no defense in any action brought against the manufacturer, seller, lessor or supplier of goods to recover damages for breach of warranty, express or implied, or for negligence, although the plaintiff did not purchase the goods from the defendant if the plaintiff was a person whom the manufacturer, seller, lessor or supplier might reasonably have expected to use, consume or be affected by the goods. . . ."

Privity of estate. Mutual or successive relation to the same right in property such as that which exists between lessor and lessee or their successors.

A subtenant, who is in privity of estate with the original lessor, may avail himself of any covenants in the original lease which "touch and concern" the land.

Privity of possession. Relationship which exists between parties in successive possession of real property. Such relationship becomes important in cases of adverse possession claims.

Vertical privity. Refers to the relationship between those who are in the distributive chain of a product.

Privity *or* knowledge. Under Rev.St. §§ 4283–4286 (46 U.S.C.A. §§ 183–186) withholding the right to limit liability if the shipowner had "privity or knowledge" of the fault which occasioned damages, privity or knowledge must be actual and not merely constructive, and must involve a personal participation of the owner in some fault or act of negligence causing or contributing to the injury suffered. The words import actual knowledge of the things causing or contributing to the loss, or knowledge or means of knowledge of a condition of things likely to produce or contribute to the loss without adopting proper means to prevent it.

Privy. A person who is in privity with another. One who is a partaker or has any part or interest in any action, matter, or thing. In connection with the doctrine of res judicata, one who, after the commencement of the action, has acquired an interest in the subject matter affected by the judgment through or under one of the parties, as by inheritance, succession, purchase or assignment. See Insider; Privies; Privity.

As an adjective, the word has practically the same meaning as "private."

Prize. Anything offered as a reward of contest. A reward offered to the person who, among several persons or among the public at large, shall first (or best) perform a certain undertaking or accomplish certain conditions. An award or recompense for some act done; some valuable thing offered by a person for something done by others. It is distinguished from a "bet" or "wager" in that it is known before the event who is to give either the premium or the prize, and there is but one operation until the accomplishment of the act, thing, or purpose for which it is offered.

The fair market value of a prize or award is generally includible in gross income. Certain exceptions are provided where the prize or award is made in recognition of religious, charitable, scientific, educational, artistic, literary, or civic achievement providing certain other requirements are met. I.R.C. § 74.

A vessel or cargo, belonging to one of two belligerent powers, apprehended or forcibly captured at sea by a war-vessel or privateer of the other belligerent, and claimed as enemy's property, and therefore liable to appropriation and condemnation under the laws of war. The apprehension and detention at sea of a ship or other vessel, by authority of a belligerent power, either with the design of appropriating it, with the goods and effects it contains, or with that of becoming master of the whole or a part of its cargo.

Prize courts. Courts having jurisdiction to adjudicate upon captures made at sea in time of war, and to condemn the captured property as prize if lawfully subject to that sentence. In England, the admiralty courts have jurisdiction as prize courts, distinct from the jurisdiction on the instance side. A special commission issues in time of war to the judge of the admiralty court, to enable him to hold such court. In the United States, the federal district courts have jurisdiction in cases of prize. 28 U.S.C.A. § 1333.

Prize goods. Goods which are taken on the high seas, *jure belli,* out of the hands of the enemy.

Prize law. The system of laws and rules applicable to the capture of prize at sea; its condemnation, rights of the captors, distribution of the proceeds, etc.

Prize money. A dividend from the proceeds of a captured vessel, etc., paid to the captors.

Pro. For; in respect of; on account of; in behalf of. The introductory word of many Latin phrases.

Probability. Likelihood; appearance of reality or truth; reasonable ground of presumption; verisimilitude; consonance to reason. The likelihood of a proposition or hypothesis being true, from its conformity to reason or experience, or from superior evidence or arguments adduced in its favor. A condition or state created when there is more evidence in favor of the existence of a given proposition than there is against it.

Probable. Having the appearance of truth; having the character of probability; appearing to be founded in reason or experience. Having more evidence for than against; supported by evidence which inclines the mind to believe, but leaves some room for doubt; likely. *See also* Possible.

Probable cause. Reasonable cause; having more evidence for than against. A reasonable ground for belief in certain alleged facts. A set of probabilities grounded in the factual and practical considerations which govern the decisions of reasonable and prudent persons and is more than mere suspicion but less than the quantum of evidence required for conviction. An apparent state of facts found to exist upon reasonable inquiry (that is, such inquiry as the given case renders convenient and proper), which would induce a reasonably intelligent and prudent man to believe, in a criminal case, that the accused person had committed the crime charged, or, in a civil case, that a cause of action existed. *See also* Information and belief; Reasonable and probable cause; Reasonable belief; Reasonable grounds.

Arrest, search and seizure. Reasonable grounds for belief that a person should be arrested or searched. The evidentiary criterion necessary to sustain an arrest or the issuance of an arrest or search warrant. "Probable cause" to arrest exists where facts and circumstances within officers' knowledge and of which they had reasonably trustworthy information are sufficient in themselves to warrant a person of reasonable caution in the belief that an offense has been or is being committed; it is not necessary that the officer possess knowledge of facts sufficient to establish guilt, but more than mere suspicion is required. Probable cause is the existence of circumstances which would lead a reasonably prudent man to believe in guilt of arrested party; mere suspicion or belief, unsupported by facts or circumstances, is insufficient. It permits an officer to arrest one for a felony without a warrant. Probable cause justifying officer's arrest without warrant has been defined as situation where officer has more evidence favoring suspicion that person is guilty of crime than evidence against such suspicion, but there is some room for doubt.

The finding of probable cause for issuance of an arrest warrant (as required by 4th Amend.) may be based upon hearsay evidence in whole or part. Fed.R.Crim.P. 4(b). See also Rule 5.1(a) (Preliminary examination), and Rule 41(c) (Search and seizure).

See also Arrest; Probable cause hearing; Search; Search warrant.

False imprisonment action. For arrest which must be shown as justification by defendants in action for false imprisonment is reasonable ground of suspicion supported by circumstances sufficient in themselves to warrant cautious man in believing accused to be guilty, but does not depend on actual state of case in point of fact, as it may turn out upon legal investigation, but on knowledge of facts which would be sufficient to induce reasonable belief in truth of accusation.

Malicious prosecution action. In context of civil action for malicious prosecution, is such a state of facts in mind of defendant as would lead a person of ordinary caution and prudence to believe, or entertain an honest and strong suspicion, that plaintiff had committed a crime. *See* Malicious prosecution.

Probable cause hearing. That procedural step in the criminal process at which the judge or magistrate decides whether a complaint should issue or a person should be bound over to a grand jury on a showing of probable cause. See *e.g.* Fed.R.Crim.P. 5.1(a). *See* Preliminary hearing.

Probable consequence. One that is more likely to follow its supposed cause than it is not to follow it.

Probable evidence. Presumptive evidence is so called, from its foundation in probability. *See* Presumption.

Probably. In all probability; so far as the evidence shows; presumably; likely.

Probate. Court procedure by which a will is proved to be valid or invalid; though in current usage this term has been expanded to generally refer to the legal process wherein the estate of a decedent is administered. Generally, the probate process involves collecting a decedent's assets, liquidating liabilities, paying necessary taxes, and distributing property to heirs. These activities are carried out by the executor or administrator of the estate, usually under the supervision of the probate court or other court of appropriate jurisdiction. *See* Letters; Probate court; Probate jurisdiction.

To place a convicted offender on probation. *See* Probation.

In the canon law, "probate" consisted of *probatio,* the proof of the will by the executor, and *approbatio,* the approbation given by the ecclesiastical judge to the proof.

Probate bond. One required by law to be given to the probate court or judge, as incidental to proceedings in such courts, such as the bonds of executors, administrators, and guardians.

Probate code. The body or system of law relating to all matters of which probate courts have jurisdiction; *e.g.* Uniform Probate Code.

Probate court. A court having general powers over probate of wills, administration of estates, and, in some states, empowered to appoint guardians or approve the adoption of minors. Court with similar functions is called Surrogate or Orphan's Court in certain states. *See also* Probate jurisdiction.

Probate duty. A tax laid by government on every will admitted to probate or on the gross value of the personal property of the deceased testator,

and payable out of the decedent's estate. *See also* Estate tax; Inheritance tax.

Probate estate. The property of a decedent that is subject to administration by the executor or administrator of an estate.

Probate homestead. *See* Homestead.

Probate jurisdiction. The exercise of the ordinary, generally understood power of a probate, surrogate or orphan's court, which includes the establishment of wills, settlement of decedents' estates, supervision of guardianship of infants, control of their property, and other powers and functions pertaining to such subjects. *See also* Probate court.

Probate proceeding. A general designation of the actions and proceedings whereby the law is administered upon the various subjects within "probate jurisdiction" *(q.v.).*

Probation. The evidence which proves a thing; the act of proving; proof; trial; test. Used in the latter sense when referring to the initial period of employment during which a new, transferred, or promoted employee must prove or show that he is capable of performing the required duties of the job or position before he will be considered as permanently employed in such position. As applied to teachers, term means that teacher is on trial, with his competence and suitability remaining to be finally determined.

Sentence imposed for commission of crime whereby a convicted criminal offender is released into the community under the supervision of a probation officer in lieu of incarceration. It is not a matter of right, but rather is an act of grace and clemency available only to those defendants found eligible by the court. It implies that defendant has a chance to prove himself and its purpose is reform and rehabilitation. For this purpose the defendant must agree to specified standards of conduct and the public authority operating through the court impliedly promises that if he makes good, his probation will continue; however, his violation of such standards subjects his liberty to revocation.

In determining whether the defendant is entitled to a sentence of probation, the court looks to such matters as the nature and circumstances of the offense, the history and characteristics of the defendant, and the need for the sentence imposed. See, *e.g.,* 18 U.S.C.A. §§ 3553(a), 3561 et seq.; Fed.R.Crim.P. 32.

The defendant is entitled to be represented by counsel in probation proceedings under Sixth Amendment.

Probationer. A convicted offender who is allowed to go at large, under suspension of sentence, during good behavior.

Probation officer. One who supervises a person (commonly juveniles) placed on probation by a court in a criminal proceeding. He is required to report to the court the progress of the probationer and to surrender him if he violates the terms and conditions of his probation.

Probative evidence /prówbətəv évədəns/. In the law of evidence, means having the effect of proof; tending to prove, or actually proving an issue; that which furnishes, establishes, or contributes toward proof. Testimony carrying quality of proof and having fitness to induce conviction of truth, consisting of fact and reason co-operating as co-ordinate factors. *See also* Relevant evidence.

Probative facts. In the law of evidence, facts which actually have effect of proving facts sought; evidentiary facts. Matters of evidence required to prove ultimate facts. *See* Probative evidence.

Probative value. Evidence has "probative value" if it tends to prove an issue.

Pro bono /prów bównow/. Lit. For the good; used to describe work or services (*e.g.* legal services) done or performed free of charge.

Procedendo /pròwsədéndow/. Action wherein court of superior jurisdiction orders court of inferior jurisdiction to proceed to judgment, but has no bearing on nature of judgment to be entered. A writ by which a cause which has been removed from an inferior to a superior court by *certiorari* or otherwise is sent down again to the same court, *to be proceeded in* there, where it appears to the superior court that it was removed on insufficient grounds.

More commonly, a case returned to a lower court is said to be remanded to such court.

Procedural due process. The guarantee of procedural fairness which flows from both the Fifth and Fourteenth Amendments due process clauses of the Constitution. For the guarantees of procedural due process to apply, it must first be shown that a deprivation of a significant life, liberty, or property interest has occurred. This is necessary to bring the Due Process Clause into play.

Minimal procedural due process is that parties whose rights are to be affected are entitled to be heard and, in order that they may enjoy that right, they must be notified. Fuentes v. Shevin, 407 U.S. 67, 79, 92 S.Ct. 1983, 1994, 32 L.Ed.2d 556. Procedures which due process requires beyond that minimum must be determined by a balancing analysis based on the specific factual context.

Procedural law. That which prescribes method of enforcing rights or obtaining redress for their invasion. Machinery for carrying on procedural aspects of civil or criminal action; *e.g.* Rules of Civil, Criminal, and Appellate Procedure, as adopted by the Federal and most state courts. As

a general rule, laws which fix duties, establish rights and responsibilities among and for persons, natural or otherwise, are "substantive laws" in character, while those which merely prescribe the manner in which such rights and responsibilities may be exercised and enforced in a court are "procedural laws". *See also* Procedure. *Compare* Substantive law.

Procedure. The mode of proceeding by which a legal right is enforced, as distinguished from the substantive law which gives or defines the right, and which, by means of the proceeding, the court is to administer; the machinery, as distinguished from its product. That which regulates the formal steps in an action or other judicial proceeding; a form, manner, and order of conducting suits or prosecutions; *e.g.* Rules of Civil or Criminal Procedure. The judicial process for enforcing rights and duties recognized by substantive law and for justly administering redress for infraction of them. Machinery for carrying on lawsuit including pleading, process, evidence and practice, whether in trial court or appellate court.

The law of procedure is what is commonly termed by jurists "adjective law" *(q.v.).*

See also Civil procedure; Criminal procedure; Procedural law; Rules of court. *Compare* Substantive law.

Proceeding. In a general sense, the form and manner of conducting juridical business before a court or judicial officer. Regular and orderly progress in form of law, including all possible steps in an action from its commencement to the execution of judgment. Term also refers to administrative proceedings before agencies, tribunals, bureaus, or the like.

An act which is done by the authority or direction of the court, agency, or tribunal, express or implied; an act necessary to be done in order to obtain a given end; a prescribed mode of action for carrying into effect a legal right. All the steps or measures adopted in the prosecution or defense of an action. The word may be used synonymously with "action" or "suit" to describe the entire course of an action at law or suit in equity from the issuance of the writ or filing of the complaint until the entry of a final judgment, or may be used to describe any act done by authority of a court of law and every step required to be taken in any cause by either party. The proceedings of a suit embrace *all* matters that occur in its progress judicially.

Term may refer not only to a complete remedy but also to a mere procedural step that is part of a larger action or special proceeding. A "proceeding" includes action and special proceedings before judicial tribunals as well as proceedings pending before quasi-judicial officers and boards. In a more particular sense, any application to a court of justice, however made, for aid in the enforcement of rights, for relief, for redress of injuries, for damages, or for any remedial object.

Any action, hearing, investigation, inquest, or inquiry (whether conducted by a court, administrative agency, hearing officer, arbitrator, legislative body, or any other person authorized by law) in which, pursuant to law, testimony can be compelled to be given. Calif.Evid.Code § 901.

Collateral proceeding. One in which the particular question may arise or be involved incidentally, but which is not instituted for the very purpose of deciding such question; as in the rule that a judgment cannot be attacked, or a corporation's right to exist be questioned, in any collateral proceeding. *See* Collateral estoppel doctrine.

Legal proceedings. See Legal proceedings.

Ordinary proceedings. Those founded on the regular and usual mode of carrying on a suit by due course at common law.

Special proceeding. Generic term for remedies or proceedings which are not ordinary actions; *e.g.* condemnation (Fed.R.Civil P. 71A); vesting title (Rule 70).

A "special proceeding" has reference to such proceedings as may be commenced independently of a pending action by petition or motion upon notice in order to obtain special relief, and, generally speaking, a special proceeding is confined to type of case which was not, under the common-law or equity practice, either an action at law or a suit in equity.

Summary proceeding. Any proceeding by which a controversy is settled, case disposed of, or trial conducted, in a prompt and simple manner, without the aid of a jury, without presentment or indictment, or in other respects out of the regular course of the common law. In procedure, proceedings are said to be summary when they are short and simple in comparison with regular proceedings; *e.g.* conciliation or small claims court proceedings as contrasted with usual civil trial.

Supplementary proceeding. A separate proceeding in an original action, in which the court where the action is pending is called upon to exercise its jurisdiction in aid of execution of the judgment in the action. It is a statutory equivalent in actions at law of the creditor's bill in equity, and in the majority of states where law and equity are merged, is provided as a substitute therefor. See *e.g.* Fed.R.Civil P. 69. In this proceeding the judgment debtor is summoned to appear before the court (or a referee or examiner) and submit to an oral examination touching all his property and effects, and if property subject to execution and in his possession or control is thus discovered, he is ordered to deliver it up, or a receiver may be appointed. *See* Execution; Supplementary proceedings.

Proceeds. Issues; income; yield; receipts; produce; money or articles or other thing of value arising or obtained by the sale of property; the sum, amount, or value of property sold or converted into money or into other property. Term does not necessarily mean only cash or money. That which results, proceeds, or accrues from some possession or transaction. The funds received from disposition of assets or from the issue of securities (after deduction of all costs and fees).

As used in context of debtor's sale of collateral, "proceeds" includes whatever is received upon the sale, exchange, collection or other disposition of collateral or proceeds. Insurance payable by reason of loss or damage to the collateral is proceeds, except to the extent that it is payable to a person other than a party to the security agreement. Money, checks, deposit accounts, and the like are "cash proceeds". All other proceeds are "non-cash proceeds". U.C.C. § 9–306.

Process. A series of actions, motions, or occurrences; progressive act or transaction; continuous operation; method, mode or operation, whereby a result or effect is produced; normal or actual course of procedure; regular proceeding, as, the process of vegetation or decomposition; a chemical process; processes of nature. To prepare for market or to convert into marketable form.

Patent Law

An art or method by which any particular result is produced. An act or series of acts performed upon the subject-matter to be transformed or reduced to a different state or thing. A means or method employed to produce a certain result or effect, or a mode of treatment of given materials to produce a desired result, either by chemical action, by the operation or application of some element or power of nature, or of one substance to another, irrespective of any machine or mechanical device; in this sense a "process" is patentable, though, strictly speaking, it is the art and not the process which is the subject of patent. Broadly speaking, a "process" is a definite combination of new or old elements, ingredients, operations, ways, or means to produce a new, improved or old result, and any substantial change therein by omission, to the same or better result, or by modification or substitution, with different function, to the same or better result, is a new and patentable process.

Civil and Criminal Proceedings

Process is defined as any means used by court to acquire or exercise its jurisdiction over a person or over specific property. Means whereby court compels appearance of defendant before it or a compliance with its demands.

When actions were commenced by original writ, instead of, as at present, by summons, the method of compelling the defendant to appear was by what was termed "original process," being founded on the original writ, and so called also to distinguish it from "mesne" or "intermediate" process, which was some writ or process which issued during the progress of the suit. The word "process," however, as now commonly understood, refers to a summons, or, summons and complaint, and, less commonly, to a writ. The content of the summons, and service requirements, are provided for in Rule of Civil Proc. 4.

See also Abuse (*Process*); Alias process; Compulsory process; Constructive service of process; Due process of law; Executory process; Long arm statutes; Malicious abuse of legal process; Malicious use of process; Prohibition; Service (*Service of process*); Summons.

Abuse of process. See Abuse.

Alias process. See that title.

Compulsory process. See Compulsory.

Criminal process. See Warrant.

Final process. The last process in an action; *i.e.* process issued to enforce execution of judgment.

Irregular process. Term is usually applied to process not issued in strict conformity with the law, whether the defect appears upon the face of the process, or by reference to extrinsic facts, and whether such defects render the process absolutely void or only voidable. Under current practice, a defective summons may be amended under Rule of Civil Proc. 15.

Judicial process. In a wide sense, this term may include all the acts of a court from the beginning to the end of its proceedings in a given cause; but more specifically it means the writ, summons, mandate, or other process which is used to inform the defendant of the institution of proceedings against him and to compel his appearance, in either civil or criminal cases.

Legal process. This term is sometimes used as equivalent to "lawful process." Thus, it is said that legal process means process not merely fair on its face, but in fact valid. But properly it means a summons, writ, warrant, mandate, or other process issuing from a court.

Mesne process. As distinguished from *final* process, this signifies any writ or process issued between the commencement of the action and the suing out of execution. "Mesne" in this connection may be defined as intermediate; intervening; the middle between two extremes. The writ of *capias ad respondendum* was called "mesne" to distinguish it, on the one hand, from the original process by which a suit was formerly commenced; and, on the other, from the final process of execution.

Original process. That by which a judicial proceeding is instituted; process to compel the appearance of the defendant (*i.e.* summons). Distinguished from "mesne" process, which issues, during the progress of a suit, for some subordinate or collateral purpose; and from "final" process, which is process of execution. *See* Summons.

Process of interpleader. A means of determining the right to property claimed by each of two or more persons, which is in the possession of a third. *See* Interpleader.

Process of law. See Due process of law.

Regular process. Such as is issued according to rule and the prescribed practice, or which emanates, lawfully and in a proper case, from a court or magistrate possessing jurisdiction.

Service of process. See Service.

Summary process. Such as is immediate or instantaneous, in distinction from the ordinary course, by emanating and taking effect without intermediate applications or delays. In some jurisdictions (*e.g.* Massachusetts), term used to describe action for eviction of tenant.

Trustee process. The name given in some states (particularly in New England) to the process of garnishment or foreign attachment.

Void process. Such as was issued without power in the court to award it, or which the court had not acquired jurisdiction to issue in the particular case, or which fails in some material respect to comply with the requisite form of legal process.

Process agent. Person authorized to accept service of process in behalf of another (*e.g.* on behalf of corporation).

Process costing system. An accounting system that accumulates costs by cost component in each production department; costs are assigned to units using equivalent units of production.

Process patent. A process patent describes and claims a new and useful method to produce a desired result or any new or useful improvement thereof. 35 U.S.C.A. §§ 100, 100. *See also* Process (*Patent Law*).

Process server. Person authorized by law (*e.g.* sheriff) to serve process papers on defendant.

Proclaim. To promulgate; to announce; to publish, by governmental authority, intelligence of public acts or transactions or other matters important to be known by the people. To give wide publicity to; to disclose.

Proclamation. The act of publicly proclaiming or publishing; a formal declaration; an avowal; a public announcement giving notice of a governmental act that has been done or is to be done. The act of causing some governmental matters to be published or made generally known. A written or printed document in which are contained such matters, issued by proper authority, usually by a high governmental executive (President, Governor, Mayor).

The declaration made by the bailiff, by authority of the court, that something is about to be done.

In equity practice, proclamation made by a sheriff upon a writ of attachment, summoning a defendant who has failed to appear personally to appear and answer the plaintiff's bill.

Pro confesso /pròw kǝnfésow/. For confessed; as confessed. A term applied to a bill in equity, and the decree founded upon it, where no answer is made to it by the defendant. Under rules practice, this has been replaced by a default for want of prosecution. Fed.R.Civil P. 55(a).

Procreation. The generation of children.

Proctor /próktǝr/. One appointed to manage the affairs of another or represent him in judgment. A procurator, proxy, or attorney. Formerly, an officer of the admiralty and ecclesiastical courts whose duties and business correspond exactly to those of an attorney at law or solicitor in chancery. See also Power of attorney; Procuration; Proxy.

Procuracy /prókyǝrǝsiy/. The writing or instrument which authorizes a procurator to act.

Procuration /pròkyǝréyshǝn/. Agency; proxy; the act of constituting another one's attorney in fact. The act by which one person gives power to another to act in his place, as he could do himself. Action under a power of attorney or other constitution of agency. Indorsing a bill or note "by procuration" is doing it as proxy for another or by his authority. The use of the word procuration (usually, *per procuratione,* or abbreviated to *per proc.* or *p. p.*) on a promissory note by an agent is notice that the agent has but a limited authority to sign.

An *express* procuration is one made by the express consent of the parties. An *implied* or *tacit* procuration takes place when an individual sees another managing his affairs and does not interfere to prevent it. Procurations are also divided into those which contain absolute power, or a general authority, and those which give only a limited power.

Also, the act or offence of procuring women for lewd purposes.

See also Proctor; Procure; Proxy.

Procurator /prókyǝrèytǝr/. In the civil law, a proctor; a person who acts for another by virtue of a procuration. See also Proctor; Procuration.

Procure. To initiate a proceeding; to cause a thing to be done; to instigate; to contrive, bring about, effect, or cause. To persuade, induce, pre-

vail upon, or cause a person to do something. To obtain, as a prostitute, for another. Procure connotes action and means to cause, acquire, gain, get, obtain, bring about, cause to be done. To find or introduce;—said of a broker who obtains a customer. To bring the seller and the buyer together so that the seller has an opportunity to sell. See also Finder; Pander; Procurer.

Procurement. The act of obtaining, attainment, acquisition, bringing about, effecting. See also Procure.

Procurement contract. A government contract with a manufacturer or supplier of goods or machinery or services under the terms of which a sale or service is made to the government. Such contracts, including the bidding process, are governed by government regulations, standard forms, etc. See Federal Acquisition Regulations.

Procurer /prǝkyúrǝr/. One who prevails upon, induces or persuades a person to do something. One who procures for another the gratification of his lusts; a pimp; a panderer. One who solicits trade for a prostitute or lewd woman. One that procures the seduction or prostitution of girls. The offense is punishable by statute. See *e.g.* Model Penal Code, § 251.2.

One who uses means to bring anything about, especially one who does so secretly and corruptly. As regards solicitation of crime, see Solicitation.

Procuring cause. The proximate cause; the cause originating a series of events, which, without break in their continuity, result in the accomplishment of the prime object. The inducing cause; the direct or proximate cause. Substantially synonymous with "efficient cause."

A broker will be regarded as the "procuring cause" of a sale, so as to be entitled to commission, if his or her efforts are the foundation on which the negotiations resulting in a sale are begun. A cause originating a series of events which without break in their continuity result in accomplishment of prime objective of the employment of the broker who is producing a purchaser ready, willing and able to buy real estate on the owner's terms.

See also Producing cause; Proximate cause.

Produce /pró(w)d(y)uws/, *n.* The product of natural growth, labor, or capital. Articles produced or grown from or on the soil, or found in the soil.

Produce /prǝd(y)úws/, *v.* To bring forward; to show or exhibit; to bring into view or notice; as, to present a play, including its presentation in motion pictures. To produce witnesses or documents at trial in obedience to a subpoena (Fed.R. Civil P. 45; Fed.R.Crim.P. 17); or to be compelled to produce materials subject to discovery rules (Fed.R.Civil P. 37; Fed.R.Crim.P. 16).

To make, originate, or yield, as gasoline. To bring to the surface, as oil.

To yield, as revenue. Thus, sums are "produced" by taxation, not when the tax is levied, but when the sums are collected.

Producer. One who produces, brings forth, or generates. Term is commonly used to denote person who raises agricultural products and puts them in condition for the market.

Producer price index. Measure of wholesale price changes issued monthly by U.S. Bureau of Labor Statistics. *Compare* Consumer Price Index.

Producing. Bring about; to cause to happen or take place, as an effect or result.

Producing cause. Respecting broker's commission, is act which, continuing in unbroken chain of cause and effect, produces result. A producing cause of an employee's death for which compensation is sought is that cause which, in a natural and continuous sequence, produces the death, and without which death would not have occurred. A producing cause is an efficient, existing, or contributing cause which, in natural and continuing sequence, produces the injury or damage complained of, if any. *See also* Procuring cause; Proximate cause.

Product. With reference to property, term refers to proceeds; yield; income; receipts; return. Goods produced or manufactured, either by natural means, by hand, or with tools, machinery, chemicals, or the like. Something produced by physical labor or intellectual effort or something produced naturally or as result of natural process as by generation or growth.

Production. Process or act of producing. That which is produced or made; *i.e.* goods. Fruit of labor, as the productions of the earth, comprehending all vegetables and fruits; the productions of intellect, or genius, as poems and prose compositions; the productions of art, as manufactures of every kind.

Production cost report. A report that is used in a process costing system; shows costs and units, classified by department.

Production for commerce. Within Fair Labor Standards Act, includes production of goods which, at time of production, employer, according to normal course of his business, intends or expects to move in interstate commerce immediately following initial sale. Fair Labor Standards Act of 1938, §§ 6, 7; 29 U.S.C.A. §§ 206, 207.

Product liability. Refers to the legal liability of manufacturers and sellers to compensate buyers, users, and even bystanders, for damages or injuries suffered because of defects in goods purchased. A tort which makes a manufacturer liable if his product has a defective condition that makes it unreasonably dangerous to the user or consumer.

Although the ultimate responsibility for injury or damage in a products liability case most frequently rests with the manufacturer, liability may also be imposed upon a retailer, occasionally upon a wholesaler or middleman, a bailor or lessor, and infrequently upon a party wholly outside the manufacturing and distributing process, such as a certifier. This ultimate responsibility may be imposed by an action by the plaintiff against the manufacturer directly, or by a claim for indemnification, asserted by way of a cross-claim or third party claim by the retailer or wholesaler, or others who might be held liable for the injury caused by a defective product. Under modern principles of products liability, and with the elimination of privity requirements in most instances, recovery is no longer limited to the purchaser of the product, or even to a user, but may extend to the non-user; the bystander who is injured or damaged by a defective product, for example. However, the term "products liability" normally contemplates injury or damage caused by a defective product, and if loss occurs as a result of a condition on the premises, or as a result of a service, as distinguished from loss occasioned by a defective product, a products liability claim does not ordinarily arise, even though a product may be involved.

For statutory time limits in bringing products liability actions, *see* Statute *(Statute of repose)*.

See also Economic loss; Enterprise liability; Intended use doctrine; Latent defect; Privity; Strict liability; Warranty.

Product liability insurance. Type of insurance coverage which protects manufacturers and suppliers when claims are made for injuries and damage incurred in the use of their goods or products.

Product market. In antitrust law, the product market includes all other products that can be reasonably substituted by consumers for the product of the business under investigation. The determination of the product market is important in the assessment of the market power of the business.

Pro emptore /pròw em(p)tóriy/. As a purchaser; by the title of a purchaser. A species of usucaption.

Pro facto /pròw fǽktow/. For the fact; as a fact; considered or held as a fact.

Profane. Irreverence toward God or holy things. Writing, speaking, or acting, in manifest or implied contempt of sacred things. That which has not been consecrated.

Profanity. Irreverence towards sacred things; particularly, an irreverent or blasphemous use of the name of God. Vulgar, irreverent, or coarse language. It is a federal offense to utter an obscene, indecent, or profane language on the radio. 18 U.S.C.A. § 1464. *See also* Obscenity.

Profess. To make open declaration of; to make public declaration or avowal.

Profession. A vocation or occupation requiring special, usually advanced, education, knowledge, and skill; *e.g.* law or medical professions. Also refers to whole body of such profession.

The labor and skill involved in a profession is predominantly mental or intellectual, rather than physical or manual.

The term originally contemplated only theology, law, and medicine, but as applications of science and learning are extended to other departments of affairs, other vocations also receive the name, which implies professed attainments in special knowledge as distinguished from mere skill.

Act of professing; a public declaration respecting something. Profession of faith in a religion.

Professional. One engaged in one of learned professions or in an occupation requiring a high level of training and proficiency.

Professional association. Any group of professional people organized to practice their profession together, though not necessarily in corporate or partnership form. A group of professionals organized for education, social activity, lobbying and the like; *e.g.* bar or medical association. *See also* Corporation *(Professional corporation).*

Professional conduct *or* **responsibility.** As regards the legal profession, *see* Canon; Model Rules of Professional Conduct.

Professional corporation. *See* Corporation.

Proffer. To offer or tender, as, the production of a document and offer of the same in evidence.

Proffered evidence. *See* Proffer.

Profit. Most commonly, the gross proceeds of a business transaction less the costs of the transaction; *i.e.* net proceeds. Excess of revenues over expenses for a transaction; sometimes used synonymously with net income for the period. Gain realized from business or investment over and above expenditures.

Profit means accession of good, valuable results, useful consequences, avail, gain, as an office of profit, excess of returns over expenditures or excess of income over expenditure.

The benefit, advantage, or pecuniary gain accruing to the owner or occupant of land from its actual use; as in the familiar phrase "rents, issues and profits," or in the expression "mesne profits."

A division sometimes made of incorporeal hereditaments. Profits are divided into *profits à prendre* and *profits à rendre (q.v.).*

Community of profits. See that title.

Gross profit. The difference between sales and cost of goods sold, but excluding expenses and taxes. *See also* Gross income.

Loss of profits. See that title.

Mesne profits. Intermediate profits; that is, profits which have been accruing between two given periods. Value of use or occupation of land during time it was held by one in wrongful possession and is commonly measured in terms of rents and profits. Thus, after a party has recovered the land itself in an action of ejectment, he frequently brings another action for the purpose of recovering the profits which have been accruing or arising out of the land between the time when his title to the possession accrued or was raised and the time of his recovery in the action of ejectment, and such an action is thence termed an "action for mesne profits."

Net profit. The amount arrived at by deducting from total revenue the cost of goods sold and all expenses. *See also* Net income; Net profits.

Operating profit. The profit arrived at by deducting from sales all expenses attributable to operations but excluding expenses and income related to non-operating activities such as interest payments.

Paper profit. Profit not yet realized as derived from an appreciation in value of an asset not yet sold (*e.g.* gain on an unsold stock).

Profit and loss. The gain or loss arising from goods bought or sold, or from carrying on any other business, the former of which, in bookkeeping, is placed on the creditor's side; the latter on the debtor's side. *See also* Contribution margin; Profit and loss account; Profit and loss statement.

Profit à prendre /prófət à próndər/. Called also "right of common." A right exercised by one person in the soil of another, accompanied with participation in the profits of the soil thereof. A right to take a part of the soil or produce of the land. A right to take from the soil, such as by logging, mining, drilling, etc. The taking (profit) is the distinguishing characteristic from an easement.

Profit à rendre /prófəd à róndər/. Such as is received at the hands of and rendered by another. The term comprehends rents and services.

Surplus profits. Within the meaning of a statute prohibiting the declaration of corporate dividends other than from such profits, means the excess of receipts over expenditures, or net earnings or receipts, or gross receipts, less expenses of operation. Of a corporation, the difference over and above the capital stock, debts, and liabilities.

Undistributed profits. Profits which have not been distributed to the stockholders in the form of dividends though earned by the corporation. *See also* Undistributed profits tax.

Undivided profits. See that title.

Profitability ratios. Ratios that examine an organization's operating success (or lack of success) during an accounting period.

Profit and loss account. A transfer account of all income and expense accounts which is closed into the retained earnings of a corporation or the capital account of a partnership.

Profit and loss statement. A statement showing the income, costs and expenses of a business over a specific period of time; the difference being the income or loss for the period. *See also* Income statement.

Profit center. A responsibility center in which managers are responsible for generating revenues and planning and controlling all expenses.

Profiteering. Taking advantage of unusual or exceptional circumstances to make excessive profits; *e.g.* selling of scarce or essential goods at inflated prices during time of emergency or war. *See* Insider trading.

Profit margin. Sales minus all expenses as a single amount. The ratio of income to sales revenue. Frequently used to mean the ratio of sales minus all operating expenses divided by sales. A high profit margin is desirable as it indicates that a company is receiving a good return on the cost of goods sold. *See also* Operating profit margin.

Profit-sharing plan. A plan established and maintained by an employer to provide for the participation in the profits of the company by the employees or their beneficiaries. In order to qualify for tax benefits, the plan must provide a definite predetermined formula for allocating the contributions made to the plan among the participants and for distributing the funds accumulated under the plan after a fixed number of years, the attainment of a stated age, or upon the prior occurrence of some event such as layoff, illness, disability, retirement, death, or severance of employment. Such plans are regulated by the federal Employee Retirement Income Security Act (ERISA). *See also* Employee Stock Ownership Plan (ESOP).

Qualified profit sharing plan. An employer-sponsored plan that meets the requirements of I.R.C. § 401. If these requirements are met, none of the employer's contributions to the plan will be taxed to the employee until distributed to him or her (§ 402). The employer will be allowed a deduc-

tion in the year the contributions are made (§ 404).

Pro forma /pròw fórmə/. As a matter of form or for the sake of form. Used to describe accounting, financial, and other statements or conclusions based upon assumed or anticipated facts. *See* Pro forma statement.

The phrase "pro forma," in an appealable decree or judgment, usually means that the decision was rendered, not on a conviction that it was right, but merely to facilitate further proceedings.

Pro forma statement. A financial statement showing the forecast (or projected) operating results or impact of a particular transaction.

Program budgeting. An approach to budgeting that relates resource inputs to service outputs.

Progressive tax. A type of graduated tax which applies higher tax rates as the income of the taxpayer increases. *Compare* Regressive tax.

Pro hac vice /pròw hǽk váysiy/. For this turn; for this one particular occasion. For example, an out-of-state lawyer may be admitted to practice in a local jurisdiction for a particular case only.

Prohibit. To forbid by law; to prevent;—not synonymous with "regulate." *See* Injunction.

Prohibited degrees. Those degrees of relationship by consanguinity which are so close that marriage between persons related to each other in any of such degrees is forbidden by law; *e.g.* brother and sister.

Prohibition. Inhibition; interdiction. Act or law prohibiting something, as 18th Amendment to U.S.Const. (1920) prohibited the manufacture, sale, or transportation of intoxicating liquors, except for medicinal purposes (such Prohibition Amendment was repealed by 21st Amendment in 1933).

Writ or process. Prohibition is that process by which a superior court prevents an inferior court or tribunal possessing judicial or quasi-judicial powers from exceeding its jurisdiction in matters over which it has cognizance or usurping matters not within its jurisdiction to hear or determine. A means of restraint on judicial personnel or bodies to prevent usurpation of judicial power, and its essential function is to confine inferior courts to their proper jurisdiction and to prevent them from acting without or in excess of their jurisdiction; it is preventive in nature rather than corrective.

The writ of prohibition is the counterpart of the writ of mandamus.

Prolixity /prowlíksədiy/. The unnecessary and superfluous statement of facts in pleading or in evidence.

Promise. A declaration which binds the person who makes it, either in honor, conscience, or law, to do or forbear a certain specific act, and which gives to the person to whom made a right to expect or claim the performance of some particular thing. A declaration, verbal or written, made by one person to another for a good or valuable consideration, in the nature of a covenant by which the promisor binds himself to do or forbear some act, and gives to the promisee a legal right to demand and enforce a fulfillment. An express undertaking, or agreement to carry a purpose into effect.

An undertaking, however expressed, either that something shall happen, or that something shall not happen, in the future.

A promise is a manifestation of intention to act or refrain from acting in a specified way, so made as to justify a promisee in understanding that a commitment has been made. A promise may be stated in words either oral or written, or may be inferred wholly or partly from conduct. Restatement, Second, Contracts §§ 2, 4.

While a "promise" is sometimes loosely defined as a declaration by any person of his intention to do or forbear from anything at the request or for the use of another, it is to be distinguished, on the one hand, from a mere declaration of intention involving no engagement or assurance as to the future, and, on the other, from "agreement," which is an obligation arising upon reciprocal promises, or upon a promise founded on a consideration.

See also Aleatory promise; Breach of promise; Collateral promise; Conditional promise; Gratuitous promise; Illusory promise; Implied promise; Offer; Raising a promise.

Commercial law. An undertaking to pay and it must be more than an acknowledgment of an obligation. U.C.C. § 3–102(1)(c).

Fictitious promise. Sometimes called "implied promises," or "promises implied in law," occur in the case of those contracts which were invented to enable persons in certain cases to take advantage of the old rules of pleading peculiar to contracts, and which are not now of practical importance.

Illusory promise. A promise in which the promisor does not bind himself to do anything and hence it furnishes no basis for a contract because of the lack of consideration; e.g. a promise to buy whatever goods the promisor chooses to buy.

Mutual promises. Promises simultaneously made by and between two parties; each promise being the consideration for the other.

Naked promise. One given without any consideration, equivalent, or reciprocal obligation, and for that reason not enforceable at law.

New promise. An undertaking or promise, based upon and having relation to a former promise which, for some reason, can no longer be enforced, whereby the promisor recognizes and revives such former promise and engages to fulfill it.

Parol promise. A simple contract; a verbal promise.

Promise implied in fact. Promise implied in fact is merely tacit promise, one which is inferred in whole or in part from expressions other than words by promisor.

Promise implied in law. Promise implied in law is one in which neither words nor conduct of party involved are promissory in form or justify inference of promise and term is used to indicate that party is under legally enforceable duty as he would have been, if he had in fact made promise.

Promise of marriage. A contract mutually entered into by a man and a woman that they will marry each other.

Promise to pay the debt of another. Within the statute of frauds, a promise to pay the debt of another is an undertaking by a person not before liable, for the purpose of securing or performing the same duty for which the party for whom the undertaking is made, continues liable.

Promisee. One to whom a promise has been made.

Promisor. One who makes a promise.

Promissor /prəmísər/. Lat. In the civil law, a promiser; properly the party who undertook to do a thing in answer to the interrogation of the other party, who was called the "stipulator."

Promissory /prómǝs(ò)riy/. Containing or consisting of a promise; in the nature of a promise; stipulating or engaging for a future act or course of conduct.

As to *promissory* Oath; Representation; and Warranty, see those titles.

Promissory estoppel. That which arises when there is a promise which promisor should reasonably expect to induce action or forbearance of a definite and substantial character on part of promisee, and which does induce such action or forbearance, and such promise is binding if injustice can be avoided only by enforcement of promise. Elements of a "promissory estoppel" are a promise clear and unambiguous in its terms, reliance by the party to whom the promise is made, with that reliance being both reasonable and foreseeable, and injury to the party asserting the estoppel as a result of his reliance. See Restatement, Second, Contracts, § 90.

Promissory fraud. A promise to perform made at a time when the promisor has a present intention not to perform. It is a misrepresentation of the promisor's frame of mind and is, for that reason a fact which makes it the basis of an action for deceit. It is sometimes called common law fraud.

Promissory note. A promise or engagement, in writing, to pay a specified sum at a time therein stated, or on demand, or at sight, to a person therein named, or to his order, or bearer. An unconditional written promise, signed by the maker, to pay absolutely and at all events a sum certain in money, either to the bearer or to a person therein designated or his order, at a time specified therein, or at a time which must certainly arrive.

A signed paper promising to pay another a certain sum of money. An unconditional written promise to pay a specified sum of money on demand or at a specified date. Such a note is negotiable if signed by the maker and containing an unconditional promise to pay a sum certain in money either on demand or at a definite time and payable to order or bearer. U.C.C. § 3–104.

Promissory warranty. In insurance law, a promissory warranty is an absolute undertaking by insured, contained in a policy or in an instrument properly incorporated by reference, that certain facts or conditions pertaining to the risk insured against shall continue, or shall be done or omitted.

Promote. To contribute to growth, enlargement, or prosperity of; to forward; to further; to encourage; to advance.

Promoter. One who promotes, urges on, encourages, incites, advances, etc. One promoting a plan by which it is hoped to insure the success of a business, entertainment, etc. venture.

The persons who, for themselves or others, take the preliminary steps to the founding or organization of a corporation or other venture. Those persons who first associate themselves together for the purpose of organizing the company, issuing its prospectus, procuring subscriptions to the stock, securing a charter, etc. Incorporators.

Prompt. To act immediately, responding on the instant.

Prompt delivery. Delivery as promptly as possible, all things considered.

Promptly. Adverbial form of the word "prompt," which means ready and quick to act as occasion demands. The meaning of the word depends largely on the facts in each case, for what is "prompt" in one situation may not be considered such under other circumstances or conditions. To do something "promptly" is to do it without delay and with reasonable speed.

Prompt shipment. Shipment within a reasonable time, all things considered.

Promulgate *or* **promulgation.** /pró(w)məlgeyt/prəmálgeyt/. To publish; to announce officially; to make public as important or obligatory. The formal act of announcing a statute or rule of court. An administrative order that is given to cause an agency law or regulation to become known and obligatory.

Pronounce. To utter formally, officially, and solemnly; to declare or affirm; to declare aloud and in a formal manner. In this sense a court is said to "pronounce" judgment or a sentence.

Proof. The effect of evidence; the establishment of a fact by evidence. Any fact or circumstance which leads the mind to the affirmative or negative of any proposition. The conviction or persuasion of the mind of a judge or jury, by the exhibition of evidence, of the reality of a fact alleged.

The establishment by evidence of a requisite degree of belief concerning a fact in the mind of the trier of fact or the court. Calif. Evidence Code, § 190.

See also Burden of going forward; Burden of persuasion; Burden of producing evidence; Burden of proof; Clear and convincing proof; Clear evidence or proof; Degree of proof; Evidence; Failure of proof; Inference; Offer of proof; Presumption; Reasonable doubt; Testimony.

Evidence and proof distinguished. Proof is the logically sufficient reason for assenting to the truth of a proposition advanced. In its juridical sense it is a term of wide import, and comprehends everything that may be adduced at a trial, within the legal rules, for the purpose of producing conviction in the mind of judge or jury, aside from mere argument; that is, everything that has a probative force intrinsically, and not merely as a deduction from, or combination of, original probative facts. But "evidence" is a narrower term, and includes only such kinds of proof as may be legally presented at a trial, by the act of the parties, and through the aid of such concrete facts as witnesses, records, or other documents. Thus, to urge a presumption of law in support of one's case is adducing proof, but it is not offering evidence. "Belief" is a subjective condition resulting from proof. It is a conviction of the truth of a proposition, existing in the mind, and induced by persuasion, proof, or argument addressed to the judgment. Proof is the result or effect of evidence, while evidence is the medium or means by which a fact is proved or disproved, but the words "proof" and "evidence" may be used interchangeably. Proof is the perfection of evidence; for without evidence there is no proof, although there may be evidence which does not amount to proof; for example, if a man is found murdered at a spot where another has been seen walking but a short time before, this fact will be *evidence* to show that the latter was the murderer, but, standing alone, will be very far from *proof* of it.

Affirmative proof. Evidence establishing the fact in dispute by a preponderance of the evidence. *See also* Preponderance of evidence.

Burden of proof. See that title.

Degree of proof. Refers to effect of evidence rather than medium by which truth is established, and in this sense expressions "preponderance of evidence" and "proof beyond reasonable doubt" are used. *See also* Degree of proof.

Full proof. See Full.

Half proof. See Half.

Negative proof. See Positive proof, below.

Positive proof. Direct or affirmative proof. That which directly establishes the fact in question; as opposed to *negative* proof, which establishes the fact by showing that its opposite is not or cannot be true.

Preliminary proof. See Preliminary.

Proof beyond a reasonable doubt. Such proof as precludes every reasonable hypothesis except that which it tends to support and which is wholly consistent with defendant's guilt and inconsistent with any other rational conclusion. Such is the required standard of proof in criminal cases. *See also* Reasonable doubt. *Compare* Probable cause.

Proof of claim. Statement under oath filed in a bankruptcy proceeding by a creditor in which the creditor sets forth the amount owed and sufficient detail to identify the basis for the claim. Also used in probate proceedings to submit the amount owed by the decedent to the creditor and filed with the court for payment by the fiduciary. See Bankruptcy Code § 501.

Proof of debt. The formal establishment by a creditor of his debt or claim, in some prescribed manner (as, by his affidavit or otherwise), as a preliminary to its allowance, along with others, against an estate or property to be divided, such as the estate of a bankrupt or insolvent, a deceased person or a firm or company in liquidation. *See Proof of claim, above.*

Proof of loss. A formal statement made by the policy-owner to the insurer regarding a loss, intended to give insurer enough information to enable it to determine the extent of its liability under a policy or bond.

Proof of service. Evidence submitted by a process server that he has made service on a defendant in an action. It is also called a return of service. Fed.R.Civil P. 4.

Proof of will. A term having the same meaning as "probate," *(q.v.),* and used interchangeably with it.

Standard of proof. A statement of how convincing the evidence must be in order for a party to comply with his/her burden of proof. The main standards of proof are: proof beyond a reasonable doubt (in criminal cases only), proof by clear and convincing evidence, and proof by a preponderance of the evidence.

Proper. That which is fit, suitable, appropriate, adapted, correct. Reasonably sufficient. Peculiar; naturally or essentially belonging to a person or thing; not common; appropriate; one's own. *See also* Reasonable.

Proper care. That degree of care which a prudent man should use under like circumstances.

Proper evidence. Such evidence as may be presented under the rules established by law and recognized by the courts; *i.e.* admissible evidence; material, relevant evidence. See *e.g.* Fed.R.Evid. 402.

Proper lookout. Duty, as imposed by law on all motorists, that requires motorist to use care, prudence, watchfulness, and attention of an ordinarily prudent person under same or similar circumstances. The duty of seeing that which is clearly visible or which in exercise of ordinary care would be visible, including watchfulness of movements of one's own vehicle as well as other things seen or seeable. Such lookout as person of ordinary care and prudence would have kept under same or similar conditions. *See also* Lookout.

Properly payable. Description of a check implying that the drawee-payor bank can and should pay it, and has a right to charge the amount against the drawer's account even though an overdraft results. See U.C.C. § 4–104(1)(i).

Proper party. As distinguished from a necessary party, is one who has an interest in the subject-matter of the litigation, which may be conveniently settled therein. One without whom a substantial decree may be made, but not a decree which shall completely settle all the questions which may be involved in the controversy and conclude the rights of all the persons who have any interest in the subject of the litigation. See Fed.R.Civil P. 19.

A proper party is one who may be joined in action but whose nonjoinder will not result in dismissal. Those without whom cause might proceed but whose presence will allow judgment more clearly to settle controversy among all parties. *See also* Parties.

Property. That which is peculiar or proper to any person; that which belongs exclusively to one. In the strict legal sense, an aggregate of rights which are guaranteed and protected by the government. The term is said to extend to every species of valuable right and interest. More specifically, ownership; the unrestricted and exclusive right to a thing; the right to dispose of a thing in every legal way, to possess it, to use it, and to exclude every one else from interfering with it. That dominion or indefinite right of use or disposition which one may lawfully exercise over particular things or subjects. The exclusive right of possessing, enjoying, and disposing of a thing. The highest right a man can have to anything; being used to refer to that right which one has to lands or tenements, goods or chattels, which no way depends on another man's courtesy.

The word is also commonly used to denote everything which is the subject of ownership, corporeal or incorporeal, tangible or intangible, visible or invisible, real or personal; everything that has an exchangeable value or which goes to make up wealth or estate. It extends to every species of valuable right and interest, and includes real and personal property, easements, franchises, and incorporeal hereditaments, and includes every invasion of one's property rights by actionable wrong.

Criminal law. "Property" means anything of value, including real estate, tangible and intangible personal property, contract rights, choses-in-action and other interests in or claims to wealth, admission or transportation tickets, captured or domestic animals, food and drink, electric or other power. Model Penal Code, § 223.0. *See also Property of another, below.*

See also Chattel; Community property; Incorporeal property; Intangible property; Interest; Land; Literary property; Lost property; Marital property.

Classification

Property is either: real or immovable; or, personal or movable. Calif.Civil Code, § 657.

Absolute property. In respect to chattels, personal property is said to be "absolute" where a man has, solely and exclusively, the right and also the possession of movable chattels. In the law of wills, a bequest or devise "to be the absolute property" of the beneficiary may pass a title in fee simple. Or it may mean that the property is to be held free from any limitation or condition or free from any control or disposition on the part of others. *See* Fee simple.

Common property. A term sometimes applied to lands owned by a local government and held in trust for the common use of the inhabitants. Property owned by tenants in common. Also property owned jointly by husband and wife under the community property system. *See* Community property, *also Public property, below.*

Community property. See that title.

General property. The right and property in a thing enjoyed by the *general owner. See* Owner.

Intangible property. Property which cannot be touched because it has no physical existence such as claims, interests, and rights. *See also* Intangible asset.

Literary property. See Literary.

Mislaid property. Property which the owner has voluntarily parted with, with the intention of retrieving it later, but which cannot now be found. Does not include intentionally hidden property, and is distinguished from "lost" property which the owner has parted with casually and involuntarily.

Mixed property. Property which is personal in its essential nature, but is invested by the law with certain of the characteristics and features of real property. Heirlooms, fixtures, and title-deeds to an estate are of this nature.

Movable property. Property the location of which can be changed, including things growing on, affixed to, or found in land, and documents although the rights represented thereby have no physical location. "Immovable property" is all other property. Model Penal Code, § 223.0.

Personal property. In broad and general sense, everything that is the subject of ownership, not coming under denomination of real estate. A right or interest in things personal, or right or interest less than a freehold in realty, or any right or interest which one has in things movable.

Generally, all property other than real estate; as goods, chattels, money, notes, bonds, stocks and choses in action generally, including intangible property. It is sometimes designated as personalty when real estate is termed realty. Personal property also can refer to property which is not used in a taxpayer's trade or business or held for the production or collection of income. When used in this sense, personal property could include both realty (*e.g.,* a personal residence) and personalty (*e.g.,* personal effects such as clothing and furniture).

Private property. As protected from being taken for public uses, is such property as belongs absolutely to an individual, and of which he has the exclusive right of disposition. Property of a specific, fixed and tangible nature, capable of being in possession and transmitted to another, such as houses, lands, and chattels.

Property of another. Includes property in which any person other than the actor has an interest which the actor is not privileged to infringe, regardless of the fact that the actor also has an interest in the property and regardless of the fact that the other person might be precluded from civil recovery because the property was used in an unlawful transaction or was subject to forfeiture as contraband. Property in possession of the actor shall not be deemed property of another who has only a security interest therein, even if legal title is in the creditor pursuant to a conditional sales contract or other security agreement. Model Penal Code, § 223.0.

Property tax. See that title.

Public property. This term is commonly used as a designation of those things which are *publici juris (q.v.),* and therefore considered as being owned by "the public," the entire state or community, and not restricted to the dominion of a private person. It may also apply to any subject of property owned by a state, nation, or municipal corporation as such. *See also State property, below.*

Qualified property. Property in chattels which is not in its nature permanent, but may at some times subsist and not at other times; such for example, as the property a man may have in wild animals which he has caught and keeps, and which are his only so long as he retains possession of them. Any ownership not absolute. *See also Special property, below.*

Real property. Land, and generally whatever is erected or growing upon or affixed to land. Also rights issuing out of, annexed to, and exercisable within or about land. A general term for lands, tenements, and hereditaments; property which, on the death of the owner intestate, passes to his heir.

Real or immovable property consists of: Land; that which is affixed to land; that which is incidental or appurtenant to land; that which is immovable by law; except that for the purposes of sale, emblements, industrial growing crops and things attached to or forming part of the land, which are agreed to be severed before sale or under the contract of sale, shall be treated as goods and be governed by the regulating the sales of goods. Calif.Civil Code, § 658.

Separate property. See that title.

Special property. Property of a qualified, temporary, or limited nature; as distinguished from absolute, general, or unconditional property. Such is the property of a bailee in the article bailed, of a sheriff in goods temporarily in his hands under a levy, of the finder of lost goods while looking for the owner, of a person in wild animals which he has caught. *See also Qualified property, above.*

State property. The State is the owner of all land below tide water, and below ordinary high-water mark, bordering upon tide water within the State; of all land below the water of a navigable lake or stream; of all property lawfully appropriated by it to its own use; of all property dedicated to the State; and of all property of which there is no other owner. Calif.Civil Code, § 670. *See also Public property, above.*

Tangible property. All property which is touchable and has real existence (physical) whether it is real or personal.

Unclaimed property. The majority of states have adopted the Uniform Disposition of Unclaimed Property Act.

Property of the debtor. As used in Bankruptcy Code, term includes property of which debtor has possession, either actual or constructive, and it is not limited to property title to which is in the debtor.

Property, plant and equipment. Assets with long lives acquired for use in business operations and not held for resale to customers.

Property right. A generic term which refers to any type of right to specific property whether it is personal or real property, tangible or intangible; *e.g.* professional baseball player has valuable property right in his name, photograph and image, and such right may be saleable by him.

Property settlement. Term as used in divorce parlance is used interchangeably in describing two different bases for division of marital property: (1) based upon agreement of the parties and approval by the court, and (2) based upon an award by the court after trial on the merits. Agreement made between spouses as an incident of a divorce proceeding. Such agreement may contain provisions for division of property owned or acquired by the spouses during the marriage, periodic payments by one of the spouses or a lump sum payment or one time conveyance of property. *See* Equitable distribution; Marital property; Separate property; Separation agreement. *Compare* Post-nuptial agreement; Pre-nuptial agreement.

Property tax. An *ad valorem* tax, usually levied by a city or county government, on the value of real or personal property that the taxpayer owns on a specified date. The tax is generally expressed as a uniform rate per thousand of valuation. *See* Ad valorem tax.

Property torts. Such involve injury or damage to property, real or personal, in contrast to "personal torts" which involve injuries to person, *i.e.,* the body, reputation, or feelings.

Proponent /prəpównənt/. The propounder of a thing. Thus, the proponent of a will is the party who offers it for probate *(q.v.).*

Proportional representation. A method of election which gives representation to minority interests. In connection with elections for political office, the Supreme Court has held that the Constitution does not require proportional representation.

Proportionate /prəpórshənət/. Adjusted to something else according to certain rate of comparative relation. *See* Pro rata.

Proposal. An offer; something proffered. An offer, by one person to another, of terms and conditions with reference to some work or undertaking, or for the transfer of property, the acceptance whereof will make a contract between them. Signification by one person to another of his willingness to enter into a contract with him on the terms specified in the offer.

The initial overture or preliminary statement for consideration by the other party to a proposed agreement. As so used, it is not an offer but it contemplates an offer and hence, its acceptance does not ripen into a contract. *See also* Offer.

Proposition. An offer to do a thing. *See* Offer; Proposal.

Propound. To offer; to propose. An executor or other person is said to propound a will when he takes proceedings for obtaining probate solemn form.

Prop.Reg. An abbreviation for Proposed Regulation (*e.g.* Proposed Treasury Regulation). A Regulation may first be issued in proposed form to give interested parties the opportunity for comment. When and if a Proposed Regulation is finalized, it is designated as a Regulation (abbreviated Reg.).

Propria persona /prówpriyə pərsównə/. *See* In propria persona.

Proprietary, *n.* /prəpráyət(èh)riy/. A proprietor or owner; one who has the exclusive title to a thing; one who possesses or holds the title to a thing in his own right; one who possesses the dominion or ownership of a thing in his own right. The grantees of Pennsylvania and Maryland and their heirs were called the proprietaries of those provinces.

Proprietary, *adj.* /prəpráyət(èh)riy/. Belonging to ownership; owned by a particular person; belonging or pertaining to a proprietor; relating to a certain owner or proprietor.

Proprietary capacity. Term used to describe functions of a city or town when it engages in a business-like venture as contrasted with a governmental function. *See* Proprietary functions, below.

Proprietary capital. In accounting, that account in a sole proprietorship which represents the original investment in addition to accumulated profits.

Proprietary duties. Those duties of a municipality which are not strictly governmental duties. *See also* Governmental duties.

Proprietary functions. Functions which city or town, in its discretion, may perform when considered to be for best interests of its citizens. "Governmental function" has to do with administration of some phase of government, that is to say, dispensing or exercising some element of sovereignty, while "proprietary function" is one designed to promote comfort, convenience, safety and happiness of citizens. *See also* Governmental duties; Governmental functions.

Proprietary information. In trade secret law, information in which the owner has a protectable interest.

Proprietary interest. The interest of an owner of property together with all rights appurtenant thereto such as the right to vote shares of stock and right to participate in managing if the person has a proprietary interest in the shares.

Proprietary lease. Type of lease in cooperative apartment between owner-cooperative and tenant-stockholder.

Proprietary rights. Those rights which an owner of property has by virtue of his ownership. A right customarily associated with ownership, title, and possession and is an interest or right of one who exercises dominion over a thing or property, of one who manages and controls. *See also* Proprietary interest, above.

Proprietor /prəpráyətər/. Owner of proprietorship. One who has the legal right or exclusive title to property, business, etc. In many instances it is synonymous with owner.

Proprietorship. A business which is owned by a person who has either the legal right and exclusive title, or dominion, or the ownership of that business. A business, usually unincorporated, owned and controlled exclusively by one person. Such a business is commonly designated a "sole proprietorship" (*q.v.*).

Pro rata /pròw réytə/. Proportionately; according to a certain rate, percentage, or proportion. According to measure, interest, or liability. According to a certain rule or proportion. For example, if a corporation has ten shareholders each of whom owns 10% of the stock, a pro-rata dividend distribution of $1,000 would mean that each shareholder would receive $100. *See also* Per capita; Pro rate.

Pro rata clause. Such clause commonly used as other insurance provision in automobile liability policy provides that when an insured has other insurance available, company will be liable only for proportion of loss represented by ratio between its policy limit and total limits of all available insurance. Provision in insurance policy to the effect that the insurer will not be liable for a greater proportion of any loss than the amount of the policy bears to the total amount of insurance on the property.

Pro-rata distribution clause. In fire insurance, provision in the policy that the amount of insurance written shall apply to each parcel of property in the proportion which the value of each parcel bears to the total value of all the property insured under the policy.

Pro rate. To divide, share, or distribute proportionally; to assess or apportion pro-rata.

The act of adjusting, dividing or prorating property taxes, interest, insurance premiums, rental income, etc., between buyer and seller proportionately to time of use, or the date of closing. *See also* Pro rata.

Prorogation /pròwrəgéyshən/. Prolonging or putting off to another day. The discontinuation or termination of a session of the legislature, parliament, or the like.

In the civil law, the giving time to do a thing beyond the term previously fixed.

Prorogue. To direct suspension of proceedings of parliament; to terminate a legislative session.

Pro se /pròw síy/. For one's own behalf; in person. Appearing for oneself, as in the case of one who does not retain a lawyer and appears for himself in court.

Prosecute. To follow up; to carry on an action or other judicial proceeding; to proceed against a person criminally. To "prosecute" an action is not merely to commence it, but includes following it to an ultimate conclusion. *See also* Prosecution.

Prosecuting attorney. The name of the public officer who is appointed or elected in each judicial district, circuit, or county, to conduct criminal prosecutions on behalf of the State or people. Federal prosecutors (U.S. Attorneys) represent the United States in prosecuting federal crimes.

A locally elected officer who represents the State in securing indictments and informations and in prosecuting criminal cases. Also called district or county attorney or State's attorney.

See also Prosecutor; State's Attorney; United States Attorney.

Prosecuting witness. The private person upon whose complaint or information a criminal accusation is founded and whose testimony is mainly relied on to secure a conviction at the trial. In a more particular sense, the person who was chiefly injured, in person or property, by the act constituting the alleged crime (as in case of robbery, assault, criminal negligence, bastardy, and the like), and who instigates the prosecution and gives evidence.

Prosecution. A criminal action; a proceeding instituted and carried on by due course of law, before a competent tribunal, for the purpose of determining the guilt or innocence of a person charged with crime. The continuous following up, through instrumentalities created by law, of a person accused of a public offense with a steady and fixed purpose of reaching a judicial determination of the guilt or innocence of the accused.

By an extension of its meaning, "prosecution" is also used to designate the government (state or federal) as the party proceeding in a criminal action, or the prosecutor, or counsel; as when we speak of "the evidence adduced by the prosecution."

The term is also used respecting civil litigation, and includes every step in action, from its commencement to its final determination.

The Fifth Amendment, U.S.Const., requires that all prosecutions for infamous *federal* crimes (*i.e.* federal offenses carrying a term of imprisonment in excess of one year) be commenced by grand jury indictment. This requirement, however, does not apply to *state* prosecutions for such crimes, which may be prosecuted on the basis of an information.

Malicious prosecution. See that title.

Prosecution history estoppel. An equitable tool for determining the permissible scope of patent claims. It limits the scope of patent claims based on arguments and claim amendments made during prosecution to obtain allowance of the patent. This doctrine applies both to claim amendments to overcome rejections based on prior art, and to arguments submitted to obtain the patent. *See also* File wrapper estoppel doctrine.

Prosecutor. One who prosecutes another for a crime in the name of the government. One who instigates the prosecution upon which an accused is arrested or who prefers an accusation against the party whom he suspects to be guilty, as does a district, county, or state's attorney on behalf of the state, or a United States Attorney for a federal district on behalf of the U.S. government. A District Attorney or any other public servant who represents the people in a criminal action. New York Penal Code, § 1.20(31). *See also* Independent counsel; Prosecuting attorney; Special attorney or counsel.

Private prosecutor. One who sets in motion the machinery of criminal justice against a person whom he suspects or believes to be guilty of a crime, by laying an accusation before the proper authorities, and who is not himself an officer of the government. *Compare Public prosecutor, below.*

Public prosecutor. An officer of government (such as a state's attorney or district attorney) whose function is the prosecution of criminal actions, or suits partaking of the nature of criminal actions. *See also* Prosecuting attorney.

Prosecutrix /pròsəkyúwtrəks/. A female prosecutor.

Prosequi /prósəkway/. Lat. To follow up or pursue; to sue or prosecute. *See* Nolle prosequi.

Prospective /prəspéktəv/. In the future; looking forward; contemplating the future.

Prospective damages /prəspéktəv dǽməjəz/. *See* Damages.

Prospective law /prəspéktəv ló/. One applicable only to cases which shall arise after its enactment.

Prospectus. A document published by a corporation, or by persons acting as its agents or assignees, setting forth the nature and objects of an issue of shares, debentures, or other securities created by the company or corporation, the investment or risk characteristics of the security and inviting the public to subscribe to the issue. The principal document of a registration statement required by law to be furnished an investor prior to any purchase. It is the document which is to contain all material facts concerning a company and its operations so that a prospective investor may make an informed decision as to the merit of an investment.

Federal securities laws (15 U.S.C.A. § 77a) require that corporations making public stock offerings file a copy of the prospectus with the SEC and also provide a copy to all prospective purchasers. The content of the prospectus is governed by federal securities laws and regulations.

The term "prospectus" means any prospectus, notice, circular, advertisement, letter, or communication, written or by radio or television, which offers any security for sale or confirms the sale of any security. Securities Act of 1933, § 1; 15 U.S.C.A. § 77b(10).

See also Offering circular; Red herring.

Prostitute. One who permits common indiscriminate sexual activity for hire, in distinction from sexual activity confined exclusively to one person. A person who engages or agrees or offers to engage in sexual conduct with another person in return for a fee. N.Y. Penal Law § 230.00. *See also* Pander.

The word in its most general sense means the act of setting one's self to sale, or of devoting to infamous purposes what is in one's power: as, the prostitution of talents or abilities; the prostitution of the press, etc.

Prostitution. Act of performing, or offering or agreeing to perform a sexual act for hire. Engaging in or agreeing or offering to engage in sexual conduct with another person under a fee arrangement with that person or any other person. Ariz. Crim. Code § 13–3211(5). Includes any lewd act between persons for money or other consideration. Cal. Penal Law § 647(b). Within meaning of statute proscribing prostitution, comprises conduct of all male and female persons who engage in sexual activity as a business.

A person is guilty of prostitution, a petty misdemeanor, if he or she: (a) is an inmate of a house of prostitution or otherwise engages in sexual activity as a business; or (b) loiters in or within view of any public place for the purpose of being hired to engage in sexual activity. Model Penal Code, § 251.2.

See also Mann Act; Pander.

Pro tanto /pròw tǽntow/. For so much; for as much as may be; as far as it goes. Partial payment made on a claim. Commonly used in eminent domain cases to describe a partial payment made for the taking by the government without prejudice to the right of the petitioner to bring action for the full amount that he claims is due.

Protected class. Under Title VII of the Civil Rights Act of 1964, one of the groups the law sought to protect, including groups based on race, sex, national origin, and religion.

Protection. In maritime law, the name of a document generally given by notaries public to sailors and other persons going abroad, in which it is certified that the bearer therein named is a citizen of the United States.

In public commercial law, a system by which a government imposes customs duties upon commodities of foreign origin or manufacture when imported into the country, for the purpose of stimulating and developing the home production of the same or equivalent articles, by discouraging the importation of foreign goods, or by raising the price of foreign commodities to a point at which the home producers can successfully compete with them. *See* Protective tariff.

Protection order. Order issued by court in domestic violence or abuse cases to, for example, protect spouse from physical harm by other spouse or child from abuse by parent(s). Such order may be granted immediately by court in cases where immediate and present danger of violence or abuse is shown. Such emergency orders are granted in ex parte type proceeding and are temporary in duration pending full hearing by court with all involved parties present. See *e.g.* Minn.St. § 518B.01.

Protective committee. A group of security holders or preferred stockholders appointed to protect the interest of their group at a time of liquidation or reorganization of corporation.

Protective custody. The condition of one who is held under authority of law for his own protection as in the case of a material witness whose safety is in jeopardy, or one who is drunk in public though public drunkenness may not be a criminal offense, or of a person who because of mental illness or drug addiction may harm himself or others.

Protective order. Any order or decree of a court whose purpose is to protect a person from further harassment or abusive service of process or discovery; *see e.g.* Fed.R.Civil P. 26(c); Fed.R.Crim.P. 16(d)(1). *See also* Gag order; Protection order.

Protective tariff. A law imposing duties on imports, with the purpose and the effect of discouraging the importation of competitive products of foreign origin, and consequently of stimulating and protecting the home production of the same or equivalent articles.

Protective trust. A species of spendthrift trust *(q.v.)* containing a provision for forfeiture to protect against creditors and voluntary alienation.

Pro tem /pròw tém/. Abbreviation for "pro tempore" which means, literally, for the time being. Hence, one who acts as a substitute on a temporary basis is said to serve pro tem.

Pro tempore /pròw témpəriy/. For the time being; temporarily; provisionally.

Protest. A formal declaration made by a person interested or concerned in some act about to be done, or already performed, whereby he expresses his dissent or disapproval, or affirms the act against his will. The object of such a declaration is generally to save some right which would be lost to him if his implied assent could be made out, or to exonerate himself from some responsibility which would attach to him unless he expressly negatived his assent.

A notarial act, being a formal statement in writing made by a notary under his seal of office, at the request of the holder of a bill or note, in which it is declared that the bill or note described was on a certain day presented for payment (or acceptance), and that such payment or acceptance was refused, and stating the reasons, if any, given for such refusal, whereupon the notary *protests* against all parties to such instrument, and declares that they will be held responsible for all loss or damage arising from its dishonor. It denotes also all the steps or acts accompanying dishonor necessary to charge an indorser.

A protest is a certificate of dishonor made under the hand and seal of a United States consul or a notary public or other person authorized to certify dishonor by the law of the place where dishonor occurs. It may be made upon information satisfactory to such person. U.C.C. § 3–509. *See also* Dishonor.

Protest is a condition on the liability of a drawer or indorser of any draft that on its face appears to be drawn or payable outside of the United States. U.C.C. § 3–501(3).

A formal declaration made by a minority (or by certain individuals) in a legislative body that they dissent from some act or resolution of the body, usually adding the grounds of their dissent. The term, in this sense, refers to such a proceeding in the English House of Lords.

The formal statement, usually in writing, made by a person who is called upon by public authority to pay a sum of money, in which he declares that he does not concede the legality or justice of the claim or his duty to pay it, or that he disputes the amount demanded; the object being to save his right to recover or reclaim the amount, which right would be lost by his acquiescence. Thus, taxes may be paid under "protest."

The name of a paper served on a collector of customs by an importer of merchandise, stating that he believes the sum charged as duty to be excessive, and that, although he pays such sum for the purpose of getting his goods out of the custom-house, he reserves the right to bring an action against the collector to recover the excess.

In maritime law, a written statement by the master of a vessel, attested by a proper judicial officer or a notary, to the effect that damage suffered by the ship on her voyage was caused by storms or other perils of the sea, without any negligence or misconduct on his own part.

Notice of protest. A notice given by the holder of a bill or note to the drawer or indorser that the bill has been protested for refusal of payment or acceptance. U.C.C. § 3–509.

Waiver of protest. As applied to a note or bill, a waiver of protest implies not only dispensing with the formal act known as "protest," but also with that which ordinarily must precede it, viz., demand and notice of non-payment.

Protest fee. Fee charged by banks or other financial agencies when items (such as checks) presented for collection cannot be collected.

Prothonotary /pròwtənówdəriy/pròwθə°/. The title given (in *e.g.* Pennsylvania) to an officer who officiates as principal clerk of some courts.

Protocol /prówtəkòl/. A brief summary of the text of a document. Also, the minutes of a meeting which are generally initialed by the parties present to reflect their assent to the accuracy of the minutes.

A section of the Department of State charged with the preparation of agreements and treaties. Commonly, term refers to the etiquette of diplomacy and the ranking of officials.

Provable. Susceptible of being proved.

Prove. To establish or make certain; to establish a fact or hypothesis as true by satisfactory and sufficient evidence. As used in legal matters and proceedings means to establish, to render or make certain. *See also* Proof.

Provide. To make, procure, or furnish for future use, prepare. To supply; to afford; to contribute.

Provided. The word used in introducing a proviso *(q.v.)*. Ordinarily it signifies or expresses a condition; but this is not invariable, for, according to the context, it may import a covenant, or a limitation or qualification, or a restraint, modification, or exception to something which precedes.

Provided by law. This phrase when used in a constitution or statute generally means prescribed or provided by some statute.

Province. The district into which a country has been divided; as, the province of Quebec in Canada. More loosely, a sphere of activity or a profession such as medicine or law.

Provision. Foresight of the chance of an event happening, sufficient to indicate that any present undertaking upon which its assumed realization might exert a natural and proper influence was entered upon in full contemplation of it as a future possibility.

In commercial law, funds remitted by the drawer of a bill of exchange to the drawee in order to meet the bill, or property remaining in the drawee's hands or due from him to the drawer, and appropriated to that purpose.

Provisional. Temporary; preliminary; tentative; taken or done by way of precaution or *ad interim*.

A term of the check collection process describing payment, credit or other settlement for a check or other item when the person giving the settlement reserves a right, by law or agreement, to recover the payment or credit if the item is not finally paid.

Provisional committee. A committee appointed for a temporary occasion.

Provisional court. A federal court with jurisdiction and powers governed by the order from which it derives its authority. A provisional court established in conquered or occupied territory by military authorities, or the provisional government, is a federal court deriving its existence and all its powers from the federal government.

Provisional government. One temporarily established in anticipation of and to exist and continue until another (more regular or more permanent) shall be organized and instituted in its stead.

Provisional injunction. Term sometimes used for interlocutory or temporary injunction.

Provisional remedy. A remedy provided for present need or for the immediate occasion; one adapted to meet a particular exigency. Particularly, a temporary process available to a plaintiff in a civil action, which secures him against loss, irreparable injury, dissipation of the property, etc., while the action is pending. Such include the remedies of injunction, appointment of a receiver, attachment, or arrest.

Proviso /prəváyzow/. A condition, stipulation, limitation, or provision which is inserted in a deed, lease, mortgage, or contract, and on the performance or nonperformance of which the validity of the instrument frequently depends; it usually begins with the word "provided."

A limitation or exception to a grant made or authority conferred, the effect of which is to declare that the one shall not operate, or the other be exercised, unless in the case provided.

A clause or part of a clause in a statute, the office of which is either to except something from the enacting clause, or to qualify or restrain its generality, or to exclude some possible ground of misinterpretation of its extent.

A "proviso" is used to limit, modify or explain the main part of section of statute to which it is appended. The office of a "proviso" in a statute is to restrict or make clear that which has gone before. A clause engrafted on a preceding enactment for the purpose of restraining or modifying the enacting clause or of excepting something from its operation which would otherwise have been within it.

Exception and proviso distinguished. See Exception.

Provocation. The act of inciting another to do a particular deed. That which arouses, moves, calls forth, causes, or occasions. Such conduct or actions on the part of one person towards another as tend to arouse rage, resentment, or fury in the latter against the former, and thereby cause him to do some illegal act against or in relation to the person offering the provocation. *See also* Procurer.

Provocation which will reduce killing to manslaughter must be of such character as will, in mind of average reasonable man, stir resentment likely to cause violence, obscure the reason, and lead to action from passion rather than judgment. There must be a state of passion without time to cool placing defendant beyond control of his reason. Provocation carries with it the idea of some physical aggression or some assault which suddenly arouses heat and passion in the person assaulted.

Provoke. To excite; to stimulate; to arouse. To irritate, or enrage.

Provost-Marshal. In military law, the officer acting as the head of the military police of any post, camp, city or other place in military occupation, or district under the reign of martial law. He or his assistants may, at any time, arrest and detain for trial, persons subject to military law committing offenses, and may carry into execution any punishments to be inflicted in pursuance of a court martial.

Proximate. Immediate; nearest; direct, next in order. In its legal sense, closest in causal connection. Next in relation to cause and effect.

Proximate cause. That which, in a natural and continuous sequence, unbroken by any efficient intervening cause, produces injury, and without which the result would not have occurred. That which is nearest in the order of responsible causation. That which stands next in causation to the effect, not necessarily in time or space but in causal relation. The proximate cause of an injury is the primary or moving cause, or that which, in a natural and continuous sequence, unbroken by any efficient intervening cause, produces the injury and without which the accident could not have happened, if the injury be one which might be reasonably anticipated or foreseen as a natural consequence of the wrongful act. An injury or damage is proximately caused by an act, or a failure to act, whenever it appears from the evidence in the case, that the act or omission played a substantial part in bringing about or actually causing the injury or damage; and that the injury or damage was either a direct result or a reasonably probable consequence of the act or omission.

The last negligent act contributory to an injury, without which such injury would not have resulted. The dominant, moving or producing cause. The efficient cause; the one that necessarily sets the other causes in operation. The causes that are merely incidental or instruments of a superior or controlling agency are not the proximate causes and the responsible ones, though they may be nearer in time to the result. It is only when the causes are independent of each other that the nearest is, of course, to be charged with the disaster. Act or omission immediately causing or failing to prevent injury; act or omission occurring or concurring with another, which, had it not happened, injury would not have been inflicted.

See also Concurrent causes; Efficient cause; Immediate cause; Legal cause.

Proximate consequence or result. One which succeeds naturally in the ordinary course of things. A consequence which, in addition to being in the train of physical causation, is not entirely outside the range of expectation or probability, as viewed by ordinary men. One ordinarily following from the negligence complained of, unbroken by any independent cause, which might have been reasonably foreseen. One which a prudent and experienced man, fully acquainted with all the circumstances which in fact existed, would, at time of the negligent act, have thought reasonably possible to follow, if it had occurred to his mind. A mere possibility of the injury is not sufficient, where a reasonable man would not consider injury likely to result from the act as one of its ordinary and probable results.

Proximate damages. *See* Damages.

Proximately. Directly or immediately. Pertaining to that which in an ordinary natural sequence produces a specific result, no independent disturbing agency intervening. *See* Proximate; Proximate cause.

Proximity. Kindred between two persons. Quality or state of being next in time, place, causation, influence, etc.; immediate nearness.

Proxy. (Contracted from procuracy.) A person who is substituted or deputed by another to represent him and act for him, particularly in some meeting or public body. An agent representing and acting for principal. Also the instrument containing the appointment of such person.

Written authorization given by one person to another so that the second person can act for the first, such as that given by a shareholder to someone else to represent him and vote his shares at a shareholders' meeting. Depending on the context, proxy may also refer to the grant of authority itself (the appointment), or the document granting the authority (the appointment form). *See also* Health care proxy; Power of attorney; Proxy statement; Voting trust.

Proxy contest. A battle for the control of a firm in which the dissident group seeks the right from the firm's other shareholders to vote those shareholders' shares in favor of the dissident group's slate of directors.

Proxy coupled with an interest. A proxy held by someone with an interest in the shares like a bank who has the shares pledged as security for a loan.

Proxy marriage. A marriage contracted or celebrated through agents acting on behalf of one or both parties. A proxy marriage differs from the more conventional ceremony only in that one or both of the contracting parties are represented by an agent; all the other requirements having been met.

Proxy statement. Information required by SEC to be given stockholders as a prerequisite to solicitation of proxies for a security subject to the requirements of Securities Exchange Act. The purpose of the proxy statement is to provide shareholders with the appropriate information to permit an intelligent decision on whether to permit their shares to be voted as solicited for particular matter at forthcoming stockholders meeting.

Prudence. Carefulness, precaution, attentiveness, and good judgment, as applied to action or conduct. That degree of care required by the exigencies or circumstances under which it is to be exercised. This term, in the language of the law, is commonly associated with Care and Diligence and contrasted with Negligence. See those titles.

Prudent. Sagacious in adapting means to end; circumspect in action, or in determining any line of conduct. Practically wise, judicious, careful, discreet, circumspect, sensible. In defining negligence, practically synonymous with cautious.

Prudent Man Rule. An investment standard. In some states, the law requires that a fiduciary, such as a trustee for pension funds, may invest the trust's or fund's money only in a list of securities designated by the state—the so-called legal list. In other states, the trustee may invest in a security if it is one which a prudent man of discretion and intelligence, who is seeking a reasonable income and preservation of capital, would buy. For example, under New York's "prudent man rule," trustee is bound to employ such diligence and such prudence in care and management of fund as, in general, prudent men of discretion and intelligence in such matters employ in their own like affairs. A federal "prudent man rule" which governs investment of pension funds is found in ERISA § 404(a)(1); 29 U.S.C.A. § 1104(a)(1).

Prurient interest. A shameful or morbid interest in nudity, sex, or excretion. Model Penal Code § 251.4(1). An obsessive interest in immoral and lascivious matters. An excessive or unnatural interest in sex. One of the criteria of obscenity enunciated in Miller v. California, 413 U.S. 15, 93 S.Ct. 2607, 37 L.Ed.2d 419, is whether the material appeals to the "prurient interest" in sex. *See also* Obscene; Obscenity.

P.S. An abbreviation for "Public Statutes;" also for "postscript."

Pseudo /s(y)úwdow/. False, counterfeit, pretended, spurious.

Pseudograph /s(y)úwdəgrǽf/. False writing.

PTI. *See* Previously taxed income; Pre-trial intervention.

Puberty. The earliest age at which persons are capable of begetting or bearing children. In the civil and common law, the age at which one became capable of contracting marriage. It was in boys fourteen, and in girls twelve years.

Public, *n.* The whole body politic, or the aggregate of the citizens of a state, nation, or municipality. The inhabitants of a state, county, or community. In one sense, everybody, and accordingly the body of the people at large; the community at large, without reference to the geographical limits of any corporation like a city, town, or county; the people. In another sense the word does not mean all the people, nor most of the people, nor very many of the people of a place, but so many of them as contradistinguishes them from a few. Accordingly, it has been defined or employed as meaning the inhabitants of a particular place; all the inhabitants of a particular place; the people of the neighborhood. Also, a part of the inhabitants of a community.

Public, *adj.* Pertaining to a state, nation, or whole community; proceeding from, relating to, or affecting the whole body of people or an entire community. Open to all; notorious. Common to all or many; general; open to common use. Belonging to the people at large; relating to or affecting the whole people of a state, nation, or community; not limited or restricted to any particular class of the community.

As to *public* Account; Acknowledgment; Act; Adjuster; Administrator; Agent; Attorney; Auction; Breach; Blockade; Boundary; Business; Capacity; Carrier; Charge; Charity; Company; Corporation; Debt; Document; Domain, Easement; Enemy; Ferry; Fund; Good; Grant; Health; Highway; Holiday; House; Indecent; Institution; Market; Minister; Money; Necessity; Notice; Nuisance; Office; Officer; Peace; Policy; Pond; Property; Prosecutor; Record; Revenue; River; Road; Sale; Seal; Square; Stock; Store; Tax; Trial; Trust; Trustee; Verdict; and War, see those titles.

Public accommodation. Within the meaning of the Civil Rights Act of 1964, which prohibits racial discrimination in such places, it is generally a business establishment, affecting interstate commerce or supported in its activities by State action, which provides lodging, food, entertainment or other services and is open to the public. 42 U.S.C.A. § 2000a(b).

Public accounting. A branch of accounting in which an accountant provides services to all types of persons and enterprises for fees. *See also* Accountant.

Public advocate. One who may or may not be an attorney who purports to represent the public at large in matters of public concern such as utility rates, environmental quality, and other consumer matters. *See also* Ombudsman.

Public agency. A department or agency of government which has official or quasi official status. An administrative body.

Public appointments. Public offices or positions which are to be filled by the appointment of individuals, under authority of law, instead of by election.

Publication. To make public; to make known to people in general; to bring before public; to exhibit, display, disclose or reveal. The act of publishing anything; offering it to public notice, or rendering it accessible to public scrutiny. An advising of the public; a making known of something to them for a purpose. It implies the means of conveying knowledge or notice. *See also* Notice; Proclamation; Publish.

Term is both a business term meaning printing and distribution of written materials and a legal term meaning communication of libelous matter to a third person. *See also Law of libel, below;* and Libel; Utter.

As descriptive of the publishing of laws and ordinances, it means printing or otherwise reproducing copies of them and distributing them in such a manner as to make their contents easily accessible to the public.

Copyright law. The act of making public a book, writing, chart, map, etc.; that is, offering or communicating it to the public by the sale or distribution of copies. Publication, as used in connection with common-law copyrights, is employed to denote those acts of an author or creator which evidence a dedication of his work to public and on which depends the loss of his common-law copyright. *See also* Common-law copyright.

As defined in Copyright Act, "publication" is the distribution of copies or phonorecords of a work to the public by sale or other transfer of ownership, or by rental, lease, or lending. The offering to distribute copies or phonorecords to a group of persons for purposes of further distribution, public performance, or public display, constitutes publication. A public performance or display of a work does not of itself constitute publication. 17 U.S.C.A. § 101.

Law of libel. The act of making the defamatory matter known publicly, of disseminating it, or communicating it to one or more persons (*i.e.* to third person or persons). The reduction of libelous matter to writing and its delivery to any one other than the person injuriously affected thereby. To communicate defamatory words orally or in writing or in print to some third person capable of understanding their defamatory import and in such a way that he did so understand; publication is an essential element of a libel action and, without publication, there is no libel. *See also* Libel.

Law of wills. The formal declaration made by a testator at the time of signing his will that it is his last will and testament. The act or acts of the testator by which he manifests that it is his intention to give effect to the paper as his last will and testament; any communication indicating to the witness that the testator intends to give effect to the paper as his will, by words, sign, motion, or conduct.

Service of process. Under Rules of Civil Procedure, publication of a summons is the process of giving it currency as an advertisement in a newspaper, under the conditions prescribed by law, as a means of giving notice of the suit to a defendant upon whom personal service cannot be made. See *e.g.* New York CPLR § 315. *See also* Service *(Service by publication).*

Public authority. An agency established by government though not a department thereof but subject to some governmental control, *e.g.* Mass. Port Authority.

Public building. One of which the possession and use, as well as the property in it, are in the public. Any building held, used, or controlled exclusively for public purposes by any department or branch of government, state, county, or municipal, without reference to the ownership of the building or of the realty upon which it is situated. A building belonging to or used by the public for the transaction of public or quasi public business.

Public character. An individual who asks for and desires public recognition, such as a political figure, statesman, author, artist, or inventor. *See also* Public figure.

Public contract. Any contract in which there are public funds provided though private persons may perform the contract and the subject of the contract may ultimately benefit private persons.

Public controversy. A "public controversy," in which a person must have voluntarily involved himself in order to qualify as a public figure for purposes of a libel or slander action, is not simply a matter of interest to the public but must be a real dispute, the outcome of which affects the general public or some segment of it in an appreciable way.

Public convenience and necessity. The common criterion used in public utility matters when a board or agency is faced with a petition for action at the request of the utility. In a statute requiring the issuance of a certificate of public convenience and necessity by the Public Utilities Commission for the operation of a public transportation line, "convenience" is not used in its colloquial sense as synonymous with handy or easy of access, but in accord with its regular meaning of suitable and fitting, and "public convenience" refers to something fitting or suited to the public need. *See also* Public utility.

Public corporations. An artificial person (*e.g.* municipality or a government corporation) created for the administration of public affairs. Unlike a private corporation it has no protection against legislative acts altering or even repealing its charter. Instrumentalities created by state, formed and owned by it in public interest, supported in whole or part by public funds, and governed by managers deriving their authority from state. A public corporation is an instrumentality of the state, founded and owned in the public interest, supported by public funds and governed by those deriving their authority from the state.

Term is also commonly used to distinguish a corporation whose stock is owned and traded by the public from a corporation with closely held shares (*i.e.* close or private corporation).

See also Municipal corporation.

Public defender. An attorney appointed by a court or employed by a government agency whose work consists primarily in defending indigent defendants in criminal cases. Federal Public Defender Organizations and Community Defender Organizations are provided for under 18 U.S.C.A. § 3006A. Most states also have public defender programs. *See also* Counsel, right to; Legal aid; Legal Services Corporation.

Public domain. Land and water in possession of and owned by the United States and the states individually, as distinguished from lands privately owned by individuals or corporations. *See also* Public lands.

Copyright law. Public ownership status of writings, documents, or publications that are not protected by copyrights.

Public entity. Public entity includes a nation, state, county, city and county, city, district, public authority, public agency, or any other political subdivision or public corporation, whether foreign or domestic. Calif.Evid.Code.

Public exchange offer. *See* Offering.

Public figure. For purposes of determining standard to be applied in defamation action, term includes artists, athletes, business people, dilettantes, and anyone who is famous or infamous because of who he is or what he has done. Public figures, for libel purposes, are those who have assumed roles of special prominence in society; commonly, those classed as public figures have thrust themselves to forefront of particular public controversies in order to influence resolution of issues involved. Persons so classified are required to prove actual notice to recover in libel actions.

In determining whether plaintiff in libel action is "public figure" required to show "actual malice" of publisher or broadcaster, it is preferable to look to nature and extent of his participation in particular controversy giving rise to the defamation, and he should not be deemed public personality for all aspects of his life in absence of clear evidence of general fame or notoriety in community and pervasive involvement in affairs of society. *See* Libel.

For right of privacy action purposes, includes anyone who has arrived at position where public attention is focused upon him as a person. *See* Invasion of privacy; Privacy, right of.

Public funds. Moneys belonging to government, or any department of it, in hands of public official.

Public hearing. Public hearing before any tribunal or body means right to appear and give evidence and also right to hear and examine witnesses whose testimony is presented by opposing parties.

Public interest. Something in which the public, the community at large, has some pecuniary interest, or some interest by which their legal rights or liabilities are affected. It does not mean anything so narrow as mere curiosity, or as the interests of the particular localities, which may be affected by the matters in question. Interest shared by citizens generally in affairs of local, state or national government.

If by public permission one is making use of public property and he chances to be the only one with whom the public can deal with respect to the use of that property, his business is affected with a public interest which requires him to deal with the public on reasonable terms. The circumstances which clothe a particular kind of business with a "public interest," as to be subject to regulation, must be such as to create a peculiarly close relation between the public and those engaged in it and raise implications of an affirmative obligation on their part to be reasonable in dealing with the public. One does not devote his property or business to a public use, or clothe it with a public interest, merely because he makes commodities for and sells to the public in common callings such as those of the butcher, baker, tailor, etc. A business is not affected with a public interest merely because it is large, or because the public has concern in respect of its maintenance, or derives benefit, accommodation, ease, or enjoyment from it.

Public invitee. A public invitee to whom owner of property owes duty to exercise ordinary care for his safety is person who is invited to enter or remain on land as member of public for purpose for which land is held open to public. *See also* Business *(Business invitee)*; Invitee.

Public lands. The general public domain; unappropriated lands; lands belonging to the United States and which are subject to sale or other disposal under general laws, and not reserved or held back for any special governmental or public purpose.

Public land system. Legal descriptions of land by reference to the public land survey.

Public law. A general classification of law, consisting generally of constitutional, administrative, criminal, and international law, concerned with the organization of the state, the relations between the state and the people who compose it, the responsibilities of public officers to the state, to each other, and to private persons, and the relations of states to one another. An act which relates to the public as a whole. It may be (1) general (applying to all persons within the jurisdiction), (2) local (applying to a geographical area), or (3) special (relating to an organization which is charged with a public interest).

That portion of law that defines rights and duties with either the operation of government, or the relationships between the government and individuals, associations, and corporations.

That branch or department of law which is concerned with the state in its political or sovereign capacity, including constitutional and administrative law, and with the definition, regulation, and enforcement of rights in cases where the state is regarded as the subject of the right or object of the duty,—including criminal law and criminal procedure,—and the law of the state, considered in its *quasi* private personality, *i.e.,* as capable of holding or exercising rights, or acquiring and dealing with property, in the character of an individual. That portion of law which is concerned with political conditions; that is to say, with the powers, rights, duties, capacities, and incapacities which are peculiar to political superiors, supreme and subordinate. In one sense, a designation given to international law, as distinguished from the laws of a particular nation or state. In another sense, a law or statute that applies to the people generally of the nation or state adopting or enacting it, is denominated a public law, as contradistinguished from a private law, affecting only an individual or a small number of persons.

See also General law. *Compare* Private bill; Private law; Special law.

Public liability insurance. Type of insurance coverage which protects against claims arising from the conduct, property and agents of the insured and which idemnifies against loss arising from liability.

Publicly. Openly. In public, well known, open, notorious, common, or general, as opposed to private, secluded, or secret.

Publicly held. Corporation whose stock is held by and available to the public. Shares of publicly held corporations are usually traded on a securities exchange or over-the-counter. *Compare* Corporation *(Close or closely held Corporation).*

Publicly-traded. Securities that can be traded in a public market, such as a stock market. *See* Publicly held.

Public nuisance. A condition dangerous to health, offensive to community moral standards, or unlawfully obstructing the public in the free use of public property. Any unreasonable interference with rights common to all members of community in general and encompasses public health, safety, peace, morals or convenience. It is one affecting rights enjoyed by citizens as part of public and must affect a considerable number of people or an entire community or neighborhood; although extent of damage may be unequal. *Compare* Private nuisance.

Public offense. An act or omission forbidden by law, and punishable as by law provided. Term used to describe a crime as distinguished from an infringement of private rights. A public offense, the commission of which authorizes private person to arrest another, includes misdemeanors. *See* Crime.

Public offering. *See* Offering.

Public office. Essential characteristics of "public office" are: (1) authority conferred by law, (2) fixed tenure of office, and (3) power to exercise some portion of sovereign functions of government; key element of such test is that "officer" is carrying out sovereign function. Essential elements to establish public position as "public office" are: position must be created by constitution, legislature, or through authority conferred by legislature, portion of sovereign power of government must be delegated to position, duties and powers must be defined, directly or impliedly, by legislature or through legislative authority, duties must be performed independently without control of superior power other than law, and position must have some permanency and continuity.

Public official. A person who, upon being issued a commission, taking required oath, enters upon, for a fixed tenure, a position called an office where he or she exercises in his or her own right some of the attributes of sovereign he or she serves for benefit of public. The holder of a public office though not all persons in public employment are public officials, because public official's position requires the exercise of some portion of the sovereign power, whether great or small.

Public passage. A right, subsisting in the public, to pass over a body of water, whether the land under it be public or owned by a private person. This term is synonymous with public highway, with this difference: by the latter is understood a right to pass over the land of another; by the former is meant the right of going over the water which is on another's land.

Public place. A place to which the general public has a right to resort; not necessarily a place devoted solely to the uses of the public, but a place which is in point of fact public rather than private, a place visited by many persons and usually accessible to the neighboring public (*e.g.* a park or public beach). Also, a place in which the public has an interest as affecting the safety, health, morals, and welfare of the community. A place exposed to the public, and where the public gather together or pass to and fro.

Public policy. Community common sense and common conscience, extended and applied throughout the state to matters of public morals, health, safety, welfare, and the like; it is that general and well-settled public opinion relating to man's plain, palpable duty to his fellowmen, having due regard to all circumstances of each particular relation and situation.

Public policy doctrine. Doctrine whereby a court may refuse to enforce contracts that violate law or public policy. Invoked, for example, to preclude the contractually authorized termination of an employee who refuses to participate in a violation of law. *See* Whistle-blower Acts.

Public policy limitation. A concept developed by the courts precluding an income tax deduction for certain expenses related to activities deemed to be contrary to the public welfare. In this connection, Congress has incorporated into the Internal Revenue Code specific disallowance provisions covering such items as illegal bribes, kickbacks, and fines and penalties. I.R.C. §§ 162(c) and (f).

Public purpose. In the law of taxation, eminent domain, etc., this is a term of classification to distinguish the objects for which, according to settled usage, the government is to provide, from those which, by the like usage, are left to private interest, inclination, or liberality. The constitutional requirement that the purpose of any tax, police regulation, or particular exertion of the power of eminent domain shall be the convenience, safety, or welfare of the entire community and not the welfare of a specific individual or class of persons. "Public purpose" that will justify expenditure of public money generally means such an activity as will serve as benefit to community as a body and which at same time is directly related function of government.

The term is synonymous with governmental purpose. As employed to denote the objects for which taxes may be levied, it has no relation to the urgency of the public need or to the extent of the public benefit which is to follow; the essential requisite being that a public service or use shall affect the inhabitants as a community, and not merely as individuals. A public purpose or public business has for its objective the promotion of the public health, safety, morals, general welfare, security, prosperity, and contentment of all the inhabitants or residents within a given political division, as, for example, a state, the sovereign powers of which are exercised to promote such public purpose or public business.

Public record. Public records are those records which a governmental unit is required by law to keep or which it is necessary to keep in discharge of duties imposed by law; *e.g.* records of land transactions kept at county court house; records of court cases kept by clerk of court. Elements essential to constitute a public record are that it be a written memorial, that it be made by a public officer, and that the officer be authorized by law to make it. A record is a "public record" within

purview of statute providing that books and records required by law to be kept by county clerk may be received in evidence in any court if it is a record which a public officer is required to keep and if it is filed in such a manner that it is subject to public inspection. For purposes of right-to-know law, includes decisions which establish, alter, or deny rights, privileges, immunities, duties, or obligations. *See also* Record.

Public safety. A state may exercise its police power (derivatively, a city or town) by enacting laws for the protection of the public from injury and dangers.

Public sale. Sale at auction of property upon notice to public of such. May result from *e.g.* tax foreclosure. *See also* Sheriff's sale.

Public service. A term applied to the objects and enterprises of certain kinds of corporations, which specially serve the needs of the general public or conduce to the comfort and convenience of an entire community, such as railroad, gas, water, and electric light companies; and companies furnishing public transportation. A public service or quasi public corporation is one private in its ownership, but which has an appropriate franchise from the state to provide for a necessity or convenience of the general public, incapable of being furnished by private competitive business, and dependent for its exercise on eminent domain or governmental agency. It is one of a large class of private corporations which on account of special franchises conferred on them owe a duty to the public which they may be compelled to perform. *See also* Public corporations.

Public service commission. A board or commission created by the legislature to exercise power of supervision or regulation over public utilities or public service corporations. An administrative agency established by the State legislature to regulate rates and services of electric, gas, telephone, and other public utilities. Such a commission is a legal, administrative body, provided for the administration of certain matters within the police power, with power to make regulations as to certain matters when required for the public safety and convenience, and to determine facts on which existing laws shall operate.

Public service corporation. A utility company privately owned but regulated by the government. It may sell gas, water or electricity but its rates are established by the state. It may be a broadcasting company. *See also* Public convenience and necessity; Public utility.

Public trial. Term as contemplated by Constitution (Amend. VI) is a trial which is not secret; one that the public is free to attend. To a great extent, it is a relative term and its meaning depends largely on circumstances of each particular case. Court session which is "public" is also "open", and, therefore, under normal conditions, a "public trial" is one which is open to general public at all times.

Although the right of public access to criminal trials is of constitutional stature, it is not absolute. However, the circumstances under which the press and public can be barred from a criminal trial are limited. Where the state attempts to deny the right of access in order to inhibit the disclosure of sensitive information, it must be shown that the denial is necessitated by a compelling governmental interest and is narrowly tailored to serve that interest.

Public trust. *See* Charitable trust; Trust.

Public trust doctrine. Provides that submerged and submersible lands are preserved for public use in navigation, fishing and recreation and state, as trustee for the people, bears responsibility of preserving and protecting the right of the public to the use of the waters for those purposes.

Public trustee. County official who is appointed to act for the public in administering deeds of trust.

Public use. *Eminent domain.* The constitutional and statutory basis for taking property by eminent domain. For condemnation purposes, "public use" is one which confers some benefit or advantage to the public; it is not confined to actual use by public. It is measured in terms of right of public to use proposed facilities for which condemnation is sought and, as long as public has right of use, whether exercised by one or many members of public, a "public advantage" or "public benefit" accrues sufficient to constitute a public use.

Public use, in constitutional provisions restricting the exercise of the right to take private property in virtue of eminent domain, means a use concerning the whole community as distinguished from particular individuals. But each and every member of society need not be equally interested in such use, or be personally and directly affected by it; if the object is to satisfy a great public want or exigency, that is sufficient. The term may be said to mean public usefulness, utility, or advantage, or what is productive of general benefit. It may be limited to the inhabitants of a small or restricted locality, but must be in common, and not for a particular individual. The use must be a needful one for the public, which cannot be surrendered without obvious general loss and inconvenience. A "public use" for which land may be taken defies absolute definition for it changes with varying conditions of society, new appliances in the sciences, changing conceptions of scope and functions of government, and other differing circumstances brought about by an increase in population and new modes of communication and transportation.

See also Condemnation; Eminent domain.

Patent law. Within statute providing that patent is invalid if invention was in "public use" more than one year prior to date of application for patent is defined as any nonsecret use of a completed and operative invention in its natural and intended way. In patent law, a public use is entirely different from a use by the public. If an inventor allows his machine to be used by other persons generally, either with or without compensation, or if it is, with his consent, put on sale for such use, then it will be in "public use" and on public sale.

Public utility. A privately owned and operated business whose services are so essential to the general public as to justify the grant of special franchises for the use of public property or of the right of eminent domain, in consideration of which the owners must serve all persons who apply, without discrimination. It is always a virtual monopoly.

A business or service which is engaged in regularly supplying the public with some commodity or service which is of public consequence and need, such as electricity, gas, water, transportation, or telephone or telegraph service. Any agency, instrumentality, business industry or service which is used or conducted in such manner as to affect the community at large, that is, which is not limited or restricted to any particular class of the community. The test for determining if a concern is a public utility is whether it has held itself out as ready, able and willing to serve the public. The term implies a public use of an article, product, or service, carrying with it the duty of the producer or manufacturer, or one attempting to furnish the service, to serve the public and treat all persons alike, without discrimination.

Public Utility Holding Company Act. Federal statute enacted in 1935 to protect public, investors and consumers from economic effect of complex, unwieldy and dishonest organization of public utilities and particularly from effect of false, misleading and irresponsible security advertising. 15 U.S.C.A. §§ 79–79Z.

Public Vessels Act. Federal law which provides for libel in personam against the United States or a petition impleading the United States for damages caused by public vessels of the United States. 46 U.S.C.A. § 781–790.

Public way. *See* Highway *(Public highway).*

Public welfare. The prosperity, well-being, or convenience of the public at large, or of a whole community, as distinguished from the advantage of an individual or limited class. It embraces the primary social interests of safety, order, morals, economic interest, and non-material and political interests. In the development of our civic life, the definition of "public welfare" has also developed until it has been held to bring within its purview regulations for the promotion of economic welfare and public convenience.

Publish. To make public; to circulate; to make known to people in general. To issue; to put into circulation. To utter; to present (*e.g.* a forged instrument) for payment. To declare or assert, directly or indirectly, by words or actions, that a forged instrument is genuine. An advising of the public or making known of something to the public for a purpose. *See also* Publication; Utter.

Publisher. One who by himself or his agent makes a thing publicly known. One whose business is the manufacture and sale of books, pamphlets, magazines, newspapers, or other literary productions. One who publishes, especially one who issues, or causes to be issued, from the press, and offers for sale or circulation matter printed, engraved, or the like.

P.U.C. Public Utilities Commission.

PUD. Planned Unit Development. In zoning, a device which has as its goal a self-contained mini-community, built within a zoning district, under density and use rules controlling the relation of private dwellings to open space, of homes to commercial establishments, and of high income dwellings to low and moderate income housing. *See* Planned unit development.

Pudicity /pyuwdísətiy/. Chastity; purity; continence; modesty; the abstaining from all unlawful carnal commerce or connection.

Puffer. A person employed by the owner of property which is sold at auction to attend the sale and run up the price by making spurious bids. *See also* Puffing.

Puffing. An expression of opinion by seller not made as a representation of fact. Exaggeration by a salesperson concerning quality of goods (not considered a legally binding promise); usually concerns opinions rather than facts. Advertising which merely states in general terms that advertiser's product is superior is only "puffing" and is not actionable in action by competitor.

Term also describes secret bidding at auction by or on behalf of seller.

Pullman abstention. This doctrine allows federal courts to stay proceedings before it in order to provide state courts opportunity to settle underlying, unsettled questions of state law, thus avoiding possibility of federal court's unnecessarily deciding constitutional questions.

Punishable. Deserving of or capable or liable to punishment; capable of being punished by law or right. *See* Criminal.

Punishment. Any fine, penalty, or confinement inflicted upon a person by the authority of the law and the judgment and sentence of a court, for some crime or offense committed by him, or for his omission of a duty enjoined by law. A deprivation of property or some right. But does not include a civil penalty redounding to the benefit of an individual, such as a forfeiture of interest. *See also* Sentence.

Cruel and unusual punishment. As prohibited by Eighth Amendment, is such punishment as would amount to torture or barbarity, and any cruel and degrading punishment not known to the common law, and also any punishment so disproportionate to the offense as to shock the moral sense of the community. Punishment which is excessive for the crime committed is cruel and unusual. Such punishment cannot be defined with specificity; it is flexible and tends to broaden as society tends to pay more regard to human decency and dignity and becomes, or likes to think that it becomes, more humane. The death penalty is not per se cruel and unusual punishment within the prohibition of the 8th Amendment, U.S.Const., but states must follow strict safeguards in the sentencing of one to death.

The fundamental respect for humanity underlying the Eighth Amendment requires consideration of the character and record of the individual offender and the circumstances of the particular offense as a constitutionally indispensable part of the process of inflicting the penalty of death.

See also Capital (*Capital punishment*); Corporal punishment; Excessive punishment; Hard labor; Penalty; Sentence.

Cumulative punishment. An increased punishment inflicted for a second or third conviction of the same offense, under the statutes relating to habitual criminals. To be distinguished from a "cumulative sentence," as to which *see* Sentence.

Infamous punishment. Punishment by imprisonment, particularly in a penitentiary. Sometimes, imprisonment at hard labor regardless of the place of imprisonment.

Punitive. Relating to punishment; having the character of punishment or penalty; inflicting punishment or a penalty.

Punitive damages. *See* Damages.

Punitive statute. One which creates forfeiture or imposes penalty.

Pur /pór/púr/. L. Fr. By or for. Used both as a separable particle, and in the composition of such words as "purparty," "purlieu."

Pur autre vie /pàr ó(w)tra váy/pùr ówtra víy/. For (or during) the life of another. An estate *pur autre vie* is an estate in lands which a person holds for the life of another person.

Pur cause de vicinage /pàr kóz də vəsáynəj/pùr kówz də visinázh/. By reason of neighborhood. *See* Common.

Purchase. Transmission of property from one person to another by voluntary act and agreement, founded on a valuable consideration. To own by paying or by promising to pay an agreed price which is enforceable at law. In a technical and broader meaning relative to land, generally means the acquisition of real estate by any means whatever except by descent.

Includes taking by sale, discount, negotiation, mortgage, pledge, lien, issue or re-issue, gift or any other voluntary transaction creating an interest in property. U.C.C. § 1–201(32). The term "purchase" includes any contract to purchase or otherwise acquire. Securities Exchange Act, § 3.

Words of purchase. Words which denote the person who is to take the estate. Thus, if a person grants land to A. for twenty-one years, and after the determination of that term to A.'s heirs, the word "heirs" does not denote the duration of A.'s estate, but the person who is to take the remainder on the expiration of the term, and is therefore called a "word of purchase."

Purchase agreement. An agreement between a buyer and seller of property, setting forth, in general, the price and terms of the sale. A sales agreement or contract to sell. *See also* Buy and sell agreement.

Purchase-and-sale. A method of securities distribution in which the securities firm purchases the securities from the issuer for its own account at a stated price and then resells them—as contrasted with a best-efforts sale. *See also* Offering.

Purchase method of accounting. A method of accounting for mergers in which the total value paid or exchanged for the acquired firm's assets is recorded on the acquiring firm's books. Any difference between the fair market value of the assets acquired and the purchase price is recorded as goodwill.

Purchase money. The actual money paid in cash or check initially for the property while the balance may be secured by a mortgage and note calling for periodic payments. *See also* Earnest money.

As used with reference to part performance under statute of frauds, comprehends consideration, whether it be money or property or services, for which lands are to be conveyed.

Purchase money mortgage. A mortgage or security device taken back to secure the performance of an obligation incurred in the purchase of the property. A "purchase money" security interest for personal property is controlled by Article 9 of the Uniform Commercial Code. *See also* Mortgage; Purchase money security interest.

Purchase money resulting trust. Such ordinarily arises when the purchase price of property is paid by one person and at his or her discretion the vendor transfers the property to another, who is deemed to hold the property in trust for the person furnishing the consideration. When one person furnishes the money for the purchase of property title to which is to be taken in the name of another, the party furnishing the funds is the equitable owner under a purchase money resulting trust. It is not necessary that he furnish the entire purchase price, but he must intend to acquire an interest.

Purchase money security interest. One which is taken or retained by seller of item to secure its price or taken by person who advances funds to enable one to acquire rights in collateral. A security interest is a "purchase money security interest" to the extent that it is: (a) taken or retained by the seller of the collateral to secure all or part of its price; or (b) taken by a person who by making advances or incurring an obligation gives value to enable the debtor to acquire rights in or the use of collateral if such value is in fact so used. U.C.C. § 9–107.

Purchase order. Document authorizing a seller to deliver goods with payment to be made later. A written authorization calling on a vendor or supplier to furnish goods to the person ordering such. It constitutes an offer which is accepted when the vendor supplies the quantity and quality ordered.

Purchase price. Price agreed upon as a consideration for which property or goods are sold and purchased.

Purchaser. One who acquires real property in any other mode than by descent. One who acquires either real or personal property by buying it for a price in money; a buyer; vendee. One who has contracted to purchase property or goods. Also, a successful bidder at judicial sale. A person who orders and pays for goods when the sale is for cash or who is legally obligated to pay for them if the sale is on credit. Term may be employed in broad sense to include anyone who obtains title otherwise than by descent and distribution but is more commonly used to refer to a vendee or buyer who has purchased property for valuable consideration.

One who takes by purchase which includes taking by sale, discount, negotiation, mortgage, pledge, lien, issue or re-issue, gift, or any other voluntary transaction creating an interest in property. U.C.C. § 1–201(32), (33).

The term "purchaser" means a person who, for adequate and full consideration in money or money's worth, acquires an interest (other than a lien or security interest) in property which is valid under local law against subsequent purchasers without actual notice. I.R.C. § 6323(h).

Transferee of a voluntary transfer, and includes immediate or mediate transferee of such a transferee. Bankruptcy Code § 101.

Bona fide purchaser. *See* Bona fide.

Innocent purchaser. One who acquires title to property without knowledge of any defect in the title. *See also* Innocent purchaser.

Purchaser for value. One who pays consideration for property or goods bought.

Purchases journal. A special journal used to record purchases of merchandise on account.

Pure. Absolute; complete; simple; unmixed; unqualified. Free from conditions or restrictions, as in the phrases pure charity, pure debt, pure obligation, pure plea, pure villenage, as to which see the nouns. *See also* Purity.

Pure accident. Implies that accident was caused by some unforeseen and unavoidable event over which neither party to the action had control, and excludes the idea that it was caused by carelessness or negligence of defendant. Unavoidable accident has been held to be synonymous. *See* Accident; Act of God.

Pure race statute. In some states, the first purchaser of real estate to record regardless of notice has the best claim to title and hence it is described as a race to the registry of deeds or other office for the recording of deeds and instruments of conveyance of real property. *See also* Recording acts.

Purge. To cleanse; to clear. To clear or exonerate from some charge or imputation of guilt, or from a contempt.

Purity. Within food adulteration statute is freedom from extraneous matter or anything debasing or contaminating. *See also* Pure.

Purport, n. Meaning; import; substantial meaning; substance; legal effect. The "purport" of an instrument means the substance of it as it appears on the face of the instrument, and is distinguished from "tenor," which means an exact copy.

Purport, v. To convey, imply, or profess outwardly; to have the appearance of being, intending, claiming, etc.

Purpose. That which one sets before him to accomplish or attain; an end, intention, or aim, object, plan, project. Term is synonymous with ends sought, an object to be attained, an intention, etc.

Purposely. Intentionally; designedly; consciously; knowingly. Act is done "purposely" if it is willed, is product of conscious design, intent or plan that it be done, and is done with awareness of probable consequences. A person acts purpose-ly with respect to a material element of an offense when: (i) if the element involves the nature of his conduct or a result thereof, it is his conscious object to engage in conduct of that nature or to cause such a result; and (ii) if the element involves the attendant circumstances, he is aware of the existence of such circumstances or he believes or hopes that they exist. Model Penal Code, § 2.02.

Purpresture /pərpréstyər/. An encroachment upon public rights and easements by appropriation to private use of that which belongs to public. An inclosure by a private party of a part of that which belongs to and ought to be open and free to the enjoyment of the public at large. It is not necessarily a public nuisance. A public nuisance must be something which subjects the public to some degree of inconvenience or annoyance; but a purpresture may exist without putting the public to any inconvenience whatever.

Purse. Some valuable thing, offered by a person for the doing of something by others; prize; premium. Sum of money available to winner(s) of contest or event.

Pursuant. A following after or following out. To execute or carry out in accordance with or by reason of something. To do in consequence or in prosecution of anything. "Pursuant to" means "in the course of carrying out: in conformance to or agreement with: according to" and, when used in a statute, is a restrictive term.

Pursue. To follow, prosecute, or enforce a matter judicially, as a complaining party. To pursue the practice of any profession or business, contemplates a course of business or professional practice, and not single isolated acts arising from unusual circumstances.

Pursuer. One who pursues; one who follows in order to overtake.

Pursuit. That which one engages in as an occupation, trade, or profession; that which is followed as a continued or at least extended and prolonged employment. Activity that one pursues or engages in seriously and continually or frequently as vocation or profession or as an avocation. To follow or chase in order to apprehend or overtake. *See also* Fresh pursuit.

Pursuit of happiness. As used in constitutional law, this right includes personal freedom, freedom of contract, exemption from oppression or invidious discrimination, the right to follow one's individual preference in the choice of an occupation and the application of his energies, liberty of conscience, and the right to enjoy the domestic relations and the privileges of the family and the home. The right to follow or pursue any occupation or profession without restriction and without having any burden imposed upon one that is not imposed upon others in a similar situation. While included as one of the inalienable rights in the Declaration of Independence, such right is not included in the U.S. Constitution.

Purview. Enacting part of a statute, in contradistinction to the preamble. That part of a statute commencing with the words "Be it enacted," and continuing as far as the repealing clause; and hence, the design, contemplation, purpose, or scope of the act.

Pusher. Person who sells illicit drugs. See *e.g.* 21 U.S.C.A. § 841.

Put. An option permitting its holder to sell a certain stock or commodity at a fixed price for a stated quantity and within a stated period. Such a right is purchased for a fee paid the one who agrees to accept the stock or goods if they are offered. The buyer of this right to sell expects the price of the stock or commodity to fall so that he can deliver the stock or commodity (the put) at a profit. If the price rises, the option need not be exercised. The reverse transaction is a *call*. See Put option; Put price; Puts and calls.

Putative.   Reputed;   supposed;   commonly esteemed.

Putative father. The alleged or reputed father of a child born out of wedlock.

Putative marriage. A marriage contracted in good faith and in ignorance (on one or both sides) that impediments exist which render it unlawful.

Putative spouse. One who believes in good faith that he or she is party to a valid marriage, even though marriage is invalid.

Put bond. Right of bondholder to redeem bond before maturity. *See also* Bond.

Put-call parity. The relationship between the value of a put and the value of a call.

Put in. To place in due form before a court; to place among the records of a court.

Put off. To postpone. In a bargain for the sale of goods, it may mean to postpone its completion or to procure a resale of the goods to a third person.

Put option. One under which buyer of the option may demand payment by the writer of a fixed price (the "striking" price) upon delivery by the buyer of a specified number of shares of stock. *See* Put.

Transferable put right. A right, which is transferable to others, to put common stock back to the issuer on specified terms; a form of put option issued by firms to repurchase their shares.

Put price. The price at which the asset will be sold if a put option is exercised. Also called the strike price or exercise price. *See* Put.

Puts and calls. A "put" in the language of the commodity or stock market is a privilege of delivering or not delivering the subject-matter of the sale; and a "call" is a privilege of calling or not calling for it. *See* Put; Put option.

Putting in fear. These words are used in the common-law definition of a robbery from the person; *i.e.* the offense must have been committed by *putting in fear* the person robbed. No matter how slight the cause creating the fear may be, if transaction is attended with such circumstances of terror, such threatening by word or gesture, as in common experience is likely to create an apprehension of danger and induce a man to part with his property for sake of his person, victim is put in fear.

Pyramiding. In the stock market, a device for increasing holdings of a stock by financing new holdings out of the increased margin of those already owned. In corporate finance, the use of small equity and capital to finance controlling interest in more corporations. *See also* Leverage; Margin.

Pyramid sales scheme. A device, illegal in many states, in which a buyer of goods is promised a payment for each additional buyer procured by him.

Q

Q-TIP trust. Refers to qualified terminal interest property trust. A type of marital deduction bequest in which the surviving spouse receives all of the income for life but is not given a general power of appointment. Property qualifies for marital deduction only to the extent that the executor so elects on the Federal estate tax return. I.R.C. § 2056(b)(7)(B)(i)(III). The Economic Recovery Tax Act of 1981 (ERTA) qualified the Q-TIP trust for the marital deduction.

Quadrant /kwódrənt/. An angular measure of ninety degrees. One of the quarters created by two intersecting roads or streets.

Quære /kwíriy/. A query; question; doubt. This word, occurring in the syllabus of a reported case or elsewhere, shows that a question is propounded as to what follows, or that the particular rule, decision, or statement is considered as open to question.

Qualification. The possession by an individual of the qualities, properties, or circumstances, natural or adventitious, which are inherently or legally necessary to render him eligible to fill an office or to perform a public duty or function. Thus, a "qualified voter" is one who meets the residency, age, and registration requirements.

Also, a modification or limitation of terms or language; usually intended by way of restriction of expressions which, by reason of their generality, would carry a larger meaning than was designed.

See also Qualified.

Qualified. Adapted; fitted; entitled; susceptible; capable; competent; fitting; possessing legal power or capacity; eligible; as a "qualified voter" *(q.v.).* Applied to one who has taken the steps to prepare himself for an appointment or office, as by taking oath, giving bond, etc. One who has a particular status through some endowment, acquisition, or achievement, or it may describe one who has obtained appropriate legal power or capacity by taking an oath, completing a form, or complying with some other routine requirement. One who has mental or physical ability to perform requirements of job, office, or the like. *Also* means limited; restricted; confined; modified; imperfect; or temporary.

As to *qualified* Acceptance; Estate; Fee; Indorsement; Nuisance; Oath; Profit-sharing plan; Property, see those titles. *See also* Capacity; Competency; Duly qualified; Eligible.

Qualified elector. A person who is legally qualified to vote. *See also* Qualified voter.

Qualified immunity. *See* Immunity.

Qualified opinion. A statement in an audit report accompanying financial statements which expresses exceptions or qualifications to certain items in financial statements.

Qualified pension plans. *See* Pension plan.

Qualified privilege. One defense to prima facie case of defamation is "qualified privilege," also referred to as conditional privilege, in which interest that defendant is seeking to vindicate is conditioned upon publication in reasonable manner and for proper purpose. "Absolute privilege" renders defendant absolutely immune from civil liability for his defamatory statements, while "qualified privilege" protects defendant from liability only if he uttered defamatory statements without actual malice. *See also* Privilege.

Qualified residence interest. A term relevant in determining the amount of interest expense the individual taxpayer may deduct as an itemized deduction for what otherwise would be disallowed as a component of personal interest (consumer interest). Qualified residence interest consists of interest paid on qualified residences (principal residence and one other residence) of the taxpayer.

Qualified stock option. An option to purchase shares awarded to an employee of the corporation under terms that qualify the option for special tax treatment under the Internal Revenue Code.

Qualified terminable interest property (Q-TIP). *See* Q-TIP trust.

Qualified voter. A legal voter. A person qualified to vote generally; *i.e.* one who meets the residency, age, and registration requirements. One having constitutional qualifications for privilege, who is duly registered pursuant to law, and has present right to vote at election being held.

Qualify. To make one's self fit or prepared to exercise a right, office, or franchise. To take the steps necessary to prepare one's self for an office or appointment, as by taking oath, giving bond, etc. Also to limit; to modify; to restrict. Thus, it is said that one section of a statute qualifies another.

Qualifying share. A share of common stock owned by a person in order to qualify as a director of the issuing corporation in a corporation that requires directors to be shareholders.

Quality. Quality is descriptive of organic composition of substance, expressed in definite quantitative units, and definitive of character, nature and decree of excellence of an article. In respect to persons, this term denotes comparative rank; state or condition in relation to others; social or civil position or class. In pleading, it means an attribute or characteristic by which one thing is distinguished from another. Adoptiveness, suitableness, fitness; grade; condition. Within food adulteration statute means character or nature, as belonging to or distinguishing a thing, or character with respect to excellence, fineness, etc., or grade of excellence.

Quantum. How much; as much as.

Quantum meruit /kwóntəm méhruwət/. Recovery under this doctrine means "as much as deserved," and measures recovery under implied contract to pay compensation as reasonable value of services rendered. An equitable doctrine, based on the concept that no one who benefits by the labor and materials of another should be unjustly enriched thereby; under those circumstances, the law implies a promise to pay a reasonable amount for the labor and materials furnished, even absent a specific contract therefor. Essential elements of recovery under quantum meruit are: (1) valuable services were rendered or materials furnished, (2) for person sought to be charged, (3) which services and materials were accepted by person sought to be charged, used and enjoyed by him, and (4) under such circumstances as reasonably notified person sought to be charged that plaintiff, in performing such services, was expected to be paid by person sought to be charged. *See also* Unjust enrichment doctrine.

Quantum valebant /kwóntəm vəlíybænt/. As much as they were worth. The common count in an action of *assumpsit* for goods sold and delivered, founded on an implied *assumpsit* or promise, on the part of the defendant, to pay the plaintiff *as much as* the goods *were* reasonably *worth*.

Quarantine. A period of time during which a vessel, coming from a place where a contagious or infectious disease is prevalent, is detained by authority in the harbor of her port of destination, or at a station near it, without being permitted to land or to discharge her crew or passengers. Quarantine is said to have been first established at Venice in 1484.

Isolation of person afflicted with contagious disease. The keeping of persons, when suspected of having contracted or having been exposed to an infectious disease, out of a community, or to confine them to given place therein, and to prevent intercourse between them and people generally of the community.

A provision or interest given in law to the widow in her husband's estate, such as the privilege of occupying the mansion house and curtilage without charge until her dower is assigned, and technically is a dower right, or more broadly is a part of the dower estate.

Quare /kwériy/kwohriy/. Lat. Wherefore; for what reason; on what account. Used in the Latin form of several common-law writs.

Quare clausum fregit /kwériy klózəm fríyjət/. Lat. Wherefore he broke the close. That species of the action of trespass which has for its object the recovery of damages for an unlawful entry upon another's land is termed "trespass *quare clausum fregit;*" "breaking a close" being the technical expression for an unlawful entry upon land. The language of the declaration in this form of action is "that the defendant, with force and arms, broke and entered the close" of the plaintiff. The phrase is often abbreviated to *"qu. cl. fr."* or *"q.c.f."*

Quarterly. Quarter yearly; once in a quarter year.

Quarterly report. An abbreviated form of a company's annual report, issued every three months between annual reports; it includes an unaudited balance sheet, income statement, statement of changes in financial position and a narrative of the business operations for the quarter; an interim report.

Quarter section. The quarter of a section of land according to the divisions of the government survey, laid off by dividing the section into four equal parts by north-and-south and east-and-west lines, and containing 160 acres. A quarter of a square mile of land. Amount of land originally granted to homesteader.

Quarters of coverage. Social Security benefits are dependent on number of yearly quarters in which person made contributions (*i.e.* payments) into social security fund.

Quash /kwósh/. To overthrow; to abate; to vacate; to annul; to make void; *e.g.* to quash an indictment.

Quasi /kwéysay/kwóziy/. Lat. As if; almost as it were; analogous to. This term is used in legal phraseology to indicate that one subject resembles another, with which it is compared, in certain characteristics, but that there are intrinsic and material differences between them. A term used to mark a resemblance, and supposes a difference beween two objects. It is exclusively a term of classification. It implies that conception to which it serves as index is connected with conception with which comparison is instituted by strong superficial analogy or resemblance. Moreover it negatives idea of identity, but points out that the conceptions are sufficiently similar for one to be classed as the equal of the other. It is often prefixed to English words, implying mere appearance or want of reality or having some resemblance to given thing.

As to *quasi* Affinity; Contract; Corporation; Crime; Delict; Deposit; Derelict; Easement; Entail; Fee; In rem; Municipal corporation; Offense; Partner; Personalty; Possession; Posthumous child; Purchase; Realty; Tenant; Tort; Trustee; and Usufruct, see those titles.

Quasi admission. An act or utterance, usually extrajudicial, which creates an inconsistency with and discredits to a greater or lesser degree, present claim or other evidence of person creating the inconsistency, and person who enacted or uttered it may nevertheless disprove its correctness by introduction of other evidence.

Quasi contract. An obligation which law creates in absence of agreement; it is invoked by courts where there is unjust enrichment. Sometimes referred to as implied-in-law contracts (as a legal fiction) to distinguish them from implied-in-fact contracts (voluntary agreements inferred from the parties' conduct). Function of "quasi contract" is to raise obligation in law where in fact the parties made no promise, and it is not based on apparent intention of the parties. *See also* Contract.

Quasi estoppel. This doctrine is properly invoked against a person asserting a claim inconsistent with a position previously taken by him, with knowledge of the facts and his rights, to the detriment of the person seeking application of the doctrine.

"Equitable estoppel" and "estoppel in pais" are convertible terms embracing "quasi estoppel" and embody doctrine that one may not repudiate an act done or position assumed by him where such course would work injustice to another rightfully relying thereon.

See Equitable estoppel.

Quasi in rem jurisdiction /kwéysay in rém°/. Type of jurisdiction of a court based on a person's interest in property within the jurisdiction of the court. Refers to proceedings that are brought against the defendant personally; yet it is the defendant's interest in the property that serves as the basis of the jurisdiction. There must be a connection involving minimum contact between the property and the subject matter of the action for a state to exercise quasi in rem jurisdiction. Quasi in rem proceedings is generally defined as affecting only interest of particular persons in specific property and is distinguished from proceedings in rem which determine interests in specific property as against the whole world. *See also* Jurisdiction.

Quasi judicial. A term applied to the action, discretion, etc., of public administrative officers or bodies, who are required to investigate facts, or ascertain the existence of facts, hold hearings,

weigh evidence, and draw conclusions from them, as a basis for their official action, and to exercise discretion of a judicial nature.

Quasi judicial act. A judicial act performed by one not a judge.

Quasi-judicial power. The power of an administrative agency to adjudicate the rights of persons before it.

Quasi-legislative power. The power of an administrative agency to engage in rule-making. Adm. Procedure Act, 5 U.S.C.A. § 553.

Quasi-public corporation. *See* Corporation.

Question. A subject or point of investigation, examination or debate; theme of inquiry; problem; matter to be inquired into, as subject matter of civil or criminal discovery. A point on which the parties are not agreed, and which is submitted to the decision of a judge and jury. *See also* Issue.

An interrogation put to a witness, for the purpose of having him declare the truth of certain facts as far as he knows them; *e.g.* direct or cross examination of witness at trial. *See also* Discovery; Interrogation.

Categorical question. One inviting a distinct and positive statement of fact; one which can be answered by "yes" or "no." In the plural, a series of questions, covering a particular subject-matter, arranged in a systematic and consecutive order.

Federal question. *See* Federal.

Hypothetical question. See that title.

Judicial question. *See* Judicial.

Leading question. See that title.

Political question. *See* Political.

Question of fact. An issue involving the resolution of a factual dispute and hence within the province of the jury in contrast to a question of law.

Question of law. Question concerning legal effect to be given an undisputed set of facts. An issue which involves the application or interpretation of a law and hence within the province of the judge and not the jury.

Quia timet /kwáyə táymət/. Lat. Because he fears or apprehends. In equity practice, the technical name of a bill filed by a party who seeks the aid of a court of equity, *because he fears* some future probable injury to his rights or interests, and relief granted must depend upon circumstances.

Quick asset ratio. Ratio of cash, accounts receivable and marketable securities to current liabilities. Also called the "acid test." *See also* Acid ratio test.

Quick assets. Liquid assets such as cash, marketable securities and accounts receivable which can be converted into cash without delay.

Quid pro quo /kwíd pròw kwów/. What for what; something for something. Used in law for the giving one valuable thing for another. It is nothing more than the mutual consideration which passes between the parties to a contract, and which renders it valid and binding.

Quiet, *v.* To pacify; to render secure or unassailable by the removal of disquieting causes or disputes.

Quiet, *adj.* Unmolested; tranquil; free from interference or disturbance.

Quiet enjoyment. A covenant, usually inserted in leases and conveyances on the part of the grantor, promising that the tenant or grantee shall enjoy the possession and use of the premises in peace and without disturbance. In connection with the landlord-tenant relationship, the covenant of quiet enjoyment protects the tenant's right to freedom from serious interferences with his or her tenancy. See, *e.g.,* Mass.G.L. c. 186, § 14.

Quiet title action. A proceeding to establish the plaintiff's title to land by bringing into court an adverse claimant and there compelling him either to establish his claim or be forever after estopped from asserting it. *See also* Action to quiet title; Cloud on title.

Quit, *v.* To leave; remove from; surrender possession of; as when a tenant "quits" the premises or receives a "notice to quit."

Notice to quit. A written notice given by a landlord to his tenant, stating that the former desires to repossess himself of the demised premises, and that the latter is required to quit and remove from the same at a time designated, either at the expiration of the term, if the tenant is in under a lease, or immediately, if the tenancy is at will or by sufferance.

Quit, *adj.* Clear; discharged; free; also spoken of persons absolved or acquitted of a charge.

Qui tam action /kwày tǽm ǽkshən/. Lat. "Qui tam" is abbreviation of Latin phrase "qui tam pro domino rege quam pro si ipso in hac parte sequitur" meaning "Who sues on behalf of the King as well as for himself." It is an action brought by an informer, under a statute which establishes a penalty for the commission or omission of a certain act, and provides that the same shall be recoverable in a civil action, part of the penalty to go to any person who will bring such action and the remainder to the state or some other institution. It is called a *"qui tam* action" because the plaintiff states that he sues *as well* for the state as for himself. *See also* False Claims Act; Whistleblower Acts.

Quitclaim, *v.* In conveyancing, to release or relinquish a claim; to execute a deed of quitclaim. *See* Quitclaim, *n.*

Quitclaim, *n.* A release or acquittance given to one man by another, in respect of any action that he has or might have against him. Also acquitting or giving up one's claim or title.

Quitclaim deed. A deed of conveyance operating by way of release; that is, intended to pass any title, interest, or claim which the grantor may have in the premises, but not professing that such title is valid, nor containing any warranty or covenants for title. In a number of states, a deed which purports to transfer nothing more than interest which grantor may have, if any, at time of transaction, and excludes any implication that he has any title or interest in described realty. Under the law of some states the grantor warrants in such deed that neither he nor anyone claiming under him has encumbered the property and that he will defend the title against defects arising under and through him, but as to no others. *Compare* Warranty deed.

Quorum /kwórəm/. A majority of the entire body; *e.g.,* a quorum of a state supreme court. The number of members who must be present in a deliberative body before business may be transacted. In both houses of Congress a quorum consists of a majority of those chosen and sworn.

Such a number of the members of a body as is competent to transact business in the absence of the other members. The idea of a quorum is that, when that required number of persons goes into a session as a body, such as directors of a corporation, the votes of a majority thereof are sufficient for binding action. When a committee, board of directors, meeting of shareholders, legislature or other body of persons cannot act unless a certain number at least of them are present, that number is called a "quorum." In the absence of any law or rule fixing the quorum, it consists of a majority of those entitled to act.

Quota /kwówtə/. A proportional part or share, the proportional part of a demand or liability, falling upon each of those who are collectively responsible for the whole.

An assigned goal, as a sales quota; a limiting number or percentage such as the quota of immigrants from a particular country.

See also Export quotas; Import quota.

Quotation. The presentation or production to a court or judge of the exact language of a statute, court opinion, precedent, or other authority, in support of an argument or proposition advanced.

The verbatim transcription of part of a literary composition into another book or writing.

A statement of the market price of one or more securities or commodities; or the price specified to a correspondent. Often shortened to "quote." The highest bid to buy and the lowest offer to sell a security or commodity in a given market at a given time.

Quotient verdict /kwówshənt vɔ́rdikt/. A verdict resulting from agreement whereby each juror writes down amount of damages to which he thinks party is entitled and such amounts are then added together and divided by number of jurors. A chance verdict such that no juror knows what the verdict will be when he submits his vote on damages because the final amount is calculated by a preagreed formula.

While the general rule is that the use of a quotient verdict is improper and constitutes grounds for a new trial, it has been held that evidence that the jury utilized the quotient verdict process at some point in their deliberations was not fatal to the verdict, so long as the figure reached was discussed by the jury and agreed upon as a fair expression of their opinion; and, is not objectionable if, after it is determined, the jury deliberates further and accepts the result as just.

Quo warranto /kwów wɔrǽntow/. In old English practice, a writ in the nature of a writ of right for the king, against him who claimed or usurped any office, franchise, or liberty, to inquire *by what authority* he supported his claim, in order to determine the right. It lay also in case of non-user, or long neglect of a franchise, or misuser or abuse of it; being a writ commanding the defendant to show *by what warrant* he exercises such a franchise, having never had any grant of it, or having forfeited it by neglect or abuse.

A common law writ designed to test whether a person exercising power is legally entitled to do so. An extraordinary proceeding, prerogative in nature, addressed to preventing a continued exercise of authority unlawfully asserted. It is intended to prevent exercise of powers that are not conferred by law, and is not ordinarily available to regulate the manner of exercising such powers.

An ancient prerogative right through which the state acts to protect itself and the good of public generally through its chosen agents as provided by its Constitution and laws, though sometimes it is brought at instance of and for benefit of a private individual who may have a special interest. Legal action whereby legality of exercise of powers by municipal corporation may be placed in issue.

In the law of corporations, quo warranto may be used to test whether a corporation was validly organized or whether it has power to engage in the business in which it is involved.

The federal rules are applicable to proceedings for quo warranto "to the extent that the practice in such proceedings is not set forth in statutes of the United States and has heretofore conformed to the practice in civil actions." Fed.R. Civil P. 81(a)(2). Any remedy that could have been obtained under the historic writ of quo warranto may be obtained by a civil action of that nature.

Q.V. An abbreviation of *"quod vide,"* meaning "which see".

R

Rabbinical divorce. Divorce granted under authority of rabbis.

Race. An ethnical stock; a great division of mankind having in common certain distinguishing physical peculiarities constituting a comprehensive class appearing to be derived from a distinct primitive source. A tribal or national stock; a division or subdivision of one of the great racial stocks of mankind distinguished by minor peculiarities.

Race-notice recording statutes. State laws which provide that an unrecorded conveyance is invalid as against a subsequent purchaser for value who records without knowledge of the prior unrecorded instrument. The recording of the later instrument, however, must generally be in the chain of title. Such laws combine the features of both notice and race statute. *See also* Pure race statute; Recording acts.

Race recording statutes. In a state with a race recording statute, the party who records an instrument of conveyance has the better claim regardless of notice of prior unrecorded instruments. *See* Pure race statutes; Recording acts.

Racket. Engaging in an operation to make money illegitimately, implying continuity of behavior. *See* Racketeering.

Racketeer. A person who makes money by violations of racketeering laws.

Racketeer Influenced and Corrupt Organizations Act. *See* RICO laws.

Racketeering. An organized conspiracy to commit the crimes of extortion or coercion, or attempts to commit extortion or coercion. From the standpoint of extortion, it is the obtaining of money or property from another, without his consent, induced by the wrongful use of force or fear. The fear which constitutes the legally necessary element in extortion is induced by oral or written threats to do an unlawful injury to the property of the threatened person by means of explosives, fire, or otherwise; or to kill, kidnap, or injure him or a relative of his or some member of his family. *See* Extortion.

Activities of organized criminals who extort money from legitimate businesses by violence or other forms of threats or intimidation or conduct of illegal enterprises such as gambling, narcotics traffic, or prostitution. See 18 U.S.C.A. § 1961(1) ("racketeering activity" defined).

Racketeering is demanding, soliciting or receiving anything of value from the owner, proprietor, or other person having a financial interest in a business, by means of either a threat, express or implied, or a promise, express or implied, that the person so demanding, soliciting or receiving such thing of value will: (a) Cause the competition of the person from whom the payment is demanded, solicited or received to be diminished or eliminated; or (b) Cause the price of goods or services purchased or sold in the business to be increased, decreased or maintained at a stated level; or (c) Protect the property used in the business or the person or family of the owner, proprietor or other interested person from injury by violence or other unlawful means.

For federal racketeering offenses, see 18 U.S. C.A. §§ 1951 et seq.; 1961 et seq.

See also Extortion; Hobbs Act; RICO laws.

Raffle. A form of lottery in which each participant buys a ticket for an article put up as a prize with the winner being determined by random drawing. *See also* Lottery.

Raider. An individual or corporation who attempts to take control of a target corporation by buying a controlling interest in its stock and installing new management. Raiders who accumulate 5% or more of the outstanding shares in the target company must publicly report their purchases under the Williams Act, § 14(e), 15 U.S.C.A. § 78n(e). *See also* Takeover.

Raiding. Practice whereby voters in sympathy with one party designate themselves as voters of another party so as to influence or determine results of other party's primary. *See also* Raider.

Railway Labor Act. An act of Congress (1962) designed to secure the prompt settlement of disputes between interstate railroad companies and their employees. A 1934 amendment created the National Mediation Board. 45 U.S.C.A. § 151 et seq.

Raise. To create; to infer; to create or bring to light by construction or interpretation. To cause or procure to be produced, bred or propagated. To bring together; to get together or obtain for use or service; to gather; to collect; to levy, as to raise money by levying taxes; to increase income by increasing salary, wages, or commissions. To solicit, secure or otherwise obtain funds for a given purpose, organization, charity, etc.

To alter the amount of an instrument such as a negotiable instrument by changing the face value to a higher amount. *See also* Forgery; Raised check; Rasure.

Raise an issue. To bring pleadings to an issue; to have the effect of producing an issue between the parties pleading in an action.

Raise a presumption. To give occasion or ground for a presumption; to be of such a character, or to be attended with such circumstances, as to justify an inference or presumption of law. Thus, a person's silence, in some instances, will "raise a presumption" of his consent to what is done. *See also* Presumption.

Raised check. A demand negotiable instrument, the face amount of which has been increased, generally without authority of the drawer and hence fraudulently. Such change constitutes a material alteration under U.C.C. § 3–407(1)(c). *See also* Forgery; Rasure.

Raise revenue. To levy a tax, as a means of collecting revenue; to bring together, collect, or levy revenue. *See* Levy; Tax.

Raising a promise. The act of the law in extracting from the facts and circumstances of a particular transaction a promise which was implicit therein, and postulating it as a ground of legal liability.

Rake-off. Share of profits of transaction or business, demanded, paid, or otherwise taken illegally. Illegal pay-off or bribe, or skimming of profits.

Range, *v.* To have or extend in certain direction, to correspond in direction or line, or to trend or run.

Range, *n.* In the government survey of the United States, one of the divisions of a state, consisting of a row or tier of townships as they appear on the map. A division of a state in the government survey, being a six mile wide row of townships, running North and South, and used in legal descriptions.

A tract or district of land within which domestic animals in large numbers range for subsistence; an extensive grazing ground. The term is used on the great plains of the United States to designate a tract commonly of many square miles occupied by one or different proprietors and distinctively called a cattle range, stock range, or sheep range. The animals on a range are usually left to take care of themselves during the whole year without shelter, except when periodically gathered in a round-up for counting and selection, and for branding, when the herds of several proprietors run together.

In financial terms, the difference between the highest and lowest possible values.

Ranking of creditors. *See* Preference; Priority.

Ransom. The money, price, or consideration paid or demanded for redemption of a kidnapped person or persons; a payment that releases from captivity. Whoever knowingly receives, possesses, or disposes of such commits a crime. 18 U.S.C.A. § 1202; Model Penal Code § 212.1(a). *See* Kidnapping.

In international law, the redemption of captured property from the hands of an enemy, particularly of property captured at sea. A sum paid or agreed to be paid for the redemption of captured property.

Rap. Slang for criminal conviction.

Rape. Unlawful sexual intercourse with a female without her consent. The unlawful carnal knowledge of a woman by a man forcibly and against her will. The act of sexual intercourse committed by a man with a woman not his wife and without her consent, committed when the woman's resistance is overcome by force or fear, or under other prohibitive conditions.

A male who has sexual intercourse with a female not his wife is guilty of rape if: (a) he compels her to submit by force or by threat of imminent death, serious bodily injury, extreme pain or kidnapping, to be inflicted on anyone; or (b) he has substantially impaired her power to appraise or control her conduct by administering or employing without her knowledge drugs, intoxicants or other means for the purpose of preventing resistance; or (c) the female is unconscious; or (d) the female is less than 10 years old. Model Penal Code, § 213.1.

Under some statutes, crime embraces unnatural as well as natural sexual intercourse; *e.g.* M.G. L.A. (Mass.) c. 277, § 39; and, may include intercourse between two males.

See also Assault with intent to commit rape; Carnal abuse; Carnal knowledge; Fresh complaint rule.

Statutory rape. Modern statutes, which often materially change the common-law definition, create an offense commonly known as "statutory rape," where the offense consists in having sexual intercourse with a female or male under statutory age. The offense may be either with or without the victim's consent; and mistake as to the victim's age is usually no defense. *See also* Statutory rape.

Rape shield law. *See* Shield laws.

RAR. A revenue agent's report which reflects any adjustments made by the agent as a result of an audit of the taxpayer. The RAR is mailed to the taxpayer along with the 30-day letter which outlines the appellate procedures available to the taxpayer.

Rasure /réyzhər/. The act of scraping, scratching, or shaving the surface of a written instrument, for the purpose of removing certain letters or words from it. It is to be distinguished from "obliteration," as the latter word properly denotes the crossing out of a word or letter by drawing a line through it with ink. But the two expressions are often used interchangeably. *See also* Forgery; Raise; Raised check.

Ratable. Proportional; proportionately rated upon a constant ratio adjusted to due relation. According to a measure which fixes proportions. It has no meaning unless referable to some rule or standard, and never means equality or equal division but implies unequal division as between different persons.

Ratable estate or property. Property in its quality and nature capable of being rated, *i.e.* appraised, assessed. Taxable estate; the real and personal property which the legislature designates as "taxable."

Rate. Proportional or relative value, measure, or degree. The proportion or standard by which quantity or value is adjusted. Thus, the *rate* of interest is the proportion or ratio between the principal and interest; the buildings in a town are *rated* for insurance purposes; *i.e.*, classified and individually estimated with reference to their insurable qualities. In this sense also we speak of articles as being in "first-rate" or "second-rate" condition.

Amount of charge or payment with reference to some basis of calculation. A certain quantity or amount of one thing considered in relation to another thing and used as standard or measure.

A fixed relation of quantity, amount or degree; also, a charge, valuation, payment or price fixed according to ratio, scale or standard; comparative price or amount of demands. Cost per unit of a commodity or service.

In connection with public utilities, a charge to the public for a service open to all and upon the same terms. The unit cost of a service supplied to the public by a utility. When used in connection with public utilities, such as a telephone company, generally means price stated or fixed for some commodity or service of general need or utility supplied to the public measured by specific unit or standard.

As used in the interstate commerce law, it means the net cost to the shipper of the transportation of his property; that is to say, the net amount the carrier receives from the shipper and retains.

See also Commodity rate; Confiscatory rates; Discount rate; Flat rate; Freight rate; Interest rate; Joint through rate; Meter rate; Nominal annual rate; Prime interest rate.

Class rate. A single rate applying to the transportation of a number of articles of the same general character.

Commodity rate. A rate which applies to the transportation of a specific commodity alone.

Joint rate. A single rate applied jointly by two carriers to cover shipment in which one carrier operates over only part of route and other carrier serves remaining distance to destination.

Rate base. The amount of investment on which a regulated public utility is entitled to an opportunity to earn a fair and reasonable return. It represents the total investment in or fair value of the used and useful property which it necessarily devotes to rendering the regulated services. *See also Rate of return, below.*

Rate-lock agreement/interest rate commitment. A written agreement by which a lender will hold an interest rate on a mortgage for a specified period of time. The terms and conditions of a rate-lock agreement vary from lender to lender.

Rate of exchange. In commercial law, the actual price at which a bill, drawn in one country upon another country, can be bought or obtained in the former country at any given time. Also, the price at which the money of one country may be exchanged for money of another country (*e.g.* dollars for marks).

Rate of interest. The charge imposed by a lender of money for the use of the money; the borrowing charge.

Discount rate. Rate charged to member banks by Federal Reserve Board for borrowing money from Federal Reserve.

Legal rate. The statutory maximum rate of interest which may be charged for loans. *See also* Usury.

Prime rate. The rate of interest charged for high quality commercial loans (*i.e.* rate charged by bank to its most credit worthy customers) which is pegged to the discount rate established by the Federal Reserve Board. This rate tends to establish the rate of interest charged for various types of personal and commercial loans.

Rate cap. Provision in loan agreement restricting interest rate increases. For example, in an adjustable rate mortgage (ARM), a clause which limits interest rate increases, on either an annual or a lifetime basis.

Real rate of interest. The rate of interest excluding the effect of inflation; that is, the rate that is earned in terms of constant purchase-power dollars.

Rate of return. The annual return on an investment, generally referred to in terms of a percentage of the investment. The percentage by which the rate base is multiplied to provide a figure that allows a utility to collect revenues sufficient to pay operating expenses and attract investment. In the case of common stock, is the annual dividend yield as a percentage of the purchase price. *See also* Dividend yield; Fair return on investment; Hurdle rate; Internal rate of return; Yield.

Rate of return ratios. Ratios that are designed to measure the profitability of the firm in relation to various measures of the funds invested in the firm.

Rate tariff. Statement by carrier to possible shippers that it will furnish certain services under certain conditions for certain price. *See* Tariff.

Ratification. In a broad sense, the confirmation of a previous act done either by the party himself or by another; as, confirmation of a voidable act. The affirmance by a person of a prior act which did not bind him, but which was done or professedly done on his account, whereby the act, as to some or all persons, is given effect as if originally authorized by him. The adoption by one, as binding upon himself, of an act done in such relations that he may claim it as done for his benefit, although done under such circumstances as would not bind him except for his subsequent assent. It is equivalent to a previous authorization and relates back to time when act ratified was done, except where intervening rights of third persons are concerned.

In contract law, the act of adopting or confirming a previous act which without ratification would not be an enforceable contractual obligation, or confirming an obligation by one without the authority to make or do (or who was incompetent at the time the contract was made). The act of ratification causes the obligation to be binding as if such was valid and enforceable in the first instance.

Approval, as by legislatures or conventions, of a constitutional amendment proposed by two-thirds of both houses of Congress. Approval by the electorate of a proposed State constitutional amendment.

In the law of principal and agent, the adoption and confirmation by one person with knowledge of all material facts, of an act or contract performed or entered into in his behalf by another who at the time assumed without authority to act as his agent. Essence of "ratification" by principal of act of agent is manifestation of mental determination by principal to affirm the act, and this may be manifested by written word or by spoken word or by conduct, or may be inferred from known circumstances and principal's acts in relation thereto.

Express ratifications are those made in express and direct terms of assent. *Implied* ratifications are such as the law presumes from the acts of the principal.

Estoppel and ratification distinguished, *see* Estoppel. *See also* Acknowledgment; Approval; Confirmation.

Ratify. To approve and sanction; to make valid; to confirm; to give sanction to. To authorize or otherwise approve, retroactively, an agreement or conduct either expressly or by implication. *See* Approval; Confirm; Ratification.

Rating. *See* Credit rating.

Ratio. Rate; proportion; degree. Reason, or understanding. Also a cause, or giving judgment therein. The number resulting when one number is divided by another.

Ratio analysis. The use of mathematical relationships to study a firm's liquidity, activity, profitability, and coverage of obligations.

Ratio decidendi /réysh(iy)ow dèsədénday/. The ground or reason of decision. The point in a case which determines the judgment.

Ratio legis /réysh(iy)ow líyjəs/. The reason or occasion of a law; the occasion of making a law.

Rational basis test. Under this test, an appellate court will not second-guess the legislature as to the wisdom or rationality of a particular statute if there is a rational basis for its enactment, and if the challenged law bears a reasonable relationship to the attainment of some legitimate governmental objective. The same test may be applied when a court is reviewing a decision of an administrative body because of the expertise of such body. It has been said that the protection of the public from unwise or improvident statutes is to be found at the voting polls or by referendum, not in court. This test does not apply, of course, if the statute or decision is unconstitutional.

As a standard of review for statutory enactments challenged on equal protection grounds, this test requires that classifications created by a state must be reasonable, not arbitrary, and must rest on some ground of difference having a fair and substantial relation to the object of the legislation, so that all persons similarly circumstanced shall be treated alike.

Rational doubt. A doubt based upon reasonable inferences such as are ordinarily drawn by ordinary men in the light of their experiences in ordinary life. *See also* Reasonable doubt.

Rational purpose test. *See* Rational basis test.

Ravish. To have carnal knowledge of a woman by force and against her will; to rape.

Ravisher. One who has carnal knowledge of a woman by force and against her consent. *See* Rape.

Ravishment. *See* Rape; Ravish.

Raw land. Unimproved land.

Raze /réyz/. To erase. *See* Forgery; Raise; Rasure.

RCRA. Resource Conservation and Recovery Act. 42 U.S.C.A. § 6901 et seq.

Re /ríy/. Lat. In the matter of; in the case of. A term of frequent use in designating judicial proceedings, in which there is only one party. Thus, "*Re* Vivian" signifies "In the matter of Vivian," or in "Vivian's Case."

R.E.A. Rural Electrification Administration.

Reacquired stock. *See* Treasury stock.

Readjustment. A voluntary reorganization of a corporation which is in financial difficulties by the stockholders themselves without the intervention of a receiver or a court appointed fiduciary.

Ready. Prepared for what one is about to do or experience; equipped or supplied with what is needed for some act or event; prepared for immediate movement or action. Fitted, arranged, or placed for immediate use; causing no delay for lack of being prepared or furnished.

Ready and willing. Implies capacity to act as well as disposition; *e.g.* ready, willing and able buyer.

Reaffirmation agreement. Agreement made prior to discharge in bankruptcy to pay certain debts that otherwise would be discharged through the bankruptcy proceeding. Such agreements are subject to certain requirements and limitations (*e.g.* court approval).

Real. In civil law, relating to a *thing* (whether movable or immovable), as distinguished from a person.

Relating to *land,* as distinguished from personal property. This term is applied to lands, tenements, and hereditaments.

As to *real* Account; Action; Chattel; Contract; Covenant; Estate; Issue; Obligation; Party; Privilege; Property; Representative; Right; Security; Servitude; Statute, and Wrong, see those titles.

Real authority. Authority manifested by the principal to the agent either expressly or by implication.

Real defenses. Defenses to which a holder in due course is subject in enforcing an instrument, especially defenses listed in U.C.C. § 3–305(2).

Real earnings. Wages, salaries, and other earnings adjusted for inflation to determine actual changes in purchasing power over a given period.

Real estate. Land and anything permanently affixed to the land, such as buildings, fences, and those things attached to the buildings, such as light fixtures, plumbing and heating fixtures, or other such items which would be personal property if not attached. The term is generally synonymous with real property. *See also* Property *(Real property).*

Real estate broker. *See* Broker.

Real estate investment trust (REIT). Financial device in which investors purchase shares in a trust the res of which is invested in real estate ventures. A company that invests in and manages a portfolio of real estate with the majority of its income distributed to the shareholders. A closed-end mutual fund that invests in real estate or mortgages. *See also* Massachusetts trust; Trust.

Real estate listing. *See* Listing.

Real Estate Settlement Procedures Act. *See* RESPA.

Real estate syndicate. A loose aggregation of persons who invest in real estate for common profits and gains.

Real evidence. Evidence furnished by things themselves, on view or inspection, as distinguished from a description of them by the mouth of a witness; *e.g.,* the physical appearance of a person when exhibited to the jury, marks, scars, wounds, fingerprints, etc.; also, the weapons or implements used in the commission of a crime, and other inanimate objects, and evidence of the physical appearance of a place (the scene of an accident or of the commission of a crime or of property to be taken under condemnation proceedings) as obtained by a jury when they are taken to view it. That type of evidence which is provided by producing for inspection at trial a particular item rather than having witnesses describe it. *See also* Demonstrative evidence.

Realignment. The process by which the court, for determining diversity jurisdiction, realigns the parties as plaintiffs and defendants according to the ultimate interest of each.

Real income. A measure of the real purchasing power of nominal income; real income is nominal income adjusted for changes in the general price level, or income corrected for inflation or deflation. *See also* Real earnings.

Real injury. In the civil law, an injury arising from an unlawful *act,* as distinguished from a verbal injury, which was done by words. *See* Injury.

Realize. To convert any kind of property into money; but especially to receive the returns from an investment.

Realized. Term, in tax law, means received, paid, debted or incurred, in accordance with method of accounting authorized for use by taxpayer.

Realized gain *or* **loss.** Gain (or loss) resulting from an identifiable event, such as a sale or an exchange of property. The amount of realized gain from the sale or other disposition of property is the excess of the amount realized over the adjusted basis of the property; the amount of realized loss is the excess of the property's adjusted basis over the amount realized. I.R.C. § 1001. *See also* Recognized gain or loss.

Real law. Real estate or real property law. The body of laws relating to real property. This use of the term is popular rather than technical.

In the civil law, a law which relates to specific property, whether movable or immovable.

Real money. Money which has real metalic, intrinsic value as distinguished from paper currency, checks and drafts.

Real party in interest. Person who will be entitled to benefits of action if successful, that is, the one who is actually and substantially interested in subject matter as distinguished from one who has only a nominal, formal, or technical interest in or connection with it. Under the traditional test, a party is a "real party in interest" if it has the legal right under the applicable substantive law to enforce the claim in question. Real party in interest within rule that every civil action in federal courts must be prosecuted in name of real party in interest is the one, who, under applicable substantive law, has legal right to bring suit; and not necessarily person who will ultimately benefit from the recovery.

Under Fed.R.Civil P. 17(a), a guardian, executor, bailee, and the like, may sue in his own name without joining the party for whom the action is brought.

See also Parties.

Real property. *See* Property *(Real property)*.

Real things *(or things real)*. In common law, such things as are permanent, fixed, and immovable, which cannot be carried out of their place; as lands and tenements. Things substantial and immovable, and the rights and profits annexed to or issuing out of them. *See also* Real estate.

Realtor. "Realtor" is a federally registered collective membership mark owned by the National Association of Realtors and properly used only in reference to members of the association.

Realty. A brief term for real property or real estate; also for anything which partakes of the nature of real property. *See* Property *(Real property)*.

Reapportionment. A realignment or change in legislative districts brought about by changes in population and mandated by the constitutional requirement of equality of representation (*i.e.* one person, one vote mandate). A new apportionment of seats in the House of Representatives among States "according to their respective numbers", is required by Art. 1, § 2 of the U.S. Constitution after every decennial census. A similar require-

ment as to State legislative seats is found in many State constitutions. *See* Census.

A state statute which violates the rights of persons to vote on a one man-one vote apportionment is contrary to the equal protection clause of the 14th Amend., U.S.Const. Baker v. Carr, 369 U.S. 186, 82 S.Ct. 691, 7 L.Ed.2d 663.

Reappraiser. A person who, in certain cases, is appointed to make a revaluation or second appraisement of imported goods at the customhouse.

Reargument. Purpose of reargument is to demonstrate to court that there is some decision or principle of law which would have a controlling effect and which has been overlooked, or that there has been a misapprehension of facts. *See also* Rehearing; Retrial.

Reason. A faculty of the mind by which it distinguishes truth from falsehood, good from evil, and which enables the possessor to deduce inferences from facts or from propositions. Also an inducement, motive, or ground for action, as in the phrase "reasons for an appeal."

Reasonable. Fair, proper, just, moderate, suitable under the circumstances. Fit and appropriate to the end in view. Having the faculty of reason; rational; governed by reason; under the influence of reason; agreeable to reason. Thinking, speaking, or acting according to the dictates of reason. Not immoderate or excessive, being synonymous with rational, honest, equitable, fair, suitable, moderate, tolerable.

As to *reasonable* Care; Diligence; Doubt; Notice, Skill, and Time, see those titles. *See also* Fair.

Reasonable act. Such as may fairly, justly, and reasonably be required of a party.

Reasonable and probable cause. Such grounds as justify any one in suspecting another of a crime, and placing him in custody thereon. It is a suspicion founded upon circumstances sufficiently strong to warrant reasonable man in belief that charge is true. *See also* Probable cause.

Reasonable belief. "Reasonable belief" or "probable cause" to make an arrest without a warrant exists when facts and circumstances within arresting officer's knowledge, and of which he had reasonably trustworthy information, are sufficient in themselves to justify a man of average caution in belief that a felony has been or is being committed. *See also* Probable cause; Reasonable and probable cause.

The words "reasonably believes" are used throughout the Restatement, Second, Torts to denote the fact that the actor believes that a given fact or combination of facts exists, and that the circumstances which he knows, or should know, are such as to cause a reasonable man so to believe. Sec. 11.

Reasonable care. That degree of care which a person of ordinary prudence would exercise in the same or similar circumstances. That degree of care which ordinarily prudent and competent person engaged in same line of business or endeavor should exercise under similar circumstances. Due care, or ordinary care, under all the circumstances. Failure to exercise such care is ordinary negligence. *See also* Care.

Reasonable cause. As basis for arrest without warrant, is such state of facts as would lead man of ordinary care and prudence to believe and conscientiously entertain honest and strong suspicion that person sought to be arrested is guilty of committing a crime. *See also* Probable cause; Reasonable and probable cause; Reasonable belief.

Reasonable certainty, rule of. This rule permits recovery of damages only for such future pain and suffering as is reasonably certain to result from the injury received. To authorize recovery under such rule for permanent injury, permanency of injury must be shown with reasonable certainty, which is not mere conjecture or likelihood or ever a probability of such injury.

To establish damages for lost profits due to breach of contract with "reasonable certainty" does not mean that such damages must be established in exact pecuniary amount; evidence must, however, lay some foundation enabling fact finder to make fair and reasonable estimate of amount of damage.

Reasonable compensation. Sum which would reasonably compensate person for injuries, for pain and suffering, for past, present and future expenses reasonably necessary or incidental to his efforts to alleviate his injuries and in all pecuniary losses suffered, or to be suffered, as result of inability to engage in his usual occupation.

Reasonable doubt. The standard used to determine the guilt or innocence of a person criminally charged. To be guilty of a crime, one must be proved guilty "beyond a reasonable doubt." Reasonable doubt which will justify acquittal is doubt based on reason and arising from evidence or lack of evidence, and it is doubt which reasonable man or woman might entertain, and it is not fanciful doubt, is not imagined doubt, and is not doubt that juror might conjure up to avoid performing unpleasant task or duty. Reasonable doubt is such a doubt as would cause prudent men to hesitate before acting in matters of importance to themselves. Doubt based on reason which arises from evidence or lack of evidence. *See also* Beyond a reasonable doubt; Doubt.

Reasonable expectation doctrine. Under this doctrine, when ambiguities exist in insurance policy they are to be resolved in accordance with the reasonable expectations of the insured.

Reasonable force. That degree of force which is not excessive and is appropriate in protecting oneself or one's property. When such force is used, a person is justified and is not criminally liable, nor is he liable in tort.

Reasonable grounds. Reasonable grounds within statute authorizing arrest without warrant by officer who has reasonable grounds for believing that person to be arrested has committed criminal offense means substantially probable cause. *See also* Probable cause; Reasonable and probable cause; Reasonable cause.

Reasonable inference rule. Under this rule the trier of fact may consider as evidence not only the testimony and real evidence presented at trial but also all inferences which may be reasonably drawn, though they are not necessary inferences.

Reasonable man doctrine *or* **standard.** The standard which one must observe to avoid liability for negligence is the standard of the reasonable man under all the circumstances, including the foreseeability of harm to one such as the plaintiff. *See also* Reasonable woman standard.

Reasonable needs of the business. A term used in connection with the accumulated earnings tax. A corporation may avoid a penalty on the unreasonable accumulation of earnings if it can show that there is a reasonable business need, and a definite plan for the use of the funds. I.R.C. § 535.

Reasonable notice. While the term is relative, it is notice which is plainly calculated to apprise the appropriate person of its contents. *See also* Notice.

Reasonable suspicion. Such suspicion which will justify police officer, for Fourth Amendment purposes, in stopping defendant in public place is quantum of knowledge sufficient to induce ordinarily prudent and cautious man under circumstances to believe criminal activity is at hand. It must be based on specific and articulable facts, which, taken together with rational inferences from those facts, reasonably warrant intrusion. *See also* Probable cause; Reasonable cause.

Reasonable time. Such time as is necessary conveniently to do what a contract requires to be done, and as soon as circumstances will permit. In determining what is a "reasonable time" for performance, court should consider such factors as relationships between parties, subject matter of contract, and time that a person of ordinary diligence and prudence would use under similar circumstances.

Any time which is not manifestly unreasonable may be fixed by agreement of the parties, and what is reasonable depends on the nature, purpose and circumstances of each case. U.C.C. § 1–204(1)(2). Acceptance of an offer must be made within a reasonable time if no time is specified. U.C.C. §§ 2–206(2), 207. See also U.C.C. § 2–513(1) (buyer's right to inspection of goods); § 2–610 (anticipatory repudiation); § 2–508(2) (substitution of conforming goods for rejected goods).

Where contract does not fix a time for performance, the law allows "reasonable time" for performance, defined as such time as is necessary, conveniently, to do what the contract requires to be done, as soon as circumstances will permit.

See also Time.

Reasonable use theory. A riparian owner may make reasonable use of his water for either natural or artificial wants. However, he may not so use his rights so as to affect the quantity or quality of water available to a lower riparian owner. *See also* Common enemy doctrine.

Reasonable woman standard. The standard by which conduct may be measured in cases where a female party's gender is relevant. For example, whether work place conduct constitutes sexual harassment may be determined by reference to whether a "reasonable woman" would be offended. Ellison v. Brady, C.A.Cal., 924 F.2d 872. *See also* Reasonable man doctrine *or* standard.

Reassessment. Re-estimating the value of a specific property or all property in a given area for tax assessment purposes.

Reassurance. Exists where an insurer procures the whole or a part of the sum which he has insured (*i.e.,* contracted to pay in case of loss, death, etc.) to be insured again to him by another insurer. *See also* Reinsurance.

Rebate. Discount; deduction or refund of money in consideration of prompt payment. A deduction from a stipulated premium on a policy of insurance, in pursuance of an antecedent contract. A deduction or drawback from a stipulated payment, charge, or rate (as, a rate for the transportation of freight by a railroad), not taken out in advance of payment, but handed back to the payer after he has paid the full stipulated sum.

Refund of portion of purchase price made by manufacturer to consumer to induce purchase of product. Such is commonly obtained by sending proof of purchase to manufacturer.

Portion of a transportation charge refunded to a shipper. Rebates are forbidden by the Interstate Commerce Act.

Tax rebate is an amount returned (*i.e.* refunded) to the taxpayer after he has made full payment of the tax.

See also Discount; Elkins Act; Kickback; Refund.

Rebellion. Deliberate, organized resistance, by force and arms, to the laws or operations of the government, committed by a subject. It is a federal crime to incite, assist, or engage in any rebellion or insurrection against the authority of the United States or the laws thereof. 18 U.S. C.A. § 2383.

Rebut. In pleading and evidence, to defeat, refute, or take away the effect of something. When a plaintiff in an action produces evidence which raises a presumption of the defendant's liability, and the defendant adduces evidence which shows that the presumption is ill-founded, he is said to "rebut it." *See* Rebuttable presumption; Rebuttal evidence.

Rebuttable presumption. In the law of evidence, a presumption which may be rebutted by evidence. Otherwise called a "disputable" presumption. A species of legal presumption which holds good until evidence contrary to it is introduced. It shifts burden of proof. It gives particular effect to certain group of facts in absence of further evidence, and presumption provides prima facie case which shifts to defendant the burden to go forward with evidence to contradict or rebut fact presumed. And which standing alone will support a finding against contradictory evidence. *See also* Presumption.

Rebuttal evidence. Evidence given to explain, repel, counteract, or disprove facts given in evidence by the opposing party. That which tends to explain or contradict or disprove evidence offered by the adverse party. Rebuttal occurs during the trial stage where evidence is given by one party to refute evidence introduced by the other party. Evidence which is offered by a party after he has rested his case and after the opponent has rested in order to contradict the opponent's evidence. *See also* Rejoinder.

Also evidence given in opposition to a presumption of fact or a *prima facie* case; in this sense, it may be not only counteracting evidence, but evidence sufficient to counteract, that is, conclusive. *See* Rebuttable presumption.

Rebutter. In common law pleading, a defendant's answer of fact to a plaintiff's surrejoinder; the third pleading in the series on the part of the defendant.

Recall. A method of removal of official in which power of removal is either granted to or reserved by the people. Right or procedure by which a public official may be removed from office before the end of his term of office by a vote of the people to be taken on the filing of a petition signed by required number of qualified voters. Recall may also be applicable to judges.

Under federal Consumer Product Safety Act, government has power to require recall of unsafe products for repair, replacement or refund. See 15 U.S.C.A. § 2064(c)–(f).

To summon a diplomatic minister back to his home court, at the same time depriving him of his office and functions.

Recall a judgment. To revoke, cancel, vacate, or reverse a judgment for matters of fact. When it is annulled by reason of errors of law, it is said to be "reversed."

Recant. To withdraw or repudiate formally and publicly.

Recapitalization. A process whereby stock, bonds or other securities of a corporation are adjusted or restructured as to type, amount, income or priority. A restructuring of the capital of a corporation through amendment of the articles of incorporation or a merger with a subsidiary or parent corporation. Recasting of capital structure (*e.g.* exchange of bonds for stock) within framework of existing corporation. *See also* Reorganization.

Recaption. At common law, a retaking, or taking back. A species of remedy by the mere act of the party injured (otherwise termed "reprisal"), which happens when any one has deprived another of his property in goods or chattels personal, or wrongfully detains one's wife, child, or servant. In this case, the owner of the goods, and the husband, parent, or master may lawfully claim and retake them, wherever he happens to find them, so it be not in a riotous manner, or attended with a breach of the peace. It also signifies the taking a second distress of one formerly distrained during the plea grounded on the former distress. *See also* Distraint; Distress; Ejectment; Repossession.

Also, formerly, a writ to recover damages for him whose goods, being distrained for rent in service, etc., are distrained again for the same cause, pending the plea in the county court, or before the justice.

Recapture. To recover (by IRS) the tax benefit of a deduction or a credit previously taken by tax payer. *See, e.g.,* Recapture of depreciation.

The taking from an enemy, by a force friendly to the former owner, of a vessel previously taken for prize by such enemy.

Recapture clause. In contracts, a provision for determining rates in the event that the contract rate is more favorable than anticipated. Also, a provision in a contract for recovering possession of goods. As used in leases, a clause giving the lessor a percentage of profits above a fixed amount of rent; or, in a percentage lease, a clause granting landlord right to terminate lease if tenant fails to realize minimum sales.

Recapture of depreciation. Upon the sale or disposition of depreciable property, the portion of the gain which represents the accelerated depreciation previously taken is taxed as ordinary income. Since Tax Reform Act of 1986, there is no monetary difference because capital gains and ordinary income are taxed at the same rate. The recapture of depreciation rules do not apply when the property is disposed of at a loss.

Recapture of investment tax credit. When investment credit property is disposed of or ceases to be used in the trade or business of the taxpayer, some of the investment tax credit claimed on such property may be recaptured as additional tax liability. The amount of the recapture (by IRS) is the difference between the amount of the credit originally claimed and what should have been claimed in light of the length of time the property was actually held or used for qualifying purposes. *See* Investment tax credit.

Receipt. Written acknowledgment of the receipt of money, or delivery of a thing of value, without containing any affirmative obligation upon either party to it; a mere admission of a fact, in writing. And, being a mere acknowledgment of payment, is subject to parol explanation or contradiction.

A writing which acknowledges taking or receiving either money or goods which have been paid or have been delivered. Act of receiving; also, the fact of receiving or being received; that which is received. That which comes in, in distinction from what is expended, paid out, sent away, and the like.

It requires delivery or change of possession from seller to buyer, and can only be accomplished, in absence of tortious appropriation, by affirmative assent and conduct of seller.

Receipt of goods. Taking physical possession of goods. U.C.C. § 2–103(1)(c).

Warehouse receipt. See that title.

Receivable. That which is due and owing a person or company (*e.g.* account receivable). In bookkeeping, the name of an account which reflects a debt due. *See also* Installment receivable.

Nontrade receivables. Those receivables that arise from transactions and events not directly related to the sale of goods and services.

Receivable turnover ratio. The ratio of annual credit sales to average accounts receivable.

Receive. To take into possession and control; accept custody of; collect.

To "receive" stolen property, means acquisition of control in sense of physical dominion or apparent legal power to dispose of property and envisages possession or control as an essential element. *See also* Receiving stolen goods or property.

Receiver. A person appointed by a court for the purpose of preserving property of a debtor pending an action against him, or applying the property in satisfaction of a creditor's claim, whenever there is danger that, in the absence of such an appointment, the property will be lost, removed or injured. An indifferent person between the parties to a cause, appointed by the court to receive and preserve the property or fund in litigation, and receive its rents, issues, and profits, and apply or dispose of them at the direction of the court when it does not seem reasonable that either party should hold them. A fiduciary of the court, appointed as an incident to other proceedings wherein certain ultimate relief is prayed. He is a trustee or ministerial officer representing court, and all parties in interest in litigation, and property or fund intrusted to him.

Formerly, in bankruptcy proceedings, a person empowered to take charge of the assets of an insolvent person or business and preserve them for sale and distribution to creditors. This function is now performed by a bankruptcy trustee.

A custodian of assets involved in litigation and title to assets remain in owner or owners who are parties in proceedings which lead to appointment of receiver who is managing agent of property for benefit of parties.

As to receivers appointed by federal courts, see Fed.R.Civil P. 66.

See also Receivership; Trustee.

Receiver pendente lite /rəsíyvər pendéntiy láytiy/. A person appointed to take charge of the fund or property to which the receivership extends while the case remains undecided. The title to the property is not changed by the appointment. The receiver acquires no title, but only the right of possession as the officer of the court. The title remains in those in whom it was vested when the appointment was made. The object of the appointment is to secure the property pending the litigation, so that it may be appropriated in accordance with the rights of the parties, as they may be determined by the judgment in the action.

Receivership. Legal or equitable proceeding in which a receiver is appointed for an insolvent corporation, partnership or individual to preserve its assets for benefit of affected parties. The state or condition of a corporation, partnership, financial institution, or individual over whom a receiver has been appointed for protection of its assets and for ultimate sale and distribution to creditors. *See also,* Receiver; Trustee. *Compare* Bankruptcy proceedings.

Regulatory receivership. Receivership by a governmental agency; *e.g.*, of an insolvent financial institution.

Receiving stolen goods or property. Criminal offense of receiving any property with the knowledge that it has been feloniously, or unlawfully stolen, taken, extorted, obtained, embezzled, or disposed of.

Receiving stolen property—a statutory crime separate from the crime involved in the stealing of the property—is defined in the typical statute as the receiving of stolen property knowing that it is stolen. Although most statutes do not specifically mention it, the receiver must, in addition to knowing the property is stolen, intend to deprive the owner of his property. Four elements are necessary to constitute crime of "receiving stolen goods"; (1) the property must be received; (2) it must, at time of its receipt, be stolen property; (3) the receiver must have guilty knowledge that it is

stolen property; and (4) his intent in receiving it must be fraudulent.

A person is guilty of theft if he purposely receives, retains, or disposes of movable property of another knowing that it has been stolen, or believing that it has probably been stolen, unless the property is received, retained, or disposed with purpose to restore it to the owner. "Receiving" means acquiring possession, control or title, or lending on the security of the property. Model Penal Code, § 223.6. For various federal offenses, see 18 U.S.C.A. § 2313 (receipt of stolen vehicles), § 2315 (receipt of stolen goods, money, etc.).

To "receive" stolen property, means acquisition of control in sense of physical dominion or apparent legal power to dispose of property and envisages possession or control as an essential element.

Recess. In the practice of the courts, a short interval or period of time during which the court suspends business, but without adjourning. The period between sessions of court. A temporary ajournment of a trial or a hearing that occurs after a trial or hearing has commenced.

In legislative practice, the interval, occurring in consequence of an adjournment, between the sessions of the same continuous legislative body; not the interval between the final adjournment of one body and the convening of another at the next regular session.

Compare Continuance.

Recession. The act of ceding or falling back. Term is commonly used with reference to a temporary set-back or slow-down in the economic growth of a nation, but less severe than a depression.

Recidivist /rəsídəvəst/. A habitual criminal; a criminal repeater. An incorrigible criminal. One who makes a trade of crime. *See also* Habitual criminal.

Reciprocal. Given or owed mutually as between two persons; interchanged. Reciprocal obligations are those due from one person to another and vice versa. *See also* Reciprocity.

Reciprocal contract. A contract, the parties to which enter into mutual engagements. A mutual or bilateral contract.

Reciprocal dealing arrangement. As included within prohibitions of Sherman Act and Clayton Act exists when two parties face each other as both buyer and seller and one party offers to buy other party's goods, but only if second party buys other goods from first party. *See also* Tying arrangement.

Reciprocal Enforcement of Support Act. Uniform law, adopted in most all states, by which a court in the jurisdiction of a wife or mother can commence proceedings for support against the husband or father residing in another state. The court in the jurisdiction where he lives issues process for his appearance and an order of support is made. This is transmitted to the court of the initiating state.

Reciprocal laws. Laws of one state which extend rights and privileges to citizens of another state if such state grants similar privileges to citizens of the first state; *e.g.* Reciprocal Enforcement of Support Act. *See also* Comity.

Reciprocal promises. Mutual promises exchanged between two parties. *See also* Reciprocal contract.

Reciprocal trade agreements. Agreement between two countries providing for interchange of goods between them at lower tariffs and better terms than exist between one such country and other countries; *e.g.* U.S. Reciprocal Trade Agreements Act of 1934.

Reciprocal trusts. Mutual trusts in one of which A is beneficiary of trust established by B and B is beneficiary of trust settled by A. Commonly these trusts are established by husband and wife.

Reciprocal wills. Wills made by two or more persons in which they make reciprocal testamentary provisions in favor of each other, whether they unite in one will or each executes a separate one. This may be done by one will, in which case the will is both joint and reciprocal, or it may be done by separate wills.

Reciprocity. Mutuality. The term is used to denote the relation existing between two states when each of them gives the subjects of the other certain privileges, on condition that its own subjects shall enjoy similar privileges at the hands of the latter state. Term may also refer to practice, prohibited by Sherman Antitrust Act, whereby a company, overtly or tacitly, agrees to conduct one or more aspects of its business so as to confer a benefit on the other party to the agreement, the consideration being the return promise in kind by the other party, and it is basically a policy of favoring one's customers in purchasing commodities sold by them. The legality of reciprocity agreements under the antitrust laws is analyzed in much the same way as the legality of typing arrangements. *See also* Reciprocal; Tying arrangement.

Recision of contract. *See* Rescission of contract.

Recital. The formal statement or setting forth of some matter of fact, in any deed or writing, in order to explain the reasons upon which the transaction is founded. The recitals are situated in the premises of a deed, that is, in that part of a deed between the date and the *habendum,* and they usually commence with the formal word "whereas."

In pleading, the statement of matter as introductory to some positive allegation, beginning in declarations with the words, "For that *whereas.*"

Recite. To state in a written instrument facts connected with its inception, or reasons for its being made. Also to quote or set forth the words or the contents of some other instrument or document; as, to "recite" a statute.

Reck. To take heed; have a care, mind, heed.

Reckless. Not recking; careless, heedless, inattentive; indifferent to consequences. According to circumstances it may mean desperately heedless, wanton or willful, or it may mean only careless, inattentive, or negligent. For conduct to be "reckless" it must be such as to evince disregard of, or indifference to, consequences, under circumstances involving danger to life or safety to others, although no harm was intended. *See also* Recklessly; Recklessness; Wanton.

Reckless disregard of rights of others. As used in automobile guest law, means the voluntary doing by motorist of an improper or wrongful act, or with knowledge of existing conditions, the voluntary refraining from doing a proper or prudent act when such act or failure to act evinces an entire abandonment of any care, and heedless indifference to results which may follow and the reckless taking of chance of accident happening without intent that any occur.

"Reckless disregard" so as to show actual malice in publication may be shown to exist where there exists sufficient evidence to permit conclusion that defendant in fact entertained serious doubts as to truth of his publication or where there are obvious reasons to doubt veracity of informant or accuracy of his reports.

Reckless driving. Operation of motor vehicle manifesting reckless disregard of possible consequences and indifference to others' rights. To establish statutory offense of reckless driving requires proof that defendant in management of motor vehicle intentionally did something with knowledge that injury to another was probable or acted with wanton and reckless disregard for safety of others and in reckless disregard of consequences of acts. Within meaning of statutory prohibition is a conscious and intentional driving which driver knows, or should know, creates unreasonable risk of harm to others, even though he has no actual intent to harm.

Reckless endangerment. A statutory offense committed by creating a substantial risk of death or serious injury to another.

Reckless homicide. A species of statutory homicide in some states characterized by a wilful and wanton disregard of consequences and resulting in death. In some states, it may amount to manslaughter. *See* Homicide *(Vehicular homicide).*

Recklessly. A person acts recklessly with respect to a material element of an offense when he consciously disregards a substantial and unjustifiable risk that the material element exists or will result from his conduct. The risk must be of such a nature and degree that, considering the nature and purpose of the actor's conduct and the circumstances known to him, its disregard involves a gross deviation from the standard of conduct that a law-abiding person would observe in the actor's situation. Model Penal Code, § 2.02(c).

Person acts "recklessly" within meaning of requirement for commission of involuntary manslaughter when he consciously disregards substantial and unjustifiable risk that his acts are such as are likely to cause death or great bodily harm to some individual and where such disregard constitutes gross deviation from standard of care which reasonable person would exercise in such situation.

See also Reckless.

Reckless misconduct. A person is guilty of reckless misconduct when he intentionally does an act, or fails to do an act in violation of his duty, with knowledge of serious danger to others involved in it or of facts which would disclose such danger to a reasonable man. Such misconduct means that the actor intentionally does an act or fails to do an act which it is his duty to another to do, knowing or having reason to know of facts which would lead a reasonable man to conclude that such conduct creates an unreasonable risk of bodily harm to the other.

Recklessness. Rashness; heedlessness; wanton conduct. The state of mind accompanying an act, which either pays no regard to its probably or possibly injurious consequences, or which, though forseeing such consequences, persists in spite of such knowledge. Recklessness is a stronger term than mere or ordinary negligence, and to be reckless, the conduct must be such as to evince disregard of or indifference to consequences, under circumstances involving danger to life or safety of others, although no harm was intended.

Reclaim. To claim or demand back; to ask for the return or restoration of a thing; to insist upon one's right to recover that which was one's own, but was parted with conditionally or mistakenly; as, to *reclaim* goods which were obtained from one under false pretenses.

Reclamation. The process of bringing economically unusable land to a higher dollar value by physically changing it; *e.g.* draining a swamp, irrigating desert, replanting a forest.

A banking term used to describe a draft or check set aside because of an error in the listing of the check in clearing house balance.

Reclamation Act. The Reclamation Act of 1902 (43 U.S.C.A. § 391 et seq.), authorized the Secretary of the Interior to locate, construct, operate, and maintain works for the storage, diversion, and development of waters for the reclamation of arid and semiarid lands in the Western States. To perform these functions, the Secretary in July 1902 established a Reclamation Service in the Geological Survey. In March 1907 the Reclamation Service was separated from the Survey, and in June 1923 the name was changed to Bureau of Reclamation. The basic objectives of the Federal Reclamation program, as administered by the Bureau of Reclamation, are to assist the States, local governments, and other Federal agencies to stabilize and stimulate local and regional economies, enhance and protect the environment, and improve the quality of life through development of water and related land resources throughout the 17 contiguous Western States and Hawaii.

Reclamation Bureau. *See* Reclamation Act.

Reclamation district. A subdivision of a state created by legislative authority, for the purpose of reclaiming swamp, marshy, or desert lands within its boundaries and rendering them fit for habitation or cultivation, generally with funds raised by local taxation or the issue of bonds, and sometimes with authority to make rules or ordinances for the regulation of the work in hand.

Recognition. Ratification; confirmation; an acknowledgment that something done by another person in one's name had one's authority.

Recognition of gain or loss. *See* Recognized gain or loss.

Recognizance /rəkógnəzəns/. An obligation entered into before a court or magistrate duly authorized for that purpose whereby the recognizor acknowledges that he will do some act required by law which is specified therein. The act of recognizing is performed by the recognizor's assenting to the words of the magistrate and acknowledging himself to be indebted to a certain party in a specific amount to be paid if he fails to perform the requisite act.

An obligation undertaken by a person, generally a defendant in a criminal case, to appear in court on a particular day or to keep the peace. It runs to the court and may not require a bond. In this case it is called personal recognizance. 18 U.S.C.A. § 3142; Fed.R.Crim.P. 46. *See* Release on own recognizance.

Recognize /rékəgnàyz/. To try; to examine in order to determine the truth of a matter. Also to enter into a recognizance.

Recognized. Actual and publicly known.

Recognized gain or loss. The portion of realized gain or loss that is subject to income taxation. *See also* Realized gain or loss.

Recognized market. Under Uniform Commercial Code provision (U.C.C. § 9–504(3)) allowing secured party to dispose of collateral without notification if collateral is type of property customarily sold in "recognized market," "recognized market" is one in which sales involve many items so similar that individual differences are nonexistent or immaterial, where haggling and competitive bidding are not primary factors in each sale, and where prices paid in actual sales of comparable property are currently available by quotation, for example, the New York Stock Exchange and bond and commodity markets.

Recognizee. He to whom one is bound in a recognizance.

Recognizor. He who enters into a recognizance.

Recollection. The act of recalling something to mind. In evidence, a person may use almost anything to refresh his recollection of an event in order to testify and the evidence then is his testimony not the document which has refreshed his recollection.

A memorandum or record concerning a matter about which a witness once had knowledge but now has insufficient recollection to enable him to testify fully and accurately, shown to have been made or adopted by the witness when the matter was fresh in his memory and to reflect that knowledge correctly is not excluded by the hearsay rule. If admitted, the memorandum or record may be read into evidence but may not itself be received as an exhibit unless offered by an adverse party. See Fed.Evid.Rules 612 and 803(5).

See also Past recollection recorded; Recorded past recollection; Refreshing the memory.

Recommend. To advise or counsel. *See* Counsel.

Reconciliation /rèkənsìliyéyshən/. The renewal of amicable relations between two persons who had been at enmity or variance; usually implying forgiveness of injuries on one or both sides. In law of domestic relations, a voluntary resumption of marital relations in the fullest sense. It means something more than mere resumption of cohabitation and observance of civility, and comprehends a fresh start and genuine effort by both parties to avoid pitfalls originally causing separation.

In bookkeeping, it is the practice of adjusting the bank statement with the depositor's books. Also, a statement showing the consistency of two or more other financial statements. *See also* Reconciliation statement.

Reconciliation statement. In accounting, a statement prepared to bring two or more accounts which show a discrepancy into agreement.

Reconsideration. As normally used in context of administrative adjudication, term implies reexamination, and possibly a different decision by the entity which initially decided it.

Reconsignment. A change in the terms of a consignment after the goods are in transit. Privilege extended by carriers to shippers under which goods may be forwarded to a point other than their original destination, without removal from the car and at the through rate from initial point to that of final delivery.

Reconstruct. To construct again, to rebuild, either in fact or idea, or to remodel. To form again or anew as in the imagination or to restore again as an entity the thing which was lost or destroyed. *See also* Recollection.

Reconveyance. The return of title and ownership in real estate to a party that previously held title to it.

Record, *v.* To commit to writing, to printing, to inscription, or the like. To make an official note of; to write, transcribe, or enter in a book, file, docket, register, computer tape or disc, or the like, for the purpose of preserving authentic evidence of. To transcribe a document, or enter the history of an act or series of acts, in an official volume, for the purpose of giving notice of the same, of furnishing authentic evidence, and for preservation. *See also* Recording acts.

Record, *n.* A written account of some act, court proceeding, transaction, or instrument, drawn up, under authority of law, by a proper officer, and designed to remain as a memorial or permanent evidence of the matters to which it relates. A memorandum public or private, of what has been done, ordinarily applied to public records, in which sense it is a written memorial made by a public officer. A computer printout qualifies as a "record" within business records exception to hearsay rule.

The act or fact of recording or being recorded; reduction to writing as evidence, also, the writing so made. A register, a family record, official contemporaneous writing; an authentic official copy of document entered in book or deposited in keeping of officer designated by law; an official contemporaneous memorandum stating the proceedings of a court or official copy of legal papers used in a case.

Records are generally admissable under Fed. Evid.R. 803. See also Rules 901 and 902 (authentication), and Rule 1005 (public records). *See* Business entry rule.

The term "records" means accounts, correspondence, memorandums, tapes, discs, papers, books, and other documents or transcribed information of any type, whether expressed in ordinary or machine language. Securities Exchange Act of 1934, § 3.

See also Business *(Business records)*; Congressional Record; Court *(Court of record)*; Defective record; Docket; File; Freedom of Information Act; Judgment book; Making record; Minutes book; Official record; Official Records Act; Of record; Public record; Sealing of records; Shop-book rule; Whole record test.

Arrest record. See Arrest record.

Complete record. Such encompasses clerk's record, record of proceedings and all evidence.

Court record of proceedings. The official collection of all the trial pleadings, exhibits, orders and word-for-word testimony that took place during the trial. The "record" includes pleadings, the process, the verdict, the judgment and such other matters as by some statutory or other recognized method have been made a part of it.

A written memorial of all the acts and proceedings in an action or suit, in a court of record. The official and authentic history of the cause, consisting in entries of each successive step in the proceedings, chronicling the various acts of the parties and of the court, couched in the formal language established by usage, terminating with the judgment rendered in the cause, and intended to remain as a perpetual and unimpeachable memorial of the proceedings and judgment. Such record in civil cases consists primarily of the "civil docket" (Fed.R.Civil P. 79); and in criminal cases of the "criminal docket" (Fed.R.Crim.P. 55). *See also* Docket; Transcript, and *Record on appeal, below.*

Courts of record. A court whose proceedings are recorded. Also a court of general jurisdiction. States vary as to the requirements and strata of courts qualifying as courts of record. *See also* Court *(Court of record)*.

Debts of record. Those which appear to be due by the evidence of a court of record; such as a judgment, recognizance, etc.

Diminution of record. Incompleteness of the record sent up on appeal. *See* Diminution.

Face of record. See Face of record.

Judicial record. A precise history of civil or criminal proceeding from commencement to termination. *See* Docket.

Matter of record. See that title.

Of record. See that title.

Public record. A record, memorial of some act or transaction, written evidence of something done, or document, considered as either concerning or interesting the public, affording notice or information to the public, or open to public inspection. Any "writing" prepared, owned, used or retained by any agency in pursuance of law or in connection with the transaction of public business; and, "writings" means all documents, papers, letters,

maps, books, photographs, films, sound recordings, magnetic or other tapes, electronic data-processing records, artifacts or other documentary material, regardless of physical form or characteristics.

Record date. The date on which a person must be registered as a shareholder on the stock book of a company in order to receive a declared dividend or, among other things, to vote on company affairs. Dividends are paid on payment date to those who own the stock on the record date.

Record on appeal. In the practice of appellate tribunals, refers to the history of the proceedings on the trial of the action below (with the pleadings, offers, objections to evidence, rulings of the court, exceptions, charge, etc.), in so far as the same appears in the record furnished to the appellate court in the paperbooks or other transcripts. Hence, derivatively, it means the aggregate of the various judicial steps taken on the trial below, in so far as they were taken, presented, or allowed in the formal and proper manner necessary to put them upon the record of the court. This is the meaning in such phrases as "no error in the record," "contents of the record," "outside the record," etc.

The official documentation of all the proceedings in court in a particular case, including the pleadings, exhibits and commonly the transcript of the examination of witnesses; may also include docket entries. Fed.R.App.P. 10(a).

Record owner. The person in whose name stock shares are registered on the records of the corporation. A record owner is treated as the owner of the shares by the corporation whether or not that person is the beneficial owner of the shares. As regards real property ownership, is person in whose name title appears on official records in contrast with one who claims title through unrecorded documents.

Records of a corporation. Such records include the transcript of its charter and by-laws, the minutes of its meetings—the books containing the accounts of its official doings and the written evidence of its contracts and business transactions.

Title of record. A title to real estate, evidenced and provable by one or more conveyances or other instruments all of which are duly entered on the public land records. *See also* Abstract of title.

Recordation. The act or process of recording an instrument such as a deed or mortgage in a public registry. Also, the system of recording court proceedings by stenography, voice-writing or tapes.

Recorded past recollection. In evidence, a document which was prepared at a time when the events recorded were fresh in the mind and memory of the person preparing it may be admissible as an exception to the hearsay rule if, as a preliminary matter, the judge is satisfied that it is the work of the witness and that it is the original unless such is excused under the best evidence rule. See Fed.Evid.R. 612 and 803(5). *See also* Past recollection recorded; Recollection.

Recorder, *n.* A magistrate, in the judicial systems of some of the states, who has a criminal jurisdiction analogous to that of a police judge or other committing magistrate, and usually a limited civil jurisdiction, and sometimes authority conferred by statute in special classes of proceedings. An officer appointed to make record or enrolment of deeds and other legal instruments authorized by law to be recorded. A local government officer in whose office deeds, mortgages, liens, and other instruments are registered.

Record, estoppel by. An "estoppel by record" is the preclusion to deny the truth of a matter set forth in a record, whether judicial or legislative, also to deny the facts adjudicated by a court of competent jurisdiction. An estoppel by record cannot be invoked where allegations or recitals did not conclude pleader in prior proceeding. It bars a second action between the same parties on an issue necessarily raised and decided in the first action. It exists only as between the same parties, or those in privity with them, in same case on same issues. The doctrine prevents a party not only from litigating again what was actually litigated in the former case, but litigating what might have been litigated therein.

Recording acts. Statutes enacted in the several states relative to the official recording of deeds, mortgages, security interests, etc. as notice to creditors, purchasers, encumbrancers, and others interested.

Notice acts. That type of recording statute provides that a person with notice of an unrecorded instrument is barred from claiming priority as of the date on which he received the instrument. *See also* Notice race statutes; Notice recording statutes.

Race acts. The first to record regardless of notice of an unrecorded deed earlier in time has the better rights under a race type recording statute. *See* Pure race statute.

Race-notice acts. The first to record in the chain of title without notice of a prior unrecorded deed or mortgage has the better rights under a race-notice type statute. *See* Race-notice recording statutes.

Record notice. When an instrument of conveyance or a mortgage is recorded in the appropriate public office, it is constructive notice of its contents to the whole world.

Recoup, *or* **recoupe** /rəkúwp/. To deduct, defalk, discount, set off, or keep back; to withhold part of a demand. *See* Recoupment.

Recoupment /rəkúwpmənt/. To recover a loss by a subsequent gain. In pleading, to set forth a claim against the plaintiff when an action is brought against one as a defendant. A keeping back something which is due, because there is an equitable reason to withhold it. A right of the defendant to have a deduction from the amount of the plaintiff's damages, for the reason that the plaintiff has not complied with the cross-obligations or independent covenants arising under the same contract. It implies that plaintiff has cause of action, but asserts that defendant has counter cause of action growing out of breach of some other part of same contract on which plaintiff's action is founded, or for some cause connected with contract.

The right of the defendant to have the plaintiff's monetary claim reduced by reason of some claim the defendant has against the plaintiff arising out of the very contract giving rise to plaintiff's claim. Unlike a counterclaim, recoupment only reduces plaintiff's claim; it does not allow recovery of affirmative money judgment for any excess over that claim.

Recoupment is the equivalent of the old counterclaim in which a defendant sets up a claim owed to him by the plaintiff though it need not arise out of the same transaction as the plaintiff's claim and the defendant may not recover more than the amount claimed by the plaintiff against him. Under rules practice, recoupment has been replaced by the modern counterclaim. *See also* Counterclaim.

Set-off distinguished. A "set-off" is a demand which the defendant has against the plaintiff, arising out of a transaction extrinsic to the plaintiff's cause of action, whereas a "recoupment" is a reduction or rebate by the defendant of part of the plaintiff's claim because of a right in the defendant arising out of the same transaction. *See also* Set-off.

Recourse. To recur. The right of a holder of a negotiable instrument to recover against a party secondarily liable, *e.g.,* prior endorser or guarantor. Therefore, if a prior endorser signs *without recourse*, he exempts himself from liability for payment, but not from all warranties. U.C.C. § 3–414(1). *See also* Nonrecourse; Nonrecourse loan; Recourse loan; Without recourse; With recourse.

Recourse loan. Loan on which an endorser or guarantor is liable in event of default of borrower. *See also* Recourse; With recourse. *Compare* Nonrecourse loan.

Recover. To get or obtain again, to collect, to get renewed possession of; to win back. To regain, as lost property, territory, appetite, health, courage. In a narrower sense, to be successful in a suit, to collect or obtain amount, to have judgment, to obtain a favorable or final judgment, to obtain in any legal manner in contrast to voluntary payment. *See also* Recovery.

Recoveree. In old conveyancing, the party who suffered a common recovery.

Recoverer. The demandant in a common recovery, after judgment has been given in his favor.

Recovery. In its most extensive sense, the restoration or vindication of a right existing in a person, by the formal judgment or decree of a competent court, at his instance and suit, or the obtaining, by such judgment, of some right or property which has been taken or withheld from him. This is also called a "true" recovery, to distinguish it from a "feigned" or "common" recovery.

The obtaining of a thing by the judgment of a court, as the result of an action brought for that purpose. The amount finally collected, or the amount of judgment. To be successful in a suit to obtain a judgment.

See Recoupment; Repossession; Restitution.

Final recovery. The final judgment or verdict in an action. *See* Judgment; Verdict.

Recrimination /rəkrìmənéyshən/. A charge made by an accused person against the accuser; in particular a counter-charge of adultery or cruelty made by one charged with the same offense in a suit for divorce, against the person who has charged him or her. Under doctrine of "recrimination", if conduct of both husband and wife has been such as to furnish grounds for divorce neither is entitled to relief. A showing by the defendant of any cause of divorce against the plaintiff, in bar of the plaintiff's cause of divorce. And to bar divorce, complainant's misconduct need not be of equal degree with that of defendant, but must be of same general character. The defense of recrimination has been abolished in many states with the enactment of "no-fault" divorce statutes.

Recross examination. An examination of a witness by a cross-examiner subsequent to a redirect examination of the witness. *See also* Re-examination.

Rectification. The act or process by which something is made right or by which a wrong is adjusted. *See also* Rectify; Restitution.

Rectify. To correct or define something which is erroneous or doubtful. Thus, where the parties to an agreement have determined to embody its terms in the appropriate and conclusive form, but the instrument meant to effect this purpose (*e.g.*, a conveyance, settlement, etc.) is, by mutual mistake, so framed as not to express the real inten-

tion of the parties, an action may be brought to have it rectified.

Recusal. The process by which a judge is disqualified on objection of either party (or disqualifies himself or herself) from hearing a lawsuit because of self interest, bias or prejudice. *See also* Recusation.

Recusation /rèkyəzéyshən/. *See* Recusal.

Redeem /rədíym/. To buy back. To free property or article from mortgage or pledge by paying the debt for which it stood as security. To repurchase in a literal sense; as, to redeem one's land from a tax-sale. It implies the existence of a debt and means to rid property of that incumbrance. *See also* Redemption.

Redeemable /rədíyməbəl/. Subject to redemption; admitting of redemption or repurchase; given or held under conditions admitting of reacquisition by purchase; as, a "redeemable pledge."

Redeemable bond. A bond which the issuer may call for payment pursuant to the terms of the bond and indenture; a callable bond.

Redeemable rights. Rights which return to the conveyor or disposer of land, etc., upon payment of the sum for which such rights are granted.

Redeemable stock. Capital stock, generally preferred, which, by its terms, may be called by the issuing corporation and paid.

Redelivery. A yielding and delivering back of a thing.

Redelivery bond. A bond given to a sheriff or other officer, who has attached or levied on personal property, to obtain the release and repossession of the property, conditioned to redeliver the property to the officer or pay him its value in case the levy or attachment is adjudged good.

Redemise /rìydəmáyz/. A regranting of land demised or leased.

Redemption. The realization of a right to have the title of property restored free and clear of the mortgage; performance of the mortgage obligation being essential for that purpose.

The right of a debtor, and sometimes of a debtor's other creditors, to repurchase from a buyer at a forced sale property of the debtor that was seized and sold in satisfaction of a judgment or other claim against the debtor, which right usually is limited to forced sales of real property. Also, a bankruptcy term for extinguishing a lien on exempt property by making a cash payment equal to the value of the property.

The reacquisition of a security by the issuer pursuant to a provision in the security that specifies the terms on which the reacquisition may take place. A security is called for redemption when the issuer notifies the holder that the redemption privilege has been exercised. Typically, a holder of a security that has been called for redemption will have a limited period thereafter to decide whether or not to exercise a conversion right, if one exists.

A repurchase; a buying back. The act of a vendor of property in buying it back again from the purchaser at the same or an enhanced price. The process of annulling and revoking a conditional sale of property, by performance of the conditions on which it was stipulated to be revocable.

The process of cancelling and annulling a defeasible title to land, such as is created by a mortgage or a tax-sale, by paying the debt or fulfilling the other conditions. The liberation of an estate from a mortgage. The liberation of a chattel from pledge or pawn, by paying the debt for which it stood as security.

Repurchase of notes, bonds, stock, bills, or other evidences of debt, by paying their value to their holders. The payment of principal and unpaid interest on bonds or other debt obligations.

Repurchase by corporation of its shares at a price equal to the net asset value of the shares on date a redemption request is received by the corporation. *See also* Stock *(Stock redemption)*.

See also Certificate of redemption; Equitable redemption; Equity of redemption; Right of redemption; Tax redemption.

Redemption period. A time period during which a defaulted mortgage, land contract, deed of trust, etc., can be redeemed. Such period is commonly provided for by state statute.

Redemption premium. An additional price paid on the retirement of a security.

Redemption price. The price at which a bond may be redeemed before maturity, at the option of the issuing company. Such term also applies to the price the company must pay to call in certain types of preferred stock.

Red handed. Expression used in reference to suspect caught with evidence of crime on him or in his possession.

Red herring. In securities law, a preliminary prospectus that has not yet been approved by the Securities Exchange Commission or state securities commissioners. It has a red border on its front to give notice to interested parties that the securities offering is not yet approved for final distribution. It is used as a type of advertising device to encourage securities sales. *See also* Prospectus.

Redhibition /rèd(h)əbíshən/. Avoidance of sale on account of vice or defect in thing sold which renders it either absolutely useless or its use so inconvenient and imperfect that it may be pre-

sumed that buyer would not have purchased it had he known of defects.

Redirect examination. An examination of a witness by the direct examiner subsequent to the cross-examination of the witness. *See also* Rehabilitation.

Rediscount. The act of discounting an instrument which has already been discounted as in the case of a bank which has already discounted a note and then discounts or sells it again.

Rediscount rate. The rate, fixed by the Federal Reserve Board, at which a Federal Reserve Bank can make loans to member banks on the security of commercial paper already discounted by such banks.

Redistricting. *See* Reapportionment.

Redlining. Term used to refer to a pattern of discrimination in which financial institutions refuse to make mortgage loans, regardless of credit record of the applicant, on properties in specified areas because of alleged deteriorating conditions. At one time, lenders actually outlined these areas with a red pencil. Such practice violates federal laws. 12 U.S.C. § 2801 et seq. Such practice also includes a discriminatory failure or refusal to provide property insurance on dwellings.

Redraft. A second or cross bill drafted by the original drawer after the first draft has been dishonored and protested. The amount includes the additional costs as well as the original face amount.

Redress. Satisfaction for an injury or damages sustained. Damages or equitable relief. *See* Recovery; Restitution.

Red tape. In a derivative sense, order carried to fastidious excess; system run out into trivial extremes. Term commonly refers to excessive bureaucracy.

Reduced to practice. *See* Reduction to practice.

Reduction to possession. Conversion of a right existing as a claim into actual custody and enjoyment.

Reduction to practice. As respects priority of invention for purposes of patentability is accomplished when inventor's conception is embodied in such form as to render it capable of practical and successful use for its intended purpose. But device need not be perfect or commercial success.

Redundancy. Introducing superfluous matter into a legal instrument; particularly the insertion in a pleading of matters foreign, extraneous, and irrelevant to that which it is intended to answer. Redundant matter in pleadings may be ordered stricken on motion. Fed.R. Civil P. 12(f).

Re-enact. To enact again; to revive.

Re-enactment rule. If the legislature enacts again a statute which had long continued executive construction by an agency, it can be said that the legislature has adopted that construction.

Re-entry. The act of resuming the possession of lands or tenements in pursuance of a right which party exercising it reserved to himself when he quit his former possession. The right reserved by a grantor to enter the premises on breach of a condition of the conveyance. *See also* Repossession.

Re-establish. To restore to its former position.

Re-examination. An examination of a witness after a cross-examination, upon matters arising out of such cross-examination. *See also* Recross examination.

Re-exchange. The damages or expenses caused by the dishonor and protest of a bill of exchange in a foreign country, where it was payable, and by its return to the place where it was drawn or indorsed, and its being there taken up.

Re-export. The act of exporting a product which has previously been imported and left relatively unchanged in form before exporting again.

Refer. When a case or action involves matters of account or other intricate details which require minute examination, and for that reason are not fit to be brought before a jury, it is common to *refer* the whole case, or some part of it, to the decision of an auditor, master, or referee, and the case is then said to be referred. *See* Referee; Reference.

Taking this word in its strict, technical use, it relates to a mode of determining questions which is distinguished from "arbitration," in that the latter word imports submission of a controversy without any lawsuit having been brought, while "reference" imports a lawsuit pending, and an issue framed or question raised which (and not the controversy itself) is sent out. Thus, arbitration is resorted to instead of any judicial proceeding; while reference is one mode of decision employed in the course of a judicial proceeding.

To point, allude, direct, or make reference to. This is the use of the word in conveyancing and in literature, where a word or sign introduced for the purpose of directing the reader's attention to another place in the deed, book, document, etc., is said to "refer" him to such other connection.

Referee. A person to whom a cause pending in a court is referred by the court, to take testimony, hear the parties, and report thereon to the court. Person who is appointed by court to exercise certain judicial powers, to take testimony, to hear parties, and report his findings. He is an officer exercising judicial powers, and is an arm of the court for a specific purpose. Similar functions are performed by auditors, assessors, or masters

(q.v.). See Fed.R.Civil P. 53. *See also* Magistrate; Master; Reference.

Referee in bankruptcy. An officer appointed by the courts of bankruptcy under the Bankruptcy Act of 1898 (11 U.S.C.A. § 1) corresponding to the "registers in bankruptcy" under earlier statutes having administrative and quasi-judicial functions under the bankruptcy law, and whose functions and powers were to administer proceedings under the federal Bankruptcy Act *(q.v.).* Such referees (called "bankruptcy judges" after 1973) were abolished by the 1978 Bankruptcy Code; their functions now being performed by Bankruptcy Court judges.

Reference. The act of referring a case to a referee, auditor, or master to find facts and submit report to the court. The document by which the reference is made. Fed.R.Civil P. 53. *See also* Master; Referee.

In contracts, an agreement to submit to arbitration; the act of parties in submitting their controversy to chosen referees or arbitrators.

A person who will provide information for you about your character, credit, etc. The act of sending or directing one person to another, for information or advice as to the character, solvency, standing, etc., of a third person, who desires to open business relations with the first, or to obtain credit with him.

Reference statutes. Statutes which refer to other statutes and make them applicable to the subject of legislation. Their object is to incorporate into the act of which they are a part the provisions of other statutes by reference and adoption.

Referendum /rèfəréndəm/. The process of referring to the electorate for approval a proposed new state constitution or amendment (constitutional referendum) or of a law passed by the legislature (statutory referendum). Right constitutionally reserved to people of state, or local subdivision thereof, to have submitted for their approval or rejection, under prescribed conditions, any law or part of law passed by lawmaking body. Not all state constitutions make provision for referendum process. *See also* Initiative; Plebiscite; Proposition.

In international law, a communication sent by a diplomatic representative to his home government, in regard to matters presented to him which he is unable or unwilling to decide without further instructions.

Refinance. To finance again or anew; to pay off existing debts with funds secured from new debt; to extend the maturity date and/or increase the amount of an existing debt; to arrange for a new payment schedule. The discharge of an obligation with funds acquired through the creation of a new debt, often at a different interest rate. *See also* Debt adjustment; Recapitalization.

Reform. To correct, rectify, amend, remodel. Instruments *inter partes* may be *reformed*, when defective, by a court. By this is meant that the court, after ascertaining the real and original intention of the parties to a deed or other instrument (which intention they failed to sufficiently express, through some error, mistake of fact, or inadvertence), will decree that the instrument be held and construed as if it fully and technically expressed that intention. *See also* Reformation.

Reformation. A court-ordered correction of a written instrument to cause it to reflect the true intentions of the parties. Equitable remedy used to reframe written contracts to reflect accurately real agreement between contracting parties when, either through mutual mistake or unilateral mistake coupled with actual or equitable fraud by other party, the writing does not embody contract as actually made.

If by mistake of fact as to the contents of a written agreement or conveyance, or by mistake of law as to its legal effect, the writing does not conform to the agreement of the parties to it, the writing can be reformed to accord with the agreement. Restatement, Second, Agency, § 8D.

Doing over to bring about a better result, correction or rectification.

See also Reform.

Reformatory. A penal institution for youthful offenders where the emphasis is on reformation of the juvenile's behavior.

Refreshing recollection. *See* Recollection; Recorded past recollection; Refreshing the memory.

Refreshing the memory. The act of a witness who consults his documents, memoranda, or books, to bring more distinctly to his recollection the details of past events or transactions, concerning which he is testifying. See Fed.Evid.R. 612. *See also* Past recollection recorded; Recollection; Recorded past recollection.

Refund, n. As generally referred to in connection with income taxes, is the amount a taxpayer or reporting entity would receive from the government due to an overpayment of taxes. *See also* Rebate.

Refund, v. To repay or restore; to return money in restitution or repayment; *e.g.* to refund overpaid taxes; to refund purchase price of returned goods. *See also* Rebate; Refund claim; Refunds.

To fund again or anew; specifically, finance, to borrow, usually by the sale of bonds, in order to pay off an existing loan with the proceeds. *See also* Recapitalization; Refinance.

Refundable. Eligible for refunding under the terms of the bond indenture. *See* Refunding bond.

Refund claim. A request directed to the Internal Revenue Service for repayment (*i.e.* refund) of taxes overpaid.

Refunding. Type of refinancing (*q.v.*) in which the issuer of bonds replaces outstanding bonds with a new issue. In general, any act of repayment of a loan or money advanced. *See also* Recapitalization; Refinance.

Refunding bond. A bond which replaces or pays off outstanding bond which holder surrenders in exchange for new security. Also a bond given to an executor by a legatee, upon receiving payment of the legacy, conditioned to *refund* the same, or so much of it as may be necessary, if the assets prove deficient.

Refunds. Money received by the government or its officers which, for any cause, are to be refunded or restored to the parties paying them; such as excessive duties or taxes, duties paid on goods destroyed by accident, duties received on goods which are re-exported, etc. *See also* Rebate; Refund.

Refusal. The act of one who has, by law, a right and power of having or doing something of advantage, and declines it. Also, the declination of a request or demand, or the omission to comply with some requirement of law, as the result of a positive intention to disobey. In the latter sense, the word is often coupled with "neglect," as if a party shall "neglect or refuse" to pay a tax, file an official bond, obey an order of court, etc. But "neglect" signifies a mere omission of a duty, which may happen through inattention, dilatoriness, mistake, or inability to perform, while "refusal" implies the positive denial of an application or command, or at least a mental determination not to comply. A rejection, a denial of what is asked. *See also* Rejection; Renunciation; Repudiation; Rescind.

Refuse, *v.* /rəfyúwz/. To deny, decline, reject. "Fail" is distinguished from "refuse" in that "refuse" involves an act of the will, while "fail" may be an act of inevitable necessity.

Refuse, *n.* /réfyuws/. That which is refused or rejected as useless or worthless. Worthless matter, rubbish, scum, leavings. In statute prohibiting discharge into navigable waters of refuse, "refuse" includes all foreign substances and pollutants other than liquid sewage.

Register, *v.* To record formally and exactly; to enroll; to enter precisely in a list or the like. To make correspond exactly one with another; to fit correctly in a relative position; to be in correct alignment one with another. *See also* Record.

Register, *n.* An officer authorized by law to keep a record called a "register" or "registry."

A book of public facts such as births, deaths and marriages (also called a registry), or the public official who keeps such book. Other examples of public record books are the register of patents (a list of all patents granted) and the register of ships (kept by customs). Other examples of public record keeping officials are the register of copyrights, register of deeds (land records) and the register of wills (clerk of probate court). They are often called "Recorder" or "Registrar."

See also Federal Register.

Registered. Entered or recorded in some official register or record or list.

Registered bond. A bond entered on the books of the issuing corporation or of its transfer agent in the name of the purchaser, whose name also appears on the face of the bonds. Either principal alone or both principal and interest may be registered.

A bond the number of which is recorded by the seller in the name of the purchaser and which only the latter, or one legally authorized to act for him, can redeem. Principal of such a bond and interest, if registered as to interest, is paid to the owner listed on the books of the issuer, as opposed to a bearer bond where the possessor of the bond is entitled to interest and principal.

The bonds of the United States government (and of many municipal and private corporations) are either registered or "coupon bonds." In the case of a registered bond, the name of the owner or lawful holder is entered in a register or record, and it is not negotiable or transferable except by an entry on the register, and checks or warrants are sent to the registered holder for the successive installments of interest as they fall due. A bond with interest coupons attached is transferable by mere delivery, and the coupons are payable, as due, to the person who shall present them for payment. But the bond issues of many private corporations now provide that the individual bonds "may be registered as to principal," leaving the interest coupons payable to bearer, or that they may be registered as to both principal and interest, at the option of the holder.

Registered check. A check purchased by a person at a bank and drawn on funds of the bank that have been specially set aside to cover the check, though not certified by the bank; loosely called a money order. *Compare* Money order.

Registered corporation. A publicly held corporation which has registered under section 12 of the Securities Exchange Act of 1934 (15 U.S.C.A. § 78*l*). *See also* Registration statement.

Registered mail. Type of special mailing privilege given by the U.S. Postal Service for an extra fee and which provides insurance of its delivery up to certain amount.

Registered representative. A person who has met the qualifications set by law or regulations (of *e.g.* SEC and New York Stock Exchange) to sell securities to the public.

Registered securities. *See* Registered bond; Registered stock; Registration of securities; Registration statement.

Registered stock. Stock issue that has been registered with Securities and Exchange Commission as a new issue or secondary offering. 15 U.S.C.A. § 77c et seq. *See also* Registration of securities; Registration statement.

Registered tonnage. The registered tonnage of a vessel is the capacity or cubical contents of the ship, or the amount of weight which she will carry, as ascertained in some proper manner and entered on an official register or record.

Registered trademark. A trademark filed in the United States Patent and Trademark office, with the necessary description and other statements required by the act of congress, and there duly recorded, securing its exclusive use to the person causing it to be registered. 18 U.S.C.A. § 1051. *See* Trademark.

Registered voters. Persons whose names are placed upon the registration books provided by law as the record or memorial of the duly qualified voters of the state or county. *See also* Qualified voter.

Register of deeds. The name given in some states to the officer whose duty is to record deeds, mortgages, and other instruments affecting realty in the official books provided and kept for that purpose; also commonly called "registrar" or "recorder" of deeds.

Register of ships. A register kept by the collectors of customs, in which the names, ownership, and other facts relative to merchant vessels are required by law to be entered. This register is evidence of the nationality and privileges of an American ship. The certificate of such registration, given by the collector to the owner or master of the ship, is also called the ship's register.

Register of the Treasury. An officer of the United States Treasury, whose duty is to keep all accounts of the receipt and expenditure of public money and of debts due to or from the United States, to preserve adjusted accounts with vouchers and certificates, to record warrants drawn upon the treasury, to sign and issue government securities, and take charge of the registry of vessels under United States laws. 31 U.S.C.A. § 161.

Register of wills. An officer in some of the states, whose function is to record and preserve all wills admitted to probate, to issue letters testamentary or of administration, to receive and file accounts of executors, etc., and generally to act as the clerk of the probate court.

Registrant. One who registers; particularly, one who registers anything (*e.g.*, a trademark) for the purpose of securing a right or privilege granted by law on condition of such registration.

Registrar /réjəstràr/. An officer who has the custody and charge of keeping of a registry or register. Person in educational institution in charge of registering students for enrollment, maintaining academic records, etc. Person in hospital responsible for admitting of patients.

An agent, usually a bank or trust company, appointed by a corporation to keep records of the names of bond and stockholders and distributions of earnings. *See* Registration of securities.

Registrar of deeds. A term used in some states to describe the person in charge of recorded instruments affecting land title. Also commonly called a recorder or register of deeds *(q.v.)*.

Registration. Recording; enrolling; inserting in an official register. Enrollment, as registration of voters, registration for school, etc. The act of making a list, catalogue, schedule, or register, particularly of an official character, or of making entries therein.

Any schedule containing a list of voters, the being upon which constitutes a prerequisite to vote.

Land. System by which owner of real property may petition court for certificate of title by which state certifies such title as being in the owner whose name appears on certificate of title. See, *e.g.*, Mass.G.L. c. 185, §§ 26 et seq. *See also* Torrens title system.

Registration of securities. Recording in the official books of the company of the name and address of the holder of each bond or certificate of stock, with the date of its issue, and, in the case of a transfer of stock from one holder to another, the names of both parties and such other details as will identify the transaction and preserve an official record of its essential facts. Such information is required for paying of dividends, mailing of proxies, annual reports, etc.

Statutory procedure requiring the filing with the S.E.C. of various documents including a prospectus in order for securities to be publicly offered. Clearance must be obtained from the S.E.C. before the securities may be sold. There is no ceiling relative to the number of shares or dollar amount that may be registered. 15 U.S.C. § 77f et seq. *See also* Registered stock; Registration statement; Regulation A; Shelf registration.

Registration statement. Document required by the Securities Act of 1933 of most companies wishing to issue securities to the public or by the Securities Exchange Act of 1934 of a company wishing to have its securities traded in public markets. The statement discloses financial data,

purpose of securities offering, and other items of interest to potential investors. Such statements must be submitted to and approved by the SEC. 15 U.S.C.A. § 77f et seq. *See* Letter of comment; Prospectus; Registration of securities; Regulation A.

Registry. A register, or book authorized or recognized by law, kept for the recording or registration of facts or documents.

The list or record of ships subject to the maritime regulations of a particular country. The listing of a vessel at a custom house under the name of the country whose flag it flies, though such flag is not necessarily indicative of the nationality of the owner. Generally, "registry" applies to vessels in foreign commerce, whereas "enrollment" refers to coastwise navigation.

Registry of deeds. *See* Register of deeds; Registrar of deeds.

Regress. To return, go back or re-enter. Used principally in the phrase "free entry, egress, and regress" but it is also used to signify the reentry of a person who has been disseised of land.

Regressive tax. A tax levied at rates which increase less rapidly than the increase of the tax base, thus bearing more heavily on poorer taxpayers. Tax for which the rate decreases as the taxed base, such as income, increases. *Compare* Progressive tax.

Regs. An abbreviation for U.S. Treasury Department Regulations. *See* Regulations.

Regular. Conformable to law. Steady or uniform in course, practice, or occurrence; not subject to unexplained or irrational variation. Usual, customary, normal or general. Made according to rule, duly authorized, formed after uniform type; built or arranged according to established plan, law, or principle. Antonym of "casual" or "occasional."

As to *regular* Clergy; Deposit; Election; Indorsement; Meeting; Navigation; Process; Session, and Term, see those titles.

Regular and established place of business. Under federal Judicial Code, § 48 (28 U.S.C.A. §§ 1400, 1694), permitting patent infringement suits to be brought in the district in which defendant resides or where defendant committed acts of infringement and has a regular and established place of business, a "regular" place of business is one where business is carried on regularly, and not temporarily, or for some special work or particular transaction, while an "established" place of business must be a permanent place of business, and a "regular and established place of business" is one where the same business in kind, if not in degree, as that done at the home office or principal place of business, is carried on. A foreign corporation may have a "regular and established place of business" although business therein is merely securing orders and forwarding them to the home office. *See also* Minimum contracts.

Regular course of business. This phrase within worker's compensation acts excluding from their benefits person whose employment is not in regular course of business of employer, refers to habitual or regular occupation that party is engaged in with view of winning livelihood or some gain, excluding incidental or occasional operations arising out of transaction of that business; to normal operations which constitute business.

Term used in connection with books and records kept by a business and which are admissible in evidence if the court finds as a preliminary matter that the entries therein were made in good faith, before the action was commenced, and that such records are part of the customary operation of the business.

A memorandum, report, record, or data compilation, in any form, of acts, events, conditions, opinions, or diagnoses, made at or near the time by, or from information transmitted by, a person with knowledge, if kept in the course of a regularly conducted business activity, and if it was the regular practice of that business activity to make the memorandum, report, record, or data compilation, all as shown by the testimony of the custodian or other qualified witness, is not excluded by the hearsay rule, unless the source of information or the method or circumstances of preparation indicate lack of trustworthiness. Fed.Evid.R. 803(6); 28 U.S.C.A. § 1732. *See* Business entry rule.

For purposes of the Uniform Business Records Act, "regular course of business" means in the inherent nature of the business in question, and in the method systematically employed for the conduct of the business as a business.

In commercial law, a requirement for due negotiation of a document of title that limits U.C.C. Article 7's good-faith-purchase protection to normal and usual mercantile dealings in the trade.

Term is also descriptive of sales which are ordinarily made by a business in contrast to a bulk sale.

Regular entries. Entries made in books of account in regular course of business. *See also* Regular course of business.

Regularly /régyələrliy/. At fixed and certain intervals, regular in point of time. In accordance with some consistent or periodical rule or practice.

Regular on its face. Process is "regular on its face" when it proceeds from a court, officer, or body having authority of law to issue process of that nature, and is legal in form and contains nothing to notify or fairly apprise any one that it is issued without authority.

Regular use. Term, for purposes of exclusionary language of automobile liability policy excluding coverage where automobile was "furnished for regular use," is defined as continuous use, uninterrupted normal use for all purposes, without limitation as to use, and customary use as opposed to occasional use or special use.

Regulate. To fix, establish, or control; to adjust by rule, method, or established mode; to direct by rule or restriction; to subject to governing principles or laws. For example, the power of Congress to regulate commerce is the power to enact all appropriate legislation for its protection or advancement; to adopt measures to promote its growth and insure its safety; to foster, protect, control, and restrain. It is also power to prescribe rule by which commerce is to be governed, and embraces prohibitory regulations.

To govern or direct according to rule or to bring under control of constituted authority, to limit and prohibit, to arrange in proper order, and to control that which already exists.

Regulation. The act of regulating; a rule or order prescribed for management or government; a regulating principle; a precept. Rule of order prescribed by superior or competent authority relating to action of those under its control. Regulation is rule or order having force of law issued by executive authority of government (*e.g.* by federal administrative agency). *See* Regulations.

Regulation A. This SEC regulation provides for simplified registration filing requirements for certain small issue securities offerings. Securities Act of 1933, 15 U.S.C.A. § 77c(b). *See* Registration of securities.

Regulation J. Administrative rules issued by the Board of Governors of the Federal Reserve System governing the collection of checks and transfer of funds, directly or indirectly, through federal Reserve Banks.

Regulation T. Securities and Exchange Commission regulation governing extension of credit by securities brokers to customers. *See* Margin account.

Regulation Z. Regulations of Federal Reserve Board which implement provisions of Federal Truth-in-Lending Act. *See* Truth-in-Lending Act.

Regulation charge. Charge exacted for privilege or as condition precedent to carrying on business. *See also* Privilege (*Privilege tax*).

Regulations. Rules, orders, and the like, issued by various governmental departments to carry out the intent of the law. Agencies issue regulations to guide the activity of those regulated by the agency and of their own employees and to ensure uniform application of the law. Regulations are not the work of the legislature and do not have the effect of law in theory. In practice, however, because of the intricacies of judicial review of administrative action, regulations can have an important effect in determining the outcome of cases involving regulatory activity. United States Government regulations appear first in the *Federal Register,* published five days a week, and are subsequently arranged by subject in the *Code of Federal Regulations. See* Regulatory Flexibility Act.

Treasury Regulations. Treasury Department Regulations (abbr. "Treas. Regs.") represent the position of the Internal Revenue Service as to how the Internal Revenue Code is to be interpreted. Their purpose is to provide taxpayers and I.R.S. personnel with rules of general and specific application to the various provisions of the tax law. Such regulations are published in the Federal Register and in tax services.

Truth-in-Lending Act. See Regulation Z.

Regulatory agency. *See* Administrative agency.

Regulatory Flexibility Act. Federal law designed to improve the federal administrative rulemaking process. 5 U.S.C.A. §§ 601–605.

Rehabilitation. Investing or clothing again with some right, authority, or dignity. Restoring person or thing to a former capacity; reinstating; qualifying again. Restoration of individual to his greatest potential, whether physically, mentally, socially, or vocationally. For rehabilitation of debtor, *see* Bankruptcy proceedings; Wage earner's plan.

Alimony. Term "rehabilitative alimony" contemplates sums necessary to assist a divorced person in regaining a useful and constructive role in society through vocational or therapeutic training or retraining and for the further purpose of preventing financial hardship on society or individual during the rehabilitative process.

Corporation. Attempt to conserve and administer assets of insolvent corporation in hope of its eventual return from financial stress to solvency. Term contemplates continuance of corporate life and activities, and its effort to restore and reinstate corporation to former condition of successful operation and solvency. See Bankruptcy Code, Ch. 11 (11 U.S.C.A.). *See also* Bankruptcy proceedings; Receivership; Reorganization.

Witness. After cross examination, a witness whose credibility has suffered may be examined again (redirect examination) to improve his standing with the trier of fact in matters covered on cross examination. This process is called "rehabilitation" of the witness. See Fed.R.Evid. 608(a).

Rehearing. Second consideration of cause for purpose of calling to court's or administrative board's attention any error, omission, or oversight in first consideration. A retrial of issues which presumes notice to parties entitled thereto and opportunity for them to be heard. Reconsideration of a case by the same court in which the original determination was made. Administrative decisions and determinations in social security cases may be reopened for "good cause" and other specified grounds. *See also* Reargument; Retrial; Trial *(Trial de novo).*

Rehypothecation /rìyhaypòθəkéyshən/. To pledge to another or to transfer to another a note, goods, or other collateral which have been already pledged; *e.g.* a broker may pledge securities pledged to him by a customer (under *e.g.* a margin account) to finance his borrowings from a bank.

Reification. /ríyəfəkéyshən/. The embodiment of a right to the payment of money in an instrument so that transfer of the instrument transfers also the right. The term can also refer generally to the embodiment of any other property in a writing, which writing represents the property.

Reimburse. To pay back, to make restoration, to repay that expended; to indemnify, or make whole. *See also* Restitution.

Reimbursement. With respect to a surety, the common-law right to get indemnity, or otherwise recoup, from the principal debtor the value of the surety's performance in satisfying the principal debtor's duty. Also refers to the right of an issuer of a letter of credit to recoup from its customer upon duly honoring the credit.

Reincorporation. A new incorporation of a business which had already been incorporated. Also, a new incorporation of a document by reference which had previously been incorporated by reference but subsequently disassociated.

Reinstate. To reinstall; to reestablish; to place again in a former state, condition, or office; to restore to a state or position from which the object or person had been removed.

In insurance, a restoration of the insured's rights under a policy which has lapsed or been cancelled (*e.g.* because of failure to pay premiums). To reinstate a policy holder or one who has allowed his policy to lapse does not mean new insurance or taking out a new policy, but does mean that the insured has been restored to all the benefits accruing to him under the policy contract, the original policy. *See also* Reinstate.

Reinstate a case. To place case again in same position as before dismissal.

Reinsurance. A contract by which an insurer procures a third person to insure him against loss or liability by reason of original insurance. A contract that one insurer makes with another to protect the latter from a risk already assumed. It binds the reinsurer to pay to the reinsured the whole loss sustained in respect to the subject of the insurance to the extent to which he is reinsured. Also the substitution, with the consent of the insured, of a second insurer for the first, so that the original insurer is released.

Reinsurance treaty. A bilateral contract containing mutual covenants which codify the ongoing process of one insurance company's transfer of risk to another.

Reinsured. An insurer who is insured against loss under its policies. *See* Reinsurance.

Reinsurer. An insurance carrier which insures insurers. *See* Reinsurance.

Reintegration. The restoration of a part to the whole after separation. Term may be used in connection with documents to be read or understood together.

Reissuable notes. Bank-notes which, after having been once paid, may again be put into circulation.

REIT. *See* Real estate investment trust.

Rejection. An offeree's communication to an offeror that the offeree refuses to accept the terms of the proposal made by the offeror. *See* Counteroffer; Non-acceptance; Refusal; Repudiation; Rescission of contract.

For rights of buyer to reject goods that fail to conform to contract, see U.C.C. §§ 2–602—2–604.

Rejoin. In common-law pleading, to answer a plaintiff's replication in an action at law, by some matter of fact.

Rejoinder. In common-law pleading, the second pleading on the part of the defendant, being his answer to the plaintiff's replication. Rejoinder occurs during the trial stage where the defendant answers the plaintiff's rebuttal.

Relate. To stand in some relation; to have bearing or concern; to pertain; refer; to bring into association with or connection with; with "to."

Related. Standing in relation; connected; allied; akin. Goods are "related" for trademark purposes if they are used in conjunction with one another or are associated together in some way in the minds of the consuming public. *See also* Relative.

Related claim. Related claims may be joined under Fed.R.Civil P. 18(a). Within statute permitting joinder of claim for unfair competition with substantial and related claim under patent laws is claim resting on substantially identical facts.

Related goods. Courts will find trademark infringement in cases where the goods sold by the defendant and the mark owner do not directly compete, if the goods are related. Goods are considered related if consumers would assume that, when marked with the same trademark, they come from a common source or are sponsored by the same party.

Related party transactions. The tax law places restrictions upon the recognition of gains and losses between related parties due to the potential for abuse. For example, restrictions are placed upon the deduction of losses from the sale or exchange of property between related parties. A related party includes a corporation which is controlled by the taxpayer. I.R.C. § 267.

Related proceedings. As used in bankruptcy context are those civil proceedings, that, in absence of petition in bankruptcy court, could have been brought in federal district court or state court. A "related proceeding" must in some way relate to the administration of the bankrupt estate; there must be some reason why adjudication of the claim is better placed with the bankruptcy court as opposed to a state court. *See also* Core proceeding.

Relation. A relative or kinsman; a person connected by consanguinity. A person connected with another by blood or affinity.

The words "relatives" and "relations," in their primary sense, are broad enough to include any one connected by blood or affinity, even to the remotest degree, but where used in wills, as defining and determining legal succession, are construed to include only those persons who are entitled to share in the estate as next of kin under the statute of distributions.

The connection of two persons, or their situation with respect to each other, who are associated, whether by the law, by their own agreement, or by kinship, in some social *status* or union for the purposes of domestic life; as the relation of guardian and ward, husband and wife, master and servant, parent and child; so in the phrase "domestic relations."

The doctrine of "relation" is that principle by which an act done at one time is considered by a fiction of law to have been done at some antecedent period. It is usually applied where several proceedings are essential to complete a particular transaction, such as a conveyance or deed. The last proceeding which consummates the conveyance is held for certain purposes to take effect by relation as of the day when the first proceeding was had. *See also* Relation back.

A recital, account, narrative of facts; information given. Thus, suits by *quo warranto* are entitled "on the relation of" a private person, who is called the "relator." But in this connection the word seems also to involve the idea of the suggestion, instigation, or instance of the relator.

See also Blood relations; Kin *or* kindred; Next of kin; Relative.

Relation back. General rule of "relation back" is that a pleading may not be amended to allege a new or different claim or defense unless it arose out of, or is based on or related to, claim, transaction or occurrence originally set forth or attempted to be set forth. *See also Amended pleadings, below.*

A principle that an act done today is considered to have been done at an earlier time. A document held in escrow and finally delivered is deemed to have been delivered as of the time at which it was escrowed.

See Ex post facto.

Amended pleadings. Whenever the claim or defense asserted in the amended pleading arose out of the conduct, transaction, or occurrence set forth or attempted to be set forth in the original pleading, the amendment relates back to the date of the original pleading. Fed.R.Civil P. 15(c).

Relations. A term which, in its widest sense, includes all the kindred of the person spoken of.

Relative. A kinsman; a person connected with another by blood or affinity. When used generically, includes persons connected by ties of affinity as well as consanguinity, and, when used with a restrictive meaning, refers to those only who are connected by blood.

Individual related by affinity or consanguinity within the third degree as determined by the common law, or individual in a step or adoptive relationship within such third degree. Bankruptcy Code, § 101.

A person or thing having relation or connection with some other person or thing; as, relative rights, relative powers, *infra. See also* Relation.

Relative confession. *See* Confession.

Relative fact. In the law of evidence, a fact having relation to another fact; a minor fact; a circumstance.

Relative powers. Those which relate to land; so called to distinguish them from those which are collateral to it.

Relative rights. Those rights of persons which are incident to them as members of society, and standing in various relations to each other. Those rights of persons in private life which arise from the civil and domestic relations.

Relator. An informer. The person upon whose complaint, or at whose instance certain writs are issued such as information or writ of *quo warranto,* and who is *quasi* the plaintiff in the proceeding. For example if John Smith is the relator and Jones is the defendant, the citation would read, State ex rel. John Smith v. Jones. A party in interest who is permitted to institute a proceeding in the name of the People or the Attorney General when the right to sue resides solely in that official. *See also* Ex relatione; Parens patriæ; Real party in interest.

Relatrix /rəléytrəks/. A female relator or petitioner.

Release, *v.* To discharge a claim one has against another, as for example in a tort case the plaintiff may discharge the liability of the defendant in return for a cash settlement. To lease again or grant new lease. *See* Accord and satisfaction.

Release, *n.* A writing or an oral statement manifesting an intention to discharge another from an existing or asserted duty. The relinquishment, concession, or giving up of a right, claim, or privilege, by the person in whom it exists or to whom it accrues, to the person against whom it might have been demanded or enforced. Abandonment of claim to party against whom it exists, and is a surrender of a cause of action and may be gratuitous or for consideration. Giving up or abandoning of claim or right to person against whom claim exists or against whom right is to be exercised.

A discharge of a debt by act of party, as distinguished from an extinguishment which is a discharge by operation of law, and, in distinguishing release from receipt, "receipt" is evidence that an obligation has been discharged, but "release" is itself a discharge of it.

An *express* release is one directly made in terms by deed or other suitable means. An *implied* release is one which arises from acts of the creditor or owner, without any express agreement. A *release by operation of law* is one which, though not expressly made, the law presumes in consequence of some act of the releasor; for instance, when one of several joint obligors is expressly released, the others are also released by operation of law.

Liberation, discharge, or setting free from restraint or confinement. Thus, a man unlawfully imprisoned may obtain his *release* on *habeas corpus. See also* Bail.

The abandonment to (or by) a person called as a witness in a suit of his interest in the subject-matter of the controversy, in order to qualify him to testify, under the common-law rule.

A receipt or certificate given by a ward to the guardian, on the final settlement of the latter's accounts, or by any other beneficiary on the termination of the trust administration, relinquishing all and any further rights, claims, or demands, growing out of the trust or incident to it.

In admiralty actions, when a ship, cargo, or other property has been arrested, the owner may obtain its release by giving bail, or paying the value of the property into court.

The conveyance of a person's interest or right which he has in a thing to another that has the possession thereof or some estate therein. The relinquishment of some right or benefit to a person who has already some interest in the property, and such interest as qualifies him for receiving or availing himself of the right or benefit so relinquished.

Conditional release. See that title.

Deed of release. A deed operating by way of release; but more specifically, in those states where deeds of trust are in use instead of common-law mortgages, as a means of pledging real property as security for the payment of a debt, a "deed of release" is a conveyance in fee, executed by the trustee or trustees, to the grantor in the deed of trust, which conveys back to him the legal title to the estate, and which is to be given on satisfactory proof that he has paid the secured debt in full or otherwise complied with the terms of the deed of trust.

Release of dower. The relinquishment by a married woman of her expectant dower interest or estate in a particular parcel of realty belonging to her husband, as, by joining with him in a conveyance of it to a third person.

Release of mortgage. A written document which discharges the obligation of a mortgage upon payment and which is given by mortgagee to mortgagor or holder of equity and recorded in the office where deeds and other instruments of conveyance are recorded.

Release to uses. The conveyance by a deed of release to one party to the use of another is so termed. Thus, when a conveyance of lands was effected, by those instruments of assurance termed a lease and release, from A. to B. and his heirs, to the use of C. and his heirs, in such case C. at once took the whole fee-simple in such lands; B. by the operation of the statute of uses, being made a mere conduit-pipe for conveying the estate to C.

Releasee. The person to whom a release is made.

Release on own recognizance. Pre-trial release based on the person's own promise that he will show up for trial (no bond required). A species of bail in which the defendant acknowledges personally without sureties his obligation to appear in court at the next hearing or trial date of his case. It is used in place of a bail bond when the judge or magistrate is satisfied that the defendant will appear without the need of a surety bond or other form of security. Also referred to as "release on own recognizance" or "ROR". See *e.g.* 18 U.S.C.A. § 3142; Fed.R.Crim.P. 46.

Relevancy /rélǝvǝnsiy/. *See* Material evidence; Relevant evidence.

Relevant. *See* Material; Material evidence; Relevancy; Relevant evidence.

Relevant evidence. Evidence tending to prove or disprove an alleged fact. Evidence having any tendency to make the existence of any fact that is of consequence to the determination of the action more probable or less probable than it would be without the evidence. Fed.Evid.R. 401. Evidence is "relevant" if it tends to make existence of material fact more or less probable.

Basic test for admissibility of evidence is relevancy, and testimony is "relevant" if reasonable inferences can be drawn therefrom regarding or if any light is shed upon, a contested matter. Evidence is "relevant" not only when it tends to prove or disprove precise fact in issue but when it tends to establish fact from which existence or nonexistence of fact in issue can be directly inferred.

See also Material; Material evidence; Relevancy; Unfair prejudice.

Relevant market. To establish claim of monopolization or of attempt to monopolize under the Sherman Act, plaintiff must define the "relevant market" within which defendant allegedly possesses monopoly power, and such "relevant market" is the geographic market composed of products that have reasonable interchangeability for purposes for which they are produced, considering their price, use and quality. Term, in relation to case involving alleged violation of Sherman Act, consists of both a product market and a geographic market. It is one in which product effectively competes with functionally equivalent products. *See also* Market.

Reliable. Trustworthy, worthy of confidence.

Reliance. In tort for deceit, it is necessary for plaintiff to prove that he relied on misrepresentation though such misrepresentation need not be the sole or even dominant reason for acting if it was a substantial factor in the plaintiff's decision. For fraud purposes, "reliance" might be defined as a belief which motivates an act.

The test of "reliance" on misrepresentation in sale of stock as ground for recovery under Securities Exchange Act is whether the misrepresentation is a substantial factor in determining the course of conduct which results in the recipient's loss. Where case involves primarily a failure to disclose, positive proof of reliance is not a prerequisite for recovery; all that is necessary is that the facts withheld be material in sense that reasonable investor might have considered them important in making of such decision.

Term "reliance" as used in rule imposing liability on one who volunteers to undertake action for the protection of another's person or things for failure to exercise reasonable care if harm is suffered because of the other's reliance upon the undertaking connotes dependence; it bespeaks a voluntary choice of conduct by the person harmed and infers that the person exercising it can decide between available alternatives.

See also Estoppel; Fraud; Material fact; Misrepresentation.

Reliance on promise. In promissory estoppel, the plaintiff is required to prove that he relied on promise of defendant to his damage. *See also* Promissory estoppel.

Reliction /rəlíkshən/. An increase of the land by the permanent withdrawal or retrocession of the sea or a river. Process of gradual exposure of land by permanent recession of body of water. The alteration of a boundary line due to the gradual removal of land by a stream serving as the boundary. *See also* Accretion; Dereliction.

Relief. The public or private assistance or support, pecuniary or otherwise, granted to indigent persons.

Deliverance from oppression, wrong, or injustice. In this sense it is used as a general designation of the assistance, redress, or benefit which a complainant seeks at the hands of a court, particularly in equity. It may be thus used of such remedies as specific performance, injunction, or the reformation or rescission of a contract. *See also* Cause of action; Remedy.

Relieve. To give ease, comfort, or consolation to; to give aid, help, or succor to; to alleviate, assuage, ease, mitigate.

To release from a post, station, or duty; to put another in place of, or to take the place of, in the bearing of any burden, or discharge of any duty.

Religious corporation. *See* Corporation.

Religious freedom. Within Constitution (First Amendment) embraces not only the right to worship God according to the dictates of one's conscience, but also the right to do, or forbear to do, any act, for conscience sake, the doing or forbearing of which is not inimical to the peace, good order, and morals of society. *See also* Establishment clause.

Religious liberty. *See* Liberty.

Religious use. *See* Charitable use.

Relinquish. To abandon, to give up, to surrender, to renounce some right or thing. *See* Abandonment; Release.

Relinquishment. A forsaking, abandoning, renouncing, or giving over a right. *See* Abandonment; Release.

Rem, action in. *See* In rem.

Remainder. The remnant of an estate in land, depending upon a particular prior estate created at the same time and by the same instrument, and limited to arise immediately on the determination of that estate, and not in abridgement of it. A future interest created in some person other than the grantor or transferor.

The property that passes to a beneficiary after the expiration of an intervening income interest. If, for example, G. places real estate in trust with income to A. for life and remainder to B. upon A.'s death, B. has a remainder interest.

An estate limited to take effect and be enjoyed after another estate is determined. As, if a man seised in fee-simple grants lands to A. for twenty years, and, after the determination of the said term, then to B. and his heirs forever, here A. is tenant for years, *remainder* to B. in fee. An estate in reversion is the residue of an estate, usually the fee left in the grantor and his heirs after the determination of a particular estate which he has granted out of it. The rights of the reversioner are the same as those of a vested remainderman in fee.

In will, the terms rest, residue, and remainder of estate are usually and ordinarily understood as meaning that part of the estate which is left after all of the other provisions of the will have been satisfied.

See also Cross remainder; Defeasibly vested remainder; Life estate; Reversionary interest. *Compare* Reversion *or* estate in reversion.

Charitable remainder. A gift over to a charity generally after a life estate. It may be vested or contingent.

Contingent remainder. One which is either limited to a person not in being or not certain or ascertained, or so limited to a certain person that his right to the estate depends upon some contingent event in the future.

An estate in remainder which is limited to take effect either to a dubious and uncertain person, or upon a dubious and uncertain event, by which no present or particular interest passes to the remainder-man, so that the particular estate may chance to be determined and the remainder never take effect. A remainder limited so as to depend upon an event or condition which may never happen or be performed, or which may not happen or be performed till after the determination of the preceding estate.

Cross-remainder. Where land is devised or conveyed to two or more persons as tenants in common, or where different parts of the same land are given to such persons in severalty, with such limitations that, upon the determination of the particular estate of either, his share is to pass to the other, to the entire exclusion of the ultimate remainderman or reversioner until all the particular estates shall be exhausted, the remainders so limited are called "cross-remainders." In wills, such remainders may arise by implication; but, in deeds, only by express limitation.

Executed remainder. A remainder which vests a present interest in the tenant, though the enjoyment is postponed to the future.

Executory remainder. A contingent remainder; one which exists where the estate is limited to take effect either to a dubious and uncertain person or upon a dubious and uncertain event.

Vested remainder. An estate by which a present interest passes to the party, though to be enjoyed *in futuro,* and by which the estate is invariably fixed to remain to a determinate person after the particular estate has been spent. One limited to a certain person at a certain time or upon the happening of a necessary event.

Remainder interest. The property that passes to a beneficiary after the expiration of an intervening income interest. If, for example, G places real estate in trust with income to A for life and remainder to B upon A's death, B has a remainder interest.

Remainderman. One who is entitled to the remainder of the estate after a particular estate carved out of it has expired. One who becomes entitled to estate after intervention of precedent estate or on termination by lapse of time of rights of precedent estate created at same time.

Under a will, the remainderman is the party who will receive what is left of the decedent's property after all specific bequests have been satisfied.

Remand. To send back. The act of an appellate court when it sends a case back to the trial court and orders the trial court to conduct limited new hearings or an entirely new trial, or to take some other further action. 28 U.S.C.A. § 2106. When a prisoner is brought before a judge on habeas corpus, for the purpose of obtaining liberty, the judge hears the case, and either discharges him or remands him. *See also* Procedendo.

Remargining. The furnishing of additional security when securities which were originally purchased on margin decline in value below a certain percent of their market price at the time of purchase. *See* Margin.

Remedial. Affording a remedy; giving means of obtaining redress; of the nature of a remedy; intended to remedy wrongs and abuses, abate faults, or supply defects; pertaining to or affecting remedy, as distinguished from that which affects or modifies the right. *See* Remedy.

Remedial action. One which is brought to obtain compensation or indemnity.

Remedial laws *or* statutes. Legislation providing means or method whereby causes of action may be effectuated, wrongs redressed and relief obtained is "remedial". Statutes which afford a remedy, or improve or facilitate remedies already existing for enforcement of rights and redress of injuries. Those statutes which pertain to or affect a remedy, as distinguished from those which affect or modify a substantive right or duty.

Those designed to correct imperfections in the prior law and to cure a wrong where an aggrieved party had an ineffective remedy under existing statutes. One that intends to afford a private remedy to a person injured by the wrongful act. That which is designed to correct an existing law, redress an existing grievance, or introduce regulations conducive to the public good. A statute giving a party a mode of remedy for a wrong, where he had none, or a different one, before. One which furnishes new remedy to claimant who has suffered injustice due to technical requirements of general statute.

The underlying test to be applied in determining whether a statute is penal or remedial is whether it primarily seeks to impose an arbitrary, deterring punishment upon any who might commit a wrong against the public by a violation of the requirements of the statute, or whether the purpose is to measure and define the damages which may accrue to an individual or class of individuals, as just and reasonable compensation for a possible loss having a causal connection with the breach of the legal obligation owing under the statute to such individual or class.

See also Curative *(Curative statute).*

Remedy. The means by which a right is enforced or the violation of a right is prevented, redressed, or compensated. The means employed to enforce a right or redress an injury, as distinguished from right, which is a well founded or acknowledged claim.

The rights given to a party by law or by contract which that party may exercise upon a default by the other contracting party, or upon the commission of a wrong (a tort) by another party.

Remedy means any remedial right to which an aggrieved party is entitled with or without resort to a tribunal. "Rights" includes remedies. U.C.C. § 1–201.

That which relieves or cures a disease, including a medicine or remedial treatment.

See also Administrative remedy; Alternative relief; Cause of action; Extraordinary remedies; Inadequate remedy at law; Mutuality of remedy; Provisional remedy.

Civil remedy. The remedy afforded by law to a private person in the civil courts in so far as his private and individual rights have been injured by a delict or crime; as distinguished from the remedy by criminal prosecution for the injury to the rights of the public.

Cumulative remedy. See Cumulative.

Equitable remedy. See Equity; Injunction; Performance *(Specific performance)*; Reformation.

Extraordinary remedy. See Extraordinary.

Joinder of remedies. See Joinder.

Legal remedy. A remedy available, under the particular circumstances of the case, in a court of law, as distinguished from a remedy available only in equity. Procedurally, this distinction is no longer generally relevant, for under Rules of Civil Procedure there is only one form of action known as a "civil action." Rule 2. *Compare* Equity.

Remedy over. A person who is primarily liable or responsible, but who, in turn, can demand indemnification from another, who is responsible to him, is said to have a "remedy over." For example, a city, being compelled to pay for injuries caused by a defect in the highway, has a "remedy over" against the person whose act or negligence caused the defect, and such person is said to be "liable over" to the city. *See* Subrogation.

REMIC. A Real Estate Mortgage Investment Conduit created by the 1986 Tax Reform Act for years beginning in 1987 providing a special tax vehicle for organizations that issue to investors different classes of interests which are backed by a pool of mortgages on real estate.

Remise /rəmáyz/. To remit or give up. A formal word in deeds of release and quitclaim; the usual phrase being "remise, release, and forever quitclaim."

Remission. A release or extinguishment of a debt. It is *conventional,* when it is expressly granted to the debtor by a creditor having a capacity to alienate; or *tacit,* when the creditor voluntarily surrenders to his debtor the original title, under private signature constituting the obligation.

A diminution or abatement of symptoms of a disease; also the period during which such diminution occurs.

Forgiveness or condonation of an offense or injury.

At common law, the act by which a forfeiture or penalty is forgiven.

Remit. To send or transmit; as to *remit* money. To send back, as to remit a check or refer a case back to a lower court for further consideration. To give up; to pardon or forgive; to annul; to relinquish; as to *remit* a fine, sentence, or punishment.

Remittance /rəmítəns/. Money sent by one person to another, either in specie, bill of exchange, check, or otherwise.

Remittee. A person to whom a remittance is made.

Remitter /rəmítər/. The relation back of a later defective title to an earlier valid title. *Remitter* occurs where he who has the true property or *jus proprietatis* in lands, but is out of possession thereof, and has no right to enter without recovering possession in an action, has afterwards the freehold cast upon him by some subsequent and of course defective title. In this case he is *remitted,* or sent back by operation of law, to his ancient and more certain title.

Remitting bank. Any payor or intermediary bank remitting for an item. U.C.C. § 4–105(f).

Remittitur /rəmítətər/. The procedural process by which an excessive verdict of the jury is reduced. If money damages awarded by a jury are grossly excessive as a matter of law, the judge may order the plaintiff to remit a portion of the award. In the alternative, the court may order a complete new trial or a trial limited to the issue of damages. The court may also condition a denial of a motion for new trial upon the filing by the plaintiff of a remittitur in a stated amount. Fed. R.Civil P. 59(a). *Compare* Additur.

Remittitur of record /rəmítətər əv rékərd/. The returning or sending back by a court of appeal of the record and proceedings in a cause, after its decision thereon, to the court whence the appeal came, in order that the cause may be tried anew (where it is so ordered), or that judgment may be entered in accordance with the decision on appeal, or execution be issued, or any other necessary action be taken in the court below.

Remonstrance /rəmónstrəns/. Expostulation; showing of reasons against something proposed; a representation made to a court or legislative body wherein certain persons unite in urging that a contemplated measure be not adopted or passed. A formal protest against the policy or conduct of the government or of certain officials drawn up and presented by aggrieved citizens.

Remote. At a distance; afar off; inconsiderable; slight.

Remote cause. In the law of negligence with respect to injury or accident, a cause which would not according to experience of mankind lead to the event which happened. One where the effect is uncertain, vague, or indeterminate, and where the effect does not necessarily follow. A cause operating mediately through other causes to produce effect. Improbable cause. *See also* Cause.

Proximate cause distinguished. "Proximate cause" (*q.v.*) is cause in which is involved idea of necessity, and one from which effect must follow, while "remote cause", though necessary for existence of effect, is one not necessarily implying existence of effect.

Remote damage. *See* Damages.

Remote disbursement. Technique that involves writing checks drawn on banks in remote locations so as to increase disbursement float. *See also* Float.

Remoteness. Want of close connection between a wrong and the injury which prevents the party injured from claiming compensation from the wrongdoer.

Remoteness of evidence. When the fact or facts proposed to be established as a foundation from which indirect evidence may be drawn, by way of inference, have not a visible, plain, or necessary connection with the proposition eventually to be proved, such evidence is rejected for "remoteness."

Removal. In a broad sense, the transfer of a person, thing, or case from one place to another. *See also* Asportation.

As used in statutes relative to removal from state is often limited to such absence from state as amounts to a change of residence.

See also Recall.

Removal bond. In customs law, a bond furnished for possible duties by one who removes imported goods from a warehouse for export. Also, bond required in some states when a party to pending action in one court desires to remove action to another court.

Removal from office. Deprivation of office by act of competent superior officer acting within scope of authority. "Suspension" is the temporary forced removal from the exercise of office; "removal" is the dismissal from office. *See* Election *(Recall election)*; Impeachment.

Removal of causes. The transfer of a case from one court to another; *e.g.* from one state court to another, or from state court to federal court. Commonly used of the transfer of the jurisdiction and cognizance of an action commenced but not finally determined, with all further proceedings therein, from one trial court to another trial court. More particularly, the transfer of a cause of action, before trial or final hearing thereof, from a state court to the United States District Court, under 28 U.S.C.A. § 1441 et seq.

Removing cloud from title. Acts or proceedings necessary to render title marketable. *See* Action to quiet title.

Remuneration /rəmyùwnəréyshən/. Payment; reimbursement. Reward; recompense; salary; compensation.

Render, *v.* To give up; to yield; to return; to surrender. Also to pay or perform; used of rents, services, and the like.

Render judgment. To pronounce, state, declare, or announce the judgment of the court in a given case or on a given state of facts; not used with reference to judgments by confession, and not synonymous with "entering," "docketing," or "recording" the judgment. Judgment is "rendered" when decision is officially announced, either oral-ly in open court or by memorandum filed with clerk. *See* Rendition of judgment.

Render verdict. To agree on and to report the verdict in due form. To return the written verdict into court and hand it to the trial judge who announces it in open court.

Render, *n.* In feudal law, used in connection with rents and heriots. Goods subject to rent or heriot-service were said to lie in *render,* when the lord might not only seize the identical goods, but might also distrain for them.

Rendition. The return of a fugitive to the State in which he is accused of having committed a crime, by the order of the governor of the State to which the fugitive has gone. *See also* Extradition; Interstate rendition.

Rendition of judgment. Such is effected when trial court in open court declares the decision of the law upon the matters at issue, and it is distinguishable from "entry of judgment," which is a purely ministerial act by which the judgment is made of record and preserved. A judgment is rendered as of date on which trial judge declares in open court his decision on matters submitted to him for adjudication, and oral pronouncement by the court of its decision is sufficient for "rendition of judgment".

It is the pronouncement of the court of its conclusions and decision upon the matter submitted to it for adjudication; a judgment may be rendered either orally in open court or by memorandum filed with the clerk. "Rendition" of judgment is distinguishable from its "entry" in the records. *See* Entering judgments; Judgment.

Rendition of verdict. *See* Render.

Renegotiation. Lit. To negotiate again (e.g., the terms of a contract or lease). As to government contracts, it consists of a review of a contract after its performance to determine whether excess profits have been made. If they were made, the government can recapture them.

Renegotiation Act. Federal law which provides for reexamination of government contracts to determine whether excess profits were made which can be recaptured by the government. 50 U.S.C. A.App. 1191 et seq. *See* Renegotiation Board.

Renegotiation Board. The Renegotiation Board was created as an independent establishment in the executive branch by the Renegotiation Act of 1951 (65 Stat. 7; 50 U.S.C.A.App. § 1211) and was organized on October 8, 1951. The Board's function was the elimination of excessive profits on defense and space contracts and related subcontracts. This federal agency was terminated and its property and records were transferred to General Services Administration in 1979 pursuant to Pub.L. 95–431, Title V, § 501.

Renew. To make new again; to restore to freshness; to make new spiritually; to regenerate; to begin again; to recommence; to resume; to restore to existence; to revive; to reestablish; to recreate; to replace; to grant or obtain an extension of. To "renew" a contract means to begin again or continue in force the old contract.

Renewal. The act of renewing or reviving. A revival or rehabilitation of an expiring subject; that which is made anew or re-established. The substitution of a new right or obligation for another of the same nature. A change of something old to something new. To grant or obtain extension of; to continue in force for a fresh period, as commonly used with reference to notes and bonds importing a postponement of maturity of obligations dealt with. An extension of time in which that obligation may be discharged; an obligation being "renewed" when the same obligation is carried forward by the new paper or undertaking, whatever it may be.

Renounce. To make an affirmative declaration of abandonment. To reject; cast off; repudiate; disclaim; forsake; abandon; divest one's self of a right, power, or privilege. Usually it implies an affirmative act of disclaimer or disavowal. *See also* Renunciation; Repudiation.

Will. Under law of many states, a widow may waive or relinquish her rights under the will of her husband and claim her statutory rights.

Rent. Consideration paid for use or occupation of property. In a broader sense, it is the compensation or fee paid, usually periodically, for the use of any rental property, land, buildings, equipment, etc.

At common law, term referred to compensation or return of value given at stated times for the possession of lands and tenements corporeal. A sum of money or other consideration, issuing yearly out of lands and tenements corporeal; something which a tenant renders out of the profits of the land which he enjoys; a compensation or return, being in the nature of an acknowledgment or recompense given for the possession of some corporeal inheritance.

Base rent. A specific amount used as a minimum rent in a lease which uses a percentage or overage for additional rent.

Ground rent. See that title.

Net rent. Rent after all expenses.

Rental. *See* Rent.

Rent control. A restriction or limitation imposed in certain cities upon the maximum rent that may be charged on rental property.

Rents, issues and profits. The profits arising from property generally. Rents collected by party in possession; the net profits. Phrase does not apply to rental value or value of use and occupation.

Rent strike. An organized undertaking by tenants in which rent is withheld until grievances between landlord and tenants are settled.

Renunciation. The act by which a person abandons a right acquired without transferring it to another.

The Model Penal Code (§ 5.01(4)) recognizes renunciation of criminal purpose (e.g., abandonment of effort to commit crime) as an affirmative defense. See *e.g.* 18 U.S.C.A. § 373(b). *See* Withdrawal from criminal activity.

Under the Uniform Commercial Code the unilateral act of the holder, usually, without consideration, whereby he expresses the intention of abandoning his rights on the instrument or against one or more parties thereto. U.C.C. § 1–107. A means whereby a holder discharges a party's liability on an instrument by declaring an intention to discharge in a signed and delivered writing. U.C.C. § 3–605(1)(b). Within Uniform Commercial Code it is a gratuitous abandonment or giving up of right, and does not require a consideration.

In connection with wills, the act of waiving a will and claiming a statutory share as in the case of a spouse whose share under a will is less than her statutory share. *See* Election *(law of wills)*; Election by spouse.

See also Disclaimer; Repudiation.

Renvoi doctrine. /renvóy/. The "doctrine of renvoi" is a doctrine under which court in resorting to foreign law adopts rules of foreign law as to conflict of laws, which rules may in turn refer court back to law of forum.

Reorganization. Act or process of organizing again or anew.

General term describing corporate amalgamations or readjustments occurring, for example, when one corporation acquires another in a merger or acquisition, a single corporation divides into two or more entities, or a corporation makes a substantial change in its capital structure. The exchange of stock and other securities in a corporate reorganization can be effected favorably for tax purposes if certain statutory requirements are followed strictly.

The classification of the Internal Revenue Code (§ 368(a)(1)) is widely used in general corporate literature. A Class A reorganization is a statutory merger or consolidation (i.e., pursuant to the business corporation act of a specific state). A Class B reorganization is a transaction by which one corporation exchanges its voting shares for the voting shares of another corporation. A Class C reorganization is a transaction in which one corporation exchanges its voting shares for the property and assets of another corporation. A Class D reorganization is a "spin off" of assets by one corporation to a new corporation; a Class E reorganization is a recapitalization; a Class F reorganization is a "mere change of identity, form, or place of organization, however effected." A Class G reorganization is a "transfer by a corporation of all or part of its assets to another corporation in a title 11 [bankruptcy] or similar case".

Reorganization of a corporation under Bankruptcy Code Chapter 11 proceedings involves the preparation of a plan of reorganization by the bankruptcy trustee, the submission thereof to the court, and, after a hearing, the determination of the feasibility of such plan by the court, followed by the court's approval thereof if it finds such plan is feasible and proper. *See also* Bankruptcy proceedings.

Tax free reorganization. Under the Internal Revenue Code, a corporate reorganization wherein a corporation which is a party thereto exchanges property, pursuant to a plan of reorganization, solely for stock or securities of a second corporate party, without recognition of gain or loss. I.R.C. § 361.

Repair. To mend, remedy, restore, renovate. To restore to a sound or good state after decay, injury, dilapidation, or partial destruction. The term contemplates an existing structure or thing which has become imperfect, and means to supply in the original existing structure that which is lost or destroyed, and thereby restore it to the condition in which it originally existed, as near as may be.

In accounting, repairs are chargeable to current income whereas an improvement is a capital expenditure which requires depreciation over the life of the improvement. *See also* Extraordinary repairs.

Landlord has obligation to use reasonable care to keep premises in such repair as to meet local building and sanitary code requirements. *See* Habitability; Warranty *(Warranty of habitability).*

Reparation /rèpəréyshən/. Payment for an injury or damage; redress for a wrong done. Several states have adopted the Uniform Crime Victims Reparation Act. Certain federal statutes also provide for reparations for violation of Act; *e.g.* persons suffering losses because of violations of Commodity Futures Trading Act may seek reparation under the Act against violator. 7 U.S.C.A. § 18. *See also* Restitution.

Payment made by one country to another for damages during war.

Repatriation /rìypeytriyéyshən/°pæt°/. The return or restoration of a person or object to his or its country of origin. The return of profits from foreign investments to the investor's country. *Compare* Deportation. *See also* Expatriation.

Repay. To pay back; refund; restore; return.

Repeal. The abrogation or annulling of a previously existing law by the enactment of a subsequent statute which declares that the former law shall be revoked and abrogated (which is called "express" repeal), or which contains provisions so contrary to or irreconcilable with those of the earlier law that only one of the two statutes can stand in force (called "implied" repeal). To revoke, abolish, annul, to rescind or abrogate by authority. *See also* Abrogation; Express repeal.

Amendment distinguished. "Repeal" of a law means its complete abrogation by the enactment of a subsequent statute, whereas the "amendment" of a statute means an alteration in the law already existing, leaving some part of the original still standing.

Repeaters. Persons who commit crime and are sentenced, and then commit another and are sentenced again. *See* Habitual criminal; Recidivist.

Replace. To place again; to take the place of; to restore to a former condition. Term, given its plain, ordinary meaning, means to supplant with substitute or equivalent.

Replacement cost. The present cost of replacing the improvement with one having the same utility. Cost of replacing lost, stolen or destroyed property to its former use and value.

Replacement cycle. In accounting, the frequency with which an asset is replaced by an equivalent asset.

Replacement insurance. Insurance coverage which provides that the loss will be measured by replacement of the property new. If the property is actually replaced, the measure is the difference between the depreciated value and the replacement cost.

Replacement of goods. *See* Cover.

Replead. To plead anew; to file new pleadings.

Repleader. In common law pleading, when, after issue has been joined in an action, and a verdict given thereon, the pleading is found (on examination) to have miscarried and failed to effect its proper object, viz., of raising an apt and material question between the parties, the court will, on motion of the unsuccessful party, award a *repleader;* that is, will order the parties to plead *de novo* for the purpose of obtaining a better issue. Under modern rules practice, amendments to pleadings are liberally allowed. Fed.R.Civil P. 15.

Replevin /rəplévən/. An action whereby the owner or person entitled to repossession of goods or chattels may recover those goods or chattels from one who has wrongfully distrained or taken or who wrongfully detains such goods or chattels. Also refers to a provisional remedy that is an incident of a replevin action which allows the plaintiff at any time before judgment to take the disputed property from the defendant and hold the property pendente lite. Other names for replevin include Claim and delivery, Detinue, Revendication, and Sequestration (q.v.).

Under the following conditions a buyer of goods may have the right of replevin: "The buyer has a right of replevin for goods identified to the contract if after reasonable effort he is unable to effect cover for such goods or the circumstances reasonably indicate that such effort will be unavailing or if the goods have been shipped under reservation and satisfaction of the security interest in them has been made or tendered." See U.C.C. § 2–711(2)(b); § 2–716(3).

See also Replevy; Self-help.

Personal replevin. At common law, a species of action to replevy a man out of prison or out of the custody of any private person. It took the place of the old writ *de homine replegiando;* but, as a means of examining into the legality of an imprisonment, it is now superseded by the writ of *habeas corpus.*

Replevin bond. A bond executed to indemnify the officer who executed a writ of replevin and to indemnify the defendant or person from whose custody the property was taken for such damages as he may sustain. Such bond guarantees that the replevisor will have the property in the same condition to abide the decision of the court.

Replevy /rəpléviy/. In reference to the action of replevin, to redeliver goods which have been distrained, to the original possessor of them, on his pledging or giving security to prosecute an action against the distrainor for the purpose of trying the legality of the distress. Also the bailing or liberating a man from prison on his finding bail to answer for his forthcoming at a future time. *See also* Replevin.

Replevy bond. Such bond guarantees that the replevisor will have the property in the same condition to abide the decision of the court.

Repliant, *or* **replicant** /rəpláyənt/réplɪkənt/. A litigant who replies or files or delivers a replication.

Replication. In common law pleading, a reply made by the plaintiff in an action to the defendant's plea, or in a suit in chancery to the defendant's answer. *See* Reply.

In equity practice (now obsolete in the federal and most state courts), a general replication is a general denial of the truth of defendant's plea or answer, and of the sufficiency of the matter alleged in it to bar the plaintiff's suit, and an assertion of the truth and sufficiency of the bill.

A special replication is occasioned by the defendant's introducing new matter into his plea or answer, which makes it necessary for the plaintiff to put in issue some additional fact on his part in avoidance of such new matter.

Reply. In its general sense, the plaintiff's answer to the defendant's set-off or counterclaim. Under Fed.R.Civil P. 7(a), a reply is only allowed in two situations: to a counterclaim denominated as such, or, on order of court to an answer or a third-party answer. *Compare* Answer.

Report. An official or formal statement of facts or proceedings. To give an account of, to relate, to tell, to convey or disseminate information. *See also* Annual report; Consumer report; Credit report.

The formal statement in writing made to a court by a master, clerk, or referee, as the result of his inquiries into some matter referred to him by the court. Fed.R.Civil P. 53. *See* Master's report.

A "report" of a public official is distinguished from a "return" of such official, in that "return" is typically concerned with something done or observed by officer, while "report" embodies result of officer's investigation not originally occurring within his personal knowledge.

The name is also applied (usually in the plural) to the published volumes, appearing periodically, containing accounts of the various cases argued and determined in the various courts of record with the decisions and opinions thereon. *See* Reporter; Reports *or* reporters.

Reporter. A person who reports the decisions of a court of record; also, published volumes of decisions by a court or group of courts. The "court reporter" is the person who records court proceedings in court and later transcribes such. *See also* Court reporter; Reports *or* reporters.

Reports *or* **reporters.** Published volumes of case decisions by a particular court or group of courts; *e.g.* Supreme Court Reporter, Federal Reporter, Federal Supplement.

Term includes: (1) (court reports) published judicial cases arranged according to some grouping, such as jurisdiction, court, period of time, subject matter or case significance, (2) (administrative reports or decisions) published decisions of an administrative agency, (3) annual statements of progress, activities or policy issued by an administrative agency or an association, (4) annual financial reports by publically owned corporations to shareholders.

See also Annual report; Law reporters *or* reports; Reporter; United States Reports.

Repos. An agreement in which one party sells a security to another party and agrees to repurchase it on a specified date for a specified price.

Repose statutes. *See* Statute *(Statute of repose).*

Repossession. To take back—as when a seller or bank or finance company repossesses or takes back an item if the buyer misses an installment payment. To recover goods sold on credit or in installments when the buyer fails to pay for them. U.C.C. § 9–503. The conditions for repossession are entirely statutory and due process standards must be met as to notice, manner, etc.

Self-help (*i.e.* without legal process) repossession of collateral is permitted under U.C.C. § 9–503. *See* Self-help.

Represent. To appear in the character of; personate; to exhibit; to expose before the eyes. To represent a thing is to produce it publicly. To represent a person is to stand in his place; to speak or act with authority on behalf of such person; to supply his place; to act as his substitute or agent. *See also* Agent; Power of appointment; Representative.

Representation. Any conduct capable of being turned into a statement of fact. Statement of fact made to induce another to enter into contract. As element of actionable fraud includes deeds, acts or artifices calculated to mislead another, as well as words or positive assertions. *See also* Material fact; Misrepresentation; Reliance.

Act of representing another. *See* Represent.

Attorney, right to. *See* Counsel, right to.

Contracts. A statement express or implied made by one of two contracting parties to the other, before or at the time of making the contract, in regard to some past or existing fact, circumstance, or state of facts pertinent to the contract, which is influential in bringing about the agreement.

False representation. *See* False representation; Fraud; Material fact; Misrepresentation.

Insurance. A collateral statement, either by writing not inserted in the policy or by parol, of such facts or circumstances, relative to the proposed adventure, as are necessary to be communicated to the underwriters, to enable them to form a just estimate of the risks. The allegation of any facts, by the applicant to the insurer, or *vice versa*, preliminary to making the contract, and directly bearing upon it, having a plain and evident tendency to induce the making of the policy. The statements may or may not be in writing, and may be either express or by obvious implication.

Law of distribution and descent. The principle upon which the issue of a deceased person take or inherit the share of an estate which their immediate ancestor would have taken or inherited, if living; the taking or inheriting *per stirpes*. *See* Per stirpes.

Material representation. One having been a real moving cause inducing the making of a contract. A representation is "material" if it relates directly to matter in controversy and is of such nature that ultimate result would not have followed if there had been no representation or if one who acted upon it had been aware of its falsity. To be "material", a representation must be of such character that if it had not been made, the contract or transaction would not have been entered into.

In life insurance, one that would influence a prudent insurer in determining whether or not to accept the risk, or in fixing the amount of the premium in the event of such acceptance.

See Material fact; also, *Misrepresentation, below.*

Misrepresentation. An intentional false statement respecting a matter of fact, made by one of the parties to a contract, which is material to the contract and influential in producing it. *See* False representation; Material fact; Misrepresentation.

Representation, estoppel by. Such arises when one by acts, representations, admissions, or silence when he ought to speak out, intentionally or through culpable negligence induces another to believe certain facts to exist and such other rightfully relies and acts on such belief, so that he will be prejudiced if the former is permitted to deny the existence of such facts. It differs from estoppel by record, deed, or contract, in that it is not based on agreement of parties or finding of fact which may not be disputed, and is not mutual, but applies to only one party.

See also Equitable estoppel; In pais, estoppel.

Representative. A person or thing that represents, or stands for, a number or class of persons or things, or that in some way corresponds to, stands for, replaces, or is equivalent to, another person or thing. One who represents others or another in a special capacity, as an agent, and term is interchangeable with "agent".

A person chosen by the people to represent their several interests in a legislative body; *e.g.* representative elected to serve in Congress from a state congressional district.

"Representative" includes an agent, an officer of a corporation or association, and a trustee, executor or administrator of an estate, or any other person empowered to act for another. U.C.C. § 1–201(35).

See also Agent; Class *or* representative action; Legal representative; Representative capacity.

Personal representative. Person who manages affairs of another because of incapacity or death. Includes executor, administrator, successor, personal representative, special administrator, and persons who perform substantially the same function under the law governing their status. "General personal representative" excludes special administrator. Uniform Probate Code, § 1–201(30).

Term as used within meaning of statute providing that every wrongful death action shall be brought in name of personal representative of deceased person, is used simply to designate person who may prosecute the action.

See Executor; Guardian; Legal representative; Power of attorney.

Representative action. An action is a "representative action" when it is based upon a primary or personal right belonging to the plaintiff stockholder and those in his class. See also Class or representative action; Derivative action.

Representative capacity. The office or other position an agent holds in relation to his or her principal which, along with the principal's name, should be indicated on any instrument the agent signs for the principal so that the agent herself avoids personal liability. See U.C.C. §§ 3–403(2) & (3).

Reprieve. Temporary relief from or postponement of execution of criminal punishment or sentence. It does no more than stay the execution of a sentence for a time, and it is ordinarily an act of clemency extended to a prisoner to afford him an opportunity to procure some amelioration of the sentence imposed. It differs from a commutation which is a reduction of a sentence and from a pardon which is a permanent cancellation of a sentence; Compare Clemency.

Reprimand /réprəmǽnd/. To reprove severely; to censure formally, especially with authority. A public and formal censure or severe reproof, administered to a person in fault by his superior officer or by a body or organization to which he belongs. Thus, a member of a legislative body may be reprimanded by the presiding officer, in pursuance of a vote of censure, for improper conduct in the house; similarly, an attorney might be reprimanded by the Supreme Court or Bar Association of his State for unethical or improper conduct.

Reprisal /rəpráyzəl/. In general, any action taken by one person either in spite or as a retaliation for an assumed or real wrong by another. The forcible taking by one nation of a thing that belonged to another, in return or satisfaction for an injury committed by the latter on the former.

Republication. The re-execution or reestablishment by a testator of a will which he had once revoked. A second publication of a will, either expressly or by construction. A codicil duly executed is a republication of the will. For "Express republication," see that title.

Repudiate. To put away, reject, disclaim, or renounce a right, duty, obligation, or privilege.

Repudiation. A rejection, disclaimer, or renunciation of a contract before performance is due that does not operate as an anticipatory breach unless the promisee elects to treat the rejection as a breach and brings a suit for damages. The

rejection or refusal of an offered or available right or privilege, or of a duty or relation. The act of a buyer or seller in rejecting a contract of sale either partially or totally. U.C.C. §§ 2–610, 2–703, 2–708, 2–711.

Repudiation of a contract means refusal to perform duty or obligation owed to other party. Such consists in such words or actions by contracting party as indicate that he is not going to perform his contract in the future.

Repudiation of contract is in nature of anticipatory breach before performance is due, but does not operate as anticipatory breach unless promisee elects to treat repudiation as breach, and brings suit for damages. Such repudiation is but act or declaration in advance of any actual breach and consists usually of absolute and unequivocal declaration or act amounting to declaration on part of promisor to promisee that he will not make performance on future day at which contract calls for performance.

See also Refusal; Renunciation.

Anticipatory repudiation. See Anticipatory breach of contract.

Repugnancy. An inconsistency, opposition, or contrariety between two or more clauses of the same deed, contract, or statute, or between two or more material allegations of the same pleading, or any two writings.

Within rule that repugnant counts cannot be joined in same declaration, means affirmation of causes of action in one count and the denial of that cause of action in another count.

Inconsistent defenses or claims are permitted under Rule of Civil Proc. 8.

Repugnant verdict. See Verdict.

Repurchase. See Redemption.

Repurchase agreements. See Repos.

Reputable. Worthy of repute or distinction, held in esteem, honorable, praiseworthy.

Reputation. Estimation in which one is held; the character imputed to a person by those acquainted with him. That by which we are known and is the total sum of how we are seen by others. General opinion, good or bad, held of a person by those of the community in which he resides. It is necessarily based upon hearsay, but may be admissible if falling within the established exceptions to the hearsay rule. See e.g. Fed.Evid.R. 803(19–21).

"Character" is made up of the things an individual actually is and does whereas "reputation" is what people think an individual is and what they say about him.

See also Character; General reputation.

Reputed. Accepted by general, vulgar, or public opinion.

Reputed owner. *See* Owner.

Request, *v.* To ask for something or for permission or authority to do, see, hear, etc., something; to solicit. In its ordinary or natural meaning when used in a will, is precatory and not mandatory.

Request, *n.* An asking or petition. The expression of a desire to some person for something to be granted or done, particularly for the payment of a debt or performance of a contract. Also, direction or command in law of wills. For Express request, see that title.

Request for admission. Written statements of facts concerning the case which are submitted to an adverse party and which that party is required to admit or deny; those statements which are admitted will be treated by the court as having been established and need not be proved at trial. Fed.R.Civil P. 36.

Request for instructions. At the close of the evidence or at such earlier time during the trial as the court reasonably directs, any party may file written requests that the court instruct the jury on the law as set forth in the requests. Fed.R.Civil P. 51.

Require. To direct, order, demand, instruct, command, claim, compel, request, need, exact. To be in need of. To ask for authoritatively or imperatively.

Requirement contract. One in which party promises to supply all specific goods or services which other party may need during a certain period at an agreed price, and in which other party expressly or implicitly promises he will obtain his goods or services from the first party exclusively. While such contracts were at one time void for indefiniteness of amount, they are now universally valid. UCC 2–306(1). *See also* Exclusive dealing arrangements.

Requisition. A demand in writing, or formal request or requirement. The taking or seizure of property by government.

The formal demand by one government upon another, or by the governor of one of the United States upon the governor of a sister state, of the surrender of a fugitive criminal. *See* Extradition.

Res /ríyz/. Lat. The subject matter of a trust or will. In the civil law, a thing; an object. As a term of the law, this word has a very wide and extensive signification, including not only things which are objects of property, but also such as are not capable of individual ownership. And in old English law it is said to have a general import, comprehending both corporeal and incorporeal things of whatever kind, nature, or species. By *"res,"* according to the modern civilians, is meant everything that may form an *object* of rights, in opposition to *"persona,"* which is regarded as a subject of rights. *"Res,"* therefore, in its general meaning, comprises *actions* of all kinds; while in its restricted sense it comprehends every object of right, except actions. This has reference to the fundamental division of the Institutes, that all law relates either to *persons,* to *things,* or to *actions.*

Res is everything that may form an object of rights and includes an object, subject-matter or status. The term is particularly applied to an object, subject-matter, or *status,* considered as the defendant in an action, or as the object against which, directly, proceedings are taken. Thus, in a prize case, the captured vessel is "the *res*"; and proceedings of this character are said to be *in rem.* (See In Personam; In Rem.) *"Res"* may also denote the action or proceeding, as when a cause, which is not between adversary parties, is entitled *"In re _____."*

Classification

Things (res) have been variously divided and classified in law, *e.g.,* in the following ways: (1) Corporeal and incorporeal things; (2) movables and immovables; (3) res *mancipi* and res *nec mancipi;* (4) things real and things personal; (5) things in possession and choses (*i.e.,* things) in action; (6) fungible things and things not fungible *(fungibles vel non fungibiles);* and (7) res *singulæ* (*i.e.,* individual objects) and *universitates rerum* (*i.e.,* aggregates of things). Also persons are for some purposes and in certain respects regarded as things.

Res adjudicata /ríyz æjùwdəkéytə/. A less common spelling of res *judicata. See* Res judicata, *below.*

Res gestæ /ríyz jéstiy/. Things done. The "res gestæ" rule is that where a remark is made spontaneously and concurrently with an affray, collision or the like, it carries with it inherently a degree of credibility and will be admissible because of its spontaneous nature.

A spontaneous declaration made by a person immediately after an event and before the mind has an opportunity to conjure a falsehood. It represents an exception to the hearsay rule and should be referred to as a spontaneous exclamation rather than res gestæ. See Fed.Evid.Rule 803(3). *See also* Excited utterance; Spontaneous exclamation; Verbal act doctrine.

Res gestae witness. An eyewitness to some event in the continuum of the criminal transaction and one whose testimony will aid in developing a full disclosure of the facts surrounding the alleged commission of the charged offense.

Res inter alios acta /ríyz ìntər éyl(i)yows ǽktə/. *See* Res inter alios acta.

Res ipsa loquitur /ríyz ípsə lówkwətər/. The thing speaks for itself. Rebuttable presumption or inference that defendant was negligent, which arises upon proof that instrumentality causing injury was in defendant's exclusive control, and that the accident was one which ordinarily does not happen in absence of negligence. Res ipsa loquitur is rule of evidence whereby negligence of alleged wrongdoer may be inferred from mere fact that accident happened provided character of accident and circumstances attending it lead reasonably to belief that in absence of negligence it would not have occurred and that thing which caused injury is shown to have been under management and control of alleged wrongdoer. Under this doctrine, when a thing which causes injury, without fault of injured person, is shown to be under exclusive control of defendant, and injury is such as in ordinary course of things does not occur if the one having such control uses proper care, it affords reasonable evidence, in absence of an explanation, that injury arose from defendant's want of care. *See also* Exclusive control.

Res judicata /ríyz jùwdəkéytə/. A matter adjudged; a thing judicially acted upon or decided; a thing or matter settled by judgment. Rule that a final judgment rendered by a court of competent jurisdiction on the merits is conclusive as to the rights of the parties and their privies, and, as to them, constitutes an absolute bar to a subsequent action involving the same claim, demand or cause of action. And to be applicable, requires identity in thing sued for as well as identity of cause of action, of persons and parties to action, and of quality in persons for or against whom claim is made. The sum and substance of the whole rule is that a matter once judicially decided is finally decided. *See also* Collateral estoppel doctrine; Final decision rule; Issue preclusion.

Collateral estoppel compared. "Res judicata" bars relitigation of the same cause of action between the same parties where there is a prior judgment, whereas "collateral estoppel" bars relitigation of a particular issue or determinative fact.

Estoppel and res judicata distinguished, *see* Estoppel.

Resale. Exists where a person who has sold goods or other property to a purchaser sells them again to someone else. Sometimes a vendor reserves the right of reselling if the purchaser commits default in payment of the purchase money, and in some cases (*e.g.,* on a sale of perishable articles) the vendor may do so without having reserved the right. U.C.C. § 2–706 provides the conditions under which a seller has a right of resale on breach by the buyer of the sales contract.

Term may also refer to act of retailer who purchases goods from manufacturer or wholesaler for purpose of selling such goods in normal course of business. *See also* Retail; Retailer.

Resale price maintenance. An agreement between a manufacturer and retailer that the latter should not resell below a specified minimum price. Such schemes operate to prevent price competition between the various dealers handling a given manufacturer's product with the manufacturer generally suggesting an appropriate resale price and enforcing dealer acquiescence through some form of coercive sanction. Until 1976, federal statutes exempted such state-permitted agreements from antitrust actions. *See also* Vertical price-fixing contract.

Rescission of contract. To abrogate, annul, avoid, or cancel a contract; particularly, nullifying a contract by the act of a party. The right of rescission is the right to cancel (rescind) a contract upon the occurrence of certain kinds of default by the other contracting party. To declare a contract void in its inception and to put an end to it as though it never were. A "rescission" amounts to the unmaking of a contract, or an undoing of it from the beginning, and not merely a termination, and it may be effected by mutual agreement of parties, or by one of the parties declaring rescission of contract without consent of other if a legally sufficient ground therefor exists, or by applying to courts for a decree of rescission. It necessarily involves a repudiation of the contract and a refusal of the moving party to be further bound by it. Nonetheless, not every default in a contract will give rise to a right of rescission. *See also* Cancellation; Renunciation; Repudiation; Revocation; Termination.

An action of an equitable nature in which a party seeks to be relieved of his obligations under a contract on the grounds of mutual mistake, fraud, impossibility, etc.

Rescissory damages. *See* Damages.

Rescript /ríyskript/. A written order from the court to the clerk, giving directions concerning the further disposition of a case. The written statement by an appellate court of its decision in a case, with the reasons therefor, sent down to the trial court. A short appellate opinion which does not bear the name of any justice.

Rescue. Act of saving or freeing. At common law, forcibly and knowingly freeing another from arrest, imprisonment or legal custody without any effort by prisoner to free himself. The unlawfully or forcibly taking back goods which have been taken under a distress for rent, damage feasant, etc. *See also* Repossession.

Rescue doctrine. Danger invites rescue. Under this doctrine, one who has, through his negligence, endangered safety of another may be held liable for injuries sustained by third person who attempts to save other from injury.

"Rescue", "humanitarian" or "good samaritan" doctrine is that one who sees a person in imminent and serious peril through negligence of another cannot be charged with contributory negligence, as a matter of law, in risking his own life or serious injury in attempting to effect a rescue, provided the attempt is not recklessly or rashly made. *See also* Humanitarian doctrine.

Research credit. A business tax credit, the purpose of which is to encourage research and development. It has two components: the incremental research activities credit and the basic research credit. I.R.C. § 41.

Reservation. A clause in a deed or other instrument of conveyance by which the grantor creates, and reserves to himself, some right, interest, or profit in the estate granted, which had no previous existence as such, but is first called into being by the instrument reserving it; such as rent, or an easement. Reservation occurs where granting clause of the deed operates to exclude a portion of that which would otherwise pass to the grantee by the description in the deed and "reserves" that portion unto the grantor.

A right created and retained by a grantor. The reservation may be temporary (such as a life estate) or permanent (such as an easement running with the land).

The reservation of a point of law is the act of the trial court in setting it aside for future consideration, allowing the trial to proceed meanwhile as if the question had been settled one way, but subject to alteration of the judgment in case the court *in banc* should decide it differently.

For exception and reservation distinguished, *see* and *compare* Exception.

A tract of land, more or less considerable in extent, which is by public authority withdrawn from sale or settlement, and appropriated to specific public uses; such as parks, military posts, Indian lands, etc. A tract of land (under control of the Bureau of Indian Affairs) to which an American Indian tribe retains its original title to ownership or which has been set aside for its use out of the public domain.

Reservation of claim. A draft or demand presented under a letter of credit is non-complying if there is an explicit reservation of claim. U.C.C. § 5–110.

Reserve, *v.* To keep back, to retain, to keep in store for future or special use, and to retain or hold over to a future time. To set aside funds, usually for indefinite contingencies, such as future maintenance of a structure, or to pay future claims.

Reserve, *n.* Funds set aside to cover future expenses, losses, claims, or liabilities. Sums of money an insurer is required to set aside as a fund for the liquidation of future unaccrued and contingent claims, and claims accrued, but contingent and indefinite as to amount. Reserves of insurance company are the amount treated as liability on the balance sheet which the company estimates will be sufficient to meet its policy obligations.

"With reserve" in an auction means that the thing will not be sold if the highest bid is not high enough. To "reserve title" is to keep an ownership right as security that the thing will be fully paid for.

Bad debt reserve. In accounting, a reserve set aside for losses on uncollectible accounts and notes receivable. An account for bad debts is offset by a reserve for bad debts. When accounts become uncollectible they are written off against the reserve. For tax years beginning after 1986, the Internal Revenue Service repealed the use of the bad debt reserve method for tax purposes, requiring most taxpayers to use the specific charge-off method for receivables which become uncollectible after 1986.

Contingency reserve (or fund). See that title.

Depletion reserve. An account used in connection with diminishing assets such as mines, timber, etc. to reflect the depletion of the asset.

Depreciation reserve. An account used to recover the cost of an asset by writing off a portion of the cost over the life of the asset or by some other acceptable method. The depreciation reserve is listed on the balance sheet as a reduction in the cost of the related asset.

Legal reserve. A reserve account required by law for insurance companies and banks as protection against losses.

Replacement reserve. An account set up for the actual replacement of machinery and equipment.

Required reserves. The minimum amount of reserves that must be held by banks as required by the Federal Reserve Board. The Board requires banks and other financial institutions that accept deposits to hold specified minimum reserves in the form of vault cash or deposits with the nearest Federal Reserve District Bank.

Sinking fund reserve. An account set up for the redemption of long term debt. It is commonly required by a bond indenture.

Reserve banks. Member banks of Federal Reserve System.

Reserve Board. *See* Federal Reserve Board of Governors.

Reserve clause. A clause included in contracts of professional athletes whereby the athlete's service is reserved for the team holding his contract. It represents a hold on the player by the team which has contracted with him, and such team has the exclusive right to trade the player to another team without his consent. Such reserve clauses in professional baseball contracts have long since been held to be exempt from federal antitrust laws.

Reserved. Retained, kept or set apart, for a purpose or a person.

Reserved land. Public land that has been withheld or kept back from sale or disposition. *See* Reservation.

Reserved power. A power specifically withheld because not mentioned or reasonably implied in other powers conferred by a constitution or statute. *See also* Power *(Constitutional powers)*.

Reserve fund. *See* Reserve.

Reserve ratio. In banking, the primary reserve ratio is the ratio of the balance of Federal Reserve balance of the bank plus cash in vault to the demand deposits of the bank. The secondary ratio is the ratio between the government securities of the bank and its demand deposits. There is also a ratio between time deposits and Federal Reserve balances plus cash in vault.

Res gestæ. *See* Res.

Reside. Live, dwell, abide, sojourn, stay, remain, lodge. To settle oneself or a thing in a place, to be stationed, to remain or stay, to dwell permanently or continuously, to have a settled abode for a time, to have one's residence or domicile; specifically, to be in residence, to have an abiding place, to be present as an element, to inhere as a quality, to be vested as a right. A foreign business corporation, for venue purposes, "resides" in county where its registered office and registered agent is located.

Residence. Place where one actually lives or has his home; a person's dwelling place or place of habitation; an abode; house where one's home is; a dwelling house. Personal presence at some place of abode with no present intention of definite and early removal and with purpose to remain for undetermined period, not infrequently, but not necessarily combined with design to stay permanently.

Residence implies something more than mere physical presence and something less than domicile. The terms "resident" and "residence" have no precise legal meaning; sometimes they mean domicile plus physical presence; sometimes they mean domicile; and sometimes they mean something less than domicile. *See also* Abode; Domicile; Legal residence; Principal residence.

"Domicile" compared and distinguished. As "domicile" and "residence" are usually in the same place, they are frequently used as if they had the same meaning, but they are not identical terms, for a person may have two places of residence, as in the city and country, but only one domicile. Residence means living in a particular locality, but domicile means living in that locality with intent to make it a fixed and permanent home. Residence simply requires bodily presence as an inhabitant in a given place, while domicile requires bodily presence in that place and also an intention to make it one's domicile.

Immigration law. The place of general abode; the place of general abode of a person means his or her principal, actual dwelling place in fact, without regard to intent. 8 U.S.C.A. § 1101.

Legal residence. See that title.

Residency requirements. Broad term to describe terms of residence required by states for such things as welfare benefits, admission to the bar, divorce, etc. As regards divorce and welfare prerequisites, the requirements must not be so stringent as to violate due process or equal protection. *See* Right to travel.

Resident. Any person who occupies a dwelling within the State, has a present intent to remain within the State for a period of time, and manifests the genuineness of that intent by establishing an ongoing physical presence within the State together with indicia that his presence within the State is something other than merely transitory in nature. The word "resident" when used as a noun, means a dweller, habitant or occupant; one who resides or dwells in a place for a period of more, or less, duration; it signifies one having a residence, or one who resides or abides. Word "resident" has many meanings in law, largely determined by statutory context in which it is used. *See also* Residence.

Resident agent. Person in a jurisdiction authorized to accept service of process for another, especially a corporation.

Resident alien. One, not yet a citizen of this country, who has come into the country from another with the intent to abandon his former citizenship and to reside here.

Resident freeholder. A person who resides in the particular place (town, city, county, etc.) and who owns an estate in lands therein amounting at least to a freehold interest.

Residential cluster. An area to be developed as a single entity according to a plan containing residential housing units which have a common or public open space area as an appurtenance. *See also* Planned unit development.

Residential density. The number of dwelling units per gross acre of residential land area including streets, easements and open space portions of a development.

Residential rental property. For tax purposes, buildings for which at least 80 percent of the gross rents are from dwelling units (*e.g.,* an apartment building). This type of building is distinguished from nonresidential (commercial or industrial) buildings in applying the recapture of depreciation provisions. I.R.C. §§ 168(e)(2) and 1250. *See also* Recapture of depreciation.

Residual /rəzídyuwəl/rəzíj(uw)əl/. Relating to the residue; relating to the part remaining; that which is left over. Term may also refer to deferred commissions.

Residual claim. The claim on what is left after all prior claims have been settled.

Residual method. An accounting method for allocating the purchase price for the acquisition of another firm (a merger) among the acquired assets.

Residual risk. All the (remaining) risk that is not borne by senior providers of capital; the common stockholders of a firm bear the residual risk of the firm.

Residual value. Value of depreciable asset after depreciation charges have been deducted from original cost. *See also* Salvage *(Salvage value).*

Residuary /rəzídyuwəriy/. Pertaining to the residue; constituting the residue; giving or bequeathing the residue; receiving or entitled to the residue. *See* Residue.

Residuary bequest. A bequest of all of testator's estate not otherwise effectually disposed of.

Residuary clause. Clause in will by which that part of property is disposed of which remains after satisfying bequests and devises. Any part of the will which disposes of property not expressly disposed of by other provisions of the will. *See also* Residuary estate.

Residuary devise and devisee. *See* Devise.

Residuary estate. That which remains after debts and expenses of administration, legacies, and devises have been satisfied. That portion of person's estate which has not otherwise been particularly devised or bequeathed. It consists of all that has not been legally disposed of by will, other than by residuary clause. Gross estate less all charges, debts, costs, and all other legacies. *See also* Residuary clause.

Residuary gift. *See* Legacy.

Residuary legacy. *See* Legacy.

Residuary legatee. *See* Legatee.

Residue. The surplus of a testator's estate remaining after all the debts, taxes, costs of administration, and particular legacies have been discharged. *See also* Residuary estate.

Residuum /rəzídyuwəm/. That which remains after any process of separation or deduction; a residue or balance. That which remains of a decedent's estate, after debts have been paid and legacies deducted. *See also* Residuary estate.

Residuum rule. While a decision of an administrative board may be based partly on hearsay evidence introduced at the hearing, it will be upheld on judicial review only if there is a residuum of competent evidence on which it is founded. The residuum rule has generally been rejected by the federal courts.

Resignation. Formal renouncement or relinquishment of an office. It must be made with intention of relinquishing the office accompanied by act of relinquishment.

Res inter alios acta /ríyz íntər éyliyows ǽktə/. This rule forbids the introduction of collateral facts which by their nature are incapable of affording any reasonable presumption or inference as to the principal matter in dispute, and thus evidence as to acts, transactions or occurrences to which accused is not a party or is not connected is inadmissible.

In law of evidence, a thing or event which occurs at a time different from the time in issue is generally not admissible to prove what occurred at the time in issue. Also events which involve those not parties to an action are generally not admissible because they are immaterial and commonly not relevant.

Res ipsa loquitur. *See* Res.

Resist. To oppose. This word properly describes an opposition by direct action and *quasi* forcible means.

Resistance. The act of resisting opposition. The employment of forcible means to prevent the execution of an endeavor in which force is employed; standing against; obstructing. Withstanding the force or effect of or the exertion of oneself to counteract or defeat. *See* Self-defense.

Resisting an officer. In criminal law, the offense of obstructing, opposing, and endeavoring to prevent (with or without actual force) a peace officer in the execution of a writ or in the lawful discharge of his duty while making an arrest or otherwise enforcing the peace. See *e.g.* 18 U.S. C.A. § 111. *See also* Resisting arrest.

Resisting arrest. The crime of obstructing or opposing a police officer making an arrest. See, *e.g.,* Model Penal Code, § 242.2; N.J.S.A. 2C:29–2.

Res judicata. *See* Res.

Resolution. A formal expression of the opinion or will of an official body or a public assembly, adopted by vote; as a legislative resolution. Such may be either a simple, joint or concurrent resolution.

The term is usually employed to denote the adoption of a motion, the subject-matter of which would not properly constitute a statute, such as a mere expression of opinion; an alteration of the rules; a vote of thanks or of censure, etc. Such is not law but merely a form in which a legislative body expresses an opinion.

The chief distinction between a "resolution" and a "law" is that the former is used whenever the legislative body passing it wishes merely to express an opinion as to some given matter or thing and is only to have a temporary effect on such particular thing, while by a "law" it is intended to permanently direct and control matters applying to persons or things in general.

Concurrent resolution. An action of Congress passed in the form of a resolution of one house, the other concurring, which expresses the sense of Congress on a particular subject.

Corporate resolution. Formal documentation of action taken by board of directors of corporation (*e.g.* declaration of stock dividend).

Joint resolution. A resolution adopted by both houses of congress or a legislature. When such a resolution has been approved by the president or passed with his approval, it has the effect of a law.

The distinction between a joint resolution and a concurrent resolution of congress, is that the former requires the approval of the president while the latter does not.

Ordinance distinguished. "Resolution" denotes something less formal than "ordinance"; generally, it is mere expression of opinion or mind of council concerning some matter of administration, within its official cognizance, and provides for disposition of particular item of administrative business of a municipality; it is not a law, and in substance there is no difference between resolution, order and motion.

Resolution Trust Corporation. A federal agency which succeeds the former Federal Savings and Loan Insurance Corporation (FSLIC) as conservator or receiver of federal savings and loan associations which became insolvent while insured by the FSLIC. One of agency's functions is to dispose of assets of insolvent S & L's. With the abolition of the FSLIC in 1989, such associations are now insured by the FDIC. *See also* Federal Deposit Insurance Corporation.

Resolutory condition /rəzólyət(ə)riy kəndíshən/. *See* Condition.

Resort, *v.* To frequent; to go, especially to go frequently, customarily, or usually. To have recourse; to look to for relief or help.

Resort, *n.* Recourse; a person or thing that is looked to for help. A place of frequent assembly; a haunt.

Court of last resort. A court whose decision is final and without further appeal in reference to the particular case; *e.g.* Supreme Court of the United States.

Resources. Money or any property that can be converted to meet needs; means of raising money or supplies; capabilities of raising wealth or to supply necessary wants; available means or capability of any kind. *See also* Natural resources.

RESPA (Real Estate Settlement Procedures Act). A federal statute governing disclosure of settlement costs in the sale of residential (one to four family) improved property which is to be financed by a federally insured lender. 12 U.S. C.A. § 2601 et seq. *See also* Closing.

Respective. Relating to particular persons or things, each to each; particular; several; as, their respective homes.

Respite /réspət/rəspáyt/. The temporary suspension of the execution of a sentence; a reprieve; a delay, forbearance, or continuation of time.

Respondeat superior /rəspóndiyət s(y)əpíriyər/. Let the master answer. This doctrine or maxim means that a master is liable in certain cases for the wrongful acts of his servant, and a principal for those of his agent. Under this doctrine master is responsible for want of care on servant's part toward those to whom master owes duty to use care, provided failure of servant to use such care occurred in course of his employment. Under doctrine an employer is liable for injury to person or property of another proximately resulting from acts of employee done within scope of his employment in the employer's service. Doctrine applies only when relation of master and servant existed between defendant and wrongdoer at time of injury sued for, in respect to very transaction from which it arose. Hence, doctrine is inapplicable where injury occurs while employee is acting outside legitimate scope of authority. But if deviation be only slight or incidental, employer may still be liable. *See* Scope of employment; Vicarious liability.

Respondent /rəspóndənt/. In equity practice, the party who makes an answer to a bill or other proceeding in equity. In appellate practice, the party who contends against an appeal; the party against whom the appeal is taken, *i.e.* the appellee.

In the civil law, one who answers or is security for another; a fidejussor.

Responsibility. The state of being answerable for an obligation, and includes judgment, skill, ability and capacity. The obligation to answer for an act done, and to repair or otherwise make restitution for any injury it may have caused. *See also* Liability; Responsible.

Responsible. Liable; legally accountable or answerable. Able to pay a sum for which he is or may become liable, or to discharge an obligation which he may be under.

Responsible bidder. One who is capable financially and competent to complete the job for which he is bidding. A responsible bidder is one who is not only financially responsible, but who is possessed of a judgment, skill, ability, capacity and integrity requisite and necessary to perform a public contract according to its terms.

Responsible cause. So as to relieve defendant from liability for injuries, a cause which is the culpable act of a human being who is legally responsible for such act. *See* Proximate cause.

Responsible government. This term generally designates that species of governmental system in which the responsibility for public measures or acts of state rests upon the ministry or executive council, who are under an obligation to resign when disapprobation of their course is expressed by a vote of want of confidence, in the legislative assembly, or by the defeat of an important measure advocated by them.

Responsive. Answering; constituting or comprising a complete answer. A "responsive allegation" is one which directly answers the allegation it is intended to meet.

Responsive pleading. A pleading which joins issue and replies to a prior pleading of an opponent in contrast to a dilatory plea or motion which seeks to dismiss on some ground other than the merits of the action. Though general denials are not commonly accepted today, an answer in which specific denials are set forth and an answer by way of confession and avoidance are examples of responsive pleadings. *See* Answer.

Rest, *v.* In the trial of an action, a party is said to "rest," or "rest his case," when he advises the court or intimates that he has produced all the evidence he intends to offer at that stage, and submits the case, either finally, or subject to his right to afterwards offer rebutting evidence.

Rest, *n.* Repose; cessation or intermission of motion, exertion or labor; freedom from activity; quiet. *See also* Residue.

Restatement of Law. A series of volumes authored by the American Law Institute that tell what the law in a general area is, how it is changing, and what direction the authors (who are leading legal scholars in each field covered) think this change should take; for example, Restatement of the Law of Contracts; Restatement of the Law of Torts. The various Restatements have been a formidable force in shaping the disciplines of the law covered; they are frequently cited by courts and either followed or distinguished; they represent the fruit of the labor of the best legal minds in the diverse fields of law covered.

Resting a case. *See* Rest.

Restitution. An equitable remedy under which a person is restored to his or her original position prior to loss or injury, or placed in the position he or she would have been, had the breach not occurred. Act of restoring; restoration; restoration of anything to its rightful owner; the act of making good or giving equivalent for any loss, damage or injury; and indemnification. Act of making good or giving an equivalent for or restoring something to the rightful owner. Compensation for the wrongful taking of property. Restoration of status quo and is amount which would put plaintiff in as good a position as he would have been if no contract had been made and restores to plaintiff value of what he parted with in performing contract. *See* Restatement, Second, Contracts, § 373.

A person who has been unjustly enriched at the expense of another is required to make restitution to the other. Restatement of the Law, Restitution, § 1.

In torts, restitution is essentially the measure of damages, while in contracts a person aggrieved by a breach is entitled to be placed in the position in which he would have been if the defendant had not breached.

In the law of commercial sales, the buyer's rights to restitution are governed by U.C.C. §§ 2–711 and 2–718.

See also Unjust enrichment doctrine.

Criminal law. The federal courts and many states have restitution programs under which the criminal offender is required to repay, as a condition of his sentence, the victim or society in money or services. See *e.g.* 18 U.S.C.A. §§ 3663, 3664.

Maritime law. The placing back or restoring articles which have been lost by jettison: This is done, when remainder of the cargo has been saved, at the general charge of the owners of the cargo.

Restrain. To limit, confine, abridge, narrow down, restrict, obstruct, impede, hinder, stay, destroy. To prohibit from action; to put compulsion upon; to restrict; to hold or press back. To keep in check; to hold back from acting, proceeding, or advancing, either by physical or moral force, or by interposing obstacle; to repress or suppress; to curb. To restrict a person's movements in such manner as to interfere substantially with his liberty.

To enjoin. *See* Injunction; Restraining order.

Restraining order. An order in the nature of an injunction which may issue upon filing of an application for an injunction forbidding the defendant from doing the threatened act until a hearing on the application can be had. It is distinguishable from an injunction, in that the former is intended only as a restraint until the propriety of granting an injunction can be determined and it does no more than restrain the proceeding until such determination. Such an order is limited in its operation, and extends only to such reasonable time as may be necessary to have a hearing on an order to show cause why an injunction should not issue. *See also* Injunction; Order; Temporary restraining order.

Restraining powers. Restrictions or limitations imposed upon the exercise of a power by the donor thereof.

Restraint. Confinement, abridgment, or limitation. Prohibition of action; holding or pressing back from action. Hindrance, confinement, or restriction of liberty. Obstruction, hindrance or destruction of trade or commerce. *See* Restraint of trade; Stop.

Unlawful restraint. Unlawful restraint is knowingly and without legal authority restraining another so as to interfere substantially with his liberty.

A person is "restrained" or "imprisoned" for *false imprisonment* purposes when he is deprived of either liberty of movement or freedom to remain in place of his lawful choice, and such restraint or imprisonment may be accomplished by physical force alone, by threat of force, or by conduct reasonably implying that force will be used.

Person is guilty of "unlawful restraint" if he knowingly: (1) restrains another unlawfully in circumstances exposing him to risk of serious bodily injury; or (2) holds another in a condition of involuntary servitude. 18 Pa.C.S.A. § 2902. *See also* Imprisonment *(False imprisonment);* Kidnapping.

Term may also refer to restraint of person for search or seizure without lawful warrant or probable cause. *See* Search.

Restraint of trade. Contracts or combinations which tend or are designed to eliminate or stifle competition, effect a monopoly, artificially maintain prices, or otherwise hamper or obstruct the course of trade and commerce as it would be carried on if left to the control of natural economic forces. Term as used in Sherman Act means "unreasonable restraints of trade" which are illegal per se restraints interfering with free competition in business and commercial transactions which tend to restrict production, affect prices, or otherwise control market to detriment of purchasers or consumers of goods and services, or those restraints of trade, ordinarily reasonable, but made unreasonable because accompanied with

specific intent to accomplish equivalent of a forbidden restraint. To restrain interstate trade and commerce means to interfere unreasonably with the ordinary, usual and freely-competitive pricing or distribution system of the open market in interstate trade and commerce. A conspiracy may restrain interstate commerce even though some or all of the defendants are not engaged in interstate commerce, and even though some or all of the means employed may be acts wholly within a state, if there is a substantial and direct effect on interstate commerce. Sherman Antitrust Act, § 1. *See also* Rule *(Rule of reason);* Sherman Antitrust Act.

Restraint on alienation. A provision in an instrument of conveyance which prohibits the grantee from selling or transferring the property which is the subject of the conveyance. Most such restraints are unenforceable as against public policy and the law's policy of free alienability of land. *See* Restrictive covenant.

Any provision in a trust or other instrument which, either by express terms or by implication, purports to prohibit or penalize the use of the power of alienation; the trusts usually involved are spendthrift, discretionary and support trusts. *See also* Perpetuity.

Restrict. To restrain within bounds; to limit; to confine. *See also* Restraint.

Restricted property. An arrangement whereby an employer transfers property (usually stock) to an employee at a bargain price (for less than the fair market value). If the transfer is accompanied by a substantial risk of forfeiture and the property is not transferable, no compensation results to the employee until such restrictions disappear. I.R.C. § 83.

Restricted securities. Securities acquired directly or indirectly from an issuer, or from a person in a controlled relationship with the issuer (an "affiliate") in a transaction or chain of transactions not involving any public offering. Those securities that either by contract or by law cannot be distributed to public; a "restricted security" is one that has no market. Stock that is subject to transfer restrictions.

Restricted surplus. The portion of retained earnings which cannot be distributed as dividends. The restrictions are generally due to preferred dividends in arrears, covenants in a loan agreement, or a decision by the company's board of directors.

Restriction. A limitation, often imposed in a deed or lease respecting the use to which the property may be put. *See e.g.* Restrictive covenant.

Restrictive covenant. Provision in a deed limiting the use of the property and prohibiting certain uses. In context of property law, term describes contract between grantor and grantee which restricts grantee's use and occupancy of land; generally, purpose behind restrictive covenants is to maintain or enhance value of lands adjacent to one another by controlling nature and use of surrounding lands. Covenants which restrict use of property on basis of race are unenforceable.

Also, clauses in contracts of partnership and employment which limit a contracting party after termination of the contract in performing similar work for a period of time and within a certain geographical area. If reasonable as to time and area, such clauses are enforceable.

Restrictive indorsement. An indorsement so worded as to restrict the further negotiability of the instrument. Thus, "Pay the contents to J. S. only," or "to J. S. for my use," or "For Deposit Only", are restrictive indorsements, and put an end to the negotiability of the paper.

An indorsement is restrictive which either (a) is conditional; or (b) purports to prohibit further transfer of the instrument; or (c) includes the words "for collection", "for deposit", "pay any bank", or like terms signifying a purpose of deposit or collection; or (d) otherwise states that it is for the benefit or use of the indorser or of another person. U.C.C. § 3–205.

Resulting powers. Powers of the federal government derived from a combination of several grants or the aggregate of power granted to the federal government. *See* Power *(Constitutional powers).*

Resulting trust. Trust implied in law from intentions of parties to a given transaction.

One in which a party, through no actual or constructive fraud, becomes invested with legal title, but holds that title for the benefit of another, although without expressed intent to do so, because of a presumption of such intent arising by operation of law. A "resulting trust" arises where a person makes or causes to be made a disposition of property under circumstances which raise an inference that he does not intend that person taking or holding the property should have the beneficial interest therein, unless inference is rebutted or the beneficial interest is otherwise effectively disposed of. Restatement, Second, Trusts, § 404.

Resulting use. *See* Use.

Resummons. A second summons. The calling a person a second time to answer an action, where the first summons is defeated upon any occasion; as the death of a party, or the like.

Retail, *v.* To sell by small quantities, in broken lots or parcels, not in bulk, directly to consumer. Sales made in minimal quantities to ultimate consumer to meet personal needs, rather than for

commercial or industrial users. In general, wholesalers sell to retailers who in turn sell to consumers.

Retail, *n.* A sale for final consumption in contrast to a sale for further sale or processing (*i.e.* wholesale). A sale to the ultimate consumer.

Retailer. A person engaged in making sales to ultimate consumers. One who sells personal or household goods for use or consumption.

The essential distinction between a "wholesaler" and "retailer" as respects application of the Fair Labor Standards Act is that the person buying from the retailer is the ultimate user or consumer of the article or commodity or does not sell it again whereas the one buying from a wholesaler buys only for the purpose of selling the article again.

Retail installment account. An account established by an agreement entered into pursuant to which the buyer promises to pay, in installments, to a retail seller his outstanding balance incurred in retail installment sales, whether or not a security interest in the goods sold is retained by the seller, and which provides for a finance charge which is expressed as a percent of the periodic balances to accrue thereafter providing such charge is not capitalized or stated as a dollar amount in such agreement. *See e.g.* Calif. Civil Code, § 1802.7.

Retail installment contract. Any contract for a retail installment sale between a buyer and seller, entered into or performed which provides for (a) repayment in installments, whether or not such contract contains a title retention provision, and in which the buyer agrees to pay a finance charge, or in which the buyer does not agree to pay a finance charge but the goods or services are available at a lesser price if paid for by either cash or credit card, or in which the buyer would have received any additional goods or services or any higher quality goods or services at no added cost over the total amount payable in installments if the sale had been for cash, or (b) which provides for payment in more than four installments. *See e.g.* Calif. Civil Code, § 1802.6.

Retail method. In accounting, an inventory estimation method widely used by retail establishments; derives a cost to retail ratio and applies the ratio to the retail value of ending inventory.

Retail sale. A sale in small quantities or direct to consumer, as distinguished from sale at "wholesale" in large quantity to one who intends to resell. The ordinary meaning of term "retail sale" within sales tax statutes is a sale to an ultimate consumer. *See also* Retail.

Retain. To continue to hold, have, use, recognize, etc., and to keep.

To engage the services of an attorney or counsellor to manage a specific matter or action or all legal matters in general. *See* Retainer.

Retained earnings. An account on the balance sheet which represents the accumulated earnings of a corporation less any dividend distributions (including capitalization through stock dividends). It is usually a credit balance and a component of stockholder's equity. Retained earnings are also called "undistributed profits" or "earned surplus." *See* Accumulated earnings tax; Earned surplus; Surplus; Undistributed profits.

Statement of retained earnings. In accounting, a financial statement that discloses the changes in the retained earnings account during an accounting period.

Retainer. The act of withholding what one has in one's own hands by virtue of some right. In the practice of law, when a client hires an attorney to represent him, the client is said to have retained the attorney. This act of employment is called the retainer. The retainer agreement between the client and attorney sets forth the nature of services to be performed, costs, expenses, and related matters. If the client employs the attorney for a specific case, that is called a *special retainer*. In contrast, if a client hires a lawyer for a specific length of time (*e.g.,* a year) rather than for a specific project, that is called a *general retainer*. The lawyer, during the period of the general retainer, may not accept any conflicting employment.

Retainer pay. Compensation paid to enlisted men retained in the service but not rendering active service.

Retaining fee. A fee given to an attorney on engaging his services. *See* Retainer.

Retaining lien. A possessory lien which attaches to client's papers, money and property which came into attorney's hands during course of his employment. Attorney's right to retain possession of property belonging to his client which comes into his hands within the scope of his employment until his charges are paid. *See also* Attorney's lien.

Retaking. The taking one's goods, from another, who without right has taken possession thereof. *See* Recaption; Repossession.

Retaliatory eviction. Act of landlord in commencing eviction proceedings against tenant because of tenant's complaints, participation in tenant's union, or like activities with which the landlord is not in agreement. In some states, such retaliation will bar the landlord from enforcing his normal remedies against tenant.

Retaliatory law. Restraints placed by state law on foreign companies equal to the restraints placed by such foreign jurisdictions on companies doing business in such states. Many states have such laws. For example, in Pennsylvania if by laws of any other state or foreign government any taxes, fines, penalties, license fees or other obligations or prohibitions additional to or in excess of those imposed by Pennsylvania laws on insurance companies, associations and exchanges of other states, are imposed on insurance companies, associations and exchanges of Pennsylvania doing business in such state, like obligations and prohibitions are imposed on insurance companies, associations and exchanges of such state doing business in Pennsylvania.

Retirement. Termination of employment, service, trade or occupation upon reaching retirement age, or earlier at election of employee, self-employed, or professional. Removal of fixed asset from service.

Retirement annuity. Type of pension plan paid through annuities to those who have retired. Plans differ as to the rights of survivors of the annuitant.

Retirement of securities. Cancellation of reacquired or redeemed stocks or bonds. *See also* Redemption; Stock *(Stock redemption).*

Retirement plans. General term referring to various types of retirement benefit plans provided by employers or established individually by self-employed. *See* Individual retirement account (I.R.A.); Keogh plan; Money-purchase plan; Pension plan; Retirement annuity. Most such plans are regulated by the federal Employee Retirement Income Security Act (ERISA).

Retraction. To take back. To retract an offer is to withdraw it before acceptance. In law of defamation, a formal recanting of the defamatory material. Retraction is not a defense but, under certain circumstances, it is admissible in mitigation of damages.

In probate practice, a withdrawal of a renunciation, *(q.v.).*

Retraxit /rətrǽksət/. Lat. He has withdrawn. A retraxit is a voluntary renunciation by plaintiff in open court of his suit and cause thereof, and by it plaintiff forever loses his action. Under rule practice, this is accomplished by a voluntary dismissal. Fed.R.Civil P. 41(a).

Retreat, *n.* A place for contemplation especially of a religious nature. The totality of exercises in a religious house where a person may "take stock" of himself.

Retreat, *v.* To withdraw from the world or from an encounter.

Something the defendant must sometimes do before using deadly force in self-defense or defense of others. Model Penal Code §§ 3.04(2), 3.05(2). *See* Retreat to the wall.

Retreat to the wall. A common law requirement that an endangered person use all reasonable means to avoid the necessity of taking human life before resorting to deadly force in self-defense. The requirement is abandoned now in the majority of jurisdictions, which hold that one assaulted in a place where he has a right to be is under no duty to retreat before using deadly force in self-defense. See Model Penal Code §§ 3.04(2), 3.05(2). *See also* Self defense.

Retrial. A new trial of an action which has already been once tried. *See also* Rehearing; Trial *(New trial; Trial de novo). Compare* Mistrial.

Retribution. Something given or demanded in payment. In criminal law, it is punishment based on the theory which bears its name and based strictly on the fact that every crime demands payment in the form of punishment. *See also* Restitution.

Retro /rétrow/. Lat. Back; backward; behind. *Retrofeodum,* a rerefief, or *arriere* fief.

Retroactive. Process of acting with reference to past occurrences. *See also* Retrospective.

Retroactive inference. The inferring of a previous fact from present conditions by a trier of facts.

Retroactive law. "Retroactive" or "retrospective" laws are generally defined from a legal viewpoint as those which take away or impair vested rights acquired under existing laws, create new obligations, impose a new duty, or attach a new disability in respect to the transactions or considerations already past. One which is intended to act on things that are past. A statute which creates a new obligation on transactions or considerations already past or destroys or impairs vested rights. Such laws may be unenforceable because violative of the ex post facto clause of the U.S.Const., Art. I, Sec. 9, Cl. 3. *See also* Retrospective law.

Retrospective. Looking backward; contemplating what is past; having reference to a state of things existing before the act in question.

Retrospective law. A law which looks backward or contemplates the past; one which is made to affect acts or facts occurring, or rights accruing, before it came into force. Every statute which takes away or impairs vested rights acquired under existing laws, or creates a new obligation, imposes a new duty, or attaches a new disability in respect to transactions or considerations already past. One that relates back to a previous transaction and gives it a different legal effect from that which it had under the law when it occurred. *See also* Ex post facto; Retroactive law.

Return. To bring, carry, or send back; to place in the custody of; to restore; to re-deliver. "Return" means that something which has had a prior existence will be brought or sent back.

The act of a sheriff, constable, marshall, or other ministerial officer, in delivering back to the court a writ, notice, process or other paper, which he was required to serve or execute, with a brief account of his doings under the mandate, the time and mode of service or execution, or his failure to accomplish it, as the case may be. Also the indorsement made by the officer upon the writ or other paper, stating what he has done under it, the time and mode of service, etc. Such return (proof of service) is required under Rule of Civil Procedure 4. *See False return; Return day, below.*

A schedule of information required by governmental bodies, such as the tax return required by the Internal Revenue Service. *See* Joint tax return; Tax return.

Merchandise which is brought back to the seller for credit or refund.

Profit on sale, or income from investments (usually expressed as annual percentage rate). *See* Income; Profit; Rate *(Rate of return)*; Return on assets; Return on equity; Revenue.

The report made by the court, body of magistrates, returning board, or other authority charged with the official counting of the votes cast at an election.

Fair return. See Fair return on investment.

Return day. The day named in a writ or process, upon which the officer is required to return it. Under Fed.R.Civil P. 4 the person serving the process shall make proof of service (return) to the court promptly and in any event within the time during which the person served must respond to the process.

Day on which votes cast are counted and the official result is declared.

Return of premium. The repayment of the whole or a ratable part of the premium paid for a policy of insurance, upon the cancellation of the contract before the time fixed for its expiration.

Returnable. To be returned; requiring a return. When a writ or process is said to be "returnable" on a certain day, it is meant that on that day the officer must return it.

Return day. *See* Return.

Return of capital. The recovery of the original investment in a project or investment; the return of principal.

Return of process. *See* Return.

Return on assets. Ratio of net income to total assets. *See* Return on equity.

Return on equity. The relationship of the amount of annual earnings available after all expenses are paid to the total value of all the common shareholders investment. Return on equity is calculated by dividing common stock equity (net worth as shown on the books of the corporation) at the beginning of an accounting period into net income for the period after payment of preferred stock dividends but before payment of common stock dividends. Return on equity indicates the amount earned on each dollar of invested capital; it is expressed as a percentage and is a guide to common shareholders as to how effectively their money is being employed.

Return on investment. Amount earned per year on an investment, usually expressed as percentage. *See also* Rate *(Rate of return)*; Return on assets; Return on equity.

Revaluation. The restoration of purchasing power to an inflated currency. Change in value by a government of its currency in relation to currencies of other countries. Also, the resetting of the tax base by recomputing the value of real estate subject to taxation. *See also* Devaluation.

Revenue. The gross receipts of a business, individual, government, or other reporting entity. The receipts are usually the results of product sales, services rendered, interest earned, etc. *See also* Gross revenue; Incremental revenue.

As applied to the income of a government, a broad and general term, including all public moneys which the state collects and receives, from whatever source and in whatever manner. *See Public revenues, below.*

Public revenues. The income which a government collects and receives into its treasury, and is appropriated for the payment of its expenses. Annual or periodical yield of taxes, excise, custom, dues, rents, etc., which a nation, state or a municipality collects and receives into treasury for public use; public income of whatever kind. Current income of nation, state, or local government from whatever source derived which is subject to appropriation for public uses.

Revenue bills. Legislative bills that levy or raise taxes. Bills for raising federal revenue must arise in the House of Representatives. Art. I, Sec. 7, U.S.Const. *See also* Revenue law or measure.

Revenue bonds. Type of bond issued by a state or local government repayable by the particular unit of government which issues it. Also, a bond issued for a specific public purpose such as the construction or maintenance of a bridge and repayable from income generated by such project. Term is a descriptive qualification which indicates that the instruments are payable solely from a revenue producing public project.

Revenue law or measure. Any law which provides for the assessment and collection of a tax to defray the expenses of the government. Such legislation is commonly referred to under the general term "revenue measures" or "revenue bills", and those measures include all the laws by which the government provides means for meeting its expenditures. *See also* Revenue bills.

Revenue neutral. Changes in the tax law which result in the same amount of overall total revenue (i.e., no overall increase or decrease in general revenue) though received from different sources. For example, a tax act might require corporations to pay more in taxes, but such excess revenue is offset by individuals paying less.

Revenue Procedure. A matter of procedural importance to both taxpayers and the I.R.S. concerning the administration of the tax laws is issued as a Revenue Procedure (abbreviated as "Rev. Proc."). A Revenue Procedure is first published in an Internal Revenue Bulletin (I.R.B.) and later transferred to the appropriate Cumulative Bulletin (C.B.). Both the Internal Revenue Bulletins and the Cumulative Bulletins are published by the U.S. Government Printing Office and many commercial tax services.

Revenue Ruling. A Revenue Ruling (abbreviated "Rev.Rul.") is issued by the National Office of the I.R.S. to express an official interpretation of the tax law as applied to specific transactions. Unlike a Regulation, it is more limited in application. A Revenue Ruling is first published in an Internal Revenue Bulletin (I.R.B.) and later transferred to the appropriate Cumulative Bulletin (C.B.). Both the Internal Revenue Bulletins and the Cumulative Bulletins are published by the U.S. Government Printing Office and many commercial tax services. I.R.C. § 7805. *See also* Letter ruling; Private letter ruling.

Revenue stamps. Formerly, a federal tax on sale of real property; since replaced by state tax stamps. The stamps are affixed to the conveyancing instrument (deed), or a rubber stamp is used to show the amount of the tax.

Reversal. The annulling or setting aside by an appellate court of a decision of a lower court. *See also* Overrule; Remand; Revise; Vacate.

Reverse. To overthrow, vacate, set aside, make void, annul, repeal, or revoke; as, to reverse a judgment, sentence or decree of a lower court by an appellate court, or to change to the contrary or to a former condition. To reverse a judgment means to overthrow it by contrary decision, make it void, undo or annul it for error. *See also* Reversal.

Reversed (Rev'd.). An indication that a decision of one court has been reversed by a higher court in the same case.

Reverse discrimination. Prejudice or bias exercised against a person or class for purpose of correcting a pattern of discrimination against another person or class. A type of discrimination in which majority groups are purportedly discriminated against in favor of minority groups, usually via affirmative action programs. *See also* Affirmative action programs.

Reverse stock split. The reduction in the number of corporate shares outstanding by calling in all shares and issuing a smaller number, though the capital of the corporation remains the same. It is the opposite of a stock split. Its effect is to increase the value of each share. Reverse stock splits often create fractional shares and may be used as a device to go private. *See also* Stock (*Stock split*).

Reversible error. *See* Error.

Reversing (Rev'g.). An indication that the decision of a higher court is reversing the result reached by a lower court in the same case.

Reversion *or* **estate in reversion** /(əstéyt in) rəvə́rzhən/. A future interest under which a grantor retains a present right to a future interest in property that the grantor conveys to another; usually the residue of a life estate. The residue of an estate left by operation of law in the grantor or his heirs, or in the heirs of a testator, commencing in possession on the determination of a particular estate granted or devised. Any future interest left in a transferor or his successor. It is a vested interest or estate, in as much as person entitled to it has a fixed right to future enjoyment. Any reversionary interest which is not subject to condition precedent; it arises when the owner of real estate devises or conveys an interest in it less than his own.

The term reversion has two meanings, first, as designating the estate left in the grantor during the continuance of a particular estate and also the residue left in grantor or his heirs after termination of particular estate. It differs from a remainder in that it arises by act of the law, whereas a remainder is by act of the parties. A reversion, moreover, is the remnant left in the grantor, while a remainder is the remnant of the whole estate disposed of, after a preceding part of the same has been given away.

See also Escheat; Possibility (*Possibility of reverter*); Reversionary interest. *Compare* Remainder.

Reversionary /rəvə́rzhənehriy/. That which is to be enjoyed in reversion.

Reversionary interest. The interest which a person has in the reversion of lands or other property. A right to the future enjoyment of property, at present in the possession or occupation of another. The property that reverts to the grantor after the expiration of an intervening income interest. Assume, for example, G places real estate in trust with income to A for eleven years and, upon the expiration of this term, the property returns to G. Under these circumstances, G has retained a reversionary interest in the property. A reversionary interest is the same as a remainder interest except that in the latter case the property passes to someone other than the original owner (*e.g.,* the grantor of a trust) upon the expiration of the intervening interest. *See also* Clifford trust; Remainder; Reversion *or* estate in reversion.

Reversionary lease. One to take effect *in futuro.* A second lease, to commence after the expiration of a former lease.

Reversioner /rəvə́rzhənər/. A person who is entitled to an estate in reversion. By an extension of its meaning, one who is entitled to any future estate or any property in expectancy.

Revert /rəvə́rt/. To turn back, to return to. With respect to property to go back to and lodge in former owner, who parted with it by creating estate in another which has expired, or to his heirs. As used in a deed connotes an undisposed of residue and imports that property is to return to a person who formerly owned it, but who parted with the possession or title by creating an estate in another person which has terminated by his act or by operation of law. *See also* Reversion; *or* estate in reversion; Reversionary interest.

Reverter /rəvə́rtər/. Reversion. A possibility of reverter is that species of reversionary interest which exists when the grant is so limited that it may possibly terminate.

Revest. To vest again. A seisin is said to *revest,* where it is acquired a second time by the party out of whom it has been divested. Opposed to "divest." The words "revest" and "divest" are also applicable to the mere right or title, as opposed to the possession.

Review. To re-examine judicially or administratively. A reconsideration; second view or examination; revision; consideration for purposes of correction. Used especially of the examination of a decision of a lower court or administrative body by an appellate court or appellate administrative body (*e.g.* Appeals Council in social security cases). *See* Appeal; Board of review; Rehearing; Retrial.

Bill of review. In equity practice, a bill, in the nature of a writ of error, filed to procure an examination and alteration or reversal of a decree made upon a former bill, which decree has been signed and enrolled. *See also* Bill.

Revise. To review and re-examine for correction. To go over a thing for the purpose of amending, correcting, rearranging, or otherwise improving it; as, to revise statutes, or a judgment.

Revised statutes. A body of statutes which have been revised, collected, arranged in order, and re-enacted as a whole. This is the legal title of the collections of compiled laws of several of the states, and also of the United States. Such a volume is usually cited as "Rev.Stat.," "Rev.St.," or "R.S." *See also* Code; Revision of statutes.

Revision. A re-examination or careful reading over for correction or improvement.

Revision of statutes. A "revision of law" on any subject is a restatement of the law on that subject in a correlated or improved from, which is intended as a substitute for the law as previously stated, and displaces and repeals former laws relating to same subject and within purview of revising statute. Such is more than a restatement of the substance thereof in different language, but implies a reexamination of them, and may constitute a restatement of the law in a corrected or improved form, in which case the statement may be with or without material change, and is substituted for and displaces and repeals the former law as it stood relating to the subjects within its purview. *See also* Codification; Revised statutes.

Revisor of statutes. Person or body charged with revising statutes.

Revival. The process of renewing the operative force of a judgment which has remained dormant or unexecuted for so long a time that execution cannot be issued upon it without new process to reanimate it.

The act of renewing the legal force of a contract or obligation, which had ceased to be sufficient foundation for an action, on account of the running of the statute of limitations, by giving a new promise or acknowledgment of it.

A will may be revived under certain conditions if the testator revokes an instrument which purported to revoke his or her will. Many states require republication *(q.v.)* of the former will as a requisite to revival.

Revival of action. Under certain conditions, a cause of action barred by the statute of limitations may be brought to life again. See *e.g.* 28 U.S.C.A. § 2415.

The substitution of the personal representative of a deceased party will revive an action and make it prosecutable by the substituted party. Fed.R.Civ.P. 17(a). See also *e.g.* 28 U.S.C.A. § 2404.

Revival of will. *See* Revival.

Revival statutes. State and federal laws which provide for the renewal of actions, wills and the legal effect of documents.

Revive. To renew, revivify; to make one's self liable for a debt barred by the statute of limita-

tions by acknowledging it; or for a matrimonial offense, once condoned, by committing another.

Revocable. Susceptible of being revoked, withdrawn or cancelled; *e.g.* revocable letter of credit.

Revocable credit. A credit which can be withdrawn or cancelled before its expiration date and without the consent of the person in whose favor it was drawn. Used in foreign trade. U.C.C. § 5–103(a).

Revocable letter of credit. Letter of credit which can be cancelled or withdrawn at any time. U.C.C. § 5–103(a).

Revocable transfer. A transfer of property whereby the transferor retains the right to recover the property. The creation of a revocable trust is an example of a revocable transfer. See I.R.C. § 2038. *See also* Incomplete transfer.

Revocable trust. A trust in which the settlor reserves the right to revoke. Such provision may have tax implications depending upon the time following its creation within which the settlor may revoke.

Revocation /revəkéyshən/. The withdrawal or recall of some power, authority, or thing granted, or a destroying or making void of some will, deed, or offer that had been valid until revoked. In contract law, the withdrawal by the offeree of an offer that had been valid until withdrawn. It may be either *general,* all acts and things done before; or *special,* revoking a particular thing.

Revocation by act of the party is an intentional or voluntary revocation. The principal instances occur in the case of authorities and powers of attorney and wills.

In contract law, the withdrawal of an offer by an offeror; unless the offer is irrevocable, it can be revoked at any time prior to acceptance without liability.

In criminal law, may refer to termination of a probation or parole order because of either a rule violation or a new offense, and forcing the offender to begin or continue serving his or her sentence.

A revocation in law, or constructive revocation, is produced by a rule of law, irrespectively of the intention of the parties. Thus, a power of attorney is in general revoked by the death of the principal.

See also Abrogation; Cancel; Cancellation; Rescind.

Revocation of probate. Exists where probate of a will, having been granted, is afterwards recalled by the court of probate, on proof of a subsequent will, or other sufficient cause.

Revocation of will. The recalling, annulling or rendering inoperative an existing will, by some subsequent act of the testator, which may be by the making of a new will inconsistent with the terms of the first, or by destroying the old will, or by disposing of the property to which it related, or otherwise.

Revoke. To annul or make void by recalling or taking back. To cancel, rescind, repeal, or reverse, as to revoke a license or will. *See also* Revocation.

Revolt. A revolt goes beyond insurrection in aim, being an attempt actually to overthrow the government itself, whereas insurrection has as its objective some forcible change within the government. A large-scale revolt is called a rebellion and if it is successful it becomes a revolution. *See also* Insurrection; Rebellion.

The endeavor of the crew of a vessel, or any one or more of them, to overthrow the legitimate authority of her commander, with intent to remove him from his command, or against his will to take possession of the vessel by assuming the government and navigation of her, or by transferring their obedience from the lawful commander to some other person. See 18 U.S.C.A. §§ 2192, 2193. *See also* Mutiny.

Revolution. A complete overthrow of the established government in any country or state by those who were previously subject to it. The word in its broadest significance is generally used to designate a sweeping change as applied to political change, it denotes a change in a method or system of government, or of the power which controls the government. It is frequently accomplished by or accompanied by violent acts, but it need not be violent in its methods and it does not necessarily denote force or violence. *See* Insurrection; Rebellion.

Revolutionary, *adj.* Pertaining to or connected with, characterized by, or of nature of, revolution.

Revolutionary, *n.* One who instigates or favors revolution or one taking part therein.

Revolving charge account. *See* Revolving credit.

Revolving credit. Type of consumer credit arrangement which permits a buyer or a borrower to purchase goods or secure loans on a continuing basis so long as the outstanding balance of the account does not exceed a certain limit. Loans are repaid and new loans granted in a cycle. *See also* Charge account; Open credit; Open-end credit plan.

In commercial financing, binding agreement that commits a bank to make loans to a company up to a predetermined credit limit. To obtain this type of commitment from a bank, a company usually pays a commitment fee based on the unused portion of the pledged funds.

Revolving fund. A fund from which withdrawals are made either as loans or as disbursements, with the obligation of repaying the fund (with or without interest) to keep the fund intact. A fund whose amounts are continually expended and then replenished; for example, a petty cash fund.

Revolving letter of credit. A self-renewing letter of credit. The unused portion of the credit is cumulative.

Revolving loan. A loan which is expected to be renewed (*i.e.* turned over) at maturity.

Rev. Proc. *See* Revenue Procedure.

Rev. Rul. *See* Revenue Ruling.

Reward. A recompense or premium offered or bestowed by government or an individual in return for special or extraordinary services to be performed, or for special attainments or achievements, or for some act resulting to the benefit of the public; as, a reward for useful inventions, for the discovery and apprehension of criminals, for the restoration of lost property. That which is offered or given for some service or attainment; sum of money paid or taken for doing, or forbearing to do, some act. *See also* Award; Prize.

Rex /réks/. Lat. The king. The king regarded as the party prosecuting in a criminal action; as in the form of entitling such actions, "Rex v. Doe."

R.F.C.A. Reconstruction Finance Corporation Act.

R.F.D. Rural Free Delivery.

RICO laws. Racketeer Influenced and Corrupt Organizations laws. Federal and state laws designed to investigate, control, and prosecute organized crime. 18 U.S.C.A. § 1961 et seq. Both criminal prosecution and civil actions may be brought under RICO statutes.

Federal RICO laws prohibit a person from engaging in activities which affect interstate or foreign commerce, including: (1) using income received from a pattern of racketeering to acquire an interest in an enterprise; (2) acquiring or maintaining an interest in an enterprise through a pattern of racketeering; (3) conducting or participating in the affairs of an enterprise through a pattern of racketeering; and, (4) conspiring to commit any of the above offenses. To establish a prima facie RICO claim, a civil plaintiff or prosecutor must allege the existence of seven elements: "(1) that the defendant (2) through the commission of two or more acts (3) constituting a 'pattern' (4) of 'racketeering activity' (5) directly or indirectly invests in, or maintains an interest in, or participates in (6) an 'enterprise' (7) the activities of which affect interstate or foreign commerce." 18 U.S.C.A. § 1962.

See also Pattern of racketeering activity.

Rider. A schedule or small piece of paper reflecting an amendment, addition or endorsement annexed to some part of a contract, document, insurance policy, or record. Any kind of a schedule or writing annexed to a document which cannot well be incorporated in the body of such document. Such are deemed to be incorporated into the terms of the document. Thus, in passing bills through a legislature, when a new clause or law is added after the bill has passed through committee, such new law or clause is termed a "rider." Another common example of a rider is an attachment to an insurance policy that modifies the conditions of the policy by expanding or restricting its benefits or excluding certain conditions from coverage. With the use of the rider the entire document does not have to be rewritten or redrafted again.

Rigging the market. A term of the stock-exchange, denoting the practice of inflating the price of given stocks, or enhancing their quoted value, by a system of pretended purchases, designed to give the air of an unusual demand for such stocks.

Right. As a noun, and taken in an *abstract* sense, means justice, ethical correctness, or consonance with the rules of law or the principles of morals. In this signification it answers to one meaning of the Latin *"jus,"* and serves to indicate law in the abstract, considered as the foundation of all rights, or the complex of underlying moral principles which impart the character of justice to all positive law, or give it an ethical content. As a noun, and taken in a *concrete* sense, a power, privilege, faculty, or demand, inherent in one person and incident upon another. Rights are defined generally as "powers of free action." And the primal rights pertaining to men are enjoyed by human beings purely as such, being grounded in personality, and existing antecedently to their recognition by positive law. But leaving the abstract moral sphere, and giving to the term a juristic content, a "right" is well defined as "a capacity residing in one man of controlling, with the assent and assistance of the state, the actions of others."

As an adjective, the term "right" means just, morally correct, consonant with ethical principles or rules of positive law. It is the opposite of wrong, unjust, illegal.

A power, privilege, or immunity guaranteed under a constitution, statutes or decisional laws, or claimed as a result of long usage. *See* Bill of rights; Civil liberties; Civil Rights Acts; Natural rights.

In a narrower signification, an interest or title in an object of property; a just and legal claim to hold, use, or enjoy it, or to convey or donate it, as he may please.

A legally enforceable claim of one person against another, that the other shall do a given act, or shall not do a given act. Restatement of the Law of Property, § 1.

That which one person ought to have or receive from another, it being withheld from him, or not in his possession. In this sense "right" has the force of "claim," and is properly expressed by the Latin *"jus."*

See also Conditional right; Droit; Jus; Justice; Natural rights; Power; Vested rights.

General Classification

Rights may be described as *perfect* or *imperfect,* according as their action or scope is clear, settled, and determinate, or is vague and unfixed.

Rights are also either *in personam* or *in rem.* A right *in personam* is one which imposes an obligation on a definite person. A right *in rem* is one which imposes an obligation on persons generally; *i.e.,* either on all the world or on all the world except certain determinate persons. Thus, if I am entitled to exclude all persons from a given piece of land, I have a right *in rem* in respect of that land; and, if there are one or more persons, A., B., and C., whom I am not entitled to exclude from it, my right is still a right *in rem.*

Rights may also be described as either *primary* or *secondary.* *Primary* rights are those which can be created without reference to rights already existing. *Secondary* rights can only arise for the purpose of protecting or enforcing primary rights. They are either preventive (protective) or remedial (reparative).

Preventive or *protective secondary* rights exist in order to prevent the infringement or loss of primary rights. They are judicial when they require the assistance of a court of law for their enforcement, and extrajudicial when they are capable of being exercised by the party himself. *Remedial* or *reparative secondary* rights are also either judicial or extrajudicial. They may further be divided into (1) rights of restitution or restoration, which entitle the person injured to be replaced in his original position; (2) rights of enforcement, which entitle the person injured to the performance of an act by the person bound; and (3) rights of satisfaction or compensation.

With respect to the ownership of external objects of property, rights may be classed as *absolute* and *qualified.* An absolute right gives to the person in whom it inheres the uncontrolled dominion over the object at all times and for all purposes. A qualified right gives the possessor a right to the object for certain purposes or under certain circumstances only. Such is the right of a bailee to recover the article bailed when it has been unlawfully taken from him by a stranger.

Rights are also either *legal* or *equitable.* The former is the case where the person seeking to enforce the right for his own benefit has the legal title and a remedy at law. The latter are such as are enforceable only in equity; as, at the suit of *cestui que trust.* Procedurally, under Rules of Civil Procedure, both legal and equitable rights are enforced in the same court under a single cause of action.

Constitutional Rights

Rights are also classified in constitutional law as natural, civil, and political, to which there is sometimes added the class of "personal rights."

Natural rights are those which grow out of the nature of man and depend upon personality, as distinguished from such as are created by law and depend upon civilized society; or they are those which are plainly assured by natural law; or those which, by fair deduction from the present physical, moral, social, and religious characteristics of man, he must be invested with, and which he ought to have realized for him in a jural society, in order to fulfill the ends to which his nature calls him. Such are the rights of life, liberty, privacy, and good reputation.

Civil rights are such as belong to every citizen of the state or country, or, in a wider sense, to all its inhabitants, and are not connected with the organization or administration of government. They include the rights of property, marriage, equal protection of the laws, freedom of contract, trial by jury, etc. Or, as otherwise defined, civil rights are rights appertaining to a person by virtue of his citizenship in a state or community. Such term may also refer, in its very general sense, to rights capable of being enforced or redressed in a civil action. Also, a term applied to certain rights secured to citizens of the United States by the Thirteenth and Fourteenth amendments to the Constitution, and by various acts of Congress (*e.g.* Civil Rights Acts) made in pursuance thereof. *See* Bill of rights; Civil liberties; Civil Rights Acts.

Political rights consist in the power to participate, directly or indirectly, in the establishment or administration of government, such as the right of citizenship, that of suffrage, the right to hold public office, and the right of petition.

Personal rights is a term of rather vague import, but generally it may be said to mean the right of personal security, comprising those of life, limb, body, health, reputation, and the right of personal liberty.

Other Compound and Descriptive Terms

Bill of rights. See that title.

Common right. *See* Common.

Declaration of rights. *See* Bill of rights.

Exclusive right. See that title.

Marital rights. *See* Marital.

Mere right. In the law of real estate, the mere right of property in land; the right of a proprie-

tor, but without possession or even the right of possession; the abstract right of property.

Patent right. *See* Patent.

Petition of right. *See* Petition.

Private rights. Those rights which appertain to a particular individual or individuals, and relate either to the person, or to personal or real property.

Right heir. *See* Heir.

Riparian rights. *See* Riparian.

Stock rights. *See* Stock.

Vested rights. *See* Vested.

Right and wrong test. Under this test of criminal responsibility, if, at the time of committing an act, the party was laboring under such a defect of reason from disease of the mind as not to know the nature and quality thereof, that he did not know that he was doing what was wrong, he should not be held criminally responsible for his act. *See* Insanity with respect to other criminal responsibility defenses. *See also* M'Naghten Rule.

Right in action. This is a phrase frequently used in place of *chose in action,* and having an identical meaning.

Right of action. The right to bring suit; a legal right to maintain an action, growing out of a given transaction or state of facts and based thereon. Such right pertains to remedy and relief through judicial procedure. Right of injured one to secure redress for violation of his rights. A right presently to enforce a cause of action by suit. Operative facts giving rise to a right of action comprise a "cause of action." *Compare* Cause of action.

Right of contribution. *See* Contribution.

Right of entry. The right of taking or resuming possession of land by entering on it in a peaceable manner.

Right of first refusal. Right to meet terms of proposed contract before it is executed; *e.g.* right to have first opportunity to purchase real estate when such becomes available, or right to meet any other offer. The holder of such a right has the option to purchase the grantor's real estate on the terms and conditions of sale contained in a bona fide offer by a third party to purchase such real estate, provided it is an offer that the grantor is otherwise willing to accept. *See also* First refusal; Option.

Right of local self-government. Power of citizens to govern themselves, as to matters purely local in nature, through officers of their own selection. *See* Home rule.

Right of possession. Right which may reside in one man while another has the actual possession, being the right to enter and turn out such actual occupant; *e.g.,* the right of a disseisee; right of ejectment or eviction. An apparent right of possession is one which may be defeated by a better right; an actual right of possession is one which will stand the test against all opponents. *See also* Repossession.

Right of privacy. *See* Privacy, right of.

Right of property. The mere right of property in land; the abstract right which remains to the owner after he has lost the right of possession, and to recover which the writ of right was given. United with possession, and the right of possession, this right constitutes a complete title to lands, tenements, and hereditaments.

Right of publicity. The right of individual, especially public figure or celebrity, to control commercial value and exploitation of his name or picture or likeness or to prevent others from unfairly appropriating that value for their commercial benefit.

Right of redemption. The right to disencumber property or to free it from a claim or lien; specifically, the right (granted by statute only) to free property from the encumbrance of a foreclosure or other judicial sale, or to recover the title passing thereby, by paying what is due, with interest, costs, etc. Not to be confounded with the "equity of redemption," which exists independently of statute but must be exercised before sale. *See also* Redemption.

Right of subrogation. The right of a person to substitute one person in the place of another, giving the substituted party the same legal rights that the original party had.

Right of survivorship. The right of survivor of a deceased person to the property of said deceased. A distinguishing characteristic of a joint tenancy relationship. Upon the death of any joint tenant, the deceased tenant's interest passes, not to the tenant's lawfully designated beneficiaries or heirs, but to the surviving joint tenants. *See also* Tenancy *(Joint tenancy; Tenancy by the entirety).*

Right of way. Term used to describe a right belonging to a party to pass over land of another, but it is also used to describe that strip of land upon which railroad companies construct their road bed, and, when so used, the term refers to the land itself, not the right of passage over it.

As used with reference to right to pass over another's land, it is only an easement; and grantee acquires only right to a reasonable and usual enjoyment thereof with owner of soil retaining rights and benefits of ownership consistent with the easement. *See also* Easement.

Term is also used to refer to a preference of one of two vehicles, or as between a vehicle and a pedestrian, asserting right of passage at the same place and time, but it is not an absolute right in the sense that possessor thereof is relieved from duty of exercising due care for his own safety and that of others. With respect to intersections, the term has been described as the right of one driver to cross before the other; and it has been defined by statute as the right of a vehicle to proceed uninterruptedly in a lawful manner in the direction in which it is moving in preference to another vehicle approaching from a different direction into its path.

Rights offering. The sale of new shares of common stock by distributing stock purchase *rights* to a firm's existing shareholders. This is also termed a *privileged subscription. See also* Rights-on; Rights, stock; Standby agreement.

Rights-on. Shares trading with the rights attached.

Rights, petition of. *See* Petition.

Rights, stock. Short term options to purchase shares from an issuer at a fixed price. A short-lived (typically less than 90 days) call option for purchasing additional stock in a firm, issued by the firm to all its shareholders on a pro rata basis. Rights are often issued as a substitute for a dividend or as a "sweetener" in connection with the issuance of senior or debt securities. Rights are often publicly traded. *Compare* Warranty. *See also* Rights offering; Standby agreement; Stock *(Stock rights).*

Right to attorney. *See* Counsel, right to.

Right to cure. *See* Cure.

Right to die laws. Cases and statutes which recognize in some instances the right of a dying person to decline extraordinary treatment and the right of such a person's guardian to ask the court to substitute its judgment for that of the dying person who no longer has the mental capacity to make such judgment. *See also* Death *(Natural Death Acts);* Life sustaining procedures; Medical directive; Will *(Living will).*

Right to know acts. Federal and state legislation requiring disclosure by certain businesses (*e.g.,* chemical manufacturers) to the public and to workers of information about hazardous substances in order that such persons might learn the full range of risks they face concerning their employment and living conditions.

Right to redeem. *See* Right of redemption.

Right to travel. Basic constitutional right exemplified in case of persons applying for welfare assistance in a state in which they have not resided for a prescribed period of time. It is said that to deny such a right to such persons is to inhibit their right to travel and hence to deny them equal protection of the law.

Right to work laws. Such state laws (as permitted by Sec. 14(b) of the National Labor Relations Act) that provide in general that employees are not to be required to join a union as a condition of receiving or retaining a job. The wording of these state statutes (existing in about 20 states) vary, with some states generally barring discrimination in employment so as to encourage union membership, others more vaguely barring an employment "monopoly" by a labor union, but most expressly barring the requirement of union membership (or paying dues to a union) as a condition of employment. *See also* Open shop.

Rigor juris /rígər júrəs/. Lat. Strictness of law. Distinguished from *gratia curiæ*, favor of the court.

Riot. Unlawful assembly which has developed to stage of violence. The term "riot" means a public disturbance involving (1) an act or acts of violence by one or more persons part of an assemblage of three or more persons, which act or acts shall constitute a clear and present danger of, or shall result in, damage or injury to the property of any other person or to the person of any other individual or (2) a threat or threats of the commission of an act or acts of violence by one or more persons part of an assemblage of three or more persons having, individually or collectively, the ability of immediate execution of such threat or threats, where the performance of the threatened acts or acts of violence would constitute a clear and present danger of, or would result in, damage or injury to the property of any other person or to the person of any other individual. 18 U.S.C.A. § 2102(a).

A person is guilty of riot if he participates with two or more others in a course of disorderly conduct: (a) with purpose to commit or facilitate the commission of a felony or misdemeanor; (b) with purpose to prevent or coerce official action; or (c) when the actor or any other participant to the knowledge of the actor uses or plans to use a firearm or other deadly weapon. Model Penal Code, § 250.1.

Incitement to riot. Incitement to riot is by words or conduct urging others to commit acts of force or violence against persons or property or to resist the lawful authority of law enforcement officers under circumstances which produce a clear and present danger of injury to persons or property or a breach of the public peace.

The term "to incite a riot," or "to organize, promote, encourage, participate in, or carry on a riot", includes, but is not limited to urging or instigating other persons to riot, but shall not be deemed to mean the mere oral or written (1) advocacy of ideas or (2) expression of belief, not involving advocacy of any act or acts of violence or assertion of the rightness of, or the right to commit, any such act or acts. 18 U.S.C.A. § 2102(b).

See also Unlawful assembly.

Rioter. One who encourages, promotes, or takes part in riots.

Riparian /rəpériyən/. Belonging or relating to the bank of a river or stream; of or on the bank. Land lying beyond the natural watershed of a stream is not "riparian." The term is sometimes used as relating to the shore of the sea or other tidal water, or of a lake or other considerable body of water not having the character of a watercourse. But this is not accurate. The proper word to be employed in such connections is "littoral."

Riparian land. Land so situated with respect to a body of water that, because of such location, the possessor of the land is entitled to the benefits incident to the use of the water. Parcel of land which includes therein a part of or is bounded by a natural watercourse. *See* Riparian; Riparian owner.

Riparian lease. The written instrument setting forth the terms, conditions, and the date of expiration of the rights to use lands lying between the high water mark and the low water mark.

Riparian owner. One who owns land on bank of river, or one who is owner of land along, bordering upon, bounded by, fronting upon, abutting or adjacent and contiguous to and in contact with river.

Riparian rights. The rights of the owners of lands on the banks of watercourses, relating to the water, its use, ownership of soil under the stream, accretions, etc. Term is generally defined as the right which every person through whose land a natural watercourse runs has to benefit of stream as it passes through his land for all useful purposes to which it may be applied. Such rights include those such as hunting, fishing, boating, sailing, irrigating, and growing and harvesting wild rice, which rights extend over lakes and wetlands.

Riparian water. Water which is below the highest line of normal flow of the river or stream, as distinguished from flood water.

Ripe for judgment. An action that is so far advanced, by verdict, default, confession, the determination of all pending motions, or other disposition of preliminary or disputed matters, that nothing remains for the court but to render the appropriate judgment. A case is ripe for decision by an appellate court if the legal issues involved are clear enough and well enough evolved and presented so that a clear decision can come out of the case. *See also* Ripeness doctrine.

Ripeness doctrine. The principle that the federal courts require an actual, present controversy, and therefore will not act when the issue is only hypothetical or the existence of a controversy merely speculative. The constitutional mandate of case or controversy, U.S.Const. Art. III, requires an appellate court to consider whether a case has matured or ripened into a controversy worthy of adjudication before it will determine the same.

The question in each case is whether there is a substantial controversy, between parties having adverse legal interests, of sufficient immediacy and reality to warrant the issuance of a declaratory judgment.

Basic rationale of "ripeness doctrine" arising out of courts' reluctance to apply declaratory judgment and injunctive remedies unless administrative determinations arise in context of a controversy ripe for judicial resolution, is to prevent courts, through avoidance of premature adjudication, from entangling themselves in abstract disagreements over administrative policies, and also to protect the agencies from judicial interference until an administrative decision has been formalized and its effects felt in a concrete way by the challenging parties, and court is required to evaluate both fitness of issues for judicial decision and hardship to parties of withholding court consideration.

See Case *(Cases and controversies)*; Final decision rule; Justiciable controversy; Standing.

Risk. In insurance law, the danger or hazard of a loss of the property insured; the casualty contemplated in a contract of insurance; the degree of hazard; a specified contingency or peril; and, colloquially, the specific house, factory, ship, etc., covered by the policy. Hazard, danger, peril, exposure to loss, injury, disadvantage or destruction, and comprises all elements of danger.

In general, the element of uncertainty in an undertaking; the possibility that actual future returns will deviate from expected returns. Risk may be moral, physical or economic.

Risk of loss in commercial sales contracts as between buyer and seller is governed by U.C.C. § 2–509 (e.g., financial responsibility for damage or destruction of property when transferred between seller and buyer).

See also Assumption of risk; Ex ship; Extraordinary risk; Incurred risk.

Diversifiable risk. Risk that can be eliminated by diversification.

Obvious risk. See Obvious.

Ordinary risk. See Ordinary.

Risk capital. Money or property invested in a business venture, generally in exchange for common stock in a business, or capital in a partnership, as distinguished from loans or bonded indebtedness. *See also* Seed money; Venture capital.

Risk capital test. Under this test, for determination of whether an investment is a security in the form of an investment contract, requires consideration of whether funds are being raised for business venture or enterprise, whether transaction is offered indiscriminately to the public at large, whether investors are substantially powerless to affect success of enterprise, and whether investors' money is substantially at risk because it is inadequately secured.

Risk classes. Groups of investments of comparable (sometimes only approximately) risk.

Risk incident to employment. Within workers' compensation acts, one growing out of or connected with what worker must do in fulfilling his or her contract of service, and may be either ordinary risk, directly connected with employment, or extraordinary risk indirectly connected with employment because of its special nature.

Riskless rate. The rate of return earned on a riskless investment. Typically modeled as the rate earned on 90–day U.S. Treasury bills.

Risk neutral. In investments, means insensitive to risk.

Risk of loss. *See* Risk.

Risk premium. Extra compensation paid to an employee or extra interest paid to a lender, over amounts usually considered normal, in return for their undertaking to engage in activities more risky than normal.

River. A natural stream of water, of greater volume than a creek or rivulet, flowing in a more or less permanent bed or channel, between defined banks or walls, with a current which may either be continuous in one direction or affected by the ebb and flow of the tide.

R.L. This abbreviation may stand either for "Revised Laws" or "Roman law."

Road. A highway; an open way or public passage; a line of travel or communication extending from one town or place to another; a strip of land appropriated and used for purposes of travel and communication between different places. *See also* Highway.

Law of the road. Custom or practice which has become crystallized into accepted system of rules regulating travel on highways. It relates to safety of travel, and is adjustment of rights of travelers using highway at same time. For example, "law of the road" refers to the rule which requires that vehicles meeting shall keep to the right of the middle of the highway. *See also* Right of way.

Rob. To take personalty in possession of another from his person or his presence, feloniously and against his will, by violence or by putting him in fear. *See* Robbery.

Robbery. Felonious taking of money, personal property, or any other article of value, in the possession of another, from his person or immediate presence, and against his will, accomplished by means of force or fear.

A person is guilty of robbery if, in the course of committing a theft, he: (a) inflicts serious bodily injury upon another; or (b) threatens another with or purposely puts him in fear of immediate serious bodily injury; or (c) commits or threatens immediately to commit any felony of the first or second degree. An act shall be deemed "in the course of committing a theft" if it occurs in an attempt to commit theft or in flight after the attempt or commission. Model Penal Code, § 222.1.

Most jurisdictions today divide robbery, for purposes of punishment, into simple robbery and aggravated robbery, the principal example of the latter being "armed" robbery.

For various types of federal crimes involving robbery, see 18 U.S.C.A. § 2111 et seq.

See also Assault; Armed robbery; Hobbs Act. *Compare* Burglary; Theft.

Aggravated robbery. A robbery committed by a person who is armed with a dangerous weapon or who inflicts bodily harm upon any person in the course of such robbery. *See also* Armed robbery.

Highway robbery. The crime of robbery committed upon or near a public highway. The felonious and forcible taking of property from the person of another on a highway. It differs from robbery in general only in the place where it is committed. Robbery by hold-up originally applied to the stopping and robbery of traveling parties, but the term has acquired a broader meaning. It has come to be applied to robbery in general, by the use of force or putting in fear. *See* Hijacking.

Roberts' Rules of Order. *See* Parliamentary law.

Robinson-Patman Act. Section 2(a) of the Clayton Act, as amended in 1936 by the Robinson-Patman Act (15 U.S.C.A. § 13) makes it unlawful for any seller engaged in commerce to directly or indirectly discriminate in the price charged purchasers on the sale of commodities of like grade and quality where the effect may be to injure, destroy or prevent competition with any person who grants or knowingly receives a discrimination, or the customer of either. *See also* Price discrimination.

Rod. A lineal measure of 5½ yards or 16½ feet; otherwise called a "perch." *See also* Land measure.

Rogatory letters /rógətoriy létərz/. A commission from one judge to another in a foreign country requesting him to examine a witness. See Fed.R.Civil P. 28(b); 28 U.S.C.A. § 1781. *See also* Letters rogatory.

ROI. Return on investment.

Roll, *n.* Record of the proceedings of a court or public office. *See Judgment roll, below.*

A register; list of persons belonging to particular group.

In taxation, the list or record of taxable persons and property, as compiled by assessors. *See Tax roll, below.*

Judgment roll. Such is required to be filed in certain states by the clerk when he enters judgment. It normally contains the summons, pleadings, admissions, and each judgment and each order involving the merits or necessarily affecting the final judgment. New York C.P.L.R. § 5017. In the federal and most state courts, judgments are recorded in the "civil docket" (Fed.R.Civil P. 79) or "criminal docket" (Fed.R.Crim.P. 55).

Tax roll. A schedule or list of the persons and property subject to the payment of a particular tax, with the amounts severally due, prepared and authenticated in proper form to warrant the collecting officers to proceed with the enforcement of the tax.

Roll, *v.* To rob by force.

Rolling over. Banking term for extension or renewal of short term loan from one loan period (e.g. 90 day) to another. *See also* Roll-over paper.

Term also refers to transfer or reinvestment of funds from one type of investment to another (e.g. from one type of IRA fund to another).

Roll-over paper. Short term notes which may be extended (rolled over) or converted to installment payments, after the initial due date.

Roman law. In a general sense, comprehends all the laws which prevailed among the Romans, without regard to the time of their origin, including the collections of Justinian. In a more restricted sense, the Germans understand by this term merely the law of Justinian, as adopted by them.

In England and America, it appears to be customary to use the phrase, indifferently with "the civil law," to designate the whole system of Roman jurisprudence, including the *Corpus Juris Civilis;* or, if any distinction is drawn, the expression "civil law" denotes the system of jurisprudence obtaining in those countries of continental Europe which have derived their juridical notions and principles from the Justinian collection, while "Roman law" is reserved as the proper appellation of the body of law developed under the government of Rome from the earliest times to the fall of the empire. *See* Civil law.

Root of title. The document with which an abstract of title properly commences.

ROR. *See* Release on own recognizance.

Round lot. Standard unit of trading on N.Y. Stock Exchange. For stocks, it is 100 shares; for bonds, $1000 or $5000 par value. *Compare* Odd lot.

Royalty. Compensation for the use of property, usually copyrighted material or natural resources, expressed as a percentage of receipts from using the property or as an account per unit produced. A payment which is made to an author or composer by an assignee, licensee or copyright holder in respect of each copy of his work which is sold, or to an inventor in respect of each article sold under the patent. Royalty is share of product or profit reserved by owner for permitting another to use the property.

As used in instruments in connection with production of minerals (*e.g.*, oil and gas leases) means in its popular sense a share of products or proceeds therefrom, reserved to owner of land for permitting another to use the property.

In patent law, signifies sums paid to owner of a patent for its use or for the right to operate under it, and may also refer to obligation giving rise to the right to such sums.

See also Minimum royalty clause; Overriding royalty; Shut-in royalty.

Reasonable royalty. Under patent law, a "reasonable royalty" is that amount which the trier of facts estimates a person desiring to use a patent right would be willing to pay for its use and a patent owner desiring to license the patent would be willing to accept.

Overriding royalty. A retained royalty by a lessee when the property is subleased. Common in oil and gas leases.

Royalty bonus. The consideration for oil and gas lease over and above the usual royalty.

R.S. An abbreviation for "Revised Statutes."

Rubber check. Slang for a check which has been returned by the drawee bank because of insufficient funds in the account of the drawer.

Rule, *v.* To command or require by a rule of court; as, to rule the sheriff to return the writ, to rule the defendant to plead, to rule against an objection to evidence. To settle or decide a point of law arising upon a trial, and, when it is said of a judge presiding at such a trial that he "ruled" so and so, it is meant that he laid down, settled, or decided such and such to be the law.

Rule, *n.* An established standard, guide, or regulation. Prescribed guide for conduct or action, regulation or principle. A principle or regulation set up by authority, prescribing or directing action or forbearance; as, the rules of a legislative body, of a company, court, public office, of the law, of ethics. Precept attaching a definite detailed legal consequence to a definite detailed state of facts.

An order made by a court, at the instance of one of the parties to a suit, commanding a ministerial officer, or the opposite party, to do some act, or to show cause why some act should not be done. It is usually upon some interlocutory matter. *See also* Decree; Order.

For purposes of the Administrative Procedure Act, includes each agency statement of general or particular applicability and future effect that implements, interprets, or prescribes law or policy. *See* Regulatory Flexibility Act.

A rule of law. Thus, we speak of the rule against perpetuities; the Rule in Shelley's Case, etc. *See also Rule of law, below.*

Rule against perpetuities. Principle that no interest in property is good unless it must vest, if at all, not later than 21 years, plus period of gestation, after some life or lives in being at time of creation of interest. This rule prohibits the granting of an estate which will not necessarily vest within a time limited by a life or lives then in being and 21 years thereafter together with the period of gestation necessary to cover cases of posthumous birth.

This common law rule or principle has been modified by statute in certain states; *e.g.* under some statutes an inquiry may be made as to whether the gift *did* vest in fact within the period. If it actually vested, it will be upheld. Under original rule, the inquiry was whether it *must* vest by its terms. See *e.g.* M.G.L.A. c. 184A (Mass.).

See also Perpetuity.

Rule in Shelley's Case. *See* Shelley's Case, Rule in.

Rule nisi. A rule which will become imperative and final *unless* cause be shown against it. This rule commands the party to show cause why he should not be compelled to do the act required, or why the object of the rule should not be enforced. An ex parte order directing the other party to show cause why such a temporary order should not become permanent.

Rule of four. Working rule devised by Supreme Court for determining if a case is deserving of review; the theory being that if four justices find that a legal question of general importance is raised, that is ample proof that the question has such importance.

Rule of law. A legal principle, of general application, sanctioned by the recognition of authorities, and usually expressed in the form of a maxim or logical proposition. Called a "rule," because in doubtful or unforeseen cases it is a guide or norm for their decision. The rule of law, sometimes called "the supremacy of law", provides that decisions should be made by the application of known principles or laws without the intervention of discretion in their application. *See e.g. Rule against perpetuities, above;* also, Shelley's Case, Rule in. *See also* Stare decisis.

Rule of lenity. Where the intention of Congress or state legislature is not clear from the act itself and reasonable minds might differ as to its intention, the court will adopt the less harsh meaning. The judicial doctrine by which courts decline to interpret criminal statutes so as to increase penalty imposed, absent clear evidence of legislative intent to do otherwise; in other words, where there is ambiguity in a criminal statute, doubts are resolved in favor of defendant. Under "rule of lenity," statute establishing penalty which is susceptible of more than one meaning should be construed so as to provide most lenient penalty.

Rule of reason. Under "rule of reason" test for determining whether alleged acts violated § 1 of the Sherman Anti-Trust Act [15 U.S.C.A. § 1], which declares conspiracies in restraint of trade to be illegal, fact finder must weigh all circumstances of the case to decide whether practice unreasonably restrains competition, and the test requires that plaintiff show anticompetitive effects, or actual harm to competition, and not whether the practices were unfair or tortious. Under the "rule of reason" in antitrust law the legality of restraints on trade is determined by weighing all the factors of the case such as the history of the restraint, the evil believed to exist, the reason for adopting the particular remedy and the purpose or end sought to be attained.

To constitute a crime under § 1 of the Sherman Antitrust Act, the defendant's conduct must result in an unreasonable restraint of interstate commerce. It is for the jury to determine from a consideration of all the facts and circumstances, including the economic conditions of the industry and the effect on competition, whether defendants' conduct creates an unreasonable restraint on interstate commerce. The "rule of reason" test is not however applied in instances of per se antitrust violations; *e.g.* price-fixing. *Compare* Per se doctrine; Per se violations.

Rule of road. See Right of way; Road.

Rule to show cause. A rule commanding the party to appear and show cause why he should not be compelled to do the act required, or why the object of the rule should not be enforced; a rule *nisi (q.v.). See* Show cause order.

Rule 415. SEC Rule enacted in 1982 that permits firms to file shelf registration statements. *See* Shelf registration.

Rulemaking power. Congress has from time to time conferred upon the Supreme Court power to prescribe rules of procedure to be followed by the lower trial and appellate courts of the United States. Pursuant to these statutes (28 U.S.C.A. §§ 2071–2075, re Civil, Criminal, Appellate, Bankruptcy, Evidence Rules) there are now in force rules promulgated by the Court to govern civil and criminal cases in the district courts, bankruptcy courts, courts of appeals, and proceedings before U.S. magistrates. Certain other federal courts are empowered to enact their own rules of court (*e.g.,* Tax Court, 26 U.S.C.A. § 7453). *See also* Administrative rule-making; Rules Enabling Act of 1934.

Rule of 72. Used to determine number of years it will take to double money when earning compound interest (interest rate paid on principal is divided into 72).

Rule of 78. Method of computing refunds of unearned finance charges on early payment of loan so that refund is proportional to the monthly unpaid balance. 78 is the sum of the digits of one to twelve, *i.e.,* the number of months in a one-year installment contract.

Rules Enabling Act of 1934. A federal statute that delegated comprehensive procedural rulemaking power to the Supreme Court and resulted in the Federal Rules of Civil Procedure. The statute is now, with slight changes, 28 U.S.C.A. § 2072.

Rules of Appellate Procedure. Federal Rules of Appellate Procedure govern procedure in appeals from the U.S. district courts and Tax Court to the U.S. Courts of Appeal. Fed.R.App.P. 1(a). In states which have adopted similar rules, they govern appeal procedure from the trial court to appellate courts. *See* Federal Rules of Appellate Procedure.

Rules of Bankruptcy Procedure. These federal Rules govern procedure in U.S. bankruptcy courts. They are supplemented by the Federal Rules of Civil Procedure and Federal Rules of Evidence.

Rules of Civil Procedure. Federal Rules of Civil Procedure govern procedure in the U.S. district courts in all suits of a civil nature whether cognizable as cases at law or in equity or in admiralty with some exceptions. Fed.R.Civil P. 1. Such Rules also govern adversary proceedings in federal bankruptcy courts. Many states have adopted similar rules which track the Federal Rules. *See* Federal Rules of Civil Procedure; Rules Enabling Act of 1934.

Rules of court. Such regulate practice and procedure before the various courts; *e.g.* Rules of Civil, Criminal, or Appellate Procedure; Rules of Evidence. In most jurisdictions, these rules are issued by the court itself, or by the highest court in that jurisdiction, while in others, such are adopted or enacted by the legislature. *See also* Court rule; Rulemaking power.

Rules of Criminal Procedure. Federal Rules of Criminal Procedure govern the procedure in all criminal proceedings in the U.S. district courts of the United States, including preliminary, supplementary, and special proceedings before U.S. magistrates. Fed.R.Crim.P. 1. Many states have adopted similar rules which track the Federal Rules. *See* Federal Rules of Criminal Procedure.

Rules of Decision Act. Section 34 of the Judiciary Act of 1789—the famous Rules of Decision Act—provided that "the laws of the several states, except where the constitution, treaties, or statutes of the United States shall otherwise require or provide, shall be regarded as rules of decision in trials at common law in the courts of the United States in cases where they apply." The statute has remained substantially unchanged to this day. See 28 U.S.C.A. § 1652.

Rules of Evidence. Rules of court which govern the admissibility of evidence at trials and hearings; *e.g.* Federal Rules of Evidence (applicable in U.S. district courts and federal bankruptcy courts); Uniform Rules of Evidence; Maine Rules of Evidence; California Evidence Code. The majority of states have adopted evidence rules patterned on the Federal Rules of Evidence. *See* Federal Rules of Evidence.

Rules of navigation. *See* Navigation.

Rules of Professional Conduct. The Model Rules of Professional Conduct of the American Bar Association set standards for such matters as client-lawyer relationships, fees, conflict of interest, role of lawyer as counselor and advocate, transactions with persons other than clients, responsibilities of law firms and associations, public service, and dissemination of information about legal services (including advertising). Such Rules replaced the former ABA Code of Professional Responsibility.

Rule 10b–5. This Rule of the Securities and Exchange Commission makes it unlawful, in connection with the purchase or sale of any security, to make any untrue statement of a material fact or to omit to state a material fact necessary in order to make the statements made, in the light of circumstances under which they were made, not misleading. See also Sec. 10(b) of the Securities Exchange Act, 15 U.S.C.A. § 78(j)(b). *See also* Insider; Material fact.

Ruling. A judicial or administrative interpretation of a provision of a statute, order, regulation, or ordinance; *e.g.* Revenue Rulings. May also refer to judicial determination of admissibility of evidence, allowance of motion, etc. *See also* Decree; Order; Rule.

Rumor. A current story passing from one person to another without any known authority for the truth of it. Such are not generally admissible in evidence.

Run, *v.* To have currency or legal validity in a prescribed territory; as, the writ *runs* throughout the county.

To have applicability or legal effect during a prescribed period of time; as, the statute of limitations has *run* against the claim.

To follow or accompany; to be attached to another thing in pursuing a prescribed course or direction; as, the covenant *runs* with the land.

To conduct, manage, carry on.

Run, *n.* A watercourse of small size. In business, a continuous round of manufacturing. In banking, a widespread and sudden withdrawal of deposits from a bank because of fear of the bank's collapse.

Runaway shop. An employer who moves his business to another location or temporarily closes his business for anti-union purposes.

Runner. Person who solicits business for attorney from accident victims. Also means a person employed by a bail bondsman for the purpose of assisting the bail bondsman in presenting the defendant in court when required, or to assist in apprehension and surrender of defendant to the court, or keeping defendant under necessary surveillance, or to execute bonds on behalf of the licensed bondsman when the power of attorney has been duly recorded. *See also* Ambulance chaser.

Running account. An open unsettled account, as distinguished from a stated and liquidated account. Running accounts mean mutual accounts and reciprocal demands between the parties, which accounts and demands remain open and unsettled. *See also* Charge account; Revolving credit.

Running at large. Refers to candidate for public office who seeks election from entire town or city and not just from one ward or district. Term is also applied to wandering or straying animals.

Running days. Days counted in their regular succession on the calendar, including Sundays and holidays.

Running of the statute of limitations. A metaphorical expression, by which is meant that the time specified in the statute of limitations is considered as having passed and hence the action is barred.

Running with the land. Prase referring generally to covenants that pass with transfer of the land. A covenant is said to run with the land when either the liability to perform it or the right to take advantage of it passes to the assignee of that land. Usually concerned with easements and covenants.

Rural. Concerning the country, as opposed to urban (concerning the city).

Rustler. Cattle thief.

Rustling. Larceny of cattle.

Rylands v. Fletcher case. The early English case which is the progenitor of the doctrine of absolute liability for abnormally dangerous things and activities. 3 H.L. 330. *See* Strict liability.

S

S. As an abbreviation, this letter stands for "section," "statute," and various other words of which it is the initial.

S–1. A form that must be filed with the Securities and Exchange Commission before a company's securities may be listed and traded on a national securities exchange. *See* Registration of securities.

Sabotage /sǽbətázh/. Term has reference to the wilful destruction or injury of, or defective production of, war material or national-defense material, or harm to war premises or war utilities. 18 U.S.C.A. § 2151 et seq. Term also refers to wilful and malicious destruction of employer's property during a labor dispute or interference with his normal operations.

Safe deposit box. A metal container kept by a customer in a bank in which he deposits papers, securities and other valuable items. Generally, there are two keys required to open, one retained by the bank and the other by the customer.

Safe Harbor rule. A provision in the tax code which gives a taxpayer protection as long as efforts were made to comply with the law. An example would be with estimated taxes. If an individual pays 100% of their prior year tax liability in estimated installments, they may avoid the underpayment penalty.

Safe place to work. In the law of master and servant (employer and employee), a place in which the master has eliminated all danger which in the exercise of reasonable care the master should remove or guard against. Master's duty to provide a "safe place" to work includes places to and from which the employee might be required or expected to go.

Federal, state, and local regulations and regulatory bodies require health and safety standards for workers. *See e.g.* Occupational Safety and Health Act; Right to know acts.

Safety Appliance Act. Federal Act regulating safety of equipment used by common carriers engaged in interstate commerce. 45 U.S.C.A. § 1 et seq.

Sailors. Seamen; mariners.

Sailors' Relief Act. *See* Soldiers' and Sailors' Civil Relief Act.

Sailors' will. A nuncupative or oral will which the law allows in the case of a sailor at sea. It has the power to pass personal property at death but not real estate. *See also* Nuncupative will.

Salable. Merchantable; fit for sale in usual course of trade, at usual selling prices. *See* Marketable title; Merchantability.

Salary. A reward or recompense for services performed. In a more limited sense, a fixed periodical compensation paid for services rendered. A stated compensation paid periodically as by the year, month, or other fixed period, in contrast to wages which are normally based on an hourly rate. *See also* Fixed salary; Wages.

Sale. A contract between two parties, called, respectively, the "seller" (or vendor) and the "buyer" (or purchaser), by which the former, in consideration of the payment or promise of payment of a certain price in money, transfers to the latter the title and the possession of property. Transfer of property as providing of services for consideration. A transfer of property for a fixed price in money or its equivalent. Passing of title from seller to buyer for a price. U.C.C. § 2–106(1).

A revenue transaction where goods or services are delivered to a customer in return for cash or a contractual obligation to pay. Term comprehends transfer of property from one party to another for valuable recompense.

The general law governing the sale of goods is the Uniform Commercial Code (Art. 2).

A contract whereby property is transferred from one person to another for a consideration of value, implying the passing of the general and absolute title, as distinguished from a special interest falling short of complete ownership.

To constitute a "sale," there must be parties standing to each other in the relation of buyer and seller, their minds must assent to the same proposition, and a consideration must pass.

The term "sale" includes any contract to sell or otherwise dispose of. Securities Exchange Act, § 3.

"Sale", "sell", "offer to sell", or "offer for sale" includes every contract of sale or disposition of, attempt or offer to dispose of, or solicitation of an offer to buy, a security or interest in a security, for value. Any security given or delivered with, or as a bonus on account of, any purchase of securities or any other thing, shall be conclusively presumed to constitute a part of the subject of such purchase and to have been sold for value. Investment Company Act, § 2.

Sale, as applied to relation between landowner and real estate broker working to secure purchaser of land, means procuring purchaser able, ready and willing to buy on terms fixed by seller.

See also Approval sales; Auction; Bargain and sale; Bargain sale *or* purchase; Bootstrap sale; Bulk sale; Buy and sell agreement; Cash sale; Casual sale; Consignment; Contract of sale; Credit sale; Exchange; Fire sale; Forced sale; Installment sale; Isolated sale; Judicial sale; Scalper; Sheriff's sale; Simulated sale; Symbolic delivery; Tax sale; Wash sale.

Other Terms Distinguished

The contract of "sale" is distinguished from "barter" (which applies only to goods) and "exchange" (which is used of both land and goods), in that both the latter terms denote a commutation of property for property; *i.e.,* the price or consideration is always paid in money if the transaction is a sale, but, if it is a barter or exchange, it is paid in specific property susceptible of valuation. "Sale" differs from "gift" in that the latter transaction involves no return or recompense for the thing transferred. But an onerous gift sometimes approaches the nature of a sale, at least where the charge it imposes is a payment of money. "Sale" is also to be distinguished from "bailment;" and the difference is to be found in the fact that the contract of bailment always contemplates the return to the bailor of the specific article delivered, either in its original form or in a modified or altered form, or the return of an article which, though not identical, is of the same class, and is equivalent. But sale never involves the return of the article itself, but only a consideration in money. This contract differs also from "accord and satisfaction;" because in the latter the object of transferring the property is to compromise and settle a claim, while the object of a sale is the price given.

The cardinal difference between the relation of seller and buyer and that of principal and factor is that in a "sale" title passes to the buyer, while in a "consignment" by principal to factor title remains in principal, and only possession passes to factor. Also, a "sale" is distinguished from a mortgage, in that the former is a transfer of the absolute property in the goods for a price, whereas a mortgage is at most a conditional sale of property as security for the payment of a debt or performance of some other obligation, subject to the condition that on performance title shall revest in the mortgagor.

An abandonment must be made without any desire that any other person shall acquire the thing abandoned, since if it is made for a consideration it is a "sale" or "barter," and if made without consideration, but with an intention that some other person shall become the possessor, it is a "gift."

General Classification

Absolute and conditional sales. An absolute sale is one where the property in chattels passes to the buyer upon the completion of the bargain. A conditional sale is one in which the transfer of title is made to depend on the performance of a condition, usually the payment of the price; it is a purchase for a price paid or to be paid, to become absolute on a particular event, or a purchase accompanied by an agreement to resell upon particular terms. Under a conditional sale the seller reserves title as security for payment for goods. *See also* Conditional sale contract; Secured transaction.

Auction sale. See Auction.

Bill of sale. See Bill.

Bulk sale. The sale of all or a substantial part of the seller's materials, supplies, merchandise, other inventory or in some cases equipment not in the ordinary course of business. U.C.C. § 6–102. Statutes prescribe the procedure for such sales because of the danger of fraud on the creditors of the seller.

Cash sale. A transaction whereby payment is to be in full on receipt of the goods. A sale where title is not to pass until the price is paid, or where title has passed, but possession is not to be delivered until payment is made. *Compare Sale on credit, below.*

Conditional sale. See Absolute and conditional sales, above.

Consignment sale. See Consignment.

Credit sale. See Sale on credit, below.

Exclusive sale. With respect to a real estate broker, an agreement by the owner that he will not sell the property during the life of the contract to any purchaser not procured by the broker in question. *See* Exclusive agency listing; Listing.

Executed and executory sales. An *executed* sale is one which is final and complete in all its particulars and details, nothing remaining to be done by either party to effect an absolute transfer of the subject-matter of the sale. An *executory* sale is one which has been definitely agreed on as to terms and conditions, but which has not yet been carried into full effect in respect to some of its terms or details, as where it remains to determine the price, quantity, or identity of the thing sold, or to pay installments of purchase-money, or to effect a delivery.

Execution sale. See Execution sale.

Fair sale. See Fair sale.

Forced sale. A sale made without the consent or concurrence of the owner of the property, but by virtue of judicial process, such as resulting from a writ of execution or an order under a decree of foreclosure. *See Judicial sale; Sheriff's sale; Tax-sale, below.*

Foreclosure sale. See Foreclosure.

Fraudulent sale. One made for the purpose of defrauding the creditors of the owner of the property, by covering up or removing from their reach and converting into cash property which would be subject to the satisfaction of their claims. Such sales may be voided by Bankruptcy Court.

Gross sale. In accounting, the total sales before deduction for return sales and allowances.

Installment sale. A sale in which the buyer makes periodic payments and generally the seller reserves title until full payment has been made. *See Retail installment sale; Sale on credit, below.*

Judicial sale. One made under the process of a court having competent authority to order it, by an officer duly appointed and commissioned to sell, as distinguished from a sale by an owner in virtue of his right of property. *See also Sheriff's sale; Tax-sale, below.*

Memorandum sale. That form of conditional sale in which the goods are placed in the possession of the vendee subject to his approval; the title remaining in the seller until they are either accepted or rejected by the vendee.

Net sale. Gross sales *(q.v.)* less returns and allowances.

Private sale. One negotiated and concluded privately between buyer and seller, and not made by advertisement and public notice or auction or through a broker or agent. See U.C.C. § 2–706.

Public sale. A sale made in pursuance of a notice, by auction or sheriff. See U.C.C. § 2–706. *See also Judicial sale, above*; *Sheriff's sale; Tax-sale, below.*

Retail installment sale. Sale of goods or the furnishing of services by a retail seller to a retail buyer for a deferred payment price payable in installments.

Sale and return. A species of contract by which the seller (usually a manufacturer or wholesaler) delivers a quantity of goods to the buyer, on the understanding that, if the latter should desire to retain or use or resell any portion of such goods, he will consider such part as having been sold to him, and will pay their price, and the balance he will return to the seller, or hold them, as bailee, subject to his order. Under "contract of sale and return" title vests immediately in buyer, who has privilege of rescinding sale, and until privilege is exercised title remains in him. See U.C.C. § 2–326.

Sale by auction. See Auction.

Sale by sample. A sales contract in which it is the understanding of both parties that the goods exhibited constitute the standard with which the goods not exhibited correspond and to which deliveries should conform. Any sample which is made part of the basis of the bargain creates an express warranty that the whole of the goods shall conform to the sample or model. U.C.C. § 2–313. *See also* Sample, sale by.

Sale in gross. A sale by the tract, without regard to quantity; it is in that sense a contract of hazard. *See also Gross sale, above.*

Sale-note. A memorandum of the subject and terms of a sale, given by a broker or factor to the seller, who bailed him the goods for that purpose, and to the buyer, who dealt with him. Also called "bought and sold notes."

Sale on approval. A species of conditional sale, which is to become absolute only in case the buyer, on trial, approves or is satisfied with the article sold. The approval, however, need not be express; it may be inferred from his keeping the goods beyond a reasonable time. *See also Sale or return, below;* and Approval sales.

A sale is a sale on approval if the goods may be returned by the buyer though they conform to the contract and if they are primarily delivered for use. Generally, such goods are not subject to the claims of the creditors of the buyer until acceptance. U.C.C. §§ 2–326, 2–327.

Sale on credit. A sale of property accompanied by delivery of possession, but where payment of the price is deferred to a future day. *See* Credit; *also, Installment sale, above.*

Sale or return. A type of conditional sale wherein the goods may be returned to the seller though they conform to the contract if the goods are delivered primarily for resale. U.C.C. §§ 2–326(1), (3), 2–327. A contract for sale of goods whereby title passes immediately to buyer subject to his option to rescind or return goods if he does not resell them. *See also Sale on approval, above.*

Sale with all faults. Under what is called a "sale with all faults," or "sale as is", unless the seller fraudulently and inconsistently represents the article sold to be faultless, or contrives to conceal any fault from the purchaser, the latter must take the article for better or worse.

Sale with right of redemption. A sale in which vendor reserves right to take back property by returning price paid. *See also Sale on approval; Sale or return, above.*

Sheriff's sale. A sale of property, conducted by a sheriff, or sheriff's deputy by virtue of his authority as an officer holding process. *See Forced sale;*

Judicial sale, above, also, Foreclosure; Sheriff's sale.

Short sale. *See* Short sale.

Tax-sale. A sale of land for unpaid taxes; a sale of property, by authority of law, for the collection of a tax assessed upon it, or upon its owner, which remains unpaid.

Voluntary sale. One made freely, without constraint, by the owner of the thing sold. *Contrast Forced sale, above.*

Wash sale. In security trading, a spurious transaction in which the same stock is sold and bought by the same person to create the impression of market activity or to establish a market for the stock. Such transactions are forbidden.

Sale against the box. A species of short sale *(q.v.)* at a time when the taxpayer owns substantially identical shares.

Sale and leaseback. A lease that is initiated when a firm sells an asset it owns to another firm and simultaneously leases the asset back for its own use. A sale of an asset to a vendee who immediately leases back to the vendor. The usual objectives are (1) to free cash in the amount of the purchase price for other uses by the vendor, (2) for benefits not otherwise available such a deduction by the vendor of the full value of the property for income tax purposes as rental payments over a period of time shorter than would be in depreciation where the base period is the allowable depreciable life. The rental payments total the purchase price plus interest less an estimated salvage value. Although the lease actually follows the sale, both are agreed to as part of the same transaction.

Sale of land. *See* Conveyance; Conveyancing.

Sale *or* exchange. The term used in taxation in reference to a transaction which results in a gain or loss recognized for federal tax purposes. I.R.C. § 1001.

Sales agreement *or* contract. A contract to sell goods. A contract by means of which the ownership of goods is transferred from a seller to a buyer for a fixed price in money, paid or agreed to be paid by the buyer. It may refer to a contract for sale which includes both a present sale and a contract to sell goods at a future time. U.C.C. § 2–106(1). Also, term used to describe a contract for the sale of real estate, including a contract for deed. *See also* Conditional sale contract; Sale.

Sale contract. *See* Sale; Sales agreement *or* contract.

Sales discount. A cash discount from the seller's point of view.

Sales finance company. A business engaged primarily in the purchase of accounts receivable at a discount. The company then undertakes to collect them.

Sales invoice. *See* Invoice.

Sales journal. A special journal used to record sales of merchandise on account.

Salesman. *See* Commercial traveler; Dealer; Drummer; Hawker; Peddler.

Sales mix. The relative combination of individual product sales to total sales.

Sales tax. A state or local-level tax on the retail sale of specified property or services. It is a percentage of the cost of such. Generally, the purchaser pays the tax, but the seller collects it, as an agent for the government. Various taxing jurisdictions allow exemptions for purchases of specified items, including certain foods, services, and manufacturing equipment. If the purchaser and seller are in different states, a *use tax* usually applies.

Salvage. In general, that portion of goods or property which has been saved or remains after a casualty such as fire or other loss.

In business, any property which is no longer useful (*e.g.* obsolete equipment) but which has scrap value.

In insurance, that portion of property which is taken over by the insurance company after payment of a claim for the loss. The insurance company may deduct the salvage value from the amount of the claim paid and leave the property with the insured.

In maritime law, a compensation allowed to persons by whose assistance a ship or its cargo has been saved, in whole or in part, from impending danger, or recovered from actual loss, in cases of shipwreck, derelict, or recapture. Elements necessary to valid "salvage" are marine peril, with service voluntarily rendered, when not required as existing duty, or from a special contract, and success in whole or in part, and that service rendered contributed to such success.

Salvage loss. That kind of loss which it is presumed would, but for certain services rendered and exertions made, have become a total loss. In the language of marine underwriters, this term means the difference between the amount of salvage, after deducting the charges, and the original value of the property insured.

Salvage value. That value of an asset which remains after the useful life of the asset has expired. It is commonly equivalent to scrap value and in most cases must be deducted in computing depreciation. Actual or estimated selling price, net of removal or disposal costs, of a used plant asset to be sold or otherwise retired. It may consist of the actual resale price which taxpayer can expect to realize upon disposition of asset when taxpayer's use of it in his business terminates; it is not some nominal or junk value.

The value of a building or portion of a building to be moved from one location for use at another site. Occurs in condemnation, especially for highway purposes, where large tracts of land must be cleared.

See also Net salvage value.

Same. Identical, equal, equivalent. The word, however, does not always mean "identical." It frequently means of the kind or species, not the specific thing. When preceded by the definite article, means the one just referred to.

Two offenses are "the same" under the double jeopardy clause of the Federal Constitution unless each requires proof of an additional fact that the other does not. See also Jeopardy; Same offense.

Same evidence test. The "same-evidence test" used in determining issue of double jeopardy is whether facts alleged in second indictment, if introduced in evidence, would have sustained a conviction under the first indictment or whether the same evidence would support a conviction in each case. See Double jeopardy; Same offense.

Same invention. Within reissue statute, refers to whatever invention was described in original letters patent, and appears therein to have been intended to be secured thereby. It is not to be determined by the claims of the original patent but from the description and such other evidence as the commissioner may deem relevant.

Same offense. As used in Constitution, providing that no person shall be twice put in jeopardy for the same offense, does not signify the same offense eo nomine, but the same criminal act, transaction, or omission. Term "same offense" as used in statute relating to enhancement of punishment for subsequent conviction of same offense means a similar offense, one of the same character or nature. However, under "same offense" test of double jeopardy, if there is any difference in elements to be proven, two instances are not the same offense. See also Jeopardy; Same; Same evidence test.

Sample. A specimen. A small quantity of any commodity, presented for inspection or examination as evidence of the quality of the whole; as a sample of cloth or of wheat.

Sample, sale by. A sale at which only a sample of the goods sold is exhibited to the buyer. Any sample or model which is made part of the basis of the bargain creates an express warranty that the whole of the goods shall conform to the sample or model. U.C.C. § 2–313(1)(c). See also Sale.

Sanction, *v.* To assent, concur, confirm, reprimand, or ratify. Approval or ratification.

Sanction, *n.* Penalty or other mechanism of enforcement used to provide incentives for obedience with the law or with rules and regulations. That part of a law which is designed to secure enforcement by imposing a penalty for its violation or offering a reward for its observance. For example, Fed.R.Civil P. 37 provides sanctions for failure to comply with discovery orders, and Rule 11 empowers court to impose disciplinary sanctions on attorneys for other types of improper conduct. See also Contempt; Criminal sanctions.

A punitive act taken by one nation against another nation which has violated a treaty or international law.

Sandwich lease. The first lease of property from lessor to lessee who in turn subleases to another. See Sublease.

Sanitary code. Municipal ordinances regulating sanitary conditions of establishments which produce, distribute or serve food, or provide medical services.

Sanitation. Devising and applying of measures for preserving and promoting public health; removal or neutralization of elements injurious to health; practical application of sanitary science. See Sanitary code.

Sanity. Sound understanding; the normal condition of the human mind; the reverse of insanity *(q.v.)*.

Sanity hearing. A preliminary inquiry into the mental competency of a person to stand trial, though it may be held at any time within the criminal proceeding. See 18 U.S.C.A. § 4241 et seq.; Fed.R.Crim.P. 12.2.

A proceeding to determine whether one should be confined under a civil commitment to an institution.

Sanity trial. In some states the issues of sanity and guilt may be tried separately in a bifurcated trial.

Satisfaction. Act of satisfying; the state of being satisfied. The discharge of an obligation by paying a party what is due to him (as on a mortgage, lien, note, or contract), or what is awarded to him, by the judgment of a court or otherwise. Thus, a judgment is satisfied by the payment of the amount due to the party who has recovered such judgment, or by his levying the amount. The execution or carrying into effect of an accord. The performance of a substituted obligation in return for the discharge of the original obligation.

A legacy is deemed satisfied if the testator makes an inter vivos gift to the legatee with the intent that it be in lieu of the legacy.

An entry made on the record, by which a party in whose favor a judgment was rendered declares that he has been satisfied and paid.

See also Accord and satisfaction; Payment; Performance.

Accord and satisfaction. An "accord" is an agreement whereby one of parties undertakes to give or perform, and other to accept in satisfaction of liquidated or disputed claim arising in either contract or tort something different from what he is or considers himself entitled to; and "satisfaction" is execution or performance of agreement.

Equity. The doctrine of satisfaction in equity is somewhat analogous to performance in equity, but differs from it in this respect: that satisfaction is always something given either in whole or in part as a substitute or equivalent for something else, and not (as in performance) something that may be construed as the identical thing covenanted to be done.

Satisfaction, contracts to. A class of contracts in which one party agrees to perform his promise to the satisfaction of the other. A contract for construction work "to the entire satisfaction of the owners" imports that the construction be to the satisfaction of a reasonable man and not to the personal satisfaction of owners.

Satisfaction of debt. *See* Satisfaction.

Satisfaction of judgment. A document such as an execution enforced by the judgment creditor and indicating that the judgment has been paid. *See* Execution.

Satisfaction of lien. Document signed by a lien holder in which he releases the property subject to the lien.

Satisfaction of mortgage. A discharge signed by the mortgagee or holder of the mortgage indicating that the property subject to the mortgage is released or that the mortgage debt has been paid and that all terms and conditions of the mortgage have been satisfied. *See also* Redemption.

Satisfaction piece. A memorandum in writing, entitled in a cause, stating that satisfaction is acknowledged between the parties, plaintiff and defendant. Upon this being duly acknowledged and filed in the office where the record of the judgment is, the judgment becomes satisfied, and the defendant discharged from it. See New York CPLR § 5020. Also referred to as "Certificate of Discharge." *See* Discharge.

Satisfactory. Where a contract provides that it is to be performed in a manner "satisfactory" to one of the parties, the provision must be construed as meaning that the performance must be such that the party, as a reasonable person, should be satisfied with it.

Satisfactory evidence. Such evidence as is sufficient to produce a belief that the thing is true; credible evidence. Such evidence as, in respect to its amount or weight, is adequate or sufficient to justify the court or jury in adopting the conclusion in support of which it is adduced. Sometimes called "sufficient evidence," means that amount of proof which ordinarily satisfies an unprejudiced mind beyond a reasonable doubt. *See* Relevant evidence; Sufficient evidence.

Satisfied term. A term of years in land is thus called when the purpose for which it was created has been satisfied or executed before the expiration of the set period.

Satisfy. To answer or discharge, as a claim, debt, legal demand or the like. To comply actually and fully with a demand; to extinguish, by payment or performance. To convince, as to satisfy a jury. *See also* Satisfaction.

Saturday night special. In corporate law, a surprise tender offer which expires in one week. Designed to capitalize on panic and haste, such an offer may be made Friday afternoon to take advantage of the fact that markets and most offices are closed on Saturday and Sunday. Saturday night specials have been effectively prohibited by the Williams Act, § 14(e), 15 U.S.C.A. § 78n(e). Term also used in reference to type of handgun weapon used in armed crimes.

Save. To except, reserve, or exempt; as where a statute "saves" vested rights. To toll, or suspend the running or operation of; as to "save" the statute of limitations. *See* Saving clause.

Save harmless clause. A provision in a document by which one party agrees to indemnify and hold harmless another party as to claims and suits which may be asserted against him. In some states, such clauses in leases are deemed against public policy and, hence, void. *See also* Hold harmless agreement.

Saving. Preservation from danger or loss; economy in outlay; prevention of waste; something laid up or kept from becoming expended or lost; a reservation.

Saving clause. In a statute, an exception of a special thing out of the general things mentioned in the statute. Ordinarily a restriction in a repealing act, which is intended to save rights, pending proceedings, penalties, etc., from the annihilation which would result from an unrestricted repeal. That provision in a statute which rescues the balance of the statute from a declaration of unconstitutionality if one or more clauses or parts are invalidated. It is sometimes referred to as the severability clause. Such clause continues in force the law repealed as to existing rights. *See also* Separability clause; Severable statute.

Savings account. Accounts maintained in commercial and savings banks for purpose of accumulating money, in contrast to a checking account. Savings accounts generally yield interest on the deposited funds, though the trend is to also pay interest on checking account balances.

Savings account trust. An account opened in the name of one person in trust for another; *e.g.* A in trust for B. *See also* Trust *(Totten Trust).*

Savings and loan association. One of a number of types of mutually-owned, cooperative, savings associations, originally established for the primary purpose of making loans to members and others, usually for the purchase of real estate or homes; though in the 1980's S & L's expanded into commercial and other non-mortgage loans and services. Such may be chartered by the state, or by the federal government, in which case it is known as a "Federal Savings and Loan Association." The deposits are insured by the Federal Deposit Insurance Corporation. The Financial Institution's Reform, Recovery and Enforcement Act of 1989 significantly changed the capital requirements, loan powers, and regulatory control of S & L's. *See also* Building and loan association.

A bank chartered by the Federal Home Loan Bank Board and engaged primarily in making home loan mortgages from the savings accounts of the depositors. Associations at the federal level are regulated by the Federal Home Loan Bank System.

Savings bank. *See* Bank.

Savings bank trust. *See* Trust.

Savings bond. *See* Bond.

Savings notes. Short term paper issued by a bank and bearing interest. The U.S. government issues such notes on a 90 day basis and for other periods of time.

Saving to suitors clause. That provision in 28 U.S.C.A. § 1333(1) which gives the U.S. District Courts original jurisdiction, "exclusive of the courts of the state" of any civil case of admiralty or maritime jurisdiction, "saving to suitors in all cases all other remedies to which they are otherwise entitled." The "saving to suitors" clause of the section of the Judiciary Act implementing constitutional provision extending federal judicial powers to cases of admiralty and maritime jurisdiction means that a suitor asserting an in personam admiralty claim may elect to sue in a "common law" state court through an ordinary civil action, and in such actions, the state courts must apply the same substantive law as would be applied had the suit been instituted in admiralty in a federal court.

S.B. Senate Bill.

S.B.A. Small Business Administration.

S.B.I.C. Small Business Investment Company.

S.C. Abbreviation for "same case." Inserted between two citations, it indicates that the same case is reported in both places. Also an abbreviation for "supreme court."

Scab. Person who works for lower wages than or under conditions contrary to those prescribed by a trade union; also one who takes the place of a worker who is on strike. Non-union workers who pass through a union picket line. A worker who works under non-union conditions.

Scale order. An order to buy (or sell) a security which specifies the total amount to be bought (or sold) and the amount to be bought (or sold) at specified price variations.

Scalper. In securities business, a small operator who takes his profits on slight fluctuations in the market. A small scale speculator. One who sells tickets to sporting, theatre and other entertainment events at prices in excess of face price (*i.e.* box office price) of ticket.

Scandal. Defamatory reports or rumors; aspersion or slanderous talk, uttered recklessly or maliciously. Scandalous matter may be ordered stricken from the pleadings by a motion to strike. Fed.R.Civ.P. 12(f). *See also* Defamation.

Scandalous matter. Within federal rule providing for striking scandalous matter from pleadings, "scandalous matter" is matter which improperly casts a derogatory light on someone, usually a party to the action, with respect to moral character or uses repulsive language.

Scenes a faire. /sén afér/. Fr. A copyright law doctrine referring to incidents, characters or settings which are as a practical matter indispensable, or at least standard, in the treatment of a given topic. Such material, in an otherwise copyrightable work, is considered unprotected by copyright because it would be natural for it to appear in works dealing with similar subjects or situations. See 17 U.S.C.A. § 102(b).

Schedule. A sheet of paper annexed to a statute, deed, deposition, tax return, or other instrument, exhibiting in detail the matters mentioned or referred to in the principal document; *e.g.* schedule of assets and liabilities (debts) in bankruptcy proceeding. *See* Tax rate schedules.

Any list of planned events to take place on a regular basis such as a train schedule or a schedule of work to be performed in a factory.

Scheduled injuries. Certain types of injuries involving partial disability that are specifically covered in state workers' compensation statutes, each of which has a predetermined amount of compensation that will be paid for an employee experiencing that injury.

Scheduled property. In insurance, a list of property and the value of each piece of such property for which the insurer will pay in the event of loss or damage.

SCHEME   **936**

Scheme. A design or plan formed to accomplish some purpose; a system. When used in a bad sense, term corresponds with "trick" or "fraud".

Scheme *or* **artifice to defraud.** For purposes of fraudulent representation statutes, consists of forming plan or devising some trick to perpetrate fraud upon another. Such connotes a plan or pattern of conduct which is intended to or is reasonably calculated to deceive persons of ordinary prudence and comprehension. "Scheme to defraud" within meaning of mail fraud statute (18 U.S.C.A. § 1341) is the intentional use of false or fraudulent representations for the purpose of gaining a valuable undue advantage or working some injury to something of value held by another. *See also* Artifice; Fraud; Mail fraud.

Schism /sízəm/. A division of a union into two factions resulting in one group leaving the union.

Scienter /sayéntər/. Lat. Knowingly. The term is used in pleading to signify an allegation (or that part of the declaration or indictment which contains it) setting out the defendant's previous knowledge of the cause which led to the injury complained of, or rather his previous knowledge of a state of facts which it was his duty to guard against, and his omission to do which has led to the injury complained of. The term is frequently used to signify the defendant's guilty knowledge.

Knowledge by the misrepresenting party that material facts have been falsely represented or omitted with an intent to deceive.

The term "scienter," as applied to conduct necessary to give rise to an action for civil damages under Securities Exchange Act of 1934 and Rule 10b–5 refers to a mental state embracing intent to deceive, manipulate or defraud.

Sci. fa. /sáy féy/. An abbreviation for *"scire facias" (q.v.).*

Scilicet /síləsət/sáyləsət/. Lat. To-wit; that is to say. A word used in pleadings and other instruments, as introductory to a more particular statement of matters previously mentioned in general terms.

Scintilla /sintílə/. Lat. A spark; a remaining particle; a trifle; the least particle.

Scintilla of evidence rule /sintílə əv évədəns/. A spark of evidence. A metaphorical expression to describe a very insignificant or trifling item or particle of evidence; used in the statement of the common-law rule that if there is any evidence at all in a case, even a mere *scintilla*, tending to support a material issue, the case cannot be taken from the jury, but must be left to their decision.

This rule requires that if there is even a scintilla of evidence presented to support the nonmoving party's position, summary judgment should not be granted. With regard to precluding summary judgment for defendant, "scintilla rule" requires only that the evidence, or reasonable inferences therefrom, furnish a mere gleam, glimmer, spark, the least bit, the smallest trace, in support of plaintiff's complaint.

Any material evidence that, if true, would tend to establish issue in mind of reasonable juror. Something of substance and relevant consequence and not vague, uncertain, or irrelevant matter not carrying quality of proof or having fitness to induce conviction. Courts differ as to what constitutes a "scintilla," and some courts do not accept the rule. For example, it has been held that while the cogency of evidence is not dependent on its quantity, if the party with the burden of proof has introduced only a *scintilla* of evidence on an essential element of his case, a judge may direct a verdict against him. Such evidence is inadequate as a matter of law. It has also been held that it is the duty of trial court to instruct a verdict, though there is slight testimony, if its probative force is so weak that it only raises suspicion of existence of facts sought to be established, since such testimony falls short of being "evidence".

Scire facias /sáyriy féysh(iy)əs/. Lat. A judicial writ, founded upon some matter of record, such as a judgment or recognizance and requiring the person against whom it is brought to show cause why the party bringing it should not have advantage of such record, or (in the case of a *scire facias* to repeal letters patent) why the record should not be annulled and vacated. The name is used to designate both the writ and the whole proceeding. A judicial writ directing a debtor to appear and show cause why a dormant judgment against him should not be revived. The most common application of this writ is as a process to revive a judgment, after the lapse of a certain time, or on a change of parties, or otherwise to have execution of the judgment, in which cases it is merely a continuation of the original action. It is used more rarely as a mode of proceeding against special bail on their recognizance, and as a means of repealing letters patent, in which cases it is an original proceeding. Under current rules practice in most states, this writ has been abolished; *e.g.* Mass.R.Civil P. 81.

A legal, as opposed to equitable, form of judicial foreclosure. After mortgagor default, the mortgagee obtains a writ of Scire Facias, which is an order to show cause why the mortgaged property should not be sold to satisfy the mortgage debt. If mortgagee prevails, the court will issue a writ of levari facias directing an execution sale of the mortgaged real estate.

Scire feci /sáyriy fíysay/. Lat. The name given to the sheriff's return to a writ of *scire facias* that he has caused notice to be given to the party or parties against whom the writ was issued.

Scope of a patent. The boundaries or limits of the invention protected by the patent, which are not matters of metes and bounds and can never be defined in the definite sense employed in thinking of physical things, but must be determined by methods based upon established principles of patent law.

Scope of authority. In law of agency, includes not only actual authorization conferred upon agent by his principal, but also that which has apparently or impliedly been delegated to agent. Under doctrine of respondeat superior *(q.v.)* a principal is liable for the contracts of his agent if the agent contracted within the scope of his actual or apparent authority. *See also* Authority; Scope of employment.

Scope of employment. The activities in which an employee engages in the carrying out of the employer's business which are reasonably foreseeable by the employer. Under doctrine of respondeat superior *(q.v.)*, a principal is liable for the torts of his agent committed within the scope, actual or apparent, of his employment.

An employee acts in scope of his employment, for purpose of invoking a doctrine of respondeat superior, when he is doing something in furtherance of duties he owes to his employer and where employer is, or could be, exercising some control, directly or indirectly, over employee's activities. Employee is in "scope of employment," such that corporate employer is liable to third party for his torts, whenever he is engaged in activities that fairly and reasonably may be said to be incident of the employment or logically and naturally connected with it.

See also Respondeat superior; Vicarious liability.

S Corporation. *See* Corporation *(S Corporation).*

Scrip. A document which entitles the holder to receive something of value. It is ultimately exchanged for money or some privilege. In corporations, when a stock dividend is declared, scrip is issued in place of fractional shares and when the holder has sufficient scrip he may exchange the scrip for a share.

Paper money issued for temporary use.

The term has also formerly been applied to warrants, certificates, or other like orders drawn on a municipal treasury showing the holder to be entitled to a certain portion or allotment of public or state lands, and also to the fractional paper currency issued by the United States during the period of the Civil War.

Scrip dividend. Type of deferred dividend commonly in the form of a promissory note which is redeemable in stock or cash at a future time. *See also* Dividend.

Script. Something written (*e.g.* manuscript). The original of an instrument or document. Where instruments are executed in part and counterpart, the original or principal is so called.

Scrivener /skrív(ə)nər/. A writer; scribe; conveyancer. One whose occupation is to draw contracts, write deeds and mortgages, and prepare other species of written instruments. Also an agent to whom property is intrusted by others for the purpose of lending it out at an interest payable to his principal, and for a commission or bonus for himself, whereby he gains his livelihood. Term is seldom used in United States.

Scroll *or* **scrawl.** A mark intended to supply the place of a seal, made with a pen or other instrument of writing.

A paper or parchment containing some writing, and rolled up so as to conceal it.

S.D. Southern District; *e.g.* U.S. District Court for Southern District of New York.

S/D B/L. The abbreviation "S/D B/L" in a contract of sale means sight draft—bill of lading attached.

SDWA. Safe Drinking Water Act. 42 U.S.C.A. §§ 300h–1 to 5.

Sea. The ocean; the great mass of water which surrounds the land. In marine insurance "sea" includes not only the high seas but the bays, inlets, and rivers as high up as the tide ebbs and flows. The "navigable sea" is divided into three zones: (1) nearest to the nation's shores are its internal or "inland waters"; (2) beyond the inland waters, and measured from their seaward edge, is a belt known as the marginal or "territorial sea"; and (3) outside the territorial sea are the "high seas". U. S. v. State of La., 89 S.Ct. 773, 781. *See also* Seaworthy.

High seas. The ocean; public waters. According to the English doctrine, the high sea begins at the distance of three miles from the coast of any country; according to the American view, at low-water mark, except in the case of small harbors and roadsteads inclosed within the *fauces terræ.* The open ocean outside of the *fauces terræ*, as distinguished from arms of the sea; the waters of the ocean without the boundary of any country. Any waters on the sea-coast which are without the boundaries of low-water mark. Waters outside of territorial jurisdiction of nation.

Sea-shore. The margin of the sea in its usual and ordinary state. When the tide is out, low-water mark is the margin of the sea; and, when the sea is full, the margin is high-water mark. The sea-shore is therefore all the ground between the ordinary high-water mark and low-water mark. It cannot be considered as including any ground always covered by the sea, for then it would have no definite limit on the sea-board. Neither can it include any part of the upland, for the same reason. That space of land over which the waters of the sea are spread in the highest water during the winter season.

Seal. An impression upon wax, wafer, or some other tenacious substance capable of being impressed. In current practice, a particular sign (*e.g.* L.S.) or the word "seal" is made in lieu of an actual seal to attest the execution of the instrument.

As regards sealing of records, means to close by any kind of fastening that must be broken before access can be obtained. *See* Sealing of records.

See also Contract under seal.

Corporate seal. A seal adopted and used by a corporation for authenticating its corporate acts and executing legal instruments.

Great seal. The United States and also each of the states has and uses a seal, always carefully described by law, and sometimes officially called the "great" seal, though in some instances known simply as "the seal of the United States," or "the seal of the state."

Private seal. The seal (however made) of a private person or corporation, as distinguished from a seal employed by a state or government or any of its bureaus or departments.

Public seal. A seal belonging to and used by one of the bureaus or departments of government, for authenticating or attesting documents, process, or records. An impression made of some device, by means of a piece of metal or other hard substance, kept and used by public authority. *See also* State seal.

Sealed. Authenticated by a seal; executed by the affixing of a seal.

Sealed and delivered. These words, followed by the signatures of the witnesses, constitute the usual formula for the attestation of conveyances.

Sealed bid. A method for submitting a bid to buy or to perform work on a proposed contract. In general, each party interested submits a bid in a sealed envelope, and all such bids are opened at the same time and the most favorable responsible bid is accepted.

Sealed instrument. An instrument of writing to which the party to be bound has affixed not only his name, but also his seal. *See also* Seal.

The affixing of a seal to a contract for sale or an offer to buy or sell goods does not make the writing a sealed instrument and the law of sealed instruments does not apply to such contract. U.C.C. § 2–203.

Sealed verdict. When the jury have agreed upon a verdict, if the court is not in session at the time, they are permitted (usually) to put their written finding in a sealed envelope, and then separate. This verdict they return when the court again convenes. The verdict thus returned has the same effect, and must be treated in the same manner, as if returned in open court before any separation of the jury had taken place.

Sealing of records. Statutes in some states permit a person's criminal record to be sealed and thereafter such records cannot be examined except by order of the court or by designated officials. Such statutes commonly pertain to juvenile offenders.

Seaman's will. *See* Sailors' will.

Seamen. Sailors; mariners; persons whose business is navigating ships, or who are connected with the ship as such and in some capacity assist in its conduct, maintenance or service. Commonly exclusive of the officers of a ship. One whose occupation is to navigate vessels upon the sea including all those on board whose labor contributes to the accomplishment of the main object in which the vessel is engaged. Term includes anyone who, in course of his work about a ship, exposes himself to risks traditionally associated with maritime duties of a member of ship's crew.

A "seaman" under the Jones Act is an employee whose duties contribute to the function of the vessel on which he works or the accomplishment of its mission. *See also* Jones Act; Longshoreman.

Seance /seyóns/séyons/. In French law, a session; as of some public body.

Search. Looking for or seeking out that which is otherwise concealed from view. An examination of a person's house or other buildings or premises, or of his person, or of his vehicle, aircraft, etc., with a view to the discovery of contraband or illicit or stolen property, or some evidence of guilt to be used in the prosecution of a criminal action for some crime or offense with which he is charged. A "search" implies prying into hidden places for that which is concealed and that the object searched for had been hidden or intentionally put out of the way; merely looking at that which is open to view is not a search. It consists of probing or exploration for something that is concealed or hidden from searcher; an invasion, a quest with some sort of force, either actual or constructive. Visual observation which infringes upon a person's reasonable expectation of privacy constitutes a "search" in the constitutional sense.

Unreasonable searches and seizures are prohibited by the Fourth Amendment, U.S. Const.

See also Border search; Consent search; Exclusionary Rule; Exigent circumstances; Fruit of poisonous tree doctrine; Illegally obtained evidence; Incident to arrest; Inspection searches; Inventory search; Knock and announce rule; Mapp v. Ohio; McNabb–Mallory Rule; Mere evidence rule; Plain view doctrine; Poisonous tree doctrine; Probable cause; Reasonable suspicion; Search warrant; Seizure; Stop and frisk; Totality of circumstances test; Warrant.

International law. The right of search is the right on the part of ships of war to visit and search merchant vessels during war, in order to ascertain whether the ship or cargo is liable to seizure. Resistance to visitation and search by a neutral vessel makes the vessel and cargo liable to confiscation. Numerous treaties regulate the manner in which the right of search must be exercised.

Title search. An examination of the official books, records and dockets, made in the process of investigating a title to land, for the purpose of discovering if there are any mortgages, judgments, tax-liens, or other incumbrances upon it. *See also* Abstract of title.

Unlawful or unreasonable search. Within constitutional immunity (Fourth Amendment) from unreasonable searches and seizures, an examination or inspection without authority of law of premises or person with view to discovery of stolen, contraband, or illicit property, or for some evidence of guilt to be used in prosecution of criminal action. *See* Exclusionary Rule; Fruit of poisonous tree doctrine; Probable cause; Search warrant.

Voluntary search. As used in context of consent to search, means that consent was not result of duress or coercion, express or implied, or any other form of undue influence exercised against defendant. *See* Consent search.

Search incident to arrest. A police officer who has the right to arrest a person either with or without a warrant may search his person and the immediate area of the arrest for weapons. Chimel v. California, 395 U.S. 752, 89 S.Ct. 2034, 23 L.Ed.2d 685. *See* Search Warrant *(Search without warrant).*

Search warrant. An order in writing, issued by a justice or other magistrate, in the name of the state, directed to a sheriff, constable, or other officer, authorizing him to search for and seize any property that constitutes evidence of the commission of a crime, contraband, the fruits of crime, or things otherwise criminally possessed; or, property designed or intended for use or which is or has been used as the means of committing a crime. A warrant may be issued upon an affidavit or sworn oral testimony. Fed.R.Crim.P. 41; 18 U.S.C.A. § 3101 et seq.

The Fourth Amendment to U.S. Constitution provides that "no warrants shall issue, but upon probable cause, supported by oath or affirmation, and particularly describing the place to be searched, and the persons or things to be seized."

See also Anticipatory search warrant; Blanket search warrant; Exclusionary Rule; Exigent circumstances; Probable cause; Search.

Search without warrant. A search without a warrant but incidental to an arrest is permitted if it does not extend beyond the person of the accused and the area into which the accused might reach in order to grab a weapon or other evidentiary items. Chimel v. California, 395 U.S. 752, 89 S.Ct. 2034, 23 L.Ed.2d 685. *See also* Search incident to arrest; Stop and frisk.

Seashore. That portion of land adjacent to the sea which is alternately covered and left dry by the ordinary flux and reflux of the tides.

Seasonable. In commercial law, an action is seasonable when taken within the time agreed or if no time is agreed within a reasonable time. U.C.C. § 1–204.

Seasonal employment. As used in compensation laws, as basis for determining right to and amount of compensation, refers to occupations which can be carried on only at certain seasons or fairly definite portions of the year, and does not include such occupations as may be carried on throughout entire year.

Seat. Membership on securities or commodities exchange.

Seat of government. The state capitol or the town within a district or county where the principal government offices and officers are located; *e.g.* "county seat."

Seaworthy. Ability to withstand ordinary stress of wind, waves and other weather which the vessel might normally be expected to encounter. This adjective, as applied to a vessel, signifies that she is properly constructed, prepared, manned, equipped, and provided, for the voyage intended. A seaworthy vessel must, in general, be sufficiently strong and staunch and equipped with appropriate appurtenances to allow it to safely engage in trade for which it was intended.

It is an implied condition of all policies of marine insurance, unless otherwise expressly stipulated, that the vessel shall be seaworthy. In marine insurance, a warranty of seaworthiness means that the vessel is competent to resist the ordinary attacks of wind and weather, and is competently equipped and manned for the voyage, with a sufficient crew, and with sufficient means to sustain them, and with a captain of general good character and nautical skill.

A warranty of seaworthiness extends not only to the condition of the structure of the ship itself, but requires that it be properly laden, and provided with a competent master, a sufficient number of competent officers and seamen, and the requisite appurtenances and equipments, such as ballast, cables and anchors, cordage and sails, food, water, fuel, and lights, and other necessary or proper stores and implements for the voyage.

See also Unseaworthy.

S.E.C. Securities and Exchange Commission.

Secession. The act of withdrawing from membership in a group. Certain states attempted unsuccessfully to secede from the United States at the time of the Civil War.

Seck. A want of remedy by distress. Want of present fruit or profit, as in the case of the reversion without rent or other service, except fealty. *See* Rent.

Second. This term, as used in law, may denote either sequence in point of time or inferiority or postponement in respect to rank, lien, order, or privilege.

As to *second* Cousin; Deliverance; Distress; Mortgage; and Surcharge, see those titles.

Second Amendment. The Second Amendment to the U.S. Constitution provides that a well regulated militia, being necessary to the security of a free state, the right of the people to keep and bear arms shall not be infringed. State and federal laws however regulate the sale, transportation and possession of firearms.

Secondary, *adj.* Of a subsequent, subordinate, or inferior kind or class; generally opposed to "primary."

As to *secondary* Conveyance; Easement; Evidence; Franchise; Meaning; and Use, see those titles.

Secondary beneficiary. The beneficiary next in line to collect should the primary beneficiary be unable to do so.

Secondary boycott. Any combination if its purpose and effect are to coerce customers or patrons, or suppliers through fear of loss or bodily harm, to withhold or withdraw their business relations from employer who is under attack. Term refers to refusal to work for, purchase from or handle products of secondary employer with whom union has no dispute, with object of forcing such employer to stop doing business with primary employer with whom union has dispute. While secondary boycotts are generally prohibited by federal labor laws, such are allowed by transportation workers under the National Railway Labor Act. *See also* Boycott; Secondary picketing.

Secondary distribution. In securities, the new distribution of stock after it has been initially sold by the issuing corporation. It is not a new issue, but rather a public sale of stock which has previously been issued and held by large corporations and investors. Also, the sale of a large block of stock after the close of business of the exchange. *See also* Offering; Secondary offering.

Secondary easement. An easement to accomplish the intended purposes of the primary easement. One which is appurtenant to the primary or actual easement.

Secondary evidence. That which is inferior to primary or best evidence. Thus, a copy of an instrument, or oral evidence of its contents, is secondary evidence of the instrument and contents. It is that species of evidence which becomes admissible, when the primary or best evidence of the fact in question is lost or inaccessible; as when a witness details orally the contents of an instrument which is lost or destroyed. *See also* Circumstantial evidence; Hearsay; Second-hand evidence. *Compare* Best evidence; Primary evidence.

Secondary lender. A wholesale mortgage buyer who purchases first mortgages from banks and savings and loan associations, enabling them to restock their money supply and loan more money.

Secondary liability. A liability which does not attach until or except upon the fulfillment of certain conditions; as that of a surety, or that of an accommodation indorser. *Compare* Primary liability.

Secondary market. Securities exchanges and over-the-counter markets where securities are bought and sold after their original issue (which took place in the primary market). Proceeds of secondary market sales accrue to selling investors not to the company that originally issued the securities. *See also* Primary market.

Secondary meaning. Some words or other devices used as trademarks may not be distinctive when first adopted, but may acquire distinctiveness over time. When such a mark has come to signify that an item is produced or sponsored by a particular merchant it is said that the mark has secondary meaning. Types of marks requiring secondary meaning before they will be protected include (1) descriptive and misdescriptive terms; (2) geographically descriptive and misdescriptive terms and (3) surnames. Under the Lanham Act, five years of exclusive use of a mark is deemed prima facie evidence of secondary meaning.

Secondary mortgage market. A national market in which existing mortgages are bought and sold; usually on a package basis. Contrasts with the primary market where mortgages are originated.

Secondary offering. *See* Offering; Secondary distribution.

Secondary parties. Parties secondarily liable on negotiable instruments; a drawer or endorser. U.C.C. § 3–102(1)(d).

Secondary picketing. A form of picketing in which pressure is put on one business establishment with which there is no dispute in order to induce such business to put pressure on the business establishment with which the employees have a primary dispute. *See also* Secondary boycott; Secondary strike.

Secondary strike. A strike against firms which supply goods and materials to the firm with which there is a primary dispute. *See also* Secondary boycott.

Second degree crime. A crime of lesser gravity than a first degree crime. Some states have first, second and third degree crimes and the punishment for each varies according to the degree. *See e.g.* Second degree murder.

Second degree murder. The unlawful taking of human life with malice, but without the other aggravating elements of first degree murder; *i.e.* without deliberation or premeditation.

Second-hand evidence. Evidence which has passed through one or more media before reaching the witness; hearsay evidence. *See also* Circumstantial evidence; Hearsay; Secondary evidence.

Second lien. One which takes rank immediately after a first lien on the same property and is next entitled to satisfaction out of the proceeds.

Second mortgage. A mortgage on property which ranks in priority below a first mortgage. In title states, it is the transfer of the mortgagor's equity of redemption to secure a debt.

Secrecy. The quality or condition of being concealed or secret, as the proceedings of a grand jury are to be held in secrecy.

Secret. Concealed; hidden; not made public; particularly, in law, kept from the knowledge or notice of persons liable to be affected by the act, transaction, deed, or other thing spoken of. Something known only to one or a few and kept from others.

As to *secret* Committee; Equity; Partnership; and Trust, see those titles. *See also* Secrete; Trade secret.

Secretary. In reference to a corporation or association, refers to an officer charged with the direction and management of that part of the business of the company which is concerned with keeping the records, the official correspondence, with giving and receiving notices, countersigning documents, etc. Also known sometimes as clerk of the corporation.

Also a name given to several of the heads of executive departments in the government of the United States; as the "Secretary of State", "Secretary of the Interior," etc.

Secretary General. The chief administrative officer of the United Nations, who is nominated by the Security Council and elected by the General Assembly.

Secretary of Embassy. A diplomatic officer appointed as secretary or assistant to an ambassador or minister plenipotentiary.

Secretary of Legation. An officer employed to attend a foreign mission and to perform certain duties as clerk.

Secretary of State. The Secretary of State, as principal foreign policy adviser to the President, is responsible for the overall direction, coordination, and supervision of U.S. foreign relations and for the interdepartmental activities of the U.S. Government overseas. The Secretary is the first-ranking member of the Cabinet, a member of the National Security Council, and is in charge of the operations of the Department, including the Foreign Service.

In most state governments, the official who is responsible for many types of formal state business, such as the licensing of corporations, filing of security agreements, etc.

Secrete. To conceal or hide away. Particularly, to put property out of the reach of creditors, either by corporally hiding it, or putting the title in another's name, or otherwise hindering creditors from levying on it or attaching it. *See* Concealment.

Secret lien. A lien reserved by the vendor of chattels, who has delivered them to the vendee, to secure the payment of the price, which is concealed from all third persons.

Secret Service. The major powers and responsibilities of the U.S. Secret Service are defined in section 3056, Title 18, United States Code. The investigative responsibilities are to detect and arrest persons committing any offense against the laws of the United States relating to coins obligations, and securities of the United States and of foreign governments; and to detect and arrest persons violating certain laws relating to the Federal Deposit Insurance Corporation, Federal land banks, electronic fund transfer frauds, credit and debit card frauds, false identification documents. The protective responsibilities include protection of the President of the United States and the members of his immediate family; the President-elect and the members of his immediate family unless the members decline such protection; the Vice President or other officer next in the order of succession to the Office of the President, and the members of his immediate family unless the members decline such protection; the Vice President-elect, and the members of his immediate family unless the members decline such protection; a former President and his wife during his lifetime; the widow of a former President until her death or remarriage; the minor children of a former President until they reach 16 years of age, unless such protection is declined; a visiting head of a foreign state or foreign government and, at the direction of the President, other distinguished foreign visitors to the United States and official representatives of the United States performing special missions abroad. In addition, 18 U.S.C.A. § 3056 authorizes the Secret Service to protect major Presidential and Vice Presidential candidates, unless such protection is declined; the spouse of a major Presidential or Vice Presidential nominee, except that such protection shall not commence more than 120 days prior to the general Presidential election.

Section of land. A division or parcel of land, on the government survey, comprising one square mile or 640 acres. Each "township" (six miles square) is divided by straight lines into thirty-six sections, and these are again divided into half-sections and quarter-sections. *See also* Quarter section.

Secular. Not spiritual; not ecclesiastical; relating to affairs of the present (temporal) world.

Secundum /səkə́ndəm/. Lat. Next to; beside; immediately after. In the civil and common law, according to. Occurring in many Latin phrases and titles; *e.g. Corpus Juris Secundum.*

Secure. To give security; to assure of payment, performance, or indemnity; to guaranty or make certain the payment of a debt or discharge of an obligation. One "secures" his creditor by giving him a lien, mortgage, pledge, or other security, to be used in case the debtor fails to make payment.

Also, not exposed to danger; safe; so strong, stable or firm as to insure safety and financial security.

See also Security.

Secured. Supported or backed by security or collateral such as a secured debt for which property has been pledged or mortgaged. *See* Security.

Secured bond. Bond backed by collateral, mortgage, or other type of security. *Compare* Debenture.

Secured creditor. A creditor who holds some special pecuniary assurance of payment of his debt, such as a mortgage, collateral, or lien. *See* Secured party; Security interest.

Secured debt. Debt that identifies specific assets that can be taken over by the debtholder in case of default. *See also* Secured loan.

Secured loan. A loan for which some form of property has been pledged or mortgaged, as in the case of an automobile loan in which title to the vehicle is held as security by lender. *See* Collateral; Mortgage.

Secured party. A lender, seller or other person in whose favor there is a security interest, including a person to whom accounts or chattel paper have been sold. When the holders of obligations issued under an indenture of trust, equipment trust agreement or the like are represented by a trustee or other person, the representative is the secured party. Section 9–105(1)(m) of the 1972

U.C.C. Code; § 9–105(1)(i) of the 1962 U.C.C. Code. The term also includes the assignee of the right to proceeds under a letter of credit. U.C.C. § 5–116(2).

Secured transaction. Any transaction, regardless of its form, that is intended to create a security interest in personal property or fixtures, including goods, documents, and other intangibles. A transaction which is founded on a security agreement. Such agreement creates or provides for a security interest. U.C.C. § 9–105(h). *See* Security agreement.

Securities. Stocks, bonds, notes, convertible debentures, warrants, or other documents that represent a share in a company or a debt owed by a company or government entity. Evidences of obligations to pay money or of rights to participate in earnings and distribution of corporate assets. Instruments giving to their legal holders rights to money or other property; they are therefore instruments which have intrinsic value and are recognized and used as such in the regular channels of commerce.

See also Bond; Consolidated securities; Convertible securities; Debenture; Distribution; Federal agency securities; Growth stock; Letter stock; Listed security; Marketable securities; Municipal securities; Registration of securities; Security; Stock; Treasury stock; Watered stock. For marshalling of securities, *see* Marshalling assets.

Coupon securities. See Coupons.

Exempt securities. Those securities which need not be registered under provisions of Securities Act of 1933, § 3; 15 U.S.C.A. §§ 77c, 78c(12).

Securities Act of 1933. Federal law which provides for registration of securities which are to be sold to the public and for complete information as to the issuer and the stock offering. 15 U.S.C.A. § 77a *et seq. See also* Registration of securities; Securities Exchange Act of 1934.

Securities Acts. Federal and state statutes governing the registration, offering, sale, etc. of securities. Major federal acts include the Securities Act of 1933 and the Securities Exchange Act of 1934 *(q.v.).* Such federal acts are administered by the Securities and Exchange Commission. The majority of the states have adopted the Uniform Securities Act. *See* Registration of securities.

Securities and Exchange Commission. The federal agency which administers such laws as the Securities Act of 1933, the Securities Exchange Act of 1934, the Trust Indenture Act of 1939, the Public Utility Holding Company Act of 1935, the Investment Adviser's Act of 1940 and the Investment Company Act of 1940. 15 U.S.C.A. § 78(d).

Securities broker. *See* Broker.

Securities Exchange Act of 1934. A federal law which governs the operation of stock exchanges and over the counter trading. It requires, among other things, publication of information concerning stocks which are listed on these exchanges. 15 U.S.C.A. § 78 *et seq. See also* Securities Act of 1933.

Securities exchanges. Markets for the purchase and sale of traditional securities at which brokers for purchasers and sellers may affect transactions. The best known and largest securities exchange is the New York Stock Exchange.

Securities Investor Protection Act. Federal law which established Securities Investor Protection Corp., which, though not an agency of the U.S. Government, is designed to protect investors and help brokers and dealers in financial trouble. 15 U.S.C.A. §§ 78aaa *et seq.*

Securities offering. *See* Formula basis; Issue *(Securities);* Offering; Purchase-and-sale; Registration of securities; Underwrite.

Security. Protection; assurance; indemnification. The term is usually applied to an obligation, pledge, mortgage, deposit, lien, etc., given by a debtor in order to assure the payment or performance of his debt, by furnishing the creditor with a resource to be used in case of failure in the principal obligation. Collateral given by debtor to secure loan. Document that indicates evidence of indebtedness. The name is also sometimes given to one who becomes surety or guarantor for another.

Test for a "security" under securities laws is whether the scheme involves an investment of money in a common enterprise with profits to come solely from the efforts of others so that whenever an investor relinquishes control over his funds and submits their control to another for the purpose and hopeful expectation of deriving profits therefrom he is in fact investing his funds in a security. "Security" under Securities Act of 1933, means investment in common enterprise in which investors are purchasing interest and where growth of that investment is to result from efforts of promoter, and the label attached to the transaction is not determinative.

"Security" includes any note, stock, treasury stock, bond, debenture, evidence of indebtedness, certificate of interest or participation in an oil, gas or mining title or lease or in payments out of production under such a title or lease, collateral trust certificate, transferable share, voting trust certificate or, in general, any interest or instrument commonly known as a security, or any certificate of interest or participation, any temporary or interim certificate, receipt or certificate of deposit for, or any warrant or right to subscribe to or purchase, any of the foregoing. Uniform Probate Code, § 1–201.

For purposes of the Securities Act of 1933 and the Securities Exchange Act of 1934, the term "security" embraces all investment contracts, and the test is whether the investment is made in a common enterprise which is premised upon the reasonable expectation of profits solely from the managerial or entrepreneurial efforts of others; such test contains three elements: the investment of money; a common enterprise; and profits or returns derived solely from efforts of others. See 15 U.S.C.A. §§ 77b(1), 78c(10).

A note may be a security, and subject to federal securities laws, even if it has no fixed term and is payable on demand, depending on the economic realities of the transaction.

The term "security" means any bond, debenture, note or certificate or other evidence of indebtedness, issued by a corporation or a government or political subdivision thereof, with interest coupons or in registered form, share of stock, voting trust certificate, or any certificate of interest or participation in, certificate of deposit or receipt for, temporary or interim certificate for, or warrant or right to subscribe to or purchase, any of the foregoing; negotiable instrument; or money. I.R.C. § 6323(h)(4).

As defined in the Bankruptcy Code § 101, "security" includes: note, stock, treasury stock, bond, debenture, collateral trust certificate, preorganization certificate or subscription, transferable share, voting-trust certificate, certificate of deposit, investment contract or certificate of interest, etc.

Under the U.C.C. (§ 8–102), a security is either a "certificated" or "uncertificated" security. See these terms below.

See also Collateral; Equity security; Hybrid securities; Internal security acts; Investment security; Junior security issue; Lien; Listed security; Pledge; Risk capital test; Securities; Stock.

Assessable security. A security on which a charge or assessment for the obligations of the issuing company may be made. In many instances, bank and insurance company stocks are assessable.

Certificated security. A "certificated security" is a share, participation, or other interest in property of or an enterprise of the issuer or an obligation of the issuer which is (i) represented by an instrument issued in bearer or registered form; (ii) of a type commonly dealt in on securities exchanges or markets or commonly recognized in any area in which it is issued or dealt in as a medium for investment; and (iii) either one of a class or series or by its terms divisible into a class or series of shares, participations, interests, or obligations. U.C.C. § 8–102(1)(a).

Collateral security. Property which has been pledged or mortgaged to secure a loan or a sale.

Convertible security. See Convertible securities.

Equity security. The term "equity security" means any stock or similar security; or any security convertible, with or without consideration, into such a security; or carrying any warrant or right to subscribe to or purchase such a security; or any such warrant or right; or any other security which the Securities and Exchange Commission shall deem to be of similar nature and consider necessary or appropriate, by such rules and regulations as it may prescribe in the public interest or for the protection of investors, to treat as an equity security. Securities Exchange Act, § 3; 15 U.S.C.A. § 78c(11).

(A) share in a corporation, whether or not transferable or denominated "stock", or similar security; (B) interest of a limited partner in a limited partnership; or (C) warrant or right, other than a right to convert, to purchase, sell, or subscribe to a share, security, or interest of a kind specified in subparagraph (A) or (B) of this paragraph. Bankruptcy Code § 101.

Exempted security. A security which is not required to be registered under the provisions of the Securities Exchange Act. 15 U.S.C.A. §§ 77c, 78c(12).

Government security. Any security issued or guaranteed as to principal or interest by the United States, or by a person controlled or supervised by and acting as an instrumentality of the Government of the United States pursuant to authority granted by the Congress of the United States; or any certificate of deposit for any of the foregoing. Investment Company Act, § 2; 15 U.S.C.A. § 80a–2(a)(16).

Hybrid security. A security which combines features of both debt and equity; *i.e.* of both bond and stock. *See also* Hybrid securities.

Junior security. Security with priority claim on assets and income subordinate to senior security.

Listed security. A security which has been listed for trading on one of the stock exchanges or which has been listed with the Securities and Exchange Commission.

Marketable security. A security which is of reasonable investment caliber and which can be easily sold on the market.

Non-marketable security. A security which cannot be sold on the market such as certain government bonds and notes. It can only be redeemed by the holder. Also, a security which is not of investment quality.

Outstanding security. A security which is held by an investor and which has not been redeemed or purchased back by the issuing corporation.

Personal security. An obligation to repay a debt evidenced by a pledge, note or bond in contrast to

collateral security. Evidences of debt which bind the person of the debtor, not real property.

Public security. Bonds, notes, certificates of indebtedness, and other negotiable or transferable instruments evidencing the public debt of a state or government.

Real security. The security of mortgages or other liens or encumbrances upon land. *See also* Collateral; Mortgage.

Redeemable security. Any security, other than short-term paper, under the terms of which the holder upon its presentation to the issuer or to a person designated by the issuer, is entitled (whether absolutely or only out of surplus) to receive approximately his proportionate share of the issuer's current net assets, or the cash equivalent thereof. Investment Company Act, § 2; 15 U.S.C.A. § 80a–2(a)(32).

Security for costs. *See* Security for costs.

Security for good behavior. A bond or recognizance which the magistrate exacts from a defendant brought before him on a charge of disorderly conduct or threatening violence, conditioned upon his being of good behavior, or keeping the peace, for a prescribed period, towards all people in general and the complainant in particular. A peace bond.

Senior security. A security with rights that take precedence over those of other securities in a given capital structure.

Short term security. A bond or note which matures in and is payable within a short span of time. Such securities are purchased by institutional investors for income rather than for growth potential.

Treasury securities. *See* Treasury stock.

Uncertificated security. An "uncertificated security" is a share, participation, or other interest in property or an enterprise of the issuer or an obligation of the issuer which is (i) not represented by an instrument and the transfer of which is registered upon books maintained for that purpose by or on behalf of the issuer; (ii) of a type commonly dealt in on securities exchanges or markets; and (iii) either one of a class or series or by its terms divisible into a class or series of shares, participations, interests, or obligations. U.C.C. § 8–102(1)(b).

Unlisted security. An over the counter security which is not listed on a stock exchange.

Voting security. Any security presently entitling the owner or holder thereof to vote for the election of directors of a company. Investment Company Act, § 2; 15 U.S.C.A. § 80a–2(a)(42).

Security agreement. An agreement which creates or provides for a security interest between the debtor and a secured party. U.C.C. § 9–105(h); Bankruptcy Code § 101. An agreement granting a creditor a security interest in personal property, which security interest is normally perfected either by the creditor taking possession of the collateral or by filing financing statements in the proper public records. *See* Perfection of security interest; Purchase money security interest; Secured transaction; Security interest.

Security Council. The executive body of the United Nations, charged with the duty of preventing or stopping wars by diplomatic, economic or military action. It is composed of five permanent members and six additional members elected at stated intervals.

Security deposit. Money deposited by tenant with landlord as security for full and faithful performance by tenant of terms of lease, including damages to premises. It is refundable unless the tenant has caused damage or injury to the property or has breached the terms of the tenancy or the laws governing the tenancy. Such deposits are regulated by statute in most states. Certain states also require the landlord to make a security deposit to cover essential repairs required on rental property.

Security for costs. Payment into court in the form of cash, property or bond by a plaintiff or an appellant to secure the payment of costs if such person does not prevail; *e.g.* Fed.R.Civ.P. 65(c) requires adequate security when restraining order or preliminary injunction is issued.

Security fund. *See* Client security fund.

Security interest. Interest in property obtained pursuant to security agreement. A form of interest in property which provides that the property may be sold on default in order to satisfy the obligation for which the security interest is given. A mortgage is used to grant a security interest in real property. An interest in personal property or fixtures which secures payment or performance of an obligation, U.C.C. §§ 1–201(37), 9–102, including the interest of an assignee of the proceeds of a letter of credit, § 5–116(2). Lien created by an agreement. Bankruptcy Code § 101.

Often, the term "lien" is used as a synonym, although lien most commonly refers only to interests providing security that are created by operation of law, not through agreement of the debtor and creditor. *Compare* Lien.

In tax law, means any interest in property acquired by contract for the purpose of securing payment or performance of an obligation or indemnifying against loss or liability. A security interest exists at any time, (A) if, at such time, the property is in existence and the interest has become protected under local law against a subsequent judgment lien arising out of an unsecured

obligation, and (B) to the extent that, at such time, the holder has parted with money or money's worth. I.R.C. § 6323(h).

Purchase money security interest. A secured interest which is created when a buyer uses the money of the lender to make the purchase and immediately gives to the lender a security interest. U.C.C. § 9–107. *See* Mortgage *(Purchase money mortgage).*

Sedimentation. The deposition of soil that has been transported from its site of origin by water, ice, wind, gravity or other natural means as a product of erosion.

Sedition. Communication or agreement which has as its objective the stirring up of treason or certain lesser commotions, or the defamation of the government. Sedition is advocating, or with knowledge of its contents knowingly publishing, selling or distributing any document which advocates, or, with knowledge of its purpose, knowingly becoming a member of any organization which advocates the overthrow or reformation of the existing form of government of this state by violence or unlawful means. An insurrectionary movement tending towards treason, but wanting an overt act; attempts made by meetings or speeches, or by publications, to disturb the tranquillity of the state. See 18 U.S.C.A. § 2383 *et seq. See also* Alien and sedition laws; Smith Act.

Seditious conspiracy. Under federal statute, it is a crime for two or more persons in any State or Territory to conspire to overthrow or put down or destroy by force the Government of the United States. 18 U.S.C.A. § 2384.

Seditious libel. A communication written with the intent to incite the people to change the government otherwise than by lawful means, or to advocate the overthrow of the government by force or violence. Smith Act, 18 U.S.C.A. § 2385. *See* Alien and sedition laws.

Seduce. To induce to surrender chastity. To lead away or astray. *See also* Seduction.

Seduction. The act of seducing. Act of man enticing woman to have unlawful intercourse with him by means of persuasion, solicitation, promises, bribes or other means without employment of force. See *e.g.* Model Penal Code § 213.3(1)(d) (inducement by promise of marriage). Many statutes provide that a subsequent marriage is a bar to prosecution. Also, by statute in some states, actions for seduction of a person over age of legal consent are prohibited. *See* Heart balm statutes.

Seed money. A venture capitalist's initial contribution toward the financing or capital requirements of a new business. Seed money frequently takes the form of a subordinated loan or an investment in convertible bonds or convertible preferred shares. Seed money provides the basis for additional capitalization to accommodate growth. *See also* Venture capital.

Segmented market. A market in which participants provide or demand products with only certain attributes; for example, debt of a particular maturity, firms with a particular capital structure, or firms with a particular dividend policy.

Segment reporting. In accounting, the disclosure of selected information when a company is involved in several distinct business activities.

Segregation. The act or process of separation. The unconstitutional policy and practice of separating people on the basis of color, nationality, religion, etc. in housing and schooling. *See* De facto segregation; De jure segregation.

Seisin /síyzən/. Possession of real property under claim of freehold estate. The completion of the feudal investiture, by which the tenant was admitted into the feud, and performed the rights of homage and fealty. Possession with an intent on the part of him who holds it to claim a freehold interest. Right to immediate possession according to the nature of the estate.

Actual seisin. Possession of the freehold by the *pedis positio* of one's self or one's tenant or agent, or by construction of law, as in the case of a state grant or a conveyance under the statutes of uses, or (probably) of grant or devise where there is no actual adverse possession; it means actual possession as distinguished from constructive possession or possession in law.

Constructive seisin. Seisin in law where there is no seisin in fact; as where the state issues a patent to a person who never takes any sort of possession of the lands granted, he has constructive seisin of all the land in his grant, though another person is at the time in actual possession.

Covenant of seisin. *See* Covenant.

Equitable seisin. A seisin which is analogous to legal seisin; that is, seisin of an equitable estate in land. Thus a mortgagor is said to have equitable seisin of the land by receipt of the rents.

Livery of seisin. Delivery of possession; called "investiture." *See* Livery of seisin.

Seisin in deed. Actual possession of the freehold; the same as actual seisin or seisin in fact.

Seisin in fact. Possession with intent on the part of him who holds it to claim a freehold interest; the same as actual seisin.

Seisin in law. A right of immediate possession according to the nature of the estate. As the old doctrine of corporeal investiture is no longer in force, the delivery of a deed gives seisin in law.

Seize /síyz/. To put in possession, invest with fee simple, be seized of or in, be legal possessor of, or

be holder in fee simple. To "seize" means to take possession of forcibly, to grasp, to snatch or to put in possession. *See* Seisin.

Seized. A person is "seized" within Fourth Amendment when police officer restrains person's freedom to walk away. It exists when reasonable person would feel that he was not free to leave. *See* Seizure.

The status of legally owning and possessing real estate. *See* Seisin.

Seizin /síyzən/. *See* Seisin.

Seizure. The act of taking possession of property, *e.g.,* for a violation of law or by virtue of an execution of a judgment. Term implies a taking or removal of something from the possession, actual or constructive, of another person or persons.

The act performed by an officer of the law, under the authority and exigence of a writ, in taking into the custody of the law the property, real or personal, of a person against whom the judgment of a competent court has passed, condemning him to pay a certain sum of money, in order that such property may be sold, by authority and due course of law, to satisfy the judgment. Or the act of taking possession of goods in consequence of a violation of public law.

A "seizure" of property (under Fourth Amendment) occurs when there is some meaningful interference with an individual's possessory interest in that property.

Seizure of an individual, within the Fourth Amendment, connotes the taking of one physically or constructively into custody and detaining him, thus causing a deprivation of his freedom in a significant way, with real interruption of his liberty of movement. Such occurs not only when an officer arrests an individual, but whenever he restrains the individual's freedom to walk away. See Fed.R.Crim.P. 41; 18 U.S.C.A. § 3101 et seq. *See also* Search.

See also Attachment; Capture; Confiscate; Forfeiture; Garnishment; Impound; Levy.

"Search" distinguished. A "search" is a probing or exploration for something that is concealed or hidden from the searcher, whereas a "seizure" is a forcible or secretive dispossession of something against the will of the possessor or owner. *See also* Search.

Select. To take by preference from among others; to pick out; to cull.

Select council. The name given, in some states, to the upper house or branch of the council of a city.

Selective service system. An executive branch agency charged with the registration, examination, classification, selection, assignment, delivery for induction, and maintenance of records of persons subject to military service. It is maintained as an active standby organization when military personnel needs are met by a volunteer program. 50 U.S.C.A.App. § 460.

Selectmen. The name of certain municipal officers, in the New England states, elected by the towns to transact their general public business, and possessing certain executive powers.

Self-dealing. Exists where person in fiduciary or confidential relationship uses property of another for his own personal benefit. For example, where a trustee, acting for himself and also as "trustee," a relation which demands strict fidelity to others, seeks to consummate a deal wherein self-interest is opposed to duty. Cestui que trust has in such case the election to affirm or disaffirm, unless countervailing equities have intervened. *See also* Conflict of interest; Insider; Insider trading.

Self-defense. The protection of one's person or property against some injury attempted by another. The right of such protection. An excuse for the use of force in resisting an attack on the person.

Various state criminal statutes define the conditions of self defense. The Model Penal Code provides: "A person is justified in the use of force against an aggressor when and to the extent it appears to him and he reasonably believes that such conduct is necessary to defend himself or another against such aggressor's imminent use of unlawful force. One who is not the aggressor in an encounter is justified in using a reasonable amount of force against his adversary when he reasonably believes: (a) that he is in immediate danger of unlawful bodily harm from his adversary and (b) that the use of such force is necessary to avoid this danger. It may be reasonable to use nondeadly force against the adversary's nondeadly attack (*i.e.*, one threatening only bodily harm), and to use deadly force against his deadly attack (an attack threatening death or serious bodily harm), but it is never reasonable to use deadly force against his nondeadly attack." Model Penal Code § 3.04.

The principles of self-defense as a justification for the torts or assault and battery are very similar to those governing self-defense as a justification in the criminal law. See Restatement, Second, Torts, §§ 633, 65, 67 (1965).

See also Apparent danger; Defense of others; Imminent danger; Justification; Reasonable force; Retreat to the wall.

Self–Employment Retirement Plan. A designation for retirement plans available to self-employed taxpayers. Also referred to as H.R. 10 and Keogh plans. *See* Keogh Plan.

Self-employment tax. The social security tax imposed on the net earnings of a self-employed individual. The self-employment tax is assessed in addition to an income tax up to an annual maximum, which is reduced by any wages previously subject to social security taxes.

Self-executing. Anything (*e.g.*, a document or legislation) which is effective immediately without the need of intervening court action, ancillary legislation, or other type of implementing action.

Self-executing constitutional provision. Term has reference to provisions which are immediately effective without the necessity of ancillary legislation. Constitutional provision is "self-executing" if it supplies sufficient rule by which right given may be enjoyed or duty imposed enforced; constitutional provision is not "self-executing" when it merely indicates principles without laying down rules giving them force of law.

Self-executing judgments. Those requiring no affirmative action of the court or action under process issued by the court to execute them.

Self-help. Taking an action in person or by a representative outside of the normal legal process with legal consequences, whether the action is legal or not. For example, a "self-help eviction" may be a landlord's removing the tenant's property from an apartment and locking the door against the tenant; or tenant might utilize "self-help" by making necessary repairs that landlord refuses to make and deduct such costs from rent (see *e.g.* Uniform Residential Landlord & Tenant Act). Self-help repossession (*i.e.* without judicial process) of goods by creditor on default is permitted under U.C.C. § 9–503, if such can be done "without breach of the peace."

Self-incrimination. Acts or declarations either as testimony at trial or prior to trial by which one implicates himself in a crime. The Fifth Amendment, U.S.Const., as well as provisions in many state constitutions and laws, prohibit the government from requiring a person to be a witness against himself involuntarily or to furnish evidence against himself. It is the burden of the government to accuse and to carry the burden of proof of guilt. The defendant cannot be compelled to aid the government in this regard. See 18 U.S.C.A. § 6001 et seq. *See also* Compulsory self-incrimination; Link-in-chain; Privilege against self-incrimination; Taking the Fifth.

Self-insurance. The practice of setting aside a fund to meet losses instead of insuring against such through insurance. A common practice of business is to self-insure up to a certain amount, and then to cover any excess with insurance. Workers' compensation obligations may also be met through this method if statutory requirements are met.

Self-murder, self-destruction, *or* **self-slaughter.** *See* Suicide.

Self serving declaration. A species of hearsay evidence consisting of an extrajudicial declaration by a party to an action, the import of which is to prove an essential element of his case. Such statements are inadmissible unless they fall under a recognized category of exception to the hearsay rule such as a business entry, declaration of a deceased party, etc., or unless they are offered for a non-hearsay purpose such as the fact that the party made the statement and not for the truth of the statement. Statement, oral or written, or equivalent act, by or on behalf of a party which if admitted would constitute evidence in his favor. See Fed.Evid.R. 803.

Sell. To dispose of by sale (q.v.). To transfer title or possession of property to another in exchange for valuable consideration.

Seller. Vendor; one who has contracted to sell property. A person who sells or contracts to sell goods. U.C.C. § 2–103(1)(d).

One who sells anything; the party who transfers property in the contract of sale. The correlative is "buyer," or "purchaser." These terms are, however, generally not used in reference to the persons concerned in a transfer of real estate, it being more customary to use "vendor" and "purchaser," or "vendee" in that case.

Test of whether a person is a "seller" of unregistered securities, so as to be liable to the buyer under the Securities Act, is whether such person is the "proximate cause" of the sale.

Seller's market. A description of a market in which there is more demand for a security, product, or property than there is available supply. Prices rise in a seller's market.

Selling stocks short. See Short sale.

Sell order. A directive to broker to sell one or more financial securities.

Semble. L. Fr. It seems; it would appear. This expression is often used in the reports to preface a statement by the court upon a point of law which is not directly decided, when such statement is intended as an intimation of what the decision would be if the point were necessary to be passed upon. It is also used to introduce a suggestion by the reporter, or his understanding of the point decided when it is not free from obscurity.

Semper /sémpǝr/. Lat. Always. A word which introduces several Latin maxims, of which some are also used without this prefix.

Senate. The name of the upper chamber, or less numerous branch, of the Congress of the United States. Also the name of a similar body in the legislatures of most of the states.

The U.S. Senate is composed of 100 Members, 2 from each State, who are elected to serve for a term of 6 years. Senators were originally chosen by the State legislatures. This procedure was changed by the Seventeenth Amendment to the Constitution, adopted in 1913, which made the election of Senators a function of the people. One-third of the Senate is elected every 2 years.

Senator. One who is a member of a senate, either of the United States or of a state. See Seventeenth Amendment.

Send. Term in connection with any writing or notice means to deposit in the mail or deliver for transmission by any other usual means of communication with postage or cost of transmission provided for and properly addressed and in the case of an instrument to an address specified thereon or otherwise agreed, or if there be none, to any address reasonable under the circumstances. The receipt of any writing or notice within the time at which it would have arrived if properly sent has the effect of a proper sending. U.C.C. § 1–201(38).

Senior. The elder. An addition to the name of the elder of two persons in the same family having the same name.

With reference to debt or security interests, means preference over junior obligations as to claims and payment; e.g. first or senior mortgage.

Senior counsel. Of two or more counsel retained on the same side of a cause, he is the "senior" who is the elder, or more important in rank or estimation, or who is charged with the more difficult or important parts of the management of the case. May also refer to "lead" counsel in a class or multi-district action.

Senior interest. A debt security or preferred share that has a claim prior to that of junior obligations or common shares on a corporation's assets and earnings. An interest or right that takes effect or has preference over that of others; e.g. a person with a perfected security interest has a senior interest over other security holders in same property. Compare Junior interest.

Seniority. Precedence or preference in position over others similarly situated. As used, for example, with reference to job seniority, worker with most years of service is first promoted within range of jobs subject to seniority, and is the last laid off, proceeding so on down the line to the youngest in point of service. Term may also refer to the priority of a lien or encumbrance. See also Dovetail seniority; Priority.

Seniority system. Any system or arrangement which recognizes length of service in promotions, layoffs, etc.

Senior judge. Of several judges composing a court, the one who holds the oldest commission, or who has served the longest time under his present commission. A judge in the federal system who qualifies for senior status and who chooses such status rather than retirement; e.g. senior judge of

U.S. District Court or Court of Appeals. See 28 U.S.C.A. § 136.

Senior lien. A prior lien which has precedence as to the property under the lien over another lien or encumbrance. *Compare* Junior lien. *See also* Senior interest.

Senior mortgage. A mortgage which is of superior priority over others; above those which are often referred to as junior mortgages. *Compare* Junior mortgage.

Sentence. The judgment formally pronounced by the court or judge upon the defendant after his conviction in a criminal prosecution, imposing the punishment to be inflicted, usually in the form of a fine, incarceration, or probation. See *e.g.* 18 U.S.C.A. § 3551. Judgment of court formally advising accused of legal consequences of guilt which he has confessed or of which he has been convicted. Sentencing may be carried out by a judge, jury, or sentencing council (panel or judges), depending on the statutes of the jurisdiction. The word is properly confined to criminal proceedings. In *Civil* cases, the terms "judgment," "decision," "award," "finding," etc., are used.

For review of sentence of federal prisoner, *see* Post-conviction remedies.

See also Accumulative sentence; Community service; Commutation; Concurrent sentences; Consecutive sentences; Cumulative sentence; Definite sentence; Diversion program; Jail credit; Mitigation of punishment; Pardon; Pre-sentence hearing; Pre-sentence investigation; Pre-sentence report; Probation; Punishment; Reprieve; Sentencing; Sentencing guidelines; Split sentence; Suspended sentence.

Concurrent sentence. A sentence imposed which is to be served at the same time as another sentence imposed earlier or at the same proceeding.

Consecutive sentence. See *Cumulative sentences, below.*

Cumulative sentences. Separate sentences (each additional to the others) imposed upon a defendant who has been convicted upon an indictment containing several counts, each of such counts charging a distinct offense, or who is under conviction at the same time for several distinct offenses; one of such sentences being made to begin at the expiration of another.

Deferred sentence. A sentence, the execution of which is postponed until a future time.

Definite sentence. Sentence set by law with no discretion for the judge or correctional officials to individualize punishment. *See Fixed sentence, below.*

Determinate sentence. A sentence for a fixed period of time. *Also* called *Definite sentence, above.* See *Fixed sentence, below.*

Final sentence. One which puts an end to a case. Distinguished from interlocutory.

A definite sentence is one which puts an end to the suit, and regards the principal matter in question as concluded. An interlocutory sentence determines only some incidental matter in the proceedings.

Fixed sentence. Fixed sentencing statutes specify the exact penalty that will follow conviction of each offense. *See Mandatory sentence, below.* See *also* Sentencing guidelines.

Indeterminate (indefinite) sentence. A form of sentence to imprisonment upon conviction of crime, authorized by statute in several states, which, instead of fixing rigidly the duration of the imprisonment, declares that it shall be for a period "not less than" so many years "nor more than" so many years, or not less than the minimum period prescribed by statute as the punishment for the particular offense nor more than the maximum period, the exact length of the term being afterwards fixed, within the limits assigned by the court or the statute, by an executive authority (the governor, board of pardons, etc.), on consideration of the previous record of the convict, his behavior while in prison or while out on parole, the apparent prospect of reformation and other such considerations. *See also Presumptive sentence, below.*

A sentence to incarceration with a spread of time between a minimum date of parole eligibility and a maximum discharge date. A completely indeterminate sentence has a minimum of one day and a maximum of natural life.

Interlocutory sentence. A temporary sentence imposed pending final sentencing. In the civil law, a sentence on some indirect question arising from the principal cause.

Life sentence. The disposition of a serious criminal case (*e.g.* capital offenses) by which the convicted defendant is sentenced to spend the rest of his natural life in prison.

Mandatory sentence. Statutes in some jurisdictions require a judge to sentence a convicted defendant to a penal institution for a prescribed time for the specific crime and furnish little or no room for discretion. These statutes generally provide that the sentence may not be suspended and that no probation may be imposed, leaving the judge with no alternative but commitment. *See Fixed sentence, above,* and Sentencing guidelines.

Maximum sentence. A maximum sentence sets the outer limit beyond which a prisoner cannot be held in custody.

Merger of sentences. See Merger.

Minimum sentence. The minimum time which an offender must spend in prison before becoming eligible for parole or release.

Presumptive sentence. A sentence in which the judge is given guidelines that control the extent of the prison term. There is a presumptive average sentence for each type of offense which can be raised or lowered depending on the presence of mitigating or aggravating circumstances. *See also Indeterminate (indefinite) sentence, above.*

Sentence in absentia. Sentencing of defendant in his absence.

Split sentence. A sentence in which part of the time is served in confinement and the balance is served on probation or on terms imposed by the court. *See also* Split sentence.

Straight or flat sentence. Fixed sentence without a maximum or minimum.

Suspension of sentence. This term may mean either a withholding or postponing the sentencing of a prisoner after the conviction, or a postponing of the execution of the sentence after it has been pronounced. In the latter case, it may, for reasons addressing themselves to the discretion of the court, be indefinite as to time, or during the good behavior of the prisoner. *See* Suspended sentence.

Withheld sentence. Sentence not imposed.

Sentencing. The postconviction stage of the criminal justice process in which the defendant is brought before the court for imposition of sentence. Usually a trial judge imposes sentence, but in some jurisdictions sentencing is performed by jury or by sentencing councils.

For federal crimes, an individual may be sentenced either to a term of probation, a term of imprisonment, or be required to pay a fine. 18 U.S.C.A. § 3551.

Sentencing has been held to be a "critical stage" of a criminal proceeding requiring assistance of appointed counsel.

See also Fatico hearing; Pre-sentence hearing; Pre-sentence investigation; Pre-sentence report; Sentencing guidelines; Victim impact statement.

Imposition of sentence. Sentence shall be imposed without unreasonable delay. Before imposing sentence, the court shall afford counsel an opportunity to speak on behalf of the defendant and shall address the defendant personally and ask him if he wishes to make a statement in his own behalf and to present any information in mitigation of punishment. The attorney for the government shall have an equivalent opportunity to speak to the court. Fed.R.Crim.P. 32(a).

For federal crimes, the court, in determining the particular sentence to be imposed, shall consider: the nature and circumstances of the offense and the history and characteristics of the defendant; the need for the sentence imposed; and the kinds and sentencing range established under the sentencing guidelines. 18 U.S.C.A. § 3553. *See also* Sentencing guidelines.

Sentencing council. A panel of three or more judges which confers to determine a criminal sentence. Sentencing councils are not as commonly used as sentencing by a trial judge.

Sentencing guidelines. Guidelines established by the U.S. Sentencing Commission to be followed by federal courts in the sentencing of those convicted of federal offenses. The Guidelines prescribe a range of sentences for each class of convicted persons as determined by categories of offense behavior and offender characteristics. 18 U.S.C.A. § 3551 et seq. Mistretta v. U.S., 109 S.Ct. 647, 102 L.Ed.2d 714.

Sentencing hearings. *See* Pre-sentencing hearing.

Sententia /senténsh(iy)ə/. Lat. In the civil law, sense; import; as distinguished from mere words. The deliberate expression of one's will or intention. The sentence of a judge or court.

SEP. *See* Simplified Employee Pension Plan.

Separability clause. A clause commonly found in contracts which provides that in the event that one or more provisions are declared void the balance of the contract remains in force. Such a provision is also commonly found in legislation. *See also* Saving clause; Severable contract; Severable statute.

Separable. Capable of being separated, disjoined, or divided.

Separable controversy. With respect to removal of case from state to federal court, 28 U.S.C.A. § 1441(c) provides: "Whenever a separate and independent claim or cause of action, which would be removable if sued upon alone, is joined with one or more otherwise non-removable claims or causes of action, the entire case may be removed and the district court may determine all issues therein, or, in its discretion, may remand all matters not otherwise within its original jurisdiction."

Separate, *v.* To disunite, divide, disconnect, or sever. *See* Sever.

Separate. Individual; distinct; particular; disconnected. Generally used in law as opposed to "joint," though the more usual antithesis of the latter term is "several." Either of these words implies division, distribution, disconnection, or aloofness. As to *separate* Acknowledgment and Covenant, see those titles.

Separate action. As opposed to a *joint* action, an action brought alone by each of several complainants who are all concerned in the same transaction, but cannot legally join in the suit. *See also* Joinder; Separate trial.

Separate but equal doctrine. The doctrine first enunciated in Plessy v. Ferguson, 163 U.S. 537, 16 S.Ct. 1138, 41 L.Ed. 256, to the effect that equality of treatment is accorded when the races are provided substantially equal facilities even though these facilities be separate. This rule was declared to be unconstitutional with respect to educational facilities in Brown v. Board of Education, etc., 347 U.S. 483, 74 S.Ct. 686, 98 L.Ed. 873, and as to other public facilities by other Supreme Court decisions and by various Civil Rights Acts.

Separate counts. Two or more criminal charges contained within one indictment, each count, in actuality, constituting a separate indictment for which the accused may be tried.

Separate estate. The individual property of one of two persons who stand in a marital or business relation, as distinguished from that which they own jointly or are jointly interested in. *See also* Community property; Separate property.

Separate maintenance. Money paid by one married person to the other for support if they are no longer living as husband and wife. Commonly it is referred to as separate support and follows from a court order. *See also* Alimony; Support.

Separate offenses. A person may be tried, convicted and sentenced for offenses which, though sharing many elements, are distinct. A particular act may offend more than one law and hence a person may be subjected to more than one punishment for acts arising out of the same event.

Separate property. Property owned by married person in his or her own right during marriage. State statutes commonly protect such separate property rights of each spouse. See e.g. Mass. Gen.L.A. c. 209, § 1. *See also Separate and marital property, below.*

Under statute governing distribution of property in marital dissolution proceeding includes property owned before marriage and maintained in separate names during marriage, property acquired during marriage solely from exchange of premarriage property and separately retained, any increase in value of separate property, gift or inheritance received and separately held, and property described in statute. *See* Equitable distribution.

Community property. In a community property jurisdiction, separate property is that property which belongs entirely to one of the spouses. Generally, it is property acquired before marriage or acquired after marriage by gift or inheritance. For purposes of community property settlement, "separate property" consists of all property brought to marriage by either spouse or acquired during marriage by gift, bequest, devise or de-

scent, together with its rents, issues and profits. *See also* Community property.

Separate and marital property. A number of state divorce statutes use the concept of separate and marital property for purposes of dividing assets of the spouses on divorce. Such statutes generally define separate property as those assets owned by either spouse prior to the marriage and those acquired afterwards by gift, devise, or exchange for other separate property, and as marital property all assets acquired by either spouse during marriage except those which can be shown to be separate. On divorce, the court is required to set aside to each spouse his or her separate property, and make an equitable division of marital property.

Separate return. *See* Tax return.

Separate support. *See* Separate maintenance.

Separate trial. The separate and individual trial of each of several persons jointly accused of a crime. Fed.R.Crim.P. 14. Court may also order separate trials in civil actions (*e.g.* Fed.R.Civil P. 42) in furtherance of convenience or to avoid prejudice, or when separate trials will be conducive to expedition and economy. *Compare* Bifurcated trial; Severance of actions *or* claims.

Separation. The living apart of a husband and wife. If court ordered it is a "legal separation," in which event the details of support and maintenance are often spelled out specifically in a document issued by the court.

Separation agreement. Written arrangements concerning custody, child support, alimony and property division made by a married couple who are usually about to get a divorce or legal separation.

Separation a mensa et thoro /sèpəréyshən èy ménsə èt θórow/. A partial dissolution of the marriage relation.

Separation from bed and board. A species of separation not amounting to a dissolution of the marriage. Same as separation a mensa et thoro (*q.v.*).

Separation of jury. After a case has been given to the jury for deliberation, they are not permitted to separate until a verdict is reached except under the control of the court through officers and sheriffs. In civil cases in some jurisdictions this rule is relaxed generally with admonition from the judge not to discuss the case with anybody. *See also* Sequester.

Separation of powers. The governments of states and the United States are divided into three departments or branches: the legislative, which is empowered to make laws, the executive which is required to carry out the laws, and the judicial which is charged with interpreting the laws and adjudicating disputes under the laws. Under this constitutional doctrine of "separation of powers, one branch is not permitted to encroach on the domain or exercise the powers of another branch. See U.S. Constitution, Articles I–III. *See also* Power *(Constitutional powers)*.

Separation of spouses. A cessation of cohabitation of husband and wife by mutual agreement, or, in the case of "judicial separation," under the decree of a court. Separation of spouses for a statutorily prescribed period is a prerequisite to "no-fault" divorce in many states. *See also* Living separate and apart; Separation agreement; Separation order.

Separation of witnesses. An order of the court requiring all witnesses, except the plaintiff and defendant, to remain outside the courtroom until each is called to testify.

Separation order. In domestic relations law, a decree or judgment of a court authorizing spouses to separate and generally included is an order respecting custody of children and support.

Sequester, *v.* To separate or isolate; *e.g.* to sequester jurors is to isolate them from contact with the public during the course of a sensational trial. *See* Jury.

Sequestered account. In accounting, an account which has been ordered separated and impounded by order of the court. No disbursements may be made from this account without order of the court.

Sequestration /sèkwəstréyshən/siy°/. In general, the process by which property or funds are attached pending the outcome of litigation. The separation or removal of property from the person in possession, pending some further action or proceedings affecting the property. *See also* Sequester.

Term is also used to refer to impoundment or stoppage of use of budget funds by governmental agencies as a result of, for example, spending restrictions. *See* Gramm-Rudman-Hollings amendment.

Debtor-creditor relations. In the law of creditors' rights, most often refers to an equitable form of attachment, although occasionally used (or misused) to identify a replevin-like process; very broad meaning implies any setting aside of a person's property to answer for the demands of another.

Jury. See Jury; Sequester.

Sequestrator /sékwəstrèyər/síy°/. One to whom a sequestration is made. One appointed or chosen to perform a sequestration, or execute a writ of sequestration.

Serf. In the feudal polity, a class of persons whose social condition was servile, and who were bound to labor and perform onerous duties at the will of their lords. They differed from slaves only in that they were bound to their native soil, instead of being the absolute property of a master.

Sergeant-at-arms. Officer appointed by, and attending on, a legislative body or court, whose principal duties are to preserve order during the sessions of such body.

Serial bonds. A serial bond issue consists of a number of bonds issued at the same time but with different maturity dates (serially due), usually with interest rates varying for the different maturity dates. To be distinguished from the *series bonds (q.v.)*. An issue of bonds that mature in part on one date, another part on another date, and so on; the various maturity dates usually are equally spaced. *Compare* Series bonds.

Serial note. A promissory note payable in installments.

Serial right. A right reserved in a publishing contract between author and publisher giving the author or publisher the right to have the manuscript published in installments in a magazine or periodical before or after the publication of the book.

Series bonds. Groups of bonds (for example, series A, series B) usually issued at different times and with different maturities but under the authority of the same indenture. To be distinguished from *serial bonds (q.v.)*.

Serious. Important; weighty; momentous, grave, great, as in the phrases "serious bodily harm," "serious personal injury," etc.

Serious crime. For purpose of determining right to jury trial, crimes carrying more than six-month sentences are "serious crimes" and those carrying less are "petty crimes." *See* Felony.

Serious illness. In life insurance, an illness that permanently or materially impairs, or is likely to permanently or materially impair, the health of the applicant. Not every illness is serious. An illness may be alarming at the time, or thought to be serious by the one afflicted, and yet not be serious in the sense of that term as used in insurance contracts. An illness that is temporary in its duration, and entirely passes away, and is not attended, nor likely to be attended, by a permanent or material impairment of the health or constitution, is not a serious illness. It is not sufficient that the illness was thought serious at the time it occurred, or that it might have resulted in permanently impairing the health.

Serjeant-at-arms. *See* Sergeant-at-arms.

Serrated. Notched on the edge; cut in notches like the teeth of a saw. This was anciently the method of trimming the top or edge of a deed of indenture. *See* Indent, *v.*

Servant. An employee. One employed to perform service in master's affairs, whose physical conduct in performance of the service is controlled or is subject to right to control by the master. Restatement, Second, Agency, § 2. A person in the employ of another and subject to his control as to what work shall be done and the means by which it shall be accomplished. One who is employed to render personal service to another otherwise than in the pursuit of an independent calling, and who, in such service, remains entirely under control and direction of employer. A person of whatever rank or position in employ and subject to direction or control of another in any department of labor or business. A servant, for purposes of doctrine of vicarious liability, is one who is employed to perform services for another, and who is subject to such other's "control" or "right to control" as regards his physical conduct in the performance of such services.

The term is often given special meanings by statutes and like other words is greatly influenced by context in wills and other documents.

See also Agent; Employee; Fellow servant; Master and servant; Subservant. *Compare* Independent contractor.

Service. This term has a variety of meanings, dependent upon the context or the sense in which used.

Contracts. Duty or labor to be rendered by one person to another, the former being bound to submit his will to the direction and control of the latter. The act of serving the labor performed or the duties required. Occupation, condition, or status of a servant, etc. Performance of labor for benefit of another, or at another's command; attendance of an inferior, hired helper, etc. "Service" and "employment" generally imply that the employer, or person to whom the service is due, both selects and compensates the employee, or person rendering the service.

The term is used also for employment in one of the offices, departments, or agencies of the government; as in the phrases "civil service," "public service," "military service," etc.

Trial Practice. The exhibition or delivery of a writ, summons and complaint, criminal summons, notice, order, etc., by an authorized person, to a person who is thereby officially notified of some action or proceeding in which he is concerned, and is thereby advised or warned of some action or step which he is commanded to take or to forbear. Fed.R.Civil Proc. 4 and 5; Fed.R.Crim.P. 4 and 49. Pleadings, motions, orders, etc., after the initial summons are normally served on the party's attorney unless otherwise ordered by court. *See Service of process, below.*

General Classification

Civil service. See that title.

Service of process. The service of writs, complaints, summonses, etc., signifies the delivering to or leaving them with the party to whom or with whom they ought to be delivered or left; and, when they are so delivered, they are then said to have been served. In the pleading stage of litigation, is the delivery of the complaint to the defendant either to him personally or, in most jurisdictions, by leaving it with a responsible person at his place of residence. Usually a copy only is served and the original is shown. The service must furnish reasonable notice to defendant of proceedings to afford him opportunity to appear and be heard. Fed.R.Civil P. 4; Fed.R.Crim.P. 4. The various types of service of process are as follows:

Constructive service of process. Any form of service other than actual personal service. Notification of an action or of some proceeding therein, given to a person affected by sending it to him in the mails or causing it to be published in a newspaper. Fed.R.Civil P. 4(e). *See also Service by publication; Substituted service, below.*

Long arm statutes. Laws enacted in most states which permit courts to acquire personal jurisdiction of non-residents by virtue of activity within the state. *See* Foreign service; Long arm statutes; Minimum contacts.

Personal service. Actual delivery of process to person to whom it is directed or to someone authorized to receive it in his behalf. Personal service is made by delivering a copy of the summons and complaint to the person named or by leaving copies thereof at his dwelling or usual place of abode with some responsible person or by delivering a copy to an agent authorized to receive such. Special rules are also provided for service on infants, incompetents, corporations, the United States or officers or agencies thereof, etc. Fed.R.Civil P. 4(d); Fed.R.Crim.P. 4(d). *See also* Found; Usual place of abode.

Proof of service. See Proof.

Service by publication. Service of a summons or other process upon an absent or nonresident defendant, by publishing the same as an advertisement in a designated newspaper, with such other efforts to give him actual notice as the particular statute may prescribe. *See also Substituted service, below.*

Substituted service. Any form of service of process other than personal service, such as service by mail or by publication in a newspaper; service of a writ or notice on some person other than the one directly concerned, for example, his attorney of record, who has authority to represent him or to accept service for him. Fed.R. Civil P. 4(d). *See also* Long arm statutes.

Service charge. That charge assessed by bank against the expense of maintaining a customer's demand deposit or checking account, and is calculated on basis of a formula whereby bank's cost of maintaining account for customer is determined.

"Credit service charge" means the sum of (1) all charges payable directly or indirectly by the buyer and imposed directly or indirectly by the seller as an incident to the extension of credit, including any of the following types of charges which are applicable: time price differential, service, carrying or other charge, however denominated, premium or other charge for any guarantee or insurance protecting the seller against the buyer's default or other credit loss; and (2) charges incurred for investigating the collateral or credit-worthiness of the buyer or for commissions or brokerage for obtaining the credit, irrespective of the person to whom the charges are paid or payable, unless the seller had no notice of the charges when the credit was granted. Uniform Consumer Credit Code, § 2.109.

Service contract. A written agreement to perform maintenance or repair (or both) service on a consumer product for a specified duration. 15 U.S.C.A. § 2301. *See* Warranty *(Extended service warranty)*.

Service life. Period of expected usefulness of an asset; such may not necessarily coincide with depreciable life for income tax purposes.

Service mark. A mark used in the sale or advertising of services to identify the services of one person and distinguish them from the services of others.

The term "service mark" means any word, name, symbol, or device, or any combination thereof—(1) used by a person, or (2) which a person has a bona fide intention to use in commerce and applies to register on the principal register established by the Trademark Act, to identify and distinguish the services of one person, including a unique service, from the services of others and to indicate the source of the services, even if that source is unknown. Titles, character names, and other distinctive features of radio or television programs may be registered as service marks notwithstanding that they, or the programs, may advertise the goods of the sponsor. 15 U.S.C.A. § 1127. *Compare* Trademark; Tradename.

Service occupation tax. Tax imposed on persons making sales of service and is computed as a percentage of net cost to serviceperson of tangible personal property transferred as an incident to such sale.

Service of process. *See* Service.

Services. Things purchased by consumers that do not have physical characteristics (*e.g.*, services of doctors, lawyers, dentists, repair personnel).

Service warranty. *See* Warranty *(Extended service warranty)*.

Servicing. *See* Service charge.

Servient /sə́rv(i)yənt/. Serving; subject to a service or servitude. A *servient* estate is one which is burdened with a servitude.

Servient tenement /sə́rv(i)yənt ténəmənt/. The person whose land is subject to an easement. An estate in respect of which a service is owing, as the *dominant tenement* is that to which the service is due. An estate burdened with a servitude. Most commonly a parcel of land subject to an easement for the benefit of another parcel (dominant tenement). *See also* Dominant estate *or* tenement.

Servitium /sərvísh(iy)əm/. Lat. In feudal and old English law, the duty of obedience and performance which a tenant was bound to render to his lord, by reason of his fee.

Servitude. The state of a person who is subjected, voluntarily or otherwise, to another person as his servant. A charge or burden resting upon one estate for the benefit or advantage of another; a species of incorporeal right derived from the civil law (see Servitus) and closely corresponding to the "easement" of the common-law, except that "servitude" rather has relation to the burden or the estate burdened, while "easement" refers to the benefit or advantage or the estate to which it accrues.

Session. The sitting of a court, legislature, council, commission, etc., for the transaction of its proper business. Hence, the period of time, within any one day, during which such body is assembled in form, and engaged in the transaction of business, or, in a more extended sense, the whole space of time from its first assembling to its prorogation or adjournment *sine die*. Either a day or a period of days in which a court, legislature, etc. carries on its business.

Strictly speaking, the word "session," as applied to a court of justice, is not synonymous with the word "term." The "session" of a court is the time during which it actually sits for the transaction of judicial business, and hence terminates each day with the rising of the court. A "term", or "sitting" in current English practice, of court, is the period fixed by law, usually embracing many days or weeks, during which it shall be open for the transaction of judicial business and during which it may hold sessions from day to day. But this distinction is not always observed, many authorities using the two words interchangeably.

See also Extra session; Extraordinary session; Lame duck session; Term.

Biennial session. See that title.

Joint session. Meeting together and commingling of the two houses of a legislative body, sitting and acting together as one body, instead of separately in their respective houses.

Regular session. An ordinary, general, or stated session (as of a legislative body), as distinguished from a special or extra session.

Session laws. The name commonly given to the body of laws enacted by a state legislature at one of its annual or biennial sessions. So called to distinguish them from the "compiled laws" or "revised statutes" of the state. Published laws of a state enacted by each assembly and separately bound for the session and for extra sessions. The session laws are normally published on a periodic basis, in a pamphlet format, throughout the legislative session and then at the end of the session are bound, in the order of their enactment, into a more permanent form. Such session laws in addition are incorporated into state and federal annotated or unannotated statute publications.

Set aside. To reverse, vacate, cancel, annul, or revoke a judgment, order, etc.

Setback. A distance from a curb, property line, or structure, within which building is prohibited. Setback requirements are normally provided for by ordinances or building codes. Provision in zoning ordinance regulating the distance from the lot line to the point where improvements may be constructed.

Set down. To "set down" a cause for trial or hearing at a given term is to enter its title in the calendar, list, or docket of causes which are to be brought on at that term.

Seti. As used in mining laws, a lease.

Set of exchange. In commercial law, foreign bills are usually drawn in duplicate or triplicate, the several parts being called respectively "first of exchange," "second of exchange," etc., and these parts together constitute a "set of exchange." Any one of them being paid, the others become void.

Set-off. A counter-claim demand which defendant holds against plaintiff, arising out of a transaction extrinsic of plaintiff's cause of action. Remedy employed by defendant to discharge or reduce plaintiff's demand by an opposite one arising from transaction which is extrinsic to plaintiff's cause of action.

A claim filed by a defendant against the plaintiff when sued and in which he seeks to cancel the amount due from him or to recover an amount in excess of the plaintiff's claim against him. In equity practice it is commenced by a declaration in set-off, though under rules practice (which

merged law and equity) it has been displaced by the counterclaim. Fed.R.Civil P. 13.

The equitable right to cancel or offset mutual debts or cross demands, commonly used by a bank in reducing a customer's checking or other deposit account in satisfaction of a debt the customer owes the bank.

For the distinction between set-off and recoupment, *see* Recoupment. *See also* Counterclaim; Offset.

Set out. To recite or narrate facts or circumstances; to allege or aver; to describe or to incorporate; as, to set out a deed or contract.

Settle. A word of equivocal meaning; meaning different things in different connections, and the particular sense in which it is used may be explained by the context or the circumstances. Accordingly, the term may be employed as meaning to agree, to approve, to arrange, to ascertain, to liquidate, to come to or reach an agreement, to determine, to establish, to fix, to free from uncertainty, to place, or to regulate.

Parties are said to *settle* an account when they go over its items and ascertain and agree upon the balance due from one to the other. And, when the party indebted pays such balance, he is also said to settle it.

Under U.C.C. § 4–104(j), "settle" means to pay in cash, by clearing house settlement, in a charge or credit or by remittance, or otherwise as instructed. A settlement may be either provisional or final.

See also Adjust; Liquidate; Settlement.

Settled estate. See Estate.

Settle up. A term, colloquial rather than legal, which is applied to the final collection, adjustment, and distribution of the estate of a decedent, a bankrupt, or an insolvent corporation. It includes the processes of collecting the property, paying debts and charges, and turning over the balance to those entitled to receive it.

Settlement. Act or process of adjusting or determining; an adjusting; an adjustment between persons concerning their dealings or difficulties; an agreement by which parties having disputed matters between them reach or ascertain what is coming from one to the other; arrangement of difficulties; composure of doubts or differences; determination by agreement; and liquidation. Payment or satisfaction. In legal parlance, implies meeting of minds of parties to transaction or controversy; an adjustment of differences or accounts; a coming to an agreement. To fix or resolve conclusively; to make or arrange for final disposition. Agreement to terminate or forestall all or part of a lawsuit.

Closing; the culmination of a particular transaction involving real property, such as the purchase and sale of the property, the execution of a lease or the making of a mortgage loan. *See also* Closing.

See also Adjust; Closing; Liquidate; Mary Carter agreement; Out-of-court settlement; Settle.

Contracts. Adjustment or liquidation of mutual accounts; the act by which parties who have been dealing together arrange their accounts and strike a balance. Also full and final payment or discharge of an account.

Estates. The settlement of an estate consists in its administration by the executor or administrator carried so far that all debts and legacies have been paid and the individual shares of distributees in the corpus of the estate, or the residuary portion, as the case may be, definitely ascertained and determined, and accounts filed and passed, so that nothing remains but to make final distribution. "Settlement," in reference to a decedent's estate, includes the full process of administration, distribution and closing. Uniform Probate Code, § 1–201. *See also Final settlement, below.*

Family settlement. See Family settlement.

Final settlement. This term, as applied to the administration of an estate, is usually understood to have reference to the order of court approving the account which closes the business of the estate, and which finally discharges the executor or administrator from the duties of his trust.

Structured settlement. Type of damages settlement whereby Defendant agrees to make periodic payments to injured Plaintiff over his or her life. Commonly such settlement consists of an initial lump-sum payment with future periodic payments funded with an annuity.

Voluntary settlement. A settlement of property upon a wife or other beneficiary, made gratuitously or without valuable consideration.

Settlement date. In stock transactions, the date upon which an executed order must be settled by the buyer paying for the securities with cash and by the seller delivering the securities sold.

Settlement option. In life insurance, a provision that provides for optional methods of payment of benefits or proceeds to beneficiary or insured such as lump sum, periodic payments, and the like.

Settlement statement. A statement prepared by an escrow agent or lender, giving a complete breakdown of costs involved in a real estate sale. A separate statement is prepared for the seller and buyer. Such statements are regulated by the federal Real Estate Settlement Procedures Act. *See also* Closing Statement; RESPA.

Settler. A person who, for the purpose of acquiring a pre-emption right, has gone upon the land in question, and is actually resident there.

Settlor. The grantor or donor in a deed of settlement. Also, one who creates a trust. Restatement, Second, Trusts § 3(1). One who furnishes the consideration (res) for the creation of a trust, though in form the trust is created by another.

See also Donor; Grantor.

Set up. To bring forward or allege, as something relied upon or deemed sufficient. To propose or interpose, by way of defense, explanation, or justification; as, to set up the statute of limitations, *i.e.,* offer and rely upon it as a defense to a claim.

Seventeenth Amendment. An Amendment of 1913 to the U.S. Constitution which transferred the election of U.S. Senators from the State legislature to the voters of the State, but provided that the legislature may impower the governor to make a temporary appointment to fill a vacancy until an election can be held.

Seventh Amendment. In suits at common law, where the value in controversy shall exceed twenty dollars, the right of trial by jury shall be preserved, and no fact tried by a jury, shall be otherwise reexamined in any Court of the United States, than according to the rules of the common law. This constitutional right of trial by jury is preserved by Fed.R.Civil P. 38. *See also* Trial *(Trial by jury).*

Seven years' absence. When a person has been missing and his whereabouts unknown for seven or more years, he is presumed by law in most states to be dead.

Sever. To separate, as one from another; to cut off from something; to divide. To part in any way, especially by violence, as by cutting, rending, etc.; as, to sever the head from the body. To cut or break open or apart; to divide into parts. To cut through; to disjoin. In practice, to insist upon a plea distinct from that of other codefendants. To separate the cases of multiple defendants in such a way as to allow separate trials for each or for fewer than all.

Relief from prejudicial joinder. If it appears that a defendant or the government is prejudiced by a joinder of offenses or of defendants in an indictment or information or by such joinder for trial together, the court may order an election or separate trials of counts, grant a severance of defendants or provide whatever other relief justice requires. In ruling on a motion by a defendant for severance the court may order the attorney for the government to deliver to the court for inspection *in camera* any statements or confessions made by the defendants which the government intends to introduce in evidence at the trial. Fed. R.Crim.P. 14.

Severability clause. *See* Saving clause; Severable statute.

Severability doctrine. If promise sued on is related to an illegal transaction, but is not illegal in and of itself, "severability doctrine" applies, and recovery should not be denied, if aid of illegal transaction is not relied on or required, or if promise sued on is remote from or collateral to illegal transaction, or is supported by independent consideration.

Severable. Admitting of severance or separation; capable of being divided; separable; capable of being severed from other things to which it was joined, and yet maintaining a complete and independent existence. Capable of carrying on an independent existence; for example, a severable statute is one that can still be valid even if one part of it is struck down as invalid by a court. It is common for statutes to have a severability or savings clause *(q.v.)*.

Severable contract. A contract which includes two or more promises which can be acted on separately such that the failure to perform one promise does not necessarily put the promisor in breach of the entire agreement. A contract, the nature and purpose of which is susceptible of division and apportionment, having two or more parts, in respect to matters and things contemplated and embraced by it, not necessarily dependent upon each other, or intended by parties as being dependent. *See* Separability clause.

When a contract is severable, a breach may be found to constitute a default as to only the specific part breached, thus relieving the defaulting party from liability for damages for breach of the entire contract. See *e.g.*, U.C.C. § 2–612 with respect to installment contracts.

See also Installment contract.

Severable statute. A statute if after an invalid portion of it has been stricken out, that which remains is self-sustaining and capable of separate enforcement without regard to the stricken portion, in which case that which remains should be sustained. *See* Saving clause; Separability clause.

Several. More than two, often used to designate a number greater than one. Each particular, or a small number singly taken. Separate; individual; independent; severable. In this sense the word is distinguished from "joint." Also exclusive; individual; appropriated. In this sense it is opposed to "common."

As to *several* Count; Covenant; Demise; Tail, and Tenancy, see those titles. *See also* Contribution; Joint and several liability; Joint tort-feasors.

Several actions. Where a separate and distinct action is brought against each of two or more persons who are all liable to the plaintiff in respect to the same subject-matter, the actions are said to be "several." If all the persons are joined as defendants in one and the same action, it is called a "joint" action.

Several inheritance. An inheritance conveyed so as to descend to two persons severally, by moieties, etc.

Several liability. Liability separate and distinct from liability of another to the extent that an independent action may be brought without joinder of others. Exists where each of the parties specifically promises to be individually bound, using language such as "each of us makes this promise severally, not jointly."

Severally. Distinctly, separately, apart from others. When applied to a number of persons the expression *severally liable* usually implies that each one is liable alone.

Severalty. Owning real or personal property without anyone else sharing in the ownership. A state of separation. An estate in *severalty* is one that is held by a person in his own right only, without any other person being joined or connected with him, in point of interest, during his estate therein.

Severalty, estate in. An estate which is held by the tenant in his own right only, without any other being joined or connected with him in point of interest during the continuance of his estate.

Severance. Act of severing, or state of being severed; partition; separation; *e.g.* a claim against a party may be severed and proceeded with separately. Fed.R.Civil P. 21. Separation of cases so that they can be tried separately. Severance divides lawsuit into two or more independent causes, each of which terminates in separate, final and enforceable judgment. *See also* Severance of actions *or* claims.

The conversion of a joint tenancy into a tenancy in common. The destruction of any one of the unities of a joint tenancy. It is so called because the estate is no longer a joint tenancy, but is severed. Term may also refer to cutting of the crops, such as corn, wheat, etc., or the separating of anything from the realty.

Severance damages. Essence of severance damages is the loss in value to the remainder tract by reason of a partial taking of land and this is predicated on the enhanced value of the remainder tract because of its relationship to whole prior to the taking. If only part of single tract is taken, owner's compensation for taking includes any and all elements of value arising out of relation of part taken to entire tract and such damages are often called severance damages.

Severance of actions *or* claims. An action of a court in separating the claims of multiple parties and permitting separate actions on each claim or on fewer than all claims at one time. Fed.R. Civ.P. 21. "Severance" divides lawsuit into two or more independent causes, each of which terminates in separate, final and enforceable judgment.

See also Severance. *Compare* Bifurcated trial; Separate trial.

Severance pay. Payment by an employer to employee beyond his wages on termination of his employment. Such pay represents a form of compensation for the termination of the employment relation, for reasons other than the displaced employee's misconduct, primarily to alleviate the consequent need for economic readjustment but also to recompense the employee for certain losses attributable to the dismissal. Generally, it is paid when the termination is not due to employee's fault and many union contracts provide for it. *See also* Golden parachute.

Severance tax. A tax on mineral or forest products at the time they are removed or severed from the soil and usually regarded as a form of property taxation. Excise taxes upon privilege or right to sever natural resources from soil and are paid by owner of resource at time it is produced.

Sexual abuse. Illegal sex acts performed against a minor by a parent, guardian, relative, acquaintance, or other person.

Sexual battery. Term used in certain state statutes for crimes of rape. *See* Rape.

Sexual harassment. As type of employment discrimination, includes sexual advances, requests for sexual favors, and other verbal or physical conduct of a sexual nature in the course of employment prohibited by Federal law (Title VII of 1964 Civil Rights Act) and commonly by state statutes; *e.g.,* Mass.G.L. c. 151B, § 1(18).

Shakedown. Extortion of money with threats of physical harm or, in case of police officer, threat of arrest. *See also* Blackmail; Extortion.

Shall. As used in statutes, contracts, or the like, this word is generally imperative or mandatory. In common or ordinary parlance, and in its ordinary signification, the term "shall" is a word of command, and one which has always or which must be given a compulsory meaning; as denoting obligation. The word in ordinary usage means "must" and is inconsistent with a concept of discretion. It has the invariable significance of excluding the idea of discretion, and has the significance of operating to impose a duty which may be enforced, particularly if public policy is in favor of this meaning, or when addressed to public officials, or where a public interest is involved, or where the public or persons have rights which ought to be exercised or enforced, unless a contrary intent appears.

But it may be construed as merely permissive or directory (as equivalent to "may"), to carry out the legislative intention and in cases where no right or benefit to any one depends on its being taken in the imperative sense, and where no public or private right is impaired by its interpretation in the other sense.

Sham pleading. Those which are inherently false and must have been known by interposing party to be untrue. A "sham pleading", subject to motion to strike (Fed.R.Civil P. 12(f)), is one that is good in form, but false in fact, and not pleaded in good faith. A pleading is "sham" only when it is so clearly false that it does not raise any bona fide issue. Pleading may be stricken as "sham" when its allegations appear false on the face of the pleading.

Sham transaction. False dealings. Transactions that appear to be contracts but are not and exist only to deceive creditors or the government. In taxation, a transaction without substance that will be disregarded for tax purposes. *See also* Dummy.

Shanghaiing sailors. /shèŋháy/. Practice of drugging, tricking, intoxicating or otherwise forcing persons to become sailors—usually to secure advance money or a premium.

Under federal law, the offense of procuring or inducing, or attempting to do so, by force, or threats, or by representations which one knows or believes to be untrue, or while the person is intoxicated or under the influence of any drug, to go on board of any vessel, or agree to do so, to perform service or labor thereon, such vessel being engaged in interstate or foreign commerce, on the high seas or any navigable water of the United States, or knowingly to detain on board such vessel such person, so procured or induced, or knowingly aiding or abetting such things. 18 U.S.C.A. § 2194.

Share, v. To partake; enjoy with others; have a portion of.

Share, n. A part or definite portion of a thing owned by a number of persons in common and contemplates something owned in common by two or more persons and has reference to that part of the undivided interest which belongs to some one of them. A unit of stock representing ownership in a corporation. "Share" means the unit into which the proprietary interests in a corporation are divided. Rev. Model Bus. Corp. Act, § 1.40. *See also* Distributive share; Share of corporate stock; Stock.

Share and share alike. In equal shares or proportions. The words commonly indicate per capita division; and they may be applied to a division between classes as well as to a division among individuals. *See* Per capita.

Share certificate. An instrument of a corporation certifying that the person therein named is entitled to a certain number of shares; it is prima facie evidence of his title thereto. Document which evidences participation in a voting trust of shares of a corporation.

Sharecropper. Type of tenant farmer who lives on and works the land of another, his compensation being a portion of the crops minus any advances for seed, food, tools, etc.

Sharecropping. Type of agricultural arrangement in which the landowner leases land and equipment to tenant or sharecropper who, in turn, gives to the landlord a percentage of the crops as rent.

Share draft. Instrument used to withdraw funds from a credit union.

Shareholder. *See* Stockholder (shareholder).

Share of corporate stock. The unit into which the proprietary interests in a corporation are divided. Rev. Model Bus. Corp. Act. § 1.40. A proportional part of certain rights in a corporation during its existence, and in the assets upon dissolution, and evidence of the stockholder's ratable share in the distribution of the assets on the winding up of the corporation's business. *See* Share certificate; Stock.

Share split. *See* Stock (*Stock split*).

Share-warrant to bearer. A warrant or certificate of a corporation, stating that the bearer of the warrant is entitled to a certain number or amount of fully paid up shares or stock. Coupons for payment of dividends may be annexed to it. Delivery of the share-warrant operates as a transfer of the shares or stock.

Shark repellent. A slang term that refers to measures undertaken by a corporation to discourage unwanted takeover attempts. *See also* Poison pill; White knight.

Sharp clause. Name used to describe a clause in a mortgage or other security (or the whole instrument described as "sharp") which empowers the creditor to take prompt and summary action upon default in payment or breach of other conditions. *See* Cognovit note.

Shelf issue. The process of issuing securities that have previously been registered by filing shelf registration statement.

Shelf registration. A procedure whereby a company is permitted to register (with SEC) all the debt and equity securities it plans to sell over the next several years. The company can then sell these securities whenever it chooses (*e.g.*, in the most favorable market) without a registration delay. See SEC Rule 415.

Shelley's Case, Rule in. "When the ancestor, by any gift or conveyance, taketh an estate of freehold, and in the same gift or conveyance an estate is limited, either mediately or immediately, to his heirs in fee or in tail, 'the heirs' are words of

limitation of the estate, and not words of purchase." 1 Co.Rep. 93b (1581). This rule has also been expressed as follows: "Where a person takes an estate of freehold, legally, or equitably, under a deed, will, or other writing, and in the same instrument there is a limitation by way of remainder, either with or without the interposition of another estate, of any interest of the same legal or equitable quality to his heirs, or heirs of his body, as a class of persons to take in succession from generation to generation, the limitation to the heirs entitles the ancestor to the whole estate."

Intimately connected with the quantity of estate which a tenant may hold in realty is the antique feudal doctrine generally known as the "Rule in Shelley's Case," which is reported by Lord Coke in 1 Coke, 93*b* (23 Eliz. in C.B.). This rule was not first laid down or established in that case, but was then simply admitted in argument as a well-founded and settled rule of law, and has always since been quoted as the "Rule in Shelley's Case." The rule was adopted as a part of the common law of this country, though it has long since been abolished by most states.

Shelter. In statutes relating to the provision of food, clothing, and shelter for one's children, term generally refers to a home with proper environments, as well as protection from the weather.

Sheriff. Constitutionally elected officer having responsibilities of law enforcement and administration of sheriff's department. The chief executive and administrative officer of a county, being chosen by popular election. His principal duties are in aid of the criminal courts and civil courts of record; such as serving process, summoning juries, executing judgments, holding judicial sales and the like. He is also the chief conservator of the peace within his territorial jurisdiction. When used in statutes, the term may include a deputy sheriff. He is in general charge of the county jail in most states. *See also* Constable; Marshal.

Deputy sheriff. *See* Deputy.

Sheriff's deed. A document giving ownership rights in property to a buyer at a sheriff's sale (*i.e.* a sale held by a sheriff to pay a court judgment against the owner of the property). Deed given at sheriff's sale in foreclosure of a mortgage. The giving of said deed begins a statutory redemption period.

Sheriff's sale. A sale, commonly by auction, conducted by a sheriff or other court officer to carry out a decree of execution or foreclosure issued by a court. Examples include sales pursuant to attachments, liens and mortgage defaults. *See also* Judicial sale.

Sherman Antitrust Act. Such Act (15 U.S.C.A. §§ 1–7) prohibits any unreasonable interference, by contract, or combination, or conspiracy, with the ordinary, usual and freely-competitive pricing or distribution system of the open market in interstate trade. *See also* Clayton Act; Monopoly; Price-fixing; Restraint of trade; Robinson-Patman Act; Rule *(Rule of reason).*

Shield laws. Statutes affording a privilege to journalists not to disclose in legal proceedings confidential information or sources of information obtained by them in their professional capacities. Most states have such laws. Cf. N.Y. McKinney's Civil Rights Law § 79–h.

Statutes which restrict or prohibit the use of evidence respecting the chastity of the victim of a rape or other sexual offense. Cf. Fed.R.Evid. 412.

Shifting. Changing; varying; passing from one person to another by substitution.

Shifting clause. In a settlement at common law, a clause by which some other mode of devolution is substituted for that primarily prescribed. Examples of shifting clauses are: The ordinary name and arms clause, and the clause of less frequent occurrence by which a settled estate is destined as the foundation of a second family, in the event of the elder branch becoming otherwise enriched. These shifting clauses take effect under the statute of uses.

Shifting income. Device used by taxpayers in high tax brackets to move income from themselves to their children and others who are in a lower bracket. Short term or Clifford trusts, as well as gifts to minors, were among the devices used to accomplish this purpose. However, since the Tax Reform Act of 1986 the process of shifting income has become more restrictive. For example, unearned income in excess of a minimal amount of children under the age of 14 is taxed at their parents' highest rate. The Clifford Trust rules have also changed and earnings on assets put into a trust subsequent to March, 1986 is taxed at the grantor's rate.

Shifting risk. In insurance, a risk created by a contract of insurance on a stock of merchandise, or other similar property, which is kept for sale, or is subject to change in items by purchase and sale; the policy being conditioned to cover the goods in the stock at any and all times and not to be affected by changes in its composition.

Shifting severalty. *See* Severalty.

Shifting stock of merchandise. A stock of merchandise subject to change from time to time, in the course of trade by purchases, sales, or other transactions.

Shifting the burden of proof. Transferring it from one party to the other, or from one side of the case to the other, when he upon whom it rested originally has made out a *prima facie* case or defense by evidence, of such a character that it

then becomes incumbent upon the other to rebut it by contradictory or defensive evidence. *See* Burden of proof.

Shifting use. *See* Use.

Ship, *v.* To put on board a ship; to send by ship. To place (goods) on board a vessel for the purchaser or consignee, to be transported at his risk. In a broader sense, to transport; to deliver to a carrier (public or private) for transportation. To send away, to get rid of. To send by established mode of transportation, as to "carry," "convey," or "transport." *See also* Send; Shipment; Shipping.

Ship, *n.* A vessel of any kind employed in navigation. *See* Shipping.

Shipment contract. Any agreement for the sale of goods under which the seller is authorized or required only to bear the expense of putting the goods in the hands of a common carrier and bears the risk of loss only up to that point. A contract for the sale of goods which is silent on a delivery term is presumed to be a shipment contract. *See* U.C.C. §§ 2–319, 2–504, 2–509(1).

Ship Mortgage Act. Federal statute regulating mortgages on ships registered as U.S. vessels. It provides for enforcement of maritime liens in favor of those who furnish supplies or maintenance to such vessels. 46 U.S.C.A. § 911 *et seq.*

Shipper. One who ships goods to another. One who engages the services of a carrier of goods. One who tenders goods to a carrier for transportation; a consignor. The owner or person for whose account the carriage of goods is undertaken. *See also* Consignor.

Shipping. Ships in general; ships or vessels of any kind intended for navigation. Relating to ships; as, shipping interests, shipping affairs, shipping business, shipping concerns. Putting on board a ship or vessel, or receiving on board a ship or vessel.

Law of shipping. A comprehensive term for all that part of the maritime law which relates to ships and the persons employed in or about them. It embraces such subjects as the building and equipment of vessels, their registration and nationality, their ownership and inspection, their employment (including charter-parties, freight, demurrage, towage, and salvage), and their sale, transfer, and mortgage; also, the employment, rights, powers, and duties of masters and mariners; and the law relating to ship-brokers, ship-agents, pilots, etc. *See* Jones Act; Longshore and Harbor Workers' Compensation Act; Maritime.

Shipping articles. A written agreement between the master of a vessel and the mariners, specifying the voyage or term for which the latter are shipped, and the rate of wages. 46 U.S.C.A. § 564.

Shipping document. Generic term to describe all papers which cover a shipment in foreign or inland trade such as bill of lading, letter of credit, certificate of insurance and the like.

Shipping order. Copy of bill of lading which carries shipper's instructions to carrier as to the disposition of the goods.

Shipping papers. *See* Shipping document.

Shire /shay(ə)r/. A Saxon word which signified a division; it was made up of an indefinite number of hundreds—later called a county *(Comitatus)*.

In England, a county. So called because every county or shire is divided and parted by certain metes and bounds from another.

Shop-book rule. An exception to the hearsay evidence rule, permitting the introduction in evidence of books of original entry made in the usual course of business, and introduced by one with custody of them, and upon general authentication. Fed.R.Evid. 803(6), (7); 28 U.S.C.A. § 1732.

Shop-books. Books of original entry kept by merchants, shop-keepers, mechanics, and the like, in which are entered their accounts and charges for goods sold, work done, etc., commonly called "account-books," or "books of account." *See* Shop-book rule.

Shoplifting. Larceny of merchandise from a store or business establishment. Essential constituents of "shoplifting" are (1) willfully taking possession of merchandise offered for sale in mercantile establishment, (2) with intention of converting merchandise to taker's own use without paying purchase price thereof.

Shop right rule. In patent law, the right of an employer to use employee's invention in employer's business without payment of royalty. The "shop right" doctrine is that, where an employee during his hours of employment working with his employer's materials and appliances conceives and perfects an invention for which he obtains a patent, he must accord his employer a nonexclusive right to practice the invention. The employer, however, is not entitled to a conveyance of the invention, this remains the right of the employee-inventor.

Shop steward. A union official elected to represent members in a plant or particular department. His duties include collection of dues, recruitment of new members and initial negotiations for settlement of grievances.

Shore. Strictly and technically, lands adjacent to the sea or other tidal waters. The lands adjoining navigable waters, where the tide flows and reflows, which at high tides are submerged, and at low tides are bare. The space bounded by the high and low water marks. And this is also true even though the lands may lie along nonnavigable bodies of water. The term is synonymous with the term "beach."

Under the civil law the "shore line" boundary of lands adjoining navigable waters is the line marked by the highest tide.

In connection with salvage, "shore" means the land on which the waters have deposited things which are the subject of salvage, whether below or above ordinary high-water mark.

Shore lands. Those lands lying between the lines of high and low water mark. Lands bordering on the shores of navigable lakes and rivers below the line of ordinary high water.

Short. Not long; of brief length or duration; not coming up to a measure, standard, requirement, or the like.

A term of common use in the stock and commodity markets. To say that one is "short," in the vernacular of the exchanges, implies only that one has less of a commodity than may be necessary to meet demands and obligations. It does not imply that commodity cannot or will not be supplied upon demand.

In finance and commodity futures, a person is short when he has sold securities or commodities which he does not own at the time of the sale, though he expects to buy them back at a lower price than that at which he sold them. *See also* Short sale.

Short covering. Buying stock to return stock previously borrowed to make delivery on a short sale.

Short form merger. *See* Merger.

Short interest. A short sale is the sale of borrowed stock. The seller expects a price decline that would enable him to purchase an equal number of shares later at a lower price for return to the lender. The "short interest" is the number of shares that haven't been purchased for return to lenders. *See also* Short sale.

Short lease. A term applied colloquially, but without much precision, to a lease for a short term (as a month or a year), as distinguished from one running for a long period.

Shortly after. In point of time, a relative term, meaning in a short or brief time or manner; soon; presently; quickly.

Short position. A short position maybe created when an investor borrows a stock in order to sell it, figuring the price of the stock will decline. The investor is in a "short position" until he purchases stock to repay the lender. *See* Short sale.

Short sale. A contract for sale of shares of stock which the seller does not own, or certificates for which are not within his control, so as to be available for delivery at the time when, under rules of the exchange, delivery must be made. A short sale occurs where a taxpayer sells borrowed property (usually stock) and repays the lender with substantially identical property either held on the date of the short sale or purchased after the sale (expecting to be able to buy the stocks later at a lower price). *See also* Short interest; Short position.

Short sale against the box. A short sale where the investor owns enough shares of the security involved to cover the borrowed securities, if necessary. The "box" referred to is the hypothetical safe deposit box in which the certificates are kept. A short sale against the box is not as risky as a regular short sale.

Short summons. A process, authorized in some of the states, to be issued against an absconding, fraudulent, or nonresident debtor, which is returnable within a less number of days than an ordinary writ of summons.

Short swing profits. Profits made by an "insider" on the purchase and sale of stock of a corporation within a six-month period. *See* Insider.

Short-term. Current; ordinarily, due within one year.

Capital gains or losses. See Capital *(Capital gain)*; Capital *(Capital loss).*

Short-term debt. Debt obligations which are due and payable on demand or within a year of issuance. Bonds with short maturity dates (*e.g.* one or two years).

Should. The past tense of shall; ordinarily implying duty or obligation; although usually no more than an obligation of propriety or expediency, or a moral obligation, thereby distinguishing it from "ought." It is not normally synonymous with "may," and although often interchangeable with the word "would," it does not ordinarily express certainty as "will" sometimes does.

Show, *n.* Something that one views or at which one looks and at the same time hears.

Show, *v.* To make apparent or clear by evidence, to prove.

Show cause order. Court order, decree, execution, etc., to appear as directed, and present to the court such reasons and considerations as one has to offer why a particular order, decree, etc., should not be confirmed, take effect, be executed, or as the case may be. See *e.g.* 28 U.S.C.A. § 2243 (habeas corpus).

An order to a person or corporation, on motion of opposing party, to appear in court and explain why the court should not take a proposed action. If the person or corporation fails to appear or to give sufficient reasons why the court should take no action, the court will take the action.

Shower. One who accompanies a jury to the scene to call the attention of the jurors to specific objects to be noted. *See also* View.

Show-up. One-to-one confrontation between suspect and witness to crime. A type of pre-trial identification procedure in which a suspect is confronted by or exposed to the victim of or witness to a crime. It is less formal than a lineup but its purpose is the same. Commonly, it occurs within a short time after the crime or under circumstances which would make a lineup impracticable or impossible. Due process standards must be met if evidence of such identification is to be admissible in court. *Compare* Lineup.

Shut down. To stop work; usually said of a factory, etc.

Shut-in royalty. In oil and gas leases, a royalty payment made to keep the lease in force though there is no production.

Sic /sík/. Lat. Thus; so; in such manner.

Sick leave. Period allowed by an employer to an employee for the employee's sickness either with or without pay but with no loss of seniority or other benefits.

Side. The margin, edge, verge, or border of a surface; any one of the bounding lines of the surface.

The party or parties collectively to a lawsuit considered in relation to his or their opponents, *i.e.,* the plaintiff side, or the defendant side. *See* Parties.

A province or field of jurisdiction of courts. Thus, the same court is sometimes said to have different *sides,* as an "equity side" and a "law side"; though with the procedural merger of law and equity in most states such side distinctions have been abolished.

Side-bar. Refers to position at side of the judge's bench where trial counsel and judge discuss matters out of hearing of jury. It is important that such conferences be recorded if they are to be considered on appeal.

Side reports. A term sometimes applied to unofficial volumes or series of reports, as contrasted with those prepared by the official reporter of the court, or to collections of cases omitted from the official reports.

Sight draft. An instrument payable on proper presentment (*i.e.* payable on demand). U.C.C. § 3–108. A bill of exchange for the immediate collection of money.

Bills of exchange are frequently drawn payable at sight or certain number of days or months after sight. U.C.C. § 3–109(1)(b).

A demand for payment drawn by a person to whom money is owed. The draft is presented to the borrower's (the debtor's) bank in expectation that the borrower will authorize its bank to disburse the funds.

See also Demand *(Demand note).*

Sign. To affix one's name to a writing or instrument, for the purpose of authenticating or executing it, or to give it effect as one's act. To attach a name or cause it to be attached to a writing by any of the known methods of impressing a name on paper. To affix a signature to; to ratify by hand or seal; to subscribe in one's own handwriting. To make any mark, as upon a document, in token of knowledge, approval acceptance, or obligation. *See also* Cross; Execution; Mark; Signature.

All pleadings must be signed by attorney of record. Fed.R.Civil P. 11.

Signatory /sígnət(o)riy/. A term used in diplomacy to indicate a nation which is a party to a treaty. In general, a person who signs a document personally or through his agent and who becomes a party thereto.

Signature. The act of putting one's name at the end of an instrument to attest its validity; the name thus written. A signature may be written by hand, printed, stamped, typewritten, engraved, photographed, or cut from one instrument and attached to another, and a signature lithographed on an instrument by a party is sufficient for the purpose of signing it; it being immaterial with what kind of instrument a signature is made. And whatever mark, symbol, or device one may choose to employ as representative of himself is sufficient.

The name or mark of a person, written by that person at his or her direction. In commercial law, any name, word, or mark used with the intention to authenticate a writing constitutes a signature. UCC §§ 1–201(39), 3–401(2). *See also* Cross; Sign; Signed.

A signature is made by use of any name, including any trade or assumed name, upon an instrument, or by any word or mark used in lieu of a written signature. U.C.C. § 3–401.

The signature to a deed may be made either by the grantor affixing his own signature, or by adopting one written for him, or by making his mark, or impressing some other sign or symbol on the paper by which the signature, though written by another for him, may be identified.

Public Officials. Many states have adopted the Uniform Facsimile Signatures of Public Officials Act.

Unauthorized signature. One made without actual, implied or apparent authority and includes a forgery. U.C.C. § 1–201(43).

Signature card. A card which a bank or other financial institution requires of its customers and on which the customer puts his signature and other information. It becomes a permanent file and permits the bank to compare the signature on the card with a signature on checks, withdrawal slips and other documents.

Signed. Includes any symbol executed or adopted by a party with present intention to authenticate a writing. U.C.C. § 1–201(39). *See also* Signature.

Signify. To make known by signs or words; express; communicate; announce; declare.

Signing judgment. *See* Sign.

Silence. The state of a person who does not speak, or of one who refrains from speaking. In the law of estoppel, "silence" implies knowledge and an opportunity to act upon it.

Silence, estoppel by. Such estoppel arises where person is under duty to another to speak or failure to speak is inconsistent with honest dealings. Silence, to work "estoppel", must amount to bad faith, and, elements or essentials of such estoppel include: change of position to prejudice of person claiming estoppel; damages if the estoppel is denied; duty and opportunity to speak; inducing person claiming estoppel to alter his position; knowledge of facts and of rights by person estopped; misleading of party claiming estoppel; reliance upon silence of party sought to be estopped.

Silent partner. An investor in a firm who takes no active part in its management but who shares in its profits and losses. A dormant or limited partner; one whose name does not appear in the firm, and who takes no active part in the business, but who has an interest in the concern, and shares the profits, and thereby becomes a partner, either absolutely, or as respects third persons. *See* Limited partner.

Silver certificates. Species of paper money formerly in circulation in this country and which was redeemable in silver. Silver certificates have been replaced by federal reserve notes.

Silver parachute. Payout compensation provisions for corporate employees that take effect in the event of a corporate takeover. *See also* Golden parachute.

Similar. Nearly corresponding; resembling in many respects; somewhat like; having a general likeness, although allowing for some degree of difference. Word is generally interpreted to mean that one thing has a resemblance in many respects, nearly corresponds, is somewhat like, or has a general likeness to some other thing but is not identical in form and substance, although in some cases "similar" may mean identical or exactly alike. It is a word with different meanings depending on context in which it is used.

Similar happenings. In law of evidence, generally things that happened at a time different from the time in dispute in the suit are not admissible because they are not material or relevant to what occurred at the disputed time. Where such happenings are admissible, the proof is limited to such issues as control of premises, or conditions which may have persisted.

Similar sales. In law of evidence, when market value is in issue, sales of similar property is admissible to prove value.

There is no specific rule to determine the degree of similarity necessary for evidence of a sale of other property to be admissible in a condemnation action. "Similar" does not mean "identical," and other sales need be only sufficiently similar in character and locality to provide the jury some reasonable basis for comparison. "Similarity" necessary to permit evidence of sale of one property to establish market value of another does not mean identical, but does require reasonable resemblance taking into consideration such factors as location, size and sale price; conditions surrounding sale, such as date and character of sale; business and residential advantages or disadvantages; and unimproved, improved or developed nature of land.

Simple. Pure; unmixed; not compounded; not aggravated; not evidenced by sealed writing or record.

As to *simple* Assault; Average; Battery; Blockade; Bond; Confession; Contract; Deposit; Imprisonment; Interest; Larceny; Obligation; and Trust, see those titles.

Simple kidnapping. A statutory form of unlawful imprisonment of a person which is not aggravated as in the case of child stealing or kidnapping for ransom. *See also* Kidnapping.

Simple negligence. Such consists of failure to exercise for protection of others that degree of care and caution that would, under prevailing circumstances, be exercised by ordinarily prudent person. Inadvertence or mistake, usually caused by heedlessness or carelessness on the face of a risk which reasonable person would not take. *See* Negligence.

Simple robbery. Gist of crime is the putting in fear and taking of property of another by force or intimidation. *See also* Robbery.

Simplified Employee Pension Plan (SEP). An individual retirement account or individual retirement annuity which an employer establishes for his or her employees. See I.R.C. § 408(k). *See also* Individual Retirement Account (I.R.A.).

Simulate. To assume the mere appearance of, without the reality; to assume the signs or indications of, falsely; to counterfeit; feign; imitate; pretend. To engage, usually with the co-opera-

tion or connivance of another person, in an act or series of acts, which are apparently transacted in good faith, and intended to be followed by their ordinary legal consequences, but which in reality conceal a fraudulent purpose of the party to gain thereby some advantage to which he is not entitled, or to injure, delay, or defraud others.

Simulated contract. One which, though clothed in concrete form, has no existence in fact. It may at any time and at the demand of any person in interest be declared a sham and may be ignored by creditors of the apparent vendor.

Simulated fact. In the law of evidence, a fabricated fact; an appearance given to things by human device, with a view to deceive and mislead.

Simulated judgment. One which is apparently rendered in good faith, upon an actual debt, and intended to be collected by the usual process of law, but which in reality is entered by the fraudulent contrivance of the parties, for the purpose of giving to one of them an advantage to which he is not entitled, or of defrauding or delaying third persons.

Simulated sale. One which has all the appearance of an actual sale in good faith, intended to transfer the ownership of property for a consideration, but which in reality covers a collusive design of the parties to put the property beyond the reach of creditors, or proceeds from some other fraudulent purpose. It results when parties execute a formal act of sale of a thing for which no price is paid or is intended to be paid, and such sale has no legal effect and no title is transferred thereby. If there exists an actual consideration for transfer evidenced by alleged act of sale, no matter how inadequate it be, the transaction is not a "simulated sale", and, even though it be charged to be in fraud of vendor's creditors, such transfer cannot be set aside as a simulation although it may be subject to annulment on the ground of fraud or the giving of undue preference.

Simulation. Assumption of appearance which was feigned, false, deceptive, or counterfeit. *See also* Personate; Impersonation; Simulate.

Simultaneous. A word of comparison meaning that two or more occurrences or happenings are identical in time.

Simultaneous Death Act. A Uniform State Law (adopted by most states) which provides that where passage of title to property depends upon the time of one's death, if there is insufficient evidence that persons have died otherwise than simultaneously, the property of each person shall be disposed of as if he had survived unless the Act provides otherwise. See also Uniform Probate Code, § 2–104.

Simultaneous death clause. A clause in a will which provides for the disposition of property in the event that there is no evidence as to the priority of time of death of the testator and another, commonly the testator's spouse. See Uniform Probate Code, § 2–104.

Since. This word's proper signification is "after," and in its apparent sense it includes the whole period between the event and the present time. "Since" a day named, does not necessarily include that day.

Sine /sáyniy/. Lat. Without.

Sine die /sáyniy dáy(iy)/. Without day; without assigning a day for a further meeting or hearing. Hence, a legislative body adjourns sine die when it adjourns without appointing a day on which to appear or assemble again.

Sine qua non /sáyniy kwèy nón/. Without which not. That without which the thing cannot be. An indispensable requisite or condition.

Single. One only, being an individual unit; alone; one which is abstracted from others. Unitary; detached; individual; affecting only one person; containing only one part, article, condition, or covenant. Unmarried; the term being also applicable to a widow, and occasionally even to a married woman living apart from her husband. Sometimes, principal; dominating.

As to *single* Adultery; Bill; Bond; Demise; Entry; Escheat; Obligation; Original; and Tract of land, see those titles.

Single creditor. One having a lien only on a single fund;—distinguished from double creditor, who is one having a lien on two funds.

Single-entry bookkeeping. In accounting, a simple system of recordkeeping in which each transaction is recorded in a single record, such as a checkbook or a list of accounts receivable.

Single juror charge. The charge that, if there is any juror who is not reasonably satisfied from the evidence that plaintiff should recover a verdict against the defendant, jury cannot find against defendant.

Single publication rule. Under the "single publication rule," where an issue of a newspaper or magazine, or an edition of a book, contains a libelous statement, plaintiff has a single cause of action and the number of copies distributed is considered as relevant for damages but not as a basis for a new cause of action. General theory of this rule is that a defendant should be subject to suit only once for each mass publication of libel, but that in that one action plaintiff may introduce evidence of all sales in all jurisdictions to show extent of his injury.

Singular. Each; as in the expression "all and singular." Also, individual. In grammar, the singular is used to express only one. In law, the singular frequently includes the plural. As to *singular* Successor; and Title, see those titles.

Sinking fund. Assets and their earnings earmarked for the retirement of bonds or other long-term obligations. An obligation sometimes imposed pursuant to the issuance of debt securities or preferred shares by which the issuer is required each year to set aside a certain amount to enable the issuer to retire the securities when they mature. A sinking fund may be allowed to accumulate or may be used each year to redeem a portion of the outstanding securities.

A fund (usually invested), which will be used to replace improvements as needed. Most commonly set aside from the income of income producing property.

A fund arising from particular taxes, imposts or duties, which is appropriated toward the payment of the interest due on a public loan, and for the payment of the principal.

In general accounting, segregated assets that are being accumulated for a specific purpose. In governmental accounting, a fund established to accumulate resources for the retirement of bonds but not for the payment of interest, which is handled through the general fund or a special revenue fund.

Sinking fund debenture. A type of debenture which is backed by a provision for sinking fund *(q.v.)*.

Sinking fund method of depreciation. The periodic charge is an amount so that when the charges are considered to be an annuity, the value of the annuity at the end of depreciable life is equal to the acquisition cost of the asset. In theory, the charge for a period ought also to include interest on the accumulated depreciation at the start of the period as well. A fund of cash is not necessarily, or even usually, accumulated.

SIPC. *See* Securities Investor Protection Act.

Sister. A woman who has the same father and mother with another, or has one of them only. In the first case, she is called sister, simply; in the second, half-sister. The word is the correlative of "brother."

Sister corporation. Two corporations having common or substantially common ownership by same shareholders.

Sister-in-law. Sister of one's spouse; wife of one's brother; wife of one's spouse's brother.

Sit. To hold court; to do any act of a judicial nature. To hold a session, as of a court, grand jury, legislative body, etc. To be formally organized and proceeding with the transaction of business.

Sit-down strike. A strike in which the workers stay in the plant but refuse to work.

Site /sáyt/. A plot of ground suitable or set apart for some specific use. A seat or ground plot. The term does not of itself necessarily mean a place or tract of land fixed by definite boundaries. *See also* site; Situs.

Sitting. The part of the year in which judicial business is transacted. A session or term of court; usually plural. *See* Session.

Sitting in bank *or* **en banc.** A session of the court in which all judges or at least a quorum of judges sit and hear cases. Under current practice, the term is reserved almost exclusively for appellate courts and in this connection it is contrasted with single justice sitting. *See* En banc.

Sittings in camera. *See* Chamber.

Situate. To give a specific position to; fix a site for; to place in certain position.

Situation of danger. Within the meaning of the last clear chance rule as applicable to a plaintiff operating a moving vehicle, is reached only when plaintiff, in moving toward path of an on-coming train or vehicle has reached a position from which he cannot escape by ordinary care, and it is not enough that plaintiff was merely approaching a position of danger. *See* Last clear chance doctrine.

Situs /sáytəs/. Lat. Situation; location; *e.g.* location or place of crime or business. Site; position; the place where a thing is considered, for example, with reference to jurisdiction over it, or the right or power to tax it. It imports fixedness of location. Situs of property, for tax purposes, is determined by whether the taxing state has sufficient contact with the personal property sought to be taxed to justify in fairness the particular tax. Generally, personal property has its taxable "situs" in that state where owner of it is domiciled. Situs of a trust means place of performance of active duties of trustee.

For business situs, *see* Business. *See also* Place.

Sixteenth Amendment. An amendment of 1913 to the U.S. Constitution, which permits Congress to tax incomes, "from whatever source derived, without apportionment among the several states, and without regard to any census or enumeration." The amendment was adopted in response to the Supreme Court's decision in Pollock v. Farmers' Loan and Trust Co., which held that the 1894 federal income tax was unconstitutional as applied to rental income from land. The thrust of the amendment was to remove the apportionment requirement for taxes on income.

Sixth Amendment. The Sixth Amendment of the U.S. Constitution includes such rights as the right to speedy and public trial by an impartial jury, right to be informed of the nature of the accusation, the right to confront witnesses, the right to assistance of counsel and compulsory process.

Sixty-day notice. Under Taft-Hartley Act, notice which must be given by either party to a collective bargaining agreement for reopening or terminating the contract. During such period, strikes and lockouts are prohibited. See 29 U.S.C.A. § 158(d).

Skeleton bill. One drawn, indorsed, or accepted in blank.

Skill. Practical and familiar knowledge of the principles and processes of an art, science, or trade, combined with the ability to apply them in practice in a proper and approved manner and with readiness and dexterity.

Skilled witnesses. One possessing knowledge and experience as to particular subject which are not acquired by ordinary persons. Such witness is allowed to give evidence on matters of opinion and abstract fact. *See also* Expert witness.

Skiptracing. Service which assists creditors in locating delinquent debtors or persons who have fled to avoid prosecution. Also, such services may include location of missing heirs, witnesses, stockholders, bondholders, spouses, assets, bank accounts, or the like.

S.L. Abbreviation for "session [or statute] laws."

Slander. The speaking of base and defamatory words tending to prejudice another in his reputation, community standing, office, trade, business, or means of livelihood. Oral defamation; the speaking of false and malicious words concerning another, whereby injury results to his reputation. The essential elements of slander are: (a) a false and defamatory statement concerning another; (b) an unprivileged communication to a third party; (c) fault amounting at least to negligence on the part of the publisher; and (d) either actionability of the statement irrespective of harm or the existence of special harm caused by the publication. Restatement, Second, Torts § 558.

"Libel" and "slander" are both methods of defamation; the former being expressed by print, writing, pictures, or signs; the latter by oral expressions or transitory gestures. See Restatement, Second, Torts, § 568.

See also Actionable per quod; Actionable per se; Per quod; Per se; Slanderous per se. *Compare* Libel.

Slanderer. One who commits slander. *See* Slander.

Slander of title. A false and malicious statement, oral or written, made in disparagement of a person's title to real or personal property, or of some right of his causing him special damage.

Slanderous per quod. *See* Per quod.

Slanderous per se. Slanderous in itself; such words as are deemed slanderous without proof of special damages. Words which intrinsically, without innuendo, import injury, and are words from which damage, by consent of men generally, flows as a natural consequence. Generally an utterance is deemed "slanderous per se" when publication (a) charges the commission of a crime; (b) imputes some offensive or loathsome disease which would tend to deprive a person of society; (c) charges a woman is not chaste; or (d) tends to injure a party in his trade, business, office or occupation. See Restatement, Second, Torts, § 570.

Slate. List of candidates for public office or for positions on board of directors.

Slayer's rule. Under this doctrine, person who kills another and persons claiming through or under that person may not share in distribution of decedent's estate as heirs, devisees, or legatees and may not collect proceeds as beneficiaries under decedent's life policy when homicide was felonious and intentional, but may share in distribution and collect proceeds when homicide was unintentional, even if it was result of gross negligence. See also Son of Sam law.

Sleeping or **silent partner.** See Silent partner.

Slight. A word of indeterminate meaning, variously defined as inconsiderable; unimportant; trifle; remote; insignificant. As to *slight* Care; Evidence; Fault and Negligence, see those titles.

Slip law. A legislative enactment which is separately and promptly published in pamphlet or in single sheet format after its passage.

Slip law print. An annotated pamphlet print (called a slip law print) of each public and private law enacted by Congress as issued shortly after being signed by the President. Slip laws are cumulated into the U.S. Statutes at Large. See Statute (*Statutes at large*).

Slip opinion. An individual court decision published separately soon after it is rendered.

Slowdown. An organized effort by workers in a plant by which production is slowed from normal pace to bring pressure on the employer for better terms and conditions of working.

Slush fund. Money collected or spent for corrupt purposes such as illegal lobbying or the like.

Small Business Administration. The fundamental purposes of the federal Small Business Administration (SBA) are to: aid, counsel, assist, and protect the interests of small business; insure that small business concerns receive a fair proportion of Government purchases, contracts, and subcontracts, as well as of the sales of Government property; make loans to small business concerns, State and local development companies, and the victims of floods or other catastrophes, or of certain types of economic injury; license, regulate,

and make loans to small business investment companies; improve the management skills of small business owners, potential owners, and managers; conduct studies of the economic environment; and guarantee leases entered into by small business concerns as well as surety bonds issued to them.

Small business corporation. A corporation which satisfies the definition of I.R.C. § 1361(b), § 1244(c)(2), or both. Satisfaction of I.R.C. § 1361(b) permits an S corporation election, and satisfaction of § 1244 enables the shareholders of the corporation to claim an ordinary loss on the worthlessness of the stock. See Corporation (S Corporation).

Small Business Investment Act. Federal legislation enacted in 1958 under which investment companies may be organized for supplying long term equity capital to small businesses. Such Act is implemented by the Small Business Administration.

Small claims court. A special court (sometimes also called "Conciliation Court") which provides expeditious, informal, and inexpensive adjudication of small claims. Jurisdiction of such courts is usually limited to collection of small debts and accounts. Proceedings are very informal with parties normally representing themselves. These courts of limited jurisdiction are often divisions or departments of courts of general jurisdiction.

Small estate probate. See Estate.

Small loan acts. Statutes in effect in nearly all the States fixing the maximum legal rate of interest and other terms on short-term loans by banks and finance companies.

Smart-money. Vindictive, punitive or exemplary damages given by way of punishment and example, in cases of gross misconduct of defendant. See Damages.

Smith Act. Federal law which punishes, among other activities, the advocacy of the overthrow of the government by force or violence. An anti-sedition law. 18 U.S.C.A. § 2385. See Sedition.

Smuggling. The offense of importing or exporting prohibited articles without paying the duties chargeable upon them. The fraudulent taking into a country, or out of it, merchandise which is lawfully prohibited. See 18 U.S.C.A. §§ 545, 546. See also Contraband.

Smut. See Obscene.

Sobriety checkpoint. A public place at which police maintain a roadblock to detain motorists briefly to determine whether they have been operating a motor vehicle under the influence of liquor. Such roadblocks do not violate Fourth Amendment search and seizure protections.

Sobriety tests. *See* Blood alcohol count; Breathalyzer test; Field sobriety tests; Intoximeter; Intoxilyzer; Sobriety checkpoint.

Social guest. For purpose of determining landowner's duty of care, "social guest" is person who goes onto property of another for companionship, diversion and enjoyment of hospitality and is treated as licensee. *See also* Guest.

Social insurance. *See* Insurance.

Social Security Act. Federal legislation creating the Social Security Administration *(q.v.)*. 42 U.S. C.A. § 301 *et seq. See also* Federal Insurance Contributions Act.

Social Security Administration. An agency of the Department of Health and Human Services under the direction of the Commissioner of Social Security which administers a national program of contributory social insurance whereby employees, employers, and the self-employed pay contributions which are pooled in special trust funds. When earnings stop or are reduced because the worker retires, dies, or becomes disabled, monthly cash benefits are paid to replace part of the earnings the person or family has lost. In addition to administering the various retirement, survivors, disability, and supplemental security income (SSI) benefit programs, the SSA oversees the administrative hearing and appeals process involving benefit claims.

Society. An association or company of persons (generally unincorporated) united together by mutual consent, in order to deliberate, determine, and act jointly for some common purpose. In a wider sense, the community or public; the people in general.

Sodomy. While variously defined in state criminal statutes, is generally oral or anal copulation between humans, or between humans and animals.

Soft dollars. Securities industry term for credits that brokers give big investors, such as pension funds and their money managers, in return for their stock trading business.

Soil bank. A federal agricultural program under which farmers are paid for not growing crops, or for growing noncommercial vegetation, in order to preserve the quality of the soil and stabilize commodity prices by avoiding surpluses.

Soldiers' and Sailors' Civil Relief Act. A Federal law that suspends or modifies a military person's civil liabilities and requires persons who want to enforce their claims against persons in the service to follow certain procedures. 50 U.S. C.A. App. § 501 et seq.

Soldier's will. Similar to a seaman's will which is informal in nature and may dispose only of the personal property of the testator. A nuncupative will *(q.v.)*.

Sole. Single; individual; separate; the opposite of joint; as a *sole tenant*. Comprising only one person; the opposite of aggregate; as a *corporation sole*. Without another or others.

Unmarried; as a *feme sole*.

Sole actor doctrine. Under this doctrine a principal is charged with the knowledge of his agent. It contemplates that agent must have ostensibly endeavored to benefit his principal, and even though he did not do so and his acts were for his personal benefit, possibly through defalcation, the third party who obligated himself must have been under the impression that he was dealing with the principal. It is based on the presumption that by reason of the relationship between an agent and his principal the principal is presumed to have been told everything the agent has done and presumed to have known of his actions and promises.

Sole and unconditional owner. *See* Owner.

Sole cause. As respects negligence of plaintiff or third party as the sole cause of injury so as to relieve defendant from liability, means the act or negligence of plaintiff or a third party directly causing the injury without any concurring or contributory negligence of defendant. Term means the act or negligence of the plaintiff or a third party directly causing the injury without any concurring or contributory negligence of defendant. *See also* Proximate cause.

Solemn /sóləm/. Formal; in regular form; with all the forms of a proceeding. As to *solemn* oath, *see* Corporal oath; as to *solemn* war, *see* War.

Solemnization. To enter marriage publicly before witnesses in contrast to a clandestine or common law marriage.

Solemn occasion. Within constitutional provision empowering the legislature to require the opinion of the justices on important questions of law means occasion when such questions of law are necessary to be determined by the body making the inquiry in the exercise of the power intrusted to it by the Constitution or laws.

Sole proprietorship. A form of business in which one person owns all the assets of the business in contrast to a partnership, trust or corporation. The sole proprietor is solely liable for all the debts of the business.

Sole source rule. In suits for false advertising at common law, the plaintiff may not recover unless it can demonstrate that it has a monopoly in the sale of goods possessing the advertised trait, because only in that situation were the common law courts confident that the plaintiff would be harmed by the defendant's false advertising.

This restrictive doctrine is known as the sole source rule.

Solicit. To appeal for something; to apply to for obtaining something; to ask earnestly; to ask for the purpose of receiving; to endeavor to obtain by asking or pleading; to entreat, implore, or importune; to make petition to; to plead for; to try to obtain; and though the word implies a serious request, it requires no particular degree of importunity, entreaty, imploration, or supplication. To awake or incite to action by acts or conduct intended to and calculated to incite the act of giving. The term implies personal petition and importunity addressed to a particular individual to do some particular thing.

As used in context of solicitation to commit a crime, term means to command, authorize, urge, incite, request, or advise another to commit a crime. *See also* Solicitation.

Solicitation. Asking; enticing; urgent request. The inchoate offense of requesting or encouraging someone to engage in illegal conduct. Any action which the relation of the parties justifies in construing into a serious request. Thus "solicitation of prostitution" is the asking or urging a person to engage in prostitution. The word is also used in such phrases as "solicitation to larceny," to bribery, etc.

For the crime of solicitation to be completed, it is only necessary that the actor, with intent that another person commit a crime, have enticed, advised, incited, ordered or otherwise encouraged that person to commit a crime. The crime solicited need not be committed.

A person is guilty of solicitation to commit a crime if with the purpose of promoting or facilitating its commission he commands, encourages or requests another person to engage in specific conduct which would constitute such crime or an attempt to commit such crime or which would establish his complicity in its commission or attempted commission. Model Penal Code, § 5.02. See also *e.g.* 18 U.S.C.A. § 373 (solicitation to commit a violent crime).

Under Model Penal Code, § 5.05, solicitation of a crime is of the same grade and degree as the most serious offense solicited.

Solicitation of bribe. Asking, or enticing, or requesting of another to commit crime of bribery. See *e.g.* 18 U.S.C.A. § 201.

Soliciting agent. In insurance law, a special agent generally having authority only to solicit insurance, submit applications to company and perform such acts as are incident to that power.

Solicitor. Chief law officer of city, town, or other governmental body or department; *see e.g.* Solicitor General.

In England, to become a solicitor a person must be articled to a practicing solicitor, pass the necessary examinations conducted by the Law Society, and be admitted by the Master of the Rolls. A solicitor may practice in the Bankruptcy Court, county courts, petty sessions, certain proceedings in the Crown Court, most inferior courts, and also in chambers of the Supreme Court. Such are controlled by the Solicitors Act of 1974. *See also* Barrister.

Solicitor General. The Solicitor General of the United States is in charge of representing the Government in suits and appeals in the Supreme Court and as well in lower federal trial and appellate courts in cases involving the interests of the United States. He decides what cases the Government should ask the Supreme Court to review and what position the Government should take in cases before the Court. He supervises the preparation of the Government's Supreme Court briefs and other legal documents and the conduct of the oral arguments in the Court and argues most of the important cases himself. The Solicitor General's duties also include deciding whether the United States should appeal in all cases it loses before the lower federal courts. 28 U.S.C.A. §§ 505, 517, 518.

Solitary confinement. In a general sense, the separate confinement of a prisoner, with only occasional access of any other person, and that only at the discretion of the jailer. In a stricter sense, the complete isolation of a prisoner from all human society, and his confinement in a cell so arranged that he has no direct intercourse with or sight of any human being, and no employment or instruction.

Solvency. Ability to pay debts as they mature and become due. Ability to pay debts in the usual and ordinary course of business. Present ability of debtor to pay out of his estate all his debts. Excess of assets over liabilities. Within Bankruptcy Code, presupposes ability to make ultimate payment of obligations then owed from assets then owned. The opposite of *insolvency (q.v.)*.

Solvent. *See* Solvency.

Son. Male offspring. An immediate male descendant. In a broad use, term may be employed as designating any young male person, as a pupil, a ward, an adopted male child or dependent.

Son-in-law. The husband of one's daughter.

Son of Sam law. Colloquial name, referring to well-known serial killer, for state statutes providing that any share a criminal might otherwise have in proceeds from a book or other presentation about his crime must be placed into an escrow account for the benefit of any victims of the crime. Cf. N.Y. McKinney's Executive Law § 632–a. *See also* Slayer's rule.

Soon. Within a reasonable time; as soon as practicable; as soon as; as soon as may be.

Sound, *v.* To have reference or relation to; to aim at. An action is technically said to *sound in tort or damages* where it is brought not for the specific recovery of a thing, but for damages only. *See* Sounding in damages.

Sound, *adj.* Whole; in good condition; marketable. *See* Warranty.

Free from disease; healthy; physically and mentally fit. The term may also mean free from danger to the life, safety, and welfare.

Sound and disposing mind and memory. Testamentary capacity. Such mind and memory as enables testator to know and understand business in which he is engaged at time of making will. *See also* Capacity, and *Sound mind, below.*

Sound health. In insurance law, means that the applicant has no grave impairment or serious disease, and is free from any ailment that seriously affects the general soundness and healthfulness of the system. A state of health unimpaired by any serious malady of which the person himself is conscious.

Sound judicial discretion. Discretion exercised on full and fair consideration of the facts presented to the judge by the well-known and established mode of procedure. Discretion exercised not arbitrarily or willfully but with regard to what is right and equitable under the circumstances.

Sound mind. The normal condition of the human mind,—that state in which its faculties of perception and judgment are ordinarily well developed, and not impaired by mania, insanity, or other mental disorder. In the law of wills means that testator must have been able to understand and carry in mind, in a general way, nature and situation of his property, his relations to those having claim to his remembrance, and nature of his act. The "sound mind" necessary to execute a will means ability of testator to mentally understand in a general way nature and extent of property to be disposed of, and testator's relation to those who would naturally claim a substantial benefit from will, as well as general understanding of practical effect of will as executed. *See also* Capacity.

Sounding in damages. When an action is brought, not for the recovery of lands, goods, or sums of money (as is the case in real or mixed actions or the personal action of debt or detinue), but for damages only, as in covenant, trespass, etc., the action is said to be "sounding in damages."

Soundness. General good health; freedom from any permanent disease or illness. *See* Sound.

Source. That from which any act, movement, information, or effect proceeds. A person or thing that originates, sets in motion, or is a primary agency in producing any course of action or result. An originator; creator; origin. A place where something is found or whence it is taken or derived. *See also* Cause.

Source document. A document, such as an inventory receiving report, bill from supplier, receipt, or customer sales slip, that provides evidence that a transaction has occurred.

Sources of the law. The origins from which particular positive laws derive their authority and coercive force; such are constitutions, treaties, statutes, usages, and customs.

In another sense, the authoritative or reliable works, records, documents, edicts, etc., to which we are to look for an understanding of what constitutes the law. Such, for example, with reference to the Roman law, are the compilations of Justinian and the treatise of Gaius; and such, with reference to the common law, are especially the ancient reports and the works of such writers as Bracton, Littleton, Coke, Fleta, Blackstone, and others.

Sovereign. A person, body, or state in which independent and supreme authority is vested; a chief ruler with supreme power; a king or other ruler in a monarchy. *See also* Sovereignty.

Sovereign immunity. A judicial doctrine which precludes bringing suit against the government without its consent. Founded on the ancient principle that "the King can do no wrong," it bars holding the government or its political subdivisions liable for the torts of its officers or agents unless such immunity is expressly waived by statute or by necessary inference from legislative enactment. The federal government has generally waived its non-tort action immunity in the Tucker Act, 28 U.S.C.A. § 1346(a)(2), 1491, and its tort immunity in the Federal Tort Claims Act, 28 U.S.C.A. § 1346(b), 2674. Most states have also waived immunity in various degrees at both the state and local government levels.

The immunity from certain suits in federal court granted to states by the Eleventh Amendment to the United States Constitution.

See also Foreign immunity; Federal Tort Claims Act; Suits in Admiralty Act; Tucker Act.

Foreign Sovereign Immunity Act. Subject to existing international agreements to which the U.S. is a party, and to certain statutorily prescribed exceptions, a foreign nation is immune from the jurisdiction of federal and state courts. 28 U.S.C.A. § 1601–1611.

Sovereign people. The political body, consisting of the entire number of citizens and qualified electors, who, in their collective capacity, possess the powers of sovereignty and exercise them through their chosen representatives.

Sovereign power *or* **sovereign prerogative.** That power in a state to which none other is superior or equal, and which includes all the specific powers necessary to accomplish the legitimate ends and purposes of government.

Sovereign right. A right which the state alone, or some of its governmental agencies, can possess, and which it possesses in the character of a sovereign, for the common benefit, and to enable it to carry out its proper functions; distinguished from such "proprietary" rights as a state, like any private person, may have in property or demands which it owns.

Sovereign states. States whose subjects or citizens are in the habit of obedience to them, and which are not themselves subject to any other (or paramount) state in any respect. The state is said to be semi-sovereign only, and not sovereign, when in any respect or respects it is liable to be controlled by a paramount government. In the intercourse of nations, certain states have a position of entire independence of others, and can perform all those acts which it is possible for any state to perform in this particular sphere. These same states have also entire power of self-government; that is, of independence upon all other states as far as their own territory and citizens not living abroad are concerned. No foreign power or law can have control except by convention. This power of independent action in external and internal relations constitutes complete sovereignty.

Sovereignty. The supreme, absolute, and uncontrollable power by which any independent state is governed; supreme political authority; the supreme will; paramount control of the constitution and frame of government and its administration; the self-sufficient source of political power, from which all specific political powers are derived; the international independence of a state, combined with the right and power of regulating its internal affairs without foreign dictation; also a political society, or state, which is sovereign and independent.

The power to do everything in a state without accountability,—to make laws, to execute and to apply them, to impose and collect taxes and levy contributions, to make war or peace, to form treaties of alliance or of commerce with foreign nations, and the like.

Speaker. The official designation of the president or chairman of certain legislative bodies, particularly of the House of Representatives in the Congress of the United States, and of one or both branches of several of the state legislatures, *i.e.* Speaker of the House.

Speaking demurrer. A demurrer which introduces a new fact that does not appear from face of bill or complaint is a "speaking demurrer," and cannot be sustained. A speaking demurrer is a special exception which, instead of limiting itself to the allegations of the petition and pointing out defects therein, states factual propositions not appearing in the petition and, in reliance upon such facts, seeks to challenge the plaintiff's right to recovery. *See also* Demurrer.

Speaking motion. A motion which requires consideration of matters outside the pleadings. Formerly, such motions were prohibited but under Fed.R.Civ.P. 12(b) such motions are now entertained.

Special. Relating to or designating a species, kind, individual, thing, or sort; designed for a particular purpose; confined to a particular purpose, object, person, or class. Unusual, extraordinary.

As to *special* Acceptance; Administration; Agent; Allocatur; Allowance; Appearance; Assessment; Assumpsit; Bail; Bailiff; Benefit; Calendar; Charge; Constable; Contract; Count; Covenant; Customs; Damage; Demurrer; Deposit; Deputy; Election; Finding; Guaranty; Guardian; Indorsement; Injunction; Insurance; Issue; Jury; Legacy; Letter of credit; License; Limitation; Malice; Master; Meeting; Mortgage; Motion; Occupant; Owner; Partner; Partnership; Plea; Pleader; Pleadings; Power; Power of appointment; Privilege; Proceeding; Property; Replication; Request; Restraint of trade; Retainer; Rule; Service; Session; Statute; Stock; Tail; Term; Traverse; Trust; Verdict, and Warranty, see those titles.

Special act. A private statute; an act which operates only upon particular persons or private concerns. *See* Special law.

Special attorney *or* **counsel.** An attorney employed by the Attorney General of the United States or of a state to assist in a particular case where the public interest so requires. 28 U.S.C.A. § 543. *See also* Independent counsel.

Special district. A limited governmental structure created to bypass normal borrowing limitations, to insulate certain activities from traditional political influence, to allocate functions to entities reflecting particular expertise, to provide services in otherwise unincorporated areas, or to accomplish a primarily local benefit or improvement, *e.g.* parks and planning, mosquito control, sewage removal.

Special errors. In common law pleading, special pleas in error are such as, instead of joining in error, alleging some extraneous matter as a ground of defeating the writ of error, *e.g.*, a release of errors, expiration of the time within which error might be brought, or the like. To these, the plaintiff in error may either reply or demur.

Special exception. An objection to the form in which a cause of action is stated. *See* Demurrer.

Special exception to municipal zoning ordinance refers to special uses which are permissive in particular zone under ordinance and are neither nonconforming uses nor akin to a variance and refers to special use which is considered by local legislative body to be essential or desirable for welfare of community and its citizenry and which is entirely appropriate and not essentially incompatible with basic uses in zone involved, but not at every or any location therein or without restriction or conditions being imposed on such use. A special exception allows property owner to put his property to use which regulations expressly permit under conditions specified in zoning regulations themselves.

Such use is also known as a conditional use, special permit, or special use. *See* Special use permit. *Compare* Variance.

Special execution. A copy of a judgment with a direction to the sheriff indorsed thereon to execute it. One that directs a levy upon some special property. *See* Execution.

Special executor. One whose power and office are limited, either in respect to the time or place of their exercise, or restricted to a particular portion of the decedent's estate. One only empowered by will to take charge of a limited portion of the estate, or such part as may lie in one place, or to carry on the administration only to a prescribed point. *See* Executor.

Special grand jury. A grand jury convened to hear a particular case or series of cases involving similar crimes. 18 U.S.C.A. § 3331 *et seq.*

Special interest groups. Groups in society that have a special interest in common. Special interest groups generally attempt to influence government legislation to benefit their own particular group interests. *See* Lobbying.

Special interrogatories. Written questions on one or more issues of fact submitted to a jury. The answers to these are necessary to a verdict. Fed.R.Civ.P. 49(b).

Specialist. Stock broker who remains at one post of exchange where particular stocks are dealt in and executes orders of other brokers, for which he receives commission; one who specializes in limited group of stocks.

Special jurisdiction. A court authorized to take cognizance of only some few kinds of causes or proceedings expressly designated by statute is called a court of special or limited jurisdiction. Power of a court over only a limited type of case (*e.g.* Probate court) or over only property and not the person or the defendant.

Special law. One relating to particular persons or things; one made for individual cases or for particular places or districts; one operating upon a selected class, rather than upon the public generally. A private law. A law is "special" when it is different from others of the same general kind or designed for a particular purpose, or limited in range or confined to a prescribed field of action or operation. One which relates to either particular persons, places, or things or to persons, places, or things which, though not particularized, are separated by any method of selection from the whole class to which the law might, but not such legislation, be applied. A special law applies only to an individual or a number of individuals out of a single class similarly situated and affected, or to a special locality. *See also* Private bill; Private law. *Compare* General law; Public law.

Special lien. A special lien is in the nature of a particular lien, being a lien upon particular property. A lien which the holder can enforce only as security for the performance of a particular act or obligation and of obligations incidental thereto. *See also* Lien.

Special matter. In common law pleading, under a plea of the general issue, the defendant is allowed to give special matter in evidence, usually after notice to the plaintiff of the nature of such matter, thus sparing him the necessity of pleading it specially.

Special permit. *See* Special use permit.

Special registration. In election laws, registration for particular election only which does not entitle elector to vote at any succeeding election.

Special session. An extraordinary session. *See* Session.

Specialty. A contract under seal. A writing sealed and delivered, containing some agreement. A special contract. A writing sealed and delivered, which is given as a security for the payment of a debt, in which such debt is particularly specified. *See* Contract (*Special contract*).

Special use permit. Permitted exception to zoning ordinance; *e.g.* church, hospital, etc. A special use permit allows property owner to use his property in a way which the zoning regulations expressly permit under the conditions specified in the regulations themselves. "Special permit" and "special exception" have the same meaning and can be used interchangeably. *See also* Special exception; *Compare* Variance.

Special use valuation. An option which permits the executor of an estate to value, for death tax purposes, real estate used in a farming activity or in connection with a closely-held business at its current use value rather than at its most suitable or highest and best use value. Under this option, a farm would be valued at its value for farming purposes even though, for example, the property might have a higher value as a potential shopping center. In order for the executor of an estate to elect special use valuation, the conditions of I.R.C. § 2032A must be satisfied.

Special warranty. A covenant of "special warranty" is one the operation of which is limited to certain persons or claims. *See also* Warranty.

Special warranty deed. A deed in which the grantor only covenants to warrant and defend the title against claims and demands of the grantor and all persons claiming by, through and under him. In some jurisdictions, such deed is called a quitclaim deed (*q.v.*).

Specie /spíyshiy(iy)/. Coin of the precious metals, of a certain weight and fineness, and bearing the stamp of the government, denoting its value as currency. Metallic money; *e.g.* gold or silver coins.

When spoken of a contract, the expression "performance *in specie*" means strictly, or according to the exact terms. As applied to things, it signifies individuality or identity. Thus, on a bequest of a specific picture, the legatee would be said to be entitled to the delivery of the picture *in specie; i.e.,* of the very thing. Whether a thing is due *in genere* or *in specie* depends, in each case, on the will of the transacting parties.

Specific. Precisely formulated or restricted; definite; explicit; of an exact or particular nature. Having a certain form or designation; observing a certain form; particular; precise; tending to specify, or to make particular, definite, limited or precise.

As to *specific* Denial; Devise; Legacy, and Performance, see those titles.

Specification. As used in the law relating to patents, manufacturing, and construction contracts, a particular or detailed statement, account, description, or listing of the various elements, materials, dimensions, etc. involved.

Specific bequest (*or* devise). A testamentary gift of specific personal property (*e.g.* "my old rocking chair") or of a specific amount of cash. A specific bequest (or devise) is a gift by will of a specific article or part of testator's estate, which is identified and distinguished from all things of same kind and which may be satisfied by delivery of particular things. *See also* Devise; Legacy *(Specific legacy).*

Specific devise. *See* Devise; Specific bequest (*or* devise).

Specific intent. The mental purpose to accomplish a specific act prohibited by law. The most common usage of "specific intent" is to designate a special mental element which is required above and beyond any mental state required with respect to the *actus reus* of the crime. Common law larceny, for example, requires the taking and carrying away of the property of another, and the defendant's mental state as to this act must be established, but in addition it must be shown that there was an "intent to steal" the property. Similarly, common law burglary requires a breaking and entry into the dwelling of another, but in addition to the mental state connected with these acts it must also be established that the defendant acted "with intent to commit a felony therein." The subjective desire or knowledge that the prohibited result will occur. *See also* Criminal *(Criminal intent)*; Mens rea.

Specific intent crime. Crime in which defendant must not only intend the act charged, but also intend to violate law. One in which a particular intent is a necessary element of the crime itself. *See also* Mens rea; Specific intent.

Specific legatee. The recipient of designated property under a will and transferred by the death of the owner.

Specific performance. *See* Performance.

Specify. To mention specifically; to state in full and explicit terms; to point out; to tell or state precisely or in detail; to particularize, or to distinguish by words one thing from another.

Specimen. A sample; a part of something intended to exhibit the kind and quality of the whole.

Spectrograph. Voice print analysis is a method of identification based on the comparison of graphic representations or "spectrograms" made of human voices. Such method utilizes a machine known as a "spectrograph" which separates the sound of human voices into the three component elements of time, frequency and intensity. Using a series of lines or bars, the machine plots the variables across electronically sensitive paper and the result is a "spectrogram" of the acoustical signal of the speaker, with the horizontal axis representing the time lapse, the vertical axis indicating frequency, and the thickness of the lines disclosing the intensity of the voice. An increasing number of courts are permitting the admissibility of spectrograph results into evidence to identify voices. *See also* Voice exemplars; Voice-print.

Speculation. Buying or selling with expectation of profiting by a rise or fall in price. Also, engaging in hazardous business transactions, or investing in risky securities or commodities, with the hope of an unusually large profit.

Speculation, upon which neither court in nonjury case nor jurors in jury case may base verdict, is the art of theorizing about a matter as to which evidence is not sufficient for certain knowledge.

Speculative damages. *See* Damages.

Speculator. One who engages in a speculative activity by taking a position (for example, in a security) in the hope of earning an extraordinary return. *See* Speculation.

Speech. Freedom of speech is right guaranteed by First Amendment, U.S.Const. *See also* Commercial speech doctrine; Freedom of speech; Liberty; Symbolic speech.

Speech or debate clause. Art. 1, § 6, cl. 1 of U.S. Constitution grants congressmen immunity "for any speech or debate in either House." The courts have extended this privilege to matters beyond pure speech and debate in either House, but only when necessary to prevent indirect impairment of such deliberations. *See also* Legislative immunity.

Speedy remedy. One which, having in mind the subject-matter involved, can be pursued with expedition and without essential detriment to the party aggrieved; *e.g.* Restraining order. *See* Speedy trial.

Speedy trial. The right of the accused to a speedy trial is guaranteed by the Sixth Amendment of the Constitution and such right is implemented by 18 U.S.C.A. § 3161 et seq. and Fed.R.Crim.P. 50. Barker v. Wingo, 407 U.S. 514, 92 S.Ct. 2182, 33 L.Ed.2d 101, lists four factors to be considered in determining whether delay was unreasonable: (1) Length of delay; (2) the government's justification for the delay; (3) whether and how the defendant asserted his right to a speedy trial; and (4) prejudice caused by the delay, such as lengthened pre-trial incarceration. A trial had as soon after indictment as prosecution, with reasonable diligence, can prepare for it; a trial according to fixed rules, free from capricious and oppressive delays, but the time within which it must be had to satisfy the guaranty depends on the circumstances. What constitutes a "speedy trial" depends on circumstances of each case. *See* Prejudice *(Speedy trial)*; Speedy Trial Act.

Speedy Trial Act. Federal Act of 1974 establishing a set of time limits for carrying out the major events *(e.g.* information, indictment, arraignment) in the prosecution of federal criminal cases. 18 U.S.C.A. § 3161 *et seq.*

In any case involving a defendant charged with an offense, the appropriate judicial officer, at the earliest practicable time, shall, after consultation with the counsel for the defendant and the attorney for the Government, set the case for trial on a day certain, or list it for trial on a weekly or other short-term trial calendar at a place within the judicial district, so as to assure a speedy trial. 18 U.S.C.A. § 3161(a). See also Fed.R.Crim.P. 50.

Spend. To consume by using in any manner; to use up, to exhaust, distribute, as to expend money or any other possession.

Spendthrift. One who spends money profusely and improvidently; a prodigal; one who lavishes or wastes his estate. By statute, a person who by excessive drinking, gaming, idleness, or debauchery of any kind shall so spend, waste, or lessen his estate as to expose himself or his family to want or suffering, or expose the government to charge or expense for the support of himself or family, or is liable to be put under guardianship on account of such excesses. *See* Spendthrift trust.

Spendthrift trust. A trust created to provide a fund for the maintenance of a beneficiary and at the same time to secure the fund against his improvidence or incapacity; provisions against alienation of the trust fund by the voluntary act of the beneficiary or by his creditors are its usual incidents. One which provides a fund for benefit of another than settlor, secures it against beneficiary's own improvidence, and places it beyond his creditors' reach. A trust set up to protect a beneficiary from spending all of the money that he is entitled to. Only a certain portion of the total amount is given to him at any one time. Most states permit spendthrift trust provisions that prohibit creditors from attaching a spendthrift trust.

Spin-off. A form of corporate divestiture that results in a subsidiary or division of a corporation becoming an independent company. Spin-off occurs where part of assets of corporation is transferred to a new corporation and stock of transferee is distributed to shareholders of transferor without surrender by them of stock in transferor. A type of reorganization wherein, for example, A Corporation transfers some assets to B Corporation in exchange for enough B stock to represent control. A Corporation then distributes the B stock to its shareholders. *See also* Split-off; Split-up.

Spiritual. Relating to religious or ecclesiastical persons or affairs, as distinguished from "secular" or lay, worldly, or business matters.

As to *spiritual* Corporation; Court, and Lord, see those titles.

Spite fence. A fence of no beneficial use to person erecting and maintaining it on his land and maintained solely for purpose of annoying owner of adjoining land. A high and unsightly fence erected to annoy a neighbor or adjoining landowner by obstructing his air, light or view.

Split gift. *See* Gift.

Split income. Congress, in 1948, enacted new joint tax return legislation and a new set of rates to remove the considerable disparity between tax treatment of married couples in community property and common-law states, and thereby to remove the considerable pressure on the common-law states to adopt community-property systems. By law enacted that year, married couples in all states were given the privilege to split their income, that is to have it taxed on a joint return at a rate equal to that which would apply if each had earned one-half the amount and were taxed on a separate return. In 1969, however, Congress retained but reduced the disparity between rates imposed on single persons and married couples with the same incomes. This reduction took the form of a new and lower rate schedule for single persons, which took effect beginning in 1971. See I.R.C. § 1(c). *See also* Gift splitting election.

Split-off. When a corporation sets up and funds a new corporation and gives the shares of this new corporation to the old corporation's stockholders in exchange for some of their shares in the old company, this new company is a "split-off" and the process is a split-off. A type of reorganization whereby, for example, A Corporation transfers assets to B Corporation in exchange for enough B stock to represent control. A Corporation then distributes the B stock to its shareholders in exchange for some of their A stock. *See also* Spinoff; Split-up.

Split order. An order to a broker directing him to buy or sell some stock at one price and some at another.

Split sentence. One where penalty of fine and imprisonment, as provided by statute, is imposed and imprisonment part is suspended and fine part enforced. It is also exemplified in a sentence by which the defendant serves some time and the balance of the sentence is suspended.

Splitting cause of action. Dividing a single or indivisible cause of action into several parts or claims and bringing several actions thereon. Commencement of action for only part of the cause of action. Rule against "splitting cause of action" applies only when several actions are brought as result of dividing single or indivisible cause of action.

There is no "splitting of causes" where demand which is subject of second action was not due at time of the first action. The rule against "splitting causes of action" does not mean that plaintiff cannot sue for less than is his due but means merely that if he does so he may be precluded from maintaining another action for the remainder of the same demand.

See also Joinder; Misjoinder; Multiplicity of actions *or* suits.

Split-up. When a corporation divides into two or more separate new corporations, gives its shareholders the shares of these new corporations, and goes out of business, this process is termed a "split-up." A type of reorganization whereby, for example, A Corporation transfers some assets to B Corporation and the remainder to Z Corporation in return for which it receives enough B and Z stock to represent control of each corporation.

The B and Z stock is then distributed by A Corporation to its shareholders in return for all of their A stock. The result of the split-up is that A Corporation is liquidated and its shareholders now have control of B and Z Corporations.

Spoilage. An occurrence in the production process that causes units to be produced that are not acceptable.

Continuous spoilage. Spoilage that is assumed to occur uniformly throughout the production process.

Spoliation /spòwliyéyshən/. The intentional destruction of evidence and when it is established, fact finder may draw inference that evidence destroyed was unfavorable to party responsible for its spoliation. Such act constitutes an obstruction of justice. The destruction, or the significant and meaningful alteration of a document or instrument.

Any change made on a written instrument by a person *not* a party to the instrument. Such a change will have no effect, provided that the original tenor of the instrument can still be ascertained.

Spontaneous declarations. A statement is admissible as a "spontaneous declaration" if there was an occurrence sufficiently startling to produce a spontaneous and unreflecting statement, if there was an absence of time to fabricate, and if the statement related to the circumstances of the occurrence. *See* Spontaneous exclamation.

Spontaneous exclamation. Within res gestae rule, a statement or exclamation made immediately after some exciting occasion by a participant or spectator and asserting the circumstances of that occasion as it is observed by him, is admissible as a spontaneous and sincere response to actual perceptions produced by shock. One exception to the Hearsay Rule is the exclamation made by one under the stress of excitement or at the very moment of an event before the mind has an opportunity to contrive a false statement; *cf.* Fed. Evid. Rule 803(2). Sometimes called the *res gestæ* exception to Hearsay Rule. *See* Res *(Res gestæ)*.

Spot. In commodity trading and in foreign exchange, immediate delivery in contrast to a future delivery.

Spot exchange rate. Exchange rate at which one currency can be converted into another currency for immediate delivery.

Spot market. *See* Spot trading.

Spot price. The selling price of commodities or goods in spot market. *See* Spot trading.

Spot trading. In commodities market, cash sales for immediate delivery in contrast to trading in futures.

Spot zoning. Granting of a zoning classification to a piece of land that differs from that of the other land in the immediate area. Term refers to zoning which singles out an area for treatment different from that of similar surrounding land and which cannot be justified on the bases of health, safety, morals or general welfare of the community and which is not in accordance with a comprehensive plan.

Spousal abuse. *See* Battered Woman Syndrome.

Spousal disqualification. *See* Marital communications privilege.

Spouse. One's husband or wife, and "surviving spouse" is one of a married pair who outlive the other.

Spread. In general, a difference between two amounts. In stock and commodity trading, the difference between the bid and asked price. In arbitrage *(q.v.)*, the difference between two markets in the price or value of a currency. In futures trading, is the difference between delivery months in the same or different markets. In fixed-income securities, is the difference between yields on securities of the same quality but different maturities or the difference between yields on securities of the same maturity but different quality. In banking, is difference between bank's cost of obtaining funds and rate it charges on loaning out funds.

Spread sheet. A multicolumned worksheet used by accountants and auditors to summarize and analyze transactions.

Springing use. *See* Use.

Sprinkling trust. *See* Trust.

Spurious. False, counterfeit, not genuine.

Spurious class action. One of the former categories of class action in which interests of members of class were several and not interdependent, and where joinder was a matter of efficiency to avoid multiplicity of suits. This category of class action no longer exists under Federal Rule of Civil Procedure 23 as revised. *See also* Class *or* representative action.

Spying. To watch or listen to secretly. *See* Eavesdropping; Wiretapping.

Gathering, transmitting, or losing defense information with intent or reason to believe such information will be used to the injury of the United States is a federal crime. 18 U.S.C.A. § 793 *et seq. See* Espionage.

Square. As used to designate a certain portion of land within the limits of a city or town, this term may be synonymous with "block," that is, the smallest subdivision which is bounded on all sides by principal streets, or it may denote a space (more or less rectangular) not built upon, and set apart for public passage, use, recreation, or ornamentation, in the nature of a "park" but smaller.

Under government survey system, an area measuring 24 × 24 miles.

Just; settled; fair.

Squatter. One who settles on another's land, without legal title or authority. A person entering upon lands, not claiming in good faith the right to do so by virtue of any title of his own or by virtue of some agreement with another whom he believes to hold the title. Under former laws, one who settled on public land in order to acquire title to the land.

Squatter's right. *See* Adverse possession.

Squeeze-out. Techniques by which a minority interest in a corporation is eliminated or reduced. Squeeze-outs may occur in a variety of contexts, *e.g.*, in a "going private" transaction in which minority shareholders are compelled to accept cash for their shares, or the issuance of new shares to existing shareholders in which minority shareholders are given the unpleasant choice of having their proportionate interest in the corporation reduced significantly or of investing a large amount of additional or new capital over which they have no control and for which they receive little or no return. Many squeeze-outs involve the use of cash mergers. "Squeeze-out" is often used synonymously with "freeze-out" *(q.v.)*.

Squire. A contraction of "esquire."

SS. An abbreviation used in that part of a record, pleading, or affidavit, called the "statement of the venue." Commonly translated or read, "to-wit," and supposed to be a contraction of *"scilicet."*

S.S.A. Social Security Administration.

S.S.S. Selective Service System.

Stacking. In insurance, refers to ability of insured, when covered by more than one insurance policy, to obtain benefits from second policy on same claim when recovery from first policy alone would be inadequate.

Stake. A deposit made to answer an event, as on a wager. Something deposited by two persons with the third on condition that it is to be delivered to the one who shall become entitled to it by the happening of a specified contingency. *See also* Stakeholder.

A boundary marker used for land survey purposes.

Stakeholder. Generally, a stakeholder is a third party chosen by two or more persons to keep on deposit property or money the right or possession of which is contested between them, and to be delivered to one who shall establish his right to it; and it is one who is entitled to interplead rival or contesting claimants to property or funds in his hands. A person who is or may be exposed to multiple liability as the result of adverse claims. A stakeholder may commence an action of interpleader against two or more claimants. New York C.P.L.R. § 1006. *See also* Interpleader.

A person with whom money is deposited pending the decision of a bet or wager *(q.v.)*. His function is to receive the sums wagered and hold them against the determining event, whether that event be a horse race or otherwise, and then pay them over to the winner.

Staking. Identification of boundaries of parcel of land by placing stakes in ground at boundary points.

Stale, *n.* In Saxon law, larceny.

Stale check. A check which bears a date of issue very much earlier than the date of its presentation or negotiation. A check which has been outstanding too long.

A check, other than a certified check, that is presented for payment more than six months after its date. U.C.C. § 4–404.

Stale demand *or* **claim.** A demand or claim that has long remained unasserted; one that is first asserted after an unexplained delay which is so long as to render it difficult or impossible for the court to ascertain the truth of the matters in controversy and do justice between the parties, or as to create a presumption against the existence or validity of the claim, or a presumption that the claim has been abandoned or satisfied. It implies a greater lapse of time than is necessary to "laches." The doctrine is purely an equitable one, and arises only when, from lapse of time and laches of plaintiff, it would be inequitable to allow a party to enforce his legal rights. *See also* Limitation *(Statute of limitations)*.

Stamp. Stamped or printed paper affixed to official or legal documents, stock certificates, etc. as evidence that tax has been paid as required by law. A small label or strip of paper, printed and sold by the government, and required to be attached to mail-matter, and to certain other documents and articles *(e.g.* liquor, cigarettes) subject to duty or excise. *See* Documentary stamp; Revenue stamps; Stamp tax.

A mark, design, seal, etc., which indicates ownership, approval, etc. An identifying or characterizing mark or impression.

Stamp acts. In English law, acts regulating the stamps upon deeds, contracts, agreements, papers in law proceedings, bills and notes, letters, receipts, and other papers. English Act of 1765 requiring that revenue stamps be affixed to all official documents in American colonies.

Stamp tax. The cost of stamps which are required to be affixed to legal documents such as deeds,

certificates, and the like. *See* Documentary stamp; Revenue stamps; Stamp.

Stand. To cease from movement or progress; to pause, remain stationary or inactive.

To abide; to submit to; as "to *stand* a trial." To appear in court.

To remain as a thing is; to remain in force. Pleadings objected to and held good are allowed to *stand.*

Standard. Stability, general recognition, and conformity to established practice. A type, model, or combination of elements accepted as correct or perfect. A measure or rule applicable in legal cases such as the "standard of care" in tort actions. *See* Double standard; Reasonable man doctrine *or* standard; Reasonable woman standard; Standard of care.

An ensign or flag used in war.

Standard deduction. *See* Deduction.

Standard established by law. That of a reasonable man under like circumstances. *See* Reasonable man doctrine *or* standard; Standard of care.

Standard of care. In law of negligence, that degree of care which a reasonably prudent person should exercise in same or similar circumstances. If a person's conduct falls below such standard, he may be liable in damages for injuries or damages resulting from his conduct. *See* Negligence; Reasonable man doctrine *or* standard.

In medical, legal, etc., malpractice cases a standard of care is applied to measure the competence of the professional. The traditional standard for doctors is that he exercise the "average degree of skill, care, and diligence exercised by members of the same profession, practicing in the same or a similar locality in light of the present state of medical and surgical science." With increased specialization, however, certain courts have disregarded geographical considerations holding that in the practice of a board-certified medical or surgical specialty, the standard should be that of a reasonable specialist practicing medicine or surgery in the same special field. *See also* Malpractice.

Standard of need. In public assistance law, total needs of an individual or family stipulated by the state, which, when unsatisfied by relevant resources, makes the individual or family in need for public assistance purposes.

Standard of performance. Regulations of Environmental Protection Agency, under authority of Clean Air Act, which set standards on what new sources of air pollution can do to the environment.

Standard of proof. The burden of proof required in a particular type of case, as in a criminal case where the prosecution has the standard (*i.e.* burden) of proof beyond a reasonable doubt, and in most civil cases where proof by a fair preponderance of the evidence is required. *See* Burden of proof.

Standard of weight, or measure. A weight or measure fixed and prescribed by law, to which all other weights and measures are required to correspond.

Standard opinion. *See* Unqualified opinion.

Standby agreement. Agreement under which a securities firm agrees to stand ready to buy any unsold shares at a predetermined price following a rights offering or to buy any shares resulting from bonds that were not converted during a forced conversion, also at a predetermined price.

Standby fee. A fee paid to an underwriter in connection with an underwritten rights offering or an underwritten forced conversion to compensate the underwriter for standing ready (standing by) to take up rights or acquire convertible bonds, exercise the options, and sell the shares obtained upon exercise.

Standing. One's place in the community in the estimation of others; his relative position in social, commercial, or moral relations; his repute, grade, or rank. *See* Reputation; Standing to sue doctrine; Status.

Standing master. An officer of the court appointed on a regular basis to hear and determine matters within his jurisdiction for which a master may be appointed, as a master in chancery. *See also* Master.

Standing mute. Such exists in criminal case when defendant refuses to plead to the charge against him. If a defendant refuses to plead, the court shall enter a plea of not guilty. Fed.R. Crim.P. 11(a).

Standing orders. Rules adopted by particular courts for governing practice before them. In some states, the presiding judge has authority to adopt standing orders for his court alone. They may include rules as to the time at which court commences each day, a procedure for requesting continuances of cases and a method by which cases are placed on the trial list of the particular court. They may be system wide or affect only a particular court in the system.

Standing to be sued. Capacity of a person or governmental body to be a party defendant in an action. A state as sovereign has no capacity to be sued except in cases in which it has consented to suit. *See* Sovereign immunity.

Standing to sue doctrine. "Standing to sue" means that party has sufficient stake in an otherwise justiciable controversy to obtain judicial resolution of that controversy. Standing is a concept utilized to determine if a party is sufficiently affected so as to insure that a justiciable contro-

versy is presented to the court; it is the right to take the initial step that frames legal issues for ultimate adjudication by court or jury. The requirement of "standing" is satisfied if it can be said that the plaintiff has a legally protectible and tangible interest at stake in the litigation. Standing is a jurisdictional issue which concerns power of federal courts to hear and decide cases and does not concern ultimate merits of substantive claims involved in the action. The doctrine emanates from the case or controversy requirement of the Constitution and from general principles of judicial administration, and seeks to insure that the plaintiff has alleged such a personal stake in the outcome of the controversy as to assure concrete adverseness.

Standing is a requirement that the plaintiffs have been injured or been threatened with injury by governmental action complained of, and focuses on the question of whether the litigant is the proper party to fight the lawsuit, not whether the issue itself is justiciable. Essence of standing is that no person is entitled to assail the constitutionality of an ordinance or statute except as he himself is adversely affected by it. *See also* Case *(Cases and controversies)*; Justiciable controversy; Ripeness doctrine.

Administrative Procedure Act. Such Act authorizes actions against federal officers by "any person suffering legal wrong because of agency action, or adversely affected or aggrieved by agency action within the meaning of a relevant statute." 5 U.S.C.A. § 702.

Staple. A major commodity grown, traded and demanded; *e.g.* grain, salt, flour. Such commodity is usually very important to the local economy where it is grown or produced. Raw material.

Stare decisis /stériy dəsáysəs/. Lat. To abide by, or adhere to, decided cases.

Policy of courts to stand by precedent and not to disturb settled point. Doctrine that, when court has once laid down a principle of law as applicable to a certain state of facts, it will adhere to that principle, and apply it to all future cases, where facts are substantially the same; regardless of whether the parties and property are the same. Under doctrine a deliberate or solemn decision of court made after argument on question of law fairly arising in the case, and necessary to its determination, is an authority, or binding precedent in the same court, or in other courts of equal or lower rank in subsequent cases where the very point is again in controversy. Doctrine is one of policy, grounded on theory that security and certainty require that accepted and established legal principle, under which rights may accrue, be recognized and followed, though later found to be not legally sound, but whether previous holding of court shall be adhered to, modified, or overruled is within court's discretion under circumstances of case before it. Under doctrine, when point of law has been settled by decision, it forms precedent which is not afterwards to be departed from, and, while it should ordinarily be strictly adhered to, there are occasions when departure is rendered necessary to vindicate plain, obvious principles of law and remedy continued injustice. The doctrine is not ordinarily departed from where decision is of long-standing and rights have been acquired under it, unless considerations of public policy demand it. The doctrine is limited to actual determinations in respect to litigated and necessarily decided questions, and is not applicable to dicta or obiter dicta.

See also Precedent; Res *(Res judicata)*.

State, *n.* A people permanently occupying a fixed territory bound together by common-law habits and custom into one body politic exercising, through the medium of an organized government, independent sovereignty and control over all persons and things within its boundaries, capable of making war and peace and of entering into international relations with other communities of the globe. The organization of social life which exercises sovereign power in behalf of the people. In its largest sense, a "state" is a body politic or a society of men. A body of people occupying a definite territory and politically organized under one government. A territorial unit with a distinct general body of law. Restatement, Second, Conflicts, § 3. Term may refer either to body politic of a nation (*e.g.* United States) or to an individual governmental unit of such nation (*e.g.* California).

The section of territory occupied by one of the United States. One of the component commonwealths or states of the United States of America. The term is sometimes applied also to governmental agencies authorized by state, such as municipal corporations. Any state of the United States, the District of Columbia, the Commonwealth of Puerto Rico, and any territory or possession subject to the legislative authority of the United States. Uniform Probate Code, § 1–201(40).

The people of a state, in their collective capacity, considered as the party wronged by a criminal deed; the public; as in the title of a cause, "The State vs. A. B."

Term "state" as used in rules providing when a state may appeal in a criminal case is all inclusive and intended to include not only the state but its political subdivisions, counties and cities.

The circumstances or condition of a being or thing at a given time.

Foreign state. A foreign country or nation. The several United States are considered "foreign" to each other except as regards their relations as common members of the Union.

State officers. Those whose duties concern the state at large or the general public, or who are authorized to exercise their official functions throughout the entire state, without limitation to any political subdivision of the state. In another sense, officers belonging to or exercising authority under one of the states of the Union, as distinguished from the officers of the United States.

State offices. See Office.

State paper. A document prepared by, or relating to, the political department of the government of a state or nation, and concerning or affecting the administration of its government or its political or international relations. Also, a newspaper, designated by public authority, as the organ for the publication of public statutes, resolutions, notices, and advertisements.

State revenue. Current income of state from whatever source derived that is subject to appropriation for public uses.

State's evidence. See that title.

State tax. A tax the proceeds of which are to be devoted to the expenses of the state, as distinguished from taxation for federal, local or municipal purposes; *e.g.* state income or sales tax.

State, *v.* To express the particulars of a thing in writing or in words; to set down or set forth in detail; to aver, allege, or declare. To set down in gross; to mention in general terms, or by way of reference; to refer.

State action. In general, term used in connection with claims under due process clause and Civil Rights Act for which a private citizen is seeking damages or redress because of improper governmental intrusion into his life. In determining whether an action complained of constitutes "state action" within purview of Fourteenth Amendment, court must examine whether sufficiently close nexus exists between state and challenged action so that the action may fairly be treated as that of the state itself. There is no practical distinction between what constitutes "state action" for purposes of Fourteenth Amendment and what is required to fulfill "under color of state law" provision of 42 U.S.C.A. § 1983. *See* Color of law.

State auditor. The elected or appointed official in a state who is responsible for auditing the accounts of state agencies.

State banks. Those banks chartered by a state in contrast to federally chartered banks. Banks under the supervision and jurisdiction of state agencies. *See also* Bank.

State courts. Those courts which constitute the state judicial system in contrast to federal courts. City and county courts may or may not be part of the state system of courts, depending upon the jurisdiction.

Stated. Determined, fixed, or settled.

Stated account. Term signifies an agreed balance between the parties to a settlement; that is, that they have agreed after an investigation of their accounts that a certain balance is due from one to the other.

Stated capital. Amount of capital contributed by stockholders. Sometimes used to mean legal capital.

The capital or equity of a corporation as it appears in the balance sheet. The sum of the par value of all par value shares issued, the entire amount received for no-par shares, and any amounts transferred by a stock dividend or other corporate action from surplus to stated capital. In some jurisdictions, only a portion of the amount received for no-par shares need be included in stated capital and the remainder may be credited to paid-in surplus and be distributed as a dividend.

State Department. That department in the executive branch of the federal government, headed by the Secretary of State, which is principally responsible for foreign affairs and foreign trade. The Department determines and analyzes the facts relating to our overseas interests, makes recommendations on policy and future action, and takes the necessary steps to carry out established policy. In so doing, the Department engages in continuous consultations with other states; negotiates treaties and agreements with foreign nations; speaks for the United States in the United Nations and in numerous major international organizations in which the United States participates; and represents the United States at numerous major international organizations in which the United States participates; and represents the United States at numerous international conferences annually.

Stated value. A term used in accounting in reference to the value assigned to a corporation's stock, similar to par value. There is no relation between the stated value and the market value of stock. Stated value is the legal capital of the company. *See also* Par value.

State law. Refers to laws of a state or ordinances of city or town, all as distinguished from Federal law which is the supreme law of the land under Art. VI of the U.S. Constitution. However, in matters which are not necessarily governed by Federal law, the Federal courts will look to state law and be governed by it. *See* Erie v. Tompkins. *Compare* Federal Acts.

Statement. In a general sense, an allegation; a declaration of matters of fact. The term has come to be used of a variety of formal narratives

of facts, required by law in various jurisdictions as the foundation of judicial or official proceedings and in a limited sense is a formal, exact, detailed presentation.

An oral or written assertion, or nonverbal conduct of a person, if it is intended by him as an assertion. Fed.R.Evid. 801(a). Oral or written verbal expression, or nonverbal conduct of a person intended by him as a substitute for oral or written verbal expression. Calif.Evid.Code § 225.

A hearsay declarant's nonverbal conduct may qualify as a "statement" for purpose of exclusion under the hearsay rule if the conduct was intended by the declarant as a substitute for oral or written verbal expression.

See also Closing statement; False statement; Financial statement; Opening statement of counsel; Prior inconsistent statements; Registration statement; Voluntary statement.

Bank statement. See Statement of account.

Financial statement. See Balance *(Balance sheet)*; Financial statement; Income statement; Profit and loss statement; Statement of affairs.

Statement of account. A report issued monthly or periodically by a bank or creditor to a customer setting forth the amounts billed, credits given and balance due. A bank statement includes the checks drawn and cleared, the deposits made, the charges debited, and account balance. *See also* Financial statement.

Statement of affairs. Document which must be filed in bankruptcy proceedings, setting forth answers to questions about the past and present financial situation of the debtor. A balance sheet showing immediate liquidation amounts, rather than historical costs, usually prepared when insolvency or bankruptcy is imminent. *See also* Financial statement; Income statement; Statement of condition.

Statement of claim. *See* Claim; Complaint.

Statement of condition. A balance sheet which shows the assets, liabilities, reserves and capital of a person, business, or a financial institution, as of a given date. *See also* Balance *(Balance sheet)*; Financial statement; Statement of affairs.

Statement of confession. Oftentimes referred to as a "power of attorney", "cognovit note", or "confession of judgment", is written authority of debtor and his direction to enter judgment against debtor as stated therein. *See* Cognovit judgment; Judgment *(Confession of judgment)*.

Statement of defense. *See* Answer; Reply.

Statement of income. *See* Financial statement; Income statement; Profit and loss statement.

Statement of particulars. *See* Bill. *(Bill of particulars)*.

State of art. *See* State of the art.

State officer. One who holds elective or appointive position in state government, *e.g.* state attorney general.

State of mind. A person's reasons and motives for acting as he did. Term used in connection with evidence. *See* Mens rea; Mental state; State of mind exception.

State of mind exception. Under the "state of mind exception" to the hearsay rule, an out of court declaration of a present existing motive or reason for acting is admissible even though the declarant is available to testify. See Fed.Evid.R. 803(3).

State of the art. In context of products liability case means level of pertinent scientific and technical knowledge existing at time of manufacture.

State of the case. In general, the posture of litigation at a given point in time. It may be ready for trial, in the process of trial, or pending appeal.

State police. A department or agency of a state government empowered with authority of police throughout a state and commonly trained and governed in a quasi-military fashion.

State police power. Every state has power to enact laws for the protection of its citizens' health, welfare, morals and safety and such power is derived from the 10th Amendment, U.S.Const. This power is upheld if exercised in a manner consistent with its ends and if the means used are reasonably calculated to protect one of these legitimate ends. *See also* Police power.

State's attorney. An officer who represents the State in securing indictments and in prosecuting criminal cases. Also called District or County Attorney or Prosecuting Attorney. Commonly he is elected in a county election and his authority is county wide.

State seal. The official die or signet having a raised emblem and used by state officials on documents of importance. Every state has its own such seal.

State secret. A governmental secret relating to national defense or international relations of United States and, once established, government has a privilege to refuse to disclose the secret in civil litigation and to prevent any litigant from disclosing the secret.

State secrets privilege. This is a long-standing evidentiary privilege that permits government to resist discovery of evidence if disclosure reasonably could be seen as threat to military or diplomatic interest of nation; when properly invoked, privilege is absolute, and no showing of need can overcome it.

State's evidence. A popular term for testimony given by an accomplice or joint participant in the commission of a crime tending to criminate or convict the others, and given under an actual or implied promise of immunity or lesser sentence for himself.

State sovereignty. The right of a state to self-government. The role of supreme authority or rule exercised by every state within the Union. *See also* Sovereign states.

State's rights. Rights not conferred on the federal government or forbidden to the States according to the 10th Amendment, U.S. Constitution.

Stating an account. Exhibiting, or listing in their order, the items which make up an account.

Station. Social position or status. *See* Standing; Status.

Status. Standing; state or condition; social position. The legal relation of individual to rest of the community. The rights, duties, capacities and incapacities which determine a person to a given class. A legal personal relationship, not temporary in its nature nor terminable at the mere will of the parties, with which third persons and the state are concerned. While term implies relation it is not a mere relation.

Status crime. A class of crime which consists not in proscribed action or inaction, but in the accused's having a certain personal condition or being a person of a specified character. An example of a status crime is vagrancy. Status crimes are constitutionally suspect. For example, being a drug addict is no longer a punishable offense.

Status quo /stéytəs kwów/. The existing state of things at any given date. *Status quo ante bellum,* the state of things before the war. "Status quo" to be preserved by a preliminary injunction is the last actual, peaceable, uncontested status which preceded the pending controversy.

Statutable, *or* **statutory** /stǽtyuwtəbəl/stǽtyət (ò)riy/. That which is introduced or governed by statutory law, as opposed to the common law or equity. Thus, a court is said to have statutory jurisdiction when jurisdiction is given to it in certain matters by act of the legislature.

Statute, *n.* A formal written enactment of a legislative body, whether federal, state, city, or county. An act of the legislature declaring, commanding, or prohibiting something; a particular law enacted and established by the will of the legislative department of government; the written will of the legislature, solemnly expressed according to the forms necessary to constitute it the law of the state. Such may be public or private, declaratory, mandatory, directory, or enabling, in nature. For mandatory and directory statutes, *see* Directory; Mandatory statutes.

Depending upon its context in usage, a statute may mean a single act of a legislature or a body of acts which are collected and arranged according to a scheme or for a session of a legislature or parliament.

This word is used to designate the legislatively created laws in contradistinction to court decided or unwritten laws. *See* Common law.

See also Codification; Mandatory statutes; Revised statutes; Slip law; Slip law print; Special law.

Affirmative statute. See that title.

Criminal statute. An act of the Legislature as an organized body relating to crime or its punishment. *See* Crime; Criminal law; Penal code; Penal laws.

Declaratory statute. See that title.

Enabling statute. See that title.

Expository statute. See that title.

General statute. A statute relating to the whole community, or concerning all persons generally, as distinguished from a private or special statute.

Local statute. See Local law.

Negative statute. A statute expressed in negative terms; a statute which prohibits a thing from being done, or declares what shall *not* be done.

Penal statute. *See* Crime; Criminal law; Penal code; Penal laws; Punitive statute.

Perpetual statute. One which is to remain in force without limitation as to time; one which contains no provision for its repeal, abrogation, or expiration at any future time.

Personal statutes. In foreign and modern civil law, those statutes which have principally for their object the *person,* and treat of property only incidentally. A personal statute, in this sense of the term, is a law, ordinance, regulation, or custom, the disposition of which affects the person and clothes him with a capacity or incapacity, which he does not change with every change of abode, but which, upon principles of justice and policy, he is assumed to carry with him wherever he goes. The term is also applied to statutes which, instead of being general, are confined in their operation to one person or group of persons. *See* Private law; Special law.

Private statute. A statute which operates only upon particular persons, and private concerns. An act which relates to certain individuals, or to particular classes of men. *See* Private law; Special law.

Public statute. A statute enacting a universal rule which regards the whole community, as distinguished from one which concerns only particular individuals and affects only their private rights. *See* Public law. *See also General statute, above.*

Punitive statute. See that title.

Real statutes. In the civil law, statutes which have principally for their object property, and which do not speak of persons, except in relation to property.

Reference statutes. See that title.

Remedial statute. *See* Remedial laws *or* statutes.

Revised statutes. See that title.

Special statute. One which operates only upon particular persons and private concerns. A private statute. Distinguished from a general or public statute. *See* Special law.

Statute of frauds. *See* Frauds, Statute of.

Statute of limitations. *See* Limitation *(Statute of limitation).*

Statute of repose. "Statutes of limitations" extinguish, after period of time, right to prosecute accrued cause of action; "statute of repose," by contrast, limits potential liability by limiting time during which cause of action can arise. It is distinguishable from statute of limitations, in that statute of repose cuts off right of action after specified time measured from delivery of product or completion of work, regardless of time of accrual of cause of action or of notice of invasion of legal rights.

Statute of uses. *See* Use.

Statutes at large. An official compilation of the acts and resolutions of each session of Congress published by the Office of the Federal Register in the National Archives and Records Service. It consists of two parts, the first comprising public acts and joint resolutions, the second, private acts and joint resolutions, concurrent resolutions, treatises, proposed and ratified amendments to Constitution, and Presidential proclamations. The arrangement is currently by Public Law number, and by chapter number in pre-1951 volumes. This is the official print of the law for citation purposes where titles of the United States Code have not been enacted into positive law.

Validating statute. See that title.

Statutes at large. *See* Statute.

Statutory. Relating to a statute; created or defined by a statute; required by a statute; conforming to a statute.

Statutory agent. Corporate agent entitled to receive legal documents in litigation and other legal notices for the corporation.

Statutory bond. One that either literally or substantially meets requirements of statute.

Statutory construction. That branch of the law dealing with the interpretation of laws enacted by a legislature. A judicial function required when a statute is invoked and different interpretations are in contention. Where legislature attempts to do several things one of which is invalid, it may be discarded if remainder of the act is workable and in no way depends upon invalid portion, but if that portion is an integral part of the act, and its excision changes the manifest intent of the act by broadening its scope to include subject matter or territory which was not included therein as enacted, such excision is "judicial legislation" and not "statutory construction". *See* Construction; Strict construction.

Statutory crime. *See* Crime; Penal code; Penal laws.

Statutory dedication. *See* Dedication.

Statutory exception. A provision in a statute exempting certain conduct or persons from the thrust of the law enacted.

Statutory exposition. When the language of a statute is ambiguous, and any subsequent enactment involves a particular interpretation of the former act, it is said to contain a *statutory* exposition of the former act.

Statutory extortion. The unlawful extraction of money or other value by means of a threat not sufficient for robbery, or a communication for the purpose of such extraction. See *e.g.* 18 U.S.C.A. § 871 et seq. *See also* Extortion.

Statutory foreclosure. *See* Foreclosure.

Statutory law. That body of law created by acts of the legislature in contrast to constitutional law and law generated by decisions of courts and administrative bodies. *See* Statute.

Statutory lien. A lien arising solely by force of statute upon specified circumstances or conditions, but does not include any lien provided by or dependent upon an agreement to give security, whether or not such lien is also provided by or is also dependent upon statute and whether or not the agreement or lien is made fully effective by statute. Bankruptcy Code § 101.

Statutory merger. *See* Merger *(Corporations)*.

Statutory obligation. An obligation—whether to pay money, perform certain acts, or discharge certain duties—which is created by or arises out of a statute, as distinguished from one founded upon acts between parties or jural relationships.

Statutory offense. *See* Crime; Penal code; Penal laws.

Statutory partnership association. *See* Partnership.

Statutory penalty. One imposed against the offender for some statutory violation by him. One which an individual is allowed to recover against a wrongdoer as satisfaction for wrong or injury suffered, without reference to actual damage sustained. In a civil sense, a "statutory penalty" is a

pecuniary punition, imposed for doing some act which is prohibited or for omitting to do some act which is required to be done; *e.g.* Copyright Act provides statutory damages for copyright infringement. 17 U.S.C.A. § 504(c); 18 U.S.C.A. § 2319. *See also* Penalty.

Statutory rape. The unlawful sexual intercourse with a female under the age of consent which may be 16, 17 or 18 years of age, depending upon the state statute. The government is not required to prove that intercourse was without the consent of the female because she is conclusively presumed to be incapable of consent by reason of her tender age. *See also* Rape.

Statutory successor. A statutory successor is the person to whom all assets of a corporation pass upon its dissolution under the provisions of a statute of the state of incorporation which is in force at the time of the dissolution. See Restatement, Second, Conflicts, § 388.

Stay, *v.* To stop, arrest, or forbear. To "stay" an order or decree means to hold it in abeyance, or refrain from enforcing it.

Stay, *n.* A stopping; the act of arresting a judicial proceeding by the order of a court. Also that which holds, restrains, or supports.

A stay is a suspension of the case or some designated proceedings within it. It is a kind of injunction with which a court freezes its proceedings at a particular point. It can be used to stop the prosecution of the action altogether, or to hold up only some phase of it, such as an execution about to be levied on a judgment.

Automatic stay in bankruptcy. *See* Automatic stay.

Stay laws. Acts of the legislature prescribing a stay of execution in certain cases, or a stay of foreclosure of mortgages, or closing the courts for a limited period, or providing that suits shall not be instituted until a certain time after the cause of action arose, or otherwise suspending legal remedies; designed for the relief of debtors, in times of general distress or financial trouble.

Stay of execution. The stopping or arresting of execution on a judgment, that is, of the judgment-creditor's right to issue execution, for a limited period. This is given by statute in many jurisdictions, as a privilege to the debtor, usually on his furnishing bail for the debt, costs, and interest. Or it may take place by agreement of the parties. See *e.g.* Fed.R.Civil P. 62. Term may also refer to the stopping of the execution of capital punishment, commonly to permit further appeals by defendant. See *e.g.* Fed.R.Crim.P. 38(a).

Stay of proceedings. The temporary suspension of the regular order of proceedings in a cause, by direction or order of the court, usually to await the action of one of the parties in regard to some omitted step or some act which the court has required him to perform as incidental to the suit; as where a nonresident plaintiff has been ruled to give security for costs. It is similar to an injunction with which a court freezes its proceedings at a particular point. It can be used to stop the prosecution of the action altogether, or to hold up only some phase of it, such as an execution about to be levied on a judgment. *See also* Automatic stay.

A "stay" does not reverse, annul, undo or suspend what already had been done or what is not specifically stayed nor pass on the merits of orders of the trial court, but merely suspends the time required for performance of the particular mandates stayed, to preserve a status quo pending appeal.

See Fed.R.Civil P. 62, "Stay of Proceedings to Enforce Judgment". *See also* Injunction; Restraining order.

Steal. This term is commonly used in indictments for larceny ("take, *steal,* and carry away"), and denotes the commission of theft, that is, the felonious taking and carrying away of the personal property of another, and without right and without leave or consent of owner, and with intent to keep or make use wrongfully. Or, it may denote the criminal taking of personal property either by larceny, embezzlement, or false pretenses. But, in popular usage "stealing" may include the unlawful appropriation of things which are not technically the subject of larceny, *e.g.,* immovables. *See also* Larceny; Robbery; Shoplifting; Theft.

Stealing children. *See* Kidnapping.

Stealth /stélθ/. The quality or condition of being secret or furtive. The act of stealing when the victim is unaware of the theft is stealing by stealth. Any secret, sly or clandestine act to avoid discovery and to gain entrance into or to remain within residence of another without permission.

Step. When used as prefix in conjunction with a degree of kinship, is repugnant to blood relationship, and is indicative of a relationship by affinity.

In accounting, a distinct change in cost because of increased activity.

Step-child. The child of one of the spouses by a former marriage. A child who has a parent by his natural parent's second marriage and has not been adopted by that parent.

Step-down in basis. A reduction in the income tax basis of property. *See also* Step-up in basis.

Step-father. The husband of one's mother by virtue of a marriage subsequent to that of which the person spoken of is the offspring.

Step-mother. The wife of one's father by virtue of a marriage subsequent to that of which the person spoken of is the offspring.

Step-parent. The mother or father of a child born during a previous marriage of the other parent and hence, not the natural parent of such child.

Step-son. The son of one's wife by a former husband, or of one's husband by a former wife.

Step-transaction approach. Method used by the Internal Revenue Service to determine tax liability by disregarding one or more transactions of a taxpayer to arrive at the final result. The objective of the step-transaction approach is to review the substance and not just the form of a transaction in determining the tax liability of the individual or entity.

Step-up in basis. An increase in the income tax basis of property. The classic step-up in basis occurs when a decedent dies owning appreciated property. The property is valued on the date of death or the alternate valuation date. The estate tax is based on the property values on the date elected; therefore the heirs receive property with a step-up in basis.

Steward. A man appointed in the place or stead of another. A union official who represents other union employees in grievances with management and who oversees the carrying out of the union contract.

Stick up. To rob at the point of a gun; armed robbery.

Sting. An undercover police operation in which police pose as criminals to trap law violators. *Compare* Entrapment.

Stipend /stáypənd/. A salary; settled pay; fixed or regular payment. Offering made to clergyman.

Stipital /stípətəl/. Relating to stipes, roots, or stocks. *See* Stirpital.

Stipulate. Arrange or settle definitely, as an agreement or covenant. *See* Stipulation.

Stipulated damage. Liquidated damage *(q.v.).*

Stipulation. A material condition, requirement, or article in an agreement.

The name given to any agreement made by the attorneys engaged on opposite sides of a cause (especially if in writing), regulating any matter incidental to the proceedings or trial, which falls within their jurisdiction. Voluntary agreement between opposing counsel concerning disposition of some relevant point so as to obviate need for proof or to narrow range of litigable issues. An agreement, admission or confession made in a judicial proceeding by the parties thereto or their attorneys. Such are evidentiary devices used to simplify and expedite trials by dispensing with the need to prove formally uncontested factual issues.

Stipulations made during the course of trial may involve jury of less than twelve (Fed.R.Civil P. 48), master's findings (Rule 53(e)(4)), dismissal of action (Rule 41(a)), or *discovery, see below.*

See also Admission; Pre-trial conference; Proviso.

Discovery. Unless the court orders otherwise, the parties may by written stipulation (1) provide that depositions may be taken before any person, at any time or place, upon any notice, and in any manner and when so taken may be used like other depositions, and (2) modify the procedures provided by these rules for other methods of discovery, except that stipulations extending the time provided in Rules 33, 34, and 36 for responses to discovery may be made only with the approval of the court. Fed.R.Civil P. 29.

Stirpes /stə́rpiyz/. Lat. Descents. The root-stem, or stock of a tree. Figuratively, it signifies in law that person from whom a family is descended, and also the kindred or family. Taking property by right of representation is called "succession *per stirpes,*" in opposition to taking in one's own right, or as a principal, which is termed "taking *per capita.*" *See also* Per stirpes and Representation.

Stirpital /stə́rpətəl/. Relating to *stirpes,* roots, or stocks. "Stirpital distribution" of property is distribution *per stirpes;* that is, by right of representation.

Stock. The goods and wares of a merchant or tradesman, kept for sale and traffic. In a larger sense, the capital of a merchant or other person, including his merchandise, money, and credits, or, in other words, the entire property employed in business. *See* Inventory.

Corporation Law

The term is used in various senses. It may mean the capital or principal fund of a corporation or joint-stock company, formed by the contributions of subscribers or the sale of shares; the aggregate of a certain number of shares severally owned by the members or stockholders of the corporation or the proportional share of an individual stockholder; also the incorporeal property which is represented by the holding of a certificate of stock; and in a wider and more remote sense, the right of a shareholder to participate in the general management of the company and to share proportionally in its net profits or earnings or in the distribution of assets on dissolution. The term "stock" has also been held to embrace not only capital stock of a corporation but all corporate wealth and resources, subject to all corporate liabilities and obligations.

"Stock" is distinguished from "bonds" and, ordinarily, from "debentures," in that it gives right of ownership in part of assets of corporation and right to interest in any surplus after payment of debt. "Stock" in a corporation is an equity, and it represents an ownership interest, and it is to be distinguished from obligations such as notes or bonds which are not equities and represent no ownership interest.

See also Certificate of stock; Discount shares; Equity security; Par value; Registration of securities; Securities; Security; Share of corporate stock.

Classes and Types of Corporate Stock

Preferred stock is a separate portion or class of the stock of a corporation, which is accorded, by the charter or by-laws, a preference or priority in respect to dividends, over the remainder of the stock of the corporation, which in that case is called *common stock.* That is, holders of the preferred stock are entitled to receive dividends at a fixed annual rate, out of the net earnings or profits of the corporation, before any distribution of earnings is made to the common stock. If the earnings applicable to the payment of dividends are not more than sufficient for such fixed annual dividend, they will be entirely absorbed by the preferred stock. If they are more than sufficient for the purpose, the remainder may be given entirely to the common stock (which is the more usual custom) or such remainder may be distributed pro rata to both classes of the stock, in which case the preferred stock is said to "participate" with the common. The fixed dividend on preferred stock may be "cumulative" or "non-cumulative." In the former case, if the stipulated dividend on preferred stock is not earned or paid in any one year, it becomes a charge upon the surplus earnings of the next and succeeding years, and all such accumulated and unpaid dividends on the preferred stock must be paid off before the common stock is entitled to receive dividends. In the case of "non-cumulative" preferred stock, its preference for any given year is extinguished by the failure to earn or pay its dividend in that year. If a corporation has no class of preferred stock, all its stock is common stock. The word "common" in this connection signifies that all the holders of such stock are entitled to an equal pro rata division of profits or net earnings, if any there be, without any preference or priority among themselves. *Deferred stock* is rarely issued by American corporations, though it is not uncommon in England. This kind of stock is distinguished by the fact that the payment of dividends upon it is expressly postponed until some other class of stock has received a dividend, or until some certain liability or obligation of the corporation is discharged. If there is a class of "preferred" stock, the common stock may in this sense be said to be "deferred," and the term is sometimes used as equivalent to "common" stock. But it is not impossible that a corporation should have three classes of stock: (1) Preferred, (2) common, and (3) deferred; the latter class being post-poned, in respect to participation in profits, until both the preferred and the common stock had received dividends at a fixed rate.

Assented stock. Stock which an owner deposits with a third person in accordance with an agreement by which the owner voluntarily accepts a change in the securities of the corporation.

Assessable stock. Stock which requires the owner to pay more than its cost if the needs of the corporation require.

Authorized stock. That amount of stock which the corporate charter permits the corporation to issue. The shares described in the articles of incorporation which a corporation may issue. Modern corporate practice recommends authorization of more shares than it is currently planned to issue. *See also* Authorized stock issue.

Blue-chip stock. Stock of a listed company which has a high grade financial record. *See Listed stock, below.*

Bonus stock. Stock given to an underwriter as compensation for services. Stock given to purchasers as an inducement. *See also* Bonus stock.

Callable preferred stock. Preferred stock which may be called by the issuing corporation at a prestated price.

Capital stock. *See* Capital *(Capital stock).*

Common stock. Securities which represent an ownership interest in a corporation. If the company has also issued preferred stock, both common and preferred have ownership rights. The preferred normally is limited to a fixed dividend but has prior claim on dividends and, in the event of liquidation, assets. Claims of both common and preferred stockholders are junior to claims of bondholders or other creditors of the company. Common stockholders assume the greater risk, but generally exercise the greater control and may gain the greater reward in the form of dividends and capital appreciation. The terms common stock and capital stock are often used interchangeably when the company has no preferred stock. *See also* Common stock.

Control stock. That amount of capital stock which permits the owner to control the corporation. It is not necessarily a majority of the shares.

Convertible stock. Stock which may be changed or converted into common stock.

Cumulative preferred. A stock having a provision that if one or more dividends are omitted, the omitted dividends must be paid before dividends may be paid on the company's common stock.

Cumulative stock. A type of stock on which unpaid dividends accumulate until paid. They must

be paid totally before the common stockholders receive their dividends. *See Cumulative preferred, above.*

Donated stock. Stock transferred to the corporation by the stockholders for resale.

Floating stock. That part of a corporation's stock which is on the open market for speculation. Stock not yet bought by public holders.

Growth stock. Stock purchased with a view towards appreciation in value rather than dividend income.

Guaranteed stock. Usually preferred stock on which dividends are guaranteed by another company, under much the same circumstances as a bond is guaranteed.

Guaranty stock. Stock in a savings and loan association in some states which yields all dividends to the holders after dividends to depositors or savers.

Issued stock. Stock which has been authorized and actually sold to subscribers. It may include treasury stock.

Shares that are currently owned by investors (outstanding shares) or have been at one time owned by investors (treasury shares).

Letter stock. Stock received by a buyer who gives the seller a letter stating that he will hold such stock and not reoffer it to others. Such stock need not be registered under the Securities Act of 1933. *See also* Letter stock.

Listed stock. The stock of a company which is traded on a securities exchange, and for which a listing application and a registration statement, giving detailed information about the company and its operations, have been filed with the Securities and Exchange Commission, unless otherwise exempted, and with the exchange itself. The various stock exchanges have different standards for listing.

Nonassessable stock. Stock which cannot be assessed (*i.e.* holder cannot be assessed) in the event of failure or insolvency of the corporation. Most all stock is nonassessable.

Noncumulative preferred stock. Type of preferred stock which yields no dividend once the dividend is passed. *Contrast Cumulative preferred, above.*

Noncumulative stock. A preferred stock on which unpaid dividends do not accrue. Omitted dividends are, as a rule, gone forever.

Nonvoting stock. Stock to which no rights to vote attach. Such shares may be created in most states; in some states, however, nonvoting shares may be entitled to vote as a class on certain proposed changes adversely affecting that class as such.

No par stock. Stock without par value but which represents a proportionate share of the ownership of a corporation based on the number of shares. Such shares are issued for the consideration designated by the board of directors; such consideration is allocated to stated capital unless the directors or shareholders determine to allocate a portion to capital surplus. A corporation may have both par and no par value stock.

Outstanding stock. Stock issued and in the hands of stockholders and such does not include treasury stock.

Paid up stock. Stock for which full payment has been made to the corporation.

Participation preferred stock. A preferred stock which is entitled to its stated dividend and, also, to additional dividends on a specified basis upon payment of dividends on the common stock.

Participation stock. In general, stock which permits the holder to participate in the profits and surplus.

Par value stock. Stock which originally had a fixed value arrived at by dividing the total value of capital stock by the number of shares to be issued. The par value does not bear a necessary relation to the actual value of the stock because of the part which surplus plays in valuation. *See also* Par value.

Penny stock. Generally, highly speculative stock which can be purchased for under a dollar a share.

Preferred stock. A class of stock with a claim on the company's earnings before payment may be made on the common stock and usually entitled to priority over common stock if company liquidates. Usually entitled to dividends at a specified rate— when declared by the Board of Directors and before payment of a dividend on the common stock—depending upon the terms of the issue.

Premium stock. Stock which carries a premium for trading as in the case of short selling.

Redeemable stock. Generally preferred stock which can be called in and retired. It is redeemable at par. *See also* Redeemable stock.

Registered stock. Stock registered under federal Securities Act. *See also* Listed stock, above.

Restricted stock. Stock to which is attached restrictions as to transferability.

Stock options. See Stock option, below.

Stock redemption. See Stock redemption, below.

Stock rights. See Stock rights, below.

Stock split. See Stock split, below.

Subscribed stock. See that title.

Treasury stock. Stock issued by a company but later re-acquired. It may be held in the company's treasury indefinitely, reissued to the public, or retired. Treasury stock receives no dividends and has no vote while held by the company. The Revised Model Business Corporation Act and the statutes of several states have eliminated the concept of treasury shares.

Unissued stock. Stock authorized by the corporate charter but not yet distributed to stockholders and subscribers.

Unlisted stock. Stock not listed on one of the stock exchanges but traded over the counter or privately.

Voting stock. Stock which carries the right to vote for directors, etc. *See also* Voting stock.

Watered stock. Stock issued for inadequate consideration. *See also* Watered stock.

Law of Descent

The term is used, metaphorically, to denote the original progenitor of a family, or the ancestor from whom the persons in question are all descended; such descendants being called "branches."

Generally

Capital stock. See Capital (Capital stock).

Certificate of stock. See Certificate; Share certificate.

Exchange of stock. See Exchange.

Public stocks. The funded or bonded debt of a government or state; though this term is commonly used to refer to stocks of publicly traded corporations.

Stock association. A joint-stock company (q.v.).

Stock attribution. See Attribution.

Stock bailout. A species of stock redemption in the form of a preferred stock dividend formerly tax free, but now governed by I.R.C. § 306.

Stockbroker. One who buys or sells stock as agent of another. *See also* Broker.

Stock certificate. See Certificate of stock; Share certificate.

Stock control. Type of inventory management by which a business maintains perpetual records of its inventory.

Stock corporation. A corporation having a capital stock divided into shares, and which is authorized by law to distribute to the holders thereof dividends or shares of the surplus profits of the corporation.

Stock dividend. Distributing stock as a dividend. It is a proportional distribution of shares without payment of consideration to existing shareholders. If the dividend is common stock declared on common stock, the only result other than to reduce the value of each share of common and to maintain the proportionate interest of each stockholder is to transfer part of surplus to the stock account. To be distinguished from a cash dividend or a stock split (*see below*). *See also* Dividend.

Stock exchange. The place at which shares of stock are bought and sold. Any organization, association, or group of persons, whether incorporated or unincorporated, which constitutes, maintains, or provides a marketplace or facilities for bringing together purchasers and sellers of securities. *See Stock market, below.*

Stock insurance company. An insurance company whose shares are held by the public and which pays dividends in contrast to a mutual insurance company whose assets are owned by the policyholders who receive dividends when available.

Stock in trade. The inventory carried by a retail business for sale in the ordinary course of business. Also, the tools and equipment owned and used by a tradesman.

Stock jobber. A dealer in stock; one who buys and sells stock on his own account on speculation.

Stock life insurance company. One in which capital stock investment is made by subscribers to stock, and business is thereafter conducted by board of directors elected by its stockholders, and, subject to statutes, distribution of earnings or profits, as between stockholders and policyholders, is determined by board of directors.

Stock market. The organized trading of securities through the various stock exchanges and over-the-counter markets. The largest stock market in the United States is the New York Stock Exchange. *See also* Fourth market; Over-the-counter market.

Stock merger. See Merger.

Stock note. The term has no technical meaning, and may as well apply to a note given on the sale of stock which the bank had purchased or taken in the payment of doubtful debts as to a note given on account of an original subscription to stock.

Stock option. The right to buy a designated stock, if holder of option chooses, at any time within specified period, at determinable price, or to sell designated stock within an agreed period at determinable price. In addition to its use for investment purposes, such options are often granted to management and key employees as a form of incentive compensation. The term "stock option" is used when the right is issued other than pro rata to all existing shareholders. When so issued to all existing stockholders, the option is called a "stock right." For "restricted," "qualified," and

"nonqualified" stock options, *see* Option. *See also* Call; Incentive stock option; Option; Put; Put option; Warrant.

Stock option contract. A negotiable instrument which gives the holder the right to buy or sell a certain number of shares of the corporation's stock within a fixed period of time for a certain price. *See also* Option.

Stock power. A power of attorney permitting a person other than the owner of the stock to transfer legally the title of ownership to a third party.

Stock purchase plan. A plan by which employees of a corporation are allowed to purchase shares of corporate stock.

Stock redemption. A partial or complete liquidation of corporate stock by the corporation with varying tax consequences depending upon the type of redemption. It generally consists in the buy back by the corporation of its own stock. The redemption of the stock of a shareholder by the issuing corporation is generally treated as a sale or exchange of the stock unless the redemption is a dividend. I.R.C. §§ 301 and 302. A public corporation might redeem its stock for the purpose of "going private", or as a defense to a hostile takeover attempt. *See also Stock bailout, above.*

Stock repurchase plan. A program by which a corporation buys back its own shares in the open market. It is usually done when the corporation believes its shares are undervalued by the market.

Stock restrictions. Prohibitions on certain types of transfers of stock (usually set forth on stock certificate).

Stock rights. The privilege to subscribe to new stock issues or to purchase stock. Usually, rights are contained in securities called warrants and the warrants can be sold to others. A right to purchase stock issued pro rata to existing shareholders. Sometimes issued on a "when, as, and if" basis, that is, the holder can buy the stock when it is issued, on such basis or of such kind as is issued, and if it is issued.

A document (*i.e.* negotiable certificate) which gives an existing stockholder the privilege of buying additional stock of a corporation. The right has a value of its own because generally the holder may buy such additional stock at a price less than the market quotation. Rights are traded in the market. A stock right differs from a warrant to the extent that a right gives a privilege of buying additional stock of the same kind whereas a warrant may permit a preferred stockholder to buy common stock.

See also Preemptive right; Standby agreement; Warrant (*Stock warrant*).

Stock split. The issuance of a number of new shares in exchange for each old share held by a stockholder resulting in a proportional change in the number of shares owned by each stockholder. Share splits, or stock splits, may be (a) split-ups, where one share is split into a larger number of shares, or (b) reverse splits, or split-downs, where a number of shares are combined to form a smaller number of shares. Share splits involve no transfer from surplus to stated capital or any changes except adjustments in par value or stated value per share, when applicable, so that the same stated capital which represented the issued shares before the split properly represents the changed number of shares after the split. A split-up requires not only board of directors action, but often requires advance shareholder approval as well when the articles of incorporation must be amended to change the par value or stated value of shares and also, when necessary, to authorize additional shares. The usual accounting treatment for a share split is to do nothing except to reflect the different (usually increased) number of issued shares and any changes in par or stated value.

A common purpose of a stock split is to reduce the per share market price in order to make for wider trading and a resulting higher per share value (*i.e.* price).

See also Reverse stock split.

Stock subscription. An agreement (by a subscriber) with the corporation to purchase its stock. *See Stock rights, above. See also* Subscribed stock; Subscriber; Subscription.

Stock swap. In corporate reorganization, an exchange of stock in one corporation for the stock of another corporation. *See also* Swaps.

Stock transfer agent. See Transfer agent.

Stock transfer tax. A tax imposed on the transfer of stock and based on the market value of the stock.

Stock warrant. A certificate evidencing the right to buy shares of stock and commonly attached to preferred stock and bonds. It generally has an expiration date before which the warrant must be exercised. *See also* Warrant.

Tainted stock. Stock owned by a person who is disqualified for some reason from serving as a plaintiff in a derivative action. The shares are "tainted" because for policy reasons a good faith transferee of such shares will also be disqualified from serving as a plaintiff.

Stockholder (Shareholder). A person who owns shares of stock in a corporation or joint-stock company. Referred to as "Shareholder" under Rev. Model Bus.Corp. Act and a number of state statutes, and defined in Model Act (§ 1.40) as "the person in whose name shares are registered in the records of a corporation or the beneficial owner of shares to the extent of the rights granted by a nominee certificate on file with a corporation." *See also* Beneficial holders of securities; Majority stockholder; Minority stockholder.

Watered stock. See that title.

Stockholder's derivative action. An action by a stockholder for purpose of sustaining in his own name a right of action existing in corporation itself, where corporation would be an appropriate plaintiff. It is based upon two distinct wrongs: The act whereby corporation was caused to suffer damage, and act of corporation itself in refusing to redress such act. Procedure in such actions is governed by Fed.R.Civil P. 23.1.

Stockholder's equity. The total of a firm's stock at par, contributed capital in excess of par, and retained earnings accounts summarized on the balance sheet. It is sometimes called the *book value* of the firm, *owners' equity,* or *net worth.*

Stockholder's liability. Phrase is frequently employed to denote stockholder's statutory, added or double liability for corporation's debts, notwithstanding full payment for stock, but is often employed where stockholder, agreeing to pay full par value of stock, obtained stock certificate before complete payment or where stock, only partly paid for, is intentionally issued by corporation as fully paid up and all or part of purported consideration therefor is entirely fictitious.

Stockholders' representative action. An action brought or maintained by a stockholder in behalf of himself and all others similarly situated. *See also* Stockholder's derivative action.

Stock insurance company. Also known as a "joint stock insurance company," it is an insurance company that has issued capital stock and which is controlled by stockholders who take the profits. It may be distinguished from a "mutual insurance company" which is owned by policy holders. *See also* Mutual insurance company.

Stockout. The condition of not having inventory available upon need or request. *See* Back order.

Stolen. Acquired, or possessed, as a result of some wrongful or dishonest act or taking, whereby a person willfully obtains or retains possession of property which belongs to another, without or beyond any permission given, and with the intent to deprive the owner of the benefit of ownership (or possession) permanently.

The word as used in the crime of interstate transportation of stolen motor vehicles includes all wrongful and dishonest takings of motor vehicles with the intent to deprive the owner of the rights and benefits of ownership, regardless of whether theft constitutes common-law larceny; and felonious taking may be effected by diverse means known to both common and statutory law, such as larceny, embezzlement, false pretenses, larceny by trick and other types of wrongful acquisition. It is not necessary that the taking of the vehicle be unlawful. Even if possession of the vehicle be unlawful. Even if possession of the vehicle is lawfully acquired, the vehicle will be deemed "stolen" if the defendant thereafter forms the intent to deprive the owner of the rights and benefits of ownership, and converts the vehicle to his own use.

See also Larceny; Receiving stolen goods or property; Robbery; Theft.

Stop. Within statutes requiring a motorist striking a person with automobile to stop, requires a definite cessation of movement for a sufficient length of time for a person of ordinary powers of observation to fully understand the surroundings of the accident.

"Stop" occurs when police officer restrains person's liberty by physical force or show of authority. As used within term "stop and frisk," is temporary restraint of person's freedom to walk away and is a permissible seizure within Fourth Amendment dimensions when such person is suspected of being involved in past, present or pending criminal activity. Terry v. Ohio, 392 U.S. 1, 88 S.Ct. 1868, 20 L.Ed.2d 889. *See also* Stop and frisk.

Stop and frisk. The situation where police officers who are suspicious of an individual run their hands lightly over the suspect's outer garments to determine if the person is carrying a concealed weapon. Also called a "patdown" or "threshold inquiry," a stop and frisk is intended to stop short of any activity that could be considered a violation of Fourth Amendment rights.

A police officer has the right to stop and pat down a person suspected of contemplating the commission of a crime. Reasonable suspicion which is sufficient for stop and frisk is more than a mere hunch but less than probable cause. The scope of the search must be strictly tied to and justified by the circumstances which rendered the initiation of the stop justified. Terry v. Ohio, 392 U.S. 1, 88 S.Ct. 1868, 20 L.Ed.2d 889. *See* Frisk; Investigatory stop; Stop.

Stop-limit order. In securities trading, a stop order in which a specific price is set below which the stock may not be sold and above which it may not be purchased.

Stop-loss order. An order given to a stockbroker to buy or sell certain securities when the market reaches a particular price.

Stop notice statute. An alternative to the mechanics' lien remedy that allows contractors, suppliers and workers to make and enforce a claim against the construction lender, and in some instances, the owner, for a portion of the undisbursed construction loan proceeds. *See also* Mechanic's lien.

Stop order. An order to buy securities at a price above the current market. Stop buy orders are generally used to limit loss or protect unrealized profits on a short sale. Stop sell orders are generally used to protect unrealized profits or limit loss on a holding. A stop order becomes a market order when the stock sells at or beyond the specified price and, thus, may not necessarily be executed at that price. *See also* Stop-limit order; Stop payment order.

Stoppage. In the civil law, compensation or set-off.

Stoppage in transit /stópəj in trǽnzət(y). The act by which the unpaid vendor of goods stops their progress and resumes possession of them, while they are in course of transit from him to the purchaser, and not yet actually delivered to the latter. The right of stoppage *in transitu* is that which the vendor has, when he sells goods on credit to another, of resuming the possession of the goods while they are in the possession of a carrier or middle-man, in the transit to the consignee or vendee, and before they arrive into their actual possession, or the destination he has appointed for them on their becoming bankrupt and insolvent. The right which arises to an unpaid vendor to resume the possession, with which he has parted, of goods sold upon credit, before they come into the possession of a buyer who has become insolvent, bankrupt, or pecuniarily embarrassed. See U.C.C. § 2–705(1).

Stop payment order. A customer's demand to a payor bank that the bank dishonor a check payable for the customer's account. See U.C.C. § 4–403.

Storage. Safekeeping of goods in a warehouse or other depository. *See also* Bailment; Warehouseman; Warehouse system.

Store, *v.* To keep merchandise for safe custody, to be delivered in the same condition as when received, where the safe-keeping is the principal object of deposit, and not the consumption or sale.

Store, *n.* Any place where goods are deposited and sold by one engaged in buying and selling them.

Stowage. In maritime law, the storing, packing, or arranging of the cargo in a ship, in such a manner as to protect the goods from friction, bruising, or damage from leakage.

Money paid for a room where goods are laid; housage.

Stowaway. One who conceals himself aboard an out-going vessel or aircraft for the purpose of obtaining free passage. See 18 U.S.C.A. § 2199.

Straddle. A strategy consisting of the combination of an equal number of put options and call options on the same underlying share, index, or commodity future. A straddle is a type of hedge. In stockbrokers' parlance the term means the double option position of a "put" and a "call" in the same underlying stock, and secures to the holder the right to demand of the seller at a certain price within a certain time a certain number of shares of specified stock, or to require him to take, at the same price within the same time, the same shares of stock. *See* Call; Option; Put option. *Compare* Hedging.

Straight-line. In accounting, an amount divided into equal per period amounts over some number of periods; for example, straight-line depreciation. *See* Depreciation.

Straight-line depreciation. *See* Depreciation.

Stranger(s). As used with reference to the subject of subrogation, one who, in no event resulting from the existing state of affairs, can become liable for the debt, and whose property is not charged with the payment thereof and cannot be sold therefor.

By this term is intended third persons generally. In its general legal signification the term is opposed to the word "privy." Those who are in no way parties to a covenant or transaction, nor bound by it, are said to be strangers to the covenant or transaction.

Straw bail. *See* Bail.

Straw man *or* **party.** A "front"; a third party who is put up in name only to take part in a transaction. Nominal party to a transaction; one who acts as an agent for another for the purpose of taking title to real property and executing whatever documents and instruments the principal may direct respecting the property. Person who purchases property for another to conceal identity of real purchaser, or to accomplish some purpose otherwise not allowed.

Stray. *See* Estray.

Stream of commerce. Term used to describe goods which remain in interstate commerce though held within a state for a short period of time. If such goods remain in the stream of commerce, they are not subject to local taxation.

In Commerce Clause analysis, local activities which are part of the current or stream of interstate commerce are considered part of the interstate movement. Congress can regulate such local incidents directly under its commerce power.

Street name. Securities held in the name of a broker instead of his customer's name are said to be carried in a "street name." This occurs when the securities have been bought on margin or when the customer wishes the security to be held by the broker. The name of a broker or bank appearing on a corporate security with *blank endorsement* by the broker or bank. The security can then be transferred merely by delivery since the endorsement is well known. Street name is used for convenience or to shield identity of the true owner.

Strict. Exact; accurate; precise; undeviating; governed or governing by exact rules.

As to *strict* Settlement, see that title.

Strict construction. A close or rigid reading and interpretation of a law. It is said that criminal statutes must be strictly construed. Rule of "strict construction" has no definite or precise meaning, has only relative application, is not opposite of liberal construction, and does not require such strained or narrow interpretation of language as to defeat object of statute.

Rule of "strict construction" means that criminal statute will not be enlarged by implication or intendment beyond fair meaning of language used, or what their terms reasonably justify, and will not be held to include offenses and persons other than those which are clearly described and provided for, although court in interpreting and employing particular statutes may think legislature should have made them more comprehensive. "Strict construction of a statute" is that which refuses to expand the law by implications or equitable considerations, but confines its operation to cases which are clearly within the letter of the statute as well as within its spirit or reason, resolving all reasonable doubts against applicability of statute to particular case.

See also Construction; Strictly construed.

Strict foreclosure. *See* Foreclosure.

Strict liability. Liability without fault. A concept applied by the courts in product liability cases in which seller is liable for any and all defective or hazardous products which unduly threaten a consumer's personal safety. This doctrine poses strict liability on one who sells product in defective condition unreasonably dangerous to user or consumer for harm caused to ultimate user or consumer if seller is engaged in business of selling such product, and product is expected to and does reach user or consumer without substantial change in condition in which it is sold.

Concept of strict liability in tort is founded on the premise that when manufacturer presents his goods to the public for sale, he represents they are suitable for their intended use, and to invoke such doctrine it is essential to prove that the product was defective when placed in the stream of commerce.

(1) One who sells any product in a defective condition unreasonably dangerous to the user or consumer or to his property is subject to liability for physical harm thereby caused to the ultimate user or consumer, or to his property, if (a) the seller is engaged in the business of selling such a product, and (b) it is expected to and does reach the user or consumer without substantial change

in the condition in which it is sold. (2) The rule stated in Subsection (1) applies although (a) the seller has exercised all possible care in the preparation and sale of his product, and (b) the user or consumer has not bought the product from or entered into any contractual relation with the seller. Restatement, Second, Torts, § 402A.

See also Product liability; Warranty.

Strict liability crimes. Unlawful acts whose elements do not contain the need for criminal intent or *mens rea*. These crimes are usually acts that endanger the public welfare, such as illegal dumping of toxic wastes. *See* Per se violations.

Strictly /stríktliy/. A strict manner; closely, precisely, rigorously; stringently; positively.

Strictly construed. Requirement that a penal statute be strictly construed means that the court will not extend punishment to cases not plainly within the language used, but at the same time such statutes are to be fairly and reasonably construed, and will not be given such a narrow and strained construction as to exclude from their operation cases plainly within their scope and meaning. *See also* Strict construction.

Strict scrutiny test. Under this test for determining if there has been a denial of equal protection, burden is on government to establish necessity of the statutory classification. Measure which is found to affect adversely a fundamental right will be subject to "strict scrutiny" test which requires state to establish that it has compelling interest justifying the law and that distinctions created by law are necessary to further some governmental purpose.

Strike. The act of quitting work by a body of workers for the purpose of coercing their employer to accede to some demand they have made upon him, and which he has refused. A combination to obtain higher wages, shorter hours of employment, better working conditions or some other concession from employer by the employees stopping work at a preconcerted time, and it involves a combination of persons and not a single individual. A cessation of work by employees as a means of enforcing compliance with some demand upon the employer. A combined effort among workers to compel their employer to the concession of a certain demand, by preventing the conduct of his business until compliance with the demand.

The term "strike" includes any strike or other concerted stoppage of work by employees (including a stoppage by reason of the expiration of a collective-bargaining agreement) and any concerted slow-down or other concerted interruption of operations by employees. Labor Management Relations Act, § 501(2).

See also No-strike clause; Rent strike; Slowdown; Wildcat strike. *Compare* Lockout.

Economic strike. A cessation of work by employees to enforce economic demands upon the employer in contrast to a strike caused by an unfair labor charge.

General strike. Cessation of work by employees effective throughout an entire industry or country.

Jurisdictional strike. Cessation of work as result of dispute by members of one union or craft against members of another union or craft as to assignment of work.

Secondary strike. Cessation of work by union members of one employer who has business dealings with another employer whose employees are on strike.

Sit-down strike. Cessation of work by employees who do not leave employer's premises but who refuse to work.

Sympathy strike. A strike in which a union strikes not to gain concessions for itself, but to aid another union's objectives. A sympathy strike involves two unions; one is striking to force some concession from the employer; the other strikes in sympathy with the first's objectives. Sympathy strikes are a common manifestation of traditional union solidarity.

Wildcat strike. Cessation of work by group of employees without authorization of union officials.

Strikebreaker. One who takes the place of workman who has left his work in an effort to force the striking employee to agree to demands of employer. *See also* Scab.

Strike off. In common parlance, and in the language of the auction-room, property is understood to be "struck off" or "knocked down," when the auctioneer, by the fall of his hammer, or by any other audible or visible announcement, signifies to the bidder that he is entitled to the property on paying the amount of his bid, according to the terms of the sale.

A court is said to "strike off" a case when it directs the removal of the case from the record or docket, as being one over which it has no jurisdiction and no power to hear and determine it.

Strike price. The price for which the asset will be exchanged in an option contract if the option is exercised. Also called the exercise price, call price, or put price.

Strike suits. Shareholder derivative action begun with hope of winning large attorney fees or private settlements, and with no intention of benefiting corporation on behalf of which suit is theoretically brought.

Striking a jury. The selecting or nominating a jury out of the whole number returned as jurors on the panel. It is especially used of the selection of a *special* jury, where a panel is prepared by the proper officer, and the parties, in turn, strike off a certain number of names, until the list is reduced to twelve. A jury thus chosen is called a "struck jury." *See also* Impanel; Jury panel.

Striking off the roll. The disbarring of an attorney.

Striking price. Price at which an option (*e.g.*, to purchase stock) is exercised. The price at which named stock can be put or called is ordinarily the market price when option is written and is termed the "striking price".

Strip. The act of spoiling or unlawfully taking away anything from the land, by the tenant for life or years, or by one holding an estate in the land less than the entire fee.

Separating coupons from corpus of bonds, which, in turn, are sold separately.

Struck. In common law pleading, a word essential in an indictment for murder, when the death arose from any wounding, beating, or bruising.

Struck jury. A special jury. *See also* Striking a jury.

Structured settlement. *See* Settlement.

Suable /s(y)úwəbəl/. Capable of being, or liable to be, sued. A suable cause of action is the matured cause of action. *See* Cause of action; Ripeness doctrine.

Sua sponte /s(y)úwə spóntiy/. Lat. Of his or its own will or motion; voluntarily; without prompting or suggestion.

Sub /sə́b/. Lat. Under; upon. For example: "sub judice" means "under judicial consideration" or in court and not yet decided, and "sublet" means to rent out something you yourself are renting.

Subagent /sə́bèyjənt/. A party to whom an agent delegates his or her authority. An under-agent; a substituted agent; an agent appointed by one who is himself an agent. A person appointed by an agent to perform some duty, or the whole of the business, relating to his agency. A person employed by an agent to assist him in transacting the affairs of his principal. A subagent is a person appointed by an agent empowered to do so, to perform functions undertaken by the agent for the principal, but for whose conduct the agent agrees with the principal to be primarily responsible. Restatement, Second, Agency, § 5. *See also* Agent.

Subchapter C corporation. *See* Corporation (C corporation).

Subchapter S corporation. *See* Corporation (S Corporation).

Subcontract. *See* Contract.

Subcontractor. One who takes portion of a contract from principal contractor or another subcontractor. One who has entered into a contract, express or implied, for the performance of an act with the person who has already contracted for its performance. One who takes from the principal or prime contractor a specific part of the work undertaken by the principal contractor.

Subdivide. To divide a part into smaller parts; to separate into smaller divisions. As, where an estate is to be taken by some of the heirs *per stirpes,* it is divided and subdivided according to the number of takers in the nearest degree and those in the more remote degree respectively.

Subdivision. Division into smaller parts of the same thing or subject-matter. The division of a lot, tract or parcel of land into two or more lots, tracts, parcels or other divisions of land for sale or development.

Resubdivision. The further division or relocation of lot lines of any lot or lots within a subdivision previously made and approved or recorded according to law; or, the alteration of any streets or the establishment of any new streets within any subdivision previously made and approved or recorded according to law, but does not include conveyances so as to combine existing lots by deed or other instrument.

Subdivision map. A map showing how a larger parcel of land is to be divided into smaller lots, and generally also showing the layout of streets, utilities, etc.

Subinfeudation /sə̀binfyuwdéyshən/. The system which the feudal tenants introduced of granting smaller estates out of those which they held of their lord, to be held of themselves as inferior lords. As this system was proceeding downward *ad infinitum,* and depriving the lords of their feudal profits, it was entirely suppressed by the statute *Quia Emptores,* 18 Edw. I, c. 1, and instead of it alienation in the modern sense was introduced, so that thenceforth the alienee held of the same chief lord and by the same services that his alienor before him held.

Subjacent support /səbjéysənt səpórt/. The right of land to be supported by the land which lies under it; distinguished from lateral (side) support. *See also* Support.

Subject. *Constitutional law.* One that owes allegiance to a sovereign and is governed by his laws. The natives of Great Britain are *subjects* of the British government. Men in free governments are subjects as well as *citizens;* as citizens they enjoy rights and franchises; as subjects they are bound to obey the laws. The term is little used, in this sense, in countries enjoying a republican form of government.

Legislation. The matter of public or private concern for which law is enacted. Thing legislated about or matters on which legislature operates to accomplish a definite object or objects reasonably related one to the other. The matter or thing forming the groundwork of the act.

The constitutions of several of the states require that every act of the legislature shall relate to but one *subject,* which shall be expressed in the title of the statute. But term "subject" within such constitutional provisions is to be given a broad and extensive meaning so as to allow legislature full scope to include in one act all matters having a logical or natural connection.

Subject-matter. The subject, or matter presented for consideration; the thing in dispute; the right which one party claims as against the other, as the right to divorce; of ejectment; to recover money; to have foreclosure. Nature of cause of action, and of relief sought. In trusts, the *res* or the things themselves which are held in trust. Restatement, Second, Trusts, § 2.

Subject matter jurisdiction. Term refers to court's power to hear and determine cases of the general class or category to which proceedings in question belong; the power to deal with the general subject involved in the action. *See also* Jurisdiction of the subject matter.

Sub judice. /sәb júwdәsiy/. Under or before a judge or court; under judicial consideration; undetermined.

Sublease. A lease executed by the lessee of land or premises to a third person, conveying the same interest which the lessee enjoys, but for a shorter term than that for which the lessee holds (as compared to assignment, where the lessee transfers the entire unexpired term of the leasehold to a third party). Transaction whereby tenant grants interests in leased premises less than his own, or reserves to himself reversionary interest in term. *See also* Lease; Sandwich lease; Subtenant.

A lease of goods the right to possession and use of which was acquired by the lessor as a lessee under an existing lease. U.C.C. § 2A–103(1)(w).

Subletting. *See also* Sublease.

Submerged lands. Land lying under water. Land lying oceanside of the tideland.

Submission. A yielding to authority; *e.g.* a citizen is bound to submit to the laws; a child to his parents.

A contract between two or more parties whereby they agree to refer the subject in dispute to others and to be bound by their award. *See also* Arbitration; Mediation.

Submission bond. The bond by which the parties agree to submit their matters to arbitration, and by which they bind themselves to abide by the award of the arbitrator.

Submission to jury. The act or process by which a judge gives to the jury the case on trial for their consideration and verdict. *See* Jury instructions.

Submit. To commit to the discretion of another. To yield to the will of another. To propound; to present for determination; as an advocate *submits* a proposition for the approval of the court. *See also* Submission.

Submortgage. When a person who holds a mortgage as security for a loan which he has made, procures a loan to himself from a third person, and pledges his mortgage as security, he effects what is called a "submortgage."

Sub nomine /sәb nómәniy/. Under the name; in the name of; under the title of.

Subordinate. Placed in a lower order, class, or rank; occupying a lower position in a regular descending series; inferior in order, nature, dignity, power, importance, or the like; belonging to an inferior order in classification, and having a lower position in a recognized scale; secondary, minor.

Subordinated bonds *or* **debentures.** A bond that has a claim on the issuing firm's assets that is junior to other forms of debt in the event of a liquidation. The claims of subordinated debenture holders can be met only *after* all the claims of senior creditors have been met. Usually such bonds or debentures are not subordinate to general creditors but only to debt owed to a financial institution.

Subordinate debt. Debt that is junior in status of claims to other types or classes of debts.

Subordinate officer. One who performs duties imposed on him under direction of a principal or superior officer or he may be an independent officer subject only to such directions as the statute lays on him.

Subordination. The act or process by which a person's rights or claims are ranked below those of others; *e.g.* a second mortgagee's rights are subordinate to those of the first mortgagee.

Subordination agreement. An agreement by which one holding an otherwise senior lien or other real estate interest consents to a reduction in priority vis-a-vis another person holding an interest in the same real estate. An agreement by which the subordinating party agrees that its interest in real property should have a lower priority than the interest to which it is being subordinated.

Subordination clause. A covenant in a junior mortgage enabling the first lien to keep its priority in case of renewal or refinancing.

Suborn. To prepare, provide, or procure especially in a secret or underhand manner. In criminal law, to procure another to commit perjury.

Subornation of perjury. The offense of procuring another to take such a false oath as would constitute perjury in the principal. 18 U.S.C.A. § 1622. *See also* Perjury.

Suborner. One who suborns or procures another to commit any crime, particularly to commit perjury.

Subpartner. *See* Partner.

Subpoena /sə(b)píynə/. A subpoena is a command to appear at a certain time and place to give testimony upon a certain matter. A subpoena duces tecum requires production of books, papers and other things. Subpoenas in federal criminal cases are governed by Fed.R.Crim.P. 17, and in civil cases by Fed.R.Civil P. 45. *See also* Alias subpoena.

Subpoena ad testificandum /sə(b)píynə æd tèstəfəkǽndəm/. Lat. Subpoena to testify. A technical and descriptive term for the ordinary subpoena. *See* Subpoena.

Subpoena duces tecum /sə(b)píynə d(y)úwsiyz tíykəm/. A court process, initiated by party in litigation, compelling production of certain specific documents and other items, material and relevant to facts in issue in a pending judicial proceeding, which documents and items are in custody and control of person or body served with process. See Fed.R.Civil P. 45, and Fed.R.Crim.P. 17.

Subrogation. The substitution of one person in the place of another with reference to a lawful claim, demand or right, so that he who is substituted succeeds to the rights of the other in relation to the debt or claim, and its rights, remedies, or securities. Subrogation denotes the exchange of a third person who has paid a debt in the place of the creditor to whom he has paid it, so that he may exercise against the debtor all the rights which the creditor, if unpaid, might have done. Subrogation appears commonly in construction contracts, insurance contracts, suretyship, and negotiable instrument law. Insurance companies, guarantors and bonding companies generally have the right to step into the shoes of the party whom they compensate and sue any party whom the compensated party could have sued.

The right of one who has paid an obligation which another should have paid to be indemnified by the other. A device adopted by equity to compel ultimate discharge of an obligation by him who in good conscience ought to pay it.

Subrogation is of two kinds, either conventional or legal; the former being where the subrogation is express, by the acts of the creditor and the third person; the latter being (as in the case of sureties) where the subrogation is effected or implied by the operation of the law. *See also* Equitable subrogation; Legal subrogation.

Subrogee /sə̀browjíy/°gíy/. A person who is subrogated; one who succeeds to the rights of another by subrogation.

Subrogor. The person who substitutes another for himself; one who performs the subrogation.

Sub rosa /sə̀b rówzə/. Confidential, secret, not for publication.

Subscribe. Literally to write underneath, as one's name. To sign at the end of a document. Also, to agree in writing to furnish money or its equivalent, or to agree to purchase some initial stock in a corporation. *See also* Attest; Subscriber; Subscription.

Subscribed capital. The total amount of stock or capital for which there are contracts of purchase or subscriptions.

Subscribed stock. A stockholders' equity account showing the capital that will be contributed as the subscription price is collected. A subscription is a legal contract so that an entry is made debiting a receivable and crediting subscribed stock as soon as the stock is subscribed. *See also* Subscriber; Subscription.

Subscriber. One who writes his name under a written instrument; one who affixes his signature to any document, whether for the purpose of authenticating or attesting it, of adopting its terms as his own expressions, or of binding himself by an engagement which it contains.

One who becomes bound by a subscription to the capital stock of a corporation. One who has agreed to purchase stock from the corporation on the original issue of such stock, whether before or after incorporation. Rev.Model Bus.Corp. Act, § 1.40. One who agrees to buy securities of a corporation, either bonds or stocks.

Subscribing witness. He who witnesses or attests the signature of a party to an instrument, and in testimony thereof subscribes his own name to the document. One who sees a writing executed, or hears it acknowledged, and at the request of the party thereupon signs his name as a witness. *See* Attestation.

Subscription. The act of writing one's name under a written instrument; the affixing one's signature to any document, whether for the purpose of authenticating or attesting it, of adopting its terms as one's own expressions, or of binding one's self by an engagement which it contains.

A written contract by which one engages to take and pay for capital stock of a corporation, or to contribute a sum of money for a designated purpose, either gratuitously, as in the case of subscribing to a charity, or in consideration of an equivalent to be rendered, as a subscription to a periodical, a forthcoming book, a series of entertainments, or the like. *See also* Subscribed stock; Subscriber, and compound terms below.

Subscription contract. In general, any contract by which one becomes bound to buy. In particular, a contract for the purchase of securities. *See* Subscription.

Subscription list. A list of subscribers to some agreement with each other or a third person. A list of subscribers to a periodical or series of publications or to some type of service.

Subscription period. The time until the option to subscriber to stock offering expires.

Subscription price. The price at which an investor can subscribe to stock offering.

Subscription rights. Rights of existing stockholders to purchase additional stock, generally at a price under market and in an amount proportionate to their existing holdings. Also, the certificates evidencing such rights. *See also* Stock *(Stock rights).*

Subsequent condition. *See* Condition.

Subservant. In law of agency, the servant or agent of another servant or agent. Generally, such agent or servant is principal as to the subservant. *See also* Subagent.

Subsidiary. Under another's control. Term is often short for "subsidiary corporation"; *i.e.* one that is run and owned by another company which is called the "parent." *See* Subsidiary corporation.

Of secondary importance.

Subsidiary corporation. One in which another corporation (*i.e.* parent corporation) owns at least a majority of the shares, and thus has control. Said of a company more than 50 percent of whose voting stock is owned by another.

Subsidy. A grant of money made by government in aid of the promoters of any enterprise, work, or improvement in which the government desires to participate, or which is considered a proper subject for government aid, because such purpose is likely to be of benefit to the public.

Sub silentio /sɔ́b səlénsh(iy)ow/. Under silence; without any notice being taken. Passing a thing *sub silentio* may be evidence of consent.

Subsistence. Support. Means of support, provisions, or that which procures provisions or livelihood. *See* Necessaries; Support.

Substance. Essence; the material or essential part of a thing, as distinguished from "form." That which is essential.

Substance vs. form concept. A standard used, commonly in taxation, to ascertain the true reality of what has occurred.

Substantial. Of real worth and importance; of considerable value; valuable. Belonging to substance; actually existing; real; not seeming or imaginary; not illusive; solid; true; veritable.

Something worthwhile as distinguished from something without value or merely nominal. Synonymous with material.

Substantial capacity test. Term used in the definition of legal insanity proposed by the Model Penal Code (§ 4.01) to the effect that a person is not responsible for criminal conduct if at the time of such conduct as a result of mental disease or defect he lacks substantial capacity either to appreciate the criminality (wrongfulness) of his conduct or to conform his conduct to the requirements of law. *See also* Insanity.

Substantial compliance rule. Compliance with the essential requirements, whether of a contract or of a statute. In life insurance law is that where insured has done substantially all he is required to do under policy to effect change in beneficiary and mere ministerial acts of insurer's officers and agents only remain to be done, change will take effect. *See* Substantial performance doctrine.

Substantial damages. *See* Damages.

Substantial equivalent of patented device. Same as thing itself, so that if two devices do same work in substantially same way, and accomplish substantially same results, they are equivalent, even though differing in name, form, or shape.

Substantial evidence rule. Such evidence that a reasonable mind might accept as adequate to support a conclusion. It is that quality of evidence necessary for a court to affirm a decision of an administrative board. Under the "substantial evidence rule," reviewing courts will defer to an agency determination so long as, upon an examination of the whole record, there is substantial evidence upon which the agency could reasonably base its decision.

Substantial evidence is evidence possessing something of substance and relevant consequence and which furnishes substantial basis of fact from which issues tendered can be reasonably resolved. Evidence which a reasoning mind would accept as sufficient to support a particular conclusion and consists of more than a mere scintilla of evidence but may be somewhat less than a preponderance. For purposes of considering sufficiency of evidence in criminal case, "substantial evidence" means evidence from which trier of fact reasonably could find issue in harmony therewith.

Under the substantial evidence rule, as applied in administrative proceedings, all evidence is competent and may be considered, regardless of its source and nature, if it is the kind of evidence that a reasonable mind might accept as adequate to support a conclusion. In other words, the competency of evidence for purposes of administrative agency adjudicatory proceedings is made to rest upon the logical persuasiveness of such evidence to the reasonable mind in using it to support a conclusion. It is more than a mere scintilla and means such relevant evidence as a reasonable mind might accept as adequate to support a conclusion.

See also Whole record test.

Substantially. Essentially; without material qualification; in the main; in substance; materially; in a substantial manner. About, actually, competently, and essentially.

Substantially justified. Test for whether government's litigation position is "substantially justified" within meaning of Equal Access to Justice Act provision governing award of attorney fees (28 U.S.C.A. § 2412(d)(1)(A)) is one of reasonableness, under which government is required to establish that its position has reasonable basis both in law and in fact. Following 1985 amendments to Equal Access to Justice Act, in order to show that its position was "substantially justified" and thus be relieved from liability for fees of a prevailing opponent, Government must show not merely that its position was marginally reasonable, but that its position was clearly reasonable, well founded in law and fact, and solid though not necessarily correct. *See* Equal Access to Justice Act.

Substantial performance doctrine. A doctrine in commercial reasonableness which recognizes that the rendering of a performance which does not exactly meet the terms of the agreement (slight deviation) will be looked upon as fulfillment of the obligation, less the damages which result from any deviation from the promised performance. This doctrine, which is widely applied in building contracts and which is intended to prevent unjust enrichment, provides that where contract is made for agreed exchange of two performances, one of which is to be rendered first, substantial performance, rather than strict, exact or literal performance, by first party of terms of contract is sufficient to entitle such party to recover on such performance.

Substantial performance of a contract is shown when party alleging substantial performance has made an honest endeavor in good faith to perform his part of the contract, when results of his endeavor are beneficial to other party, and when such benefits are retained by the other party; if any one of these circumstances is not established the performance is not substantial, and the party has no right of recovery.

Substantiate /səbstǽnshiyèyt/. To establish the existence or truth of, by true or competent evidence, or to verify. *See* Burden of proof.

Substantive. An essential part or constituent or relating to what is essential.

Substantive due process. Doctrine that due process clauses of the Fifth and Fourteenth Amendments to the United States Constitution require legislation to be fair and reasonable in content as well as application. Such may be broadly defined as the constitutional guarantee that no person shall be arbitrarily deprived of his life, liberty or property. The essence of substantive due process is protection from arbitrary and unreasonable action. *See* Due process of law.

Substantive evidence. That adduced for the purpose of proving a fact in issue, as opposed to evidence given for the purpose of discrediting a witness (*i.e.*, showing that he is unworthy of belief), or of corroborating his testimony. *See also* Substantial evidence rule.

Substantive felony. An independent felony; one not dependent upon the conviction of another person for another crime.

Substantive law. That part of law which creates, defines, and regulates rights and duties of parties, as opposed to "adjective, procedural, or remedial law," which prescribes method of enforcing the rights or obtaining redress for their invasion. The basic law of rights and duties (contract law, criminal law, tort law, law of wills, etc.) as opposed to procedural law (law of pleading, law of evidence, law of jurisdiction, etc.). *Compare* Adjective law; Procedural law.

Substantive offense. One which is complete of itself and not dependent upon another.

Substantive rights. A right to the equal enjoyment of fundamental rights, privileges and immunities; distinguished from procedural right.

Substitute, *n.* /sə́bstət(y)ùwt/. One who or that which stands in the place of another; that which stands in lieu of something else. A person hired by one who has been drafted into the military service of the country, to go to the front and serve in the army in his stead.

Substitute, *v.* To put in the place of another person or thing; to exchange.

Substituted basis. In taxation, the basis of an asset determined by reference to the basis in the hands of a transferor, donor or grantor or by reference to other property held at any time by the person for whom the basis is to be determined. I.R.C. § 1016(b). *See also* Basis.

Substitute defendant. One who takes the place of another in the same suit or controversy and not one who is sued upon an entirely different cause of action. *See* Substitution of parties.

Substituted executor. One appointed to act in the place of another executor upon the happening of a certain event; *e.g.*, if the latter should refuse the office.

Substituted service. Service of process upon a defendant in any manner, authorized by statute or rule, other than personal service within the jurisdiction; as by publication, by mailing a copy to his last known address, or by personal service in another state. See Fed.R.Civil P. 4. *See also* Service.

Substitution of judgment doctrine. Such doctrine, where permitted, allows the court, upon petition of an incompetent's guardian, to approve an estate plan designed to produce tax savings. Uniform Probate Code, § 5–408.

Substitution of parties. In pleading, the replacement of one party to an action by another party because of death, incompetency, transfer of interest, or in case of a public official who is a party to an action, his death or separation from office. Fed.R.Civ.P. 17(a), 25. *See also* Real party in interest; Revival of action.

Subsurface rights. Rights of landowners in the minerals and water below their property.

Subtenant /sɔbténənt/. An under-tenant; one who leases all or a part of the rented premises from the original lessee for a term less than that held by the latter. *See* Sublease.

Subterfuge /sɔbtəfyùwj/. That to which one resorts for escape or concealment. *See also* Artifice.

Subversion. The act or process of overthrowing, destroying, or corrupting. Used in connection with activities designed to undermine and overthrow the government, state and federal. *See* Subversive activities.

Subversive activities. Acts directed toward the overthrow of the government, including treason, sedition and sabotage. Such acts are federal crimes. 18 U.S.C.A. § 2381 *et seq.*; 50 U.S.C.A. § 781 *et seq.* *See* Espionage; Smith Act.

Successful party. For purposes of rule allowing "successful party" to recover costs, is one who obtains judgment of competent court vindicating civil claim of right. *See also* Prevailing party.

Succession. The devolution of title to property under the law of descent and distribution. The act or right of legal or official investment with a predecessor's office, dignity, possession, or functions; also the legal or actual order of so succeeding from that which is or is to be vested or taken. The word when applied to realty denotes persons who take by will or inheritance and excludes those who take by deed, grant, gift, or any form of purchase or contract.

Although "succession" is defined in statute as the acquisition of title to the property of one who dies without disposing of it by will, the word frequently possesses the somewhat broader mean-

ing of the acquisition of rights upon the death of another.

The right by which one group of persons may, by succeeding another group, acquire a property in all the goods, movables, and other chattels of a corporation. The power of perpetual *succession* is one of the peculiar properties of a corporation. *See* Perpetual.

See also Descent; Devise; Inheritance; Intestate; Successor; Testamentary.

Intestate succession. The succession of an heir at law to the property and estate of his ancestor when the latter has died intestate, or leaving a will which has been annulled or set aside. *See also* Descent; Devise; Inheritance; Intestate.

Legal succession. That which the law establishes in favor of the nearest relation of a deceased person. *See* Descent.

Natural succession. Succession taking place between natural persons, for example, in descent on the death of an ancestor.

Testamentary succession. In the civil law, that which results from the institution of an heir in a testament executed in the form prescribed by law. *See* Testamentary.

Testate succession. Passing of property to another by will.

Succession duty or tax. A tax placed on the gratuitous acquisition of property passing on the death of any person by transfer from one person to another. A tax imposed upon the privilege of receiving property from a decedent by devise or inheritance. *See* Inheritance tax.

Successor. One that succeeds or follows; one who takes the place that another has left, and sustains the like part or character; one who takes the place of another by succession. One who has been appointed or elected to hold an office after the term of the present incumbent.

Term with reference to corporations, generally means another corporation which, through amalgamation, consolidation, or other legal succession, becomes invested with rights and assumes burdens of first corporation.

Successor in interest. One who follows another in ownership or control of property. In order to be a "successor in interest", a party must continue to retain the same rights as original owner without change in ownership and there must be change in form only and not in substance, and transferee is not a "successor in interest." In case of corporations, the term ordinarily indicates statutory succession as, for instance, when corporation changes its name but retains same property.

Successors. Those persons, other than creditors, who are entitled to property of a decedent under his will or succession statute. Uniform Probate Code, § 1–201(42).

Successor trustee. A trustee who follows or succeeds an earlier trustee and who generally has all the powers of the earlier trustee. Trusts generally make provisions for appointment of successor trustees.

Sudden emergency doctrine. When a person finds himself confronted with a sudden emergency, which was not brought about by his own negligence or want of care, such person has the legal right to do what appears to him at the time he should do, so long as he acts in a reasonably prudent manner as any other person would have done under like or similar circumstances, to avoid any injury, and if he does so act, he will not be deemed to have been negligent even though it might afterwards be apparent that some other course of action would have been safer. Under sudden emergency doctrine, one placed in position of sudden emergency or peril other than by his own negligence, is not held to same degree of care and prudence as one who has time for thought and reflection. *See also* Emergency doctrine; Sudden peril rule.

Sudden heat of passion. In the common-law definition of manslaughter, this phrase means an excess of rage or anger, suddenly arising from a contemporary provocation. It means that the provocation must arise at the time of the killing, and that the passion is not the result of a former provocation, and the act must be directly caused by the passion arising out of the provocation at the time of the homicide. *See also* Heat of passion.

Sudden *or* **violent injury.** Injury occurring unexpectedly and not naturally or in the ordinary course of events.

Sudden peril rule. Under this rule, a defendant who is guilty of primary negligence is not liable in case of sudden peril where the peril or alarm was caused by the negligence of the opposite party, apprehension of peril from the standpoint of defendant seeking to excuse his primary negligence was reasonable, and appearance of danger was so imminent as to leave no time for deliberation. But rule cannot be invoked by one bringing emergency on or not using due care, to avoid it. *See also* Sudden emergency doctrine.

Sue. To commence or to continue legal proceedings for recovery of a right; to proceed with as an action, and follow it up to its proper termination; to gain by legal process. To commence and carry out legal action against another. Word includes a proceeding instituted by confession of judgment. *See also* Suit.

Sue out. To obtain by application; to petition for and take out. Properly the term is applied only to the obtaining and issuing of such process as is only accorded upon an application first made; but conventionally it is also used of the taking out of process which issues of course. The term is occasionally used of instruments other than writs.

Suffer. To allow, to admit, or to permit. It includes knowledge of what is to be done under sufferance. To suffer an act to be done or a condition to exist is to permit or consent to it; to approve of it, and not to hinder it. It implies knowledge, a willingness of the mind and responsible control or ability to prevent.

Sufferance /sə́f(ə)rənts/. Toleration; negative permission by not forbidding; passive consent; license implied from the omission or neglect to enforce an adverse right.

Sufficiency of evidence test. Term refers to test prescribed by rule providing that grand jury ought to find an indictment when all the evidence taken together, if unexplained or uncontradicted, would warrant a conviction by the trier of the offense.

Barring plain error, an appellate court may not grant a directed verdict or a judgment n. o. v. absent an appropriate motion in the trial court; that is to say, it may not review the "sufficiency of the evidence" and grant a final judgment in favor of a party who failed to move; and "sufficiency" is a term of art meaning that legal standard which is applied to determine whether the case may go to the jury or whether the evidence is legally sufficient to support the jury verdict as a matter of law.

See also Burden of proof; Substantial evidence rule; Sufficient evidence. *Compare* Insufficiency of evidence to support verdict.

Sufficient. Adequate, enough, as much as may be necessary, equal or fit for end proposed, and that which may be necessary to accomplish an object. Of such quality, number, force, or value as to serve a need or purpose. As to *sufficient* Consideration, see that title.

Sufficient cause. Such cause as to hold defendant to answer charges is reasonable or probable cause or that state of facts as would lead a man of ordinary caution to conscientiously entertain strong suspicion of defendant's guilt. *See also* Probable cause.

Sufficient evidence. Adequate evidence; such evidence, in character, weight, or amount, as will legally justify the judicial or official action demanded; according to circumstances, it may be "prima facie" or "satisfactory" evidence. Sufficient evidence is that which is satisfactory for the purpose; that amount of proof which ordinarily satisfies an unprejudiced mind, beyond a reasonable doubt. The term is not synonymous with "conclusive;" but it may be used interchangeably with the term "weight of evidence." *See also*

Burden of proof; Evidence; Satisfactory evidence; Substantial evidence rule; Sufficiency of evidence.

Suffrage /sə́frəj/. A vote; the act of voting; the right or privilege of casting a vote at public elections. The last is the meaning of the term in such phrases as "the extension of the suffrage," "universal suffrage," etc. Right of "suffrage" is right of a man to vote for whom he pleases. *See* Nineteenth Amendment.

Suggestion. A suggesting; presentation of an idea especially indirectly, as through association of ideas, bringing before the mind for consideration, action, solution, or the like. It is in the nature of a hint or insinuation, and lacks the element of probability. Facts which merely suggest do not raise an inference of the existence of the fact suggested, and therefore a suggestion is much less than an inference or presumption. *See* Leading question.

In litigation practice, a statement, formally entered on the record, of some fact or circumstance which will materially affect the further proceedings in the cause, or which is necessary to be brought to the knowledge of the court in order to its right disposition of the action, but which, for some reason, cannot be pleaded. Thus, if one of the parties dies after issue and before trial, his death may be *suggested* on the record.

Suicide. Self-destruction; the deliberate termination of one's own life.

Attempted suicide is a crime in some jurisdictions, but not in others. Some jurisdictions hold an attempted suicide which kills an innocent bystander or would-be rescuer to be murder, others manslaughter, others no crime. Some jurisdictions hold it to be murder for one person to persuade or aid another to commit suicide; some (by statute) make it manslaughter or a separate crime.

Suicide clause. Provision in life insurance policy that denies recovery if the insured commits suicide.

Sui generis /s(y)úway jénərəs/. Lat. Of its own kind or class; *i.e.*, the *only one* of its own kind; peculiar.

Sui juris /s(y)úway júrəs/. Lat. Of his own right; possessing full social and civil rights; not under any legal disability, or the power of another, or guardianship.

Having capacity to manage one's own affairs; not under legal disability to act for one's self.

See Emancipation; Majority.

Suit. A generic term, of comprehensive signification, referring to any proceeding by one person or persons against another or others in a court of law in which the plaintiff pursues, in such court, the remedy which the law affords him for the redress of an injury or the enforcement of a right, whether at law or in equity. It is, however, seldom applied to a criminal prosecution. And it was formerly sometimes restricted to the designation of a proceeding in equity, to distinguish such proceeding from an action at law. Term "suit" has generally been replaced by term "action"; which includes both actions at law and in equity. Fed.R.Civil P. 2. For Ancillary suit and suit In rem see those titles. *See also* Action; Cause of action; Litigation; Proceeding.

Class suits. *See* Class *or* representative action.

Derivative suit. *See* Stockholder's derivative action.

Suit against state. Suit in which relief against the state is sought. *See* Sovereign immunity; Tort claims acts.

Suit money. Counsel fees allowed or awarded by court to party. An allowance, in the nature of temporary alimony, authorized by statute in some states to be made to a wife on the institution of her suit for divorce, intended to cover the reasonable expenses of the suit and to provide her with means for the efficient preparation and trial of her case. Many federal statutes provide for allowance of attorney fees for actions brought under respective statutes; *e.g.*, actions to recover social security disability benefits. *See also* American rule; Equal Access to Justice Act; Fee.

Suit of a civil nature. A suit for the remedy of a private wrong, called a "civil action". Fed.R.Civil P. 2. *See* Action.

Suits or proceedings at law or in chancery. Suits instituted and carried or in substantial conformity with the forms and modes prescribed by the common law or by the rules in chancery excluding cases instituted and carried on solely in accordance with statutory provisions. Under current rules practice in the federal and most state courts, there is now only one form of action called a "civil action", which embraces both actions at law and in equity. Fed.R.Civil P. 2.

Suitable. Fit and appropriate for the end in view. *See* Suable.

Suitor. A party who brings an action; a petitioner; a plaintiff. In its ancient sense, "suitor" meant one who was bound to attend the county court; also one who formed part of the *secta*.

Suits in Admiralty Act. Federal statute giving injured parties the right to sue the government in admiralty. 46 U.S.C.A. §§ 741–752. *See also* Sovereign immunity.

Sum certain. A requisite of a negotiable instrument is that it contains an unconditional promise to pay a "sum certain." U.C.C. § 3–104(1)(b). In law of negotiable instruments, the sum payable is a sum certain even though it is to be paid (a) with stated interest or by stated installments; or (b) with stated different rates of interest before and after default or a specified date; or (c) with a stated discount or addition if paid before or after the date fixed for payment; or (d) with exchange or less exchange, whether at a fixed rate or at the current rate; or (e) with costs of collection or an attorney's fee or both upon default. U.C.C. § 3–106(1).

Amount in contract or negotiable instrument, or measure of damages in litigation, that is fixed, settled, exact, or stated. Default judgment may be entered only for a "sum certain," which is a sum susceptible to reliable computation or determined by the court after an accounting.

Sum in gross. *See* In gross.

Summarily. Without ceremony or delay, short or concise.

Summary, *n.* An abridgment; brief; compendium; digest; also a short application to a court or judge, without the formality of a full proceeding.

Summary, *adj.* Short; concise; immediate; peremptory; off-hand; without a jury; provisional; statutory. The term as used in connection with legal proceedings means a short, concise, and immediate proceeding.

Summary conviction. *See* Conviction.

Summary courts martial. *See* Court-Martial.

Summary ejectment. *See* Process *(Summary process).*

Summary eviction. *See* Process *(Summary process).*

Summary judgment. See that title.

Summary jurisdiction. The jurisdiction of a court to give a judgment or make an order itself forthwith; *e.g.,* to commit to prison for contempt. In the case of justices of the peace, a jurisdiction to convict an offender themselves instead of committing him for trial by a jury.

Summary proceeding. *See* Proceeding *(Summary proceeding).*

Summary trial. *See* Proceeding *(Summary proceeding).*

Summary process. *See* Process.

Summary judgment. Procedural device available for prompt and expeditious disposition of controversy without trial when there is no dispute as to either material fact or inferences to be drawn from undisputed facts, or if only question of law is involved. Federal Rule of Civil Procedure 56 permits any party to a civil action to move for a summary judgment on a claim, counterclaim, or cross-claim when he believes that there is no genuine issue of material fact and that he is entitled to prevail as a matter of law. The motion may be directed toward all or part of a claim or defense and it may be made on the basis of the

pleadings or other portions of the record in the case or it may be supported by affidavits and a variety of outside material. *See also* Genuine issue; Material fact.

Summation. *See* Summing up.

Summing up. On the trial of an action to a jury, a recapitulation by attorneys and, sometimes, judge of the evidence adduced, in order to draw the attention of the jury to the salient points at issue. The counsel for each party has the right of summing up his evidence, if he has adduced any, and the judge sometimes sums up the whole in his charge to the jury. *See* Closing argument.

Summon. To serve a summons; to cite a defendant to appear in court to answer a suit which has been begun against him; to notify the defendant that an action has been instituted against him, and that he is required to answer to it at a time and place named. *See* Summons.

Summons. Instrument used to commence a civil action or special proceeding and is a means of acquiring jurisdiction over a party. Writ or process directed to the sheriff or other proper officer, requiring him to notify the person named that an action has been commenced against him in the court from where the process issues, and that he is required to appear, on a day named, and answer the complaint in such action. Upon the filing of the complaint the clerk is required to issue a summons and deliver it for service to the marshal or to a person specially appointed to serve it. Fed.R.Civil P. 4(a). *See also* Alias summons; Process; Service.

In criminal law, an alternative to arrest generally used for petty or traffic offenses; a written order notifying an individual that he or she has been charged with an offense. A summons directs the person to appear in court to answer the charge. It is used primarily in instances of low risk, where the person will not be required to appear at a later date. See *e.g.* Fed.R.Crim.P. 4, 9.

Form and content of summons. The summons shall be signed by the clerk, be under the seal of the court, contain the name of the court and the names of the parties, be directed to the defendant, state the name and address of the plaintiff's attorney, if any, otherwise the plaintiff's address, and the time within which these rules require the defendant to appear and defend, and shall notify him that in case of his failure to do so judgment by default will be rendered against him for the relief demanded in the complaint. When service is made pursuant to a statute or rule of court of a state, the summons, or notice, or order in lieu of summons shall correspond as nearly as may be to that required by the statute or rule. Fed.R.Civil P. 4(b). For form of summons in criminal cases, see Fed.R.Crim.P. 4, 9.

John Doe summons. An order of the court to appear in a proceeding to one whose name is unknown. A description of the person so ordered is required to appear on the summons to satisfy due process requirements.

Summons ad respondendum /sə́mənz æd rèspondéndəm/. Process issuing in a civil case at law notifying defendant therein named that he must appear on day designated and thereupon make answer to plaintiff's statement of his cause of action.

Sum-of-the-years'-digits. A method of computing depreciation expense. *See* Depreciation.

Sum payable. As used within negotiable instruments law is the amount for which, by the terms of the instrument, the maker becomes liable, and which he might tender and pay in full satisfaction of his obligation. *See also* Sum certain.

Sunday closing laws. Laws and ordinances which restrict certain types of business or commercial activities from operating on Sunday. Also called "blue laws".

Sunset law. A statute or provision in a law that requires periodic review of the rationale for the continued existence of the particular law or the specific administrative agency or other governmental function. The legislature must take positive steps to allow the law, agency, or functions to continue in existence by a certain date or such will cease to exist.

Sunshine law. Laws which require that meetings of governmental agencies and departments be open to public with reasonable access to the records of such proceedings. 5 U.S.C.A. § 552b. *See also* Freedom of Information Act.

Super /s(y)úwpər/. Lat. Upon; above; over; higher, as in quantity, quality and degree; more than; as in super-essential, super-natural or super-standard.

Superfund. Popular name for the Comprehensive Environmental Response, Compensation, and Liability Act of 1980, 42 U.S.C.A. § 9601 et seq., which holds responsible parties liable for the cost of cleaning up hazardous waste sites. The name derives from a trust fund initially created by the Act for meeting clean up costs pending reimbursement from responsible parties. Many states have passed similar laws. Cf. McKinney's Environmental Conservation Law §§ 71–2701 et seq. *See also* Toxic waste.

Superior, *n.* One who has a right to command; one who holds a superior rank.

Superior, *adj.* Higher; belonging to a higher grade. More elevated in rank or office. Possessing larger power. Entitled to command, influence, or control over another.

In estates, some are superior to others. An estate entitled to a servitude or easement over another estate is called the "superior" or "dominant," and the other, the "inferior" or "servient," estate.

Superior courts. Courts of general or extensive jurisdiction, as distinguished from the inferior courts. As the official style of a tribunal, the term "superior court" bears a different meaning in different states. In some it is a court of intermediate jurisdiction between the trial courts and the chief appellate court; elsewhere it is the designation of the trial courts. *See also* Court.

Superior force. In the law of bailments and of negligence, an uncontrollable and irresistible force, of human agency, producing results which the person in question could not avoid; equivalent to the Latin phrase *"vis major."* *See* Force majeure; Vis.

Supersede /s(y)ùwpərsíyd/. Obliterate, set aside, annul, replace, make void, inefficacious or useless, repeal. To set aside, render unnecessary, suspend, or stay.

Supersedeas /s(y)ùwpərsíydiyəs/. The name of a writ containing a command to stay the proceedings at law. A suspension of the power of a trial court to issue an execution on judgment appealed from, or, if writ of execution has issued, it is a prohibition emanating from court of appeal against execution of writ. An auxiliary process designed to supersede enforcement of trial court's judgment brought up for review, and its application is limited to the judgment from which an appeal is taken.

Originally it was a writ directed to an officer, commanding him to desist from enforcing the execution of another writ which he was about to execute, or which might come in his hands. In modern times the term is often used synonymously with a "stay of proceedings," and is employed to designate the effect of an act or proceeding which of itself suspends the enforcement of a judgment.

Supersedeas bond. A bond required of one who petitions to set aside a judgment or execution and from which the other party may be made whole if the action is unsuccessful. See Fed.R.Civil P. 62; Fed.R.App.P. 7 and 8.

Superseding cause. An act of a third person or other force which by its intervention prevents the actor from being liable for harm to another which his antecedent negligence is a substantial factor in bringing about. An intervening act or acts of negligence which operate to insulate an antecedent tort-feasor from liability for negligently causing a dangerous condition which results in injury. *See also* Intervening cause; Supervening negligence.

Supervening cause. A new effective cause which, operating independently of anything else, becomes proximate cause of accident. *See also* Intervening cause; Superseding cause.

Supervening negligence. To come within the doctrine of last clear chance or supervening negligence, four conditions must coexist, to wit: (1) the injured party has already come into a position of peril; (2) the injuring party then or thereafter becomes, or in the exercise of ordinary prudence ought to have become, aware, not only of that fact, but also that the party in peril either reasonably cannot escape from it or apparently will not avail himself of opportunities open to him for doing so; (3) the injuring party subsequently has the opportunity by the exercise of reasonable care to save the other from harm; and (4) he fails to exercise such care. *See also* Intervening cause; Last clear chance doctrine; Superseding cause.

Supervisor. A surveyor or overseer. Also, in some states, the chief officer of a town; one of a board of county officers.

In a broad sense, one having authority over others, to superintend and direct.

The term "supervisor" means any individual having authority, in the interest of the employer, to hire, transfer, suspend, lay off, recall, promote, discharge, assign, reward, or discipline other employees, or responsibly to direct them, or to adjust their grievances, or effectively to recommend such action, if in connection with the foregoing the exercise of such authority is not of a merely routine or clerical nature, but requires the use of independent judgment. National Labor Relations Act, § 2(11); 12 U.S.C.A. § 152.

Supervisory control. Control exercised by courts to compel inferior tribunals to act within their jurisdiction, to prohibit them from acting outside their jurisdiction, and to reverse their extrajurisdictional acts. *See* Mandamus.

Supplemental. That which is added to a thing or act to complete it. *See also* Amendment.

Supplemental act. That which supplies a deficiency, adds to or completes, or extends that which is already in existence without changing or modifying the original. Act designed to improve an existing statute by adding something thereto without changing the original text.

Supplemental affidavit. An affidavit made in addition to a previous one, in order to supply some deficiency in it.

Supplemental answer. One which was filed for the purpose of correcting, adding to, and explaining an answer already filed. *See* Supplemental pleading.

Supplemental claim. A further claim which is filed when further relief is sought after the bringing of a claim. *See* Supplemental complaint.

Supplemental complaint. Under the Rules of Civil Procedure in the federal and most state courts, is a complaint filed in an action to bring to the notice of the court and the opposite party matters occurring after the commencement of action and which may affect the rights asserted. Fed.R.Civil P. 15(d).

It is distinguished from an "amended complaint," in that an "amended complaint" is one which corrects merely faults and errors of a pleading.

Supplemental jurisdiction. A federal court's discretionary power to hear and determine matters related to claims within the court's original jurisdiction. 28 U.S.C.A. § 1367. Claims are related if they are part of the same case or controversy under Art. III of the Constitution. Courts also have supplemental jurisdiction over related claims that involve the joinder or intervention of additional parties, provided the plaintiffs are not merely trying to avoid the complete diversity requirement of 28 U.S.C.A. § 1332. *See also* Jurisdiction.

Supplemental pleading. One consisting of facts arising since filing of the original. Supplemental pleadings relate to occurrences, transactions and events which may have happened since the date of the pleadings sought to be supplemented. Fed. R.Civil P. 15(d). *Compare* Amendment *(Practice and pleading)*.

Supplementary. Added as a supplement; additional; being, or serving as, a supplement.

Supplementary Employee Retirement Plan (SERP). An agreement whereby an employer agrees to pay employees retirement benefits out of operating profits. Such plans are not prefunded or guaranteed, and contributions are not tax-deductible.

Supplementary proceedings. Proceedings supplementary to an execution, directed to the discovery of the debtor's property and its application to the debt for which the execution is issued. Post-judgment remedies provided by statute or procedural rules that allow discovery against persons who might have information on the whereabouts of nonexempt assets of the debtor (supplemental discovery) and that facilitate application of these assets in satisfaction of the judgment (supplemental relief). *See also* Execution.

After an execution on a judgment has issued, the judgment creditor may commence new proceedings to collect the debt. This process includes a summons to the judgment debtor to appear and to submit to an examination as to his property and the court is empowered under statutes to enter an order for payment, for violation of which the debtor may be cited for contempt and imprisoned; *e.g.* M.G.L.A. (Mass.) c. 246, § 6; Mass.R. Civil P. 4.3(b). See also Fed.R. Civil P. 69(a).

Suppletory oath. *See* Oath.

Supplier. Any person engaged in the business of making a consumer product directly or indirectly available to consumers; includes all persons in the chain of production and distribution of a consumer product including the producer or manufacturer, component supplier, wholesaler, distributor, and retailer. 15 U.S.C.A. § 2301.

Support, *v.* Furnishing funds or means for maintenance; to maintain; to provide for; to enable to continue; to carry on. To provide a means of livelihood. To vindicate, to maintain, to defend, to uphold with aid or countenance.

Support, *n.* That which furnishes a livelihood; a source or means of living; subsistence, sustenance, maintenance, or living. In a broad sense the term includes all such means of living as would enable one to live in the degree of comfort suitable and becoming to his station of life. It is said to include anything requisite to housing, feeding, clothing, health, proper recreation, vacation, traveling expense, or other proper cognate purposes; also, proper care, nursing, and medical attendance in sickness, and suitable burial at death. *See also* Maintenance.

Support also signifies the right to have one's ground supported so that it will not cave in, when an adjoining owner makes an excavation. This support is of two kinds, *lateral* and *subjacent.* Lateral support is the right of land to be supported by the land which lies next to it. Subjacent support is the right of land to be supported by the land which lies under it.

See also Family expense statutes; Legal duty; Legal obligation; Maintenance; Necessaries; Nonsupport; Reciprocal Enforcement of Support Act; Separate maintenance.

Crime of non-support. A person commits a misdemeanor if he persistently fails to provide support which he can provide and which he knows he is legally obliged to provide to a spouse, child or other dependent. Model Penal Code, § 230.5.

Ground for divorce. Non-support of spouse, if able to so provide, is a ground for divorce under many state statutes.

Legal duty. Most all states have statutes which impose obligation to support spouse and children; *e.g.* "Every individual shall support his or her spouse and child, and shall support his or her parent when in need." Calif.Civil Code, § 242.

Interstate enforcement. The majority of states have adopted the "Uniform Reciprocal Enforcement of Support Act" as a means of interstate enforcement of support obligations.

Supposition. A conjecture based upon possibility or probability that a thing could or may have occurred, without proof that it did occur.

Suppress. To put a stop to a thing actually existing; to prohibit, put down; to prevent, subdue, or end by force. To "suppress evidence" is to keep it from being used in a trial by showing that it was either gathered illegally or that it is irrelevant. *See* Suppression hearing; Suppression of evidence.

Suppression. Conscious effort to control and conceal unacceptable impulses, thoughts, feelings or acts.

Suppression hearing. A pretrial proceeding in criminal cases in which a defendant seeks to prevent the introduction of evidence alleged to have been seized illegally. The ruling of the court then prevails at the trial. Fed.R.Crim.P. 5.1(a), 12, and 41. *See also* Exclusionary Rule.

Suppression of evidence. The ruling of a trial judge to the effect that evidence sought to be admitted should be excluded because it was illegally acquired. Motions to suppress illegally obtained evidence are governed by Fed.R.Crim.P. 5.1(a), 12, and 41. *See also* Exclusionary Rule; Motion to suppress.

The crime of compounding a felony by refusing to give evidence or to testify in a criminal proceeding.

Concept of "suppression" as that term is used in rule that suppression by the prosecution of material evidence favorable to an accused on request violates due process, implies that the government has information in its possession of which the defendant lacks knowledge and which the defendant would benefit from knowing. *See also* Withholding of evidence.

Supra /s(y)úwprə/. Lat. Above; upon. This word occurring by itself in a book refers the reader to a previous part of the book, like *"ante;"* it is also the initial word of several Latin phrases.

Supra protest /s(y)úwprə prówtèst/. *See* Protest.

Supremacy. The state of being supreme, or in the highest station of power; paramount authority; sovereignty; sovereign power.

Supremacy clause. The clause of Art. VI of the U.S. Constitution which declares that all laws made in pursuance of the Constitution and all treaties made under the authority of the United States shall be the "supreme law of the land" and shall enjoy legal superiority over any conflicting provision of a State constitution or law. *See also* Preemption.

Supreme. Superior to all other things.

Supreme court. An appellate court existing in most of the states. In the federal court system, and in most states, it is the highest appellate court or court of last resort. In others (such as New York) the supreme court is a court of general original jurisdiction, possessing also (in New

York) some appellate jurisdiction, but not the court of last resort. *See also* Court of Appeals.

Supreme court of errors. Formerly, the court of last resort in Connecticut, now called "Supreme Court".

Supreme Court of the United States. The U.S. Supreme Court comprises the Chief Justice of the United States and such number of Associate Justices as may be fixed by Congress. Under that authority, and by virtue of the act of June 25, 1948 (62 Stat. 869; 28 U.S.C.A. 1), the number of Associate Justices is eight. Power to nominate the Justices is vested in the President of the United States, and appointments are made by and with the advice and consent of the Senate. Article III, section 1, of the Constitution further provides that "the Judges, both of the supreme and inferior Courts, shall hold their Offices during good Behaviour, and shall, at stated Times, receive for their Services, a Compensation, which shall not be diminished during their Continuance in Office." See 28 U.S.C.A. § 1251 et seq.

Supreme Judicial Court. Highest appellate court in Maine and Massachusetts.

Supreme law of the land. *See* Supremacy clause.

Supreme power. The highest authority in a state, all other powers in it being inferior thereto.

Surcharge, *n.* An overcharge; an exaction, impost, or encumbrance beyond what is just and right, or beyond one's authority or power. Term may also refer to a second or further mortgage.

The amount with which a court may charge a fiduciary who has breached his trust through intentional or negligent conduct. The imposition of personal liability on a fiduciary for such conduct.

Overprint on a stamp that changes the denomination.

An additional tax or cost onto an existing tax, cost, or charge. *See* Surtax.

Surcharge, *v.* The imposition of personal liability on a fiduciary for wilful or negligent misconduct in the administration of his fiduciary duties.

In equity practice, to show that a particular item, in favor of the party surcharging, ought to have been included, but was not, in an account which is alleged to be settled or complete. To prove the omission of an item from an account which is before the court as complete, which should be inserted to the credit of the party surcharging.

The imposition of an additional tax, impost, or cost. *See* Surtax.

Surety. One who at the request of another, and for the purpose of securing to him a benefit, becomes responsible for the performance by the latter of some act in favor of a third person, or hypothecates property as security therefor. One who undertakes to pay money or to do any other act in event that his principal fails therein. A person who is primarily liable for payment of debt or performance of obligation of another. One bound with his principal for the payment of a sum of money or for the performance of some duty or promise and who is entitled to be indemnified by some one who ought to have paid or performed if payment or performance be enforced against him. Term includes a guarantor. U.C.C. § 1–201(40). *See also* Suretyship; Suretyship, contract of.

Guarantor and surety compared. A surety and guarantor have this in common, that they are both bound for another person; yet there are points of difference between them. A surety is usually bound with his principal by the same instrument, executed at the same time and on the same consideration. He is an original promisor and debtor from the beginning, and is held ordinarily to every known default of his principal. On the other hand, the contract of guarantor is his own separate undertaking, in which the principal does not join. It is usually entered into before or after that of the principal, and is often founded on a separate consideration from that supporting the contract of the principal. The original contract of the principal is not the guarantor's contract, and the guarantor is not bound to take notice of its nonperformance. The surety joins in the same promise as his principal and is primarily liable; the guarantor makes a separate and individual promise and is only secondarily liable. His liability is contingent on the default of his principal, and he only becomes absolutely liable when such default takes place and he is notified thereof. "Surety" and "guarantor" are both answerable for debt, default, or miscarriage of another, but liability of guarantor is, strictly speaking, secondary and collateral, while that of surety is original, primary, and direct. In case of suretyship there is but one contract, and surety is bound by the same agreement which binds his principal, while in case of guaranty there are two contracts, and guarantor is bound by independent undertaking. A surety is an insurer of the debt or obligation of another; a guarantor is an insurer of the solvency of the principal debtor or of his ability to pay. Under U.C.C., term "surety" includes a guarantor. § 1–201(40). *See also* Guarantor.

Surety bond. *See* Bond.

Surety company. A company, usually incorporated, whose business is to assume the responsibility of a surety on the bonds of officers, trustees, executors, guardians, etc., in consideration of a fee proportioned to the amount of the security required.

Surety insurance. This phrase is generally used as synonymous with "guaranty insurance."

Suretyship. The relationship among three parties whereby one person (the surety) guarantees payment of a debtor's debt owed to a creditor or acts as a co-debtor. Generally speaking, "the relation which exists where one person has undertaken an obligation and another person is also under an obligation or other duty to the obligee, who is entitled to but one performance, and as between the two who are bound, one rather than the other should perform." Restatement of Security, § 82 (1941). *See also* Surety; Suretyship, contract of.

Suretyship, contract of. Contract whereby one party engages to be answerable for debt, default, or miscarriage of another and arises when one is liable to pay debt or discharge obligation, and party is entitled to indemnity from person who should have made the payment in the first instance before surety was so compelled. A contract whereby one person engages to be answerable for the debt, default, or miscarriage of another. An accessory promise by which a person binds himself for another already bound, and agrees with the creditor to satisfy the obligation, if the debtor does not. A lending of credit to aid a principal having insufficient credit of his own; the one expected to pay, having the primary obligation, being the "principal," and the one bound to pay, if the principal does not, being the "surety." *See also* Surety.

Suretyship defenses. Defenses of a surety against the creditor that are dependent on the surety's status as such and that are tied to the conduct of the creditor that alters or modifies the principal debtor's obligation or impairs collateral for the obligation.

Surface rights. A right or easement granted with mineral rights, enabling the possessor of the mineral rights to drill or mine through the surface.

Surgeon General. The chief medical officer of the United States Public Health Service.

Surplus. That which remains of a fund appropriated for a particular purpose; the remainder of a thing; the overplus; the residue. Ordinarily, surplus means residue or excess of assets after liabilities, including capital, have been deducted.

A general term in corporate accounting that usually refers to either the excess of assets over liabilities or that amount further reduced by the stated capital represented by issued shares. Surplus has a more definite meaning when combined with a descriptive adjective from par value statutes, *e.g.*, earned surplus, capital surplus or reduction surplus.

As to *surplus* Earnings, and Profit, see those titles.

Accumulated surplus. That surplus which results from the accumulation of profits.

Acquired surplus. Surplus acquired by the purchase of one business by another.

Appreciation surplus. Surplus which results from the revaluation of the assets of a business.

Appropriated surplus. That portion of surplus which is earmarked or set aside for a specific purpose.

Capital surplus. All surplus which does not arise from the accumulation of profits. It may be created by a financial reorganization or by gifts to the corporation. The entire surplus of a corporation other than its earned surplus.

Earned surplus. The portion of the surplus of a corporation equal to the balance of its net profits, income, gains and losses from the date of incorporation, or from the latest date when a deficit was eliminated by an application of its capital surplus or stated capital or otherwise, after deducting subsequent distributions to shareholders and transfers to stated capital and capital surplus to the extent such distributions and transfers are made out of earned surplus. Earned surplus also includes also any portion of surplus allocated to earned surplus in mergers, consolidations or acquisitions of all or substantially all of the outstanding shares or of the property and assets of another corporation, domestic or foreign. *See also* Earned surplus.

Initial surplus. That surplus which appears on the financial statement at the commencement of an accounting period and which does not reflect the operations for the period covered by the statement.

Paid-in surplus. Surplus paid in by stockholders as contrasted to earned surplus that arises from profits. Such being the difference between the par value and price received for the stock by the corporation. If the stock is no-par; it is the amount received that is allocated to paid-in surplus. *See also* Paid-in-capital.

Reserved surplus. See Appropriated surplus, above.

Restricted surplus. That portion of surplus which is limited or restricted as to its use.

Surplusage. Extraneous, impertinent, superfluous, or unnecessary matter. Matter in any instrument which is unnecessary to its meaning and does not affect its validity; whatever is extraneous, impertinent, superfluous or unnecessary, and in procedure means matter which is not necessary or relevant to the case.

The remainder or surplus of money left. *See also* Surplus.

Pleading. Allegations of matter wholly foreign and impertinent to the cause. All matter beyond the circumstances necessary to constitute the action. Any allegation without which the pleading would yet be adequate. On motion, the court may order stricken from the pleadings any insufficient defense, redundant, immaterial, or scandalous matter. Fed.R.Civil P. 12(f).

Surprise. Act of taking unawares; sudden confusion or perplexity. In its legal acceptation, denotes an unforeseen disappointment against which ordinary prudence would not have afforded protection.

On motion and upon such terms as are just, the court may relieve a party or his legal representative from a final judgment, order, or proceeding because of surprise. Fed.R.Civil P. 60(b).

Ground for new trial. As a ground for a new trial, that situation in which a party is unexpectedly placed without fault on his part, which will work injury to his interests. He must show himself to have been diligent at every stage of the proceedings, and that the event was one which ordinary prudence could not have guarded against. A situation or result produced, having a substantive basis of fact and reason, from which the court may justly deduce, as a legal conclusion, that the party will suffer a judicial wrong if not relieved from his mistake. The general rule is that when a party or his counsel is "taken by surprise," in a material point or circumstance which could not have been anticipated, and when want of skill, care, or attention cannot be justly imputed, and injustice has been done, a new trial should be granted.

Surrebutter /sə̀rəbə́tər/. In common law pleading, the plaintiff's answer of fact to the defendant's rebutter. It is governed by the same rules as the replication. It is no longer required under modern pleading.

Surrejoinder /sə̀rəjóyndər/. In common law pleading, the plaintiff's answer of fact to the defendant's rejoinder. It is governed in every respect by the same rules as the replication.

Surrender. To give back; yield; render up; restore; and in law, the giving up of an estate to the person who has it in reversion or remainder, so as to merge it in the larger estate. A yielding up of an estate for life or years to him who has an immediate estate in reversion or remainder, wherein the estate for life or years may drown by mutual agreement between them. To relinquish, to deliver into lawful custody, or to give up completely in favor of another.

In commercial law, a means whereby a holder discharges a party's liability on an instrument by delivering possession of the instrument with the intention to release the person from liability. The term also refers to the act of a holder of a negotiable document in presenting the document to the bailee upon taking possession of the goods.

In landlord-tenant law, surrender exists when the tenant voluntarily gives up possession of the premises prior to the full term of the lease and the landlord accepts possession with intent that the lease be terminated. It differs from "abandonment," as applied to leased premises, inasmuch as the latter is simply an act on the part of the lessee alone; but to show a surrender, a mutual agreement between lessor and lessee that the lease is terminated must be clearly proved. *See* Surrender by operation of law.

Surrender by operation of law. This phrase is properly applied to cases where the tenant for life or years has been a party to some act the validity of which he is by law afterwards estopped from disputing, and which would not be valid if his particular estate continued to exist. An implied surrender occurs when an estate incompatible with the existing estate is accepted, or the lessee takes a new lease of the same lands.

Any acts which are equivalent to an agreement on the part of the tenant to abandon, and on the part of the landlord to resume the possession of the demised premises, amount to a "surrender by operation of law." The rule may be said to be that a surrender is created by operation of law, when the parties to a lease do some act so inconsistent with the subsisting relation of landlord and tenant as to imply that they have both agreed to consider the surrender as made.

Surrenderee. The person to whom a surrender is made.

Surrender of a preference. In bankruptcy practice, the surrender to the assignee in bankruptcy, by a preferred creditor, of anything he may have received under his preference and any advantage it gives him, which he must do before he can share in the dividend. The word as generally defined may denote either compelled or voluntary action. See Bankruptcy Code, § 547.

Surrender of criminals. The act by which the public authorities deliver a person accused of a crime, and who is found in their jurisdiction, to the authorities within whose jurisdiction it is alleged the crime has been committed. *See* Extradition; Rendition.

Surrender value. In insurance, the current value of a policy which will be paid to the policyholder when he elects to surrender the policy.

Surreptitious /sə̀rəptíshəs/. Stealthily or fraudulently done, taken away, or introduced.

Surrogate /sə́hrəgət/. The name given in some of the states to the judge or judicial officer who has jurisdiction over the administration of probate matters, guardianships, etc. In other states he is called judge of probate, register, judge of the orphans' court, etc. He is ordinarily a county officer, with a local jurisdiction limited to his county. *See* Surrogate court.

Surrogate court. Name of court in certain states with jurisdiction similar to that of probate court.

In New York the Surrogate's Court has jurisdiction over all actions and proceedings relating to the affairs of decedents, probate of wills, administration of estates and actions and proceedings arising thereunder or pertaining thereto, guardianship of the property of minors, and such other actions and proceedings, not within the exclusive jurisdiction of the supreme court, as may be provided by law.

Surrogate mother. A woman who is artificially inseminated with the semen of another woman's husband. She conceives a child, carries the child to term, and after the birth assigns her parental rights to the birth father and his wife. *See* Surrogate parenting agreement.

Surrogate parent. A person other than a parent who stands in loco parentis to the child by virtue of his or her voluntary assumption of parental rights and responsibilities. The person appointed by a juvenile court as a child's advocate in the educational decision-making process in place of the child's natural parents or guardian.

Surrogate parenting agreement. Agreement wherein a woman agrees to be artificially inseminated with the semen of another woman's husband; she is to conceive a child, carry the child to term and after the birth, assign her parental rights to the birth father and his wife. The intent of the contract is that the child's birth mother will thereafter be forever separated from her child. The wife is to adopt the child, and she and the birth father are to be regarded as the child's parents for all purposes. Such contracts have been held illegal and invalid where a woman agrees to act as a surrogate for payment of money with a binding agreement to assign her parental rights to her child. Matter of Baby M, 109 N.J. 396, 537 A.2d 1227, 1234–35.

Surround. To inclose on all sides; to encompass.

Surrounding circumstances. Such as may permit inference of culpability on part of defendant under res ipsa loquitur rule, refers not to circumstances directly tending to show lack of care, but only to mere neutral circumstances of control and management by defendant, which may, when explained, appear to be entirely consistent with due care.

Surtax. Any tax that is levied in addition to some "normal" tax rate. An additional tax on what has already been taxed. A tax on a tax; for example: if person must pay a hundred dollar tax on a one thousand dollar income (ten percent), a ten percent surtax would be an additional ten dollars, not an additional hundred dollars.

Surtax exemption. The portion of taxable income not subject to the surtax.

Surveillance /sərvéy(l)əns/. Oversight, superintendence, supervision. Police investigative technique involving visual or electronic observation or listening directed at a person or place (*e.g.*, stakeout, tailing of suspects, wiretapping). Its objective is to gather evidence of a crime or merely to accumulate intelligence about suspected criminal activity. *See also* Eavesdropping; Pen register; Wiretapping.

Survey, *v.* To survey land is to ascertain corners, boundaries, and divisions, with distances and directions, and not necessarily to compute areas included within defined boundaries. To appraise as to value or condition.

Survey, *n.* The process by which a parcel of land is measured and its boundaries and contents ascertained; also a map, plat, or statement of the result of such survey, with the courses and distances and the quantity of the land. *See also* Corner; Government survey system; Meander lines.

An investigation or examination. In insurance law, the term has acquired a general meaning, inclusive of what is commonly called the "application," which contains the questions propounded on behalf of the company, and the answers of the assured.

Polling or questioning of public regarding their views on issues, candidates, etc.

Topographical survey. A survey of land to determine its elevation levels in relation to sea level.

Surveyor. One who makes surveys, determines area of portion of earth's surface, length and direction of boundary lines, and contour of surface.

Survival actions. Term refers to actions for personal injuries which by statute survives death of injured person. An action or cause of action which does not become extinguished with the death of the party claiming the action. *See* Survival statutes; Wrongful death statutes.

Survival statutes. Statutory provision for the survival, after death of the injured person, of certain causes of action for injury to the person whether death results from the injury or from some other cause. The cause of action which survives is for the wrong to the injured person. A type of statute, that allows an action to continue, notwithstanding the death of the one who originally had a right to bring the action. Such a right usually may be enforced by or against the estate of the decedent. Some survival statutes cover death of both injured party (plaintiff) and death of defendant. *See also* Wrongful death statutes.

Survive. To continue to live or exist beyond the life, or existence of; to live through in spite of; live on after passing through; to remain alive; exist in force or operation beyond any period or event specified.

Surviving. Remaining alive. Living beyond the life of another or beyond the happening of some event so as to be entitled to a distribution of property or income. *See* Survival actions.

Surviving corporation. The corporation which, through a merger or takeover, acquires the assets and liabilities of another corporation.

Surviving spouse. The spouse who outlives (survives) the other spouse. Term commonly found in statutes dealing with probate, administration of estates and estate and inheritance taxes.

A taxpayer classification which, generally, describes an unmarried taxpayer whose spouse died within either of the past two taxable years and who provides a home for his dependent(s). I.R.C. § 2(a).

Survivor. One who survives another; one who outlives another; one who lives beyond some happening; one of two or more persons who lives after the death of the other or others. The word "survivor," however, in connection with the power of one of two trustees to act, is used not only with reference to a condition arising where one of such trustees dies, but also as indicating a trustee who continues to administer the trust after his cotrustee is disqualified, has been removed, renounces, or refuses to act.

Survivorship. The living of one of two or more persons after the death of the other or others. Survivorship is where a person becomes entitled to property by reason of his having survived another person who had an interest in it. A feature of joint tenancy and tenancy by the entirety, whereby the surviving co-owner takes the entire interest in preference to heirs or devisees of the deceased co-owner. *See also* Presumption of survivorship; Tenancy *(Joint tenancy; Tenancy by the entirety)*.

Survivorship annuity. Type of annuity contract which provides for payments beyond the life of the annuitant, as for example, to a widow of the annuitant.

Susceptible. Capable.

Suspect. To have a slight or even vague idea concerning;—not necessarily involving knowledge or belief or likelihood. "Suspect" with reference to probable cause as grounds for arrest without warrant is commonly used in place of the word believe. A person reputed or suspected to be involved in a crime. *See also* Probable cause; Suspicion.

Suspect classifications. A court will employ the "strict scrutiny" standard under the Equal Protection Clause in determining the legitimacy of classifications that are based upon a trait which itself seems to contravene established constitutional principles so that any purposeful use of the classification may be deemed "suspect." Examples include race, sex, national origin and alienage (with exceptions).

Suspend. To interrupt; to cause to cease for a time; to postpone; to stay, delay, or hinder; to discontinue temporarily, but with an expectation or purpose of resumption. As a form of censure or discipline, to forbid a public officer, attorney, employee, or ecclesiastical person from performing his duties or exercising his functions for a more or less definite interval of time.

To postpone, as a judicial sentence. To cause a temporary cessation, as of work by an employee; to lay off.

See also Suspension.

Suspended sentence. A conviction of a crime followed by a sentence that is given formally, but not actually served. A suspended sentence in criminal law means in effect that defendant is not required at the time sentence is imposed to serve the sentence. *See also* Sentence *(Suspension of sentence)*.

Suspension. A temporary stop, a temporary delay, interruption, or cessation. Thus, we speak of a *suspension* of the writ of *habeas corpus,* of a statute, of the power of alienating an estate, of a person in office, etc.

A temporary cutting off or debarring one, as from the privileges of one's profession.

Temporary withdrawal or cessation from employment as distinguished from permanent severance accomplished by removal; "removal" being, however, the broader term, which may on occasion include suspension.

Suspicion. The act of suspecting, or the state of being suspected; imagination, generally of something ill; distrust; mistrust; doubt. The apprehension of something without proof or upon slight evidence. Suspicion implies a belief or opinion based upon facts or circumstances which do not amount to proof.

Suspicious character. In the criminal laws of some of the states, a person who is known or strongly suspected to be an habitual criminal, or against whom there is reasonable cause to believe that he has committed a crime or is planning or intending to commit one, or whose actions and behavior give good account of himself, and who may therefore be arrested or required to give security for good behavior.

Sustain. To carry on; to maintain. To affirm, uphold or approve, as when an appellate court sustains the decision of a lower court. To grant, as when a judge sustains an objection to testimony or evidence, he or she agrees with the objection and gives it effect.

To support; to warrant;—said of evidence in connection with a verdict, decision, etc.

To suffer; bear; undergo. To endure or undergo without failing or yielding; to bear up under.

Swaps. The exchange of one security for another. A swap may be executed to change the maturities of a bond portfolio or the quality of the issues in a share or bond portfolio, or because investment objectives have shifted. Swap agreements are used by corporations and financial institutions to hedge against changes in interest and foreign exchange rates. *See also* Currency swap.

Swear. To put on oath; to administer an oath to a person. To take an oath; to become bound by an oath duly administered. To declare on oath the truth (of a pleading, etc.). *See also* Affirmation; False swearing; Oath.

To use obscene or profane language. Its use in public places is an offense in many states.

Swearing in. The administration of an oath as to a trial witness or to a public official or one about to become a public official, as in the case of a person who becomes a judge. *See* Oath.

Swearing the peace. Showing to a magistrate that one has just cause to be afraid of another in consequence of his menaces, in order to have him bound over to keep the peace.

Sweat equity. Financial equity created in property through labor of owner in making improvements to property.

Sweat shop. A business whose employees are overworked and paid low wages, or a place where employees are required to work to an extent hardly endurable, and in the public mind the term imputes unsavory and illegal business practices. Sweat shops resulted in the enactment of wage and hour laws, child labor laws, minimum wage laws, etc.

Sweep account. A non-interest-bearing transaction bank account out of which all funds remaining at the end of each business day are automatically "swept" and deposited into an interest-bearing account or invested in some other manner that the account holder has previously specified.

Sweepstakes. Term initially referring to a type of horse race in which the winner's prize was the sum of the stakes which subscribers agreed to pay for each horse nominated. Currently refers generally to contests, often conducted for promotional purposes, which award prizes based on the random selection of entries. Federal law prohibits conducting a scheme for obtaining money or prop-

erty through the mail by means of false representations. 39 U.S.C.A. § 3005. *See also* Lottery.

Sweeteners. Inducement to a brokerage firm to enter into an underwriting arrangement with an issuer.

Sweetheart contract. Derogatory term used to describe a contract between a union and an employer in which concessions are granted to one or to the other for purpose of keeping a rival union out.

Swift v. Tyson Case. An early case decided in 1842 by the U.S. Supreme Court, 41 (16 Pet.) U.S. 1, 10 L.Ed. 865, which held that federal courts in suits founded on diversity of citizenship were free to exercise an independent judgment in matters of "general" law; *i.e.* matters not at all dependent upon local statutes or local usages of a fixed and permanent operation. Swift v. Tyson was overruled by Erie R.R. Co. v. Tompkins, 304 U.S. 64, 58 S.Ct. 817, 82 L.Ed. 1188 which requires the application of state law in diversity actions under most circumstances. *See* Erie v. Tompkins; Federal common law.

Swift witness. A term colloquially applied to a witness who is unduly zealous or partial for the side which calls him, and who betrays his bias by his extreme readiness to answer questions or volunteer information.

Swindle. A scheme for cheating or defrauding.

Swindler. A cheat; one guilty of defrauding divers persons.

Swindling. Cheating and defrauding with deliberate artifice. Usually applied to a transaction where the guilty party procures the delivery to him, under a pretended contract, of the personal property of another, with the felonious design of appropriating it to his own use. The acquisition of any personal or movable property, money, or instrument of writing conveying or securing a valuable right, by means of some false or deceitful pretense or device, or fraudulent representation, with intent to appropriate the same to the use of the party so acquiring, or of destroying or impairing the rights of the party justly entitled to the same.

To make out offense of "cheating" and "swindling" by false representations, government must prove that representations were made, that representations were knowingly and designedly false, that such were made with intent to defraud, that such did defraud, that representations related to existing fact or past event, and that party to whom representations were made, relying on their truth, was thereby induced to part with his property. See *e.g.* 18 U.S.C.A. §§ 1341, 1342 (mail swindles).

See False pretenses; Fraud.

Sworn. Frequently used interchangeably with "verified." *See* Affirmation; Oath; Swear; Verify.

Sworn statement. Listing by contractor-builder of all of his suppliers and sub-contractors and their respective bids. Such is required by lending institution for interim construction financing.

Syllabus. An abstract; a headnote; a note prefixed to the report or opinion of an adjudged case, containing an epitome or brief statement of the rulings of the court upon the point or points decided in the case. The syllabus (in Supreme Court decisions) constitutes no part of the opinion of the Court but is prepared by the Reporter of Decisions for the convenience of the reader. Ordinarily, where a headnote, even though prepared by the court, is given no special force by statute or rule of court, the opinion is to be looked to for the original and authentic statement of the grounds of decision. *See also* Digest; Headnote.

Symbolic delivery. The constructive delivery of the subject-matter of a sale or gift, where it is cumbersome or inaccessible, by the actual delivery of some article which is conventionally accepted as the symbol or representative of it, or which renders access to it possible, or which is evidence of the purchaser's or donee's title to it. Thus, a present gift of the contents of a box in a bank vault, accompanied by a transfer of the key thereto, is valid as a symbolical delivery.

Symbolic speech. A person's conduct which expresses opinions or thoughts about a subject and which may or may not be protected by the First Amendment. Actions which have as their primary purpose the expression of ideas as in the case of students who wore black arm bands to protest the war in Viet Nam. Such conduct is generally protected under the First Amendment as "pure speech" because very little conduct is involved. However, not all such conduct is protected; *e.g.* the burning of a draft card has been held to not be protected speech because of the government's substantial interest. *See* Flag desecration.

Sympathy strike. A boycott. *See* Boycott; Strike.

Syndicalism /síndəkəlìzəm/. The theory, plan, or practice of trade-union action which aims by the general strike and direct action to establish control by local organizations of workers over the means and processes of production.

Criminal syndicalism. Any doctrine or precept advocating, teaching, or aiding and abetting the commission of crime, sabotage (defined in the act as willful and malicious physical damage or injury to physical property), or unlawful acts of force and violence or unlawful methods of terrorism, as a means of accomplishing a change in industrial ownership, or control, or effecting any political change. *See also* Criminal.

Syndicate /síndəkət/. An association of individuals, formed for the purpose of conducting and carrying out some particular business transaction, ordinarily of a financial character, in which the members are mutually interested. An organization formed for some temporary purpose, such as the organization of a real estate trust and the sale of shares to the public. Syndicates may exist as corporations or partnerships (either general or limited).

A group of investment bankers who together underwrite and distribute a new issue of securities or a large block of an outstanding issue. A syndicate is formed in such instances because the capital commitment or risk involved for any single investor, financial institution or broker is too great. An association of securities broker-dealers, usually in writing, who assist the principal underwriter in the controlled distribution of the securities of an issuer.

Syndicating. Gathering materials suitable for newspaper publication from writers and artists and distributing the same at regular intervals to newspapers throughout the country for publication on the same day.

Syndication. Act or process of forming a syndicate.

Synonymous. Expressing the same or nearly the same idea.

Synopsis. A brief or partial statement, less than the whole; an epitome; synonymous with summary. *See* Abstract; Digest; Syllabus.

T

T. As an abbreviation, this letter may stand for such terms as "term", "territory", "title", "table".

Table, *v.* To suspend consideration of a pending legislative bill or other measure.

Table, *n.* A synopsis, condensed statement or listing bringing together numerous items or details so as to be comprehended in a single view; as genealogical tables, exhibiting the names and relationships of all the persons composing a family; life and annuity tables, used by actuaries; interest tables, etc. Term may also refer to an alphabetical, numerical, etc. listing of cases, statutes, court rules, and the like, cited or referred to in a legal publication. *See* Table of cases.

Table of cases. An alphabetical list of the adjudged cases cited, referred to, or digested in a legal text-book, volume of reports, or digest, with references to the sections, pages, or paragraphs where they are respectively cited, etc., which is commonly either prefixed or appended to the volume.

T–account. Account form shaped like the letter T with an account name above the horizontal line. Debits are shown to the left of the vertical line; credits, to the right. In bookkeeping, an original form of account in which debits and credits may be recorded on the appropriate side of the "T".

Tacit /tǽsət/. Existing, inferred, or understood without being openly expressed or stated; implied by silence or silent acquiescence, as a tacit agreement or a tacit understanding. Done or made in silence, implied or indicated, but not actually expressed. Manifested by the refraining from contradiction or objection; inferred from the situation and circumstances, in the absence of express matter.

Tacit admissions. An acknowledgment or concession of a fact inferred from either silence or from the substance of what one has said.

Tack. To annex some junior lien to a first lien, thereby acquiring priority over an intermediate one. *See* Tacking.

Tacking. The term is applied especially to the process of establishing title to land by adverse possession, when the present occupant and claimant has not been in possession for the full statutory period, but adds or "tacks" to his own possession that of previous occupants under whom he claims. That doctrine which permits an adverse possessor to add his period of possession to that of a prior adverse possessor in order to establish a continuous possession for the statutory period.

The term is also used in a number of other connections, as of possessions, disabilities, or items in accounts or other dealings. In these several cases the purpose of the proposed tacking is to avoid the bar of a statute of limitations.

The uniting of securities given at different times, so as to prevent any intermediate purchaser from claiming a title to redeem or otherwise discharge one lien, which is prior, without redeeming or discharging the other liens also, which are subsequent to his own title. The term is particularly applied to the action of a third mortgagee who, by buying the first lien and uniting it to his own, gets priority over the second mortgagee.

Taft-Hartley Act. The Wagner Act was amended in 1947 by the Taft-Hartley Act to balance some of the advantages given to unions under the Wagner Act by imposing corresponding duties on unions. Principal changes imposed by the Act included the following: abolishment of the closed shop, but permitting the union shop under conditions specified in the Act; exempting supervisors from coverage of the Act; requiring the N.L.R.B. to accord equal treatment to both independent and affiliated unions; permitting the employer to file a representation petition even though only one union seeks to represent the employees; granting employees the right not only to organize and bargain collectively but also to refrain from such activities; permitting employees to file decertification petitions for elections to determine whether or not employees desire to revoke a union's designation as their bargaining agent; declaring certain activities engaged in by unions to be unfair labor practices; giving to employers, employees, and unions new guarantees of the right of free speech; providing for settlement by the N.L.R.B. of certain jurisdictional disputes; vested in the General Counsel, rather than in the Board the authority to investigate and prosecute unfair labor practices. 29 U.S.C.A. § 141 et seq.

Tail. Limited; abridged; reduced; curtailed, as a fee or estate in fee, to a certain order of succession, or to certain heirs.

Tail, estate in. An estate of inheritance, which, instead of descending to heirs generally, goes to the heirs of the donee's body, which means his lawful issue, his children, and through them to his grandchildren in a direct line, so long as his posterity endures in a regular order and course of descent, and upon the death of the first owner without issue, the estate determines.

Taint. A conviction of felony, or the person so convicted.

Take. The word "take" has many shades of meaning, with the precise meaning which it is to bear in any case depending on the subject with respect to which it is used; *e.g.* eminent domain; larceny; arrest.

To lay hold of; to gain or receive into possession; to seize; to deprive one of the use or possession of; to assume ownership. Thus, constitutions generally provide that a person's property shall not be taken for public uses without just compensation. Fifth Amend., U.S.Const. *See* De facto taking; Taking.

In the law of larceny, to obtain or assume possession of a chattel unlawfully, and without the owner's consent; to appropriate things to one's own use with felonious intent. Thus, an actual taking is essential to constitute larceny. The element of "taking" in robbery does not require robber's manual possession of property; it is sufficient if robber has acquired dominion and control over property. A "taking" may occur when a person with a preconceived design to appropriate property to his own use obtains possession of it by means of fraud or trickery; and, such taking may be accomplished by the use of an innocent agent acting under the control and direction of the taker where the goods finally come into possession of the taker and are converted to his use.

To seize or apprehend a person; to arrest the body of a person by virtue of lawful process. Thus, a *capias* commands the officer to *take* the body of the defendant. *See* Seize.

To acquire the title to an estate; to receive or be entitled to an estate in lands from another person by virtue of some species of title. Thus one is said to "*take* by purchase," "*take* by descent," "*take* a life-interest under the devise," etc.

Profit from a transaction, lottery, etc. Person open to taking bribes (*i.e.* "on the take".)

See also Taking as regards eminent domain proceedings.

Take back. To revoke; to retract; as, to take back one's promise.

Take care of. To support; maintain; look after (a person). To pay (a debt). To attend to.

Take effect. To become operative or executed. To be in force, or go into operation.

Take-home pay. The net amount of a paycheck; gross earned wages or salary reduced by deductions for income taxes, Social Security taxes, contributions to fringe benefit plans, union dues, and so on.

Take or pay contracts. A contract that obligates the purchaser to take any product that is offered to it (and pay the cash purchase price) or pay a specified amount if it refuses to take the product. *See also* Tied product.

Takeover. To assume control or management of; not necessarily involving the transfer of absolute title. *See* Takeover bid; Tender offer.

Takeover bid. An attempt by an outside corporation or group, usually called the aggressor or "insurgent," to wrest control away from incumbent management of target corporation. A takeover attempt may involve purchase of shares, a tender offer, a sale of assets or a proposal that the target merge voluntarily into the aggressor. *See* Golden parachute; Greenmail; Leveraged buyout; Poison pill; Target company; Tender offer; White knight.

Takeover defenses. Tactics or devices used to prevent unwanted takeover bid; *see e.g.* Poison pill; White knight.

Taker. One who takes or acquires; particularly, one who takes an estate by devise. When an estate is granted subject to a remainder or executory devise, the devisee of the immediate interest is called the "first taker."

Take up. To pay or discharge, as a note. Also, sometimes, to purchase a note. To retire a negotiable instrument; to discharge one's liability on it;—said particularly of an indorser or acceptor. A party to a negotiable instrument, particularly an indorser or acceptor, is said to "take up" the paper, or to "retire" it, when he pays its amount, or substitutes other security for it, and receives it again into his own hands.

Take-up fee. A fee paid to an underwriter in connection with an underwritten rights offering or an underwritten forced conversion as compensation for each share of common stock the underwriter obtains and must resell upon exercise or rights or conversion of bonds.

Taking. In criminal law and torts, the act of laying hold upon an article, with or without removing the same. It implies a transfer of possession, dominion, or control.

Under various statutes relating to sexual offenses, such as the abduction of a girl under the age of 18 years for the purpose of carnal intercourse, to constitute a "taking" no force, actual or constructive, need be exercised. The "taking" may be effected by persuasion, enticement, or inducement. And it is not necessary that the girl be taken from the control or against the will of those having lawful authority over her.

There is a "taking" of property when government action directly interferes with or substantially disturbs the owner's use and enjoyment of the property. To constitute a "taking, within constitutional limitation, it is not essential that there be physical seizure or appropriation, and any actual or material interference with private property rights constitutes a taking. For example, the noise of jet aircraft in process of landing or taking off can amount to a "taking" or "damaging" of property for which the constitution requires that compensation be made. Also, "taking" of property is affected if application of zoning law denies property owner of economically viable use of his land, which can consist of preventing best use of land or extinguishing fundamental attribute of ownership. *See also* Condemnation; Constructive taking; Eminent domain; Take.

As element of crime of larceny, *see* Take.

Taking case from jury. Directing a verdict; a situation in which a court grants a motion to sustain a judgment. *See* Directed verdict.

Taking delivery. Receiving actual delivery of commodity under futures contract or spot market contract, or of securities recently purchased.

Taking the Fifth. The practice of witnesses or suspects in refusing to answer a question because of the Fifth Amendment right in the U.S. Constitution to refuse to furnish information implicating one's self in a crime. *See* Fifth Amendment; Self-incrimination.

Talesman. A person summoned to act as a juror from among the by-standers in the court. A person summoned as one of the tales added to a jury.

Tamper. To meddle so as to alter a thing, especially to make illegal, corrupting or perverting changes; as, to tamper with a document or a text; to interfere improperly; to meddle; to busy oneself rashly; to try trifling or foolish experiments. To illegally change as to tamper with the mileage reading on an odometer of a motor vehicle, or a motor vehicle identification number (18 U.S.C.A. §§ 511, 512), or consumer products (18 U.S.C.A. § 1365), or a witness or victim (18 U.S.C.A. § 1512 et seq.).

Tampering with jury. Embracery. The act of attempting to influence a juror corruptly by promises, threats, persuasions, entreaties, money or any other means except the production of evidence in open court. Such act is a criminal offense. See *e.g.* 18 U.S.C.A. §§ 1503, 1504.

Tampering with records. *See* Falsifying a record.

Tangible. Having or possessing physical form. Capable of being touched and seen; perceptible to the touch; tactile; palpable; capable of being possessed or realized; readily apprehensible by the mind; real; substantial.

Tangible assets. Assets with physical existence (*e.g.*, cash, real estate, equipment) and which are not held for resale. Although accounts receivable do not appear to have a physical existence, they are considered to be tangible assets on the balance sheet.

Tangible cost. A term used in connection with the costs associated with oil and gas drilling. Tangible costs include the materials and land in contrast to such costs as drilling or testing costs which are considered intangible costs.

Tangible evidence. Evidence which consists of something which can be seen or touched, *e.g.* gun in homicide trial. In contrast to testimonial evidence, tangible evidence is real evidence. *See* Evidence.

Tangible property. Property that has physical form and substance and is not intangible. That which may be felt or touched, and is necessarily corporeal, although it may be either real or personal (*e.g.* ring or watch). *Compare* Intangible property.

Tapping. The interception of a telephonic or telegraphic message by connecting a device to the lines, permitting a person to hear the message. It is regulated by federal and state statutes and normally requires prior judicial approval. See 18 U.S.C.A. § 2510 et seq. *See also* Eavesdropping; Pen register; Surveillance; Wiretapping.

Target company. Company attempted to be taken over in tender offer, leveraged buyout, or other type of takeover or acquisition attempt. *See* Takeover bid; Tender offer.

Target offense. In crime of conspiracy, the crime contemplated by the illegal agreement.

Target witness. A person whose testimony the investigating body is principally seeking as in the case of a grand jury which has, as its objective, the information which such a person may give. A witness called before a grand jury against whom the government is seeking an indictment.

Tariff /tǽrəf/. The list or schedule of articles on which a duty is imposed upon their importation into the United States, with the rates at which they are severally taxed. Also the custom or duty payable on such articles. 19 U.S.C.A. And, derivatively, the system of imposing duties or taxes on the importation of foreign merchandise.

A series of schedules or rates of duties or taxes on imported goods. Tariffs are for revenue if their primary objects are fiscal; protective if designed to relieve domestic businesses from effective foreign competition; discriminatory if they apply unequally to products of different countries; and retaliatory if they are designed to compel a country to remove artificial trade barriers against the entry of another nation's products.

A public document setting forth services of common carrier being offered, rates and charges with respect to services and governing rules, regulations and practices relating to those services.

See also Customs duties; GATT; Most favored nation clause.

Antidumping tariff. A tariff calculated to prevent the dumping or unloading of imported goods below cost by fixing the tariff at the difference between the price at which the goods commonly sell in the country of origin and the price at which it is to be sold in the importing country. *See also* Dumping Act.

Autonomous tariff. Tariff set by legislation and not by commercial treaties.

Joint tariff. Schedule of rates established by two or more carriers covering shipments between places requiring the use of facilities owned by such carriers.

Preferential tariff. Tariff aimed at favoring the products of one country over those of another. *See also* Most favored nation clause; Preferential tariff.

Protective tariff. Tariff designed to protect or encourage domestic goods by imposing a high rate on imported goods of a similar nature. *See also* Protective tariff.

Revenue tariff. Tariff designed primarily to raise revenues and to support the customs service instead of encouraging production of imported goods.

Tax. A charge by the government on the income of an individual, corporation, or trust, as well as on the value of an estate or gift or property. The objective in assessing the tax is to generate revenue to be used for the needs of the public.

A pecuniary burden laid upon individuals or property to support the government, and is a payment exacted by legislative authority. Essential characteristics of a tax are that it is not a voluntary payment or donation, but an enforced contribution, exacted pursuant to legislative authority.

In a general sense, any contribution imposed by government upon individuals, for the use and service of the state, whether under the name of toll, tribute, tallage, gabel, impost, duty, custom, excise, subsidy, aid, supply, or other name.

See also Accumulated earnings tax; Estate tax; Estimated tax; Excess profits tax; Excise tax; Gift tax; Holding company tax; Income tax; Inheritance tax; Intangibles tax; Investment tax credit; Levy; License fee *or* tax; Occupation tax; Payroll tax; Poll-tax; Progressive tax; Property tax; Regressive tax; Sales tax; Service occupation tax; Surtax; Taxation; Toll; Transfer tax; Undistributed profits tax; Use tax; Withholding.

Synonyms

In a broad sense, *taxes* undoubtedly include *assessments,* and the right to impose assessments has its foundation in the taxing power of the government; and yet, in practice and as generally understood, there is a broad distinction between the two terms. "Taxes," as the term is generally used, are public burdens imposed generally upon the inhabitants of the whole state, or upon some civil division thereof, for governmental purposes, without reference to peculiar benefits to particular individuals or property. "Assessments" have reference to impositions for improvements which are specially beneficial to particular individuals or property, and which are imposed in proportion to the particular benefits supposed to be conferred. They are justified only because the improvements confer special benefits, and are just only when they are divided in proportion to such benefits. As distinguished from other kinds of taxation, "assessments" are those special and local impositions upon property in the immediate vicinity of municipal improvements which are necessary to pay for the improvement, and are laid with reference to the special benefit which the property is supposed to have derived therefrom.

Taxes differ from *subsidies,* in being certain and orderly, and from forced contributions, etc., in that they are levied by authority of law, and by some rule of proportion which is intended to insure uniformity of contribution, and a just apportionment of the burdens of government.

Generally

Ad valorem tax. See that title.

Amusement tax. See that title.

Bracket creep. The process by which inflation pushes income earners into higher marginal tax brackets. The significance of the bracket creep changed with the Tax Reform Act of 1986 which substantially reduced the number of brackets.

Capital gains tax. *See* Capital.

Capital stock tax. Tax assessed as a percentage of par or assigned value of capital stock of a corporation.

Capitation tax. See that title.

Collateral inheritance tax. See that title.

Consumption tax. Tax imposed on sales of consumption goods and services.

Customs tax. *See* Customs duties.

Estate tax. A tax imposed upon the right to transfer property at death, while an inheritance tax is a tax upon the right to receive. *See also* Estate tax; Inheritance tax.

Excess profits tax. Tax imposed on all income beyond the normal amount calculated on either a normal return on invested capital or on the average of income of previous years. Such tax is commonly imposed in war time. *See* Excess profits tax; also, *Undistributed profits tax, below.*

Excise tax. See that title.

Flat tax. Tax imposed at same rate to all levels of income.

Floor tax. A tax on all the distilled spirits "on the floor" of a warehouse, *i.e.,* in the warehouse.

Franchise tax. *See* Franchise.

Gift tax. A tax imposed on the transfer of assets without adequate consideration. The federal gift tax is levied on the donor; however, some states impose a gift tax on the donee. *See also* Gift tax.

Graduated tax. A tax so structured that the rate increases as the amount of the income or value of the property increases.

Gross receipts tax. A tax based on total sales rather than on net profits.

Head tax. A flat tax imposed on a per person basis.

Income tax. See that title.

Inheritance tax. See that title and Estate tax.

Land tax. See that title and Ad valorem tax; Property tax.

License tax. *See* License fee *or* tax.

Local taxes. Taxes imposed by municipalities such as local property taxes or city income or sales taxes.

Occupation tax. See that title.

Payroll tax. A type of tax which is collected by deduction from an employee's wages. Federal, state and half of the social security tax is paid by employees, with the social security tax matched by the employer.

Personal property tax. A tax assessed against personal property by cities and towns. The tax is commonly referred to as an excise tax and is levied against such items as automobiles, boats, etc.

Poll-tax. See that title.

Progressive tax. See that title. *Compare Regressive tax, below.*

Property tax. Generic term describing a tax levied on the basis of the value of either personal or real property owned by the taxpayer. *See also* Ad valorem tax; Property tax; and *Real estate tax, below.*

Proportional taxes. Taxes are "proportional" when the proportion paid by each taxpayer bears the same ratio to the amount to be raised that the

value of his property bears to the total taxable value, and in the case of a special tax when that is apportioned according to the benefits received.

Real estate tax. Tax levied by local taxing authority against the ownership of real estate for purposes of financing the operations of the local government. *See also* Ad valorem tax; Property tax.

Regressive tax. A tax system in which higher-income groups pay a smaller percentage of their income to taxes than do lower-income groups; that is, the marginal rate is below the average rate. The average rate falls as income increases. *Compare* Progressive tax.

Sales tax. Tax levied in most states on the sale of goods and based on their value. It may be a direct tax which is paid by the purchaser or a turnover tax paid by the seller on the gross sales of his business. *See also* Sales tax.

Severance tax. Tax levied on the mining or extraction of some natural resource such as oil or coal. It may be assessed on the value of the product extracted or on the volume.

Sinking fund tax. *See* Fund *or* funds.

Specific tax. A tax imposed as a fixed sum on each article or item or property of a given class or kind, without regard to its value (*e.g.* sales tax); opposed to *ad valorem* tax.

Stamp tax. Tax collected through the sale of stamps which must be affixed to certain documents such as deeds, stock certificates, etc. *See* Revenue stamps.

Stock transfer tax. Tax levied by the federal government and by certain states on the transfer or sale of shares of stock.

Succession tax. *See* Succession duty or tax.

Surtax. An additional tax imposed on incomes exceeding a specified amount. *See also* Surtax.

Tax abatement. *See* Abatement.

Tax assessment. *See* Assessment; Tax assessment.

Tax certificate. A certificate of the purchase of land at a tax sale thereof, given by the officer making the sale, and which is evidence of the holder's right to receive a deed of the land if it is not redeemed within the time limited by law.

Tax-deed. The deed given upon a sale of real property made for non-payment of taxes. The deed whereby the officer of the law undertakes to convey the title of the property to the purchaser at the tax-sale. *See also* Tax certificate; Tax deed; and *Tax-title, below.*

Tax deficiency. *See* Deficiency assessment.

Taxing district. The district throughout which a particular tax or assessment is ratably apportioned and levied upon the inhabitants; it may comprise the whole state, one county, a city, a ward, or part of a street.

Tax lease. The instrument (or estate) given to the purchaser of land at a tax sale, where the law does not permit the sale of the estate in fee for non-payment of taxes, but instead thereof directs the sale of an estate for years.

Tax levy. The total sum to be raised by a tax. Also the bill, enactment, or measure of legislation by which an annual or general tax is imposed. *See also* Assessment; Levy.

Tax lien. A statutory lien, existing in favor of the state or municipality, upon the lands of a person charged with taxes, binding the same either for the taxes assessed upon the specific tract of land or (in some jurisdictions) for all the taxes due from the individual, and which may be foreclosed for non-payment, by judgment of a court or sale of the land. *See also* Tax lien.

Taxpayer. A person whose income is subject to taxation; one from whom government demands a pecuniary contribution towards its support.

Taxpayers' lists. Written exhibits required to be made out by the taxpayers resident in a district, enumerating all the property owned by them and subject to taxation, to be handed to the assessors, at a specified date or at regular periods, as a basis for assessment and valuation. *See also* Roll *(Tax roll).*

Tax roll. *See* Roll.

Tax sale. *See* Sale.

Tax-title. The title by which one holds land which he purchased at a tax sale. That species of title which is inaugurated by a successful bid for land at a collector's sale of the same for nonpayment of taxes, completed by the failure of those entitled to redeem within the specified time, and evidenced by the deed executed to the tax purchaser, or his assignee, by the proper officer.

Tonnage tax. *See* Tonnage-duty.

Transfer tax. *See* Stock transfer tax, above.

Undistributed profits tax. A tax imposed on the accumulated surplus of specific types of corporations when such surplus reaches a certain level. The objective of such a tax is to discourage the formation of a corporation for the purpose of preventing the imposition of an income tax on the shareholder through accumulated earnings instead of making distributions thru dividends. I.R.C. § 531. *See* Accumulated earnings tax.

Unemployment tax. Tax required by the Federal Unemployment Tax Act (FUTA) to cover the cost of unemployment insurance. The federal statute provides for a tax based on a percentage of em-

ployee earnings but allows a credit for amounts paid in state unemployment taxes.

Taxes paid by employers to state governments. The taxes are disbursed to the unemployed through the various state programs.

Unitary tax. A method of determining the locally taxable income of businesses that transact business with affiliated companies outside the state. *See also* Unitary business; Unitary theory.

Use tax. Tax generally imposed by a state on the use of certain goods which are not subject to a sales tax. It is commonly designed to discourage people from going out of state and purchasing goods which are not subject to sales tax at the point of purchase. *See also* Use tax.

Value-added tax (VAT). A tax assessed on goods and services on the value added by each producing unit. The value added is generally the sum of all wages, interest, rent, and profits. Otherwise stated, it is the total sale price of output minus the cost of raw materials and intermediate goods purchased from other firms. The amount of the tax is a percentage of the value of the goods or services. Such a tax exists in many European countries, but not as yet in the U.S.

Withholding tax. A tax which is collected by deducting it from the wages of an employee, *e.g.* federal income taxes. *See also* Payroll tax.

Taxable. Subject to taxation; liable to be assessed, along with others, for a share in a tax. Something of value, subject to assessment, and to be levied upon and sold for taxes.

As applied to costs in an action, the term means proper to be taxed or charged up; legally chargeable or assessable. *See also* Taxation *(Taxation of costs).*

Taxable acquisition. A merger or consolidation that is not a tax-free acquisition. *Compare* Tax-free acquisition.

Taxable estate. As defined in I.R.C. § 2051, the taxable estate is the gross estate of a decedent reduced by the deductions allowed by §§ 2053–2057 (*e.g.,* administration expenses, marital, charitable and ESOP deductions). The taxable estate is the amount that is subject to the unified transfer tax at death. *See also* Adjusted gross estate; Gross estate.

Taxable gift. As defined in I.R.C. § 2503, a taxable gift is the gift that is subject to the unified transfer tax. Thus, a taxable gift has been adjusted by the annual exclusion and other appropriate deductions (*e.g.,* marital and charitable deductions).

Taxable income. Under the federal tax law, taxable income is gross income reduced by adjustments and allowable deductions. It is the income against which tax rates are applied to compute an individual or entity's tax liability. Essence of "taxable income" is the accrual of some gain, profit or benefit to taxpayer. *See* Gross income; Net income.

Taxable transaction. Any transaction that is not tax-free to the parties involved, such as a taxable acquisition (*q.v.*).

Taxable year. The taxable period for computing the Federal or state income tax liability; generally it is either the calendar year or a fiscal year of 12 months ending on the last day of a month other than December. I.R.C. § 441(b). *See also* Accounting period; Fiscal year.

Tax accounting. The accounting (timing) rules and methods used in determining a taxpayer's tax liability.

Tax anticipation bill (TAB). Short term obligations issued by the federal government, the objective of which is to meet the cash flow needs of the government. TABs generally mature one week after corporate estimated taxes are due and are popular because they are accepted by the government at par value on the tax due date without forfeiting any interest income.

Tax anticipation note (TAN). Short-term obligations issued by state or local governments to finance current expenditures. TANs generally mature once individual and corporate taxes are received by the local government.

Tax anticipation warrants. A method of raising public money by the issuance of warrants payable out of tax receipts when collected.

Tax assessment. The value given to the property which is being taxed. Multiplying the assessed valuation by the tax rate yields the tax paid. *See also* Assessment.

Tax assessor. The official responsible for tax valuation of property. *See also* Assessor.

Taxation. The process of taxing or imposing a tax. *See* Assessment; Equalization; Tax; Withholding.

Double taxation. *See* Double taxation.

Progressive taxation. A taxing system in which the higher one's income, the higher the tax bracket one is put in.

Proportional taxation. A system of taxation in which the rate of taxation is uniform no matter what the size of income. *Compare Regressive taxation, below.*

Regressive taxation. A system in which, unlike progressive taxation, as more and more income is earned, the tax rate falls.

Taxation of costs. The process of ascertaining and charging up the amount of costs and fees in an action to which a party is legally entitled, or

which are legally chargeable. See *e.g.* Fed.R.Civil P. 54(d); 28 U.S.C.A. § 1920.

Tax audit. *See* Audit.

Tax avoidance. The minimization of one's tax liability by taking advantage of legally available tax planning opportunities. Tax avoidance may be contrasted with tax evasion which entails the reduction of tax liability by using illegal means. *Compare* Tax evasion.

Tax base. The total assessed value of all the property in a given area which determines the rate at which an individual property is assessed.

Tax basis. *See* Basis.

Tax benefit rule. A rule which limits the recognition of income from the recovery of an expense or loss properly deducted in a prior tax year to the amount of the deduction that generated a tax savings. Under the "tax benefit rule" if an amount deducted from gross income in a prior taxable year is recovered in a later year, the recovery is income in the later year.

Tax bracket. A specified interval of income to which a specific tax rate is applied.

Marginal tax rate. The point where the highest level of income falls.

Tax certificate. Instrument issued to the buyer of property at a tax sale which entitles the holder to the property thus purchased if it is not redeemed within the period provided by law. *See also* Tax deed.

Tax clawback agreement. An agreement to contribute as equity to a project the value of all previously realized project-related tax benefits (not already clawed back) to the extent required to cover any cash deficiency of the project.

Tax court. The United States Tax Court is a court of record under Article I of the Constitution of the United States (*see* I.R.C. § 7441). The Tax Court tries and adjudicates controversies involving the existence of deficiencies or overpayments in income, estate, and gift taxes in cases where deficiencies have been determined by the Commissioner of Internal Revenue.

At the option of the individual taxpayer, simplified procedures may be utilized for the trials of small tax cases, provided that in a case conducted under these procedures the decision of the court would be final and not subject to review by any court. All decisions other than small tax cases are subject to review by the United States Courts of Appeals and thereafter by the Supreme Court of the United States upon the granting of a writ of certiorari.

State tax courts. Such courts exist in certain states, *e.g.* Maryland, Minnesota, New Jersey, Oklahoma, Oregon. Generally, court has jurisdiction to hear appeals in all tax cases and has power to modify or change any valuation, assessment, classification, tax or final order appealed from. Certain of these tax courts (*e.g.* Minnesota) have small claims sessions at which citizens can argue their own cases without attorneys.

Tax credit. An amount subtracted from an individual's or entity's tax liability to arrive at the total tax liability. A tax credit reduces the taxpayer's liability dollar for dollar, compared to a deduction which reduces taxable income—upon which the tax liability is calculated. A credit differs from a deduction to the extent that the former is subtracted from the tax while the latter is subtracted from income before the tax is computed.

Foreign tax credit. If a U.S. citizen or resident incurs or pays income taxes to a foreign country on income subject to U.S. tax, the taxpayer may be able to claim some of these taxes as a deduction or as a credit against the U.S. income.

Investment tax credit. A reduction in federal taxes for purchasing certain property—primarily equipment. The objective in providing the credit was to encourage companies to make acquisitions resulting in a stronger economy. The Tax Reform Act of 1986 repealed the investment tax credit for property acquired after January 1, 1986 with some exceptions for transition property.

Tax deduction. A subtraction from gross income in arriving at taxable income. A deduction differs from a tax credit in that a deduction reduces taxable income and a credit reduces tax liability. *See also* Deduction.

Tax deed. A proof of ownership of land given to the purchaser by the government after the land has been taken from another person by the government and sold for failure to pay taxes. *See also* Tax certificate.

Tax deficiency notice. *See* Ninety (90) day letter.

Tax evasion. Illegally paying less in taxes than the law permits; committing fraud in filing or paying taxes. An example includes reporting less income than actually received or deducting fictitious expenses. Such act is a crime and may result in an underpayment penalty. See I.R.C. § 7201. *Compare* Tax avoidance. *See also* Fraud *(Tax fraud).*

Tax exempt. Term pertains to property used for educational, religious, or charitable purposes which is ordinarily exempted by law from assessment for taxes; or to certain bonds issued by the federal government or a State or one of its subdivisions. Interest on State and local government bonds is exempt from federal income taxation, and interest on bonds of the United States or its instrumentalities is correspondingly exempt from State income taxation. *See also* Charitable organizations; Tax exempt securities.

Tax exemption. Immunity from the obligation of paying taxes in whole or in part.

Tax exempt securities. Investments that yield income that is tax exempt. Generally, tax exempts are municipal bonds with interest that is not taxed by the federal government. *See also* Tax exempt.

Tax foreclosure. Seizure and sale by public authority of property for non-payment of taxes.

Tax fraud. *See* Fraud.

Tax-free acquisition. A merger or consolidation in which (1) the acquiror's tax basis in each asset whose ownership is transferred in the transaction is generally the same as the acquiree's and (2) each seller who receives only stock does not have to pay any tax on the gain he realizes until the shares are sold.

Tax-free exchange. Transfers of property specifically exempted from income tax consequences by the tax law. Examples are a transfer of property to a controlled corporation under I.R.C. § 351(a) and a like-kind exchange under § 1031(a).

Tax haven. A country that imposes little or no tax on the profits from the transactions carried on from that country.

Tax home. Since travel expenses of an employee are deductible only if the taxpayer is away from home, the deductibility of such expenses rests upon the definition of "tax home". The IRS position is that "tax home" is the business location, post or station of the taxpayer.

Tax incentive. Government taxing policy intended to encourage a particular activity (*e.g.* mortgage financing of real estate sales).

Tax increment financing. Technique used by municipalities to finance commercial developments. Typically, the municipality issues bonds to finance land acquisition and other up-front costs and then uses the additional property taxes generated from the new development to service the debt.

Taxing master. *See* Master.

Taxing power. The governmental power to levy and collect taxes. U.S. Const., Art. I, § 8, cl. 1. *See also* Sixteenth Amendment.

Tax injunction act. A statute that mandates that federal district courts not interfere with the assessment or collection of any state tax where a plain, speedy and efficient remedy is available in the state courts. 28 U.S.C.A. § 1341.

Tax liability. The amount which a taxpayer owes under the tax law after properly computing gross income and deductions, using the appropriate tax rate and subtracting any applicable tax credits.

Tax loophole. A legal method of reducing tax liabilities, properly called tax avoidance. Tax avoidance should not be confused with tax evasion, which is illegal and punishable by penalties, fines, and imprisonment. *See* Tax avoidance.

Tax laws. *See* Internal Revenue Code; Letter ruling.

Tax levy. The order for payment of taxes. Also, the determination of the total receipts to be collected by the tax. *See* Assessment; Levy.

Tax lien. A lien on real estate in favor of a state or local government which may be foreclosed for nonpayment of taxes. The majority of the states have adopted the Uniform Federal Tax Lien Registration Act. *See also* Tax *(Tax lien)*.

Federal tax lien. A lien placed on property and all rights to property by the federal government for unpaid federal taxes. See I.R.C. § 6321.

Tax loss carryback, carryforward. A provision in the Internal Revenue Code which allows an individual or corporation to apply current year losses against prior or subsequent year income to reduce their tax liability.

Tax-option corporation. *See* Corporation *(S Corporation)*.

Taxpayer. One who is subject to a tax on income, regardless of whether he or she pays the tax. I.R.C. § 7701(a)(14).

Taxpayer bill of rights. Provisions of the Technical and Miscellaneous Revenue Act of 1988 granting taxpayers specific legal rights when dealing with the IRS, including the right to: receive an explanation of the examination and collection processes; have representation; make audio recordings of interviews with IRS personnel; rely on the IRS's written advice; file an application for relief with the IRS Ombudsman; and receive written notice of levy 30 days prior to enforcement. Pub.L. 100–647, § 6226 et seq.

Tax preference items. Certain items which must be considered in calculating a taxpayer's alternative minimum tax. Such items are deducted in arriving at taxable income for regular tax purposes, and added back in arriving at taxable income for alternative minimum tax purposes. I.R.C. § 55–58. *See* Alternative minimum tax.

Tax rate. Amount of tax imposed on personal or corporate income, capital gains, gifts, estates, sales, etc. *See also* Average rate of tax; Breakeven tax rate; Tax rate schedules.

Marginal tax rate. The tax rate on the last (or each additional) dollar of taxable income earned by an individual or firm.

Tax rate schedules. Schedules used to determine the tax on a given level of taxable income. Separate rate schedules are provided for married individuals filing jointly, unmarried individuals who maintain a household, single taxpayers, estates

and trusts, and married taxpayers filing separate returns. *See also* Tax tables.

Tax rebate. Amount of money remitted by taxing authority after payment of taxes. *See* Rebate.

Tax redemption. The act by which a taxpayer reclaims property which has been taken for nonpayment of taxes. He does so by paying the delinquent taxes in addition to interest, costs and penalties.

Tax return. The form on which an individual, corporation or other entity reports income, deductions, and exemptions and calculates their tax liability. A tax return is generally for a one year period, however, in some cases, the period may be less than a year. A federal tax return is filed with the Internal Revenue Service, and a state return is filed with the revenue department of the state. *See also* Return.

Amended return. A tax return filed after the original return generally due to a correction of an error.

Consolidated returns. A procedure whereby certain affiliated corporations may file a single return, combine the tax transactions of each corporation, and arrive at a single income tax liability for the group. The election to file a consolidated return is usually binding on future years.

Declaration of estimated taxes. The amount of tax expected to be paid for the year. Self-employed individuals, and those whose withheld taxes are not adequate to cover their tax liability, as well as corporations, estates, and trusts, must make estimated payments quarterly.

Information return. A tax return filed by an entity listing the income, expenses, assets, and liabilities of the entity. A tax liability is generally not calculated on an information return, instead, it is a vehicle used to report the financial results of an entity for the tax period. An example of an information return is a partnership return (Form 1065). I.R.C. § 6031 et seq.

Joint return. Tax return filed jointly by both spouses; permitted even though only one had income. *See* Split income.

Separate return. Tax return filed by only one spouse and covering only his or her income.

Tax roll. The official record maintained by cities and towns listing the names of taxpayers and the assessed property. *See also* Roll.

Tax sale. Sale of property for nonpayment of taxes. *See also* Tax certificate.

Tax shelter. A device used by a taxpayer to reduce or defer payment of taxes. Common forms or tax shelters include: limited partnership interests, real estate investments which have deductions such as depreciation, interest, taxes, etc.

The Tax Reform Act of 1986 limited the benefits of tax shelters significantly by classifying losses from such shelters as passive and ruling that passive losses can only offset passive income in arriving at taxable income (with a few exceptions). Any excess losses are suspended and may be deducted in the year the investment is sold or otherwise disposed of.

Tax "situs". A state or jurisdiction which has a substantial relationship to assets subject to taxation.

Tax straddle rule. The commodities straddle rule prevents a taxpayer from deferring income by requiring a loss on an identified straddle to be recognized when the offsetting position is closed. The straddle rules generally relate to intangibles such as rights to future events in contrast to more tangible assets such as stock. See I.R.C. §§ 165(c)(2), 1092.

Tax surcharge. Tax added to another tax. *See also* Surcharge; Surtax.

Tax tables. Tables established by taxing authorities from which taxes may be computed. The federal income tax system provides for separate rates for single taxpayers, married taxpayers filing a joint return, head of household, and married taxpayers filing separate returns. *See also* Tax rate schedules.

Tax title. Title held by one who purchases property at a tax sale. *See also* Tax certificate; Tax deed.

Tax warrant. Official process for collecting unpaid taxes and under which property may be seized and sold.

Tax year. The period covered by a tax return. Individuals generally file on a calendar year while corporations, trusts, and other entities may file on a fiscal year. *See* Accounting period; Fiscal year.

Tax withholding. *See* Income tax withholdings.

T.C. An abbreviation for the U.S. Tax Court. It is used to cite a Regular Decision of the U.S. Tax Court.

T.C. Memo. An abbreviation used to refer to a Memorandum Decision of the U.S. Tax Court.

Technical errors. Errors committed in course of trial which have not prejudiced the party and hence are not grounds for reversal. Fed.R.Civil P. 61; Fed.R.Crim.P. 52. *See also* Harmless error doctrine.

Temporary. That which is to last for a limited time only, as distinguished from that which is perpetual, or indefinite, in its duration. Opposite of permanent. Thus, temporary alimony is granted for the support of the wife pending the action for divorce; a temporary receiver is one appointed to take charge of property until a hearing is had and an adjudication made.

As to *temporary* Disability; Insanity; Injunction; and Statute, see those titles.

Temporary administration. Fiduciary appointed by court to administer the affairs of a decedent estate for a short period of time before an administrator or executor can be appointed and qualified.

Temporary alimony. Interim order of payment to spouse pending final outcome of action for divorce. *See also* Alimony.

Temporary detention. Temporary exercise of custody pending final determination on merits of criminal case.

Temporary disability. Healing period during which claimant is totally or partially unable to work due to injury, and continues as long as recovery or lasting improvement of injured person's condition can reasonably be expected. *See also* Disability; Temporary total disability.

Temporary Emergency Court of Appeals. The Economic Stabilization Act Amendments of 1971 (85 Stat. 743) created a special court known as the Temporary Emergency Court of Appeals of the United States. The court has exclusive jurisdiction of all appeals from the district courts of the United States in cases and controversies arising under the economic stabilization laws, and consists of eight district and circuit judges appointed by the Chief Justice of the Supreme Court.

Temporary injunction. *See* Injunction; Preliminary injunction; Temporary restraining order.

Temporary (nominal) accounts. Accounts that are reduced to zero at the end of the accounting period via the closing process.

Temporary restraining order (TRO). An emergency judicial remedy of brief duration which may issue only in exceptional circumstances and only until the trial court can hear arguments or evidence, as the circumstances require, on the subject matter of the controversy and otherwise determine what relief is appropriate. Court order which is issued to maintain status quo pending a hearing on an application for an injunction.

A temporary restraining order may be granted without written or oral notice to the adverse party or his attorney only if (1) it clearly appears from specific facts shown by affidavit or by the verified complaint that immediate and irreparable injury, loss, or damage will result to the applicant before the adverse party or his attorney can be heard in opposition, and (2) the applicant's attorney certifies to the court in writing the efforts, if any, which have been made to give the notice and the reasons supporting his claim that notice should not be required. Fed.R.Civil P. 65(b).

See also Injunction; Injury *(Irreparable injury)*; Preliminary injunction.

Temporary total disability. As used in workers' compensation law, means inability to return to substantial gainful employment requiring skills or activities comparable to those of one's previous gainful employment during healing or recovery period after injury. Total disability which is not permanent. *See also* Disability; Total disability.

Tenancy. A tenancy involves an interest in realty which passes to the tenant, and a possession exclusive even of that of landlord, except as lease permits landlord's entry, and saving his right to enter to demand rent or to make repairs. Possession or occupancy of land or premises under lease. Period of tenant's possession or occupancy. To constitute tenancy, tenant must acquire some definite control and possession of premises.

See also Periodic tenancy; Tenant.

General tenancy. A tenancy which is not fixed and made certain in point of duration by the agreement of the parties.

Joint tenancy. An estate in fee-simple, fee-tail, for life, for years, or at will, arising by purchase or grant to two or more persons. Joint tenants have one and the same interest, accruing by one and the same conveyance, commencing at one and the same time, and held by one and the same undivided possession. The primary incident of joint tenancy is survivorship, by which the entire tenancy on the decease of any joint tenant remains to the survivors, and at length to the last survivor.

Type of ownership of real or personal property by two or more persons in which each owns an undivided interest in the whole and attached to which is the right of survivorship. Single estate in property owned by two or more persons under one instrument or act. An estate held by two or more persons jointly, each having an individual interest in the whole and an equal right to its enjoyment during his or her life.

See also Cotenancy.

Periodic tenancy. See that term.

Several tenancy. A tenancy which is separate, and not held jointly with another person.

Tenancy at sufferance. *See* Tenant.

Tenancy at will. *See* Tenant.

Tenancy by the entirety. A tenancy which is created between a husband and wife and by which together they hold title to the whole with right of survivorship so that, upon death of either, other takes whole to exclusion of deceased heirs. It is essentially a "joint tenancy," modified by the common-law theory that husband and wife are one person, and survivorship is the predominant and distinguishing feature of each. Neither party can alienate or encumber the property without the consent of the other. It is inherited by the survivor of the two, and dissolution of marriage transforms it to tenancy in common.

Tenancy for a period. A tenancy for years or for some fixed period.

Tenancy for years. See Tenant.

Tenancy from month to month. *See* Tenant *(Tenant at will)*.

Tenancy from period to period. A periodic tenancy which runs from month to month or from year to year (though term usually refers to period of less than one year).

Tenancy from year to year. A periodic tenancy which runs from one year to the next. *See* Periodic tenancy.

Tenancy in common. A form of ownership whereby each tenant (*i.e.*, owner) holds an undivided interest in property. Unlike a joint tenancy or a tenancy by the entirety, the interest of a tenant in common does not terminate upon his or her prior death (*i.e.*, there is no right of survivorship). Assume, for example, B and C acquire real estate as equal tenants in common, each having furnished one-half of the purchase price. Upon B's prior death, his one-half interest in the property passes to his estate or heirs.

Interest in which there is unity of possession, but separate and distinct titles. The relationship exists where property is held by several distinct titles by unity of possession, and is not an estate but a relation between persons, the only essential being a possessory right, as to which all are entitled to equal use and possession.

See also Cotenancy; Partition.

Tenancy in coparcenary. Of historical value only today; formerly it was a form of concurrent ownership in which property was acquired by intestacy by the female line of heirs and arose only by descent. Today, it is governed by the rules of tenancy in common.

Tenancy in partnership. Real estate held by partnership. See Uniform Partnership Act, § 25.

Tenant. In the broadest sense, one who holds or possesses lands or tenements by any kind of right or title, whether in fee, for life, for years, at will, or otherwise. In a more restricted sense, one who holds lands of another; one who has the temporary use and occupation of real property owned by another person (called the "landlord"), the duration and terms of his tenancy being usually fixed by an instrument called a "lease." One who occupies another's land or premises in subordination to such other's title and with his assent, express or implied. One renting land and paying for it either in money or part of crop or equivalent.

See also Holdover tenant; Lessee; Tenancy.

Feudal law. One who holds of another (called "lord" or "superior") by some service; as fealty or rent.

Joint tenants. Two or more persons to whom are granted lands or tenements to hold in fee-simple, fee-tail, for life, for years, or at will. Persons who own lands by a joint title created expressly by one and the same deed or will. Joint tenants have one and the same interest, accruing by one and the same conveyance, commencing at one and the same time, and held by one and the same undivided possession. *See also* Tenancy *(Joint tenancy)*.

Land tenant. See that title.

Prime tenant. Commercial or professional tenant with established reputation that leases substantial, and usually most preferred, space in office building, shopping center, etc. Such type tenant is important in securing construction financing and in attracting other quality tenants.

Sole tenant. He that holds lands by his own right only, without any other person being joined with him.

Tenant at sufferance. Such tenancy arises when one comes into the possession of property by lawful title, but wrongfully holds over after the termination of his interest. He has no estate nor title but only naked possession without right and wrongfully, and stands in no privity to landlord and is not entitled to notice to quit, and is a bare licensee to whom landlord owes merely duty not wantonly nor willfully to injure him.

Tenant at will. One who holds possession of premises by permission of owner or landlord, but without fixed term. Characteristics of a "tenancy at will," whether created by express contract or by implication of law, are uncertain duration and right of either party to terminate on proper notice.

Tenant for life. One who holds lands or tenements for the term of his own life, or for that of any other person (in which case he is called *"pur auter vie"*), or for more lives than one.

Tenant for years. One who has the temporary use and possession of lands or tenements not his own, by virtue of a lease or demise granted to him by the owner, for a determinate period of time, as for a year or a fixed number of years.

Tenant from year to year. One who holds lands or tenements under the demise of another, where no certain term has been mentioned, but an annual rent has been reserved. One who holds over, by consent given either expressly or constructively, after the determination of a lease for years. *See also* Tenancy.

Tenant in common. Tenants who hold the same land together by several and distinct titles, but by unity of possession, because none knows his own severalty, and therefore they all occupy promiscuously. Where two or more hold the same land, with interests accruing under different titles, or accruing under the same title, but at different periods, or conferred by words of limitation importing that the grantees are to take in distinct shares. *See also* Tenancy *(Tenancy in common)*.

Tenant in tail. One who holds an estate in fee-tail, that is, an estate which, by the instrument creating it, is limited to some particular heirs, exclusive of others; as to the heirs of *his body* or to the heirs, *male* or *female,* of his body.

Tenantable repair. Such a repair as will render premises fit for present habitation. *See* Habitability *(Warranty of habitability)*; Self-help.

Tender. An offer of money. The act by which one produces and offers to a person holding a claim or demand against him the amount of money which he considers and admits to be due, in satisfaction of such claim or demand, without any stipulation or condition. As used in determining whether one party may place the other in breach of contract for failure to perform, means a readiness and willingness to perform in case of concurrent performance by other party, with present ability to do so, and notice to other party of such readiness. Essential characteristics of tender are unconditional offer to perform coupled with manifested ability to carry out the offer and production of subject matter of tender.

At a settlement under an agreement of sale the seller tenders the executed deed to the purchaser, who tenders the remainder of the purchase price to the seller.

The actual proffer of money, as distinguished from mere proposal or proposition to proffer it. Hence mere written proposal to pay money, without offer of cash, is not "tender."

Tender, though usually used in connection with an offer to pay money, is properly used in connection with offer of property or performance of duty other than payment of money.

Tender, in common law pleading, is a plea by defendant that he has been always ready to pay the debt demanded, and before the commencement of the action tendered it to the plaintiff, and now brings it into court ready to be paid to him, etc.

Legal tender is that kind of coin, money, or circulating medium which the law compels a creditor to accept in payment of his debt, when tendered by the debtor in the right amount. *See also* Legal tender.

See also Legally sufficient tender.

Tender of issue. A form of words in common law pleading, by which a party offers to refer the question raised upon it to the appropriate mode of decision. The common tender of an issue of fact by a defendant is expressed by the words, "and of this he puts himself upon the country."

Tender of delivery. Tender of delivery requires that the seller put and hold conforming goods at the buyer's disposition and give the buyer any notification reasonably necessary to enable him to take delivery. The manner, time and place for tender are determined by the agreement and Article 2 of the Uniform Commercial Code. See U.C.C. § 2–503. Tender connotes such performance by the tendering party as puts the other party in default if he fails to proceed in some manner. U.C.C. § 2–503, Comment 1.

Tender offer. A public announcement by a company or individual indicating that it will pay a price above the current market price for the shares "tendered" of a company it wishes to acquire or take control of. An offer to purchase shares made by one company direct to the stockholders of another company, sometimes subject to a minimum and/or a maximum that the offeror will accept, communicated to the shareholders by means of newspaper advertisements and (if the offeror can obtain the shareholders list, which is not often unless it is a friendly tender) by a general mailing to the entire list of shareholders, with a view to acquiring control of the second company. Such purchase offer is used in an effort to go around the management of the second company, which is resisting acquisition.

Tender offers are one of several types of corporate takeover techniques, and are regulated by state and federal securities laws; e.g., Williams Act § 14(e), 15 U.S.C.A. § 78n(e). See also Aggressor corporation; Leveraged buyout; Saturday night special; Takeover bid.

Tender of performance. Offer to perform which is commonly necessary to hold the defaulting party to a contract liable for breach. See also Tender.

Tender years doctrine. Under this doctrine courts generally award custody of children of tender years to mother unless she is found to be unfit. However, in many states this doctrine has been abolished by statute, e.g., N.Y.Dom.Rel.L. § 240, or by judicial decisions, e.g., Arnold v. Arnold, 95 Nev. 951, 604 P.2d 109.

Tenement /ténəmənt/. This term, in its common acceptation, is only applied to houses and other buildings, but in its original, proper, and legal sense it signifies everything that may be *holden*, provided it be of a permanent nature, whether it be of a substantial and sensible, or of an unsubstantial, ideal, kind. Thus, *liberum tenementum*, frank tenement, or freehold, is applicable not only to lands and other solid objects, but also to offices, rents, commons, advowsons, franchises, peerages, etc. At common law, "tenements" included lands,

other inheritances, capable of being held in freehold, and rents.

Dominant tenement. One for the benefit or advantage of which an easement exists or is enjoyed.

Servient tenement. One which is subject to the burden of an easement existing for or enjoyed by another tenement. See Easement.

10–K. The name of the annual financial report required by the SEC of nearly all publicly-held corporations. This report contains more information than the annual report to stockholders. Corporations must send a copy of the 10–K to those stockholders who request it. See also 10–Q.

10–Q. A quarterly report that must be filed with the Securities and Exchange Commission by any company whose securities are traded on a national or over-the-counter market. See also 10–K.

Tenth Amendment. An amendment to the U.S. Constitution (1791) which provides that the powers not delegated to the federal government are reserved to the States or to the people.

Tenure /tényər/. Generally, tenure is a right, term, or mode of holding or occupying, and "tenure of an office" means the manner in which it is held, especially with regard to time.

Status afforded to teacher or professor upon completion of trial period, thus protecting him or her from summary dismissal without sufficient cause or economic reasons. A faculty appointment for an indefinite period of time. Tenure denotes relinquishment of the employer's unfettered power to terminate the employee's services.

Term of office. Duration of holding public or private office. The tenure of federal judges is during life and good behavior. The tenure of merit system employees is during satisfactory performance of duties until a fixed age of retirement unless the position is discontinued.

Feudal law. The mode or system of holding lands or tenements in subordination to some superior which, in feudal ages, was the leading characteristic of real property.

Tenure is the direct result of feudalism, which separated the *dominium directum* (the dominion of the soil), which is placed mediately or immediately in the crown, from the *dominion utile* (the possessory title), the right to the use and profits in the soil, designated by the term "seisin," which is the highest interest a subject can acquire.

Term. A word or phrase; an expression; particularly one which possesses a fixed and known meaning in some science, art, or profession.

A fixed and definite period of time; implying a period of time with some definite termination. Period of determined or prescribed duration. A specified period of time; e.g. term of lease, loan, contract, court session, public office, sentence.

In civil law, a space of time granted to a debtor for discharging his obligation.

Bounds, limitation, or extent of time for which an estate is granted; as when a man holds an estate for any limited or specific number of years, which is called his "term," and he himself is called, with reference to the term he so holds, the "termor," or "tenant of the term."

Word, phrase, or condition in a contract, instrument, or agreement which relates to a particular matter. U.C.C. § 1–201(42). *See also* Open price term.

When used with reference to a court, signifies the space of time during which the court holds a session. A *session* signifies the time during the term when the court sits for the transaction of business, and the session commences when the court convenes for the term, and continues until final adjournment, either before or at the expiration of the term. The *term* of the court is the time prescribed by law during which it may be in *session*. The *session* of the court is the time of its actual sitting. But "term" and "session" are often used interchangeably. *See also* Session; and *Term of court, below.*

General term. A phrase used in some jurisdictions to denote the ordinary session of a court, for the trial and determination of causes, as distinguished from a *special* term, for the hearing of motions or arguments or the despatch of various kinds of formal business, or the trial of a special list or class of cases. Or it may denote a sitting of the court *in banc.*

Regular term. A term begun at the time appointed by law, and continued, in the discretion of the court, to such time as it may appoint, consistent with the law.

Special term. In court practice in certain states, that branch of the court which is held by a single judge for hearing and deciding in the first instance motions and causes of equitable nature is called the "special term," as opposed to the "general term," held by three judges (usually) to hear appeals.

Peculiar or unusual conditions imposed on a party before granting some application to the favor of the court.

Term bonds. A bond issue whose component bonds all mature at the same time. Contrast with "serial bonds." *See also* Bond.

Term for years. An *estate for years* and the *time* during which such estate is to be held are each called a "term;" hence the term may expire before the time, as by a surrender.

Term in gross. A term of years is said to be either in gross (outstanding) or attendant upon the inheritance. It is outstanding, or in gross, when it is unattached or disconnected from the estate or inheritance, as where it is in the hands of some third party having no interest in the inheritance; it is attendant, when vested in some trustee in trust for the owner of the inheritance.

Term life insurance. See Insurance.

Term loan. A loan with a specified maturity date, as opposed to a demand loan which is due whenever the lender requests payment.

Term of court. The period of time prescribed by law during which a court holds session. The Supreme Court sits in an annual term that begins on the first Monday in October and in recent years ordinarily has ended in the first week of July. The Court may also hold special terms as necessary. The U.S. district courts do not have formal terms, but rather the times for holding regular sessions are determined by local rules of the respective courts. 28 U.S.C.A. §§ 2, 138, 139. *See also General term; Regular term; Special term, above.*

Term of lease. The word "term," when used in connection with a lease, means the period which is granted for the lessee to occupy the premises, and does not include the time between the making of the lease and the tenant's entry.

Term of office. The period during which elected officer or appointee is entitled to hold office, perform its functions, and enjoy its privileges and emoluments.

Terminable interest. An interest in property which terminates upon the death of the holder or upon the occurrence of some other specified event. The transfer of a terminable interest by one spouse to the other spouse may not qualify for the marital deduction.

Terminable property. Name sometimes given to property of such a nature that its duration is not perpetual or indefinite, but is limited or liable to terminate upon the happening of an event or the expiration of a fixed term; *e.g.*, a leasehold, a life-annuity, etc.

Terminate. To put an end to; to make to cease; to end.

Termination. End in time or existence; close; cessation; conclusion.

Word for purposes of insurance, refers to the expiration of a policy by lapse of the policy.

With respect to a lease or contract, term refers to an ending, usually before the end of the anticipated term of the lease or contract, which termination may be by mutual agreement or may be by exercise of one party of one of his remedies due to the default of the other party. As regards a partnership, term refers to a winding up and cessation of the business as opposed to only a technical ending (as upon the death of a partner) which is a dissolution. A dissolved partnership may terminate or may be continued by a partnership of the remaining partners, including perhaps the estate or heirs of the deceased partner.

Under the Uniform Commercial Code, "termination" means legally ending a contract without its being broken by either side. U.C.C. § 2–106.

See also Dissolution; Expiration; Lapse.

Termination of employment. Within policies providing that insurance should cease immediately upon termination of employment, means a complete severance of relationship of employer and employee. *See also* Employment at will; Wrongful discharge.

Term life insurance. *See* Insurance.

Terms. Conditions, obligations, rights, price, etc., as specified in contract or instrument. *See also* Term.

Terms of trust. The phrase "terms of the trust" means the manifestation of intention of the settlor with respect to the trust expressed in a manner which admits of its proof in judicial proceedings. Restatement, Second, Trusts § 4.

Terra /téhrə/. Lat. Earth; soil; arable land.

Territorial. Having to do with a particular area; for example, territorial jurisdiction is the power of a court to take cases from within a particular geographical area.

Territorial courts. U.S. courts in each territory, such as the Virgin Islands. They serve as both Federal and state courts. Created under U.S. Const., Art. IV, Sec. 3, cl. 2.

Territorial jurisdiction. Territory over which a government or a subdivision thereof, or court, has jurisdiction. Jurisdiction considered as limited to cases arising or persons residing within a defined territory, as, a county, a judicial district, etc. The authority of any court is limited by the boundaries thus fixed. *See also* Extraterritorial jurisdiction; Jurisdiction.

Territorial property. The land and water over which the state has jurisdiction and control whether the legal title be in the state itself or in private individuals. Lakes and waters wholly within the state are its property and also the marginal sea within the three-mile limit, but bays and gulfs are not always recognized as state property.

Territorial; territoriality. These terms are used to signify connection with, or limitation with reference to, a particular country or territory. Thus, "territorial law" is the correct expression for the law of a particular country or state, although "municipal law" is more common.

Territorial waters. Term refers to all inland waters, all waters between line of mean high tide and line of ordinary low water, and all waters seaward to a line three geographical miles distant from the coast line. That part of the sea adjacent to the coast of a given country which is by international law deemed to be within the sovereignty of that country, so that its courts have jurisdiction over offenses committed on those waters, even by a person on board a foreign ship. *See* Three-mile limit.

Territory. A part of a country separated from the rest, and subject to a particular jurisdiction. Geographical area under the jurisdiction of another country or sovereign power.

A portion of the United States, not within the limits of any state, which has not yet been admitted as a state of the Union, but is organized, with a separate legislature, and with executive and judicial officers appointed by the president. *See* Trust territory.

An assigned geographical area of responsibility; *e.g.* salesman's territory.

Territory of a judge. The territorial jurisdiction of a judge; the bounds, or district, within which he may lawfully exercise his judicial authority. See *e.g.* 28 U.S.C.A. § 81 et seq. (territorial composition of federal district courts). *See also* Jurisdiction.

Terror. Alarm; fright; dread; the state of mind induced by the apprehension of hurt from some hostile or threatening event or manifestation; fear caused by the appearance of danger. In an indictment for riot at common law, it must have been charged that the acts done were "to the *terror* of the people."

As element of offense of aggravated kidnapping, is any act which is done to fill with intense fear or to coerce by threat or force.

Terrorism. "Act of terrorism" means an activity that involves a violent act or an act dangerous to human life that is a violation of the criminal laws of the United States or of any State, or that would be a criminal violation if committed within the jurisdiction of the United States or of any State; and appears to be intended—(i) to intimidate or coerce a civilian population; (ii) to influence the policy of a government by intimidation or coercion, or (iii) to affect the conduct of a government by assassination or kidnapping. 18 U.S.C.A. § 3077.

Terroristic threats. A person is guilty of a felony if he threatens to commit any crime of violence with purpose to terrorize another or to cause evacuation of a building, place of assembly, or facility of public transportation, or otherwise to cause serious public inconvenience, or in reckless disregard of the risk of causing such terror or inconvenience. 18 U.S.C.A. § 3077; Model Penal Code, § 211.3. *See also* Terrorism.

Terry-stop. *See* Stop and frisk.

Test. To bring one to a trial and examination, or to ascertain the truth or the quality or fitness of a thing. Something by which to ascertain the truth respecting another thing; a criterion, gauge, standard, or norm.

In public law, an inquiry or examination addressed to a person appointed or elected to a public office, to ascertain his qualifications therefor, but particularly a scrutiny of his political, religious, or social views, or his attitude of past and present loyalty or disloyalty to the government under which he is to act.

See also Competitive civil service examination; Examination.

Discovery. Requests for permission to test tangible things in civil actions are governed by Fed.R. Civil P. 34. Requests for reports or results of examinations or tests are governed by Fed.R.Civil P. 35, and Fed.R.Crim.P. 16.

Testable. A person is said to be testable when he or she has capacity to make a will. In general, person of eighteen years of age and of sane mind is testable. Uniform Probate Code, § 2–501. *See also* Testamentary (*Testamentary capacity*).

Test action *or* **case.** An action selected out of a considerable number of suits, concurrently depending in the same court, brought by several plaintiffs against the same defendant, or by one plaintiff against different defendants, all similar in their circumstances, and embracing the same questions, and to be supported by the same evidence, the selected action to go first to trial (under an order of court equivalent to consolidation), and its decision to serve as a *test* of the right of recovery in the others, all parties agreeing to be bound by the result of the test action. A lawsuit brought to establish an important legal principle or right.

Testacy /téstəsiy/. The state or condition of leaving a will at one's death. Opposed to "intestacy."

Testament. Under the early English law, a term that referred to the disposition of *personal* property by will; *i.e.* by "last will and testament." The words "and testament" are no longer necessary since a will now relates to both real and personal property.

Testamentary. Pertaining to a will or testament; as *testamentary* causes. Derived from, founded on, or appointed by a testament or will; as a *testamentary* guardian, letters *testamentary*, etc.

A paper, instrument, document, gift, appointment, etc., is said to be "testamentary" when it is written or made so as not to take effect until after the death of the person making it, and to be

revocable and retain the property under his control during his life, although he may have believed that it would operate as an instrument of a different character.

Letters testamentary. The formal instrument of authority and appointment given to an executor by the proper court, upon the admission of the will to probate, empowering him to enter upon the discharge of his office as executor.

Testamentary capacity. That measure of mental ability which is recognized in law as sufficient for the making of a will. A testator to have such capacity must have sufficient mind and memory to intelligently understand the nature of business in which he is engaged, to comprehend generally the nature and extent of property which constitutes his estate, and which he intends to dispose of, and to recollect the objects of his bounty. *See also* Capacity.

Testamentary character. Of the nature or pertaining to a disposition of property at death.

Testamentary class. Body of persons, uncertain in number at time of gift, ascertainable in future, and each taking in equal or in other definite proportions. A "testamentary class gift" is a gift to a group whose number at the time of the gift is uncertain but which will be ascertained at some future time when all who constitute the class will take an equal or other definite portion, the amount of the share of each being dependent upon the number that ultimately constitutes the class.

Testamentary disposition. The passing of property to another upon the death of the owner. A disposition of property by way of gift, will or deed which is not to take effect unless the grantor dies or until that event.

Testamentary gift. Gift made by will.

Testamentary guardian. A guardian appointed by the last will of parent for the person and real and personal estate of child until the latter arrives of full age.

Testamentary intent. Requirement for a valid will that the testator must intend that the instrument presently operate as his or her last will and testament.

Testamentary paper or instrument. An instrument in the nature of a will; an unprobated will; a paper writing which is of the character of a will, though not formally such, and, if allowed as a testament, will have the effect of a will upon the devolution and distribution of property.

Testamentary power of appointment. A power of appointment that can be exercised only through the will (*i.e.*, upon the death) of the holder. Restatement, Property, § 321(1). *See also* Power of appointment.

Testamentary trust. A trust created by a will which takes effect only upon the testator's death. The trust must satisfy requirements of both a valid trust and a valid will. *See also* Trust.

Testamentary trustee. See Trustee.

Testate /tésteyt/. One who has made a will; one who dies leaving a will. *See* Testator; *Compare* Intestate.

Testate succession. Acquisition of property or rights through a will.

Testation /testéyshən/. Witness; evidence.

Testator(-trix) /testéytər/. One who makes or has made a testament or will; one who dies leaving a will. This term is borrowed from the civil law.

Testatrix /testéytrəks/. A woman who makes a will; a woman who dies leaving a will; a female testator.

Testatum /testéytəm/. The name of a writ which is issued by the court of one county to the sheriff of another county in the same state, when defendant cannot be found in the county where the court is located: for example, after a judgment has been obtained, and a *ca. sa.* has been issued, which has been returned *non est inventus,* a testatum *ca. sa.* may be issued to the sheriff of the county where the defendant is.

In conveyancing, that part of a deed which commences with the words, "This indenture witnesseth."

Testatum writ /testéytəm rìt/. In practice, a writ containing a *testatum* clause; such as a *testatum capias,* a *testatum fi. fa.,* and a *testatum ca. sa. See* Testatum.

Test case. *See* Test action *or* case.

Teste. To bear witness formally.

Testify. To bear witness; to give evidence as a witness; to make a solemn declaration, under oath or affirmation, in a judicial inquiry, for the purpose of establishing or proving some fact.

Testimonial. In the nature of testimony. Evidence is said to be testimonial when elicited from a witness in contrast to documentary evidence or real evidence.

Testimonial evidence. Evidence elicited from a witness in contrast to documentary or real evidence. *See also* Evidence; Testimony.

Testimonium clause /tèstəmówn(i)yəm klóz/. In conveyancing, that clause of a deed or instrument with which it concludes; "In witness whereof, the parties to these presents have hereunto set their hands and seals." A clause in the instrument reciting the date on which the instrument was executed and by whom.

Testimony. Evidence given by a competent witness under oath or affirmation; as distinguished from evidence derived from writings, and other sources. Testimony is particular kind of evidence that comes to tribunal through live witnesses speaking under oath or affirmation in presence of tribunal, judicial or quasi-judicial.

In common parlance, "testimony" and "evidence" are synonymous. Testimony properly means only such evidence as is delivered by a witness on the trial of a cause, either orally or in the form of affidavits or depositions.

See also Character evidence; Evidence; Failure to testify; Opinion evidence *or* testimony; Perpetuating testimony.

Expert testimony. See Evidence *(Expert evidence)*; Expert witness.

Testis /téstəs/. Lat. A witness; one who gives evidence in court, or who witnesses a document.

Test oath. An oath required to be taken as a criterion of the fitness of the person to fill a public or political office; but particularly an oath of fidelity and allegiance (past or present) to the established government. *See also* Loyalty oath.

Tests. *See* Test.

Textbook. A legal text or treatise which presents principles on any branch of the law. *See also* Hornbook.

Theft. A popular name for larceny. The act of stealing. The taking of property without the owner's consent. The fraudulent taking of personal property belonging to another, from his possession, or from the possession of some person holding the same for him, without his consent, with intent to deprive the owner of the value of the same, and to appropriate it to the use or benefit of the person taking.

It is also said that theft is a wider term than larceny and that it includes swindling and embezzlement and that generally, one who obtains possession of property by lawful means and thereafter appropriates the property to the taker's own use is guilty of a "theft".

Theft is any of the following acts done with intent to deprive the owner permanently of the possession, use or benefit of his property: (a) Obtaining or exerting unauthorized control over property; or (b) Obtaining by deception control over property; or (c) Obtaining by threat control over property; or (d) Obtaining control over stolen property knowing the property to have been stolen by another.

See also Auto theft; Embezzlement; Extortion; Intimidation; Larceny; Robbery; Shoplifting; Steal.

Theft by deception. Under Model Penal Code § 223.3, a person is guilty of theft by deception if he purposely obtains property of another by deception.

Theft by false pretext. Obtaining property by means of false pretext with intent to deprive owner of value of property without his consent and to appropriate it to own use, followed by such appropriation.

Theft of services. Obtaining services from another by deception, threat, coercion, stealth, mechanical tampering or use of false token or device.

Theory of case. Facts on which the right of action is claimed to exist. The basis of liability or grounds of defense. *See* Cause of action.

Theory of law. The legal premise or set of principles on which a case rests.

Theory of pleading doctrine. The pre-code principle that one must prove his case as pleaded. Otherwise, he fails though he has set forth facts sufficient to sustain his case on a theory different from his pleadings. The various codes and rules of civil procedure have abolished this strict pleading and proof requirement; see *e.g.* Fed.R.Civil P. 15 which permits amendment of pleadings to conform to evidence.

Thief. One who steals; one who commits theft or larceny. *See also* Common thief.

Thin capitalization. When debt owed by a corporation to its shareholders is large in relationship to its capital structure (*i.e.,* stock and shareholder equity), the I.R.S. may contend that the corporation is thinly capitalized. In effect, this means that some or all of the debt will be reclassified as equity. The immediate result is to disallow any interest deduction to the corporation on the reclassified debt. To the extent of the corporation's earnings and profits, interest payments and loan repayments are treated as dividends to the shareholders. I.R.C. § 385.

Thin corporation. A corporation with an excessive amount of debt in its capitalization. A thin corporation is primarily a tax concept. *See* Thin capitalization.

Things personal. Goods, money, and all other movables, which may attend the owner's person wherever he may go. *See also* Property *(Personal property)*.

Things real. Such things as are permanent, fixed, and immovable, which cannot be carried out of their place; as lands and tenements and hereditaments. *See also* Property *(Real property)*.

Thinly traded. Infrequently traded securities.

Third conviction. *See* Habitual criminal; Recidivist.

Third degree. Term used to describe the process of securing a confession or information from a suspect or prisoner by prolonged questioning, the use of threats, or actual violence. *See* Confession; Interrogation; Miranda Rule.

Term is also sometimes used as a classification of crime (*e.g.* murder in the third degree).

Third market. *See* Over-the-counter market.

Third party. One not a party to an agreement, a transaction, or an action but who may have rights therein. *See also* Party; Privity *or* knowledge.

Third party action. A proceeding distinct from the main action. It is in the nature of an indemnity or contribution, the purpose of which is to bring into the lawsuit a party who is or may be liable to defendant for all or part of plaintiff's claim against defendant. *See* Third party complaint; Third-party practice.

Third party beneficiary. One for whose benefit a promise is made in a contract but who is not a party to the contract. A person not a party to an insurance contract who has legally enforceable rights thereunder. A prime requisite to the status of "third party beneficiary" under a contract is that the parties to the contract must have intended to benefit the third party, who must be something more than a mere incidental beneficiary. *See also* Privity *or* knowledge.

Third-party-beneficiary contract. A contract between two or more parties, the performance of which is intended to benefit directly a third party, thus giving the third party a right to file suit for breach of contract by either of the original contract parties.

Third party check. Check which the payee endorses to another party, *e.g.* as when a person endorses a check received from a customer and endorses it to the IRS. A person who takes a third-party check in good faith and without notice of a security interest can be a holder in due course.

Third party claim proceedings. A summary proceeding to determine title to attached property. *See e.g.* Cal.Code Civ.Proc. § 689.

Third party complaint. A complaint filed by the defendant against a third-party (*i.e.,* a person not presently a party to the lawsuit). This complaint alleges that the third party is or may be liable for all or part of the damages which the plaintiff may win from the defendant. See Fed.R.Civil P. 14. For requisite content of third party claim under Federal Rules of Civil Procedure, *see* Complaint. *See also* Third-party practice.

Third-party practice. Under rules practice, a defendant may, after the main action has been commenced, institute an action against a person not a party to the action for all or part of the plaintiff's claim against him. See Fed.R.Civ.P. 14. Procedural device whereby defendant in an action may bring in additional party in claim against such party because of a claim that is being asserted against the defendant. *See also* Impleader; Third-party complaint; Vouching-in.

Thirteenth Amendment. Amendment to U.S. Constitution which abolished slavery and involuntary servitude in 1865.

Thirty-day letter. A letter which accompanies a revenue agent's report (RAR) issued as a result of an Internal Revenue Service audit of a taxpayer (or the rejection of a taxpayer's claim for refund). The letter outlines the taxpayer's appeal procedure before the Internal Revenue Service. If the taxpayer does not request any such procedures within the 30-day period, the Internal Revenue Service will issue a statutory notice of deficiency (the "90-day letter"). *See also* Ninety (90) day letter.

Threat. A communicated intent to inflict physical or other harm on any person or on property. A declaration of an intention to injure another or his property by some unlawful act. A declaration of intention or determination to inflict punishment, loss, or pain on another, or to injure another or his property by the commission of some unlawful act. A menace; especially, any menace of such a nature and extent as to unsettle the mind of the person on whom it operates, and to take away from his acts that free and voluntary action which alone constitutes consent. A declaration of one's purpose or intention to work injury to the person, property, or rights of another, with a view of restraining such person's freedom of action.

An avowed present determination or intent to injure presently or in the future. A statement may constitute a threat even though it is subject to a possible contingency in the maker's control. The prosecution must establish a "true threat," which means a serious threat as distinguished from words uttered as mere political argument, idle talk or jest. In determining whether words were uttered as a threat the context in which they were spoken must be considered.

Threats against the President and successors to the President, mailing of threatening communications, and other extortionate acts, are federal offenses. 18 U.S.C.A. § 871 *et seq.*

See also Coercion; Duress; Extortion.

Terroristic threat. Any threat to commit violence communicated with intent to terrorize another, or to cause the evacuation of any building, place of assembly or facility of transportation, or in wanton disregard of the risk of causing such terror or evacuation. See Model Penal Code § 211.3; 18 U.S.C.A. § 3077. *See also* Terroristic threats.

Threatening letters. Mailing of threatening communications is a federal offense. 18 U.S.C.A. §§ 876, 877.

Three-judge courts. Most cases in federal district courts are heard and determined by only a single judge. For many years, however, Congress has provided for a special three-judge panel in certain categories of cases thought to require special safeguards against arbitrary action, with direct review in the Supreme Court. Three judges are required in condemnation suits involving the TVA, 16 U.S.C.A. Section 831X, and in certain actions under the 1964 Civil Rights and 1965 Voting Rights Acts, 42 U.S.C.A. Sections 1971(g), 1973h(c), 2000a–5(b). Of most significance, however, were 28 U.S.C.A. Sections 2281 and 2282, which required three judges in suits to enjoin enforcement of state or federal statutes, or state administrative orders, on constitutional grounds. Sections 2281 and 2282 were however repealed in 1976 and § 2284 amended to restrict the convening of three-judge courts to when otherwise required by Congress, or to when an action is filed challenging the constitutionality of congressional apportionment or the apportionment of any statewide legislative body.

Three-mile limit. The distance of one marine league or three miles offshore normally recognized as the limit of territorial jurisdiction. *See* Territorial waters.

Thrift institutions. *See* Bank; Savings and loan association.

Through bill of lading. That species of bill of lading which is used when more than one carrier is required for shipping.

Through lot. A lot that abuts upon a street at each end.

Through rate. Total shipping costs when two or more shippers (carriers) are involved. *See* Joint through rate; Rate.

Throwback Rule. In taxation of trusts, the throwback rule requires that the amount distributed in any tax year which is in excess of that year's distributable net income must be "thrown back" to the preceding year and treated as if it had then been distributed. The beneficiary is taxed in the current year although the computation is made as if the excess had been distributed in the previous year. If the trust did not have undistributed accumulated income in the preceding year, the amount of the throwback is tested against each of the preceding years; in other words, the throwback rule may require consideration of the trust income and its distributions for all of the years preceding the tax year. I.R.C. §§ 665–668.

As term is also used in taxation, if there is no income tax in the state to which a sale would otherwise be assigned for apportionment purposes, the sale essentially is exempt from state income tax, even though the seller is domiciled in a state that levies an income tax. Nonetheless, if the seller's state has adopted a throwback rule, the sale is attributed to the *seller's* state, and the transaction is subjected to a state-level tax. *See also* Apportionment.

Throw out. To ignore (*e.g.* a bill of indictment) or dismiss a cause of action. *See also* Dismissal.

Ticket. In contracts, a slip of paper containing a certificate that the person to whom it is issued, or the holder, is entitled to some right or privilege therein mentioned or described; such, for example, are railroad tickets, theater tickets, pawn tickets, lottery tickets, etc.

Citation or summons issued to violator of motor vehicle law. *See also* Citation.

In election law, a list of candidates for particular offices to be submitted to the voters at an election; a ballot.

Tidal. Affected by or having tides. In order that a river may be "tidal" at a given spot, it may not be necessary that the water should be salt, but the spot must be one where the tide, in the ordinary and regular course of things, flows and reflows.

Tide. The ebb and flow of the sea. As affecting determination of upland boundary of shore, "tide" is rising and falling of water of the sea that is produced by attraction of sun and moon, uninfluenced by special winds, seasons or other circumstances, and meteorological influences should be distinguished as "meterological tides," and "atmospheric meteorological tides" should be distinguished. *See also* Mean high tide; Mean low tide.

Tie, *v.* To bind.

Tie, *n.* When, at an election, neither candidate receives a majority of the votes cast, but each has the same number, there is said to be a "tie." Exists also when the number of votes cast in favor of any measure, in a legislative or deliberative body, is equal to the number cast against it. The Vice President of the United States has the deciding vote in the event of tie votes in the Senate. Art. I, § 3, U.S.Const.

Tied product. Tying arrangement exists when a person agrees to sell one product, the "tying product," only on the condition that the vendee also purchase another product, the "tied product." *See* Take-or-pay contracts; Tying arrangement.

Tie-in arrangement. *See* Tied product; Tying arrangement.

TIF. *See* Tax increment financing.

Tight. As colloquially applied to a note, bond, mortgage, lease, etc., this term signifies that the clauses providing the creditor's remedy in case of default (as, by foreclosure, execution, distress, etc.) are summary and stringent.

Tight money. Banking or finance expression meaning that financial institutions are only loaning money to the most creditworthy customers.

Timber lease. Lease of real property which contemplates that the lessee will cut timber on the demised premises. *See also* Timber rights.

Timber rights. A profit a prendre, the owner of which is entitled to cut and remove timber from the real property described therein. *See also* Profit (*Profit à prendre*); Timber lease.

Time. The measure of duration. The word is expressive both of a precise *point* or *terminus* and of an *interval* between two points.

A point in or space of duration at or during which some fact is alleged to have been committed.

See also Computation of time; Enlargement of time.

Cooling time. *See* Cooling off period.

Reasonable time. Such length of time as may fairly, properly, and reasonably be allowed or required, having regard to the nature of the act or duty, or of the subject-matter, and to the attending circumstances. *See also* Reasonable time.

Time-bargain. In the language of the stock exchange, an agreement to buy or sell stock at a future time, or within a fixed time, at a certain price. It is in reality nothing more than a bargain to pay differences.

Time bill. A bill of exchange which contains a definite or determinable date for payment in contrast to a demand or sight bill.

Time charter. A time charter is a specific and express contract by which the owner lets a vessel or some particular part thereof to another person for a specified time or use; the owner continues to operate the vessel, contracting to render services by his master and crew to carry goods loaded on the vessel, and the master and crew remain servants of the owner. A lease of vessel under which owner provides captain and crew who remain subject to owner's control. *Compare* Bareboat charter.

Time credit. A letter of credit that is duly honored by the issuer accepting drafts drawn thereunder. Essentially synonymous with "usance credit" and "acceptance credit."

Time deposit. Another term for a savings account or certificate of deposit in a commercial bank. It is so called because in theory (though no longer in practice) a person must wait a certain amount of time after notice of desire to withdraw part or all of his or her savings. Certificates of deposit usually carry penalties for early withdrawal. Cash in a bank earning interest; contrast with demand deposit. *See* Deposit.

Time draft. A draft payable at a definite time in the future. *See also Time bill, above.*

Time immemorial. Time whereof the memory of a man is not to the contrary.

Time is the essence of contract. Means that performance by one party at time or within period specified in contract is essential to enable him to require performance by other party. When this phrase is in a contract, it means that a failure to do what is required by the time specified is a breach of the contract.

Time order. An order which becomes a market or limited price order at a specified time.

Time out of memory. Time beyond memory; time out of mind; time to which memory does not extend.

Time-policy. A policy of marine insurance in which the risk is limited, not to a given voyage, but to a certain fixed term or period of time.

Time value. The price associated with the length of time an investor must wait until an investment matures or the related income is earned. *See also* Yield *(Yield to maturity).*

Time value of money. The concept that a dollar today is worth more than a dollar in the future because the dollar received today can earn interest up until the time the future dollar is received.

Timeliness. The importance of fulfilling the terms of a contract by the date provided for in the agreement. *See,* Time *(Time is the essence of contract).*

Time-price differential. Term which refers to a figure representing the difference between the cash price of an item and the total cost of purchasing that item on credit. Method by which seller charges one price for immediate cash payment and a different (advance in) price when payment is made at future date or in installments and the former is the cash price and the latter the "time-price" or credit price and difference in price is the "time-price differential".

Timesharing. Form of shared property ownership, commonly in vacation or recreation condominium property, wherein rights vest in several owners to use property for specified period each year (*e.g.,* two weeks each year).

Times interest earned. A coverage ratio computed by dividing net income before taxes and interest by a firm's interest charges.

Time to expiration. The time remaining until a financial security or contract (*e.g.,* an option) expires. Also called the time to maturity.

Time to maturity. *See* Time to expiration.

Tip. A sum of money given, as to a servant, waiter, bellman, or the like, over and above actual cost or charge for services rendered, with the amount commonly varying upon the quality of such service. A form of gratuity for extra services rendered. Tip income is taxable. I.R.C. § 61(a).

In securities law, refers to advance or inside information passed by one person (a "tipper") to another (a "tippee") as a basis for a decision to buy or sell a security. Such information is presumed to be of material value and not available to the general public. The SEC prohibits trading on the basis of such information by insiders. *See also* Insider; Insider trading; Tippees; Tipper.

Tippees. In securities law, person who acquires material nonpublic information from another who enjoys a fiduciary relationship with the company to which such information pertains. Persons given information by insiders in breach of trust. The purpose of SEC Rule 10b–5 *(q.v.)* is to prevent corporate insiders and their "tippees" from taking unfair advantage of the uninformed outsiders. *See also* Insider; Tip; Tipper.

Tipper. A person who possesses material inside information and who makes selective disclosure of such information for trading or other personal purposes; "tippee" is one who receives such information from "tipper." *See also* Insider; Tip; Tippees.

Tithe. A tenth part of one's income, contributed for charitable or religious purposes. Broadly, any tax or assessment of one tenth. *See also* Tithes.

Tither /táyðər/. One who gathers tithes.

Tithes /táyðz/. In English law, the *tenth* part of the increase, yearly arising and renewing from the profits of lands, the stock upon lands, and the personal industry of the inhabitants. 2 Bl.Comm. 24. A species of incorporeal hereditament, being an ecclesiastical inheritance collateral to the estate of the land, and due only to an ecclesiastical person by ecclesiastical law. *See also* Tithe.

Title. A mark, style, or designation; a distinctive appellation; the name by which anything is known. Thus, in the law of persons, a title is an appellation of dignity or distinction, a name denoting the social rank of the person bearing it; as "duke" or "count." So, in legislation, the title of a statute is the heading or preliminary part, furnishing the name by which the act is individually known. It is usually prefixed to the statute in the form of a brief summary of its contents; as "An act for the prevention of gaming." Again, the title of a patent is the short description of the invention, which is copied in the letters patent from the inventor's petition; *e.g.,* "a new and improved method of drying and preparing malt."

The title of a book, or any literary composition, is its name; that is, the heading or caption prefixed to it, and disclosing the distinctive appellation by which it is to be known. This usually comprises a brief description of its subject-matter and the name of its author.

See also Abstract of title; Action to quiet title; Bad title; Cloud on title; Color of title; Defective title; Disparagement of title; Doubtful title; Good title; Indicia of title; Just title; Legal title; Marketable title; Marketable Title Acts; Merchantable title; Muniments of title; Non-merchantable title; Onerous title; Owner; Ownership; Paramount title; Possession; Recording acts; Torrens title system; Worthier title doctrine.

Law of Trademarks

A title may become a subject of property; as one who has adopted a particular title for a newspaper, or other business enterprise, may, by long and prior usage, or by compliance with statutory provisions as to registration and notice, acquire a right to be protected in the exclusive use of it. *See* Trademark.

Real Property Law

The formal right of ownership of property. Title is the means whereby the owner of lands has the just possession of his property. The union of all the elements which constitute ownership. Full independent and fee ownership. The right to or ownership in land; also, the evidence of such ownership. Such ownership may be held individually, jointly, in common, or in cooperate or partnership form.

One who holds vested rights in property is said to have title whether he holds them for his own benefit or for the benefit of another. Restatement, Second, Trusts, § 2, Comment d.

See also Deed; Estate.

Procedure

Every action, petition, or other proceeding has a title, which consists of the name of the court in which it is pending, the names of the parties, etc. Administration actions are further distinguished by the name of the deceased person whose estate is being administered. Every pleading, summons, affidavit, etc., commences with the title. In many cases it is sufficient to give what is called the "short title" of an action, namely, the court, the reference to the record, and the surnames of the first plaintiff and the first defendant. *See also* Caption.

Generally

Absolute title. As applied to title to land, an exclusive title, or at least a title which excludes all others not compatible with it. An absolute title to land cannot exist at the same time in different persons or in different governments. *See also* Fee simple.

Abstract of title. See that title.

Adverse title. A title set up in opposition to or defeasance of another title, or one acquired or claimed by adverse possession. *See* Adverse possession.

Bad title. See that title.

Bond for title. *See* Bond.

By accession. Title acquired by additions innocently acquired such as in the case of intermingling of another's property with one's own. *See* Accession.

By accretion. Title acquired by additions to one's property as in the case of deposits of soil from a stream. *See* Accretion.

By adverse possession. *See* Adverse possession.

Chain of title. See that title; *also* Abstract of title.

Clear title, good title, merchantable title, marketable title, are synonymous; "clear title" meaning that the land is free from incumbrances, "good title" being one free from litigation, palpable defects, and grave doubts, comprising both legal and equitable titles and fairly deducible of record. *See* Marketable title.

Clear title of record, or clear record title. Title free from apparent defects, grave doubts, and litigious uncertainties, and is such title as a reasonably prudent person, with full knowledge, would accept. A title dependent for its validity on extraneous evidence, ex parte affidavits, or written guaranties against the results of litigation is not a clear title of record, and is not such title as equity will require a purchaser to accept. *See* Marketable title.

Cloud on title. See that title.

Color of title. See that title.

Covenants for title. Covenants usually inserted in a conveyance of land, on the part of the grantor, and binding him for the completeness, security, and continuance of the title transferred to the grantee. They comprise "covenants for seisin, for right to convey, against incumbrances, for quiet enjoyment, sometimes for further assurance, and almost always of warranty." *See* Covenant.

Defective title. Title which has some defect or is subject to litigation and hence may not be transferred to another. *See* Unmarketable title.

Document of title. *See* Deed; Document.

Doubtful title. See that title.

Equitable title. A right in the party to whom it belongs to have the legal title transferred to him; or the beneficial interest of one person whom equity regards as the real owner, although the legal title is vested in another. *See also* Equitable ownership.

Examination of title. See Examination; Title search.

Good title. Title which is free of defects and litigation and hence may be transferred to another. See Marketable title.

Imperfect title. One which requires a further exercise of the granting power to pass the fee in land, or which does not convey full and absolute dominion.

Legal title. See that title.

Lucrative title. In the civil law, title acquired without the giving of anything in exchange for it. The title by which a person acquires anything which comes to him as a clear gain, as, for instance, by gift, descent, or devise. Opposed to *Onerous title,* as to which see *below.*

Marketable title. See that title.

Onerous title. In the civil law, title to property acquired by the giving of a valuable consideration for it, such as the payment of money, the rendition of services, the performance of conditions, the assumption of obligations, or the discharge of liens on the property; opposed to "lucrative" title, or one acquired by gift or otherwise without the giving of an equivalent.

Paper title. A title to land evidenced by a conveyance or chain of conveyances; the term generally implying that such title, while it has color or plausibility, is without substantial validity.

Paramount title. See that title.

Perfect title. Various meanings have been attached to this term: (1) One which shows the absolute right of possession and of property in a particular person. See Fee simple. (2) A grant of land which requires no further act from the legal authority to constitute an absolute title to the land taking effect at once. (3) A title which does not disclose a patent defect suggesting the possibility of a lawsuit to defend it; a title such as a well-informed and prudent man paying full value for the property would be willing to take. (4) A title which is good both at law and in equity. (5) One which is good and valid beyond all reasonable doubt. (6) A marketable or merchantable title. See Marketable title.

Presumptive title. A barely presumptive title, which is of the very lowest order, arises out of the mere occupation or simple possession of property (*jus possessionis*), without any apparent right, or any pretense of right, to hold and continue such possession.

Quiet title. See Quiet title action.

Record title. See Record.

Root of title. Root of title means that conveyance or other title transaction or other link in the chain of title of a person, purporting to create the interest claimed by such person, upon which he relies as a basis for the marketability of his title, and which was the most recent to be recorded or established as of a date forty years prior to the time when marketability is being determined. The effective date of the "root of title" is the date on which it is recorded. See Chain of title.

Singular title. The title by which a party acquires property as a singular successor.

Tax title. See Tax.

Title by adverse possession or prescription. The right which a possessor acquires to property by reason of his adverse possession during a period of time fixed by law. See Adverse possession.

The elements of title by prescription are open, visible and continuous use under a claim of right, adverse to and with knowledge of owner. Such title is equivalent to a "title by deed" and cannot be lost or divested except in the same manner, and mere recognition of title in another after such acquisition will not operate to divest the adverse claimant of that which he has acquired.

Title by descent. That title which one acquires by law as heir to the deceased owner.

Title by prescription. See *Title by adverse possession or prescription, above.*

Title deeds. Deeds which constitute or are the evidence of title to lands. See Deed.

Title defective in form. Title on face of which some defect appears, not one that may prove defective by circumstances or evidence dehors the instrument. Title defective in form cannot be basis of prescription.

Title insurance. See Insurance.

Title of a cause. The distinctive appellation by which any cause in court, or other juridical proceeding, is known and distinguished from others. See Caption.

Title of an act. The heading, or introductory clause, of a statute, wherein is briefly recited its purpose or nature, or the subject to which it relates.

Title of declaration. That preliminary clause of a declaration which states the name of the court and the term to which the process is returnable. See also Caption.

Title of entry. The right to enter upon lands.

Title of record. Evidence that real property is in the lawful possession of owner. Such title is acquired through a deed, a will, adverse possession, or eminent domain. The conditions of the title are found in a title search. See Abstract of title.

Title registration. See Torrens title system.

Title retention. A form of lien, in the nature of a chattel mortgage, to secure the purchase price. *See* Security interest.

Unity of title. See that title.

Unmarketable title. See that title.

Warranty of title. *See* Warranty.

Title company. Company that examines real estate titles and, commonly, issues title insurance. *See* Title search.

Title documents. Those instruments necessary for establishing or for conveying good title; *e.g.* deed.

Title guaranty company. A business organization which searches title to determine whether any defects or encumbrances are recorded and which then gives the buyer of the property or the mortgagee a guaranty of the title.

Title insurance. *See* Insurance.

Title opinion. An opinion (usually by an attorney or title company) on the legal state of the title of specific real property. It should reflect any clouds on title such as rights of way, servitudes and easements. *See also* Title search.

Title search. An examination of the records of the registry of deeds or other office which contains records of title documents to determine whether title to the property is good; *i.e.* whether there are any defects in the title. The examiner then prepares an abstract of the documents examined. *See also* Abstract of title; Back title letter; Examination; Title company.

Title standards. Criteria by which a title to real estate may be evaluated to determine whether it is defective or marketable. Many states through associations of conveyancers and real estate attorneys have adopted such standards.

Title theory. A mortgage law theory that holds that from the date of the mortgage execution until the mortgage is satisfied or foreclosed, legal title belongs to the mortgagee and the right to possession belongs to the mortgager while mortgage is not in default.

Title transaction. Any transaction affecting title to any interest in land, including title by will or descent, title by tax deed, or deed by trustee, referee, guardian, executor, administrator, master in chancery, sheriff, or any other form of deed, or decree of any court, as well as warranty deed, quitclaim deed, mortgage, or transfer or conveyance of any kind.

To have and to hold. The words in a conveyance which show the estate intended to be conveyed. Thus, in a conveyance of land in fee-simple, the grant is to "A. and his heirs, to have and to hold the said [land] unto and to the use of the said A., his heirs and assigns forever."

Strictly speaking, however, the words "to have" denote the estate to be taken, while the words "to hold" signify that it is to be held of some superior lord, *i.e.*, by way of tenure *(q.v.)*. The former clause is called the *"habendum;"* the latter, the *"tenendum."*

Toll, *v.* To bar, defeat, or take away; thus, to toll the entry means to deny or take away the right of entry.

To suspend or stop temporarily as the statute of limitations is tolled during the defendant's absence from the jurisdiction and during the plaintiff's minority.

Toll, *n.* A sum of money for the use of something, generally referring to the consideration paid for the use of a road, highway, bridge, or the like, of a public nature. Charge for long-distance telephone calls.

Tollage. Payment of toll; money charged or paid as toll; the liberty or franchise of charging toll.

Tolls. In a general sense, any manner of customs, subsidy, prestation, imposition, or sum of money demanded for exporting or importing of any goods or merchandise to be taken of the buyer. *See also* Customs duties; Tariff; Toll.

Tombstone ad. A notice, circular or advertisement placed in newspaper of a stock offering containing basic information and language to the effect that the announcement is neither an offer to sell nor a solicitation of an offer to buy any of the securities listed. The actual securities offer is made only by means of the prospectus. *See also* Red herring.

Tonnage-duty. A tax laid upon vessels according to their tonnage or cubical capacity. The vital principle of a tonnage duty is that it is imposed, whatever the subject, solely according to the rule of weight, either as to the capacity to carry or the actual weight of the thing itself. 46 U.S.C.A. § 121 et seq.

Tontine /tontíyn/. A financial arrangement (such as an insurance policy) in which a group of participants share advantages on such terms that upon the default or death of any participant, his advantages are distributed among the remaining participants until only one remains, whereupon the whole goes to him; or on the expiration of an agreed period, the whole goes to those participants remaining at that time. Under the "Tontine" plan of insurance, no accumulation or earnings are credited to the policy unless it remains in force for the Tontine period of a specified number of years. Thus those who survive the period and keep their policies in force share in the accumulated funds and those who die or permit their policies to lapse during period do not; neither do their beneficiaries participate in such accumulation.

Top lease. A lease made before the prior lease has expired; therefore the term of the new lease overlaps the term of the old lease. A subsequent oil and gas lease which covers one or more mineral interests that are subject to a valid, subsisting prior lease.

Torrens title system /tóhrənz táytəl sistəm/. A system for registration of land under which, upon the landowner's application, the court may, after appropriate proceedings, direct the issuance of a certificate of title. With exceptions, this certificate is conclusive as to applicant's estate in land. System of registration of land title as distinguished from registration or recording of evidence of such title. The originator of the system was Sir Richard Torrens, 1814–1884, reformer of Australian Land Laws.

Tort (from Lat. torquere, to twist, tortus, twisted, wrested aside). A private or civil wrong or injury, including action for bad faith breach of contract, for which the court will provide a remedy in the form of an action for damages. A violation of a duty imposed by general law or otherwise upon all persons occupying the relation to each other which is involved in a given transaction. There must always be a violation of some duty owing to plaintiff, and generally such duty must arise by operation of law and not by mere agreement of the parties.

A legal wrong committed upon the person or property independent of contract. It may be either (1) a direct invasion of some legal right of the individual; (2) the infraction of some public duty by which special damage accrues to the individual; (3) the violation of some private obligation by which like damage accrues to the individual.

See also Federal Tort Claims Act; Government tort; Husband-wife tort actions; Joint tort-feasors; Liability; Negligence; Parental liability; Privilege; Privity *or* knowledge; Product liability; Sovereign immunity; Strict liability; Warranty.

Children. *See* Parental liability.

Constitutional tort. Federal statute providing that every person who under color of any statute, ordinance, regulation, custom, or usage, of any state or territory, subjects, or causes to be subjected, any citizen of the United States or any other person within the jurisdiction thereof to the deprivation of any rights, privileges, or immunities secured by the Constitution and laws, shall be liable to the party injured in an action at law, suit in equity, or other proper proceeding for redress. 42 U.S.C.A. § 1983. *See also* Color of law.

Intentional tort. Tort or wrong perpetrated by one who intends to do that which the law has declared wrong as contrasted with negligence in which the tortfeasor fails to exercise that degree

of care in doing what is otherwise permissible. *See also* Willful tort.

Maritime tort. *See* Jones Act; Longshore and Harbor Workers' Compensation Act; Maritime.

Negligence. The tort of negligence consists of the existence of a legal duty owed the plaintiff by the defendant, breach of the duty, proximate causal relationship between the breach and plaintiff's injury, and damages. *See also* Negligence.

Personal tort. One involving or consisting in an injury to the person or to the reputation or feelings, as distinguished from an injury or damage to real or personal property, called a "property tort."

Prenatal injuries. *See* Child; Unborn child; Viable child.

Quasi tort. Though not a recognized term of English law, may be conveniently used in those cases where a man who has not committed a tort is liable as if he had. Thus a master is liable for wrongful acts done by his servant in the course of his employment.

Strict tort liability. *See* Strict liability.

Wilful tort. *See Intentional tort, above;* also Willful tort.

Tort claims acts. *See* Federal Tort Claims Act; Sovereign immunity.

Tort-feasor. A wrong-doer; an individual or business that commits or is guilty of a tort. *See also* Joint tort-feasors.

Tortious /tórshəs/. Wrongful; of the nature of a tort. The word "tortious" is used throughout the Restatement, Second, Torts, to denote the fact that conduct whether of act or omission is of such a character as to subject the actor to liability, under the principles of the law of torts. (§ 6). To establish "tortious act" plaintiff must prove not only existence of actionable wrong, but also that damages resulted therefrom. As used in state long-arm statutes, such acts may afford a basis for jurisdiction over a nondomiciliary. *E.g.* N.Y. CPLR § 302(a)(2)(3).

Formerly certain modes of conveyance (*e.g.,* feoffments, fines, etc.) had the effect of passing not merely the estate of the person making the conveyance, but the whole fee-simple, to the injury of the person really entitled to the fee; and they were hence called "tortious conveyances."

Total disability. A person is "totally disabled" if his physical condition, in combination with his age, training, and experience, and the type of work available in his community, causes him to be unable to secure anything more than sporadic employment resulting in an insubstantial income.

Within meaning of workers' compensation acts, means lack of ability to follow continuously some substantially gainful occupation without serious discomfort or pain and without material injury to health or danger to life. *See also* Disability; Temporary total disability.

Total Incapacity. *See* Total disability.

Totality of circumstances test. Test used to determine the constitutionality of various search and seizure procedures, *e.g.* issuance of a search warrant or investigative stops. This standard focuses on all the circumstances of a particular case, rather than any one factor.

Total loss. The complete destruction of the insured property by fire, so that nothing of value remains from it; as distinguished from a *partial* loss, where the property is damaged, but not entirely destroyed.

Totten trust. *See* Trust.

To wit. That is to say; namely; *scilicet; videlicet.*

Town. A community which is smaller and less organized than a city; a small municipality. A civil and political division of a state, varying in extent and importance, but usually one of the divisions of a county. In the New England states, the town is the political unit, and is a municipal corporation. In some other states, where the county is the unit, the town is merely one of its subdivisions, but possesses some powers of local self-government. In still other states, such subdivisions of a county are called "townships," and "town" is the name of a village, borough, or smaller city. The word "town" is quite commonly used as a generic term and as including both cities and villages.

Town house. Type of dwelling unit normally having two, but sometimes three, stories; usually connected to a similar structure by a common wall, and commonly (particularly in planned unit developments) sharing and owning in common the surrounding grounds.

Town-meeting. Under the municipal organization of the New England states, the town-meeting is a legal assembly of the qualified voters of a town, held at stated intervals or on call, for the purpose of electing town officers, and of discussing and deciding on questions relating to the public business, property, and expenses of the town.

Town or city tax. Such tax as a town or city may levy for its peculiar expenses; as distinguished from a county or state tax; *e.g.*, New York City tax.

Township. Township, in government survey, is square tract six miles on each side containing thirty-six square miles of land. In some of the states, this is the name given to the civil and political subdivisions of a county.

Toxic /tóksək/. Poisonous; having the character or producing the effects of a poison; referable to a

poison; produced by or resulting from a poison. *See* Toxin.

Toxicology. The science of poisons; that department of medical science which treats of poisons, their effect, their recognition, their antidotes, and generally of the diagnosis and therapeutics of poisoning.

Toxic waste. Hazardous, poisonous substances such as PCB's, and DDT. Several federal laws regulate the use, transportation, and disposal of toxic material; *e.g.*, The Resource Conservation and Recovery Act of 1976, 42 U.S.C.A. §§ 6901–6987, The Toxic Substances Control Act of 1976, 15 U.S.C.A. §§ 2601–2629, amended by 15 U.S. C.A. §§ 2642–2654, the Comprehensive Environmental Response Compensation and Liability Act of 1980 (CERCLA), 42 U.S.C.A. §§ 9601–9657. Most states also have similar laws regulating the handling and disposing of toxic wastes. *See also* Superfund.

Toxin. In its widest sense, this term may denote any poison or toxicant; but as used in pathology and medical jurisprudence it signifies, in general, any diffusible alkaloidal substance (as, the ptomaines, abrin, brucin, or serpent venoms), and in particular the poisonous products of pathogenic (disease-producing) bacteria.

Tract of land. A lot, piece or parcel of land, of greater or less size, the term not importing, in itself, any precise dimension, though term generally refers to a large piece of land. Term is synonymous with parcel of land and does not have reference to size but to contiguous quantity of land. *See also* Parcel.

Tract index. A page or set of pages in an index book devoted to listing all documents which affect a particular tract of land.

Trade. The act or the business of buying and selling for money; traffic; barter. Purchase and sale of goods and services between businesses, states or nations. Trade is not a technical word and is ordinarily used in three senses: (1) in that of exchanging goods or commodities by barter or by buying and selling for money; (2) in that of a business occupation generally; (3) in that of a mechanical employment, in contradistinction to the learned professions, agriculture, or the liberal arts.

An occupation or regular means of livelihood; the business one practices or the work in which one engages regularly. One's calling; occupation; gainful employment; means of livelihood. *See also* Trade or business.

Transaction involving purchase and sale of stocks, bonds, or other securities.

See also Balance *(Balance of trade)*; Commerce; Trade and commerce; Trade or business.

Trade acceptance. A draft or bill of exchange drawn by the seller on the purchaser of goods sold, and accepted by such purchaser, and its purpose is to make the book account liquid, and permit the seller to raise money on it before it is due under the terms of the sale, and its principal function is to take the place of selling goods on an open account and when properly drawn, it is negotiable.

A draft drawn by a seller which is presented for signature (acceptance) to the buyer at the time goods are purchased and which then becomes the equivalent of a note receivable of the seller and the note payable of the buyer.

A bill of exchange or draft drawn by the seller of goods on the purchaser and accepted by such purchaser. Once accepted, the purchaser becomes primarily liable to pay the draft. See U.C.C. § 3–413(1).

Trade agreement. Agreement between two countries or among many nations concerning buying and selling of each country's goods. See also Collective bargaining agreement; GATT; Most favored nation clause; Reciprocal trade agreements.

Trade and commerce. The words "trade" and "commerce," when used in juxtaposition impart to each other enlarged signification, so as to include practically every business occupation carried on for subsistence or profit and into which the elements of bargain and sale, barter, exchange, or traffic, enter. See Commerce.

Trade association. An association of business organizations having similar problems and engaged in similar fields formed for mutual protection, interchange of ideas and statistics and for maintenance of standards within their industry.

Trade claims. The unpaid bills of a bankrupt company's creditors. There is a market for these with investors.

Trade commission. See Federal Trade Commission.

Trade credit. Credit that firms extend to other firms in the ordinary course of business through the creation of receivables/payables.

Trade deficit or surplus. Excess of nations imports over exports (trade deficit) or exports over imports (trade surplus). Such determines a nation's balance of trade (positive or negative). See Balance (Balance of trade).

Trade discount. A discount from list price offered to all customers of a given type; e.g. discount offered by lumber dealer to building contractor. Difference between seller's list price and the price at which he actually sells goods to the trade. Contrast with a discount offered for prompt payment and quantity discount.

Trade dress. The total appearance and image of a product, including features such as size, texture, shape, color or color combinations, graphics, and even particular advertising and marketing techniques used to promote its sale. Duplication of the trade dress of another's goods is actionable as passing off at common law and under Trademark Act. 15 U.S.C.A. § 1125(a). Commercial prints and labels constituting key elements of trade dress may be protectible under the copyright laws as well.

Trade fixtures. Personal property used by tenants in carrying on business. Such fixtures retain the character of personal property; e.g. shelves used to display merchandise. See also Fixture.

Trade libel. Intentional disparagement of quality of property, which results in pecuniary damage to plaintiff. The distinction between "libel" and "trade libel" is that the former concerns the person or reputation of plaintiff and the latter relates to his goods.

Trademark. Generally speaking, a distinctive mark of authenticity, through which the products of particular manufacturers or the vendible commodities of particular merchants may be distinguished from those of others. It may consist in any symbol or in any form of words, but, as its office is to point out distinctively the origin or ownership of the articles to which it is affixed, it follows that no sign or form of words can be appropriated as a valid trademark which, from the nature of the fact conveyed by its primary meaning, others may employ with equal truth and with equal right for the same purpose.

A distinctive mark, motto, device, or emblem, which a manufacturer stamps, prints, or otherwise affixes to the goods he produces, so that they may be identified in the market, and their origin be vouched for. Exclusive rights to use a trademark are granted by the federal government for ten years, with the possibility of additional ten year renewal periods. 15 U.S.C.A. §§ 1058, 1059.

The term "trademark" includes any word, name, symbol, or device, or any combination thereof—(1) used by a person, or (2) which a person has a bona fide intention to use in commerce and applies to register on the principal register established by the Trademark Act, to identify and distinguish his or her goods, including a unique product, from those manufactured or sold by others and to indicate the source of the goods, even if that source is unknown. 15 U.S.C.A. § 1127.

See also Certification mark; Collective mark; Common descriptive name; Descriptive mark; Distinctiveness; Functionality; Infringement; Likelihood of confusion; Official Gazette; Patent and Trademark Office; Related goods; Secondary meaning;

Service mark; Trade dress; Trade name; Use in commerce.

Descriptive and suggestive trademarks. Distinction between descriptive and suggestive trademarks is that "suggestive" terms are those which require the buyer to use thought, imagination, or perception to connect the mark with the goods, while "descriptive" terms are those which directly convey to the buyer the ingredients, qualities, or characteristics of the product.

Fanciful mark. A trademark consisting of a made-up or coined word is said to be "fanciful." Such marks are considered inherently distinctive, and thus are protected at common law, and are eligible for Trademark Act registration, from the time of first use.

Geographically descriptive mark. A geographic word used as a trademark that indicates where the goods are grown or manufactured is considered geographically descriptive. Such marks will only be protected at common law and registered under the Trademark Act upon proof of secondary meaning. *See* Secondary meaning.

Strong trademark. For purposes of determining the likelihood of confusion between marks, is a mark which is generally fictitious, arbitrary or fanciful and is inherently distinctive. A strong mark is entitled to a greater degree of protection from infringing uses than is a weak one, because of its unique usage. *Compare Weak trademark, below.*

Suggestive mark or term. One that suggests, rather than describes, some particular characteristic of goods and services to which it applies and requires consumer to exercise imagination in order to draw conclusion as to nature of goods or services.

Trade name distinguished. A "trade name" is a descriptive of a manufacturer or dealer and applies to business and its goodwill, whereas "trademark" is applicable only to vendable commodities. Corporate or business name symbolizing the reputation of a business as a whole, whereas a "trademark" is a term identifying and distinguishing a business' products. *See* Trade name.

Weak trademark. A mark that is a meaningful word in common usage or is merely a suggestive or descriptive trademark, and is entitled to protection only if it has acquired a secondary meaning. *See also* Secondary meaning. *Compare Strong trademark, above.*

Trade name. That name which is used by manufacturers, industrialists and merchants to identify their businesses, which actually symbolizes reputation of business. The name or title lawfully adopted and used by a particular organization engaged in commerce, which can be used in advertising, promotion, and to generate publicity for the business.

The terms "trade name" and "commercial name" include individual names and surnames, firm names and trade names used by manufacturers, industrialists, merchants, agriculturists, and others to identify their businesses, vocations, or occupations; the names or titles lawfully adopted and used by persons, firms, associations, corporations, companies, unions, and any manufacturing, industrial, commercial, agricultural, or other organizations engaged in trade or commerce and capable of suing and being sued in a court of law. 15 U.S.C.A. § 1127.

See also Certification mark; Collective mark. *Compare* Service mark; Trademark.

Trade or business. Any business or professional activity conducted by a taxpayer, the objective of which is to earn a profit. General test for determining whether person is engaged in "trade or business" so as to be entitled to deduct expenses as trade or business expenses under Internal Revenue Code is whether taxpayer's primary purpose and intention in engaging in the activity is to make a profit.

Trader. A merchant; a retailer. One who makes it his business to buy merchandise, goods, or chattels to sell the same at a profit. One who sells goods substantially in the form in which they are bought; one who has not converted them into another form of property by his skill and labor. *See also* Dealer; Merchant.

In securities, one who as a member of a stock exchange buys and sells on the floor of the exchange either for brokers or on his own account. Likewise, in commodity market, one who buys and sells commodities (*e.g.* grain) and commodity futures for others and for his own account in anticipation of a speculative profit. *See also* Broker; Dealer.

Trade secret. A "trade secret," as protected from misappropriation, may consist of any formula, pattern, device of compilation of information which is used in one's business, and which gives person an opportunity to obtain an advantage over competitors who do not know or use it; or, it may be a formula or a chemical compound, a process of manufacturing, treating or preserving materials, a pattern for a machine or other device, or a list of customers.

A plan or process, tool, mechanism, or compound known only to its owner and those of his employees to whom it is necessary to confide it. A secret formula or process not patented, but known only to certain individuals using it in compounding some article of trade having a commercial value.

Tradesman. A mechanic, craftsman, or artificer of any kind, whose livelihood depends primarily on the labor of his hands.

Trade-union. A combination of workers of the same trade or of several allied trades, for the purpose of securing by united action the most favorable conditions regarding wages, hours of labor, etc., for its members. *See also* Union.

Trade usage. The usage or customs commonly observed by persons conversant in, or connected with, a particular trade.

A usage of trade is any practice or method of dealing having such regularity of observance in a place, vocation or trade as to justify an expectation that it will be observed with respect to the transaction in question. The existence and scope of such a usage are to be proved as facts. If it is established that such a usage is embodied in a written trade code or similar writing the interpretation of the writing is for the court. U.C.C. § 1–205(2). *Compare* Course of dealing. *See also* Usage *(Usage of trade)*.

Trading. Engaging in trade *(q.v.)*; pursuing the business or occupation of trade or of a trader.

Trading corporation. *See* Corporation.

Trading on the equity. The process of securing funds at fixed interest and preferred dividend rates and investing the funds to earn a return greater than their cost; also called leverage.

Trading partnership. A firm the nature of whose business, according to the usual modes of conducting it, imports the necessity of buying and selling.

Trading posts. The posts on the floor of a stock exchange where the specialists stand and securities are traded.

Trading with the enemy. Offense of carrying on commerce with a country or with a subject of a nation with whom the U.S. is at war. Federal laws prohibit commercial intercourse with nations and with subjects and allies of nations with whom the U.S. is at war. 50 U.S.C.A. App. § 1 et seq.

Traffic. Commerce; trade; sale or exchange of merchandise, bills, money, and the like. The passing or exchange of goods or commodities from one person to another for an equivalent in goods or money. The subjects of transportation on a route, as persons or goods; the passing to and fro of persons, animals, vehicles, or vessels, along a route of transportation, as along a street, highway, etc. *See* Commerce.

Traffic balances. Balances of moneys collected in payment for the transportation of passengers and freight.

Trafficking. Trading or dealing in certain goods and commonly used in connection with illegal narcotic sales.

Traitor. One who, being trusted, betrays; one guilty of treason *(q.v.)*.

Transact. To undertake negotiations; to carry on business; to have dealings; to carry through; bring about; perform; to carry on or conduct; to pass back and forth as in negotiations or trade; to bring into actuality or existence. The word embraces in its meaning the carrying on or prosecution of business negotiations, but it is a broader term than the word "contract" and may involve business negotiations which have been either wholly or partly brought to a conclusion. *See also* Negotiate; Transaction.

Transacting business. Term as used in statute providing that no foreign corporation transacting business in State without a certificate of authority shall maintain an action in State if it has not obtained a certificate of authority, is not susceptible of precise definition automatically resolving every case; each case must be dealt with on its own circumstances to determine if foreign corporation has engaged in local activity or only in interstate commerce.

Test of whether or not a corporation is transacting business, in a district, for purpose of section of the Clayton Act providing that an action may be brought against a corporation in any district wherein it transacts business, is the practical everyday business or commercial concept of doing business of any substantial character. *See also* Doing business; Minimum contacts.

Transaction. Act of transacting or conducting any business; between two or more persons; negotiation; that which is done; an affair. An act, agreement, or several acts or agreements between or among parties whereby a cause of action or alteration of legal rights occur. It may involve selling, leasing, borrowing, mortgaging or lending. Something which has taken place, whereby a cause of action has arisen. It must therefore consist of an act or agreement, or several acts or agreements having some connection with each other, in which more than one person is concerned, and by which the legal relations of such persons between themselves are altered. It is a broader term than "contract". *See also* Closed transaction; Trade; Transact.

Transactional immunity. *See* Immunity *(Immunity from prosecution)*.

Transaction or occurrence test. Fed.R.Civil P. 13(a) provides that a claim qualifies as a *compulsory* counterclaim if it arises out of the "transaction or occurrence" that is the subject matter of the opposing party's claim. Courts generally have agreed that these words should be interpreted liberally in order to further the general policies of the federal rules which are to avoid multiple suits and to encourage the determination of the entire controversy among the parties. Thus, the "transaction" test does not require the court to differentiate between opposing legal and equitable claims or between claims in tort and those in contract. Most courts, rather than attempting to define the key terms of Rule 13(a) precisely, have preferred to suggest standards by which the compulsory or permissive nature of specific counterclaims can be determined. Four tests have been suggested: (1) Are the issues of fact and law raised by the claim and counterclaim largely the same? (2) Would res judicata bar a subsequent suit on defendant's claim absent the compulsory counterclaim rule? (3) Will substantially the same evidence support or refute plaintiff's claim as well as defendant's counterclaim? (4) Is there any logical relation between the claim and the counterclaim? *See* Counterclaim *(Compulsory counterclaim).*

Cross-claims. Most courts have held that the above standards used for dealing with the "transaction or occurrence" test for compulsory counterclaims also apply to cross-claims under Fed.R.Civil P. 13(g). *See* Cross-claim.

Transactions approach. In accounting, an approach to determining and measuring net income by focusing on business transactions, which have produced changes in the entity's assets, liabilities, and/or owner's equity.

Transcript. That which has been transcribed. A copy of any kind, though commonly the term refers to a copy of the record of a trial, hearing or other proceeding as prepared by a court reporter. A writing made from or after an original. A copy of an original writing or deed and suggests the idea of an original writing.

An official copy of the record of proceedings in a trial or hearing. Word-for-word typing of everything that was said "on the record" during the trial. The stenographer (court reporter) types this transcription which is paid for by the parties requesting it.

Transcript of record. Refers to the printed record as made up in each case of the proceedings and pleadings necessary for the appellate court to review the history of the case.

Transfer, v. To convey or remove from one place, person, etc., to another; pass or hand over from one to another; specifically, to change over the possession or control of (as, to transfer a title to land).

Transfer, n. An act of the parties, or of the law, by which the title to property is conveyed from one person to another. The sale and every other method, direct or indirect, of disposing of or parting with property or with an interest therein, or with the possession thereof, or of fixing a lien upon property or upon an interest therein, absolutely or conditionally, voluntarily or involuntarily, by or without judicial proceedings, as a conveyance, sale, payment, pledge, mortgage, lien, encumbrance, gift, security or otherwise. The word

is one of general meaning and may include the act of giving property by will.

The assignment or conveyance of property, including an instrument or document, that vests in the transferee such rights as the transferor had therein. See U.C.C. §§ 3–201(1) & 7–504(1). Transfer is the all-encompassing term used by the Uniform Commercial Code to describe the act which passes an interest in an instrument to another.

Transfer means every mode, direct or indirect, absolute or conditional, voluntary or involuntary, of disposing of or parting with property or with an interest in property, including retention of title as a security interest and foreclosure of the debtor's equity of redemption. Bankruptcy Code § 101.

See Barter; Constructive transfer; Exchange; Gift; Sale; Will.

Transferable. A term used in a *quasi* legal sense, to indicate that the character of assignability or negotiability attaches to the particular instrument, or that it may pass from hand to hand, carrying all rights of the original holder. The words "not transferable" are sometimes printed upon a ticket, receipt, or bill of lading, to show that the same will not be good in the hands of any person other than the one to whom first issued.

Transfer agent. An organization, usually a bank, that handles transfers of shares for a publicly held corporation. Generally, a transfer agent assures that certificates submitted for transfer are properly endorsed and that there is appropriate documentation of the right to transfer. The transfer agent issues new certificates and oversees the cancellation of the old ones. Transfer agents also usually maintain the record of shareholders for the corporation and mail dividend checks.

Transferee. He to whom a transfer is made.

Transferee liability. Under certain conditions, if the Internal Revenue Service is unable to collect taxes owed by a transferor of property, it may pursue its claim against the transferee of such property. The transferee's liability for taxes is limited to the extent of the value of the assets transferred. For example, the Internal Revenue Service can force a donee to pay the gift tax when such tax cannot be paid by the donor making the transfer. I.R.C. §§ 6901–6905.

Transfer in contemplation of death. A transfer made under a present apprehension on the part of the transferor, from some existing bodily or mental condition or impending peril, creating a reasonable fear that death is near at hand. *See* Contemplation of death.

Transfer of a cause. The removal of a case from the jurisdiction of one court or judge to another by lawful authority. 28 U.S.C.A. §§ 1404(a),

1406(a), 1631. *See* Forum non conveniens; Removal of causes.

Transferor. One who makes a transfer.

Transfer payments. Payments made by the government to individuals for which no services are concurrently rendered in return. A transfer payment might be a Social Security check or an unemployment check.

Transfer price. In accounting, internal charge established for the exchange of goods and services between organizational units of the same company.

Transferred intent doctrine. If an illegal yet unintended act results from the intent to commit a crime, that act is also considered illegal. Under doctrine of "transferred intent," original malice is transferred from one against whom it was entertained to person who actually suffers consequence of unlawful act. For example, if a person intentionally directs force against one person wrongfully but, instead, hits another, his intent is said to be transferred from one to the other and he is liable to the other though he did not intend it in the first instance. *See also* Intent *(Transferred intent)*.

Transfers to Minors Act. The Uniform Transfers to Minors Act (UTMA) revises and replaces the Uniform Gifts to Minors Act (UGMA). As expanded, the Act allows the transfer of any type of property, real or personal, tangible or intangible, and wheresoever located (within or without the state) to a custodianship. In addition, the UTMA permits (in addition to outright lifetime gifts) transfers from trusts, estates, and guardianships even if the trust, will, etc., instrument does not expressly permit such transfers. Transfers from persons indebted to the minor also may be made to the custodianship if the minor does not have a conservator. The UTMA also permits the legal representative of the minor to transfer other property of the minor to the custodianship for the purpose of convenience or economy.

Many states have repealed the former UGMA and substituted this new UTMA. *See also* Gifts (or Transfers) to Minors Act.

Transfer tax. A tax upon the passing of the title to property or a valuable interest therein out of or from the estate of a decedent, by inheritance, devise, or bequest. *See* Estate tax; Inheritance tax; Unified transfer tax.

Tax on the transfer of property, particularly of an incorporeal nature, such as bonds or shares of stock, between living persons. A tax imposed by New York State when a security is sold or transferred from one person to another. Also, a tax imposed by states on each deed conveying real estate. The tax is paid by the seller. *See also* Revenue stamps.

Transit. A stop-over privilege on a continuous journey granted by carrier by which a break de facto in continuity of carriage of goods is disregarded and two legs of a journey are treated as though covered without interruption, uniting both legs into a through route for which a joint rate can be published. Within policy covering goods in transit, term has significance of activity and of motion and direction; literally it means in course of passing from point to point, and ordinarily goods in transit would imply that foods will lawfully be picked up at given place and hauled to place designated by owner or one with authority to so designate. Term may also be applied to a check which is mailed for collection while it is still in the mails and uncollected. *See also* In transitu; Stoppage in transit.

Transportation of goods or persons from one place to another. Passage; act of passing.

Transitory. Passing from place to place; that which may pass or be changed from one place to another; the opposite of "local." *See* Transitory action.

Transitory action. An action that is personal; *i.e.*, brought against the person of the defendant— and brought in any county in which service of process upon the defendant is obtained. A lawsuit that may be brought in any one of many places. Actions are "transitory" when transaction on which they are based might take place anywhere, and are "local" when they could not occur except in some particular place; the distinction being in nature of subject of injury and not in means used or place at which cause of action arises. *See also* In personam; In rem.

Transmit. To send or transfer from one person or place to another, or to communicate.

Transmittal letter. Non-substantive document which establishes a record of delivery; *e.g.* letter to the SEC which accompanies a preliminary filing.

Transport, *v.* To carry or convey from one place to another.

Trap. A device, as a pitfall, snare, or machine that shuts suddenly as with a spring, for taking game and other animals. Hence, any device or contrivance by which one may be caught unawares, strategem; snare; gin. It imports an affirmative intent or design either malicious or mischievous, to cause injury. The doctrine of "trap" as ground for recovery by trespasser is rested upon theory that owner expected trespasser and prepared an injury. *See also* Entrapment.

Trauma /tráwmə/trómə/. A physical injury caused by a blow, or fall, or a psychologically damaging emotional experience. An injury, wound, shock, or the resulting condition or neurosis.

Travel Act. Federal act prohibiting travel in interstate or foreign commerce to further unlawful gambling, prostitution, extortion, bribery or arson, as well as illegal transactions involving liquor or narcotics. 18 U.S.C.A. § 1952.

Traveler's check. Instrument purchased from bank, express company, or the like, in various denominations, which can be used as cash upon second signature by purchaser. It has the characteristics of a cashier's check of the issuer. It requires the signature of the purchaser at the time he buys it and also at the time when he uses it.

Traveler's letter of credit. A type of letter of credit which is addressed to a correspondent bank. When the traveler wishes to draw credit on the correspondent bank, he identifies himself as the person in whose favor the credit is drawn. *See also* Letter of credit (*Traveler's letter*).

Traverse. In common law pleading, a traverse signifies a denial. Thus, where a defendant denies any material allegation of fact in the plaintiff's declaration, he is said to traverse it, and the plea itself is thence frequently termed a "traverse." *See also* Denial.

Treason. A breach of allegiance to one's government, usually committed through levying war against such government or by giving aid or comfort to the enemy. The offense of attempting by overt acts to overthrow the government of the state to which the offender owes allegiance; or of betraying the state into the hands of a foreign power. Treason consists of two elements: adherence to the enemy, and rendering him aid and comfort. See 18 U.S.C.A. § 2381. A person can be convicted of treason only on the testimony of two witnesses, or confession in open court. Art. III, Sec. 3, U.S. Constitution.

Treasonable. Having the nature or guilt of treason. *See* Treason.

Treasure. A thing hidden or buried in the earth, on which no one can prove his property, and which is discovered by chance. *See* Treasure-trove.

Treasurer. An officer of a public or private corporation, company, or government, charged with the receipt, custody, investment, and disbursement of its moneys or funds.

Treasurer of the United States. *See* Treasury Department.

Treasure-trove. Literally, treasure found. Money or coin, gold, silver, plate or bullion *found* hidden in the earth or other private place, the owner thereof being unknown. Finder of treasure trove, is entitled thereto as against owner of land where such treasure is found and all the world save the true owner, in absence of statute.

Treasuries. Debt obligations of U.S. government backed by Full Faith and Credit of government. *See* Treasury bill; Treasury bond; Treasury note.

Treasury. A place or building in which stores of wealth are reposited; particularly, a place where the public revenues are deposited and kept, and where money is disbursed to defray the expenses of government.

That department of government which is charged with the receipt, custody, and disbursement (pursuant to appropriations) of the public revenues or funds.

Treasury bill. Short-term obligations of the federal government. Treasury bills are for specified terms of three, six and twelve months.

An obligation of the U.S. Treasury with a maturity date less than one year from the date of issue and bearing no interest but sold at a discount. Distinguished from a *certificate of indebtedness,* which also is of a maturity of one year or less but bears interest. *Compare* Treasury bond; Treasury certificate; Treasury note.

Treasury bond. A bond issued by a corporation and then reacquired; such bonds are treated as retired when reacquired and an extraordinary gain or loss on reacquisition is recognized. *Compare* Treasury stock.

Long term debt instruments of U.S. government.

Treasury certificate. An obligation of the U.S. generally maturing in one year on which interest is paid on a coupon basis. *Compare* Treasury bill.

Treasury Department. The Treasury Department was created by act of Congress approved September 2, 1789. Many subsequent acts have figured in the development of the Department delegating new duties to its charge and establishing the numerous bureaus and divisions which now compose the Treasury. The Department of the Treasury performs four basic types of functions: formulating and recommending financial, tax, and fiscal policies; serving as financial agent for the U.S. Government; law enforcement; and manufacturing coins and currency. *See also* Internal Revenue Service.

Treasury note. An obligation of the federal government, with a maturity of one to ten years, on which interest is paid by coupon. *Compare* Treasury bill; Treasury bond.

Treasury Regulations. *See* Regulations.

Treasury securities. *See* Treasury stock.

Treasury shares. *See* Treasury stock.

Treasury stock. Stock which has been issued as fully paid to stockholders and subsequently reacquired by the corporation to be used by it in furtherance of its corporate purposes; stock which is merely to be held as unsubscribed for and unissued is not usually regarded as "treasury stock". The Revised Model Business Corporation Act and the statutes of several states have eliminated the concept of treasury shares; reacquired shares automatically having the status of authorized but unissued shares. *Compare* Treasury bond.

Treasury warrant. Order in check form on U.S. Treasury on which treasury (*i.e.* government) disbursements are paid.

Treating physician rule. This rule states that social security disability claimant's treating physician's diagnoses and findings regarding degree of claimant's impairment are binding on administrative law judge unless there is substantial contrary evidence.

Treaty. An agreement, league, or contract between two or more nations or sovereigns, with a view to the public welfare, formally signed by commissioners properly authorized, and solemnly ratified by the several sovereigns or the supreme power of each state. A treaty is not only a law but also a contract between two nations and must, if possible, be so construed as to give full force and effect to all its parts. The term has a far more restricted meaning under U.S. Constitution than under international law. *See also* Compact.

United States treaties may be made by the President, by and with the advice and consent of the Senate. Art. II, Sec. 2, U.S. Const. States may not enter into treaties (Art. I, Sec. 10, cl. 1), and, once made, shall be binding on the states as the supreme law of the land (Art. VI, cl. 2). *See* Supremacy clause; Treaty clause.

Treaty clause. The provision in the U.S. Constitution, Art. II, Sec. 2, which gives to the President the power "by and with the consent of the Senate, to make treaties, provided two thirds of the Senators present concur."

Treaty power. *See* Treaty clause.

Treble costs. *See* Cost.

Treble damages. *See* Damages.

Trespass. An unlawful interference with one's person, property, or rights. At common law, trespass was a form of action brought to recover damages for any injury to one's person or property or relationship with another.

Any unauthorized intrusion or invasion of private premises or land of another. Trespass comprehends any misfeasance, transgression or offense which damages another person's health, reputation or property. Doing of unlawful act or of lawful act in unlawful manner to injury of another's person or property. An unlawful act committed with violence, actual or implied, causing injury to the person, property, or relative rights of another. It comprehends not only forc-

ible wrongs, but also acts the consequences of which make them tortious.

See also Forcible trespass; Intruder.

Continuing trespass. One which is in its nature a permanent invasion of the rights of another; as, where a person builds on his own land so that a part of the building overhangs his neighbor's land or dumps rubbish on the land of another. In such a case, there is a continuing wrong so long as the offending object remains.

A trespass may be committed by the continued presence on the land of a structure, chattel, or other thing which the actor or his predecessor in legal interest has placed on the land: (a) with the consent of the person then in possession of the land, if the actor fails to remove it after the consent has been effectively terminated, or (b) pursuant to a privilege conferred on the actor irrespective of the possessor's consent, if the actor fails to remove it after the privilege has been terminated, by the accomplishment of its purpose or otherwise. Restatement, Second, Torts, § 160.

Criminal trespass. Criminal trespass is entering or remaining upon or in any land, structure, vehicle, aircraft or watercraft by one who knows he is not authorized or privileged to do so; and (a) He enters or remains therein in defiance of an order not to enter or to leave such premises or property personally communicated to him by the owner thereof or other authorized person; or (b) Such premises or property are posted in a manner reasonably likely to come to the attention of intruders, or are fenced or otherwise enclosed. *See also* Criminal.

Joint trespass. Exists where two or more persons unite in committing it, or where some actually commit the tort, the others command, encourage or direct it.

Trespass on the case. The form of action, at common law, adapted to the recovery of damages for some injury resulting to a party from the wrongful act of another, unaccompanied by direct or immediate force, or which is the indirect or secondary consequence of defendant's act. Such action is the ancestor of the present day action for negligence where problems of legal and factual cause arise. Commonly called, by abbreviation, "Case."

Trespass to land. At common law, every unauthorized and direct breach of the boundaries of another's land was an actionable trespass. It is a wrong against one who has this right to possession, not necessarily against the person who has title but no immediate right to possession. No intent to commit a trespass was required. All that was necessary was that the act resulting in the trespass be volitional, and that the resulting trespass be direct and immediate. Nor did actual damage need be shown. Any trespass justified at least nominal damages. The present prevailing position of the courts, and Restatement of Torts, finds liability for trespass only in the case of intentional intrusion, or negligence, or some "abnormally dangerous activity" on the part of the defendant. Restatement, Second, Torts, § 166. *Compare* Nuisance.

Extent of trespasser's liability for harm. A trespass on land subjects the trespasser to liability for physical harm to the possessor of the land at the time of the trespass, or to the land or to his things, or to members of his household or to their things, caused by any act done, activity carried on, or condition created by the trespasser, irrespective of whether his conduct is such as would subject him to liability were he not a trespasser. Restatement, Second, Torts, § 162.

Failure to remove thing tortiously placed on land. A trespass may be committed by the continued presence on the land of a structure, chattel, or other thing which the actor has tortiously placed there, whether or not the actor has the ability to remove it. A trespass may be committed by the continued presence on the land of a structure, chattel, or other thing which the actor's predecessor in legal interest therein has tortiously placed there, if the actor, having acquired his legal interest in the thing with knowledge of such tortious conduct or having thereafter learned of it, fails to remove the thing. Restatement, Second, Torts, § 161.

Intrusions upon, beneath, and above surface of land. (1) Except as stated in Subsection (2), a trespass may be committed on, beneath, or above the surface of the earth. (2) Flight by aircraft in the air space above the land of another is a trespass if, but only if, (a) it enters into the immediate reaches of the air space next to the land, and (b) it interferes substantially with the other's use and enjoyment of his land. Restatement, Second, Torts, § 159.

Liability for intentional intrusions on land. One is subject to liability to another for trespass, irrespective of whether he thereby causes harm to any legally protected interest of the other, if he intentionally (a) enters land in the possession of the other, or causes a thing or a third person to do so, or (b) remains on the land, or (c) fails to remove from the land a thing which he is under a duty to remove. Restatement, Second, Torts, § 158.

Trespass to try title. The name of the action used in several of the states for the recovery of the possession of real property unlawfully withheld, from an owner who has a right of immediate possession, with damages for any trespass committed upon the same by the defendant. A procedure by which rival claims to title or right to possession of land may be adjudicated, and as an incident partition may also be had when the contro-versy concerning title or right to possession is settled. It is different from "trespass *quare clausum fregit (see above),*" in that title must be proved. *See also* Ejectment.

Trespasser. One who has committed trespass. One who intentionally and without consent or privilege enters another's property. One who enters upon property of another without any right, lawful authority, or express or implied invitation, permission, or license, not in performance of any duties to owner, but merely for his own purpose, pleasure or convenience.

Innocent trespasser. See that title.

Joint trespassers. Two or more who unite in committing a trespass.

Trial. A judicial examination and determination of issues between parties to action, whether they be issues of law or of fact, before a court that has jurisdiction. A judicial examination, in accordance with law of the land, of a cause, either civil or criminal, of the issues between the parties, whether of law or fact, before a court that has proper jurisdiction.

See also Bifurcated trial; Civil jury trial; Examining trial; Fair and impartial trial; Mini-trial; Mistrial; Speedy trial; Trifurcated trial.

Bench trial. See *Trial by court or judge, below.*

New trial. A re-examination in the same court of an issue of fact, or some part or portions thereof, after the verdict by a jury, report of a referee, or a decision by the court. See Fed.R.Civil P. 59; Fed. R.Crim.P. 33. See *Trial de novo, below.* See also Motion for new trial; Plain error rule; Venire facias.

Nonjury trial. See *Trial by court or judge, below.*

Public trial. A trial held in public, in the presence of the public, or in a place accessible and open to the attendance of the public at large, or of persons who may properly be admitted. The Sixth Amendment, U.S.Const., affords the accused the right to a speedy and "public" trial. *See,* however, *Trial by news media, below.*

Separate trial. See that title.

Speedy trial. See that title.

State trial. See State.

Trial balance. In bookkeeping, a listing of debit and credit balances of all ledger accounts. The listing is generally taken at end of an accounting period to check as to whether all entries have been made in both debit and credit accounts, though such listing need not prove accuracy of accounts if an error has been made in both the debit and credit entry.

A listing of account balances; all accounts with debit balances are totaled separately from accounts with credit balances. The two totals should be equal. Trial balances are taken as a partial check of the arithmetic accuracy of the entries previously made. *See also* Post-closing trial balance.

Trial by court or judge. Trial before judge alone, in contrast to trial before jury and judge. A jury waived trial.

Trial by jury. A trial in which the issues of fact are to be determined by the verdict of a jury, duly selected, impaneled, and sworn. The terms "jury" and "trial by jury" were used at the adoption of the Constitution, and have their source in the English legal system. A jury for the trial of a cause was a body of twelve men, described as upright, well-qualified, and lawful men, disinterested and impartial, not of kin nor personal dependents of either of the parties, having their homes within the jurisdictional limits of the court, drawn and selected by officers free from all bias in favor of or against either party, duly impaneled under the direction of a competent court, sworn to render a true verdict according to the law and the evidence given them, who, after hearing the parties and their evidence, and receiving the instructions of the court relative to the law involved in the trial, and deliberating, when necessary, apart from all extraneous influences, must return their unanimous verdict upon the issue submitted to them. In federal court, and as well in many state courts, the parties may stipulate that the jury shall consist of less than twelve members or that a verdict of a stated majority of the jurors shall be taken as the verdict of the jury. See Fed.R.Civil P. 48; Fed.R.Crim.P. 23.

The Seventh Amendment to Federal Constitution provides that "In suits at common law, where the value in controversy shall exceed twenty dollars, the right of trial by jury shall be preserved." See also Fed.R.Civil P. 38(a). The right to a jury trial is also preserved in state constitutions. In *civil* cases in federal court, a jury trial must be expressly demanded or such right will be deemed waived (Fed.R.Civil P. 38); while in *criminal* cases the right exists unless expressly waived and approved by court and government (Fed.R.Crim.P. 23(a)). *See also* Jury trial.

Summary jury trial. A settlement technique designed to resolve disputes. Attorneys present abbreviated arguments to jurors who render an informal nonbinding verdict that guides the settlement of the case. Normally, six mock jurors are chosen after a brief voir dire conducted by the court. Following short opening statements, all evidence is presented in the form of a descriptive summary to the mock jury through the parties' attorneys. Live witnesses do not testify, and evidentiary objections are discouraged. *See also* Mini-trial.

Trial by news media. The process by which the news media in reporting an investigation of a person on trial leads its readers to act as judge and jury in determining guilt, liability or innocence before the person is tried in a judicial forum. Failure to protect accused from inherently prejudicial publicity may constitute deprivation of right to fair and impartial trial as guaranteed by due process clause of Fourteenth Amendment. Sheppard v. Maxwell, 384 U.S. 333, 86 S.Ct. 1507, 16 L.Ed.2d 600.

Local court rules have been widely adopted, seeking to set a proper balance between a free press and a fair trial by putting restrictions on the release of information by attorneys and courthouse personnel, making special provision for the conduct of proceedings in extensively publicized and sensational cases, and barring photography, radio, and television equipment from the courtroom and its environs.

See also Gag order.

Trial court. The court of original jurisdiction; the first court to consider litigation.

Trial de novo. A new trial or retrial had in which the whole case is retried as if no trial whatever had been had in the first instance. A trial of the entire case anew, both on law and on facts. *See New trial, above. See also* Motion for new trial; Plain error rule.

Trial jury. See Jury.

Trial list. A list of cases marked down for trial for any one term. *See* Trial calendar.

Trial calendar. Comprehensive list of cases awaiting trial and containing the dates for trial, names of counsel, expected time required for trial, etc. In some states it is maintained by the trial judge and in others, by the clerk of court. See *e.g.* Fed.R.Civil P. 79. *See also* Calendar; Docket.

Trial court. The court of original jurisdiction where all evidence is first received and considered; the first court to consider litigation. Used in contract to appellate court.

In federal tax cases, trial courts include U.S. District Courts, the U.S. Tax Court, and U.S. Claims Court.

Trial on merits. Trial of substantive issues in case. Term used in contrast to a hearing on motion or on other interlocutory matters.

Tribal lands. Lands of Indian reservation which are not allotted to or occupied by individual Indians but rather the unallotted or common lands of the nation.

Land allotted in severalty to a restricted Indian is no longer part of the "reservation" nor is it "tribal land" but the virtual fee is in the allottee with certain restrictions on the right of alienation.

See also Indian country; Indian lands; Indian reservation; Indian tribal property.

Tribunal. The seat of a judge; a court of law; the place where he administers justice. The whole body of judges who compose a jurisdiction; a judicial court; the jurisdiction which the judges exercise.

Trier of fact. Term includes (a) the jury and (b) the court when the court is trying an issue of fact other than one relating to the admissibility of evidence. Calif.Evid.Code. Commonly refers to judge in jury waived trial or jury which, in either case, has the exclusive obligation to make findings of fact in contrast to rulings of law which must be made by judge. Also may refer to hearing officer or judge in administrative proceeding.

Trifurcated trial. A trial which is divided into three stages or parts as for example, a trial on issue of liability, trial for general damages, and trial for special damages.

TRO. *See* Temporary restraining order.

Trover /tróvvər/. In common-law practice, the action of trover (or trover and conversion) is a species of action on the case, and originally lay for the recovery of damages against a person who had *found* another's goods and wrongfully converted them to his own use. Subsequently the allegation of the loss of the goods by the plaintiff and the finding of them by the defendant was merely fictitious, and the action became the remedy for any wrongful interference with or detention of the goods of another. In form a fiction; in substance, a remedy to recover the value of personal chattels *wrongfully* converted by another to his own use. Common-law form of action to recover value of goods or chattels by reason of an alleged unlawful interference with possessory right of another, by assertion or exercise of possession or dominion over the chattels, which is adverse and hostile to rightful possessor. Such remedy lies only for wrongful appropriation of goods, chattels, or personal property which is specific enough to be identified. *See also* Conversion; Detinue; Replevin.

Truancy. Wilful and unjustified failure to attend school by one who is required to attend. It is a punishable offense within the juvenile system in some states and, in others, it is the basis of a petition for a child in need of services.

True. Conformable to fact; correct; exact; actual; genuine; honest. In one sense, that only is "true" which is conformable to the actual state of things. In that sense, a statement is "untrue" which does not express things exactly as they are. But in another and broader sense the word "true" is often used as a synonym of "honest", "sincere", not "fraudulent."

True bill. The endorsement made by a grand jury upon a bill of indictment, when they find it sustained by the evidence laid before them, and are satisfied of the truth of the accusation. The endorsement made by a grand jury when they find sufficient evidence to warrant a criminal charge. An indictment.

True copy. A true copy does not mean an absolutely exact copy but means that the copy shall be so true that anybody can understand it. *See* Certified copy; Copy; Copying.

True value. For tax assessment purposes, term refers to the market value of the property at fair and bona fide sale at private contract, and is in essence the value property has in exchange for money. In condemnation proceedings, is market value or price which would be agreed upon at voluntary sale between willing seller and willing purchaser, taking into consideration all available uses to which land might be put, as well as all factors, which lead to reimbursement for loss caused by taking. *See also* Market value; Value.

True verdict. The voluntary conclusion of the jury after deliberate consideration, and it is none the less a true verdict because the respective jurors may have been liberal in concessions to each other, if conscientiously and freely made. A verdict is not a "true verdict," when it is the result of any arbitrary rule or order, whether imposed by themselves, or by the court or officer in charge. *See* Verdict.

Trust. A legal entity created by a grantor for the benefit of designated beneficiaries under the laws of the state and the valid trust instrument. The trustee holds a fiduciary responsibility to manage the trust's corpus assets and income for the economic benefit of all of the the beneficiaries. A confidence reposed in one person, who is termed trustee, for the benefit of another, who is called the cestui que trust, respecting property which is held by the trustee for the benefit of the cestui que trust. Any arrangement whereby property is transferred with intention that it be administered by trustee for another's benefit. A fiduciary relationship in which one person is the holder of the title to property subject to an equitable obligation to keep or use the property for the benefit of another.

Essential elements of trust are designated beneficiary and trustee, fund sufficiently identified to enable title to pass to trustee, and actual delivery to trustee with intention of passing title.

An association or organization of persons or corporations having the intention and power, or the tendency, to create a monopoly, control production, interfere with the free course of trade or transportation, or to fix and regulate the supply and the price of commodities. In the history of economic development, the "trust" was originally a device by which several corporations engaged in the same general line of business might combine for their mutual advantage, in the direction of eliminating destructive competition, controlling the output of their commodity, and regulating and maintaining its price, but at the same time preserving their separate individual existence, and without any consolidation or merger. This device was the erection of a central committee or board, composed, perhaps, of the presidents or general managers of the different corporations, and the transfer to them of a majority of the stock in each of the corporations, to be held "in trust" for the several stockholders so assigning their holdings. These stockholders received in return "trust certificates" showing that they were entitled to receive the dividends on their assigned stock, though the voting power of it had passed to the trustees. This last feature enabled the trustees or committee to elect all the directors of all the corporations, and through them the officers, and thereby to exercise an absolutely controlling influence over the policy and operations of each constituent company, to the ends and with the purposes above mentioned. Though the "trust," in this sense, is now seldom if ever resorted to as a form of corporate organization, having given place to the "holding corporation" and other devices, the word became current in statute laws as well as popular speech, to designate almost any form of combination of a monopolistic character or tendency.

In a looser sense the term is applied to any combination of establishments in the same line of business for securing the same ends by holding the individual interests of each subservient to a common authority for the common interests of all.

A trust, as the term is used in the Restatement, when not qualified by the word "charitable," "resulting" or "constructive," is a fiduciary relationship with respect to property, subjecting the person by whom the title to the property is held to equitable duties to deal with the property for the benefit of another person, which arises as a result of a manifestation of an intention to create it. Restatement, Second, Trusts § 2.

See also Breach of trust; Charitable trust; Claflin trust; Common-law trust; Complex trust; Constructive trust; Declaration *(Declaration of trust)*; Deed *(Deed of trust)*; Equipment; Executory trust; Generation-skipping trust; Governmental trusts; Grantor trusts; Illusory trust; Indestructible trust; Investment trust; Involuntary trust; Land trust; Life insurance trust; Life interest; Nominal trust; Nominee trust; Oral trust; Pension trust; Precatory trust; Purchase money resulting trust; Reciprocal trusts; Resulting trust; Revocable trust; Spendthrift trust; Terms of trust; Unitrust; Voting trust.

Accumulation trust. Trust in which trustees are directed to accumulate income and gains from sales of trust assets for ultimate disposition when the trust is terminated. Many states have laws governing the time over which accumulations may be made. *See also* Accumulation trust.

Active trust. One which imposes upon the trustee the duty of taking active measures in the execution of the trust, as, where property is conveyed to trustees with directions to sell and distribute the proceeds among creditors of the grantor; distinguished from a "passive" or "dry" trust.

In a "passive trust" the legal and equitable titles are merged in the beneficiaries and beneficial use is converted into legal ownership, while in an "active trust" the title remains in trustee for purpose of the trust.

Alimony trust. Device used to secure obligation of husband to pay support or alimony for wife. Transfer by husband to trustee of property from which wife as beneficiary will be supported after divorce or separation.

Annuity trust. An annuity trust is a trust from which the trustee is required to pay a sum certain annually to one or more individual beneficiaries for their respective lives or for a term of years, and thereafter either transfer the remainder to or for the use of a qualified charity or retain the remainder for such a use. The sum certain must not be less than 5% of the initial fair market value of the property transferred to the trust by the donor. A qualified annuity trust must comply with the basic statutory requirements of I.R.C. § 664. *See also* Annuity trust.

Blind trust. Device used to give management of one's investments to an outside person over whom the beneficiary has no control. For example, to avoid the possibility of disqualification a judge could utilize a blind trust with respect to his or her investments.

Bond trust. A trust, the *res* of which consists in bonds which yield interest income.

Business trust. See Business; Massachusetts trust; Trust estates as business companies.

Bypass trust. Also known as a credit trust, credit shelter trust or exemption equivalent trust, it is an estate planning tool whereby a deceased spouse's estate passes to a trust rather than to the surviving spouse, thereby reducing the likelihood that the surviving spouse's subsequent estate will exceed the estate tax threshold. Typically, the surviving spouse is given a life estate in the trust.

Cestui que trust. The person for whose benefit a trust is created or who is to enjoy the income or the avails of it. *See* Beneficiary.

Charitable remainder trust. A trust which consists of assets which are paid over to the trust after the expiration of a life estate or intermediate estates and designated for charitable purposes. *See also* Charitable remainder annuity trust.

Charitable trusts. Trusts designed for the benefit of a class or the public generally. They are essentially different from private trusts in that the beneficiaries are uncertain. In general, such must be created for charitable, educational, religious or scientific purposes. *See Public trust, below.*

Clifford trust. Under this tax planning device, a transfer of income-producing property is made to a trust which provides that the income is either to be paid or accumulated for the benefit of a beneficiary other than the grantor for a period of more than ten years, at which time the trust is to terminate and the property reverts back to the grantor. This transfer is made at the cost of a gift tax and if the gift tax paid is less than the income tax which will be saved as the result of the shifting of the income from the high-bracket grantor to the low-bracket beneficiary, the technique has merit from a tax point of view. Helvering v. Clifford, 309 U.S. 331, 60 S.Ct. 554, 84 L.Ed. 788; I.R.C. §§ 671–678. The Tax Reform Act of 1986 changed the laws with respect to the Clifford Trust and for transfers made after March 1, 1986, the trust is subject to taxation at the grantor's rate, which effectively eliminates the benefits of the Clifford Trust.

Community trust. An agency organized for the permanent administration of funds placed in trust for public health, educational and charitable purposes.

Complete voluntary trust. One completely created, the subject-matter being designated, the trustee and beneficiary being named, and the limitations and trusts being fully and perfectly declared.

Complex trust. A complex trust is any trust other than a simple trust. One in which the trustees have discretion as to whether to distribute and discretion as to amounts distributed. Such trusts are governed for tax purposes by I.R.C. §§ 661–663.

Constructive trust. A trust raised by construction of law, or arising by operation of law, as distinguished from an express trust. Wherever the circumstances of a transaction are such that the person who takes the legal estate in property cannot also enjoy the beneficial interest without necessarily violating some established principle of equity, the court will immediately raise a *constructive trust,* and fasten it upon the conscience of the legal owner, so as to convert him into a trustee for the parties who in equity are entitled to the beneficial enjoyment.

Constructive trusts do not arise by agreement or from intention, but by operation of law, and fraud, active or constructive, is their essential element. Actual fraud is not necessary, but such a trust will arise whenever circumstances under which property was acquired made it inequitable that it should be retained by him who holds the legal title. Constructive trusts have been said to arise through the application of the doctrine of equitable estoppel, or under the broad doctrine that equity regards and treats as done what in good conscience ought to be done, and such trusts are also known as "trusts ex maleficio" or "ex delicto" or "involuntary trusts" and their forms and varieties are practically without limit, being raised by courts of equity whenever it becomes necessary to prevent a failure of justice. *See also Involuntary trust; Trust ex maleficio, below.*

Contingent trust. An express trust depending for its operation upon a future event.

Creation of trust. A trust may be created by: (a) a declaration by the owner of property that he holds it as trustee for another person; or (b) a transfer inter vivos by the owner of property to another person as trustee for the transferor or for a third person; or (c) a transfer by will by the owner of property to another person as trustee for a third person; or (d) an appointment by one person having a power of appointment to another person as trustee for the donee of the power or for a third person; or (e) a promise by one person to another person whose rights thereunder are to be held in trust for a third person. Restatement, Second, Trusts § 17.

Credit trust. See Bypass trust, above.

Declaration of trust. See Declaration.

Deed of trust. See Deed.

Directory trust. One which is not completely and finally settled by the instrument creating it, but only defined in its general purpose and to be carried into detail according to later specific directions.

Direct trust. An express trust, as distinguished from a constructive or implied trust. *See Express trust below.*

Discretionary trust. Trust in which trustees have discretion as to types of investment and also as to whether and when distributions may be made to beneficiaries. Trusts under which the trustee or another party has the right to accumulate (rather than pay out) the income for each year. Depending on the terms of the trust instrument, such income may be accumulated for future distributions to the income beneficiaries or added to corpus for the benefit of the remainderperson.

Dry trust. One which merely vests the legal title in the trustee, and does not require the performance of any active duty on his part to carry out the trust.

Educational trusts. Trusts for the founding, endowing, and supporting schools for the advancement of all useful branches of learning, which are not strictly private.

Equipment trust. Financing method commonly used by railroads in which the equipment's title is transferred to trustees as security for the financing.

Estate trust. An estate trust is a trust, for all or part of the income of which is to be accumulated during the surviving spouse's life and added to corpus, with the accumulated income and corpus being paid to the estate of the surviving spouse at death. This type of trust is commonly used to qualify property for the marital deduction.

Executed trust. A trust of which the scheme has in the outset been completely declared. A trust in which the estates and interest in the subject-matter of the trust are completely limited and defined by the instrument creating the trust, and require no further instruments to complete them.

Executory trust. One which requires the execution of some further instrument, or the doing of some further act, on the part of the creator of the trust or of the trustee, towards its complete creation or full effect.

Express active trust. Where will confers upon executor authority to generally manage property of estate and pay over net income to devisees or legatees, such authority creates an "express active trust".

Express private passive trust. Such exists where land is conveyed to or held by one person in trust for another, without any power being expressly or impliedly given trustee to take actual possession of land or exercise acts of ownership over it, except by beneficiary's direction.

Express trust. A direct trust. A trust created or declared in express terms, and usually in writing, as distinguished from one inferred by the law from the conduct or dealings of the parties. A trust directly created for specific purposes in contrast to a constructive or resulting trust which arises by implication of law or the demands of equity. Trusts which are created by the direct and positive acts of the parties, by some writing, or deed, or will, or by words expressly or impliedly evincing an intention to create a trust.

Fixed trust. A non-discretionary trust in which the trustee may not exercise his own judgment.

Foreign situs trust. A trust which owes its existence to foreign law. It is treated for tax purposes as a non-resident alien individual.

Foreign trust. A trust created and administered under foreign law.

Grantor trust. A trust in which the grantor transfers or conveys property in trust for his own benefit alone or for himself and another.

Honorary trust. Trust for specific non-charitable purposes where there is no definite ascertainable beneficiary and hence unenforceable in the absence of statute.

Illusory trust. A trust arrangement which takes the form of a trust, but because of powers retained in the settlor has no real substance and in reality is not a completed trust.

Imperfect trust. An executory trust *(q.v.); see also Executed trust, above.*

Implied trust. A trust raised or created by implication of law; a trust implied or presumed from circumstances. Constructive and resulting trusts are implied trusts because they arise by implication of law or by demands of equity. Such arise by operation of law when the circumstances of a transaction are such that the court finds it inequitable for the legal owner to enjoy the beneficial interest.

Indestructible trust. A trust which may not be terminated or revoked. *See* Claflin trust.

Instrumental trust. See Ministerial trusts, below.

Insurance trust. A trust, the res of which consists of insurance policies or their proceeds. *See also* Insurance.

Inter vivos trust. Trust created by an instrument which becomes operative during the settlor's lifetime as contrasted with a testamentary trust which takes effect on the death of the settlor. A *Living trust (q.v.).*

Involuntary trust. Involuntary or "constructive" trusts embrace all those instances in which a trust is raised by the doctrines of equity, for the purpose of working out justice in the most efficient manner, when there is no intention of the parties to create a trust relation. This class of trusts may usually be referred to fraud, either actual or constructive, as an essential element.

Irrevocable trust. Trust which may not be revoked after its creation as in the case of a deposit of money by one in the name of another as trustee for the benefit of a third person (beneficiary).

Land trust. See Land trust.

Limited trust. Trust created for a limited period of time in contrast to a perpetual trust.

Liquidation trust. Trust created for purpose of terminating a business or other undertaking and for distributing the *res.*

Living trust. An inter vivos trust created and operative during the lifetime of the settlor and commonly for benefit or support of another person.

Marital deduction trust. A testamentary trust created to take full advantage of the marital deduction *(q.v.)* provisions of the Int.Rev.Code.

Massachusetts or business trusts. See Business; Massachusetts trust; Trust estates as business companies.

Ministerial trusts. (Also called "instrumental trusts.") Those which demand no further exercise of reason or understanding than every intelligent agent must necessarily employ; as to convey an estate. They are a species of special trusts, distinguished from discretionary trusts, which necessarily require much exercise of the understanding.

Mixed trust. Trusts established to benefit both private individuals and charities.

Naked trust. A dry or passive trust; one which requires no action on the part of the trustee, beyond turning over money or property to the *cestui que trust.*

Nominee trust. An arrangement for holding title to real property under which one or more persons or corporations, pursuant to a written declaration of trust, declare that they will hold any property that they acquire as trustees for the benefit of one or more undisclosed beneficiaries.

Non-discretionary trust. A fixed trust under which the trustees may exercise no judgment or discretion at least as to distributions.

Oral trust. See Oral trust.

Passive trust. A trust as to which the trustee has no active duty to perform. "Passive trust," which equity court may terminate before it ends by its terms, is one in which the trustee does not have responsibilities or discretionary duties to perform.

Perpetual trust. A trust which is to continue as long as the need for it continues as for the lifetime of a beneficiary or the term of a particular charity.

Personal trust. Trusts created by and for individuals and their families in contrast to business or charitable trusts.

Pour-over trust. A provision in a will in which the testator leaves the residue of his estate to a trustee of a living trust for purpose of that pour-over trust.

Power of appointment trust. Type of trust used to qualify property for the marital deduction. Property is left in trust for a surviving spouse. The trustee is required to distribute income to the spouse for life and the spouse is given an unqualified power to appoint the property to herself or to her estate.

Precatory trust. Where words employed in a will or other instrument do not amount to a positive command or to a distinct testamentary disposition, but are terms of entreaty, request, recommendation, or expectation, they are termed "precatory words," and from such words the law will raise a trust, called a "precatory trust," to carry out the wishes of the testator or grantor.

Private trust. One established or created for the benefit of a certain designated individual or individuals, or a known person or class of persons, clearly identified or capable of identification by the terms of the instrument creating the trust, as distinguished from trusts for public institutions or charitable uses.

Public trust. One constituted for the benefit either of the public at large or of some considerable portion of it answering a particular description; public trusts and charitable trusts may be considered in general as synonymous expressions. *See also Charitable trusts, above.*

Q–TIP trust. See that title.

Real estate investment trust (REIT). Type of tax shelter wherein investors purchase certificates of ownership in trust which invests such funds in real estate and then distributes profits to investors.

Reciprocal trust. Trust which one person creates for the benefit of another who in turn creates a trust for the benefit of the first party.

Resulting trust. One that arises by implication of law, or by the operation and construction of equity, and which is established as consonant to the presumed intention of the parties as gathered from the nature of the transaction. It arises where the legal estate in property is disposed of, conveyed, or transferred, but the intent appears or is inferred from the terms of the disposition, or from the accompanying facts and circumstances, that the beneficial interest is not to go or be enjoyed with the legal title.

Revocable trust. A trust in which the settlor reserves the right to revoke.

Savings bank trust. A Totten trust *(q.v.).*

Secret trusts. Where a testator gives property to a person, on a verbal promise by the legatee or devisee that he will hold it in trust for another person.

Shifting trust. An express trust which is so settled that it may operate in favor of beneficiaries additional to, or substituted for, those first named, upon specified contingencies.

Short term trust. Trust which by its terms is to be administered for a short period of time and then terminated.

Simple trust. A simple trust corresponds with the ancient use, and arises where property is simply vested in one person for the use of another, and the nature of the trust, not being qualified by the settlor, is left to the construction of law. A simple trust is a trust which provides that all of its income is required to be distributed currently, even if it is not in fact distributed, does not provide that any amounts are to be paid, permanently set aside, or used for charitable purposes; and does not distribute any amount other than current income.

Simple trusts are those that are not complex trusts. Such trusts may not have a charitable beneficiary, accumulate income, nor distribute corpus.

Special trust. One in which a trustee is interposed for the execution of some purpose particularly pointed out, and is not, as in case of a simple trust, a mere passive depositary of the estate, but is required to exert himself actively in the execution of the settlor's intention; as, where a conveyance is made to trustees upon trust to reconvey, or to sell for the payment of debts.

Special trusts have been divided into (1) ministerial (or instrumental) and (2) discretionary. The former, such as demand no further exercise of reason or understanding than every intelligent agent must necessarily employ; the latter, such as cannot be duly administered without the application of a certain degree of prudence and judgment.

Spendthrift trust. See Spendthrift trust.

Split-interest trust. Type of charitable trust commonly consisting of a life estate to an individual and a remainder to a charity. The Tax Reform Act of 1969 has placed restrictions on this type of trust.

Sprinkling trust. When a trustee has the discretion to either distribute or accumulate the entity accounting income of the trust and to distribute it among the trust's income beneficiaries in varying magnitudes, a sprinkling trust exists. The trustee can "sprinkle" the income of the trust.

Support trust. A trust in which the trustee has the power to pay the beneficiary only so much of the trust income as is necessary for the beneficiary's support, education and maintenance. *See also Spendthrift trust, above.*

Tentative trust. See Totten trust, below.

Testamentary trust. Trust created within a will and executed with the formalities required of a will in contrast to an inter vivos trust which is created by the grantor during his lifetime. A trust which does not take effect until the death of the settlor. Nearly all states have adopted the Uniform Testamentary Additions to Trust Act.

Totten trust. Device used to pass property in bank account after depositor's death to designated person through vehicle of trust rather than through process of probate. It is a tentative trust revocable at will until the depositor dies or completes the gift in his lifetime by some unequivocal act or declaration such as delivery of the passbook or notice to the beneficiary. If the depositor dies

before the beneficiary without revocation or some decisive act or declaration of disaffirmance the presumption arises that an absolute trust was created as to the balance on hand at the death of the depositor.

Transgressive trust. A name sometimes applied to a trust which transgresses or violates the rule against perpetuities.

Trust allotments. Allotments to Indians, in which a certificate or trust patent is issued declaring that the United States will hold the land for a designated period in trust for the allottee.

Trust certificate. An obligation issued to finance railroad equipment and by which title to the equipment is held by trustees as security for repayment of the money invested.

Trust company. A corporation formed for the purpose of taking, executing, and administering all such trusts as may be lawfully committed to it, and acting as testamentary trustee, executor, guardian, etc. To these functions are sometimes (but not necessarily) added the business of acting as fiscal agent for corporations, attending to the registration and transfer of their stock and bonds, serving as trustee for their bond or mortgage creditors, engaging in fiduciary investment and estate planning functions, and transacting a general banking and loan business. A bank which is authorized to serve in fiduciary capacity as executor, administrator, etc. Such companies are commonly associated or combined with commercial banks.

Trust deed. The document by which one creates a trust. An indenture by which property is transferred to a trust. May also include a deed from the trustees. In some states, a mortgage deed.

A species of mortgage given to a trustee for the purpose of securing a numerous class of creditors, as the bondholders of a railroad corporation, with power to foreclose and sell on failure of the payment of their bonds, notes, or other claims. In some of the states, a trust deed or deed of trust is a security resembling a mortgage, being a conveyance of lands to trustees to secure the payment of a debt, with a power of sale upon default, and upon a trustee to apply the net proceeds to paying the debt and to turn over the surplus to the grantor.

A trust deed on real estate as security for a bond issue is, in effect, a mortgage on property executed by the mortgagor to a third person as trustee to hold as security for the mortgage debt as evidenced by the bonds, for the benefit of the purchasers of the bonds as lenders.

See also Deed *(Deed of trust)*; Mortgage.

Trust deposit. Where money or property is deposited to be kept intact and not commingled with other funds or property of bank and is to be returned in kind to depositor or devoted to particular purpose or requirement of depositor or payment of particular debts or obligations of depositor. Also called *special deposit*. *See also* Deposit.

Trust estate. This term may mean either the estate of the trustee,—that is, the legal title,—or the estate of the beneficiary, or the corpus of the property which is the subject of the trust.

Trust ex delicto. See Trust ex maleficio, below.

Trust ex maleficio. Where actual fraud is practiced in acquiring legal title, the arising trust is referred to as a "trust ex maleficio."

A "constructive trust," otherwise known as "trust ex maleficio," a "trust ex delicto," a "trust de son tort," an "involuntary trust" or an "implied trust" is a trust by operation of law which arises against one who, by fraud, actual or constructive, by duress or abuse of confidence, by commission of a wrong or by any form of unconscionable conduct, artifice, concealment or questionable means and against good conscience, either has obtained or holds right to property which he ought not in equity and good conscience hold and enjoy. *See also Constructive trust, above.*

Trust fund. A fund held by a trustee for the specific purposes of the trust; in a more general sense, a fund which, legally or equitably, is subject to be devoted to a particular purpose and cannot or should not be diverted therefrom. In this sense it is often said that the assets of a corporation are a "trust fund" for the payment of its debts. *See also* Trust fund.

Trust fund doctrine. In substance, where corporation transfers all its assets with a view to going out of business and nothing is left with which to pay debts, transferee is charged with notice of the circumstances of the transaction, and takes the assets subject to an equitable lien for the unpaid debts of the transferring company; the property of a corporation being a fund subject to be first applied to the payment of debts.

Under such doctrine, if insolvent corporation's assets are distributed among its stockholders before its debts are paid, each stockholder is liable to creditors for full amount received by him.

See Common trust fund; Trust fund; Trust fund theory or doctrine.

Trust in invitum. A constructive trust imposed by equity, contrary to the trustee's intention and will, upon property in his hands.

Trust legacy. See Legacy.

Trust receipt. See Trust receipt.

Unitrust. A unitrust is a trust from which the trustee is required, at least annually, to pay a fixed percentage which is not less than five percent of the net fair market value of the trust assets, valued annually, to one or more beneficiaries, at least one of which is not a charity, for life or for a term of years, with an irrevocable remainder interest to be held for the benefit of, or paid over to, charity. A qualified unitrust must comply with the basic statutory requirements of I.R.C. § 664.

Vertical trust. In antitrust law, a combination which gathers together under a single ownership a number of businesses or plants engaged in successive stages of production or marketing.

Voluntary trust. An obligation arising out of a personal confidence reposed in, and voluntarily accepted by, one for the benefit of another, as distinguished from an "involuntary" trust, which is created by operation of law. According to another use of the term, "voluntary" trusts are such as are made in favor of a volunteer, that is, a person who gives nothing in exchange for the trust, but receives it as a pure gift; and in this use the term is distinguished from "trusts for value," the latter being such as are in favor of purchasers, mortgagees, etc. A "voluntary trust" is an equitable gift, and in order to be enforceable by the beneficiaries must be complete. The difference between a "gift inter vivos" and a "voluntary trust" is that, in a gift, the thing itself with title passes to the donee, while, in a voluntary trust, the actual title passes to a cestui que trust while the legal title is retained by the settlor, to be held by him for the purposes of the trust or is by the settlor transferred to another to hold for the purposes of the trust.

Voting trust. A trust which holds the voting rights to stock in a corporation. It is a useful device when a majority of the shareholders in a corporation cannot agree on corporate policy. *See also* Voting trust.

Trustee. Person holding property in trust. Restatement, Second, Trusts, § 3(3). The person appointed, or required by law, to execute a trust. One in whom an estate, interest, or power is vested, under an express or implied agreement to administer or exercise it for the benefit or to the use of another. One who holds legal title to property "in trust" for the benefit of another person (beneficiary) and who must carry out specific duties with regard to the property. The trustee owes a fiduciary duty to the beneficiary.

See also Bare trustee.

Bankruptcy trustee. See Bankruptcy proceedings *(Bankruptcy trustee).*

Bond offering. The bondholders' representative in a public debt offering. The trustee is responsible for monitoring the borrower's compliance with the terms of the indenture.

Joint trustees. Two or more persons who are intrusted with property for the benefit of one or more others.

Judicial trustee. One appointed by a decree of court to execute a trust, as distinguished from one appointed by the instrument creating the trust.

Testamentary trustee. A trustee appointed by or acting under a will; one appointed to carry out a trust created by a will. The term does not ordinarily include an executor or an administrator with the will annexed, or a guardian, except when they act in the execution of a trust created by the will and which is separable from their functions as executors, etc.

Trustee ad litem. Trustee appointed by a court in contrast to a trustee selected by a settlor or executor.

Trustee de son tort. Person who is treated as a trustee because of his wrongdoing with respect to property entrusted to him or over which he exercised authority which he lacked.

Trustee ex maleficio. A person who, being guilty of wrongful or fraudulent conduct, is held by equity to the duty and liability of a trustee, in relation to the subject-matter, to prevent him from profiting by his own wrong. *See* Trust *(Trust ex maleficio).*

Trustee in bankruptcy. A person in whom the property of a debtor is vested in trust for the creditors. See Bankruptcy Code, § 321 *et seq.;* 28 U.S.C.A. § 581 *et seq.*

Trustee process. The name given, in certain New England states, to the process of garnishment or foreign attachment. *See* Garnishment; Process.

Unit investment trust. A trust established whereby funds are pooled and invested in income-producing securities such as bonds, preferred stock, etc. Units of the trust are sold to investors who maintain an interest in the trust in proportion to their investment.

Trusteeship. Fiduciary relationship between trustee and beneficiary wherein trustee holds title to property for the benefit of the beneficiary.

Trust estates as business companies. A practice originating in Massachusetts of vesting a business or certain real estate in a group of trustees, who manage it for the benefit of the beneficial owners; the ownership of the latter is evidenced by negotiable (or transferable) shares. *See also* Massachusetts trust.

Trust fund. Money or property set aside as a trust for the benefit of another and held by a trustee. The majority of states have adopted the Uniform Common Trust Fund Act. *See also* Common trust fund; Trust *(Trust fund; Trust fund doctrine);* Trust fund theory or doctrine.

Trust fund theory or doctrine. Generic term used in many contexts to describe the imposition of fiduciary obligations on persons who control money or property of another under certain circumstances. A creature of equity which operates to treat officers, directors, or majority shareholders of a corporation as holding in trust for the benefit of creditors such corporate assets as have been improperly appropriated. *See also* Common trust fund; Trust *(Trust fund; Trust fund doctrine).*

Trust indenture. The document which contains the terms and conditions which govern the conduct of the trustee and the rights of the beneficiaries. Commonly used when a corporation floats bonds. *See* Indenture.

Trust Indenture Act. Federal Act (1939) designed to protect investors in certain types of bonds by requiring that the trust indenture be approved by the SEC and include certain protective clauses and exclude certain exculpatory clauses, and that trustees be independent of the issuing company. 15 U.S.C.A. § 77aaa et seq. *See also* Indenture.

Trust instrument. The formal document which creates the trust and contains the powers of the trustees and the rights of the beneficiaries. It may be a deed in trust or a formal declaration of trust. *See also* Trust *(Trust deed).*

Trust officer. The official or officer in a trust company who has direct charge of funds administered by it in its capacity as trustee.

Trustor. One who creates a trust. Also called settlor.

Trust property. The property which is the subject matter of the trust. The trust *res (q.v.). See also* Principal.

Trust receipt. A pre-U.C.C. security device now governed by Article 9 of the Code. A receipt stating that the wholesale buyer has possession of the goods for the benefit of the financier. Today there usually must be a security agreement coupled with the filing of a financing statement. Method of financing commercial transactions by means of which title passes directly from manufacturer or seller to banker or lender who as owner delivers goods to dealer in whose behalf he is acting secondarily, and to whom title goes ultimately when primary right of banker or lender has been satisfied.

Trust res. The property of which the trust consists. It may be real or personal and the trustee has legal title. *See also* Principal.

Trust territory. A territory or colony placed under the administration of a country by the United Nations.

Trusty. A prisoner who, because of good conduct, is given some measure of freedom in and around the prison.

Truth. There are three conceptions as to what constitutes "truth": agreement of thought and reality; eventual verification; and consistency of thought with itself. For "Fact" and "truth" distinguished, *see* Fact.

Truth-in-Lending Act. The purpose of the Truth-in-Lending Act (15 U.S.C.A. § 1601 et seq.) is to assure that every customer who has need for consumer credit is given meaningful information with respect to the cost of that credit. In most cases the credit cost must be expressed in the dollar amount of finance charges, and as an annual percentage rate computed on the unpaid balance of the amount financed. Other relevant credit information must also be disclosed so that the customer may compare the various credit terms available to him from different sources and avoid the uninformed use of credit. The Act further provides a customer the right, in certain circumstances, to cancel a credit transaction which involves a lien on his residence. The intent of the Act is to promote the informed use of consumer credit. The requirements of the Act are implemented by Regulation Z of the Federal Reserve Board, 12 CFR pt. 226. Many states have their own Truth-in-Lending Acts, *e.g.*, Mass.G.L. ch. 140D. *See also* Consumer Credit Protection Act; Regulation Z; Uniform Consumer Credit Code.

Try. To examine judicially. To examine and investigate a controversy, by the legal method called "trial," for the purpose of determining the issues it involves.

TSCA. Toxic Substances Control Act. 42 U.S.C.A. § 2601 *et seq.*

Tucker Act. The Tucker Act, which was passed in 1887, was a response by Congress to the inadequacies of the original Court of Claims legislation. By this act, the jurisdiction of the court was extended to include claims founded upon the Constitution, act of Congress, or executive department regulation, as well as claims for liquidated or unliquidated damages in cases not sounding in tort, in addition to all claims within the scope of the earlier statutes. The present provisions of the Tucker Act are embodied in 28 U.S.C.A. §§ 1346(a)(2), 1491. *See also* Claims Court, U.S.; Court of Claims.

Turncoat witness. A witness whose testimony was expected to be favorable but who turns around and becomes an adverse witness. *See also* Adverse witness.

Turning State's evidence. *See* State's evidence.

Turn-key contract. Project in which all owner need do is "turn the key" in the lock to open the building with nothing remaining to be done and all risks to be assumed by contractor. Term used in building trade to designate those contracts in which builder agrees to complete work of building and installation to point of readiness for occupancy. It ordinarily means that builder will complete work to certain specified point, such as

building a complete house ready for occupancy as a dwelling, and that builder agrees to assume all risk.

In oil drilling industry a job wherein driller of oil well undertakes to furnish everything and does all work required to complete well, place it on production, and turn it over ready to turn the key and start oil running into tanks. A turn-key contract to drill a well involves the testing of the formation contemplated by the parties and completion of a producing well or its abandonment as a dry hole, all done for an agreed-upon total consideration, putting the risk of rising costs, well trouble, weather, and the like upon the driller, but it does not, in the absence of a clear expression, require the driller to guarantee a producing well.

Turntable doctrine. Also termed "attractive nuisance" doctrine. This doctrine requires the owner of premises not to attract or lure children into unsuspected danger or great bodily harm, by keeping thereon attractive machinery or dangerous instrumentalities in an exposed and unguarded condition, and where injuries have been received by a child so enticed the entry is not regarded as unlawful, and does not necessarily preclude a recovery of damages; the attractiveness of the machine or structure amounting to an implied invitation to enter. It imposes a liability on a property owner for injuries to a child of tender years, resulting from something on his premises that can be operated by such a child and made dangerous by him, and which is attractive to him and calculated to induce him to use it, where he fails to protect the thing so that a child of tender years cannot be hurt by it.

The dangerous and alluring qualities of a railroad turntable gave the "attractive nuisance rule" the name of "Turntable Doctrine."

See also Attractive nuisance doctrine.

Turpitude /tɜ́rpət(y)ùwd/. In its ordinary sense, inherent baseness or vileness of principle or action; shameful wickedness; depravity. In its legal sense, everything done contrary to justice, honesty, modesty, or good morals. An action showing gross depravity.

Moral turpitude. A term of frequent occurrence in statutes, especially those providing that a witness' conviction of a crime involving moral turpitude may be shown as tending to impeach his credibility. In general, it means neither more nor less than "turpitude," *i.e.*, anything done contrary to justice, honesty, modesty, or good morals. It is also commonly defined as an act of baseness, vileness, or depravity in the private and social duties which a man owes to his fellow man or to society in general, contrary to the accepted and customary rule of right and duty between man and man. Although a vague term, it implies something immoral in itself, regardless of its being punishable by law. Thus excluding unintentional wrong, or an improper act done without unlawful or improper intent. It is also said to be restricted to the gravest offenses, consisting of felonies, infamous crimes, and those that are *malum in se* and disclose a depraved mind. *See also* Moral turpitude.

Tutelage /t(y)úwtələj/. Guardianship; state of being under a guardian.

Tutorship. The office and power of a tutor. The power which an individual, *sui juris,* has to take care of the person of one who is unable to take care of himself. There are four sorts of tutorships: Tutorship by nature; tutorship by will; tutorship by the effect of the law; tutorship by the appointment of the judge. Civ.Code La. art. 247.

T.V.A. Tennessee Valley Authority.

Twelfth Amendment. Amendment to the U.S. Constitution (1804) which altered the method of voting in presidential elections by requiring each elector to vote for President and Vice President on separate ballots instead of voting for two persons for President on single ballot as before.

Twentieth Amendment. The so-called lame duck Amendment to the U.S. Constitution (1933) which changed the beginning of Presidential and Vice-Presidential terms from March 4 to January 20, and of Congressional terms from March 4 to January 3, thereby eliminating the short session of Congress which had formerly convened early in December in even-numbered years, and in which a number of Congressmen sat who had not been re-elected to office. The Amendment also provides for Presidential succession under certain circumstances.

Twenty-Fifth Amendment. Amendment to U.S. Constitution (1967) which provides for filling vacancy in offices of President and Vice-President on the death, removal, or resignation of the office holders.

Twenty-First Amendment. Amendment to the Constitution (1933) which repealed Prohibition Amendment (18th) but prohibited the importation of intoxicating beverages into any State where delivery or use of such beverages violated the State's laws.

Twenty-Fourth Amendment. Amendment to the Constitution (1964) which prohibits federal or State denial of right to vote in any primary or other election for federal elective officers because of the prospective voter's failure to pay any poll tax or other tax. *See* Poll-tax.

Twenty-Second Amendment. Amendment to the Constitution (1951) which prevents any person from being elected President more than twice, or, if he has succeeded to the Presidency before the midpoint of his predecessor's term, from being elected more than once.

Twenty-Sixth Amendment. Amendment to U.S. Constitution (1971) which established voting age at 18.

Twenty-Third Amendment. Amendment to the Constitution (1961) which allots to the District of Columbia presidential electors, to be appointed as Congress directs, equal in number to those of a State of equivalent population but never more than the number of electors allotted to the least populous State.

Twice in jeopardy. *See* Jeopardy; Once in jeopardy.

Two issue rule. Under this rule, whenever multiple issues are submitted to a jury for resolution in a general verdict and one of them is free from prejudicial error, it will be presumed that all issues were decided in favor of prevailing party and a judgment will be affirmed. This rule is also a short-cut way of stating that in perjury trial, evidence must consist of something more convincing than one man's word against another's.

Two witness rule. This rule requires that falsity element of a perjury conviction be supported either by direct testimony of two witnesses or by direct testimony of one witness plus independent corroborating evidence. *See also* Treason.

Tying. A term which, as used in a contract of lease of patented machinery means that the lessee has secured only limited rights of use, and that if he exceeds such limited rights by agreeing not to use the machines of others he may lose his lease. *See also* Tying arrangement.

Tying arrangement. A condition imposed by a seller or lessor that a buyer or lessee may obtain a desired product (the "tying" product) only if it also agrees to take an additional product (the "tied" product), which may or may not be desired. Some tying arrangements violate either § 3 of the Clayton Act or § 1 of the Sherman Act. *See also* Reciprocal dealing arrangement; Tied product.

Tyranny /tíhrəniy/. Arbitrary or despotic government; the severe and autocratic exercise of sovereign power, either vested constitutionally in one ruler, or usurped by him by breaking down the division and distribution of governmental powers.

U

U.C.C. *See* Uniform Commercial Code.

U.C.C.C. *See* Uniform Consumer Credit Code.

U.C.C.J.A. Uniform Child Custody Jurisdiction Act. *See* Custody of children.

U.C.M.J. Uniform Code of Military Justice; consisting of rules of conduct and criminal behavior for members of the Armed Forces. *See* Code of Military Justice.

UCP. *See* Uniform Customs and Practice for Commercial Documentary Credits.

U.C.R. Uniform Crime Reports as compiled by the Federal Bureau of Investigation.

UDITPA. The Uniform Division of Income for Tax Purposes Act has been adopted in some form by many of the states. The Act develops criteria by which the total taxable income of a multistate corporation can be assigned to specific states. *See* Unitary business; Tax *(Unitary tax)*.

UFCA. Uniform Fraudulent Conveyance Act, which many states have adopted. *See* Fraudulent conveyance.

UFTA. Uniform Fraudulent Transfer Act (1984), which is the successor to the UFCA.

ULA. *See* Uniform Laws *or* Acts.

Ultimate facts. Issuable facts; facts essential to the right of action or matter of defense. Facts necessary and essential for decision by court. Facts which are necessary to determine issues in case, as distinguished from evidentiary facts supporting them. The logical conclusions deduced from certain primary evidentiary facts. Final facts required to establish plaintiff's cause of action or defendant's defense.

One that is essential to the right of action or matter of defense, and the trial court is under the duty of submitting only ultimate or controlling issues.

Ultimate issue. That question which must finally be answered as, for example, the defendant's negligence is the ultimate issue in a personal injury action. *See also* Ultimate facts.

Ultra vires /ə́ltrə váyriyz/. An act performed without any authority to act on subject. Acts beyond the scope of the powers of a corporation, as defined by its charter or laws of state of incorporation. The term has a broad application and includes not only acts prohibited by the charter, but acts which are in excess of powers granted and not prohibited, and generally applied either when a corporation has no power whatever to do an act, or when the corporation has the power but exercises it irregularly. Act is ultra vires when corporation is without authority to perform it under any circumstances or for any purpose. By doctrine of ultra vires a contract made by a corporation beyond the scope of its corporate powers is unlawful. Ultra vires act of municipality is one which is beyond powers conferred upon it by law.

Umbrella policy. *See* Insurance.

Umpire /ə́mpay(ə)r/. Third party selected to arbitrate labor dispute. One clothed with authority to act alone in rendering a decision where arbitrators have disagreed. When matters in dispute are submitted to two or more arbitrators, and they do not agree in their decision, it is usual for another person to be called in as "umpire," to whose sole judgment it is then referred. An umpire, strictly speaking, makes his award independently of that of the arbitrators. *See also* Arbitrator; Mediator.

Un-. A prefix used indiscriminately, and may mean simply "not." Thus, "unlawful" means "not authorized by law."

Unaccrued /ənəkrúwd/. Not become due, as rent on a lease.

Unadjusted /ənəjə́stəd/. Uncertain; not agreed upon.

Unalienable /ənéyl(i)yənəbəl/. Inalienable; incapable of being aliened, that is, sold and transferred.

Inalienable rights. Rights which can never be abridged because they are so fundamental.

Unambiguous /ənæmbígyuwəs/. Susceptible of but one meaning. A contract provision is "unambiguous" if its meaning is so clear as to preclude doubt by a reasonable person.

Unanimity /yùwnənímətiy/. Agreement of all the persons concerned, in holding one and the same opinion or determination of any matter or question; as the concurrence of a jury in deciding upon their verdict or of judges in concurring in their decision. *See* Unanimous.

Unanimous /yənǽnəməs/. To say that a proposition was adopted by a "unanimous" vote does not always mean that every one present voted for the proposition, but it may, and generally does, mean, when a *viva voce* vote is taken, that no one voted in the negative. *See also* Unanimity.

Unauthorized. That which is done without authority, as a signature or indorsement made without actual, implied or apparent authority and this includes a forgery. U.C.C. § 1–201(43).

Unauthorized use. The criminal offense of use of a motor vehicle without authority of the owner, knowing that such use is without his permission. It differs from larceny to the extent that in the crime of unauthorized use, the government need not prove the intent to deprive permanently the owner of the vehicle. *See* Joyriding.

Unavailability. In law of evidence, on a showing that a witness or his testimony is not available, prior reported testimony of that witness which can be faithfully reproduced is admissible as an exception to the hearsay rule. A witness is unavailable if he is dead, insane or beyond reach of a summons. Unavailability as a witness also includes situations in which the declarant is exempted by ruling of the court on the ground of privilege from testifying concerning the subject matter of the declarant's statement. See Fed. Evid.R. 804.

Unavailability as defined in rule providing for admission of prior testimony, requires, among other things, either that the witness be beyond the jurisdiction of the court's process to compel his appearance, or that the proponent of the prior statement be unable, despite due diligence, to obtain the attendance of the witness.

Unavoidable. Not avoidable, incapable of being shunned or prevented, inevitable, and necessary.

Unavoidable accident. An inevitable accident; one which could not have been prevented by exercise of due care by both parties under circumstances prevailing. Not necessarily an accident which was physically impossible, in the nature of things for the person to have prevented, but one not occasioned in any degree, either remotely or directly, by the want of such care or skill as the law holds every person bound to exercise. Such type accident is present when an event occurs which was not proximately caused by the negligence of any party to the event. *See also* Accident; Act of God.

Unavoidable casualty. An event or accident which human prudence, foresight, and sagacity cannot prevent, happening against will and without negligence. Within the meaning of statutes in several states relating to the vacation of judgments, means some casualty or misfortune growing out of conditions or circumstances that prevented the party or his attorney from doing something that, except therefor, would have been done, and does not include mistakes or errors of judgment growing out of misconstruction or understanding of the law, or the failure of parties or counsel through mistake to avail themselves of remedies, which if resorted to would have pre-

vented the casualty or misfortune. If by any care, prudence, or foresight a thing could have been guarded against, it is not unavoidable. The term is not ordinarily limited to an act of God. *See also* Accident; Act of God; Unavoidable accident.

Unavoidable cause. A cause which reasonably prudent and careful men under like circumstances do not and would not ordinarily anticipate, and whose effects, under similar circumstances, they do not and would not ordinarily avoid. *See also* Unavoidable accident.

Unborn beneficiaries. Those persons named in a general way as sharing in an estate or gift though not yet born. Commonly, a court appoints a guardian ad litem to protect and to represent their interests.

Unborn child. The individual human life in existence and developing prior to birth.

A child not yet born at the happening of an event. A child not born at the time of an injury to his mother which causes the child to suffer an injury may recover in most jurisdictions after birth if the child were viable in his mother's womb at the time of the defendant's wrongdoing. In the majority of states, injuries sustained by a viable, unborn child which cause the child's death may form the basis of a wrongful death action brought by the estate of the stillborn child.

See also Child; Viable child; Wrongful death statutes.

Unbroken. Continuous, as in requisite for adverse possession.

Uncertainty. The state or quality of being unknown or vague. Such vagueness, obscurity, or confusion in any written instrument, *e.g.,* a will, as to render it unintelligible to those who are called upon to execute or interpret it, so that no definite meaning can be extracted from it. *See also* Ambiguity.

Unclean hands doctrine. Doctrine simply means that in equity, as in law, plaintiff's fault, like defendant's, may be relevant to question of what, if any, remedy plaintiff is entitled to. Principle that one who has unclean hands is not entitled to relief in equity. Doctrine means no more than that one who has defrauded his adversary in the subject matter of the action will not be heard to assert right in equity. Under this doctrine, a court of equity may deny relief to a party whose conduct has been inequitable, unfair, and deceitful, but doctrine applies only when the reprehensible conduct complained of pertains to the controversy at issue.

Uncollected funds. A credit, such as an increase in the balance of a checking or other deposit account in a bank, that is given on the basis of a check or other right to payment that has not been paid by the drawee or other payor.

Unconditional. Not limited or affected by any condition; applied especially to the quality of an insured's estate in the property insured. *See* Owner *(Sole and unconditional owner).*

Unconditional discharge. One whose term of confinement has expired is unconditionally discharged if there are attached no parole provisions to his release.

A release from liability without any terms or delimiting conditions attached.

Unconscionability. A doctrine under which courts may deny enforcement of unfair or oppressive contracts because of procedural abuses arising out of the contract formation, or because of substantive abuses relating to terms of the contract, such as terms which violate reasonable expectations of parties or which involve gross disparities in price; either abuse can be the basis for a finding of unconscionability.

Basic test of "unconscionability" of contract is whether under circumstances existing at time of making of contract and in light of general commercial background and commercial needs of particular trade or case, clauses involved are so one-sided as to oppress or unfairly surprise party. Unconscionability is generally recognized to include an absence of meaningful choice on the part of one of the parties, to a contract together with contract terms which are unreasonably favorable to the other party.

Typically the cases in which unconscionability is found involve gross overall one-sidedness or gross one-sidedness of a term disclaiming a warranty, limiting damages, or granting procedural advantages. In these cases one-sidedness is often coupled with the fact that the imbalance is buried in small print and often couched in language unintelligible to even a person of moderate education. Often the seller deals with a particularly susceptible clientele.

Uniform Commercial Code. (1) If the court as a matter of law finds the contract or any clause of the contract to have been unconscionable at the time it was made the court may refuse to enforce the contract, or it may enforce the remainder of the contract without the unconscionable clause, or it may so limit the application of any unconscionable clause as to avoid any unconscionable result. (2) When it is claimed or appears to the court that the contract or any clause thereof may be unconscionable the parties shall be afforded a reasonable opportunity to present evidence as to its commercial setting, purpose and effect to aid the court in making the determination. U.C.C. § 2–302.

Section 2–302 should be considered in conjunction with the obligation of good faith imposed at several places in the Code. See *e.g.* U.C.C. § 1–203.

Restatement of Contracts. If a contract or term thereof is unconscionable at the time the contract is made a court may refuse to enforce the contract, or may enforce the remainder of the contract without the unconscionable term, or may so limit the application of any unconscionable term as to avoid any unconscionable result. Restatement, Second, Contracts, § 208.

Unconscionable bargain *or* **contract.** A contract, or a clause in a contract, that is so grossly unfair to one of the parties because of stronger bargaining powers of the other party; usually held to be void as against public policy. One which no man in his senses, not under delusion, would make, on the one hand, and which no fair and honest man would accept, on the other. *See also* Unconscionability.

Unconscious. Not possessed of mind. A state of mind of persons of sound mind suffering from some voluntary or involuntary agency rendering them unaware of their acts. Insensible to the reception of any stimuli and incapable of performing or experiencing any controlled functions.

As a criminal defense, one who engages in what would otherwise be criminal conduct is not guilty of a crime if he does so in a state of unconsciousness. See *e.g.* Calif. Penal Code § 26(4). *See also* Automatism.

Unconstitutional. That which is contrary to or in conflict with a constitution. The opposite of "constitutional." (*q.v.*)

This word is used in two different senses. One, which may be called the English sense, is that the legislation conflicts with some recognized general principle. This is no more than to say that it is unwise, or is based upon a wrong or unsound principle, or conflicts with a generally accepted policy. The other, which may be called the American sense, is that the legislation conflicts with some provision of our written Constitution, which it is beyond the power of a legislative body to change.

See also Unlawful.

Uncontestable clause. Provision in a life insurance policy that prevents the carrier from contesting a claim if the policy has been in force for a certain number of years (commonly two years). *See also* Contestable clause.

Uncontrollable. Incapable of being controlled or ungovernable.

Uncontrollable impulse. As an excuse for the commission of an act otherwise criminal, this term means an impulse towards its commission of such fixity and intensity that it cannot be resisted by the person subject to it, in the enfeebled condition of his will and moral sense resulting from derangement or mania. *See* Insanity.

Under. Sometimes used in its literal sense of below in position, beneath, but more frequently in its secondary meaning of "inferior" or "subordinate." Also according to; as, "under the testimony."

Under and subject. Words frequently used in conveyances of land which is subject to a mortgage, to show that the grantee takes subject to such mortgage.

Undercapitalization. A term used in reference to a business which does not have enough cash or "capital" to effectively carry on the business. *See also* Thin capitalization.

Under color of law. *See* Color of law.

Under control. This phrase does not necessarily mean the ability to stop instanter under any and all circumstances, an automobile being "under control" within the meaning of the law if it is moving at such a rate, and the mechanism and power under such control, that it can be brought to a stop with a reasonable degree of celerity. And motorist is only bound to use that degree of care, caution, and prudence that an ordinarily careful, cautious, and prudent man would have used at the time under same or similar circumstances in operation of said automobile. In general, as applied to street cars or railroad trains, the term denotes the control and preparation appropriate to probable emergencies. It is such control as will enable a train to be stopped promptly if need should arise. It implies the ability to stop within the distance the track is seen to be clear. *See also* Control; Lookout.

Undercover agent. A person who works as an agent without disclosing his role as an agent. In police work, one who makes contact with suspected criminals without disclosing his role as an agent of the police. He gathers evidence of criminal activity which may later be used at trial of the criminals. Such agents are commonly used in narcotic investigations. *See also* Informer.

Under insurance. Insurance coverage in an amount less than the value of the property insured or less than the risk exposure.

Underinsured motorist coverage. Such insurance provides for situations in which offending motorist does not carry enough coverage to pay damages incurred by the injured party. Over half of the states have statutes providing for some form of underinsured coverage. It is not designed to relieve an insured or his family from the failure to purchase adequate liability coverage. *Compare* Uninsured motorist coverage.

Under-lease. Exists where lessee lets premises for less time than period of his unexpired term; a sub-lease. Also the transfer of a part only of the lands, though for the whole term.

Under protest. A payment made or an act done under compulsion while the payor or actor asserts that he waives no rights by making the payment or by doing the act. U.C.C. § 1–207. *See* Protest.

Undersigned, the. The person whose name is signed or the persons whose names are signed at the end of a document; the subscriber or subscribers.

Understand. To know; to apprehend the meaning; to appreciate; as, to understand the nature and effect of an act. To have a full and clear knowledge of; to comprehend. Thus, to invalidate a deed on the ground that the grantor did not understand the nature of the act, the grantor must be incapable of comprehending that the effect of the act would divest him of the title to the land set forth in the deed. As used in connection with the execution of wills and other instruments, the term includes the realization of the practical effects and consequences of the proposed act. *See* Capacity.

Understanding. In the law of contracts, an agreement. An implied agreement resulting from the express terms of another agreement, whether written or oral. An informal agreement, or a concurrence as to its terms. A valid contract engagement of a somewhat informal character. This is a loose and ambiguous term, unless it be accompanied by some expression to show that it constituted a meeting of the minds of parties upon something respecting which they intended to be bound. *See* Agreement; Contract.

Understood. The phrase "it is understood," when employed as a word of contract in a written agreement, has the ᴖame general force as the words "it is agreed."

Undertake. To take on oneself; to engage in; to enter upon; to take in hand; set about; attempt; as, to undertake a task or a journey; and, specifically, to take upon oneself solemnly or expressly. To lay oneself under obligation or to enter into stipulation; to perform or to execute; to covenant; to contract. Hence, to guarantee; be surety for; promise; to accept or take over as a charge; to accept responsibility for the care of. To engage to look after or attend to, as to undertake a patient or guest. To endeavor to perform or try; to promise, engage, agree, or assume an obligation.

Undertaking. A promise, engagement, or stipulation. An engagement by one of the parties to a contract to the other, as distinguished from the mutual engagement of the parties to each other. It does not necessarily imply a consideration. In a somewhat special sense, a promise given in the course of legal proceedings by a party or his counsel, generally as a condition to obtaining some concession from the court or the opposite party. A promise or security in any form. *See* Stipulation.

Under-tenant. A tenant under one who is himself a tenant; one who holds by under-lease. *See also* Under-lease.

Under the influence of intoxicating liquor *or* drugs. Phrase as used in statutes or ordinances prohibiting the operation of motor vehicle by a party under the influence of intoxicating liquor or drugs covers not only all well-known and easily recognized conditions and degrees of intoxication, but any abnormal mental or physical condition which is the result of indulging in any degree in intoxicating liquors or drugs, and which tends to deprive one of that clearness of intellect and control of himself which he would otherwise possess. Any condition where intoxicating liquor or drugs has so far affected the nervous system, brain or muscles of the driver as to impair, to an appreciable degree, his ability to operate a motor vehicle in the manner that an ordinary, prudent and cautious man, in full possession of his faculties, using reasonable care, would operate or drive under like conditions. A condition that makes a person less able, either mentally or physically, or both, to exercise clear judgment, and with steady hands and nerves, to operate an automobile with safety to himself and to the public. *See also* Intoxication.

Undertook. Agreed; promised; assumed. This is the technical word to be used in alleging the promise which forms the basis of an action of *assumpsit*.

Underwrite. To insure life or property. *See* Insurance.

To agree to sell bonds, etc., to the public, or to furnish the necessary money for such securities, and to buy those which cannot be sold. An underwriting contract, aside from its use in insurance, is an agreement, made before corporate shares are brought before the public, that in the event of the public not taking all the shares of the number mentioned in the agreement, the underwriter will take the shares which the public do not take; "underwriting" being a purchase, together with a guaranty of a sale of the bonds. *See also* Offering *(Public offerings)*; Prospectus; Standby agreement; Standby fee; Take–up fee; Underwriter.

Underwriter. Any person, banker, or syndicate that guarantees to furnish a definite sum of money by a definite date to a business or government entity in return for an issue of bonds or stock. A professional firm (*e.g.*, investment banker) that handles the marketing of a corporate or government security offering to the public; it either buys all of a new security offering for a specified price and then sells it to the public, either directly or through dealers, or takes a commission on the securities it actually sells.

Term refers to any person who has purchased from an issuer with a view to, or sells for an issuer in connection with, the distribution of any security, or participates or has a direct or indirect participation in any such undertaking, or participates or has a participation in the direct or indirect underwriting of any such undertaking; but such term shall not include a person whose interest is limited to a commission from an underwriter or dealer not in excess of the usual and customary distributor's or seller's commission. Investment Company Act, § 2, 15 U.S.C.A. § 80a–2(40).

See also Investment banker; Underwrite.

In insurance, the party assuming a risk in return for the payment of a premium (the insurer).

Underwriting agreement. Agreement between corporation and underwriter covering terms and conditions of new issue of securities to be offered to public. *See* Standby agreement; Take-up fee; Underwriter.

Underwriting fee. The portion of the gross underwriting spread that compensates the securities firms who underwrite a public offering for their underwriting risk.

Underwriting spread. The difference between the selling price to the public of a new security offering and the proceeds received by the offering firm. This is also termed an *underwriting discount*.

Undisclosed agency. Exists where agent deals with a third person without notifying that person of the agency. An agency relationship in which the third party has no knowledge of the existence of the agency.

Undisclosed principal. A principal whose identity is unknown by a third person, and the third person has no knowledge that the agent is acting in an agency capacity at the time the contract is made. *See also* Principal.

Undisputed. Not questioned or challenged; uncontested.

Undisputed fact. An admitted fact, which the court has not deemed sufficiently material to add to the finding, or has inadvertently omitted from it; a fact not found by the court does not become an "undisputed fact," merely because one or more witnesses testify to it without direct contradiction.

Undistributed profits. *See* Undivided profits.

Undistributed profits tax. Tax imposed on the unreasonable accumulation of profits by a corporation which has sufficient surplus for expansion and other needs beyond the amount which it could but does not pay out in dividends. I.R.C. § 531 et seq. *See also* Accumulated earnings tax.

Undivided interest. *See* Tenancy *(Joint tenancy; Tenancy by the entirety; Tenancy in common).*

Undivided profits. Profits which have not been distributed as dividends or set aside as surplus. Current undistributed earnings.

Undivided right. An undivided right or title, or a title to an undivided portion of an estate, is that owned by one of two or more tenants in common or joint tenants before partition. Held by the same title by two or more persons, whether their rights are equal as to value or quantity, or unequal.

Undue. More than necessary; not proper; illegal. It denotes something wrong, according to the standard of morals which the law enforces in relations of men, and in fact illegal, and qualifies the purpose with which influence is exercised or result which it accomplishes.

Undue influence. Persuasion, pressure, or influence short of actual force, but stronger than mere advice, that so overpowers the dominated party's free will or judgment that he or she cannot act intelligently and voluntarily, but acts, instead, subject to the will or purposes of the dominating party.

Any improper or wrongful constraint, machination, or urgency of persuasion whereby the will of a person is overpowered and he is induced to do or forbear an act which he would not do or would do if left to act freely. Influence which deprives person influenced of free agency or destroys freedom of his will and renders it more the will of another than his own. Misuse of position of confidence or taking advantage of a person's weakness, infirmity, or distress to change improperly that person's actions or decisions.

Term refers to conduct by which a person, through his power over mind of testator, makes the latter's desires conform to his own, thereby overmastering the volition of the testator. For purpose of executing instruments, such exists when there was such dominion and control exercised over mind of person executing such instruments, under facts and circumstances then existing, as to overcome his free agency and free will and to substitute will of another so as to cause him to do what he would not otherwise have done but for such dominion and control.

See also Coercion; Duress.

Unearned income. *See* Income.

Unearned interest. Interest generally received by a financial institution in advance of the time in which it is earned.

Unearned premium. Portion of original premium not yet earned by insurance company and

therefore due policyholder if the policy should be cancelled.

Unearned revenue. Future revenue that has been collected but not as yet earned. *See also* Income *(Unearned income).*

Unearned surplus. As distinguished from "earned surplus" includes: (a) "paid-in surplus"—amounts contributed for or assigned to shares in excess of stated capital applicable thereto; (b) "revaluation surplus"—surplus arising from a revaluation of assets above cost, and (c) "donated surplus"—contributions other than for shares, whether from shareholders or others. *See also* Surplus.

Unemployment. State of not being employed; lack of employment. *See also* Seasonal employment.

Structural unemployment. Unemployment that results when there is a shift in the demand for a particular product or service such that certain skills and jobs are no longer needed or desired.

Unemployment tax. *See* Tax.

Unencumbered. Without any impediments, *e.g.,* an unencumbered title to property.

Unenforceable contract. A contract having no legal effect or force in a court action. *See* Void contract. *Compare* Valid contract.

Unequal. Not uniform. Ill-balanced; uneven; partial; discriminatory; prejudicial; unfair;—not synonymous with inappropriate, which means unsuitable, unfit, or improper. *See* Discrimination; Separate but equal doctrine.

Unequivocal. Clear; plain; capable of being understood in only one way, or as clearly demonstrated. Free from uncertainty, or without doubt; and, when used with reference to the burden of proof, it implies proof of the highest possible character and it imports proof of the nature of mathematical certainty. *See also* Unambiguous.

Unethical. Not ethical; hence, colloquially, not according to business or professional standards.

Unethical conduct. *See* Rules of Professional Conduct.

Unexpected. Not expected, coming without warning, sudden. *See* Act of God; Accident.

Unexpired term. Remainder of a period prescribed by law or provided for in lease after a portion of such time has passed, and phrase is not synonymous with "vacancy."

Unfair competition. A term which may be applied generally to all dishonest or fraudulent rivalry in trade and commerce, but is particularly applied to the practice of endeavoring to substitute one's own goods or products in the markets for those of another, having an established reputation and extensive sale, by means of imitating or counterfeiting the name, title, size, shape, or distinctive peculiarities of the article, or the shape, color, label, wrapper, or general appearance of the package, or other such simulations, the imitation being carried far enough to mislead the general public or deceive an unwary purchaser, and yet not amounting to an absolute counterfeit or to the infringement of a trade-mark or trade-name. Tort involving the misappropriation for commercial advantage of a benefit or property right belonging to another.

The simulation by one person of the name, materials, color scheme, symbols, patterns, or devices employed by another for purpose of deceiving the public, or substitution of goods, or wares of one person for those of another, thus falsely inducing purchase of goods and obtaining benefits belonging to competitor. Passing off, or attempting to pass off upon the public the goods or business of one person as the goods or business of another. The selling of another's product as one's own. Also, deceitful advertising which injures a competitor, bribery of employees, secret rebates and concessions, and other devices of unfair trade.

See also Antitrust acts; Unfair methods of competition; Uniform Deceptive Trade Practices Act.

Unfair hearing. Where the defect, or the practice complained of, was such as might have led to a denial of justice, or where there was absent one of the elements deemed essential to due process.

Unfair labor practice. Within National Labor Relations Act, it is an unfair labor practice for an employer: (1) To interfere with, restrain, or coerce employees in the exercise of their rights to self-organization, to form, join or assist labor organizations, to bargain collectively through representatives of their own choosing, and to engage in concerted activities, for the purpose of collective bargaining or other mutual aid or protection. (2) To dominate or interfere with the formation or administration of any labor organization or contribute financial or other support to it. (3) By discrimination in regard to hire or tenure of employment or any term or condition of employment to encourage or discourage membership in any labor organization. (4) To discharge or otherwise discriminate against an employee because he has filed charges or given testimony under the Act. (5) To refuse to bargain collectively with the representatives of his employees. National Labor Relations Act, §§ 7, 8; 29 U.S.C.A. §§ 102 et seq., 157, 158.

Unfair methods of competition. This phrase within Federal Trade Commission Act has broader meaning than common-law term "unfair competition," but its scope cannot be precisely defined, and what constitutes "unfair methods of competition" must be determined in particular instances, upon evidence, in light of particular competitive conditions and of what is found to be a specific and substantial public interest. Federal Trade Commission Act § 5, 15 U.S.C.A. § 45. *See also* Antitrust acts; Unfair competition; Uniform Deceptive Trade Practices Act; Vertical restraints of trade.

Unfair prejudice. Within context of rule regarding admission of evidence means undue tendency to suggest decision on improper basis, commonly, though not necessarily, emotional one. Generally, danger of unfair prejudice in admission of evidence always exists where it is used for something other than its logical probative force. Such is caused by evidence that is likely to arouse emotional response rather than rational decision among jurors.

Unfair trade practices. *See* Unfair competition; Unfair methods of competition.

Unfaithful. Characterized by bad faith; not synonymous with "illegal," which means unlawful or contrary to law, nor with "improper," which, as applied to conduct, implies such conduct as a man of ordinary and reasonable prudence would not, under the circumstances, have been guilty of.

Unfinished. Not completed; not brought to an end; imperfect; the last effort, as a final touch is given to a work.

Unfit. Unsuitable; incompetent; not adapted or qualified for a particular use or service; having no fitness. As applied to relation of rational parents to their child, word "unfit" usually, though not necessarily, imports something of moral delinquency, but, unsuitability for any reason, apart from moral defects, may render a parent unfit for custody.

Unforeseen. Not foreseen, not expected. *See also* Unexpected.

Unharmed. Within provision of Federal Kidnapping Act that death sentence shall not be imposed if kidnapped person has been liberated unharmed, means uninjured. Federal Kidnapping Act § 1 et seq., as amended, 18 U.S.C.A. § 1201 et seq.

Unified. Made one. *See* Consolidation; Joinder; Merger.

Unified bar. *See* Integrated bar.

Unified estate and gift tax. *See* Unified transfer tax.

Unified tax credit. A credit against the federal Unified Transfer Tax, replacing the former lifetime gift tax exemption and the estate tax exemption. I.R.C. §§ 2010–2505.

Unified transfer tax. A federal tax levied on the transfer of property through an estate at the time of death or on a taxable transfer by gift. The estate or the donor is responsible for payment of the tax. The unified credit may be applied against the unified transfer tax.

Uniform. Conforming to one rule, mode, pattern, or unvarying standard; not different at different times or places; applicable to all places or divisions of a country. Equable; applying alike to all within a class; sameness.

A statute is general and uniform in its operation when it operates equally upon all persons who are brought within the relations and circumstances provided for; when all persons under the same conditions and in the same circumstances are treated alike, and classification is reasonable and naturally inherent in the subject-matter. The words "general" and "uniform" as applied to laws have a meaning antithetical to special or discriminatory laws.

Taxation. The burdens of taxation, to be uniform, must have the essential of equality, and must bear alike upon all the property within the limits of the unit wherein it is lawful to levy taxes for a purpose, whether that unit be the state, county, or a municipality. And requirement is met when tax is equal on all persons belonging to described class on which tax is imposed. With reference to locality, a tax is "uniform" when it operates with equal force and effect in every place where the subject of it is found, and with reference to classification, it is uniform when it operates without distinction or discrimination upon all persons composing the described class. Uniformity in taxation implies equality in the burden of taxation, which cannot exist without uniformity in the mode of assessment, as well as in the rate of taxation. Further, the uniformity must be coextensive with the territory to which it applies. And it must be extended to all property subject to taxation, so that all property may be taxed alike and equally.

Uniform Child Custody Jurisdiction Act. *See* Custody of children.

Uniform Code of Military Justice. The body of law which governs military persons in their conduct as military personnel. 10 U.S.C.A. §§ 801–940. *See* Code of Military Justice.

Uniform Commercial Code. One of the Uniform Laws drafted by the National Conference of Commissioners on Uniform State Laws and the American Law Institute governing commercial transactions (including sales and leasing of goods, transfer of funds, commercial paper, bank deposits and collections, letters of credit, bulk transfers, warehouse receipts, bills of lading, investment securities, and secured transactions). The U.C.C. has been adopted in whole or substantially by all states.

Uniform Consumer Credit Code. (Also called the "U.3C.") A Uniform Law, adopted by some states: (a) to simplify, clarify, and modernize the law governing consumer credit and usury; (b) to provide rate ceilings to assure an adequate supply of credit to consumers; (c) to further consumer understanding of the terms of credit transactions and to foster competition among suppliers of consumer credit so that consumers may obtain credit at reasonable cost; (d) to protect consumers against unfair practices by some suppliers of consumer credit, having due regard for the interests of legitimate and scrupulous creditors; (e) to permit and encourage the development of fair and economically sound consumer credit practices; (f) to conform the regulation of disclosure in consumer credit transactions to the Federal Truth-in-Lending Act; and (g) to make uniform the law, including administrative rules, among the various jurisdictions. *See also* Consumer Credit Protection Act; Truth-in-Lending Act.

Uniform Controlled Substances Act. A uniform and comprehensive law governing use, sale, and distribution of drugs and narcotics adopted by most states, including Puerto Rico and the Virgin Islands. See 21 U.S.C.A. § 801 *et seq.* for federal Act. *See also* Controlled Substance Acts.

Uniform Customs and Practice for Commercial Documentary Credits (UCP). A publication of the International Chamber of Commerce which codifies the widespread understanding of bankers and merchants about the mechanics and operations of letters of credit. The UCP is law in the sense that the typical commercial credit is issued subject to the UCP, and courts refer to the UCP to interpret and supplement primary sources of credit law, such as U.C.C. Article 5.

Uniform Deceptive Trade Practices Act. One version of a "baby" F.T.C. Act that provides private remedies for a variety of unfair and deceptive acts, including false advertising and disparagement. The remedies under this particular uniform statute, as enacted by certain states, are limited to injunctive relief.

Uniform Divorce Recognition Act. One of the Uniform Laws adopted by some states governing questions of full faith and credit and recognition of divorces of sister states.

Uniform Gifts to Minors Act. *See* Gifts (or Transfers) to Minors Act; Transfers to Minors Act.

Uniformity. *See* Uniform.

Uniform Laws *or* **Acts.** Laws in various subject areas, approved by the Commissioners on Uniform State Laws, that are often adopted, in whole or substantially, by individual states; their purpose being to make the laws on various subjects uniform throughout the states. Examples are the Uniform Anatomical Gifts Act; Uniform Partnership Act; and the Uniform Commercial Code. These various laws are published in Uniform Laws Annotated. *See also* Model act.

Uniform Principal and Income Act. One of the Uniform Laws adopted by some states governing allocation of principal and income in trusts and estates.

Uniform Residential Landlord and Tenant Act. Uniform statute, adopted in certain states, governing landlord/tenant relationships.

Uniform Simultaneous Death Act. *See* Simultaneous Death Act.

Uniform State Laws. *See* Model act; Uniform Laws *or* Acts.

Uniform Transfers to Minors Act. *See* Transfers to Minors Act.

Unify. To cause to be one; to make into a unit; to unite; to become one; to consolidate.

Unilateral. One-sided; ex parte; having relation to only one of two or more persons or things.

Unilateral contract. *See* Contract.

Unilateral mistake. A mistake or misunderstanding as to the terms or effect of a contract, made or entertained by one of the parties to it but not by the other.

Unilateral record. Records are unilateral when offered to show a particular fact, as a *prima facie* case, either for or against a stranger.

Unimproved land. A statutory term which includes lands, once improved, that have reverted to a state of nature, as well as lands that have never been improved.

Unincorporated association. Voluntary group of persons, without a charter, formed by mutual consent for purpose of promoting common enterprise or prosecuting common objective. An organization composed of a body of persons united with a charter for the prosecution of a common enterprise. *See also* Partnership.

Uninsured motorist coverage. Protection afforded an insured by first party insurance against bodily injury inflicted by an uninsured motorist, after the liability of the uninsured motorist for the injury has been established. Purpose is to guarantee that the injured insured will be in the same position in the event of injury attributable to negligence of an uninsured motorist as the insured would be if he were injured through the negligence of a motorist carrying liability insurance. *See also* Unsatisfied judgment funds. *Compare* Underinsured motorist coverage.

Unintelligible. That which cannot be understood.

Union. An organization of workers, formed for the purpose of negotiating with employers on matters of wages, seniority, working conditions, fringe benefits, and the like.

A league; a federation; an unincorporated association of persons for a common purpose; as, a trade or labor union. A joinder of separate entities (*see* Merger).

A popular term in America for the United States; also, in Great Britain, for the consolidated governments of England and Scotland, or for the political tie between Great Britain and Ireland.

See also Agency shop; Bargaining unit; Craft union; Credit union; Labor organization; Labor union; Open shop; Preferential shop; Right to work laws.

Closed union. Union with highly restrictive membership requirements such as high initiation fees, and long apprenticeship periods. *See also* Closed shop; *compare Open union, below.*

Company union. Union formed or sponsored by the employer. For all practical purposes, such union is now illegal because employers are prohibited from interfering with union representation by the National Labor Relations Act.

Craft union. Union composed of members of the same trade or craft, as carpenters, plumbers, etc. regardless of the company for which they work.

Horizontal union. A craft union which cuts across employer or industry lines.

Independent union. Union formed by employees of a particular employer without affiliation with an international union.

Industrial union. Union composed of workers in a particular industry regardless of their particular trade or craft, as for example, the United Automobile Workers union.

International union. A parent union with affiliates in other countries such as Canada and Mexico.

Local union. A union of workers in one plant or location but affiliated with a parent or larger union. The local is the bargaining unit of the union.

National union. A parent union with locals in various parts of the United States, though not outside the country.

Open union. A union whose admission requirements are relatively easy to meet. *See also* Open shop; *compare Closed union, above.*

Trade union. Generically, a labor union. Restrictively, a craft union.

Union shop. Exists where all workers, once employed, must become union members within a specified period of time as a condition of their continued employment. *See also* Closed shop; Open shop; Right to work laws.

Vertical union. An industrial union organized along lines of industry and not craft.

Union certification. The process by which an official, governmental body such as the National Labor Relations Board declares that a particular union has qualified as the bargaining representative of the employees of a company or industry by reason of a majority vote of the workers.

Union contract. A written agreement between the union and employer covering such matters as wages, seniority rights and working conditions.

Union mortgage clause. A clause, as in a fire policy (together with the rider making the loss, if any, payable to the mortgagee), which provides that if the policy is made payable to a mortgagee of the insured real estate, no act or default of any person other than such mortgagee, or his agents or those claiming under him, shall affect his right to recover in case of loss on such real estate. Such clause creates independent contract between insurer and mortgagee and is distinguished from "open mortgage clause" in that latter clause simply provides that policy is payable to mortgagee as his interest may appear. And mortgagee under such latter clause is merely an appointee to receive fund recoverable in case of loss to extent of his interest.

Union rate. The wage scale set by a union as a minimum wage to be paid and generally expressed as an hourly rate or piece-work rate.

Union security clause. Provision in union contract which establishes status of union in a plant. It provides for the relation of the union to the workers and their positions. Any contract clause requiring some or all employees represented by a union to become or remain members of the union as a condition of employment.

Unissued stock. Stock of a corporation which has been authorized but is not outstanding (*i.e.* not issued).

Unit. A single thing of any kind. A term sometimes used in the sense of a share, as in an oil syndicate, or as equivalent to an investment security. With respect to labor unit, *see* Bargaining unit.

Unitary business. "Unitary business operation," to which unitary apportionment method of reporting business income is applied, is one in which there is high degree of interrelationship and interdependence between, typically, one corporation, which generally is a parent corporation, and its corporate subsidiaries or otherwise associated corporations, which are usually engaged in multistate, and in some instances in international, business operations. For purpose of determining taxable corporate income, recognized test for a "unitary business" is whether operation of portion of business within the state is dependent upon or contributory to operation of the business outside the state. *See also* Tax *(Unitary tax)*; UDITPA; Unitary theory.

Unitary tax. *See* Unitary business; Tax *(Unitary tax)*; UDITPA.

Unitary theory. Under the unitary theory, the sales, property, and payroll of related corporations are combined for nexus and apportionment purposes, and the worldwide income of the unitary entity is apportioned to the state. Subsidiaries and other affiliated corporations that are found to be part of the corporation's unitary business (because they are subject to overlapping ownership, operation, or management) are included in the apportionment procedure. *See also* Tax *(Unitary tax)*; Unitary business.

Unite. To join in an act; to concur; to act in concert.

United in interest. A statutory term applicable to codefendants only when they are similarly interested in and will be similarly affected by the determination of the issues involved in the action; *e.g.,* joint obligors upon a guaranty.

United Nations. An organization started by the allied powers in World War II for the stated purposes of preventing war, providing justice and promoting welfare and human rights of peoples. Its membership is made up of nearly all nations of the world. New members may be admitted by a two-thirds vote of the General Assembly. It consists of a Security Council and a General Assembly and subordinate agencies.

United States. This term has several meanings. It may be merely the name of a sovereign occupying the position analogous to that of other sovereigns in family of nations, it may designate territory over which sovereignty of United States extends, or it may be collective name of the states which are united by and under the Constitution.

United States Attorney. A United States Attorney is appointed by the President for each judicial district. The general duties of U.S. attorneys are to: prosecute for all offenses against the United States; prosecute or defend, for the Government, all civil actions, suits or proceedings in which the United States is concerned; appear in behalf of the defendants in all civil actions, suits or proceedings pending in his district against collectors, or other officers of the revenue or customs for any act done by them or for the recovery of any money exacted by or paid to these officers, and by them paid into the Treasury; institute and prosecute proceedings for the collection of fines, penalties, and forfeitures incurred for violation of any revenue law, unless satisfied on investigation that justice does not require the proceedings. 28 U.S. C.A. § 547.

United States Code. Prior to 1926, the positive law for federal legislation was contained in the one volume of the Revised Statutes of 1875 and then in each subsequent volume of the Statutes at Large. In 1925, Congress authorized the preparation of the United States Code. This was prepared by a Revisor of Statutes appointed by Congress, who extracted all sections of the Revised Statutes of 1875 that had not been repealed and then all of the public and general laws from the Statutes at Large since 1873 that were still in force. These were then rearranged into fifty titles and published as the United States Code, 1926 ed., in four volumes. Each year thereafter a cumulative supplement containing the laws passed since 1926 was published. In 1932 a new edition was issued which incorporated the cumulated supplements to the 1926 edition, and this became the United States Code, 1932 ed. Every six years a new edition of the U.S. Code is published with cumulative supplement volumes being issued during the intervening years.

United States Code Annotated. This multi-volume publication includes the complete text of the United States Code, together with case notes of state and federal decisions which construe and apply specific Code sections, cross references to related sections, historical notes, and library references. U.S.C.A. is further supplemented with the United States Code Congressional and Administrative News and periodic pamphlet supplements containing laws as passed by Congress during the current session.

United States Commissioners. *See* Magistrate.

United States Courts. Except in the case of impeachments, the judicial power of the United States is vested by the Constitution in a Supreme Court and such other inferior courts as may be from time to time established by congress. All the judges are appointed by the President, with the advice and consent of the senate, to hold office during good behavior, and their compensation cannot be diminished during their term of office. Art. III, U.S.Const. Such "inferior" courts include the Courts of Appeals, District Courts, Claims Court, Bankruptcy Courts, and Tax Court. 28 U.S.C.A. § 1 *et seq. See* Legislative courts. See also specific courts.

United States currency. Commonly understood to include every form of currency authorized by the United States government, whether issued directly by it or under its authority. *See* Legal tender.

United States Government Securities. *See* Government securities.

United States Magistrates. *See* Magistrate.

United States notes. *See* Treasury bill; Treasury note.

United States officer. Usually and strictly, in United States statutes, a person appointed in the manner declared under Art. II, § 2, U.S.Const., providing for the appointment of officers, either by the President and the Senate, the President alone, the courts of law, or the heads of departments.

United States Reports. The official printed record of cases heard and decided by the U.S. Supreme Court which usually includes a syllabus of each case, the opinion of the Court, concurring and dissenting opinions, if any, the disposition made of each case, and orders of the Court. Originally a series of Reports was issued during the incumbency of each successive court reporter and such were cited as Dallas (1790–1800); Cranch (1801–1815); Wheaton (1816–1827); Peters (1828–1843); Howard (1843–1860); Black (1861–1862); and Wallace (1863–1874). By 1874, when the number of volumes totalled 90, the practice began of eliminating the reporter's name and citing them as United States Reports.

United States Supreme Court. *See* Supreme Court.

United States trustee. *See* Bankruptcy proceedings *(Bankruptcy trustee).*

Unit investment trust. An investment company organized under a trust indenture, contract of custodianship or agency or similar instrument. 15 U.S.C.A. § 80a–4(2). The most common form of organization is the trust indenture. The holder of shares in this investment vehicle has an undivided interest in a fixed pool of securities held by the trustee or custodian.

Unit ownership acts. State laws governing condominium ownership. *See* Planned unit development.

Unit pricing. System under which contract items are priced per unit and not on the basis of a flat contract price.

Unit rule. A method of valuing securities by multiplying the total number of shares held by the sale price of one share sold on a licensed stock exchange, ignoring all other facts regarding value.

Unitrust. A trust from which a fixed percentage of the net fair market value of the trust's assets, valued annually, is paid each year to the beneficiary. *See also* Trust.

Unity. Under common law, "four unities" had to be present to create a joint tenancy: *interest*—the tenants must have one and the same interest; *title*—the interests must accrue by one and the same instrument or conveyance; *time*—the interests must commence at one and the same time; and *possession*—the property must be held by one and the same undivided possession. If any one of these unities were lacking, the estate was not one in joint tenancy. *See also* these specific unities, infra.

Unity of interest. As required in case of joint tenancy, means that interests must accrue by one and same conveyance. It also signifies that the interests must be equal; that is, no one of joint tenants can have a greater interest in the property than each of the others, while, in the case of tenants in common, one of them may have a larger share than any of the others. However, this unity of interest requisite refers to equality among the cotenants only as to their interests in the estate; it does not relate to quality in contribution of purchase money. *See* Unity.

Unity of possession. Joint possession of two rights by several titles. Exists for example where a person takes a lease of land from another at a certain rent, and afterwards purchases the fee-simple of such land. By this he acquires unity of possession, by which the lease is extinguished. It is also one of the essential properties of a joint estate, requiring that the joint tenants must hold the same undivided possession of the whole and enjoy same rights until death of one. *See* Unity.

Unity of seisin. Exists where a person seised of land which is subject to an easement, *profit à prendre,* or similar right, also becomes seised of the land to which the easement or other right is annexed.

Unity of time. One of the four unities recognized at common law to create a joint tenancy. The interests of the parties commence at one and the same time. *See also* Unity.

Unity of title. As applied to joint tenants, signifies that they hold their property by one and the same title, while tenants in common may take property by several titles. *See* Unity.

The majority rule regarding water rights that all land within the watershed that forms a part of a contiguous whole belonging to one person and bordering on the water is riparian land regardless of when ownership of the part was acquired.

Universal. Having relation to the whole or an entirety; pertaining to all without exception; a term more extensive than "general," which latter may admit of exceptions.

Universal agent. One who is appointed to do all the acts which the principal can personally do, and which he may lawfully delegate the power to another to do. *See also* Agent.

Universal legacy. *See* Legacy.

Universal partnership. *See* Partnership.

Unjust. Contrary to right and justice, or to the enjoyment of his rights by another, or to the standards of conduct furnished by the laws.

Unjust enrichment doctrine. General principle that one person should not be permitted unjustly to enrich himself at expense of another, but should be required to make restitution of or for property or benefits received, retained or appropriated, where it is just and equitable that such restitution be made, and where such action involves no violation or frustration of law or opposition to public policy, either directly or indirectly. Unjust enrichment of a person occurs when he

has and retains money or benefits which in justice and equity belong to another.

Three elements must be established in order to sustain a claim based on unjust enrichment: A benefit conferred upon the defendant by the plaintiff; an appreciation or knowledge by the defendant of the benefit; and the acceptance or retention by the defendant of the benefit under such circumstances as to make it inequitable for the defendant to retain the benefit without the payment of its value. *See also* Quantum meruit.

Unknown injury rule. *See* Injury.

Unknown persons. Persons whose identities cannot be ascertained. *See* John Doe.

Unlawful. That which is contrary to, prohibited, or unauthorized by law. That which is not lawful. The acting contrary to, or in defiance of the law; disobeying or disregarding the law. Term is equivalent to "without excuse or justification." While necessarily not implying the element of criminality, it is broad enough to include it. *See* Crime; Criminal.

Term as applied to agreements and the like, denotes they are ineffectual in law, for they involve acts which, though not positively forbidden, are disapproved by law and are therefore not recognized as ground of legal rights because they are against public policy. *See* Illegal.

Unlawful act. An illegal act. Act contrary to law, and presupposes that there must be an existing law. A violation of some prohibitory law and includes all willful, actionable violations of civil rights, and is not confined to criminal acts. *See also* Unconstitutional.

Unlawful assembly. At common law, the meeting together of three or more persons, to the disturbance of the public peace, and with the intention of co-operating in the forcible and violent execution of some unlawful private enterprise. If they take steps towards the performance of their purpose, it becomes a *rout;* and, if they put their design into actual execution, it is a *riot.* An unlawful assembly is a meeting of three or more persons with a common plan in mind which, if carried out, will result in a riot. In other words, it is such a meeting with intent to (a) commit a crime by open force, or (b) execute a common design lawful or unlawful, in an unauthorized manner likely to cause courageous persons to apprehend a breach of the peace.

Unlawful assembly is the meeting or coming together of not less than five (5) persons for the purpose of engaging in conduct constituting either disorderly conduct, or a riot, or when in a lawful assembly of not less than five (5) persons, agreeing to engage in such conduct. Kansas Criminal Code, 21–4102.

See also Assembly, right of; Riot.

Unlawful detainer. The unjustifiable retention of the possession of real property by one whose original entry was lawful and of right, but whose right to the possession has terminated and who refuses to quit, as in the case of a tenant holding over after the termination of the lease and in spite of a demand for possession by the landlord. Actions of "unlawful detainer" concern only right of possession of realty, and differ from ejectment in that no ultimate question of title or estate can be determined. *See also* Detainer; Ejectment; Eviction; Forcible detainer; Forcible entry and detainer; Process *(Summary process).*

Unlawful detainer proceeding. A statutory procedure by which a landlord can legally evict a tenant in default on his or her rent. *See* Unlawful detainer.

Unlawful entry. An entry upon lands effected peaceably and without force, but which is without color of title and is accomplished by means of fraud or some other willful wrong.

Unlawfully. Illegally; wrongfully. *See* Criminal; Unlawful; Unlawful act.

This word is frequently used in indictments in the description of the offence; it was formerly necessary when the crime did not exist at common law, and when a statute, in describing an offence which it created, used the word; but was unnecessary whenever the crime existed at common law and was manifestly illegal.

Unlawful picketing. Picketing which involves false statements or misrepresentations of facts. Such exists when force or violence is used to persuade or prevent workers from continuing their employment. Examples include secondary picketing in violation of 29 U.S.C.A. § 158(b)(4)(ii)(B); and recognitional picketing in violation of 29 U.S.C.A. § 158(b)(7)(A) and (C). *See also* Secondary boycott; Picketing.

Unless. If it be not that; if it be not the case that; if not; supposing not; if it be not; except. A reservation or option to change one's mind provided a certain event happens, a conditional promise. A subordinate conjunction in common usage, connecting a dependent or subordinate clause to the main clause of a sentence.

Unlimited. Without confines, unrestricted, boundless.

Unliquidated. Not ascertained in amount; not determined; remaining unassessed or unsettled, as unliquidated damages.

Unliquidated claim or demand. A claim which has not been finally determined either as to liability or amount of damages. A disputed claim. Under the law of accord and satisfaction, a claim or debt will be regarded as unliquidated if it is in dispute as to the proper amount. For purposes of rule that prejudgment interest is allowed if a

claim is liquidated but not if a claim is unliquidated, claim is "unliquidated" when the amount of the damages cannot be computed except on conflicting evidence, inferences and interpretations. *See also* Unliquidated.

Unliquidated damages. Damages which have not been determined or calculated. Those which are not yet reduced to a certainty in respect to amount, nothing more being established than the plaintiff's right to recover, or such as cannot be fixed by a mere mathematical calculation from ascertainable data in the case. *See also* Damages.

Unliquidated debt. An obligation which has not been reduced to a specific money amount; also, there may be a bona fide dispute between the parties as to this undetermined amount. *See also* Unliquidated claim or demand. *Compare* Liquidated debt.

Unlisted security. Security that is not listed on an organized exchange (*e.g.,* New York Stock Exchange) and, as such, is traded on over-the-counter markets.

Unloading. Act of discharging a cargo; taking a load from; disburdening or removing from.

An unloading clause in an automobile liability policy covers the entire process involved in the movement of articles by and from a motor vehicle to the place where they are turned over to the one to whom the insured is to make delivery, if the clause is construed in accordance with what may be called the "complete operation" rule. There are, however, two other rules or doctrines used by various courts in applying the unloading clause of such a policy. One is known as the "coming to rest" rule, and the other is the "continuous passage" rule. But the complete operation rule is said to be the modern doctrine, supported by the trend of the later cases.

Unmarketable title. Exists when for vendee to accept title proffered such would lay him open to fair probability of vexatious litigation with possibility of serious loss. It being sufficient to render it so if ordinarily prudent man with knowledge of the facts and aware of legal questions involved would not accept it in the ordinary course of business but title need not be bad in fact. Exists where some defect of substantial character exists and facts are known which fairly raise reasonable doubt as to title. Title is "unmarketable" where it is of such a character as to expose the purchaser to the hazards of litigation and where there are outstanding possible interests in third persons. And mere quibbles and pecadilloes which the ingenuity of counsel can raise against a title do not alone render it an "unmarketable title". *Compare* Marketable title.

Unnatural offense. The infamous crime against nature; *i.e.,* sodomy or buggery.

Unnatural will. An expression applied to disposition of estate or large portion thereof to strangers, to exclusion of natural objects of testator's bounty without apparent reason.

Unnecessary. Not required by the circumstances of the case.

Unnecessary hardship. As considered, sufficient to establish basis for granting zoning variance, is shown by establishing that: physical characteristics of property are such that it could not be used for any permitted purpose; property could be so used only at prohibitive expense; or that characteristics of area are such that property has no value or any distress value for any permitted purpose. *See also* Variance (Zoning).

Unoccupied. Within fire policy exempting insurer from liability in case dwelling is "unoccupied," means when it is not used as a residence, when it is no longer used for the accustomed and ordinary purposes of a dwelling or place of abode, or when it is not the place of usual return and habitual stoppage. Hence a mere temporary absence of occupants of dwelling house from such premises, with intention to return thereto does not render dwelling "unoccupied". *See* Occupation.

Unprecedented. Having no precedent or example, novel, new, unexampled. Unusual and extraordinary; affording no reasonable warning or expectation of recurrence.

Unprofessional conduct. That which is by general opinion considered to be unprofessional because immoral, unethical or dishonorable. That which violates ethical code or rules of profession (*e.g.* Model Rules of Professional Conduct) or such conduct which is unbecoming member of profession in good standing. It involves breach of duty which professional ethics enjoin. Within statutes, rules, etc., promulgating standards of professional conduct for attorneys denotes conduct which it is recommended be made subject to disciplinary sanctions. *See* Rules of Professional Conduct.

Unqualified opinion. The version of an audit opinion rendered when a certified public accountant is satisfied that the financial statements are fairly presented and are consistent with those of the preceding year, and that the audit was performed in accordance with generally accepted auditing standards.

Unrealized profit or loss. A profit or loss that has not yet materialized. An example of an unrealized profit would be in the appreciation of stock. Although the stock price has increased, if the stock is not sold, the profit is considered a "paper" profit or unrealized profit.

Unrealized receivables. Amounts earned by a cash basis taxpayer but not yet received. Because of the method of accounting used by the taxpayer, such amounts have no income tax basis.

Unreasonable. Not reasonable; immoderate; exorbitant; capricious; arbitrary; confiscatory.

Unreasonable appreciation. An unrealized holding gain; frequently used in the context of investment property or marketable securities. A paper profit (*q.v.*). *See also* Equity.

Unreasonable compensation. Under the Internal Revenue Code, a deduction is allowed for "reasonable" salaries or other compensation for personal services actually rendered. To the extent compensation is "excessive" (*i.e.,* "unreasonable"), no deduction will be allowed. The problem of unreasonable compensation usually is limited to closely-held corporations where the motivation is to pay out profits in some form deductible to the corporation. Deductible compensation, therefore, becomes an attractive substitute for nondeductible dividends when the shareholders also are employed by the corporation.

Unreasonable decision. Term can be applied to an administrative agency's decision only when it is determined that the evidence presented leaves no room for difference of opinion among reasonable minds.

Unreasonable restraint of trade. Restraint of trade is "unreasonable," for purpose of Sherman Anti-Trust Act (15 U.S.C.A. § 1), only where it produces significant anitcompetitive effect. A conclusion that a restraint of trade is unreasonable may be based either (1) on the nature or character of the contracts, or (2) on surrounding circumstances giving rise to the inference or presumption that they were intended to restrain trade and enhance prices. Under either branch of the test, the inquiry is confined to a consideration of impact on competitive conditions. Within Sherman Act, term includes agreements for price maintenance of articles moving in interstate commerce. That is, any combination or conspiracy that operates directly on prices or price structure and has for its purpose the fixing of prices. *See* Price-fixing; Restraint of trade; Robinson-Patman Act.

Unreasonable restraint on alienation. Such act is brought about by gift of absolute ownership in property followed by such condition as takes away incidents of such ownership.

Unreasonable search and seizure. *See* Exclusionary Rule; Fourth Amendment; Probable cause; Search.

Unrelated business income. Income recognized by an exempt organization that is generated from activities not related to the exempt purpose of the entity. For instance, the pharmacy located in a hospital often generates unrelated business income. I.R.C. § 511.

In order for income of tax exempt organization to be "unrelated business taxable income" income must be derived from an activity which is a trade or business, the trade or business must not be substantially related to the exempt purposes of the organization and the exempt organization must regularly carry on the trade or business.

Unrelated business income tax. Tax levied on the unrelated business taxable income of an exempt organization. *See* Unrelated business income.

Unrelated offenses. A violation of law which is independent of the offense being charged. Evidence of other crimes, wrongs, or acts is not admissible to prove the character of a person in order to show that he acted in conformity therewith. It may, however, be admissible for other purposes, such as proof of motive, opportunity, intent, preparation, plan, knowledge, identity, or absence of mistake or accident. Fed.Evid.R. 404(b).

Unresponsive evidence. In evidence, an answer to a question which is irrelevant to the question asked.

Unsafe. Dangerous; not secure.

Unsatisfied judgment funds. Fund created by state law in several states to reimburse persons having claims arising out of automobile accidents who have been unable to collect from the party responsible for the accident because such party is not insured or is financially not able to pay. *See also* Uninsured motorist coverage.

Unseaworthy. A vessel which is unable to withstand the perils of an ordinary voyage at sea. *Compare* Seaworthy.

Unsecured debt. Debt obligations that are not backed by pledged collateral or security agreement.

Unsolemn will. In the civil law, one in which an executor is not appointed.

Unsound mind. Non-legal term referring to one who from infirmity of mind is incapable of managing himself or his affairs. The term, therefore, includes insane persons (*see* Insanity). It exists where there is an essential deprivation of the reasoning faculties, or where a person is incapable of understanding and acting with discretion in the ordinary affairs of life. But eccentricity, uncleanliness, slovenliness, neglect of person and clothing, and offensive and disgusting personal habits do not constitute unsoundness of mind. *See also* Capacity.

Untenantable. Term frequently used in landlord-tenant law to mean the condition of leased premises that are not fit for occupancy or rental. *See also* Warranty (*Warranty of habitability*).

Until. Up to time of. A word of limitation, used ordinarily to restrict that which precedes to what immediately follows it, and its office is to fix some point of time or some event upon the arrival or occurrence of which what precedes will cease to exist.

Untrue. *Prima facie* inaccurate, but not necessarily wilfully false. A statement is "untrue" which does not express things exactly as they are. *See* Misrepresentation.

Unusual. Uncommon; not usual, rare.

Unusual punishment. *See* Corporal punishment; Punishment (*Cruel and unusual punishment*).

Unvalued policy. In insurance, one where the value of property insured is not settled in policy, and in case of loss must be agreed on or proved.

Unwholesome food. Food not fit to be eaten; food which if eaten would be injurious. *See* Adulteration.

Unworthy. Unbecoming; discreditable; not having suitable qualities or value.

Unwritten law. All that portion of the law, observed and administered in the courts, which has not been enacted or promulgated in the form of a statute or ordinance, including the unenacted portions of the common law, general and particular customs having the force of law, and the rules, principles, and maxims established by judicial precedents or the successive like decisions of the courts. *See also* Natural law.

UPA. Uniform Partnership Act.

Upkeep. The act of keeping up or maintaining; maintenance, repair. *See* Maintenance.

Upset price. The price at which any subject, as lands or goods, is exposed to sale by auction, below which it is not to be sold. In a final decree in foreclosure, the decree should name an upset price large enough to cover costs and all allowances made by the court, receiver's certificates and interest, liens prior to the bonds, amounts diverted from the earnings, and all undetermined claims which will be settled before the confirmation and sale.

Upstreaming. Practice by parent corporation of using cash flow or other assets of subsidiary for its own use or for purposes not necessarily tied to those of subsidiary.

UREDA. Uniform Reciprocal Enforcement of Divorce Act.

U.S. An abbreviation for "United States."

Usage. A reasonable and lawful public custom in a locality concerning particular transactions which is either known to the parties, or so well established, general, and uniform that they must be presumed to have acted with reference thereto. Practice in fact. Uniform practice or course of conduct followed in certain lines of business or professions or some procedure or phase thereof. Usage cannot be proved by isolated instances, but must be certain, uniform and notorious. Habitual or customary practice which prevails within geographical or sociological area, and is course of conduct based upon series of actual occurrences, and in order to be controlling upon parties to contract, it must be adopted by them, or be well known to parties or to persons in their circumstances. *See also* Custom and usage; Local usage; Trade usage.

"Custom" distinguished. "Usage" is a repetition of acts, and differs from "custom" in that the latter is the law or general rule which arises from such repetition; while there may be usage without custom, there cannot be a custom without a usage accompanying or preceding it.

Fair usage. See Fair use doctrine.

General usage. One which prevails generally throughout the country, or is followed generally by a given profession or trade, and is not local in its nature or observance.

Usage of trade. The prevailing and accepted customs within a particular trade or industry. It is implied that merchants are cognizant of the usage of their trade. A usage of trade is any practice or method of dealing having such regularity of observance in a place, vocation, or trade as to justify an expectation that it will be observed with respect to the transaction in question. See U.C.C. § 1–205(2). *See also* Course of dealing; Trade usage.

U.S.C. *See* United States Code.

U.S.C.A. *See* United States Code Annotated.

U.S.D.C. United States District Court.

Use, *v.* To make use of; to convert to one's service; to employ; to avail oneself of; to utilize; to carry out a purpose or action by means of; to put into action or service, especially to attain an end.

Term "use" of narcotics, for purposes of statute defining offense of narcotics use, refers to act of injecting or ingesting controlled substance or narcotic.

Use, *n.* Act of employing everything, or state of being employed; application, as the use of a pen, or his machines are in use. Also the fact of being used or employed habitually; usage, as, the wear and tear resulting from ordinary use. The purpose served; a purpose, object or end for useful or advantageous nature. That enjoyment of property which consists in its employment, occupation, exercise or practice.

A confidence reposed in another, who was made tenant of the land, or terre-tenant, that he would dispose of the land according to the intention of the *cestui que use,* or him to whose use it was granted, and suffer him to take the profits.

A right in one person, called the *"cestui que use,"* to take the profits of land of which another

has the legal title and possession, together with the duty of defending the same, and of making estates thereof according to the direction of the *cestui que use.*

Uses and *trusts* are not so much different things as different aspects of the same subject. A use regards principally the beneficial interest; a trust regards principally the nominal ownership. The usage of the two terms is, however, widely different. The word "use" is employed to denote either an estate vested since the statute of uses, and by force of that statute, or to denote such an estate created before the statute as, had it been created since, would have become a legal estate by force of the statute. The word "trust" is employed since that statute to denote the relation between the party invested with the legal estate (whether by force of that statute or independently of it) and the party beneficially entitled, who has hitherto been said to have the equitable estate.

See also Beneficial use; Best use; Charitable use; Conforming use; Exclusive use; Highest and best use; Nonconforming use; Public use; Unauthorized use.

Civil law. A right of receiving so much of the natural profits of a thing as is necessary to daily sustenance. It differs from "usufruct," which is a right not only to use, but to enjoy.

Conveyancing. "Use" literally means "benefit;" thus, in an ordinary assignment of chattels, the assignor transfers the property to the assignee for his "absolute use and benefit." In the expressions "separate use," "superstitious use," and "charitable use," "use" has the same meaning.

Useful. The basic quid pro quo contemplated by the Constitution and the congress for granting a patent monopoly is the benefit derived by the public from an invention with substantial utility. Specific benefit must exist in currently available form. By "useful" is meant such an invention as may be applied to some beneficial use in society, in contradistinction to an invention which is illegal, injurious to morals or against public policy.

Useful life. In accounting and taxation, the period of time for which an asset is capable of being used for the production of income.

For income tax purposes, the "useful life" of depreciable property is period over which asset may reasonably be expected to be useful to taxpayer in his trade or business or in production of income, and such is necessarily an estimate made at time when property is first put to use. Useful life for depreciation purposes is an estimate; length of the useful period must be shown by evidence that allows it to be estimated with reasonable accuracy.

Usefulness. Capabilities for use. The word pertains to the future as well as to the past.

Use immunity. Term generally refers to order of court which compels witness to give testimony of self-incriminating nature but provides that such testimony may not be used as evidence in subsequent prosecution of such witness. Such immunity protects a witness only against actual use of his compelled testimony and evidence derived directly or indirectly therefrom, while "transactional immunity" protects the person against all later prosecutions relating to matters about which he testifies. *See also* Immunity.

Use in commerce. A prerequisite for trademark registration. An applicant must show a bona fide intention to use the mark in commerce with respect to the goods or services for which registration is sought and not merely to reserve any rights in a mark. 15 U.S.C.A. § 1051(b). *See also* Trademark.

User. The actual exercise or enjoyment of any right, property, drugs, franchise, etc.

Adverse user. Such a use of the property under claim of right as the owner himself would make, asking no permission, and disregarding all other claims to it, so far as they conflict with this use. *See also* Adverse possession.

User fee. Charges imposed on persons for the use of a particular facility. A charge designed only to make the user of state-provided facilities pay a reasonable fee to help defray the costs of their construction and maintenance may be constitutionally imposed on interstate and domestic users alike. Such charges are usually upheld as long as they are neither discriminatory nor excessive.

Use tax. A sales tax that is collectible by the seller where the purchaser is domiciled in a different state. A tax on the use, consumption, or storage of tangible property, usually at the same rate as the sales tax, and levied for the purpose of preventing tax avoidance by the purchase of articles in a state or taxing jurisdiction which does not levy sales taxes or has a lower rate. A tax on the use, consumption, or storage of tangible property, usually at the same rate as the sales tax, and levied for the purpose of preventing tax avoidance by the purchase of articles in a state or taxing jurisdiction which does not levy sales taxes or has a lower rate.

A levy on privilege of using, within taxing state, property purchased outside the state, if the property would have been subject to the sales tax had it been purchased at home. Such tax ordinarily serves to complement sales tax by eliminating incentive to make major purchases in states with lower sales taxes; it requires resident who shops out-of-state to pay use tax equal to sales tax savings.

Use variance. *See* Variance.

Using mail to defraud. The elements of this offense are the formation of a scheme or artifice to defraud, and use of mails for purpose of executing or attempting to execute such scheme or artifice; the latter element being gist of the offense. 18 U.S.C.A. § 1341. The crime is complete when mails are used in such scheme, and what happened subsequently is not controlling. *See* Mail fraud.

Usual. Habitual; ordinary; customary; according to usage or custom; commonly established, observed, or practiced. That which happens in common use or occurs in ordinary practice or course of events. Synonymous with custom, common, normal, regular.

Usual covenants. *See* Covenant.

Usual place of abode. Within meaning of statute or rule relating to service of process is place where defendant is actually living at time of service; is place where person would most likely have knowledge of service of process and is generally considered to be place where person is living at time of service. *See* Domicile; Residence; Service *(Service of process).*

Usufruct /yúwz(y)əfrə́kt/. In the civil law, a real right of limited duration on the property of another. The features of the right vary with the nature of the things subject to it as consumables or nonconsumables. Civ. Code La. art. 535. The right of using and enjoying and receiving the profits of property that belongs to another, and a "usufructuary" is a person who has the usufruct or right of enjoying anything in which he has no property interest.

There are three types of "usufructs": natural profits produced by the subject of the usufruct, industrial profits produced by cultivation, and civil profits, which are rents, freights and revenues from annuities and from other effects or rights. *See also* Legal usufruct.

Usufructuary /yùwz(y)əfrə́ktyuwəriy/. In the civil law, one who has the usufruct or right of enjoying anything in which he has no property.

Usurious /yuwzhúriyəs/. Pertaining to usury; partaking of the nature of usury; involving usury; tainted with usury; as, a usurious contract. *See* Usury.

Usurious contract. A contract where interest to be paid exceeds the rate established by statute. *See also* Usury.

Usurp /yuwsə́rp/. To seize and hold any office by force, and without right; applied to seizure of office, place, functions, powers, rights, etc. of another.

Usurpation /yùwsərpéyshən/. The unlawful encroachment or assumption of the use of property, power or authority which belongs to another. An interruption or the disturbing a man in his right and possession.

The unlawful seizure or assumption of sovereign power. The assumption of government or supreme power by force or illegally, in derogation of the constitution and of the rights of the lawful ruler.

Usurpation for which writ of prohibition may be granted involves attempted exercise of power not possessed by inferior officer.

Usurpation of franchise or office /yùwsərpéyshən əv frǽnchayz ər ófəs/. The unjustly intruding upon or exercising any office, franchise, or liberty belonging to another. *See also* Usurpation; Usurper of a public office.

Usurped power. *See* Usurp; Usurpation.

Usurper. One who assumes the right of government by force, contrary to and in violation of the constitution of the country.

Usurper of a public office. One who either intrudes into a vacant office or ousts the incumbent without any color of title. One who intrudes on office and assumes to exercise its functions without legal title or color of right thereto. Any person attempting to fill pretended office attempted to be created by an unconstitutional law.

Usury. Charging an illegal rate of interest. Collectively, the laws of a jurisdiction regulating the charging of interest rates. A usurious loan is one whose interest rates are determined to be in excess of those permitted by the usury laws. An illegal contract for a loan or forbearance of money, goods, or things in action, by which illegal interest is reserved, or agreed to be reserved or taken. An unconscionable and exorbitant rate or amount of interest. An unlawful contract upon the loan of money, to receive the same again with exorbitant increase. The reserving and taking, or contracting to reserve and take, either directly or by indirection, a greater sum for the use of money than the lawful interest. *See also* Legal interest; Loansharking; Usury laws.

Usury laws. Statutes that prohibit finance charges (interest and other forms of compensation for loaning money) above a certain level for debt. See 18 U.S.C.A. § 891 *et seq.* with respect to

extortionate credit transactions. *See also* Loan sharking; Usury.

Utility. In patent law, a patent applicant must demonstrate that his invention performs some function that is of benefit to society. This utility requirement is in addition to the requirements of non-obviousness and novelty.

Utmost care. Term is substantially synonymous with "highest care."

Utmost resistance. This term, under the rule that to constitute rape there must be utmost resistance by the woman, is a relative rather than a positive term, and means that greatest effort of which she is capable must be used to foil assailant. Most states have eliminated this as a requirement to prove nonconsent in rape cases.

Utter, *v.* To put or send (as a forged check) into circulation; to publish or put forth; to offer. To utter and publish an instrument, as a counterfeit note, is to declare or assert, directly or indirectly, by words or actions, that it is good; uttering it is a declaration that it is good, with an intention or offer to pass it. To utter, as used in a statute against forgery and counterfeiting, means to offer, whether accepted or not, a forged instrument, with the representation, by words or actions, that the same is genuine.

The phrase "utters or publishes as true", as used in federal forgery statute, means to make or attempt any use of a written or printed instrument or document, such as an attempt to place a check in circulation (as when it is presented for payment), whereby, or in connection with which, some assertion, representation or claim is made to another in some way or manner, directly or indirectly, expressly or impliedly, or by words or conduct, that the check or document is genuine.

Uttering a forged instrument. The crime of passing a false or worthless instrument, such as a check, or counterfeit security, with the intent to defraud or injure the recipient. See *e.g.* 18 U.S. C.A. §§ 472, 479, 483. *See* Counterfeit; Forgery; Utter.

Utter, *adj.* Entire; complete; absolute; total.

Utterance. *See* Excited utterance; Spontaneous declarations.

V

v. Abbreviation of "versus" (against) in titles of legal actions and reported cases.

V.A. Veterans Affairs (Department of); Veterans Administration. *See* Veterans Administration.

Vacancy. A place or position which is empty, unfilled, or unoccupied. An unoccupied or unfilled post, position, or office. An existing office, etc., without an incumbent. The state of being destitute of an incumbent, or a proper or legally qualified officer. The term is principally applied to an interruption in the incumbency of an office, or to cases where the office is not occupied by one who has a legal right to hold it and to exercise the rights and perform the duties pertaining thereto. The word "vacancy," when applied to official positions, means, in its ordinary and popular sense, that an office is unoccupied, and that there is no incumbent who has a lawful right to continue therein until the happening of a future event, though the word is sometimes used with reference to an office temporarily filled. *See also* Vacant.

Vacant. Empty; unoccupied; as, a "vacant" office or parcel of land. Deprived of contents, without inanimate objects. It implies entire abandonment, nonoccupancy for any purpose. Absolutely free, unclaimed, and unoccupied.

See also Vacancy, and as to *vacant* Possession and Succession, see those titles.

Vacate. To annul; to set aside; to cancel or rescind. To render an act void; as, to vacate an entry of record, or a judgment. As applied to a judgment or decree it is not synonymous with "suspend" which means to stay enforcement of judgment or decree.

To put an end to; as, to vacate a street. To move out; to make vacant or empty; to leave; especially, to surrender possession by removal; to cease from occupancy.

See also Annul; Reverse; Vacancy.

Vacatio /vəkéysh(iy)ow/. Lat. In the civil law, exemption; immunity; privilege; dispensation; exemption from the burden of office.

Vacation of judgment. The setting aside of a judgment on grounds that it was issued by mistake, inadvertence, surprise, excusable neglect or fraud. While the term "vacate" has been replaced by Fed.R.Civil P. 60, the basis for relief from judgment is the same as formerly when one sought to vacate a judgment.

Vacation of term. That period of time between the end of one term of court and the beginning of another. *Compare* Recess.

Vagrancy. At common law, the act of going about from place to place by a person without visible means of support, who is idle, and who, though able to work for his or her maintenance, refuses to do so, but lives without labor or on the charity of others.

As defined by Kansas Criminal Code, vagrancy is: (a) Engaging in an unlawful occupation; or (b) Being of the age of eighteen (18) years or over and able to work and without lawful means of support and failing or refusing to seek employment; or (c) Loitering in any community without visible means of support; or (d) Loitering on the streets or in a place open to the public with intent to solicit for immoral purposes; or (e) Deriving support in whole or in part from begging. KSA 21–4108. State vagrancy statutes, however, vary greatly, and many have been declared unconstitutional because, as drawn, they purport to punish conduct which is not criminal or are worded too vaguely to inform persons of the nature of the act declared criminal.

Vagrancy laws. *See* Vagrancy; Visible means of support.

Vague. Indefinite. Uncertain; not susceptible of being understood. For purposes of determining whether statute is constitutionally infirm by reason of being vague, statute is "vague" if its prohibitions are not clearly defined; or if it does not provide explicit standards for its enforcement. *See also* Vagueness doctrine.

Vagueness doctrine. Under this principle, a law (*e.g.*, criminal statute) which does not fairly inform a person of what is commanded or prohibited is unconstitutional as violative of due process. The doctrine originates in due process clause of Fourteenth Amendment, and is basis for striking down legislation which contains insufficient warning of what conduct is unlawful. It requires that penal statutes give notice to ordinary person of what is prohibited and provide definite standards to guide discretionary actions of police officers so as to prevent arbitrary and discriminatory law enforcement. *See also* Vague; Void for vagueness doctrine.

Valid. Having legal strength or force, executed with proper formalities, incapable of being rightfully overthrown or set aside. Founded on truth of fact; capable of being justified; supported, or defended; not weak or defective. Of binding force; legally sufficient or efficacious; authorized by law. Good or sufficient in point of law; efficacious; executed with the proper formalities; incapable of being rightfully overthrown or set aside; sustainable and effective in law, as distinguished from that which exists or took place in fact or appearance, but has not the requisites to enable it to be recognized and enforced by law. A deed, will, or other instrument, which has received all the formalities required by law, is said to be valid.

Meritorious, as, a *valid* defense.

See also Legal.

Validate. To make valid; confirm; sanction; affirm.

Validating statute. A statute, purpose of which is to cure past errors and omissions and thus make valid what was invalid, but it grants no indulgence for the correction of future errors.

Validation. Process of gathering evidence to show job-relatedness of employment test or selection device.

Valid contract. A contract in which all of the elements of a contract are present and, therefore, enforceable at law by the parties. A properly constituted contract having legal force. *Compare* Unenforceable contract.

Validity. Legal sufficiency, in contradistinction to mere regularity.

Valuable. Of financial or market value; commanding or worth a good price; of considerable worth in any respect, whether monetary or intrinsic.

Valuable consideration. A class of consideration upon which a promise may be founded, which entitles the promisee to enforce his claim against an unwilling promisor. For contract, may consist either in some right, interest, profit, or benefit accruing to one party, or some forbearance, detriment, loss, or responsibility given, suffered, or undertaken by the other. A gain or loss to either party is not essential, it is sufficient if the party in whose favor the contract is made parts with a right which he might otherwise exert. It need not be translatable into dollars and cents, but is sufficient if it consists of performance, or promise thereof, which promisor treats and considers of value to him. It is not essential that the person to whom the consideration moves should be benefited, provided the person from whom it moves is, in a legal sense, injured. The injury may consist of a compromise of a disputed claim or forbearance to exercise a legal right, the alteration in position being regarded as a detriment that forms a consideration independent of the actual value of the right forborne. Mutual promises in contract

is sufficient. For Fair and valuable consideration, see that title. *See also* Consideration.

Valuation. The act of ascertaining the worth of a thing. The estimated worth or price of a thing. *See also* Appraisal; Assessed valuation; Fair value; Special use valuation; Value.

Value. The utility of an object in satisfying, directly or indirectly, the needs or desires of human beings, called by economists "value in use," or its worth consisting in the power of purchasing other objects, called "value in exchange." Also the estimated or appraised worth of any object or property, calculated in money. To estimate the worth of; to rate at a certain price; to appraise; or to place a certain estimate of worth on in a scale of values.

Any consideration sufficient to support a simple contract. The term is often used as an abbreviation for "valuable consideration," especially in the phrases "purchaser for value," "holder for value," etc. *See* Consideration; Valuable consideration.

In economic consideration, the word "value," when used in reference to property, has a variety of significations, according to the connection in which the word is employed. It may mean the cost of a production or reproduction of the property in question, when it is sometimes called "sound value;" or it may mean the purchasing power of the property, or the amount of money which the property will command in exchange, if sold, this being called its "market value," which in the case of any particular property may be more or less than either the cost of its production or its value measured by its utility to the present or some other owner; or the word may mean the subjective value of property, having in view its profitableness for some particular purpose, sometimes termed its "value for use."

Salable value, actual value, market value, fair value, reasonable value, and cash value may all mean the same thing and may be designed to effect the same purpose.

"Value," as used in Art. I, § 8, U.S.Const., giving Congress power to coin money and regulate the value thereof, is the true, inherent, and essential value, not depending upon accident, place, or person, but the same everywhere and to every one, and in this sense regulating the value of the coinage is merely determining and maintaining coinage composed of certain coins within certain limitations at a certain specific composition and weight.

For taxation purposes, "value" is the worth established by bargaining process of willing buyer and willing seller. *See* Fair market value.

Value as it relates to stolen property is the market value at the time and place of the taking, or, in case of property without a market value, the cost of replacing it. The National Stolen

Property Act defines value as "face, par or market value, whichever is the greatest ..." 18 U.S.C.A. § 2311.

Value as used in eminent domain proceeding means market value *(q.v.)*. *See also* Just compensation; Market value.

Most generally, a legal basis for enforcing a transfer of property or an undertaking, including a promise or other commitment, which is different from common-law consideration. For purposes of the U.C.C. generally, see U.C.C. § 1–201(44); for purposes of due-course status, see U.C.C. §§ 3–303; 4–208 & 4–209.

Under U.C.C. § 1–201(44), a person gives "value" for rights if he acquires them: (a) in return for a binding commitment to extend credit or for the extension of immediately available credit whether or not drawn upon and whether or not a chargeback is provided for in the event of difficulties in collection; or (b) as security for or in total or partial satisfaction of a pre-existing claim; or (c) by accepting delivery pursuant to a pre-existing contract for purchase; or (d) generally, in return for any consideration sufficient to support a simple contract.

See also Actual value; Agreed value; Annual value; Appraisal; Assess; Cash value; Commuted value; Consideration; Diminution in value; Face value; Fair cash market value; Fair cash value; Fair market value; Fair value; Going concern value; Improved value; Insurable value; Intrinsic value; Just compensation; Leasehold value; Market value; Net asset value; Par value; Policy value; Present value; Present value index.

Actual cash value. In insurance, its customary meaning is replacement cost new less normal depreciation, though it may be determined by current market value of similar property or by the cost to replace or repair the property.

Book value. The value at which assets of a business are carried on the books of the company. The book value of fixed assets is arrived at by subtracting accumulated depreciation from the cost of the fixed assets. It may also refer to the net worth of a business arrived at by subtracting liabilities from assets. *See also* Book.

Cash surrender value. In life insurance, the amount which the insurer will pay before death when the policy is cancelled. *See also* Cash value.

Intrinsic value. The value which a thing has as of itself, and not the value reflecting extrinsic factors such as market conditions.

Liquidation value. The value of a business or of an asset when it is sold other than in the ordinary course of business as in the liquidation of a business.

Market value. Fair value of property as between one who wants to purchase it and another who desires to sell it. What willing purchaser will give for property under fair market conditions. Not what the owner could realize at a forced sale, but the price he could obtain after reasonable and ample time, such as would ordinarily be taken by an owner to make a sale of like property. *See* Fair cash market value; Fair market value; Fair value; Just compensation.

Net value. The "reserve" or "net value" of a life insurance policy is the fund accumulated out of the net premiums during the earlier years of the policy where the premium throughout life or a term of years exceeds the actual value of the risk. The "net value" of a policy is equivalent to "reserve," and means that part of the annual premium paid by insured which, according to the American Experience Table of Mortality, must be set apart to meet or mature the company's obligations to insured, the net value of a policy on a given date being its actual value, its reserve.

No par value. Stock of a corporation which has no par value but which represents a proportionate share of the ownership of the corporation.

Optimal use value. Synonym for Most suitable use value *(q.v.)*.

Par value. The nominal value of stock arrived at by dividing the total stated capital stock by the number of shares authorized.

Residual value. Amount expected to be obtained when a fixed asset is disposed of at the end of its useful life (also called scrap or salvage value).

Scrap value. The value of the constituent materials and components of a thing; not its value for the purpose for which it was made.

Stated value. The dollar value of no par stock established by the corporation as constituting the capital of the corporation.

Surrender value. See Cash surrender value, above.

Terminal value. In accounting, value of the project remaining at the end of the project's useful life.

True value. As referring to value at which property must be assessed, is price which would be paid therefor on assessing date to willing seller, not compelled to sell, by willing purchaser, not compelled to purchase.

Use value. The value established by the usefulness of an object and not its value for sale or exchange.

Value of matter in controversy. See Amount in controversy; Jurisdictional amount.

Value received. A phrase usually employed in a bill of exchange or promissory note, to denote that a lawful consideration has been given for it. It is prima facie evidence of consideration, although not necessarily in money.

Value added tax. *See* Tax.

Valued policy. Insurance policy in which a definite valuation is by agreement of both parties put on the subject-matter of the insurance and written in the face of the policy and such value, in the absence of fraud or mistake, is conclusive on the parties. One in which both property insured and loss are valued. It is distinguished from an "open policy", which is one where the value of the property insured is not settled in the policy.

Valueless. Worthless.

Vandalism. Such willful or malicious acts as are intended to damage or destroy property. Willful or ignorant destruction of property of another, commonly referring to artistic or literary treasures. Hostility to or contempt for what is beautiful or venerable. Vandalism connotes act of vandal and in ordinary usage is not limited to destruction of works of art, but has broadened its meaning to include destruction of property generally. Within dwelling policy means the willful and malicious destruction of property generally, and the destruction must have been intentional or in such reckless and wanton disregard of rights of others as to be equivalent of intent, and malice may be inferred from act of destruction. *See also* Deface; Desecrate.

Variable annuity. An annuity whose periodic payments depend upon some uncertain outcome, such as stock market prices. An annuity contract in which the premiums or payments are invested in securities to keep pace with inflation. The payments, therefore, which the annuitant receives vary from time to time. *See also* Annuity.

Variable interest rate. Interest rate that is set according to fluctuation in the prime rate; it is a floating rate.

Variable-rate mortgage. *See* Mortgage.

Variance. *Civil and criminal practice.* A discrepancy or disagreement between two instruments or two pleading allegations in the same cause, which should by law be entirely consonant. Thus, if the evidence adduced by the plaintiff does not agree with the allegations of his pleadings, it is a variance. A disagreement between the allegations and the proof in some matter which, in point of law, is essential to the charge or claim. The test of materiality of "variance" in an information is whether the pleading so fully and correctly informs a defendant of offense with which he is charged that, taking into account proof which is introduced against him, he is not misled in making his defense.

To constitute a fatal variance, there must be a real and tangible difference between the allegations in the pleading and the proof offered in its support. The difference must be substantial and material. It must be one that actually misleads the adverse party to his prejudice in maintaining his action or defense on the merits; or, in criminal cases, one which might mislead the defense or expose a defendant to being put twice in jeopardy for the same offense, as, *e.g.*, when evidence offered at trial proves facts materially different from those alleged in the indictment.

Stipulations to vary discovery procedures are governed by Fed.R. Civil P. 29.

The assertion of "variance" or discrepancy between the pleadings and proof has essentially been eliminated in *civil* cases by Fed.R.Civil P. 15(b) which permits liberal amendment of the pleadings to conform to the evidence. This same rule is followed by most state courts. In *criminal* cases, variances that do not affect the substantial rights of the accused will be disregarded. *See* Fed.R.Crim.P. 7(c), (e), 52(a).

See also Area variance; Departure; Fatal variance; Error *(Harmless error)*; Irregularity.

Accounting. In accounting, a variance is the difference between the actual and standard cost of such things as direct materials, direct labor, and overhead. An unfavorable variance generally means that the actual costs incurred exceeded the budgeted amounts.

Zoning. Permission to depart from the literal requirements of a zoning ordinance by virtue of unique hardship due to special circumstances regarding person's property. It is in the nature of a waiver of the strict letter of the zoning law upon substantial compliance with it and without sacrificing its spirit and purpose. An authorization to a property owner to depart from literal requirements of zoning regulations in utilization of his property in cases in which strict enforcement of the zoning regulations would cause undue hardship. A "use variance" is a variance permitting a use other than that permitted in particular district by zoning ordinance. *Compare* Area variance; Special exception; Special use permit; Unnecessary hardship.

VAT. Value added tax. *See* Tax.

Vehicular crimes. Criminal acts committed while operating a motor vehicle, *e.g.* vehicular manslaughter (N.Y.Penal Law 125.13), vehicular assault (N.Y.Penal Law 120.04). *See also* Vehicular homicide.

Vehicular homicide. Homicide caused by the unlawful and negligent operation of a motor vehicle. Both intentional conduct and negligence may be the basis for such charge though statutes vary from state to state as to the elements of the crime. See e.g. Model Penal Code § 210.4 (negligent homicide); N.Y. Penal Law 125.13 (vehicular manslaughter). *See also* Homicide.

Vend. To transfer to another for a pecuniary equivalent; to make an object of trade, especially by hawking or peddling; to sell. The term is not commonly applied to the sale of real estate, although its derivatives "vendor" and "vendee" are.

Vendee. A purchaser or buyer; one to whom anything is sold. Generally used of the purchaser of real property, one who acquires goods by sale being generally called a "buyer." *Compare* Vendor.

Vendor. The person who transfers property or goods by sale. A seller of goods or services. A merchant, retail dealer, supplier, importer, wholesale distributor; one who buys to sell; a seller. *Compare* Vendee.

Vendor's lien. A creature of equity, being a lien impliedly belonging to a vendor for the unpaid purchase price of land, where he has not taken any other lien or security beyond the personal obligation of the purchaser. An equitable security which arises from the fact that a vendee has received from his vendor property for which he has not paid the full consideration, and such lien exists independently of any express agreement. Also, a lien existing in the unpaid vendor of chattels, the same remaining in his hands, to the extent of the purchase price, where the sale was for cash, or on a term of credit which has expired, or on an agreement by which the seller is to retain possession.

In English and American law a vendor's lien is exceptional in character, and is an importation from the civil law, which found its recognition through courts of chancery, on the equitable principle that the person who had secured the estate of another ought not in conscience to be allowed to keep it and not pay full consideration money, and that to enforce that payment it was just that the vendor should have a lien upon the property.

Venire /vənáyriy/. Lat. To come; to appear in court. The group of citizens from whom a jury is chosen in a given case. Sometimes used as the name of the writ for summoning a jury, more commonly called a "venire facias." *See also* Jury panel. A special venire is sometimes prepared for a protracted case.

Venire facias /vənáyriy féysh(iy)əs/. Lat. A judicial writ, directed to the sheriff of the county in which a cause is to be tried, commanding him that he "cause to come" before the court, on a certain day therein mentioned, twelve good and lawful men of the body of his county, qualified according to law, by whom the truth of the matter may be the better known, and who are in no wise of kin either to the plaintiff or to the defendant, to make a jury of the county between the parties in the action, because as well the plaintiff as the defendant, between whom the matter in variance is, have put themselves upon that jury, and that he return the names of the jurors, etc.

Venireman /vənáyriymən/. A member of a panel of jurors; a prospective juror. Before becoming a juror, a person must pass voir dire examination. *See* Jury.

Venture, v. To take (the) chances.

Venture, n. An undertaking attended with risk, especially one aiming at making money; business speculation. *See also* Joint enterprise; Joint venture.

Venture capital. Funding for new companies or others embarking on new or turnaround ventures that entails some investment risk but offers the potential for above average future profits. Venture capital is often provided by firms that specialize in financing new ventures with capital supplied by investors interested in speculative or high risk investments. *See also* Risk capital; Seed money.

Venue. Formerly spelled *visne*. In common law pleading and practice, a neighborhood; the neighborhood, place, or county in which an injury is declared to have been done, or fact declared to have happened.

The particular county, or geographical area, in which a court with jurisdiction may hear and determine a case. Venue deals with locality of suit, that is, with question of which court, or courts, of those that possess adequate personal and subject matter jurisdiction may hear the specific suit in question. It relates only to place where or territory within which either party may require case to be tried. It has relation to convenience of litigants and may be waived or laid by consent of parties.

In the federal courts, the term refers to the district in which the suit is brought. Venue may be determined by where the action arose or where the parties reside or conduct their business. The venue statute for civil actions in federal district courts is 28 U.S.C.A. § 1391.

In federal cases the prosecutor's discretion regarding the location of the prosecution is limited by Article III, § 2, U.S.Const., which requires trial in the state where the offense "shall have been committed," and the Sixth Amendment, which guarantees an impartial jury "of the state and district wherein the crime shall have been committed." *See also Federal criminal cases, below.*

Venue does not refer to jurisdiction at all. "Jurisdiction" of the court means the inherent power to decide a case, whereas "venue" designates the particular county or city in which a court with jurisdiction may hear and determine the case. As such, while a defect in venue may be waived by the parties, lack of jurisdiction may not.

See also Change of venue; Forum conveniens; Forum non conveniens.

Federal criminal cases. Except as otherwise permitted by statute or by the rules, the prosecution shall be had in a district in which the offense was committed. The court shall fix the place of trial within the district with due regard to the convenience of the defendant and the witnesses. Fed.R. Crim.P. 18 *et seq.*

Venue facts. Facts to be established at hearing on plea of privilege. Facts which by statute constitute an exception to the general right of a defendant to be sued in the county of his residence.

Venue jurisdiction. Power of the particular court to function. *See also* Venue.

Veracity. Truthfulness; accuracy.

Verba /vɜrbə/. Lat. (Plural of *verbum.*) Words.

Verbal. Strictly, of or pertaining to words; expressed in words, whether spoken or written, but commonly in spoken words; hence, by confusion, spoken; oral. Parol; by word of mouth; as, verbal agreement, verbal evidence; or written, but not signed, or not executed with the formalities required for a deed or prescribed by statute in particular cases.

Verbal act doctrine. Under this doctrine, utterances accompanying some act or conduct to which it is desired to give legal effect are admissible where conduct to be characterized by words is material to issue and equivocal in its nature, and words accompany conduct and aid in giving it legal significance. Under this doctrine, where declarations of an individual are so connected with his acts as to derive a degree of credit from such connection, independently of the declaration, the declaration becomes part of the transaction and is admissible. The "verbal act doctrine" and the "res gestæ doctrine" coincide practically and serve equally to admit certain sorts of statements, but they are nevertheless wholly distinct in their nature and in their right to exist. *See also* Excited utterance; Res *(Res gestae)*; Verbal acts.

Verbal acts. Situations in which legal consequences flow from the fact that words were said, *e.g.* the words of offer and acceptance which create a contract, or words of slander upon which an action for damages is based. The rule against hearsay does not apply to proof of relevant verbal acts because evidence of such acts is being offered to prove something other than the truth of an out of court assertion. *See* Excited utterance; Res *(Res gestae)*; Verbal act doctrine.

Verbal assaults. *See* Threat.

Verbal contract. An oral, nonwritten agreement; a parol contract. *See also* Contract *(Parol contract)*; Oral contract.

Verdict. From the Latin "veredictum," a true declaration. The formal decision or finding made

by a jury, impaneled and sworn for the trial of a cause, and reported to the court (and accepted by it), upon the matters or questions duly submitted to them upon the trial. The definitive answer given by the jury to the court concerning the matters of fact committed to the jury for their deliberation and determination.

The usual verdict, one where the jury decides which side wins (and how much, sometimes), is called a general verdict. When the jury is asked to answer specific questions of fact, it is called a special verdict. *See General verdict* and *Special verdict below.*

In criminal cases the verdict shall be unanimous, and shall be returned by the jury to the judge in open court. Fed.R.Crim.P. 31. In civil cases the parties may stipulate that a verdict of a stated majority of the jurors shall be taken as the verdict of the jury. Fed.R.Civil P. 48.

See also Polling the jury.

Chance verdict. One determined by hazard or lot, and not by the deliberate understanding and agreement of the jury. While formerly used, such are now illegal.

Compromise verdict. One which is the result, not of justifiable concession of views, but of improper compromise of the vital principles which should have controlled the decision. Although it is proper for jurors to harmonize their views and reach a verdict with proper regard for each other's opinions, it is not proper for any juror to surrender his conscientious convictions on any material issue in return for a relinquishment by others of their like settled opinions on another issue, producing a result which does not command the approval of the whole panel.

Directed verdict. Verdict ordered by the judge as a matter of law when he rules that the party with the burden of proof has failed to make out a prima facie case. The judge under these circumstances orders the jury to return a verdict for the other party. See Fed.R.Civil P. 50. Motion for judgment of acquittal is used in place of directed verdict in criminal cases. See Fed.R.Crim.P. 29.

Excessive verdict. See that title.

General verdict. A verdict whereby the jury find either for the plaintiff or for the defendant in general terms; the ordinary form of a verdict. A finding by the jury in the terms of the issue, or all the issues, referred to them. That by which they pronounce generally upon all or any of the issues, either in favor of the plaintiff or defendant;—distinguished from a special verdict, which is that by which the jury finds facts only.

General verdict with interrogatories. The court may submit to the jury, together with appropriate forms for a general verdict, written interrogatories upon one or more issues of fact the decision of which is necessary to a verdict. The court shall give such explanation or instruction as may be necessary to enable the jury both to make answers to the interrogatories and to render a general verdict, and the court shall direct the jury both to make written answers and to render a general verdict. When the general verdict and the answers are harmonious, the appropriate judgment upon the verdict and answers shall be entered. When the answers are consistent with each other but one or more is inconsistent with the general verdict, judgment may be entered in accordance with the answers, notwithstanding the general verdict, or the court may return the jury for further consideration of its answers and verdict or may order a new trial. When the answers are inconsistent with each other and one or more is likewise inconsistent with the general verdict, judgment shall not be entered, but the court shall return the jury for further consideration of its answers and verdict or shall order a new trial. Fed.R.Civil P. 49(b).

Instructed verdict. *See Directed verdict, above.*

Joint verdict. See that title.

Judgment notwithstanding verdict. *See* Non obstante veredicto.

Open verdict. A verdict of a coroner's jury which finds that the subject "came to his death by means to the jury unknown," or "came to his death at the hands of a person or persons to the jury unknown," that is, one which leaves open either the question whether any crime was committed or the identity of the criminal.

Partial verdict. In criminal law, a verdict by which the jury acquits the defendant as to a part of the accusation and finds him guilty as to the residue.

Privy verdict. One given after the judge has left or adjourned the court, and the jury, being agreed, in order to be delivered from their confinement, obtain leave to give their verdict privily to the judge out of court. Such a verdict is of no force unless afterwards affirmed by a public verdict given openly in court. This practice is now superseded by that of rendering a sealed verdict.

Public verdict. A verdict openly delivered by the jury in court. Such is usually required; *e.g.* Fed. R.Crim.P. 31(a).

Quotient verdict. See that title.

Repugnant verdict. Verdicts are "repugnant" when there are charges of two crimes, each of which has identical elements, and there is finding of guilt on one but not on the other.

Sealed verdict. *See* Sealed.

Several defendants. If there are two or more defendants, the jury at any time during its deliberations may return a verdict or verdicts with respect to a defendant or defendants as to whom it has agreed; if the jury cannot agree with respect to all, the defendant or defendants as to whom it does not agree may be tried again. Fed. R.Crim.P. 31(b).

Special verdict. A special finding of the facts of a case by a jury, leaving to the court the application of the law to the facts thus found. The "special" verdict is a statement by the jury of the facts it has found—in essence, the jury's answers to questions submitted to it; the court determines which party, based on those answers, is to have judgment. With the advent of the apportionment rule among tortfeasors, closely followed by the adoption of a rule of comparative negligence to replace the traditional rule of contributory negligence, the need to have the jury reveal its specific findings of percentages of fault in personal injury and wrongful death cases has given rise to the increased use of the special verdict.

The court may require a jury to return only a special verdict in the form of a special written finding upon each issue of fact. In that event, the court may submit to the jury written questions susceptible of categorical or other brief answer or may submit written forms of the several special findings which might properly be made under the pleadings and evidence; or it may use such other method of submitting the issues and requiring the written findings thereon as it deems most appropriate. The court shall give to the jury such explanation and instructions concerning the matter thus submitted as may be necessary to enable the jury to make its findings upon each issue. Fed.R.Civil P. 49(a).

Split verdict. A verdict in which one party prevails on some claims in issue while the other party prevails on other claims. In criminal law, a verdict finding a defendant guilty of one charge but innocent of another, or finding one defendant guilty while acquitting a codefendant. See *e.g.* Fed.R.Crim.P. 31.

Stipulation on majority verdict. The parties may stipulate that a verdict of a stated majority of the jurors shall be taken as the verdict of the jury. Fed.R.Civil P. 48.

Verdict by lot. *See Chance verdict, above.*

Verdict contrary to law. A verdict which law does not authorize jury to render on evidence because conclusion drawn is not justified thereby. One which is contrary to the principles of law as applied to the facts which the jury were called upon to try and contrary to the principles of law which should govern the cause. *See* Non obstante veredicto.

Verdict for lesser offense. *See* Lesser included offense.

Verdict subject to opinion of court. A verdict returned by the jury, the entry of judgment upon which is subject to the determination of points of law reserved by the court upon the trial.

Verdict, estoppel by. Rule that where some controlling fact or question material to determination of both causes has been adjudicated in former suit by court of competent jurisdiction, and same fact or question is again an issue between the same parties, adjudication in first cause will, if properly presented, be conclusive of the same question in later suit, irrespective of whether cause of action is the same in both suits. "Estoppel by verdict" or "collateral estoppel" provides that prior judgment must be deemed conclusive as to all right of parties and their privies when same parties or their privies are involved with same issues actually or necessarily finally determined by court of competent jurisdiction in earlier, but different, cause of action. *See also* Collateral estoppel doctrine; Judgment, estoppel by; Res *(Res judicata)*.

Verification. Confirmation of correctness, truth, or authenticity, by affidavit, oath, or deposition. Affidavit of truth of matter stated and object of verification is to assure good faith in averments or statements of party. Sworn or equivalent confirmation of truth. For example, a verified complaint typically has an attached affidavit of plaintiff to the effect that the complaint is true. In accounting, the process of substantiating entries in books of account. *See also* Acknowledgment; Affidavit; Authentication; Certification; Confirmation; Oath; Verify.

Verified copy. Copy of document which is shown by independent evidence to be true. A copy, if successive witnesses trace the original into the hands of a witness who made or compared the copy.

Verified names. Names verified by county clerk in accordance with his duty to check names of signers against official registration lists.

Verify. To confirm or substantiate by oath or affidavit. Particularly used of making formal oath to accounts, petitions, pleadings, and other papers. The word "verified," when used in a statute, ordinarily imports a verity attested by the sanctity of an oath. It is frequently used interchangeably with "sworn."

To prove to be true; to confirm or establish the truth or truthfulness of; to check or test the accuracy or exactness of; to confirm or establish the authenticity of; to authenticate; to maintain; to affirm; to support; second; back as a friend.

See also Verification.

Verily /véhrəliy/. In very truth; beyond doubt or question; in fact; certainly; truly; confidently; really.

Versus /vórsəs/. Lat. Against. In the title of a cause, the name of the plaintiff is put first, followed by the word *"versus,"* then the defendant's name. Thus, "Fletcher *versus* Peck," or "Fletcher *against* Peck." The word is commonly abbreviated *"vs."* or *"v."* Vs. and *versus* have become ingrafted upon the English language; their meaning is as well understood and their use quite as appropriate as the word *against* could be.

Vertical. Pertaining to a relationship between a buyer and a seller—*e.g.,* an agreement between a supplier and a retail dealer is called a vertical agreement. *See also* related terms below.

Vertical analysis. In accounting, an analysis in which each figure on a financial statement is related to a relevant total and stated as a percentage of that total.

Vertical integration. Ownership or control of network of production and distribution of goods from raw materials to sale to ultimate consumer.

Vertical merger. Merger between two business firms that have a buyer-seller relationship; that is, one produces a product that is then sold to the other. Acquisition of one company which buys product sold by acquiring company or which sells product bought by acquiring company. If a producer or wholesaler acquires a retailer, it is a *forward* merger. If a retailer or distributor acquires its producer, it is a *backward* merger. *See also* Merger. *Compare* Horizontal merger.

Vertical price-fixing contract. An illegal agreement to maintain prices between producers and wholesalers or distributors, between producers and retailers, or between wholesalers or distributors and retailers. An agreement between a supplier and a distributor, relating to the price at which the distributor will resell the supplier's product; also known as resale price maintenance, it exists if manufacturer or wholesaler suggests resale prices to his retailer and then secures compliance with those prices by doing more than announcing his price policy and refusing to deal. Such agreements are prohibited by antitrust laws. *See also* Price-fixing; Resale price maintenance. *Compare* Horizontal price-fixing.

Vertical restraints of trade. Anticompetitive agreements between entities operating at different levels of market structure, such as manufacturers and distributors (*e.g.,* vertical price-fixing; tying arrangement). *See also* Tying arrangement; Vertical price-fixing contract. *Compare* Horizontal restraints of trade.

Vertical nonprice restraint. A vertical restriction imposed by a supplier on its dealers, which does not govern the resale price. *See* Tying arrangement.

Vertical price restraint. A vertical restriction imposed by a supplier on its dealers, which governs the price at which the product can be resold. *See* Resale price maintenance; Vertical price-fixing contract.

Vest. To give an immediate, fixed right of present or future enjoyment. To accrue to; to be fixed; to take effect.

To clothe with possession; to deliver full possession of land or of an estate; to give seisin; to enfeoff. *See also* Vested.

Vested. Fixed; accrued; settled; absolute; complete. Having the character or given the rights of absolute ownership; not contingent; not subject to be defeated by a condition precedent. Rights are "vested" when right to enjoyment, present or prospective, has become property of some particular person or persons as present interest; mere expectancy of future benefits, or contingent interest in property founded on anticipated continuance of existing laws, does not constitute "vested right." *See also* Accrue; Vest, and specific types of vested interests, *infra.*

Vested devise. *See* Devise.

Vested estate. An interest clothed with a present, legal, and existing right of alienation. Any estate, whether in possession or not, which is not subject to any condition precedent and unperformed. The interest may be either a present and immediate interest, or it may be a future but uncontingent, and therefore transmissible, interest. Estate by which present interest is invariably fixed to remain to determinate person on determination of preceding freehold estate. An estate, when the person or the class which takes the remainder is in existence or is capable of being ascertained when the prior estate vests; or when there is an immediate right of present enjoyment or a present right of future enjoyment.

Vested gift. A gift that is absolute and not contingent or conditional. A gift is vested if it is immediate, notwithstanding that its enjoyment may be postponed. A future gift when the right to receive it is not subject to a condition precedent.

Vested in interest. A legal term applied to a present fixed right of future enjoyment; as reversions, vested remainders, such executory devises, future uses, conditional limitations, and other future interests as are not referred to, or made to depend on, a period or event that is uncertain.

Vested in possession. A legal term applied to a right of present enjoyment actually existing. *See* Vest.

Vested interest. A present right or title to a thing, which carries with it an existing right of alienation, even though the right to possession or enjoyment may be postponed to some uncertain time in the future, as distinguished from a future right, which may never materialize or ripen into

title, and it matters not how long or for what length of time the future possession or right of enjoyment may be postponed, if the present right exists to alienate and pass title. A future interest not dependent on an uncertain period or event, or a fixed present right of future enjoyment. When a person has a right to immediate possession on determination of preceding or particular estate. One in which there is a present fixed right, either of present enjoyment or of future enjoyment.

Vested legacy. A legacy given in such terms that there is a fixed, indefeasible right to its payment. A legacy payable at a future time, certain to arrive, and not subject to conditions precedent, is vested, where there is a person in esse at the testator's death capable of taking when the time arrives, though his interest may be altogether defeated by his own death. A legacy is said to be vested when the words of the testator making the bequest convey a transmissible interest, whether present or future, to the legatee in the legacy. Thus a legacy to one to be paid when he attains the age of twenty-one years is a vested legacy, because it is given unconditionally and absolutely, and therefore vests an immediate interest in the legatee, of which the enjoyment only is deferred or postponed.

Vested pension. Said of a pension plan when an employee (or his or her estate) has rights to all the benefits purchased with the employer's contributions to the plan even if the employee is not employed by this employer at the time of retirement. One in which the right to be paid is not subject to forfeiture if the employment relationship terminates before the employee retires. Vesting of qualified pension plans is governed by the Employees Retirement Income Security Act (ERISA). *See also* Vesting.

Vested remainder. *See* Remainder.

Vested rights. In constitutional law, rights which have so completely and definitely accrued to or settled in a person that they are not subject to be defeated or canceled by the act of any other private person, and which it is right and equitable that the government should recognize and protect, as being lawful in themselves, and settled according to the then current rules of law, and of which the individual could not be deprived arbitrarily without injustice, or of which he could not justly be deprived otherwise than by the established methods of procedure and for the public welfare. Such interests as cannot be interfered with by retrospective laws; interests which it is proper for state to recognize and protect and of which individual cannot be deprived arbitrarily without injustice.

Vesting. Right that employee acquires to various employer-contributed benefits (*e.g.*, pension) after having been employed for requisite number of years. Federal laws (*e.g.*, ERISA) govern vesting rights. *See also* Vested pension.

Veterans Administration. An independent federal agency that administers a system of benefit programs for veterans and their dependents. These benefits include compensation payments for disabilities or death related to military service; pensions; education and rehabilitation; home loan guaranty programs; burial, including cemeteries, markers, flags, etc.; and a comprehensive medical program involving a widespread system of nursing homes, clinics, and hospitals. Effective in 1989 the former Veterans Administration became the Department of Veterans Affairs, and was elevated to cabinet level status. *See also* Court of Veterans Appeals.

Veterans Affairs Department. *See* Veterans Administration.

Veterans Appeals Court. *See* Court of Veterans Appeals.

Veto /víytow/. (Lat. I forbid.) The refusal of assent by the executive officer whose assent is necessary to perfect a law which has been passed by the legislative body, and the message which is usually sent to such body by the executive, stating such refusal and the reasons therefor. A refusal by the president or a governor to sign into law a bill that has been passed by a legislature. In the case of a presidential veto, the bill can still become a law if two-thirds of each House of Congress votes to override the veto. Art. I, § 7, U.S.Const.

It is either absolute or qualified, according as the effect of its exercise is either to destroy the bill finally, or to prevent its becoming law unless again passed by a stated proportion of votes or with other formalities. Or the veto may be merely suspensive.

Line item veto. The power which governors possess in most States to veto items in appropriation bills without affecting any other provisions of such bills.

Overriding veto. Passing a law again that has already been vetoed (turned down and left unsigned) by a government official such as a governor, president, etc. In the federal government, a bill vetoed by the President must receive two-thirds majority in Congress to override the veto and enact the measure into law.

Pocket veto. Non-approval of a legislative act by the president or state governor, with the result that it fails to become a law. Such is not the result of a written disapproval (a veto in the ordinary form), but rather by remaining silent until the adjournment of the legislative body, when that adjournment takes place before the expiration of the period allowed by the constitution for the examination of the bill by the executive.

Inaction on the part of the President when sent a bill just passed by Congress which has the effect of vetoing it. While Presidential inaction for ten days after a bill's presentment normally results in the bill becoming law just as if signed, inaction by the President results in a "pocket veto" if Congress adjourns and thereby prevents the bill's return within the ten-day period after presentment. U.S. Const., Art. I, § 7.

Veto power. Executive's power conditionally to prevent acts passed by legislature, which have not yet become law, from becoming law. *See* Veto.

Vexatious /vekséyshəs/. Without reasonable or probable cause or excuse.

Viability. Capability of living. A term used to denote the power a new-born child possesses of continuing its independent existence. That stage of fetal development when the life of the unborn child may be continued indefinitely outside the womb by natural or artificial life-supportive systems. The constitutionality of this statutory definition (V.A.M.S. (Mo.), § 188.015) was upheld in Planned Parenthood of Central Mo. v. Danforth, 428 U.S. 52, 96 S.Ct. 2831, 49 L.Ed.2d 788.

For purposes of abortion regulation, viability is reached when, in the judgment of the attending physician on the particular facts of the case before him, there is a reasonable likelihood of the fetus' sustained survival outside the womb, with or without artificial support. *See also* Viable; Viable child.

Viable. Livable; having the appearance of being able to live; capable of life. This term is applied to a newly-born infant, and especially to one prematurely born, which is not only born alive, but in such a state of organic development as to make possible the continuance of its life. *See* Viability; Viable child.

Viable child. Unborn child who is capable of independent existence outside his or her mother's womb, even if only in an incubator. In most states a viable unborn child is considered a person under the wrongful death statute, and in some states is considered to be a person under a homicide statute. *See also* Child; Children (*Rights of unborn child*); Unborn child; Viability; Wrongful death statutes.

Vicarious liability. The imposition of liability on one person for the actionable conduct of another, based solely on a relationship between the two persons. Indirect or imputed legal responsibility for acts of another; for example, the liability of an employer for the acts of an employee, or, a principal for torts and contracts of an agent. *See also* Imputed negligence; Respondeat superior. *Compare* Strict liability.

Vice, *n.* A fault, defect, or imperfection. Immoral conduct, practice or habit; *e.g.* prostitution.

Vice crimes. Generic term applied to crimes of immoral conduct such as prostitution, gambling, pornography.

Vicinage /vísənəj/. Neighborhood; near dwelling; vicinity. In modern usage, it means the county or particular area where a trial is had, a crime committed, etc. At common law, accused had the right to be tried by jury of the neighborhood or "vicinage," which was interpreted to mean the county where the crime was committed.

Vicinity. Quality or state of being near, or not remote; nearness; propinquity; proximity; a region about, near or adjacent; adjoining space or country. Neighborhood; etymologically, by common understanding, it admits of a wider latitude than proximity or contiguity, and may embrace a more extended space than that lying contiguous to the place in question; and, as applied to towns and other territorial divisions, may embrace those not adjacent.

Victim. The person who is the object of a crime or tort, as the victim of a robbery is the person robbed. Person who has suffered damages as result of defendant's criminal activities; that person may be individual, public or private corporation, government, partnership, or unincorporated association. *See also* Restitution.

Victim impact statement. Statement read into the record during the sentencing phase of a criminal trial to inform the court about the impact of the crime on the victim or victim's family.

Victimless crimes. Term applied to a crime which generally involves only the criminal, and which has no direct victim, as in the crime of illegal possession of drugs.

View. The common law right of prospect; the outlook or prospect from the windows of one's house. A species of urban servitude which prohibits the obstruction of such prospect.

The act or proceeding by which tribunal goes to an object which cannot be produced in court because it is immovable or inconvenient to remove, and there observes it. An inspection by the jury of property in controversy, of an accident scene, of a place where a crime has been committed, etc. An inspection by the fact finding tribunal which is a species of real evidence.

The appropriate procedures to be followed in connection with views are widely regulated by state statute. At common law, and generally in civil cases today, the presence of the trial judge at a view is not required, the more common practice being for the jury to be conducted to the scene by "showers," expressly commissioned for the purpose. Attendance at the view by the parties and their counsel is generally permitted though subject to the discretion of the trial judge. In criminal cases, the rights of the defendant to have the

judge present at the view, and to be present himself, are frequently provided for by statute.

See also Inspection; Plain view doctrine; Viewers.

Viewers. Persons appointed by a court to make an investigation of certain matters, or to examine a particular locality (as, the proposed site of a new road), and to report to the court the result of their inspection, with their opinion on the same.

View of an inquest. A view or inspection taken by a jury, summoned upon an inquisition or inquest, of the place or property to which the inquisition or inquiry refers.

Village. Traditionally, word "village" has connoted an area possessed of some attributes of a community, and is not a technical word, or one having a peculiar meaning, but is a common word in general usage and is merely an assemblage or community of people, a nucleus or cluster for residential and business purposes, a collective body of inhabitants, gathered together in one group. Term refers to any small assemblage of houses for dwellings or business, or both, whether they are situated on regularly laid out streets and alleys, or not.

In some states, this is the legal description of a class of municipal corporations of smaller population than "cities" and having a simpler form of government, and corresponding to "towns" and "boroughs," as these terms are employed elsewhere.

Vindicate. To clear of suspicion, blame, or doubt.

Violation. Injury; infringement; breach of right, duty or law; ravishment; seduction. The act of breaking, infringing, or transgressing the law.

A classification used by the Model Penal Code for public welfare offenses. A violation is not a crime. M.P.C. § 1.04(5).

Violence. Unjust or unwarranted exercise of force, usually with the accompaniment of vehemence, outrage or fury. Physical force unlawfully exercised; abuse of force; that force which is employed against common right, against the laws, and against public liberty. The exertion of any physical force so as to injure, damage or abuse. *See e.g.* Assault.

Violent. Moving, acting, or characterized, by physical force, especially by extreme and sudden or by unjust or improper force. Furious, vehement; as a violent storm or wind. A violent attack marked by, or due to, strong mental excitement. Vehement, passionate; as, violent speech. Violent reproaches produced or effected by force, not spontaneous or natural; as, a violent death. Displaying or proceeding from extreme or intense force; caused by unexpected unnatural causes.

Violent death. Death caused by violent external means, as distinguished from natural death as caused by disease or the wasting of the vital forces. Death is "violent" within accident policy if it results from external agency and is not in ordinary course of nature. *See e. g.* Murder.

Violent offenses. Crimes characterized by extreme physical force such as murder, forcible rape, and assault and battery by means of a dangerous weapon.

Vires /váyriyz/. Lat. (The plural of *"vis."*) Powers; forces; capabilities; natural powers; powers granted or limited. *See* Ultra vires.

Vis /vis/. Lat. Any kind of force, violence, or disturbance relating to a man's person or his property. The plural is *vires (q.v.)*.

Visa /víyzə/. An official endorsement made out on a passport, denoting that it has been examined and that the bearer is permitted to proceed. A recognition by the country in which the holder of a passport desires to travel of that passport's validity. A visa is generally required for the admission of aliens into the United States. Cf. 8 U.S.C.A. §§ 1181, 1184. *See also* Alien; Passport.

Vis à vis /vìyzavíy/. Face to face. One of two persons or things opposite or corresponding to each other. In relation to each other.

Visible. Perceptible, discernible, clear, distinct, evident, open, conspicuous.

Visible means of support. Term used in vagrancy statutes to indicate that person was without any ostensible ability to support himself, though he is able bodied.

Visitation rights. In a marriage dissolution or custody action, permission granted by court to a noncustodial parent to visit child or children. May also refer to visitation rights extended to grandparents in a number of states.

Visitor. One who goes or comes to see a particular person or place. For "business visitor", *see* Business.

Vis major /vís méyjər/. A greater or superior force; an irresistible force. A loss that results immediately from a natural cause without the intervention of man, and could not have been prevented by the exercise of prudence, diligence, and care. A natural and inevitable necessity, and one arising wholly above the control of human agencies, and which occurs independently of human action or neglect. In the civil law, this term is sometimes used as synonymous with *"vis divina,"* or the act of God. *See* Act of God.

Vital statistics. Public records kept by a state, city or other governmental subdivision, under a statutory provision, of births, marriages, deaths, diseases, and the like. For admissibility of, see Fed.Evid.R. 803. *See also* Census.

Vitiate. To impair; to make void or voidable; to cause to fail of force or effect. To destroy or annul, either entirely or in part, the legal efficacy and binding force of an act or instrument; as when it is said that fraud *vitiates a contract.*

Viva voce /váyvə vówsiy/. Lat. With the living voice; by word of mouth. As applied to the examination of witnesses, this phrase is equivalent to "orally." It is used in contradistinction to evidence on affidavits or depositions. As descriptive of a species of voting, it signifies voting by speech or outcry, as distinguished from voting by a written or printed ballot.

Voice exemplars. Type of test in which one's voice is compared to the voice heard on some particular occasion. Used in trial of cases as type of scientific evidence. An order compelling a defendant in a criminal case to furnish a sample of his voice does not violate the privilege against self-incrimination. While voiceprint identification was formerly not admissible, the trend in recent years has been towards admissibility under restricted conditions. See Fed.Evid.R. 901. *See also* Spectrograph; Voiceprint.

Voice identification. In evidence, one may testify that he heard a person's voice if he is familiar with that voice. See Fed.Evid.R. 901(5). *See also* Spectrograph; Voiceprint.

Voiceprint. An instrument known as a spectrograph produces "prints" of one's voice for use in comparing such readings with the actual voice of the person involved to determine whether such person uttered the material words. Used in trial of cases which require identification of voices. *See* Spectrograph; Voice exemplars.

Void. Null; ineffectual; nugatory; having no legal force or binding effect; unable, in law, to support the purpose for which it was intended. An instrument or transaction which is wholly ineffective, inoperative, and incapable of ratification and which thus has no force or effect so that nothing can cure it.

There is this difference between the two words "void" and "voidable": *void* in the strict sense means that an instrument or transaction is nugatory and ineffectual so that nothing can cure it; *voidable* exists when an imperfection or defect can be cured by the act or confirmation of him who could take advantage of it. The term "void," however, as applicable to conveyances or other agreements, has not at all times been used with technical precision, nor restricted to its peculiar and limited sense, as contradistinguished from "voidable"; it being frequently introduced, even by legal writers and jurists, when the purpose is nothing further than to indicate that a contract was invalid, and not binding in law. But the distinction between the terms "void" and "voidable," in their application to contracts, is often one of great practical importance; and, whenever entire technical accuracy is required, the term "void" can only be properly applied to those contracts that are of no effect whatsoever, such as are a mere nullity, and incapable of confirmation or ratification.

The word "void," in its strictest sense, means that which has no force and effect, is without legal efficacy, is incapable of being enforced by law, or has no legal or binding force, but frequently the word is used and construed as having the more liberal meaning of "voidable."

The word "void" is used in statutes in the sense of utterly void so as to be incapable of ratification, and also in the sense of voidable and resort must be had to the rules of construction in many cases to determine in which sense the Legislature intended to use it. An act or contract neither wrong in itself nor against public policy, which has been declared void by statute for the protection or benefit of a certain party, or class of parties, is voidable only.

Compare Voidable.

Void ab initio. A contract is null from the beginning if it seriously offends law or public policy in contrast to a contract which is merely voidable at the election of one of the parties to the contract. *See also* Void contract; Void marriage.

Voidable. That which may be avoided, or declared void; not absolutely void, or void in itself. It imports a valid act which may be avoided rather than an invalid act which may be ratified. *See also* Voidable contract. *Compare* Void.

Voidable contract. A contract that is valid, but which may be legally voided at the option of one of the parties. One which is void as to wrongdoer but not void as to wronged party, unless he elects to so treat it. One which can be avoided (cancelled) by one party because right of rescission exists as a result of some defect or illegality (*e.g.*, fraud or incompetence). *See also* Void contract.

A voidable contract is one where one or more parties have the power, by a manifestation of election to do so, to avoid the legal relations created by the contract, or by ratification of the contract to extinguish the power of avoidance. Restatement, Second, Contracts § 7.

Voidable judgment. One apparently valid, but in truth wanting in some material respect. One rendered by a court having jurisdiction but which is irregularly and erroneously rendered. *See also* Void judgment.

Voidable marriage. One which is valid (not void) when entered into and which remains valid until either party secures lawful court order dissolving the marital relationship. Major difference between "void marriage" and "voidable marriage" is that latter is treated as binding until its nullity is

ascertained and declared by competent court, whereas former does not require such judgment because parties could not enter into valid marital relationship. *See also* Void marriage.

Voidable preference. Under Bankruptcy Code, such exists where person while insolvent transfers property, the effect of which will be to enable one creditor to obtain greater percentage of his debt than other creditors of same class. A preference given to one creditor over another by a bankrupt, usually manifested by a payment to that creditor just prior to the bankruptcy declaration, that may be set aside by the trustee in bankruptcy. See Bankruptcy Code § 547. *See also* Preference.

Void contract. A contract that does not exist at law; a contract having no legal force or binding effect. Expression denotes that the parties to the transaction have gone through the form of making a contract, but that none has been made in law because of lack of some essential element of a contract, and such contract creates no legal rights and either party thereto may ignore it at his pleasure, in so far as it is executory. *See also* Voidable contract.

Void for vagueness doctrine. A law which is so obscure in its promulgation that a reasonable person could not determine from a reading what the law purports to command or prohibit is void as violative of due process. The doctrine means that criminal responsibility should not attach where one could not reasonably understand that his contemplated conduct is proscribed. Also, the First Amendment requires special clarity so that protected expression will not be chilled or suppressed.

Void judgment. One which has no legal force or effect, invalidity of which may be asserted by any person whose rights are affected at any time and at any place directly or collaterally. One which, from its inception is and forever continues to be absolutely null, without legal efficacy, ineffectual to bind parties or support a right, of no legal force and effect whatever, and incapable of confirmation, ratification, or enforcement in any manner or to any degree. Judgment is a "void judgment" if court that rendered judgment lacked jurisdiction of the subject matter, or of the parties, or acted in a manner inconsistent with due process. *See also* Voidable judgment.

Void marriage. One not good for any legal purpose, the invalidity of which may be maintained in any proceeding between any parties, while a "voidable marriage" is one where there is an imperfection which can be inquired into only during the lives of both of the parties in a proceeding to obtain a judgment declaring it void. Such marriage is invalid from its inception, and parties thereto may simply separate without benefit of court order of divorce or annulment. A "voidable marriage" is valid and not ipso facto void, until sentence of nullity is obtained; a "void marriage" is void ab initio. *See* Annulment.

Void on its face. An instrument is void on its face when an inspection will reveal its defects and invalidity.

Void transaction. One that has no force and effect and is incapable of legal enforcement. *See* Void; Void contract.

Voir dire /vwár dír/. L. Fr. To speak the truth. This phrase denotes the preliminary examination which the court and attorneys make of prospective jurors to determine their qualification and suitability to serve as jurors. Peremptory challenges or challenges for cause many result from such examination. *See* Challenge.

Volenti non fit injuria /vowléntay nón fit injúriyə/. The maxim "volenti non fit injuria" means that if one, knowing and comprehending the danger, voluntarily exposes himself to it, though not negligent in so doing, he is deemed to have assumed the risk and is precluded from a recovery for an injury resulting therefrom. This is an affirmative defense that should be pleaded under Fed.R.Civil P. 8. *See also* Assumption of risk; Voluntary exposure to unnecessary danger.

Volstead Act. A now repealed Federal law prohibiting the manufacture, sale, or transportation of liquor. The law was passed under the Eighteenth Amendment to the U.S. Constitution which was repealed by Twenty-First Amendment.

Voluntary. Unconstrained by interference; unimpelled by another's influence; spontaneous; acting of oneself. Done by design or intention. Proceeding from the free and unrestrained will of the person. Produced in or by an act of choice. Resulting from free choice, without compulsion or solicitation. The word, especially in statutes, often implies knowledge of essential facts. Without valuable consideration; gratuitous, as a *voluntary* conveyance. Also, having a merely nominal consideration; as, a *voluntary* deed.

As to *voluntary* Answer; Assignment; Confession; Conveyance; Deposit; Dismissal; Escape; Indebtedness; Intoxication; Manslaughter; Nonsuit; Oath; Payment; Redemption; Sale; Search; Settlement; Trust, and Waste, see 'those titles. For *voluntary* bankruptcy, *see* Bankruptcy proceedings.

Voluntary abandonment. As statutory ground for divorce, exists if there is a final departure, without consent of other party, without sufficient reason and without intent to return. As used in adoption statute, the term "voluntarily abandoned" means a willful act or course of conduct such as would imply a conscious disregard or indifference to such child in respect to the parental obligation owed to the child. *See also* Abandonment; Desertion.

Voluntary bankruptcy. A bankruptcy proceeding that is initiated by the debtor. *See* Bankruptcy proceedings.

Voluntary discontinuance. Voluntary action on part of plaintiff, whereby his case is dismissed without decision on merits. Fed.R.Civil P. 41(a). *See* Dismissal.

Voluntary dismissal. *See* Dismissal.

Voluntary exposure to unnecessary danger. An intentional act which reasonable and ordinary prudence would pronounce dangerous. Intentional exposure to unnecessary danger, implying a conscious knowledge of the danger. The voluntary doing of an act which is not necessary to be done, but which requires exposure to known danger to which one would not be exposed if unnecessary act is not done. The term implies a conscious, intentional exposure, something of which one is conscious but willing to take the risk. *See* Assumption of risk; Volenti non fit injuria.

Voluntary statement. A statement made that is free from duress, coercion or inducement.

Volunteer. A person who gives his services without any express or implied promise of remuneration. One who intrudes himself into a matter which does not concern him, or one who pays the debt of another without request, when he is not legally or morally bound to do so, and when he has no interest to protect in making such payment. A person who pays the debt of another without a request, when not legally or morally bound to do so and not in the protection of his own interest.

Vote. Suffrage; the expression of one's will, preference, or choice, formally manifested by a member of a legislative or deliberative body, or of a constituency or a body of qualified electors, in regard to the decision to be made by the body as a whole upon any proposed measure or proceeding or in passing laws, rules or regulations, or the selection of an officer or representative.

See also Absentee voting; Apportionment; Ballot; Canvass; Cumulative voting; Fifteenth Amendment; Franchise; Gerrymander; Majority vote; Nineteenth Amendment; Noncumulative voting; Twenty-Fourth Amendment; Twenty-Sixth Amendment; Twenty-Third Amendment; Voting Rights Act.

Voter. The word has two meanings—a person who performs act of voting, and a person who has the qualifications entitling him to vote. Its meaning depends on the connections in which it is used, and is not always equivalent to electors. In a limited sense a voter is a person having the legal right to vote, sometimes called a legal voter. *See* Legal voter.

Voting by ballot. The term is used to distinguish open voting from secret voting. The privilege of secrecy is of the essence of "voting by ballot." *See* Ballot.

Voting group. A term defined in the Revised Model Business Corporation Act (§ 1.40(26)) to describe the right of shares of different classes to vote separately at shareholders meetings on fundamental corporate changes that adversely affect the rights or privileges of that class. The scope of the right to vote by voting groups is defined by statute. The right is of particular value to classes of shares with limited or no voting rights under the articles of incorporation. Most older state statutes use the terms "class voting" or "voting by class" to refer essentially to the same concept. *See also* Voting trust.

Voting Rights Act. Federal law which guarantees the right of citizens to vote without discrimination based on race, color or previous condition of servitude. The Attorney General is authorized to file proper proceedings for preventive relief to protect this right. 42 U.S.C.A. § 1971 et seq. *See also* Poll-tax.

Voting stock. In corporations, that type of stock which gives the holder the right to vote for directors and other matters in contrast to non-voting stock which simply entitles the holder to dividends, if any. Common stock is normally voting stock. *See also* Stock.

Voting stock rights. The stockholder's right to vote his stock in the affairs of his company. Most common shares have one vote each. Preferred stock usually has the right to vote when preferred dividends are in default for a specified period. The right to vote may be delegated by the stockholder to another person. *See also* Cumulative voting; Majority voting; Noncumulative voting; Voting group; Voting stock.

Voting tax. *See* Poll-tax.

Voting trust. The transfer of title by stockholders of shares of a corporation to a trustee who is authorized to vote the shares on their behalf. One created by an agreement between a group of the stockholders of a corporation and the trustee, or by a group of identical agreements between individual stockholders and a common trustee, whereby it is provided that for a term of years, or for a period contingent upon a certain event, or until the agreement is terminated, control over the stock owned by such stockholders, either for certain purposes or for all, shall be lodged in the trustee, with or without a reservation to the owner or persons designated by them of the power to direct how such control shall be used. A device whereby two or more persons, owning stock with voting powers, divorce voting rights thereof from ownership, retaining to all intents and purposes the latter in themselves and transferring the former to trustees in whom voting rights of all depositors in the trust are pooled.

Agreement accumulating several owners' stock in hands of one or more persons in trust for voting purposes in order to control corporate business and affairs. It differs from proxy or reciprocal proxy in that it does not make either party the other's agent.

See also Voting group; Voting trust certificates.

Voting trust certificates. Certificates issued by voting trustees to the beneficial holders of shares held by the voting trust. Such certificates may be as readily transferable as the underlying shares, carrying with them all the incidents of ownership of the underlying shares except the power to vote.

Vouch /váwch/. To call upon; to call in to warranty; to call upon the grantor or warrantor to defend the title to an estate; to call upon witness to give warranty of title. To substantiate with evidence; to verify.

To give personal assurance or serve as a guarantee. To call upon, rely on, or quote as an authority. Thus, formerly, to vouch a case or report was to quote it as an authority.

See also Impleader; Third-party practice; Vouching-in.

Voucher /váwchər/. A receipt, acquittance, or release, which may serve as evidence of payment or discharge of a debt, or to certify the correctness of accounts. An account-book containing the acquittances or receipts showing the accountant's discharge of his obligations. When used in connection with disbursement of money, is a written or printed instrument in the nature of an account, receipt, or acquittance, that shows on its face the fact, authority, and purpose of disbursement.

A document that serves to recognize a liability and authorize the disbursement of cash. Sometimes used to refer to the written evidence documenting an accounting entry, as in the term journal voucher. *See also* Voucher register.

Voucher register. A multicolumn journal in which vouchers are recorded.

Vouching-in. Common law procedural device whereby person against whom action is brought may give notice of suit to third party who is liable over to him with respect to matter sued upon, and third party thereafter will be bound by decision in appropriate circumstances. Though largely supplanted by third-party practice, vouching-in remains marginally viable under the federal rules. *See* Impleader; Intervention; Third-party practice.

In commercial law, inviting a person who is liable over to a defendant in a lawsuit to intervene in the suit and defend so that, if the invitation is denied and the defendant later sues the person invited, the latter is bound by any determination of fact common to the two litigations. See, *e.g.,* U.C.C. §§ 2–607, 3–803.

Voyage charter. The document in admiralty which sets forth the arrangements and contractual engagements entered into between the charterer and the owner of the ship. Under "voyage charter," ship is engaged to carry full cargo on specific voyage, and ship is manned, controlled and navigated by owner.

Voyage policy. *See* Policy of insurance.

Voyeurism. The condition of one who derives sexual satisfaction from observing the sexual organs or acts of others, generally from a secret vantage point.

vs. An abbreviation for *versus* (against), used in legal proceedings, and especially in entitling cases.

W

W. As an abbreviation, this letter frequently stands for "west," or "western."

Wage and hour laws. General term describing federal and state laws governing the maximum hours which may be worked and the minimum wage to be paid. In particular, the federal law known as Fair Labor Standards Act of 1938 which regulates wages, hours and other conditions of labor. 29 U.S.C.A. § 201 *et seq. See also* Eight hour laws; Fair Labor Standards Act; Wages; Walsh-Healey Act.

Wage and price controls. A system of government-mandated maximum prices that can be charged for different goods and services, and maximum wages that can be paid to different workers in different jobs.

Wage assignments. The transfer or assignment in advance of one's wages generally in connection with a debt or judgment. Such assignments are governed by statutes in most states. *See also* Assignment (*Assignment for benefit of creditors*).

Wage earner's plan. A type of partial bankruptcy in which a person keeps his or her property and pays off a court-established proportion of debt to creditors over a period of time and under court supervision. See Bankruptcy Code Ch. 13, "Adjustment of Debts of An Individual With Regular Income". *See also* Bankruptcy proceedings.

Wage garnishment. *See* Garnishment.

Wager. A contract by which two or more parties agree that a certain sum of money or other thing shall be paid or delivered to one of them or that they shall gain or lose on the happening of an uncertain event or upon the ascertainment of a fact in dispute, where the parties have no interest in the event except that arising from the possibility of such gain or loss. The word "wagering" is practically synonymous with the words betting and gambling, and the terms are so used in common parlance and in statutory and constitutional enactments. *See also* Bet; Bookmaking; Gambling; Pari-mutuel betting.

Wagering contract. One in which the parties stipulate that they shall gain or lose, upon the happening of an uncertain event, in which they have no interest except that arising from the possibility of such gain or loss. *See also* Wager.

Wager policy. *See* Policy of insurance.

Wages. A compensation given to a hired person for his or her services. Compensation paid to employees based on time worked or output of production.

Every form of remuneration payable for a given period to an individual for personal services, including salaries, commissions, vacation pay, dismissal wages, bonuses and reasonable value of board, rent, housing, lodging, payments in kind, tips, and any other similar advantage received from the individual's employer or directly with respect to work for him. Term should be broadly defined and includes not only periodic monetary earnings but all compensation for services rendered without regard to manner in which such compensation is computed.

Real wages. Money wages divided by a price index. Real wages are different from money or nominal wages because they represent the true purchasing power of the dollars paid to workers. *See* Consumer Price Index.

See also Compensation; Current wages; Front wages; Minimum wage; Salary; Tip.

Wagner Act. A Federal law, passed in 1935, that established most basic union rights. It prohibited several employer actions (such as attempting to force employees to stay out of a union) and labeled these actions "unfair labor practices." It also set up the National Labor Relations Board to help enforce the new labor laws. 29 U.S.C.A. § 151 et seq.

Waiting period. Time period that must expire before some legal right or remedy can be undertaken or enforced. The period during which an insurance policy is not in effect or for which nothing will be paid on the policy. For example, if there is a waiting period of 30 days under a particular disability policy, the insured will have to be disabled for 30 days before a payment is made for loss of earnings.

In labor law, a period following a notice of intention to strike during which a strike may not lawfully take place. See 29 U.S.C.A. § 158(d). *See also* Cooling off period.

In securities law, the period following registration of a security with Securities and Exchange Commission during which the security may not be sold to the public.

Waive, *v.* To abandon, throw away, renounce, repudiate, or surrender a claim, a privilege, a right, or the opportunity to take advantage of some defect, irregularity, or wrong. To give up right or claim voluntarily.

A person is said to waive a benefit when he renounces or disclaims it, and he is said to waive a tort or injury when he abandons the remedy which the law gives him for it.

In order for person to "waive" a right, he or she must do it knowingly and be possessed of the facts.

Waiver. The intentional or voluntary relinquishment of a known right, or such conduct as warrants an inference of the relinquishment of such right, or when one dispenses with the performance of something he is entitled to exact or when one in possession of any right, whether conferred by law or by contract, with full knowledge of the material facts, does or forbears to do something the doing of which or the failure of forbearance to do which is inconsistent with the right, or his intention to rely upon it. The renunciation, repudiation, abandonment, or surrender of some claim, right, privilege, or of the opportunity to take advantage of some defect, irregularity, or wrong. An express or implied relinquishment of a legal right. A doctrine resting upon an equitable principle, which courts of law will recognize.

Waiver is essentially unilateral, resulting as legal consequence from some act or conduct of party against whom it operates, and no act of party in whose favor it is made is necessary to complete it. And may be shown by acts and conduct and sometimes by nonaction.

The term is often used in the context of waiving one's right to counsel (for example, *Miranda* warning) or waiving certain steps in the criminal justice process (for example, the preliminary hearing). Essential to waiver is the voluntary consent of the individual. See *e.g.* Fed.R.Crim.P. 44(a).

Terms "estoppel" and "waiver" are not synonymous; "waiver" means the voluntary, intentional relinquishment of a known right, and "estoppel" rests upon principle that, where anyone has done an act, or made a statement, which would be a fraud on his part to controvert or impair, because other party has acted upon it in belief that what was done or said was true, conscience and honest dealing require that he not be permitted to repudiate his act or gainsay his statement.

See also Abandonment; Estoppel; Forfeiture.

Express waiver. The voluntary, intentional relinquishment of a known right.

Implied waiver. A waiver is implied where one party has pursued such a course of conduct with reference to the other party as to evidence an intention to waive his rights or the advantage to which he may be entitled, or where the conduct pursued is inconsistent with any other honest intention than an intention of such waiver, pro-

vided that the other party concerned has been induced by such conduct to act upon the belief that there has been a waiver, and has incurred trouble or expense thereby. To make out a case of implied "waiver" of a legal right, there must be a clear, unequivocal and decisive act of the party showing such purpose, or acts amounting to an estoppel on his part. See also Estoppel.

Insurance law. Substance of doctrine of "waiver" in insurance law is that if insurer, with knowledge of facts which would bar existing primary liability, recognizes such primary liability by treating policy as in force, it will not thereafter be allowed to plead such facts to avoid its primary liability.

Lien waiver. See that title.

Waiver by election of remedies, doctrine of. Doctrine applies if there exist two or more coexisting remedies between which there is right of election, inconsistency as to such available remedies, and actual bringing of action or doing some other decisive act, with knowledge of facts, whereby party electing indicates his choice between such inconsistent remedies.

Waiver of claims and defenses. A term in an instrument or other contract whereby the maker, drawer or other obligor explicitly agrees not to assert against an assignee of the contract any claim or defense the obligor has against the assignor.

Waiver of exemption. A clause inserted in a note, bond, lease, etc., expressly waiving the benefit of the laws exempting limited amounts of personal property from levy and sale on judicial process, so far as concerns the enforcement of the particular debt or obligation.

Waiver of immunity. A means authorized by statutes by which a witness, in advance of giving testimony or producing evidence, may renounce the fundamental right guaranteed to him by constitutions, that no person shall be compelled in any criminal case to be a witness against himself. See Immunity.

Waiver of premium clause. Provision in insurance policy providing for waiver of premium payments upon disability of insured. Commonly such waiver only takes effect after a certain time period of disability; *e.g.* six months.

Waiver of protest. An agreement by the indorser of a note or bill to be bound in his character of indorser without the formality of a protest in case of non-payment, or, in the case of paper which cannot or is not required to be protested, dispensing with the necessity of a demand and notice.

Waiver of tort. The election, by an injured party, for purposes of redress, to treat the facts as establishing an implied contract, which he may enforce, instead of an injury by fraud or wrong, for the committing of which he may demand damages, compensatory or exemplary.

Walsh-Healey Act. Federal Act (1936) which provides that government contractors should pay not less than the prevailing minimum wage, observe the eight-hour day and the forty-hour week, employ no convict labor and no female under 18 years of age or male under 16 years of age, and allow no hazardous or unsanitary working conditions in their plants. 41 U.S.C.A. §§ 35–45.

Want of consideration. In the general law of contracts, this term means a total lack of any valid consideration for a contract, while "failure of consideration" is the neglect, refusal or failure of one of the parties to perform or furnish the consideration agreed on. *See also* Failure of consideration.

Want of jurisdiction. Lack of jurisdiction over person or subject matter. A lack of authority to exercise in a particular manner a power which board or tribunal has; the doing of something in excess of authority possessed. *See also* Lack of jurisdiction.

Wanton. Reckless, heedless, malicious; characterized by extreme recklessness or foolhardiness; recklessly disregardful of the rights or safety of others or of consequences. Means undisciplined, unruly, marked by arrogant recklessness of justice, feelings of others, or the like; willful and malicious. In its ordinarily accepted sense connotes perverseness exhibited by deliberate and uncalled for conduct, recklessness, disregardful of rights and an unjustifiable course of action. *See also* Reckless; Wanton act; Wantonness.

Wanton act. One done in malicious or reckless disregard of the rights of others, evincing a reckless indifference to consequences to the life, or limb, or health, or reputation or property rights of another, and is more than negligence, more than gross negligence, and is such conduct as indicates a reckless disregard of the just rights or safety of others or of the consequences of action, equivalent in its results to wilful misconduct. *See also* Wanton and reckless misconduct.

Wanton acts and omissions. Those of such character or done in such manner or under such circumstances as to indicate that a person of ordinary intelligence actuated by normal and natural concern for the welfare and safety of his fellowmen who might be affected by them could not be guilty of them unless wholly indifferent to their probable injurious effect or consequences. *See also* Wanton act.

Wanton and reckless misconduct. Occurs when a person, with no intent to cause harm, intentionally performs an act so unreasonable and dangerous that he knows, or should know, that it is highly probable that harm will result. As used in punitive damages statute, consists of conduct that creates a substantial risk of harm to another and is purposely performed with an awareness of the risk and disregard of the consequences. *See also* Wanton misconduct.

Wanton conduct. *See* Wanton misconduct.

Wanton injury. Injury produced by conscious and intentional wrongful act, or omission of known duty with reckless indifference to consequences. It must be predicated upon actual knowledge of another's peril and a failure to take available preventative action knowing that such failure will probably result in injury.

Wanton misconduct. Act or failure to act, when there is a duty to act, in reckless disregard of rights of another, coupled with a consciousness that injury is a probable consequence of act or omission. Term refers to intentional act of unreasonable character performed in disregard of risk known to him or so obvious that he must be taken to have been aware of it and so great as to make it highly probable that harm would follow and it is usually accompanied by conscious indifference to the consequences. *See also* Wanton and reckless misconduct; Willful and wanton misconduct.

Wanton negligence. Heedless and reckless disregard for another's rights with consciousness that act or omission to act may result in injury to another. *See also* Negligence; Recklessness.

Wantonness. *See* Recklessness; Wanton.

War. Hostile contention by means of armed forces, carried on between nations, states, or rulers, or between citizens in the same nation or state.

Articles of war. See that title.

Civil war. An internecine war. A war carried on between opposing citizens of the same country or nation.

War clauses. Art. I, § 8 (Clauses 11–16) U.S. Const., provides, inter alia, that Congress shall have power to declare war, and raise and support military forces. Art. II, § 1, provides, inter alia, that the President is the Commander-in-Chief of the armed forces. *See also* Commander-in-Chief; War power; War powers resolution.

War crimes. Crimes committed by countries in violation of the international laws governing wars. At Nuremberg after World War II, crimes committed by the Nazis were so tried.

Ward. Guarding, caring, protecting.

A division of a city or town for elections, police, and other governmental purposes. A corridor, room, or other division of a prison, hospital, or similar institution.

A person, especially a child or incompetent, placed by the court under the care and supervision of a guardian or conservator. *See* Guardian; Guardianship.

Warehouseman. One engaged in business of receiving and storing goods of others for compensation or profit; person who receives goods and merchandise to be stored in his warehouse for hire. U.C.C. § 7–102. The business is public or private as it may be conducted for storage of goods of general public or for those of certain persons. The general commercial laws governing rights and liabilities of warehousemen are provided in U.C.C. § 7–201 *et seq.*

Warehousemen's lien. Right of warehouseman to retain possession of goods until storage charges have been paid. See U.C.C. §§ 7–209, 7–210.

Warehouse receipt. A document in the form of "a receipt issued by a person engaged in the business of storing goods for hire." U.C.C. § 1–201(45). It is evidence of title to goods thereby represented. § 1–210(15). For form and content of warehouse receipt, see U.C.C. § 7–202. As regards altered warehouse receipts, see § 7–208. *See also* Field warehouse receipt.

Warehouse system. A system of public stores or warehouses, established or authorized by law, called "bonded warehouses," in which an importer may deposit goods imported, in the custody of the revenue officers, paying storage, but not being required to pay the customs duties until the goods are finally removed for consumption in the home market, and with the privilege of withdrawing the goods from store for the purpose of re-exportation without paying any duties.

Bonded warehouse. Special type of private warehouse used to store products on which a federal tax must be paid before they can be sold.

Warehousing. Practice of mortgage banker of holding mortgages until the market for their resale improves. Term also refers to situation when a corporation gives advance notice of its intention to launch a tender offer to institutional investors who are then able to purchase stock in the target company before the tender offer is made public and the price of shares rises.

Warning. A pointing out of danger. Also a protest against incurring it. The purpose of a "warning" is to apprise a party of the existence of danger of which he is not aware to enable him to protect himself against it, and where the party is aware of the danger, the warning will serve no useful purpose and is unnecessary, and there is no duty to warn against risks which are open and obvious.

Federal laws require warning labels to be affixed to potentially dangerous products, clothes, drugs, tools, and the like. See *e.g.* 21 U.S.C.A. § 825.

See also Caveat; Caveat emptor.

War power. Authority granted by U.S. Constitution to Congress and President to declare and conduct war. While Congress has power to declare war (Art. I, § 8, U.S.Const.), the President, as Commander in Chief, has ultimate power over conduct of war including tactics and strategy (Art. II, § 1). *See also* War clauses; War powers resolution.

War powers resolution. Passed by Congress over a Presidential veto in 1973; restricts the President's authority to involve the U.S. in foreign controversies without Congressional approval. Specific provisions ensure that the President has authority to send the military into combat without requesting authorization from Congress if the United States or one of her territories is attacked. 50 U.S.C.A. §§ 1541–48.

Warrant, *v.* In contracts, to engage or promise that a certain fact or state of facts, in relation to the subject-matter, is, or shall be, as it is represented to be.

In conveyancing, to assure the title to property sold, by an express covenant to that effect in the deed of conveyance. To stipulate by an express covenant that the title of a grantee shall be good, and his possession undisturbed.

See also Warranty.

Warrant, *n.* An order by which the drawer authorizes one person to pay a particular sum of money.

An authority issued to a collector of taxes, empowering him to collect the taxes extended on the assessment roll, and to make distress and sale of goods or land in default of payment.

A command of a council, board, or official whose duty it is to pass upon the validity and determine the amount of a claim against the municipality, to the treasurer to pay money out of any funds in the municipal treasury, which are or may become available for the purpose specified, to a designated person whose claim therefor has been duly adjusted and allowed.

See also Detachable warrant; Land warrant; Possessory warrant; Probable cause; Search warrant; Share-warrant to bearer.

Arrest warrant. A written order of the court which is made on behalf of the state, or United States, and is based upon a complaint issued pursuant to statute and/or court rule and which commands law enforcement officer to arrest a person and bring him before magistrate. See Fed.R.Crim.P. 4 and 9.

Form. The warrant shall be signed by the magistrate and shall contain the name of the defendant or, if his name is unknown, any name or description by which he can be identified with reasonable certainty. It shall describe the offense charged in the complaint. It shall command that the defendant be arrested and brought before the nearest available magistrate. Fed.R.Crim.P. 4(c).

Issuance. If it appears from the complaint, or from an affidavit or affidavits filed with the complaint, that there is probable cause to believe that an offense has been committed and that the defendant has committed it, a warrant for the arrest of the defendant shall issue to any officer authorized by law to execute it. Upon the request of the attorney for the government a summons instead of a warrant shall issue. More than one warrant or summons may issue on the same complaint. If a defendant fails to appear in response to the summons, a warrant shall issue. Fed.R.Crim.P. 4(a).

See also Arrest; Probable cause; Search warrant; Warrantless arrest.

Bench warrant. *See* Bench.

Death warrant. A warrant issued generally by the chief executive authority of a state, directed to the sheriff or other proper local officer or the warden of a jail, commanding him at a certain time to proceed to carry into execution a sentence of death imposed by the court upon a convicted criminal.

Distress warrant. *See* Distress.

General warrant. A search or arrest warrant that is not particular as to the person to be arrested or the property to be seized.

Interest warrant. Order drawn by a corporation on its bank directing the bank to pay a bondholder who is entitled to interest.

Landlord's warrant. *See* Landlord.

Land warrant. See that title.

Outstanding warrant. An order for arrest of a person which has not yet been executed.

Search warrant. See that title.

Stock warrants. Certificates entitling the owner to buy a specified amount of stock at a specified time(s) for a specified price. Such differ from stock options only in that options are generally granted to employees and warrants are sold to the public. Warrants are typically long period options, are freely transferable, and if the underlying shares are listed on a securities exchange, are also publicly traded. *See also* Detachable warrant; Stock *(Stock rights)*.

Warrant creditor. *See* Creditor.

Warrant of arrest. *See* Arrest warrant, above.

Warrant of attorney. An instrument in writing, addressed to one or more attorneys therein named, authorizing them, generally, to appear in any court, or in some specified court, on behalf of the person giving it, and to confess judgment in favor of some particular person therein named, in an action of debt. It usually contains a stipulation not to bring any action, or any writ of error, or file a bill in equity, so as to delay him; such writing usually being given as security for obligation on which judgment was authorized, and in such procedure service of process is not essential. *See* Judgment *(Confession of judgment).*

Warrant of commitment. A written authority committing a person to custody.

Warrant officers. In the United States army, navy, coast and geodetic survey, coast guard, marine corps and air force, these are a class of inferior officers who hold their rank by virtue of a written warrant instead of a commission.

Warrant of merchantability. *See also* Warranty.

Warrant upon indictment or information. *See* Fed.R.Crim.P. 9. *See also* Indictment; Information.

Warrantee. A person to whom a warranty is made.

Warrantless arrest. Arrest of a person without a warrant. It is generally permissible if the arresting officer has reasonable grounds to believe that the person has committed a felony or if the person has committed a misdemeanor amounting to a breach of the peace in the officer's presence. Wong Sun v. U.S., 371 U.S. 471, 83 S.Ct. 407, 9 L.Ed.2d 441. If probable cause exists, no warrant is required to apprehend a suspected felon in a public place. *See also* Arrest.

Warrantor. One who makes a warranty. Any supplier or other person who gives or offers to give a written warranty or who is or may be obligated under an implied warranty. 15 U.S. C.A. § 2301.

Warranty. A promise that a proposition of fact is true. An assurance by one party to agreement of existence of fact upon which other party may rely. It is intended precisely to relieve promisee of any duty to ascertain facts for himself, and amounts to promise to indemnify promisee for any loss if the fact warranted proves untrue. A promise that certain facts are truly as they are represented to be and that they will remain so, subject to any specified limitations. In certain circumstances a warranty will be presumed, known as an "implied" warranty.

Commercial Transactions

An assurance or guaranty, either express in the form of a statement by a seller of goods, or implied by law, having reference to and ensuring the character, quality, or fitness of purpose of the goods. A warranty is a statement or representation made by seller of goods, contemporaneously with and as a part of contract of sale, though collateral to express object of sale, having reference to character, quality, fitness, or title of goods, and by which seller promises or undertakes to insure that certain facts are or shall be as he then represents them. A promise or agreement by seller that article sold has certain qualities or that seller has good title thereto. A statement of fact respecting the quality or character of goods sold, made by the seller to induce the sale, and relied on by the buyer.

See also Magnuson-Moss Warranty Act; Privity; Promissory warranty; Special warranty.

Express warranty. A promise, ancillary to an underlying sales agreement, which is included in the written or oral terms of the sales agreement under which the promisor assures the quality, description, or performance of the goods. (1) Express warranties by the seller are created as follows: (a) Any affirmation of fact or promise made by the seller to the buyer which relates to the goods and becomes part of the basis of the bargain creates an express warranty that the goods shall conform to the affirmation or promise. (b) Any description of the goods which is made part of the basis of the bargain creates an express warranty that the goods shall conform to the description. (c) Any sample or model which is made part of the basis of the bargain creates an express warranty that the whole of the goods shall conform to the sample or model. (2) It is not necessary to the creation of an express warranty that the seller use formal words such as "warrant" or "guarantee" or that he have a specific intention to make a warranty, but an affirmation merely of the value of the goods or a statement purporting to be merely the seller's opinion or commendation of the goods does not create a warranty. U.C.C. § 2–313.

A written statement arising out of a sale to the consumer of a consumer good pursuant to which the manufacturer, distributor, or retailer undertakes to preserve or maintain the utility or performance of the consumer good or provide compensation if there is a failure in utility or performance; or in the event of any sample or model, that the whole of the goods conforms to such sample or model. It is not necessary to the creation of an express warranty that formal words such as "warrant" or "guarantee" be used, but if such words are used then an express warranty is created. An affirmation merely of the value of the goods or a statement purporting to be merely an opinion or commendation of the goods does not create a warranty. Statements or representations such as expressions of general policy concerning customer satisfaction which are not subject to any limitation do not create an express warranty. Calif.Civil Code, § 1791.2.

See also Written warranty, below.

Extended service warranty. Type of additional warranty sold with purchase of appliances, motor vehicles, and other consumer goods to cover repair costs not otherwise covered by manufactur-

er's standard warranty. Also known as an extended service contract, such either extends the coverage period or extends the range of potential defects covered beyond the protection furnished in the contract of sale.

Full warranty. A warranty as to full performance covering generally both labor and materials. Under a full warranty, the warrantor must remedy the consumer product within a reasonable time and without charge after notice of a defect or malfunction. 15 U.S.C.A. § 2304. *Compare Limited warranty, below.*

Implied warranty of merchantability or fitness for particular purpose. A promise arising by operation of law, that something which is sold shall be merchantable and fit for the purpose for which the seller has reason to know that it is required. (a) Unless excluded or modified, a warranty that the goods shall be merchantable is implied in a contract for their sale, if the seller is a merchant with respect to goods of that kind. The serving for value of food or drink to be consumed either on the premises or elsewhere is a sale for this purpose. U.C.C. § 2–314(1). (b) Where the seller, at the time of contracting, has reason to know any particular purpose for which the goods are required, and that the buyer is relying on the seller's skill or judgment to select or furnish suitable goods, there is, unless excluded or modified, an implied warranty that the goods shall be fit for such purpose. U.C.C. § 2–315.

"Implied warranty of fitness" means that when the retailer, distributor, or manufacturer has reason to know any particular purpose for which the consumer goods are required, and further, that the buyer is relying on the skill and judgment of the seller to select and furnish suitable goods, then there is an implied warranty that the goods shall be fit for such purpose and that when there is a sale of an assistive device sold at retail in the state, then there is an implied warranty by the retailer that the device is specifically fit for the particular needs of the buyer. Calif.Civil Code, § 1791.1.

"Implied warranty of merchantability" or "implied warranty that goods are merchantable" means that the consumer goods meet each of the following: (1) Pass without objection in the trade under the contract description; (2) Are fit for the ordinary purposes for which such goods are used; (3) Are adequately contained, packaged, and labeled; (4) Conform to the promises or affirmations of fact made on the container or label. Calif.Civil Code, § 1791.1.

See also Fitness for particular purpose; Merchantability; Merchantable.

Limited warranty. A written warranty which fails to meet one or more of the minimum standards for a "full" warranty. 15 U.S.C.A. § 2303.

Warranty limited to labor or to materials for a specified time, commonly given by automobile dealers in connection with sale of used cars. *Compare Full warranty, above.*

Presentment warranties. Implied-in-law promises concerning the title and credibility of an instrument which are made by certain persons to a payor or acceptor upon presentment of the instrument for payment or acceptance. See U.C.C. §§ 3–417(1), 3–418, 4–207(1).

Third party beneficiaries of warranties. See Privity.

Transfer warranties. With respect to instruments, implied-in-law promises concerning title to, and credibility of, an instrument which a transferor of the instrument for consideration gives her transferee and, if the transfer is by indorsement, to remote transferees. U.C.C. §§ 3–417(2) & 4–207(2). A transferee of a document of title also makes transfer warranties, upon transferring a document for value, to her immediate transferee. See U.C.C. § 7–507.

Warranty of title. In a sale of goods an implied promise exists that the seller owns the item offered for sale. (1) Subject to subsection (2) there is in a contract for sale a warranty by the seller that (a) the title conveyed shall be good, and its transfer rightful; and (b) the goods shall be delivered free from any security interest or other lien or encumbrance of which the buyer at the time of contracting has no knowledge. (2) A warranty under subsection (1) will be excluded or modified only by specified language or by circumstances which give the buyer reason to know that the person selling does not claim title in himself or that he is purporting to sell only such right or title as he or a third person may have. (3) Unless otherwise agreed a seller who is a merchant regularly dealing in goods of the kind warrants that the goods shall be delivered free of the rightful claim of any third person by way of infringement or the like but a buyer who furnishes specifications to the seller must hold the seller harmless against any such claim which arises out of compliance with the specifications. U.C.C. § 2–312.

Written warranty. Any written affirmation of fact or written promise made in connection with the sale of a consumer product by a supplier to a buyer which relates to the nature of the material or workmanship and affirms or promises that such material or workmanship is defect free or will meet a specified period of time, or any undertaking in writing in connection with the sale by a supplier of a consumer product to refund, repair, replace, or take other remedial action with respect to such product in the event that such product fails to meet with the specifications set forth in the undertaking, which written affirmation, promise, or undertaking becomes part of the basis of the bargain between a supplier and a buyer for purposes other than resale of such product. 15 U.S.C.A. § 2301. *See also Express warranty, above.*

Insurance

A warranty in the law of insurance consists of a statement by insured upon the literal truth of which the validity of the contract depends. Statement, made in insurance contract by insured, which is susceptible of no construction other than that parties mutually intended that policy should not be binding, unless such statement be literally true.

A statement, description or undertaking on the part of insured, appearing in the policy or in another instrument properly incorporated in the policy and relating contractually to the risk insured against.

Affirmative warranty. In the law of insurance, warranties may be either affirmative or promissory. Affirmative warranties may be either express or implied, but they usually consist of positive representations in the policy of the existence of some fact or state of things at the time, or previous to the time, of the making of the policy; they are, in general, conditions precedent, and if untrue, whether material to the risk or not, the policy does not attach, as it is not the contract of the insurer.

Express warranty. An agreement expressed in a policy, whereby the assured stipulates that certain facts relating to the risk are or shall be true, or certain acts relating to the same subject have been or shall be done.

Promissory warranty. In the law of insurance, a warranty which requires the performance or omission of certain things or the existence of certain facts after the beginning of the contract of insurance and during its continuance, and the breach of which will avoid the policy. *See also* Promissory warranty.

Generally

Construction warranty. An undertaking or promise made by seller or building contractor of new home that such home is fit for the purpose intended; *i.e.* free from structural, electrical, plumbing, etc. defects. Many states have statutes which provide the purchaser with such warranty protection. *See* Home Owners Warranty; *also, Warranty of habitability, below.*

Continuing warranty. One which applies to the whole period during which the contract is in force; *e.g.*, an undertaking in a charter-party that a vessel shall continue to be of the same class that she was at the time the charter-party was made.

Covenant of warranty. See Covenant.

Cumulation and conflict of warranties. Warranties whether express or implied shall be construed as consistent with each other and as cumulative, but if such construction is unreasonable the intention of the parties shall determine which warranty is dominant. In ascertaining that intention the following rules apply: (a) Exact or technical specifications displace an inconsistent sample or model or general language of description. (b) A sample from an existing bulk displaces inconsistent general language of description. (c) Express warranties displace inconsistent implied warranties other than an implied warranty of fitness for a particular purpose. U.C.C. § 2–317.

General warranty. The name of a covenant of warranty inserted in deeds, by which the grantor binds himself, his heirs, etc., to "warrant and forever defend" to the grantee, his heirs, etc., the title thereby conveyed, against the lawful claims of all persons whatsoever. Where the warranty is only against the claims of persons claiming "by, through, or under" the grantor or his heirs, it is called a "special warranty."

Implied warranty. Exists when the law derives it by implication or inference from the nature of the transaction or the relative situation or circumstances of the parties. *See also* this topic under "Commercial Transactions", *above.*

Personal warranty. One available in personal actions, and arising from the obligation which one has contracted to pay the whole or part of a debt due by another to a third person.

Special warranty. A clause of warranty inserted in a deed of lands, by which the grantor covenants, for himself and his heirs, to "warrant and forever defend" the title to the same, to the grantee and his heirs, etc., against all persons claiming "by, through, or under" the grantor or his heirs. If the warranty is against the claims of all persons whatsoever, it is called a "general" warranty. *See also* Covenant.

Warranty deed. See that title.

Warranty of fitness. Warranty by seller that goods sold are suitable for special purpose of buyer. *See also Implied warranty of fitness* under "Commercial Transactions", *above.*

Warranty of habitability. Implied warranty of landlord that the leased premises are properly maintained and are fit for habitation at time of letting and will remain so during term of tenancy.

Under "implied warranty of habitability," applicable to new housing, builder-vendor warrants that he has complied with the building code of the area in which the structure is located and that the residence was built in a workmanlike manner and is suitable for habitation. *See also* Habitability.

Warranty deed. Deed in which grantor warrants good, clear title. A deed which explicitly contains covenants concerning the quality of title it conveys. In some states, statutes impute warranties or covenants from the use of specific words, such as "grant." The usual covenants of title are warranties of seisin, quiet enjoyment, right to convey, freedom from encumbrances and defense of title as to all claims. *Compare* Quitclaim deed.

War risk insurance. *See* Insurance.

Wash sale. The offsetting sale and purchase of the same or similar asset within a short time period. For income tax purposes, losses on a sale of stock may not be recognized if equivalent stock is purchased within thirty days before or thirty days after the date of sale. I.R.C. § 1091.

Transactions resulting in no change in beneficial ownership. A fictitious kind of sale, disallowed on stock and other exchanges, in which a broker who has received orders from one person to buy and from another person to sell a particular amount or quantity of some particular stock or commodity simply transfers the stock or commodity from one principal to the other and pockets the difference, instead of executing both orders separately to the best advantage in each case, as is required by the rules of the different exchanges. Such practices of wash sales and matched orders by brokers to give impression of active trading in such securities are prohibited by SEC. 15 U.S.C.A. § 78i(a)(1). *See also* Sale.

Wash transaction. *See* Wash sale.

Waste. Action or inaction by a possessor of land causing unreasonable injury to the holders of other estates in the same land. An abuse or destructive use of property by one in rightful possession. Spoil or destruction, done or permitted, to lands, houses, gardens, trees, or other corporeal hereditaments, by the tenant thereof, to the prejudice of the heir, or of him in reversion or remainder. An unreasonable or improper use, abuse, mismanagement, or omission of duty touching real estate by one rightfully in possession, which results in its substantial injury. Unreasonable conduct by owner of possessory estate that results in physical damage to real estate and substantial diminution in value of estates in which others have an interest.

A residual output of a production process that must be disposed of because it has no sales value.

Ameliorating waste. Change in the physical characteristics of property by an unauthorized act of the tenant but an act which adds value and improves the property. A tenant is usually not liable for such waste.

Permissive waste. That kind of waste which is a matter of omission only, as by tenant letting premises fall into disrepair by not making reasonable maintenance repairs expected of tenant.

Voluntary waste. Active or positive waste; waste done or committed, in contradistinction to that which results from mere negligence, which is called "permissive" waste. Voluntary waste is the willful destruction or carrying away of something attached to the freehold, and "permissive waste" is the failure to take reasonable care of the premises. Voluntary or commissive waste consists of injury to the demised premises or some part thereof, when occasioned by some deliberate or voluntary act, as, for instance, the pulling down of a house or removal of floors, windows, doors, furnaces, shelves, or other things affixed to and forming part of the freehold. Contrasted with *"permissive"* waste (*above*).

Wasting asset. A natural resource having a limited useful life and, hence, subject to amortization called depletion. An asset that will be exhausted through its use. Examples are timberland, oil and gas wells, and ore deposits. *See also* Depletion; Wasting property.

Wasting property. Includes such property as leasehold interests; royalties; patent rights; interests in things the substance of which is consumed, such as mines, oil and gas wells, quarries and timberlands; interests in things which are consumed in the using or are worn out by use, such as machinery and farm implements. *See also* Wasting asset.

Wasting trust. A trust in which the trustee may apply a part of the principal to make good a deficiency of income. Trust, the res of which consists in whole or in part of property which is gradually being consumed (*i.e.* consisting of wasting assets).

Water course. A running stream of water; a natural stream fed from permanent or natural sources, including rivers, creeks, runs, and rivulets. There must be a stream, usually flowing in a particular direction, though it need not flow continuously. It may sometimes be dry. It must flow in a definite channel, having a bed and banks, and usually discharges itself into some other stream or body of water. It must be something more than a mere surface drainage over the entire face of the tract of land, occasioned by unusual freshets or other extraordinary causes. *See also* Ancient water course.

Natural water course. A natural stream flowing in a defined bed or channel; one formed by the natural flow of the water, as determined by the general superficies or conformation of the surrounding country, as distinguished from an "artificial" water course, formed by the work of man, such as a ditch or canal.

Water district. Official geographical areas which are supplied water under regulation of a body of commissioners or other officials.

Watered stock. Stock issued by corporation for less than full and adequate consideration. Stock which is issued by a corporation as fully paid-up stock, when in fact the whole amount of the par value thereof has not been paid in. Stock issued as bonus or otherwise without consideration or issued for a sum of money less than par value, or issued for labor, services, or property which at a fair valuation is less than the par value.

Water-mark. A mark indicating the highest point to which water rises, or the lowest point to which it sinks.

Transparent design or symbol which can be seen when paper is held up to the light and is used to identify the manufacturer of the paper or the genuineness of the document such as a check or stamp.

High-water mark. This term is properly applicable to tidal waters, and designates the line on the shore reached by the water at the high or flood tide. With reference to the waters of artificial ponds or lakes, created by dams in unnavigable streams, it denotes the highest point on the shores to which the dams can raise the water in ordinary circumstances. The high-water mark of a river, not subject to tide, is the line which the river impresses on the soil by covering it for sufficient periods to deprive it of vegetation, and to destroy its value for agriculture.

Low-water mark. That line on the shore of the sea which marks the edge of the waters at the lowest point of the ordinary ebb tide. The "low-water mark," of a river is the point to which the water recedes at its lowest stage.

Water rights. A legal right, in the nature of a corporeal hereditament, to use the water of a natural stream or water furnished through a ditch or canal, for general or specific purposes, such as irrigation, mining, power, or domestic use, either to its full capacity or to a measured extent or during a defined portion of the time. A usufruct in a stream consisting in the right to have the water flow so that some portion of it may be reduced to possession and be made private property of individual; the right to divert water from natural stream by artificial means and apply the same to beneficial use. It includes right to change the place of diversion, storage, or use of water if rights of other water users will not be injured. It was also said to be real property which may be sold and transferred separately from land on which it has been used. *See also* Common enemy doctrine; Drainage rights; Implied reservation of water doctrine; Littoral rights; Mill privilege; Overlying right; Reasonable use theory; Riparian rights; Territorial waters.

Waterway. *See* Water course.

Way. A passage, path, road, or street. In a technical sense, a *right* of passage over land. *See also* Easement.

Private way. A right which a person has of passing over the land of another. In another sense (chiefly in New England) a private way is one laid out by the local public authorities for the accommodation of individuals and wholly or chiefly at their expense, but not restricted to their exclusive use, being subject, like highways, to the public easement of passage.

Right of way. See that title.

Way of necessity. Exists where land granted is completely environed by land of the grantor, or partially by his land and the land of strangers. The law implies from these facts that a private right of way over the grantor's land was granted to the grantee as appurtenant to the estate. It is not merely one of convenience, and never exists where person may reach highway over his own land. The extent of a "way of necessity" is a way such as is required for complete and beneficial use of land to which the way is impliedly attached.

Way-bill. Written document made out by carrier listing point of origin and destination, consignor and consignee, and describing goods included in shipment and transportation costs. Such constitutes the written description of the shipment in the event of any claim by or against common carrier. *See also* Bill of lading.

Ways and means. In a legislative body, the "committee on ways and means" is a committee appointed to inquire into and consider the methods and sources for raising revenue, and to propose means for providing the funds needed by the government. In Congress it is a standing committee of the House of Representatives responsible for supervising legislation dealing with financial matters.

W.D. An abbreviation for "Western District;" *e.g.* U.S. District Court for Western District of Kentucky.

Weapon. An instrument of offensive or defensive combat, or anything used, or designed to be used, in destroying, defeating, threatening, or injuring a person. The term is chiefly used, in law, in the statutes prohibiting the carrying or using of "concealed" or "deadly" weapons. *See also* Dangerous weapon; Deadly weapon; Offensive weapon.

Wear and tear. "Natural wear and tear" means deterioration or depreciation in value by ordinary and reasonable use of the subject-matter. *See* Depreciation.

Webb-Pomerene Act. Federal Act (1918) which provides a qualified exemption for an export association from the prohibitions of the antitrust laws. The Act is administered by the Federal Trade Commission.

Weight of evidence. The balance or preponderance of evidence; the inclination of the greater amount of credible evidence, offered in a trial, to support one side of the issue rather than the other. It indicates clearly to the jury that the party having the burden of proof will be entitled to their verdict, if, on weighing the evidence in their minds, they shall find the greater amount of credible evidence sustains the issue which is to be established before them. Weight is not a question of mathematics, but depends on its effect in inducing belief. *See also* Burden of proof; Preponderance of evidence.

Welfare clause. Constitutional provision (Art. I, § 8) permitting the federal government to enact laws for the overall general welfare of the people. It is the basis for the exercise of implied powers necessary to carry out the express provisions of the Constitution.

Weregild, *or* **wergild** /wírgild/wórgild/. This was the price of homicide, or other atrocious personal offense, paid partly to the king for the loss of a subject, partly to the lord for the loss of a vassal, and partly to the next of kin of the injured person. In the Anglo-Saxon laws, the amount of compensation varied with the degree or rank of the party slain.

WESTLAW. A computer-assisted legal research service provided by West Publishing Company. WESTLAW provides on-line access to a database of legal information including federal and state caselaw, statutes, and administrative, regulatory, and secondary materials.

W-4 form. The "Employee's Withholding Allowance Certificate," indicating the number of exemptions that the employee is claiming, used by the employer in determining the amount to be withheld for federal income taxes. *See also* W-2 form.

Wharfage /(h)wórfəj/. The money paid for landing goods upon, or loading them from, a wharf. Charge for use of wharf by way of rent or compensation.

Wharton Rule. In criminal law of conspiracy, the rule that an agreement by two persons to commit a particular crime cannot be prosecuted as a conspiracy when the crime is of such a nature as to require necessarily the participation of the two persons, *e.g.* adultery. It is named after the criminal law author, Francis Wharton. Iannelli v. U. S., 420 U.S. 770, 95 S.Ct. 1284, 1288, 43 L.Ed.2d 616. Also called "concert of action" rules.

When issued. Abbreviated term in securities law for "when, as and if issued" in connection with a stock not yet authorized for issuance. The term refers to a conditional transaction in which one indicates a desire to buy when the security is available for sale after its authorization.

Whereas. When in fact. A "whereas" clause of a contract is but an introductory or prefatory statement meaning "considering that" or "that being the case", and is not an essential part of the operating portions of the contract.

Whereby. By or through which; by the help of which; in accordance with which.

Whereupon. Upon which; after which.

Whim. Passing fancy; an impulse or caprice. Used in jury instruction in cautioning the jurors to avoid returning a verdict based on anything but the evidence and its strength, not on the personal whim or caprice of the jurors.

Whistle-blower. An employee who refuses to engage in and/or reports illegal or wrongful activities of his employer or fellow employees. Employer retaliation against whistle blowers is often statutorily prohibited. *See also* False Claims Act; Whistle-blower Acts; Wrongful discharge.

Whistle-blower Acts. Federal and state statutes designed to protect employees from retaliation for a disclosure of an employer's misconduct. The Civil Service Reform Act, 5 U.S.C.A. § 2302(b), protects federal employees who disclose mismanagement or illegal conduct. Several other federal laws protect employees who disclose regulatory violations; *e.g.* OSHA violations, 29 U.S.C.A. § 660(c). Many states also protect private and/or public sector whistle-blowers. Cf. California Labor Code § 1102.5. *See also* False Claims Act; Qui tam action; Wrongful discharge.

White acre. A fictitious name given to a piece of land for purposes of illustrating real property transactions.

White collar crimes. Term signifying various types of unlawful, nonviolent conduct committed by corporations and individuals including theft or fraud and other violations of trust committed in the course of the offender's occupation (*e.g.,* embezzlement, commercial bribery, racketeering, anti-trust violations, price-fixing, stock manipulation, insider trading, and the like). RICO laws are used to prosecute many types of white collar crimes. *See* RICO laws.

White knight. In corporate law, a potential acquirer usually sought out by the target of an unfriendly takeover to rescue it from the unwanted bidder's takeover. A word of art used to describe potential merger partners with whom a target company negotiates toward the realization of a merger on terms which the target company management finds acceptable. The white knight

pursues ownership by means of a "sweetheart deal" with the incumbent management, while an unwanted bidder deals directly with the shareholders. *See also* Golden parachute; Lockup; Poison pill; Porcupine provisions; Raider; Saturday night special.

White slave. A term formerly used in the United States statutes to indicate a female with reference to whom an offense is committed under the so-called Mann White Slave Traffic Act of June 25, 1910, prohibiting the transportation in interstate and foreign commerce for immoral purposes of women and girls. A 1986 amendment to the federal Criminal Code substituted "Transportation for Illegal Sexual Activity and Related Crimes" for "White Slave Traffic" as the description for this crime. 18 U.S.C.A. § 2421 et seq. *See* Mann Act.

Whole blood. *See* Blood relations.

Whole life insurance. *See* Insurance (*Life insurance*).

Whole record test. Test used by court to review sufficiency of an administrative board's findings of fact. It does not allow a reviewing court to replace board's judgment between two reasonably conflicting views, although court could have justifiably reached different result had matter been before it de novo. *See also* Substantial evidence rule.

Wholesale. Selling to retailers or jobbers rather than to consumers. A sale in large quantity to one who intends to resell.

Wholesale dealer. One whose business is the selling of goods in gross to retail dealers, and not by the small quantity or parcel to consumers thereof. *See* Jobber; Wholesaler.

Wholesale price. That which retailer pays in expectation of obtaining higher price by way of profit from resale to ultimate consumer.

Wholesale price index. A statistical measure compiled monthly which compares the price changes of a large group of commodities (weighted by their relative importance) to prices in a base year. *See also* Consumer Price Index; Producer price index.

Wholesaler. One who buys in comparatively large quantities, and then resells, usually in smaller quantities, but never to the ultimate consumer. He sells either to a "jobber," a sort of middleman, or to a "retailer," who in turn sells to the consumer. *See also* Jobber.

Wholly disabled. These words within accident policy do not mean a state of complete physical and mental incapacity or utter helplessness but mean rather inability to do all the substantial and material acts necessary to carry on a certain business or occupation or any business or occupation in a customary and usual manner and which acts the insured would be able to perform in such manner but for the disability. Total disability. *See also* Disability; Total disability.

Widow's allowance. The amount of money or property which a widow may claim from her husband's estate, free of all claims. State statutes govern the amount and conditions of the allowance. It is for her support and maintenance.

Widow's election. In most states, a widow may either take her share under her husband's will or waive his will and claim her statutory share which commonly is an amount equal to what she would receive if he had died intestate. *See* Election by spouse.

Wildcat strike. A strike called without authorization from the union or in violation of a no-strike clause in the collective bargaining agreement. *See also* Strike.

Will, *v.* An auxiliary verb commonly having the mandatory sense of "shall" or "must." It is a word of certainty, while the word "may" is one of speculation and uncertainty.

Will, *n.* Wish; desire; pleasure; inclination; choice; the faculty of conscious, and especially of deliberate, action. When a person expresses his "will" that a particular disposition be made of his property, his words are words of command, and the word "will" as so used is mandatory, comprehensive, and dispositive in nature.

An instrument, executed with the formalities of state statutes, by which a person makes a disposition of his real and personal property, to take effect after his death, and which by its own nature is ambulatory and revocable during his lifetime. For competency to make a will, *see* Competent.

See also Codicil; Conditional will; Last will; Lost will; Mariner's will; Mutual wills; No contest clause; Nuncupative will; Publication; Reciprocal wills; Revocation of will; Sailors' will; Simultaneous death clause; Will contest; Witness (*Witness to will*).

Ambulatory will. A changeable will (*ambulatoria voluntas*), the phrase merely denoting the power which a testator possesses of altering his will during his life-time.

Antenuptial will. See that title.

Conditional will. A conditional disposition is one which depends upon the occurrence of some uncertain event, by which it is either to take effect or to be defeated. If the happening of an event named in a will is the reason for making the will, it is "unconditional"; but, if the testator intends to dispose of his property in case the event happens, the will is "conditional."

Conjoint will. *See Joint will, below.*

Contingent will. A will which is to take effect only upon the happening of a specified contingency.

Counter wills. Another name for "double," "mutual," or "reciprocal" wills.

Double will. Called also a "counter," "mutual," or "reciprocal" will. *See* Double will.

Estate at will. This estate entitles the grantee or lessee to the possession of land during the pleasure of both the grantor and himself, yet it creates no sure or durable right, and is bounded by no definite limits as to duration. It must be at the reciprocal will of both parties (for, if it be at the will of the lessor only, it is a lease for life), and the dissent of either determines it.

Holographic will. One that is entirely written, dated, and signed by the hand of the testator himself. Sometimes spelled "olographic." *See* Holograph.

Joint and mutual (or reciprocal) will. One executed jointly by two persons with reciprocal provisions, which shows on its face that the devises are made one in consideration of the other. Joint will is one in which the same instrument is executed by two persons as their respective wills; mutual wills are the separate wills of two persons, more or less reciprocal in their provisions. Word "joint" goes to form, and word "mutual" goes to substance of what is called "joint and mutual will." *See also Mutual will, below.*

Joint will. One where the same instrument is made the will of two or more persons and is jointly signed by them. Such wills are usually executed to make testamentary disposition of joint property. A joint or conjoint will is a testamentary instrument executed by two or more persons, in pursuance of a common intention, for the purpose of disposing of their several interests in property owned by them in common, or of their separate property treated as a common fund, to a third person or persons.

Living will. A document which governs the withholding or withdrawal of life-sustaining treatment from an individual in the event of an incurable or irreversible condition that will cause death within a relatively short time, and when such person is no longer able to make decisions regarding his or her medical treatment. Living wills are permitted by statute in most states. *See* Uniform Rights of the Terminally Ill Act (Uniform Laws Annotated). *See also* Health care proxy; Life sustaining procedures; Medical directives; Patient Self Determination Act; Power of attorney (*Durable power of attorney*); Right to die laws.

Mutual and reciprocal will. *See Joint and mutual (or reciprocal) will, above; also Mutual will, below.*

Mutual will. One in which two or more persons make mutual or reciprocal provisions in favor of each other. "Mutual wills" are the separate wills of two persons which are reciprocal in their provisions, and such a will may be both joint and mutual. Sometimes called a "reciprocal," "double," or "counter" will. *See also Joint and mutual (or reciprocal) will, above.*

Non-intervention will. In some jurisdictions, one authorizing the executor to act without bond and to manage, control, and settle the estate without the intervention of any court whatsoever.

Nuncupative will. See that title.

Reciprocal will. One in which two or more persons make mutual or reciprocal provisions in favor of each other. Also known as a "mutual," "double," or "counter" will. *See Joint and mutual (or reciprocal) will; Mutual will, above.*

Renunciation of will. See Renunciation.

Self-proved wills. A will which eliminates some of the formalities of proof by execution in compliance with statute. It is made self-proved by affidavit of attesting witnesses in the form prescribed by statute. Most statutes provide that, unless contested, such a will may be admitted to probate without testimony of subscribing witnesses. See *e.g.* Uniform Probate Code, § 2–504.

Criminal Law

The power of the mind which directs the action of a man. *See* Willful.

Will contest. A direct attack upon a decree admitting a will to probate. Any kind of litigated controversy concerning the eligibility of an instrument to probate as distinguished from validity of the contents of the will. Will contests are commonly governed by state statutes; *e.g.* Uniform Probate Code § 3–407, burden of proof.

Willful. Proceeding from a conscious motion of the will; voluntary; knowingly; deliberate. Intending the result which actually comes to pass; designed; intentional; purposeful; not accidental or involuntary.

Premeditated; malicious; done with evil intent, or with a bad motive or purpose, or with indifference to the natural consequences; unlawful; without legal justification.

An act or omission is "willfully" done, if done voluntarily and intentionally and with the specific intent to do something the law forbids, or with the specific intent to fail to do something the law requires to be done; that is to say, with bad purpose either to disobey or to disregard the law. It is a word of many meanings, with its construction often influenced by its context.

Under the Model Penal Code, a requirement that an offense be committed "willfully" is satis-

fied if a person acts knowingly with respect to the material elements of the offense, unless a purpose to impose further requirements appears. M.P.C. § 2.02(8). *See also* Criminal *(Criminal intent)*; Mens rea; Motive; Premeditation.

In civil actions, the word [willfully] often denotes an act which is intentional, or knowing, or voluntary, as distinguished from accidental. But when used in a criminal context it generally means an act done with a bad purpose; without justifiable excuse; stubbornly, obstinately, perversely. The word is also employed to characterize a thing done without ground for believing it is lawful or conduct marked by a careless disregard whether or not one has the right so to act.

Willful and malicious injury. For such to exist there must be an intent to commit a wrong either through actual malice or from which malice will be implied. Such an injury does not necessarily involve hatred or ill will, as a state of mind, but arises from intentional wrong committed without just cause or excuse. It may involve merely a willful disregard of what one knows to be his duty, an act which is against good morals and wrongful in and of itself, and which necessarily causes injury and is done intentionally. *See also* Willful and wanton misconduct.

Willful and wanton act. *See* Willful and wanton misconduct.

Willful and wanton injury. *See* Willful and wanton misconduct.

Willful and wanton misconduct. Conduct which is committed with an intentional or reckless disregard for the safety of others or with an intentional disregard of a duty necessary to the safety of another's property. *See also* Wanton misconduct.

Willful and wanton negligence. Failure to exercise ordinary care to prevent injury to a person who is actually known to be, or reasonably is expected to be, within range of a known danger. *See also* Negligence; Willful and wanton misconduct.

Willful blindness. In criminal law, a term used to refer to a situation where the defendant tries to avoid knowing something that will incriminate. It is usually held in this situation that the defendant "knows" anyway because he is aware of a high probability of its existence. See Model Penal Code § 2.02(7). *See also* Recklessly.

Willful, deliberate and premeditated. A criterion used in many jurisdictions to separate first from second degree murder. The Model Penal Code rejects this concept. *See* Premeditation.

Willful indifference to the safety of others. *See* Willful and wanton misconduct.

Willfully and knowingly. An act is done willfully and knowingly when the actor intends to do it and knows the nature of the act. Deliberately. *See* Willful.

Willful misconduct of employee. Under workers' compensation acts, precluding compensation, means more than mere negligence, and contemplates the intentional doing of something with knowledge that it is likely to result in serious injuries, or with reckless disregard of its probable consequences.

Willful murder. The unlawful and intentional killing of another without excuse or mitigating circumstances. *See also* Murder; Premeditation.

Willful negligence. *See* Negligence; *also* Wanton negligence.

Willfulness. *See* Willful.

Willful tort. Term implies intent or purpose to injure. It involves elements of intent or purpose and malice or ill will, but malice or ill will may be shown by indifference to safety of others, with knowledge of their danger, or failure to use ordinary care to avoid injury after acquiring such knowledge. *See also* Tort (*Intentional tort*).

Williams Act. *See* Tender offer.

Willingly. Voluntarily; unreluctantly; without reluctance, and of one's own free choice. *See* Willful.

As used in an instruction that one cannot invoke the doctrine of self-defense if he enters a fight willingly, it means voluntarily, aggressively, and without legal excuse.

Will substitutes. Documents which purportedly accomplish what a will is designed to accomplish, *e.g.* trusts, life insurance, joint ownership of property.

Windfall profits tax. A tax imposed on a business or industry as a result of an extraordinary sudden increase in the profits of the business. An example includes the tax imposed on oil companies in 1980, due to the windfall profits from the Arab oil embargo.

Winding up. Process of settling the accounts and liquidating the assets of a partnership or corporation, for the purpose of making distribution of net assets to shareholders or partners and dissolving the concern. *See* Liquidation.

Wind up. *See* Winding up.

Wiretapping. A form of electronic or mechanical eavesdropping where, upon court order, law enforcement officials surreptitiously listen to phone calls or other conversations or communications of persons. Federal (18 U.S.C.A. § 2510 et seq.) and similar state statutes govern the circumstances and procedures under which wiretaps will be permitted. *See also* Eavesdropping; Pen register.

Wish. Eager desire; longing; expression of desire; a thing desired; an object of desire. As used in wills, it is sometimes merely directory or precatory; and sometimes mandatory; being equivalent to "will," to "give" or "devise."

With all faults. This phrase, used in a contract of sale, implies that the purchaser assumes the risk of all defects and imperfections, provided they do not destroy the identity of the thing sold. *See also* As is.

Withdraw. To take away what has been enjoyed; to take from. To remove, as deposits from bank, or oneself from competition, candidacy, etc.

Withdrawal. Removal of money or securities from a bank or other place of deposit.

Withdrawal from criminal activity. A person is not legally accountable for the criminal conduct of another if before the commission of the offense, he terminates his efforts to promote such commission and gives a warning to law enforcement officials or makes a proper effort to prevent the criminal activity. Ill.Ann.St. ¶ 5–2(c)(3). Under Model Penal Code, § 5.01(4), withdrawal is an affirmative defense which requires a showing of a complete and voluntary renunciation of defendant's criminal purpose.

Withdrawal from a conspiracy requires either making a clean breast to authorities or communicating the abandonment of the conspiracy in manner reasonably calculated to reach co-conspirators.

Withdrawal of charges. A failure to prosecute by the person preferring charges—distinguished from a dismissal, which is a determination of their invalidity by the tribunal hearing them. *See* Nolle prosequi.

Withhold. To retain in one's possession that which belongs to or is claimed or sought by another. To omit to disclose upon request; as, to withhold information. To refrain from paying that which is due.

Withholding. Deductions from salaries or wages, usually for income taxes and social security contributions, to be remitted by the employer, in the employee's name, to the taxing authority.

Withholding of evidence. It is an obstruction of justice to stifle, suppress or destroy evidence knowing that it may be wanted in a judicial proceeding or is being sought by investigating officers, or to remove records from the jurisdiction of the court, knowing they will be called for by the grand jury in its investigation. See *e.g.* 18 U.S.C.A. §§ 1506, 1512. *See also* Suppression of evidence.

Withholding tax. *See* Withholding.

Without delay. Instantly; at once. Also, within the time allowed by law.

Without notice. As used of purchasers, etc., such language is equivalent to "in good faith." To be a holder in due course, one must take a bill or note "without notice" that it is overdue or has been dishonored or of any defense against or claim to it on the part of any person. See U.C.C. §§ 3–302(1)(c), 3–304(3). *See also* Good faith; Notice.

Without prejudice. Where an offer or admission is made "without prejudice," or a motion is denied or a suit dismissed "without prejudice," it is meant as a declaration that no rights or privileges of the party concerned are to be considered as thereby waived or lost except in so far as may be expressly conceded or decided. The words "without prejudice" import into any transaction that the parties have agreed that as between themselves the receipt of money by one and its payment by the other shall not of themselves have any legal effect on the rights of the parties, but they shall be open to settlement by legal controversy as if the money had not been paid.

A dismissal "without prejudice" allows a new suit to be brought on the same cause of action. The words "without prejudice", as used in judgment, ordinarily import the contemplation of further proceedings, and, when they appear in an order or decree, it shows that the judicial act is not intended to be res judicata of the merits of the controversy.

Compare With prejudice.

Without recourse. Words that may be used by a drawer in signing a draft or check so as to eliminate completely the drawer's secondary liability. This phrase, used in making a qualified indorsement of a negotiable instrument, signifies that the indorser means to save himself from liability to subsequent holders, and is a notification that, if payment is refused by the parties primarily liable, recourse cannot be had to him. See U.C.C. § 3–414(1).

An indorser "without recourse" specially declines to assume any responsibility for payment. He assumes no contractual liability by virtue of the indorsement itself, and becomes a mere assignor of the title to the paper, but such an indorsement does not indicate that the indorsee takes with notice of defects, or that he does not take on credit of the other parties to the note.

See also Nonrecourse; Nonrecourse loan; With recourse.

Without reserve. A term applied to a sale by auction, indicating that no price is reserved.

With prejudice. Phrase "with prejudice," as used in context in which an action is dismissed with prejudice, means an adjudication on merits and final disposition, barring right to bring or main-

tain an action on same claim or cause. Addition of the words "with prejudice" to order granting motion to dismiss complaint indicates finality for purposes of appeal. *Compare* Without prejudice.

With recourse. Term which may be used in indorsing negotiable instrument and by which the indorser indicates that he remains liable for payment of the instrument. *See also* Recourse; *Compare* Without recourse.

Witness, *v.* To subscribe one's name to a deed, will, or other document, for the purpose of attesting its authenticity, and proving its execution, if required, by bearing witness thereto. *See also* Affirmation; Attest; Jurat; Verification.

Witness, *n.* In general, one who, being present, personally sees or perceives a thing; a beholder, spectator, or eyewitness. One who testifies to what he has seen, heard, or otherwise observed.

A person whose declaration under oath (or affirmation) is received as evidence for any purpose, whether such declaration be made on oral examination or by deposition or affidavit. Code Civ. Proc.Cal. § 1878.

A person attesting genuineness of signature to document by adding his signature.

One who is called upon to be present at a transaction, or the making of a will. He may thereafter, if necessary, testify to the transaction.

See also Accomplice witness; Competency; Competent witness; Expert witness; Hostile *or* adverse witness; Lay witness; Prosecuting witness; Subscribing witness; Swift witness; Target witness; Witness Protection Act; Witness tampering.

Adverse witness. *See* Adverse witness; Hostile *or* adverse witness.

Alibi witness. *See* Fed.R.Crim.P. 12.1. *See also* Alibi.

Attesting witness. *See* Attestation.

Character witness. In criminal cases, the accused is entitled to use character evidence in presenting the defense. The accused is entitled to show character traits inconsistent with the crime charged. Fed.R.Evid. 404(a)(1). The Federal Rules of Evidence and a majority of jurisdictions permit proof of character either by reputation or by receiving the opinion of persons who are sufficiently familiar with the accused to be able to testify concerning the trait in question. Fed.R. Evid. 405(a).

Both the reputation witness who testifies as to the accused person's community reputation and the opinion witness who testifies that in his opinion the accused possesses certain character traits are generically referred to as "character witnesses." See also Fed.R.Evid. 607–609.

Competent witness. *See* Competency; Competent witness.

Credible witness. *See* Competency; Competent witness; Credible.

Grand jury witness. A person called to give evidence regarding matters under inquiry by the grand jury.

Immunity of witnesses. *See* Immunity.

Material witness. In criminal trial, a witness whose testimony is crucial to either the defense or prosecution. In most states, he may be required to furnish bond for his appearance and, for want of surety, he may be confined until he testifies. *See also* Material witness.

Witness to will. One who has attested the will by subscribing his name thereto. The trend in state statutes is to require two witnesses to attest to the signing of the will. See *e.g.* Uniform Probate Code § 2–502. *See also* Attestation clause.

Witness against oneself. *See* Immunity; Self-incrimination.

Witnessing part. In a deed or other formal instrument, is that part which comes after the recitals, or, where there are no recitals, after the parties. It usually commences with a reference to the agreement or intention to be effectuated, then states or refers to the consideration, and concludes with the operative words and parcels, if any. Where a deed effectuates two distinct objects, there are two witnessing parts. *See also* Attestation; Attestation clause.

Witness Protection Act. Federal law which establishes the manner in which the Attorney General may provide for relocation and other protection of a witness or a potential witness for the federal government or for a state government in an official proceeding concerning an organized criminal activity or other serious offense. See 18 U.S.C.A. § 3521 et seq.

Witness tampering. The federal Victim and Witness Protection Act prohibits the intimidation and harassment of witnesses before they testify, as well as prohibiting retaliation, or threats of retaliation, against witnesses after they testify. 18 U.S.C.A. § 1512–1515.

Wittingly. With knowledge and by design, excluding only cases which are the result of accident or forgetfulness, and including cases where one does an unlawful act through an erroneous belief of his right.

Words actionable in themselves. In libel and slander, refer to words which are libelous or slanderous per se. *See* Actionable per se; Libelous per se.

Words of art. The vocabulary or terminology of a particular art, science, or profession, and especially those expressions which are idiomatic or peculiar to it. For example, in law "Taking the Fifth" means that a person is asserting his or her Fifth Amendment protection against self-incrimination.

Words of limitation. *See* Limitation.

Words of negotiability. The language used in making an instrument payable to order or to bearer. See U.C.C. §§ 3–110 & 3–111. As applied to documents, language therein providing that the goods are to be delivered to bearer or to the order of a named person. See U.C.C. § 7–104(1)(a). *See also* Negotiable instruments.

Words of procreation. To create an estate tail by deed, it is necessary that words of procreation should be used in order to confine the estate to the descendants of the first grantee, as in the usual form of limitation,—"to A. and the heirs of his body."

Words of purchase. *See* Purchase.

Workers' Compensation Acts. State and federal statutes which provide for fixed awards to employees or their dependents in case of employment related accidents and diseases, dispensing with need by employee to bring legal action and prove negligence on part of the employer. Some of the statutes go beyond the simple determination of the right to compensation, and provide insurance systems, either under state supervision or otherwise. The various state acts vary as to extent of workers and employment covered, amount and duration of benefits, etc.

The effect of most workers' compensation acts is to make the employer strictly liable to an employee for injuries sustained by the employee which arise out of and in the course of employment, without regard to the negligence of the employer or that of the employee. Where the statute applies, it has been uniformly held that this remedy is exclusive and bars any common-law remedy which the employee may have had, the compensation scheduled under the act being the sole measure of damage.

Federal employees are covered by the Federal Employees Compensation Act; seamen by the Jones Act; longshore and harbor workers by the Longshore and Harbor Workers' Compensation Act. The FECA and LHWCA are administered by the federal Office of Workers' Compensation Programs. Additional benefits to disabled workers are provided under Title II of the Social Security Act.

See also Employers' liability acts.

Workers' compensation boards or courts. Such exist in most states with jurisdiction to review cases arising under workers' compensation acts and related rules and regulations.

Workers' compensation insurance. Insurance coverage purchased by employers to cover risks under workers' compensation laws. Such is usually mandated by state acts, unless the employer is self-insured. *See also* Insurance.

Work furlough. A prison treatment program that allows inmates to be released during the day to work in the community.

Workhouse. Place of confinement for persons convicted of lesser offenses. Such imprisonment is usually for a relatively short duration.

Working capital. A firm's investment in current assets, such as cash, accounts receivable, inventory, etc. The net working capital is the difference between the current assets and current liabilities. Such represents the amount of cash, materials, and supplies ordinarily required by a business in its day-to-day business operation to meet current expenses and such contingencies as may typically develop.

Working interest. The rights to the mineral interest granted by an oil and gas lease, so-called because the lessee acquires the right to work on the lease property to search, develop and produce oil and gas and the obligation to pay all costs). *See also* Royalty.

Working papers. Valid employment certificate. By statute in certain states, such document must be filed by one employing a minor; *e.g.* N.Y. Labor Law, § 132(2). *See also* Work permit.

In accounting, the records kept by an independent auditor of the procedures followed, tests performed, information obtained, and conclusions reached pertinent to his or her examination.

Discovery. See Work product rule.

Work-in-process. Products being manufactured or assembled, but not yet completed.

Work made for hire. As defined by the Copyright Act (17 U.S.C.A. § 101), is: (1) a work prepared by an employee within the scope of his or her employment; or (2) a work specially ordered or commissioned for use as a contribution to a collective work, as a part of a motion picture or other audiovisual work, as a translation, as a supplementary work, as a compilation, as an instructional text, as a test, as answer material for a test, or as an atlas, if the parties expressly agree in a written instrument signed by them that the work shall be considered a work made for hire.

Workout. In bankruptcy, an out-of-court negotiation with creditors whereby a debtor enters into an agreement with a creditor or creditors for a payment or plan to discharge the debtor's debt(s). *See also* Bankruptcy proceedings.

Term is also used to refer to restructuring or refinancing by banks of nonperforming or overdue loans of creditors.

Work permit. Documentary authorization to work given to an alien by the Immigration and Naturalization Service (INS). It is unlawful for an employer to hire an alien who lacks INS work authorization. Immigration Reform and Control Act of 1986 (IRCA), 8 U.S.C.A. § 1324a(a)(1). *See also* Working papers.

Work product rule. Under this rule any notes, working papers, memoranda or similar materials, prepared by an attorney in anticipation of litigation, are protected from discovery. Fed.R.Civ. Proc. 26(b)(3). See Hickman v. Taylor, 329 U.S. 495, 67 S.Ct. 385, 91 L.Ed. 451. Most states have codified the work product rule in some form either by statute or court rule. This rule has been interpreted to include private memoranda, written statements of witnesses and mental impressions of personal recollections prepared or formed by attorney in anticipation of litigation or for trial.

Work release program. Correctional programs which allow an inmate to leave the institution for the purpose of continuing regular employment during the daytime, but reporting back to lockup nights and weekends.

Work sheet. In accounting, columnar form that aids in the construction of the financial statements and assists in the performance of other end-of-period tasks.

World Bank. The International Bank for Reconstruction and Development, commonly referred to as the World Bank, is an international financial institution whose purposes include assisting the development of its member nations' territories, promoting and supplementing private foreign investment, and promoting long range balanced growth in international trade. See 22 U.S.C.A. § 286.

World Court. *See* International Court of Justice.

Worth. The quality or value of a thing which gives it value. Although "worth" in some connections may mean more than pecuniary value, in law it means that sum of valuable qualities which renders a thing valuable and useful expressed in the current medium of the country. Furnishing an equivalent for. *See also* Net worth; Value.

Worthier title doctrine /wə́rðiyər táytəl/. At common law where testator undertook to devise to an heir exactly same interest in land as such heir would take by descent, descent was regarded as the "worthier title" and heir took by descent rather than by devise. Doctrine of worthier title provides that conveyance by grantor with limitation over to grantor's heirs creates reversion in grantor, not remainder interest in heirs, and to take by descent rather than by purchase, is said to create a worthier title. To the extent that it exists today in the United States (the doctrine has been abolished in many states), it is a rule of construction. That is, applying it is said to turn on the intention of the transferor.

Worthless. Destitute of worth, of no value or use.

Worthless check. A check drawn on a bank account which is no longer open or on an account with funds insufficient to cover the check.

Giving a worthless check is the making, drawing, issuing or delivering or causing or directing the making, drawing, issuing or delivering of any check, order or draft on any bank or depository for the payment of money or its equivalent with intent to defraud and knowing, at the time of the making, drawing, issuing or delivering of such check, order or draft as aforesaid, that the maker or drawer has no deposit in or credits with such bank or depository or has not sufficient funds in, or credits with, such bank or depository for the payment of such check, order or draft in full upon its presentation. Such act is a misdemeanor in most states. See e.g. Model Penal Code, § 224.5. *See also* Bad check; Check kiting.

Worthless securities. A loss (usually capital) is allowed for a security that becomes worthless during the year. The loss is deemed to have occurred on the last day of the year. Special rules apply to securities of affiliated companies and small business stock. See I.R.C. § 165.

Wraparound mortgage. A second mortgage which wraps around or exists in addition to a first or other mortgages. Form of secondary financing typically used on older properties having first mortgages with low interest rates in which a lender assumes the developer's first mortgage obligation and also loans additional money, taking back from developer a junior mortgage in total amount at an intermediate interest rate.

Writ. A written judicial order to perform a specified act, or giving authority to have it done, as in a writ of mandamus or certiorari, or as in an "original writ" for instituting an action at common law. A written court order or a judicial process, directing that a sheriff or other judicial officer do what is commanded by the writ; or giving authority and commission to have it done. *See also* Order; Prerogative writs; Process.

In old English law, an instrument in the form of a letter; a letter or letters of attorney. This is a very ancient sense of the word.

In the old books, "writ" is used as equivalent to "action;" hence writs are sometimes divided into real, personal, and mixed.

For the names and description of various particular writs, see the titles below.

Alias writ. A second writ issued in the same cause, where a former writ of the same kind has been issued without effect.

All Writs Act. Federal Act which permits federal appellate courts to "issue all writs necessary or appropriate in aid of their respective jurisdictions and agreeable to the usages and principles of law." 28 U.S.C.A. § 1651.

Prerogative writs. Those issued by the exercise of the extraordinary power of the crown (the court, in modern practice) on proper cause shown; namely, the writs of *procedendo, mandamus, prohibition, quo warranto, habeas corpus,* and *certiorari.*

Writ system. The common-law procedural system, under which plaintiffs commenced most actions by obtaining the appropriate kind of original writ. This pigeonholed approach shaped both procedural and substantive law. *See* Forms of action.

Write-down. In accounting, to transfer a portion of the balance of an asset to an expense account due to a decrease in the value of an asset. *See also* Write-off.

Write-off. To remove from the books of account an asset which has become worthless. Most often referred to in connection with accounts or notes receivable which are deemed worthless or uncollectible. *See* Bad debt.

Write-up. To increase the valuation of an asset in a financial statement to reflect current value. With a few exceptions, this is not generally permitted in accounting.

Writing. The expression of ideas by letters visible to the eye. The giving an outward and objective form to a contract, will, etc., by means of words or marks placed upon paper, parchment, or other material substance.

Any intentional reduction to tangible form of an agreement, commitment, right to payment, property rights, or other abstraction. See U.C.C. § 1–201(46) (definition of "written" or "writing").

In the most general sense of the word, "writing" denotes a document, whether manuscript or printed, as opposed to mere spoken words. Writing is essential to the validity of certain contracts and other transactions.

"Writings" consist of letters, words, or numbers, or their equivalent, set down by handwriting, typewriting, printing, photostating, photographing, magnetic impulse, mechanical or electronic recording, or other form of data compilation. Fed.Evid.R. 1001(1).

"Writing" means handwriting, typewriting, printing, photostating, photographing, and every other means of recording upon any tangible thing any form of communication or representation, including letters, words, pictures, sounds, or symbols, or combinations thereof. Calif.Evid.Code, § 250.

See also Ancient writings; Instrument.

Writing obligatory. The technical name by which a *bond* is described in pleading.

Writ of assistance. Writs of Assistance exist to enforce judgment of court directing specific act. An equitable remedy normally used to transfer real property, the title of which has been previously adjudicated, as a means of enforcing the court's own decree. It is essentially a mandatory injunction, the effect of which is to bring about a change in the possession of realty; it dispossesses the occupant and gives possession to one adjudged entitled thereto by the court.

Despite merger of law and equity in rules practice, provision is made for writ of assistance in Fed.R.Civ.P. 70.

Writ of attachment. An order to seize a debtor's property so as to secure the claim of a creditor. A writ employed to enforce obedience to an order or judgment of the court. It may take the form of taking or seizing property to bring it under control of the court. In its generic sense, any mesne civil process in the nature of a writ on which property may be attached, including trustee process. *See also* Attachment.

Writ of capias. *See* Capias.

Writ of certiorari. An order by the appellate court which is used by that court when it has discretion on whether or not to hear an appeal from a lower court. If the writ is denied, the court refuses to hear the appeal and, in effect, the judgment below stands unchanged. If the writ is granted, then it has the effect of ordering the lower court to certify the record and send it up to the higher court which has used its discretion to hear the appeal. *See also* Certiorari.

In the U.S. Supreme Court, a review on writ of certiorari is not a matter of right, but of judicial discretion, and will be granted only when there are special and important reasons therefor. 28 U.S.C.A. §§ 1254, 1257; Sup.Ct.Rules 10 et seq.

Writ of coram nobis. *See* Coram nobis.

Writ of ejectment. The writ in an action of ejectment, for the recovery of lands. *See* Ejectment.

Writ of entry. A real action to recover the possession of land where the tenant (or owner) has been disseised or otherwise wrongfully dispossessed. Under rules practice, such writ has been abolished in favor of a civil action which grants similar relief, *e.g.* Mass.R.Civ.P. 81(b).

Writ of error. A writ issued from a court of appellate jurisdiction, directed to the judge or judges of a court of record, requiring them to remit to the appellate court the record of an action before them, in which a final judgment has been entered, in order that examination may be made of certain errors alleged to have been committed, and that the judgment may be reversed, corrected, or affirmed, as the case may require.

It is brought for supposed error in law apparent on record and takes case to higher tribunal, which affirms or reverses. It is commencement of new suit to set aside judgment, and is not continuation of suit to which it relates. And unless abolished by statute, is writ of right applicable to all cases in which jurisdiction is exercised according to course of common law, but is inapplicable to cases not known to or in derogation of common law, unless otherwise provided by statute. *See also* Writ of error coram nobis; Writ of error coram vobis.

Writ of error coram nobis /rít əv éhrər kórəm nówbəs/. *See* Coram nobis.

Writ of error coram vobis /rít əv éhrər kórəm vówbəs/. This writ, at the English common law, is distinguished from "writ of error coram nobis," in that the former issued from the Court of King's Bench to a judgment of the Court of Common Pleas, whereas the latter issued from the Court of King's Bench to a judgment of that court. *See also* Coram vobis.

Writ of execution. A writ to put in force the judgment or decree of a court. Formal, written command of a court directing a sheriff or other official to enforce a judgment through process of execution. *See* Execution; Pluries.

Writ of habeas corpus. *See* Habeas corpus.

Writ of inquiry. In common-law practice, a writ which issued after the plaintiff in an action had obtained a judgment by default, on an unliquidated claim, directing the sheriff, with the aid of a jury, to inquire into the amount of the plaintiff's demand and assess his damages.

Writ of mandamus. *See* Mandamus.

Writ of possession. Writ of execution employed to enforce a judgment to recover the possession of land. It commands the sheriff to enter the land and give possession of it to the person entitled under the judgment. For a distinction between this writ and the Writ of assistance, see that title. *See also* Ejectment.

Writ of process. *See* Action; Process.

Writ of prohibition. *See* Prohibition.

Writ of replevin. *See* Replevin.

Writ of review. A general designation of any form of process issuing from an appellate court and intended to bring up for review the record or decision of the court below. *See* Writ of certiorari.

Writ of supersedeas /rít əv s(y)ùwpərsíydiyəs/. *See* Supersedeas.

Writ of supervisory control. A writ which is issued only to correct erroneous rulings made by the lower court within its jurisdiction, where there is no appeal, or the remedy by appeal cannot afford adequate relief, and gross injustice is threatened as the result of such rulings. It is in nature of summary appeal to control course of litigation in trial court when necessary to prevent miscarriage of justice, and may be employed to prevent extended and needless litigation.

Written contract. *See* Contract.

Written instrument. Something reduced to writing as a means of evidence, and as the means of giving formal expression to some act or contract. *See* Instrument.

Written law. Statutory law; *i.e.* law deriving its force from express legislative enactment. Also, a constitution or treaty. *See* Common law; Constitution; Statute; Treaty.

Wrong. A violation of the legal rights of another; an invasion of right to the damage of the parties who suffer it, especially a tort. It usually signifies injury to person, property or relative noncontractual rights of another than wrongdoer, with or without force, but, in more extended sense, includes violation of contract.

Wrongdoer. One who commits an injury; a *tortfeasor*. The term ordinarily imports an invasion of right to the damage of the party who suffers such invasion.

Wrongful. Injurious, heedless, unjust, reckless, unfair; it implies the infringement of some right, and may result from disobedience to lawful authority. *See also* Crime; Criminal; Negligence; Tort.

Wrongful abuse of process. *See* Abuse *(process)*; Malicious abuse of legal process.

Wrongful act. Any act which in the ordinary course will infringe upon the rights of another to his damage, unless it is done in the exercise of an equal or superior right. Term is occasionally equated to term "negligent," but generally has been considered more comprehensive term, including criminal, wilful, wanton, reckless and all other acts which in ordinary course will infringe upon rights of another to his damage. *See e.g.* Crime; Tort.

Wrongful birth. A medical malpractice claim brought by the parents of an impaired child, alleging that negligent treatment or advice deprived them of the opportunity to avoid conception or terminate the pregnancy. *See also* Wrongful conception; Wrongful life.

Wrongful conception. Also know as wrongful pregnancy, it is a claim by parents for damages arising from the negligent performance of a sterilization procedure or abortion, and the subsequent birth of a child. *See also* Wrongful birth; Wrongful life.

Wrongful conduct. Conduct which contravenes some duty which law attaches to relation between parties affected. *See* Wrongful act.

Wrongful death action. Type of lawsuit brought on behalf of a deceased person's beneficiaries that alleges that death was attributable to the willful or negligent act of another. Such action is original and distinct claim for damages sustained by statutory beneficiaries and is not derivative of or continuation of claim existing in decedent. *See* Kilberg doctrine; Wrongful death statutes.

Wrongful death statutes. Such statutes, which exist in all states, provide a cause of action in favor of the decedent's personal representative for the benefit of certain beneficiaries (*e.g.* spouse, parent, children) against person who negligently caused death of spouse, child, parent, etc. Statutory provision which operates upon the common-law rule that the death of a human being may not be complained of as an injury in a civil court. The cause of action for wrongful death permitted under such statutes is for the wrong to the beneficiaries. Most such statutes are compensatory though some states retain statutes which measure damages in terms of culpability and some statutes reflect a combination of both. *See also* Death on High Seas Act; Lord Campbell Act; Survival statutes; Unborn child; Wrongful death action.

Wrongful discharge. An at-will employee's cause of action against his former employer, alleging that his discharge was in violation of state or federal anti-discrimination statutes (cf. 42 U.S. C.A. §§ 2000e to 2000e–17), public policy, an implied employment contract, or an implied covenant of good faith and fair dealing. *See also* Employment at will; Whistle-blower Acts.

Wrongful dishonor. *See* Dishonor.

Wrongful levy. Such as will entitle the owner of property levied on to damages for wrongful execution, exists where there has been done to a third person's personalty those acts that would constitute a valid and complete levy if the debtor's property had been seized.

Wrongful life. Refers to type of medical malpractice claim brought on behalf of a child born with birth defects, alleging that the child would not have been born but for negligent advice to, or treatment of, the parents. *See also* Wrongful birth; Wrongful conception.

Wrongfully. In a wrong manner; unjustly; in a manner contrary to the moral law, or to justice. *See also* Wrongful; Wrongful act.

W–2 form. A statement of earnings and taxes withheld (including federal, state, and local income taxes and FICA tax) during the year, prepared for and provided to each employee and also filed with the Internal Revenue Service by employer. *See also* W–4 form.

X

X. A mark used in place of a signature by one who is unable to otherwise affix his or her signature. *See* Mark.

Symbol used in financial newspapers to indicate that a stock is trading ex dividend (*i.e.* without dividend).

Y

Year and a day rule. At common law, death could not be attributed to defendant's wrongful conduct unless it occurred within a year and a day of the conduct. The rationale for this rule was the lack of medical precision in determining cause after such a long period of time, coupled with the very real probability of an intervening cause being responsible for the death. In view of the medical advances of the twentieth century, it can be argued that the year and a day rule is obsolete and should be discarded. Although some jurisdictions have done this either by legislation or judicial decision, most jurisdictions have not.

Year end. In accounting, the close of a fiscal period of a business.

Yearly. *See* Annual; Annually.

Year to year tenancy. *See* Tenancy.

Yeas and nays. The affirmative and negative votes on a bill or measure before a legislative assembly. "Calling the yeas and nays" is calling for the individual and oral vote of each member, usually upon a call of the roll.

Yellow dog contract. An employment practice by which employer requires employee to sign an agreement promising as condition of employment that he will not join a union, and will be discharged if he does join. Such contracts are prohibited by the National Labor Relations Act, the Norris LaGuardia Act, the Railway Labor Act, and as well by the laws of most states. 29 U.S. C.A. § 103.

Yellow journalism. Type of journalism which distorts and exploits the news by sensationalism in order to sell copies of the newspapers or magazines.

Yield. To give up, relinquish, or surrender.

Current return from an investment or expenditure as a percentage of price of investment or expenditure. The stock dividends or bond interest paid expressed as a percentage of the current price. As to bonds or stock, is coupon or dividend rate divided by purchase price. *See also* Bond equivalent yield; Coupon equivalent yield; Net yield; Rate *(Rate of return)*.

Current yield. On bonds, the annual interest paid divided by the current market price of the bond. As interest rates fall, the market price of the bond rises; as they rise, bond prices fall. The actual rate of return on a bond. For example, a 10% bond with a face value of $500 purchased for $450

earns $50 of interest in the first year. The current yield on the bond is 11.11% while the coupon rate on the bond remains at 10%.

Nominal yield. The annual income received from a fixed-income security divided by the par or face value of the security. It is stated as a percentage figure.

Reoffering yield. In purchase-and-sale, the yield to maturity at which the underwriter offers to see the bonds to investors.

Yield ratio. The relationship that should or does exist between input and output.

Yield spread. Yield differences between various issues of securities.

Yield to maturity. On bonds, a complex calculation that reflects the overall rate of return an investor would receive from a bond if the bond is held to maturity and the interest payments reinvested at the same rate. It takes into account purchase price, coupon yield, time to maturity and the time between interest payments.

Yield upon investment. *See* Yield.

York-Antwerp rules /yórk ǽntwərp rùwlz/. Certain rules relating to uniform bills of lading and also governing settlement of maritime losses among the several interests such as ship owners, cargo owners, etc. These rules are commonly incorporated in contracts of affreightment. They are the result of conferences of representatives of mercantile interests from several countries, in the interest of uniformity of law. They have no statutory authority.

Younger doctrine. The principle, developed by the Supreme Court in Younger v. Harris, 401 U.S. 37, 91 S.Ct. 746, 27 L.Ed.2d 669 and other cases, that federal courts should not interfere with an ongoing state criminal proceeding, either by injunction or declaratory relief, unless the prosecution has been brought in bad faith or as harassment. The *Younger* doctrine has also been applied in civil actions where the state is a party and important state substantive goals are implicated.

Youthful offenders. Status classification of youths and young adults, generally older than juveniles (18–25 age range), who are given special sentencing consideration. The purpose of federal and state statutes granting youthful offender status is to improve the chances of correction and successful return to the community of young offenders sentenced to imprisonment by providing them with vocational, education, counseling, or public service opportunities and by preventing their association with older and more experienced criminals during the terms of their confinement; see *e.g.* Fla. St. § 958.011; 18 U.S.C.A. § 5001 *et seq.*; 5031 *et seq.* The determination of whether or not to grant youthful offender status rests within the discretion of the sentencing court. *See also* Delinquent child.

Z

Zero-balance account. A bank account that is managed so as to have just enough cash to cover checks that will be presented for payment during the day, which results in the balance returning to zero at the end of each business day.

Zero bracket amount. A tax deduction available to individual taxpayers whether or not the individual itemizes his or her deductions. The zero bracket amount was replaced with the standard deduction, effective for tax years beginning after 1986. Each of these are factored into the tax tables. *See* Standard deduction.

Zoning. The division of a city or town by legislative regulation into districts and the prescription and application in each district of regulations having to do with structural and architectural designs of buildings and of regulations prescribing use to which buildings within designated districts may be put. Division of land into zones, and within those zones, regulation of both the nature of land usage and the physical dimensions of uses including height setbacks and minimum area.

See also Buffer-zone; Cluster zoning; Comprehensive zoning plan; Conforming use; Land use planning; Master plan; Official map; Planned unit development; Special exception; Special use permit; Spot zoning; Variance.

Aesthetic zoning. Zoning regulations designed to preserve the aesthetic features or values of an area.

Cluster zoning. *See* Cluster zoning; Planned unit development.

Conditional zoning. The imposition of specific restrictions upon the landowner as a condition of full realization of the benefit of rezoning. A zoning change which permits use of particular property subject to conditions not generally applicable to land similarly zoned. *See* Special exception; Use.

Contract zoning. Rezoning of a property to a less restrictive zoning classification subject to an agreement by the landowner to observe certain specified limitations on the uses and physical development of the property that other properties in the zone are not required to observe. This device is used particularly in dealing with property located in a more restrictive zone but on the border-line of the less restrictive zone, for which classification the rezoning is sought.

Density zoning. Type of cluster zoning which regulates open spaces, density of population and use of land. Density zoning requires state enabling legislation. Under this device, the city council determines what percentage of a particular district must be devoted to open space and what percentage may be used for dwelling units. The task of locating in the particular district the housing and open spaces devolves upon the planning commission working in conjunction with the developer. The latter will submit a series of plans and seek approval to go forward at each stage. *See also* Planned unit development.

Euclidean zoning. Type of zoning based on district-and-use. It envisions the specification of determined geographic areas separated according to zoning districts with the uses permitted in each district set forth in the ordinances. Thus, a property owner could from the zoning map determine in what type of district the property was located and by reference to the district's restrictions what uses are permitted.

Exclusionary zoning. Type of zoning which has been challenged on the grounds that it serves to erect exclusionary walls on the municipality's boundary according to local selfishness for socially improper goals which are beyond the legitimate purpose of zoning. The trend in the courts is to strike down such zoning.

Floating zone. In an attempt to avoid the inflexibility of mapped districts, some communities have created exceptional use districts to allow small tracts for such uses as shopping centers, garden type apartments or light industry. At time of ordinance approval the district is unlocated. *See also* Floating Zone.

Holding zone. A form of low density zoning employed for a temporary purpose until the community decides how to rezone the area.

Spot zoning. Changing the zoning of a particular piece of land without regard to the zoning plan for the area. *See also* Spot zoning.

Zoning map. The map created by a zoning ordinance which displays the various zoning districts.

Zoning variance. *See* Variance.

APPENDICES

*

1115

TABLE OF ABBREVIATIONS

Note: *This is a listing of the most commonly used abbreviations in the Dictionary. Many other abbreviations of legal words and terms, as well as their definitions, are contained in the main body of the Dictionary.*

Fed.Evid.R. ....Federal Rules of Evidence

Fed.R.App.P. ....Federal Rules of Appellate Procedure

Fed.R.Civil P. ....Federal Rules of Civil Procedure

Fed.R.Crim.P. ....Federal Rules of Criminal Procedure

I.R.C. ....Internal Revenue Code

I.R.S. ....Internal Revenue Service

U.C.C. ....Uniform Commercial Code

U.S.C.A. ....United States Code Annotated

*

THE CONSTITUTION OF THE UNITED STATES

PREAMBLE

We the People of the United States, in Order to form a more perfect Union, establish Justice, insure domestic Tranquility, provide for the common defence, promote the general Welfare, and secure the Blessings of Liberty to ourselves and our Posterity, do ordain and establish this Constitution for the United States of America.

ARTICLE I

Section 1. All legislative Powers herein granted shall be vested in a Congress of the United States, which shall consist of a Senate and House of Representatives.

Section 2. [1] The House of Representatives shall be composed of Members chosen every second Year by the People of the several States, and the Electors in each State shall have the Qualifications requisite for Electors of the most numerous Branch of the State Legislature.

[2] No Person shall be a Representative who shall not have attained to the Age of twenty five Years, and been seven Years a Citizen of the United States, and who shall not, when elected, be an Inhabitant of that State in which he shall be chosen.

[3] Representatives and direct Taxes shall be apportioned among the several States which may be included within this Union, according to their respective Numbers, which shall be determined by adding to the whole Number of free Persons, including those bound to Service for a Term of Years, and excluding Indians not taxed, three fifths of all other Persons. The actual Enumeration shall be made within three Years after the first Meeting of the Congress of the United States, and within every subsequent Term of ten Years, in such Manner as they shall by Law direct. The Number of Representatives shall not exceed one for every thirty Thousand, but each State shall have at Least one Representative; and until such enumeration shall be made, the State of New Hampshire shall be entitled to chuse three, Massachusetts eight, Rhode Island and Providence Plantations one, Connecticut five, New York six, New Jersey four, Pennsylvania eight, Delaware one, Maryland six, Virginia ten, North Carolina five, South Carolina five, and Georgia three.

[4] When vacancies happen in the Representation from any State, the Executive Authority thereof shall issue Writs of Election to fill such Vacancies.

[5] The House of Representatives shall chuse their Speaker and other Officers; and shall have the sole Power of Impeachment.

Section 3. [1] The Senate of the United States shall be composed of two Senators from each State, chosen by the Legislature thereof, for six Years; and each Senator shall have one Vote.

[2] Immediately after they shall be assembled in Consequence of the first Election, they shall be divided as equally as may be into three Classes. The Seats of the Senators of the first Class shall be vacated at the Expiration of the Second Year, of the second Class at the Expiration of the fourth Year, and of the third Class at the Expiration of the sixth Year, so that one third may be chosen every second Year; and if Vacancies happen by Resignation, or otherwise, during the Recess of the Legislature of any State, the Executive thereof may make temporary Appointments until the next Meeting of the Legislature, which shall then fill such Vacancies.

[3] No Person shall be a Senator who shall not have attained to the Age of thirty Years, and been nine Years a Citizen of the United States, and who shall not, when elected, be an Inhabitant of that State for which he shall be chosen.

[4] The Vice President of the United States shall be President of the Senate, but shall have no Vote, unless they be equally divided.

[5] The Senate shall chuse their other Officers, and also a President pro tempore, in the Absence of the Vice President, or when he shall exercise the Office of President of the United States.

[6] The Senate shall have the sole Power to try all Impeachments. When sitting for that Purpose, they shall be on Oath or Affirmation. When the President of the United States is tried, the Chief Justice shall preside: And no Person shall be convicted without the Concurrence of two thirds of the Members present.

[7] Judgment in Cases of Impeachment shall not extend further than to removal from Office, and disqualification to hold and enjoy any Office of honor, Trust, or Profit under the United States: but the Party convicted shall nevertheless be liable and subject to Indictment, Trial, Judgment, and Punishment, according to Law.

Section 4. [1] The Times, Places and Manner of holding Elections for Senators and Representatives, shall be prescribed in each State by the Legislature thereof; but the Congress may at any time by Law make or alter such Regulations, except as to the Places of chusing Senators.

[2] The Congress shall assemble at least once in every Year, and such Meeting shall be on the first Monday in December, unless they shall by Law appoint a different Day.

Section 5. [1] Each House shall be the Judge of the Elections, Returns, and Qualifications of its own Members, and a Majority of each shall constitute a Quorum to do Business; but a smaller Number may adjourn from day to day, and may be authorized to compel the Attendance of absent Members, in such Manner, and under such Penalties as each House may provide.

[2] Each House may determine the Rules of its Proceedings, punish its Members for disorderly Behavior, and, with the Concurrence of two thirds, expel a Member.

[3] Each House shall keep a Journal of its Proceedings, and from time to time publish the same, excepting such Parts as may in their Judgment require Secrecy; and the Yeas and Nays of the Members of either House on any question shall, at the Desire of one fifth of those Present, be entered on the Journal.

[4] Neither House, during the Session of Congress, shall, without the Consent of the other, adjourn for more than three days, nor to any other Place than that in which the two Houses shall be sitting.

Section 6. [1] The Senators and Representatives shall receive a Compensation for their Services, to be ascertained by Law, and paid out of the Treasury of the United States. They shall in all Cases, except Treason, Felony and Breach of the Peace, be privileged from Arrest during their Attendance at the Session of their respective Houses, and in going to and returning from the same; and for any Speech or Debate in either House, they shall not be questioned in any other Place.

[2] No Senator or Representative shall, during the Time for which he was elected, be appointed to any civil Office under the Authority of the United States, which shall have been created, or the Emoluments whereof shall have been increased during such time and no Person holding any Office under the United States, shall be a Member of either House during his Continuance in Office.

Section 7. [1] All Bills for raising Revenue shall originate in the House of Representatives; but the Senate may propose or concur with Amendments as on other Bills.

[2] Every Bill which shall have passed the House of Representatives and the Senate, shall, before it become a Law, be presented to the President of the United States; If he approve he shall sign it, but if not he shall return it, with his Objections to the House in which it shall have originated, who shall enter the Objections at large on their Journal, and proceed to reconsider it. If after such Reconsideration two thirds of that House shall agree to pass the Bill, it shall be sent together with the Objections, to the other House, by which it shall likewise be reconsidered, and if approved by two thirds of that House, it shall become a Law. But in all such Cases the Votes of both Houses shall be determined by Yeas and Nays, and the Names of the Persons voting for and against the Bill shall be entered on the Journal of each House respectively. If any Bill shall not be returned by the President within ten Days (Sundays excepted) after it shall have been presented to him, the Same shall be a Law, in like Manner as if he had signed it, unless the Congress by their Adjournment prevent its Return in which Case it shall not be a Law.

[3] Every Order, Resolution, or Vote, to Which the Concurrence of the Senate and House of Representatives may be necessary (except on a question of Adjournment) shall be presented to the President of the United States; and before the Same shall take Effect, shall be approved by him, or being disapproved by him, shall be repassed by two thirds of the Senate and House of Representatives, according to the Rules and Limitations prescribed in the Case of a Bill.

Section 8. [1] The Congress shall have Power To lay and collect Taxes, Duties, Imposts and Excises, to pay the Debts and provide for the common Defence and general Welfare of the United States; but all Duties, Imposts and Excises shall be uniform throughout the United States;

[2] To borrow money on the credit of the United States;

[3] To regulate Commerce with foreign Nations, and among the several States, and with the Indian Tribes;

[4] To establish an uniform Rule of Naturalization, and uniform Laws on the subject of Bankruptcies throughout the United States;

[5] To coin Money, regulate the Value thereof, and of foreign Coin, and fix the Standard of Weights and Measures;

[6] To provide for the Punishment of counterfeiting the Securities and current Coin of the United States;

[7] To Establish Post Offices and Post Roads;

[8] To promote the Progress of Science and useful Arts, by securing for limited Times to Authors and Inventors the exclusive Right to their respective Writings and Discoveries;

[9] To constitute Tribunals inferior to the supreme Court;

[10] To define and punish Piracies and Felonies committed on the high Seas, and Offenses against the Law of Nations;

[11] To declare War, grant Letters of Marque and Reprisal, and make Rules concerning Captures on Land and Water;

[12] To raise and support Armies, but no Appropriation of Money to that Use shall be for a longer Term than two Years;

[13] To provide and maintain a Navy;

[14] To make Rules for the Government and Regulation of the land and naval Forces;

[15] To provide for calling forth the Militia to execute the Laws of the Union, suppress Insurrections and repel Invasions;

[16] To provide for organizing, arming, and disciplining, the Militia, and for governing such Part of them as may be employed in the Service of the United States, reserving to the States respectively, the Appointment of the Officers, and the Authority of training the Militia according to the discipline prescribed by Congress;

[17] To exercise exclusive Legislation in all Cases whatsoever, over such District (not exceeding ten Miles square) as may, by Cession of particular States, and the Acceptance of Congress, become the Seat of the Government of the United States, and to exercise like Authority over all Places purchased by the Consent of the Legislature of the State in which the Same shall be, for the Erection of Forts, Magazines, Arsenals, dock-Yards, and other needful Buildings;—And

[18] To make all Laws which shall be necessary and proper for carrying into Execution the foregoing Powers, and all other Powers vested by this Constitution in the Government of the United States, or in any Department or Officer thereof.

Section 9. [1] The Migration or Importation of Such Persons as any of the States now existing shall think proper to admit, shall not be prohibited by the Congress prior to the Year one thousand eight hundred and eight, but a Tax or duty may be imposed on such Importation, not exceeding ten dollars for each Person.

[2] The privilege of the Writ of Habeas Corpus shall not be suspended, unless when in Cases of Rebellion or Invasion the public Safety may require it.

[3] No Bill of Attainder or ex post facto Law shall be passed.

[4] No Capitation, or other direct, Tax shall be laid, unless in Proportion to the Census or Enumeration herein before directed to be taken.

[5] No Tax or Duty shall be laid on Articles exported from any State.

[6] No Preference shall be given by any Regulation of Commerce or Revenue to the Ports of one State over those of another: nor shall Vessels bound to, or from, one State be obliged to enter, clear, or pay Duties in another.

[7] No money shall be drawn from the Treasury, but in Consequence of Appropriations made by Law; and a regular Statement and Account of the Receipts and Expenditures of all public Money shall be published from time to time.

[8] No Title of Nobility shall be granted by the United States: And no Person holding any Office of Profit or Trust under them, shall, without the Consent of the Congress, accept of any present, Emolument, Office, or Title, of any kind whatever, from any King, Prince, or foreign State.

Section 10. [1] No State shall enter into any Treaty, Alliance, or Confederation; grant Letters of Marque and Reprisal; coin Money; emit Bills of Credit; make any Thing but gold and silver Coin a Tender in Payment of Debts; pass any Bill of Attainder, ex post facto Law, or Law impairing the Obligation of Contracts, or grant any Title of Nobility.

[2] No State shall, without the Consent of the Congress, lay any Imposts or Duties on Imports or Exports, except what may be absolutely necessary for executing its inspection Laws: and the net Produce of all Duties and Imposts, laid by any State on Imports or Exports, shall be for the Use of the Treasury of the United States; and all such Laws shall be subject to the Revision and Control of the Congress.

[3] No State shall, without the Consent of Congress, lay any Duty of Tonnage, keep Troops, or Ships of War in time of Peace, enter into any Agreement or Compact with another State, or with a foreign Power, or engage in War, unless actually invaded, or in such imminent Danger as will not admit of delay.

ARTICLE II

Section 1. [1] The executive Power shall be vested in a President of the United States of America. He shall hold his Office during the Term of four Years, and, together with the Vice President, chosen for the same Term, be elected, as follows:

[2] Each State shall appoint, in such Manner as the Legislature thereof may direct, a Number of Electors, equal to the whole Number of Senators and Representatives to which the State may be entitled in the Congress; but no Senator or Representative, or Person holding an Office of Trust or Profit under the United States, shall be appointed an Elector.

[3] The Electors shall meet in their respective States, and vote by Ballot for two Persons, of whom one at least shall not be an Inhabitant of the same State with themselves. And they shall make a List of all the Persons voted for, and of the Number of Votes for each; which List they shall sign and certify, and transmit sealed to the Seat of the Government of the United States, directed to the President of the Senate. The President of the Senate shall, in the Presence of the Senate and House of Representatives, open all the Certificates, and the Votes shall then be counted. The Person having the greatest Number of Votes shall be the President, if such Number be a Majority of the whole Number of Electors appointed; and if there be more than one who have such Majority, and have an equal Number of Votes, then the House of Representatives shall immediately chuse by Ballot one of them for President; and if no Person have a Majority, then from the five highest on the List the said House shall in like Manner chuse the President. But in chusing the President, the Votes shall be taken by States the Representation from each State having one Vote; A quorum for this Purpose shall consist of a Member or Members from two thirds of the States, and a Majority of all the States shall be necessary to a Choice. In every Case, after the Choice of the President, the Person having the greater Number of Votes of the Electors shall be the Vice President. But if there should remain two or more who have equal Votes, the Senate shall chuse from them by Ballot the Vice President.

[4] The Congress may determine the Time of chusing the Electors, and the Day on which they shall give their Votes; which Day shall be the same throughout the United States.

[5] No person except a natural born Citizen, or a Citizen of the United States, at the time of the Adoption of this Constitution, shall be eligible to the Office of President; neither shall any Person be eligible to that Office who shall not have attained to the Age of thirty five Years, and been fourteen Years a Resident within the United States.

[6] In case of the removal of the President from Office, or of his Death, Resignation or Inability to discharge the Powers and Duties of the said Office, the Same shall devolve on the Vice President, and the Congress may by Law provide for the Case of Removal, Death, Resignation or Inability, both of the President and Vice President, declaring what Officer shall then act as President, and such Officer shall act accordingly, until the Disability be removed, or a President shall be elected.

[7] The President shall, at stated Times, receive for his Services, a Compensation, which shall neither be increased nor diminished during the Period for which he shall have been elected, and he shall not receive within that Period any other Emolument from the United States, or any of them.

[8] Before he enter on the Execution of his Office, he shall take the following Oath or Affirmation: "I do solemnly swear (or affirm) that I will faithfully execute the Office of President of the United States, and will to the best of my Ability, preserve, protect and defend the Constitution of the United States."

Section 2. [1] The President shall be Commander in Chief of the Army and Navy of the United States, and of the militia of the several States, when called into the actual Service of the United States; he may require the Opinion, in writing, of the principal Officer in each of the Executive Departments, upon any Subject relating to the Duties of their respective

Offices, and he shall have Power to grant Reprieves and Pardons for Offenses against the United States, except in Cases of Impeachment.

[2] He shall have Power, by and with the Advice and Consent of the Senate to make Treaties, provided two thirds of the Senators present concur; and he shall nominate, and by and with the Advice and Consent of the Senate, shall appoint Ambassadors, other public Ministers and Consuls, Judges of the Supreme Court, and all other Officers of the United States, whose Appointments are not herein otherwise provided for, and which shall be established by Law; but the Congress may by Law vest the Appointment of such inferior Officers, as they think proper, in the President alone, in the Courts of Law, or in the Heads of Departments.

[3] The President shall have Power to fill up all Vacancies that may happen during the Recess of the Senate, by granting Commissions which shall expire at the End of their next Session.

Section 3. He shall from time to time give to the Congress Information of the State of the Union, and recommend to their Consideration such Measures as he shall judge necessary and expedient; he may, on extraordinary Occasions, convene both Houses, or either of them, and in Case of Disagreement between them, with Respect to the Time of Adjournment, he may adjourn them to such Time as he shall think proper; he shall receive Ambassadors and other public Ministers; he shall take Care that the Laws be faithfully executed, and shall Commission all the Officers of the United States.

Section 4. The President, Vice President and all civil Officers of the United States, shall be removed from Office on Impeachment for, and Conviction of, Treason, Bribery, or other high Crimes and Misdemeanors.

ARTICLE III

Section 1. The judicial Power of the United States, shall be vested in one supreme Court, and in such inferior Courts as the Congress may from time to time ordain and establish. The Judges, both of the supreme and inferior Courts, shall hold their Offices during good Behaviour, and shall, at stated Times, receive for their Services a Compensation, which shall not be diminished during their Continuance in Office.

Section 2. [1] The judicial Power shall extend to all Cases, in Law and Equity, arising under this Constitution, the Laws of the United States, and Treaties made, or which shall be made, under their Authority;—to all Cases affecting Ambassadors, other public Ministers and Consuls;—to all Cases of admiralty and maritime Jurisdiction;—to Controversies to which the United States shall be a Party;—to Controversies between two or more States;—between a State and Citizens of another State;—between Citizens of different States;—between Citizens of the same State claiming Lands under the Grants of different States, and between a State, or the Citizens thereof, and foreign States, Citizens or Subjects.

[2] In all Cases affecting Ambassadors, other public Ministers and Consuls, and those in which a State shall be a Party, the supreme Court shall have original Jurisdiction. In all the other Cases before mentioned, the supreme Court shall have appellate Jurisdiction, both as to Law and Fact, with such Exceptions, and under such Regulations as the Congress shall make.

[3] The trial of all Crimes, except in Cases of Impeachment, shall be by Jury; and such Trial shall be held in the State where the said Crimes shall have been committed; but when not committed within any State, the Trial shall be at such Place or Places as the Congress may by Law have directed.

Section 3. [1] Treason against the United States, shall consist only in levying War against them, or, in adhering to their Enemies, giving them Aid and Comfort. No Person shall be convicted of Treason unless on the Testimony of two Witnesses to the same overt Act, or on Confession in open Court.

[2] The Congress shall have Power to declare the Punishment of Treason, but no Attainder of Treason shall work Corruption of Blood, or Forfeiture except during the Life of the Person attainted.

ARTICLE IV

Section 1. Full Faith and Credit shall be given in each State to the public Acts, Records, and judicial Proceedings of every other State. And the Congress may by general Laws prescribe the Manner in which such Acts, Records and Proceedings shall be proved, and the Effect thereof.

Section 2. [1] The Citizens of each State shall be entitled to all Privileges and Immunities of Citizens in the several States.

[2] A Person charged in any State with Treason, Felony, or other Crime, who shall flee from Justice, and be found in another State, shall on demand of the executive Authority of the State from which he fled, be delivered up, to be removed to the State having Jurisdiction of the Crime.

[3] No Person held to Service or Labour in one State, under the Laws thereof, escaping into another, shall, in Consequence of any Law or Regulation therein, be discharged from such Service or Labour, but shall be delivered up on Claim of the Party to whom such Service or Labour may be due.

Section 3. [1] New States may be admitted by the Congress into this Union; but no new State shall be formed or erected within the Jurisdiction of any other State; nor any State be formed by the Junction of two or more States, or Parts of States, without the Consent of the Legislatures of the States concerned as well as of the Congress.

[2] The Congress shall have Power to dispose of and make all needful Rules and Regulations respecting the Territory or other Property belonging to the United States; and nothing in this Constitution shall be so construed as to Prejudice any Claims of the United States, or of any particular State.

Section 4. The United States shall guarantee to every State in this Union a Republican Form of Government, and shall protect each of them against Invasion; and on Application of the Legislature, or of the Executive (when the Legislature cannot be convened) against domestic Violence.

ARTICLE V

The Congress, whenever two thirds of both Houses shall deem it necessary, shall propose Amendments to this Constitution, or, on the Application of the Legislatures of two thirds of the several States, shall call a Convention for proposing Amendments, which, in either Case, shall be valid to all Intents and Purposes, as part of this Constitution, when ratified by the Legislatures of three fourths of the several States, or by Conventions in three fourths thereof, as the one or the other Mode of Ratification may be proposed by the Congress; Provided that no Amendment which may be made prior to the Year One thousand eight hundred and eight shall in any Manner affect the first and fourth Clauses in the Ninth Section of the first Article; and that no State, without its Consent, shall be deprived of its equal Suffrage in the Senate.

ARTICLE VI

[1] All Debts contracted and Engagements entered into, before the Adoption of this Constitution shall be as valid against the United States under this Constitution, as under the Confederation.

[2]   This Constitution, and the Laws of the United States which shall be made in Pursuance thereof; and all Treaties made, or which shall be made, under the Authority of the United States, shall be the supreme Law of the Land; and the Judges in every State shall be bound thereby, any Thing in the Constitution or Laws of any State to the Contrary notwithstanding.

[3]   The Senators and Representatives before mentioned, and the Members of the several State Legislatures, and all executive and judicial Officers, both of the United States and of the several States, shall be bound by Oath or Affirmation, to support this Constitution; but no religious Test shall ever be required as a Qualification to any Office or public Trust under the United States.

ARTICLE VII

The Ratification of the Conventions of nine States shall be sufficient for the Establishment of this Constitution between the States so ratifying the Same.

ARTICLES IN ADDITION TO, AND AMENDMENT OF, THE CONSTITUTION OF THE UNITED STATES OF AMERICA, PROPOSED BY CONGRESS, AND RATIFIED BY THE LEGISLATURES OF THE SEVERAL STATES PURSUANT TO THE FIFTH ARTICLE OF THE ORIGINAL CONSTITUTION.

AMENDMENT I   [1791]

Congress shall make no law respecting an establishment of religion, or prohibiting the free exercise thereof; or abridging the freedom of speech, or of the press; or the right of the people peaceably to assemble, and to petition the Government for a redress of grievances.

AMENDMENT II   [1791]

A well regulated Militia, being necessary to the security of a free State, the right of the people to keep and bear Arms, shall not be infringed.

AMENDMENT III   [1791]

No Soldier shall, in time of peace be quartered in any house, without the consent of the Owner, nor in time of war, but in a manner to be prescribed by law.

AMENDMENT IV   [1791]

The right of the people to be secure in their persons, houses, papers, and effects, against unreasonable searches and seizures, shall not be violated, and no Warrants shall issue, but upon probable cause, supported by Oath or affirmation, and particularly describing the place to be searched, and the persons or things to be seized.

AMENDMENT V   [1791]

No person shall be held to answer for a capital, or otherwise infamous crime, unless on a presentment or indictment of a Grand Jury, except in cases arising in the land or naval forces, or in the Militia, when in actual service in time of War or public danger; nor shall any person be subject for the same offence to be twice put in jeopardy of life or limb; nor shall be compelled in any criminal case to be a witness against himself, nor be deprived of life, liberty, or property, without due process of law; nor shall private property be taken for public use, without just compensation.

AMENDMENT VI [1791]

In all criminal prosecutions, the accused shall enjoy the right to a speedy and public trial, by an impartial jury of the State and district wherein the crime shall have been committed, which district shall have been previously ascertained by law, and to be informed of the nature and cause of the accusation; to be confronted with the witnesses against him; to have compulsory process for obtaining witnesses in his favor, and to have the Assistance of Counsel for his defence.

AMENDMENT VII [1791]

In Suits at common law, where the value in controversy shall exceed twenty dollars, the right of trial by jury shall be preserved, and no fact tried by jury, shall be otherwise re-examined in any Court of the United States, than according to the rules of the common law.

AMENDMENT VIII [1791]

Excessive bail shall not be required, nor excessive fines imposed, nor cruel and unusual punishments inflicted.

AMENDMENT IX [1791]

The enumeration in the Constitution, of certain rights, shall not be construed to deny or disparage others retained by the people.

AMENDMENT X [1791]

The powers not delegated to the United States by the Constitution, nor prohibited by it to the States, are reserved to the States respectively, or to the people.

AMENDMENT XI [1798]

The Judicial power of the United States shall not be construed to extend to any suit in law or equity, commenced or prosecuted against one of the United States by Citizens of another State, or by Citizens or Subjects of any Foreign State.

AMENDMENT XII [1804]

The Electors shall meet in their respective states and vote by ballot for President and Vice–President, one of whom, at least, shall not be an inhabitant of the same state with themselves; they shall name in their ballots the person voted for as President, and in distinct ballots the person voted for as Vice–President, and they shall make distinct lists of all persons voted for as President, and of all persons voted for as Vice–President, and of the number of votes for each, which lists they shall sign and certify, and transmit sealed to the seat of the government of the United States, directed to the President of the Senate;—The President of the Senate shall, in the presence of the Senate and House of Representatives, open all the certificates and the votes shall then be counted;—The person having the greatest number of votes for President, shall be the President, if such number be a majority of the whole number of Electors appointed; and if no person have such majority, then from the persons having the highest numbers not exceeding three on the list of those voted for as President, the House of Representatives shall choose immediately, by ballot, the President. But in choosing the President, the votes shall be taken by states, the representation from each state having one vote; a quorum for this purpose shall consist of a member or members from two-thirds of the states, and a majority of all the states shall be necessary to a choice. And if the House of

Representatives shall not choose a President whenever the right of choice shall devolve upon them before the fourth day of March next following, then the Vice–President shall act as President, as in the case of the death or other constitutional disability of the President.—The person having the greatest number of votes as Vice–President, shall be the Vice–President, if such number be a majority of the whole number of Electors appointed, and if no person have a majority, then from the two highest numbers on the list, the Senate shall choose the Vice–President; a quorum for the purpose shall consist of two-thirds of the whole number of Senators, and a majority of the whole number shall be necessary to a choice. But no person constitutionally ineligible to the office of President shall be eligible to that of Vice–President of the United States.

AMENDMENT XIII [1865]

Section 1. Neither slavery nor involuntary servitude, except as a punishment for crime whereof the party shall have been duly convicted, shall exist within the United States, or any place subject to their jurisdiction.

Section 2. Congress shall have power to enforce this article by appropriate legislation.

AMENDMENT XIV [1868]

Section 1. All persons born or naturalized in the United States, and subject to the jurisdiction thereof, are citizens of the United States and of the State wherein they reside. No State shall make or enforce any law which shall abridge the privileges or immunities of citizens of the United States; nor shall any State deprive any person of life, liberty, or property, without due process of law; nor deny to any person within its jurisdiction the equal protection of the laws.

Section 2. Representatives shall be apportioned among the several States according to their respective numbers, counting the whole number of persons in each State excluding Indians not taxed. But when the right to vote at any election for the choice of electors for President and Vice President of the United States, Representatives in Congress, the Executive and Judicial officers of a State, or the members of the Legislature thereof, is denied to any of the male inhabitants of such State, being twenty-one years of age, and citizens of the United States, or in any way abridged, except for participation in rebellion, or other crime, the basis of representation therein shall be reduced in the proportion which the number of such male citizens shall bear to the whole number of male citizens twenty-one years of age in such State.

Section 3. No person shall be a Senator or Representative in Congress, or elector of President and Vice President, or hold any office, civil or military, under the United States, or under any State, who having previously taken an oath, as a member of Congress, or as an officer of the United States, or as a member of any State legislature, or as an executive or judicial officer of any State, to support the Constitution of the United States, shall have engaged in insurrection or rebellion against the same, or given aid or comfort to the enemies thereof. But Congress may by a vote of two-thirds of each House, remove such disability.

Section 4. The validity of the public debt of the United States, authorized by law, including debts incurred for payment of pensions and bounties for services in suppressing insurrection or rebellion, shall not be questioned. But neither the United States nor any State shall assume or pay any debt or obligation incurred in aid of insurrection or rebellion against the United States, or any claim for the loss or emancipation of any slave; but all such debts, obligations and claims shall be held illegal and void.

Section 5. The Congress shall have power to enforce, by appropriate legislation, the provisions of this article.

AMENDMENT XV   [1870]

Section 1.   The right of citizens of the United States to vote shall not be denied or abridged by the United States or by any State on account of race, color, or previous condition of servitude.

Section 2.   The Congress shall have power to enforce this article by appropriate legislation.

AMENDMENT XVI [1913]

The Congress shall have power to lay and collect taxes on incomes, from whatever source derived, without apportionment among the several States, and without regard to any census or enumeration.

AMENDMENT XVII [1913]

[1] The Senate of the United States shall be composed of two Senators from each State, elected by the people thereof, for six years; and each Senator shall have one vote.   The electors in each State shall have the qualifications requisite for electors of the most numerous branch of the State legislatures.

[2] When vacancies happen in the representation of any State in the Senate, the executive authority of such State shall issue writs of election to fill such vacancies: *Provided,* That the legislature of any State may empower the executive thereof to make temporary appointments until the people fill the vacancies by election as the legislature may direct.

[3] This amendment shall not be so construed as to affect the election or term of any Senator chosen before it becomes valid as part of the Constitution.

AMENDMENT XVIII [1919]

Section 1.   After one year from the ratification of this article the manufacture, sale, or transportation of intoxicating liquors within, the importation thereof into, or the exportation thereof from the United States and all territory subject to the jurisdiction thereof for beverage purposes is hereby prohibited.

Section 2.   The Congress and the several States shall have concurrent power to enforce this article by appropriate legislation.

Section 3.   This article shall be inoperative unless it shall have been ratified as an amendment to the Constitution by the legislatures of the several States, as provided in the Constitution, within seven years from the date of the submission hereof to the States by the Congress.

AMENDMENT XIX [1920]

[1] The right of citizens of the United States to vote shall not be denied or abridged by the United States or by any State on account of sex.

[2] Congress shall have power to enforce this article by appropriate legislation.

AMENDMENT XX [1933]

Section 1.   The terms of the President and Vice President shall end at noon on the 20th day of January, and the terms of Senators and Representatives at noon on the 3d day of

January, of the years in which such terms would have ended if this article had not been ratified; and the terms of their successors shall then begin.

Section 2. The Congress shall assemble at least once in every year, and such meeting shall begin at noon on the 3d day of January, unless they shall by law appoint a different day.

Section 3. If, at the time fixed for the beginning of the term of the President, the President elect shall have died, the Vice President elect shall become President. If the President shall not have been chosen before the time fixed for the beginning of his term, or if the President elect shall have failed to qualify, then the Vice President elect shall act as President until a President shall have qualified; and the Congress may by law provide for the case wherein neither a President elect nor a Vice President elect shall have qualified, declaring who shall then act as President, or the manner in which one who is to act shall be selected, and such person shall act accordingly until a President or Vice President shall have qualified.

Section 4. The Congress may by law provide for the case of the death of any of the persons from whom the House of Representatives may choose a President whenever the right of choice shall have devolved upon them, and for the case of the death of any of the persons from whom the Senate may choose a Vice President whenever the right of choice shall have devolved upon them.

Section 5. Sections 1 and 2 shall take effect on the 15th day of October following the ratification of this article.

Section 6. This article shall be inoperative unless it shall have been ratified as an amendment to the Constitution by the legislatures of three-fourths of the several States within seven years from the date of its submission.

Amendment XXI [1933]

Section 1. The eighteenth article of amendment to the Constitution of the United States is hereby repealed.

Section 2. The transportation or importation into any State, Territory, or possession of the United States for delivery or use therein of intoxicating liquors, in violation of the laws thereof, is hereby prohibited.

Section 3. This article shall be inoperative unless it shall have been ratified as an amendment to the Constitution by conventions in the several States, as provided in the Constitution, within seven years from the date of the submission hereof to the States by the Congress.

Amendment XXII [1951]

Section 1. No person shall be elected to the office of the President more than twice, and no person who has held the office of President, or acted as President, for more than two years of a term to which some other person was elected President shall be elected to the office of President more than once. But this Article shall not apply to any person holding the office of President when this Article was proposed by the Congress, and shall not prevent any person who may be holding the office of President, or acting as President, during the term within which this Article becomes operative from holding the office of President or acting as President during the remainder of such term.

Section 2. This article shall be inoperative unless it shall have been ratified as an amendment to the Constitution by the legislatures of three-fourths of the several States within seven years from the date of its submission to the States by the Congress.

Amendment XXIII [1961]

Section 1.   The District constituting the seat of Government of the United States shall appoint in such manner as the Congress may direct:

A number of electors of President and Vice President equal to the whole number of Senators and Representatives in Congress to which the District would be entitled if it were a State, but in no event more than the least populous state; they shall be in addition to those appointed by the states, but they shall be considered, for the purposes of the election of President and Vice President, to be electors appointed by a state; and they shall meet in the District and perform such duties as provided by the twelfth article of amendment.

Section 2.   The Congress shall have power to enforce this article by appropriate legislation.

Amendment XXIV [1964]

Section 1.   The right of citizens of the United States to vote in any primary or other election for President or Vice President, for electors for President or Vice President, or for Senator or Representative in Congress, shall not be denied or abridged by the United States, or any State by reason of failure to pay any poll tax or other tax.

Section 2.   The Congress shall have power to enforce this article by appropriate legislation.

Amendment XXV [1967]

Section 1.   In case of the removal of the President from office or of his death or resignation, the Vice President shall become President.

Section 2.   Whenever there is a vacancy in the office of the Vice President, the President shall nominate a Vice President who shall take office upon confirmation by a majority vote of both Houses of Congress.

Section 3.   Whenever the President transmits to the President pro tempore of the Senate and the Speaker of the House of Representatives his written declaration that he is unable to discharge the powers and duties of his office, and until he transmits to them a written declaration to the contrary, such powers and duties shall be discharged by the Vice President as Acting President.

Section 4.   Whenever the Vice President and a majority of either the principal officers of the executive departments or of such other body as Congress may by law provide, transmit to the President pro tempore of the Senate and the Speaker of the House of Representatives their written declaration that the President is unable to discharge the powers and duties of his office, the Vice President shall immediately assume the powers and duties of the office as Acting President.

Thereafter, when the President transmits to the President pro tempore of the Senate and the Speaker of the House of Representatives his written declaration that no inability exists, he shall resume the powers and duties of his office unless the Vice President and a majority of either the principal officers of the executive department or of such other body as Congress may by law provide, transmit within four days to the President pro tempore of the Senate and the Speaker of the House of Representatives their written declaration and the President is unable to discharge the powers and duties of his office.   Thereupon Congress shall decide the issue, assembling within forty-eight hours for that purpose if not in session.   If the Congress, within twenty-one days after receipt of the latter written declaration, or, if Congress is not in session, within twenty-one days after Congress is required to assemble, determines by two-thirds vote of both Houses that the President is unable to discharge the power and duties of his office, the Vice President shall continue to discharge the same as Acting President; otherwise, the President shall resume the powers and duties of his office.

AMENDMENT XXVI [1971]

Section 1. The right of citizens of the United States, who are eighteen years of age or older, to vote shall not be denied or abridged by the United States or by any State on account of age.

Section 2. The Congress shall have power to enforce this article by appropriate legislation.

TIME CHART OF THE UNITED STATES SUPREME COURT [†]

The following table is designed to aid the user in identifying the composition of the Court at any given time in American history. Each listing is headed by the Chief Justice, whose name is italicized. Associate Justices are listed following the Chief Justice in order of seniority. In addition to dates of appointment, the table provides information on political party affiliation. Following each Justice is a symbol representing his party affiliation at the time of appointment:

F = Federalist	W = Whig
DR = Democratic Republican	R = Republican
(Jeffersonian)	I = Independent
D = Democrat	

1789	**1796–97**	**1806**	**1826–28**
Jay (F)	*Ellsworth* (F)	*J. Marshall* (F)	*J. Marshall* (F)
J. Rutledge (F)	Cushing (F)	Cushing (F)	Washington (F)
Cushing (F)	Wilson (F)	S. Chase (F)	W. Johnson (DR)
Wilson (F)	Iredell (F)	Washington (F)	Duval (DR)
Blair (F)	Paterson (F)	W. Johnson (DR)	Story (DR)
	S. Chase (F)	Livingston (DR)	Thompson (DR)
1790–91			Trimble (DR)
Jay (F)	**1798–99**	**1807–10**	
J. Rutledge (F)	*Ellsworth* (F)	*J. Marshall* (F)	**1829**
Cushing (F)	Cushing (F)	Cushing (F)	*J. Marshall* (F)
Wilson (F)	Iredell (F)	S. Chase (F)	Washington (F)
Blair (F)	Paterson (F)	Washington (F)	W. Johnson (DR)
Iredell (F)	S. Chase (F)	W. Johnson (DR)	Duval (DR)
	Washington (F)	Livingston (DR)	Story (DR)
1792		Todd (DR)	Thompson (DR)
Jay (F)	**1800**		McLean (D)
Cushing (F)	*Ellsworth* (F)	**1811–22**	
Wilson (F)	Cushing (F)	*J. Marshall* (F)	**1830–34**
Blair (F)	Paterson (F)	Washington (F)	*J. Marshall* (F)
Iredell (F)	S. Chase (F)	W. Johnson (DR)	W. Johnson (DR)
T. Johnson (F)	Washington (F)	Livingston (DR)	Duval (DR)
	Moore (F)	Todd (DR)	Story (DR)
1793–94		Duval (DR)	Thompson (DR)
Jay (F)	**1801–03**	Story (DR)	McLean (D)
Cushing (F)	*J. Marshall* (F)		Baldwin (D)
Wilson (F)	Cushing (F)	**1823–25**	
Blair (F)	Paterson (F)	*J. Marshall* (F)	**1835**
Iredell (F)	S. Chase (F)	Washington (F)	*J. Marshall* (F)
Paterson (F)	Washington (F)	W. Johnson (DR)	Duval (DR)
	Moore (F)	Todd (DR)	Story (DR)
		Duval (DR)	Thompson (DR)
1795	**1804–05**	Story (DR)	McLean (D)
J. Rutledge (F)*	*J. Marshall* (F)	Thompson (DR)	Baldwin (D)
Cushing (F)	Cushing (F)		Wayne (D)
Wilson (F)	Paterson (F)		
Blair (F)	S. Chase (F)		
Iredell (F)	Washington (F)		
Paterson (F)	W. Johnson (DR)		

[†] Source: Ducat and Chase, Constitutional Interpretation, 4th Edition, published in 1988 by West Publishing Co.

1836
Taney (D)
Story (DR)
Thompson (DR)
McLean (D)
Baldwin (D)
Wayne (D)
Barbour (D)

1837–40
Taney (D)
Story (DR)
Thompson (DR)
McLean (D)
Baldwin (D)
Wayne (D)
Barbour (D)
Catron (D)
McKinley (D)

1841–43
Taney (D)
Story (DR)
Thompson (DR)
McLean (D)
Baldwin (D)
Wayne (D)
Catron (D)
McKinley (D)
Daniel (D)

1844
Taney (D)
Story (DR)
McLean (D)
Baldwin (D)
Wayne (D)
Catron (D)
McKinley (D)
Daniel (D)

1845
Taney (D)
McLean (D)
Wayne (D)
Catron (D)
McKinley (D)
Daniel (D)
Nelson (D)
Woodbury (D)

1846–50
Taney (D)
McLean (D)
Wayne (D)
Catron (D)
McKinley (D)
Daniel (D)
Nelson (D)
Woodbury (D)
Grier (D)

1851–52
Taney (D)
McLean (D)
Wayne (D)
Catron (D)
McKinley (D)
Daniel (D)
Nelson (D)
Grier (D)
Curtis (W)

1853–57
Taney (D)
McLean (D)
Wayne (D)
Catron (D)
Daniel (D)
Nelson (D)
Grier (D)
Curtis (W)
Campbell (D)

1858–60
Taney (D)
McLean (D)
Wayne (D)
Catron (D)
Daniel (D)
Nelson (D)
Grier (D)
Campbell (D)
Clifford (D)

1861
Taney (D)
McLean (D)
Wayne (D)
Catron (D)
Nelson (D)
Grier (D)
Campbell (D)
Clifford (D)

1862
Taney (D)
Wayne (D)
Catron (D)
Nelson (D)
Grier (D)
Clifford (D)
Swayne (R)
Miller (R)
Davis (R)

1863
Taney (D)
Wayne (D)
Catron (D)
Nelson (D)
Grier (D)
Clifford (D)
Swayne (R)
Miller (R)
Davis (R)
Field (D)

1864–65
S. P. Chase (R)
Wayne (D)
Catron (D)* *
Nelson (D)
Grier (D)
Clifford (D)
Swayne (R)
Miller (R)
Davis (R)
Field (D)

1866
S. P. Chase (R)
Wayne (D)* *
Nelson (D)
Grier (D)
Clifford (D)
Swayne (R)
Miller (R)
Davis (R)
Field (D)

1867–69
S. P. Chase (R)
Nelson (D)
Grier (D)
Clifford (D)
Swayne (R)
Miller (R)
Davis (R)
Field (D)

1870–71
S. P. Chase (R)
Nelson (D)
Clifford (D)
Swayne (R)
Miller (R)
Davis (R)
Field (D)
Strong (R)
Bradley (R)

1872–73
S. P. Chase (R)
Clifford (D)
Swayne (R)
Miller (R)
Davis (R)
Field (D)
Strong (R)
Bradley (R)
Hunt (R)

1874–76
Waite (R)
Clifford D)
Swayne (R)
Miller (R)
Davis (R)
Field (D)
Strong (R)
Bradley (R)
Hunt (R)

1877–79
Waite (R)
Clifford (D)
Swayne (R)
Miller (R)
Field (D)
Strong (R)
Bradley (R)
Hunt (R)
Harlan (Ky.) (R)

1880
Waite (R)
Clifford (D)
Swayne (R)
Miller (R)
Field (D)
Bradley (R)
Hunt (R)
Harlan (Ky.) (R)
Woods (R)

1881
Waite (R)
Miller (R)
Field (D)
Bradley (R)
Hunt (R)
Harlan (Ky.) (R)
Woods (R)
Matthews (R)
Gray (R)

1882–87
Waite (R)
Miller (R)
Field (D)
Bradley (R)
Harlan (Ky.) (R)
Woods (R)
Matthews (R)
Gray (R)
Blatchford (R)

1888
Fuller (D)
Miller (R)
Field (D)
Bradley (R)
Harlan (Ky.) (R)
Matthews (R)
Gray (R)
Blatchford (R)
L. Lamar (D)

1889
Fuller (D)
Miller (R)
Field (D)
Bradley (R)
Harlan (Ky.) (R)
Gray (R)
Blatchford (R)
L. Lamar (D)
Brewer (R)

1890–91	**1902**	**1914–15**	**1930–31**
Fuller (D)	*Fuller* (D)	*E. White* (D)	*Hughes* (R)
Field (D)	Harlan (Ky.) (R)	McKenna (R)	Holmes (R)
Bradley (R)	Brewer (R)	Holmes (R)	Van Devanter (R)
Harlan (Ky.) (R)	Brown (R)	Day (R)	McReynolds (D)
Gray (R)	Shiras (R)	Hughes (R)	Brandeis (R)
Blatchford (R)	E. White (D)	Van Devanter (R)	Sutherland (R)
L. Lamar (D)	Peckham (D)	J. Lamar (D)	Butler (D)
Brewer (R)	McKenna (R)	Pitney (R)	Stone (R)'
Brown (R)	Holmes (R)	McReynolds (D)	Roberts (R)

1892	**1903–05**	**1916–20**	**1932–36**
Fuller (D)	*Fuller* (D)	*E. White* (D)	*Hughes* (R)
Field (D)	Harlan (Ky.) (R)	McKenna (R)	Van Devanter (R)
Harlan (Ky.) (R)	Brewer (R)	Holmes (R)	McReynolds (D)
Gray (R)	Brown (R)	Day (R)	Brandeis (R)
Blatchford (R)	E. White (D)	Van Devanter (R)	Sutherland (R)
L. Lamar (D)	Peckham (D)	Pitney (R)	Butler (D)
Brewer (R)	McKenna (R)	McReynolds (D)	Stone (R)
Brown (R)	Holmes (R)	Brandeis (R)* * *	Roberts (R)
Shiras (R)	Day (R)	Clarke (D)	Cardozo (D)

1893	**1906–08**	**1921**	**1937**
Fuller (D)	*Fuller* (D)	*Taft* (R)	*Hughes* (R)
Field (D)	Harlan (Ky.) (R)	McKenna (R)	McReynolds (D)
Harlan (Ky.) (R)	Brewer (R)	Holmes (R)	Brandeis (R)
Gray (R)	E. White (D)	Day (R)	Sutherland (R)
Blatchford (R)	Peckham (D)	Van Devanter (R)	Butler (D)
Brewer R)	McKenna (R)	Pitney (R)	Stone (R)
Brown (R)	Holmes (R)	McReynolds (D)	Roberts (R)
Shiras (R)	Day (R)	Brandeis (R)	Cardozo (D)
H. Jackson (D)	Moody (R)	Clarke (D)	Black (D)

1894	**1909**	**1922**	**1938**
Fuller (D)	*Fuller* (D)	*Taft* (R)	*Hughes* (R)
Field (D)	Harlan (Ky.) (R)	McKenna (R)	McReynolds (D)
Harlan (Ky.) (R)	Brewer (R)	Holmes (R)	Brandeis (R)
Gray (R)	E. White (D)	Van Devanter (R)	Butler (D)
Brewer (R)	McKenna (R)	Pitney (R)	Stone (R)
Brown (R)	Holmes (R)	McReynolds (D)	Roberts (R)
Shiras (R)	Day (R)	Brandeis (R)	Cardozo (D)
H. Jackson (D)	Moody (R)	Sutherland (R)	Black (D)
E. White (D)	Lurton (D)	Butler (D)	Reed (D)

1895–97	**1910–11**	**1923–24**	**1939**
Fuller (D)	*E. White* (D)	*Taft* (R)	*Hughes* (R)
Field (D)	Harlan (Ky.) (R)	McKenna (R)	McReynolds (D)
Harlan (Ky.) (R)	McKenna (R)	Holmes (R)	Butler (D)
Gray (R)	Holmes (R)	Van Devanter (R)	Stone (R)
Brewer (R)	Day (R)	McReynolds (D)	Roberts (R)
Brown (R)	Lurton (D)	Brandeis (R)	Black (D)
Shiras (R)	Hughes (R)	Sutherland (R)	Reed (D)
E. White (D)	Van Devanter (R)	Butler (D)	Frankfurter (I)
Peckham (D)	J. Lamar (D)	Sanford (R)	Douglas (D)

1898–1901	**1912–13**	**1925–29**	**1940**
Fuller (D)	*E. White* (D)	*Taft* (R)	*Hughes* (R)
Harlan (Ky.) (R)	McKenna (R)	Holmes (R)	McReynolds (D)
Gray (R)	Holmes (R)	Van Devanter (R)	Stone (R)
Brewer (R)	Day (R)	McReynolds (D)	Roberts (R)
Brown (R)	Lurton (D)	Brandeis (R)	Black (D)
Shiras (R)	Hughes (R)	Sutherland (R)	Reed (D)
E. White (D)	Van Devanter (R)	Butler (D)	Frankfurter (I)
Peckham (D)	J. Lamar (D)	Sanford (R)	Douglas (D)
McKenna (R)	Pitney (R)	Stone (R)	Murphy (D)

1941–42
Stone (R)
Roberts (R)
Black (D)
Reed (D)
Frankfurter (I)
Douglas (D)
Murphy (D)
Byrnes (D)
R. Jackson (D)

1943–44
Stone (R)
Roberts (R)
Black (D)
Reed (D)
Frankfurter (I)
Douglas (D)
Murphy (D)
R. Jackson (D)
W. Rutledge (D)

1945
Stone (R)
Black (D)
Reed (D)
Frankfurter (I)
Douglas (D)
Murphy (D)
R. Jackson (D)
W. Rutledge (D)
Burton (R)

1946–48
Vinson (D)
Black (D)
Reed (D)
Frankfurter (I)
Douglas (D)
Murphy (D)
R. Jackson (D)
W. Rutledge (D)
Burton (R)

1949–52
Vinson (D)
Black (D)
Reed (D)
Frankfurter (I)
Douglas (D)
R. Jackson (D)
Burton (R)
Clark (D)
Minton (D)

1953–54
Warren (R)
Black (D)
Reed (D)
Frankfurter (I)
Douglas (D)
R. Jackson (D)
Burton (R)

Clark (D)
Minton (D)

1955
Warren (R)
Black (D)
Reed (D)
Frankfurter (I)
Douglas (D)
Burton (R)
Clark (D)
Minton (D)
Harlan (N.Y.) (R)

1956
Warren (R)
Black (D)
Reed (D)
Frankfurter (I)
Douglas (D)
Burton (R)
Clark (D)
Harlan (N.Y.) (R)
Brennan (D)

1957
Warren (R)
Black (D)
Frankfurter (I)
Douglas (D)
Burton (R)
Clark (D)
Harlan (N.Y.) (R)
Brennan (D)
Whittaker (R)

1958–61
Warren (R)
Black (D)
Frankfurter (I)
Douglas (D)
Clark (D)
Harlan (N.Y.) (R)
Brennan (D)
Whittaker (R)
Stewart (R)

1962–65
Warren (R)
Black (D)
Douglas (D)
Clark (D)
Harlan (N.Y.) (R)
Brennan (D)
Stewart (R)
B. White (D)
Goldberg (D)

1965–67
Warren (R)
Black (D)
Douglas (D)
Clark (D)

Harlan (N.Y.) (R)
Brennan (D)
Stewart (R)
B. White (D)
Fortas (D)

1967–69
Warren (R)
Black (D)
Douglas (D)
Harlan (N.Y.) (R)
Brennan (D)
Stewart (R)
B. White (D)
Fortas (D)
T. Marshall (D)

1969
Burger (R)
Black (D)
Douglas (D)
Harlan (N.Y.) (R)
Brennan (D)
Stewart (R)
B. White (D)
Fortas (D)
T. Marshall (D)

1969–70
Burger (R)
Black (D)
Douglas (D)
Harlan (N.Y.) (R)
Brennan (D)
Stewart (R)
B. White (D)
T. Marshall (D)

1970
Burger (R)
Black (D)
Douglas (D)
Harlan (N.Y.) (R)
Brennan (D)
Stewart (R)
B. White (D)
T. Marshall (D)
Blackmun (R)

1971
Burger (R)
Douglas (D)
Brennan (D)
Stewart (R)
B. White (D)
T. Marshall (D)
Blackmun (R)

1972–75
Burger (R)
Douglas (D)
Brennan (D)
Stewart (R)

B. White (D)
T. Marshall (D)
Blackmun (R)
Powell (D)
Rehnquist (R)

1975–81
Burger (R)
Brennan (D)
Stewart (R)
B. White (D)
T. Marshall (D)
Blackmun (R)
Powell (D)
Rehnquist (R)
Stevens (R)

1981–1986
Burger (R)
Brennan (D)
B. White (D)
T. Marshall (D)
Blackmun (R)
Powell (D)
Rehnquist (R)
J. Stevens (R)
O'Connor (R)

1986–1988
Rehnquist (R)
Brennan (D)
B. White (D)
T. Marshall (D)
Blackmun (R)
Powell (D)
J. Stevens (R)
O'Connor (R)
Scalia (R)

1988–1990
Rehnquist (R)
Brennan (D)
B. White (D)
T. Marshall (D)
Blackmun (R)
J. Stevens (R)
O'Connor (R)
Scalia (R)
Kennedy (R)

1990–
Rehnquist (R)
B. White (D)
T. Marshall (D)
Blackmun (R)
J. Stevens (R)
O'Connor (R)
Scalia (R)
Kennedy (R)
Souter (R)

---

[*] Rutledge was a recess appointment whose confirmation was rejected by the Senate after the 1795 Term.

[**] Upon the death of Catron in 1865 and Wayne in 1867 their positions were abolished according to a congressional act of 1866. The Court's membership was reduced to eight until a new position was created by Congress in 1869. The new seat has generally been regarded as a re-creation of Wayne's seat.

[***] According to Professor Henry Abraham, "Many—and with some justice—consider Brandeis a Democrat; however, he was in fact a registered Republican when nominated." Freedom and the Court 455 (3d ed., 1977).

†